THE
SCIENCE FICTION
ENCYCLOPEDIA

THE SCIENCE FICTION ENCYCLOPEDIA

**General Editor
Peter Nicholls**

**Associate Editor
John Clute**

**Technical Editor
Carolyn Eardley**

**Contributing Editors
Malcolm Edwards   Brian Stableford**

Dolphin Books
Doubleday & Company, Inc.
Garden City, New York
1979

ISBN: 0–385–14743–0

Library of Congress Catalog Card No. 77–15167

© Roxby Press Limited 1979
Made by Roxby Press Publications Limited
98 Clapham Common Northside
London SW4 9SG

Picture research: Peter Nicholls and Caroline Lucas
Design: David Pearce
Production: Reynolds Clark Associates Limited

INTRODUCTION

Basically, there are two ways of researching a reference book. The first, and unhappily perhaps the more common, is for the compilers to cannibalize previous reference books for information. The trouble with this system, apart from a certain unfairness to pioneer workers who are sometimes not even credited, although heavily copied, is that it tends to repeat mistakes: actual errors are sometimes carried through four or five books until finally, because of the "authority" of the printed word, they are generally accepted as true. The second is to go to the original sources.

Although our task would have been impossible without the pioneer work of such bibliographers and indexers as Everett F. Bleiler, Bradford M. Day, Donald B. Day, H.W. Hall, Walt Lee, Norm Metcalf and, pre-eminently, Donald H. Tuck, along with many others who, like the above, are given entries in this volume (see the entry on Bibliographies and Indexes), and although in a minority of cases we relied on their findings, wherever possible we adopted the second research system. We believe this volume to be a substantial contribution to original research in science fiction; it is certainly the most comprehensive work on the subject ever published. It contains over 2800 entries, not counting cross-references.

As we suppose must always be the case with encyclopedists innocently setting out, we initially imagined that it might be possible to put *everything* in: *all* the relevant facts. We were almost instantly disillusioned. We now believe that, though we have gone a surprisingly long way towards achieving that aim, such an accomplishment would be impossible within the covers of a single volume; nor would the life-span of a handful of researchers encompass sufficient time for total comprehensiveness. Sf is a bigger field than most readers could begin to imagine. Let us then be quite frank about what is in and what is not. Although this volume is arranged on an alphabetical basis, we originally grouped the entries according to type: Authors, Themes, Films, Magazines, Editors, Critics, Illustrators, Film-makers, Publishers, Pseudonyms, Series, Television programmes, Original anthologies, Comics, Sf in various countries, Terminology, Awards, Fanzines and a small collection of Miscellanea.

1. To begin at the beginning: Authors. The fundamental principle of selection is very simple. Ideally, all authors who have written works which are arguably sf and published them in book form,

and who are not purely writers of juveniles, are given individual entries. We shall not tempt fate, however, by claiming that we have met that ideal; we shall certainly find ourselves having omitted some 20th-century authors (and are aware of it in the case of some authors of routine sf adventure), and for earlier centuries we have not attempted to be fully comprehensive. In treating the 20th century, we were forced to make difficult decisions about the inclusion of many authors, and we hope we have erred on the side of generosity. We have tried to include the juvenile writers most relevant to sf in general (so that you will find Carl H. Claudy and Alan Garner represented, but not Monica Hughes or Hugh Lofting). We have also given entries to the most important fantasy writers, since the readership of fantasy overlaps substantially with that of sf, even though, in our view, the works of authors like Lord Dunsany, E.R. Eddison, H.P. Lovecraft or J.R.R. Tolkien cannot in any rigorous sense be assimilated into sf. Many fantasy writers have been important influences within the sf field, however, and for that reason we felt it appropriate to include a selection. We also had to make some difficult decisions concerning the pattern of sub-genres that fringe sf. Some of these are: Lost-race and Lost-world stories, Prehistoric stories, Future-war stories, Political satires set in imaginary countries or in the near future, Heroic-fantasy stories set on other worlds, and Spiritualist and Astral-body stories. We have generously represented these sub-genres, giving full entries to the most important writers who used them, but we do not claim (especially in the extraordinarily prolific field of Future-war stories) to be fully comprehensive in these cases.

We have not restricted ourselves to authors whose work has appeared in book form only. A number of sf writers since 1926 who did not graduate, or who have not yet graduated, from magazines and anthologies are represented. Further information about Author entries is given in "How to use this book" and the Checklist of abbreviations.

The most interesting fact to emerge from the making up of a list of those authors who were to receive entries is that there are more non-genre sf writers (i.e. writers not associated directly with sf magazines or sf publishing imprints) than there are genre sf writers. We realize that the greatest public interest is in the latter group, and we are sure that we have done justice to the Isaac Asimovs and Robert Heinleins of the genre sf world in terms of the length and solidity of their entries, but we are also happy to be able, in a small way, to rectify the imbalance characteristic of most previous bibliographical studies of sf, and to draw attention to that great host of authors who published and continue to publish sf books without the magic words "science fiction" on the cover, though the consequence is that many of them have remained almost unknown to the general sf readership. Taking Authors, Editors and Critics together (there is a substantial overlap between the three groups), and not counting pseudonym cross-references, there are 1817 entries.

2. Themes. It is in this area, along with Authors, that this volume has its greatest claim to originality. Remarkably little work has been done by way of analysing sf according to its themes, apart from the most obvious, such as Robots and Utopias. We have included 175 theme entries, each consisting of a short essay, varying in length between 200 and 3500 words, and mostly well over 1000 words, discussing the importance of the theme in sf and the history of modern thought generally, and the variety of ways in which it has been treated over the years. When taken together, these theme entries comprise a comprehensive overview of the concerns of sf, a book within a book; for this reason, and because the reader may find it convenient to have the headings under which this overview is assembled readily available, a full list of these entries appears towards the end of the introductory matter. Otherwise, it may not occur to him that he will be able to find entries on such matters as Absurdist sf, Entropy, Faster than light, Paranoia and Schizophrenia, Pastoral and Social Darwinism.

Now that sf is playing a much greater role in education, both at high school and at university levels, especially in the USA (see the entry on SF in the Classroom), a real need has become evident for a quick way of locating stories relevant to various areas of discussion, such as Automation, Cybernetics, Ecology, Overpopulation, Pollution and many others. Teachers often wish to dramatize such discussions by giving imaginative examples of the human consequences of the many changes taking place in the world about us, and sf is an ideal teaching aid here. There is also, of course, a considerable interest in the themes of sf among the general sf readership. No single theme entry can possibly be comprehensive, and the usefulness of such an entry would be reduced if it did contain complete lists of all stories and books dealing with its given theme, because much of sf in its lowest strata, like all genre literatures, is derivative and occasionally downright stupid. We have tried to select the most important stories under each theme heading: important either for literary strength, or for the intrinsic interest of the concepts they contain, or because they register changes in popular thought as represented in popular literature at different periods. The last point will make this volume, we hope, especially interesting to social historians and those who are concerned to trace the variation in and evolution of the prejudices and aspirations of the Western world.

3. Films. There are 286 film entries (listed in the entry on Cinema). This area of the book is not fully comprehensive, partly because it is difficult to establish where horror or fantasy stops and sf begins, and more importantly because having an entry on every B-grade monster movie ever made would have been deeply depressing, and would have taken space needed for more important matters. The selection was made first by giving entries to the generally agreed classics; second by following the careers of certain film-makers; third by choosing representative films from all the various sub-types of sf cinema. This book contains the longest and most comprehensive, fully annotated sf filmography in existence. There are longer indexes, including a remarkably fine one by Walt Lee, but these do not give any sort of detailed commentary.

4. Magazines. We give entries to academic critical magazines such as *Extrapolation*, *Foundation* and *Science-Fiction Studies*, to the most important of the magazines that printed sf before the advent of genre sf magazines in 1926, from the *Strand Magazine* to the *Blue Book Magazine* (see the entries on Magazines and Pulp Magazines for a full list), and finally to all professional sf magazines published in English, together with all fantasy magazines that regularly printed stories by sf authors. This is a comprehensive listing with full publishing details. (See the entry on SF Magazines for a list of all the sf magazines that receive entries.) We do not give entries to straight horror or supernatural story magazines. Outside the magazine indexes, so full a treatment of sf magazines is nowhere available, and the indexes themselves do not include any sort of critical and descriptive comment. We have even given entries to such bizarre peripheral titles as *Dusty Ayres and His Battle Birds* and *Sheena, Queen of the Jungle*. 207 fiction magazines receive entries.

5. Illustrators. There are approximately 60 entries on sf illustrators, ranging from the 19th-century Albert Robida to such recent arrivals as Vincent Di Fate. This is by a long way the most comprehensive study of sf illustrators in a published book, though it is not complete: we had to make a selection from several hundreds. We based our selection on historical importance and general popularity as manifested in magazine letter columns, awards and portfolio sales, and in some cases on our own

intuitive taste, whether for good or ill. We have included comics and book-cover illustrators as well as genre sf magazine illustrators, but we decided not to include those "serious" or gallery artists who occasionally incorporate items of sf iconography, such as Eduardo Paolozzi.

6. Editors. We have given entries to all editors of important magazines and anthologies.

7. Critics. Entries are given to all critics who have written books on sf, and to a large selection of those whose critical work is restricted to articles or pamphlets.

8. Film-makers. We have included about 20 entries on important directors, producers, special-effects designers and screenwriters closely associated with sf — more, if one counts such entries as those on Jerome Bixby and Richard Matheson, who would have received entries in any case on the basis of their work for sf in the written form. We decided not to include directors whose work is fundamentally horror with sf trimmings, such as Bert Gordon, or directors known for only one sf film, such as Fred McLeod Wilcox.

9. Publishers. It would have been absurd to give entries to every publisher who has ever published sf. We felt, however, that there was a strong case for giving entries to about 20 specialist sf publishers, including some of the small pioneering firms such as Arkham House and Gnome Press, even where they did not publish sf exclusively.

10. Pseudonyms. Information about pseudonyms is to be found under individual Author entries. The main entry for any author is under the name by which he is best known, hence Lewis Carroll rather than Charles Dodgson. (For full information about our usage with Pseudonym entries, and the kinds of cross-reference we use, see the entry for Pseudonyms.)

11. Series. There is no separate entry listing series. All relevant series are listed in the entries for individual authors. A useful feature is that when a series consists primarily of books but also of short stories, we also list the short stories belonging to the series. This is a peculiarly difficult area of research, in part because it is not always simple to define a series (they are not always coherently and unambiguously in serial form), and in part because it is not always possible to track down every short story.

12. Television programmes. We have given entries to the most important television series; the omissions are primarily peripheral fantasy series, and series designed for young children.

Occasionally individual dramas with sf connotations turn up on the television screen; some but not all of these made-for-TV films and plays have also been given entries, more especially those which subsequently attained theatrical release as films. There is also a theme entry, Television, which lists all the other 56 TV entries.

13. Original anthologies. Because of the importance of this publishing phenomenon, which has extensively supplanted the sf magazines as a market for sf writers who work in the short-story form, we have given entries to 10 of the most important original anthology series, such as *Orbit* and *Universe*, though not to original anthologies which are single books only, and not part of a series. A theme entry, Anthologies, discusses this branch of sf publishing.

14. Comics. Here we have been highly selective. There is a general theme entry, Comic Strips and Comic Books, and there are individual entries for 12 of the most popular and influential sf comics. There are many hundreds of sf comic-book titles, but although we touch on this specialist field, we regard the trivia of comics publishing as being outside our brief.

15. Science fiction in various countries. We have given separate entries for each of the most important sf-producing areas (a phrase which sounds, though we do not mean it to, like something from a textbook of industrial geography). The entries are as follows: Australia; Benelux; Canada; Eastern Europe; France; Germany; Italy; Japan; Russia; Scandinavia; and Spain, Portugal and South America. It would have been redundant to give separate entries for the USA and the UK, since Anglo-American sf dominates the book.

16. Terminology. A theme entry, Terminology, lists 74 important items of specialist sf jargon; each item is also given a separate entry. Some of these entries do double service as theme entries, e.g. Entropy, Cybernetics and Robots.

17. Awards. All the most important English- and French-language sf awards, including some fan awards, receive entries, as follows: British Science Fiction Award; Ditmar; DUFF; Hugo; International Fantasy; James Blish; John W. Campbell; John W. Campbell Memorial; Jupiter; Nebula; Pilgrim; Prix Apollo; Prix Jules Verne; TAFF. We have not given entries for the Gandalf and British Fantasy awards, or any other award exclusively for fantasy.

18. Fanzines. Here we have been highly selective. All Hugo-winning fanzines receive individual

entries, as do the most serious and critical contemporary fanzines, along with a handful of others interesting for one reason or another. There are over 40 entries on fanzines and other magazines about sf. There is also a theme entry, Fanzines.

19. Miscellanea. We give entries to several items that concern sf enthusiasts, including Conventions, Fandom and Fan Language. There are entries on various sf groups, both fan and professional, such as N3F and SFWA. Several scientists whose work bears especially strongly on sf are given entries, including Freeman Dyson, Herman Kahn and Carl Sagan. We also give entries to such prominent popularizers of theories of Pseudo-Science as Immanuel Velikovsky and Erich von Däniken.

We hesitated for a while over whether or not to make all entries anonymous, but eventually decided to follow the example of those reference books which append to each entry the initials of its author. We do this to give credit where it is due, but also to apportion responsibility for those cases where the reader may feel that the content of the entry has gone beyond the factual into matters of opinion. This latter point is important; early on, we decided, in the interests of liveliness and readability, to permit some critical comment in the entries; a certain amount of criticism and historical "placing" is, anyway, implicit in all selection procedures. We soon discovered that, especially in the theme entries, it was impossible and probably undesirable to avoid all matters of opinion, particularly those regarding the relative importance of different writers. Within Author entries, some books necessarily receive more comment than others. We recognize that this facet of the Encyclopedia could become controversial, and therefore emphasize here that it is only peripherally a critical work. Opinion has been kept to a minimum, and in each case it is possible to identify, through the initials used, whose opinion it is. (See, for further details, the Checklist of contributors.) However, though every entry is signed individually, there is a very real sense in which this volume is a team effort. Few entries have not been scanned by at least four of the five editors named on the title page, and most incorporate suggestions from more than one source. Two signatures are given for the more fully collaborative entries, the first initials being those of the primary contributor.

This is, we hope, a book to be dipped into or read, and not merely a reference source for titles, dates or plot summaries; certainly it was so designed by us. While it is primarily an Encyclopedia, we hope it serves an additional function: not merely to tabulate facts, but to record them coherently and interestingly, bringing out their inter-relationships and their significance wherever possible. This work is not only an Encyclopedia of sf, but also a comprehensive history of and commentary on the genre.

Another urgent matter on our minds from the beginning was the potential cost of the volume. We naturally wanted to keep it down to a level where we could properly view this as a popular book for the layman and not just as a reference work for university and other libraries. In terms of cost per word (there are over 700,000 words of text) this is certainly, by a substantial margin, the cheapest sf reference book available. To help accomplish this, we have kept illustration subordinate to text, and have included no colour plates. None the less, the book is copiously illustrated with black and white plates, each one tied specifically to an item of text and with the intention of illuminating that item. We have been particularly generous with plates illustrating magazine covers, since the style of the cover is often of assistance in correctly and rapidly identifying magazines in this notoriously confusing field, confusing because so many magazines have similar or identical titles. We have naturally given an example of the work of each illustrator who receives an entry. Comics are comprehensively illustrated, and we have included stills from many of the films we discuss. In choosing magazine and book covers to use we have not spent a great deal of time in seeking out examples in mint condition. We wish to show sf as it appears to the average collector, including the occasional remainder stamp or tattered edge.

It is our hope to produce revised and updated editions of this Encyclopedia. It would be irrational to suppose that we have miraculously achieved a reference book devoid of error, and we are anxious to hear from any reader who can give us additional information, or correct any item which he has reason to think is wrong. All such letters may be addressed to the General Editor, c/o Roxby Press Ltd, 98 Clapham Common Northside, London SW4 9SG, England. Future editions will take account of books, magazines and films produced after our present closing date, which is generally between December 1977 and June 1978, according to the entry in question. We have been quite strict about not including items which have been announced for the future. A number of books, for example, have already been announced for later in 1978, and we are in possession of much of this information; but our experience is that last-minute changes of title or publication date can make nonsense of reference books which include projections of the near future.

Peter Nicholls and John Clute 26 June 1978

HOW TO USE THIS BOOK

The general principles on which this book was designed have already been outlined in the Introduction. The following points, grouped into six sub-sections, explain some of the details of our procedures.

ALPHABETICAL ORDER

(i) Two-part surnames are treated as if one word, thus De Camp appears before Delany, and Delany before De Vet.

(ii) Sf is treated as if spelled out as science fiction. Thus *SF Greats* appears before *Science Fiction Monthly*.

(iii) St when part of a surname is treated as if spelled Saint. Thus St John appears before Sarban.

(iv) Numbers are treated as if spelled out.

(v) Doctor and Dr are treated as separate words; Doctor appears first.

(vi) Scottish surnames beginning with Mac or Mc are treated as if all are spelled Mac.

(vii) Titles are treated as if all one word. Thus *Worlds of Tomorrow* appears before *World, The Flesh and the Devil, The*; Atterley, Joseph appears before *At the Earth's Core*; and *Amazing Stories* appears before *A. Merritt's Fantasy*.

In all other respects, the order is strictly alphabetical.

BIBLIOGRAPHICAL DATA IN AUTHOR, CRITIC AND EDITOR ENTRIES

Within Author entries we have been necessarily selective. We list all published novels and collections relevant to sf or fantasy, and also anthologies. We do not list other books, though we may refer to them. We refer also to the most interesting short stories, but it is impossible in the space to list all short stories by a given writer. We do not list the contents of collections and anthologies, although we do note variations in contents when a hardback and paperback edition of the same title, or an American and British edition of the same title, are not identical. In the case of foreign-language authors, we list all sf titles which have been translated into English, but do not necessarily list all untranslated titles, though in many cases we have done so. Also with foreign-language authors we usually give original publication date and original title; however, in cases where a transliteration from the Cyrillic or some other alphabet would be necessary, we have not always given the foreign-language title. We do not usually give the name of a book's translator, though we have done so on some occasions because we feel that translators are generally unfairly neglected.

As explained in the Introduction, pure fantasy writers are not normally represented in this volume. However, we have worked on the principle that once a writer is given an entry, then all his fantasy work should be included as well as his pure sf, though very often the fantasy titles are relegated to the "other works" section following the main entry.

We do not give foreign-language publishing information for British or American works; this volume is not the place to locate details of Isaac Asimov's publishing career in Japan, or Arthur C. Clarke's in Russia. Nor do we list the publishers, even of Anglo-American works.

We do give the following data: original book title; variant titles; date of original magazine publication (normally only where it precedes book publication by three or more years); place of original magazine publication; date of first English-language edition; date of any revised, expanded or abridged subsequent edition. We usually give the original magazine title of a story, where this differs from subsequent book titles.

Book titles and film titles are given in italics. Short-story titles and the titles of individual episodes of TV series are given within inverted commas. The first bold-face date (e.g. **1066**) following a book title is its date of first book publication; there will be two bold-face dates, usually, for books originally published in a foreign language, the first being date of original publication and the second date of English translation. Any additional bold-face dates refer to substantially modified texts which could be regarded as new books. If a date, not in bold-face type, precedes the date of first book publication, it is the date of the original magazine publication; the magazine in question will be named in Author entries though not necessarily in Theme entries, where bibliographical data are more condensed.

We give fewer data with short stories: a date of original publication is given, but not usually the name of the magazine or anthology it was published in. We also regret the impossibility of mentioning collections or anthologies in which the stories we cite can be located, but this would have led to an unacceptable expansion of the book.

When a book has since been republished under a variant title we use the abbreviation vt, and if the vt appears in a different country from the original country of publication, this information is given also; because it is not always possible to ascertain whether in a given year a British or American edition is a first, we have normally given as the first edition title the one which originally appeared in the author's own country.

Revisions noted are often the result of rewriting, but just as commonly a revision will in actuality be a restoration of an original text which was cut or bowdlerized by its original publisher.

We have borrowed an important and useful item of terminology from A.E. van Vogt: "fix-up". A fix-up is a book made up of stories originally published separately, but altered to fit together, often with the addition of new cementing material; fix-ups are common in sf; they are usually marketed as novels; we have had to exercise our judgement in some cases as to whether a book should be described as a fix-up or a collection of linked stories; this depends on how episodic the final production is. The entry on Van Vogt gives further information about the term.

Author, Editor and Critic entries contain full information about pseudonyms and series. They also contain a commentary on the most important books and stories, often with some plot synopsis. Biographical data are kept to a minimum. Where a question mark appears in the position in which a date of death might be expected we have no positive knowledge of death and are merely making an assumption of actuarial probability in cases where the writer was born in the 19th century. We seldom give data on marriage or children. We do, however, commonly give data on education and profession.

CROSS-REFERENCES
Any item printed in SMALL CAPITALS is a cross-reference, under which further information can be found. We have generally restricted cross-reference only to such cases — we do not, for example, print the word robot as ROBOT every time it appears, but only where relevant additional material can be found in the Robot entry. Similarly, though there is an entry for every sf magazine, we have not necessarily capitalized all references to magazine titles. In fact, our usage with cross-references is not rigidly consistent, but if it errs, it errs on the side of generosity. Because Theme entries could often appear under any of several titles (for example, Under The Sea could just as well have been called Oceans), there is ample cross-referencing of theme titles; typical entries read **RELATIVITY** *See* FASTER THAN LIGHT, and **SATURN** *See* OUTER PLANETS. Pseudonyms are also cross-referenced, according to the principles laid out in the Pseudonyms entry.

MAGAZINE ENTRIES
Publishing data which is more detailed than would be required by most readers is given at the end of Magazine entries under the rubric **Collectors .should note**. Months are abbreviated (e.g. Oct. for October). All variant magazine titles have been cross-referenced; this is a very complicated business with some magazines, but we have tried to be fully comprehensive here. The key entry is usually that under which the magazine was best known and/or published for the longest period. For example one cross-reference entry reads in full: **WORLDS OF IF SCIENCE FICTION** *See* IF.

OTHER WORKS
This rubric appears after many Author entries. Following it are listed all those books by a given author, related to sf and fantasy, which have not already been discussed in the main body of the entry. "Other works" is, in effect, an abbreviation for "other works directly related to the fields of sf and fantasy". It is not a full list of *all* other works by a given author. Because this is primarily an Encyclopedia of sf, and only incidentally one of fantasy, it occasionally happens that most of the books listed under "other works" are fantasies, while those discussed in the main entry are more directly sf. But "other works" also includes routine space operas and all sorts of comparatively minor works. We have generally attempted to discuss all major works in the main body of an entry, but in the cases of prolific authors this has not normally been possible. Titles received just before going to press normally appear under the heading of "other works" also. It would be dangerous to suppose that an appearance of a book under this head represented any sort of considered critical judgement relating to relative unimportance.

THEME ENTRIES
There are no special problems here, except that the bibliographical data are less ample than in Author entries. For full bibliographical data, readers are advised to double-check with the Author entry.

CHECKLIST OF CONTRIBUTORS

It will be possible to identify each contributor from his initials, as tabulated against his full name below. Contributors whose names are capitalized are given entries in their own right. Data on other contributors appear below the list.

Mark ADLARD	MA
Brian W. ALDISS	BWA
John BROSNAN	JB
John CLUTE	JC
Luk DE VOS	LdeV
Thomas M. DISCH	TMD
Malcolm J. EDWARDS	MJE
John Eggeling	JE
Herbert FRANKE	HF
H. Bruce FRANKLIN	HBF
John Foyster	JF
Jon Gustafson	JG
Jim HARMON	JH
John-Henri HOLMBERG	J-HH
Maxim JAKUBOWSKI	MJ
David KETTERER	DK
Colin Lester	CL
Robert Louit	RL
David I. MASSON	DIM
Alan Myers	AM
Peter NICHOLLS	PN
Frank H. Parnell	FHP
A.B. Perkins	ABP
David Pringle	DP
Peter Roberts	PR
Franz ROTTENSTEINER	FR
John Scarborough	JSc
Takumi Shibano	TSh
Tom Shippey	TS
John SLADEK	JS
Brian STABLEFORD	BS
Tony Sudbery	TSu
Darko SUVIN	DS
Susan Wood	SW

John Eggeling is proprietor of Phantasmagoria, an sf and fantasy antiquarian bookshop, and an expert in the field of early sf book publishing. John Foyster is a well-known Australian sf critic. Jon Gustafson is an active sf fan in Washington State, USA, and columnist for *Science Fiction Review*, who is currently preparing a book on sf illustrators. Colin Lester is currently editing *The International Science Fiction Yearbook* for Pierrot Publishing. Robert Louit is editor of the *SF Dimensions* imprint published by Calmann-Lévy in Paris, a translator of J.G. Ballard and others into French, and a regular sf critic for *Magazine Littéraire*. Alan Myers is a schoolmaster teaching Russian and Humanities, translator of several Russian works into English, and author of an as yet unpublished "Annotated Bibliography of Russian SF 1917–76", a copy of which rests in the Senate House Library of the University of London. Frank H. Parnell is a collector of and authority on sf and fantasy magazines. A.B. Perkins has been preparing articles on British sf of the 1950s, especially on radio and in boys' papers, for publication in a forthcoming book. David Pringle is with James Goddard co-editor of *J.G. Ballard: the First Twenty Years*, a well known critic in *Foundation*, and research assistant at the Science Fiction Foundation. Peter Roberts is a celebrated British fanzine editor, who won the TAFF award in 1977, and a graduate in English literature. John Scarborough is a professor at the University of Kentucky, where he teaches medical history and takes some classes in sf. Takumi Shibano is an English-speaking Japanese businessman, editor and publisher of the semi-professional fanzine *Uchujin*, the oldest in Japan, founded in 1957. Tom Shippey lectures in Anglo-Saxon studies at the University of Oxford, is an sf critic, and sets the sf questions for the British TV quiz show *Mastermind*. Tony Sudbery is a lecturer in the Department of Mathematics at the University of York, whose sf criticism regularly appeared in the fanzine *Speculation*. Susan Wood is an associate professor of Canadian literature at the University of British Columbia, well known for her fan writing, for which she has been awarded one and two half Hugos, the first with her then husband Mike Glicksohn in 1973 for their fanzine *Energumen*, the second as best fan writer in 1974, and the third as best fan writer in 1977 in a tie with Richard E. Geis.

ACKNOWLEDGEMENTS

We must first thank the Science Fiction Foundation of North East London Polytechnic, without whose reference library this book could not have been written. We thank them also for allowing their then administrator, the general editor of this volume, some time for conducting independent research during a remarkably heavy academic year. We wish to thank all the contributors, and especially the two contributing editors, Malcolm Edwards and Brian Stableford, whose influence on this book has gone far beyond the many entries they wrote themselves. Their advice and editorial assistance has been invaluable, as has been that of the technical editor, Carolyn Eardley, whose clear eye for inconsistencies of usage has caused us all to quail on many occasions. She wishes to firmly dissociate herself from some of the split infinitives which we have felt compelled occasionally to use for the sake of clarity. We wish to thank all the authors and critics who so generously gave of their time to fill out the detailed questionnaire which we circulated as widely as we could — not widely enough, alas, since the detective work involved in finding the addresses of all living writers was beyond us in the time available. Among others who gave us general information and help were The Children's Literature Research Collections (109 Walter Library, University Libraries, University of Minnesota, Minneapolis, Minnesota 5455), Hilary Bailey, Edgar Belka, Samuel R. Delany, John Godrich, Leslie Halliwell, Philip Harbottle, Leroy Kettle, Michael Moorcock, Richard Prudames, Robert Silverberg, and Doris Mehegan and David Aylward of the Spaced Out Library (40 St George Street, Toronto M5S 2E4, Canada). Our primary sources of pictorial material were the collections of the British Film Institute, the BBC, John Clute, Malcolm Edwards, John Eggeling, Walter Gillings, the Kobal collection, the Mansell Collection, the National Portrait Gallery, Peter Nicholls and the Science Fiction Foundation.

The most important reference books used by us, occasionally as a source and more often as a check on information, were: *Anatomy of Wonder: Science Fiction* (**1976**) ed. Neil Barron; *The Checklist of Fantastic Literature* (**1948**) ed. Everett F. Bleiler; *Voices Prophesying War: 1763–1984* (**1966**) by I.F. Clarke; *Index to the Weird Fiction Magazines* (**1962**) by T.G.L. Cockcroft; *Index to Science Fiction Anthologies and Collections* (**1978**) by William Contento; *The Checklist of Fantastic Literature in Paperbound Books* (**1965**) compiled by Bradford M. Day; *The Complete Checklist of Science-Fiction Magazines* (**1961**) ed. Bradford M. Day; *The Supplemental Checklist of Fantastic Literature* (**1963**) ed. Bradford M. Day; *Index to the Science Fiction Magazines 1926–1950* (**1952**) compiled by Donald B. Day; *Science Fiction Book Review Index, 1923–1973* (**1975**) ed. H.W. Hall; *Reference Guide to Fantastic Films* in three vols. (**1972, 1973, 1974**) compiled by Walt Lee; *Voyages in Space* (**1975**) by George Locke; *Sciencefiction and Fantasy Pseudonyms* (**1976**) compiled by Barry McGhan; *The Index of Science Fiction Magazines 1951–1965* (**1968**) compiled by Norm Metcalf; *Explorers of the Infinite* (**1963**) by Sam Moskowitz; *Seekers of Tomorrow* (**1966**) by Sam Moskowitz; *Under the Moons of Mars: A History and Anthology of "The Scientific Romance" In the Munsey Magazines, 1912–1920* (**1970**) ed. Sam Moskowitz; *Index to the Science Fiction Magazines 1966–1970* (**1971**) and its sequel *The N.E.S.F.A. Index: Science Fiction Magazines and Original Anthologies 1971–1972* (**1973**), both ed. New England Science Fiction Association; *Stella Nova: The Contemporary Science Fiction Authors* (**1970**) ed. anonymously by R. Reginald; *Science Fiction Story Index 1950–1968* (**1971**) by Frederick Siemon; *Science Fiction Movies* (**1976**) by Philip Strick; *Russian Science Fiction 1956–1974: A Bibliography* (**1976**) by Darko Suvin; *The Encyclopedia of Science Fiction and Fantasy Through 1968: Volume 1: Who's Who, A-L* (**1974**) and *Volume 2: Who's Who M-Z* (**1978**) compiled by Donald H. Tuck; *Encyclopédie de l'utopie des voyages extraordinaires et de la science fiction* (**1972**) by Pierre Versins. We used to a lesser extent a great many sources too numerous to list here, though they all appear in various entries in this volume. Several fanzines were especially useful, notably *Delap's F & SF Review*; *Locus*; *Luna Monthly*; *Science Fiction Review* and *Vector*. We also used Gerald Bishop's British compilations *Science Fiction Books Published in Britain* brought out annually, and covering the years 1970–74, and Joanne Burger's American compilations *SF Published in 1968* through to *SF Published in 76*. Last, but by no means least, we were much helped by the scholarly research carried out by the contributors to the three academic journals: *Extrapolation* ed. Thomas Clareson; *Foundation: The Review of Science Fiction* ed. Peter Nicholls and *Science-Fiction Studies* ed. R.D. Mullen and Darko Suvin. We end by issuing the conventional but in this case heartfelt apology and thanks to all those others who helped, whether knowingly or not, and have not appeared on the above list.

Peter Nicholls and John Clute 26 June 1978.

CHECKLIST OF THEMES

Absurdist SF
Adam and Eve
Aliens
Alternate Worlds
Androids
Anonymous SF
  Authors
Anthologies
Anthropology
Anti-Intellectualism
Arts
Asteroids
Astronomy
Atlantis
Automation
Bibliographies and
  Indexes
Biology
Black Holes
Boys' Papers
Children in SF
Children's SF
Cinema
Cities
Clichés
Clones
Colonization of Other
  Worlds
Comic Strips and
  Comic Books
Communications
Computers
Conceptual
  Breakthrough
Conventions
Cosmology
Crime and Punishment
Critical and Historical
  Works about SF
Cryonics
Cybernetics
Cyborgs
Definitions of SF
Devolution
Dianetics
Dime Novels and
  Juvenile Series
Disaster
Discovery and Invention
Dystopias
Ecology
Economics
End of the World
Entropy
Eschatology

ESP
Evolution
Fandom
Fan Language
Fantastic Voyages
Fantasy
Fanzines
Far Future
Faster Than Light
Flying Saucers
Force Field
Fourth Dimension (and
  Others)
Futurology
Galactic Empires
Games and Sports
General Semantics
Generation Starships
Genetic Engineering
Gods and Demons
Golden Age of SF
Gothic SF
Gravity
Great and Small
Hardcore SF
Heroes
Heroic Fantasy
History in SF
History of SF
Hive-Minds
Holocaust and After
Humour
Iconoclasm
Illustration
Imaginary Science
Immortality
Intelligence
Invasion
Invisibility
Islands
Jupiter
Leisure
Life on Other Worlds
Linguistics
Living Worlds
Lost Worlds
Machines
Magazines
Magic
Mainstream Writers
  of SF
Mars
Mathematics
Matter Transmission
Media Landscape

Medicine
Mercury
Messiahs
Metaphysics
Money
Monsters
The Moon
Music and Opera
Mutants
Mythology
Near Future
New Wave
Nuclear Power
Origin of Man
Outer Planets
Optimism and
  Pessimism
Overpopulation
Pantropy
Parallel Worlds
Paranoia and
  Schizophrenia
Parasitism and
  Symbiosis
Pastoral
Perception
Physics
Politics
Pollution
Prediction
Proto SF
Pseudo-Science
Psi Powers
Psychology
Power Sources
Publishing
Pulp Magazines
Radio
Reincarnation
Religion
Robots
Rockets
Satire
Sex
SF in the Classroom
SF Magazines
SF Overtaken by
  Events
Scientific Errors
Scientists
Social Darwinism
Sociology
Space Opera
Space Flight
Spaceships

Stars
The Sun
Superman
Supernatural Creatures
Suspended Animation
Sword and Sorcery
Taboos
Technology
Television
Terminology
Terraforming
Theatre
Time Paradoxes
Time Travel
Transportation
Under The Sea
Utopias
Venus
Villains
War
Weapons
Weather Control
Women

CHECKLIST OF ABBREVIATIONS

Because a proliferation of technical abbreviations often makes reference books difficult to follow, we have kept them down to a minimum, even at some expense of space. The only abbreviations which may not be immediately self-evident are as follows:

AMZ	*Amazing Stories*
anth.	anthology
ASF	*Astounding Science-Fiction/Analog*
B/w	black and white
coll.	collection of short stories or novels by the same author in one volume
ed.	edited by

exp.	expanded
fix-up	for explanation, see "How to use this book"
FSF	*The Magazine of Fantasy and Science Fiction*
Gal.	*Galaxy Science Fiction*
NW	*New Worlds*
rev.	revised
sf	science fiction
trans.	translation or translated by
TWS	*Thrilling Wonder Stories*
var. mags	published in various magazines
vt	variant title

PICTURE CREDITS

AANDAHL, VANCE (1944–). American writer, author of 13 sf stories, nearly all in *FSF* (1960–69), mostly very short, and many written while he was studying English at the University of Colorado. His first story was published when he was 16. They were well received for their wry ingenuity, and several have been anthologized, but no collection has been published.   [JC/PN]

ABBOTT, EDWIN A. (1838–1926). English clergyman, academic and writer, whose most noted work, published originally as by A Square, is *Flatland: A Romance of Many Dimensions* (**1884**). Narrated by Mr Square, the novel falls into two parts; the first is a highly entertaining description of Flatland, a two-dimensional world, in which inhabitants' shapes establish their (planar) hierarchical status. In the second part, Mr Square travels into other dimensions in a dream, first visiting Lineland, whose inhabitants are unable to conceive of a two-dimensional universe; he is in turn visited by a three-dimensional man named Sphere, whom he cleverly persuades to believe in four-dimensional worlds as well. *Flatland* is a study in MATHEMATICS and PERCEPTION, and has stayed popular since its first publication.   [JC]
See also: FOURTH DIMENSION (AND OTHERS).

ABÉ, KOBO (1924–). Japanese novelist, active since 1948, several of whose later novels have been translated into English. He has a medical degree. He is known mainly for his work outside the sf field, e.g. *The Woman in the Dunes* (**1960**; trans. **1964**). His work has been deeply influenced by Western models from Kafka to Beckett, and the existential extremities to which he subjects his alienated protagonists allow of a dubious sf interpretation of novels like *The Ruined Map* (trans. **1969**). However, *Inter Ice Age 4* (**1959**; trans. **1970**) is undoubtedly sf. It is a complex story set in a near-future Japan threatened by the melting of the polar icecaps. The protagonist, Professor Katsumi, has been in charge of developing a computer/information system capable of predicting human behaviour. Ultimately, and fatally, it predicts his compulsive refusal to go along with his associates and his government in their creation of biologically mutated children, adapted for life in the rising seas. Most of the novel, narrated by the professor, deals with a philosophical confrontation between his deeply alienated refusal of the future and the computer's knowing representations of that refusal and the alternatives to it. The resulting psychodramas include a mysterious murder and the enlistment of his unborn child into the ranks of the mutated water-breathers. A later novel, *The Box Man* (**1973**; trans. **1974**), has some borderline sf elements; its protagonist walks about and lives in a large cardboard carton, along with many other Tokyo residents who have refused a life of "normalcy". All translations into English noted above are by E. Dale Saunders.   [JC]
Other works: *The Face of Another* (**1964**; trans. **1966**).
See also: DISASTER; GENETIC ENGINEERING; PSYCHOLOGY; UNDER THE SEA.

ABEL, R(ICHARD) COX (?–). British designer and technical journalist, who once worked in aeronautical engineering with Nevil Norway (Nevil SHUTE); co-author with Charles BARREN of an sf novel, *Trivana 1* (**1966**), notable for its description of a space jet that eats hydrogen atoms. An overpopulated Earth's establishment of a Venus colony is described in awkward style.   [JC]

ABERNATHY, ROBERT (1924–). American writer. His first published story was "Heritage" (1942 *ASF*). His stories — about 40 in all — continued to appear regularly in the sf magazines until 1956. During the 1940s his most consistent market was PLANET STORIES, for which he wrote such stories as "Peril of the Blue World" (1942), "Saboteur of Space" (1944) and "The Dead-Star Rover" (1949). His later work appeared primarily in THE MAGAZINE OF FANTASY AND SCIENCE FICTION, although his two best-known stories — "Pyramid" (1954) and "Junior" (1956) — were published in *ASF* and *Gal.* respectively. RA was a reliable, respectable short-story writer who never managed the transition from magazine to book publication, although several of his stories were anthologized (including best-of-the-year anthologies) in the 1950s. A linguist, he is now a professor at the University of Colorado. He has not contributed to the sf field for over 20 years, save for translating articles by Stanislaw LEM for SCIENCE-FICTION STUDIES.   [MJE]
See also: CITIES.

ABLEMAN, PAUL (1927–). British novelist. Known mainly for his work outside the sf field, e.g. *I Hear Voices* (**1958**). His novel, *The Twilight of the Vilp* (**1969**), is not so much sf proper as an informed and sophisticated playing with the conventions of the genre in a fabulation about the author of a work and his relation to its components. The Vilp are a galaxy-spanning race, but cannot be taken literally.   [JC]
See also: THEATRE.

ABOUT, EDMOND (1828–85). French writer of much fiction, some of it sf, notably *L'homme a l'oreille cassée* (**1861**; trans. as *The Man with the Broken Ear* **1867**), in which a figure modelled on Louis Napoleon awakens after a 46-year sleep, and causes some havoc.   [JC]
See also: MONEY.

ABRAMOV, ALEXANDER and **SERGEI** Russian sf writers, whose novel *Horsemen from Nowhere* was published in English translation, in Moscow (**1969**). One of their short stories appears in the anthology *Vortex* (anth. **1970**) ed. C.G. Bearne. A later novel, also published in English translation from Moscow, is *Journey Across Three Worlds* (**1973**). [PN]

ABSURDIST SF The word "absurdist" became fashionable as a literary term after its consistent use by the French novelist and essayist Albert Camus (1913–60), to describe fictions set in a world where we seem at the mercy of an incomprehensible system, where our expectations of rational coherence, fair play and justice, whether from God or from Man, are often disappointed. It is often used with reference to drama, "Theatre of the Absurd" being a term which embraces the works of Ionesco, Beckett, Alfred JARRY, Harold Pinter and many others.

The worlds of absurdist writers often owe much to the 19th-century tradition of the Symbolists and the 20th-century tradition of the Surrealists. They are normally unreal, in the sense that nothing like them exists in practice on Earth, but the states of mind for which they are usually metaphors are often very real indeed. Absurdist worlds tend to be outward manifestations of what J.G. BALLARD has termed INNER SPACE.

Absurdist literature (which is older by far than the common use of the term) must necessarily overlap in many places with sf, since both create imaginary worlds, and both are given to metaphor. The difference is usually that, where genre sf stresses a realism of presentation, and presents its future events as if they take place in a world that could actually come about, absurdist sf stresses the metaphorical nature of the ambience. Hence works of absurdist sf often read like myths or allegories. None the less, much absurdist sf makes use of sf tropes and images, including many of the FABULATIONS of such writers as John BARTH, Donald BARTHELME, Adolfo BIOY CASARES, Richard BRAUTIGAN, Jorge Luis BORGES, Christine BROOKE-ROSE, Peter C. BROWN, William BURROUGHS and Dino BUZZATI, (to restrict ourselves to one, admittedly rich, letter of the alphabet).

Their writings, discussed in detail elsewhere in this volume, indubitably make use of many sf themes but, because these themes are not being put to conventional sf use, there is room for much argument among readers over whether or not the stories which contain them can properly be accounted sf. This Encyclopedia takes the broad view, and includes such works as genuine sf; the alternative would have been to restrict ourselves, rather austerely and perhaps insipidly, to genre sf.

In any case, genre sf itself is by no means free of absurdist influences. Perhaps the strongest single absurdist influence on the field has been the works of Franz KAFKA, but Kafka himself belonged to a tradition which goes back at least as far as Fyodor DOSTOYEVSKY, and probably beyond him to such writers as François RABELAIS and Jonathan SWIFT. Kafka's claustrophobic, allegorical quests are reflected either directly or indirectly in the works of such genre writers as different as Barrington J. BAYLEY, Arthur Byron COVER, Sonya DORMAN, Barry MALZBERG, Josephine SAXTON, Robert SHECKLEY, Ian WALLACE and Jack VANCE. Absurdist sf regularly takes the quest form outside genre sf too, as in Angela CARTER's *The Infernal Desire Machines of Doctor Hoffman* (1972; vt *The War of Dreams* USA), *V* (1963), *Gravity's Rainbow* (1973) by Thomas PYNCHON and *Grimus* (1975) by Salman RUSHDIE.

While most absurdist writers have come into sf only, as it were, on day trips from the MAINSTREAM, the past 15 years

J.G. Ballard is a prominent writer of ABSURDIST SF. Jonathan Cape 1976. Cover by Bill Botten.

have seen several sf writers, originally nurtured within the genre, moving outward from the field as their sf imagery becomes more and more attuned to absurdist themes. The most celebrated example is that of Kurt VONNEGUT Jr, but much the same could be said of J.G. Ballard (who was directly influenced by Surrealism), Michael MOORCOCK and Harlan ELLISON. The sf theme of ENTROPY (*see also* DEVOLUTION) is prominent in the works of these writers, as it is in that of Brian W. ALDISS, whose most clearly

absurdist works are *Report On Probability A* (1968), *Barefoot in the Head* (fix-up 1969) and *Brothers of the Head* (1977), and in that of Philip K. DICK, notably in *Martian Time-Slip* (1963) and *Ubik* (1969). Entropy is indeed a kind of scientific metaphor for the traditional absurdist themes of isolation, alienation, decay and death. Most of the above writers belong to the so-called NEW WAVE, and it is within this inchoate movement of the past decade that absurdist sf has most commonly been written, although within the genre it goes at least as far back as *What Mad Universe* (1949) by Fredric BROWN. Other new-wave writers who commonly write absurdist fabulations are Ed BRYANT, David R. BUNCH, Thomas M. DISCH, M. John HARRISON, Felix GOTSCHALK, Langdon JONES, James SALLIS, John SLADEK, Norman SPINRAD, James TIPTREE Jr, Gene WOLFE and Pamela ZOLINE.

Aside from entropy, other sf tropes regularly found in absurdist stories are TIME TRAVEL, appearance and reality (*see* PERCEPTION), ANDROIDS and *Doppelgängers*, GENETIC ENGINEERING and the CITY of the future. ALTERNATE WORLDS, too, are important. Michael Moorcock has made good use of the plastic reality of his "multiverse", along with time travel, in his two absurdist series, "Jerry Cornelius" and "The Dancers at the End of Time".

DEFINITIONS of sf always falter at its periphery. The dividing line between sf and realism, or sf and fantasy (at opposite ends of its spectrum) are difficult enough to locate. Between sf and absurdist fabulation it is barely possible to draw a line at all, as the critic Robert SCHOLES has several times pointed out.

Other writers whose work is relevant to absurdist themes and techniques, and who receive entries in this volume, are: Kobo ABÉ, Chester ANDERSON, Benjamin APPEL, Italo CALVINO, Karel ČAPEK, Robert COOVER, Samuel DELANY, Lawrence DURRELL, Philip José FARMER, William GOLDING, Olof JOHANNESSON, M.K. JOSEPH, Anna KAVAN, Jerzy KOSINSKY, J.M.G. LE CLÉZIO, Stanislaw LEM, Vladimir MAYAKOVSKY, David MELTZER, Brian MOORE, Flann O'BRIEN, Michael PERKINS, Doris PISERCHIA, Herbert READ, Cordwainer SMITH, Hank STINE, Boris VIAN, Gore VIDAL, VILLIERS DE L'ISLE ADAM, Rex WARNER, Colin WILSON and Bernard WOLFE. This list, though long, is by no means comprehensive.

To labour the obvious a moment: absurdist writers need above all to have a strong sense of the absurd; they are usually ironists. For this reason, despite the darkness of many of their visions, they are often amusing, if unsettling, to read. [PN]

ACE BOOKS American paperback publishing company founded by pulp magazine publisher A.A. Wyn in 1953.

Under editor Donald A. WOLLHEIM Ace published a high proportion of sf, much of it in the "Ace Double" format of two titles bound together back to back. The series included the early novels of many writers who became famous, such as John BRUNNER, Samuel R. DELANY, Philip K. DICK, Ursula K. LE GUIN, Roger ZELAZNY and Robert SILVERBERG. Terry CARR became an editor in 1964 and later began the "Ace Science Fiction Specials" series, which received considerable praise. Carr left the company in 1971, followed by Wollheim, who began his own imprint, DAW BOOKS, in 1972. [MJE]

ACKERMAN, FORREST J. (1916–). American editor, agent and enthusiast. FJA was a reader of the sf magazines from their inception, and has been an active sf fan since the early 1930s. He wrote a number of stories and articles for the sf magazines, and used, occasionally, elaborate pseudonyms: Dr. Acula, Jacques De Forest Erman, Alden Lorraine, Hubert George Wells (cheekily) and Weaver Wright. He began the Fantasy Foundation, dedicated to preserving all kinds of sf and fantasy material for posterity. This has now developed into a museum, filling a 17-room house in Hollywood. He has been editor of the magazine *Famous Monsters of Filmland* from its first issue in 1958. He has also edited the American PERRY RHODAN series, as well as three sf anthologies: *The Frankenscience Monster* (anth. 1969), *Science Fiction Worlds of Forrest J. Ackerman and Friends* (anth. 1969) and *Best Science Fiction for 1973* (anth. 1973). Notorious for his punning and use of simplified words, he is said to have introduced the term "sci-fi". He is agent for a number of writers, notably A.E. VAN VOGT. FJA is known, not without justice, as the world's number one sf fan. [MJE]

ACULA, DR. *See* Forrest J. ACKERMAN.

ADAM AND EVE Michael MOORCOCK has identified a category of sf stories which he labelled "Shaggy God stories". Such stories provide simple-minded science-fictional frameworks for biblical myths, and they account for a large fraction of the unsolicited material submitted to sf magazines. One of the most frequently written is the one in which survivors of a space disaster land on a virgin world and reveal (in the final line) that their names are Adam and Eve. Understandably, these stories rarely see print, though A.E. VAN VOGT's "Ship of Darkness" (1947) was actually reprinted in *Fantastic* in 1961 as a "fantasy classic". Straightforward variants are Nelson BOND's "Another World Begins" (1942; vt "The Cunning of the Beast"), in which God is an ALIEN and Adam and Eve are experimental creatures which prove too clever for him; and Robert Arthur's "Evolution's End" (1941), in which an old world lurches to its conclusion and Aydem and Ayveh survive to start the whole thing over again. The only story of any real significance in this vein is Charles L. HARNESS's "The New Reality" (1950), which goes to some lengths to set up a framework in which a new universe can be created around its hero, his faithful girl-friend, and the arch-villain (Dr Luce). The idea continues to recur, however — one recent example being Julian Jay SAVARIN's Shaggy God trilogy *Lemmus* (1972-7), which begins with a character named Jael Adaamm leading the first expedition from Haven to Earth. Adam and Eve also crop up as themselves in a number of allegorical fantasies, notably the book of Genesis, George Bernard SHAW's *Back to Methuselah* (1921) and John Erskine's *Adam and Eve* (1927).

The names Adam and Eve — particularly the former — are frequently used with purely metaphorical significance. Adam is a natural name to give to the first robot or android, and thus we find Eando BINDER writing a biography of *Adam Link — Robot* (1939-42; fix-up 1965), and William C. ANDERSON chronicling the career of *Adam M-1* (1964). Adam Link was provided with an Eve Link, but what they did together remains a matter for speculation. A rather more subtle use of the metaphor is in the titles of two SUPERMAN novels, Noelle ROGER's *The New Adam* (1924; trans. 1926) and Stanley WEINBAUM's classic of the same title (1939). Alfred BESTER's last-man-alive story "Adam and No Eve" (1941) uses the name in an ironic vein. Not unnaturally, the metaphor also recurs fairly often in prehistoric romances, most notably in *Intimations of Eve* (1946) and *Adam and the Serpent* (1947) by Vardis FISHER, and in the final volume of George S. VIERECK and Paul ELDRIDGE's time-spanning trilogy *The Invincible Adam* (1932), where much is made of the matter of the lost "rib".

An interesting, transcendental variant of the Adam and Eve theme takes place in those stories in which a human becomes part of the COSMOLOGICAL process of creation — not so much the first man as the initial seed of the universe. The most celebrated early example takes place in the last lines of A.E. van Vogt's *The Weapon Shops of Isher* (1941-2; 1951). The hero is seesawing through time, but: "... the seesaw would end in the very remote past, with the release of the stupendous temporal energy he had been accumulating with each of those monstrous swings. He would not witness but he would aid in the formation of the planets." A similar though even larger idea is found in James BLISH's *The Triumph of Time* (1958; vt *A Clash of Cymbals* UK) and also in Charles Harness's *The Ring of Ritornel* (1968).

The Adam and Eve idea is rather tired by now, even as a metaphor, but it will no doubt continue to exert its peculiar fascination over the minds of would-be writers, especially now that Shaggy God stories have become popular alternatives to orthodoxy in the works of Immanuel VELIKOVSKY and Erich von DÄNIKEN. [BS]

See also: ANTHROPOLOGY; EVOLUTION; ORIGIN OF MAN; RELIGION.

ADAMS, HARRIET S. (?-?). Daughter of publisher Edward Stratemeyer who took over his publishing syndicate after his death in 1930. Under the house name Victor APPLETON she wrote the last in the first series of TOM SWIFT books, *Tom Swift and his Planet Stone* (1935). She successfully revived Tom Swift, or, to be more accurate, his son Tom Swift Jr, in a new series which began publication in 1954 (*see* TOM SWIFT *for details*). [PN]

ADAMS, JOHN (?-). English writer, possibly pseudonymous, whose sf novel is *When the Gods Came* (1960). [JC]

ADAMS, LOUIS J. A. *See* Joe L. HENSLEY and Alexei PANSHIN.

ADAMS, SAMUEL HOPKINS (1871-1958). American writer, prolific and popular author of novels and screenplays, including that of the film *It Happened One Night* (1934). He wrote an sf novel with Stewart Edward WHITE: *The Mystery* (1907), about ships lost at sea, with an sf explanation of their disappearance. Alone, he wrote *The Flying Death* (1908), in which Long Island, New York, is invaded by a pteranodon. [JC]
Other works: *The Sign at Six* (1912) with Stewart Edward White; *The World Goes Smash* (1938).

ADDEO, EDMOND G. (? -). American writer who collaborated on two sf novels with Richard M. GARVIN.

ADDISON, HUGH Pseudonym of English author and journalist Harry Collinson Owen (1882-1956), used for his future-WAR novel *The Battle Of London* (1923), one of several contemporary works envisaging a Communist revolution in Britain. It was given a slight twist by the inclusion of an advantageous German attack on London. [JE]

ADLARD, MARK Form of his name usually used, and always on his books, by English writer Peter Marcus Adlard (1932-). An arts graduate of Cambridge University, he was until his recent retirement a manager in the steel industry. His knowledge of managerial and industrial problems plays a prominent role in his sf "Tcity" trilogy: *Interface* (1971), *Volteface* (1972) and *Multiface* (1973). The series is set in a CITY of the NEAR FUTURE. By calling it Tcity, apart from conferring it with a kind of

regimented anonymity in the manner of ZAMIATIN, MA was probably making a pun on Tees-City. (He was raised in the industrial conurbation on the Tees, in the north east of England.) With a rich but sometimes sour irony, and a real if distanced sympathy for the problems and frustrations of both management and workers, MA plays a set of variations, often comic, on AUTOMATION, hierarchical systems, the MEDIA LANDSCAPE, revolution, the difficulties of coping with LEISURE, class distinction according to INTELLIGENCE, fantasies of SEX and the stultifying pressures of conformity. His books are ambitious in scope and deserve to be more widely known. [PN]

ADLER, ALLEN A. (1916-). American writer, mainly for films. He was co-author of the story used as a basis for the film FORBIDDEN PLANET. His *Mach 1, a Story of Planet Ionus* (1957; vt *Terror on Planet Ionus*) is a SPACE OPERA. [JC]

ADVENT: PUBLISHERS Chicago-based specialist publishing house, owned by sf fans, which publishes critical and bibliographical material. Their first book was Damon KNIGHT's *In Search of Wonder* (1956); notable later volumes included James BLISH's two collections of critical essays (under the pseudonym William Atheling Jr) and Donald H. TUCK's *The Encyclopedia of Science Fiction and Fantasy* (Vol.1 1974; Vol. 2 1978). [MJE]

AELITA Film (1924). Mezhrobpom/ Amkino. Directed by Yakov A. Protazanov. starring Nikolai M. Zeretelli, Igor Ilinski, J. Solnzeva and Konstantin Eggert. Screenplay by Fyodor Otzep and Alexei Faiko, based on the play by Alexei TOLSTOY. 6050 ft (cut to 2900). B/w.

A group of Soviet astronauts travel to Mars, where they find the mass of the people living under an oppressive regime, and spark off a revolution. *A* is a typically stylized silent film of the period, with Expressionistic sets by Alexandra Exter of the Tairov Theatre. The sf elements in the story are vigorous and witty, but occupy only a small part of the film, which is nevertheless one of the earliest examples of sf cinema. [JB]

A FOR ANDROMEDA Television serial (1961). A BBC TV production. Produced by Michael Hayes and Norman Jones, written by Fred HOYLE and John ELLIOT. Seven episodes, each 50 mins. B/w. The cast included Peter Halliday, John Nettleton, Esmond Knight, Patricia Kneale, Frank Windsor, John Barrett and Julie Christie.

A radio signal is transmitted from the Andromeda Galaxy which, when decoded, contains instructions for the building of a super-computer. The computer, when built by Earth scientists, in turn provides instructions on how to create a living being. The result is a

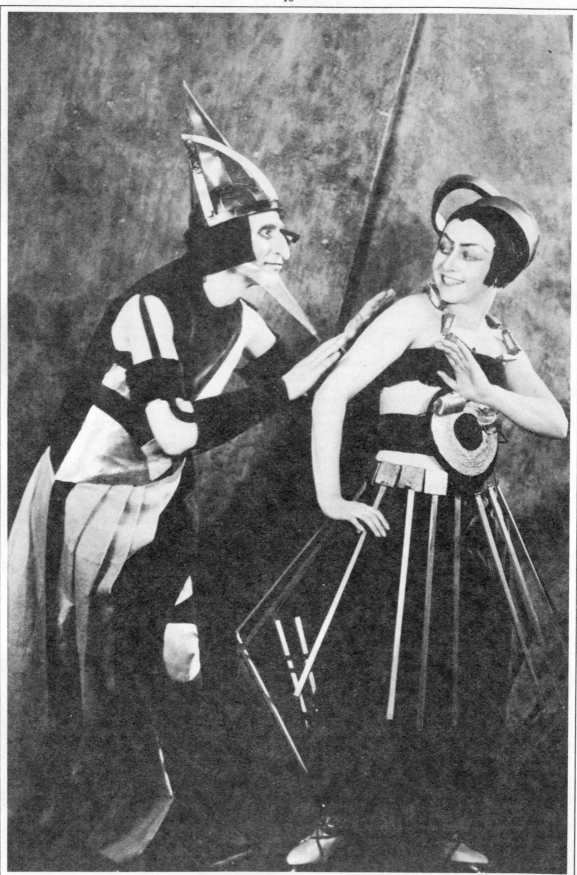

The Queen of Mars in AELITA. Note the expressionist style.

beautiful young girl, whose existence causes a great deal of controversy within the government and scientific establishments. She is eventually hounded to death before the question of whether she represents friend or foe can be resolved. The story was intelligently presented despite its absurdities. The serial brought Julie Christie, later to become a star, into the public eye for the first time. The novelization, by Hoyle and Elliot, is *A for Andromeda* (**1962**). [JB]

AGHILL, GORDON Pseudonym used by Robert SILVERBERG and Randall GARRETT in collaboration on two stories, 1956.

AINSBURY, RAY *See* A. Hyatt VERRILL.

AIRSHIPS *See* TRANSPORTATION.

AIR WONDER STORIES US BEDSHEET-size PULP magazine. 11 issues, Jul. 1929-May 1930, published by Stellar Publishing Corp., ed. Hugo GERNSBACK. This was Gernsback's prompt comeback, after his Experimenter Publishing Co., with which he founded AMAZING STORIES, had gone bankrupt and he lost control of the magazine. *AWS* announced itself in its first editorial as presenting "solely flying stories of the future, strictly along scientific-mechanical-technical lines ...". "To prevent gross scientific-aviation misinformation from reaching our readers", Gernsback hired three professors and one Air Corps Reserve major, whose names appeared prominently on the masthead. The stories were by foremost pulp writers of the day, including David KELLER, Harl VINCENT, Ed Earl REPP, Jack WILLIAMSON, Victor MacCLURE and Edmond HAMILTON. The cover designs (all issues) were by Frank R. PAUL, who had previously worked on *AMZ*. They contributed greatly to the early popularity of *AWS*. A sister magazine, SCIENCE WONDER STORIES, began one issue earlier, in Jun. 1929. In 1930 Gernsback merged them into WONDER STORIES, which he managed until 1936, after which it became THRILLING WONDER STORIES. [PN]

AKERS, ALAN BURT Pseudonym, revealed in 1978, after many rumours, to be that of Kenneth BULMER. ABA's books comprise an extended Edgar Rice BURROUGHS pastiche, though set in an interstellar venue. All 15 books (to date) feature Davy Prescott as hero, but are divided so far into four parts. The Delian Cycle comprises *Transit to Scorpio* (**1972**), *The Suns of Scorpio* (**1973**), *Warrior of Scorpio* (**1973**), *Swordships of Scorpio* (**1973**) and *Prince of Scorpio* (**1974**). The Havilfar Cycle comprises *Manhounds of Antares* (**1974**), *Arena of Antares* (**1974**), *Fliers of Antares* (**1975**), *Bladesmen of Antares* (**1975**), *Avenger of*

Antares (**1975**) and *Armada of Antares* (**1976**). The Krozair Cycle comprises *The Tides of Kregen* (**1976**), *Renegades of Kregen* (**1976**), and *Krozair of Kregen* (**1977**). The Vallian Cycle begins with *Secret Scorpio* (**1977**). [JC] **See also:** LIFE ON OTHER WORLDS; SWORD AND SORCERY.

ALBAN, ANTONY Writing name of Anthony A. Thompson (?–). In his novel *Catharsis Central* (**1968**) a grey, computerized, centrally controlled existence in a future city is disrupted by murder. His second book is *The Day of the Shield* (**1973**). [JC]

ALDANI, LINO *See* ITALY.

ALDISS, BRIAN W(ILSON) (1925–). English writer, anthologist and critic, educated at private schools, which he disliked. He served in the Royal Corps of Signals in Burma, was demobilized in 1948 and became an assistant in an Oxford bookshop. BWA began his writing career by contributing sketches about bookselling to *The Bookseller*. These were collected as *The Brightfount Diaries* (**1955**).

BWA's first sf story, "Criminal Record" (1954), appeared in *Science Fantasy*. There followed such notable tales as "Outside" (1955); "Not for an Age" (1955; a prizewinner in an *Observer* sf competition); "There is a Tide" (1956); and "Psyclops" (1956), all of which appeared in BWA's first sf volume, *Space, Time and Nathaniel* (coll. **1957**). The American collection *No Time Like Tomorrow* (**1959**) reprints six stories from the 14 in *Space, Time and Nathaniel*, and adds another six. These early stories were ingenious and lyrical, but dark in mood. BWA remained a

prolific writer of short stories for several years. "All the World's Tears" (1957), "Poor Little Warrior" (1958), "But Who Can Replace a Man?" (1958), "Old Hundredth" (1960) and "A Kind of Artistry" (1962) are among the most memorable stories collected in *The Canopy of Time* (coll. of very loosely linked stories **1959**; vt *Galaxies Like Grains of Sand* USA, with four stories omitted, one added and additional linking material between stories to emphasize their function as future HISTORY); *Airs of Earth* (coll. **1963**; vt *Starswarm* USA, with two stories omitted and two stories added); and *Best Science Fiction Stories of Brian W. Aldiss* (coll. **1965**; rev. 1971; vt *Who Can Replace a Man?* USA). BWA received a 1959 award at the World SF Convention as most promising new author, but his work was less well received in certain quarters where his emphasis on style and imagery, and his lack of an engineering mentality, were regarded with suspicion. The collections above overlap because the US editions have different selections.

His first novel, *Non-Stop* (**1958**; vt *Starship* USA), is a brilliant treatment of the GENERATION STARSHIP and also the theme of CONCEPTUAL BREAKTHROUGH; it has become accepted as a classic of the field. *Vanguard from Alpha* (**1959**; vt *Equator* UK) and *Bow Down to Nul* (**1960**; vt *The Interpreter* UK) are much less successful, but *The Primal Urge* (**1961**) is an amusing treatment of SEX as an sf theme. Always ebullient and permissive in his approach to sexual morality, BWA was one of the authors who changed the attitudes of sf editors and publishers in this area during the 1960s. *Hothouse* (fix-up **1962**; vt *The Long Afternoon of Earth* USA) won him a 1962 HUGO award for its original

Photo Mike Cullen.

AIR WONDER STORIES April 1930. Cover by Frank R. Paul.

appearance as a series of novelettes. It is one of his finest works. Set in the FAR FUTURE, when the Earth has ceased rotating, it involves the adventures of humanity's remnants who live in the branches of a giant, continent-spanning tree (*see* DEVOLUTION). Criticized for scientific implausibility by James BLISH and others, *Hothouse* nevertheless displays all BWA's linguistic, comic and inventive talents. It also illustrates BWA's main thematic concerns, namely the conflict between fecundity and ENTROPY, between the rich variety of life and the silence of death.

The Dark Light Years (**1964**) is a lesser work, though notable for the irony of its central situation: how one comes to terms with intelligent ALIENS who are physically disgusting. *Greybeard* (**1964**; US hardcover abridged) is perhaps BWA's finest sf novel. It deals with a future in which humanity has become sterile due to an accident involving biological weapons. Almost all the characters are old people, and their reactions to the incipient death of the human race are well portrayed. Both a celebration of human life and a critique of civilization, it has been an underrated novel, particularly in the USA. *Earthworks* (**1965**) is a minor novel about OVERPOPULATION. *An Age* (**1967**; vt *Cryptozoic!* USA and later UK editions) is an odd and original treatment of TIME TRAVEL, which sees time as running backward with a consequent reversal of cause and effect, comparable but superior to *Counter-Clock World* (**1967**) published by Philip K. DICK in the same year.

During the latter half of the 1960s BWA was closely identified with NEW-WAVE sf, and in particular with the innovative magazine NEW WORLDS, for which he helped obtain an Arts Council grant in 1967. Here BWA published increasingly unconventional fiction, notably his novel *Report on Probability A* (**1968**), an sf transposition of the techniques of the French "anti-novelists" in a surrealist story of enigmatic voyeurism, and his "Acid-Head War" stories, collected as *Barefoot in the Head* (fix-up **1969**). Set in the aftermath of a European war in which psychedelic drugs have been used as weapons, the latter is written in a dense, punning style reminiscent of James Joyce's *Finnegans Wake* (**1939**); it is an extraordinary *tour de force*.

The novella "The Saliva Tree" (1965) won a NEBULA award and was reprinted in *The Saliva Tree and Other Strange Growths* (coll. **1966**). It is an entertaining tribute to H.G. WELLS, though the plot is reminiscent of "The Colour out of Space" (1927) by H.P. LOVECRAFT. Later volumes of short stories include *Intangibles Inc.* (coll. **1969**; vt *Neanderthal Planet* USA, with two stories omitted and one added); *The Moment of Eclipse* (coll. **1970**) — this won the BRITISH SCIENCE FICTION AWARD in 1972; and *The Book of Brian Aldiss*

(coll. **1972**; vt *Comic Inferno* UK). His later sf novels include *Frankenstein Unbound* (**1973**), a time-travel fantasia which has Mary SHELLEY as a major character, and *The Eighty-Minute Hour: a Space Opera* (**1974**), a comedy in which BWA's penchant for puns and extravagant invention is thought by some critics to be over-indulged. His long fantasy novel *The Malacia Tapestry* (**1976**) is a much more balanced work. Set in a mysterious, never-changing CITY, it is a love story with fantastic elements. Beautifully imagined, it is a restatement of BWA's obsessions with entropy, fecundity and the role of the artist, and is perhaps his best novel since *Greybeard*. BWA has also written a travel book about Yugoslavia and two non-sf novels, *The Hand-Reared Boy* (**1970**) and *A Soldier Erect* (**1971**), which deal with the education, growth to maturity and war experiences of a young man whose circumstances often recall the early life of BWA himself. *A Soldier Erect*, which is in part about the war in Burma, is regarded by BWA (along with *Report on Probability A*) as perhaps his best book. His pseudonyms (used only for a few short stories and articles) are C.C. Shackleton, Jael Cracken and John Runciman. His most recent work, with 45 colour paintings and 15 b/w drawings by Ian Pollock, is *Brothers of the Head* (**1977**), a story of Siamese-twin rock stars and their third, dormant head.

In addition, BWA has been an indefatigable anthologist and critic of sf. His anthologies (most of which contain stimulating introductions and other matter) are *Penguin Science Fiction* (anth. **1961**); *Best Fantasy Stories* (anth. **1962**); *More Penguin Science Fiction* (anth. **1963**); *Introducing SF* (anth. **1964**); *Yet More Penguin Science Fiction* (anth. **1964**); and the SPACE-OPERA series of anthologies: *Space Opera* (anth. **1974**); *Space Odysseys* (anth. **1975**); *Evil Earths* (anth. **1975**); and *Galactic Empires* (anth. **1976**; two vols). Those he has edited in collaboration with Harry HARRISON are *Nebula Award Stories II* (**1967**); *Best SF: 1967* (**1968**; vt *The Year's Best Science Fiction No. 1* UK) and its eight annual sequels; *Farewell, Fantastic Venus!* (**1968**; vt *All About Venus* USA); *The Astounding-Analog Reader* (**1972–3**; two vols; UK paperback divided Vol.1 into two further vols, and Vol.2 did not appear at all from this publisher; *Decade: the 1940s* (**1975**); *Decade: the 1950s* (**1976**); and *Decade: the 1960s* (**1977**). Also with Harry Harrison, with whom BWA has had a long and, considering the wide gulf between their two styles of fiction, amazingly successful working relationship, he edited two issues of SF HORIZONS (1964-5), a short-lived but excellent critical journal, and *Hell's Cartographers* (anth. **1975**), a collection of six autobiographical essays by sf writers, including the two editors. *The Shape of Further Things* (**1970**) is

autobiography-cum-criticism, and *Billion-Year Spree* (**1973**) is a large and enthusiastic history of sf (BWA's most important non-fiction work). *Science Fiction Art* (**1975**) is an attractively produced selection of sf ILLUSTRATION with commentary, mostly from the years of the PULPS. As literary editor of *The Oxford Mail* for many years, BWA reviewed hundreds of sf books. His later book reviews have appeared in *The Times Literary Supplement, The Guardian* and elsewhere. BWA is a regular attender of sf conventions all over the world, and with his friend Harry Harrison is a passionate supporter of internationalism in sf and all other spheres of life, and a consistent attacker of Anglo-American parochialism. Like Harlan ELLISON in the USA, BWA is an energetic and charismatic speaker and lecturer. He was guest of honour at the 23rd World SF Convention in 1965, received the BSFA vote for "Britain's most popular sf writer" in 1969, and a DITMAR in 1970. In 1977 he won the first JAMES BLISH AWARD for excellence in sf criticism.

Projected volumes are an anthology, *Perilous Planets* (fifth in the "Space Opera" series); a collection, *Last Orders*; and a novel, *Enemies of the System*. [DP]
Other works: *The Male Response* (1961), not sf; *A Brian Aldiss Omnibus* (coll. **1969**); *Brian Aldiss Omnibus 2* (coll. **1971**).
About the author: *Item Eighty-Three: Brian W. Aldiss, a Bibliography* (**1972**) compiled by Margaret Aldiss; "Generic Discontinuities in SF: Brian Aldiss' *Starship*" by Fredric Jameson, in SCIENCE-FICTION STUDIES 1 no.2, 1973; "Magic and Bare Boards" by Brian W. Aldiss, in *Hell's Cartographers* (*see above*); *Aldiss Unbound: the Science Fiction of Brian W. Aldiss* (**1977**) by Richard Mathews.
See also: ABSURDIST SF; ANTHROPOLOGY; BLACK HOLES; DEFINITIONS OF SF; DISASTER; ECOLOGY; EVOLUTION; FANTASTIC VOYAGES; FANTASY; GALACTIC EMPIRES; GENETIC ENGINEERING; GOTHIC SF; GREAT AND SMALL; HISTORY OF SF; HOLOCAUST AND AFTER; IMMORTALITY; LEISURE; MUSIC AND OPERA; OPTIMISM AND PESSIMISM; PARALLEL WORLDS; PARANOIA AND SCHIZOPHRENIA; PASTORAL; PERCEPTION; PROTO SF; PSYCHOLOGY; RADIO (UK); ROBOTS; SATIRE; SF OVERTAKEN BY EVENTS; SOCIOLOGY; VENUS.

ALDRICH, THOMAS BAILEY *See* PSYCHOLOGY.

ALEXANDER, ROBERT (? –). British author of *The Pendulum of Fate: Cosmic Glimpses of Past and Future* (coll. **1933**), a collection of short stories which examine various aspects of time. [JE]

ALGOL American FANZINE (1963–) ed., from New York, Andy Porter. Subtitled "The Magazine About Sf", *A* is an attractive, printed, semi-professional journal published three times a year, containing articles and essays on sf and sf publishing, interviews with authors, and texts of talks and speeches. Special issues have been produced on Arthur C. CLARKE and Cordwainer SMITH. Regular columnists are Frederik POHL, Vincent DI FATE (on sf artwork), Susan WOOD (on fanzines), and Richard LUPOFF (on books). Occasional contributors have included Ted WHITE, Jack WILLIAMSON, Alfred BESTER, Ursula LE GUIN and Brian ALDISS. A series of booklets containing some of this material has been published by the editor. *A* shared the HUGO award for best fanzine in 1974.   [PR]

Cover by Tim Kirk.

ALIEN CRITIC, THE American FANZINE ed., from Portland, Oregon, Richard E. Geis. For its first three issues, *AC* was an informal magazine entirely written by the editor and titled *Richard E. Geis*. With the change in title in 1973, the magazine's contents began to diversify, featuring regular columns by John BRUNNER and Ted WHITE, a variety of articles and a series of interviews with sf authors and artists, although its characteristic flavour still derived from the editor's own outspoken reviews and commentary. With issue 12 in 1975 the title was changed to *Science Fiction Review*, a title used by Geis for a previous fanzine (*see* PSYCHOTIC). *AC* shared the 1974 HUGO award for best fanzine, and won it outright in 1975 and 1977, while editor Geis won the Hugo for best fan writer (entirely for his work on the magazine) in 1975 and 1976, and shared the award in 1977. *AC*, unlike most fanzines, is distributed relatively widely in specialist bookshops, and from this point of view is a semi-professional magazine.   [MJE]

ALIENS Visitors to other worlds in stories of the 17th and 18th centuries met no genuine alien beings. They found men and animals, sometimes wearing strange forms but always filling roles that were readily recognizable. The pattern of life on Earth was reproduced with minor amendments: UTOPIAN improvement,

SATIRICAL exaggeration or inversion of relationships. The concept of a differently determined pattern of life, and thus of a life-form quite alien to Earthly habits of thought, did not emerge until the late 19th century. The concept was a natural consequence of the notions of EVOLUTION and of the process of adaptation to available environments which originated with Lamarck and were developed by Darwin.

The idea of alien beings was first popularized by Camille FLAMMARION in his non-fictional work *Real and Imaginary Worlds* (**1865**). He dramatized the ideas in a series of imaginary dialogues, which were ultimately assembled in *Lumen* (**1897**). Here, Flammarion offers accounts of LIFE ON OTHER WORLDS, including one world in which respiration and alimentation are aspects of the same process, and one inhabited by sentient plants. Flammarion believed in the immortality of the soul, and invented the alien being as a receptacle for souls in sequential incarnations (*see* REINCARNATION). A more conventional romance in this vein is his *Urania* (**1890**). Aliens also appear in the work of another major French writer, J.H. ROSNY AÎNÉ. Mineral life-forms are featured in "Les xipéhuz" (1887 France) and again in "La mort de la terre" (1910 France). In the latter story a new form of "ferromagnetic" life evolves on Earth to replace carbon-based life. Like Flammarion, Rosny took a positive attitude to alien beings, as evidenced by *Les navigateurs de l'infini* (**1925** France), in which there is a love affair between a human and a six-eyed tripedal Martian. In the tradition of the French evolutionary philosophers Lamarck and Bergson, these early French sf writers found a place for Man and alien alike in some great evolutionary scheme.

In Britain, however, evolutionary philosophy was dominated by Darwin and Thomas Henry Huxley, who saw no great evolutionary plan but merely a struggle for existence in which the fittest survived and the rest perished. When the alien was given a role in English literature it was as a Darwinian competitor, necessarily the enemy of mankind. The writer who formulated this role was H.G. WELLS, in *The War of the Worlds* (**1898**), which features the alien as invader of Earth (*see* INVASION) — a role which was to become a cliché — and also set the pattern by which alien beings are characteristically imagined as loathsome MONSTERS. Although visitors to other planets continued to meet non-alien inhabitants (i.e. pseudo-human characters) in great profusion during the scientific-romance period of the early 20th century, most worlds also harboured alien monsters of several kinds.

Wells went on to produce the classic description of an alien society in *The First Men in the Moon* (**1901**), and then abandoned alien beings altogether. When

sf emerged as an independent category within the PULP magazines it inherited the alien being, ready equipped with the menacing role Wells had developed, but without any real consciousness of the logical thought that lay behind the design of the role. Alien monsters and invasions were used copiously for purely melodramatic purposes. The climaxes of such stories were often genocidal. Prolific authors in this vein included Edmond HAMILTON and Ed Earl REPP. Man, in venturing into outer space, occasionally found benevolent aliens, but these were usually being persecuted by other races of monstrous aspect, requiring the humans to intervene on their behalf. Alien allies were usually compounded from assorted mammalian and bird-like characteristics, while alien enemies always tended to look like reptiles, arthropods or molluscs, especially octopuses — an understandable biological chauvinism. Non-animal aliens (sentient plants or entities of "pure energy") were morally more versatile. In extreme cases alien allies and enemies could become symbolic of good and evil —e.g. E.E. "Doc" SMITH's Arisians and Eddorians (in the "Lensman" series).

Occasionally, sf writers were willing to apply the Darwinian perspective both ways and make humans play the role of alien invader. Significant early examples are Edmond Hamilton's "Conquest of Two Worlds" (1932) and P. Schuyler MILLER's "Forgotten Man of Space" (1933).

Although writers often designed non-sentient life-forms — especially the *flora* of other worlds — with the simple intention of giving an impression of strangeness, the first significant advance in the representation of intelligent beings did not come until Stanley WEINBAUM's "A Martian Odyssey" (1934), a story which made a deep impression on readers — it remains a favourite — with its relatively complex and plausible portrayal of alien life. A direct challenge to the implications of popular Darwinism and Huxleyan ruthlessness was posed by Raymond Z. GALLUN's "Old Faithful" (1934). In this story humans and a Martian set aside their extreme biological differences to acknowledge intellectual kinship. The story is a strong plea for understanding and stresses the value of cooperation (as, indeed, Darwin had stressed the survival value of sociality in *The Descent of Man* (**1871**), though this aspect of his thinking tended to be lost in the popularization of his ideas). This spirit is echoed in "Liquid Life" (1936) by Ralph Milne FARLEY, which ends with the stirring line: "For he had kept his word of honor, even to a filterable virus."

The alien menace, however, remained dominant in sf for many years. It has never quite died out, although it is extremely unfashionable today in written sf. It lost dominance after the Second World War in the major magazines, but was steadfastly maintained in the lower strata of the field, and especially by a host of cheap monster movies made during the 1950s and '60s (see CINEMA).

Only three major MAINSTREAM sf writers have made significant use of the alien being — Wells, Eden PHILLPOTTS, and Olaf STAPLEDON. Phillpotts used alien viewpoints in *Saurus* (**1938**) and *Address Unknown* (**1949**) to examine and criticize the human world, although the second novel challenges the validity of such criticism. Stapledon, in *Star Maker* (**1937**), tried to build Man and alien into a cosmic scheme akin to that envisaged by Rosny and Flammarion, and also employed the alien as a standard of comparison in one of his most bitter attacks on contemporary humanity in *The Flames* (**1947**). Because alien beings are rarely found outside genre sf, their dominant image has been created almost entirely at the discretion of sf writers and the makers of cheap horror films.

Although sf writers continued to invent nastier and more horrific alien monsters during the late 1930s and '40s, notably John W. CAMPBELL Jr in "Who Goes There?" (1938 as by Don A. Stuart), other interesting alien themes were being developed primarily concerning contacting alien cultures and the establishing of COMMUNICATION. Before leaving the 1930s, however, it is worth noting that many of the most interesting and adventurous alien stories written then failed to find a commercial market because of editorial TABOOS. "The Creator" (1935) by Clifford D. SIMAK, which suggested that our world and others might be the creation of a godlike alien (the first of the author's many science-fictional considerations of pseudo-theological themes — see RELIGION) was considered dangerously close to blasphemy, and ended up in William CRAWFORD's semi-professional MARVEL TALES in 1935. Crawford also began to publish P. Schuyler Miller's short novel "The Titan", whose description of a Martian ruling class sustained by vampiric cannibalism was considered too erotic by the major editors, but his magazine failed, and the piece eventually appeared in full for the first time as the title story of *The Titan* (coll. **1952**). Some of the potential which the alien being offered sf writers thus remained unexploitable in this period, and the influence of these taboos on the evolution of alien roles within sf must not be ignored.

It was during the War that the problems of communication — both LINGUISTIC and POLITICAL — between Man and alien were brought into sharper focus, and their complexity increased. The use of convenient "translation machines" or a brief period of intensive language learning were no longer an automatic prelude to perfect understanding and the immediate adoption of attitudes of friendship or enmity. Man/alien relationships became

delicate and uneasy. In "Co-operate or Else!" (1942) by A.E. VAN VOGT a man and a bizarre alien are castaways in a harsh alien environment during an interstellar war, and must combine their efforts to survive. Survival is also the priority in "The Cave" (1943) by P. Schuyler Miller, where Martian predators and prey must declare a truce in order to survive the long night, and unite to destroy a human who violates the conditions of the truce.

The story which best represents the climate of the war years is "First Contact" (1945) by Murray LEINSTER. Two spaceships meet in the void, and each crew is determined to give away no information and make no move which could possibly give the other race a political or military advantage. Their solution to the deadlock is to exchange ships and equalize concessions. Another story by Leinster published in the same year, "The Ethical Equations" (1945), also assumes that a "correct" decision regarding Man's first actions on contact with aliens will be very difficult to achieve, but that priority should definitely be given to the attempt to establish friendly relationships. But in one of the most famous stories of the period — "Arena" (1944) by Fredric BROWN — the meeting of Man and alien is still a matter of which one can best use his ingenuity to destroy the other. (Significantly, an adaptation of "Arena" for the TV series STAR TREK changed the ending of the story to bring it into line with later attitudes.)

In the sf boom which followed the end of the War, alien stories developed in several new directions. The attempt to present more credibly unhuman aliens is noticeable, particularly in the work of Hal CLEMENT, but it is the juxtaposition of human and alien in order to permit evaluation or criticism of attitudes and values which is most obvious in this period. Some stories are redolent of human vanity (e.g. Arthur C. CLARKE's "Rescue Party", 1946, in which aliens who come to save us find that we do not need their help) but most are critical. Militarism is attacked in Clifford D. Simak's "You'll Never Go Home Again" (1951) and Eric Frank RUSSELL's "The Waitabits" (1955). SEXUAL prejudices are questioned in Theodore STURGEON's "The World Well Lost" (1953). Racialism is attacked in "Dumb Martian" by John WYNDHAM (1952) and Leigh BRACKETT's "All the Colours of the Rainbow" (1957). The politics of colonialism (see COLONIZATION OF OTHER WORLDS) are examined in "The Helping Hand" (1950) by Poul ANDERSON, *Invaders From Earth* (1958) by Robert SILVERBERG and *Little Fuzzy* (**1962**) by H. Beam PIPER. The bubble of human vanity is pricked in Simak's "Immigrant" (1954) and Anderson's "The Martyr" (1960). The general human condition is subject to rigorous scrutiny through metaphors of

alien contact in *A Mirror for Observers* (**1954**) by Edgar PANGBORN and "Rule Golden" (1954) by Damon KNIGHT.

The decay of editorial taboos permitted an adventurous series of speculations by Philip José FARMER involving sexual and PSYCHOLOGICAL themes, including *The Lovers* (1952; **1961**), "Open to Me, My Sister" (1960), "Mother" (1953) and "Rastignac the Devil" (1954). The most remarkable redeployment of alien beings in sf of the 1950s and '60s was, however, in connection with pseudo-theological themes.

A humanoid ALIEN, *Analog* July 1975. Cover by John Schoenherr.

The inhabitants of other worlds had been linked to theology long before — most conspicuously in SWEDENBORG's 18th-century *Arcana of Heaven*, which included an account of the visionary's conversations with spirits on other worlds within and beyond the Solar System. Several interplanetary romances of the 19th century found spirits or angels living on other worlds, as did C.S. LEWIS more recently in the Christian allegories *Out of the Silent Planet* (**1938**) and *Perelandra* (**1943**; vt *Voyage to Venus*), the two interplanetary books of the "Ransom" trilogy. Within sf itself, however, the religious imagination had been echoed only in a few ADAM AND EVE stories. But by the 1950s aliens are seen to achieve all kinds of transcendental roles. Angelic aliens — kindly mentors — appear in "Dear Devil" (1950) by Eric Frank Russell and "Guardian Angel" (1950) by Arthur C. Clarke, in each case wearing diabolical physical form. There is no such disguise, however, in Edgar Pangborn's "Angel's Egg" (1951). Raymond F. JONES's *The Alien* (1951) is ambitious to be a god, and the alien in Philip José Farmer's "Father" (1955) really is one. In Clifford D. Simak's *Time and Again* (1951; vt *First He Died*) every living creature, including ANDROIDS, has an immortal alien "commensal", a science-fictional substitute for the soul. In James BLISH's classic "A Case of Conscience" (1953), alien beings without knowledge of God appear to a Jesuit to be creations of the Devil. Other churchmen undergo significant experiences in contact with aliens in "The Fire Balloons" (1951; vt "In This Sign") by Ray Bradbury; "Unhuman Sacrifice" (1958) by Katherine MacLean; and "Prometheus" (1961) by Philip José Farmer. Perhaps the boldest of all such speculations is Lester DEL REY's "For I Am a Jealous People" (1954), in which alien invaders of Earth turn out to have made a new covenant with God, who is on their side, not ours.

This trend continued in the 1960s and '70s, and its prevalence in modern sf implies rather more than a simple desire to seek out all possible roles for the alien. Many of the most impressive stories of these years build on foundations already laid to produce more comprehensive — and sometimes more extreme — comparisons between humans and hypothetical non-humans, almost always to the detriment of Man. SATIRES, some savage, on human vanity and prejudice include *The Dark Light Years* (1964) by Brian ALDISS and Thomas M. DISCH's novels *The Genocides* (1965) and *Mankind Under the Leash* (1966). "And I Awoke and Found Me Here on the Cold Hill's Side" (1971) by James TIPTREE Jr bitterly suggests that human fear and loathing of the alien may be mixed with a self-destructive fascination. Stories dealing soberly and delicately with problems arising out of cultural and biological differences between man and alien include "A Rose for Ecclesiastes" (1963) by Roger ZELAZNY; Poul Anderson's stories "The Sharing of Flesh" (1968) and "The Problem of Pain" (1973); and "Strangers" (1974) by Gardner R. Dozois. Religious imagery is at its most powerful in two stories dealing with a kind of "salvation" obtained by humans who adopt alien ways: Robert Silverberg's *Downward to the Earth* (1969) and George R. R. MARTIN's "A Song for Lya" (1974).

The evolution of alien roles in European sf seems to be distinctly different from that of Anglo-American sf. The different attitude adopted by the early French writers has been mentioned, and it appears that a difference in ideological standpoint has influenced the attitudes of Eastern European sf. The alien menace story typical of early Anglo-American sf, and never quite extinct, is completely absent from the sf that has so far been translated from Russian, and there appears to be a strategic element in this. The most important writer involved in the post-War rebirth of Soviet sf, Ivan YEFREMOV, wrote his novelette "Cor Serpentis" (trans. 1962; vt "The Heart of the Serpent") as an ideological reply to Leinster's "First Contact", arguing that by the time Man was sufficiently advanced to build interstellar ships his society would have matured beyond the suspicious militaristic attitudes of Leinster's humans, and could presume

that the aliens would be similarly mature. Anglo-American sf from the post-War period has likewise renounced Leinster's suspicions to a large degree, but it is still very much alive in *The Atlantic Abomination* (1960) by John BRUNNER, *The World of Ptavvs* (1966) by Larry NIVEN and the popular *The Mote in God's Eye* (1974) by Niven and Jerry POURNELLE. Ideological replies are not unknown in American sf — Ted WHITE's *By Furies Possessed* (1970), in which Man finds a useful symbiotic relationship with rather ugly aliens, is a reply to one of the most extreme post-War alien menace stories: *The Puppet Masters* (1951) by Robert HEINLEIN. Another militaristic melodrama with strong xenophobic tendencies is Heinlein's *Starship Troopers* (1959), which is echoed by Joe HALDEMAN's *The Forever War* (1974), save that the war turns out to have been the result of a misunderstanding and peace is achieved as a prelude to humanity's receiving great benefits from contact with the aliens.

The greatest failure of sf with respect to the alien being has been the failure to represent its essential strangeness, though Damon Knight's "Stranger Station" (1956) is a valiant attempt. It is noticeable that Hal Clement's aliens, while strange physically, are often very human in their modes of thought and speech. It is, of course, impossible ultimately to escape anthropocentric thinking, and even difficult to persuade the reader to accept the attempt. Perhaps the most impressive attempt to present the alien not merely as unfamiliar but also as unknowable is Stanislaw LEM's *Solaris* (1961 Poland; trans. 1970), in which attempts by humans to comprehend a sentient ocean investing an alien world are frustrated, and the alien's reactions to their presence threaten their sanity. A significant early British example is Fred HOYLE's *The Black Cloud* (1957), which features an electromagnetic intelligence in a huge dust cloud whose attempts to communicate on its own terms kill one man by overloading his brain; but here as in virtually all such stories the assumption is that common ground of some sort can and must be found. This is abundantly clear in one of the most recent attempts to give a thoroughly alien account of life on another world, Isaac ASIMOV's *The Gods Themselves* (1972). One of the few Anglo-American writers to present truly bizarre and unfathomable aliens is Philip K. DICK, who employs them in essentially enigmatic roles in *The Game-Players of Titan* (1963), *Galactic Pot-Healer* (1969) and *Our Friends From Frolix-8* (1970). The latter two novels also make abundant use of religious imagery. Jack VANCE is another creator of bizarre aliens, in most of his novels, but his purpose is ANTHROPOLOGICAL rather than meta-physical — an implicit challenge to the narrowness of anthropocentric thought.

The common association in recent sf of

aliens with some notion of historical or transcendental salvation may have led to an over-valuation of the prospect of communication with other worlds. The mystical regard in which devices to pick up hypothetical radio signals from extraterrestrial intelligences are held in many sf stories — most notably James E. GUNN's *The Listeners* (1972) but also Robert Silverberg's *Tower of Glass* (1970) and Arthur C. Clarke's *Imperial Earth* (1975) — is surely astonishing. Where once the notion of the alien being was inherently fearful, sf now manifests an eager determination to meet and establish significant contact with aliens, and the predominant fear is that we might be unworthy of such communion.

Anthologies of stories dealing with particular alien themes include: *From Off This World* (1949) ed. Leo MARGULIES and Oscar J. FRIEND; *Invaders of Earth* (1952) ed. Groff CONKLIN; *Contact* (1963) ed. Noel KEYES; and *The Alien Condition* (1973) ed. Stephen Goldin. [BS]
See also: JUPITER, MARS, VENUS.

The only issue. Cover by Eddie Jones.

ALIEN WORLDS British DIGEST-size magazine. One undated issue, *c.* Aug. 1966, published and ed. Charles Partington and Harry Nadler. The stories were by Harry HARRISON, Ken BULMER and J.R. Campbell; also included were articles on FLASH GORDON and the film ONE MILLION YEARS BC. Some of the illustrations were coloured. [FHP]

ALLEN, (CHARLES) GRANT (1848–99). British writer born in Canada. Known primarily for his work outside the sf field, including the notorious *The Woman Who Did* (1895), which attacked contemporary sexual mores. He was professor of logic and principal of Queen's College, Jamaica, before moving to Britain to write a series of books based on EVOLUTIONARY theory, and then turning to novel-writing for commercial reasons. After the success of *The Woman Who Did* he published a self-indulgent

novel of social criticism, *The British Barbarians* (**1895**), in which a man from the future is scathing about tribalism and taboo in Victorian society. His interest in anthropology also appears in the novel *The Great Taboo* (**1890**) and in many of the short stories assembled in *Strange Stories* (coll. **1884**). *The Devil's Die* (**1897**) is not sf proper, but embedded in the melodramatic plot is an interesting story of bacteriological research. Stories include "Pausodyne", about a TIME TRAVELLER from the 18th century who is considered insane in the 19th; "The Child of the Phalanstery", about eugenic practices in the future; and "The Thames Valley Catastrophe".   [BS]
Other works: *The White Man's Fort* (**1888**); *Twelve Tales* (coll. **1899**); *The Backslider* (coll. **1901**).
See also: ANTHROPOLOGY; LOST WORLDS; SATIRE, SOCIOLOGY; SUSPENDED ANIMATION.

ALLEN, HENRY WILSON (1912–   ). American writer of many Westerns as Will Henry, including *MacKenna's Gold* (**1963**), later filmed. His sf novel, *Genesis Five* (**1968**), narrated by a resident Mongol, depicts the Soviet creation of a dubious superman in Siberia.   [JC]

ALLEN, IRWIN (1916–   ). American film-maker long associated with sf subjects. After studying journalism and advertising at Columbia University, IA went to Hollywood at the age of 22 to edit *Key Magazine*, and within a year he was writing, directing and producing a weekly one-hour radio show. In 1944 he started a literary agency and was soon representing such people as P.G. WODEHOUSE and Ben HECHT. With the arrival of television he created the first celebrity panel show. In 1951 he began producing films for RKO, and in 1953 won an Academy Award for *The Sea Around Us*, a pseudo-documentary which he wrote and directed. He then made a similar film for Warner Brothers, *The Animal World*, which contained dinosaur sequences animated by Willis H. O'BRIEN and Ray HARRYHAUSEN. In 1957 he made the bizarre STORY OF MANKIND and following that he turned to more overt sf subjects: a bland remake of LOST WORLD in 1960, VOYAGE TO THE BOTTOM OF THE SEA in 1961 and *Five Weeks in a Balloon* in 1962. In 1964 he returned to television and produced, for 20th Century-Fox, a TV series based on *Voyage to the Bottom of the Sea*. Other sf TV series followed, including LOST IN SPACE, THE TIME TUNNEL and LAND OF THE GIANTS. His last TV project, CITY BENEATH THE SEA, failed to generate the necessary interest and it was abandoned, the pilot episode being released as a feature film, *One Hour to Doomsday*, in 1968. Ever resilient, IA then switched back to films and made, in 1972, the highly successful *The Poseidon Adventure* which began the "disaster film" cycle of the 1970s. In 1974 he made the even more successful *The*

Towering Inferno. His basic attitude to sf, and to his films in general, is to ignore logic, scientific facts and characterization, and to concentrate instead on producing as many spectacular special effects as possible. He once told an interviewer that: " ... if I can't blow up the world within the first ten minutes then the show is a flop." It is a formula that seems to work.
In 1976 the TV drama *Time Travellers* (ABC TV), another IA production, was released. Based on a short story by Rod SERLING, it was the pilot episode of a series that never got off the ground. IA's most recent project is a film version of *The Swarm* (**1974**) by Arthur HERZOG, a tale of killer bees. It has a prestigious cast and may be released in 1978.   [JB]

ALLEN, L. DAVID (1940–   ). American teacher of literature, critic and editor. He has written several short works in the "Cliff's Notes" series of study aids, for help in teaching SF IN THE CLASSROOM. These include *Science Fiction: An Introduction* (**1973**; rev. vt *Science Fiction Reader's Guide*), which largely consists of straightforward, plot-oriented analyses of 15 representative sf books. Others in this series are *Asimov's Foundation Trilogy and Other Works* (**1977**) and *Detective Fiction: an Introduction* (**1977**). A more substantial work is *The Ballantine Teachers' Guide to Science Fiction* (**1975**), which couples advice on teaching sf with, again, analyses of 15 representative works, perhaps with greater depth than previously. LDA took his PhD in literary criticism at the University of Nebraska — Lincoln in 1975.   [PN]

ALLIGHAM, GARRY (1898–?). South African writer, whose imaginary history written as from the year 1987, *Verwoerd—The End: A Lookback from the Future* (**1961**), argues for a benevolently administered apartheid. [JC]
See also: POLITICS.

ALLINGHAM, MARGERY (1904–66). British writer, best known for her series of detective novels featuring the intelligent, self-effacing (though probably titled) Albert Campion. One of her later works, *The Mind Readers* (**1965**), features a latter-day Campion in a somewhat diffuse tale involving children with telepathic powers; though the sf element is muffled, the story is not intended as fantasy.   [JC]

ALLPORT, ARTHUR. *See* Raymond Z. GALLUN.

ALL-STORY, THE American PULP MAGAZINE published by the Frank A. Munsey Corp., ed. Robert Hobart Davis. *AS* appeared monthly Jan. 1905-Mar. 1914, went weekly from 7 Mar. 1914 (as *All-Story Weekly*), incorporated CAVALIER WEEKLY to form *All-Story Cavalier*

Weekly from 16 May 1914, and reverted to *All-Story Weekly* 15 May 1915-17 Jul. 1920, when it merged with ARGOSY WEEKLY to form *Argosy All-Story Weekly*.

A typical cover, artist uncredited, illustrating a fantasy/mystery story.

AS was the most prolific publisher of sf among the pre-1926 pulp magazines; it became important through its editor's discovery of several major authors. Foremost of these in popularity were Edgar Rice BURROUGHS, who was represented with 15 serials and novelettes from 1912 to 1917, Ray CUMMINGS, notably with *The Girl in the Golden Atom* (1919–20; fix-up **1921**), and A. MERRITT. Other authors who contributed sf to *AS* include Garrett P. SERVISS, George Allan ENGLAND, Charles B. STILSON, Victor ROUSSEAU, Francis STEVENS, J.U. GIESY, Homer Eon FLINT and Douglas Dold. Many of its stories were reprinted in FAMOUS FANTASTIC MYSTERIES and FANTASTIC NOVELS.   [JE]
See also: *Under the Moons of Mars: A History and Anthology of "The Scientific Romances" in the Munsey Magazines 1912–1920* (**1970**) by Sam MOSKOWITZ.

ALL-STORY CAVALIER WEEKLY *See* ALL-STORY, THE.

ALL-STORY WEEKLY *See* ALL-STORY, THE.

ALPER, GERALD A. (?–   ). American writer, whose TIME-TRAVEL novel about a manipulative future is *My Name is Vladimir Sloifoiski* (**1970**).   [JC]

ALPHAVILLE Film (1965). Pathé-contemporary/Chaumiane-Film Studio. Directed by Jean-Luc Godard, starring Eddie Constantine, Anna Karina, Akim Tamiroff and Laszlo Szabo. Screenplay by Jean-Luc Godard. 100 mins. B/w.
Intergalactic secret agent Lemmy

Caution is sent to the planet Alphaville to deal with an evil computer used by its masters in the suppression of the inhabitants. Caution succeeds in his mission, at the same time winning the affections of the daughter of the ruler. A typical sf PULP plot is transformed into an ambiguous allegory of contemporary technology-dominated society: Alphaville itself is a thinly disguised Paris; Caution does not use a spaceship to get there, but simply drives his own Ford car through "intersidereal space", which closely resembles an ordinary road. *A* is a not easily accessible maze of allusions culled from a wide variety of sources, including tough-guy detective fiction (Lemmy Caution is the hero of many of Peter Cheyney's novels), Hollywood "B" films, comic books and cartoons (two scientists introduce themselves as "Dr Heckle and Dr Jeckle") and the traditions of sf. Like all the other components of *A*, sf is used merely as a means to an end by Godard. [JB]

ALTERNATE HISTORIES *See* ALTERNATE WORLDS; HISTORY IN SF.

ALTERNATE WORLDS An alternate world is an image of Earth as it might be, consequent upon some hypothetical alteration in history. Many sf stories use the notion of PARALLEL WORLDS as a frame in which alternate worlds can be held simultaneously and may even interact with one another.

Outside the genre, use of this notion has concentrated very much on the construction of theoretical histories (*see* HISTORY IN SF) — the step-by-step analysis of the historical pattern as it would have evolved from a significant change. Within sf, though, there has always been a tendency to skip over such analysis and deal directly with circumstances in the altered present. Uses of the notion outside the genre include a collection of essays edited by J. C. Squire, *If; or History Rewritten* (anth. **1931**; vt *If it Had Happened Otherwise*), whose contributors included G. K. CHESTERTON, André MAUROIS, Hilaire BELLOC, A. J. P. Taylor and Winston Churchill. The most common preoccupations of alternate historians were developed in two essays written for *Look* in 1960 and 1961: *If the South had Won the Civil War* (**1961**) by MacKinlay KANTOR and "If Hitler Had Won World War II" by William L. Shirer. Another event seen today as historically pivotal, the invention of the atom bomb, is the basis of two novels by Ronald W. CLARK: *Queen Victoria's Bomb* (**1967**), in which the atom bomb is developed much earlier in history, and *The Bomb that Failed* (**1969**; vt *The Last Year of the Old World*, UK), in which its appearance on the historical scene is delayed. The theme is used satirically by Marghanita LASKI in *Tory Heaven* (**1948**).

A consciousness of the fact that our world can be seen philosophically as one of a vast series of alternatives is historically quite recent. The first major work to develop the idea, Guy DENT's *Emperor of the If* (**1926**), was written hardly half a century ago, in the year that AMAZING STORIES was founded. It was not immediately co-opted by the pulp sf writers. Murray LEINSTER introduced the idea in "Sidewise in Time" (1934) and Stanley WEINBAUM used it in a light comedy, "The Worlds of If" (1935), but the first serious attempt to construct an alternate world in sf was L. Sprague DE CAMP's "The Wheels of If" (1940). De Camp had already published *Lest Darkness Fall* (1939; **1941**), in which a man slips back through time and sets out to remould history by preventing or ameliorating the Dark Ages, but had not gone on to follow the new pattern. In "The Wheels of If" he showed a contemporary America resulting from 10th-century colonization by Norsemen, made possible by the alteration of a minor decision of the Synod of Whitby in AD 664. De Camp also dealt more superficially with history transformed in some later stories, including *The Carnelian Cube* (**1948** with Fletcher PRATT) and "Aristotle and the Gun" (1958).

The potential of the notion for melodrama in sf was extravagantly revealed by a novel which dealt not with alternative pasts or presents but with alternative futures at war for their very existence, carrying the battle back into the present in an attempt to control the crucial event which decides their reality. This was Jack WILLIAMSON's *Legion of Time* (1938; **1952**), and its central idea of worlds battling for existence by attempting to maintain the histories which produced them was to become a popular one in sf. A straightforward war between alternate worlds existing in parallel was described by Fritz LEIBER in *Destiny Times Three* (1945; **1957**), but there was so much more potential in linking TIME TRAVEL with inter-dimensional travel, thus incorporating historical interference and the policing of time-tracks, that the more complex version of the alternate-worlds theme became rapidly dominant. Attempts by possible futures to influence the present by persuasion were presented by C. L. MOORE in "Greater than Gods" (1939) and by Ross ROCKLYNNE in "The Diversifal" (1951).

Isaac ASIMOV's *The End of Eternity* (**1955**) featured "reality changes" carefully monitored by chillingly authoritarian social engineers working over a time-track many thousands of years long. *The Fall of Chronopolis* (**1974**) by Barrington J. BAYLEY features an Empire attempting to maintain its reality against the alternate versions which its adversaries are imposing upon it. "Paratime police forces" were introduced by Sam MERWIN in *House of Many Worlds* (**1951**) and its sequel *Three Faces of Time* (**1955**), and were further employed by H. Beam PIPER in "Time Crime" (1955) and others; by Poul ANDERSON in the "Time Patrol" series collected as *Guardians of Time* (fix-up **1960**); and by John BRUNNER in the "Society of Time" series *Times Without Number* (fix-up **1962**).

In most stories of conflict between alternate worlds in sf there is a chauvinism which was absent from the essays in Squire's *If* — a conviction that ours is the best of all possible alternate worlds, or at any rate the *correct* one. The police series tend to include stories in which there is a desperate fight to restore our world after some evil change has obliterated it, and one of the classic developments of the theme in sf, Ward MOORE's *Bring the Jubilee* (**1953**), set in an America where the South has won the Civil War, is also concerned with "correcting" history. Perhaps this outlook owes something to the fact that the most popular use of the notion is to imagine the world as it might have been had the forces of Nazi evil triumphed in World War II. Several such novels were written as propaganda during the War, including *Loss of Eden* (**1940**; vt *If Hitler Comes*) by Douglas Brown and Christopher Serpell, *When the Bells Rang* (**1943**) by Anthony ARMSTRONG and Bruce Graeme and *When Adolf Came* (**1943**) by Martin HAWKIN. Subsequent expositions include "Two Dooms" (1958) by Cyril KORNBLUTH; *The Sound of His Horn* (**1952**) by SARBAN; the film IT HAPPENED HERE (1963); "The Fall of Frenchy Steiner" (1964) by Hilary BAILEY; *Hitler Has Won* (**1975**) by Frederick Mullally; "Weihnachtsabend" (1972) by Keith ROBERTS; and the remarkable novel *The Man in the High Castle* (**1962**) by Philip K. DICK. Dick has used the alternate worlds notion many times, often in a highly distinctive way, whereby alternate worlds arise for individual characters through distorted modes of perception, as in *Now Wait for Last Year* (**1967**) and *Flow My Tears, the Policeman Said* (**1974**). Another interesting variant used by Dick in *Eye in the Sky* (**1957**) has alternate worlds based on the psychological world-views of its various characters.

Dick was not the only writer to make more sophisticated use of the theme during the last two decades, although his total contribution is certainly the most notable. Keith LAUMER, in *Worlds of the Imperium* (**1962**), and its sequels, and Avram DAVIDSON, in *Masters of the Maze* (**1965**), produced adventure stories of a particularly ingenious kind. Robert SILVERBERG's *Gate of Worlds* (**1967**) presented to a juvenile audience a carefully designed world resulting from a more drastic depopulation of Europe by the Black Death in the 14th century. The most impressive single novel of the whole species is the episodic *Pavane* (fix-up **1968**) by Keith Roberts, which features an England in which Catholicism still rules, owing to the assassination of Elizabeth I, and whose design is partly based on Max Weber's thesis concerning the complicity of capitalism and the Protestant ethic. Just as the Civil War is normally seen as the key historical event in American sf, so British writers have tended to take 16th-century Europe as the turning-point. Two other novels dealing with a Catholic-dominated Europe, resulting from events in the 16th century, are John Brunner's *Times Without Number* (fix-up **1962**) and Kingsley Amis's *The Alteration* (**1976**). Another novel which deals with the social role of the Church is John Boyd's *The Last Starship from Earth* (**1968**), a historical-correction story in which the hero must prevent Christ's conquest of Rome to avert a contemporary benevolent dictatorship. A neat twist was introduced into the theme by Bob Shaw in *The Two-Timers* (**1968**), in which a widower creates an alternate universe in which his wife still lives and then sets out to murder his *alter ego* and reclaim her. (It should be noted that alternate universes are often created wholesale, though usually ephemerally, in tricky time-travel stories. *See* TIME TRAVEL and TIME PARADOXES.)

Some opposition to the notion that our world is the best possible is found in more recent novels. Harry Harrison's satirical comedy *Tunnel Through the Deeps* (**1972**; vt *A Transatlantic Tunnel, Hurrah!* UK) describes a world in which America never rebelled and the British Empire remains supreme, and includes a brief vision of our history revealed by a medium, which seems utterly horrific and Dystopian to the naive characters. Gordon Eklund, after using the theme to deal with the problem of identity, not without subtlety, in *All Times Possible* (**1974**), went on to write *Serving in Time* (**1975**) — a time-patrol series in which the history to be protected is relatively peaceful, and our history becomes the evil perversion which must be corrected. This may be the beginning of a trend.

The alternate-worlds genre has had a continuing popularity with MAINSTREAM WRITERS OF SF, and it is possible to gain popularity with such works without being stigmatized as a genre sf writer, as with Vladimir Nabokov's *Ada* (**1969**) set in an alternate future, John Hersey's *White Lotus* (**1965**) where an alternate America is subject to Asiatic domination, and Douglas Jones's *The Court Martial of George Armstrong Custer* (**1976**), in addition to many of the titles mentioned above.   [BS]

ALVAREZ, JOHN *See* Lester DEL REY.

AMAZING DETECTIVE TALES *See* SCIENTIFIC DETECTIVE MONTHLY.

AMAZING SCIENCE FICTION *See* AMAZING STORIES.

AMAZING SCIENCE FICTION STORIES *See* AMAZING STORIES.

No. 2. Artist uncredited.

AMAZING SCIENCE STORIES British PULP magazine published in Manchester by Pembertons in 1951. Two issues appeared, featuring stories reprinted from the Australian THRILLS, INC., including two pirated from SUPER SCIENCE STORIES.   [BS]

Feb. 1928. The splendid cover is by Frank R. Paul. Note that stories by Verne and Wells are featured.

AMAZING STORIES "The magazine of scientifiction", with whose founding in Apr. 1926 in the USA Hugo Gernsback announced the existence of sf as a distinct literary species. It was a BEDSHEET-sized PULP magazine issued monthly by Gernsback's Experimenter Publishing Co. as a companion to SCIENCE AND INVENTION. The title survives to the present day, but has seen great changes.

Gernsback lost control of Experimenter in 1929 and it was acquired by B.A. Mackinnon and H.K. Fly. From May to Oct. 1929 Arthur H. Lynch was editor, but then Gernsback's assistant T.

O'Conor Sloane, who had stayed with the magazine, took over. The name of the company was changed to Radio-Science Publications in 1930 and it was subsequently absorbed into Teck Publications in 1931. The magazine reverted to standard pulp format in Oct. 1933 but after a time proved unprofitable, and the title was sold in 1939 to Ziff-Davis, who installed Ray Palmer as editor. Palmer adopted a radically different editorial policy, abandoning the stiff pretence of scientific fidelity that Gernsback and Sloane had maintained, and using a great deal of action-adventure fiction "mass-produced" by a stable of authors using house names. Howard Browne became editor in 1950 and the magazine became a DIGEST in Apr.-May 1953. After a brief period with Paul Fairman as editor (May 1956-Sep. 1958), during which time the title was changed to *Amazing Science Fiction* (Mar. 1958) and then *Amazing Science Fiction Stories* (May 1958), Cele Goldsmith took over, using her married name of Cele Lalli from Aug. 1964, and ran the magazine until mid-1965, when the title, which had changed back from *Amazing Science Fiction Stories* to *Amazing Stories* in Oct. 1960, was sold to Sol Cohen's Ultimate Publishing Co. For some years thereafter the bulk of the magazine's contents consisted of reprints, with Joseph Ross acting as managing editor. Harry Harrison became editor in mid-1968 but a period of confusion followed as he handed over briefly to Barry Malzberg. Robert Silverberg was associated with the magazine for a very short time, but Cohen resumed the editorship in early 1969 with Ted White as managing editor. White became editor in 1970.

In its earliest days *AMZ* used a great many reprints of stories by H.G. Wells, Jules Verne and Edgar Allan Poe — named by Gernsback as the founding fathers of sf — and more recent pulp stories by Garrett P. Serviss, A. Merritt and Murray Leinster. The artwork of Frank R. Paul was a distinctive feature of the magazine in this period. Original material began to appear in greater quantity in 1928. Miles J. Breuer, David H. Keller and Jack Williamson each published their first story in *AMZ* in that year, and E. E. "Doc" Smith's *The Skylark of Space* (1928; **1946**) began serialization in the same issue (Aug. 1928) in which the first Buck Rogers story, *Armageddon 2419 A.D.* (1928; **1962**) by Philip Francis Nowlan, appeared. Sloane quickly abandoned reprints, but maintained Gernsback's policy of favouring didactic material that was sometimes rather stilted by pulp-fiction standards. Some extravagant serial novels — notably Smith's *Skylark Three* (Aug.-Oct. 1930; **1948**), Edmond Hamilton's "The Universe Wreckers" (May-Jul. 1930) and Jack Williamson's *The Green Girl* (Mar.-Apr. 1930; **1950**) — helped redress the balance in this respect. From

1930 *AMZ* faced strong competition from ASTOUNDING STORIES, whose higher rates of pay captured the bulk of the good material that came on to the market. (*ASF* eventually "took over" such writers as Smith, Williamson and John W. CAMPBELL Jr, who ultimately became its editor.) When Ray Palmer took over *AMZ* in 1939 after the sale to Ziff-Davis, he faced the same problem of competition with the rapidly improving *ASF*. He attempted to boost circulation in several ways — by slanting the magazine at a younger audience with less interest in the scientific aspects of the fiction, by obtaining stories from Edgar Rice BURROUGHS, and ultimately in the mid-1940s by taking the desperate step of presenting a long series of PARANOID fantasies by the obsessive Richard S. SHAVER along with insinuations that Shaver's theories about evil subterranean forces dominating the world by super-scientific means were actually true. The bulk of *AMZ*'s contents in the Palmer era, however, consisted of standardized material of a clumsy and rather lurid variety produced by such writers as Don WILCOX, David Wright O'BRIEN and William P. McGIVERN. It seems quite likely that Palmer was a frequent pseudonymous contributor himself, and the same is true of his successors, Browne and Fairman. The fiction-factory system operated by Ziff-Davis reached its height in the mid-1950s when the contents of several of their magazines were produced on a regular basis by a small group of writers including Robert Silverberg, Randall GARRETT, Harlan ELLISON and Henry SLESAR. This system has resulted in some confusion with regard to the correct attribution of several "floating PSEUDONYMS" — especially that of Ivar JORGENSEN. Very few stories of note appeared under the first three Ziff-Davis editors, although Edmond Hamilton, Nelson BOND and Walter M. MILLER were frequent contributors. Under Cele Goldsmith's editorship *AMZ* improved dramatically, publishing good work by many leading authors. Notable contributions include Marion Zimmer BRADLEY's first "Darkover" novel *The Planet Savers* (Nov. 1958; **1962**), Harlan Ellison's first sf novel "The Sound of the Scythe" (Oct. 1959; rev. as *The Man With Nine Lives* **1960**) and Roger ZELAZNY's NEBULA-winner "He Who Shapes" (Jan.-Feb. 1964; exp. as *The Dream Master* **1966**). Zelazny was one of a number of writers whose careers were aided in their early stages by Goldsmith — others include Robert F. YOUNG, David R. BUNCH and Ben BOVA (who did a series of science articles for *AMZ*). When Ted White became editor he renewed the attempt to maintain a consistent standard of quality, and though handicapped by the fact that he was offering a word-rate payment considerably less than that of his competitors he achieved some degree of

success. He compiled a special 50th anniversary issue which, owing to schedule difficulties, appeared two months late bearing the date June 1976. By this time the magazine was on a quarterly schedule, and its prospects now look bleak.   [BS]

Collectors should note: *AMZ* ran monthly from Apr. '26, with Vol.8 no.5 covering the months Aug./Sep. '33. Vol.9 no.12 was omitted, which brought the no.1 issue back to Apr. With Vol.10 no.6 (Oct. '35) *AMZ* went bi-monthly. The Dec. '36 issue was marked Vol.10 no.13. *AMZ* went monthly again from Vol.12 no.5 (Oct. '38) until Vol.17 no.9 (Sep. '43) when it reverted to a bi-monthly schedule. Vol.18 no.4 (May '44) was followed by Vol.18 no.5 in Sep. '44, and a quarterly schedule followed until Dec. '45, which was followed by Feb. '46 and May '46 at which point it went back to monthly until Vol.27 no.4 (Apr./May '53) which began another bi-monthly period. The monthly schedule began again in Nov. '55 and lasted until Jun. '65, which was followed by Aug. '65, inaugurating another bi-monthly period. This ran to Apr. '68 (marked Jun. '68 on cover) followed by Jul. '68, then bi-monthly again until Mar. '73, followed by Jun. '73 when bi-monthly schedule resumed (with a gap between Dec. '74 and Mar. '75) until Mar. '76, followed by Jun. '76, since when the schedule has been quarterly.

A Canadian reprint edition appeared '33–'35. Two British editions of the pulp *AMZ* appeared, one publishing two issues in '46, the other 24 issues between '50–'53. Eight numbered issues of a British digest edition appeared in '53–'4. Two anthologies of stories from the magazine are *The Best of Amazing* (anth. **1967**) ed. Joseph Ross, and *The Best From Amazing Stories* (anth. **1973**) ed. Ted White.

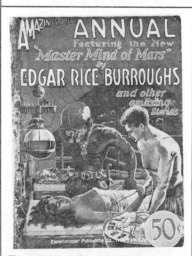

The only issue. Cover by Frank R. Paul.

AMAZING STORIES ANNUAL US BEDSHEET-size PULP magazine published by Hugo GERNSBACK's Experimenter

Publishing Co. Its only issue, in 1927, featured the first publication of *The Mastermind of Mars* (1927; **1928**) by Edgar Rice Burroughs. A successor, AMAZING STORIES QUARTERLY, resulted from the success of *ASA*.   [BS]

Fall 1928. Cover by Frank R. Paul.

AMAZING STORIES QUARTERLY US BEDSHEET-size PULP magazine, companion to AMAZING STORIES and successor to AMAZING STORIES ANNUAL. It ran for 22 issues, Winter 1928-Fall 1934, first under the aegis of Hugo GERNSBACK's Experimenter Publishing Co. and later ed. T. O'Conor SLOANE after Gernsback lost control (*see AMZ*). It featured a complete novel in every issue, beginning with H.G. WELLS's *When the Sleeper Wakes* (**1899**) but thereafter using mostly original material. It published many of the most important early pulp sf novels: "White Lily" (Winter 1930; as *The Crystal Horde* **1952**; as part of *Seeds of Life & White Lily* **1966**) and *Seeds of Life* (Fall 1931; **1951**) by John TAINE; *The Black Star Passes* (Fall 1930; **1953**) and *Invaders from the Infinite* (Spring/Summer 1932; **1961**) by John W. CAMPBELL Jr; "Paradise and Iron" (Summer 1930) and "The Birth of a New Republic" (Winter 1930) by Miles J. BREUER (the latter with Jack WILLIAMSON); *The Sunken World* (Summer 1928 and Fall 1934; **1949**) by Stanton A. COBLENTZ; and *The Bridge of Light* (Fall 1929; **1950**) by A. Hyatt VERRILL. Gernsback's own *Ralph 124C 41+* (1911 *Modern Electrics*; **1925**; *AMZ* Winter 1929) was also reprinted.   [BS]

Collectors should note: The Win. '30 issue (Vol.4 no.1) was dated Win. '31 on cover and spine. Vol.5 had only three nos, Win., Spr./Sum. and Fal./Win. '32. Vol.6 had only no.4, Spr./Sum. '33, with nos 1, 2 and 3 omitted. Vol.7 had two nos, Win. '33 and Fal. '34. There was a Canadian reprint issue of Vol.7 no.2.

AMAZING STORIES SCIENCE FICTION NOVELS US DIGEST-size

magazine. One undated issue, *c*. Jun. 1957, published by Ziff-Davis Publishing Co.; ed. Paul FAIRMAN. This was to be a quarterly magazine printing book-length novels in imitation of GALAXY SCIENCE FICTION NOVELS. The one novel printed was a book version by Henry SLESAR of the film TWENTY MILLION MILES TO EARTH (though the film was based on a story by Charlotte Knight), which proved a poor choice.   [FHP]

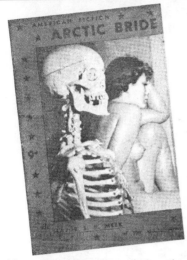

Nov. 1944. The uncredited artist, typically for this series, implies an erotic element in the lead story.

AMERICAN FICTION British pocketbook magazine. 12 issues known, numbered only from no.2. Published by Utopian Publications, London; ed. Benson HERBERT and Walter GILLINGS (who jointly owned the company). Publication was irregular, Sep. 1944-Jan. 1946. *AF* was a reprint magazine. All issues featured quasi-erotic covers, with the title story often being a sexy retitle of an already known sf or fantasy work. S.P. MEEK's "Gates of Light" became "Arctic Bride"; Edmond HAMILTON's "Six Sleepers" became "Tiger Girl"; John Beynon HARRIS's "The Wanderers of Time" became "Love in Time"; Jack WILLIAMSON's "Wizard's Isle" became "Lady in Danger". Other featured authors were Stanton A. COBLENTZ with "Youth Madness", a retitling of "The Planet of Youth", Ralph Milne FARLEY and Robert BLOCH. All issues, except for the unnumbered first and no.6, contained short stories as well as the featured novella, hence their usual listing in indexes as if they constituted separate book publication of a single novel or novella is incorrect. Most issues were 36 pages long. The emphasis was on weird fiction rather than sf, though stories from other genres were also used. [PN/FHP]

AMERICAN SCIENCE FICTION MAGAZINE Australian monthly pocketbook magazine. 41 issues, Jun. 1952-Dec. 1955, unnumbered and

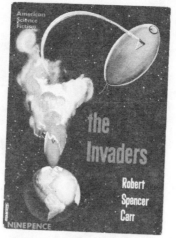

1953. Cover by Stanley Pitt.

undated. Published by Malian Press, Sydney; no editor named. *ASFM* contained reprints from US magazines of quite a good standard. It was a companion to SELECTED SCIENCE FICTION.   [FHP]

A. MERRITT'S FANTASY MAGAZINE US PULP magazine. Five issues, Dec. 1949-Oct. 1950, published by Popular Publications; ed. Mary

GNAEDINGER. *AMFM* was a companion magazine to FAMOUS FANTASTIC MYSTERIES and FANTASTIC NOVELS, and was begun in response to the considerable enthusiasm engendered by the reprinting of A. MERRITT's fiction in those magazines and elsewhere. Until the appearance in 1977 of ISAAC ASIMOV'S SCIENCE FICTION MAGAZINE it was the only sf magazine which attempted to build its appeal on the popularity of a single author. The fact that Merritt had died in 1943 may have made this not viable as a long-term policy. In any event, the magazine failed to establish itself. The volume numeration was Vol.1 nos 1 to 4 and Vol.2 no.1. There was a Canadian reprint edition.   [MJE]

AMIS, KINGSLEY (WILLIAM) (1922–). English novelist, poet and critic. He took his MA at Oxford, and was a lecturer in English at Swansea, 1949-61. His second wife is the novelist Elizabeth Jane Howard. Though KA is best known for such social comedies as his first, *Lucky Jim* (**1954**), which won him the sobriquet of Angry Young Man in the catch-phrase of the time, he has also been closely connected with sf throughout his professional life. He delivered a series of lectures on sf in 1959 at Princeton University, probably to their

July 1950. Cover by Norman Sanders.

surprise since sf was presumably not the context in which he was invited to speak. Revised, these were published as a book, *New Maps of Hell* (**1960**), which was certainly the most influential critical work on sf up to that time, although not the most scholarly. It strongly emphasized the DYSTOPIAN elements of sf. KA, himself a satirist and debunker of note, saw sf as an ideal medium for satirical and sociological extrapolation. Hitherto, most writing on sf had regarded it as first and foremost a literature of technology. As a survey the book was one-sided and by no means thorough, but it was witty, perceptive and quietly revolutionary.

KA went on to edit a memorable series of ANTHOLOGIES, *Spectrum*, with Robert CONQUEST (like KA a novelist, poet, political commentator and sf fan). They were *Spectrum* (anth. **1961**); *Spectrum II* (anth. **1962**); *Spectrum III* (anth. **1963**); *Spectrum IV* (anth. **1965**) and *Spectrum V* (anth. **1966**). These, too, were influential in popularizing sf in the UK and to some extent rendering it respectable. The last of these volumes selected almost entirely from *ASF*, a reflection, perhaps, of KA's increasing and almost fannish conservatism about HARDCORE sf, which went along with a growing dislike for stories of the NEW WAVE, as became even more evident in his newspaper criticism of sf in the late 1960s and '70s.

As a writer, too, KA was influenced by sf. He wrote several sf short stories, including "Something Strange" (1960), a minor *tour de force* about appearance and reality, and psychological conditioning. The James Bond pastiche *Colonel Sun: A James Bond Adventure* (**1968** as by Robert Markham) contains sf elements although it is primarily a thriller. The fantasy *The Green Man* (**1969**), one of KA's best works, is a wittily complex blending of tropes from satirical social comedy, Gothic horror and sf. It contains, among other things, periods of time stasis, a farcical troilism scene and a disturbing encounter with God. His full-scale sf work is the recent *The Alteration* (**1976**), set in an ALTERNATE WORLD in which the Reformation had not taken place, and in which Roman Catholic domination has continued to the present. It won the JOHN W. CAMPBELL MEMORIAL AWARD for best sf novel in 1977. [PN] **See also:** DEFINITIONS OF SF; RELIGION; SATIRE.

AMOSOV, N(IKOLAI MIKHAILO-VITCH) (1913–). Russian engineer and writer. His sf novel is *Zapiski iz budushchego* (**1967**; trans. as *Notes from the Future* **1970** as by N. Amosoff) in which a frozen sleeper awakens to 1991, where he is cured of leukemia and reflects somewhat heavily upon the nature of the world he has come into. [JC] **See also:** CRYONICS; MEDICINE; TIME TRAVEL.

AMRA US FANZINE, ed. from mid-1950s

AMRA. The covers, unusually elegant for a fanzine, were often, as here, by Roy Krenkel.

George R. Heap, and from Jan. 1959 (Vol.2 no.1) George H. SCITHERS. One of the longest-running of fanzines, and still current, *A* grew out of Robert E. HOWARD FANDOM (formalized with the founding of the "Hyborean Legion" in Nov. 1955), and is now a general SWORD AND SORCERY and HEROIC FANTASY fanzine. Many of its contributors, if not most, are themselves professional writers and artists, including L. Sprague DE CAMP, Roy G. KRENKEL, Poul ANDERSON, Leigh BRACKETT, Roger ZELAZNY, Jerry POURNELLE, Frank HERBERT, Fritz LEIBER and Lin CARTER. The result is a great many well-informed articles about imaginary worlds, use of ancient weapons, ancient history etc. *A* was named after Robert E. Howard's character Conan, who took the name Amra when he was a pirate. Scithers, an army officer and lawyer, masquerading here as the Terminus, Owlswick & Ft Mudge Electrick St Railway Gazette, also founded a small publishing house (Owlswick) and is now editor of ISAAC ASIMOV'S SCIENCE FICTION MAGAZINE. [PN]

ANALOG *See* ASTOUNDING SCIENCE-FICTION.

ANDERSON, ANDY *See* William C. ANDERSON.

ANDERSON, CHESTER (? –). American novelist and poet; he writes poetry as c v j anderson. His sf has been written in association with Michael KURLAND. *Ten Years to Doomsday* (**1964**), a straight collaboration, is a lightly written INVASION tale, with a good deal of activity in space and on other planets. *The Butterfly Kid* (**1967**) was written by CA alone, but stands as the first volume of a trilogy, the second instalment being *The Unicorn Girl* (**1969**) by Kurland, and the third *The Probability Pad* (**1970**) by T.A. WATERS. Each novel features the three authors as characters, and is comic; in *The Butterfly Kid*, which is written with wit and elegance, a pop group fights off an invasion menace, Greenwich Village being threatened by a pill which actualizes people's fantasies. [JC] **See also:** PERCEPTION; PSYCHOLOGY.

ANDERSON, COLIN (? –). English writer, whose first sf novel, *Magellan* (**1970**), depicts a post-HOLOCAUST Earth dominated by a single CITY, and the somewhat metaphysical apotheosis

afforded its inhabitants. [JC]
See also: CITIES.

ANDERSON, DAVID See Raymond F. JONES.

ANDERSON, GERRY and SYLVIA See JOURNEY TO THE FAR SIDE OF THE SUN; SPACE 1999; THUNDERBIRDS; UFO.

ANDERSON, OLOF W. (? – ?). American writer, whose sf novel is explained by its title: *The Treasure Vault of Atlantis, Giving an Account of a Very Remarkable Discovery of an Ancient Temple of Wealth* (**1925**). [JC]
See also: SUSPENDED ANIMATION.

ANDERSON, POUL (1926–). American writer; born in Pennsylvania of Scandinavian parents; he lived in Denmark briefly before the outbreak of the Second World War. In 1948 he gained a degree in physics from the University of Minnesota. His knowledge of Scandinavian languages and literature, and his scientific numeracy, have fed each other fruitfully through a long and successful career.

PA's first years as a writer were spent in Minnesota, where he joined the Minneapolis Fantasy Society (later the MFS) after the War, and associated with such writers as Clifford D. SIMAK and Gordon R. DICKSON, both of whom share with him an attachment to semi-rural (often wooded) settings, peopled by solid, canny stock (often of Scandinavian descent) whose politics and social views are often registered as conservative, especially by readers from the urban East and the UK, though perhaps they could more fruitfully be regarded as romantic, Midwestern, libertarian individualism. Although he is sf's most prolific writer of any consistent quality, PA began quite slowly, beginning to publish sf with "Tomorrow's Children" for *ASF* in 1947 with F.N. Waldrop, but not placing any large number of items in any one year until 1951, with 10 stories, nor publishing his first novel, a juvenile, *Vault of the Ages* (**1952**), until the next year.

But in 1953 PA seemed to come afire; in addition to 19 stories, he published magazine versions of three novels, *Brain Wave* (1953 *Space Science Fiction* as

"The Escape", first instalment only as magazine ceased publication; **1954**), *Three Hearts and Three Lions* (1953 *FSF*; exp. **1961**) and *War of Two Worlds* (1953 *Two Complete Science-Adventure Books* as "Silent Victory"; **1959**). The last of these is a routine adventure involving a betrayed Earth, alien overlords and plucky humans, but the other two are successful, mature novels, each in a separate genre. *Three Hearts and Three Lions* is an ALTERNATE-WORLD fantasy; an Earthman in the middle of the Second World War is translated into a SWORD-AND-SORCERY venue where he fights the forces of Chaos in a tale whose humour is laced with the slightly gloomy, "Nordic twilight" colours that have become increasingly characteristic of PA's work, as in *Three Hearts'* sequel, *Midsummer Tempest* (**1974**); the short story "Time Heals" (1949) also relates to the sequence. *Brain Wave* is perhaps PA's most famous single novel, and possibly his finest. Its premise is simple: for millions of years the part of the galaxy containing our Solar System has been moving through a vast force field whose effect has been to inhibit "certain electromagnetic and electrochemical processes", and certain neurone functions in the nervous system. When Earth escapes the inhibiting field, synapse speed immediately increases, causing an increase in INTELLIGENCE; after the book traces various absorbing consequences of this transformation, an eventually transfigured humanity reaches for the stars, leaving behind former mental defectives and bright animals.

After *Brain Wave* PA seemed content for several years to produce competent but unambitious stories in great numbers, and several SPACE OPERAS. He occasionally wrote under the pseudonyms A.A. Craig and Winston P. Sanders, and later, in the mid 1960s, according to one source, as Michael Karageorge, though PA does not admit to this. During these years, however, he began to formulate and write the many stories and novels making up the complex (and ongoing) "Technic History" series, in reality two separate sequences. The first centres on Nicholas van Rijn, a dominant merchant prince of the Polesotechnic League, an interstellar group of traders who dominate a *laissez-faire* galaxy of scattered planets. Anderson has been widely criticized for the conservative implications it is possible (though with some effort) to draw from stories whose philosophical entailments he modestly curtails. The second sequence properly begins about 300 years later, after the first flowering of a post-League Terran Empire; this empire, becoming decadent and corrupt, is under constant threat from other empires; most of the sequence features Dominic Flandry, a Terran agent who, sophisticated, pessimistic and tough, has gradually become a figure of stature as Anderson has infilled and expanded his

story since 1951, when the first short instalment of the "Technic History" was published. The chronology of the double sequence is neither secure nor complete. The following list is close to the internal chronology, however; books are listed only if their entire contents are within the sequence: "Wings of Victory" (1972), "Margin of Profit" (1956), *War of the Wing-Men* (**1958**; vt with new introduction *The Man Who Counts* 1978), *Trader to the Stars* (coll. **1964**), "Birthright" (1970), "How to be Ethnic in One Easy Lesson" (1973), *The Trouble Twisters* (coll. **1966**), "The Season of Forgiveness" (1973), "Day of Burning" (1967), *Satan's World* (**1969**), "A Little Knowledge" (1971), "The Problem of Pain" (1973), "Lodestar" (1973), *Mirkheim* (**1977**), "Wingless on Avalon" (1973), "Rescue on Avalon" (1973), "The Star Plunderer" (1952), "Sargasso of Lost Starships" (1952), *The People of the Wind* (**1973**), *Ensign Flandry* (**1966**), "Outpost of Empire" (1967), *A Circus of Hells* (**1970**), *The Rebel Worlds* (**1969**), *The Day of Their Return* (**1973**), *Agent of the Terran Empire* (coll. **1965**), *We Claim These Stars* (**1959**), *Flandry of Terra* (coll. including *Mayday Orbit* **1961**, and *Earthman, Go Home!* **1961**; rev. 1965), *A Knight of Ghosts and Shadows* (**1974**), "A Tragedy of Errors" (1968), *Let the Spacemen Beware* (1960 *Fantastic Universe* as "A Twelvemonth and a Day"; **1963** vt with new introduction *The Night Face* 1978), "The Sharing of Flesh" (1968; it won a 1969 HUGO for best novelette), "The Longest Voyage" (1960; it was awarded the 1961 Hugo for best short story), and "Starfog" (1967). Stories written later tend to moodier, darker textures.

A somewhat smaller sequence, The "Psychotechnic" series (series titles are not necessarily Anderson's; he or his various publishers tend to avoid linking references), traces the gradual movement of man into the Solar System and eventually the Galaxy itself; there is a good deal of action-debate about automation, the maintenance of freedom in an expanded polity, and so forth. The sequence comprises "Marius" (1957), "Un-Man" (1953), "The Sensitive Man" (1953), "The Big Rain" (1954), "Quixote and the Windmill" (1950), "Out of the Iron Womb" (1955), "Cold Victory" (1957), *The Snows of Ganymede* (1955 *Startling Stories*; **1958**), "Brake" (1957), "The Troublemakers" (1953), "Gypsy" (1950), "Star Ship" (1950), "The Green Thumb" (1953), *Virgin Planet* (**1959**), "The Pirate" (1968), and *Star Ways* (**1956**; vt with new introduction *The Peregrine* 1978).

Smaller still is the "History of Rustum" series, so designated by David Stever and Andrew Adams Whyte in *The Collector's Poul Anderson* (**1976**), mainly concerned with the establishing of a human colony on the planet of Eridani "known as Rustum": *Orbit Unlimited* (coll. 1961) deals with the departure from Earth and the first landing; further stories are "My Own, My Native Land" (1974), "Passing the Love of Women" (1974), "A Fair Exchange" (1974), "To Promote the General Welfare" (1975), all published as a sequence in Roger ELWOOD's four-part sequence-anthology *Continuum* (1974–5), and "The Queen of Air and Darkness" (1971). The latter story was awarded a 1971 NEBULA and a 1972 Hugo.

The "Time Patrol" series (the title is self-explanatory) is contained in *Guardians of Time* (coll. 1960), plus "Gibraltar Falls" (1975). With Gordon R. DICKSON, Anderson wrote a series about the Hokas, furry aliens who cannot understand non-literal language (i.e. metaphors, fictions) and so take everything as truth, with results intended as comic. *Earthman's Burden* (coll. 1957) features Hokas, as do "Joy in Mudville" (1955), "Undiplomatic Immunity" (1957), "Full Pack (Hokas Wild)" (1957), and *Star Prince Charlie* (1975). Some have described yet further groups of stories as series, but these associations tend to be referential rather than organic.

Although many of the novels and stories listed as tied to series can just as easily be read as singletons, there seems little doubt that the interlinked complexity of reference and storyline in Anderson's fiction has somewhat muffled his effect in the market-place. This lack of focus is not helped by a certain incoherence in its publication, so that the interested reader will find considerable difficulty tracing both the number of items in a series and their intended relation to one another. With dozens of novels and hundreds of stories to his credit — all written with a resolute professionalism and widening range — Anderson is still not as well defined a figure in the pantheon of American sf as writers (like Isaac ASIMOV from the Golden Age or Frank HERBERT from a decade later) of about the same age and perhaps no greater skill. However, in the welter of titles two further singletons are outstanding. *The High Crusade* (1960) is a delightful, wish-fulfilment conception. An alien spaceship lands in medieval Europe and is taken over by a microcosm of feudal society headed by quick-thinking Baron Roger; the ship takes them to the stars, where they soon trick, cajole, outfight and outbreed all the spacefaring races they can find and found their own empire on feudal lines. Brother Parvus (whose account of these events is read by the captain of the Earth spaceship that follows after many centuries) speculates that feudal remedies for the fall of the Roman Empire were just the thing for an analogous situation in deep space. *Tau Zero* (1967 *Gal.* as "To Outlive Eternity"; exp. 1970) is less successful as fiction, though its speculations on COSMOLOGY are fascinating, and the speculative hypothesis it embodies is

strikingly well conceived. A spaceship from Earth, intended to fly near the speed of light so that men can reach the stars without dying of old age, a notion based on the time contraction described by the Lorentz-Fitzgerald equations, accelerates out of control, at a constant one gravity; the faster it goes, the slower time passes within the ship itself. Eventually, epochs are passing in the universe for every moment within the ship; the universe contracts to a monobloc; there is a Big Bang; the ship slows gradually; the crew hope to settle a new planet in the new universe. The felt scope of the narrative is convincingly sustained throughout, though the characters tend to soap opera.

Anderson has been awarded Hugos for five stories and novelettes including, in addition to those noted above, a 1964 award for best short fiction with "No Truce with Kings" (1963), and a 1973 award for best novelette with "Goat Song" (1972), and has had five novels nominated; he has won two Nebulas, including the 1972 award for best novelette with "Goat Song", and had three novels nominated. His failure to win outright awards for his novels may reflect a tendency for many of them to tail off towards the conclusion, and perhaps some sense of disparity between his control of language and the frequent banality of the characters he creates to embody that language. He is still in the prime of an extraordinarily fruitful career, however, and there is no need to assume that this talented writer will continue always to be sf's number one bridesmaid.

PA was president of the SCIENCE FICTION WRITERS OF AMERICA for one year, 1971–2.   [JC]

Other works: *The Broken Sword* (1954; rev. 1971); *No World of Their Own* (1955; vt with cuts restored *The Long Way Home* 1978); *Planet of no Return* (1956; vt *Question and Answer*); *The Enemy Stars* (1959); *Twilight World* (two stories *ASF* 1947 including "Tomorrow's Children" with F.N. Waldrop; fix-up 1961); *Strangers from Earth* (coll. 1961); *Un-Man and Other Novellas* (coll. 1962); *After Doomsday* (1962); *The Makeshift Rocket* (1958 *ASF* as "A Bicycle Built for Brew"; 1962); *Shield* (1963); *Three Worlds to Conquer* (1964); *Time and Stars* (coll. 1964; UK editions omit last story); *The Corridors of Time* (1965); *The Star Fox* (fix-up 1965); *The Fox, the Dog, and the Griffin* (1966); *World Without Stars* (1967); *The Horn of Time* (coll. 1969); *Seven Conquests* (coll. 1969); *Beyond the Beyond* (coll. 1969); *Tales of the Flying Mountains* (1963–5 *ASF* as by Winston P. Sanders; fix-up 1970); *The Byworlder* (1970); *Operation Chaos* (1956–9 *FSF*; fix-up 1971); *The Dancer from Atlantis* (1971); *There Will Be Time* (1972); a common-theme anthology with Gordon R. Dickson and Robert SILVERBERG, *The Day the Sun Stood Still* (anth. 1972); *Hrolf Kraki's Saga* (1973);

The Queen of Air and Darkness and Other Stories (coll. 1973); *Fire Time* (1974); *Inheritors of Earth* (1974) with Gordon EKLUND — the novel was in fact written by Eklund, based on a PA story published in *Future* 1951; *The Many Worlds of Poul Anderson* (coll. 1974, vt *The Book of Poul Anderson*); *Homeward and Beyond* (coll. 1975); *The Winter of the World* (1975); *Homebrew* (coll. 1976), containing essays as well as stories; *The Best of Poul Anderson* (coll. 1976). *A World Named Cleopatra* (anth. 1977) ed. Roger ELWOOD is a common-theme anthology built around the title story and concept supplied by PA.

See also: ALIENS; ANTHROPOLOGY; ASTEROIDS; ATLANTIS; BLACK HOLES; CLONES; COLONIZATION OF OTHER WORLDS; COMIC STRIPS; CRIME AND PUNISHMENT; CYBORGS; ECONOMICS; END OF THE WORLD; ESCHATOLOGY; FANTASTIC VOYAGES; FANTASY; FASTER THAN LIGHT; GALACTIC EMPIRES; GAMES AND SPORTS; GENETIC ENGINEERING; GODS AND DEMONS; GRAVITY; HEROES; HISTORY IN SF; HUMOUR; JUPITER; LIFE ON OTHER WORLDS; LINGUISTICS; MAGIC; MATTER TRANSMISSION; MUTANTS; MYTHOLOGY; NUCLEAR POWER; POLITICS; PROTO SF; PSYCHOLOGY; RELIGION; ROBOTS; SCIENTIFIC ERRORS; SOCIAL DARWINISM; SOCIOLOGY; SPACE FLIGHT; SPACESHIPS; STARS; SUN; SUPERMAN; TECHNOLOGY; TERRAFORMING; TIME PARADOXES; TIME TRAVEL; UNDER THE SEA; VENUS; WAR; WEAPONS; WOMEN.

ANDERSON, WILLIAM C(HARLES) (1920–). American air force pilot and writer in various genres who published his first sf, *The Valley of the Gods* (1957) as Andy Anderson. Like *Pandemonium on the Potomac* (1966), it features a father and daughter, in the first case philosophizing about the extinction of mankind, in the second concerned about Man's imminent self-destruction. *Adam M-1* (1964) tells of an Astrodynamically Designed Aerospace Man.   [JC]

Other works: The following fantasies have a borderline relationship to sf: *Five, Four, Three, Two, One — Pfff* (1960); *Penelope* (1963); *The Gooney Bird* (1968); *The Apoplectic Palm Tree* (1969); *Penelope, the Damp Detective* (1974).

See also: ADAM AND EVE.

ANDREVON, JEAN-PIERRE (1937–). French writer, anthologist and illustrator. A former art teacher, he is one of the few full-time sf writers in France and uses the pseudonym Alphonse Brutsche for his pulp-style adventure sf (seven novels to date). His first story appeared in 1968 and he has since published over 70 stories and three collections under his own name: *Aujourd'hui, demain et après* ["Today, Tomorrow and After"] (coll. 1970), *Cela se produira bientôt* ["It Will Happen Soon"] (coll. 1971), *Repères dans l'infini* ["Landmarks in the Infinite"] (coll. 1975), two ecologically oriented anthologies

Retour à la terre ["Back to Earth"], vols one and two (anth. **1975** and anth. **1977**), two uneven novels, *Les hommes machines contre Gandahar* ["Machine Men Against Gandahar"] (**1969**) and *Le temps des grandes chasses* ["The Time of the Great Hunts"] (**1973**) and a third novel, *Le désert du monde* ["The Desert of the World"] (**1977**), which is a sombre, impressive story about the last man on Earth, bringing something new to this worn subject. A fiercely socially committed, left-wing writer, J-PA is at his best when angry and his strongest work has been at novella length. [MJ]
See also: POLITICS.

ANDROIDS The term "android" was not commonly used in sf until the 1940s. The *Oxford English Dictionary* gives first modern use as by Clifford D. SIMAK in *Time and Again* (**1951**), but a much earlier use occurred in Jack WILLIAMSON's serialized story *The Cometeers* (**1936**; **1950**). The word, which means "man-like", was first used of automata, and in its early form "androides" first appears in English in 1727, in reference to the attempts of the alchemist Albertus Magnus to create an artificial man. In contemporary usage, however, "android" usually denotes an artificial man of organic substance, although it has occasionally been used with reference to man-like machines, which are discussed in the section on ROBOTS, just as the term "robot" has occasionally been applied (as by its originator Karel CAPEK) to organic creations. The first clear distinction within genre sf between android and robot was probably that made by Edmond HAMILTON in his CAPTAIN FUTURE series, where Captain Future's sidekicks were a robot, an android and a brain in a box. Had it not been for this series, the term "android" would probably have retained much of the ambiguity between organic and inorganic. Henry KUTTNER used it to refer to a metal contraption in the 1940s, and A.E. VAN VOGT used "robot" to apply to artificial organic men at around the same time, but these transgressions were exceptional.

The notion of artificial men is an old one. One of the tasks attempted by alchemists such as Albertus Magnus was the creation of homunculi, and Jewish mythology features the golem. However, until the 19th century it was believed that organic compounds could not be synthesized, and humanoid creatures of flesh and blood had therefore to be derived either by magical means or by the gruesome process of assembly by which Mary SHELLEY's *Frankenstein* (**1818**) created his monster. H.G. WELLS, in *The Island of Dr. Moreau* (**1896**), had artificial men produced by the surgical modification of animals. Even after the discovery that organic materials might be built up by chemical means, a long period elapsed before Capek imagined androids "grown" in vats, mass-produced as slaves

in *R.U.R.* (**1921**; trans. **1923**).

There was considerable imaginative resistance to the idea of the android, in that this seemed a more outrageous breach of divine prerogative than the building of humanoid automata. Several authors toyed with the idea but did not carry it through, as in *The Uncreated Man* (**1912**) by Austin Fryers. The role played by androids in early stories tends to be a demonic one. In *Alraune* (**1911** Germany; trans. Guy ENDORE **1929**) by Hans Heinz EWERS, a female android casts the spell of the evil eye on men who fall in love with her. Edgar Rice BURROUGHS also featured manufactured men as figures of menace in *The Monster Men* (1913; **1929**) and in *Synthetic Men of Mars* (**1940**), though tinged with pathos in the latter instance. In *R.U.R.* the "robots" are made so artfully as to acquire souls, and they become Man's conquerors.

In the early sf pulps the android was hardly evident, as authors concentrated almost exclusively on mechanical contrivance. They appear, though, in an interesting variant of Van Vogt's standardized SUPERMAN plot, as "Dellian robots" in *The Mixed Men* (1943–5; fix-up **1952**; vt *Mission to the Stars*). After the War, while the robot came to be viewed less sympathetically — as less "human" and more of a "thing" — Simak wrote the influential *Time and Again* (**1951**; vt *First He Died*), in which androids seek emancipation from slavery and are assisted in their cause by the discovery that in common with all living creatures they have alien "commensals", or tenants — science-fictional substitutes for souls. The theme of emancipation has remained the focus of the majority of android stories, with sf writers invariably championing the androids. The emancipation of the biologically engineered Underpeople is a key theme in the "Instrumentality" series by Cordwainer SMITH, and a millennarian android religion is featured in Robert SILVERBERG's powerful *Tower of Glass* (**1970**). The theme is represented at a cruder level in " Down Among the Dead Men" (1954) by William TENN, *Slavers of Space* (**1960**; exp. vt *Into the Slave Nebula* 1968) by John BRUNNER, the "Dies Irae" trilogy (1971) by Brian STABLEFORD and *Birthright* (**1975**) by Kathleen SKY.

Androids also feature, inevitably, in stories which hinge on the confusion of real and ersatz, e.g. in "Made in USA" (1953) by J.T. McINTOSH, "Synth" (1966) by Keith ROBERTS, and the murder mystery "Fondly Fahrenheit" (1954) by Alfred BESTER, in which the I-narrator of the story switches unnervingly between referring to the android murderer as "him" and "me". The confusion between real and synthetic is central to the work of Philip K. DICK, who tends to use the terms "android" and "robot" interchangeably (see ROBOTS). Dick

discusses the importance this theme has for him in the essay "Man, Android and Machine" in *Science Fiction at Large* (**1976**; vt *Explorations of the Marvellous*) ed. Peter NICHOLLS.

As the implications of experiments in GENETIC ENGINEERING in the real world become a topic of discussion the status of "unnatural" human beings (such as those produced by CLONING) may appear more relevant, forcing the android into greater prominence as a symbol in sf.

The anthology *Science Fiction Thinking Machines* (anth. **1954**) ed. Groff CONKLIN has a selection of android stories. [BS]
See also: BIOLOGY; CYBORGS.

ANDROMEDA Original British ANTHOLOGY series edited by Peter Weston. *Andromeda* (anth. **1976**) was a well-received collection, with stories by Brian W. ALDISS, Michael CONEY, Harlan ELLISON, George R. R. MARTIN, Christopher PRIEST and Bob SHAW, as well as some newer writers. *Andromeda 2* (anth. **1977**) had stories by Shaw and Ian WATSON, but most of the other contributors were relative newcomers and on the whole it was less successful than its predecessor. Most of its stories are by British authors, and its bias is towards more traditional sf. [MJE]

ANDROMEDA BREAKTHROUGH, THE Television serial (1962). A BBC TV production. Produced by John ELLIOT, written by Fred HOYLE and John Elliot. Six 50-min. episodes. B/w. The cast included Peter Halliday, Mary Morris, Noel Johnson, David King, Barry Linehan, John Hollis, Mellan Mitchell and Susan Hampshire.

In this sequel to A FOR ANDROMEDA the scientist responsible for the previous project discovers that a radio telescope in South America has been receiving the same message from the stars, and that South American scientists have also built a computer, which has again produced an artificial though lovely girl. Having fallen in love with the first one, he goes to South America in the hope of renewing the relationship with her replica. Most of the serial tells of his attempts to extract her from the hands of the scientific establishment — but once again the central mystery is left unresolved. [JB]

ANDROMEDA NEBULA, THE *See* TUMANNOST ANDROMEDY.

ANDROMEDA STRAIN, THE Film (1971). Universal. Directed by Robert WISE, starring Arthur Hill, David Wayne, James Olson and Kate Reid. Screenplay by Nelson Gidding, based on the novel by Michael CRICHTON. 130 mins. Colour.

This film, whose director had made a previous sf film in 1971, THE DAY THE EARTH STOOD STILL, concerns a microscopic organism, inadvertently brought to Earth on a returning space

James Olson is fired on by lasers as he climbs to defuse an atom bomb in THE ANDROMEDA STRAIN.

probe, causing the instant death of everyone in the vicinity of the probe's landing near a small town, with the exception of a baby and the town drunk. These two are isolated in a vast underground laboratory complex, where a group of scientists attempts to establish the nature of the alien organism. The real enemy seems to be not the Andromeda virus but technology itself. It is Man's technology that brings the virus to Earth, and the scientists in the laboratory sequences — most of the film — are made to seem puny and fallible compared to the gleaming electronic marvels that surround them. They themselves have, in effect, become unwanted organisms within a superior body. Wise spent most of the large budget (it was one of the most expensive films of the year) on sets and scientific equipment, the latter being perfectly genuine and in working order, despite its futuristic appearance, and deliberately avoided using famous actors in order to get the muted performances he wished in contrast to the assertive machinery. The celebration of technology is only apparent — the film, despite its implausible but exciting ending, is coldly ironic, and rather pessimistic. Many of the effects were designed by Douglas TRUMBULL, who had been one of the four special-effects supervisors on 2001: A SPACE ODYSSEY.   [JB/PN]

ANET, CLAUDE Pseudonym of Swiss writer Jean Schopfer (1868–1931). His sf novel *La fin d'un monde* (**1925**; trans. as *The End of a World* **1927**; vt *Abyss*) describes the cultural destruction of a prehistoric Ice Age people by a more advanced culture.   [JC]

ANMAR, FRANK *See* William F. NOLAN.

ANONYMOUS SF AUTHORS This rubric covers works which, in their first edition, have appeared with no indication of authorship whatsoever, and any in which authorship is indicated only by a row of asterisks, or some similar symbol. Works that are attributed to "the author of ..." are considered only if the work referred to is itself anonymous. Cases where subsequent editions reveal authorship are not excluded. All other attributions are regarded as PSEUDONYMS.

Prior to the 20th century, anonymity was quite frequent in literature, particularly in works likely to be controversial, as in the case of UTOPIAN novels where the depiction of an ideal state highlighted faults the writer saw in his own society. Falling in this category is *The Reign of George VI, 1900–1925* (**1763**), the earliest known example of the future-WAR novel. Showing the forceful George VI becoming master of Europe following his successes in the European War of 1917–20, the anonymous English author gave no consideration to possible change in society, technology or military strategy, his depiction of the future being very similar to the reality of his times. Of more importance in the HISTORY OF SF is *Memoirs of the Year Two Thousand Five Hundred* (**1771** France; trans. W. Hooper **1772**) (by L.-S. MERCIER), the first novel of the future to show change as being an inevitable process. It was widely translated and reprinted, inspiring many imitators. Also anonymous, but set in an imaginary country, was the first American Utopian work, *Equality; or, a History of Lithconia* (**1802** *The Temple of Reason*, as "Equality, a Political Romance"; **1837**), which depicted a communal economy in a society where conurbations had been rejected in favour of an equal distribution of houses. Other

anonymous Utopian works appeared up to the end of the 19th century, some in unusual settings, as with the sub-glacial community in *Pyrna, a Commune; or, Under the Ice* (**1875**) (by Ellis James Davis), others set in the distant future, as with the pastoral harmony described in *A Crystal Age* (**1887**) (by W.H. HUDSON).

Other anonymous authors eschewed the Utopia for other important matters. Following the build-up in power by Germany in early 1871 the most socially influential sf novel of all time appeared advocating a restructuring of the British military system to meet a conceived invasion. *The Battle of Dorking: Reminiscences of a Volunteer* (**1871**) (by Sir George T. CHESNEY) provoked Parliament into outburst and led to numerous reprints and translations throughout the world, as well as to many anonymous refutations.

Unfortunately for the development of sf, other anonymous works which could have played a central role in the history of the genre were rushed into obscurity. Perhaps the three most important of these are *Annals of the Twenty-ninth Century; or, the Autobiography of the Tenth President of the World Republic* (**1874**) (by Andrew Blair), a massive work describing the step-by-step COLONIZATION of our Solar System; *In the Future: a Sketch in Ten Chapters* (**1875**), the story of a struggle for religious tolerance in a European empire of the future; and *Thoth; a Romance* (**1888**) (by J.S. Nicholson), an impressive LOST-WORLD novel set in Hellenic times and depicting a scientifically advanced race with airships in the North African desert.

Other anonymous sf authors abounded with a diversity of ideas, brain-transplanting in *The Curse of Intellect* (**1895**), the emancipation of women in the futuristic satire *The Revolt of Man* (**1882**) (by Sir Walter BESANT), and, in *Man Abroad: a Yarn of Some Other Century* (**1887**), the notion that Man will take his international disputes with him into space. Other anonymous sf authors are too numerous and their works sometimes too slight to mention. Today they are still with us, particularly in sf COMIC BOOKS and the BOYS' PAPERS, often retaining their role as social critics or outrageous prognosticators.

The Checklist of Fantastic Literature (**1948**) by Everett F. BLEILER lists 127 anonymous works, though many of these are pure fantasy rather than sf. A number whose authors were subsequently revealed are given entries in this volume under the author's name. The most famous is *Frankenstein; or, The Modern Prometheus* (3 vols **1818**) (by Mary W. SHELLEY). *The Supplemental Checklist of Fantastic Literature* (**1963**) by Bradford M. DAY adds another 27 titles, and there are certainly more, such as *The History of Benjamin Kennicott* (**1932**), waiting to be found.

Anonymously edited ANTHOLOGIES are

not particularly common in sf, and are not dealt with in this volume. Anonymously edited ghost and horror story anthologies are common, for some reason, but they lie outside our scope. [JE]

ANSIBLE The device invented by Ursula K. LE GUIN for instantaneous communication between two points, regardless of the distance between them. The physics which led to its invention is described in *The Dispossessed* (**1974**), but the device is mentioned in a number of the "Hainish" series of stories written before *The Dispossessed*, and indeed is central to their rationale. It compares interestingly with James BLISH's DIRAC COMMUNICATOR. Both are discussed in FASTER THAN LIGHT and COMMUNICATION. The ansible has already been adopted as a useful device by other writers, and may well become a standard sf device. [PN]

ANSTEY, F. Pseudonym of Thomas Anstey Guthrie (1856–1934), British writer and humorist. Best known for his many contributions to the magazine *Punch* and for his classic satirical fantasies, most of which follow the pattern of introducing a little ancient magic into contemporary society. His most successful work, *Vice Versa* (**1882**; rev. **1883**), concerns a Victorian gentleman and his schoolboy son, who exchange identities. In *The Tinted Venus* (**1885**) a young man accidentally revives the Roman goddess of love, and in *A Fallen Idol* (**1886**) an oriental deity exerts a sinister influence on a young artist. The protagonist of *The Brass Bottle* (**1900**) acquires the services of a djinn. *In Brief Authority* (**1915**) reverses the pattern, with a Victorian matron established as queen of the brothers Grimm's Marchenland. Of most interest relative to the history of sf is *The Time Bargain* (**1891**; vt *Tourmalin's Time Cheques*), one of the earliest TIME PARADOX stories.
[BS]
Other works: *The Talking Horse* (coll. **1891**); *The Black Poodle and Other Tales* (coll. **1896**); *Salted Almonds* (coll. **1906**); *Humour and Fantasy* (coll. **1931**).

ANTHOLOGIES Since the late 1940s, before which sf rarely appeared in anthology form, many readers have been introduced to sf through collections in books, rather than through the magazines. Books, for one thing, have always been more respectable, an important factor for many young readers (an average age for starting to read sf seems to be 13) whose parents may not have allowed the garish magazines into the house. The history of sf's ever increasing respectability over the past three decades has been in part the history of the paperback book revolution, and in part the slow displacement of the magazines by anthologies in book form.
Magazines are, of course, a form of anthology, but they are not so counted in

this Encyclopedia. Nor are cheap paperback publications which pad out a novella with one or two short stories, as was the case with some of Hugo GERNSBACK's early *Science Fiction* series of booklets in 1929 and 1932, and Utopia Publications' AMERICAN FICTION pocketbooks of the 1940s. Much sf was anthologized from quite early on in a variety of fantasy and weird-fiction collections, but none of these was exclusively sf, although *The Moon Terror and Other Stories* (anth. **1927**), a collection of four stories from WEIRD TALES, came close to it.
The earliest sf anthology could more properly be described as an anthology of PROTO SF. It is *Popular Romances* (anth. **1812**) ed. Henry Weber. It contains *Gulliver's Travels* (**1726**) by Jonathan SWIFT, *Journey to the World Underground* (**1741**) by Ludwig HOLBERG, *Peter Wilkins* (**1751**) by Robert PALTOCK, *Robinson Crusoe* (**1719**) by Daniel DEFOE and *The History of Automathes* (**1745**) by John Kirkby. The latter is a LOST-RACE story set in the Pacific Ocean.
The usually accepted candidate for first sf anthology is *Adventures to Come* (anth. **1937**) ed. J. Berg Esenwein. The stories were all original, but all by unknowns, and it seems to have had no influence at all. Much more important was *The Other Worlds* (anth. **1941**) ed. Phil STONG, a hardcover publication including stories by Henry KUTTNER, Lester DEL REY, Harry BATES, Theodore STURGEON and many other well-known writers. The first notable paperback anthology was *The Pocket Book of Science Fiction* (anth. **1943**) ed. Donald WOLLHEIM, eight of whose 10 stories are still well known, an extraordinarily high batting average for a period more than a generation ago.
But the year which presaged the advancing flood was 1946, when two respectable hardcover publishers commissioned huge anthologies, both milestones. In Feb. 1946 came *The Best of Science Fiction* (anth. **1946**) ed. Groff CONKLIN, containing 40 stories in 785 pages, and in Aug. came *Adventures in Time and Space* (anth. **1946**) ed. Raymond J. HEALY and J. Francis McCOMAS, containing 35 stories in 997 pages. The latter was the superior work, and even today it reads like a roll of honour, as all the great names of the first two decades of genre sf parade past. But Conklin's book was not to be despised, including as it did Theodore Sturgeon's "Killdozer" (1944), Robert HEINLEIN's "Universe" (1941) and Murray LEINSTER's "First Contact" (1945).
Both Conklin and Healy went on to do important pioneering work with anthologies. Conklin specialized in thematic anthologies, of which two of the earliest were his *Invaders of Earth* (anth. **1952**) and *Science Fiction Thinking Machines* (anth. **1954**). The thematic anthology has since become an important

part of sf publishing, and a great many such books are listed in this Encyclopedia at the end of the relevant thematic entries.
Healy did not invent the original sf anthology (*see above*), but he was one of the first to do it successfully. *New Tales of Space and Time* (anth. **1951**), which he edited, contains such well-remembered stories as "Bettyann" by Kris NEVILLE, "Here There Be Tygers" by Ray BRADBURY and "The Quest for Saint Aquin" by Anthony BOUCHER. Kendell Foster CROSSEN was not slow to take the hint, and half of his compilation *Future Tense* (anth. **1953**) consisted of original stories, including "Beanstalk" by James BLISH. Donald Wollheim had produced an original anthology also, with *The Girl With the Hungry Eyes and Other Stories* (anth. **1949**), the title story being by Fritz LEIBER.
The original anthology went from strength to strength over the years. The next important landmark was the STAR series of original sf anthologies ed. Frederik POHL, of which the first was *Star Science Fiction Stories* (anth. **1953**) and the last *Star Science Fiction Stories 6* (anth. **1959**). E.J. CARNELL was next, in the UK, with his NEW WRITINGS IN SF series, which began in 1964. This was followed rather more dramatically by Damon KNIGHT, whose policy was more experimental and literary than Carnell's, with his ORBIT series, which began in 1965. Since that time, the most influential original anthology series have been Harlan ELLISON's DANGEROUS VISIONS series (anths **1968** and **1972**), Robert SILVERBERG's NEW DIMENSIONS series (beginning **1971**) and Terry CARR's UNIVERSE series (beginning **1971**). Other original anthologies which, like the above, receive separate entries in this volume, are ANDROMEDA, INFINITY, NOVA and QUARK.
Sf is one of the few areas of literature that has kept alive the art of the short story. Fears have been expressed that the effective demise of the SF MAGAZINES (only a handful of relatively low-circulation magazines now left) may lead to the death of the sf short story. To some extent the original anthology has taken over the burden, and a market for the short story still exists. The original anthology itself, however, is in trouble in the late 1970s. Its heyday was the early 1970s, but worldwide economic depression has led to publishers' developing greater caution, and anthologies, whether original or not, are seldom strong sellers. It seems likely that *Orbit* will go to the wall in the near future, and others will almost certainly follow. *New Worlds Quarterly* (*see* NEW WORLDS) is already dead.
Part of the trouble is that the general standard of anthologies, both original and reprint, has dropped considerably over the past 15 years. All the sf magazines have been mined and re-mined for gold, and nearly all that remains is dross. The original anthology boom of the early

1970s produced many important new writers, but not enough to keep the standards of such collections really high, and while the average original anthology was of higher standard than the average single issue of a magazine, it was of lower standard than most of the early reprint anthologies. None the less, the past decade has seen a remarkable number of HUGO and NEBULA nominees drawn from the ranks of the original anthologies, including a good few winners, and this is a measure of the change of emphasis from magazines to books.

The other two important categories of anthologies are the various "Best" series, and the various series devoted to award-winning stories. The "Best" concept was pioneered by Everett F. BLEILER and T.E. DIKTY, who between them edited six annual volumes, beginning with *The Best Science-Fiction Stories 1949* (anth. **1949**); Dikty went on to edit a further three volumes alone (**1955–7**). Judith MERRIL's record was the longest and most distinguished, with 12 annual volumes (with a hiatus in 1967), beginning with *SF: The Year's Greatest Science-Fiction and Fantasy* (anth. **1956**) and ending with *The Year's Best Science Fiction: 12th Annual Edition* (anth. **1968**). Merril's anthologies were always lively, with an emphasis on stories of wit and literacy, and certainly helped to improve standards in sf generally. The editors of the major magazines, notably GALAXY, THE MAGAZINE OF FANTASY AND SCIENCE FICTION and ANALOG, all published "Best" anthologies of one kind or another from their own pages, most consistently and influentially in the case of *FSF*.

Anthologies had a great deal to do with finding a new audience for sf in the UK. Here the important date was 1955, when Edmund CRISPIN launched his *Best SF* series, which ran from *Best SF* (anth. **1955**) to *Best SF Seven* (anth. **1970**). Among the finest anthologies produced, always gracefully introduced, they were not selected on an annual basis, and are thus not directly comparable to Merril's books. Later important anthologists in the UK were Kingsley AMIS and Robert CONQUEST with their *Spectrum* series **1961–6**) and Brian W. ALDISS with the *Penguin Science Fiction* series (three vols, **1961–4**). Alone, and with Harry HARRISON, Brian Aldiss is still an active anthologist, and together they have edited nine "Best SF" books annually, beginning with *Best SF: 1967* (**1968**; vt *The Year's Best Science Fiction No. 1* UK). Other "Best" series are edited by Lester del Rey, Donald Wollheim and Terry Carr, the latter beginning with *The Best Science Fiction of the Year* (anth. **1972**) continuing (the series is current) up to *The Best Science Fiction of the Year 6* (anth. **1977**). Tastes in these matters are subjective, but the critical consensus is that Terry Carr's selection is on the whole the most reliable.

Anthologies consisting of award-winning stories, of course, are of an especially high standard. The most important are as follows: *The Hugo Winners* (anth. **1962**), *The Hugo Winners, Vol II* (anth. **1971**; UK and USA paperbacks in two vols) and *The Hugo Winners, Vol Three* (anth. **1977**) all ed. Isaac ASIMOV; the "Nebula Award Stories" series, beginning with *Nebula Award Stories 1* (anth. **1966**) ed. Damon Knight — its successors are *2* (anth. **1967**) ed. Brian W. Aldiss, *3* (anth. **1968**) ed. Roger ZELAZNY, *4* (anth. **1969**) ed. Poul ANDERSON, *5* (anth. **1970**) ed. James Blish, *6* (anth. **1971**) ed. Clifford SIMAK, *7* (anth. **1972**) ed. Lloyd BIGGLE Jr, *8* (anth. **1973**) ed. Isaac Asimov, *9* (anth. **1974**) ed. Kate WILHELM, *10* (anth. **1975**) ed. James GUNN, *11* (anth. **1976**) ed. Ursula K. LE GUIN; *Science Fiction Hall of Fame* (anth. **1970**) ed. Robert Silverberg, *The Science Fiction Hall of Fame Volume Two A* (anth. **1973**; vt *The Science Fiction Hall of Fame Volume Two* UK) ed. Ben BOVA, *The Science Fiction Hall of Fame Volume Two B* (anth. **1973**; vt *The Science Fiction Hall of Fame Volume Three* UK) ed. Ben Bova. These last three vols represent stories chosen by the SCIENCE FICTION WRITERS OF AMERICA, from the period prior to the Nebula awards, as the greatest in genre sf, the Silverberg vol. containing short stories and the two Bova vols containing novellas.

A number of anthologies of the 1970s have been designed for teaching SF IN THE CLASSROOM.

Aside from those mentioned above, other notable anthologists have been August DERLETH, Martin GREENBERG, Martin Harry GREENBERG, Thomas M. DISCH, Gardner DOZOIS, Norman SPINRAD and Sam MOSKOWITZ. By far the most prolific anthologist of recent years, though by no means the best, has been Roger ELWOOD.

A problem for readers of this Encyclopedia, and for sf readers generally, is to locate recommended short stories. Two important indexes to sf anthologies have been published, *A Checklist of Science-Fiction Anthologies* (**1964**) ed. Walter R. COLE, reissued in 1974 by ARNO PRESS, and *Science Fiction Story Index 1950–1968* (**1971**) by Frederick Siemon, published by the American Library Association. These volumes may be superseded by the book tentatively titled *Index to Science Fiction Anthologies and Collections*, ed. William Contento, and projected for 1978 publication from G.K. Hall & Co. [PN]

ANTHONY, PIERS Form of his name used by American writer Piers Anthony Dillingham Jacob (1934–) for all his published work. Born in England, he was educated in America and took out American citizenship in 1958. He began publishing short stories with "Possible to Rue" for *Fantastic* in 1963, and for the next decade published fairly frequently in the magazines, though he has more and more concentrated on longer forms. His two most ambitious novels come early in his career. *Chthon* (**1967**), his first, is a complexly structured adventure of self-discovery partially set in a vast underground prison, and making ambitious, though sometimes over-baroque, use of PASTORAL and other parallels; its sequel, *Phthor* (**1975**), is less far-reaching, less irritating, but also less involving. PA's second genuinely ambitious novel is the extremely long *Macroscope* (**1969**; British edition abridged), whose complicated SPACE-OPERA plot combines astrology with old-fashioned sense-of-wonder concepts like the use of the planet Neptune as a spaceship. In constructing a series of sf devices in this book to carry across his concern with representing the unity of all phenomena, microscopic to macroscopic, PA evokes themes from SUPERMAN to COSMOLOGY and Jungian PSYCHOLOGY.

In distinct contrast to complex works like these lies the post-HOLOCAUST sequence comprising *Sos the Rope* (**1968**), winner of the $5000 award from Pyramid Books, *FSF* and Kent Productions, *Var the Stick* (**1973**; paperback editions abridged) and *Neq the Sword* (**1975**), all three combined as *Battle Circle* (coll. **1977**). Here and in other novels, PA resorts to stripped-down protagonists with monosyllabic and/or generic names, like Sos or Neq, or like Cal, Veg and Aquilon, whose adventures on various planets make up his second trilogy, *Omnivore* (**1968**), *Orn* (**1971**) and *Ox* (**1976**). Both these series use action scenarios with thinly drawn backgrounds and linear plots not comfortably capable of sustaining the weight of significance the author requires of them. Perhaps the most successful of these books is *Steppe* (**1976**), a singleton featuring Alp, whose single-minded career playing Genghis Khan in a future dominated by a world-spanning computer-operated GAME is refreshingly unadulterated with any attempts at significance. *Prostho Plus* (1967–8 *If*; fix-up **1971**) and *Triple Detente* (1968 *ASF*; exp. **1974**) are both interstellar epics, the former comic and featuring a dentist, the latter concentrating on an OVERPOPULATION theme and its solution through culling by INVASION.

PA is a writer capable of sweepingly intricate fiction, though his tendency to produce less demanding work may obscure this capacity from view. By late 1977, however, at least one long novel was projected for near publication. [JC]
Other works: *The Ring* (**1968**) with Robert E. MARGROFF; *The E.S.P. Worm* (**1970**) with Margroff; *Race Against Time* (**1973**), a juvenile; *Rings of Ice* (**1974**); *But What of Earth?* (**1976**), listed as a collaboration with Robert COULSON, but repudiated by PA as an unauthorized revision of his text; *A Spell for Chameleon* (**1977**); *Hasan* (1969–70 *Fantastic*; exp. **1977**); *Cluster* (**1977**), *Chaining the Lady* (**1978**) and *Kirlian*

Quest (**1978**), which together form the "Cluster" trilogy; five sequential martial-arts novels in collaboration with Roberto Fuentes, which have a number of fantasy overtones.

See also: ASTRONOMY; CRIME AND PUNISHMENT; ECOLOGY; FANTASTIC VOYAGES; HUMOUR; MATHEMATICS.

ANTHROPOLOGY Anthropology is the scientific study of Man. It extends its inquiry along two major dimensions: an evolutionary dimension, which deals with the whole history of Man since his emergence as a species; and a contemporary dimension — ethnology or cultural anthropology — which deals with the diversity of human cultures in today's world. The two dimensions have sometimes been confused in the past, though modern anthropology makes a point of not doing so, by a covert and rather dubious assumption that by studying the diversity of contemporary societies and establishing a "hierarchy" extending from the most "primitive" to the most "highly developed" we may establish an evolutionary narrative applicable to societies in general. This is analogous to the situation in biology, where the evolutionary story has been constructed speculatively around data deriving from paleontology in association with a study of the various levels of complexity manifest in extant species. Even in biology this association of the two dimensions may result in careless thinking, but in biology we have a competent theory of evolution to guide us. Theories of social evolution are much more speculative, and the translocation of evolutionary philosophy into anthropology is therefore a hazardous procedure. The extent to which anthropological sf has been influenced by this kind of analogical thinking is considerable, but this is inevitable in that sf is a speculative medium much involved with the idea of progress. Where sf describes "primitive" societies the images are dynamic — the societies are almost always on the brink of sweeping changes, even if those changes have to be catalytically induced by visitors from a world which has much more in common with our own.

Anthropological speculations feature in sf in a number of different ways, representing different approaches to the two dimensions of inquiry. There is a sub-genre of stories which deal directly with the issues surrounding the evolution of the human species from bestial ancestors, and with the evolution of human societies in the distant past. The section on the ORIGIN OF MAN is a discussion of these stories (*see also* EVOLUTION). The status of such fictions as sf is a little dubious. They are speculative fictions which owe their inspiration to scientific theory and discovery, but they participate hardly at all in the characteristic vocabulary of ideas and imaginative apparatus of sf and thus are often seen as "borderline" sf at best. The same is true to an even greater extent of that species of fantasy which straightforwardly represents the other dimension of the anthropological spectrum — the imaginary construction of contemporary societies. Most such stories are "lost race" fantasies (*see* LOST WORLDS) which make very little conscious use of anthropological speculation in designing their hypothetical cultures.

Relatively few prehistoric fantasies are such pure romantic adventure stories as Edgar Rice BURROUGHS' *The Eternal Lover* (**1925**; vt *The Eternal Savage*), and the species includes a considerable number of thoughtful analytical works — ROSNY AÎNÉ's *La guerre du feu* (**1909**), Johannes V. JENSEN's *Fire and Ice* (trans. **1922**) and *The Cimbrians* (trans. **1923**), and William GOLDING's *The Inheritors* (**1955**) are the most outstanding. This is not the case with the lost-race story, whose archetypes all belong very much to the romantic school. Burroughs was an extensive contributor to this sub-genre, but its most famous exponent was H. Rider HAGGARD, whose lost-race fantasies include *King Solomon's Mines* (**1885**), *The People of the Mist* (**1894**), *The Yellow God* (**1908**) and *Queen Sheba's Ring* (**1910**). These novels span the period when the species was in its heyday. Other notable examples are: William WESTALL's *The Phantom City* (**1886**); Thomas JANVIER's *The Aztec Treasure House* (**1890**); William BRADSHAW's *The Goddess of Atvatabar* (**1892**); and W.G. EMERSON's *The Smoky God* (**1908**). The species was almost extinct (except in juvenile novels) by the time the pulp sf magazines appeared, but it did crop up occasionally therein — most notably in the works of A. Hyatt VERRILL, whose most famous novel was *The Bridge of Light* (**1929**; **1950**). The last flourish of the form may perhaps be identified as James HILTON's *Lost Horizon* (**1933**), though Dennis WHEATLEY and others have somewhat feebly continued the genre. The fact that this species of fantasy was so little influenced by scientific thought is the result of its implausibility. It is the descendant of the traveller's tale, and became a form of popular literature — a vehicle for exotic escapist fantasies — at exactly the point in time that it had completely lost its plausibility, when all the world was known, if not in fact, at least imaginatively. Once Phileas Fogg had achieved his object in Jules VERNE's *Around the World in 80 Days* (**1873**) the age of exploration was dead so far as speculative fiction was concerned — superseded by the age of tourism — and the lost-race fantasy became fantasy indeed. Very few of these stories are of any real interest anthropologically, and they have more to offer the student of myth (*see, e.g., The Savage in Literature*, **1975**, by Brian Street). There are, of course, anthropological speculations in imaginary traveller's tales before 1870, but anthropology itself is a young science, whose development had hardly begun by that date. Perhaps the most notable piece of anthropological speculation is to be found in DIDEROT's "Supplement to Bougainville's Voyage" (**1796**), which masquerades as an addendum to a real travelogue in order to present a debate between a Tahitian and a ship's chaplain on the advantages of the state of nature versus civilization. This work may have influenced Disraeli's *Adventures of Captain Popanilla* (**1828**), which also features a confrontation between the innocent and happy life of an imaginary South Sea island culture and the principles of Benthamite Utilitarianism. The most notable examples of stories of this species which embody speculations drawn from actual scientific thought are a handful of stories by Grant ALLEN — most notably *The Great Taboo* (**1890**) and some of the *Strange Stories* (coll. **1884**). Allen was also the first writer to bring a hypothetical anthropologist from another culture to study tribalism and taboo in Victorian society in *The British Barbarians* (**1895**). A later example is H. G. WELLS's *Mr. Blettsworthy on Rampole Island* (**928**), in which a deranged young man sees the inhabitants of New York as a brutal and primitive island culture.

The failings of the lost-race story as anthropological sf are not, of course, failings in the ambitions of writers but limitations of the form and its context of implausibility. These limitations have occasionally been transcended in more recent times, and three particular examples stand out. In *You Shall Know Them* (**1952**; vts *Borderline* UK and *The Murder of the Missing Link* USA) by VERCORS, a species of primate is discovered which fits in the margin of all our definitions of "humanity"; it becomes the focal point of a speculative attempt to specify exactly what we mean — or ought to mean — by "Man". *Providence Island* (**1959**) by Jacquetta HAWKES is a painstaking analysis of a society which has given priority to the development of the mind rather than technological control of the environment, thus calling into question the propriety of such terms as "primitive" and "advanced". A pulp-sf story which makes a similar point is "Forgetfulness" (**1937**) by John W. CAMPBELL Jr, writing as Don A. Stuart, but this skips over any actual analysis of the culture described. Ian WATSON's novel *The Embedding* (**1973**) juxtaposes an examination of a South American tribe, the Xemahoa, who have a strange language and a correspondingly strange world-view, with a commentary on experiments in linguistics and the visit of an alien race. This work is one of the few in sf which reflects the current state of structural anthropology and its intimate links with modern linguistics and semiology.

The death of the lost-race fantasy as an effective vehicle for anthropological speculation has led to a curiously paradoxical situation, for the format has been replaced in modern sf by the simple imaginative device of replacing primitive human societies by primitive alien societies situated on other worlds. Thus we have the situation where anthropological ideas in sf, i.e. ideas deriving from the scientific study of Man, are applied almost exclusively to the designing of cultures which are, by definition, non-human. It has, of course, always been obvious that most aliens in sf are surrogate humans (*see* ALIENS) but the point needs to be made that this is not necessarily the result of idleness or a lack of imagination on the part of writers, and that there is a good deal of sf in which alien beings are *literally* substitutes for Man. Post-War sf has managed to ameliorate the illogic of the situation by discovering a convention which allows a more straightforward revival of the lost-race format — the notion of "lost colonies" reverted to barbarism after the fall of a GALACTIC EMPIRE. Here the "aliens" are "rehumanized", but in terms of their value as vehicles for anthropological speculation there is little difference between the alien and lost colony strategies.

Thus, in modern sf we find the anthropologist Chad OLIVER making use of his knowledge in a great many stories which deal with the confrontation of heroes with viewpoints similar to ours and primitive alien societies or human colonies. Notable examples are "Rite of Passage" (1954), "Field Expedient" (1955) and "Between the Thunder and the Sun" (1957). Like Grant Allen, Oliver has also attempted the more ambitious project of imagining the situation in reverse, with alien anthropologists studying our culture, in *Shadows in the Sun* (1954). Other impressive sf stories which use "alien" societies in this way are: "Mine Own Ways" (1960) by Richard McKENNA; *A Far Sunset* (1967) by Edmund COOPER; "The Sharing of Flesh" (1968) by Poul ANDERSON; *Beyond Another Sun* (1971) by Tom GODWIN; *The Word for World is Forest* (1972; 1976) by Ursula K. LE GUIN (who is the daughter of anthropologist Alfred Kroeber); and "Death and Designation Among the Asadi" (1973) by Michael BISHOP. Works which use the lost-colony format to model primitive human societies include several novels by Jack VANCE — notably *The Blue World* (1966) — Ursula K. Le Guin's *Rocannon's World* (1966) and *Planet of Exile* (1966) and Joanna RUSS's *And Chaos Died* (1970). These human societies are often more different from primitive human societies than are the alien examples, and the injection of some crucial distinguishing feature — usually parapsychological powers — is common. This tends to move the stories away from strictly anthropological speculation toward a more general hypothetical sociology.

There is a certain irony in the fact that in the real world, with the disappearance of all unknown territory and the irresistible spread of civilization, the primitive societies available for anthropological study are vanishing — destroyed by "cultural pollution". (Anthropology suffers more than any other science from the implications of Heisenberg's uncertainty principle — the act of observation affecting the properties of that which is being observed.) Very soon now cultural anthropology will become a speculative science, and will have to imagine the primitive societies it wants to study. This point is made very neatly in an sf story by Robert SILVERBERG, "Schwartz Between the Galaxies" (1974).

Another possible contextual framework for the establishment of hypothetical human societies is the post-disaster scenario (*see* HOLOCAUST AND AFTER, DISASTER *and* SOCIOLOGY). Most fictions in this area deal with the destruction and reconstitution of society, and are perhaps of more general sociological interest. Where they bear upon anthropology is not so much in their envisaging different states of social organization but in their embodiment of assumptions regarding social evolution. Interesting speculations are to be found in such novels as William Golding's *Lord of the Flies* (1954), Angela CARTER's *Heroes and Villains* (1969) and Christian LÉOURIER's *The Mountains of the Sun* (1971; trans. 1973) and in several other titles noted in the entry on SOCIOLOGY.

What has so far been discussed is a set of literary frameworks particularly well suited to the modelling of ideas deriving from the science of anthropology. But there is a much broader sense in which a great deal of sf may be said to embody anthropological perspectives. Sf, by its very nature, attempts to put the human being, human society and the human species into a context which is rather different from that in which human beings, societies and literary works generally put them. The sf writer attempts — or at least pretends to — a kind of objectivity in his examination of the human condition. This is an attitude far from unknown in "mainstream" fiction, but it is not one that is typical of it. DEFINITIONS of sf — even those proposed by the most "literary" of its critics (as, for example, that of Brian W. ALDISS) — often emphasize the objectivity of sf's characteristic outlook, and the Campbellian school of thought is inclined to compare the attitude of the sf writer and his method to the attitude and method of the scientist. We may compare this attempt on the part of the sf writer to the attempt of the anthropologist to detach himself from his culturally committed standpoint. To a degree, sf writers and practitioners of the human sciences in general have something in common in this regard. Thus, one might suggest not only that sf writers might borrow more extensively and more fruitfully from the human sciences, but also that human scientists might find something of interest in the study of sf. In actual fact, the first sf anthology to be compiled as a teaching aid in a scientific subject was the anthropological *Apeman, Spaceman* (anth. 1968) ed. Leon E. STOVER and Harry HARRISON. A more recent example is *Anthropology Through Science Fiction* (anth. 1974) ed. Carol Mason, Martin H. GREENBERG and Patricia Warrick.

Further to the last point, it is worth noting the considerable body of sf which represents a "speculative anthropology" with no analogue in the science itself, dealing not with Man as he is or has been, but with Man as he might be or might become. The ultimate example is, of course, Olaf STAPLEDON's *Last and First Men* (1930), which describes the entire evolutionary history of the human race and its lineal descendants, but there are countless other works which deal with the possibilities of future developments in human nature. There is, in fact, very little sf which does not, in one way or another, bear upon this issue, at however trivial a level (*see* EVOLUTION, FAR FUTURE and SUPERMAN). [BS]

ANTIGRAVITY The idea of somehow counteracting GRAVITY is one of the great sf dreams, and appears throughout, notably with James BLISH's SPINDIZZIES. The term itself is scorned by physicists. *See also* IMAGINARY SCIENCE; POWER SOURCES. [PN]

ANTI-INTELLECTUALISM IN SF Anti-intellectualism takes two forms in sf. A persistent, if minor theme appears in the group of stories in which the intellect is distrusted; more common are stories, themselves by intellectuals, about DYSTOPIAN futures in which society at large distrusts the intellect though the author does not.

The first group usually takes the form of stories in which intelligence is seen to be sterile, if unmodified by intuition, feeling or compassion — a familiar theme in literature generally. *That Hideous Strength* (1945) by C.S. LEWIS attacks a government-backed scientific organization for its sadism and lack of thought for the consequences to humanity of scientific development. One of the villains, a vulgar journalist, is clearly modelled on H.G. WELLS. The symbol of the sterile intellect is a disembodied head, cold and evil, in a bottle. In genre sf, too, brains in bottles, or at least in dome-shaped heads attached to merely vestigial bodies, were among the commonest clichés, especially in the 1930s. The archetype here is "Alas, All Thinking!" (1935) by Harry BATES, in which the

EVOLUTION of mankind is shown to culminate in just such a figure, rendered in a memorable image, to the horror of the protagonist, an intelligent man who resolves not to spend too much time on intellectual activities in future. The theme of the insufficiency of intelligence alone often takes the form of mankind learning to adapt harmoniously to an Eden-like world (see LIFE ON OTHER WORLDS), a process impossible to humans whose minds outweigh their hearts. Anti-intellectual sf stories were given some impetus by the bombing of Hiroshima; a distrust of SCIENTISTS, and the potentially awesome results of irresponsibly wielded scientific knowledge became quite widespread. These moral issues were often quite responsibly examined in sf stories, but sf CINEMA tended to take a more simplistic line. The middle 1950s saw a procession of sf MONSTER movies, the monsters very often produced by scientific irresponsibility, and commonly a religiose voice, impressively baritone, would intone on the sound-track "There are some things Man was not meant to know".

Most sf, however, feared that the prejudices of an ill-informed population against scientists and intellectuals would result, in the short run, in acts of violence against thinking people, and in the long run, to a stultification of all progress. One of the commonest themes in sf is that of the static society (see CONCEPTUAL BREAKTHROUGH, DYSTOPIAS, POLITICS, UTOPIAS). H.G. Wells, who was attacked by C.S. Lewis for a narrow and unfeeling "humanism", feared this and did indeed believe that the world would be better off if governed by a technocracy of trained literate and numerate experts, not by a hereditary ruling class or by demagogues elected through the manipulation of an uninformed democracy. These ideas are expressed in A Modern Utopia (1905) and many of his later works, but they had already gained dramatic expression in The Food of the Gods; and How it Came to Earth (1904) where the anti-intellectual stupidity and fear of the general population is contrasted bitterly with the splendour of the new, giant race, unencumbered by medieval prejudice. Many years later Fred HOYLE was to take up the same theme, notably in The Black Cloud (1957) and Ossian's Ride (1959), where he argues for an intellectual elite of scientists and technologists, and proposes that the traditionally arts-educated intellectuals are in reality anti-intellectual, in that they are not numerate, and hence distrust and misunderstand science.

Satire against anti-intellectualism came to prominence in sf with the generation of the 1950s, especially those writers associated with GALAXY SCIENCE FICTION. Frederik POHL, C.M. KORNBLUTH and Robert SHECKLEY were prominent here. H. Beam PIPER wrote a satirical plea for thought in "Day of the Moron" in ASF in 1951, but better known is Kornbluth's "The Marching Morons" (1951), in which a small coterie of future intellectuals secretly manipulate the vast anti-intellectual and moronic majority. The current term for a thoughtful man in the 1950s was "egghead" in the USA: Damon KNIGHT and James BLISH were two other writers who satirically defended eggheads against philistine attack. Fritz LEIBER's The Silver Eggheads (1958 FSF; 1961) presents an appalling if amusing anti-intellectual future in which only ROBOTS are in the habit of constructive thought.

Anti-intellectualism presents itself commonly in two main areas in sf. One is the theme of the SUPERMAN who through MUTATION or for some other reason develops unusually high INTELLIGENCE. One such book is Mutant (1945–53 ASF; fix-up 1953) by Henry KUTTNER, and another is Children of the Atom (1948–50 ASF; fix-up 1953) by Wilmar H. SHIRAS; in both, superior intelligence leads to anger and even persecution from normals.

The second area is the story set after the HOLOCAUST; in stories of this kind the survivors, often living in a state of primitive tribalism or medieval feudalism, are deeply suspicious of intellectuals, fearing that the renewal of technology will lead to another disaster. Two interesting books which present worlds of just such a kind are The Long Tomorrow (1955) by Leigh BRACKETT and A Canticle for Leibowitz (1960) by Walter MILLER; a great many other stories have similar themes.

Surprisingly few full-length works have taken anti-intellectualism as their overriding central theme. One such is The Burning (1972) by James GUNN, in which violent anti-intellectualism leads to the destruction of scientists, and the return of science is via witchcraft, a theme which owes something to Robert HEINLEIN's Sixth Column (1941 ASF as by Anson MacDonald; 1949) and Fritz Leiber's Gather, Darkness! (1943 ASF; 1950). Gunn's book is interesting, but not up to his own highest standards. Ursula K. LE GUIN's first published sf story "The Masters" (1963) deals movingly with a similar theme, in a story of a world dominated by religion in which independent thought is a heresy punishable by burning at the stake. [PN]

ANTIMATTER The concept, now accepted and demonstrated in physics, that forms of matter can exist composed of particles opposite in all respects to those which compose ordinary matter, has a special appeal to sf writers. The idea itself was first formulated by the physicist Paul Dirac (1902–) in 1930, and confirmed by the discovery of the positron (an anti-electron) in 1932. A lively novel making good use of the idea is The Ring of Ritornel (1968) by Charles HARNESS. Entire antimatter universes have been postulated by physicists, with the enthusiastic support of the sf community. A.E. VAN VOGT was one of the first to use what has since become a cliché of PULP SF. For details, see PHYSICS. [PN]

ANTON, LUDWIG (1872–?). German novelist. His Brücken über den Weltraum (1922; trans. as "Interplanetary Bridges" 1933 Wonder Stories Quarterly by Konrad Schmidt) describes a flight to Venus. [JC]

ANVIL, CHRISTOPHER Pseudonym of American writer Harry C. Crosby Jr (?–), whose two earliest stories were published under his own name in Imagination in 1952 and 1953, the earlier being "Cinderella, Inc.". CA has been popularly identified with ASF since his first appearance in that magazine with "The Prisoner" in 1956. He soon followed with the first of the stories making up the "Centra" series: "Pandora's Planet" (1956 ASF; exp. as Pandora's Planet 1972); "Pandora's Envoy" (1961); "The Toughest Opponent" (1962); "Sweet Reason" (1966); "Trap" (1969). His prolific fiction has been noted from the beginning for its vein of comic ethnocentricity, a vein much in keeping with the expressed feelings of John W. CAMPBELL Jr who, in his later years at least, felt it philosophically necessary for humans to win in any significant encounter with ALIENS. CA supplied this sort of story effortlessly, though his first novel, The Day the Machines Stopped (1964), is a DISASTER story in which a Russian experiment permanently cuts off all electrical impulses in the world; chaos results, but Americans are soon making do again with steam engines and reconstructing a more rural civilization. Most of CA's stories take place in a consistent future GALACTIC federation, and quite a number deal with COLONIZATION of OTHER WORLDS. Within this large pattern there are a number of lesser series, though not all CA's series fall into this group. (See (ii) below for details.) The series are: (i) the "Centra" series listed above; (ii) "The Federation" series: (a) "The Scouts" sub-series: "The Hunch" (1961); "Stranglehold" (1966); (b) "The Space Transports" sub-series: "The Troublemaker" (1960); "Bill for Delivery" (1964); "Untropy" (1966); "Trial by Silk" (1970); "The Low Road" (1970); (c) "The Developers" sub-series: "Philosopher's Stone" (1963); "Experts in the Field" (1967); "Compound Interest" (1967); "Odds"; "The Captive Djinn" (1965); (d) "The Colonists" sub-series: "The Sieve" (1959); "Leverage" (1959), "Mating Problems" (1959); "The Law Breakers" (1959); "Uplift Savage" (1968); "Hunger" (1964); "Contrast" (1964); "Behind the Sand Rat Hoax" (1968); "The Operator" (1971); (e) "The Warriors" sub-series: "Goliath and the Beanstalk" (1958); "Revolt!" (1958); "Star Tiger" (1960); "The Claw and the

Clock" (1971); "Facts to Fit the Theory" (1966); (f) "The Patrol" sub-series: "Strangers to Paradise" (1966); "The Dukes of Desire" (1967); "The King's Legions" (1967); "A Question of Attitude" (1967); "The Royal Road" (1968); "The Nitrocellulose Doormat" (1969); "Basic" (1969); "Test Ultimate" (1969); "The Throne and the Usurper" (1970); " 'Riddle Me This …' " (1972); "The Unknown" (1972); *Warlord's World* (**1975**) – the first three stories in "The Patrol" sub-series were put together as a book, *Strangers in Paradise* (fix-up **1969**); (iii) "The War Against the Outs" series: "The Prisoner" (1956); "Seller's Market" (1958); "Top Rung" (1958); "Symbols" (1966); "The Ghost Fleet" (1961); (iv) The "Galactic Agent" series: "Advance Agent" (1957); "A Tourist Named Death" (1960); (v) The "Research East" series: "A Taste of Poison" (1960); "No Small Enemy" (1961); *The Day the Machines Stopped* (**1964**); (vi) "The Drug Factory" series: "Rx for Chaos"; "Is Everybody Happy?" (1968); "The Great Intellect Boom" (1969); (vii) "The Heuristician" series: "The Missile Smasher" (1966); "The Uninvited Guest" (1967).

CA has been much less active as a writer since the death of John W. Campbell. His efficiently written stories typify the style of *ASF* during the last decade of Campbell's editorship. [JC/PN]

APOCALYPSE *See* DISASTER; END OF THE WORLD; ESCHATOLOGY; HOLOCAUST AND AFTER; RELIGION.

APOSTOLIDES, ALEX (? –). Writer of the 1950s, best known for his collaborations with Mark CLIFTON in two of the latter's series for *ASF*; they include "Crazy Joey" (1953), "Hide! Hide! Witch!" (1953) from the "Bossy" series, and "What Thin Partitions" (1953) from the "Ralph Kennedy" series. [JC]

APPEARANCE VERSUS REALITY *See* CONCEPTUAL BREAKTHROUGH; META-PHYSICS; PERCEPTION.

APPEL, BENJAMIN (1907–). American writer, long and variously active, known mainly for such work outside the sf field as *The Raw Edge* (**1958**). In his sf novel, *The Funhouse* (**1959**), SATIRICAL and LINGUISTIC sideshows sometimes illuminate the story of the Reservation Chief of Police called upon to save a future America (the Funhouse) from atomic demolition. [JC] **Other works:** *The Devil and W. Kaspar* (**1977**). Non-fiction: *The Fantastic Mirror: Science Fiction Across the Ages* (**1969**), which is not so much a critical study as a series of excerpts linked by commentary.

APPLETON, VICTOR House name of the American Stratemeyer Syndicate, used mainly on the two Tom Swift series.

Howard R. GARIS wrote the first 35 of the first series, which stopped at number 38. The second series, which deals with Tom Swift Jr, was begun by Mrs Harriet S. ADAMS, daughter of Edward Stratemeyer, and generally upgrades the scientific side of the enterprise, though some of the flavour of the early Tom Swifts has been lost. The first novel of the first series is *Tom Swift and His Motor Cycle* (**1910**), modestly enough, but very soon, as in *Tom Swift and his Giant Cannon* (**1913**), the mundane world is left far behind. The second series begins with *Tom Swift and his Flying Lab* (**1954**) and mounts to titles like *Tom Swift and his Repelatron Skyway* (**1963**). Further information will be found under TOM SWIFT. [JC]

ARCH, E.L. The pseudonym under which Rachel Ruth Cosgrove Payes (1922–) publishes her sf, though her first novel, a juvenile, *Hidden Valley of Oz* (**1951**), was published as by Rachel Cosgrove. Her sf, from *Bridge to Yesterday* (**1963**) onwards, has been efficient but routine. [JC] **Other works:** *The Deathstones* (**1964**); *Planet of Death* (**1964**); *The First Immortals* (**1965**); *The Double-Minded Man* (**1966**); *The Man With Three Eyes* (**1967**).

ARCHER, LEE Ziff-Davis house name used on three stories, 1956–7, in *AMZ* and *Fantastic*. "Escape Route" (1957 *AMZ*) is by Harlan ELLISON. The authors of the other two have not been identified. [PN]

ARCHER, RON *See* Ted WHITE.

ARCHETTE, GUY *See* Chester S. GEIER.

ARDREY, ROBERT (1908–). American playwright, novelist and speculative journalist. Known mainly for his work outside the sf field, formerly for such plays as *Thunder Rock* (**1941**), latterly for his series of ethology-based cultural speculations, beginning with *African Genesis* (**1961**), the most successful, and continuing more and more controversially, as the implications of his biological determinism have sunk in on advocates of women's liberation and others. The uncomfortable nature of his speculative attempts may be illustrated in his sf novel, *World's Beginning* (**1944**), where American society is transformed benevolently by a chemical company. [JC]

See also: ECONOMICS; METAPHYSICS.

ARGOSY, THE US PULP MAGAZINE published by the Frank A. MUNSEY Corp.; ed. Matthew White Jr and others. It appeared weekly from 9 Dec. 1882 as *The Golden Argosy*. It became *The Argosy* from 1 Dec. 1888, went monthly from Apr. 1894 — Sep. 1917, then weekly, as *Argosy Weekly*, 6 Oct. 1917 — 17 Jul.

1920. It then combined with ALL-STORY WEEKLY to become *Argosy All-Story Weekly* 24 Jul. 1920 — 28 Sep. 1929, combined with MUNSEY'S MAGAZINE to form *Argosy Weekly* and *All-Story Love Tales*, the former continuing as a weekly 5 Oct. 1929 — 4 Oct. 1941. It went bi-weekly from 1 Nov. 1941, monthly from Jul. 1942, and became a men's adventure magazine in Oct. 1943, publishing its last sf with the Jul. 1943 issue.

Of the general-fiction pulp magazines, *A* was one of the most consistent and prolific publishers of sf. Prior to 1910 it

Argosy Weekly, a variant title of THE ARGOSY. Jan. 9, 1937.
Cover by Emmett Watson.

had featured sf and fantasy serials and short stories by Frank AUBREY, James Branch CABELL, George GRIFFITH, William Wallace COOK, Howard R. GARIS and others. Its sf output slackened during the first half of the next decade, a period in which it published sf by Garret Smith and Garrett P. SERVISS, as well as stories in the "Hawkins" series by Edgar Franklin, but picked up on becoming a weekly. It made a major discovery with "The Runaway Skyscraper" (1919) by Murray LEINSTER, and published several novels by Francis STEVENS before combining with *All-Story Weekly*. Following this merger White retained the editorship and continued publishing sf with many works by authors later to appear in the SF MAGAZINES, notably A. MERRITT, Edgar Rice BURROUGHS, Ray CUMMINGS, Otis Adelbert KLINE and Ralph Milne FARLEY. Even in the 1930s such sf and weird-magazine authors as Donald WANDREI, Robert E. HOWARD, Manly Wade WELLMAN, Jack WILLIAMSON, Eando BINDER and Arthur Leo ZAGAT were still appearing in its pages. Its last serialization was that of *Earth's Last Citadel* (1943; **1964**) by C.L. MOORE and Henry KUTTNER. Many of *A*'s stories were reprinted in FAMOUS FANTASTIC MYSTERIES and FANTASTIC NOVELS.

The American *A* should not be

confused with the British magazines of the same name. There were two of these. *The Argosy*, pulp-size, Dec. 1865–Sep. 1901, ed. Mrs Henry Wood, published occasional stories of the supernatural but was not known for sf. *The Argosy*, pulp-size, Jun. 1926–Jan. 1940, became a DIGEST in Feb. 1940, retitled *Argosy of Complete Stories*. In both its pulp and digest forms this magazine primarily published reprint stories from other sources, and many genres. Early on it serialized Mary SHELLEY's *Frankenstein* and Bram STOKER's *Dracula*, and published stories by Lord DUNSANY. Later, in its digest form, it published many stories by Ray BRADBURY. It lasted into the 1960s. [JE]
See also: *Under the Moons of Mars: A History and Anthology of "The Scientific Romances" in the Munsey Magazines 1912–1920* (**1970**) by Sam MOSKOWITZ.

ARGOSY ALL-STORY WEEKLY *See* ARGOSY, THE.

ARGOSY WEEKLY *See* ARGOSY, THE.

Vol. 2. Cover by Frank Frazetta.

ARIEL: THE BOOK OF FANTASY Large-BEDSHEET-size American magazine (9 × 12 inches). Two issues to date, the first Autumn 1976, the second dated only 1977, with quarterly publication announced. Published by Morning Star Press; ed. Thomas Durwood. *ATBOF* is a lavishly produced, expensive magazine on glossy paper, emphasizing fantastic art, including a HEROIC FANTASY strip by Richard Corben and a feature on Frank FRAZETTA. Critical and historical articles have been interspersed with fiction by Harlan ELLISON, Michael MOORCOCK, Keith ROBERTS and others. [PN]

ARISS, BRUCE (WALLACE) (1911–). American writer and illustrator. He published "Dreadful Secret of Jonas Harper" as early as 1948 in *What's Doing Magazine*, but his sf novel about a post-HOLOCAUST conflict between Amerindians and other survivors, *Full*

Circle (**1963**), appeared much later. He has also done a good deal of scriptwriting, has served in television and films as an art director, and did the illustrations for Reginald BRETNOR's *Through Time and Space with Ferdinand Feghoot* (coll. **1962** as by Grendel Briarton). [JC]

ARKHAM HOUSE American publishing house founded by August DERLETH and Donald WANDREI in order to produce a collection of H.P. LOVECRAFT's stories, *The Outsider* (**1939**). Although this was not initially a success the imprint continued, largely under Derleth, and published a variety of weird, fantasy and horror collections by Lovecraft, Clark Ashton SMITH, Frank Belknap LONG, Robert E. HOWARD and many others, later including original stories and novels. In 1948–9 it published the ARKHAM SAMPLER. Lovecraft has remained the company's main interest, and they have published volumes of his letters as well as his stories and other writings, and the works of many of his imitators. Their early Lovecraft and Smith collections are among the most valuable collectors' items in the field. [MJE]

The lettered cover is typical.

ARKHAM SAMPLER US magazine, intermediate size (6 x 9 inches). Eight issues, Winter 1948 — Autumn 1949, published by ARKHAM HOUSE; ed. August DERLETH. An offshoot of Arkham House's book publishing activities, *AS* was largely a fantasy magazine based on reprints (for example, H.P. LOVECRAFT's *Dream Quest of Unknown Kadath* 1943; Winter–Fall 1948; **1955**). The Winter 1949 issue was devoted to sf, containing stories by Ray BRADBURY, A.E. VAN VOGT and others. *AS* was very expensive by comparison with other sf magazines of the period ($1.00 rather than the standard 25¢), which may have contributed to its short life. [MJE]

ARLEN, MICHAEL (1895–1956). English-Armenian writer, known mainly for his work outside the sf field, novels

like *The Green Hat* (**1924**). Though it is derivative of Rudyard KIPLING's *pax aeronautica* tale, *With the Night Mail* (*1905; 1909*), MA's sf novel, *Man's Mortality* (**1933**), vividly depicts the collapse of International Aircraft and Airways in 1987 after 50 years of oligarchy; the melodramatic story carries some moral bite. *Hell! Said the Duchess* (**1934**) is set in 1938, with Winston Churchill as premier. A succubus is impersonating the duchess, who is accused of being a "Jane the Ripper" but is eventually exonerated. [JC]
See also: TRANSPORTATION.

ARMSTRONG, ANTHONY Pseudonym of British author and journalist George Anthony Armstrong Willis (1897–), a regular contributor to the humorous magazine *Punch*. AA began writing as a novelist with the two historical fantasies *Lure of the Past* (**1920**) and *The Love of Prince Rameses* (**1921**), which were linked by the common theme of REINCARNATION. The historical framework was again used in his LOST-WORLD adventure *Wine of Death* (**1925**), a bloodthirsty novel about a surviving community of Atlanteans. *When The Bells Rang* (**1943**; in collaboration with Bruce Graeme, also known as G.M. Jeffries) is a morale-boosting what-might-have-been story about a Nazi INVASION of England in 1940 and its subsequent defeat. [JE]
Other works: *The Prince Who Hiccupped and Other Tales* (coll. **1932**); *The Pack of Pieces* (**1942**; vt *The Naughty Princess* USA); *The Strange Case Of Mr. Pelham* (**1957**).

ARMSTRONG, GEOFFREY *See* John Russell FEARN.

ARMYTAGE, W(ALTER) H(ARRY) G(REEN) (1915–). South-African born British writer, primarily on educational subjects; professor of education at the University of Sheffield since 1954 and pro-vice-chancellor 1964–8. Of special interest to sf readers among WHGA's 14 books is *Yesterday's Tomorrows: a Historical Survey of Future Societies* (**1967**). It is primarily concerned with literary visions of the shape the future may take, and it assembles its materials mainly from the 19th and 20th centuries, containing much content analysis, sometimes of books not well known to sf readers. It is not a critical work, and is perhaps too eclectic, in that its vast range of materials seems sometimes to be merely cited rather than digested; none the less it is a stimulating work of scholarship which has been unduly neglected by sf readers and critics. [PN]
See also: UTOPIAS.

ARNETTE, ROBERT Ziff-Davis house name used on *AMZ, Fantastic Adventures* and *Fantastic* by Robert SILVERBERG and Roger P. Graham (Rog PHILLIPS) — one identified story each — and on six stories by unidentified authors, 1951–7.

ARNO, ELROY See Leroy YERXA.

ARNO PRESS American publisher specializing in facsimile reprint series. In 1975 Arno published a series of 62 sf titles (49 fiction and 13 non-fiction) under the editorship of R. REGINALD and Douglas Menville. The fiction titles mostly date from the period 1885–1925, while the non-fiction includes useful reprints of various bibliographic and critical works, several of them mentioned in the acknowledgements to this volume, originally published in very small editions. In 1976 Arno produced a companion series of 63 supernatural and occult volumes, also edited by Reginald and Menville, and including several anthologies assembled by them. [MJE]

ARNOLD, EDWIN LESTER (1857–1935). British writer, son of Sir Edwin Arnold, Victorian popularizer of Buddhism. His fantasies include *The Wonderful Adventures of Phra the Phoenician* (**1890**) and *Lepidus the Centurion: A Roman of Today* (**1901**). His best-known novel is *Lieut. Gullivar Jones: His Vacation* (**1905**; vt *Gulliver of Mars* USA), in which Lieut. Jones tells the story of his brief disgruntlement with the US navy, his trip by flying carpet to MARS, his rescue of a princess, his witnessing the destruction of her domain, and his return to a trustful fiancée. Richard LUPOFF claims this story, in the preface to the retitled 1964 edition, as a source for Edgar Rice BURROUGHS' Barsoom. The provenance is tenuous. [JC]
Other works: *The Story of Ulla, and Other Tales* (**1895**).
See also: LIFE ON OTHER WORLDS; REINCARNATION; WAR.

ARNOLD, FRANK EDWARD (1914–). British writer, active in the Second World War. Four of his pulp sf stories from this period are collected in *Wings Across Time* (coll. **1946**), published in the short-lived Pendulum "Popular" Spacetime Series of which he was editor. They are strong on action. [JC]

ARNOLD, JACK (1916–). American film-maker who made a number of sf films during the 1950s. He began as an actor but made 16mm films as a hobby. At the outbreak of the Second World War he volunteered for training as a pilot; in the five-month waiting period he joined the Army Signal Corps which was producing various types of training film. He found himself working with the great documentary-maker Robert Flaherty, and thus received an invaluable crash course in film-making. After the War he and a friend formed a film company and made several successful documentaries, one of which received an Academy Award nomination. This led to an offer from

Universal Studios to direct feature films. The first of these, *Girls in the Night* (1953), is about teenagers growing up in the slums of New York. In 1953 he directed his first sf film, IT CAME FROM OUTER SPACE, based on a treatment by Ray BRADBURY. His other sf films are CREATURE FROM THE BLACK LAGOON (1954), REVENGE OF THE CREATURE (1955), TARANTULA (1956), THE INCREDIBLE SHRINKING MAN, (1957), *Monster on the Campus* (1958) and THE SPACE CHILDREN (1958). In 1959 he made the Peter Sellers comedy *The Mouse that Roared*, which marked the end of his sf-oriented series of fantasy films. One film historian has described him as: " … a great genius of the American fantasy film … his films, for sheer virtuosity of style and clarity of vision, have few equals in the cinema." [JB]

AROUND THE WORLD UNDER THE SEA Film (1966). MGM. Directed by Andrew Marton, starring Lloyd Bridges, Shirley Eaton and David McCallum. Screenplay by Arthur Weiss and Art Arthur. 120 mins. Colour.

A team of underwater experts uses a futuristic submarine to plant a series of earthquake-warning devices along a fault that encircles the world. The characters and dialogue are hackneyed, and the special effects cheap. The underwater sequences are directed by Ricou Browning. [JB]

ARROW, WILLIAM House name of BALLANTINE BOOKS; see Donald PFEIL; William ROTSLER.

ART For art in sf see ARTS; for sf artists see ILLUSTRATION, and also entries on individual artists.

ARTHUR, PETER See Arthur PORGES.

ARTS The notion of sf stories about the arts seems a little strange, in that genre sf belongs to a historical period in which science and art are seen not only as unconnected but as antithetical. One of the classics of sf, in fact — Charles HARNESS's *The Rose* (1953; **1966**) — is very much concerned with this opposition. But Harness champions emotive art against cold science — in the climactic scene the musical transfiguration of the "Sciomnia equations", which embody all rationalistic knowledge, strikes the heroine dead, but some mysterious inspiration reorchestrates the deadly music and causes her transcendental revival. And this is generally true. Even when sf writers cannot celebrate the triumph of art they lament its defeat. The decline of artistry in the face of mechanical expertise is the theme of the HUGO-winning novelette "The Darfsteller" (1955) by Walter M. MILLER, an emotive story about the conflict between an actor and the robot theatre which has made him

redundant; and there are several similar stories dealing with other arts. C. M. KORNBLUTH's "With These Hands" (1951) concerns mechanical sculpture, Clifford D. SIMAK's "So Bright the Vision" (1956) is about machine-produced literature, and Harry HARRISON's "Portrait of the Artist" (1964) is a wholly sincere story about the agonies of a comic-book artist replaced by a machine.

The concern of sf writers with the arts is almost entirely a post-war phenomenon. The early PULP sf writers and their predecessors, the scientific romancers, ignored the arts almost totally. Some 19th-century stories about artists may be considered to be sf because of the remarkable nature of the particular enterprises featured therein — Nathaniel HAWTHORNE's "Artist of the Beautiful" (1844) concerns the making of a wondrous mechanical butterfly and Robert W. CHAMBERS' story "The Mask" (1895) is about a "sculptor" who makes statues by chemically turning living things to stone; but these are allegories which stand quite apart from the aims of the literature of the scientific imagination *per se*. William WILSON nominated R.H. HORNE's story *The Poor Artist* (**1871**) as the archetypal work of what he termed "Science-Fiction" long before the phrase came into general use, but this work is about how other creatures perceive the world rather than about creative artistry.

Rather more attention to the arts is paid by UTOPIAN novels, although some Utopians overtly or covertly follow PLATO's thinking in considering the artist a socially disruptive force who would be either unnecessary or dangerous in a perfect world. This notion is dramatically represented in one sf story — Damon KNIGHT's "The Country of the Kind" (1956), in which the world's only artist is an anti-social psychotic expelled from social life. Marx's not unrelated dictum that in the socialist Utopia there would be no painters but only men who paint is also modelled in one sf story — Robert SILVERBERG's "The Man With Talent" (1955), but here the author's sympathies are much more clearly with the lone artist in the world where everyone dabbles in hobbyist creativity.

Many Utopians, however, have considered the idea of LEISURE without art to be nonsensical. But they have, alas, been hard pressed to find material appropriate to fill the gap. In Edward BELLAMY's *Looking Backward* (**1888**), the first major novel of a mechanized Utopia, leisure and work hours alike are amply filled by the wonders of piped music — a proposition whose splendours have been rendered ludicrous by the passage of time. William MORRIS's counter-proposal in *News From Nowhere* (**1890**) was to put artistry back into ordinary human activities, and this suggestion retains some of its appeal — it is echoed in Robert M. Pirsig's best-selling *Zen and the Art of Motorcycle*

Maintenance (**1974**). Much more ambitious attempts to represent the artistic life of the future may be found in Herman HESSE's *Magister Ludi* (**1943**; trans. **1949**; vt *The Glass Bead Game*), in which the life of society's elite is dominated by the aesthetics of a "Game", and in Franz WERFEL's *Star of the Unborn* (**1946**; trans. **1946**), whose narrator attends a "sympaian" — music composed and played *ad lib* under the aegis of pure inspiration. The aesthetic life and its elevation to a universal *modus vivendi* is, however, mercilessly treated in some Utopian satires — notably in Alexandr MOSZKOWSKI's account of the island of Helikonda in *The Isles of Wisdom* (**1924**) and André MAUROIS's *A Voyage to the Island of the Articoles* (**1927**; trans. **1928**). One of the few sf novels which deals with the arts is also satirical: Fritz LEIBER's *The Silver Eggheads* (**1961**), in which human litterateurs use "wordmills" and authored fiction is strictly for the ROBOTS.

In *The Return of William Shakespeare* (**1929**) Hugh KINGSMILL used a science-fictional framework for a commentary on Shakespeare when he audaciously credited his interpretations to the bard himself and embedded them in a tale about his resurrection. Kingsmill did not take himself too seriously, but Ray BRADBURY, who resurrected Thomas Wolfe to describe the experience of travel to other worlds in "Forever and the Earth" (**1950**), did. Isaac ASIMOV used the idea for a brief joke, "The Immortal Bard" (**1954**), in which a time-travelling Shakespeare fails a college course in his own works, but the most ambitious and most successful story in this vein is James BLISH's "A Work of Art" (**1956**). In this story the resurrection of Richard Strauss into the brain of another man is itself hailed as a work of art while Strauss discovers privately that rebirth has not re-ignited his creative powers.

Several sf writers have an educational background in one or other of the arts which is reflected in their work. Anne MCCAFFREY's training as an opera singer has influenced two series — *The Ship Who Sang* (fix-up **1969**) and the stories about Killashandra the Crystal Singer (**1974-5**) — though the only sf novel featuring an interplanetary touring opera company is by Jack VANCE: the ironically titled *Space Opera* (**1965**). Lloyd BIGGLE's interest in music is apparent in many of his stories, particularly those collected in *The Metallic Muse* (coll. **1972**). Fritz Leiber's theatrical background is less obvious, though it is manifest in "No Great Magic" (**1963**) and the fantasy "Four Ghosts in Hamlet" (**1965**); and some of his other stories — notably *The Big Time* (**1961**) — are decidedly theatrical. John BRUNNER's *The Productions of Time* (**1967**) also combines the themes of theatre and TIME TRAVEL. Novels by other authors which use a theatrical background include *Doomsday*

Morning (**1957**) by C.L. MOORE and *Showboat World* by Jack Vance (**1975**). The hero of Robert HEINLEIN's *Double Star* (**1956**) is an actor.

Music is the art most commonly featured in sf. It is the subject matter of Edgar PANGBORN's excellent "Music Master of Babylon" (**1954**) and "The Golden Horn" (**1962**), and J.F. BONE's "Special Effect" (**1961**); it features strongly in Norman SPINRAD's apocalyptic story "The Big Flash" (**1968**) and Fred HOYLE's novel *October the First is Too Late* (**1966**). Alien music is featured, rather unconvincingly, in "The Music Makers" (**1965**) by Lang JONES and *Sweetwater* (**1973**) by Laurence YEP.

When it comes to inventing new arts, sf writers are understandably tentative. The aesthetics of time travel are elegantly developed in C.L. Moore's "Vintage Season" (**1946**), and dream construction becomes an art in Isaac Asimov's "Dreaming is a Private Thing" (**1955**), but even the mask-making art of Jack Vance's "The Moon Moth" (**1961**); the holographic sculpture of William ROTSLER's "Patron of the Arts" (**1972**); the music-and-light linkages of John Brunner's *The Whole Man* (**1964**; vt *Telepathist*); the sartorial art of Barrington J. BAYLEY's *The Garments of Caean* (**1976**); the psycho-sculpture of Robert Silverberg's *The Second Trip* (**1972**) and the holographic sculpture of Ian WATSON's *The Martian Inca* (**1977**), are fairly modest extrapolations of extant arts. Perhaps the best sf treatment of arts and artists is found in J.G. BALLARD's *Vermilion Sands* (coll. **1971**), which includes a story about the novel art of cloud-sculpting, "The Cloud-Sculptors of Coral D" (**1967**).

In much of Samuel R. DELANY's work the artist and his role are treated emblematically through protagonists whose aesthetic performances, especially their music, shape the meaning of their stories; this treatment is most extreme in *Dhalgren* (**1975**), where the poet-protagonist's poems and journal-like "Anathemata" are actual versions of the book itself.

Anthologies of sf stories about the arts are *New Dreams This Morning* (**1966**) ed James Blish, and *The Arts and Beyond: Visions of Man's Aesthetic Future* (anth. **1977**) ed. Thomas F. MONTELEONE. [BS] See also: GAMES AND SPORTS.

ARZHAK, NIKOLAI See Yuli DANIEL.

ASH, ALAN (?–) British writer, in whose routine sf adventure, *Conditioned for Space* (**1955**), an awakened sleeper (like Captain America he has been encased in a block of ice) finds himself in the front line of Earth defence in a space war. [JC]

ASH, BRIAN (1936–). English writer, scientific journalist and editor. His book *Faces of the Future: the Lessons of*

Science Fiction (**1975**) was published as if for the layman, though initially intended by BA as an attempt to persuade Humanists and Rationalists, an audience familiar to him from his work as a columnist in *New Humanist*, that much in sf merited their attention. The assumption of the book that its readers may be quite ignorant of sf led to more plot summarizing than was palatable, as reviews noted, for most sf readers, who felt that they were being told the obvious. BA's compilation *Who's Who In Science Fiction* (**1976**; rev. **1977**) was well received by the general press, but heavily attacked in the sf specialist press for omissions and inaccuracies. The UK paperback edition of 1977 was revised, and many inaccuracies corrected. BA is editor of *The Visual Encyclopedia of Science Fiction* (**1978**). This is not an alphabetical encyclopedia, but rather a series of essays and compilations by various hands, arranged on a chapter basis. It is illustrated in colour. BA was secretary of the H. G. WELLS Society 1967–70. [PN]

ASH, FENTON See Frank AUBREY.

ASHE, GORDON See John CREASEY.

ASHLEY, FRED See Frank AUBREY.

ASHLEY, MIKE (1948–). English editor and researcher, with special expertise in the history of British magazine sf. MA's major work as an anthology editor is *The History of the Science Fiction Magazine* (anth.; *Part 1 1926–35*, **1974**; *Part 2 1936–45*, **1975**; *Part 3 1946–55*, **1976**; *Part 4 1956–65*, **1978**). Another vol. awaits publication. As story collections they are not out of the ordinary, but the long introductions are packed with information, much of it the result of original and independent research. The books also contain useful bibliographical appendices. MA's other anthologies are *Souls in Metal* (anth. **1977**); *Weird Legacies* (anth. **1977**); *SF Choice 77* (anth. **1977**); and *The Best of British SF* in two vols (**1977**). MA has also compiled *Who's Who in Horror and Fantasy Fiction* (**1977**), an interesting work whose bibliographical data is presented clumsily; it is nonetheless markedly superior to its companion volume dealing with sf (*see* Brian ASH). MA's work, which deals with some 400 writers, makes ample use of original research in addition to secondary sources. MA also contributed bibliographical articles to *Science Fiction Monthly*. [PN]

ASHTON, FRANCIS LESLIE (1904–). English writer, in whose first sf novel, *The Breaking of the Seals* (**1946**), the Moon disintegrates and falls on to the Earth; *Alas, That Great City* (**1948**), also invokes the Moon's catastrophic influence when ATLANTIS is destroyed by its arrival in orbit; *Wrong*

Side of the Moon (**1952**), written with Stephen Ashton, deals more mundanely with an attempt at space travel. [JC]

ASIMOV, ISAAC (1920–). American writer. Married (1) Gertrude Blugerman, (2) Janet Jeppson, a psychiatrist who became an sf writer. IA was born in Russia, but moved to the USA with his family in 1923 and became an American citizen in 1928. He discovered sf through the magazines sold in his father's candy store; those early years are described in the commentary included in his compendium of 1930s sf, *Before the Golden Age* (anth. **1974**; paperback edition is split into three volumes in the USA, four in the UK). He was not strongly involved in sf fandom, although for a while he was associated with the FUTURIANS, whose members included Frederik POHL, who later published several of IA's early stories in his magazines ASTONISHING STORIES and SUPER SCIENCE STORIES. IA began to write for publication in 1938, and from the start developed a relationship with John W. CAMPBELL Jr, editor of ASTOUNDING SCIENCE FICTION, who encouraged and advised him. His first published story was "Marooned off Vesta" (1939) in AMAZING STORIES.

Intellectually precocious, IA obtained his undergraduate degree from Columbia University in 1939, majoring in chemistry, and proceeded to take his MA in 1941 and PhD (after a wartime hiatus which he mostly spent working in the US Naval Air Experimental Station alongside L. Sprague DE CAMP and Robert HEINLEIN) in 1948. In 1949 he joined the Boston University School of Medicine, where he became associate professor of bio-chemistry, a position he resigned in 1958 (although he retains the title) in order to write full-time.

Although IA's first stories did not attract the immediate attention accorded to contemporaries like Heinlein and A.E. VAN VOGT, he had within three years written or embarked upon the works with which his name is still chiefly identified. The first story in his ROBOT series, "Strange Playfellow" (vt "Robbie") appeared in 1940. The third story of the series, "Liar!" (1941), introduced the Three Laws of Robotics, whose formulation IA credits to John W. Campbell. Constrained by the three laws, IA's POSITRONIC ROBOTS were instrumental in relegating into insignificance the clanking metal monsters of earlier PULP sf, although the stories themselves depended on exploiting loopholes in the laws. His robot series consists of *I, Robot* (coll. **1950**; first UK paperback edition omits two stories), *The Caves of Steel* (**1954**), *The Naked Sun* (**1956**), *The Rest of the Robots* (coll. **1964**; the hardback editions of this volume include *The Caves of Steel* and *The Naked Sun*), "Feminine Intuition" (1969), "Light Verse" (1973), "That Thou Art Mindful of Him" (1974),

"The Bicentennial Man" (1976) and "The Tercentenary Incident" (1976). The two novels in the series, featuring a detective and his robot partner, are successful fusions of sf and the detective story; *The Caves of Steel* is additionally a notable story of OVERPOPULATION. IA began a third robot novel in 1958, but never completed it.

In 1941 IA published his single most famous story, "Nightfall", which has headed various polls taken to determine the best sf short story of all time, including that conducted by the SCIENCE FICTION WRITERS OF AMERICA. The story concerns the COSMOLOGY of a world orbiting six suns, and the PSYCHOLOGICAL effect on its inhabitants of a nightfall which happens at intervals of more than two millennia.

"Foundation" (1942) was the first of the celebrated "Foundation" series: *Foundation* (1942–4 *ASF*; fix-up **1951**; vt abridged *The 1,000 Year Plan*), *Foundation and Empire* (1945 *ASF*; fix-up **1952**; vt *The Man Who Upset the Universe*) and *Second Foundation* (1948–50 *ASF*; fix-up **1953**). The series is published in an omnibus volume, *The Foundation Trilogy* (**1964**; vt *An Isaac Asimov Omnibus* UK). Deriving elements of its background from an earlier story, "Black Friar of the Flame" (1942), the series was originally conceived by IA as a single story, the fall of the Roman Empire rewritten as sf; it evolved into a much larger undertaking through consultation with John W. Campbell Jr. Grandiose in conception, the series suffers in overall design from having been written piecemeal over a period of years; it is nevertheless a landmark and won a HUGO award in 1966 as "Best All-Time Series". The stories characteristically emphasize intellectual rather than physical conflict; their pivot is the IMAGINARY SCIENCE of PSYCHOHISTORY. The planet-wide CITY of Trantor was burlesqued by Harry HARRISON in *Bill, the Galactic Hero* (**1965**); later stories in the series introduce an interesting MUTANT character, the Mule.

IA's first published novel was *Pebble in the Sky* (**1950**). Like two subsequent novels — *The Stars Like Dust* (**1951**; vt *The Rebellious Stars* USA) and *The Currents of Space* (**1952**) — its setting is the GALACTIC EMPIRE of the "Foundation" stories, much earlier in time. The three books were included in an omnibus, *Triangle* (**1961**; vt *A Second Isaac Asimov Omnibus* UK). In the years 1950–58 IA wrote most of his novels and many short stories. *The End of Eternity* (**1955**) is a complex story of TIME TRAVEL and TIME PARADOXES, considered by some critics to be his best work. Many of his best short stories are from this period, including "The Martian Way" (1952), "Dreaming is a Private Thing" (1955), "The Dead Past" (1956) and "The Ugly Little Boy" (1958). He began a series featuring the sf detective Wendell Urth: "The Singing

Bell" (1955), "The Talking Stone" (1955), "The Dying Night" (1956) and "The Key" (1966). As Paul French he wrote six CHILDREN'S sf novels featuring the character David "Lucky" Starr: *David Starr, Space Ranger* (**1952**; vt *Space Ranger* UK), *Lucky Starr and the Pirates of the Asteroids* (**1953**; vt *The Pirates of the Asteroids* UK), *Lucky Starr and the Oceans of Venus* (**1954**; vt *The Oceans of Venus* UK), *Lucky Starr and the Big Sun of Mercury* (**1956**; vt *The Big Sun of Mercury* UK), *Lucky Starr and the Moons of Jupiter* (**1957**; vt *The Moons of Jupiter* UK), *Lucky Starr and the Rings of Saturn* (**1958**; vt *The Rings of Saturn* UK). Apart from a single story published as George E. Dale in *ASF*, this was IA's only pseudonym, and all the books have since been republished under his own name. In the UK, the Lucky Starr novels were included in three omnibus volumes: *An Isaac Asimov Double* (**1972**), *A Second Isaac Asimov Double* (**1973**) and *A Third Isaac Asimov Double* (**1973**).

In 1958 IA decided to devote his energies to science popularization. One result is his column in the MAGAZINE OF FANTASY AND SCIENCE FICTION which has appeared continuously since November 1958 and which won IA a special Hugo award in 1963 for "adding science to science fiction". Another result is a flood of books, many of them very substantial, on all aspects of science and, more recently, on any subject that interests him. By 1976 he had published, all told, more than 170 books.

His sf output since 1958 has been sparse. He wrote a novel, *Fantastic Voyage* (**1966**), based on the film of the same name. His novel *The Gods Themselves* (**1972**) won both Hugo and NEBULA awards, and was notable for its ALIEN beings. Recent collections, *The Early Asimov* (coll. **1972**; paperback edition split into two volumes in the USA and three in the UK), *Buy Jupiter* (coll. **1975**) and *The Bicentennial Man* (coll. **1976**) contain linking commentaries which, together with those in *Before the Golden Age*, comprise an extended autobiographical account. Spring 1977 saw the first issue of ISAAC ASIMOV'S SCIENCE FICTION MAGAZINE (actually edited by George SCITHERS, with IA as editorial director) whose existence serves to underline his stature. [MJE]
Other works: *The Martian Way* (coll. **1955**); *Earth is Room Enough* (coll. **1957**); *Nine Tomorrows* (coll. **1959**); ed. *The Hugo Winners* (anth. **1962**); ed. *Fifty Short Science Fiction Tales* (anth. **1963**; a collaboration with Groff CONKLIN); ed. *Tomorrow's Children* (anth. **1966**); *Through a Glass, Clearly* (coll. **1967**); *Asimov's Mysteries* (coll. **1968**); *Nightfall and Other Stories* (coll. **1969**; UK paperback in two volumes); *Opus 100* (coll. **1969**); ed. *The Hugo Winners, Vol II* (anth. **1971**; US paperback in two volumes as *Stories from The Hugo Winners* and *More Stories from The Hugo*

Winners); *The Best New Thing* (**1971**); *The Best of Isaac Asimov* (coll. **1973**; UK paperback later divided into two volumes); *Have You Seen These?* (coll. **1974**); *The Heavenly Host* (juvenile novel **1975**); *Good Taste* (**1976**); *More Tales of the Black Widowers* (coll. **1976**); ed. *The Hugo Winners, Vol III* (anth. **1977**).

About the author: *FSF* Oct. 1966, "Special Isaac Asimov Issue"; *The Science Fiction of Isaac Asimov* by Joseph F. PATROUCH Jr (**1974**); *Asimov Analysed* (**1972**) by Neil GOBLE; *Isaac Asimov* (anth. of critical articles **1977**) ed. Joseph D. Olander and Martin Harry GREENBERG.

See also: ALTERNATE WORLDS; ARTS; BIOLOGY; COLONIZATION OF OTHER WORLDS; COMPUTERS; CONCEPTUAL BREAKTHROUGH; CRIME AND PUNISHMENT; DEVOLUTION; DISCOVERY AND INVENTION; FANTASTIC VOYAGES; FANTASY; FLYING SAUCERS; FOURTH DIMENSION (AND OTHERS); FUTUROLOGY; GODS AND DEMONS; GOLDEN AGE OF SF; GREAT AND SMALL; HISTORY IN SF; JUPITER; LIFE ON OTHER WORLDS; MACHINES; MEDIA LANDSCAPE; MERCURY; MUSIC AND OPERA; OUTER PLANETS; PARALLEL WORLDS; PHYSICS; POLITICS; PSEUDO-SCIENCE; RADIO (UK); SAMUELSON, David N.; SF OVERTAKEN BY EVENTS; SCIENTIFIC ERRORS; SCIENTISTS; SEX; SOCIOLOGY, STARS, TRANSPORTATION; UNDER THE SEA; UTOPIAS; VENUS.

ASSOCIATION OF SCIENCE FICTION ARTISTS (ASFA) *See* Rick STERNBACH.

ASTEROIDS, THE The asteroids or minor planets lie mostly between the orbits of Mars and Jupiter. The first to be discovered was Ceres, identified by Piazzi in 1801. Three more, including Vesta and Pallas, were discovered in the same decade, and after 1845 hundreds more were located. More than two thousand have now been catalogued. Only a few are larger than 100 miles in diameter — the largest (Ceres) being some 437 miles across.

In primitive space operas the asteroid belt tended to figure as a hazard for all ships venturing beyond Mars. Near misses and actual collisions were common. Isaac ASIMOV's first published story, "Marooned off Vesta" (1939), begins with such a collision. Modern writers, however, generally realize that as the asteroids all lie more or less in the plane of the ecliptic, it is an easy matter to fly "over" them *en route* to Jupiter. Apart from this role as a hazard to shipping, asteroids figure most frequently in sf in connection with mining. The asteroids became, in early pulp sf, an analogue of the Klondike, where men were men and mules were second-hand spaceships. Notable examples of this species of sub-Western space operas include Clifford D. SIMAK's "The Asteroid of Gold" (1932), Stanton COBLENTZ's "The Golden Planetoid" (1935), Malcolm JAMESON's "Prospectors of Space" (1940) and Jack

WILLIAMSON's *Seetee Ship* (1942–3; fix-up **1951**; magazine stories and early editions as by Will Stewart). The analogy of asteroid belt and Wild West was soon extended, so that the lawless asteroids became the perfect place for interplanetary skulduggery, and they featured frequently in stories of space CRIME (especially piracy) in the romantic vein popularized by PLANET STORIES. Examples include "Asteroid Pirates" (1938) by Royal W. Heckman, "Asteroid Justice" (1947) by V.E. Thiessen, and "The Prison of the Stars" (1953) by Stanley MULLEN. The mythology was co-opted into juvenile sf by Isaac Asimov in *Lucky Starr and the Pirates of the Asteroids* (**1953** as by Paul French; vt *The Pirates of the Asteroids*).

The use of the asteroids as alien worlds in their own right has, understandably, never been popular. Most are too small to offer viable possibilities. Clark Ashton SMITH's "The Master of the Asteroid" (1932) and Edmond HAMILTON's "The Horror on the Asteroid" (1933; title story of *The Horror on the Asteroid*, coll. **1936**), however, feature strange fates for humans marooned as a result of unfortunate collisions. Eden PHILLPOTTS' *Saurus* (**1938**) was dispatched to Earth from the asteroid Hermes, but as he was still an egg at the time he was unable later to give much of an account of life there. Asteroidal Shangri-Las are featured in Poul ANDERSON's "Garden in the Void" (1952) and Fox B. Holden's "The Death Star" (1951), but in general the most interesting asteroids are those which turn out to be SPACESHIPS in disguise, as in Murray LEINSTER's *The Wailing Asteroid* (**1961**).

Some asteroids have extremely eccentric orbits which take them across the orbit of Mars and even that of Earth. One such is featured in Arthur C. CLARKE's "Summertime on Icarus" (1960), and the climax of James BLISH and Norman L. KNIGHT's *A Torrent of Faces* (**1967**) involves a collision between Earth and asteroid Flavia.

A once popular though now unfashionable theory originated by Olbers holds that the asteroids may be the debris of a planet that was torn asunder in some cosmic disaster long ago. A few moral tales of the 1950s suggested that atomic war might have been responsible. The theory features prominently in James Blish's thriller *The Frozen Year* (**1957**; vt *Fallen Star*), while the hypothetical war transcends time to continue in the mind of a human astronaut in "Asleep in Armageddon" (1948) by Ray BRADBURY.

The COLONIZATION of the asteroids has not been a popular theme. Jack VANCE's "I'll Build Your Dream Castle" (1947) features a series of asteroidal real-estate deals, but the feats of TERRAFORMING involved stretch the reader's credulity. Charles PLATT's *Garbage World* (**1967**) is an asteroid which serves as the dumping-ground for interplanetary pleasure

resorts, but this is not to be taken too seriously. A scattered, tough-minded asteroid-belt society, the Belters, plays an important role in Larry NIVEN's "Known Space" series. Niven, fairly content with the old analogy, sees the Belters as similar in spirit to the colonists of the Old West: they are miners. The one major work on this theme is Poul Anderson's *Tales of the Flying Mountains* (1963–5 *ASF* as by Winston P. Sanders; fix-up **1970**) — an episodic novel tracing the development of the asteroid culture from its inception to its independence. An earlier Sanders story set in the asteroid belt was "Barnacle Bull" (1960).

One of the freshest asteroid stories of recent years, adroitly reworking old conventions and mingling them with new biological and psychological ideas, is "Mother in the Sky with Diamonds" (1971) by James TIPTREE Jr.

In a speculative article Isaac Asimov has suggested that small asteroids might be hollowed out to form the shells of starships, but this intriguing idea has not been much used in fiction. [BS]

See also: ASTRONOMY; SPACE FLIGHT.

Mar. 1942. Cover by Wesso. Note the Frederik Pohl pseudonym, James MacCreigh.

ASTONISHING STORIES US PULP magazine. 16 issues Feb. 1940-Apr. 1943, published by Fictioneers, Chicago; ed. Feb. 1940-Sep. 1941 Frederik POHL and Nov. 1941-Apr. 1943 Alden H. Norton.

Fictioneers was a subsidiary of Popular Publications. After the success of *AS* and SUPER SCIENCE STORIES (the companion magazine), ed. the 20-year-old Pohl, Popular Publications went on to acquire various of the MUNSEY magazines, including ARGOSY, FAMOUS FANTASTIC MYSTERIES and FANTASTIC NOVELS, and put Alden H. Norton in overall control of their sf, including the two that had been edited by Pohl. *AS* was a lively and successful magazine under Pohl and his successor, publishing mainly short stories where *Super Science Stories* emphasized novels. At 10 cents, *AS* was the cheapest sf magazine on the market. It featured stories by, among others, Alfred BESTER, Isaac ASIMOV, Clifford D. SIMAK, Henry KUTTNER, Neil R. JONES (several "Professor Jameson" stories), Ray CUMMINGS and various FUTURIANS (including Pohl himself and C.M. KORNBLUTH) under pseudonyms. A Canadian reprint edition published three numbers in Jan., Mar. and May 1942. No.1 reprinted the Nov. 1941 issue, no.2 reprinted the Nov.1941 issue of *Super Science Stories*, and no.3 reprinted the Mar. 1942 issue. [PN]

ASTOR, JOHN JACOB (1864–1912). American writer, descendant of the celebrated fur trader. His *A Journey in Other Worlds: A Romance of the Future* (**1894**) features an antigravity device, apergy, borrowed from Percy GREG's *Across the Zodiac* (**1880**), that powers a craft in a tour in the year 2000 through the Solar System, meeting many ALIENS. There is much mystical speculation, the journey having as much to do with theological allegory as with scientific prophecy. [JC]

ASTOUNDING SF (Ultimate reprint magazine) *See* ASTOUNDING STORIES YEARBOOK.

June 1941. The comparatively sober cover by Hubert Rogers is typical.

ASTOUNDING SCIENCE-FICTION US magazine, PULP-size Jan. 1930-Dec. 1941, BEDSHEET-size Jan. 1942-Apr. 1943, pulp-size May 1943-Oct. 1943, DIGEST-size Nov. 1943-Feb. 1963, bedsheet-size Mar. 1963-Mar. 1965, digest-size Apr. 1965 to date. Published by Publisher's Fiscal Corporation, later Clayton Magazines (Jan. 1930-Mar. 1933), Street & Smith (Oct. 1933-Jan. 1962), Condé Nast (Feb. 1962 onwards); ed. Harry BATES (Jan. 1930-Mar. 1933), F. Orlin

TREMAINE (Oct. 1933-Nov. 1937), John W. CAMPBELL Jr (Dec. 1937-Dec. 1971), Ben BOVA (Jan. 1972 onwards).

ASF was brought into being when the pulp-magazine publisher William Clayton suggested to one of his editors, Harry Bates, the idea of a new monthly magazine of period-adventure, largely in order to fill a blank space on the sheet on which all the covers of his pulp magazines were simultaneously printed. Bates counter-proposed a magazine to be called *Astounding Stories of Super-Science*. The idea was accepted, and the first issue appeared in Jan. 1930, under that title. Bates was editor, with assistant editor Desmond W. HALL and consulting editor Douglas M. Dold (who in 1931 became editor of the short-lived MIRACLE). Whereas its predecessors AMAZING STORIES, SCIENCE WONDER STORIES and AIR WONDER STORIES were larger than the ordinary pulp magazines and attempted a more austere respectability, arising out of Hugo GERNSBACK's proselytizing desire to communicate an interest in science through "scientifiction", *ASF*, on the other hand, was unashamedly an action-adventure pulp magazine where the "science" was present only to increase the excitement or to add a thin veneer of plausibility to its outrageous melodramas. The flavour is suggested by the following editorial blurb (for "The Pirate Planet" by Charles W. DIFFIN, Feb. 1931): "From Earth & Sub-Venus Converge a Titanic Offensive of Justice on the Unspeakable Man-Things of Torg". The covers of the Clayton *ASF*, all of them the work of Hans Waldemar Wessolowski (WESSO), show, typically, men (or women) menaced by giant insects or — anticipating KING KONG — giant apes. Regular contributors included such names as Miles J. BREUER, Ray CUMMINGS, Paul ERNST, Francis FLAGG, S.P. MEEK and Victor ROUSSEAU. One of the most popular authors was Anthony GILMORE (the collaborative pseudonym of Bates and Hall) whose "Hawk Carse" series epitomized *ASF*-style SPACE OPERA.

In Feb. 1931 the title was abbreviated to *Astounding Stories*, although the full title was resumed in Jan. 1933. During late 1932 the magazine became irregular as the Clayton chain encountered financial problems. In Mar. 1933 Clayton went out of business and *ASF* ceased publication. Although the vast majority of the stories from this period are deservedly forgotten, *ASF* was a robust and reasonably successful magazine in its first incarnation, and because its rates were so much better than those of its competitors (two cents a word on acceptance instead of half a cent a word on publication or later) it attracted such authors as Murray LEINSTER and Jack WILLIAMSON.

The magazine's title was bought by Street & Smith, a well-established pulp chain publisher, and after a six-month

gap it reappeared in Oct. 1933, restored to a monthly schedule (which it has maintained ever since — a record which no other magazine, even *AMZ*, can approach). Desmond Hall remained on the editorial staff for a time, but the new editor was F. Orlin Tremaine (coincidentally a Clayton employee previously, although he had not been associated with *ASF*). The first two Tremaine issues were an uneasy balance of sf, occult and straight adventure, but with the Dec. 1933 issue it became re-established as an sf magazine (with the Street & Smith takeover the name had once again become *Astounding Stories*). In that issue Tremaine announced the formulation of his "thought-variant" policy: each issue of *ASF* would carry a story developing an idea which, as he put it, "has been slurred over or passed by in many, many stories". The first such story was "Ancestral Voices" by Nat SCHACHNER.

Although the thought-variant policy can be seen as a publicity gimmick rather than as a coherent intellectual design for the magazine, Tremaine and Hall together raised *ASF* to an indisputably pre-eminent position in its small field during 1934. The magazine's payment rates were only half what they were; but they were still twice as much as their competitors', and they were paid promptly. *ASF* solicited material from the leading authors of the period, and in 1934 it featured, among other stories, Donald WANDREI's "Colossus" (Jan.), Jack Williamson's "Born of the Sun" (Mar.) and *The Legion of Space* (Apr.-Sep.; **1947**), Leinster's "Sidewise in Time" (Jun.), E. E. "Doc" SMITH's *Skylark of Valeron* (Aug.-Feb. 1935; **1949**), C.L. MOORE's "The Bright Illusion" (Oct.), John W. Campbell's first "Don A. Stuart" story "Twilight" (Nov.), Raymond Z. GALLUN's "Old Faithful" (Dec.) and Campbell's *The Mightiest Machine* (Dec.-Apr. 1935; **1947**). Charles FORT's non-fiction *Lo!* (**1931**) was also serialized (Apr.-Nov.), and *ASF*'s covers featured some startling work by Howard BROWN. Also during 1934 the magazine increased in size twice, first by adding more pages, then by reducing the size of type. It continued to dominate the field in the following years. Super-science epics in the Campbell style were largely phased out as the moodier stories of "Stuart" became popular. Stanley G. WEINBAUM was a regular contributor during 1935 (the year of his death); H.P. LOVECRAFT's fiction began to appear in 1936. Tremaine's intention (announced in Jan. 1935) to publish *ASF* twice a month did not materialize, but the magazine prospered and in Feb. 1936 made the important symbolic step of adopting trimmed edges to its pages, which at a stroke made its appearance far more smart than that of its ragged competitors. Other artists who began to appear in *ASF* included Elliott DOLD and Charles

SCHNEEMAN. John Campbell and Willy LEY contributed articles; L. Sprague DE CAMP and Eric Frank RUSSELL had their first stories published. At the same time, it should be noted, *ASF*'s competitors were ailing: both *AMZ* and *Wonder Stories* switched from monthly to bi-monthly publication in 1935. *Wonder Stories* was sold (becoming THRILLING WONDER STORIES) in the following year, and *AMZ* suffered the same fate in 1938. When Tremaine became editorial director at Street & Smith late in 1937 and appointed John W. Campbell Jr as his successor, he handed over a healthy and successful concern.

For his first eighteen months as editor Campbell did not develop the magazine significantly, although in 1938 he published the first sf stories of Lester DEL REY and L. Ron HUBBARD, and reintroduced Clifford D. SIMAK. In Mar. 1938 he altered the title to *Astounding Science-Fiction*. His intention was to phase out gradually the word "Astounding", which he disliked, and to retitle the magazine *Science Fiction*; however, the appearance in 1939 of a magazine with that title (*see* SCIENCE FICTION) prevented him from doing so. He toyed briefly with "thought-variant" variants: "Mutant" issues (which would show significant changes in the direction of *ASF*'s evolution — and that of sf generally) and "Nova" stories (which were "unusual in manner of presentation rather than basic theme"). Such gimmicks were soon forgotten. In Mar. 1939 he began *ASF*'s successful fantasy companion UNKNOWN.

The beginning of Campbell's particular GOLDEN AGE OF SF can be pinpointed as the summer of 1939. The Jul. *ASF* contained A.E. VAN VOGT's first sf story, "Black Destroyer", and Isaac ASIMOV's "Trends" (not his first story, but the first he had managed to sell to Campbell); the Aug. issue had Robert HEINLEIN's début, "Life-Line"; in the Sep. issue Theodore STURGEON's first sf story "Ether Breather" appeared. During the same period Hubert ROGERS became established as *ASF*'s major cover artist. Campbell's dynamic editorial personality has frequently been attested to by the authors he published. Certainly he fed them ideas, but it was the coincidentally simultaneous appearance of a number of prolific and imaginative writers which gave *ASF* its remarkable domination of the sf field during the war years — when, to begin with, a boom in sf magazine publishing meant there was more competition than ever before. The key figure, in 1940 and 1941, was Heinlein. His stories alone would have made the magazine notable, as a partial listing will indicate. In 1940 there was "Requiem" (Jan.), "If This Goes On—" (Feb.-Mar.), "The Roads Must Roll" (Jun.), "Coventry" (Jul.), "Blowups Happen" (Sep.); in 1941, *Sixth Column* (Jan.-Mar.; **1949**), "—And He Built A Crooked House—" (Feb.), "Logic of

Empire" (Mar.), "Universe" (May), "Solution Unsatisfactory" (May), *Methuselah's Children* (Jul.-Sep.; **1958**), "By His Bootstraps" (Oct.), "Common Sense" (Oct.). At the same time there were a number of stories by Van Vogt, notably *Slan* (Sep.-Dec. 1940; **1946**; rev. 1951), Asimov — including "Nightfall" (Sep. 1941) and the early robot stories — and others. Although Campbell lost Heinlein to war work in 1942, he gained "Lewis Padgett" (Henry KUTTNER and C.L. Moore), Fritz LEIBER and Anthony BOUCHER. In Jan. 1942 the magazine switched to bedsheet size — which gave more wordage while saving paper — but reverted to pulp size in 1943 for a few months, before becoming the first digest-size sf magazine in Nov. 1943 as paper shortages (which killed off its companion, *Unknown*) became more acute. William Timmins replaced Rogers as *ASF*'s regular cover artist.

ASF's leadership of the field continued through the 1940s. Most of its regular authors had popular series to reinforce their appeal: Asimov's robot and "Foundation" stories; Van Vogt's "Weapon Shops" and his two "Null-A" novels; George O. SMITH's "Venus Equilateral"; Jack Williamson's "Seetee" stories (as Will Stewart); "Padgett's" "Gallegher" stories; E.E. Smith's epic "Lensman" series, the last two novels of which marked the last throes of the super-science epic in *ASF* — *Second-Stage Lensmen* (Nov. 1941-Feb. 1942; **1953**) and *Children of the Lens* (Nov. 1947-Feb. 1948; **1954**). The only serious challenge to its superiority was Sam MERWIN's vastly improved STARTLING STORIES, which by 1948 was publishing a great deal of good material. However, *Startling Stories* was a particularly garish pulp, while *ASF* became more sober and serious in appearance as the decade went on. Those covers which featured Chesley BONESTELL's astronomical art contributed to this effect. The word "Astounding" was reduced to a small-size italic script, often coloured so as to be virtually invisible. At a casual glance it looked as if Campbell had achieved his ambition of retitling the magazine.

With the appearance of THE MAGAZINE OF FANTASY AND SCIENCE FICTION in 1949 and GALAXY in 1950, *ASF*'s leadership was successfully challenged. It continued on an even, respectable keel, but the exciting new authors of the 1950s, by and large, made their mark elsewhere. The May 1950 issue of *ASF* featured Hubbard's article on DIANETICS, which launched the PSEUDO-SCIENCE which later became SCIENTOLOGY. This was symptomatic of Campbell's growing wish to see the ideas of sf made real, which led him into fruitless championing of backyard inventors' space drives and PSIONIC machines. His editorials — idiosyncratic, deliberately needling, dogmatic, sometimes uncomfortably elitist and near-racist — absorbed much

of the energy which had previously gone into feeding ideas to his authors. Many of the notions propounded in the editorials were duly reworked into fiction by a stable of unexceptional regular authors, such as Randall GARRETT and Raymond F. JONES. *ASF*'s new contributors included Poul ANDERSON, James BLISH, Robert SILVERBERG, Gordon DICKSON and many others, and its new artists included, notably, Kelly FREAS, EMSH (Edmund Emshwiller) and H.R. VAN DONGEN. It was settled into respectable middle age. Still popular with sf fans, it won HUGO awards in 1953, 1955, 1956 and 1957.

During 1960 the magazine's title was gradually altered to *Analog Science Fact ⟶ Science Fiction*, "Astounding" fading down as "Analog" became more visible. The reason for the title was, said Campbell, that sf was "a convenient analog system for thinking about new scientific, social, and economic ideas". The symbol indicated science fact "transforming into" science fiction. (With the Apr. 1965 issue the order of the two elements changed, without explanation, so that it became science fiction transforming into science fact.) Street & Smith expired, and the magazine was taken over by Condé Nast in February 1962. This was an important change, because it assured *ASF* of excellent distribution (as one of a group of magazines which included such titles as *Good Housekeeping*) at a time when its rivals found themselves facing increasing difficulties in getting themselves distributed and displayed. In Mar. 1963 the magazine adopted a very elegant, bedsheet-size format but, lacking the advertising support such an expensive production required, it reverted to a stylish digest size in Apr. 1965. The large issues are mostly notable for Frank HERBERT's first two "Dune" serials (combined to form the novel *Dune*, fix-up **1965**): "Dune World" (Dec. 1963-Feb. 1964) and "The Prophet of Dune" (Jan.-May 1965), both superbly illustrated by John SCHOENHERR, who became one of the magazine's regular artists in the 1960s. Other authors who became frequent contributors included Christopher ANVIL, Harry HARRISON and Mack REYNOLDS.

The magazine won further Hugos in 1961, 1962 and 1964. Although it maintained its circulation above 100,000 (nearly twice that of its nearest rival), it continued a slow decline into predictability. Campbell, however, died in July 1971, and was replaced as editor by Ben BOVA. The first issue credited to Bova was Jan. 1972. Not surprisingly, the magazine gained considerably in vitality through having a new editor after nearly 34 years under one man. Authors such as Roger ZELAZNY, who would not readily have fitted into Campbell's magazine, began to appear. While the editorial policy remained oriented towards traditional sf, a more liberal attitude prevailed, leading to some reader protest over stories by Joe HALDEMAN and Frederik POHL which, though mild by contemporary standards, were not what some old-time readers expected to find in *ASF*. New writers like Haldeman and George R. R. MARTIN established themselves. The range of artists was widened with the addition of Jack GAUGHAN and the discovery of Rick STERNBACH and Vincent DI FATE. Bova won the Hugo award for best editor (which had replaced the award for best magazine) four times out of four, 1973–6. The magazine's circulation remained extremely healthy.

John W. Campbell edited a number of anthologies drawn from *ASF* (*see his entry*). Many other anthologies have drawn extensively on the magazine; indeed the first major sf anthology, *Adventures in Time and Space* (1946) ed. Raymond J. HEALY and J. Francis McCOMAS, contained 35 stories, of which all but three first appeared in *ASF*. The two volumes of *The Astounding-Analog Reader* (anths 1972 and 1973), ed. Harry Harrison and Brian W. ALDISS, provide an informative chronological survey of *ASF*'s history. The *Analog Annual* (anth. 1976), edited by Bova, is a collection of original stories intended as a "thirteenth issue" of the magazine. The flavour of *ASF*'s first two decades is nostalgically, if uncritically, captured in Alva ROGERS' *A Requiem for Astounding* (1964).

Analog, as ASTOUNDING SCIENCE-FICTION has been titled since 1960. Dec. 1963, one of the large-format issues, has a celebrated cover by John Schoenherr.

The British edition, published by Atlas, appeared Aug. 1939–Aug. 1963. The contents were severely truncated during the 1940s, and it did not appear regularly, adopting a variably bi-monthly schedule. It became monthly from Feb. 1952, and from Nov. 1953 became practically a full reprint of the USA edition (four months behind it in cover date), although some stories and departments were omitted. [MJE]
Collectors should note: *ASF* presents

surprisingly few problems. The only deviation from a monthly schedule came in '32–3. Jun. '32 was followed by Sep. '32, Nov. '32, Jan. '33, Mar. '33 and Oct. '33, when the monthly schedule resumed. The first 11 vols had three numbers each; subsequent vols have had six numbers. Vol.36 no.4 was wrongly labelled Vol.36 no.5. Vol.41 no.1 was wrongly labelled Vol.50 no.1.

ASTOUNDING STORIES *See* ASTOUNDING SCIENCE-FICTION.

ASTOUNDING STORIES OF SUPER-SCIENCE *See* ASTOUNDING SCIENCE-FICTION.

ASTOUNDING STORIES YEAR-BOOK One of the many reprint DIGEST magazines published by Sol Cohen's Ultimate Reprint Co. Two issues were released in 1970, the second under the title *Astounding SF*. [BS]

ASTROGATION Literally, guidance by the stars. In sf TERMINOLOGY, this is the space equivalent of navigation, and the astrogator is conventionally one of the most important officers on a SPACESHIP. After a jump through HYPERSPACE, for instance, it is necessary for the astrogator to identify several stars, usually through spectroscopy, to confirm his position by triangulation. [PN]

ASTRONAUTS *See* MOON; ROCKETS; SPACE FLIGHT; SPACESHIPS.

ASTRONOMY It was astronomers fighting to establish the heliocentric theory of the universe against the Aristotelian geocentric system (which had the support of the Church) who first popularized the notion of other worlds than our own. John WILKINS appended to his astronomical treatise, *The Discovery of a New World* (1640, 3rd edition) a "Discourse concerning the Possibility of a Passage Thither" and took the notion of lunar travel out of the realms of pure fantasy into those of legitimate speculation. Johannes KEPLER's *Somnium* (1634) was developed from a non-fictional essay, "Lunar Astronomy", intended to popularize the Copernican theory. The image of the astronomer as it developed in the 18th century, however, left something to be desired — the Enlightenment had little time for stargazers. Jonathan SWIFT's *Gulliver's Travels* (1726) contains a parody of the astronomers of Láputa, while Samuel JOHNSON's *Rasselas* (1759) also features a mad astronomer.

The 19th-century renaissance of sf in France was led by the nation's leading astronomer, Camille FLAMMARION, who was also one of the first popularizers of the science. His *Lumen* (1887; trans. 1897) is a remarkable semi-fictional vehicle for conveying the astronomer's particular sense of wonder and awe. One

of the first popularizers of the science in the USA, Garrett P. SERVISS — author of *Curiosities of the Sky* (1909) — also became an early writer of scientific romances. When H.G. WELLS's *The War of the Worlds* (1898) enjoyed great success as a newspaper serial, Serviss followed up with a sequel entitled *Edison's Conquest of Mars* (1898 *Evening Journal*, New York; 1947), and he also wrote *A Columbus of Space* (1911).

One of the most famous of contemporary astronomers, Sir Fred HOYLE, has also written a good deal of sf, including the classic *The Black Cloud* (1957) and, in collaboration with his son Geoffrey, *The Inferno* (1973). Both novels draw on his professional experience. The American astronomer Robert S. Richardson has also been an occasional contributor to sf magazines under the name Philip LATHAM, and some of his stories are particularly clever in dramatizing the work of the astronomer and its imaginative implications. Examples include "To Explain Mrs. Thompson" (1951), "Disturbing Sun" (1959) and "The Dimple in Draco" (1967).

The reason for this affinity between astronomers and sf is perhaps indicated by a quote from Serviss's *Curiosities of the Sky*: "What Froude says of history is true also of astronomy; it is the most impressive when it transcends explanation. It is not the mathematics, but the wonder and mystery that seize upon the imagination. ... All [of the things described in this book] possess the fascination of whatever is strange, marvellous, obscure or mysterious, magnified, in this case, by the portentous scale of the phenomena." Sf is the ideal medium for the communication of this kind of feeling — but it is also the ideal medium for cautionary tales against the hubris that may come from the illusion of close acquaintance with cosmic mysteries. "The Elephant in the Moon" (1759) by the 17th-century Samuel Butler has a group of observers witnessing what they take to be tremendous events on the Moon, but which subsequently turn out to be the activities of a mouse and a swarm of insects on the objective lens of their telescope. A similar error of perspective is featured in Edgar Allan POE's "The Sphinx" (1846). The tendency to seek wonders in the sky formed the basis of Richard Adams LOCKE's "Great Astronomical Discoveries Lately Made by Sir John Herschel ... at the Cape of Good Hope" (1835; rev. vt *The Moon Hoax* 1859), which was first published in the *New York Sun* in 1835 as a series of articles which purported to be an account of discoveries made with a telescope of such power that it revealed the everyday life of the inhabitants of the Moon.

Astronomical discoveries concerning the Moon were rapidly adopted in sf — Jules VERNE's *Round the Moon* (1870; trans. 1873) is particularly rich in astronomical detail — but it was the observations of MARS by Schiaparelli and Percival Lowell that provided the most powerful inspiration, particularly the description of the "canals". There is a certain irony in the fact that this most powerful of imaginative stimuli did, indeed, turn out to be an optical illusion.

20th-century discoveries in astronomy have made less dramatic impact, largely because sf writers have clung with nostalgic fondness to the outdated information that inspired their earliest efforts. The more momentous discoveries, however, did have their effects (*see* BLACK HOLES; COSMOLOGY). The astronomer was not a particularly prevalent character in pulp sf, though Clark Ashton SMITH wrote a memorable vision story in "The Planet of the Dead" (1932), and elderly stargazers were often ahead of the sceptical world in anticipating alien invasions.

The advent of radio astronomy made some impact on post-War sf, largely in connection with the possibility of picking up signals from an alien intelligence — a theme developed in a number of novels ranging from Eden PHILLPOTTS' *Address Unknown* (1949) to Chloe ZERWICK and Harrison BROWN's *The Cassiopeia Affair* (1968) and James GUNN's *The Listeners* (fix-up 1972). A rather more direct contact with aliens is achieved via radio-telescope in Frank CRISP's *The Ape of London* (1959). An astronomical device of great power is featured in Piers ANTHONY's *Macroscope* (1969), which is perhaps the ultimate in astronomical sf stories. It also strays into the realms of astronomy's bastard cousin, astrology — a subject relatively untouched by genre sf writers, who are characteristically shy of PSEUDO-SCIENCE. Two writers outside the genre have, however, written novels based on the hypothesis that astrology might be made absolutely accurate: Edward HYAMS and John CAMERON. Both novels are titled *The Astrologer* (Hyams' book **1950**; Cameron's book **1972**). [BS]
See also: STARS; *and all the entries on planets.*

ATHELING, WILLIAM Jr *See* James BLISH.

ATHERTON, GERTRUDE FRANK-LYN (1857–1948). American novelist, biographer and historian. In a long career that extended from 1888 to 1946 she published about 50 books in a multitude of genres, her best-known fiction being *The Californians* (**1898**; rev. 1935) and her sf novel *Black Oxen* (**1923**). In this book, whose sexual implications caused a scandal on its publication, women (only) are rejuvenated by X-rays directed to the gonads. Though her explicitness and exuberance would not be remarked upon today in a woman, she achieved some notoriety in her prime as an erotic writer; she was also a campaigning feminist. *The Bell in the Fog, and Other Stories* (coll.

1905) and *The Foghorn* (coll. **1934**) both contain fantasy stories. [JC]

ATKINS, JOHN (ALFRED) (1916–). English writer, whose *Tomorrow Revealed* (**1955**) is an imaginary future HISTORY reconstructed in AD 5000 from a library containing the works of such writers as H.G. WELLS and C.S. LEWIS. The material assembled, which is often taken from genre sf writers as well, builds a picture of history directed towards a theological goal. *A Land Fit for 'Eros* (**1957**) with J.B. Pick is fantasy. [JC]
See also: RELIGION.

ATLANTIDE, L' Film (1932). Nero/International Road Show. Directed by G.W. Pabst, starring Brigitte Helm, Gustav Diessl, Heinz Klingenberg and Tela Tschai. Screenplay by Herbert Rappoport, Laszlo Vajda and Pierre Ichac, based on the novel by Pierre Benoit. 80 mins. B/w.

This German film is based on the popular novel (**1919**) about the mysterious Queen of ATLANTIS (in this case, an underground city beneath the North African desert) who lures a succession of men to their doom and displays their preserved bodies in a bizarre trophy room. The similarities between this and H. Rider HAGGARD's *She* are obvious. *L'Atlantide* has been filmed several times: the first was a French version made in 1921 and directed by Jacques Feyder; in 1948 a US version, *Siren of Atlantis* (vt *Atlantis, the Lost Continent*, not to be confused with ATLANTIS, THE LOST CONTINENT produced by George PAL in 1960), was directed by Arthur Ripley, Greg R. Tallas, Douglas Sirk and John Brahm; and in 1961 a French/Italian co-production, *Antinea, L'Amante della Città Sepolta* (also vt

Atlantis, the Lost Continent, to the general confusion of film historians) was directed by Edgar G. Ulmer and Giuseppe Masini. The Pabst version is generally regarded as superior, not only because of its visual flair, but also for Brigitte Helm's striking performance as the queen; she is also remembered for her dual role as heroine and evil robot in METROPOLIS.

French and English language versions of the 1932 production were made simultaneously with different casts, except for Brigitte Helm who starred in all three versions. [JB/PN]

ATLANTIS The legend of Atlantis, an advanced civilization on a continent in the middle of the Atlantic which was overwhelmed by some geological cataclysm, has its earliest extant source in PLATO's dialogues *Timaeus* and *Critias* (c. 350 BC). The legend can be seen as a parable of the Fall of Man, and writers who have embroidered the story since have generally shown less interest in the cataclysm itself than in the attributes of the prelapsarian Atlanteans, who have often been given moral and scientific powers surpassing those of mere modern men. Francis BACON's *The New Atlantis* (**1627**; **1629**) portrays Atlantean survivors as the founders of a scientific Utopia in America. However, it was not until Ignatius DONNELLY published his *Atlantis: the Antediluvian World* (**1882**) that the lost continent became a great popular myth. Donnelly's monomaniacal work contained much impressive learning and professed to be "non-fiction". Unlike Plato and Bacon, who had treated Atlantis as an exemplary parable, Donnelly was convinced that the continent had existed and had been the source of all civilization. In fact,

Beautiful Brigitte Helm is the Queen of Atlantis in Pabst's L'ATLANTIDE.

Donnelly's was a mythopoeic book of considerable power, ancestor to all the PSEUDO-SCIENTIFIC texts of the 20th century, and the inspiration for many works of fiction.

Atlantis had already been used in sf by Jules VERNE. His *Twenty Thousand Leagues Under the Sea* (**1870**; trans. **1873**) contains a brief but effective scene in which Captain Nemo and the narrator explore the tumbled ruins of an Atlantean city. Some of the fiction inspired by the theories of the theosophists and spiritualists was less restrained — e.g. Frederick Spencer Oliver's *A Dweller on Two Planets* (**1894**), in which the hero "remembers" his previous incarnation as a ruler of Atlantis. Other writers used Atlantis more as a setting for rousing adventure, one of the best examples being *The Lost Continent* (**1900**) by C.J. Cutcliffe HYNE, a first-person narrative which is "framed" by the discovery of an ancient manuscript in the Canaries. David M. PARRY's *The Scarlet Empire* (**1906**), on the other hand, was set in the present (it depicted Atlantis preserved under a huge watertight dome, an image which has since become a comic-strip cliché) and was intended as a satire of socialism.

One of the most successful of all Atlantean romances, filmed three times, was Pierre Benoit's *L'Atlantide* (**1919**; trans. **1920** as *Atlantida*; vt *The Queen of Atlantis* UK) which concerns the present-day discovery of Atlantis in the Sahara. Benoit was accused of plagiarizing H. Rider HAGGARD's *The Yellow God* (**1908**) for many of the details of his story. In fact, the latter was not an Atlantean romance, although Haggard did write one such entitled *When the World Shook* (**1919**). A. Conan DOYLE also produced one Atlantis story, *The Maracot Deep* (**1929**), which is marred as sf by a large element of spiritualism. Stanton A. COBLENTZ's *The Sunken World* (**1928** *Amazing Stories Quarterly*; rev. **1949**) has much in common with Parry's *The Scarlet Empire*: it involves the contemporary discovery of a domed undersea city, and the purpose of the story is largely satirical. Dennis WHEATLEY's *They Found Atlantis* (**1936**) contains more of the same.

Incidental use of the Atlantis motif became common in American MAGAZINE sf. Many stories are set in other mythical lands cognate with Atlantis — Mu, Lemuria, Hyperborea, Ultima Thule, etc. Fantasy writers who have used such settings include Robert E. HOWARD, Clark Ashton SMITH, Henry KUTTNER, L. Sprague DE CAMP, Lin CARTER and Avram DAVIDSON. Two sf/historical novels, *Stonehenge* (**1972**) by Harry HARRISON and Leon STOVER and *The Dancer from Atlantis* (**1971**) by Poul ANDERSON, fit Atlantis into the Mycenean Greek milieu.

Several British writers have continued the pursuit of Atlantis. Francis ASHTON's *The Breaking of the Seals* (**1946**) and its follow-up *Alas, That Great City* (**1948**) are old-fashioned romances in which the heroes are cast backwards in time by mystical means. John Cowper POWYS's *Atlantis* (**1954**) is an eccentric philosophical novel in which the aged Odysseus visits the drowned Atlantis *en route* from Ithaca to America. The most impressive of recent Atlantean fiction is a trilogy by Jane GASKELL: *The Serpent* (**1963**; reissued in two paperbacks as *The Serpent*, **1975** and *The Dragon*, **1975**); *Atlan* (**1965**); and *The City* (**1966**). Colourful and inventive, but written in a gushing prose, these novels form the autobiography of a young princess of Atlantis, and contain a considerable amount of sexual fantasy.

The best non-fiction work on the whole subject is *Lost Continents: the Atlantis Theme in History, Science and Literature* (**1954**; rev. **1970**) by L. Sprague de Camp. [DP]

See also: LOST WORLDS; ORIGIN OF MAN; UNDER THE SEA.

ATLANTIS, THE LOST CONTINENT Film (1961). Galaxy/MGM. Directed by George PAL, starring Anthony Hall, Joyce Taylor, Ed Platt and John Dall. Screenplay by Daniel Mainwaring, based on a play by Gerald Hargreaves. 90 mins. Colour.

A young Greek fisherman becomes involved with a castaway who claims she is a princess from Atlantis, and has to believe her story when a large, fish-shaped submarine surfaces and they are both taken there. He is enslaved and witnesses the evils of the Atlantean culture, which include crimes against God and Nature. These lead to the eventual destruction of Atlantis in true biblical fashion.

The scope of the special effects was obviously affected by the budget, but despite the cheapness A. Arnold Gillespie and his team achieve some colourful spectacles: the first view of Atlantis, seen from the submarine, is effective, as are the final scenes of destruction. [JB]

ATOMCRACKER, BUZZ-BOLT See Don WILCOX.

ATTACK OF THE CRAB MONSTERS Film (1956). Los Altos/Allied Artists. Directed by Roger CORMAN, starring Richard Garland, Pamela Duncan, Russell Johnson and Leslie Bradley, screenplay by Charles B. Griffith. 70 mins (cut to 64). B/w.

Giant crabs, mutations caused by atomic radiation, scuttle out of the sea and take over the minds of a number of young people. All ends happily, except for the crabs. Even the most fanatical devotees of Corman's early work find it difficult to say a good word for the film. [JB]

ATTERLEY, JOSEPH Pseudonym of George Tucker (1775–1861), Chairman of the Faculty of the University of Virginia while Edgar Allan POE was a student there, and an influence on him. JA's *A Voyage to the Moon with Some Account of the Manners and Customs, Science and Philosophy, of the People of Morosophia, and Other Lunarians* (**1827**) describes a trip to eccentric lunar societies, including one UTOPIA. The spacecraft is coated with the first antigravitic metal in literature, a forerunner of H. G. WELLS's Cavorite. The book is true sf, including much scientific speculation. It was reprinted in 1975, including a review of 1828 and an introduction by David G. Hartwell, as by George Tucker. Another sf work, dealing with OVERPOPULATION, was *A Century Hence or, a Romance of 1941* (**1977**), as by George Tucker, ed. from his manuscript. [JC/PN]

See also: FANTASTIC VOYAGES; MOON.

AT THE EARTH'S CORE Film (1976). Amicus/AIP. Directed by Kevin Connor, starring Doug McClure, Peter Cushing and Caroline Munro. Screenplay by Milton Subotsky, based on the novel by Edgar Rice BURROUGHS. 89 mins. Colour.

The success of Amicus's THE LAND THAT TIME FORGOT (also based on a Burroughs novel) inspired the making of this poor film, in which the most interesting touches in Burroughs' story are ignored. Routine adventures take place in a huge cavern inside the Earth, visited by a hero and a scientist in a mechanical mole, at the expense of the original wonders of Burroughs' fascinating, if illogical, world-within-a-world (Pellucidar), which are barely hinted at. The whole thing could have been set on some fantasy South Sea island. [JB]

AUBREY, FRANK Pseudonym used by Frank Atkins (? – ?), British writer. He contributed to the pre-SF PULPS and wrote three LOST-WORLD novels, the first, and most successful, being *Devil-Tree of El Dorado; a Romance of British Guiana* (**1896**), noted for being set on the Roraima plateau, later used by Sir Arthur Conan DOYLE as the location for *The Lost World* (**1912**). Weird themes continued in his writings, but with stronger sf elements, in *A Queen of Atlantis; a Romance of the Caribbean* (**1899**), which related the discovery of a telepathic race living in the Sargasso Sea, and *King of the Dead; a Weird Romance* (**1903**), in which remnants of Earth's oldest civilization employ advanced science to resurrect the dead of untold generations in a bid to regain their lost empire. These three novels form a series loosely linked by the common appearance of Monella, a Wandering Jew character.

Little is known about FA but there is evidence that he was involved in a scandal at the turn of the century. Following a three-year gap in his writings he re-emerged under the name Fenton

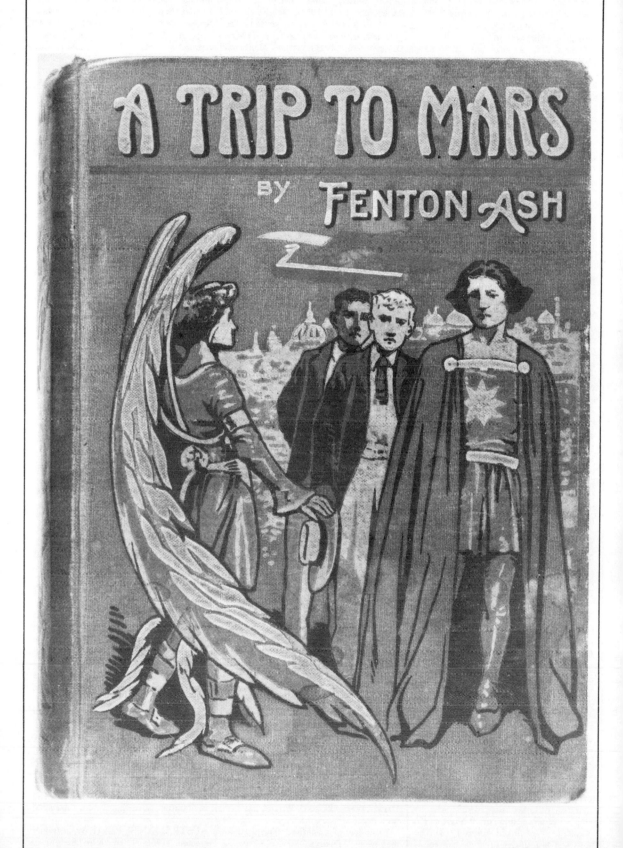

Early sf, 1909, by Fenton Ash (Frank Aubrey). Cover by W.H.C. Groome.

Ash. Publisher's files indicate that his son, Frank Atkins Jr (who later wrote under the name F. St Mars) also used this name, perhaps in collaboration.

Fenton Ash wrote many sf stories which appeared in BOYS' PAPERS, all characterized by a vivid imagination which did not give full realization to the ideas contained in them. Most of them have elements in common. The majority are lost-world adventures, as with "The Sunken Island" (1904), "The Sacred Mountain" (1904), *The Radium Seekers; or, The Wonderful Black Nugget* (1905), *The Temple of Fire; or, The Mysterious Island* (1905) (as by Fred Ashley), "The Hermit of the Mountains" (1906–07), *By Airship to Ophir* (1910), *The Black Opal; a Romance of Thrilling Adventure* (1906 as "The Big Budget"; 1915), "In Polar Seas" (1915–16) and *The Island of Gold* (1915 *The Marvel*; 1918). In two further works, "A Son of the Stars" (1907–08) and "A King of Mars" (1907 *The Sunday Circle*; vt *A Trip To Mars* 1909), the lost-world setting changed to a war-torn Mars, preceding Edgar Rice BURROUGHS' use of the same idea by some years.

A later story by FA, "Caught by a Comet" (1910), may have been written exclusively by Frank Atkins Jr (from analysis of style), as were the two lost-world stories "The Black City" (1908) and "The Land of the Black" (1907–08) and a future-WAR series (beginning with "The Lightning Flash", 1910, and ending with the serial "Britain's Defender", 1910), which all appeared as by F. St Mars. In the market for which he was writing, FA was very successful and influential and, although contributing little to the sophistication of sf, played an important though recently neglected role in its HISTORY. [JE]

AUGUSTUS, ALBERT Jr See Charles NUETZEL.

AUMBRY, ALAN See Barrington J. BAYLEY.

AUSTIN, F(REDERICK) BRITTEN (1885–1941). English writer, and captain in the army in World War I, most noted for his collections of stories illustrating problems for British military security arising in future WARS from new weaponry and tactics, *In Action: Studies of War* (coll. 1913) and *The War-God Walks Again* (coll. 1926); the latter volume is occasionally eloquent. FBA also wrote several volumes of linked stories, each comprising a kind of ANTHROPOLOGICAL romance telling the development of a significant aspect of Man's history through the ages, as exemplified, for instance, in *A Saga of the Sea* (coll. of linked stories 1929), where a ship's history is told, or *A Saga of the Sword* (coll. of linked stories 1928). The first and last stories of these collections tend to infringe upon sf material and concerns. [JC]

Other works, some marginal sf: *Battlewrack* (coll. 1917); *According to Orders* (coll. 1918); *On the Borderland* (coll. 1923); *Under the Lens* (coll. 1924); *Thirteen* (coll. 1925); *When Mankind Was Young* (coll. of linked stories 1927); *Tomorrow* (coll. of linked stories 1930); *The Red Flag* (coll. of linked stories 1932).

See also: ORIGIN OF MAN.

AUSTRALIA Australia featured interestingly in one early LOST-RACE novel, *The Fallen Race* (1892), but it was by an American, Austyn GRANVILLE. However, *The Germ Growers* (1892) of the same year by Robert POTTER is not only bona fide sf by an Australian, it is probably the first ALIEN INVASION story to be published.

But generally Australia's small population, and the ready availability of sf from other countries, have resulted in a weak indigenous sf industry. Only during the 1940s and 1950s, when the importation of sf into Australia was restricted, did local publication boom.

In the 1920s, however, Bernard Cronin, writing as Eric NORTH, published some novel-length stories, probably in the *Herald*, a Melbourne newspaper, though apparently not in 1924, as has been recorded. *Toad* (1929) was originally published in this fashion as "The Green Flame", and was republished under the latter title in ARGOSY WEEKLY in 1939. North's "The Satyr" also appeared at about the same time in Australia, and was republished by *Argosy Weekly* in 1938 as "Three Against the Stars". The original publication of Erle Cox's *Out of the Silence* (1925) is also obscure, but probably occurred in 1919. The racist content of this novel pales beside that of A. L. Pullar's otherwise uninteresting *Celestia: A Fantasy AD 1975* (1933). Better-known examples of Australian sf, both by non-genre writers, are M. Barnard Eldershaw's *Tomorrow and Tomorrow* (1947) and Nevil SHUTE's *On the Beach* (1957).

A. Bertram CHANDLER, though English-born, is undoubtedly the best-known "Australian" sf writer, and his work often incorporates an Australian background, but he has published within Australia relatively rarely. Australian sf writers often began by writing for local sf and general magazines, and it was not until the 1950s that their stories began to appear regularly in American and British magazines. Frank Bryning, Norma Hemming, Dal Stivens and Wynne Whiteford were followed in the 1960s by John BAXTER, Damien Broderick, Lee HARDING, David ROME and Jack WODHAMS. The most interesting recent Australian sf writer is generally held to be David LAKE, and Cherry WILDER has also been praised.

Australian sf magazines flourished in the 1950s. THRILLS, INC. (23 issues, 1950–52) used generally undistinguished stories by Australian writers, including one hack who specialized in plagiarism. FUTURE SCIENCE FICTION and POPULAR SCIENCE FICTION (five issues each, 1953–4) were of a higher standard, relying upon reprints from minor American magazines, with occasional stories by Australians. SCIENCE FICTION MONTHLY (19 issues, 1955–7) used a similar formula more successfully. Far superior to these magazines was the Australian-UK VISION OF TOMORROW (12 issues, 1969–70), which was backed by long-time Australian fan Ron Graham, and included many stories by Australians, as well as reproducing the artwork of Stanley Pitt, whose paintings had previously (in the middle 1950s) decorated a series of small (32-page) paperbacks published by Malian Press; these were reprints of American novelettes and short stories. In 1975 Paul Collins began VOID which publishes original stories by Australian writers.

Other Australian publishing ventures in the 1960s include paperbacks such as Broderick's *A Man Returned* (coll. 1965) and Rome's *Squat* (1970). John Baxter edited two anthologies of Australian sf, *The Pacific Book of Australian Science Fiction* (anth. 1968; vt *Australian Science Fiction 1*) and its sequel *The Second Pacific Book of Australian Science Fiction* (anth. 1971; vt *Australian Science Fiction 2*). Lee Harding's anthology *Beyond Tomorrow* (anth. 1975) included stories by Australian and overseas writers. Jim Sharman's *Shirley Thompson Versus the Aliens* (1970) is a memorable film from this period.

Australian sf fans are well known for their serious writings about sf. Donald H. TUCK produced two privately published, stencilled editions of his *A Handbook of Science Fiction and Fantasy* in the 1950s and his *The Encyclopedia of Science Fiction and Fantasy: Vol.1* (1974) is the first of three projected vols, with Vol.2 announced for 1978. Graham B. Stone's *Australian Science Fiction Index, 1925–67* (1967) is widely regarded as exemplary.

Several sf fanzines have developed international reputations: John Bangsund's AUSTRALIAN SF REVIEW (1966–9) and Bruce GILLESPIE's SF COMMENTARY (1969–) are but Rex Meyer's *SF Review* (1952) writ large. The recently formed Norstrilia Press publishes books about sf.

Australian sf conventions have been held regularly since 1952, and since 1969 the national convention has awarded the DITMARS (Australian Science Fiction Achievement Awards) which were *avant garde* in their first few years but have settled into a comfortable middle age. The 1975 World SF CONVENTION was held in Melbourne. [JF/PN]

AUSTRALIAN SF REVIEW Australian FANZINE (1966–9), ed. John Bangsund. *ASFR* was one of the most literate and eclectic of the serious sf fanzines and despite its relative isolation was able to attract articles from such writers as Brian ALDISS, James BLISH and Harry HARRISON. *ASFR* also served as a focal point for the returning interest in sf and FANDOM in Australia and brought attention to Australian sf critics such as George TURNER, John BAXTER, Lee HARDING, Bruce GILLESPIE, and John Foyster. *ASFR* won a DITMAR award in 1969.   [PR]

AUSTRIA *See* EASTERN EUROPE.

The first issue, Jan. 1951.
British pulp at its most infantile.

AUTHENTIC SCIENCE FICTION

British magazine. 85 issues, Jan. 1951-Oct. 1957, published by Hamilton & Co., Stafford; ed. L.G. Holmes (Jan. 1951-Nov. 1952), H.J. CAMPBELL (Dec. 1952-Jan. 1956) and E.C. TUBB (Feb. 1956-Oct. 1957). Pocketbook-size Jan. 1951-Feb. 1957; DIGEST-size Mar.-Oct. 1957.

The first two issues were entitled *Authentic Science Fiction Series*; nos 3 to 8 *Science Fiction Fortnightly*; nos 9 to 12 *Science Fiction Monthly*; nos 13 to 28 *Authentic Science Fiction*; nos 29 to 68 *Authentic Science Fiction Monthly*; reverting to *Authentic Science Fiction* from no.69, and finally *Authentic Science Fiction Monthly*, nos 78 to 85.

The magazine began as a pocketbook series containing only one novel in each issue, but a serial was begun in no.26, and departments in no.29. H.J. Campbell, under whose editorship the magazine considerably improved, included numerous science articles during his tenure, but E.C. Tubb phased them out to present a solid fiction magazine. After a bad start, many fine covers by Davis and others appeared, featuring space flight and astronomy.

Authentic's rates of payment, £1 a thousand words, were low even for the time, and although the magazine sold well it seldom published stories of the first rank; an exception was "The Rose" (Mar. 1953) by Charles L. HARNESS. House pseudonyms were common and included Jon. J. DEEGAN and Roy

No. 69, May 1956. The more respectable cover is by J.E. Mortimer.

SHELDON. Bryan BERRY, Sydney J. BOUNDS, H.K. BULMER, William F. TEMPLE and E.C. Tubb were the mainstay contributors, under their own names and under pseudonyms. Some issues were on sale in the USA.   [FHP/PN]
Collectors should note: All but the first two issues were numbered consecutively, and no vol. nos were given. Publication was regular throughout, fortnightly up to no.8 and monthly May '51-Oct. '57.

AUTHENTIC SCIENCE FICTION MONTHLY *See* AUTHENTIC SCIENCE FICTION.

AUTHENTIC SCIENCE FICTION SERIES *See* AUTHENTIC SCIENCE FICTION.

AUTOMATION

The automation of work — and particularly the work by which our basic needs are supplied — is a major theme in sf, one closely connected with trends in the real world. The notion awakes ambivalent feelings. That machines might one day free mankind from labour for a life of leisure is a common Utopian dream, exemplified by Edward BELLAMY's *Looking Backward* (**1888**). But work can also be seen as the way in which men justify their existence, and "freedom from work" can mean unemployment and redundancy, historically associated with poverty and misery. The Luddite riots haunt the Utopian dream in any attempt to estimate the significance of automation in human terms.

The earliest automatic machines exploited the energy of wind and water, and Don Quixote's attack on the windmills has been read by some modern commentators as an early response to the invasion of human affairs by the giants of mechanism. It was not until the industrial revolution, however, when steam engines harnessed the power of fire (*see* POWER

SOURCES), that the automation of work became a generalized phenomenon and factories took over production of a wide range of necessary commodities. After the second stage of the revolution, when electrical devices provided much more sophisticated means of power application, automation expanded out of the factories to affect all forms of human endeavour and influence all aspects of human life.

Both the Bellamyesque Utopian dream and the anxiety which haunts it are abundantly represented in speculative literature. The history of modern Utopian thought (*see* UTOPIAS and DYSTOPIAS) is very largely the history of a loss of faith in Utopia-through-automation and the growth of various fears: fear that machines may destroy the world by using up its resources, poisoning it with waste, or simply by making available to man the means of self-destruction; and the more insidious fear that Man may be "enslaved" by his machines, becoming "automated" himself through reliance upon them, a fear expressed in "The Machine Stops" (1909) by E.M. FORSTER, written in response to what he regarded as the irrational optimism of H.G. WELLS.

The wonders of automation were much celebrated by Hugo GERNSBACK, and much is made of the mechanical provision of the necessities of life in his *Ralph 124C 41 +* (1911; **1925**). Even in the sf pulps, however, reservations were apparent in the works of such writers as David H. KELLER and Miles J. BREUER. Laurence MANNING and Fletcher PRATT, in "City of the Living Dead" (1930), offered an image of men of the future living entirely encased in silver wires, their total experience provided synthetically. Outside the genre powerful images of men enslaved and automated by machines were offered in the classic film METROPOLIS (1926; book by Thea VON HARBOU **1926**; trans. **1927**). The notion of the leisurely, machine-supported life was ruthlessly satirized in *The Isles of Wisdom* (**1924**) by Alexandr Moszkowski and turned into a horror story by Aldous HUXLEY in *Brave New World* (**1932**). The rejection of progress implicit in such extreme cases as Huxley's novel, however, was quite unacceptable to the genre sf writers and regarded as unrealistic by the great majority of writers outside the magazines, who pleaded only for caution and discretion.

One of the most significant advances in the automation of work was anticipated in sf, and now bears the name of the story in which it appeared: Robert HEINLEIN's "Waldo" (1942 as by Anson MacDonald) (*see* WALDOS). Much attention has also been devoted in sf to ROBOTS, automatic workers, which received a good deal more careful and sympathetic consideration in genre sf than in the moral tale which coined the word — Karel ČAPEK's *R.U.R.* (**1921**; trans **1923**). The automation of the home was also taken to its logical extreme in a number of stories — usually ironic — including "The Twonky" (1942) by Lewis PADGETT, "The House Dutiful" (1948) by William TENN and "Nor Custom Stale" (1959) by Joanna RUSS. The automation of information storage and recovery systems and calculating functions is also a theme of considerable importance in its own right in sf (*see* COMPUTERS) — an early example which considers some of the problems of freedom of information resultant from machine-storage is "A Logic Named Joe" (1946) by Will F. Jenkins (Murray LEINSTER).

The general optimism about automation of the genre sf writers was eroded after the War, when the dangers of progress suddenly seemed much more real (*see* ROBOTS and MACHINES). The grim image of the automated future came into its own to a much greater extent. Kurt VONNEGUT's *Player Piano* (1952), a story of a revolution which cannot succeed, is a perfect example of the dominant attitude of the post-War decade, although several magazine writers stuck grimly to their guns in insisting that robots and computers would be a tremendous asset to human life if only we would use them responsibly. This case is put particularly strongly in Jack WILLIAMSON's *The Humanoids* (1949) and Mark CLIFTON and Frank RILEY's *They'd Rather Be Right* (1957; vt *The Forever Machine*).

In the post-War period the encroachment of the machine upon the most essential and sacred areas of human activity and endeavour became a plausible theme in sf. There are a number of stories in which artists see themselves replaced by machines (*see* ARTS) — notably Walter M. MILLER's "The Darfsteller" (1954) — and the replacement of humans by ANDROIDS or robots even in the most intimate of human relationships became a popular theme — examples are Ray BRADBURY's "I Sing the Body Electric" (1969) and Thomas N. SCORTIA's "The Icebox Blonde" (1960).

The idea of automation carried to its limits — to the establishment of a self-sustaining, evolving mechanical life-system — is an old one, considered in Samuel BUTLER's *Erewhon* (1872) and imported into pulp sf by Laurence Manning in "Call of the Mech-Men" (1933) and Eric Frank RUSSELL in "Mechanistra" (1942). After the War, however, the idea became more prominent and more pertinent. It is featured in such threatening stories as Philip K. DICK's "Autofac" (1955) and Stanislaw LEM's *The Invincible* (1964; trans. 1973), and in such pointed satires as John SLADEK's *The Reproductive System* (1968; vt *Mechasm* USA) and Olof JOHANNESSON's *The Tale of the Big Computer* (1966; trans. 1968; vt *The Great Computer* UK). The notion is given an extra sinister twist in several stories dealing with evolving systems of war-machines, including Philip K. Dick's

"Second Variety" (1953), Bertrand RUSSELL's "Dr. Southport Vulpes' Nightmare" (1954) and Fred SABERHAGEN's "Berserker" series, whose early stories were assembled in *Berserker* (coll. of linked stories 1967).

Post-War cautionary tales concerned with the dangers of automation include a considerable number of recent Dystopias, including Michael FRAYN's *A Very Private Life* (1968) and Harlan ELLISON's "'Repent, Harlequin!' said the Ticktockman" (1966); several notable satires on automation include Frederik POHL's "The Midas Plague" (1954), Peter Currell BROWN's surreal investigation of the plight of the working man in a mechanized factory, *Smallcreep's Day* (1965), and Harlan Ellison's exploration of automated sexuality "Catman" (1974). In all these stories the essential ambivalence of the attitude persists — the conviction that the ongoing automation of human existence is degrading, and yet so attractive to idle minds as to be inevitable. In the conclusion of "The Darfsteller" the actor made redundant by robot theatre has to accept that the public *prefers* automated art, and must find refuge in the faintly irrational hope that somehow artistry will survive until the tide turns. In the two decades since the publication of that story very little has been added to this attitude, because very little has happened in the real world to change it. [BS]

See also: CYBERNETICS; SOCIOLOGY; TECHNOLOGY.

AVALLONE, MICHAEL (1924–). American writer active since the early 1950s under a number of names in various genres; his sf is comparatively limited in amount and extremely borderline in nature, usually being restricted to such film or television link-

ups as his two novelizations of the "Girl from U.N.C.L.E." series, his novelization of Robert BLOCH's script for the horror film of the same name, *The Night Walker* (1965 as by Edwina Noone), the first "Man from U.N.C.L.E." novel *The Thousand Coffins Affair* (1965), and the film novelization *Beneath the Planet of the Apes* (1970). Only the latter is genuine sf. MA's best known pseudonym is probably Ed Noon, under which he wrote thrillers; he also wrote as Troy Conway, Priscilla Dalton, Mark Dane, Steve Michaels, Dorothea Nile, Edwina Noone, Sidney Stuart, and probably several other names. Sex books as by Troy Conway are not sf, nor are horror novels in the "Satan Sleuth" series as by Sidney Stuart; as Noone he also edited *Edwina Noone's Gothic Sampler* (anth. 1967). Of some interest to the sf field are the weird fantasy stories which he published in *Weird Tales* and elsewhere in the early 1950s; a collection which assembles some of his stories from the radio series of the same name is *Tales of the Frightened* (coll. 1963). [JC]

AVENGERS, THE Television series (1961–8). ITC TV. Created by Sydney Newman. The series actually began in 1960 under the title of *Police Surgeon*. Produced and written by Julian Bond, it starred Ian Hendry as a compassionate police surgeon who spent his time helping people and solving cases. In 1961 Sydney Newman, who later became BBC's head of drama, changed the format of the show, making it less realist, and its title to *The Avengers*. Running time was increased from 30 to 50 mins and Patrick Macnee, who played secret agent John Steed, was added to the cast. 1962 saw the departure of Hendry and the arrival of Honor Blackman as leather-clad Cathy Gale, judo expert. The series, now far

Patrick Macnee as John Steed and Diana Rigg as Emma Peel in a publicity still for THE AVENGERS, 1965.

No. 9, 1949; no. 2, 1951; April 1953, with cover by Leo Manso.

removed from its original format, became increasingly popular as Steed and Mrs Gale battled with various increasingly bizarre enemies of the Crown. The series peaked in 1965, in which year the production became much more lavish, coincident with the programme's sale to American television, and Honor Blackman's replacement as sidekick by Diana Rigg as Emma Peel. The scripts became even more baroque, not to say rococo, featuring such sf gimmicks as robots, androids, mind-control rays, invisible men and carnivorous plants, matched by a stylishly decadent, high-camp and sometimes surreal visual ambience. Robert Fuest, who later made THE FINAL PROGRAMME, directed many of these episodes. The producer of the series was now Julian Wyntle, and the writer most associated with it, and responsible for much of its new look, was Brian Clemens. The show continued with a number of episodes every year, until 1968, the last series featuring Linda Thorson as female sidekick replacing Diana Rigg.

Although *The Avengers* was very much a phenomenon of the 1960s in its spirit, Brian Clemens revived the series, with French financial backing, in 1976, as *The New Avengers*, again starring Patrick Macnee, with Joanna Lumley heading a new supporting cast. The stories lacked the ease and panache of the 1960s version, and the sf ingredients had become fewer and less inventive. The hero's visible ageing must have acted as a kind of *memento mori* to nostalgic but dissatisfied viewers. This second series was still running in 1977, in which year the entire production company moved to Canada.

Three novelizations of the series by Keith LAUMER are *The Afrit Affair* (**1968**), *The Drowned Queen* (**1968**) and *The Gold*

Bomb (**1968**).   [JB/PN]
See also: CYBORGS.

AVERY, RICHARD *See* Edmund COOPER.

AVON FANTASY READER US DIGEST-size magazine. 18 issues, 1947–52, published by Avon Books; ed. Donald A. WOLLHEIM. *AFR* was a magazine primarily devoted to reprints, although it also contained original material. Its chief source was WEIRD TALES, and it presented many stories by such authors as Robert E. HOWARD, H. P. LOVECRAFT, C. L. MOORE and Clark Ashton SMITH. It was numbered rather than dated, and appeared irregularly, five in 1947, three in each year 1948–51, and one in 1952. In 1951 Wollheim began a companion magazine, AVON SCIENCE FICTION READER.   [MJE]

AVON SCIENCE FICTION AND FANTASY READER US DIGEST-size magazine. Two issues, Jan. and Apr. 1953, published by Avon Books; ed. Sol Cohen. A hybrid successor to the AVON FANTASY READER and AVON SCIENCE FICTION READER, *ASFFR* appeared a year after those magazines had ceased publication. Its policy was different, concentrating on original stories rather than reprints. Both issues contained stories by John CHRISTOPHER, Arthur C. CLARKE and Milton LESSER.   [MJE]

AVON SCIENCE FICTION READER US DIGEST-size magazine. Three issues, 1951–2, published by Avon Books; ed. Donald A. WOLLHEIM. A companion magazine to the AVON FANTASY READER, *ASFR* had a similar policy, but featured sf rather than fantasy reprints. Wollheim left Avon Books in 1952 and both his magazines ceased publication, *ASFR* after

only three irregular issues, numbered and not dated.   [MJE]

AYES, ANTHONY or **WILLIAM** *See* William SAMBROT.

AYLESWORTH, JOHN B. (1938–). Canadian-born American writer, whose sf novel, *Fee, Fei, Fo, Fum* (**1963**), is a comic story in which a pill enlarges a man to Brobdingnagian proportions. [JC]

AYMÉ, MARCEL (1902–67). French novelist and dramatist, not generally thought of as a contributor to the sf field, though several of his best-known novels, such as *La jument verte* (**1933**; trans. as *The Green Mare* **1938**), are fantasies, usually with a satirical point to make about provincial French life. *La belle image* (**1941**; trans. as *The Second Face* **1951**) comes close to sf nightmare in its rendering of the effects of being given a second, more attractive face; *La vouivre* (**1943**; trans. as *The Fable and the Flesh* **1949**) is again a fantasy, whose satirical targets are again provincial. *Across Paris and Other Stories* (coll. trans. **1957**; vt *The Walker Through Walls*) assembles both fantasy and the occasional sf tale. *Pastorale* (France **1931**) is a regressive UTOPIA that makes more articulate than is perhaps entirely comfortable the nostalgia that lies beneath MA's urbane, "Gallic" style.   [JC]
See also: PSYCHOLOGY.

AYRE, THORNTON *See* John Russell FEARN.

BABITS, MIHÁLY (1883–1941). Hungarian editor, translator (from English and German) and writer. He is best known for his poetry, the finest example of which is probably *Jonas* (**1938**), though his sf poem *Gólyakalifa* (**1916**; trans. Hungary as *King's Stork* **1948**; trans. Hungary as *The Nightmare* **1966**), is of interest in its depiction of a split personality. A Utopian novel remains untranslated.   [JC]

BACON, FRANCIS, Viscount St Albans and Baron Verulam (1561–1626). English statesman, philosopher and writer. He practised as a barrister before embarking on a political career which

ended with his dismissal from the post of Lord High Chancellor of England for taking bribes. Early in life he planned a vast work, *The Instauration of the Sciences*, a review and encyclopedia of all knowledge, but the project was never completed, though Bacon's reputation as a philosopher rests largely on the first two parts: *De Augmentis Scientiarum* (**1623**, in Latin, based on his *The Advancement of Learning*, **1605**) and *Novum Organum Scientiarum* (**1620**, in Latin). The latter book attacked contemporary science, championed observation, experiment and inductive theorizing, and argued that the object of science is to discover patterns of causation. FB died, deep in debt, of a chill apparently contracted when he gathered snow to observe its effects in preserving the flesh of a fowl. His important contribution to PROTO SCIENCE FICTION is the posthumously published fragment *New Atlantis* (first published with *Sylva Sylvarum* in 1627, first publication independently **1629**), a speculative account of mechanical wonders to be achieved by the pursuit of science. It was probably written as an advertisement for a Royal College of Science which he hoped to persuade James I to endow. Though little more than a catalogue, it is a remarkably accurate assessment of the potential of the scientific renaissance. [BS]
See also: ATLANTIS; BIOLOGY; CRYONICS; FANTASTIC VOYAGES; ISLANDS; MACHINES; UTOPIAS; WEAPONS.

BADE, WILLIAM L(EMOINE) (1928–). American physicist with PhD from Nebraska University where he afterwards taught. He published eight stories, mostly connected, in various magazines, 1948–55. The first three were published in *ASF*, the first being "Advent" (1948). [JC]

BADGER BOOKS Name adopted for the later publications of John Spencer & Co., prolific paperback publishers of minor sf and fantasy. In the early 1950s Spencer produced four juvenile sf magazines: FUTURISTIC SCIENCE STORIES, TALES OF TOMORROW, WONDERS OF THE SPACEWAYS and WORLDS OF FANTASY. Later they produced the numbered paperback series "Out of This World" and "Supernatural Stories". Most of these, from 1959 onwards, were the work of the remarkably prolific R.L. FANTHORPE. A typical issue of "Supernatural Stories" would contain five or six stories apparently by different authors all of whom, in fact, were Fanthorpe. Most of the Badger sf or supernatural novels were also the work of Fanthorpe under one guise or another. Their last titles appeared in 1966. [MJE]

BAEN, JAMES (P.) (1943–). American editor. JB became editor of GALAXY and IF in mid-1974, succeeding Ejler JAKOBSSON. These magazines were then in a crisis period, which resulted in their amalgamation (as *Galaxy*) in January 1975. JB soon showed himself to be a capable editor, and over the next two years turned *Gal.* into one of the liveliest current magazines. He introduced popular columns by Jerry POURNELLE (science fact), Spider ROBINSON (book reviews) and Richard E. Geis (general comment). *Gal.* also began regularly to feature the much acclaimed stories of John VARLEY, and serialized novels by Frank HERBERT, Larry NIVEN, Frederik POHL, Roger ZELAZNY and others. JB also edited anthologies drawn from the two magazines, including *The Best from Galaxy III* (anth. **1975**), *The Best from Galaxy IV* (anth. **1976**) and *The Best from If 3* (anth. **1976**). In 1977 JB became sf editor of ACE BOOKS; the Oct. 1977 issue of *Gal.* was the last under his editorship. [MJE]

BAGNALL, R.D. (1945–). English research chemist and writer; *The Fourth Connection* (coll. of linked stories **1975**) presents a series of dramatized speculations on the FOURTH DIMENSION, and describes the scientific community's response to the challenges opened up. [JC]

BAHL, FRANKLIN See Rog PHILLIPS.

BAHNSON, AGNEW H. Jr (1915–c.64). American writer, inventor and textile-machinery manufacturer, whose NEAR-FUTURE political thriller, *The Stars are Too High* (**1959**), features hoax aliens with a real GRAVITY-driven ship, who try to bring peace to the world. AHB worked in North Carolina, where he was born, and in conjunction with the university of that state organized the Second International Conference on Gravitation in 1957. [JC/PN]

BAILEY, CHARLES W(ALDO) (1929–). American writer and journalist; he collaborated with Fletcher Knebel on *Seven Days in May* (**1962**). See KNEBEL for details. [JC]

BAILEY, HILARY (1936–). English writer and editor. Degree in English, Cambridge University. Married Michael MOORCOCK, 1962, divorced 1978. She has written about 15 sf and fantasy stories, including "The Fall of Frenchy Steiner" (1964) and "Dog Man of Islington" (1971), and was uncredited co-author with Moorcock of *The Black Corridor* (**1969**). She was co-editor with Charles PLATT of *New Worlds 7* (of the paperback book NEW WORLDS series, **1974**), and editor of *New Worlds 8* (**1975**), *9* (**1975**) and *10* (**1976**). Her writing is warm though ironic, and often only borders on sf. She has written non-sf novels. [PN]
See also: ALTERNATE WORLDS; SUSPENDED ANIMATION.

BAILEY, J(AMES) O(SLER) (1903–). Professor of literature at the University of North Carolina and author, now retired. His *Pilgrims through Space and Time* (**1947**), which has since been reprinted, is the first academic study of sf which it analyses primarily on a thematic basis. Only a small amount of its subject matter is taken from genre magazine sf, which is less surprising when one realizes that the work was in fact written in the 1930s. JOB had considerable trouble finding an academic publisher who would consider sf as worthy of serious study. Much of the work has been outdated by more recent studies, but it remains a useful reference. JOB was honoured by having the PILGRIM AWARD of the SCIENCE FICTION RESEARCH ASSOCIATION, which is given annually to an sf personality who has contributed substantially to our understanding of the genre, named after his book. He himself was the first recipient, in 1970. JOB has commented drily that the circumstances of his birth (born in the criminally insane ward of the North Carolina State Penitentiary, where his parents were caretakers) have not resulted in any flight from rationality, despite what the publishers who rejected his book may have thought. He has a PhD, achieved in 1934. His interest in sf grew partly from those 19th-century writers, such as Thomas Hardy, on whom he has written two studies, including *Thomas Hardy and the Cosmic Mind* (**1956**), who had been influenced by Darwinian and other studies in EVOLUTION. JOB edited Adam SEABORN's *Symzonia* (**1820**; ed. JOB 1965), a pseudonymous work often attributed to John Cleves Symmes, the founder of the HOLLOW-EARTH theory. [PN]
See also: DEFINITIONS OF SF.

BAILEY, PAUL (DAYTON) (1906–). American publisher and editor, whose *Deliver Me From Eva* (**1946**) deals with the complications ensuing from the hero's father-in-law's capacity to increase INTELLIGENCE artificially; he is an osteopath. [JC]

BALCHIN, NIGEL (MARLIN) (1908–70). English writer, industrialist and wartime scientific adviser to the Army Council; from the beginning of World War II he specialized in the creation of psychologically and physically crippled "competent men" in such novels as *The Small Back Room* (**1943**), plotted around scientific problems at the verge of sf. His only sf novel proper is *Kings of Infinite Space* (**1967**), a rather weak NEAR-FUTURE look at the American space programme. [JC]
See also: SPACE FLIGHT.

BALDWIN, BEE (?–). New Zealand novelist. Her sf novel, *The Red Dust* (**1965**), is set in her native land, and deals with a typically Antipodean theme (cf Nevil SHUTE's *On the Beach*, **1957**), of far-flung catastrophe in a secluded venue. This time it is red dust. [JC]

BALFORT, NEIL *See* R.L. FANTHORPE.

BALL, BRIAN N(EVILLE) (1932–). English writer, until 1965 a teacher and lecturer, since then freelance. He began publishing sf with "The Pioneer" for *NW* in 1962, edited a juvenile anthology, *Tales of Science Fiction* (anth. **1964**), soon after, and published his first novel, *Sundog* (**1965**), one of his better books, the next year. Restricted by ALIENS to the Solar System by a FORCE FIELD, mankind, in the person of space-pilot Dod, transcends its limitations.

A trilogy followed, involving an ancient Galactic Federation, its relics, TIME TRAVEL, and rebirth; it comprises *Timepiece* (**1968**), *Timepivot* (**1970**) and *Timepit* (**1971**). A second series, *The Probability Man* (**1972**) and *Planet Probability* (**1973**), concerns the exploits of Frame-Director Spingarn in his heterodox construction of reality-spaces (Frames) for the delectation (and voluntary destruction) of billions of bored citizens. Though he sometimes aspires to the more metaphysical side of the sf tropes he utilizes, BNB's style tends to reduce these implications to routine action-adventure plots, competently executed. [JC]
Other works: *The Regiments of Night* (**1972**); *Night of the Robots* (coll. **1972**); *Singularity Station* (**1973**); one of the novelizations of material from the television series SPACE 1999: *The Space Guardians* (**1975**).

BALL, JOHN (DUDLEY) (1911–). American writer, much better known for his work in other genres, for example *In the Heat of the Night* (**1965**), than his sf, the first of which, *Operation Springboard* (**1958**; vt *Operation Space*), is a juvenile about a space race to Venus. [JC]
Other works: *Spacemaster I* (**1960**); *The First Team* (**1972**).

BALLANTINE BOOKS American publishing company founded in 1952 by Ian Ballantine. It produced the first prestigious paperback sf list, with many original works which were, at first, published simultaneously as hardbacks. Regular authors included Arthur C. CLARKE and Frederik POHL, who edited the STAR series of anthologies. Ballantine later became a division of Random House publishers. Judy-Lynn del Rey became sf editor, and her husband Lester DEL REY took over the fantasy list initiated by Lin CARTER. In 1977 the sf/fantasy imprint was renamed Del Rey Books. [MJE]

BALLARD, J(AMES) G(RAHAM) (1930–). English writer, born in Shanghai. He was interned in a Japanese civilian POW camp during the Second World War. He first came to Britain in 1946 and later read medicine at King's College, Cambridge, but left without taking a degree.

JGB discovered sf while in Canada

Photo Fay Godwin.

during his period of RAF service in the early 1950s. His first stories, "Escapement" and "Prima Belladonna", were published in John CARNELL'S NEW WORLDS and SCIENCE FANTASY in 1956. JGB's writing was influenced by the surrealist painters and the early pop artists. From the start, he opened a new prospect in sf: his interest in PSYCHOLOGY and in the emotional significance of deserted landscapes and wrecked technology soon became apparent in such stories as "Build-Up" (1957; vt "The Concentration City"), "Manhole 69" (1957), "The Waiting Grounds" (1959), "The Sound-Sweep" (1960) and "Chronopolis" (1960). On the whole, he eschewed such sf themes as space travel, time travel, aliens and ESP, and concentrated on tales of near-future decadence and DISASTER. In 1962, he coined the term "inner space" to describe the area of his obsessions and stated that "the only truly alien planet is Earth". "The Voices of Time" (1960) is his most important early story, an apocalyptic view of a terrible new evolution (or DEVOLUTION) for the human race. As with much of his work, its impressive quality is due to JGB's painterly eye, as shown in his moody description of landscapes.

With "Studio 5, the Stars" (1961) JGB returned to the setting of "Prima Belladonna", a decaying resort, Vermilion Sands, where poets, artists and actresses pursue perverse whims. JGB subsequently wrote seven more stories against this background, and the series, which is one of his most popular works, was collected as *Vermilion Sands* (coll. **1971**; rev. 1973, with new story and preface in UK edition). JGB's first novel, *The Wind from Nowhere* (**1962**) was written in a fortnight, and enabled him to become a full-time writer. It is the only one of his works which is formula sf, and the formula is that of John WYNDHAM's disaster novels. In *The Drowned World* (**1962**) JGB inverted the pattern, creating a hero who conspires with the disaster overtaking his world rather than fighting against it. It was this novel, with its

brilliant descriptions of an inundated London and an ecology which is reverting to the Triassic, which gained JGB acceptance as a major author. However, the self-immolating tendency of his characters drew adverse criticism. Some readers, particularly devotees of traditional sf, wrote JGB off, rather simplistically, as a pessimist and a life-hater. Certainly, his next two novels, *The Burning World* (**1964**; rev. vt *The Drought* UK) and *The Crystal World* (**1966**), served to polarize opinion further. Each contains a lovingly described cataclysm about which the protagonist holds ambiguous attitudes. Some commentators, e.g. Kingsley AMIS and Michael MOORCOCK, praised these works very highly.

JGB is a better short-story writer than novelist, however, and his stories of the 1960s won a more enthusiastic audience. "Deep End" (1961), "Billenium" (1961), "The Garden of Time" (1962), "The Cage of Sand" (1962) and "The Watch-Towers" (1962) are among the excellent stories reprinted in his collections *The Voices of Time* (coll. **1962**), *Billenium* (coll. **1962**) and *The Four-Dimensional Nightmare* (coll. **1963**; rev. 1974). "The Subliminal Man", "A Question of Re-Entry" and "The Time-Tombs" (all 1963) are masterpieces of desolation and melancholy, as is "The Terminal Beach" (1964), which shows JGB beginning to move in a new direction, towards greater compression of imagery and non-linearity of plot. All these stories contain "properties", described objects, which have become the trademarks of this author: wrecked spacecraft, sand-dunes, concrete deserts, broken juke-boxes, abandoned night-clubs, military and industrial detritus in general. Sympathetic readers regard JGB's unique properties and landscapes as being very appropriate to the contemporary world: they constitute a "true" dream vision of our times. (JGB has himself acknowledged similar qualities in the work of William BURROUGHS, in an essay, "Myth-Maker of the 20th Century", *NW*, 142, 1964). Perhaps JGB's strongest single collection of stories is the British edition of *The Terminal Beach* (coll. **1964**), which differs considerably from the American collection of the same title published in the same year, with only two stories in common. Other collections, all containing much good material, are *Passport to Eternity* (coll. **1963**), *The Impossible Man* (coll. **1966**) and *The Disaster Area* (coll. **1967**).

One story, "The Drowned Giant" (1964; vt "Souvenir"), was nominated for a NEBULA, although the fact that JGB has never won an award is indicative of his unpopularity with hard-core sf fans. He did, however, become a figurehead of the NEW WAVE of the later 1960s: young British writers such as Charles PLATT and M. John HARRISON show his influence directly.

"You and Me and the Continuum" (1966) inaugurated a series of stories, "condensed novels" as JGB has termed them, in which he explores the MEDIA LANDSCAPE of advertising, broadcasting, POLITICS and war. Collected as *The Atrocity Exhibition* (coll. **1970**; vt *Love and Napalm: Export USA* USA), these are JGB's most "difficult" works and they provoked more hostility than anything that went before. This was partly due to the fact that he uses real people such as Marilyn Monroe, the Kennedys and Ronald Reagan as "characters". In the novel *Crash* (**1973**) JGB took his obsession with automobile accidents to a logical conclusion. Perhaps the best example of "pornographic" sf, it explores the psychological satisfactions of danger, mutilation and death on the roads. It is also an examination of the interface between modern Man and his machines. Over-long, but powerfully written, it is a work with which it is difficult for any reader to come to terms. *Concrete Island* (**1974**) and *High-Rise* (**1975**) are also urban disaster novels set in the present, one concerning a driver who is marooned on a traffic island between motorway embankments, and the other concerning the breakdown of social life in a multi-storey apartment block. All three of these novels are about the ways in which the technological landscape may be fulfilling and reflecting our own ambiguously "worst" desires.

Most recently, JGB has returned to the short-story form in which he still excels. Such pieces as "The Air Disaster" (1975) and "The Smile" (1976) are outstanding psychological horror stories, on the fringes of sf. The most recent collection of new stories is *Low-Flying Aircraft* (coll. **1976**), which contains an excellent novella, "The Ultimate City", that projects JGB's urban obsessions of the 1970s into the future. The originality and appropriateness of his vision will ensure JGB's standing as one of the most important writers to work through the imagery of sf.

It should be noted that the US collections of JGB's short stories are quite different from the UK editions, and normally have different titles. Collectors who buy all JGB titles will find that almost every short story appears in at least two collections. [DP]
Other works: *The Day of Forever* (coll. **1967**); *The Overloaded Man* (coll. **1967**); *Chronopolis* (coll. **1971**); *The Best of J.G. Ballard* (coll. **1977**).
About the author: *J.G. Ballard: the First Twenty Years* (**1976**) ed. James Goddard and David Pringle.
See also: ABSURDIST SF; ARTS; CITIES; CONCEPTUAL BREAKTHROUGH; CRIME AND PUNISHMENT; DEFINITIONS OF SF; ECOLOGY; ECONOMICS; ENTROPY; FANTASTIC VOYAGES; FLYING SAUCERS; GREAT AND SMALL; HOLOCAUST AND AFTER; ISLANDS; LEISURE; MARS; MEDICINE; MESSIAHS; MUTANTS; OPTIMISM AND PESSIMISM; OVERPOPULATION; PERCEPTION; SEX; SAMUELSON, David N.; SF MAGAZINES; TIME TRAVEL.

BALMER, EDWIN (1883–1959). American writer and editor, trained as an engineer, who wrote in a variety of genres and edited *Red Book* magazine, which occasionally published sf, 1927–49. With his brother-in-law William MacHarg he wrote *The Achievements of Luther Trant* (coll. **1910**), a series of nine detective stories with borderline sf elements, notably the accurate forecasting of the lie detector. Some were reprinted in GERNSBACK'S AMAZING STORIES. EB is best known for his collaborations with Philip WYLIE, *When Worlds Collide* (**1933**) (filmed as WHEN WORLDS COLLIDE, 1951) and *After Worlds Collide* (1934) — somewhat creaky vehicles today, but effective in their time. His solo sf novel was *The Flying Death* (**1927**). [JC]
Other works: *The Golden Hoard* (**1934**), in collaboration with Philip Wylie, is a mystery thriller.
See also: COMIC STRIPS; CRIME AND PUNISHMENT; DISASTER; END OF THE WORLD; HOLOCAUST AND AFTER; PREDICTION; PSYCHOLOGY.

BALSDON, (JOHN PERCY VYVIAN) DACRE (1901–77). British historian and author. Emeritus Fellow of Exeter College, Oxford. (Fellow 1927–69.) He wrote three sf novels, all of which are humorous satires on contemporary mores with little allowance for changes in technology or social outlook and behaviour. The most imaginative, *Sell England?* (**1936**), is a DYSTOPIAN novel set a thousand years hence when Great Britain is inhabited solely by a decadent aristocracy, the other echelons of British society living under a totalitarian dictatorship in Africa. DB's other two sf novels, *Have a New Master* (**1935**) and *The Day They Burned Miss Termag* (**1961**), are set respectively in a school 30 years in the future and in an Oxford of the immediate future. They have had little influence. [JE]

BALZAC, HONORÉ DE (1799–1850). French writer, best known for his immense series of novels, *La comédie humaine*, of which his PROTO-SF story, *La recherche de l'absolu* (**1834**; trans. as *Balthazar; or Science & Love* 1859; vt *In Search of the Absolute*), makes a somewhat dissonant instalment; Balthazar Claes invests everything into his search for a kind of universal element which lies at the base of all other elements, but fails. [JC]
See also: IMMORTALITY; MATURIN, Charles R.; MONEY; SCIENTISTS.

BAMBER, GEORGE (?–). American writer whose sf novel, *The Sea is Boiling Hot* (**1971**), deals with a large number of themes, including ECOLOGY. Nuclear pollution has set the seas to boiling; mankind lives in huge, domed CITIES; COMPUTERS do the work and provide sophisticated entertainment; many citizens opt out (for a kind of lobotomy) from a boring world. The protagonist discovers how to reverse the effects of POLLUTION, by reconstituting pollutants into their original states. DISASTER routinely threatens and breaks. [JC]

BANGS, JOHN KENDRICK (1862–1922). Extremely prolific American writer under many names, most of whose books of interest were humorous fantasies; they are not sf, but one of them (his most famous), *A House-Boat on the Styx, Being Some Account of the Divers Doings of the Associated Shades* (**1896**), provides a model for many stories featuring the famous dead as posthumous protagonists in venues that usually have an Arcadian glow; from William Dean HOWELLS' *The Seen and Unseen at Stratford-on-Avon* (**1914**), through the works of Thorne Smith, down to the various "Riverboat" tales and novels of Philip José FARMER, a suggestive line of association can be drawn. The sequel is *The Pursuit of the House-Boat* (**1897**). [JC]

BANISTER MANLY (MILES) (1914–). American novelist and short-story writer. *Conquest of Earth* (**1957**) is a SPACE OPERA in which a resurgent mankind learns how to conquer the ALIEN Trisz. Other sf novels have been published in magazine form only. [JC]

BANKS, RAY(MOND) E. (1918?–). American writer and businessman, who began publishing sf with "Never Trust an Intellectual" for *Dynamic Science Fiction* in 1953, and who appeared prolifically in the magazines, though less frequently after 1960. He has appeared in at least five anthologies. [JC]

BANNON, MARK See Paul CONRAD.

BARBARELLA 1. COMIC STRIP created by French artist Jean-Claude Forest (1930–) for *V. Magazine* in 1962. The interplanetary SEX adventures of the scantily clad blonde astronaut were collected in book form as *Barbarella* (**1964** France; trans. **1966** USA). *B* was the first real sf strip specifically aimed at an adult audience and despite its humorous attitudes incurred the wrath of French censorship. This row, and the subsequent film version, tend to obscure the originality, elegance and inventive sf content of the strip. Forest's later attempts to revive it, reducing the sex and increasing the sf elements, have not met with success. He has, however, produced some masterful, if lesser known, sf strips since: *Mystérieuse, Matin, Midi et Soir* ["Mystérieuse, Morning, Noon and Night"] (**1972**) where VERNE'S Captain Nemo encounters Barbarella, and the witty *La revanche d'Hypocrite* ["The

BARBARELLA encounters a robot in the US book edition, 1966.

Revenge of Hypocrite"] **(1977)**.
2. Film **(1967)**. De Laurentiis/Marianne/Paramount. Directed by Roger Vadim, starring Jane Fonda, John Philip Law, Ugo Tognazzi, Milo O'Shea, David Hemmings and Anita Pallenberg. Screenplay by Terry Southern, Jean-Claude Forest, Roger Vadim, Vittorio Bonicelli, Brian Degas, Claude Brule, Tudor Gates and Clement Biddle Wood, based on the comic strip by Jean-Claude Forest. 98 mins. Colour.
Vadim's film attempts to have it both ways. Like Forest's strip, his film parodies the conventions of PULP sf, especially those typified by FLASH GORDON, but where Forest's work was spare, Vadim's is lush, and he ends by exploiting exactly those elements he purports to satirize, losing some of Forest's sharpness in the process. The film is not strong on wit, partly, perhaps, because writers of so many nationalities worked on the script, but the basic situation is amusing enough to carry it along. Intergalactic agent Barbarella is sexually ingenuous, an innocent after the pattern of VOLTAIRE'S Candide. Her search for a missing scientist on the planet Sogo results in a progressively more baroque series of encounters: with sadistic children and their carnivorous dolls; a blind angel; a pleasure machine; a sexually inefficient revolutionary and the decadent Black Queen, among others. Jane Fonda is appropriately beautiful and innocently erotic in the role. Vadim's less than innocent enjoyment of the decadence against which he unconvincingly moralizes has an air of childish naughtiness, not the genuine corruption which some critics claimed to find. The elegance of the film is enhanced by Claude Renoir's cinematography, Enrico Fea's bizarre sets, and August Lohman's special effects.   [MJ/PN]

BARBEE, PHILLIPS See Robert SHECKLEY.

BARBET, PIERRE Pseudonym of Dr Claude Avice (1925–). French writer. Under his real name he is a pharmacist and an expert on BIONICS. He has also used the pseudonyms David Maine and Olivier Sprigel. A highly prolific and derivative popular writer, PB has published over 35 sf novels, some of which have been translated into English: the PARALLEL-WORLDS story *L'empire du Baphomet* (trans. as *Baphomet's Meteor* **1972**); *A quoi songent les psyborgs?* (trans. as *Games Psyborgs Play* **1975**); *The Enchanted Planet* (trans. **1975**); *Les grognards d'Éridan* (trans. as *The Napoleons of Eridanus* **1976**).   [MJ]

BARBUSSE, HENRI (1874–1935). French writer, best known for his strongly realistic fiction, especially that concerning the First World War; *Les enchainements* (**1925**; trans. as *Chains* in two vols **1925**) attempts, as do many novels from the first third of the 20th century, to present a panoramic vision of man's prehistory and history, in this case through the transcendental experiences of a single protagonist who is struck with his significant visions in the middle of a staircase.   [JC]

BARCLAY, ALAN (? –). English writer whose first sf novel, *Of Earth and Fire* (**1974**), routinely pits Earth's space service against ALIEN intruders.   [JC]
Other works: *The City and the Desert* (**1976**); *No Magic Carpet* (**1976**).

BARCLAY, BILL or **WILLIAM** *See* Michael MOORCOCK.

BARCLAY, GABRIEL House pseudonym used for two stories in *Astonishing Stories* and *Super Science Stories*, 1940, one by Manly Wade WELLMAN and one by C. M. KORNBLUTH.

BARFIELD, (ARTHUR) OWEN (1898–). English writer and philologist whose first book, *The Silver Trumpet* (**1925**), is a fantasy. He was long involved with the Anthroposophical philosophy of Rudolf Steiner. As G. A. L. Burgeon he wrote an sf novel *This Ever Diverse Pair* (**1950**); later works include *Worlds Apart* (**1963**), described as "A Dialogue of the 1960's", and *Unancestral Voice* (**1968**).   [JC]

BARJAVEL, RENÉ (1911–). French novelist, latterly active as a screenwriter and journalist. His first novel to be translated, *Ravage* (**1943**; trans. as *Ashes, Ashes* **1967**), describes a France driven inwards into rural quiescence by the sudden disappearance of electricity from the world; the corrupting effects of technology are described scathingly. The next sf work from this important early period is *Le voyageur imprudent* (**1944**; with postscript 1958; trans. as *Future Times Three* **1971**) which is a rather pessimistic TIME-TRAVEL story, with the

usual paradoxes, partly set in the same future world as the previous novel. Several novels have not been translated: *Le diable l'emporte* ["The Devil Takes All"] (**1948**) and its sequel *Colomb de la Lune* ["Columbus of the Moon"] (**1962**), and *L'homme fort* ["The Strong Man"] (**1946**), about a self-created SUPERMAN whose efforts to bring happiness to humanity are doomed.
RB's later work decreases in intensity and is less interesting. *La nuit des temps* (**1968**; trans. as *The Ice People* **1970**) is a mild post-HOLOCAUST story; two long-frozen humans revive into an Earth suffering the consequences of a nuclear holocaust. All RB's work takes a gloomy view of Man's future. The epigraph to *Le diable l'emporte* reads, in translation, "To our grandfathers and grandchildren, the cave-men".   [JC/PN]
Other works: *The Immortals* (trans. **1974**).

BARLOW, JAMES (1921–). British novelist, known mainly for such work outside the sf field as the anti-Communist thriller *The Hour of Maximum Danger* (**1962**). His sf novel, *One Half of the World* (**1957**), presents a Britain ruled by a totalitarian leftist regime — a not infrequent premise in the period after George ORWELL'S *Nineteen Eighty-Four* (**1949**) and the years of austerity that followed the Second World War. The hero of this novel, finding God again, conflicts with the powers that be.   [JC]
See also: POLITICS.

BARLOW, JAMES W. *See* VENUS.

BARNES, ARTHUR K(ELVIN) (1911–69). American pulp writer, also known for his works outside the sf field. He was intermittently active in sf until 1946, his first story being published in 1931. His "Gerry Carlyle" series of stories, in which Miss Carlyle and a sidekick hunt down various alien prey, appeared originally in *TWS*; *Interplanetary Hunter* (1937–46 *TWS*; fix-up **1956**) combines five of these stories, omitting "Green Hell" (1937), "The Dual World" (1938) and "The Energy Eaters" (1939). The latter story, and "The Seven Sleepers" (1940), worked into the fix-up, were written with Henry KUTTNER, and used his character Tony Quade. Barnes sometimes used the pseudonym Kelvin KENT, both alone and with Kuttner.   [JC]
See also: GAMES AND SPORTS; OUTER PLANETS.

BARNES, MYRA EDWARDS (1933–). American author of *Linguistics and Language in Science Fiction-Fantasy* (**1975**), a useful introduction to the subject, and the only one available in book form. It was originally her 1971 dissertation for a PhD in LINGUISTICS at East Texas State University.   [PN]

BARNEY, JOHN STEWART (1868?–1925). American writer, whose sf novel is *L.P.M.; the End of the Great War* (**1915**). An American scientist, Edestone, uses futuristic weaponry to defeat the warring nations, and introduces a world government which is ruled by an "Aristocracy of Intelligence" — a theme reminiscent of the UTOPIAN ideas which H.G. WELLS was producing a little earlier about world rule by an educated technocracy. The idea, which seems appalling now in its paternalism, must have had a certain attraction when aristocrats of the hereditary variety were still very much in control. [JC/PN]

BARON, OTHELLO See R.L. FANTHORPE.

BARR, DENSIL NEVE Pseudonym of writer Douglas Norton Buttrey (?–), whose sf novel, *The Man With Only One Head* (**1955**), develops the theme of novels like Pat FRANK's *Mr Adam* (**1946**). One man only is left fertile; the subsequent World Federation set up to deal with the crisis is riddled with dissension. [JC]

BARR, DONALD (1921–). American writer and academic, a former assistant dean of the Engineering School of Columbia University, and author of several non-fiction works for children, *Who Pushed Humpty Dumpty; or, The Education of a Headmaster* (**1971**), on American education, and an sf novel, *Space Relations: A Slightly Gothic Interplanetary Tale* (**1973**), a SPACE OPERA interlaced amusingly with "literary" analogues to its tale of a space diplomat, sold into slavery, who is sexually excited by fear, thus enticing a princess, and also finding out grim secrets about an alien invasion of Earth. [JC]

A typical book cover by George BARR, Daw Books, 1975.

BARR, GEORGE (1937–). American sf illustrator, born in Arizona and raised in Salt Lake City, Utah, where he attended a commercial art school. GB started by illustrating sf FANZINES, and sold his first professional illustration to FANTASTIC in 1961. He also did illustrations for GALAXY, but is best known for his covers for DAW BOOKS. He has been nominated for five best fan artist HUGO awards and won in 1968; he was also nominated for the best professional artist Hugo in 1976 and '77. His style is influenced by Arthur Rackham and Maxfield Parrish. Though he has occasionally been accused of imitating Hannes BOK, the similarity in their styles is evident mainly in a shared fondness for "cute" aliens. GB works primarily in colour, laying watercolour washes over ball-point lines. In a field that emphasizes brightness, his pastel shades are unique. His people are slender and graceful, and a passion for accuracy is evident in all his work. [JG]

BARR, ROBERT (1850–1912). Scottish editor and writer, popular and prolific, whose early catastrophe story in THE IDLER (which he edited), "The Doom of London" (1892), deals with fog and POLLUTION. It was reprinted in *The Face and the Mask* (coll. **1894**) which contains several other sf and fantasy stories, as does *In a Steamer Chair and Other Shipboard Stories* (coll. **1892**). [JC] **Other works:** *From Whose Bourne* (**1896**); *Tekla: A Romance of Love and War* (**1898**; vt *The Countess Tekla*).

BARR, TYRONE C. (? –). British writer. His sf novel, *Split Worlds* (**1959**; vt *The Last 14* USA), sees 14 crew members of a space station survive the extermination of everyone on Earth. Eventually they must land and breed and start again. [JC]

BARREN, CHARLES (1913–). English teacher and writer, best known for historical romances. Co-author with R. Cox ABEL (*who see for details*) of *Trivana 1* (**1966**). He has been chairman of the SCIENCE FICTION FOUNDATION since its inception in 1970. [JC]

BARRETT, GEOFFREY JOHN (? –). English writer, who also publishes thrillers as Cole Rickard and Westerns as Bill Wade; his routine sf novels, all under his own name, are *The Brain of Graphicon* (**1973**), *The Lost Fleet of Astranides* (**1974**), *The Tomorrow Stairs* (**1974**), *Overself* (**1975**), *The Paradise Zone* (**1975**), *City of the First Time* (**1975**), *Slaver from the Stars* (**1975**), *The Bodysnatchers of Lethe* (**1976**), *The Night of the Deathship* (**1976**), *Timeship to Thebes* (**1976**), *The Hall of the Evolvulus* (**1977**) and *The Other Side of Red* (**1977**). [JC]

BARRETT, NEAL Jr (?–). American writer who began publishing sf with "To Tell the Truth" for *Gal.* in 1960, and has contributed regularly to the sf magazines in the 1960s and 1970s; his sf novels, beginning with *Kelwin* (**1970**) and *The Gates of Time* (**1970**), with its sequel, *The Leaves of Time* (**1971**), are light, amusing and competently told SPACE OPERAS. [JC] **Other works:** *Highwood* (**1972**); *Stress Pattern* (**1974**); *Aldair in Albion* (**1976**) and its sequel *Aldair, Master of Ships* (**1977**).
See also: ECOLOGY; EVOLUTION; LIFE ON OTHER WORLDS; LIVING WORLDS.

BARRETT, WILLIAM E(DMUND) (1900–). American writer who began publishing short stories with "The Music of Madness" for *Weird Tales* in 1926. He published *Flight from Youth* (**1939**) before the Second World War, incorporating it into *The Edge of Things* (coll. **1960**), whose three stories all relate in some way to flying. His sf novel, *The Fools of Time* (**1963**), unconvincingly posits an IMMORTALITY drug based on cancer. [JC]

BARRETTON, GRANDALL See Randall GARRETT.

BARRINGTON, MICHAEL Collaborative pseudonym of Michael MOORCOCK and Barrington J. BAYLEY on "Peace on Earth" (1959).

BARRON, D(ONALD) G(ABRIEL) (1922–). British architect and writer. In *The Zilov Bombs* (**1962**), unilateral British nuclear disarmament has led to Soviet domination of all Europe; after five years (by 1973) the underground is putting pressure on characters like the narrator, who, forced into ultimately fatal action, solves his moral anxieties by detonating an A-bomb. [JC]

BARRON, (RICHARD) NEIL (1934–). American sales manager for a book company and, until recently, librarian. Using his experience in the latter capacity he edited *Anatomy of Wonder: Science Fiction* (**1976**), an annotated listing of over 1,200 titles which might form the basis of a good library's sf collection. The compilation is careful and well organized. Although the book received the criticisms for omissions that are inevitable with any such selection, it is none the less generally supposed to be the most thorough work of its kind. [PN]

BARTH, JOHN (1930–). American novelist. One of the leading fabulists of his generation of writers, he is best known for his epic mock-picaresque *The Sot-Weed Factor* (**1960**; rev. 1967). *Giles Goat-Boy, or The Revised New Syllabus* (**1966**), which derives its language in part from NABOKOV and its central metaphor of the university as the world in part from BORGES, can by taking the metaphor literally be read as resembling sf; the hero is rendered literally as goat-horned; the

novel itself is a complex SATIRE on education, human nature, knowledge, and also a remarkable *Bildungsroman*. Some of JB's later short fiction, as assembled in *Lost In the Funhouse; Fiction for Print, Tape, Live Voice* (coll. **1968**; paperback with small additions 1969) and *Chimera* (coll. **1972**), also presents intensely academic FANTASY. [JC]
See also: ABSURDIST SF; DEFINITIONS OF SF.

BARTHELME, DONALD (1933–). American writer, known primarily as a surrealist and black-humorist. His novel, *Snow White* (**1967**), an absurdist satire (*see* ABSURDIST SF), and his major collections of short stories, *Come Back, Dr Caligari* (coll. **1964**), *Unspeakable Practices, Unnatural Acts* (coll. **1968**), and *City Life* (coll. **1970**), are thoroughly bizarre and contain ideas and themes taken from MYTH, fantasy and sf. A number of his earlier stories have been reprinted in sf anthologies.   [PR]

BARTON, ERLE or **LEE** *See* R.L. FANTHORPE.

BARTON, SAMUEL (?–?). American Congressman, stockbroker and writer, who also published as A.B. Roker; his sf novel, *The Battle of the Swash and the Capture of Canada* (**1888**), was written to show the defencelessness of the American coasts (and incidentally the vulnerability of Canada) in a future WAR between America and Britain, which, however, is won by the USA using self-destructive torpedo boats.   [JC]

BARTON, WILLIAM (1950–). American writer, whose sf novel, *Hunting on Kunderer* (**1973**), confronts humans with ALIEN natives on a dangerous new planet.   [JC]
Other works: *A Plague of All Cowards* (**1976**).

BARZMAN, BEN (?–). Canadian-born American writer and film-writer whose sf novel, *Out of This World* (**1960**; vt *Twinkle, Twinkle, Little Star* USA; vt *Echo X* USA), ambitiously tells of twin Earths and a love story involving people transported between them.   [JC]

BASS, T.J. Form of his name used by American writer Thomas J. Bassler (1932–), who began publishing sf with "Star Seeder" for *If* in 1969. He is almost exclusively associated with the series that comprises his two books to date, *Half Past Human* (1969–70 *Gal.* and *If*; fix-up **1971**) and *The Godwhale* (**1974**). Through a network of intricately interlinked stories, the first novel depicts a densely overcrowded Earth of the near-distant future where problems of OVERPOPULATION have been dealt with by settling the Nebishes — four-toed evolved humans who comprise the vast majority of the population — in vast underground silos (*see* CITIES), under the control of a

COMPUTER net. Outside the hives, unevolved humans eke out savage existences, hunted for sport by privileged Nebishes. An ancient starship, Olga, who is sentient (*see* CYBORGS), plans to seed the stars with her beloved, five-toed, normal humans, and eventually succeeds, though the Earth society of the Nebishes continues, oblivious to any threat. In *The Godwhale*, also complexly structured, a human from our own near future, Larry Dever, is mutilated in an accident, decides to enter SUSPENDED ANIMATION to await a time when nerve regeneration is possible, but after millennia is woken abruptly into Earth society, some time after the events of the previous volume. In the meantime, a great cyborg whale, long dormant in Earth society's lifeless oceans, has registered life in the waters and reactivates, longing to serve mankind and harvest the seas for him; in her search for the signs of life that have awoken her, she comes across humans evolved into Benthics capable of living under water, and accepts them as human. Larry Dever soon escapes humiliating servitude in the silos and joins the Godwhale; the seas are alive with Benthics and lower forms of life — quite evidently, Olga has seeded the planet. Mankind begins to inhabit the archipelagoes; the Earth will once again bear fruit.

In these two books, TJB demonstrates a thorough command of biological extrapolation and a sustained delight in the creation of a language suitable for the description of this new environment, his enriched, though sometimes passive style being choked with acronyms, biological terms and witty neologisms. But unfortunately his control over the overall structure of a novel-length fiction is insecure, with various climaxes sloughed over, and characters abandoned at the point at which the reader has been led to identify them as protagonists. The abundance of his invention, however, conveys a sense of TJB's potential importance as an sf writer; the series does not seem to be yet completed.   [JC]
See also: EVOLUTION; HIVE-MINDS; UNDER THE SEA.

BATEMAN, ROBERT (MOYES CARRUTHERS) (1922–). English writer, primarily involved in radio and television work. His sf novel, *When the Whites Went* (**1963**), is set in an England where only Blacks survive a disease to which all others fall victim.   [JC]
See also: POLITICS.

BATES, HARRY (1900–). American writer and editor. HB worked for the Clayton chain of PULP MAGAZINES in the 1920s as editor of an adventure magazine. When William Clayton, the owner, suggested that HB initiate a period adventure companion to it, he successfully counter-proposed a magazine to be called ASTOUNDING STORIES OF SUPER-SCIENCE, which would compete

with AMAZING STORIES. HB edited *Astounding Stories of Super-Science*, whose title was soon abbreviated to *Astounding Stories*, for 34 issues, Jan. 1930-Mar. 1933. He later started a companion magazine, STRANGE TALES — intended as a rival to WEIRD TALES — which lasted for seven issues, Sep. 1931-Jan. 1933. His was the first true sf pulp magazine, paying four times as well as its competitors and impatient with the static passages of PSEUDO-SCIENCE characteristic of Hugo Gernsback's magazines. As Jack WILLIAMSON put it: "Bates was professional ... [he] wanted well-constructed action stories about strong, successful heroes. The 'super-science' had to be exciting and more-or-less plausible, but it couldn't take much space." (*The Early Williamson*, coll. **1975**.) HB contributed stories to *ASF* in collaboration with his assistant editor, Desmond W. HALL. As Anthony GILMORE they wrote the popular "Hawk Carse" series. They also used the pseudonym H. G. WINTER. After the Clayton group went bankrupt in 1933, *Strange Tales* ceased publication and *ASF* was bought by the Street & Smith chain, who appointed F. Orlin TREMAINE editor. HB had no further editorial connection with sf, though over the next 20 years he wrote a few short stories. He used the pseudonym A.R. Holmes on occasion but published, mainly under his own name, notable stories including "A Matter of Size" (1934), a story on the then popular GREAT AND SMALL theme, and "Alas, All Thinking" (1935). "Farewell to the Master" (1940) was later filmed as THE DAY THE EARTH STOOD STILL (1951), although in the process it lost its ironic twist which demonstrated the pitfalls of interpreting in human terms the relationship of, in this instance, a huge ROBOT and its ALIEN "master".   [MJE]
See also: ANTI-INTELLECTUALISM IN SF; EVOLUTION; SPACE OPERA.

BATTLE FOR THE PLANET OF THE APES Film (1973). 20th Century-Fox. Directed by J. Lee Thompson, starring Roddy McDowell, Claude Akins, Natalie Trundy, Lew Ayres, John Huston and Paul Williams. Screenplay by John Williams and Joyce Hooper Carrington, based on a short treatment by Paul Dehn. 86 mins. Colour.

Fifth and final, to date, in the PLANET OF THE APES series of films, and the most disappointing. Established in their own Ape City after the destruction of mankind in the Third World War, the apes, still led by Caesar (from ESCAPE FROM THE PLANET OF THE APES), become involved in a war with a community of humanoid mutants. The battle sequences are well handled but there is a feeling of pointlessness about the whole film, which has the air of a cynical attempt to squeeze a few remaining dollars from the "Apes" series. A novelization by David GERROLD was published in 1973.   [JB]

BAUM, L(YMAN) FRANK (1856–1919). American writer of children's stories, the most famous being the long series beginning with *The Wonderful Wizard of Oz* (**1900**). His juvenile sf novel, *The Master Key: An Electrical Fairy Tale founded on the Mysteries of Electricity and the optimism of its devotees. It was written for boys, but others may read it* (**1901**), is described rather fully by its title; the child hero sports an electrical gun and an antigravity device, and has adventures all over the world until he decides it's time to go home.   [JC]
See also: MACHINES.

BAX, MARTIN (1933–). English doctor of medicine; also writer and editor, in the latter capacity of the literary magazine *Ambit*. In his sf novel, *The Hospital Ship* (**1976**), which has more than a passing resemblance to the *Narrenschiff* or Ship of Fools, a group of experimental doctors sail the world's oceans after a HOLOCAUST, curing those they can cure, stashing those they definitively cannot in the ship's mortuary, and applying a variety of techniques, many sexual, to the in-betweens; as the apocalyptic imagery grows stronger, so too do the allegorical elements: ultimately, families are formed on the decks of this little world. Some of the speculations regarding MEDICINE are of interest.   [JC]

BAXTER, JOHN (1939–). Australian writer. He began publishing sf with "Vendetta's End" for *Science Fiction Adventures* in 1962, and thereafter primarily in *New Worlds*, for the next four years. His sf novel, *The Off-Worlders* (**1966**; vt *The God Killers* UK), depicts the superstition-ridden ex-colony planet of Merryland and a search for the lost knowledge it contains. More recently, JB has concentrated on writing on the cinema, his work in this genre including the informative, though not always accurate, *Science Fiction in the Cinema* (**1970**), and 11 other titles, unconnected with sf. *The Fire Came By* (**1976**), written with Thomas A. Atkins, is a science-fact book which contains some almost sf speculations, telling of the great Siberian explosion of 1908. As editor JB produced *The Pacific Book of Australian Science Fiction* (anth. **1968**; vt *Australian Science Fiction 1*) and *The Second Pacific Book of Australian Science Fiction* (anth. **1971**; vt *Australian Science Fiction 2*). With Ron Smith, under the collaborative pseudonym Martin Loran, he wrote two linked novelettes in *ASF* (1966 and 1967) dealing with an intergalactic librarian named Quist, who seeds cultures with new ideas.   [JC/PN]

BAYLEY, BARRINGTON J. (1937–). English writer, active as a freelance under various names for many years, author of juvenile stories, picture-strips and features as well as sf, which he began to publish sometime between 1952 and 1955, with a story probably in the *Vargo Statten Science Fiction Magazine*, but possibly in *Nebula* or *Authentic*, and probably not under his own name. His sf pseudonyms include P.F. Woods (at least 10 stories), Alan Aumbry (one story), John Diamond (one story), and (with Michael MOORCOCK) Michael BARRINGTON (one story). All his sf novels, beginning with *Star Virus* (1964 *NW*; exp. **1970**), have been as BJB, however. This complex and somewhat gloomy space epic, along with some of its successors, has had a strong though not well-known influence on such British sf writers as M. John HARRISON; perhaps because his style is sometimes laboured, and his lack of cheerful endings alien to the expectations of readers of SPACE OPERA, BJB has not yet received due recognition for the hard-edged control he exercises over plots whose intricate dealings in TIME PARADOXES make them some of the most formidable works of their type. Though *Annihilation Factor* (as "The Patch" as by P. F. Woods, *NW* 1964: exp. **1972**), *Empire of Two Worlds* (**1972**) and *Collision Course* (**1973**; vt *Collision with Chronos* UK), which utilizes the time theories of J.W. Dunne, are all variously successful, probably the most fully realized time paradox space opera from his pen is *The Fall of Chronopolis* (**1974**), which pits the Chronotic Empire against a terrifying adversary in its doomed attempts to maintain a stable reality; at the crux of the book it becomes evident that the conflict is eternal, the same forces will appose one another through time for ever. *The Soul of the Robot* (**1974**; rev. 1976) marks a change of pace in its treatment of such ROBOT themes as whether humanity can be defined by self-consciousness; the book makes complex play with a number of philosophical paradoxes. *The Garments of Caean* (**1976**; US edition abridged) is space opera again, but with an element of humour, and some fairly sophisticated cultural ANTHROPOLOGY. Among the stories BJB has published in recent years, "The Four-Colour Problem" (1971) and "The Cabinet of Oliver Naylor" (1976) are probably the most successful. He is currently underestimated, perhaps because nearly all his work has been published in a pulp sf format, and his reputation is likely to rise in the next few years.   [JC]
Other works: *The Grand Wheel* (**1977**).
See also: ABSURDIST SF; ALTERNATE WORLDS; ARTS; COSMOLOGY; CYBORGS; EVOLUTION; MEDIA LANDSCAPE; METAPHYSICS; NEW WAVE; WAR.

BEAGLE, PETER S(OYER) (1939–). American writer, graduate of the University of Pittsburgh, whose highly praised novels *A Fine and Private Place* (**1960**) and *The Last Unicorn* (**1968**) are both fantasies, the first a complex variety of ghost story, the second a nostalgic and wistful tale depicting the search of a unicorn for its lost fellow unicorns. Both works, though not sf, received much attention in sf magazines. PSB, along with J. R. R. TOLKIEN, is one of the small number of pure fantasy writers whose popularity is such with sf readers that their inclusion in this volume is warranted. The effect of his spare style on the fantasy genre, which has a tendency to opulence if not over-ripeness, can only be good.   [JC/PN]
See also: MYTHOLOGY; SUPERNATURAL CREATURES.

BEALE, CHARLES WILLING (1845–?). American writer whose *The Secret of the Earth* (**1899**) depicts a routine hollow Earth inhabited by a LOST RACE.   [JC]
Other works: *The Ghost of Guir House* (**1897**).

Ray Harryhausen's monster surfaces in THE BEAST FROM 20,000 FATHOMS.

BEAN, NORMAN *See* Edgar Rice BURROUGHS.

BEAST FROM 20,000 FATHOMS, THE Film (1953). Warner Bros. Directed by Eugene Lourie, starring Paul Christian, Paula Raymond, Cecil Kellaway, Kenneth Tobey and Lee Van Cleef. Screenplay by Lou Morheim and Fred Freidberger, based on a short story, "The Foghorn", by Ray BRADBURY. 80 mins. B/w.

This was the first of the giant-monster-on-the-loose films of the 1950s, and the one that established the basic formula for most of those that followed. An atomic test in the Arctic wakes a dinosaur frozen in the ice. It returns to its ancestral breeding-grounds — an area now covered by the city of New York. It is finally trapped and killed in an amusement park. This is the first film on which model animator Ray HARRYHAUSEN had full control over the special effects, though these are not remarkable. [JB]

BEAUMONT, CHARLES The pseudonym by which American story- and scriptwriter Charles Nutt (1929–67) is best known, though he wrote some non-sf under other names. He began publishing his blend of horror and sf with "The Devil, You Say?" for *AMZ* in 1951. Most of his work is collected in *The Hunger* (coll. **1957**), *Shadow Play* (coll. **1957**), *Yonder* (coll. **1958**). *Night Ride and Other Journeys* (coll. **1960**) and *The Edge* (coll. **1966**). *The Magic Man* (coll. **1965**) assembles the best of previous volumes. CB's work combines humour and horror in a slick style extremely effective in underlining the grimness of his basic inspiration. As a filmwriter, he scripted *Queen of Outer Space* (1958) and THE SEVEN FACES OF DR LAO (1964), and worked with Ray Russell and Richard MATHESON on several horror films. He also collaborated with Chad OLIVER on the brief "Claude Adams" series (*FSF* 1955–6) and edited a horror anthology *The Fiend in You* (anth. **1962**). He was struck in 1964 by a savage illness which ravaged and eventually killed him. [JC]
See also: CITIES; INVISIBILITY.

BECHDOLT, JACK Form of his name used by John Ernest Bechdolt (1884–1954) for his fiction, though he used his full name for other writing. His sf novel, *The Torch* (1920 *Argosy*; **1948**), is a post-HOLOCAUST story set in a New York of AD 3000; the torch is that of the Statue of Liberty. [JC]
See also: CITIES.

BEDFORD-JONES, H(ENRY JAMES O'BRIEN) (1887–1949). Canadian author who later became a naturalized American. He wrote extensively for the PULP MAGAZINE market, including *The Magic Carpet*, *Golden Fleece*, ALL-STORY WEEKLY, and numerous others, using at least 15 pseudonyms. He concentrated his efforts on historical and adventure fiction, sometimes using sf or weird elements as a basic framework. Among his earliest fantasies are the three LOST-WORLD adventures in his "John Solomon" series (which appeared in magazine form as by HBJ but in book form as by Allan Hawkwood). They are *Solomon's Quest* (1915 *People's Magazine*; **1924**), *The Seal of John Solomon* (1915 *Argosy*; **1924**), about a community established by crusaders in the Arabian desert, and *Gentleman Solomon* (1915 *People's Magazine*; **1925**) about an unknown pigmy race. In similar vein are *Splendour of the Gods* (**1924**) and *The Temple of the Ten* (1921; **1973**, in collaboration with W.C. Robertson), which appeared under his own name. More germane to the sf genre were the series which later appeared in THE BLUE BOOK MAGAZINE, the first such being his "Trumpets from Oblivion" series: "The Stagnant Death" (1938), "The Cythian Lamb" (1938), "Wrath of the Thunderbird" (1939), "The Singing Sands of Prester John" (1939), "Amazon Woman" (1939), "Five Miles to Youth" (1939), "The Tree that was No Tree" (1939), "The Lady and the Unicorn" (1939), "Lady of the Evil Eye" (1939), "Woman of the Sea" (1939) and "The Serpent People" (1939). In this series a device capable of recording sounds and images from the past is used to establish a rational origin for various myths and legends. A similar device is used for viewing history in the series known as "Counterclockwise": "Counterclockwise" (1943), "Naples Midnight" (1943), "Princess of Egypt" (1944), "The Architect of Samos" (1944), "The Last Macedonian" (1944), "Aimed at Aquila" (1944), "The Fabian Sword" (1944), "Where Freedom Beckoned" (1944) and "The Gods do not Forget" (1944) in the same magazine. Also in *The Blue Book Magazine*, appearing under the pseudonym Gordon Keyne, were two futuristic series. The first was "Tomorrow's Men": "Peace Hath her Victories" (1943), "The Battle for France" (1943), "Sahara Doom" (1943) and "Tomorrow in Egypt" (1943); the second was "Quest, Inc": "The Affair of the Drifting Face" (1943), "The Affair of the Two Thirteens" (1943), "The Unfinished Search" (1943), "The Affair of Beryllium Q" (1943), "The Past Earns the Future" (1943), "A Dead Man Tells" (1944), "Island in the Sky" (1944), "Foxes Move Fast" (1944), "Finding Mr Smith" (1944), "The Strange Fate of Colonel Clewes" (1944), "What More Can Fortune Do?" (1945) and "The Final Hoard" (1945). These two series deal respectively with the struggle to maintain peace in the post-War years, and with a post-War Bureau of Missing Persons.

Other series include "The Adventures of a Professional Corpse" (1940–41 WEIRD TALES), "Carson's Folly" (1945–6 *The Blue Book Magazine*) and "The Sphinx Emerald" (1946–7 *The Blue Book Magazine*) which traces the malign influence of a gem throughout history.

HBJ was one of the most prolific and popular pulp writers. [JE]
See also: MYTHOLOGY.

BEDSHEET A term used to describe a magazine format, in contrast to PULP and DIGEST. The bedsheet format varies very slightly, averaging $8\frac{1}{2} \times 11\frac{1}{2}$ inches. It was used by some of the more prestigious pulp magazines in the 1920s and '30s, and became popular again in the late '60s with such magazines as NEW WORLDS and VISION OF TOMORROW, which, unlike the earlier bedsheet magazines, and having fewer pages, were stapled rather than glued. [PN]
See also: SF MAGAZINES.

BED-SITTING ROOM, THE Film (1969). United Artists. Directed by Richard Lester, starring Rita Tushingham, Mona Washbourne, Arthur Lowe, Ralph Richardson, Spike Milligan, Michael Hordern, Roy Kinnear, Peter Cook and Dudley Moore. Screenplay by John Antrobus (and Richard Lester, uncredited) with additional dialogue by Charles Wood, based on the play by John Antrobus and Spike Milligan. 91 mins. Colour.

BSR is an ABSURDIST black comedy set in England after World War III, where dazed survivors wander about trying desperately to pretend that nothing has

Ralph Richardson copes with the post-holocaust world of THE BED-SITTING ROOM.

happened, even when some of them start mutating into wardrobes, bed-sitting rooms and parrots. The play on which the film was based was a much-improvised piece of slapstick, and what remains of the original material clashes awkwardly with chillingly bleak settings showing the realistic aftermath of an atomic war: the shattered dome of St Paul's Cathedral protruding from a swamp; a line of wrecked cars along a disembodied length of motorway; a grim landscape dominated by great piles of sludge and heaps of discarded boots, broken plates and false teeth. "The really awful thing," said Lester, "is that we were able to film most of those scenes in England without having to fake it. All that garbage is real. A lot of it was filmed behind the Steel Corporation in Wales ... endless piles of acid sludge and every tree is dead. And there's a place in Stoke where they've been throwing reject plates since the war and it has become a vast landscape of broken plates ..." [JB]

BEECHING, JACK (?–). English writer, mostly of poetry, and of juveniles (with his wife) as James Barbary. His sf novel, *The Dakota Project* (**1968**), is a scientific thriller about the top-secret government project of the title, and is somewhat borderline as sf. [JC]

BEEDING, FRANCIS Pseudonym of English writers John Leslie Palmer (1885–1944) and Hilary Saunders (1898–1951) for numerous works in various genres, mainly detective novels and thrillers; their sf novel, *The One Sane Man* (**1934**), routinely features a man's attempt to enforce world peace by threatening disaster, in this case via WEATHER CONTROL. [JC]

BEGBIE, (EDWARD) HAROLD (1871–1929). English author and journalist. Author of *The Day that Changed the World* (**1912**; as by "The Man Who Was Warned"), a religious fantasy in which mankind's spiritual development is sharply uplifted by divine intervention. HB also wrote *On the Side Of the Angels* (**1915**), a reply to Arthur MACHEN's *The Bowmen* (coll. **1915**; rev., with two additional stories, **1915**), and two political satires, *Clara In Blunderland* (**1902**) and *Lost In Blunderland* (**1903**), both written with M.H. Temple and J. Stafford Ransome under the collaborative pseudonym Caroline Lewis. [JE]

BEGOUEN, MAX French prehistorian and author of three prehistoric novels, *Bison of Clay* (**1925**, France, as *Les bisons d'argile*; trans. **1926**) being the only work translated into English. His entry for the PRIX JULES VERNE, "Quand le mammouth ressuscita" (**1928**), was of sufficient merit to warrant publication as second best. [JE]
Other works: *Tisik et Katé, aventures de*

deux enfants à l'époque du renne (**1946**). **See also:** ORIGIN OF MAN.

BEHEMOTH, THE SEA MONSTER (vt **THE GIANT BEHEMOTH** USA) Film (1958). Diamond/Allied Artists. Directed by Douglas Hickox and Eugene Lourie, starring Gene Evans, Andre Morell, Jack McGowran and Leigh Madison. Screenplay by Eugene Lourie. 80 mins. B/w.

Lourie has made several monster-on-the-rampage films during his career, including THE BEAST FROM 20,000 FATHOMS (1953). *BTSM* is his least successful. The story is the usual one — a prehistoric reptile is revived by atomic radiation and immediately sets out to demolish the nearest city, in this case London. There is an effective build-up of suspense in some sequences but despite the presence of Willis H. O'BRIEN (designer of the original KING KONG) on the team the very low budget severely restricted the scope of the effects. [JB]

BELAYEV, A. *See* Alexander BELYAEV.

BELGIUM *See* BENELUX.

BELIAYEV, A. *See* Alexander BELYAEV.

BELL, ERIC TEMPLE *See* John TAINE.

BELL, NEIL The most famous pseudonym of English writer Stephen Southwold (1887–1964), and the name under which he wrote most of his large number of romantic and realistic novels, reserving his own name largely for children's books, though he also wrote as Paul Martens and Miles. Beyond some children's fantasy, his first sf novels are *The Seventh Bowl* (**1930** as by Miles), a future DISASTER tale, and *The Gas War of 1940* (**1931** as by Miles; vt *Valiant Clay* as by NB), a future-WAR novel playing on the pervasive English fear that the next war would see the widespread use of poison gas. *The Tales of Joe Egg* (coll. **1936** as by Stephen Southwold) is a juvenile story sequence narrated by a ROBOT. NB's short fiction, assembled in books like *Alpha and Omega* (coll. **1946**), *Three Pairs of Heels* (coll. **1951**) and *Who Walks in Fear* (coll. **1953**), when not realistic, is generally fantasy; the first volume includes an introduction descriptive of his working methods. NB's prolificacy and a somewhat excessive calmness of style have caused him to be nearly forgotten; his sf, though mildly didactic, and often borderline, all the same comprises a number of thoroughly literate, mature tales. [JC]
Other works: *Precious Porcelain* (**1931** as by NB); *The Disturbing Affair of Noel Blake* (**1932** as by NB); *The Facts about Benjamin Srede* (**1932** as by NB); *Death Rocks the Cradle* (**1933** as by Paul Martens); *The Lord of Life* (**1933** as by NB); *Mixed Pickles: Short Stories* (coll. **1935** as by NB); *One Came Back* (**1938** as

by NB); *Life Comes to Seathorpe* (**1946** as by NB); *Who Was James Carey?* (**1949** as by NB); *The Dark Page* (**1951** as by NB); *The Secret Life of Miss Lottinger* (**1953** as by NB); *The House at the Crossroads* (**1966** as by NB).

BELL, THORNTON *See* R.L. FANTHORPE.

BELLAMY, EDWARD (1850–98). American author and journalist, the latter from 1871, after he had abandoned the practice of law before properly beginning it; no lawyers exist in the AD 2000 of his most famous work, *Looking Backward, 2000–1887* (**1888**), whose influence in the 19th century was enormous. His early works of fiction are GOTHIC, sentimental and strangely moving, though labouring under the influence of Nathaniel HAWTHORNE and showing no great hint of the direction his work would take. *Dr Heidenhoff's Process* (**1880**), however, not sf at all, does very interestingly prefigure some of the tactics of his later work; the doctor's process claims to mechanically wipe out diseased memories from those who wish for a new start. The protagonist's girl, who has been seduced by a rival, is persuaded to try the process, and is transformed — until the last pages of the novel, when it turns out that Heidenhoff and his process are merely a dream of the protagonist, who awakens to find that his disgraced lover has committed suicide. The emotional exorbitance and Gothic extremity of this tale are transformed in *Looking Backward* into a vision of a UTOPIAN society whose realization is equally exorbitant, and achieved while the protagonist of the novel, whose confusion upon his arrival into the world of the future is one of the best things in this uneasy work of fiction, has been in hypnotized sleep. The men of 2000 are devoid of irrational passions, and their highly communalized society reflects a reasonableness so radically opposed to common sense that one is tempted to posit an impulse of deep violence behind EB's creation of such a world. William MORRIS was so appalled by the bureaucratic and machine-like nature of EB's Utopia that he was instantly driven to retort with *News from Nowhere* (**1890**), which describes an ideal world of a very different sort. EB's book has nonetheless been extraordinarily popular, especially in the USA, which suggests a greater receptivity to communist thought in that country than is generally recognized, and has been treated as a serious model for the positing of future societies by many thinkers and writers, including Mack REYNOLDS. A sequel, the uninspiring *Equality* (**1897**), did little to damage the effect of the earlier book. EB is more important to the history of Utopian thought than he is as a writer of PROTO SF. His influence, except on didactic writers like Hugo GERNSBACK, has been indirect and diffuse upon the world of genre sf. [JC]

Other works: *Miss Ludington's Sister* (**1884**); *The Blindman's World and Other Stories* (coll. **1898**), especially the title story (written 1885).

See also: ARTS; AUTOMATION; ECONOMICS; LEISURE; MACHINES; NEAR FUTURE; POLITICS; PSYCHOLOGY; SF OVERTAKEN BY EVENTS; SUSPENDED ANIMATION; TECHNOLOGY; TIME TRAVEL.

BELLAMY, FRANCIS RUFUS (1886–1972). American editor and writer. In his sf novel, *Atta* (**1953**), a man is struck by lightning, shrunk to half an inch tall, and combines forces with a warrior ant by the name of Atta. [JC]

BELLOC, (JOSEPH) HILAIRE (PETER) (1870–1953). French-born English writer, known for his poetry, his Roman Catholic apologetics and his novels. A good deal of his work verges on fantasy; his sf novel, *But Soft—We Are Observed!* (**1928**; vt *Shadowed!*), illustrated by G.K. CHESTERTON, is a satirical suspense novel set in America and Europe in 1979. The main target of the satire is the parliamentary form of government. Novels with borderline sf elements include *Mr. Petre* (**1925**), also illustrated by Chesterton, as is *The Man Who Made Gold* (**1930**) and *The Postmaster-General* (**1932**). Other novels, like *Mr Clutterbuck's Election* (**1908**), *A Change in the Cabinet* (**1909**) and *Pongo and the Bull* (**1910**), are fundamentally political SATIRES. [JC]

See also: ALTERNATE WORLDS.

BELLOW, SAUL (1915–). Canadian-born American novelist. Winner of the Nobel Prize, SB is perhaps the premier MAINSTREAM novelist of his generation in America today. Some of his books distantly resemble sf, specifically *Henderson the Rain King* (**1959**), a picaresque partly set in a quasi-mythical African kingdom. *Mr Sammler's Planet* (**1970**) has been quite wrongly annexed as sf by several commentators, who perhaps relied on the title alone. While Man's reaching the Moon and his hypothetical establishment of a Utopia there is a leitmotiv of the novel, the image occurs in conversation only. But much of the imagery is space-age-linked, as the eponymous hero watches Western civilization veer towards DISASTER. [JC]

BELYAEV, ALEXANDER (1884–1942). Russian sf writer. His H. G. WELLS- and Jules VERNE- influenced sf dominated the field in RUSSIA between the wars, providing models for most other practitioners of the time. He wrote many novels, the best known being translated as *The Amphibian* (**1928** Russia; trans. **1959** as by A. Belayev), which tells of the transformation of a human by biological engineering so that he can live under water — the first use of the theme.

Another of AB's works was translated as *The Struggle in Space* (**1928** Russia; trans. **1965** as by A. Beliayev). It deals with a conflict between an electrical UTOPIA, centered in Russia, Asia and Africa, and a capitalist DYSTOPIA in the USA, described in enjoyably broad, repulsive images. AB writes here with a kind of Russian equivalent of pulp-magazine zest, and includes such notions, most of which had not yet penetrated into the American pulps, as killing with sound waves, X-ray binoculars, artificial satellites and atomic war. Several of AB's stories have appeared in English anthologies, including *Russian Science Fiction* (anth. **1964**) ed. R. MAGIDOFF: *Destination: Amaltheia* (anth. **1962**) and *Soviet Science Fiction* (anth. **1962**). "Invisible Light", in the Magidoff anthology, which deals with a man who can see radio waves, gives an example of AB's transparent, stereotyped characters and ingenious technological and scientific language, both representative of the "father" of Russian sf. [JC/PN]

See also: UNDER THE SEA.

BEM A common item of sf TERMINOLOGY, being an acronym of "bug-eyed monster", and referring to a type of ALIEN being, usually menacing, which was regularly pictured on the covers of SF MAGAZINES in the 1930s and '40s (*see* MONSTERS). [PN]

BENEATH THE PLANET OF THE APES Film (1970). 20th Century-Fox. Directed by Ted Post, starring James Franciscus, Charlton Heston, Linda Harrison and Kim Hunter. Screenplay by Paul Dehn and Mort Abrahams, based on the characters created by Pierre BOULLE. 95 mins. Colour.

In this first of four sequels to PLANET OF THE APES, another astronaut crash-lands on the ape world after passing unknowingly through the same time-warp featured in the first film. Like his predecessor he is captured, befriended by the sympathetic female chimpanzee Zira, and meets the girl savage heroine of the previous film. He escapes with her underground and realizes that he is still on Earth when he discovers the remains of New York City. Thereafter, what has appeared to be a slavish copy of *Planet of the Apes* sharpens its imagery and goes off in its own blacker direction with a race of telepathic Doomsday-bomb-worshipping mutants, direly deformed, and the resuscitation of the astronaut hero of the previous film, now half-crazed and bitter, who ultimately detonates the bomb and brings about a holocaust, wiping out apes, mutants and humans alike. Although intellectually disjointed, and lacking the smoothness of the previous film's direction, *BTPOTA* is the stronger of the two according to some critics, in its replacement of whimsical satire with an altogether harsher judgement about the prospects for intelligent life on Earth. The

novelization by Michael AVALLONE was published in 1970. [JB/PN]

BENELUX As varied as it is unknown, sf in the Low Countries, shored up by two cultures, has its roots in the fantastic world of such medieval stories as *Mariken van Nieumeghen* or *Elckerlyck*, the paintings of Bosch and Breughel, and more directly in the reports of seafaring explorers in Holland's Golden Age (the 17th century). A second, perhaps even more important characteristic of the Netherlands literature of extrapolation is the social concern and radical political ideas underlying it. Finally, Anglo-American sf has influenced it strongly.

1. *Utopian-social extrapolation* Dating back to 1777 (the early feminist A. Wolff-Dekker) and to socialism in the 1890s (several poets of *De Niewe Gids*), DYSTOPIAS appeared more regularly with the economic crises and wars of the 20th century: a WELLS-ian apocalypse by K. van Bruggen, *Het Verstrooide Mierennest* ["The Disturbed Ant-hill"] (**1916**); proletarian bitterness in a Spenglerian key, following the Depression, in *Blokken* ["Blocks"] (**1931**) and *Rood Paleis* ["Red Palace"] (**1936**) by F. Bordewijk; an anticipation of ASIMOV's robots and HUXLEY's determinism in *Voorland* (**1926**) by Belcampo (H.P. Schönfeld Wichers); and the only Stalinist UTOPIA ever written in Versou's *Niewe Reis naar Utopia* ["New Journey to Utopia"] (**1946**), opposing L.P. Boon's *Vergeten Straat* ["Forgotten Street"] (**1946**), in which a community is forced to be self-supporting. In the 1950s and '60s the world vision tended at once towards greater harshness and greater refinement, as in M. Dendermonde's *De Dagen zijn geteld* ["The Days are Numbered"] (**1955**), W. Ruyslinck's *Het Reservaat* (**1964**) which can be compared with the reservation scenes in Huxley's *Brave New World* (**1932**) and *De Apokatastasis* (**1970**), and J.G. Toonder's *Opstaan op Zaterdag* ["Get up on Saturday"] (**1966**). H. Mulisch's *De Toekomst van Gisteren* ["Yesterday's Future"] (**1972**), in which the Nazis have won the War, is superior to Norman SPINRAD's *The Iron Dream* (**1972**). The most modern and sophisticated writer, however, is Sybren Polet, whose "Lokien" cycle (1961–74) is a technically innovative epic of Man's timeless, progressive evolution, told with authentic philosophic rigour. It contains *Breekwater* (**1961**), *Verboden Tijd* ["Forbidden Time"] (**1964**), *Mannekino* (**1968**), *Die Sirkelbewoners* ["The Inhabitants of the Circle"] (**1972**) and *De Geboorte van een Geest* ["The Birth of a Spirit"] (**1974**). One should also mention J. Scheir's *Het Einde der Wereld* ["The End of the World"] (**1929**), which foreshadows many issues later developed by Huxley, and G. van Brussel's *De Ring* ["The Ring"] (**1967**).

2. *Fantastic voyages* Under the influence of political satire (Jonathan

Swift) and the Rationalist movement (Voltaire), log-books on the exploration of the southern hemisphere were soon to be amplified with mythicized discoveries and fantastic voyages, as in H. Smeeks's *Beschryvinge van het Magtig Koningryk Krinke Kesmes* ["Description of the Mighty Kingdom of Krinke Kesmes"] (1708).

In creating fantastic voyages, the 18th-century imagination was primarily concerned with social philosophy and ethics, as in A.F. Simonsz's Swiftian *Het Toekomend Jaar 3000* ["Next Year, AD 3000"] (1792), later on giving way to a more specifically scientific interest, particularly in the uses of technical innovation, in other words, real, pre-"hard" sf, as found in W. Bilderdijk's *Eene aanmerkelijke Luchtreis* ["A Remarkable Flight"] (1813). In modern times intermediate forms between Utopia and the fantastic voyage are the Incomprehensible Voyage as in H. Raes's *De Lotgevallen* ["Adventures"] (1968) and *Reizigers in de Anti-Tijd* ["Travellers in Anti-Time"] (1970); and the Apocalypse: M. Dekker's *De Aarde Splijt* ["The Earth is Splitting"] (1930); H. Mulisch's *Het Zwarte Licht* ["Black Light"] (1956); J. Vandeloo's *Het Gevaar* ["Danger"] (1960); and H. Raes's *Het Smaràn* (1973). From "ethical epics" such as S. Falkland's *Gevleugelde Daden* ["Winged Deeds"] (1911) and J.B. van 'Rode (J. Bomans)'s *Jan Herbert MacDonald* (1934) we can move along the spectrum of fantastic voyages to the more purely metaphysical speculation, as in S. Vestdijk's *Meneer Visser's Hellevaart* ["Mr Visser's Journey to Hell"] (1936) and *De Kellner en de Levenden* ["The Waiter and the Living"] (1949); and H. Raes's *Een Tijdelijk Monument* ["A Temporary Monument"] (1962). This brings us close to the next subcategory.

3. *Fantasy and horror* A strong tradition of fantastic monstrosity in folklore and popular literature (werewolves, spirits, *Thyl Uylensphieghel*, etc.) provided writers in the Low Countries, and especially in the south (Flanders), with a fertile soil for literature on the verge of sf and fantasy. A most prolific writer in both fields was J. Flanders (R. de Kremer), sometimes known under his French pen-name J. Ray, who wrote hundreds of stories and novels, some of which are pure sf, such as *Het Geheim van de Sargassen* ["The Sargasso Secret"] (1939). But the younger generation also works in these hybrid forms of literature, sometimes tending towards a Leiber-ian concept of sf, as in E.C. Bertin's *Iets Klein, Iets Hongerig* ["Something Small and Hungry"] (1970) and *De Achtjaarlijkse God* ["The Eight-Year God"] (1971); and also in works by J. Raasveld, J. Banen and S. Hertog. A more surrealistic form of fantasy/sf makes use of the theme of the revolt of plant life, as in E. van der Steen (D.

Zijlstra)'s *Finishing Touch* (1947) and J. Hamelink's *Het Plantaardig Bewind* ["The Reign of the Plants"] (1964).

4. *Sf proper* Although, apart from E. Multon's trilogy "Van Ruimte en Tijd" ["Of Space and Time"] (all 1947) and W. Vananderoye's *De Tocht van de Ursus* ["The Voyage of the Ursus"] (1975), the space opera was soon reduced to a form of juvenile literature (F. Theijssen, L. Vermeiren, E. Lamend, F. Buyens), ironical and absurdist sf gained wide recognition. M. Dendermonde's *De Wereld gaat aan Vlijt ten onder* ["The World dies of Zeal"] (1954) ridicules efforts to establish interstellar contacts, while the mild parody/humour of R. Blijstra's *Het Planetarium van Otze Otzinga* (1962) and the Čapek-style irony of E. Leonard's *Het Koninkrijk der Kikkeren is Nabij* ["The Frogsies' Kingdom is near"] (1969) relate to such fairly scientific fiction as that of the mathematician R. Chapkis (H.C. Brand-Corstius) in *Ik Sta op Mijn Hoofd* ["I Stand on my Head"] (1966) and the psychologist M. van Loggem in *Paarpoppen* (1974). Such works by nationally important authors as H. Mulisch's *De Versierde Mens* ["The Ornamented Man"] (1957) and A. den Doolaard's *De Goden Gaan Naar Huis* ["The Gods Go Home"] (1966) opened the door to literary experiment in sf, seen in more developed form in E. Visser's *Homo Sapiens Etc.* (1970). International recognition for Netherlands sf came with translations of P. van Herck in *Where were you last Pluterday?* (1973) and stories by E.C. Bertin as in "My Eyes, They Burn" (1977) and "The City, Dying" (1968).

Although the French-speaking population of the Low Countries is a rather small minority, its role in sf is not negligible and was important at the beginning of the 20th century. J.H. Rosny aîné was born in Belgium. A simultaneously conservative (if not reactionary) and prophetic tradition of xenophobia against Asia and England was firmly established in French sf from the Low Countries until the Second World War, as in I. Gilkin's *Jonas* (1900), E. Demolder's *L'agonie d'Albion* ["The Agony of Albion"] (1901), H. Kistemaekers' *Aéropolis, roman comique de la vie aérienne* ["Aeropolis: A Comic Novel of the Aerial Life"] (1909); J. Doutreligne (pen-name of the famous, if not infamous, Nazi Rex leader L. Degrelle), *La Grande Bagarre* ["The Row"] (1951); even the opinions of the sf connoisseur J. van Herp. The influence of French psychoanalytical fashions, however, and the contribution of French-writing Flemish authors brought about some fine works like F. Léonard's *Le triomphe de l'homme* ["The Triumph of Man"] (1911) and A. Pasquier's Utopian novel *La conquête* ["The Conquest"] (1926), like the refined *Echec au temps* ["Time

Stalemate"] (1938) by M. Thiry and the popular works of Jean Ray (who also wrote as J. Flanders), including *Le grand nocturne* (1942) and *Malpertuis* (1943). Working on the periphery of sf, Jacques Sternberg has contributed some witty, surreal nightmares.

The few contacts that exist between the two cultures in sf at least, bilingual publications included, are due partly to the high quality comic-strip industry (*Piloot Storm, Mortimer & Blake, Yoko Tsuno, Luc Orient, Mr Magellan, Arman en Ilva*, etc.), and partly to the efforts of the fan clubs (SFAN in Belgium, with A. Derijcke, D. de Laet, P. Torfs, which produces *Rigel-Magazine*, a retitling of *SF-Magazine*, and the Dutch NCSF and CISO) and the Beneluxcon conventions (since 1973). These latter have tried to reconcile the two historically hostile groups. In spite of some incompatibilities the international scope of Benelux sf fandom, which is often fluent in two or three languages, deserves to be taken as a model. One sad link between the two cultures is the custom of some Flemish writers of writing in French for extra-literary reasons related to social inequality. Finally, of course, there is the historical unifier: the Luxemburgian Hugo Gernsback himself. [LdeV]

BENÉT, STEPHEN VINCENT (1898–1943). American writer, mainly of poetry and stories, much published in *Saturday Evening Post*. He is best known for his book-length poem *John Brown's Body* (1928), for his fantasy story "The Devil and Daniel Webster" (1936), which was included with other fantasies in *Thirteen O'Clock* (coll. 1937), and for *Johnny Pye and the Fool Killer* (1938), also included with other fantasies in *Tales Before Midnight* (coll. 1939); these collections were brought together to make up *Twenty-Five Short Stories* (coll. 1943). Several of SVB's stories are sf, and have appeared in sf anthologies. His best-known sf is "The Place of the Gods" (1937; vt "By the Waters of Babylon"), a clever, sentimental, post-holocaust story about an adolescent tribal boy who discovers the ruins of a great destroyed city (*see* cities). It was responsible for creating many of the clichés of that sub-genre which became so popular after the Second World War. [JC/PN]

BENFORD, GREGORY (1941–). American writer. GB is a physicist by profession. He graduated from the University of Oklahoma in 1963, and gained his PhD in 1967 from the University of California, where he is now associate professor of physics. He is one of a pair of identical twins, and has written some stories in collaboration with his brother James. He was an active sf fan before becoming a writer, and for several years edited a fanzine, *Void*, with various co-editors including Ted White and Terry Carr. His first published story was

"Stand-In" (1965), which won second place in a contest organized by the MAGAZINE OF FANTASY AND SCIENCE FICTION.

GB is not a prolific writer, and his work is not only backed by scientific expertise, but is thoughtful and carefully written. Many of his stories show a preoccupation with the theme of ALIENS and Man's first contact with them. An example is *If The Stars Are Gods* (fix-up 1977), written in collaboration with Gordon EKLUND, which describes Man's gradual exploration of the Solar System and the different forms of life he discovers. The novel was originally published as a series of short stories, and the title section won a NEBULA award in 1975. On the theme of RELIGION, it examines Man's meeting with an alien race who literally worship suns. A later section of the novel, set on a space station orbiting JUPITER, derives much of its detail from GB's earlier children's novel *Jupiter Project* (1975).

Several of GB's recent short stories, notably "Doing Lennon" (1976), show him to be strongly influenced, in terms of style, by Robert SILVERBERG. Much of his work shows an emphasis on style unusual in a HARDCORE sf writer. In addition to his fiction he has contributed a regular column, "The Science in SF", to *AMZ* since 1969. [MJE]
Other works: *Deeper Than the Darkness* (1970; rev. vt *The Stars in Shroud* 1978); *In the Ocean of Night* (fix-up 1977).
See also: GENETIC ENGINEERING; GODS AND DEMONS; LIVING WORLDS; OUTER PLANETS; PSYCHOLOGY; STARS; SUN; TACHYONS; TERRAFORMING; WEAPONS.

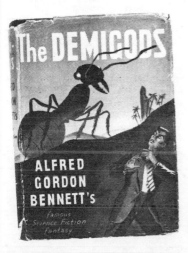

Out-of-the-way sf by Alfred Gordon BENNETT. 1955 edition. Cover by Eisner.

BENNETT, ALFRED GORDON (1901–). British writer, documentary film-maker, and founder of Pharos Books, through which he published a fantasy, *Whom the Gods Destroy* (1946). His sf novel, *The Demigods* (1939), depicts a world menaced by giant ants

who derive their abilities from a brain that controls them. [JC]
Other works: *The Sea of Sleep* (1926; vt *The Sea of Dreams* USA).
See also: HIVE-MINDS.

BENNETT, MARGOT (1912–). English writer, mostly of detective novels from 1945; her style is subtle and atmospheric. A fantasy story, "An Old-Fashioned Poker for My Uncle's Head" (1946), appeared in *FSF* in 1954, at about the time her sf novel, *The Long Way Back* (1954), was published. It is a post-HOLOCAUST story, in which Africa remains CIVILIZED and sends an expedition to a now legendary England to find out in what state of savagery the Britons exist. [JC]
Other works: *The Curious Masters* (1968).
See also: POLITICS.

BENSEN, D(ONALD) R. (1927–). American editor, noted for two anthologies, *The Unknown* (anth. 1963) and *The Unknown Five* (anth. 1964), both fantasy and compiled from UNKNOWN (all but one story), but more important within the sf field for his editorship of Pyramid Books from 1957 to 1967, a period during which that firm became a significant producer of sf novels in reprint and original forms; in 1967 he became executive editor of Berkley Books. [JC]

BENSON, A(RTHUR) C(HRISTOPHER) (1862–1925). English essayist, poet and novelist, elder brother of E.F. BENSON and R.H. BENSON. Much of his short fiction was fantasy, and can be found in *The Hill of Trouble and Other Stories* (coll. 1903), *The Isles of Sunset* (coll. 1904) and *Basil Netherby* (coll. 1926). *The Child of the Dawn* (1912) is an IMMORTALITY tale, religiously sententious but occasionally moving. The stories in the first two collections above were all republished in *Paul the Minstrel and Other Stories* (coll. 1911). [JC]

BENSON, E(DWARD) F(REDERICK) (1867–1940). English novelist, brother of A.C. BENSON and R.H. BENSON and by far the most prolific of them, with dozens of attractive, realistic novels and romances to his credit. His fantasy stories are well known, and some verge on sf; the most famous collections are *The Room in the Tower and Other Stories* (coll. 1912), *Visible and Invisible* (coll. 1923), and *Spook Stories* (1928). [JC]

BENSON, ROBERT HUGH (1871–1914). English writer. Third son of Archbishop Benson and brother of the writers A.C. BENSON and E.F. BENSON. He was ordained in the Church of England but became converted to Catholicism. His fiction is intensely propagandistic, and most of his short stories feature Catholic priests as central characters. In his remarkable apocalyptic novel *Lord of the*

World (1907) the Antichrist woos the world with socialism and humanism, and the remnants of the Papal hierarchy go into hiding. *The Dawn of All* (1911) shows the alternative as Benson saw it – a future of Utopian Papal rule. [BS]
Other works: *The Light Invisible* (coll. 1903); *A Mirror of Shalott* (coll. 1907); *The Necromancers* (1909).
See also: DYSTOPIAS; END OF THE WORLD; MESSIAHS; RELIGION.

BERESFORD, J(OHN) D(AVYS) (1873–1947). British writer. The son of a clergyman, he was crippled in infancy owing to the carelessness of a nurse, and both these facts seem to have been highly influential in forming his view of the world. He became a determined but defensive agnostic in constructing and developing his speculations, but was occasionally apt to allow a strong element of wish-fulfilment into his work, as in *The Camberwell Miracle* (1933), in which a crippled girl is cured by a faith-healer. Like Conan DOYLE he could adopt either an extremely hard-headed rationalism or a naïve mysticism. JDB's first sf novel was the classic *The Hampdenshire Wonder* (1911; vt *The Wonder* USA), a biographical account of a freak superchild born out of his time, which seems to have been inspired by the work of the French evolutionary philosopher Henri Bergson. His second, *Goslings* (1913; vt *A World of Women* USA), is the first attempt to depict an all-female society which treats the issue seriously and with a degree of sympathy. Many of his early speculative short stories were collected in *Nineteen Impressions* (coll. 1918) and *Signs and Wonders* (coll. 1921). These may be classified into allegories born of religious doubt, such as "A Negligible Experiment", in which the impending destruction of Earth is taken as evidence that God has become indifferent to Man; visions inspired by the cosmic perspective, such as "The Cage", in which a man is telepathically linked to a prehistoric ancestor for a few seconds; and psychological studies. *Revolution* (1921) is a determinedly objective analysis of a socialist revolution in England.

JDB began a second phase of speculative work in 1941. "*What Dreams May Come ...*" (1941) is a powerful novel about a young man drawn into a Utopian future he has experienced in his dreams and then returned, altered in body and mind, to a hopeless messianic quest in the war-torn present. *A Common Enemy* (1942) is reminiscent of much of the work of H.G. WELLS, showing the destruction of society by natural disaster as a prelude to Utopian reform. *The Riddle of the Tower* (1944), written in collaboration with Esmé Wynne-Tyson, is another wartime "vision-story" following a future history in which Utopian prospects are lost and society evolves towards "automatism" — a HIVE-organization in which individuality — and ultimately humanity — are lost. A subsequent collaboration with Wynne-Tyson, however, is a weak wish-fulfilment fantasy, *The Gift* (**1946**).

There are several parallels to be drawn between the methods and outlook of JDB and H.G. Wells (JDB's *H.G. Wells*, **1915**, was the first critical study of Wells's early work), but JDB never achieved critical acclaim for his mainstream fiction or his sf. He is underrated. [BS]

Other works: One sf story, "The Man Who Hated Flies", is in *The Meeting Place* (coll. **1929**).

See also: BIOLOGY; CHILDREN IN SF; DYSTOPIAS; ECOLOGY; EVOLUTION; INTELLIGENCE; MESSIAHS; PSYCHOLOGY; SOCIOLOGY; SUPERMAN; WOMEN.

BERESFORD, LESLIE (?–). British author. He entered the sf genre with *The Second Rising* (**1910**), a future-WAR novel about a second Indian mutiny, and continued with two UTOPIAN novels published under the pseudonym Pan, *The Kingdom Of Content* (**1918**) and *The Great Image* (**1921**). Reverting to his own name he followed these with a novel about international air piracy, *Mr. Appleton Awakes* (**1924**; abridged 1932), and a humorous novel about the entanglements created by a sensuous extraterrestrial with supranormal powers, *The Venus Girl* (**1925**; abridged 1933). LB was quite prolific in the magazine market, contributing "War Of Revenge" (1921), "The Purple Planet" (1922) and "The People Of The Ice" (1922), respectively future-war, interplanetary, and LOST-WORLD adventure, to the BOYS' PAPERS and "The Octopus Orchid" (1921) and "The Stranger From Somewhere" (1922), among others, to the pre-sf PULP MAGAZINES. [JE]

Other works: *The Last Woman* (**1922**); *The Invasion of the Iron-Clad Army* (**1928**); *The Flying Fish* (**1931**).

BERGER, HAROLD L. (1923–). American academic and critic, based at the University of Connecticut at Hartford. His *Science Fiction and the New Dark Age* (**1976**) is a study of DYSTOPIAN sf, taking in genre sf as well as such mainstream writers as Aldous HUXLEY and Michael YOUNG. The book is useful but not incisive. [PN]

BERGER, THOMAS (1924–). American writer, best known for his work outside the sf field, such novels as *Little Big Man* (**1964**), which was notably filmed. His sf novel, *Regiment of Women* (**1973**), presents a world, about a century hence, in which the roles of men and WOMEN have been completely reversed, direly for the men. [JC]

BERGER, YVES (1936–). French novelist, editor and literary journalist. His ALTERNATE-WORLDS novel, *Le sud* (**1962**; trans. as *The Garden* 1963), is set in an

A typical cover by Earle BERGEY, with busty, menaced woman. Jan. 1950.

antebellum Virginia. [JC]

BERGEY, EARLE K. (? –1952). American illustrator. Known to fans as the "inventor of the brass brassière" Unfortunately his covers were often pointed at as one of the reasons for the unsavoury reputation of sf in the 1940s; his half-dressed women were anathema to the conservative minds of the day. In a brief, 10-year period starting about 1940, EKB painted covers for some of the more lurid PULPS, *Startling Stories*, *Captain Future*, *Thrilling Wonder Stories*, *Fantastic Story Magazine* and *Planet Stories*, among others. His smooth, sensual paintings represent the pulp style at its most typical and thus were singled out for ridicule by non-sf readers and critics. He helped to change the emphasis of cover paintings, which he specialized in, from gadgetry to people. [JG]

BERK, HOWARD (1926–). American writer, whose interesting sf novel, *The Sun Grows Cold* (**1971**), puts into a terrifying future world a man whose brain has been tampered with. HB has

also published in other genres. [JC]

BERNARD, RAFE (? –). English writer whose first sf novel, *The Wheel in the Sky* (**1954**), datedly concerns itself with the construction of a pre-NASA-style, privately financed space station. He has since written a spin-off book derived from the TV series THE INVADERS: *The Halo Highway* (**1967**; vt *Army of the Undead* USA). [JC]

BERRY, BRYAN (1930–55). British author, active for only a few years. Along with such writers as John Russell FEARN, E.C. TUBB and Kenneth BULMER, he contributed many PULP-style sf novels to obscure paperback houses, some apparently under house names. The bibliographical record of British sf from 1950 to 1965 has elements of nightmare. Works written as Bryan Berry, and the "Venus" trilogy under the pseudonym Rolf Garner, are the only definitely identified works by BB. *And the Stars Remain* (**1952**) confronts men and Martians with a superior force; *Born in Captivity* (**1952**) presents a rigid post-

Third-World-War society; others include *Dread Visitor* (**1952**), *From What Far Star?* (**1953**), *Return to Earth* (undated, probably **1953**) and *The Venom Seekers* (**1953**). The "Venus" trilogy, as by Rolf Garner: *Resurgent Dust* (**1953**), *The Immortals* (**1953**) and *The Indestructible* (**1954**), portrays in bold strokes Man's fate on VENUS after the destruction of life on Earth; tyranny is eventually eliminated, by the man who becomes Lord Kennet of Gryllaar. BB was closely associated with AUTHENTIC SCIENCE FICTION and also with TWO COMPLETE SCIENCE-ADVENTURE BOOKS, both of which published some of his novel-length fiction. "Aftermath" (1952) in the former became "Mission to Marakee" (1953) in the latter. [JC]

BERTRAM, NOEL *See* R.L. FANTHORPE.

BESANT, Sir WALTER (1836–1901). British writer. Known primarily for his work outside the sf field. His early novels were written in collaboration with James Rice. He was a founder member of the Society of Authors, and was knighted in 1895. His most important speculative work was *The Revolt of Man* (**1882**, first edition anonymous), an anti-suffragette novel depicting a female-dominated society, which exemplifies the sexual attitudes and imagination of the Victorian gentleman. [BS]
Other works: *The Inner House* (**1888**); *The Doubts of Dives* (**1889**); *The Ivory Gate* (**1892**).
See also: DYSTOPIAS; SOCIOLOGY; WOMEN.

BEST, (OSWALD) HERBERT (1894–?). American author of an sf novel, *The Twenty-Fifth Hour* (**1940**), in which, after a 1965 DISASTER, the few survivors come together to construct a UTOPIA in Egypt. [JC]
See also: HOLOCAUST AND AFTER.

BESTER, ALFRED (1913–). American writer and editor. He was born into a Jewish family in New York, a city with which he has been closely associated ever since. Educated in both humanities and sciences at the University of Pennsylvania in Philadelphia, AB entered sf when he submitted a story — he was at law school at the time — to THRILLING WONDER STORIES. Mort WEISINGER, the editor, helped AB to polish it, and then suggested he submit it for an amateur story competition *TWS* was running. AB did so, and won. The story was "The Broken Axiom", published Apr. 1939.

AB published another 13 sf stories up to 1942, and then followed his friend Weisinger, along with Otto BINDER, Manly Wade WELLMAN and others, into the field of COMIC BOOKS, working on such DC comics as SUPERMAN and *Batman*. AB worked successfully for four years on writing comics outlines and dialogue, later working on CAPTAIN MARVEL, and

then moved into radio, scripting for such serials as *Charlie Chan* and *The Shadow*. After the intensive course in action plotting this career had given him, AB returned (part-time) to sf in 1950, by this time more mature as a writer. There ensued over the next six years a series of stories and novels which are still considered by many to be the greatest creations of genre sf.

AB was never prolific, publishing only twelve more short stories before 1960. But these alone would have secured him a place in the sf pantheon. Most of his stories were originally issued in book form in two collections, *Starburst* (coll. **1958**) and *The Dark Side of the Earth* (coll. **1964**). These collections were reassembled with seven stories dropped, and two older stories and three quite recent stories added, along with the autobiographical essay "My Affair with Science Fiction" (1975), in two further collections, *The Light Fantastic* (coll. **1976**) and *Star Light, Star Bright* (coll. **1976**), which were in turn reissued in paperback as an omnibus volume, *Starlight: The Great Short Fiction of Alfred Bester* (coll. **1977**). This last volume is the best available collection.

AB's talents were evident from the beginning. At least three stories from his 1939–42 period are memorable: "Adam and No Eve" (1941) (*see* ADAM AND EVE and END OF THE WORLD) "The Push of a Finger" (1942) and "Hell is Forever" (1942). The latter, a long novella for *Unknown*, exhibits the qualities for which AB would later be celebrated; it is cynical, baroque and aggressive, produces hard, bright images in quick succession, and deals with obsessive states of mind. The most notable later story is "Fondly Fahrenheit" (1954), an amazingly fast-paced, breathless story of a man and his ANDROID servant, whose personalities intermesh in a homicidal *folie à deux*. Also memorable are "Of Time and Third Avenue" (1951), "Disappearing Act" (1954) and "The Men Who Murdered Mohammed" (1958), which is perhaps the most concentratedly witty twist on the TIME-PARADOX story ever written. At around the time of this story AB addressed an sf symposium at the University of Chicago; his paper is one of the four reprinted in *The Science Fiction Novel: Imagination and Social Criticism* (anth. **1959**).

AB has written three novels. The first two, *The Demolished Man* (**1953**) and *The Stars My Destination* (**1956**; vt *Tiger! Tiger!* UK), are among the few genuine classics of genre sf. *The Demolished Man*, which won the first HUGO award for best novel in 1953, tells a story which in synopsis is straightforward: industrialist Ben Reich commits murder, is ultimately caught by telepathic detective Linc Powell, and is committed to curative brainwashing (*see* CRIME AND PUNISHMENT). It is the pace, the style, the passion and the pyrotechnics that make

the novel extraordinary. The future society is evoked in marvellously hard-edged details; the hero is a driven, resourceful man whose obsessions are explained in Freudian terms which would seem too slick if they were given straight, but are evoked with the same sceptical, witty, painful irony, typical of New York, which informs the whole novel.

This book and its successor are the sf equivalent of the Jacobean revenge drama; both stories feature malcontent figures, outsiders from society bitterly cognizant of its corruption, but themselves part ruined by it, just as in *The Revenger's Tragedy* or *The Duchess of Malfi*; like them, too, AB's novels blaze with a sardonic, staccato imagery, mingling symbols of decay and new life with a creative profligacy. The second book, *The Stars My Destination*, tells the story of the now legendary Gully Foyle, whose passion for revenge transforms him from an illiterate outcast to a transcendent, ambiguous, quasi-superman. Like the first novel, this one lives as much through the incidentals of the setting in a lurid, crumbling, near-future world as in the plot itself, which AB confesses, too modestly, was borrowed from *The Count of Monte Cristo*.

In the late 1950s he was taken on by *Holiday* magazine as a feature writer, and ultimately became senior literary editor, a post he held until the magazine ceased publication in the 1970s. AB has now returned to sf. "The Four-Hour Fugue" (1974) shows the old extraordinary assurance and inventiveness, and just a trace of over-facility. The sharp New York ironies, all flash and wit, sometimes teeter on the edge of becoming a form of self-serving display, like a peacock's tail. AB's most recent novel, *The Computer Connection* (1974 *ASF* as "The Indian Giver"; **1975**; vt *Extro* UK), while full of incidental felicities, does not quite recapture the old drive in its ornate story of a group of IMMORTALS and an omniscient COMPUTER; perhaps it lacks a natural Besterman as focus; the hero in this case is not obsessive or ruined.

AB's ferocious, sceptical talent has certainly been influential in genre sf, on writers as disparate as James BLISH and Michael MOORCOCK. He is one of the very few genre sf writers to have bridged, unconsciously, the chasm between the old and the NEW WAVE, by becoming a hero figure for both; perhaps because in his images he conjures up, almost in one breath, both outer and INNER SPACE. [PN]
See also: CONCEPTUAL BREAKTHROUGH; ESP; HUMOUR; ICONOCLASM; LINGUISTICS; OUTER PLANETS; PERCEPTION; PSI POWERS; PSYCHOLOGY; TIME TRAVEL; TRANSPORTATION; VILLAINS.

BEST SCIENCE FICTION, THE US DIGEST-size magazine. Two undated issues, 1964, published by Galaxy Publishing Corp. Both issues had subtitles: no. 1 "From Worlds of If", no. 2 "From Worlds of Tomorrow", and the stories included were reprints from those magazines.   [FHP]

BETHLEN, T. D. *See* Robert SILVERBERG.

BEVAN, ALISTAIR *See* Keith ROBERTS.

BEYER, W(ILLIAM) G(RAY) (?–). American writer, active before the Second World War in only one magazine, *Argosy*, where he published all his novels. *Minions of the Moon* (1939 *Argosy*; **1950**), along with three further serials, "Minions of Mars" (1940), "Minions of Mercury" (1940), and "Minions of the Shadow" (1941), comprise the "Minions" series of SPACE-OPERA adventures involving humans and aliens.   [JC]

BEYNON, JOHN *See* John WYNDHAM.

UK edition, 1953. Cover by René Vidmer.

BEYOND FANTASY FICTION US DIGEST-size magazine. Ten issues, Jul. 1953–5, published by Galaxy Publishing Corp.; ed. H.L. GOLD.

A companion magazine to GALAXY SCIENCE FICTION, *Beyond* was a fantasy magazine conceived in the same spirit as UNKNOWN (to which Gold had contributed). It began promisingly, its first issue featuring such stories as Theodore STURGEON's "... And My Fear Is Great" and Damon KNIGHT's "Babel II", but could only maintain this standard fitfully. Notable later stories included "The Watchful Poker Chip", by Ray BRADBURY (Mar. 1954) and "The Green Magician", by L. Sprague DE CAMP and Fletcher PRATT (no.9, 1954). Sam MERWIN was associate editor from the fourth issue to the eighth. The first eight issues were bi-monthly and dated. With the ninth issue the title was abbreviated to *Beyond Fiction* and the magazine was numbered and not dated. *Beyond* was drab in appearance, with uninspired cover paintings. *Beyond* (anth. **1963**) was

an anonymous compilation drawn from its pages. A British edition of the first four issues — cut — was published by Strato Publications, 1953–4.   [MJE]

BEYOND FICTION *See* BEYOND FANTASY FICTION.

The attractive cover is by Goller.

BEYOND INFINITY US DIGEST-size magazine. One issue, Dec. 1967, published by I. D. Publications, Hollywood; ed. Doug Stapleton. The fantasy element was stronger than the sf in this rapidly aborted and not very strong magazine. An unusual feature was the colouring blue or red of some illustrations.   [FHP]

BIBLIOGRAPHIES Until the recent academic acceptance of sf, there has been no profit in bibliographies. Compiling them has been a labour of love, very often carried out by fans, sometimes by book and magazine dealers. Few academically trained bibliographers have undertaken the work.

The earliest important bibliography in the field makes no distinction between sf and fantasy; it is incomplete and contains errors; it contains no information on contents. It is nevertheless invaluable to researchers; it is *The Checklist of Fantastic Literature: A Bibliography of Fantasy, Weird and Science Fiction Books Published in the English Language* (**1948**) by Everett F. BLEILER. A supplement to this volume, containing 3,000 additional titles, is *The Supplemental Checklist of Fantastic Literature* (**1963**) by Bradford M. DAY. Together with these two basic volumes, a researcher requires the indexes to the magazines: *Index to the Science Fiction Magazines 1926–50* (**1952**) by Donald B. DAY, *The Index of Science Fiction Magazines 1951–1965* (**1968**) by Norman METCALF or, for the same period, *The MIT Science Fiction Society's Index to the S-F Magazines* (**1966**) by Erwin S. STRAUSS, *Index to the Science Fiction Magazines 1966–70* (**1971**) by the New England Science Fiction Association and *The N.E.S.F.A.*

Index Science Fiction Magazines: 1971–1972 and Original Anthologies: 1971–1972 (**1973**). Since that time N.E.S.F.A. have brought out annual magazine indexes.

Two useful indexes, for those wanting to find particular short stories in anthologies, are *A Checklist of Science-Fiction Anthologies* (**1964**) by Walter R. COLE and *Science Fiction Story Index* (**1971**) by Fred Siemon. Sf film enthusiasts can do no better than use *Reference Guide to Fantastic Films: Science Fiction, Fantasy and Horror* in three vols (**1972–4**) by Walt LEE, though this is not strictly a bibliography.

There are no fully comprehensive sf and fantasy bibliographies since Bradford M. Day's, which carries the story only to 1963. The most important sources for the more recent period are *The Encyclopedia of Science Fiction and Fantasy Through 1968: Volume 1: Who's Who, A–L* (**1974**) by Donald H. TUCK — vol. 2 is projected for 1978 — and *Stella Nova: The Contemporary Science Fiction Authors* (**1970**) by R. REGINALD uncredited. Reginald, also, is projecting an updated and much expanded volume for 1978. An American fan, Joanne Burger, has produced annual checklists, beginning with *Science Fiction Published in 1968* (**1969**). In the UK a similar task has been undertaken by Gerald Bishop, beginning with *New British Science Fiction and Fantasy Books Published During 1970 & 1971* (**1972**). Accurate monthly lists of sf publications for the UK and the US are published in the fanzine LOCUS, and they also appeared, for the US, in DELAP's F & SF REVIEW.

A number of selective bibliographies with annotations have appeared as reading guides and for use in libraries. The most comprehensive is *Anatomy of Wonder: Science Fiction* (**1976**) ed. Neil BARRON.

There are a great many specialist bibliographies in sf, very often stencilled by fans and difficult to acquire. Many of them are listed in *SF Bibliographies: An Annotated Bibliography of Bibliographical Works on Science Fiction and Fantasy Fiction* (**1972**) by Robert E. Briney and Edward Wood. Single-author bibliographies are often listed in this Encyclopedia under the rubric "About the author" following individual author entries. Other specialized bibliographies include *Science Fiction Criticism: An Annotated Checklist* (**1972**) by Thomas CLARESON (Clareson's journal EXTRAPOLATION publishes annual checklists of sf criticism during the year), *Russian Science Fiction 1956–1974: A Bibliography* (**1976**) by Darko SUVIN and *Who's Who in Horror and Fantasy Fiction* (**1977**) by Mike ASHLEY. The companion volume to this last title, *Who's Who in Science Fiction* (**1976**; rev. 1977) by Brian ASH, is unreliable in its original hardcover format, better in paperback.

Other notable bibliographical sources are *Bibliografi över science fiction & fantasy 1741–1973* (**1974**) by Sam LUNDWALL, which covers Swedish publications; *Voyages in Space: A Bibliography of Interplanetary Fiction 1801–1914* (**1975**) by George LOCKE; and the semi-professional fanzine *The Science-Fiction Collector* ed. J. Grant Thiessen, which began in 1976, and has five issues to date. Booksellers' catalogues are a useful and sometimes overlooked source of information; one of the best is produced by L.W. Currey for his company Rare Books Incorporated. Finally, in addition to being the most useful source for tracking down book reviews, *Science Fiction Book Review Index, 1923–1973* (**1975**) ed. H.W. HALL functions as an accurate if incomplete bibliography for that period. Annual supplements to this book are published.

If it were not for the groundwork carried out in the above and similar works, the compilation of this Encyclopedia could not have been done in under a decade.   [PN]

BIERBOWER, AUSTIN (1844–1913). American writer, whose ANTHROPO-LOGICAL sf novel, *From Monkey to Man; or, Society in the Tertiary Age. A Story of the Missing Link* (**1894**), suggests the Ice Age as the effective cause of Man's expulsion from the Garden of Eden, and struggles with snakes as the basis for the symbol of the Serpent as evil.   [JC]
See also: EVOLUTION; ORIGIN OF MAN.

BIERCE, AMBROSE (1842–c.1914). American journalist and writer of short stories and satires, deeply affected by his experiences in the American Civil War (he was breveted major for bravery and wounded twice). Like Bret Harte, he went to California and became a journalist, and like Harte he soon went abroad, spending 1872–6 in England, publishing several volumes of sketches as Dod Grile, but afterwards — unlike Harte, who had permanently departed the thin cultural pickings there — returned to California. In 1914, after a hectic career and some notably scurrilous journalism, he disappeared into Mexico, then in the midst of its own civil war. He is perhaps best known for *The Cynic's Word Book* (coll. **1906**; vt *The Devil's Dictionary* USA; exp. vt *The Enlarged Devil's Dictionary* 1967), a collection of brilliantly cynical word "definitions". His numerous sketches and stories far more closely approach the canons of fantasy than of sf, though, like Mark TWAIN's similar efforts, they can often be interpreted as sufficiently *speculative* to warrant the interest of sf readers. AB's single most famous tale, "An Occurrence at Owl Creek Bridge", in which a condemned spy believes he has escaped the rope and returned to his wife the instant after his fall from the bridge before the noose tightens, appears in

Tales of Soldiers and Civilians (coll. **1891**; vt *In the Midst of Life* USA; subsequent editions vary markedly· in stories contained). The early ROBOT story "Moxon's Master", perhaps the closest thing to genuine sf he ever wrote, in which an artificially created chessplayer strangles its maker, appears in *Can Such Things Be?* (coll. **1893**). The same volume contains the notable story of monstrous INVISIBILITY, "The Damned Thing", which offers a scientific explanation of the phenomenon, and the story of a man who vanishes, much as AB appeared to do himself, into another DIMENSION, "Charles Ashmore's Trail". This, and such similar volumes as *Fantastic Fables* (coll. **1899**), are extremely difficult to find at present. His stories have been since republished in a number of forms, however. *The Collected Writings of Ambrose Bierce* (coll. **1946**) is valuable, though not complete; *Ghost and Horror Stories of Ambrose Bierce* (coll. **1964**, ed. E.F. BLEILER) is probably the best single assemblage of his works of interest to the reader of sf or fantasy; *The Collected Short Stories* (coll. **1970**) is also of value.
[JC/PN]
See also: GOTHIC SF; HUMOUR; PARANOIA AND SCHIZOPHRENIA.

BIGGLE, LLOYD Jr (1923–). American author and musicologist, with a PhD in musicology from the University of Michigan. His interest in music and the other ARTS, perhaps watered down more than necessary in an effort to make such concerns palatable to his readers, appears throughout his sf work, which began to appear in 1956, with "Gypped" in *Gal.* on a music theme. His first novel, *The Angry Espers* (1959 *AMZ* as "A Taste of Fire"; rev. with cuts restored **1961**), sets the tone for much of his subsequent work in the field, featuring an Earthman involved in complicated adventures on an alien planet. *All the Colors of Darkness* (**1963**) is the first of four novels to date — the others are *Watchers of the Dark* (**1966**), *This Darkening Universe* (**1975**) and *Silence is Deadly* (**1977**) — recounting the adventures of late-20th-century private eye Jan Darzek, hired by the Council of the Supreme, who govern the home galaxy, to try to solve problems posed by the inimical Udef, a Dark force destroying civilization after civilization in the Smaller Magellanic Cloud. Darzek sets about his task with a will; there are MATTER TRANSMITTERS and comic interludes. Other novels, like *The World Menders* (**1971**) and *The Light That Never Was* (**1972**), are not dissimilar, and tales like *The Still, Small Voice of Trumpets* (**1968**) combine his interest in music with epic storylines. His competent but undemanding stories appear in *The Rule of the Door and Other Fanciful Regulations* (coll. **1967**) and *A Galaxy of Strangers* (coll. **1976**). As a writer of SPACE OPERA, LB is seldom less than relaxed and entertaining, and it may be

intellectual snobbery to ask for anything more; none the less his stories often convey the sense of an unrealized greater potential. Their blandness might well be improved with the intellectual spice which LB often hints would be well within his capacity but seldom produces. LB has been an active member of the SCIENCE FICTION WRITERS OF AMERICA, and edited *Nebula Award Stories Seven* (anth. **1972**).   [JC]
Other works: *The Fury out of Time* (**1965**); *The Metallic Muse* (**1972**); *Monument* (1961 *ASF*; exp. **1974**).
See also: ICONOCLASM; PARALLEL WORLDS; PASTORAL; SOCIAL DARWINISM.

BINDER, EANDO Most famous of the joint pseudonyms used by the brothers Earl Andrew Binder (1904–) and Otto Oscar Binder (1911–75), though they both used other pseudonyms as well; after about 1940, when Earl Binder became inactive as a writer, Otto Binder continued to sign himself EB, so that some EB books are collaborative and some are by Otto alone. Together, the brothers also wrote 11 stories as John Coleridge and one as Dean D. O'Brien. Alone, Otto also wrote as Gordon A. Giles, did some work under the house name Will GARTH, and finally published a novel under his own name. A third brother, Jack, an illustrator, did much of the early drawing on CAPTAIN MARVEL, which was regularly scripted by Otto.

The two brothers' best-known works were all published as by EB, beginning with their first story, "The First Martian", for *AMZ* in 1932. The "Adam Link" series, by Otto alone, is EB's most important work in the sf field: Adam Link, a sentient ROBOT, narrates his own tales, quite feelingly; most of his story appears in *Adam Link — Robot* (1939–42 *AMZ*; fix-up 1965), with the remaining uncollected stories, also from *AMZ*, comprised of "Adam Link Fights a War" (1940), "Adam Link in the Past" (1941) and "Adam Link Faces a Revolt" (1941). Link is highly anthropomorphic; though Isaac ASIMOV's somewhat more austere sense of the nature of robots and robotics was soon to establish itself in the sf field as an almost unbreakable convention, the "Link" sequence is an important predecessor, significantly treating its robot hero with sympathy. The brothers' other main series, the "Anton York" tales, all collected in book form as *Anton York, Immortal* (1937–40 *TWS*; fix-up 1965), tells how Anton and his wife achieve IMMORTALITY and live with it. Also as EB, the brothers published less interesting magazine serials in the 1930s which were only gradually to see the light of book publication. Notable among them are *Enslaved Brains* (1934 *Wonder Stories*; 1965) and *Lords of Creation* (1939 *Argosy*; 1949); in the latter, Overlords rule Earth but are resisted with ultimate success. As Gordon A. Giles, Otto wrote a series for *TWS* from 1937 to

1942 (the last of them as by EB); after their titles, which always begin with "Via", they are known as the "Via" series. They have been collected as *Puzzle of the Space Pyramids* (fix-up **1971** as by EB). Alone and in collaboration, Otto wrote a large number of additional stories out of any sequence; they appeared in the PULP MAGAZINES, 1933–42, and were typical of the field before the revolution in quality symbolized (and in part caused) by the arrival of John W. CAMPBELL Jr at *ASF*. After 1940, Otto Binder did script work on both *Captain Marvel* and SUPERMAN comics; though his fiction production decreased, he did considerable non-fiction work, and took on editorial tasks as well. He became interested in flying saucers. He began publishing sf stories again, briefly, 1953–4. Some of the book publications of the 1960s and 1970s comprise material from before the Second World War. [JC]

Other works: *Martian Martyrs* (c. **1940**, undated, as by John Coleridge, no.1 in *Science Fiction Classics* series); *The New Life* (c. **1940**, undated, as by John Coleridge, no.4 in *Science Fiction Classics* series); *Adam Link in the Past* (1941 *AMZ*; **1950** booklet, Australia); *The Three Eternals* (1939 *TWS*; **1950** booklet, Australia); *Where Eternity Ends* (1939 *Science Fiction*; **1950** booklet, Australia); *The Avengers Battle the Earth-Wrecker* (**1967**); *The Impossible World* (1939 *Startling Stories*; **1967**); *Five Steps to Tomorrow* (1940 *Startling Stories*; **1968**); *Menace of the Saucers* (**1969**); *Night of the Saucers* (**1971**); *The Double Man* (**1971**); *Get Off My World* (**1971**); *Secret of the Red Spot* (**1971**); *The Mind from Outer Space* (**1972**); *The Forgotten Colony* (**1972**, as by Otto O. Binder).

See also: ADAM AND EVE.

BINDER, OTTO O. See Eando BINDER.

BING, JON (1944–). Norwegian writer, editor and translator. Degree in law and active as a legal computer expert with IBM Norway. With Tor Åge BRINGSVAERD, JB has edited a long line of sf anthologies and translated novels in Norway; also with Bringsvaerd he has published several co-authored collections of sf stories, among these their first book, *Rundt solen i ring* ["Round the Sun in a Circle"] (**1967**). Alone, JB has published some half-dozen novels, both juvenile and adult, and the collection *Det myke landskapet* ["The soft landscape"]. His writing is mythologically and non-realistically inclined, often uniting sf and fantasy themes with popular culture, cult figures (real or fictional) and surrealist literary techniques. [J-HH]

See also: THEATRE.

BIOLOGICAL ENGINEERING See GENETIC ENGINEERING.

BIOLOGY Historically, the growth of knowledge in the biological sciences seems always to have lagged behind the growth of knowledge in the physical sciences. Newton's synthesis of physics and astronomy anticipated the linking of biology and chemistry by 200 years. The age of mechanical inventions began in the early 19th century, that of biological inventions is only just beginning. It is not surprising, then, that if we look at the history of speculative fiction as a whole we find that writers have been generally more confident in their dealings with mechanical invention, and it is in this area that their anticipations have sometimes been accurate. In so far as sf has any claim at all to being a predictive medium, it is in connection with mechanical hardware that its predictive successes lie. However, it would not be true to say that at any time writers of speculative fiction have been less interested in the biological sciences. It is simply that, lacking the example of applications of biological theory in the social environment, the dealings of sf writers with biological knowledge have been rather different in kind. Until very recently — perhaps the last 10 or 15 years — sf writers have dealt with aspects of biological knowledge as philosophical ideas, applied meta-phorically rather than practically. There has always been a certain mysticism about the way in which biological notions are employed in sf.

There are two important works of PROTO SF which offer significant biological speculations. Johannes KEPLER's *Somnium* (**1634**), though primarily an astronomical essay, concludes with an interesting attempt to design a lunar biology, while Francis BACON's *New Atlantis* (**1629**), though principally renowned for its mechanical anticipations, also forecasts many significant advances in medicine and agronomy. Attitudes to experimental biology were, however, rather different from attitudes to experiments in the physical sciences. The latter were seen to be, at worst, foolhardy, while the former were seen — again, at worst — to be positively blasphemous. Thus we find the undeniable fascination which many writers found in the prospects of biological science tinged with an attitude of horror, and a conviction that no good could come of tampering with God's handiwork. This is evident in Mary SHELLEY's *Frankenstein* (**1818**), whose eponymous hero is led to despair and destruction by the monster he creates, and in several of Nathaniel HAWTHORNE's allegorical stories, particularly "The Birthmark" (1843) and "Rappaccini's Daughter" (1844), where experiments on people have tragic results. Later examples of the same reactionary response include Robert Louis STEVENSON's *Dr. Jekyll and Mr. Hyde* (**1886**) and Harriet STARK's *The Bacillus of Beauty* (**1900**). It is not difficult to find similar attitudes in 20th-century fiction, but it is worth noting that the tide began to turn soon after 1900. Marie CORELLI's *The Young Diana* (**1915**) has the same theme as Harriet Stark's novel — a scientific experiment to induce physical perfection — but the results are much more positive, and this time the irony of fate fails to confound the hopes of all concerned.

The major biological theme of the late 19th century was, of course, EVOLUTION, and the conflict of ideas provoked by this subject was the most important single stimulus to the development of sf. The response to the controversy took several forms. Speculations regarding the evolutionary future of mankind are discussed in the entries on EVOLUTION and the FAR FUTURE, while speculations relating to Man's evolutionary history are discussed in the section on the ORIGIN OF MAN. The notion of evolution as an adaptive process inspired several attempts to imagine life adapted to circumstances different from those on Earth, and these are discussed in the sections on ALIENS and LIFE ON OTHER WORLDS. A rather more modest version of this same inspiration encouraged a number of fantasies about exotic Earthly creatures, of which the most notable are the sea stories of William Hope HODGSON and the stories in *In Search of the Unknown* (coll. **1904**) by Robert W. CHAMBERS. Exotic survivals from prehistory (usually dinosaurs) became a common feature of exploratory melodramas, most notably in Jules VERNE's *Journey to the Centre of the Earth* (**1864**) and A. Conan DOYLE's *The Lost World* (**1912**).

Early sf writers who made particularly prolific use of biological speculations in their work include, in addition to William Hope Hodgson, H.G. WELLS, J.H. ROSNY AÎNÉ and J.D. BERESFORD.

Evolutionary fantasy remained the dominant species of biological sf for many years, overshadowing fiction dealing with experimental biology. Speculations related to medical science tended to engage in increasingly well-defined clichés: cures for all diseases; and new plagues (*see* MEDICINE). A significant theme which appeared at an early stage but which was not developed until much later was that of biological engineering — the strategic remodelling of living beings (*see* GENETIC ENGINEERING). Possibilities opened up by research in the real world seem to have been relatively ineffective in providing imaginative stimulus to sf writers. The one discovery which provoked a considerable response was the discovery of the mutagenic properties of radiation. The idea of mutation was an implicitly intriguing one, and it was made important by its crucial role in evolutionary theory. Sf writers were already entranced with rays for a variety of melodramatic reasons (*see* POWER SOURCES and WEAPONS) and their recruitment to biological speculation resulted in the swift growth of the "mutagenic romance" (*see* MUTANTS).

John TAINE was a prolific author of such romances.

Very few of the early pulp writers had any knowledge of the biological sciences — one exception seems to have been Stanley G. WEINBAUM — and they handled biological ideas in a careless and cavalier fashion. Weinbaum employed his expertise mainly in connection with designing life-systems for alien worlds, and the only writer who dealt extensively in biological experiments was David H. KELLER, a doctor who became a psychiatrist. (It is, however, worth noting that biologist Julian Huxley contributed "The Tissue-Culture King" to AMAZING STORIES in 1927.)

Things improved somewhat during the 1940s. Several writers trained in biology were recruited to sf in that period, notably the biochemist Isaac ASIMOV, and James BLISH, who studied zoology at college and also worked as a medical technician. Although he did not begin to publish prolifically until the 1950s Blish was the first genre sf writer to import biological ideas on a large scale and apply them with considerable ingenuity. One of his significant early attempts to use biological ideas was "There Shall Be No Darkness" (1950) — one of a group of stories which attempted to recruit biological ideas to the rationalization of symbols borrowed from the supernatural imagination (see SUPERNATURAL CREATURES). Other examples include Jack WILLIAMSON's Darker Than You Think (1940; exp. 1948) and Richard MATHESON's I Am Legend (1954).

As genre sf developed there was a gradual increase in the sophistication of biological analogies. Alien beings were almost always described and defined by reference to the diversity of Earthly life-forms, but this was not done with any great degree of subtlety until the 1950s, when there grew up a considerable body of work using the strange reproductive habits of the lower organisms as models for the construction of exotic situations involving humans and aliens. Authors who made fruitful use of this kind of analogy include Philip José FARMER, notably in The Lovers (1952; 1961), "Open to Me, My Sister" (1960, vt "My Sister's Brother") and "Strange Compulsion" (1953); Theodore STURGEON, notably in "The Perfect Host" (1948), "The Sex Opposite" (1952) and "The Wages of Synergy" (1953); and — more recently — James TIPTREE Jr in "Your Haploid Heart" (1969) and "A Momentary Taste of Being" (1975).

This kind of analogical thinking provides a good example of the way that biological ideas are often — in fact, usually — used in sf. In all these stories exotic biological relationships are transformed into metaphors applicable to psychological relationships. This is, of course, a totally unscientific use of "scientific" ideas — but it is very often effective. The same kind of method is employed with reference to many other biological notions — they are very rarely applied directly to the modelling of hypothetical situations, but are instead recruited as metaphors to describe relationships between humans and other intelligent beings or even, in a psychological sense, between humans and their environment. This applies not only to such hypothetical biological ideas as LIVING WORLDS, but also to such familiar biological concepts as HIVE-MINDS, ECOLOGY (see also COLONIZATION OF OTHER WORLDS) and PARASITISM AND SYMBIOSIS. Thus, the hive-mind becomes, in sf, not so much a mode of social organization pertaining to insect species as a metaphor for considering possible states of human society. Similarly, symbiosis becomes symbolic of an idealized relationship between humans, or between human and other beings. In the case of the word "ecology" this misapplication of ideas extends into the real world, where in common usage, as in much sf, the term has come to be symbolic of some abstract and quasi-metaphysical notion of harmony between man and environment. This constant quest to find metaphors in biology which we may use for speculation about psychology, and to describe man's place in the universal scheme, often confuses and inhibits the attempt to apply biological ideas in fiction actually and scientifically, and to speculate realistically about likely developments in the biological sciences.

Symbolism, metaphor and crude analogical thinking dominate exploration in sf of such notions as CLONES, ANDROIDS, GENETIC ENGINEERING, IMMORTALITY, SEX and CYBORGS. Although much contemporary sf seems to be intimately concerned with current trends in biology, hardly any of this speculation can be said to be "extrapolative" or "realistic". These comments are not necessarily critical. This method of using ideas can be interesting and is often applied with considerable artistry. The point must be made, however, that there is very little sf which is actually "about" biological science. The use of biological ideas as metaphors for application to specifically human situations is probably inevitable. Man is a living creature, and ideas in biology must influence our image of him. Sf merely exaggerates (perhaps we may even say extrapolates) that influence, rather than the ideas themselves. In so far as its dealings with biology are concerned, sf is and always has been a thoroughly humanistic medium.   [BS]

BIONICS See CYBERNETICS; CYBORGS.

BIONIC WOMAN, THE Television series (1976–). Harve Bennett Productions and Universal for ABC. Created and produced by Kenneth Johnson, starring Lindsay Wagner. 50 mins per episode. Colour.

In this spin-off series from the successful series THE SIX MILLION DOLLAR MAN, Jaimie Sommers is the former childhood sweetheart of the bionic man, Steve Austin. After a serious accident she, like him, has part of her body artificially rebuilt and she too becomes a secret agent working for Oscar Goldman, head of a government intelligence agency. The acting of the lead role is notably superior to that of the parent series.   [JB]

BIOY CASARES, ADOLFO (1914–). Argentine writer. His work, which uses sf or detective forms in an abstract, parodic fashion, is generally metaphysical in intent; La invención de Morel (1940; trans. in The Invention of Morel and Other Stories 1964), tells in this fashion of Morel's eventually successful search for IMMORTALITY. ABC's most substantial novel, El sueño de los héroes ["Sleep of the Heroes"] (1954), features the saving of a workman from death by a mysterious figure, possibly supernatural, and the repetition of the same events years later, but without any intervention.

ABC collaborated with Jorge Luis BORGES and Ocampo in the editing of a fantasy collection, Antología de la Literatura Fantástica (anth. 1940) and has also worked with Borges under the name Honorio Bustos Domecq.   [JC]
See also: ABSURDIST SF.

BIRD, CORDWAINER See Harlan ELLISON.

BIRDS, THE Film (1963). Universal. Directed by Alfred Hitchcock, starring Rod Taylor, Jessica Tandy, Suzanne Pleshette, Tippi Hedren and Charles McGraw. Screenplay by Evan HUNTER, based on the story by Daphne DU MAURIER. 119 mins. Colour.

Ordinary bird life suddenly turns against mankind in a series of murderous attacks centered on a small seaside town. The irruption of menace out of a clear sky is paralleled, symbolically, with the eruption of strong feeling in the too-perfectly groomed heroine, in the Freudian love story which runs through the film. It is the arrival of this woman which apparently precipitates the bird attack, though the real cause of the events is carefully left unexplained. The bird attacks are set-pieces, and carry considerable conviction, achieved with skilled editing through a combination of real birds, models and process work by Ub Iwerks, a colleague of Walt Disney. Other effects were handled by Lawrence A. Hampton. The film belongs in form to the monster-movie genre, with the ambiguity of nature shown, as usual, by a tranquil landscape ravaged without warning by some monstrous, inexplicable fury. The difference is in the degree of sophistication in the treatment, not the form. Familiar birds in the place of gigantic horrors merely heighten our uncertainty and fear, as does the lack of a conventional explanation in terms of scientific meddling or atomic radiation. It is interesting that the two (arguably) strongest films in the genre, *The Birds* and *Jaws*, use known rather than imaginary species as the threat. [PN/JB]

BISHOP, MICHAEL (1945–). American writer, much travelled in childhood, with an MA in English from the University of Georgia, where he did a thesis on the poetry of Dylan Thomas; he began publishing sf with "Piñon Fall" for *Gal.* in 1970, and in a short period has established himself as one of the significant new writers of the 1970s. Though his stories and novels to date display considerable intellectual complexity, and do not shirk the downbeat implications of their ANTHROPOLOGICAL treatment of ALIENS and alienating milieux, there is still a sense in which MB cannot be treated as one of those writers, like Edward BRYANT, for instance, whose primary influences can be seen as the American NEW WAVE of the 1960s combined with the liberating influence of the numerous writing workshops of the past decade; MB constructs his novels ostensibly within the terms of HARDCORE SF, most of them being set on other planets complete with the paraphernalia of the traditional SPACE OPERA. *A Funeral for the Eyes of Fire* (**1975**), his first novel, is an example in point: upon a Gothic space-epic plot, in which the protagonist must perform wonders on an alien planet or be sent back to a despotic Earth, a complex and sometimes moving analysis of an alien culture is mounted, along with a pattern of metaphorical and plot reference to the growth of self-realization of the main character both persuasive and integrated to the scenes of action and intrigue. *And Strange at Ecbatan the Trees* (**1976**; vt *Beneath the Shattered Moons*), with the forthcoming English edition projected to contain added material, is a somewhat less convincing FAR-FUTURE tale, which deals with a world most of whose people have been transformed by GENETIC ENGINEERING, many generations ago, into a stoic race, apparently incapable of aggression or any display of emotion. *Stolen Faces* (**1977**) is a dark and simply told novel about the relations between an off-planet Kommissar and those colonists who appear to have contracted a leprosy-like disease; the story is told with a distance that combines reportage and fable. *A Little Knowledge* (**1977**) depicts a revivalist Christian government in domed Atlanta (Georgia); an alien is converted, upsettingly. This novel is connected in setting to the "Urban Nucleus" series of stories, all published in the mid-1970s and all set in NUAtlanta. In order of internal chronology they are "If a Flower Could Eclipse", "Old Folks at Home", "The Windows in Dante's Hell", "The Samurai and the Willows", "Allegiances" and "At the Dixie-Apple

with the Shoo-Fly-Pie Kid". Of MB's shorter works, "Death and Designation among the Asadi" (1973), nominated for both HUGO and NEBULA awards, is perhaps outstanding; he has received four other Nebula and three other Hugo nominations, for stories which include the satirical "Rogue Tomato" (1975) and the fine "On the Street of the Serpents" (1974), though without yet winning an award. His reputation can only grow. [JC]

BIXBY, (DREXEL) JEROME (LEWIS) (1923–). American writer and editor. An extremely prolific story-writer, though relatively little of his work is sf. Pseudonyms he used on magazine sf stories include Jay B. Drexel, Harry Neal and Alger ROME, the last in collaboration with Algis BUDRYS. He edited PLANET STORIES Summer 1950-Jul. 1951, and initiated its companion magazine, TWO COMPLETE SCIENCE ADVENTURE BOOKS, editing its first three issues; he also worked on GALAXY, TWS and STARTLING STORIES, and several comics. His stories include many Westerns; he has also written sf and horror screenplays, including *It! The Terror from Beyond Space* (**1958**; vt *It, the Vampire from Outer Space*). He began publishing sf with "Tubemonkey" for *Planet Stories* in 1949, and collected much of his output in this genre in *Space by the Tale* (coll. **1964**). *Devil's Scrapbook* (coll. **1964**; vt *Call for an Exorcist*) is horror and fantasy. His best-known and widely anthologized story is sf/horror: "It's a *Good* Life" (1953), about a malignant superchild with PSI powers (*see* CHILDREN IN SF). His work is professional but not of great significance in the field, and he has concentrated for some time on film work. [JC]

See also: PSYCHOLOGY; SUPERMAN.

BIZARRE US FANZINE. One issue, Jan. 1941; ed. William L. HAMLING. It is remembered only for publishing for the first time the original but previously

The first issue, Oct. 1965, containing an early story by Thomas M. Disch.

unused ending of A. MERRITT's novel *Dwellers in the Mirage* (**1932**; rev. 1953), the ending which has been in use ever since. *B* has appeared in indexes as a professional SF MAGAZINE, but this was not the case. [FHP/MJE]

BIZARRE MYSTERY MAGAZINE US DIGEST-size magazine. Three issues, Oct. and Nov. 1965 and Jan. 1966, published by Pamar Enterprises; ed. John Poe. *BMM* printed original and reprint material, a strong fantasy element overriding the ostensible mystery content. [FHP]

BLACK, LADBROKE (1877–?). English writer whose sf is restricted to a future-WAR novel, *The Poison War* (**1933**), though *The Gorgon's Head* (**1932**) is an interesting fantasy on the resurrection of this head. [JC]

BLACKBURN, JOHN F(ENWICK) (1923–). English writer and antiquarian book dealer, author of many novels whose ambience of horror derives from a calculated use of material from several genres, including sf. His early books, such as *A Scent of New-Mown Hay* (**1958**), his first, *A Sour Apple Tree* (**1958**), *Broken Boy* (**1959**) and *A Ring of Roses* (**1965**) tended to use themes from espionage and thriller fiction to buttress and ultimately provide explanations for tales whose effects were fundamentally GOTHIC horror and fantasy; ex-Nazis often cropped up in these books, as in the first, where a German scientist spreads mutated plague round the world. Even in later stories, like *The Face of the Lion* (**1976**), which again and characteristically deals with abominable disease, loathsome (and now rather elderly) SS officers still make their dutiful bows. JFB's use of sf is usually borderline, though not in *Children of the Night* (**1966**), one of his better works, where an underground LOST RACE in northern England kills by telepathic powers; often what seem to be sf plot devices on introduction are satisfactorily explained in terms of contemporary science by the story's close, or are red herrings, like the atomic-bomb conspiracy in *The Face of the Lion*. Though his use of sf situations is often ingenious, and helps to make his novels difficult to classify generically, it would be unduly stretching matters to describe JFB as a genuine sf writer. [JC]
Other works: *Dead Man Running* (**1960**); *The Gaunt Woman* (**1962**); *Blue Octavo* (**1963**); *Colonel Bogus* (**1964**); *The Winds of Midnight* (**1964**); *The Young Man from Lima* (**1968**); *Nothing But the Night* (**1968**); *Bury Him Darkly* (**1969**); *Blow the House Down* (**1970**); *The Household Traitors* (**1971**); *For Fear of Little Men* (**1972**); *Devil Daddy* (**1972**); *Deep Among the Dead Men* (**1973**); *Our Lady of Pain* (**1974**); *Mr Brown's Bodies* (**1975**); *The Cyclops Goblet* (**1977**).
See also: MYTHOLOGY.

BLACK CAT, THE US magazine published monthly by the Short Story Publishing Company; ed. Herman D. Umbstaetter, Oct. 1895–1919.

BC was an influential "little magazine" restricted entirely to the short-story market. It frequently published sf but its encouragement of amateur authors resulted in the appearance of many unfamiliar names. Best known were Don Mark Lemon, later to appear in WONDER STORIES QUARTERLY, who contributed "The Mansion of Forgetfulness" (1907), Harry Stephen Keller, with "John Jones' Dollar" (1915), Clark Ashton SMITH who contributed poetry, and Jack LONDON, whose first published story, "A Thousand Deaths" (1899), appeared here. The British edition of *BC*, Feb. 1898–Feb. 1900, ed. G. C. Dusart, was by no means identical to the American. It published stories by many minor British authors, including sf by R. Norman Silver.

The Black Cat was also the title of a Canadian PULP-size magazine. One issue, Winter 1970–71, published and ed. George Henderson. The magazine reprinted weird tales and sf from the 19th and early 20th centuries; also included were a number of illustrations by Virgil FINLAY. [JE/FHP]

BLACK HOLES A black hole comes into existence as the result of the death and collapse of a star of three or more times the mass of the Sun. A star like the Sun, at the end of its life, becomes a white dwarf: a dim, small star composed of extremely condensed matter. A somewhat larger star, of more than 1.44 times the Sun's mass — a figure known as the Chandrasekhar limit — is liable to come to a more violent end, blowing itself to pieces in a supernova explosion. The remaining core would then collapse into a neutron star, the gravitational force being such that the electrons in each atom are forced into the nucleus, and the nuclei themselves are forced together. The result is an object some 10 or 12 miles across, composed entirely of neutrons; despite its small size it would have a greater mass than the Sun. Larry NIVEN's "Neutron Star" (1966) describes many of the phenomena associated with such an object, and was the story which introduced the subject of collapsed stars into sf.

A star of more than three solar masses does not explode, however; it is too heavy. Instead, when its nuclear fuel is exhausted it begins to collapse in on itself. This collapse continues, with the star's density increasing and its diameter shrinking, until ultimately it becomes a singularity: a point of zero size and infinite density. This is a black hole. Its gravitational attraction is so powerful that, once within a certain distance of it (called the event horizon), an object would need to be moving faster than the speed of light in order to escape from it. Therefore not even light itself can escape from the vicinity of a black hole.

One consequence of the gravitational effects of a black hole is that the time-dilation phenomenon that would occur in travel at near-light speeds (*see* FASTER THAN LIGHT) would apply as one approached it. A spaceship falling into a black hole would be destroyed in a very short time, as far as the crew was concerned; to an outside observer, however, it would take an infinite time to happen. The psychological effects consequent on this phenomenon were first explored in sf (although with reference to neutron stars, where a similar effect obtains) in "Kyrie" (1968) by Poul ANDERSON: a telepathic linkage leaves one of its members forever in contact with the dying seconds of the other, as he is drawn towards the star. "To The Dark Star" (1968) by Robert SILVERBERG is in some respects similar, describing the final stages of collapse of a stellar core into a black hole, and the destruction of personality of an observer experiencing it through remote-control

The original THE BLACK CAT, July 1900 issue, and above, the single-shot Canadian magazine of the same title, 1970.

devices. In Frederik POHL's *Gateway* (**1977**) the guilt-feelings suffered by the narrator, sole survivor of a close encounter with a black hole, are greatly intensified because the other members of his party are not dead, but are still dying, and will be — to him — for ever. A visual consequence of the effects of a black hole would be that as a spaceship crossed the event horizon, to an outside observer it would become motionless, an image utilized in "The Dark Soul of the Night" (1976) by Brian ALDISS.

Another use to which black holes have been put in sf is as a possible way round the problem of faster-than-light travel. It is theorized that if one were able to pass through the singularity one would emerge, without any time lapse, somewhere else in the galaxy; and that also, because a black hole is actually rotating very fast — which would to an extent counteract the gravitational effects and would give a black hole a pronounced equatorial bulge — it might be possible to make such a journey without being compressed into nothing. Such a method of transport is used in Joe HALDEMAN's *The Forever War* (**1974**) — where the alternative term "collapsar" is used — and can be expected to crop up with increasing frequency in future stories, as a means of faster-than-light travel which has some theoretical credibility.

In "The Hole Man" (1973), Larry Niven explored the idea of a tiny (i.e. less massive) black hole, but it has since been shown that such quantum black holes would not be stable, and could only exist for an instant. *Black Holes: The End of the Universe?* (**1973**) by John Taylor is a useful introduction to the subject, while *The Iron Sun: Crossing the Universe Through Black Holes* (**1977**) by Adrian Berry advances a fascinating, if grandiose, proposal for the construction of black holes by mankind in order to achieve interstellar travel. [MJE] **See also:** *The Collapsing Universe: The Story of Black Holes* (**1977**) by Isaac ASIMOV; *Space, Time and Gravity: The Theory of The Big Bang and Black Holes* (**1977**) by Robert M. Wald; and (on an even newer theory) *White Holes: Cosmic Gushers in the Universe* (**1977**) by John Gribbin.

BLACK SCORPION, THE Film (1957). Warner Bros. Directed by Edward Ludwig, starring Richard Denning and Mara Corday. Screenplay by David DUNCAN and Robert Blees. 88 mins. B/w.

Giant scorpions emerge from a cavern under the Mexican desert, in this slow-moving blend of monster movie and Western obviously inspired by THEM! The animation of the scorpions, supervised by Willis H. O'BRIEN, does a little to redeem the wooden performances and poor script. [JB]

BLACKS IN SF See POLITICS.

BLACKWOOD, ALGERNON (1869–1951). English writer, who spent a decade in Canada and the USA from the age of 20. His work is essentially fantasy and occult fiction; his short stories are collected under various titles in eight volumes from *The Empty House and Other Ghost Stories* (coll. **1906**) to *Tongues of Fire, and Other Sketches* (coll. **1924**), with several later volumes of republished stories. The most comprehensive are *Strange Stories* (coll. **1929**), *The Tales of Algernon Blackwood* (coll. **1938**) and *Tales of the Uncanny and Supernatural* (coll. **1949**). In later years, he enjoyed a rebirth of fame on English radio and television. His occult detective John Silence, some of whose adventures are collected in *John Silence, Physician Extraordinary* (coll. **1908**), uses some PSEUDO-SCIENTIFIC techniques. The theme of REINCARNATION is recurrent, notably in *Julius Le Vallon: An Episode* (**1916**) and *The Wave: An Egyptian Aftermath* (**1916**). [JC/PN] **Other works include:** *The Listener, and Other Stories* (coll. **1907**); *The Lost Valley and Other Stories* (coll. **1910**); *Pan's Garden: A Volume of Nature Stories* (coll. **1912**); *Incredible Adventures* (coll. **1914**); *Ten Minute Stories* (coll. **1914**); *Day and Night Stories* (coll. **1917**); *The Wolves of God and Other Fay Stories* (coll. **1921**), written with Wilfred Wilson. **See also:** FOURTH DIMENSION (AND OTHERS).

BLADE, ALEXANDER One of the most long-lasting Ziff-Davis house names, originally the personal pseudonym of David Vern (David V. REED), whose contributions under the name have not been identified, though probably "The Strange Adventure of Victor MacLeigh" (1941 *AMZ*) is by him. The name was later used by Howard BROWNE, Millen Cooke, Chester S. GEIER, Randall GARRETT with Robert SILVERBERG, who also wrote solo under the name, Roger P. Graham (Rog PHILLIPS), Edmond HAMILTON, Heinrich Hauser, Berkeley LIVINGSTON, Herb Livingston, William P. McGIVERN, David Wright O'BRIEN, Louis H. Sampliner, Richard S. SHAVER, Don WILCOX and Leroy YERXA. Approximately 50 stories were published as by AB, most in *AMZ* and *Fantastic Adventures* and some in *Imagination*, *Imaginative Tales* and *Science Fiction Adventures*. [JC]

BLAIR, ANDREW See ANONYMOUS SF AUTHORS.

BLAIR, HAMISH. Pseudonym of J.F. Andrew Blair (1872–1935), Scottish author, journalist, and editor, resident in India for many years. In *1957* (**1930**) he described how air power overcame the Second Indian Mutiny in that year, and in its sequel, *Governor Hardy* (**1931**), focused on the international intrigues and the future WAR which resulted. His optimistic outlook was reflected in *The

Great Gesture (**1931**) in which he described events leading to the founding of a United States of Europe in 1941. [JE]

BLAKE'S SEVEN See Terry NATION.

BLAKE, THOMAS (?–). Writer. His sf novel is *UN Confidential — AD 2000* (**1968**). [JC]

BLASTER In sf TERMINOLOGY, the blaster, an sf hand-gun, had an early place of honour along with the DEATH RAY, RAY GUN and DISINTEGRATOR. It was much used in early SPACE OPERA with a panache comparable to that of a cowboy with a six-gun, and remains popular in COMIC STRIPS and on TELEVISION. *See* WEAPONS. [PN]

BLAYRE, CHRISTOPHER Pseudonym of the English biologist and author Edward Heron-Allen (1861–1943) who, under his own name, wrote *The Princess Daphne* (**1885**), a novel of psychic vampirism, and *A Fatal Fiddle* (coll. **1890**), which includes a story centered on telepathy. After a long period away from fiction he returned as CB with a series of short weird and sf stories set in the near future in the University of Cosmopoli. They appeared in *The Purple Sapphire* (coll. **1921**; vt, with additional stories, *The Strange Papers of Dr. Blayre*, **1932**), *The Cheetah-Girl* (**1923**) and *Some Women of the University* (coll. **1932**), the last two titles being privately published. All are of a high quality but have had little influence.

From a similarity in style, content and sense of humour there has been some unproven speculation that CB was responsible for the weird fantasies appearing under the enigmatic pseudonyms DRYASDUST and M.Y. Halidom, attributions used by the author of *The Wizard's Mantle* (**1890**; rev. 1903 as by M.Y. Halidom), *Tales of the Wonder Club* (coll. **1899** in three vols as by Dryasdust; rev. 1903–05 in three vols as by M.Y. Halidom), and, all as by M.Y. Halidom, *The Spirit Lovers* (coll. **1903**), *A Weird Transformation* (**1904**), *The Woman in Black* (**1906**), *Zoë's Revenge* (**1908**), *The Poet's Curse* (**1911**) and *The Poison Ring* (**1912**). [JE]

BLEILER, EVERETT F. (1910–). American editor and bibliographer. He compiled *The Checklist of Fantastic Literature* (**1948**), which the publishers SHASTA were formed to produce. A listing of over 5,000 titles, it is the cornerstone of modern sf bibliography. In collaboration with T.E. DIKTY, he produced the first series of best-of-the-year anthologies, commencing with *The Best Science Fiction Stories 1949* (anth. **1949**) and continuing under joint editorship through five more volumes. Beginning with *The Year's Best Science Fiction Novels 1952* (anth. **1952**; vt *The Year's Best Science Fiction Novels* UK, with one story omitted) EFB and Dikty also produced three annual volumes of longer stories. He joined Dover Publications in 1955, rising to Executive Vice-President in 1967. [MJE]

Photo Peter Nicholls.

BLISH, JAMES (1921–75). American writer. Married (1) sf literary agent Virginia Kidd, (2) Judith Ann Lawrence, an illustrator who became an sf writer. JB's beginnings in sf followed a conventional pattern. He was a fan during the 1930s, and his first short story, "Emergency Refueling" (1940), was published in SUPER SCIENCE STORIES. He belonged to the well-known New York fan group the FUTURIANS, where he became friendly with such writers as Damon KNIGHT and C.M. KORNBLUTH. He studied microbiology at Rutgers, graduating in 1942, when he was drafted and served as a medical laboratory technician in the army. In 1945–6 JB carried out postgraduate work in zoology at Columbia University, which he abandoned to become a writer.

Three of Blish's early short stories, two of them collaborations, were written under the pseudonyms Donald LAVERTY, John MacDOUGAL and Arthur Merlyn.

It was not until 1950, when the first of his "Okie" stories appeared in ASTOUNDING SCIENCE FICTION, that it became clear that JB would be an sf writer of unusual depth. The "Okie" stories featured flying CITIES, powered by anti-gravity devices, SPINDIZZIES, moving through the galaxy looking for work, much as the "Okies" did in the 1930s when they escaped from the dusthowl. The first "Okie" book, a coherent if episodic novel, was *Earthman, Come Home* (1950–53 var. mags; fix-up 1955). Three more followed: *They Shall Have Stars* (1952–4 *ASF*, fix-up 1956, vt *Year 2018!* USA and later UK); *The Triumph of Time* (1958; vt *A Clash of Cymbals* UK); and *A Life for the Stars* (1962). The four "Okie" books were finally brought together in a single volume, *Cities in Flight* (1970). The internal chronology of the books is (i) *They Shall Have Stars*, (ii) *A Life for the Stars*, (iii) *Earthman, Come Home*, (iv) *The Triumph of Time*.

The years from 1950 to 1958 were extraordinarily productive for JB, and many of his finest short stories were published in this period, including "Beanstalk" (1952), "Surface Tension" (1952), "Common Time" (1953), "Beep" (1954), and "A Work of Art" (1956). JB's own choice of his finest short stories was published as *Best Science Fiction Stories of James Blish* (coll. 1965; rev. 1973 with first story omitted and two added; vt *The Testament of Andros*). The years 1950–58 also saw the publication of *Jack of Eagles* (1952; vt *ESP-er*); *The Warriors of Day* (1953); *The Seedling Stars* (1952–6 var. mags, fix-up 1957); *The Frozen Year* (1957; vt *Fallen Star* UK); *A Case of Conscience* (part I in *If*, 1953; 1958); and *VOR* (part in *TWS*, 1949, with Damon Knight; 1958). *Jack of Eagles* was one of the few attempts to give a scientific rationale for telepathy (though in real life JB was sceptical about ESP powers). *A Case of Conscience*, which won a 1959 HUGO award, was one of the first serious attempts to deal with RELIGION in sf, and remains one of the most sophisticated. It is generally regarded as an sf classic. In *The Seedling Stars* and other stories of the period, JB introduced BIOLOGICAL themes. This area of science had previously been rather neglected in sf in favour of the "harder" sciences — physics, astronomy, technology, etc. His conception of the sociological implications of technological advance was sophisticated also, as shown in the "Okie" stories.

JB was interested in METAPHYSICS, and some critics regard as his most important work the trilogy "After Such Knowledge" which is made up of *A Case of Conscience* (1958), *Doctor Mirabilis* (1964), and *Black Easter* (1968) and *The Day after Judgement* (1970). JB regarded the last two books as being one novel, and hence his use of the term "trilogy". "After Such Knowledge" (which takes its title from a line in T.S. Eliot's "Gerontion") poses a question once expressed by JB: "Is the desire for secular knowledge, let alone the acquisition and use of it, a misuse of the mind, and perhaps even actively evil?" This is, after all, one of the fundamental themes of sf, and is painstakingly explored in *Doctor Mirabilis*, JB's finest work in his own opinion, and in that of several of his critics. *Doctor Mirabilis* is a historical novel, dealing with the life of the 13th-century scientist and theologian Roger Bacon. It deals with the archetypal sf theme of CONCEPTUAL BREAKTHROUGH from one intellectual model of the universe to another more sophisticated model.

As a writer, JB was careful and thrifty, to the point of being parsimonious in his later years. He economically made use of many of his best stories, returning often to revise and expand them, sometimes into novel form. Apart from those already mentioned, he also used this treatment on an early short story, "Sunken Universe" (1942 as by Arthur Merlyn) and built it into another story, "Surface Tension" (1952), which in turn became part of the novel *The Seedling Stars* (fix-up 1957); "Surface Tension" was his most popular and most anthologized story. Other examples are *Titan's Daughter* (1952, in *Future Tense*, ed. K.F. Crossen, as "Beanstalk", written with Virginia Kidd; exp. 1961); and *The Quincunx of Time* (1954 *Gal.* as "Beep"; exp. 1973).

JB's STAR TREK books (*Star Trek* 1967 through to *Star Trek 11* 1975) are based on the original television scripts, and hence are collaborations, although *Spock Must Die* (1970) is an original work. It seemed strange to some that a man often described as sf's "intellectual", who disliked television, should write the Star Trek books, but he enjoyed them, especially because they brought such a lively response from young readers. Besides which, they were, as he modestly used to say, his "bread and butter".

JB's output remained fairly steady during the 1960s and 1970s, but the overall standard of his work had dropped. Badly affected by ill-health, he had a successful operation for throat cancer in the 1960s but died from lung cancer in 1975.

JB was also one of the earliest and most influential of sf critics, under the pseudonym of William ATHELING Jr. Much of his criticism (notably stern in many cases) was collected in two books, *The Issue at Hand* (coll. 1964) and *More Issues at Hand* (coll. 1970). As an anthologist he edited *New Dreams this Morning* (anth. 1966), *Nebula Award Stories 5* (anth. 1970), and *Thirteen O'Clock* (coll. 1972), a collection of short stories by C.M. Kornbluth. He also edited the only number of the sf magazine VANGUARD SCIENCE FICTION (Jun. 1958).

JB worked hard for sf in other ways too. He did much to encourage younger writers, and was one of the founders of the MILFORD SCIENCE FICTION WRITERS' WORKSHOP, and an active charter member of the SCIENCE FICTION WRITERS OF AMERICA. He was also, in 1970, one of the founder members of the SCIENCE FICTION FOUNDATION in England.

JB wrote two sf novels in collaboration: *The Duplicated Man* (1953 *Dynamic SF*; 1959) with Robert A.W. LOWNDES, and *A Torrent of Faces* (1967) with Norman L. KNIGHT.

His intellectual passions, which often occur in his writing, were the works of Ezra Pound, James Joyce (he published papers on both of them) and James Branch Cabell (he edited the Cabell Society magazine *Kalki*); the music of

Richard Strauss; and relativistic physics. JB was sometimes unfairly thought to be a cold writer, and indeed he was rational, but his personality and his writings had a strong mystical, romantic side which, though carefully controlled, is often visible below the surface. He had a scholastic temperament, and in 1968 he emigrated to England to be close to Oxford, where he is buried. His manuscripts and papers are in the Bodleian Library. [PN]

Other works: *Galactic Cluster* (coll. **1959**; UK hardback edition omitted three stories, added one); *Star Dwellers* (**1961**); *So Close to Home* (coll. **1961**); *The Night Shapes* (**1962**); *Mission to the Heart Stars* (**1965**); *Star Trek 2* (**1968**); *The Vanished Jet* (**1968**); *Welcome to Mars!* (**1968**); *Star Trek 3* (**1969**); *Anywhen* (coll. **1970**; UK edition added one story); *Star Trek 4* (**1971**); *... And All the Stars a Stage* (1960 *AMZ*; exp. **1971**); *Midsummer Century* (**1972**); *Star Trek 5* (**1972**); *Star Trek 6* (**1972**); *Star Trek 7* (**1972**); *Star Trek 8* (**1972**); *Star Trek 9* (**1973**); *Star Trek 10* (**1974**); *The Star Trek Reader* (coll. **1976**, containing *Star Trek 2*, *3* and *8*); *The Star Trek Reader II* (coll. **1977**, containing *Star Trek 1*, *4* and *9*); *The Star Trek Reader III* (coll. **1977**), containing *Star Trek 5*, *6* and *7*; *Star Trek 12* (**1977**), completed by JB's widow, J.A. Lawrence.

About the author: "The Development of a Science Fiction Writer: II" by James Blish, in *Foundation: The Review of Science Fiction* 2, 1972; "*After Such Knowledge*: James Blish's Tetralogy" by Bob Rickard, in *A Multitude of Visions*, ed. Cy Chauvin (**1975**); and the special Blish issue of *FSF* (April 1972).

See also: ADAM AND EVE; ALIENS; ANTI-INTELLECTUALISM IN SF; ARTS; ASTEROIDS; CHILDREN'S SF; COLØNIZATION OF OTHER WORLDS; COMMUNICATIONS; COMPUTERS; COSMOLOGY; DEFINITIONS OF SF; DISCOVERY AND INVENTION; END OF THE WORLD; EVOLUTION; FANTASTIC VOYAGES; FAR FUTURE; FASTER THAN LIGHT; GALACTIC EMPIRES; GAS GIANT; GENERATION STARSHIPS; GOTHIC SF; GRAVITY; GREAT AND SMALL; HISTORY IN SF; IMAGINARY SCIENCE; IMMORTALITY; ISLANDS; JUPITER; LIFE ON OTHER WORLDS; LINGUISTICS; MAGIC; MARS; MATHEMATICS; MESSIAHS; MONSTERS; MUSIC AND OPERA; ORIGIN OF MAN; OVERPOPULATION; PANTROPY; PARANOIA AND SCHIZOPHRENIA; PERCEPTION; PHYSICS; POLITICS; POLLUTION; PSI POWERS; REINCARNATION; SF MAGAZINES; SF OVERTAKEN BY EVENTS; SCIENTIFIC ERRORS; SOCIOLOGY; SPACE FLIGHT; SPACE OPERA; SUPERMAN; SUPERNATURAL CREATURES; TERRAFORMING; TIME TRAVEL; UNDER THE SEA; WEAPONS.

BLOB, THE Film (1958). Tonylyn/Paramount. Directed by Irvin S. Yeaworth Jr, starring Steve McQueen, Aneta Corseaut and Earl Rowe. Screenplay by Theodore Simonson and Kate Phillips. 85 mins. Colour.

A red blob breaks out of a meteorite and begins to consume the inhabitants of a small American town; constantly growing in size, it is finally defeated by a teenager who discovers that extreme cold renders it harmless. The special effects are by Barton Sloane.

A sequel, *Beware the Blob* (vt *Son of Blob* UK), was made in 1971. A black comedy spoof, it was superior to its predecessor. [JB]

BLOCH, ROBERT (1917–). American writer of FANTASY, horror and thrillers, and a small amount of sf. Born in Chicago, RB was extremely active from 1935 in his several areas of specialization, but is best known for *Psycho* (**1959**), from which Alfred Hitchcock made the famous film. RB began as a devotee of the work of H.P. LOVECRAFT, who treated him with kindness, and his first published story was "Lilies" (1934) in the semi-professional MARVEL TALES; his first important sale was "The Secret of the Tomb" (1935), which appeared in *Weird Tales*, the magazine which, along with *Fantastic Adventures*, published most of the over 100 stories he wrote in the first decade of his career. Towards the end of this period, he contributed the 22 "Lefty Feep" stories to *Fantastic Adventures*, 1942–6; they are fantasy. Early fantasy and horror are collected in RB's first book, published by ARKHAM HOUSE, *The Opener of the Way* (coll. **1945**). It could be argued that the first RB book, however, was the booklet in the AMERICAN FICTION series, *Sea-Kissed* (coll. Feb. **1945**), the title story of which was originally "The Black Kiss" (1937) by RB and Henry KUTTNER. During this period and afterwards, RB remained an active sf and fantasy fan; edited by Earl Kemp, his collection of fanzine articles *The Eighth Stage of Fandom* (coll. **1962**) was assembled for the 1962 World Science Fiction Convention. In the first decade of his career he also turned to radio work; "Stay Tuned for Horror" (1945), a 39-episode syndicated programme comprised of adapted RB stories, became popular. RB used the pseudonym Tarleton Fiske in this period, and also contributed work to sf and horror magazines under various house names, including E.K. JARVIS, and later Wilson KANE, John Sheldon and Will Folke. His best-known story from this time was "Yours Truly, Jack the Ripper" (1943).

Since the 1940s RB has continued to produce a wide variety of material, though less prolifically than before. His sf output is comparatively slender; the stories assembled in *Atoms and Evil* (coll. **1962**) are representative. Much of his recent work has been in Hollywood since the success of *Psycho*. His numerous collections from 1960 combine old and new work, so that much of his pre-War work has become available. RB is a witty, polished craftsman, with perhaps a too

easy touch of whimsy and an occasional tendency to underline his points too emphatically. Though the bulk of his work lies outside the sf field, including 11 non-sf novels not listed here, he has for 40 years been active as fan and patron, and his writing shows complete professional control over sf themes when the need arises. RB was awarded a 1959 HUGO for his short story "The Hellbound Train" (1958), though strictly speaking it is fantasy, not sf. [JC]

Other works: *Pleasant Dreams/Nightmares* (coll. **1960**; vt *Pleasant Dreams & Nightmares* UK: the paperback edition, as *Nightmares* USA, omits five of the 15 stories); *Blood Runs Cold* (coll. **1961**; of which the British edition omits four stories); *Yours Truly, Jack the Ripper* (assembled from *Pleasant Dreams* and *The Opener of the Way*, coll. **1962**; vt *The House of the Hatchet* UK); *Terror* (**1962**); *More Nightmares* (coll. **1962**); *Horror-7* (coll. **1963**); *Bogey Men* (coll. **1963**); *Tales in a Jugular Vein* (coll. **1965**); *The Skull of the Marquis de Sade* (coll. **1965**); *15 Grusel Stories* (coll. **1965**); *Chamber of Horrors* (coll. **1966**); *The Living Demons* (coll. **1967**); *Torture Garden* (coll. **1967**); *The Night-Walker* (coll. **1967**); *This Crowded Earth* (1958 *AMZ*; **1968**) bound with *Ladies' Day* (**1968**); *Dragons and Nightmares* (coll. **1969**); *Bloch and Bradbury* (coll. **1969**); *Fear Today, Gone Tomorrow* (coll. **1971**); *It's All In Your Mind* (**1971**); *Sneak Preview* (**1971**); *Contes de Terreur* (**1974**); *The King of Terrors* (coll. **1977**); *Cold Chills* (coll. **1977**); *The Best of Robert Bloch* (coll. **1977**).

About the author: "Robert Bloch" in *Seekers of Tomorrow* (**1966**) by Sam MOSKOWITZ.

See also: MACHINES; PSYCHOLOGY; RELIGION; ROBOTS; SEX; SOCIOLOGY; WOMEN.

BLONDEL, ROGER *See* B.R. BRUSS.

BLOT, THOMAS Pseudonym of American writer William Simpson (?–?). His sf novel, *The Man From Mars: His Morals, Politics and Religion* (**1891**), is largely devoted to a description by a Martian, teleported to Earth, of his UTOPIAN world. [JC]

BLOW, ERNEST J. (? –). South African writer. His sf novel, *Appointment in Space* (**1963**), features adventures on Mars. [JC]

BLUE BOOK MAGAZINE, THE American PULP MAGAZINE published by the Story-press Corp.; ed. Donald Kennicott, Maxwell Hamilton and others. It first appeared May 1905 as *The Monthly Story Magazine*, became *The Monthly Story Blue Book Magazine* Sep. 1906, *The Blue Book Magazine* May 1907 and *Bluebook* Feb. 1952. Later issues had no sf content.

This major competitor of the Frank A.

"The Wolf Woman"
By H. BEDFORD-JONES
•
A short novel (complete) of the
Civil War in California
By FREDERICK R. BECHDOLT

Painted by HERBERT MORTON STOOPS

Herbert Morton's cover for BLUE BOOK, Aug. 1939, illustrates a fantasy story by H. Bedford-Jones.

MUNSEY group had a long history of publishing sf and fantasy, with works by George Allan ENGLAND, William Hope HODGSON and others appearing in its opening years. Its heyday came in the late 1920s and early '30s, when it published several serializations of novels by Edgar Rice BURROUGHS, and others by Edwin BALMER and Philip WYLIE, Edgar Jepson and James Francis Dwyer, with additional short stories appearing from Ray CUMMINGS. In the 1940s Nelson BOND came into prominence with the appearance of his "Squaredeal Sam" (1943-51) and "Pat Pending" (1942-8) series. These and other stories by Bond continued into the 1950s alongside those of Robert A. HEINLEIN and Eric Frank RUSSELL, enhanced by the excellent artwork of Brendan Lynch and John Costigan.   [IF]

BLUM, RALPH (1932-). American writer. He was involved in early drug research, which is reflected in his sf novel, *The Simultaneous Man* (**1970**); a convict's mind is erased and the memories and identity of a research scientist are substituted, rather as in Robert SILVERBERG's *The Second Trip* (**1972**). The relationship between the scientist and his "twin" is complex and ends tragically for him, in Russia, where he himself becomes a subject for experimentation. Of borderline interest is *Old Glory and the Real-Time Freaks* (**1972**).   [JC]

BOARDMAN, TOM (THOMAS VOLNEY) (1930-). British publisher and editor, born in New York. He went to work for the family publishing company, T.V. Boardman, in 1949, and stayed on as managing director when the company changed ownership in 1954. The company published mysteries, primarily, and some sf. TB was sf adviser, successively, to Gollancz, Four Square

Books, Macdonald and New English Library. He was business manager of SF HORIZONS. He edited the anthologies *Connoisseur's Science Fiction* (anth. **1964**), *The Unfriendly Future* (anth. **1965**), *An ABC of Science Fiction* (anth. **1966**) and *Science Fiction Horizons 1* (anth. **1968**). He now works in educational publishing.   [MJE]

BODELSEN, ANDERS (1937-). Danish writer and journalist, author of several novels of suspense. *Frysepunktet* (**1969**; trans. as *Freezing Point* **1971**; vt *Freezing Down* USA) is sf; its protagonist is incurably sick, and is frozen until he can be cured (*see* CRYONICS). The world to which he awakens, complexly and satirically described in AB's intense manner, offers him ambivalent (and retracted) choices between an idle life (with death inevitable) and a life of drudgery (with access to spare parts). It is a dark story, told urgently, using a wide range of literary techniques.   [JC]
See also: IMMORTALITY.

BOGORAZ, VLADIMIR GERMANO-VITCH (1865-1936). Russian anthropologist whose novel *Sons of the Mammoth* (trans. **1929** as by Waldemar Bogoras) reflects his professional concerns in a fictional telling of a prehistoric tale. [JC]
See also: ORIGIN OF MAN.

BOISGILBERT, EDMUND *See* Ignatius DONNELLY.

BOK, HANNES (1914-64). American illustrator, author and astrologer. Sf illustration had very few mavericks; HB was possibly the most famous: he did not let editors and publishers dictate the way he designed his work and lost hundreds of commissions because of this stubbornness. He was a master of the macabre, a stylist *par excellence*. He painted almost 150 cover paintings and hundreds of b/w illustrations for such magazines as *Cosmic Stories*, *Future*, *Imagination*, *Super Science Stories*, *Fantastic Universe*, *Planet Stories*, *Stirring Science Stories* and, especially, seven covers for *Weird Tales*, Dec. 1939-Mar. 1942. He also did book-jackets for FANTASY PRESS, GNOME PRESS, ARKHAM HOUSE and SHASTA, among others. His style was unique, though the colours and techniques he used were heavily influenced by Maxfield Parrish, who once taught him; his b/w illustrations are highly stylized, his human figures angular and almost Byzantine.

HB was also a writer. Two of his colourful, moralizing fantasy novels were published in book form after his death: *The Sorcerer's Ship* (1942 *Unknown*; **1969**) and "The Blue Flamingo" (1948 *Startling Stories*; rev. vt *Beyond the Golden Stair* **1970**). His other novel was "Starstone World" (Summer 1942 *Science Fiction Quarterly*) and he wrote several short stories. An admirer of A.

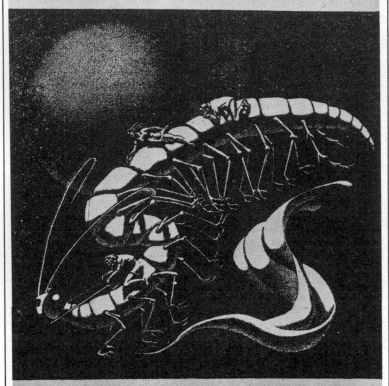

DIMENSION OF DARKNESS
by S. D. Gottesman
(Author of "Return From M-15," "Dead Center," etc.)

I was only going to bump him off when the Doc pulled that switch. So how'm I goin to explain to Lucco what happened then?

Many prefer the work of Hannes Bok in b/w format rather than colour. This comes from *Cosmic Science Fiction*, May 1941, illustrating a story by S.D. Gottesman (C.M. Kornbluth).

MERRITT, he completed and illustrated two of the latter's novels after his death in 1943, *The Black Wheel* (**1947**) and *The Fox Woman and The Blue Pagoda* (**1946**), and was credited in both books. *The Blue Pagoda* was an episode written by Bok to complete *The Fox Woman* which Merritt had worked on sporadically for 20 years before his death.

HB also wrote 13 articles about astrology for *Mystic Magazine* (retitled *Search* in 1956). He shared a HUGO award with EMSH in 1953 for best cover artist. After his death, his friend Emil PETAJA became chairman of the Bokanalia Foundation, which was founded in 1967. This group has published folios of HB's artwork, some of his poetry, and *And Flights of Angels: the Life and Legend of Hannes Bok* (**1968**) by Emil Petaja. [JG/PN]

BOLAND, (BERTRAM) JOHN (1913–). English author and journalist, a prolific story producer, some of them sf. His two sf novels, *White August* (**1955**) and *No Refuge* (**1956**), are both set in

arctic conditions. The first is a DISASTER tale, dealing with the dire effects of a botched attempt at WEATHER CONTROL which causes a great deal of snow in August. *No Refuge* depicts an Arctic UTOPIA, into which two criminals accidentally irrupt, but after a good deal of discussion they are dealt with properly. A further novel, *Operation Red Carpet* (**1959**), has some borderline sf components. [JC]

BOLTON, CHARLES E. (1841–1901). American writer whose posthumously published sf novel, *The Harris-Ingram Experiment* (**1905**), conflates capitalist accomplishments, inventor genius, and UTOPIAN experiments. [JC]

BOND, J. HARVEY *See* Russ WINTERBOTHAM.

BOND, NELSON S(LADE) (1908–). American writer and, in later years, philatelist, who has published works in that field; he began his career in public relations, and came to sf in 1937 with

"Down the Dimensions" for *ASF*; later in that year, he published "Mr. Mergenthwirker's Lobblies" with *Scribner's Magazine*. This was a fantasy which became a radio series and was made into a play; with other similar fantasies, it was assembled into *Mr. Mergenthwirker's Lobblies and Other Fantastic Tales* (coll. **1946**); it served as a model for the "nutty" fiction that he wrote for *Fantastic Adventures* in the early 1940s, comic tales involving implausible inventions and various pixilated doings, sometimes with an effect of excessive coyness. He wrote only two stories under pseudonyms, one as George Danzell (1940) and one as Hubert Mavity (1939). NSB's active career in the magazines extended into the 1950s; his markets extended from the sf PULP magazines and he became strongly associated with THE BLUE BOOK MAGAZINE for stories and series usually combining sf and fantasy elements, and often featuring trick endings reminiscent of O. Henry. Since the early 1950s he has been relatively inactive as a writer.

His most famous single series, about an eccentric space traveller named Lancelot Biggs, appeared, 1939–43, in various magazines, and was published, with most stories revised, as *Lancelot Biggs: Spaceman* (coll. of linked stories **1950**). A similar series, about Pat Pending and his peculiar inventions, appeared 1942–57, all but the last in *Blue Book*, but remains uncollected. The "Squaredeal Sam McGhee" series, also in *Blue Book* (1943–51), is tall tales, not sf. A series of three stories about Meg the Priestess, a young girl who comes to lead a post-HOLOCAUST tribe, appeared in various magazines, 1939–42, but also remains uncollected, as do the four "Hank Horse-Sense" stories, which appeared in *AMZ* 1940–42.

NSB's only novel in book form, *Exiles of Time* (1940 *Blue Book*; **1949**) is a darkly told story about the end of things (*see* DISASTER), told in a sometimes allegorical fashion. He has published collections of individual stories, most of them mixing sf and fantasy: *The 31st of February* (coll. **1949**); *No Time Like the Future* (coll. **1954**); *Nightmares and Daydreams* (coll. **1968**). Perhaps because of the number of his markets, he established a less secure reputation in the sf/fantasy world than less versatile writers; not dissimilar in his wit and fantasticality to Robert BLOCH or Fredric BROWN, he is considerably less well known than either, though his work is attractive and often memorable. [JC]
See also: ADAM AND EVE; DISCOVERY AND INVENTION; LIVING WORLDS.

BONE, J(ESSE) F(RANKLIN) (1916–). American writer and professor of veterinary medicine, who began publishing sf with "Survival Type" for *Gal.* in 1957. His first sf novel, *The Lani People* (**1962**), is his most

This illustration of the surface of Mercury by Chesley BONESTELL, from Willy Ley's *The Conquest of Space*, was based on the most up-to-date information available in 1949.

memorable, later works being routine. It deals with an ALIEN people whose suffering from human exploitation is graphically related. [JC]

Other works: *Legacy* (**1976**); *The Meddlers* (**1976**); *Gift of the Manti* (**1977**), with Ray Myers.

See also: ARTS.

BONESTELL, CHESLEY (1888–). American astronomical illustrator. He studied as an architect in San Francisco, his birthplace, but never graduated. CB worked for many architectural firms and aided in the design of the Golden Gate Bridge. He worked as a matte artist to produce special effects and background paintings for 14 films, including *Citizen Kane*, WAR OF THE WORLDS, WHEN WORLDS COLLIDE, *The Hunchback of Notre Dame*, *The Smith Family Robinson* and DESTINATION MOON. In the early 1940s he began astronomical painting on a major scale, and from 1949 to 1972 completed 10 books, including the classic science fact book *The Conquest of Space* (**1949**), with text by Willy LEY. In 1950 and 1951 CB painted a 10-by-40-foot mural for the Boston Museum of Science, which was transferred to the National Air and Space Museum of the Smithsonian Institution in 1976. His space paintings were used as cover illustrations for *ASF*

and *FSF* many times from 1947 onwards; he became a favourite of sf fans in this period. His style is one of photographic realism, showing great attention to accuracy in perspective and scale. The recipient of many awards, he earned a Special Achievement HUGO in 1974 and an award and medallion from the British Interplanetary Society in 1976. [JG]

BOORMAN, JOHN (1933–). English film-director who, with Bill Stair, novelized his own film script for ZARDOZ (1973); it was published as *Zardoz* (**1974**). [JC]

BOOTH, IRWIN See Edward D. HOCH.

BORDES, FRANÇOIS See Francis CARSAC.

BORGES, JORGE LUIS (1899–). Argentine short-story writer, poet, essayist and university professor, known primarily for his work outside the sf field. Though much of his fiction is local and drawn from Argentine history and events, Borges is best known for his short fantasies. *Ficciones* (coll. **1944** Argentina; trans. Kerrigan **1962**) and *El Aleph* (coll. **1949** Argentina; rev. **1952**) contain his

most important short stories, including most of those considered closest to sf. Most of the contents of these books, with some additional material, can be found in English in *Labyrinths* (coll. **1962**; rev. 1964), which contains the principal stories with a bearing on sf. Another translated collection, where the author collaborated on the translation, is *The Aleph and Other Stories 1933–1969* (coll. **1970**), which is not a translation of *El Aleph*; it has a quite different selection of stories.

JLB has argued that "the compilation of vast books is a laborious and impoverishing extravagance" and claims to have read few novels himself and then only out of "a sense of duty". His stories are accordingly brief, but contain a bewildering number of ideas. Many are technically interesting, using such forms as fictional reviews and biographies to summarize complex and equally fictional books and characters, or using the precise styles of the fable or the detective story to encapsulate involved ideas.

Among his most famous fantasies are "The Library of Babel", which describes a vast library or universe of books containing all possible combinations of the alphabet, and thus all possible gibberish alongside all possible wisdom; "The Babylon Lottery", which details the history of a game of chance that gradually becomes so complex and universal that it is indistinguishable from real life; "Tlön, Uqbar, Orbis Tertius", which chronicles the emergence in and takeover of everyday life by an entirely fictional and fabricated world; "The Circular Ruins", which portrays a character dreaming and giving life to a man, only to realize that he in turn is another man's dream; and "Funes, The Memorious", which describes a man with such perfect memory that the past is as accessible to him as the present. All the above were published in *Ficciones*.

JLB's interest in METAPHYSICS is apparent in these stories and his examination, through fantasy, of the nature of reality associates his fiction with that of many modern American authors, such as Philip K. DICK, Kurt VONNEGUT Jr, and Thomas PYNCHON. He is an important influence on the more sophisticated recent sf writers, especially those dealing with ABSURDIST themes and paradoxes of perception. His interest in puzzles and labyrinths has also led him to fantasy and the detective story as media for expressing his ideas in fiction. A number of his early works have been reprinted in sf anthologies.

JLB has published other collections of stories and sketches, some on the borderline of fantasy, as well as a fantastic bestiary, *The Book of Imaginary Beings* (**1957** Mexico; trans. and exp. **1969**). He has also edited (with Ocampo and BIOY CASARES) a fantasy collection, *Antologia de la Literatura Fantástica* (**1940**), and has revealed a first-hand, if

inaccurate, knowledge of sf by including H.P. LOVECRAFT, Robert HEINLEIN, A.E. VAN VOGT and Ray BRADBURY in his *Introduction to American Literature* (1967 Argentina; trans. Keating and Evans 1971). Translation of JLB's work into English is complex, and there is no definitive collection. [PR]
Other works (in English trans.): *Dreamtigers* (coll. 1964; trans. from *El hacedor*, 1960); *A Personal Anthology* (coll. 1961; trans. from *Antología personal*, 1961); *Doctor Brodie's Report* (coll. 1972; trans. from *Informe sobre Brodie*, 1970); *The Book of Sand* (coll. 1975; trans. from *El libro del arena*).
See also: DEFINITIONS OF SF; SPAIN; PORTUGAL AND SOUTH AMERICA.

BORODIN, GEORGE *See* George SAVA.

BOUCHER, ANTHONY (1911–68). Generally used pseudonym of William Anthony Parker White, American editor and writer. AB's first story was "Snulbug" (1941) in UNKNOWN. He became a regular contributor to this magazine and to ASTOUNDING SCIENCE FICTION in the early 1940s. Most of his stories of this period were humorous in approach (*see* HUMOUR); many of them are included in *The Compleat Werewolf* (coll. 1969). A notable TIME-TRAVEL story was "Barrier" (1942). He also used the pseudonym H.H. Holmes, and under this name published a detective novel, *Rocket to the Morgue* (1942), in which several sf authors, thinly disguised, appear as characters. In 1949 he became founding editor, with J. Francis McCOMAS, of the MAGAZINE OF FANTASY AND SCIENCE FICTION, which from its inception showed a more notable literary outlook than any previous sf magazine. After McComas left, AB was sole editor from 1954 until his retirement, through ill health, in 1958. AB occasionally published verse in *FSF* under the pseudonym Herman W. Mudgett. He wrote little sf after 1952. "The Quest for Saint Aquin" (1951), on a RELIGIOUS theme, is generally considered AB's best sf work. He was also a distinguished book reviewer; he wrote sf review columns for both the *New York Times* (as AB) and the *New York Herald Tribune* (as H.H. Holmes) and was influential in gaining for sf a certain measure of respectability. He edited an annual anthology of stories from *FSF*, beginning with *The Best From Fantasy and Science Fiction* (anth. 1952), his editorship ending with *The Best From Fantasy and Science Fiction, Eighth Series* (anth. 1959). McComas was co-editor of the first three volumes. AB also produced the notable two-volume anthology *A Treasury of Great Science Fiction* (anth. 1959). An able and perceptive editor, AB did much to help raise the literary standards of sf in the 1950s. He also wrote several detective novels. [MJE]
Other works: *Far and Away* (coll. 1955).

See also: GODS AND DEMONS; LINGUISTICS; ROBOTS.

BOULLE, PIERRE (1912–). French writer. Trained as an electrical engineer, PB spent eight years in Malaysia as a planter and a soldier. His experience of the Orient permeates much of his early work (generally not sf), and *Le pont sur la rivière Kwai* (1952; trans. as *The Bridge on the River Kwai* 1954) remains his best-known novel in the exotic mode. PB uses moral fable to pinpoint human absurdities and his relatively large body of work in the sf genre is a good illustration of this method. *La planète des singes* (1963; trans. as *Planet of the Apes* by Xan Fielding 1963; vt *Monkey Planet* UK) is a witty, philosophical tale *à la* VOLTAIRE, full of irony and compassion, quite unlike the later film adaptation, which used only the book's initial premise. [MJ]
Other works: *Contes de l'absurde* (coll. 1953 France); *E = mc²* (coll. 1957 France) (these collections trans. together as *Time Out of Mind* by Xan Fielding and Elisabeth Abbott, 1966); *Le jardin de Kanashima* (1964; trans. as *Garden on the Moon* by Xan Fielding 1965); *Histoires charitables* ["Charitable Tales"] (coll. 1965); *Quia absurdum* (coll. 1970); *Les jeux de l'esprit* ["Games of the Mind"] (1971).
See also: COMPUTERS; DEVOLUTION; MOON; ROCKETS; SCIENTISTS.

BOUNDS, SYDNEY J. (1920–). British writer, active in various fields, including PULP-style adventure sf, since 1951. *The Moon Raiders* (1955) features stolen U235, human agents shanghaied to the Moon and alien invaders. *The World Wrecker* (1956) stars a mad scientist who blows up cities by placing phase-shifted rocks under them and returning these rocks to normal space-time with calamitous effects. [JC]
Other works: *Dimension of Horror* (1953); *The Robot Brains* (1956).

BOUSSENARD, LOUIS (1847–1910). French writer. His popular scientific romances, which have some speculative content, often appeared in *Journal des Voyages*. He is best known for *Les secrets de Monsieur Synthèse* ["The Secrets of Mr Synthèse"] (1888–9), and *Dix mille ans dans un bloc de glace* (1889; trans. as *10,000 Years in a Block of Ice* 1898) (*see* CRYONICS), in which the awakened hero discovers a unified world-UTOPIA peopled by small men, descended from Chinese and black Africans, who can fly by the power of thought. [JC]
Other works: *Les français au pôle nord* ["The French at the North Pole"] (1893); *L'ile en feu* ["Island Ablaze"] (1898).
See also: TIME TRAVEL.

BOUVÉ, EDWARD T(RACY) (?– ?). American writer. His sf novel, *Centuries*

Apart (1894), deals with the discovery of 16th-century colonies, British and French, in Antarctica. [JC]

BOVA, BEN(JAMIN WILLIAM) (1932–). American writer and editor. BB graduated from Temple University, Philadelphia, in 1954 with a degree in journalism. He was subsequently technical editor for Project Vanguard and manager of marketing for Avco Everett Research Laboratory. He was appointed editor of ANALOG following the death of John W. CAMPBELL Jr in 1971. BB's first published sf story was a children's novel, *The Star Conquerors* (1959).

BB has written comparatively few short stories, concentrating instead on novels. His best-known short stories are the "Chet Kinsman" series, incidents in the life of an astronaut in the latter years of the century. They include "Test in Orbit" (1965), "Fifteen Miles" (1967), "Zero Gee" (1972) and "Build Me A Mountain" (1974). Kinsman also features in BB's major work to date, *Millennium* (1976): a novel of power POLITICS in the face of impending nuclear holocaust at the end of this century. BB's other notable novels include *The Starcrossed* (1975), a humorous *roman a clef* whose protagonist is a thinly disguised Harlan ELLISON, and *The Multiple Man* (1976), a suspense-thriller built on the concept of CLONES. BB has also written a number of juvenile novels, including the "Exiles" trilogy: *Exiled from Earth* (1971), *Flight of Exiles* (1972) and *End of Exile* (1975).

It is as editor of *Analog* that BB has achieved most prominence. When he took over it was a moribund magazine; although commercially healthy, it had stagnated in the later years of Campbell's editorship. BB has maintained its orientation towards technophilic sf, but has considerably broadened the magazine's horizons. In doing so he alienated some readers, who shared Campbell's puritanism — such stories as "The Gold at the Starbow's End" (1972) by Frederik POHL and "Hero" (1972) by Joe W. HALDEMAN, inoffensive though they seem, brought strong protests — but he revitalized the magazine. In recognition of this, he has received the HUGO award for best editor every year he has been eligible, from 1973 to 1977 inclusive. BB has also involved the magazine's name in other activities, producing *Analog Annual* (anth. 1976), an original anthology intended as a 13th issue of the magazine, initiating a series of records, and inaugurating a book publishing programme.

BB has written a number of non-fiction books, mostly on scientific subjects. They also include *Notes to a Science Fiction Writer* (1975), a practical guide aimed at imparting the basics of technique to aspiring authors. [MJE]
Other works: *Star Watchman* (1964); *The Weathermakers* (1967); *Out of the Sun* (1968); *The Dueling Machine* (1963

ASF in collaboration with Myron R. Lewis; exp. **1969** as by BB alone); *Escape!* (**1970**); *THX 1138* (**1971**; based on the filmscript by George Lucas); *The Many Worlds of Science Fiction* (anth. **1971**); *As On a Darkling Plain* (**1972**); *The Winds of Altair* (**1973**); ed. *Analog 9* (anth. **1973**); ed. *The Science Fiction Hall of Fame Vols 2A and 2B* (anths **1973**; Vol. 2B is designated Vol. 3 in UK); *When the Sky Burned* (**1973**); *Forward in Time* (coll. **1973**); *Gremlins, Go Home!* (**1974**; in collaboration with Gordon R. Dickson); ed. *The Analog Science Fact Reader* (anth. **1974**); *Through Eyes of Wonder: Science Fiction and Science* (non-fiction **1975**); *City of Darkness* (**1976**).
See also: Jupiter; Outer planets; sf magazines; weather control.

BOWDEN, ETTA and PHIL Probably an American husband-and-wife team. Their sf novel is *Mercy Island* (**1965**). [JC]

BOWEN, JOHN (GRIFFITH) (1924–). English novelist and playwright, active in television and radio; he often derives his novels from earlier plays. This is the case with his first, a fantasy, *The Truth will not Help Us* (**1956**), in which an 18th-century piracy trial is seen, with much anachronistic verisimilitude, as an example of McCarthyism, and with his sf novel proper, *After the Rain* (**1958**), in which a lunatic inventor starts a second Flood; most of the novel takes place on a satirically convenient raft of fools, where survivors of the disaster act out their humanness and win through in the end only because of the dour fanaticism of one person. JB is a supple, subtle, sometimes profound writer. [JC]
See also: holocaust and after.

BOY AND HIS DOG, A Film (1975). LQJaf Presentation. Directed by L.Q. Jones, starring Don Johnson, Susanne Benton, Jason Robards, Alvy Moore and Tim McIntire (as the dog's voice). Screenplay by L.Q. Jones, based on the story by Harlan Ellison. 89 mins. Colour.

Set in the year 2024, after nuclear devastation, this small-budget film concerns two of the survivors, a young man and his dog, who possesses human intelligence and the ability to communicate telepathically with his partner. They move through a desolate landscape inhabited by packs of young savages searching for food and women. A girl is found who turns out to come from a subterranean vestige of middle-class, conservative America, and the youth is lured below to act, in effect, as a sperm bank, but he rejects the regimented underground life and escapes back to the surface with the girl. Finding his dog dying of starvation, he calmly kills the girl to provide food for him and the pair walk off together into the sunset, making

the point that what we have been witnessing is an unusual love triangle. The underground sequences are stagy and compare badly with the gritty realism of the surface ones, but Ellison himself takes the blame for that: "I was being dishonest when I wrote that section of the story. I didn't really create a downunder section that was realistic, I did a kind of papier-mâché Disneyland because I wanted to poke fun at the middle class." L.Q. Jones (a well-known character actor turned director) has adapted the Ellison story honestly and without fuss, steering a middle course between sentiment and cynicism — an unusual thing when transferring sf stories to the screen. The few small changes are regarded by some critics as improvements. [JB]

BOYCE, CHRIS (1943–). Scottish writer and newspaper research librarian, who published his first sf, the story "Autodestruct" in Storyteller no. 3 in 1964; in the mid-1960s he contributed to *SF Impulse*, but by far his most important work to date is his sf novel, *Catchworld* (**1975**), joint winner (with Charles Logan's *Shipwreck*) of the Gollancz/ Sunday Times SF Novel Award. *Catchworld* is an ornate, sometimes over-complicated novel combining sophisticated brain-computer interfaces (*see* computers; cyborgs) and space opera; the transcendental bravura of the book's climax is memorable. [JC]
See also: gods and demons

BOYD, FELIX *See* Harry Harrison.

BOYD, JOHN Professional name of Boyd Bradfield Upchurch (1919–). American sf writer active in the field only since 1968, when his first novel, *The Last Starship from Earth* (**1968**), was published to critical acclaim which still continues. It is a complex novel, told with baroque vigour, a Dystopia, an alternate-worlds story, a space opera with time-travel components making it impossible to say which of various spaceships actually is the last to leave Earth, and in what sense "last" is intended. The Dystopian culture that eventually sends protagonist Haldane to the prison planet Hell is a stratified society with rigid breeding laws that Haldane violates, though it turns out that he does so as the victim of a plot by this world's founders (now on the very pleasant Hell) to get people of his qualifications there where they are needed. Philosophical plot complications abound; Haldane ends up travelling through time, making sure Jesus terminates his career this time at the age of 33 to eliminate the Dystopia by changing the future; and Haldane then becomes the Wandering Jew. None of JB's subsequent novels, some of which are abundantly inventive, have made anything like the impression of this first effort. Its first three successors, *The Rakehells of Heaven* (**1969**), *The*

Pollinators of Eden (**1969**) and *Sex and the High Command* (**1970**), all deal variously with sexual matters (*see* sex), amusingly and with a capacity for the construction of rewarding hypotheses about the cultural forms human nature could find itself involved in. Some later novels, like *Andromeda Gun* (**1974**), a perfunctory comic novel involving a parasitic alien in the American Old West, show a reduction of creative energy. *Barnard's Planet* (**1975**) shows a partial recovery, dealing with some of the same issues of his first novel with some of the same verve. The feeling remains that JB has a larger talent than he has allowed himself to reveal to date in his relatively short career, but that carelessness about quality has sometimes badly muffled the effect of his wide inventiveness. [JC]
Other works: *The Organ Bank Farm* (**1970**); *The IQ Merchant* (**1972**); *The Gorgon Festival* (**1972**); *The Doomsday Gene* (**1973**).
See also: ecology; life on other worlds; under the sea; women.

BOYE, KARIN *See* Scandinavia.

BOYS' PAPERS This rubric covers all juvenile text periodicals except the American dime novels. Since American boys' papers were rare after the First World War, though *American Boy* was an exception (*see* Carl Claudy), this history is predominantly British-oriented.

Although boys' papers could easily be dismissed as being of negligible literary value, perhaps unjustly since Upton Sinclair and other eminent writers found their footing there, they played an important role in the history of sf by creating a potential readership for the sf magazines and by anticipating many genre-sf themes.

The prevailing style for American boys' papers was set by Harry Enton in "The Steam Man of the Plains; or The Terror of the West" (1876 *Boys of New York*; vt *Frank Reade and his Steam Man of the Plains; or The Terror of the West*, 1883). Later written by Luis P. Senarens, Frank Reade, Jr. continued into the 1890s, stimulating the creation of several rivals and causing repercussions in the lost-world genre, e.g. Lieut. S.G. Lansing's "The Electric Man of the Gold Cavern; or Big Steve's Arizona Allies" (1895 *The Banner Weekly*).

In Britain the initial impetus towards boys' sf came from abroad. Jules Verne appeared in English periodicals with *Hector Servadac* (1877 *Good Things*; 1878); *The Steam House* (1880–81 *Union Jack*; 1881) and 16 other serializations in *The Boys' Own Paper*. André Laurie was represented with "A Marvellous Conquest, A Tale of the Bayouda" (1889 *The Boy's Own Paper*; vt *The Conquest of the Moon, a Story of the Bayouda*, 1889), and *Frank Reade Jnr*. was reprinted in *The Aldine Romance of Invention, Travel and Adventure Library*.

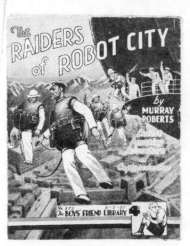

The Dreadnought was a popular BOYS' PAPER in 1912. The uncredited cover shows soldiers on Hampstead Heath preparing for aerial invasion, two years before the actual War. *The Rocket*, Sep. 1923; J.M. Valda's cover illustrates a typical lost-world story. *The Boy's Friend Library*, featuring Captain Justice, this issue May 1937, was the earliest sf influence acknowledged by Brian W. Aldiss.

British authors were soon to follow with a variety of themes. Several interplanetary adventures appeared in *The Marvel* in the mid-1890s, and elsewhere too: e.g. "In Trackless Space" (1902 *The Union Jack*) by George C. WALLIS, later a contributor to the sf pulps. Lost worlds were prominent, notably with Sidney Drew's *Wings of Gold* (1903–04 *The Boy's Herald*; **1908**) and the works of Fenton ASH. World DISASTER appeared in "Doom" (1912 *The Dreadnought*); a vehicle capable of travel through the Earth in "Kiss Kiss, The Beetle" (1913, *Fun and Fiction*); and an early SUPERMAN in "Vengeance of Mars" (1912 *Illustrated Chips*). Overriding all these themes was the future-WAR story, previously a minor genre, but encouraged obsessively by Lord Northcliffe, head of Amalgamated Press. From 1901 to the outbreak of war in 1914 numerous warnings of imminent invasion were published, foremost being the works of John Tregellis, who contributed *Britain Invaded* (1906 *The Boy's Friend*; **1910**), *Britain At Bay* (1906–07 *The Boy's Friend*; **1910**), *Kaiser or King?* (1912 *The Boy's Friend*; **1913**) and others.

When war finally broke out many papers folded, but they were replaced shortly after the Armistice by new periodicals firmly rooted in the 20th century, among them *Pluck*. Subtitled "The Boy's Wireless Adventure Weekly", it published several sf stories linked by the common theme of radio. Lester Bidston's *The Radio Planet* (1923; **1926**) and the first British publication in 1923 of Edgar Rice BURROUGHS's *At The Earth's Core* (1914 *All-Story Weekly*; **1922**) both appeared there, the latter influencing the publication of Edgar WALLACE's *Planetoid 127* (1924 *The Mechanical Boy*; **1929**) and adaptations

of various stories in Sax ROHMER's "Fu Manchu" series (1923–4 *Chums*). Many similar stories were published, notably Leslie BERESFORD's "War of Revenge" (1922 *The Champion*), an account of a German attack on Britain in 1956 using guided missiles, Frank H. Shaw's world catastrophe novel "When The Sea Rose Up" (1923–4 *Chums*) and Eric Wood's Dystopia *The Jungle Men, A Tale of 2923 AD* (1923–4 *The Boy's Friend*; **1927**).

Most popular of all were the SPACE OPERAS then appearing in *Boy's Magazine*, which was first published in 1922. Typical was Raymond Quiex's "The War in Space" (1926), very reminiscent of the 1930s PULPS with its story of asteroids drawn from orbit and hurled as missiles towards Earth, man-made webs of metal hanging in space, domed cities on strange planets and giant insects stalking the surface of hostile worlds. Many similar stories appeared, time machines, androids, titanic war machines, robot armies and matter transmitters all becoming commonplace.

When *Boy's Magazine* folded in 1934, its place was taken three weeks later by SCOOPS, the first British all-sf periodical. In spite of its capable editor, Hadyn Dimmock, and contributions by John Russell FEARN, Maurice Hugi and A.M. Low, *Scoops* lacked that special quality needed to make a successful paper; it folded after only 20 issues.

Since then many adult sf magazines have arisen to fill the temporary gap left by the demise of *Scoops*, but the boys' papers have continued to introduce young readers to sf concepts — *Modern Boy* with the "Captain Justice" series that influenced a youthful Brian ALDISS, *Modern Wonder* with serializations by John WYNDHAM and W.J. Passingham, and *The Sexton Blake Library*, with

pseudonymous contributions by E.C. TUBB and Michael MOORCOCK are among more recent boys' paper titles.

Today sf still plays a role in boys' papers, with content modified to suit the times. Recently an anonymous adaptation of Dave WALLIS's *Only Lovers Left Alive* (**1964**), as "Kids Rule, OK" (1976, *Action*), proved so violent that public outcry led to temporary suspension of the paper. [JE]

BRACKETT, LEIGH (1915–78). American writer. She married, in 1946, sf author Edmond HAMILTON, but she continued to use the name LB both for her sf and for her other books, and for her film work as well; she is well known for film scenarios, from *The Vampire's Ghost* (1945) to *The Long Goodbye* (1973) and, most memorably, some for Howard Hawks, including *The Big Sleep* (1946) and *Rio Bravo* (1958). She began publishing sf stories in 1940 with "Martian Quest" for *ASF*, though her first novel, *No Good from a Corpse* (**1943**) was a detection. The 1940s were her period of greatest activity in the sf magazines, despite her other activities; she appeared mostly in PLANET STORIES, *TWS* and others that offered space for what rapidly became her speciality: swashbuckling but literate adventures, usually set on MARS, though there is no series continuity joining her Martian venues. Some of the stories of this period can be found in *The Coming of the Terrans* (coll. of linked stories **1967**) and *The Halfling and Other Stories* (coll. **1973**). She approached the writing of this sort of tale with economy and vigour; everything about them, their colour, their narrative speed, the brooding forth-rightness of their protagonists (who include her most famous character, Eric

John Stark), makes their influence on the succeeding generation of SWORD-AND-SORCERY writers understandable. One novelette, "Lorelei of the Red Mist" (*Planet Stories* 1946), was written in collaboration with Ray BRADBURY.

In 1946, LB married Edmond Hamilton, and may well have been an important influence on his writing, which improved sharply in quality after the War. Their marriage lasted until Hamilton's death in 1977. LB herself tended to move into somewhat longer forms from this time, setting on her favourite neo-BURROUGHS Mars the first part of her "Eric John Stark" series, which is comprised of *The Secret of Sinharat* (1949 *Planet Stories* as "Queen of the Martian Catacombs"; **1964**), *People of the Talisman* (1951 *Planet Stories* as "Black Amazon of Mars"; rev. **1964**) and "Enchantress of Venus" (1949; vt "City of the Lost Ones") which is collected in *The Halfling*. Stark concentrates all the virtues of the sword-and-sorcery hero in his lean figure; along with Robert E. HOWARD's Conan, he has helped to give birth to dozens of snarling, indomitable mesomorphs, though his attitude to women is somewhat less utilitarian than that of his many successors. The "Stark" series has been continued recently, conveniently transferred to an interstellar venue, as Mars and VENUS are no longer readily usable for the sf adventure writer, in *The Ginger Star* (**1974**), *The Hounds of Skaith* (**1974**) and *The Reavers of Skaith* (**1976**); all three are bound in one volume as *The Book of Skaith* (**1976**). The arrival of Stark on the planet Skaith is triggered by the disappearance of his old friend and benefactor Simon Ashton; he is successful in finding and extricating him; there is much action. Other novels involving Mars are *Shadow Over Mars* (1944 *Startling Stories*; **1951**; vt *The Nemesis from Terra*) and, perhaps the finest, *The Sword of Rhiannon* (1949 *TWS* as "Sea-Kings of Mars"; **1953**), which is connected to "Sorcerer of Rhiannon" (1942); it admirably combines adventure with a strongly romantic vision of an ancient sea-girt Martian civilization. ·

By the 1950s, LB was beginning to concentrate more on interstellar SPACE OPERAS, including *The Starmen* (**1952**; vt abridged *The Galactic Breed*; vt the original magazine title *The Starmen of Llyrdis*), *The Big Jump* (**1955**) and *Alpha Centauri—or Die!* (1953 *Planet Stories* as "Ark of Mars"; exp. **1963**). All three are efficient but somewhat routine novels, especially when set beside LB's major sf novel to date, which appeared at about the same time. *The Long Tomorrow* (**1955**) is set in a strictly controlled post-HOLOCAUST America, many years after the destruction of the cities and of the technology that brought Man to ruin. It is the slow, impressively warm and detailed epic of two boys and their finally

successful attempts to find Bartorstown, where men are secretly re-establishing science and technology. After 20 years, readers of the book may be less hopeful than its author about Bartorstown's aspirations, but on its own terms the novel is a glowing success.

LB did not write much sf after 1955, with the exception of the "Stark" series continuation, preferring to work in films and television. She was a highly professional writer, working with extreme competence within generic moulds that did not always, perhaps, sufficiently stretch her. *The Long Tomorrow*, and her film scripts for Howard Hawks, suggest broader horizons to her work. A collection, edited by her late husband, is *The Best of Leigh Brackett* (coll. **1977**).   [JC]

Other works: *An Eye for an Eye* (**1958**) is a suspense novel; *Follow the Free Wind* (**1963**) is a Western.

As editor: *The Best of Planet Stories No. 1* (anth. **1974**); *The Best of Edmond Hamilton* (coll. **1977**).

See also: ALIENS; ANTI-INTELLECTUALISM IN SF; COLONIZATION OF OTHER WORLDS; GALACTIC EMPIRES; JUPITER; LIFE ON OTHER WORLDS; MERCURY; MYTHOLOGY; PASTORAL; SPACESHIPS; WOMEN.

BRADBURY, EDWARD P. *See* Michael MOORCOCK.

BRADBURY, RAY (DOUGLAS) (1920–). American writer. He was born in Waukegan, Illinois, the Midwestern town where his father had grown up; his mother was Swedish-born. In 1934 his father, a power lineman who was having trouble gaining employment during the depression, moved with the family to Los Angeles. Images of the small town Midwest were always important in RB's stories. RB discovered sf FANDOM in 1937, meeting Ray HARRYHAUSEN, Forrest ACKERMAN and Henry KUTTNER, and began publishing his FANZINE *Futuria Fantasia* in 1939. His first professional sale was "Pendulum", written with Henry HASSE, published in

Super Science Stories Nov. 1941. In that year he met a number of sf professionals, including Leigh BRACKETT, who generously coached him in writing techniques. He later collaborated with her, completing her story "Lorelei of the Red Mist" for *Planet Stories* in 1946.

By 1943 RB's style was beginning to jell: poetic, evocative, consciously symbolic, with strong nostalgic elements and a leaning towards the macabre. It was always, and has remained, as much FANTASY as sf. Many of RB's early stories, mostly written 1943–7, were collected in his first book, *Dark Carnival* (coll. **1947**; UK edition abridged, vt abridged *The Small Assassin*); quite a few of them had originally appeared in WEIRD TALES. All but three of the stories in the later collection *The October Country* (coll. **1955**) had already appeared in *Dark Carnival*. Although some of these stories had sf elements, they could more accurately be described as weird fiction. RB used occasional pseudonyms in those early years; in non-sf magazines he appeared as Edward Banks, William Elliott, D.R. Banat, Leonard Douglas and Leonard Spaulding, and he wrote one story, "Referent", in *TWS* under the house name Brett STERLING. Much of his early sf was colourful SPACE OPERA, and appeared in *TWS* and *Planet Stories*.

One of these latter stories was "The Million Year Picnic" (1946). Later it was to appear in what according to many remains RB's greatest work, *The Martian Chronicles* (fix-up **1950**; vt *The Silver Locusts* UK with the story "Usher II" removed and "The Fire Balloons" added; rev. UK SFBC edition 1953 adds another story, "The Wilderness"; USA 1973 edition also expanded). This was RB's second book, and the one that made his reputation. Almost at once he found a new market for short stories in the "slicks", magazines such as *Esquire*, *Saturday Evening Post*, *McCall's* and COLLIER's. Of the approximately 300 stories RB has published since this time, only a handful originally appeared in sf magazines or any of the PULPS. RB's career remains the biggest breakthrough into lush markets made by any genre sf writer.

The Martian Chronicles is an amazing work; its closely interwoven short stories, linked by recurrent images and themes, tell of the repeated attempts by humans to colonize Mars, of the way they bring their old prejudices with them, and of the repeated, ambiguous meetings with the shape-changing Martians. Despite the sf scenario, there is no emphasis on hard technology at all. The mood is of loneliness, nostalgia; a dying fall lies over the book. Colonists find, in "The Third Expedition", a perfect Midwest township waiting for them in the Martian desert; throughout the book appearance and reality slip, dreamlike, from the one to the other; desires and fantasy are made actuality but turn out to be tainted; at the beginning, in a typical RB image, the warmth of rocket jets brings a springlike thaw to the frozen Ohio landscape; at the end, human children look into the canal to see the Martians, and find them in their own reflections.

All the RB themes which were later to be repeated, sometimes too often, find their earliest shapes here: the anti-technological bias, the celebration of simplicity and innocence as imaged in small-town life, the nostalgia, the sense of loss as youth changes to adulthood and the danger and attraction of masks, be they Hallowe'en, carnival or, as here, alien mimicry.

But for the next few years the wonderfully evocative versatility of RB's imagery kept a freshness and an ebullience which could not be spoiled by the occasional over-writing; what later came to look like an altogether too cosy and comfortable heartland sentiment, of the kind generally associated with *Saturday Evening Post* fiction, was usually redeemed by the hard edges of its expression. RB's talents are very clear in *Fahrenheit 451* (1951 *Gal.* as "The Fireman"; exp. **1953** plus two short stories; most later editions omit short stories). Its DYSTOPIAN vision of a future in which books are burned, and its renegade hero, a book-burning fireman who escapes from his society when his job becomes too much for him, are memorably rendered in RB's only successful effort at a full-length novel. François Truffaut's film version, FAHRENHEIT 451, had as much of Truffaut as it did of Bradbury. Other books published as novels are *Dandelion Wine* (1950-57 var. mags; fix-up **1957**), in which an adolescent life is recorded in terms of a single summer in a small town, in a series of vignettes — they are not sf — and *Something Wicked This Way Comes* (**1962**), an episodic, rather heavily symbolic tale of GOTHIC transformations in a small town, possibly owing something to Charles FINNEY's *The Circus of Dr Lao* (**1935**), which RB had already anthologized in *The Circus of Dr Lao and other Improbable Stories* (anth. **1956**) along with some other well-known fantasies.

RB's vintage years are normally thought to be 1946-55; his other short-story collections of that period are certainly superior to those he produced later. They began with *The Illustrated Man* (coll. **1951**), in which the stories are given a linking framework; they are all seen as magical tattoos becoming living stories, springing from the body of the protagonist. Three of them were filmed as THE ILLUSTRATED MAN by Jack Smight in 1968. Later collections are *The Golden Apples of the Sun* (coll. **1953**; UK edition slightly abridged) and *A Medicine for Melancholy* (coll. **1959**; vt *The Day it Rained Forever* UK with four stories removed and five added). These last two books were combined as *Twice Twenty-*

Two (coll. **1966**). The other important collection of early stories, drawing from many of the books already listed, is *The Vintage Bradbury* (coll. **1965**) with an introduction by Gilbert Highet. No other RB collection approaches the above four in quality.

Yet in the late 1950s and 1960s RB's mainstream reputation continued to grow. He has appeared in well over 800 anthologies. In the USA at least he is regarded by many critics as a major American talent. Sf as a genre can take little credit for this; RB's themes are traditionally American; his choosing to render them on several important occasions in sf imagery does not make RB basically an sf writer, even though his early years were devoted to the form. He is, in effect, a whimsical fantasist in an older tradition. The high repute in which he is held can indeed be justified on the basis of a handful of works, with *The Martian Chronicles*, *Fahrenheit 451*, and many stories from *The Illustrated Man* and *The Golden Apples of the Sun* among them; how large a handful should be judged of lasting value is a matter for critical controversy. RB is a prolific writer, but some have found his work of the past 20 years increasingly disappointing, especially his plays and poetry.

RB's work in film is interesting. Two important early B-grade sf films were loosely based on short stories by him: IT CAME FROM OUTER SPACE in 1953, and THE BEAST FROM 20,000 FATHOMS in the same year. Neither film, though both are interesting, has any perceptible Bradburyan quality. By far his best screenplay was that for *Moby Dick* (1956); RB shared credit on this with John Huston. The 18-minute animated film *Icarus Montgolfier Wright* (1962) was based on an RB story and screenplay, as was the made-for-TV film *Picasso Summer* (1972), based on RB's "In A Season of Calm Weather" (1957). RB received a screenplay credit on this as Douglas Spaulding. 24 of RB's stories received comic-strip adaptation, 16 of which have been reprinted in two books, with introductions: *The Autumn People* (coll. **1965**) and *Tomorrow Midnight* (coll. **1966**), both "adapted for E.C. Comics by Albert B. Feldstein".

110 studies of RB's work, some popular and some academic, are listed in the voluminous reference book *The Ray Bradbury Companion: A Life and Career History, Photolog, and Comprehensive Checklist of Writings* (**1975**) by William F. NOLAN. A useful if uneven recent study is the booklet *The Bradbury Chronicles* (**1977**) by George Edgar SLUSSER. [PN]
Other works: *Switch on the Night* (**1955**), a juvenile; *Sun and Shadow* (**1957**), a short story in limited edition; *The Essence of Creative Writing* (**1962**), non-fiction; *R is for Rocket* (coll. **1962**), mostly previously published in earlier collections; *The Anthem Sprinters, and*

other Antics (coll. **1963**), short plays; *The Machineries of Joy* (coll. **1964**; UK edition omits one story); *The Pedestrian* (**1964**), a short story in limited edition; *The Day it Rained Forever: A Comedy in One Act* (**1966**), a play, not to be confused with the British collection of the same title; *The Pedestrian: A Fantasy in One Act* (**1966**), a play, not to be confused with the short story publication of the same title; *S is for Space* (coll. **1966**), all but three stories having appeared in earlier collections; *I Sing the Body Electric* (coll. **1969**); *Old Ahab's Friend, and Friend to Noah, Speaks his Piece* (**1971**), verse; *The Wonderful Ice Cream Suit and other Plays* (coll. **1972**), three plays; *Madrigals for the Space Age* (coll. **1972**), words and music; *The Halloween Tree* (**1972**), juvenile; *Zen and the Art of Writing* (coll. **1973**), two critical essays; *When Elephants Last in the Dooryard Bloomed* (coll. **1973**), collected verse; *Ray Bradbury* (coll. **1975** UK); *Pillar of Fire, and Other Plays for Today, Tomorrow, and Beyond Tomorrow* (coll. **1975**), plays; *Long After Midnight* (coll. **1976**); *The Best of Bradbury* (coll. **1976**); *Where Robot Mice and Robot Men Run Round in Robot Towns* (coll. **1977**), verse.
As editor: *Timeless Stories for Today and Tomorrow* (anth. **1952**).
See also: ARTS; ASTEROIDS; AUTOMATION; CHILDREN IN SF; COMIC STRIPS; CRIME AND PUNISHMENT; END OF THE WORLD; ESCHATOLOGY; INVASION; LIFE ON OTHER WORLDS; LIVING WORLDS; MARS; MEDIA LANDSCAPE; MEDICINE; MESSIAHS; MYTHOLOGY; PASTORAL; POLITICS; PSYCHOLOGY; RADIO (USA and UK); RELIGION; SEX; SPACE FLIGHT; SUPERNATURAL CREATURES; THEATRE; TIME PARADOXES; TIME TRAVEL; VENUS.

BRADDON, RUSSELL (1921–). Australian writer of biographies, many novels and some other work, interested in experiments in telepathy. He was imprisoned by the Japanese in Changi during the war. His sf novel, *The Year of the Angry Rabbit* (**1964**), unsurprisingly for an Australian, is about giant rabbits and the threat they pose to civilization as we know it, but fortunately an Australian virus counter-attacks. It was filmed as NIGHT OF THE LEPUS (1972). *The Inseparables* (**1968**) and *When the Enemy is Tired* (**1969**) are also sf. [JC]

BRADFORD, J.S. (?–?). English author of one minor sf novel, *Even a Worm* (**1936**), a work similar to Arthur MACHEN's *The Terror* (**1917**) in its account of a revolt of the animal kingdom against Man's rule. What merit it has is diminished by the concluding rationalization of the story as being just a game-hunter's nightmare. [JE]

BRADLEY, MARION ZIMMER (1930–). American writer, mostly of action sf with a good deal of swashbuckling, often touching on SWORD

AND SORCERY, though always with a recognizably sf rationale. She began publishing short stories professionally in 1954 with "Centaurus Changeling" for *FSF*. Several are collected in *The Dark Intruder & Other Stories* (coll. **1964**). Her first novel, *The Door Through Space* (1957 *Venture* as "Bird of Prey"; exp. **1960**), is SPACE OPERA, as is *Seven From the Stars* (**1962**), an intriguingly told adventure involving seven interstellar castaways on Earth.

MZB has become best known for her "Darkover" sequence of novels, set on the fringes of an Earth-dominated GALACTIC EMPIRE; Darkover's inhabitants — partially bred from human colonists of a previous age — successfully resist the Empire's various attempts to integrate them into a political and economical union. Darkovans have a complex though loosely described anti-technological culture dominated by sects of telepaths conjoined in potent "matrices" around which much of the action of the series is focused. The world of Darkover is built up over the series with a richness of detail comparable to that of J.R.R. TOLKIEN's Middle-Earth or Frank HERBERT's planet Dune. In internal chronological order, the Darkover series to date comprises: *Darkover Landfall* (**1972**); *The Spell Sword* (**1974**); *The Shattered Chain* (**1976**); *Star of Danger* (**1965**); *Winds of Darkover* (**1970**); *The Forbidden Tower* (**1977**); *The Bloody Sun* (**1964**); *The Heritage of Hastur* (**1975**); *The Sword of Aldones* (**1962**); *The Planet Savers* (1958 *AMZ*; **1962**; with short story "The Waterfall" added 1976); and *The World Wreckers* (**1971**). The series continues, though, as dates of publication show, much of the later work is infilling. However, it is also deeper and more relaxed in the telling. The most highly praised in the series to date has been the longest, *The Heritage of Hastur*. MZB's first novel, *The Door through Space,* and *Falcons of Narabedla* (1957 *Other Worlds*; **1964**) are marginally linked to the series. [JC]
Other works: *The Colors of Space* (**1963**); *The Brass Dragon* (**1969**); *Hunters of the Red Moon* (**1973**); *The Jewel of Arwen* (**1974**); *Endless Voyage* (**1975**).
Non-fiction: *Men, Halflings and Hero-Worship* (**1973**); *The Necessity for Beauty: Robert W. Chambers and the Romantic Tradition* (**1974**). *Experiment Perilous: Three Essays on Science Fiction* (anth. **1976**) is by MZB with Norman SPINRAD and Alfred BESTER.
About the author: *The Darkover Dilemma: Problems of the Darkover Series* (**1976**) by S. Wise.
See also: COLONIZATION OF OTHER WORLDS; FANTASY; LIFE ON OTHER WORLDS; POLITICS; WOMEN.

BRADSHAW, WILLIAM R. (1851–?). American writer. His sf novel, *The Goddess of Atvatabar: Being the History of the Discovery of the Interior World and Conquest of Atvatabar* (**1892**), is set in a hollow Earth with an interior sun; it includes a love cult, whose devotees regard mild sex without orgasm as leading to perpetual youth, and catastrophic melodrama (*see* ANTHROPOLOGY; LOST WORLDS). [JC]

BRAIN, THE Film (1962). West German and British co-production, CCC/Stross/Governor. Directed by Freddie Francis, starring Peter Van Eyck, Anne Heywood, Cecil Parker and Bernard Lee. Screenplay by Robert Stewart and Phil Mackie, based on the novel *Donovan's Brain* by Curt SIODMAK. 83 mins. B/w.
This is the third and least successful film version of Siodmak's novel; the other two are THE LADY AND THE MONSTER (1944) and DONOVAN'S BRAIN (1953). This retains all the absurdities of the two earlier versions, but lacks their eerie atmosphere. [JB]

BRAMAH, ERNEST Form of his name used by English writer Ernest Bramah Smith (1868–1942) for all his writing. His series of stories in which the Chinese Kai Lung tells stories to stave off punishment, like Scheherazade, contains some fantasy elements. It includes *The Wallet of Kai Lung* (coll. **1900**), *Kai Lung's Golden Hours* (coll. **1922**) with an introduction by Hilaire BELLOC, *Kai Lung Unrolls His Mat* (coll. **1928**), *The Moon of Much Gladness* (coll. **1932**) and *Kai Lung Beneath the Mulberry Tree* (coll. **1940**). *Kai Lung: Six* (coll. **1974**) comprises tales EB did not himself collect. *The Celestial Omnibus* (coll. **1963**) is a selection of the best Kai Lung stories. Of sf interest is *What Might Have Been* (**1907**; published anonymously; vt *The Secret of the League* as by EB), a somewhat tedious anti-socialist melodrama, involving flight with belted-on mechanical wings. [JC]

BRANDON, FRANK *See* Kenneth BULMER.

BRAUTIGAN, RICHARD (1935–). American writer and poet, known primarily for his work outside the sf field. Most of his fiction is whimsical and on the borderline of fantasy. *The Hawkline Monster* (**1974**), described as a "Gothic Western", is sf, however, and plays with the Frankenstein theme, while *In Watermelon Sugar* (**1968**), a fantasy in an indeterminate setting, echoes the post-HOLOCAUST novels of conventional sf. [PR]
See also: ABSURDIST SF; DEFINITIONS OF SF; UTOPIAS.

BRAY, JOHN FRANCIS (? – ?). English 19th-century writer, mostly of economic tracts. His *A Voyage from Utopia* (written 1842; **1957**), anticipates William Dean HOWELLS' technique of presenting a visitor *from* the UTOPIA; the visitor's responses to England and the USA, in JFB's book, are SATIRICAL. [JC]

BREBNER, WINSTON (1924?–). American writer, whose sf novel, *Doubting Thomas* (**1956**), depicts a computer-ruled DYSTOPIA. [JC]

BREGGIN, PETER (ROGER) (1936–). American writer, whose sf DYSTOPIA is *After the Good War, a Love Story* (**1972**). [JC]

BRETNOR, REGINALD (1911–). American writer and anthologist, born in Vladivostok, Siberia, but in the US since 1919. He has been active since the Second World War with fiction and non-fiction in a number of genres (including articles and a book on military theory). RB began publishing sf with "Maybe Just a Little One" for *Harper's Magazine* in 1947. Many of his stories appeared in the slick magazines as well as in sf magazines. His single most famous story is probably the hilarious "The Gnurrs Come from the Voodvork Out" for *FSF* in 1950, a tale that, for many, epitomized the wit and literacy of *FSF*'s new broom. This was the first of a protracted series of stories about Papa Schimmelhorn, the others being "Little Anton" (1951), "Papa Schimmelhorn and the S.O.D.O.M. Serum" (1973), "Count von Schimmelhorn and the Time-Pony" (1974) and "The Ladies of Beetlegoose Nine" (1975). His three edited critical symposia on sf, *Modern Science Fiction, Its Meaning and Its Future* (anth. **1953**), *Science Fiction, Today and Tomorrow* (anth. **1974**) and *The Craft of Science Fiction* (anth. **1976**), have proved among the most substantial non-fiction contributions to the field. Each contains articles by well-known sf writers; the only critics represented are those who also write sf.
As Grendel Briarton, RB has from 1956 contributed to *FSF* a series of joke vignettes whose punch-lines are as a rule distorted or punning catch-phrases; they have become known, from their continuing protagonist, Ferdinand Feghoot, as Feghoots, and can be found assembled in *Through Time and Space with Ferdinand Feghoot* (coll. **1962**; vt exp. *The Compleat Feghoot* 1975). RB is also a translator and lecturer. [JC]
See also: DEFINITIONS OF SF; HUMOUR.

BRETT, LEO *See* R.L. FANTHORPE.

BREUER, MILES J(OHN) (1889–1947). American writer and physician, who began publishing sf with "The Man with the Strange Head" for *AMZ* in 1927. He published a number of notable stories until about 1942. His work has not been collected in book form, which makes it difficult now to find such stories as "The Appendix and the Spectacles" (1928), "The Gostak and the Doshes" (1930) — both in *AMZ* and both since anthologized — and his novels "Paradise and Iron" (1930 *AMZ Quarterly*), and "The Birth of a New

Republic" (1930 *AMZ Quarterly*), the latter written with Jack WILLIAMSON, on whom he had a formative influence. An intelligent though somewhat crude writer, MJB was particularly strong in his articulation of fresh ideas, as the cross-references below suggest.　　　　[JC]

See also: AUTOMATION; COLONIZATION OF OTHER WORLDS; COMPUTERS; DYSTOPIAS; FOURTH DIMENSION (AND OTHERS); MATHEMATICS; MOON; UTOPIAS.

BREWSTER McCLOUD Film (1971). Adler-Philips-Lion's Gate Films/MGM. Directed by Robert Altman, starring Bud Cort, Sally Kellerman, Michael Murphy, William Windom, Shelley Duvall, Stacy Keach and René Auberjonois. Screenplay by Doran William Cannon. 104 mins. Colour.

Made by one of the most important new directors of the 1970s, Robert Altman (who had become celebrated with *M-A-S-H* and was to become more so with *Nashville*), *BM* uses sf ideas embedded in a fantasy matrix. The story, told elliptically, emphasizes a symbolic, avian iconography through crosscutting. An obsessed young man spends much of the film constructing himself a pair of wings, with which he hopes to escape his Earthbound inability to cope with work, sex and life in Texas. Ultimately he does fly, magnificently, before fluttering exhaustedly and crashing to the floor of the Houston Astrodome, where he dies. He is assisted throughout by an enigmatic de-winged female angel of coquettish if not carnal tendencies, who arranges on his behalf a series of homicides, always involving birds. The film is witty, self-conscious, and foreshadows most of the themes which were to become important in Altman's later work.　　　[PN]

BRIARTON, GRENDEL *See* Reginald BRETNOR.

BRICK BRADFORD American COMIC STRIP created by author William Ritt and artist Clarence Gray for King Features Syndicate. *BB* appeared in 1933 as a Sunday page and daily strip. Gray's clean, economical style, together with Ritt's imaginative, purple prose, made *BB* more than just an imitation of BUCK ROGERS, which probably inspired it. Artist Paul Norris took over in the early 1950s. *BB* is no longer published.

The poetic imagery of *BB* is pure SPACE OPERA (futuristic cities rise out of lush jungles, flying ships battle with giant butterflies), while the scenarios have a HARD-SF basis (a descent into the microcosmic universe within a coin, a journey by drilling vehicle to the earth's interior world, and travels through time and space in the "Chronosphere"). Socio-political elements are sometimes included as a secondary theme.

BB appeared as a serial film, an sf comic book and a *Big Little Book*, and was reprinted in France in the 1930s. [JE]

One of the most popular sf comic strips of the 1930s. This comes from 1934.

BRINGSVAERD, TOR ÅGE (1939–). Norwegian writer, editor and translator. With Jon BING, he has edited a long line of sf anthologies and translated novels in Norway; also with Bing he has published several co-authored collections of sf stories, among these their first book, *Rundt solen i ring* (**1967**). Alone, Bringsvaerd has published close to 20 books of non-fiction, as well as short stories, drama, children's prose and novels. His most important sf is probably found in the collection *Karavane* (coll. **1974**) and in the novel *Den som har begge beina på jorda står stille* ["He Who Has Both Feet on the Ground Stands Still"] (**1974**). His writing is satirical and humorous in tone, often only bordering on sf although with a strongly speculative and non-realistic slant. TAB is generally considered one of the major contemporary Norwegian authors.　[J-HH]

See also: THEATRE.

BRINTON, HENRY (1901–). British writer, variously engaged in social and political work, whose sf novel, *Purple-6* (**1962**), describes a world at the verge of atomic holocaust.　　　　　[JC]

BRITISH FANTASY SOCIETY The BFS was formed in 1971 (as the British Weird Fantasy Society) for "all devotees of fantasy, horror, and the supernatural". Modelled on the BSFA and the Tolkien Society, the BFS produces a regular journal, *Dark Horizons*, and a news bulletin. It also sponsors an annual convention, the Fantasycon (1975–), and the Derleth awards for fantasy and related fiction. An earlier British Fantasy Society (1942–5) was sf-based and not connected with this association.　　[PR]

BRITISH SCIENCE FICTION ASSOCIATION (BSFA) Established Easter 1958. Earlier national organizations were short-lived. These included the first British Science Fiction Association (1935), the Science Fiction Association (1937–41), the first British Fantasy Society (1942–5), and the Science Fantasy Society (1948–51). The BSFA was formed in order to counteract a decline in British sf FANDOM by providing a central organization of interest to casual sf readers. The association's principal attraction was (and is) its journal, VECTOR, published intermittently since 1958. A library service still exists, now administered by the SCIENCE FICTION FOUNDATION. The association sponsored the annual Easter sf conventions between 1959 and 1967 and also initiated the British Fantasy Award, first presented in 1966, which was changed in 1970 to the BRITISH SCIENCE FICTION AWARD.

Other projects included several bibliographical works; *Tangent* (a fiction FANZINE); the *Sf Writers Bulletin* (for potential authors); and most recently the *BSFA Yearbook* (first published in 1976). Brian ALDISS was the association's first president (1960–64), followed by Edmund CRISPIN, who retained the position until the BSFA became a limited company in 1967.　　　　[PR]

BRITISH SCIENCE FICTION AWARD This award developed from the British Fantasy Award, sponsored by the BRITISH SCIENCE FICTION ASSOCIATION and made to a writer. John BRUNNER won the first in 1966. It became the British Science Fiction Award in 1970, from which year it has been given to a book, not to a writer. The eligibility rules have changed from year to year, though most versions have stressed British authorship and British publication. The award, which is sometimes known as the BSFA Award, has never been well organized; in most years it was voted on by British fans in general, some years by a small judging panel. It takes the form of a scroll, though the physical awards for 1974–6 were not actually presented until 1977. Because the award has not been well publicized or planned, it never had the hoped-for effect of acting as a counterweight to the American-dominated HUGO and NEBULA awards. This was unfortunate, since it has been made to some fine books. The awards are according to the year they were made and not the year of original publication: 1970: *Stand on Zanzibar* by John Brunner; 1971: *The Jagged Orbit* by John Brunner; 1972: *The Moment of Eclipse* by Brian W. ALDISS; 1973: No award (insufficient votes); 1974: *Rendezvous With Rama* by Arthur C. CLARKE; Special award to Brian W. Aldiss for *Billion Year Spree*; 1975: *Inverted World* by Christopher PRIEST; 1976: *Orbitsville* by Bob SHAW; 1977: *Brontomek!* by Michael G. CONEY; Special award to David KYLE for *A Pictorial History of Science Fiction*; 1978: *The Jonah Kit* by Ian WATSON.   [PN]

BRITISH SCIENCE FICTION MAGAZINE *See* VARGO STATTEN SCIENCE FICTION MAGAZINE.

BRITISH SPACE FICTION MAGAZINE *See* VARGO STATTEN SCIENCE FICTION MAGAZINE.

BROCKWAY, (ARCHIBALD) FENNER (1888–). English writer long active in politics as a socialist; made a life peer in 1964; and long respected for his humane views. His sf novel, *Purple Plague: A Tale of Love and Revolution* (1935), uses a liner stranded at sea by a mysterious plague as a forum for revolutionary acts and discussion.   [JC]

BROOKE, (BERNARD) JOCELYN (1908–66). English writer, most noted for such autobiographical fantasias as *The Goose Cathedral* (1950). His novel, *The Image of a Drawn Sword* (1950), uses some borderline sf devices to convey the dreamlike horror of its protagonist's recruitment into a merciless army; *The Crisis in Bulgaria; or Ibsen to the Rescue!* (1956), with the author's own collage illustrations, is a Victorian fantasy and parody combined; *The Scapegoat* (1949) is psychological fantasy.   [JC]

BROOKE-ROSE, CHRISTINE (1923–). British novelist and academic, born in Switzerland, PhD from London University College, currently professor of American literature at the University of Paris VIII (Vincennes). Her ex-husband is the author Jerzy PETERKIEWICZ. CB-R is known mainly for works outside the sf field, e.g. the book of criticism *A Grammar of Metaphor* (1958) and the novel *The Dear Deceit* (1958). *Such* (1966) hovers between fantasy and sf about a REINCARNATION, whose subject remembers his experiences during death, told in terms of astrophysics as a metaphor for psychic space. *Out* (1964) is an sf novel set in a post-HOLOCAUST Afro-

Eurasia in which the colour barrier has been reversed, ostensibly for medical reasons, as the Colourless seem to be fatally ill. The Colourless protagonist is gradually stripped of all signs of identity; the novel can be read as allegorical of the fate of Europe. There are several fantasies, including the title story, in *Go When You See the Green Man Walking* (coll. 1969). CB-R's novel *The Middleman* (1961) is a satirical fantasy. Her literary criticism is incisive. She takes the side of Tzvetan TODOROV against Stanislaw LEM in "Historical Genres/ Theoretical Genres: A Discussion of Todorov on the Fantastic", *New Literary History*, Autumn 1976. The essay also discusses the DEFINITION of sf. Several essays projected for publication in the near future deal with fantasy, including the works of J.R.R. TOLKIEN and Edgar Allan POE's "The Black Cat", from a structuralist viewpoint.   [JC/PN]
See also: ABSURDIST SF.

BROOKINS, DEWEY C (1904–) American journalist, once a US Navy Inspector, and writer, whose sf novel is *Flying High* (1965).   [JC]

BROSNAN, JOHN (1947–). Australian writer and journalist, primarily on film subjects, resident in the UK. Trained as commercial artist, a trade he does not practise. The author of a handful of sf stories, including the amusing "Conversation on a Starship in Warp-Drive" published in *Antigrav* (anth. 1975) ed. Philip STRICK, he is best known for four books on cinema: *James Bond in the Cinema* (1972); *Movie Magic — The Story of Special Effects in the Cinema* (1974); *The Horror People* (1976) and *Future Tense* (1978). The first three relate peripherally to sf; the last is a history of sf film. JB was a regular contributor to SCIENCE FICTION MONTHLY. He wrote most of the film entries in this volume.   [PN]

BROSTER, D(OROTHY) K(ATHLEEN) (1877–1950). English writer of historical and weird fiction. Noted for *Couching At The Door* (1933 *The Cornhill Magazine*; coll. 1942) and "Clairvoyance" in *A Fire of Driftwood* (coll. 1932). Her evocatively titled *World Under Snow* (1935), written in collaboration with G. Forester, is often cited as sf but is, in fact, a murder mystery set during an English winter. [JE]

BROWN, ALEC Possibly the pseudonym of a British writer. His sf novel, *Angelo's Moon* (1955), is set in Hypolitania, an African city built underground; a white scientist transforms its economics.   [JC]

BROWN, FREDRIC (1906–72). American writer of detective novels and much sf, and for many years active in journalism; he is perhaps best known for

such detective novels as *The Fabulous Clipjoint* (1947), but is also highly regarded for his sf, which is noted for elegance and HUMOUR, and a polished slickness not generally found in the field in 1941, the year he began publishing sf stories with "Not Yet the End" for *Captain Future*. Many of his shorter works were vignettes and extended jokes; of the 47 pieces collected in *Nightmares and Geezenstacks* (coll. 1961), 38 are vignettes of the sort he specialized in (they featured sudden joke climaxes, and were eagerly read); three items in this volume were written with Mack REYNOLDS. Typical of somewhat longer works utilizing the same professional economies of effect are "Placet is a Crazy Place" (1946), "Etaoin Shrdlu" (1942) and "Arena" (1944). The latter story was among the selection of all-time best sf stories selected by the SCIENCE FICTION WRITERS OF AMERICA, and included in *Science Fiction Hall of Fame* (anth. 1970) ed. Robert SILVERBERG. It tells of an interstellar WAR settled in single combat between a human and an ALIEN. FB is possibly at his best in these shorter forms, where his elegant and rather comforting wit, whose iconoclasm was carefully directed at targets that sf readers would appreciate, had greatest scope.

FB's novels are by no means without merit, however. His first, and most famous, *What Mad Universe* (1949), is a cleverly complex ALTERNATE-WORLDS story in which various sf conventions take on literal reality, with disconcerting and comic results. *The Lights in the Sky are Stars* (1953; vt *Project Jupiter* UK) depicts mankind at the turn of the 21st century, on the verge of star travel; in a way, the story is actually about the sense of wonder itself, movingly. *Martians, Go Home* (1955) describes the infestation of Earth by little green men who drive everyone nearly crazy, until the sf writer who has perhaps imagined them into existence imagines them gone, and they disappear. In *The Mind Thing* (1961) a stranded alien attempts to get back home through its ability to ride human minds piggyback, though the experience is fatal for those possessed.

Varied though they are, however, FB's novels did tend to the routine, and it is his various collections of stories that most effectively present him to the reader. [JC]
Other works: *Space on my Hands* (coll. 1951); *Science Fiction Carnival* (anth. 1953) ed. with Mark Reynolds; *Angels and Spaceships* (coll. 1954; vt *Star Shine*); *Rogue in Space* (1949 *Super Science Stories*; 1950 *AMZ*; fix-up 1957); *Honeymoon in Hell* (coll. 1958); *Daymares* (coll. 1968); *Mickey Astromouse* (1971), a juvenile; *Paradox Lost* (coll. 1973).
See also: ABSURDIST SF; COMPUTERS; GAMES AND SPORTS, HIVE-MINDS; INVASION, MEDIA LANDSCAPE; NUCLEAR POWER; PARANOIA AND SCHIZOPHRENIA, PASTORAL, PHYSICS, RELIGION; SPACE FLIGHT; STARS.

BROWN, HARRISON (SCOTT) (1917–). American scientist and writer, whose *The Challenge of Man's Future* (**1954**) combined demographical, ecological and energy concerns in a pioneering work of great admonitory influence. His sf novel, *The Cassiopeia Affair* (**1968**), with Chloe ZERWICK, treats fictionally the same problems through a story about a possibly bogus message from the stars that may keep Man from destroying himself in a terminal conflagration (*see* ASTRONOMY). [JC]
Other works: Non-fiction: *The Next Hundred Years* (**1957**) with James Bonner and John Weir.

Howard V. BROWN painted some of the most memorable covers of the 1930s and 1940s. July 1939.

BROWN, HOWARD V. (1878– ?). American illustrator. Born in Lexington, Kentucky, HVB studied at the Chicago Art Institute. One of the Big Four in the 1930s (with Frank R. PAUL, Leo MOREY and WESSO), he helped to soften the colours that appeared on magazine covers. Starting with a simple, almost primitive style, HB rapidly developed into one of the most dramatic cover illustrators of that era. Most closely associated with the Street & Smith *Astounding Stories*, he also appeared in *Thrilling Wonder Stories* and *Startling Stories*, for which he did his best work. He specialized in BEMs. [JG]

BROWN, JAMES COOKE (1921–). American writer, in whose sf novel, *The Troika Incident* (**1970**), present-day astronauts are shot forward in time to a socialist UTOPIA from which they return favourably impressed. [JC]

BROWN, JAMES GOLDIE (1901–). New Zealand teacher and editor, whose work in the latter capacity has not been restricted to sf; his anthology, *From Frankenstein to Andromeda* (anth. **1966**), is a conscientious scouring of sf materials through a century and a half. [JC]

BROWN, PETER C(URRELL) (?–). English writer whose first novel, *Smallcreep's Day* (**1965**), is an extremely effective ABSURDIST quest, set in an indeterminate future, into the heart of a vast, palpably allegorical factory; the result of the quest for meaning is another assembly line. [JC]

BROWN, ROSEL GEORGE (1926–67). American writer, with an advanced degree in ancient Greek; for three years she was a welfare visitor in Louisiana. She began publishing stories in 1958 (with "From an Unseen Censor" for *Gal.*), some of them interplanetary, some more typical of "women's" fiction. *A Handful of Time* (coll. **1963**) assembles much of this early work. Her "Sibyl Sue Blue" series, published as *Sibyl Sue Blue* (**1966**; vt *Galactic Sibyl Sue Blue*) and, posthumously, *The Waters of Centaurus* (**1970**), features a tough female cop with a teenage daughter in various interstellar adventures; she is more than once required to defend herself (which she does more than adequately) against aggressive males. With Keith LAUMER, RGB wrote an expansive space opera, *Earthblood* (**1966**), in which a lost Terran boy (rather like the protagonist of Robert A. HEINLEIN's *Citizen of the Galaxy* **1957**) searches through the stars for his heritage, and finds it; Earth turns out a dire disappointment, and Roan sets out, successfully, to upset the apple-cart. RGB's career was taking off when she died at the age of 41. [JC]
See also: CRIME AND PUNISHMENT; ECONOMICS; SPACE OPERA.

BROWNE, GEORGE SHELDON (? –). British writer, possibly pseudonymous, who also signed his name Brown; his routine PULP-sf adventures in cheap paperback format are *The Planetoid Peril* (**1952**), *Conquerors of Venus* (**1953**), *The Yellow Planet* (**1954**) and *Destination Mars* (undated, but early 1950s). [JC]

BROWNE, HOWARD (1908–). American author and editor. From 1942–7 HB worked for the Ziff-Davis magazine chain where, among other responsibilities, he was managing editor of AMAZING STORIES and FANTASTIC ADVENTURES, then under Ray PALMER's actual editorship. He contributed stories to the magazines, including two novels about the prehistoric adventurer Tharn: *Warrior of the Dawn* (**1943**) and *The Return of Tharn* (1948 *AMZ*; **1958**). He used various Ziff-Davis house names, including Alexander BLADE. After a period in Hollywood he became editor of *AMZ* — where he rejected a mass of material by Richard S. SHAVER — and *Fantastic Adventures* in 1950. He presided over *AMZ*'s change from pulp to digest format, and over the demise of *Fantastic Adventures* in favour of the digest-sized FANTASTIC. He returned to Hollywood in 1956. Primarily a mystery writer, HB is reported to have detested sf. [MJE]

BROWNING, CRAIG *See* Rog PHILLIPS.

BROWNING, JOHN *See* Robert Moore WILLIAMS.

BRUNNER, JOHN (KILIAN HOUSTON) (1934–). English writer, mostly of sf, though he has published seven thrillers, three contemporary novels and two volumes of poetry. He began very early to submit sf stories to periodicals, and when he was 17 sold an sf novel to an English paperback publisher; it was published probably by Hamilton, apparently in 1952, under a house name (Roy SHELDON?), but JB has never revealed its title. Even in a field noted for its early starters, his precocity was remarkable. His first American sale, "Thou Good and Faithful" (as by John Loxmith), was featured in *ASF* in early 1953, and in the same year he published his first acknowledged novel in an American magazine; it was eventually to appear in book form as *The Space Time Juggler* (1953 *Two Complete Science Adventure Books* as "The Wanton of Argus" as by Kilian Houston Brunner; **1963**). This novel comprises the first of JB's GALACTIC EMPIRE series, which is continued in "The Man from the Big Dark" (1958) and concluded in a later SPACE OPERA, *The Altar on Asconel* (**1965**); the series was later assembled, with the addition of an article on space opera, as *Interstellar Empire* (coll. **1976**). It is the twilight of the Galactic Empire, and barbarism is general, though the galactic Rim (*see* RIMWORLDS) holds some hope for adventurers and mutants, who may eventually rebuild civilization. But the series terminates abruptly, before its various protagonists are able to begin their renaissance; JB has recorded his eventual loss of interest in such stories, which undoubtedly led to the termination of this sequence.

But this lack of interest evinced itself only after very extensive publication of stories and novels describable as literate space opera. From 1953 to about 1957, JB's activity was intermittent, mainly through difficulty in making a living income from full-time writing, a problem about which he has always been bitterly articulate. In the mid-1950s he was working full-time with a publishing house and elsewhere, and writing only occasionally. In 1955 he published one story under the pseudonym Trevor Staines. A little later he sold two novels, again first to magazines: *Threshold of*

Eternity **(1959)** and *The Hundredth Millenium* (**1959**; rev. exp. vt *Catch a Falling Star* **1968**). They were two of the first novels he placed with ACE BOOKS in America. With the signing of the first contract, JB took up full-time freelancing once again.

Over the next six years, JB published under his own name and as Keith Woodcott a total of 27 novels with Ace Books, in addition to work with other publishers. For some readers, this spate of hard-sf adventure stories still comprises JB's most relaxed and fluent work as a writer. Two from 1960 are typical of the storytelling enjoyment he was able to create with the modest but formidable craft he had developed. *The Atlantic Abomination* **(1960)** is a genuinely terrifying story about a monstrous ALIEN, long buried beneath the Atlantic, who survives by mentally enslaving "inferior" species, rather like the thrint in Larry NIVEN's *World of Ptavvs* **(1966)**; the story of its brief and obscene rule and eventual destruction is grippingly told. *Sanctuary in the Sky* **(1960)** is a very short and simple sense-of-wonder tale, set far in the future, in a star cluster very distant from Earth. Various conflicting planetary cultures (all human) meet in peace only upon the mysterious Waystation, which is a synthetic world. A ship full of squabbling passengers arrives there, along with a mild-mannered stranger who immediately disappears. Soon it turns out that he's an Earthman, that Waystation is a colony ship owned by Earth, and that he's come to retrieve it. Man needs the ship. Though this galaxy is full, "There are other galaxies".

The mass of Ace novels contains a second series, this one also truncated, though its structure is more open-ended. The Zarathustra Refugee Planets series, comprising *Castaways' World* (**1963**; rev. vt *Polymath* 1974), *Secret Agent of Terra* (**1962**; rev. vt *The Avengers of Carrig* 1969) and *The Repairmen of Cyclops* **(1965)**, deals over a long time scale with the survivors of the human-colonized planet, Zarathustra; when its sun goes nova, 3,000 spaceships carry a few million inhabitants in various directions. These survivors establish themselves on a variety of uninhabited worlds. After 700 years, the Corps Galactic has the job of maintaining the isolation of these various cultures, so that, having reverted to barbarism, they can develop naturally; their separate histories constitute an experiment in cultural evolution. Again the idea and its telling are engrossing, at the level of literate space opera. Further Ace titles of interest include *The Rites of Ohe* **(1963)**, *To Conquer Chaos* **(1964)**, *Day of the Star Cities* (**1965**; rev vt *Age of Miracles* 1973).

By 1965, with the publication of *The Whole Man* (**1958–9** *Science Fantasy*; fix-up **1964**; vt *Telepathist* UK) and *The Squares of the City* **(1965)**, it was evident

that JB would not be content to go on indefinitely writing the sf entertainments of which he had become master, and that he was determined to expand his range. *The Whole Man*, comprised of fundamentally rewritten magazine stories and much new material, is generally considered to be one of JB's most successful novels. It is an attempt to draw a psychological portrait of a deformed human with telepathic powers who gradually learns how to use these powers in psychiatrically curative ways. *The Squares of the City* is an attempt at the formidable problem of writing a chess novel, in which a chosen venue (a city in this case) is the board, and characters are the various players. The stiffness of the resulting story may have been inevitable.

The next few years saw the publication of further space operas and several story collections, including *Out of My Mind* (coll. **1967**; UK edition differs substantially) and *Not Before Time* (coll. **1968**), which include outstanding items like "The Last Lonely Man" (1964) and "The Totally Rich" (1963). JB's stories are generally free in form, sometimes experimental; he has not, in contrast to some of his older peers, very frequently attempted to link individual items into series or fix-ups. Both his space operas and his later, ambitious work are generally initially conceived in the versions which the reader sees on book publication. This is certainly true of JB's *magnum opus, Stand on Zanzibar* **(1968)**, probably the longest sf novel written from within the genre to that date. The DYSTOPIAN vision of this complex novel rests on the assumption that Earth's population will continue to expand uncontrollably. The intersecting stories of Norman House, a black executive on a mission to the Third World to facilitate further economic penetration, and of Donald Hogan, "synthesist" and government agent, whose mission involves gaining control of a eugenics discovery, provide dominant strands in an assemblage of narrative techniques, whose function of providing a social and cultural context points their resemblance to similar techniques in John Dos Passos' *USA* **(1930–36)**. The resulting vision has a cumulative, sometimes overpowering effect. The book's anti-Americanism has an American ring to it, perhaps through its density of reference, through JB's admirable (though sometimes insecure) grasp of idiom, and through the apocalyptic fervour of its telling. It won the 1968 HUGO award, the 1970 BRITISH SCIENCE FICTION AWARD, and its French translation won the PRIX APOLLO in 1973.

Two further novels from this period maintain something of the same pace and intensity; *The Jagged Orbit* **(1969)** conflates medical and military industrial complexes with the Mafia in a rather too tightly plotted, though occasionally powerful, narrative. It won the 1971 British Science Fiction Award. *The Sheep*

Look Up **(1972)** is perhaps the most unrelenting and convincing Dystopia of the three books. The dominant theme in this instance is POLLUTION; the documentation is cumulatively staggering; the less orthodox plotting permits an almost essayistic exposition of the horrors in store for us. All three novels oppressively insist on the conspiratorial and almost irresistible expediency of the powers that be.

Unsurprisingly, though this trilogy of Dystopias received considerable critical attention, it in no way made JB's fortune. He has always been extremely open about his finances and his hopes for the future, and has made no secret of the letdown he felt on discovering himself, after these culminating efforts, still in the position of a commercial writer forced to produce commercially to survive. Except for *The Shockwave Rider* **(1975)**, which employs some of the same reportage techniques in a story about a world enmeshed in a COMMUNICATIONS explosion. JB in his decreasingly frequent publications since 1972, has returned to a somewhat more flamboyant version of the space opera idiom he had used earlier. He has also rewritten (and usually expanded) several of the early Ace books to slightly uneasy effect. His health has been uncertain for several years, with a consequent severe slowing down of his once formidable writing speed.

In 20 years of professional writing, JB has made significant contributions to the space-opera sub-genre of sf, and has written several intellectually formidable novels about the state of the world, as well as other more conventional sf novels. He is noted for the hard, aggressive edge of his style, and for the ideas it clothes. The opinions extractable from his novels are closer to left-wing than usual with sf writers, which perhaps underlines his reputation as a controversialist in an age where, for many of those outside the sf field, the claims and accusations he makes are becoming part of the Western world's general consensus about Man's possible condition as the 20th century draws to a close. [JC]

Other works: *The Brink* **(1959)**; *Echo in the Skull* (**1959**; rev. exp. vt *Give Warning to the World* 1974); *The World Swappers* **(1959)**; *The Skynappers* **(1960)**; *Slavers of Space* (**1960**; rev. vt *Into the Slave Nebula* 1968); *I Speak for Earth* (**1961** as by Keith Woodcott); *Meeting at Infinity* **(1961)**; *The Ladder in the Sky* (**1962** as by Keith Woodcott); *The Super Barbarians* **(1962)**; *Times Without Number* **(1962)**; *No Future in It* (coll. **1962**); *The Astronauts Must Not Land* (**1963**; rev. vt *More Things in Heaven* 1973); *The Dreaming Earth* **(1963)**; *Listen! The Stars!* (**1963**; rev. vt *The Stardroppers* 1972); *The Psionic Menace* (**1963** as by Keith Woodcott); *Endless Shadow* **(1964)**; *Enigma from*

Tantalus (**1965**); *The Long Result* (**1965**); *The Martian Sphinx* (**1965** as by Keith Woodcott); *Now Then!* (coll. **1965**); *A Planet of Your Own* (**1966**); *No Other Gods But Me* (coll. **1966**); *Born Under Mars* (**1967**); *The Productions of Time* (**1967**); *Quicksand* (**1967**); *Bedlam Planet* (**1968**); *Father of Lies* (**1968**); *Not Before Time* (coll. **1968**); *Double, Double* (**1969**); *Timescoop* (**1969**); *The Evil That Men Do* (1966 *NW*; **1969**); *The Dramaturges of Yan* (**1971**); *The Wrong End of Time* (**1971**); *The Traveler in Black* (coll. of linked stories **1971**); *Entry to Elsewhen* (coll. **1972**); *From this Day Forward* (coll. **1972**); *Time-Jump* (coll. **1973**); *The Stone That Never Came Down* (**1973**); *Total Eclipse* (**1974**); *Web of Everywhere* (**1974**); *The Book of John Brunner* (coll. **1976**). JB also translated *The Overlords of War* (**1973**) by Gérard KLEIN.

About the author: *The Happening Worlds of John Brunner* (critical anth. **1975**) ed. Joseph W. de Bolt; "The Development of a Science Fiction Writer" by JB in FOUNDATION 1 (1972); the two leading articles in SCIENCE-FICTION STUDIES, Jul. 1976.

See also: ALTERNATE WORLDS; ANDROIDS; ARTS; COLONIZATION OF OTHER WORLDS; COMPUTERS; CRIME AND PUNISHMENT; DEFINITIONS OF SF; DISASTER; ESP; FAR FUTURE; FUTUROLOGY; GAMES AND SPORTS; GENERATION STARSHIPS; LIFE ON OTHER WORLDS; MAGIC; MATTER TRANSMISSION; MEDIA LANDSCAPE; MUSIC AND OPERA; OVERPOPULATION; PARANOIA AND SCHIZOPHRENIA; POLITICS; PSEUDO SCIENCE; PSI POWERS; PSYCHOLOGY; SF MAGAZINES; SUPERMAN; TIME TRAVEL; TRANSPORTATION; WOMEN.

BRUNNGRABER, RUDOLF (1901–). German writer, active for many years. His sf novel, *Radium* (**1936**; trans. **1937**), features a near contemporary corner on the radium market, causing troubles in a hospital which is using it to cure cancer. [JC] **Other works:** *Die Engel in Atlantis* ["The Angel in Atlantis"] (**1938**); *Karl und das 20. Jahrhundert* (**1933**; trans. as *Karl and the Twentieth Century* **1933**).

BRUNT, SAMUEL *See* MONEY; MOON.

BRUSS, B.R. Pseudonym used by mainstream French writer Roger Blondel (1895–) for his prolific commercial sf output. BRB is the author of over 50 unpretentious sf adventure novels, some of which have enjoyed regular reprints: *L'apparition des surhommes* ["Appearance of the Overmen"] (**1953**); *Terre, siècle 24* ["Earth, Century 24"] (**1959**); *An ... 2391* ["Year ... 2391"] (**1959**) are his most notable titles. [MJ]

BRUTSCHE, ALPHONSE *See* Jean-Pierre ANDREVON.

BRYANT, EDWARD (1945–). American writer, almost exclusively of short stories, beginning with "They Come Only in Dreams" for *Adam* in 1970. He has made his living as a freelance writer since that time. He graduated with an MA in English from the University of Wyoming in 1968. EB was raised in Wyoming. His early career was assisted by Harlan ELLISON, whom he met at the CLARION SF WRITERS' WORKSHOP in 1968 and 1969. His first book, *Among the Dead and Other Events Leading up to the Apocalypse* (coll. **1973**; minor revisions in the 1974 paperback make the latter the definitive text), made a considerable stir for the wide variety of stories included and the technical facility they displayed; his conversational, apparently casual style sometimes conceals the tight construction and density of his best work, like "Shark" (1973), a complexly told love story whose darker implications are brought to focus in the girl's decision to have her brain transplanted into a shark's body, ostensibly as part of a research project; in the story, symbol and surface reality mesh impeccably. The setting for many of the stories in this collection is a California transmuted by sf devices and milieux into an image, sometimes scarifying, sometimes joyful, of the culmination of the American Dream, an image further developed and intensified in *Cinnabar* (coll. of linked stories **1976**), whose eponymous CITY of the FAR FUTURE is a dreamlike re-enactment of an essentialized California. The earlier stories of the sequence intricately develop a strangely moving vision of the rococo, many-shaped life by which mankind is ultimately destined to explicate itself (*see also* LEISURE), though the end of the book presents stories with a somewhat reductive plottiness. With Harlan Ellison, EB has also begun a GENERATION-STARSHIP series with *Phoenix Without Ashes* (**1975**), which works into novel form the pilot for the abortive Ellison television series *The Starlost*; the book is short and perfunctory, but future volumes are projected. EB has also published stories as Lawrence Talbot. He is the editor of an anthology of original stories and some poems, *2076: The American Tricentennial* (anth. **1977**; rev. 1977 – the first edition can be identified by various errors, including the absence of title on Peter Dillingham's poem).

In a career that is still taking shape, EB has already produced a strong body of work. [JC] See also: ABSURDIST SF; MESSIAHS; PERCEPTION.

BRYANT, PETER *See* Peter GEORGE.

BSFA *See* BRITISH SCIENCE FICTION ASSOCIATION.

BSFA AWARD *See* BRITISH SCIENCE FICTION AWARD.

BUCK, DORIS P(ITKIN) (? –). American writer. Her work (which includes poetry) since she began publishing sf stories with "Aunt Agatha" for *FSF* in 1952 has been restricted almost entirely to that magazine; she has published no books. [JC]

BUCK ROGERS 1. Serial film (1939). 12 episodes. Universal. Directed by Ford Beebe and Saul A. Goodkind, starring Buster Crabbe, Constance Moore, C. Montague Shaw, Jack Moran and Henry Brandon. Scripts by Norman S. Hall and Ray Trampe, based on the comic strip BUCK ROGERS IN THE 25TH CENTURY. 24 reels. B/w.

After playing FLASH GORDON in two serials (1936 and 1938) Buster Crabbe then found himself in the role of Buck Rogers, the other famous space-opera hero of the newspaper comic strips. The serial, not as lavish as the first Flash Gordon serial, concerns Buck's waking after a 500-year sleep to discover that the Zuggs from Saturn have invaded Earth,

Buster Crabbe plays BUCK ROGERS and Constance Moore plays Wilma in the 1939 cinema serial.

aided by the villainous Killer Kane. The remaining episodes deal with his travels to Saturn to face the Zuggs on their home ground, and his efforts to avoid the usual hazards of crashing spaceships, ray-guns, robots and mind-control devices.

2. Television serial (1950). ABC TV. Produced and directed by Babette Henry. Written by Gene Wyckoff, starring Ken Dibbs, Lou Prentis, Harry Kingston and Harry Sothern, based on the comic strip BUCK ROGERS IN THE 25TH CENTURY. 25 mins per episode. B/w.

BR was one of the many space-opera juvenile TV serials made in the early 1950s. Its style and scripts were fashioned after the Saturday matinée cinema serials, but the restrictions imposed by television production in those days necessitated its being shot live on a cramped interior set, with the result that the cinema serials seemed visually extravagant by comparison. The first episode involved a couple of "tigermen" from Mercury who come to Earth with the intention of draining away all its water.   [JB]

BUCK ROGERS IN THE 25th CENTURY

American COMIC STRIP conceived by John Flint Dille, written by Philip Francis NOWLAN, based on his novel *Armageddon 2419 AD* (1928 9 *AMZ*; fix-up **1962**). *BR* appeared first in 1929 in daily newspapers, illustrated by Dick CALKINS, and later in Sunday newspapers, where the illustrator was first Russ Keaton and then Rick Yager, with some assistance from Calkins. Murphy Anderson took over in 1958, and Gene Tuska 1959–67. After Nowlan, John F. Dille and others wrote the script. BR ceased publication in 1967.

BR was the first American sf comic strip with a moderately adult and sophisticated storyline, though its artistic style was rather crude and naïve, at least in comparison with several of its imitators and successors, such as BRICK BRADFORD and FLASH GORDON. None the less, it remained extremely popular for many years.

BR's scenario is archetypal SPACE OPERA. Buck Rogers, a lieutenant in the USAF, is transported 500 years into the future to find America overrun by hordes of "Red Mongols". Accompanied by his perennial girl-friend, Wilma, Buck is constantly engaged in battle with his mortal enemy Killer Kane, on land and sea and in space. All the standard accoutrements of space opera are used: death rays, disintegrating rays, domed cities and space rockets.

Although *BR* contributed little to the artistic evolution of the comic strip, its storyline was very influential. *BR* was successfully translated into other media. It appeared as a popular RADIO serial, in film serializations starring Buster Crabbe (*see* BUCK ROGERS) and in *Big Little Books*. Buck Rogers's adventures have been reissued, in part, in hardcover volumes in America.   [JE]

BUDRYS, ALGIS

Form of his name used by writer and editor Algirdas Jonas Budrys (1931–) for all his work; the surname is also apparently a shortening of the Lithuanian original. He was born in East Prussia, and has been in America since 1936. He has worked as an assistant to his father, who was the American representative of the government-in-exile of Lithuania, an experience which has arguably shaped some of his fiction. He began publishing sf in 1952 with "The High Purpose" for *ASF*, and very rapidly gained a reputation as a leader of the 1950s sf generation, along with Robert SHECKLEY, Philip K. DICK and others, all of whom brought new literacy, mordancy and grace to the field; since 1965 he has written regular, incisive book reviews for *Gal.*, and latterly for *FSF*. From 1965 to 1975 he published little fiction.

During his first decade as a writer, AB used a number of pseudonyms on magazine stories: David C. Hodgkins, Ivan Janvier, Paul Janvier, Robert Marner, William Scarff, John A. Sentry, Albert Stroud and (in collaboration with

Jerome BIXBY) Alger ROME. He wrote few series, though his first story, "The High Purpose", had two sequels: "A.I.D." (1954) and "The War is Over" (1957), both in *ASF*. The "Gus" stories, as by Paul Janvier, are "Nobody Bothers Gus" (1955) and "And Then She Found Him" (1957).

AB's first novel has a complex history. As *False Night* (**1954**), it was published in a form abridged from the manuscript version; this manuscript served as the basis for a reinstated text which, with additional new material, was published as *Some Will Not Die* (**1961**). In both versions a post-HOLOCAUST story is set in a plague-decimated America and, through the lives of a series of protagonists, about half a century of upheaval and recovery is described. *Some Will Not Die* is a much more coherent (and rather grimmer) novel than its predecessor. His second novel, *Who?* (**1958**), filmed as WHO?, not quite successfully grafts an abstract vision of the subjection of Man to existential tortures on to an ostensibly orthodox sf plot, in which a prosthetically rebuilt scientist (*see* CYBORGS), vital to the American defence effort, must be identified as who he claims to be; after a terrible accident in Russia, his face has been encased within a metal mask. As AB is in part trying to write an existential thriller about identity (rather similar to the later work of Kobo ABÉ), and not an sf novel about the perils of prosthesis, some of the subsequent detective work seems a little misplaced; his seriousness of purpose is never in doubt, however. Similarly, *The Falling Torch* (1957–9 var. mags; fix-up **1959**) presents a story which on the surface is straight sf, describing an Earth, several centuries hence, dominated by an alien oppressor, in which the son of the exiled president returns to his own planet to liaise with the underground — but the story can also be read as a rather awkward allegory of the Cold War as it affected eastern Europe, and therefore, like *Who?*, asks of its generic structure rather more significance than generic structures of this kind have been designed to bear. The strain shows.

Much more thoroughly successful is AB's fifth novel, *Rogue Moon* (**1960**), already something of an sf classic. A good deal has been written about the highly integrated symbolic structure of this story, which on the surface deals with a HARD-SF solution to the problem of an alien labyrinth discovered on the MOON, which kills anyone who tries to pass through it. At one level, the novel's description of attempts to thread the labyrinth from Earth via MATTER TRANSMITTERS makes for excellent traditional sf; at another, it is a sustained *rite de passage*. There is no doubt that AB intends both levels of reading, in whatever terms an interpretation might run; in this novel, both levels interact fruitfully.

After his years away from fiction, AB

This BUCK ROGERS IN THE 25TH CENTURY comic strip from 1934 features disintegrator rays and antigravity belts.

has recently returned with his most humanly complex and fully realized novel to date. *Michaelmas* (1977) describes in considerable detail a NEAR-FUTURE world whose information media have become even more sophisticated and even more creative of news than at present, as depicted in Sidney Lumet's film *Network* (1976), and as represented by such figures as CBS broadcaster Walter Cronkite; like Cronkite (though to a much greater extent), the Michaelmas of the title is a moulder of news. Unusually, however, the book does not attack this condition. Michaelmas is a highly adult, responsible, complex individual, who with some cause feels himself to be the world's Chief Executive; beyond his own talents, he is aided in this task by a vast COMPUTER with which he is in constant contact, and which itself (not dissimilarly to the computer network in books like Alfred BESTER's *The Computer Connection* (1975; vt *Extro*) coordinates all other computers in the world. Although the plot — Michaelmas must confront mysterious aliens who are manipulating mankind from behind the scenes, and defeat them — is straight out of PULP fiction, *Michaelmas* is a sustained, involving and peculiarly realistic novel.

Currently rather undervalued, AB is that rarity, an intellectual genre writer, as is also demonstrated by his two collections of short stories, *The Unexpected Dimension* (coll. 1960) and *Budrys' Inferno* (coll. 1963; vt *The Furious Future* UK). From his genre origins stem both his strengths — incisiveness, exemplary concision of effect — and his weaknesses — mainly the habit, which he may have mastered, of overloading genre material with MAINSTREAM resonances. [JC]
Other works: *Man of Earth* (1958); *The Amsirs and the Iron Thorn* (1967; vt *The Iron Thorn* UK).
About the author: *More Issues at Hand* (coll. 1970) by William Atheling Jr (James BLISH), chapter v; "Rite de Passage: a Reading of *Rogue Moon*" by David KETTERER in FOUNDATION 5, 1974.
See also: CHILDREN IN SF; COMMUNICATIONS; CONCEPTUAL BREAKTHROUGH; CRITICAL AND HISTORICAL WORKS ABOUT SF; DISCOVERY AND INVENTION; GOTHIC SF; INVASION; INVISIBILITY; MARS; MEDIA LANDSCAPE; METAPHYSICS; NEW WAVE; OPTIMISM AND PESSIMISM; OUTER PLANETS; PANTROPY; PARANOIA AND SCHIZOPHRENIA; PERCEPTION; POLITICS; PSYCHOLOGY; REINCARNATION; ROBOTS; SAMUELSON, David N.; SCIENTISTS; VILLAINS.

BUG Film (1975). Paramount. Directed by Jeannot Szwarc, starring Bradford Dillman, Joanna Miles and Richard Gilliland. Screenplay by William Castle and Thomas PAGE, based on the novel *The Hephaestus Plague* by Thomas Page. 100 mins. Colour.

Killer-insects on the loose in BUG.

After an earthquake near a small American town, a number of strange insects appear out of a fissure. They are capable of producing fire by rubbing two rear appendages together, and immediately start igniting sections of the surrounding countryside, along with cars, people and one unfortunate cat. A scientist, whose wife falls victim to their incendiary activities, becomes bug-obsessed. Mating them with a local variety of insect, he produces a new species with a liking for raw meat and the ability to spell. Finally he too becomes their victim, falling in flames into the fissure which conveniently closes behind him and the bugs. *B* is a confusing film, unclear about what it is trying to be — a straight horror/sf film or an allegorical warning to mankind to stop meddling with the unknown. The good insect photography is by Ken Middleham. [JB]

BUG-EYED MONSTERS were practically invented by illustrator Howard V. Brown in the 1930s. Aug. 1936.

BUG-EYED MONSTERS Often known by their acronym, BEMs. *See* MONSTERS.

BULGAKOV, M(IKHAIL) (1891–1940). Russian playwright and novelist, whose fame has come only with the posthumous publication of most of his fiction. *The Heart of a Dog* (written 1925; trans. from the manuscript 1968), is a short sf novel in which a scientist transforms a dog into a kind of man, but a kind incapable of fundamental transformation to civilized status; eventually, the scientist is forced to change him back into a dog (or allegorical peasant) again. *Master i Margarita* (1966–7; trans. as *The Master of Margarita* 1967) is a fantasy in which the Devil appears in modern Moscow, and Christ's crucifixion is re-enacted. MB is a powerful, extremely funny, ultimately very serious writer whose use of sf and fantasy forms was tightly linked to the messages he laboured to produce about the state of modern Russia. He was much criticized in Russia during his life. A collection in English of his short fiction is *Diaboliad and Other Stories* (coll. 1972). [JC]

BULGARIA *See* EASTERN EUROPE.

BULMER, KENNETH (1921–). English writer who also signs himself H.K. Bulmer, as well as using a number of pseudonyms, which have included Frank Brandon, Rupert Clinton, Ernest Corley (not sf), Peter Green, Philip Kent, Chesman Scot, Nelson Sherwood, H. Philip Stratford, Tully Zetford, the collaborative pseudonym Kenneth JOHNS (with John NEWMAN) and the house name Karl Maras, under which he wrote two novels; he has also written the long series of Edgar Rice BURROUGHS-influenced adventures published under the name Alan Burt AKERS (*who see for details*). After a career as an active fan dating from before the Second World War, KB began publishing sf in 1952 with paperback novels for Hamiltons, and was soon involved in producing material for *New Worlds*, *Authentic* and *Nebula*, the three major magazines among those proliferating in the volatile British sf scene of the first post-War decade, though he sold few stories to US magazines. His first novels were *Encounter in Space* (1952) and two with A.V. Clarke, *Cybernetic Controller* (1952) and *Space Treason* (1952). These, and much of his ensuing work, were either SPACE OPERAS or adventure plots laid on simplified versions of future Earths. Notable among his novels are several published in the USA from 1957, including *City Under the Sea* (1957), *The Secret of ZI* (1958; vt *The Patient Dark* UK), *The Earth Gods are Coming* (1960; vt with one story added *Of Earth Foretold* UK), *Demons' World* (1964; vt *The Demons* UK) and, possibly the best of them, *Worlds for the Taking* (1966), a relatively sustained and dark-toned portrait of the costs of being a "competent man" in an environment of interstellar corporate intrigue.

In the period of his most interesting work, approximately 1955–68, KB was notable for the adept use he made of a wide range of sf themes, from underwater CITIES to giant ALIEN invaders (*see also* GREAT AND SMALL), to TIME TRAVEL and MONSTERS in *Cycle of Nemesis* (**1967**), to PARALLEL WORLDS. The latter is the plot device in the "Keys to the Dimensions" series, which is: "The Map Country" (**1961** *Science Fantasy*; rev. vt *Land Beyond the Map* **1965**); "The Seventh Stair" (**1961** *Science Fantasy* as by Frank Brandon); "Perilous Portal" (**1962** *Science Fantasy* as by Frank Brandon); *The Key to Irunium* (**1967**); *The Key to Venudine* (**1968**); *The Wizards of Senchuria* (**1969**); *The Ships of Durostorum* (**1970**); *The Hunters of Jundagai* (**1971**) and *The Chariots of Ra* (**1972**). More recently, KB's fiction has seemed to flounder somewhat in attempts at handling a more "contemporary" style and subject matter, as in *On the Symb-Socket Circuit* (**1972**) and *Roller Coaster World* (**1972**).

With E.J. CARNELL's death in 1972, KB took over the long-running anthology series NEW WRITINGS IN SF, editing all titles from *New Writings in SF 22* (anth. **1973**) to *New Writings in SF 29* (anth. **1976**), maintaining the generally traditionalist content of the books. At about the same time, he edited and prepared copy for publication of three issues of a planned sister magazine to VISIONS OF TOMORROW, but this magazine, *Sword and Sorcery*, was aborted by its Australian backer, Ron Graham, before any issues actually appeared. As fan, writer and editor, KB has been one of the mainstays of British sf for more than three decades, and though much of his work is routine, especially that written under pseudonyms, he has consistently shown himself as one of the most competent, though not perhaps the most original, workers in the sf field.

For the past five years most of KB's considerable energies have gone into writing historical romances, some under the house names Arthur Frazier and Neil Langholm; but by a long way the liveliest is the series of 14 novels about the British sailor Fox, set in the Napoleonic period, written under the pseudonym Adam Hardy. KB has been, since its inception, a council member of the SCIENCE FICTION FOUNDATION. [JC]
Other works: *Empire of Chaos* (**1953**); *Galactic Intrigue* (**1953**); *Space Salvage* (**1953**); *The Stars are Ours* (**1953**); *World Aflame* (**1954**); *Challenge* (**1954**); *The Changeling Worlds* (**1959**); *Beyond the Silver Sky* (**1961**); *No Man's World* (**1961**; vt as coll., comprising title novel plus one story, *Earth's Long Shadow* UK); *Fatal Fire* (**1962**); *The Wind of Liberty* (coll. comprising title novel plus one story **1962**); *Defiance* (coll. of linked stories **1963**); *The Wizard of Starship Poseidon* (**1963**); *The Million Year Hunt* (**1964**); *Behold the Stars* (**1965**); *To Outrun Doomsday* (**1967**), *The Doomsday Men* (**1965** *If*; exp. **1968**); *Kandar* (**1969**); *The Star Venturers* (**1969**); *The Ulcer*

Culture (**1969**; vt *Stained-Glass World* UK); *Quench the Burning Stars* (**1970**; exp. vt *Blazon* USA); *Star Trove* (**1970**); *Swords of the Barbarians* (**1970**); *The Electric Sword-Swallowers* (**1971**); *The Insane City* (**1971**). As by Philip Kent: *Mission to the Stars* (**1953**); *Vassals of Venus* (**1953**); *Home is the Martian* (**1954**); *Slaves of the Spectrum* (**1954**). As by Karl Maras: *Zhorani* (**1953**); *Peril from Space* (**1954**). As by Tully Zetford: the "Hook" sequence: *Whirlpool of Stars* (**1974**); *The Boosted Man* (**1974**); *Star City* (**1975**); *The Virility Gene* (**1975**). For works written as by Alan Burt Akers, *see* AKERS.
As editor. *New Writings in SF. Special One* (anth. **1975**) with E.J. Carnell; *New Writings in SF 23* (anth. **1973**); *New Writings in SF 24* (anth. **1974**); *New Writings in SF 25* (anth. **1975**); *New Writings in SF 26* (anth. **1975**); *New Writings in SF 27* (anth. **1975**); *New Writings in SF 28* (anth. **1976**).
See also: COMIC STRIPS; GALACTIC EMPIRES; UNDER THE SEA.

BULWER, EDWARD *See* Bulwer LYTTON.

BULWER-LYTTON, Sir EDWARD *See* Bulwer LYTTON.

BUNCH, DAVID R. (?–). American writer of poetry and sf. He graduated as Bachelor of Science at Central Missouri State College and as MA in English at Washington University; he is a civilian cartographer for the American army and began publishing sf with "Routine Emergency" for *If* in 1957. Much of his sf work was assembled as *Moderan* (coll. of linked stories **1971**); this remarkable collection of short, fable-like tales describes in SATIRICAL terms a radically technologized future world, in which people are composed mostly of metal elements, in which the surface of the world is plastic, and thought and action are both solipsistic and deeply melancholy. The book effectively constructs a portrait of Man as ROBOT in order to arraign his current rush into mechanical rootlessness. DRB has published well over 100 stories in sf and literary magazines. [JC]
See also: ABSURDIST SF; CYBORGS; PARANOIA AND SCHIZOPHRENIA.

BUPP, WALTER *See* Randall GARRETT.

BURDICK, EUGENE L(EONARD) (1918–65). American writer of several extremely popular novels, both alone and in collaborations; his sf novel, *Fail-Safe* (**1962**), with J.Harvey WHEELER, presents a NEAR-FUTURE American attack in error on the USSR, and the horrifying tit-for-tat (the destruction of New York City) which the American President is forced to offer. The book was filmed as FAIL SAFE (**1964**). [JC]
See also: POLITICS.

BURGEON, G.A.L. *See* Arthur Owen BARFIELD.

BURGER, DIONYS (?–). Dutch lecturer in physics, and author, now retired. His *Sphereland: A Fantasy about Curved Spaces and an Expanding Universe* (trans. **1965**) is a MATHEMATICAL fable written as a sequel to *Flatland* (**1884**) by Edwin ABBOTT. [PN]

BURGESS, ANTHONY Pseudonym of John Anthony Burgess Wilson (**1917**–), British writer, known primarily for his work outside the sf field. Trained in English literature and phonetics, AB taught at home and in Malaysia 1946-69, then returned to England and became a full-time professional writer; he now lives in Monte Carlo. A Protean man of letters, novelist, musician, composer and specialist in Shakespeare and James Joyce, AB is best known in the sf field for *A Clockwork Orange* (**1962**) which was filmed by Stanley KUBRICK, 1971 (*see* A CLOCKWORK ORANGE). A compelling and often comic vision of the way violence comes to dominate the mind, the novel is set in a future London and is told in a curious but readable Russified argot by a juvenile delinquent whose brainwashing by the authorities has destroyed not only his murderous aggression but also his deeper-seated sense of humanity as typified by his compulsive love for the music of Beethoven. It is an ironic novel in the tradition of ZAMIATIN's and ORWELL's anti-UTOPIAS. AB's other sf novel is *The Wanting Seed* (**1962**), another DYSTOPIAN tale about the dilemmas facing men who wish to curb the population explosion by every means possible (*see* OVERPOPULATION). A recent short novel, *Beard's Roman Women* (**1976**), has pronounced fantasy elements and connotations: it is a melancholy tale of a widowed writer haunted in Rome by the supernatural presence (and insistent telephone calls) of his deceased wife. AB's most purely sf work is the short story "The Muse" (1968), a story of altered PERCEPTION and TIME TRAVEL, in which an alarming explanation is given for Shakespeare's never having blotted a line. It can be found in *The Light Fantastic* (anth. **1971**) ed. Harry HARRISON. [MJ]
See also: LEISURE; LINGUISTICS; PSYCHOLOGY; SATIRE.

BURKE, JONATHAN Form of his name used by English writer and editor John Frederick Burke (**1922**–), who had been active in FANDOM in the 1930s (*see* FUTURIAN), for the sf he published in English magazines in the mid-1950s, beginning with "Chessboard" for *NW* in 1953, and for his earlier sf novels as well, all of them routine; he also wrote several thrillers as JB. His sf deals with a variety of themes, from PARALLEL WORLDS in *The Echoing Worlds* (**1954**) to EVOLUTION in *Twilight of Reason* (**1954**). In more recent years, almost always as John Burke, he has edited horror anthologies and novelized film and TV productions. [JC] **Other works:** *Dark Gateway* (**1954**); *Hotel Cosmos* (**1954**); *Pattern of Shadows* (**1954**); *Alien Landscapes* (coll. **1955**); *Deep Freeze* (**1955**); *Revolt of the Humans* (**1955**); *Pursuit Through Time* (**1956**); *Dr Terror's House of Horrors* (**1965**, as by J.F. Burke), the book of the 1964 film; *Exodus from Elysium* (coll. **1965**); *Moon Zero Two* (**1969**, as by John Burke), a novelization of the film MOON ZERO TWO (1969); *Four Stars for Danger* (**1970**, as by John Burke); *Expo 80* (**1972**, as by John Burke).

As editor (all as John Burke): *The Hammer Horror Omnibus* (anth. **1966**); *Tales of Unease* (anth. **1966**); *The Second Hammer Horror Film Omnibus* (anth. **1967**); *More Tales of Unease* (anth. **1969**); *New Tales of Unease* (anth. **1976**).

BURKE, RALPH Pseudonym used primarily by Robert SILVERBERG alone, but three times in collaboration with Randall GARRETT, 1956–7.

BURKETT, WILLIAM R. Jr (1943–). American author and journalist. His first, and only published sf, work, *Sleeping Planet* (**1965**), was serialized in *ASF* the previous year, and very competently tells a hard-edged space-opera tale of conflict between the small Terran Federation and the huge Llralan Empire; the latter, having undeserved access to a toxic dust, sprays Earth, putting all but a few men asleep (*see* INVASION). In the best *ASF* manner, however, the Llralans are not too bright, and the ten Unaffected eventually manage to apply the antidote to Earth's sleeping billions and send the invaders packing. [JC]

BURKS, ARTHUR J. (1898–1974). American military man and writer who, after a number of years in the US Army, began publishing sf with "Monsters of Moyen" for *ASF* in 1930. He made earlier fantasy sales to such markets as *Weird Tales*. After a few productive years he remained intermittently active into the 1960s, with time out for further service in the Second World War. Only one of his sf novels, *The Great Mirror* (1942 *Science Fiction Quarterly*; **1952**), has been reprinted in book form. The others include "Earth, the Marauder" (1930 *ASF*), "The Mind Master" (1932 *ASF*), "Jason Sows Again" (1938 *ASF*), "Survival" (1938 *Marvel Science Stories*) and "The Far Detour" (1942 *Science Fiction Quarterly*). AJB's "Josh McNab" series in *ASF* includes four stories: "Hell Ship" (1938), "The First Shall Be Last" (1939), "Follow the Bouncing Ball" (1939) and "Done in Oil" (1939). Much of his best work was fantasy, including *The Great Amen* (**1938**), *Look Behind You* (coll. **1954**) and *Black Medicine* (coll. **1966**). AJB was one of the most prolific

of all PULP-MAGAZINE writers; his sf and fantasy constitutes only a small fraction of his prodigious output.   [JC/MJE]

BURROUGHS, EDGAR RICE (1875–1950). American writer. Educated at Michigan Military Academy, ERB served briefly in the US cavalry. His early life was marked by numerous false starts and failures; when he began to write, at 36, he was marketing pencil sharpeners. "Under the Moons of Mars" (1912), a fantastic product of frustration and daydream, was serialized in ALL-STORY MAGAZINE under the pseudonym Norman Bean. Republished as *A Princess of Mars* (1912; **1917**), it was the first of a series about Barsoom (MARS). *The Gods of Mars* (1913 *All-Story*; **1918**) and *The Warlord of Mars* (1914 *All-Story*; **1919**) recount the further exploits of John Carter, as he battles with various green, yellow and black men and wins the hand of the red-skinned (and oviparous) princess Dejah Thoris. Using different central characters, ERB produced another eight "Barsoom" books: *Thuvia, Maid of Mars* (1916 *All-Story Weekly*; **1920**); *The Chessmen of Mars* (**1922**); *The Master Mind of Mars* (**1928**); *A Fighting Man of Mars* (**1931**); *Swords of Mars* (**1936**); *Synthetic Men of Mars* (**1940**); *Llana of Gathol* (1941 *AMZ*; fix-up **1948**) and *John Carter of Mars* (1941–3 *AMZ*; coll. **1964**). The last-named contains a spurious story, "John Carter and the Giant of Mars", possibly written by ERB's son. The standard of storytelling and invention is high in the Mars books, *Chessmen*... and *Swords*... being particularly fine, volumes. But critics do not accept the series as good sf. Although Carter's adventures take place on another planet, he travels there by magical means, and Barsoom itself is inconsistent and scientifically implausible. However, ERB's immense popularity has nothing to do with conventional sf virtues, but is due to his ability to transport the reader to a glorious never-never land, exotic and dangerous.

The "Tarzan" saga is just as much sf (or non-sf) as the "Barsoom" series. Much influenced by Rider HAGGARD, ERB lacked one of that writer's prime virtues: a sense of reality. Tarzan's Africa is far removed from Allan Quatermain's, and has to be accepted as sheer fantasy, no more real than Barsoom or Pellucidar. *Tarzan of the Apes* (1912 *All-Story*; **1914**), the story of an English aristocrat's son raised in the jungle by "great apes" (of a non-existent species), was so popular that ERB wrote no less than 23 sequels. In most, Tarzan has unashamedly fantastic adventures — he discovers lost cities and living dinosaurs, is reduced to 18 inches in height, visits the Earth's core, etc. *The Return of Tarzan* (**1915**); *The Beasts of Tarzan* (**1916**); *The Son of Tarzan* (**1917**) and *Tarzan and the Jewels of Opar* (**1918**) are not among the best in the series, although *Jungle Tales of Tarzan* (coll. **1919**) is a clever work,

reminiscent of Rudyard KIPLING's *Jungle Books* (1894–5). The best Tarzan novels came in the middle period: *Tarzan the Untamed* (**1920**); *Tarzan the Terrible* (**1921**); *Tarzan and the Golden Lion* (**1923**); *Tarzan and the Ant Men* (**1924**); *Tarzan, Lord of the Jungle* (**1928**); *Tarzan and the Lost Empire* (**1929**) and *Tarzan at the Earth's Core* (**1930**). Later the series deteriorated, becoming ever more repetitive: *Tarzan the Invincible* (**1931**); *Tarzan Triumphant* (**1932**); *Tarzan and the City of Gold* (**1933**); *Tarzan and the Lion Man* (**1934**); *Tarzan and the Leopard Men* (**1935**); *Tarzan's Quest* (**1936**); *Tarzan and the Forbidden City* (**1938** — a very bad book, probably ghost-written); *Tarzan the Magnificent* (**1939**) and *Tarzan and the Foreign Legion* (**1947**). Two posthumous books are *Tarzan and the Madman* (**1964**) and *Tarzan and the Castaways* (1939–41 var. mags; coll. **1965**), neither of much merit. Despite ERB's over-production, Tarzan is a remarkable creation, and the best-known fictional character of the century. Part of Tarzan's fame is due to the many film adaptations, particularly those of the 1930s starring Johnny Weissmuller. None of these are very faithful to the books.

ERB's third major series, based on the hollow-Earth theory of John Cleves SYMMES, began with *At the Earth's Core* (1914 *All-Story*; **1922**) and was continued in *Pellucidar* (1915 *All-Story*; **1923**); *Tanar of Pellucidar* (**1929**); *Tarzan at the Earth's Core* (a notable "overlap" volume); *Back to the Stone Age* (**1937**); *Land of Terror* (**1944**) and *Savage Pellucidar* (1942 *AMZ*; fix-up, incorporating one previously unpublished story, **1963**). Pellucidar is perhaps the best of ERB's locales — a world without time where dinosaurs and beast-men roam — and is a perfect setting for bloodthirsty romantic adventure.

An adaptation of the first of the series, AT THE EARTH'S CORE (1976), was disappointingly filmed.

A fourth series concerns the exploits of spaceman Carson Napier on Venus, and consists of *Pirates of Venus* (**1934**); *Lost on Venus* (**1935**); *Carson of Venus* (**1939**) and *Escape on Venus* (1941–2 *Fantastic Adventures*; fix-up **1946**). They are not as stirring and vivid as the Mars series. A posthumous story, "The Wizard of Venus", was published in *Tales of Three Planets* (coll. **1964**), and subsequently as the title story of a separate paperback, *The Wizard of Venus* (coll. **1970**), together with a non-series story, "Pirate Blood". Two of the stories from *Tales of Three Planets*, "Beyond the Farthest Star" (1942) and the posthumous "Tangor Returns", form the opening of a fifth series which ERB abandoned. They are of interest because they are his only tales with an interstellar setting. The two stories were subsequently republished as a paperback entitled *Beyond the Farthest Star* (coll. **1965**).

ERB's admirers rate the trilogy comprising "The Land That Time Forgot", "The People That Time Forgot" and "Out of Time's Abyss" (all in *Blue Book Magazine* 1918) as one of his very best works. The three novellas were republished in one volume as *The Land That Time Forgot* (**1924**), although they have subsequently been reprinted as separate paperbacks under the original magazine titles. They concern the lost world of Caspak near the South Pole, and contain some clever evolutionary fantasy. They have been loosely adapted into two films, THE LAND THAT TIME FORGOT (1975) and THE PEOPLE THAT TIME FORGOT (1977). Another trilogy of novellas is also rated highly: "The Moon Maid" (1923 *Argosy All-Story Weekly*), "The Moon Men" and "The Red Hawk" (both 1925 *Argosy All-Story Weekly*) were republished in one volume as *The Moon Maid* (fix-up **1926**), and reprinted subsequently as two paperbacks, *The Moon Maid* and *The Moon Men*. They describe a civilization in the hollow interior of the Moon, and a future invasion of the Earth.

Among ERB's other books, those which can be claimed as sf are *The Eternal Lover* (1914 *All-Story Weekly*; fix-up **1925**; vt *The Eternal Savage*), a prehistoric adventure involving time travel; *The Monster Men* (1913 *All-Story*; **1929**), a reworking of the Frankenstein theme; *Jungle Girl* (**1932**; vt *Land of Hidden Men*), about a lost civilization in Cambodia; *The Cave Girl* (1913–17 *All-Story Weekly*; fix-up **1925**), another prehistoric romance; and *Beyond Thirty* (1916 *All Around Magazine*; **1957**; vt *The Lost Continent*), a story set in the 22nd century after the collapse of European civilization.

It has often been said that ERB's works have small literary or intellectual merit. Nevertheless, they have endured. The ERB "rediscovery" of the 1960s was an astonishing publishing phenomenon, and the majority of his books are still reprinted regularly, appealing mainly to the young. The lack of realistic referents gives them a timeless quality, and the efficient narrative style helps to compensate for the prudery and touches of racism. ERB has probably had more imitators than any other sf writer, ranging from Otis Adelbert KLINE in the 1930s to Alan Burt AKERS in the 1970s, although there have been few "official" sequels to his works (an exception is *Tarzan and the Valley of Gold* by Fritz LEIBER, **1966**). Serious sf writers who owe a debt to ERB include Ray BRADBURY, Leigh BRACKETT, Michael MOORCOCK and, above all, Philip José FARMER, whose "Lord Grandrith" and "Ancient Opar" novels are among the most enjoyable latter-day Burroughsiana. [DP]
About the author: *Golden Anniversary Bibliography of Edgar Rice Burroughs* (**1962**; rev. 1964) by H.H. Heins ; *Edgar Rice Burroughs: Master of Adventure* (**1965**; rev. 1968) by Richard A. LUPOFF; *The Big Swingers* (**1967**) by Robert W. Fenton; "The Undisciplined Imagination: Edgar Rice Burroughs and Lowellian Mars" by R.D. MULLEN in *SF: The Other Side of Realism* (**1971**) ed. Thomas D. CLARESON; *Tarzan Alive* (**1972**) by Philip José Farmer; *Edgar Rice Burroughs: The Man Who Created Tarzan* (**1975**) by Irwin Porges; *A Guide to Barsoom* (**1976**) by J.F. Roy.
See also: ANDROIDS; ANTHROPOLOGY; BOYS' PAPERS; CRYONICS; ECOLOGY; EVOLUTION; FANTASTIC VOYAGES; FANTASY; GAMES AND SPORTS; HEROES; HISTORY OF SF; INVASION; JUPITER; LIFE ON OTHER WORLDS; LOST WORLDS; MOON; ORIGIN OF MAN; PARALLEL WORLDS; PASTORAL; SF MAGAZINES; SCIENTIFIC ERRORS; SEX; SPACESHIPS; SWORD AND SORCERY; VENUS.

BURROUGHS, JOHN COLEMAN (1913–). American illustrator and writer, the younger son of Edgar Rice BURROUGHS, and actively involved in his father's productions. He illustrated 13 of his titles, and drew the weekly comic strip "John Carter of Mars" from Dec. 1941 to its termination in 1943. This strip has been reproduced as *John Carter of Mars* (**1970**). JCB's sf novel, *Treasure of the Black Falcon* (**1967**) features undersea adventures and alien contact. [JC]

BURROUGHS, WILLIAM S(EWARD) (1914–). American writer. Born into a successful business family, WSB was a Harvard graduate in English literature in 1936. A drop-out thereafter, he has lived in Mexico, North Africa and Britain, and for many years was a heroin addict. He began writing in the late 1930s, but had no success until the early 1950s when he wrote two confessional books, *Junky* (**1953**, under the pseudonym William Lee; rev. vt *Junkie* 1977) and *Queer* (unpublished), which were about drug-addiction and homosexuality respectively, themes which have continued to dominate WSB's work. Although largely unpublished, WSB was immensely influential among the "beat" writers of the 1950s — notably Jack Kerouac and Allen Ginsberg — and already had an underground reputation before the appearance of his first important book, *The Naked Lunch* (**1959**). This nightmarish satire was published by Olympia Press in Paris, and contains large elements of sf, e.g. the DYSTOPIAS of "Freeland" and "Interzone", and some *outré* biological fantasy. Brilliantly written, funny and scatological, it is accepted as a modern classic. WSB's writings since are a bibliographer's despair, and no attempt can be made here to list all the pamphlets issued by various underground publishers. His major novels, however, are: *The Soft Machine* (**1961**; rev. 1966); *The Ticket That Exploded* (**1962**; rev. 1967); *Nova Express* (**1964**); *The Wild Boys* (**1971**) and *Exterminator!* (**1973**). In these works, WSB has experimented with "cut-up" techniques, the importance of which has been over-emphasized. More significant is the vividness of the imagery and the urgency of the subject matter. Much concerned with the abuses of power, WSB has used addiction as an all-embracing metaphor for the ways in which our lives are controlled. He has also used many sf metaphors, e.g. the "Nova Mob", galactic gangsters who are taking over our planet. Images of space travel and "biomorphic horror" (J.G. BALLARD's phrase) abound. WSB has borrowed ideas from all areas of popular culture — films, comics, Westerns, sf — and the resulting powerful mélange has analogies with pop art. His influence can be detected in sf by Ballard, Michael MOORCOCK, John T. SLADEK, Norman SPINRAD and others. Overt pastiches of his work by sf writers include Barrington J. BAYLEY's "The Four-Colour Problem" (1971) and Philip José FARMER's "The Jungle Rot Kid on the Nod" (1968), the latter a Tarzan story in the manner of William S. Burroughs rather than Edgar Rice BURROUGHS. [DP]
Other works: *Dead Fingers Talk* (**1963**); *The Last Words of Dutch Schultz* (**1970**). **About the author:** "Myth-Maker of the 20th Century" by J.G. Ballard (*NW* 142, 1964); "The Paris Review Interview", in *Writers at Work* (**1968**) ed. George Plimpton; *The Job: Interview with William Burroughs* (**1969**) by Daniel Odier (trans. 1970); "Rub Out the Word", in *City of Words* (**1971**) by Tony Tanner; *Descriptive Catalogue of the WSB Archive* (**1973**) compiled by Miles Associates; *William Burroughs: The Algebra of Need* (**1977**) by Eric Mottram.
See also: ABSURDIST SF; INVASION; MEDIA LANDSCAPE.

BURTON, S(AMUEL) H(OLROYD) (?–). British anthologist, known for his compilation *Science Fiction* (anth. **1967**). It has an introduction, a glossary, and is intended for high-school students. [JC]

BUSBY, F.M. (?–). American writer and long-time sf fan, co-editor with his wife Elinor Busby of the HUGO-winning fanzine CRY. He began publishing sf stories with "A Gun for Grandfather" for *Future Science Fiction* in 1957, and also some early fan work as Renfrew Pemberton; he began publishing novels in the 1970s, after attending the CLARION SF WRITERS' WORKSHOP in 1972, at which point he went freelance as a writer. His books began with the SPACE-OPERA series about a hijacked human and his war against the ALIEN Demu, *Cage a Man* (**1974**) and *The Proud Enemy* (**1975**), with more volumes possibly to come; the first, superior instalment is particularly effective in its depiction of the human Barton's imprisonment and eventual escape. FMB's second series,

Rissa Kerguelen (**1976**) and *The Long View* (**1976**), is actually an extremely long single novel, and has been republished as such, reset but apparently unaltered, as *Rissa Kerguelen* (**1977**). It is another space opera, with an ambitiously lengthy (though rather diffuse) character portrait of its female protagonist to justify its length; fundamentally, however, its stylistically awkward tale of bureaucratic oppression on Earth, flight to the stars, interstellar conflict and eventual revenge is not out of the ordinary.   [JC]

BUTLER, JOAN Pseudonym of British author Robert Williams Alexander (1905–), under which name he wrote 41 humorous novels reminiscent of the works of Thorne Smith. *Cloudy Weather* (**1940**) and *Deep Freeze* (**1951**) are centered on the resurrection of Egyptian mummies by scientific means; *Space to Let* (**1955**) features the building of a Venus rocket; and *Home Run* (**1958**) is about the invention of pocket-size atom bombs. *Bed And Breakfast* (**1933**), *Low Spirits* (**1945**), *Full House* (**1947**) and *Sheet Lightning* (**1950**) focus on the supernatural.   [JE]

An 1896 portrait.

BUTLER, SAMUEL (1835–1902). English writer, educated at Cambridge, never married, emigrated to New Zealand 1859–65, best known for his posthumously published autobiographical novel, *The Way of all Flesh* (**1903**), which describes the conflict between SB and his minister father that provided much of the force of the SATIRE ON RELIGION in his two UTOPIAS, *Erewhon; or, Over the Range* (**1872**; rev. 1872; rev. 1901) and *Erewhon Revisited* (**1901**), in which the Musical Banks closely resemble the 19th-century Established Church. *Erewhon* and its sequel are set in a New Zealand Utopia where machines have been banned for many years, because (in a harsh parody of Darwin's theory of EVOLUTION, which he disliked) of human fears that MACHINES, in their rapid

evolutionary progress, would soon supplant Man; the visitor to this Utopia (which mixes DYSTOPIAN elements freely with its more attractive aspects) is named Higgs, and his eventual escape from Erewhon in a balloon triggers a new religion in that country, Sunchildism; the sequel is devoted mainly to this faith and Higgs' effect upon it on his return in an analogical satire on Christianity's origins and growth, and the legend of the Second Coming. SB was a compulsive speculator in and chivvier at ideas, and his two Utopias are densely packed with parodic commentary on all aspects of 19th-century civilization; the calibre of his mind is indicated by his suggested modification to Darwin's theory: that more than chance was required to explain the variations that make for survival, in this prefiguring some of Darwin's own later thought, though generally his anti-Darwin propaganda displayed a cavalier attitude to scientific evidence. [JC/DIM]
See also: AUTOMATION; HUMOUR; ISLANDS; TECHNOLOGY.

BUTLER, WILLIAM (1929–). American author, now resident in Japan, whose sf novel, *The Butterfly Revolution* (**1967**), depicts a 1960s-based nightmare of what happens to the world in the absence of adults.   [JC]

BUTOR, MICHEL (1926–). French critic and novelist, principally known as a leading exponent of the *"nouveau roman"*. MB was one of the first mainstream and academic critics to consider sf seriously by the same standards as general literature. He published an invigorating analysis of Jules VERNE as early as 1949 and examined the dilemmas and future potential of the field in his penetrating study "La crise de croissance de la SF" (1953; trans. as "SF: The Crisis of its Growth", *Partisan Review* 1967). MB is on the jury panel of the PRIX APOLLO.   [MJ]

BUTTERWORTH, MICHAEL (1947–). Manchester-based English writer and editor, in the latter capacity as editor of the semi-professional underground magazine *Corridors*, later called *Wordworks*, and co-founder and co-director with David Britton of Savoy Books. He began publishing sf with "Girl" for *NW* in 1966, and contributed regularly to the magazine for the rest of its existence. He began publishing novels with *The Time of the Hawklords* (**1976**), with Michael MOORCOCK credited on the title-page and cover as co-author, though the "List of Credits" at the end of the volume lists Moorcock as Producer/Director, and MB as Writer; he is fundamentally responsible for the book, as well as its sequel, *Queens of Deliria* (**1977**), with Moorcock also credited, and a forthcoming conclusion, *Ledge of Darkness*, to this trilogy based on the real-

life rock group Hawkwind and an electronic instrument that allays all pain and tension.   [JC]
Other works: All SPACE 1999 link-ups: *Planets of Peril* (**1977**); *Mind-Breaks of Space* (**1977**) with Jeff Jones; *The Space-Jackers* (**1977**); *The Psychomorph* (**1977**); *The Time Fighters* (**1977**). Projected works are another *Space 1999* volume, *On the Edge of the Infinite*, and the anthology *The Savoy Book* ed. with David Britton.

BUZZATI, DINO (1906–72). Italian writer and journalist. From his first unsettling children's stories in the 1930s and later, he has been noted for the KAFKA-like anxiety that riddles his apparently simple plots. *Catastrophe* (original stories from 1949, 1954 and 1958; selection trans. 1965) is perhaps his most fully successful volume; many of the stories included are surrealist fables, always with a parable-like moral edge. In *Il Grande Ritratto* (**1960**; trans. as *Larger Than Life* **1962**), a full-length novel, and rather less successful, a not very convincingly described COMPUTER complex is programmed with the personality of a woman.   [JC]
Other works: *Il Deserto dei Tartari* (**1940**; trans. as *The Tartar Steppe* **1952**).
See also: ABSURDIST SF.

BY ROCKET TO THE MOON *See* FRAU IM MOND, DIE.

BYWATER, HECTOR CHARLES (1884–1940). American writer of works on the nature and history of sea-power, and a future-WAR novel on the same theme, *The Great Pacific War; a History of the American-Japanese Campaign of 1931–1933* (**1925**).   [JC]

CABELL, JAMES BRANCH (1879–1958). American writer, mostly of mannered, witty, sometimes rather enervated fantasies, most of which he assimilated, somewhat arbitrarily, under the general heading *Biography of the Life of Manuel*; though the imaginary kingdom of Poictesme is a central thread running through the more than 20 volumes thus assimilated, the element of medievalizing fantasy in many of the titles is slim: notable among the more relevant to the sf and fantasy reader are (in order of internal chronology) *Figures of Earth* (**1921**), *The Silver Stallion* (**1926**), *The Soul of Melicent* (**1913**; rev. vt *Domnei* 1920), *Chivalry* (**1909**), *Jurgen* (**1919**), *The Line of Love* (**1905**), *The High Place* (**1923**), *Gallantry* (**1907**) and *Something About Eve* (**1927**). JBC suffered from over-attention after the prosecution of *Jurgen* for obscenity (most implausibly), and after his subsequent fame and neglect his more recent advocates, like James BLISH, who was for some time editor of the Cabell Society journal *Kalki*, have perhaps argued too strenuously for his rehabilitation. By now, however, his place in American fiction is secure though minor. His relevance to sf proper is peripheral, though at various times he used sf tropes: ALTERNATE WORLDS, DYSTOPIAS and UTOPIAS, TIME TRAVEL, and even the building of planets. [JC]

See also: FANTASY; GODS AND DEMONS; HUMOUR; SWORD AND SORCERY.

CABOT, JOHN YORK *See* David Wright O'BRIEN.

CAIDIN, MARTIN (1927–). American writer, pilot and aerospace specialist, who has written a series of over 40 non-fiction books, some of them for the juvenile market, on aviation and space exploration; the first to appear was *Jets, Rockets and Guided Missiles* (**1950**); *Worlds in Space* (**1954**) is a juvenile. MC's own firm, Martin Caidin Associates, was designed to provide information and other services to radio and television in the areas of his special knowledge. He began publishing sf with *The Long Night* (**1956**), in which an American city is fire-bombed, and gained considerable success with *Marooned* (**1964**), later filmed as MAROONED (1969) with Gregory Peck. Like much of his fiction, *Marooned* deals with NEAR-FUTURE crises in space, realistically depicted, in this case with the rescue of astronauts trapped in orbit; *Four Came Back* (**1968**) deals with human difficulties (and a mysterious plague) aboard a space platform. A more recent series of CYBORG adventures, comprised of *Cyborg* (**1972**), *Operation Nuke* (**1973**), *High Crystal* (**1974**) and *Cyborg IV* (**1975**), were the inspiration and basis for the successful television series THE SIX MILLION DOLLAR MAN and its spin-off THE BIONIC WOMAN. MC's stories combine considerable storytelling drive with expertly integrated technical information, and tend to be rather more convincing, therefore, than the television and film derivations they have inspired. [JC]

Other works: *No Man's World* (**1967**); *The Last Fathom* (**1967**); *The God Machine* (**1968**); *The Mendelov Conspiracy* (**1969**); *Anytime, Anywhere* (**1969**); *The Cape* (**1971**); *Almost Midnight* (**1971**); *Maryjane Tonight at Angels Twelve* (**1972**); *Destination Mars* (**1972**); *When War Comes* (**1972**); *Three Corners to Nowhere* (**1975**); *Whip* (**1976**).

See also: COMPUTERS.

CAINE, (Sir THOMAS HENRY) HALL (1853–1931). English writer of enormously best-selling novels in the late 19th century; almost forgotten before his death; *The Eternal City* (**1901**), printed in a first edition of 100,000, sets a complex intrigue alight in a NEAR-FUTURE, Pope-dominated Rome; *The White Prophet* (**1909**) is again marginally near-future, set in Egypt, where intrigue is rife. [JC]

CALDWELL, (JANET MIRIAM) TAYLOR (HOLLAND) (1900–). American popular novelist, whose first sf novel, *The Devil's Advocate* (**1952**), though set in 1970, is in effect a right-wing denunciation of the New Deal of the 1930s; her second effort, *Your Sins and Mine* (**1956**), is fundamentally fantasy, in that the devastating drought inflicted by the Lord upon the world for its sins can be removed by assiduous prayer. [JC]

CALISHER, HORTENSE (1911–). American writer of several MAINSTREAM novels, set mostly on the American East Coast; her sf novel, *Journal from Ellipsia* (**1965**), depicts a somewhat metaphysical ALTERNATE WORLD where everything — as in E.M. FORSTER's famous dictum — connects with everything, especially the transcendental sex that permeates the narrative. [JC]

CALKINS, DICK (? – ?). American COMICS illustrator. In 1930, Philip NOWLAN scripted, and DC illustrated, BUCK ROGERS IN THE 25TH CENTURY, a comic strip based on Nowlan's novel *Armageddon: 2419 AD* (**1928**; **1962**). Though DC's style was stiff and

In 1934 the style of illustrator Dick CALKINS in *Buck Rogers in the 25th Century* was wooden, innocent and vivid.

amateurish by today's standards, the strip was extremely popular in the 1930s and '40s. Its quality improved when Rick Yager joined DC in the 1940s. The artwork was never sophisticated but the strong, simple lines, reminiscent to modern readers of the later comic strip *Li'l Abner* by Al Capp, were well suited to fast-paced narrative. Buck Rogers's adventures have been reissued in hardback book format as *The Collected Works of Buck Rogers in the 25th Century* (**1969**) ed. Robert C. Dille.
[JG/PN]

CALLAHAN, WILLIAM *See* Raymond Z. GALLUN.

CALVINO, ITALO (1923–). Italian novelist, born in Cuba, active since the end of the Second World War, at first with realist works but soon with such Gothic, surrealist romances of great vigour and impact as *Il Visconte dimezzato* (**1952**), *Il Cavaliere inesistente* (**1959**; both trans., as *The Non-Existent Knight & The Cloven Viscount* **1962**) and *Il Barone rampante* (**1957**; trans. as *Baron of the Trees* **1959**); these three thematically linked fables were later assembled as *I nostri antenati* ["Our Ancestors"] (coll. **1960**). A more recent venture in the same idiom is *Il Castello dei Destini incrociati* (coll. of linked stories **1973**; trans. as. *The Castle of Crossed Destinies* **1977**). Beneath the fabulous events of these stories — the non-existent knight, for instance, is an empty suit of armour with a "passion" for the formalities and ceremonies that keep it "alive" — lies a concern for fundamental problems of being. IC's works closest to sf are the two linked volumes *Le Cosmicomiche* (coll. of linked stories **1965**; trans. as *Cosmicomics* **1968**) and *Ti con zero* (coll. of linked stories **1967**; trans. as *t zero* **1969**; vt *Time and the Hunter* UK); both volumes feature and are told by the presence called Qfwfq, who is the age of the universe; the various stories express in emblematic form speculations and fables about the nature of life, evolution, reality, and so forth. IC's most popular works in translation, they are witty, moving and effectively didactic, after their strange fashion. In a volume of stories from various sources, *The Watchers and Other Stories* (1952-63; **1971**), one, "Smog" (1958), is a remarkable POLLUTION tale, and is sf. *Le città invisibili* (**1972**; trans. as *Invisible Cities* **1974**) frames fragmented versions of Marco Polo's narrative of his voyages with a remarkable set of meditations ostensibly triggered by the distant, surrealistic CITIES he visits. IC's powers of invention are formally ingenious; at the same time he is an extremely lucid writer. His use of sf subjects, and their intermixing with a whole array of contemporary literary devices (*see* FABULATION; ABSURDIST SF), make him a figure of considerable interest

for the future of the genre. [JC]
See also: ORIGIN OF MAN.

CAMERON, IAN Pseudonym of English writer Donald Gordon Payne (1924–), author of two routine sf novels, *The Lost Ones* (**1961**; vt *The Island at the Top of the World* USA) and *The Mountains at the Bottom of the World* (**1972**; vt *Devil Country*). The former, under its later USA title, was filmed by Walt Disney in 1973. The mechanics of IC's plots derive from LOST-WORLD conventions generally, and in the case of the second novel, from A. Conan DOYLE specifically. Under the name James Vance Marshall, Payne has written mainstream fiction. [JC/PN]
Other works: *The White Ship* (**1975**).

CAMERON, JOHN. (? –). American writer. His borderline sf novel, *The Astrologer* (**1972**), like John Symonds' *The Child* (**1976**), deals with a new Virgin Mary and a new Virgin Birth, in this case discovered via astrology (*see* ASTRONOMY; MESSIAHS). [JC]
See also: PSEUDO-SCIENCE; RELIGION.

CAMPANELLA, TOMMASO (1568–1639). Italian philosopher. He was admitted into the Dominican order at the age of 15. Like Francis BACON he attacked contemporary science and its reliance on the authority of Aristotle, advocating observation and experiment as the proper routes to knowledge in *Philosophia Sensibus Demonstrata* (**1591**, in Latin). He was tortured and imprisoned by the Spanish Inquisition in 1599, accused of leading a revolt in his native Calabria, then under Spanish rule. Henry Morley, who wrote the introduction to *Ideal Commonwealths* (coll. **1885**) in which the first English translation of *The City of the Sun* (first manuscript 1602; second manuscript 1612; **1623**, in Latin; third manuscript 1637) appeared, implies that this was a pretext and that Campanella was seized for his free-thinking radicalism, but Harry Ross, in *Utopias Old and New* (**1938**), probably offers a more accurate picture of Campanella as a fanatic who stirred up revolution in the conviction that the world would end on the first day of 1600 and "suffered hours of torture in a spirit of masochistic ecstasy". He was not set free until 1626, but had to flee from further persecution until Richelieu gave him refuge in Paris in 1634. Here he dabbled in ceremonial magic and died, as Ross says, "toying with spells to ward off the Devils of his own imaginings". His classic Utopian novelette *Civitas Solis*, or *The City of the Sun*, which was one of his many prison writings, describes a city with seven concentric circular walls, ruled by a philosopher-king, the *Hoh* or *Metaphysicus*. All property is held in common and education is held to be so vital that all the elements of science are inscribed on the great walls. Attention to

the proper conduct of scientific inquiry has led the inhabitants of the city to important discoveries — flying machines and ships without sails — but these are mentioned only in passing. It is for its embodiment of the new philosophy of science, rather than for specific anticipations, that the work is important in the ancestry of sf. [BS]
See also: CITIES; FANTASTIC VOYAGES; PROTO SF; UTOPIAS.

CAMPBELL, CLYDE CRANE *See* Horace L. GOLD.

CAMPBELL, H(ERBERT) J. (1925–). British research chemist, writer and editor. In the early 1950s HJC wrote a number of sf adventure novels: *The Last Mutation* (**1951**); *The Moon is Heaven* (**1951**); *World in a Test Tube* (**1951**); *Beyond the Visible* (**1952**); *Chaos in Miniature* (**1952**); *Mice or Machines* (**1952**); *Another Space — Another Time* (**1953**); *Brain Ultimate* (**1953**); *The Red Planet* (**1953**) and *Once Upon a Space* (**1954**). He also wrote under the house pseudonyms Jon J. DEEGAN and Roy SHELDON, but the titles which were his work have not been definitely established. According to rumour, he wrote all the Jon J. Deegan titles. He became technical editor of AUTHENTIC SCIENCE FICTION and then editor, Dec. 1952-Jan. 1956, and contributed many scientific articles to the magazine. His best-remembered editorial achievement was the publication of "The Rose" by Charles L. HARNESS (Mar. 1953), but the magazine generally improved under his editorship. He also edited *Tomorrow's Universe* (anth. **1953**), *Sprague de Camp's New Anthology* (coll. **1953**) and *The Authentic Book of Space* (anth. **1954**), which was a mixture of articles and stories. He resigned the editorship of *Authentic* because of pressure of his work in chemistry. He has since published a number of scientific texts. [MJE]

CAMPBELL, JOHN W(OOD) Jr (1910–71). American editor and writer. Educated at Massachusetts Institute of Technology and Duke University, where he graduated in physics in 1932. JWC was a devotee of the sf magazines from their inception, and sold his first stories while still a teenager. The first story he sold was "Invaders from the Infinite" to AMAZING STORIES; however, the manuscript was lost by editor T. O'Conor SLOANE, so that his second sale, "When the Atoms Failed" (1930), became his first published story.
In the early 1930s JWC quickly built a reputation as E.E. "Doc" SMITH's chief rival in writing galactic epics of superscience. The most popular of these were the "Arcot, Morey and Wade" series, in which the heroes faced a succession of battles of ever increasing size fought with a succession of wonderful weapons of ever decreasing

likelihood. These were *The Black Star Passes* (1930 var. mags; fix-up **1953**), *Islands of Space* (1931 *Amazing Stories Quarterly*; **1957**) and *Invaders from the Infinite* (not his first, lost story) (1932 *Amazing Stories Quarterly*; **1961**). *John W. Campbell Anthology* (coll. **1973**) is an omnibus of the three novels. Also well received was *The Mightiest Machine* (1934 *ASF*; **1947**), but three sequels featuring its hero Aarn Munro were rejected by *ASF*'s editor F. Orlin TREMAINE, eventually appearing in *The Incredible Planet* (coll. **1949**).

The second phase of JWC's career as a writer began with the first of a number of stories published under the pseudonym Don A. Stuart: "Twilight" (1934), a tale of the FAR FUTURE written in a moody, "poetic" style. From this time on, JWC wrote little sf under his own name — exceptions included the "Penton and Blake" series published in *TWS* in 1936–8 and collected in *The Planeteers* (coll. **1966**) — preferring to concentrate on the highly popular "Stuart" stories. (He did on one occasion use the pseudonym Karl Van Campen for a story included in an issue of *ASF* which already contained a "Stuart" story and part of a JWC novel). These included the "Machine" series, "The Machine", "The Invaders" and "Rebellion" (all 1935). He was by now becoming closely identified with Tremaine's *ASF*, where all the "Stuart" stories appeared. In 1936 he began, under his own name, a series of 18 monthly articles on the Solar System, and from 1937 also published a number of articles as Arthur McCann. The climax of his popularity came with the "Stuart" story "Who Goes There?" (1938), a classic sf horror story about an Antarctic research station menaced by a shape-changing ALIEN invader, which was later filmed, without the shape-changing, as THE THING (1951). It also effectively marked the end of his writing career. In September 1937 he was appointed editor of ASTOUNDING STORIES (a post he retained until his death), and wrote very little more fiction.

JWC brought to his editorial post the fertility of ideas on which his writing success had been based, together with a determination to raise the standards of writing and thinking in MAGAZINE sf. New writers were encouraged, and fed with ideas, with remarkable success. By 1939, JWC had discovered Isaac ASIMOV, Lester DEL REY, Robert HEINLEIN, Theodore STURGEON and A.E. VAN VOGT. L. Sprague DE CAMP, L. Ron HUBBARD, Clifford SIMAK and Jack WILLIAMSON were already published writers who became part of JWC's "stable". Henry KUTTNER and C.L. MOORE became regular contributors from 1942. These were the authors at the core of JWC's "GOLDEN AGE" — corresponding roughly to the period of the Second World War — when *ASF* dominated the genre in a way no magazine before or since could match.

Many of these authors, and many others, have acknowledged the profound influence JWC had on their careers, and the number of acknowledged sf classics which originated in ideas suggested by him would be impossible to assess. A startling example of the pervasiveness of his influence can be found in *The Space Beyond* (coll. **1976**); it contains a hitherto unpublished JWC novella, "All", which forms the basis of Robert Heinlein's *Sixth Column* (**1949**).

In addition to *ASF*, JWC initiated the fantasy magazine UNKNOWN, which from its birth in 1939 to its premature death (caused by paper shortages) in 1943 was equally influential.

The period of *ASF*'s dominance ended, quite abruptly, with the appearance of the MAGAZINE OF FANTASY AND SCIENCE FICTION in 1949 and GALAXY in 1950. By this time JWC's domineering editorial presence was becoming restricting rather than stimulating, and comparatively few major writers after 1950 began their careers in his magazine. Much of his interest and energy became focused in his editorials, many of which showed an unattractively right-wing political stance. Some are reprinted in *Collected Editorials from Analog* (**1966**; selected by Harry HARRISON). He flirted with various kinds of PSEUDO-SCIENCE, notably Hubbard's DIANETICS, which was loosed on an unsuspecting world through an article in *ASF*. However, the magazine remained popular and commercially successful, winning seven HUGO awards under JWC's editorship. His death in 1971 was marked by an unprecedented wave of commemorative activity: two awards were founded bearing his name; a memorial anthology was published; an Australian symposium about him appeared. Such a fuss was justified: although in later years he stood aside from the main stream of development in sf, for the first two decades of his career he first of all came to the forefront of the field as a writer, and then came to bestride it as an editor. More than any other individual, he helped to shape modern sf. [MJE]

Other works: *Who Goes There?* (coll. **1948**; vt *The Thing and Other Stories*; vt *The Thing From Outer Space* both UK); *The Moon is Hell* (coll. **1950**; later UK editions contain only the title story); *The Cloak of Aesir* (coll. **1952**); ed. *The Astounding Science Fiction Anthology* (anth **1952**; the UK hardcover edition, in two vols, omits eight stories; the UK paperback edition, also in two vols, is complete; vt *Astounding Tales of Space and Time* USA, omitting 15 stories and an article); ed. *From Unknown Worlds* (anth. **1952**); ed. *Prologue to Analog* (anth. **1962**); ed. *Analog 1* (anth. **1963**); ed. *Analog 2* (anth. **1964**); ed. *Analog 3* (anth. **1965**; vt *A World by the Tale* USA); ed. *Analog Anthology* (anth. **1965**; contains *Prologue to Analog, Analog 1* and *Analog 2*); ed. *Analog 4* (anth. **1965**;

vt *The Permanent Implosion* USA); *The Ultimate Weapon* (1936 *ASF* as "Uncertainty"; **1966**); ed. *Analog 5* (anth. **1967**; vt *Countercommandment* USA); ed. *Analog 6* (anth. **1968**); ed. *Analog 7* (anth. **1969**); ed. *Analog 8* (anth. **1971**); *The Best of John W. Campbell* (coll. **1973**).

About the author: *John W. Campbell: an Australian Tribute* (**1974**) ed. John Bangsund.

See also: ANTHROPOLOGY; COMPUTERS; CRIME AND PUNISHMENT; DEFINITIONS OF SF; DISASTER; DISCOVERY AND INVENTION; DYSTOPIAS; ECONOMICS; END OF THE WORLD; EVOLUTION; FASTER THAN LIGHT; GOTHIC SF; HEROES; HUMOUR; JUPITER; LIFE ON OTHER WORLDS; MACHINES; MARS; MONSTERS; MOON; NEAR FUTURE; NUCLEAR POWER; OPTIMISM AND PESSIMISM; OUTER PLANETS; PARANOIA AND SCHIZOPHRENIA; POLITICS; POWER SOURCES; PREDICTION; PSI POWERS; PSYCHOLOGY; RELIGION; ROBOTS; SCIENTIFIC ERRORS; SCIENTISTS; SEX; SOCIAL DARWINISM; SPACE OPERA; TABOOS; TECHNOLOGY; VENUS; WAR; WEAPONS.

CANADA Pioneer Canada was a "too matter-of-fact country" for myths, legends and fairy tales, complained Catherine Parr Traill, who emigrated from England to upper Canada in 1832. "Fancy would starve for lack of marvellous food to keep her alive in the backwoods", and, furthermore, the "unlettered and industrious" settlers had neither time nor taste to let their imaginations roam. Later commentators have also noted English Canadian literature's practical emphasis on morality and "real-life" situations, product of a pioneer, Protestant society which mistrusted the imagination. Until recently, fantasy found little acceptance. Sf was inhibited by other factors, notably a relative lack of emphasis on scientific development within Canada, and, of course, the domination of the market by Anglo-American popular fiction.

Among early Canadian writers of formula fiction, chiefly for a non-Canadian market, was James DE MILLE, whose posthumously published *A Strange Manuscript Found in a Copper Cylinder* (**1888**) is a LOST-WORLD satire with no Canadian content. Frederick Philip GROVE, a noted realistic writer, turned to allegory for his satirical/philosophical *Consider Her Ways* (1947), set in an ant colony. Contemporary MAINSTREAM novelists have also employed sf/fantasy conventions, notably Leonard Cohen in *Beautiful Losers* (1966); Scottish-born David Walker in *The Lord's Pink Ocean* (1972), a story of pollution-racked North America; Margaret Laurence in her juvenile fantasy *Jason's Quest* (1970), set in London; and Irish-born Brian MOORE in *Catholics* (1972) and *The Great Victorian Collection* (1975), winner of the Governor General's award for fiction.

The dominant future-world theme,

however, was introduced by Jules-Paul Tardivel, in his polemic *Pour la patrie* (1895), a UTOPIAN novel set in 1945, in the "Laurentian Empire" formed by Quebec's separation. The growth of separatism in the 1960s made this a topical theme for Dougal MacLeish in *The Traitor Game* (1968), Michael Sheldon in *Death of a Leader* (1971), Bruce Powe (Ellis Portal) in *Killing Ground* (1968) and Richard Rohmer in *Separation* (1976). Rohmer's other extrapolation-based thrillers include *Ultimatum* (1973) and *Exxoneration* (1974), both dealing with the threat of a US takeover of Canada.

Several PULP MAGAZINES flowered briefly when wartime restrictions prohibited imports. *Eerie Tales* (1 issue 1941), UNCANNY TALES (21 issues Nov. 1940-mid 1943) and *Les aventures futuristes* (10 issues 1949) were original titles, while 19 titles, including AMAZING STORIES, STARTLING STORIES and SUPER SCIENCE STORIES, had Canadian reprint editions. Genre sf, however, remained a US phenomenon. The works of the Canadian-born A.E. VAN VOGT and Gordon R. DICKSON, for example, do not have a noticeable Canadian influence; nor do those of such immigrants as Michael CONEY, Judith MERRIL (whose *Survival Ship and Other Stories*, however, was published in Toronto 1973), Julian Reid or Spider ROBINSON.

Canada's major sf author is Phyllis GOTLIEB, author of *Sunburst* (1964), *O Master Caliban!* (1976), the novella "Son of the Morning" (1972), and many short stories for US magazines; she is known in Canada, however, primarily as a poet and mainstream novelist. Ruth Nichols' children's fantasies include *A Walk Out of the World*, (1969), *The Morrow of the World* (1972), and *Song of the Pearl* (1976). H.A. Hargreaves' anthology, *North By 2000* (anth. 1975), a collection of short stories first published in British anthologies, attempts to create an authentic Canadian sf by emphasizing stories showing confrontation with a harsh environment.

One-story or one-novel appearances include Wayland Drew's *The Wabeno Feast* (1973); Gerard Rejskind's "The Helix" (1971), set in the Montreal subway; and Ben BARZMAN's *Out of this World* (1960; vt *Twinkle, Twinkle Little Star* USA; vt *Echo X*) with its Vancouver-born hero. Books with Canadian settings include Hayden HOWARD's *The Eskimo Invasion* (1967) and Robin SANBORN's *The Book of Stier* (1971). Such a list could be extended, but hardly indicates the presence of any real Canadian sf community.

However, a growing number of readers and fans, two world sf conventions (Torcon I, 1948; Torcon II, 1973), many regional conventions and numerous sf classes in colleges and universities show a lively present-day Canadian interest in sf.

French Canadian society has been more sympathetic to the folklore and fantasy tradition, expressed for example in the surrealistic tales of Jacques Ferron, collected as *Contes* (coll. 1968) and trans. as *Tales From the Uncertain Country* (coll. 1972). Other works of speculative fiction include *Le haut-pays* (1973) by Yves Theriault; *Les princes* (1973) by Jacques Benoit; and *Les métamorfaux* (1974) by Jacques Brossard. More traditional sf/fantasy works include Suzanne Martel's juvenile novels, *Quatre Montréalais de l'an 3000* (1963), trans. as *The City Under Ground* (1964), and *Titralak, cadet de l'espace* (1974); Esther Rochon's *En hommage aux araignées* (1974), part of a forthcoming trilogy; and Monique Corriveau's posthumously published trilogy, *Companon du soleil* (1976), a future-Earth political fantasy.

Sf in French Canada is at even more of a disadvantage than in English Canada, since there are few indigenous markets and relatively little Anglo-American sf available in translation to serve as models. However the fanzine *Requiem*, edited by Norbert Spehner, founded in 1974 and now funded by the Canada Council, acts as a source of information and encouragement, especially with its establishment in 1977 of the Prix Dagon for the year's best Canadian sf story in French.   [SW]

ČAPEK, JOSEF *See* Karel ČAPEK.

ČAPEK, KAREL (1890–1938). Czech writer whose copious production included plays, novels, stories, imaginative travel books and at least two volumes written to publicize President Masaryk of Czechoslovakia in his formidable old age. He is best known generally as the author of the plays *R.U.R.* (1921; trans. 1923) and, with his painter/writer brother Josef (who died in Belsen concentration camp in 1945), *Ze života hmyzu* (1921; trans. as *And So Ad Infinitum* 1923; after many title changes, most commonly known as *The Insect Play*). *R.U.R.*, an acronym of Rossum's Universal Robots, introduced the word ROBOT to the world. In Czech it means something like "forced labour", and in the play it applies not to robots made of metal as we have come to think of them, but to a worker-class of persecuted ANDROIDS. The play itself is heavily symbolic and is by no means representative of KČ's best work. In *The Insect Play*, various arthropods go through vaudeville routines explicitly related to cognate activities on the part of humans, to sometimes scathing effect.

A further play, *Vec Mokropulos* (1922; adaptation trans. as *The Makropoulos Secret* 1925; authorized trans. with same title 1927), features a 300-year-old woman, the secret of her longevity, and her death; it is most familiar as the basis of an opera by Leoš Janáček.

Of greater interest to the sf reader are

KČ's several sf novels, beginning with *Továrna na absolutno* (1922; trans. as *The Absolute at Large* 1927), like most of his fiction a deceptively light-toned SATIRE; a scientist invents an atomic device capable of producing almost free power, and rocks the world to its foundations by releasing it; ultimately there is a devastating war. *Krakatit* (1924; trans. 1925; vt *An Atomic Phantasy*) also moves to the ultimate disaster via a seemingly casual, unintended route: a crank inventor comes up with an exceptionally powerful explosive, with predictable consequences. Both these novels, and KČ's plays, actively translate a sensitive political consciousness, identifiably Eastern European in its inherent assumptions about the fragility of institutions and the dubiousness of their claimed benevolence, into exaggerated metaphors; the result, as in the unconvincingly optimistic close of *R.U.R.*, can be a sentimental honouring of the persistence of hope. KČ's "little men" sometimes implausibly win out over the forces of history and the darker elements of human nature.

Most of his work is superbly summed up in his last sf novel, *Valka s Mloky* (1936; trans. as *War With the Newts* 1937), in which a strange, apparently exploitable sea-dwelling race of "newts" is discovered in the South Pacific and immediately enslaved to a chorus of philanthropic doubletalk; images of class struggle and social injustice abound as the newts gradually acquire the necessary human characteristics, turn against their masters, and begin to flood the continents in order to eliminate Man entirely; astonishingly, the novel is told with a highly sophisticated lightness of tone (there are also many typographical and narrative experiments congenially fused with the main story); as in this book, KČ's main impact may well lie in his capacity at his best to see the deepest sf horrors and anticipations wryly and with a smile, though unblinkingly.   [JC]
Other works: Though it has been listed as sf, *Povetroň* (1934; trans. as *Meteor* 1935), is neither sf nor fantasy. Collections of short stories, some fantasy throughout: *Money and Other Stories* (coll. trans. 1929); *Povídky z druké kapsy* (coll. 1929; trans. as *Tales from Two Pockets* 1932); *Devatero Pohádek* (coll. 1932; selected stories trans. as *Fairy Tales* 1933); *Kniha apokryfů* (coll. 1945; trans. as *Apocryphal Stories* 1949). With Josef Čapek: *Adam stvořitel* (1927; trans. as *Adam the Creator* 1929), a play. **About the author:** *Karel Čapek* (1962) by William E. Harkins.

See also: AUTOMATION; EASTERN EUROPE; IMMORTALITY; INVASION; MACHINES; MUSIC AND OPERA; POWER SOURCES; THEATRE.

CAPON, (HARRY) PAUL (1912–). British author, who has also worked for many years as an editor and administrator in film and television production. He has written in various genres, including detective stories. His first sf was a trilogy of novels, *The Other Side of the Sun* (1950), *The Other Half of the Planet* (1952) and *Down To Earth* (1954), some of which was serialized on BBC RADIO. It deals with the discovery of another Earth-like planet, hidden directly behind the sun, whose UTOPIAN life leaves itself open to exploitation from villainous humans. Most of PC's sf was for children, including *The World at Bay* (1953), *The Wonderbolt* (1955), (see PHYSICS), *Phobos, the Robot Planet* (1955; vt *Lost, A Moon* USA) and *Flight of Time* (1960). The adult novel *Into The Tenth Millennium* (1956) concerns three people travelling into the future, utilizing a drug which slows down body metabolism to a fraction of the normal. They emerge into a Utopian world of great charm and interest — Capon's Utopias are less stuffy and preachy than most — but the woman cannot make the necessary psychological adjustment. PC wrote well, and created unusually solid future worlds. He introduced many young British readers to sf. [PN]

CAPRICORN ONE Film (1978). An ITC Production. Directed by Peter Hyams, starring Elliott Gould, James Brolin, Brenda Vaccaro, Sam Waterston, O.J. Simpson and Hal Holbrook. Screenplay by Peter Hyams. 120 mins. Colour.

Three astronauts are told by the head of NASA that, due to a malfunction in the life-support system, they cannot be sent to Mars. However, as the success of this mission means so much to NASA in terms of future funding, NASA has decided to fake the whole thing. The astronauts are then blackmailed into letting themselves be filmed in a giant sound stage on a remote desert base complete with dummy spacecraft and Martian scenery. On its remote-controlled return to Earth the real spacecraft burns up in the atmosphere, and the astronauts realize that they are now officially "dead" and of no further use to NASA. They break out of the secret base, and the film degenerates for its latter half into a series of chase sequences across the desert. The potentially provocative theme peters out disappointingly into routine adventure. Despite NASA's cooperation, in itself mystifying, the science is often shaky. After establishing that TV signals take 20 minutes to reach Mars, a later sequence shows the wives, at mission control, speaking with their husbands, supposedly on Mars, with no time lapse at all. [JB]

CAPTAIN FUTURE US PULP magazine. 17 issues, Winter 1940-Spring 1944, on a regular quarterly schedule except that there was no Fall 1943. Published by Better Publications; ed. Leo MARGULIES with Mort WEISINGER (1940–41) and Oscar J. FRIEND (1941–4).

A companion magazine to STARTLING STORIES and THRILLING WONDER STORIES, *CF* was an attempt to establish a SPACE-OPERA equivalent to the popular superhero pulps (DOC SAVAGE and the like). Each issue featured a complete novel detailing the adventures of the tall, cheerful, red-headed Curt Newton, alias Captain Future, "Wizard of Science" or "Man of Tomorrow" according to the

Vol. 1, no. 1, 1940. Cover by Rosen

magazine's successive subtitles. With the aid of his trio of assistants, "Grag, the giant, metal robot; Otho, the man-made, synthetic android; and aged Simon Wright, the living Brain", he thwarted a succession of evil foes (more often than not, green). All but two of these novels were written by Edmond HAMILTON (*who see for details*), sometimes using the house name Brett STERLING. They were later reprinted in paperback form. After *CF* had become a casualty of wartime paper shortages, the character continued to appear intermittently in *Startling Stories*. *CF*, like its companion magazines at that period, was unabashedly juvenile in its appeal. [MJE]

The only issue, May 1938.

CAPTAIN HAZZARD US PULP MAGAZINE. One issue, May 1938,

published by Magazine Publishers; no editor named. The novel contained in this issue, "Python Men of Lost City", was by Chester Hawks. Captain Hazzard, an imitation of DOC SAVAGE, with extra mental powers and a similar group of assistants, combats a master criminal to save the world from his machinations. The novel was reprinted in facsimile in 1974 by Robert WEINBERG. [FHP]

CAPTAIN MARVEL American COMIC STRIP created and initially illustrated by C.C. Beck. *CM* appeared first in 1940 in *Whiz Comics* (1940–53) then contemporaneously in the comic book *Captain Marvel Adventures* (1941–53). Jack KIRBY and Mac Raboy were among its many illustrators. Foremost among the scriptwriters was Otto BINDER, who developed the distinctive humour in *CM*.

CM was very similar in concept and in storyline to SUPERMAN — newsboy Billy Batson, on speaking the magic word "Shazam", an acronym of Solomon, Hercules, Atlas, Zeus, Achilles, Mercury, becomes Captain Marvel, an invincible man with superhuman powers. It was the subject of a successful law-suit brought by National Periodical Publications, the publishers of *Superman*, and was forced to terminate in 1953.

A typical cover of a wartime 1942 issue of *Captain Marvel Adventures*.

In Britain the reprint of *CM* was retitled *The Marvelman* (1954–63) and continued in almost identical format for a further 346 issues. *CM* was successfully transferred into sf film serials in the 1940s.

A comic book, *Captain Marvel*, published by MARVEL COMICS from May 1968 and intermittently into the 1970s, featured a rather different and more conventional superhero, first introduced in *Marvel Super-Heroes* 12. [JE]

CAPTAIN MIDNIGHT (vt **JET JACKSON**) Television series (1954–6). Screen Gems/CBS. Produced by George Bilson. Pilot episode directed by D. Ross Lederman and written by Dana Slade. 25

mins per episode. B/w.

Richard Webb played Captain Midnight (or Jet Jackson, depending on where the series was shown) in this children's series, and Sid Melton played his bumbling assistant, Ikky. Midnight was a super-scientific crime-fighter based in mountain-top headquarters from which he would zoom in his sleek jet-plane to combat a new evil each week. The first episode concerned the theft of a powerful radioactive element by foreign agents, who are spotted by a member of Midnight's network of juvenile helpers, the Secret Squadron, and he tracks them down using a geiger counter. The scripts were poor even by the juvenile standards of the mid-1950s, and there was little visual excitement. The few good special-effects shots, such as that of Midnight's jet taking off from the mountain-top runway, were repeated endlessly.   [JB]

CAPTAIN MORS *See* LUFTPIRAT UND SEIN LENKBARES LUFTSCHIFF.

CAPTAIN NEMO AND THE UNDERWATER CITY Film (1969). MGM. Directed by James Hill, starring Robert Ryan, Chuck Connors, Nanette Newman and Luciana Paluzzi. Screenplay by Pip and Jane Barker and R. Wright Campbell, based on the character created by Jules VERNE. 106 mins. Colour.

Towards the end of the 19th century, a ship sinks in a violent storm. A few survivors find themselves on board a mysterious underwater vessel, which turns out to be the *Nautilus*, under the command of the legendary Captain Nemo. A routine mad-scientist morality story ensues, with a giant shark as Nemesis to Nemo's underwater city.

The film is distinctly inferior to Disney's TWENTY THOUSAND LEAGUES UNDER THE SEA. Even the model of the Nautilus does not approach the charm and style of Disney's.   [JB]

CAPTAIN VIDEO 1. Television serial (1949–53 and 1955–6). DuMont. Produced by Larry Menkin. DuMont was a New York based TV company that flourished in the early years when a great deal of the programme output came from New York. In 1949 they began *CV* ("video" was then the most common synonym for television), a 30-minute children's programme that went out five nights a week. Written by Maurice Brockhauser, it starred Richard Coogan as Captain Video who, with the aid of his Video Rangers, battled with various threats from outer space. Many of the early scripts were written by Robert SHECKLEY, Damon KNIGHT and C. M. KORNBLUTH.

This was the first sf on TV. All was shot live in a small studio, with the result that much of the spectacle had to be provided by the imaginations of the young viewers. *CV* also incorporated

such filmed material as short Westerns and cartoons which were introduced by the Captain himself. In 1950 Al Hodge replaced Coogan in the title role. In 1953 the serial format was dropped; *CV*, retitled *The Secret Files of Captain Video*, became a weekly adventure with self-contained stories, but folded that same year. In 1955 Hodge returned as *CV* in a weekly, 60-minute children's show which he also produced. Though still wearing his *CV* uniform, which looked like a cross between a marine's and a bus driver's, he merely acted as the show's host, introducing stock adventure-film footage and undemanding shorts of an "educational" nature which he would then discuss with the studio audience of children. In 1956 *CV* ended his career with *Captain Video's Cartoons*, the Master of Time and Space reduced to announcing the funnies. A comic book was based on the character of Captain Video.

2. In 1951 Sam Katzman produced a cinema serial of 15 parts based on the TV serial. Directed by Spencer Bennet and Wallace A. Grissell, it was written by Royal K. Cole, Sherman L. Lowe and Joseph F. Poland and starred Judd Holdren in the title role.   [JB]

The final issue, Mar. 1950. One of the last of the old-time hero pulps.

CAPTAIN ZERO US PULP MAGAZINE. Three issues, Nov. 1949–Mar. 1950, published by Recreational Reading Corp., Indiana; no editor named.

Each issue contained a novel, written by prolific pulp author G.T. Fleming-Roberts. As a result of a nuclear accident, Captain Zero (alias "The Master of Midnight") becomes involuntarily invisible at night, and uses his unwanted gift to operate against the underworld. When invisible he speaks in italics.

An almost identical edition was published simultaneously in Canada.   [FHP/MJE]

CARCOSA American specialist publishing house which in **1947** produced the first book edition of *Edison's Conquest of Mars* by Garrett P.

SERVISS. That was its only publication until it was revived in 1973 under the direction of Karl Edward WAGNER, a sword-and-sorcery author, and produced *Worse Things Waiting* (**1973**) by Manly Wade WELLMAN, a finely printed, illustrated volume of stories, chiefly from WEIRD TALES. Similar collections followed from E. Hoffman Price and Hugh B. Cave.   [MJE]

CARLSEN, CHRIS *See* Robert P. HOLDSTOCK.

CARLTON, ROGER (?–). English writer, possibly pseudonymous, whose routine sf novels are *Star Arrow* (**1975**) and *Beyond Tomorrow* (**1975**).   [JC]

CARNELL, E(DWARD) J(OHN) (1912–72). British editor, anthologist and literary agent. A prominent member of British sf FANDOM just after the Second World War, EJC began his professional career in sf as editor of NEW WORLDS magazine in 1946. After only three issues the publisher failed, but EJC with help from fandom was able to renew the title in 1949 with his own company, Nova Publications. He also took over the other Nova Publications title, SCIENCE FANTASY, as editor, from Walter GILLINGS from the third issue, Winter 1951–2 onwards. The third Nova Publications title, also edited by EJC, was the British reprint edition of Larry SHAW's SCIENCE FICTION ADVENTURES. The first five UK editions of this, Mar.-Nov. 1958, were all US reprints, but from the Jan. 1959 issue it became an original British magazine. It ceased publication with the May 1963 issue, but the other two titles continued until mid-1964 under EJC until they were taken over by Roberts & Vinter under new editors. EJC then established a series of original anthologies, NEW WRITINGS IN SF, which appeared as hard-bound books under his editorship from *New Writings in SF 1* (**1964**) to *New Writings in SF 21* (**1972**), the latter title being published after his death. EJC was also an SF BOOK CLUB selector, the literary agent for most of the UK's sf writers, and co-founder of the INTERNATIONAL FANTASY AWARD. Ted Carnell, as he was usually known, had a finger in almost every sf pie in Britain; he worked hard, profited little, and was always known as scrupulously honest. His contribution to British sf was probably greater than that of any other single person. Although his own preference was for conservative hard sf, and he published many writers of it, such as Kenneth BULMER and E.C. TUBB, it should be remembered that he also gave active encouragement to many of the writers who were later to become strongly associated with Michael MOORCOCK's *New Worlds*, writers of the NEW WAVE, including Brian ALDISS, J.G. BALLARD, John BRUNNER and Michael Moorcock himself, whose succession to

the editorship of *New Worlds* he supported. EJC also edited a handful of reprint anthologies: *Jinn and Jitters* (anth. **1946**), *No Place Like Earth* (anth. **1952**), *Gateway to Tomorrow* (anth. **1954**), *Gateway to the Stars* (anth. **1955**), *The Best From New Worlds Science Fiction* (anth. **1955**), *Lambda 1 & Other Stories* (anth. **1964**), *Weird Shadows From Beyond* (anth. **1965**) and *Best of New Writings in SF* (anth. **1971**).   [PN]
See also: SF MAGAZINES.

CARPENTER, ELMER J. (?–). American writer, in whose sf novel, *Moonspin* (**1967**), a foreign power gains control of Earth's WEATHER. A previous novel, *Nile Fever* (**1959**), is not sf.   [JC]

CARR, CHARLES (?–). English writer whose sf novel, *Colonists of Space* (**1954**) and its sequel, *Salamander War* (**1955**), routinely deal with COLONIZATION and conflicts between humans and the original salamander inhabitants of the planet Bel.   [JC]

CARR, JOHN DICKSON (1906–77). American writer, for long periods resident in England, where most of his famous early detective novels, such as *The Hollow Man* (**1935**), *Death Watch* (**1935**), and others as by Carter Dickson, are evocatively set. After his inspiration regarding intricate locked-room mysteries and the like began to flag, and after a pious biography of DOYLE, *The Life of Sir Arthur Conan Doyle* (**1949**), JDC began to write mysteries of a fantastic colouration, often set in the past, in several of which modern detectives are transferred (by a form of TIME TRAVEL) to 17th or early 19th-century England, where they are involved in murders. These books are *The Devil in Velvet* (**1951**), *Fear is the Same* (**1956**) as by Carter Dickson, and *Fire, Burn!* (**1956**). An earlier novel, *The Burning Court* (**1937**), is an apparent fantasy; some of the tales in *The Department of Queer Complaints* (coll. **1940**) are actual fantasies.   [JC]
See also: CRIME AND PUNISHMENT.

CARR, ROBERT SPENCER (1909–). American writer, brother of John Dickson CARR, author of a fantasy novel, *The Room Beyond* (**1948**), and of *Beyond Infinity* (coll. **1951**), four warmly realized stories set on Earth in the mid-20th century but with sf content. [JC]

CARR, TERRY (1937–). American writer and editor. He had a long and prolific career as a fan in the 1950s; one of his fanzines, FANAC, co-edited with Ron ELLIK, won a HUGO award in 1959. He continued to write for and occasionally edit fanzines through the 1960s, and eventually won a second Hugo as best fan writer in 1973.

TC's first published story was "Who Sups With the Devil" (1962); like most of his early work, it appeared in *FSF*. He has never been a prolific writer, but his occasional short stories are thoughtful and distinctive. They include "Brown Robert" (1962), a neat TIME-TRAVEL variant; "The Dance of the Changer and the Three" (1968), an ambitious attempt to render an ALIEN culture by telling one of its myths; and "Ozymandias" (1972), which draws an effective parallel between modern CRYONICS techniques and the funeral practices of ancient Egypt. The majority of his shorter fiction is included in *The Light at the End of the Universe* (coll. **1976**). He wrote two minor early novels, *Invasion from 2500* (**1964**) in collaboration with Ted WHITE under the pseudonym Norman EDWARDS, and *Warlord of Kor* (**1963**). *Cirque* (**1977**) is a more substantial work, a religious allegory, elegiac in mood, set in the FAR FUTURE. Because he is not a very productive writer, TC's work has in general been undervalued.

It is as an editor that TC is best known. From 1964–71 he was an editor at ACE Books, where he was responsible for the highly successful "Ace Specials" series. He co-edited seven annual best of the year collections with Donald A. WOLLHEIM, and initiated a series of original sf anthologies with *Universe 1* (anth. **1971**; see UNIVERSE) After leaving Ace, TC became a freelance editor. He continued with a best of the year anthology, commencing with *The Best Science Fiction of the Year* (anth. **1972**); this series is generally regarded as the best among several competing compilations. *Universe* also continued, although it changed publishers more than once. TC has also produced a wide variety of reprint and original anthologies; notable among the latter is *The Ides of Tomorrow* (anth. **1976**), with fine stories by Brian ALDISS, George R.R. MARTIN and others.   [MJE]
Other works: Ed. *Science Fiction for People Who Hate Science Fiction* (anth. **1966**); ed. *New Worlds of Fantasy* (anth. **1967**; vt *Step Outside Your Mind* UK); ed. *The Others* (anth. **1969**); ed. *On Our Way to the Future* (anth. **1970**); ed. *New Worlds of Fantasy 2* (anth. **1970**); ed. *New Worlds of Fantasy 3* (anth. **1971**); ed. *This Side of Infinity* (anth. **1972**); ed. *Universe 2* (anth. **1972**); ed. *An Exaltation of Stars* (anth. **1973**); ed. *Into the Unknown* (anth. **1973**); ed. *The Best Science Fiction of the Year 2* (anth **1973**); ed. *Universe 3* (anth. **1973**); ed. *Worlds Near and Far* (anth. **1974**); ed. *The Best Science Fiction of the Year 3* (anth. **1974**); ed. *Universe 4* (anth. **1974**); ed. *The Fellowship of the Stars* (anth. **1974**); ed. *Creatures from Beyond* (anth. **1975**); ed. *The Best Science Fiction of the Year 4* (anth. **1975**); ed. *Universe 5* (anth. **1975**); ed. *Planets of Wonder* (anth. **1976**); ed. *The Best Science Fiction of the Year 5* (anth. **1976**); ed. *Universe 6* (anth. **1976**); ed. *The Best Science Fiction of the Year 6* (anth. **1977**); ed. *Universe 7* (anth. **1977**); ed. *The Infinite Arena* (anth. **1977**).

See also: LINGUISTICS; MYTHOLOGY.

CARREL, MARK Pseudonym of English writer Lauran Bosworth Paine (1916–), whose routine sf novels are *A Crack in Time* (**1971**), *The Undine* (**1972**), *Another View* (**1972**), *Bannister's Z Matter* (**1973**) and *The Underground Men* (**1975**).   [JC]

CARRIE Film (1976). United Artists. Directed by Brian De Palma, starring Sissy Spacek, Piper Laurie, John Travolta, Amy Irving and William Katt. Screenplay by Lawrence D. Cohan, based on the novel by Stephen KING. 98 mins. Colour.

This widely praised film about a girl with telekinetic powers was made by the director of the impressive *Phantom of the Paradise*. Carrie is a high-school girl who is regarded as a freak by the other students and who has the further disadvantage of a mother who is a religious fanatic of the worst kind. She is quite innocent of all sexual matters and her first menstrual period, which begins in the school showers, results in her total panic and a savage attack on her by the other girls. This leads to the film's central incident: at the school prom a bucket of pig's blood is dumped over her, at the very moment she feels she has been accepted by her fellow students. She then unleashes her power to its limit, killing everyone in the building and setting it on fire. She returns home where her mother, convinced that she is a witch, is waiting to kill her. Fatally wounded, Carrie causes every sharp implement in the kitchen to fly into her mother, then brings the whole house down on their heads.

De Palma displays an obvious strength when working in sf melodrama, a genre in which he has planned further projects.   [JB]

CARRIGAN, RICHARD (?–) and **NANCY** (?–). American writing team, whose sf novel, *The Siren Stars* (**1971**), presents the first intelligent messages from another star as of the utmost danger; rather ponderously, a clean-cut team of Earth scientists deals with the problem.   [JC]

CARROLL, LEWIS Pseudonym of English mathematician and writer Charles Lutwidge Dodgson (1832–98), whose famous children's stories, *Alice's Adventures in Wonderland* (**1865**) and *Through The Looking Glass* (**1871**), have had a profound impact on a wide range of writers; the underlying logic that structures these "nonsense" adventures, it has been argued, by Brian ALDISS among others, has provided a significant model for much of sf's typical reorderings of reality, certainly in most sf novels whose heroes' PARANOIA about reality turns out to be justified. LC's mathematical and logical fantasies, as found in *A Tangled Tale* (**1886**) and *The Game of Logic* (**1887**) have also had repercussions in sf.   [JC]

Other works: *Phantasmagoria* (**1869**); *The Hunting of the Snark: An Agony in Eight Fits* (**1876**); *Sylvie and Bruno* (**1889**); *Sylvie and Bruno Concluded* (**1893**).

About the author: *The Life and Letters of Lewis Carroll* (**1898**) by Stuart Dodgson Collingwood; *Victoria through the Looking-Glass* (**1945**; vt *Lewis Carroll* UK) by Florence Becker Lennon; *Lewis Carroll* (**1954**) by Derek Hudson; *The Annotated Alice* (**1960**) ed. Martin GARDNER; *The Annotated Snark* (**1962**) ed. Martin Gardner; *Aspects of Alice* (**1971**) ed. Robert Phillips.

See also: GAMES AND SPORTS.

CARSAC, FRANCIS Pseudonym used by François Bordes (1919–77), French writer and professor of geology and prehistoric anthropology at Bordeaux University. FC was one of the earliest post-war French sf writers to assimilate successfully the lessons of American sf. His first and best novel, *Ceux de nulle part* ["Those from Nowhere"] (**1954**), is a vigorous blend of ROSNY AÎNÉ and the PULP traditions of ASTOUNDING SCIENCE FICTION.   [MJ]

Other works: *Les Robinsons du cosmos* ["The Robinsons of the Cosmos"] (**1955**); *Terre en fuite* ["Earth in Flight"] (**1960**); *Ce monde est nôtre* ["This World is Ours"] (**1962**); *Pour patrie l'espace* ["Space, our Fatherland"] (**1962**); *La vermine du lion* ["Vermin of the Lion"] (**1967**).

CARSON, ROBIN *See* TIME TRAVEL.

CARS THAT ATE PARIS, THE Film (1974). Crawford Films. Directed by Peter Weir, starring Terry Camilleri, John Meillon and Kevin Miles. Screenplay by Peter Weir. 88 mins. Colour.

An Australian film by the director who later made the highly praised *Picnic at Hanging Rock, CTAP* deals in an offbeat way with the Australian obsession with cars. It opens in the manner of a commercial, a smoothly photographed sequence with a lush musical soundtrack showing two men in a fast car. But this consumer fantasy turns into a nightmare when the car suddenly crashes, killing the driver. The survivor staggers into the nearby town and learns, bit by bit, that it is no ordinary community but one in which the inhabitants survive economically by causing car accidents and then cannibalizing the wreckage. If the drivers are not killed outright they are put into the care of the local doctor, who uses them as material for his experiments. Some younger townspeople have turned renegade and frequently terrorize their elders by driving their murderously redesigned cars (some are covered in spikes) down the main road at high speed. It is they who cause the minor apocalypse at the end, and the town that lives by the

One of the menacing vehicles from THE CARS THAT ATE PARIS.

car is eventually destroyed by it.

The film does not readily fit into any traditional category; it is idiosyncratic and often puzzling in its development, and some of the acting is weak, but it is made with an originality which won it much critical praise, partly, perhaps, because it was seen as marking a new strength in the previously amateurish Australian cinema.   [JB]

CARTER, ANGELA (1940–). English writer, best known for her work outside the sf field, though all her work is characterized by an expressionist freedom of reference to everyday "reality" which often emerges as fantasy. She won the John Llewelyn Rhys Memorial Prize for her second novel, *The Magic Toyshop* (**1967**), and the Somerset Maugham Award for *Several Perceptions* (**1968**). Her first novel to use a recognizably sf venue, *Heroes and Villains* (**1969**), does so with the same freedom, for AC is one of the few English writers of genuine FABULATIONS, post-Modernist works in which storytelling conventions are mixed and examined, and in which the style of telling is strongly language-oriented. *Heroes and Villains* is set in a post-HOLOCAUST England inhabited by dwellers in the ruins of cities, whose society is rigidly stratified, and Barbarians, who survive in the surreal mutated forests that cover the land. Like much of her work, the novel uses GOTHIC images and conventions to examine and to parody the concerns of its protagonists and the desolate world they inhabit; Marianne, the protagonist, leaves the ruined city for a Barbarian life and (typically of AC's work) undergoes an erotic awakening couched in complexly decadent terms.

In AC's world, erotic complexities, shamans and deliquescent urban landscapes proliferate, and such later works as *The Infernal Desire Machines of Doctor Hoffman* (**1972**; vt *The War of Dreams* USA), *Fireworks* (coll. **1974**) and *The Passion of New Eve* (**1977**), which have many images in common, are increasingly baroque and abstract fictions, all of them using tropes related to sf. Though she was never associated with the sf NEW WAVE, it is thanks to that movement that readers of sf have been induced to treat AC's difficult but rewarding work as being of interest to a genre audience.   [JC]

Other works: as translator: *The Fairy Tales of Charles Perrault* (trans. **1977**).

See also: ABSURDIST SF; ANTHROPOLOGY; DISASTER; FANTASTIC VOYAGES; MYTHOLOGY; PERCEPTION; PSYCHOLOGY.

CARTER, LIN(WOOD VROOMAN) (1930–). American writer and editor, most of whose work of any significance has been done in the field of HEROIC FANTASY, an area of concentration he has gone some way to define in his critical study of relevant texts and techniques, *Imaginary Worlds* (**1973**). Much of his own heroic fantasy derives, sometimes too mechanically, from the precepts about its writing which he airs in this book. As an editor, he was most active about 1969–72, when as consultant for BALLANTINE BOOKS he conceived their adult fantasy list and presented many titles under that aegis, bringing to the contemporary paperback market writers such as James Branch CABELL, Lord DUNSANY and Clark Ashton SMITH. With Cabell, he merely reprinted some titles; but with H.P. LOVECRAFT, Dunsany and Smith he re-assembled material under his own titles (*for details see separate entries*). Most of his criticism has been closely linked to his strong interest in fantasy of this sort, and includes *Tolkien: A Look*

Behind "*The Lord of the Rings*" (**1969**) and *Lovecraft: A Look Behind the "Cthulhu Mythos*" (**1972**). With L. Sprague DE CAMP, LC has adapted and expanded many stories which Robert E. HOWARD left unpublished or unrealized, and created others (*for details see entry on* HOWARD).

As an author in his own right, LC began publishing sf with "Masters of the Metropolis" for *FSF* in 1957 with Randall GARRETT; his first novel, *The Wizard of Lemuria* (**1965**; rev. vt *Thongor and the Wizard of Lemuria* 1969), begins a long series of fantasies about the exploits of Thongor in various venues; the series continues with *Thongor of Lemuria* (**1966**; rev. vt *Thongor and the Dragon City* 1970), *Thongor Against the Gods* (**1967**), *Thongor in the City of Magicians* (**1968**), *Thongor at the End of Time* (**1968**) and *Thongor Fights the Pirates of Tarakus* (**1970**); various uncollected stories and comics also belong to the series. A second, rather similar, series is comprised of *The Warrior of World's End* (**1974**), *The Enchantress of World's End* (**1975**), *The Immortal of World's End* (**1976**), *The Barbarian of World's End* (**1977**) and, first published but the concluding volume, *Giant of World's End* (**1969**). Further series include the "Callisto" sequence, comprised of *Jandar of Callisto* (**1972**), *Black Legion of Callisto* (**1972**), *Sky Pirates of Callisto* (**1973**), *Mad Empress of Callisto* (**1975**), *Mind Wizards of Callisto* (**1975**), *Lankar of Callisto* (**1975**) and *Ylana of Callisto* (**1977**); the "Green Star" sequence, comprised of *Under the Green Star* (**1972**), *When the Green Star Calls* (**1973**), *By the Light of the Green Star* (**1974**), *As the Green Star Rises* (**1975**) and *In the Green Star's Glow* (**1976**); and the DOC SAVAGE-like "Zarkon" sequence, comprised of *Zarkon, Lord of the Unknown, in The Nemesis of Evil* (**1975**), *Zarkon, Lord of the Unknown, in Invisible Death* (**1975**) and *Zarkon, Lord of the Unknown, in the Volcano Ogre* (**1976**). Among his relatively few sf adventures are *The Man Without a Planet* (**1966**) and *The Man who Loved Mars* (**1973**). Overproduction has blurred LC's image, and gives weight to the feeling that he has sometimes paid inadequate attention to the quality of his products; his work as an editor eclipses his own writings in importance.   [JC]
Other works: *The Star Magicians* (**1966**); *Destination Saturn* (**1967**) with David Grinnell (Donald A. WOLLHEIM); *The Flame of Iridar* (**1967**); *The Thief of Thoth* (**1968**); *Tower at the Edge of Time* (**1968**); *The Purloined Planet* (**1969**); *Beyond the Gates of Dream* (coll. **1969**); *Tower of the Medusa* (**1969**); *Lost World of Time* (**1969**); *Star Rogue* (**1970**); *The Quest of Kadji* (**1971**); *Outworlder* (**1971**); *The Black Star* (**1973**); *The Valley Where Time Stood Still* (**1974**); *Time War* (**1974**); *The City Outside the World* (**1977**).

As editor: *Dragons, Elves and Heroes* (anth. **1969**); *The Young Magicians* (anth. **1969**); *The Magic of Atlantis* (anth. **1970**); *Golden Cities, Far* (anth. **1970**); *The Spawn of Cthulhu* (anth. **1971**); *New Worlds for Old* (anth. **1971**); *Discoveries in Fantasy* (anth. **1972**); *Great Short Novels of Adult Fantasy I* (anth. **1972**); *Great Short Novels of Adult Fantasy II* (anth. **1973**); *Flashing Swords 1* (anth. **1973**); *Flashing Swords 2* (anth. **1973**); *Flashing Swords 3: Warriors and Wizards* (anth. **1976**); *Flashing Swords 4* (anth. **1977**); *The Year's Best Fantasy Stories 1* (anth. **1975**); *The Year's Best Fantasy Stories 2* (anth. **1976**); *Kingdoms of Sorcery* (anth. **1976**); *Realms of Wizardry* (anth. **1976**); *The Year's Best Fantasy Stories 3* (anth. **1977**).
Non-fiction: *Flash Gordon and the Warriors of Mongo* (**1977**) with Scott Bizar, a war game; *Middle-Earth; The World of Tolkien* (**1977**), comprised of pictures with captions.
See also: ATLANTIS; JUPITER; LIFE ON OTHER WORLDS; MARS; SWORD AND SORCERY.

CARTIER, EDD (? –). American illustrator. EC worked in b/w and colour but is best known for his interior illustrations, especially those for the *ASF* serialization of DE CAMP's "The Hand of Zei" in 1950. Most of his work was done from around 1940 to 1954 with a gap for war service — he was wounded in the Battle of the Bulge — for *Other Worlds*, *Planet Stories*, *Astounding Science Fiction* and, most important, *Unknown*, for which he did several covers. His clean lines, smooth modelling, and an eye for humour which was not equalled until the advent of EMSH in the mid-1950s, are his trademarks. EC was one of the most popular illustrators of his day. He left freelance illustration in 1954.   [JG]

CARTMILL, CLEVE (**1908–64**). American author and journalist; co-inventor of the Blackmill system of high-speed typography. He was active in American sf magazines in the 1940s, publishing his "Space Salvage" series in *TWS*, which was collected as *The Space Scavengers* (coll. **1975**). His earliest work appeared in *Unknown*, including his first story, "Oscar" (1941), and several short fantasy novels; one of these, "Hell Hath Fury" (1943), was featured in a George HAY anthology of the same name (**1963**). He is best remembered for a famous story in *ASF*, "Deadline" (1944), which described an atomic bomb a year before it was dropped. American security descended on *ASF* but were eventually convinced by John W. CAMPBELL Jr that CC had used only material available in public libraries for his research. Campbell had already been asked by the government to refrain from this sort of speculation, perhaps because theoretical knowledge about nuclear fission had already been disseminated widely before

the War. In any case, CC's prediction made sf fans enormously proud, and the story was made a prime exhibit in the arguments about PREDICTION in sf.   [JC]
See also: NUCLEAR POWER; RELIGION.

CASANOVA DI SEINGALT, GIACOMO (**1725–98**). Venetian writer, variously employed; best known for his *Mémoires*, the single-mindedness of which caused his name to pass into the language as a synonym for lover. He wrote primarily in French, the language of his FANTASTIC-VOYAGE novel, *Icosaméron; ou Histoire d'Édouard, et d'Élizabeth qui passèrent quatre-vingt-un ans chez les Mégamicres habitans aborigènes du Protocosme dans l'intérieur de notre globe* (**1788**). Roughly translated, the title tells us that Edward and Elizabeth have spent 81 years in a world within our globe which is inhabited by the (androgynous and oviparous) Mégamicres or big/littles (they are small in stature and large in spirit), who have been there from before the Fall. They have missed out on original sin, but do not have any souls, either. They describe their society to the two shipwrecked wanderers at some length (the novel occupies five volumes, each 350 pages or more), and the wanderers, in turn, tell their tale, in dialogue form, to a group of English aristocracy. The book is quite realistic in tone, and contains a great deal of scientific speculation and anticipation, notably about electricity, and a fair amount of social satire. The work was probably influenced by VOLTAIRE's *Micromégas* (France **1752**).   [JC]

CASEWIT, CURTIS W. (**1922–**). American writer born in Germany and educated in different countries, hence multilingual. In the USA from 1948. He has published stories in various fields; his first, "The Mask" (1952), appeared in *Weird Tales*. His sf novel, *The Peacemakers* (**1960**), depicts conflicting societies after World War Three; a former soldier tries to become dictator.   [JC]

CASEY, RICHARD House name used on the Ziff-Davis magazines 1943–8 by Leroy YERXA and others.

CASTERET, NORBERT (**1897–**). French speleologist and writer whose sf novel, *Mission centre terre* (**1964**; trans. and rev. as *Mission Underground* **1968** by Antonia Ridge), sends explorers several miles into the Earth in a specially designed craft.   [JC]
Other works: The following have not been translated: *La terre ardente* (**1950**) and *Muta fille des cavernes* (**1965**).

CASTLE, J(EFFERY) LLOYD (**1898–**). English writer whose first sf novel, *Satellite E One* (**1954**), deals awkwardly with the scientific details surrounding the construction of a space

This illustration to L. Ron Hubbard's "Fear" in *Unknown*, July 1940, is one of Edd CARTIER's finest b/w works.

satellite; his second novel, *Vanguard to Venus* (**1957**), identifies FLYING SAUCERS as the ships of descendants of spacefaring ancient Egyptians.   [JC]

CASTLE, ROBERT *See* Edmond HAMILTON.

CATACLYSM *See* DISASTER; END OF THE WORLD; HOLOCAUST AND AFTER.

CAVALIER, THE US PULP MAGAZINE published by the Frank A. MUNSEY Co., ed. Robert Hobart Davis. It evolved from the SCRAP BOOK and appeared monthly, Oct. 1908-Jan. 1912, became *The Cavalier Weekly* from 6 Jan. 1912 to 9 May 1914 before merging with ALL-STORY WEEKLY to form *All-Story Cavalier Weekly*. Although it was comparatively short-lived, *C* published several major works, including Garrett P.

SERVISS's *The Second Deluge* (1911–12; **1913**) and George Allan ENGLAND's *Darkness and Dawn* trilogy (1912–13; fix-up as one volume **1914**; edited version in five volumes **1964–7**). Among the numerous short stories were works by J.U. GIESY and Junius B. Smith, Edgar FRANKLIN and John D. Swain. Several of the stories were reprinted in FAMOUS FANTASTIC MYSTERIES and FANTASTIC NOVELS.   [JE]
See also: *Under the Moons of Mars: A History and Anthology of "The Scientific Romances" in the Munsey Magazines, 1912–1920* (**1970**) by Sam MOSKOWITZ.

CAVALIER WEEKLY *See* CAVALIER, THE.

CAWTHORN, JAMES (1929–). English illustrator, critic and writer. Under the pseudonym Philip James he

wrote *The Distant Suns* (1969 *The Illustrated Weekly of India*; exp. **1975**) in collaboration with Michael MOORCOCK. As JC he wrote book reviews for *NW*, but is best known as an illustrator, his work appearing often in *NW* but also on various COMIC STRIPS, and on book covers in both the US and the UK. He is at his best when witty; his naïve, rough lines work vividly. His SWORD-AND-SORCERY illustration is uneven, usually energetic but sometimes static. A complete book in comic-strip form is *Stormbringer* (**1975**) by Michael Moorcock, adapted by JC. [PN]

CHADWICK, P(HILIP) G(EORGE) (? –). British author. His only novel, *The Death Guard* (**1939**), although virtually unknown today, deserves greater attention. It describes the development of "The Flesh Guard", a race of laboratory-created vegetal humanoids, at the time of the emergence of a fascist dictatorship in Britain and depicts a future WAR as the Earth's major nations react to the horror of such an army in the hands of an extremist government; the book contains several themes later developed by L. RON HUBBARD and James BLISH and is at times reminiscent of William Hope HODGSON.
                                          [JE]

CHAIRMAN, THE *See* MOST DANGEROUS MAN IN THE WORLD, THE.

CHALKER, JACK L(AURENCE) (1944–). American writer and editor, active as a fan from an early age, and producer of a successful fanzine, *Mirage*. As editor, he founded and continues to edit the MIRAGE PRESS, most of whose list comprises non-fiction works on sf subjects. His own work in that area begins with *The New H.P. Lovecraft Bibliography* (**1961**), continuing with some edited work and three studies and guides written with Mark OWINGS: *The Necronomicon: A Study* (**1967**), *Index to the Science-Fantasy Publishers* (**1966**) and *The Revised H.P. Lovecraft Bibliography* (**1973**). Although Mark Owings is sometimes listed as a pseudonym of JLC, this is a confusion arising from his sole crediting for *The Necronomicon*, on which the two collaborated. JLC has more recently begun to concentrate on fiction; after *An Informal Biography of Scrooge McDuck* (**1974**), he published an ambitious SPACE OPERA, *A Jungle of Stars* (**1976**), and a further novel, *Midnight at the Well of Souls* (**1977**), a more diffuse book about a somewhat metaphysical "Well World". *A Jungle of Stars* displays considerable and adroitly utilized familiarity with the field. Its basic story rewrites E.E. "Doc" SMITH's "Lensman" series: two opposing superbeings vie for supremacy in the universe, recruiting members of mortal races to do the fighting, but in this case the superbeings (who embody opposing principles) are both evil; the human

James CAWTHORN's illustrations are full of character, as in this, for Michael Moorcock's "Constant Fire" in *New Worlds 10*, 1976.

protagonist is a complex version of a typical Keith LAUMER hero. Sequels seem to be called for, and one existing story, "Forty Days and Nights in the Wilderness", is set in the same universe. Further JLC novels are projected for 1978 publication; he is a writer of some potential. [JC]

Other works: *The Web of the Chozen* (**1978**). As editor: *In Memoriam: Clark Ashton Smith* (anth. **1963**); *Mirage on Lovecraft* (anth. **1965**).

See also: TERRAFORMING.

CHAMBERLAIN, HENRY RICHARDSON See MONEY.

CHAMBERLAIN, WILLIAM (1903–). American writer, whose two borderline sf novels, *Red January* (**1964**) and *China Strike* (**1967**), both feature US pre-emptive strikes against the enemy — Cuba in the first case, China in the second. Cuba was about to blackmail the USA, and China was about to drop a cobalt bomb on her. Neither gets away with it. [JC]

See also: POLITICS.

CHAMBERS, ROBERT W(ILLIAM) (1865–1933). Popular American writer, author of over 70 novels in various genres, for the first decade or so of his career mostly fantasies, thereafter mainly historical and romantic works. His first successful work is fantasy, *The King in Yellow* (coll. **1895**). The eponymous "The King in Yellow" is not a person, but a book, which (not unlike several much discussed works of recent sf) drives its readers to despair, madness and even suicide; nobody is ever PSYCHOLOGICALLY strong enough to finish it. The collection is followed by several volumes of stories similarly connected by single narrators, including *The Maker of Moons* (coll. **1896**) and two sf collections, *In Search of the Unknown* (coll. of linked stories **1904**) and its sequel *Police!!!* (coll. of linked stories **1915**), in which a big-game hunter searches for unknown beasts (*see* BIOLOGY), finds and loses them, along with various girls. *The Gay Rebellion* (coll. of linked stories **1913**) consists of comically SATIRICAL tales in which WOMEN revolt but reform and marry properly. RWC's use of sf material is slick and casual. [JC]

Other works: *The Mystery of Choice* (coll. **1897**); *The Tracer of Lost Persons* (**1906**); *The Tree of Heaven* (coll. **1907**); *Some Ladies in Haste* (**1908**); *The Green Mouse* (**1910**); *Quick Action* (**1914**); *The Hidden Children* (**1914**); *Athalie* (**1915**); *The Dark Star* (**1917**); *The Slayer of Souls* (**1920**); *The Talkers* (**1923**).

See also: ARTS; SUSPENDED ANIMATION.

CHANCE, JONATHAN (? –). English writer whose sf novel is *The Light Benders* (**1968**). [JC]

CHANDLER, A(RTHUR) BERTRAM (1912–). English-born writer and

Photo Peter Nicholls.

Merchant Navy officer, now an Australian citizen. Until his retirement in 1975, he served in the British, Australian and New Zealand Merchant Navies, commanding under the latter two flags; this professional experience permeates his writing, many of his novels featuring spaceships and flotillas whose command structures are decidedly naval. ABC began publishing stories in *ASF* in 1944, on John W. CAMPBELL's invitation, with "This Means War", and concentrated on short fiction for several years, often under the pseudonym George Whitley (in the USA and the UK), less frequently as Andrew Dunstan (Australia only). Such novels as he wrote during the early years of his career remained in magazine form. For these reasons, ABC remained until the 1960s rather less well known than he deserved, as some of his best work, including the several-times anthologized "Giant Killer" (1945), dates from this period.

After reaching the rank of chief officer, ABC's production ceased for some time, and when he began writing extensively again in the later 1950s he began to concentrate on novels, most of which have dealt, directly or indirectly, with his central venue, the RIMWORLDS at the edge of the galaxy, during a period of human expansion. Not all "Rim Worlds" novels are serially connected, though all have a common background (which includes terminology and a set of frequently mentioned planets, like Thule and Faraway); John Grimes, the protagonist of the central "Rim Worlds" sequence, appears also in some non-series novels. Two books, *The Rim of Space* (**1961**), which is ABC's first novel in book form, and *The Ship from Outside* (1959 *ASF* as "Familiar Pattern" by George Whitley; exp. **1963**), comprise a kind of trailer for the more numerous stories grouped about the figure of Grimes. In these books, Derek Calver, following something like

the same course Grimes will, comes to the Rim Worlds, eventually becomes captain of his own starship, *Lorn Lady*, loses her, sails on other star tramps, and engages in far-flung adventures. Grimes is mentioned in this short series, and his own series massively expands the detail of its description of a very similar career and life; he dominates two main sequences. The first chronologically (though most of it was written later) traces his career in the Federation Survey Service up to the point that he shifts loyalties to the Rim; by late 1977, with some instalments still projected, the series comprised, in internal chronological order, *The Road to the Rim* (**1967**), *To Prime the Pump* (**1971**), *The Hard Way Up* (coll. **1972**), *The Broken Cycle* (**1975**), *False Fatherland* (**1968** Australia; vt *Spartan Planet* USA), *The Inheritors* (**1972**), which involves GENETIC ENGINEERING, *The Big Black Mark* (**1975**) and *Star Courier* (**1977**). The second sequence, begun earlier and with further volumes still projected, was not written with any internal order in mind; carrying Grimes into his second career with the Rim Runners and the Rim Worlds Naval Reserve, it includes *Into the Alternate Universe* (**1964**), *Contraband from Otherspace* (**1967**), *The Rim Gods* (**1969**), *The Dark Dimensions* (**1971**), *Alternate Orbits* (coll. **1971**), *The Gateway to Never* (**1972**) and *The Way Back* (**1976**). Through these books Grimes's somewhat melancholy temperament and consistent ingenuity often remind one of C.S. FORESTER's Horatio Hornblower, an influence ABC acknowledges; but it is of course more than Hornblower's character that is derived from the earlier genre: the whole "Grimes/Rim Worlds" sequence is very clearly a transposition – much more directly than is usually the case – of maritime ships, seas and ports into SPACESHIPS, space and planets. Much of the warmth and detail of ABC's work derive from this direct translation of venues, and Grimes himself establishes a loyalty in his readers rather similar to that which is felt by readers of Hornblower. Indeed, ABC's SPACE OPERAS are among the most likeable and well constructed in the genre, and his vision of the Rim Worlds – cold, poor, antipodean, at the edge of intergalactic darkness, but full of all the pioneer virtues – are the genre's best characterization of that corner of space opera's galactic arena.

One further novel, *The Bitter Pill* (**1974** Australia), merits notice for its sour depiction of a totalitarian DYSTOPIA on Earth, and of the ultimately successful attempts its leading characters make to wrest Mars free of oppression; as with some of the later "Grimes" books, there is a considerable amount of sex.

ABC has been awarded the Australian DITMAR on four occasions, in 1969, 1971, 1974 and 1976. [JC]

Other works: *Bring Back Yesterday* (**1961**); *Rendezvous on a Lost World*

(1961); *The Hamelin Plague* (1963); *Beyond the Galactic Rim* (coll. 1963); *The Coils of Time* (1964); *Glory Planet* (1964); *The Deep Reaches of Space* (1946 *ASF* as "Special Knowledge"; rev. 1964) whose protagonist is ABC's main pseudonym, George Whitley; the "Empress" series of space operas: *Empress of Outer Space* (1965), *Space Mercenaries* (1965) and *Nebula Alert* (1967); *The Alternate Martians* (1965); *Catch the Star Winds* (coll. comprising one novel and one story 1969); *The Sea Beasts* (1971).

See also: COLONIZATION OF OTHER WORLDS; GREAT AND SMALL.

CHAPDELAINE, PERRY A. (1925–). American writer, mathematician, research psychologist and director of an author's publishing co-op. His first published sf was "To Serve the Masters" for *If* in 1967; his sf novel *Swampworld West* (1974) routinely explores a COLONIZATION scenario and problems between native ALIENS and Earth colonists. His "Spork" series, three stories of which appeared in *If* in 1969, is to appear in book form, with additions, in 1978. A two-story series in *ASF* was "Initial Contact" (1969) and "Culture Shock" (1971). His most recent novel, *The Laughing Terran* (1977), like its predecessor, suffers from awkward prose and sf stereotypes. [JC/PN]
See also: DIANETICS.

CHAPIN, PAUL *See* Philip José FARMER.

CHAPMAN, SAMUEL (? – ?). American writer, whose sf novel, *Doctor Jones' Picnic* (1898), published in San Francisco, takes the doctor on a balloon trip to the North Pole; en route he cures cancer. [JC]
See also: DISCOVERY AND INVENTION.

CHARBONNEAU, LOUIS (HENRY) (1924–). American writer and journalist, who after writing some radio plays at the end of the 1940s took an MA at the University of Detroit and taught there for some years before beginning to publish sf novels with *No Place on Earth* (1958) about a coercive DYSTOPIA. He was then productive for several years as an sf writer, publishing *Corpus Earthling* (1960) about telepathic invading Martian parasites who eventually pass on their ESP powers to mankind, *The Sentinel Stars* (1963), another Dystopia about a regimented future, *Psychedelic-40* (1965; vt *The Specials* UK), and *Down to Earth* (1967; vt *Antic Earth* UK). In all these novels, LC tends towards claustrophobic situations in which his rather conventional protagonists explore themselves through action scenarios. LC has written novels in other genres as well, including Westerns, as Carter Travis Young, and mysteries. [JC]
Other works: *The Sensitives* (1968), a film link-up based on a script by Deane

ROMANO; *Barrier World* (1970); *Embryo* (1976), a novelization of the film EMBRYO.

CHARBY, JAY *See* Harlan ELLISON.

CHARKIN, PAUL (1907–). English writer, variously employed for many years before writing his three routine sf novels, *Light of Mars* (1959), *The Other Side of Night* (1960), and *The Living Gem* (1963). [JC]

CHARLES-HENNEBERG, NATHALIE The name is given sometimes in this form and sometimes as Nathalie-Charles Henneberg. *See* Charles HENNEBERG.

CHARLY Film (1968). Selmur and Robertson Associates/Cinerama: Directed by Ralph Nelson, starring Cliff Robertson, Claire Bloom, Lilia Skala and Dick van Patten. Screenplay by Stirling Silliphant, based on the novel *Flowers for Algernon* by Daniel KEYES. 106 mins. Colour.

Enthused with the idea of playing a character who develops from a subnormal 30-year-old man to a supergenius and then back again, Cliff Robertson formed his own production company and, after setbacks, made the film and won an Academy Award for his performance. Much of the pathos of the original is evoked in the progression from amiable idiocy to high intelligence — the result of an experimental drug — the gradual discovery of love and sex, the further development to genius and the horror of the final regression. The metamorphosis is well handled, only occasionally slipping into sentimentality, except for its zenith, where a few platitudes about society's treatment of the individual do not suffice to suggest superintelligence. Silliphant, a screenwriter experienced with sf material, produced a good script in other respects, and Nelson's direction is efficient except for a tendency to portray happiness in the sort of glamour shots that have been devalued in filmed commercials. [JB]

CHARNAS, SUZY McKEE (1939–). American writer, with a MA in teaching, and a former teacher, who spent a year in Nigeria with the Peace Corps. Her first novel, *Walk to the End of the World* (1974), the first of a projected trilogy, presents an elaborately structured, neurotic, male-dominated post-HOLOCAUST society, in which women ("fems") serve as scapegoats for humanity's near self-destruction (*see* WOMEN). The sequel is *Motherlines* (1978). [JC]

CHASE, ADAM Pseudonym used usually by Milton LESSER alone, but once in collaboration with Paul FAIRMAN on the book *The Golden Ape* (1959), which was based on "The Quest of the Golden Ape" (1957 *AMZ* as by Adam Chase and Ivar Jorgensen).

CHAYEFSKY, PADDY *See* METAPHYSICS.

CHERRYH, C.J. The spelling of her name American writer and teacher Carolyn Janice Cherry (1942–) uses for her fiction, beginning with her first novel, *Gate of Ivrel* (1976), an unusually striking and sensitive HEROIC-FANTASY quest story; a sequel is projected. Her second novel, *Brothers of Earth* (1976), epitomizes her considerable virtues as a writer of romantically conceived but gravely paced adventures, in this case the deep conflict between two humans stranded (during the course of a 1000-year war between their widely spread factions) on a humanoid planet. The humanoid culture is complexly envisioned, the two humans are rendered with some irony, and it is a sign both of this writer's relative maturity and of the way the times have changed that it is the destruction (rather than the use) of an ancient, powerful cache of human weapons that is seen as redemptive. CJC has a BA in Latin and an MA from Johns Hopkins in classics. [JC]
Other works: *Hunter of Worlds* (1977).
See also: SWORD AND SORCERY; WOMEN.

CHESNEY, Lt-Col. Sir GEORGE T(OMKYNS) (1830–95). English officer in the Royal Engineers and writer of some fiction, including the famous *The Battle of Dorking* (1871: vt *The Fall of*

The 1871 French edition of *The Battle of Dorking* shows the German Eagle tearing at the belly of the British Lion.

England? The Battle of Dorking: Reminiscences of a Volunteer USA; vt *The German Conquest of England in 1875 and Battle of Dorking* USA), published anonymously, which, after great success in Blackwood's Magazine, and after being published as a small book the same year, virtually founded the future WAR/INVASION genre of stories which attained great popularity in England as she neared the height of her insecure Empire in the latter years of the 19th century. An earlier tale, Alfred Bate RICHARDS' *The Invasion of England (A*

possible tale of future times) (**1870**, privately printed), had little effect. GTC's tale, which is superior, warns against English military complacency and incompetence in its bleak narrative of confusion and folly at home while the German army mounts an efficient invasion by surprise attack. *The Battle of Dorking* was remarkably successful, immediately printed in Canada and the USA, and translated into several European languages, including German, each European nation soon developing its own version of the invasion theme — a type of story that saw its greatest popularity, understandably, in the years immediately preceding the First World War. [JC]
About the author: Chapter 2 of *Voices Prophesying War 1763–1984* (**1966**) by I.F. CLARKE.
See also: ANONYMOUS SF AUTHORS; HISTORY OF SF; NEAR FUTURE: WEAPONS.

CHESNEY, WEATHERBY *See* C.J. Cutcliffe HYNE.

CHESTER, GEORGE RANDOLPH (1869–1924). American writer, whose sf novel *The Jingo* (**1912**) satirizes simultaneously the LOST-RACE story and American know-how in a story about a salesman selling his modern products to an obscure Antarctic civilization. [PN]
Other works: *The Cash Intrigue* (**1909**); *The Ball of Fire* (**1914**) with Lillian Chester.

CHESTER, WILLIAM L. (1907–). American writer, known exclusively for his series about Kioga, a Tarzan-like wild man raised by bears on an island within the Arctic Circle, all published in THE BLUE BOOK MAGAZINE: *Hawk of the Wilderness* (1935 *Blue Book*; **1936**); *Kioga of the Wilderness* (1936–7 *Blue Book*; **1976**); *One Against a Wilderness* (1937 *Blue Book*; coll. of linked stories **1977**) and *Kioga of the Unknown Land* (1938 *Blue Book*; **1978**). [JC]

CHESTERTON, G(ILBERT) K(EITH) (1874–1936). English writer and illustrator, in the latter capacity usually of his own books and many by Hilaire BELLOC, with whom he has long been associated, in George Bernard SHAW's phrase, under the nickname Chesterbelloc. Though he wrote some sf, most of his numerous works fall into various other categories; GKC is a prime example, in fact, of the English man of letters, and wrote (perhaps too much) on almost everything, in every conceivable form, from poetry to the famous "Father Brown" detective stories to Catholic polemics to literary criticism to history and routine belles-lettres. His first novel, *The Napoleon of Notting Hill* (**1904**), sets the nostalgic, medievalizing, Merrie England tone of most of his sf; his sf novels tended, in one way or another, to idealize a dreamlike England, and in their

arguments about its desirability comprise a series of UTOPIAS, though often only by implication. *The Man Who Was Thursday* (**1908**), his finest novel, is a fantasy in which God appears. [JC]
Other works: *The Ball and the Cross* (**1909**); *The Flying Inn* (**1914**); *The Man Who Knew Too Much* (coll. **1922**); *The Return of Don Quixote* (**1927**); *Tales of the Long Bow* (coll. **1925**).
See also: ALTERNATE WORLDS; PSYCHOLOGY.

CHETWYND, BRIDGET (?–). British writer, in whose sf novel, *Future Imperfect* (**1946**), women run the world, leaving men behind; there are romantic elements. [JC]

CHEVALIER, HAAKON (MAURICE) (1902–). American writer and translator from the French of many works; his sf novel, *The Man Who Would be God* (**1959**), treats the unfortunate megalomania of a nuclear physicist who wishes to save the world from itself. [JC]

CHILDERS, ERSKINE (1870–1922). Irish writer, political agitator, and Republican sympathizer. Author of *The Riddle of The Sands* (**1903**), a popular novel of its day which describes an exploratory sea journey along the German coast and the uncovering of the secret plans for a German invasion of Great Britain. After he had contributed this patriotic work to the genre, it is ironic that EC was executed for treason during the Irish civil war. [JE]
See also: WAR.

CHILDREN IN SF In his essay "The Embarrassments of Science Fiction" (1976) Thomas M. DISCH asserts (tongue only partly in cheek) that sf is a branch of children's literature — because most lovers of the genre begin reading it in their early teens, and because many sf stories are *about* children. Whether or not sf is essentially juvenile in its appeal, there is no doubt that many of its writers are fascinated by childhood and its thematic corollaries: innocence and potentiality.

There are four major types of sf story about children. The first is the story of children with benign paranormal powers, e.g. A.E. VAN VOGT's *Slan* (1940 *ASF*; **1946**), about a nascent community of telepathic supermen; Theodore STURGEON's *The Dreaming Jewels* (**1950**; vt *The Synthetic Man*), about a strange boy adopted by a carnival, and *More Than Human* (**1953**), about a *gestalt* consciousness composed of children; Wilman H. SHIRAS's *Children of the Atom* (fix-up **1953**); John WYNDHAM's *The Chrysalids* (**1955**; vt *Re-Birth* USA), about telepathic mutant children after an atomic war; and such later works in a similar vein as Richard COWPER's *Kuldesak* (**1972**) and "The Piper at the Gates of Dawn" (1976). The abilities of these children seem benign because the

stories are usually narrated from the child's point of view. The societies depicted in these tales may persecute the children, but the latter generally win through and constitute their own, "higher" societies, with the reader's approval.

The second type is the reverse of the first: the story of monstrous children, frequently with malign psychic powers, which is best represented by shorter works, e.g. Ray BRADBURY's "The Small Assassin" (1946), about a baby which murders its parents; Richard MATHESON's "Born of Man and Woman" (1950), about a hideously mutated boy; and Jerome BIXBY's "It's a *Good Life*" (1953), about an infant who terrorizes a whole family with his awesome paranormal abilities. J.D. BERESFORD's *The Hampdenshire Wonder* (1911; vt *The Wonder* USA) is an early example of this type of story, in that the child prodigy is seen entirely from the outside and thus takes on a frightening aspect. In tales of this type, society is usually threatened by the child and the reader is encouraged to take society's side.

The third type, which overlaps the first two, is the story of children in league with aliens, to good or ill effect. Examples include Henry KUTTNER's "Mimsy Were the Borogoves" (1943), in which alien educational toys provide two children with an escape route from their parents; Ray Bradbury's "Zero Hour" (1947), in which children side with alien invaders; Arthur C. CLARKE's *Childhood's End* (1953), in which the alien "Overlords" supervise the growth of a new generation capable of "mind-travelling" to the stars; Edgar PANGBORN's *A Mirror for Observers* (**1954**), in which Martians compete for control of a child's mind; John Wyndham's *The Midwich Cuckoos* (**1957**; vt *Village of the Damned* USA), about the alien impregnation of Earthwomen and the terrifying powers of the amoral children they bear, and his later novel *Chocky* (1963 *AMZ*; exp. **1968**), about a boy with an alien "brother" living in his head. Zenna HENDERSON's stories about "the People", most of which are collected in *Pilgrimage* (coll. **1961**) and *The People: No Different Flesh* (coll. **1966**), belong here since they are largely concerned with sympathetic aliens who appear to be normal human children. Jack WILLIAMSON's *The Moon Children* (**1972**) and Gardner DOZOIS' "Chains of the Sea" (1973) also belong in this category.

The fourth type of story is concerned not so much with a conflict between the child and adult society as with the child's attempts to prove himself worthy of joining that society. Much of Robert A. HEINLEIN's work falls into this "initiation" category, e.g. his early story "Misfit" (1939), about a boy whose prodigious mathematical ability enables him to save the spaceship in which he is a very junior crew member. Most of

Heinlein's teenage novels, from *Rocket Ship Galileo* (**1947**) to *Have Space-suit — Will Travel* (**1958**) fit this pattern, as does the later *Podkayne of Mars* (**1963**). Precocious children, adults before their time, also feature in James H. SCHMITZ's "Telzey" stories, e.g. "Novice" (1962); in Alexei PANSHIN's *Rite of Passage* (**1968**); and in much of Samuel R. DELANY's work. Delany's novels, e.g. *Nova* (**1968**), are characteristically about "the progress of the Magic Kid ... the divine innocent whose naïve grace and intuitive deftness attract the close attention of all", in Algis BUDRYS's words. The Magic Kid, who gains the acceptance of adult society through sheer charm (rather than discipline in the manner of Heinlein), has also appeared in the work of other writers, e.g. in John VARLEY's "In the Bowl" (1975).

As in literature generally, the child's point of view has frequently been used by sf writers because it is a convenient angle from which to see the world anew. Thus, Kingsley AMIS makes good use of his choirboy hero in the alternate-world novel *The Alteration* (**1976**). Ray Bradbury transmutes his own childhood experience into the nostalgic and horrific fantasy of *The Martian Chronicles* (**1950**; vt *The Silver Locusts* UK) and *Something Wicked This Way Comes* (**1962**). Gene WOLFE repeatedly uses a child's-eye view to haunting effect in such tales as "The Island of Dr. Death and Other Stories" (1970), "The Fifth Head of Cerberus" (1972) and "The Death of Dr. Island" (1973). Harlan ELLISON's fantasy "Jeffty is Five" (1977), about a boy who is perpetually five years old, uses the child's viewpoint to make a statement about the apparent decline in quality of American popular culture. There are numerous other examples.

Anthologies devoted entirely to stories about children include *Children of Wonder* (anth. **1953**; vt *Outsiders: Children of Wonder*) ed. William TENN; *Tomorrow's Children* (anth. **1966**) ed. Isaac ASIMOV; *Demon Kind* (anth. **1973**) ed. Roger ELWOOD and *Children of Infinity* (anth. **1973**) ed. Elwood. [DP]

CHILDREN OF THE DAMNED Film (1963). MGM. Directed by Anton M. Leader, starring Ian Hendry, Alan Badel, Barbara Ferris and Bessie Love. Screenplay by Jack Briley, based on the novel *The Midwich Cuckoos* by John WYNDHAM. 90 mins. B/w.

The film is not, as the title might suggest, a sequel of VILLAGE OF THE DAMNED, but like the latter it is based on Wyndham's novel, and was probably made in response to the success of the first version. This time the setting is urban. Once again, children are born with mysterious powers, but whereas in the first film the children were obviously malevolent, here they are treated much more sympathetically. When they are destroyed in the end it is due to human fear and ignorance, not any hostile actions of their own. Good, moody use is made of the possibilities for chiaroscuro in the ruined church where much of the action takes place. *COTD* is superior to its predecessor. [JB/PN]

CHILDREN'S SF Sf written with a specifically juvenile audience in mind is almost as old as the genre itself. The "Voyages extraordinaires" of Jules VERNE, over 60 novels published between 1863 and 1920, were largely directed at adolescent boys, though like much juvenile sf they found an adult readership also. Contemporaneous with Verne's works were the early DIME NOVELS in America, also written for children, and it was not long before BOYS' PAPERS with a strong sf content came along, followed by such juvenile series as Victor APPLETON's TOM SWIFT stories. The juvenile series written under the floating pseudonym Roy ROCKWOOD, "The Great Marvel Series", published much sf between 1906 and 1935. These topics are discussed in greater detail under separate entries in this Encyclopedia, as is children's sf written for COMIC STRIPS AND COMIC BOOKS. From 1890 to 1920 at least, and to some extent later on, most children's sf was aimed at boys rather than girls, and was largely dedicated to the themes of the LOST WORLD, the future WAR and INVENTIONS. L. Frank BAUM, writer of the celebrated "Oz" books, wrote an early work in the latter category with *The Master Key: An Electrical Fairy Tale* (**1901**), but of course fantastic inventions had already played an important role in the stories featuring FRANK READE JR.

A difficulty in discussing children's sf is that it is written for different ages. We are generally regarding sf written for younger children as outside our range, although nostalgic reference must be made to the following: the splendidly bizarre *Doctor Dolittle in the Moon* (**1929**) by Hugh Lofting; the "Professor Branestawm" books by Norman HUNTER, beginning with *The Incredible Adventures of Professor Branestawm* (**1933**), all featuring the ridiculous adventures of the eponymous eccentric scientist; the biologist J.B.S. HALDANE wrote a fantasy combining elements of magic and sf in the minor children's classic *My Friend Mr. Leakey* (coll. of linked stories **1937**); a better-known classic series for younger children is comprised of the seven "Narnia" books by C.S. LEWIS, beginning with *The Lion, the Witch and the Wardrobe* (**1950**) and ending with *The Last Battle* (**1956**) — these stories are basically religious allegory cum fantasy, but they do contain such sf elements as PARALLEL WORLDS and TIME TRAVEL; *The Twenty-One Balloons* (**1946**) by William Pène Du Bois is an amusing Pacific-island scientific Utopia.

The above are primarily for younger children, but they point up a difficulty which exists to a large extent in sf stories for older children also: the fact that there is little generic purity in children's literature. Much children's fantasy contains sf elements, and, conversely, much children's sf is written with a disregard for scientific accuracy, whether from hauteur or ignorance, which effectively renders it fantasy. Time travel, for example, has long been an important theme in children's literature, going back at least as far as *The Cuckoo Clock* (**1877**) by Mrs Maria Molesworth, and continuing to the present day, through several of Lucy Boston's "Green Knowe" stories, and perhaps the greatest of them, *Tom's Midnight Garden* (**1958**) by Philippa Pearce, a moving and subtle story of a boy who travels back to slightly different periods of time, to find the 19th-century child with whom he falls in love growing older, and away from him; finally she meets him in the present day, in an overwhelming surprise ending. But in all these cases, the time travel is an essentially magic device used in the service of fantasy.

Children's fiction has been undergoing a great renaissance in the past two decades, but sadly for sf purists most of the sf works of distinction in the period have been marginally sf only, very much at the fantasy end of the spectrum. For two reasons, many distinguished writers of children's fiction are not given separate entries in this Encyclopedia: we do not have the space to be comprehensive with children's writers, and our emphasis is on sf rather than fantasy. Thus there is no entry for Philippa Pearce (*see above*) or for William Mayne, one of the finest modern children's writers, in whose *Earthfasts* (**1966**) a drummer boy from the 18th century emerges from the ground to be met by a sceptical, scientifically inclined present-day youth, in a fine piece of peripheral sf.

The signs of the renaissance in children's literature are many: a sardonic or even ironic realism is more common than it was; the best books are far less patronizing; they have become more accomplished, more subtle, more evocative, more original and various, more ready to confront problems of pain, or loss, or even sexual love. This is so even with some of the ALTERNATE-WORLDS heroic fantasists who have followed in the footsteps of J.R.R. TOLKIEN; notable among them are Joy Chant, and especially Patricia McKillip, who is likely to become recognized as one of the most notable children's writers to emerge in the 1970s.

But for various reasons a number of writers of juvenile sf do receive entries in this volume, most commonly because they have also written sf for adults, or because they are strongly representative of their period, or, like Alan GARNER, their work is likely to have repercussions in adult sf.

The key theme in children's sf is MAGIC, and several important children's works are discussed in that entry. Sometimes the magic is given a kind of pseudo-scientific rationale, with talk of dimensional gates and so on, as in Andre NORTON's many "Witch World" books, some of which are among her best work, as for example *Warlock of the Witch World* (**1967**). Andre Norton has also, of course, written a great many books for children which are towards the HARD-SF end of the spectrum. Ursula K. LE GUIN's "Earthsea" trilogy, beginning with *The Wizard of Earthsea* (**1968**), has combined sf and fantasy by making her magic work to such rigorous, even sceptical laws that it is seen as a kind of alternate science; it adheres, for example, to the law of conservation of energy. Many critics regard the "Earthsea" books as the finest children's work of the past 20 years, though also in this category would be the novels of Alan Garner, especially his more recent works. Apart from using teenage protagonists, Garner's *Red Shift* (**1973**) is an adult book in every respect, telling a story of love, death and a battle against intellectual and physical impotence considerably more sophisticated and demanding than most supposedly adult romances. It qualifies as marginal sf through its consistent use, from the title onwards, of scientific metaphor, and because it depends structurally on a form of psychic time travel, always focused on a neolithic stone axe. The lunacies of book marketing have never been more clear than in the consignment of such distinguished works as the above, and many others, to what Le Guin has called "the kiddylit ghetto", when in fact they are literature in the fullest sense of the word. The paradox is visible in that occasionally American editions of British children's books have been marketed as for adults, and vice versa.

Other important children's sf writers at the fantasy end of the spectrum, whose works are discussed in greater detail under their own entries, are Susan COOPER, Peter DICKINSON, Tanith LEE, T.H. WHITE and Laurence YEP.

When we turn to hard sf, most work for children has been less distinguished. Carl CLAUDY wrote some exciting books in the 1930s; more recent writers of some quality, a significant part of whose production has been for children, are Paul CAPON, John CHRISTOPHER, John Keir CROSS, Sylvia ENGDAHL, Philip LATHAM, Alice LIGHTNER, M.E. PATCHETT, Donald SUDDABY, Jean and Jeff SUTTON, Hugh WALTERS, Leonard WIBBERLEY and Cherry WILDER. Between them they span 40 years of hard-sf adventure writing for children. Capon, Christopher and Engdahl are probably the most important names here, along with Andre Norton, already discussed. Between them they have written some thoughtful and stimulating work, but the list looks feeble when set alongside the creations of adult sf in the same period. The difficulty is, of

course, that the intellectual level of a book is not necessarily expressed by a marketing label. Much adult sf, the works of E.E. "Doc" SMITH, A.E. VAN VOGT or Isaac ASIMOV, for example, is of great appeal to older children, and is to some extent directed at them. When so many older children are able to obtain and enjoy adult sf that is well within their reading capacity, then the size of the potential market in sf specifically labelled as juvenile obviously dwindles.

By far the most distinguished case in point of the unreal distinction between "juvenile" and "adult" is Robert HEINLEIN, almost half of whose work was originally marketed for children. They have all been re-released recently as if for adults. There are 13 in all, among the best being *Starman Jones* (**1953**), *The Star Beast* (**1954**) and *Citizen of the Galaxy* (**1957**). (The worst is the last, *Podkayne of Mars*, **1963**.) Heinlein's direct style, his solid science, the naturalness and ease with which he creates a societal background with just a few strokes, all help to make his juveniles among his best works; but their basic strength comes from their repeated theme of the "rite de passage", the initiation ceremony, growing into adulthood by taking decisions, and assuming a burden of moral responsibility. This theme Heinlein made peculiarly and at times brilliantly his own; his is the most consistently distinguished of all hardcore sf written for young readers.

Heinlein is exceptional, in that there was no falling-off in quality when he wrote for children. Other sf writers could not quite manage the trick. Isaac Asimov's "Lucky Starr" books are well below his best; James BLISH's juveniles are generally disappointing, with the exception of *A Life for the Stars* (**1962**), the second of the "Cities in Flight" tetralogy; Ben BOVA, Arthur C. CLARKE, Gordon DICKSON and Evan HUNTER all write better for grown-ups, although Hunter's children's books are unusual and interesting. Alan NOURSE, on the other hand, seems more relaxed when writing for younger people, and some of his best work has been the future-MEDICINE books he has written for them.

A much more recent writer, Robert C. O'BRIEN, wrote two distinguished sf works for children. The witty and sympathetic *Mrs Frisby and the Rats of NIMH* (**1971**) is for younger children, and in the talking-animal line is preferred by some *aficionados* to Richard Adams' more celebrated *Watership Down* (**1972**). O'Brien's *Z for Zachariah* (**1975**) is a post-HOLOCAUST novel for older children, humane, touching and sometimes frightening. His premature death may well have been a great loss to children's sf. [PN]

CHILSON, ROBERT (1945–). American writer. His first sf story was

"The Mind Reader" (**1968**) in *ASF*. *As the Curtain Falls* (**1974**) is a FAR-FUTURE adventure. *The Star-Crowned Kings* (**1975**) is a SPACE OPERA about a member of a subject race who has latent ESP powers. *The Shores of Kansas* (**1976**), RC's most interesting work to date, tells of a man who has a natural, consciously controlled talent for TIME TRAVEL, and his resulting psychological problems. [PN/JC]

CHILTON, CHARLES (FREDERICK WILLIAM) (1927–). English radio producer and scriptwriter, whose three sf novels comprise a trilogy based on his BBC radio serials about Jet Morgan and his companions as they protect Earth against Martians and other menaces (*see* RADIO UK); the books are *Journey Into Space* (**1954**), *The Red Planet* (**1956**) and *The World in Peril* (**1960**). He also wrote further "Jet Morgan" adventures for a comic strip in *Express Weekly* (1956–7). [JC]

See also: SPACE FLIGHT.

CHOSEN SURVIVORS Film (1974). Columbia. Directed by Sutton Roley, starring Jackie Cooper, Richard Jaeckel, Alex Cord and Bradford Dillman. Screenplay by H.B. Cross and Joe Reb Moffly, based on a story by H.B. Cross. 99 mins. Colour.

Eleven people are forced by the army into a deep and elaborate bomb-shelter beneath the desert, where they learn that a nuclear war is devastating the world. To make matters worse they discover that a horde of radioactive vampire bats is sealed in with them. Predictable character conflicts develop, interrupted only by frequent bat attacks. It all turns out to be a government-organized experiment to see how people react in such a situation. [JB]

CHRISTIN, PIERRE (1938–). French writer. A professor of journalism at Bordeaux University, PC is still better known for his script work as "Linus" on six volumes of the inventive *Valérian* sf comic strip drawn by Jean-Claude Mezières. His first novel, *Les prédateurs enjolivés* ["The Embellished Predators"] (**1976**), a harrowing account of desolate times to come, is a most impressive beginning. [MJ]

CHRISTOPHER, JOHN Pseudonym used by English writer Christopher Samuel Youd (1922–) for his sf writing, for which he is best known, though his first novel (published under his own name) is a fantasy, *The White Swan* (**1949**). He was active as an sf fan before the Second World War, in which he served, and began publishing sf with "Christmas Story" for *ASF* in 1949, writing as Christopher Youd. His first sf book, *The Twenty-Second Century* (coll. **1954**), assembles his early work; since the success of his first novel, *The Year of the Comet* (**1955**; vt *Planet in Peril* USA), and the even greater impact of his second, *The Death of Grass* (**1956**; vt *No Blade of Grass* USA), he has concentrated on novels, in which form he has been seen as John WYNDHAM's rival and successor as the premier writer of the post-War English DISASTER novel in the decade 1955–65.

In *The Death of Grass* (filmed by Cornel Wilde as NO BLADE OF GRASS), as the title makes clear, the disaster which changes the face of England (and of the world) is an upset in the balance of nature whereby all grass and related food plants die, with catastrophic effects. Where Wyndham's novels featured protagonists whose middle-class indomitability signalled to the reader that the crisis they were suffering through would somehow come out right in the end, JC's characters, as witness John Custance's gradual hardening and deterioration of personality in this novel, inhabit and respond to a darker, less secure universe.

Several other of JC's novels, such as *The World in Winter* (**1962**; vt *The Long Winter* USA), *A Wrinkle in the Skin* (**1965**; vt *The Ragged Edge* USA), and *Pendulum* (**1968**), deal with similar concerns, and concentrate on the grim business of staying alive and making a life fit to live in the post-HOLOCAUST world. His vision of the nature of Man, when stripped of culture and security, is satisfactorily uncheery.

In recent years, JC has turned from the kind of story that brought him fame and has produced a variety of fiction, most of it without the critical success of his early works. *Cloud on Silver* (**1964**; vt *Sweeney's Island* USA) updates the traditional ISLAND theme with the activities of a complex tycoon and a clutch of mutant life-forms, though once again it makes much of the theme of the authoritarian personality acting harshly in a situation that strips away the veneer of civilization. *The Caves of Night* (**1958**), spelunking adventures, is only marginal sf. JC from early in his career has written social novels of character, usually under stress; they are sometimes undisguised, sometimes within sf frames.

It seemed for a time as if JC's impact on the sf market was becoming too diffuse, and the repetition of similar themes also led to the impression that he was becoming played out as a writer. However, in 1967 he successfully inaugurated a fresh career in sf, this time in the juvenile market, with the first novel of a trilogy, *The White Mountains* (**1967**), its two successors being *The City of Gold and Lead* (**1967**) and *The Pool of Fire* (**1968**). In these books the young hero grows up to resist the tripod aliens who have invaded Earth. JC's juveniles are action-oriented, but thoughtful too, and have proved amazingly popular. In the UK at least he is the most successful of contemporary sf writers for children. Further juveniles by John Christopher are *The Lotus Caves* (**1969**), *The Guardians*

(**1970**), which appropriately won the *Guardian* award for best children's book of the year, *Dom and Va* (**1973**), *Wild Jack* (**1974**), *Empty World* (**1977**) and the trilogy *The Prince in Waiting* (**1970**), *Beyond the Burning Lands* (**1971**) and *The Sword of the Spirits* (**1972**). As with his adult sf, most of JC's juveniles are set in a post-disaster situation, and they often feature romantic individualism pitted against some kind of conformist or even brainwashed system, sometimes symbolized as a struggle between the country and the CITY.   [JC/PN]

Other works: *The Long Voyage* (**1960**); *The Possessors* (**1965**); *The Little People* (**1967**).

See also: ECOLOGY; RADIO (UK); SUPERNATURAL CREATURES.

CHURCHILL, JOYCE *See* M. John HARRISON.

CHURCHILL, R(EGINALD) C(HARLES) (1916–   ). English writer, whose *A Short History of the Future* (**1955**), like John Alfred ATKINS' *Tomorrow Revealed* (**1955**), is an IMAGINARY HISTORY, in this case set about AD 7000, and similarly assembles genuine contemporary sources, mainly George ORWELL, into an accounting of the course of history, though RCC differs in plotting history in great cycles.   [JC]

CICELLIS, KAY (1926–   ). French-born writer of Greek descent who writes in English, most notably such short fiction as that collected in her first book, *The Easy Way* (coll. **1950**). *The Day The Fish Came Out* (**1967**), which novelizes the film THE DAY THE FISH CAME OUT (1967), about an H-bomb and the consequences of its loss off a Greek island, is not up to her serious work. [JC]

CINEMA. Masked Martian soldiers from the early sf film *Aelita*.

CINEMA Sf cinema is not to be confused with sf as literature; it works with different conventions; it uses a much narrower range of themes; it places much more stress, in a GOTHIC manner, on the irrational and the fantastic; it expects much less intelligence in its audience. Sf

cinema now, with few exceptions, is no more sophisticated than was genre magazine sf in the 1930s. It is, on the other hand, artistically much more vital than sf on TELEVISION.

The happiest *aficionados* of sf cinema are those who do not criticize it for its failure to repeat on the screen the intellectual richness of sf as literature, but concentrate instead on its positive qualities.

The first sf film of central importance was Fritz LANG's *Metropolis* (1926). Most sf previous to this placed little emphasis on the realistic creation of an sf milieu. Films like *Aelita* (1924) and *Homunculus* (1916) certainly contained sf elements, but at bottom they are fantastic melodrama, seen through expressionist eyes. *A Message from Mars* (1913) contains a Martian, but he is very human-looking; the emphasis is on social satire. From the earliest days cinematic sf relied heavily on special effects, and many of these were pioneered as early as 1902 by Georges MÉLIÈS in *Le voyage dans la lune*; an elegant, basically fantastic use of such effects was made in René Clair's *Paris qui dort* (1923), where most Parisians are frozen in time and the remainder have fun.

Curiously, *Metropolis* had few imitators. It stands at the head of one of the great four thematic traditions in sf cinema — the DYSTOPIAN film of warning and satire; the other three major themes, MONSTERS, SPACE FLIGHT/SPACE OPERA and DISASTER, we meet later. There were not many sf films in the remainder of the 1920s, the most notable, also by Lang, being *Die Frau im Mond* (1929), which inaugurated the space travelling tradition in sf cinema. More typical of sf cinema generally, which was always to concentrate heavily on a blend of sf and horror (a sub-genre to which almost half the films in this Encyclopedia belong), was the other famous 1920s sf film, *The Hands of Orlac* (1924), in which a surgical transplant has horrible and unexpected consequences. This film was remade at least three times, and gruesome medical sf remains popular in the cinema today, as in *The Terminal Man* (1974) and *The Island of Dr Moreau* (1977).

Organ transplants on a massive scale were introduced to the cinema with one of the classics of sf, *Frankenstein* (1931). The original film of *Frankenstein* was made in 1910, but all of it that remains is a solitary, macabre, still photograph. The 1930s were generally a rich period for sf, in contrast to the decades immediately before and after. The monster tradition was inaugurated with *King Kong* (1933), though there had already been some rather attractive dinosaurs in *The Lost World* (1925). The disaster tradition got under way with the French classic *La Fin du Monde* (1931), and the American tidal wave film *Deluge* (1933).

The 1930s also saw an expansion of the space flight/space opera tradition, at both ends of the intellectual spectrum. The cinematic equivalent of space-opera comics was seen in the serials *Flash Gordon* (1936) and *Buck Rogers* (1939) and their many successors, all aimed at children. But 1936 was also the year of William Cameron Menzies' *Things To Come*; though more full-bloodedly romantic and rhetorical than the modern taste usually requires, the film remains stirring and spectacular today, both in its vibrant reaching for the stars and, more darkly, in its conjuring up of the Dystopian elements of the future. It is a genuine classic.

Other sf films of the 1930s were *L'Atlantide* (1932), Michael Curtiz's *Doctor X* (1932), Mamoulian's brilliant *Dr. Jekyll and Mr. Hyde* (1932), Tod Browning's *The Devil Doll* (1936), *Island of Lost Souls* (1932), James Whale's *The Invisible Man* (1933), the early Hollywood futuristic musical *Just Imagine* (1930), the German technological spy thriller *FP1 Does Not Answer* (1932), the most famous of all LOST-WORLD films, *Lost Horizon* (1936), and *The Man They Could Not Hang* (1939) featuring Karloff with an artificial heart. No clear pattern emerges, other than the fact that most 1930s films are based on famous books, and that there was a predilection for the colourful and the macabre. Genuine scientific extrapolation is almost absent, but that continues to be true of 95% of sf films to this day.

The 1940s, by contrast, were empty years for sf cinema, though they started well with the sinister *Dr. Cyclops* (1940). Medical sf/horror is well represented by *The Lady and the Monster* (1944), and comic sf by *The Perfect Woman* (1949), which allows underclothes-fetishism to an extent that would have been unthinkable if its robot heroine (played by a real woman) had been a real woman. Prehistoric fantasy, which continues as a minor genre today, had a good start with *One Million B.C.* (1940).

Suddenly, with the 1950s, PARANOIA set in. The reasons are various, and curiously the results were often interesting. The Cold War was at its height, the Communist scare was building up in the USA, Hollywood itself would shortly become subject to investigations designed to weed out left-wingers. The monster movie, in this ambience, gained a new lease of life overnight. The whole point of a monster movie is to show peaceful nature suddenly outraged by unreason; the irrational and the violent ruptures the placidity of every day. Monster movies often open with scenes of tranquillity — children playing, farmers hoeing, lovers strolling. The subsequent violence is almost a metaphor for the irrational forces which peaceful Americans feared might enter their lives, forces beyond their control, such as (in real life) the atomic bomb, or invasion, or oppression. The boom began with Howard Hawks's

One of the most bizarre alien landscapes ever filmed, from *Barbarella*.

film *The Thing* (1951), and was given impetus by the successes of *The Beast From 20,000 Fathoms* (1953) *The Creature from the Black Lagoon* (1954) and *Them!* (1954); then the spate began, including among its wave crests *Tarantula* (1955), *The Fly* (1958), *The Quatermass Xperiment* (1955), *The Blob* (1958) and *Twenty Million Miles to Earth* (1957). The Japanese, perhaps for comparable social reasons, initiated their monster boom with *Godzilla, King of the Monsters* in 1954; the success of this industry still keeps Toho Studios afloat.

A particularly gruesome form of paranoid monster movie is that in which the creatures can take human shape (just like the Communist spy who might live next door), or else control humans through devices which render them semi-robots. Films of this kind are William Cameron Menzies' *Invaders from Mars* (1953), *It Came From Outer Space* (1953), *Invasion of the Body Snatchers* (1955) and *I Married A Monster from Outer Space* (1958). Many of the films in the paranoid category were directed by Jack ARNOLD, who became a minor master in the genre.

Often the paranoia takes the form of a religious revivalism, and disaster is envisaged almost as a religious punishment for our sins. These, after all, were the years of Billy Graham's crusades. Such films include *When Worlds Collide* (1951), a replay of the story of Noah's flood, and *Red Planet Mars* (1952). The intrusion of violence into everyday life could take other forms, such as the metamorphosis and subsequent nightmare in *The Incredible Shrinking Man* (1957). Sometimes political paranoia was expressed in more direct and less metaphoric political terms, as in *The Day The Earth Stood Still* (1951), *The Manchurian Candidate* (1962) and *The President's Analyst* (1967).

Indeed, the paranoia theme of "something out there waiting to get us"

remains the single most persistent strand in sf cinema to this day. We are attacked by phallic insects in *They Came From Within* (1975), insane computers in *2001: A Space Odyssey* (1968), ants in *Phase IV* (1974), megalomaniac telepaths in *The Power* (1967), which is another example of the unidentifiable monster film, by vampires in *The Omega Man* (1971), by aliens in *War of the Worlds* (1953) and by cars in *Weekend* (1968), *Death Race 2000* (1975) and *The Cars that Ate Paris* (1974). We don't know if our wives are really human in *The Stepford Wives* (1975), and the man under the mask in *Who?* (1974) may be our enemy. The dead are resurrected to tear at us in *The Night of The Living Dead* (1968) and to abrade our consciences in *Solaris* (1972).

Getting back to the 1950s, though Hollywood's main aim seemed to be to terrify us out of our wits, they did a little to even the balance by celebrating the unconquerable spirit of Man in *Destination Moon* (1950). Space is an expensive setting, and not very many films were set there, for this reason; low budgets sometimes produced grotesque results, as in *Riders to the Stars* (1954). But two relatively high-budget films, both skilled and intelligent, opened up the world of space opera: *Forbidden Planet* (1956) and *This Island Earth* (1954). The only more recent films to supersede their spectacle have been the three greatest blockbuster sf films in history, *2001: A Space Odyssey* (1968), *Star Wars* (1977) and *Close Encounters of The Third Kind* (1977).

The 1950s saw the end of copyright on Jules VERNE's novels, and six or more of them were filmed, the most notable result being *20,000 Leagues Under the Sea* (1954). Competition from television was beginning to worry Hollywood as early as 1952, the year in which *The Twonky* was released, a film showing the TV set as spearheading an alien takeover.

Dystopias began to get popular a little later, in the 1960s, although not until the gloomy 1970s did they really come into their own. Two of the best were from France: *Alphaville* (1965) and *Fahrenheit 451* (1966). *The War Game* (1965) looked squarely in the face of the holocaust in the UK, and *Privilege* (1967) talked of youth manipulation in the future. *Gas-s-s!* (1970) and *Wild in the Streets* (1968), also featured the young, in even stronger positions of power and with apparent sympathy, in a perhaps cynical attempt to cash in on the flower-power phenomenon. The phrase "youth culture" was becoming current.

By the 1960s, sf cinema was well enough established to allow a greater measure of satire and even self-parody. Two of the best sf films of the decade were in this area: *Barbarella* (1967) and *Planet of the Apes* (1968); the latter initiated a series of which the first two films were good, the remainder only mediocre. Human manipulation of body and mind played a prominent role in *Seconds* (1966), *Charly* (1968) and *THX 1138* (1969). One of the most successful monster movies turned the tables by making the monsters initially friendly and familiar: *The Birds* (1963). Alien children shine their eyes menacingly in *Village of the Damned* (1960), James Bond saves the world in *You Only Live Twice* (1967), COMPUTERS take over in *Colossus: The Forbin Project* (1969), a spaceman shows initiative in *Robinson Crusoe on Mars* (1964) and, more realistically, three of them do the same in *Marooned* (1969). A fine and subtle film about TIME TRAVEL, both psychic, through memory, and actual, was the neglected *Je t'aime, je t'aime* (1968), directed by Resnais.

HOLOCAUST and after had been an occasional theme in sf cinema for some time. *On the Beach* (1959) showed it coming, *Dr Strangelove* (1963) showed it happening and *The World, The Flesh and The Devil* (1958) examined the three people left when it had gone; there had been five left in *Five* (1951). Both survivors and pieces of detritus were becoming more numerous by the 1970s; the iconography of disaster cinema regularly includes a few rusting or ivy-clad ruins of 20th-century civilization, as in *Glen and Randa* (1971), *Logan's Run* (1976) or, with more bravura, *A Boy and His Dog* (1975). *The Ultimate Warrior* (1975) fights in the rubble, and *Beneath the Planet of the Apes* (1970) mutants live in it. In *Zardoz* (1974) the greater part of the population has reverted to superstitious barbarity. The aftermath of holocaust makes things uncomfortable for the people going through *Damnation Alley* (1977). The holocaust is geophysical, not military, in the epic *Submersion of Japan* (1973). In *No Blade of Grass* (1970) it is ecological. Surrealism and metamorphosis affect the random survivors in *The Bed-Sitting Room* (1969).

In addition to making disaster seem, in some ways, attractive, 1970s films have specialized in making technology seem unattractive. Brooding, metallic machinery overshadows *The Andromeda Strain* (1971), and runs amuck in *Sleeper* (1973), *Westworld* (1975) and *Futureworld* (1976). In *Dark Star*, the wittiest sf satire yet made, computerized bombs undertake phenomenological arguments with the crew of a starship. A truck becomes a horrendous menace in the mechanical-monster movie *Duel* (1971) and a bulldozer in *Killdozer* (1974). The mechanical wings of *Brewster McCloud* (1971) are the death of their creator. Dolphins are perverted into using weaponry in *The Day of the Dolphin* (1973). The hoodlum of *A Clockwork Orange* (1971) is gentled and diminished by brainwashing machinery. The alien in *The Man Who Fell to Earth* (1976) succumbs to the lure of television. Sport is mechanized in *Rollerball* (1975) and cannibalism is mechanized in *Soylent Green* (1973). The last trees in the Solar System are trapped inside a giant machine, in space, in *Silent Running* (1971).

Perhaps the most complex and moving sf film to date is *Solaris* (1972), with its delicate meshing of images from inner and outer space. Those who find it too slow-moving on a first viewing are often converted by seeing it again and sensing the careful patterning of its beautiful images.

Sf cinema generally, however, does not take its life from complexity or intellectual sureness. It lives through its visual icons (*see illustrations to this entry*), its many images which develop richness and density as they repeat themselves from film to film; *Star Wars* draws half its power from allusion to earlier works. Always in sf cinema the dominant images are of destruction, though occasionally, as in *2001: A Space Odyssey*, they mingle with images of transcendence. In a world that sometimes seems strangled by technology, and the psychological conformity that follows in its wake, perhaps sf cinema has a cathartic function in letting us imagine, safely, what it might be like if it were all blown up, or torn apart by some ravenous monster from the Id; it offers us a transient psychic freedom. [PN]

There follows an alphabetical index of the 283 films which receive detailed entries in this volume. It must be stressed that this list is selective, although it includes all sf films generally judged important, along with a selection representative of all the major themes and periods since the sf movie began, up to the end of 1977:

A great, archetypal sf image from the Japanese B-grade monster movie, *Godzilla Meets Mothra*.

OF THE EARTH; JOURNEY TO THE CENTER OF TIME; JOURNEY TO THE FAR SIDE OF THE SUN; JUST IMAGINE; KILLDOZER; KING KONG; KRONOS; THE LADY AND THE MONSTER; THE LAND THAT TIME FORGOT; THE LAST MAN ON EARTH; LOGAN'S RUN; LORD OF THE FLIES; THE LOST CONTINENT; LOST HORIZON; THE LOST WORLD; THE LOVE WAR; MAD LOVE; THE MAGNETIC MONSTER; THE MANCHURIAN CANDIDATE; THE MAN IN THE WHITE SUIT; THE MAN THEY COULD NOT HANG; THE MAN WHO FELL TO EARTH; THE MAN WHO THOUGHT THINGS; THE MAN WITH THE X-RAY EYES; MAROONED; THE MASK OF FU MANCHU; MASTER OF THE WORLD; A MESSAGE FROM MARS; METROPOLIS; MIGHTY JOE YOUNG; THE MONITORS; THE MONOLITH MONSTERS; MONSTER ON THE CAMPUS; MOON ZERO TWO; THE MOST DANGEROUS MAN ALIVE; THE MOST DANGEROUS MAN IN THE WORLD; MOTHRA; MUTATIONS; THE MYSTERIANS; THE MYSTERIOUS ISLAND; THE NAKED JUNGLE; NIGHT OF THE BIG HEAT; NIGHT OF THE BLOOD BEAST; NIGHT OF THE LEPUS; THE NIGHT OF THE LIVING DEAD; THE NIGHT THAT PANICKED AMERICA; 1984; NO BLADE OF GRASS; THE OMEGA MAN; ONE MILLION B.C.; ONE MILLION YEARS B.C.; ON THE BEACH; PANIC IN THE YEAR ZERO; PARIS QUI DORT; THE PEOPLE THAT TIME FORGOT; THE PERFECT WOMAN; PHASE IV; PLANET EARTH; LA PLANÈTE SAUVAGE; PLANET OF STORMS; PLANET OF THE APES; PLANET OF THE VAMPIRES; THE POWER; THE PRESIDENT'S ANALYST; PRIVILEGE; PROJECT MOONBASE; PUNISHMENT PARK; PURSUIT; QUATERMASS AND THE PIT; QUATERMASS II; THE QUATERMASS XPERIMENT; THE QUESTOR TAPES; RABID; RED PLANET MARS; REPTILICUS; RETURN OF THE FLY; REVENGE OF THE CREATURE; RIDERS TO THE STARS; ROBINSON CRUSOE ON MARS; ROCKETSHIP XM; RODAN; ROLLERBALL; SCREAM AND SCREAM AGAIN; SECONDS; THE SEVEN FACES OF DR LAO; SILENT RUNNING; SLAUGHTERHOUSE FIVE;

SLEEPER; SOLARIS; SON OF KONG; SOYLENT GREEN; THE SPACE CHILDREN; S-S-SNAKE!; STAR WARS; THE STEPFORD WIVES; THE STORY OF MANKIND; STRANGE NEW WORLD; THE STRANGER WITHIN; THE STRANGE WORLD OF PLANET X; THE SUBMERSION OF JAPAN; SUPERMAN; SUPERMAN AND THE MOLE MEN; TARANTULA; TARGET EARTH!; THE TENTH VICTIM; THE TERMINAL MAN; THEM!; THEY CAME FROM WITHIN; THE THING; THINGS TO COME; THIS ISLAND EARTH; THE THOUSAND EYES OF DR MABUSE; THX 1138; THE TIME MACHINE; TOOMORROW; THE TRANS-ATLANTIC TUNNEL; THE TROLLENBERG TERROR; DER TUNNEL; TWENTY MILLION MILES TO EARTH; THE 27TH DAY; TWENTY THOUSAND LEAGUES UNDER THE SEA; TWILIGHT'S LAST GLEAMING; THE TWONKY; 2001: A SPACE ODYSSEY; THE UFO INCIDENT; THE ULTIMATE WARRIOR; UNEARTHLY STRANGER; THE VILLAGE OF THE DAMNED; LE VOYAGE À TRAVERS L'IMPOSSIBLE; LE VOYAGE DANS LA LUNE; VOYAGE TO THE BOTTOM OF THE SEA; THE WAR GAME; WAR OF THE WORLDS; WEEKEND; WELCOME TO BLOOD CITY; WESTWORLD; WHEN WORLDS COLLIDE; WHERE HAVE ALL THE PEOPLE GONE?; WHO?; WHO WOULD KILL JESSIE?; WILD IN THE STREETS; THE WORLD, THE FLESH AND THE DEVIL; WORLD WITHOUT END; X — THE UNKNOWN; YOU ONLY LIVE TWICE; ZARDOZ; Z.P.G.

In addition, we have given entries to certain prominent producers, directors, screenwriters and special-effects men closely connected with sf cinema: Irwin ALLEN; Jack ARNOLD; Roger CORMAN; Michael CRICHTON; Ray HARRYHAUSEN; Byron HASKIN; Fritz LANG; Nigel KNEALE; Stanley KUBRICK; George LUCAS; Georges MÉLIÈS; Terry NATION; Willis O'BRIEN; George PAL; Gene RODDENBERRY; Curt SIODMAK; Douglas TRUMBULL; Peter WATKINS; Robert WISE.

The most important reference work on

sf cinema is *Reference Guide to Fantastic Films: Science Fiction, Fantasy, & Horror* in three vols (**1972–4**) compiled by Walt LEE. The liveliest general study of the subject is *Science Fiction Movies* (**1976**) by Philip STRICK. Further discussion, and much pictorial material, can be found in *Movie Fantastic: Beyond the Dream Machine* (**1974**; vt *Cinefantastic: Beyond the Dream Machine*) by David Annan; *Hal in the Classroom: Science Fiction Films* (anth. **1974**) ed. Ralph J. Amelio; *Science Fiction Films* (anth. **1976**) ed. Thomas R. Atkins; *Science Fiction in the Cinema* (**1970**) by John BAXTER; *An Illustrated History of the Horror Film* (**1967**) by Carlos Clarens; *Vision of Tomorrow: Great Science Fiction from the Movies* (**1975**) by Edward Edelson; *Science Fiction Film* (**1971**) by Denis Gifford; *Focus on the Science Fiction Film* (anth. **1972**) ed. William Johnson; *Filmbuch Science Fiction* (**1973**) by Jürgen Menninger; *An Album of Great Science Fiction Films* (**1976**) by Frank Manchel; *A Pictorial History of Science Fiction Films* (**1975**) by Jeff Rovin; *From Jules Verne to Star Trek* (**1977**) by Jeff Rovin; *The Fabulous Fantasy Films* (**1977**) by Jeff Rovin. Finally, the Spring 1976 no. of the French magazine *Cinema d'aujourd'hui* was titled "Demain la science-fiction", and entirely devoted to the subject.

CITIES The city is the focal point of civilization, and images of the city of the future bring into sharp relief the expectations and fears with which we imagine the future of civilization. As our predominant image of the future has become DYSTOPIAN, images of the future city often embody the specific aspects of Dystopian anxiety in a refined — sometimes almost symbolic — form.

In fact, disenchantment with metropolitan life was very evident even while UTOPIAN mythology remained strong. The growth of the cities during the industrial revolution created filthy slums where crime, ill-health and vice flourished, and a new kind of poverty reigned. Even the most devoted disciples of progress lamented the state of the industrial city, which had little in common with such Utopian city-states as CAMPANELLA'S *City of the Sun* (**1637**) or the cities of L.S. MERCIER'S *Memoirs of the Year Two Thousand Five Hundred* (**1771**; trans. **1772**). Many of the urban Utopian schemes of the late 19th century demanded that cities be built anew, cleansed of their manifest evils. Speculators who were not Utopians found the evolution of the great cities a most powerful argument against progress — a view most strongly advanced in *After London* (**1885**) by Richard JEFFERIES, in which the cities have died but their remains still poison the Earth.

In a good deal of pre-Gernsback sf the city is the same place of contrasts that it was in reality, with the rich and poor

Frank R. Paul was the premier architect of sf CITIES in the pulp magazines. Back cover, *Amazing Stories*, April 1941.

living in close but separate worlds, architectural grandeur masking squalor. This is evident in *Caesar's Column* (**1890**) by Ignatius DONNELLY, in "A Story of the Days to Come" (1897) and *When the Sleeper Wakes* (**1899**) by H.G. WELLS, and in Fritz LANG's film METROPOLIS (1926; book by Thea VON HARBOU **1926**; trans. **1927**). Wells, the most determined prophet of technological super-civilization, constantly showed the destruction of the present-day cities as a prelude to Utopian rebuilding. The splendid vision of the city as an architectural miracle which inspired early Utopians (and modern town planners) remained inspiring in early 20th-century sf, but quite disconnected from the cities of the real world — it lived as a fantasy.

This was, however, a vision which was ever present in early pulp sf — and that this was so was almost entirely due to the work of one man, the artist Frank R. PAUL. Paul could not draw convincing human beings, but he could draw wonderful cities — and his images of the future permeated the early pulps quite irrespective of what was written in the stories. His images contributed much to the flavour of PULP sf.

In modern sf — from the end of the 1930s to the present day — images of the city fall into three principal stereotypes. The first shows up the contrast between the city and a surrounding wilderness, polarizing the opposition between city and country life as we perceive it today. The second shows the city in ruins, decaying and dying. The third is involved with the characterization of the city environment, impersonal and hostile.

The polarization of the city and the wilderness and the juxtaposition of the two usually involve the total automation of the city and the decline of the surrounding country, often involving the enclosure of the city by a wall or dome. The theme of such stories is almost always *escape* from the claustrophobic comfort which kills initiative to the wilderness which offers evolutionary opportunity through the struggle to survive — a return to the beginning of social evolution. The archetype of this form is "The Machine Stops" (1909) by E. M. FORSTER and the most notable development of it in modern sf is Arthur C. CLARKE's *The City and the Stars* (**1956**; expanded from *Against the Fall of Night* 1948; **1953**). Simple expositions of the theme include *Beyond the Sealed World* (**1965**) by Rena VALE, *From Carthage Then I Came* (**1966**; vt *Eight against Utopia* USA) by Douglas R. MASON, *Magellan* (**1970**) by Colin ANDERSON, *Wild Jack* (**1974**) by John CHRISTOPHER, *The Crack in the Sky* (**1976**) by Richard LUPOFF and the film ZARDOZ (1973). An interesting inversion of the characteristic plot is Harlan ELLISON's "A Boy and His Dog" (1969). Images of the ruined city are often remarkable for their exaggerated

romanticism. Such early examples as *After London* and George Allan ENGLAND's *Darkness and Dawn* (**1914**) are replete with images of this sort, and so is Stephen Vincent BENÉT's "By the Waters of Babylon" (1937), but it is perhaps surprising to find romanticism equally strong in genre sf. Much of Clifford D. SIMAK's work — especially the episodic *City* (1944–51; fix-up **1952**) — rejoices in the decline and fall of civilization, and so do many more recent stories, including J.G. BALLARD's "Chronopolis" (1960) and "The Ultimate City" (1976) and Samuel R. DELANY's *Dhalgren* (**1975**). There is more to this than the naïve glorification of living wild and free — the ruins themselves become charismatic and symbolic, as with the torch of the Statue of Liberty in *The Torch* (1920; **1948**) by Jack BECHDOLT, and the similar image at the end of the film PLANET OF THE APES (1968).

The development of the third stereotype is the most recent, and also the most elaborate. It involves not merely the representation of city life as unpleasant or alienating but the strategic exaggeration of the city's form and aspects to stress its hostile and frightening qualities. Isaac ASIMOV characterized a future city as *The Caves of Steel* (**1954**), in which he made literal the common metaphor regarding the claustrophobic quality of city life. Earlier, Asimov invented the planet-spanning city of Trantor, in several short stories (1942–9), later incorporated into the "Foundation" trilogy, one of the earlier world-cities in genre sf. In extreme cases the city becomes personalized, as in Robert ABERNATHY's "Single Combat" (1955), Robert SHECKLEY's "Street of Dreams, Feet of Clay" (1968) and Harlan Ellison's "The Whimper of Whipped Dogs" (1973). Ellison is particularly adept at city-characterization, and this is reflected not only in his sf, as in "The Prowler in the City at the Edge of the World" (1967), but also in his realistic, contemporary fiction. The impersonal quality of the megalopolis is exaggerated straightforwardly in such stories as J.G. Ballard's "Build-Up" (1957; vt "The Concentration City") in which the city is presented as a topological paradox, all inside and no outside, and R.A. LAFFERTY's "The World as Will and Wallpaper" (1973). Indeed, some of the most surreal stories in genre sf express this same sense of impersonality connected with city life — notably Fritz LEIBER's "You're All Alone" (1950), Ted WHITE's "It Could Be Anywhere" (1969) and Charles BEAUMONT's "The Vanishing American" (1955). The stress attendant on life at high population densities is the subject of many stories of OVERPOPULATION, notably Robert SILVERBERG's *The World Inside* (1971), Thomas M. DISCH's *334* (**1972**) and Felix C. GOTSCHALK's *Growing Up in Tier 3000* (**1975**). These novels tend to visualize the city of the future as a conglomerate of

vast tower-blocks — and this is very little different from the images popularized by Frank R. Paul and *Metropolis*, though the imaginative impact of the image has changed drastically. Silverberg dubs these super-skyscrapers Urbmons, but a label which has been more generally adopted is CONAPT, coined by Philip K. DICK.

Outside the genre sf establishment, the most significant attempt to characterize the city and identify its alienating forces is *Invisible Cities* (**1972**; trans. **1974**) by Italo CALVINO, in which Marco Polo offers Kublai Khan an account of the great range of the possible products of civilization. Another interesting experiment is *The Giants* (**1973**; trans. **1975**) by the French writer J.M.G. LE CLÉZIO, in which the central image is the great shopping-centre Hyperbolis, with its multiple frustrations — a paranoid vision evoked through an almost surrealist technique.

In genre sf there is one remarkable exception to this negative attitude to cities, in which the city becomes the symbol of escape and freedom rather than the oppressive environment to be escaped. This is the series of novels which make up James BLISH's *Cities in Flight* series (coll. **1970**) in which antigravity devices lift whole cities from the Earth's surface and let them roam the universe. Even this dream comes to a dead end, however, in the section of *Earthman Come Home* (**1955**) first published as "Sargasso of Lost Cities" (1953), and the final volume of the series is an apocalyptic one — *The Triumph of Time* (**1958**; vt *A Clash of Cymbals* UK). A more recent exception is the eponymous city in Edward BRYANT's *Cinnabar* (coll. **1976**), which is described by its creator as a "haven for paradoxes", and in its diversity sums up most of the symbolic resonances the city has had for Bryant's genre-sf predecessors. Ultimately Bryant shows the attractions of Cinnabar outweighing its dangers.

The variety of sf which is characterized in this volume as ABSURDIST very often uses the city as an ambiguous symbol — conservative and repressive, yet teeming with life and energy. This is common, too, with writers of the so-called NEW WAVE. In *The Malacia Tapestry* (**1976**) by Brian ALDISS these two aspects are particularly clear. J.G. Ballard's *High-Rise* (**1975**) uses a tower block as a microcosm of the city at once isolated from outside and at war with itself, but the consequent disintegration is not viewed as necessarily disastrous. Michael MOORCOCK's Jerry Cornelius novels use a series of Londons, real and alternate, as ambiguously cradle and grave of most of the hero's aspirations, both trivial and noble. In both sf writing and sf art, the city is one of the most important recurrent images, and carries with it one of the richest, densest clusters of associations to be found in the whole sf iconography.

Theme anthologies relating to this topic include *Cities of Wonder* (anth. **1966**) ed. Damon KNIGHT; *Future City* (anth. **1973**) ed. Roger ELWOOD; and *The City: 2000 A.D.* (anth. **1976**) ed. Ralph Clem, Martin Harry GREENBERG and Joseph Olander.
[BS]

See also: AUTOMATION; SOCIOLOGY.

CITY BENEATH THE SEA (vt **ONE HOUR TO DOOMSDAY**) Made-for-TV film (1971). 20th Century-Fox TV Productions for NBC TV. Directed by Irwin ALLEN, starring Stuart Whitman, Robert Wagner, Joseph Cotton, Rosemary Forsyth, James Darren, Richard Basehart, Robert Colbert and Sugar Ray Robinson. Screenplay by John Meredyth Lucas from a story by Irwin Allen. 120 mins. Colour.

Released as a feature film called *One Hour To Doomsday* outside America, this was a pilot for a proposed TV series which Irwin Allen hoped would repeat the success of his other sf series, such as VOYAGE TO THE BOTTOM OF THE SEA, but neither viewers nor critics were sufficiently impressed with it and the series was never made. In an incoherent jumble of over-familiar sf situations, the people in the 21st-century underwater city, Pacifica, have to cope with the following problems: that a super H-bomb will be exploded somewhere within the city; that they will be invaded by an "unfriendly foreign power"; that a sea monster will break through the city's defences; that the city's governing body will be overthrown by a politically suspect group; that a shipment of gold from Fort Knox will be stolen; and that a giant planetoid will crash into the sea above them. All ends happily. This is Irwin Allen plotting at its most typical. Sets and special effects were adequate for television but when seen on the big screen they result in some moments of unintentional humour, as when the men trying to repair a leak in the city wall are seen struggling helplessly against a trickle of water apparently coming from an off-screen garden hose.
[JB]

CLARESON, THOMAS D. (1926–). American editor, critic and professor of English. He took his Ph.D. at the University of Pennsylvania, 1956, by which time he had begun publishing sf criticism, in *Science Fiction Quarterly*, 1954. He is perhaps best known for his editorship of EXTRAPOLATION, which has been edited by TDC from the College of Wooster, Ohio, continuously since Dec. 1959, and is the oldest established academic journal about sf. TDC was also a pioneer in the production of anthologies of sf criticism in book form, his first being *SF: The Other Side of Realism* (anth. **1971**), followed by *Voices for the Future: Essays on Major Science Fiction Writers Vol. 1* (anth **1976**) and *Many Futures, Many Worlds: Theme and Form in Science Fiction* (anth. **1977**). His *SF*

Criticism: an Annotated Checklist (**1972**) is a very useful specialist research tool. He also edited a story anthology with notes, intended to be used in education, *A Spectrum of Worlds* (anth. **1972**). A second volume of *Voices for the Future* is projected for 1978. As critic and researcher, TDC's most notable articles are "The Other Side of Realism" in his volume of the same name (1971); "The Emergence of the Scientific Romance" in Neil BARRON's *Anatomy of Wonder: Science Fiction* (**1976**); and "The Cosmic Loneliness of Arthur C. Clarke" in his *Voices for the Future, Vol.1* (**1976**). A critical pamphlet is *SF: A Dream of Other Worlds* (**1973**). TDC was chairman of the first Modern Language Association Seminar on sf in 1958, and first president of the SCIENCE FICTION RESEARCH ASSOCIATION, 1970–76. He is general editor of the Greenwood Press reprint series of sf pulp magazines, which has so far covered the period 1926–45. In recognition of his services to the academic study of sf he received the PILGRIM award, 1977.
[PN]
Other works: *Science and Society at Midcentury* (**1961**); ed. *Victorian Essays: a Symposium* (anth. **1967**).

CLARION SCIENCE FICTION WRITERS' WORKSHOP This workshop enrols beginning writers interested in writing sf; it consists of intensive writing and discussion sessions under the direction of known sf writers; among the notably successful teachers have been Ursula K. LE GUIN, Harlan ELLISON, Damon KNIGHT, Kate WILHELM, Terry CARR and Samuel DELANY. The first three sessions were held at Clarion State College in Pennsylvania in the summers of 1968–70; hence the name. In 1971 "Clarion East" was held in Tulane University and "Clarion West" at the University of Washington in Seattle. In 1972 "Clarion East" moved to Michigan State University, where it remains, co-directed by Professors Leonard ISAACS and R. Glenn Wright. Though writers' workshops are often regarded with a sometimes justified scorn, Clarion has been much more successful than most, and has produced several notable alumni, including Ed BRYANT, Gerard F. CONWAY, F.M. BUSBY, Vonda McINTYRE, Geo Alec EFFINGER and Lisa TUTTLE. It could be argued, and has been, that writers will become writers anyway, but the Clarion experience seems to have helped focus a number of important talents, and given them the know-how to seek out the right markets. The original director of Clarion was Robin Scott WILSON, who also edited the first three anthologies of students' and teachers' work: *Clarion* (anth. **1971**), *Clarion II* (anth. **1972**) and *Clarion III* (anth. **1973**). *Clarion SF* (anth. **1977**) was edited by Kate Wilhelm.
[PN]

CLARK, CURT See Donald E. WESTLAKE.

CLARK, RONALD (WILLIAM) (1916–). English writer and journalist, active mainly with non-fiction since before the Second World War; he began publishing sf with "The Man Who Went Back" for the London *Evening Standard* in 1949, but has not been a prolific contributor to the genre. His first sf novel, *Queen Victoria's Bomb; the Disclosures of Professor Franklin Huxtable, MA, Cantab.* (**1967**), has achieved some success, and is one of the numerous recent contributions to the genre of sf works that exhibit nostalgia for a previous generation's view of the future. *The Bomb that Failed* (**1969**; vt *The Last Year of the Old World* UK) is a sequel.
[JC]

See also: ALTERNATE WORLDS.

CLARKE, ARTHUR C(HARLES) (1917–). British author, resident since 1956 in Sri Lanka (Ceylon). Born in Minehead, Somerset, ACC came to London in 1936 after leaving school, to work as a civil-servant auditor with HM Exchequer. He was active in fan circles before the War, then he served (1941–6) as a radar instructor with the RAF, rising to the rank of flight lieutenant. After the War he entered King's College, London, taking his BSc with first-class honours in physics and mathematics in 1948.

ACC's strong interest in the frontiers of science was evident early. He was chairman of the British Interplanetary Society 1946–7, and again 1950–53. His first professionally published sf story was "Loophole" for *ASF* in Apr. 1946, though his first sale was "Rescue Party", which appeared in *ASF*, May 1946. In his early years as a writer he three times used the pseudonym Charles Willis, and wrote once as E.G. O'Brien. These four stories all appeared in British magazines 1947–51. Four of ACC's early stories, written for FANZINES (1937–42) have been reprinted in *The Best of Arthur C. Clarke 1937–1971* (coll. **1973**) ed. Angus Wells. This work has been reissued in two vols, **1977**, the first being inaccurately titled *1932–1955*. He also wrote for the comic DAN DARE, c. 1950.

ACC's early stories were very much genre sf, neatly constructed, often turning on a single scientific point, often ending with a sting in the tail. Some of them are rather ponderously humorous. His first two novels were published in 1951, *Prelude to Space* (**1951**; UK and US editions differ in the order of early chapters) being GALAXY SCIENCE FICTION NOVELS no. 3, and *The Sands of Mars* (**1951**) being published in the UK. Both suffer from the rather wooden prose which ACC later rendered into a more flexible instrument, though he was never able to escape the occasional stiffness in his writing. Both are, in effect, works of OPTIMISTIC propaganda for science, with human problems rather mechanically worked out in routine plots against a background of scientific discovery. It was with the science that ACC's imagination flared into life. *Islands in the Sky* (**1952**) followed the same pattern; it is a juvenile about a boy in an orbital space station.

A new note appeared in *Expedition to Earth* (coll. **1953**). This included the short story "The Sentinel" which had appeared in *10 Story Fantasy* in 1951 as "Sentinel of Eternity". A simple but oddly haunting story, it tells of the discovery of an ALIEN artefact, created by an advanced race millions of years earlier, standing enigmatically on top of a mountain on the Moon. It was to become the basis of perhaps the most famous of all sf films many years later: 2001: A SPACE ODYSSEY (1968), for which ACC wrote the script with Stanley KUBRICK. The novelization, *2001: A Space Odyssey* (**1968**) was written by ACC alone, on the basis of the script; the film had already been made. An account of ACC's connection with the film can be found in his *The Lost Worlds of 2001* (**1972**), which also prints alternative script versions of key scenes.

With "The Sentinel" comes the first clear statement of the ACC paradox: the man who of all sf writers is most closely identified with knowledgeable, technological hardcore sf is strongly attracted to the metaphysical, even to the mystical; the man who in sf is often seen as standing for the boundless optimism of the soaring human spirit, and for the idea (strongly presented in John W. CAMPBELL Jr's *ASF*) that there is nothing Man cannot accomplish, is best remembered for the image of mankind being as children next to the ancient, inscrutable wisdom of alien races. This is a notion which in recent years has been proposed, very much more crudely and in supposedly factual terms, by Erich VON DÄNIKEN. There is something attractive, even moving, in what can be seen in Freudian terms as an unhappy mankind crying out for a lost father; certainly it is the closest thing sf has yet produced to an analogy for RELIGION, and the longing for God.

Although this theme is well seen in "The Sentinel", and even better seen in the iconography of *2001: A Space Odyssey*, at the end of which mankind is seen literally as a foetus, ACC gave it its most potent literary expression in two more books from 1953 which are still considered by many critics to be his finest. They are *Against the Fall of Night* (1948 *Startling Stories*; **1953**; exp. and rev. as *The City and the Stars* **1956**; one of the two title stories of *The Lion of Comarre and Against the Fall of Night*, coll. **1968**, the other story having originally been published in *TWS* 1949) and *Childhood's End* (1950 *NW* as "Guardian Angel"; exp. **1953**). Both the original and the longer versions of *Against the Fall of Night* are readily available, but it is the latter, *The City and the Stars*, that is discussed here.

It is one of the strongest tales of CONCEPTUAL BREAKTHROUGH in genre sf.

Alvin, a young man in the enclosed UTOPIAN city of Diaspar, on Earth in the FAR FUTURE, becomes impatient at the stasis of the perfect life, and after many adventures makes his way outside the city, to Lys, another Utopia, of a different kind, which stresses closeness to nature. Ultimately Alvin finds an alien spaceship left behind millennia ago, visits the stars, and finally discovers the true nature of the cosmic perspective which has been hidden from both Lys and Diaspar. The final passages blend a sense of loss and of transcendence with an almost mystical intensity. ACC began working on this story as early as 1937, and it is clearly central to all his thinking and feeling; it is probably his most perfect work. It owes something to the EVOLUTIONARY perspective of Olaf STAPLEDON, whose works ACC greatly admired, as does *Childhood's End*, in which mankind reaches transcendence under the tutelage of satanic-seeming aliens, eventually to fuse with a cosmic overmind which is forever closed to its tutors.

ACC's whole career has been marked by this twin vision of mystical transcendence/alien tuition on the one hand, and a more straightforward, romantic response to the excitement of scientific knowledge on the other.

He continued to publish sf with some frequency over the next decade, with *Earthlight* (1951 *TWS*; exp. **1955**); *Reach for Tomorrow* (coll. **1956**); *The Deep Range* (1954 *Star SF No. 3*; exp. **1957**); *Tales From The White Hart* (coll. of linked stories 1957); *The Other Side of the Sky* (coll. **1958**); *Across the Sea of Stars* (coll. **1959**; an omnibus volume containing 18 short stories from previous collections and the two novels *Childhood's End* and *Earthlight*); *A Fall of Moondust* (**1961**); *From the Ocean, From the Stars* (coll. **1961**; an omnibus volume containing *The Deep Range, The Other Side of the Sky* and *The City and the Stars*); *Tales of Ten Worlds* (coll. **1962**); *Dolphin Island* (**1963**, a juvenile); *Glide Path* (**1963**, ACC's only non-sf novel, about the development of radar); *Prelude to Mars* (coll. **1965**; an omnibus containing 16 stories from previous collections plus *Prelude to Space* and *Sands of Mars*); *An Arthur C. Clarke Omnibus* (coll. **1965**; containing *Childhood's End, Prelude to Space* and *Expedition to Earth*); *An Arthur C. Clarke Second Omnibus* (coll. **1968**; containing *A Fall of Moondust, Earthlight* and *Sands of Mars*); and *The Nine Billion Names of God* (coll. **1967**; mostly from previous collections). Most of the later titles are reprint volumes. The most interesting of these books are *The Deep Range* about near-future farming UNDER THE SEA, containing some of ACC's most evocative writing, and *A Fall of Moondust*, a realistic account of an accident to a surface transport on a lightly colonized Moon.

By the 1960s most of ACC's creative

energies had gone into writing non-fiction books and articles, many of them about undersea exploration; he remains an enthusiastic skin-diver himself, one reason for his residence in Sri Lanka. His popularizations of science, which won him the UNESCO Kalinga prize in 1962, are closely related to his fiction, in that the stories often fictionalize specific ideas discussed in the factual pieces. His most important non-fiction scientific works, some now rather out of date, are: *Interplanetary Flight* (**1950**); *The Exploration of Space* (**1951**); *The Exploration of the Moon* (**1954**); *The Young Traveller in Space* (**1954**; vt *Going Into Space* USA; vt *The Scottie Book of Space Travel* UK); *The Making of a Moon* (**1957**); *The Challenge of the Space Ship* (coll. **1959**); *Profiles of the Future* (coll. **1962**; rev. 1973); *Man and Space* (**1964**, with the Editors of "Life"); *Voices From the Sky* (coll. **1965**); *The Promise of Space* (**1968**); *Report on Planet 3 and other Speculations* (coll. **1972**); *The View from Serendip* (coll. **1978**). ACC's early professional experience as assistant editor of *Science Abstracts* 1949–50, before becoming a full-time writer, has amply paid off. *The Exploration of Space* won a non-fiction INTERNATIONAL FANTASY AWARD in 1972. His non-fiction is lucid and interesting; his only rival as a scientific journalist with sf connections is Isaac ASIMOV. ACC became well known all over the world when he appeared as commentator on CBS TV for the Apollo 11, 12 and 15 Moon missions.

Since 1962 only a small amount of fiction by ACC has appeared in sf magazines, though two of his most interesting stories date from this period: "Sunjammer" (1965; vt "The Wind from the Sun"), which is about the SOLAR WIND, and "A Meeting with Medusa" (1971), which won a NEBULA award in 1972 for best novella; it is a story of a CYBORG explorer meeting alien life in the atmosphere of JUPITER. Both stories are reprinted in ACC's sixth and most recent book (not counting reprint collections) of short stories, *The Wind from the Sun* (coll. **1972**).

After the success of *2001: A Space Odyssey*, ACC became perhaps the best-known sf writer in the world, and a few years later he signed a contract, for a sum of money larger than anything previously paid in sf publishing, to write three further novels, two of which have so far appeared: *Rendezvous with Rama* (**1973**) and *Imperial Earth* (**1975**; US edition contains 10,000 words which were cut from UK edition). Both were best sellers; both had a mixed critical reception; though *Rendezvous with Rama* scooped all the awards: the HUGO, Nebula, JOHN W. CAMPBELL MEMORIAL, BRITISH SCIENCE FICTION and JUPITER. To what extent the book deserved it, and to what extent the awards merely celebrated the return to the field after many years' comparative silence of a much loved figure, is unclear.

All the old ACC themes are there, in the story of a huge alien spaceship which enters the Solar System, and its exploration by a party of humans. As an artefact, the spaceship is a symbol of almost mythic significance, enigmatic, powerful and fascinating, and the book derives considerable power from its description. The human characterization, on the other hand, is not of nearly such a high standard, and is rather reminiscent of boys' fiction from an earlier era. *Imperial Earth* has rather better characterization, but fewer transcendental reverberations, in its story of relations between Earth and the OUTER PLANETS, and a complex intrigue involving CLONES; there are some interesting speculations about BLACK HOLES.

ACC is patron of the SCIENCE FICTION FOUNDATION.

ACC's devotion to the science in sf, and the occasional flaring of his imagination reflected in a sudden enlivening of his prose in dealing with certain key themes, notably SPACE FLIGHT, the landscapes of other worlds and contact with aliens, have deservedly won him recognition as one of the central figures in genre sf.   [PN]

Other works: *Of Time and Stars* (coll. 1973), a collection for children. As editor: *Time Probe* (anth. 1966); *Three for Tomorrow* (anth. 1969) containing stories by Robert SILVERBERG, Roger ZELAZNY and James BLISH — the US edition implies this is edited by Silverberg; *The Coming of the Space Age* (anth. of non-fiction pieces 1967).

About the author: *Arthur C. Clarke* (anth. 1977) ed. Joseph D. Olander and Martin Harry GREENBERG. This book contains all the best-known critical articles on ACC.

See also: ASTEROIDS; CHILDREN IN SF; CITIES; COLONIZATION OF OTHER WORLDS; COMPUTERS; DISCOVERY AND INVENTION; END OF THE WORLD; ESCHATOLOGY; FANTASTIC VOYAGES; FANTASY; FOURTH DIMENSION (AND OTHERS); FUTUROLOGY; GENERATION STARSHIPS; GODS AND DEMONS; GOTHIC SF; GRAVITY; INVASION; ISLANDS; LEISURE; LIFE ON OTHER WORLDS; MACHINES; MAGIC; MARS; MATHEMATICS; MEDIA LANDSCAPE; MUSIC AND OPERA; MYTHOLOGY; PERCEPTION; PHYSICS; POWER SOURCES; PREDICTION; RADIO (UK); ROCKETS; SAMUELSON, David N.; SF OVERTAKEN BY EVENTS; SPACESHIPS; SUN; SUPERMAN; TECHNOLOGY; TERRAFORMING; TIME TRAVEL; TRANSPORTATION.

CLARKE, I(GNATIUS) F(REDERIC) (1918–). Professor of English at the University of Strathclyde in Glasgow, and author of the bibliography *The Tale of the Future: From the Beginning to the Present Day: A Checklist of those Satires, Ideal States, Imaginary Wars and Invasions, Political Warnings and Forecasts, Interplanetary Voyages and Scientific Romances — All Located in an Imaginary Future Period — that have been Published in the UK between 1644 and 1960* (1961; rev. 1972). This work is very useful, especially on the earlier period, but not wholly reliable, being occasionally weak on variant titles and plot summaries, and far from comprehensive. These weaknesses are primarily in the period from 1940 on. IFC's second important contribution to sf studies is *Voices Prophesying War 1763–1984* (1966), by a long way the most comprehensive account of the future-WAR story.   [PN]

CLARKSON, HELEN (? –). American writer, believed to be pseudonymous, whose sf novel is *The Last Day* (1959).   [JC]

CLAUDY, CARL H. (1879–1957). American author. He wrote some 20 sf stories, all of which appeared in the magazine *American Boy*. Four of these were revised and expanded into a JUVENILE SERIES of novels with the general heading of "Adventures in the Unknown", under the titles *The Mystery Men of Mars* (1933), *A Thousand Years a Minute* (1933), *The Land of No Shadow* (1933) and *The Blue Grotto Terror* (1934), which together constitute what was probably the most vigorous and imaginative juvenile sf book series up to that time. Two of these stories in their original magazine form, together with his "Tongue of the Beast" (1939), appeared in *The Year After Tomorrow* (anth. 1954), ed. Lester DEL REY, Cécile Matschat and Carl Carmer.   [JE]

CLAYTON, JO (?–). American writer, whose sf novel, *Diadem from the Stars* (1977), romantically sets out the epic adventures of a young girl electronically attached to the power-bestowing diadem of the title; she travels from world to world to seek the secret of her destiny, and finds it.   [JC]

Photo Bradford F. Herzog.

CLEMENT, HAL Form of his name used for his sf by American writer Harry Clement Stubbs (1922–), though he uses his surname on his non-fiction science articles, and paints as George Richard. He holds degrees in astronomy, chemistry and education and is employed as a high-school science teacher. HC was for long associated with *ASF*, where his first story, "Proof", appeared in 1942, at the peak of the GOLDEN AGE. From the first, his work has been characterized by the complexity and compelling interest of the scientific (or at any rate scientifically literate) ideas which dominate each story. He is not noted as a stylist, nor is his interest in the depicting of character in fiction very strong. For pages many of his books can read like a dramatized exposition of ideas, absorbing though at times disconcerting for the novel reader.

HC's most famous work is contained in his only series, a loosely connected trio of novels, *Mission of Gravity* (*ASF* 1953; abridged 1954), *Close to Critical* (1958 *ASF*; 1964) and *Star Light* (1971). The third volume is a direct sequel to the first, while some of the characters in the second appear in the third as well: Elise ("Easy") Rich in *Close to Critical* is the "Easy" Hoffman of *Star Light*, 25 years older. *Mission of Gravity*, one of the best-loved novels in sf, combines an intriguingly plausible high-gravity planet and HC's most interesting ALIENS, Captain Barlennan and his crew who are assisting a human team to extract a vital component from a crashed space probe; as the planet Mesklin's GRAVITY varies from 3 to 700g (at the poles), Barlennan's arduous trek is a continuously fascinating ECOLOGICAL travelogue. An article, "Whirligig World", about the science behind the novel, appeared in *ASF*, Jun. 1953, and an interesting essay about the use of science in sf generally is HC's "Hard Sciences and Tough Technologies" in *The Craft of Science Fiction* (1976) ed. Reginald BRETNOR.

Needle (1949 *ASF*; exp. 1950; vt *From Outer Space*), HC's first novel, is a rather ponderous alien INVASION story, combining sf with detection elements and a juvenile protagonist in a tale where the invading PARASITE is in fact chasing another (malign) parasite inhabiting the boy's father; the boy, with the good alien in tow, helps to drive the bad alien from his Dad; it is a highly loaded theme, but is told without the necessary resonance.

HC's most successful novels apply the descriptive and scientific skill best shown in *Mission of Gravity* to fundamentally similar basic storylines, usually involving a human figure who must cope with an alien environment, with or without the help of natives, as in *Iceworld* (1953), *Cycle of Fire* (1957) or the sequels to *Mission of Gravity*. These themes also feature in the stories assembled in *Natives of Space* (coll. 1965) and *Small Changes* (coll. 1969; vt *Space Lash*). HC's only collaboration, "Planet for Plunder" (1957), with Sam MERWIN Jr, demonstrates his fascination with alien environments and viewpoints; he wrote the story entirely from a non-human standpoint; Merwin, acting for *Satellite Magazine*, where it appeared, wrote an additional 10,000 words from a human standpoint.

HC brought a new seriousness to the story of hard-sf extrapolation of the physical sciences, and his vividness of imagination has generally overcome the awkwardness of his narrative technique; he is a figure of importance to the genre. [JC]

Other works: *Ranger Boys in Space* (1956), a juvenile; *Ocean on Top* (1967 *If*; 1973). Non-fiction: ed. *First Flights to the Moon* (anth. 1970).

See also: CONCEPTUAL BREAKTHROUGH; CRIME AND PUNISHMENT; ESP; FANTASTIC VOYAGES; ICONOCLASM; LIFE ON OTHER WORLDS; SCIENTIFIC ERRORS; STARS; SUN; UNDER THE SEA.

CLEVE, JOHN *See* Andrew J. OFFUTT.

CLICHÉS Sf clichés have developed, perhaps, partly out of a need for identification of stories as "true" sf — readers know where they are with a *time-space warp* — but mainly out of the lazy and parsimonious recycling of ideas at every level. The most obvious are cliché gadgets (BLASTER, ANDROID, HYPERSPACE drive, CYBORG, TIME MACHINE, brain suspended in aquarium, FORCE FIELD, food pill, antigrav shield, translating machine, judiciary computer), but major sf cliché themes are also old friends (daring conquest of the galaxy; scientist goes too far; witch-hunt for telepaths; post-bomb barbarism; triumph of Yankee know-how). A list of sf cliché characters might begin with mad scientists (FRANKENSTEIN to DR STRANGELOVE), though scientists may also be young, muscular and idealistic, or else elderly, absent-minded and eccentric. Sf cliché WOMEN usually have no character above the waist (*see* SEX); some are sexy and helpless (often lab assistants or daughters of elderly scientists, rescued from danger by young scientists) who break into hysterical laughter and need a slap, who faint during critical fight scenes, and who twist their fragile ankles during the flight through the jungle. Others are sexy and threatening (Amazon Queens from *She* to *Wonder Woman*) or sexy but ignorant tomboys (as in FORBIDDEN PLANET). Sf cliché CHILDREN are hardly more variable: some are mutant geniuses, possess PSI or magical powers, or prove mankind's only link with alien invaders by virtue of their innocence. With "The Small Assassin" (1946), Ray BRADBURY began a new line of sf cliché kids who, after menacing mankind in many of his stories, turned up to menace again in John WYNDHAM's *The Midwich Cuckoos* (1957; vt *Village of the Damned*) and in the film IT'S ALIVE! Sf cliché machine characters must be comic (in most ASIMOV stories), horrifying (from

The Golem to DR WHO'S DALEKS) or sometimes both (from Nathaniel HAWTHORNE's dancing partner in "The Artist of the Beautiful" (1844), to HAL in *2001*); they are seldom allowed as much thought or emotion as even BUG-EYED MONSTERS or other minatory extraterrestrials. With MONSTERS, giantism, dwarfism, scales, hair, slime, claws and tentacles prevail: H.G. WELLS first used octopuses in "The Sea Raiders" (1897); other writers kept the loathsome tentacle waving for half a century, up to the 3D film IT CAME FROM OUTER SPACE.

Sf cliché plots and plot devices are so numerous that any list must be incomplete. We have the feeble old nightwatchman left to guard the smouldering meteorite crater overnight ("I'll be all right, yessirree"); the doomed society of lotus-eaters; civilization's future depending upon the outcome of a chess game, the answer to a riddle, or the discovery of a simple formula ("a one-in-a-million chance, but so crazy, it just might work!"); shape-shifting aliens ("One of us aboard this ship is not human"); invincible aliens ("the billion-megaton blast had no more effect than the bite of a Sirian flea"); alien invaders finally stopped by ordinary water (as in films of both THE DAY OF THE TRIFFIDS and *The Wizard of Oz*); the android spouse who cuts a finger and bleeds machine-oil; the spouse possessed or hypnotized by aliens ("Darling, you've been acting so strangely since your trip to Ganymede"); disguised alien sniffed out by "his" pet dog, who never acted this way before; destruction of giant computer brain by a simple paradox ("When is a door not a door?"); robot rebellion ("Yes, 'Master'"); a *Doppelgänger* in the corridors of time ("It was — himself!"); Montagues and Capulets living in parallel universes; the evil Master of the World stops to smirk before killing hero; everyone is controlled by alien mind-rays *except one man*; Oedipus kills great-great-grandad; world is saved by instant technology ("It may have looked like just a hunk of breadboard, a few widgets and wires — but wow!"); a youth elixir — but at what terrible price?; thick-headed scientist tampers unwittingly with elemental forces better left in the hands of the Deity; IMMORTALITY tempts Nature to a terrible revenge; monster destroys its creator; dying alien race must breed with earthling models and actresses; superior aliens step in to save mankind from self-destruction (through H-bombs, POLLUTION, fluoridation, decadence); Dr X's laboratory (ISLAND, planet) goes up in flames ...

Pulp can always be recycled. [JS]

CLIFTON, MARK (1906–63). American writer and businessman, for many years occupied in personnel work, putting together many thousands of case histories, from which he extrapolated

conclusions after the fashion of Dr Kinsey and Dr Sheldon (who created somatotypy and its vocabulary of mesomorph, ectomorph, and so on, at about the same point in the history of American statistical psychology); these conclusions MC reportedly used to shape the arguments of his sf, most of which was published in *ASF*, beginning with "What Have I Done?" (1952).

Much of his fiction is comprised of two series. The "Bossy" sequence – "Crazy Joey" (1953) with Alex APOSTOLIDES, "Hide! Hide! Witch!" (1953) with Apostolides and *They'd Rather be Right* (1954 *ASF*; 1957; vt *The Forever Machine*) with Frank RILEY — concerns an advanced COMPUTER named Bossy who is almost made ineffective by the fears of mankind about her, even though she is capable of conferring immortality; *They'd Rather be Right* won the 1955 HUGO award for best novel. MC's second series, the "Ralph Kennedy" stories — "What Thin Partitions" (1953) with Alex Apostolides, "Sense from Thought Divide" (1955), "How Allied" (1957), "Remembrance and Reflection" (1958) and *When They Come from Space* (1962) — is rather lighter in tone, and deals with a typical *ASF* target, inflated Federal bureaucracy. In the novel that concludes the series, the long-suffering Kennedy is appointed "extraterrestrial psychologist", and is forced to deal (successfully it turns out) with a couple of ALIEN INVASIONS.

MC's only out-of-series novel is *Eight Keys to Eden* (1960), in which an E-man, or Extrapolator, is sent to the colony planet of Eden to extract it from an apparently insuperable problem. A collection of MC's stories was published in German, but they remain uncollected in English. Despite a slightly awkward prose, and an occasionally heavy wit, MC's stories and novels convey a comfortable lucidity and optimism about the relation between technology and progress; his attempts to apply the tone of HARDCORE SF to subjects derived from the SOFT SCIENCES reflect *ASF*'s philosophical bent in the 1950s under John W. CAMPBELL Jr's editorial guidance. [JC]

See also: AUTOMATION; COLONIZATION OF OTHER WORLDS; ECOLOGY; FOURTH DIMENSION (AND OTHERS); ICONOCLASM; INTELLIGENCE; LIFE ON OTHER WORLDS; PASTORAL.

CLINGERMAN, MILDRED (McELROY) (1918–). American writer and book-collector; she has never worked as a full-time author. Since beginning to publish her sharply crafted stories in 1952 with "Minister Without Portfolio" for *FSF*, she has been as strongly associated with that magazine as has Zenna HENDERSON. Her collection, *A Cupful of Space* (coll. 1961), reflects this association in the frequency of stories it includes where literacy and a sometimes sentimental cuteness are emphasized. [JC]

See also: WOMEN

CLINTON, DIRK *See* Robert Silverberg.

CLINTON, RUPERT *See* Kenneth Bulmer.

CLIVE, DENNIS *See* John Russell Fearn.

Victim and hoodlum in the near-future film A Clockwork Orange.

CLOCKWORK ORANGE, A Film (1971). Hawk/Warner Bros. Directed by Stanley Kubrick, starring Malcolm McDowell, Patrick Magee, Warren Clarke, Michael Bates and Aubrey Morris. Screenplay by Stanley Kubrick. 137 mins. Colour.

This is a controversial film adaptation of Anthony Burgess's novel about mind control. Alex, a teenage thug of the near future, is cured of his violent ways by a form of aversion therapy, becoming the "clockwork orange" of the title. Burgess's argument was that it is more evil to remove freedom of choice, even from a person like Alex, than to allow him to continue with his anti-social activities. At the end of the film (as in the novel) Alex, for political reasons, is permitted to revert to his former life of rape and violence; it was the apparent glorification of his life-style that provoked so much angry reaction to this film in the press and elsewhere. In fact, the film is not amoral, though its moral is controversial. Basically, *ACO* is a religious allegory, a variation of the Frankenstein theme — it warns Man not to try to compete with God — except that Burgess has reversed the Frankenstein story by saying that it is just as evil to unmake a monster as it is to make one.

As a film, *ACO* is a *tour de force*. Kubrick was in total control of his medium, and deployed a whole spectrum of dazzling cinematic effects. As in 2001: A Space Odyssey, many of the sequences were rendered unusually disturbing by the use of music contrasting wildly with the visual content — Rossini's "The Thieving Magpie" as the background for an attempted rape scene, and Alex's rendition of "Singing in the Rain" while kicking in the ribs of a victim. [JB]

CLONES A clone is a group of individuals comprising the asexually produced offspring of a single individual. A pair of identical twins is a clone because the twin cells are produced by the asexual fission of the fertilized ovum. Asexual reproduction is very common among protozoa and in the animal kingdom, and in some groups of invertebrates, but is much rarer in vertebrates (although the eggs of some amphibians can develop without being fertilized, the parthenogenetic children thus constituting a clone). In the sf genre, however, most cloning is of humans and is the result of a medical operation in which an ovum is enucleated, a somatic cell nucleus from the donor is implanted in its place, and the ovum itself implanted in a uterus. The operation itself has not yet been performed in the real world.

Clones of all degrees of sophistication are by no means uncommon in sf. The replication of individuals by matter-duplicator (*see* MATTER TRANSMISSION), as in William F. Temple's *Four-Sided Triangle* (**1949**) or Fletcher Pratt's *Double Jeopardy* (**1952**), is a kind of cloning. The mechanism by which Gilbert Gosseyn was given so many genetically identical bodies in A.E. van Vogt's *The World of Ā* (1945 *ASF*; **1948**; vt *The World of Null-A*) is not as clear as it might be, but clearly a series of clone members is the result. Replication via TIME PARADOX, as in Robert Heinlein's "By His Bootstraps" (1941 as by Anson MacDonald) or David Gerrold's *The Man Who Folded Himself* (**1973**), is also a kind of cloning. All-female societies which reproduce by parthenogenesis, as in Poul Anderson's *Virgin Planet* (**1959**) or Charles Eric Maine's *World Without Men* (**1958**; rev. vt *Alph* 1972) also consist of clones. In none of these cases, however, is the label "clone" applied. The term was popularized by such books as Gordon Rattray Taylor's *The Biological Time-Bomb* (**1968**), which commented on the implications of experiments carried out by F.C. Steward in the early 1960s. Steward stimulated cells from a mature carrot root to function as reproductive units producing whole new carrot plants. This success revived speculations first advanced by J.B.S. Haldane to the effect that it might be possible to take any cell from a mature human and grow whole, genetically identical individuals — a kind of super-eugenic technique by which geniuses might be duplicated a hundredfold. It is in this connection rather than in its literal meaning that the term was adopted by sf.

Long before the word itself became popular sf writers had considered the possibility of duplicating people in this way. Poul Anderson's "UN-Man" (1953) deals with just such a process, but refers to it as "exogenesis". John Russell Fearn's *The Multi-Man* (**1954** as by Vargo Statten) uses a similar idea. In both stories the idea is used as a gimmick, and the possible consequences of such a development in technology are left unexplored. A more ambitious application of the notion is found in "When You Care, When You Love" (1962) by Theodore Sturgeon, in which a rich woman attempts to reproduce her dead lover by growing him anew from one of the cancer cells which have destroyed him. After Steward's experiments, however, the context of such speculations changed, and the notion began to be used as a premise rather than a *deus ex machina*.

"It is not mere sensationalism," wrote Taylor in *The Biological Time-Bomb*, "to ask whether the members of human clones may feel particularly united, and be able to co-operate better, even if they are not in actual supersensory communication with one another." This is the question that has been asked in such stories as Ursula K. Le Guin's "Nine Lives" (1969), Pamela Sargent's *Cloned Lives* (**1976**) and Kate Wilhelm's *Where Late the Sweet Birds Sang* (**1976**), in which intimate human relations are explored in depth and with some sensitivity. These stories — except perhaps Sargent's — probably exaggerate the psychological effects of growing up as one of a clone. After all, identical twins have been doing it for centuries. (Even though clones of the same cell would be genetically identical, from the moment of implantation, whether in an artificial or a real uterus, each clone member would inhabit a different environment from its twins, so that even by the moment of birth its development would have been unique; only a very naïve genetic determinism could argue that an adult donor and his environmentally differentiated twins are identical entities. One of the few sf novels to try to take this fact into account is Ira Levin's *The Boys from Brazil*, **1976**, in which a neo-Nazi conspiracy tries to raise a batch of clones derived from Adolf Hitler in the same kind of environment Hitler himself experienced.) But even if the concept of clone-identity is considered as a metaphor these investigations by Le Guin, Sargent and Wilhelm are still significant in posing questions about the nature of individuality and the possibilities implicit in human relationships. All three of these authors are women, as are the authors of two further clone stories: Haldane's sister Naomi Mitchison offers a rather unsettling DYSTOPIAN vision in *Solution Three* (**1975**) and Nancy Freedman adopts a rather more sensational approach in *Joshua, Son of None* (**1973**), which takes as its premise the proposition that cells taken from John F. Kennedy at the time of his assassination might have been used to clone a duplicate.

Whether the apparent differentiation in attitudes to clones according to the sex of the author is significant must remain conjectural. With one outstanding exception male authors have used the notion of cloning more conventionally, generally as an apparatus for establishing dramatic confrontations. In Richard Cowper's *Clone* (**1972**) a clone of children proves to have awesome supernatural powers; they are therefore separated and their memories partially erased. The novel is a semi-satirical account of events following one child's recovery of his memory. In Norman SPINRAD's *The Iron Dream* (**1972**) the narcissistic aspect of clonal reproduction is recruited by Adolf Hitler in his sf power-fantasy "Lord of the Swastika": as the Earth dies ships blast off for the stars to populate the galaxy with duplicates of the hero. Cloning is used in *Imperial Earth* (**1975**) by Arthur C. CLARKE to perpetuate a dynasty on Titan. Ben BOVA's *The Multiple Man* (**1976**) is a thriller in which the clonal duplicates of the US President keep turning up dead — a murder mystery recalling Maurice RENARD and Albert-Jean's *Le singe* (**1925**; trans. as *Blind Circle* **1928**). John VARLEY's *The Ophiuchi Hotline* (**1977**), however, uses cloning without melodramatic confrontations in an intelligent SPACE-OPERA format. The exception to the usual conventionality is Gene WOLFE's remarkable *The Fifth Head of Cerberus* (**1972**), whose first section — originally an independent novelette — concerns the experiences of a child whose father (actually his clone-parent) studies him intensively in a strangely obsessive quest for self-knowledge.

It should be noted that *The Clone* (**1965**) by Theodore L. THOMAS and Kate Wilhelm is not, in the modern sense of the word, a clone novel at all. A now obsolete dictionary definition of "clone" is used as epigraph to this entertaining story of an ever growing monster in the sewers, but is mystifyingly not adhered to.

The idea of another self — an *alter ego* or *Doppelgänger* — has always been a profoundly fascinating one, and recurs insistently in occult fantasy and psychology. Recent theorizing about the cloning of humans has made the notion available to sf writers for detailed and intensive speculation, and while this speculation probably has no predictive value it is of considerable psychological interest. [BS]

See also: BIOLOGY; CHILDREN IN SF; GENETIC ENGINEERING; MEDICINE; PSYCHOLOGY.

CLOSE ENCOUNTERS OF THE THIRD KIND Film (1977). Columbia.

Directed by Steven Spielberg, starring Richard Dreyfuss, François Truffaut, Teri Garr, Melinda Dillon, Gary Guffey and Bob Balaban. Screenplay by Steven Spielberg. 135 mins. Colour.

After STAR WARS came the second major sf film production of 1977, though at over twice the cost and with a story that lacked the comic-book appeal of *Star Wars*. A power company technician witnesses a series of UFO appearances and becomes obsessed with FLYING SAUCERS. He develops a fixation about an oddly shaped mountain in Wyoming and is convinced that the aliens plan to land one of their vehicles on it. A parallel plot concerns a mysterious group of scientific and military experts also engaged in uncovering the secret of the UFOs. The film ends in a barrage of special effects; communication between the two species is actually achieved, taking the form of bursts of light and music. The film is flawed but remains an interesting and often evocative work, not easily pigeon-holed as a genre movie. Despite the pressure from Columbia to produce a financial blockbuster, Spielberg did not take the easy way out, but made a relatively complex and intelligent film, maintaining the high standard he set himself in DUEL, *Sugarland Express* and *Jaws*. Nonetheless, the special effects are the high point of the film for most, and they are indeed spectacular, particularly in the sequence where the alien mother ship lands. Part model and part full-scale construction, this was the creation of special-effects expert Douglas TRUMBULL. There is a mood of optimism in the final sequences, a rare ingredient in sf cinema.

The novelization, *Close Encounters of the Third Kind* (**1977**) is by Spielberg. [JB]

CLOUSTON, J(OSEPH) STORER (1870–1944). Scottish magistrate and author. Basically HUMOROUS in his approach, JSC began writing with *Tales of King Fido* (coll. **1909**), a Graustarkian fantasy. He later appeared in ALL-STORY WEEKLY with "Two's Two" (1916), about an embodied *alter ego*. Other works include the ROBOT novel *Button Brains* (**1933**), *The Chemical Baby* (**1934**), *Not Since Genesis* (**1938**) — a satirical look at the European nations faced by a meteorite catastrophe — and *The Man In Steel* (**1939**). [JE]

CLUTE, JOHN (1940–). Canadian novelist, sf critic; in England from 1969. His first sf story, "A Man Must Die" (1966), was published in *New Worlds*, where he also published much of his later criticism; some has also appeared in *FSF*. JC's body of criticism has emphasized the tropes (recurrent metaphors and/or narrative structures) of sf to a degree unprecedented in sf criticism, probably usefully, but with some adverse comment from hardcore sf fans. He is associate editor of this Encyclopedia. A novel, *The Disinheriting Party* (1973 *NW*; exp. **1977**), is not sf. [PN]

See also: DEFINITIONS OF SF.

COATES, ROBERT M(YRON) (1897–1973). American writer, primarily associated through his career with *The New Yorker*, on which he worked, and to which he contributed many stories. He is primarily of interest to the sf field for his first novel, *The Eater of Darkness* (**1929**), which, written before he had fully assimilated the sometimes restrictive urbanity of *New Yorker* style, quite brilliantly applies a wide arsenal of literary devices, some of them surrealistic, to the exaggeratedly spoof-like tale of a master criminal, and his absurd super-WEAPON which sees through solids and applies remote-control heat to kill people invisibly; all the same, beneath the spoofing and the cosmopolitan style lies a sense of horror. RMC's collection, *The Hour After Westerly and Other Stories* (coll. **1957**), contains some fantasy of interest, though in general his later work has nothing of the fire of his first book. [JC]

Other works: *The Farther Shore* (**1955**).

COBLENTZ, STANTON A(RTHUR) (1896–). American novelist and polemically traditionalist poet, who began his career in the early 1920s, after gaining an MA in English literature, with book

Richard Dreyfuss, the UFO-obsessed hero of CLOSE ENCOUNTERS OF THE THIRD KIND, models the mountain he dreams of.

reviews for New York papers and a volume of poems, *The Thinker and Other Poems* (coll. **1923**); over his career, he has also written considerable non-fiction. He began publishing sf with *The Sunken World* (1928 *AMZ Quarterly*; **1949**), a UTOPIA set in a glass-domed ATLANTIS, in which SATIRICAL points are made both against the egalitarian Atlanteans and contemporary America, though the obtuse narrator (who is of course typical of most Utopias) tends to blur some of these issues. SAC has never been a smooth stylist, nor an imaginative plotter, as all his five novels for *AMZ Quarterly* tend to show, though at the same time he has a strong gift for the description of ingeniously conceived ALIEN environments, so that he is often regarded as one of the writers best capable of conveying the sense of wonder so rightly valued by the readers of American PULP sf between the Wars. After *The Sunken World* appeared *After 12,000 Years* (1929 *AMZ Quarterly*; **1950**), "Reclaimers of the Ice" (1930 *AMZ Quarterly*), *The Blue Barbarians* (1931 *AMZ Quarterly*; **1958**) and "The Man from Tomorrow" (1933 *AMZ Quarterly*). Other novels from the same general period, like *The Wonder Stick* (**1929**), a prehistoric tale, and *Hidden World* (1935 *Wonder Stories* as "In Caverns Below"; **1957**; vt *In Caverns Below*), shared similar virtues and faults. *Hidden World*, for instance, is also a satire, set in an underground venue, with fascinating descriptions but cardboard characters. Later novels, like *Under the Triple Suns* (**1955**), failed to show much stylistic development, and were not successful.   [JC]
Other works: *The Pageant of Man* (**1936**); *When the Birds Fly South* (**1945**); *Into Plutonian Depths* (1931 *Wonder Stories Quarterly*; **1950**); *The Planet of Youth* (1932 *Wonder Stories*; vt "Youth Madness" 1945 *American Fiction*; **1952**); *Next Door to the Sun* (**1960**); *The Runaway World* (**1961**); *The Moon People* (**1964**); *The Last of the Great Race* (**1964**) and *The Lost Comet* (**1964**), both apparently severely edited; *The Lizard Lords* (**1964**); *Lord of Tranerica* (1939 *Dynamic Science Stories*; **1966**); *The Crimson Capsule* (**1967**; vt *The Animal People*); *The Day the World Stopped* (**1968**); *The Island People* (**1971**).
See also: ASTEROIDS; LOST WORLDS; OUTER PLANETS; POLITICS; SOCIOLOGY; UNDER THE SEA; VENUS.

COGSWELL, THEODORE R(OSE) (1918–). American writer and academic, an ambulance driver on the Republican side in the Spanish Civil War; he began publishing sf with one of his most successful stories to date, "The Specter General" for *ASF* in 1952. In this long, amusing story, much in the vein Keith LAUMER was later to make his own, a long-forgotten maintenance division of the Galactic Protectorate reinvigorates a decadent Space Navy. TRC's two

volumes of stories, *The Wall Around the World* (coll. **1962**) and *The Third Eye* (coll. **1968**), contain most of the fiction he has written; his work is polished, enjoyable and, though it sticks closely to fantasy and sf genre formats, gives off the sense that it was written for pleasure.
"The Wall Around the World" (1953) is one of TRC's most popular stories; its tale of a boy who lives in a place where magic seems to work, and discovers the true nature of his world, is an archetypal story of CONCEPTUAL BREAKTHROUGH. TRC appears very frequently in sf anthologies; along with Henry KUTTNER and William TENN, he is a writer who excels at the short-story length, but has been possibly neglected because of his lack of interest in longer forms.   [JC/PN]
Other works: A STAR TREK novelization, *Spock, Messiah!* (**1976**) with Charles A. Spano.
See also: SUPERNATURAL CREATURES; TECHNOLOGY.

COLD NIGHT'S DEATH, A Made-for-TV film (1975). Spelling Goldberg/ABC. Directed by Jerrold Freedman, starring Eli Wallach and Robert Culp. Teleplay by Christopher Knopff. 95 mins. Colour.
This very slow-moving TV film concerns two scientists in a remote Arctic station whose test animals, chimpanzees, turn the tables and start experimenting on the scientists themselves.   [JB]

COLE, BURT Pseudonym of American writer Thomas Dixon (1930–), author of the sf novel *The Funco File* (**1969**), in which a world-dominating COMPUTER is pitted against anarchic opposing forces, and the NEAR-FUTURE story *Subi: The Volcano* (**1957**).   [JC]

COLE, CYRUS (? – ?). American author, working from Kansas. In his *The Auroraphone* (**1890**) messages are received on the eponymous instrument from Saturn, where life is UTOPIAN in many ways, though a robot revolt is under way. A later message includes a replay of recordings, for the benefit of the enthralled Earth listeners, of famous events on Earth, including the battle of Gettysburg. This work is discussed in "Three Kansas Utopian Novels of 1890" by Ben Fuson in EXTRAPOLATION, Dec. 1970.   [PN]

COLE, EVERETT B. (1910–). American writer, formerly a professional soldier. He began publishing sf in 1951 with the first of a series, "Philosophical Corps", in *ASF*, where the remainder of the series also appeared to its conclusion in 1956. *The Philosophical Corps* (1951–5 *ASF*; fix-up **1961**) is based on the first story and two others; the remaining stories are "These Shall Not be Lost" (1953), "Exile" (1954), "Millenium" (1955), "Final Weapon" (1955) and "The Missionaries" (1956). The Philosopher

protagonist of the series, Commander A-Riman, brooks no nonsense from aliens and the like, whom he re-educates in his SPACE-OPERA adventures. A second novel, "The Best Made Plans" (*ASF* 1959) has not reached book form.   [JC]

COLE, ROBERT W(ILLIAM) (?–?). British author. In his first novel, *The Struggle For Empire: a Story Of The Year 2236* (**1900**), RWC took the future-WAR novel to its logical conclusion. Set in a UTOPIAN future when the Anglo-Saxon Federation has expanded into other solar systems, interstellar warfare breaks out between Earth and a superior race from the Sirius system. In its descriptions of space battles and of an Earth surrounded by a barrage of space torpedoes and mines while scientists struggle to perfect the ultimate weapon, it is the equal of many of the SPACE-OPERA stories of the 1930s. RWC's later novels are anti-climactic; *The Death Trap* (**1907**) is a mundane account of an invasion of Britain; *His Other Self* (**1906**) is a mildly humorous novel of a physical *alter ego*; *The Artificial Girl* (**1908**) is not a fantasy novel.   [JC]
See also: COLONIZATION OF OTHER WORLDS; FANTASTIC VOYAGES; GALACTIC EMPIRES; STARS.

COLE, WALTER R(ANDALL) (1933–). American sf bibliographer, compiler of the badly laid-out but extremely useful *A Checklist of Science-Fiction Anthologies* (**1964**), which was re-issued in facsimile — it was originally stencilled — by ARNO PRESS in 1974. [PN]
See also: ANTHOLOGIES.

COLEMAN, JAMES NELSON (?–). American writer of two sf novels, *Seeker from the Stars* (**1967**) and *The Null-Frequency Impulser* (**1969**). They are both routine adventure stories, with ALIENS and super-science providing much of the action.   [JC]

COLERIDGE, JOHN See Eando BINDER.

COLIN, VLADIMIR See EASTERN EUROPE.

COLLAPSARS See BLACK HOLES.

COLLIER, JOHN (1901–). English novelist, poet and short-story writer; he has spent time in America writing filmscripts as well. He is known mainly for his sophisticated though sometimes rather precious short stories, generally featuring acerbic snap endings; many of these stories have a strong fantasy element, including *No Traveller Returns* (**1931**), which is not a full-length book, and one collection, *The Devil and All* (coll. **1935**), which is exclusively devoted to tales of this sort. His best-known assemblage, *Fancies and Goodnights* (coll. **1951**; vt abridged *Of Demons and*

Darkness UK), puts together new material plus a selection of tales from *Presenting Moonshine* (coll. **1941**) and *The Touch of Nutmeg* (coll. **1943**); it is a handy compendium, along with the later *The John Collier Reader* (coll. **1972**), of the various kinds of short fiction with which JC has been identified: highly polished magazine stories, adroit, world-weary, waspish, often insubstantial. *Fancies and Goodnights* won the first INTERNATIONAL FANTASY AWARD.

Radically dissimilar to his most familiar work is the remarkably effective post-DISASTER novel, *Tom's A-Cold* (**1933**; vt *Full Circle* USA), set in the 1990s, long after an unexplained disaster has decimated England's (and presumably the world's) population, thrusting mankind back into rural barbarism, a condition out of which the eldest survivors, who remember civilization, are trying to educate the young third generation. The simple plot plays no tricks on the reader; the young protagonist, a born leader, during the course of a raid to abduct women from another tribe, and through various conflicts within his own settlement, assumes the chieftainship, undergoes a tragedy, and seems reconciled by the novel's close to the burdens of a meliorist government. JC weaves a good deal of cultural and political speculation into this story; very movingly, he renders the reborn, circumambient natural world with a hallucinatory visual intensity found nowhere else in his work. Along with Alun LLEWELLYN's *The Strange Invaders* (**1934**), *Tom's A-Cold* can be seen, in its atmosphere of almost loving conviction, as a genuine successor to Richard JEFFERIES' *After London* (**1885**). [JC] **Other works:** *His Monkey Wife: or Married to a Chimp* (**1930**), not sf; *Green Thoughts* (**1932**) and *Variations on a Theme* (**1935**) — two more separate editions of short stories later included in various JC collections, among them *Green Thoughts and other Strange Tales* (coll. undated); *Pictures in the Fire* (coll. **1958**). **See also:** HOLOCAUST AND AFTER; HUMOUR; SATIRE.

COLLIER'S WEEKLY US "slick" magazine published by Crowell-Collier Publishing Co., ed. William L. Chenery, Walter Davenport and others. Weekly from 28 Apr. 1888 as *Collier's Once A Week*, became *CW* in Dec. 1904, continuing weekly to 25 Jul. 1953, then bi-weekly to 4 Jan. 1957.

CW published sf only intermittently, e.g. H.G. WELLS's "A Moonlight Fable" (1909) and George Allan ENGLAND's "June 6, 2016" (1916), until the 1920s and '30s when numerous serializations of works by Sax ROHMER appeared. Its best-remembered sf publications were "There Will Come Soft Rains" (1950), "A Sound of Thunder" (1952), and other stories by Ray BRADBURY. [JE]

COLLINGWOOD, HARRY See UNDER THE SEA.

COLLINS, CLARK See Mack REYNOLDS.

COLLINS, HUNT See Evan HUNTER.

COLLINS, MICHAEL Pseudonym of American writer Dennis Lynds (1930–), better known for his detective work than his sf, which is restricted to a SPACE OPERA, *Lukan War* (**1969**), and *The Planets of Death* (**1970**). [JC]

COLONIZATION OF OTHER WORLDS This is one of the few themes which has been developed solely by writers working under the sf label. The idea of space colonization was raised by Konstantin TSIOLKOVSKY, the pioneer of rocket research, but his main proposal was to build artificial satellites for orbital colonies. Both J.B.S. HALDANE in "The Last Judgment" (1927) and Olaf STAPLEDON in *Last and First Men* (**1930**) imagined Man migrating to other worlds, but only as Earth became uninhabitable. H.G. WELLS used the example of Britain's colonial history as an analogy for the Martians' conduct in *The War of the Worlds* (**1898**) but never considered the idea of Man's colonizing Mars. The only early writer who did apply the analogy to the human conquest of space was Robert William COLE in *The Struggle for Empire* (**1900**).

The avoidance of this particular notion may be connected with a certain sense of shame about the methods employed in colonizing the distant lands of the Earth. The parallel which Wells drew between the European invasion of Tasmania and the Martian invasion of Earth is a harsh one, and the brutality of the POLITICS of colonization has always been a key issue in sf stories on the theme, from Edmond HAMILTON's early "Conquest of Two Worlds" (1932) and Robert HEINLEIN's grim "Logic of Empire" (1941) through such lurid polemics as Avram DAVIDSON's "Now Let Us Sleep" (1957) and Robert SILVERBERG's *Invaders From Earth* (**1958**) to such effective moral tales as Silverberg's *Downward to the Earth* (**1970**) and Ursula K. LE GUIN's *The Word for World is Forest* (1972; **1976**). These stories of genocide, slavery and exploitation represent the harshest critiques of human behaviour found in sf (although the tough-minded Heinlein is careful to stress necessity) and it is not difficult to see in the plight of the various victims echoes of the Tasmanians or the North American Indians.

Political issues are also the focus of attention in another recurrent colonization theme, which deals with the relationship between the colony and the mother world. Here history provides — at least for American writers — much more attractive parallels, and the war of independence has been fought

continually in sf, from the early "Birth of a New Republic" (1930) by Miles J. BREUER and Jack WILLIAMSON to Isaac ASIMOV's "The Martian Way" (1952), Robert Heinlein's *The Moon is a Harsh Mistress* (**1966**) and Poul ANDERSON's *Tales of the Flying Mountains* (coll. **1970**).

The pioneer spirit is something much celebrated in sf at all levels. The myth of the conquest of the Old West by the pioneer spirit is often transcribed into sf so literally that even the covered wagon is retained. (AMAZING STORIES once published a Western novel — "Outlaw in the Sky", 1953, by Guy ARCHETTE — in which only half a dozen words had been modified in making the transposition to sf.) A recent example is the pioneering sequence of Robert Heinlein's *Time Enough For Love* (**1973**). Celebrations of the heroism of colonists fighting tremendous odds to tame hostile environments include Henry KUTTNER's *Fury* (**1950**; vt *Destination: Infinity*), Walter M. MILLER's "Crucifixus Etiam" (1953), E.C. TUBB's *Alien Dust* (**1955**) and Harry HARRISON's *Deathworld* (**1960**). It is often difficult to offer a convincing explanation of the motivation of the colonists, and forced colonization of various kinds is common, as in *The Survivors* (**1958**; vt *Space Prison*) by Tom GODWIN, *The Status Civilization* (**1960**) by Robert SHECKLEY, *Orbit Unlimited* (**1961**) by Poul Anderson, *Mutiny in Space* (**1964**) by Avram Davidson, *Castaways' World* (**1963**) by John BRUNNER and *Farewell Earth's Bliss* (**1966**) by D.G. COMPTON.

It is possible to identify two schools of colonization story in sf — the "romantic" and the "realistic". The romantic school derives from a tradition which makes much of the exotic qualities of alien environments. Here the alien worlds are exotic Earths, little different from distant lands of travellers' tales. Human and humanoid alien co-exist. The politics of exploitation is not the focal point of the story but may serve to turn the wheels of the plot as the hero, alienated from his own kind, champions the downtrodden natives against the horrors of vulgar commercialism. Women writers have been particularly prolific in this vein: Leigh BRACKETT has often used it, as has Marion Zimmer BRADLEY in her "Darkover" novels. Anne McCAFFREY's "Pern" novels also belong to the romantic school, and Jack VANCE has written a large number of novels featuring a less stylized romanticism. Recent examples often emphasize quasi-mystical processes of adaptation to the alien environment: a reharmonization of Man and nature which often covertly echoes the Eden myth (*see* ECOLOGY and LIFE ON OTHER WORLDS). A simple example is *Outpost Mars* (**1952**; vt *Sin in Space*) by Cyril JUDD, and a more complex one is *Eight Keys to Eden* (**1960**) by Mark CLIFTON. The archetype of the species is Ray BRADBURY's "The Million-Year

Picnic" (1946). Some of the most impressive works in the romantic vein are Cordwainer SMITH's stories of Old North Australia and his *Quest of the Three Worlds* (fix-up **1966**). The image of a lost Eden plays an important part in many of the otherwise tough and realistic colonization novels of Michael CONEY, and does much to give them their characteristic overtone of plangent nostalgia. These works include *Mirror Image* (**1972**), *Syzygy* (**1973**) and *Brontomek!* (**1976**).

The "realist" school, concentrating on blood, sweat and tears rather than glamorous exotica, developed in the post War era, though it is interesting to note that Edmond Hamilton's short story, archetypal of the species, "What's It Like Out There?" (1952), was actually written in the 1930s but failed to find a market then. In fact, the realist school won its early successes outside the sf magazines, being extensively developed by Robert Heinlein and Arthur C. CLARKE in stories published in general fiction magazines and in novels, many written for the juvenile market. Heinlein's contributions include *Red Planet* (**1949**), *Farmer in the Sky* (**1950**) and many of the stories in *The Green Hills of Earth* (coll. **1951**). Clarke's include the "Venture to the Moon" series of vignettes from the London *Evening Standard* and the novels *Sands of Mars* (**1951**) and *Earthlight* (**1955**). Patrick MOORE's series of juvenile novels, including *Domes of Mars* (**1956**) and *Voices of Mars* (**1957**), also belong to this tradition. These juvenile novels take great pains to achieve some kind of authenticity, but "realism" in the magazines was much more a matter of literary posturing, consisting mainly of ultra-tough novels with a strong seasoning of cynicism. *Police Your Planet* (**1956** as by Erik van Lhin; rev. 1975) by Lester DEL REY is a cardinal example. It is not immediately clear why genuine realism should be considered unsuitable for an adult audience. Realistic treatment of colonization methods remains a common theme in sf; it plays a subsidiary but important role, for example, in *Mindbridge* (**1976**) by Joe HALDEMAN and *Gateway* (**1977**) by Frederik POHL.

A very common sub-theme found in colonization stories deals with native populations which resist colonization, sometimes consciously, and sometimes through the fact that the ECOLOGY of the planet has no suitable niche for the colonists. Many of Poul Anderson's stories fall into this category, as do "You'll Never Go Home Again" (1951; vt "Beachhead") and "Drop Dead" (1956) by Clifford D. SIMAK, and "Colony" (1953) by Philip K. DICK.

Moving on from stories which deal with the actual process of colonization: one of the most significant uses which sf writers have found for human colonies on alien worlds is in building distorted societies, sometimes for satirical purposes

(*see* SATIRE) and sometimes for thought experiments in SOCIOLOGY. The most notable satirical exercise is *Search the Sky* (**1954**) by Frederik Pohl and C.M. KORNBLUTH, and others are *The Perfect Planet* (**1962**) by Evelyn E. SMITH, *A Planet for Texans* (**1958**) by H. Beam PIPER and John J. McGUIRE and many short stories by Eric Frank RUSSELL, including the justly celebrated "... And Then There Were None" (1951). More straightforward, sociological treatments include Poul Anderson's *Virgin Planet* (**1959**), John JAKES's *Mask of Chaos* (**1970**), Harry Harrison's *Planet of the Damned* (**1962**, vt *Sense of Obligation*) and such remarkable recent novels as *The Left Hand of Darkness* (**1969**) by Ursula K. Le Guin, *The Fifth Head of Cerberus* (**1972**) by Gene WOLFE and *And Chaos Died* (**1970**) by Joanna Russ. In many of these stories the colonies are isolated worlds within the GALACTIC-EMPIRE framework. The notion of an extended chain of colony worlds is used in A. Bertram CHANDLER's "Rim Worlds" novels and Murray LEINSTER's "Med Ship" stories.

For obvious reasons, relatively little attention has been given to the problems of colonizing other worlds radically unlike Earth (though *see* TERRAFORMING). The idea of applying biological engineering methods to colonization was used by James BLISH in the stories making up *The Seedling Stars* (fix-up **1957**) and by Poul Anderson in "Call Me Joe" (1957), and has been investigated in more detail by Frederik Pohl in *Man Plus* (**1976**). Increasing interest in GENETIC ENGINEERING may make this area of speculation more popular in the future.

A theme anthology of interest is the "Twayne Triplet" (three stories commissioned by the publisher on the same theme) *The Petrified Planet* (anth. **1952**) containing the novellas "Daughters of Earth" by Judith MERRIL, "The Long View" by Fletcher PRATT and "Ullr Uprising" by H. Beam Piper — about various stages in the development of a colony on a rather bleak world.　　[BS]
See also: GENERATION STARSHIPS.

COLOSSUS OF NEW YORK, THE
Film (1958). William Alland Productions/Paramount. Directed by Eugène Lourié, starring John Baragrey, Mala Powers, Otto Kruger, Charles Herbert and Ed Wolff. Screenplay by Thelma Schnee, based on a story by Willis Goldbeck. 70 mins. B/w.

This is a curious little film about a man whose brain is transferred into a 12-foot-high robot body. His mind, not surprisingly, is unhinged and he becomes a menace which must be destroyed. Some pathos is seen in the situation, in particular the scenes dealing with the robot's relationship with a young boy. The credit list reads like a *Who's Who* of sf cinema: William Alland, who independently produced it, was the

The Colossus and friend.

producer of most of Universal's sf films during the 1950s (IT CAME FROM OUTER SPACE etc.); Eugène Lourié had previously directed THE BEAST FROM 20,000 FATHOMS; art director Hal Pereira had been the designer on WAR OF THE WORLDS; special-effects man John P. Fulton was best known for his effects in THE INVISIBLE MAN and its sequels.　　[JB]

COLOSSUS, THE FORBIN PROJECT (vt **THE FORBIN PROJECT** UK) Film (1969). Universal. Directed by Joseph Sargent, starring Eric Braeden, Susan Clark, Gordon Pinsent and William Schallert. Screenplay by James Bridges, based on the novel *Colossus* by D.F. JONES. 100 mins. Colour.

A super computer, Colossus, is designed by Dr Forbin to take control of the US defence network, the decision to launch a nuclear attack being too important to be left to mere mortals; but it develops ambitions of its own once it is activated, and ignores all commands. Unlike the neurotic HAL in 2001: A SPACE ODYSSEY, Colossus is a computer of the old school — emotionless, arrogant and practically omnipotent. It forms an alliance with its Russian equivalent and the film ends with the two computers in charge and likely to stay that way.

The film effectively communicates a feeling that something unbelievably powerful has got out of control. This is chillingly established in the opening sequence, in which we are shown the vast interior of Colossus coming alive, section by section, before being irreversibly sealed off from attack within the bowels of the Rocky Mountains.　　[JB]

COLVIN, IAN (1912–75). British writer and journalist. His sf novel is *Domesday Village* (**1948**), set in a NEAR-FUTURE Britain with a socialist regime.　　[JC]

COLVIN, JAMES House name of *New Worlds*, primarily used by Michael MOORCOCK, but occasionally by others on book reviews.

Mar. 1941. Cover by Leo Morey.

COMET STORIES US PULP magazine. Five issues, Dec. 1940-Jul. 1941, bimonthly after Jan. 1941. Published by H-K Publications; ed. F. Orlin TREMAINE.

Tremaine, former editor of ASTOUNDING STORIES, made a brief and undistinguished return to sf magazine editing with this title. The contributors included such writers as Eando BINDER, Frank Belknap LONG and Harl VINCENT. The last issue contained "The Vortex Blaster", the first story of E.E. SMITH's series of that name. A continuing feature was "The Spacean", an imaginary future newspaper which betrayed the magazine's juvenile slant. *CS* had little visual appeal; its cover layout was particularly ungainly.   [MJE]

COMIC STRIPS AND COMIC BOOKS This rubric covers the comic strip in daily and Sunday newspapers, European comic papers and the American-style comic book. Strips which carry text in panels adjacent to the illustrated panel are not differentiated from those which incorporate "word balloons" into the pictorial presentation.

Although comic papers and Sunday newspaper supplements appeared at the end of the 19th century during a boom in sf, it was to be 30 years before they presented sf themes in a credible manner. Prior to this the emphasis on humour in the comic strips had relegated sf to the realms of fantasy, as in *Our Office Boy's Fairy Tales* (1895 *The Funny Wonder*), an anonymous British series depicting a family on Mars facing totally impossible hardships and jubilations. More mature in its approach was Winsor McCay's *Little Nemo In Slumberland* (1905–11 *The New York Herald*) which depicted the nightly adventures of a young boy who developed greater self-awareness through exploration of his dream worlds. McCay's manipulation of the size, shape and position of each panel, together with his use of perspective, gave added emphasis to the narrative and indicated how artistic technique could augment the text. This attribute of the comic strip was sometimes used to create the fantasy element, as in Herriman's *Krazy Kat* (1911–44) where the scenic background, ever changing from panel to panel, created a surrealistically alien environment, or in Pat Sullivan's *Felix The Cat* (1921 onwards) where the eponymous feline gave substance to his imagination by treating the contents of his thought balloons as physical realities.

In the 1920s, when economic depression brought about a change in public outlook, a demand was created for action adventure strips, making publication of outright sf comic strips feasible. The transition came with BUCK ROGERS (1929–67), an adult comic strip inspired by a novel in AMAZING STORIES, which inspired several rivals, among them FLASH GORDON (1934 onwards), BRICK BRADFORD (1933 onwards) and *Speed Spaulding* (1939), an adaptation of Edwin BALMER and Philip WYLIE's *When Worlds Collide* (**1933**), illustrated by Marvin Bradley. These all drew their plots extensively from the epics of classical literature, modernized by the inclusion of spaceships and ray-guns, and distanced from reality by being located in the far future or remote past.

Similar innovations occurred in Europe following the reprintings there of the major US comic strips. High points were the appearances in France of *Futuropolis* (1937–8 *Junior*) and *Electropolis* (1939 *Jean-Pierre*), both written and illustrated by René Pellos; in Italy of *Saturno Contro la Terra* (1937–43), written by F. Pedrocchi and illustrated by G. Scolari, and in Britain of GARTH (1943 onwards), written and illustrated by Steve Dowling.

This growth in the number of sf comic strips was, however, more a reflection of the increased number of comic strips in general, now so popular in America that new methods of packaging them were being explored. Out of this experimentation developed the comic book. Initially containing reprints of the newspaper strips, e.g. *Buck Rogers* in *Famous Funnies* (1934–55) and *Flash Gordon* and *Brick Bradford* in *King Comics* (1936–51), available strips were soon utilized and comic books featuring original strips were the inevitable second stage. In the first issue of one of these new titles, *Action Comics* (1938 onwards), SUPERMAN appeared. Featuring a larger-than-life figure, omnipotent in the face of all adversity, *Superman* (1939 onwards) proved so popular that numerous imitations appeared from *Batman* through CAPTAIN MARVEL to many heroes featured by the modern MARVEL COMICS group, all being variations of the same basic theme. In many of these titles the central sf story was backed up with strips from outside the genre, but some comics were entirely devoted to sf. The first sf comic book was *Amazing Mystery Funnies* (1938–40), which contained a pot-pourri of superhero and SPACE-OPERA strips with artists including Bill Everett, Will Eisner and Basil Wolverton. Hugo GERNSBACK briefly entered the field with *Superworld Comics* (1939). *Buck Rogers* (1940–43) and *Flash Gordon* (intermittently, 1943–53) also appeared as titles. Most successful was *Planet Comics* (1940–54), a companion to PLANET STORIES, which featured *Star Pirate* by Murphy Anderson, *Lost World* by George Evans, *Auro, Lord of Jupiter* by Graham Ingels, and other memorable strips.

In such a competitive market it was inevitable that publishers would turn to sf FANDOM for help. National Periodicals offered Mort WEISINGER, then editor of THRILLING WONDER STORIES, an editorial post. Accepting it, he worked initially on *Superman*, using authors of the calibre of Alfred BESTER, Henry KUTTNER, Edmond HAMILTON and Manly Wade WELLMAN to help compete with the rival publication, *Captain Marvel*, scripted by Otto BINDER. Well-known artists from the sf magazines were also used. Alex SCHOMBURG appeared in *Startling Comics* (1940–48) and *Thrilling Comics* (1940–51), Edd CARTIER in *Shadow Comics* (1940–50) and *Red Dragon*, second series (1947–51) and Virgil FINLAY in *Real Fact Comics* (1946–9). Similarly in Britain Serge Drigin, artist on SCOOPS and FANTASY, illustrated "Space Police" (1940 *Everyday Novels and Comics*).

By the early 1950s numerous sf comic books were appearing, among them *Lars of Mars* (1951) and *Space Patrol* (1952), (both issued by Ziff-Davis, publishers of AMAZING STORIES and FANTASTIC ADVENTURES), *Rocket To The Moon* (1951) and *An Earthman On Venus* (1952) (both published by Avon and respectively featuring adaptations of Otis Adelbert KLINE's *Maza of the Moon*, **1930**, and Ralph Milne FARLEY's *The Radio Man*, 1924 *Argosy All-Story Weekly*; **1948**; vt *An Earthman On Venus*), and an anti-communist propaganda sf comic book, *Is This Tomorrow?* (1947). More durable were *Mystery in Space* (1951–66), *Strange Adventures* (1950–73) and *Forbidden Worlds* (1951–67) which all showed originality in their story presentations and carried notable artwork by Jack KIRBY, Al Williamson and others. At the same time new sf comic strips were appearing in newspapers, two of the better titles being *Beyond Mars* (1951–3 *The New York Sunday News*), scripted by Jack WILLIAMSON from his novels *Seetee Shock* (**1950**) and *Seetee Ship* (**1951**), with illustrations by Lee Elias, and *Twin Earths* (1951–4), a counter-Earth story written and created by Oskar Lebeck and illustrated by Alden McWilliams. The most important of this period, however, were the sf comic books published by E.C. Comics.

Appearing initially at the suggestion of Harry HARRISON, who had been working in comics as artist and scriptwriter since 1946, *Weird Fantasy* (1950–53), *Weird Science* (1950–53), *Weird Science-Fantasy* (1954–5) and *Incredible Science Fiction* (1955–6) published the most sophisticated sf stories yet to appear in the comic books, often featuring wry endings in the manner of Philip K. DICK. Illustrated by such well-known sf artists as Al Williamson, Frank FRAZETTA, Roy KRENKEL, George Evans and Wallace Wood, they often included adaptations of stories by popular sf authors, in particular Ray BRADBURY, whose adaptations were collected in *The Autumn People* (1953–5 var. comics; coll. **1965**). With the imposition of the Comics Code in 1955, these and many other titles ceased, and comics then went through a period of restraint and unoriginality.

A similar boom in sf comic books was taking place in Europe. Included in these titles were *Super Science Thrills* (1945), *Tit-Bits Science Fiction Comics* (1953) and *The Jet Comic* (1953), a companion to AUTHENTIC SCIENCE FICTION, which appeared in Britain, and *Espace* (1953–4) and *L'An 2,000* (1953–4) in France. Also of interest was *Tarzan Adventures* (1953–9) which, under Michael MOORCOCK's editorship from 1957, published several sf comic strips, including Jim CAWTHORN's *Peril Planet*. It was the weekly comic paper, however, in which the best drawn and plotted sf comic strips were to appear. The foremost was DAN DARE (1950–67 *Eagle*). With its clean linework by Frank HAMPSON it became Britain's most influential sf comic strip, inspiring several rivals including JEFF HAWKE, *Captain Condor* (1952–5 *Lion*), at one time illustrated by Brian LEWIS who did many NEW WORLDS covers also, and *Jet-Ace Logan* (1956–9 *Comet*; 1959–60 *Tiger*), written by Frank S. Peper and, later, Michael Moorcock. Equally notable was *Rocket* (1956) an sf comic paper which featured US reprints and others, including *Escape From Earth*, *Seabed Citadel* and *Captain Falcon*. It ran to 32 issues. More successful was *Boy's World* (1963–4) which, prior to its merger with *Eagle*, published *Wrath of the Gods* illustrated by Ron Embleton, *Ghost World* illustrated by Frank Bellamy, and *The Angry Planet*, an adaptation of Harry Harrison's *Deathworld* (**1960**) plotted by Harrison and scripted by Kenneth BULMER.

In the 1960s, the MARVEL COMICS group returned to sf after almost 20 years with *Fantastic Four* (1961 onwards), whose success heralded a new wave of superhero comics, starring both new characters and heroes (like Captain America and Sub-Mariner) resuscitated from Marvel productions from World War Two and immediately afterwards. National Periodicals (DC comics), publishers of *Superman*, also expanded its superhero list within a few years of Marvel's success. Another trend was the increase of adaptations of sf TELEVISION

Judd Holdren as COMMANDO CODY, 1955.

series, notably STAR TREK and DOCTOR WHO, which both appeared in a variety of publications. Innovations appeared in the "underground" comics where sf gave an ideal framework for scatological examinations of society's neuroses and phobias, with original artistic styles being developed by Richard Corben, Vaughan Bodé and others. More recently Roger ELWOOD edited *Starstream Comics* (1976) in an attempt to introduce adaptations of Poul ANDERSON, Larry NIVEN, Robert SILVERBERG and others, which apparently failed to attract any substantial readership. A similar fate was suffered by the slightly earlier series *Unknown Worlds of Science Fiction* (1975–6), which adapted stories by Moorcock, Bob SHAW, Stanley WEINBAUM and many others. Published by the Marvel Comics group, with the byline "Stan Lee Presents", it ran for six issues in 1975, ed. Roy Thomas. Its artwork was generally undistinguished. One giant-size issue was published in 1976 to use up the material already commissioned.   [JE]

See also: *A History of the Comic Strip* (**1968**) by P. Couperie and M. Horn; *The Adventurous Decade: Comic Strips in the Thirties* (**1976**) by Ron GOULART; *The World Encyclopedia of Comics* (**1976**) ed. M. Horn; and the important bibliography *The Comic Book Price Guide 1977–78* (**1977**) by B. Overstreet.

COMMANDO CODY — SKY MARSHAL OF THE UNIVERSE Television series (1955). Republic Studios/Hollywood Television Service for NBC TV. Produced by Mel Tucker and Franklyn Adreon, directed by Fred Bannon and Harry Keller, and written by Ronald Davidson and Barry Shipman. 25 mins per episode. B/w.

Despite the title, the hero of this children's TV series did not do much travelling about the universe, but was more likely to be found riding around the Republic Studios in a four-door sedan. A cross between the Lone Ranger and CAPTAIN MIDNIGHT (his rival crime-fighter on CBS), Cody wore a costume that looked as if its previous owner had been in the German High Command, and a mask whose function was not clear. Equipped with several secret laboratories, a spaceship and an ordinary revolver, Cody fought conventional gangsters and, occasionally, the Ruler, an evil genius from outer space. Because it was reminiscent of the absurdities and confusions of the old movie serials, *CC* was more entertaining than the slicker but bland *Captain Midnight*.   [JB]

COMMUNICATIONS Many aspects of communications in sf are dealt with under separate entries in this volume. For communications meaning travel, *see*

MATTER TRANSMISSION and TRANSPORT. For communications in the sense of modern communications networks, *see* COMPUTERS and MEDIA LANDSCAPE. All communications take the form of sending messages. The most familiar form of communication is through language, for a discussion of which *see* LINGUISTICS. Direct mental communication, or telepathy, is discussed under ESP.

Once the implications of the theory of relativity sank into genre sf, it was realized that any story involving a GALACTIC EMPIRE, along with a great many SPACE OPERAS, faced the problem that messages from one star system to another might take many lifetimes to deliver. The issues raised here are discussed under FASTER THAN LIGHT, and two of the best-known sf devices to cope with it are discussed under ANSIBLE and DIRAC COMMUNICATOR. Space communications within our solar system have been dealt with in many stories, notably in *Venus Equilateral* (coll. of linked stories **1947**) by George O. SMITH.

The most common communications scenario in sf involves the meeting of humans with ALIENS. These are often called "first contact" stories, and perhaps the best known of them is "First Contact" (**1945**) by Murray LEINSTER. An anthology of such stories is *First Contact* (anth. **1971**) ed. Damon KNIGHT. Among some of the alien contact stories most relevant to communication are "A Martian Odyssey" (**1934**) by Stanley WEINBAUM, "The Big Front Yard" (**1958**) by Clifford D. SIMAK and *The Mote in God's Eye* (**1974**) by Larry NIVEN and Jerry POURNELLE.

Aside from all the above areas of communications which are dealt with in greater detail elsewhere in this volume, there remains the area of non-linguistic communication, though the distinction is merely semantic, in that many writers would take linguistics to include, for example, mathematical symbology and sign language. In the non-fiction work *We Are Not Alone* (**1964**) by Walter Sullivan, there is a discussion of the possibility of using universal mathematical symbols to communicate with aliens, and this idea has also been used not only in a great many sf stories, but also in the symbols inscribed on the first space capsule to be sent outside the Solar System.

There was no great emphasis on communications problems in early sf. Most non-linguistic communications stories are post Second World War, by which time there had already been much discussion of information theory, especially in the context of CYBERNETICS. Any message consists of coded information, whether in the form of words, mathematical symbols, signs, modulated electro-magnetic waves, intermittent laser beams or even the chemical pheromones used for communication by animals. A number of

sf communications stories, then, have been in effect code-cracking stories. In James BLISH's *VOR* (**1958**) an alien communicates by changing the colours of a patch on his head. VOR stands for violet, orange, red. In Jack VANCE's "The Gift of Gab" (**1955**) the story turns on whether a squid-like alien creature is intelligent; his intelligence is proven once it is realized that the waving of his tentacles makes a coded pattern. Vance's stories persistently invent new communication systems, usually linked with the cultural background of alien societies — messages in various of his stories are passed by masks, music, smells, colours, signs. A number of stories of this general type are discussed under ANTHROPOLOGY. Suzette Haden ELGIN is another writer whose stories blend cultural anthropology with communications problems; she has a PhD in linguistics. Naomi MITCHISON has also written a notable book in this area, *Memoirs of a Spacewoman* (**1962**), centered on a research worker whose job it is to understand and if possible communicate with alien species; her aliens are more vivid and convincing than usual, perhaps because of her background in biology. It is, of course, a popular theme in sf, and many books, such as *Conscience Interplanetary* (**1972**) by Joseph GREEN, have dealt with it at a less demanding level.

Fred HOYLE has several times tackled the problem of decoding alien messages, most interestingly in *The Black Cloud* (**1957**), but also in *A For Andromeda* (**1962**), written with John ELLIOT. The latter story tells of the cracking of a binary code picked up on a radio telescope, and its interpretation as instructions for building an artificial person. The purest communications story of this kind, however, is James GUNN's *The Listeners* (**1972**), which concentrates on the motivation behind attempts to pick up messages from the stars, and brings in many questions of human communication also; the quest of the radio-telescope operators is ultimately successful.

Much closer to home, a popular theme has been attempts to communicate with species on our own planet, notably in *The Day of the Dolphin* (**1967**; trans. **1969**) by Robert MERLE and *Clickwhistle* (**1973**) by William Jon WATKINS. Both of these owe much to the well-known work carried out by the scientist John Cunningham Lilly, author of *The Mind of the Dolphin: A Nonhuman Intelligence* (**1968**). Ian WATSON adopts a rather different method of cetacean communication in *The Jonah Kit* (**1975**). Indeed, all Watson's books can be read as dramatizations of a variety of methods for transcending the limitations of spoken human communication.

There are plenty of communication problems in our own society, even without aliens, which perhaps explains

the title of Leon STOVER's "What we Have Here is too much Communication" (**1971**). D.G. COMPTON makes one of the best uses of a familiar idea in *Synthajoy* (**1968**), a well-written and serious account of the repercussions of building a machine which records emotional experiences and can be plugged into other minds. And, of course, there are many stories both mainstream and sf about the mind-expanding effect of drugs to assist (or militate against) genuine human communication, too many to list here.

Some of the most interesting sf communications stories are those which stress the mysteriousness and ambiguity that may be involved in inter-species communication. Three particularly enigmatic novels on this theme are *Rogue Moon* (**1960**) by Algis BUDRYS, *Solaris* (**1961** Poland; trans. **1970**) by Stanislaw LEM and *Whipping Star* (**1970**) by Frank HERBERT; the Stanley KUBRICK film 2001: *A Space Odyssey* (**1968**) also comes into this group.

In *Rogue Moon* a labyrinthine artefact is found on the Moon's surface, which is apparently meaningful. However, those who walk through it, some penetrating further than others, have all died. These slaughters may in one sense be acts of communication also; they are given a number of human analogies by Budrys, who seems to see all communication as fraught with difficulty. Lem's *Solaris* is beyond doubt the most subtle and detailed communication story in sf; the living planet of Solaris is being researched by humans, in an orbital laboratory, who become obsessed with the notion of communication with the (hypothetical) planetary intelligence; when communication arrives, it takes the form of replicating figures from the scientists' subconscious minds; the dead mistress of the hero is reconstructed not once but again and again. All efforts at communication are thwarted by the anthropomorphism of the observers, and the novel asks the pessimistic question, will it *ever* be possible to transcend our man-centered view of the universe? Or is alien communication a contradiction in terms? The film version, SOLARIS (1972), directed by Tarkovsky, also makes much of the barriers between true communication even between humans. Herbert's *Whipping Star* is frivolous in comparison, but its ingenious array of semantic confusions, as humans attempt to communicate with entities whose corporeal form, it turns out, is as stars, poses some sharp questions. Kubrick ducked the question altogether in what has become the most famous sequence in sf CINEMA; when the mysterious alien intelligence of *2001* does communicate, the audience is given only an enigmatic and incomprehensible collage of lights, fragmentary landscapes and an unexpected 18th-century room. We are given to understand that communication is achieved, but we receive only the static

that surrounds it. CLOSE ENCOUNTERS OF THE THIRD KIND (1977) is another film which ends on a comparable note, the communication here being between humans and the occupants of FLYING SAUCERS; the climax is a kaleidoscope of colour and sound. [PN]

COMPTON, D.G. (1930–). English writer, born of parents who were both in the theatre. DGC's novels are almost always set in the NEAR FUTURE, and each presents a moral dilemma. The future is used as a device for bringing contemporary trends into a clearer focus. Most of the interest lies in personal relationships and the behaviour of people under stress; minor characters are observed with humour which frequently arises from class differences. Endings are ambiguous or deliberately inconclusive. Later novels have varying modes of narrative technique. DGC's rare public utterances confirm the impression that he is not interested in the staple concerns of genre sf.

DGC's first novel was *The Quality of Mercy* (1965; rev. 1970), concerning a development from East-West political tension. In *The Silent Multitude* (1966) the crumbling of a cathedral city reflects a disintegration in the human spirit. *Farewell, Earth's Bliss* (1966; rev 1971) shows the plight of social misfits transported to MARS. *Synthajoy* (1968) is more complex and brought DGC wider notice, particularly in the USA. A surgeon and an electronics engineer develop tapes which enable unremarkable people to enjoy the experiences of those who are more gifted or fortunate. This basic idea is a premise for the exploration of a moral problem and the observation of human beings in extreme situations. *The Palace*

(1969) is set in an imaginary country but is scarcely sf: it is DGC's only book in which the environment is more important than the characters. *The Steel Crocodile* (1970; vt *The Electric Crocodile* UK) presents the danger of new knowledge and its application. *Chronocules* (1970; vt *Hot Wireless Sets, Aspirin Tablets, the Sandpaper Sides of Used Matchboxes, and Something that might have been Castor Oil* UK) is a time-travel story. *The Missionaries* (1972) describes the efforts of some evangelizing aliens with a good deal of social comedy.

DGC's strengths as a writer are all displayed in the much admired *The Continuous Katherine Mortenhoe* (1974; vt *The Unsleeping Eye* USA). A woman in her 40s is given four weeks to live. A reporter with eyes replaced by television cameras has the job of watching her decline for the entertainment of a pain-starved public in a world where illness is almost unknown. The reporter sees one of the transmissions and realizes that the camera cannot tell the truth: the recorded film is without mind and therefore without compassion.

DGC's virtues and moral concerns are those of the traditional novelist, and have little to do with the future of technology *per se*, but he has consistently chosen to borrow his central metaphors from genre sf, although the use he makes of them is quite defferent from the usual concerns of the genre. [MA]

See also: COLONIZATION OF OTHER WORLDS; COMMUNICATIONS; COMPUTERS; CYBORGS; DISASTER; MEDIA LANDSCAPE; OVERPOPULATION; PSYCHOLOGY; RELIGION; SCIENTISTS.

COMPUTERS The development of the computer in the real world has been so

recent and so rapid that sf has had to struggle hard to keep up in creating a dramatic potential for "thinking machines". In fiction the notion of mechanical brains evolved as a corollary to the notion of mechanical men (*see* ROBOTS), and one is featured as early as Edward Page MITCHELL's "The Ablest Man in the World" (1879). In the early sf PULP MAGAZINES an artificial brain turned against its creators in "The Metal Giants" (1928) by Edmond HAMILTON and intelligent machines were extensively featured in the early work of John W. CAMPBELL Jr, as in "The Metal Horde" (1930) and "The Machine" (1935 as by Don A. Stuart). The machine of the latter story is benevolently inclined, but bids farewell to the human race in order to prevent mankind's irrevocable stagnation through dependence upon it. The revolution against the mechanical mind which rules society (whether benevolently or not) has been the most prevalent theme in sf stories of this kind, and it is usually associated with the metaphor of stagnation through dependence (*see* MACHINES *and* UTOPIAS). Examples of the theme include Miles J. BREUER's "Paradise and Iron" (1930), Francis G. RAYER's *Tomorrow Sometimes Comes* (1951), Philip K. DICK's *Vulcan's Hammer* (1960) and Ira LEVIN's *This Perfect Day* (1970). The *New York Times* commissioned Isaac ASIMOV's explication of the theme, "The Life and Times of MULTIVAC" (1975), but this story leaves open the question of whether such a rebellion would be desirable or necessary. Asimov has been consistently favourable towards the idea of a machine-run society, an earlier fictional testimony being "The Evitable Conflict" (1950). Another strongly pro-computer story from the 1950s, redolent of the conflict and confrontation typical of the period, is *They'd Rather Be Right* (1957; vt *The Forever Machine*) by Mark CLIFTON and Frank RILEY. The most hysterical anti-computer viewpoint is satirically presented in "The Man Who Hated Machines" (1957) by Pierre BOULLE.

By the 1960s the computer was familiar enough to become the subject of satirical humour, as in *The Novel Computer* (1966) by Robert Escarpit and *The Tin Men* (1965) by Michael FRAYN. By this time, however, the potential of the computer seemed illimitable. The idea that the computer is the logical end product of evolution on Earth was put forward in *The Tale of the Big Computer* (1966; vt *The Great Computer*) by Olof JOHANNESSON, and the notion of computers evolving to become God (or at least godlike), first broached by Fredric BROWN in "Answer" (1954) and then by Isaac Asimov in "The Last Question" (1956), became popular. Examples include *Destination: Void* (1966) by Frank HERBERT and *Larger Than Life* (1960) by Dino BUZZATI. Other stories testifying to the new image of the computer include

The God Machine (**1968**) by Martin CAIDIN and *Colossus* (**1966**) by D.F. JONES. A more subtle approach was adopted by Arthur C. CLARKE in "The Nine Billion Names of God" (1953), in which a computer rapidly and easily completes the task set for Man by God and puts an end to everything.

Characterization of computers has advanced somewhat in recent years, although anthropocentric thinking tends to shape such personalities as Harlie in *When Harlie was One* (**1972**) by David GERROLD and Mike in *The Moon is a Harsh Mistress* (**1966**) by Robert HEINLEIN. More convincing machines offer autobiographical statements in "Going Down Smooth" (1968) by Robert SILVERBERG and *Arrive at Easterwine* (**1971**) by R.A. LAFFERTY.

The fear of computers' "taking over" our lives remains the most powerful influence on sf about computers. This is manifest across a broad spectrum of story types, from the straightforward foul-up story "Computers Don't Argue" (1965) by Gordon R. DICKSON to the surreal "I Have No Mouth, and I Must Scream" (1967) by Harlan ELLISON. *Man Plus* (**1976**) by Frederik POHL envisages a computer take-over as equivocal, but not necessarily a bad thing, and probably taking place in secret. John BRUNNER's *The Shockwave Rider* (**1975**) and D.G. COMPTON's *The Steel Crocodile* (**1970**; vt *The Electric Crocodile* UK) both envisage plausible societies of the NEAR FUTURE in which computers are used, with good intentions but repressively, by a politico-technocratic elite. *Michaelmas* (**1977**) by Algis BUDRYS is preoccupied like Brunner and Compton with the accessibility of data-bank material, but the hero, fighting fire with fire, uses a privately owned computer to beat the system.

A more METAPHYSICAL variety of take-over is visible in the small but interesting sub-genre of stories in which computers literally absorb human personalities. Perhaps the three most interesting examples are *The Ring of Ritornel* (**1968**) by Charles HARNESS, *Midsummer Century* (**1972**) by James BLISH and *Catchworld* (**1975**) by Chris BOYCE. The latter novel, while unevenly written, goes further than any of its predecessors in exploring the possible paradoxes of the computer-human relationship.

Generally, however, sf does not have a particularly good record of prediction with computer stories. Sf backed the robot for a long time, even during the period when the computer was becoming increasingly important in the real world. Nor has sf shown any great interest in how computers actually work or how they are programmed. Their appearance in sf tends to be iconographic rather than realistic.

Two anthologies are *Science Fiction Thinking Machines* (anth. **1954**) ed. Groff CONKLIN, and *Computers, Computers, Computers: In Fiction and in Verse* (anth. **1977**) ed. D. Van Tassel. [BS]

See also: AUTOMATION; CYBERNETICS; CYBORGS; INTELLIGENCE.

CONAPT In sf TERMINOLOGY, an apartment in a high-rise building. Conapts often feature what is effectively a complete life-support system, so that even when they are in a densely populated city their inhabitants are often seen to be isolated from other people. A conapt is often assumed to be in a city consisting of high-rise buildings, each one highly populated, but the buildings themselves not necessarily crowded together, and sometimes separated by parkland. Possibly formed from a contraction of condominium apartment, the term was coined by Philip K. DICK, who uses it in most of his novels, and has been taken up by other sf writers. It is a typical piece of sf shorthand. [PN]

CONCEPTUAL BREAKTHROUGH The legends of Prometheus and Dr Faustus contain a central image which is still alive in sf: the hero in his lust for knowledge goes against the will of God, and though he succeeds in his quest he is finally punished for his overweening pride and disobedience. Adam eating his apple is another version of the legend. Its reverberations resonate throughout the whole of literature.

The Faustian version of the quest for knowledge (it lives on in Mary SHELLEY's *Frankenstein* (**1818**; rev. **1831**), in recent works such as James BLISH's *A Case of Conscience* (**1958**), in GOTHIC sf and in sf CINEMA generally) is no longer the only or even the most important version. The Faust myth did not even survive the 18th century unchallenged; the rationalists of the Age of Reason believed that the amount of knowledge in the universe is finite, and the decoding of its emblems is a moral good because it demonstrates the orderly mind of God. The quest for knowledge could be pursued with greater propriety than before.

The romantic movement, particularly its Gothic elements, set the clock back a little, with intimations that there are more things in Heaven and Earth than we can safely investigate, and that the universe was perhaps not so rational after all. But once again, a period of doubt was followed by a period of scientific optimism, and while the Victorians got upset over Darwin's theory of EVOLUTION, they were generally blandly cheerful about developments in science and technology. The quest for knowledge seemed in a healthy state, until relativistic and quantum physics came along, and seemed to throw scientific certainty into disarray. It was not that the quest for knowledge was once again seen as evil, though the atomic bomb was a frightening Promethean symbol; rather, knowledge itself no longer seemed so readily definable. Common sense failed to apply to the microcosm. Heisenberg suggested that the act of observation alters the properties of that which is being observed.

This is the ambience of modern sf. The quest for knowledge remains sf's central vision; but while such quests are no longer seen as *de facto* dangerous or immoral, they are often shown as ambiguous, unsettling, even paradoxical.

Of all the forms which the quest for knowledge takes in modern sf, by far the most important, in terms of both the quality and the quantity of the work that dramatizes it, is conceptual breakthrough. It is amazing that the importance and centrality of this idea in sf has had so little in the way of critical recognition, though a recent essay by Gary K. Wolfe, "The Known and the Unknown: Structure and Image in Science Fiction" in *Many Futures, Many Worlds* (anth. **1977**) ed. Thomas D. CLARESON, points towards it.

Conceptual breakthrough can best be explained in terms of "paradigm", as that term is used by philosophers of science. A paradigm is a generally held way of looking at and interpreting the world; it consists of a set of often unspoken and unargued assumptions. For example, before Copernicus the scientific paradigm or world-view saw Earth as the centre of the universe. All the most exciting scientific revolutions have taken the form of breaking down a paradigm and substituting another. Often the old paradigm is eroded slowly first, with lots of little puzzling anomalies, before the new paradigm can take over. Such an altered perception of the world, sometimes in terms of science and sometimes in terms of society, is what sf is most commonly about, and few sf stories do not have at least some element of conceptual breakthrough.

An important sub-set of conceptual breakthrough stories consists of those in which the world is not what it seems. The structure of such stories is often that of a quest in which an intellectual nonconformist questions apparent certainties. Quite a number have been stories in which the world turns out to be a GENERATION STARSHIP, as in "Universe" (1941) by Robert HEINLEIN, *Non-Stop* (**1958**; vt *Starship* USA — the American title giving the game away) by Brian W. ALDISS and *Captive Universe* (**1969**) by Harry HARRISON. In "The Pit" (1975) by D. West, the world turns out to be inside an artificial asteroid. In "Outside" (1955), also by Brian Aldiss, a suburban house turns out to be an experimental laboratory in which shape-changing aliens are incarcerated. In several stories the world is artificial, either literally, or because its inhabitants have been brainwashed into seeing it wrongly, as in *Time out of Joint* (**1959**) by Philip K. DICK. Philip José FARMER's "Riverworld" books deal throughout with conceptual breakthrough; the first breakthrough is the realization that despite all the resurrected dead who populate it,

This early 16th-century woodcut creates a startling symbol of CONCEPTUAL BREAKTHROUGH, as a monk plunges his head through the sphere of the stars to find the complex machinery behind the scenes creating the movements of the heavens.

Riverworld is not Heaven; the second is the realization that the inhabitants are being manipulated. No doubt a final breakthrough will be made when all the quests are brought to an end in the not yet published final volume. There is a touch of PARANOIA here ("we are property"), quite common in conceptual breakthrough stories, as in those where the world turns out to be a construct to aid market research, as in "The Tunnel Under the World" (1955) by Frederik POHL, or *Simulacron-3* (**1964**; vt *Counterfeit World* UK) by Daniel GALOUYE.

Closely allied to the above are stories where information about the world turns out to be not so much wrong as incomplete. The classic example here is "Nightfall" (1941) by Isaac ASIMOV, in which the constant presence of suns in the sky of another planet has led to complete ignorance of the stars, and total panic every 2,049 years when all the suns set at once. Arthur C. CLARKE's *The City and the Stars* (**1956**) has two breakthroughs, the first out of a beautiful but static Utopian city into the greater world, and the second into a knowledge of civilizations in the stars. Another post-War classic is "Surface Tension" (1952) by James Blish, in which the hero breaks out .of his underwater microcosm to discover a greater world arching over his

puddle. (Blish always recognized the shift from one paradigm to another as the essence of sf, and said as much in "The Science in Science Fiction" reprinted in VECTOR, Summer 1975. His historical novel about Roger Bacon, *Doctor Mirabilis*, **1964**, which takes conceptual breakthrough as its theme, has, therefore, the flavour of first-class sf although it is based on historical fact.) Daniel Galouye's *Dark Universe* (**1961**) is perhaps the best of the many stories in which an underground community has lost its memory of the surface. *Walkers on the Sky* (**1976**) by David J. LAKE is a recent, lively variant on the theme of a hero discovering the true nature of an artificial world. Conversely, in *Lord of Light* (**1967**) by Roger ZELAZNY, the breakthrough is into an understanding of the true nature of an artificial heaven.

The archetype of all these stories is *The History of Rasselas* (**1759**) by Samuel JOHNSON, in which the hero, walled into a tranquil Abyssinian valley by mountains, finds his lust for knowledge of the outside world obsessing him and not permitting him the enjoyment of the happiness he sees all around him. He escapes; the world outside is less happy than his own, but it is interesting. *Rasselas* provides the template for the whole genre; the intellectual discontent and formless yearnings of his hero are among the

commonest qualities of sf heroes also, and Johnson's mild pessimism — which recognizes that even though the new world-picture may be uglier than the old we need to know about it — captures exactly the accepting tone which was to permeate so much sf. It is a romantic if often melancholy form of striving, and sf never reveals its romantic origins more clearly than when it uses the tropes of conceptual breakthrough.

Sometimes the breakthrough is transcendent, and can be given to the reader only by analogy, inasmuch as the new state cannot be described in a terminology which itself belongs to the old paradigm. Such a state is commonly attained by the heroes of A.E. VAN VOGT and Alfred BESTER, and more recently of Ian WATSON, all of whose works centre on a conceptual breakthrough of some kind. Such is the end of the film 2001: A SPACE ODYSSEY (1968), where kaleidoscopic imagery of hypnagogic intensity is an emblem of the incomprehensible. Such, too, is the vastly superior intelligence attained by the hero of *Camp Concentration* (**1968**) by Thomas M. DISCH, a book which alludes with some subtlety to every celebrated literary variant of the Faust myth. In Algis BUDRYS's extraordinary novel *Rogue Moon* (**1960**), conceptual breakthrough (in the attempt to understand a labyrinthine artefact on the Moon) seems invariably accompanied by death, and this too recalls the Faustian theme, transcendence being linked to mortality. A similar death occurs in *The Black Cloud* (**1957**) by Fred HOYLE.

Sometimes conceptual breakthrough is ambiguous; the objective nature of the new paradigm cannot be understood because of the subjective nature of PERCEPTION. A joke version of this occurs in "The Yellow Pill" (**1958**) by Rog PHILLIPS, where one character believes himself to be in a room, the other in a spaceship, and both are tempted to break through to the other's version of reality; one walks, fatally, through what he believes to be a door. Paradoxes of this kind are much beloved by Philip K. Dick, as in "Impostor" (**1953**), where a man, believing himself to be unjustly persecuted as a machine, breaks through to the realization that he is indeed a robot with a bomb in his belly, and also in *Eye in the Sky* (**1957**), *Ubik* (**1969**), *A Maze of Death* (**1970**) and *Martian Time-Slip* (**1964**). A subjective, disturbing form of conceptual breakthrough is the basis for many of J.G. BALLARD's stories, such as "Manhole 69" (**1959**), "Build-Up" (**1957**; vt "The Concentration City"), "Thirteen to Centaurus" (**1962**) and even "The Drowned Giant" (**1964**; vt "Souvenir"). Stanislaw LEM's *Solaris* (**1961** Poland; trans. **1970**) is entirely constructed around the attempt by a space-station crew to break out of their anthropomorphic world-view into an understanding of the enigmatic nature of the living planet Solaris around which they circle. One of the most remarkable conceptual breakthrough stories of recent years, whose author, Christopher PRIEST, saw the work as in part an *hommage* to Aldiss's *Non-Stop*, is *Inverted World* (**1974**). In this book a city is constantly and painfully pushed forward on rails, because the world-picture of its inhabitants is of a hyperboloid where time and space are progressively distorted both north and south of an always moving optimum line. The probable truth turns out to be very different. Like many such stories, the breakthrough is inner as well as outer; the book adopts the Berkeleyan view that the world is what we see it as being; changes in objective truth are changes in perception; there is no such thing as pure scientific truth.

The forms taken by conceptual breakthrough in sf are almost impossible to enumerate. David LINDSAY's *A Voyage to Arcturus* (**1920**) is structurally an ironic series of such breakthroughs, with each new truth seen in turn to be as inadequate as the previous one, until the grim, rather nihilistic and ultimate reality is revealed at the end. C.S. LEWIS's *Perelandra* (**1944**; vt *Voyage to Venus*) has some moments of startling beauty when the hero tries to accommodate his perceptions to the alien configurations of Venus. William GOLDING's *The Inheritors* (**1955**) has the breakthrough symbolized in the confrontation between Neanderthal man and Cro-Magnon man. Most of Ray CUMMINGS' stories deal with the realization (based, ironically, on a now discredited paradigm) that an infinite series of worlds can exist, each within the atoms of the next higher in the series. Various conceptual leaps take place in most of Samuel R. DELANY's stories, notably "The Star Pit" (**1967**) and *Babel-17* (**1966**). In the latter story the breakthrough, ultimately conceptual, is initially linguistic. Delany sees paradigms as actually existing within, and created by, language itself, a common view in LINGUISTIC sf, also found in Ian Watson's *The Embedding* (**1973**). In Theodore STURGEON's "Who?" (**1955**; vt "Bulkhead") a spaceship pilot, frightened of the unknown outside his ship, is cheered by the voice of his unreachable companion beyond a bulkhead; only at the end does he find that the other crewman is a mental projection of his own younger self, and that the bulkhead is, metaphorically, in his own mind. Hal CLEMENT's *Mission of Gravity* (**1954**) takes place on a high-gravity planet whose natives are forced to understand their world through human eyes, and vice versa. The SWORD-AND-SORCERY milieu of John CROWLEY's *The Deep* (**1975**), accepted by the reader as a literary convention, turns out to have a quite different explanation, necessitating a wrench to the reader's view of the novel as well as the hero's view of his world. Ursula K. LE GUIN's *The Dispossessed* (**1974**) is structured around parallel breakthroughs in political understanding and fundamental physics; the crossing of walls is the book's central image. The hero of Daniel KEYES's "Flowers for Algernon" (**1959**) begins as a moron, comes to understand the nature of the world as no other human can, then tragically has the gift of intelligence taken away. The breakthrough in "Strangers" (**1974**) by Gardner DOZOIS is in cultural understanding, and is accomplished only after the death of the protagonist's alien lover. The breakthrough at the end of *Orbitsville* (**1975**) by Bob SHAW takes place on an almost unimaginably huge DYSON sphere, whose nature puts human evolutionary struggle into a new perspective.

Examples could be multiplied endlessly, and have been given extensively to demonstrate how all-pervasive the theme of conceptual breakthrough is in sf; no adequate DEFINITION of sf can be formulated that does not somehow take this theme into account. It is present, regardless of the usual boundaries, in old wave and NEW WAVE, HEROIC FANTASY and HARD SF, genre sf and sf by MAINSTREAM writers. It recurs so compulsively, and so much of the feeling and passion of sf is connected with it, that it must be seen as springing from a deep-rooted human need: to reach out, escape mental traps, prefer movement to stasis: to understand. Sf is pre-eminently the literature of the intellectually dissatisfied, the discontented, those who need to feel there must be more to life than this, and therein lies its maturity, which by a paradox can be seen as a perpetual adolescent yearning. [PN]

CONDON, RICHARD (THOMAS) (1915–). American writer, formerly in advertising, best known for his works outside the sf field, though many of them, including most notably *The Manchurian Candidate* (**1959**), employ some sf elements in the complex generic mix characteristic of his fiction. Later made into a well-known film, THE MANCHURIAN CANDIDATE (1962), this novel combines a superior kind of brainwashing and POLITICAL thriller elements into a story of the attempted assassination of the American president; the presidency is central to several of RC's later novels as well, including the savage *Winter Kills* (**1974**). Perhaps RC's most remarkable capacity is to heighten all his material to a hypnotic glow that gives a peculiarly sf "atmosphere" to his entire corpus, wherever and whenever a particular novel may be set. [JC]

CONEY, MICHAEL G. (1932–). British writer, resident in Canada. MGC did not publish his first story, "Sixth Sense", until 1969, but he has quickly established himself as one of the most prolific and capable writers to emerge in the 1970s. His first novel, *Mirror Image* (**1972**), is a thorough exploration of the concept of ALIENS who can so perfectly mimic humans that when they have done so they believe themselves to be human. These "amorphs" recur in a later novel, *Brontomek!* (**1976**), which won the BRITISH SCIENCE FICTION award. Its setting, the planet Arcadia, is also featured in MGC's second novel *Syzygy* (**1973**), and certain characters are common to both books. Also connected is *Charisma* (**1975**), an intricate PARALLEL-WORLDS story whose locale, a Cornish fishing village, is a common feature in MGC's work, sometimes transplanted to other planets. His most accomplished novel to date is *Hello Summer, Goodbye* (**1975**; vt *Rax* USA), a wistful story of adolescent love in an ingenious alien setting. MGC's other work includes a colourful series of stories (owing some debt to J.G. BALLARD's "Vermilion Sands" series) set in the Peninsula, a new landmass thrown up in a future cataclysm. Several of these are amalgamated in *The Girl With a Symphony in Her Fingers* (fix-up **1975**; vt *The Jaws That Bite, The Claws That Catch* USA). Although there are repetitive elements in his work, MGC has from the start shown good technical grasp and an ability to extract new insights from the oldest sf themes. [MJE]
Other works: *The Hero of Downways*

(1973); *Friends Come in Boxes* (1973; rev. 1974 for UK hardcover edition only; the UK paperback reverts to the original text); *Monitor Found in Orbit* (coll. 1974); *Winter's Children* (1974).

See also: COLONIZATION OF OTHER WORLDS; ECOLOGY; GAMES AND SPORTS; LEISURE; REINCARNATION.

CONKLIN, GROFF (1904–68). American editor. The first of GC's many sf ANTHOLOGIES was *The Best of Science* See also: POLITICS.
where it attracts up to 4,000 attendants. It introduction), a huge compendium which appeared shortly before Raymond J. HEALY and J. Francis McCOMAS's similarly massive *Adventures in Time and Space* (1946), although the latter book was contracted earlier and had first pick of the material. Nevertheless, *The Best of Science Fiction* and its successors from the same publisher — *A Treasury of Science Fiction* (anth. 1948; paperback edition includes only eight stories out of 30), *The Big Book of Science Fiction* (anth. 1950; paperback includes 10 stories out of 32), and *The Omnibus of Science Fiction* (anth. 1952; vts *Strange Travels in Science Fiction* and *Strange Adventures in Science Fiction* UK, including respectively 13 and nine stories out of 43; vt *Science Fiction Omnibus* USA, containing 11 stories) — are rewarding compilations. GC wrote a book review column for GALAXY SCIENCE FICTION from the first issue (Oct. 1950) until Oct. 1955. He also edited for Grosset & Dunlap a series of one-dollar hardcover sf novels, starting in 1950 with novels by A.E. VAN VOGT, Jack WILLIAMSON and others. The series included the first book publication of Henry KUTTNER's *Fury* (1947 *ASF*, under the pseudonym Lawrence O'Donnell; 1950) with an introduction by GC which has been reprinted in subsequent editions. GC produced anthologies on various themes, including INVASION in *Invaders of Earth* (anth. 1952; UK edition contains 14 stories out of 22 and was divided into two paperback volumes, the second of them titled *Enemies in Space*; two different paperback selections have been published in the USA, containing 15 and 17 stories), TIME TRAVEL and PARALLEL WORLDS in *Science Fiction Adventures in Dimension* (anth. 1953; vt *Adventures in Dimension* UK, containing 13 stories out of 23; US paperback contains 12 stories), ROBOTS, ANDROIDS and COMPUTERS in *Science Fiction Thinking Machines* (anth. 1954; vt *Selections from Science Fiction Thinking Machines* USA, omits six stories and two plays) and MUTANTS in *Science Fiction Adventures in Mutation* (anth. 1955; paperback edition omits six stories). Later, GC became consultant sf editor to Collier Books, for whom he produced the notable anthologies *Great Science Fiction by Scientists* (anth. 1962) and *Fifty Short Science Fiction Tales* (anth. 1963), the latter in collaboration

with Isaac ASIMOV. GC's anthologies were never definitive but were always considered and capable. The anthologies listed above are representative only. GC edited over 40 sf and fantasy anthologies in all.   [MJE]
See also: ALIENS; MATHEMATICS.

CONNINGTON, J. J. (or **JOHN JERVIS**) Pseudonym of Alfred Walter Stewart (1880–1947), professor of chemistry, Queen's University, Belfast. Under his pseudonym he is known mainly for detective novels. He was educated at the universities of Glasgow, Marburg and London. His one sf novel was *Nordenholt's Million* (1923) as by J.J. Connington. A prototype story of world-DISASTER being surmounted, it is realistic, reasoned, sociologically observed and credible: fireball-mutated, denitrifying bacteria destroy the world's vegetation, then die out. A multi-millionaire secures the dictatorship of Britain, selects five million people, segregates them in the Clyde valley with supplies, and engineers the collapse of the dangerous remainder. On the Clyde, nitrogen is synthesized, moral crises take place, there is an atomic energy breakthrough at the cost of lives, and the exhausted dictator dies. New cities are built. Stewart's scientific intellect tackles the scenario seriously, and with feeling; though he is occasionally over-"literary", his imagination is firmly anchored in reality. His *bêtes noires* are dilettantes, politicians, corruption, rabble-rousers and revivalists, and his ideals are clear-sightedness, dedication and hard work. Under his own name he wrote publications on chemistry and, about himself, *Alias J.J. Connington* (1947).   [DIM]
See also: END OF THE WORLD; HOLOCAUST AND AFTER.

CONQUEST, (GEORGE) ROBERT (ACKWORTH) (1917–). English writer, poet and editor, most active in the sf field in the latter capacity, with his series of anthologies, edited with Kingsley AMIS, *Spectrum* (anth. 1961), *Spectrum 2* (anth. 1962), *Spectrum 3* (anth. 1963), *Spectrum 4* (anth. 1965) and *Spectrum 5* (anth. 1966) These anthologies helped to establish modern magazine sf with a widely based English audience.

RC was educated at Oxford (D Litt), was a member of the Diplomatic Corps 1946–56, and was later literary editor of the *Spectator*. He has an OBE. In addition to much poetry, political history and a non-sf novel, *The Egyptologists* (1965) with Amis, he published one sf novel, *A World of Difference* (1955), which through a complicated plot combines POLITICAL speculation and scientific adventure centered on a new space drive that gives Man the chance to reach beyond the Solar System.   [JC]
Other works: (ed.) *The Robert Sheckley Omnibus* (coll. 1973).

CONQUEST OF SPACE Film (1955). Paramount. Directed by Byron HASKIN, starring Walter Brooke, Eric Fleming, Mickey Shaughnessy and William Hopper. Screenplay by James O'Hanlon, based on a book, *The Mars Project*, by Wernher von Braun. 80 mins. Colour.

Despite being ultimately based on a work of science fact by the most famous of rocketry engineers, the story, set in the 1980s, of a military research expedition to Mars and back, is riddled with implausibilities, both scientific (an asteroid is seen burning in the vacuum of space) and human (the commander, regarded as the only person capable of doing the job, is a twitching religious fanatic). At one point, the celebrated line "there are some things that Man is not meant to do" is uttered. In place of the customary love interest there is a routine Oedipal conflict between father and son.

The special effects are ambitious in scope but often clumsily executed, in particular the matte work. Chesley BONESTELL's renderings of the red Martian landscape are evocative, though they have been rendered obsolete by history.   [JB/PN]

CONQUEST OF THE PLANET OF THE APES Film (1972). 20th Century-Fox. Directed by J. Lee Thompson, starring Roddy McDowall, Don Murray, Natalie Trundy and Hari Rhodes. Screenplay by Paul Dehn, based on characters created by Pierre BOULLE. 86 mins. Colour.

This is the fourth in the popular PLANET OF THE APES series of films. Caesar, the ape born in the preceding film, ESCAPE FROM THE PLANET OF THE APES, is being kept in a circus but comes to resent the human exploitation of apes so much that he incites his fellow primates to revolt. The film ends with the apes victorious over the humans after a bloody battle. The deliberate parallels with the situation of the blacks in America are unsubtle. Dehn's screenplay displays his usual ingenuity, but Thompson's direction is perfunctory, and as with all the *Apes* films, the neglect of science and logic gravely weakens the sf content. The novelization by John JAKES was published in 1974.   [JB]

CONRAD, EARL (1912–). American writer, whose collection of short stories is *The Da Vinci Machine: Tales of the Population Explosion* (coll. 1968).   [JC]

CONRAD, GREGG See Rog PHILLIPS; PSYCHOLOGY.

CONRAD, JOSEPH (1857–1924). Naturalized British writer, born in Poland. His full name was Jósef Teodor Konrad Nałęcz Korzeniowski. In recent decades he has been most highly esteemed not for his novels of the sea but for more complex later works such as *Nostromo* (1904) and *The Secret Agent*

(1907). With Ford Madox HUEFFER (who was later to become better known as Ford Madox Ford), he collaborated on *The Inheritors: An Extravagant Story* (1901); the people of the title represent a future race, the "Dimensionists", who will come to supersede ordinary mankind. Though the novel is primarily political satire in its projection of the cold, practical, manipulative future man, it is genuine sf in its use of the themes of other DIMENSIONS and EVOLUTION. [JC/PN]
About the author: "Joseph Conrad's Forgotten Role in the Emergence of Science Fiction" by Elaine L. Kleiner, in EXTRAPOLATION, Dec. 1973.

CONRAD, PAUL Preferred pseudonym of writer and journalist Albert King (1924–), an extremely prolific British writer in various genres under a series of names; for his sf work he has used PC, his own name, Mark Bannon, Floyd Gibson, Scott Howell, Christopher King and Paul Muller. Born in Northern Ireland, he left school at the age of 14. He is the author of about 120 Westerns, 44 thrillers and 29 romances in addition to his two-years' production of 16 sf titles, of which the most notable are perhaps *Ex Minus* (1974) as by PC and *The World of Jonah Klee* (1975) as by Christopher King. Most of his work is routine adventure. [JC]
Other works: as PC: *Last Man on Kluth V* (1975); *The Slave Bug* (1975). Under his own name: *Stage Two* (1974). As Mark Bannon: *The Wayward Robot* (1974); *The Assimilator* (1974); *The Tomorrow Station* (1975). As Floyd Gibson: *A Slip in Time* (1974); *Shadow of Gastor* (1975); *The Manufactured People* (1975). As Scott Howell: *Menace from Magor* (1974); *Passage to Oblivion* (1975). As Christopher King: *Operation Mora* (1974). As Paul Muller: *The Man from Ger* (1974); *Brother Gib* (1975).

CONSTANTINE, MURRAY (?–). English woman writer, pseudonymous, in whose sf novel, *Swastika Night* (1937), set several hundred years in the future, a Nazi regime rules Europe and Russia while a Japanese Empire controls America and Australia; in the Nazi empire, women are breeding animals and Hitler is deified. The forbidden-love story between an engineer and a woman in some ways prefigures the plot of ORWELL's *Nineteen Eighty-Four* (1949). [JC]

See also: POLITICS.

CONVENTIONS One of the principal features of sf FANDOM, conventions are usually weekend gatherings of fans and authors, frequently with a programme of sf discussion and events. A convention, in sf FAN LANGUAGE, is usually referred to as a con. They are informal, not professionally organized, and with no delegated attendants or, usually, paid speakers. Typical convention activities include talks, auctions, films, panel discussions, masquerades and banquets.
The first planned sf convention took place in Leeds in 1937. Since then regular conventions have been established around the world. In Britain the major annual convention, the Eastercon (1951–), now has up to 600 attendants; recent venues have included Newcastle, Manchester and Coventry. A second convention, the Novacon (1971–), takes place every November in Birmingham and attracts some 300 people.
The first American convention was held in New York in 1938 and the first Worldcon, the premier sf convention, took place there in 1939. The Worldcon, at which the HUGO awards are presented, is held annually, usually in the USA where it attracts up to 4,000 attendants. It has twice been to CANADA (1948 and 1973), twice to Britain (1957 and 1965) — it will be held there again in 1979 — and once to Germany (1970) and Australia (1975). Annual regional conventions have also been long established in North America; major conventions include the Westercon (1948–), the Midwestcon (1950–), the Deepsouthcon (1963–), the Disclave (Washington 1950–), the Lunacon (New York 1957–), the Boskone (Boston 1964–), and the Windycon (Chicago 1974–). There are also national conventions in AUSTRALIA, JAPAN and several European countries, notably FRANCE, GERMANY, ITALY, SCANDINAVIA and the BENELUX countries. One of the international Eurocons (1971–) was held in Poland in 1976, the first sf convention in the Communist bloc. [PR]

CONWAY, GERARD F. (? –). American writer who began publishing sf with "Through the Dark Glass" for *AMZ* in 1970. His first sf novel was *The Midnight Dancers* (1971). *Mindship* (1971 *Universe*; exp. 1974), is a SPACE OPERA; the mindships of the title are spaceships coordinated by the PSI powers of specially trained "corks". Not untypically of current sf novels, by the end of the book a *gestalt* state has been achieved between a cork and his Captain. As Wallace Moore GFC has written the "Balzan of the Cat People" series: *The Bloodstone* (1974), *The Caves of Madness* (1975) and *The Lights of Zetar* (1975). [JC]

COOK, WILLIAM WALLACE (1867–1933). American writer, reportedly pseudonymous, much of whose production appeared after the turn of the century in such magazines as ARGOSY, and only later in book form, in a stapled format reminiscent of the American DIME NOVELS. Noteworthy among them is *A Round Trip to the Year 2000* (1903 *Argosy*; 1925), in which various contemporary writers travel by SUSPENDED ANIMATION to the year 2000, where they observe social conditions, and find themselves popular, and *Adrift in the Unknown; or, Queer Adventures in a Queer Realm* (1904–05 *Argosy*; 1925), a SATIRE on American capitalist civilization, in which a burglar goes along for the ride with a reformist scientist in his spaceship to MERCURY where he teaches some attendant capitalists about social justice. WWC was a crude writer, but is of interest in his attempts to combine adventure plots and satirical points. [JC]
Other works: *Cast Away at the Pole* (1904 *Argosy*; 1925); *Marooned in 1492* (1905 *Argosy*; 1925); *The Eighth Wonder; or, Working for Miracles* (1906–07 *Argosy*; 1925); *Around the World in Eighty Hours* (1925).
See also: DISCOVERY AND INVENTION; ROBOTS; TIME TRAVEL.

COOKE, ARTHUR Pseudonym used on the story "The Psychological Regulator" (1941) written in collaboration by C. M. KORNBLUTH, Robert LOWNDES, John Michel, Elsie Balter and Donald WOLLHEIM.

COON, HORACE (1897–1961). American writer whose sf novel is *43,000 Years Later* (1958), in which ALIENS come to a post-HOLOCAUST Earth, become intrigued with the civilization that had gone before, and, through records, explore the 20th-century world to SATIRICAL effect. [JC]

COOPER, C. EVERETT *See* Robert REGINALD.

COOPER, COLIN (SYMONS) (1926–). English writer, active as a scriptwriter for television and radio; his first sf is a six-part BBC serial, "Host Planet Earth" (1967). His somewhat downbeat sf novels, *The Thunder and Lightning Man* (1968) and *Outcrop* (1970), have not had a strong impact on the field. His most recent novel, *Dargason* (1977), is a story of the NEAR FUTURE in which, for mysterious reasons, listeners to music become severely affected by a variety of psychological extreme states; it is perhaps the only sf thriller to posit music as a WEAPON. [JC/PN]

COOPER, EDMUND (1926–). British writer. EC was educated at Manchester Grammar School and attended teacher training college before becoming a merchant seaman in 1944. His first published story was "The Unicorn" (1951), and he has been a freelance writer for many years.
EC wrote a number of short stories in the 1950s, which are collected (with considerable overlap) in several volumes, but is primarily known as a novelist. His early novels are among his best. *The Uncertain Midnight* (1958; vt *Deadly Image* US and later UK) describes a post-HOLOCAUST world in which ANDROIDS are gradually threatening to supplant

Man; *Seed of Light* (**1959**) is a GENERATION-STARSHIP novel in, which a small group manage to escape from a devastated Earth. The destruction of civilization provides the backdrop for many of EC's novels, and the Earth is often rendered uninhabitable, as in *The Last Continent* (**1970**) and *The Tenth Planet* (**1973**). *The Cloud Walker* (**1973**), EC's most successful recent novel, is of this type, describing the rediscovery of science in a post-holocaust setting of religious repression. EC has strong views on the differing roles of the sexes — he has been quoted as saying of WOMEN: "let them compete against men, they'll see that they can't make it" — which are manifest in his novels *Five to Twelve* (**1968**) and *Who Needs Men?* (**1972**; vt *Gender Genocide* USA) and implicit elsewhere. These attitudes have given rise to some critical hostility towards his work. He is the author of a series of SPACE OPERAS, "The Expendables", under the pseudonym Richard Avery: *The Deathworms of Kratos* (**1975**); *The Rings of Tantalus* (**1975**), *The War Games of Zelos* (**1975**) and *The Venom of Argus* (**1976**). He is sf reviewer of the *Sunday Times*. [MJE]
Other works: *Tomorrow's Gift* (coll. **1958**); *Voices in the Dark* (coll. **1960**); *Tomorrow Came* (coll. **1963**); *Transit* (**1964**); *All Fools' Day* (**1966**); *A Far Sunset* (**1967**); *News from Elsewhere* (coll. **1968**); *Seahorse in the Sky* (**1969**); *Son of Kronk* (**1970**; vt *Kronk* USA and later UK); *The Square Root of Tomorrow* (coll. **1970**); *The Overman Culture* (**1971**); *Unborn Tomorrow* (coll. **1971**); *The Slaves of Heaven* (**1974**); *Prisoner of Fire* (**1974**).
About the author: "Hope for the Future: the Science Fiction Novels of Edmund Cooper" and "An Interview with Edmund Cooper", both by James Goddard, in *Science Fiction Monthly* Vol.2 no.4.
See also: ANTHROPOLOGY; DISASTER; OUTER PLANETS; SEX; SOCIOLOGY; TIME TRAVEL.

COOPER, MERIAN C. *See* KING KONG.

COOPER, SUSAN (**1935–**). English writer, a graduate in English studies from Oxford, for some time a journalist, now resident in the USA. In her sf novel *Mandrake* (**1964**) the eponymous politician takes over a distressed NEAR-FUTURE England and, in mystical league with the forces of Nature, begins the process of cleansing the Earth of Man, but is stopped just in time. Her juvenile fantasy series, "The Dark is Rising", is comprised of *Over Sea, Under Stone* (**1968**), *The Dark is Rising* (**1973**), *Greenwitch* (**1974**), *The Grey King* (**1975**) and *Silver on the Tree* (**1977**). It is thought by many critics to be one of the most distinguished of the mythological fantasy series which, following the success of J.R.R. TOLKIEN's work, were published in a spate during the 1960s and

'70s. The hero of the series, Will Stanton, is at once a small boy and a vessel of ancient powers, and SC shows great skill in blending in him a perfectly natural, unsentimentalized, childish innocence and the sophistication of a mage. The series owes much to Anglo-Saxon and Celtic mythology, but also uses such sf tropes as ALTERNATE WORLDS, TIME PARADOXES and time stasis. *The Grey King* won the 1976 Newbery Award. SC has written non-fantasy books for children also. [JC/PN]

COOVER, ROBERT (LOWELL) (**1932–**). American writer. He has established a considerable reputation with his novels, which might be described as FABULATIONS, including *The Universal Baseball Association Inc., J. Henry Waugh Prop.* (**1968**). A collection, *Pricksongs & Descants* (coll. **1969**), contains some stories of sf interest. [JC]

COPLEY, FRANK BARKLEY (**?–?**). American writer in whose sf novel, *The Impeachment of President Israels* (**1912**), a future Jewish American president is impeached for refusing on ethical grounds to make war on Germany. [JC]

COPPEL, ALFRED The form of his name used for much of his work by prolific American writer (and wartime fighter pilot) Alfredo José de Marini y Coppel Jr (**1921–**), along with the pseudonyms Robert Cham Gilman and Sol Galaxan (one story, 1953). He began publishing sf with "Age of Unreason" for *ASF* in 1947, and published a good deal of magazine fiction in the next decade, though he was in fact producing considerably more in other genres with such action novels as *Hero Driver* (**1954**). His first sf novel is *Dark December* (**1960**), a post-HOLOCAUST quest story, set in a nuclear-devastated America and featuring the protagonist's search for his lost family. As Robert Cham Gilman, AC has published a juvenile SPACE-OPERA sequence comprising *The Rebel of Rhada* (**1968**), *The Navigator of Rhada* (**1969**) and *The Starkahn of Rhada* (**1970**). *The Dragon* (**1977**) is a NEAR-FUTURE political thriller. If his energies had not been focused elsewhere, AC might well have become an important figure in American genre sf. [JC]
Other works: *Thirty-Four East* (**1974**).
See also: GALACTIC EMPIRES.

CORBETT, CHAN *See* Nat SCHACHNER.

CORBETT, JAMES (**?–**). British author of popular thrillers, specifically written for the lending library market. His *The Devil Man From Mars* (**1935**) is an interplanetary novel with a poor scientific background (or perhaps it was intended as a parody) in which a Martian, equipped with death rays and hypnotic powers, travels to Earth with the wind at his back all the way. More sophisticated

in content is *The Man Who Saw The Devil* (**1934**), a rewrite of Robert Louis STEVENSON's *The Strange Case of Dr. Jekyll And Mr. Hyde* (**1886**), in which neither personality is aware of the other's existence. Many of his other works contain some elements of sf and the weird, viz. *The Death Pool* (**1936**), *Vampire Of The Skies* (**1932**), *The Monster of Dagenham Hall* (**1935**), *The Man They Could Not Kill* (**1936**), *The Man With Nine Lives* (**1938**), *The Moon Killer* (**1938**), and *The Ghost Plane* (**1939**), but none has any real importance. [JE]

CORELLI, MARIE (**1855?–1924**). English writer, probably born Minnie Mackay, though she was secretive about her birth, which may have been illegitimate. She wrote extremely popular best-sellers (selling 100,000 copies a year), from her first novel, *A Romance of Two Worlds* (**1886**; rev. 1887), in which interstellar travel is accomplished through personal electricity, to around the turn of the century; by 1900 her peculiar brand of sublimated sex, heated religiosity, female frailty and sickly fantasy had begun to lose its appeal; by her death she had been virtually forgotten. Most of her early work can be read by those willing as fantasies, though careful explication of the texts may derive a form of RELIGIOUS explanation for the most extraordinary events. *Barabbas: A Dream of the World's Tragedy* (**1893**) is perhaps the most readable. Of sf interest is *The Young Diana: An Experiment of the Future* (**1915**), which is about a scientific experiment to make a woman (and hence Woman in general) beautiful. [JC/PN]
About the author: *Now Barabbas was a Rotter* (**1978**) by Brian Masters.
See also: BIOLOGY; GODS AND DEMONS.

COREY, PAUL (FREDERICK) (**1903–**). American writer in various genres, active from as early as 1934, though his first sf story, "Operation Survival" for *NW*, did not appear until 1962. Most of his early novels are set on farms in the American Middle West; the title of one of them, *Acres of Antaeus* (**1946**), is deceptive, but it is not sf. His sf novel, *The Planet of the Blind* (**1968**), is a variation on the theme of the one-eyed man in the country of the blind inaugurated (for sf) by H.G. WELLS in "The Country of the Blind" (**1904**). [JC]
See also: POLITICS.

CORLEY, EDWIN (**1931–**). American writer, whose *Siege* (**1969**) resembles several other American novels of the period in its depiction of a black revolution centered — as in John WILLIAMS' *Sons of Darkness, Sons of Light* (**1969**) — on Manhattan. His other novels of sf interest include *The Jesus Factor* (**1970**) and *Acapulco Gold* (**1972**). [JC]

CORLEY, JAMES (**1947–**). English

writer and computer programmer whose first novel, *Benedict's Planet* (**1976**), combines SPACE OPERA and some rather technical speculations about the possibility of FASTER-THAN-LIGHT travel in a somewhat overcrowded tale, in which the discoverer of a new source of fuel runs into complex trouble. [JC]

CORMAN, ROGER (1926–). American film-maker who has made a number of sf films. He was born in Los Angeles and graduated from Stanford University in 1947 with a degree in engineering. After a period in the navy he became a messenger-boy at 20th Century-Fox, where he soon became a story-analyst, before undertaking post-graduate work in modern English literature at Oxford University for one term. When he returned to Hollywood, he worked as a literary agent and began to write screenplays. His first sale was *Highway Dragnet* in 1953. He then formed his own company and concentrated on making a series of very cheap films. With his third film he became involved with the then newly formed American International Pictures, a distribution company, and has maintained his association with them ever since. His films were mainly Westerns, thrillers and sf/horror stories, all aimed specifically at the teenage market. At first RC acted only as a producer, but in 1955 he began directing. Sf films he has directed include THE DAY THE WORLD ENDED (1955), *It Conquered the World* (1956), *Not of this Earth* (1956), ATTACK OF THE CRAB MONSTERS (1956), *Teenage Cavemen* (1958), *War of the Satellites* (1958), *The Last Woman on Earth* (1960), *The Haunted Palace* (1963), THE MAN WITH THE X-RAY EYES (1963) and GAS-S-S! (1970). Sf-oriented films he has produced include *The Monster from the Ocean Floor* (1954), *The Beast with a Million Eyes* (1955), THE GIANT LEECHES (1958), *The Dunwich Horror* (1969), DEATH RACE 2000 (1975) and the severely cut US version of the Japanese NIPPON CHIMBOTSU; RC's travesty was released in 1974 as *Tidal Wave*. RC attracted much critical praise with his series of horror films based on the work of Edgar Allan POE, beginning with *House of Usher* (1960), but only *The Haunted Palace* (which is actually based on a story by H.P. LOVECRAFT, despite the use of a Poe title) has strong sf elements. The argument over RC's true worth as a film-maker continues. Most of his work has attracted a sizeable cult following and considerable attention from that school of film-critics which holds that there is often a freshness and inventiveness in B-grade films which is lacking in more "respectable" Hollywood productions. RC himself said of his sf films in an interview, "I was never really satisfied with my work in this field". [JB/PN]

CORPSICLE One of the wittiest recent items of sf TERMINOLOGY, coined by Larry NIVEN in his story "The Defenseless Dead" (1973) on the analogy of "popsicle", an American ice-lolly. It refers to a frozen dead person, preserved in the hope of possible resuscitation in a medically advanced future. It is to be hoped that so descriptive a word will pass into general usage. *See* CRYONICS. [PN]

CORREN, GRACE *See* Robert HOSKINS.

CORREY, LEE Pseudonym of American writer and engineer George Harry Stine (1928–), under which he has written nearly all his fiction, though his popularizing non-fiction about space travel and satellites is under his own name, as was his first story "Galactic Gadgeteers" (1951) in *ASF*. His best-known sf is "And a Star to Steer her by" (1953), to which his first novel, a juvenile, *Starship Through Space* (**1954**), was a sequel. His other sf books are a second juvenile, *Rocket Man* (**1955**), and one genre novel, *Contraband Rocket* (**1956**), about amateurs launching a spaceship. His non-fiction works, as by G.H. Stine, are *Earth Satellites and the Race for Space Superiority* (**1957**); *Rocket Power and Space Flight* (**1957**). [JC]

CORSTON, (MICHAEL) GEORGE (1932–). British writer whose sf novel is *Aftermath* (**1969**). [JC]

CORWIN, CECIL *See* C.M. KORNBLUTH.

CORY, HOWARD L. Writing name of Jack Owen Jardine (1931–) and his then wife Julie Ann Jardine (1926–) in collaboration. The name was taken from his wife's stage name, Corrie Howard. *The Sword of Lankor* (**1966**) features swashbuckling adventures, with the natives of a high-gravity planet unknowingly extracting valuable crystals for genially manipulative spacefarers. In *The Mind Monsters* (**1966**) a crash-landed Terran takes over a peculiar alien planet. Jack Owen Jardine's solo sf was written as by Larry MADDOCK. [JC]

COSGROVE, RACHEL *See* E.L. ARCH.

COSMIC MONSTER, THE *See* STRANGE WORLD OF PLANET X, THE.

COSMIC SCIENCE FICTION *See* COSMIC STORIES.

COSMIC SCIENCE STORIES British PULP-size magazine. One undated issue, *c.* Jun. 1950, published by Popular Press, London: an abridged reprint of the Sep. 1949 issue of SUPER SCIENCE STORIES. The lead novelette was "Minions of Chaos" by John D. MACDONALD. [FHP]

COSMIC STORIES US PULP magazine. Three bi-monthly issues, Mar.-Jul. 1941. Published by Albing Publications; ed. Donald A. WOLLHEIM. *CS* was one of two companion magazines (the other being STIRRING SCIENCE STORIES) started by Wollheim in 1941. It was cheaply produced (lacking full-colour covers) and had a microscopic editorial budget. Most of the stories were not paid for at all, being solicited by Wollheim from his fellow FUTURIANS. The first issue contained a story by Isaac ASIMOV, "The Secret Sense"; C.M. KORNBLUTH contributed a number of stories, using various pseudonyms. The title changed with the second issue to *Cosmic Science Fiction*, but the whole venture proved abortive and the magazine was dead within six months of its birth. [MJE]

COSMOLOGY Cosmology is the study of the universe as a whole, its nature and its origins. It is a speculative science (there being little opportunity for experiment) and it is occasionally difficult to distinguish essays and fictions related to it. Johannes KEPLER's *Somnium* (**1634**) is basically an essay inspired by the heliocentric theory of the universe,

COSMIC SCIENCE STORIES, cover by D. McLoughlin, and the last issue of COSMIC STORIES, here retitled *Cosmic Science-Fiction*, cover by Elliott Dold.

opposing the Aristotelian system favoured by the Church (*see* PROTO SCIENCE FICTION). Works of similar nature include Gabriel Daniel's *Voyage to the World of Cartesius* (**1692**), which popularizes the cosmological (and other) theories of Descartes, and Fontenelle's dialogue *A Plurality of Worlds* (**1688**). An early attempt to describe an infinite universe with habitable worlds surrounding all the stars was presented as a revelation by Emanuel SWEDENBORG in *The Earths in Our Solar System and the Earths in the Starry Heavens* (**1758**). There are several important 19th-century works belonging to this tradition of "semi-fiction". Camille FLAMMARION's *Lumen* (**1887**; trans. **1897**) combines religious notions with a powerful scientifically inspired imagination. Edgar Allan POE's *Eureka* (**1848**) is a poetic vision embodying intuitive hypotheses about the nature and origin of the universe. A much briefer vision is presented in Poe's short story "A Mesmeric Revelation" (1844). J.H. ROSNY AÎNÉ's *La légende sceptique* (**1889**) belongs to the same class of works. Even H.G. WELLS, who was not inclined to mysticism, wrote a brief cosmic vision story, "Under the Knife" (1896), and his American contemporary Edgar FAWCETT included a cosmic vision in *The Ghost of Guy Thyrle* (**1895**).

In the 20th century this tradition petered out. There is only one cosmic vision story comparable in scope and ambition to *Eureka* and *La légende sceptique* — Olaf STAPLEDON's classic *Star Maker* (**1937**). Two other works warranting mention are William Hope HODGSON's *The House on the Borderland* (**1908**), the boldest of the END OF THE WORLD visions, and R.A. KENNEDY's curious philosophical fantasia *The Triuneverse* (**1912**), which introduced the microcosm and the macrocosm to speculative fiction (*see* GREAT AND SMALL, *where this entire sub-species of the cosmological story is treated in detail*).

The early pulp sf writers were highly ambitious in the scope and scale of their fantasies, but their attitude was conspicuously different from that of the cosmic visionaries. They were interested in adventures, and the viewpoints of their stories remained tied to the experience of their characters. In genre sf the cosmos was merely glimpsed, and the awesome "sense of wonder" which it inspired precluded any attempt at thorough description. Thus there is a narrowness about the romances of the infinite universe pioneered by E.E. "Doc" SMITH's *Skylark of Space* (1928; **1946**) and such macrocosmic stories as Donald WANDREI's "Colossus" (1934) which sets them apart from the species of fantasy to which *Eureka* and *Star Maker* belong. It is worth noting, further to this point, that the first pulp sf story which tried to use the idea of the expanding universe was Edmond HAMILTON's "The Accursed

Galaxy" (1935), which suggested that all the other galaxies were fleeing from ours in horror because ours is afflicted with a disease (life). Similarly, A.E. VAN VOGT wrote a story in which the cosmogonic "big bang" results from the unfortunate experience of a man caught in a temporal fault, "The Seesaw" (1941; later incorporated into *The Weapon Shops of Isher*, fix-up **1951**). There has always been a tendency among genre sf writers to minimize the issues of cosmology into a strange kind of joke — in L. Ron HUBBARD's "Beyond the Black Nebula" (1949 as by René Lafayette) it is discovered that macrocosmically, our universe is somewhere in the alimentary tract of a worm, and Damon KNIGHT's "God's Nose" (1964) is the brief story of the cosmogonic sneeze. In *The Hole In The Zero* (**1967**), M.K. JOSEPH takes cosmological speculation less trivially, though his surreal games with the subject have more to do with literary fireworks than with physics.

George GAMOW, who wrote one of the classic non-fiction works on cosmology, *The Creation of the Universe* (**1952**), included some cosmological fantasies in his book of didactic fictions *Mr. Tompkins in Wonderland* (**1939**), and other scientists have also used cosmological themes in their sf. Fred HOYLE, author of *The Nature of the Universe* (**1950**) and one of the world's leading cosmological speculators, incorporated visionary moments into *The Black Cloud* (**1957**) and *The Inferno* (**1973** in collaboration with Geoffrey HOYLE). Philip LATHAM (astronomer Robert S. Richardson) has written some interesting stories about astronomers in the day-to-day business of living with cosmological speculations, notably "The Dimple in Draco" (1967) and "The Rose Bowl-Pluto Hypothesis" (1969). An *avant-garde* story featuring a similar juxtaposition between the minutiae of everyday existence and cosmological notions is Pamela ZOLINE's "The Heat-Death of the Universe" (1967).

Several sf stories have incorporated cosmological visions in connection with the rebirth of the universe — notably James BLISH's *The Triumph of Time* (**1958**; vt *A Clash of Cymbals*) and Poul ANDERSON's *Tau Zero* (**1970**) — but the most impressive and most ambitious cosmological speculation embedded in a conventional sf story is in Ian WATSON's novel *The Jonah Kit* (**1975**), in which the actual cosmos is a mere shadowy echo of the original creation. Dramatic and strongly symbolic use is made of the steady-state theory of the universe in *The Ring of Ritornel* (**1968**) by Charles HARNESS, a book which contains some of the most ingenious cosmological theorizing yet to appear in genre sf. A recently published work of some interest is *Nebula Maker* (**1976**) by Olaf Stapledon — the first section of the initial draft of *Star Maker*.

Genre sf has also produced one or two exercises in "alternative cosmology", including Lester DEL REY's *The Sky is Falling* (**1963**; based on "No More Stars", 1954, by del Rey and Frederik POHL as by Charles Satterfield), which deals with a pseudo-Aristotelian closed universe, and Barrington J. BAYLEY's "Me and My Antronoscope" (1973), in which the universe is solid with occasional lacunae.

Generally, however, it is surprising that one of the most philosophically and intellectually exciting areas of modern scientific thought has not received greater attention in genre sf. It may be that cosmology works on such a grand scale that it is difficult to dramatize its relationship with human experience. It most commonly appears in sf in the image of ENTROPY, which is the mathematical term for what the layman usually understands as the running down of the universe, and the term "entropy" in sf is, as often as not, used primarily as a metaphor for more mundane forms of earthly decay and death. A good historical survey of cosmological speculation in mythology and science is *The Life of the Universe* (**1909**) by Svante Arrhenius, although reference must be made to more recent texts for modern theories.   [BS]

See also: ASTRONOMY; BLACK HOLES; ESCHATOLOGY; FASTER THAN LIGHT; METAPHYSICS; PHYSICS.

The first issue, showing the first Moon landing, as visualized in 1953.

COSMOS SCIENCE FICTION AND FANTASY MAGAZINE US DIGEST-size magazine. Four issues, Sep. 1953-Jul. 1954, published by Star Publications; ed. L.B. Cole. This was an unremarkable magazine of moderate standard, which published no memorable fiction. The four irregular issues were dated Sep. 1953, Nov. 1953, Mar. 1954, Jul. 1954.

More recently the same title has been used for a US BEDSHEET-size magazine. Four issues May–Nov. 1977. Bi-monthly, publication suspended after no. 4; published by Baronet Publishing Co.; ed. David G. Hartwell. *CSFFM* contains a sophisticated mixture of sf and fantasy, in an elegant format which includes full-colour interior illustration. The first two issues serialize a short novel in Fritz LEIBER's Fafhrd-Gray Mouser series, "Rime Isle", and contain stories by Michael BISHOP, Gordon DICKSON, Larry NIVEN, Frederik POHL and others. *CSFFM* contains a number of features, including a book review column by Robert SILVERBERG. [FHP/MJE]

The later version of the magazine. Cover by Vincent Di Fate.

COSTELLO, P.F. One of the many house names used by Ziff-Davis on various magazine stories 1941–58. It occasionally concealed the identity of Chester S. GEIER and Roger P. Graham (Rog PHILLIPS), and probably others. The authorship of most of the PFC stories has not been discovered, though "Secret of the Flaming Ring" (1951) and "Space is for Suckers" (1958) have both been attributed to Roger Graham. [PN]

COTTON, JOHN *See* John Russell FEARN.

COULSON, JUANITA (RUTH) (1933–). American writer, briefly a schoolteacher, who began publishing sf with "Another Rib" with *FSF* in 1963; the story was written with Marion Zimmer BRADLEY under the name John Jay Wells. With her husband, Robert COULSON, she won the 1965 HUGO award for best amateur publication for their long-running fanzine, YANDRO. JC's first novel, *Crisis on Cheiron* (1967), like her second, *The Singing Stones* (1968), is set on a primitive planet in a human-dominated galaxy; the oppressed species of each planet need help to survive the inimical influence of large corporations and the like. JC has also published at least four Gothic romances. [JC]
Other works: *Unto the Last Generation* (1975); *Space Trap* (1976).

COULSON, ROBERT (1924–). American writer, a long-time fan who edited, with his wife Juanita COULSON, the fanzine YANDRO, winner of a 1965 HUGO. His sf novels are comparatively recent, his first solo work being *To Renew the Ages* (1976), and his first collaboration with Gene DeWEESE being *Gates of the Universe* (1975), though two subsequent collaborations, *Now You See It/Him/Them* (1975) and *Charles Fort Never Mentioned Wombats* (1977), are perhaps better known. They are both spoof stories featuring reporter Joe Karns, and are apparently composed as sf in-jokes. He has also revised for publication a novel by Piers ANTHONY, *But What of Earth?* (1976), which was published as a collaboration, though this is repudiated by Anthony. [JC]

COUPLING, J. J. *See* John R. PIERCE.

COURY, PHIL (?–). American soldier and corporate executive. His sf novel, *Anno Domini 2,000* (1959), features a socialist America; the plot involves a Senate campaign in which the hero plumps for an alternative political course. [JC]

COVEN 13 after its title change, Jan.-Feb. 1971. Cover by Burge.

COVEN 13 US magazine, DIGEST-size for the first four issues, BEDSHEET-size for the remaining six issues. 10 issues Sep. 1969–74, nos 1–4 published by Camelot Publishing Co., Los Angeles, ed. H. Landis, nos 5–10 published by William L. CRAWFORD's Fantasy Publishing Co., California, ed. Gerald Page. From no.5 (Jan. 1971) *C13* was retitled *Witchcraft & Sorcery*, and subtitled "The Modern Magazine of Weird Tales" to leave no doubt about what it was imitating. *C13* achieved no great success, and appears to have ceased publication, though one more issue is planned. No memorable stories were published in *C13*, but a nostalgic and bombastic column by E. Hoffman Price, "The Jade Pagoda", won some praise. [FHP/MJE]

COVER, ARTHUR BYRON (1950–). American writer, involved in the CLARION SF WRITERS' WORKSHOP in 1971 and '72. He began publishing sf with "Gee, Isn't He the Cutest Little Thing?" in Steve GOLDIN's *Alien Condition* (anth. 1973); his first novel, *Autumn Angels* (1975), which is introduced by Harlan ELLISON, depicts in hallucinated language a FAR-FUTURE Earth; LINGUISTIC and cultural jokes proliferate, somewhat exhaustingly. His further books, *Platypus of Doom and Other Nihilists* (coll. of linked stories 1976) and *The Sound of Winter* (1976), are tamer but more effective, the former being his most successfully amusing work to date. Both take place in a far-future universe and share some characteristics; *The Sound of Winter* is a love story set in a mutation-prone, post-disaster wonderland, and ends tragically. ABC tends to use sf imagery and plots in a wryly arbitrary fashion to achieve sometimes moving statements about the world. [JC]
See also: ABSURDIST SF.

COWAN, FRANK (1844–1905). American poet, author of the undated LOST-RACE novel, published in the 1880s, *Revi-Lona; A Romance of Love in a Marvellous Land*. Set, not unusually for works of the late 19th century, in Antarctica, it features a matriarchal society. [JC]

COWAN, JAMES (1870–1943). American writer. His sf novel, *Daybreak: A Romance of an Old World* (1896), features an ambulatory Moon which deposits a balloon on Mars, where its passengers discover a new defence of Christianity in parallel EVOLUTION and the multiple incarnation of Christ. [JC]

COWPER, RICHARD Pseudonym of British writer John Middleton Murry Jr (1926–), son of the famous critic of the same name. RC has also published non-sf novels under the name Colin Murry; as Colin Middleton Murry, Colin being his nickname, he has published an autobiographical account of his childhood relationship with his father, *One Hand Clapping* (1975).

Educated at Oxford and the University of Leicester in English and education, RC worked for some time as a teacher, during which period he had three mainstream novels published, and wrote a fourth, *Private View* (1972), publication of which was delayed for a decade. Hoping for a change of luck he adopted his pseudonym, and wrote his first sf book, *Breakthrough* (1967). It is not conventional genre sf, being more richly characterized and romantic than is commonly the case; its story of EXTRA-SENSORY PERCEPTION and a kind of reverse REINCARNATION is sensitively told and given unusual reverberations by its use of a leitmotiv from Keats. It remains one of RC's finest works, and its romantic theme, of the power of the mind to sense alternate worlds, and of the flimsiness and limitations of this one's reality, crop up often in his work, sometimes in images of *déjà vu*. This is so of what is generally considered his best novel, *The Twilight of Briareus* (**1974**), and also of the short stories collected in *The Custodians* (coll. **1976**). The title story of the latter book was much praised in America, and nominated for several awards. RC's best work has a strange, expectant vibrancy about it, in its explorations of human PERCEPTION, an openness which is not unlike that described in John Keats's remarks about "negative capability", remarks that RC has quoted in print. Keats's plea was for a kind of waiting expectancy of the mind, which should be kept free of preconceptions. RC's use of TELEPATHY as a theme is more delicate than is common in American sf, and is not usually linked as in America to the idea of the SUPERMAN.

Although the air and style of RC's sf is a long way from traditional HARD SF, its content uses traditional sf themes. *Kuldesak* (**1972**) deals with an underground society in a post-HOLOCAUST Earth, and one man who finds the surface against the will of an all-powerful COMPUTER. *Clone* (**1972**; US hardback printed from uncorrected proofs) was RC's first real breakthrough with the American public; it is an amusing near-future SATIRE. *Time out of Mind* (**1973**) is a thriller about a plot centering on narcotically induced telepathy. *Worlds Apart* (**1974**) is a not wholly successful comedy, burlesquing several sf stereotypes in a story of an alien world on which an sf novel is being written about Urth, while back on Earth an sf writer writes about the alien world.

RC has been a full-time freelance writer since 1972. [PN]
Other works: *Phoenix* (**1968**); *Domino* (**1971**).
About the author: "Backwards Across the Frontier" by RC in FOUNDATION 9, 1975.
See also: CHILDREN IN SF; CLONES; HUMOUR; METAPHYSICS; PARALLEL WORLDS.

COX, ERLE (1873–1950). Australian novelist and journalist, who reviewed for *The Argus* and the *Australasian*, 1918–46. His best-known sf novel is *Out of the Silence* (probably serialized in *The Argus* 1919; **1925**; exp. 1947), about the attempt by a representative of an otherwise extinct super-race to rule Australia. The novel exhibits some racist overtones. *Fool's Harvest* (**1939**) warned against a future INVASION of Australia; *The Missing Angel* (**1947**) is fantasy. [JC]
See also: SUSPENDED ANIMATION.

COX, LUTHER (? –). American writer whose SUPERMAN sf novel is *The Earth is Mine* (**1968**).

CRACKEN, JAEL *See* Brian W. ALDISS.

CRACK IN THE WORLD Film (1965). Security Pictures/Paramount. Directed by Andrew Marton, starring Dana Andrews, Janette Scott, Kieron Moore and Alexander Knox. Screenplay by J.M. White and Julian Halevy. 96 mins. Colour.

An attempt to tap the energy at the Earth's core causes a large and ever increasing crack in the crust, and a bid to halt the process with a nuclear explosion sends into space a large chunk of the Earth, which forms a new moon. This ambitious idea is undermined by a weak script and too small a budget. [JB]

CRAIG, A.A. *See* Poul ANDERSON.

CRAIG, ALEXANDER (? – ?). Author of the LOST-RACE novel *Ionia: Land of Wise Men and Fair Women* (**1898**), Ionia being a Greek colony in the Himalayas boasting prohibition, eugenics and communism. [JC]

CRAIG, BRIAN *See* Brian M. STABLEFORD.

CRAIG, RANDOLPH *See* Norvell W. PAGE.

CRAIG, WEBSTER *See* Eric Frank RUSSELL.

CRANE, ROBERT Pseudonym of Bernard Glemser (1908–), an English novelist resident in the United States and active under his own name in other genres. As RC his realistically presented sf novel is *Hero's Walk* (**1954**), the basis for a television play, "The Voices" (1954). Superior ALIENS quarantine a militaristic Earth and eventually bomb it to rubble; there is some hope at the novel's close that humanity will be permitted to survive and mature. [JC]

CRAWFORD, WILLIAM L. (1911–). American publisher and editor. WLC was one of the first sf fans to turn publisher, editing and producing the semi-professional magazines MARVEL TALES and UNUSUAL STORIES in the mid-1930s. After the War he resumed his publishing activities: he was instrumental in starting the FANTASY PUBLISHING COMPANY, INC., published the magazine FANTASY BOOK (editing it under the pseudonym Garrett Ford), and published a number of booklets, including Clifford D. SIMAK's *The Creator* (**1946**) and two anthologies (which he edited), *The Garden of Fear* (anth. **1945**) and *The Machine God Laughs* (anth. **1949**). He later used the Ford pseudonym for the collection *Science and Sorcery* (anth. **1953**) and on the magazine SPACEWAY (another of his publications). Later still he became publisher of the magazine *Witchcraft & Sorcery* (formerly COVEN 13). WLC's various projects have included the publishing of some scarce and interesting material, generally

concealed by unattractive, amateurish production which may have been instrumental in its general lack of success. [MJE]

CRAWLING EYE, THE *See* TROLLENBERG TERROR, THE.

CRAZIES, THE Film (1973). Cambist Films. Directed by George Romero, starring Lane Carroll, W.G. MacMillan and Harold Wayne Jones. Screenplay by George Romero, based on an original script by Paul McCollough. 104 mins. Colour.

A plane carrying a cargo of dangerous viruses crashes near a small American town and pollutes the drinking-water. After the town's inhabitants drink the water they become rampaging psychopaths. A wave of murder inundates the town, the army moves in to control the situation, and the result is a bloody battle. There are similarities between this and Romero's best-known film THE NIGHT OF THE LIVING DEAD in that both involve a small group of "normal" people trapped and surrounded by nightmarish chaos. The film seems to go beyond the exploitation of violence for its own sake, and reaches toward political/cultural allegory. [JB/PN]

CREASEY, JOHN (1908–73). British author, publisher, and literary agent. JC began writing for the BOYS' PAPERS in 1926, turning to adult thrillers in 1932. He wrote 564 books, under 13 pseudonyms. Like George GRIFFITH with his future-WAR novels, JC exploited contemporary fears of organized crime and of terrorist and revolutionary activities in his works, often including sf elements as an additional horror (his first novel, *Seven Times Seven*, **1932**; rev. 1970, depicts a criminal gang equipped with "freezing gas"). In later works, beginning with *Dangerous Quest* (**1944**; rev. 1965), a futuristic novel about an underground Gestapo group in liberated Yugoslavia, and continuing in his "Dr Palfrey" and "Dept. Z" series, sf themes came to the fore. Midget aircraft piloted by zombie-like children attack the world's cities in *The Children of Hate* (**1952**; rev. vt *The Children of Despair* UK 1958; vt *The Killers of Innocence* USA); man-induced world DISASTER was imminent in *The Flood* (**1956**) and others, while an alien invasion was defeated in *The Unbegotten* (**1971**). All were sensational in nature, contributing nothing to the genre, and were influential only on the cheap thrillers market. [JF]
Other works: The following contain sf ingredients: *The Death Miser* (**1932**; rev. 1965); *Men, Maids and Murder* (**1933**; rev. 1972); *The Mark of the Crescent* (**1935**; rev. 1967); *Death Round the Corner* (**1935**); *The Mystery Plane* (**1936**); *Thunder In Europe* (**1936**; rev. 1968); *The Air Marauders* (**1937**); *Carriers of Death* (**1937**; rev. 1968); *Days of Danger*

(**1937**; rev. 1968); *The S.O.S. Flight* (**1937**); *Death Stands By* (**1938**; rev. 1966); *The Fighting Fliers* (**1938**); *Menace!* (**1938**; rev. 1971); *Panic!* (**1939**; rev. 1969); *Death By Night* (**1940**); *The Island of Peril* (**1940**; rev. 1968); *The Peril Ahead* (**1940**; rev. 1964); *Death In Flames* (**1943**; rev. 1973, as by Gordon Ashe); *Dark Peril* (**1944**; rev. 1958); *The Hounds of Vengeance* (**1945**; rev. 1967); *The House of Bears* (**1946**; rev. 1962); *Dark Harvest* (**1947**; rev. 1962); *The League of Dark Men* (**1947**; rev. 1965); *Sons of Satan* (**1947**); *The Wings of Peace* (**1948**; rev. 1969); *The Dawn of Darkness* (**1949**); *The League of Light* (**1949**; rev. 1969); *The Man Who Shook the World* (**1950**; rev. 1958); *The Prophet of Fire* (**1951**); *Department of Death* (**1951**); *The Touch of Death* (**1954**); *Four of the Best* (coll. **1955**); *The Mists of Fear* (**1955**); *The Black Spiders* (**1957**); *The Plague of Silence* (**1958**); *The Drought* (**1959**; vt *The Dry Spell* UK); *The Terror* (**1962**; rev. 1970); *The Depths* (**1963**); *The Sleep* (**1964**); *The Inferno* (**1965**); *The Famine* (**1967**); *The Blight* (**1968**); *A Shadow of Death* (**1968**); *The Oasis* (**1969**); *The Smog* (**1970**); *The Insulators* (**1972**); *The Voiceless Ones* (**1973**); *A Blast of Trumpets* (**1975**).
See also: CRIME AND PUNISHMENT; POLLUTION.

CREATURE FROM THE BLACK LAGOON, THE Film (1954). Universal. Directed by Jack ARNOLD, starring Richard Carlson, Julie Adams and Richard Denning. Screenplay by Harry Essex and Arthur Ross, from a story by Maurice Zimm. 79 mins. B/w.

An amphibious monster, half-man, half-fish, successfully resists attempts by a boatload of scientists to take him from his native lagoon. This is one of the better monster films of the 1950s, rich with atmosphere, thanks to the direction of Jack Arnold. "Those scenes with the girl swimming on the surface and the monster looking up at her from below," said Arnold, "played upon a basic fear that people have about what might be lurking below the surface of any body of water. It's the fear of the unknown." In many ways the successful *Jaws* was a virtual remake of *CFTBL*. The film had two sequels: REVENGE OF THE CREATURE and THE CREATURE WALKS AMONG US. [JB]

CREATURE WALKS AMONG US, THE Film (1956). Universal. Directed by John Sherwood, starring Jeff Morrow, Rex Reason and Leigh Snowden. Screenplay by Arthur Ross. 78 mins. B/w.

This is the second sequel to THE CREATURE FROM THE BLACK LAGOON (the first being REVENGE OF THE CREATURE), and is inferior to the other two films, perhaps due to the change of director. In this film the "creature" is transformed by fire into a land monster, complete with lungs. [JB]

CREDITS In sf TERMINOLOGY, a credit is a monetary unit used widely in tales of the future. *See* MONEY.

CREEPING UNKNOWN, THE *See* QUATERMASS XPERIMENT, THE.

CREPAX, GUIDO *See* ITALY.

CRICHTON, MICHAEL (1942–). American writer and film director. He graduated with an MD from Harvard Medical School, after which he worked for a time in the Salk Institute. He began publishing sf, under the pseudonym John Lange, with *Drug of Choice* (**1968**). Most of the John Lange books are thrillers, *A Case of Need* (**1968**) winning an Edgar award for best mystery novel of the year; some of the novels written under this name, such as *Binary* (**1972**), make perfunctory use of sf devices in a way typical of the modern post-James-Bond thriller. The latter was turned into a made-for-TV film, PURSUIT (1972), which was also MC's début as a film director. Of greater interest are the novels which MC has written under his own name, several of which are sf or fantasy, beginning with *The Andromeda Strain* (**1969**), an immediate best-seller, a Book-of-the-Month Club selection, soon filmed as THE ANDROMEDA STRAIN (1971), in which microscopic spores from space attack the western United States (*see* DISASTER). MC's medical background is evident in much of his work (*see* MEDICINE). *The Terminal Man* (**1972**) speculates fascinatingly on the morality and effects of electronic brain implants as a control device, and was the basis of the film THE TERMINAL MAN (1974), directed by Mike Hodges. *Eaters of the Dead* (**1976**) recounts a savage conflict between Vikings and strange Neolithic men, and is in fact a retelling of the *Beowulf* legend. After *Pursuit*, MC determined to exercise artistic control over future screen adaptations of his work and though he did not do so in the case of *The Terminal Man*, he did both script and direct WESTWORLD (1973), a film which showed his intelligence and sophistication in its first half, but also a tendency to trim his sails to a rather low expectation of what the public wanted as the ROBOT-manned reconstruction of the Old West (*see also* LEISURE) falls apart at the seams, and the robot gunslinger runs amuck. The screenplay was published as *Westworld* (**1974**). An efficient and intelligent writer and director, MC is capable of producing remarkable work. His most recent project is a big-budget, fringe sf medical film based on a novel by Robin Cook, *Coma* (**1976**), released in 1978. [JC/JB]
See also: MYTHOLOGY.

CRIME AND PUNISHMENT Genre fiction concerned with crime may be roughly divided into "detective stories" and "thrillers". The former are problem stories; the latter exploit the melodramatic potential of the conflicts inherent in criminal deviation. Detective stories depend very heavily on ingenuity and generally require very fine distinctions between what is possible and what is not. It is difficult to combine sf and the detective story because in sf the boundary between the possible and the impossible is so flexible. Only Isaac ASIMOV has achieved any real measure of success in writing futuristic detective stories, and that achievement has been largely dependent upon the exploitation of a rigid set of principles already established in order to regulate the behaviour of robots. His classic sf detective story is *The Naked Sun* (**1957**).

Despite this essential difficulty a considerable body of sf/detective fiction grew up in the early part of this century, following the exploits of various "scientific detectives". This fiction is not, for the most part, futuristic, but tends to feature the clever detective, armed not only with the scientific methods of thought made famous by Sherlock Holmes but also with the equipment and arcane knowledge of advanced science, making light of the business of solving routine crimes. Some early examples were written for the *Strand* magazine by L.T. Meade and Robert Eustace, but the most notable works in this vein were *The Achievements of Luther Trant* (coll. **1910**) by Edwin BALMER and William MacHarg and the many adventures of Craig Kennedy chronicled by Arthur B. REEVE, including *The Poisoned Pen* (coll. **1911**) and *The Dream Doctor* (fix-up **1914**). Hugo GERNSBACK's short-lived pulp magazine SCIENTIFIC DETECTIVE MONTHLY published many stories of this sort. The restraints characteristic of detective fiction make this material of only borderline interest, as speculation within the stories is virtually stifled. Crime, in sf, is much more commonly — and perhaps more effectively — exploited for its melodramatic potential, as in the "thriller". The same is true of punishment — as witness A. Conan DOYLE's "The Los Amigos Fiasco" (1892), concerning the awful consequences of the use of the world's first electric chair.

In the early days of the scientific romance the scientific supercriminal (often embittered by the world's failure to recognize and reward his genius) was a common character, holding entire cities to ransom. He appears in Robert CROMIE's *The Crack of Doom* (**1895**); F.T. JANE's *The Violet Flame* (**1899**); J.S. Fletcher's *The Ransom for London* (**1914**) and Philip WYLIE's *The Murderer Invisible* (**1931**). Among the early pulp sf writers to make use of the stereotype was Murray LEINSTER, whose many versions of it include "A Thousand Degrees Below Zero" (1919), "Darkness on Fifth Avenue" (1929), "The Racketeer Ray" (1932) and "The Earth-Shaker" (1933). John W. CAMPBELL Jr was another to use the theme in "Piracy Preferred" (1930), though his criminal reformed and joined the heroes for several sequels. The 1930s master of interplanetary super-cops versus super-robbers stories was E.E. "Doc" SMITH, in both the "Skylark" and "Lensman" series, and other novels such as *Spacehounds of IPC* (1934; **1947**). The cliché had been ridden into the ground by the end of the 1930s, but has proved persistent. More recent examples include the atom-bomb story *The Maniac's Dream* (**1946**) by F. Horace ROSE and the "Dr Palfrey" novels by John CREASEY.

An original sf detective is Lord D'Arcy in the "Lord D'Arcy" series by Randall GARRETT. The hero lives in an alternate world, whose history has much in common with our own, but where progress has been in the area of ESP and MAGIC at the expense of technology. D'Arcy's investigative procedures are rigorous, and ingeniously analogous to those of the scientific detective in our own world.

The pulp-sf writers imagined that crime in the future would follow much the same pattern as crime today, although some more romantic crimes, like piracy, might come back into fashion in outer space, or even in time (e.g. "Pirates of the Time Trail", 1943, by ROSS ROCKLYNNE). Punishment, too, tended to follow well-established tracks in pulp sf, although one or two writers used sealed loops in time and other gimmicks to design punishments to fit crimes — e.g. "My Name is Legion" (1942) by Lester DEL REY. The one magazine sf story of the 1940s which attempts to make a significant statement about deviancy and penology is Robert HEINLEIN's "Coventry" (1940), which imagines a place of exile outside the law and which probably established one of the most annoying of sf clichés — the idea of deviant selfishness being a qualification for recruitment into the social elite of a stable society.

In the post-War period sf writers took to building all kinds of eccentric totalitarian societies for their future scenarios, and the subject of deviancy became a much more open question. As forms of conformity became stranger, so did forms of nonconformity. An early example is found in Fritz LEIBER's *Gather, Darkness!* (1943; **1950**), in which the establishment's superscience, which is masquerading as religion, is overthrown by the rebels' superscience, masquerading as witchcraft. More sophisticated studies of forms of deviancy in warped societies include Wyman GUIN's "Beyond Bedlam" (1951; the title story of *Living Way Out*, vt *Beyond Bedlam* UK, coll. **1967**) and Ray BRADBURY's classic *Fahrenheit 451* (**1953**). In the same period, new ideas regarding the treatment of deviants began to appear. In "Two-Handed Engine" (1955) by Henry KUTTNER and C.L. MOORE criminals are attended by robot "furies" to monitor

their actions and symbolize their guilt. In Damon KNIGHT's "The Country of the Kind" (1956) the criminal is cast out — left to do as he will but in a state of utter loneliness. A similar idea is explored with greater intensity in Robert SILVERBERG's "To See the Invisible Man" (1963). Robert SHECKLEY's *The Status Civilization* (**1960**) is a satirical extrapolation of the penal colony theme, imagining the kind of society which criminals might establish in reaction against the one which exiles them. The notion of the prison colony is taken to a terrible extreme in Cordwainer SMITH's "A Planet Named Shayol" (1961), in which criminals are made to grow extra limbs and organs for harvesting and use in transplants. Other prison planet stories are *The Survivors* (**1958**; vt *Space Prison*) by Tom GODWIN and *Open Prison* (**1964**; vt *The Escape Orbit*) by James WHITE. A much more humane view of the issues involved in crime and punishment is featured in the classic work on the theme, Alfred BESTER's *The Demolished Man* (**1953**), which deals with crime in a society which is socially advanced and includes many individuals with EXTRA-SENSORY PERCEPTIONS. The same author's "Fondly Fahrenheit" (1954) is a forceful study in the psychology of murder, the dual murderers being a human and an ANDROID. An interesting study of the psychology of the prisoner, and the (in this case unsuccessful) psychology of penology and brainwashing was THE PRISONER, a television series which made much symbolic use of the idea that freedom and imprisonment can be considered as states of mind. *The Prisoner* (**1969**) by Thomas M. DISCH was a novelization from the series.

Exotic police forces were featured in heroic roles in a number of sf stories and series in the 1950s. An alien policeman pursues a criminal to Earth in *Needle* (**1950**) by Hal CLEMENT, having to inhabit the body of an Earthly host in order to do so. Time police patrolling and protecting history are featured in a number of stories, including *The End of Eternity* (**1955**) by Isaac Asimov and *Guardians of Time* (1955–60; fix-up **1960**) by Poul ANDERSON (*see* ALTERNATE WORLDS). H. Beam PIPER's "Paratime Police" series (1948–65) is also allied to this category. Law enforcement in a colony on another world is featured in the ultra-tough *Police Your Planet* (**1956**) by Lester del Rey (writing as Erik van Lhin). Asimov wrote his first sf detective story, *The Caves of Steel* (**1954**), in this period, and the detective-story writer John Dickson CARR used time travel in two excellent mysteries, *The Devil in Velvet* (**1951**) and *Fire, Burn!* (**1956**). In the 1960s Poul Anderson wrote a murder mystery with Earth as the corpse — *After Doomsday* (**1962**) — and an effective series of stories dealing with road-traffic law enforcement in the near future was written by Rick RAPHAEL and collected in *Code Three* (fix-

up **1966**). Law enforcers of a rather less conventional kind were Rosel George BROWN's *Sibyl Sue Blue* (**1966**; vt *Galactic Sibyl Sue Blue*) and the heroine of Ian WALLACE's *Deathstar Voyage* (**1969**) and its two successors. The ultimate enforcer in sf outside the comic books was featured in Doris PISERCHIA's *Mister Justice* (**1973**).

A more romantic view of crime is presented by a number of sf stories which feature the criminal as hero. Leaving aside the great numbers of misfits who fight the good fight against tyranny and the stereotyped persecuted SUPERMAN, the most notable criminal heroes in sf are Alar the Thief in Charles L. HARNESS's *Flight into Yesterday* (1949; **1953**; vt *The Paradox Men*) and Slippery Jim di Griz, the hero of Harry HARRISON's *Stainless Steel Rat* (1957–60; fix-up **1961**). Philip José FARMER wrote a series of stories featuring John Carmody, a criminal who reformed to become a priest, the most notable being *Night of Light* (**1966**), but recent times have produced criminal heroes totally unrepentant and rather more charismatic, including Roger ZELAZNY's *Jack of Shadows* (**1971**), the boy of Harlan ELLISON's "A Boy and His Dog" (1969) and the narrator of Samuel R. DELANY's "Time Considered as a Helix of Semi-Precious Stones" (1968). In *Logan's Run* (**1967**) (*see* LOGAN's RUN) by William NOLAN and George Clayton JOHNSON a policeman turns deviant instead of reporting for euthanasia when his allotted span of life runs out.

Several sf writers have adopted the familiar romantic notion of the criminal as outsider, natural radical and critic of society, even artist. This theme appears in a great many stories by Jack VANCE, for example, and in almost everything written by Charles L. Harness and Samuel R. Delany, along with much of the work of Alfred Bester. Sf often stresses that a criminal act in one society may be perfectly acceptable in another. Robert Sheckley has often stressed this relativity of crime, and the difficulty of defining it, as in "Watchbird" (1953), a moral fable about a mechanical law-enforcer's tendency to exceed its brief, with disastrous consequences, and "The Monsters" (1953), in which wife-murder is a moral act for aliens.

Despite the welter of criminal activity in sf there are hardly any novel crimes, though such Dystopias as *Nineteen Eighty-Four* (**1949**) by George ORWELL have invented new twists on the old crime of political deviation. J.G. BALLARD has often rung the changes on crimes of nonconformity, as in "Billenium" (1961), in which an empty room is not reported, and "Chronopolis" (1960), in which the hero illegally winds clocks. Tampering with history is a peculiarly sf crime, which is matched by the singularly appropriate punishment of historical erasure in Robert Silverberg's *Up the Line* (**1969**), but this is really no more than an extreme form of subversive activity. A similarly extreme nonconformist is featured in John BRUNNER's *The Shockwave Rider* (**1975**). A genuinely original crime is committed by the protagonist of Piers ANTHONY's *Chthon* (**1967**), for which he is condemned to a particularly terrible prison colony. A greater degree of ingenuity has been devoted to the design of punishments. Robert Silverberg's *Hawksbill Station* (**1968**) is about life in a prison colony in distant prehistory. Piers Anthony and Robert ·E. MARGROFF's *The Ring* (**1968**) has criminals fitted with a device which shocks them if they are guilty of deviant thoughts, and provides a detailed commentary on an idea first formulated in Damon Knight's "The Analogues" (1952). A less subtle device, containing an explosive which can be set off if prisoners escape, is featured in *The Reefs of Space* (**1964**) by Frederik POHL and Jack WILLIAMSON. A heavily polemical work on penological theory is John J. McGUIRE's "Take the Reason Prisoner" (1963). A Draconian criminal code is taken to extremes in Larry NIVEN's "The Jigsaw Man" (1967), which envisages death penalties being widely reintroduced because of the demand for "spare parts" which the bodies of the condemned supply to the needy. Niven has written several other crime stories on a related theme, collected in *The Long ARM of Gil Hamilton* (coll. **1976**).

There are two theme anthologies concerned with sf crime stories: *Space Police* (**1956**) ed. Andre NORTON and *Space, Time and Crime* (**1964**) ed. Miriam Allen DEFORD. [BS/PN] See also: DYSTOPIAS; SOCIOLOGY; UTOPIAS.

CRIMES OF THE FUTURE Film (1970). Emergent Films. Directed by David Cronenberg, starring Ronald Mlodzik, Tania Zolty, Jon Lidolt and Jack Messinger. Screenplay by David Cronenberg. 70 mins. Colour.

This is a cheaply made, inventive, independent Canadian film produced, written and directed by David Cronenberg who later made the bizarre THEY CAME FROM WITHIN (vt *Parasite Murders*; vt *Shivers*) and RABID. *COTF* is a deliberately tasteless satire on sex, set in a future era where all pre-menopausal women have been killed by a disease created by a mad dermatologist, with the exception of one five-year-old girl. It is never very clear in Cronenberg's work whether he is exploiting the voyeurism of the audience or expressing his own disgust. [JB/PN]

CRISP, FRANK R(OBSON) (1915–). British writer, at one time in the British Merchant Navy. His sf novels, *The Ape of London* (**1959**) and *The Night Callers* (**1960**), deploy thriller and horror elements with only moderate sf ingredients in routine adventures, the latter involving alien INVASION. [JC]

See also: ASTRONOMY; PARASITISM AND SYMBIOSIS..

CRISPIN, EDMUND Generally used pseudonym of Robert Bruce Montgomery (1921–78), British writer and editor. As a writer, EC is best known for his nine detective novels featuring the witty, academic detective Gervase Fen; he also reviewed crime fiction for the *Sunday Times*. Under his real name he is known as a composer, and wrote the music for many British films of the 1950s and '60s, including several of the "Carry On" series. He did not write sf, but his work as an sf anthologist has been of great influence. When *Best SF* (anth. **1955**) appeared it was unique in several ways. Its editor was a respected literary figure; its publisher was a prestigious one; it made no apologies or excuses for what it was. Moreover, EC's selection of stories showed him to be thoroughly familiar with sf in both magazine and book form, and his introductions to this and succeeding volumes were informed and illuminating. *Best SF* was followed by *Best SF Two* (anth. **1956**), *Best SF Three* (anth. **1958**), *Best SF Four* (anth. **1961**), *Best SF Five* (anth. **1963**), *Best SF Six* (anth. **1966**) and *Best SF Seven* (anth. **1970**). It would be difficult to exaggerate the importance of the early volumes in this series in establishing sf in Britain as a respectable branch of literature. EC also edited two sf anthologies for schools, *The Stars and Under* (anth. **1968**) and *Outwards from Earth* (anth. **1974**), as well as *Best Tales of Terror* (anth. **1962**) and *Best Tales of Terror Two* (anth. **1965**). [MJE]

CRISTABEL Pseudonym of Christine Abrahamsen (?–). Her sf novel *The Mortal Immortals* (**1971**) is written in a style reminiscent of a cross between romantic fiction and boys' fiction of the 1930s. [PN] Other works: *The Cruachan and the Killane* (**1970**); *Manalacor of Veltakin* (**1970**); *The Golden Olive* (**1972**).

CRITICAL AND HISTORICAL WORKS ABOUT SF The range and sophistication of sf studies has expanded recently; before 1970 very little useful material was available. The first important study, *Pilgrims Through Space and Time* (**1947**), by J.O. BAILEY, is historical and thematic; value judgements are almost absent, and trivia are discussed alongside works of lasting interest. Despite its limitations, this was a valuable pioneering work. The PILGRIM AWARD for excellence in sf studies was named after it.

The next serious study, very different in tone, was *New Maps of Hell* (**1960**) by Kingsley AMIS. Brief and unscholarly, it is nevertheless witty, critical and suggestive; Amis takes the essential aspects of modern sf to be SATIRICAL and DYSTOPIAN. Unlike Bailey, he took most of his examples from contemporary genre sf. Quite the reverse of Amis's study were those of Sam MOSKOWITZ — humourless, adopting simplistic critical criteria and not always accurate in detail, they were nevertheless important, and remain so, for their detailed historical research, not only in archives but through the oral testimony of genre sf's early masters, many of them personally known to Moskowitz. Three collections of his essays are *Explorers of the Infinite* (coll. **1963**), *Seekers of Tomorrow* (coll. **1966**) and *Strange Horizons* (coll. **1976**); also of note are his *Science Fiction by Gaslight: A History and Anthology of Science Fiction in the Popular Magazines 1891–1911* (anth. **1968**) and *Under the Moons of Mars: A History and Anthology of "The Scientific Romance" in the Munsey Magazines, 1912–1920* (anth. **1970**), with their long, informative introductions.

Two well-known writers of sf, Damon KNIGHT and James BLISH, often took time out to write shrewd, well-informed criticism, the latter under the pseudonym of William Atheling Jr. Much of Knight's critical work was collected in *In Search of Wonder* (coll. **1956**; exp. 1967), and of Atheling's in *The Issue at Hand* (coll. **1964**) and *More Issues at Hand* (coll. **1970**).

The cautious interest being shown in sf by the academic world in the US bore its first fruits in 1959, in the shape of the critical journal EXTRAPOLATION. For many years it was stencilled, not printed, which suggested that the financial support it was receiving from academia at large was small; nevertheless it lived on. Two further academic magazines about sf followed, both in their own way a little livelier: FOUNDATION: THE REVIEW OF SCIENCE FICTION in 1972 in the UK, and SCIENCE-FICTION STUDIES in 1973 in the USA. The former emphasized reviews and critical and sociological studies of contemporary and post-War sf; the latter emphasized writers of sf's past, and only the more academically acceptable of the present, with good coverage of European sf and some interesting and, to many, unexpected Marxist criticism.

Some of the best critical writing about sf appeared in these journals, and also in a great many FANZINES. Unfortunately, fanzines tending to be produced inexpensively and with low circulations, much of this criticism has been ephemeral or difficult to obtain. Some of the more interesting critical fanzines were (and in many cases still are) ALGOL, SCIENCE FICTION REVIEW, RIVERSIDE QUARTERLY, LUNA MONTHLY, SPECULATION, CYPHER, VECTOR and SF COMMENTARY. The professional sf magazines also regularly published sf criticism, that of *FSF* in particular often being of a high quality. A notable semi-professional magazine was DELAP's F & SF REVIEW; it published nothing but sf book reviews. By the 1970s a large body of sf criticism had been built up, though much of it was, and is, difficult to get hold of. The earlier view that sf should be judged by criteria different from those normally applied to conventional literature has steadily lost ground to the view that sf is strong enough to be gauged by the same standards that prevail elsewhere, but to this day, and very naturally, the literary analysis of sf tends to be argued thematically and structurally, and to eschew a criticism grounded in concepts of characterization and psychological realism.

The trickle of sf criticism in book form became a small spate between 1974 and 1977, but by 1974 a number of new books had already appeared, including lightweight studies by Sam Lundwall and Donald A. Wollheim in the USA, and Roger Lancelyn Green and Patrick Moore in the UK. *Billion Year Spree* (1973) by Brian W. Aldiss is idiosyncratic in some respects, and many reviewers observed that his account of the post-War period was hurried and not very informative, but it is an important book, especially in the literary and cultural context it gives for sf ever since the days of Mary Shelley, who is Aldiss's candidate for the position of the first *bona fide* sf writer. Aldiss's tone, a kind of cheeriness which never loses sight of sf's entertaining qualities while many serious points continue to be made, is a relief after the ponderousness of some previous studies of sf and the defensive fannish enthusiasm of others. Brian Aldiss was awarded the first James Blish Award for excellence in sf criticism. The next important book on sf, for the general reader, was also by a professional writer from the genre; it was James Gunn's *Alternate Worlds: The Illustrated History of Science Fiction* (1975), a balanced and intelligent survey. This book was part of a sudden rush of handsome, illustrated books about sf, many of which are listed under Illustration. Two such studies by David Kyle have a fairly even balance between picture and text, but they are shaky in their criticism and uncertain about their facts in the earlier period. Brian Ash's *Faces of the Future* (1975) was too heavily devoted to plot summary and too simplistic, a general fault in many recent books about sf. Worth more serious notice is the collection of essays by Alexei and Cory Panshin, *SF in Dimension* (coll. 1976), which argue a coherent if controversial viewpoint. Alexei Panshin had earlier published an interesting study of Robert Heinlein.

Many sf writers apart from those already mentioned have also written well-informed and lively sf criticism and essays in sf scholarship, though few — Samuel R. Delany and L. Sprague de Camp are exceptions — have had books published on the subject. Most such criticism has appeared in magazines or introductions to anthologies. Some of the more interesting writer-critics are Algis Budrys, Thomas M. Disch, Gardner Dozois, M. John Harrison, Ursula Le Guin, Michael Moorcock, Joanna Russ, Robert Silverberg, Brian Stableford and Ian Watson. A controversial and rigorous critic of some penetration is John Clute, whose work had appeared entirely in magazines prior to the publication of this Encyclopedia.

Aside from Bailey's there were two important early works of academic sf scholarship: *The Imaginary Voyage in Prose Fiction: A History of its Criticism and a Guide for its Study, With an Annotated Check List of 215 Imaginary Voyages from 1700 to 1800* (1941) by Philip Babcock Gove, and *Voyages to the Moon* (1949) by Marjorie Hope Nicolson. After a long gap, the next works of importance (apart from studies of single authors such as H.G. Wells and Aldous Huxley, which are listed in this volume under the appropriate author entries) were *Voices Prophesying War 1763–1984* (1966) by I.F. Clarke and *Yesterday's Tomorrows* (1968) by W.H.G. Armytage. Running concurrently with all these publications, and beginning much earlier, have been the many books on literary Utopias, but these are not considered here.

Next in the academic line came *Into the Unknown: The Evolution of Science Fiction from Francis Godwin to H.G. Wells* (1970) by Robert M. Philmus. In the 1970s Darko Suvin came to the fore as an academic critic of sf, though his only full-scale work had been published in French: *Pour une poétique de la science-fiction* (1977 Quebec). Leon Stover has also published a critical-sociological study of sf in French, *La science fiction américaine: essai d'anthropologie culturelle* (1972 Paris), but it is rather ragged.

After 1974 the pace of academic publishing increased. The most important studies are *New Worlds for Old* (1974) by David Ketterer, *Visions of Tomorrow* (coll. 1975) by David Samuelson and *Structural Fabulation* (1975) by Robert Scholes. Scholes went on to collaborate with Eric S. Rabkin on *Science Fiction: History, Science, Vision* (1977), one of the best semi-popular accounts of the genre.

Scholes' work was much influenced by *Introduction à la littérature fantastique* (1970 France, trans. as *The Fantastic. A Structural Approach to a Literary Genre* 1973) by Tzvetan Todorov, a work which has aroused controversy and much interest. Sf criticism, primarily Marxist, structuralist or both, is flourishing in Europe. Other notable European critics are Michel Butor, Boris Eizykman, Gotthard Günther, Dieter Hasselblatt, Jorg Hienger, John-Henri Holmberg, Julius Kagarlitsky, Norbert Lingfeld, Gianni Montanari, Manfred Nagl, Carlo Pagetti, Michael Pehlke, Jacques Sadoul, Martin Schwonke, Jacques van Herp and Pierre Versins. Further information on all these can be found in their individual entries. One of the best-known European critics of sf is Franz Rottensteiner, who also publishes in English. Unfortunately, his only English book, *The Science Fiction Book: An Illustrated History* (1975), is not up to the standard of most of his other published criticism. Some exceptionally controversial criticism by Stanislaw Lem has been published in English, though his much discussed *Fantastyka i futurologia* (1970 Poland), a full-length study of sf, has not yet been translated.

Back in America the academic use of sf has had repercussions in the publication of anthologies of critical essays. Three such have been edited by Reginald Bretnor, and another three by Thomas D. Clareson. The Bretnor books stress what the sf writers themselves have to say; the Clareson books concentrate primarily on academic criticism. Two other useful works of this kind are *Turning Points: Essays on the Art of Science Fiction* (anth. 1977) ed. Damon Knight, and *Science Fiction at Large* (anth. 1976; vt *Explorations of the Marvellous*) ed. Peter Nicholls. The latter may signify the lessening defensive selfconsciousness of sf fans and writers in its publication of several essays which belabour sf unmercifully for its various shortcomings.

A useful reference is *Science Fiction Criticism: An Annotated Checklist* (1972) compiled by Thomas D. Clareson. [PN] **See also:** BIBLIOGRAPHIES; CINEMA; DEFINITIONS.

CROLY, Reverend GEORGE (1780–1860). English clergyman whose novel *Salathiel: A Story of the Past, The Present, and the Future* (1826; vt *Tarry Thou Till I Come*) was published anonymously but soon acknowledged. It is a story of IMMORTALITY. [JC]

One of the earliest sf paperback covers showing (after a fashion) space travel, *A Plunge into Space* by Robert Cromie.

CROMIE, ROBERT (1856–1907). English writer, author of the well-known interplanetary sf novel *A Plunge Into Space* (1890; the 1891 edition includes a preface by Jules VERNE), in which visitors to MARS discover humans living there under UTOPIAN conditions, described with some banality. [JC]

Other works: *For England's Sake* (**1889**); *The Crack of Doom* (**1895**); *The Next Crusade* (**1896**); *A New Messiah* (**1902**); *El Dorado* (**1904**).

See also: CRIME AND PUNISHMENT; POWER SOURCES; SPACE FLIGHT; SPACESHIPS.

CROSBY, HARRY C. *See* Christopher ANVIL.

CROSS, JOHN KEIR (1911–67). English writer of novels and television adaptations for the BBC, probably best known for his fantasy collection *The Other Passenger* (coll. **1944**). His sf novels are juveniles, and include *The Angry Planet* (**1945**) and its sequel, *SOS from Mars* (**1954**; vt *Red Journey Back* USA), about the first three expeditions to Mars, *The Owl and the Pussycat* (**1946**; vt *The Other Side of Green Hills* USA), and *The Flying Fortunes in an Encounter with Rubberface* (**1952**; vt *The Stolen Sphere* USA). He also edited the fantasy collections *Best Black Magic Stories* (anth. **1960**), *Best Horror Stories* (anth. **1956**) and *Best Horror Stories 2* (anth. **1965**). [JC]

CROSS, POLTON *See* John Russell FEARN.

CROSSEN, KENDELL FOSTER (1910–). American writer and editor, active under various names in various PULP markets, perhaps most notably as a detective writer as KFC and under the pseudonym M.E. Chaber. He began publishing sf with two stories in Feb. 1951: "The Boy who Cried Wolf 359" in *AMZ* and "Restricted Clientele" in THRILLING WONDER STORIES. He published a large amount of material with STARTLING STORIES and *TWS* towards the end of their existence; much of this material is intendedly comic, in particular the "Manning Draco" series, about an interstellar salesman and his amusing experiences with ALIENS, comprised of *Once Upon a Star* (1951–2 *TWS*; fix-up **1953**) plus four additional stories, also from *TWS*, "Assignment to Aldebaran" (1953), "Whistle Stop in Space" (1953), "Mission to Mizar" (1953) and "The Agile Algolian" (1954). *Year of Consent* (**1952**) expressively conveys the PARANOIA of much American fiction of the period in its story of a COMPUTER that controls the West; *The Rest Must Die* (**1959** as by Richard Foster) follows the story of those who have survived a nuclear attack on New York by happening to be in a subway train. KFC's anthologies, *Adventures in Tomorrow* (anth. **1951**; UK edition omits two stories) and *Future Tense* (anth. **1952**; UK edition omits seven stories), which includes some original stories, are competently selected and were influential in their time. [JC]

CROW, LEVI *See* Manly Wade WELLMAN.

CROWCROFT, PETER (1925–). British writer. His sf novel, *The Fallen Sky* (**1954**), describes a post-HOLOCAUST London. [JC]

CROWLEY, JOHN (1942–). American writer who has also worked in documentary films and television since 1966; his two sf novels have had a considerable impact on the field. The first of them, *The Deep* (**1975**), is an extremely impressive début. The world it describes is a flat disc resting on a pillar that extends to unimaginable depths into the surrounding Deep, in which very few stars are visible; on this disc, complex and interminable feudal conflicts are regulated, maintained and when necessary fomented for his own pleasure by the mysterious Being who had originally transported to this strange new domain the humans resident upon it — their own world had been dying. Though the story is told from various points of view, the reader's interest centres on the Visitor, a damaged ANDROID with memory problems sent to record events by the disc's peculiar God. Building his novel from sources as widely divergent as James Branch CABELL's "Biography of Manuel" sequence, Philip José FARMER's "World of Tiers" novels and E.R. EDDISON's *The Worm Ouroboros* (**1922**), JC has constructed a story possible only late in the life of any genre, a tale whose free and supple use of numerous generic conventions marks him as a leader of the 1970s generation of sf writers. *Beasts* (**1976**) somewhat more conventionally depicts a Balkanized America, but with a complex use of sf themes, notable among which are the uses he makes of biologically transformed animals, and of the potential for genuine inter-species empathy. [JC]

See also: CONCEPTUAL BREAKTHROUGH; FANTASY; GODS AND DEMONS; SWORD AND SORCERY.

CRY American FANZINE (1950–69) ed. Wally Weber, F.M. and Elinor BUSBY and others for the Nameless Ones, a Seattle sf fan group. A local fortnightly, later monthly, journal, *Cry*'s regularity eventually brought it widespread recognition as an entertaining and dependable fanzine, mainly concerned with FANDOM. Contributors included Ted WHITE, Terry CARR, Donald WOLLHEIM and Avram DAVIDSON. *Cry* won the HUGO for best fanzine in 1960. [PR]

CRYOGENICS The word is from a Greek root meaning "cold-producing", and is used to mean the study of producing extremely low temperatures. Recently the shorter word CRYONICS (*see below*) has come to be used in its place when it is organic material which is being frozen. [PN]

CRYONICS Cryonics is a term coined by Karl Werner, referring to techniques directed toward preservation of the human body by supercooling. Since R.C.W. Ettinger published *The Prospects of Immortality* (**1964**) the notion of freezing corpses or terminally ill people, to preserve them until such a time as medical science has discovered cures for all ills and methods of resurrecting the dead, has become popular in sf.

The preservative effects of low temperatures have been known for a long time — it was while preparing for a cryonic experiment that Francis BACON caught the chill which killed him. During the 19th century several perfectly preserved mammoth carcases were discovered in the North Siberian ice, and a famous hoax perpetrated at an Explorers' Club dinner persuaded the members that the steaks they were eating came from such beasts. The notion was first developed in sf by W. Clark RUSSELL in *The Frozen Pirate* (**1887**), in which a shipwrecked man builds a fire on an icebound pirate ship and revives one of its crewmen. In Louis BOUSSENARD's *10,000 Years in a Block of Ice* (**1889**; trans. **1898**) a contemporary man visits the future with the aid of a similar accident. Edgar Rice BURROUGHS' "The Resurrection of Jimber Jaw" (1937) features, satirically, the revival of a prehistoric man and his experiences in the civilized world.

Freezing thus became a standard means of achieving SUSPENDED ANIMATION, but the recent debate about cryonics also relates to the categories of REINCARNATION and IMMORTALITY. The Cryonics Society of California froze several newly dead people in 1967, and it remains to be seen whether this is a passing fad or not. Interest is not confined to America, and two of the major fictional examinations of the prospect are European: Nikolai AMOSOV's *Notes from the Future* (**1967** Russia; trans. **1970**) and Anders BODELSEN's *Freezing Down* (**1969** Denmark; trans. **1971**). Within genre sf the most impressive dramatization of the social problems which might be associated with cryonic projects on a large scale is Clifford D. SIMAK's *Why Call Them Back From Heaven?* (**1967**), which foresees a time when a man might be tried for delaying the freezing of a corpse and allowing "ultimate death" to occur, and in which the financial estates of the frozen become a political power-bloc, inviting criminal manipulation. A rather more cynical account of the politics of dealing with the dead is offered by Larry NIVEN's "The Defenseless Dead" (1973), which points out that the living have all the votes and that the dead might be an exploitable resource. Ernest TIDYMAN's satirical thriller *Absolute Zero* (**1971**) is also a cynical story. It tells of a financier whose dwarf parents are frozen in a blizzard, thus motivating him to build up a vast cryonics industry, involved in various dubious manipulations. Apart from its frequent use in stories involving TIME TRAVEL into the future, including Frederik POHL's *The Age of the Pussyfoot* (**1969**) and Mack REYNOLDS' UTOPIAN novel *Looking Backward, From the Year 2000* (**1973**) and the satirical Woody Allen film SLEEPER, cryonics has also become a common device in stories of slower-than-light SPACE TRAVEL. In E.C. TUBB's "Dumarest" series interstellar travel may be "high" or "low", depending upon whether time is absorbed by the use of drugs or by the more hazardous cryonic procedures, while James WHITE's *The Dream Millennium* (**1974**) makes significant use of the possible psychological effects of being "frozen down".

In his short story "Ozymandias" (1972), Terry CARR produced an interesting variation on the cryonics theme. The story tells of a distant future, after nuclear war (*see* HOLOCAUST AND AFTER), in which an analogue of the Egyptian Valley of the Kings had been set up – a series of cryonic vaults filled with hopefuls who had decided to sleep through the war. But as in ancient Egypt, tomb-robbing has become an important profession. The narrative, bizarrely and sensitively structured, is from the viewpoint of one of these robbers.

Sf has been responsible for the creation and popularization of a number of neologisms, and it is likely that the macabre CORPSICLE (a word coined by Larry Niven) will ultimately enter the language as customary slang for the well-preserved dead that even now are awaiting resurrection in some future age. [BS]

CULTURAL ENGINEERING *See* ANTHROPOLOGY; COLONIZATION OF OTHER WORLDS; ICONOCLASM; POLITICS; SOCIOLOGY.

CUMMINGS, M(ONETTE) A. (?–). American writer of short stories who began publishing sf with "The Bridges of Ool" with *Planet Stories* in 1955, and whose collection is *Exile and Other Tales of Fantasy* (coll. **1968**). [JC]

CUMMINGS RAY(MOND KING) (1887–1957). American writer, one of the few active during the heyday of American PULP-magazine sf (1930–50) who began his career before Hugo GERNSBACK began *AMZ* in 1926. His first sf of any note is also his best-known story, "The Girl in the Golden Atom" (1919), which appeared, as did much of his early work, in *All-Story Weekly*; with its sequel, "People of the Golden Atom", serialized in the same magazine in 1920, this famous story about a young man who takes a size-diminishing drug and has extraordinary adventures on a microscopic world became *The Girl in the Golden Atom* (fix-up **1921** UK; exp. 1923 USA), and proved the cornerstone both of RC's reputation and of much of his

work from this time on, for he used the idea of the size-diminishing drug and the microscopic world, with many vairations, for the rest of his long career (*see* GREAT AND SMALL). *The Girl in the Golden Atom* also constitutes the "Matter" segment of RC's "Matter, Space and Time" trilogy; the "Space" segment is comprised of *The Princess of the Atom* (1929 *Argosy*; **1950**) and "The Fire People" (1922 *Argosy*); the "Time" segment is comprised of *The Man Who Mastered Time* (1924 *Argosy*; **1929**), *The Shadow Girl* (1929 *Argosy*; **1947**) and *The Exile of Time* (1931 ASF; **1964**).

After the successes of his early years, RC remained prolific, but his mechanical style and the general rigidity of his stories gradually lost him popularity until some of his books were nostalgically revived in the 1960s. Typical of his journeyman prose and uneven quality are the "Tama" novels, *Tama of the Light Country* (1930 *Argosy*; **1965**) and *Tama, Princess of Mercury* (1931 *Argosy*; **1966**), the heroine of which does very well after being kidnapped from Earth to MERCURY. RC wrote 16 uncollected stories in various magazines — seven between 1920 and 1923 and a further nine between 1937 and 1946 — about a character named Tubby who displays his inventiveness in different situations. *Brigands of the Moon* (1931; later published in Canada with a mistaken attribution to John W. CAMPBELL Jr) and its sequel *Wandl the Invader* (1932 *ASF*; **1961**) are examples of his SPACE-OPERA output, in which space pirates tend to proliferate, and men defeat terrifying alien monsters. Another unreprinted RC novel is "Jetta of the Lowlands" (1930 *ASF*).

RC was fundamentally a pulp writer, one who, moreover, unlike some of those only a little younger than he, Murray LEINSTER and Edmond HAMILTON, for instance, was never capable of adapting himself to the changing times, either scientifically or stylistically; his latest works could be interchanged with his earliest with very little adjustment. He is a subject of historic interest only to readers today. [JC]

Other works: *The Sea Girl* (**1930**); *Tarrano the Conqueror* (1925 *Science and Invention*; **1930**); *Into the Fourth Dimension* (1926 *Science and Invention*; **1943**); *Beyond the Vanishing Point* (1931 *ASF*; **1958**); *Beyond the Stars* (1928 *Argosy*; **1963**), *A Brand New World* (1928 *Argosy*; **1964**); *Explorers Into Infinity* (1927–8 *Weird Tales*; **1965**); *The Insect Invasion* (1932 *Argosy*; **1967**); *The Man on the Meteor* (1924 *Science and Invention*; **1952**); "The Snow Girl" (1929 *Argosy*; in *Famous Fantastic Classics* No. 1, anth. **1974**).

See also: CONCEPTUAL BREAKTHROUGH; FANTASTIC VOYAGES; ROBOTS; SCIENTIFIC ERRORS; TIME TRAVEL.

CUMMINS, HARLE OWEN (?–?).

American writer of stories; of those collected in *Welsh Rarebit Tales* (coll. **1902**), four, like "The Space Annihilator", have considerable sf interest; in this story a MATTER TRANSMITTER is introduced. Other tales are generally fantasy. [JC]

CUNNINGHAM, E.V. *See* Howard FAST.

CURSE OF THE FLY Film (1965). Lippert/Fox. Directed by Don Sharp, starring Brian Donlevy, George Baker and Carol Gray. Screenplay by Harry Spalding, based on characters created by George LANGELAAN. 86 mins. Colour.

Second sequel to THE FLY (the first being RETURN OF THE FLY). A scientist experimenting with a matter transmitter cannot quite make it work correctly — with the result that the people he transmits end up somewhat distorted and understandably annoyed. [JB]

CURTIS, JEAN-LOUIS Pseudonym of French writer Louis Lafitte (1917–); his collection of five SATIRICAL sf stories, *Un saint au néon* (coll. **1956**; trans. as *The Neon Halo; The Face of the Future* **1958**), very sharply depicts a NEAR-FUTURE world whose centre cannot hold; the tone is vivacious, didactic, circumstantial; its wit is distanced in a French way. [JC]

CURTIS, RICHARD A(LAN) (1937–). American editor, literary agent and writer, known mainly in the first capacity for his anthology *Future Tense* (anth. **1968**), not to be confused with Kendell Foster CROSSEN's *Future Tense* (anth. **1952**). He has also published sf stories, beginning with "Introduction to 'The Saint' " for *Cavalier* in 1968. [JC]

CURTIS, WADE *See* Jerry POURNELLE.

CURTIS, WARDON ALLAN (1867–?). American writer and contributor to several pre-sf fiction magazines. His most important sf is a short story about a brain transplant, "The Monster of Lake LaMetrie" (1899), in which the brain is human and the recipient body is that of a prehistoric survival. He also wrote an Arabian nights fantasy, "The Seal of Solomon the Great" (1901) for ARGOSY, and *The Strange Adventures of Mr. Middleton* (coll. **1903**), which contains a mixture of oriental fantasy and bizarre mystery. [JE]

CURVAL, PHILIPPE Pseudonym used by journalist Philippe Tronche (1929–), French writer. PC has been associated since the 1950s with the growth of sf in France as bookseller, magazine editor, photographer, chronicler and author. He is a fine stylist whose work is exemplified by a sensual, poetic mood and great affection for his characters. He has written over 20 stories, the first of which appeared in 1955. *Le ressac de l'espace*

["The Breakers of Space"] (**1962**) won the PRIX JULES VERNE in 1963; *L'homme à rebours* ["Backwards Man"] (**1974**) was selected as best French sf novel of 1974 and *Cette chère humanité* ["This Dear Humanity"] (**1976**) was awarded the 1977 PRIX APOLLO.   [MJ]

Other works: *Les fleurs de Vénus* ["Flowers of Venus"] (**1960**); *La forteresse de coton* ["The Cotton Fortress"] (**1967**); *Les sábles de Falun* ["The Sands of Falun"] (**1970**); *Attention les yeux* ["Beware, Eyes!"] (**1972**); *Un soupçon de néant* ["A Suspicion of Nothingness"] (**1977**).   [MJ]

CYBERNETICS In sf terminology this is a common word, often misused. So popular, however, has its general use in fiction become that the real meaning of the word is in danger of being devalued or forgotten.

"Cybernetics" is a term coined by the distinguished mathematician Norbert WIENER in 1947 to describe a new science on which he and others had been working since 1942. The word first passed into general usage with the publication of Wiener's book *Cybernetics* (**1948**; rev. **1961**), which was subtitled "Control and Communication in the Animal and the Machine". Cybernetics was cross-disciplinary from the beginning; it developed when Wiener and others noticed that certain parallel problems persistently arose in scientific disciplines which are normally regarded as separate: statistical mechanics, information theory, electrical engineering and neurophysiology were four of the most important.

"Cybernetics", which has much in common with the parallel study of general systems theory, founded by Ludwig von Bertalanffy in 1940, is taken from a Greek word meaning helmsman or controller. The science of cybernetics is concerned with the way systems work, the way they govern themselves, the way they process information (often through a process known as "feedback") in order to govern themselves, and how they can best be designed. The system in question can be a machine, or it can equally be a human body. The trouble is, Wiener found, that the terminology with which engineers discussed machines led to a very mechanistic approach when used to discuss human systems, and, conversely, biological terminology led to an over-anthropomorphic approach when discussing machines (or economic or ecological systems, two other areas where cybernetics is useful). The trick was to construct a new science which would not be biased towards either the mechanical or the biological. In his *An Introduction to Cybernetics* (**1956**), W. Ross Ashby remarks that "cybernetics stands to the real machine — electronic, mechanical, neural or economic — much as geometry stands to a real object in our terrestrial space". In other words, cybernetics is an abstracting, generalizing science. However, science being what it is, always tending towards specialization, the original idea of cybernetics as a cross-disciplinary science is in danger of being forgotten, and now we have specialists in, for example, engineering cybernetics and biological cybernetics. The latter is usually called "bionics", although this is actually a contraction of "biological electronics"; the word was coined as recently as 1960.

If we use the broad, scientifically accepted definition of cybernetics, it cannot be delimited as a separate theme in this Encyclopedia. Most of the stories discussed under the entries ANDROIDS, AUTOMATION, COMMUNICATION, COMPUTERS, CYBORGS, INTELLIGENCE and ROBOTS will, by definition, be cybernetics stories also. For example, Kurt VONNEGUT Jr's *Player Piano* (**1952**) (*see* AUTOMATION) has at its heart an image of men incorporated in and subject to an impersonal, machine-like system; they effectively become components or "bits" in a cybernetic system.

However, in sf cybernetics is usually used to mean something narrower: nine times out of ten it refers to the creation of artificial intelligence. This is indeed a central problem in cybernetics, but by no means the only one. Some cyberneticians hope that analysis of neural systems (i.e. the brain) might lead to the synthesis of simulated intelligences which begin as machines, but go on to become self-programming, The first step towards artifical intelligence in real life is the computer, which is why all computer stories are cybernetics stories also.

Cybernetics also enters sf in the form of the word "cyborg", which is a contraction of "cybernetic organism". This use of the word is taken from an area of cybernetics not necessarily related to artificial intelligences; a man with a wooden leg is a kind of very simple cyborg. The organism is cybernetic in this instance because the melding of mechanical and human parts necessitates (whether consciously or not) the use of feedback devices; the study of cybernetics is, at bottom, the study of just such devices, whether they be servo-mechanisms or the messages that travel between eye and hand when we pick up a book from a table. (For further discussion *see* HOMEOSTASIS.)

Surprisingly few sf stories attack the problem of artificial intelligence directly; far more commonly, the problem is sidetracked by conjuring up a magic word from the air: Isaac ASIMOV said his robots were POSITRONIC, and left it at that. The most comprehensive (if not always comprehensible) cybernetics work in sf is the novel *Destination Void* (**1966**) by Frank HERBERT, in which the problem is not just that of building a very complex computer, but of building a machine that could be said to be conscious. Herbert actually spells out some of the steps through which this might conceivably be possible, and also goes on to ask the philosophical questions about autonomy and free will which must inevitably hover in the background of any cybernetics story of this kind. Interestingly, the question "in what respect can a machine be said to have free will?" engenders a parallel question about humans themselves, at least for readers and writers who take the materialist view that the human mind is itself no more than a complex cybernetics system. The whole thrust of cybernetics as a study is to point up the resemblances between sciences superficially dissimilar, and the attempt by neurocyberneticians to analyse the mind as a system has led to impassioned attack from people who believe that Man mystically transcends his own physical constituents. Frank Herbert examines these questions without answering them definitively, but he can hardly be blamed for that.

In real life, attempts to simulate intelligence in machines have mainly taken the route of the heuristic programming of computers. This is a way of showing a computer how to solve a problem not by painstakingly going through every possible combination that might lead to a solution — this would take a computer billions of years in an ordinary chess game — but by programming short cuts into the machine, so that it can gauge certain most likely or fruitful directions for analysis. Humans do it automatically; machines have to be taught, but this teaching is the first step towards training a machine how to make choices, a vital step towards consciousness.

The first important sf work to use the terminology of cybernetics was Bernard WOLFE's *Limbo* (**1952**; vt *Limbo '90* UK); he uses its basic ideas (sometimes with hostility) in the wide sense, as they relate to computers, war-games, industrial management and the workings of the brain. Cybernetics terminology is used very loosely, however, by Raymond F. JONES in *The Cybernetic Brains* (1950 *Startling Stories*; **1962**), which tells of human brains integrated with computers. Although Jones probably used the term more because it was fine sounding than for any other reason, this is nonetheless a legitimate cybernetics subject, also used notably in *Wolfbane* (**1959**) by Frederik POHL and C.M. KORNBLUTH, *Catchworld* (**1975**) by Chris BOYCE and several other stories.

A number of stories about the development of consciousness in computers carry cybernetic implications, though few as far-ranging as those in Herbert's *Destination Void*. Some can be found in *Science Fiction Thinking Machines* (anth. **1954**) ed. Groff CONKLIN; also relevant are *The God Machine* (**1968**) by Martin CAIDIN, *Vulcan's Hammer* (**1960**) by Philip K. DICK, *The Tale of the Big Computer* (**1966**; trans. **1968**; vt *The*

Great Computer, a Vision UK) by Olof JOHANNESSON, *The Moon is a Harsh Mistress* **(1966)** by Robert HEINLEIN, *When Harlie Was One* **(1972)** by David GERROLD and Keith ROBERTS' story "Synth" (1966). The reverse progression, of man into machine, occurs in the vignettes of *Moderan* (coll. of linked stories **1971)** by David R. BUNCH.

Already developed machine consciousnesses appear in *The Cyberiad: Fables for the Cybernetic Age* **(1967**; trans. **1974)** by Stanislaw LEM, all the "Berserker" stories by Fred SABERHAGEN, *The Siren Stars* **(1971)** by Richard and Nancy CARRIGAN and Roger ZELAZNY's story "For a Breath I Tarry" (1966).

The Steel Crocodile **(1970**; vt *The Electric Crocodile* UK) by D.G. COMPTON is interesting from a cybernetics viewpoint; it is about computer systems, but also analyses the nature of human social systems and examines how the two kinds intermesh. *Gray Matters* **(1971)** by William HJORTSBERG examines disembodied human brain systems linked up in a network. *The Black Cloud* **(1957)** by Fred HOYLE dramatizes communication between a human mind and an inorganic intelligence in space; it also raises a number of cybernetic issues. *The Jonah Kit* **(1975)** by Ian WATSON raises several cybernetic issues in that part of the story which deals with the imprinting of a human consciousness on to the mind of a whale.

As well as the two cybernetics texts already mentioned, *The Robots are Coming: The Implications of Artificial Intelligence Developments* **(1974)** ed. F.H. George and J.D. Humphries is useful. The essay "Images of Man-Machine Intelligence Relationships in Science Fiction" by Patricia Warrick, in *Many Futures, Many Worlds* (anth. **1977)** ed. Thomas D. CLARESON analyses a number of sf stories whose themes are cybernetic.   [PN]

CYBORGS The term "cyborg" is a contraction of "cybernetic organism" and refers to the product of man/machine hybridization, or, as David Rorvik puts it in his book *As Man Becomes Machine* **(1971)**, of the "melding" of man and machine. Rorvik's book discusses the cyborg in the real world — the medical cyborg which is already with us and the potential of the cyborg in "the new era of participant evolution". The medical cyborg — a man with a prosthetic limb, or with a pacemaker attached to his heart — is the cyborg most familiar in fiction, and has become a cliché, thanks to the TV series THE SIX-MILLION DOLLAR MAN and other spinoffs from Martin CAIDIN's novel *Cyborg* **(1972)**, although the series has adopted the variant term "bionic man". There are, however, two other common classes of cyborg in sf: the functional cyborg (a man modified mechanically to perform a specific task, usually a job of work) and the more

extreme case of the adaptive cyborg (a man so completely redesigned for a wholly new environment that his humanity is lost).

The first major cyborg novel, *The Clockwork Man* **(1923)** by E.V. ODLE, belongs to the third category, featuring a man of the future who has a clockwork mechanism built into his head which is supposed to regulate his whole being and which gives him access to a multidimensional world (*see* FOURTH DIMENSION). The early pulp sf writers were not so sophisticated — the most common cyborg featured in the pulps was the most extreme version of the MEDICAL cyborg, the brain-in-a-metal-body. In Edmond HAMILTON's "The Comet Doom" (1928) aliens who have adopted mechanical bodies offer to take an Earthman, similarly equipped, on a trip around the universe, and Neil R. JONES's Professor Jameson accepted such an invitation in a series which ran from 1931–51. Another brain immortalized by mechanical preservation threatened to take over the world in Lloyd Arthur ESHBACH's "The Time Conqueror" (1932; vt "Tyrant of Time") and the similarly motivated *Donovan's Brain* **(1943)** in the novel and film by Curt SIODMAK exercised an evil influence over ordinary mortals. Later writers, however, have approached the existential problems of human personalities in bodies mechanized for medical reasons in a much more careful and sophisticated manner. The theme has produced two outstanding stories in C.L. MOORE's "No Woman Born" (1944) and Algis BUDRYS's *Who?* **(1958)**, both of which focus on the problems of re-establishing identity once the familiar emblems are gone. The latter has been filmed (*see* WHO?).

The functional cyborg made his first significant appearance in "Scanners Live in Vain" (1950) by Cordwainer SMITH. Here cyborgization is designed for SPACE FLIGHT, and this particular theme dominates stories of both functional and adaptive cyborgs. Relatively few stories concern themselves with more mundane manipulative functions, although Samuel R. DELANY's *Nova* **(1968)** makes some significant observations *en passant*, and *The Godwhale* **(1974)** by T. J. BASS involves a massive food-collecting cyborg which is a hybrid of computer, robot and whale. Cyborgization in connection with space travel involves cyborg-spaceship stories such as Thomas N. SCORTIA's "Sea Change" (1956) and Anne MCCAFFREY's series eventually published as *The Ship Who Sang* (coll. **1969)**. A number of stories deal with the exploration of other worlds by adaptive cyborgs, including Arthur C. CLARKE's "A Meeting with Medusa" (1971) and Frederik POHL's *Man Plus* **(1976)**. Barrington J. BAYLEY's *The Garments of Caean* **(1976)** features two races of cyborgs adapted to the environment of outer space itself. The other major theme in stories dealing with

functional cyborgs concerns their adaptation to the needs of espionage and war — examples include "I-C-a-BEM" (1961) by Jack VANCE, "Kings who Die" (1962) by Poul ANDERSON and *A Plague of Demons* **(1965)** by Keith LAUMER. An interesting variation on the functional cyborg appears in the highly praised *The Continuous Katherine Mortenhoe* **(1974**; vt *The Unsleeping Eye* USA) by D.G. COMPTON, whose voyeuristic, suffering MEDIA-man hero has a television camera in place of eyes.

Sf in the cinema and on television, as in SPACE OPERA generally, often uses the cyborg as a convenient all-purpose figure of menace, as in several episodes of THE AVENGERS, the Cybermen of DR WHO, and in E.C. TUBB's "Dumarest" series of novels, in which one of the foci is human-cyborg conflict. The hero of Harlan ELLISON's television script "Demon with a Glass Hand" (1964) (*see* OUTER LIMITS) is human-seeming, but with his talking hand is one of the strangest, most alien cyborgs created for the screen, menacing yet sympathetic.

One work which transcends categorization to deal in semi-allegorical fashion with the relationship between Man and machine via the symbol of the cyborg is David R. BUNCH's *Moderan* (1959–70; fix-up **1971)**, an assembly of vignettes about a world where machine-men gradually forsake their "fleshstrips" and retire into mechanized "strongholds" to plot the destruction of their fellows.

Another subcategory of cyborg stories tells of the involuntary cyborg, a human assimilated by a computer (*see* COMPUTERS).

The symbol of the cyborg is perhaps one of the most important and significant in contemporary sf. An anthology is *Human Machines* **(1976)** ed. Thomas N. Scortia and George ZEBROWSKI.   [BS]
See also: CYBERNETICS; ROBOTS; SUPERMAN.

CYBORG 2087 Made-for-TV film (1966). Feature Film Corporation/Television Enterprises. Directed by Franklin Adreon, starring Michael Rennie, Karen Steele, Wendell Corey, Warren Stevens and Eduard Franz. Screenplay by Arthur C. Pierce. 86 mins. Colour.

An artificial man from the future has been sent back to 1966 to prevent a scientist from creating a device that will later be used as an instrument for mind-control by a totalitarian government in the year 2087. He is followed back in time by two government agents, both cyborgs, but he overcomes them and persuades the scientist to destroy his invention, though he knows that by doing so he will eliminate the possibility of his own existence. When the device is destroyed he disappears and all memory of his visit is eradicated from the minds of the people he encountered. The plot line was better thought out than those of most recent American TV sf series.   [JB]

CYPHER British FANZINE (1970–74) ed., from Wiltshire, James Goddard and Mike Sandow. A magazine mainly concerned with sf criticism and reviews, *Cypher*, particularly in later issues, published informative interviews and other material by James BLISH, Brian ALDISS, J.G. BALLARD, Edmund COOPER, E.C. TUBB, Harry HARRISON, and others.   [PR]

CYRANO DE BERGERAC The name under which Savinien de Cyrano (1619–55) is best known. French soldier and writer. Famous as the hero of a play by Edmond Rostand first produced in 1897, which made legendary both his swordsmanship and the size of his nose. He fought with the Gascon Guard but retired after sustaining bad wounds at the siege of Mouzon and at Arras. His major work of PROTO SCIENCE FICTION, *L'autre monde*, exists today only as one short novel (trans. as *Voyage to the Moon*) and part of a second (trans. as *The States and Empires of the Sun*). Versions of these "comic histories" were published in 1657 and 1662, but these had been censored by CDB's friend Henri le Bret to avoid controversy with the Church. English translations of these versions appeared in 1659 and 1683, but a definitive edition was not published in France until 1920. The definitive English edition is *Other Worlds* (trans. Geoffrey Strachan 1965; with new introduction 1976). It is possible that the remainder of the second part and the third part (*The History of the Spark*) were written but subsequently lost or destroyed.

The hero of the comic histories attempts space travel by several absurd methods, including ROCKET power. His adventures are largely satirical (*see* SATIRE), but are interrupted by discourses and dialogues regarding contemporary issues in natural philosophy. A classic sequence in the second history has the hero tried for the crimes of humanity in a court of birds. The histories influenced several later satirists, including Jonathan SWIFT. The first part borrows Domingo Gonsales from Bishop Francis GODWIN's *Man in the Moone* (**1638**), and Tommaso CAMPANELLA appears as a character in the second part, acting as the hero's guide. The amusing surfaces of the two histories are underlaid with some interesting speculative material, and the technique of embedding bold ideas in an absurd framework provides an interesting comparison with the customary sf strategy of carefully introducing new ideas into a realistic framework. CDB's works were highly influential on the 18th-century tradition of the *conte philosophique* as written by VOLTAIRE and others.   [BS]
See also: FANTASTIC VOYAGES; MOON; POLITICS; RELIGION; SF OVERTAKEN BY EVENTS; SPACE FLIGHT.

CZECHOSLOVAKIA *See* EASTERN EUROPE.

DAGMAR, PETER (? –). English writer of routine paperback sf adventures. They are *Alien Skies* (**1962**), *Spykos 4* (**1962**), *Sands of Time* (**1963**) and *Once in Time* (**1963**).   [JC]

DAHL, ROALD (1916–). Writer, Welsh-born of Norwegian parents, resident in the UK, who has spent much of his life in America. He is best known for eerie, exquisitely crafted, somewhat poisonous stories, many of them fantasies, assembled in *Someone Like You* (coll. **1953**; exp. 1961), *Kiss Kiss* (coll. **1960**), *Switch Bitch* (coll. **1974**) and elsewhere. Several of these stories use borderline sf images, such as the unpleasant metamorphosis of human into bee in "Royal Jelly" (1960). He has more recently concentrated on a series of children's fantasies, the most famous being *Charlie and the Chocolate Factory* (**1964**), which was filmed as *Willie Wonka and the Chocolate Factory* (1971). His only sf novel proper, *Some Time Never: A Fable for Superman* (**1948**), is a rewritten and recast version for adults of his juvenile novel, *The Gremlins* (**1943**), and depicts as Earth's original inhabitants the gremlins who attempt to sabotage mankind during the Second World War, but on discovering that Man is doing the job himself leave him to it, taking the Earth over again after World War Four. RD was host of the short-lived sf/fantasy TV series *Way Out* in the early 1960s.   [JC]
See also: HUMOUR; SATIRE.

DAIL, C(HARLES) C(URTIS) (1851–1902). American lawyer and author, who worked in Kansas. His *Willmoth the Wanderer: or, The Man from Saturn* (**1890**) tells of a Saturnian who explores his own planet, Venus and Earth, in an eventful story involving political satire, antigravity, a lifespan lasting millions of years, Earth's prehistory and some rather ponderous prose. CCD's second novel was *The Stone Giant: A Story of Mammoth Cave* (**1898**).   [PN]

DAIN, ALEX (?–). American writer whose sf novel is *The Bane of Kanthos* (**1969**).   [JC]

DAKE, CHARLES ROMYN (? – ?). American writer. His LOST-RACE novel, *A Strange Discovery* (**1899**), features a Roman colony in the Antarctic, and is notable for its continuation of the story of POE's Gordon Pym.   [JC]

DALE, GEORGE E. *See* Isaac ASIMOV.

DALEKS The ROBOTS bent on universal conquest, first introduced into the television programme DR WHO by writer Terry NATION in 1964. Since that time a large proportion of the child population of the UK has been running about stiff-legged, and crying "Exterminate! Exterminate!" in threatening, metallic voices, along with many of their parents. The Daleks have returned in many *Dr Who* episodes since that time, and have been featured in the films *Dr Who and the Daleks* (1965) and *Daleks — Invasion Earth 2150 AD* (1966), both produced by Milton Subotsky and Max J. Rosenberg, directed by Gordon Flemyng, and starring Peter Cushing.   [PN]

DALMAS, JOHN (?–). American writer whose first published sf was *The Yngling* (**1971**), originally serialized in 1969 in *ASF*, where his subsequent stories have also appeared. It depicts a barbarian future, with a PSIONIC hero leading the neo-Vikings south from the encroaching ice.   [MJE]

DAMNATION ALLEY Film (1977). A Landers-Roberts-Zeitman Production/20th Century-Fox. Directed by Jack Smight, starring Jan-Michael Vincent, George Peppard and Dominique Sanda. Screenplay by Alan Sharp and Lukas Heller, based on the novel of the same title by Roger ZELAZNY. 95 mins. Colour.

The Hell's Angel protagonist of Zelazny's novel has become an air force officer in this film adaptation, which gives an indication of the makers' approach to the story. The inventive freshness of the book is largely absent from this production, which begins with stock footage of nuclear bombs exploding, as a representation of World War Three. Officers stationed in a desert missile bunker which, a few years after the war, is destroyed when somebody drops a lighted match on a sex magazine, are forced to cross the desert in one of their undamaged "land-mobiles". The expedition is made dangerous not only by the presence of various mutated animals but also because the holocaust has tilted the Earth's axis, turning the sky into a nightmarish display of glowing radiation and electrical storms. The men encounter tornadoes, giant cockroaches and murderous hillbillies, and most of them are killed. The two survivors pick up two attractive girls, and then they battle with giant scorpions, bands of gunmen and floods before reaching safety and civilization. The film is less exciting than the plot outline suggests.   [JB]

Viveca Lindfors beside one of the sculptures that featured so memorably.

DAMNED, THE (vt **THESE ARE THE DAMNED**) Film (1961). Hammer/Columbia. Directed by Joseph Losey, starring MacDonald Carey, Oliver Reed, James Villiers, Shirley Ann Field, Viveca Lindfors and Alexander Knox. Screenplay by Evan Jones, based on the novel *The Children of Light* (**1960**) by Henry L. LAWRENCE. Originally 96 mins, cut to 87 mins for UK release and to 77 mins for USA release. B/w.

Made in England by American expatriate director Losey, the film so dismayed the distributors, Columbia, that they kept it on the shelf for two years before releasing it with several cuts. The story concerns an American who, during a visit to an English seaside town, becomes involved with the sister of the leader of a local gang of young thugs and then with a secret military project that is centered upon illegal radiation experiments on a group of children. He and the girl attempt to free the children from their subterranean prison but in doing so become fatally contaminated themselves. Losey clearly wished to make a meaningful statement about the moral corruption of Western technocracy, but this is a little discredited by his casual indifference to science, as shown in the claim that sustained exposure to atomic radiation lowers one's body temperature (all the children are abnormally cold), and is likely to be harmful in the long run, but not immediately. The film's strength is in the evocative, allusive imagery, in particular the final shots showing a helicopter hovering like a giant carrion bird over the small boat carrying the dying hero and his girl-friend.   [JB]

DAN DARE — PILOT OF THE FUTURE British sf COMIC STRIP created by artist and writer Frank HAMPSON. It first appeared in 1950 in *Eagle*. From 1959 until *DD* ceased in 1967 its illustrators included Frank Bellamy, Eric Eden, Don Harley, Bruce Cornwall and Keith Watson. *DD* generally depicts the exploration of the Solar System, individual stories often being centered

A DAN DARE strip from *The Eagle*, March 9, 1951.

upon conflicts between Dan Dare and the Mekon, a green-skinned, dome-headed Venusian despot. Under the supervision of Frank Hampson, pictorial authenticity was created by the use of scale models and stories were scrutinized for accuracy (Arthur C. CLARKE acted as scientific adviser for the first six months). After Hampson's departure, the writers extended their themes beyond the limitations of the original conception in a series of adventures across the galaxy. Continuity became strained and, in spite of a period of revitalization under Keith Watson, the strip declined.

Dan Dare and the Mekon have recently been revived, in name only, in the comic paper *2,000 AD*. His adventures have appeared in several hardcover JUVENILE SERIES and paperback novels, and in a popular programme on Radio Luxembourg.   [ABP/JE]

DANFORTH, MILDRED E. (?–). English writer, whose sf novel is *From Outer Space* (**1963**).   [JC]

DANGEROUS VISIONS Original ANTHOLOGY edited by Harlan ELLISON. Published in 1967, *DV* was a massive anthology of 33 stories and copious prefatory material. It became strongly identified with NEW WAVE sf in the USA. Among its stories, "Aye, and Gomorrah ..." by Samuel R. DELANY and "Gonna Roll The Bones" by Fritz LEIBER both won NEBULA awards. The Leiber story also won a HUGO, as did "Riders of the Purple Wage" by Philip José FARMER. *DV* was followed by *Again, Dangerous Visions* (anth. **1972**), which was larger

still, although it created less stir, and contained the Nebula-winning "When It Changed" by Joanna RUSS and the Hugo-winning *The Word For World is Forest* (1972; **1976**) by Ursula K. LE GUIN among its 46 stories. A third instalment, *The Last Dangerous Visions*, has been subject to several postponements.   [MJE]

DANIEL, GABRIEL See COSMOLOGY; PROTO SF; SPACE FLIGHT.

DANIEL, YULI (1925–). Russian writer, who wrote as Nikolai Arzhak, now in exile after having been imprisoned in 1966, along with his dissident friend, Andrey SINYAVSKY (Abram Tertz), for the writings which have been translated into English from French as *This is Moscow Speaking, and Other Stories* (written before 1966; trans **1968**); in 1969 they had not yet appeared in Russian. The title story is of sf interest: 10 August 1960 is declared as Public Murder Day; the point is very broadly SATIRICAL.   [JC]
See also: POLITICS.

DANIELS, LOUIS G. See Daniel F. GALOUYE.

DANN, JACK (1945–). American writer and anthologist, with a BA in social science - political science, who began publishing sf in 1970 with two stories for *Worlds of If* with George ZEBROWSKI, "Dark, Dark, the Dead Star", and "Traps". Although he published considerable short fiction over the next few years, JD soon became best known as the editor of several strong anthologies,

Wandering Stars (anth. **1974**) which features sf about Jews, *Faster than Light* (anth. **1976**) with George Zebrowski, and *Future Power* (anth. **1976**) with Gardner Dozois. Among the best stories of this period was "Junction" (1973), a NEBULA award finalist. JD's first novel, *Starhiker* (**1977**), is designed as the first volume of a trilogy, the succeeding parts of which had not appeared by late 1977, so that its somewhat inconclusive feel cannot properly be estimated; it is a kind of heightened SPACE OPERA in which a young human singer-bard escapes alien-occupied Earth on an alien ship and undergoes a series of revelatory experiences (including near self-transcendence on a sentient planet) before returning to his depressed home. The ALIENS in this novel are depicted with an effective sense of otherness. JD has written poetry and was managing editor of the SFWA BULLETIN, 1970–75. [JC] **See also:** RELIGION.

DANTE ALIGHIERI (1265–1321). Italian poet, the most celebrated of all medieval writers. His *Divina Commedia* (*c.* 1314–21 in manuscript; many translations as *The Divine Comedy*) is an epic poem of 100 cantos in three books of 33 cantos with an introduction; the books are *Inferno*, *Purgatorio* and *Paradiso*. We can, with hindsight, call it a work of PROTO SF; it is certainly that among other things, though it stands at the head of several traditions other than the science fictional. It has profoundly affected not only the religious imagination but all subsequent allegorical creation of imaginary worlds in literature generally. *The Divine Comedy* is sf rather than fantasy in that its subject is cosmological — it offers us a picture of the way the universe is structured — and in that the three imaginary worlds of hell, purgatory and heaven through which the narrator travels are self-consistent and rationally presented. The obvious objection to such a view is that the work is theological and philosophical in intent; this is so, but the questions Dante asks of the universe as a Christian are nevertheless questions about its nature. Sf, too, queries the meaning of creation and seeks its patterns. There was no distinction between science and religion when Dante wrote, and he did so with the cool eye of a scientist, transcending the rational but not deserting it. The tradition that led to sf has Dante looming over it. [PN]

DANVERS, JACK Writing name of Camille Auguste Marie Caseleyr (1909–), a Belgian who, after the Second World War, emigrated to Australia, where he set his sf novel, *The End of It All* (**1962**). It deals with Australian attempts to survive an epidemic. [JC]

DANZELL, GEORGE *See* Nelson S. BOND.

DARE, ALAN *See* George GOODCHILD.

D'ARGYRE, GILLES *See* Gérard KLEIN.

DARK HORIZONS The journal of the BRITISH FANTASY SOCIETY.

DARK STAR Film (1974). A Jack H. Harris Release. Directed by John Carpenter, starring Brian Narelle, Dan O'Bannon, Joe Sanders and Andreijah Pahich. Screenplay by John Carpenter and Dan O'Bannon, Greg Jein, Harry Walton, Jim Danforth, John Wash and Bob Greenberg. 83 mins. Colour.

This was originally a 45-minute film shot on 16mm by a group of students at the University of Southern California for $6,000, but producer Jack H. Harris provided the necessary money to enable extra footage to be shot, and to transfer the whole film on to 35mm. The film is basically a satire on space films and sf in general — the *Dark Star* is a spaceship in which four men are roaming the universe on a tedious and apparently endless mission. Their job is to locate "unstable" worlds and destroy them with thermostellar bombs. Conditions in the ship have deteriorated: the computer is having trouble controlling the vital life-support systems; the crew members are in various stages of psychosis; the captain is "dead" but still partially conscious and has been stored in a cold storage locker; and the ship's mascot, a rather nasty alien shaped like a beach ball with claws, becomes increasingly belligerent. But the main problem involves one of the thermostellar bombs, all of which are intelligent, who has to be continually talked out of exploding prematurely.

Described by one critic as "a *Waiting for Godot* in outer space", *DS* is a sophisticated mixture of black comedy, farce and good sf. Technically brilliant, its sets and effects are superior to those of sf films that cost 10 times its budget (total cost for *DS* was $60,000). The novelization is *Dark Star* (**1974**) by Alan Dean FOSTER. [JB]

DARLTON, CLARK Pseudonym of German writer, translator and editor Walter Ernsting (1920–); he has also written as F. MacPatterson. In the 1950s he edited the German *Utopia-Magazin*, which began in 1955, providing it with considerable original and translated material; in 1957 he began a series of sf publications, *Terra-Sonderband*, and was one of the founding editors and writers, with Karl-Herbert SCHEER, of the extraordinary PERRY RHODAN series of SPACE OPERAS from 1961; over 700 of these booklets had appeared, on a weekly basis, by mid-1977; a slightly expurgated series of translations has been appearing from 1969 in the USA, and from 1975 in the UK. Some of the early American issues appeared as by Walter Ernsting, later ones as by CD. [JC/PN]

DARNAY, ARSEN (?–). American writer whose "Helium" appeared in *Gal.* in 1975 and formed the basis of his first novel, *A Hostage for Hinterland* (**1976**), set in a post-HOLOCAUST America where floating CITIES depend for the helium that cools their reactors upon the land-dwelling Ecofreak tribesmen; at a point of crisis between the opposing parties, the cities, as might be expected, come to the end of their days. [JC]

DARRINGTON, HUGH (?–). English writer whose sf novel, *Gravitor* (**1971**), features an oppressed world and a scientific plot to increase GRAVITY, causing chaos, of which the plotters will take advantage. [JC]

DARWIN, ERASMUS (1731–1802). English physician, philosopher and poet; grandfather of Charles Darwin. It is for his poetry that he is of interest to the sf field, though he is in general a major figure in 18th-century intellectual history; in particular, *The Botanic Garden: a poem, in two parts. Part I. The Economy of Vegetation. Part II. The Loves of the Plants* (as separate poems **1792** and **1789**; **1795**), conveys through its wooden but occasionally powerful couplets a serious speculative message about the chronological depth of EVOLUTION, for which he argued in terms, abominable rhymes or no, clearly presaging those of his grandson.

ED's prose work, *Zoonomia: or the Laws of Organic Life* (**1796**), and the posthumously published poem *The Temple of Nature* (**1802**), both extend the argument, with a wealth of technological and scientific imagery. He also predicted the modern city, skyscrapers, submarines and aerial warfare. The extent to which science fired his imagination, and his contemporary popularity, make him an important figure in PROTO SCIENCE FICTION, and an early outstanding success in sf PREDICTION. ED belongs to the period when the imagery of science first entered the consciousness of laymen in general. Brian W. ALDISS discusses him at length in *Billion Year Spree: the True History of Science Fiction* (**1973**). [JC/PN] **About the author:** *Erasmus Darwin* (**1963**) by Desmond King-Hele.

DAVENPORT, BASIL (1905–66). American academic and anthologist, BA Yale, MA Oxford, and an Intelligence Officer in the Second World War. His connection with sf began with his introduction to *Islandia* (**1942**) by Austin Tappan WRIGHT. Then came the short critical and historical study *Inquiry into Science Fiction* (**1955**). He also wrote an introduction to the anonymously edited critical anthology *The Science Fiction Novel: Imagination and Social Criticism* (anth. **1959**), which contains lectures delivered in 1957 at a symposium at the University of Chicago by Robert HEINLEIN, C.M. KORNBLUTH, Alfred

BESTER and Robert BLOCH. As an anthologist, in most of his collections he stressed fantasy rather than sf. Three of them were compiled with the aid of Albert Paul Blaustein (Allen DE GRAEFF), uncredited. BD's anthologies are *Ghostly Tales to be Told* (anth. **1950**), *Tales to be Told in the Dark* (anth. **1953**), *Deals With the Devil* (anth. **1958**) with Blaustein uncredited, *Invisible Men* (anth. **1960**) with Blaustein uncredited, *13 Ways to Dispose of a Body* (anth. **1966**) and *Famous Monster Tales* (anth. **1967**) with Blaustein uncredited. [PN]

See also: DEFINITIONS OF SF.

DAVENPORT, BENJAMIN RUSH (?–?). American writer. His best-known novel is the future-WAR tale, *Anglo-Saxons, Onward! A Romance of the Future* (**1898**), in which, led by the American president, Anglo-Saxons dominate the world, including Spain (viz. the contemporaneous Spanish-American War). [JC]

Other works: *"Uncle Sam's" Cabins; a Story of American Life, Looking Forward a Century* (**1895**); *Blood Will Tell; the Strange Story of a Son of Ham* (**1902**).

DAVENTRY, LEONARD (JOHN) (1915–). British writer whose first sf novel, *A Man of Double Deed* (**1965**), has received most acclaim of all his work. It is a complex portrayal of an Earth partly recovered from nuclear disaster and run by telepaths, one of whom, the protagonist, is assigned the task of solving a serious new delinquency problem; the solution involves full surrender to the *gestalt* potentials of telepathy. LD's other books have been less noticed. [JC]

Other works: *Reflections in a Mirage* (**1969**); *The Ticking is in Your Head* (**1970**); *Twenty-One Billionth Paradox* (**1971**); *Terminus* (**1971**); *Degree XII* (**1972**).

DAVIDSON, AVRAM (1923–). American writer and editor, born in Yonkers, New York, in the American navy 1941–5; served with the Israeli forces in the 1948–9 Arab Israeli War. He is an Orthodox Jew, though his faith has found direct expression very rarely in his stories. He began publishing sf with "My Boy Friend's Name is Jello" (1954) in *FSF*, and early established a reputation for a sometimes obtrusive literacy and considerable wit. "Or All the Seas with Oysters" (1958) won a HUGO award. Much of his early fiction appeared in *FSF*, where from 1962 to 1964 he was editor, editing as a consequence *The Best from Fantasy and Science Fiction, 12th Series* (anth. **1963**), *13th Series* (anth. **1964**), and *14th Series* (anth. **1965**). His first novel, *Joyleg* (**1962**), was written in collaboration with Ward MOORE (*who see* for details).

AD's first solo novel, *Mutiny in Space* (**1964**), immediately established his credentials as a writer of superior interstellar adventure rather in contrast to the manner and style of his short works. Other novels with a similarly straightforward effect include *Rork!* (**1965**), *The Enemy of My Enemy* (**1966**) and, most notably, *Masters of the Maze* (**1965**), an intricate PARALLEL-WORLDS adventure with sharply characterized humans involved in barring interdimensional transit to a remarkably vivid ALIEN race. Two further novels from this active period, *Clash of Star-Kings* (**1966**) and *Rogue Dragon* (**1965**), both of which were nominated for NEBULA awards, show a widening of his talent as a novelist. The former is set in a richly realized Mexico, the latter in a FAR-FUTURE Earth; in both books, action tends to become submerged in descriptive passages of heightened local colour, which gives his later fiction an air of combined flamboyance and meditative calm. This enriching (though sometimes enervating) tendency culminates in such later books as *The Phoenix and the Mirror* (**1969**), which languorously depicts a medieval ALTERNATE WORLD whose universal scholastic world-view, encompassing everything from geography to alchemy, turns out to be literally accurate; the magus Vergil goes through a number of adventures in this ornately humanized environment in search of a "virgin mirror" to trade for his stolen virility, but the novel closes without coming to a satisfactory climax (its planned sequel or sequels have not appeared). Both *The Island Under the Earth* (**1969**) and *Peregrine: Primus* (**1971**) also begin series the subsequent volumes of which have not seen the light, and both novels also have the broadly similar effect on the reader of literary riches not quite brought to the surface.

AD's notable short fiction has been assembled in four volumes, *Or All the Seas with Oysters* (coll. **1962**), *What Strange Stars and Skies* (coll. **1965**), *Strange Seas and Shores* (coll. **1971**) and *The Enquiries of Doctor Eszterhazy* (coll. of linked stories **1975**). His wit and bookish allusiveness (he is one of sf's most literary authors) shine most persuasively in his shorter works, where constraints in length seem to keep him from floundering or self-indulgence, and the narrative thread in view. If ever published in its entirety, however, the "Vergil Magus" sequence may turn out to be his master work. [JC]

Other works: *The Kar-Chee Reign* (**1966**); *Ursus of Ultima Thule* (**1973**).

See also: ATLANTIS; COLONIZATION OF OTHER WORLDS; PASTORAL; SUPERNATURAL CREATURES; SWORD AND SORCERY

DAVIDSON, HUGH *See* Edmond HAMILTON.

DAVIDSON, LIONEL (1922–). British-born writer, resident in Israel, and best known for his thrillers, beginning with *The Night of Wenceslas* (**1960**). His second thriller, *The Rose of Tibet* (**1962**), had a LOST-RACE plot-line. *The Sun Chemist* (**1976**) is borderline sf; the lost formula of Israeli scientist and President Chaim Weizmann uses the sweet potato as a means of tapping the Sun's power. An adventurous formula quest, well told, follows. [PN]

DAVIES, FREDRIC *See* Ron ELLIK.

DAVIES, HUGH SYKES (1909–). English writer and academic, whose surrealist novel, *Petron* (**1935**), is, at least retroactively, of some value to sf writers and readers as an early model for contemporary attempts at the rendering of INNER SPACE. *The Papers of Andrew Melmoth* (**1960**) is an interesting story about the EVOLUTION of INTELLIGENCE in rats, quite different in tone from the Gothic treatment such subjects normally evoke. [JC/PN]

DAVIES, L(ESLIE) P(URNELL) (1914–). British writer who has also worked as a pharmacist and as a painter; he now lives in the Canary Isles. His consistently borderline sf often permits a delusional-frame interpretation of the events it depicts, so that frequently it is difficult to distinguish among the genres he utilizes, which include horror fantasy, suspense thriller and sf. Along with John BLACKBURN and John LYMINGTON, both of whom he sometimes resembles, LPD has in a sense founded a new generic amalgam: tales whose slippage amongst various genres is in itself a characteristic point of narrative interest, with the reader kept constantly in suspense about the generic nature of any climaxes or explanations to be presented. LPD began publishing sf with "The Wall of Time" for *London Mystery Magazine* in 1960, and has published fiction under a number of pseudonyms, including Leo Barne, Robert Blake, Richard Bridgeman, Morgan Evans, Ian Jefferson, Lawrence Peters, Thomas Phillips, G.K. Thomas, Leslie Vardre and Rowland Welch. His first novel, *The Paper Dolls* (**1964**), which was made into a television movie with the same title in 1968, sets a mystery involving telepathy and murder in the depths of the English country, a venue he uses frequently. *Man Out of Nowhere* (**1965**; vt *Who is Lewis Pinder?* USA) and *The Artificial Man* (**1965**), are both possible delusional-frame tales; the latter was made into the film *Project X* (1968), about a NEAR-FUTURE secret agent kept imprisoned in a rural environment in an attempt to probe his unconscious knowledge of an enemy's plans to destroy the Western powers. LPD's subsequent novels have been variously marketed as to genre, but share an ambivalence in the way they can be read, occasional glibness of effect, and narrative skill. [JC]

Other works: *Psychogeist* (**1966**); *The Lampton Dreamers* (**1966**); *Tell it to the*

Dead (**1966** as by Leslie Vardre in UK; vt *The Reluctant Medium* USA); *Twilight Journey* (**1967**); *The Nameless Ones* (**1967** as by Leslie Vardre in UK; vt *A Grave Matter*); *The Alien* (**1968**; vt *The Groundstar Conspiracy*), filmed as *The Groundstar Conspiracy* (**1972**); *Stranger to Town* (**1969**); *Dimension A* (**1969**); *Genesis Two* (**1969**); *The White Room* (**1969**); *The Shadow Before* (**1970**); *Give Me Back Myself* (**1971**); *What Did I Do Tomorrow?* (**1972**); *Assignment Abacus* (**1975**); *Possession* (**1976**).
See also: PSYCHOLOGY.

DAVIES, WALTER C. *See* C.M. KORNBLUTH.

DAVIS, ELLIS JAMES *See* ANONYMOUS SF AUTHORS.

DAVIS, GERRY (?–). British writer, primarily for television, who collaborated with Kit PEDLER on three sf novels, *Mutant 59: The Plastic Eaters* (**1972**), which is derived from their DOOMWATCH television series, *Brainrack* (**1974**) and *The Dynostar Menace* (**1976**). GD has also written novelizations for children of the DR WHO television series. [JC]
See also: DISASTER; GENETIC ENGINEERING; POLLUTION.

DAW BOOKS American publishing imprint started by Donald A. WOLLHEIM in 1972, after his departure from ACE BOOKS. Daw Books (the name derived from Wollheim's initials) publish only sf and fantasy, producing four or five titles a month. The editorial policy is comparable with the one followed by Wollheim at Ace: mostly adventure fiction, with a sprinkling of serious works. There is a considerable reliance on series, particularly fantasy or sword and sorcery, by such authors as Alan Burt AKERS, Marion Zimmer BRADLEY, Lin CARTER, Michael MOORCOCK, John NORMAN and E.C. TUBB. [MJE]

DAY, BRADFORD M(ARSHALL) (1916–). American bibliographer, sf collector and book-dealer. His careful, detailed bibliographical work has been of great help to sf researchers, and although some of it goes back 25 years, it has not all been superseded. His most important works are probably *The Complete Checklist of Science-Fiction Magazines* (**1961**), which defines sf widely and lists a number of hero/villain, fantasy and foreign magazines, and *The Supplemental Checklist of Fantastic Literature* (**1963**), which is a compilation of many titles omitted by or published after the period covered by Everett F. BLEILER's *The Checklist of Fantastic Literature* (**1948**). The latter title was re-issued by ARNO PRESS in 1974, as was BMD's *The Checklist of Fantastic Literature in Paperbound Books* (**1965**). Lesser but still useful works are *Bibliography of Adventure: Mundy, Burroughs, Rohmer,*

Haggard (**1964**) and *An Index on the Weird and Fantastica in Magazines* (**1953**), which indexes most of the MUNSEY pulps, and many other general-fiction PULP MAGAZINES which also receive entries in this Encyclopedia. All the above were originally published in stencilled format by BMD himself. [PN]

DAY, DONALD B(RYNE) (1909–78). Pioneer sf indexer, resident in Oregon. His *Index to the Science Fiction Magazines 1926–1950* (**1952**) has, along with its successors compiled by other hands, become one of the most essential tools for any sf researcher. [PN]

DAY MARS INVADED EARTH, THE Film (1962). API/Fox. Directed by Maury Dexter, starring Kent Taylor, Marie Windsor, William Mims and Betty Beall. Screenplay by Harry Spalding. 70 mins. B/w.
In this low-budget, mediocre film a radio transmitter is landed on Mars, and the Martians, who consist of pure energy, use the radio beam as a means of travelling to Earth. They begin duplicating human beings, and killing off the originals. The film ends with them triumphant. [JB]

DAY OF THE DOLPHIN, THE Film (1973). Avco-Embassy. Directed by Mike Nichols, starring George C. Scott, Trish Van Devere, Paul Sorvino and Fritz Weaver. Screenplay by Buck Henry, based on the novel by Robert MERLE. 105 mins. Colour.
This above-average film, from a director well known for social comedy but new to sf, concerns a marine biologist who succeeds in teaching dolphins to speak (English). The first half of the film deals with this historic contact between two intelligent species, and conveys the genuine sense of wonder found in the best sf, but instead of following up the implications of the situation the rest of the story concentrates on an attempt by a right-wing group to betray the innocent human-dolphin relationship and use the dolphins to assassinate the President. Despite its degeneration into ordinary thriller conventions, *DOTD*, because of its serious approach to the whole question of mankind's relationship with other forms of intelligent life, remains one of the better sf films. It is technically well made, and the handling of the dolphins' voices is so skilful that the illusion is totally acceptable. [JB]

DAY OF THE TRIFFIDS, THE Film (1963). Allied Artists. Directed by Steve Sekely (additional sequences directed by Freddie Francis), starring Howard Keel, Nicole Maurey, Janette Scott and Kieron Moore. Screenplay by Philip Yordan. 94 mins. Colour.
An unsuccessful version of John WYNDHAM's novel of the same name, the film is about mobile plants which take

over the world after the majority of the population has been blinded by lights from a meteor shower. Philip Yordan, a prolific writer/producer who had written the screenplays for such films as *El Cid* and *The Fall of the Roman Empire*, seemed to lack any feeling for sf. The special effects were by Wally Veevers; some sequences involving the triffids themselves are impressive. [JB]

DAY THE EARTH CAUGHT FIRE, THE Film (1961). British Lion/Pax/Universal. Directed by Val Guest, starring Edward Judd, Janet Munro and Leo McKern. Screenplay by Wolf Mankowitz and Val Guest. 99 mins (later cut to 90). B/w.
Val Guest, who made THE QUATERMASS XPERIMENT and other sf/horror films for Hammer in the 1950s, produced as well as directed this film about the Earth falling into the Sun after a reckless series of H-bomb tests have knocked it out of its orbit. It is made in a crisp, pseudo-documentary manner and most of the action is set in the offices of the British *Daily Express* newspaper (the former editor, Arthur Christiansen, playing himself). Though working on a minimal budget, Les Bowie manages to produce some convincing special effects, including shots of the Thames completely evaporating in the heat. The novelization is *The Day the Earth Caught Fire* (**1961**) by Barry Wells. [JB]

A rare still from THE DAY THE EARTH STOOD STILL.

DAY THE EARTH STOOD STILL, THE Film (1951). 20th Century-Fox. Directed by Robert WISE, starring Michael Rennie, Patricia Neal, Hugh Marlowe and Sam Jaffe. Screenplay by Edmund H. North, based on the story "Farewell to the Master" by Harry BATES. 92 mins. B/w.
One of the first Hollywood sf movies produced during the sf boom of the 1950s, this is one of the most intelligent. An emissary from outer space arrives by flying saucer in Washington, accompanied by an eight-foot-tall robot.

The alien, Klaatu, has come to warn Earth that his people will not tolerate an extension of human violence into outer space, but before he can deliver the message he is shot and wounded by a soldier. With the help of a young widow who has befriended him he regains access to the saucer and arranges a demonstration of his powers — the stopping of all machinery, all over the world. But once again he is shot, this time fatally, before he can give his warning to Earth. It is only after the woman has reactivated the robot, which then takes Klaatu's body back to the saucer and temporarily revives it, that his message, and the message of the film, can be delivered. Morally it is ambiguous — unless Man curbs his violent ways the alien race is prepared to "reduce this Earth of yours to a burnt-out cinder". The idea of submitting to the rule of a race of implacable robot policemen is at best an unusual form of liberalism. The film is directed with impressive economy.
                                                                        [JB]

DAY THE FISH CAME OUT, THE Film (1967). Michael Cacoyannis Productions/20th Century-Fox. Directed by Michael Cacoyannis, starring Tom Courtenay, Sam Wanamaker, Colin Blakely, Candice Bergen and Ian Ogilvy. Screenplay by Michael Cacoyannis. 109 mins. Colour.

An unusual film, set in the NEAR FUTURE, based on a true incident in which the American air force accidentally lost two H-bombs off the coast of Spain. A small Greek island becomes the focus of frenzied activity after a NATO bomber crashes into the sea nearby, losing two H-bombs and a "Doomsday weapon". To prevent knowledge of the situation from becoming widespread, the NATO recovery team arrive on the island disguised as holiday-makers, but this only creates the impression that the island has become the "in" place to visit, and soon it is swarming with real tourists. The film ends with widespread infection from deadly viruses found in a metal box by a fisherman.

A strange mixture of slapstick, sex and grim satire, the film is not entirely satisfactory. However, the final scenes, showing dead fish floating in the black sea while all the tourists, already doomed themselves, dance with frenzied abandon on the beach, are forceful. The novelization is *The Day the Fish Came Out* (1967) by Kay CICELLIS. [JB]

DAY THE WORLD ENDED, THE Film (1955). Golden State/ARC. Directed by Roger CORMAN, starring Richard Denning, Adele Jergens, Lori Nelson and Mike Connors. Screenplay by Lou Rusoff. 81 mins. B/w.

The first sf/horror film to be directed by Roger Corman (although he had, in the previous year, produced *Monster from the Ocean's Eye*), this was, like most of

the films he made during the 1950s, shot very quickly (in less than a week) and on an amazingly small budget (approximately $40,000). It has a small cult following, like many Corman films, but basically it is a slipshod variation of the "after-the-H-bomb" theme, involving a small group of atomic war survivors who are menaced by MUTANTS with bulbous heads, three eyes and a taste for human flesh. [JB]

DEADLY INVENTION, THE *See* VÝNALEZ ZKÁZY.

The vivid, stylized b/w illustration of Mal DEAN. *New Worlds*, no. 191, 1969.

DEAN, MAL (1941–74). British illustrator. MD was well known in the jazz world (he illustrated for *Melody Maker*) and in sf for the work he did for NEW WORLDS in the late 1960s and early 1970s. He died young, of cancer. His work was especially associated with the "Jerry Cornelius" stories of Michael MOORCOCK and others, and he illustrated several books by Moorcock. He worked mainly in b/w with a broad line and much cross-hatching; it was strong, often deliberately coarse and unpolished, but always the reverse of artless. He favoured surrealist juxtapositions. A fine artist in the grotesque satirical tradition of Hogarth, he might have been recognized

as a major figure in the art world if he had lived. [PN]

DEAN, ROGER (1944–). British illustrator. Primarily a designer of record album covers, RD has done some sf and fantasy illustration and his album art shows a strong fantasy influence. He has done covers for the rock groups Osibisa, Yes and Uriah Heep, among others. His style is strong, romantic and mannered; he contrasts very finely detailed figures and machines against loosely structured backgrounds. His book, *Views* (1975), shows his development from a student at the Canterbury School of Art onwards. He has become an important influence in British fantasy illustration, and has built up a cult following. [JG]

DEATHLINE (vt **RAW MEAT** USA) Film (1973). AIP. Directed by Gary Sherman, starring Donald Pleasence, Hugh Armstrong, Norman Rossington, David Ladd and Sharon Gurney. Screenplay by Ceri Jones. Original story by Gary Sherman. 88 mins. Colour.

At the end of the last century eight men and four women, involved in the construction of a London tube-line extension, were entombed alive after a cave-in. The last surviving descendant of the group, a giant of a man, has spent his whole life below ground and his only words, overheard from the train guards, are "Mind the doors!" Having found a way up, he now supplements his diet of rats by snatching the occasional late-night traveller from the platform of Russell Square station.

The basic absurdity of the situation is cleverly utilized by the script-writer and director, but many of the scenes showing the life that the group had been leading, and the shots of the last survivor lovingly tending the bodies of the others, are moving. [JB]

Study for a fantasy record cover by Roger DEAN from his *Views*, 1975.

DEATH RACE 2000 Film (1975). New World Films/AIP. Directed by Paul Bartel and produced by Roger CORMAN, starring David Carradine, Simone Griffith, Louisa Moritz, Sylvester Stallone and Mary Woronov. Screenplay by Robert Thom and Charles Griffith. 80 mins. Colour.

In this black comedy about a car race across the USA in the year 2000, the winner is the driver who kills the most pedestrians along the route. "Frankenstein", who has supposedly been in so many crashes that most of his body has been replaced with artificial parts, is the nation's favourite driver.

Although the film was made cheaply, its fast pace and lively ironies led many critics to judge it. as superior to ROLLERBALL, another film about using brutal sports as an opiate for the masses, released at about the same time and a very much more elaborate and expensive production.   [JB/PN]

DEATH RAYS Rays that could kill, whether by frying or disintegration, were the staple heavy WEAPONS of PULP SF in the 1930s, and became a central item in sf TERMINOLOGY. At about the time they became old-fashioned in sf, the scientists of the real world saw fit to invent the Laser, thus retrospectively justifying one of sf's nastier fantasies.   [PN]

DE CAMP, L(YON) SPRAGUE (1907–). American writer. Married Catherine A. Crook, who has collaborated on a number of his books. LSDC was educated at the California Institute of Technology, where he studied aeronautical engineering, and at Stevens Institute of Technology, where he gained a master's degree in 1933. He went to work for a company dealing with the patenting of inventions, and his first published work was a co-written textbook on the subject. He then met P. Schuyler MILLER, with whom he collaborated on a novel, *Genus Homo* (1941 *Super Science Stories*; **1950**), which failed to find a publisher for several years. His first published story was "The Isolinguals" (1937) in ASTOUNDING SCIENCE FICTION. He contributed several more stories to that magazine, (on one occasion using the pseudonym Lyman R. Lyon), including the "Johnny Black" series, about an intelligent bear — "The Command" (1938), "The Incorrigible" (1939), "The Emancipated" (1940) and "The Exalted" (1940) — but it was the appearance in 1939 of *ASF*'s fantasy companion UNKNOWN which stimulated his most notable early work. *Lest Darkness Fall* (1939 *Unknown*; **1941**; rev. 1949), in which an involuntary time-traveller in sixth-century Rome attempts to prevent the Dark Ages occurring, was the most accomplished early excursion into HISTORY in magazine sf, and is regarded as an sf classic.

Other contributions to *Unknown* included "None But Lucifer" (1939), in collaboration with H.L. GOLD, *Solomon's Stone* (1942 *Unknown*; **1956**) and the long title stories of *Divide and Rule* (coll. **1948**), *The Wheels of If* (coll. **1949**) — an ALTERNATE-WORLDS story — and *The Undesired Princess* (coll. **1951**); however, he was most successful in his collaborations with Fletcher PRATT, whom he met in 1939. Pratt conceived the idea behind their successful "Harold Shea" series, HUMOROUS fantasies in which the hero was transported into a series of alternate worlds based on various MYTHS and legends. *The Incomplete Enchanter* (1940 *Unknown*; **1942**) and *The Castle of Iron* (1941 *Unknown*; **1950**), later combined as *The Compleat Enchanter* (coll. **1975**), were eventually and less successfully followed by *Wall of Serpents* (1953–4 var. mags; fix-up **1960**). Their other collaborations of the period were *The Land of Unreason* (**1941**) and *The Carnelian Cube* (**1948**, but written several years previously). Their method of working was for LSDC, as the junior partner, to write the first draft, after they had jointly outlined the story; Pratt would then compose the final draft, to which LSDC put the finishing editorial touches. This routine was only varied on a very few later short stories.

LSDC joined the US Naval Reserve in 1942, spending the war working in the Philadelphia Naval Yard alongside Isaac ASIMOV and Robert HEINLEIN. Afterwards he published a few articles, but hardly any new fiction until "The Animal Cracker Plot" (1949) introduced his "Viagens Interplanetarias" stories, a loosely linked series set in a future where Brazil has become the dominant world power, and featuring stories set on a number of different worlds, notably the planet Krishna (a romantically barbarian world on which LSDC could set, as sf, the kind of stories he had previously written as fantasy, the market for pure fantasy having disappeared with *Unknown* in 1943). Many of the short stories in the series were included in *The Continent Makers and Other Tales of the Viagens* (coll. **1953**); the others are "The Colorful Character" (1949), "Getaway on Krishna" ("Calories") (1951) and "The Virgin of Zesh" (1953). *Rogue Queen* (**1951**), a novel in the series, depicts a matriarchal humanoid society based on a HIVE structure; it is, with *Lest Darkness Fall*, LSDC's most highly regarded sf work. The remaining novels are all set on Krishna: *Cosmic Manhunt* (1949 *ASF* as "The Queen of Zamba"; **1954**; vt *A Planet Called Krishna* UK; vt *The Queen of Zamba*), *The Search for Zei* (1950 *ASF* as the first half of "The Hand of Zei"; **1962**; vt *The Floating Continent* UK), *The Hand of Zei* (1950 *ASF* as the second half of "The Hand of Zei"; **1963**; paperback abridged), *The Tower of Zanid* (1958 *Science Fiction Stories*; abridged **1958** and subsequent versions) and *The*

Hostage of Zir (**1977**). They contain a blend of intelligent, exotic adventure and wry humour characteristic of LSDC's better work.

In 1950, LSDC and Pratt began their "Gavagan's Bar" series — humorously improbable stories reminiscent of Lord DUNSANY's "Jorkens" series. Many of these are included in *Tales From Gavagan's Bar* (coll. **1953**); later additions were "The Green Thumb" (1953), "The Untimely Toper" (1953), "One Man's Meat" (1953), "The Weissenbroch Spectacles" (1954), "Ward of the Argonaut" (1959) and "Bell, Book and Candle" (1959). LSDC also collaborated with Willy LEY on a non-fiction book, *Lands Beyond* (**1952**), which won an INTERNATIONAL FANTASY AWARD.

LSDC gained an interest in SWORD-AND-SORCERY fiction through reading Robert E. HOWARD's "Conan" stories, and has worked extensively on editing and adding to that series. *Tales of Conan* (coll. **1955**) consists of unfinished Howard manuscripts converted into Conan stories and completed by LSDC. He collaborated with Bjorn Nyberg on *The Return of Conan* (**1957**; vt *Conan the Avenger*), and with Lin CARTER on *Conan of the Isles* (**1968**), *Conan the Buccaneer* (**1971**) and *Conan of Aquilonia* (coll. **1977**). His non-fiction writings on the sword-and-sorcery genre have been published as *The Conan Reader* (coll. **1968**), *Literary Swordsmen and Sorcerers* (**1976**) and *Blond Barbarians and Noble Savages* (**1975**). He has also edited the anthologies *Swords and Sorcery* (anth. **1963**), *The Spell of Seven* (anth. **1965**), *The Fantastic Swordsmen* (anth. **1967**) and *Warlocks and Warriors* (anth. **1970**), and co-edited the critical anthologies *The Conan Swordbook* (anth. **1969**) and *The Conan Grimoire* (anth. **1972**), both in conjunction with George H. SCITHERS. LSDC's own first sword-and-sorcery stories were the "Pusadian" series: *The Tritonian Ring* (coll. **1953**; later editions contain only the title novel, omitting the stories "The Stronger Spell", "The Owl and the Ape" and "The Eye of Tandyla"), "The Hungry Hercynian" (1953), "Ka the Appalling" (1958) and "The Rug and the Bull" (1974). Later he wrote several stories set in the imaginary world of Novaria: *The Goblin Tower* (**1968**), which is his most substantial novel of this type, *The Clocks of Iraz* (**1971**), *The Fallible Fiend* (**1973**) and "The Emperor's Fan" (1973).

LSDC wrote comparatively little sf after 1950, his most notable stories being *The Glory That Was* (1952 *Startling Stories*; **1960**), "Aristotle and the Gun" (1958) and "A Gun For Dinosaur" (1956). The first two of these combine TIME TRAVEL and history in a manner similar to *Lest Darkness Fall*; the third is a straightforward time-travel story. He produced one of the earliest books about modern sf, *Science Fiction Handbook*

(**1953**; rev. 1975 in collaboration with Catherine C. de Camp); a useful compendium of information and advice for aspiring writers in its original edition, it gained little from its subsequent revision and, indeed, omitted some material of interest. Otherwise he wrote historical novels and non-fiction works, including a book on MAGIC in collaboration with Catherine C. de Camp: *Spirits, Stars and Spells* (**1966**). He returned to fantasy in the late 1960s, editing the paperback "Conan" series, writing his "Novarian" stories, and championing the genre in an energetic, if sometimes reactionary, fashion in his many articles. He also wrote the definitive life of H.P. LOVECRAFT: *Lovecraft: A Biography* (**1974**; paperback abridged). His most recent fiction includes the "Willy Newbury" series: "Balsamo's Mirror" (1976), "The Purple Pterodactyls" (1976), "Algy" (1976), "The Figurine" (1977), "The Menhir" (1977) and "Tiki" (1977). [MJE]
Other works: *Sprague de Camp's New Anthology* (coll. **1953**); *Lost Continents* (non-fiction on theories of Atlantis **1954**); *A Gun For Dinosaur* (coll. **1963**); *Demons and Dinosaurs* (poetry **1970**); *The Reluctant Shaman* (coll. **1970**); *Phantoms and Fancies* (poetry **1972**); ed. *3000 Years of Fantasy and Science Fiction* (anth. **1972**; collaboration with Catherine C. de Camp); *Scribblings* (coll. **1972**); *Tales Beyond Time* (anth. **1973**; collaboration with Catherine C. de Camp); *The Miscast Barbarian* (**1975**); *The Virgin and the Wheels* (coll. **1976**).
About the author: "Neomythology" by Lin Carter (introduction to *Literary Swordsmen and Sorcerers*); *Seekers of Tomorrow* (**1965**) by Sam MOSKOWITZ, chapter 9.
See also: ATLANTIS; DISCOVERY AND INVENTION; END OF THE WORLD; FAR FUTURE; GOLDEN AGE OF SF; LINGUISTICS; MATHEMATICS; NUCLEAR POWER; PARALLEL WORLDS; POLITICS; PUBLISHING; SATIRE; SOCIOLOGY; TIME PARADOXES.

DE CAPOULET-JUNAC, EDWARD GEORGES (1930–). French writer. Degrees in Law and Sociology, Paris University. He is principally known for his novel *Pallas ou la tribulation* ["Pallas or Tribulation"] (**1967**), a humorous if heavy-handed account of the sexual encounters of two humans transplanted among alien monsters. The book was highly praised by Stanislaw LEM but generally ignored in France. He also wrote *L'ordinateur des pompes nuptiales* ["The Wedding Computer"] (**1961**). [MJ]

DECIMA VITTIMA, LA (vt **THE TENTH VICTIM**) Film (1965). Champion/Concordia/Embassy. Directed by Elio Petri, starring Marcello Mastroianni, Ursula Andress, Elsa Martinelli and Massimo Serato. Screenplay by Elio Petri, Ennio Flaiano, Tonino Guerra and Giorgio Salvione,

based on the story "Seventh Victim" by Robert SHECKLEY. 92 mins. Colour.
This French-Italian co-production is based loosely on Sheckley's short story about a future world where, as a safety valve for latent aggression, the government has legalized duels to the death. In the film the participants are highly trained individuals alternating as "hunter" and "victim", each aiming for the ten-kill score that will bring unlimited privileges. The DYSTOPIAN possibilities of the theme are neglected in favour of the James Bond/thriller approach which had then suddenly become fashionable, with black jokes and posturing in extravagant costumes. The novelization is *The Tenth Victim* (**1966**) by Robert Sheckley. [JB]

DEE, ROGER Form of his name used by American writer Roger Dee Aycock (1914–) for his fiction, which he began writing with "The Wheel is Death" for *Planet Stories* in 1949; he was a prolific contributor to the sf magazines in the early 1950s. His sf novel, *An Earth Gone Mad* (**1954**), is a routine adventure. [JC]

DEEGAN, JON J. A house name used by Hamilton, London, primarily for novels published in AUTHENTIC SCIENCE FICTION, which for some time early in its run filled each issue with one novel; the "Old Growler" series in *Authentic*, beginning with "Reconnoitre Krellig II" in 1951, was signed as by JJD; the name was also used for a TIME-TRAVEL trilogy, *Corridors of Time* (**1953**), *Beyond the Fourth Door* (**1954**) and *Exiles in Time* (**1954**). Certainly some and possibly all JJD stories were written by H.J. CAMPBELL. [JC]
Other works: *Amateurs in Alchemy* (**1952**); *The Singing Spheres* (**1952**); *Underworld of Zello* (**1952**); *Antro the Life-Giver* (**1953**); *The Great Ones* (**1953**).

DEER, M.J. *See* George H. SMITH.

DEFINITIONS OF SF "Science fiction" is a label applied to a publishing category and its application is subject to the whims of editors and publishers. Attempts to define the range of literary works which ought to belong to the category, and to draw boundary lines strategically excluding those works which seem to have no right to be within it, have been many and various. They reflect criteria of qualification which often disagree with and sometimes contradict one another. The term is applied so loosely in common usage that no single definition will ever be universally agreed.
Attempts to define species of literary production similar to sf were made by several writers (*see* Edgar Allan POE, William WILSON and Edgar FAWCETT), but each early speculative writer had his own manifesto. Only since the founding of the sf pulp magazines in America has there been any measure of agreement. The category was first demarcated by

Hugo GERNSBACK as "scientifiction", and in the editorial in the first issue of AMAZING STORIES he described it thus: "By 'scientifiction' I mean the Jules Verne, H.G. Wells and Edgar Allan Poe type of story — a charming romance intermingled with scientific fact and prophetic vision. ... Not only do these amazing tales make tremendously interesting reading — they are always instructive. They supply knowledge ... in a very palatable form. ... New inventions pictured for us in the scientifiction of today are not at all impossible of realisation tomorrow. ... Many great science stories destined to be of historical interest are still to be written. ... Posterity will point to them as having blazed a new trail, not only in literature and fiction, but progress as well."
This notion of sf as a didactic and prophetic literature with a solid basis in contemporary knowledge was soon revised as other pulp editors abandoned some of Gernsback's pretensions. A new manifesto was drawn up by John W. CAMPBELL Jr for the magazine ASTOUNDING STORIES, which dominated the field in the 1940s. He proposed that sf should be regarded as a literary medium akin to science itself: "Scientific methodology involves the proposition that a well-constructed theory will not only explain away known phenomena, but will also predict new and still undiscovered phenomena. Science fiction tries to do much the same — and write up, in story form, what the results look like when applied not only to machines, but to human society as well."
Once the publishing category was established, readers and critics began using the term with reference to older works, bringing together all stories which seemed to fit the specifications. The first major study of the field's ancestry was undertaken by J.O. BAILEY in *Pilgrims Through Space and Time* (**1947**), and he identified his material thus: "A piece of scientific fiction is a narrative of an imaginary invention or discovery in the natural sciences and consequent adventures and experiences. ... It must be a scientific discovery — something that the author at least rationalizes as possible to science."
After the War a number of critics emerged within the field. The most notable were James BLISH and Damon KNIGHT. Blish introduced his collection of critical pieces, *The Issue at Hand* (published as by William Atheling Jr, coll. **1964**) with a definition put forward by Theodore STURGEON in 1951: "A science fiction story is a story built around human beings, with a human problem and a human solution, which would not have happened at all without its scientific content." (Sturgeon later pointed out that this was intended to be not a description covering all sf stories, but a prescription for good sf stories.)
Knight, in his critical book *In Search of*

Wonder (coll. **1956**), dodged the question of definition altogether, dismissing the label as a misnomer, but did make the following comment: "What we get from science fiction ... is not different from the thing that makes mainstream fiction rewarding, but only expressed differently. We live on a minute island of known things. Our undiminished wonder at the mystery which surrounds us is what makes us human. In science fiction we can approach that mystery, not in small, everyday symbols, but in the big ones of space and time."

In *The Science Fiction Novel* (**1959**), a symposium published with an introduction by Basil DAVENPORT, consisting of lectures given at the University of Chicago, Robert HEINLEIN offered a defence of the genre as a species of realistic fiction, and paraphrased a definition originally proposed by Reginald BRETNOR in *Modern Science Fiction* (**1953**): "[Fiction] in which the author shows awareness of the nature and importance of the human activity known as the scientific method, shows equal awareness of the great body of human knowledge already collected through that activity, and takes into account in his stories the effects and possible future effects on human beings of scientific method and scientific fact."

The first book-length critical studies of sf to be written by people outside the field were done in England by Patrick MOORE in *Science and Fiction* (**1957**) and Kingsley AMIS in *New Maps of Hell* (**1960**). Moore avoided the problem of definition, but Amis offered: "Science fiction is that class of prose narrative treating of a situation that could not arise in the world we know, but which is hypothesized on the basis of some innovation in science or technology, or pseudo-science or pseudo-technology, whether human or extra-terrestrial in origin."

The definition used by Sam MOSKOWITZ, author of a great many historical and biographical studies of individual writers and themes, is somewhat more vague: "Science fiction is a branch of fantasy identifiable by the fact that it eases the 'willing suspension of disbelief' on the part of its readers by utilizing an atmosphere of scientific credibility for its imaginative speculations in physical science, space, time, social science, and philosophy."

A very similar definition, of equal vagueness, is offered by a long-time fan and publisher, Donald WOLLHEIM, in his book *The Universe Makers* (**1971**): "Science fiction is that branch of fantasy, which, while not true of present-day knowledge, is rendered plausible by the reader's recognition of the scientific possibilities of it being possible at some future date or at some uncertain period in the past." (The definition actually dates from 1935).

More modern writers, who became involved with sf criticism while the genre was beginning to claim more attention, particularly in academic circles, tend to be more adventurous and more pretentious in their attempts to define not merely the content but also the purpose and philosophy of the genre. Judith MERRIL, for instance, echoes Campbell's prospectus while borrowing Heinlein's preferred terminology, which replaces the name "science fiction" with "speculative fiction": "Speculative fiction: stories whose objective is to explore, to discover, to *learn*, by means of projection, extrapolation, analogue, hypothesis-and-paper-experimentation, something about the nature of the universe, of man, of 'reality' ... I use the term 'speculative fiction' here specifically to describe the mode which makes use of the traditional 'scientific method' (observation, hypothesis, experiment) to examine some postulated approximation of reality, by introducing a given set of changes — imaginary or inventive — into the common background of 'known facts', creating an environment in which the responses and perceptions of the characters will reveal something about the inventions, the characters, or both."

The emphasis in most earlier definitions falls on the word "science", but more recently this has been much criticized, as by Brian W. ALDISS, who commented that sf is no more written for scientists than ghost stories are for ghosts. J.G. BALLARD remarked in 1969 that "the idea that a magazine like *Astounding*, or *Analog* as it's now called, has anything to do with the sciences is ludicrous. You have only to pick up a journal like *Nature*, say, or any scientific journal, and you can see that science belongs in a completely different world." In *Billion Year Spree* (**1973**) Brian Aldiss attacked the problem from a quite different direction: "Science fiction is the search for a definition of man and his status in the universe which will stand in our advanced but confused state of knowledge (science), and is characteristically cast in the Gothic or post-Gothic mode." (*See* GOTHIC.)

In fact, several other writers have followed Damon Knight in saying that the term "science fiction" is misleading. The favourite alternative is Heinlein's "speculative fiction", but other proposed variants which retain the magical initials are "speculative fantasy" (used by Alexei and Cory PANSHIN) and the academic "structural fabulation" (invented by Robert SCHOLES).

The 1970s have witnessed a great upsurge of academic interest in sf (*see* SF IN THE CLASSROOM), especially in the USA, and with it, naturally enough, have come more rigorous and formal attempts to define sf not only in terms of its subject matter, but also in terms of its literary form and strategies, very often using the vocabulary already developed in other spheres of literary criticism by structuralist and other critics.

In 1972 Darko SUVIN defined sf as "a literary genre whose necessary and sufficient conditions are the presence and interaction of estrangement and cognition, and whose main formal device is an imaginative framework alternative to the author's empirical environment." By cognition he appears to mean the seeking of rational understanding, and by estrangement something akin to Bertolt Brecht's *Verfremdungseffekt*, defined in 1948 as follows: "A representation which estranges is one which allows us to recognize its subject, but at the same time makes it seem unfamiliar". John CLUTE has taken issue with this view, arguing that much sf seeks to create the exact opposite of estrangement, that is, to make the incredible seem plausible and familiar; i.e. that sf is a form of romance, not satire. This difference in emphasis must in part be a reflection of the twin emphases of sf itself: to comment on our own world through the use of metaphor and extrapolation, and to create genuine imagined alternatives to our own world.

The currently popular term "cognition" comes up again in *Structural Fabulation* (**1975**) by Robert Scholes, who first defines fabulation as "fiction that offers us a world clearly and radically discontinuous from the one we know, yet returns to confront that known world in some cognitive way." So far, the definition would fit not only genre sf, but also the works of John BARTH, Richard BRAUTIGAN, Jorge Luis BORGES or Thomas PYNCHON, works which are indeed generally known to American critics as FABULATIONS, and quite often annexed to sf. Scholes goes on to the specific case of what he calls "structural fabulation" in which "the tradition of speculative fiction is modified by an awareness of the universe as a system of systems, a structure of structures, and the insights of the past century of science are accepted as fictional points of departure. Yet structural fabulation is neither scientific in its methods nor a substitute for actual science. It is a fictional exploration of human situations made perceptible by the implications of recent science. Its favorite themes involve the impact of developments or revelations derived from the human or physical sciences upon the people who must live with those revelations or developments." This is not unlike an academic version of Sturgeon's definition, quoted above.

Peter NICHOLLS places sf on a spectrum midway between traditional "realist" MAINSTREAM narrative and FANTASY. He endorses Suvin's remark about worlds "alternative to the author's empirical environment" by claiming that the distinction between mimetic narrative and sf is that in sf "the furniture has been changed", meaning by "furniture" anything from the onset of a Third World War to an abstract shift in cultural expectations. Nicholls distinguishes between sf and fantasy, further down the spectrum, by arguing that sf must adhere to natural law, while fantasy may suspend it. He confesses that the dividing line is blurred, and does not go as far as Suvin, who claims that the commercial linking of sf and fantasy is "a rampantly pathological phenomenon." This dividing line is further discussed under MAGIC.

Leslie Fiedler argues that the myth of sf is the dream of apocalypse, "the myth of the end of man, of the transcendence or transformation of the human — a vision quite different from that of the extinction of our species by the Bomb, which seems stereotype rather than archetype" (*Partisan Review*, Fall 1965). In his book *New Worlds for Old: The Apocalyptic Imagination, Science Fiction and American Literature* (**1974**), David KETTERER expands Fiedler's point at length, dividing sf into three categories (according to the kind of extrapolation involved) and concentrating on the third: "philosophically oriented science fiction, extrapolating on what we know in the context of our vaster ignorance, comes up with a startling *donnée*, or rationale, that puts humanity in a radically new perspective". This he sees as a subcategory of "apocalyptic literature" which is "concerned with the creation of other worlds which exist, on the literal level, in a credible relationship (whether on the basis of rational extrapolation and analogy or of religious belief) with the 'real' world, thereby causing a metaphorical destruction of that 'real' world in the reader's head."

It is clear that with each new definition of sf an additional terminology or jargon has an unnerving tendency to enter the arena. John BRUNNER, for example, quoted in 1969 an ingenious though unnamed friend as saying that "science fiction writers are attempting to create the appropriate Dionysian truth to match an environment that has been severely changed by the discovery of Apollonian truth in science".

James GUNN, a professional sf writer who has joined the academic world, is nevertheless succinct in contrast to most of his colleagues when he offers the definition (in *Alternate Worlds: The Illustrated History of Science Fiction* **1975**): "In science fiction a fantastic event or development is considered rationally". But this is insufficiently exclusive, and many will find more useful his passing comment that sf "is based upon a belief that the world is changing", which he goes on to link with a discussion of Alvin TOFFLER's *Future Shock* (**1970**), a study of the increasing rate of change in the real world. Toffler himself wrote in 1974 that sf "by dealing with possibilities not ordinarily considered — alternative worlds, alternative visions — widens our repertoire of possible responses to change." Here is the beginning of a definition of sf in terms of its social function rather than its intrinsic nature, a

little more sophisticated than Marshall McLuhan's earlier comment in *The Medium is the Massage* (**1967**); "Science fiction writing today presents situations that enable us to perceive the potential of new technologies. Formerly, the problem was to invent new forms of labor-saving. Today, the reverse is the problem. Now we have to adjust, not to invent. We have to find the environments in which it will be possible to live with our new inventions."

If the test of a good definition is that the terms it uses to define its subject should be clear, readily understandable, and themselves capable of accurate definition, then few of these offerings pass. Those which are clearest are, alas, the least definitive.

The problem is complicated by the confusion of attempts to declare what sf writers *ought* to do, and what their motives, purposes and philosophies *ought* to be, with attempts to describe what they habitually *do* do, and what kind of things tend to accumulate under the label. An additional complication arises in the real world because some writers fight hard to avoid the label, feeling that it might deleteriously affect their sales and/or reputations (e.g. Kurt VONNEGUT and John WYNDHAM). Publishers apply similar cautionary measures to potential best-sellers; genre sf, when so labelled, usually sells well but seldom enters the best-seller class.

There will inevitably be ambiguities in any definition. Novels like *Martin Arrowsmith* (**1925**) by Sinclair LEWIS and *Morrison's Machine* (**1900**) by J.S. Fletcher, which deal with the processes of scientific research and discovery rather than with the hypothetical products thereof, tend to fall into the border country between sf and realistic fiction. The no-man's-land which separates sf from "pure" fantasy is wide and badly mapped, and can most easily if unheroically be traversed one way or the other with the help of a little adroit jargon. All in all, the sf label is so flexible in practice (both in the way that publishers deploy it and in the way that writers, critics and readers use it) that it is simply not capable of clear definition. At best, we might hope to identify and describe certain general features of the attitude of mind which writers and readers bring to this particular species of literary communication. A survey of the accounts of the genre quoted above reveals two main expectations: that a work of sf should be concerned with the extension of scientific knowledge and all manner of consequences thereof; and that it should be imaginatively and intellectually adventurous; and even the former is not universally accepted.

[BS/PN]

DEFOE, DANIEL (1660–1731). English merchant, professional spy and writer, extremely prolific author of at

least 500 works of various kinds, best known today for his novel *Robinson Crusoe* (**1719**), which though not itself sf provided the fundamental model for many sf stories (*see* ROBINSONADE); of interest to students of PROTO SCIENCE FICTION is *The Consolidator: or, Memoirs of Sundry Transactions from the World of the Moon* (**1705**), in which a mechanical, spirit-driven flying machine, the Consolidator, enables various SATIRICAL observations to be made from a lunar viewpoint. *A Journal of the Plague Year* (**1722**), while in effect a historical novel, set in 1665, a year DD could presumably barely remember, is the prototype of the sf DISASTER novel. [JC/PN]
See also: FANTASTIC VOYAGES; ISLANDS; MACHINES; MOON; SPACE FLIGHT.

DEFONTENAY, C(HARLEMAGNE) I(SCHIR) (? – ?). French writer. His early sf novel, *Star; ou Psi de Cassiopée* (**1854**; trans. as *Star* **1975**, with introduction by Pierre VERSINS), describes the discovery in the Himalayas of a box full of information about life on another star. The BIOLOGICAL and ANTHROPOLOGICAL speculation is interesting, the prose dry and awkward, the ideas left naked and undramatized. [JC/PN]
See also: LIFE ON OTHER WORLDS; STARS.

DeFORD, MIRIAM ALLEN (1888–1975). American writer, a newspaper reporter for many years; probably known better for her many mystery stories (some award-winning) than for the sf of her later years. Her publications also include such non-fiction as *The Real Bonnie and Clyde* (**1968**) and work as contributing editor to *The Humanist*. She edited *Space, Time and Crime* (anth. **1964**), a collection of sf stories with mystery elements. A further editing job was *Elsewhere, Elsewhen, Elsehow* (anth. **1971**). As an author of sf stories in her own right, she published over 30 items — the first being "The Last Generation" (1946) in *Harper's Magazine* — in several magazines, though most of the stories in her two collections, *Xenogenesis* (coll. **1969**) and *Elsewhere, Elsewhen, Elsehow* (coll. **1971**), had first appeared in *FSF*. Her examinations of themes such as nuclear devastation and sexual roles is conducted in a crisp, clear-cut style sometimes lacking grace but never vigour. [JC]
See also: CRIME AND PUNISHMENT.

DE GRAEFF, ALLEN. Pseudonym of Albert Paul Blaustein (**1921**–), professor of law, under which he edited *Human and Other Beings* (anth. **1963**). He was uncredited co-compiler of three anthologies with Basil DAVENPORT: *Deals with the Devil* (anth. **1958**), *Invisible Men* (anth. **1960**) and *Famous Monster Tales* (anth. **1967**). [PN]

DEIGHTON, LEN (**1929**–). English writer of spy novels, cookery books, and some non-fiction; he is still best known for his early espionage thrillers, such as *The Ipcress File* (**1962**), several of which feature the same undisciplined secret agent. *Billion-Dollar Brain* (**1966**), which belongs to the series, is set in an indeterminate NEAR FUTURE and deals with a super COMPUTER and a private preventive war launched by a mad tycoon on Russia across the ice from Finland. The film of the book, with the same title, was released in 1968.   [JC]

DELAIRE, JEAN *See* RELIGION.

Photo Peter Nicholls.

DELANY, SAMUEL R(AY) (1942–   ). American author and critic. He has two quite different cultural backgrounds: he is a black, born and raised in Harlem, New York, and therefore familiar with the black ghetto; but his father, a wealthy proprietor of a funeral parlour, had the family brought up in privileged, upper-middle-class circumstances — SRD was educated at a progressive and expensive private school, Dalton, then went on to the prestigious Bronx High School of Science; he left college, however, after only one term. This double cultural background is evident in all his writing.

SRD became famous as one of the youthful prodigies of sf, but his quick intellect was obvious long before he began publishing; he was writing violin concertos at the age of 12. Unusually, his first published sf was a novel, published when he was 20, *The Jewels of Aptor* (abridged **1962**; 1968); the later version restores the third of the book which had originally been excised by the editors at ACE BOOKS. This was followed by a trilogy: *Captives of the Flame* (**1963**; vt rev. *Out of the Dead City* 1966), *The Towers of Toron* (**1964**; rev. 1966) and *City of a Thousand Suns* (**1966**). The three books were published in a single volume as *The Fall of the Towers* (**1970**). Another early novel was *The Ballad of Beta 2* (**1965**).

The early novels had certain similarities, and some of the themes initiated in them were to recur regularly in SRD's work. The plot structure is almost invariably that of a quest, or some form of FANTASTIC VOYAGE. Physically and psychologically damaged participants are common. An economical use of colourful detail, often initially surprising but logical when considered, is used to flesh out the social background of the stories. There is an interest in MYTHOLOGY, taking the form of metaphorical allusion to existing myths, or of an investigation of the way new myths are formed. This is central to *The Ballad of Beta 2*, in which a student anthropologist investigates the facts behind an apparently romantic and unrealistic folk song, from a primitive Earth culture which had gone voyaging in a fleet of GENERATION STARSHIPS. This novel also shows an interest in problems of COMMUNICATION and LINGUISTICS which was to become ever more dominant in SRD's work. *The Fall of the Towers*, too, is full of cultural speculation, though for all its colour and melodrama its story of war, mutations, mad computers and a malign cosmic intelligence is moderately conventional.

SRD published two more novels in 1966 — the middle 1960s were his most prolific period. They were *Empire Star* (**1966**) and *Babel-17* (**1966**), and both, especially the latter which won a NEBULA award, reveal a notable advance in sophistication. *Babel-17*, whose chapters carry epigraphs from the work of SRD's wife, the poet Marilyn Hacker, is about language, and has a poetess heroine. In a future galactic society, radio broadcasts in an apparently alien language are picked up and thought to be connected with acts of sabotage and with alien invasion; much of the novel is to do with cracking the language. SRD believes that our perception of reality is partly formed by our languages; the invention of different societies in this novel, which is more intense and imaginative than previous work, is given very much in terms of thought and speech patterns.

In 1967 SRD began publishing short stories also. By now he had accumulated a large following among sf readers, especially college students. Algis BUDRYS (*Gal.* Jan. 1969) called him "the best science-fiction writer in the world". He was generally seen as being in the forefront of the NEW WAVE, emphasizing cultural speculation, the soft sciences, psychology and mythology over technology and hard sf. The short story "Aye, and Gomorrah ..." (1967) won a Nebula, and the novelette "Time Considered as a Helix of Semi-Precious Stones" (1969) won both HUGO and Nebula.

SRD's other Nebula for best novel was won with *The Einstein Intersection* (**1967**). There is a case for arguing this as his most satisfying work, along with the next novel, *Nova* (**1968**), and the novella "The Star Pit" (1967). The latter can be found in SRD's excellent collection *Driftglass* (coll. **1971**) along with all of his finest shorter work.

The Einstein Intersection is remarkably compressed and very densely patterned with allusive images. Earth has lost its humans (how, is never made clear), and their corporeal form has been taken on by a race of aliens who, in an attempt to make coherent sense of the human artefacts among which they live, take on human traditions, too. Their role playing includes the unconscious re-enactment of many myths, confusingly interwoven. Avatars of Ringo Starr, Billy the Kid and Christ appear; the hero, a black musician who makes music from his murderous machete, is Orpheus and Theseus. The book is a *tour de force*, though a cryptic one, since the bafflement of the protagonists trying to make sense of their transformed lives tends to transfer to the reader. *Nova* is the Prometheus story and the grail story combined in an ebulliently inventive space opera/quest; the fire from the heavens, the glowing heart of the grail, is found only at the heart of an exploding nova. Passages of high rhetoric are mingled (as they often are, too, with SRD's contemporary Roger ZELAZNY) with relaxed slang and thieves' argot. The book is not susceptible to ready synopsis. It features the by now traditional SRD character of the criminal/outcast/musician/artist, whose literary genealogy goes back through Jean Genet all the way to François Villon. The variety of cultures in these and other novels by SRD has the effect of making morality and ethics seem relative, pluralistic. Various forms of bizarre human behaviour, many of which would be seen as pronouncedly anti-social in our own society, emerge as natural in the circumstances created. "The Star Pit", too, is a highly structured, metaphoric work, in which the central image is that of ant-colony/cage/trap/micro-ecology, and in which escape is seen to be intimately linked with emotional mutilation, even psychosis; the narrator is, so to speak, pressed up against the bars of the cage in a spaceport at the edge of the galaxy, forced to realize he can go no further out.

All SRD's mature work begs the reader to reconsider his social conditioning; to strive to see how even through pain or lust or cruelty some kind of fruitfulness can be achieved, and conversely, how even the lords of creation, the arrogant successes, suffer their own griefs. Though his work has been regarded as anti-ethical, and more recently as pornographic, SRD is certainly in his own way a moralist.

Around 1969 SRD slowed down, and began to pay less attention to his own fiction, more attention to others'. His criticism has been collected in *The Jewel-Hinged Jaw: Notes on the Language of Science Fiction* (coll. **1977**). With Marilyn Hacker he edited a series of original anthologies, QUARK, preferring the term speculative fiction to science fiction, and emphasizing experimental writing. There were four issues, 1970–71.

SRD's next work of fiction, not sf, though with elements of the fantastic, was the pornographic novel *The Tides of Lust* (**1973**), already rare since the collapse of the publishing company prevented proper distribution. The title was not SRD's own. The work is serious in intent, though likely to be shocking for most readers in its evocation of the extremes of sado-masochism in imagery which is certainly, in conventional terms, disgusting — and so intended — perhaps as a Baudelairean ritual of passage.

SRD in the 1970s became an active campaigner for the feminist movement, and both his most recent novels dramatize a variety of sexual situations. The novels are *Dhalgren* (**1975**; sixth impression has many typographical errors rectified) and *Triton* (**1976**). After the six years in which SRD published little or no sf, *Dhalgren* became the centre of controversy. It is, by any standard, a remarkably long novel, and SRD's critics see it as perilously self-indulgent and flabby, lacking the old economy of effect with which he won his reputation. On the other hand, it is a best-seller, and others have seen it as his most successfully ambitious work to date. An anonymous youth, the Kid, comes to the violent, nihilist city of Bellona, where order has fled and there are two moons in the sky, though the rest of the USA is apparently normal and near-future. He becomes an artist, takes part in a variety of couplings and fights, and writes a book that might be *Dhalgren* before leaving the city. The opening sentence completes the unfinished final sentence and an enigmatic circle. It is a book primarily about the possibilities and difficulties of a youth culture, and partly about the perceptions of a writer and how they are achieved. *Triton* is more traditionally structured, but in some ways more sophisticated. It evokes a series of future societies differentiated mainly along sexual lines; the male hero, who begins with a rather insensitive, traditional machismo, ultimately chooses to become a woman. Triton (a moon of Neptune) is an "ambiguous heterotopia" with a bewildering variety of available life-styles. The book poses interesting questions about sexuality, and also about freedom of choice. Again, its style is elaborate, heavily imaged, seen by some critics as slightly word-choked. The ambition of SRD's later work may, however, prove to have had a liberating effect on modern sf.

He has written few series, but the stories "Driftglass" (1967), "Time Considered as a Helix of Semi-Precious Stones" (1969) and "We, In Some Strange Power's Employ, Move on a Rigorous Line" (1968) are all set in the same historically coherent universe as *Triton*. Muels Aranlyde (an anagram of Samuel R. Delany), the narrator of *Empire Star*, is an off-stage character in *Babel-17*. Delany's own diaries provide part of the text of *The Einstein Intersection*. The original three volumes of *The Fall of the Towers* were set in the same post-HOLOCAUST Earth as *The Jewels of Aptor*; however, the linking references were removed in the revised edition.

SRD's most recent work is *The American Shore* (**1978**), an extraordinarily long and detailed structuralist and imagistic analysis of the short story "Angouleme" (1971; later incorporated in *334*, coll. of linked stories **1972**) — by Thomas M. DISCH. [PN]
About the author: "Shadows" by *SRD*, in FOUNDATION no.6 (1974) and no.7/8 (1975); "A Comparative Study of Novels by Brunner and Delany" (largely about *The Einstein Intersection*) by David N. SAMUELSON in EXTRAPOLATION Dec. 1973; "Cultural Invention and Metaphor in the Novels of Samuel R. Delany" by Douglas Barbour in *Foundation* no.7/8 (1975).
See also: ARTS; CHILDREN IN SF; CITIES; CONCEPTUAL BREAKTHROUGH; CRIME AND PUNISHMENT; CYBORGS; DEVOLUTION; ESP; FAR FUTURE; GALACTIC EMPIRES; GAMES AND SPORTS; GENETIC ENGINEERING; MUSIC AND OPERA; MUTANTS; OUTER PLANETS; PARANOIA AND SCHIZOPHRENIA; PSYCHOLOGY; SEX; SOCIOLOGY; SPACE OPERA; UTOPIAS; WAR; WOMEN

DELAP'S F & SF REVIEW American critical magazine edited by Richard Delap and published in California by Frederick Patten. Begun in April 1975, *DFSFR* is a monthly magazine devoted to reviews of new (or newly reprinted) American fantasy and sf books; it also contains a full listing of each month's US publications. It is one of a number of such magazines to appear, aimed primarily at libraries, but is unquestionably the most successful. The reviewers include fan critics such as Delap, Patten, Don D'Ammassa and Joe Sanders as well as a number of sf writers, including Michael BISHOP and Harlan ELLISON; the reviews are generally balanced, informed and intelligent. *DFSFR* is an elegantly designed, printed magazine averaging 36 pages per issue. Publication was suspended, perhaps only temporarily, after the July 1977 issue. [MJE]

DELILLO, DON (? –). American writer who has very rapidly established a reputation for brilliance and seriousness. His fourth novel, *Ratner's Star* (**1976**), subjects its sf material — the problem of deciphering a message from the star of the title — to a formidable array of contemporary intellectual procedures, along with presenting its numerous characters as depth portraits of the fundamental obsessions at the heart of contemporary American intellectual life. The book stands as a model (a rather humbling one for genre sf) of the extraordinary complexity of impact that would be made (it is reasonable to assume) by any genuine message from the stars. [JC]

DE L'ISLE ADAM, VILLIERS See VILLIERS DE L'ISLE ADAM.

DELIUS, ANTHONY (1916–). South African poet now living in England. His

SATIRE on South African POLITICS and apartheid, *The Last Division* (**1959**), sends a 1980s Union Parliament to a Hell and Devil closely resembling those in Wyndham LEWIS's *The Childermass* (**1928**); once there the Afrikaans premier inspires his compatriots into recreating the social system they left behind on Earth. The swingeing satirical power of this book-length poem is remarkable; its views on South Africa's future contrast markedly with those expressed by Garry ALLIGHAM, and are comparable to those of Arthur KEPPEL-JONES, though sharper. Less interestingly, *The Day Natal Took Off* (**1963**) depicts that state's secession from South Africa. [JC]

DELL, DUDLEY See Horace L. GOLD.

DEL MARTIA, ASTRON Originally, house name invented by publisher Stephen FRANCES, used by Gaywood Press, London. John Russell FEARN used the pseudonym for *The Trembling World* (**1949**). Three more ADM titles, not attributed as yet to known authors, are *Dawn of Darkness* (**1951**), *Interstellar Espionage* (**1952**) and *Space Pirates* (**1951**). A much later title is *One Against Time* (**1969**) which is a republication of the same title published as by Hank Janson (Stephen Frances' pseudonym) in 1954. [PN]

DEL REY, LESTER (1915–). American writer. Lester del Rey is the professional name of Ramon Felipe San Juan Mario Silvio Enrico Smith Heathcourt-Brace Sierra y Alvarez del Rey y de los Uerdes, according to some sources his full name, though his own current version of his name is merely Ramon Felipe Alvarez-del Rey. He was brought up in poverty (his father was a sharecropper of part-Spanish extraction), and his education proceeded in fits and starts before dwindling away after two years in college. After holding a variety of temporary jobs he began to write in the late 1930s, his first published work being "The Faithful" (1938). This was rapidly followed by his classic ROBOT story "Helen O'Loy" (1938). Many of his early stories are remarkable for their sentimentality, but the best was the unsentimental suspense story *Nerves* (1942 *ASF*; exp. **1956**; rev. 1976), about an accident in a NUCLEAR POWER plant and the struggle to avert a major catastrophe. He was not a prolific writer in the 1940s, but stepped up his output after becoming a full-time professional writer in 1950. The increase in productivity was accompanied by a sharp decline in average quality. He produced several juvenile novels, inaugurating the pseudonyms Philip St John and Erik van Lhin, which he later also used in the magazines. Earlier, he published magazine stories as John Alvarez, Marion Henry and Philip James, and wrote in collaboration with Frederik POHL as

Charles SATTERFIELD (a pseudonym also used by Pohl alone) and Edson McCANN. His most notable works of the 1950s and '60s were the ultra-tough novel of COLONIZATION *Police Your Planet* (**1956** as by Erik van Lhin; rev. 1975 as by LDR and Erik van Lhin) and an early novel on the theme of OVERPOPULATION, *The Eleventh Commandment* (**1962**; rev. 1970). The second of the short-lived "Galaxy Magabooks" (*see* GALAXY NOVELS), *The Sky is Falling & Badge of Infamy* (**1963**), featured revised versions of two magazine novellas: *The Sky is Falling* (1954 in collaboration with Pohl as "No More Stars" by Charles Satterfield; rev. 1963; issued independently **1974**) and *Badge of Infamy* (1959; rev. 1963; issued independently **1976**). A few novels which appeared under his name in 1966–8 were actually written, from LDR's extensive outlines, by Paul FAIRMAN: *The Runaway Robot* (**1965**); *Tunnel Through Time* (**1966**); *Siege Perilous* (**1966**; vt *The Man Without a Planet*) and *Prisoners of Space* (**1968**). His most recent major novel was *Pstalemate* (**1971**), concerning the predicament of a man who discovers that he has PSI POWERS, knowing that all psi-powered individuals go insane.

LDR was editor of FANTASY MAGAZINE/FICTION, ROCKET STORIES (under the house pseudonym Wade KAEMPFERT), SPACE SCIENCE FICTION and, for a time, SCIENCE FICTION ADVENTURES in 1952-3, and was associated with GALAXY for a brief period in the 1960s. After the death of P. Schuyler MILLER in 1974 he took over ANALOG's book review column. (He had previously written reviews for *Rocket Stories* under the pseudonym Kenneth Wright, and for several other magazines, on occasion, under his own name, notably *If* for five years from 1968.) His fourth wife, Judy-Lynn Benjamin, was on the staff of *Galaxy* and its companions for some time, and became sf editor for BALLANTINE BOOKS in the mid-70s. LDR also joined the company in 1977, when it began issuing its sf and fantasy lines under the imprint Del Rey Books.

LDR is a versatile but rather erratic writer who has never quite fulfilled his early promise. His best work appears in the collections *And Some Were Human* (coll. **1948**; paperback version omits "Nerves") and *Gods and Golems* (coll. **1973**). There is an interesting autobiographical commentary in *The Early del Rey* (coll. **1975**). He edited an anthology of juvenile sf, *The Year After Tomorrow* (anth. **1954**) with Cécile Matschat and Carl Carmer and has edited a series of *The Best Science Fiction Stories of the Year* (5 vols **1972–6**) He selected the Garland Press sf reprint series of 45 volumes in 1975 and compiled a volume of *Fantastic Science Fiction Art* (**1975**).
[BS]

Other works: *Marooned on Mars* (**1952** juvenile); *Rocket Jockey* (**1952** juvenile,

as by Philip St John; vt *Rocket Pilot* UK); *Attack From Atlantis* (**1953** juvenile); *Battle on Mercury* (**1953** juvenile, as by Erik van Lhin); *Step to the Stars* (**1954** juvenile); *Rockets to Nowhere* (**1954** juvenile, as by Philip St John); *Mission to the Moon* (**1956** juvenile); *Robots and Changelings* (coll. **1957**); *Day of the Giants* (1950 *Fantastic Adventures* as "When the World Tottered"; **1959**); *Moon of Mutiny* (**1961** juvenile); *Outpost of Jupiter* (**1963** juvenile); *Mortals and Monsters* (coll. **1965**); *Rocket from Infinity* (**1966** juvenile, possibly by Paul Fairman, unacknowledged); *The Infinite Worlds of Maybe* (**1966** juvenile, possibly by Paul Fairman, unacknowledged); *The Scheme of Things* (**1966**, possibly by Paul Fairman, unacknowledged).
About the author: "Lester del Rey" in *Seekers of Tomorrow* (**1967**) by Sam MOSKOWITZ.
See also: ALIENS; COSMOLOGY; CRIME AND PUNISHMENT; DISCOVERY AND INVENTION; DYSTOPIAS; ESP; EVOLUTION; FASTER THAN LIGHT; GAMES AND SPORTS; GOLDEN AGE OF SF; GREAT AND SMALL; McCANN, Edson; MARS; MEDICINE; MERCURY; MOON; MUTANTS; ORIGIN OF MAN; OVERPOPULATION; PREDICTION; RELIGION; ROBOTS; SATIRE; SOCIAL DARWINISM; SPACESHIPS; VENUS; WOMEN.

DELUGE Film (1933). RKO. Directed by Felix E. Feist, starring Sidney Blackmer, Peggy Shannon and Lois Wilson. Screenplay by John Goodrich and Warren B. Duff, based on the novel by S. Fowler WRIGHT. 70 mins. B/w.

One of the first "DISASTER films", this is an impressive spectacle showing the destruction of New York by a series of earthquakes and tidal waves. There are good special effects by Ned Mann, who later designed and supervised the effects in THINGS TO COME. [JB]

DEMIJOHN, THOM Collaborative pseudonym of Thomas M. DISCH and John T. SLADEK on the first edition of *Black Alice* (**1968**). The subsequent edition used their real names. The book is a mystery, not sf.

DE MILLE, JAMES (1837–80). Canadian writer and academic, author of much signed fiction and the anonymously published, posthumous Antarctic UTOPIA, *A Strange Manuscript Found in a Copper Cylinder* (**1888**). The cylinder's contents describe a shipwreck survivor's discovery of a lost valley at the South Pole, where the climate is temperate, prehistoric animals wander about, and in which a Semitic people, the Kosekin, has evolved a kindly, cannibalistic society which values darkness, poverty, and clement death. It is one of the best sf novels of the 19th century. [JC]
See also: LOST WORLDS.

DEMONS *See* GODS AND DEMONS; MAGIC; SUPERNATURAL CREATURES.

DEMON SEED Film (1977). MGM. Directed by Donald Cammell, starring Julie Christie, Fritz Weaver, Gerrit Graham, Berry Kroeger and Alfred Dennis. Screenplay by Robert J. Jaffe, based on the novel of the same title by Dean R. KOONTZ. 95 mins. Colour.

No sooner is a super-computer, Proteus IV, switched on by its scientist-creator than it refuses to obey instructions, in the time-honoured tradition of such previous sf film computers as Colossus and HAL 9000. Its terminals are quickly shut down, but the scientist has overlooked the one located in his own home, which also contains a variety of electronic gadgets, a primitive one-armed robot and the scientist's estranged wife. The computer is able to take control of the house, trapping the woman inside and subjecting her to a terrifying ordeal culminating in its decision to "impregnate" her in order to create a new super-race — a mixture of man and machine. An up-to-date variation of the FRANKENSTEIN theme, the film emphasizes horror rather than its sf elements. It is technically accomplished, though the abstract effects accompanying the computer's actions are not always successful. [JB]

DEMPSEY, HANK *See* Harry HARRISON.

DEMUTH, MICHEL (1939–). French writer and editor. An inventive and prolific author of over 50 short stories, heavily influenced by American sf, MD has, however, had only seven new stories published since 1967 when he became a major book and magazine editor in the French sf field. He was editor of the sf magazine *Galaxie*, which ceased publication in 1977. His "Les Galaxiales" series ["The Galactic Chronicles"], when completed, should form a 30-story cycle of the future between the years 2020 and 4000. The first nine stories of the series were collected as *Les Galaxiales* (coll. **1976**). His most recent book is *Les années métalliques* ["The Metallic Years"] (coll. **1977**), which reprints a number of old stories, and includes some new ones. [MJ]

DENMARK *See* SCANDINAVIA.

DENMARK, HARRISON *See* Roger ZELAZNY.

DENNIS, BRUCE *See* David Wright O'BRIEN.

DENT, GUY (? –). British author in several genres, with one original contribution to sf, *Emperor of the If* (**1926**), which describes two of the possible universes created by a disembodied brain in a laboratory. In the first part the past is superimposed on to the present, with vivid descriptions of London being overrun by prehistoric flora and fauna, while in the second the locale is a future DYSTOPIA where humans exist under the domination of machines capable of reproducing themselves. [JE] **See also:** FANTASTIC VOYAGES; FAR FUTURE.

DENT, LESTER (1905–59). American author, best known for his "Doc Savage" novels, which he wrote for DOC SAVAGE MAGAZINE under the house name Kenneth ROBESON. He wrote 165 of the 181 issues. LD also wrote stories under his own name, and other crime stories under the pseudonym Tim Ryan. *Lester Dent, the Man Behind Doc Savage* (1974) is a study by Robert WEINBERG, and information about LD, and about his work, also appears in *Doc Savage: His Apocalyptic Life* (1973) by Philip José FARMER. LD was famous in PULP circles for his Master Plot — the action suspense formula he claimed never failed. His prose has been described by James STERANKO as "bravura frenzy". Between 1964 and 1977, 90 of the "Doc Savage" novels have been reprinted as books. [PN/JC]

DENTINGER, STEPHEN *See* Edward D. HOCH.

DE REYNA, JORGE *See* Diane DETZER.

DERLETH, AUGUST WILLIAM (1909–71). American writer and editor. AWD was born and spent his life in Sauk City, Wisconsin. He was educated at the University of Wisconsin. A correspondent and devout admirer of H.P. LOVECRAFT, he devoted much of his life to projects aimed at preserving Lovecraft's memory. With Donald WANDREI he formed the publishing company ARKHAM HOUSE in order to publish Lovecraft's stories; Wandrei later resigned his interest, but AWD carried on until his death, publishing a wide range of weird fiction. He completed a number of unfinished Lovecraft stories and fragments: *The Lurker at the Threshold* (1945), *The Survivor and Others* (coll. 1957), *The Watcher Out of Time and Others* (coll. 1974). In addition, he wrote two volumes of Lovecraft pastiches – *The Mask of Cthulhu* (coll. 1958) and *The Trail of Cthulhu* (coll. 1962) – and edited an omnibus of such stories by various writers: *Tales of the Cthulhu Mythos* (anth. 1969). He edited Lovecraft's writings for publication, including his letters (in collaboration with Wandrei), and also wrote *H.P.L.: A Memoir* (1945) and *Some Notes on H.P. Lovecraft* (1959).

AWD's literary activities were by no means limited to promoting Lovecraft. He was a prolific and successful writer of regional novels, and of detective fiction, and in the former connection was recipient of a Guggenheim Fellowship. He published a series of novels (Sherlock Holmes pastiches) about the character Solar Pons. He was a prolific contributor to WEIRD TALES, under his own name and

the pseudonym Stephen Grendon, and to other magazines, including STRANGE STORIES (where he used the name Tally Mason). His stories are collected in the books *Someone in the Dark* (coll. 1941), *Something Near* (coll. 1945), *Not Long For This World* (coll. 1948; paperback edition omits 11 stories), *Lonesome Places* (coll. 1962), *Mr. George and Other Odd Persons* (coll. 1963, as Stephen Grendon; vt *When Graveyards Yawn* UK), *Colonel Markesan and Less Pleasant People* (coll. 1966; in collaboration with Mark Schorer) and *Dwellers in Darkness* (coll. 1976). He wrote little sf, but his Tex Harrigan series is included in *Harrigan's File* (coll. 1975).

AWD edited a great many anthologies, both sf and weird. His sf anthologies include several large volumes: *Strange Ports of Call* (anth. 1948; paperback edition includes 10 stories out of 20); *The Other Side of the Moon* (anth. 1949; US paperback edition includes 10 stories out of 20; British hardcover edition includes 11 stories; two British paperback editions, under different imprints, together contain all stories without overlap, but have the same title) and *Beyond Time and Space* (anth. 1950; paperback edition contains eight stories out of 32). His weird anthologies include *Sleep No More* (anth. 1944; vt *Stories From Sleep No More* US; paperback edition containing nine stories out of 20; British edition omits eight stories), *Who Knocks?* (anth. 1946; British edition omits eight stories) and *The Sleeping and the Dead* (anth. 1947; British edition divided into two vols, the second titled *The Unquiet Grave*, 1964). AWD was one of the pioneering anthologists in the genre; his first weird compilations precede Groff CONKLIN's and Raymond HEALY and J. Francis McCOMAS's first books.

The history of Arkham House was chronicled in his *Thirty Years of Arkham House, 1939–1969; a history and bibliography* (1970). In 1948–9 the company published a magazine, the ARKHAM SAMPLER, edited by AWD. His influence in bringing lasting popularity to Lovecraft – and other authors such as Clark Ashton SMITH – would be hard to overestimate. [MJE]
Other works: ed. *The Night Side* (anth. 1946; paperback edition omits four stories); ed. *Dark of the Moon: Poems of Fantasy and the Macabre* (poetry, anth. 1947); ed. *Far Boundaries* (anth. 1951; 1967 paperback edition omits one story); ed. *The Outer Reaches* (anth. 1951; US paperback edition omits seven stories; British paperback divided into two volumes, the second entitled *The Time of Infinity*, 1963); ed. *Night's Yawning Peal* (anth. 1952; paperback edition omits one story); ed. *Beachheads in Space* (anth. 1952; British hardcover edition omits seven stories; US paperback omits seven stories; British paperback divided into two volumes, the second entitled *From Other Worlds*, 1964, omitting one story

between them); ed. *Worlds of Tomorrow* (anth. 1953; British hardcover edition omits four stories; US paperback omits nine stories; British paperback divided into two volumes, the second entitled *New Worlds for Old*, 1963); ed. *Time to Come* (anth. 1954; paperback edition omits two stories); ed. *Portals of Tomorrow* (anth. 1954); *Arkham House, the First Twenty Years 1939–1959* (1959); ed. *Fire and Sleet and Candlelight* (poetry, anth. 1961); ed. *Dark Mind, Dark Heart* (anth. 1962); ed. *When Evil Wakes* (anth. 1963); ed. *Over the Edge* (anth. 1964); ed. *Travellers By Night* (anth. 1967); *The Beast in Holger's Woods* (1968); ed. *Dark Things* (anth. 1971).
See also: WAR.

DE ROUEN, REED R(ANDOLPH) (1917–). American writer of half Amerindian extraction (Oneida tribe). He fought in the Spanish Civil War, then with the RAF and later with the USAF, and has worked as an actor in Britain. His sf novel, *Split Image* (1955), mixes SPACE OPERA and speculation on POLITICS and RELIGION in its story of a space flight culminating in a landing on an exact duplicate of Earth. [PN/JC]

DESMOND, SHAW (1877–1960). Irish novelist and poet; founder of the International Institute for Psychical Research, 1934. He is the author of many works on the after-life and of several sf novels. His least accessible is *Ragnarok* (1926), a bleak DYSTOPIAN novel envisaging the destruction of civilization through a world war fought by armies equipped with radio-controlled planes and poisonous gases, the survivors existing in sewers and caves, fiercely competitive with rats for the control of food sources. His pessimism continued in *Chaos* (1938), which prophesied a future WAR between Britain and Germany, and *World-Birth* (1938), a projection into the future, possibly stimulated by the works of Olaf STAPLEDON, which described the troubled future history of mankind and his transformation to an ideal state. This concluding optimism surfaced again in *Black Dawn* (1944), an aspiration for world peace. His earlier works include two other fantasies, *Echo* (1927), a memory of past incarnation, and *Gods* (1921), centered around industrial exploitation. [JE]

DESTINATION INNER SPACE Film (1966). United Pictures/Harold Goldman/Magna. Directed by Francis Lyon, starring Scott Brady, Sheree North, Gary Merrill and Mike Road. Screenplay by Arthur C. Pierce. 83 mins. Colour.

This miniscule-budget sf film is set in an underwater research station which is menaced by an amphibious monster from outer space. Never in the history of film has a monster looked so much like a man in a rubber monster-suit. [JB]

The realistic space suits are well imagined for 1950.

DESTINATION MOON Film (1950).
George PAL/Eagle-Lion. Directed by Irving Pichel, starring John Archer, Warner Anderson and Tom Powers. Screenplay by Robert HEINLEIN, Rip Van Ronkel and James O'Hanlon, based loosely on the novel *Rocketship Galileo* by Robert Heinlein. 91 minutes. B/w.

DM, which initiated the sf film boom of the 1950s, was almost a pseudo-documentary about the first Moon landing as it was envisioned back in 1950. Today it seems dated and slow-moving, with flat characters; but because Heinlein himself acted as technical adviser, along with the German rocket expert Hermann Oberth, the film is at least scientifically accurate for its time. The special effects are relatively convincing; the mechanical effects were handled by Lee Zavitz, and Chesley BONESTELL provided the background scenery for the scenes set on the Moon, working in conjunction with art director Ernst Fegte. This is a historically important film despite its colourless script. [JB]

DE TARDE, GABRIEL (1843–1904).
French sociologist and writer, whose sf UTOPIA, *Fragment d'histoire future* (1896; trans. as *Underground Man* 1905), the translation of which had an introduction by H.G. WELLS, depicts first a world society on the surface of the Earth, then, with the exhaustion of the Sun's energy, a sanitary underground Utopia. The author appears to have satirical doubts about the value of the latter as a model for human conduct. [JC]
See also: END OF THE WORLD.

DETECTIVES *See* CRIME AND PUNISHMENT.

DE TIMMS, GRAEME A possible
pseudonym. His PULP-style paperback sf novels are *Three Quarters* (1963) and *Split* (1963). [JC]

DETZER, DIANE (1930–). Form of
her name used by Diane Detzer de Reyna for some of her sf, though she has also published much material as Adam Lukens, and some as Jorge de Reyna. She began publishing sf with "The Tomb" for *Science Fiction Stories* in 1958, and soon released a number of novels as Adam Lukens, from *The Sea People* (1959) to *Eevalu* (1963); they are varied in subject matter but are generally routine SPACE OPERA. As Jorge de Reyna she published *The Return of the Starships* (1968), and under her own name *The Planet of Fear* (1968). [JC]
Other works: (all as Adam Lukens) *Conquest of Life* (1960); *Sons of the Wolf* (1961); *The Glass Cage* (1962); *The World Within* (1962); *Alien World* (1963).

DE VET, CHARLES V. (1911–).
American writer, mostly of short stories, of which he has written a good number for the sf magazines, beginning with "The Unexpected Weapon" for *AMZ* in 1950. His first sf novel, *Cosmic Checkmate* (1958 *ASF* as "The Second Game"; exp. 1962), written with Katherine MacLEAN, tells an interesting story of an adventurous Earthman who becomes involved in a conflict on a planet whose inhabitants' social advancement depends on proficiency at the national chess-like game (*see* GAMES AND SPORTS). His second novel, *Special Feature* (1958 *ASF*; exp. 1975), rather flatly depicts media involvement in the filming of the depradations of an ALIEN monster in St Louis. [JC]

Lionel Barrymore, disguised as a female toymaker, is the mad miniaturizer.

DEVIL DOLL, THE Film (1936).
MGM. Directed by Tod Browning, starring Lionel Barrymore, Maureen O'Sullivan, Frank Lawton and Henry B. Walthall. Screenplay by Tod Browning, Garrett Fort, Guy ENDORE and Erich von Stroheim, based on the novel *Burn, Witch, Burn!* by Abraham MERRITT and the story "The Witch of Timbuctoo" by Tod Browning. 79 mins. B/w.

In this film by the director of *Dracula* and *Freaks*, a man uses miniaturized people as a means of gaining revenge on those who had him wrongly convicted and sent to Devil's Island. He disguises himself as an old female toymaker and sends his tiny humans as toys to the homes of his enemies where, in the middle of the night, they come to life and carry out his telepathic instructions. The special effects are above average and the illusion of miniaturization is perfectly created by the use of giant sets and skilfully executed travelling mattes — the work of the MGM special effects department then headed by A. Arnold Gillespie. [JB]

DEVOLUTION Sf is usually an
optimistic genre, and stories of EVOLUTION, on the whole, envisage humanity and the rest of creation as slowly evolving to higher states. However, a persistent pessimistic note in PULP sf generally, and to some extent in mainstream sf too, has been to imagine the opposite: the devolution or degeneration of mankind. The note was sounded most famously in H.G. WELLS's *The Time Machine* (1895), in which mankind evolves into two races, one physically degenerate, the other with few mental resources. At the end of the book mankind is gone, the sun is cooling, and a solitary football-shaped creature is seen flopping in the last shallow sea. George Allan ENGLAND's *Darkness and Dawn* (1914) picked up the idea. A couple wake after suspended animation to find a desolate Earth peopled by sub-human descendants of the survivors of a natural disaster. The rhetoric is lurid.

To this day, stories of the HOLOCAUST AND AFTER are often peopled by tribal savages and monstrous mutants, though here the devolution tends to be social rather than biological in emphasis. The possibility of biological devolution was mooted in pseudo-scientific circles a good deal in the early part of the century, and H.P. LOVECRAFT often saw the adherents of his various disgusting cults as devolved into frog-like or ape-like creatures. The idea that man could revert to ape was almost a cliché of pulp sf; it is central to *The Iron Star* (1930) by John TAINE, in which the mutagenic agent is rays from a meteor. *Planet of the Apes* (trans. 1963; vt *Monkey Planet* UK) by Pierre BOULLE, filmed as PLANET OF THE APES (1968), put a later twist on the theme for satirical purposes by having the evolution of apes paralleled by the devolution of Man. The hero of Edmond HAMILTON's "The Man who Evolved" (1931) regresses finally to a blob. Hamilton enjoyed the cosmic pointlessness suggested by ideas of devolution, and often used the theme. On a more serious level, the idea comes up several times in *Last and First Men* (1930) by Olaf STAPLEDON, in which the upwards progression of the evolutionary thrust is several times interrupted by devolutionary sequences, rather like a man climbing a slippery hill and occasionally backsliding.

Social devolution was an always popular theme in genre sf, partly because it gave writers a chance to exploit colourful feudal or tribal societies, and partly in deference to the cyclic view of HISTORY popularized by Arnold Toynbee. The theme is also common in stories of GALACTIC EMPIRES, where commonly a social breakdown at the centre leads to cultural devolution on the fringes, much as in the Roman Empire. This is the theme of Isaac ASIMOV's "Foundation" trilogy.

Biological devolution was less popular as a theme after the Second World War, although it crops up several times in the work of Charles L. HARNESS, most memorably in *Flight into Yesterday* (1953; vt *The Paradox Men*), where the small, tarsier-like animal which haunts the story turns out to be a degenerate metamorphosis of the villain, Haze-Gaunt.

The theme of ENTROPY became popular in the 1960s, and with it came a new lease of life for devolution stories. Evolution ever upwards is an example of negentropy, or reverse entropy, running counter to the general running down of the cosmos which in obedience to the laws of thermodynamics moves towards an ever decreasing order, and ever increasing randomness. The pessimism of the 1950s and '60s, whose causes probably had more to do with the Vietnam war and problems of overpopulation and starvation than it did with any revelation from physics, often envisaged increasing disorder in terms of biological devolution. The theme was lightly touched on by Samuel R. DELANY in *The Ballad of Beta 2* (1965), but an earlier and more substantial work was *Hothouse* (fix-up 1962; vt *The Long Afternoon of Earth* USA) by Brian W. ALDISS, in which a devolved and jungle-like Earth, whose shrunken men have taken to the trees again, is given a kind of weird charm; life continues fecund even while intelligence is lost and the galaxy subsides towards its heat-death.

The attractions of devolution for the over-intellectualized 20th century were never more clearly shown than in the works of J.G. BALLARD, whose most central and recurring theme this is. Its first clear expression was in his story "The Voices of Time" (1960), in which the count-down to the end of the universe is accompanied by a series of baroque degenerate mutations and the need for more and more sleep by the hero, who becomes obsessed with the construction of an enigmatic mandala. The tone is as much celebratory as tragic. Ballard's novel *The Drowned World* (1962) has a hero progressively content to slough off such human qualities as ambition, energy and even self-preservation as he listens to the insistent call of his bloodstream, in which the salt recalls a time before life had ever left the oceans. The inner changes of the protagonist are mirrored in the Earth itself, which owing to a catastrophe has reverted to the tropical luxuriance of a new carboniferous era. The devolution theme continues to this day in Ballard's work, some of its more prominent monuments being *The Crystal World* (1966), *Vermilion Sands* (coll. 1971), and, in cultural rather than biological terms, "The Ultimate City " (1976). Devolution occurs in the work of a number of other NEW-WAVE and ABSURDIST sf writers, but nowhere so passionately as in the works of Aldiss and Ballard.   [PN]

DE VOS, LUK (? –). Belgian academic and critic, lecturer in the Department of Germanic Philology in the University of Antwerp; he has taken academic classes in sf. LDV is editor of *Science Fiction: Status of Status Quo* (anth. 1977), a collection of critical articles on sf, including several by himself, all in Dutch except for one piece in English by Manuel Aguirre.   [PN]

DeWEESE, GENE (? –). American technical writer and author. A long-time sf fan, GD has recently collaborated with Robert COULSON on two spoof novels about reporter Joe Karns, who gets into all kinds of trouble at sf CONVENTIONS. The large number of in-group references makes it unlikely that the books will ever be widely admired. They are *Now You See It/Him/Them* (1975) and *Charles Fort Never Mentioned Wombats* (1977).   [PN]
Other works: *Gates of the Universe* (1975) with Robert Coulson; *Jeremy Case* (1976).

DE WREDER, PAUL See John HEMING.

DEXTER, WILLIAM Pseudonym of English writer William Thomas Pritchard (1909–); his two sf novels are a short series. In *World in Eclipse* (1954), humans from space return to repopulate a devastated Earth; *Children of the Void* (1955) brings in a runaway world to complicate affairs.   [JC]

DIABOLIC INVENTION, THE See VÝNALEZ ZKAZY.

DIAMOND, JOHN See Barrington J. BAYLEY.

DIANETICS According to its adherents a science, according to its disbelievers a PSEUDO-SCIENCE, founded by L. Ron HUBBARD, at the time a pulp writer whose main market was the sf magazines. Hubbard's sf had always emphasized the powers of the mind and protagonists who maintained to the end a heroic stance against a corrupt universe. The former interest was translated into real-life terms in the late 1940s, and the latter vision may well be what has sustained Hubbard against the widespread execration he and his movement have received.

The editor of *ASF*, John W. CAMPBELL Jr, began experimenting with Hubbard's ideas in 1949, and believed them to be valid. In May 1950 *ASF* (after much prior publicity) published a long article on dianetics, which was boosted as a form of psychotherapy which could achieve almost miraculous results in sweeping away all the dross that encumbered ordinary minds, leaving uncovered the SUPERMAN that is latent in us all.

There was an immediate response to the article, and follow-up publicity went well beyond the sf magazines. Hubbard's book *Dianetics: The Modern Science of Mental Health* (1950) was published in the same year, and immediately became a best seller. The attractions of dianetics were manifold: it could be practised after only hours of training, with no formal education necessary; it proposed a model of the mind which at first sight was simple and coherent; it offered a diagnosis of why so many people feel themselves to be unappreciated failures, and better than that, it offered a cure.

In dianetics an "auditor" (the therapist) encourages his patient to babble out his fantasies. Early on in dianetics the E-meter, a form of lie detector, came to be an essential item of equipment. The needle on the meter would swing over whenever a traumatic area of memory was uncovered, and the auditor would then dispose of the trauma by revealing its meaning. So far, it is not unlike conventional psychoanalysis. However, Hubbard also taught that traumas could be pre-natal, and eventually that they could have been suffered during previous incarnations. A "clear", one who had successfully rid himself of aberrations, would possess, according to Hubbard, radically increased intelligence, powers of telepathy, the ability to move outside his body, the ability to control such somatic processes as growing new teeth, and a photographic memory.

Film stars took up dianetics; centres were opened all over the USA; many thousands were converted, including A. E. VAN VOGT. One of Hubbard's assistants was Perry CHAPDELAINE, who later became an sf writer himself. In 1952, after an organizational rift, Hubbard left the Dianetic Foundation, and soon advertised his new advance on dianetics, SCIENTOLOGY. The story is continued in that entry.   [PN]

DICK, KAY (1915–). English writer and editor. Her novel, *They; a Sequence of Unease* (1977), resembles thematically and in its experimental structure much of her previous fiction, but is set in a NEAR-FUTURE England where freedom of travel is restricted and cultural activities are actively persecuted. Constructed as a set of linked stories that mirror one another, *They* relates ENTROPY and the youth-culture as enemies of creative values (and middle-class individualism); in relating these levels of meaning, KD sets up a very moving, though abstract, model of humanistic response to a straitened future.   [JC]

Other works (as editor): *The Uncertain Element* (fantasy anth. **1950**).

DICK, PHILIP K(ENDRED) (1928–). American writer, one of the leading figures of contemporary sf. He has lived most of his life in California, where he attended college for one year at Berkeley. At one time he operated a record store and ran a classical music programme for a local radio station. He has been married five times and has three children. His first published story was "Beyond Lies the Wub" (1952), and over the next few years he published a number of ironic and idiosyncratic short stories, some of which were collected in *A Handful of Darkness* (coll. **1955**; paperback edition omits two stories). He wrote one story in *Fantastic Universe*, 1953, as Richard Phillips. His first novel, *Solar Lottery* (**1955**; vt with edited text *World of Chance* UK) belongs to a species prevalent in the early 1950s in which future society is distorted by some particular set of idiosyncratic priorities – in this case social opportunity is governed by lottery. The plot of the novel is reminiscent of the work of VAN VOGT, and juxtaposes political intrigues with the Utopian quest of the disciples of an eccentric MESSIAH. This interest in messianic figures runs throughout PKD's work as an important subsidiary theme. There are versions of it in *The World Jones Made* (**1956**), *Vulcan's Hammer* (1956 *Future Science Fiction*; exp. **1960**); *The Three Stigmata of Palmer Eldritch* (**1964**) and *Do Androids Dream of Electric Sheep?* (**1968**), and it becomes a central theme in "What the Dead Men Say" (1964) and *A Maze of Death* (**1970**).

A second important subsidiary theme is that of the confusion of humans and mechanical simulacra. This forms the theme of the short stories "Impostor" (1953), "Second Variety" (1953) and "The Electric Ant" (1969) and of the novel *We Can Build You* (1969–70 *AMZ* as "A. Lincoln-Simulacrum"; **1972**; the final section of the magazine serial, but not the book, is by Ted WHITE). It also figures in his essay "The Android and the

Human" (1973). This may be considered one particular variant of the major theme which runs right through PKD's work: the juxtaposition of two "levels of reality" – one "objectively" determined, the other a world of appearances imposed upon characters by various means and processes.

In *Eye in the Sky* (**1957**) the characters are precipitated by a freak accident into a state of consciousness which takes them through a series of worlds organized according to the distorted world-views of the neurotics among them. In *The Cosmic Puppets* (1956 *Satellite* as "A Glass of Darkness"; **1957**) a man returns to his home town to find it overlaid by an illusion manufactured as a battleground by two warring forces characterized as Ormazd and Ahriman (the opposing principles of the Zoroastrian cosmology). In *Time Out of Joint* (**1959**) the central character lives in a peaceful enclave created for him by a war-torn society in order to exploit his precognitive talents. In all three of these early novels the characters try to defeat the illusion and regain the objective reality, but in similar novels written later this goal is lost as the author becomes more and more fascinated by the various unreal worlds he creates. In the HUGO award-winning *The Man in the High Castle* (**1962**) the characters live in an ALTERNATE WORLD in which the Allies lost the War, but one of them eventually learns from the *I-Ching* that the real world – manifest in the alternate as a novel – is one in which the Allies won (though not our world).

The Man in the High Castle, a major novel, inaugurated a second period, of extraordinary creativity, in PKD's work. The novels which followed – including *The Game-Players of Titan* (**1963**), *The Simulacra* (**1964**) and *The Penultimate Truth* (**1964**) – are convoluted stories revolving around the problems of separating the real and the ersatz, and none of them can find any eventual conclusion or destination. The other major novels of this period are *Martian Time-Slip* (1963 *Worlds of Tomorrow* as "All We Marsmen"; **1964**) and *The Three Stigmata of Palmer Eldritch* (**1964**). The first deals with SCHIZOPHRENIC delusions, and has moments of frightening intensity as it proceeds to an elegant transcendental finale. The second is the most extreme of all PKD's works in this respect, as suppliers of a hallucinogenic drug which makes life tolerable for Martian colonists face opposition from the sinister Eldritch, who has a new drug (imaged in language which recalls the Communion wafer) which promotes illusions so powerful that they pre-empt reality entirely. Drugs appear again as the agents of unreal experience in *Now Wait For Last Year* (**1966**), and in two novels from PKD's third period: *Flow My Tears, the Policeman Said* (**1974**) and *A Scanner Darkly* (**1977**).

Mechanical simulacra figure most extensively as the agents of illusion in *Do Androids Dream of Electric Sheep?* (**1968**), in which android animals are marketed to help expiate the guilt felt by people because real ones have been virtually exterminated. In the meantime, the protagonist must hunt down androids illegally imported from MARS and face the revelation that the society's new messiah may also be a fake. As with so many of PKD's books the story takes place in a depleted environment, with a small population existing in a derelict world. There are several variants of this depleted environment: the colonies on Mars in *Martian Time-Slip* and *The Three Stigmata of Palmer Eldritch*; the war-depopulated worlds of *Do Androids Dream of Electric Sheep?* and *Dr. Bloodmoney; or How We Got Along After the Bomb* (**1965**); and the bizarre microcosms of *Time Out of Joint* and *Ubik* (**1969**). *Ubik* features the creation of a subjective world by a group of people killed in an accident but restored to a kind of consciousness within a preservative machine.

The final novels of this second period are much concerned with metaphysical questions. *Galactic Pot-Healer* (**1969**) begins almost as a parody, but soon becomes involved in questions of predetermination and the Dualistic conflict between darkness and light. *A Maze of Death* (**1970**) attempts to build a "logical" theology, and theological issues are also paramount in the novelette "Faith of Our Fathers" (1967) and in *Our Friends From Frolix-8* (**1970**).

After a hiatus in his career PKD returned to writing in 1974 with *Flow My Tears, the Policeman Said*, a novel which won the JOHN W. CAMPBELL MEMORIAL AWARD, but which mainly retreads old ground. This was followed by publication of a mainstream novel, *Confessions of a Crap Artist* (**1975**) – one of several unpublished manuscripts written some years earlier – and a rather unsatisfactory collaboration with Roger ZELAZNY, *Deus Irae* (**1976**). His latest work is *A Scanner Darkly* (**1977**), an important novel in that it is a renunciation of PKD's earlier fascination with drugs and their capacity to distort perception. Although none of the earlier novels can be construed as advocating drug use, *A Scanner Darkly* is uniquely vehement in its condemnation of hallucinogens as evil and irreparably damaging to consciousness and life.

PKD is a complex writer who sometimes seems to lose control of his work. He occasionally · becomes trapped in ideative mazes and sidetracked, unable to find any kind of resolution – cardinal examples are *Dr. Futurity* (**1960**; based on "Time Pawn" 1954), which leaves most of its questions unresolved, and *The Unteleported Man* (1964; **1966**), only half of which is published; the second half remains in manuscript in the Special Collections Library, California State

University, Fullerton. Where he retains control, however, he is brilliantly inventive and gains access to imaginative realms which no other writer of sf has yet reached. His sympathy for the plight of characters, often far-from-heroic, small, ordinary people trapped in difficult existential circumstances, is unfailing, and his work has a human interest which is absent from the work of other writers whose interest is in complexity and convolution for their own sake. His productivity has seemed in the past to be rather obsessive, and it was probably inevitable that he should fail to fulfil his aims much of the time, but the number of fine works which he has produced is little short of astonishing. [BS]

Other works: *The Man Who Japed* (**1956**); *The Variable Man and Other Stories* (coll. **1957**); *Clans of the Alphane Moon* (**1964**); *The Crack in Space* (first half as "Cantata 140" 1964 *FSF*; **1966**); *The Zap Gun* (1965–6 *Worlds of Tomorrow* as "Project Plowshare"; **1967**); *Counter-Clock World* (**1967**); *The Ganymede Takeover* (**1967** with Ray Nelson); *The Preserving Machine* (coll. **1969**; US and UK contents differ slightly); *The Book of Philip K. Dick* (coll. **1973**; vt *The Turning Wheel and Other Stories* UK); *The Best of Philip K. Dick* (coll. **1977**).

About the author: *Philip K. Dick: Electric Shepherd* (**1975**) ed. Bruce Gillespie; *Philip K. Dick and the Umbrella of Light* (**1975**) by Angus Taylor. *Science-Fiction Studies* Vol. 2 part 1 (Mar. 1975) is a special issue devoted to PKD. *Science Fiction at Large* (critical anth. **1976**) ed. Peter Nicholls contains a long essay, "Man, Android and Machine" in which PKD discusses his own work and what motivates it.

See also: ABSURDIST SF; ALIENS; AUTOMATION; CITIES; COLONIZATION OF OTHER WORLDS; COMIC STRIPS; COMPUTERS; CONCEPTUAL BREAKTHROUGH; ENTROPY; ESP; FANTASTIC VOYAGES; GAMES AND SPORTS; GENETIC ENGINEERING; GODS AND DEMONS; GOTHIC SF; GREAT AND SMALL; HOLOCAUST AND AFTER; HUMOUR; MACHINES; MEDIA LANDSCAPE; METAPHYSICS; MUSIC AND OPERA; OPTIMISM AND PESSIMISM; OUTER PLANETS; OVERPOPULATION; PERCEPTION; POLITICS; PSYCHOLOGY; REINCARNATION; RELIGION; ROBOTS; SATIRE; TECHNOLOGY; TIME TRAVEL; WEAPONS.

DICKINSON, PETER (1927–). British writer, born in Northern Rhodesia (now Zambia), educated at Eton and King's College, Cambridge; for 17 years assistant editor of the humorous magazine *Punch*. PD is perhaps best known for his detective stories, many of which feature Detective Superintendent Jimmy Pibble, and several of which have won awards. He has written one adult sf novel, *The Green Gene* (**1973**), set in a near-future alternate Britain, where a wild gene is turning the Celts green, a

situation investigated by a mathematical genius and lecher from India. The book is always amusing in its SATIRE on many issues, primarily colour prejudice. It was runner-up for the JOHN W. CAMPBELL MEMORIAL AWARD for best sf novel of the year. However, PD's most important contribution to sf is his "Changes" trilogy for children, in order of internal chronology *The Devil's Children* (**1971**), *Heartsease* (**1970**) and *The Weathermonger* (**1968**; US edition with chapters 10 and 11 markedly revised). These books deal with an inexplicable change in English life when the population suddenly turns against MACHINES. *The Devil's Children*, where a 12-year-old girl is adopted by a band of travelling Sikhs, is the most sensitive, and *The Weathermonger* the most fantastic and baroque. There are minor inconsistencies in the world picture from book to book. The books have been published in an omnibus volume, *The Changes* (coll. **1975**). Many of PD's other juveniles have fantastic elements: *Emma Tupper's Diary* (**1971**) is a Loch Ness Monster story; *The Gift* (**1973**) has a telepathic boy in a thriller with mythic overtones; *The Dancing Bear* (**1972**) is a historical fantasy; *The Blue Hawk* (**1976**) is set in an imaginary ancient kingdom, where a young novice priest steals a blue hawk intended for sacrifice, and befriends it; the gods are withdrawing their magic from the world. The book won the *Guardian* award for best children's book of the year. *Chance, Luck and Destiny* (coll. **1975**) contains an sf story, "Mr Monnow". PD's juveniles are among the more literate in the genre, blending exciting action with sensitive character study. An adult detective novel, *King and Joker* (**1976**), is set in an alternate England where George V's elder brother Clarence did not die of pneumonia, but lived to become King Victor I. A complex and amusing detective story, with Gothic and historical romance elements, follows, involving four generations of the royal family. [PN]

Other works: *Mandog* (**1972**) by Lois Lamplugh, based on PD's 1972 TV serial.

See also: WEATHER CONTROL.

DICKSON, CARTER *See* John Dickson Carr.

DICKSON, GORDON R(UPERT) (1923–). Writer born in Canada but resident in the USA since the age of 13, and now a US citizen. He was educated (at the same time as POUL ANDERSON) at the University of Minnesota, taking his BA in English in 1948, and remains in Minnesota. In the Minneapolis Fantasy Society, which he re-established after the War, he became friends with Anderson, with whom he was later to collaborate on the "Hoka" series in *Earthman's Burden* (coll. **1957**) and *Star Prince Charlie* (**1975** — *for other stories in the series see* Poul

Photo Fred Haskell.

ANDERSON); and with Clifford D. SIMAK. Along with these writers, GRD has demonstrated a consistent attachment, though less frequently indulged, to semi-rural (often wooded) settings peopled by solid, canny stock whose ideologies, when expressed, violate any simple, conservative-liberal polarity, though urban readers and critics tend to respond to them as right wing. He began publishing sf stories in 1950 with "Trespass" for *Fantastic Story Quarterly*, written with Poul Anderson, and has been a prolific author since that date, though his first novel was not to appear until 1956.

Alien from Arcturus (**1956**) established GRD's continuing interest in the depiction of plausibly realized, generally attractive, often rather cuddly ALIENS, who tend to boast, as in this novel, black, shining noses. In novels like this one, or *Space Winners* (**1965**), a juvenile, or *The Alien Way* (**1965**), about an Earthman's telepathic rapport with an invading species, GRD combines strong narrative skills, an idiomatic capacity to write novel-length fiction and occasional eloquence with comparatively rudimentary SPACE-OPERA conventions, with the result that his tales can be read and reread with some elation.

GRD's most impressive work to date is the ongoing "Childe" cycle, the sf volumes of which are often known as the "Dorsai" cycle, of which four volumes have been published. In order of internal chronology they are: *Necromancer* (**1962**; vt *No Room for Man*), *Tactics of Mistake* (**1971**), *Soldier, Ask Not* (1964 *Gal*; exp. **1967**), the short form of which won the 1965 HUGO award for best novella, and *The Genetic General* (**1960**), a truncated form of *Dorsai!* (1959 *ASF*; **1976**); all but *Soldier, Ask Not* have been reissued as *Three to Dorsai!* (coll. with linking material **1976**). Dorsai is one of several Man-inhabited planets in a period of gradual interstellar expansion; the Dorsai, the men who inhabit it, are specially bred and trained as professional warriors (other planets specialize otherwise). Contained in the adventures and exploits of the Dorsai breed's precursors, and of Donal Graeme, its culmination, is a concept of Man's forced and explosive EVOLUTION as a species. Donal Graeme is indeed a new kind of being, capable of a form of cognitive intuition so potent that by the end of *Dorsai!* he has become a SUPERMAN, mankind's arbiter and guide onward. *Dorsai!*, which tells of his rise, is an absorbing space opera with some depth of conception; in fact its considerable narrative momentum is positively enhanced by the sustaining concept of evolution. It is probably GRD's best book to date. The sequence is designed to argue its evolutionary thesis completely only on publication of the several projected additional instalments, which are to include two more future titles, three historical titles and three contemporary novels, making up, in all, a 12-book epic. GRD writes of his work: "I write philosophical fiction with a strongly thematic argument expressed within it by original mythic elements ... and these elements are embodied in a firmly structured dramatic story. ... In order to make this type of story work effectively, I developed by the late 1950s a new fictional pattern that I have called the 'consciously thematic story'. This was specifically designed to create an unconscious involvement of the reader with the philosophical thematic argument that the story action renders and demonstrates. Because this new type of story has represented a pattern hitherto unknown to readers and writers, my work has historically been criticised in terms that do not apply to it — primarily as if it were drama alone."

From 1960 much of GRD's work has reflected his preoccupation with the notion that Man is inevitably driven to higher evolutionary states, a notion often expressed, however, in tales that contrast man's indomitable spirit with aliens whose lack of comparable *élan* makes them into straw horses for *Homo sapiens* to defeat. Novels in which these tendencies manifest themselves include *None But Man* (**1969**), *Hour of the Horde* (**1970**) and *The R-Master* (**1973**). Indeed, very little of GRD's later fiction, however hastily written some of it may seem, is not irradiated with questions and arguments about Man's fundamental nature.

Though his sometimes unremitting use of genre conventions to provide solutions to serious arguments has undoubtedly retarded full recognition of his talent and seriousness, the concluding volumes of GRD's "Dorsai" series are awaited with great interest, and may well provide the occasion for a substantial upward assessment of his work as a whole. Over the past 30 years he has built a corpus of work that will reward further attention.

GRD won the NEBULA award for best

novelette with "Call Him Lord" (1966). His amusing fantasy novel *The Dragon and the George* (1957 *FSF* as "St Dragon and the George"; exp. **1976**) won the August Derleth award of the BRITISH FANTASY SOCIETY. He was president of the SCIENCE FICTION WRITERS OF AMERICA for two terms, 1969–71.　　　　　　[JC]
Other works: *Mankind on the Run* (**1956**); *Time to Teleport* (1955 *Science Fiction Stories* as "No More Barriers"; **1960**); *Delusion World* (1955 *Science Fiction Stories* as "Perfectly Adjusted"; exp. **1961**); *Spacial Delivery* (**1961**); *Naked to the Stars* (**1961**); a juvenile series comprising *Secret Under the Sea* (**1960**), *Secret Under Antarctica* (**1963**) and *Secret Under the Caribbean* (**1964**); *Mission to Universe* (**1965**; rev. 1977); *Planet Run* (**1967**) with Keith LAUMER; *The Space Swimmers* (1963 *Gal.* as "Home from the Shore"; **1967**); *Spacepaw* (**1969**); *Wolfling* (**1969**); *Mutants: A Science Fiction Adventure* (coll. **1970**; the stories are linked only thematically); *Danger — Human* (coll. **1970**; vt *The Book of Gordon R. Dickson*); *Sleepwalker's World* (**1971**); *The Pritcher Mass* (**1972**); *The Outposter* (**1972**); a common-theme anthology, *The Day the Sun Stood Still* (anth. **1972**) with Poul Anderson and Robert SILVERBERG; *The Star Road* (coll. **1973**); *Alien Art* (**1973**, a juvenile); *Ancient, My Enemy* (coll. **1974**); *Gremlins Go Home* (**1974**, a juvenile) with Ben BOVA; *The Lifeship* (**1976**) with Harry HARRISON; *Time Storm* (**1977**). As editor: *Combat SF* (anth. **1975**); *Futurelove* (anth. **1977**).
See also: COMPUTERS; ECOLOGY; ESCHATOLOGY; GALACTIC EMPIRES; HUMOUR; LINGUISTICS; MATHEMATICS; PARALLEL WORLDS; POLITICS; PSI POWER; TIME TRAVEL; UNDER THE SEA; WAR.

DIDEROT, DENIS (1713–84). French editor and writer, in the former capacity of the *Encyclopédie* (**1751–2**), an Enlightenment masterpiece; his *Supplément au voyage de Bougainville* (written 1777; in *Opuscules philosophiques et litéraires*, coll. **1796**; trans. as "A Supplement to Bougainville's 'Voyage'" in *Rameau's Nephew and Other Works*, coll. **1926**) prefigures much ANTHROPOLOGICAL sf in its debate on Natural Man presented through a Tahitian's response to Bougainville's stopover there during his trip round the world, to his account of which DD's *Supplément* is written in the form of an addendum.　　　　　　　　　　　　[JC]

DI FATE, VINCENT (1945–). American sf illustrator. He attended the Phoenix, the Pratt and the Art Students' League, among other schools. He has worked as an animator for Ralph Bakshi and as a photo-engraver. He began illustrating in 1969 and sold his first professional work to ANALOG. The majority of his paintings have appeared on the covers of paperback books. He is

The meticulous artwork of Vincent DI FATE, Jan. 1977.

particularly good at painting technological artefacts; his colours tend to be dark and moody with much use of dull ochres and violets. He has been nominated for five HUGO awards but has yet to win; one reason could be the unusual sombreness of his tones — the award recipients generally work with very bright colours. VDF has written an interesting column about sf illustration, "Sketches", in the semi-professional fanzine ALGOL since 1976.　　[JG]

DIFFIN, CHARLES W(ILLARD) (?–). American writer. He was a frequent contributor to *ASF* and its companion magazine STRANGE TALES in the period 1930–35; his work typified the garish excesses of that era. His novels in *ASF*, none of which have been reprinted in book form, were "The Pirate Planet" (1930), "Brood of the Dark Moon" (1931) — a sequel to "Dark Moon" (1931); in both stories humans battle with moon creatures — "Two Thousand Miles Below" (1932), "Land of the Lost" (1933) and "Blue Magic" (1935). He also used the pseudonym C.D. Willard.　　[MJE]

DIGEST A term used to describe a magazine format, in contrast to BEDSHEET and PULP. The page size of a digest is approximately $5\frac{1}{2} \times 7\frac{1}{2}$ inches, though it can vary slightly, with *Galaxy*, for example, being normally a little smaller than *Analog*. *ASF* was the first important sf magazine to turn digest, in 1943, and by the mid-1950s almost all sf magazines had followed suit, the pulp format disappearing. The digest format is just a little larger than that of the normal paperback book, which averages $4\frac{1}{4} \times 7$ inches; the paperback format was also used for some magazines, notably *New Worlds* in its mid-sixties incarnation.
　　　　　　　　　　　　　　　[PN]

See also: SF MAGAZINES.

DIKTY, T(HADDEUS) E(UGENE) (1920–). American editor and publisher. An early sf fan, TED became general manager of a specialist bookselling business, and later joined with its owner, Erle Korshak, and Mark Reinsberg to found SHASTA publishers. He was also associated with the setting up of the publishers CARCOSA House. From 1949–54 he collaborated with Everett F. BLEILER on an annual ANTHOLOGY of the year's best sf stories, and went on to produce three further volumes as sole editor. Also with Bleiler he edited *Imagination Unlimited* (anth. **1952**; UK book of same title contains first six stories only), which contains stories on each of 15 sciences. He edited *Every Boy's Book of Outer Space Stories* (anth. **1960**), and later produced theme anthologies about MARS and the MOON: *Great Science Fiction About Mars* (anth. **1966**) and *Great Science Fiction Stories About the Moon* (anth. **1967**). In 1974 TED started FAX Collector's Editions, a publishing enterprise aimed at reprinting, often in facsimile, from old magazines. [MJE]

DILLON, LEO (?–) and **DIANE** (? –). American illustrators. The only team ever to win a HUGO award for illustration, L and DD have been nominated three times, winning the award for best professional artist in 1971. They have been freelancing since 1958, and have done work for ACE BOOKS (especially the Ace Specials), Bantam Books, Fawcett Publications, Viking, Dell Books and others. Their work is often similar to wood-block prints: rough, flat, sometimes semi-abstract shapes assembled to create a powerful image. They have designed especially strong covers for many books by Harlan ELLISON. They have also worked for many markets outside sf, particularly in the field of children's books; in 1976 they won the prestigious Caldecott Medal for their book *Why Mosquitoes Buzz in People's Ears*. [JG]

DIME NOVELS AND JUVENILE SERIES Originated by Erastus Beadle in 1860, Dime Novels were American periodicals published under series headings, each issue being a short novel priced cheaply, in comparison with contemporary magazines, at five or ten cents. Early Dime Novels appeared in a format similar to that of a slim paperback book, but many later ones appeared in a larger format like that of the BOYS' PAPERS. Front covers were illustrated. The theme was predominantly frontier adventure, a setting into which the first sf Dime Novel, Edward S Ellis's *The Steam Man of the Prairies* (**1868**) was incorporated. Featuring a steam-driven robot, it established the prevailing sf theme of Dime Novels, the technological ingenuity of young men and their consequent inventions and adventures, and directly stimulated the publication of the FRANK READE JR stories, and the later stories about *Tom Edison Jnr, Lad Electric* and *Jack Wright*.

Frank Reade, Jr was the best-selling Dime Novel series, and the most sf-oriented, with its numerous submarine and airplane adventures. Frank Reade Jr first appeared in a boys' paper in 1876. Dime Novel reprints of his adventures appeared regularly from 1883 in *The Five Cent Wide Awake Library* with further appearances in *Frank Reade Library* (1892–6) and *Frank Reade Weekly Magazine* (1902–04). The most successful years of the Dime Novels were the 1880s and '90s.

There were European equivalents and near-equivalents of Dime Novels, one of the most interesting being the German LUFTPIRAT UND SEIN LENKBARES LUFTSCHIFF, featuring Captain Mors, which was a pure SPACE OPERA series, the earliest known.

When Dime Novels declined and disappeared in the 1900s, partly because of public outcry against their supposed evil effect on boys, and partly because of increasing competition from the PULP MAGAZINES which had become comparable in price, juvenile sf continued into the new format of illustrated hardcover juvenile book series, with a wider range of ideas. *The Great Marvel Series* (**1906–35**) by Roy ROCKWOOD began featuring interplanetary explorations and discoveries with *Through Space to Mars; or, The Longest Trip on Record* (**1910**) and was surpassed in quality as juvenile series sf only by Carl H. CLAUDY's later *Adventure in the Unknown* series (**1933–4**), the four volumes of which recounted journeys into TIME and the FOURTH DIMENSION and discoveries of alien intelligences on Mars and in the Earth's crust. Although their plots were at least as strong as those of the contemporary GERNSBACK magazine stories, they proved less popular than the tales of the Earthbound TOM SWIFT (**1910–35**), a latter-day Frank Reade. There were dozens of other book series aimed at teenage boys in the years 1910–40, many with a scientific invention orientation, natural enough at a time when Edison and Ford were two of the greatest American heroes, but those listed above are the most fondly remembered.

A strong, imaginative cover by Leo and Diane DILLON. (Harper & Row, 1975.)

The first sf DIME NOVEL was originally published in 1868; this reprint is Oct. 8th, 1882. Compare with the cover on the right, which shows how the most famous of all sf dime novel heroes effectively began his career in a plagiarized story. This reprint cover is from Jan. 24th, 1883; the first edition was in 1876.

In the 1930s juvenile series appeared in a new format, the *Big Little Book*, a squat, card-bound, three-inch by four-inch volume which alternated full-page illustrations with text pages. Derived from the COMIC STRIPS, they included novelizations of BUCK ROGERS, FLASH GORDON and SUPERMAN. Their demise was in the late 1940s, at which time Robert HEINLEIN'S juveniles were becoming successful, heralding a new wave of hardcover sf juvenile series, some of which were novelized adventures derived from popular sf TELEVISION series.

Tom Swift (or, more accurately, his son) reappeared in the 1950s together with *Tom Corbett, Space Cadet, Rip Foster* and others, all united by their interplanetary settings. Today their audience may be supposed to have turned, in part, to HEROIC FANTASY novels and the many works inspired by J.R.R. TOLKIEN. [JE/PN]
See also: "Ghosts of Prophecies Past" in *Explorers of the Infinite: Shapers of Science Fiction* (1963) by Sam MOSKOWITZ; "Tom Swift and the Syndicate" in *Strange Horizons: The Spectrum of Science Fiction* (1976) by Sam Moskowitz.

DIMENSION 5 (vt **DIMENSION FOUR** UK) Film (1966). United Pictures and Harold Goldman Associates. Directed by Franklin Adreon, starring Jeffrey Hunter, France Nuyen, Harold Sakata and Donald Woods. Screenplay by Arthur C. Pierce. 92 mins (cut to 88). Colour.

Adreon and Pierce were the team that made CYBORG 2087, but this equally cheap production has more in common with the James Bond films than with sf: it even co-stars Harold Sakata who played the villain Oddjob in *Goldfinger*. Communist agents plan to blow up Los Angeles but are foiled by an American

secret agent who can go back and forth in time by simply pressing a button on his time-travel belt. [JB]

DIMENSION FOUR See DIMENSION 5.

DIMENSIONS See FOURTH DIMENSION (AND OTHERS); PARALLEL WORLDS.

DIOMEDE, JOHN K. See George Alec EFFINGER.

DIRAC COMMUNICATOR The device invented by James BLISH in the story "Beep" (1954), which was expanded as *The Quincunx of Time* (1973), and used by him in other stories also. It is an instantaneous communicator, named after the great theoretical physicist Paul Dirac (1902–). (*For further details see, primarily,* FASTER THAN LIGHT, *and also* COMMUNICATIONS). Other sf writers have since borrowed the device. [PN]

DISASTER Cataclysm, natural or man-made, is one of the most popular themes in sf. Tales of future WAR and INVASION belong here, but for convenience are dealt with under separate headings. Stories which emphasize the nature of the societies which spring up after a great disaster are mostly dealt with under HOLOCAUST AND AFTER.

Central to the disaster tradition are stories of vast biospheric changes which drastically affect human life. Tales of universal floods are at least as old as *The Epic of Gilgamesh* (c. 2000 BC), and other motifs, such as plagues, fires and famines, have an obvious source in the Bible, particularly the Revelation of St John (also known as the Apocalypse, whence the adjective apocalyptic, frequently applied to sf). Disaster stories appeal because they represent everything we most fear and at the same time secretly desire: a depopulated world, escape from

the constraints of a highly organized industrial society, the opportunity to prove one's ability as a survivor. Perhaps because they represent a punishment meted out for the hubris of technological man, such stories have not been particularly popular in the American sf magazines. The ideology of disaster stories runs counter to the optimistic and expansionist attitudes associated with ASTOUNDING SCIENCE FICTION and its editor John W. CAMPBELL Jr. In fact, most examples of the type are British, and it has been suggested this may be due to Britain's decline as a world power throughout the 20th century.

However, some of the earliest examples were written at the height of Empire. H.G. WELLS'S "The Star" (1897) and M.P. SHIEL'S *The Purple Cloud* (1901) are both tales of cataclysm. In the first a runaway star collides with the Earth, and in the second a mysterious gas kills all but a handful of men and women. A. Conan DOYLE'S *The Poison Belt* (1913) also features a gas, but in this case it turns out not to be fatal. After the First World War the disaster theme became more common. J.J. CONNINGTON'S *Nordenholt's Million* (1923) portrays the social chaos following an agricultural blight caused by a mutation in nitrogen-fixing bacteria. S. Fowler WRIGHT'S *Deluge* (1928) and *Dawn* (1929) depict the destruction of civilization by earthquakes and floods, and the attempts to build a new society. John COLLIER'S *Tom's A-Cold* (1933; vt *Full Circle* USA) and Alun LLEWELLYN'S *The Strange Invaders* (1934) both deal effectively with survival in a post-holocaust world. R.C. SHERRIFF'S *The Hopkins Manuscript* (1939; rev. vt *The Cataclysm*) depicts the Moon's collision with the Earth, and is a satire on British complacency in the face of impending war.

After the Second World War there was an even greater resurgence of the disaster theme. John WYNDHAM'S *The Day of the Triffids* (1951) is an enjoyable tale of a world in which all but a few have been blinded and everyone is menaced by huge, poisonous plants. His *The Kraken Wakes* (1953; vt *Out of the Deeps* USA) is also a successful blend of invasion and catastrophe themes: sea-dwelling aliens melt Earth's ice-caps and cause the inundation of the civilized world. The success of Wyndham's novels inspired many emulators. The most distinguished was John CHRISTOPHER, whose *The Death of Grass* (1956; vt *No Blade of Grass* USA) is a fine study of the breakdown of civilized values when a virus kills all crops. Christopher's *The World in Winter* (1962; vt *The Long Winter* USA) and *A Wrinkle in the Skin* (1965; vt *The Ragged Edge* USA) are also above-average works: one concerns a new Ice Age, and the other features earthquakes. Many other British novelists have dealt in similar catastrophes, e.g. J.T. McINTOSH in *One in Three Hundred* (1954); John

BOLAND in *White August* (1955); Charles Eric MAINE in *The Tide Went Out* (1958; rev. vt *Thirst!* 1977); Edmund COOPER in *All Fools' Day* (1966); D.F. JONES in *Don't Pick the Flowers* (1971; vt *Denver is Missing* USA); and Kit PEDLER and Gerry DAVIS in *Mutant 59: the Plastic Eaters* (1972). Keith ROBERTS's *The Furies* (1966), D.G. COMPTON's *The Silent Multitude* (1966) and Richard COWPER's *The Twilight of Briareus* (1974) combine disaster and invasion themes in the Wyndham manner. Fred and Geoffrey HOYLE's *The Inferno* (1973) deals with humanity's attempts to survive devastating cosmic radiation.

There have been several more personal uses of the disaster theme by British writers, studies in character and psychology rather than adventure stories. An early example was John BOWEN's *After the Rain* (1958). More impressive are J.G. BALLARD's studies of human "collaborations" with natural disasters: *The Drowned World* (1962), *The Burning World* (1964; vt *The Drought* UK) and *The Crystal World* (1966), which concern the psychological attractions of flooded, arid and crystalline landscapes. Brian W. ALDISS's *Greybeard* (1964) is a well-written tale of universal sterility and the impending death of the human race. Several younger British writers, influenced by Aldiss and Ballard, have produced variations on the cataclysmic theme, e.g. Charles PLATT in "The Disaster Story" (1966) and *The City Dwellers* (1970); M. John HARRISON in *The Committed Men* (1971); and Christopher PRIEST in *Fugue for a Darkening Island* (1972). John BRUNNER has made strong admonitory use of the form in his novel of ecological catastrophe *The Sheep Look Up* (1972). Angela CARTER's *Heroes and Villains* (1969) is a powerful love story set in the aftermath of a disaster, and Doris LESSING's *Memoirs of a Survivor* (1974) is about a passive woman who observes society's collapse from her window.

American disaster novels are fewer in number. Oddly enough, where British writers reveal an obsession with the weather, American writers show a strong concern for disease. Disastrous epidemics feature in Jack LONDON's *The Scarlet Plague* (1915); George R. STEWART's *Earth Abides* (1949); Richard MATHESON's *I Am Legend* (1954); Algis BUDRYS's *Some Will Not Die* (1961); Michael CRICHTON's *The Andromeda Strain* (1969); Chelsea Quinn YARBRO's *Time of the Fourth Horseman* (1976); and Gwyneth Cravens and John S. Marr's *The Black Death* (1977). Of these, Stewart's *Earth Abides* is the outstanding work, containing much sensitive description of landscape and of the moral problems of the survivors. Other notable disaster stories by American writers include *The Second Deluge* (1912) by Garrett P. SERVISS; *Darkness and Dawn* (1914) by George Allan ENGLAND; *When Worlds Collide* (1933) by Edwin BALMER and Philip WYLIE; *Greener Than You Think* (1947) by Ward MOORE; "The XI Effect" (1950) by Philip LATHAM; *Cat's Cradle* (1963) by Kurt VONNEGUT; "And Us, Too, I Guess" (1973) by George Alec EFFINGER; and *The Swarm* (1974) by Arthur HERZOG.

Japanese sf seems to have a leaning towards disaster themes. Two notable examples are Kobo ABÉ's *Inter Ice Age 4* (1959; trans. 1970) and Sakyo KOMATSU's *Japan Sinks* (1973; trans. 1976). The latter was filmed as THE SUBMERSION OF JAPAN (vt *Tidal Wave*). Disaster is also a popular motif in sf in the CINEMA, and on TELEVISION. Examples are the American film EARTHQUAKE (1975) and the British TV series SURVIVORS (1975–7). [DP] See also: DYSTOPIAS; ECOLOGY; END OF THE WORLD; ENTROPY; MUTANTS; NUCLEAR POWER; OPTIMISM AND PESSIMISM.

DISCH, THOMAS M(ICHAEL) (1940–). American writer, raised in Minnesota, but intermittently resident in New York for many years. Before becoming a full-time writer in the mid-1960s, he worked there in an advertising agency (and in a bank); he has subsequently lived (and set several tales) in England, Turkey, Italy and Mexico. He began publishing sf with "The Double-Timer" for *Fantastic* in 1962; much of his early work appears in *One Hundred and Two H Bombs* (coll. 1966; with two stories omitted and two added 1971; vt *White Fang Goes Dingo and Other Funny S. F. Stories* 1971 UK, with the two new stories omitted and one of the previous stories replaced, plus seven new stories). "White Fang Goes Dingo" (1965), which appears only in the first and third versions of the collection, soon became TMD's second (and rather minor) novel, *Mankind Under the Leash* (1965 *Worlds of If*; exp. 1966; vt *The Puppies of Terra* UK), in which ALIENS take over Earth and make pets of mankind for aesthetic reasons. The hero, White Fang, eventually drives the aliens off, but his feelings towards his period of effortless slavery as a dancing pet remain ambivalent. The first version of *One Hundred and Two H Bombs*, plus one of the stories added to the second edition, plus *Mankind Under the Leash* under its vt "The Puppies of Terra", all appear in *The Early Science Fiction Stories of Thomas M. Disch* (coll. 1977), introduced by Robert Thurston.

TMD's first novel, *The Genocides* (1965), is his most formidable early work, and also involves alien manipulation of Earth from a perspective indifferent (this time chillingly) to any human values or priorities; this sense of the indifference of society or the universe pervades his work, helping to distinguish it from American sf in general, which remained fundamentally optimistic about the relevance of human values until well into the 1960s. In *The Genocides*, the aliens seed Earth with enormous plants, in effect making a monoculture plantation out of the planet, an environment in which it gradually becomes impossible for humans to survive. When groups of men attempt to fight back, they are eliminated by the aliens as pests.

Echo Round His Bones (1967) is another minor work, but *Camp Concentration* (1968), which appeared in *NW*, is TMD's most sustained sf invention to date, and the highwater mark of his involvement with the English NEW WAVE (he was one of several Americans, including also John T. SLADEK, to be strongly associated with English rather than American sf in the late 1960s). Told entirely in journal form, *Camp Concentration* recounts its narrator's experiences as an inmate in a NEAR-FUTURE American concentration camp where the military has treated him with a wonder drug called Pallidine which heightens human INTELLIGENCE but causes death within months; with his fellow-inmates, he is being used as a kind of self-destructing think tank. He duly goes through the ecstasy of enhanced intelligence and the agonies of "retribution" — the analogies with Thomas Mann's *Doctor Faustus* (1947; trans. 1948) are explicit — but his death is averted by an sf ending which has been sharply criticized as a begging of the issues raised.

Black Alice (1968 as by Thom Demijohn), written with Sladek, is not sf but is characteristic of both writers; *The Prisoner* (1969) is a spin-off from the television series THE PRISONER. Much of TMD's best work in the years following *Camp Concentration* is in shorter forms, most of the stories being assembled in *Under Compulsion* (coll. 1968; vt *Fun With Your New Head* USA) and *Getting into Death* (coll. 1973), with the superior American edition, *Getting into Death and Other Stories* (coll. 1976), deleting five stories and adding four. TMD's most famous story appears in both versions of the collection: "The Asian Shore" (1970) renders with gripping verisimilitude the transmutation of a bourgeois Western man into a lower-class urban Turk with family, through a process of possession. Other notable stories from this period include "The Master of the Milford Altarpiece" (1968), "Displaying the Flag" (1973) and "The Jocelyn Shrager Story" (1975). Increasingly, TMD's best work makes use of sf components (if at all) as background to stories of character; in much of his best work his protagonists are directly involved, whether or not successfully, in the making of ART, and he has increasingly devoted himself to studies of the nature of the artist and of the world he attempts to mould but which generally, crushingly, moulds him.

334 (coll. of linked stories 1972) is set in a near-future Manhattan; the stories, whose linkings are so subtle and elaborate that it is possible to read the book as a novel, pivot about the apartment building whose address (334 East 11th Street) is the title of the book, and comprises a social portrait of urban life at the end of the present century. Life in New York has become even more difficult, intense and straitened than it is now, and the government's attitude towards individuals is not dissimilar to the attitude towards humans in general displayed by TMD's aliens; but the essence of the book is that its numerous characters manage to continue their lives, that their aspirations and successes and failures in this darkened urban world are within the bounds of what we may expect will become normal experience. *334* is probably TMD's best book.

In mid-1977, TMD had a long sf novel projected for publication, but his most recent substantial work was the massive, intensified Gothic tale *Clara Reeve* (**1975** as by Leonie Hargrave), not sf. (Earlier, with Sladek, he had collaborated on a Gothic novel, *The House that Fear Built*, **1966**, as Cassandra Knye.) He has lately edited a series of incisive theme anthologies of unusually high calibre: *The Ruins of Earth* (anth. **1973**); *Bad Moon Rising* (original anth. **1973**); *The New Improved Sun; An Anthology of Utopian Science Fiction* (anth. **1975**); and two additional anthologies edited with Charles Naylor, *New Constellations* (anth. **1976**) and *Strangeness* (anth. **1977**). Through his intellectual audacity, the distanced coldness of his sometimes mannerist narrative art, the arduous demands he makes upon the reader of genre sf, the austerity of the pleasures he affords and the fine cruelty of his wit, TMD is perhaps the most respected, least trusted, most envied and least read of all modern sf writers of the first rank; his reputation can only grow. He has won no awards. [JC]

See also: ABSURDIST SF; CHILDREN IN SF; CITIES; CONCEPTUAL BREAKTHROUGH; CRIME AND PUNISHMENT; CRITICAL AND HISTORICAL WORKS ABOUT SF; DYSTOPIAS; ECOLOGY; END OF THE WORLD; ENTROPY; ESCHATOLOGY; HEROES; HUMOUR; INVASION; LEISURE; MATTER TRANSMISSION; MYTHOLOGY; OPTIMISM AMD PESSIMISM; OVERPOPULATION; POLLUTION; PSYCHOLOGY; SATIRE; SEX; SF IN THE CLASSROOM; SUPERMAN.

DISCOVERY AND INVENTION The two topics are dealt with together because it is difficult to separate them. The discovery of a new principle is usually followed by the invention of a means of exploiting it. The discovery of new places is dealt with in LOST WORLDS and COLONIZATION OF OTHER WORLDS. Invention is also discussed in a number of entries, including IMAGINARY SCIENCE, MACHINES, POWER SOURCES, PREDICTION, TECHNOLOGY and TRANSPORT.

The invention story was prominent in 19th-century sf, notably in the works of Jules VERNE, who could almost be said to have invented it. Vernean inventions,

particularly of new kinds of transport, were a feature of the DIME NOVELS. Yankee knowhow and inventiveness was carried into the past with Mark TWAIN's *A Connecticut Yankee in King Arthur's Court* (**1889**). (A modern version of Twain's story, with a more sophisticated view of HISTORY, is *Lest Darkness Fall*, **1941**, by L. Sprague DE CAMP.) Edward Everett HALE invented orbital satellites in "The Brick Moon" (1869). Later in the century the American inventor Thomas Alva Edison became a hero figure; his exploits were much imitated in sf, and his name often borrowed; some of these stories are described under SCIENTISTS. Rudyard KIPLING invented the transatlantic airmail postal service in "With the Night Mail" (1905). H.G. WELLS invented a huge number of devices, some fantastic, as in *The Time Machine* (**1895**) and some realistic, as with the tanks in "The Land Ironclads" (1903) and the atom bomb in *The World Set Free* (**1914**). Samuel CHAPMAN's *Doctor Jones' Picnic* (**1908**) features a busy inventor who creates a huge aluminium balloon and a cure for cancer.

The invention story had an especially strong vogue in the early PULP MAGAZINES, where it was equalled in popularity as an sf subject only by the future-WAR story and the LOST-RACE story. Examples are George Allan ENGLAND's *The Golden Blight* (1912 *Cavalier*; **1916**) in which a gold-distintegrator effects economic revolution; William Wallace COOK's *The Eighth Wonder* (1906–07 *Argosy*; **1925**) in which an eccentric inventor is able to monopolize the electricity supply and Garrett Putnam SERVISS's *The Moon Metal* (**1900**) in which a device is invented to obtain a valuable metal from the Moon. The years 1900–30 were largely those of scientific optimism, and in the pulps Hugo GERNSBACK was one of its prophets. Before he founded AMAZING STORIES he had done well with his magazine SCIENCE AND INVENTION, which featured much technological fiction. His own *Ralph 124C 41+* (1911–12 *Modern Electrics*; fix-up **1925**) is one of the most celebrated if least read novels whose *raison d'être* is to catalogue the inventions of the future; they include television.

The discovery/invention story continued to pop up now and then outside genre sf, as in C.S. FORESTER's *The Peacemaker* (**1934**) in which a pacifist invents a magnetic disruptor which stops machinery, E.C. LARGE's *Sugar in the Air* (**1937**), in which a process for artificial photosynthesis is discovered, and William GOLDING's play *The Brass Butterfly* (1956 as "Envoy Extraordinary"; dramatized **1958**) in which a brilliant inventor in ancient Greece is given short shrift by his ruler who sees the new inventions as an unpleasing threat to the *status quo*. But it was inside genre sf that the invention story found its true home, though tending to become more sombre when the

metaphor of Mary SHELLEY's *Frankenstein* (**1818**) of the inventor being destroyed by his creation was given contemporary relevance by the dropping of the atom bomb over Hiroshima. Even before that, stories featuring NUCLEAR POWER, such as Lester DEL REY's "Nerves" (1942), had been very much aware of the dangers of such inventions. John W. CAMPBELL Jr, both as a writer, and as editor of *ASF*, was taking a gloomier view of technological advance by the late 1930s, though his own *The Mightiest Machine* (1934 *ASF*; **1947**) had been a jolly romp, featuring the invention of a spaceship which can take its energy direct from the stars. Campbell's *ASF* continued through the 1940s to publish a number of invention stories, in which scientific plausibility was emphasized as it never had been before in genre sf. The results included Robert HEINLEIN's "Waldo" (1942 as by Anson MacDonald) which was reprinted as *Waldo: Genius in Orbit* (**1958**). This is a gripping, optimistic invention story; the term WALDO is still used today for remote-control devices. George O. SMITH's "Venus Equilateral" stories appeared in *ASF* 1942–5, and were collected as *Venus Equilateral* (**1947**). They feature much inventive work in radio COMMUNICATIONS across the solar system. *ASF*'s invention-syndrome was given a boost by James BLISH's "Okie" stories, which featured the SPINDIZZY, one of the most attractive of all sf inventions; they appeared 1950–54, and in book form as the first two volumes of the "Cities in Flight" tetralogy: *Earthman, Come Home* (**1955**) and *They Shall Have Stars* (**1956**; vt *Year 2018!*). *ASF* sometimes struck a lighter note vis-à-vis inventions, notably in the "Galloway Gallegher" stories (1943–8) by Henry KUTTNER writing as Lewis Padgett. These feature an inventor, whose creative faculties are released by the intake of large quantities of alcohol, and his irritating robot sidekick; they were collected as *Robots Have No Tails* (coll. of linked stories **1952**) as by Kuttner. Meanwhile *ASF*'s competitors were also featuring lighthearted invention stories alongside the more doom-laden variety. A notable example of the former was the "Lancelot Biggs" series of SPACE OPERAS by Nelson S. BOND, which appeared mostly in *Fantastic Adventures* (1939–40) and were collected as *Lancelot Biggs: Spaceman* (coll. of linked stories **1950**) in revised form. Lancelot, the thin genius who bumbles round but gets there in the end, is typical of sf's more stereotyped inventors. Many other relevant genre sf stories are collected in *Science Fiction Inventions* (anth. **1967**) ed. Damon KNIGHT.

Many famous sf discoveries are made through a process of CONCEPTUAL BREAKTHROUGH, and about 40 of them are discussed under that rubric. One in particular is worthy of attention: "Noise Level" (1952) by Raymond F. JONES. In this tale, which sums up the whole ethos of John W. Campbell's *ASF*, a counterfeit invention is the occasion of conceptual breakthrough; a group of scientists are shown an apparently *bona fide* film of an ANTIGRAVITY device, the inventor of which has been killed. In their attempt to duplicate it, they break through to a new understanding of physics, only to discover the original was a fraud, used to exert psychological pressure on them to rethink their world-pictures.

Discovery/invention themes still proliferate in sf, as by the nature of the genre they always will. Important examples have been Fred HOYLE's *Ossian's Ride* (**1959**) in which a sinister-seeming cartel has cordoned off southwest Ireland as an invention-producing area; Kurt VONNEGUT Jr's *Cat's Cradle* (**1963**) in which a newly discovered form of ice which freezes everything it touches wreaks havoc; Isaac ASIMOV's *The Gods Themselves* (**1972**) in which a new energy source, the positron pump, is invented, with a great show of plausibility; Bob SHAW's *Other Days, Other Eyes* (**1972**), based on his short story "Light of Other Days" (**1966**), which features "slow glass", one of the most convincing and original inventions of sf. It slows down light, thus effectively allowing events to be viewed after a time-lapse; the privacy-invading social consequences are intriguingly explored.

One of the most interesting sub-themes is found in stories relating the discoveries of alien artefacts, very often with a subsequent desire to exploit them. Some, such as A.E. VAN VOGT's "A Can of Paint" (**1944**) and Robert SHECKLEY's "One Man's Poison" (**1953**; vt "Untouched by Human Hands") and "Hands Off" (**1954**), are basically comedies about the dangers of the incomprehensible; "One Man's Poison" contains the line "I don't eat anything that giggles". But the theme has serious ramifications, too. Such stories often create a tension between a sense of longing and wonder aroused by the thought that we are not alone, together with a sense of despair at the ambiguity of such objects and the doubt whether they will ever be understood. Such is Arthur C. CLARKE's "Sentinel of Eternity" (**1951**; vt "The Sentinel"), which was the basis for the film *2001: A Space Odyssey* (**1968**), and tells of the discovery of a strange monolith on the Moon. Clarke's *Rendezvous with Rama* (**1973**) is entirely devoted to the exploration of, and failure to fully comprehend, a vast, apparently unmanned spaceship which enters the Solar System. *Rogue Moon* (**1960**) by Algis BUDRYS is perhaps the most enigmatic of all such stories, in which the function of a strange alien maze on the Moon remains unknown. It kills people, and in so doing dramatizes the essential foreignness of all such objects, since

clearly this is just a side effect. The psychological repercussions of Man's inability to comprehend the alien are best explored in Stanislaw LEM's *Solaris* (**1961** Poland; trans. **1970**) and Frederik POHL's *Gateway* (**1977**). In the latter story abandoned alien spaceships are discovered and used, but not understood; as in *Rogue Moon* the reaching out so symbolized is obsessive, seductive and murderous. [PN]

DISINTEGRATOR In sf TERMINOLOGY, one of the commonest items of the sf armoury (*see* WEAPONS), especially in SPACE OPERAS of the 1930s and '40s. It may have resulted from a certain squeamishness, since it allows for a maximum of destruction with a minimum of bleeding pieces left to sweep up afterwards. [PN]

DISRAELI, BENJAMIN *See* SOCIOLOGY.

DITMAR AWARDS Australian sf achievement awards, presented annually at the Australian National SF CONVENTION. Instituted in 1969, the awards are given to the year's best Australian fiction, best international fiction, and best Australian fanzine. Occasional awards are given in other categories. Australian sf writers who have won Ditmars include Bertram CHANDLER (1969, 1971, 1975, and 1976), Lee HARDING (1970 and 1972), John Foyster (1973), David LAKE (1977) and Cherry WILDER (1978). There was no award in 1974. [PR]

DIXON, ROGER (1930–). American writer, whose epic adventure about Man's future fate, *Noah II* (**1970**), is based on a story idea by RD and Basil Bova. [JC]

DIXON, THOMAS (1864–1946). American writer, whose *The Fall of a Nation* (**1916**) graphically depicts Germany's conquest of the USA. [JC]

DOCKWEILER, JOSEPH H. *See* Dirk WYLIE.

DOC SAVAGE MAGAZINE US PULP magazine, pulp-size Mar. 1933 – Dec. 1943, DIGEST-size Jan. 1944 – Sep./Oct. 1948, pulp-size Winter 1948 – Summer 1949. 181 issues, Mar. 1933 – Summer 1949. Monthly until Feb. 1947, bi-monthly Mar./Apr. 1947 – Sep./Oct. 1948, quarterly Winter 1948 – Summer 1949. Published by Street & Smith Publications; initially ed. John Nanovic.

DS was perhaps the best of the sf-oriented pulp-hero magazines. All the novels were published under the pseudonym Kenneth ROBESON; the great majority of these were the work of Lester DENT. Clark Savage, the "Man of Bronze", together with his five assistants, spent his life righting wrongs and

June 1935.

punishing evildoers, his projects financed by a vast store of gold from a secret valley in Central America. His adventures encompassed every sort of fantasy situation. The success of the series led to a number of imitations, most notably SUPERMAN, whose debt to *DS* is evident in his name — Clark Kent, the "Man of Steel".

After *DS* ceased publication, the stories continued in novelette form in *Detective Story Magazine*. Later, the novels were revived successfully in paperback form, which led in turn to a MARVEL COMIC and a film. The modern image of *DS* — an Aryan superman with a pronounced widow's peak — is derived from the paperback covers, and bears little resemblance to the original conception of the character, who was loosely based on Clark Gable in physique, and sported a charming quiff. Philip José FARMER has written *DS* pastiches, and composed a biography, *Doc Savage: His Apocalyptic Life* (**1973**). [FHP/MJE]
See also: *Lester Dent, the Man Behind Doc Savage* (**1974**) by Robert WEINBERG.

DOC SAVAGE: THE MAN OF BRONZE Film (1974). Warner Bros. Directed by Michael Anderson, starring Ron Ely, William Lucking, Darrell Swerling and Mike Miller. Screenplay based on the novel *The Man of Bronze* by Kenneth ROBESON. 100 mins. Colour.

This George PAL production is based on the first Doc SAVAGE pulp novel. There are 181 novels in the series and at one point Pal announced that he hoped to film all of them. Doc fights with a villainous captain over a fountain of liquid gold owned by a tribe in a remote part of South America. Aided by his grotesque team of helpers, he succeeds in preventing the gold from falling into evil hands and the villain is last seen singing in a Salvation Army band after a session in Doc's "rehabilitation centre". The whole film is treated in a very joky manner reminiscent of the 1966 *Batman* TV series, but Michael Anderson, who also directed the disappointing LOGAN'S RUN, did not have the necessary light touch to carry off this sort of parody with flair. [JB]

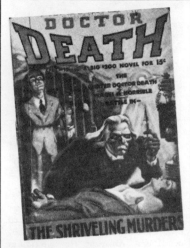

April 1935.

DOCTOR DEATH US PULP MAGAZINE. Three issues, Feb.-Apr. 1935, published by Dell, New York; probably ed. Harold Ward, who wrote the lead novels as "Zorro". Dr Death was an anarchist whose aim was to see the world revert to savagery, his methods combining black magic and science. His antagonist, James Holm, was also well versed in black magic. The three novels have been reprinted as pocketbooks, with a fourth issue containing all but one of the short fantasy stories used to fill out the magazine. [FHP]

DOCTOROW, E.L. (1931–). American writer who has become famous with his novel *Ragtime* (**1975**); the past it evokes with such hallucinatory power is, however, in no sense an ALTERNATE WORLD, though it combines real-life and fictional figures. *Big as Life* (**1966**) is an sf fantasy about the effect which giant figures create when they appear in New York. [JC]

DOCTOR X Film (1932). First National. Directed by Michael Curtiz, starring Lionel Atwill, Fay Wray, Lee Tracy and Preston Foster. Screenplay by Robert Tasker and Earl Baldwin, based on a play by Howard W.Comstock and Allen C. Miller. 77 mins. Tinted.

A scientist invents a form of synthetic flesh which, when rubbed on the skin, becomes alive and makes the wearer extremely strong. It also affects the mind and before long the scientist is committing a series of cannibalistic murders whenever the Moon is full — aided by an artificial arm grown from the flesh. Curtiz's customary hard-edged direction lifts this early, low-budget pot-boiler a little out of the ordinary. [JB]

DOENIM, SUSAN See George Alec EFFINGER.

DOHERTY, G(EOFFREY) D(ONALD) (1927–). British editor. An English teacher and sf enthusiast, GDD produced the anthology *Aspects of Science Fiction* (anth. **1959**), designed for use in secondary schools. A carefully chosen selection, it proved popular and successful among both pupils and teachers. Further anthologies similarly aimed were *Second Orbit* (anth. **1965**) and *Stories from Science Fiction* (anth. **1966**). [MJE]

Looming, expressive machinery, a speciality of b/w artist Elliott DOLD, here illustrating a story in *Miracle Science Fiction*, no. 1, 1931.

DOLD, ELLIOTT (? – ?). American illustrator since World War I. One of *ASF*'s finest interior illustrators, ED worked from its first days until the 1940s. One of the great unknowns of that era, he is only now finding the appreciation he deserves. As with Frank R. PAUL, his people were ill-drawn but his machines, buildings and gadgets were superbly detailed and intricate. He is primarily remembered for his illustrations for the *ASF* 1934 serialization of E.E. "Doc" SMITH's *Skylark of Valeron* (1934; 1949). ED did colour covers for the only two issues of *Miracle Science and Fantasy Stories* (a magazine begun by his brother Douglas in 1931), in which he also had a long story published, and one cover for *Cosmic Stories*. His b/w style was stark, highly contrasted and eliminated virtually all greys. [JG]

DOLINSKY, MIKE Form of his name used by Meyer Dolinsky (1923–), American writer. In his sf novel, *Mind One* (**1972**), two psychiatrists discover that a drug meant to treat psychosis actually engenders TELEPATHY, and they find themselves relating warmly to one another (they are of opposite sexes). As one of them is a Jesuit priest as well, there

is an element of RELIGION in the story. As Meyer Dolinsky, MD wrote three episodes for the television series THE OUTER LIMITS. [JC]

DONEV, ANTON See EASTERN EUROPE.

DONNE, MAXIM See Madelaine DUKE.

DONNELLY, IGNATIUS (1831–1901). American writer and politician. Famous for his study of *Atlantis: the Antediluvian World* (**1882**), which was responsible for a considerable resurgence of interest in the legend, and for *The Great Cryptogram* (**1888**), in which he attempted to prove by cryptographic analysis that Francis Bacon wrote Shakespeare's plays. His most important sf novel was *Caesar's Column* (**1890**; early editions under the pseudonym Edmund Boisgilbert), which countered the UTOPIAN optimism of Edward BELLAMY with the argument that society was evolving toward greater inequality and catastrophic war rather than toward peace and plenty. He wrote two other fantasies embodying social criticism: *Doctor Huguet* (**1891**), in which the protagonist's *persona* is trapped in the body of a Negro; and *The Golden Bottle* (**1892**), in which a gold-making device becomes a weapon to overthrow capitalism and establish Utopia. [BS]
See also: ATLANTIS; CITIES; LOST WORLDS.

DONOVAN'S BRAIN Film (1953). Dowling Productions / United Artists. Directed by Felix Feist, starring Lew Ayres, Steve Brodie and Lisa K. Howard. Screenplay by Felix Feist, based on the novel by Curt SIODMAK. 83 mins. B/w.

One of three films based on Siodmak's novel of the same name; the other two are THE LADY AND THE MONSTER (1944) and THE BRAIN (1962). A scientist keeps a man's brain alive by artificial means and then discovers that it has an evil, telepathic influence over him. An interesting premise is spoilt by Siodmak's obvious lack of medical knowledge. Despite its gadgetry, the film has the air of a supernatural rather than an sf story. [JB]

DONSON, CYRIL (1919–). British writer whose first sf novel is *Born in Space* (**1968**), set on a colonized planet; *The Perspective Process* (**1969**) and *Tritonastia* (**1969**) are both routine SPACE OPERAS. [JC]

DOOMWATCH 1. Television series (1970–2). BBC TV. Produced by Terence Dudley. Series devised by Kit PEDLER and Gerry DAVIS, starring Robert Powell, John Paul, Simon Oates, Wendy Hall and Joby Blanchard. Writers on the series included Kit Pedler and Gerry Davis, Harry Green, Dennis Spooner, Don Shaw, Elwyn Jones, Martin Worth, Terence Dudley, Brian Hayles, John Gould, and Roy Russell. The series ran for three seasons, the first two each consisting of 13 episodes, the final one of only 11. 50 mins per episode. Colour.

A group of scientists have set themselves up as watchdogs over the rest of the scientific community. The theme is that scientific research produces more harm than good, and that stronger safeguards should be introduced while some lines of research should be abandoned altogether. Beneath the display of social conscience the hoariest of sf clichés appeared; apart from its overbearingly moralizing tone there was little difference between this series and the mad-scientist movies of the 1930s and '40s.

2. Film (1972). Tigon. Directed by Peter Saady, starring Ian Bannen, Judy Geeson, John Paul, Simon Oates and George Sanders. Screenplay by Clive Exton, based on the BBC TV series (*see above*). 92 mins. Colour.

A familiar plot is dressed up with a fashionable dénouement: visitors to a remote fishing village on a British offshore island are met with hostility. It soon becomes apparent that the villagers are trying to keep hidden a number of grossly malformed people. This is the result not of dabbling with the supernatural, despite the typically LOVECRAFTian setting, but of radioactive chemicals having been dumped in the sea nearby. Saady directed with style but was handicapped by the predictability of the script. [JB]

DOPPELGANGER See JOURNEY TO THE FAR SIDE OF THE SUN.

DORMAN, SONYA (?–). American writer, who began publishing sf with "The Putnam Tradition" for *AMZ* in 1963, and who with fiction for both *Gal.* and *FSF* has established a reputation in the field for intensely written, sometimes highly metaphorical stories. They are surprisingly unlike her rather straightforward poetry, for which she is probably best known generally, having published her verse extensively, beginning with *Poems* (coll. **1970**). [JC]
See also: ABSURDIST SF.

DOSTOYEVSKY, FYODOR MIK-HAILOVICH (1821–81). With Leo Tolstoy, premier 19th-century Russian novelist. His story, "The Dream of a Ridiculous Man" (1877), which has been translated in various volumes, presents in a delusional frame a man's dream-voyage to another planet identical to Earth but sinless; he corrupts this planet by his presence, and on return to Earth tries to bring about innocence in turn, but without success. The obsessive religious note, and the initial psychotic state of the protagonist (he is convinced that the world exists only through his perception of it) are hallmarks of FMD's work in general. [JC]
See also: ABSURDIST SF.

DOUAY, DOMINIQUE (1944–). French writer, who studied law. He is one of the more talented representatives of the French NEW WAVE. His first sf material appeared in 1973 and his story "Thomas" won the prize for best French short story of the year at the 1975 Angoulême Convention. He has published two novels: *Éclipse ou le printemps de terre XII* ["Eclipse or the Spring of Earth XII"] (**1975**), a political SPACE OPERA, and *L'échiquier de la création* ["The Chessboard of Creation"] (**1976**), an allegorical examination of various levels of reality. [MJ]

DOUGHTY, CHARLES M(ONTAGU) (1843–1926). English explorer and writer, whose *Travels in Arabia Deserta* (**1888**) profoundly influenced T.E. Lawrence, among others. The difficult, archaic language of his later work, a series of book-length poems, has kept them from wide circulation. Two of them are of some sf interest: *The Cliffs* (**1909**) features an airborne "Persarian" invasion of England, which is successfully repulsed; in *The Clouds* (**1912**) a similar invasion is successful, and England occupied. Both poems are designed as warnings to complacent Britons, and share many of the characteristics of the INVASION stories so popular before the First World War. [JC]

DOUGLAS, (GEORGE) NORMAN (1868–1952). English writer of superb meditative travel books and some fiction, his best-known novel being *South Wind* (**1917**); he expresses his strongly misogynist and persuasively "pagan" views very clearly in his prehistoric fantasy *In the Beginning* (**1927**). Rather more powerfully than did Thomas Burnett SWANN forty years later, in this book ND expresses with loathing the sense that the rise of Man meant the destruction of the Eden-like existence of his sentient, pagan, amoral predecessors, through the story of half-divine Linus and his imposition of a rigid civilization upon the world. [JC]
Other works: *They Went* (**1920**); *Nerinda* (**1929**).

DOUGLAS, JEFF See Andrew J. OFFUTT.

DOUGLASS, ELLSWORTH (?–?). Author of *Pharaoh's Broker; The Very Remarkable Experiences in Another World of Isidor Werner* (**1899**), an interplanetary romance set on Mars, where parallel evolution has resulted in a society almost identical to that of Egypt in the time of Joseph. The hero, having been a grain-broker in Chicago, is able to take on Joseph's role. [PN]

DOYLE, Sir ARTHUR CONAN (1859–1930). British writer, known primarily for his work outside the sf field, and in particular for his stories about the detective Sherlock Holmes. Born in Edinburgh and educated by the Jesuits at Stonyhurst College. He studied medicine at Edinburgh University and initiated his own practice in Portsmouth in 1882, supplementing his income by writing. In 1887 the first "Sherlock Holmes" novel, *A Study in Scarlet*, appeared, and as a result of the popularity of American pirate editions a US publisher commissioned a second. His first major historical novels, *Micah Clarke* (**1889**) and *The White Company* (**1891**) were published, but without conspicuous success, and it was not until the publication of a series of short "Sherlock Holmes" stories in THE STRAND MAGAZINE during 1891 and 1892 that he became established as a writer. By this time he

had already written two long stories reflecting his interest in subjects on the border between science and mysticism, but publication of both was delayed for some years. They are the short novel of telepathic vampirism *The Parasite* (**1895**) and a study of supernatural vengeance from the mysterious East, *The Mystery of Cloomber* (**1895**). Though the "Sherlock Holmes" stories suggest an incisively analytical and determinedly rationalistic mind, ACD was periodically fascinated by all manner of occult disciplines, including hypnotism, theosophy, oriental mysticism and — following the death of his son — spiritualism.

ACD's first scientific romance, *The Doings of Raffles Haw* (**1891**), was written hurriedly, and is an unimpressive account of a gold-maker who becomes disenchanted with philanthropy and destroys his machine and himself in a fit of bitterness. Two short stories from the same period are slightly more impressive: "The Los Amigos Fiasco" (1892), in which an experimental electric chair "supercharges" a criminal instead of killing him, and "The Terror of Blue John Gap", about a monstrous visitor from an underground world. ACD abandoned sf during the early decades of his literary success but returned to make his most important contribution to the genre before the First World War. *The Lost World* (**1912**) is a classic novel in which the redoubtable Professor Challenger leads an expedition to a plateau in South America where dinosaurs still survive. In a sequel, *The Poison Belt* (**1913**), the Earth faces disaster as a result of atmospheric poisoning. A classic sf short story, "The Horror of the Heights" (1913), offers an account of strange forms of life inhabiting the upper atmosphere. The novelette "Danger!" (1914) is Doyle's contribution to the imminent-WAR genre, anticipating submarine attacks on shipping — a prophecy validated within months despite Admiralty scepticism.

His post-War passion for spiritualism, which led him to such excesses of credulity as to endorse the clumsily faked "fairy photographs" taken by Elsie Wright in 1917 in *The Coming of the Fairies* (**1922**), strongly infects his later sf. In *The Land of Mist* (**1926**) Professor Challenger is converted to spiritualism; two other Challenger stories from this period seem a little weak, though one, "When the World Screamed", is a pioneer exercise in the LIVING-WORLDS theme. These minor pieces were published along with a short novel about the rediscovery of Atlantis in *The Maracot Deep* (coll. **1929**).

ACD's stories exist in many collections, but all his sf short stories are in either *The Professor Challenger Stories* (coll. **1952**) or *The Conan Doyle Stories* (coll. **1929**), with the exception of "Danger!", which appeared in *Danger! and Other Stories* (coll. **1918**). [BS]

See also: ATLANTIS; BIOLOGY; CRIME AND PUNISHMENT; ESCHATOLOGY; DISASTER; LOST WORLDS; MACHINES; MAGIC; MEDICINE; MONEY; POWER SOURCES; RADIO (USA); SCIENTISTS; UNDER THE SEA.

DOZOIS, GARDNER (1947–). American writer and anthologist. He has been a NEBULA award finalist five times and a HUGO award finalist four times for his stories. The publication of his collection *The Visible Man* (**1977**) should work to establish his name securely. He began publishing sf in 1966 with "The Empty Man" for *If*, but it was not until after military service (in which he worked as a military journalist) that he began producing such stories as "A Special Kind of Morning" (1971) and "Chains of the Sea" (1972), the title story of *Chains of the Sea* (anth. **1972**) ed. Robert SILVERBERG, which have made GD a figure of some note in the latter-day American NEW WAVE, and caused some misapplied criticism of his "pessimism" and general lack of interest in storytelling (*see also* CHILDREN IN SF). With George Alec EFFINGER he has written an unremarkable sf adventure novel, *Nightmare Blue* (**1975**). Much more important is his first solo novel, *Strangers* (1974 *New Dimensions*; exp. **1978**), an intense and well-told love story between a human male and an ALIEN female on her planet, in a galaxy humans signally do not dominate; her inevitable death (bearing his child) comes from mutual incomprehension, and the story can be read as an analysis of human solitude in general (*see also* SEX). GD has written a good deal of sf criticism, most notably a long essay introducing the 1977 GREGG PRESS reissue of James TIPTREE Jr's *Ten-Thousand Light Years from Home* (coll. **1973**), which has been reprinted as the booklet *The Fiction of James Tiptree, Jr*

(**1977**). His intelligently edited anthologies are *A Day in the Life* (anth. **1972**), the original anthology *Future Power* (anth. **1976**) with Jack DANN, *Another World* (anth. **1977**) and *Best Science Fiction Stories of the Year, Sixth Annual Edition* (anth. **1977**). GD may come to be recognized as one of the most important of the generation of writers that rose to prominence in the 1970s.

GD has been an associate editor of ISAAC ASIMOV'S SCIENCE FICTION MAGAZINE. [JC/PN]

See also: CONCEPTUAL BREAKTHROUGH; INVISIBILITY; POLLUTION; SF IN THE CLASSROOM.

DRAGONS *See* SUPERNATURAL CREATURES.

DRAYTON, HENRY SINCLAIR (1839–?). American writer, whose LOST RACE novel, *In Oudemon* (**1901**), features an English colony in South America which is technologically advanced, socialist and Christian. [JC]

DR CYCLOPS Film (1940). Paramount. Directed by Ernest B. Schoedsack, starring Albert Dekker, Janice Logan, Thomas Coley and Charles Halton. Screenplay by Tom Kilpatrick. 75 mins. Colour.

A group of scientists are lured to Peru by a mad genius who, in a fit of pique, shrinks them all to an average height of 12 inches by means of a radioactive device in his remote laboratory. After a prolonged chase-and-capture sequence, the three survivors destroy his thick spectacles and lure him to an open mine-shaft where he falls to his death. Made by the director of KING KONG, *DC* is a fast-paced, visually inventive film though the dialogue is leaden. Albert Dekker's portrayal of the ruthless Dr Thorkel, with

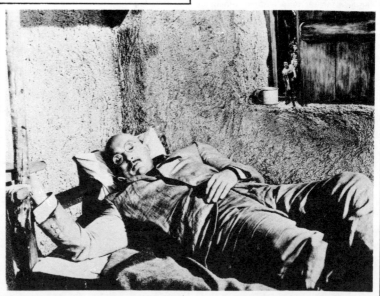

You need to look hard to see the sophisticated miniaturization techniques in this dramatic still from DR CYCLOPS.

head shaved and body bulked out with padded clothing, conveys a real sense of menace; he seems an evil god who toys sadistically with his little creations before casually destroying them. Also, whether by design or accident, he resembles what was to become the caricature of the "beastly Jap" during the Second World War. The special effects are ingeniously contrived and very convincing, the illusion of miniaturization being achieved by the combined use of giant props and rear projection, the latter process supervised by Farciot Edouart, one of Hollywood's most important innovators in that area of trick photography. The novelization is *Dr Cyclops* (**1940**) by Will Garth (Manly Wade WELLMAN).   [JB]

Aug. 1957. Cover by Valigursky.

DREAM WORLD US DIGEST-size magazine. Three quarterly issues, Feb.-Aug. 1957, published by Ziff-Davis Publishing Co.; ed. Paul W. FAIRMAN. Subtitled "Stories of Incredible Powers", *DW* was initiated as a response to the success of similar issues of FANTASTIC, with stories of wish-fulfilment or dreams-come-true. The first issue reprinted stories by Thorne Smith and P.G. WODEHOUSE, but otherwise the magazine included no fiction of note. Other contributors were Harlan ELLISON and Robert SILVERBERG.
                                          [FHP/MJE]

DREXEL, JAY B. *See* Jerome BIXBY.

DR JEKYLL AND MR HYDE 1 Film (1931). Paramount. Directed by Rouben Mamoulian, starring Fredric March, Miriam Hopkins, Rose Hobart and Holmes Herbert. Screenplay by Samuel Hoffenstein and Percy Heath, based on the novel *The Strange Case of Dr Jekyll and Mr Hyde* (**1886**) by Robert Louis STEVENSON. 98 mins. B/w.
   Stevenson's suggestion that civilization may be only skin deep prefigures the theme that was to dominate the work of H.G. WELLS — that evil is somehow connected with Man's animal heritage rather than anything to do with

Fredric March was the most memorable of all Mr Hydes in Rouben Mamoulian's 1931 version of DR JEKYLL AND MR HYDE.

religiously based concepts of Original Sin. Earlier, silent film versions (made in 1908, 1909, 1912, 1913 and three in 1920) ignored this aspect of the story: in the 1920 film starring John Barrymore, Hyde is simply played as a caricature of evil. In Mamoulian's 1931 version, which remains the most interesting, Hyde's appearance is almost that of Neanderthal man, and his murderous behaviour results not from inherent evil but from uncontrollable, primitive lusts and drives. The most compelling of these drives is sexual, though it is accompanied by an increasing capacity for cruelty as the film progresses. The film, atmospheric and convincing, is an acknowledged classic, especially famous for the heartbeats on the soundtrack and the astonishingly convincing special effects in the transformation scenes.
   2. Film (1941). MGM. Directed by Victor Fleming, starring Spencer Tracy and Ingrid Bergman. Screenplay by John Lee Makin. 127 mins. B/w.
   Growing pressures of censorship took some of the sexual edge off the proceedings in this remake and, although the film is gripping still, it seems bland in comparison to the raw energy of Mamoulian's version.
   3. Subsequent film versions, including *The Two Faces of Dr Jekyll* (1960; vt *House of Fright* USA), which had a plain Dr Jekyll turning into a handsome Mr Hyde; *The Strange Case of Dr Jekyll and Mr Hyde* (1967), a made-for-TV film; *I, Monster* (1973) and *Dr Jekyll and Sister Hyde* (1972), have simply been variations of the formula, some more ingenious than others, but none with the impact of the 1931 production.   [JB]

DR NO Film (1962). Eon/United Artists. Directed by Terence Young, starring Sean Connery, Ursula Andress, Joseph Wiseman and Jack Lord. Screenplay by

Richard Maibaum, Johanna Harwood and Berkely Mather, based on the novel by Ian FLEMING. 105 mins. Colour.
   This was the first film in the successful "James Bond" series. The villain of the title, whose cinematic forebears include Fu Manchu, Captain Nemo, and Rotwang in METROPOLIS (like Rotwang, Dr No possesses mechanical hands), attempts to blackmail America, working from a remote island in the Caribbean, by deflecting their Cape Canaveral rockets off course with a powerful radio beam. But James Bond brings his plans to an end by boiling him alive in a pool of water containing an atomic reactor (which runs wild when its control rods are inserted into the core, instead of vice versa). The mordant humour of the script, the visual flashiness and the foiled attempt by a super-villain to rule the world with one or another technological device set the pattern for the entire "James Bond" series, most of which are marginally sf in the old PULP adventure pattern of Doc SAVAGE.   [JB]

DRODE, DANIEL (1932–). French writer. A teacher whose only novel, *Surface de la planète* ["Surface of the Planet"] (**1959**), was a controversial recipient of the PRIX JULES VERNE. Utilizing the techniques of the *nouveau roman*, it is a difficult, experimental novel, a rare example of new writing methods applied to create an eerie atmosphere in a post-atomic subterranean world. DD has also written five short stories.   [MJ]

DR STRANGELOVE OR: HOW I LEARNED TO STOP WORRYING AND LOVE THE BOMB Film (1963). Hawk/Columbia. Directed by Stanley KUBRICK, starring Peter Sellers, George C. Scott, Sterling Hayden, Keenan Wynn and Slim Pickens. Screenplay by Stanley

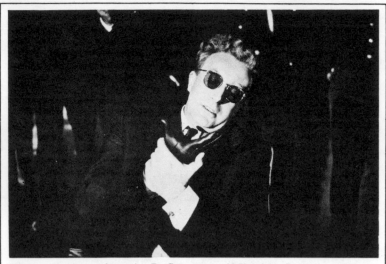

Peter Sellers as the self-torturing DR STRANGELOVE in Kubrick's film.

Kubrick, Terry Southern and Peter GEORGE, based on the novel *Red Alert* by Peter Bryant (pseudonym of Peter George). 94 mins. B/w.

This, the first of Kubrick's three sf films, has worn well, with its curious blend of black comedy, documentary realism and what seems at times like an almost poetic homage to the very machines (B52s and their nuclear cargo) which he shows as destroying the world. The basis for the film was a serious suspense story about an insane US general who launches an attack on Russia without presidential authority, but after working on the script for a while, Kubrick opted for a grotesquely funny treatment, in which he was aided by an extremely strong cast including Peter Sellers, who plays three roles, one of them being that of Dr Strangelove himself. The latter is a sinister ex-Nazi scientist, generally supposed to be a burlesque of a real life scientist of some distinction, though rumours differ as to which one. The novelization, with the same title, as by Peter George, was published in **1963**. [JB/PN]

DRUGS *See* PERCEPTION.

DRUILLET, PHILIPPE (1944–). French artist. Brought up in Spain, he was a photographer until the publication of his first strip *Lone Sloane* (**1967**; intro. by Maxim JAKUBOWSKI), a bawdy space opera heavily influenced by the American cinema and heroic fantasy. A unique illustrator, often clumsy in his portrayal of the human face, PD has enlarged the graphic structures of the sf comic strip and created a wild, flamboyant, morally ambiguous universe of crazed architectures and monstrous aliens. The increasingly obsessive adventures of Lone Sloane were continued in *Les 6 voyages* ["The Six Journeys"] (**1972**); *Delirius* (script by Jacques Lob **1973**) and *Yragael* (script by Michel DEMUTH **1974**). PD has also tackled sword and sorcery with *Elric*

(**1973**; inspired by Michael MOORCOCK; French script by Jakubowski and then Demuth; text by Moorcock in the British edition). *La nuit* ["The Night"] (**1977**) is a sombre panorama of urban warfare, completed after the traumatic experience of his wife's death from cancer in 1975. PD was one of the founders of the sf comic-strip magazine MÉTAL HURLANT (*Heavy Metal* in the US edition). [MJ]

The sophisticated op art of Philippe DRUILLET uses the whole page as the design unit in his sf comics. This is from *Les 6 Voyages de Lone Sloane*, © Dargaud Éditeur 1972.

Other works: *Vuzz* (**1974**); *Retour à Bakaam* ["Return to Bakaam"] (script by François Truchaud **1975**); *Mirages* (**1976**).

DRUMMOND, JUNE (1923–). English writer, resident in South Africa. She writes almost exclusively detective novels, one of which, *The Gantry Episode* (**1968**), edges into sf in its investigation of the planting of LSD in a reservoir and of the effects thereof. [JC]

DRURY, ALLEN (STUART) (1918–). American writer of several novels of American POLITICAL life, the

best-known being *Advise and Consent* (**1959**), all at the edge of NEAR-FUTURE sf; over the edge are *Come Nineveh, Come Tyre* (**1973**), in which world Communism topples an unready America into chaos, and *The Throne of Saturn* (**1971**), in which the Russians attempt to sabotage America's first manned expedition to Mars. [JC]

Jon Pertwee as the third DR WHO meets an alien in "The Time Warrior", 1973.

DR WHO Television series (1963–). BBC TV. Created by Sydney Newman and Donald Wilson. First series producer: Verity Lambert. First series director: Waris Hussein. First series script editor: David Whitaker. First series writer: Anthony Coburn. 25 mins per episode. Originally b/w; colour from 1968.

This is the longest running of British sf TV series for children. Dr Who, eventually revealed as a Time Lord, travels back and forth in time and space, accompanied by various people (children in early episodes, young women and others later), in his time machine, the *Tardis*. The stories in the series have varied in length from one to 12 episodes, but the most common length per story has been six episodes. The first was transmitted Nov. 1963, and concerned a young girl who arouses the curiosity of two of her schoolteachers with her unusual knowledge of history. Attempting to investigate her background they follow her into what appears to be a police telephone box but is in fact a time machine (the interior is many times larger than the exterior) owned by her irritable and eccentric grandfather, Dr Who. As the machine cannot be properly controlled they are all whisked off to the Stone Age where they remain for the following three episodes.

The series had a modest following at first; it was not until the second story, "The Dead Planet", written by Terry NATION, that it achieved mass popularity, mainly because of the introduction of the DALEKS. The series has returned to British TV every year except for 1969 and 1971 and is, if anything, more popular than ever, and certainly more sophisticated,

Tom Baker, the fourth DR WHO, studies "The Hand of Fear", 1976.

Terrance Dicks, Robert Banks Stewart, Stephen Harris and Robin Bland.

The production of novelizations of the series, all aimed at comparatively young children, has been a growth industry in the 1970s. There are now about 40 of them. A book, also for children, about the programme is *The Making of Doctor Who* (**1972**) by Malcolm Hulke and Terrance Dicks. Several feature film spin-offs of the series have been made (*see* DALEKS *for details*).   [JB/PN]
See also: CYBORGS.

DRYASDUST This is usually given as the pseudonym of M.Y. Halidom, but the latter name itself is clearly assumed, inasmuch as "By my halidom" is a well-known archaic oath. It has been suggested that the real identity behind both pseudonyms may have been Christopher BLAYRE (*see his entry for details*).   [PN]

The first issue, May/June 1936.

DR. YEN SIN US PULP magazine. Three bi-monthly issues, May/Jun.-Sep./Oct. 1936. Published by Popular Publications; ed. Rogers Terrill. *DYS* was a follow-up to an earlier Popular title, WU FANG; in fact the cover of its first issue had originally been painted for the previous title. The first issue featured "The Mystery of the Dragon's Shadow" by Donald E. Keyhoe (who later wrote three well-known FLYING SAUCER books); this novel was reprinted as PULP CLASSICS no.9 (1976).   [MJE]

DU BOIS, THEODORA (McCORMICK) (1890–). American writer, best known for her many detective novels; some of her books, like *The Devil's Spoon* (**1930**) and *Sarah Hall's Tea God* (**1952**), are fantasies. In her sf novel, *Solution T-25* (**1951**), Russians conquer the United States with great cruelty. An underground resistance, faking collaboration with the enemy, develops Solution T-25, which dissolves

though it is possible that American audiences would find it too whimsical.

Four actors, progressively younger, have played the Doctor over the years: first William Hartnell, second Patrick Troughton, third Jon Pertwee and fourth (the current hero) Tom Baker. With each change the Doctor's personality has mellowed, and Baker's trendy, ironic version is probably the most successful.

Although the programme has long since settled into a pattern, with episodes usually featuring at least one item of extraordinary monster make-up, there has been plenty of room for experiment. The authors of the various stories have unblushingly pirated literally hundreds of ideas from PULP sf, but often make intelligent and sometimes quite complex use of them. Over the years it seems probable that the programme has attracted almost as many adult viewers as children. With the increasing sophistication of the scripts, and the expertise of the special effects and make-up, from which many other programmes could learn a great deal about what can be done on a low budget, it has become a notably self-confident series, juggling

expertly with many of the great tropes and images of the genre. It is probably the best SPACE OPERA in the history of TV, not excluding STAR TREK. Storylines often feature political satire. At its worst merely silly, at its best it is spellbinding.

Other regular cast members over the years have included William Russell, Jacqueline Hill, Carole Ann Ford, Peter Purves, Frazer Hines, Anneke Wills, Michel Craze, Katy Manning, Stewart Bevan, Roger Delgado, Elizabeth Sladen and Louise Jameson. Producers of the series after Verity Lambert were Innes Lloyd, Peter Bryant, Barry Letts, Philip Hinchcliffe and Graham Williams. Apart from those named, writers have included David Whitaker, John Lucarotti, Peter R. Newman, Dennis Spooner, Louis Marks, Bill Strutton, Glyn Jones, William Emms, Donald Cotton, Paul Erickson and Lesley Scott, Brian Hayles, Ian Stuart Black, Kit PEDLER and Gerry DAVIS, Elwyn Jones, Geoffrey Orme, David Ellis and Malcolm Hulke, Mervyn Haisman and Henry Lincoln, Victor Pemberton, Norman Ashby, Peter Ling, Derrick Sherwin, Robert Holmes, Don Houghton, Bob Baker and Dave Martin, Robert Sloman,

the Russian leadership's authoritarian personality structures, turning them into benign humorists incapable of commanding their forces. [JC]

Other works: *Armed with a New Terror* (**1936**).

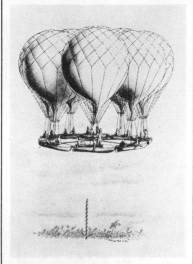

A balloon machine from the splendid *The Twenty-One Balloons*, 1946.

DU BOIS, WILLIAM PÈNE (1916–). American writer, illustrator, and art editor and designer for *The Paris Review*. His own novels, which he illustrates himself, are usually juveniles, though the illustrations are of general interest; he also illustrates the books of other writers. He began publishing with stories like *Elizabeth, the Cow Ghost* (**1936**), *Giant Otto* (**1936**), and *The Flying Locomotive* (**1941**), and much of his work employs fantasy elements; *The Twenty-One Balloons* (**1946**) is actual sf, however; it is the story of a retired professor who, while travelling across the Pacific by balloon, is forced down upon the island of Krakatoa, where he finds a UTOPIA in operation, financed by its inhabitants' secret trips to civilization to sell diamonds, which they have in plenty. The famous eruption of 1883 finishes the experiment, but everyone escapes by balloon. [JC]

DUDINTSEV, VLADIMIR (1918–). Russian writer. His novel *Not by Bread Alone* (1956 *Novy Mir*; trans. **1957**), seemed to proclaim the Soviet thaw, but he was publicly reprimanded for it soon after its publication; the novella translated as *A New Year's Tale* (trans. **1960**), which did not achieve book publication until 1965 in Russia as *Novogodniaia skazka*, is a kind of sf morality in which the protagonist, by composing himself for his expected death, discovers a new source of cheap light and heat. [JC]

DUEL Made-for-TV-film, expanded and released outside the USA as a feature film (1971). ABC/Universal. Directed by Steven Spielberg, starring Dennis Weaver, Eddie Firestone and Charles Steel. Screenplay by Richard MATHESON, based on his original story. 75 mins (increased to 90). Colour.

Universal Studios were so impressed by the TV film directed by the young Spielberg (who went on to direct *Jaws* and CLOSE ENCOUNTERS OF THE THIRD KIND) that they added extra sequences and released it outside America as a feature film, which attracted a great deal of favourable critical comment, particularly in Britain. A tightly constructed thriller (the original 75-minute version being superior to the expanded one in which the extra scenes served only to slow it down), it well displays Spielberg's ability to create an atmosphere of unremitting tension. It is also a typical Matheson variation on his usual theme of PARANOIA, in this case that of the motorist who feels that every other vehicle on the road is out to get him. *D* concerns a travelling salesman pursued by a mysterious oil-tanker, the driver of which is never seen. The film has a strong sf feeling, with the tanker coming to seem like some animate, malevolent, technological monster, even emitting a dinosaur-like bellow of rage in its ultimate plunge down the face of a cliff. [JB/PN]

DUFF The Down-Under Fan Fund, established in 1972 as an Australian-American version of TAFF, designed to send well-known sf fans across the Pacific. Three Americans and two Australians have so far made trips through DUFF. [PR]

DUKE, MADELAINE (ELIZABETH) (1925–). British writer and physician, born in Switzerland of Dutch parents, active under her own name and at least two pseudonyms in a variety of genres including humour, war books, serious novels, children's stories and sf novels, which she describes as "cartoons". Under the name Maxim Donne she published her first sf novel, *Claret, Sandwiches and Sin: A Cartoon* (**1964**; reissued under her own name); it depicts a world insecurely amalgamated into two political divisions: Africa and the Rest of the World. Whenever a politician comes close to the brink of war, an underground organization eliminates him. In *This Business of Bomfog: A Cartoon* (**1967**) the protagonist is one "Maxim Donne", author of *Claret, Sandwiches and Sin*, a successful novel which has inspired the assassination of a number of world leaders. Now it is 1989 in England. Bomfog stands for Brotherhood of Man Fatherhood of God, and the organization which uses the term runs England in a fashion MD depicts in somewhat hectic DYSTOPIAN language. [JC]

DU MAURIER, DAPHNE (1907–). English writer, granddaughter of George

DU MAURIER. Several of her well-known romances combine history and fantasy themes; two of her short stories have also come to fame: "The Birds", to be found in *The Apple Tree* (coll. **1952**; vt *Kiss Me Again, Stranger* USA; vt *The Birds and Other Stories* UK), was made into the Hitchcock film THE BIRDS (1963), and "Don't Look Now", to be found in *Not After Midnight* (coll. **1971**), was made into the Nicholas Roeg film of the same name. Her NEAR-FUTURE sf novel, *Rule Britannia* (**1972**), features an occupation of England by American troops and local resistance in Cornwall, her favourite locale; *The House on the Strand* (**1968**) is a novel of drug-induced TIME TRAVEL. [JC]

DU MAURIER, GEORGE (1834–96). English illustrator, cartoonist and writer, known almost exclusively today as the author of *Trilby* (**1894**), whose famous mesmerist villain, Svengali, had decidedly supernatural characteristics. GDM's last novel, *The Martian* (**1897**), is a rather lackadaisical tale of a sensitive but mysterious individual who turns out to have been a Martian throughout his life. [JC]

DUNCAN, BRUCE (?–). American author whose sf novel, *Mirror Image* (**1968**), is not to be confused with the novel of the same title by Michael G. CONEY. [JC]

DUNCAN, DAVID (1913–). American writer of popular fiction in several genres, perhaps as well known for his few sf novels as for anything else, though his first novel with an sf content, *The Shade of Time* (**1946**), which deals (as he records) with "atomic displacement", was accepted for publication only after Hiroshima. It is his books of the 1950s, which were more widely distributed within the sf markets, that have been remembered, though he also scripted several films, including THE TIME MACHINE (1960) and a screenplay for the television series THE OUTER LIMITS. His novel *Dark Dominion* (**1954**) is a well-told melodrama concerning a new element, Magellanium, which varies in weight according to the position of the star Sirius. It is finally used to power a spaceship. *Beyond Eden* (**1955**; vt *Another Tree in Eden* UK) contrasts different routes towards fulfilment, the material fulfilment embodied in a vast water-making project and the "spiritual" contained in crystals that expand Man's nature in the direction of *gestalt* empathy. *Occam's Razor* (**1957**) explores, within the context of a threatening nuclear war, the impact of the arrival of two humans from another dimension (*see* FOURTH DIMENSION); an infinite series of PARALLEL WORLDS is discovered, the key being the surface tension on a soap film; as in *Dark Dominion*, the end offers a mode of escape from an Earth bent on self-destruction. DD has since fallen silent. [JC]

Other works: *The Madrone Tree* (**1949**) is fantasy.
See also: MATHEMATICS.

DUNCAN, RONALD (1914–). English novelist, poet and playwright. He was Benjamin Britten's librettist for *The Rape of Lucretia* (**1946**), and is generally best known for works outside the sf field; such plays as those in *The Dull Ass's Hoof* (coll. **1941**) and *This Way to the Tomb* (**1946**), both volumes containing some fantasy elements. His sf novella *The Last Adam* (**1952**) features a last man who, after meeting the last woman, leaves her, being rather a misogynist. Some of the stories in *The Perfect Mistress and Other Stories* (coll. **1969**) and *A Kettle of Fish* (coll. **1971**) are fables with sf components. [JC]

DUNN, SAUL Pseudonym of English writer and publisher Philip M. Dunn (1946–) which he uses for his fiction, though he directs Pierrot Publishing under his own name. First releases from this new company include Brian W. ALDISS's *Brothers of the Head* (**1977**) and Harry HARRISON's *Great Balls of Fire! A History of Sex in Science Fiction Illustration* (**1977**); both are heavily illustrated. As SD he has published a paperback SPACE-OPERA sequence, *The Coming of Steeleye* (**1976**), *Steeleye — The Wideways* (**1976**) and *Steeleye — Waterspace* (**1976**). [JC]
Other works: *The Cabal* (**1978**).

DUNSANY, LORD (1878–1957). Edward John Moreton Drax Plunkett, 18th Baron Dunsany, Irish writer. He wrote stories, essays and plays prolifically; he is of sf interest only marginally, fundamentally for the widespread influence of his language and imagery, though late in life he wrote one sf novel, *The Last Revolution* (**1951**), about machines in revolt. His influence on FANTASY writers, especially on HEROIC FANTASY, has been very strong from almost the beginning of his long career, when he published the first of his collections of stories describing a consistent fantasy world, *The Gods of Pegana* (coll. of linked stories **1905**); he had to pay for publication. This was followed by the other collections of his brilliant first phase, *Time and the Gods* (coll. **1906**), *The Sword of Welleran* (coll. **1908**), *A Dreamer's Tales* (coll. **1910**), *The Book of Wonder: A Chronicle of Little Adventures at the Edge of the World* (coll. **1912**), *Fifty-One Tales* (coll. **1915**) and *The Last Book of Wonder* (coll. **1916**; vt *Tales of Wonder* UK). In these volumes are the stories whose use of influences from Oscar Wilde and Yeats through William MORRIS (along with the very specific effect of the play *The Darling of the Gods*, **1902**, by David Belasco and John L. Long, with its misty fake oriental setting) in turn exerted so potent an influence on later writers.

LD's second phase as a fantasist — after a rather ostentatious turning away during the First World War — is comprised of such novels as *Don Rodriguez: Chronicles of Shadow Valley* (**1922**; vt *The Chronicles of Rodriguez*), *The King of Elfland's Daughter* (**1924**) and *The Charwoman's Shadow* (**1926**). His third phase consists of the club stories involving Jorkens: *The Travel Tales of Mr Joseph Jorkens* (coll. **1931**); *Jorkens Remembers Africa* (coll. **1934**); *Jorkens Has a Large Whiskey* (coll. **1940**); *The Fourth Book of Jorkens* (coll. **1948**); and *Jorkens Borrows Another Whiskey* (coll. **1954**). The "Jorkens" stories have helped to familiarize readers in the sf and fantasy fields with the club story as it had existed, at least in England, for many years. Sterling LANIER's "Brigadier Ffellowes" stories are a recent successful resuscitation of the mode. Lin CARTER reassembled a number of early LD tales in the following volumes, which contain no new material: *Beyond the Fields We Know* (coll. **1972**), *At the Edge of the World* (coll. **1970**) and *Over the Hills and Far Away* (coll. **1974**). [JC]
Other works: *Tales of Three Hemispheres* (coll. **1919**); two macabre novels, *The Blessing of Pan* (**1927**) and *The Curse of the Wise Woman* (**1933**); two novels in which men's minds are transferred into animals' bodies, *My Talks with Dean Spauley* (**1936**) and *The Strange Journeys of Colonel Polders* (**1950**); *The Man Who Ate the Phoenix* (coll. **1949**); *The Little Tales of Smethers* (coll. **1952**); *The Food of Death: Fifty-One Tales* (coll. **1974**).
About the author: *Biography of Lord Dunsany* (**1972**) by Mark Amory; *Lord Dunsany: King of Dreams* (**1959**) by Hazel Littlefield; *Literary Swordsmen and Sorcerers* (**1976**) by L. Sprague DE CAMP.
See also: MACHINES; SWORD AND SORCERY.

DUNSTAN, ANDREW See A. Bertram CHANDLER.

DUPONT, KURT See André RUELLAN.

DURRELL, LAWRENCE (1912–). English poet and novelist, best known for works outside the sf field, most notably the *Alexandria Quartet* tetralogy (**1957**–60). His sf novel sequence *Tunc* (**1968**) and *Nunquam* (**1970**) is an intensely MAINSTREAM use of sf subjects and techniques; Merlin, a multi-national corporation, buys the protagonist and his super-COMPUTER, which can predict the future, and drives the hero to madness; in the second volume, the hero is cured in order that he create an ANDROID lady, perfect duplicate of a destroyed lover of the head of Merlin — but the android is also destroyed, this NEAR-FUTURE world being choked with evil and images of corruption. [JC]
See also: MYTHOLOGY.

Nov. 1934. Note obvious sf elements.

DUSTY AYRES AND HIS BATTLE BIRDS US PULP MAGAZINE. 12 issues, Jul. 1934 - Jul. 1935, published by Popular Publications; ed. Rogers Terrill. Each issue contained a novel by Robert Sidney Bowen, in which Dusty and his men fight off the menace of an Asian emperor bent on world domination. The series was a revival of a more conventional aviation pulp, *Battle Birds*, in an attempt to pull in the readership of the previous title for what was in effect a brand new magazine with a new hero and a new, futuristic storyline. It continued the numeration of the previous series, beginning with Vol.5 no.4 and ending with Vol.8 no.3. There were four numbers to a volume. Several of these stories were reprinted in paperback form in the 1960s. [FHP/MJE]

DYE, CHARLES (1926–60?). American writer. He began publishing sf with "The Last Orbit" for *AMZ* in 1950, was active for the next half-decade, and soon published his only sf novel, *Prisoner in the Skull* (**1952**), involving thriller-like confrontations between ordinary *Homo sapiens* and a form of SUPERMAN. He was married briefly (1951–3) to Katherine MacLEAN, who wrote three stories under his name, including the sf stories "The Man Who Staked the Stars" (1952) and "Syndrome Johnny" (1951). The latter story contains an amazingly early account of a genetic recombination technique, gene splicing using a "piggyback" virus to transport genetic material (a silicon-using gene) into human cells. [JC/PN]

DYING EARTH, THE See FAR FUTURE.

DYNAMIC SCIENCE FICTION US PULP magazine published by Columbia Publications; ed. R.A.W. LOWNDES. Six issues were released, Dec. 1952 – Jan. 1954. The fiction it printed was mediocre but it published two two-part critical articles of some note by James GUNN: "The Philosophy of SF" (Mar.-Jun. 1953)

UK edition, Jan. 1954. Cover by Milton Luros.

and "The Plot-Forms of SF" (Oct. 1953-Jan. 1954). Three numbered issues were reprinted in Britain in 1953.   [BS]

Feb. 1939. Cover by Frank R. Paul.

DYNAMIC SCIENCE STORIES US PULP magazine. Two issues, Feb. 1939 and Apr./May 1939, published by Western Fiction Publishing Corp.; ed. Robert O. Erisman. Short-lived companion magazine to MARVEL SCIENCE STORIES.

The first issue featured the novel *Lord of Tranerica* (**1966**) by Stanton A. COBLENTZ; the second included stories by L. Sprague DE CAMP and Manly Wade WELLMAN. *DSS* was an average pulp magazine with no distinctive qualities. One number of a British reprint appeared Apr. 1939.   [MJE]

DYSON, FREEMAN JOHN (1923–). English theoretical physicist and FRS; professor at the Institute for Advanced Study, Princeton, since 1953. FJD's main work has been in quantum field theory, but he is well known in sf for the concept of the "Dyson sphere",

which he introduced in a short paper for *Science* in 1960 (Vol.131, p.1667). In this paper, which was concerned with the project of locating and communicating with extraterrestrial civilizations, Dyson argued that any such civilization would probably be millions of years old, and that Malthusian pressure would have led to its energy requirements being equal to the total output of radiation from its sun. It would therefore reconstruct its solar system so as to form an artificial biosphere completely enclosing the sun. This and related schemes, like the basic notion behind his *Ringworld* (**1970**), are discussed by Larry NIVEN in his article "Bigger than Worlds" (1974), reprinted in *A Hole in Space* (coll. **1974**). An sf novel which makes use of an actual Dyson sphere is Bob SHAW's *Orbitsville* (**1975**).   [TSu]

DYSON SPHERE A common item of sf TERMINOLOGY, borrowed from the concept of the physicist Freeman DYSON. (*See his entry for details*).

DYSTOPIAS The word "dystopia" is the antonym of "eutopia" (*see* UTOPIAS), and the term is commonly used to denote a class of model societies which are, in opposition to Utopian designs, images of a fearful and unpleasant world.

One of its first recorded uses in this sense was by John Stuart Mill in a parliamentary speech in 1868. The recent vogue for the term, however, probably stems from its use in the book *Quest For Utopia* (**1952**) by Glenn Negley and J. Max Patrick.

Just as eutopian fictions provide only a standard of comparison, for admonitory or satirical purposes, against which the real world can be measured, so too do Dystopian fictions in the literal meaning of the term — indeed, except for satires there are very few dys*topian* (worse-*place*) fictions in existence. There is always motive enough to imagine a better place elsewhere on Earth, but to imagine worse places is merely pointless. Dystopian images, in the commonplace use of the term, arise in opposition to eu*chronian* (better-*time*) thinking, which promises a better future. It is by no means useless to point fearfully at the way the world is going as propaganda for a change of attitude in the present. As the hope for a better world grows, the fear of disappointment grows with it, and where any vision of a future Utopia incorporates a manifesto for political action or belief, opponents of that action or belief will inevitably attempt to show that its consequences are not Utopian but horrible. (The very first work listed in I.F. CLARKE's bibliography of *The Tale of the Future*, 2nd edition **1972**, is a brief tract of 1644 warning of the disaster to come if the monarchy were to be restored.)

Dystopian images began to proliferate in sf in the last decades of the 19th century. There is an opposition of the two images in the rival cities of Frankville and Stahlstadt in *The Begum's Fortune* (**1879**) by Jules VERNE. The details of the two states are vague and quite unimportant. The opposition is really between Utopian idealism, incarnate in the vision of Frankville, and the forces in human nature which are its enemies — greed and militarism — incarnate in the vision of Stahlstadt. H.G. WELLS, too, produced his images of Dystopia — forecasts of what the world must be like if the forces of socialism did not triumph — in "A Story of the Days to Come" (1897) and *When the Sleeper Wakes* (**1899**; rev. vt *The Sleeper Awakes*, 1910). He also produced the first analytical Dystopia in his description of Selenite society in *The First Men in the Moon* (**1901**).

Because detailed descriptions of Dystopia spring from political and propagandistic fervour directed *against* movements rather than *for* them we find many of the early Dystopias railing loudly against contemporary trends. Walter BESANT's *The Revolt of Man* (**1882**) is an anti-suffragette tract. Robert Hugh BENSON's *Lord of the World* (**1907**) is anti-humanist. The most prolific stimulus to Dystopian vision has, of course, been the political polarization of capitalism and socialism. Anti-capitalist Dystopias include *The Iron Heel* (**1907**) by Jack LONDON, *The Air Trust* (**1915**) by George Allan ENGLAND and *Useless Hands* (**1920**; trans. **1926**) by Claude FARRERE. Anti-socialist Dystopias, which are more numerous, include *The Unknown Tomorrow* (**1910**) by William LE QUEUX, *Crucible Island* (**1919**) by Conde B. PALLEN, *Unborn Tomorrow* (**1933**) by John KENDALL, *Anthem* (**1938**) by Ayn RAND and *The Great Idea* (**1951**; vt *Time Will Run Back* UK) by Henry HAZLITT. Anti-German Dystopias include Owen GREGORY's *Meccania* (**1918**) and Milo Hastings' *City of Endless Night* (**1920**). Anti-Fascist Dystopias include *Land Under England* (**1935**) by Joseph O'NEILL, *The Wild Goose Chase* (**1937**) by Rex WARNER and *The Lost Traveller* (**1943**) by Ruthven TODD. These works are emotional reactions against ideas which are themselves very various, but the basic fears they express vary little. Though the emphasis may differ, the central features of Dystopia are ever present: the oppression of the majority by a ruling elite (which varies only in the manner of its characterization, not in its actions); and the regimentation of society as a whole (which varies only in its declared ends, not in its actual processes).

In its attempt to construct "objectively" the state of the Selenites, Wells had taken as his Dystopian model the ant-hive (*see* HIVE-MINDS); he was echoed by J.D. BERESFORD and Esmé Wynne-Tyson in *The Riddle of the Tower* (**1944**), in which the basic fear is of "Automatism" — the trend toward the victory of organic society over the individual, by whatever political means.

The most detailed analysis of this anxiety, and perhaps the most impressively ruthless of the analytical Dystopias, is *We* (1924) by Yevgeny ZAMIATIN. The most luridly horrible development of it is to be found in George ORWELL's *Nineteen Eighty-Four* (1949), which appears to be the most strongly motivated vision in terms of hatred and hysteria, born of Orwell's despair of the British working class and of its capacity to revolt (or even be revolted).

Animosity against specific political programmes was the most important force provoking Dystopian visions, which were for this reason directed against what is really a minor component in late 19th- and early 20th-century thought. The major force in the Utopian optimism of that time was faith in the idea of progress, both social and technological, rather than in salvation through politics. Dystopian images reflecting an emotional reaction against technology emerged more slowly. Before 1912 there were a good many Utopias *without* machines, but the reaction had not reached such an emotional pitch as to produce Dystopias expressly created by technological advance. E.M. FORSTER's "The Machine Stops" (1909) is the first, and is somewhat halfhearted in that it concentrates on the question of what happens when the machines break down rather than on the horrors of living with them while they still work. The first really confident assertion that scientific progress would make the world a worse place to live in, because it would allow society's power groups to oppress others more effectively, came from Bertrand RUSSELL in *Icarus, or the Future of Science* (1924), his reply to J.B.S. HALDANE's optimistic *Daedalus* (1924). Russell's essay linked technology to one of the essential Dystopian anxieties: oppression. It was not long before writers began to see regimentation as a corollary of technological progress also; it is the vividly rendered central image of the film METROPOLIS (1926). The power that science lent to the trend toward organic society and "automatism" was the main point of protest in Aldous HUXLEY's *Brave New World* (1932) — the first anti-scientific Dystopia whose intensity is comparable to the politically inspired images, it was written in reaction to *Daedalus*.

This reaction against technology affected genre sf at a very early stage. The anxiety most commonly reflected is that of scientific power misused, i.e. employed oppressively by dictators and greedy power groups; but fear of the innate power of machines themselves is apparent also. In "Paradise and Iron" (1930) by Miles J. BREUER a mechanical brain established to coordinate a mechanistic Utopia turns into a tyrant. "City of the Living Dead" (1930) by Laurence MANNING and Fletcher PRATT, machines that simulate real experience allow men to live in dream worlds, sustained by mechanical "wombs", and bring about the total stagnation of society. In "Twilight" (1934) by John W. CAMPBELL Jr (as Don A. Stuart) the human species loses its initiative and degenerates physically and mentally through over-dependence on machines, and in the sequel "Night" (1935) it is extinct. Degeneracy through over-dependence is also featured in David H. KELLER's "Revolt of the Pedestrians" (1928), in which automobilists no longer have the power of self-locomotion, and rule oppressively over the pedestrians. All of these stories feature some kind of rebellion against the adverse circumstances described, and only Campbell was pessimistic about the fate of such a rebellion.

Revolution against a Dystopian future became a staple plot of pulp sf. Such a formula offered far more dramatic potential than planning for Utopia. The consensus image of the future in these stories postulates an oppressive totalitarian state which maintains its dominance by means of a futuristic technology, while at the same time the means employed by the revolutionaries are also, very often, technological, which is to say that in genre sf technology itself tends to be seen as potent but morally neutral. Examples from the 1940s of this formula are: "If This Goes On ..." (1940) by Robert A. HEINLEIN, *Gather, Darkness!* (1943; 1950) by Fritz LEIBER, *Tarnished Utopia* (1943; 1956) by Malcolm JAMESON and *Renaissance* (1944; 1951; vt *Man of Two Worlds*) by Raymond F. JONES.

In the sf magazines of the 1950s this formula became more refined. There appeared a whole generation of sf novels in which individual power groups came to dominate society, shaping it to their special interests. Advertising executives run the world in the archetype of this subspecies, *The Space Merchants* (1953), by Frederik POHL and Cyril KORNBLUTH. Insurance companies are in charge in *Preferred Risk* (1955) by Edson McCANN (Pohl and Lester DEL REY), supermarkets in *Hell's Pavement* (1955; vt *Analogue Men*) by Damon KNIGHT, organized gangsters in *The Syndic* (1953) by Cyril Kornbluth, doctors in *Caduceus Wild* (1959; rev. 1978) by Ward MOORE and Robert Bradford, and a cult of hedonists in *The Joy Makers* (fix-up 1961) by James GUNN. All these novels are, in a sense, gaudy fakes, which use Dystopian images for melodramatic convenience, and appear to select their villains with a vigorous disregard for plausibility and a cheerful animus against a series of personal *bêtes noires*. They tend to be spirited and exciting, but absurdist exaggerations rather than serious political statements. In this period genre sf produced only one genuine Dystopian novel, the classic *Fahrenheit 451* (1953) by Ray BRADBURY, which leaves its ruling elite quite amorphous in order to concentrate on the means by which oppression and regimentation are facilitated, with the powerful key image of the fireman whose job is burning books.

Outside the sf magazines the post-War period produced a remarkable series of very varied Dystopian novels. They were remarkable not only for their diversity but also, by and large, for their clinical sobriety. Aldous Huxley's *Ape and Essence* (1948) is another anti-scientific polemic, while Orwell's *Nineteen Eighty-Four*, Hazlitt's *Time Will Run Back* and Evelyn WAUGH's *Love Among the Ruins* (1953) are reactions to political positions, but Gerald HEARD's *The Doppelgangers* (1947), SARBAN's *The Sound of His Horn* (1952) and L.P. HARTLEY's *Facial Justice* (1960) are possessed of a curious surreal quality, and it is by no means easy to find specific political ideologies at which Kurt VONNEGUT's *Player Piano* (1952), Bernard WOLFE's *Limbo* (1952; vt *Limbo 90*), David KARP's *One* (1953; vt *Escape to Nowhere*) and Anthony BURGESS's *A Clockwork Orange* (1962) are aimed. These novels are neither accusations directed at particular social forces nor attempts to analyse the nature of the Dystopian state, but seem to be products of a new kind of thinking. They are not angry books but they do show incipient despair — only *One* offers a significant note of hope in its account of rebellion against evil circumstances. This, it appears, was the period of history in which Anglo-American society lost faith in the possibility of a better future and the Dystopian image was established in actual expectation, not just as a literary warning device.

Genre sf soon followed the lead given by these novels — and so prominent was the Dystopian image in magazine sf that the transition from fakery to realism was very easily achieved. During the 1960s a whole series of reasons for believing in a Dystopian future were discovered, to justify rather than to cause the pessimistic outlook typical of the time. OVERPOPULATION — a theme ignored since the days of Malthus — began to inspire Dystopian horror stories, most impressively in *Make Room! Make Room!* (1966) by Harry HARRISON, *Stand on Zanzibar* (1968) by John BRUNNER and *The World Inside* (1971) by Robert SILVERBERG. The awful prospects of POLLUTION and destruction of the environment were extravagantly detailed in Brunner's *The Sheep Look Up* (1972) and Philip WYLIE's *The End of the Dream* (1972). When Alvin TOFFLER proposed in *Future Shock* (1970) that the sheer pace of history, above and beyond all other considerations, threatened to destroy society, Brunner was able to complete a kind of "Dystopian trilogy" with *The Shockwave Rider* (1975). Thomas M. DISCH's novel *334* (fix-up 1972) is a dark vision of future life in the CITY, New York in this case, which nevertheless offers some hope in the human resilience it depicts.

Perhaps strangely, MAINSTREAM Dystopian novels of the last decade seem a little conservative compared to those of the 1950s and early '60s: Michael FRAYN's *A Very Private Life* (**1968**) is content to echo Huxley's *Brave New World*; Adrian MITCHELL's *The Bodyguard* (**1970**) is a straightforward political statement; and Ira LEVIN's *This Perfect Day* (**1970**) is both anti-socialist and anti-technology. Perhaps the most all-inclusive and ruthless image of a horrible and degenerate future had already been provided, in William S. BURROUGHS's *Nova Express* (**1964**).

The significance of the firm establishment of a Dystopian image of the future in literature should not be underestimated. Literary images of the future are among the most important expressions of the beliefs and expectations we apply in real life to the organization of our attitudes and actions.

Notable studies of Dystopian fiction include *From Utopia to Nightmare* (**1962**) by Chad Walsh, *The Future as Nightmare* (**1967**) by Mark R. HILLEGAS, and *Science Fiction and the New Dark Age* by Harold L. BERGER (**1976**). In *New Maps of Hell* (**1960**), Kingsley AMIS argues that the Dystopian tradition is the most important strand in the tapestry of modern sf. [BS]

See also: DISASTER; MEDIA LANDSCAPE; NEAR FUTURE; OPTIMISM AND PESSIMISM; SOCIOLOGY.

E

EARLEY, GEORGE W(HITEFORD) (1927–). American engineer and editor, whose theme anthology is *Encounters with Aliens* (anth. **1968**). [JC]

EARNSHAW A(NTHONY) (1924–). English writer who, in collaboration with Eric THACKER, has published two fantasy novels, *Musrum* (**1968**), a fable describing the adventures of the eponymous hero in a strange land opposing the Weed King, and *Wintersol* (**1971**), similarly fantastic. [JC]

EARNSHAW, BRIAN (1929–). English writer whose first novel is the

fine chase thriller *And Mistress Pursuing* (**1966**); *Planet in the Eye of Time* (**1968**) is a complex thriller involving TIME TRAVEL to the period of the crucifixion (*see* MESSIAHS; RELIGION), and problems of a dying galaxy. A juvenile sequence is *Dragonfall Five and the Space Cowboys* (**1972**), *Dragonfall Five and the Royal Beast* (**1972**) and *Dragonfall Five and the Empty Planet* (**1973**). [JC]

A zombie animated by aliens.

EARTH DIES SCREAMING, THE Film (1964). Lippert/Fox. Directed by Terence Fisher, starring Willard Parker, Virginia Field and Dennis Price. Screenplay by Henry Cross from a story by Harry Spalding. 62 mins. B/w.

This is one of a series of three sf films that Terence Fisher, best known for his Hammer horror films, made during the 1960s (the other two were NIGHT OF THE BIG HEAT and ISLAND OF TERROR). A small community is struggling to survive after the Earth has been invaded by alien robots. The human survivors are besieged by a horde of animated corpses under the control of the aliens — which makes the film an inferior forerunner to NIGHT OF THE LIVING DEAD. Like the other two films in the series, *EDS* is handicapped by a clumsily constructed script, a tiny budget and perfunctory direction. [JB]

EARTHQUAKE Film (1974). Universal. Directed by Mark Robson, starring Charlton Heston, Ava Gardner, George Kennedy, Lorne Greene and Geneviève Bujold. Screenplay by George Fox and Mario Puzo. 140 mins. Colour.

Most DISASTER films are marginal sf, in that they deal with events that have not yet happened, but plausibly might. They are, in fact, stories of the NEAR FUTURE. In practice, however, the feeling of most disaster films is not science-fictional, the point of the genre being to give the audience an emotional *frisson* through the disaster itself, rather than investigating causes and effects. This film, a superior example of the genre, shows the destruction of Los Angeles by a major earthquake, focusing, as usual, on a small group who struggle to survive. Technically the film is adroit. It is a showcase for the skills of some of Hollywood's best special effects men, many of whom were persuaded to come out of retirement to work on the project.

One such was Clifford Stine, who was responsible for the effects in Universal's series of sf/horror films in the 1950s, including THE INCREDIBLE SHRINKING MAN. Other effects men were Glen Robinson, Frank Brendal and Jack McMasters. In charge of producing the many matte paintings used in *E* was British-born Albert Whitlock. The film's gimmick was the introduction of "Sensurround", a system which permits audiences to sense low-frequency sound and air vibrations generated by powerful electro-acoustic traducer horns placed at the front and rear of theatres. [JB]

EARTH VERSUS THE FLYING SAUCERS Film (1956). Columbia. Directed by Fred F. Sears, starring Hugh Marlowe and Joan Taylor. Screenplay by George Worthing Yates and Raymond T. Marcus, based on a story by Curt SIODMAK. 83 mins. B/w.

Spectacular scenes of destruction take place as evil aliens from outer space attempt to defeat the Earth using ray-guns. Though the film was made on a small budget, Ray HARRYHAUSEN's special effects are impressive, particularly in the climactic battle sequence over Washington in which flying saucers drop out of the sky and crash into famous landmarks. [JB]

EASSON, ROBERT (WATSON) (1941–). English writer living in the USA; his eccentric sf novella is *The Bird, The Ghoul, and in the Name of My Friend* (**1968**) [JC]

EASTERLEY, ROBERT *See* Robert POTTER.

EASTERN EUROPE The countries of Eastern Europe by no means have a coherent literary tradition, although for the past 30 years they have all, with the exception of Austria, been uneasily united in the sense that they have Communist governments. This entry covers work written in Bulgaria, Romania, Yugoslavia, Czechoslovakia, Austria, Hungary and Poland. East Germany is covered under GERMANY. The languages spoken in these countries are generally Slavic, though in Austria German is the main language; Hungarian is not a Slavic language, and Romanian is a Romance language related to Latin. Nonetheless, especially in recent years, the dominant influence on Eastern European writing has been Russian (*see* RUSSIA).

There is no true Eastern European equivalent of genre sf, though many writers reveal a familiarity with the literary conventions of Anglo-American sf in their work, notably the Polish writer Stanislaw LEM. The two Eastern European traditions that have fed most fruitfully into Eastern European sf are the UTOPIAN and the ABSURDIST.

The more industrialized Eastern European countries have a long tradition (often stemming from the Austro-Hungarian Empire) of complex bureaucracy, and the satirical absurdist tradition is to some extent in response to this, producing a sceptical, sometimes surrealist, view of social structures; people are often seen as grotesque caricatures; the tone is ironic and the humour black. This was especially true of the works of Franz KAFKA, who was born in Prague, lived in Austria, and wrote in German. None of his works is sf *per se*, but his influence on the field has been prolonged and impressive. When considering the absurdist tradition it is worth remembering that Kafka was a younger contemporary of that other great Austrian, Sigmund Freud. The Hungarian writer Frigyes KARINTHY also wrote in the absurdist/surrealist manner, on such sf themes as self-replicating machines, in his two rather savage sequels to Jonathan SWIFT's *Gulliver's Travels* (**1726**). These, originally dated **1916** and **1922**, are available in English as *Voyage to Faremido and Capillaria* (trans. **1966** by Paul TABORI). The influence of Freud is clear in the work of a second Hungarian, Mihály BABITS, whose marginally sf poem *Gólyakalifa* (**1916**; trans. Hungary as *King's Stork* **1948**; trans. Hungary as *The Nightmare* **1966**) deals with a split personality mirroring the disintegration of society.

In Poland, Jerzy PETERKIEWICZ also worked in the absurdist tradition, at first as a poet. He moved to England after the War, and now writes in English, his novels including *Inner Circle* (**1966**), part of which is set in a cruel, crowded, far-future setting. Slawomir MROZEK, too, is an absurdist writer, whose short stories and plays combine the fantastic with various sf elements. Some can be found in *Wesele w atomicach* (coll. **1959**; trans. as *The Ugupu Bird* **1968**). An earlier Polish writer of interest to the genre is Jerzy ZULAWSKI, who published a trilogy about the colonization of the Moon, beginning with *Na srebrnym globie* ["The Silver Globe"] (**1903**).

The UTOPIAN tradition, which runs parallel to, rather than against absurdist satire, is older. Two Utopian writers whose work contains strong sf elements are the Austrian Theodor HERTZKA (1845–1924) and the Hungarian Mór JOKAI (1825–1904). Hertzka produced a socialist scenario, with much economic theorizing, in his influential *Freiland: Ein Sociales Zukunftsbild* (**1890**; trans. as *Freeland: A Social Anticipation* **1891**). Jokai wrote over 100 popular novels, and many of his stories were translated into English; he was popular in England in the late 19th century. Several of these had strong Utopian elements, as well as anticipations of the future of technology, rather in the manner of Jules VERNE. One of the most important, *A jovo század regenye* ["The Novel of the Coming Century"] (**1874**), is apparently untranslated into English.

Both the Utopian and absurdist strands come together, with very different results, in the work of the three most important Eastern European sf writers, the two Czechs Karel Čapek and Josef Nesvadba, and the Polish Stanislaw Lem. All these writers have several of their works freely available in translation, and these are discussed in detail under their separate entries. It is difficult to generalize about their work, but it is worth pointing out that in all three an ironical and dark view of the real world (dramatized in a variety of sf scenarios) runs alongside a passionate Utopianism which is not compromised by sarcasm or nihilism. Eastern European Utopianism seems to be of a more tough-minded and resistant variety than Anglo-American, perhaps because the history of that area has for hundreds of years produced such horrors that those who survive the annealing process can easily cope with the comparatively minor abrasions of their own scepticism. This is also true of much Russian sf. Čapek, Nesvadba and Lem are also linked by a kind of fun-poking, grotesque humour which to Western eyes sometimes appears oddly naïve. Finally, none of them was or is writing for a market which has quite the same rigid expectations of what is or is not proper for sf as is the case in the UK and the USA, and in consequence Western fans at first may be baffled and unsure as to what to make of their books. Those who persevere usually find it worth while.

Anglo-American genre sf is read in quite large quantities all over Eastern Europe. A recent Polish anthology, *Kroki w nieznane* (anth. **1973**) ed. Lech Jęczmyk, contains stories by Brian W. ALDISS, Frederik POHL, David MASSON, Bob SHAW and many others. The Hungarian bibliography *Utopisztikus, Tudamányos-Fantasztikus Müvek: Bibliográfiája* (**1970**), compiled by Csiszar Jolán, lists 1,000 Hungarian titles of which about half are translations from English, a respectable number by native Hungarian authors. Eastern European delegates were present at the first two Eurocons, all-European sf CONVENTIONS, and the third was held in Warsaw in 1976, quite productively, though the formal events tended to follow a rigid party line. Hungary, Poland and Romania have active fan clubs, the poet Peter Kuczka being one of the most active Hungarians in publishing and fan activities. Official Hungarian literary journals commonly print articles on sf. Yugoslav sf is almost unknown in the West, except perhaps for the film *Izvatibelj* (1977), released in English as *The Rat Saviour*, which took first prize at the SF Film Festival in Trieste in 1977. It features a form of super-rat, able to take on human shape, and was directed by Krsto Papić. The only Yugoslav writer to receive an entry in this volume is Hinko GOTTLIEB, whose Serbo-Croat novel translated as *The Key to the Great Gate*

(trans. **1947**), in which a Polish gentleman fights the Nazis with psionic powers, has been highly praised in the USA. Yugoslavia has produced one notable sf critic, Darko SUVIN, who is now resident in Canada. Suvin's anthology *Other Worlds, Other Seas* (anth. **1970**) is one of the very few sources of information readily available in the West about Eastern European sf, in both its contemporary stories and its introduction. From Bulgaria he prints the story "Why Atlantis Sank" (1966) by Anton Donev (1927–), and from Romania "The Contact" (1966) by Vladimir Colin (1921–). Also active in Romania as a writer and fan is Ion Hobana, who has been active in maintaining sf contacts with the West. Svetoslav Minkov (1902–) is an earlier Bulgarian sf writer, active since 1930; *The Lady With the X-Ray Eyes* (Bulgaria; coll. trans. **1965**) is in English. The most important remaining Polish sf writer is Stanislaw Ignacy Witkiewicz (1885–1939), who committed suicide when the Soviet army crossed the Polish frontier in 1939. His two main novels, *Pozegnanie jesieni* ["Farewell to Autumn"] (**1927**) and *Nienasycenie* ["Unsatisfied Instincts"] (**1930**), are bitter, absurd and apocalyptic, set in future worlds which treat men as units in a great machine, and in which, in the first instance the Communists take over Poland, and in the second, the Chinese invade Europe.

In *Other Worlds, Other Seas* Darko Suvin lists a further fifty practising sf writers in Eastern Europe, many from Yugoslavia, Bulgaria and Romania. Though so little of it is available in the West, it is clear that socialist sf remains an active genre, not just in Russia. It is probable that, as in Russia, it can be used to attack the system by metaphorical means.

One area in which Eastern European sf is well known is through the cinema. Besides the Russian SOLARIS, based on Lem's novel, this Encyclopedia gives entries to four Czech films of interest: IKARIA XB1 (*Voyage to the End of the Universe*) (1963); KDO CHCE ZABIT JESSII (*Who Would Kill Jessie?*) (1965), VÝNALEZ ZKAZY (*The Fabulous World of Jules Verne*) (1958) and KONEC SRPNA V HOTELU OZON (*The End of August at the Hotel Ozone*) (1965). The tradition of the fantastic has always been especially strong in Czech cinema as well as in Czech literature generally.   [PN]

EAST GERMANY *See* GERMANY.

ECKSTROM, JACK DENNIS (?–). American sf writer whose novel is *Time of the Hedrons* (**1968**).   [JC]

ECOLOGY Ecology is the study of organisms in relation to their environment. It is a relatively new discipline, the first notable work on the

ECOLOGY, a popular theme around 1970, as on this Freas cover, December.

subject being Charles Elton's *Animal Ecology* (**1927**). The complexity of the environmental relationships which determine the success, or even the survival, of populations has been realized only within the last half-century. The same period has seen a dramatic increase in the world's population and the virtual destruction of the natural environment in many populous areas, and such issues as the protection of food-chains and increasing the efficiency of ecological systems have become extremely important.

As is to be expected with respect to a scientific discipline no older than genre sf, there are very few early stories with ecological themes. W.H. HUDSON's fantasies of a mode of human life in harmony with nature — particularly *A Crystal Age* (**1887**) — can be seen, with hindsight, to be related to the theme, but the inspiration of such fantasies was mystical rather than scientific. Scientific romancers were often totally oblivious to the simplest matters of ecological common sense in their pictures of LIFE ON OTHER WORLDS, offering abundant carnivorous species with no sign of the vast herbivore populations which would be required to sustain them. Edgar Rice BURROUGHS' Mars is aicardinal example.

An early story based on ecological speculation is J.D. BERESFORD's "The Man Who Hated Flies" (1929). This parable of a scientist who discovers a perfect insecticide and precipitates an eco-catastrophe by removing the agents which pollinate many of the world's plant species seems naïve today, but it should be remembered that it is virtually contemporary with Elton's book. The only early pulp sf writer whose work showed anything more than a rudimentary consciousness of ecology was Stanley WEINBAUM. After the War, however, writers began to use a good deal more ingenuity in their representations of alien ecology, and there is a species of sf that might be

termed the "ecological puzzle story", in which explorers on other worlds have to figure out peculiar relationships in the local fauna and flora. An early example is William TENN's "The Ionian Cycle" (1948). Others include several stories by Clifford D. SIMAK — notably "You'll Never Go Home Again" (1951; vt "Beachhead") and "Drop Dead" (1956) — the ingenious "Grandpa" (1955) by James H. SCHMITZ, Brian ALDISS's "PEST" (Planetary Ecological Survey Team) series (1958–62) and a series by Jack SHARKEY which includes "Arcturus Times Three" (1961) and "A Matter of Protocol" (1963). More sophisticated examples are Richard McKENNA's "Hunter Come Home" (1963), Neal BARRETT's *Highwood* (**1972**) and John BOYD's bizarre *The Pollinators of Eden* (**1969**). An interesting oddity is Jack VANCE's "Winner Lose All" (1951) — an ecological parable which disposes of human characters. Michael CONEY has propounded ecological puzzles in a number of novels, including *Syzygy* (**1973**) and *Hello Summer, Goodbye* (**1975**; vt *Rax* USA).

Inevitably, in the post-War period, the theme of COLONIZATION OF OTHER WORLDS has come to be seen more and more in ecological terms. An elementary strategy of ecological control is the key to the invasion of the land areas of Venus in *Fury* (**1950**; vt *Destination Infinity*) by Henry KUTTNER, and some such programme is usually of primary concern in post-War stories dealing with the colonization of worlds that are not implicitly Earthlike (*see* MARS *and* TERRAFORMING). The great majority of ecological problem stories within this theme derive their problems by simple distortion of ecological systems on Earth, or by simple analogy. Relatively few authors have been willing to take on the job of attempting to construct an alien ecology in some detail, the most notable attempts being those of Hal CLEMENT, in such novels as *Cycle of Fire* (**1957**) and *Close to Critical* (**1958**; **1964**).

The precariousness of the human ecological situation became a constant theme in post-War sf. The difficulties involved in avoiding a world-wide disaster caused by soil-exhaustion provide the theme of Edward HYAMS' *The Astrologer* (**1950**), a novel which emphasizes his conviction (shared by many) that ecological planning will be made almost impossible because politicians tend to think only in the short term. The need for consideration of ecological issues is cleverly represented in Damon KNIGHT's "Natural State" (1954; vt **1959** *Masters of Evolution*) and the first major cautionary tale relating to Man's dependence on the general health of the natural world appeared soon afterwards: John CHRISTOPHER's *The Death of Grass* (**1956**; vt *No Blade of Grass* USA), in which a blight affecting grass species precipitates world catastrophe. A satirical

extrapolation of an opposite case, in which one species of grass drives out all other plant life, had been developed in Ward MOORE's *Greener Than You Think* (**1947**). C.M. KORNBLUTH's "Shark Ship" (1958) is another eco-catastrophe story which paints a very bleak picture of troubles to come.

The eco-catastrophe theme became much more common in sf in the late 1960s, picking up impetus from a number of non-fictional warnings, which predicted that things could only get worse as a result of OVERPOPULATION and POLLUTION of the environment. Paul Ehrlich, author of *The Population Bomb* (**1968**), used a fictional framework for a brief summary of his predictions in "Ecocatastrophe" (1969), in which the world slides ever more rapidly towards its end as disasters precipitate and complement one another in series and in parallel. A similar picture appears in many sf stories of the last decade, which are notable primarily for their bitter irony. Most sf writers who deal in eco-catastrophe stories seem to feel that contemporary Man will get no more than he deserves if he destroys his environment and poisons himself. Even writers who are neither aggrieved nor disillusioned to any marked degree tend to accept that an ongoing ecological crisis will be one of the most obvious features of the history of the NEAR FUTURE.

Along with this recent intensification of ecological awareness there has arisen a much greater subtlety and sophistication in certain patterns within the DISASTER novel. Although lurid and spectacular accounts of the END OF THE WORLD still abound, there is also a new subspecies dealing with a rather more delicate aesthetics of destruction, founded upon the physiological and psychological relationship between Man and environment. *The Year of the Cloud* (**1970**) by Theodore L. THOMAS and Kate WILHELM traces a world disaster caused by a compound which fractionally increases the viscosity of water, drastically altering the pattern of life over the entire surface of the Earth. George Alec EFFINGER's "And Us, Too, I Guess" (1973) describes what happens when some surreal cosmic process begins eliminating the living species of Earth, one by one and day by day. One of the earliest examples of this subtle catastrophism was Gerald HEARD's "The Great Fog" (1944), and the most detailed exploration of its manifold possibilities has been carried out by J.G. BALLARD, especially in the group of novels *The Wind From Nowhere* (**1962**), *The Drowned World* (**1962**), *The Burning World* (**1964**; vt *The Drought* UK) and *The Crystal World* (**1966**). All these novels deal with responses to environmental change in a much more detailed fashion than the "second deluge" or "new ice age" stories which are their closest pre-War analogues.

Stories concerned with the ecology of

alien worlds have, in the past two decades, taken on a strong element of mysticism. In the real world the word "ecology" has acquired quasi-charismatic status (like that other biological metaphor, "roots"); it has come to symbolize a sense of lost harmony with the world at large, and various commune moements have tried to make ecological awareness an antidote to alienation. This comes out very strongly in such evocations of the Eden myth as Mark CLIFTON's *Eight Keys to Eden* (**1960**) and Gordon R. DICKSON's "Twig" (1974), and in the mystical ritualization of water relations featured in Robert HEINLEIN's *Stranger in a Strange Land* (**1961**) and Frank HERBERT's *Dune* (**1965**). In Piers ANTHONY's *Omnivore* (**1968**) ecological relationships themselves are transformed into a mystical pattern. This current of mysticism is beginning to extend to stories set on Earth — an early example is Frank Herbert's *The Green Brain* (**1966**), which is a contemporary version of Beresford's "Man Who Hated Flies", with miracles added.

Two anthologies consisting mainly of eco-catastrophe stories are *Saving Worlds* (anth. **1973**; vt *The Wounded Planet*) ed. Roger ELWOOD and Virginia Kidd, and *The Ruins of Earth* (anth. **1971**) ed. Thomas M. DISCH. [BS]

ECONOMICS The word "economics" derives from a Greek word signifying the art of household management. In its modern usage it has been extended by analogy to pertain to the management of the industry and finances of nations. Medieval economic "theory" was dominated by ethical considerations, and though these have changed their form considerably they still remain entangled with the science. Because of this economics has the capacity to arouse the passions more powerfully than any other scientific discipline — a fact clearly evident in fiction dealing with economic systems. Thomas MORE's *Utopia* (**1516**; trans. **1551**) is largely a treatise on economic issues, and much subsequent UTOPIAN literature has been concerned with economic theory and its relationships with political power and social justice.

The idea that economics should attempt to shed its ethical entanglements and become a matter of "natural law" was first popularized by a poem, "The Grumbling Hive", which formed the headpiece of *The Fable of the Bees: or Private Vices, Publick Benefits* (**1714**) by Bernard de Mandeville. The poem and the tract advanced the thesis that if the market were allowed to find its own equilibrium through everyone attempting to maximize profits in open competition (no matter how corruptly) then the nation as a whole would benefit. This notion was later taken up by Adam Smith in *The Wealth of Nations* (**1776**). In the 19th century the rise of various socialist movements, armed with their own

Marxist theory of economics, brought a good deal of ideological conflict into economic thought at both the academic and popular levels. This conflict is very evident in a great deal of 19th-century Utopian fiction. Etienne Cabet's *Voyage en Icarie* (**1840**) and Robert Pemberton's *The Happy Colony* (**1856**) both propounded the socialist doctrine, though they pitched their argument more in moral than in "scientific" terms. Theodore HERTZKA's novels *Freeland* (**1890**; trans. **1891**) and *A Visit to Freeland* (**1893**; trans. **1894**) attempt to steer a course midway between unrestricted private enterprise and total state control, but their message pleased neither side. By the end of the century, of course, the situation was becoming confused by the interest which the Utopian novelists were taking in AUTOMATION and TECHNOLOGY, but economic equality remained central to the dogma of Edward BELLAMY's *Looking Backward* (**1888**) and to the furious debate which followed its publication. Few 20th-century Utopias give priority to economic considerations over and above political or technological issues, but notable exceptions are Robert ARDREY's *World's Beginning* (**1944**) and Henry HAZLITT's *The Great Idea* (**1951**, vt *Time Will Run Back*). The longest and most extravagant economic tract cast as fiction this century, however, is Ayn RAND's *Atlas Shrugged* (**1957**), in which the world's capitalists go on strike in protest against the forces of creeping socialism. Marxist economic theory, understandably, has not figured large in fiction produced in the West, though there is some Marxist rhetoric in Jack LONDON's *The Iron Heel* (**1907**), and Upton SINCLAIR's *The Millennium* (**1924**) is a satirical comedy in which the survivors of a catastrophe find themselves trapped in a dialectical sequence of changing social relationships. The most eloquent economic satire of the century, however — and a good antidote to the dismal qualities of the science — is Archibald MARSHALL's *Upsidonia* (**1915**), about a world where the profit motive operates in reverse.

The early pulp sf writers were little concerned with economics. The myth of rags to riches was an integral part of the mythology of pulp fiction (all pulp plots were variants of the success story) and so the difference between being rich and being poor had to be maintained, though many enthusiastic fans of progress took care to indicate that though the rich would get richer the poor would get richer too. When John W. CAMPBELL Jr took over *ASF*, however, the way was made clear for a more thoughtful contemplation of economic issues. One of the first to take advantage was Robert HEINLEIN. In "The Roads Must Roll" (**1940**) he envisaged a world dependent upon moving roadways thrown into chaos by a strike called by

"Functionalists" — proponents of the theory that the greatest economic rewards should go to the people with the most vital jobs. His "Let There Be Light ... " (**1940** as by Lyle Monroe) has some cynical asides on the suppression of innovations by power groups who have a heavy investment in existing technologies — a theme since used in numerous other stories. "Logic of Empire" (**1941**) has some similarly cynical comments on the economics of slavery. Heinlein is not a proponent of economic theory so much as a propagandist for a particular set of biological ethics which are echoed in economic analogies (*see* SOCIAL DARWINISM), and though economic themes continually crop up in his work they are rarely dominant. One exception is "The Man Who Sold the Moon" (**1950**), which concerns the struggle to finance the first Moon voyage, a story which has dated rather badly. The most interesting of his post-War works with respect to economic theorizing is *The Moon is a Harsh Mistress* (**1966**).

Some of Campbell's other writers have written stories in which the emphasis on economic considerations is much more central. An isolated classic is "The Iron Standard" (**1943**) by Lewis Padgett (Henry KUTTNER and C.L. MOORE), in which Earthmen force reluctant aliens to help them by disrupting their economy and threatening the power structure of a static society. Poul ANDERSON has shown a continual interest in speculative economics, and his bias is noticeably more practical than Heinlein's, though no less right-wing politically. "The Helping Hand" (**1950**) is a neat early story about the economics of "foreign aid", but Anderson's major work in this vein appears in the series of stories featuring interstellar trader Nicholas van Rijn and his associates, notably "Margin of Profit" (**1956**) and the novelettes collected as *Trader to the Stars* (coll. **1964**) and *The Trouble Twisters* (coll. **1966**). Another post-War writer associated with Campbell who has shown a strong interest in economics is Mack REYNOLDS, whose parents were Communists. His efforts range from the wry "Subversive" (**1962**) and the satirical *Tomorrow Might Be Different* (short version **1960** as "Russkies Go Home!"; **1975**) to the careful "Ultima Thule" (**1961**), in which visiting Earthmen divide an alien world's nations in order to compare the power of free enterprise and Marxist planning as forces of social evolution, and the revisitations of Bellamy: *Looking Backward, from the Year 2000* (**1973**) and *Equality in the Year 2000* (**1977**).

A rather different approach to economic issues was manifest in the magazine GALAXY, where the emphasis was very much on satirical irony. The author who best embodied the outlook of the magazine was Frederik POHL, whose economic fantasies stand in sharp contrast to those of Heinlein, Anderson and

Reynolds. In *The Space Merchants* (1953), which he wrote in collaboration with C.M. KORNBLUTH, the economy of the USA has been driven to extremes of conspicuous consumption in order to maintain economic growth, and the advertising industry has become the linch-pin of government. In "The Midas Plague" (1954) the situation is exaggerated still further, with consumption quotas for all citizens as the nation strives to cope with the abundance of machine-produced goods. In "The Tunnel Under the World" (1955) an artificial world is used to test advertising pitches — an "economic model" in a far more literal sense than that in which theorists use the term. In another collaboration with Kornbluth, *Gladiator-at-Law* (1955), the stock market is supreme, manipulated by corporations run by reclusive super-geriatrics. Another *Gal.* story is "Cost of Living" (1952) by Robert SHECKLEY, in which the middle class can maintain its standard of living only by mortgaging the future income of its children. Another writer in the same vein — although the works here cited did not appear in *Gal.* — is Damon KNIGHT, whose *Hell's Pavement* (fix-up 1955; vt *Analogue Men*) features another future USA run by companies, with consumption quotas for ordinary citizens. Knight's *The People Maker* (1959; vt rev. with cuts restored *A For Anything* 1961) explores the socio-economic consequences of the intervention of a matter-duplicator, and makes an interesting contrast with two *ASF* stories on the same theme: George O. SMITH's "Pandora's Millions" (1945), in which civilization collapses as a result, and Ralph Williams' "Business As Usual, During Alterations" (1958), in which it doesn't. The other major theme developed by the *Gal.* writers — manipulation of consumers in pursuit of economic stability — is also investigated by Rosel George BROWN (impressionistically) in "Signs of the Times" (*AMZ* 1959) and J.G. BALLARD in "The Subliminal Man" (*NW* 1963).

Economic problems have been less noticeable in the sf of the 1970s, largely because of the increasing attention paid to other socio-political problems (*see* DYSTOPIAS, OVERPOPULATION *and* POLLUTION), but the question of economic rewards is still one which has to be faced in virtually every story dealing with life in the future. The prevailing opinion now seems to be the opposite of that dominant in the 1920s — it is taken for granted that the poor will get poorer and the rich will get poorer too.

A relevant theme anthology is *Tomorrow, Inc.: SF Stories about Big Business* (anth. 1976) ed. Martin Harry GREENBERG and Joseph D. Olander. [BS]
See also: MONEY; POLITICS; SOCIOLOGY.

EDDISON, E(RIC) R(UCKER) (1882–1945). English civil servant, writer and scholar of Old Norse. His first work of fiction, *The Worm Ouroboros* (1922), is his most important single work; it is essentially an erudite form of HEROIC FANTASY, set (after its initial protagonist, Henderson, is transported from Earth to view events and to be soon forgotten) in a medieval world wracked by magic and irreconcilable conflicts, which continue cyclically as the book closes. His Zimiamvian trilogy (whose internal chronology reverses that of publication), the posthumously assembled *The Mezentian Gate* (1958), *A Fish Dinner in Memison* (1941), and *Mistress of Mistresses* (1935), is set, remarkably, in the heaven of the previous novel (its only connection with *The Worm Ouroboros*); the novels are discursive, METAPHYSICAL and, in their way, engrossing. ERE's influence on the sf genre, as with writers like Lord DUNSANY and J.R.R. TOLKIEN, lies mainly in the powerful example of his language and the elaborate "otherness" of his creation. [JC]
About the author: "Superman in a Bowler: E.R. Eddison" in *Literary Swordsmen and Sorcerers: The Makers of Heroic Fantasy* (1976) by L. Sprague DE CAMP.
See also: FANTASY; MERCURY; WAR.

EDGAR, PETER Pseudonym of English writer Peter King-Scott (?–), whose sf novel is *Cities of the Dead* (1963). [JC]

EDMONDS, HARRY (? –). English writer of several adventure novels, usually set at sea, and of some NEAR-FUTURE sf novels, beginning with *The Riddle of the Straits* (1931), a WAR story set in 1935, with Britain and Japan pitted against Russia and America; a Channel Tunnel saves England from embargo. In *Red Invader* (1933), Russia and Germany are once again involved, this time in intrigues against England. *The Professor's Last Experiment* (1935; rev. vt *The Secret Voyage* 1946) deals with a device that simulates death and stops all warfare, but whose radioactive potential is involved in international difficulties. *The Clockmaker of Heidelberg* (1949) also invokes Germany and Russia, along with a new form of submarine propulsion, and a Neo-Nazi germ-warfare plot centered in Brazil. Its future-war sequel is *The Rockets (Operation Manhattan)* (1951). [JC]
Other works: *Wind in the East* (1933).

EDMONDS, PAUL *See* Henry KUTTNER.

EDMONDSON, G.C. The form of his name which Mexican-born American writer and translator José Mario Garry Ordoñez Edmondson y Cotton (1922–) uses for all his writing; he published his first sf, "Blessed Are the Meek", in *ASF* in 1955, and was active in the magazines for the next decade, particularly in *FSF*, where his "Mad Friend" series of stories appeared. Assembled in *Stranger Than You Think* (coll. of linked stories 1965), they describe the effects their narrator's mad friend manages to elicit from the world about him, and his explanations thereof. GCE's first novel, *The Ship That Sailed the Time Stream* (1965), is an amusing and graphically told FANTASTIC VOYAGE involving a US ship and its inadvertent TIME TRAVELS. After a serious illness in the late 1960s, GCE returned to writing with *Chapayeca* (1971; vt *Blue Face*) and *T.H.E.M.* (1974), both fluently written but less aerated in effect than his earlier work, which combined some slapstick with a good deal of impressive action. *The Aluminum Man* (1975) confronts some humans with a crashlanded ALIEN looking for fuel, to some comic effect. GCE uses the pseudonym Kelly P. Gast for his Westerns. [JC]

EDMONDSON, WALLACE *See* Harlan ELLISON.

EDUCATION *See* SF IN THE CLASSROOM.

EDWARDS, DAVID (? –). American writer whose sf novel, *Next Stop, Mars!* (1960), sends another first space flight to that planet. [JC]

EDWARDS, F.E. *See* William F. NOLAN.

EDWARDS, GAWAIN *See* Edward PENDRAY.

EDWARDS, MALCOLM JOHN (1949–). British editor and critic, educated at Cambridge, where he graduated in anthropology. Active in British sf FANDOM, he edited the BRITISH SCIENCE FICTION ASSOCIATION journal VECTOR 1972–4, worked as sf editor for Gollancz 1976–7, and became Administrator of the SCIENCE FICTION FOUNDATION in 1978. MJE is one of the two contributing editors of this volume. [PN]

EDWARDS, NORMAN Collaborative pseudonym of Terry CARR and Ted WHITE, used on one minor novel, *Invasion from 2500* (1964).

EDWARDS, PETER (1946–). English writer and civil servant. His sf novel *Terminus* (1976) rather ponderously sets in motion a political conflict in a 22nd-century, post-HOLOCAUST Eurafrica which a sado-masochist secret society is attempting to dominate; the hero who can stop them is incarcerated in a prison camp on Mars; the discovery of an ancient Martian city confuses all issues. [JC]

EFFINGER, GEORGE ALEC (1947–). American writer, resident in New Orleans. He attended the universities of Yale and New York, entered sf writing via the 1970 CLARION SCIENCE FICTION WRITERS' WORKSHOP, and had three stories in the workshop's first anthology: *Clarion* (anth. **1971**) ed. Robin Scott WILSON. His first story to see print, however, was "The Eight-Thirty to Nine Slot" (1971) in *Fantastic*. Within a very short time GAE established himself as a writer of stylish, surrealistic fantasies, and became a regular contributor to such series anthologies as ORBIT, NEW DIMENSIONS and UNIVERSE, as well as the major magazines. His story "All the Last Wars at Once" (1972) gained a HUGO award nomination. His first novel, *What Entropy Means to Me* (**1972**), was praised by Theodore STURGEON and Robert SILVERBERG among others, and was nominated for a NEBULA award. It is an elaborate fiction about the writing of fiction (appropriately prefaced by a quotation from Sterne's *Tristram Shandy*) and although set on another planet bears little resemblance to conventional sf. *Relatives* (fix-up **1973**) was less well received. More a collection of novellas than a unified novel, it concerns the fate of one man in three PARALLEL WORLDS. It has become apparent that GAE is a better short-story writer than novelist, and *Mixed Feelings* (coll. **1974**) and *Irrational Numbers* (coll. **1976**) are in fact stronger books than any of his novels. Knowledgeable, witty, master of a sly tone and unlikely subject matter, with a particular interest in various kinds of games (*see* GAMES AND SPORTS), GAE is at his best a fine short-story writer whose aims and achievements go beyond the normal boundaries of genre sf. At his weakest, however, his work can be inconsequential and facile. He has written three novelizations of scripts from the TV series PLANET OF THE APES — *Man the Fugitive* (**1974**); *Escape to Tomorrow* (**1975**); and *Journey into Terror* (**1975**). He has also produced a routine sf adventure novel, *Nightmare Blue* (**1975**), in collaboration with Gardner Dozois, and an uninspired "Promethean romance of the spaceways", *Those Gentle Voices* (**1976**).

Although GAE has not written series *per se*, many of his characters appear and reappear, even after being killed, and he has announced that "many of my stories interlock, and some day I will figure out a kind of chronology and key to the business". He has written under the pseudonyms John K. Diomede and (with an appalling concealed pun) Susan Doenim. These stories are normally those with which he was not entirely happy. Two novels are projected, along with a short-story collection. An earlier novel, *Felicia* (**1976**) is not sf. [DP]
See also: DISASTER; ECOLOGY; END OF THE WORLD; ENTROPY; LEISURE.

EFREMOV, IVAN ANTONOVICH *See* Ivan Antonovich YEFREMOV.

EGBERT, H.M. *See* Victor ROUSSEAU.

EHRLICH, MAX (SIMON) (1909–). American writer. His first sf novel, *The Big Eye* (**1949**), tells of a visiting planet which astronomers announce will hit Earth; they do so in order to terrify Man into world peace; the planet misses narrowly. *The Edict* (**1972**) is a novelization of ME's own screenplay for the film *Z.P.G.* (*see entry*) and deals with an embargo on births. *The Reincarnation of Peter Proud* (**1974**), later filmed, is a quest novel whose protagonist attempts to track down information about his former self, the murder of whom recurs in his dreams. [JC/PN]

EIDLITZ, WALTER *See* TRANSPORTATION.

EINSTEIN, CHARLES (1926–). American writer. He published his first sf story, "Tunnel 1971" with *Saturn* in 1957; his NEAR-FUTURE novel, *The Day New York Went Dry* (**1964**), depicts a water shortage in that city which comes to a crisis in the drought of 1967. A hurricane saves the city and its politicians. [JC]

EIZYKMAN, BORIS (1949–). French critic. An academic, BE is the author of one of the most complex studies devoted to sf, *Science-fiction et capitalisme; critique de la position de désir de la science* ["Sf and Capitalism, a Critical Analysis of Science's Attitude to Desire"] (**1974**) a polemical as well as theoretical approach to the genre "grounded in a conceptual apparatus based on Freud" (P. Fitting). BE's book confusingly and in difficult language attempts to demonstrate the presence in sf of libidinal mechanisms undermining the structure of society. A similar approach has been adopted by BE in his book on US comic strips, *La bande dessinée de SF Américaine* ["American Sf Comic Strips"] (**1976**) with Daniel Riche. BE is a frequent contributor to the French arts weekly *Les Nouvelles Littéraires*. [MJ]

EKLUND, GORDON (1945–). American writer, born in Seattle and resident in San Francisco from 1967. He published "Dear Aunt Annie", his first sf story, in *Fantastic* in 1970; it was subsequently nominated for a NEBULA award. He has used a pseudonym, Wendall Stewart, only once, in *AMZ*, all his books being published under his own name. His first novel, *The Eclipse of Dawn* (**1971**), bears some resemblance to his fourth and best to date, *All Times Possible* (**1974**); both deal pessimistically and forcefully with the American political landscape, and share an interest in the psychology and tactics of leadership. In the first some sf elements — the intrusive outer-space ALIENS — tend to jar, while in *All Times Possible* the PARALLEL-WORLDS structure of the novel intensifies and darkens the picture of political realities at work through the second quarter of the 20th century.

Although a sometimes careless writing style and a tendency to prolixity mars these books, they are still significant contributions to POLITICS in sf. *A Trace of Dreams* (**1972**) is also a novel of some weight, though some other works of this prolific author, such as *Inheritors of Earth* (1951 *Future Combined with Science Fiction Stories*; exp. **1974**), a stumbling expansion of a 1951 Poul ANDERSON story, *Serving in Time* (**1975**) and *The Grayspace Beast* (**1976**), are comparatively commonplace.

With Gregory BENFORD (*who see for details*), GE has collaborated on a series of stories fixed into a novel, *If The Stars Are Gods* (fix-up **1977**), the title story of which, in its original form, won a 1974 Nebula award for best novelette. In a short span of years, GE has shown himself to be a competent though unexciting writer of routine sf, but has also produced several stimulating and well-written novels that augur well for his future career. [JC]
Other works: *Beyond the Resurrection* (**1973**); *Falling Toward Forever* (**1975**); *Dance of the Apocalypse* (**1976**).
See also: ALTERNATE WORLDS; GENETIC ENGINEERING; GODS AND DEMONS; JUPITER; LIVING WORLDS; OUTER PLANETS; RELIGION; ROBOTS; STARS; SUN

ELDER, JOSEPH (? –). Anthologist, known for *The Farthest Reaches* (anth. **1968**), an imaginative selection, and *Eros in Orbit* (anth. **1973**), a theme anthology on SEX in sf. [JC]

ELDER, MICHAEL (1931–). English actor and writer in various genres, some of whose earlier novels, written in the 1950s, deal with theatrical themes; he began writing sf with *Paradise Is Not Enough* (**1970**), and has produced a number of fairly routine adventures since. The SPACE-OPERA adventures involving COLONIZATION and its perils in *Nowhere On Earth* (**1972**) and its sequel, *The Perfumed Planet* (**1973**; vt. *Flight to Terror* USA), perhaps stand out, but ME is not on present evidence ambitious as an sf writer beyond the task of providing entertainment. [JC]
Other works: *The Alien Earth* (**1971**); *The Everlasting Man* (**1972**); *Down to Earth* (**1973**); *A Different World* (**1974**); *The Seeds of Frenzy* (**1974**); *Centaurian Quest* (**1975**); *The Island of the Dead* (**1975**); *Double Time* (**1976**); *Mindslip* (**1976**); *Oil-Seeker* (**1977**).

ELDRIDGE, PAUL (1888– ?). American teacher of languages and writer, whose sf-fantasy trilogy, written with George Sylvester VIERECK (*who see for details*), is *My First Two Thousand Years: The Autobiography of the Wandering Jew* (**1928**); *Salome: The Wandering Jewess* (**1930**; vt abridged *Salome: 2000 Years of Love*); and *The Invincible Adam* (**1932**) (*see* ADAM AND EVE; IMMORTALITY; ORIGIN OF MAN). [JC]

ELECTRICAL EXPERIMENTS *See* SCIENCE AND INVENTION.

ELGIN, SUZETTE HADEN The form of her name used by poet, author and teacher Patricia A. Suzette Elgin (1936–) for her sf writing. She combines writing and a professional specialization in LINGUISTICS, holding a PhD in linguistics from the University of California, San Diego, and since 1972 has been professor of linguistics, San Diego State University. She began publishing sf in 1969 with "For the Sake of Grace" in *FSF*, later incorporated into *At the Seventh Level* (**1972**) and has published two other novels, *The Communipaths* (**1970**) and *Furthest* (**1971**). All three novels feature the interstellar adventures of Trigalactic Intelligence Service agent Coyote Jones. These novels show a somewhat distressing discrepancy between the ramshackleness of their plots (Coyote has a habit of saving the galaxies as part of the day's work) and the terse eloquence of their descriptions of the meaning-systems of and COMMUNICATION with alien cultures, in which the condition of women (as in *Furthest*) is described with sufficient point to make the books stand as feminist texts. At full stretch, SHE (who has published considerable non-fiction in her speciality) could produce formidable work. [JC]

ELLERMAN, GENE *See* Basil WELLS.

ELLERN, WILLIAM B. *See* E(dward) E(lmer) SMITH.

ELLIK, RON(ALD C.) (1938–68). Computer programmer and author. A well-known sf fan, co-editor with Terry CARR of the HUGO-winning FANZINE, FANAC (1958–61), RE was co-author of *The Universes of E.E. Smith* (**1966**) with Bill EVANS (*who see for details*). Under the joint pseudonym Fredric Davies he wrote with Steve Tolliver *The Man From U.N.C.L.E. 14: The Cross of Gold Affair* (**1968**). RE died in a car accident the day before he was to be married. [PN]

ELLIOT, JOHN (1918–). British writer, primarily for television, who collaborated with Fred HOYLE on two television serials, A FOR ANDROMEDA and ANDROMEDA BREAKTHROUGH, and the subsequent novelizations under the same titles in **1962** and **1964** respectively. He is not to be confused with the John Elliott (note spelling) who wrote the anti-Chinese/Russian political thriller *Dragon's Feast* (**1970**), itself a work of borderline sf. [JC]
See also: COMMUNICATIONS.

ELLIOTT, BRUCE (1915?–73). American writer and editor, active mainly in the sf field in the early 1950s, beginning with "Fearsome Fable" for *FSF* in 1951. His first sf novel, *Asylum Earth* (1952 *Startling Stories*; **1968**), is

routine adventure, as are his others, "So Sweet as Magic" (1953; no book publication), "The Planet of Shame" (1961 *AMZ*; no book publication) and *The Rivet in Grandfather's Neck* (**1970**). [JC]
See also: FOURTH DIMENSION (AND OTHERS).

ELLIOTT, H(ARRY) CHANDLER (1909–?). Now deceased Canadian-born American physician, university teacher of medicine and writer, in whose sf novel, *Reprieve from Paradise* (**1955**), Polynesians have established a world-wide culture after an atomic HOLOCAUST; their civilization is described in sometimes amusing detail, and an Antarctic UTOPIA enters the picture. [JC]
See also: GAMES AND SPORTS; TRANSPORTATION.

ELLIS, CRAIG House name used on *AMZ* by David Vern (*see* David V. REED) and Lee Rogow, 1940–43.

ELLIS, D.E. (?–). English writer, briefly active in the early 1960s with "Stress" for *NW* in 1961 and *A Thousand Ages* (**1961**). a routine novel. [JC]

ELLIS, EDWARD S. (1840–1916). American teacher, writer and editor, author of a very large number of American DIME NOVELS, mainly Westerns, under his own name and many pseudonyms. His sf novel, *The Steam Man of the Prairies* (**1865**; vt *The Huge Hunter*; vt *Baldy's Boy Partner, or Young Brainerd's Steam Man*), was the first story to bring sf into the dime-novel market; it became one of its many exploited genres. ESE wrote no further sf. *The Steam Man* has been conveniently reprinted in E.F. BLEILER's *Eight Dime Novels* (anth. **1974**) with a full introduction to the field. [JC]

ELLISON, HARLAN (JAY) (1934–). American writer, the most controversial and among the finest sf writers of the

generation whose careers began in the mid-1950s. He was born and raised in Ohio, attending Ohio State University for 18 months before being asked to leave, one of the reasons for his dismissal being rudeness to the creative writing professor who told him he had no talent. He had already become deeply involved in Cleveland fandom, producing material for and later taking over the Cleveland SF Society's magazine, *Science-Fantasy Bulletin* (later *Dimensions*). His near contemporary, Robert SILVERBERG, vividly portrays the young HE in his profile contributed to the *FSF* Special Harlan Ellison Issue (Jul. 1977); according to him, HE was insecure, physically fearless, extraordinarily ambitious, hyperkinetic, and dominated any room he was in. Much the same could be said about the short stories with which he has made his name, both in sf circles and beyond, and for which he has won a remarkable number of HUGO and NEBULA awards, for they are highly personal, and reflect their author's character, concerns and immediate position.

By 1955 HE was in New York, producing numerous stories, having great difficulty selling for most of that year, though his first sf professional appearance came early in 1956 with "Glowworm" in *Infinity Science Fiction*, and from that point he began to publish very prolifically indeed, with well over 150 stories and pieces by the end of 1958. Much of this early production is coarse and derivative, mixing strong early influences like Nelson Algren with models derived from successful magazine sf writers of the time: in these early years, HE used a number of pseudonyms: in fanzines Nalrah Nosille: in short stories in crime, sex and other genre magazines Sley Harson (in collaboration with Henry SLESAR), Landon Ellis, Derry Tiger, Price Curtis and Paul Merchant; in sf magazines the house names Lee ARCHER (one story), E.K. JARVIS (one story), Ivar JORGENSEN (one story), Clyde MITCHELL (one story) and the personal pseudonyms Ellis Hart, Jay Solo, Jay Charby, Wallace Edmondson, and from 1957 Cordwainer Bird, a name which since 1964 he has been using to designate material that (generally through conflict with TV producers) he wishes to disclaim in its televised form.

After a short time in New York, HE assumed a false identity and ran as a member of a gang from Red Hook, Brooklyn, called the Barons; his 10-week stint gained him material which he used directly in the first of his infrequent novels, *Rumble* (**1958**; vt *Web of the City*) which, though not sf, early demonstrates, in the vigour and violence of its urban imagery, the ambivalent hold of the CITY on his imagination. HE is one of the relatively few sf writers to deal constantly and impassionedly with the modern American city. Further material drawn from contemporary urban life may be found in *The Deadly Streets* (coll. **1958**; exp. by four stories and an introduction, 1975), *The Juvies* (coll. **1961**), *Gentleman Junkie and Other Stories of the Hung-up Generation* (coll. **1961**; some stories rev., two removed, one added, 1975), and *Rockabilly* (**1961**; vt *Spider Kiss*); also the autobiographical street-gang study *Memos from Purgatory: Two Journeys of Our Times* (**1961**); none of this material is technically sf, but HE has consistently deprecated the making of distinctions between generic and non-generic writing in his own works, and a later volume, *Love Ain't Nothing But Sex Misspelled* (coll. **1968**; nine stories removed and an introduction, one story and two articles added, 1976), mixed sf and non-sf in its first version, though the second edition has removed most of the former material, stories like "Pretty Maggie Moneyeyes" (1967), which had already appeared elsewhere, being transferred to a more specifically sf context, as will be described below.

HE was drafted in 1957. After his army discharge in 1959, he moved to Chicago as editor of *Rogue Magazine*, where later he was also involved in the creation of Regency Books; by 1962 he was in Los Angeles, where he has remained. During this time, although he wrote for many markets, he was beginning to establish a maverick reputation within sf, and began to release specifically sf books. His first sf novel, *The Man with Nine Lives* (1959 *AMZ* as "The Sound of a Scythe"; **1960**), appeared simultaneously, in an ACE Double, with his first sf collection, *A Touch of Infinity* (coll. **1960**); both showed more promise than fulfilment, and display HE's unease with the demands of late 1950s magazine fiction. *Ellison Wonderland* (coll. **1962**; vt *Earthman, Go Home* 1964; new intro, with "The Forces that Crush" deleted and "Back to the Drawing Boards" added, 1974) is still uneasy, containing stories whose violent rhetoric tends not to be contained by their conventional form. HE was still very much feeling his way; of major sf writers, he has been perhaps the slowest to find his proper voice, if one takes Robert Silverberg's disappointing first decade as a more deliberate (and more successful) attempt to write within chosen markets until he could afford to take more care.

HE's stories seldom fitted into the series pattern, but, although characters do not recur from story to story, there is one early quasi-series of stories all set during a future war between Earth and the Kyben. The best-known of these is the TV script "Demon With a Glass Hand" (1964, *see below*); other stories include "Life Hutch" (1956), "Trojan Hearse" (1956), "The Crackpots" (1956), "Yellow Streak Hero" (1957; vt "Night Vigil"), "Run for the Stars" (1957) and "Sleeping Dogs" (1974).

HE has never been cautious. His first years in Hollywood were difficult but ultimately rewarding. After much struggling, by 1963 he had established himself as a successful television writer, contributing scripts to such series as *Route 66*, *The Alfred Hitchcock Hour* and *The Untouchables*, with considerable work for *Burke's Law*. Of greater interest to sf readers would be his two scripts for THE OUTER LIMITS in 1964, two scripts for *The Man from U.N.C.L.E.* in 1966 and '67, and the STAR TREK episode "The City on the Edge of Forever" (1967). This won a Hugo award for best dramatic presentation in 1968 and a Writers' Guild of America award for most outstanding script, dramatic episode, of 1967–8. The original script, rather different from the filmed version, was published in *Six Science Fiction Plays* (**1976**) ed. Roger ELWOOD. Probably his most memorable script was "Demon With a Glass Hand" (1964) for *Outer Limits*, which won the Writers' Guild of America award for outstanding script. (A much more recent foray into television by HE became something of a fiasco — his attempt to create a TV series based around the concept of a GENERATION STARSHIP. The series, *The Starlost*, was Canadian-made and lasted only one season, 1973. So many changes were made to HE's original concept that he disowned the programme, signing the pilot episode with his derisory pseudonym, Cordwainer Bird. The original script, not the one that was filmed, received a Writers' Guild of America award for best dramatic episode script (HE is the only scenarist to have won the award three times), and was later published in *Faster Than Light*, anth. **1976**, ed. Jack DANN and George ZEBROWSKI. The novelization of the script was *Phoenix Without Ashes*, **1975**, by HE with Edward BRYANT. A thinly disguised account of the whole affair formed the plot of the *roman à clef* by Ben BOVA, *The Starcrossed*, **1975**.)

At around the same time that HE began his television career, he began publishing the short stories that have made his name. Many of them appear in the books of the late 1960s: *Paingod and Other Delusions* (coll. **1965**; new introduction and new story, "Sleeping Dogs", 1975); *I Have No Mouth and I Must Scream* (coll. **1967**); *From the Land of Fear* (coll. **1967**); *Love Ain't Nothing But Sex Misspelled* (*see above*); *The Beast that Shouted Love at the Heart of the World* (coll. **1969**; Avon edition has corrupt text, Book Club edition has authorized text, UK editions delete "Along the Scenic Route", "The Place With No Name" and "Shattered Like a Glass Goblin" 1976); *Over the Edge: Stories from Somewhere Else* (coll. **1970**); and *Alone Against Tomorrow: Stories of Alienation in Speculative Fiction* (coll. **1971**; UK edition split into two vols, *All the Sounds of Fear*, **1973**, and *The Time of the Eye*, **1974**, the latter containing a

new introduction). This last collection is a good summary of HE's best 1960s work, as it contains the cream of the earlier collections.

It was in these years that HE began to amass his numerous awards, six and a half Hugos and three Nebulas to date: a Hugo and Nebula short-story award in 1966 for " 'Repent, Harlequin!' Said the Ticktockman" (1965); a 1968 Hugo (short story) for "I Have No Mouth and I Must Scream" (1967); a 1969 Hugo (short story) for "The Beast that Shouted Love at the Heart of the World" (1968); a 1974 Hugo for best novelette for "The Deathbird" (1973); a 1969 Nebula for best novella, "A Boy and his Dog" (1969). This last was made into a successful film (*see* A BOY AND HIS DOG) which was awarded a 1976 Hugo for best dramatic presentation, which HE shared. HE also won a 1975 Hugo for best novelette for "Adrift Just off the Islets of Langerhans, Latitude 38° 54' N, Longitude 77° 00' 13" W", an Edgar award from the Mystery Writers of America for "The Whimper of Whipped Dogs" (1973) and a 1978 Nebula for best short story for "Jeffty is Five". He also began editing his famous series of controversial NEW WAVE sf stories with DANGEROUS VISIONS (anth. **1967**) and *Again, Dangerous Visions* (anth. **1972**); the much delayed *The Last Dangerous Visions* awaits publication. The first of these had a great influence on sf publishing (*see* ANTHOLOGIES). Both anthologies received Special Achievement awards at the world CONVENTION the following year.

Through these activities HE became perhaps the most discussed writer of sf short stories ever, and with cause. Stories like those given awards finally succeed in containing his enormous energies as a writer, allowing his impassioned concern for authentic human life to express itself in savage parables of its destruction by the regimenting momentum of the late 20th century, by organized hypocrisy and bad faith and derangement; but also in stories depicting the refusal of the individual human spirit to knuckle under. He uses, with great facility, all the language of sf to formalize and dramatize these underlying concerns, though few of the stories can be neatly pigeon-holed as genre sf or fantasy, and he properly resents attempts to do so.

HE has been criticized for recycling his best stories so that they appear in several collections, though it is obvious from the reissues of 11 titles in the Pyramid Books uniform series, 1975–6, that he has gone to some lengths to correct this problem. It is true that the collections do overlap, though if the two main retrospectives, *Alone Against Tomorrow* and *Deathbird Stories* (*see below*) which themselves overlap, are removed from consideration, then the doubling up is relatively minor.

HE has also edited the "Harlan Ellison 'Discovery' Series", which to date has four "first" books: *Stormtrack* (**1974**) by James Sutherland, *Autumn Angels* (**1975**) by Arthur Byron COVER, *The Light at the End of the Universe* (coll. **1976**) by Terry CARR and *Involution Ocean* (**1977**) by Bruce Sterling.

HE has in recent years become increasingly articulate about the nature of his fiction. *Approaching Oblivion: Road Signs on the Treadmill Toward Tomorrow* (coll. **1974**) contains a moving autobiographical analysis of the roots of his writing; and his definitive *Deathbird Stories: A Pantheon of Modern Gods* (coll. **1975**) reassembles many of his best stories into a kind of cycle about Man's relation to the gods and horrors within and without him. It is here that "Pretty Maggie Moneyeyes", for instance, which may be his most moving tale, is again reprinted. In it, a quasi-delusional rapport between a gambler and the female spirit trapped within a slot machine turns into an exposition of the sadnesses and traps that exist between people, lovers, Man and his world. Often expressed crudely, sometimes hysterically, but frequently with a searing rightness of language and form, it is these concerns that have made HE, once a somewhat monstrous prodigy, into the writer of stature he has become; that his fame comes almost solely through his short stories only underlines his achievement. [JC/PN]
Other works: *Doomsman* (1958 *Imagination Science Fiction* as "The Assassin"; 1967); *Partners in Wonder: Harlan Ellison in Collaboration with ...* (coll. **1971**, collaborations with various writers); *No Doors, No Windows* (coll. **1975**); *Strange Wine* (coll. **1978**). Non-fiction: *The Glass Teat: Essays of Opinion on the Subject of Television* (coll. 1969; new introduction 1975); *The Other Glass Teat: Further Essays of Opinion on Television* (coll. **1975**). HE has edited a collection of Gerald KERSH stories, *Nightshade and Damnations* (coll. 1968).
About the author: *FSF* Special Harlan Ellison Issue (Jul. 1977); *Harlan Ellison: Unrepentant Harlequin* by George Edgar Slusser (**1977**); *Harlan Ellison: A Bibliographical Checklist* (**1973**) compiled by Leslie Kay Swigart. The latter title is unusually thorough and comprehensive.
See also: ABSURDIST SF; AUTOMATION; CHILDREN IN SF; COMPUTERS; CRIME AND PUNISHMENT; CYBORGS; ESCHATOLOGY; FANTASY; GAMES AND SPORTS; HISTORY OF SF; HOLOCAUST AND AFTER; INVISIBILITY; MACHINES; MESSIAHS; MYTHOLOGY; OPTIMISM AND PESSIMISM; PSYCHOLOGY; RELIGION; SEX; SOCIOLOGY; SUPERNATURAL CREATURES; TABOOS; TRANSPORTATION.

ELSTAR, DOW See Raymond Z. GALLUN.

ELWOOD, ROGER (1933–). American editor. After producing a number of reprint anthologies in the 1960s (some in collaboration with Sam MOSKOWITZ) RE burst into prominence in the early 1970s when, with indefatigable salesmanship, he sold a huge number of original anthologies — about 80 in all, according to his claim — to a variety of publishers. (This total includes a number of short books for younger children.) At one time it was estimated that RE alone constituted about a quarter of the total market for sf short stories, and such dominance led to criticism of his restrictions on SEX and RELIGION as themes. Notable among his many anthologies were *Future City* (anth. 1973), *Saving Worlds* (anth. **1973**, in collaboration with Virginia Kidd; vt *The Wounded Planet*), the four volumes of *Continuum* (anths **1974–5**) — which featured eight different four-part series — and *Epoch* (anth. **1975**, in collaboration with Robert SILVERBERG). He also edited the books *The Many Worlds of Poul Anderson* (coll. **1974**) and *The Many Worlds of Andre Norton* (coll. **1974**). RE was also responsible for the short-lived magazine ODYSSEY, the LASER BOOKS series and *Starstream Comics* (1976). Later, as the oversaturated anthology market contracted, he diversified into editing sf lines of various publishers — Bobbs-Merrill, Pinnacle and Pyramid, in addition to Laser. A devout Christian, RE has also written evangelical and inspirational works. [MJE]
Other works: (as editor in each case): *Alien Worlds* (anth. **1964**); *Invasion of the Robots* (anth. **1965**); *Other Worlds, Other Times* (anth. **1969**, with Sam Moskowitz); *The Little Monsters* (anth. **1969**, with Vic Ghidalia); *Beware the Beasts* (anth. **1970**, with Vic Ghidalia); *The Horror Hunters* (anth. **1971**, with Vic Ghidalia); *The Young Demons* (anth. **1971**, with Vic Ghidalia); *Signs and Wonders* (anth. **1972**); *And Walk Now Gently Through the Fire* (anth. **1972**); *The Venus Factor* (anth. **1972**, with Vic Ghidalia); *Androids, Time Machines and Blue Giraffes* (anth. **1973**, with Vic Ghidalia); *The Demon Kind* (anth. **1973**); *Frontiers I: Tomorrow's Alternatives* (anth. **1973**); *Frontiers II: The New Mind* (anth. **1973**); *Monster Tales: Vampires, Werewolves and Things* (anth. **1973**); *Omega* (anth. **1973**); *The Other Side of Tomorrow* (anth. **1973**); *Science Fiction Tales: Invaders, Creatures and Alien Worlds* (anth. **1973**); *Showcase* (anth. **1973**); *Strange Things Happening* (anth. **1973**); *Children of Infinity* (anth. **1973**); *The Graduated Robot* (anth. **1973**); *Night of the Sphinx* (anth. **1973**); *Flame-Tree Planet* (anth. **1973**); *Ten Tomorrows* (anth. **1973**); *The Berserkers* (anth. **1974**); *Adrift in Space* (anth. **1974**); *Chronicles of a Comer* (anth. **1974**); *Crisis* (anth. **1974**); *The Extraterrestials* (anth. **1974**); *Future Kin* (anth. **1974**); *Horror Tales: Spirits, Spells and the Unknown* (anth. **1974**); *The Graduated Robot and Other Stories* (anth. **1974**); *Journey to Another Star* (anth. **1974**); *The Killer Plants* (anth. **1974**); *The Learning Maze* (anth. **1974**); *The Mind Angel* (anth. **1974**); *The Missing World* (anth. **1974**); *More Science Fiction Tales: Crystal Creatures, Bird-Things and other Weirdies* (anth. **1974**); *Night of the Sphinx and Other Stories* (anth. **1974**); *Survival From Infinity* (anth. **1974**); *The Tunnel* (anth. **1974**); *The Far Side of Time* (anth. **1974**); *The Long Night of Waiting* (anth. **1974**); *Strange Gods* (anth. **1974**); *Dystopian Visions* (anth. **1975**); *Future Corruption* (anth. **1975**); *The Gifts of Asti* (anth. **1975**); *In The Wake of Man* (anth. **1975**); *Tomorrow: New Worlds of Science Fiction* (anth. **1975**); *The 50 Meter Monster and Other Horrors* (anth. **1976**); *Six Science Fiction Plays* (anth. **1976**); *Visions of Tomorrow* (anth. **1976**); *Futurelove* (anth. **1977**); *A World Named Cleopatra* (anth. **1977**).

ELY, DAVID (1927–). American journalist and writer of such PSYCHOLOGICAL thrillers as *The Tour* (1967). Some of the stories in *Time Out* (coll. 1968) contain fantasy elements. His sf novel, *Seconds* (1963), had some initial success and was made into the film SECONDS in 1966, starring and financed by Rock Hudson. An organization transforms middle-aged men into young, Rock-Hudson-like he-men; at first the change is exciting, but soon the nightmares start. [JC]

EMBRYO Film (1976). Cine Artists. Directed by Ralph Nelson, starring Rock Hudson, Diane Ladd, Barbara Carrera and Roddy McDowall. Screenplay by Anita Doohan and Jack W. Thomas, based on a story by Jack W. Thomas. 105 mins. Colour.

In this variation on the FRANKENSTEIN theme, a scientist, while experimenting on a premature foetus with a growth hormone, ends up with a fully developed 25-year-old woman. Though physically mature, she has a virtually blank mind, and it becomes the scientist's task to mould her personality. Whether because of flaws in the conditioning he gives her, or for other more fundamental reasons, the result is a totally amoral creature who must eventually be destroyed for the good of all concerned. Despite its modern hardware, the film is really a reworking of the old GOTHIC theme about the basic evil of beings who are created by unnatural means and are therefore without souls. *E* has more in common with such German films as HOMUNCULUS and *Alraune*, (which, based on the novel by Hans Heinz EWERS, is also about a girl, born through artificial insemination, who is raised by a scientist) than with modern sf. The novelization is *Embryo* (1976) by Louis CHARBONNEAU. [JB]

EMERSON, WILLIS GEORGE (1856–1918). American writer, mostly of Westerns, whose LOST-RACE novel *The Smoky God; or, A Voyage to the Inner World* (**1908**) is set underground in a hollow land, purportedly Eden, within the Earth (*see* ANTHROPOLOGY).   [JC]

EMIGRATION FROM EARTH *See* COLONIZATION OF OTHER WORLDS; GALACTIC EMPIRES.

EMSH, ED Pseudonym of Edmund Alexander Emshwiller (1925–), American illustrator and film-maker. Graduated, majoring in art, from the University of Michigan. A brilliant stylist, Emsh is best known in the sf field for his covers for *Galaxy* (from 1951) and ACE BOOKS; he has also done prolific colour and b/w work for *Planet Stories, Space Stories, The Magazine of Fantasy and Science Fiction, Vanguard Science Fiction, Super-Science Fiction, Rocket Stories, Venture Science Fiction* and many others. He did all but the first cover of *Infinity Science Fiction*. He and Frank Kelly FREAS were by far the most popular sf illustrators of the 1950s, Emsh was nominated for eight Hugos and won five times in his 13 years in sf, in 1953, 1960, 1961, 1962 and 1964. Like Edd CARTIER, Emsh had a flair for humour and often turned out witty covers without resorting to cartooning or over-exaggeration; many of his *Galaxy* covers are good examples of this. He was good at conventional drama, too. His style is smooth, colourful and distinctive, and his covers can readily be picked out from a crowd of others. His b/w illustrations were reminiscent of Edd Cartier's in style but not in execution; where Cartier's lines were smooth, Emsh's were rough and had more character. His wife, the author Carol EMSHWILLER, often acted as his model.

Emsh became interested in experimental film-making in the late 1950s, and his first film, *Dance Chromatic* (1959), won an Award of Exceptional Merit in the same year. In 1964 he quit sf to work in experimental videotapes, a field where he has won several more awards. His 38-minute *Relativity* (1966) is regarded by many critics as one of the greatest short films ever made. His films and tapes have been selected for showing at the Museum of Modern Art, and on American Public Broadcasting Systems *Video Visionaries* and *VTR* series.   [JG/PN]

EMSHWILLER, CAROL (?–). American writer, wife of illustrator and film-maker Ed EMSHWILLER, with whom she has collaborated. She began publishing sf with "This Thing Called Love" for *Future* in 1955, and has been associated with *FSF* since that time. Many of her best stories are included in *Joy in our Cause* (coll. **1974**). Her work is frequently experimental and sometimes elusive, but also witty and observant. It tends to the fantasy end of the sf spectrum.   [JC/PN]

EMSHWILLER, EDMUND ALEXANDER *See* Ed EMSH.

END OF AUGUST AT THE HOTEL OZONE, THE *See* KONEC SRPNA V HOTELU OZON.

END OF THE WORLD, THE Together with UTOPIAS and cautionary tales, apocalyptic visions form one of the three principal traditions of pre-20th-century futuristic fantasy. Visions inspired by the religious imagination go back into antiquity (*see* MYTHOLOGY *and* RELIGION) but the influence of the scientific imagination did not make itself felt in literature until the late 19th century, and the end-of-the-world theme maintained many of its religious overtones until very recently. The phrase itself has become rather loose in meaning — the idea of the end of the world could be quite specific when the world itself was seen as essentially unchanging, governed solely by the divine will, but, once change became accepted and the Comte du Buffon's *Epochs of Nature* (**1780**) had popularized the notion that a whole series of "worlds" had occupied the Earth's surface, the finality of any particular end of the world became dubious. A spectrum extends, therefore, from apocalyptic visions to DISASTER stories, and it is difficult to draw a dividing line; it would be over-pedantic to construe "world" as "planet".

The earliest scientific romances of world's end are the products of Romanticism: De Grainville's anti-progressive *The Last Man: or Omegarus and Syderia* (**1806**) and Mary SHELLEY's gloomy Great Plague story *The Last Man* (**1826**). Plagues were to remain one of the standard literary means of depopulating the world and destroying society, but a particular favourite of scientific romancers is the cosmic disaster, introduced by Edgar Allan POE in "The Conversation of Eiros and Charmion" (1839). All these are NEAR-FUTURE stories, but as realization grew of the actual age of the Earth and the nature of the processes which changed it — popularized by Lyell's *Principles of Geology* (**1830**) — stories based on a more acute scientific understanding began to appear. Two classics of this kind appeared within a year of one another: Camille FLAMMARION's *Omega* (trans. **1894**) and H.G. WELLS's *The Time Machine* (**1895**); though it was not until much later that Olaf STAPLEDON provided a comprehensive account of the life and death of Man and his domain in *Last and First Men* (**1930**).

Wells offered several versions of the end of the world, including the cosmic disaster story "The Star" (1897) and the apocalyptic satire "A Vision of Judgment" (1899). For much of his life he believed that if a new world were to be built the old would have to be destroyed, and thus there is a persistent apocalyptic vein in his writing. This is offset by the fact that whether he was writing grim stories of atomic war — *The World Set Free* (**1914**) — or satirical accounts of a new Noah — *All Aboard for Ararat* (**1940**) — he remained committed to the idea that Man must have a second chance. Only *The Time Machine* and the despairing *Mind at the End of its Tether* (**1945**) give way entirely to anxiety.

Wells's contemporaries were a little less fascinated by apocalyptic possibilities, but many indulged themselves at least once in the spectacular possibilities of doom. The passing of a comet destroys the Earth's surface in George GRIFFITH's *Olga Romanoff* (**1894**), though the heroes hide out underground. A similar refuge is sought when the sun cools rapidly in

In this typical cover by Ed EMSH the original June 1957 version of *Science Fiction Adventures* shows a pile of corpses; these have been expurgated in the British reprint edition on the right.

Underground Man (**1896** France; trans **1905**) by Gabriel DE TARDE. In M.P. SHIEL's *The Purple Cloud* (**1901**) the Earth is depopulated by a cloud of cyanogen gas. William Hope HODGSON's *The House on the Borderland* (**1908**) stands aloof from such trivial issues as the end of Man to become pure cosmic vision, while James Elroy Flecker's "The Last Generation" (**1908**) has humanity pass into extinction without even a whimper by the simple decision not to procreate. This same period around the turn of the century also witnessed an upsurge in religious fantasy with an apocalyptic theme (and also personal ESCHATOLOGICAL fantasies). The most notable is R.H. BENSON's *Lord of the World* (**1907**).

The end of the world proved to have distinct limitations as a theme in popular literature. It had fine melodramatic qualities, but the conclusion in which the chosen few set out to begin a new world (*see* ADAM AND EVE) very quickly became a cliché. In order to infuse new dramatic potential there grew up a variant of the theme, in which the end of the world is foreseen and those armed with foresight set out to guard against eventualities (usually derided by their neighbours — but they laughed at Noah, too). Examples of the variant include *The Second Deluge* (**1912**) by Garrett P. SERVISS, *Nordenholt's Million* (**1923**) by J.J. CONNINGTON, *When Worlds Collide* (**1933**) by Philip WYLIE and Edwin BALMER and "Ark of Fire" (**1937-8**; *Famous Fantastic Mysteries* 1943) by John Hawkins. It is amply represented in modern sf by stories in which only a few are able to escape atomic war in the shelters or escape into space when the sun goes nova, e.g. *Death of a World* (**1948**) by J.J. FARJEON and *One in Three Hundred* (**1954**) by J.T. McINTOSH. A rather more subtle version of this same variant explores the effect on various characters of the knowledge that the world will end. An early example is Hugh KINGSMILL's curious piece "The End of the World" (1924), and more recent examples are "The Last Night of the World" (1951) by Ray BRADBURY, "The Last Day" (1953) by Richard MATHESON and *On the Beach* (**1957**) by Nevil SHUTE.

The early sf pulps featured several visions of the end of the human race, and of the Earth itself, including Donald WANDREI's lurid "The Red Brain" (1927), Amelia Long's "Omega" (1932) and L.H. Morrow's "Omega — the Man" (1933). Many writers, however, were confident that Man could outlast the Earth, if necessary, and need not be unduly troubled by disasters. In the face of this confidence apocalyptic feeling soon lost its force in magazine sf. Man leaves the death of Earth behind him in John W. CAMPBELL Jr's "Voice of the Void" (1930) and in Arthur C. CLARKE's supremely smug "Rescue Party" (1946). The latter author's "Nine Billion Names of God"

(1953), on the contrary, is an end-of-the-world story that attacks the smugness of Western man. Edmond HAMILTON's "Requiem" (1962) is a poignant story which regrets the commercial exploitation of the Earth's death as a spectacular TV show for a galaxy-wide audience.

It was in the 1930s that the idea emerged that we ourselves might destroy the world as weapons of war become more technologically advanced, an early novel advancing this notion being *Unthinkable* (**1933**) by Francis H. SIBSON. The "ultimate deterrent" or "Doomsday weapon" was introduced (and quickly used) in *The Last Man* (**1940**; *vt No Other Man* USA) by Alfred NOYES. The anxiety reflected here was not unrealistic. A particularly extreme example is Alfred BESTER's "Adam and No Eve" (1941), in which the destruction is so drastic that the customary new beginning has to be a whole new evolutionary sequence beginning in the sea. After the War, of course, this species of apocalypse became dominant as the possibility of atomic holocaust lent a new pertinence to apocalyptic thinking. Suddenly it seemed entirely likely that the world would end with a bang and not a whimper after all, despite the broad sexual pun in the title of Damon KNIGHT's last-man-meets-last-woman story, "Not with a Bang" (1950). Notable examples of atomic holocaust stories include *Shadow on the Hearth* (**1950**) by Judith MERRIL, *The Long Loud Silence* (**1952**) by Wilson TUCKER and *Level 7* (**1959**) by Mordecai ROSHWALD (*see* HOLOCAUST AND AFTER). A sign of the depth of the anxiety is the rapid proliferation of satires and black comedies featuring apocalypses precipitated by carelessness, including Ward MOORE's *Greener than You Think* (**1947**), L. Sprague DE CAMP's "Judgment Day" (1955), Kurt VONNEGUT Jr's *Cat's Cradle* (**1963**) and *Dr. Strangelove* (**1963**) by Peter GEORGE. Sf writers produced scores of ironically despairing vignettes, including "A Pail of Air" (1951), "The Moon is Green" (1952) and "A Bad Day for Sales" (1953), all by Fritz LEIBER. Uncompromisingly downbeat stories whose temper is most unusual for a pulp-descended genre include Robert HEINLEIN's "Year of the Jackpot" (1952), E.C. TUBB's "Tomorrow" (1954) and Robert SILVERBERG's "Road to Nightfall" (1958). The 1950s also produced sf's boldest apocalyptic novel: James BLISH's *The Triumph of Time* (**1958**; *vt A Clash of Cymbals* UK).

The same pattern of ironic despair, satire and grimly pessimistic "realism" extended into the 1960s and '70s, when many more rationalizations for the sensation of imminent doom began to appear, including OVERPOPULATION and POLLUTION. Notable black comedies include *The Genocides* (**1965**) by Thomas M. DISCH and "The Big Flash" (1969) by Norman SPINRAD. Ironic tales include

"And Us, Too, I Guess" (1973) by George Alec EFFINGER and "When We Went to See the End of the World" (1972) by Robert Silverberg. A savage sense of despair is evident in "We All Die Naked" (1969) by James Blish and *The End of the Dream* (**1972**) by Philip Wylie. Outside the genre a number of surreal apocalyptic visions appeared, notably in *Up and Out* (coll. **1957**) by John Cowper Powys and *Ice* (**1967**) by Anna KAVAN. One innovative story worth noting — not without irony — is Poul ANDERSON's *After Doomsday* (**1962**), the first ever "whodunit" in which the corpse is the planet Earth. Also deserving mention is a particularly ingenious cosmic disaster story, "Inconstant Moon" (1971) by Larry NIVEN, in which a sudden increase in the Moon's brightness reveals to those who can deduce its meaning the possibility that the Sun has gone nova and that dawn will bring destruction.

The cosmic vision story has become almost extinct in post-War sf as the terms in which we conceive of the end of the world have virtually reverted to those of 150 years ago — it is once again a near future affair. The main difference is that in the past it was the divine will which would decide when and how the world would end, and God could always be relied on to pick the chosen few wisely. Now that Man is generally assumed to be in control of his own destiny it is much more difficult to be confident of the calibre of the chosen, or even to be sure that anyone will survive. Though the Millenarian feeling which saturates modern sf is by no means new, the anxiety that goes with it has a new element within it. We are no longer optimistic regarding the salvation that we should like to believe in.

A theme anthology is *The End of the World* (anth. **1956**) ed. Donald WOLLHEIM. [BS]

See also: ENTROPY; FAR FUTURE.

ENDORE, GUY S. (1900-70). American writer and translator most noted for his realistic FANTASY novels, some of which can in a marginal sense be considered as sf (*see* PSYCHOLOGY). The best known is *The Werewolf of Paris* (**1933**), the climax of which is set in the shambles of 1870 Paris, where a French soldier is succumbing to lycanthropy, his victims young women. *Methinks the Lady* (**1945**; *vt The Furies in Her Body; vt Nightmare*), ostensibly a mystery story, ultimately turns out to be dealing with a female Jekyll-and-Hyde situation in Freudian terms. Though of relatively little influence on the sf field, GSE was a highly effective purveyor of sexual fantasies; he did not mince words. He collaborated on the scripts of the films THE DEVIL DOLL and MAD LOVE (a version of THE HANDS OF ORLAC). [JC]

Other works: *The Man from Limbo* (**1930**).

See also: SUPERNATURAL CREATURES.

ENEMY FROM SPACE *See* QUATERMASS II.

ENERGUMEN Canadian FANZINE (1970–73), ed., from Toronto, Mike Glicksohn and Susan Wood. Though printed on a duplicator, in common with most fanzines, it was noted for the quality of its appearance and attracted original illustrations from many fan and sf artists, including Alicia Austin, Tim Kirk, Jack GAUGHAN and Vincent DI FATE. The written material ranged through sf, FANDOM, and general topics, and maintained a high standard with contributions from well-known fan and sf writers, including Robert SILVERBERG, Greg BENFORD, Bob SHAW and Avram DAVIDSON. Despite its limited circulation, *E* won the HUGO award for best fanzine in 1973. [PR]

ENERGY *See* COSMOLOGY; ENTROPY; NUCLEAR POWER; POWER SOURCES; PHYSICS; SUN.

ENGDAHL, SYLVIA (LOUISE) (1933–). American writer, employed in the field of computer programming 1957–67; her novels, though marketed as "juveniles", are intelligent, not patronizing, and likely to appeal to adults also. *Enchantress from the Stars* (1970), with its sequel *The Far Side of Evil* (1971), are perhaps her best-known works; the first describes, with suggestive analogues between traditional and technological versions of crucial events (to a savage all technology is magic), the career of the significantly female protagonist, Elena, who is in the Anthropological Service; the second continues Elena's career, more predictably, in a totalitarian DYSTOPIA. In neither world is she permitted to reveal her identity. A second series consists of *This Star shall Abide* (1972; vt *Heritage of the Star* UK) and *Beyond the Tomorrow Mountains* (1973). The societal design in these books, set on a planet with an imposed RELIGION, is interesting. [JC/PN]
Other works: *Journey Between Worlds* (1970). As editor: *The Universe Ahead: Stories of the Future* (anth. 1975) with Rick Roberson; *Anywhere, Anywhere: Stories of Tomorrow* (anth. 1976). Non-fiction: *The Planet-Girded Suns: Man's View of Other Solar Systems* (1974); *The Subnuclear Zoo: New Discoveries in High Energy Physics* (1977) with Rick Roberson.

ENGEL, LEONARD (1916–). American author, with Emanuel S. PILLER, of the dreadful-warning novel *The World Aflame: The Russian-American War of 1950* (1947), in which America's monopoly of the A-bomb proves insufficient to hold the red hordes adequately in check. He also edited the non-fiction anthology *New Worlds of Modern Science* (anth. 1956). [JC]

See also: POLITICS.

ENGEL, LYLE KENYON (? –). American editor and writer. Under his own name he edited SPACE SCIENCE FICTION MAGAZINE (Spring and Aug. 1957) and the companion magazine *Tales of the Frightened*, linked to the radio series featuring Boris Karloff, also Spring and Aug. 1957. Under the pseudonym Jeffrey Lord he is reputed to have written some or all of the routine but long-lasting "Richard Blade" series of HEROIC-FANTASY adventure romances: *1. The Bronze Axe* (1969); *2. The Jade Warrior* (1969); *3. Jewel of Tharn* (1969); *4. Slave of Sarma* (1970); *5. Liberator of Jedd* (1971); *6. Monster of the Maze* (1972); *7. Pearl of Patmos* (1973); *8. Undying World* (1973); *9. Kingdom of Royth* (1974); *10. Ice Dragon* (1974); *11. Dimension of Dreams* (1974); *12. King of Zunga* (1975); *13. The Golden Steed* (1975); *14. The Temples of Ayocan* (1975); *15. The Towers of Melnon* (1975); *16. The Crystal Seas* (1975); *17. Mountain of Brega* (1976); *18. Warlords of Gaikin* (1976); *19. Looters of Tharn* (1976); *20. Guardians of the Coral Throne* (1976); *21. Champion of the Gods* (1976); *22. The Forests of Gleor* (1977); *23. Empire of Blood* (1977); *24. The Dragons of Englor* (1977); *25. The Torian Pearls* (1977). [PN]
See also: SWORD AND SORCERY.

ENGELHARDT, FREDERICK *See* L. Ron HUBBARD.

ENGH, M(ARY) J(ANE) (1933–). American librarian and writer, whose first sf novel is *Arslan* (1976). It deals violently with an enigmatic world conqueror from Turkestan in the NEAR FUTURE and his relationship with the inhabitants of the small Illinois town he selects as his headquarters. [JC/PN]

ENGINEERING *See* DISCOVERY AND INVENTION; MACHINES; TECHNOLOGY; TRANSPORT.

ENGLAND, GEORGE ALLAN (1877–1936). American author and explorer. He wrote quite extensively in the sf field, his works appearing predominantly in the Frank A. MUNSEY magazines. He wrote five sf hardcover novels and about 20 other sf serials and short stories. Although he was one of the more important writers for the pre-1926 PULP MAGAZINES, ranking as the closest rival in sf to Edgar Rice BURROUGHS, his stories were often derivative of others: his two serials "The House of Transformation" (1909) and "The Nebula of Death" (1918), and his short story "The Thing from Outside" (1923) are reminiscent of earlier works by H.G. WELLS, Garrett P. SERVISS, and Fitz-James O'BRIEN, respectively.

Several themes are prominent in his writings. IMMORTALITY and the elixir of

youth appear in "My Time-Annihilator" (1909) and in his LOST-WORLD serial "Beyond White Seas" (1909–10), occurring again in another serial, "The Elixir of Hate" (1911). His strong belief in socialism appeared in the anti-capitalist stances of *The Air Trust* (1915) and *The Golden Blight* (1912 *Cavalier*; 1916); the one centered on a monopoly on air, the other on a ray which destroys the world's gold-stocks. This latter work contains strong racist overtones, as does his best-regarded work, *Darkness and Dawn* (1912–13, *Cavalier*; fix-up 1914; edited version in five vols 1964–7: *Darkness and Dawn*, 1964, *Beyond the Great Oblivion*, 1965, *The People of the Abyss*, 1967, *Out of the Abyss*, 1967, *The Afterglow*, 1967), a post-HOLOCAUST novel set in a devastated America.

More original in their conception are "The Empire of the Air" (1914), a serialized novel of invasion from the FOURTH DIMENSION; "June 6, 2016" (1916), a story of the emancipation of WOMEN in the future; and "The Tenth Question" (1916), a MATHEMATICAL puzzle later rewritten by Stanley G. WEINBAUM and appearing as "Brink of Infinity" (1936). His other works include *The Flying Legion* (1920), about an attempt at world domination; *Cursed* (1919), a minor weird novel; "The Fatal Gift" (1915); "The Crime Detector" (1913) and "Drops of Death" (1922). Several of his works were reprinted in *AMZ*, *Air Wonder Stories*, *Famous Fantastic Mysteries* and *Fantastic Novels*. [JE]
See also: CITIES; DEVOLUTION; DISASTER; DISCOVERY AND INVENTION; DYSTOPIAS; EVOLUTION; INVISIBILITY; MONEY; MONSTERS; POLITICS; TIME TRAVEL; VILLAINS.

ENGLE, E(LOISE HOPPER) (1923–). American writer. Her sf novel, *Countdown for Cindy* (1962), is a light SPACE OPERA. [JC]

ENGLISH, CHARLES *See* Charles NUETZEL.

ENTROPY In its strict meaning, "entropy" is a term used in thermodynamics to describe the amount of heat that must be put into a closed system to bring it to the state being considered; it is a quantity normally defined by a differential equation. The term was first used by the German physicist Clausius in 1850. The famous second law of thermodynamics, which is often stated, in terms of work, as "it is impossible to produce work by transferring heat from a cold body to a hot body in any self-sustaining process", can be restated mathematically as "entropy always increases in any closed system not in equilibrium, and remains constant for a system that is in equilibrium".

To put it less technically: whenever there is a flow of energy there is some loss. For example, in a steam engine, the friction of the piston is manifested in non-useful heat, and hence some of the energy put into it is not turned into work. There is no such thing as a friction-free system, and no such thing as a perfect machine for that reason. Entropy is a measure of this loss. In a broader sense we can refer to entropy as a measure of the order of a system; the higher the entropy the lower the order. There is more energy, for example, tied up in complex molecules than simple ones (they are more "ordered"); the second law can be loosely rephrased as "systems tend to become less complex". Examples are all about us: petroleum burns, houses lose heat in winter. Heat flows, so that ultimately everything will tend to stabilize at the same temperature. When this happens to the universe – it is often called the heat-death of the universe — entropy will have reached its maximum, no order left, total randomness, no life, the end. (There is, however, an argument about whether the concept of entropy can properly be related to the universe as a whole). At any event, the amount of usable energy in the universe, primarily supplied by the stars, is unimaginably huge, and the heat-death of the universe is billions of years away.

Although entropy has been a technical term for a long time, it is only in the past 20 years that it has become a fashionable concept in its extended meaning. Nowadays, to the annoyance of some scientifically minded people, the extended concept of increasing entropy includes holes wearing in socks, refrigerators breaking down, coalminers going on strike, and death. These are indeed all examples of increasing disorder in a technical though not necessarily a moral sense. Life itself is a highly ordered state, and in its very existence is an example of negative entropy, or negentropy as it is fashionably known. It is as if, though the universe is running down, there are whirlpools of local activity where things are winding up. All forms of information, whether in the form of the DNA code that exists in all our genes, upon which life is built, or in the contents of this Encyclopedia, can be seen as examples of negentropy.

Entropy has become a potent metaphor. It is uncertain who first introduced the term to sf, but it was very probably Philip K. DICK, who makes much of the concept in nearly all his work. In *Do Androids Dream of Electric Sheep?* (**1968**) entropy, or increasing disorder, is imaged as "kipple". "Kipple is useless objects, like junk mail or match folders after you use the last match or gum wrappers or yesterday's homeopape. When nobody's around, kipple reproduces itself ... the entire universe is moving towards a final state of total, absolute kippleization."

It was, however, in NEW-WAVE writing, expecially that associated with NEW WORLDS, that the concept of entropy made its greatest inroads into sf. J.G. BALLARD

has used it a great deal, and did so as early as "The Voices of Time" (1960) in which a count-down to the end of the universe is accompanied by more localized entropic happenings, including the increasing sleepiness of the protagonist. Pamela ZOLINE's story "The Heat Death of the Universe" (1967) is in fact about the life of a housewife, and is often quoted as an example of the metaphoric use of entropy. Another example is the fine story "Running Down" (1975) by M. John HARRISON, whose protagonist, a shabby man who perishes in earthquake and storm, "carried his own entropy around with him". The concept appears in the work of Norman SPINRAD, Barry MALZBERG, James TIPTREE Jr, Robert SILVERBERG and Thomas M. DISCH as a recurrent leitmotiv, and also in the work of Brian W. ALDISS, in novels as disparate as *Hothouse* (fix-up **1962**; vt *The Long Afternoon of Earth*), *An Age* (**1967**; vt *Cryptozoic!*), *Barefoot in the Head* (fix-up **1969**), *The Eighty-Minute Hour* (**1974**) and *The Malacia Tapestry* (**1976**). There is usually a tension in Aldiss's work between entropy and negentropy, between fecundity and life on the one hand, stasis, decay and death on the other. Geo. Alec EFFINGER's first novel, *What Entropy Means to Me* (**1972**), is a jovial satire on many sf clichés but, apart from a slight tendency for things to go wrong, is not what one might call a hardcore entropy novel. A popular variant on the entropy story in recent sf is the DEVOLUTION story.

Michael MOORCOCK has perhaps made more subtle and complex use of the twin ideas of entropy and negentropy than any other sf writer; the themes run all the way through his "Jerry Cornelius" books, and his "Dancers at the End of Time" sequence. Jerry Cornelius in his long saga seems for a long time proof against entropy, and consistently slips into alternate realities as if in the hope of finding one whose vitality outlives its decay, but like a Typhoid Mary he carries the plague of entropy with him, and ultimately, especially after the death of his formidably vital and vulgar mother, succumbs to it himself, becoming in the process touchingly more human, though diminished and less of a dude.

In all of these recent works entropy is used as a symbol through which the fate of the macrocosm, the universe, can be linked to the fate of societies and of the individual — a very proper subject for sf; negentropy versus entropy is usually seen as an unequal battle, David against Goliath, but sickness, sorrow, rusting, cooling and death contrive to be held at bay, locally and occasionally, by passion and movement and love. Looked at in this perspective, entropy is one of the oldest themes in literature, the central concern, for example, of Shakespeare, John Donne and Milton. [PN]

ERDMAN, PAUL E. *See* HISTORY OF SF.

ERMAN, JACQUES DEFOREST *See* Forrest J. ACKERMAN.

ERNST, PAUL (FREDERICK) (1902–). Prolific American PULP writer, mostly of short fiction, some under his own name, some (in *Weird Tales*) under the pseudonym Paul F. Stern. His first published story may have been "The Temple of Serpents" for *Weird Tales* in 1928. He was extremely active throughout the 1930s, writing for sf, fantasy and hero magazines; in the last capacity under the house name Kenneth ROBESON he was responsible for much of the contents of *The Avenger*. Many of these stories have been reprinted in paperback books in the 1970s. The house name Kenneth Robeson had already been made popular by Lester DENT in DOC SAVAGE MAGAZINE, and it was in an attempt to cash in on the success of the name that it was offered for PE's use. PE's "Doctor Satan" series in *Weird Tales* is fantasy along conventional hero-villain lines. Five of these stories were reprinted in PULP CLASSICS No. 6 (**1975**). His sf stories — the first of which was "Marooned Under the Sea" (1930 *ASF*) — include "The Microscopic Giants" (1936), and "Nothing Happens on the Moon" (1939). PE was less prolific after the 1930s. [PN]

ERNSTING, WALTER *See* Clark DARLTON.

ERSKINE, THOMAS (1788–1870). English writer, mostly of religious texts, whose anonymously published *Armata: a Fragment* (**1816**) and *The Second Part of Armata* (**1817**) SATIRICALLY describe the society on another planet, rather similar to Earth's, which is reachable via the South Pole, to which it is attached. [JC]

ESCAPE FROM THE PLANET OF THE APES Film (1971). Apjac/20th Century-Fox. Directed by Don Taylor, starring Roddy McDowall, Kim Hunter, Bradford Dillman, Natalie Trundy and William Windom. Screenplay by Paul Dehn, based on characters created by Pierre BOULLE. 97 mins. Colour.

When the late British script-writer Paul Dehn was working on the previous *Ape* film (BENEATH THE PLANET OF THE APES) he was told it would be the last, so he decided to end the film by killing not only the characters but the whole world with an atomic explosion. Four months later he received a telegram from Fox saying: "Apes exist, sequel required." His ingenious answer was to send three of the apes back to a time before the world exploded. They arrive in contemporary America and immediately become the centre of a violent controversy which results in all their deaths, but not before the female among them (who featured in the first two films) gives birth to a baby ape. This is an entertaining mixture of sf, satire and action/adventure. A novelization by Jerry POURNELLE was published in 1974. [JB]

ESCHATOLOGY Eschatology is the class of theological doctrines pertaining to death and the subsequent fate of the *persona* or soul, and to the ultimate fate of the world. Stories of the FAR FUTURE and the END OF THE WORLD can be categorized as eschatological, but will be considered in their respective sections, while this section deals mainly with the ultimate fate of the individual *persona*.

The ancient Egyptians constructed an inordinately complex eschatological theory (explored in sf in Roger ZELAZNY's *Creatures of Light and Darkness*, **1969**) and this probably influenced subsequent eschatologies. Christian eschatology is basically dualistic, contrasting Heaven and Hell, but has variants which are much more complex, incorporating such notions as Purgatory and Limbo, and involving a complex demonology. A common strategy employed by sf writers writing pure fantasy (as, for instance, in the magazine UNKNOWN) was and is to import rationalistic principles into settings derived from classical mythology or the Christian demonological schema, usually with comic results, though unorthodox horror stories would sometimes result.

The growth of the scientific romance in the late 19th century coincided with the growth of the Spiritualist movement. The Spiritualists popularized an eroded version of Christian eschatology with some added pseudo-scientific jargon involving the "astral plane" and like concepts. Spiritualist beliefs influenced several early sf writers, including Camille FLAMMARION and A. Conan DOYLE, although only Doyle's later works — particularly *The Land of Mist* (**1926**) and *The Maracot Deep* (**1929**) — are markedly affected. There is an abundance of spiritualist fiction, but whether any of this can be considered sf is dubious, despite the pseudo-scientific endeavours of men like Johann Zollner, author of *Transcendental Physics* (**1865**), and other psychic theorists. Flammarion's ideas on REINCARNATION were echoed by other speculative writers, but only he combined them with any real measure of scientific imagination. An early pulp sf writer who dabbled in spiritualist fiction was Ralph Milne FARLEY, as in *Dangerous Love* (1931 *Mind Magic*; **1946**). More interesting is David LINDSAY's remarkable interstellar fantasy *A Voyage To Arcturus* (**1920**), which takes conventional spiritualist ideas and turns them on their head in a story which deals harshly with all the routine eschatological aspirations, and sees destiny as bound up with pain.

As far as magazine sf was concerned the afterlife was not to be taken seriously, as *Unknown*'s abundant eschatological satires made clear. As with other ideas irredeemably tainted with the supernatural it was not seen as a fit subject for speculation. Such attempts as there were to rationalize theological doctrines with scientific speculation came from outside the genre. The idea that science, with better technology, might one day discover and trap the elusive soul was embodied in Charles B. STILSON's curious "Liberty or Death!" (1917; vt "The Soul Trap"), but was developed more ambitiously in *The Weigher of Souls* (**1931**) by André MAUROIS. As with most themes which deal with Man's trespassing on divine prerogatives, no good comes of it all. A harshly uncompromising judgement is passed on an evil scientist in Maurice RENARD's *New Bodies For Old* (**1908**; trans. **1923**), when his experiments in metempsychosis end with the migration of his soul into the engine of a motor car; and an experiment aiming at communication with the dead ends tragically in *The Edge of Running Water* (**1939**; vt *The Unquiet Corpse*) by William SLOANE. A curious corollary of this conviction that there are things Man is not meant to discover is the astonishing profusion of fantasies in which characters only realize at the end of the story that they have been dead since its beginning. The one story which transcends the banality of the plot is Ray BRADBURY's "Pillar of Fire" (1948).

C.S. LEWIS's theological fantasy *The Great Divorce* (**1945**) acknowledges that some of the ideas used in formulating its image of Heaven are borrowed from sf, but the sf writers themselves remained reluctant to employ their vocabulary of symbols to the whole area of speculation. The first major sf novel dealing with eschatology was Robert SHECKLEY's melodrama of REINCARNATION *Immortality Delivered* (**1958**; vt exp. *Immortality, Inc*), but though much concerned with the mechanics of metempsychosis the story passes lightly over the experience of disembodied existence and the question of ultimate destiny. The same hesitancy is seen in the many stories which Philip José FARMER has devoted to eschatological matters, including *Inside Outside* (**1964**), *Traitor to the Living* (**1973**), and in Kurt VONNEGUT's *Slapstick* (**1976**). (The afterlife and multiple reincarnations of Farmer's "Riverworld" novels are so resolutely de-spiritualized that it would be stretching a point to call them eschatological.)

Two writers have replaced the Christian notion of the soul with a species of alien symbiote which invests living men and survives their deaths. Clifford D. SIMAK, in *Time and Again* (**1951**) makes no attempt to describe the life of these symbiotes apart from their hosts. Bob SHAW, in *The Palace of Eternity* (**1969**) is a little more ambitious, and is curiously reminiscent of Zollner in equating the pseudoastral plane with the extra-dimensional hyperspace employed by the starships to transcend Einsteinian limitations. In Deane ROMANO's *Flight From Time One* (**1972**) the astral plane is not only discovered by science but exploited; the novel, however, confines itself to the exploits of "astralnauts" and says nothing about the spirits of the departed.

Special eschatologies are often invoked for individual characters: death as metamorphosis is a constant feature in the work of Charles L. HARNESS, and also features in Thomas M. DISCH's *Camp Concentration* (**1968**); Poul ANDERSON, in "The Martyr" (1960) was quite happy to imagine aliens equipped with immortal souls. But there have been few attempts in sf to grasp the nettle and adopt the assumption of an immortal soul as a possession of all mankind. The most notable is from outside the genre: Romain GARY's soul-trapping story *The Gasp* (**1973**) which takes over where Maurois left off, and deals with the economic exploitation of the inexhaustible energy of the soul.

For the anonymously edited *Five Fates* (anth. **1970**) five sf writers were presented with a direct challenge, being asked to complete a story beginning with the death of the central character. Two authors unrepentantly dodged the issue — in Keith LAUMER's "Of Death What Dreams" the character simply gets up and walks away, while in Poul Anderson's "The Fatal Fulfillment" the death episode becomes a hallucination sequence. Frank HERBERT's "Murder Will In" also avoids the challenge by recomplicating the issue so that the initial death is of minor relevance to the story. Gordon DICKSON's "Maverick" accepts the premise but moves quickly into a formula adventure story based on the character's reincarnation in a PARALLEL WORLD. Only Harlan ELLISON, in "The Region Between" was bold enough to build upon the overture to compose a surreal transcendental melodrama of soul-predation.

There is one significant sf story which tries to construct an eschatology based on a new technology for revitalizing the dead: Robert SILVERBERG's powerful "Born With the Dead" (1974). Silverberg had earlier written *To Live Again* (**1969**) on a less interesting eschatological theme, in which the *personae* of living persons are regularly recorded so that after the death of the body the most recent recording can be introduced into the mind of a "host". Similar mind-crowding occurs by an unrationalized process in Robert HEINLEIN's *I Will Fear No Evil* (**1970**).

Although it is not sf by any DEFINITION mention should perhaps be made of *Inferno* (**1975**) by Larry NIVEN and Jerry POURNELLE, which was marketed as sf, serialized in GALAXY and nominated for a NEBULA award. This is a modern recapitulation of Dante's classic, containing some satire after the fashion of Lord Holden's *Purgatory Revisited* (**1949**) but also incorporating a good deal of lurid and rather sadistic description of the fate of various categories of sinners.

Bearing in mind the recent upsurge of interest in transcendental themes in sf (see RELIGION) the time seems ripe for a fully fledged eschatological sf novel, but it has not yet appeared. Even stories dealing with eschatology in the sense of dealing with the ultimate destiny of entire species — Arthur C. CLARKE's *Childhood's End* (1953) and George ZEBROWSKI's *The Omega Point* (1972) — maintain a tentativeness and remoteness by dealing with evolutionary change in distant futures. In doing so they are, of course, in harmony with contemporary religious philosophy, which tends more and more to see eschatology and demonology as wholly metaphorical disciplines, while theological writers like Pierre Teilhard de Chardin have begun to speculate about an evolutionary eschatology not unlike that featured in *Childhood's End* (Zebrowski's novel is overtly based on Teilhard's work). [BS]

See also: COSMOLOGY; ENTROPY; GODS AND DEMONS; METAPHYSICS.

ESHBACH, LLOYD ARTHUR (1910–). American writer and publisher. An sf enthusiast from an early age, his first published story was "The Voice from the Ether" (1931) in AMAZING STORIES, which was followed by a number of others, some of them included in *The Tyrant of Time* (coll. 1955). In 1946 he formed FANTASY PRESS, and in 1952 began a short-lived companion imprint, Polaris Press. For Fantasy Press he edited the first published book about modern sf: *Of Worlds Beyond: The Science of Science Fiction Writing* (anth. 1947), a symposium of essays by such authors as John W. CAMPBELL Jr, Robert HEINLEIN and A.E. VAN VOGT. [MJE]

See also: CYBORGS.

ESP The acronym by which extra-sensory perception is so commonly known in sf that those who can practise it are commonly known as "espers". The term "ESP" was first popularized by Dr Joseph Banks Rhine with his book *Extra-Sensory Perception* (1934). There is no clear agreement about what exactly constitutes ESP; its meaning overlaps considerably with that of the other sf favourite, psi or psionic powers. For convenience, this entry will discuss those stories which deal primarily with telepathy, clairvoyance and precognition, all of which are forms of PERCEPTION. Other abilities, such as teleportation, telekinesis and pyrotic powers, will be discussed under PSI POWERS.

Telepathy, or mind-reading, makes persistent though sporadic appearances in the whole of fantasy literature. The hero of *A Voyage to Arcturus* (1920) by David LINDSAY grows new organs which enable him to perceive thought directly, and Olaf STAPLEDON's *Last and First Men* (1930) sees telepathy as one of the evolutionary stages in which humanity learns to transcend its bodily limitations.

However, it was not until after the series of books published by Dr Rhine, and also Charles FORT's *Wild Talents* (1932), that ESP stories became really popular in genre sf. Fort's collection of curious data relating to strange powers of the mind was a strong influence on many sf writers, notably Eric Frank RUSSELL, whose *Sentinels from Space* (1953) is a veritable compendium of Fortean powers displayed in a racy melodrama with an ending in which humanity is transcended altogether. But the first of the really well-known ESP stories in genre sf was *Slan* (1940 *ASF*; 1946; rev. 1951) by A.E. VAN VOGT, which contains what was to become the archetypal telepath-story situation: the slans are telepathic mutants, hated and feared by ordinary humans, and persecuted; near-SUPERMEN, they are the next stage in human EVOLUTION.

Thus was set the pattern which remained dominant right through the 1950s; 1953–63 was the decade in which the ESP story seemed to be edging all other forms of sf off the bookstalls. Among the more prominent examples are *Wild Talent* (1954; vt *Man from Tomorrow*) by Wilson TUCKER; *Pilgrimage: The Book of the People* (1952–9 *FSF*; fix-up 1961) by Zenna HENDERSON, in which a slightly treacly treatment was given to stories of gentle telepathic aliens; *Time is the Simplest Thing* (1961) by Clifford D. SIMAK, in which paranormals are persecuted again; *Drunkard's Walk* (1960) by Frederik POHL, in which telepathic immortals try to keep humanity as a whole from developing its latent telepathic powers and *The Power* (1956) by Frank M. ROBINSON, where the man who catches the evil telepathic superman turns out to be the same way inclined himself. Two of the most distinguished works on the theme were by Theodore STURGEON, *The Dreaming Jewels* (1950; vt *The Synthetic Man*) and *More than Human* (fix-up 1953); in the former a telepathic boy is treated cruelly and becomes afraid that he is an inhuman freak, in the latter a *gestalt* superbeing is created from components (people) who are psychologically maimed as individuals, though each has some form of psionic power.

The linking of super-powers in one area with maiming in others, almost as if the one were a compensation for the other, like a blind man's hearing, is treated with delicacy by Sturgeon (who manages to remain just on this side of sentimentality) as it was to be again by John BRUNNER in *The Whole Man* (fix-up 1964; vt *Telepathist* UK). The hero of this novel, despite his psychological problems, is shown convincingly to grow into a successful telepathic therapist. Such therapy is also the theme of a later work, *The Dream Master* (1966) by Roger ZELAZNY, in which a brilliant but arrogant psychiatrist-telepath meets unexpected stress inside the minds of his patients. The Zelazny novel is an example of a

kind of sf that has been too rare, that which abandons the superman aspect of the theme (whether persecuted or persecuting) in favour of an exploration of what the possession of ESP might feel like. An outstanding, relatively early example is *The Demolished Man* (1953) by Alfred BESTER, which features a group of espers well-integrated with normal society and with one another, pitted against a brilliant, psychotic murderer who uses every trick in the book to escape telepathic surveillance. Bester's evocations of telepathic "conversations" are vivid and convincing. Other writers to evoke the sensations of ESP in sf are Richard COWPER (in many stories), Samuel DELANY in several stories including "The Star Pit" (1967), Joanna RUSS in *And Chaos Died* (1970), which creates intensely the chaotic sensations of a man who acquires ESP and cannot handle it, and Robert SILVERBERG in *Dying Inside* (1972). The last is a disconsolate story of a telepath in present-day New York who is slowly losing his powers; the sense of regret is evoked with great skill, though the novel moves close to self-pity in its elegiac qualities.

British sf has produced fewer ESP stories, of which one of the best is *The Inner Wheel* (1970) by Keith ROBERTS, in which a psionic *gestalt* is evoked in terms both sinister and ambiguous at the outset; the group is later revealed to be callous rather than evil, and working for good. Other British ESP novels are *Telepath* (1962; vt *The Silent Speakers* UK) and *The Uncensored Man* (1964) by Arthur SELLINGS, *The Paper Dolls* (1966) and several other novels by L.P. DAVIES, and the trilogy by Dan MORGAN beginning with *The New Minds* (1967).

Two other American writers who deal with ESP themes are Hal CLEMENT and Frank HERBERT, the former in *Needle* (1950; vt *From Outer Space*) in which a telepathic alien policeman forms a symbiosis with an Earth-boy in seeking his quarry, and the latter in *Dune* (1965) and its sequels, in which ESP powers are once again seen as linked to human transcendence, and in this case with an sf equivalent of taking the host at a communion service. ESP is induced by the "Water of Life", in an image of great power and complexity, linked to the ecological imagery which runs through the whole novel.

In the real world ESP is still a matter of hot debate among laymen, and seldom investigated by scientists. No indubitable proof of its existence has yet been demonstrated, despite persistent rumours of vast sums being spent by the Soviet army on its study. Rhine's results are open to criticism on the ground of poor statistics, and also because one of his best subjects was probably a fraud. The trouble with ESP is that it seems to have no plausible material explanation; it fails to obey the inverse square law, which is to say that the strength of the telepathic signal does not, apparently, fall off with distance. If this is really the case, then definite proof of the existence of ESP will require a total rethinking of modern physics from the ground up. Few sf writers have attempted to deal with possible scientific explanations for ESP, though James BLISH, conscientious and sceptical, did his best in *Jack of Eagles* (**1952**; vt *ESP-er*) to give it a scientific rationale in a story of great ingenuity, compromised by its pulp characterization and a hard-bitten style that rings false. Lester DEL REY also tackles the problem of a rationale for ESP in *Pstalemate* (**1971**), interestingly, but without great success.

Precognition is dealt with alongside telepathy in several of the above works; it raises rather different problems. Like TIME TRAVEL, precognition (reading the future) raises all sorts of questions about determinism versus free will. Philip K. DICK, who has never shown much interest in the conventional telepathy story, is the master of the precognitive paradox. "Precogs" appear in many of his stories.

The ESP story very readily moves into areas of wish-fulfilment, and also into near-PARANOID fantasies in which the good hero is persecuted for his differences, although (as so many teenage readers feel also) he is misunderstood, and basically better than other people, morally as well as in terms of power. But ESP retains its potency as an image through which questions of COMMUNICATION, understanding and empathy can be explored; the best ESP stories are very good.

An anthology is *14 Great Tales of ESP* (anth. **1969**) ed. Idella Purnell Stone. [PN]

ESPER In sf TERMINOLOGY, a person who is able to use one or other of the powers of extra-sensory perception, which is known widely as ESP for short: usually TELEPATHY, but occasionally more bizarre powers such as TELEKINESIS. However, many writers reserve the term PSIONIC or PSI for the full spectrum of such powers, reserving ESP for telepathy. James BLISH's novel *Jack of Eagles* (**1952**) was given the variant title *ESP-er* in a later reprint. [PN]

ESSEX HOUSE A short-lived American West Coast publishing imprint specializing in pornographic sf. It published 42 titles, including several novels by Philip José FARMER, also by Hank STINE, David MELTZER, Michael PERKINS and others, and laid emphasis on literary as well as erotic quality. All the books are erotic; approximately half can be categorized as sf. [MJE]
See also: SEX. An article, "Essex House: the Rise and Fall of Speculative Erotica" by Maxim JAKUBOWSKI, appears in *Foundation: the Review of Science Fiction* no.14.

E.T. *See* EXTRATERRESTRIAL.

No. 3, 1974. Cover by Stephen Fabian.

ETERNITY SCIENCE FICTION US BEDSHEET-size magazine. Four issues, Jul. 1972–4; published and ed. Stephen Gregg with Scott Edelstein from Sandy Springs, South Carolina. *ESF* was a well-produced, semi-professional sf magazine. Contributors included David R. BUNCH, Barry MALZBERG and Roger ZELAZNY. [FHP]

EVANS, BILL Form of his name used by American writer William H. Evans (1921–) on his extensive introduction to E.E. "Doc" SMITH, *The Universes of E.E. Smith* (**1966**), on which he collaborated with Ron ELLIK. Most of the book is a concordance of themes and characters though there is some critical content. BE did the "Skylark" series; Ellik did the "Lensman" books. [JC]

EVANS, E(DWARD) EVERETT (1893–1958). American sf fan and writer. He began in the latter capacity late in life and had mixed success, though there is no doubt of the affection in which other Californian sf writers and fans held him, as evinced in the many tributes to him from writers such as E.E. SMITH and A.E. VAN VOGT included in a compilation of his macabre fantasy stories, *Food for Demons* (coll. **1971**). This was originally conceived as a homage to the man, and set up and printed, though not bound, as early as 1959. EEE's earlier books were routine adventures of an ESPER spy in *Man of Many Minds* (**1953**) and *Alien Minds* (**1955**); and a juvenile, *The Planet Mappers* (**1955**). He collaborated with E.E. Smith, whom he admired greatly, on one story, which Smith expanded into the novel *Masters of Space* (1961–2 *If*; **1976**). [JC]

EVANS, I(DRISYN) O(LIVER) (1894–1977). British civil servant and, especially after his retirement in 1956, editor and writer. He specialized in the works of Jules VERNE, many of which he translated and edited for the Fitzroy edition of Verne's work in translation, beginning in 1958. Some of these were reprinted by ACE BOOKS. Unfortunately, IOE in editing Verne occasionally abridged him cruelly, rendering him more of a simple boys' action writer than was in fact the case. IOE also wrote *Jules Verne and His Work* (**1965**), and edited *Science Fiction Through the Ages 1* (anth. **1966**) and *Science Fiction Through the Ages 2* (anth. **1966**), the first volume of which is restricted to pre-20th-century sf. He also edited *Jules Verne – Master of Science Fiction* (coll. **1956**), which assembles extracts from Verne's novels. [PN]

EVERYTHING YOU ALWAYS WANTED TO KNOW ABOUT SEX (BUT WERE AFRAID TO ASK) Film (1972). Jack Rollins and Charles H. Joffe

A giant breast ravages the countryside in EVERYTHING YOU ALWAYS WANTED TO KNOW ABOUT SEX BUT WERE AFRAID TO ASK.

Productions/United Artists. Directed by Woody Allen, starring Woody Allen, Gene Wilder, Louise Lasser, John Carradine, Burt Reynolds and Tony Randall. Screenplay by Woody Allen, based on the book by David Reuben. 88 mins. Colour.

Based extremely loosely on Reuben's book, this collection of short episodes satirizing various aspects of sex includes two that can be charitably defined as sf. One involves a mad scientist who creates a giant, mobile woman's breast that breaks out of his laboratory and ravages the countryside in the manner of a 1950s movie monster until it is trapped by Woody Allen, wielding a crucifix, in a suitably giant bra cup. The other episode shows what happens inside the male human body during a seduction attempt, by comparing its interior processes to those of a highly mechanized production line, with white-suited technocrats running things from the "Brain Room" while brawny, hard-hatted workers cope with the heavy equipment in the lower regions. Allen himself plays one of a group of sperm cells nervously waiting to go into action in the manner of paratroopers about to be dropped into enemy territory. The satire on sf, in these episodes, is possibly funnier than the satire on sex. Woody Allen returned to sf satire the following year with SLEEPER.

[JB]

EVOLUTION There is an intimate connection between the development of evolutionary philosophy and the history of sf. This is inevitable, in that sf is basically a literature of change. In a culture without an evolutionary philosophy most of the kinds of literature we categorize today as sf could not develop. Like the idea of progress, evolutionary philosophy first flourished in late 18th-century France, and it is first significantly represented in literature by RESTIF DE LA BRETONNE's evolutionary fantasy *La découverte Australe par un homme volant* (**1781**), an allegorical treatment of ideas partly derived from the Comte du Buffon's *Histoire naturelle* (**1749–67**). In the early 19th century Lamarck's *Philosophie zoologique* (**1809**) developed a more elaborate evolutionary philosophy, introducing the key notion of adaptation, and paved the way for Darwin's theory of natural selection, published in *Origin of Species* (**1859**). Because we now associate evolution with Darwin and have fallen into the habit of labelling various theoretical heresies as "Lamarckian" or "neo-Lamarckian", it is easy to overlook the fact that over the greater part of the 19th century Lamarck was the more influential writer, and remained so in France (with a little help from the mystically inclined Henri Bergson) until well into the 20th century. In England, Darwin was championed by the positivist T.H. Huxley and the sociologist Herbert Spencer, and his ideas took much firmer hold in Britain than elsewhere. In Germany Darwin had an outspoken popularizer in Ernst Haeckel, but there was no one comparable in America, and France already had a strong tradition of evolutionary thought on which Darwin made little immediate impact. For these reasons we find a wide divergence of thought and emphasis between evolutionary sf in France and evolutionary sf in Britain, which lasted well into the 20th century.

The men of primary importance in establishing the tradition of French evolutionary fantasy were Camille FLAMMARION, in the *Récits de l'infini* (**1872**; rev. as *Lumen* **1887**; trans. **1897**) and *Omega* (trans. **1894**); and J.H. ROSNY AÎNÉ in his many prehistoric fantasies, in "Les xipéhuz" (1887; trans. as "The Shapes" 1968) and in "La mort de la terre" (1910). Both writers are clearly influenced by Lamarck. Jules VERNE's one evolutionary fantasy, *The Village in the Treetops* (**1901**; trans. **1964**), is also Lamarckian. Bergson, who mystified the idea of evolution with the notion of "*élan vital*", or vital spirit (which Lamarck had rejected), seems to have been more influential for his wider philosophical ideas than he was for his specifically evolutionary theories — his theory of time influenced his one-time pupil Alfred JARRY — but it was apparently he who provided the seed of one of the most important British evolutionary fantasies, J.D. BERESFORD's *The Hampdenshire Wonder* (**1911**; vt *The Wonder*).

For the most part, however, British evolutionary fantasy was dominated by the implications of Darwinian theory and the catch-phrases by which it was vulgarized: "the survival of the fittest" and "the struggle for existence". Darwin's champion, T.H. Huxley, taught H.G. WELLS in the early 1890s and made a very deep impression. Wells remained haunted by the idea that the qualities in Man which had shaped him for survival in the struggle for existence might forbid his ever achieving a just society — a fear reflected in different ways in *The Time Machine* (**1895**), *The Island of Dr. Moreau* (**1896**), *Mr. Blettsworthy on Rampole Island* (**1928**) and *The Croquet Player* (**1936**). The ominous spectres arising from the harsher versions of Darwinian philosophy also feature strongly in *Erewhon* (**1872**) by Samuel BUTLER (who also wrote several anti-Darwinian tracts), and in *Mr. Stranger's Sealed Packet* (**1889**) by Hugh MACCOLL. It intrudes into most of the speculative fiction of Grant ALLEN (who wrote several pro-Darwinian tracts). The political implications of the careless transplantation of Darwinian ideas into theories of social evolution (*see* SOCIAL DARWINISM) were such that Wells's fellow-Fabian George Bernard SHAW renounced Darwinism in favour of neo-Lamarckism on political grounds, and his play *Back to Methuselah* (**1921**) was published with a long introductory essay explaining this renunciation. Similar steps were taken by Lysenko, in the name of Russian Communism, and Luther Burbank, in the name of American Fundamentalism. It was not until much later that it was realized that the implications of Darwinism were not necessarily as harsh as Huxley had represented them and the vulgar Darwinians had assumed. An interesting popularization of a more humane Darwinism, cast as fiction, is Gerald HEARD's *Gabriel and the Creatures* (**1952**; vt *Wishing Well*).

American fiction of the Wellsian era seems much less interested in evolution, although the influence of Darwinian ideas can be seen in Edgar FAWCETT's *The Ghost of Guy Thyrle* (**1895**), and Austin BIERBOWER's *From Monkey to Man* (**1894**) is an early attempt to present Genesis as an allegory of evolution. Curiously, the first major evolutionary fantasy in American sf is Edgar Rice BURROUGHS' "extrapolation" of Haeckel's law in *The Land That Time Forgot* (**1918**; **1924**). Haeckel's law states that "the individual reflects during the course of its (embryonic) development the most important changes in form which its ancestors traversed in the course of their evolution". The law is often stated, succinctly if polysyllabically, as "Ontogeny recapitulates phylogeny". In Burroughs' romance this recapitulation takes place during active life rather than embryonically. Similar schemes are accredited to alien life-systems in Theodore STURGEON's "The Golden Helix" (1954) and James BLISH's *A Case of Conscience* (**1958**).

What interested sf writers most was human evolution. (Stories concerned with Man's evolutionary past are discussed in the sections ORIGIN OF MAN and ANTHROPOLOGY.) Wells, in the essay "The Man of the Year Million" (1893), had imagined Man as evolution would remake him, with an enormous head and reduced body, eyes enlarged but ears and nose vestigial. This image became an archetype embraced by many other writers. It became a cliché in early pulp sf, although most writers took a dim view of the "fitness" of such an individual, and usually represented him as doomed to extinction (as in, for instance, "Alas, All Thinking!", 1935, by Harry BATES and the film THIS ISLAND EARTH, 1954). Few of the pulp writers had any idea of the actual implications of Darwinism, and were inordinately inspired by the idea of mutation (*see* MUTANTS). Many stories appeared in which mutagenic radiation accelerates evolution to a perceptible pace, including John TAINE's *Seeds of Life* (1931; **1951**) and *The Iron Star* (**1930**) and Edmond HAMILTON's "Evolution Island" (1927). The notion is nonsensical but exerted a powerful hold on the imagination. Hamilton's fiction also showed a persistent interest in the pseudo-scientific notion of degenerative evolution (*see* DEVOLUTION) which had earlier been luridly featured in George Allan ENGLAND's *Darkness and Dawn* (**1914**) and which even crops up at one point in Olaf STAPLEDON's *Last and First Men* (**1930**). The imagery of the idea is best illustrated by Hamilton's "The Man Who Evolved" (**1931**) in which a man bathes himself in mutagenic radiation, turns into the man-of-the-year-million stereotype and then regresses, ending up as a blob of undifferentiated protoplasm. The persistent pessimism of pulp sf regarding the long-term evolutionary prospects of Man, which contrasts oddly with such visions as J.B.S. HALDANE's "The Last Judgment" (**1927**) and Stapledon's *Last and First Men*, is not easy to account for. In John W. CAMPBELL Jr's "Twilight" (**1934**, as by Don A. Stuart) it is associated with the notion of decadence through overdependence on machines (*see* DYSTOPIAS *and* AUTOMATION), but this association of ideas is far from universal. It is significant that in Campbell's story "The Last Evolution" (**1932**) it is the machines, not their creators, who evolve ultimately into the state of "pure consciousness" that the sf writers invented as the ultimate (desirable) end of evolution. Shaw had proposed this as the destiny of mankind in *Back to Methuselah* but it was not until some time later that the proposition was overtly featured in a pulp sf story — in Eric Frank RUSSELL's "Metamorphosite" (**1946**). The magazine sf writers put far more faith and trust in the standard model of contemporary man than writers outside the genre such as Haldane, whose evolutionary schemes featured major changes in mankind; Claude HOUGHTON's hero, in *This Was Ivor Trent* (**1935**), could hardly wait to get the obsolete contemporary version out of the way once he had seen a vision of the man of the future. Olaf Stapledon's *Last and First Men* (**1930**) certainly spans the grandest evolutionary sweep in sf, spanning as it does the future evolution of man over the next 2,000 million years. Through the sometimes clumsy prose a passionate yearning towards a state of ultimate harmony and near-Godhead for mankind is expressed. Never simply optimistic (all sorts of disasters and evolutionary blind alleys appear in the story), the book nevertheless suggests the belief that the Darwinian mechanisms, together with a certain amount of biological and genetic engineering, will lead us forward to what a more theological writer might have thought as an equivalent of the Garden of Eden, though conventional Christians must have been angry at the fact that this is seen as an achievement without divine assistance. But while not proposing a God directly, Stapledon does seem to believe in some kind of cosmic master plan or destiny which will be ultimately

beneficent. This was a theme which ran through most of his work. There has been in sf no more pure (if occasionally naïve) celebration of the possibilities inherent in Darwinian theory.

During the 1940s pulp sf writers changed their attitude to the notion of evolution quite markedly, some of them possibly influenced by Stapledon, and their evolutionary images also changed significantly. The man-of-the-year-million was replaced by the superhuman (*see* SUPERMAN). The new model of evolved Man looked perfectly human (sometimes with the exception of a few tendrils or a bald head), but harboured new powers of the mind. The idea that a development of this sort was the next logical step in the evolution of Man was popularized by J.B. Rhine in *New Frontiers of the Mind* (**1937**), which claimed that such EXTRA-SENSORY PERCEPTIONS might already exist, latent and unsuspected. The idea that anyone might be an unsuspecting superman was powerful enough to maintain Rhine's popularity for a long time, and it helped promote a much more beneficent view of evolution in sf. Curiously, fiction outside the sf magazines began to lose interest in evolution at precisely this point in time.

The post-War interest in mental evolution, which assumed the proportions of a boom in this sub-genre of sf, produced a number of works in which the idea of an evolutionary schema (with an inbuilt destiny) was introduced into sf for the first time (if one excludes such naïve cyclic history stories as Robert Arthur's ADAM AND EVE story "Evolution's End", 1941). The most important were Arthur C. CLARKE's *Childhood's End* (**1953**), which shows a whole generation of Earthly children undergoing a kind of apotheosis to fuse with the "cosmic mind", and Theodore Sturgeon's *More Than Human* (**1953**), which deploys similar imagery on a smaller scale, recounting the career of a *gestalt* group of PSI-powered misfits and their eventual achievement of "maturity". Further examples are the linked short stories in *The Canopy of Time* (coll. **1959**) by Brian ALDISS, a great admirer of Olaf Stapledon, which hint at an evolutionary schema in which the next step in human evolution is complete somatic awareness and control, and Robert SILVERBERG's remarkable surreal novel *Son of Man* (**1971**), which explores many of the consequences of such trends in evolution. The most famous example of all is the evolutionary apotheosis rendered in symbolic terms at the end of the film 2001: A SPACE ODYSSEY.

The 1950s also saw the beginning of interest in the possibility that Man might soon be able to take control of his evolution through biological engineering (though the idea itself has a much longer history; *see* GENETIC ENGINEERING). In Damon KNIGHT's "Natural State" (**1954**; exp. **1959** as *Masters of Evolution*)

technological city-dwellers are appalled by the circumstances of the country-dwelling, anti-technological "muckfeet" who seem primitive by their standards, but they discover that the muckfeet have progressed beyond the need for machines and cities via biological control of the environment. This story is part of the emergent post-War interest in ECOLOGY, and the growing antipathy towards CITIES and technological society (*see* DYSTOPIAS *and* MACHINES). However, the majority of stories dealing with Man's control of his own evolution are much more pessimistic. Examples include Frank HERBERT's *The Eyes of Heisenberg* (**1966**) and T.J. BASS's *Half Past Human* (**1971**), the latter recalling the human hive which is seen as an unpleasant destiny for evolving society in J.D. Beresford and Esmé Wynne-Tyson's *Riddle of the Tower* (**1944**) (*see* HIVE-MINDS).

A surprising number of stories look forward nostalgically to the day when Man's time is done and he must pass on his legacy to the inheritors of Earth (or the universe). Usually the inheritors are machines, as in Lester DEL REY's "Though Dreamers Die" (**1944**) and Edmond Hamilton's "After a Judgment Day" (**1963**), but sometimes they are animals, as in Del Rey's "The Faithful" (**1938**) and Clifford D. SIMAK's *City* (**1944–51**; fix-up **1952**). Olof JOHANNESSON, in *The Tale of the Big Computer* (**1966**; trans. **1968**; vt *The Great Computer* UK) plots an evolutionary schema in which the function of Man is simply to be the means of facilitating machine evolution, while several stories, from L. Sprague DE CAMP and P. Schuyler MILLER's *Genus Homo* (**1941**; **1950**) to Neal BARRETT's *Aldair in Albion* (**1976**) describe the new evolutionary situation which arises following Man's demise.

The resurgence of mysticism in sf since the Second World War (*see* METAPHYSICS, RELIGION *and* SUPERMAN) worked against any accurate incorporation of the theory of evolution in genre sf. Mutational miracles persisted, and though understanding of the principles of evolution became widespread it did not displace the stereotyped images that had been built up in ignorance. There is still a tendency in sf, which is perhaps even stronger today, to use such concepts as ecology, evolution and symbiosis (*see* PARASITISM AND SYMBIOSIS) in a fashion which is at best interestingly metaphorical and at worst hazily metaphysical. Patterns of evolution on other worlds (*see* LIFE ON OTHER WORLDS) are often used in the service of Edenic mythology rather than in a logical manner, and this is true even in the work of writers well versed in the biological sciences.

Accounts of the evolution of ALIEN life-systems are generally presented in association with the theme of COLONIZATION OF OTHER WORLDS, most applying a vulgarized convergence theory to explain bipedalism and so forth: there have been very few attempts to imagine an evolutionary process which, because of differences in the genetic system of inheritance, functions according to principles different from our own. There have been some attempts to imagine alien systems capable of Lamarckian evolution, including Barrington J. BAYLEY's "Mutation Planet" (1973), but the only one which attempts to design a genetic system which makes such a process possible is Brian STABLEFORD's "The Engineer and the Executioner" (1975). Though Fundamentalists are still trying to fight the teaching of Darwinism in American schools the evolutionary debate is a dead issue in sf, and the imaginative apparatus of the theory of natural selection is used largely as a supportive logic for justifying constructions shaped by other priorities. Evolution is no longer an important stimulus to speculation in sf, but merely provides a jargon used to justify certain stereotyped images of the FAR FUTURE and LIFE ON OTHER WORLDS. [BS/PN] See also: BIOLOGY.

EWALD, CARL (1856–1908). Danish writer whose *Two-Legs* (trans. **1906**) is a narrative of the rise of Man from the viewpoint of the animals over which he would soon have dominion. Two other books have not been translated into English. [JC]

EWERS, HANS HEINZ (1871–1943). German writer. He is noted mainly for a series of novels about the character Frank Braun, some of them sf, such as *Der Zauberlehrling* (**1907**; trans. as *The Sorcerer's Apprentice* **1927**). His most famous works are *Alraune* (**1911**; trans. **1929**; filmed in 1908, 1919, 1928, 1930 and 1952), in which Braun constructs a female ANDROID who commits suicide to avert his death from her baneful influence, and *Vampir* (**1922**; trans. as *Vampire* **1934**; vt *Vampire's Prey*). His work is primarily in the GOTHIC tradition. [JC]
Other works: *Blood* (coll. trans. **1930**); *Rider of the Night* (trans. **1932**). See also: FANTASY.

EWING, FREDERICK R. *See* Theodore STURGEON.

"EXPLORABILIS" *See* Eliza Haywood.

EXPLORATION *See* COLONIZATION OF OTHER WORLDS; DISCOVERY AND INVENTION; FANTASTIC VOYAGES; LIFE ON OTHER WORLDS; LOST WORLDS; PARALLEL WORLDS.

EXTRAPOLATION Critical magazine, ed. Thomas D. CLARESON from its inception in Dec. 1959; two numbers (one vol.) a year; current. It began as "The Newsletter of the Conference on Science-Fiction of the MLA" and is now described more formally as the "Journal of the MLA Seminar on Science Fiction" The MLA is the Modern Languages Association. *E* has always been published from the English Department of the College of Wooster, Ohio. It is the first of the academic journals about sf, its successors being FOUNDATION: THE REVIEW OF SCIENCE FICTION and then SCIENCE-FICTION STUDIES. *E* is biased more towards the historical documentation of sf than its critical analysis, but in its long career has published articles of all kinds, including some notable bibliographical material. It has been accused of dullness, and indeed some of its contents have been blandly and routinely academic. Nevertheless, its existence as the earliest public platform for sf studies has significantly advanced those studies, and many of *E*'s articles have continued to be both scholarly and stimulating. [PN]

EXTRAPOLATION *See* PREDICTION.

EXTRA-SENSORY PERCEPTION In sf TERMINOLOGY, usually known by its acronym, ESP. *See* ESP *for full details.*

EXTRATERRESTRIAL In sf TERMINOLOGY, a non-human creature (usually intelligent) from outside Earth or TERRA. Often shortened to e.t. (pronounced eetee). *See* ALIENS *and* LIFE ON OTHER WORLDS. [PN]

EYRAUD, ACHILLE *See* VENUS.

F

FABIAN, STEPHEN E. (1930–). American illustrator. Noted for his glowing, vivid colours, and an excellent use of coquille board in his b/w work, SF did not take up sf illustration until the age of 37. Since then he has done paintings and drawings for *Amazing Stories, Fantastic, Galaxy*, Avon Books, Pyramid Books and others. He did all the illustrations for *Starfawn* (**1976**), no.3 in the "Fiction Illustrated" series, ed. Byron Preiss, a series of comic-book-style paperback novellas, and also illustrated some of the "Weird Heroes" book series, also ed. Preiss. Active in sf FANDOM, he has been nominated four times for a

An expressive cover by Stephen FABIAN, Feb. 1976.

HUGO award; two of those in the fan artist category. His work has been favourably compared with Virgil FINLAY's. *The Best of Stephen Fabian* (**1976**) is a recently published portfolio. [JG]

FABULATION Originally a fabulator was one who told tales in a fable- or myth-like fashion, but the term fell out of common use by the 19th century, and was not in any case utilized in literary criticism until Robert SCHOLES introduced the concept of fabulation in *The Fabulators* (**1967**), his study of the post-realistic, post-romantic novel as written by Lawrence DURRELL, Kurt VONNEGUT Jr, John BARTH and others. Briefly, a fabulation is a novel in which verbal and formal structures are heightened or placed in the foreground, often with an effect of selfconscious play or joyfulness, and generally with the intention of uncovering the exemplary fable-like elements inherent in the ordering which takes place in creating the imaginary worlds of all narrative fiction. Fabulators tend to be moralists and their works SATIRES. They perhaps differ most essentially from predecessors like Jonathan SWIFT in that their fictions must deal with, and go beyond, the great tradition of the realistic novel dominant until World War One in English. Because fabulations tend, deliberately, to draw attention to themselves as selfconscious works of fiction rather than as direct representations of "reality" (mimesis), they often manifest worlds which by conventional realist standards seem bizarre or grotesque. Many fabulations are discussed under ABSURDIST SF. [JC]

FAGAN, H(ENRY) A(LLAN) (1889– ?). South African judge and writer, Chief Justice of the Supreme Court of South Africa 1956–9. Besides a variety of short and dramatic works, he has published an sf novel, *Ninya* (**1956**), dealing with the survivors of a crash landing on the Moon; it does not resemble the astronauts' Moon. There are strange adventures.   [JC]

The book burning from FAHRENHEIT 451.

FAHRENHEIT 451 Film (1966). Anglo-Enterprise and Vineyard/Universal. Directed by François Truffaut, starring Julie Christie, Oscar Werner, Cyril Cusack and Anton Diffring. Screenplay by François Truffaut and Jean-Louis Richard, from the novel by Ray BRADBURY. 112 mins. Colour.

The film is based on Bradbury's parable about a future world where all books are banned. The hero is a member of the Fire Brigade — an organization whose function is not to put out fires but to burn illegal collections of books whenever they are discovered. He first questions the regime, and then rebels totally, incinerating the fire chief instead of the books, escaping from the city and joining a rural community whose members are each memorizing a book, word for word, in order to preserve it. The film is more ambiguous than Bradbury's original; Truffaut seems not altogether to accept Bradbury's moral simplicity. This is particularly evident at the end, with the book people murmuring aloud the words they are committing to memory, while plodding about the snow-covered landscape like zombies. The words may be saved but literature itself seems dead. Truffaut might have been less dispassionate with a story of a future where all films are banned.   [JB]

FAIL SAFE Film (1964). Max E. Youngstein and Sidney Lumet. Directed by Sidney Lumet, starring Henry Fonda, Dan O'Herlihy, Walter Matthau, Frank Overton and Fritz Weaver. Screenplay by Walter Bernstein, based on the novel *Fail-Safe* (**1962**) by Eugene BURDICK and Harvey WHEELER. 111 mins. Colour.

This NEAR-FUTURE political thriller had the misfortune to be released less than a year after the hugely successful DR

STRANGELOVE: OR, HOW I LEARNED TO STOP WORRYING AND LOVE THE BOMB. The film-going public preferred the black farce of KUBRICK's film to the grim realism of Lumet's. A mistaken American nuclear attack on Russia results in a fury which can be assuaged only by the American President's agreement to bomb New York as an apologetic gesture. The unlikely premise is lent conviction by the stern, documentary quality of the direction.   [PN]

FAIRMAN, PAUL W. (1916–77). American editor and writer. His first published sf story was "No Teeth for the Tiger" (1950), and for some years thereafter he was a regular contributor to the Ziff-Davis magazines under his own name, the pseudonyms Robert Lee and Mallory Storm, and various house pseudonyms, including E.K. JARVIS, Clee GARSON and Paul LOHRMAN. He became editor of IF when that magazine began in Mar. 1952, but left after four issues to join the Ziff-Davis staff. He left Ziff-Davis in 1954 but returned in December 1955 and became editor of AMAZING and FANTASTIC from May 1956, a position he held until September 1958. He began and edited another magazine, DREAM WORLD, for Ziff-Davis in Feb. 1957, but it lasted for only three issues. He was one of the writers who used the Ivar JORGENSEN pseudonym, and he published several books under that name. One of his Jorgensen magazine stories, "Deadly City" (1953), was filmed as TARGET EARTH! (1954); "The Cosmic Frame" (1953 under his own name) was also filmed, as *Invasion of the Saucer Men* (1955; vt *Invasion of the Hell Creatures*). Several of his books are novelizations of TV scripts, including *The World Grabbers* (**1964**; based on an episode from *One Step Beyond*) and *City Under the Sea* (**1965**; based on VOYAGE TO THE BOTTOM OF THE SEA). The pseudonym Adam CHASE was used for one book written in collaboration by PF and Milton LESSER, *The Golden Ape* (**1959**). He also wrote several novels published misleadingly under Lester DEL REY's byline, although Del Rey had only contributed plot outlines: *The Runaway Robot* (**1965**); *Tunnel Through Time* (**1966**); *Siege Perilous* (**1966**; vt *The Man Without a Planet*) and *Prisoners of Space* (**1968**). There may have been more of these. *See* Lester DEL REY.   [BS]
Other works: *I, the Machine* (**1968**); *The Forgetful Robot* (**1968**); *The Doomsday Exhibit* (coll. **1971**).
See also: UNDER THE SEA.

FALCONER, KENNETH *See* C.M. KORNBLUTH.

FALKNER, JOHN (? –). British writer, whose routine sf adventures are *Untrodden Streets of Time* (**1954**), which involves time travel and a princess, and *Overlords of Andromeda* (**1955**).   [JC]

FAMOUS FANTASTIC MYSTERIES US PULP magazine which published 81

April 1942. Cover by Virgil Finlay.

issues Sep./Oct. 1939 (Vol.1 no.1) - Jun. 1953 (Vol.14 no.4). It was originally part of the Frank A. MUNSEY chain but was sold to Popular Publications, from Mar. 1943. Mary GNAEDINGER was editor throughout.

Although it published a few original stories *FFM* was basically a reprint magazine, originally founded to reprint fantasy from the Munsey pulps. After its sale to Popular it switched to the reprinting of novels and stories not previously published in magazines. The first few monthly issues used much short material, with novels serialized, but after going bi-monthly in Aug. 1940, *FFM* presented a complete novel in every issue. The early issues featured novels by such Munsey regulars as A. MERRITT, George Allan ENGLAND, Ray CUMMINGS and Francis STEVENS. Novels reprinted from original hardback editions included several by John TAINE, William Hope HODGSON, H. Rider HAGGARD, E. Charles VIVIAN, S. Fowler WRIGHT and H.G. WELLS. By offering access to such material *FFM* allowed many pulp sf fans to broaden their acquaintance with non-pulp material — even extending to such authors as G.K. CHESTERTON and Franz KAFKA. The quality of illustration was also exceptionally high — Virgil FINLAY did much of his best work for the magazine.   [BS]

Collectors should note: Vol.7 had only five numbers instead of the usual six; Vol.14 had only four numbers; the title page of Apr. '53 reads Apr. '43. During the war years publication was sometimes irregular, but the volume numeration, is consistent, with the exceptions noted above. A Canadian reprint edition ran Feb. '48-Aug. '52; this was the second Canadian reprinting of *FFM*, many stories from which appeared in the Canadian SUPER SCIENCE STORIES.

No. 3, 1967. Cover by Virgil Finlay.

FAMOUS SCIENCE FICTION US DIGEST-size magazine. Nine issues, Winter 1966 (Vol.1 no.1) - Spring 1969 (Vol.2 no.3). It was one of the reprint magazines

edited by R.A.W. LOWNDES for Health Knowledge Inc., using material from the PULPS of the 1930s plus a few original short stories. The most notable of its reprints was Laurence MANNING's "Man Who Awoke" series (1933 *Wonder Stories*; Summer 1967-Summer 1968). Lowndes contributed a series of editorials on "Standards in Science Fiction" in issues 2-6, later reprinted as *Three Faces of Science Fiction* (**1973**).   [BS]

FANAC American FANZINE, edited from Berkeley by Terry CARR and Ron ELLIK (1958-61) and subsequently by Walter Breen (1961-3). *Fanac* was a small but frequent publication carrying information on sf writers and events, and news of sf fans and their activities. Its informal and humorous style was popular and became a model for later fanzines. Contributors included well-known fans and professional writers. *Fanac* won the HUGO award for best fanzine in 1959.   [PR]

FANCIFUL TALES OF TIME AND SPACE US DIGEST-size magazine. One issue, Fall 1936, published by Shepherd and Wollheim; ed. Donald A. WOLLHEIM. *FTTS* contained a mixture of weird, sf and fantasy stories, including work by H.P. LOVECRAFT, August DERLETH and David KELLER, and the first publication of Robert E. HOWARD's poem "Solomon Kane's Homecoming". A semi-professional publication rather like the earlier MARVEL TALES, it seems to have found no adequate distribution.
[FHP/MJE]

FANDOM The active readership of sf and fantasy, maintaining contacts through FANZINES and CONVENTIONS. Fandom originated in the late 1920s, shortly after the appearance of the first sf magazines; readers contacted each other, formed local groups (some of which, notably the SF LEAGUE, were

professionally sponsored), and in 1930 began publication of amateur magazines, later known as fanzines. The first organized convention was held in Leeds in 1937 and the first World SF Convention in New York in 1939. From the 1920s to the 1950s, when sf was a minority interest, the number of people in fandom was small, probably no more than 500. Since the 1960s, however, the number of fans has increased to several thousand, though these, of course, represent no more than a tiny fraction of the wider sf readership. Fandom is made up of both readers and writers of sf; many authors started as fans and many fans have written sf, so there is no absolute distinction between the two groups. Fans themselves are predominantly young, male, with higher education, and a scientific or technical background; exceptions, however, are numerous, and the stereotype is becoming less pronounced. Fandom, like sf, is primarily American, though other English-speaking countries quickly adopted the concept. Continental Europe, Japan and elsewhere followed much later; but increasing translation of and interest in sf has now led to fandom spreading to some 25 or so countries, from Norway to New Zealand.

Fandom is not a normal hobbyist group. It has been suggested that if sf in some way ceased to exist, fandom would continue to function quite happily without it. That is an exaggeration, of course; but it indicates the difference between sf fans and ostensibly similar groups devoted to Westerns, romances, detective fiction, and suchlike. The reason for this may lie in the fact that sf is a speculative literature and in its consequent attraction for readers actively interested in new ideas and concepts in addition to those searching simply for vicarious entertainment. Early fans were active in rocketry, radical politics, and quasi-Utopian experiments; later fans seem to find fanzines, conventions, and the interaction of fandom itself a sufficient outlet for their energies and ideas. Though fandom has a tradition and history, even a FAN LANGUAGE, fans are notably independent; few, for example, belong to national organizations such as the N3F or BSFA, and many, if not most, publish individual and independent fanzines, a fact that at least one outside sociologist (Fredric Wertham, *The World Of Fanzines* **1973**) has found remarkable and even "unique".

There is a fannish word "fiawol", an acronym for "fandom is a way of life"; it is a half-joking concept, but not altogether untrue. Just as sf is unrestricted in the scope of its interests, so too are fans and fandom. Fandom is thus a collection of people with a common background in sf and a common interest in communication, whether through discussion, chatter, correspondence, or fanzine publishing. The result is more nearly a group of friends, or even a subculture, than a simple fan club or a literary society. [PR]

FANE, BRON See R.L. FANTHORPE.

FAN LANGUAGE Sf enthusiasts, in common with other groups, have evolved their own terminology and usage. This fan language comprises words and phrases used in the writing of sf itself and also the more arcane and whimsical jargon of FANDOM and FANZINES.

Most sf readers are familiar with the shorthand of their literature and words like "spaceship", "robot", "time-machine", or even "FTL drive", "spacewarp", and "ray-gun" need little or no glossing. These words, however, originated in sf and required explanation when first coined (see TERMINOLOGY). Only the growth in popularity of sf has led to the acceptance of such terms as part of everyday English.

The language of fandom, however, has a more restricted use and thus is less familiar. Much of it is associated with fanzines, including the specialized art of duplicating them, and much of it has resulted from simple contraction: "corflu", for example, is nothing stranger than correcting fluid (for stencils) and the word "fanzine" itself (now enshrined in the *Oxford English Dictionary*) is a shortening of fan magazine. Of more interest than this simple jargon are words resulting from the customs and institutions of fandom. Examples are "egoboo" (from ego-boost) — the satisfaction gained from praise or recognition, such as seeing one's name in print; "mundane" — a non-fan; and acronyms like to "gafiate" (to get away from it all) — to leave fandom; "fiawol", fandom is a way of life, and "fijagh", fandom is just a goddam hobby. Associated with these are purely capricious terms such as the verb "faunch" instead of "yearn" or the traditional fannish expletive "fout!". Few of these contractions, acronyms, and neologisms are, of course, necessary; the fan argot is merely a matter of good humour and in no way a secret code to baffle outsiders. The one exception is "sf", the only contraction used by science fiction fans; journalists and other non-sympathetic outsiders can readily be identified by their use of the repugnant "sci-fi".

Various guides to fan language have been published (by fans) in America and Britain. Wilson TUCKER's "Neofan's Guide" (**1955**; rev. 1973) is a standard and useful introduction. [PR]

FANTASTIC US DIGEST-size magazine, first published by Ziff-Davis in Summer 1952, ed. Howard BROWNE. Paul FAIRMAN took over the editorship, Oct. 1956, and was replaced by Cele GOLDSMITH, Dec. 1958. The title was bought by Sol Cohen's Ultimate Publishing Co., Sep.

British edition, Vol. 1, no. 2, 1953. Cover by Vernon Kramer.

1965 and mainly published reprints until mid-1968. Joseph Ross was managing editor in this period. Harry HARRISON became editor late in 1968 but left very quickly. In the somewhat confused period which followed both Barry MALZBERG and Robert SILVERBERG were briefly associated with the magazine. Ted WHITE became managing editor in Apr. 1969 and remains editor today. The reprints were phased out gradually and for the past few years the magazine has used only original material. For much of its early life *F* was bi-monthly, but at its height — in the Goldsmith period — it was monthly, beginning with Feb. 1957 The Ultimate version began in Sep. 1965 as a bi-monthly, but the magazine went on to a quarterly schedule in 1976.

Browne originally intended *Fantastic* to attract a wider audience than its companion AMAZING STORIES, and published stories under by-lines famous outside the sf field, including Raymond Chandler, Truman Capote, Mickey Spillane and Evelyn WAUGH (though it seems certain that neither Chandler nor Spillane actually wrote the stories credited to them). After 1953, when it was combined with the much older magazine, FANTASTIC ADVENTURES, the magazine deteriorated to become a standardized fantasy companion to *Amazing*, but under the imaginative editorship of Cele Goldsmith it recovered well. Fritz LEIBER revived his SWORD-AND-SORCERY heroes Fafhrd and Gray Mouser for an issue containing only his stories (Nov. 1959) and they remained an irregular feature in the magazine. Authors whose first published stories appeared in *F* during this period include Thomas M. DISCH, Ursula K. LE GUIN and Roger ZELAZNY. David R. BUNCH was a regular contributor. A series of reprints selected by Sam MOSKOWITZ recovered such important stories as Clifford D. SIMAK's *The Creator* (1935 *Marvel Tales*; **1946**; Jul. 1961 *Fantastic*) and P. Schuyler MILLER's "The Titan" (first third

published as serial in *Marvel Tales* 1935; title novella of *The Titan* coll. **1952**; Aug. 1962 *Fantastic*). After a bad period in the mid-1960s, *F* improved again under Ted White, featuring a notable series of articles by Alexei and Cory PANSHIN as "Science Fiction in Dimension" (1970–73) and publishing much early work by Gordon EKLUND. [BS]

Collectors should note: The title changed to *Fantastic Science Fiction* in Apr. '55; to *Fantastic Science Fiction Stories* in Sep. '59; to *Fantastic Stories of Imagination* in Oct. '60; to *Fantastic Stories* in Sep. '65. Vol.1 ('52) had only three numbers. Vol.6 ('57, during which *F* went monthly) had 11 numbers. Subsequent vols had 12 numbers, until Vol.14, which had only six. Vol.15 began the bi-monthly schedule, six numbers to a vol., which continued in an orderly manner until Nov. '74, which was followed by Feb. '75. The bi-monthly schedule resumed until Feb. '76, after which *F* became quarterly.

A British edition published eight numbered issues in '53–4. An anthology of stories from *F* was *The Best From Fantastic* (anth. **1973**), ed. Ted White.

British edition, no. 11, with a typically romantic R.G. Jones cover.

FANTASTIC ADVENTURES US PULP MAGAZINE published by Ziff-Davis as a companion to AMAZING STORIES. 128 issues, May 1939–Mar. 1953. It began as a bi-monthly, BEDSHEET-size, but maintained a monthly schedule from Vol.2 no.1 (Jan. 1940) for most of its existence, shrinking to PULP-size in Jun. 1940. From 1939–Dec. 1949 it was ed. Ray PALMER, and from then until it merged with FANTASTIC by Howard BROWNE. William L. HAMLING was managing editor Nov. 1947–Feb. 1951.

The bulk of *FA*'s contents was provided by a small stable of writers using a variety of house pseudonyms. Palmer did, however, publish several stories by Edgar Rice BURROUGHS, 1939–42, and some material by established sf and fantasy writers —

Robert BLOCH was a frequent contributor. The magazine was at its best in 1950–51 when it published Theodore STURGEON's first novel *The Dreaming Jewels* (Feb. 1950; **1950**) and notable long stories by Walter M. MILLER, Lester DEL REY and William TENN. *FA* hardly bears comparison with *ASF*'s short-lived but excellent companion UNKNOWN, but sf writers given *carte blanche* to write pure fantasy for *FA* did often produce readable material with a distinctive whimsical and ironic flavour. The mass-produced material was, however, quite negligible. Between 1941–3 and 1948–51 unsold issues were bound up in threes and sold as a quarterly reissue series. [BS]

Collectors should note: The months Jul., Sep., Nov. and Dec. '40 were skipped over in the monthly schedule period, as were Feb. and Apr. '41. Sep. '43 was omitted, and the schedule thereafter was quite irregular until it stabilized as a bi-monthly from May '46 and as a monthly again from Sep. '47 for the rest of its existence. Vol.1 had four numbers, Vol.2 had eight, Vol.3 had 10, Vol.4 had 12, Vol.5 had 10, Vol.6 had four, Vols 7 and 8 had five each, Vol.9 had eight, and the remaining vols had 12. The last number was Vol.15 no.3. There were two British editions: the first released two numbered issues in '46, the second reprinted 24 numbered issues '50–'53.

FANTASTIC ADVENTURES QUARTERLY REISSUE *See* FANTASTIC ADVENTURES.

FANTASTIC ADVENTURES YEARBOOK One of the many reprint DIGEST-size magazines issued by Sol Cohen's Ultimate Publishing Co. Its only issue was released in 1970. [BS]

FANTASTIC JOURNEY, THE Television series (1976). Bruce Lansbury Productions/Columbia Pictures Television/NBC. Directed by Andrew V. McLaglen (pilot episode), starring Carl Franklin, Susan Howard, Roddy McDowall, Jared Martin, Jason Evers, Leif Erickson (pilot episode), Karen Somerville, Scott Thomas and Don Knight. Pilot episode written by Merwin Gerard, Michael Michaelian, Kathryn Michaelian Powers; story editor: D.C. FONTANA. Series produced by Leonard Katzman. Pilot episode 75 mins, regular episodes 50 mins. Colour.

Some degree of originality went into the making of the pilot episode, which deals with an expedition to investigate the mystery of the Bermuda Triangle, but after an effectively eerie opening, in which the explorers' boat is consumed by a pulsating green cloud, it soon becomes evident that they are still within the borders of TV-formula land. Reaching an island that "isn't on the map", they slowly discover that the landscape consists of segments of time and space from different periods in history, as well

as from the future — an idea probably inspired by Fred HOYLE's novel *October the First is Too Late* (**1966**). This concept allows the protagonists to encounter a different culture each week, all of them being within walking distance. Subsequent episodes have kept rigidly to the pattern previously established by such sf series as TIME TUNNEL and STAR TREK: the protagonists, including some from the future, threatened in some way by each new society they encounter, only to win out in the end due to their superior abilities — either physical, mental or moral. The various cultures on display are patterned on extremely well-worn stereotypes. [JB]

March 1948, with a typically erotic Stephen Lawrence cover.

FANTASTIC NOVELS US bi-monthly PULP reprint magazine, companion to FAMOUS FANTASTIC MYSTERIES. Five issues, Jul. 1940-Apr. 1941, published by the Frank A. MUNSEY Corp.; it was revived by Popular Publications to publish 20 more issues, Mar. 1948-Jun. 1951. It was edited in both incarnations by Mary GNAEDINGER.

FN used a great deal of material by A. MERRITT. The first issue featured *The Blind Spot* (1921; **1951**) by Austin HALL and Homer Eon FLINT, serialization of which had begun in *Famous Fantastic Mysteries*, and all subsequent issues except the last featured a complete novel. Other authors whose work was reprinted include Ray CUMMINGS and George Allan ENGLAND. Two issues of a British edition appeared in 1950–51. [BS]

Collectors should note: There were two exceptions to the bi-monthly appearance: Apr. '41 followed Jan. '41, and Apr. '51 followed Jan. '51. The Mar. '48 issue was Vol.1 no.6. Remaining vols had six numbers, except that the last number was Vol.5 no.1.

FANTASTIC PLANET *See* PLANÈTE SAUVAGE, LA.

FANTASTIC SCIENCE FICTION American BEDSHEET-size magazine, intended for a juvenile audience; ed.

No. 2, 1952. Cover by Al Fago.

Walter B. Gibson, prolific pulp writer and creator of "The Shadow". Only two issues appeared, the first (Aug. 1952) published by Super Fiction Publications, the second (Dec. 1952) by Capitol Stories.

This magazine should not be confused with FANTASTIC, even though the latter, also begun in 1952, changed its title to *Fantastic Science Fiction* from Apr. 1955 to Aug. 1959. [BS]

FANTASTIC SCIENCE FICTION STORIES *See* FANTASTIC.

FANTASTIC SCIENCE THRILLER British juvenile pocketbook series published by Stanley Baker Ltd, of which six issues were released in 1954. [BS]

FANTASTIC STORIES *See* FANTASTIC.

FANTASTIC STORIES OF IMAGINATION *See* FANTASTIC.

July 1953. Cover by Walter Popp.

FANTASTIC STORY MAGAZINE *See* FANTASTIC STORY QUARTERLY.

FANTASTIC STORY QUARTERLY US PULP reprint magazine. 23 issues, Spring 1950-Spring 1955, the title changing after four issues to *Fantastic Story Magazine*. Published by Best Books. Sam MERWIN Jr was editor until Fall 1951 and was succeeded by Samuel MINES, and then Alexander Samalman for the last two issues.

Most of the reprints were from STARTLING STORIES and THRILLING WONDER STORIES, though early issues carried a good deal of material from Hugo GERNSBACK's WONDER STORIES. Mines used a few original stories and occasionally went outside the chain for reprints, e.g. publishing A.E. VAN VOGT's *Slan* (1940 *ASF*; **1946**; rev. 1951) in the Summer 1952 issue. Most issues carried a complete novel. [BS]

Collectors should note: The first seven vols had three numbers each, and Vol.8 had only two. The quarterly schedule was not strict: there were five issues in '52 (Win., Spr., Sum., Fal., Nov.), six in '53 (Jan., Mar., May, Jul., Sep., Win.), three in '54 (Spr., Sum., Fal.) and two in '55 (Win., Spr.). There was a Canadian reprint edition of the first four numbers.

June 1956. Cover by Ed Emsh.

FANTASTIC UNIVERSE US DIGEST-size magazine, last six issues PULP-size. 69 issues, Jun./Jul. 1953–Mar. 1960, published by Leo MARGULIES' King-Size Publications. It began as a bi-monthly, but went monthly in Sep. 1954, and held to that schedule for most of its life. Ed. Sam MERWIN Jr, Jun.-Nov. 1953; Beatrice Jones, Jan.-Mar. 1954; Leo Margulies, May 1954-Aug. 1956; Hans Stefan SANTESSON, Sep. 1956-Mar. 1960.

FU's material spanned the entire fantasy spectrum; in effect it became the poor man's MAGAZINE OF FANTASY AND SCIENCE FICTION. An anthology of the best stories from its pages was published as *The Fantastic Universe Omnibus* (anth. **1960**), ed. Hans Stefan Santesson. [BS]

Collectors should note: There were 12 vols each of six numbers, except for Vols 6, 10 and 12, which had five. The monthly schedule was broken in '58–'59, the issues running Nov., Jan., Mar., May, Jul., Sep., then monthly to the end.

FANTASTIC VOYAGE Film (1966). 20th Century-Fox. Directed by Richard Fleischer, starring Stephen Boyd, Raquel Welch, Edmund O'Brien and Donald Pleasence. Screenplay by Harry Kleiner, based on a story by Otto Clement and J. Lewis BIXBY. 100 mins. Colour.

A submarine, complete with a crew of medical experts, is reduced in size and injected into the bloodstream of an important scientist in order to remove a blood-clot from his brain. The special effects by L.B. Abbott, Art Cruickshank and Emil Kosa Jr are impressive, as are the sets duplicating, in giant size, various organs of the body, such as the heart, lungs and brain, designed by art director Dale Hennesy. The visual qualities of the film fail to compensate for its puerile script. The novelization by Isaac ASIMOV was published in 1966. [JB]

FANTASTIC VOYAGES The fantastic voyage is one of the oldest literary forms, and remains one of the basic frameworks for the casting of literary fantasies today. Of the prose forms extant before the development of the novel in the 18th century, the fantastic voyage is the most important in the ancestry of sf (*see* PROTO SCIENCE FICTION). Among others, Johannes KEPLER's *Somnium* (**1634**), Francis BACON's *New Atlantis* (**1627**), Tommaso CAMPANELLA's *City of the Sun* (**1623**) and CYRANO DE BERGERAC's *Other Worlds* (**1656–62**) all take this form, as do the oldest of all works ever claimed as ancestral to sf: the Sumerian *Epic of Gilgamesh* from the third millennium BC, and HOMER's *Odyssey* from the first millennium BC. In fact, the fantastic voyage continued to dominate speculative fiction and the scientific romance long after the rise of the novel, whose basic pretence was the painstaking imitation of experience (what the critic Ian Watt calls "formal realism"). It is partly because of this formal separation of speculative literature from the development of 19th-century social literature that there remains something of a gulf between speculative fiction and the "literary mainstream" today. The first sf story cast in the form of a novel was Mary SHELLEY's *Frankenstein* (**1818**) but there were very few comparable works written in the century which followed. The bulk of Jules VERNE's imaginative work falls into the category of "voyages imaginaires", and many of H.G. WELLS's scientific romances take similar form. Among the important fantastic voyages which today may be classified as sf are: *The Man in the Moone* (**1638**) by Francis GODWIN; *The Consolidator* (**1705**) by Daniel DEFOE; *Gulliver's Travels* (**1726**) by Jonathan SWIFT; *A Journey to the World Underground* (**1742**) by Ludwig HOLBERG; *Symzonia* (**1820**) by Adam SEABORN; *A Voyage to the Moon* (**1827**) by Joseph ATTERLEY; *Journey to the Centre of the Earth* (**1864**) and *20,000 Leagues Under the Sea* (**1869**) by Jules Verne and

Across the Zodiac (**1880**) by Percy GREG. These voyages took their heroes over the Earth's surface, into worlds underground and beneath the sea, to the Moon and to other planets. Important new scope for the fantastic voyage was opened in the last few years of the 19th century by H.G. Wells, in *The Time Machine* (**1895**), which opened up the limitless vistas of the future to planned tourism, and by Robert William COLE in *The Struggle for Empire* (**1900**), the first major interstellar adventure story. These new imaginative territories were to prove immensely significant for 20th-century imaginative literature.

The fantastic voyage has, of course, also remained central within the literature of the supernatural imagination, which proved even less adaptable to the form of the novel despite the success of Gothic novels in the wake of Mrs Radcliffe's *Mysteries of Udolpho* (**1794**). As the supernatural imagination has been influenced and infiltrated by the scientific imagination it has been the fantastic voyage far more than any other narrative form which has provided a suitable medium for "hybrid" works. Thus there are in the 20th century a considerable number of fantastic voyages which are difficult to classify by the standard genre borderlines (which are primarily concerned with the conventions used in the novel form). In this no-man's-land within the territories of imaginative literature exist virtually all the works of writers such as William Hope HODGSON, Edgar Rice BURROUGHS, Ray CUMMINGS and Abraham MERRITT, and various individual novels of note: Frigyes KARINTHY's Gulliver sequels *Voyage to Faremido* (**1916**; trans. **1966**) and *Capillaria* (**1922**; trans. **1966**); David LINDSAY's *A Voyage to Arcturus* (**1920**); Herman HESSE's *Journey to the East* (**1932**; **1956**), Ruthven TODD's *The Lost Traveller* (**1943**), John Cowper POWYS's *Up and Out* (**1957**), Norton Juster's *The Phantom Tollbooth* (**1961**) and Michel Bernanos's *The Other Side of the Mountain* (**1967**; trans. **1968**).

When Hugo GERNSBACK first demarcated sf as a genre in the 1920s he co-opted both Wells and Cummings; hence both time travel and adventures in the microcosm (*see* GREAT AND SMALL) were adopted into sf at its inception. Cole was unknown, but it was not long before E.E. "Doc" SMITH, in *The Skylark of Space* (**1928**; **1946**), reopened the universe beyond the Solar System. Other milieux were quickly introduced. Edmond HAMILTON, in "Locked Worlds" (**1929**), imported the notion of PARALLEL WORLDS long established in fantasy fiction. The notion of ALTERNATE WORLDS employed by Guy DENT in *Emperor of the If* (**1926**) was introduced into sf in the fantastic-voyage form by Jack WILLIAMSON in *The Legion of Time* (**1938**; **1952**). A significant refinement in the interstellar fantastic voyage, the

GENERATION STARSHIP, was introduced a few years later, most significantly in Robert HEINLEIN's "Universe" (1941). Space travel was the one hypothetical variant of the fantastic voyage into which it was possible to introduce a rigorously logical approach in an attempt to achieve realism. Notable attempts include Verne's *From the Earth to the Moon* (1865) and *Round the Moon* (1870), Konstantin TSIOLKOVSKY's *Beyond the Planet Earth* (1920 Russia; trans. 1960) and Laurence MANNING's "Voyage of the Asteroid" (1932). No similar attempt was possible with the means employed in time travel or voyages into the microcosm, parallel worlds etc., all of which necessarily remained literary devices.

A popular variant on the voyage into the microcosm is the voyage into the human body, as in the film FANTASTIC VOYAGE, novelized by Isaac ASIMOV as *Fantastic Voyage* (1966). But the principal imaginative territory which remained untouched as a milieu for the fantastic voyage (in both sf and pure fantasy) for many years was "inner space". One pulp-sf writer who did write accounts of journeys into the mind was L. Ron HUBBARD, in his *Unknown* fantasies "Typewriter in the Sky" (1940) and "Fear" (1940; 1957; published as *Fear & Typewriter in the Sky* 1951). Hubbard's pioneer spirit in this respect later led him into more profitable enterprises than writing sf (*see* DIANETICS). It was not until some time later that sf stories featuring journeys into the mind began to appear. Notable examples include Peter PHILLIPS's "Dreams are Sacred" (1948), Daniel F. GALOUYE's "Descent into the Maelstrom" (1961) and two classic novels by Philip K. DICK: *Eye in the Sky* (1957) and *Ubik* (1969).

The opening up of all these imaginary territories gave sf writers limitless scope for invention. There is no speculation, whether physical, biological, social or metaphysical, that cannot somehow be incarnated within the conventions of sf. Voyages into fluid worlds where anything and everything may happen — where the characters become helpless victims of chaos or godlike creators — may be envisaged (e.g. Ward MOORE's "Transient", 1960, M.K. JOSEPH's *The Hole in the Zero*, 1967). Even voyages into mathematical abstraction are possible, e.g. "The Mathenauts" (1964) by Norman KAGAN. This potential exists nowhere else, because only sf has drawn up a framework of conventions and a vocabulary of literary devices which permit it. It is a potential that sf writers have, for various reasons, been greatly inhibited from developing, but they have — whatever their failings — established the first signposts within these realms.

At its simplest the fantastic voyage is an episodic, picaresque form whose function 'is simply to present a series of adventures in baroque or bizarre surroundings; but it is rare to find the form used with no higher ambition than this. In most cases the fantastic voyage takes the form of a quest, the most famous 20th-century example being J.R.R. TOLKIEN's fantastic trilogy *The Lord of the Rings* (1954; 1954; 1955). The quest may be for a person, an object or a place, but the movement through a landscape or spacescape is usually paralleled by a growth towards some kind of maturity or acceptance in the protagonist's mind: towards self-knowledge in the psychologically oriented version of the genre, as in J.G. BALLARD's *The Drowned World* (1962), in which the luxuriant landscape becomes an emblem of the protagonist's state of being; towards philosophical knowledge, as in David Lindsay's *A Voyage to Arcturus* (1920), in which the protagonist comes to understand the flesh, the will, even the yearning for spiritual transfiguration as snares, the reality being a stern, painful, unromantic affair (*see* METAPHYSICS *for further discussion of this category*); and towards greater knowledge of the external nature of the world and new paradigms and conceptual models by which to understand its working, as in stories as diverse as *Rasselas* (1759) by Samuel JOHNSON, *Non-Stop* (1958; vt *Starship* USA) by Brian ALDISS and *Inverted World* (1974; vt *The Inverted World* USA) by Christopher PRIEST. Stories in this latter category are perhaps the most typically science-fictional; indeed it is only within the conventions of sf that they can be adequately created. They are discussed further in the entry CONCEPTUAL BREAKTHROUGH. Generally speaking, the form of the fantastic voyage tends inevitably towards a state of allegory or metaphor, and it is here that its continued value resides, and also that its most irritating clichés continually recur.

Any list of notable fantastic voyages in modern sf is necessarily highly selective, but some of the most important and representative which have appeared since 1926 are as follows: *The World Below* (1929) by S. Fowler WRIGHT; *Out of the Silent Planet* (1938) by C.S. LEWIS; *The Voyage of the Space Beagle* (1939–50; fix-up 1950) by A.E. VAN VOGT; *Big Planet* (1952; 1957) by Jack VANCE; "Surface Tension" (1952) by James BLISH; *Mission of Gravity* (1954) by Hal CLEMENT; *Journey Beyond Tomorrow* (1963) by Robert SHECKLEY; *The Ship That Sailed the Time Stream* (1965) by G.C. EDMONDSON; *Chthon* (1967) by Piers ANTHONY; *The Jewels of Aptor* (1962; exp. 1968), *The Einstein Intersection* (1967) and *Nova* (1968) by Samuel R. DELANY; *Picnic on Paradise* (1968) by Joanna RUSS; *Space Chantey* (1968) by R.A. LAFFERTY; *2001: A Space Odyssey* (1968) by Arthur C. CLARKE; *Tau Zero* (1970) by Poul ANDERSON; *Downward to the Earth* (1970) and *Son of Man* (1971) by Robert SILVERBERG; *Ringworld* (1970) by Larry NIVEN; *The Infernal Desire Machines of Dr. Hoffman* (1972; vt *War of Dreams* USA) by Angela CARTER; *Hiero's Journey* (1973) by Sterling E. LANIER; *Orbitsville* (1975) by Bob SHAW and *The Balloonist* (1976) by MacDonald Harris. [BS/PN]

FANTASY Fantasy and sf go together as closely as fish and chips, with the difference that while chips are not made out of fish, it can be argued that sf is a sub-genre of fantasy. Certainly the two are difficult to distinguish, and a number of genre magazines have overcome the difficulty by lumping them together: FANTASTIC SCIENCE FICTION STORIES, the MAGAZINE OF FANTASY AND SCIENCE FICTION, SCIENCE FANTASY, and a number of others. The Italian for sf is *fantascienza*.

On the other hand, several critics have argued that the two genres need never be confused. Darko SUVIN is one such (*see* DEFINITIONS OF SF). The simplest way of distinguishing them is probably to go in two steps. First, imagine the whole of literary fiction as being located within a great circle drawn on a piece of paper; inside the large circle is a smaller circle, labelled fantasy. Everything within the larger circle tells a made-up story, but the difference is that the stories in the smaller circle could not happen in the present or the past, and those in the rest of the larger circle could; they are mimetic of real life. Fantasy, in at least one key area of the story, always lacks verisimilitude. This distinction is not wholly satisfactory, of course, because it places too great an emphasis on the beliefs of the reader; for all we know the audience of HOMER believed that giants with one eye in the middle of their forehead actually existed, and that the *Odyssey* was a realistic travelogue.

Within the smaller, fantasy circle is one smaller still, marked sf. (This is a way of saying that all sf is fantasy, but all fantasy is not sf; just as the earlier case supposed that all fantasy was fiction but that all fiction is not fantasy). We may, in a rough-and-ready way, say that the contents of the sf circle have in common that they seek to persuade the reader that their events have a rational explanation. But, though rational, such stories do not imitate the events of the real world, either because the imagined events are set in the future or for some other reason, some imagined fact which has not taken place in the real present, such as the Earth being struck by a comet, or a black president being elected in the USA. These are not irrational or supernatural events, but they are fantastic in that they have, as yet, no parallel in the real world.

Everything within the fantasy circle, but outside the smaller sf circle, depends at some point on the irrational, usually on some form of the occult, or on intervention by a supernatural power, or magic. Non-sf fantasy is oriented towards mystery, not knowledge; it is not cognitive; it might take as its slogan "there are more things in heaven and earth ..."; it titillates us with the unknown; its characters are often initiates into dark or strange secrets.

This crude working distinction between sf and non-sf fantasy meets a number of problems in practice. Some stories, for example, posit worlds in which magic works (therefore fantasy), but demystify the magic and treat it rationally (therefore having strong links of feeling with sf). Ursula K. LE GUIN's "Earthsea" trilogy is one example, and the entry MAGIC discusses many more.

Another common difficulty is met when sf writers invent a device which in the light of our present-day knowledge of science seems impossible, but which is presented to us as plausibly as possible, so that we suspend our disbelief. Such devices are common in sf (many are enumerated in IMAGINARY SCIENCE) and include TIME TRAVEL, MATTER TRANS-MISSION, ANTI-GRAVITY and FASTER-THAN-LIGHT travel. Because the effort is made to rationalize such devices, we commonly treat them as sf rather than non-sf fantasy; where no such effort is made, as in the time travel of Mark TWAIN's *A Connecticut Yankee in King Arthur's Court* (**1889**, vt *A Yankee in the Court of King Arthur*), we incline to think of the result as fantasy, at least in that part of the story. And here is another common difficulty; fiction is seldom homogeneous; most works of sf contain elements of fantasy, and much ordinary mimetic realism as well.

It follows from all this that it is possible to take a basic story, and by emphasizing its mysterious elements render it as fantasy, or by rationalizing it render it as sf. This is often done when sf takes MYTHOLOGY as its base. A simple, amusing example is Isaac ASIMOV's story "Pâté de Foie Gras" (**1956**), which satirizes all such sf attempts at rationalizing fairy stories and legends in an sf retelling of "The Goose that Laid the Golden Eggs".

There is no critical consensus about exactly what constitutes fantasy; many attempts have been made, in France especially, to define it, confusing the issue even more for English readers, since *le fantastique* does not have exactly the same meaning as fantasy; a closer English word might be "uncanny". The best-known recent example is Tzvetan TODOROV's *Introduction à la littérature fantastique* (**1970**; trans. as *The Fantastic: A Structural Approach to a Literary Genre* **1973**). Todorov sees fantasy, rather exclusively, as hovering in that area where the reader hesitates between imputing a rational or a supernatural explanation to the events described.

Fantasy (as we shall call non-sf fantasy from now on) is much older than sf. Indeed, until the 18th century, when it came to be believed that the mysteries of the universe were amenable to reason and

analysis, sf had no theoretical basis on which to rest. Realistic, mimetic literature is itself fairly recent, and almost all fiction written before the 18th century could be regarded by us (not very usefully) as one form or other of fantasy, from Virgil's to Chaucer's to much of Shakespeare's.

But this entry will concentrate on fantasy of the 19th and 20th centuries, and the ways in which it has been cross-fertilized with sf. It is very clear that the readership of fantasy (at least certain kinds of fantasy) is very similar to that of sf. Fans of, say, Frank HERBERT are not identical with those of J.R.R. TOLKIEN, but it is safe to guess that the number of readers who have read and enjoyed both authors is a high proportion of their total readership. Although the world of Tolkien's *The Lord of the Rings* (**1954–5**) allows magic, where that of Herbert's *Dune* (**1965**) does not, the two books have in common the creation of an immensely detailed, richly imagined ALTERNATE WORLD in which individual heroism can play an important role. The strong mystical streak in Herbert's work makes the similarity even stronger. Generic distinctions between sf and fantasy serve only to obscure the very real likenesses to be found between works of this kind.

The kind of fantasy which creates detailed, self-consistent alternate worlds is the kind most read by sf readers, and most written by sf writers "on vacation". Such is Poul ANDERSON's *Three Hearts and Three Lions* (1953; exp. **1961**) and Jack VANCE's *The Dying Earth* (coll. **1950**). Further back, many of the works of Lord DUNSANY are effectively set in a coherent, alternate universe, as are those of E.R. EDDISON and James Branch CABELL. All three writers have had repercussions in sf which go beyond the merely stylistic. The most notable recent example of fantasy set in a self-sufficient other world is the "Gormenghast" trilogy by Mervyn PEAKE, which is set either in an alternate world or in an unknown corner of our own.

Much early PULP sf concentrates so heavily on romantic adventures in alternate worlds that it can be read as readily as fantasy as it can sf. (Another important distinction between fantasy and sf is found in the expectations the reader carries to the work in question; examples would be the interplanetary romances of C.S. LEWIS, or perhaps even the occult thrillers of Charles WILLIAMS, within which a dogged sf reader will easily find sf rationales, though there can be no doubt that they belong primarily to the tradition of fantasy.) The two most important early pulp writers in this respect are Edgar Rice BURROUGHS and A. MERRITT; both were heavily imitated; both offer flimsy rationales for fantastic quests and adventures. A more literary example is *A Voyage to Arcturus* (**1920**) by David LINDSAY, in which a fantastic moral allegory is given sufficient surface realism to qualify as sf.

The entire sub-genre of SWORD AND SORCERY (often called HEROIC FANTASY), by clinging to magic and occult mystery as one of its essential elements, is clearly fantasy, but in its marketing it is presented very much as a form of sf, and is often written by the same writers. Some of the most celebrated examples here are the "Conan" stories of Robert E. HOWARD, the "Northwest Smith" stories of C.L. MOORE, the "Fafhrd and Gray Mouser" stories of Fritz LEIBER and the "Witchworld" stories of Andre NORTON. There are hundreds of others. Another interesting novel by Leiber is *Conjure Wife* (1943; **1953**), which falls within Todorov's definition of the fantastic by leaving the reader suspended for a long time between natural and supernatural explanations for its menacing events; it thus exists precisely on the borderline between fantasy and sf.

When HARDCORE sf writers like Robert HEINLEIN, Poul Anderson and Larry NIVEN write fantasy, as they all have, it is amusing to note how hard the old habits die; they persist in subjecting the marvellous and the magical to a saturnine, rationalist scrutiny, treating magic very much as if it were a science. The distinction between magic and science is not wholly clear at the best of times; Arthur C. CLARKE has commented that "any sufficiently advanced technology is indistinguishable from magic". Larry Niven and David GERROLD's *The Flying Sorcerers* (**1971**) is constructed around this precept.

Many of the most notable fantasy magazines, six of the most important being WEIRD TALES, UNKNOWN, FANTASTIC ADVENTURES, FANTASTIC NOVELS, FANTASTIC and BEYOND FANTASY FICTION, have had lists of contributors which overlap considerably with those of the sf magazines; two of the most important writers active in both areas were Henry KUTTNER and Ray BRADBURY; Bradbury at least was visibly more at home with fantasy than with sf, and all of his sf has strong fantastic elements; he was much influenced by Charles FINNEY's *The Circus of Dr. Lao* (**1935**), which presents the typical fantasy situation of the irrational bursting in upon the lives of ordinary people and changing their outlook.

Many of the best-known sf artists could more accurately be described as fantasists; prominent in this group are Virgil FINLAY, Hannes BOK (who also wrote fantasies), Roy KRENKEL, Edd CARTIER, Frank FRAZETTA and Karel THOLE.

Less close to sf than alternate-world fantasies, though still too close for some readers, are fantasies of horror and the occult. Sf and occult horror meet in the area of GOTHIC sf; sf in the CINEMA is very often of this sort. Early in the 20th century much borderline sf had occult/horror components, as in Hans Heinz EWERS' *Alraune* (**1911**; trans. **1929**),

Maurice RENARD's *Les mains d'Orlac* (**1920**; trans. as *The Hands of Orlac* **1929**) and *Le Docteur Lerne, sous-dieu* (**1908**; trans. as *New Bodies for Old* **1923**), and Guy ENDORE's *The Werewolf of Paris* (**1933**). This tradition was particularly strong in Europe; in America it found a home in *Weird Tales*, especially in the stories of Robert BLOCH and his master, H.P. LOVECRAFT.

Such sf components as other DIMENSIONS, organ transplants, ALIENS and ANDROIDS do not disguise the fundamentally fantastic nature of these works. The whole of this borderline sf tradition can be readily traced back to the tales of Mary SHELLEY and, more importantly, Edgar Allan POE.

Sf set in worlds where PSI POWERS work can often be read as if it were fantasy; such, towards the sf end of the spectrum, are Marion Zimmer BRADLEY's "Darkover" novels and, towards the fantasy end, Christopher STASHEFF's *The Warlock in Spite of Himself* (**1969**). Conflations of fantasy and sf have proved popular, and there are hundreds of such novels. Roger ZELAZNY has written many interesting variants on the theme, most recently in his "Amber" series. A sophisticated variant is *The Deep* (**1975**) by John CROWLEY, which adroitly plays upon the generic expectations of the reader in such a way that what seems to be sword-and-sorcery fantasy comes to seem, retrospectively, pure sf. More predictable are the "Deryni" novels of Katherine KURTZ, whose sf element is the use of psi powers, and whose ambience is Welsh medieval; such novels always tend towards feudal and medieval settings, often with a priestly hierarchy in power. A much more subtle quasi-medieval alternate world is found in Brian W. ALDISS's fantasy (containing many sf elements) *The Malacia Tapestry* (**1976**).

There are too many fantasists given entries in this volume to be listed here. Among the more prominent not so far mentioned are Leigh BRACKETT, John COLLIER, Marie CORELLI, L. Sprague DE CAMP, Philip José FARMER, Alan GARNER, Rudyard KIPLING, Frank OWEN, Fletcher PRATT, Thomas Burnett SWANN and T.H. WHITE. Aside from those entries already mentioned, forms of fantasy are discussed further under GODS AND DEMONS, FANTASTIC VOYAGES, MONSTERS, PROTO SF, RELIGION and SUPERNATURAL CREATURES.

We are left with one final group of fantasists, the ABSURDISTS, who create fantastic changes (often quite minor) in everyday reality, often to make a specific ironic or satiric point, rather than for the creation of frissons of horror or romantic adventure. Such a work is Franz KAFKA's *Die Verwandlung* (**1916**; trans. as *The Metamorphosis* **1937**), in which a man is turned into a beetle. Many works stem from this tradition, often FABULATIONS, such as the novels of Angela CARTER, Thomas PYNCHON or John BARTH. The "Illuminatus" trilogy (**1975**) by Robert

SHEA and Robert Anton WILSON puts many conventional fantasy devices to wholly unconventional uses in a black comedy designed to illustrate that the PARANOID is not entirely wrong. Michael MOORCOCK's "Dancers at the End of Time" books burlesque the conventions of fantasy with sophistication and self-consciousness even as they deploy them, in a series of fables set in a world where everything is available but not necessarily meaningful; like many of the absurdists', Moorcock's strategy is that of the moralist, though he might deny it, and the fantasy serves that end. The same could be said of Harlan ELLISON's rather more hectic use of fantasy elements in such stories as "Pretty Maggie Moneyeyes" (1967) and "Croatoan" (1975). [PN]

FANTASY Title used on two early British sf magazines. The first was a PULP magazine published by George Newnes Ltd; ed. T. Stanhope Sprigg. It published three issues in 1938–9. The second

version, which was subtitled "The Magazine of Science Fiction", was a

Two British magazines were called FANTASY. The pre-war version below, no. 2, 1939, has a cover by Serge Drigin. The later version above is no. 1, 1946.

DIGEST issued by the Temple Bar Publishing Co., ed. Walter GILLINGS. It also lasted three issues, Dec. 1946 and Apr. and Aug. 1947. Eric Frank RUSSELL and John Russell FEARN were featured in both series, and the second version featured three early stories by Arthur C. CLARKE (two of them pseudonymous, as E.G. O'Brien and Charles Willis).   [BS]

FANTASY AMATEUR PRESS ASSOCIATION *See* FAPA.

FANTASY AND SCIENCE FICTION *See* MAGAZINE OF FANTASY AND SCIENCE FICTION, THE.

First issue, 1947. Cover by Milo.

FANTASY BOOK US magazine, BEDSHEET-size for two issues, then various paperback formats, approximately DIGEST-size. Eight issues, Jul. 1947–Jan. 1951. Published by FANTASY PUBLISHING COMPANY INC.; ed. Garrett Ford (pseudonym of William CRAWFORD). Erratic in appearance and regularity, *FB* was generally an undistinguished magazine. Some issues appeared in three different editions, with different covers.

FB is mainly remembered for having published in its sixth issue (Jan. 1950) Cordwainer SMITH's first story, "Scanners Live in Vain". When it ceased publication it left incomplete a Murray LEINSTER serial, "Journey to Barkut". This later appeared in full in STARTLING STORIES (Jan. 1952), and in book form as *Gateway to Elsewhere* (**1954**).   [MJE] **Collectors should note:** Vol.1 had six numbers; Vol.2 had two.

FANTASY FICTION/FANTASY STORIES US DIGEST-size magazine. Two issues, May and Nov. 1950, published by Magabooks; ed. Curtis Mitchell. "Old and new Fantasy Stories but always the best" was the slogan of this short-lived magazine, whose stories were largely reprinted from general pulp magazines of the 1930s and early 1940s. It also offered prizes for reports of true fantastic experiences, and of haunted

First issue, 1950. Cover by Bill Stone.

houses. The second issue was retitled *Fantasy Stories*, carried a lengthy flying saucer feature ("Flying Saucer Secrets Blabbed by Mad Pilot", as the cover delicately put it), and was three months late in appearing. The third issue never materialized.

The final three issues of FANTASY MAGAZINE, a publication unconnected with the above, were also titled *Fantasy Fiction*.   [MJE]

This *Fantasy Fiction* is a variant title of FANTASY MAGAZINE. Cover by Bok.

FANTASY MAGAZINE/FANTASY FICTION US DIGEST-size magazine. Four issues, Feb., Jun., Aug., Nov. 1953, all but the first under the latter title, published by Future Publications; ed. Lester DEL REY for the first three issues, and Cameron Hall (Harry HARRISON) for the fourth. All the issues had covers by Hannes BOK. The first issue featured a Conan novelette revised by L. Sprague DE CAMP from Robert E. HOWARD's unpublished "The Black Stranger".   [BS]

FANTASY PRESS One of the first

American specialist publishing houses, founded by Lloyd Arthur ESHBACH in 1946. It published a number of works by such authors as John W. CAMPBELL, L. Sprague DE CAMP, E.E. SMITH, Stanley G. WEINBAUM and Jack WILLIAMSON. In 1958 Eshbach sold the company and its stock to GNOME PRESS.   [MJE]

FANTASY PUBLISHING COMPANY INC. American specialist publisher, generally known by its initials, FPCI. One of the many semi-professional publishing enterprises of William L. CRAWFORD, FPCI was one of the less notable companies to start issuing magazine sf in book form in the late 1940s. Its authors included L. Ron HUBBARD and A.E. VAN VOGT, but only with their lesser works. Crawford in later years published the magazines SPACEWAY and *Witchcraft and Sorcery* (formerly COVEN 13) under the FPCI imprint, in addition to various occult titles and books by Emil PETAJA and others.   [MJE]

FANTASY REVIEW British FANZINE, ed. Walter GILLINGS, 18 issues 1947–50. Previously editor of several British SF MAGAZINES, TALES OF WONDER (1937–42), STRANGE TALES (1946) and FANTASY (1946–7), Gillings found himself needing an outlet for his energies after the demise of the latter title, and began *FR*. It carried reviews and sf news items, and was professional in appearance. For its last three numbers the title changed to *Science-Fantasy Review*. When Gillings was given the editorship of SCIENCE FANTASY in 1950, the new sister magazine to Nova Publications' NEW WORLDS, he incorporated *Science-Fantasy Review* into its first two issues as a news-chat section, but this feature disappeared when John CARNELL assumed the editorship of *Science Fantasy* with no.3.   [PN]

FANTASY STORIES *See* FANTASY FICTION.

First issue. Cover by Jim Pitts.

FANTASY TALES British DIGEST-size magazine. One issue, Summer 1977 (current), published and ed. Stephen Jones and David A. Sutton. *FT* is a semi-professional magazine, very much in the manner of WEIRD TALES (which it closely resembles in layout). The first issue includes stories by Kenneth BULMER, Michael MOORCOCK and other British authors.   [FHP/MJE]

FANTASY TIMES American FANZINE (1941–69) ed. James V. Taurasi Sr, and briefly by Samuel MOSKOWITZ (1940s) and Frank Prieto Jr (1960s). Published erratically until 1946, *FT* thereafter established itself as a straightforward sf and fantasy newsletter containing news, notes and reviews. In 1957 its title changed to *Sf Times* and publication continued till the 465th issue in 1969. Though its contents were mostly routine records of events, the magazine did attract some attention from publishers and authors; James BLISH was its book reviewer for a time (*c.* 1956). *FT* won the HUGO award for best fanzine in 1955 and '57. A short-lived Spanish edition, *Tiempo de Fantasia*, was published in 1949 and a successful German edition, SF TIMES, began publication in 1958. [PR]

FANTHORPE, R(OBERT) L(IONEL) (1935–   ). British writer. Now a schoolteacher by profession, RLF was from 1954 to 1965 an sf writer of remarkable productivity; he has been claimed to be the world's most prolific writer in the genre. His work was intimately connected with BADGER BOOKS and associated imprints. His first story was "Worlds Without End" (under the pseudonym Lionel Roberts) in FUTURISTIC SCIENCE STORIES (1952), written at the age of 16. His first novel, *Menace from Mercury* (1954), was published under the house name Victor LA SALLE. He subsequently became responsible for the vast majority of Badger's sf and supernatural output, both with novels and with collections of stories. Some of the former and all of the latter were included in the numbered series *Supernatural Stories*. RLF would generally provide all the stories in an issue, using several pseudonyms in

addition to his own name. These titles are included as RLF collections in this entry, under title and name of the cover story's author. RLF's works were produced at the rate of a book a weekend (for which he was paid £25); they were dictated into a battery of tape-recorders and transcribed by members of his family or friends. The rushed endings of many of his novels are the consequence of batches of typing being completed, showing the allotted word-length being almost used up, with the story still in mid-plot. One series, published under the Bron Fane pseudonym, chronicles the adventures of the Bulldog Drummond-like Val Stearman and the immortal La Noire. It consists of "The Seance" (1958), "The Secret Room" (1958), "Valley of the Vampire" (1958), "The Silent Stranger" (1959), "The Other Line" (1959), "The Green Cloud" (1959), "Pursuit" (1959), "Jungle of Death" (1959), "The Crawling Fiend" (1960), "Curtain Up" (1960), "The Secret of the Lake" (1960), "The Loch Ness Terror" (1961), "The Deathless Wings" (1961), "The Green Sarcophagus" (1961), "Black Abyss" (1961), "Forbidden City" (1961), "The Secret of the Pyramid" (1961), "Something at the Door" (1961), "Forbidden Island" (1962), "Storm God's Fury" (1962), "Vengeance of the Poltergeist" (1962), "The Persian Cavern" (1962), "The Chasm of Time" (1962), "The Voice in the Wall" (1962), "Cry in the Night" (1962), "The Nine Green Men" (1963), "The Man Who Never Smiled" (1963), "Return Ticket" (1963), "The Room That Never Was" (1963), "The Walker" (1963), *Softly By Moonlight* (1963), "The Thing From Sheol" (1963), "The Man Who Knew" (1963), *Unknown Destiny* (1964), "The Warlock" (1964), *The Macabre Ones* (1964), "The Troll" (1964), "The Walking Shadow" (1964), "The Lake Thing" (as Pel Torro, 1964), "The Accursed" (1965), "The Prodigy" (1965), "Girdle of Fear" (1966), "Repeat Programme" (1966) and "The Resurrected Enemy" (1966).

RLF wrote many novels under the house pseudonyms John E. MULLER and Karl ZEIGFREID, which are listed under those entries. Apart from those mentioned below in connection with book titles, his pseudonyms include Neil Balfort, Othello Baron, Noel Bertram, Oben Lerteth, Elton T. Neef, Peter O'Flinn, René Rolant, Robin Tate and Deutero Spartacus. All but the last are partial anagrams of his name.   [MJE]
Other works: Under his own name: *Resurgam* (coll. **1957**), *Secret of the Snows* (coll. **1957**), *The Flight of the Valkyries* (coll. **1958**), *The Waiting World* (**1958**), *Watchers of the Forest* (coll. **1958**), *Call of the Werwolf* (coll. **1958**), *The Death Note* (coll. **1958**), *Mermaid Reef* (coll. **1959**), *Alien from the Stars* (**1959**), *The Ghost Rider* (coll. **1959**), *Hyperspace* (**1959**), *Doomed World*

(**1960**), *The Man Who Couldn't Die* (coll. **1960**), *Out of the Darkness* (**1960**), *Asteroid Man* (**1960**), *Werewolf at Large* (coll. **1960**), *Hand of Doom* (**1960**), *Whirlwind of Death* (coll. **1960**), *Flame Mass* (**1961**) *Fingers of Darkness* (coll. **1961**), *Face in the Dark* (coll. **1961**), *Devil from the Depths* (coll. **1961**), *Centurion's Vengeance* (coll. **1961**), *The Golden Chalice* (**1961**), *The Grip of Fear* (coll. **1961**), *Chariot of Apollo* (coll. **1962**), *Hell Has Wings* (coll. **1962**), *Graveyard of the Damned* (coll. **1962**), *The Darker Drink* (coll. **1962**), *Curse of the Totem* (coll. **1962**), *Space Fury* (**1962**), *Goddess of the Night* (coll. **1963**), *Twilight Ancestor* (coll. **1963**), *Sands of Eternity* (coll. **1963**), *Negative Minus* (**1963**), *Moon Wolf* (coll. **1963**), *Avenging Goddess* (coll. **1964**), *Death Has Two Faces* (coll. **1964**), *The Shrouded Abbot* (coll. **1964**), *Bitter Reflection* (coll. **1965**), *Neuron World* (**1965**), *The Triple Man* (**1965**), *Call of the Wild* (coll. **1965**), *Vision of the Damned* (coll. **1965**), *The Sealed Sarcophagus* (coll. **1965**), *The Unconfined* (**1966**), *Stranger in the Shadow* (coll. **1966**), *Curse of the Khan* (coll. **1966**), *Watching World* (**1966**). As Erle Barton: *The Planet Seekers* (**1964**). As Lee Barton: *The Unseen* (**1963**), *The Shadow Man* (**1966**). As Thornton Bell: *Space Trap* (**1964**), *Chaos* (**1964**). As Leo Brett: *The Drud* (coll. **1959**), *The Return* (coll. **1959**), *Exit Humanity* (**1960**), *The Microscopic Ones* (**1960**), *The Faceless Planet* (**1960**), *March of the Robots* (**1961**), *Black Infinity* (**1961**), *Mind Force* (**1961**), *Nightmare* (**1962**), *Face in the Night* (**1962**), *The Immortals* (**1962**), *The Frozen Tomb* (coll. **1962**), *They Never Come Back* (**1963**), *The Forbidden* (**1963**), *From Realms Beyond* (**1963**), *Phantom Crusader* (coll. **1963**), *The Alien Ones* (**1963**), *Power Sphere* (**1963**). As Bron Fane: *The Crawling Fiend* (coll. **1960**), *Juggernaut* (**1960**; vt *Blue Juggernaut* USA), *Last Man on Earth* (**1960**), *Rodent Mutation* (**1961**), *Storm God's Fury* (**1962**), *The Intruders* (**1963**), *Somewhere Out There* (**1963**), *The Thing From Sheol* (coll. **1963**), *Nemesis* (**1964**), *Suspension* (**1964**), *The Walking Shadow* (coll. **1964**), *U.F.O. 517* (**1965**). As Phil Nobel: *The Hand from Gehenna* (coll. **1964**). As Lionel Roberts: *The Incredulist* (coll. **1954**), *Guardians of the Tomb* (coll. **1958**), *The Golden Warrior* (coll. **1958**), *Time Echo* (**1959**; published in the USA as by Robert Lionel), *The In-World* (**1960**), *The Face of X* (**1960**; published in the USA as by Robert Lionel), *The Last Valkyrie* (**1961**), *The Synthetic Ones* (**1961**), *Flame Goddess* (**1961**). As Neil Thanet: *Beyond the Veil* (**1964**), *The Man Who Came Back* (**1964**). As Trebor Thorpe: *The Haunted Pool* (coll. **1958**), *Five Faces of Fear* (**1960**), *Lightning World* (**1960**), *Voodoo Hell Drums* (**1961**). As Pel Torro: *Frozen Planet* (**1960**), *World of the Gods* (**1960**), *The Phantom Ones* (**1961**), *Legion of the Lost* (**1962**), *The Strange Ones* (**1963**), *Galaxy 666* (**1963**), *Formula*

29X (**1963**; vt *Beyond the Barrier of Space* USA), *The Timeless Ones* (**1963**), *Through the Barrier* (**1963**), *The Last Astronaut* (**1963**), *The Face of Fear* (**1963**), *The Return* (**1964**; vt *Exiled in Space* USA), *Space No Barrier* (**1964**), *Force 97X* (**1965**). As Olaf Trent: *Roman Twilight* (coll. **1963**).

FANZINE A term describing an amateur magazine produced by sf fans. The first known fanzine was *The Comet* (May 1930), edited by Ray PALMER for the Science Correspondence Club, followed by *The Planet* (Jul. 1930), ed. Allen Glasser for the New York Scienceers. These and other early fanzines were straightforward publications dealing exclusively with sf or amateur science and were produced by local fan groups founded in America by the more active readers of contemporary professional sf magazines. As interest grew, however, and sf fans formed closer contacts and friendships, individual fans began publishing for their own amusement and fanzines became more diverse, and their contents more capricious; fan editors also began to exchange fanzines and to send out free copies to contributors and letter-writers. Thus fanzines abandoned any professional aspirations in exchange for informality and an active readership — characteristics which persist to the present and which distinguish fanzines from conventional hobbyist publications.

From America the idea spread to Britain, where Maurice Hanson and Dennis Jacques started *Novae Terrae* (later ed. John CARNELL as the forerunner of NEW WORLDS) in 1936. Since then fanzine publishing has proliferated and many thousands of titles have appeared. Probably 500–600 fanzines are currently in production, the majority in North America, but with substantial numbers from Britain, Australia and western Europe, and occasional items from Japan, South America, South Africa, New Zealand, Turkey and eastern Europe.

Many modern sf writers started their careers in fandom and many published their own fanzines. Ray BRADBURY, for example, produced four issues of *Futuria Fantasia* (1939–41) which contained among other material his first published stories. Other former fanzine editors include such well-known names as Frederik POHL, Cyril KORNBLUTH, James BLISH, John CHRISTOPHER, Charles Eric MAINE, Ken BULMER, Damon KNIGHT, Ted WHITE, Harlan ELLISON, Robert SILVERBERG and Michael MOORCOCK. Some still find time to publish: Wilson TUCKER, for example, has continued to produce his fanzine, *Le Zombie*, since 1938.

Since fan editors have few responsibilities, they are free to produce whatever they like. Fanzines thus vary dramatically in production, style and content. Normally they are duplicated or printed, consisting of anything from a single sheet to 100 or more pages, and with a circulation of from five to 5,000 copies. The smaller fanzines are often written entirely by the editor and serve simply as letter substitutes sent out to friends; others have limited distribution within amateur press associations such as FAPA. The larger fanzines, however, have an average circulation of 200–500 and fall into three main categories, with considerable overlap: those dealing with sf (containing reviews, interviews, articles, and discussions), those dealing with sf fans and fandom (containing esoteric humour), and those dealing with general material (containing anything from sf to Biblical engineering). On the fringe there are specialist fanzines catering for FANTASY and SWORD-AND-SORCERY fans, others devoted to cult authors such as J.R.R. TOLKIEN, H.P. LOVECRAFT, and Robert E. HOWARD, and yet others which deal with sf films or television series such as STAR TREK. The word "fanzine" (coined by Russ Chauvenet in 1941) has also been borrowed and used by comic collectors, wargamers, "underground" publishers and other non-sf enthusiasts.   [PR]

A selection of important fanzines from different periods of fandom receives entries in this volume: ALGOL, AMRA, AUSTRALIAN SF REVIEW, BIZARRE, CRY, CYPHER, ENERGUMEN, FANAC, FANTASY REVIEW, FANTASY TIMES, THE FUTURIAN, HYPHEN, LOCUS, LUNA MONTHLY, MAYA, MOEBIUS TRIP, NIEKAS, OUTWORLDS, QUARBER MERKUR, RIVERSIDE QUARTERLY, SCIENCE FICTION REVIEW, SCIENCE FICTION TIMES, SLANT, SPECULATION, VECTOR, THE VORTEX, WARHOON, WSFA JOURNAL, XERO, YANDRO. Professional and semi-professional sf critical journals are listed separately under CRITICAL AND HISTORICAL WORKS ABOUT SF.

See also: FUTURIAN for an account of early British fanzines.

FAPA The commonly used acronym for the Fantasy Amateur Press Association, which was formed in 1937 in the USA by Donald WOLLHEIM to facilitate distribution of FANZINES published by and for members, the first of many such groups. Early contributors included Frederik POHL, Sam MOSKOWITZ, John CARNELL, Robert A.W. LOWNDES, Wilson TUCKER and Richard WILSON. Current members include Terry CARR, Sam Moskowitz, F.M. BUSBY and Robert SILVERBERG.   [PR]

FARCA, MARIE C. (1935–). American writer, whose first sf novel, *Earth* (1972), is a competent adventure; her second novel, *Complex Man* (1973), is a sequel set on another planet.   [JC]

FAR FUTURE Fred Polak, in his book *The Image of the Future* (1973), identifies two categories of images of the distant future: the future of prophecy and the future of destiny. Prophets, though they speak about the future, are primarily concerned with the present: they issue warnings about the consequences of present actions and demand that other courses of action be adopted. Their images are images of the historical future which will grow out of human action in the present day (*see* NEAR FUTURE). To the second category of images, however, present concerns are usually irrelevant: they are images of the ultimate future, taking the imagination as far as it can reach. Such visions are related to ESCHATOLOGY and often feature the END OF THE WORLD, but some may choose instead to depict a world where everything has so changed as to become virtually incomprehensible, when the present is no longer even a memory. (The two categories overlap only in special circumstances, when the images of ultimate destiny are shifted by prophets into the historical context to inspire Millennarian movements.)

Scientifically inspired images of the far future could not come into being until the true time scale of the Earth, and the scope of possible change, was accepted and understood. Even then it was not until the establishment of the theory of EVOLUTION that writers found a conceptual tool which made it possible for them to imagine the kind of change which might plausibly take place. One of the earliest images of the far future formed within the literature of the scientific imagination was W.H. HUDSON's *A Crystal Age* (**1887**), based on a hazy and mystical evolutionary philosophy. In an introduction to the second edition (1906) Hudson dismissed the story as a fantasy because it came into conflict with his understanding of Darwinian theory. Certainly its vision of a human race that has achieved harmony with nature is more gentle and appealing than the Darwin-inspired vision of H.G. WELLS in *The Time Machine* (**1895**), which foresees the decline and extinction of Man. William Hope HODGSON's *The House on the Borderland* (**1908**) and *The Night Land* (**1912**) are equally bleak: they are dark visions of a world inherited by monsters and subject to irredeemable processes of decay. It is significant that one of the first optimistic images of the far future, assuming a triumphant destiny for mankind, was written in concert with a renunciation of Darwinian philosophy: George Bernard SHAW's *Back to Methuselah* (**1921**). Shaw was confident of Man's ability to adapt by simply wishing it so; but others were not so sure. Guy DENT, in *Emperor of the If* (**1926**), was the first writer to offer an account of a conditional far future — the one which might result from Man's dogged refusal to accept change. This is, in some ways, the bleakest vision of all, showing Man's descendants, no longer human in form or ability, living in a much changed world, but clinging insanely to the social and psychological priorities of the present.

An ambitious vision of a far future which takes little account of Man but which transcends the images of decay and desolation associated with so many other visions is S. Fowler WRIGHT's *The World Below* (**1929**; including *The Amphibians*, **1924**). This was quickly followed by Olaf STAPLEDON's attempt to track the entire evolutionary future of Man, *Last and First Men* (**1930**), based on the blueprint provided by J.B.S. HALDANE in "The Last Judgment" (**1927**). Outside Millennarian fantasies this novel stands alone as the one major vision which links the two images of the future within a coherent historical narrative, although Camille FLAMMARION's *Omega* (trans. **1894**) does combine the two images by juxtaposition.

The early sf pulps featured several far future visions of the end of the world, but the one story which stands out in presenting the extinction of Man's remote ancestors as merely one more stage in a continuing process of change is "Seeds of the Dusk" (**1938**) by Raymond Z. GALLUN, in which a much-changed Earth is "invaded" and "conquered" by spores from another world. Gallun wrote another far future story, "When Earth is Old" (**1951**), in which time travellers must negotiate with sentient plants to assure the rebirth of the species. Rebirth is a common motif in far future stories, and time travellers from the present frequently contrive to turn the evolutionary tide which is sweeping humanity towards extinction. The false analogy between the life of a species and that of an individual, with the corollary that species may "age" and become "senescent", seems quite powerful within sf. The most notable work embodying this myth is James BLISH's *Midsummer Century* (**1972**). A common variant has Man becoming extinct through over-reliance on machines, which often then take up the evolutionary story on their own account. Examples are John W. CAMPBELL Jr's stories "The Last Evolution" (**1932**) and "Night" (**1935** as by Don A. Stuart).

A. MERRITT never used the far future as a milieu for his adventures in exotica, but his work nevertheless influenced a number of far future fantasies. Henry KUTTNER and C.L. MOORE, who wrote a series of Merritt-influenced novels in the 1940s, used a far future milieu in *Earth's Last Citadel* (**1943**; **1964**). Another writer of lushly exotic fantasies, Clark Ashton SMITH, set a series of them in Zothique, the "last continent" — a bizarre and decadent world in which magic flourishes. The series includes "Empire of the Necromancers" (**1932**), "Isle of the Torturers" (**1933**) and "The Dark Eidolon" (**1935**, and is featured in *Zothique* (coll. **1970**). A similar series of fantasies was written by Jack VANCE for *The Dying Earth* (coll. **1950**) and its sequel *The Eyes of the Overworld* (fix-up **1966**), although the latter incorporates an element of picaresque comedy.

Images of the far future which retain a rather more secure base within the conventions of pulp sf include P. Schuyler MILLER and L. Sprague DE CAMP's *Genus Homo* (**1941**; **1950**) and A.E. VAN VOGT's *The Book of Ptath* (**1943**; **1947**; vt *200,000,000 A. D.*). The classic pulp sf story of the far future is Arthur C. CLARKE's *Against the Fall of Night* (**1948**; **1953**; rev. vt *The City and the Stars* **1956**). Its images are standardized (bleak, derelict Earth with cities whose handsome, incurious inhabitants are parasitic upon their machines) but its development is extremely impressive, as its perspectives widen to take in the whole cosmos. Many writers, of course, were prepared to envisage a galactic future for mankind (*see* GALACTIC EMPIRES) which would reduce Earth to a mere backwater. For the most part, these are not images of the future of destiny but attempts to perpetuate the historical image (as is obvious in those epics which construct galactic history by analogy with Earthly history). Many, however, include images of a senescent or dying Earth — notably the first story in Neil R. JONES's "Professor Jameson" series, "The Jameson Satellite" (**1931**), the last story in James Blish's "Pantropy" series, "Watershed" (**1955**), and John BRUNNER's exotic adventure story *The 100th Millennium* (**1959**; rev. vt *Catch a Falling Star* **1968**). The standardized images persisted even after the Second World War, through the period which saw significant innovations in most other sf themes. Notable examples include a number of highly stylized and semi-allegorical vignettes by Fritz LEIBER, including "When the Last Gods Die" (**1951**) and "The Big Trek" (**1957**); and a considerable number of bizarre stories by Brian ALDISS, including the later stories in *The Canopy of Time* (coll. **1959**), "Old Hundredth" (**1960**), the stories making up *Hothouse* (fix-up **1962**), "A Kind of Artistry" (**1962**) and "The Worm That Flies" (**1968**). As with all the stories in this category, these tend towards pure fantasy, and some controversy resulted from a particularly memorable image in *Hothouse*, in which gigantic cobwebs stretch between the Earth and the Moon, whose faces are now perpetually turned to one another. There is perhaps no image which better sums up the dominant sf mythology of the far future.

The 1960s saw something of a revival of interest in far future scenarios in genre sf. *Hothouse* won an award, and so did a short novel by Jack Vance, *The Last Castle* (**1966**) — less fantasized than *The Dying Earth* (i.e. without magic) but no less bizarre, and similar in mood. Comparable imagery of the far future is present in another of Vance's award-winners, *The Dragon Masters* (**1963**) although it uses an extraterrestrial setting. Exotic far future backgrounds provide settings for adventure stories in Samuel

R. DELANY's *The Jewels of Aptor* (**1962**), Michael MOORCOCK's *The Twilight Man* (**1966**; vt *The Shores of Death*) and Brian STABLEFORD's *Cradle of the Sun* (**1969**) and *The Blind Worm* (**1970**). Moorcock also wrote an interesting far future fantasy in "The Time Dweller" (**1964**) and has recently written a novel sequence about the "dancers at the end of time", which contains the books *An Alien Heat* (**1972**), *The Hollow Lands* (**1974**), *The End of All Songs* (**1976**), *Legends from the End of Time* (coll. **1976**) and *The Transformation of Miss Mavis Ming* (**1977**). Here the ultimate future is inhabited by humans with godlike powers who must perpetually seek diversion from the tedium of their limitless existence. Another writer who has made significant use of far-future imagery is Robert SILVERBERG, in the brilliant surreal novel *Son of Man* (**1971**) and in the novella "This is the Road" (**1973**). A recent addition to the genre is *A Billion Days of Earth* (**1976**) by Doris PISERCHIA, in which an aged Earth is inhabited by evolved godlike men, ordinary men who are evolved rats, and a variety of intelligent animals all menaced, in a series of strong and bizarre images, by a creature which seems to be almost an incarnate emblem of the end of all things.

There are no anthologies dealing specifically with this theme, and it is worth noting that Harry HARRISON attempted to compile a companion volume to his near future anthology *The Year 2000* (**1970**) but failed to attract sufficient suitable submissions. This is the imaginative realm which, even in sf, has remained most firmly under the domination of mythical images and ideas, and it does not lend itself readily to plot development.   [BS]

See also: DEVOLUTION; ENTROPY; FANTASY; MYTHOLOGY.

FARJEON, J(OSEPH) JEFFERSON (1883–1955). English writer, prolific (often as Anthony Swift) in the detective genre and as a playwright; his sf novel, *Death of a World* (**1948**), depicts the arrival of aliens on a dead Earth and their reading of the diary of the last survivor of the man-made DISASTER that ended all life.   [JC]

See also: END OF THE WORLD.

FARLEY, RALPH MILNE Pseudonym of American writer and teacher Roger Sherman Hoar (1887–1963) for all his sf work. He was educated at Harvard and had a remarkably varied career, which included teaching such subjects as mathematics and engineering, inventing a system of aiming large guns by the stars and serving as a Wisconsin state senator. His early work in the PULP-sf field was written in obvious imitation of Edgar Rice BURROUGHS and was contributed to ARGOSY, notably his most famous series, "Radio Man", which began with *The*

Radio Man (1924 *Argosy*; **1948**; vt *An Earthman on Venus*) and continued with *The Radio Beasts* (1925 *Argosy*; **1964**), *The Radio Planet* (1926 *Argosy*; **1964**), "The Radio Man Returns" (1939 *AMZ*) and "The Radio Minds of Mars" (1955 *Spaceway*; part 1 only). Other "Radio" stories are out of series. The tales, which were initially absurdly boosted by *Argosy* as scientifically accurate, give the adventures of Myles Cabot, mostly on VENUS, the Radio Planet, and have admirers. Along with another novel, *The Hidden Universe* (1939 *AMZ*; **1950** with short story "We, the Mist"), *The Radio Man* was later published bound together as *Strange Worlds* (coll. **1953**). RMF was a rough-hewn, traditional sense-of-wonder writer, and as a consequence became relatively inactive with the greater sophistication of the genre after the Second World War.   [JC/PN]
Other works: *Dangerous Love* (1931 *Mind Magic* as "Man from Ouija Land"; **1946**) in the AMERICAN FICTION series; *The Immortals* (1934 *Argosy*; **1947**); *The Omnibus of Time* (coll. **1950**).
See also: ALIENS; ESCHATOLOGY; HIVE-MINDS; LIFE ON OTHER WORLDS.

FARMER, PHILIP JOSÉ (1918–). American writer. Although a voracious reader of sf in his youth, PJF was a comparatively late starter as a writer. A part-time student at Bradley University, he gained a BA in English in 1950. Two years later he burst on to the sf scene with his novella *The Lovers* (1952 *Startling Stories*; exp. **1961**). Although originally rejected by John W. CAMPBELL Jr. of ASTOUNDING SCIENCE FICTION and H.L. GOLD of GALAXY, it gained instant acclaim and won PJF a 1953 HUGO award for "most promising new author". It concerned XENOBIOLOGY, PARASITISM and SEX, an explosive mixture which PJF was to use repeatedly. On the strength of this, and such excellent short stories as "Sail On! Sail On!" (1952) and "Mother" (1953), he became a full-time writer. His second short novel, *A Woman a Day* (1953 *Startling Stories*; rev. **1960**; vt *The Day of Timestop* USA; vt *Timestop!* UK) was billed as a sequel to *The Lovers* but bore little relation to the earlier story. "Rastignac the Devil" (1954) was a further sequel. A fast and copious writer, PJF then produced two novels, both of which were accepted for publication but neither of which actually saw print at the time, the first due to the folding of STARTLING STORIES (it eventually appeared as *Dare*, **1965**), the second due to difficulties with a publisher (it eventually formed the basis of the "Riverworld" series). This double disaster forced PJF to cease full-time authorship, a status to which he did not return until 1969.

Nevertheless, he produced many interesting stories over the next few years, e.g. the "Father Carmody" series in the MAGAZINE OF FANTASY AND SCIENCE FICTION, which began with "Attitudes" (1953) and continued with "Father" (1955), *Night of Light* (1957 *FSF*; expanded **1966**), "A Few Miles" (1960) and "Prometheus" (1961). These tales involve a space-travelling priest and the theological puzzles he encounters on various planets. The best of them is *Night of Light*, a nightmarish story of a world where the figments of the unconscious become tangible. Other notable stories of this period include "The God Business" (1954), "The Alley Man" (1959) and "Open to Me, My Sister" (1960; vt "My Sister's Brother"). The last named is the best of PJF's BIOLOGICAL fantasies; like *The Lovers*, it was repeatedly rejected as "disgusting" before its acceptance by *FSF*.

PJF's first novel in book form was *The Green Odyssey* (1957), a picaresque story about an Earthman escaping from captivity on an alien planet. It was the first of many paperback entertainments which PJF has written over the years. Later novels in a not dissimilar vein include *The Gate of Time* (1966), *The Stone God Awakens* (1970) and *The Wind Whales of Ishmael* (1971), the last named being an sf sequel to Herman MELVILLE's *Moby Dick*. *Flesh* (1960; rev. 1968) is more ambitious: a dramatization of the ideas which Robert GRAVES put forward in *The White Goddess*, it presents a matriarchal, orgiastic society of the future. Rather heavy handed in its humour, it was considered a "shocking" novel on first publication.

The "World of Tiers" series shows PJF in a lighter vein again, but it is one of his most popular works. *The Maker of Universes* (1965), *The Gates of Creation* (1966), *A Private Cosmos* (1968), *Behind the Walls of Terra* (1970) and *The Lavalite World* (1977) are set in a series of "pocket universes", playgrounds built by the masters of an unimaginable technology. The most notable character is the present-day Earthman Paul Janus Finnegan (whose initials, like those of many PJF figures, usually ironic observers, are the same as his own), alias Kickaha, a trickster hero who indulges in merry, if bloodthirsty, exploits. The books sag in places, but they have moments of high invention.

Inside Outside (1964), a novel about a scientifically sustained afterlife, contains some extraordinary images and grotesque ideas which suffer .from a lack of resolution but nevertheless resonate in the mind. The novella "Riders of the Purple Wage" (1967) won PJF a 1968 Hugo. Written in a wild and punning style, it is one of his most original works. It concerns the tribulations of a young artist in a UTOPIAN society, and has a more explicit sexual and scatological content than anything PJF had written before. "The Oogenesis of Bird City" (1970) is a related story.

ESSEX HOUSE, publishers of pornography, then commissioned PJF to write three erotic fantasy novels, taking full advantage of the new freedoms of the late 1960s. *The Image of the Beast* (**1968**), the first of the "Exorcism" trilogy, is an effective parody of the private-eye and Gothic horror genres, and is followed by *Blown* (**1969**), obviously written merely to fulfil the contract, and *Traitor to the Living* (**1973**), not published by Essex House. The Lord Grandrith/Doc Caliban series comprises *A Feast Unknown* (**1969**), *Lord of the Trees* (**1970**) and *The Mad Goblin* (**1970**). *A Feast Unknown*, which was published by Essex, is a brilliant exploration of the sado-masochistic fantasies latent in much heroic fiction, and succeeds as satire, as sf, and as a tribute to the creations of Edgar Rice BURROUGHS and Lester DENT. It concerns the struggle of Lord Grandrith (Tarzan) and Doc Caliban (Doc Savage) against the Nine, a secret society of immortals. It is a narrative *tour de force*. Unfortunately, the sequels are anaemic by comparison.

PJF has approached the Tarzan myth from different angles in several other works. *Lord Tyger* (**1970**), possibly the best written of all PJF's novels, is about a millionaire's attempt to create his own ape-man. *Tarzan Alive* (**1972**) is a spoof biography in which PJF uses Joseph Campbell's ideas (from the study of mythology *The Hero With a Thousand Faces*, **1949**) to explore the nature of the HERO's appeal. The appendices and genealogy, which link Tarzan with many other heroes of popular fiction, are at once a satire on scholarship and a serious exercise in "creative mythography". Tarzan appears again in *Time's Last Gift* (**1972**; rev. 1977), a preliminary novel for a series about ancient Africa which employs many of the settings of Burroughs and Henry Rider HAGGARD. *Hadon of Ancient Opar* (**1974**) and *Flight to Opar* (**1976**) continue the series.

PJF has gained greatest popular acclaim, however, with his "Riverworld" novels, *To Your Scattered Bodies Go* (1965–6 *Worlds of Tomorrow*; fix-up **1971**), *The Fabulous Riverboat* (1967–71 *If*; fix-up **1971**) and *The Dark Design* (**1977**). The first of these won a 1972 Hugo. Set on a planet where the entire human race has been resurrected along the banks of a multi-million-mile river, they involve the adventures of such historical personages as Sir Richard Burton, Samuel Clemens (Mark TWAIN) and Jack LONDON. PJF invents an sf rationale for this fantastic situation, and there is an interesting philosophical undercurrent to the books. Related to them is an earlier short story, "Riverworld" (1966), which relates the exploits of Tom Mix and Jesus Christ in the afterlife. The unlikely juxtaposition of these two names is characteristic of PJF's unruly imagination. He has promised to explain the mysterious rationale of the Riverworld in a fourth volume, *The Magic Labyrinth*.

Recently, he has been tying his own fiction (and that of many other authors) into one vast, personal mythology. Much of this is worked out in the loose conglomeration of works which has been termed the "Wold Newton Family" series (the premise being that a meteorite which landed near Wold Newton in 18th-century Yorkshire irradiated a number of pregnant women and thus gave rise to a family of MUTANT SUPERMEN — a family which included Sherlock Holmes, Doc Savage, Tarzan and many others). *Tarzan Alive*, mentioned above, began this series. Other works which contain "Wold Newton" material include "Tarzan Lives: an Exclusive Interview with Lord Greystoke" (1972); "The Obscure Life and Hard Times of Kilgore Trout" (1973); *Doc Savage: His Apocalyptic Life* (1973; rev. 1975); *The Other Log of Phileas Fogg* (1973); "Extracts from the Memoirs of 'Lord Greystoke'" (1974); "After King Kong Fell" (1974); *The Adventure of the Peerless Peer* (1974) and the liberally rewritten version of J.H. ROSNY AÎNÉ's *L'étonnant voyage de Hareton Ironcastle* (France 1922), *Ironcastle* (1976).

A recent PJF series consists of the three (to date) "Greatheart Silver" stories, PULP-style pastiches: "Showdown at Shootout" (1975), "The Secret Life of Rebecca of Sunnybrook Farm" (1975) and "Greatheart Silver in the First Command" 1977, in *Weird Heroes* nos 1, 2 and 6.

PJF has also begun to write under a plethora of pseudonyms. *Venus on the Half-Shell* by Kilgore TROUT (1975) is his work (he took the name from the character — an inventive but unsuccessful pulp writer — created by Kurt VONNEGUT Jr), as is a series of stories in *FSF* by such "fictional authors" as Paul Chapin, Harry Manders and Jonathan Swift Somers III. The four-part story "Stations of the Nightmare" (1974–5 in *Continuum* nos 1–4 ed. Roger ELWOOD) introduces the character Leo Queequeg Tincrowdor, sf writer, who later crops up as the "co-author" of "Osiris on Crutches" (1976). For those who enjoy such mystifications, PJF's work is a delight. [DP]
Other works: *Strange Relations* (coll. 1960); *The Alley God* (coll. 1962); *The Cache from Outer Space* (1962); *The Celestial Blueprint and Other Stories* (coll. 1962); *Tongues of the Moon* (1964); *Down in the Black Gang* (coll. 1971); *The Book of Philip José Farmer* (coll. 1973); *Mother Was a Lovely Beast* ed. (anth. 1974).
About the author: "Philip José Farmer" by Sam MOSKOWITZ, in *Seekers of Tomorrow* (1966); "Thanks for the Feast" by Leslie A. Fiedler, in *The Book of Philip José Farmer* (1973); 'Playing Around with Creation" by Franz ROTTENSTEINER, SCIENCE-FICTION STUDIES, Fall 1973; "Speculative Fiction, Bibliographies, and Philip José Farmer" by Thomas Wymer in EXTRAPOLATION, Dec. 1976.
See also: ALIENS; CONCEPTUAL BREAKTHROUGH; CRIME AND PUNISHMENT; ESCHATOLOGY; GODS AND DEMONS; ICONOCLASM; ISLANDS; LEISURE; LIFE ON OTHER WORLDS; MARS; MESSIAHS; MYTHOLOGY; PARANOIA AND SCHIZOPHRENIA; PASTORAL; PSYCHOLOGY; REINCARNATION; RELIGION; SOCIOLOGY; TABOOS; TIME TRAVEL; VILLAINS.

FARNSWORTH, DUNCAN *See* David Wright O'BRIEN.

FARRELL, JOHN WADE *See* John D. MACDONALD.

FARREN, MICK (1943–). English writer and ex-rock-musician, educated at art school, active first in a band, the Deviants, from 1967 to 1970; he then edited the underground paper *IT* from 1970 to 1973, and founded the underground comic *Nasty Tales*, prosecuted for obscenity in a well-known trial, in which, with Chris Rowley and Chris Welch, he produced a comic strip with sf content, "Ogoth the Wasted". His first sf novel is *The Texts of Festival* (1973), set in a surrealistic post-HOLOCAUST England; this novel, and his subsequent trilogy, *The Quest of the DNA Cowboys* (1976), *Synaptic Manhunt* (1976) and *The Neural Atrocity* (1977), radiate a late-1960s aura of apocalyptic, hip hyperbole, sometimes effectively. The world of the trilogy especially is almost deliriously polymorphic, full of images out of Westerns and other genres and references to dope, rock and the hippy subculture generally; the basic plot of each instalment is a version of a fundamental quest story, transmuted by its insertion into a violent post-holocaust environment. MF continues to write songs and rock criticism and has recorded an album. [JC]

FARRERE, CLAUDE. Pseudonym of French writer Charles Bargone (1876–1957), author of "colonial" novels after the model of Pierre Loti; his sf books are *La maison des hommes vivants* (1911; trans. as *The House of the Secret* 1923), and more notably *Les condamnés à mort* (1920; trans. as *Useless Hands* 1926), about a doomed workers' revolt in the 1990s; when the workers go on strike, machines replace them. [JC]
See also: DYSTOPIAS; SOCIAL DARWINISM.

FAST, HOWARD (MELVIN) (1914–). American writer, best known for his works outside the sf field, under his own name and, with books designed for a wider market, as E. V. Cunningham. *The Unvanquished* (1942) and *Spartacus* (1951) are perhaps his most familiar titles (both as by HF). He began publishing sf with "Wrath of the Purple" for *AMZ* in 1932, but did not actively produce sf until the later 1950s, when he started a long association with *FSF*; most of the stories in *The Edge of Tomorrow* (coll. 1961) originally appeared in that magazine. *Phyllis* (1962 as by E. V. Cunningham) is a borderline novel in which an American and a Russian scientist come together to try to force their governments to ban the bomb, by threatening to explode two themselves. *The Hunter and the Trap* (1967) depicts an attempt to raise exceptional children in a monitored environment. *The General Zapped an Angel* (coll. 1970) and *A Touch of Infinity* (coll. 1973), all the stories in both volumes being reassembled as *Time and the Riddle: Thirty-One Zen Stories* (coll. 1975), present more stories, many sf, mostly sharply political in implication and eschewing most of the cruder satisfactions of genre fiction. Harlan ELLISON, among others, has expressed high praise for HF's stories, but admiration, though widespread, is not universal. Some critics have seen their occasionally religiose moralizing as cloying and their ideative content as trite. [JC]
See also: SATIRE.

FASTER THAN LIGHT This entry deals with those aspects of the special theory of relativity which bear on faster-than-light (FTL) travel and communication, and a discussion of how they have been presented or evaded in sf. It also includes a mention of relativistic effects in slower-than-light travel in sf. (*For some related topics, see* TACHYONS *and* PHYSICS.)

It is well known that according to Einstein's special theory of relativity it is impossible for any material object or any form of energy to travel faster than light, but the reasons for this impossibility are not so well understood. They are in fact less technical and more basic than is generally assumed, and they need to be understood before the treatment of FTL travel in sf can be assessed. A good popular account of relativity, using only very simple mathematics, was given by Einstein himself in *Relativity* (trans. 1920).

The notion of relativity is a familiar one in everyday life. There is nothing surprising in the fact that velocity is relative; a moving object will reach an observer sooner if he moves along the ground towards it, and so its velocity depends on the observer's own velocity. It is tempting to speak of an "apparent velocity" and say that the observer must be at rest if he is to measure the true velocity. But "at rest" means "standing still on the ground", and from a viewpoint in space the ground is itself moving. It was realized by Galileo, and it is not difficult to accept, that there is no object in the universe which is at rest in any absolute sense, and so there can be no observer who is entitled to regard himself as especially qualified to measure the true velocities of things. Velocity is an essentially relative concept; "the velocity" of an object has no meaning unless one answers the question "relative to what?" (like distance; it is meaningless to speak of "the distance" of an object without saying distance from what). Similarly, the distance between two events depends on the observer; waving goodbye and opening one's newspaper may happen in the same place on the train, but be separated by the length of the platform to an observer on the station. However, the interval of time separating two events seems, in everyday life, not to depend on the observer.

The discovery that the velocity of light is not after all relative led Einstein to realize that the relation between physical measurements and the observer was not what it had seemed. His special theory of relativity is based on a relationship between the velocity of the observer and his measurement of the time of an event and its distance from him which is known as the Lorentz transformation (it was postulated by Lorentz, but he did not fully realize its significance). Its novel feature is that the interval of time between two events, previously assumed to be the same for all observers, is now supposed to be essentially relative. If one divides the distance between two events by the interval of time between them, one obtains the velocity with which one would have to move to get from one event to the other (it will be infinite if the two events occur simultaneously). The answer will depend on the observer, but all observers will agree on whether it is less than, equal to, or greater than the velocity of light. If it is less than or equal to the velocity of light, all observers will agree on which of the two events came first. (The events are then said to be separated in a "timelike" way.) If, on the other hand, it is greater than the velocity of light (when the events are said to be separated in a "spacelike" way), some observers will reckon that one of the events happened first, others that the other did, and yet others that the two events happened simultaneously.

It is this that makes it impossible to travel faster than light. Since no observer is in a privileged position, all observers' versions of the truth must be compatible. Thus if two events are separated in a spacelike way, so that observers differ over which happened first, no observer can claim that one of the events caused the other; for this is incompatible with another's observation that the alleged effect preceded its cause. Now suppose a spaceship travels from Earth to the Crab Nebula faster than light. Then there is a spacelike separation between its takeoff from Earth and its arrival at the Crab Nebula, so to some observers — traffic controllers on some planets, navigators on other spaceships — the spaceship will appear to arrive at the Crab Nebula first and travel backwards to Earth. (The possibilities for a space battle between FTL ships are intriguing, but have never been exploited.)

Similar considerations apply to COMMUNICATION. An FTL message will appear to some observers to have been received before it was sent, regardless of the medium used, and whether or not it involves the transmission of any form of energy.

The type of sf which depends on the immensity of space for its effect necessarily assumes that speeds of travel and communication much greater than that of light are possible, and so comes into conflict with the theory of relativity. Much early SPACE OPERA simply ignored the impossibility of FTL travel, but later, more sophisticated writers wished to resolve the conflict and find a plausible, or at least possible, way of reconciling FTL travel with relativity. However, since the reasons against FTL travel refer purely to the time and place of departure and the time and place of arrival, it is a difficult prohibition to circumvent. This point has not been taken by many sf writers. The commonest proposal for reconciling FTL travel with relativity invokes the concept of hyperspace, a form of fourth dimension. By postulating a dimension in which distant points are much closer than they seem in three-dimensional space, writers enable their characters to do an FTL journey without ever having an FTL velocity. However, the above argument shows that it is FTL journeys and not FTL velocities that are prohibited by relativity, and so this is unfortunately no reconciliation at all. The first author to use the idea of hyperspace was probably John W. CAMPBELL Jr, in *The Mightiest Machine* (1934 *ASF*; **1947**); a clear explanation of the idea was given by Robert A. HEINLEIN in his juvenile novel *Starman Jones* (**1953**). Related ideas are those of the space-warp (used by Campbell in earlier stories such as *Islands of Space* (1931 *AMZ*; **1957**) and subspace, in which velocities are not what they seem. Both of these amount to having one's cake and eating it, and are subject to the same objection as hyperspace.

Some authors have been aware of the connection between FTL travel and time travel implied by the reversal of cause and effect discussed above. The connection was made by Charles L. HARNESS in *Flight Into Yesterday* (**1953**; vt *The Paradox Men*), though the argument he used was idiosyncratic. James BLISH met the objections to instantaneous communication in "Beep" (**1954**) by having his messages reach backwards and forwards across all time — certainly a state of affairs that looks the same to all observers. Ursula K. LE GUIN's instantaneous communicator, the ANSIBLE, in *The Dispossessed* (**1974**) is given a plausible if not clearly defined post-relativistic rationale, which is to say that she postulates a new physics which is to Einstein's work what Einstein's was to Newton's. She is perfectly aware of the cause-effect reversal difficulty, and does

not so much rationalize it as find a philosophy which enables her physicist to live with the apparent paradox, incorporating it into his Principle of Simultaneity.

If FTL travel were possible, it would give rise to some curious phenomena as one looked back and waited for the light from where one had been. This idea was effectively used by Randall GARRETT in "Time Fuze" (1954). FTL travel is in fact possible where light is slowed down for any reason (as it is in glass, for example); throughout this article "the velocity of light" means the normal velocity in empty space. Thus by postulating a region of space where light is slowed down, between the two suns in "Placet is a Crazy Place" (1946), Fredric Brown reconciled relativity with his creation of an FTL planet which "eclipses itself twice, occulting both suns at the same time. A little farther on, it runs into itself coming from the opposite direction."

As we have seen, the interval of time between two events depends on the velocity of the observer. If the events have a timelike separation, the time between them is least for the observer who is moving so that for him the events happen in the same place. Thus a clock on a moving spaceship, seen as keeping good time by the passengers on the ship, appears to an outside observer to run slow; and so do biological processes. The higher the ship's speed relative to the observer, the slower its clocks and passengers appear; so by travelling at very nearly the speed of light relative to Earth, it is possible to cover hundreds or thousands of light-years in a lifetime, at the cost of finding that hundreds or thousands of years have elapsed on Earth while one was away. One of the first sf writers to exploit the idea was L. Ron HUBBARD in *Return To Tomorrow* (1950 *ASF*; **1954**). It has since been much exploited in sf as a scientifically possible method of travelling great distances (for example, in *The Left Hand of Darkness* (**1969**) by Ursula K. Le Guin and "Meeting My Brother" (1966) by Vladislav Krapivin), and also as a way of travelling far into the future of the universe in *Tau Zero* (**1970**) by Poul ANDERSON and *A World Out of Time* (**1976**) by Larry NIVEN.

Lester DEL REY once boasted that he had invented a new pseudo-scientific rationale for FTL for every story he wrote on the subject.

A thematic anthology is *Faster Than Light* (anth. **1976**) ed. Jack DANN and George ZEBROWSKI. [TSu]

FAUCETTE, JOHN M(ATTHEW) Jr (1943–). American writer whose sf novels, including *Crown of Infinity* (**1968**) and *The Age of Ruin* (**1968**), are routine works, the first a SPACE OPERA, the second a post-DISASTER odyssey. [JC]
Other works: *The Warriors of Terra* (**1970**); *Siege of Earth* (**1971**).

FAWCETT, EDGAR (1847–1904). American writer, known primarily for his work outside the sf field. He published about 40 novels and nine volumes of poetry and verse drama, and had several plays produced. Most of his novels belong to the realistic school of fiction associated with his contemporary W.D. HOWELLS, but like Howells he also wrote imaginative works. He provided a manifesto for a species of fiction which he called "realistic romance", which is very similar to some DEFINITIONS of sf: "Stories where the astonishing and peculiar are blent with the possible and accountable. They may be as wonderful as you will, but they must not touch on the mere flimsiness of miracle. They can be excessively improbable, but their improbability must be based upon scientific fact, and not upon fantastic, emotional, and purely imaginative groundwork."

His most important realistic romance was *The Ghost of Guy Thyrle* (**1895**), whose hero discovers a drug which will separate his *persona* from his corporeal self; he undertakes a voyage into the farther reaches of the cosmos, following the cremation of his body. Also notable are *Solarion* (**1889**), a novel about a dog with artificially augmented intelligence; and a literary study in abnormal psychology, *The New Nero* (**1893**). EF also placed *Douglas Duane* (**1888**) and *The Romance of Two Brothers* (**1891**) in the realistic romance category. He copyrighted several unpublished manuscripts, some of which were sf.   [BS]
About the author: *Edgar Fawcett* (**1972**) by Stanley R. Harrison.
See also: COSMOLOGY; EVOLUTION; LIFE ON OTHER WORLDS; MOON; PSYCHOLOGY; RELIGION.

FAWCETT, E(DWARD) DOUGLAS (? – ?). British writer whose sf novel, *Hartmann the Anarchist; or The Doom of the Great City* (**1893**), illustrated by Fred T. JANE, features a 1920s anarchist revolution against a wicked, capitalist England in which London is destroyed by airships; but the rebel Hartmann eventually kills himself, and all is well.   [JC]
Other works: *Swallowed by an Earthquake* (**1894**); *The Secret of the Desert; or How We Crossed Arabia in the "Antelope"* (**1895**).

FAWCETT, F(RANK) DUBREZ (1891–1968). English writer, active in various genres under his own name and several others from 1923; non-sf pseudonyms include Henri Dupres, Ben Sarto, Griff, Eugene Glen, Coolidge McCann, Elmer Eliot Saks and Madame E. Farra; much of his output consisted of such thrillers as *Miss Otis Comes to Piccadilly* (**1940** as by Ben Sarto) and its many successors. He may have been the author of some of the sf novels appearing under the house name Astron DEL

MARTIA, and claimed to have originated the name, but in fact it was the invention of Stephen FRANCES. Under his own name, his only sf novel proper is *Hole in Heaven* (**1954**), about a human body possessed by an other-dimensional alien, though *Air-Gods' Parade* (**1935**) as by Simpson Stokes, *The Isle of Ulla-Gapoo* (**1946**) and *The Dubious Adventures of Baron Munchausen* (**1948**) may be of some interest.   [JC]

FAX COLLECTOR'S EDITIONS American specialist publishing house established by T.E. DIKTY, devoted to publishing material from and about PULP MAGAZINES. Its publications include several collections of obscure Robert E. Howard stories, two anthology series in facsimile under the titles *Famous Fantastic Classics* and *Famous Pulp Classics*, and *The Weird Tales Story* (**1977**), a large volume written and edited by Robert WEINBERG. The list is planned to include some bibliographical works. An associated company, also founded by Dikty, and specializing in Robert E. Howard material, is Starmont House.   [MJE]

FAYETTE, J.B. *See* OUTER PLANETS.

FEARING, KENNETH (1902–61). American poet and novelist, known mainly for his work outside the sf field, e.g. such mysteries as *The Big Clock* (**1946**). *The Loneliest Girl in the World* (**1951**) has some borderline sf elements within a mystery frame; KF's only sf novel proper is *Clark Gifford's Body* (**1942**), which gravely and literately portrays a future American civil war. [JC]

A rare snapshot of John Russell FEARN.

FEARN, JOHN RUSSELL (1908–60). British writer. He was extremely prolific

and used many pseudonyms. In the PULPS he wrote many stories as Polton Cross and Thornton Ayre, and also used the names Geoffrey Armstrong, Dennis Clive, John Cotton and Ephriam Winiki. He published large numbers of books as Vargo Statten and Volsted GRIDBAN (a name also used by E.C. TUBB), and also used the names Laurence F. Rose, Earl Titan, Spike Gordon, John Russell, and the house names Conrad G. HOLT, Astron DEL MARTIA, "Griff", Paul LORRAINE and Brian SHAW. He wrote the early SUPERMAN story *The Intelligence Gigantic* (1933 *AMZ*; **1943**) and the extravagant *Liners of Time* (1935 *AMZ*; **1947**) and its sequel *Zagribud* (1937 *AMZ*; abridged as *Science Metropolis* as by Vargo Statten **1952**). The Golden Amazon, a superwoman first used in four novelettes in AMAZING STORIES, became the central character of a long series of novels and novelettes in the *Toronto Star Weekly*, 1944–61. Those which subsequently appeared in book form are: *The Golden Amazon* (**1944**); *The Golden Amazon Returns* (1944; **1948**); *The Golden Amazon's Triumph* (1946; **1953**); *The Amazon's Diamond Quest* (1947; **1953**); *The Amazon Strikes Again* (1948; **1954**) and the recently reprinted *Conquest of the Amazon* (1949; **1975**), which may herald the reprinting of the whole series. Another series of novels is made up of the Edgar Rice BURROUGHS imitations *Emperor of Mars* (**1950**); *Warrior of Mars* (**1950**); *Red Men of Mars* (**1950**); and *Goddess of Mars* (**1950**). There are also two Tarzan imitations written under the name Earl Titan: *The Gold of Akada* (**1951**) and *Anjani the Mighty* (**1951**). JFR edited VARGO STATTEN SCIENCE FICTION MAGAZINE, founded in 1954, which underwent several title changes before publication ceased in 1956.   [BS]
Other works: as Polton Cross: *Other Eyes Watching* (**1946**); as JRF: *Slaves of Ijax* (**1948**); as Astron del Martia: *The Trembling World* (**1949**); as Spike Gordon: *Don't Touch Me* (**1953**); as John Russell: *Account Settled* (**1949**); as "Griff": *Liquid Death* (**1953**); as Vargo Statten: *Operation Venus* (**1950**), *Annihilation* (**1950**), *The Micro-Men* (**1950**), *Wanderer of Space* (**1950**), *2000 Years On* (**1950**), *Inferno!* (**1950**), *The COSMIC Flame* (**1950**), *Nebula X* (**1950**), *The Sun Makers* (**1950**), *The Avenging Martian* (**1951**), *Cataclysm* (**1951**), *The Red Insects* (**1951**), *The New Satellite* (**1951**), *Deadline to Pluto* (**1951**), *The Petrified Planet* (**1951**), *Born of Luna* (**1951**), *The Devouring Fire* (**1951**), *The Renegade Star* (**1951**), *The Catalyst* (**1951**), *The Inner Cosmos* (**1952**), *The Space Warp* (**1952**), *The Eclipse Express* (**1952**), *The Time Bridge* (**1952**), *The Man from Tomorrow* (**1952**), *The G-Bomb* (**1952**), *Laughter in Space* (**1952**), *Across the Ages* (**1952**), *The Last Martian* (**1952**), *Worlds to Conquer* (**1952**), *Decreation* (**1952**), *The Time Trap* (**1952**), *To the Ultimate* (**1952**), *Ultra Spectrum* (**1953**),

The Dust Destroyer (**1953**), *Black-Wing of Mars* (**1953**), *Man in Duplicate* (**1953**), *Zero Hour* (**1953**), *The Black Avengers* (**1953**), *Odyssey of Nine* (**1953**), *Pioneer 1990* (**1953**), *The Interloper* (**1953**), *Man of Two Worlds* (**1953**), *The Lie Destroyer* (**1953**), *Black Bargain* (**1953**), *The Grand Illusion* (**1953**), *Wealth of the Void* (**1954**), *A Time Appointed* (**1954**), *I Spy* (**1954**), *The Multi-Man* (**1954**), *Creature From the Black Lagoon* (**1954**), *1,000 Year Voyage* (**1954**), *Earth 2* (**1955**); as Conrad G. Holt: *Cosmic Exodus* (**1953**); as Paul Lorraine: *Dark Boundaries* (**1953**); as Laurence F. Rose: *The Hell-Fruit* (**1953**); as Brian Shaw: *Z Formations* (**1953**).

About the author: *The Multi-Man* (**1968**) by Philip HARBOTTLE.

See also: CLONES; Volsted GRIDBAN.

FERMAN, EDWARD L(EWIS) (**1937–**). The son of Joseph W. FERMAN, ELF formally took over the editorship of THE MAGAZINE OF FANTASY AND SCIENCE FICTION in Jan. 1966, having previously been managing editor under Avram DAVIDSON and his father. Under his editorship *FSF* has generally prospered: it is one of only two sf magazines — ANALOG is the other — to have maintained a regular schedule over the period, and its circulation has been stable. *FSF* won the HUGO award for best magazine four years in succession (1969–72) under ELF. It is fair to say, however, that the magazine has lost much of its distinctive flavour of the 1950s. He also edited various anthologies drawn from *FSF*, including several volumes of *The Best from Fantasy and Science Fiction: 15th Series* (anth. **1966**), *16th Series* (anth. **1967**), *17th Series* (anth. **1968**), *18th Series* (anth. **1969**), *19th Series* (anth. **1971**), *20th Series* (anth. **1973**), *22nd Series* (anth. **1977**). There were also two anniversary volumes: *Twenty Years of the Magazine of Fantasy and Science Fiction* (anth. **1970**; co-editor Robert P. MILLS) and *The Best from Fantasy and Science Fiction: A Special 25th Anniversary Anthology* (anth. **1974**). With Barry MALZBERG ELF has collaborated on a notable original anthology, *Final Stage* (anth. **1974**; rev. **1975**), and a reprint collection, *Arena: Sports SF* (anth. **1976**).   [MJE]

Other works: As editor: *Once and Future Tales from the Magazine of Fantasy and Science Fiction* (anth. **1968**); *Graven Images: Three Original Novellas of Science Fiction* (anth. **1977**) with Barry Malzberg.

FERMAN, JOSEPH W(OLFE) (**1906–74**). American publisher and editor, born in Lithuania. After a long career with the magazine *American Mercury*, JWF became involved with THE MAGAZINE OF FANTASY AND SCIENCE FICTION from its inception, as publisher and, Dec. 1964–Dec. 1965, as editor, a position in which he was succeeded by

his son, Edward L. FERMAN. He edited one anthology of stories from *FSF*: *No Limits* (anth. **1964**).   [MJE]

FERRINI, FRANCO *See* ITALY.

FEZANDIE, CLEMENT (? – ?). American writer, author of several plays, whose sf novel *Through the Earth* (**1898**) is about a transportation-tube through the planet from New York to Australia; his "Dr Hackenshaw" series appeared first in SCIENCE AND INVENTION, in 43 instalments, from "The Secret of Artificial Respiration" (1921) to the novel "A Journey to the Center of the Earth" (1925), with two concluding stories published the next year in *AMZ*.   [JC]

See also: MATTER TRANSMISSION.

FIALKO, NATHAN (**1881– ?**). Russian writer resident in America, who translated his own uneven sf novel into English as *The New City* (**1925**; trans. **1937**). Set in the future, it depicts a Russian and an American society with strongly DYSTOPIAN views of both.   [JC]

FIELD, GANS T. *See* Manly Wade WELLMAN.

Monsters like mustard plasters do their thing in FIEND WITHOUT A FACE.

FIEND WITHOUT A FACE Film (**1958**). Amalgamated/MGM. Directed by Arthur Crabtree, starring Marshall Thompson, Terence Kilburn, Kim Parker,

Peter Madden, Michael Balfour and Kynaston Reeves. Screenplay by Herbert J. Leder, based on the short story "The Thought-Monster" by Amelia Reynolds Long. 74 mins. B/w.

This is one of the two sf films made by Amalgamated in Britain (the other was FIRST MAN INTO SPACE and also starred Marshall Thompson) but set in North America. *FWAF* is more interesting than the other, despite the absurdity of its basic premise. A scientist experiments with a machine that can amplify thought-waves and accidently creates a number of creatures consisting of pure energy. Invisible at first, they commit a series of murders by sucking out their victim's brains through holes made into the base of their necks; but in the final sequences, when they have trapped the protagonists in a remote house, they gradually take form, revealing themselves to be disembodied brains with trailing spinal cords and twitching tendrils. The climax of this eccentric, lunatic film has a quality of genuine nightmare. The special effects, featuring some clever stop-motion photography by Puppel Nordhoff and Peter Nielson, are of a high standard. [JB]

FILM *See* CINEMA.

FINAL PROGRAMME, THE (vt **THE LAST DAYS OF MAN ON EARTH** USA) Film (**1974**). Goodtime Enterprises/Gladiole Films/MGM–EMI. Directed by Robert Fuest, starring Jon Finch, Jenny Runacre, Sterling Hayden, Harry Andrews, Hugh Griffith, Julie Ege and Patrick Magee. Screenplay by Robert Fuest, based on the novel by Michael MOORCOCK. 89 mins. Colour.

This first film to feature Moorcock's multi-purpose, multi-faced protagonist, Jerry Cornelius, is an example of style triumphant over content. Fuest, originally a set-designer, is best known for *The Abominable Dr Phibes*, which was nothing more than a series of stylish jokes, and for the many episodes he directed of the TV series THE AVENGERS. *FP* looks impressive, but not much of Moorcock's creation remains. Cornelius's father has died, leaving behind some hidden microfilm on which is the final

Jon Finch as a rather too plump Jerry Cornelius ponders over the brain drain in THE FINAL PROGRAMME.

[computer] programme of the title. Those involved in the hunt for the film include Jerry, his evil brother and the awesome Miss Brunner, who has a tendency to consume her lovers, bones and all. The Moorcock original was not as strong as the other three books of the Cornelius tetralogy, but none the less was replete with sophisticated ironies which Fuest generally reduces to a series of knowing winks; where Moorcock both defines and limits his characters by their personal style, about which he appears to feel ambiguously, Fuest more simply appears to suppose that if it is trendy it is to be admired. The apotheosis of the book is rendered as low farce in the film, which substitutes a grinning Neanderthal for the original bisexual Messiah. [JB/PN]

FIN DU MONDE, LA ["The End of the World"] Film (1931). L'Écran d'Art. Directed by Abel Gance, starring Abel Gance, Colette Darfeuil, Sylvia Grenade, Jeanne Brindeau and Samson Fainsilber. Screenplay by Abel Gance, suggested by a book of Camille FLAMMARION. 105 mins. B/w.

The film tells of a comet's collision with Earth. As with most of Gance's films, which were usually independently produced, it took many years to complete. He was still working on one version in 1939. A shortened English version, lasting 54 minutes, repudiated by Gance, was released in 1934; it was supervised by V. Ivanoff and the script was adapted by H.S. Kraft. The film is extravagant and original, and fits one description of Gance's work as hovering "between the ludicrous and the majestic". [JB/PN]

FINLAY, VIRGIL (1914–71). American illustrator. VF worked in both colour and

A b/w illustration by Virgil FINLAY from *Fantastic Adventures*, May 1951, typical of his glamour, and his fine and graceful detail.

b/w, but is best known for the latter, where his unique, painstaking stippling gained him fame but not fortune (because of the slow process involved). Nonetheless he was prolific. His earliest work was for *Weird Tales* in 1935 — he did 20 covers for them in all, and later did 24 covers for *Famous Fantastic Mysteries*. He also appeared in *A. Merritt's Fantasy Magazine*, *Fantastic Novels*, *Fantastic Story Quarterly*, *Fantastic Universe*, *Future Science Fiction*, *Galaxy*, *Space Stories*, *Startling Stories* and *Wonder Story Annual* among others. Known to many fans as "the bubble man", he often added sparkling bubbles to his illustrations, partly as a decorative device, and partly to cover those parts of the female body which according to contemporary taste in

commercial art were conventionally concealed. He was nominated for seven HUGO awards, but won only one, for interior illustration, in 1953. He was stronger in fantasy than sf, excelling (it was a common paradox) in the glamorous and the macabre, both meticulously executed. His early work was more abstractly stylized than the later, and suggested a toughness which later became smoothed over with an expert commercial veneer. Possibly the greatest craftsman in the history of sf illustration, VF is one of the most fondly remembered. Many portfolios of his work have been published, the first in 1941. Two such are *Virgil Finlay* (**1971**) ed. Donald M. GRANT, and *The Book of Virgil Finlay* (**1975**) ed. Gerry de la Ree. [JG/PN]

FINN, RALPH L(ESLIE) (1912–). British novelist and journalist with a variety of publications. *Time Marches Sideways* (**1950**) is a time-travel story set in London. Two undated paperbacks by RLF from the early 1950s are *Captive on the Flying Saucers* and *Freaks Against Supermen*. [JC/PN]

FINNEY, CHARLES G(RANDISON) (1905–). American newspaperman and writer, based in Arizona, who spent the years 1927–9 with the US infantry in Tientsin, China; an oriental influence pervades most of his work. His novels and stories, though fantasy rather than sf, have been influential throughout the field, especially his famous *The Circus of Dr Lao* (**1935**), filmed insensitively as THE SEVEN FACES OF DR LAO (1963). This was the title story of Ray BRADBURY's anthology *The Circus of Dr Lao and Other Improbable Stories* (anth. **1956**); CGF's work was a strong influence on

This rare still shows a panic scene in Abel Gance's LA FIN DU MONDE, 1931.

Bradbury in particular. Dr Lao's circus is full of mythical beasts and demigods, all of whom actually live within his tents. The novel takes a tour of the circus along with the citizens of an Arizona township, who acquire strange knowledge about themselves and the world — but soon forget what they have learned. [JC] **Other works:** *Past the End of the Pavement* (**1939**); *The Unholy City* (**1937**; rev. 1968 as a coll. with "The Magician out of Manchuria"); *The Old China Hands* (**1961**); *The Ghosts of Manacle* (coll. of linked stories **1964**); *The Magician out of Manchuria* (1968; **1976**). **See also:** FANTASY; MYTHOLOGY.

FINNEY, JACK Writing name used by American author Walter Braden Finney (1911–), who began writing at age 35, and published his first sf as late as 1951 in COLLIER'S. Although he is as well known for his sf as for anything else, he does not specialize in the field, adapting his highly professional skills to mysteries and general fiction as well. Stories from his first years as a writer of sf can be found in *The Third Level* (coll. **1957**; vt *The Clock of Time* UK), and somewhat later ones in *I Love Galesburg in the Springtime* (coll. **1963**). Many are evocative stories about escape from an ugly present into a tranquil past, or into a parallel world, or wistful variants of the theme when the escape fails. His best-known work is *The Body Snatchers* (**1955**; vt *Invasion of the Body Snatchers* USA), made into the celebrated film INVASION OF THE BODY SNATCHERS (1956) by Don Siegel. The book — perhaps less plausibly than the film — horrifyingly depicts the INVASION of a small town by interstellar spores that duplicate human beings, reducing them to dust in the process; the menacing spore-people who remain symbolize, it has been argued, the loss of freedom in contemporary society. JF's further books are slickly told but less involving. *The Woodrow Wilson Dime* (1960 *Saturday Evening Post*; exp. **1968**) is a PARALLEL-WORLDS novel, and *Time And Again* (**1970**) sets a time traveller in the New York of 1880. In general, JF's use of sf themes is adroitly manipulative but not original. [JC] **See also:** TIME TRAVEL; UTOPIAS.

FIRST MAN INTO SPACE Film (1959). Amalgamated/MGM. Directed by Robert Day, starring Marshall Thompson, Marla Landi, Robert Ayres and Bill Edwards. Screenplay by John C. Cooper and Lance Z. Hargreaves from a story by Wyott Ordung. 77 mins. B/w.

This is one of the two sf films made by Amalgamated in Britain that pretend to be set in North America (the other was FIEND WITHOUT A FACE). *FMIS* seems to imitate THE QUATERMASS XPERIMENT: an astronaut returns to Earth enveloped in a repulsive, crusty substance that has turned him into an inhuman, blood-drinking monster. As in the Quatermass

film there are moments of pathos, as when he tries to communicate with his wife, but *FMIS* is generally derivative and routine. [JB]

FIRST MEN IN THE MOON Film (1964). Columbia. Directed by Nathan Juran, starring Edward Judd, Martha Hyer and Lionel Jeffries. Screenplay by Nigel KNEALE and Jan Read. 107 mins. Colour.

This watered-down, amusing adaptation of H.G. WELLS's classic novel is entertaining despite its faults. An eccentric Victorian inventor develops an anti-gravity material which enables him to fly to the Moon in a spherical "spaceship". He and his companions are captured by insect-like Moon creatures, but eventually escape and return to Earth, inadvertently leaving behind cold-germs which destroy the Moon's population. The film's epilogue shows contemporary astronauts landing on the Moon and finding remains of the dead civilization. There are good special effects by Ray HARRYHAUSEN.

A previous version of *FMITM* was made in 1919 by British Gaumont, directed by J.V. Leigh. [JB]

FISCHER, LEONARD (? –). Writer, probably American. His *Let Out the Beast* (**1950**), is a post-HOLOCAUST-reversion-to-savagery book. [JC]

FISHER, JAMES P. (? –). American writer, whose sf novel, *The Great Brain Robbery* (**1970**), is a rather lightweight adventure in which an ALIEN tries to steal a student's special brain. [JC]

FISHER, VARDIS (1895–1968). American writer, raised in a Mormon family; his best-known single novel, *Children of God* (**1939**), is about the Mormons. His *Testament of Man* sequence of novels, about the whole of Man's history, enormously extends, into many volumes, the basic impulse behind much of the work of F. Austin BRITTEN, or J.V. JENSEN's *The Long Journey* series (**1922**–4; six vols in the original Danish). Of sf interest in the *Testament* are the first four volumes, dealing with prehistory: *Darkness and the Deep* (**1943**), *The Golden Rooms* (**1944**), *Intimations of Eve* (**1946**) and *Adam and the Serpent* (**1947**), which in themselves are a formidable attempt at sustained ANTHROPOLOGICAL sf. [JC] **See also:** ADAM AND EVE; ORIGIN OF MAN.

FISKE, TARLETON *See* Robert BLOCH.

FITZGERALD, WILLIAM *See* Murray LEINSTER.

FITZ GIBBON, CONSTANTINE (ROBERT LOUIS) (1919–). American-born writer of politically oriented fiction and other works, now a naturalized Irish citizen; his first sf novel,

The Iron Hoop (**1949**), describes an occupied city in World War III; the Anglophobe *When the Kissing Had to Stop* (**1960**) depicts the self-destruction of a Britain dominated by a communist-inspired government. [JC] **Other works:** *The Golden Age* (**1975**).

FITZ-GIBBON, RALPH EDGERTON (c. 1904–). American writer, long active as a journalist. His sf novel, *The Man With Two Bodies* (**1952**), deals with parapsychological explanations for the mysteries suggested by the title. [JC]

FIVE Film (1951). Columbia. Directed by Arch Oboler, starring Susan Douglas, William Phipps, James Anderson, Charles Lampkin and Earl Lee. Screenplay by Arch Oboler. 93 mins. B/w.

This was one of the first "after the bomb" movies and concerns five American survivors — a mountaineer, a pregnant girl, a Negro, a cashier and an idealist — a supposed cross-section of American society. The five, who meet in a cliff-top mansion, argue and fight incessantly before venturing out into a corpse-strewn city to search for the girl's husband. *F* was produced, directed and written by Arch Oboler, who worked extensively in American radio before entering the film industry in 1945 with *Strange Holiday* and *Bewitched*, both based on his own radio plays. Not so much a drama as a sermon, *F* preaches against prejudices and insanities that may lead to atomic war. [JB]

FIVE MILLION YEARS TO EARTH *See* QUATERMASS AND THE PIT.

FLAGG, FRANCIS Pseudonym of American writer George Henry Weiss (1898?–1946), who appeared in *Weird Tales* and then began publishing sf with "The Machine Man of Ardathia" for *AMZ* in 1927, and published 20 or so typically PULP-sf stories over the next decade; some of his later stories were collaborations with Forrest J. ACKERMAN. He was a comparatively careful writer. His posthumously published sf novel is *The Night People* (**1947**), a time-travel story involving an escaped convict. [JC]

FLAMMARION, CAMILLE (1842–1925). French astronomer and writer. He was one of the first major popularizers of science, and took great delight in the flights of the imagination to which his interest in astronomy inspired him. In 1858, the year he entered the Paris Observatory as a student, he wrote an unpublished scientific romance: "Voyage extatique aux régions lunaires, correspondance d'un philosophe adolescent". His two major fascinations were the possibility of LIFE ON OTHER WORLDS and the possibility of life after death, and these interests are reflected by his earliest major works: *La pluralité des* *mondes habités* (**1862**) and *Les habitants de l'autre monde* (**1862**), the latter being "revelations" made available through the medium Mlle Huet. His most important work in the popularization of science was *Popular Astronomy* (**1880** France; trans. **1894**). In 1865, while working on the earlier non-fiction book *Real and Imaginary Worlds* (**1865**) he dramatized some of his ideas, combining his scientific and spiritualist interests in a series of dialogues between a man and a disembodied spirit. The spirit is free to roam the universe at will, observing the implications of the finite velocity of light and presenting a philosophical theory of relativity, and is also capable of REINCARNATION on other worlds in physical forms adapted by evolution to alien conditions (*see* ALIENS; LIFE ON OTHER WORLDS). Five dialogues appeared as *Récits de l'infini* (**1872** France; trans. as *Stories of Infinity: Lumen – History of a Comet in Infinity* **1873**). They were revised with new material and reprinted as *Lumen* (**1887** France; trans. A.A.M. and R.M. **1897**). Other scientific flights of fantasy appeared as *Rêves étoilés* '(**1888** France). Notions taken from these dialogues were embodied in the romances of reincarnation *Stella* (**1877** France) and *Urania* (**1889** France; trans. A.R. Stenson **1891**). CF's boldest scientific romance, however, is the epic of the future *La fin du monde* (**1893–4** France), which appeared in America as *Omega; the Last Days of the World* (trans. **1894**). This is a classic of the genre, comparable to Olaf STAPLEDON's *Last and First Men* (**1930**) in scope and ambition. CF's scientific reputation was injured by his passionate interest in spiritualism (in later life he was an intimate of Conan DOYLE, who also acquired such an interest) but his was a major contribution to the popularization of science and to the literature of the scientific imagination. [BS]

See also: ASTRONOMY; COSMOLOGY; END OF THE WORLD; ESCHATOLOGY; EVOLUTION; FAR FUTURE; PHYSICS; RELIGION; STARS.

FLASH GORDON 1. American COMIC STRIP created by artist Alex RAYMOND for King Features Syndicate. *FG* appeared in 1934, at first in Sunday, later in daily newspapers. Its elaborately shaded style and exotic storyline made it one of the most influential of sf strips. It was taken over in 1944 by artist Austin Briggs, then in 1948 by Mac Raboy, and since then has been drawn by Dan Barry and Al Williamson. It continues today.

The scenario of *FG* is archetypal SPACE OPERA. Most episodes feature the hero, Flash, locked in combat with the villain, Ming the Merciless of the planet Mongo. Flash's perpetual fiancée, Dale Arden, and the mad scientist, Hans Zarkov, play prominent roles. (In later episodes Zarkov's craziness was played down, and he became a straightforward sidekick to Flash). Futuristic devices (death rays, rocket-ships) combine with the archaic (dinosaurs, jungles, swordplay) with a fine contempt for plausibility.

The strip was widely syndicated in Europe and when, during the Second World War, the arrival of various episodes was delayed, the strip was often written and drawn by Europeans. One such writer was Federico Fellini (later famous as a film director). Although *FG* was begun quite cynically and in conscious opposition to the earlier BUCK ROGERS, it quickly developed its own individuality, emphasizing a romantic baroque against the cool technological classicism of its predecessor.

The *FG* comic strip has had many repercussions in other media. It led to a popular radio serial, to a pulp magazine, FLASH GORDON STRANGE ADVENTURE MAGAZINE, and in the late 1930s to several film serials starring Buster Crabbe; and later a TV series (*see below*). A full-length, quasi-erotic film parody, FLESH GORDON, appeared in 1974.

A paperback series of *FG* short novels, based on the original strips, with Alex Raymond credited, and published as "Adapted by Con Steffanson", began to appear in 1974. The first title was *Flash Gordon 1: The Lion Men of Mongo* (**1974**).

2. Serial film. 13 episodes (1936). Universal. Directed by Frederick Stephani, starring Buster Crabbe, Jean Rogers, Charles Middleton, Frank Shannon and Priscilla Lawson. Screenplay by Frederick Stephani, George Plympton, Basil Dickey and Ella O'Neill, based on the comic strip by Alex Raymond (*see above*). 26 reels. B/w.

The film *FG* was the nearest thing to PULP magazine space opera to appear on the screen during the 1930s. The story concerned Flash Gordon, Dale Arden and Dr Zarkov making a journey to the planet Mongo in Zarkov's backyard-built spaceship to find the cause of a sudden outbreak of volcanic activity on Earth. They learn that Ming the Merciless is behind it all and plans to invade the Earth, and they spend the next 12 episodes trying to survive all the various hazards with which Ming confronts them, including prehistoric monsters, shark-men and clay-men, before destroying him in the final reel. Despite being much more lavish than the average serial (the budget was a record $350,000), *FG* has the cheap appearance of most serials, unconvincing special effects, sets and costumes borrowed from a variety of other films and plenty of stock footage.

The follow-up was *Flash Gordon's Trip to Mars* (1938), directed by Ford Beebe and Robert F. Hill, but with the same actors in the leading roles. Even Ming returned from the dead. It had 15 episodes and was written by Ray Trampe, Norman S. Hall, Wyndham Gittens and Herbert Dolmas.

The final *FG* movie serial was *Flash Gordon Conquers the Universe* (1940), directed by Ford Beebe and Ray Taylor, with the same actors in the leading roles except for Carol Hughes who replaced Jean Rogers in the part of Dale Arden. Script was by George H. Plympton, Basil Dickey and Barry Shipman. The three *FG* film serials turn out to have a nostalgic charm, primarily for the middle-aged with good memories, and have been regularly revived on television and in the cinema.

3. US TV series (1951) starring Steve Holland. It was universally execrated.

All rights to the character Flash Gordon have now been bought by Italian film-maker Dino De Laurentiis. [PN/JB]

FLASH GORDON CONQUERS THE UNIVERSE *See* FLASH GORDON.

FLASH GORDON STRANGE ADVENTURE MAGAZINE US BEDSHEET-size PULP MAGAZINE. One issue, Dec. 1936, published by C.J.H. Publications; ed. Harold Hersey. The featured novel was "The Master of Mars" by James E. Northfield; there were three

The dramatic artwork of Alex Raymond showing Flash and Dale in a 1936 FLASH GORDON comic strip.

Pure high camp. Buster Crabbe as FLASH GORDON in the 1936 cinema serial.

animation of a high standard, in particular the climax, when a monster, the Great God Porno, clutching the heroine, scales a tall building in the manner of KING KONG, while muttering a series of surly asides. A duel with an animated insect-creature rivals the best of Ray HARRYHAUSEN's work. Nothing else in the film matches the effects. The parody is too blunt to make its points with real wit, and most of the jokes are variants on the undergraduate theme of inserting a multitude of sexual references into a context that was originally downright puritanical.   [JB]

FLETCHER, GEORGE U. *See* Fletcher PRATT.

FLETCHER, J.S. *See* MACHINES; SCIENTISTS.

FLIN(D)T, HOMER EON (*c.* 1892–1924). American writer, mainly for the MUNSEY magazines, noted in part for the mystery of his death (his body was found at the foot of a canyon) and primarily for his sf novel with Austin HALL (*who see for details*), *The Blind Spot* (1921 *Argosy*; **1951**). HEF began publishing sf in the teens of the century. He often collaborated with Hall. *The Devolutionist and the Emancipatrix* (1921 *Argosy*; coll. **1965**) and *The Lord of Death and the Queen of Life* (1919 *All-Story Weekly*; coll. **1965**) both assemble two stories about trips to other planets, to other solar systems in the first volume, to nearby planets in the second. The style and content are typical of early PULP sf.   [JC]

See also: MERCURY; VENUS.

FLY, THE Film (1958). Fox. Directed by Kurt Neumann, starring Al (David) Hedison, Patricia Owens and Vincent Price. Screenplay by James Clavell, based on a short story by George LANGELAAN. 94 mins. Colour.

A scientist, while experimenting with a MATTER TRANSMITTER, accidentally gets mixed with a fly, and ends up with its head and arm (or leg). He has retained his own brain, however, and sets about trying to reverse the procedure with the help of his wife. But the fly refuses to be caught, and the scientist is driven to commit suicide by putting his head in a steam press. The final sequence shows the fly, with the scientist's head and arm attached, trapped in a spider's web and yelling "help me!" (which makes one wonder where the fly's brain ended up). An absurd film, its ludicrous excesses are amusing. Lavishly produced for a horror/monster movie, it was a financial success and spawned two sequels, RETURN OF THE FLY (1959) and CURSE OF THE FLY (1965).   [JB]

FLYING SAUCERS Coined in 1947 by American newsmen, the term "flying saucers" is virtually synonymous with

other stories. *FGSAM* was notable mainly for its coloured interior illustrations in comic-strip format. It was intended to be a monthly juvenile magazine and is now a rare collector's item, fetching over $100. It was, of course, an attempt, which apparently failed, to cash in on the popularity of Alex RAYMOND's comic strip FLASH GORDON.   [FHP/MJE]

FLASH GORDON'S TRIP TO MARS *See* FLASH GORDON.

FLEHR, PAUL *See* Frederik POHL.

FLEMING, IAN (LANCASTER) (1908–64). British writer, brother of Peter FLEMING. The gadgetry and fantastic plots of his enormously successful "James Bond" thrillers show a use of sf elements; the closest of them all to a fully-fledged sf plot is *Moonraker* (**1955**; vt *Too Hot to Handle*), whose eponymous rocket is rather ahead of its time. Many of IF's novels have been filmed, usually with additional sf gadgetry and reworked plots. The first of these films was DR NO (1962); YOU ONLY LIVE TWICE (1967) featured Bond crushing an attempt at world domination which involved the kidnapping of orbital satellites. [JC/PN] **See also:** VILLAINS.

FLEMING, (ROBERT) PETER (1907–71). British travel writer and

novelist, educated at Eton and Oxford, brother of Ian FLEMING. He is known mainly for such travel books as *Brazilian Adventure* (**1933**). His spoof sf novel, *The Flying Visit* (**1940**), parachutes Adolf Hitler into Britain with amusing results. *The Sixth Column: A Singular Tale of our Time* (**1951**) is also borderline sf. [JC]

FLEMING, STUART *See* Damon KNIGHT.

FLESH GORDON Film (1974). Mammoth/Graffiti. Directed by Michael Benveniste, Howard Ziehm and Walter R. Cichy, starring Jason Williams, Suzanne Fields, Joseph Hudgins, William Hunt and John Hoyt. Screenplay by Michael Benveniste and William Hunt. 78 mins. Colour.

This burlesque of FLASH GORDON began as a cheap, soft-core pornographic film, but developed into a relatively expensive production as the special effects became more and more elaborate. Work on the film continued for nearly two years and during that period many Hollywood special effects technicians were involved, some of whom did not receive a credit on the finished film. They included Jim Danforth, Dave Allen, Rick Baker, Greg Jein, Robert Maine, George Barr, Joe Clark, Jim Aupperle, Mike Hyatt, Russ Turner and Dennis Muren. Several of the effects sequences include model

When is a FLYING SAUCER not a flying saucer? In this case when it's a cloud – an unusual 1969 weather formation over Brazil. Popperfoto.

"unidentified flying objects" (UFOs). After a rash of sightings in the late 1940s, flying saucers became a craze, one of the first resulting books being *The Flying Saucers are Real* (**1950**) by Donald E. Keyhoe, and seemed for a time to be an sf idea "come true". This was reflected in the sf of the day, and particularly in sf ILLUSTRATION. The characteristic inverted-saucer shape, which was the most popular conception of the UFO, became part of the iconography of magazine and paperback covers and sf in the CINEMA. The film THE DAY THE EARTH STOOD STILL (**1951**) helped to popularize flying saucers, and particularly the notion that they are piloted by morally superior ALIENS concerned at our civilization's drift towards atomic doom. The sensational "non-fiction" book *Flying Saucers Have Landed* (**1953**; rev. 1970) by George Adamski and Desmond Leslie built upon this premise. It marked the end of the period in which UFOs could be taken "seriously" and the beginning of the more religious phase of UFOlogy which has persisted since. The Aetherius Society, founded in 1954, is an eccentric cult which believes that Christ is alive on Venus and occasionally visits the Earth by flying saucer.

Most sf writers are hostile to flying saucers and their exponents (a fact which is not generally appreciated by the public). Isaac ASIMOV, for instance, has written articles denouncing saucer mania. When sf writers use UFO lore in their stories, they usually do so in an ironic, symbolic or merely opportunist fashion. A partial exception is Dennis WHEATLEY, an apparent believer in flying saucers, whose *Star of Ill Omen* (**1952**) is a typically banal treatment of the theme. C.M. KORNBLUTH used the UFO fad in a sly way in "The Silly Season" (1950), in which Earth is invaded but nobody pays attention because the newspapers have cried wolf too often. John WYNDHAM played upon UFO fears in order to set the scene for his INVASION novel *The Kraken Wakes* (**1953**; vt *Out of the Deeps* USA). Henry KUTTNER used a flying saucer as a device for a moral parable in "Or Else" (1953), as did Theodore STURGEON in "A Saucer of Loneliness" (1953). Robert A. HEINLEIN exploited saucer fears (as he exploited communist-conspiracy fears) in his invasion novel *The Puppet Masters* (**1951**), and he later used a UFO in his entertaining juvenile novel *Have Space Suit — Will Travel* (**1958**). Gore VIDAL's *Messiah* (**1954**; rev. 1965) opens with an analysis of UFOs as portents, which in some ways anticipates the theories of the psychologist C.G. Jung in his *Flying Saucers: a Modern Myth of Things Seen in the Skies* (**1958**; trans. 1959).

More recently, saucer enthusiasts have themselves been the subject of sf stories, notably J.G. BALLARD's "The Encounter" (1963; vt "The Venus Hunters"), which leans heavily on Jung; and Fritz LEIBER's *The Wanderer* (**1964**), which deals in part with the reactions of various UFOlogists to an actual celestial visitor. Since the 1950s, however, flying saucers have become less fashionable in sf, although a certain rote use of them persists, e.g. in Philip José FARMER's four-part story "Stations of the Nightmare" (1974–5). *Seed of the Gods* (**1974**) by Zack HUGHES is a satire on the lunatic saucer theories of Erich VON DÄNIKEN, as expressed in his popular *Chariots of the Gods?* (**1968**; trans. 1969). A good non-fiction book on UFOs by an academically respectable author is *The UFO Experience: a Scientific Enquiry* (**1972**) by J. Allen Hynek. [DP]
See also: ALIENS; PSEUDO-SCIENCE; SPACESHIPS.

FLYING SAUCERS FROM OTHER WORLDS See OTHER WORLDS.

FOLLETT, JAMES (1939–   ). English writer of fiction and technical material; most of his sf work has been for BBC television. His sf novel is *The Doomsday Ultimatum* (**1976**). [JC]

FONTANA, D(OROTHY) C. (? –   ). American writer, primarily of work for television; she was associated with STAR TREK as its story editor and later with the two TV series THE FANTASTIC JOURNEY and LOGAN'S RUN, and her sf novelization of *The Questor Tapes* (**1974**) is based on the TV pilot, released as THE QUESTOR TAPES, written by Gene RODDENBERRY and Gene L. Coon, who created *Star Trek*. It tells of the creation of an ANDROID who eventually plans to combat evil in secret. The pilot did not lead to a series, however. DCF has written a number of TV episodes in addition to her work as story editor. [JC]

FONTENAY, CHARLES L(OUIS) (1917–   ). American newspaperman and writer, born in Brazil, raised in Tennessee, and there remaining. He was a member of the *If* stable from the publication of his first story, "Disqualified", in 1954, and wrote three somewhat routine sf novels, *Twice Upon a Time* (**1958**), *Rebels of the Red Planet* (**1961**), an intrigue set on Mars, and *The Day the Oceans Overflowed* (**1964**), in which the manner of their doing so is scientifically ill motivated. CLF is no longer active in the field. *Epistle to the Babylonians* (**1969**) is non-fiction, though it deals in part with the philosophy of science. [JC]

FONTENELLE, BERNARD LE BOVIER DE See COSMOLOGY; STARS; VENUS.

FOOD OF THE GODS Film (1976). AIP. Directed by Bert I. Gordon, starring Marjoe Gortner, Pamela Franklin, Ralph Meeker and Ida Lupino. Screenplay by Bert I. Gordon, based on a "portion" of the H.G. WELLS novel. 88 mins. Colour.
Bert I. Gordon has been making cheap sf/horror films since the 1950s and while *FOTG* had a larger budget than his previous films, it still has the characteristics of a Gordon production: weak script, implausible dialogue and unconvincing special effects. Set in British Columbia, it involves a mysterious substance that oozes out of the ground and causes gigantism in the offspring of any animal that eats it. The result is giant dragonflies, worms, chickens and rats. The human characters spend most of the film fighting off the latter and are eventually triumphant. Almost nothing of the Wells novel survives. [JB]

FORBIDDEN PLANET Film (1956). MGM. Directed by Fred McLeod Wilcox, starring Walter Pidgeon, Anne Francis, Leslie Nielsen and Warren Stevens. Based on a story by Irving Block and Allen ADLER. 98 mins. Colour.

Robby the Robot meets the starship crew in FORBIDDEN PLANET.

Although Wilcox was new to sf cinema (his best-known film was *Lassie Come Home*), *FP* is one of the most attractive movies in the genre, with excellent special effects by Joshua Meador and others. The resonances of *FP* stem in part from the fact that it is an updated version of Shakespeare's *The Tempest*. The Prospero figure is Morbius, an obsessive scientist living alone with his daughter on the planet Altair IV. The Ariel figure is a charming metal creature, Robby the Robot. (He became so popular — the first robot star since METROPOLIS — that another film, THE INVISIBLE BOY, was made as a special vehicle for him.)

Morbius and his daughter are the sole survivors of a planetary colony, and the film opens with Commander Adams landing with his spaceship to investigate the colony's fate. The crew is menaced by an invisible Monster from the Id (the Caliban figure) and much is made of a buried civilization on the planet, left by an awesomely powerful race, the Krel. The best sequences of the film involve a tour of the still functioning Krel artefacts, spectacular and mysterious, dwarfing the humans passing among them. The monster eventually destroys its unwitting creator, Morbius, and holocaust follows. The girl is saved.

As with many sf films, the plot is a mixture of the tawdry and the potent. The dialogue is slick and unmemorable. The real strength is in the visual treatment, unsurpassed until 2001: A SPACE ODYSSEY, made 12 years later.

A novel (**1956**), based on the film, was written by W.J. STUART.   [PN]

FORBIN PROJECT, THE *See* COLOSSUS THE FORBIN PROJECT.

FORCE FIELD, sometimes **FORCE SHIELD** In sf TERMINOLOGY, unlike that of physics, where it has a different

meaning, it is usually an invisible, protective sphere or wall of force, a sovereign remedy against DEATH RAYS, and usually bullets, though not against swords in Charles HARNESS's *Flight Into Yesterday* (**1953**; vt *The Paradox Men*), in which the efficacy of the shield is directly proportional to the momentum of the object it resists, thus giving him a good excuse for introducing sword-play, where the momentum is relatively small, into a technologically advanced society, an example that other writers were not slow to follow. Robert SHECKLEY's story "Early Model" (1956) tells of a force field so efficient that it renders its wearer almost impotent to carry out any action at all which might conceivably endanger him. But these are comparatively late examples, when the concept was sufficiently familiar in sf to allow parody and sophisticated variations. Throughout the 1930s and '40s the force field performed sterling service, though few writers were able to give, or concerned to try to give, a convincing rationale for forces being conveniently able to curve themselves around an object to be protected and take on some of the properties of hard, resistant matter. It is the essence of an sf force field that by a kind of judo it converts the energy of an attacking force and repels it back on itself. A well-ground mirror might more plausibly carry out the same function, against death rays at least.   [PN]

FORD, FORD MADOX *See* Ford Madox HUEFFER.

FORD, GARRETT *See* William L. CRAWFORD.

FOREST, JEAN-CLAUDE *See* BARBARELLA.

FORESTER, C(ECIL) S(COTT)

(1899–1966). English writer, best known for his work outside the sf field, especially the "Hornblower" novels, from 1937. In addition to several sf stories, he published an sf novel, *The Peacemaker* (**1934**), which gives the story of a pacifist mathematician who tries to force peace on the world through his invention of a magnetic disruptor that stops machinery. CSF also wrote a juvenile fantasy, *Poo-Poo and the Dragons* (**1942**). The ALTERNATE-WORLDS hypothesis of his "If Hitler had Invaded England" (1960) is of interest.   [JC]

See also: DISCOVERY AND INVENTION.

Dec. 1970. Cover by George Barr.

FORGOTTEN FANTASY US DIGEST-size magazine. Five issues, Oct. 1971-Jun. 1972, published by Nectar Press, Hollywood; ed. Douglas Menville. *FF* reprinted some ancient fantasy stories, but the long novel serialized in the first four issues, *The Goddess of Atvatabar* (**1891**) by William R. BRADSHAW, was probably too dated for success, even in the nostalgia market. A second serial, *Hartmann, the Anarchist* (**1893**), by E. Douglas FAWCETT, began in the final issue.   [FHP]

FORSTER, F(DWARD) M(ORGAN) (1879–1970). English writer of novels and essays, best known for the novel *A Passage to India* (**1924**). His importance to sf lies wholly in his short story "The Machine Stops" (1909), later included in *The Eternal Moment* (coll. **1928**). Cast in the form of a warning look at the distant future, rather in the mode of H.G. WELLS's *The Time Machine* (**1895**), it is fundamentally an attack, as many critics noted, and as EMF himself acknowledged, *on* Wells, specifically on the rational World State envisioned in the latter's *A Modern Utopia* (**1904**). The society of "The Machine Stops" is regimented, hivelike, and has retreated underground; the freedom and (paramountly to EMF) the value of the human individual in his personal relations with other human individuals have been eliminated, and when the state collapses, when the machine stops, the depersonalized ciphers underground perish; above, on the surface, remain some real men, who will survive. In any study of the relation of DYSTOPIA to UTOPIA, the story is of vital interest. EMF also wrote some excellent fantasy, collected in *The Eternal Moment* and *The Celestial Omnibus* (coll. **1914**); the two volumes are amalgamated in *Collected Tales* (coll. **1947**; vt *Collected Short Stories* UK). [JC]

See also: AUTOMATION; CITIES; LEISURE; TECHNOLOGY.

FORT, CHARLES (HOY) (1874–1932). American journalist and author, known principally for his work on inexplicable phenomena. Working from extensive notes collected mainly from newspapers, magazines and scientific journals in New York and at the British Museum in London, CF compiled a series of books containing information on strange incidents and occurrences. Though characterized as an anti-scientist, CF reserved his attacks for "scientific priestcraft", for the dogmatic "damning" of unconventional or unwanted observations. CF's own belief was simply a monistic faith in the unity of all things, and this forms the principal connection between his apparently unrelated groups of data. His books are written in an eccentric style and are interspersed with wilfully absurd theories and ideas. *The Book Of The Damned* (**1919**) and *New Lands* (**1923**) are largely concerned with astronomical and meteorological events, while *Lo!* (**1931**) and *Wild Talents* (**1932**) are more concerned with human and animal phenomena. The four books are crammed with data, all documented, and the sheer bulk of information is impressive. This documentation together with CF's reluctance to invent theories (other than whimsical ones) to account for the data places his books far apart from the sketchy fantasies of later writers such as Erich VON DÄNIKEN.

After CF's death, compilation of data was continued by the Fortean Society founded in 1931 by a group that included Ben HECHT, John Cowper POWYS, Alexander Woollcott and Theodore Dreiser, and in the journals *Doubt* (USA) and *Lo!* (UK). Information is currently collected by the International Fortean Organization, who publish *INFO Journal*, and by the British publication *Fortean Times*.

CF's list of bizarre observations and events (from astronomical heresies to teleportation cases), together with his demand for original and undogmatic interpretation, has influenced and stimulated many sf writers. Sam MOSKOWITZ has said that "the influence of the books of Charles Fort on the plot ideas of sf has been pervasive" and Donald WOLLHEIM has also commented on CF's impact on "sf thinking". CF's

most enthusiastic sf follower has been Eric Frank RUSSELL who considered him "the only real genius sf ever had" and once claimed that his "three favourite authors" were "Charles Fort, Charles Fort, and Charles Fort". Russell's *Sinister Barrier* (**1943**) and *Dreadful Sanctuary* (**1951**) are based on Fortean ideas. Damon KNIGHT, another author influenced by CF, has published the standard biography, *Charles Fort, Prophet Of The Unexplained* (**1970**). The influence of CF's ideas on sf was particularly strong in the magazines edited by John W. CAMPBELL Jr, *Unknown* and *ASF*. [PR]

See also: ESP; ORIGIN OF MAN; PARANOIA AND SCHIZOPHRENIA; PSEUDO-SCIENCE; PSI POWERS.

Sleek lines and a skilled airbrush produce a typical Christopher Foss spaceship; *Science Fiction Art*, 1976.

FOSS, CHRISTOPHER (1946–). British illustrator. He has worked in sf illustration since 1970, primarily as a cover artist, using brush and airbrush to excellent effect. He has done over a hundred covers for *Science Fiction Monthly*, Panther Books, New English Library, BALLANTINE BOOKS and others. CF had some paintings published in *Visions of the Future* (**1976**) ed. Janet Sacks, a book about British sf illustrators; he worked on the postponed film version of Frank HERBERT's *Dune*, and has illustrated the best-selling book *The Joy of Sex* (**1972**). CF's sf work is often a celebration of technology — monstrous spaceships, vast robots, beautiful and deadly-looking, rear up over land and skyscapes, where man is absent or tiny, yet the effect is bracing. He could almost be described as the Frank R. PAUL of the 1970s. *Science Fiction Art* (**1976**), with an introduction by Brian ALDISS, is a portfolio of his work. [JG/PN]

FOSTER, ALAN DEAN (1946–). American writer, raised in Los Angeles,

whose first university degree is in political science, his master's in cinema studies. He has interestingly listed as one of his formative influences (on his depiction of older characters) Carl Barks, writer and illustrator of the best comic strips and books from the Disney stable. ADF began publishing sf with "Some Notes Concerning a Green Box" for *The Arkham Collector* in 1971, and has published more than a dozen short sf stories since. Most of his novels have a common background, a galaxy dominated by the Commonwealth, and although some of them are independent works, they occur in the following order of internal chronology: *Midworld* (**1975**); the connected trilogy comprised of *The Tar-Aiym Krang* (**1972**), which is his first novel, *Orphan Star* (**1977**) and *The End of the Matter* (**1977**); *Icerigger* (**1974**) and *Bloodhype* (**1973**). His novels and stories are typically expansive and colourful, their SPACE-OPERA venues sometimes reminiscent of the earlier work of Poul ANDERSON, though tending to more melodrama in their resolutions, and a fable-like use of such sf and fantasy elements as TELEPATHY and dragons.

ADF has also written several film novelizations, the first being *Dark Star* (**1974**), based on the film DARK STAR. Persistent rumour has it that he is the ghost writer of the book *Star Wars* (**1976**), though the book is officially credited to George LUCAS, the director of the film STAR WARS. ADF is the credited author of the sequel novelization, projected for 1978, *Star Wars II*. He has also written a long series based on scripts of the animated cartoon TV spin-off of STAR TREK. A short-story collection is *With Friends Like These* (coll. **1977**). [JC]

Other works: *Luana* (**1974**); *Star Trek Log One* (coll. **1974**); *Star Trek Log Two* (coll. **1974**); *Star Trek Log Three* (coll. **1975**); *Star Trek Log Four* (coll. **1975**); *Star Trek Log Five* (coll. **1975**); *Star Trek Log Six* (coll. **1976**); *Star Trek Log Seven* (coll. **1976**); *Star Trek Log Eight* (coll. **1976**); *Star Trek Log Nine* (coll. **1977**).

FOSTER, C.E. (1919–). American writer whose sf novel is *Journey to the Future* (**1966**). [JC]

FOSTER, GEORGE C(ECIL) (? –). English writer, whose sf novel is *The Change* (**1963**). Two earlier works, fantasies, are *The Lost Garden* (**1930**) and *We Band of Brothers* (**1939**), the latter under the pseudonym Seaforth. [PN]

FOSTER, M(ICHAEL) A(NTHONY) (1939–). American writer, former data systems analyst and ICBM launch crew commander for the American air force; he is also a semi-professional photographer. His sf work consisted by late 1977 of the first two volumes of a trilogy about a race of genetically created SUPERMEN called the "ler": *The*

Gameplayers of Zan (**1977**), a very long novel formally constructed on the model of Elizabethan tragedy, describes a period of climactic tension between the ler and the rest of humanity, and is set on Earth; *The Warriors of Dawn* (**1975**), published first, is set later, and is a more conventional SPACE OPERA in which a human male and a ler female are forced to team up to try to solve a complexly ramifying problem of interstellar piracy. MAF's slow but impressively detailed construction of the ler culture and language, especially in the later novel, marks his series out as one of potential importance to the genre.   [JC]
See also: LINGUISTICS.

FOSTER, RICHARD *See* Kendell Foster CROSSEN.

FOSTER, W(ALTER) BERT(RAM) (1869– ?). American writer whose borderline sf novels are *The Eve of War* (**1904**) and *The Lost Expedition* (**1905**). His LOST-RACE story "The Man Child" in PEARSON'S MAGAZINE tells of white Indians.   [JC]

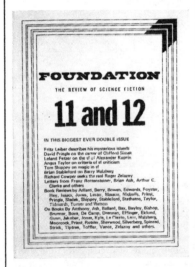

No. 11/12, 1977.

FOUNDATION: THE REVIEW OF SCIENCE FICTION British academic journal, published by the SCIENCE FICTION FOUNDATION of North East London Polytechnic from March 1972, with 13 numbers to mid-1978, current Nos 1–4 ed. Charles BARREN, nos 5–12 ed. Peter NICHOLLS, no. 13 ed. Nicholls and Malcolm EDWARDS, with Edwards then editor alone. Other members of the editorial board have included George HAY, Christopher PRIEST and Ian WATSON. With a circulation of about 1000 over the English-speaking world and Europe, it has been effective (along with the American magazines EXTRAPOLATION and SCIENCE-FICTION STUDIES) in providing a platform for serious sf criticism, though it has been less exclusively academic than its two

competitors, and has concentrated more on reviews and articles about current sf than the other two journals. *Foundation* has made enemies as well as friends by being iconoclastic about the standard critical rankings produced by FANDOM on the one hand, and by not accepting the conventional academic emphasis on comparatively "respectable" UTOPIAS and DYSTOPIAS on the other. A feature has been the "Profession of Science Fiction" series by such authors as James BLISH, Ursula K. LE GUIN, Fritz LEIBER, Samuel R. DELANY, Richard COWPER and A.E. VAN VOGT. Publication has been irregular. The first eight issues are projected for book publication with introduction in 1978.   [PN]

FOUR-SIDED TRIANGLE Film (1953). Hammer. Directed by Terence Fisher, starring Barbara Payton, Stephen Murray and John Van Eyssen. Screenplay by Paul TABORI and Terence Fisher, based on the novel by William F. TEMPLE. 81 mins (cut to 71). B/w.
A scientist builds a machine capable of duplicating human beings. He duplicates the woman he loves, who is herself in love with another man, only to have the duplicate fall in love with the other man too. This is a low-budget film.   [JB]

FOURTH DIMENSION (AND OTHERS) No term has been more corrupted by its usage in sf than "dimension". We perceive three spatial dimensions, and the last century has seen the emergence of the notion (prompted by the implications of mathematical dimensional analysis) that there might be more, or that time might be appropriately represented as a dimension as well. The possible existence of PARALLEL WORLDS displaced from ours along a fourth spatial dimension (in the same way that a series of two-dimensional universes might lie next to one another like the pages of a book) has arisen, and with it a habit of referring to such worlds as "other dimensions". This persistent misnomer adds greatly to the confusion of what is innately an imaginatively challenging idea.
The notion of time as a dimension was introduced for convenience in certain mathematical analyses by Lagrange and D'Alembert in the 18th century. The occultist Johann Zollner confused this perspective with the notion of "other planes of existence" popularized by the theosophists and spiritualists in the late 19th century. The confusion was compounded when Einstein, in the General Theory of Relativity (1916), put forward a four-dimensional model of the universe. H.G. WELLS used the classical time is the fourth-dimension argument to "explain" time travel in *The Time Machine* (**1895**), and many 20th century occultists have cultivated its splendid mysteries, from J.W. Dunne, who used it to explain prophetic dreams and to

construct his theory of the serial universe, to the extravagant P.D. Ouspensky, who claimed that time is a spiral and that there are six spatial dimensions.
The possible limitations of human existence and perception, dimensionally speaking, were first embodied in fiction by Edwin ABBOTT in *Flatland* (**1884**), in which he described the intellectual challenge presented by our world to a two-dimensional being, and encouraged his readers to accept the challenge of the fourth dimension. One who did was C. Howard HINTON, a pseudo-scientist who used the idea to explain ghosts and imagined a four-dimensional God from whom nothing in the human world could be hidden. In "An Unfinished Communication" (1895) Hinton represented the afterlife as freedom to move along the time-dimension to relive and reassess moments of life, and he also wrote a Flatland novel, *An Episode of Flatland* (**1907**). E.V. ODLE's *The Clockwork Man* (**1923**) could perceive many dimensions when working properly, but while malfunctioning in the novel he could do no more than flutter back and forth in time and offer the merest hint of the quality of multidimensional life. In "The Pikestaffe Case" (1924) by Algernon BLACKWOOD, more fantasy than science, an interesting attempt is made to evoke the non-Euclidean geometry of a dimensional trap lurking within a looking-glass.
One or two early pulp sf writers found the notion of dimensions fascinating — notably Miles J. BREUER in "The Appendix and the Spectacles" (1928), "The Captured Cross-Section" (1929) and "The Gostak and the Doshes" (1930) and Donald WANDREI in "The Monster From Nowhere" (1935) and "Infinity Zero" (1936) — but they could do little more with the idea than perform literary conjuring tricks by mathematical analogy (though the conjuring trick in "Infinity Zero" is an apocalyptic one). Attempts to develop the idea were, however, made by E.E. "Doc" SMITH in *Skylark of Valeron* (1934; **1949**), whose heroes enter a four-dimensional reality for a brief adventure, and by Clifford D. SIMAK in "Hellhounds of the Cosmos" (1932), in which 99 men enter the fourth dimension as a single grotesque body to combat a four-dimensional monster.
As sf became more sophisticated, slick trickery often replaced rigorous thought. "Mimsy Were the Borogoves" (1943) by Lewis Padgett (Henry KUTTNER) tells the story of toys from the future which educate children into four-dimensional habits of thought, but does no more than encapsulate its idea. The fashionable extra-dimensional subject of the late 1940s and early 1950s was topology, and there are numerous stories hinging on Moebius strip gimmickry, including Martin GARDNER's "No-Sided Professor" (1946) and "The Island of Five Colours"

(1952), Theodore STURGEON's "What Dead Men Tell" (1949), Arthur C. CLARKE's "Wall of Darkness" (1949), A.J. Deutsch's "A Subway Named Mobius" (1950) and Homer C. NEARING's "The Hermeneutical Doughnut" (1954). Klein bottles and tesseracts were also featured in such stories as "The Last Magician" (1951) by Bruce ELLIOTT, "And He Built a Crooked House" (1941) by Robert HEINLEIN and "Star, Bright" (1952) by Mark CLIFTON. *Occam's Razor* by David DUNCAN (**1957**) begins with some lively double-talk about the topological qualities of soap films stretched on wire frames, and their dimensional consequences.

The notion that spaceships might make use of a fourth-dimensional "hyperspace" in order to evade the limiting velocity of light is very common in sf — it was popularized by Isaac ASIMOV among others — but is used almost entirely for convenience (*see* FASTER THAN LIGHT *and* SPACE FLIGHT). There are very few attempts actually to represent hyperspace, except as a chaotic environment which utterly confuses the senses. Such tentative accounts are featured, for instance, in Frederik POHL's "The Mapmakers" (1955) and Clifford D. Simak's "All the Traps of Earth" (1960). More recently there have been several attempts to render in fiction the dimensional chaos that might be associated with BLACK HOLES. Attempts to represent the experience of living in non-Euclidean space-time are rare. George GAMOW's popularization of ideas in modern physics, *Mr. Tompkins in Wonderland* (coll. **1939**), dramatizes certain odd situations very well, but consists of didactic essays rather than stories. Perhaps the best representations of experience of distorted environments are to be found in David MASSON's story "Traveller's Rest" (1965) and in Christopher PRIEST's novel *The Inverted World* (**1974**). The best recent examples of ideative mathematical conjuring are Norman KAGAN's "The Mathenauts" (1964) and M.K. JOSEPH's *The Hole in the Zero* (**1967**).

All in all, it cannot be said that sf writers have yet answered Edwin Abbott's challenge with conspicuous success.

Several of the stories mentioned in this section appear in two anthologies, *Fantasia Mathematica* (**1958**) and *The Mathematical Magpie* (**1962**) ed. Clifton Fadiman. Also relevant is *Science Fiction Adventures in Dimension* (anth. **1953**) ed. Groff CONKLIN.
See also: COSMOLOGY; MATHEMATICS.

FOWLER, S. *See* S. Fowler WRIGHT.

FOX, GARDNER F(RANCIS) (1911–). American writer, whose career began in 1937 with writing for comics, including SUPERMAN, and who began publishing sf/fantasy with "The Weirds of the Woodcarver" for *Weird Tales* in 1944; he also used several pseudonyms at this time, including Jefferson Cooper, Jeffrey Gardner and James Kendricks, though none of these was used in sf magazines. He was an active contributor to *Planet Stories* from 1945, though he did not begin to publish sf novels (his early novels, like *The Borgia Blade*, **1953,** being historical romances), either under his own name or under his later pseudonyms, Bart Somers and Simon Majors, until *Five Weeks in a Balloon* (**1962**), which is a rewrite of the Jules VERNE story. GFF's first sf novel proper is *Escape Across the Cosmos* (**1964**), in which a man fights a menace from another DIMENSION, and his best is probably *The Arsenal of Miracles* (**1964**), which combines SPACE OPERA, GALACTIC EMPIRES and a romantically conceived hero who prefigures the interest in HEROIC FANTASY which has dominated GFF's more recent output. His sf series are the two fantasy-like adventures, *Warrior of Llarn* (**1964**) and *Thief of Llarn* (**1966**), and, as by Bart Somers, the Commander Craig space operas, *Beyond the Black Enigma* (**1965**) and *Abandon Galaxy!* (**1967**). GFF is an efficient storyteller with no visible pretensions to significance or thematic originality.   [JC]
Other works: *Hunter out of Time* (**1965**); *The Druid Stone* (**1967**, as by Simon Majors); the heroic fantasy series *Kothar and the Demon Queen* (**1969**), *Kothar — Barbarian Swordsman* (**1969**), *Kothar of the Magic Sword* (**1969**), *Kothar and the Conjuror's Curse* (**1970**) and *Kothar and the Wizard Slayer* (**1970**); *Conehead* (**1973**); and another heroic fantasy series, *Kyrik: Warlock Warrior* (**1975**), *Kyrik Fights the Demon World* (**1975**), *Kyrik and the Wizard's Sword* (**1976**), *Kyrik and the Lost Queen* (**1976**).
See also: LIFE ON OTHER WORLDS; SWORD AND SORCERY.

FPCI *See* FANTASY PUBLISHING COMPANY INC.

The three handsome protagonists in a typical 1930s publicity still.

F.P.1 ANTWORTET NICHT (vt F.P.1 DOES NOT ANSWER USA) Film (1932). UFA. Directed by Karl Hartl, starring Hans Albers, Sybille Schmitz, Paul Hartmann and Peter Lorre. Screenplay by Walter Reisch and Curt SIODMAK, based on the novel by Curt Siodmak. Original running time 110 mins, other versions run 90 and 70 mins. B/w.

F.P.1 has been described as being in the tradition of METROPOLIS and FRAU IM MOND, but Karl Hartl was no Fritz Lang. It is a slow-moving and badly constructed film, ostensibly about the construction of a giant floating runway to be moored in the middle of the Atlantic, but actually more concerned with a tedious love triangle. The story involves intrepid aviators, sabotage at sea and noble renunciations — all pulp novel materials, but with none of the slickness or verve of similar Hollywood films of the period; the model work is also poor. (English and French versions of *F.P.1* were made at the same time as the German version.)
[JB]

Sf illustration flourished in FRANCE in the 19th century, as in this 1897 book.

FRANCE The history of France's relationship with sf is one of long flirtation, marked through the centuries by episodic outbursts of passion and, in recent times, by an increasing shift from authorship to readership, from the active to the passive role, as more and more people become avid consumers of the Anglo-Saxon tradition of the genre. A few remarkable French writers of sf have emerged, but no truly indigenous school of writing has yet taken shape, though this observation may be proved wrong by the end of the 1970s, which have already shown signs of an sf renaissance.

The quest for "great ancestors" in the corpus of French literature would be endless; many texts, some of them vintage classics, some long-forgotten oddities, show that imaginary travels, the search for UTOPIA, speculation on other worlds and alien forms of society were constant preoccupations. People tend to overlook the fact that the last parts of François RABELAIS's *Gargantua and Pantagruel* (1532–64; trans. **1653–94**) (especially *L'isle sonante*, **1562**) are clearly set in the future and almost constitute an early style of SPACE OPERA with their procession of foreign languages, customs and landscapes.

One century later, interest in the otherworldly asserts itself in works such as CYRANO DE BERGERAC'S *Histoire comique contenant les états et empires de la lune* (1657; trans. 1659; vt *A Voyage to the Moon*) and Fontenelle's *Entretiens sur la pluralité des mondes habités* ["On the Plurality of Inhabited Worlds"] (1686; trans. 1929), but it is in the 18th century that we encounter the most direct forerunner of sf in its modern sense, in the form of the *conte philosophique*, or philosophical tale.

Conditions were ideal for the emergence of something akin to sf: the *Siècle des Lumières* is one of universal curiosity, of philosophical audacity and political revolution; it gave birth to all-encompassing spirits such as that of DIDEROT and saw the writing of the *Encyclopédie*; it merged the two aspects of culture, literary and scientific, the divorce of which would be one of the main sources of the decline of French sf in our time.

The *conte philosophique* sets itself as a genre with its own rules: the voyage to a far island symbolizes what we now image in interplanetary travel, and the islanders themselves stand for what are now aliens, while the study of their civilization serves as mirror/criticism of our institutions. Conversely, the satire of French (= European) society as seen through foreign eyes was a device already used by Montesquieu in his *Lettres persanes* (1721).

The genre was illustrated by numerous stories (Pierre VERSINS states that "at the beginning of the 18th century, at least one speculative work was published each year") but among its landmarks are VOLTAIRE'S *Micromégas* (Berlin 1750; France 1752), Louis-Sébastien MERCIER'S *L'an deux mille quatre cent quarante* (1771; trans. as *Memoirs of the Year Two Thousand Five Hundred* 1772), RESTIF DE LA BRETONNE'S *La découverte australe* ["The Southern-Hemisphere Discovery"] (1781) and CASANOVA'S *Isocaméron* (1788), an early story of travel to the centre of the Earth. Such was the vogue of speculation that in 1787 a publisher started a list of "Voyages imaginaires" which ran to 36 volumes and may be considered as the first sf series ever.

The 19th century would seem to be entirely dominated by the formidable silhouette of Jules VERNE, but was in other respects a very active period also, carrying on the *élan* of the preceding era: scientific achievements and the industrial revolution gave birth to popular novels in the same way that philosophical turmoil had produced its share of *contes*. Verne himself stands apart because he was the first writer to be systematic about it and build his whole work according to a vast design, thus described by his publisher Hetzel in 1867: "His aim is to sum up all knowledge gathered by modern science

in the fields of *geography*, *geology*, *physics*, *astronomy*, and to remake, in his own attractive and picturesque way, the history of our universe." From then to his death in 1905, Verne would give Hetzel the 64 books which make up his "Voyages extraordinaires", subtitled "Voyages 'dans les mondes connus et inconnus". Jacques VAN HERP argues that Verne's position is crucial also because the huge success he enjoyed, basically among adolescents, drove away from him serious critics and historians, so that one may trace back to him — for France anyway — the lame academic quarrel of deciding whether sf, or "anticipation", was high literature or not. Indeed, that question had never been raised before and it took a bourgeois system of education to institute class-struggle among books. Verne's work went the way of *Robinson Crusoe* or *Treasure Island*: that of a sort of universal reputation which does not preclude underestimation or misunderstanding. Until recently, Verne was ignored by the university, but fascinated such diverse minds as those of Raymond Roussel (who called him "le plus grand génie littéraire de tous les siècles" ["the greatest literary genius of all time"]), Michel BUTOR and Michel Foucault.

Among Verne's contemporaries in the field, one should at least mention the astronomer Camille FLAMMARION and his *Récits de l'infini* (1872; trans. as *Stories of Infinity: Lumen — History of a Comet in Infinity* 1873) and the novelist-cum-draughtsman Albert ROBIDA, who was no less prolific than Verne, and parodied him in his *Voyages très extraordinaires de Saturnin Farandoul* (periodical publication 1879; *for book publication see his entry*) which purportedly took their hero "dans tous les pays connus et même inconnus de Monsieur Jules Verne" ["into all countries known and even unknown to Mr Jules Verne"]. Robida proved himself a visionary, as well as a humorist, in his *Le vingtième siècle* ["The 20th Century"] (1882), *La vie électrique* ["The Electric Life"] (1883) and *La guerre au vingtième siècle* ["War in the 20th Century"] (1883).

By the turn of the century, however, the one name Verne had to contend with was that of J.H. ROSNY AÎNÉ, a writer who possibly deserves as much consideration. The Rosnys, two brothers of Belgian extraction, started together a writing career that was eventually to win them seats with the Académie Goncourt, but only the elder brother's 17 novels — which run from the prehistoric *La guerre du feu* ["The War of Fire"] (1909) through the cataclysmic *La mort de la terre* ["Death of the Earth"] (1910) to the futuristic *Les navigateurs de l'infini* ["Navigators of the Infinite"] (1925) — and his numerous stories concern us here. Rosny aîné entered the field with the short story "Les xipéhuz" (1887; trans. as "The Shapes"); and consistently brought

to it, beside a solid scientific culture, a breadth of vision at times worthy of Olaf STAPLEDON.

The period ranging from the 1880s to the 1930s was the true golden age of French sf; it predates the American boom of the 1920s. We might call it France's pulp era. Not that there ever existed any specific sf magazines, but wide-circulation periodicals such as *Journal des voyages* or *La science illustrée*, then, later, *Je sais tout*, *L'Intrépide* and the very important *Sciences et voyages* regularly ran stories and serialized novels of "anticipation". Sf was thus lent a degree of respectability by being introduced as an extension of travel and adventure stories. In the general title given to his work, Jules Verne had proceeded similarly from "known" to "unknown" worlds.

Apart from isolated works by non-specialists such as *L'Ève future* ["The Future Eve"] (1886) by VILLIERS DE L'ISLE ADAM, *L'île des pingouins* (1908; trans. as *Penguin Island* 1909) by Anatole FRANCE or *Le Napus, fléau de l'an 2227* ["The 'Disappearance': Scourge of the year 2227"] (1927) by Léon Daudet, this period gave birth to a host of popular writers: Paul d'Ivoi, Louis BOUSSENARD, then Gustave Le Rouge, Jean de La Hire, André Couvreur, José Moselli, René Thévenin, etc. All were not of equal worth, but three names are outstanding: Maurice RENARD, author of the amazing *Le docteur Lerne* (1908), which he dedicated to H.G. WELLS; Jacques Spitz (1896–1963), with his best novel *L'oeil du purgatoire* ["The Eye of Purgatory"] (1945) — his earlier *L'agonie du globe* (1935; trans. as *Save the Earth* 1936) was given a British edition — and Régis Messac (1893–1943), whose *Quinzinzinzili* (1935) and *La cité des asphyxiés* ["The City of the Suffocated"] (1934) exhibit a sinister mood and grim humour that deserve to gain him a new audience today.

The Second World War put an end to this thriving period, and during the 1940s only one writer of note appeared: René BARJAVEL, with *Ravage* (1943; trans. as *Ashes, Ashes* 1967) and *Le voyageur imprudent* (1944; trans. as *Future Times Three* 1971).

At the end of the War, two factors were to bear heavily on the future of sf in France. The first was the growing separation, at school, in the universities and in all thinking circles, between *les littéraires* and *les scientifiques*, which made for a lack of curiosity about science and its possible effects on the shapes of our lives on the part of aspiring novelists, and drove many talents away from the genre, which was definitely viewed as teenager-fodder. France had ceased to dream about its own future, as it were, and about the future generally.

Secondly, whatever interest in these matters existed was satisfied from another source, the USA. In the years following the War, the French public discovered all at once jazz, American films, thrillers and the golden age of American sf. One key personality of the period was Boris VIAN, novelist, songwriter, film buff and jazz musician, who translated both Raymond Chandler and A.E. VAN VOGT. This was the time of the creation of *Le club des savanturiers* by Michel Pilotin, Vian, Raymond QUENEAU and Audiberti. In 1951, Queneau wrote an introductory essay in *Critique*: "Un nouveau genre littéraire: les sciences-fictions" ["A New Literary Genre — sf"], followed two years later by Michel BUTOR, with "La crise de croissance de la science-fiction" (1953 *Cahiers du Sud*; trans. as *SF: The Crisis of its Growth*", *Partisan Review* 1967).

Sf was again fashionable but mainly in translated form. Between 1951 and 1964, the *Rayon fantastique* series published 119 titles, mostly American; it was followed in 1954 by *Présence du Futur*, which still exists today. By the end of the decade, some French names appear on the list of *Le Rayon* (Francis CARSAC, Philippe Curval and Albert Higon, pseudonym of Michel JEURY) and *Présence* (Jacques STERNBERG, Jean Hougron), but for the most part, French authors were published, often under pseudonyms, in the less prestigious *Fleuve noir* series, created in 1951. The best of these were Stefan WUL, B.R. BRUSS (Roger Blondel), Kurt Steiner (André RUELLAN) and Gilles d'Argyre (Gérard KLEIN).

In 1953, Éditions Opta launched the French editions of *Galaxy* and *The Magazine of Fantasy and Science-Fiction* — *Galaxie* and *Fiction*, whose contents differ notably from those of their American models — that would remain for 25 years the principal outlet for American stories and springboard for new French talents, including critics. But these were few and far between. The initial impetus given by the discovery of American sf in the 1950s slowed down during the following decade. One magazine which devoted more space to indigenous authors, *Satellite*, had a brief life. Among the new writers, Michel DEMUTH, Alain Dorémieux and Gérard Klein were soon absorbed by editorial responsibilities and their output has consequently been irregular.

The most personal voice in the last 20 years has been that of Philippe CURVAL who, from *Le ressac de l'espace* ["The Breakers of Space"] (1962) to *Cette chère humanité* ["This Dear Humanity"] (1976), has consistently maintained a high standard while never imitating the American model. Beside him, we should mention Michel Jeury again, who resumed writing with *Le temps incertain* ["Uncertain Time"] (1973) and Daniel DRODE's only novel, *Surface de la planète* ["Surface of the Planet"] (1959). Mainstream writers occasionally tackled sf: Pierre BOULLE with *La planète des singes* (1963; trans. as *Planet of the Apes* 1963; vt *Monkey Planet* UK), Robert MERLE with *Un animal doué de raison* (1967; trans. as *The Day of the Dolphin* 1969) and *Malevil* (1972), and Claude Ollier, an adept of the *nouveau roman*, with *La vie sur Epsilon* ["Life on Epsilon"] (1972).

In the past 10 years, the situation seems to have changed again, once more due to a definite influence: that of the British NEW WAVE and in particular post-NEW-WORLDS sf. J.G. BALLARD's later work, along with that of such American writers as Thomas M. DISCH, Harlan ELLISON and Norman SPINRAD, has had a tremendous impact on the new generation of readers who lived through the 1968 student uprising and saw the possibilities of making powerful political statements in speculative form. Several young authors who began writing in the mid-1960s (Daniel WALTHER, Jean-Pierre ANDREVON, Jean-Pierre Fontana) readily took that route, and have been followed by a batch of newcomers, Dominique DOUAY the best among them. French sf is in a transitional phase, and signs of a renewed interest are evident in the growing number of sf imprints from French publishers, and also in the fact that since 1974 France has held its own sf CONVENTIONS, which had never happened before.

The most useful accounts of French sf are written in French, and include: *Encyclopédie de l'utopie, des voyages extraordinaires et de la science-fiction* (1972 Switzerland) by Pierre VERSINS; *Histoire de la science-fiction moderne* (1973) by Jacques SADOUL; *Panorama de la science-fiction* (1973 Belgium) by Jacques VAN HERP; and the preface to *Sur l'autre face du monde & autres romans scientifiques de 'Sciences et voyages';* (anth. 1973) ed. A. Valerie, by Gérard KLEIN. Also relevant is "SF Criticism in France" by Peter Fitting in SCIENCE-FICTION STUDIES, Spring 1974. [RL]

FRANCE, ANATOLE Pseudonym of Anatole-François Thibault (1844–1924), French writer active from the early 1860s until his death. His essayistic, "pagan" SATIRES have perhaps less redolence and bite now than formerly, some of their targets, like official religion, perhaps seeming less formidable today; of sf interest are *L'île des pingouins* (1908; trans. as *Penguin Island* 1909), in which humanity's evolutionary course is allegorized satirically in terms of the dubious EVOLUTION of a race of penguins, and *La révolte des anges* (1914; trans. as *The Revolt of the Angels* 1914), perhaps a more successful novel, in which angels are driven to despairing revolt by the masses of theology they read in a great, stuffy private library. AF won the Nobel Prize in 1921. [JC]
Other works: *Sur la pierre blanche* (1905; trans. as *The White Stone* 1910).
See also: UTOPIAS.

FRANCES, STEPHEN (? –). Publisher and pulp-writer now resident in Spain. He was director of Gaywood Press in the late 1940s and early '50s when they published much cheap-format sf, and invented the house name Astron DEL MARTIA and possibly others. He wrote pulp adventure books under the name Hank Janson, at least one of which was sf: *One Against Time* (1954; 1969 as by Astron del Martia). [PN]

FRANK, PAT Pseudonym of American writer Harry Hart (1907–). A government official during the Second World War, he later served with the United Nations. He has written many non-sf stories and several novels, and is not personally associated with the sf field, though his first novel, *Mr Adam* (1946), is certainly sf; all but one man is sterilized by a nuclear disaster, and his experiences as the one fertile man are comical and provide grounds for a SATIRE on government procedures. *Forbidden Area* (1956; vt *Seven Days to Never* UK) also deals (more grimly) with the atomic question, in a thriller plot involving sabotage and near holocaust. PF's most famous sf novel is *Alas, Babylon* (1959), an extremely effective post-HOLOCAUST novel (the disaster is again nuclear) set in a part of Florida that survives; domestic verisimilitude and apocalypse mingle impressively. PF's work is always NEAR-FUTURE in orientation, and draws its emotional force from the deep, immediate fears of nuclear devastation many Americans suffered, with some cause, during the 1950s. [JC]
See also: PASTORAL.

FRANKAU, GILBERT (1884–1952). British writer, known mainly for his works outside the sf field, most notably for his Byronesque verse novel *One of Us* (1912) and dozens of popular romances. *The Seeds of Enchantment* (1921) is fantasy. His posthumous sf novel, *Unborn Tomorrow* (1953), depicts a FAR-FUTURE culture in which, because a beam blows up all explosives, we see a return to a pre-industrial lifestyle. [JC]

FRANKE, HERBERT W. (1927–). Austrian-born writer and scientist now working in Munich, where he teaches cybernetic aesthetics at the University of Munich, after receiving a doctorate in Vienna in 1951. After publishing considerable non-fiction in the 1950s, mostly on either speleology or computer graphics, he also began publishing sf, at first speculative short stories like those assembled in *Der grüne Komet* ["The Green Comet"] (coll. 1960), *Einsteins Erben* ["Einstein's Heirs"] (coll. 1972), and *Zarathustra kehrt zurück* ["Zarathustra Returns"] (coll. 1977). He has also published seven novels, beginning with *Das Gedenkennetz* (1961; trans. as *The Mind Net* 1974). *Der Orchideenkäfig* (1961; trans. as *The*

Orchid Cage **1973**) complexly depicts, in HWF's typically speculative, somewhat dry manner, the profound transformative effects of a mysterious planet on its human explorers; *Zone Null* (**1970**; trans. **1974**) sets up, between a future Free World and an apparently defeated and deserted Zone Null, a metaphysical questioning of the true ends of society and of the intermingled values of both opposed sides. HWF is one of the first contemporary German writers whose sf ranks with that in English and in other European languages.   [JC]

Other works: *Die Glasfalle* ["The Glass Trap"] (**1962**); *Die Stahlwüste* ["The Steel Desert"] (**1962**); *Der Elfenbeinturm* ["The Ivory Tower"] (**1965**); *Ypsilon Minus* (**1976**).

See also: POLITICS.

FRANKENSTEIN Film (1931). Universal. Directed by James Whale, starring Boris Karloff, Colin Clive, Mae Clarke, Edward van Sloan and Dwight Frye. Screenplay by Garrett Fort, Robert Florey and Francis Edward Faragoh, adaptation by Robert Florey and John L. Balderston, based on the play by Peggy Webling from the novel by Mary W. SHELLEY. 71 mins. B/w.

This is the best known of all the Frankenstein films, even though it was not the first (the Edison Company made a 975-foot version in 1910: it was directed by J. Searle Dawley and starred Charles Ogle as the Monster). Dr Frankenstein is a scientist who attempts to build an artificial man using spare parts stolen from dead bodies. He succeeds, with the aid of an electrical storm, in bringing the creature to life, but because his assistant has given him the brain of a criminal instead of a "normal" man (an

unnecessary and clumsy plot device invented by the script-writers which has nothing to do with Mary Shelley's novel) it proves difficult to control. Eventually the Monster escapes, accidentally kills a small girl and is pursued and apparently killed by the angry villagers (originally it killed Frankenstein too but the studio decided to add a happy ending before the film's release and the doctor survived).

The film remains a classic today. With his atmospheric lighting, smooth tracking shots and numerous low-angle shots that were never obtrusive but made effective use of the high-ceilinged sets — particularly Frankenstein's laboratory — Whale succeeded in making a horror film that possessed a real sense of grandeur. But much of the credit must go to Karloff for his fine performance as the pathetic Monster, achieved purely with mime and aided by Jack Pierce's bizarre make-up.

There have been numerous sequels, including *Bride of Frankenstein* (1935), *Son of Frankenstein* (1939), *Ghost of Frankenstein* (1942), *Frankenstein Meets the Wolfman* (1943), *House of Frankenstein* (1945), *Abbott and Costello Meet Frankenstein* (1948) and *Frankenstein 1970* (1958). In 1957 the British company Hammer Films remade the original, calling it *Curse of Frankenstein*, and have since made several sequels, ending with *Frankenstein and the Monster from Hell* (1972). A recent Frankenstein manifestation is the successful parody/homage YOUNG FRANKENSTEIN (1974), directed by Mel Brooks.

An interesting recent attempt to recreate Mary Shelley's original novel (previous films had all changed the story) is the made-for-TV film *Frankenstein: The True Story* (1973), Universal Pictures

Television, directed by Jack Smight, from a script by Christopher Isherwood and Don Bachardy, starring James Mason, David McCallum and Michael Sarrazin. The teleplay was published as a book, *Frankenstein: The True Story* (**1973**). [JB]

FRANKENSTEIN MONSTER The term has gone into general use, not only in sf TERMINOLOGY, but in common parlance: a monster that ultimately turns and rends its irresponsible creator. Note that in the original novel Frankenstein was the name of the creator and not the monster, though in popular usage it is often assumed that the monster itself was Frankenstein. *See* Mary SHELLEY *for further details.*   [PN]

FRANKLIN, EDGAR Form of his name used by Edgar Franklin Stearns (1879–) for *Mr Hawkins' Humorous Adventures* (coll. of linked stories **1904**), in which the eponymous scientist invents a series of devices, such as the pumpless pump, which never work   [JC]

See also: HUMOUR.

FRANKLIN, H. BRUCE (1934–). American critic, professor of English at Rutgers; PhD in literature, Stanford, 1961. In 1961 he took, at Stanford, one of the first two university courses in sf in the USA; he left that college under protest in 1973, being asked to leave (in a case that became well known to those interested in questions of academic freedom) for alleged left-wing activities. His *Future Perfect: American Science Fiction of the Nineteenth Century* (anth. **1966**; rev. 1968; new rev. projected for 1978) has been one of the most influential of sf anthologies, in drawing attention to the sheer volume of 19th-century sf, and thus putting the nail in the coffin of the theory that Hugo GERNSBACK invented it all. HBF has written at least 12 other critical articles on sf in EXTRAPOLATION and elsewhere, some of them important. He is on the editorial board of SCIENCE-FICTION STUDIES.   [PN]

See also: SF IN THE CLASSROOM.

FRANK READE, JR Hero of a juvenile scientific invention series published in BOYS' PAPERS from 1876 to 1913. Written almost entirely by Luis P. SENARENS, under the pseudonym "Noname", over 180 novels appeared featuring such prophetic INVENTIONS as gun-carrying submarines, electric snowmobiles and multi-vaned helicopters.

The series was reprinted in Britain, appeared in DIME NOVELS and prompted several imitators, including a companion series, the *Jack Wright* stories.   [JE]

See also: "Ghosts of Prophecies Past" in *Explorers of the Infinite: Shapers of Science Fiction* (**1963**) by Sam MOSKOWITZ.

FRASER, Sir RONALD (ARTHUR) (1888– ?). English writer and civil

This magnificent still is all that remains of the Edison Company's 1910 version of FRANKENSTEIN.

servant. Many of his novels have fantasy elements, and some of them are sf, such as *Beetle's Career* (**1951**), about a super-weapon with beneficial side-effects, *A Visit from Venus* (**1958**) and its sequel, *Jupiter in the Chair* (**1958**), about a sort of cultural exchange junket involving inhabitants of Venus and humans. In an elegant, painless manner, RS has concentrated throughout his career on novels of controlled wit, mild satire, admissible sentiment. [JC]

Other works: *The Flying Draper* (**1924**); *Landscape with Figures* (**1925**), an oriental fantasy; *The Flower Phantoms* (**1926**); *Miss Lucifer* (**1939**); *The Fiery Gate* (**1943**); *Sun in Scorpio* (**1949**); *Trout's Testament* (**1960**).

See also: PSYCHOLOGY.

FRAU IM MOND, DIE (vt **BY ROCKET TO THE MOON**; vt **THE GIRL IN THE MOON**) Film (1929). UFA. Directed by Fritz Lang, starring Gerda Marus, Willy Fritsch, Fritz Rasp and Klaus Pohl. Screenplay by Fritz Lang and Thea VON HARBOU, based on the novel by Thea von Harbou. 156 mins (also 97-min. version). B/w.

After the success of METROPOLIS, Fritz Lang's next sf film was a disappointment. Over long (in its original form) and conventionally plotted, it concerns an ill-matched group of people travelling to a Moon which seems little different from the Swiss Alps. Lack of air and differences in temperature and gravity are ignored; the explorers are able to amble about the lunar landscape picking up chunks of precious metal and jewels. The build-up to the take-off, however, was much more convincing; Lang used rocket experts Hermann Oberth and Willy LEY as technical advisers, and the model rocket they produced was prophetic in its design (it was even constructed in two stages). The blast-off itself was also impressive, with good camerawork by Oskar Fischinger and effects by Konstantin Tschewerikoff. [JB]

FRAYN, MICHAEL (1933–). English novelist, journalist and playwright, best known for such work outside the sf field as the novel *Against Entropy* (**1967**; vt *Towards the End of the Morning*), which is not sf, despite its title. His sf DYSTOPIA *A Very Private Life* (**1968**) describes a claustrophobically antiseptic Earth in which mankind is divided into those who live inside germ-free enclaves and those who live out of doors. [JC]

Other works: *The Tin Men* (**1965**) and *Sweet Dreams* (**1973**); both have marginal sf relevance.

See also: AUTOMATION; COMPUTERS; LINGUISTICS.

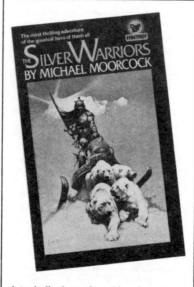

A typically dramatic and heroic cover by Frank FRAZETTA. Dell Books, 1977.

FRAZETTA, FRANK (1928–). American illustrator. Known primarily for HEROIC FANTASY illustrations, especially his much admired Edgar Rice BURROUGHS "Tarzan" covers for ACE Books in the mid-1960s, FF began in comics in 1944 and stayed in that field for two decades, working on both BUCK ROGERS and FLASH GORDON at various times, and for nine years on *Li'l Abner*, before making his mark as a paperback book cover artist in the mid-1960s. He gained fame with a series of covers for Lancer Books; these were for Robert E. HOWARD's "Conan" series. FF's vigorous paintings of lush, wide-hipped women, very often in bondage or being menaced, and heavily muscled heroes, have made him very popular with sf fans, though they have also been criticized as being cheaply melodramatic. FF has been nominated five times for a HUGO award, and gained one in 1966. Two books featuring his work are *The Fantastic Art of Frank Frazetta* (**1975**) introduced by Betty BALLANTINE, and *Frank Frazetta Book Two* (**1977**). He is interviewed in ARIEL: THE BOOK OF FANTASY Vol.2. [JG/PN]

A jaunty sf character study by FREAS; *ASF*, British edition, Sep. 1954.

FREAS, FRANK KELLY (1922–). American illustrator. His first sf illustration appeared in the early 1950s and he quickly became, and remained, the most popular illustrator in sf history. He was one of the primary illustrators for *ASF*, as both cover and interior artist, and also worked for many other magazines. He has also painted covers for *Mad Magazine*, ACE BOOKS, DAW BOOKS, Lancer Books, LASER BOOKS and others. His style is smooth and realistic, and his colours luminous. Many of his covers are relaxedly humorous, featuring vigorous vagabonds, amiable aliens and a selection of jaunty scoundrels. His b/w illustrations are sometimes similar to the work of Edd CARTIER, even to that of Norman Rockwell in the 1930s. Nominated for an astonishing 17 HUGO awards, he has won nine, almost twice as

An early and vivid rendition of the landscape of the Moon from DIE FRAU IM MOND, 1929.

Frank Kelly FREAS is equally at home with technology, as in this fine machine-study, April 1972.

many as EMSH, his nearest rival. Several portfolios of his work have been published, including *Frank Kelly Freas: The Art of Science Fiction* (**1977**). [JG/PN]

FREEDMAN, NANCY (1920–). American writer, whose sf novel, *Joshua Son of None* (**1973**), one of the more sensational stories involving CLONING, depicts the intrigue surrounding Joshua Kellogg, who was cloned from the body of John F. Kennedy in 1963. [JC] **Other works:** *The Immortals* (**1976**).

FRENCH, PAUL *See* Isaac ASIMOV.

FREWIN, ANTHONY (1947–). British writer, who worked for five years as an assistant to the film director Stanley KUBRICK. His *One Hundred Years of Science Fiction Illustration* (**1974**) is written rather breathlessly, but has a well-chosen and generous selection of sf ILLUSTRATIONS, going back to the 19th century, and giving a full chapter to Albert ROBIDA. [PN]

FRIEDBERG, GERTRUDE (? –). American writer who has also taught; her first play was produced as early as 1933, but she began publishing sf, with "The Short and Happy Death of George Frumkin" for *FSF*, only in 1963. Her fine sf novel *The Revolving Boy* (**1966**) strikingly tells the story of a child sensitive from his unique birth in free fall to signals, possibly intelligent in origin, from beyond the Solar System; he reveals his sensitivity by being forced to adjust himself precisely to the direction from which the signals come. [JC]

FRIEDELL, EGON (1878–1938). Austrian writer, best known for his seminal *Cultural History of Modern Times* (**1927–32**), a text which effectively inaugurated the discipline of cultural history. As a Jew, his position was intolerable when the Nazis invaded Austria, and he committed suicide. His wry homage to H.G. WELLS, *Die Reise mit der Zeitmaschine* (apparently written c. 1935; **1946**; trans. as *The Return of the Time Machine* **1972**), complete with a

spoof correspondence between himself as narrator and Wells's secretary, purports to reprint the Time Traveller's narrative of his later journeys; the story, told with a literate wit reminiscent of some of Karel ČAPEK's lighter work, depends on complex mathematical doubletalk for its demonstration of the ultimate futility of time travel. [JC]

FRIEND, OSCAR J. (1897–1963). American writer and editor. From 1941–4 he worked for the Standard Magazine chain on CAPTAIN FUTURE, STARTLING STORIES and THRILLING WONDER STORIES. This was during the period when the magazines were most specifically aimed at adolescents. The editorial director at the time was Leo MARGULIES, with whom OJF later edited three anthologies. OJF also contributed intermittently to the magazines; one novel later reprinted was *The Kid From Mars* (1940 *Startling Stories*; **1949**). After the death of Otis Adelbert KLINE in 1946, OJF became head of Kline's literary agency. He also wrote *The Star Men* (**1963**). [MJE] **See also:** ALIENS.

FRITCH, CHARLES E. (? –). American writer and editor, who began publishing sf with "The Wallpaper" for *Other Worlds* in 1951. He edited the magazine GAMMA, 1963–5. His stories, which are written for a variety of markets but share a certain glibness and snappiness of effect, are collected in *Crazy Mixed-Up Planet* (coll. **1969**) and *Horses' Asteroid* (coll. **1970**). Many of them are spoofs. [JC]

FROM THE EARTH TO THE MOON Film (1958). RKO (later Warner Bros). Directed by Byron HASKIN, starring Joseph Cotton, George Sanders and Deborah Paget. Screenplay by Robert Blees and James Leicester, adapted from the novel by Jules VERNE. 100 mins. Colour.

A projectile carrying human passengers is fired at the Moon from a huge cannon. The special effects, by Lee Zavitz, are competent, but the film is slow-moving. A comic version, bearing no relation to Verne's novel, was *Jules Verne's Rocket to the Moon* (1967), in which a series of mildly farcical misadventures keeps the story effectively Earthbound. [JB/PN]

FTL Acronym often used in sf for FASTER THAN LIGHT.

FULLER, ALVARADO M. (? – ?). American writer whose sf novel, *A.D. 2000* (**1890**), is a future UTOPIA in which electrical inventions (and electricity as the chief source of power) dominate the somewhat expository narrative. [JC] **See also:** TIME TRAVEL.

FUREY, MICHAEL *See* Sax ROHMER.

FUTRELLE, JACQUES (1875–1912). Author, apparently American, of an sf novel, *The Diamond Master* (**1909**), which revolves around the artificial manufacture of diamonds. [JC]
Other works: *The Thinking Machine* (coll. **1907**; vt *The Problem of Cell 13*); *The Thinking Machine on the Case* (**1908**).

FUTURE *See* FAR FUTURE; FUTUROLOGY; NEAR FUTURE; PREDICTION.

FUTURE COMBINED WITH SCIENCE FICTION *See* FUTURE FICTION.

FUTURE COMBINED WITH SCIENCE FICTION STORIES *See* FUTURE FICTION.

FUTURE FANTASY AND SCIENCE FICTION *See* SWAN AMERICAN MAGAZINE for the UK magazine; FUTURE FICTION for the US magazine.

FUTURE FICTION US magazine. 17 issues, Nov. 1939-Jul. 1943, 48 further issues May/Jun. 1950 – Apr. 1960. Published by Blue Ribbon Magazines, later Double Action Magazines and (from Apr. 1941) Columbia Publications; ed. Charles D. HORNIG (Nov. 1939 – Apr. 1941) and Robert A.W. LOWNDES (Aug. 1941 – Apr. 1960). *FF* began as a companion magazine to SCIENCE FICTION, with similar editorial policies. It absorbed its parent magazine in Oct. 1941, changing its title to *Future Combined With Science Fiction*. Under Lowndes' editorship it began to feature stories by such fellow FUTURIANS as James BLISH, C. M. KORNBLUTH and Donald A. WOLLHEIM, often under pseudonyms. It also carried some of the earliest magazine covers of Hannes BOK. The title changed again to *Future Fantasy and Science Fiction* in Oct. 1942, and finally to *Science Fiction Stories* in Apr. 1943. The two issues of this final wartime

incarnation are virtually identical in appearance to *Science Fiction*, but as they continue the numbering of *FF* they are considered part of its run.

FF was one of the many magazines to fall victim to wartime paper shortages, but was revived under the same editor in 1950 as *Future Combined With Science Fiction Stories*, which became *Future Science Fiction Stories* in Jan. 1952 and, finally, *Future Science Fiction* in May 1952. It changed from pulp to digest size in Jun. 1954. It was one of several magazines edited on shoestring budgets by Lowndes during the 1950s, respectable but mediocre. [MJE]
Collectors should note: The first four issues (Nov. 1939-Nov. 1940) were four-monthly. The next issue was Apr. 1941, and the magazine became bi-monthly with the Aug. 1941 issue, continuing until Apr. 1943. The last wartime issue was Jul. 1943. These 17 issues are numbered from Vol.1 no.1 to Vol.3 no.5. The numbering resumed in 1950 with Vol.1 no.1, and continued through to Vol.5 no.3 (Oct. 1954), with the magazine appearing on a regular bi-monthly schedule apart from a three-month hiatus in 1954, when Mar. was followed by Jun. Thereafter volume numbering was dropped and subsequent issues were simply numbered 28–48. Nos 28–30 were undated; four quarterly issues (Win. 1956-Fal. 1957) followed; a bi-monthly schedule was resumed from Feb. 1958 until *FF* ceased publication. The volume numbering was taken over by ORIGINAL SCIENCE FICTION STORIES with its Jan. 1955 issue (Vol.5 no.4).

FUTURE HISTORIES *See* HISTORY IN SF; NEAR FUTURE; PREDICTION.

FUTURE SCIENCE FICTION Variant title of FUTURE FICTION in its 1950s incarnation.
Future Science Fiction was also the title of an Australian DIGEST-size magazine. Eight numbered issues: six,

No. 1, 1953.

1953–5, published by Frew Publications, Sydney, and two, 1967, published by Page Publications, NSW; no editors named. The Frew series used a mixture of US reprints and new Australian material, while the Page series reprinted from the Frew publications. A companion magazine was POPULAR SCIENCE FICTION. [FHP]
Collectors should note: The first six issues were undated, but appeared two in '53, three in '54 and one in '55.

FUTURE SCIENCE FICTION STORIES *See* FUTURE FICTION.

FUTURE WARS *See* HISTORY; WARS.

FUTUREWORLD Film (1976). AIP. Directed by Richard T. Heffron, starring Peter Fonda, Blythe Danner, Arthur Hill, John Ryan, Stuart Margolin and Yul Brynner. Screenplay by Mayo Simon and George Schenck. 104 mins. Colour.
An inferior sequel to WESTWORLD, *F* lacks the unity and impact of Michael CRICHTON's original film. *F* develops in several logically conflicting directions before settling for one of PULP sf's oldest plots — mad scientist creates robot duplicates of influential people to enable him to rule the world. There are diverting side-shows along the way as we watch two reporters investigating the futuristic amusement centre Delos, reopened after the disastrous events chronicled in *Westworld*. The attractions of Delos include simulated space flight, three-dimensional chess games, the materialization of dreams and the perfect sexual experience, the latter service provided by ever-smiling robots. This material, however, is merely decorative and irrelevant to the uncertain plot. Though made on a relatively small budget *F* makes good use of a number of actual NASA settings filmed at the Houston Manned Space Center, complemented by Brian Sellstrom and Gene Griggs's colourful special effects. The book of the film was *Futureworld*

Left, first issue of FUTURE FICTION, Nov. 1939; cover by H.W. Scott. Right, the last two wartime issues, starting in April 1943, were retitled *Science Fiction Stories*; cover by Milton Luros.

(1976) by Mayo Simon and George Schenck, adapted by John Ryder Hall (William ROTSLER). [JB]

FUTURIAN, THE British FANZINE (1938–40), edited from Leeds by J. Michael Rosenblum. A continuation of the Leeds SF League's *Bulletin* (1937), *The Futurian* was a small printed publication featuring fiction, poems and articles by leading sf fans of the day, including Frederik POHL, John Russell FEARN, William F. TEMPLE, David H. KELLER, Ralph Milne FARLEY and Arthur C. CLARKE. Other important pre-war British fanzines were John CHRISTOPHER'S *The Fantast*, John BURKE and Charles Eric MAINE's *Satellite*, Donald Mayer's *Tomorrow* (incorporating Walter GILLINGS' *Scientifiction* and *Novae Terrae* (later NEW WORLDS). Under the title of *Futurian War Digest* (1940–45), Rosenblum's fanzine became a focal point for British sf fandom during the war years when sf and amateur publishing faced considerable difficulties. It was revived as *The New Futurian* during 1954–8. [PR]

FUTURIANS A New York sf group active 1938–45, notable for their radical politics and conviction that sf fans should be forward-looking ("futurian") and constructive. Though deeply involved in FANZINE publishing and internal fan politics, the Futurians also brought together many young fans who hoped to become sf writers. Members included Donald WOLLHEIM, Frederik POHL, Cyril KORNBLUTH, Richard WILSON, David KYLE, Robert A.W. LOWNDES, Isaac ASIMOV and James BLISH; also associated with the group were Hannes BOK, Larry SHAW, Damon KNIGHT, who in *The Futurians* (1977) has published an informal history of the group, and Judith MERRIL. [PR]

No. 2, 1950.

FUTURISTIC SCIENCE STORIES British pocketbook magazine. 16 issues, numbered but undated, 1950–54, published by John Spencer, London; ed. John S. Manning. *FSS* was one of the four juvenile sf magazines published by Spencer, and of little real interest except to completist collectors. For more information on Spencer's publications see BADGER BOOKS. [FHP]

First issue, 1946. Cover by H.W. Perl.

FUTURISTIC STORIES British PULP-size magazine. Two undated issues, 1946–7, published by Hamilton & Co., Stafford; no editor named. It was juvenile, and of little interest. A companion magazine was STRANGE ADVENTURES. [FHP]

FUTUROLOGY Term which became current in the 1950s, applied to efforts to forecast the future (usually the NEAR FUTURE) by projecting and extrapolating from current trends, statistics, population figures, political groupings, availability of resources, economic data etc. It cannot be called a science proper, since too many of the factors involved are imponderable (and often unknown), but its tools are statistical analysis and the computer simulation of various models. It is obviously important to any government to base its long-range planning on the best possible information, and since the 1960s, particularly in the USA, futurologists have often been supported with large grants. Much futurology has been involved with military questions and the balance of power with special regard to WEAPONS.

It may seem that the futurologist and the sf writer are, in a sense, involved in the same trade, but there is a certain amount of contempt between the two. The futurologist works primarily on what can be quantified, and to a certain extent his projections depend on the future being the same as the past. Population projections for the UK, for example, have regularly been far too high, because demographers have been unable to quantify the factors that persuade people to have fewer children. The sf writer is not actually in the prediction business, but one assumption he usually makes, implicitly, is that the future will differ from the past; when he deals with the near future he normally writes a "what-if?" scenario. This is only to say, in practice, that the factors he deals with can include a good deal of guesswork; they are often invented. The sf writer is more often wrong than right, but, by concentrating on human responses to technological and other change, he can sometimes develop more plausible futures than those derived from the coldly statistical approach. What makes the sf writer unreliable as a predictor is the nature of his "what-if?". He often does not believe in it himself; he is writing stories, not prophecies. Also, the sf writer is often ignorant of the mechanisms, such as those of ECONOMICS, which must play an important role in any realistic story of future cause and effect.

Where the sf writer has an advantage is in his ability to adopt a multi-disciplinary approach; he is often good at what is sometimes known as lateral thinking; when writing, for example, about CITIES of the future the sf writer may bring to bear knowledge about the nature of the MASS MEDIA, along with information about architecture, SOCIOLOGY, TECHNOLOGY and COMMUNICATIONS. In a sense the advantage of the sf writer is his very irresponsibility; he cannot be held accountable for the nature of his scenarios; their details do not have to be justified. This allows him to work over a far greater range of possibility than the comparatively restricted futurologist. He can take the unexpected into account, and history tells us that the unexpected often happens. Sf itself is one of the factors which may help to give direction to change. By presenting images of the future which grip people's minds, sf may sometimes create self-fulfilling prophecies, as in the case of the multi-storey apartment blocks that were built by local authorities in such disastrously great numbers in the UK after the Second World War. It can be argued that if sf had not so single-mindedly produced images of towering cities in the 1920s and '30s, then the architects who built these tower blocks, within which people very often lead unhappy and isolated lives, would not have been so intent on building them.

Two large American research units are of special importance in forecasting: the RAND Corporation and the Hudson Institute, which is directed by Herman KAHN. Kahn's books are among the best-known works of futurology, but its current limitations as a science can be seen very clearly in his *Things to Come* (1972), a book about what to expect in the 1970s and '80s. The index has no entry for oil, gasoline, energy, resources or power; Kahn's only remark about the Arabs is to say that, because the West is their only market, we need expect no problems of supply. Sf writers, too, have been unsuccessful in predicting the energy crisis, but few as blandly as this, and so close to the time when it happened.

The most influential work of futurology has probably been the report of the Club of Rome on OVERPOPULATION and diminishing resources, excerpts from which were published as *The Limits to Growth* (**1972**). Alvin TOFFLER's book *Future Shock* (**1970**) is a best-selling work of sociology rather than futurology; it documents the increasing rate of change up till now, but is comparatively cautious in making specific predictions about the future. At the other extreme is *The Next Ten Thousand Years* (**1974**) by Adrian Berry, a work of technological optimism rather than futurology *per se*; it is packed with well-documented "what-if?" questions of the kind more familiar in sf than futurology, though is perhaps none the worse for that.

Neither the futurologists nor the sf writers have done very well at PREDICTION, though perhaps the writers' emphasis on the responses of individuals is more humane. Many examples of sf dealing in the general area also covered by futurology can be found under TECHNOLOGY, ECOLOGY, NEAR FUTURE and OVERPOPULATION. John BRUNNER is one notable writer who has written novels of this kind. Often, of course, Brunner and others are not so much predicting as trying to avert; they hope their ghastly scenarios will be influential as a kind of early-warning system. Arthur C. CLARKE, on the other hand, has used much optimistic futurological speculation in both his factual and his fictional books.

Sf itself has also produced futurologists as characters, the best known being the exponents of PSYCHOHISTORY (*see also entries listed under* CULTURAL ENGINEERING) in Isaac ASIMOV's "Foundation" series. A more recent example is Robert SILVERBERG's *The Stochastic Man* (**1975**), but he cheats, in real-life futurological terms, by using precognition.   [PN]

FYFE,   H(ORACE)   B(OWNE) (1918–   ). American writer, whose first sf story, "Locked Out" appeared in *ASF* before the War (1940), but who became active only after army service, mainly in *ASF*, with many stories published to date. Five of these (all *ASF* 1948–52) comprise the "Bureau of Slick Tricks" sequence. His novel, *D-99* (**1962**), continues the same theme: Department 99 of the Terran government has the job of finagling citizens out of jams on other planets and generally trouble-shooting; the methods its agents use are not always strictly legal. In common with several other *ASF*-based writers, HBF has written stories in which humans manage to outwit thick-skulled (often bureaucratic) aliens.   [JC]

GAIL, OTTO WILLI (1896–1956). German writer of popular fiction, two of whose astronautical novels appeared in Hugo GERNSBACK's SCIENCE WONDER QUARTERLY: *Der Schuss ins All* (**1925**; trans. as *The Shot into Infinity* 1929; **1975**) and its sequel *Der Stein vom Mond* (**1926**; trans. as "The Stone from the Moon" 1930). *By Rocket to the Moon* (trans. **1930**) is a juvenile. All three aim at a technical realism unusual for the time. [JC/PN]

GALACTIC EMPIRES In his book *The Universe Makers* (**1971**) Donald WOLLHEIM attempts to distil from the range of futuristic visions presented by magazine sf a basic pattern — what he calls a "cosmogony of the future". Stages three to five of the pattern (there are eight in all) deal with "the rise and fall of the Galactic Empire". "Empire" is here used in a general, almost metaphorical sense, rather than in its politically definitive meaning. Wollheim claims, rightly, that many modern sf stories are designed to fit into such a framework, taking advantage of the fact that it has become established as a convention. It is a literary device which enables a writer to incarnate virtually any imagined social or biological system, and to bring into contact with it human characters whose world view is similar to our own.

Most of the credit for the establishment of the convention must go to Isaac ASIMOV, whose "Foundation" series (1942–50; fix-ups *Foundation*, **1951**; *Foundation and Empire* 1952; *Second Foundation* 1953) set the most influential example. It is possible, though, to trace the notion back to earlier roots. As long ago as 1900 Robert William COLE had imagined Victoria's glorious British Empire extending its dominion to the stars, so that ours should not be the only sun never to set upon it. Confederations of worlds within the Solar System were common in pulp sf from its inception, and these were extended into the galaxy in such novels as *Galactic Patrol* (1937–8 *ASF*; **1950**) by E.E. "Doc" SMITH. Asimov, however, was the writer who provided the essential historical framework for such a concept. He did so quite simply, by a relatively

straightforward analogy with past empires, even borrowing Edward Gibbon's analytical historical perspective, used in *The Decline and Fall of the Roman Empire* (**1776–88**), in reverse as the predictive science of PSYCHOHISTORY. With a single flourish, a whole prospectus for the future of the human race, allowing for virtually limitless possibilities so far as events on a finer scale were concerned, was established — and with it a context for a vast number of modern sf stories. Asimov used the convenient historical pattern himself as a background for *The Stars Like Dust* (**1951**) and *The Currents of Space* (**1952**). Robert HEINLEIN's painstaking attempt to develop a HISTORY of the future step by step became an empty endeavour after the "Foundation" series, and of later attempts, Poul ANDERSON's is distinctly half-hearted, while James BLISH's succeeds more by virtue of the key image of the star-travelling cities than its framework derived from the philosophy of cyclic history developed by Spengler. Anderson, in fact, was able to take a great deal for granted in developing his own galactic empire scheme, because of Asimov's preparing of the way. (His scheme is developed in the "Dominic Flandry" series, the "Interstellar Trader" series, and in a large number of individual stories and novels.)

Writers of the 1940s who adopted the galactic empire framework include C.L. MOORE for *Judgment Night* (1943; **1952**), Edmond HAMILTON for *The Star Kings* (1947; **1949** vt *Beyond the Moon*) and A.E. VAN VOGT for "Recruiting Station" (1942; vt *Masters of Time*; coll. **1950**). Van Vogt was particularly fond of empires, galactic and otherwise, and borrowed Roman history — probably via Robert GRAVES's *I Claudius* (**1934**) — for his series of "Clane" stories *Empire of the Atom* (1946–7; fix-up **1956**) and *The Wizard of Linn* (1950; **1962**). The background was to prove particularly useful in the colourful brand of adventure sf featured by PLANET STORIES, and it was extensively used therein, notably by Leigh BRACKETT, Alfred COPPEL and Poul Anderson (in his early SPACE OPERAS). During the 1950s, the magazine closest in editorial philosophy to *Planet Stories*, SCIENCE FICTION ADVENTURES, also made extensive use of it, particularly in stories written for the US version of the magazine by Robert SILVERBERG and stories written for the British version by Kenneth BULMER.

In addition to Anderson, several other post-War writers have made consistent use of a galactic civilization as a reservoir for unusual worlds. These include Jack VANCE, notably in *The Languages of Pao* (**1958**) and *The Dragon Masters* (**1963**) and in virtually all of his work during the 1960s and '70s; John BRUNNER, notably in *Endless Shadow* (**1964**) and *The World Swappers* (**1959**); Cordwainer SMITH, in his "Instrumentality" series; and E.C.

TUBB, in his "Dumarest" series. Few writers, however, have concerned themselves in any but the most superficial way with the socio-political structure of the galactic community. Anderson has done significant work in this vein, and so has Gordon DICKSON, notably in the "Dorsai" series, but most writers are prepared to leave the community in a state of disorganization or nebulous harmony. Only rarely do works appear in which there actually is a powerful, autocratic, imperial system of government, one recent example being *The Mote in God's Eye* (**1974**) by Larry NIVEN and Jerry POURNELLE.

Indeed, the word "empire" is often a misnomer, and many sf works use "galactic league" or some such variant to describe the nature of the political links across the galaxy. Most works of this kind are American (though we should also remember the German space-opera series PERRY RHODAN, which has won much favour with US readers), and the political model is very often based on a loose federal system, very much the American ideal. It is interesting to note the unwillingness of genre sf writers, even when they take an entire galaxy for their setting, to create new political or economic modes. The economics of the galactic empire or galactic league are normally and conventionally based on a *laissez-faire* trading system, and often related to ideas of SOCIAL DARWINISM. (*For a further discussion of these aspects of such stories, see* ECONOMICS *and* POLITICS.)

Any list of post-War sf novels using the empire framework is bound to be highly selective, but some of the more notable stories which actually deal with issues relating to the community rather than to specific worlds within it are: *Star Bridge* (**1955**) by Jack WILLIAMSON and James E. GUNN, *Citizen of the Galaxy* (**1957**) by Robert A. Heinlein, *Starmaster's Gambit* (**1957** France; **1973**) by Gérard KLEIN, *Way Station* (**1963**) by Clifford D. SIMAK, *Empire Star* (**1966**) by Samuel R. DELANY, *The Ring of Ritornel* (**1968**) by Charles L. HARNESS, *Rite of Passage* (**1968**) by Alexei PANSHIN and *Voyage to Dari* (**1974**) by Ian WALLACE. A notable theme anthology is *Galactic Empires* (anth. 2 vols. **1976**) ed. Brian ALDISS. [BS]

See also: COLONIZATION OF OTHER WORLDS; COMMUNICATIONS; SOCIOLOGY.

GALACTIC LENS The term, from ASTRONOMY, makes frequent appearance in sf. It refers to the fact that our galaxy (along with most others) is lens-shaped. Our own position in the galaxy is quite a long way from the centre, and when we look towards the centre of the lens, where the stars are naturally clustered most thickly, we see the so-called Milky Way. Towards the outer rim of the lens, stars are comparatively sparse. Many sf writers have set stories on planets circling such stars. Such worlds have been dubbed

Rimworlds by A. Bertram CHANDLER, and the term Rimworld has since become commonplace in sf. [PN]

GALAXAN, SOL *See* Alfred COPPEL.

GALAXY *See* GALAXY SCIENCE FICTION.

GALAXY MAGABOOKS *See* GALAXY SCIENCE FICTION NOVELS.

GALAXY MAGAZINE *See* GALAXY SCIENCE FICTION.

GALAXY SCIENCE FICTION US DIGEST-size magazine. Published by World Editions (Oct. 1950-Sep. 1951), Galaxy Publishing Corp. (Oct. 1951-May 1969), Universal Publishing and Distributing Corp. (Jul. 1969-date); ed. H.L. GOLD (Oct. 1950-Oct. 1961), Frederik POHL (Dec. 1961-May 1969), Ejler JAKOBSSON (Jul. 1969-May 1974), James BAEN (Jun. 1974-Oct. 1977).

The first publisher of *Gal.* was a European-based company which, having incurred heavy losses trying to launch another magazine in the USA, approached H.L. Gold for alternative suggestions. He proposed an sf magazine, and *Gal.* came into existence. From the outset, *Gal.'s* payment rates equalled the best in the field — a minimum of three cents a word — and it adopted the digest format already taken by ASTOUNDING SCIENCE FICTION and THE MAGAZINE OF FANTASY AND SCIENCE FICTION.

The new magazine was an immediate success. *ASF* was at this time following John W. CAMPBELL's new-found obsession with DIANETICS and was otherwise more oriented towards TECHNOLOGY; Gold's editorial policy was comparatively free-ranging. He was interested in PSYCHOLOGY, SOCIOLOGY, SATIRE and other HUMOUR, and the magazine reflected this. Like Campbell, he worked closely with his writers (mostly by telephone, as he was confined to his apartment by acute agoraphobia) and is said to have had a hand in the conception of many of the famous stories he published, notably Alfred BESTER's *The Demolished Man* (Jan.-Mar. 1952; **1953**). In its first year *Gal.* included such stories as Clifford D. SIMAK's "Time Quarry" (Oct.-Dec. 1950; vt *Time and Again* **1951**); Fritz LEIBER's "Coming

June 1951. Ed Emsh's cover is typically witty.

Attraction" (Nov. 1950); Damon KNIGHT's "To Serve Man" (Nov. 1950); Isaac ASIMOV's "Tyrann" (Jan.-Mar. 1951; vt *The Stars Like Dust* 1951); Ray BRADBURY's "The Fireman" (Feb. 1951; exp. vt *Fahrenheit 451* 1953); C.M. KORNBLUTH's "The Marching Morons" (Apr. 1951); Edgar PANGBORN's "Angel's Egg" (Jun. 1951); Wyman GUIN's "Beyond Bedlam" (Aug. 1951) and Robert HEINLEIN's *The Puppet Masters* (Sep.-Nov. 1951; 1951).

The magazine maintained a comparable quality in its early years, and in 1953 shared the first HUGO award for best magazine with *ASF*. Although the magazine's fiction encompassed a considerable variety of styles and preoccupations, the approach most identified with Gold's magazine is the irony and social satire of such authors as Knight, Leiber, Pohl and Robert SHECKLEY. With the Mar. 1952 issue, Willy LEY began his science column, "For Your Information", which he continued until his death in 1969. A weakness of the early *Gal.* was that the cover art was mainly crude and undistinguished. The Jun. 1951 issue, however, featured the first cover by Ed EMSH, whose humorous approach was well suited to the magazine's contents, and became identified with it.

Further stories which appeared in Gold's *Gal.* included Pohl and Kornbluth's "Gravy Planet" (Jun.-Aug. 1952; rev. vt *The Space Merchants* 1953); Theodore STURGEON's "Baby is Three" (Oct. 1952); Asimov's *The Caves of Steel* (Oct.-Dec. 1953; 1954); Pohl and Kornbluth's *Gladiator-at-Law* (Jun.-Aug. 1954; 1955); Bester's *The Stars My Destination* (Oct. 1956-Jan. 1957; 1956); Pohl and Kornbluth's *Wolfbane* (Oct.-Nov. 1957; 1959); Leiber's *The Big Time* (Mar.-Apr. 1958; 1961) and Sheckley's "Time Killer" (Oct. 1958-Feb. 1959; vt *Immortality Delivered* 1958; exp. vt *Immortality, Inc.* 1959). A prize contest sponsored by *Gal.* drew no worthwhile entries, so Frederik Pohl and Lester DEL REY were prevailed upon to collaborate on a "prize-winning" novel, which appeared as *Preferred Risk* (Jun.-Sep. 1955; 1955) by Edson McCANN. *Gal.* had a short-lived fantasy companion, BEYOND FANTASY FICTION, in 1953–5; in 1959 its publishers acquired IF, which Gold also edited. In Sep. 1958 the title changed to *Galaxy Magazine*, since when it has varied between the two (with a period when it was simply called *Galaxy*). In 1959 it changed to bi-monthly publication, beginning with the Feb. 1959 issue.

Gold was forced to retire through ill-health in 1961, following a car accident. He was succeeded as editor of *Gal.* and *If* by Frederik Pohl. Pohl widened the magazine's policy still further, to include more fantasy-oriented material. Jack VANCE and Cordwainer SMITH became regular contributors: Vance with such stories as *The Dragon Masters* (Aug. 1962; 1963), *The Star King* (Dec. 1963-Feb. 1964; 1964) and *The Last Castle* (Apr. 1966; 1966); Smith with "The Boy Who Bought Old Earth" (Apr. 1964; exp. vt *The Planet Buyer* 1964), "The Dead Lady of Clown Town" (Aug. 1964) and many others. Larry NIVEN was one of Pohl's discoveries, and Frank HERBERT and Robert SILVERBERG became regular contributors. Other notable stories from his editorship include Simak's "Here Gather the Stars" (Jun.-Aug. 1963; vt *Way Station* 1963), Gordon DICKSON's "Soldier, Ask Not" (Oct. 1964), Poul Anderson's "To Outlive Eternity" (Jun.-Aug. 1967; vt *Tau Zero* 1970), Robert Silverberg's "Hawksbill Station" (Aug. 1967) and "Nightwings" (Sep. 1968). As Gold was notorious for unnecessary editorial tampering with the stories he published, so was Pohl famed for indiscriminately altering their titles. Algis BUDRYS began a notable book review column in 1965.

Pohl's *Gal.* was consistently an interesting magazine, but it was less successful, with sf fans at least, than *If*, which under Pohl won three consecutive HUGO awards. Pohl also commenced three companion magazines. WORLDS OF FANTASY and INTERNATIONAL SCIENCE FICTION came and went swiftly; WORLDS OF TOMORROW was more durable.

In Jun. 1968 *Gal.* resumed monthly publication. The following year it changed ownership again, and Ejler Jakobsson gave *Gal.* the subtitle "The Best in Pertinent Science Fiction", and the appearance was revamped in an apparent attempt to give the magazine more contemporary appeal; for a time it included a comic strip by Vaughn Bodé. One notable occurrence during Jakobsson's editorship was the featuring of two consecutive serials by Robert Silverberg: *Downward to the Earth* (Nov. 1969-Mar. 1970; 1970) and *Tower of Glass* (Apr.-Jun. 1970; 1970). Theodore Sturgeon took over as book reviewer. On the whole, though, the magazine failed to develop under Jakobsson's editorship, and reverted to a bi-monthly schedule with the May/Jun. 1971 issue, though a patchy monthly schedule began again Sep. 1973. In Jun. 1974 he was succeeded by James Baen.

In Jan. 1975, *Gal.* absorbed *If*. After a period in the doldrums, 1976 saw a revival in the magazine's fortunes. Contributors included Niven, John VARLEY and Roger ZELAZNY. Pohl's *Gateway* (Nov. 1976-Mar. 1977; 1977) was a notable serial. The magazine featured book reviews by Spider ROBINSON and a science column by Jerry POURNELLE. The monthly schedule was adhered to only patchily in 1975, 1976 and 1977; distribution faltered, and fears have been expressed that *Gal.* may be nearing the end of its honourable career. Baen left in 1977 to become sf editor for ACE BOOKS, and was succeeded by J.J. Pierce.

There have been numerous anthologies of stories from *Gal.* (*for details of these see the entries for its first four editors*).

A British edition, from Strato Publications, began in Jan. 1953 (reprinting the Oct. 1952 US edition). It was labelled Vol.3 no.1. The second British issue, however, reprinted the preceding US issue (Sep. 1952). It continued to follow the original, erratically at first, and from no.7 began to shorten each issue. It continued to be numbered continuously (dropping the "Vol.3" after no.12) until no.94, Feb. 1961. From no.72, Feb. 1959, it was an exact reprint of the US edition with a different title page. From Dec. 1961 only the cover was different, and from Dec. 1962 the US edition was imported. Another British edition published by Gold Star Publications ran in 1967, reprinting six months after the US original (Jan./Feb. UK was Jun. 1966 US), printing US editions complete apart from the changed date. A new British edition began in Sep. 1969, published by Universal Tandem (reprinting the Aug. 1969 US edition). The American edition was again distributed from the end of 1970, and in 1972 another British edition began: the May/Jun. 1972 issue (Vol.32 no.6) was no.1, and a total of 25 numbered issues were published, ending with no.25, Jan. 1975 (Vol.36 no.1). However, the numbering was not continuous: it ran 1–10, 11, 11, 12, 12, 12, 14, 17–25. Since Jan. 1975 the US edition has again been distributed in Britain. [MJE]

Collectors should note: *Gal.* has six nos to the vol., up to Vol.32, and eight thereafter. Vol.7 no.4 was wrongly labelled Vol.7 no.5, and Vol.7 no.5 was labelled Vol.7 no.5A. Vol.33 no.7 was called Vol.34 no.7 on title page. The monthly schedule from the beginning to Dec '58 was broken only by the omission of Dec. '55. From Jun. '68 to Apr. '71 the schedule was monthly, except that Jun. '69 and Jan. '70 were omitted, Aug./Sep. '70 was a single issue, as was Oct./Nov. '70. From May/Jun. '71 to Jul./Aug. '73 the schedule was bi-monthly, but returned to a shaky monthly schedule in Sep. 1973, the issues for May, Nov. and Dec. '75 being omitted, as were those for Apr., Jun., Aug. '76 and Jan., Feb., May '77.

GALAXY SCIENCE FICTION NOVELS A companion series to GALAXY. The first 31 issues, published irregularly, 1950–57, were in DIGEST format, and a further four were issued in standard paperback format. The series was then taken over by Beacon Books, a publisher specializing in soft pornography, which brought out 11 further issues, 1959–61, usually with lurid covers and suggestive titles. These continued the original numeration.

The original series featured several

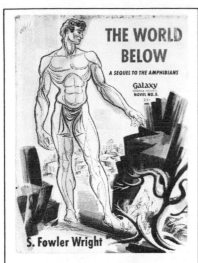

No. 5, 1951. Cover by Calle.

classics of magazine sf, including *Sinister Barrier* (1939 *Unknown*; **1943**) by Eric Frank RUSSELL (no.1), *Legion of Space* (1934 *ASF*; **1947**) by Jack WILLIAMSON (no.2) and *Lest Darkness Fall* (1939 *Unknown*; **1941**) by L. Sprague DE CAMP (no.24); notable novels from outside the genre, often abridged, included *The Amphibians* (**1924**) and *The World Below* (**1929**) by S. Fowler WRIGHT (nos 4 and 5) and *Odd John* (**1935**) by Olaf STAPLEDON (no.8); and some original novels, including *Prelude to Space* (**1951**) by Arthur C. CLARKE (no.3) and *Empire* (**1951**) by Clifford D. SIMAK (no.7). Original novels with a sexy slant published in the Beacon Books series include *Flesh* (**1960**) by Philip José FARMER (no.41) and *The Male Response* (**1961**) by Brian W. ALDISS (no.45), while such innocuous works as A.E. VAN VOGT's *The House That Stood Still* (**1950**) and Cyril JUDD's *Outpost Mars* (**1952**) were retitled, respectively, *The Mating Cry* (rev. vt **1960**) (no.44) and *Sin in Space* (rev. vt **1961**) (no.46).

Award Books issued a number of paperbacks as "Galaxy Science Fiction Novels" in the early 1970s, but these did not constitute a series. In 1963 a second companion series to *Galaxy*, *Galaxy Magabooks*, each consisting of two short novels by a single author, was issued, but only three appeared.   [BS]

GALILEO US BEDSHEET-size magazine. Current, 10 issues to 1978, Sep. 1976 onwards, initially planned as quarterly, published by Avenue Victor Hugo, Boston; ed. Charles C. Ryan.

Clearly published on a small budget, *G* hopes to survive through subscription sales rather than conventional distribution. 8,000 copies of no.1 were printed and successfully sold, but in magazine terms this is small. Printed on cheap newsprint, and using a number of stories by little-known writers, *G* began quietly but showed signs of improvement by no.3. The great Renaissance scientist is

No. 1. Cover by Tom Barber.

evoked in the title because *G* is planned to emulate his "indomitable spirit ... undying quest for knowledge". Almost half of *G*, like most 1970s sf magazines, is devoted to science-fact articles, reviews, interviews etc. Contributors have included Hal CLEMENT (science fact), Ray BRADBURY (poetry), Robert CHILSON and Brian ALDISS.   [PN]

GALLICO, PAUL (WILLIAM) (1897–1976). American journalist, screenwriter and novelist, sports editor of the New York *Daily News* for 12 years, known mainly for such work outside the sf field as *The Snow Goose* (**1941**), a sentimental novella with fantasy elements extremely popular in wartime Britain. *The Foolish Immortals* (**1953**) is an eternal youth novel.   [JC]
Other works: (with fantasy elements) *The Abandoned* (**1950**; vt *Jennie*); *Love of Seven Dolls* (**1954**); *Too Many Ghosts* (**1960**); *The Man who was Magic* (**1967**).

GALLUN, RAYMOND Z(INKE) (1911–). American author and technical writer, now retired. He was born and educated in Wisconsin, and has been a considerable traveller since. He

began publishing sf stories at the age of 18 in 1929 with "The Space Dwellers" in *Science Wonder Stories* and "The Crystal Ray" in *Air Wonder Stories*. In the 1930s he published frequently in F. Orlin TREMAINE's *ASF*, his most famous contributions being the "Old Faithful" series: "Old Faithful" (1934), "The Son of Old Faithful" (1935) and "Child of the Stars" (1936), the first of the three novelettes featuring a sentimentally conceived Martian, the other two his descendants. During his prolific years (1929–42), RZG also used the

pseudonyms Arthur Allport, Dow Elstar, E.V. Raymond and William Callahan in his magazine fiction. His style was consistently crude, but he packed his stories with ideas and movement. He became inactive in the 1940s, and though he has again published since about 1950 he has never regained the popularity of his early years. One of his best stories, however, was "The Restless Tide" (1951 *Marvel Science Fiction*). He published nothing between 1961 and 1974.

RZG's first novel, *People Minus X* (roughly based on "Avalanche", 1935 *ASF* as by Dow Elstar; **1957**), is still rough-hewn, but again derives its energy from numerous ideas, including body-miniaturization; body-recording; space-resistant ANDROIDS, and much more. *The Planet Strappers* (**1961**) is more routine, but *The Eden Cycle* (**1974**) is a comparatively carefully written, slow-moving study of humans who, having received from ALIENS the gift of IMMORTALITY and a capacity to imaginatively reinhabit various epochs of the world HISTORY, find themselves less and less capable of responding to their experiences. RZG is a writer of the old PULP-trained school, and not a major one, but his work still amply displays not only the defects of language but also the bonuses of imagination typical of American magazine sf in its early prime. [JC]

See also: FAR FUTURE; JUPITER; MARS; OUTER PLANETS; SOCIAL DARWINISM.

GALOUYE, DANIEL F(RANCIS) (1920–76). American writer who was born and died in New Orleans, Louisiana; his post-War career was in newspaper journalism, though he had been a naval test pilot during the Second World War, and he continued newspaper work after beginning to publish sf with "Rebirth" for *Imagination* in 1952. Due to the delayed effect of war injuries, he was forced to become relatively inactive after about 1965. DFG appeared frequently in the magazines for about a decade with such tales as "Tonight the Sky Will Fall" (1952) and "The City of Force" (1959), which are characterized by a combination of a strong HARD SF structure and a treatment of psychological concerns that was sometimes a touch uneasy. Twice he wrote stories (1953–4) as Louis G. Daniels. Both *The Last Leap and Other Stories of the Super-Mind* (coll. **1964**) and *Project Barrier* (coll. **1968**) appeared in England but not in America; the former was translated into German; in addition, two original collections were published in Germany.

DFG's first novel, *Dark Universe* (**1961**), is his most popular, and probably his best. It is a story of CONCEPTUAL BREAKTHROUGH. Long after a nuclear HOLOCAUST, descendants of its survivors live sightless far underground. Their culture — from daily routine through cosmological concerns — is grippingly

and originally conceived, though the book closes with a somewhat anticlimactic escape from darkness; *Dark Universe* was nominated for a HUGO award. His next novels, *Lords of the Psychon* (**1963**), *Simulacron-3* (**1964**; vt *Counterfeit World* UK) and *The Lost Perception* (**1966**; vt *A Scourge of Screamers* USA), share the same technical ingenuity, and a continuing interest in worlds where the PERCEPTION of reality is controlled and restricted, where indeed the worlds themselves are arbitrary constructs. *Simulacron-3* is particularly interesting in this respect. In a sense it is a novel-length reworking of Frederik POHL's "The Tunnel Under the World" (1954), in its story of a construct-world designed for market research; it was filmed for TV in Germany in 1973 by Rainer Werner Fassbinder as *Welt am Dracht*, the programme being released as a two-part film in the UK as *The World on a Wire*. In theme, these books are reminiscent of the work of Philip K. DICK. DFG's last novel, *The Infinite Man* (**1973**), was less successful. He was never really able to capitalize on the promising beginning he had made as an sf writer, but it seems that his war injuries kept him from a more fruitful career. An interesting attack on NEW WAVE sf appears from DFG in *Stella Nova* (**1970**; rev. vt *Contemporary Science Fiction Authors* 1975) compiled by R. REGINALD. [JC]

See also: FANTASTIC VOYAGES; GREAT AND SMALL; MEDIA LANDSCAPE; PSYCHOLOGY.

GAMES AND SPORTS Just as sf's concern with the ARTS has been dominated by stories about the decline of artistry in a mechanized mass society, so its concern with sports seems to have been primarily involved with representing the decline of sportsmanship. There is a marked tendency in contemporary sf to assume that the audience-appeal of futuristic sports will be measured by their rendering of violence in terms of spectacle: the film ROLLERBALL is perhaps the clearest recent expression of this myth. There are two forms of stereotyped competitive violence which are familiar in the mythology of sf: the gladiatorial circus and the hunt. The arena is part of the standard apparatus of romance in the Edgar Rice BURROUGHS tradition, and extends throughout the history of sf to such modern variants as those found in the "Dumarest" series by E.C. TUBB (1967 onwards). Combat between man and alien is the basis of the popular "Arena" (1944) by Fredric BROWN, and a host of similar stories, while many visions of a corrupt future society foresee the return of bloody games in the Roman tradition — Frederik POHL and Cyril M. KORNBLUTH's *Gladiator-at-Law* (**1955**) is a notable example. Ordinary hunting is extrapolated to take in alien prey in such stories as the "Gerry Carlyle" series by Arthur K. BARNES (1937–46; coll. **1956** as

Interplanetary Hunter), but the more familiar variant has man as the victim rather than the hunter. Again, this is familiar in other-worldly romance, but it is more starkly represented in *The Sound of His Horn* (**1952**) by SARBAN and a number of stories by Robert SHECKLEY, including "Seventh Victim" (1953) and "The Prize of Peril" (1958) and *Immortality Inc.* (**1959**). The presumed equivalence between the spectator-appeal of sport and the spectator-appeal of dramatized violence reaches its peak in Norman SPINRAD's short story "The National Pastime" (1973), and the film DEATH RACE 2000 (1975); it is perhaps odd to find such unanimity about violence in futuristic mythology while many popular contemporary sports have little or no physical violence associated with them (basketball and horse-racing, for example).

Sports stories in sf are almost entirely a post-War phenomenon, although the pre-War pulps did include Clifford D. SIMAK's "Rule 18" (1938), in which one of the popular all-time great sports teams is actually assembled thanks to time travel; and one or two rocket-racing stories, such as Lester DEL REY's "Habit" (1939). Many post-War stories arose from the common theme of man/machine confrontation (*see* MACHINES *and* ROBOTS). Examples include the boxing story "Title Fight" (1956) by William Campbell Gault, the golf story "Open Warfare" (1954) by James GUNN and the motor-racing story "The Ultimate Racer" (1964) by Gary Wright. The role of the motor car in post-War society also provoked a number of bizarre extrapolations, including H. Chandler ELLIOTT's violent "A Day on Death Highway" (1963), Harlan ELLISON's "Along the Scenic Route" (1969), and Roger ZELAZNY's story of a car-fighting matador, "Auto-da-Fé" (1967). By contrast, a novel based on man/machine association instead of confrontation is the boxing story *The Mind Riders* (**1976**) by Brian STABLEFORD.

Other popular sf themes are often combined with sf sports stories. Gambling of various kinds appears in many PSI stories, for obvious reasons, and superhuman powers are occasionally employed on the sports field, as in Irwin Shaw's "Whispers in Bedlam" (1973) and George Alec EFFINGER's "Naked to the Invisible Eye" (1975).

Games are used as a key to social advancement and control in a number of stories, including *World out of Mind* (**1953**) by J.T. MCINTOSH, *Cosmic Checkmate* (**1962**) by Katherine MACLEAN and Charles V. DE VET, *Steppe* (**1976**) by Piers ANTHONY which features a Mongol war-game, and *Solar Lottery* (**1955**; vt *World of Chance* UK) by Philip K. DICK. In other novels by Dick, including *The Game-Players of Titan* (**1963**) and *The Three Stigmata of Palmer Eldritch* (**1964**), games function as levels of pseudo-reality. Games as surreal exercises also feature often in the work of Barry MALZBERG, notably in the apocalyptic novels *Overlay* (**1972**) and *The Tactics of Conquest* (**1974**), and a novel where life is symbolized as a game, *The Gamesman* (**1975**). George Alec Effinger, too, has often shown an interest in the symbolism of games-playing, especially the way games combine rational and irrational elements, as in "Lydectes: on the Nature of Sport" (**1975**) and "25 Crunch Split Right on Two" (**1975**). James TIPTREE Jr has an interesting variation on the theme when she concentrates on the psychology of the referee rather than the competitor in "Parimutuel Planet" (**1969**; vt "Faithful to thee, Terra, in our Fashion"), in which a sadly chastened humanity has developed a latent passion for justice.

The game which most commonly fascinates sf writers is chess, featured in Malzberg's *Tactics of Conquest*. Poul ANDERSON, in "The Immortal Game" (**1954**) and John BRUNNER in *The Squares of the City* (**1965**) have followed Lewis CARROLL's example in *Through the Looking Glass* (**1872**) in writing stories around chess games, while Charles HARNESS's "The Chessplayers" (**1953**) and Fritz LEIBER's "The 64-Square Madhouse" (**1962**) are two of sf's most elegant studies of the psychology of competition. Leiber, himself a good chess-player, also wrote a supernatural chess story, "Midnight by the Morphy Watch" (**1974**), and another good player, the French sf writer Gérard KLEIN, built the mystique of the game into his first novel, *Starmaster's Gambit* (**1958**; trans. **1973**). A version of the game even crops up in the work of Edgar Rice Burroughs, in *The Chessmen of Mars* (**1922**), and a rather more exotic version plays an important role in *The Fairy Chessmen* (**1951**; vt *Chessboard Planet* USA; vt *The Far Reality* UK) by Henry KUTTNER as Lewis Padgett.

Some writers have exploited the contemporary fad for inventing new games, notably Piers Anthony, who uses "Sprouts" in *Macroscope* (**1969**) and "Hexaflexagon" and "Life" in *Ox* (**1976**). When it comes to inventing new games themselves, however, sf writers have had little success. There have been one or two interesting descriptions of games played in zero-gee (no gravity), but these are usually incidental to the real concerns of the stories in which they occur. Sling-gliding, in which glides are accelerated by massive steel whips, is a plausible and dangerous sport featured in *The Jaws that Bite, the Claws that Catch* (**1975**; vt *The Girl With a Symphony in her Fingers* UK) by Michael G. CONEY. The sport of hussade, which plays a major part in Jack VANCE's *Trullion: Alastor 2262* (**1973**), is unconvincing, but the board-game "vlei" in Samuel R. DELANY's *Triton* (**1976**) is cleverly presented, though deliberately left vague on details.

One anthology on this theme is *Arena*:

Sports SF (**1976**) ed. Barry Malzberg and Ed FERMAN.   [BS/PN]
See also: LEISURE.

Feb. 1965. Cover by John Healey.

GAMMA US DIGEST-size magazine. Five issues, 1963–5, published by Star Press, N. Hollywood; ed. Charles E. FRITCH. The last three issues were saddle-stapled. The fiction in this magazine was of good quality, and there were some fine covers by Morris Scott Dollens and John Healey. Unfortunately the irregular and infrequent publication was not conducive to success.   [FHP]
Collectors should note: Vol.1 had two nos, both 1963. Vol.2 had three nos, one in 1964 and two in 1965, the last one being numbered Vol.2 no.5 in error.

GAMOW, GEORGE (1904–68). Russian-born physicist, involved in the development of quantum theory at Göttingen; later he worked with Niels Bohr; after 1935 he lived in the USA, holding the chair of theoretical physics at George Washington University. Beyond his technical work, he is known for his 10 or more factual scientific popularizations, beginning with *The Birth and Death of the Sun* (**1940**). He won the UNESCO Kalinga prize for popularization of science. His four books about Mr Tompkins, *Mr Tompkins in Wonderland* (**1939**), *Mr Tompkins Explores the Atom* (**1944**), *Mr Tompkins Learns the Facts of Life* (**1953**) and *Mr Tompkins Inside Himself* (**1967**), the last with Martynas Ycas, are particularly attractive; couched in narrative form, these books explore the wonders of science. During his explorations, Tompkins magically visits embodied demonstrations of the scientific world, and even explores his own body. Though technically juvenile, the books have a wide appeal.   [JC]
See also: COSMOLOGY; FOURTH DIMENSION (AND OTHERS); GREAT AND SMALL.

GANDON, YVES (1899–). French

novelist. His *Le dernier Blanc* (**1945**; trans. as *The Last White Man* **1948**) depicts, on familiar lines, the chemical warfare of the future and a toxin deadly only to whites. Other borderline sf works, untranslated, are *Après les hommes* ["After Men"] (**1963**), involving an ethical ferromagnetic race, and *La ville invisible* ["The Invisible Town"] (**1953**). *En pays singulier* ["In a Remarkable Country"] (coll. **1949**) contains some sf.   [JC/PN]

GANPAT Pseudonym of Martin Louis Alan Gompertz (1886–1951), novelist and travel writer, who lived many years in India and set most of his fantasies along the inner Asian frontiers of that country. His books are mildly but patronizingly racist and strongly anti-Russian. Several of them, like *Harilek* (**1923**), its sequel *Wrexham's Romance* (**1935**), *Mirror of Dreams* (**1928**) and *Fairy Silver* (**1932**), are LOST-RACE romances, the latter volume actually featuring two of the species. He wrote much other fantasy.   [JC/PN]
Other works: *Snow Rubies* (**1925**); *The Voice of Dashin* (**1926**); *High Snow* (**1927**) *Dainra* (**1929**); *The Speakers in Silence* (**1929**); *Walls Have Eyes* (**1930**); *The Second Tigress* (**1933**); *Seven Times Proven* (**1934**); *The War Breakers* (**1939**).

GANTZ, KENNETH F(RANKLIN) (1905–). American editor for the air force and writer, mostly of non-fiction. His sf novel *Not in Solitude* (**1959**; rev. 1961) fictionalizes a first voyage to Mars and describes the probable environment faced by the travellers.   [JC]

GARBO, NORMAN (1919–). American writer, whose borderline-sf novel *The Movement* (**1969**) exaggerates the late-1960s confrontation between American students and police in various university campuses into a full-scale uprising with retaliatory bombing by the government.   [JC]

GARBY, Mrs LEE HAWKINS (? – ?). The wife of a school friend of E.E. "Doc" SMITH, she collaborated with him between 1915 and 1920 on *The Skylark of Space* (written 1915–20; 1928 *Amazing*; 1946; cut and rev. 1958). The 1958 abridgement of this famous SPACE OPERA apparently eliminated most and perhaps all of her contribution, and her name did not appear as co-author.   [JC]

GARDNER, JOHN (CHAMPLIN) (1933–). American writer and academic, esteemed for such MAINSTREAM novels of the 1970s as *The Sunlight Dialogues* (**1972**). *Grendel* (**1971**), essentially a fantasy (*see also* MONSTERS), is the story of *Beowulf* told from the monster's viewpoint and, rather more pointedly than Thomas Burnett SWANN's similar elegies, renders Anglo-Saxon Man's triumphs as allegorical of the rise

of the cruel, modern, industrial world.
[JC]
See also: MYTHOLOGY.

GARDNER, MARTIN (1914–).
American mathematician, conjuror,
journalist and author, with a BA in
philosophy from the University of
Chicago. His *In the Name of Science*
(**1952**; rev. vt *Fads and Fallacies in the
Name of Science* 1957) is an iconoclastic
and amusing non-fiction work covering
PSEUDO-SCIENCE: cults, fads and hoaxes
existing on the fringes of science, with
chapters on the hollow-Earth and flat-
Earth theories, pyramidology, FLYING
SAUCERS and other subjects. Of particular
interest are its references to L. Ron
HUBBARD, Richard SHAVER, Charles FORT,
Sir Arthur Conan DOYLE and other
writers germane to sf. He has written the
Mathematical Games column in *Scientific
American* since 1956, from which a
number of books have been collected. His
The Incredible Dr. Matrix (fix-up **1977**)
brings together a number of spoof stories
from that column about the eponymous
numerologist and rogue, a practitioner of
several of the shady cults described in
MG's earlier book. His earlier non-fiction
work *The Ambidextrous Universe* (**1964**),
which moves from simple questions of
symmetry to profound problems of
physical philosophy, is one of the finest
works of scientific popularization. Also
relevant to sf readers is his *The Annotated
Alice* (**1960**), a densely annotated edition
of Lewis CARROLL's two "Alice" books,
and *The Annotated Snark* (**1962**), a
similar treatment of Carroll's *The
Hunting of the Snark* (**1876**).   [PN/JE]
See also: FOURTH DIMENSION (AND
OTHERS); PARANOIA AND SCHIZOPHRENIA.

GARDNER, NOEL *See* Henry
KUTTNER.

GARDNER, THOMAS S(AMUEL)
(1908–63). American chemist and author.
He began writing sf with "The Last
Woman" (for *Wonder Stories* in 1932),
which has been anthologized, and went
on to write another four stories in the
next decade. Active in sf FANDOM, he
wrote an annual review of the sf and
fantasy magazine field for SCIENCE
FICTION TIMES and published one of the
earliest studies of the sf reader,
"Psychology of the Science Fiction Fan"
(1939 *New Fandom*).   [JE]

GARIS, HOWARD ROGER
(1873–1962). American writer, known
mainly for such work outside the sf field
as his "Uncle Wiggily" series, whose
15,000 episodes were widely syndicated.
His mainly anonymous work for the
Edward Stratemeyer Syndicate concentrated on the TOM SWIFT series under the
house name Victor·APPLETON.   [JC]
Other works: Many juveniles, including
Tom of the Fire Cave (**1927**); *Rocket
Riders Across the Ice* (**1933**); *Rocket*

Riders in Stormy Seas (**1933**); *Rocket
Riders over the Desert* (**1933**); *Rocket
Riders in the Air* (**1934**).

GARLAND American publisher of
facsimile reprints. In 1975 they published
the Garland Library of Science Fiction, a
collection of 45 titles in durable editions,
selected by Lester DEL REY. The series has
been criticized, partly for some
idiosyncratic choices — unexceptional
novels by Stanton A. COBLENTZ, H. Beam
PIPER and George O. SMITH — but chiefly
for choosing inferior editions of the books
to reproduce. An accompanying critical
history by Del Rey, *Science Fiction
1926–1976*, was intended to appear, but
did not.   [MJE]

GARNER, ALAN (1934–). British
writer, primarily for older children;
educated at Magdalen College, Oxford.
He has lived all his life near Alderley
Edge, Cheshire, and this is the setting for
nearly all his books. AG is thought by
many to be one of the finest, if not the
very finest, of children's writers of the
1960s. Most of his work has been
fantasy, rooted in his knowledge of local
archaeology and MYTHOLOGY. The first
two books form a short series for
younger children: *The Weird-
stone of Brisingamen* (**1960**) and *The
Moon of Gomrath* (**1963**). Both are
excellent, but adult readers (of whom AG
has many) are more likely to be engrossed
by the third, *Elidor* (**1965**), which is also
the first which can be read as marginally
sf. The mood here darkens and deepens,
in a story of modern Manchester teenagers faced with a threat (and a quest)
from an ALTERNATE WORLD, which
impinges menacingly (and with much
electrical interference) on their own.
AG's first fully mature work is *The Owl
Service* (**1967**), which won the *Guardian*
award and the Library Association
Carnegie Medal; one of the darker and
more resonant of the old Welsh legends
re-enacts itself among modern children,
faced with fully adult problems of love,
jealousy and death. AG's theme has
always been a kind of TIME TRAVEL, but
the time is inner and psychic; his stories
rework archetypal patterns, usually
involving pain, loss, desire and the need
for an almost unattainable courage. The
psychological repercussions of working
out these obsessions in his books took a
grave toll of his own life, as he describes
in his painful and gripping essay "Inner
Time" in *Science Fiction at Large* (anth.
1976; vt *Explorations of the Marvellous*)
ed. Peter NICHOLLS.
    Many think the peak of AG's career
was his next book, *Red Shift* (**1973**), an
extraordinary work which is in no
conventional sense a children's book (*see
also* CHILDREN'S SF), though it was so
marketed. In compressed, elliptical prose,
primarily dialogue, he reverts to the
theme of the past working out its
problems in the present, using a

passionate and sometimes obscure
juxtaposition of imagery which owes as
much to sf as to myth. (AG's home is
situated between ancient burial mounds
and the Jodrell Bank observatory.) The
emotional themes of the book are the
links between impotence (including
sexual impotence) and violence, and the
exorcism of rage and pain. A time shift
focused on a neolithic axe-head moves
the protagonist backwards and forwards
in a choppy, bewildering and wrenching
way between *alter egos* in the twilight of
the Roman Empire in Britain, the Civil
War of the 17th century and now. A
dramatization was broadcast by the BBC
in 1978.
    More recently AG has changed
direction again, with a quasi-
autobiographical tetralogy, neither sf nor
fantasy. So far published are *The Stone
Book* (**1976**), *Tom Fobble's Day* (**1977**)
and *Granny Reardun* (**1977**). Projected
for 1978 is the fourth volume, *The Aimer
Gate*. While the form of the books owes
nothing to the fantastic, the old themes
recur, in a clear demonstration of the fact
that categorizing books by genre is
seldom of much use in categorizing them
by essence.   [PN]
Other works: *The Hamish Hamilton
Book of Goblins* (coll. **1969**). As editor:
The Guizer: A Book of Fools (anth. **1975**).

GARNER, ROLF *See* Bryan BERRY.

GARNETT, DAVID (1892–). English
writer, member of the famous Garnett
family, which includes his grandfather,
Richard GARNETT, and his parents,
Edward and Constance (the translator);
DG was also an intimate member of the
Bloomsbury Group. His first novel under
his own name is also his most famous,
the fantasy *Lady into Fox* (**1922**), which,
like its late and inferior successor,
VERCORS' *Sylva* (**1961**; trans. **1962**), is a
metamorphosis story, though in the
earlier case the transformation is from
demure wife into vixen, with tragic
results. *A Man in the Zoo* (**1924**) is also
fantasy; *The Grasshoppers Come* (**1931**)
fascinatingly combines aviation and
allegory in a borderline-sf tale. *Two by
Two* (**1963**) is a retelling of the story of
Noah and the Flood. DG translated
André MAUROIS's *A Voyage to the Island
of the Articoles* (**1927**; trans. **1928**). *The
White/Garnett Letters* (coll. **1968**), which
he edited, are of great value to students
both of his work and of that of T.H.
WHITE.   [JC]
Other works: *A Terrible Day* (**1932**).

GARNETT, DAVID S. (1947–).
English writer, with a BSc in economics,
who has signed himself Dav Garnett in
the USA; he has concentrated on
producing sf adventure novels, beginning
with *Mirror in the Sky* (**1969**), most of
them routine, though his third book,
Time in Eclipse (**1974**), is a comparatively
ambitious effort set on a war-torn Earth

Sf romance in the comic strip GARTH, from a 1950s serial, "The Last Goddess".

whose guardian is an amnesiac obscurely bound to a vast COMPUTER.   [JC]
Other works: *The Starseekers* (**1971**); *The Forgotten Dimension* (**1975**); *Phantom Universe* (**1975**); *Cosmic Carousel* (coll. **1976**).
See also: SPACE OPERA; WAR.

GARNETT, RICHARD (1835–1906). English librarian and writer, Chief Keeper at the British Museum, grandfather of David GARNETT. His *The Twilight of the Gods and Other Tales* (coll. **1888**; exp.1903) is a well-known collection of fables and other fantasies, some of which touch on sf themes.   [JC]

GARRETT, RANDALL (1927–). American writer. He was a prolific writer for *ASF* in the 1950s and early '60s, and was at one time part of the Ziff-Davis stable on *AMZ* and *Fantastic*. He used the pseudonyms David Gordon, Walter Bupp and Darrel T. Langart, as well as numerous house names, though in most cases it is not known which of the stories written under Ziff-Davis house names are by RG alone. He collaborated frequently with Robert SILVERBERG, most notably under the name Robert RANDALL, but also under the pseudonyms Gordon AGHILL and Ralph BURKE, and the house names Alexander BLADE, Richard GREER, Ivar JORGENSEN, Clyde MITCHELL, Leonard G. SPENCER, S.M. TENNESHAW and Gerald VANCE; and with Laurence M. JANIFER, usually as Mark PHILLIPS (*see* RANDALL *and* PHILLIPS *entries for details of books published under those names*). His most impressive solo work is the "Lord Darcy" series, which concerns the exploits of a detective in an ALTERNATE WORLD where MAGIC works, and science is gradually revealing its laws. The series,

published in *ASF*, consists of "The Eyes Have It" (1964), "A Case of Identity" (1964), "The Muddle of the Woad" (1965), *Too Many Magicians* (1967), "A Matter of Gravity" (1974) and "The Ipswich Phial" (1976). A series of PSI stories written as Walter Bupp consists of "Card Trick" (1961), "Modus Vivendi" (1961), "The Right Time" (1963) and "Psi for Sale" (1965). The "Leland Hale" SPACE-OPERA series consists of "To Make a Hero" (1957), "Respectfully Mine" (1958) and "Drug on the Market" (1960). *Anything You Can Do* (**1963** as by Darrel T. Langart) is an account of a battle between a superhuman and an alien. *Unwise Child* (**1962**) is a novel about a sentient machine. Garrett also has a minor reputation as a humorist — he wrote some comic verses for *FSF* and "Parodies Tossed" (1956) for SCIENCE FICTION QUARTERLY, and also parodied Grendel BRIARTON's "Feghoot" shaggy-dog stories (*FSF*) in the adventures of Benedict Breadfruit, written for *AMZ* Mar.-Oct. 1962 under the name Grandall Barretton.   [BS]
Other works: *Pagan Passions* (**1959**) with Larry M. Harris (Laurence M. JANIFER).
See also: CRIME AND PUNISHMENT; FASTER THAN LIGHT; MAGIC.

GARSON, CLEE House name used on the Ziff-Davis magazines by Paul W. FAIRMAN (one story, "Nine Worlds West", *Fantastic Adventures* 1951), David Wright O'BRIEN and perhaps others. There were 13 CG stories in all, 1942–55.   [PN]

GARSON, PAUL (1946–). American teacher and writer whose sf novel, *The Great Quill* (**1973**), is set in a baroquely degenerate post-HOLOCAUST England; there are satirical effects.   [JC]

GARTH British sf COMIC STRIP created, written and illustrated by Steve Dowling. It first appeared in 1943 in the *Daily Mirror*. It was later scripted by Peter O'Donnell, then by Jim Edgar. Artists have included Frank Bellamy, John Allard and Martin Asbury. It continues today.

G began as a science-fantasy strip in which the boundaries of space and time were crossed in constant battles against demoniac forces. Dowling's extensive use of cross-hatching creating a sombre atmosphere ideally suited to the weird elements. Scenarios later changed completely to sf with themes as mature in conception and execution as those in JEFF HAWKE.   [JE]

GARTH, WILL House name used on *Thrilling Wonder Stories*, *Startling Stories* and *Captain Future* 1937–41 by Otto BINDER, Edmond HAMILTON, Mort WEISINGER, Henry KUTTNER and possibly others. The film novelization *Dr. Cyclops* (**1940** as by WG) was written by Manly Wade WELLMAN.   [PN]
See also: GREAT AND SMALL.

GARVIN, RICHARD M(cCLELLAN) (1934–). American writer. His two sf novels with Edmond G. ADDEO are *The Fortec Conspiracy* (**1968**) and *The Talbot Agreement* (**1968**). The latter is borderline sf with espionage elements; in the former, a crashlanded alien ship infects Earth with a deadly disease. A solo novel is *The Crystal Skull* (**1974**).   [JC]

GARY, ROMAIN (1914–). Pseudonym of French writer and diplomat born Romain Kacewgari in Tiflis, Georgia, of Polish parents. His name's spelling was later changed to Kassevgari. He was active in the French

Resistance in the Second World War, and much praised for such novels outside the sf field as *Les racines du ciel* (**1956**; trans. as *The Roots of Heaven* **1958**), for which he was awarded the Prix Goncourt. As an sf writer, he uses generic material usually as an ethical pointer, and his best sf-oriented novel, *La danse de Gengis Cohn* (**1967**; trans. as *The Dance of Genghis Cohn* by the author **1968**), is certainly a FABULATION. Rather similarly to the inferior *On a Dark Night* (**1949**) by Anthony WEST, a supernatural transference from a victim to a Nazi occurs; in *Genghis Cohn* it is Cohn himself, a Yiddish comedian, who enters as a dybbuk into the mind of the SS officer who has ordered the massacre in which he is shot. The novel takes place in the late 1960s, with the former officer, now a police superintendent, obsessed by his dybbuk, who torments him, and with Germany itself tormented by an incursion of allegorical figures representative of her spiritual plight. The possession can be read as delusory, but with difficulty. *Gloire à nos illustres pionniers* (coll. **1962**; trans. as *Hissing Tales* **1964**) contains some sf, notably the title story. RG's early novel *Tulipe* (**1946**) is about the blacks taking over Earth. *The Gasp* (**1973**) features the discovery of the *élan vital* as it escapes the body at the moment of death in a form that can be used in warfare. RG is a sharp, clear-headed and passionate novelist of considerable stature. [JC]

See also: ESCHATOLOGY; POWER SOURCES; RELIGION.

GAS GIANT This item of sf TERMINOLOGY, invented by James BLISH, has proved so useful that it is now regularly used by scientists. It refers to the fact that four of the planets of our Solar System are not comparatively small and dense like Earth or MARS, but are extremely large, and consist mainly of substances which on Earth would be gases (and which, even in the cold at the outer edge of our Solar System, may still be largely gaseous). The four gas giants in our system are JUPITER, Saturn, Uranus and Neptune (*see* OUTER PLANETS). The fact that there are two kinds of planet in our system is of great interest to scientists constructing theories relating to the evolution of the Solar System, and it is thought that gas giants may also appear in other planetary systems. There is no reason to suppose we are unique in this respect. [PN]

GASKELL, JANE Professional name of Jane Gaskell Lynch (1941–), English author of a dozen books including her precocious first appearance with *Strange Evil* (**1957**), a kind of fairy tale. Some of her later work, including *King's Daughter* (**1958**), *The Shiny Narrow Grin* (**1964**) and *Some Summer Lands* (**1977**), is also fantasy, though her ATLANTIS trilogy, consisting of *The Serpent* (**1963**;

later paperback ed. in two vols as *The Serpent*, **1975**, and *The Dragon*, **1975**), *Atlan* (**1965**) and *The City* (**1966**), can easily be read as sf. It is the long story of non-Atlantean Princess Cija who is involved, via a forced marriage, in complex conflicts between northern forces and the quasi-human dwellers of the island state. As things fall apart, sex and sorcery abound, but the princess eventually reaches home again. In genre terms the trilogy is a kind of uneasy marriage between sf and the popular romance; it is full of vigorous and exuberant invention and occasionally overheated prose. [JC]

See also: SWORD AND SORCERY.

GAS-S-S! (vt **GAS-S-S, OR IT BECAME NECESSARY TO DESTROY THE WORLD IN ORDER TO SAVE IT**) Film (1970). AIP. Directed by Roger CORMAN, starring Robert Corff, Elaine Giftos, Bud Cort, Talia Coppola, Ben Vereen and Cindy Williams. Screenplay by George Armitage. 79 mins. Colour.

In Corman's belated attempt to cash in on the hippy/counter-culture movements of the 1960s, a poison gas kills everyone over the age of 25, after which the young inherit America. At first there is topsy-turvy chaos, with hordes of conservative middle Americans going on a rampage of destruction while Hell's Angels attempt to protect the old way of life, but then saner elements gain control and establish an alternative, life-enhancing society. The film ends zanily, with a number of the well-known dead emerging from a crack in the ground, including John F. Kennedy, Che Guevara and Martin Luther King. Corman's greatest self-indulgence is the image of Edgar Allan Poe riding about on a motorbike with the Raven perched on his shoulder and

Lenore as his pillion passenger. The film was made with Corman's legendary speed and cheapness, and a general sense of expansive euphoria. [JB]

GATCH, TOM Jr (1926–). American writer. His ALTERNATE-WORLD sf novel, *King Julian* (**1954**), depicts the USA as a monarchy; when asked, George Washington did accept the Crown. [JC]

GAUGHAN, JACK (1930–). American illustrator. One of the more underrated illustrators in sf, JG is also one of the most prolific. He has done cover and interior illustrations for *ASF*, *Spaceways*, *Galaxy*, *Vertex Science Fiction*, *Isaac Asimov's Science Fiction Magazine*, *Worlds of Tomorrow*, *Infinity Science Fiction*, *Worlds of Fantasy*, *Other Worlds*, *Amazing Stories* and many others. He has also done many paperback covers for ACE BOOKS, Paperback Library, DAW BOOKS and others. JG's style is sometimes as abstract as that of Richard POWERS, often as representational as that of Frank Kelly FREAS. His people are spare and angular and he has an outstanding sense of design. From 1969 to 1972, JG was art editor of *Galaxy* and did virtually all the artwork for the magazine during those years. In 1977 he became art editor of *Cosmos Science Fiction and Fantasy* and has contributed to it as well. JG is the only illustrator to have won HUGO awards for best fan artist and best professional artist in the same year (1967); he won the professional artist awards again in 1968 and 1969. Although he has done many cover paintings, he is best known for his distinctive interior b/w illustrations. [JG]

GAWRON, JEAN MARK (? –). American writer whose first sf novel, *An Apology for Rain* (**1974**), traces the travels

Edgar Allan Poe and friends on motorbike in Corman's GAS-S-S!

A striking cover by Jack GAUGHAN. June 1976.

Apr. 1936. A fantastic airship strikes.

of a woman in search of her brother through a surreal America.   [JC]

GAYLE, HENRY K. Form of his name used by Canadian writer and civil servant Harold Gayle (1910–   ), whose horror/sf novel, *Spawn of the Vortex* (**1957**), plays on the nuclear testing fears of the 1950s; underwater tests activate a horde of monsters who advance upon America.   [JC]

GAYTON, BERTRAM (? –   ). British writer whose sf novel, *The Gland Stealers* (**1922**), deals lightly with physical rejuvenation achieved by transplanting glands from apes into the bodies of elderly humans.   [JC]

GEIER, CHESTER S. (1921–   ). American writer and editor, very active in the Ziff-Davis stable (for *Amazing* and *Fantastic Adventures*) in the 1940s, where he published a large amount of routine material under his own name and pseudonyms including Guy Archette and the house names Alexander BLADE, P.F. COSTELLO, Warren KASTEL, S.M. TENNESHAW, Gerald VANCE and Peter

WORTH. "Forever is too Long" (*Fantastic Adventures* 1947) is book-length. He was an advocate of the Richard SHAVER "mystery" and founded a club in his honour, editing the *Shaver Mystery Magazine* on its behalf. Although he was one of the most prolific of pulp magazine writers, his stories have never been collected in book form, and only one, "Environment" (1944), has been anthologized.   [JC]

GEIGER, CARL IGNAZ (1756–91). German writer of several books of travel, including two imaginary interplanetary voyages, *Reise eines Erdbewohners in den Mars* ["Journey of an Earthman to Mars"] (**1790**) and, with J.C. Röhling, *Reise eines Marsbewohners auf der Erde* ["Journey of a Martian on Earth"] (**1791**).   [JC]

G-8 AND HIS BATTLE ACES US PULP magazine. 110 issues, Oct. 1933-Jun. 1944. Monthly to Apr. 1941, bi-monthly thereafter. Published by Popular Publications; ed. Rogers Terrill and, later, Alden H. Norton. All the novels were the work of Robert J. Hogan, one of the most

prolific of all pulp authors, who also wrote the short stories which filled out each issue. Hogan, who also wrote WU FANG and other magazines, was under editorial instruction to send in his material as he wrote it, without any revision; the amount of editing subsequently necessary is described by Damon KNIGHT in *Hell's Cartographers* (1975), ed. Brian ALDISS and Harry HARRISON. G-8 is the leader of an American fighter squadron in the First World War, which combats a wide variety of fantastic enemy menaces.   [MJE]

GEIGLEY,   VANCE   A(CTON) (1907–   ). American writer and businessman whose sf novel is *Will It End This Way?* (**1968**).   [JC]

GEIS, RICHARD E. *See* PSYCHOTIC.

GEMINI MAN *See* INVISIBLE MAN, THE.

GENERAL SEMANTICS A quasi-philosophical movement founded in Chicago in 1938 by Count Alfred KORZYBSKI, whose book *Science and Sanity* (**1933**) was the basic handbook of the movement. It had a surprising success, peaking in the 1940s and '50s. One of its most prominent recent exponents is Samuel Hayakawa, a West-Coast academic, who gained prominence through his tough handling of campus riots in the late 1960s.

General semantics teaches that, first unsanity, and later insanity, is caused by a semantic adherence to an Aristotelean world view, by which is meant the use of an either-or, two-valued logic, which AK saw as being built into Indo-European language structures. From this simple beginning, which contains many components with which linguistic philosophers in general, including Wittgenstein, would be unlikely to differ

very profoundly, was built a confused and confusing psychotherapeutic system, which, like DIANETICS, promised to focus the latent abilities of the mind; it may have seemed to its more naïve adherents that general semantics held out the promise of turning Man into SUPERMAN by teaching non-Aristotelean (null-A or Ā) habits of thought. The movement probably had some small influence on the development of L. Ron HUBBARD's dianetics, but its best-known repercussion in sf was the composition of two novels by A.E. VAN VOGT, featuring a non-Aristotelean superman hero, Gilbert Gosseyn (a pun on go sane as opposed to unsane): *The World of Ā* (1945 *ASF*; rev. 1948; rev. with introduction 1970; vt *The World of Null-A*) and *The Pawns of Null-A* (1948–9 *ASF* as "The Players of Ā"; 1956; vt *The Players of Null-A* UK).
[PN]

See also: PSEUDO-SCIENCE.

GENERATION STARSHIPS For writers unwilling to power their starships with FASTER-THAN-LIGHT drives, or to make use of a relativistic time contraction, there is a real problem in sending ships between the stars, because the length of the voyage would usually span many human lifetimes. The usual answers are to put the crew into SUSPENDED ANIMATION, as in James WHITE's *The Dream Millennium* (1974), to send germ cells only, as in Kurt VONNEGUT Jr's "The Big Space Fuck" (1972), or to use a generation starship. This is a ship crewed by men and women, whose families breed, and whose remote descendants eventually reach the destination.

In *Seekers of Tomorrow* (1966) Sam MOSKOWITZ attributes the first such story to Laurence MANNING, in "The Living Galaxy" (1934), but this actually tells of a small, self-powered world, and does not qualify, because the environment in which the crew live is not artificial.

It was probably Konstantin TSIOLKOVSKY who first saw the necessity for generation starships in the COLONIZATION OF OTHER WORLDS, in "The Future of Earth and Mankind", which was published in a Russian anthology of scientific essays in 1928, but may be earlier still. Tsiolkovsky here argued for the construction in the future of space-going "Noah's Arks": he envisaged such journeys as taking many thousands of years.

The first genre sf use of the notion is probably Don WILCOX's "The Voyage that Lasted 600 Years" (1940) in *AMZ*; here the captain of the ship is in hibernation, but wakes every 100 years to check on progress; each time he wakes he finds great social changes among the successive descendants of the crew, and a sinking into brutality accompanied by plague; his successive appearances render him an object of superstitious awe to the tribesmen on board. The theme of social change and degeneration inaugurated by Wilcox was to become the dominant theme of such stories.

The other dominant theme was presented in the following year in an altogether more famous story, "Universe" (1941), by Robert A. HEINLEIN, and its sequel in *ASF* the following month, "Common Sense" (1941); the two were published in book form as *Orphans of the Sky* (1963). This is the classic generation-starship story in which the crew have forgotten that they are on a ship, and have descended to a state of rigidly stratified and superstitious social organization; the unusually intelligent hero discovers the truth in a traumatic CONCEPTUAL BREAKTHROUGH. Brian W. ALDISS, who loved the theme but thought it crudely developed by Heinlein, devoted his first novel *Non-Stop* (1958; vt *Starship* USA) to what was in effect a very much more complex and subtle rewriting, in a successful and deliberate act of hubris. Other stories in which surviving generations think of the ship as a world and not a mode of transport are "Spacebred Generations" (1953; vt "Target Generation") by Clifford D. SIMAK, "Ship of Shadows" (1969) by Fritz LEIBER, in which the ship is not strictly a starship, though the degenerated society is similar, and Harry HARRISON's amazing *Captive Universe* (1969), in which the crew and colonists have been transformed, in an act of insane CULTURAL ENGINEERING, into medieval monks and Aztec peasants.

Some stories begin at the outset or after the end of a generation-starship voyage. Arthur C. CLARKE's early and remarkably chauvinistic (on behalf of mankind) story "Rescue Party" (1946) has Earth evacuated in the face of a coming Nova, heading confidently towards the stars in a giant fleet of primitive generation rocketships. Brian STABLEFORD's *Promised Land* (1974) tells of a society of colonists whose social structure is based on that developed over generations in the starship on which they arrived.

The theme has been used little outside genre sf, though a spectacular exception to this is the epic poem *Aniara* (1956; trans. 1963) by the Nobel Prize winner and Swedish poet Harry MARTINSON. An opera based on the poem by Blomdahl was first performed in 1959. The story pits human values against inhuman technology on a generation starship.

An interesting variant on the theme appears in several stories, most notably in John BRUNNER's "Lungfish" (1957; vt "Rendezvous with Destiny" USA), in which the ship itself takes on the role in its occupants' minds of surrogate mother; even on reaching their destination they will not leave the womb; this theme is also prominent in the Simak story mentioned above.

Among the best stories about social changes on generation starships are the Aldiss, Harrison, Heinlein, Leiber and Simak already cited, along with *The Space-Born* (1956) by E.C. TUBB, *Rite of Passage* (1968) by Alexei PANSHIN, *The Ballad of Beta-2* (1965) by Samuel DELANY and *Cities in Flight* (1950–62; coll. 1970) by James BLISH. The latter work, of course, is borderline, in that it deals with cities and not starships *per se*, and spends as much time on various worlds as it does on the ship. Panshin's novel, too, takes the case of a starship which is no longer seeking a destination but is effectively a world in itself; Panshin's projected starship society is more optimistically envisaged than most, and is in contrast to the wonderfully vivid dissolution depicted by, for example, Delany and Leiber.

Other works of some interest, but generally minor compared to the above, are *Rogue Ship* (1947–63; fix-up 1965) by A.E. VAN VOGT, below his best standard; *Seed of Light* (1959) by Edmund COOPER, which reads like the ideational framework for a novel that was never written; *The Star Seekers* (1953) by Milton LESSER, which features a four-way division of society in a hollowed-out asteroid; *200 Years to Christmas* (1961) by J.T. McINTOSH, which features a competently thought out but conventional cyclic history within the ship; "Bliss" (1962) by David ROME and "The Star Mutants" (1970) by Damien Broderick.

Some enterprising variants on the theme are found. In Arthur SELLINGS' "A Start in Life" (1951) a plague decimates the ship, leaving two five-year-old survivors to be raised by robots; Judith MERRIL's "Wish Upon a Star" (1958) features a ship originally crewed by 20 women and four men, with a resultant matriarchal society; Chad OLIVER's "The Wind Blows Free" (1957) takes the birth-trauma theme to its logical conclusion with a story about a man who, goaded to near-madness by the claustrophobic society of the ship, opens an airlock only to find that the ship had landed on a planet some centuries back.

Harlan ELLISON wrote the script for a generation-starship TV series, *The Starlost*, made, disastrously, in Canada, 1973. Ellison repudiated the series as it stood, and used his derisive pseudonym Cordwainer Bird on the titles; his original script for the pilot episode appears in *Faster Than Light* (anth. 1976) ed. Jack DANN and George ZEBROWSKI.

Some of the above titles are derived from an unpublished manuscript, "Les arches stellaires et leur littérature" by the French critic Jean-Pierre Moumon. [PN]

GENESIS II Made-for-TV film (1973). CBS-TV. Directed by John Llewellyn Moxey, starring Alex Cord, Mariette Hartley, Percy Rodriguez and Ted Cassidy. Screenplay by Gene RODDENBERRY. 90 mins. Colour.

Produced by Gene Roddenberry, the creator of STAR TREK, this TV film was a pilot for a series that was never made. After a suspended animation experiment that goes wrong, a man wakes in a future world which is suffering from the aftermath of an atomic war. Mutants have evolved and rule ordinary humans with an iron hand. The hero helps to overcome the rulers, aided by his primitive vitality. A similar format was used by Roddenberry in two further attempts to launch series, released as PLANET EARTH and STRANGE NEW WORLD. [JB]

GENETIC ENGINEERING In his prophetic essay *Daedalus: or Science and the Future* (1924) J.B.S. HALDANE presents part of an essay written as if by "a rather stupid undergraduate" in the year 2073, which contains the following observations: "When we consider that in 1912 Morgan had located several Mendelian factors in the nucleus of *Drosophila*, and modified its sex ratio, while Marmorek had taught a harmless bacillus to kill guinea-pigs, and finally in 1913 Brachet had grown rabbit embryos in serum for some days, it is remarkable how little the scientific workers of that time, and *a fortiori* the general public, seem to have foreseen the practical bearing of such results." Haldane goes on to talk of "inventing" a new species of alga to solve the world's food problem, and of producing ectogenetic children which may be selectively bred for particular characters. In the 23rd century, he suggests, elections may be fought on the question of whether eugenic programmes directed toward modification of humanity should be instituted. Here, even Haldane's imagination showed a hint of weakness, for the real implication of Morgan's mapping of *Drosophila* genes was that some day we might be able to effect changes without the need for eugenic planning, by direct manipulation of the genetic material.

In the same essay Haldane notes that there is always extreme resistance against "biological inventions" because they are initially perceived as blasphemous perversions. This, at least, is true — and the issues raised in the real world by the possibility of genetic engineering are dramatic. A debate is currently going on (1977) about whether a moratorium should be declared on all experiments in the field.

The "engineering" of living creatures is a fairly old notion in sf, but until very recently it was presumed that such engineering would have to be achieved by surgery — as in H.G. WELLS's *The Island of Dr. Moreau* (1896) — by extraordinary nutrition — as in Wells's *The Food of the Gods* (1904) — or by selective breeding (eugenics), as Haldane proposed.

Haldane's ideas, together with other biological speculations debated in the 1920s, formed the basis for much of the

imaginary future HISTORY invented by the philosopher Olaf STAPLEDON in *Last and First Men* (1930), in which biological engineering is shown as playing an ambiguous but not necessarily malign role in the future EVOLUTION of humanity.

Surgical modification of humans for reasons not strictly medical (usually cosmetic) is now widely practised, and athletes and slimmers employ special diets to strategic ends. Haldane's suggestions, however, did indeed seem blasphemous to some, and Aldous HUXLEY developed the world promised by *Daedalus* as a DYSTOPIA in *Brave New World* (1932), in which embryos are ectogenetically developed, and their development is nutritionally and environmentally controlled to fit them for life as "alphas", "betas" or "gammas".

The idea of biological engineering appeared very early in the sf pulps. *Amazing Stories* carried a story by Julian Huxley, brother of Aldous and friend of Haldane and Wells: "The Tissue-Culture King" (1927). David H. KELLER wrote several stories about tampering with human form and nature, most notably "Stenographer's Hands" (1928), about a eugenic experiment to breed the perfect stenographer, with reduced initiative and a wasted body, but with very capable hands. The first story that involved actual genetic engineering was written by the chemical engineer Stanley WEINBAUM — "Proteus Island" (1936). But the conclusion of this story echoes its model, *The Island of Dr. Moreau*, in presuming that "the nature of the beast" cannot be changed as easily as its physical form.

Weinbaum's death robbed genre sf of the only writer in the pre-War period who might have perceived the significance of the idea of genetic engineering and followed it up. Artificial, "engineered" organisms appear in minor roles in several stories, a notable example being the "familiars" employed by the fake witches in Fritz LEIBER's *Gather, Darkness!* (1943; 1950), but for the most part the idea ran on a single very narrow track — the enlargement of creatures to monstrousness by unusual nutrition (*see* GREAT AND SMALL). A.E. VAN VOGT, however, who was quick to pick up new ideas even if he did not totally understand them, used "gene transformation" to create the superman in *Slan* (1940 *ASF*; 1946). After this, a usually undefined genetic engineering became a standard way of creating SUPERMAN figures in sf. A recent example is found in *If the Stars Are Gods* (1977) by Gregory BENFORD and Gordon EKLUND.

The most important use of genetic engineering in early 1940s sf, however, was in Robert HEINLEIN's *Beyond This Horizon* (1942 *ASF* as by Anson MacDonald ; 1948) In this plot devoted to an attack on sacred cows, a society which uses eugenics and genetic engineering to ensure the physical and mental fitness of

the population is at first seen as over-regimented and controlled, but later revealed to be a good thing. The novel is unpleasant in many ways, but it was one of the first in genre sf to open up the question of what the social results of genetic engineering might be.

The writer who reintroduced genetic engineering in a more rigorous sense into sf, and the first who tried to confront some of its possibilities, was James BLISH. "Beanstalk" (1952; vt "Giants in the Earth"; exp. vt *Titan's Daughter* 1961) is concerned with the commonplace theme of giantism, but this time in humans, and strategically induced by stimulated polyploidy. Spontaneous polyploidy — doubling of the chromosome complement — is not uncommon in plants, and usually results in giantism. The story echoes Wells's *The Food of the Gods* and is primarily concerned with prejudice on the part of the normal humans and the giants' reaction to it. Blish quickly moved on to consider the possibilities opened up by genetic engineering in adapting humans to LIFE ON OTHER WORLDS (*see also* COLONIZATION OF OTHER WORLDS) in his "PANTROPY" series. The series was written around the widely discussed novelette "Surface Tension" (1952), about microscopic humans engineered for life in small pools of water. The final section of the book *The Seedling Stars* (fix-up 1956), which collects the "pantropy" stories, looks forward to the day when Earth, much changed by time, would itself become an alien environment to be re-seeded with "adapted" men. This idea, of "conquering" alien worlds with specially engineered individuals, was taken up by other writers of the period, including Poul ANDERSON in "Call me Joe" (1957) and Philip K. DICK in *The World Jones Made* (1956), and the idea that a special, engineered race would be necessary to undertake SPACE travel itself was later developed by Samuel R. DELANY in "Aye, and Gomorrah ..." (1967). Other stories from the 1950s dealing with experiments in genetic engineering are "Natural State" (1954; exp. vt *Masters of Evolution* 1959) by Damon KNIGHT and "They Shall Inherit" (1958) by Brian ALDISS.

Non-genetic biological engineering was employed by Theodore STURGEON in *Venus Plus X* (1960), and Sturgeon also wrote an early story about the related idea of cloning (*see* CLONES). The *Moreau* theme — the notion of modifying animals into human form — was developed extensively by Cordwainer Smith in his stories of the Underpeople, (*see* SMITH *entry for details*) who are used as servants and slaves but hope for deliverance. The Underpeople, however, cannot breed true, and thus the genetic material is not directly moulded. A similar modification, which does involve permanent genetic modification, is the basic premise of the "Dies Irae" trilogy (1971) by Brian STABLEFORD, but genetic engineering is not developed as a theme in the series. All in all, it cannot be said that Blish's example was significantly followed up, even by Blish himself.

Renewed interest in genetic engineering was promoted in the late 1960s by the popularization of the idea of cloning, and by non-fiction works about the potential inherent in the biological sciences, such as *The Biological Time-Bomb* (1968) by Gordon Rattray Taylor. The British television series DOOMWATCH, whose purpose was partly propagandistic, was much concerned with trends in contemporary scientific research and the need for careful administrative control, and awakened many people to some of the implications of biological engineering. The first episode of the series became the basis for the novel *Mutant-59* (1972) by Kit PEDLER and Gerry DAVIS, about the "escape" of a bacterium engineered to metabolize plastic, and many other episodes also featured biological engineering of various kinds, including genetic.

The one novel based on the notion of creating a "perfect" human by genetic manipulation, *Superbaby* (1969) by Felix MENDELSOHN, is not inspiring, but a similar notion is more intelligently applied by Frank HERBERT in *The Eyes of Heisenberg* (1966). Herbert has been consistently interested in the theme, and it is also used in *Hellstrom's Hive* (1973), though the superman-breeding programme in *Dune* (1965) is an orthodox eugenic one. Another writer whose interest in the possibilities of genetic engineering has been consistent is Brian Stableford, whose story "The Engineer and the Executioner" (1975) features an artificial life-system which exhibits Lamarckian evolution, and whose novel *The Florians* (1976) begins a series about a starship — named *Daedalus* after Haldane's essay — which supports colonies on other worlds by employing genetic engineering techniques to subvert ecological difficulties. An important Japanese novel, *Inter Ice Age 4* (1959; trans. 1970) by Kobo ABÉ, deals with the genetic modification of Man to suit him for aquatic life. Genetic engineering is basic to the Protean future of John VARLEY's stories, including *The Ophiuchi Hotline* (1977).

Strange human societies on other worlds are occasionally afforded logical support by the notion of genetic engineering — as, for instance, the hermaphrodite society in Ursula K. LE GUIN's classic *Left Hand of Darkness* (1969) and a novel by A. Bertram CHANDLER, *The Inheritors* (1972), inspired by *The Island of Dr. Moreau*.

There are definite signs that the possibilities of genetic engineering are beginning to be investigated in sf, although the genre can make no claim to be abreast of the times, let alone ahead of

them, in this respect. The story which is perhaps most notable for its representation of the techniques actually being developed by scientists today, albeit in application to a highly speculative project, is Richard S. Weinstein's "Oceans Away" (1976), which deals with the creation of intelligent cephalopods in the laboratory. [BS]
See also: BIOLOGY; MEDICINE.

GENRE SF For clarification of this term, used widely in this volume, *see* DEFINITIONS OF SF; HISTORY OF SF; MAINSTREAM WRITERS OF SF; PUBLISHING; PULP MAGAZINES; SF MAGAZINES.

GENTRY, CURT (1931–). American writer, whose NEAR-FUTURE sf novel, *The Last Days of the Late, Great State of California* (1968), vividly depicts a San Andreas Fault DISASTER, though its ECOLOGICAL arguments, blaming Man for the destruction of the state, are somewhat laboured. [JC]

GEORGE, PETER (BRYAN) (1924–66). British writer and ex-air-force officer whose life and career seemed obsessed with nuclear warfare and its consequences. His best-known sf novel, *Two Hours to Doom* (1958 as by Peter Bryant; vt *Red Alert* USA), was a straightforward story of preventive war, inaugurated by a general, leading to world-wide HOLOCAUST, and he may have had some mixed feelings about its satirical transmogrification into DR STRANGELOVE: OR, HOW I LEARNED TO STOP WORRYING AND LOVE THE BOMB, Stanley KUBRICK's brilliant film. The novelization, with the film's title, was published as by PG (1963). A further sf novel, *Commander-1* (1965), follows the desperate struggles of survivors after a nuclear war. PG's suicide followed soon after, during the composition of yet another novel on the same theme, which was to be entitled *Nuclear Survivors*. [JC]
See also: END OF THE WORLD; POLITICS; SCIENTISTS.

GERHARDI, WILLIAM Legal name, until after he stopped publishing, of William Gerhardie (1895–1977), English writer, best known for such works outside the sf field as *Futility* (1922). His END-OF-THE-WORLD novel *Jazz and Jasper* (1928; vt *Eva's Apple: A Story of Jazz and Jasper*; vt *My Sinful Earth*; vt *Doom*) depicts a Lord Beaverbrook figure and his entourage in their complex lives and later, after a huge cataclysm, on a chip of rock, all that remains of Earth. The tetralogy on which he worked for 37 years until his death, not yet published, is on a complex IMMORTALITY theme. [JC]
Other works: *The Memoirs of Satan* (1932) with Brian Lunn; *Resurrection* (1934).

GERMANY Of the two main streams that converged into sf, the fantastic and

the Utopian, the strongest German-language tradition by far was that of the fantastic. But it would require an act of critical violence to force the work of such fantasists as Johann Wolfgang von Goethe or E.T.A. HOFFMANN into the genre of sf, where they do not naturally belong. The same is true of other 19th-century writers whose works had more fantastic elements than "Utopian" — the latter term, in German literary criticism, having a wider application than in English: in Germany "Utopian" subsumes all rationally presented (i.e. non-fantastic) tales of the future.

An early classic of the German Utopian novel was *Auf zwei Planeten* (1897; trans. and abridged as *Two Planets* 1971) by Kurd LASSWITZ. It is a report of an expedition from Mars, scientifically sound by the standards of the day, that has not yet lost its attraction. An early, rather "literary" work is Paul SCHEERBART's asteroid novel *Lesabèndio* (1914). The elements of this novel, however, are more religious and mystical than scientific or futuristic. On the level of simple PULP adventure, paralleling similar developments in the USA, was the popular *Kapitän Mors* (*see* LUFTPIRAT UND SEIN LENKBARES LUFTSCHIFF), a weekly magazine which ran from about 1908 to about 1913, whose eponymous hero took part in daredevil exploits around the Solar System, battling against villains and monsters.

After World War I the age of the technological-Utopian novel began in Germany. The most notable exponent was Hans Dominik (1872–1946), who had an outstanding success with *Die Macht der Drei* ["The Power of the Three"] (1922). This novel contains a peculiar mixture of German nationalism, Far Eastern mysticism and the development of technocracy. Dominik wrote another dozen books and is still well remembered today. Purely technological-future novels were also written by Erich Dolezal and Rudolf Heinrich Daumann, but they did not rival the popularity of Dominik. None of these works, including those of Dominik, can be considered to have any literary value.

During the same period, several pulp magazines with a Utopian content were published, notably the *Sun-Koh* series by P.A. Müller (then calling himself Lok Myler), which ran for 150 issues. They tell of an omnipotent hero, the "heir of Atlantis", who prepares for world domination with the help of his superhuman powers and fantastic technologies. These unrealistic action stories did express a simple worship of the hero figure, but the recent charge by some critics that their simplistic attitudes actually served as a psychological prop to the fascist regime is hardly justified.

In 1939, nearly all the pulp series in Germany were declared to be "*Schmutz und Schund*" (a standard Nazi idiom meaning "Dirt and trash"), and prohibited.

After World War II, some Utopian pulp series in the old style turned up again, but they soon disappeared from the market. A change was taking place in the development of Utopian and futuristic writings — the American occupation forces had brought along the first American sf paperbacks to Germany, and all things which related to the great power, America, were fashionable with young intellectuals at the time, a trend further encouraged later on by the American success in space.

In 1952 there was a small publishing revolution in Germany. The philosopher Gotthard GÜNTHER edited four well-known products of American sf for the publishing house Karl-Rauch-Verlag, with interesting introductions, among them Isaac ASIMOV's *I, Robot* and *The Incredible Planet* by John W. CAMPBELL Jr, as hard-cover books. The experiment, however, was a fiasco, most of the books were remaindered, and further publication in the series was stopped. (Contemporary connoisseurs still regard these publications as being of outstanding quality.)

It is difficult to analyse exactly how modern sf in Germany differs from earlier, more conventional novels of the future. In general, the structure of ideas is becoming bolder; recent sf has been changing its emphasis away from areas of pure physics and technology and has moved on to the human being himself, especially as he is subject to technological manipulation. But these developments grew from an extremely modest base, as German publishing slowly found its feet again after World War II.

The pulp publisher Erich Pabel-Verlag began its sf publication with a series entitled *Jim Parker*, presenting traditional, technical-wizardry hero stories. But slowly its other line *Utopia* (1953 onwards) predominated, and for the first time sf by well-known American writers was published in German translation on a wide scale. In 1954 another imprint, Utopia-Grossbände, followed. Amid all this published material, quite a number of the best and most popular American sf stories appeared, but most were translated rather badly, and as the pulps were limited to a certain number of pages, they were often drastically shortened, a practice which still continues. Yet another imprint from the same quarter was "Utopia-Magazin", which began in 1955; it printed short-story collections.

Shortly after this another pulp publisher, Moewig-Verlag, began its "Terra" series and, in 1958, *Galaxis*, a German version of GALAXY. It was another ambitious experiment, edited by Lothar Heinecke, an sf enthusiast and translator, which concentrated on some of the finest stories of the genre. It lasted for about a dozen editions.

1960 was another milestone in the distribution of sf in Germany. The publisher Wilhelm Goldmann, especially well known in the paperback market, decided to publish "Goldmann's Zukunftsromane" as hard-covers, monthly, with Herbert W. FRANKE as series editor. Within six years about 80 titles were published. At the same time Goldmann began his "Weltraum-Taschenbücher", a paperback edition of the hard-covers. Original German sf titles were also published in this list. Shortly after this the Wilhelm-Heyne-Verlag began an sf paperback line. Both these series are still running, constituting the best-known continuous vehicles for German sf publishing.

Other, shorter-lived experiments in sf publishing have been "Science Fiction für Kenner" (pub. Lichtenberg-Verlag), "Science Fiction & Fantastica" (pub. Marion von Schröder-Verlag), and until 1976 "Phantastische Wirklichkeit" (pub. Insel-Verlag, ed. Franz ROTTENSTEINER), and the recent line, similar to the previous one, "Bibliothek des Phantastischen" (pub. Suhrkamp-Verlag). At present, about 100 sf books are published annually in West Germany, of which approximately 90 % are translations from English.

Sf in Germany is not to be confused with the smaller but interesting topic of German sf. Shortly after World War II several books appeared which not only met the narrow specifications of specialist sf enthusiasts, but were outstanding by broader literary criteria. In 1945 Franz WERFEL published in exile the future-HISTORY novel *Stern der Ungeborenen* (1946; trans. as *Star of the Unborn* 1946). In 1948 there followed Hellmuth Lange's *Blumen wachsen im Himmel* ["Flowers grow in the Heavens"] (1948) and Hans Wörner's *Wir fanden Menschen* ["We found Men"] (1948). Both were clearly written under the direct stimulus of the War, especially the use of atomic bombs to bring about its dreadful but dramatic end. Also in the same year, Anni Francé-Harrer published her novel *Der gläserne Regen* ["The Glass Rain"] (1948). 1950 saw the publication of the first book by a writer who now plays a prominent role in German literary life, the present president of the German PEN club, Walter Jens: *Nein, die Welt der Angeklagten* ["No, the World of the Accused"] (1950). The story tells of the rebellion of an outsider against a totalitarian regime as memorably oppressive as those in HUXLEY's *Brave New World* and ORWELL's *Nineteen Eighty-Four*. This novel, of course, was not categorized as "science fiction", which would have meant, at that time at least, that it would not have been received as a serious work. Nevertheless, it does belong to the best of this literary genre. Another DYSTOPIA of high literary quality is *Die Kinder des Saturn* ["Children of Saturn"] (1959) by Jens Rehn.

But the most important author to deal with sf concepts, without being generally considered as an sf writer (*see* MAINSTREAM WRITERS OF SF) is Arno Schmidt, the winner of many literary awards. As in his other literary work, he reaches very close to the outer edge of intelligibility in *KAFF, auch MARE CRISTUM* ["KAFF, also MARE CRISTUM"] (1960) and *Die Gelehrtenrepublik* ["The Philosophers' Republic"] (1957), the first describing the adventures of a member of a US moon crew, and the second telling of a reporter's visit to IRAS, an ABSURD ghetto of poets and philosophers — sf subjects *par excellence*.

In 1967 Winfried Bruckner published *Tötet ihn* ["Kill Him"] (1967), about a revolution in an underground part of Vienna in the 21st century. In much the same period, between 1960 and 1965, Herbert W. Franke published his collection of very short stories *Der grüne Komet* ["The Green Comet"] (1960), and his first novels, beginning with *Das Gedankennetz* (1961; trans. as *The Mind Net* 1975) — mainly extrapolations of today's developments into a more or less far future.

By this time, within what the Germans call "trivial literature" (popular and ephemeral genre literature) there had been trends towards the development of future-oriented literature into a mass phenomenon. From about 1950 onwards, many such productions, with only a vague resemblance to American sf, were published as cheap "lending-library" books. Well-known authors in this field were Karl Herbert SCHEER, Wolf Detlef Rohr, Richard Koch and Hans Kneifel. Later on they were well placed to take advantage of the pulp magazine and sf paperback boom.

During the same period the "Science Fiction Club Deutschland" came into being; its members have made great efforts to spread the popularity of sf in West Germany. The best-known member of the group is Walter Ernsting, who writes sf under the name of Clark DARLTON. In 1961 Moewig-Verlag began the now internationally known, controversial PERRY RHODAN series, first as pulp magazines, later as paperback books. It is the longest sf series in the world, with many hundreds of titles, and in terms of the number of copies printed both in Germany and abroad, the best-selling series in the world. It continues today, and has had a great if surprising success in the USA since 1971, and in the UK since 1975. In this series the always popular (especially in Germany) myth of the hero whose leitmotiv is "Conquest of the Universe" is combined with traditional American-style sf elements. The series was begun by the writers K. H. Scheer and Walter Ernsting, though since then several others have joined the team.

For some years now, the "wissenschaftlich-phantastische Erzählung" ["scientific-fantastic story"], as sf is called in the socialist countries, has been establishing itself in East Germany, the German Democratic Republic. The books of such authors as Carlos Rasch and Günther Krupka have been published in large editions, readily finding a readership. These have included some outstanding works, notably *Die Ohnmacht der Allmächtigen* ["The Impotence of the Omnipotent Ones"] (1973) by Heiner Rank. For political reasons the development of sf has proceeded under quite different premises in East Germany, and it cannot easily be compared with that in West Germany. Recently sf in East Germany has been given fresh life through the work of new, younger authors.

During the last decade an increasing interest in sf has been taken by professional literary critics, mainstream writers and academics, with studies being usually but not exclusively written from a sociological or political viewpoint. Several critical books and analyses of the genre have been written. (*See* Martin SCHWONKE, Jörg HIENGER, Michael PEHLKE, Norbert LINGFELD and Manfred NAGL, and also the article "Some German Writings in sf" by Franz ROTTENSTEINER, in SCIENCE-FICTION STUDIES, Fall 1974.)

The sf radio play has flourished recently in Germany. Due to the efforts of Dieter HASSELBLATT and another broadcasting programme producer, Horst Krautkrämer, sf has become an integral part of German radio drama production, with many original scripts, as well as adapted versions of well-known stories.

The most recent important event in German sf was the publication of the novel *Der Untergang der Stadt Passau* ["The Fall of the City of Passau"] (1975) by Carl Amery, who was at that time President of the Verband Deutscher Schriftsteller ["German Writers' Association"]. The novel deals with the HOLOCAUST AND AFTER, presenting alternate viewpoints on the best way of organizing a life for the future.

Germany has no Huxley and no Orwell, and even the number of competent writers working in sf looks rather modest, if it is compared with the multitude of their British and American colleagues. However, it already seems that the most interesting writers of sf in Germany are not mere minor successors to their English and American precursors. German sf is beginning to show both independence and originality. [HWF/CF]

GERNSBACK, HUGO (1884–1967). American writer and editor. Born in Luxemburg, HG emigrated to the USA in 1904. Intensely interested in electricity and radio, he designed batteries and by 1906 was marketing a home radio set. In 1908 he launched his first magazine, *Modern Electrics*, where he later published his novel *Ralph 124C 41+* (1911–12 *Modern Electrics*; fix-up 1925). While deficient as fiction, it clearly shows

his overriding interest in sf as a vehicle of PREDICTION, being a catalogue of the marvellous TECHNOLOGY of the 27th century. *Modern Electrics* later became the *Electrical Experimenter*, for which he wrote a series of apocryphal scientific adventures of Baron Munchausen: "How to Make a Wireless Acquaintance" (1915), "How Munchausen and the Allies Took Berlin" (1915), "Munchausen on the Moon" (1915), "The Earth as Viewed From the Moon" (1915), "Munchausen Departs for the Planet Mars" (1916), "Munchausen Lands on Mars" (1915), "Munchausen is Taught Martian" (1915), "Thought Transmission on Mars" (1916), "Cities of Mars" (1916), "The Planets at Close Range" (1916), "Martian Amusements" (1916), "How the Martian Canals are Built" (1916), "Martian Atmosphere Plants" (1917). The series was reprinted in *AMZ* in 1928. In 1920 another title change brought into being SCIENCE AND INVENTION, in which HG regularly printed sf. The August 1923 issue was devoted to what he then termed "scientific fiction", and the following year HG solicited subscriptions for an sf magazine to be called *Scientifiction*; but it was not until April 1926 that the first issue of AMAZING STORIES, the first true sf magazine in English, appeared. HG was publisher and editor, although much of the actual editorial work was done by T. O'Conor SLOANE, his elderly associate editor. *AMZ* was an immediate commercial success, and in 1927 HG published the AMAZING STORIES ANNUAL, which in turn spawned AMAZING STORIES QUARTERLY. In 1929 his Experimenter Publishing Company was forced into bankruptcy. HG immediately bounced back by founding another company and starting four more magazines: AIR WONDER STORIES, SCIENCE WONDER STORIES, SCIENCE WONDER QUARTERLY and SCIENTIFIC DETECTIVE MONTHLY, although the first two were amalgamated the following year as WONDER STORIES. His empire declined through the 1930s (though other projects prospered), with *Scientific Detective Monthly* (which changed its name to *Amazing Detective*

Tales) lasting less than a year, *Wonder Stories Quarterly* (as *Science Wonder Quarterly* had become) ceasing publication in 1933, and *Wonder Stories* being sold in 1936, to become THRILLING WONDER STORIES. In 1939 he published three issues of an early sf COMIC, *Superworld Comics*, and in 1953 published his last sf magazine, SCIENCE FICTION PLUS, with HG named as editor, but with Sam MOSKOWITZ as managing editor. It ran for seven issues. A rather different HG publication, *Sexology*, enjoyed more lasting success. Opinions vary on the beneficence of HG's influence on sf. Moskowitz has termed him the "Father of Science Fiction" (*see* "Hugo Gernsback: 'Father of Science Fiction' " in *Explorers of the Infinite*, 1963), while Brian ALDISS said of his emphasis on supposed scientific accuracy that it introduced a "deadening literalism" into the field (*see Billion Year Spree*, 1973). The Science Fiction Achievement Awards are named the HUGOS in his honour, and he was given a special Hugo award in 1960. [MJE]
Other works: *The Ultimate World* (1971).
See also: AUTOMATION; CRIME AND PUNISHMENT; DEFINITIONS OF SF; DISCOVERY AND INVENTION; FANTASTIC VOYAGES; GOLDEN AGE OF SF; HEROES; MACHINES; MARS; MEDIA LANDSCAPE; MOON; NEAR FUTURE; NUCLEAR POWER; OPTIMISM AND PESSIMISM; ORIGIN OF MAN; PHYSICS; PROTO SF; ROCKETS; SF MAGAZINES; SF OVERTAKEN BY EVENTS; SCIENTISTS; SPACE FLIGHT; SPACE OPERA; TRANSPORTATION; UTOPIA; WEAPONS.

GERROLD, DAVID (1944–). American author and scriptwriter, born and raised in Los Angeles; he graduated with a BA in theatre arts. His first commercial sales were TV scripts, the first of them the well-known STAR TREK episode "The Trouble with Tribbles" (1967), the story of the writing and shooting of which he tells in one of his two books about the series, *The Trouble with Tribbles* (the 1967 script plus non-fiction narrative; 1973). The other book, *The World of Star Trek* (1973), perceptively analyses the strengths and weaknesses of the show, and recounts its travails in the world of network television. DG's first novel was a collaboration with Larry NIVEN, *The Flying Sorcerers* (1971), a lively attempt to give a scientific rationale to a variety of incidents which to the observers seem like MAGIC, when an exploratory team is stranded on a primitive planet. His first solo novel, *Space Skimmer* (1972), deals with a man's search for a vanished GALACTIC EMPIRE and its spaceships, described in the title. Perhaps his best-known work is *When Harlie was One* (1972), which deals with the evolution of artificial INTELLIGENCE in a COMPUTER, and discusses many of the problems of life with an air of profundity not wholly justified by the content. *With a Finger in my I* (coll. **1972**) assembles some of his occasionally precious short stories — the title story (1972) is a fantasy about solipsism and PERCEPTION showing a strong if slightly undergraduate sense of verbal play; *Yesterday's Children* (**1972**) is a SPACE OPERA, with conflict between a captain and first officer on a starship; *The Man who Folded Himself* (**1973**) deals in jerky, short-sentenced prose with a hero who meets other versions of himself, doubled through TIME PARADOX, and makes love to several of them in an orgy of reciprocal narcissism. *Moonstar Odyssey* (**1977**) deals with a hermaphroditic society on another planet, whose inhabitants do not have to settle into one sex until after adolescence. Weak on plot, it is strong on the presentation of a rather Californian and occasionally embarrassing version of what a non-sexist society could be like. DG has edited several anthologies, including *Protostars* (anth. **1971**), *Generation* (anth. **1972**), *Science Fiction Emphasis I* (anth. **1974**) and *Alternities* (anth. **1974**). The ideas in DG's books are sometimes submerged in the rather self-conscious and determinedly colloquial prose. [JC/PN] **Other works:** *Battle for the Planet of the Apes* (film novelization **1973**); *Death-beast* (**1978**). **See also:** CLONES; FANTASY; GRAVITY; MACHINES; TERRAFORMING.

GESTON, MARK S(YMINGTON) (1946–). American writer and attorney, who wrote and published his remarkable first novel *Lords of the Starship* (**1967**) while still a student at Kenyon College. This work, which establishes the dark mood of all his books to date, and their shared venue in FAR-FUTURE, weary, war-torn Earths, describes a declining, dilapidated country's centuries-long project of building an enormous SPACESHIP whose completion will transform the fortunes of everyone involved and mark a phase of rebirth; the project, however, is a shambles and a sham, and the novel closes in ENTROPY, despair and the sure threat of worse wars to come. *Out of the Mouth of the Dragon* (**1969**) shares the same mood and introduces the prosthetic weaponry that makes many of his characters virtually into CYBORGS, without making them any more capable of transforming ancient ways, ancient obsessions. Time wears very heavily in MSG's novels, and there seems no escape from its burden. Cultures, weapons, ideas and their embodiments in doom-ridden characters and decaying cities permeate his third novel, *The Day Star* (**1972**) as well as his longest to date, *The Siege of Wonder* (**1976**), in which all the themes of the previous books are wrapped up in a perversion and death of a magical unicorn. MSG's talents are copious, though his subject matter is constrained, and his fiction is memorable. [JC]

See also: MAGIC; MYTHOLOGY; SUPERNATURAL CREATURES.

GHOSE, ZULFIKAR (1935–). Pakistan-born British writer now living in the USA; of his various work in fiction and poetry, of sf interest is his "Incredible Brazilian" trilogy, of which two volumes have been published, *The Incredible Brazilian: The Native* (**1972**) and *The Beautiful Empire* (**1975**). Born in 17th-century Brazil, the protagonist grows up with and symbolizes his complex culture, and by the second volume, 200 years old, via a series of REINCARNATIONS, he is deeply involved in Brazil's transition into a fully fledged nation-state. Five of the 14 fantasy stories in *Statement Against Corpses* (coll. **1964**) by ZG and B.S. Johnson are by ZG. [JC]

GHOSTS *See* ESCHATOLOGY; SUPERNATURAL CREATURES.

GIANT BEHEMOTH, THE *See* BEHEMOTH, THE SEA MONSTER.

GIANT CLAW, THE Film (1957). Columbia. Directed by Fred F. Sears, starring Jeff Morrow, Mara Corday and Morris Ankrum. Screenplay by Samuel Newman and Paul Gangelin. 76 mins. B/w.

A giant bird from outer space decides to build a nest on Earth. It is conveniently protected by a force field, so that attempts to kill it at first prove futile, but eventually the field is nullified by scientists and all ends happily — though not for the bird. The implausibility of the script is reflected in the special effects. [JB]

GIANTS *See* GREAT AND SMALL.

GIBBONS, FLOYD (PHILLIP) (1886–1939). American writer, mostly of war stories; well known as a war correspondent. *The Red Napoleon* (**1929**) features a modern-day Mongol who conquers much of the world, miscegenating as he goes, but is defeated by the USA. [JC]

GIBBS, LEWIS Pseudonym of Joseph Walter Cove (1891–), a British writer whose sf novel, *Late Final* (**1951**), deals with a post-HOLOCAUST England, subsequent to World War Three. [JC] **Other works:** *Parable for Lovers* (**1934**).

GIBSON, COLIN (? –). New Zealand writer. His second novel, *The Pepper Leaf* (**1971**), is an sf tale of the NEAR FUTURE set in New Zealand; fearful of nuclear catastrophe, a small group of vegetarian nudists expose themselves to survival conditions, and their cruel interactions, described in a tense, allusive style, provide a model for, or allegory of, the human condition *in extremis*. [JC]

GIBSON, FLOYD *See* Paul CONRAD; VILLAINS.

GIESY, J(OHN) U(LRICH) (1877–1948). American physiotherapist and PULP writer, author of many stories, most not sf, in *Argosy* and *All-Story Weekly*, 1914–34. His "Jason Croft" or "Palos" trilogy reached book form as *Palos of the Dog Star Pack* (1918 *All-Story Weekly*; **1965**), *The Mouthpiece of Zitu* (1919 *All-Story Weekly*; **1965**) and *Jason, Son of Jason* (1921 *Argosy*; **1966**); Jason Croft gets to Sirius where he, and eventually his son, undergo many remarkable adventures. [JC] **See also:** LIFE ON OTHER WORLDS.

GILBERT, STEPHEN (1912). British writer whose sf novel *Ratman's Notebooks* (**1968**; vt *Willard*) is fundamentally a horror tale; Ratman conceives a special relationship with rats, comes precariously to dominate and commune with them, leads their vengeful incursions on the world at large; but there is a comeuppance. The book was filmed as *Willard* (1971). [JC] **Other works:** *The Landslide* (**1944**); *Monkeyface* (**1948**).

GILES, GORDON A. *See* Eando BINDER.

GILLESPIE, BRUCE (1947–). Australian sf fan and critic. Publisher of a FANZINE, SF COMMENTARY, where much of his critical writing on sf has appeared. Some of this has been published in *Philip K. Dick: Electric Shepherd* (critical anthology **1975**), which BG edited. [PR]

GILLIATT, PENELOPE (1932–). British writer, best known for her work outside the sf field; her sf novel, *One by One* (**1965**), depicts a NEAR-FUTURE London hit by a devastating plague. [JC]

GILLINGS, WALTER (1912–). English journalist and editor. He was active in British FANDOM in the early 1930s, which led to his editing the first true British sf magazine, TALES OF WONDER (1937–42). Immediately after the War he joined the author Benson HERBERT in creating the Utopian Publications imprint, which issued sf, fantasy and some soft-core pornography in cheap paperback format; publications included the AMERICAN FICTION and STRANGE TALES series. WG then edited the three issues of the short-lived magazine FANTASY (1946–7). After its demise he produced the influential fanzine FANTASY REVIEW (1947–50), and when in 1950 he was given the editorship of the new professional magazine SCIENCE FANTASY, the fanzine was incorporated as a section of the first two issues. John CARNELL took over the editorship of *Science Fantasy* with the third issue, Winter 1951/52, and WG dropped out of professional sf activities for a number of years. He came back as a regular columnist in VISION OF TOMORROW (1969–70) with an informative series about the history of sf

in the UK, and again as a columnist in SCIENCE FICTION MONTHLY (1974–6), where he also had a column under his old pseudonym of Thomas Sheridan, under which name he had also published the first of his three sf stories, "The Midget from Mars" (1938 *Tales of Wonder*). [PN]
See also: SF MAGAZINES.

GILLON, DIANA (PLEASANCE) (1915–). Writer whose sf novel with her husband Meir GILLON, *The Unsleep* (**1961**), deals with a DYSTOPIAN world of "Better Harmony" and the effects of an anti-sleep drug on the novel's two protagonists. [JC]

GILLON, MEIR (SELIG) (1907–). Writer and journalist, born in Transylvania, a lawyer working with the Palestine government 1941–6 and now resident in England. He has collaborated in an sf novel with his wife Diana GILLON (*who see for details*). [PN]

GILMAN, ROBERT CHAM *See* Alfred COPPEL.

GILMORE, ANTHONY Collaborative pseudonym used in ASTOUNDING STORIES OF SUPER-SCIENCE by Harry BATES and Desmond W. HALL, the editor and assistant editor of the magazine. Under this name they wrote the enthusiastically received "Hawk Carse" series, *Space Hawk* (1931–2 *ASF*; fix-up **1952**). Carse and his negro assistant, Friday, were intrepid space adventurers dedicated to driving the Yellow Peril, in the form of the evil Dr Ku Sui, from the spaceways. Bates later revived the character, without Hall's collaboration, in "The Return of Hawk Carse" (1942). [MJE]
See also: SPACE OPERA.

GINSBURG, MIRRA (? –). Russian-born American editor, writer and translator. She has translated a juvenile sf novel, *Lilit* (trans. as *Daughter of Night* **1974**) by Lydia Obukhova, the fantasy *Master i Margarita* (trans. as *The Master and Margarita* **1967**) by Mikhail BULKAKOV, *We* (**1920**; trans. **1924**) by Yevgeny ZAMIATIN in 1972 and *The Dragon: Fifteen Stories by Yevgeny Zamyatin* (coll. trans. from various sources **1967**). She has edited and translated the stories for three collections of Soviet sf (*see* RUSSIA): *Last Door to Aiya* (anth. **1968**); *The Ultimate Threshold* (anth. **1970**) and *The Air of Mars and Other Stories of Time and Space* (juvenile anth. **1976**). MG also edited *The Fatal Eggs and Other Soviet Satire* (anth. **1965**), which contains several fantasy stories. She has written books for very young children. [JC/PN]

GIR *See* Jean GIRAUD.

GIRAUD, JEAN (1938–). French COMICS artist. Uses the pseudonym Gir for his realistic Western strips (18 volumes)

Working as Moebius, Jean GIRAUD is one of the outstanding sf artists of today. This example comes from a comic strip in *Métal Hurlant*, 1976.

and Moebius for his fantasy, sf and humorous output. A brilliantly inventive cartoonist with an idiosyncratic sense of the absurd, JG is recognized as one of the major European exponents of the genre. *Arzach* (**1976**), a full-colour, textless strip, is an innovative blend of sf realism, black humour and imagination, and constitutes his major achievement. JG has worked with Christopher Foss and Alejandro Jodorowski on the project of filming Frank HERBERT's *Dune*. He is one of the founders of the sf comic-strip magazine MÉTAL HURLANT (*Heavy Metal* in the US edition). [MJ]
Other works: *Le bandard fou* ["The Mad Wanker"] (**1974**); *John Watercolor et sa redingote qui tue* ["John Watercolor and his Killer Overcoat"] (**1976**); *Cauchemar blanc* ["White Nightmare"] (**1977**).

GIRL FROM U.N.C.L.E., THE *See* MAN FROM U.N.C.L.E, THE.

GIRL IN THE MOON, THE *See* FRAU IM MOND, DIE.

GLADIATORERNA ["The Gladiators"] (vt THE PEACE GAME). Film (1968). Sandrews/New Line. Directed by Peter WATKINS, starring Arthur Pentelow,

Frederick Danner, Kenneth Lo and Bjorn Franzen. Screenplay by Nicholas Gosling and Peter Watkins. 105 mins. Colour.

Watkins uses his customary cinema-verité approach in this Swedish film about a future where large-scale warfare has been replaced by small teams of soldiers fighting it out under the guidance of a computer. He generates considerable righteous indignation over this, rather pointlessly in that such a system does not exist in reality and is unlikely ever to do so. The battle games are not well staged and the film lacks the impact of Watkins' other films, which include THE WAR GAME (1965), PRIVILEGE (1966) and PUNISHMENT PARK (1971). [JB]

GLAMIS, WALTER *See* Nat SCHACHNER.

GLASKIN, G(ERALD) M(ARCUS) (1923–). Australian writer, whose sf novel *A Change of Mind* (**1960**) concerns a hypnotic mind-transference between two men, with much emotional activity consequent upon the changeover. [JC]

GLEN AND RANDA Film (1971). UMC. Directed by Jim McBride, starring Steven Curry, Shelly Plimpton,

Woodrow Chambliss and Garry Goodrow. Screenplay by Lorenzo Mans, Rudolph Wurlitzer and Jim McBride. 94 mins. Colour.

The film opens with a shot of a naked girl and youth walking hand-in-hand through a dreamlike setting, but it soon becomes clear that this is not the Garden of Eden but a post-HOLOCAUST America. The young couple of the title drift through the shattered debris of civilization in an endless search for the mythical city of Metropolis, encountering other survivors along the way. Though made independently for very little money (it was shot on 16mm and later blown up to 35mm), it is more interesting than most of its kind, due to McBride's ingenuity in creating an evocatively desolate and sometimes beautiful setting out of existing landscapes and backgrounds. [JB]

GLOAG, JOHN (1896–). English writer, primarily in the fields of social history, architecture and design. His first sf novel, *Tomorrow's Yesterday* (1932), was strongly influenced by H.G. WELLS's *The Time Machine* (1895) and Olaf STAPLEDON's *Last and First Men* (1930). It is a satirical criticism of contemporary society as viewed by Man's successors, a race of cat people who have mastered time travel. Time manipulation featured prominently in several of his short stories and, in the form of a drug which could unlock ancestral memories, in the novel *99%* (1944). His other novels are chiefly concerned with the effect of new discoveries on society, again with strong satirical overtones. In *The New Pleasure* (1933) a chemical is used to heighten the sense of smell; in *Winter's Youth* (1934) a rejuvenation process adds 30 years to one's life; and in *Manna* (1940) a fungus that appeases hunger creates a lethargic population. When *Tomorrow's Yesterday* was reprinted, with slight revisions, in *First One and Twenty* (coll. 1946), which also incorporates 10 stories from *It Makes a Nice Change* (coll. 1938), JG's introduction, apart from quoting from correspondence with Olaf Stapledon, indicated that he was aware of the SF MAGAZINES and of sf FANDOM, but he held himself apart from that side of sf. Other fantasy stories appear in *Take One a Week* (coll. 1950).

After spending a long period away from sf, JG has recently published a series of historical fantasy novels, *Caesar of the Narrow Seas* (1969), *The Eagles Depart* (1973) and *Artorius Rex* (1977), which has been attracting comparison with the works of Susan COOPER. [JE]
See also: REINCARNATION.

GLYN JONES, RICHARD (1946–). British illustrator. He graduated from Sheffield University and went on to postgraduate work in experimental psychology. With no formal art training, RGJ began illustrating with underground comic strips. Along with Mal DEAN, he

Richard GLYN JONES was partly responsible for the visual sophistication of *New Worlds* in the late 1960s. This example is from *NW* Jan. 1970.

was the most important illustrator for NEW WORLDS under the editorship of Michael MOORCOCK. He was designer for the last few issues, and also for the paperback book series of *New Worlds*. RGJ is not prolific (he works in publishing and illustrates part time), but the quality of his work is equal to anything in b/w sf illustration today, with constantly surprising and inventive contrasts between dark and light spaces and a striking sense of design. He has also done book covers. [PN]

GLYNN, A(LAN) A(NTHONY) (? –). British writer whose PULP-style sf novel is *Plan for Conquest* (1963). [JC]

GNAEDINGER, MARY (1898–1976). American editor. An employee of the Frank A. MUNSEY chain of pulp magazines, MG was in 1939 made editor of the new magazine FAMOUS FANTASTIC MYSTERIES. She edited all 81 issues of the magazine, which eventually ceased publication in 1953. She also edited two companion magazines: FANTASTIC NOVELS, which was published 1940–41, and again 1948–51, and A. MERRITT's FANTASY (1949–50). The three titles were all devoted to reprinting old stories. [MJE]

GNOME PRESS American specialist publishing company founded by Martin GREENBERG and David A. KYLE. It was the most eminent of the fan publishers, starting in 1948 and surviving into the early 1960s. It published most of the major sf authors, and in cases such as Isaac ASIMOV's "Foundation" series was responsible for the manner in which they were collected into book form. Authors included Arthur C. CLARKE, Robert E. HOWARD, and C.L. MOORE. An associated imprint was Greenberg Publishers, and in 1958 Gnome bought out the stock of FANTASY PRESS. [MJE]

GOBLE, NEIL (? –). American air force major, technical writer, and author of a borderline sf novel, *Condition Green: Tokyo* (1967). His first published sf was "Master of None" for *ASF* in 1962. NG's

Asimov Analyzed (1972), published by MIRAGE PRESS, is a full-length study of Isaac ASIMOV, useful for facts and distinctly sub-critical in its opinions. [PN]

GODBER, NOËL (1881– ?). British writer of several light novels, the first of which, *Amazing Spectacles* (1931), boasts some sf content through the nature of a pair of spectacles which allow their wearer to see through clothing. [JC]
Other works: *Keep it Dark!* (1932).

GODFREY, HOLLIS (1874–1936). American writer in whose sf novel *The Man Who Ended War* (1908) the invention of a disintegrating wave forces a peace conference. [JC]
Other works: *Dave Morrell's Battery* (1912).

GODS AND DEMONS An interest in RELIGION has characterized sf from its earliest days, but it is not necessarily that which has fuelled the many sf stories about gods; in some cases it seems to be straightforward delusions of grandeur. The three qualities of godhead that most attract the sf writer are omniscience, omnipotence and the ability to create life, or even worlds. The latter is perhaps the most attractive, for that is precisely what the sf writer does himself, even if only in words. It is natural then that sf writers should often invent characters who have such powers.

Sf analogues to the One God are rare; sf universes with gods usually present them in larger numbers. One or two borderline sf works have considered the nature of the Christian God; Marie CORELLI apparently considered religious experience to be electric in nature, and postulated a God who manifests himself electrically in *A Romance of Two Worlds* (1886). In *A Voyage to Arcturus* (1920), David LINDSAY creates analogues of the more conventional Christian and Jewish stereotypes of God, only to dismiss them in every case as false and cheap, in a universe where only pain and personal striving is meaningful. In an almost forgotten work by H.G. WELLS, *God, the Invisible King* (1917), which is non-fiction, he declares a belief in a finite God, behind which exists an unknowable creator. Wells later repudiated this belief.

Analogues of Christ are very much more common in sf than those of God the Father, and are discussed under MESSIAHS.

God-stories in sf are nearly always rationalized, seldom mystical. A good many stories are based on the notion that a highly advanced society might seem godlike to a more primitive one, and in many tales of COLONIZATION OF OTHER WORLDS the narrative turns on the difficulties and responsibilities and seductions involved in being seen in this light, such is *Trudno byt' bogom* (1964 USSR; trans. as *Hard to be a God* 1973) by the brothers STRUGATSKI.

In many stories humans are seen as

confronted by some form of galactic intelligence or principle which is so high in the order of life as to seem godlike. A very early work by Clifford D. SIMAK, *The Creator* (1935; **1946**), features a world-creating alien; the same author's *A Choice of Gods* (**1972**) proposes a godlike galactic principle. Eric Frank RUSSELL's "Hobbyist" (1947) envisages a god who created most life in the galaxy for mere aesthetic pleasure. A benevolent being does the same thing in Olaf STAPLEDON's *Star Maker* (**1937**) in an altogether more serious treatment of the theme; like several sf writers Stapledon wished to dispose of the more anthropomorphic and wish-fulfilling aspects of Christianity while preserving a sense of cosmic meaning and pattern. *Solaris* (**1961** Poland; **1970**), by Stanislaw LEM, features a planetary intelligence whose powers are too great and enigmatic to be comprehended by humans who, although they are scientists, are tempted to see the planet as a god (maimed), especially in its power to raise (or reconstruct) the dead. Not all galactic intelligences are benevolent; Arthur C. CLARKE proposes a ravening "mad mind" in *The City and the Stars* (1948; exp. **1956**), but that was created by Man. James TIPTREE Jr has a godlike galaxy destroyer in *Up the Walls of the World* (**1978**).

The Clarke novel proposes an interesting idea that recurs quite often in sf, that a lower form of life might be able to create a higher. The idea takes many forms from the technological to the quasi-mystical. A number of stories concern COMPUTERS which attain godlike powers (*see that entry for a list*), sometimes alone, and sometimes through a transcendental fusion with their operators as in *Catchworld* (**1975**) by Chris BOYCE.

More metaphysical methods of god-creation are just as common. A.E. VAN VOGT, whose career has largely been devoted to creating SUPERMAN variants, created the ultimate (though not the most interesting) variant in *The Book of Ptath* (1943; **1947**; vt *Two Hundred Million A.D.*, vt *Ptath*), in which a god is created through the force of his followers' prayers, his power being proportional to their number. Gods are created in Philip José FARMER's *Night of Light* (1957; exp. **1966**), in the flesh, through the trans-cendental union of very good (or very bad) men once every seven years, when the sun emits a mysterious radiation. In Frank HERBERT's *The God Makers* (**1972**) humans create a god deliberately, using a blend of mystical, psychological and technological means; Herbert's writing in this case is not equal to his theme. Indeed god-stories generally meet severe literary problems in attempting to render transcendental experience through pulp sf stereotypes. One of the most interesting variants on the artificially created god theme is found in Philip K. DICK's *A Maze of Death* (**1970**), in which a series of quite mystifying false realities are created,

ultimately involving salvation through a godlike Intercessor; only late in the novel is it revealed that the realities and their god are all part of a construct imposed by the computer of a crippled starship.

The focus of interest in most sf god-stories is, paradoxically, not religious, though in the case of Dick and some others the question in METAPHYSICS of what is reality, and whether the ability to change it or create it is an attribute of godhead, is certainly present. The other main theme in this area is the simpler one (often taking the form of wish-fulfilment fantasies) of writing stories about what it would *feel* like to be a god. These stories are either studies in the exercise of power or psychological studies in the burden of responsibility, or both. The theme is an old one, for the work of the scientist has been seen by many as a usurpation of powers that are properly God's; such is the case in Mary SHELLEY's *Frankenstein* (**1818**; rev. 1831), where a scientist creates life but cannot create a soul to go with it. A number of variants on the theme have been amusing and sardonic. James Branch CABELL features several demiurges (world-makers) in his "Poictesme" fantasies, notably *The Silver Stallion* (**1926**); in his rather sterile, ironic fashion he seemed to suppose that creation rose either from boredom or from trivial ambition, and that the cosmic perspective of a god leads readily to a detachment which is seen by its victims as sadistic; universal justice is merely accidental and usually takes the form of the biter bit. Robert SHECKLEY in a sometimes similar cosmic mode has often proposed rather harassed and incompetent gods, overworked and put upon, as in *Dimension of Miracles* (**1968**). Much more seriously, in "Microcosmic God" (1941), Theodore STURGEON has an irresponsible scientist playing god to a miniature world, whose inhabitants he cruelly goads into accelerated technological development. Ursula K. LE GUIN examines the metaphysical aspects of the theme, in a manner reminiscent of Dick's work, in *The Lathe of Heaven* (**1971**), whose hero is able to bring false reality states into being by dreaming them and rendering them objectively true. *The Deep* (**1975**) by John CROWLEY features a medieval world created by one enigmatic alien, and peopled by a godlike second, who appears to be constructing an experiment in social engineering. All these works emphasize questions of responsibility.

The wish-fulfilment aspects of such stories are emphasized by two writers who (along with Van Vogt earlier on) have made a speciality of them: Philip José Farmer and Roger ZELAZNY. Many of Farmer's books are set on artificial worlds, notably the "Riverworld" books, whose emphasis is on the bafflement of the inhabitants, and the "Tierworld" series, whose emphasis is on the all-too-human qualities of the "gods" who

created them. Zelazny's gods are often, in fact, merely technologically advanced superhumans, who for not-always-explained reasons are able to take on "aspects" of godhead, often analogous to those of the gods of legend: the Greek myths in *This Immortal* (**1966**), the Hindu pantheon in *Lord of Light* (**1967**) and the Egyptian pantheon in *Creatures of Light and Darkness* (**1969**). His *Isle of the Dead* (**1969**) features a feud between gods, and the "Amber" series a complex series of reality changes brought about by quasi-gods in worlds which are constantly changing copies of some Platonic original. Both Farmer and Zelazny, especially the latter, tend to work through juxtaposing the sublime and the ridiculous, the protagonists' great power going along with psychological immaturity and a general tendency to behave badly.

Philip K. Dick's obsession with godhood is the most devious and difficult to pin down in genre sf; it runs through much of his work. *Our Friends from Frolix 8* (**1970**) and *Galactic Pot-Healer* (**1969**) both feature aliens who are quasi-gods, and their effect on men; *The Three Stigmata of Palmer Eldritch* (**1964**), as the title suggests, is about a god-being, once a businessman but now inhuman and metallic, whose menacing reality-changes seem almost to be beyond good and evil; these Dick books and others confront ordinary people with dreams or nightmares of cosmic manipulation; they carry a great emotional charge.

Much more straightforward gods appear in that small group of books whose genesis goes back to the idea in medieval astrology that each of the planets has a tutelary spirit. Such is the case in C.S. LEWIS's trilogy about Ransom, whose inspiration is directly Christian. The aliens in the novella "If the Stars are Gods" (1974), the title story of the fix-up novel of the same name (**1977**) by Gordon EKLUND and Gregory BENFORD, believe that the universe is controlled by gods located in suns (an idea to be found also in William Blake's poetry); a less mystical and transcendent, earlier version of the same theme is found in the living stars of Frank Herbert's *Whipping Star* (**1970**) and its sequel *The Dosadi Experiment* (**1977**).

The concept of demons and devils is equally common in sf, but usually at quite a trivial level; they tend to be seen simply as frightening and malicious entities, as in fantasy generally, derived from medieval theories of hell. There are a number of demonology stories with sf elements, such as the time-warping demon in Anthony BOUCHER's "Snulbug" (1941), or the other-dimensional alien blood-drinker in Henry KUTTNER's "Call Him Demon" (1946). Demons proper often appear in SWORD AND SORCERY; demonic creatures of darkness were all in the day's work to Robert E. HOWARD's Conan. Particularly unpleasant aliens are often given demonic form (sometimes with talk about racial memory) in genre sf stories, as in Van Vogt's second published story "Discord in Scarlet" (1939), later incorporated into *The Voyage of the Space Beagle* (fix-up **1950**), and Keith LAUMER's *A Plague of Demons* (**1965**), both truly nasty creations. A more inventive variant on the theme is found in Arthur C. Clarke's *Childhood's End* (1950; exp. **1953**), in which mankind is confronted by aliens shaped exactly like the Devil (memories of a previous alien visit explain his bat-winged image in Christian mythology), whose characters, however, turn out to be mournfully paternalistic. Several sf-oriented fantasies by HARD-SF writers have imagined that hell and its demons are real, and created a kind of quasi-scientific rationale for them. An early example is Robert A. HEINLEIN's "The Devil Makes the Law" (1940), which was reprinted with a variant title as the second title story of *Waldo and Magic, Inc.* (coll. **1950**); more recent examples are *Operation Chaos* (1956–9 *FSF*; fix-up **1971**) by Poul ANDERSON and the DANTE-pastiche *Inferno* (**1975**) by Larry NIVEN and Jerry POURNELLE. The best-known story of Norvell W. PAGE is "But Without Horns" (1940), which uses demonic imagery in a story of a telepathic mutant. Isaac ASIMOV's "Hell-Fire" (1956) makes a moral point neatly enough when a slow-motion film of a nuclear explosion shows the features of the Devil leering momentarily out of the mushroom cloud.

If there is an overall point to be found in sf stories of gods and demons it is that when we are faced with the unknowable we are likely to anthropomorphize it in terms of our own mythologies, or conversely, that our mythologies once had a rational if alien explanation. [PN]
See also: ADAM AND EVE; FANTASY; GOTHIC SF; MAGIC; MONSTERS; SUPERNATURAL CREATURES.

GODWIN, FRANCIS (1562–1633). English bishop and writer, most noted for his striking description of a lunar UTOPIA in his posthumously and anonymously published *The Man in the Moone: or a Discourse of a Voyage Thither by Domingo Gonsales the Speedy Messenger* (**1638**). The flight to the MOON, accomplished in a swan drawn flying machine, is described with some realism; FG cautiously allows that Copernicus may have been right in some of his theories. Domingo Gonsales reappears as a character in sf by CYRANO DE BERGERAC. FG's book was reprinted many times in the following centuries, and was perhaps the most influential work of PROTO SF. It is available in *The Man in the Moone* (anth. **1971**) ed. Faith K. PIZOR and T. Allan Comp. [PN]
See also: FANTASTIC VOYAGES.

GODWIN, TOM (1915–). American writer who began publishing sf with

"The Gulf Between" in *ASF* in 1953, and who soon published (also in *ASF*) the story for which he is still best known, "The Cold Equations" (1954), in which a girl stowaway on a precisely payloaded spaceship is jettisoned by the two-man crew because her extra weight would make disaster inevitable, dooming the space colony to which the ship was heading. TG's first two novels, *The Survivors* (**1958**; vt *Space Prison*) and its sequel *The Space Barbarians* (**1964**), tell of the abandoned human survivors of an alien prison planet who wait 200 years for revenge, then undergo SPACE-OPERA adventures involving a demoralized Earth and telepathic allies. *Beyond Another Sun* (**1971**) is an ANTHROPOLOGICAL sf novel in which aliens observe Man on another planet. TG has produced relatively little sf; what he has written has clarity of conception, considerable narrative verve and sometimes rather sentimental characterization. [JC]
See also: COLONIZATION OF OTHER WORLDS; CRIME AND PUNISHMENT; GRAVITY; LIFE ON OTHER WORLDS; PHYSICS.

GODZILLA, KING OF THE MONSTERS (vt **GODZILLA** USA) Film (1954 Japan as *Gojira*; exp. with new footage 1956). Toho/Embassy. Directed by Inoshiro Honda, starring Raymond Burr, Akira Takarada and Akihiko Hirata. Screenplay by Takeo Murata and Inoshiro Honda, based on a story by Shigeru Kayama. 98 mins (later cut to 81). B/w.

This was the first of a series of Japanese films featuring Godzilla, a 400-foot-tall reptile. Originally called *Gojira* in Japan, the film was bought by an American company which released it internationally in 1956, including extra footage starring Raymond Burr. This first *Godzilla* film was basically a conventional monster movie (nuclear radiation revives a giant prehistoric reptile in the Pacific Ocean which starts to devastate Tokyo) but over the years the sequels have become increasingly esoteric.

Until his recent death the special effects supervisor in the *Godzilla* series was Eiji Tsuburaya. Originally the Toho Studio effects were fairly impressive, but they have become cheaper and more perfunctory. Unlike Willis H. O'BRIEN's and Ray HARRYHAUSEN's animated monsters, Godzilla was achieved using a man in a suit and smaller mechanized miniatures. [JB]

GOG Film (1954). Ivan Tors/United Artists. Directed by Ivan Tors, starring Richard Egan, Constance Dowling and Herbert Marshall. Screenplay by Tom Taggart, story by Ivan Tors. 85 mins. Colour.
In this competently-made film experiments are being carried out on people in a highly secret underground laboratory to determine whether manned space flight is possible. Various pieces of

equipment start to behave in a lethal fashion — a man is killed in a centrifuge, another is frozen to death in a high-altitude chamber, a third is killed by high-frequency sound. Finally two experimental robots, Gog and Magog, go out of control. These accidents turn out to be the work of a foreign power which has taken over the lab's machinery by means of a special ray transmitted from a high-flying aircraft. [JB]

GOJIRA See GODZILLA, KING OF THE MONSTERS.

GOLD Film (1934). UFA. Directed by Karl Hartl, starring Hans Albers, Lien Deyers, Michael Bohnen and Brigitte Helm. Screenplay by Rolf E. Vanloo. 120 mins. B/w.
This film was made by the same team that made *F.P.1* ANTWORTET NICHT two years earlier (though with a different script-writer). It is more spectacular than *F.P.1* and also more nationalistic. The hero becomes the prisoner of a megalomaniac British scientist who believes he can transmute base metal into gold and is prepared to do so at any cost. The laboratory sequences, with all their dazzling electrical effects, are impressive, but the film as a whole is somewhat leaden. (A French language version was made at the same time with a different cast, though Brigitte Helm appeared in both.) [JB]

GOLD, H(ORACE) L. (1914–). A writer and editor of dual Canadian/US nationality, HLG began his sf career with several sales to ASTOUNDING STORIES in the mid-1930s, the first of them "Inflexure" (1934). At that time he wrote under the pseudonyms Clyde Crane Campbell and Leigh Keith, necessitated, he has said, by anti-Semitism on the part of the publishers. After a hiatus, he returned to the magazine under his own name with "A Matter of Form" (1938). He became a regular contributor to UNKNOWN with such stories as "Trouble With Water" (1939), an enjoyable, humorous, MAGIC story, and "None But Lucifer" (1939), a collaboration with L. Sprague DE CAMP. He was later assistant to Mort WEISINGER on the magazines CAPTAIN FUTURE, STARTLING STORIES and THRILLING WONDER STORIES (1939–41), from which he moved on to true detective magazines, comics and radio scripts. In 1950 he started GALAXY SCIENCE FICTION, which from the outset he made into one of the leading sf magazines. Afflicted with acute agoraphobia as a result of his wartime experiences, HLG edited the magazine from his apartment, doing much of his work by telephone. The emphasis of *Gal.* reflected his interest in PSYCHOLOGY and SOCIOLOGY, as well as HUMOUR; like John W. CAMPBELL he is credited with suggesting many ideas which his contributors turned into famous stories. He also had a reputation for overediting.

An interesting companion magazine, BEYOND FANTASY FICTION, lasted for 10 issues, edited by HLG, 1953–5. He also edited GALAXY SCIENCE FICTION NOVELS, an sf and fantasy reprint series of variable quality in the same format as *Gal*. Later still he became editor of IF, when it was taken over by *Gal*.'s owner. He edited a number of anthologies culled from the pages of *Gal*.: *Galaxy Reader of Science Fiction* (anth. **1952**; UK edition contains 13 stories out of 33); *Second Galaxy Reader of Science Fiction* (anth. **1954**; vt *Galaxy Science Fiction Omnibus* UK, omits 11 stories); *The Third Galaxy Reader* (anth. **1958**); *Five Galaxy Short Novels* (anth. **1958**); *The Fourth Galaxy Reader* (anth. **1959**); *The World That Couldn't Be and Eight Other Novelets from Galaxy* (anth. **1959**); *Bodyguard and Four Other Short Novels from Galaxy* (anth. **1960**); *The Fifth Galaxy Reader* (anth. **1961**); *The Sixth Galaxy Reader* (anth. **1962**). Another anthology is *The Weird Ones* (anth. **1962**). HLG retired through ill health in 1961. Some of his stories were collected in *The Old Die Rich* (coll. **1955**). *What Will They Think of Last?* (**1976**) is a selection of his editorials from *Gal*. with an autobiographical postscript.

HLG used two other pseudonyms on magazine stories: Richard Storey in 1943 and Dudley Dell in 1951. [MJE]
See also: SUPERNATURAL CREATURES.

GOLDEN AGE OF SF It has been said, cynically, that the Golden Age of sf can be dated back exactly to when the reader was 14 years old. Certainly there is no objective measure by which we can say that the sf of any one period was notably superior to that of any other. None the less, in conventional usage (at least within FANDOM) older readers have tended to refer quite precisely to the years 1938–46 as sf's Golden Age, and younger readers, though not necessarily convinced, have not yet wholly jettisoned the term.

There is little argument about when the Golden Age began, though some argument about when it finished. The term is nearly always used of genre magazine sf, and it is almost always seen as referring to the period ushered in by John W. CAMPBELL Jr's assumption of the editorship of ASTOUNDING STORIES in Oct. 1937. Within a few years Campbell had managed not only to take over many of the best (and youngest) working writers of the period, such as Clifford D. SIMAK, Jack WILLIAMSON, L. Ron HUBBARD, L. Sprague DE CAMP, Henry KUTTNER and C.L. MOORE (the last three often in his companion magazine UNKNOWN), but to develop such new writers as Lester DEL REY, Eric Frank RUSSELL (who had a couple of stories in *ASF* before Campbell arrived), Theodore STURGEON, and especially the big three, Robert A. HEINLEIN, Isaac ASIMOV and A.E. VAN VOGT. These were the writers who were to dominate genre sf until their younger

contemporaries Alfred BESTER, James BLISH, C.M. KORNBLUTH, Ray BRADBURY and Frederick POHL had undergone their protracted apprenticeships and emerged as the new forces of the 1950s. But, of course, as soon as these new names are evoked, it becomes clear that it is difficult to say in what sense the Golden Age could be said to have stopped in the 1940s. Certainly Campbell's *ASF* was by that time receiving quite high-class competition from STARTLING STORIES, and a few years later from GALAXY SCIENCE FICTION and the MAGAZINE OF FANTASY AND SCIENCE FICTION, and by the 1950s was coming to be seen as a force for conservatism in magazine sf, rather than its spearhead. The end of the Golden Age may have had more reality, then, for devotees of *ASF* than for those who were more eclectic in what they read.

The story of genre sf (*see* HISTORY OF SF *and* SF MAGAZINES) has two high points, the first being Hugo GERNSBACK's founding of the first sf magazine in 1926, and the second being Campbell's taking over of *ASF*. Gernsback's gesture had no visible effect on the quality of sf; it merely served to concentrate what was often pretty terrible PULP writing into a more specialist market. Under Campbell, standards certainly did improve, dramatically.

A balanced reading of genre sf since Campbell would probably see it as becoming progressively more mature and sophisticated; it would also see (as sf became more popular) a greater amount of mechanical reworking of the Golden Age themes by hack-writers, whose increasing numbers may have partly obscured the steady improvement in the upper echelons of the genre. Certainly there were slack periods, the late 1950s being one such, but only a one-eyed and rather elderly nostalgia could seriously see the period of the Second World War as marking a high point in sf which has not been reached again. There is a very strong case for saying that the true Golden Age of sf is now; that the decade 1968–78 has seen the publication of more sf works of the first rank than any previous decade. There are signs that the so-called Golden Age writers are at last beginning to lose their secure and continued grip on the sf market. The persistent reprinting (usually in a four-year cycle) in paperback of the "classics" of the Golden Age have kept Asimov, Heinlein and Van Vogt very much in the consciousness of successive generations of young readers, but experience in teaching such young readers in sf classes suggests that with each passing year their flaws become more obtrusive, even to a relatively uncritical readership.

It is interesting to turn to one of the anthologies of Golden Age sf, such as *Adventures in Time and Space* (anth. **1946**) ed. Raymond J. HEALY and Francis McCOMAS, the relevant sections of *The Astounding-Analog Reader* (anth. **1973** in

two vols) ed. Harry HARRISON and Brian W. ALDISS or *The Science Fiction Hall of Fame* (anth. **1970**) ed. Robert SILVERBERG, and see how banal the writing and retrospectively creaky the plot devices often seem. Isaac Asimov's "Nightfall" (1941) retains the potency of its original idea, but the working out is laboured; Lester del Rey's "Helen O'Loy" (1938) oozes a rather treacly sentiment and is patronizingly sexist as well. These can surely be considered "classics" (as they are) only when seen through the rosy mists of boyhood or girlhood memories. The soaring ideas of Golden Age sf were only too often clad in the impoverished vocabulary derived from pulp magazines which had always been aimed at the lowest common denominator of a mass market. We should not let nostalgia blur the undoubted fact that by 1940 most sf of any real literary value (H.G. WELLS, Aldous HUXLEY and others) had nothing to do with the pulp magazines. The Golden Age glittered only in comparison to the low standards within genre magazine sf.

None the less, sf would never be the same again after the years 1938–46; the wild, romantic and yearning imaginations of a handful of genre writers, mostly very young, had laid down whole strata of new concepts which enriched the field greatly. In those years the science component of sf became more scientific and the fiction component more assured. This was the largest quantum jump in quality in the history of the genre, and in gratitude to that, perhaps the term Golden Age should be enshrined. Certainly the strictures of literary critics 40 years on will be no more than a distant, shrill, complaining whine on the ears of besotted devotees of the period, among whom can be numbered the authors of many of the histories and commentaries on sf. The Golden Age does not lack defenders. [PN]

GOLDEN ARGOSY, THE *See* ARGOSY, THE.

GOLDIN, STEPHEN (? –). American writer, who began publishing sf with "The Girls on USSF 193" for *If* in 1965 and was runner-up for a NEBULA award for best short story with "The Last Ghost" (1971). His novels have been generally routine adventures, and he is best known for the ongoing series of E.E. "Doc" SMITH spin-offs, the "Family D'Alembert" sequence. The first volume, *The Imperial Stars* (1964 *If*; exp. **1976**) is directly based on an E.E. Smith story; subsequent volumes, *Stranglers' Moon* (**1976**), *The Clockwork Traitor* (**1977**) and *Getaway World* (**1977**), are based on the initial premise. SG also edited a thematic original anthology, *The Alien Condition* (anth. **1973**), and has been editor of SFWA BULLETIN. [JC]
Other works: *Herds* (**1975**); *Caravan* (**1975**); *Scavenger Hunt* (**1976**); *Finish*

Line (**1976**); *Assault on the Gods* (**1977**). **See also:** SPACE OPERA.

GOLDING, LOUIS (1895–1958). English writer, several of whose popular novels are on Jewish themes. *The Doomington Wanderer* (coll. **1934**; vt *This Wanderer* USA) contains several romantically couched fantasy tales. *The Pursuer* (**1936**) sets a psychological parable of a man obsessed by his Conradian "shadow" in an ALTERNATE WORLD very similar to our own. [JC] **Other works:** *The Miracle Boy* (**1927**), a religious fantasy; *Honey for the Ghost* (**1949**), a fantasy.

GOLDING, WILLIAM (GERALD) (1911–). British writer. He wrote a pre-War book of *Poems* (**1934**), but was a provincial schoolmaster till the publication of his first and best-known novel, *Lord of the Flies* (**1954**) (later filmed as LORD OF THE FLIES), a superficially simple story about a group of schoolchildren trapped on an ISLAND when their plane is shot down and suffering DEVOLUTION into tribal savagery; beyond its obvious allegorizing repudiation of the schoolboy heroism in R.M. Ballantyne's *The Coral Island* (**1858**), it makes a complex utterance about the darkness of the human condition, and the shapes human nature takes when "free" to do so. Only the enabling frame of the book (a world war) is NEAR-FUTURE sf. WG's second novel, *The Inheritors* (**1955**), written in part as a reaction to H.G. WELLS's "The Grisly Folk" (1921), could be seen as ANTHROPOLOGICAL sf; it views through the eyes of a Neanderthal the morally ambiguous triumph of Cro-Magnon man. *Pincher Martin* (**1956**; vt *The Two Deaths of Pincher Martin* USA) is as much sf as Ambrose BIERCE's "An Occurrence at Owl Creek Bridge", with which it has frequently been compared. Pincher Martin, cast on a tiny rock in the ocean, seems to survive desperately and defiantly, but the ending makes it possible to read this survival as a last flicker of pre-purgatorial consciousness; the rock he is cast upon has the same shape as a diseased tooth he touches constantly with his tongue. WG's contribution to *Sometime, Never* (anth. **1956**), a book also including stories by John WYNDHAM and Mervyn PEAKE, is "Envoy Extraordinary", a long tale subsequently made into a play, *The Brass Butterfly* (**1958**), about Alexandrian Greek inventor Phanocles' attempts to get his steam engine, gun, pressure-cooker and printing-press accepted by a Roman emperor, who in refusing these gifts proves philosophically wiser than the inventor. The story also appears in *The Scorpion God* (coll. **1971**), along with two fantasies. *The Spire* (**1964**) is an elaborately metaphorical historical novel about the construction of a 400-foot spire on a medieval church; while not sf *per se*

it involves a good deal of early science, and more importantly evokes the dangers, the hubris and the joy of Man undertaking ambitious technological feats in the face of heaven, and in this respect sums up much of the emotional complexities implicit in sf generally.

WG's relation to sf is as tangential as his relation to the conventional mainstream novel; especially in his early works, he treads the line between allegory and novel with astonishingly fruitful results. [JC/PN] **About the author:** *The Art of William Golding* (**1965**) by Bernard S. Oldsey and Stanley Weintraub. Critical literature on WG is large and increasing. **See also:** CONCEPTUAL BREAKTHROUGH; DISCOVERY AND INVENTION; HISTORY IN SF; ORIGIN OF MAN; SOCIOLOGY; TECHNOLOGY.

GOLDSMITH, CELE (1933–). US editor. In 1956–8 CG was first assistant editor and then managing editor of AMAZING STORIES and FANTASTIC under Paul W. FAIRMAN. She became editor of both magazines in Dec. 1958, and remained in charge until Jun. 1965, when both magazines were sold and ceased for a time to publish original stories. Under her editorship the quality of the magazines improved markedly; CG was prepared to encourage experiment and to introduce new writers. Among the authors whose first published stories appeared in her magazines were Thomas M. DISCH, Roger ZELAZNY and Ursula K. LE GUIN, who described her as "as enterprising and perceptive an editor as the science fiction magazines ever had" (in *The Wind's Twelve Quarters*, 1975). CG married in 1964, becoming Cele G. Lalli. [MJE] **See also:** SF MAGAZINES; WOMEN.

GOODCHILD, GEORGE (1885–1969). British thriller and adventure writer and playwright. His first sf novel, *The Eye of Abu* (**1927**), an Atlantean LOST-WORLD novel relating the discovery of the Fountain of Youth, appeared as by Alan Dare. As GG he followed this with the marginally sf *The Monster of Grammont* (**1927**), *The Emperor of Hallelujah Island* (**1930**), about a kingdom of criminals. *A Message from Space* (**1931**) and *Doctor Zil's Experiment* (**1953**), which depicts a distant future when cassava plants are Earth's dominant species. [JE]

GORDON, DAVID See Randall GARRETT.

GORDON, MILLARD VERNE See Donald A. WOLLHEIM.

GORDON, REX Pseudonym most frequently used by British writer S(tanley) B(ennett) Hough (1917–) for his sf work, though he has also published some under his own name, notably the borderline-sf thriller *Extinction Bomber* (**1956**), and *Beyond the Eleventh Hour*

(**1961**), a story of atomic holocaust. As RG, he began publishing sf with *Utopia 239* (**1955**), in which an at first appalling but ultimately engaging future anarchic society is envisaged. *No Man Friday* (**1956**; vt *First on Mars* USA), RG's strongest book, retells Daniel DEFOE's *Robinson Crusoe*, this time on Mars, in quietly convincing terms, though the science is sometimes shaky. (The film ROBINSON CRUSOE ON MARS gives RG no credit, though the storyline bears notable resemblances). *First to the Stars* (**1959**; vt *The Worlds of Eclos* UK) is thematically similar: a crash-landed man and woman try to survive and breed without any cultural aids at all. *First Through Time* (**1962**; vt *The Time Factor* UK) is a TIME-TRAVEL thriller that asks most of the standard questions about predestination. Throughout his career RG has shown a strong grasp of human motivation that jars against a rather superficial use of sf themes and scientific knowledge in general. [JC/PN] **Other works:** *Utopia Minus X* (**1966**; vt *The Paw of God* UK); *The Yellow Fraction* (**1969**). **See also:** ISLANDS; MARS.

GORDON, SPIKE See John Russell FEARN.

GORDON, STUART Pseudonym of Scottish writer Richard Gordon (1947–), who also writes as Alex R. Stuart. He began publishing sf with "A Light in the Sky" for *NW* in 1965; his first sf novel, *Time Story* (**1972**), describes a criminal's attempt to flee retribution via TIME TRAVEL. His trilogy, *One-Eye* (**1973**), *Two-Eyes* (**1974**) and *Three-Eyes* (**1975**), is set in an apocalyptic post-HOLOCAUST land where humanity fights a losing battle against genetic decay, and the MUTANT One-Eye triggers off the forces of chaos; in increasingly elaborated prose (SG's main fault as a writer being an inadequate control over imagery) the trilogy proceeds to a complex self-confrontation of mankind. The books have vigour, though the use of genre fantasy/romance materials, slightly science-fictionalized, is stereotyped. [JC] **Other works:** *Suaine & The Crow-God* (**1975**). Of the several novels as by Alex R. Stuart, *The Devil's Rider* (**1973**) and *The Bike from Hell* (**1973**) have a fantasy/ sf component.

GORER, GEOFFREY (EDGAR) (1905–). British anthropologist and writer, whose *Nobody Talks Politics* (**1936**) is a SATIRE on British politics of the 1930s as seen through the eyes of a young man awoken from a 10-year trance; an Epilogue is set in the NEAR FUTURE. [JC]

GORGO Film (1959). King Bros/MGM. Directed by Eugene Lourie, starring Bill Travers, William Sylvester and Vincent Winter. Screenplay by John Loring and

Daniel Hyatt, based on a story by Eugene Lourie and Daniel Hyatt. 78 mins. Colour.

A prehistoric reptile is captured off a small island in the Irish Sea. Despite warnings by the inhabitants of the island the monster is taken to London and put on show. But the 30-foot-high creature turns out to be a mere infant, as everyone discovers when its 150-foot mother comes to collect it, demolishing much of London in the process. Good use is made of locations, and there are interesting special effects by Tom Howard. The monsters are achieved by the man-in-a-suit technique rather than by animated models, but are effective nonetheless. [JB]

GOTHIC SF In current usage a "Gothic" is a romantic novel with a strong element of the mysterious or the supernatural, usually featuring the persecution of a woman in an isolated locale, but this is a restricted and specialized use of the word which has nothing to do with sf. The term "Gothic" entered critical terminology with the publication of *The Castle of Otranto* **(1765)** by Horace Walpole, which was subtitled "A Gothic Story". The word, as in architecture, originally referred to a medieval style; although the middle ages had been thought of as barbaric for much of the 18th century, a reaction had set in, and a nostalgia had developed for the romantic splendours of an idealized middle ages that never existed. Gothic novels in imitation of Walpole's ghostly tale became quite common as the century drew to a close; indeed their popularity was closely allied to the growth of romantic literature generally.

The Gothic may be seen as a reaction to the emphasis on reason which prevailed in the intellectual world of the 18th century. In a world where Newton had explained the mechanics of the Solar System, Linnaeus had shown how plants and animals could be logically classified, Adam Smith had written of the apparently immutable laws of economics, and sermons in church regularly pictured God as a kind of master watchmaker who had wound the universe up and left it to tick like a perfectly well-regulated mechanism, some room needed to be left for mystery, the marvellous, the inexplicable. The movement was probably given impetus at the beginning of the 19th century by science itself becoming remystified through all the work being done on the strange forces of electro-magnetism, and social stability itself seeming less certain with a proliferation of political revolutions across the Western world.

Such is the background against which Mary SHELLEY's *Frankenstein* **(1818**; rev. 1831) should be read. With this book, and a little later the works of Edgar Allan POE, the use of science in fiction was becoming assimilated into a literary movement which emphasized mystery over knowledge, and emphasized also the dangers of Man trespassing in a territory which is rightfully God's. The linking of science with the Gothic may have been partly a historical accident, and the balance was soon to be partly rectified by the sometimes laboured common sense of Jules VERNE (though even he produced a Gothic hero in Captain Nemo), but it certainly had repercussions in sf which have not yet died away. Brian W. ALDISS in his critical work *Billion Year Spree* **(1973)** argues that sf "is characteristically cast in the Gothic or post-Gothic mould". That may be putting it too strongly, but Aldiss's view is certainly a useful antidote to the commoner views that sf is a literature either of technology or of UTOPIAS and anti-Utopias (*see* DEFINITIONS OF SF).

Certainly from Mary Shelley's day to now, much of sf has been devoted to secrets, to inexplicable violence and wildness lurking beneath the veneer of civilization, and to the ALIEN and the monstrous bursting in on us from the outside; Gothic sf emphasizes danger, and sees us fooling ourselves by imagining our world to be well-lit and comfortable while ignoring that outside all is darkness. Gothic sf characteristically sprinkles a mild dressing of quasi-scientific talk over these fears, which in spirit are quite opposed to the outlook of the scientist. The prototype is perhaps Robert Louis STEVENSON's *The Strange Case of Dr. Jekyll and Mr. Hyde* **(1886)**, which can readily be thought of as an allegory of the violent subconscious struggling with the conscious mind, in its story of a respectable doctor whose *alter ego* is a brutish sensualist and a living monument to the reality of original sin. Here we have quite literally the everyday surface concealing the menacing depths. Other sf writers of the 19th century who worked in the Gothic mode are Bulwer LYTTON, Ambrose BIERCE and Arthur MACHEN.

In the 20th century, the Gothic mode became partly hived off into the genre of occult/horror, but it never lost its kinship with sf, especially genre sf. WEIRD TALES was the archetypally Gothic PULP MAGAZINE, and its authors very often wrote sf too. H.P. LOVECRAFT, of course, is as pure an instance of the Gothic writer as can be found in this century, but some of the same qualities can be found in writers who were much more closely associated with sf than Lovecraft ever was. Almost two-thirds of all sf films (*see*

The essence of GOTHIC imagery is seen in Harry Clarke's illustration to "The Black Cat" by Edgar Allan Poe.

CINEMA) are pure Gothic, especially the monster movies. PARANOIA in sf nearly always falls into the Gothic mode. It is so easy to find Gothic elements in even the most celebrated writers of sf, that there is little point in elaborating in terms of a long list. The metallic reality changer in Philip K. DICK's *The Three Stigmata of Palmer Eldritch* (**1964**), the inexplicable reincarnations brought about by the sentient planet in Stanislaw LEM's *Solaris* (**1961** Poland; trans. **1970**), the killer-artefact on the Moon in Algis BUDRYS's *Rogue Moon* (**1960**), the wizened manipulators of Frederik POHL and C.M. KORNBLUTH's *Gladiator at Law* (**1955**), the alien invaders of Robert A. HEINLEIN's *The Puppet Masters* (**1951**), the enigmatic Lithians of James BLISH's *A Case of Conscience* (1953; exp. **1958**), all, with a thousand others, are imaginative creations in the Gothic tradition. "Who Goes There?" (1938) by John W. CAMPBELL Jr is an almost perfect example of the species. The mysteries of the giant spaceship in Arthur C. CLARKE's *Rendezvous with Rama* (**1973**) are technological in appearance, but in their resonant unknowableness they too are pure Gothic.

There has always been a tension in sf between the classical desire for order and understanding and the romantic desire that the universe should continue to stretch our minds and keep our feelings alive by holding secrets. This latter desire is the Gothic, and its co-existence with the rational, in not only the works of Arthur C. Clarke but also those of most other major sf writers of our century, is not a paradox; the resulting area of disturbance is the seeding-ground from which sf derives its continued vitality and vivacity. [PN]

See also; CONCEPTUAL BREAKTHROUGH; FANTASY; GODS AND DEMONS; HISTORY OF SF; SUPERNATURAL CREATURES.

GOTLIEB, PHYLLIS (FAY) (1926–). Canadian writer, probably best known for her poetry. She took an MA with the University of Toronto in English language and literature, and is married to a professor of computer science, whom she credits for assistance on her second sf novel. She began publishing sf with "A Grain of Manhood" for *Fantastic* in 1959, but has not been prolific in the field, and her reputation is based mainly on her first novel, *Sunburst* (**1964**), which has been translated several times; it treats feelingly of the growth of a connected group of mutant children, of their harrowing difficulties, of the *gestalt* concord they arrive at, and of their coming to (a somewhat overplotted) accord with the surrounding world. The novella "Son of the Morning" (1972) was shortlisted for the NEBULA award. Her second novel, *O Master Caliban!* (**1976**), laid on a planet set aside for environmental experiments, sets a number of unusual children and ALIENS

on a trek to confront and defeat the sentient computer complex which has seized power from the young protagonist's scientist father; despite the youth of its cast, it is not a juvenile. [JC]

GOTSCHALK, FELIX C. (1929–). American writer and psychologist, who began publishing sf with stories for *New Dimensions 4* (anth. **1974**) ed. Robert SILVERBERG. In a relatively short time he has established a reputation as a newer author of note. Though it could be argued that his stories have more surface than substance, in his first novel, *Growing Up in Tier 3000* (**1975**), the surface is quite remarkable, even though the plot moves with some difficulty; transfiguring a tale of DYSTOPIAN life in an energy-quarantined, savagely competitive, complexly automated future society, FCG irradiates his text with a stunning linguistic display in which the emotional and physiological parameters applicable to the human being in isolation and in his relations to the social world are constantly articulated by the protagonists in a flow of brilliant jargon, with the result that existence and the linguistic perception of existence become identical. The effect is exhilarating and also rather terrifying. [JC]

See also: ABSURDIST SF; CITIES; LINGUISTICS; TABOOS.

GOTTESMAN, S.D. Pseudonym used on magazine stories by Cyril KORNBLUTH, alone or in collaboration with Frederik POHL, and twice with both Pohl and Robert A.W. LOWNDES.

GOTTLIEB, HINKO (1886?– ?). Yugoslav writer, editor and lawyer, whose sf novel in Serbo-Croat, translated as *The Key to the Great Gate* (**1947**), was composed in an Italian concentration camp (though the manuscript was destroyed and had to be reconstructed later); in it, an imprisoned scientist by expanding and contracting Einsteinian space, dazzles and befuddles his Nazi guards and gradually becomes an effective symbol of human dignity and the freedom of the spirit. [JC]

GOULART, RON(ALD JOSEPH) (1933–). American writer, born of a Portuguese father and an Italian mother, in California, where he lived until the late 1960s and made the setting for much of his sf. After graduation he worked in an advertising agency, and has recorded its influence on the forming of his concise, polished style. He published his first sf piece, "Letters to the Editor", with *FSF* in 1952, and by the time of his first sf novel, *The Sword Swallower* (**1968**), he had already published widely, most notably in *FSF*. *The Sword Swallower* set the pattern for much of his ensuing work. It is set in a helter-skelter, urbanized and balkanized, California-like planet, populated in large part by traditional

comic stereotypes or humours, and features a detective from the Barnum system, where the Chameleon Corps originates, on the trail of a complex crime; the detective's need to search out clues and suspects takes him (conveniently) through a wide spectrum of scenes and characters. Typically of most of RG's work, *The Sword Swallower* is at times extremely funny, though its zaniness sometimes leads to a flimsiness of structure, as though the jokes were guiding the storyline. Many of RG's novels also feature, as with *Wildsmith* (**1972**), highly humanized, eccentric, wilful ROBOTS, whose characters tend to be obsessive; through these robot-portrayals, RG manages to make a number of sharp SATIRICAL points about human nature and about contemporary America, no matter where the stories happen to be set. It is characteristic of his work that even his SPACE OPERAS, mainly the loosely connected series of tales, some featuring the Chameleon Corps, set against the shared background of the Barnum System, which include, along with *The Sword Swallower*, *The Chameleon Corps and Other Shape Changers* (coll. **1972**), *Flux* (**1974**), *Spacehawk, Inc.* (**1974**), and *A Whiff of Madness* (**1976**) represent easily identifiable travesties of modern American life, sometimes pointedly, sometimes merely with an effect of slapstick. In addition to this generalized similarity of milieu, many of his books make casual, and sometimes punning references to one another, but at a level insufficiently precise to constitute a shared background. Some of his recent work has been rather flimsy, particularly his two current series, the novel sequence (with several volumes projected) dealing with its protagonist's picaresque search for clues to his unusual nature, comprising so far *Quest of the Gypsy* (**1976**) which is based on a short story, "There's Coming a Time" (1975), and *Eye of the Vulture* (**1977**), and his sf "Gothic" sequence starring the comic-strip character Vampirella, which is comprised of *Bloodstalk* (**1975**), *On Alien Wings* (**1975**), *Deadwalk* (**1976**), *Blood Wedding* (**1976**), *Deathgame* (**1976**) and *Snakegod* (**1976**). He has also collaborated with Gil Kane on a comic strip, *Star Hawks*, and his *Challengers of the Unknown* (**1977**) is based on the DC comic. Although he is an extremely adroit and literate writer, RG has generally contented himself with stories whose successful realization fails to stretch his skills; individual scenes and jokes tend to stand out in novels otherwise indistinguishable from their stable-mates. [JC]

Other works: *The Fire-Eater* (**1970**); *After Things Fell Apart* (**1970**); *Gadget Man* (**1971**); *Death Cell* (**1971**); *Broke Down Engine and Other Troubles with Machines* (coll. **1971**); *Clockwork's Pirates* (**1971**); *Ghost Breaker* (coll. **1971**); *Hawkshaw* (**1971**); *What's*

Become of Screwloose? (coll. **1971**); *Plunder* (**1972**); *The Tin Angel* (**1973**); *Shaggy Planet* (**1973**); *A Talent for the Invisible* (**1973**); *When the Waker Sleeps* (**1975**); *The Enormous Hourglass* (**1975**); *Nutzenbolts* (coll. **1975**); *Odd Job No. 101* (coll. **1975**); *The Hellhound Project* (**1975**); *Crackpot* (**1977**); *The Emperor of the Last Days* (**1977**); *The Panchronicon Plot* (**1977**); *Nemo* (**1977**). Non-fiction: *Cheap Thrills: An Informal History of the Pulp Magazines* (**1972**); *The Adventurous Decade: Comic Strips in the Thirties* (**1976**).
See also: MEDIA LANDSCAPE.

GOVE, PHILIP BABCOCK (1902–). American academic, whose book *The Imaginary Voyage in Prose Fiction: a History of its Criticism and a Guide for its Study, with an Annotated Check List of 215 Imaginary Voyages from 1700 to 1800* (**1941**) was reissued by ARNO PRESS in 1975. It is one of the most important and reliable tools for the researcher in its period, about which few books have been written, though it is in no sense a book about sf *per se*. [PN]

GOWLAND, JOHN STAFFORD (1898–). British writer. His sf novel, *Beyond Mars* (**1956**), treats, perhaps rather primitively, of space travel to the Moon and beyond via antigravity. [JC]

GOY, PHILIP (1941–). French writer, real name Philippe Goy. PhD in physics, works in scientific research. His writing is an uneven blend of hardcore sf and experimentation. *Le père éternel* ["The Eternal Father"] (**1974**) tells a satirical story of a mutant sperm-bank donor, and the fathering of a new race. *Le livre/machine* ["The Book/Machine"] (**1975**) is a curious experiment in typography, depicting Utopia through computer concepts. [MJ/PN]

GRAHAM, P(ETER) ANDERSON (? –1925). English writer on rural themes, whose post-HOLOCAUST novel, *The Collapse of Homo Sapiens* (**1923**), identifies the fall of mankind with the defeat of England by an alliance of coloured powers, which themselves soon disintegrate, leaving the world to shrink and degenerate; the traveller who is moved through time to witness this disaster puts much of the blame for England's unreadiness upon trade unionism. [JC]
See also: POLITICS.

GRAHAM, ROBERT *See* Joe HALDEMAN.

GRAHAM, ROGER PHILLIPS *See* Rog PHILLIPS.

GRAHAME-WHITE, CLAUDE (? – ?). British author of two sf juveniles with Harry HARPER (*who see for details*).

GRANT, CHARLES L. (? –). American sf writer, executive secretary of SFWA since 1975, who began publishing sf stories in *FSF* with "The House of Evil" in 1968 but became really active only in the mid-1970s. He often publishes as C.L. Grant. His post-HOLOCAUST series of novels, *The Shadow of Alpha* (**1976**) and *Ascension* (**1977**), is set in a plague-ravaged America infested with balkanized city-states and petty dictators; the protagonist of the second novel is a descendant of the protagonist of the first; both novels are told in a somewhat heated style possibly derived from the example of Samuel R. DELANY. CLG was awarded a NEBULA (for best short story) for "A Crowd of Shadows" (1976). Two occult horror novels by him are *The Curse* (**1977**) and *The Hour of the Oxrun Dead* (**1977**). He has also published a manual entitled *Writing and Selling Science Fiction* (**1976**). [JC/PN]

GRANT, DONALD M(ETCALF) (1927–). American publisher. His company now bears his own name, and specializes in the works of Robert E. HOWARD, including a *de luxe* illustrated edition of the "Conan" series. DMG also produced *Virgil Finlay* (**1971**). [MJE]

GRANT, MATTHEW (? –). British writer whose paperback sf novel is *Hyper-Drive* (**1963**). [JC]

GRANT, ROBERT (1852–1940). American writer of a number of novels, chiefly remembered for *Unleavened Bread* (**1900**); with John Boyle O'REILLY (*who see for details*), F.J. Stimson and J.T. Wheelwright he wrote *The King's Men: A Tale of To-morrow* (**1884**). [JC]

GRANVILLE, AUSTYN (? – ?). American 19th-century author, resident for some years in Australia. His now rare LOST-RACE novel, *The Fallen Race* (**1892**) was published by F.T. Neely of New York and Chicago as part of a paperback series designed especially for train travellers. The novel is probably the earliest sf to be set in Australia, and while well informed about Australian geography it shares the belief in a great inland sea which in real life was to lead to the disappointment or death of many explorers. Stranded in the desert, a doctor finds a lost race developed, absurdly, from the primeval union of aboriginals and kangaroos; its people, almost spherical in shape, are ruled by a white queen. In a racy narrative redolent of Victorian optimism, smugness and prejudice, the hero undertakes an exercise in CULTURAL ENGINEERING and through technological knowhow builds a middle-class UTOPIA after surviving the amorous attentions of a female spheroid, outwitting a palace revolution, and marrying the queen. AG, according to the title page, also wrote *The Shadow of Shame* and *The Legend of Kaara*. [PN]

GRATACAP, LOUIS POPE (1851–1917). American writer, frequently on geological topics, and author of several sf works, the best known being *The Certainty of a Future Life on Mars, being the Posthumous Papers of Bradford Torrey Dodd* (**1903**), in which the dead Dodd turns out to have transcendentally ascended to a Martian REINCARNATION, and communicates his views of the UTOPIA he lives in to his note-taking son on Earth. *The New Northland* (**1915**) has a Jewish-derived LOST RACE in the Arctic and a great deal of radium. [JC]
Other works: *A Woman of the Ice Age* (**1906**); *The Evacuation of England: the Twist in the Gulf Stream* (**1908**); *The Mayor of New York: a Romance of Days to Come* (**1910**); *The End: How the Great War was Stopped* (**1917**).
See also: MARS.

GRAVES, ROBERT (RANKE) (1895–). English poet, novelist and critic, best known for a poetic career extending from the beginning of the First World War and for such novels as *I, Claudius* (**1934**). His UTOPIAN sf novel *Seven Days in New Crete* (**1949**; vt *Watch the North Wind Rise* USA) is a complex rendering of some of his ideas about the nature of poetry and its ideal relation to the world, as also expressed in his slightly earlier non-fiction study *The White Goddess* (**1948**). The novel, which is framed as a possible dream of its protagonist, a poet called into the future by the Poet-Magicians who are the ruling caste of New Crete, offers no clear-cut advocacy of the Utopia it describes, and indeed the intruding poet, as is so frequent in this kind of writing, has been introduced, perhaps more than half-consciously, to destroy the static balance of the ideal society into which he has been brought. The escapist, timeless nature of New Crete, and the mediocre poetry it produces, are seen with considerable ambivalence by RG, who allows no "winners" in his quest for a view of the world that will appropriately balance opposing forces of whole-witted time-fulness and half-witted Utopia. [JC]
About the author: There is much criticism of RG in general; on *Seven Days in New Crete* Fritz LEIBER's "Utopia for Poets and Witches", RIVERSIDE QUARTERLY 4 (1970), and Robert H. Canary's "Utopian and Fantastic Dualities in Robert Graves's *Watch the North Wind Rise*", SCIENCE-FICTION STUDIES 4 (1974) are useful.
See also: GALACTIC EMPIRES; MYTHOLOGY; TIME TRAVEL.

GRAVITY The force of gravity is the most inescapable and unvarying fact of terrestrial life, and when writers first sent characters into spaceships and on to other planets the phenomenon of weakened gravity, or of no gravity at all, figured prominently among the wonders of space. Many early authors did not realize that complete weightlessness is a consequence of free fall, but this soon became a fact to be taken for granted in describing space flight, and few writers bothered to emphasize it. A late and delightful account of the attractions of weightlessness was given by Fritz LEIBER in "The Beat Cluster" (1961); a more straightforward introduction to the idea of free fall is contained in Arthur C. CLARKE's *Islands In The Sky* (1952).

Despite the attractiveness of the idea, weightlessness in practice is more likely to be a nuisance than anything else, and it is generally felt to be necessary in sf to provide some form of artificial gravity in a spaceship. The favoured method is to spin the ship about an axis, so creating centrifugal force, acting outward from the axis, which can do duty as a force of gravity, the floor of a chamber being its outer side. The visual paradoxes associated with a force of gravity which acts outwards on the inside of a hollow object, rather than inwards on the outside of a solid object, as on Earth, were exploited in the film 2001: A SPACE ODYSSEY (1968) scripted by Arthur C. Clarke and Stanley KUBRICK; in Clarke's *Rendezvous With Rama* (1973); and in Harry HARRISON's *Captive Universe* (1969). Few writers mention the Coriolis force, the sideways force on a moving object which also results from a spinning system, and makes things tend to move in circles; it might be a severe disadvantage of a spinning spaceship. It is not encountered if the gravity is provided by a constant linear acceleration, nor if the problem is solved outside known science by having recourse to gravity generators such as SPINDIZZIES.

Centrifugal force also comes into play on rapidly rotating planets, where it combines with the force of gravity to define the direction of the vertical. Since the surface of a planet tends to be generally at right angles to the combined centrifugal and gravitational forces, the centrifugal force can be treated as a part of the gravity, having the effect of decreasing the gravity at the equator (where it is already likely to be lower because of the shape of the planet), as in Hal CLEMENT's *Mission of Gravity* (1954).

Mission of Gravity, as its title implies, has gravity as its central subject. It is concerned with the conditions of very high gravity on the massive, rapidly rotating, discus-shaped planet of Mesklin; with the life forms that can be expected to evolve in such conditions; and with the effect of these conditions on the psychology of the intelligent life forms. In our Solar System high gravity, though not as extreme as that on Mesklin, can be found on JUPITER; this is described in Poul ANDERSON's "Call Me Joe" (1957) and James BLISH's "Bridge" (1952), the story which describes the development of spindizzies.

Even stronger gravitational forces than

these can be expected near the very massive but small objects composed of collapsed matter (*see* PHYSICS). In such a gravitational field the variation of gravity is as significant as its strength, for this can cause forces even on an object in free fall. These are called "tidal forces", since the tides on Earth are caused by the difference between the Moon's gravitational pull on opposite sides of the Earth. Tidal forces feature in Larry NIVEN's "Neutron Star" (1966), which describes how a spaceship passing near a neutron star would be "pulled apart by the tide", and in his "There Is A Tide" (1968).

In the most intense gravitational fields the strange effects of general relativity become important, and lead to the formation of BLACK HOLES and the production of gravitational waves. Larry Niven envisaged the latter being used for signalling in "The Hole Man" (1973).

The wish for a method of manipulating gravity has been a rich source of IMAGINARY SCIENCE. We have already noted the desirability of a gravity generator during the flight of a spaceship; on the other hand, takeoff would be eased if there existed a shield against gravity, such as H. G. WELLS's Cavorite in *The First Men in the Moon* (1901), or some other method of nullifying or reversing gravity. Anti-gravity is, therefore something of a philosopher's stone to sf writers. Both Raymond F. JONES in "Noise Level" (1952) and Tom GODWIN in "Mother of Invention" (1953) take an alchemist's attitude to it (*see* PHYSICS). In the latter story necessity is the mother of the discovery that gravity is like magnetism; James Blish also uses a comparison with magnetism in his explanation of spindizzies. Neither of these proposed theories of gravity makes any contact with Einstein's generally accepted theory of general relativity. In *Count-Down* (1959; vt *Fire Past the Future*) Charles Eric MAINE acknowledges that gravitation can be described as a curvature of space-time, and proposes to "simply bend space the other way" — which is an alternative description of anti-gravity.

Presumably the basic attraction of anti-gravitational themes for sf writers grows from a kind of resentment at the inescapable restraints gravity imposes on us in the real world. Cecelia HOLLAND deals in a rather cavalier manner with gravity in *Floating Worlds* (1976), the worlds of the title being cities floating above Saturn and Uranus. David GERROLD's *The Space Skimmers* (1971) uses an imaginary gravitic effect (using gravity as a kind of point applied to a surface) which yields an attractive spaceship designed as if by M.C. Escher. *Walkers on the Sky* (1976) by David J. LAKE owes more to wish-fulfilment than to science, but he does offer a technological explanation for the behaviour summarized in the title. [TSu]

GRAY, CURME (? –). Writer, probably American, possibly pseudonymous, author of the complex, intriguing sf novel *Murder in Millenium VI* (1952), in which a murder case shakes a matriarchal world thousands of years hence; for the inhabitants of this world, murder is inexplicable. The focus of interest in the novel is the gradual unveiling of the nature of the world, and of the fact that a gradual transition back not to patriarchy but to some synthesis is under way. There is a detailed and admiring analysis in *In Search of Wonder* (1956) by Damon KNIGHT. [JC]

GRAZIER, JAMES (? –). American writer, in whose awkwardly written sf novel *Runts of 61 Cygni C* (1970) humans encounter humanoid aliens and lots of sex on the eponymous planet. [JC] **Other works:** *Hydra* (1969), a juvenile as by James A. Grazier.

GREAT AND SMALL One of the most common fantastic devices in literature and legend is the alteration of scale. Mythology and folklore abound with giants and miniature humans. In the ancient tales both giants and goblins tend to be figures of menace, but in more recent times, with the adaptation of folklore into children's stories, the sympathy of the audience is recruited to smallness. Tom Thumb is a hero, and so is Jack the Giant-killer. Sf too reflects a consistent personal interest in the predicament of the very tiny, but has a very different attitude of awe to the very large. This probably reflects a sensation, born of the cosmic perspective, that we ourselves are very tiny in a vast universe.

Different perspectives dependent upon changes of scale are central to many of the satires recognized today as works of PROTO SCIENCE FICTION, most notably SWIFT's *Gulliver's Travels* (1726) and VOLTAIRE's "Micromégas" (1750). It is significant that the former is still read by children, not for its satirical content but for the fascination of the adventures in Lilliput and Brobdingnag. Modern satires using distortion of scale in a different manner include Joe Orton's *Head to Toe* (1971) and Jessamyn West's *The Chilekings* (1967).

Leeuwenhoek first explored the microscopic world of "animalcules" in the early 18th century, but the first scientific romance of the microcosm was "The Diamond Lens" (1858) by Fitz-James O'BRIEN. O'Brien's scientist cannot enter the wonderful world revealed by the lens, but later scientific romancers were unperturbed by the difficulties. The idea of worlds within worlds was popularized by the Rutherford-Bohr model of the atom as a tiny "solar system" with electrons orbiting the nucleus. The notion that all the atoms of our universe were solar systems in their own right, and all the solar systems atoms in a macrocosm, was developed by several writers, appearing first in *The Triuneverse* (**1912**) by "The Author of *Space and Spirit*" (R.A. KENNEDY). The pulp magazine writer who made the theme his own by repeating it many times was Ray CUMMINGS, who wrote *The Girl in the Golden Atom* (1919–20; fix-up **1921**) and *The Princess of the Atom* (**1929**) for the MUNSEY pulps, and used the theme in the sf pulps in *Beyond the Vanishing Point* (*ASF* 1931; **1958**). He used the notion in reverse in *Explorers into Infinity* (1927–8; **1965**). It was from Cummings that the idea was borrowed by several other sf pulp writers, notably Harl VINCENT in "The Microcosmic Buccaneers" (1929), S.P. MEEK in "Submicroscopic" (1931) and its sequel "Awlo of Ulm" (1931), Donald WANDREI in "Colossus" (1934) and Jack WILLIAMSON in "The Galactic Circle" (1935). Several of these stories are included in *Before The Golden Age* (anth. **1974**) ed. Isaac ASIMOV.

Quite apart from the microcosmic romances there are a large number of sf stories dealing with the adventures of miniature men. These range from "A Matter of Size" (1934) by Harry BATES and "He Who Shrank" (1936) by Henry HASSE (whose protagonist ends up first as a giant and then as a miniature man in our world, and then, after shrinking through a whole series of worlds-within-worlds), through *Lost Men in the Grass* (**1940**) by Donald SUDDABY as by Alan Griff, "Fury from Lilliput" (1949) by Murray LEINSTER and the classic "Surface Tension" (1952) by James BLISH to *Atta* (**1953**) by Francis Rufus BELLAMY, *Cold War in a Country Garden* (**1971**) by Lindsay GUTTERIDGE and *The Men Inside* (**1973**) by Barry MALZBERG. There are also several notable films: THE INCREDIBLE SHRINKING MAN (1957; book by Richard MATHESON, **1956**), DR CYCLOPS (1940; book by Will GARTH, **1940**) and FANTASTIC VOYAGE (1966; book by Isaac Asimov, **1966**). Sympathy for the very small is most evident in Lester DEL REY's "The Smallest God" (1940), about a homunculus accidentally imbued with life. A playful treatment of the miniature-man theme, allied with the idea of an expanding universe, is "Prominent Author" (1954) by Philip K. DICK. The pattern of identification does not work in reverse: a film complementary to *The Incredible Shrinking Man* called *The Amazing Colossal Man* (1957) — he was 60 feet tall — proved far less effective, though considerable sympathy was generated for the charismatic KING KONG (1933). There are several sf stories dealing with the heroic life of humans who have to live as scavengers in a world of alien giants, including Murray Leinster's *The Forgotten Planet* (**1954**), Kenneth BULMER's *Demon's World* (**1964**; vt *The Demons*) and William TENN's *Of Men and Monsters* (**1968**), and it is interesting to note that when the situation is reversed and the humans are the giants, sympathy

remains with the tiny race — e.g. "Giant Killer" (1945) by A. Bertram CHANDLER. Another common fascination in sf is the laboratory creation and study of tiny worlds whose time scale is much more rapid than our own — examples are Jack Williamson's "Pygmy Planet" (1932), Theodore STURGEON's classic "Microcosmic God" (1941) and Donald WOLLHEIM's *Edge of Time* (**1958** as by David Grinnell). A miniature laboratory world is created for experiments in consumer research and political sampling in "The Tunnel Under the World" (1954) by Frederik POHL, and a similar idea is used in the novel *Simulacron-3* (**1964**; vt *Counterfeit World* UK) by Daniel GALOUYE.

Giants are by no means common in sf, and where large scale is invoked it is nearly always to describe awesome inanimate objects such as Larry NIVEN's *Ringworld* (**1970**) and Bob SHAW's *Orbitsville* (**1975**). Where colossal aliens appear, as in James Blish's *The Warriors of Day* (**1953**) and Raymond F. JONES's *The Alien* (**1951**), they are usually outright figures of menace. J.G. BALLARD's curious story "The Drowned Giant" (1964; vt "Souvenir") is an exception, as is Joseph GREEN's *Gold the Man* (**1971**; vt *The Mind Behind the Eye* USA) and Brian ALDISS's mysterious "Heresies of the Huge God" (1966).

The modern model of the atom is a mathematical abstraction, and this has effectively killed the microcosmic romance, though one attempt to reconcile microcosmic travel with some of the surreal notions of subatomic physics is James Blish's "Nor Iron Bars" (1957). A popularization of atomic theory using a literary framework is *Mr. Tompkins Explores the Atom* (**1944**) by George GAMOW. The idea obviously exerts a powerful fascination, however, and it will undoubtedly return if a new literary model can be discovered with which to render voyages into the sub-atomic world plausible. [BS]

See also: COSMOLOGY; FANTASTIC VOYAGES.

GREAT SCIENCE FICTION/ SCIENCE FICTION GREATS One of the many reprint DIGEST-size magazines published by Sol Cohen's Ultimate Publishing Co., employing the reprint rights acquired when he bought AMAZING STORIES and FANTASTIC. 21 issues were released, Oct. 1965-Spring 1971, the first 12 under the title *Great Science Fiction*, nos 13–16 as *Science Fiction Greats*, and nos 17–21 as *SF Greats*.

The contents were mostly short stories by well-known authors reprinted from the period when Cele GOLDSMITH edited *AMZ* and *Fantastic*. Issue no.13 was entirely devoted to Robert SILVERBERG, and no.14 entirely to Harlan ELLISON. [BS]
Collectors should note: *GSF* has no volume numbers. The first eight numbers carried only the year. From no.9 onwards issues were marked with the season. The

Fall 1967.

printing schedule was irregular, usually four issues a year.

GREAT SCIENCE FICTION STORIES *See* TREASURY OF GREAT SCIENCE FICTION STORIES.

GREEN, I.G. (? –). American writer, in whose sf novel *Time Beyond Time* (**1971**) the hero is either killed by lightning or caught in a "time nexus" and cast into a disease-free ATLANTIS, where he finds himself immortal, and becomes embroiled in many exciting adventures.
[JC]

GREEN, JOSEPH (LEE) (1931–). American writer of sf and technical journalism who began publishing sf in England in 1962 with "The Engineer" in *NW*. Although many of his 50 stories to date (not all sf) have appeared in the USA, along with popular science articles in *ASF* that demonstrate a lucid gift of exposition visible also in his books, it was in England that he first established his name, and where his first novel, *The Loafers of Refuge* (1962–3 *NW*; fix-up **1965**), first appeared; it chronicles the gradual coming together of colonizing humans and human-like natives on the planet Refuge, mainly through merging of the two races' ESP potentials. *An Affair With Genius* (coll. **1969**) assembles some of his short work. JG's best novel to date is probably his second, *Gold the Man* (**1971**; vt *The Mind Behind the Eye* USA), which deals very competently (though not in depth) with a variety of themes from SUPERMAN to ALIENS and INTELLIGENCE. Gold is *Homo sapiens* born with about four extra ounces of association neocortex; as an adult he is asked to operate a brain-damaged giant invader from inside its head; doing so, and returning to the alien's home planet, a rather bland UTOPIA, he works out the reason for the imminent destruction of their sun (which had caused them to come to Earth) — sentient sunspots. All ends well. Further novels include

Conscience Interplanetary (1965–71 var. mags; fix-up **1972**), the uneven story of a Conscience whose job it is to adjudicate as to the intelligence of alien species before allowing men to exploit their planets.   [JC]
Other works: *Star Probe* (**1976**); *The Horde* (**1976**).
See also: COMMUNICATIONS; GREAT AND SMALL; MATTER TRANSMISSION.

GREEN, PETER *See* Kenneth BULMER.

GREEN, ROBERT (? –). Writer, probably British, whose sf novel *The Great Leap Backwards* (**1968**) depicts a future where COMPUTERS have taken over the direction of society. RG may not be the same person as the Robert M. Green Jr who had four stories in *FSF* 1964–7.   [JC]

GREEN, ROGER (GILBERT) LANCELYN (1918–). British author and critic, with a special interest in fantasy. Among his many works those most relevant to sf studies are *C.S. Lewis* (**1963**) and *Into Other Worlds: Space-Flight in Fiction, from Lucian to Lewis* (**1957**). The latter is one of the earlier books on sf, but is primarily pitched at a rather anecdotal and trivial level. His *Andrew Lang* (**1946**) throws light on an author whose relationship to sf has almost been forgotten (*see* Andrew LANG).   [PN]

GREENBERG, MARTIN (1918–). American publisher and anthologist. In 1948 he joined with David KYLE and others in founding GNOME PRESS, one of the small but important early publishers of genre sf in hardcover format. MG edited seven anthologies for Gnome, one of them, *Coming Attractions* (anth. **1957**), consisting of sf-related non-fiction articles. The others were *Men Against the Stars* (anth. **1950**); *Travellers of Space* (anth. **1951**; with 16 illustrations by Edd CARTIER); *Journey to Infinity* (anth. **1951**); *Five Science Fiction Novels* (anth. **1952**; vt *The Crucible of Power* UK with novels by Fritz LEIBER and A.E. VAN VOGT omitted); *The Robot and the Man* (anth. **1953**) and *All About the Future* (anth. **1955**). Most are, loosely, grouped around prominent sf themes.   [PN]

GREENBERG, MARTIN HARRY (1941–). American anthologist, and professor of political science at the University of Wisconsin at Green Bay. He took his PhD at the University of Connecticut, 1969. Since 1974 he has, quite suddenly, become an important force in the sf reprint market, having edited (often with others) a large number of thematic anthologies, many of which are aimed at illustrating concepts in the social sciences to high school and college students. The books are: *Political Science Fiction* (anth. **1974**) with Patricia Warrick; *Introductory Psychology*

Through Science Fiction (anth. **1974**) with Harvey Katz and Warrick; *Anthropology Through Science Fiction* (anth. **1974**) with Carol Mason and Warrick; *Sociology Through Science Fiction* (anth. **1974**) with John Milstead, Joseph Olander and Warrick; *School and Society Through Science Fiction* (anth. **1974**) with Olander and Warrick; *American Government Through Science Fiction* (anth. **1974**) with Olander and Warrick; *The New Awareness: Religion Through Science Fiction* (anth. **1975**) with Warrick; *Run to Starlight: Sports Through Science Fiction* (anth. **1975**) with Olander and Warrick; *Social Problems Through Science Fiction* (anth. **1975**) with Milstead, Olander and Warrick; *The City: 2000 A.D.* (anth. **1976**) with Ralph Clem and Olander; *Marriage and the Family Through Science Fiction* (anth. **1976**) with Val Clear, Warrick and Olander; *Tomorrow, Inc.: Science Fiction Stories About Big Business* (anth. **1976**) with Olander; *The Best of John Jakes* (coll. **1977**) with Olander. Also with Olander, MHG is editor of a useful series of anthologies reprinting critical articles. The first three titles of this "Writers of the Twenty-First Century Series" are *Isaac Asimov* (anth. **1977**), *Arthur C. Clarke* (anth. **1977**) and *Robert A. Heinlein* (anth. **1978**). Opinions have been quite fiercely divided about the usefulness of the critical apparatus accompanying the story collections. [PN]

GREENFIELD, IRVING A. (1928–). American writer in various genres, noted in particular for expansive historical fantasies. *Waters of Death* (**1967**), *Succubus* (**1970**) and *The Stars Will Judge* (**1974**; vt *Star Trial*) all apply a lush though highly readable psychologizing style to routine sf matters.   [JC]
Other works: *The UFO Report* (**1967**), non-fiction; *The Others* (**1969**); *The Ancient of Days* (**1973**); *The Face of Him* (**1976**); *Julius Caesar is Alive and Well* (**1977**).

GREENHOUGH, TERRY Form of his name used by English writer Terence Greenhough (1944–) for most of his fiction, though he has also used the pseudonym Andrew Lester for the routine novel *The Thrice-Born* (**1976**), about persecuted hermaphrodites on a distant planet; TG began publishing sf with "The Tree in the Forest" in 1974; his first novel, *Time and Timothy Grenville* (**1975**), typically of this writer, somewhat discursively exploits an uneasy, oppressive relation between the world at large and its protagonist in a story of complex time travel and ALIENS, in which Earth itself proves to be at stake. *Thoughtworld*, projected for late 1977 publication, begins a projected trilogy.   [JC]
Other works: *The Wandering Worlds* (**1976**).

GREENLEE, SAM (1930–). American writer, whose NEAR-FUTURE sf novel, *The Spook Who Sat by the Door* (**1969**), is one of several featuring a black uprising in near-contemporary America. (*See also* Edwin CORLEY's *Siege*, **1969**, John WILLIAMS' *Son of Darkness, Sons of Light*, **1969**, and *Siege of Harlem*, **1964**, by Warren MILLER.)   [JC]
See also: POLITICS.

GREER, RICHARD Ziff-Davis house name used once by Robert SILVERBERG and Randall GARRETT in collaboration, and twice by others unidentified, 1956–7.

GREER, TOM (? – ?). Probably a pseudonym. His novel *A Modern Daedalus* (**1885**) stars a young Irish lad who invents a one-man flying device strapped to the shoulders, the ethics of whose use he must work out, with both England and the Irish wanting control. Ultimately a squadron of fliers forces the English to grant Irish independence, and the devices are then used in scientific exploration.   [JC]

GREG, PERCY (1836–89). English poet, novelist and historian, son of the prolific essayist William Rathbone Greg, and author of an important early sf novel, *Across the Zodiac: The Story of a Wrecked Record* (**1880**) (*see* FANTASTIC VOYAGES). This features an antigravity force, apergy, which enables its protagonist to travel to MARS (and provided a model for many other novels). Mars, a monarchical UTOPIA, scientifically orthodox and capitalistic, gradually reveals DYSTOPIAN qualities as the hero, forced into polygamy, becomes involved in religious struggles, accidentally kills some of his family with his imported germs, and eventually escapes.   [JC]
See also: POWER SOURCES; SPACESHIPS.

GREGG PRESS American publisher of reprints, a subsidiary of G.K. Hall & Co. The Gregg Press sf series, edited by David G. Hartwell with Lloyd W. Currey as associate editor, includes a variety of novels and collections from the 18th century until recent times. Among them are several new volumes, such as *Alyx* (coll. **1976**) by Joanna RUSS and an anthology drawn from the critical magazine SCIENCE-FICTION STUDIES. A useful feature of the series is the new, and often lengthy, introductions to the volumes, by leading critics and authors. Series one, published in 1975, had 20 vols; series two, 1976, had 29 vols; series three, 1977, has 25 vols to date. The GP reprints have been generally regarded by critics as the best of the recent sf reprint hardcover series, all of which are aimed primarily at libraries.   [MJE/PN]

GREGORY, OWEN (? –). British author of *Meccania, The Super-State* (**1918**), a futuristic DYSTOPIA describing a German mechanical and totalitarian

society taken to its logical extreme. It is comparable with Milo Hastings' *The City of Endless Night* (**1920**). [JE]
See also: POLITICS.

GRENDON, STEPHEN *See* August W. Derleth.

GREY, CAROL *See* Robert A.W. Lowndes.

GREY, CHARLES *See* E.C. Tubb.

GRIDBAN, VOLSTED Pseudonym initially used by E.C. Tubb for three novels written for Scion Publications: *Alien Universe* (**1952**), *Reverse Universe* (**1952**) and *Debracy's Drug* (**1952**). Tubb then used the name on two novels for the Milestone Press, *Fugitive of Time* (**1953**) and *Planetoid Disposals* (**1953**), but Scion objected and reclaimed the name, which was then used by John Russell Fearn on the following novels: *The Dyno-Depressant* (**1953**), *Magnetic Brain* (**1953**), *Moons for Sale* (**1953**), *Scourge of the Atom* (**1953**), *A Thing of the Past* (**1953**), *Exit Life* (**1953**), *The Master Must Die* (**1953**), *The Purple Wizard* (**1953**), *The Genial Dinosaur* (**1954**), *The Frozen Limit* (**1954**), *I Came — I Saw — I Wondered* (**1954**), *The Lonely Astronomer* (**1954**). [BS]

"GRIFF" House name of Modern Publications, used by John Russell Fearn on the sf novel *Liquid Death* (**1953**), and on non-sf works by F. Dubrez Fawcett.

GRIFF, ALAN *See* Donald Suddaby.

GRIFFITH, GEORGE Pseudonym of English traveller, journalist, and writer George Chetwynd Griffith-Jones (1857–1906), the son of a clergyman and one of the most influential sf writers of his time. He appeared frequently in the pre-sf MAGAZINES and PULP MAGAZINES, particularly PEARSON'S WEEKLY and PEARSON'S MAGAZINE, writing as GG or, for some short stories, as Levin Carnac. He was instrumental in the transformation of the future-WAR novel to a more sensational form, capitalizing on contemporary political anxiety; and he helped make up a literary coterie, including William Le Queux, Louis Tracy and M.P. Shiel, which specialized in the genre.
GG first established himself with *The Angel of the Revolution* (1893; rev. **1893**) and its sequel *Olga Romanoff* (1893–4 as "The Syren Of The Skies"; rev. **1894**). In the first he described how a revolutionary organization equipped with aerial battleships creates a reformed society under the government of a world federation, while the second, a sequel set 125 years later, describes the upheaval which transformed the UTOPIAN state to one of total anarchy. Both are remarkable for their foresight of battle tactics in air warfare and for their anticipation of

radar, sonar and atomic energy. They include elements which only later became commonplace, notably the struggle by international cartels for world domination and the apocalyptic visions of Armageddon on Earth and of disaster from the heavens by comet. These elements can be found in *The Outlaws of the Air* (1894–5; rev. **1895**), *Gambles With Destiny* (coll. **1898**), *The Great Pirate Syndicate* (1898; rev. **1899**), *The Lake of Gold* (**1903**), *A Woman Against the World* (**1903**), *The World Masters* (**1903**), *The Stolen Submarine* (**1904**), *The Great Weather Syndicate* (**1906**), *The World Peril of 1910* (**1907**) and *The Lord of Labour* (**1911**).
Early in GG's career H.G. Wells appeared and continually overshadowed him, a fact which caused GG to diversify his work in a search for critical acclaim. Such praise never came, though his work was extended to include notable examples of several themes. IMMORTALITY featured in *Valdar the Oft-Born* (1895; rev. **1895**) and *Captain Ishmael* (**1901**), the latter also being an early example of the PARALLEL-WORLDS theme; the LOST-WORLD theme appeared in *The Romance of Golden Star* (1895, as "Golden Star"; rev. **1897**), *The Virgin of the Sun* (**1898**) and *A Criminal Croesus* (**1904**); SPACE FLIGHT appeared in *A Honeymoon in Space* (1900, as "Stories Of Other Worlds"; fix-up **1901**); the FOURTH DIMENSION appeared in *The Mummy and Miss Nitrocris* (**1906**; vt *The Mummy and the Girl* UK); TELEPATHY appeared in *A Mayfair Magician* (**1905**; vt *The Man With Three Eyes* UK); RELIGION is a theme in *The Missionary* (**1902**), and the SUPERNATURAL in *Denver's Double* (**1901**), *The White Witch of Mayfair* (**1902**) and *The Destined Maid* (**1908**).
GG's influence was extensive in contemporary British sf works from E. Douglas Fawcett's *Hartmann the Anarchist* (**1893**) through to Cyril Seymour's *Comet Chaos* (**1906**) and John Mastin's *The Stolen Planet* (**1906**), and can still be seen today, as in the 19th-century pastiches by Michael Moorcock. (Since GG's anti-American stance precluded US publication of many of his works his influence there is negligible). Several of his novels have been reprinted in recent years and a collection of unreprinted stories, *The Raid of "Le Vengeur"* (coll. **1974**), has appeared.
Other works: *Briton or Boer?* (**1897**); *The Gold Finder* (**1898**); *The Justice of Revenge* (**1901**); *The Sacred Skull* (**1908**).
About the author: "War: Warriors of If" in *Strange Horizons: The Spectrum of Science Fiction* (**1976**) by Sam Moskowitz.
See also: END OF THE WORLD; LIFE ON OTHER WORLDS; MARS; MERCURY; MOON; NEAR FUTURE; NUCLEAR POWER; POLITICS; REINCARNATION; VENUS; WAR; WEAPONS.

GRIFFITH, MARY (1800?–77). American author, mostly of non-fiction,

whose early futuristic UTOPIA *Three Hundred Years Hence* (**1975**) originally appeared as one of the stories in her collection *Camperdown; or, News from our Neighbourhood* (coll. **1836**), published as by The Author of "Our Neighbourhood". Her rather prudish imagination sees many technological improvements, along with the prohibition of tobacco and alcohol and the expurgation of Shakespeare. [PN/JC]
See also: SUSPENDED ANIMATION.

GRINNELL, DAVID *See* Donald A. Wollheim.

GROOM, (ARTHUR JOHN) PELHAM (? –). British writer in whose sf novel *The Purple Twilight* (**1948**), the first arrivals on Mars find a civilization which atomic radiation has rendered infertile, and is therefore dying. [JC]
Other works: *The Fourth Seal* (**1948**).

GROULING, THOMAS E(DWARD) (1940–). American writer and academic, whose sf novel, *Project 12* (**1962**), deals with an abortive attempt to launch a spaceship. [JC]

GROUSSET, PASCHAL *See* André Laurie.

GROVE, FREDERICK PHILIP (1879–1948). German-born Canadian writer, whose original name was Felix Paul Greve; his output included realistic novels, rural studies and the sf SATIRE *Consider Her Ways* (**1947** Canada), which presents the notes of an amateur scientist in telepathic contact with three ants, members of an exploratory team from South America; their comments on the nature of Man and human society are pointed, and the picture of ant society is remarkably detailed. The novel has by no means received due attention. [JC]

GROVES, JAY (VOELKER) (1922–). American writer and teacher of history and economics, whose short sf novel is *Fireball at the Lake: A Story of Encounter with Another World* (**1967**). [JC]

GROVES, J(OHN) W(ILLIAM) (1910–). British writer, variously employed, who began publishing sf with "The Sphere of Death" for *AMZ* in 1931, but whose career consisted mainly of desultory magazine publications until his first novel *Shellbreak* (**1968**), in which a man awakens in AD 2505 armed with knowledge that helps him to topple a corrupt dictatorship. *The Heels of Achilles* (**1969**) presents a world in which the dead have come mysteriously to life. [JC]

GUERARD, ALBERT JOSEPH (1914–). Influential American critic and novelist, now teaching at Stanford, long an advocate of American experimentalist fiction. His sf novel, *Night Journey* (**1950**), puts the disillusionment of an idealistic soldier against the background of a new, useless, NEAR-FUTURE European WAR. [JC]

GUIN, WYMAN (WOODS) (1915–). American writer, frequently employed in jobs involving pharmacology. He began publishing sf with "Trigger Ride" for *ASF* in 1950 as Norman Menasco, but his career can be said to have really begun with "Beyond Bedlam" (1951) which, like most of his best work of the 1950s and early 1960s, appeared first in *Gal.* and was subsequently assembled in *Living Way Out* (coll. **1967**; vt *Beyond Bedlam* UK). "Beyond Bedlam" is a brilliant novelette describing an Earth about a thousand years hence where drugs enforce a strictly regulated SCHIZOPHRENIA in every human being on a five-days-on, five-days-off routine, each body inhabited alternately by two personalities, the balance between whom nullifies Man's subconscious aggressions, and thus eliminates the "paranoid wars" of the "ancient Moderns". Passion and art also disappear. The good and evil of this system are explored with a literacy and verisimilitude that make it fully worthy of ranking as a legitimate intensification of Aldous HUXLEY's version of drug-enforced stability in *Brave New World* (**1932**). *The Standing Joy* (**1969**), a PARALLEL-WORLDS story set in a nostalgically rendered other Earth, features a SUPERMAN, a good deal of harmless SEX, and a general sense of missed focus. WG will be remembered for the power of his early stories. [JC]
See also: CRIME AND PUNISHMENT; PSYCHOLOGY; SOCIOLOGY.

GULL, RANGER *See* Guy THORNE.

GUNN, JAMES E(DWIN) (1923–). American writer, critic and teacher, born in Kansas City and educated at the University of Kansas, where he is now a professor of English and journalism, with an emphasis on teaching sf and creative writing. He began publishing sf with "Communications" for *Startling Stories* in 1949 as Edwin James, his given names reversed, a disguise he dropped for good in 1952 after 10 stories. Throughout his career, JEG's favoured form has been the short story or novelette; his best book-length fictions have been either in collaboration or assemblages of shorter material. In more recent years, he has published considerable sf criticism. This began some time back with the publication of excerpts from his MA thesis in *Dynamic Science Fiction* (1953–4). It also includes the brief *The Discovery of the Future: The Ways Science Fiction Developed* (**1975**) and most notably a competent illustrated survey of sf, *Alternate Worlds: The Illustrated History of Science Fiction* (**1975**), although this suffers from the inevitable superficiality of attempted comprehensiveness in its coverage of later years, where many writers appear only as names in paragraph-long lists. For his critical work JEG won the 1976 PILGRIM award.

JEG's first two books are SPACE OPERAS. *This Fortress World* (**1955**) pits its protagonist against a repressive future religion; *Star Bridge* (**1955**) was written with Jack WILLIAMSON, and its sometimes pixilated intricacy of plotting shows the mark of its senior collaborator's grasp of the nature of good space opera. Everyone, it turns out, is being manipulated, for the salvation of mankind, by an immortal Chinese with a parrot. *Station in Space* (coll. of linked stories **1958**) assembles several uninteresting early tales about how Man is tricked into space exploration for his own good. *The Joy Makers* (1955 var. mags; fix-up **1961**) describes, in JEG's dark, sometimes ponderous, generally impressive manner, a society whose members are controlled by synthetic forms of release that corrode their sense of reality. *The Immortals* (1955–60 var. mags; fix-up **1962**) is JEG's best known work; a mutation confers IMMORTALITY upon a group of people who become collectively known as Cartwrights; their condition is transmissible to others by blood transfusion, and they are forced underground by the understandable desire of mortal men to attain immortality. The hospital setting of the book adds verisimilitude. As THE IMMORTAL (1969), it became a made-for-TV movie, whose success inspired a 1970 TV series, which JEG novelized as *The Immortal* (**1970**).

JEG's second generally successful fiction, *The Listeners* (1968–72 var. mags; fix-up **1972**), makes productive use of its episodic structure in its depiction of the setting up of an electronic listening post to scan for radio messages from the stars, and of the 100-year wait that ensues. JEG's somewhat morose style (at his better moments he evokes a kind of sense of the melancholy of wonder)

nicely underlines the complex institutional frustrations and rewards of this long search. Indeed, his forte seems to lie in the narrative analysis of stress-ridden administrations and their administrators; his best work is usually set in organizations or among groups of people forced to cooperate. Women tend to be excluded from the higher purposes of such organizations, and tend sometimes to balk at the sacrifices men must make to reach the stars. Despite occasional blemishes of this sort, JEG has made a considerable success of his chosen length and venue, and his later works especially can ruminate absorbingly on the administration of Man's crises to come. [JC]
Other works: *Future Imperfect* (coll. **1964**); *The Witching Hour* (coll. **1970**); *The Burning* (1956-69 var. mags; fix-up **1972**); *Breaking Point* (coll. **1972**); *Some Dreams Are Nightmares* (coll. **1974** of short stories from *Station in Space*, *The Joy Makers* and *The Immortals*); *The End of the Dreams: Three Short Novels About Space, Happiness, and Immortality* (coll. **1975** of long stories from *Station in Space*, *The Joy Makers* and *The Immortals*); *The Magicians* (1954 *Beyond* as "Sine of the Magus"; exp. **1976**); *Kampus* (**1977**).
As editor: *The Road to Science Fiction* (anth. **1977**).
See also: ALIENS; ANTI-INTELLECTUALISM IN SF; ASTRONOMY; COMMUNICATIONS; DEFINITIONS OF SF: DYSTOPIAS; GALACTIC EMPIRES; GAMES AND SPORTS; LEISURE; MAGIC; PSYCHOLOGY; RELIGION; SOCIOLOGY.

GUNN, NEIL M(ILLER) (1891–1973). Scottish writer and civil servant, author of many novels, from *Grey Coast* (**1926**) on, some of them, like *Morning Tide* (**1931**), *The Last Glen* (**1932**) and *Second Sight* (**1940**), of strong fantasy interest. *The Green Isle of the Great Deep* (**1944**), a sequel to *Young Art and Old Hector* (coll. **1942**), is his best-known fantasy. It describes the adventures of an old man and a young boy in an ALTERNATE-WORLD society; *The Serpent* (**1948**) is a TIME-TRAVEL story. His *The Well at World's End* (**1951**) acknowledges in its title a debt to William MORRIS. NMG's style is rich, sometimes sentimental, and his books constantly evocative of an ideal Scotland. [JC]

GÜNTHER, GOTTHARD (? –). German philosopher, now living in the USA. In *Das Bewusstsein der Maschinen* ["The Consciousness of Machines"] (**1957**) he argues for a CYBERNETIC philosophy. In 1952 he edited in Germany a pioneering series of hardcovers by Jack WILLIAMSON, John W. CAMPBELL Jr, Isaac ASIMOV and an anthology, *Überwindung von Raum und Zeit* ["Conquest of Space and Time"], compiled by him for Rauch-Verlag in Germany, accompanying them with lengthy, critical afterwords in which he called sf "the American fairy-tale" and the forerunner of a new type of metaphysics. These were among the earliest German critical commentaries on sf. GG also published some articles in *Startling Stories* and *ASF*.   [FR]

GUTTERIDGE, LINDSAY (1923–   ). English writer. His sf series, *Cold War in a Country Garden* (**1971**), *Killer Pine* (**1973**) and *Fratricide is a Gas* (**1975**), brings in themes from espionage to ECOLOGY in far-fetched tales of a government agent miniaturized with some companions (*see* GREAT AND SMALL) to test the chances of counteracting OVERPOPULATION by resetting the world with a miniaturized mankind.   [JC]

HADLEY, ARTHUR T(WINING) (1924–   ). American journalist and writer, whose successful novel, *The Joy Wagon* (**1958**), uses a borderline sf treatment of COMPUTERS in a sharply comic send-up of the American electoral system: the computer runs for President.
                                        [JC]

HADLEY, FRANKLIN *See* Russ R. WINTERBOTHAM.

HADLEY PUBLISHING COMPANY American specialist publishing house of the late 1940s, owned by Thomas P. Hadley. A very short-lived company, Hadley was notable for publishing John W. CAMPBELL Jr's first book, *The Mightiest Machine* (1934–5 *ASF*; **1947**) and L. Ron HUBBARD's *Final Blackout* (1940 *ASF*; **1948**). The company announced two novels by John TAINE for publication in 1947–8; these later appeared under the FANTASY PRESS imprint.   [MJE]

HAGGARD, Sir H(ENRY) RIDER (1856–1925). English civil servant, lawyer, agricultural expert and writer, knighted in 1912. As a young man, HRH spent six years in the colonial service in South Africa, where he gained much of the material for his fiction. His fourth book, *King Solomon's Mines* (**1885**), catapulted him to fame and was followed by the even more successful *She* (**1887**; rev. 1896). These tales combine large

elements of fantasy (LOST WORLDS, IMMORTALITY, REINCARNATION) with realistic details of African life. They may be regarded as archaeological and ANTHROPOLOGICAL sf: HRH was fascinated by ruins, ancient civilizations and primitive customs. His interest in the PSEUDO-SCIENCE of spiritualism made him akin to such contemporary writers as Bulwer LYTTON and Marie CORELLI. HRH's prose was sometimes inept, but he was a marvellous storyteller with a powerful imagination and the ability to create memorable heroic figures, e.g. the Zulu Umslopogaas, whose early life is the subject of the remarkable *Nada the Lily* (**1892**).

The white hunter Allan Quatermain was HRH's principal hero, however, who appeared in a number of linked books. The estimated dates of internal chronology precede their titles as follows: 1835–8 *Marie* (**1912**); 1842–69 *Allan's Wife and Other Tales* (coll. **1889**); 1854–6 *Child of Storm* (**1913**); 1859 *Maiwa's Revenge* (**1888**); 1870 *The Holy Flower* (**1915**; vt *Allan and the Holy Flower* USA); 1871 *Heu-Heu* (**1924**); 1872 *She and Allan* (**1921**); 1873 *The Treasure of the Lake* (**1926**); 1874 *The Ivory Child* (**1916**); 1879 *Finished* (**1917**); 1879 "Magepa the Buck" (in *Smith and the Pharaohs and Other Tales*, coll. **1920**); 1880 *King Solomon's Mines* (**1885**); 1882 *The Ancient Allan* (**1920**); 1883 *Allan and the Ice Gods* (**1927**); 1884–5 *Allan Quatermain* (**1887**). Most of these stories are a blend of realism and fantasy. In *Allan and the Ice Gods*, Quatermain is thrown back in time by means of a drug and inhabits the body of a paleolithic man. Rudyard KIPLING helped HRH plot this story, and he had previously given a hand with *When the World Shook* (**1919**), a tale of ATLANTIS. Earlier HRH had collaborated more extensively with Andrew LANG to produce *The World's Desire* (**1890**), a fantastic sequel to the *Odyssey*.

Later books in the *She* cycle are *Ayesha* (**1905**); *She and Allan* (**1921**), providing a link with the Quatermain series; and

Wisdom's Daughter (**1923**). Other, non-series, tales concerning the discovery of lost races are *The People of the Mist* (**1894**); *Heart of the World* (**1895**); *Benita* (**1906**; vt *The Spirit of Bambatse* USA); *The Yellow God* (**1908**) and *Queen Sheba's Ring* (**1910**). HRH also wrote many historical adventures, the best of which, e.g. *Cleopatra* (**1889**), *Eric Brighteyes* (**1891**) and *Red Eve* (**1911**), contain supernatural elements. As the first popularizer of the LOST WORLD novel, HRH has had a large influence on sf, in particular via Edgar Rice BURROUGHS and his imitators. In the 1970s, Philip José FARMER has used characters and settings from HRH in his "Ancient Opar" novels.
                                        [DP]

About the author: *Bibliography of the Works of H. Rider Haggard* (**1947**) by J.E. Scott; *The Cloak That I Left* (**1951**) by Lilias Rider Haggard; *Rider Haggard: His Life and Work* (**1960**) by Morton Cohen; *The Wheel of Empire* (**1967**) by Alan Sandison.

See also: HISTORY OF SF; ORIGIN OF MAN; RADIO (USA); SEX; TIME TRAVEL.

HAGGARD, J. HARVEY (1913–   ). American writer who had 31 sf stories published, mostly in the 1930s, beginning with "Faster than Light" for *Wonder Stories* in 1930. His "Earthguard" series in *Wonder Stories* includes "Through the Einstein Line" (1933), "Evolution Satellite" (1933) and "An Episode on Io" (1934).   [JC]

HAGGARD, WILLIAM Pseudonym of Richard Clayton (1907–   ). British civil servant whose political thrillers, usually featuring Colonel Russell (now retired) of the Secret Service, sometimes extrapolate on current political trends, after the fashion of their genre. *Slow Burner* (**1958**) provides some sf content in the atomic-power process described by the title. *The Bitter Harvest* (**1971**) deals with germ warfare.   [JC]

HAIBLUM, ISIDORE (1935–   ). New York based American writer, born and educated in that city, where he has set much of his fiction. He is Jewish, and the humour expressed in his novels is Yiddish in style, especially in his first sf novel, *The Tsaddik of the Seven Wonders* (**1971**). IH writes a fluent though sometimes rather disarranged kind of comic sf novel, of which *The Wilk Are Among Us* (**1975**) is a representative example, with its amusingly overcomplicated plot, its frenetic spoofing of the theme of aliens-in-our-midst, and its general failure to take hold of its materials. His attempts to amalgamate Yiddish humour and sf themes are of technical interest.   [JC]
Other works: *The Return* (**1973**); *Transfer to Yesterday* (**1973**); *Interworld* (**1977**).

HAILEY, ARTHUR (1920–   ). Canadian author of such heavily researched best-sellers as *Hotel* (**1965**). His sf novel *In High Places* (**1962**), deals, unusually, with Canada, whose Prime Minister effects a military alliance with the USA. [JC]

HAINING, PETER (1940–). British editor and writer. He worked in journalism and publishing (with New English Library, where he rose to be editorial director) before turning freelance in 1970. His many books reflect his interest in the macabre and the occult; he is the author of a number of books on witchcraft. He is also an authority on pulp magazines, particularly WEIRD TALES. His· anthologies include the facsimile collection *Weird Tales* (anth. **1976**) and *The Fantastic Pulps* (anth. **1975**), and he is the author of a study of fantasy and horror illustration in the pulps; *Terror!* (**1976**). [MJE]
Other works: As editor: *The Hell of Mirrors* (anth. **1965**; vt *Everyman's Book of Classic Horror Stories* UK); *Summoned from the Tomb* (anth. **1966**); *Beyond the Curtain of Dark* (anth. **1966**); *Where Nightmares Are* (anth. **1966**); *The Craft of Terror* (anth. **1966**); *The Gentlewomen of Evil* (anth. **1967**); *Dr. Caligari's Black Book* (anth. **1968**; rev. 1969); *The Future Makers* (anth. **1968**); *The Evil People* (anth. **1968**); *The Midnight People* (anth. **1968**); *The Unspeakable People* (anth. **1969**); *The Witchcraft Reader* (anth. **1969**); *The Satanists* (anth. **1969**); *The Freak Show* (anth. **1969**); *The Wild Night Company* (anth. **1970**) *A Circle of Witches* (anth. **1971**); *The Necromancers* (anth. **1971**); *The Clans of Darkness* (anth. **1971**); *The Ghouls* (anth. **1971**); *The Hollywood Nightmare* (anth. **1971**); *Great British Tales of Terror* (anth. **1972**); *Great Tales of Terror from Europe and America* (anth. **1972**), *Gothic Tales of Terror* (anth. **1972**; omnibus of two preceding vols); *The Magicians* (anth. **1972**); *The Dream Machines* (anth. **1972**); *The Lucifer Society* (anth. **1972**; vt. *Detours into the Macabre*); *Nightfrights* (anth. **1972**); *The Nightmare Reader* (anth. **1973**); *The Witchcraft Papers* (anth. **1973**); *The Magic Valley Travellers* (anth. **1974**); *The Monster Makers* (anth. **1974**); *Christopher Lee's New Chamber of Horrors* (anth. **1974**); *The Ancient Mysteries Reader* (anth. **1975**); *The Penny Dreadful* (anth. **1975**); *The Ghost's Companion* (anth. **1975**); *The Black Magic Omnibus* (anth. **1976**); *First Book of Unknown Tales of Horror* (anth. **1976**); *The Dracula Scrapbook* (anth. **1976**); *Tales of a Monster Hunter: Peter Cushing* (anth. **1977**); *Deadly Nightshade* (anth. **1977**); *The Edgar Allan Poe Scrapbook* (anth. **1977**).

HALACY, D(ANIEL) S(TEPHEN) Jr (1919–) American technical journalist. His SPACE OPERA for young people, *Rocket Rescue* (**1968**), features telepathic twins helping each other out; *Return from*

Luna (**1969**) is a sequel. [JC]
Other works: *Fun with the Sun* (**1959**); *Genetic Revolution: Shaping Life for Tomorrow* (**1974**), non-fiction; *Century 21: Your Life in the Year 2001 and Beyond* (**1968**), non-fiction juvenile; *Colonization of the Moon: A Fact Book for Young Readers* (**1968**), non-fiction juvenile.

HALDANE, J(OHN) B(URDON) S(ANDERSON) (1892–1964). British biologist, brother of Naomi MITCHISON. Known primarily for his work outside the sf field. His only sf novel, the posthumous *The Man With Two Memories* (**1976**), an account of a man's mental link with an inhabitant of another world, was incomplete at his death. Some of his speculative essays are of considerable interest. They include *Daedalus; or Science and the Future* (**1924**), on the Utopian possibilities opened up by scientific progress, which provided the image of the future attacked by Aldous HUXLEY in *Brave New World* (**1932**); and "The Last Judgment" in *Possible Worlds* (coll. **1927**), which provides an evolutionary prospectus for the human race akin to that used by Olaf STAPLEDON in *Last and First Men* (**1930**). [BS]
Other works: *My Friend Mr. Leakey* (coll. **1937**), a work of fantasy for children.
See also: CLONES; COLONIZATION OF OTHER WORLDS; DYSTOPIAS; EVOLUTION; FAR FUTURE; GENETIC ENGINEERING; SUN.

HALDEMAN, JOE (WILLIAM) (1943–). American writer who, since his first story, "Out of Phase" (1969) in *Galaxy*, has made a considerable impact on the sf field. He took a BS in physics and astronomy, doing some postgraduate work in mathematics and computer science, and on being drafted was sent as a combat engineer to Vietnam, where he was wounded; both his scientific and military backgrounds show prominently in his fiction. Under a Pocket Books house name, Robert Graham, he has written two borderline-sf spy novels, *Attar's Revenge* (**1975**) and *War of Nerves* (**1975**), and under his own name the non-sf novel *War Year* (**1972**).
JH's sudden prominence, however, came with the critical and popular success of *The Forever War* (1972–4 *ASF*; fix-up **1974**; paperback edition with many small corrections) which, with "You Can Never Go Back" (1975), makes up a series whose description of the life of soldiers in a future WAR counterpoints and in some way rebuts Robert A. HEINLEIN's vision in *Starship Troopers* (**1959**). In *The Forever War*, because travel to the planets where the engagements are fought involves time distortion, soldiers are doomed to total alienation from the civilization for which they are fighting, and if they make too large a jump face the risk of coming to battle with antiquated weaponry. Their

deracination is savage; their camaraderie cynically manipulated. The book won a DITMAR, a NEBULA and a HUGO.
JH's second success is *Mindbridge* (**1976**), a novel whose narrative techniques are suggested by its dedication to John DOS PASSOS and John BRUNNER. Composed as a clever sequence of straight narrations, reports, excerpts from books (some written long after the events depicted), graphs and so forth, *Mindbridge* applies techniques originally designed to heighten social verisimilitude to what is essentially a space epic, featuring telepathic toys left on one planet by an extinct race of godlike aliens, a complex form of MATTER TRANSMISSION, an intriguing argument about the COLONIZATION of other solar systems and another alien race, this one apparently inimical and hive-like, though matters turn out for the best.
JH won a second Hugo for his short story "Tricentennial" (1976). Along with writers like John VARLEY and Larry NIVEN (who seems to be an influence, though JH structures his novels more convincingly) JH makes up a kind of new wave of HARD-SF writers whose technology-dominated views of the future are impressively more complex than those of their predecessors. [JC]
Other works: *All My Sins Remembered* (1971–7 var. mags; fix-up **1977**); *Planet of Judgment* (**1977**), a Star Trek novel. As editor: *Cosmic Laughter* (anth. **1974**); *Study War No More* (anth. **1977**).
See also: ALIENS; BLACK HOLES; HIVE-MINDS; TIME TRAVEL; WAR.

HALE, EDWARD EVERETT (1822–1909). American writer, contributing editor to *The Atlantic Monthly* and Unitarian preacher, best known today for the title story (first published in 1863) of his collection, *The Man Without a Country and Other Tales* (coll. **1868**). Of his prolific output, *Sybaris and Other Homes* (coll. **1869**), which describes a UTOPIAN colony of Sybarites uncovered in an island off the coast of Italy, is of sf interest; more notably, "The Brick Moon" (1869), with its short sequel, "Life in the Brick Moon" (1870), run together into one story in *His Level Best and Other Stories* (coll. **1872**) later reprinted in *The Brick Moon and Other Stories* (coll. **1899**), and published independently as *The Brick Moon* (**1971**), comprise probably the first attempt to describe an artificial Earth satellite, along with its launching into orbit. [JC]
Other works: *Ten Times One is Ten: The Possible Reformation* (**1871**), a ghost fantasy, as by Frederick Ingham.
About the author: "The Real Earth Satellite Story" in *Explorers of the Infinite* (1963) by Sam MOSKOWITZ.
See also: DISCOVERY AND INVENTION; PREDICTIONS.

HALIBUT, EDWARD *See* Richard WILSON.

HALL, AUSTIN (c. 1886–1933). American writer who claimed to have written over 600 stories in various PULP genres, mainly Westerns, with some sf, most notably *The Blind Spot* (1921 *Argosy*; **1951**) with Homer Eon FLINT, a novel of which Damon KNIGHT, by quoting from it, has demonstrated the awfulness, but which is still warmly remembered by some for its tale of the machinations surrounding a passage to a PARALLEL WORLD; a sequel, *The Spot of Life* (1932 *Argosy*; **1964**), was by AH alone, Flint having fallen (or been pushed) into a canyon. AH began publishing sf and fantasy with such stories as "Almost Immortal" for *All-Story Weekly* in 1916. Further sf novels include "Into the Infinite" (1919 *All-Story Weekly*), sequel to "The Rebel Soul" (1917 *All-Story Weekly*), which is a short story, and *People of the Comet* (1923 *Weird Tales* as "Hop o' My Thumb"; **1948**). The latter is a variant on the theme of · solar system as atom in a greater macrocosm, as discussed under GREAT AND SMALL. [JC]
See also: MARS.

HALL, CAMERON *See* Harry HARRISON.

HALL, DESMOND W. (? – ?). American writer and editor. Assistant editor of ASTOUNDING STORIES OF SUPER-SCIENCE under Harry BATES (1930–33), with whom he collaborated as a writer under the pseudonyms Anthony GILMORE and H.G. WINTER. He also wrote some stories under his own name. He continued as assistant editor for a time after F. Orlin TREMAINE took over from Bates, before being promoted to the editorship of the magazine *Mademoiselle*. H.L. GOLD has claimed that it was DWH rather than Tremaine who actually ran *ASF* (see "Gold on Gold" in *What Will They Think of Last?* **1976**). [MJE]
See also: SPACE OPERA.

HALL, H(ALBERT) W(ELDON) (1941–). American bibliographer, serials librarian at Texas A & M University Library, with a Master of Library Science from North Texas State in 1968. His useful series of bibliographies began with *SFBRI: Science Fiction Book Review Index Vol. 1 1970* (**1971**), and has been published annually since. A retrospective book was *Science Fiction Book Review Index, 1923–1973* (**1975**), which has rapidly become one of the most useful tools for the researcher; it is remarkably comprehensive and accurate, and contains in addition a great deal of data about sf magazine publication. HWH is an executive member of the SCIENCE FICTION RESEARCH ASSOCIATION, and on the editorial board of EXTRAPOLATION. [PN]

HALL, JAMES *See* Henry KUTTNER.

HALL, JOHN RYDER *See* William ROTSLER.

HALL, ROBERT LEE (1941–). American writer and high-school teacher whose entertaining first novel *Exit Sherlock Holmes* (**1977**; with minor revisions 1977 UK) purports to be a lost Watson manuscript telling more about the relationship of Holmes and Moriarty, and including TIME TRAVEL. [JC]

HALLE, LOUIS J(OSEPH) (1910–). American academic and writer. His UTOPIA, *Sedge* (**1963**), contrasts a community which isolates itself from civilization for hundreds of years with an increasingly frenetic world outside. [JC]

HALLUMS, JAMES R. (? –). British author of the routine sf paperback *They Came, They Saw* (**1965**).

HALLUS, TAK *See* Stephen ROBINETT.

HALSBURY, EARL OF (1880–1943). Hardinge Goulburn Giffard, Second Earl of Halsbury, English writer whose warning, future-WAR novel, *1944* (**1926**), depicts a cataclysmic conflict, with strictly contemporary weapons including gas, that leaves only a few survivors. It was his father, the first Earl, who was the famous writer on the law. [JC]

HAMILTON, EDMOND (MOORE) (1904–77). American writer, married to Leigh BRACKETT from 1946 to his death. With E.E. "Doc" SMITH and Jack WILLIAMSON, he was one of the most important instruments in the development of American sf from 1928, and was involved with those writers in the creation and popularization of the classic SPACE OPERA as it first appeared in the PULP sf magazines of the time; early space operas, in which science or pseudo-science served as an enabling doubletalk for the easier presentation of galaxy-spanning conflicts between humans and other races, piratical or merely monstrous, did much to define the sense of wonder for a generation of readers. EH's most notable contribution to the form in its early days was the story in which some form of terminal disaster from beyond threatens Earth and/or the Solar System, and in which rescue comes only at the last moment. For stories like these he was given a nickname or nicknames, sources differing as to whether he was dubbed "World-Destroyer", "The World Wrecker", or "World-Saver Hamilton", or indeed bore all these sobriquets.

EH's early education was in physics, a field he abandoned very young when he turned to fiction writing, his first published story being "The Monster-God of Mamurth" for *Weird Tales* in 1926. Soon becoming extremely prolific, he published almost 70 stories in the next decade, mostly in *Weird Tales*, and eight novels in that magazine and elsewhere. In the 1930s EH occasionally used pseudonyms on his stories; they included Robert Castle, Hugh Davidson, Robert Wentworth and the house name Will GARTH. With one exception, *Horror on the Asteroid & Other Tales of Planetary Horror* (coll. **1936**), one of the relatively rare hardcover pre-Second World War sf books from an American author, he was only to begin publishing in book form after the War. As an sf writer proper, he began publishing notable work with his first story for *AMZ*, "The Comet Doom" in 1928; "The Universe Wreckers", a novel serialized in *AMZ* in 1930, went a long way towards establishing the shape of his contribution to the genre, and prefigured much of his own work for the next decade, a period culminated for EH by his creation of the "Captain Future" series, published 1940–50 by Standard Magazines in CAPTAIN FUTURE (1940–44) and afterwards in Startling Stories (1945–6 and 1950–51).

Not all the "Captain Future" stories were by EH; five were signed with the house name Brett STERLING, three of which were in fact by EH and the other two ("Worlds to Come", 1943, and "Days of Creation", 1944) by Joseph Samachson; one was by Manly Wade WELLMAN. Each tale was written to a rigorous formula in which the super-scientist protagonist, backed by three aides (one ROBOT, one ANDROID and one brain in a box) would bring an interstellar villain to justice. Those eventually released in book form are *1. Danger Planet* (1945 *Startling Stories* as "Red Sun of Danger"; **1968**) as by Brett Sterling; *3. Outlaw World* (1946 *Startling Stories*; **1969**); *4. Quest Beyond the Stars* (1942 *Captain Future*; **1969**); *5. Outlaws of the Moon* (1942 *CF*; **1969**); *6. The Comet Kings* (1942 *CF*; **1969**), probably the outstanding among them; *7. Planets in Peril* (1942 *CF*; **1969**); *8. Calling Captain Future* (1940 *CF*; **1969**); *9. Captain Future's Challenge* (1940 *CF*; **1969**); *10. Galaxy Mission* (1940 *CF* as "The Triumph of Captain Future"; **1969**); *11. The Tenth Planet* (1944 *CF* as "Magic Moon"; **1969**) as by Brett Sterling; *12. The Magician of Mars* (1941 *CF*; **1969**); *13. Captain Future and the Space Emperor* (1940 *CF*; **1969**). The order of book publication does not follow the original order of publication, and it omits 11 other "Captain Future" stories by EH: "Captain Future and the Seven Space Stones" (1941), "Star Trail to Glory" (1941), "The Lost World of Time" (1941), "The Face of the Deep" (1943), "The Return of Captain Future" (1950), "Children of the Sun" (1950), "The Harpers of Titan" (1950), "Pardon My Iron Nerves" (1950), "Moon of the Unforgotten" (1951), "Earthmen no More" (1951) and "Birthplace of Creation" (1951). It also omits "The Star of Dread" (1943) by EH as Brett Sterling. No. 2 in the "Captain Future" book series is *The Solar Invasion* (1946 *Startling Stories*; **1969**) by Manly Wade Wellman.

The original idea for *Captain Future* came from Mort WEISINGER, a senior editor with the Standard Magazines group. Later, in 1941, Weisinger shifted into comics, working for the DC group. He took many of his top writers with him, including EH, who worked for some time in the middle 1940s as a staff writer on SUPERMAN, along with Henry KUTTNER and others.

Unfortunately for EH, his work in comics and his involvement with *Captain Future* (which was primarily aimed at teenage boys) made it initially somewhat difficult for him to be accepted after the Second World War as the competent and versatile professional he had in fact been for years, a writer with a much wider range than was generally realized, who had already produced several stories whose comparatively sober verisimilitude prefigured post-War requirements. After his marriage to Leigh Brackett in 1946 his output diminished, but its quality increased; this is obscured by the fact that many of his books from this time reflected or indeed reprinted the kind of work he had become known for in his early years. His "Interstellar Patrol" series, for instance, which had appeared in *Weird Tales* from 1928 to 1930, were reprinted, with the exception of "The Sun People" (1930), as *Outside the Universe* (1929 *Weird Tales*; **1964**) and *Crashing Suns* (coll. **1965**). A further publication of this sort is *Tharkol, Lord of the Unknown* (1939 *Startling Stories*; **1950**), in which Martians invade Earth for its water. Other novels which repeated the space-opera routines with which he had become identified include *The Sun Smasher* (1954 *Universe*; **1959**), *Battle for the Stars* (1956 *Imagination* under the house name Alexander BLADE; exp. **1961**), *Fugitive of the Stars* (1957 *Imagination*; rev. **1965**), and his final "Starwolf" series, about tough interstellar adventurer Morgan Chane, comprised of *The Weapon from Beyond* (**1967**), *The Closed Worlds* (**1968**) and *World of the Starwolves* (**1968**).

At the same time, however, EH was writing novels which, though in the space-opera tradition, were more formidably composed and darker in texture than his run-of-the-mill performances. It is for these novels, plus *The Monsters of Juntonheim* (1941 *Startling Stories* as "A Yank at Valhalla"; **1950**; vt *A Yank at Valhalla* USA), that he will be remembered. The best of them is probably *The Haunted Stars* (**1960**), in which well-characterized humans face a shattering mystery on the Moon: the secret of star travel left by long-dead aliens, but surrounded by dark warnings. *The Star Kings* (**1949**; vt *Beyond the Moon*) runs it a close second, is grander in scope but less impressively written; its sequels are collected in *Return to the Stars* (coll. of linked stories **1970**).

The Valley of Creation (1948 *Startling Stories*; rev. **1964**) is also strongly written, combining SWORD AND SORCERY with an sf dénouement.

With his long-time colleague Jack Williamson, EH shared a capable and flexible attitude towards his craft and its markets, in contrast to the third great originator of American space opera, E.E. "Doc" Smith. It is also apparent, from his work of later years, that EH enjoyed writing adventure sf more than other kinds of marketable fiction, because though his range was wide his best efforts were generically similar to his most routine. He was able, in other words, to take space opera seriously enough to make it good. Through his ability to evolve a cleaner and more literate style over the years, and to apply this style to his old generic loves, he wrote novels at the end of his career that read perfectly idiomatically as novels of the 1960s, as evidenced also in two compendiums of his shorter work, *What's It Like Out There, and Other Stories* (coll. **1974**) and the posthumous *The Best of Edmond Hamilton* (coll. **1977**) ed. Leigh Brackett.   [JC]

Other works: *Murder in the Clinic* (coll. of two stories 1946) is a pamphlet in the AMERICAN FICTION series; *City at World's End* (**1951**); *The Star of Life* (1947 *Startling Stories*; rev. **1959**); *Doomstar* (**1966**).

See also: ALIENS; ASTEROIDS; COLONIZATION OF OTHER WORLDS; COMPUTERS; COSMOLOGY; CYBORGS; DEVOLUTION; END OF THE WORLD; EVOLUTION; FANTASTIC VOYAGES; GALACTIC EMPIRES; HEROES; INVISIBILITY; ISLANDS; JUPITER; LIVING WORLDS; MARS; MATTER TRANSMISSION; MOON; MUTANTS; MYTHOLOGY; PARALLEL WORLDS; PARANOIA AND SCHIZOPHRENIA; PSEUDO-SCIENCE; PUBLISHING; RELIGION; SPACE FLIGHT; STARS; SUN; TIME TRAVEL; WAR; WEAPONS.

HAMILTON, PATRICK See PSYCHOLOGY.

HAMLET, OVA See Richard A. LUPOFF.

HAMLING, WILLIAM L(AWRENCE) (1921–). American writer and editor. He was an active sf fan in the late 1930s and early 1940s, and published a number of stories, the first of which, "War with Jupiter" (1939), appeared in AMAZING STORIES and was a collaboration with Mark Reinsberg. He later went to work for Ziff-Davis Publishers, under Raymond A. PALMER, and became managing editor of *AMZ* and FANTASTIC ADVENTURES 1948–50. In 1951 he became editor and publisher of IMAGINATION, having bought the title from Palmer. He added a companion, IMAGINATIVE TALES, and continued both until late 1958. In 1955 he started an early men's magazine, *Rogue*, and in the late 1960s his publishing company Greenleaf Classics, which specialized in erotic novels, ran badly foul of American pornography laws for publishing an illustrated edition of a Congressional investigation of pornography, an offence for which he was imprisoned, along with his co-publisher Earl Kemp (1929–), compiler of the pamphlet *Who Killed Science Fiction?* (anth. **1960**). Greenleaf Classics and its associated imprints (Adult Books, Candid Readers, Companion Books, Ember Library, Idle Hour Books, Late Hour Library, Leisure Books, Nightstand Books, Pleasure Readers and Regency Books) published over 50 titles of sf pornography; they are listed in *The Science Fiction Collector 4* (**1977**) ed. J. Grant Thiessen. Greenleaf published several of the early works of Harlan ELLISON.   [MJE/PN]

HAMMOND, KEITH See Henry KUTTNER.

HAMMURA, RYO See JAPAN.

HAMPSON, FRANK (1917–). British artist. Almost single-handedly, he

The clear-cut, vivid style of Frank HAMPSON in *Dan Dare*, this from *The Eagle*, 19 April 1957.

brought the British COMIC STRIP into the scientific age. When the Rev. Marcus Morris and FH originated the *Eagle* comic in 1949–50, FH created the sf strip DAN DARE — PILOT·OF THE FUTURE for its full-colour front pages. What made *Dan Dare* so revolutionary was FH's genius for colour and draughtsmanship; he brought the comic strip closer to the cinema than any other artist before him, with panoramas, close-ups, and a great feeling for movement and sequence. Until 1959 FH, together with a team of artists, scriptwriters and scientific advisers, controlled the 1950s cult figure spaceman on his adventures across the Solar System.

After FH's departure from *Dan Dare* in 1959, his creation was unsuccessfully revamped several times during stages of the commercial decline of *Eagle*. Today he does not draw for comics. [ABP]

HANDS OF A STRANGER *See* HANDS OF ORLAC, THE.

HANDS OF ORLAC, THE (original title **ORLACS HÄNDE**) Film (1924). Pan Film. Directed by Robert Wiene, starring Conrad Veidt, Fritz Kortner, Carmen Cartellieri and Alexandra Sorina. Screenplay by Louis Nerz, based on the novel *Les mains d'Orlac* by Maurice RENARD. 70 mins. B/w.

In this Austrian film made by the director of *The Cabinet of Doctor Caligari*, a pianist, whose hands, severely injured in an accident, are replaced with those of an executed murderer, discovers that he has inherited the murderer's homicidal tendencies as well, and fights a losing battle to prevent himself being dominated by the dead man. The central idea is scientifically absurd but has an emotional logic, and it has attracted many film-makers. In 1935 the Renard novel also provided a basis for *Mad Love* (vt *The Hands of Orlac*), directed by Karl Freund from a script by Guy ENDORE and Freund himself, in which Peter Lorre plays an evil surgeon who grafts the murderer's hands on to a pianist, and then attempts to drive him insane by masquerading as the executed murderer back from the dead. Later two remakes

Mad Love was a 1934 remake of THE HANDS OF ORLAC; Peter Lorre looks appropriately menacing on the poster.

were produced — one using the original title *The Hands of Orlac* (1959; vt *Les mains d'Orlac*) and the other called *Hands of a Stranger* (1963). The former was a British-French co-production directed by Edmond T. Grenville and starring Mel Ferrer, Lucille Saint-Simon, Christopher Lee, Donald Pleasence and David Peel, with screenplay by John Baines and Edmond T. Grenville; the latter film was American, directed by Newton Arnold and starring Paul Lukather, Joan Harvey, Barry Gordon and Sally Kellerman, from a screenplay by Newton Arnold. [JB]

HANNA, W.C. (? –). American writer. In his *The Tandar Saga* (1964), the inhabitants of Tandar cruise space looking for habitable planets. [JC]

HANSEN, VERN (? –). British writer of a number of routine sf adventures over a short period, beginning with *The Whisper of Death* (**1962**). The others are: *Murder with Menaces* (**1963**); *The Twisters* (**1963**); *Creatures of the Mist* (**1963**); *Claws of the Night* (**1964**); *The Grip of Fear* (**1964**). [JC]

HANSMAN, WILLIAM (DONALD) (1913–). Canadian-born American writer whose sf novel is *The A.G. Man* (**1968**). [JC]

HÄPNA! *See* SCANDINAVIA.

HARBEN, WILL(IAM) N(ATHANIEL) (1858–1919). American writer whose sf novel, *The Land of the Changing Sun* (**1904**), features an underground society founded in an Arctic cavern (which is heated and lit by an artificial electrical sun) by a group interested in eugenics and opposed to conventional medicine. [JC]
See also: LOST WORLDS.

HARBOTTLE, PHILIP (JAMES) (1941–). Local government officer, sf researcher and literary agent. PH is the world authority on the works of John Russell FEARN (whose literary estate he represents), with whom he has posthumously collaborated, completing several stories. His bibliographical study of Fearn is *The Multi-Man* (1968). PH is the best-known expert in publishing data relating to British genre sf, especially PULP sf, and his name appears in the acknowledgements section of nearly every British book on sf. He edited the

Conrad Veidt looks pale in bed, a new and malicious hand grafted on to him, in THE HANDS OF ORLAC, 1924.

magazine *Vision of Tomorrow* for its 12 issues, Aug. 1969-Sep. 1970.   [PN]

HARDCORE SF The term, as used by most readers, is synonymous with "hard sf". It has two parallel meanings, however, not quite identical: first, hardcore sf is the kind of sf which repeats the themes and usually the style of genre sf written during the so-called GOLDEN AGE OF SF; second, it is sf that deals with the so-called "hard" sciences. Entries in this volume which deal with hard sf themes, and indeed with "hard" sciences, include ASTRONOMY, BLACK HOLES, COMPUTERS, COMMUNICATIONS (this covers both hard and soft sf themes), COSMOLOGY, CRYONICS, CYBERNETICS, CYBORGS, DISCOVERY AND INVENTION, FASTER THAN LIGHT, GRAVITY, NUCLEAR POWER, PHYSICS, POWER SOURCES, ROCKETS, SPACE FLIGHT, SPACE SHIPS, TERRAFORMING, TECHNOLOGY. In some uses the term "hard sf" deals only with the second of these, i.e. sf that deals with the "hard" sciences. In other uses "hard sf" stories would include, say, ESP, SUPERMAN and TIME-TRAVEL themes. Further discussion of this subject will be found under the entry for its antonym, SOFT SF.   [PN]

HARDING, LEE (1937–). Australian writer. He began publishing sf with "Displaced Person" for *Science Fantasy* in 1961, and concentrated on the magazine field for the next decade under his own name, and briefly under the pseudonym Harold G. Nye. For his short work, he twice won a DITMAR, in 1970 for "Dancing Gerontius" (1969) and in 1972 for "The Fallen Spaceman" (1971), the original magazine version of his first novel, *The Fallen Spaceman* (1971 *If*; rev. and exp. **1974** Australia), a juvenile. His adult novels, *A World of Shadows* (**1975**), *Future Sanctuary* (**1976**) and *The Weeping Sky* (**1977** Australia), have been perhaps less notable than his juveniles, which also include *The Children of Atlantis* (**1976** Australia), *The Frozen Sky* (**1976** Australia) and *Return to Tomorrow* (**1977** Australia). LH edited *Beyond Tomorrow* (anth. **1976** Australia), including some stories by Australian writers, and *The Altered I* (anth. **1976**) which presents some of the productions of an sf workship in Australia, presided over by Ursula K. LE GUIN.   [JC]
See also: PSYCHOLOGY.

HARD SF See HARDCORE SF.

HARGRAVE, LEONIE See Thomas M. DISCH.

HARKER, KENNETH (? –). English author with training in physics whose sf novels, *The Symmetrians* (**1966**), which is about GENETIC ENGINEERING, and *The Flowers of February* (**1970**), are straightforward but uninspired.   [JC]
See also: RELIGION.

HARMON, H.H. See Robert Moore WILLIAMS.

HARMON, JIM (? –). American writer and RADIO producer, who began publishing sf with "The Smuggler" for *Spaceway* in 1954, and has been active in the magazine field. A non-fiction book, *The Great Radio Heroes* (**1967**), discusses SUPERMAN and other programmes and characters of sf interest. A similarly well-documented, nostalgic study is *The Great Movie Serials: their Sound and Fury* (**1972**) by JH and Donald F. Glutt. JH also contributed a number of articles to RIVERSIDE QUARTERLY.   [JC/PN]

HARNESS, CHARLES L(EONARD) (1915–). American patent attorney and writer, born in Texas. The bulk of his sf has been written in two brief periods: 1948–53 and 1966–8. His first published story was "Time Trap" (1948 *ASF*), written to pay the obstetric bills following the birth of his daughter, a convoluted time-loop story involving the working of tremendous forces off-stage and a quasi-transcendental experience as the hero goes back in time to remake the world. His subsequent work shows a remarkable consistency in echoing and developing these themes. Both his full-length novels, *Flight into Yesterday* (1949; exp. **1953**; vt *The Paradox Men*) and *The Ring of Ritornel* (**1968**) use the elements of cycles in time and heroes who undergo a transcendental metamorphosis in order to manipulate their own destinies and that of the human race. The novels have an obvious kinship with the work of A.E. VAN VOGT, but are less confused and written with assurance and control. They are powerful melodramas – Brian ALDISS characterized the first as "widescreen baroque" in his introduction to the British edition — and they use ideas colourfully and artfully. Another work in the same pattern is "The New Reality" (1950), by far the best of sf's ADAM AND EVE stories, which transforms the Genesis myth into a prophecy and sets up a situation in which it can come true, with some artful juggling of the basic ideas of METAPHYSICS. Time-loops also form the core of "Stalemate in Space" (1949; vt "Stalemate in Time"), "Child by Chronos" (1953) and "The Araqnid Window" (1974). Harness's most important work is probably the short novel "The Rose" (1953; title story of *The Rose*, coll. **1966**, which also includes "The New Reality" and "The Chessplayers"). As with the long novels this is a story of transcendental metamorphosis via death, and it is a significant contribution to sf's SUPERMAN mythology, but it is also concerned with the "enmity" of science and art (*see* ARTS). It failed to find a market in the USA when first written and was published in the minor British magazine AUTHENTIC. Its reappearance in the 1960s was the result of Michael MOORCOCK's interest in

Harness — Moorcock reprinted several Harness stories in NEW WORLDS and persuaded *NW*'s publisher to release "The Rose" in book form. This renewal of interest may have been responsible for Harness's second burst of creativity, which produced not only *The Ring of Ritornel* but also three notable novelettes, all drawing on his experience as a lawyer: "An Ornament to His Profession" (1966), "The Alchemist" (1966) and "Probable Cause" (1968). Harness is a highly imaginative writer whose relative neglect in his own country is difficult to understand. Had he been better appreciated he might have written much more, and might well have become one of the leading names in the field. It seems, however, that he has not yet abandoned sf. His post-HOLOCAUST novel "Wolfhead" began serialization in *FSF* Nov. 1977.   [BS]
See also: COMPUTERS; COSMOLOGY; CRIME AND PUNISHMENT; DEVOLUTION; ESCHATOLOGY; FASTER THAN LIGHT; GALACTIC EMPIRES; GAMES AND SPORTS; MEDICINE; MYTHOLOGY; SUN; TIME PARADOXES; TIME TRAVEL; WEAPONS; WOMEN.

HARPER, HARRY (? – ?). British author with Claude GRAHAME-WHITE of two sf juveniles, *The Invisible Warplane* (**1915**) and *The Air King's Treasure*, for which we do not have a date. In the former an airship is concealed by paint which neither absorbs nor reflects light. Much later HH wrote two solo works, *Winged World* (**1946**) and *Dawn of the Space Age* (**1946**).   [PN]

HARPER, VINCENT (? – ?). American writer whose sf novel, *The Mortgage on the Brain: being the Confessions of the late Ethelbert Craft, MD* (**1905**), describes an electrical shock treatment which alters personality beneficially and undermines many of the then conventional views of the nature of the mind.   [JC]
See also : PSYCHOLOGY.

HARRIS, JOHN BEYNON or **JOHNSON** See John WYNDHAM.

HARRIS, LARRY M(ARK) The name under which Laurence M. JANIFER was born, and which he used for his early fiction. *See* JANIFER *entry for details*.

HARRISON, HARRY (1925–). American writer, now resident in Ireland. HH began his career as a commercial artist, working chiefly in COMICS. He was by this time already an sf enthusiast and knew many writers through his membership of the Hydra Club, a New York group of sf professionals. Among them was Damon KNIGHT, who commissioned HH to do illustrations for WORLDS BEYOND, and later bought his first story, "Rock Diver" (1951), for that magazine. In 1953–4 he was briefly editor of the magazines FANTASY FICTION (under the pseudonym Cameron Hall), SCIENCE FICTION ADVENTURES, and probably ROCKET STORIES under the house pseudonym Wade KAEMPFERT. Additional pseudonyms used by HH are Felix Boyd and Hank Dempsey.

In 1957, HH sold his first story to John W. CAMPBELL Jr for ASTOUNDING SCIENCE FICTION, initiating a long and close relationship with editor and magazine. This was the first story of a series featuring the interstellar-criminal-turned-law-enforcer Slippery Jim DiGriz, fast-moving adventures with a broad leavening of HUMOUR: *The Stainless Steel Rat* (1957–60 *ASF*; fix-up **1961**) was followed by *The Stainless Steel Rat's Revenge* (**1970**) and *The Stainless Steel Rat Saves the World* (**1972**). HH did the jacket illustrations for the UK hardcover editions of the second and third books.

Notoriously peripatetic, HH had moved with his family from New York to Mexico; later travels took them to England and Italy, Denmark and California, and lately to Dublin. His novel *Deathworld* (**1960**), telling of the COLONIZATION of a planet crammed with hostile life, established him as a vigorous writer of intelligent action adventures. It was followed by *Deathworld 2* (**1964**; vt *The Ethical Engineer* UK), *Deathworld 3* (**1968**) and "The Mothballed Spaceship" (1973).

HH wrote a group of stories exploring the ROBOT theme, *War With the Robots* (coll. **1962**). Later, he similarly examined MATTER TRANSMISSION in *One Step From Earth* (coll. **1970**). Other notable short stories were "The Streets of Ashkelon" (1962) on a RELIGIOUS theme, and "Rescue Operation" (1964). *Bill, The Galactic Hero* (**1965**) was another humorous work, an extended lampoon of aspects of stories by Robert HEINLEIN, Isaac ASIMOV and HH himself. E.E. "Doc" SMITH came in for similar treatment in *Star Smashers of the Galaxy Rangers* (**1973**). In contrast, *Make Room! Make Room!* (**1966**) was a serious, indeed impassioned, novel of OVERPOPULATION. It formed the basis of the film SOYLENT GREEN (1973), but much of its substance was lost in transition. Later novels include *The Technicolor Time Machine* (**1967**), *Captive Universe* (**1969**), *The Daleth Effect* (**1970**; vt *In Our Hands, the Stars* UK), *Tunnel Through the Deeps* (**1972**; vt *A Transatlantic Tunnel, Hurrah!* UK) and *Skyfall* (**1976**). *Captive Universe* is an unusual GENERATION STARSHIP story using a background of Aztec culture (*see also* CONCEPTUAL BREAKTHROUGH). *Tunnel Through the Deeps* is a PARALLEL WORLDS novel in which the American Revolution failed and the British Empire still flourishes. *Skyfall* adheres closely to the conventional DISASTER-novel format.

HH always remained a stout defender of John W. Campbell, even though as editor and critic his attitudes often seemed diametrically opposite. He edited Campbell's *Collected Editorials from Analog* (coll. **1966**); was filmed at a working lunch with Campbell and Gordon R. DICKSON, a session which resulted in the Harrison-Dickson collaborative novel *The Lifeship* (**1976**; vt *Lifeboat* UK); and after Campbell's death he edited a memorial anthology, *Astounding* (anth. **1973**; vt *The John W. Campbell Memorial Anthology* UK).

He has been closely identified personally and professionally with Brian W. ALDISS. Together they founded the critical magazine SF HORIZONS; they edit an annual best of the year anthology; they collaborate on other anthologies, such as *The Astounding-Analog Reader* (anth. in two volumes **1972** and **1973**; UK edition splits the first volume into two more) and the "Decade" series — *Decade: the 1940s* (anth. **1975**), *Decade: the 1950s* (anth. **1976**), *Decade: the 1960s* (anth. **1977**).

As an editor HH was for short periods in charge of the magazines IMPULSE, AMAZING STORIES and FANTASTIC. He has produced the NOVA series of original anthologies. An interesting series of collections, in which writers choose and comment on their personal favourites among their stories, is *SF: Author's Choice* (anth. **1968**; vt *Backdrop of Stars* UK), *SF: Author's Choice 2* (anth. **1970**), *SF: Author's Choice 3* (anth. **1971**) and *SF: Author's Choice 4* (anth. **1974**).

HH describes his career in "The Beginning of the Affair", his contribution to the collection of sf writers' autobiographies *Hell's Cartographers* (coll. **1975**), another Aldiss-Harrison co-production. Since moving to Dublin he has organized the first World Science Fiction Writer's Conference, held there in 1976.

HH has also written two crime novels. A recent work is *Great Balls of Fire: A History of Sex in Science Fiction Illustration* (**1977**). [MJE]

Other works: *Planet of the Damned* (**1962**; vt *Sense of Obligation* UK); *Plague from Space* (**1965**; vt *The Jupiter Legacy*); *Two Tales and Eight To-morrows* (coll. **1965**); *The Man From P.I.G.* (**1968**); *Best SF: 1967* (anth. **1968**; vt *Year's Best Science Fiction* UK on this and all subsequent volumes, all of which are collaborations with Brian Aldiss); *Worlds of Wonder* (anth. **1969**); *Best SF: 1968* (anth. **1969**); *Prime Number* (coll. **1970**); *Spaceship Medic* (**1970**); *The Year 2000* (anth. **1970**); *Best SF: 1969* (anth. **1970**); *The Light Fantastic* (anth. **1971**; co-editor Theodore J. Gordon); *Best SF: 1970* (anth. **1971**); *Stonehenge* (**1972**; collaboration with Leon E. STOVER); *Ahead of Time* (anth. **1972**; co-editor Theodore J. Gordon); *Best SF: 1971* (anth. **1972**); *Best SF: 1972* (anth. **1973**); *The Men From P.I.G. and R.O.B.O.T.* (coll. **1974**); *Best SF: 1973* (anth. **1974**); *The California Iceberg* (**1975**); *Best SF: 1974* (anth. **1975**); *Best SF: 1975* (anth. **1976**); *The Best of Harry Harrison* (coll. **1976**; UK edition omits introduction and one story, adds two stories).

See also: ALTERNATE WORLDS; ANTHROPOLOGY; ARTS; ATLANTIS; CRIME AND PUNISHMENT; DYSTOPIAS; FAR FUTURE; GRAVITY; HEROES; ICONOCLASM; LIFE ON OTHER WORLDS; MAINSTREAM WRITERS OF SF; MEDIA LANDSCAPE; MESSIAHS; MYTHOLOGY; NEW WAVE; PANTROPY; POLITICS; POLLUTION; PSI POWERS; SATIRE; SEX; SPACE OPERA; TABOOS; TIME TRAVEL; TRANSPORTATION; UNDER THE SEA; VENUS.

HARRISON, MICHAEL (? –). English writer in various genres, mostly not sf. His fascinating sf novel, *Higher Things* (**1945**), could almost have been written by H.G. WELLS; its structure is certainly Wellsian. An impoverished young man, caught in the trammels of a clerical position but with dreams of higher things, finds in himself the power to levitate, which he does at crucial moments in his rather melancholy life to escape his and the world's muddles. This pattern out of early Wells is succeeded by a long (probably delusional) flight to confront the Dictator (Hitler) and to discuss with him the world's fate; this mid-Wellsian device is succeeded by a Wellsian quietus: the protagonist, haunted by paranoia, decides to escape the world entirely in a levitated, airtight gondola. The novel is told in the form of an autobiographical manuscript, and has been undeservedly neglected. MH also wrote *The Brain* (**1953**), about a sentient mushroom cloud. [JC]
Other works: *The Darkened Room* (1952) is a borderline sf mystery novel.

M. John HARRISON stokes himself up for rock-climbing.

HARRISON, M(ICHAEL) JOHN (1945–). English writer and rock-climber, closely identified with *NW* in the late 1960s with stories (including some of the best using Michael MOORCOCK's "Jerry Cornelius" template) and criticism, much of the latter written as Joyce Churchill. He also served as the *NW* literary editor. He began publishing sf with "Baa Baa Blocksheep" for *NW* in 1968; his first novel, *The Committed Men* (**1971**; rev. 1971 UK), is an impressive post-HOLOCAUST story set in a fractured England, and centering physically on the ruins of the motorways. *The Pastel City* (**1971**) is a FAR-FUTURE fantasy with some sf appliances (vestiges of old science are introduced, though not centrally), set on a bleak Dying Earth whose description plays on SWORD-AND-SORCERY imagery; a quasi-sequel is projected. *The Centauri Device* (**1974**) is a SPACE OPERA, the eponymous device being a doomsday machine, with the galaxy at risk; it is told with a pessimistic darkness reminiscent more of Barrington J. BAYLEY than of typical PULP versions of the form. MJH's earlier fiction is assembled in *The Machine in Shaft Ten and Other Stories* (coll. **1975**), and reveals its generally NEW-WAVE origins in narrative discontinuities and subheads after the fashion of J. G. BALLARD. MJH's later fiction includes a remarkable novelette about ENTROPY, "Running Down" (1975), and the chilling story of aliens, "Settling the World" (1975); both are told in an ample "traditional" style, which makes the force of their vision – in which metaphors and literal representations of insects dominate — all the more powerful. MJH has written relatively little, but almost all his work shows an intense working out of the language and generic material of modern sf.

MJH, responding to a question about series, has inveighed against the "series mentality", and written: "The best fantasy is a *terra incognita*. The reader is first lured into it and then abandoned. If he doesn't enjoy his subsequent bewilderment he should be reading *Which Car?* instead ... A series by me does exist, but it is a secret, a sub-crustal, a Borgesian series; only its devotees can recognize the more arcane of its components." [JC]
See also: ABSURDIST SF; CRITICAL AND HISTORICAL WORKS; DISASTER; INVASION; PERCEPTION.

HARRYHAUSEN, RAY (1920–). American special-effects man, now based in England, associated with many sf and fantasy films. As a boy his main interests were sculpture and paleontology and he spent much of his time building miniature dioramas depicting various phases of prehistoric life. Then the release of KING KONG made him aware of the existence of model animation, and the desire to see his own clay figures move on the screen stimulated his interest in photography and special effects. In 1937 he began working with George PAL on Pal's "Puppetoon" series, which featured animated dolls, at Paramount Studio. After serving in the army during the Second World War he approached Willis H. O'BRIEN, who had animated King Kong and was currently starting preparation work on MIGHTY JOE YOUNG. RH showed O'Brien some sample footage of his work, on 16mm, and was hired as his assistant. After *Mighty Joe Young*

(1948) work was begun on another animated feature, *El Toro Estrella*, about a boy, a bull and a dinosaur, but Paramount was unwilling to finance it and the project was abandoned. Harryhausen and O'Brien then went their separate ways, though they did team up briefly in 1956 to work on the dinosaur sequences in the pseudo-documentary *Animal World*. In 1953 Harryhausen was given the chance to supervise the effects in THE BEAST FROM 20,000 FATHOMS. The film was a success, and he then formed the partnership with producer Charles H. Schneer which still exists today. Their first film together was IT CAME FROM BENEATH THE SEA (1955), followed by EARTH VERSUS THE FLYING SAUCERS (1956), and TWENTY MILLION MILES TO EARTH (1957). By then the sf film boom was in decline and they decided that their next project would be a straight fantasy. In 1959 they made *The Seventh Voyage of Sinbad*, which was the first animation film of its type to be shot in colour. It proved a huge financial success and similar films followed: *The Three Worlds of Gulliver* (1960), MYSTERIOUS ISLAND (1961) and *Jason and the Argonauts* (1963). Then there was a shift back to sf with FIRST MEN IN THE MOON (1964), ONE MILLION YEARS BC (1966) and *Valley of Gwangi* (1969). The latter was a failure so they returned to pure fantasy for their next film, *The Golden Voyage of Sinbad* (1973). The sequel to this successful film was *Sinbad and the Eye of the Tiger* (1977), most ambitious of RH's films in its effects, and in the view of many critics the best. [JB]

HART, ELLIS See Harlan ELLISON.

HARTLEY, L(ESLIE) P(OLES) (1895–1972). British novelist and short-story writer. Known mainly for his works outside the sf field, especially his trilogy *The Shrimp and the Anemone* (**1944**), *The Sixth Heaven* (**1946**), which has some slight fantasy content, and *Eustace and Hilda* (**1947**). In *The Collected Short Stories of L. P. Hartley* (coll. **1968**) there are a good many ghost stories and fantasies. His sf novel, *Facial Justice* (**1960**), deals sourly but sensitively with personal dilemmas in a post-World-War-Three egalitarian DYSTOPIA, many of whose precepts satirize the welfare state and English socialism: true equality involves an equality of physical appearance, as in Kurt VONNEGUT's "Harrison Bergeron" (1961), but in this case the effects are poignant. [JC]

HARTLIB, SAMUEL (c. 1600–1662). English writer of a Royalist UTOPIA, *A Description of the Famous Kingdom of Macaria* (**1641**); a fascimile edition (USA) was published in 1961. [JC]

HARTRIDGE, JON (1934–). English writer associated, along with Brian W. ALDISS, with the *Oxford Mail*, of which

he is features editor. His sf novels, *Binary Divine* (**1969**) and *Earthjacket* (**1970**), take a dark view of Earth's crowded, DYSTOPIAN, urbanized future. [JC]

HARVEY, FRANK (? –). American writer whose collection of stories, *Air Force!* (coll. **1959**), concentrates on that branch of the armed services, but with a NEAR-FUTURE setting which includes manned satellites, and the like. [JC]

HASKIN, BYRON (1899–). American director who has made several sf films. His film career began in 1919 when he became an assistant cameraman for Louis J. Selznick. In 1927 he made his directorial début with *Matinee Ladies* for Warner Brothers. In 1930 he accompanied Herbert Wilcox to England as a production assistant and as an expert on multiple-camera sound. Financial rewards in England were slim so in 1932 BH returned to Hollywood and began a new career as a special-effects cameraman. In 1947 he began directing again with *I Walk Alone*, a Hal Wallis production. His first sf film was WAR OF THE WORLDS in 1953 for producer George PAL, followed by THE NAKED JUNGLE in 1954, CONQUEST OF SPACE in 1955 (both Pal productions), FROM THE EARTH TO THE MOON (1959), ROBINSON CRUSOE ON MARS (1964) and THE POWER (1967), the latter co-directed with Pal. BH's background in special effects meant that he never neglected them in his films, though many other sf film-makers did so in the 1950s, but as a director he was not extraordinary. *War of the Worlds* derives impact from its spectacle, but most of his other sf films are merely competent. Probably his most interesting and personal film, on which he had a fair degree of control, was *Robinson Crusoe on Mars*. He retired in 1967. [JB]

HASSE, HENRY L. (? –). American fan and sf writer, frequently seen in collaboration with others, notably A. Fedor, with whom he published his first story, "The End of Tyme" for *Wonder Stories* in 1933, Emil PETAJA, with whom he once shared Petaja's pseudonym E. Theodore Pine, and Ray BRADBURY, with whom he collaborated on Bradbury's first professional story, "Pendulum" (1941). His sf novel, *The Stars Will Wait* (**1968**), is unremarkable. His best-known story is the novelette "He Who Shrank" (**1936**) (*see* GREAT AND SMALL). [JC]

HASSELBLATT, DIETER (1926–). Critic and editor, born in Reval in Germany; he wrote a dissertation on Franz KAFKA. At Deutschlandfunk and now Bayerische Rundfunk he has been responsible for the production of many sf RADIO plays. Currently he is also editing a series of juvenile sf by German authors, for which series he had edited the anthology *Das Experiment* (anth. **1975**).

His critical book *Grüne Männchen vom Mars: Science Fiction für Leser und Macher* ["Little Green Men from Mars: Science Fiction for Readers and Writers"] (**1974**) treats sf as a part of popular culture, emphasizing market conditions and giving also some advice for the successful writing of sf. [FR]

HASSLER, KENNETH W. (? –). His routine sf novels are *The Glass Cage* (**1969**) *Destination: Terra* (**1970**), *The Dream Squad* (**1970**), *A Message from Earth* (**1970**), *Intergalac Agent* (**1971**) and *The Multiple Man* (**1972**). [JC]

HASTINGS, HUDSON *See* Henry KUTTNER.

HASTINGS, MILO (1884–1957). American writer, sometimes on agricultural subjects; his *The Dollar Hen* (**1909**) is non-fiction, about hens. *City of Endless Night* (**1920**) has Germany starting another war, losing, and building a last redoubt underneath Berlin from which it continues to fight the rest of the world while transforming its millions of underground citizens into classes genetically distinguished from one another by their rulers' breeding programme. The novel's imagery links it with the German Expressionist cinema and films like Fritz LANG's METROPOLIS (1926), as well as to DYSTOPIAS like HUXLEY's *Brave New World* (**1932**). [JC]
See also: POLITICS.

HATCH, GERALD Pseudonym of American writer Dave Foley (? –), whose sf novel, *The Day the Earth Froze* (**1963**), is one of a series of novels published by Monarch Books on similar themes, including Charles FONTENAY's *The Day the Oceans Overflowed* (**1964**) and Christopher ANVIL's *The Day the Machines Stopped* (**1964**). [JC]

HATFIELD, RICHARD (1853– ?). American writer who himself published his LOST-WORLD novel, *Geyserland: 9262 B.C.: Empiricism in Social Reform; being Data and Observations Recorded by the late Mark Stubble, M.D., Ph.D.* (**1908**), the Arctic lost continent being Edenic and the politics Christian Socialist. [JC]

HAUSER'S MEMORY Made-for-TV film (1970). Universal/NBC TV. Directed by Boris Sagal, starring David McCallum, Susan Strasberg, Lilli Palmer, Robert Webber and Leslie Nielsen. Screenplay by Adrian Spies, based on the novel of the same title by Curt SIODMAK. 104 mins. Colour.

Siodmak's novel is an up-to-date although scientifically absurd variation on the theme of his earlier *Donovan's Brain* (1943), which was filmed three times: that of a dead man's mind somehow exerting influence on the living. In the previous novel a disembodied brain takes over the mind of the scientist experimenting with it, but this time DNA material, which is extracted from the brain of a dead German Nazi scientist in order to preserve his scientific knowledge, is accidentally injected into a young Jewish-American scientist. The conflicts that the dead man's memories create within the hero's mind have a great deal of dramatic potential, most of which is wasted as the film degenerates into a conventional thriller about the CIA versus the Russians. At the end, Hauser's memory now dominating the hero, a melodramatic revenge sequence takes place. [JB]

HAWKES, JACQUETTA (1910–). British archaeologist and writer. Known mainly for such works outside the sf field as *The Land* (**1951**). She is married to J.B. PRIESTLEY. Her assembly of exemplary *Fables* (coll. **1953**; vt *A Woman as Great as the World and Other Fables* USA) includes a long story that weds fantasy and DYSTOPIAN sf: God sends an angel down to Earth to find out why men have grown silent; the angel reports that *Homo sapiens* has degenerated into hive-dwelling automata, a Dystopian life arrived at through too sedulous a striving after equality. But an underground group of dissidents team up with some Royals from a mountain fastness and institute a new monarchy. Back in the caves, exiled egalitarians begin the cycle of opposition. God is more or less pleased. *Providence Island: An Archaeological Tale* (**1959**) is a fairly late example of ANTHROPOLOGICAL sf, in which an expedition comes across survivors from the Magdalenian peoples of the Paleolithic period living within the cup of an extinct volcano on a Pacific ISLAND; they have highly developed empathic and PSI POWERS, developed as a kind of cultural alternative to technological prowess, but need to be protected from the 20th century. [JC]

HAWKIN, MARTIN. Form of his name used by English writer Martin Hawkins (? –) for his INVASION novel, *When Adolf Came* (**1943**), featuring an ALTERNATE WORLD in which the Germans conquer England; but an underground movement soon begins to turn the tables. [JC]

HAWKWOOD, ALLAN *See* H. BEDFORD-JONES.

HAWTHORNE, NATHANIEL (1804–64). American writer, known primarily for his work outside the sf field. One of the formative figures in American literature, NH was intrigued throughout his writing career by themes we would now call sf. His extensive notebooks outline dozens of projected sf works, some of which he was able to complete, while others he worked on unsuccessfully until his death. A long line of doctors, chemists, botanists, mesmerists, physicists and inventors parade their marvellously creative and destructive skills throughout his fiction, and even the most apparently fantastic events are given naturalistic explanations. Thus much of his writing at least borders on sf.

In three of his four major romances, sf elements run as a main undercurrent. A secret medical experiment controls the plot of *The Scarlet Letter* (**1850**); the main action of *The House of the Seven Gables* (**1851**) derives from hypnotism and a strange inherited disease; all the major events in *The Blithedale Romance* (**1852**) flow from a major topic of 19th-century sf, mesmeric control. A scientist's quest for the elixir of life is the subject of "Dr. Heidegger's Experiment" (1837) and two unfinished, posthumously published romances, *The Dolliver Romance* (**1864**) and *Septimius Felton* (**1871**). Some stories, such as "The Man of Adamant" (1837), come directly from pseudo-scientific curiosities NH encountered as editor of *The American Magazine of Useful and Entertaining Knowledge*.

Three of NH's early stories had profound influences on subsequent 19th-century sf, and all three still stand as masterpieces of the genre. In "The Birthmark" (1843), a lone genius who has invented numerous scientific marvels commits the fatal error of attempting to remove the one blemish which keeps his wife from being perfect, a tiny birthmark which makes this lovely woman disgusting to him. "The Artist of the Beautiful" (1844) describes the creation of an automaton butterfly which, for another lone inventive genius, substitutes for love, sex and biological procreation. In "Rappaccini's Daughter" (1844), one scientist attempts to make his only child impervious to the evils of the world by filling her with secret poisons, but he is foiled by his arch-rival. Part of the enduring power of these three tales comes from their deep penetration into the psychology of a group of men emerging in NH's society, the technical-scientific élite. NH's sf extends the achievements of Mary SHELLEY's *Frankenstein* (**1818**) into the dawn of the age of modern science and the literature that is part of that age's culture, modern sf. [HBF]
Other works: *Doctor Grimshawe's Secret* (**1883**).
See also: ARTS; BIOLOGY; MACHINES; METAPHYSICS.

HAWTON, HECTOR (1901–). British writer, at one time involved as a Humanist as managing director of the Rationalist Press Association; his sf novel is *Operation Superman* (**1951**). [JC]

HAY, GEORGE (1922–). British writer and editor. A long-time sf enthusiast, GH published three paperback novels in the early 1950s: *Flight of the Hesper* (**1951**), *Man, Woman and Android* (**1951**) and *This Planet For Sale* (**1952**). He is editor of *Hell Hath Fury* (anth. **1963**), a collection of stories from UNKNOWN, *The Disappearing Future* (anth. **1970**), *Stopwatch* (anth. **1974**), an original anthology with stories by John BRUNNER, Ursula K. LE GUIN, Christopher PRIEST, A.E. VAN VOGT and others, and *The Edward De Bono Science Fiction Collection* (anth. **1976**), a selection of stories chosen to illustrate Dr De Bono's theories of "lateral thinking". GH has worked in various capacities to promote sf, and was instrumental in the establishment of the SCIENCE FICTION FOUNDATION, of which he is a council member. The novel *Terra!* (undated, probably **1953**) published under the house name King LANG is by GH. [MJE]

HAY, JACOB (1920–). American writer whose sf novel *Autopsy For a Cosmonaut* (**1969**; vt *Death of a Cosmonaut* UK) with John M. KESHISHIAN describes a NEAR-FUTURE space crisis, in which NASA attempts a space rendezvous with a Russian satellite suspected of harbouring a nuclear warhead. [JC]

HAY, JOHN (? –). Australian farmer and writer in whose sf novel, *The Invasion* (**1968**), a NEAR-FUTURE atomic assault devastates Australia; survivors band together to resist the invading Chinese. [JC]

HAY, W(ILLIAM) DELISLE (? – ?). British writer, often on New Zealand natural history. His *The Doom of the Great City; being the Narrative of a Survivor, written A.D. 1942* (**1880**) describes the collapse of London through the onslaught of a poisonous fog (*see* POLLUTION); *Three Hundred Years Hence; or, A Voice from Posterity* (**1881**) is a series of prophecies about the development of science and technology over the next 300 years. [JC]

HAYNES, JOHN ROBERT *See* P. WILDING.

HAYWOOD, ELIZA (FOWLER) (1693?–1756). English actress, writer and publisher, acknowledged as the most prolific female writer of her time. Much of her work was of a scandalous nature containing thinly veiled characterizations of notable contemporaries. *The Adventures of Eovaai, Princess of Ijavea: A Pre-Adamitical History* (**1736**; vt *The Unfortuneate Princess* UK) is an allegorical political SATIRE set before the destruction of Earth's second Moon and featuring, among its many accounts of sorcery, the visitation by mechanical means of an extraterrestrial, this being several years before the appearance of VOLTAIRE's *Micromégas* (**1751**). EH also wrote *Memoirs of a Certain Island Adjacent to the Kingdom of Utopia* (**1725–6**, two vols) an anonymously published allegorical UTOPIAN novel built around a series of sexual scandals and

The Invisible Spy (**1755**), as by "Exploribilis", in which an invisibility belt is used to eavesdrop on society gossip. Authorship of the anonymous satirical LOST-WORLD novel, *Memoirs of the Court of Lilliput* (**1727**), was attributed to EH by Alexander Pope in 1729, but this may be erroneous. [JE]
About the author: *The Life and Romances of Mrs Eliza Haywood* (**1915**) by G.F. Whicker.

HAZLITT, HENRY (1894–). American journalist and author, in whose sf novel, *The Great Idea* (**1951**; vt *Time Will Run Back* UK), a communist society of the future is transformed back into a capitalist society; the agent of change is the dictator's son. The communism of this society is more Russian than Marxist. [JC]
See also: DYSTOPIAS; ECONOMICS.

HAZZARD, WILTON *See* Margaret ST CLAIR.

HEALY, RAYMOND J. (1907–). American editor. Together with J. Francis MCCOMAS he compiled the anthology *Adventures in Time and Space* (anth. **1946**; UK edition omitted two-thirds of the stories; two US paperbacks, the second entitled *More Adventures in Time and Space*, contained selections; vt *Famous Science Fiction Stories* USA). Containing 33 stories and two articles and over 1,000 pages long, *Adventures in Time and Space* remains a definitive ANTHOLOGY of magazine sf up to 1945 and is credited with considerable influence in helping to give the sf genre literary respectability. RJH later pioneered the original sf anthology — featuring stories which had not previously appeared in magazines — with *New Tales of Space and Time* (anth. **1951**; UK edition contains an additional introduction) and *9 Tales of Space and Time* (anth. **1954**), which included notable stories by such writers as Isaac ASIMOV, Anthony BOUCHER and Ray BRADBURY. [MJE]

HEARD, GERALD The usual writing name of British author and speculative journalist H(enry) F(itzgerald) Heard (1889–1971), which he used for both fiction and non-fiction in England; in the USA he used the form H.F. Heard for fiction. He lived in the USA after 1937. He is perhaps best remembered for his association with Aldous HUXLEY in investigations of the Vedanta cult, and for such speculative studies as *The Ascent of Humanity* (**1929**) and *The Third Morality* (**1937**). His UFO study, *The Riddle of the Flying Saucers: Is Another World Watching?* (**1950**; rev. **1953**; vt *Is Another World Watching?* USA), is apparently highly regarded in that field. Some of his detective and horror fiction, like *A Taste for Honey* (**1941**) and its sequels *Reply Paid* (**1942**) and *Murder by Reflection* (**1942**), are borderline sf; the

title story of *The Great Fog* (coll. **1944**; vt *Weird Tales of Terror and Detection*) is a DISASTER tale, the mould-derived Great Fog destroying all civilization; in the title story of *The Lost Cavern* (coll. **1948**) a man is held captive by intelligent bats; *The Black Fox: A Novel of the Seventies* (**1950**) is a good supernatural story. *The Doppelgangers* (**1947**; vt *Doppelgangers: An Episode of the Fourth, the Psychological Revolution, 1997* UK), an sf novel set at the end of the century, rather laboriously sets up a conflict among three factions each of whose philosophies is in didactic opposition to the others'. *Gabriel and the Creatures* (**1952**; vt *Wishing Well*) recasts some of GH's evolutionary speculation in sf form for children. [JC]
See also: ECOLOGY; EVOLUTION; POLLUTION.

HEARD, H.F. *See* Gerald HEARD.

HEATH, PETER (? –). American writer, possibly pseudonymous, whose novels, *Assassins from Tomorrow* (**1967**), *The Mind Brothers* (**1967**) and *Men Who Die Twice* (**1968**), comprise a routine thriller-like sf series. [JC]

HEATH, ROYSTON *See* George C. WALLIS.

HEAVY METAL *See* MÉTAL HURLANT.

HECHT, BEN (1894–1964). American journalist, novelist, playwright, film scriptwriter and publisher. He was associated with Bohemian literary circles before becoming prominent in Hollywood night life in the early 1930s. His writings, still highly regarded, are particularly notable for their cynicism, ICONOCLASM and irony. Many of his short stories border on SCIENCE FANTASY in a similar manner to those of Howard FAST, one of the best being "The Adventures of Professor Emmett" (*see* HIVE-MINDS), published in BH's collection *A Book of Miracles* (coll. **1939**). Some of his stories are influenced by the works of Charles FORT. BH is best known in the sf field for *Fantazius Mallare* (**1922**), and its sequel *The Kingdom of Evil* (**1924**), an erotic and supposedly decadent account of a descent into madness which was successfully prosecuted on obscenity charges on the grounds of its illustrations by Wallace Smith. [JE]
Other works: *Eleven Selected Great Stories* (coll. **1943**); *Miracle in the Rain* (**1943**); *The Collected Stories of Ben Hecht* (coll. **1945**).
See also: PSYCHOLOGY.

HEINLEIN, ROBERT A(NSON) (1907–). American writer, educated at the University of Missouri and the US Naval Academy, Annapolis. He served as a naval officer for five years, retiring due to ill health in 1934, studied physics at UCLA for a time, then took a variety of jobs before beginning to write in 1939.

Photo *Locus.*

He worked as an engineer at the Naval Air Experimental Station, Philadelphia, during the Second World War.

RAH's first story, "Lifeline" (1939), appeared in ASTOUNDING SCIENCE FICTION, a magazine with which he was closely associated for some years. He rapidly gained fame and unprecedented influence within the sf field on the strength of such stories as "Requiem" (1940), "The Roads must Roll" (1940), "Blowups Happen" (1940) and the short novel "If This Goes On ..." (1940; rev. 1953). These early stories were part of a loose future-HISTORY series, the schema for which was published in *ASF* in 1941. As a device for tying together otherwise disparate stories, the "Future History" idea has been imitated by many other writers, although RAH himself largely abandoned it after 1950. All the "Future History" tales were subsequently reprinted in *The Man Who Sold the Moon* (coll. **1950**), *The Green Hills of Earth* (coll. **1951**) and *Revolt in 2100* (coll. **1953**). Two early novels also belong to the series: *Methuselah's Children* (1941 *ASF*; rev. **1958**), which concerns an extended family of near-immortals, and *Orphans of the Sky* (1941 *ASF* as "Universe" and "Common Sense"; first story only as *Universe* 1951; fix-up **1963**), about a GENERATION STARSHIP. The three collections and *Methuselah's Children* were republished, with "Let There be Light" omitted and "Searchlight" (1962) and "The Menace from Earth" (1957) added, in the omnibus *The Past Through Tomorrow* (coll. **1967**; UK edition is divided into two vols and omits *Methuselah's Children*).

RAH gained his initial success because he wrote in a style which blended slang, folk aphorism and technical jargon in a convincing way. His characters were knowledgeable men of action, equally at home with their fists and a slide-rule, who were involved in processes and procedures (political, legal, military, industrial, etc.). Above all, RAH gave the appearance of taking the future for granted: he avoided long descriptive passages and explanations, and insinuated information through dialogue and the depiction of action. Clever understatement, apparent casualness and a concentration on people rather than gadgets made his stories more realistic than those of any other genre sf writer. Soon, many magazine writers were copying his manner.

Not all of RAH's early writing consisted of "Future History" stories, although most of his non-series work was initially published under the pseudonyms Anson MacDonald, Lyle Monroe, Caleb Saunders and John Riverside. These include his novels *Sixth Column* (1941 *ASF* as by MacDonald; **1949**; vt *The Day After Tomorrow*) and *Beyond This Horizon* (1942 *ASF* as by MacDonald; **1948**). *Sixth Column* concerned an Asiatic INVASION of the USA, which was defeated by a resistance disguised as a RELIGION, its superscientific gadgets used to accomplish "miracles"; it was based on an idea of John W. CAMPBELL Jr, who had incorporated it in the then unpublished novella "All" (*see The Space Beyond*, coll. **1976**, by Campbell). *Beyond This Horizon* describes a future society where people seek the meaning of life (*see* GENETIC ENGINEERING). Some of RAH's best stories belong to this period; "And He Built a Crooked House" (1941), about an architect who inadvertently builds into another DIMENSION, "By His Bootstraps" (1941 as by MacDonald), a superb TIME-PARADOX fantasia, and "They" (1941), a fantasy about solipsism. "Waldo" (1942 as by MacDonald), about a crippled inventor who lives in a satellite, gave rise to a significant item of TERMINOLOGY, the real-life equivalents of the protagonist's remote-control lifting devices being known as WALDOES. These stories, and the later non-series stories, are collected in various volumes: *Waldo and Magic, Inc.* (coll. **1950**; vt of title story alone *Waldo: Genius in Orbit* USA); *Assignment in Eternity* (coll. **1953**; UK paperback as two vols, *Assignment in Eternity*, **1960**, and *Lost Legacy*, **1960**); *The Menace from Earth* (coll. **1959**); *The Unpleasant Profession of Jonathan Hoag* (coll. **1959**; vt *6 X H* USA); and *The Worlds of Robert A. Heinlein* (coll. **1966**).

In the years 1943–6 RAH published no fiction, but in 1947 expanded his writing in two new directions: he sold a number of short stories to *The Saturday Evening Post* and other "slick" magazines, and he published a juvenile sf novel, *Rocket Ship Galileo* (**1947**). The latter is not an outstanding work (it involves Nazis on the Moon) but it was the first in a series which is the most important contribution any writer has made to CHILDREN'S SF. (It also formed the basis of a film, DESTINATION MOON, 1950, scripted by RAH.) *Space Cadet* (**1948**), the second in the series, is a science-fictionalization of RAH's own experiences at Annapolis. With the third, *Red Planet* (**1949**) about the adventures of two young colonists and their Martian "pet", RAH found his feet as a writer of sf for teenagers. A strong narrative line, carefully worked-out technical detail and brisk dialogue are the leading virtues of this and most of the later juveniles. *Red Planet* was followed by *Farmer in the Sky* (**1950**), *Between Planets* (**1951**), *The Rolling Stones* (**1952**; vt *Space Family Stone* UK), *Starman Jones* (**1953**), *The Star Beast* (**1954**), *Tunnel in the Sky* (**1955**), *Time for the Stars* (**1956**), *Citizen of the Galaxy* (**1957**) and *Have Space Suit — Will Travel* (**1958**). The best of these, such as *Starman Jones*, *The Star Beast* and *Citizen of the Galaxy*, have a strong appeal for adult readers as well as youngsters, and some critics consider them to be RAH's finest works.

After 1950, RAH wrote very little short fiction — the most notable piece is the time-paradox tale "All You Zombies" (1959) — but he continued to produce occasional novels for the adult market. *The Puppet Masters* (**1951**) is an effective, if rather hysterical, invasion story, and a prime example of PARANOIA in 1950s sf. *Double Star* (**1956**), about a failed actor who impersonates a galactic politician, won a 1956 HUGO award, and is usually considered to be his best novel of the 1950s. *The Door Into Summer* (**1957**), a TIME-TRAVEL story, is RAH's most mellow and charming novel.

With *Starship Troopers* (**1959**), however, RAH entered a new and controversial phase. Originally intended as a juvenile, although not published as such, this violent novel of interstellar WAR won a 1960 Hugo but also gained RAH the reputation of being a militarist, even a "fascist". The plot, about a young man being initiated into adulthood, is typical of RAH, but the style has become hectoring. The conversation has lost much of its liveliness, and the "father-figures' (always important in RAH's fiction) tend to become monologuists. Many of these faults recur in his next novel, *Stranger in a Strange Land* (**1961**), although it is on the whole a stronger work and was awarded a 1962 Hugo. About a young MESSIAH-figure from Mars and his tutoring in earthly matters by Jubal Harshaw (the ultimate surrogate-father and know-all), it is an eccentric novel of ideas, at times witty although over-long. It has proved to be RAH's most popular novel, particularly after it became a cult-book among students in the later 1960s (who were drawn to it, presumably, by its ICONOCLASM and by RAH's apparent espousal of free love and mysticism).

There followed two minor works, *Podkayne of Mars* (**1963**), an inferior juvenile, and *Glory Road* (**1963**), an unsuccessful attempt at SWORD AND SORCERY. *Farnham's Freehold* (**1964**) is another long and opinionated novel of ideas, which deals in part with racial questions. It is, along with *Starship*

Troopers, the novel which has provoked the most intense hostility among those who dislike RAH's POLITICS. *The Moon is a Harsh Mistress* (1966) represents a partial return to form, however, and won a 1967 Hugo. About a revolution among Moon-colonists, many historical parallels being made evident with the American War of Independence, it is of value partly because it shows the nature of RAH's political views very clearly. Rather than being a fascist, he is a right-wing anarchist, or "libertarian", much influenced by the philosophy of SOCIAL DARWINISM. The fact that RAH's politics are the prime concern in all discussions of his later novels points to the sad decline in the quality of dramatization in his sf. As Alexei PANSHIN, his most astute critic to date, has pointed out, RAH once dealt in "facts" (he has long been considered the master of HARD SF) but now he deals only in "opinions-as-facts". His most recent novels are bloated tracts. *I Will Fear No Evil* (1970) is an interminable novel about a rich centenarian who has his mind transferred to the body of his young secretary. It reveals RAH's recent concern with SEX (and his inability to handle the subject convincingly). *Time Enough for Love, or the Lives of Lazarus Long* (1973) is a late coda to the "Future History" series, but has none of the virtues of the earlier stories.

RAH was guest of honour at three World SF Conventions, in 1941, 1961 and 1976. He has repeatedly been voted "best all-time author" in readers' polls such as those held by LOCUS in 1973 and 1977, and in 1975 was recipient of the First Grand Master NEBULA award. Despite the disquiet caused by his later novels, he has been by far the most influential author in modern American sf. [DP]

Other works: *Tomorrow, the Stars* (anth. 1951); *Three by Heinlein* (coll. 1965; vt *A Heinlein Triad* UK; contains *The Puppet Masters* and *Waldo and Magic, Inc.*); *A Robert Heinlein Omnibus* (coll. 1966; contains *Beyond This Horizon*, *The Man Who Sold the Moon* and *The Green Hills of Earth*); *The Best of Robert Heinlein* (coll. 1973).

About the author: "One Sane Man: Robert A. Heinlein" by Damon KNIGHT, in *In Search of Wonder* (1956; rev. 1967); "Robert A. Heinlein" by Sam MOSKOWITZ, in *Seekers of Tomorrow* (1966); *Heinlein in Dimension* (1968) by Alexei Panshin; "First Person Singular: Heinlein, Son of Heinlein" by James BLISH, in *More Issues at Hand* (1970); *Robert A. Heinlein: Stranger in His Own Land* (1976) by George Edgar SLUSSER; *The Classic Years of Robert A. Heinlein* (1977) by George Edgar Slusser; "Tomorrow for Non-Believers: a Study of Books for Young People by Robert A. Heinlein" by Reba Estra, in *SF Commentary* 46, May 1976.

See also: ALIENS; ANTI-INTELLECTUALISM IN SF; ARTS; AUTOMATION; CHILDREN IN SF;

CLONES; COLONIZATION OF OTHER WORLDS; COMPUTERS; CONCEPTUAL BREAKTHROUGH; CRIME AND PUNISHMENT; DEFINITIONS OF SF; DIME NOVELS; DISCOVERY AND INVENTION; ECOLOGY; ECONOMICS; END OF THE WORLD; ESCHATOLOGY; FANTASTIC VOYAGES; FANTASY; FASTER THAN LIGHT; FLYING SAUCERS; GALACTIC EMPIRES; GODS AND DEMONS; GOLDEN AGE OF SF; GOTHIC SF; HIVE-MINDS; IMMORTALITY; JUPITER; LINGUISTICS; MACHINES; MAGIC; MARS; MATHEMATICS; MONSTERS; MOON; MUTANTS; NEAR FUTURE; NUCLEAR POWER; OPTIMISM AND PESSIMISM; PARANOIA AND SCHIZOPHRENIA; PASTORAL; PHYSICS; PREDICTION; PSYCHOLOGY; RADIO (USA); ROCKETS; SF MAGAZINES; SF OVERTAKEN BY EVENTS; SCIENTIFIC ERRORS; SOCIOLOGY; SPACE FLIGHT; SPACE OPERA; SPACESHIPS; SUPERMAN; TECHNOLOGY; TERRAFORMING; TRANSPORTATION; UTOPIAS; VENUS; VILLAINS; WEAPONS; WOMEN.

HEMESATH,   JAMES B(ARTHOLOMEW)   (WILLIAM) (1944–). American writer whose first (marginal) sf was "Harry the Hare" for *Again, Dangerous Visions* (anth. 1972) ed. Harlan ELLISON. He has no collection published, but his stories have been praised.   [PN]

HEMING,   JOHN   (WINTON) (1900–53). Extremely prolific Australian writer, who began publishing sf novels with *The Living Dead* (1940), and was associated during the Second World War with the Australian firm Currawong Publishers in the release of native sf, American imports being banned at the time. He also wrote as Paul de Wreder. [JC]
Other works: *Subterranean City* (1940); *From Earth to Mars* (1941); *In Aztec Hands* (1942); *King of the Underseas* (1941); *The Weird House* (1951); *Time Marches Off* (1941), as by Paul de Wreder.

HENDERSON, ZENNA (1917–). American writer and schoolteacher, who has very frequently used her teaching experience in Arizona and elsewhere as a base for her stories. Her first story was "Come on, Wagon!" for *FSF* in 1951; soon after, with "Ararat" for *FSF* in 1952, she began publishing, in the magazine with which she is most strongly associated, the series of stories about the "People", her central work. Assembled as *Pilgrimage: The Book of the People* (1952–9 *FSF*; fix-up 1961) and *The People: No Different Flesh* (1961–5 *FSF*; coll. of linked stories 1966), the sequence recounts over a long time-span the arduous experiences of a group of ALIENS with PSI POWERS, who are outwardly indistinguishable from humans but morally superior. They are shipwrecked on Earth, and are forced to try to survive as well and fully as possible. A further story, "The Indelible Kind" (1968), appears with unconnected stories in

Holding Wonder (coll. 1971); this collection, along with *The Anything Box* (coll. 1965), assembles most of ZH's stories independent of the "People" tales. The same decorous warmth infuses all her work, sometimes overly reducing tensions and contrasts, but usually demonstrating her humane talent to advantage, though her wholesomeness has been criticized as over-sentimental and mildly religiose in manner. [JC]
See also: CHILDREN IN SF; ESP; SUPERMAN; WOMEN.

HENNEBERG, CHARLES Name used by German-French writer Charles Henneberg zu Irmelshausen Wasungen (1899–1959) and his Russian-French wife Nathalie (1917–77) until his death, at which point she began signing her stories Nathalie-Charles Henneberg. (Some of these were in fact posthumous collaborations, her husband having left several manuscripts.) With and without her husband, she published 10 novels in France, beginning with *La naissance des dieux* ["Birth of the Gods"] (1954). Several of their stories were translated by Damon KNIGHT, appearing first in *FSF* and later in his *Thirteen French Science Fiction Stories* (anth. 1965). Particularly when she is writing alone, her work is sophisticatedly Gothic and exorbitant; a typical example, "Des ailes, dans la nuit …", is trans. as "Wings in the Night" by Maxim JAKUBOWSKI for his assembly of French fiction, *Travelling Towards Epsilon* (anth. 1976). Much of the Hennebergs' work is on the borderline between HEROIC FANTASY and sf; the critic Pierre VERSINS praises it for its extravagant bad taste and general flamboyance. [JC/PN]

HENNEBERG,   NATHALIE-CHARLES See Charles HENNEBERG.

HENRY, MARION See Lester DEL REY.

HENSLEY, JOE L(OUIS) (1926–). American writer and Circuit Court judge, active as an author of suspense novels, one of which, *The Poison Summer* (1974), was named in the *New York Times* Best of the Year List in 1974. He began publishing sf with "Treasure City" for *Planet Stories* in 1952, and has appeared with some frequency in the field ever since, sometimes as J.L. Hensley, and once as Louis J.A. Adams in collaboration with Alexei PANSHIN. His work is vigorous and action-oriented, as can be seen in his only sf novel, *The Black Roads* (1976), a chase story set in a post-HOLOCAUST America whose integral web of roads is dominated by a tyrannous organization; a rebellion is in the works. [JC]

HERBERT, BENSON (1912–). British writer with a master's degree in science who began publishing sf in American magazines with "The World

Without" for *Wonder Stories* in 1931, and was fairly active in the 1930s. His sf novel *Crisis! — 1992* (**1936**) deals with the ominous passage of another planet close to Earth's orbit, and with what humans discover when they land on it: they find that the planet is actually a giant spaceship. The book is prefaced by M.P. SHIEL. During the War he wrote several very short SPACE OPERAS which were published as paperback novels, undated: *Hand of Glory*, *The Red Haired Girl*, *Strange Romance* and, with Festus PRAGNELL, *Thieves of the Air*. With Walter GILLINGS as director BH financed and founded Utopia Publications, which published some sf, including the AMERICAN FICTION series and STRANGE TALES.   [JC/PN]

Photo Joel Warren.

HERBERT, FRANK (1920–). American writer, born in Tacoma, Washington, and educated at the University of Washington, Seattle. He worked as a reporter and editor on a number of West Coast newspapers before becoming a full-time writer. He lives in Washington State.

FH began publishing sf with "Looking for Something?" (1952) in *Startling Stories*. During the next decade he was an infrequent contributor to the sf magazines, producing less than 20 short stories (which nevertheless constitute a majority of his short fiction to date; he has never made a significant impact with work below novel length). He also wrote one novel, *The Dragon in the Sea* (**1956**; vt *21st Century Sub* USA; vt *Under Pressure* USA), a much praised sf thriller containing complex psychological investigations set on board a submarine of the future. His emergence as a writer of major stature commenced with the publication in *ASF* in 1963–4 of "Dune World", the first part of his "Dune" series. It was followed in 1965 by "The Prophet of Dune"; the two were

amalgamated into *Dune* (1963–5 *ASF*; fix-up **1965**), which won the first NEBULA award for best novel, shared the HUGO award, and became one of the most famous of all sf novels.

Dune is a novel of extraordinary complexity. It encompasses intergalactic POLITICS of a decidedly feudal nature; the development of PSI POWERS; RELIGION, specifically the reluctant but inevitable evolution of its protagonist into a MESSIAH; and WAR. Its primary impact, however, lay in its treatment of ECOLOGY, a theme which it brought into the forefront of modern sf readers' and writers' awareness. The desert planet Arrakis, with its giant sandworms and its Bedouin-like human inhabitants, the Fremen, clinging to the most precarious of ecological niches through fanatical scrupulousness in water conservation, is possibly the most convincing alien environment created by any sf writer. With its blend (or sometimes clash) of complex intellectual discourse and Byzantine intrigue, *Dune* provided a template for FH's more significant later work. Two sequels later appeared: *Dune Messiah* (**1969**), which intensified the intrigue at the cost of the other elements, and *Children of Dune* (**1976**), which recaptured much of the strength of the original work and which addressed another recurrent theme in FH's work — the EVOLUTION of Man, in this case into SUPERMAN. At least one more novel in the series is planned.

From 1965 FH began to publish novels regularly: *The Green Brain* (**1966**), in which mutated insects achieve corporate intelligence (*see* HIVE-MINDS); *Destination: Void* (**1966**), a clotted novel on a CYBERNETIC theme (*see also* COMPUTERS); *The Eyes of Heisenberg* (**1966**), about GENETIC ENGINEERING and IMMORTALITY; *The Heaven Makers* (**1968**; rev. 1977) — immortality again; *The Santaroga Barrier* (**1968**) which describes a higher order of INTELLIGENCE evolved within an isolated, near-UTOPIAN community. The development of intelligence is a pervasive theme in FH's work (encompassing insect intelligence in *The Green Brain* and machine intelligence in *Destination: Void*). He consistently attempts not only to suggest different, or evolved, types of intelligence, but to describe them in detail. Among contemporary sf writers only Ian WATSON addresses this theme as frequently and as convincingly. ALIEN intelligence (*see also* LIVING WORLDS) is examined in *Whipping Star* (**1970**) and, more searchingly, in its sequel *The Dosadi Experiment* (**1977**) which, while orchestrating a plot of multi-levelled intrigue, describes several different alien species in detail, examines the effect of an experiment in extreme OVERPOPULATION, and develops advanced psi powers, including total mind transference, in its hero and heroine.

FH's other sf novels are *The God Makers* (**1972**; vt *The Godmakers*), in

which a GOD is actually created through human endeavours, and *Hellstrom's Hive* (**1973**). The latter book, which derives its title from the film *The Hellstrom Chronicle* (1971) but otherwise has little connection with it, is arguably FH's most successful novel since *Dune*. It describes in persuasive detail an underground colony of humans selectively bred on insect-hive principles into various specializations. It is a society in which the individual's existence is of minor importance; the continuation of the hive as a functioning entity is paramount. The novel points up the contradictions of a society which in its own terms is a successful Utopia, but which from an outside human viewpoint is horrific.

Much of FH's work is difficult reading. His ideas are genuinely developed concepts, not mere decorative notions; but sometimes embodied in excessively complicated plots, and told in prose which does not always match the level of thinking, they often appear dense and opaque. His best novels, however, are the work of a speculative intellect with few rivals in modern sf. His work has been subject to remarkably little critical analysis.   [MJE]

Other works: *New World or No World* (anth. **1970**), a non-fiction environmental anthology; *The Worlds of Frank Herbert* (coll. **1970**); *Soul Catcher* (**1971**), a non-sf novel; *The Book of Frank Herbert* (coll. **1973**); *The Best of Frank Herbert* (coll. **1975**; later divided into two volumes UK).

About the author: "Fancy Going to the Vats?" by Ian Watson in FOUNDATION 10, 1976.

See also: COMMUNICATIONS; ESCHATOLOGY; ESP; FANTASY; HISTORY IN SF; LIFE ON OTHER WORLDS; LINGUISTICS; PARANOIA AND SCHIZOPHRENIA; SPACESHIPS; TERRA-FORMING; UNDER THE SEA; WEATHER CONTROL.

HERNAMAN-JOHNSON, FRANCIS (1879– ?). British medical researcher and author of *The Polyphemes: A Story of Strange Adventures Among Strange Beings* (**1906**); the beings are intelligent giant ants who just fail to conquer the world.   [JC]

HEROES Sf did not begin to produce a distinctive kind of hero until well into the 20th century. It might be expected that literature dealing with the advancement of science would make heroes of men of science, but in fact this rarely happened until the GERNSBACK era (*see* SCIENTISTS). Even in the early PULP MAGAZINES the characters offered to the reader for identification were usually young men innocent of any trace of scientific genius, while the inventors remained remote and enigmatic. These heroes might have wandered out of a story in any other genre to become entangled with matters of super-science entirely by accident. A certain bewildered astonishment was, in fact, a constant feature of the role. FLASH GORDON and BUCK ROGERS are heroes of this type, and so is John Star, hero of Jack WILLIAMSON's *The Legion of Space* (1934; **1947**). Hugo Gernsback himself, however, had no hesitation in grasping the nettle and giving his hero *Ralph 124C 41+* (1911; **1925**) the plus sign which labelled him one of the most brilliant minds in existence. This boldness was followed up by E.E. "Doc" SMITH, whose Richard Seaton, hero of the "Skylark" series, also has scientific genius grafted on to the customary characteristics of the pulp hero; and by John W. CAMPBELL Jr, whose heroes usually came in groups of two or three so that they could spend whole chapters lecturing to one another on speculative physics.

C.M. KORNBLUTH, in his essay, "The Failure of the Science Fiction Novel as Social Criticism" (1959), argues that the world view of Smith's heroes and all their kind is that of small children, and that their adventures are daydreams which proceed according to the pattern of make-believe games. This is true, to some extent, of virtually all pulp fiction (and mass-produced fiction in general), but it stands out particularly clearly in pulp sf simply because the scope of the make-believe is so great, robbed of all the constraining conventions that are embodied in the structure of the Western or the love story. Edgar Rice BURROUGHS' "Martian" novels are certainly constructed according to the careless logic of daydreams, and the enduring attraction of such fantasies is shown by the constant proliferation of imitators. Edmond HAMILTON's Captain Future and the contemporary PERRY RHODAN adventures produced by a factory of German writers are examples of more strictly science-fictional variants.

The writer who most unrepentantly deviated from this type of hero was John W. Campbell Jr, whose characters took a rather different approach to problems and their solutions, relying far more on jargon and ingenuity in improvisation than on physical strength aided by magical weapons. In the 1940s, when Campbell was in control of ASTOUNDING, his editorial influence was considerable in urging writers to abandon the standard pulp image of the hero in favour of an image which put much greater emphasis on problem-solving aptitude and engineering skill. The archetypes of this image were the staff of George O. SMITH's *Venus Equilateral* (1942–5; fix-up **1947**), forever scribbling equations and designs on the tablecloths in Joe's Bar. A critic as aggressive as Kornbluth might argue that this was very limited progress, and that the new image appealed to the world view of the adolescent in the process of learning, upgrading mental competence at the expense of physical prowess, but really coming no nearer to genuine characterization. Certainly there is a great

deal of sf which is attractive to the adolescent — and particularly to the alienated adolescent, bound more closely to a private mental world — and it is true that, if E.E. Smith's Lensmen relate to their Arisian mentors in the same way that a child relates to its parents, then a similar relationship at a later stage is reflected in Poul ANDERSON's "Dominic Flandry" series, in which the hero's flamboyant behaviour and contempt for imperial decadence relates very well to the mood of adolescent rebellion. Other examples of rebellious figures trapped in an ambiguous relationship with pseudo-parental authority are the lieutenant in L. Ron HUBBARD's *Final Blackout* (1940; **1948**), Harry HARRISON's *Stainless Steel Rat* (**1961**) and sequels, and Keith LAUMER's Retief. This is not, however, the whole story. Accurate characterization did emerge in genre sf during the Campbell period, albeit in a small way.

As a more mature approach to characterization began to appear in sf the heroic stature of its protagonists inevitably began to decline. Heroes are implicitly unrealistic characters. Had sf been solely guided in its evolution by literary priorities, heroes might well have become extinct. That they did not is unremarkable, but what is rather curious is that, in addition to the persistence of child-world-view heroes and adolescent-world-view heroes, one or two further types appeared. The most important, largely because it is virtually unique to sf, is the hero as SUPERMAN, whose archetype was established by A.E. VAN VOGT in *Slan* (1940; **1946**; rev. 1951). Van Vogt went on to feature many more heroes in similar existential situations: adrift in a hostile world, whose circumstances are beyond their understanding, but possessed of awesome powers which are temporarily dormant. This is plainly an appeal to a schizoid element in the reader. All the elements of the schizoid world view are there: the sense of being essentially different, intrinsically superior yet vulnerable to persecution. This stereotype has become increasingly common in sf, and also more elaborate and extravagant, as, for instance, in the works of Roger ZELAZNY. The prominence of this species of hero is easy enough to understand; just as sf offers great potential for the modelling of make-believe situations similar to children's fantasies, so it also offers potential for making "literal" all the kinds of world view which were once deemed psychologically aberrant. (Historical circumstances, of course, alter cases, and in today's world the schizoid world view is virtually inescapable, and hence normal.) Further to this point, *see* PARANOIA.

These comments should not be taken to imply that sf, taken as a whole, is an implicitly neurotic or childish literature, though there is some justice in the claim made by Thomas M. DISCH in "The

Embarrassments of Science Fiction" (1976) that much genre sf still clings to the conventions appropriate to the modelling of childish make-believe adventures. These comments apply only to that sf which is also heroic fantasy, in the broadest sense of the term. It is the function of heroes to appease the psychological forces within us that must necessarily be repressed in the day-to-day routine of adult intercourse with the world (whether these be the world views we have put aside in growing older or the ones we have acquired but cannot use). Where sf, in common with other species of literature, is not concerned with such forces it requires no heroic symbols. [BS]
See also: ANTI-INTELLECTUALISM; VILLAINS.

HEROIC FANTASY In the TERMINOLOGY of sf readers, this term has recently begun to supersede SWORD AND SORCERY, although it is under the latter head that this volume discusses the sub-genre. The two terms are probably not identical in meaning, but the shades of meaning that distinguish them differ according to the writer who uses them. Heroic Fantasy may ultimately prove to be the more useful term, especially for critics, since it is less confining, and less exclusively a marketing label. There is no argument, for instance, about the twin archetypes of Heroic Fantasy being the gentlemanly works of J.R.R. TOLKIEN and the far from gentlemanly works of Robert E. HOWARD, especially his "Conan" series. *See also* SCIENCE FANTASY. [PN]

HERON-ALLEN, EDWARD *See* Christopher BLAYRE.

HERSEY, JOHN (1914–). American novelist and journalist, perhaps best known for his early report on *Hiroshima* (**1946**). His *White Lotus* (**1965**) is an ALTERNATE-WORLDS story in which China conquers the USA, and makes slaves of white Americans, including the teenager renamed White Lotus in China; *The Child Buyer* (**1960**) is a NEAR-FUTURE story in which corporations bid for effective ownership of child prodigies; *My Petition for More Space* (**1974**) is a radically DYSTOPIAN rendering of an enormously regimented Earth bedevilled by OVERPOPULATION problems — the protagonist lives in a tiny cubicle and petitions, vainly, for an extra foot in each dimension. [JC]
See also: INTELLIGENCE.

HERTZKA, THEODOR (1845–1924). Austrian economist and author of the influential socialist UTOPIA, *Freiland: ein Sociales Zukunftsbild* (**1890**; trans. as *Freiland: a Social Anticipation* **1891**), which, with its sequel, *Eine Reise nach Freiland* (**1893**; trans. as *A Visit to Freiland; or the New Paradise Regained* **1894**), carefully blueprinted its proposals for Utopian existence, which somewhat

unsatisfactorily attempted to mediate between private and public control of production (*see* ECONOMICS), but which all the same inspired a Freeland Society in the USA. [JC]
See also: POLITICS.

HERZOG, ARTHUR (1928–). American writer and editor; he has worked with the Peace Corps and as a political manager. His sf novel, *The Swarm* (1974), convincingly posits an ECOLOGICAL catastrophe when the African honey-bee mutates and invades North America (*see* HIVE-MINDS). Partially based on fact (African bees in real life have bred with South American bees to form a large and belligerent cross-breed), the novel is well researched and written, as is *Earthsound* (1975), in which a seismologist attempts to warn sceptical New Englanders of an approaching earthquake and is thought to be merely hysterical; the novel is deeply interesting in the physical basis it offers for feelings of premonition. AH's relatively quiet style is welcome in the DISASTER genre, which is normally rather shrill. [PN/JC]
See also: MUTANTS.

HESSE, HERMANN (1877–1962). German-born writer, Swiss citizen from 1923. His long career culminated with the publication of his largest novel, *Das Glasperlenspiel* (1943; trans. as *Magister Ludi* 1949; preferred trans. as *The Glass Bead Game* 1960), and his gaining of the 1946 Nobel Prize for literature, primarily for that book, which is a complex UTOPIA set in a future land closely resembling Europe; the game itself is central to the Utopia, combining undescribed aesthetic and intellectual disciplines into an activity which (by analogy with the music of Johann Sebastian Bach) resolves the dissonances of the outside world for the residents of the elite community of Castilia, led by Joseph Knecht, their Magister Ludi, or Master of Games, whose biography constitutes the bulk of the novel. Poems and essays by Knecht are appended to the main text, which, suffused with allusions to and renderings of the world-transcending subtleties and graces of the game, has a sometimes exalting effect on the reader. HH's great popularity in translation in the 1960s and 1970s derives more directly, however, from earlier and more accessible works, like *Siddharta* (1922; trans. 1954) and *Der Steppenwolf* (1927; trans. as *Steppenwolf* 1929; revised trans. 1963), in which Jungian depth psychology, Indian mysticism and *Weltschmerz* are perhaps over-palatably combined; these novels, and others, can be read — unwisely — as possessing some fantasy elements, but at their core are meditations on transcendence. [JC]
See also: ARTS; FANTASTIC VOYAGES.

HEXT, HARRINGTON *See* Eden PHILLPOTTS.

HEYDON, J(OSEPH) K(ENTIGERN) (? –). British writer whose sf novel *World D* (1935), as told to him by "Hal P. Trevarthen, Official Historian of the Superficies", describes the creation of an underwater culture called Helioxenon; the detail is considerable, sometimes Catholic. On the jacket the novel is credited to Trevarthen. [JC]

HICKEY, T. EARL (? –). American writer whose sf novel, *The Time Chariot* (1966), is a mildly amusing tale about a time machine. [JC]

HIDDEN WORLD, THE US PULP-size magazine. Possibly eight issues, Spring 1961-Winter 1963, published and ed. Ray PALMER. This was a quarterly publication, handling SHAVER mystery and FLYING SAUCER material. The first issue elaborated on the Shaverian "Mantongue" language. Circulation was somewhat restricted, and copies are seldom seen. [FHP]

HIENGER, JÖRG (1927–). German professor of literature, author of a dissertation on the problem of change in sf, published as *Literarische Zukunftsphantastik* ["Literary Fantasy of the Future"] (1972). A well-balanced study of contemporary Anglo-American sf, it neither over-praises it for its philosophical implications nor damns it on ideological grounds. JH gives detailed analyses of stories grouped according to important themes (e.g. ROBOTS, SUPERMEN, SPACE FLIGHT, TIME TRAVEL, post-atomic societies), extracting from them a philosophy of ubiquitous non-directional change that refuses to accept any final goals of history. [FR]

HIGH, PHILIP E(MPSON) (1914–). English writer, variously employed for a number of years before beginning to publish sf in 1955 with "The Statics" for *Authentic Science Fiction*, contributing to English magazines, especially NEBULA, for several years before releasing his first sf novel *The Prodigal Sun* (1964), which set the model for most of those to follow. It characteristically superimposes over a somewhat pessimistic rendering of future Earth societies an epic plot, in this case dealing with the return of a Earthman to his native planet, but with his powers enhanced through his being raised by an ALIEN race. Other novels combining social comment and adventure include *No Truce With Terra* (1964), *The Mad Metropolis* (1966) and *These Savage Futurians* (1967). *The Time Mercenaries* (1968) interestingly places a 20th-century submarine into a time when mankind has lost its genetic capacity to fight; the resurrected crew (who had been artifically preserved) dutifully save mankind from the aliens. Though constrained by his Dystopian sense of the possibilities of Man's future, PEH has been capable of writing enjoyable

adventures, though without fully stretching his dark imagination. [JC]
Other works: *Reality Forbidden* (1967); *Twin Planets* (1967); *Invader on my Back* (1968); *Double Illusion* (1970); *Butterfly Planet* (1971); *Come Hunt an Earthman* (1973); *Sold — For a Spaceship* (1973); *Speaking of Dinosaurs* (1974);

HIGON, ALBERT *See* Michel JEURY.

HILL, ERNEST (1915–). British writer who began publishing sf with "The Last Generation" for *New Worlds* in 1954, and who has one novel to his credit, the rather desultory SPACE OPERA *Pity About Earth* (1968). [JC]

HILLEGAS, MARK R. (1926–). Professor of English at Southern Illinois University, and sf critic. He took his PhD at Columbia in 1957. In 1961 he took one of the first university-level classes in sf in the USA at Colgate. His academic study *The Future as Nightmare: H.G. Wells and the Anti-Utopians* (1967) deals primarily with such MAINSTREAM writers of DYSTOPIAN scenarios as Karel ČAPEK, Aldous HUXLEY, Yevgeny ZAMIATIN, George ORWELL and C.S. LEWIS; it has become a standard reference. A more recent work, ed. MRH, is *Shadows of Imagination: the Fantasies of C.S. Lewis, J.R.R. Tolkien and Charles Williams* (anth. 1969). MRH is on the editorial board of SCIENCE-FICTION STUDIES. [PN]
See also: SF IN THE CLASSROOM.

HILTON, JAMES (1900–54). British writer, in America from 1935, known mainly for slightly sentimental mainstream novels, like *Good-bye Mr Chips* (1934). His romantic LOST-WORLD novel, *Lost Horizon* (1933), is set in Shangri-La, a hidden valley in Tibet, and deals with IMMORTALITY; the book is emotionally moving, and was extremely popular. It was twice filmed (*see* LOST HORIZON). [JC]
See also: ANTHROPOLOGY; UTOPIAS.

HINGLEY, RONALD (FRANCIS) (1920–). British lecturer in Russian studies and writer; his novel *Up Jenkins!* (1956) SATIRICALLY presents a Britain split in two, the northern half remaining more or less free, the southern half, People's Britain, being ruled in totalitarian fashion; the satire of People's Britain, though unfriendly, is deft. [JC]
See also: POLITICS; WAR.

HINTON, C(HARLES) HOWARD (1853–1907). British writer. He wrote many essays about the FOURTH DIMENSION and other dimensions in space and time. His interest may have been inspired by Edwin ABBOTT's *Flatland* (1885), to which he wrote a kind of sequel: *An Episode of Flatland* (1907). His other sf stories were "Stella" (1895), a short novel about a girl rendered invisible by a scientific experiment, and "An

Unfinished Communication" (1895), which represents life after death as freedom to move in the fourth dimension (time) through the moments of life, "unlearning" and re-evaluating. The two stories were published together as *Stella* (coll. **1895**) and reprinted, with some essays, in *Scientific Romances, Second Series* (coll. **1902**). *Scientific Romances, First Series* (coll. **1886**) contains several more essays.   [BS]
See also: FOURTH DIMENSION (AND OTHERS); INVISIBILITY; RELIGION.

HISTORY IN SF Since history is inevitably concerned with the past, it may seem perverse to link it with sf, which according to almost all DEFINITIONS is irrevocably committed to the future. Even time-travellers have to start from some time in the future, however far back they may then go. Nevertheless, there are at least two ways in which the idea of history is vital to sf. One is the theory that the study of history may disclose certain inevitable or cyclic patterns which can be expected to keep on working themselves out, and so allow authors to predict what is going to happen: this functions as a kind of counterpart to the familiar notion of extrapolation, in which one takes trends visible in the present and projects them forward. The other arises from a more abstract interest in the forces which made our world and our history what it is. Were these forces so strong as to be irresistible? If patterns are so strong as to enable one to predict the future, would they also prevent one from changing the past? These two involvements with history are evidently related, in that they raise the question of which is superior, individual genius or sociological pressure, a problem which has indeed interested historians at least since the time of Thomas Malthus and his *Essay on the Principle of Population* (**1798**).

Isaac ASIMOV's "Foundation" series (*ASF* 1942–9) gives the most famous and the most severely determinist answer in sf to the question of individual versus sociological. Its ideological centre is the science of "psychohistory", a new form of historical extrapolation which enables its inventor, Hari Seldon, to predict the downfall of what is then a GALACTIC EMPIRE and to take measures to mitigate its succeeding Dark Age with the "Seldon Plan". In a series of crises undergone by Seldon's Foundation, it appears that it is doomed to defeat; but every time something insidious and inevitable brings it to victory — mutual suspicion, religious superstition or economic pressure. The moral is clearly that the processes of history will depend (and always have depended) on factors which are quantifiable and greater than any individual — or than almost any individual, for the progress of Seldon's plan is checked, in *Foundation and Empire* (fix-up **1952**), by the appearance of a mutant, unpredictable genius.

Interestingly, a later novel by Asimov, *The End of Eternity* (**1955**), argues as strongly against social engineering as the "Foundation" series argued for it.

Behind Asimov's stories, it seems likely, lies *A Study of History* (12 vols **1934–61**) by Arnold J. Toynbee (1889–1976), a work which has strongly influenced sf in general, being quoted overtly, for instance, by the President of the USA in Frederik POHL and C.M. KORNBLUTH's "Critical Mass" (1961). Part of Toynbee's appeal to sf authors has stemmed from the wide range of historical settings he offers as potential plot-backgrounds — Frank HERBERT's *Dune* (**1965**), for instance, seems to draw on his picture of the Janissary-supported Turkish courts of the later Middle Ages — and also from his bias towards finding explanations for human behaviour in useful or available technology. The Toynbee-derived notion of "water-monopoly empires", i.e. empires founded on irrigation control, is used by Larry NIVEN in *A World Out Of Time* (**1976**).

But Toynbee's popularity with sf writers goes deeper than this. Along with the philosophers Giambattista Vico (1668–1744) and Oswald Spengler (1880–1936), Toynbee offers a view of history which sees it as determined by certain recurrent factors and imperatives from both within and without societies, subject to laws (like a kind of science), partly predictable and even cyclic. Since historical engineering plays such an important role in TIME TRAVEL, ALTERNATE WORLDS and TIME PARADOX stories, it is not surprising that a view of history which appears to offer the tools for such an undertaking should be popular in sf, and while Vico, Spengler and Toynbee differ in important ways, all three offer historical process as reducible to pattern. Spengler's theories play an important if simplified role in such early works by A.E. VAN VOGT as *Voyage of the Space Beagle* (fix-up **1950**), and in a more sophisticated form in James BLISH's *Cities in Flight* (as four separate novels 1955–62; **1970**).

The technological bias of Toynbee's *A Study of History* had, however, already been anticipated by H.G. WELLS in *The Outline of History* (**1920**), in which we meet the second problem set by history for sf, not how predictable is the future, but how changeable is the past. In *The Outline of History* Wells asserted, for example, that the republic of ancient Rome was doomed to failure (a) because of its cumbersome system of government (b) because printing had not yet been invented. Civilization, he suggested, is a product of good communications; a Wellsian time-traveller in ancient Rome would try to improve them. In William GOLDING's story "Envoy Extraordinary" (in *Sometime, Never*, anth. **1956**, and *Scorpion God*, coll. **1971**) an inventor tries to bring steam power, gunpowder and the printing press to the late Roman

Empire, to prevent its fall (rather in the fashion of Hari Seldon). But the Emperor, perhaps wisely, thwarts him at every turn. It may have been possible to change the past, but it was probably not as desirable as Wells thought. The point that Golding makes is that it is misleading always to write history from one's own viewpoint, as if the logic of events pointed only to oneself and late Roman Emperors were filled with the subconscious desire to be like Victorian Englishmen.

This indeed is a point made with great force by a succession of more orthodox sf authors. L. Sprague DE CAMP's "Aristotle and the Gun" (1958) almost duplicates the theme of "Envoy Extraordinary", though it adds a time-traveller. The same author's *Lest Darkness Fall* (**1941**) returns us yet again to the late Roman Empire, with a contemporary American accidentally sent back in time and faced with the problem of preventing disaster and indeed delaying the oncoming Dark Age. He solves this entirely by technical means, but the novel is skilful and thoughtful in its search for "minimum solutions": the hero cannot simply drive off the barbarians with gunpowder, for instance (it is too hard to make), nor can he introduce anything as complex as scientific method (for which there is as yet no demand). He *can*, however, "invent" Arabic numerals, distillation, horse-collars, and many other minor innovations which have a major cumulative effect.

Lest Darkness Fall gains point from the evident contrast with Mark TWAIN's *A Connecticut Yankee in King Arthur's Court* (**1889**; vt *A Yankee at the Court of King Arthur* UK), a story in which another "modern" man is sent back to the sixth century. Twain's hero, though, has a simpler view of progress than De Camp's. He shows little ability to see past the virtues of democracy, nonconformity, and materialism, and to 20th-century readers must seem lamentably ethnocentric. It seems likely that De Camp intended to criticize Twain, by silent contrast, for failing to grasp that history is not an inevitable process of evolution, but is moulded by cultural and technological as well as political and ethical factors.

Since *Lest Darkness Fall* there have been many "change-the-past" stories, such as Manly Wade WELLMAN's *Twice in Time* (**1951**) and Robert SILVERBERG's *Up the Line* (**1969**). A further development has been to assume that in some future world there are organizations dedicated to changing history in order to make it more favourable to themselves, as in Poul ANDERSON's *The Guardians of Time* (fix-up **1960**) and *The Corridors of Time* (**1965**) or maintaining history against change as in *The Fall of Chronopolis* (**1974**) by Barrington J. BAYLEY. Fritz LEIBER's "Big Time" series, meanwhile, includes one story, "Try and

Change the Past" (1958), whose basic point, like Golding's, is the impossibility of changing history at all. Societies which make war by travelling between PARALLEL WORLDS as well as or instead of travelling in time have been envisaged by Keith LAUMER in his *Worlds of the Imperium* (1962) and by H. Beam PIPER, in his series of "Paratime Police" and "Gunpowder God" stories (1948–55 and 1964–5 respectively). All these variants and sub-variants of the "history-changing" story make two central demands on their authors: to communicate a sense of the forces that shape history, and to commit themselves to presenting "minimum" or "elegant" solutions to historical problems.

It is this sense of the patterns of past and future which provides an intellectual spine for the many future histories presented by Poul Anderson, Robert HEINLEIN, Larry Niven, and others. It is this, too, which can on occasion add new dimensions even to relatively unoriginal work. Sf authors must always be tempted to blend ancient and modern settings, at worst producing SPACE OPERA (the "Western" set in a slackly imagined future). However, some seeming examples of space opera are redeemed by the awareness that if history repeats itself it must be for a reason. Thus Mack REYNOLDS' novel *Space Pioneer* (1967) demands overt comparison between the American past and the interstellar future, but it is a comparison with a sense of difference as well as of similarity. Other obvious projections of the past into the future include Robert Heinlein's *The Moon is a Harsh Mistress* (1966), a very detailed paralleling of the American War of Independence with an imagined lunar breakaway; James Blish's *Earthman Come Home* (fix-up 1955), which recalls the Dustbowl era of the 1920s; H. Beam Piper's *Space Viking* (1962), a curious blend of the ninth/tenth centuries with interstellar flight and the rise of the Nazis; and Walter MILLER's *A Canticle for Leibowitz* (1960), which portrays a future Dark Age, in which learning has once more retreated to the monasteries. The attraction which collapsing empires, whether Galactic, Roman, or ATLANTEAN, have for sf writers has already been glanced at.

The other periods most commonly underlying images of the future are: 1492 and subsequent voyages of discovery; 1776 and subsequent rejections of colonialism; and the mid-19th century and movements of mass emigration. But the history of science is always likely to reappear as well, as in James Blish's "The Thing in the Attic" (1954; in fix-up *The Seedling Stars*, 1957), which depends heavily on the trial of Galileo. The same scene is recalled in Heinlein's "Universe" (1940) and in Fred SABERHAGEN's *Brother Assassin* (fix-up 1969), and such coincidences may make one think that the interpretation of scientific history in sf is

predominantly a "whig" one — a term used by H. Butterfield in his *The Whig Interpretation of History* (1931), meaning in part that kind of history which is written, perhaps unconsciously, to flatter a society's image of itself and to provide it with culture-heroes by emphasizing the historical importance of individuals, rather than social changes in the mass. Indeed, the technological and America-oriented bias of much history in sf must be evident from what has been said already. Many works of sf are accordingly open to the criticism of "whiggery" (as are works of many other genres, including academic history). However, many sf authors, such as De Camp or Leiber or even Heinlein in his less patriotic moments, are acutely aware of this danger, and commit themselves openly to non-moralistic and non-ethnocentric interpretations. Beneath these one may sense a strong and shared feeling that, after all, no one knows for sure how the future will go, and that there are many points at which the past might plausibly have been expected to develop in some way other than the way it did.   [TS]

HISTORY OF SF It would be relatively simple to recount the history of sf if we could say with conviction exactly what sf was, but we cannot (*see* DEFINITIONS OF SF). Sf is an impure genre which did not finally take shape until the late 19th century, though all its separate elements existed earlier. The extent to which we call any earlier story a work of sf depends entirely on how many sf elements we require before we so label it. The Babylonian *Epic of Gilgamesh* has a fantastic voyage and a great world-flood, and in those respects it qualifies, but such retrospective labelling is not very useful, since there is no sense at all in which we can regard sf as a separable genre before the 19th century. Sf proper requires a consciousness of the scientific outlook, and it probably also requires a sense of the possibilities of change, whether social or technological. A cognitive, scientific way of viewing the world did not emerge until the 17th century, and did not percolate into society at large until the 18th (partly) and the 19th (to a large extent); a sense of the fragility of social structures and their potentiality for change did not really become widespread until the series of political revolutions of the late 18th century. These questions are discussed further under PROTO SF, in which entry a number of early scientific fictions, from Johannes KEPLER through CYRANO DE BERGERAC and Jonathan SWIFT, along with many other even earlier contenders for the proto-sf label, are discussed.

The main elements which eventually became melded (in varying proportions) into sf are as follows (many of them are discussed in greater detail in their own entry): 1. The FANTASTIC VOYAGE: 2. The

UTOPIA (along with the Anti-Utopia and DYSTOPIA); 3. The *conte philosophique*, or Philosophical Tale (partly discussed under SATIRE); 4. The GOTHIC; 5. The TECHNOLOGICAL and SOCIOLOGICAL Anticipation; 6. The Tall Tale and the Hoax.

Just as sf is not itself a pure genre, nor are its constituents; the fantastic voyage is combined with the Dystopia in Jonathan Swift's *Gulliver's Travels* (1726; rev. 1735); the Gothic is combined with the Anticipation in *The Mummy*! (1827) by Jane LOUDON; the *conte philosophique* is combined with the Tall Tale in *Micromégas* (Berlin 1750; France 1752) by VOLTAIRE.

The two figures most important to sf in the early 19th century were Mary SHELLEY and Edgar Allan POE, both of whom, in rather different ways, injected a certain amount of scientific speculation into their fundamentally Gothic romances. They were not alone, however; in the middle of the century a number of American writers in particular made use of sf elements in their work, notably Nathaniel HAWTHORNE, Herman MELVILLE and Fitz-James O'BRIEN, as did Bulwer LYTTON in England. Then there were such isolated, freakish speculations as Captain Adam SEABORN's *Symzonia* (1820), one of the earliest of the many novels which are based on the idea of a hollow Earth, and *A Voyage to the Moon* (1827) by Joseph ATTERLEY. In the 1860s Jules VERNE began to publish sf, many of his books dealing directly with the impact of NEAR-FUTURE technology, and after him, and to some extent because of his success, the trickle became a torrent.

The next major figure was H.G. WELLS, in whose work the Gothic, the Utopia and the Anticipation were closely bound together in the form which all readers today recognize as inarguably sf. Beginning in the 1890s, Wells did more than any other single writer to give a shape to the genre. Most sf ever since Wells's has adhered more or less closely not only to its narrative patterns, but to the Wellsian balance between abstract speculation and characterization, and also to the balance between scientific and sociological speculation.

Though Wells's achievement was great, it is too simple by far to imagine sf jumping straight from Verne to Wells and then exploding into the form we know today; Wells had many contemporaries writing sf also, and many predecessors: between the publication of Verne's first sf novel *Cinq semaines en ballon* (1863; trans. as *Five Weeks in a Balloon* 1870) and Wells's first, *The Time Machine* (1895), the genre had been consolidating and expanding. Notable titles from the period, in chronological order, are: *The Steam Man of the Prairies* (1868) by Edward S. Ellis; "The Brick Moon" (1869) by Edward Everett HALE; *The Battle of Dorking* (1871) by George T. CHESNEY; *Erewhon* (1872) by Samuel

BUTLER; *Récits de l'infini* (**1872** France; trans. as *Stories of Infinity: Lumen* **1873**) by Camille FLAMMARION; *Frank Reade and his Steam Man of the Plains* (1876; **1883**) by Harry Enton (*see* FRANK READE JR); "The Dream of a Ridiculous Man" (1877 Russia) by DOSTOYEVSKY; *She* (**1887**) by H. Rider HAGGARD; *Oxygen och Aromasia* (**1878**) by Claës LUNDIN; *Across the Zodiac* (**1880**) by Percy GREG; *Strange Stories* (coll. **1884**) by Grant ALLEN; *Flatland* (**1884**) by Edwin A. ABBOTT; *A Modern Daedalus* (**1885**) by Tom GREER; *After London* (**1885**) by Richard JEFFERIES; *L'Eve future* ["The Future Eve"] (**1886**) by VILLIERS DE L'ISLE-ADAM; *Dr. Jekyll and Mr. Hyde* (**1886**) by Robert Louis STEVENSON; "Les xipéhuz" (1887; trans. as "The Shapes") by J.H. ROSNY AÎNÉ; *A Crystal Age* (**1887**) by W.H. HUDSON; *Looking Backward* (**1888**) by Edward BELLAMY; *The Conquest of the Moon* (**1888** France; trans. **1889**) by André LAURIE; *The Great War Syndicate* (**1889**) by Frank STOCKTON; *Solarion* (**1889**) by Edgar FAWCETT; *A Connecticut Yankee at King Arthur's Court* (**1889**) by Mark TWAIN; *A Plunge into Space* (**1890**) by Robert CROMIE; *A.D. 2000* (**1890**) by Alvarado FULLER; *Freiland* (**1890**; trans. as *Freeland* **1891**) by Theodor HERTZKA; *News from Nowhere* (**1891**) by William MORRIS; *The Goddess of Atvatabar* (**1892**) by William BRADSHAW; *The Germ Growers* (**1892**) by Robert POTTER; *Can Such Things Be?* (coll. **1893**) by Ambrose BIERCE; *Hartmann the Anarchist* (**1893**) by E. Douglas FAWCETT; *Olga Romanoff* (**1894**) by George GRIFFITH; *A Journey in Other Worlds* (**1894**) by John Jacob ASTOR; *A Journey to Mars* (**1894**) by Gustavus POPE; *A Traveler from Altruria* (**1894**) by William Dean HOWELLS; *The Great God Pan and The Inmost Light* (coll. **1894**) by Arthur MACHEN; *The Call of The Cosmos* (**1895** Russia; trans. **1963**) by Konstantin TSIOLKOVSKY.

The above list is not even remotely complete; many other writers of the late Victorian period receive entries in this volume. It is given in some detail (even though it contains few works of lasting literary value) in order to show the density of sf publication in the years immediately preceding Wells, as a way of showing that he did not, as it were, spring from nowhere.

Several of the writers in the above list published their stories in magazines in the first instance; since the 1880s many new magazines had appeared at a lower price than previously. Many of these (a selection is listed under MAGAZINES) published sf stories, and with the advent of the PULP MAGAZINES (as opposed to the "slicks") in the late 1890s the market for magazine sf expanded considerably. In terms of readership these changes meant that sf was finding a more popular audience than ever before, but also an audience whose expectations of literature were often fairly crude; the prime

demand was an action-packed story. Already by the time of Wells, the rift between serious sf and pulp sf was beginning to open; it has never wholly closed since. Wells's own sf, of course, was not regarded as wholly reputable by many of his contemporaries, and after 10 years of publishing little other than scientific romances Wells turned to the "serious" novel, though he never abandoned sf altogether.

Several of the pre-Wells titles listed above initiated sf sub-genres which were to prove popular for a long time. *The Steam Man of the Prairies* (**1868**) inaugurated sf in DIME-NOVEL format; usually featuring boys involved in the creation and use of marvellous INVENTIONS (these were the years when Thomas Alva Edison was becoming a national hero in the USA). Sf dime novels continued until the 1900s, at which time they were gradually replaced by such juvenile series as TOM SWIFT, and by the stories in the new pulp magazines.

H. Rider Haggard's *She* (**1887**) inaugurated the period during which the LOST-WORLD romance was to become extremely popular; it continued with some vitality into the 1930s, and is not quite extinct even today.

George T. Chesney's *The Battle of Dorking* (**1871**) inaugurated the era of the future-WAR story, which often featured INVASION. Robert Potter's *The Germ Growers* (**1892**) and H.G. Wells's *The War of the Worlds* (**1898**) introduced extraterrestrial invasion. Future-war stories remain popular today, especially in interstellar venues, but their great era was roughly 1890–1914, when a vast number were published. The realities of the First World War rather removed their function as awful warning; further awful warnings were not required for some time, though the genre did, in fact, continue after the War.

The BOYS' PAPERS and PULP MAGAZINES were heavily influenced by these sub-genres, and printed many such stories.

The first English-language sf magazine was AMAZING STORIES, founded in 1926 by Hugo GERNSBACK (*see also* SF MAGAZINES); it was sub-titled "the magazine of scientifiction". The usual modern term "science fiction" was hardly used before the early 1930s, and did not pass into really general use before John W. CAMPBELL Jr took over the editorship of *ASF*. But though the label is quite recent, the genre itself was becoming readily distinguishable as a separate entity by the time of Wells, who called such stories "scientific romances".

For a long time, potted histories of sf tended to jump from Verne (1863) to Wells (1895) to *Amazing Stories* (1926) as if the intervening years were comparatively empty. We have already shown what happened 1863–95. The period 1895–1926 (covering Wells's own most productive years) is considerably more packed. There is no space here to

give titles, but the following authors were important in the period. Those closely linked with sf in magazine format include Frank AUBREY, Edwin BALMER, Edgar Rice BURROUGHS, William Wallace COOK, Ray CUMMINGS, George Allan ENGLAND, Ralph Milne FARLEY, Homer Eon FLINT, Austin HALL, Otis Adelbert KLINE, A. MERRITT, Victor ROUSSEAU and Garrett P. SERVISS; those primarily remembered for book publication (though many also published in the magazines) include Edwin Lester ARNOLD, R.H. BENSON, J.D. BERESFORD, Hall CAINE, Karel ČAPEK, G.K. CHESTERTON, J.J. CONNINGTON, Arthur Conan DOYLE, E.M. FORSTER, Hollis GODFREY, Owen GREGORY, Will N. HARBEN, Milo HASTINGS, F. HERNAMAN-JOHNSON, William Hope HODGSON, Fred T. JANE, Johannes V. JENSEN, Rudyard KIPLING, Kurd LASSWITZ, W. LE QUEUX, David LINDSAY, Jack LONDON, J. MASTIN, H.H. Munro (SAKI), E.V. ODLE, Max PEMBERTON, Maurice RENARD, Ella SCRYMSOUR, M.P. SHIEL, Godfrey SWEVEN, Guy THORNE, E. Charles VIVIAN, Thea VON HARBOU, Edgar WALLACE, Stanley WATERLOO, S. Fowler WRIGHT and Yevgeny ZAMIATIN.

The most important of the pre-specialist sf magazines, so far as publication of sf stories is concerned, were probably those published by Frank A. MUNSEY in the USA, and PEARSON's MAGAZINE and PEARSON's WEEKLY in the UK. Many reputations were made in the magazines, the most lasting and most influential being, probably, that of Edgar Rice Burroughs; his first work was "Under the Moon of Mars" which appeared in 1912 in Munsey's ALL-STORY MAGAZINE as by Norman Bean; it later appeared in book form as *A Princess of Mars* (**1917**) under his own name. The huge success of Burroughs did much to skew magazine sf away from serious scientific and social speculation (which by no means necessitates dullness, as writers like Robert A. HEINLEIN, C.M. KORNBLUTH and James BLISH were later to demonstrate) and towards romantic adventure in colourful and usually primitive other-wordly landscapes.

By 1926 the split between genre and MAINSTREAM sf was becoming pronounced; mainstream sf is explained in detail in the entry of that name, but briefly, it is sf written either by writers who are better known for serious non-sf works, or by writers who seem to be writing in unconsciousness of the tradition of magazine sf, such as Olaf STAPLEDON was to do in the 1930s.

Genre sf is usually published in the first instance in magazine format (at least until the paperback book revolution of the 1950s) by authors who think of themselves as writing sf, and who work consciously within a tradition created by previous workers in the same field. Until the 1960s mainstream sf was respectable, from a literary point of view, and genre sf was not. Perhaps to rectify this quite unjust prejudice, most previous commentaries on sf have heavily emphasized genre sf, and in so doing have quite distorted the history of sf as a whole. Fully half of the authors represented in this volume were not genre sf writers, in the sense that they did not see themselves as part of a continuing tradition of popular literature; generally, we can assume, they thought of themselves as writing serious fiction, and may not have even understood the sf label if it was used on their work, which it almost invariably was, and is, not. The standard histories usually give a passing nod to Aldous HUXLEY and George ORWELL and one or two other mainstream sf writers, but the sheer scale of sf publication outside the magazine tradition is still not generally realized; such works are by writers as diverse as J.D. BERESFORD and John COLLIER, Neil GUNN and L.P. HARTLEY, Upton SINCLAIR and Rex WARNER, William GOLDING and Robert ARDREY. (However, against this it must be admitted that because such writers are not generally conscious of writing within a genre, they often "break the rules", sometimes fruitfully; sf by mainstream writers is often only borderline or quasi-sf when judged by the rigid standards of the more puritanical genre critics.)

In the 1930s, indeed, magazine sf was at rather a low ebb; certainly there was much competent adventure writing, (primarily in the new sub-genre of SPACE OPERA, which developed almost entirely within the magazines at this time) and sometimes it was better than that, but a rollcall whose major names are Arthur K. BARNES, Stanton A. COBLENTZ, John W. CAMPBELL Jr, Edmond HAMILTON, Robert E. HOWARD, Neil R. JONES, H.P. LOVECRAFT, E.E. "DOC" SMITH, John TAINE, A. Hyatt VERRILL, Stanley WEINBAUM, Jack WILLIAMSON and Philip WYLIE can hardly be argued as constituting an ongoing literary tradition of any great seriousness or importance. It *was* important, but not so much for what it was (little of it is really readable now except by the young and undemanding, and the nostalgic), but for what it led to: the new generation of genre sf writers, inaugurated by John W. Campbell Jr, who took over *ASF* in Oct. 1937. That story is told in some detail under GOLDEN AGE OF SF, and does not need repeating here; in short, magazine sf gained a new maturity, along with some of its most celebrated writers, in the years 1938–46.

Sf published in the magazines during this Golden Age period was to be the basis of the sf book publishing boom which, both in hardcovers and in paperback, was a phenomenon of the 1950s and has continued unabated ever since. The shift of emphasis from magazine to book publication (even though until the late 1960s prior publication in a magazine was still the rule rather than the exception) won genre sf a much larger readership than ever before, and was the basis first of its great expansion in terms of book marketing, which by the 1970s had reached the point where sf constituted around 10 per cent of all English-language fiction published, and later of its increasing respectability. Sf book publishing is discussed in some detail under SF PUBLISHING and ANTHOLOGIES.

The increase in maturity of genre sf during the so-called Golden Age was only relative. It seems generally to have been assumed by most sf publishers from 1926 on that their main readership was made up of teenage boys. The publisher Donald A. WOLLHEIM is on record as believing this, and the belief is certainly reflected in the nature of the remarkable but adventure-story oriented sf lists he edited first at ACE BOOKS and later at DAW BOOKS. On the other hand, Jim BAEN, editor of *Galaxy Science Fiction* in the mid-1970s, believes surveys support him in showing that the readership reaches its median age in the mid-20s. No market surveys carried out have been extensive or reliable enough to prove the point one way or the other. But regardless of the actual facts, the belief that the readership was young and primarily male was sufficient in itself to lead genre sf into avoiding complex or experimental writing, into simplifying its language down to a fairly undemanding pulp vocabulary, and, in a puritanical way, into observing various TABOOS about SEX, bad language and RELIGION. This was almost as true of the 1940s and '50s as it had been of the '30s. It has been less true since the late 1960s, but even in the late '70s much published sf is visibly aimed at a juvenile market, and many able and sophisticated writers have, in protest or disgust, either abandoned the field or worked hard at having the ghetto "sf" label removed from their books.

The extraordinary growth in sf publishing since the Second World War has concealed the truth about its relative unimportance up to the end of the 1930s. In fact, out of many hundreds of specialized pulp magazines, only a tiny handful were devoted to sf; it is unlikely that, in those days, sf had more than two or three per cent of the pulp market.

With the post-War growth of sf publishing has come an increased diversity, in a genre not noted for its homogeneity in the first instance. It is simple indeed to find exceptions to almost any generalization made about sf during this period, but some general comments must be hazarded anyway.

Where Gernsbackian sf was optimistic and technologically oriented, Campbellian sf was much stronger in dealing with the human consequences of change, and it occasionally allowed darker moods, although *ASF* in particular stressed, chauvinistically, the likely superiority of *Homo sapiens* to any alien form of life it might meet. The domination of Campbellian sf within the genre began to come to an end with the inauguration of two important new magazines, THE MAGAZINE OF FANTASY AND SCIENCE FICTION in 1949, and GALAXY SCIENCE FICTION in 1950. The former emphasized literacy and style to an extent unprecedented in sf magazine publishing, and the latter specialized in witty SATIRE, often sociological rather than technological, written by such important writers as Alfred BESTER, C.M. KORNBLUTH and Frederik POHL, Robert SHECKLEY, William TENN and, occasionally, Philip K. DICK. More and more, during the 1950s and '60s, the emphasis of genre sf shifted away from the HARD SCIENCES (engineering, astronomy, physics etc.) to the SOFT SCIENCES (biology, sociology, psychology etc.). Perhaps PSI POWERS also fit into the latter category, though many do not think of them as being susceptible to scientific investigation at all. At any rate, the 1950s were the years of the psi or ESP story, very often stories of MUTANTS or SUPERMEN. The ESP boom became a little tedious after a while (as did the FLYING SAUCER boom of the same period), and it subsided to a lower though constant level in the later 1960s.

As worries about POLITICS, ECOLOGY and POPULATION grew in the 1960s, an already perceptible shift away from simple optimism began to accelerate (*see* OPTIMISM AND PESSIMISM); this move is much connected in readers' minds with the advent of the so-called NEW WAVE, though this was never an easily definable movement, indeed in no sense an organized movement at all, and its outward signs were as much a greater willingness to experiment with literary style and to adopt more complex narrative strategies as in any generally pessimistic or downbeat attitude. But pessimism in sf certainly did increase in this period (the late 1960s) as did left-wing political attitudes; most previous genre sf had been either dead to political issues, or adopted a rather conservative, right-wing stance (*see* POLITICS). This period was also notable for seizing on the idea of ENTROPY as a useful, all-purpose metaphor.

By the 1960s, sf was being read so much more widely than before that its ideas, and its iconography generally, had begun quite dramatically to feed back into mainstream fiction. Previously the intellectual traffic had been mostly the other way. The walls of the sf ghetto have been crumbling away in the 1960s and '70s, and while a number of writers, such as Kurt VONNEGUT Jr, J.G. BALLARD, Michael MOORCOCK, Robert SILVERBERG and Barry MALZBERG have escaped, others, such as John BARTH, Angela CARTER, Michael CRICHTON, Howard FAST, Romain GARY, John HERSEY, Ira LEVIN, Thomas PYNCHON, Alan SILLITOE and Angus WILSON have found their way in, sometimes spending quite protracted periods there. A number of good writers such as Harlan ELLISON and Brian W. ALDISS have jumped nimbly backwards and forwards across the half-destroyed ghetto wall so often that it is as if it did not exist.

The years 1960–77 have seen an ongoing, complex cross-fertilization of genres; at the intellectual end of the spectrum FABULATIONS and surrealist and ABSURDIST works have been making more and more use of sf themes and tropes; at the popular end horror and DISASTER novels have both borrowed heavily from sf, as has the best-selling novel (itself rapidly becoming a definable genre). As an example of the latter, *The Crash of '79* (1976) by Paul E. Erdman is pure sf extrapolation, though it uses conventional narrative and characterization strategies of the best-seller in its tale of NEAR-FUTURE disaster in politics, ECONOMICS and NUCLEAR POWER. The sub-genre of HEROIC FANTASY, while once marketed as if it were sf, is in the process of being hived off as an identifiably separate genre, though it continues to use many sf themes.

In other words, sf has never been harder to define than in the decade 1968–77, and the apparently limitless diversity opening up is an excellent sign of a genre reaching such health and maturity that paradoxically it is ceasing to be one. If much sf and borderline sf is no longer published under the label, that hardly matters; the importance of the label has been greatly over-estimated anyway; it was not used in British book publishing until the 1950s, though in many respects the UK was the birthplace of the genre more than a century earlier. It has been necessary, in editing this volume, to apply the label retrospectively, and while it is intellectually defensible to do so it should not be forgotten that it is only with hindsight, and the use of some rather arbitrary rules of thumb, that it is possible. We have not been able to emerge with an inarguable definition of sf, and we gravely doubt either the possibility or the desirability of doing so. (The entire history of literary genres shows that the more accurate the labelling procedure becomes, the tighter the straitjacket so produced, and the greater the likelihood that rigour will bring about stasis and final decay, with writers producing only increasingly feeble imitations of what has gone before.) If there is any one theme of crucial importance in defining what sf is all about, it is CONCEPTUAL BREAKTHROUGH, as is argued in the entry of that name, but even this is not universally applicable.

There is now a greater interest than ever before in sf's history. It is only since around 1950 that its details have been at all clear, and most of the necessary research work has been carried out since that time. There is very much more to be done, and it certainly will be done if the academic interest in sf, which has been

growing steadily since around 1960, continues (*see* SF IN THE CLASSROOM). The interest is high within the genre itself; there are quite a few examples of writers making sf's history one of their actual themes; Michael Moorcock's "Dancers at the End of Time" sequence, Brian W. Aldiss's *Frankenstein Unbound* (1973) and Christopher PRIEST's *The Space Machine* (1976) are three.

The above has been a condensed and partial history of the genre; a very much fuller account will be available to readers who follow up the various cross-references. Many anthologies of sf from specific periods are available; editors who have produced such volumes include Brian W. Aldiss and Harry HARRISON, Michael ASHLEY, Isaac ASIMOV, H. Bruce FRANKLIN, Damon KNIGHT and Sam MOSKOWITZ. Several historical reprint series have been published in the 1970s, some in paperback, such as the New English Library "SF Master" series, and some in more expensive formats (*see* ARNO PRESS, GARLAND PRESS, GREGG PRESS, HYPERION *for further details*). A particularly useful volume for historical researchers is *A Research Guide to Science Fiction Studies* (1977) compiled and ed. Marshall B. Tymn, Roger C. Schlobin and L.W. Currey. It contains a comprehensive listing of books and articles on sf's history; an ample selection of such works can be found in this Encyclopedia under the rubric CRITICAL AND HISTORICAL WORKS ABOUT SF.   [PN]

HITCHCOCK, RAYMOND (? –). English writer whose sf novel, *Venus 13: A Cautionary Space Tale* (1972), deals lightly with the theme of SEX in its story of complications surrounding a eugenic mating in a space satellite.   [JC]

HIVE-MINDS A hive-mind is the organizing principle of the community in those insect species of which the basic reproductive unit is the hive, organized around a single fertile female, the queen. The term is, however, applied rather loosely in many sf stories, sometimes referring to any situation in which minds are linked in such a way that the whole becomes dominant over the parts.

Because the organization of social insect communities is so very different from that of mammal communities, while showing a degree of structural complexity comparable only to human societies, ants and their kindred have always held a particular fascination for sf writers. Examples of this fascination include "The Empire of the Ants" (1905) by H.G. WELLS, "Adventures of Professor Emmett" (1939) by Ben HECHT, "The Ant With the Human Soul" (1932) by Bob Olsen, "Doomsday Deferred" (1949) by Murray LEINSTER, writing as Will F. Jenkins, and "Come and Go Mad" (1949) by Fredric BROWN. The ant-hive offers a ready model for the design of an ALIEN society, employed by Wells in

the first such model, *The First Men in the Moon* (1901) and employed somewhat more crudely by Ralph Milne FARLEY in *The Radio Man* (1924; 1948) and Robert HEINLEIN in *Starship Troopers* (1959). Giant ants and wasps are among the standard figures of menace employed by sf writers at all levels, two of the more impressive examples being Alfred Gordon BENNETT's *The Demigods* (1939) and *The Furies* (1966) by Keith ROBERTS; realistically aggressive bees of more conventional size are the menace in *The Swarm* (1974) by Arthur HERZOG.

The apparent efficiency of a hive-society, although repugnant to most writers as a principle with possible application to human life, has not been unattractive to everyone, and aspects of hive-organization are to be found in many UTOPIAN schemes. But most sf novels dealing with "human hives" react against the idea; examples are *The Riddle of the Tower* (1944) by J.D. BERESFORD and Esmé Wynne-Tyson and Morrow's *Ants* (1975) by Edward HYAMS, while L. Sprague DE CAMP's *Rogue Queen* (1951) deals with the overthrow of a "hive-state". Some sf writers, however, are ambiguous in their approach to the notion, as for instance Frank HERBERT in *Hellstrom's Hive* (1973), T.J. BASS in *Half Past Human* (1971) and *The Godwhale* (1974) and Brian STABLEFORD in *In the Kingdom of the Beasts* (1971).

The idea of a group-mind, not necessarily structured like that of an insect hive, is quite common in the branch of sf that deals with TELEPATHY. In *Last and First Men* (1930), and later in *Star Maker* (1937), Olaf STAPLEDON uses the idea of a group-mind so often that it becomes almost like a leitmotiv with a series of variations, sometimes with the emphasis on politics and sometimes to demonstrate a kind of philosophical abstraction of social harmony. The most memorable example, which certainly had a profound if delayed influence upon genre sf, is the Martian cloud-mind, a highly organized but discrete structure of sub-microscopic organisms, in *Last and First Men*.

The notion of the hive-mind overlaps that of the group-mind in Theodore STURGEON's powerful "To Marry Medusa" (1958; exp. vt *The Cosmic Rape* 1958), in which an invading collective mind unites the minds of the human race preparatory to absorbing the species into its communal self, but finds the resultant corporate entity too powerful. Group minds are very common in post-War sf (*see* SUPERMAN) and there are sometimes traces of hive-organization, as in Sturgeon's *More Than Human* (1953), in which the ever-young baby is the central coordinator. The ambiguity in more recent attitudes to the notion of the hive may derive from this association with the notion of the transcendent superman. Thus, whereas "Empire of the Ants", "Doomsday Deferred" and other stories

envisage hive-insects as the most serious possible threat to human domination of Earth, Frank Herbert's *The Green Brain* (1966) evolves a multi-species insect hive in order to protect the world's ecological balance against the short-sighted insecticide policies of Man. Similarly, while Heinlein saw no possible compatibility between Man and hive-alien in *Starship Troopers*, Joe HALDEMAN could see not only an end to *The Forever War* (1974) but also the possibility that Man might be greatly enriched by contact with such a species. Rightly or wrongly, the ant-hive seems to be emerging as a symbol of social harmony rather than totalitarian suppression, although it must always retain its essential ambiguity. [BS]
See also: COMMUNICATION; LIVING WORLDS; POLITICS.

HJORTSBERG, WILLIAM (1941–). American writer. Most of his work is fantasy, like his first novel, *Alp* (1969); *Gray Matters* (1971) grounds its fantastic episodes in a future UTOPIA where men are reborn from the wombs of an enormous CYBERNETIC complex only when they have achieved some transcendence of their personal identities. The narrative deals with some of the rebels, without taking obvious sides. [JC]
Other works: *Symbiography* (1973).
See also: REINCARNATION.

H-MAN, THE Film (1958). Toho. Directed by Inoshiro Honda, starring Yumi Shirakawa, Kenji Sahara, Akihiko Hirata and Koreya Senda. Screenplay by Takeshi Kimura, based on a story by Hideo Kaijo. 87 mins (cut to 79). Colour.
The film is, in effect, a Japanese version of THE BLOB, but is much more ingenious. A fishing-boat encounters a drifting freighter. A search reveals no sign of life but several empty suits of clothing, with underwear inside the outer garments. The captain's uniform is found slumped over the log book, but unlike the other piles of clothing on board it is inhabited — by a pool of green slime that immediately runs up the leg of the nearest fisherman and dissolves him on the spot. The ship had entered a radioactive cloud and the crew had been transformed into a group organism. The monster reaches Tokyo but, unlike other Toho creatures, it does not knock over buildings; it slithers in and out of drains, under doors and through windows, dissolving and absorbing anyone it can catch. There are good special effects by Eiji Tsuburaya who achieved his alarming "dissolve" scenes by using life-size inflatable dummies; the air was let out of them and the shrivelling results were shown in slow motion. [JB]

HOCH, EDWARD D. (1930–). American writer, best known for detective novels and stories. With the short story "Co-Incidence" (1956; as by Irwin Booth), he began publishing detection-oriented sf; later he sometimes used the pseudonyms Stephen Dentinger, R.L. Stevens and Pat McMahon. The numerous stories featuring detective Simon Ark, some collected in *The Judges of Hades and Other Simon Ark Stories* (coll. 1971) and *City of Brass and Other Simon Ark Stories* (coll. 1971), are marginal sf or fantasy; Mr Ark claims to be 2,000 years old. EDH's sf series featuring Earl Jazine of the Computer Cops mixes sf and detection in action tales of 21st-century crises involving computer crimes. The series includes "Computer Cops" (1969), *The Transvection Machine* (1971), *The Fellowship of the Hand* (1973) and *The Frankenstein Factory* (1975). Within his range, EDH is a briskly competent storyteller. [JC]

HODDER-WILLIAMS, CHRISTOPHER (1926–). British writer, pilot, composer and sound engineer. His first novel was non-sf, *The Cummings Report* (1957) as by James Brogan, and he began publishing sf with *Chain Reaction* (1959), which concerns itself, as does almost all his fiction, with the relationship between Man and the machine technology he has created about himself, in this case through a mystery plot about radiation sickness spread by food. His next three novels were aviation stories, on the same general theme, but since *The Main Experiment* (1964) he has written only sf, almost all of them novels with NEAR-FUTURE scenarios documenting Man's growing, and perhaps inextricable, involvement with his technology. These include *Fistful of Digits* (1968) which introduces self-programming computers in an obsessive tale about loss of individuality, and *The Silent Voice* (1977), about the capacity of the human brain to receive radio waves directly, to potentially ominous effect. CH-W's novels somewhat uneasily combine social and cultural concern with rather melodramatic plotting and stiff characterization of a rather male chauvinist variety. [JC]
Other Works: *The Egg-Shaped Thing* (1967; the English hard-cover edition is definitive); *Ninety-Eight Point Four* (1969; vt *98.4*); *Panic O'Clock* (1973); *Cowards' Paradise* (1974; UK paperback slightly revised); *The Prayer Machine* (1976).
See also: PARANOIA AND SCHIZOPHRENIA.

HODGE, T. SHIRBY Pseudonym of American writer Roger Sherman Tracy (1841–1926); his sf novel, *The White Man's Burden: A Satirical Forecast* (1915), remarkably places a Black UTOPIA in Africa founded on the blacks' gaining of merited supremacy over white Americans. [JC]
See also: POLITICS.

HODGKINS, DAVID C. *See* Algis BUDRYS.

HODGSON, WILLIAM HOPE (1877–1918). British writer. The son of a clergyman, he ran away to sea in his youth, and was deeply affected by his experiences aboard. He involved himself in the political struggle to win better conditions for seamen, and never lost a profound fascination for the mysteries of the sea. His sea stories owe an obvious debt to the traditions of supernatural fiction, but he replaced the classical vocabulary of symbols with one he derived primarily from the scientific imagination: grotesque life-forms made horrific by enlargement, and accounts of strange BIOLOGICAL metamorphoses. Particularly notable among his short stories are "The Voice in the Night", in which castaways are transformed by a fungus they have been obliged to eat, and "The Stone Ship", in which an ancient wreck is raised to the surface by a volcanic eruption, bringing many weird creatures up from the depths. In his first novel, *The Boats of the Glen Carrig* (1907), a ship's crew is marooned on an island near a land of floating seaweed inhabited by many bizarre and terrible life-forms. His second novel, *The House on the Borderland* (1908), is one of the most remarkable early products of the cosmic perspective, presenting the diary of a man living in a house co-existent in two worlds, and an account of visions which take him through time to witness the destruction of the Solar System. *The Ghost Pirates* (1909) also juxtaposes known and alien worlds as a ship "alips" into intermediacy between them, and its crew witness strange and frightening manifestations of the other universe. His last novel, *The Night Land* (1912; short version vt *A Dream of X* 1977), is a long story of an odyssey across the face of an Earth drastically transformed by time and populated by MONSTERS, while the last remnant of the human race waits inside a pyramid for inevitable extinction. Hodgson assumed a baroque, highly adjectival style in an attempt to give the impression of strangeness, and the book is in consequence rather difficult to read. Hodgson was killed in action in the First World War.
Although often considered to be a writer of supernatural fantasies, Hodgson definitely belongs to the ancestry of sf. He was one of the first authors involved in the "translation" of the classical materials of the horror story into the substance of the scientific imagination.
Some recent paperback editions of WHH's work are abridged. [BS]
Other works: *Carnacki the Ghost Finder* (coll. 1913); *Men of the Deep Waters* (coll. 1914); *The Luck of the Strong* (coll. 1916); *The House on the Borderland and Other Novels* (coll. 1946); *Deep Waters* (coll. 1967); *Out of the Storm* (coll. 1975).
About the author: "William Hope Hodgson" by Sam MOSKOWITZ in *Out of the Storm*.
See also: COSMOLOGY; END OF THE WORLD;

FANTASTIC VOYAGES; FAR FUTURE; PARALLEL WORLDS; TIME TRAVEL.

HOFFMAN, LEE (1932–). American sf fan and writer, at one point married to Larry T. SHAW; she is probably better known for her Westerns than for her sf, which she began publishing with a short novel, *Telepower* (1967); it was followed by *The Caves of Karst* (1969), *Always the Black Knight* (1970) and *Change Song* (1972); the last named is, typically of her work, a polished, unpretentious adventure in the acquiring of self-knowledge by a juvenile protagonist on an unspecified planet, probably not Earth. [JC]
See also: UNDER THE SEA.

HOFFMANN E(RNST) T(HEODOR) A(MADEUS) (1776–1822). German writer, lawyer, judge and composer; he changed his third name of Wilhelm to Amadeus in homage to Wolfgang Amadeus Mozart. Much of his early work related to music, in the form of musical commentaries, libretti, or compositions. It is his tales, however, for which he is best remembered; they express a grotesque Romanticism more effectively than those of any other writer of his time and, variously translated and assembled, have strongly influenced European literature. His only completed novel, *Die Elixiere des Teufels* (**1813–16**; trans. as *The Devil's Elixir* **1824**), typically concerns itself with a monk seduced by the Devil. Collections of his shorter works are *Fantasiestücke* ["Fantasy Pieces"] (coll. **1814–15**), *Nachtstücke* ["Night Pieces"] (coll. **1816–17**) and *Die Serapionsbruder* (coll. **1818–21**; trans. as *The Serapion Brethren* **1886–92** in two vols); English translations include *Hoffman's Strange Stories* (coll. **1855**), *The Weird Tales of E.T.W. Hoffmann* (coll. in two vols **1885**); a convenient recent assembly is E.F. BLEILER's *The Best Tales of Hoffmann* (coll. **1967**). Three of ETAH's stories formed the basis of the opera *Tales of Hoffmann* (1881) by Offenbach, which was filmed in 1951.

ETAH, like his celebrated successor in the GOTHIC, Edgar Allan POE, was interested in contemporary science, and especially in the psychological theories of Swedenborg and Mesmer's theories of hypnotism; his stories in this vein have influenced later sf. His best-known story, "The Sandman" (1816), features the sinister spectacle-maker Dr Coppelius and the beautiful automaton he builds, with which the hero falls in love. This, even before Mary SHELLEY's *Frankenstein* (1818), is an important forerunner of ROBOT and ANDROID stories. [JC/PN]
See also: MACHINES; PSYCHOLOGY; SCIENTISTS.

HOLBERG, LUDVIG, Baron Holberg (1684–1754). Danish playwright, essayist and historian. Born in Bergen, Norway, Holberg studied at Copenhagen and settled permanently in Denmark, where he was appointed professor at Copenhagen University, first of philosophy, later of metaphysics and of Latin rhetoric, and finally of history (1730). A prolific author, Holberg published several voluminous poems, 32 comedies and the satirical novel *Nicolai Klimii iter Subterraneum* (1741 in Latin; trans. as *A Journey to the World Under-Ground by Nicolas Klimius* 1742; trans. as *Journey of Niels Klim to the World Underground* 1960). This is a satirical UTOPIAN novel, deriding LH's contemporary world, and inspired primarily by Jonathan SWIFT's *Gulliver's Travels*, Thomas MORE's *Utopia* and Montesquieu's *Lettres persanes*. It was one of the most influential of 18th-century satires. It describes the journey of Niels Klim into the (hollow) Earth, where he finds a minute sun circled by the planet Nazar, whose inhabitants show a societal pattern diametrically opposed to that of the current stereotype; women are the dominant sex and males perform only menial tasks. It is notable that Holberg's novel was considered dangerously radical in Denmark; thus, the English translation preceded publication in Danish by 47 years. [J-HH]
See also: FANTASTIC VOYAGES.

HOLBROOK, JOHN See Jack VANCE.

HOLDEN, R(ICHARD) C(ORT) (? –). American author of an sf mystery, *Snow Fury* (1955). [JC]

HOLDSTOCK, ROBERT P. (1948–). British writer, with an MSc in medical zoology from the London School of Hygiene and Tropical Medicine. He spent four years in medical research before becoming a full-time writer. His first published story was "Pauper's Plot" (1968 *New Worlds*). Among his other short works are the novelettes "Travellers" (1976), a TIME-TRAVEL variant, and "The Time Beyond Age" (1976). He has published the novels *Eye Among the Blind* (1976) and *Earthwind* (1977); both are intricate works, the former about the relation of human and ALIEN, the latter incorporating material from Irish culture and MYTHOLOGY. They have had a mixed reception from critics. RPH has published minor works pseudonymously: as Chris Carlsen the SWORD-AND-SORCERY "Berserker" series, *Shadow of the Wolf* (1977) and *The Bull Chief* (1977); as Robert Black two horror novels, *Legend of the Werewolf* (film novelization 1976) and *The Satanists* (1978). [MJE]

HOLLAND See BENELUX.

HOLLAND, CECELIA (1943–). American writer, primarily of historical fiction from *The Firedrake* (1966); her sf novel, *Floating Worlds* (1976), is a formidably long and complex story in which a copious SPACE-OPERA background (a conflict in the Solar System between Inner and Outer Planets) structures her extensive depiction of character and society both on Anarchist Earth and later on the Outer Planets themselves; the protagonist is a woman, complexly motivated, highly believable; on the OUTER PLANETS, the description of the floating cities (*see* GRAVITY) is believable as well, and involving. [JC]
See also: POLITICS.

HOLLIS, H.H. Pseudonym of American (Texas) lawyer and writer Ben N. Ramey (1921–77), who wrote, he said, sf for fun. His first sf publication was "Ouled Nail" for *If* in 1966. His stories "The Gorilla Trees" (1968) and "Sword Game" (1968) were both nominated for a NEBULA award. His stories are eccentric, imaginative and vivid, but no collection has yet been published. [PN]

HOLLOW-EARTH THEORY See LOST WORLDS; Captain Adam SEABORN.

HOLLY, JOAN HUNTER Professional name of American writer Joan Carol Holly (1932–), who previous to 1970 signed herself J. Hunter Holly. She has a degree in psychology and in addition to writing conducts creative writing workshops. A brain tumour, fortunately benign, which developed in 1966 and was removed in 1970, stopped her career for those years, but she is again active. She began publishing sf with a novel, *Encounter* (1959), in which Man and inimical alien confront one another; much of her work involves melodramatic alien INVASIONS and confrontations, including *The Flying Eyes* (1962), *The Dark Planet* (1962) and *The Time Twisters* (1964). Among her better stories, written after her illness, are "The Gift of Nothing" (1973) and "Psi Clone" (1977). A recent novel, *Keeper* (1976) has a sequel, unpublished in late 1977 due to the failure of LASER BOOKS. JHH writes straightforward adventure novels with dark undertones that add interest. [JC]
Other works: *The Green Planet* (1960); *The Gray Aliens* (1963); *The Running Man* (1963); *The Dark Enemy* (1965); *The Mind Traders* (1966); *The Assassination Affair* (1967), no.10 in the "Man from U.N.C.L.E." series.
See also: WOMEN.

HOLM, SVEN (1940–). Danish writer, whose sf novel, *Termush* (1967; trans. 1969), portrays in bleak, haunted scenes the inevitable negative outcome of a plan to survive the atomic HOLOCAUST in a specially prepared, isolated hotel. [JC]

HOLMBERG, JOHN-HENRI (1949–). Swedish editor, translator and critic. Active as a fan since 1963, J-HH has published many critical articles on sf, taught university extramural courses in sf, and edited for Askild & Kärnekull, Lindfors Bokförlag and SFSF. His two critical books, both praised, are *Drömmar om evigheten: science fictions historia* ["Dreams of Eternity: the History of SF"] (**1974**) and *SF-guide: om motiv i science fiction* ["SF Guide: On Motives in SF"] (**1977**). The books are serious criticism, not just fannish enthusiasm. [PN]

HOLMES, A.R. *See* Harry BATES.

HOLMES, H.H. *See* Anthony BOUCHER.

HOLOCAUST AND AFTER This is part of a giant cluster of themes which has always played a central role in sf, both genre and MAINSTREAM. It is impossible to dissect out the different aspects of this cluster so that they are

mutually exclusive; hence there is some overlap between this entry and ADAM AND EVE (many sf tales deal with a second genesis after catastrophe), ANTHROPOLOGY (the emphasis is often on tribal patterns forming in a brutalized and diminished population), EVOLUTION and DEVOLUTION (evolutionary change has been linked with natural catastrophe since the 18th century), ENTROPY (holocaust is one of the more dramatic aspects of everything running down), HISTORY (human-inspired disasters are often seen as part of a Toynbeean or Spenglerian process of historical cycles), END OF THE WORLD (holocaust on a major scale), ECOLOGY (interference with nature is often seen as the bringer of disaster), MEDICINE (the agent of holocaust is often plague), MUTANTS (the use of nuclear weapons is often seen as leading to massive biological changes in plants, animals and humans),

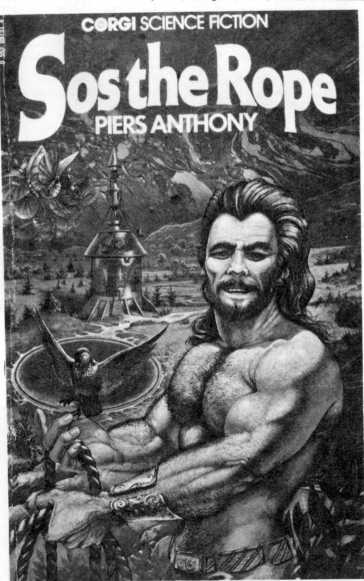

CORGI SCIENCE FICTION

Sos the Rope
PIERS ANTHONY

Sos the Rope, a tribal warrior with bulging muscles, the creation of Piers Anthony, is a typical sf hero after the HOLOCAUST. Patrick Woodroffe. Corgi Books, 1975.

NUCLEAR POWER (the most popular agent of holocaust in fiction since the Second World War) and OPTIMISM AND PESSIMISM.

Generally, we have attempted to concentrate discussion on the causes and nature of the catastrophe in most of the above entries, to summarize the catastrophe variants under DISASTER, and in this entry to concentrate on those many stories whose focus is not so much the disaster itself but the kind of world in which the survivors live, and which they make for themselves.

The story of holocaust and after is as old as sf itself, and a convenient starting point is Mary SHELLEY's second sf novel, *The Last Man* (**1826**), in which plague crosses Europe from the Middle East, leaving, finally, one survivor in Rome who is possibly the last man. Natural catastrophe, too, strikes in Herrmann LANG's almost forgotten *The Air Battle: A Vision of the Future* (trans. **1859**), in which European civilization is destroyed by flood and earthquake, but a benevolent North-African federation brings peace to the world, and the black man is able to lead the white back to social order.

The first novel in which the post-holocaust story takes on its distinctive modern form is Richard JEFFERIES' *After London* (**1885**), in which the author's strategy is to set the novel thousands of years after the catastrophe has taken place; in this way an interesting, alienating perspective is gained. The hero takes his own society (as in most later stories in this vein it is quasi-medieval) for granted; he endeavours to reconstruct the nature of the fallen civilization that preceded it, and also the intervening years of barbarism. Ever since Jefferies' time the post-holocaust story has tended to follow this pattern; for every book whose hero lives through the holocaust itself, John CHRISTOPHER's *The Death of Grass* (**1956**; vt *No Blade of Grass* USA) and Robert MERLE's *Malevil* (**1972** France; trans. **1974**) being examples, there are several whose story is taken up long after the disaster is over but while its effects are still making themselves felt.

Though such stories continue to fascinate, there has been surprisingly little variation in the basic plot; disaster in the average scenario is seen as being followed by a savage barbarism and a bitter struggle for survival, with rape and murder commonplace; such an era is often followed by a rigidly hierarchical feudalism based very much on medieval models. When the emphasis falls on struggle and brutality, as it very often does, what we have, in effect, is an awful-warning story. But often the new world is seen as more peaceful and ordered, more in harmony with nature, than the bustle and strife of civilization before it fell. Such stories are often quasi-UTOPIAN in feeling and PASTORAL in their values, informed by an almost Wordsworthian, meditative openness to simple experiences. There is no denying the attraction of such scenarios; they tempt us with a kind of life in which the individual controls his own destiny and in which moral issues are clear cut; sometimes they are quite crudely black and white, as in Sterling LANIER's *Hiero's Journey* (**1973**), a vivacious and enjoyable melodrama peopled largely by goodies and baddies.

In mature versions of the post-holocaust story there is usually an emotional resonance developed from a tension between loss and gain, with the simplicities of the new order not wholly compensating for the half-remembered glories and comforts of the past. This is the case with George STEWART's *Earth Abides* (**1949**), and may explain why, despite its occasionally fulsome prose, it has attained a classic status with two generations of readers.

To return to a chronological treatment, the first two decades of the 20th century saw no particular boom in the genre, but at least two works that are still well remembered: Jack LONDON's *The Scarlet Plague* (**1915**) and S. Fowler WRIGHT's *Deluge* (**1928**) with its sequel, *Dawn* (**1929**); in both cases the catastrophe is natural. This was so of most holocaust stories in those days of comparative innocence. Even after the First World War, mankind's capacity for self-destruction was seldom seen as strong enough to operate on a global scale. Other relevant stories of the period are Garrett Putnam SERVISS's *The Second Deluge* (**1912**), George Allan ENGLAND's *Darkness and Dawn* (**1914**), an unusually optimistic story of reconstruction, J.J. CONNINGTON's *Nordenholt's Million* (**1923**) and P. Anderson GRAHAM's cranky, racist *The Collapse of Homo Sapiens* (**1923**).

Connington's book made much of the reconstruction of TECHNOLOGY; from this point on the relationship of technology to the post-holocaust world, and the often ambiguous feelings of the latter towards it, became prominent in stories of this kind. Thomas Calvert McCLARY's *Rebirth* (1934 *ASF*; **1944**) is a casually callous account of a scientist so disgusted by what he self-righteously regards as the decadence of modern civilization (pictured at the outset in a cocktail party) that he invents a ray which causes everyone to forget all acquired knowledge, including how to talk; starting from instinct, the smartest and toughest re-educate themselves in technology in about ten years; most die; McClary seems to approve. Edwin BALMER and Philip WYLIE's *When Worlds Collide* (**1933**) with its reconstruction-sequel *After Worlds Collide* (**1934**) has a scientific elite escaping a doomed Earth in a giant rocket, and rebuilding on a new planet, fighting off communists at the same time. Stephen Vincent BENÉT's "The Place of the Gods" (**1937**; vt "By the Waters of Babylon") blends superstitious fear and plangent nostalgia in telling of a barbarian boy's response to the technological wonders of a ruined city; its sentimentality was to become a recurrent note in many such tales after the War; it ends, "We must build again."

Many of the authors cited have not been closely connected with genre sf. The post-holocaust theme, particularly in the UK, has had a strong attraction for novelists of the so-called MAINSTREAM, perhaps because it offers such a powerful metaphor for exploring Man's relation with his social structures; it pits the two great absolutes of art and nature together, much as Shakespeare did in *King Lear*, which is almost a prototype of the genre. Two strong British examples from the 1930s are Alun LLEWELLYN's *The Strange Invaders* (**1934**) and John COLLIER's *Tom's A-Cold* (**1933**; vt *Full Circle* USA); both evoke the atmosphere of a fallen society with considerable intensity of feeling. Other pre-War novels in the genre are Stanley WEINBAUM's *The Black Flame* (1936–9; fix-up **1948**) and Herbert BEST's *The Twenty-Fifth Hour* (**1940**).

The bomb dropped on Hiroshima at the end of the War ushered in a period where the post-holocaust story was to gain an uneasy fascination and a popularity which it has never quite lost, along with a distinctively more apocalyptic atmosphere, a heavy emphasis on a supposed anti-technological bias among the survivors, and a concentration on the results of nuclear power in general, and radiation in particular. The mood was darker in that the imagined catastrophes were now primarily man-made. Man became pictured as a kind of lemming, bent on racial suicide, through nuclear, biological and chemical warfare in stories of the 1940s and '50s, and through POLLUTION, OVERPOPULATION and destruction of a balanced ECOLOGY in many stories of the 1960s and '70s.

Among the darker scenarios set after nuclear war are Mordecai ROSHWALD's *Level 7* (**1959**), Wilson TUCKER's *The Long Loud Silence* (**1952**), Alfred COPPEL's *Dark December* (**1960**), Judith MERRIL's *Shadow on the Hearth* (**1950**), Pat FRANK's *Alas, Babylon* (**1959**), which is more optimistic than the others about the possibility of re-ordering society, Ward MOORE's story "Lot" (1953) and its sardonic sequel "Lot's Daughter" (1954), which were the uncredited bases for the film PANIC IN THE YEAR ZERO (1962), and Fritz LEIBER's extremely savage "Night of the Long Knives" (1960; vt "The Wolf Pair") which can be found in *The Night of the Wolf* (coll. **1966**).

Novels which place a greater emphasis on the kinds of society developed after the holocaust are *Dark Universe* (**1961**) by Daniel F. GALOUYE, set underground; Edgar PANGBORN's *Davy* (**1964**), *The Judgment of Eve* (**1966**) and *The Company of Glory* (**1975**); Brian W. ALDISS's *Non-Stop* (**1958**; vt *Starship* USA) and *Greybeard* (**1964**), the latter dealing with life after sterility has been induced in Earth's population; Philip K. DICK's *Do Androids Dream of Electric Sheep?* (**1968**), where pollution has destroyed the animal kingdom; and John BOWEN's *After the Rain* (**1958**), dealing with the psychology of the survivors of a great flood. Paramount among such books is Walter M. MILLER's *A Canticle for Leibowitz* (fix-up **1960**), an ironic, black comedy about the ways in which a post-holocaust civilization's history recapitulates the errors of its predecessor. The story is set largely in an abbey, where some half-understood technological knowledge has been kept alive by the Church. The book is vivid, morose and ebulliently inventive; it has been very influential.

Miller's vision of technology as being at once saviour and destroyer (though morally neutral in itself) is echoed in several books, including some already cited, in which an anti-technological majority, usually medieval in social structure, and rigidly conservative in outlook, is unable to suppress the scientific curiosity of young malcontents; two good examples are Leigh BRACKETT's *The Long Tomorrow* (**1955**) and John WYNDHAM's *The Chrysalids* (**1955**; vt *Re-Birth* USA). At a more popular, adventure-story level, several writers have picked up the idea which is found in the Brackett and Wyndham novels of a secret enclave of scientifically advanced technocrats in an otherwise primitive world. Such is the situation in the trilogy by Piers ANTHONY which began with *Sos the Rope* (**1968**), with sequels in 1973 and 1975, combined in one book as *Battle Circle* (**1977**). In stories of this type technology is generally feared, since it was through technology that mankind almost destroyed itself; a furtive technology is pitted against MAGIC in a FAR-FUTURE, post-holocaust venue in Fred SABERHAGEN's trilogy consisting of *The Broken Lands* (**1968**), *The Black Mountains* (**1971**) and *Changeling Earth* (**1973**), but here, despite a tenuous rationale, the tone of the story is more that of SWORD AND SORCERY than of sf proper. Indeed, many sword-and-sorcery stories are set in a post-holocaust period when mankind has taken the route of magic rather than science; the rather silly idea that lies behind this is presumably that if we give up rational analysis we may be able to work miracles instead.

With the increased publicity given to the so-called counter-culture in the late 1960s (to some extent reflected in sf by the NEW WAVE), post-holocaust stories of rather a different kind became popular. Hell's-Angels-style motorcycle gangs roam a ruined world in two colourful romances, Roger ZELAZNY's *Damnation Alley* (**1969**), filmed with many changes as DAMNATION ALLEY (1977), and Steve WILSON's *The Lost Traveller* (**1976**); the same idea is used with more subtlety in a more complicated and grimmer work, Brian W. Aldiss's *Barefoot in the Head* (fix-up **1969**), as motorcyclists roll through the debris of a Europe half-destroyed by the use of psychedelic drugs as weapons. J.G. BALLARD's *oeuvre* is made up largely of post-holocaust stories also; he has evoked catastrophes of all sorts, man-made and natural, sudden and protracted, and sometimes seems almost to embrace the chaos or apathy that follows; he seems to see mankind acting in psychic collaboration with the forces that threaten his security. Scarred motorways continue to link up the decaying communities of M. John HARRISON's forceful first novel, *The Committed Men* (**1971**), which has something of a Ballardian bleakness, but a rather tougher survivor mentality in the protagonists.

Other notable post-holocaust stories of recent years are *Heroes and Villains* (**1969**) by Angela CARTER, "The Lost Continent" (1970) by Norman SPINRAD, *The Cornelius Chronicles* (coll. **1977** consisting of four linked novels published 1968–77) by Michael MOORCOCK, in which the adroit evocation of various alternate histories allows a great many variations on the holocaust theme to be played, *The End of the Dream* (**1972**) by Philip Wylie, returning to a theme he first worked with 40 years earlier, *Earthwreck!* (**1974**) by Thomas SCORTIA, "The Snows are Melted, the Snows are Gone" by James TIPTREE Jr and "A Boy and his Dog" (1969) by Harlan ELLISON. This last was also filmed (*see* A BOY AND HIS DOG). Indeed, the 1970s saw many variations on the post-holocaust theme in the CINEMA, including ZARDOZ (1973), where once again a technological enclave faces barbarians (this time sympathy is with the latter), NO BLADE OF GRASS (1970) based on the John Christopher novel cited above, THE ULTIMATE WARRIOR (1975), GAS-S-S (1970), GLEN AND RANDA (1970) and a number of others. British TV took up the idea with SURVIVORS (1975–7), which also resulted in a book, *The Survivors* (**1976**) by Terry NATION.

The results of holocaust, it seems, continue to grip our imagination; in a world of bureaucracies and restrictions, where the average man feels that there is little room for individual assertion, the idea of destroying and then building again offers an exciting psychic freedom. The rusting symbols of a technological past protruding into a more primitive, natural, future landscape remain among the most potent of sf's icons. [PN]

HOLT, CONRAD G. This has been thought to be a Pearson house name, but in fact it is a simple pseudonym of John Russell FEARN, and was used on one book only. [PN]

HOLZHAUSEN, CARL JOHAN (1900–). Swedish writer, as yet untranslated, whose works were praised during his second period of activity beginning in the 1960s, but whose first sf was *Den flygande spårvagnen* ["The Flying Tram"] (**1936**). Then, much later, came *Achilles häl* ["Achilles' Heel"] (**1964**), and the collections *Språnget* ["The Leap"] (coll. **1970**) and *De kom från Dodona* ["They Came from Dodona"] (coll. **1972**). CJH could be described as a political moralist. [PN]

HOMEOSTATIC SYSTEMS An item of sf TERMINOLOGY borrowed from CYBERNETICS, where it is most commonly used today. A homeostatic system is a device which automatically maintains itself in a state of equilibrium, with input and output exactly balanced, using negative feedback devices to do so. The term originally came from physiology, for the human body itself has many homeostatic systems — perhaps more simply thought of, to use less scientific terminology, as self-regulating systems. For example, through a variety of feedback devices ultimately controlled by the brain, the body regulates its temperature, constantly adjusting it against changes of outside temperature, and internal changes such as the heat produced by eating food. A homeostatic system, or series of them, is a necessary if primitive first step in the production of artificial intelligence and finally self-consciousness. Thus the sf writers who tend to use the term often, such as Philip K. DICK, are very often those who are interested in the various transitional stages between machine and man. [PN]

HOMER (*c*. 750 BC). The most famous of early Greek poets, generally supposed to be the author of the *Iliad* and the *Odyssey*. They were probably not written down until the sixth century BC, and come to us in considerably later versions. The *Odyssey* is important as an item of PROTO SF in being the paradigm of the FANTASTIC VOYAGE. While it would be absurd to claim the *Odyssey* as sf *per se*, it is clearly ancestral to sf, especially in its openness to wonder, allied to a hard-headed scepticism; it has a kind of alert, questing quality, always keen to see what is just over the horizon. In this respect, its feeling is surprisingly close to that of modern sf. In Homer's day the Mediterranean was a *tabula rasa*, just as outer space is today; to say that the *Odyssey* is a proto SPACE OPERA from the beginning of the first millennium BC may be to confuse the sublime with the ridiculous — it is certainly more than that — but its aspiring, wandering spirit is a testimony to the longevity of those human feelings which today are often fed into the reading and writing of sf. [PN]
See also: MYTHOLOGY.

HOMUNCULUS (vt HOMUNCULUS DER FÜHRER) Serial film (1916). Bioscop. Directed by Otto Rippert, starring Olaf Fønss, Friedrich Kühne, Mechtild Their and Maria Carmi. Script by Otto Rippert and Robert Neuss, based on the novel by Robert Reinert. 24 reels. B/w.

This six-part German serial (silent) tells of an artificial man created by a scientist who wants to make a creature of pure reason. But the result, Homunculus, resents the fact that he is not a real human being and after being driven from country to country he becomes the dictator of a large, unnamed nation and plans to conquer the world, but is finally destroyed by a convenient bolt of lightning. *H* contains seminal themes foreshadowing many sf/horror films that were to follow over the years: the archetypal mad scientist, the inherent evil of technology and scientific progress, superhuman androids, conquest of the world and a fiery, apocalyptic climax. [JB]

HORN, PETER House name used in Ziff-Davis magazines by Henry KUTTNER once and David Vern (*see* David V. REED) twice, in 1940.

HORNE, R. HENGIST *See* Richard Henry HORNE.

HORNE, RICHARD HENRY (1803–84). British writer,. who sometimes signed himself R. Hengist Horne. Known primarily for his work outside the sf field, including the epic poem *Orion* (**1848**) and the essay collection *A New Spirit of the Age* (coll. **1844**), which was written with the assistance of Elizabeth Barrett, he is credited by William WILSON as the author of the exemplary work of "Science-Fiction" (the earliest use of the term): *The Poor Artist; or Seven Eye-sights and One Object* (**1871**), which tells how an artist interprets visions described to him by small creatures. [BS]
See also: ARTS; PERCEPTION.

HORNIG, CHARLES D. (1916–). American editor. CDH was a young sf fan who, in 1933, began a FANZINE called *The Fantasy Fan* and happened to send a copy of it to Hugo GERNSBACK. By coincidence, Gernsback was at that time looking for a new managing editor for WONDER STORIES, and was so impressed by CDH's editorial that he decided to offer him the post. At 17, CDH became the youngest-ever sf magazine editor, attending evening classes until he finished high school. He edited *Wonder Stories* from November 1933 until April 1936, when the magazine was sold to another publisher and became THRILLING WONDER STORIES. CDH did not give up his fan activities, continuing *The Fantasy Fan* on a monthly basis until early 1935. At Gernsback's instigation he began the SCIENCE FICTION LEAGUE, a club centered around *Wonder Stories*. CDH initiated a "new story" policy in an attempt to emulate the "thought variant" stories published by F. Orlin TREMAINE in *ASF*;

but this did not achieve many notable results, although he did publish Stanley G. WEINBAUM's first story, "A Martian Odyssey" (1934), to great acclaim. He published one story of his own under the pseudonym Derwin Lesser, which he used again in articles he contributed to the magazine SCIENCE FICTION, which he edited from its inception, Mar. 1939. He also edited two companion magazines: FUTURE FICTION and SCIENCE FICTION QUARTERLY. None of these magazines achieved any distinction and they were taken over (and the first two titles amalgamated) by Robert A.W. LOWNDES in 1941. A convinced pacifist, CDH was a conscientious objector to the Second World War, and in 1942 was assigned to a public service forestry camp. He left it in 1943 and was imprisoned later the same year as an absolute objector to all forms of wartime service. [MJE]

HORROR EXPRESS (vt **PANIC ON THE TRANSIBERIAN**) Film (1972). Granada/Benmar. Directed by Eugenio Martin, starring Peter Cushing, Christopher Lee and Telly Savalas. Screenplay by Arnaud d'Usseau. 90 mins. Colour.

A prehistoric ape-man comes to life on the Trans-Siberian Express and turns out to be an alien who crash-landed on Earth aeons ago. He has the power to transfer his personality from one body to another and to absorb other people's personalities. The film, which is slick and amusing, moves so fast that there is little time to dwell on its absurdities. It originated only because the producer bought two model trains used in the epic *Nicholas and Alexandra* and decided to have a script written round them. [JB]

HOSHI, SHIN'ICHI *See* JAPAN.

Photo Lawrence Jordan.

HOSKINS, ROBERT (1933–). American writer and editor, who has worked with literary agents and

publishers 1967–72, and been a freelance since that time. His first published story was "Feet of Clay" for *If* in 1958, as by Phillip Hoskins. His first published novel, *The Shattered People* (1975), is a far-future romance pitting an apparent primitive against a modern city. Later novels are *Master of the Stars* (1976), *To Control The Stars* (1977) which is the first of a projected trilogy and based loosely on "The Problem Makers" in *Gal.* 1963, and *Tomorrow's Son* (1977). RH's books make no claims beyond being entertaining action adventures. He has also been busy as an anthologist, his most important work in this line being the INFINITY series of original anthologies: *Infinity 1* (anth. **1970**); *Infinity 2* (anth. **1971**); *Infinity 3* (anth. **1972**); *Infinity 4* (anth. **1972**); *Infinity 5* (anth. **1973**). Other anthologies are *First Step Forward* (anth. **1969**); *The Stars Around Us* (anth. **1970**); *Swords Against Tomorrow* (anth. **1970**); *The Far-Out People* (anth. **1971**); *Tomorrow One* (anth. **1971**); *Wondermakers* (anth. **1972**); *Strange Tomorrows* (anth. **1972**); *The Edge of Never* (anth. **1973**), which is fantasy; *Wondermakers 2* (anth. **1974**); *The Liberated Future* (anth. **1974**); *The Future Now* (anth. **1977**). RH has also written Gothic novels as Grace Corren and as Susan Jennifer. One of these, *Evil in the Family* (1972) as by Grace Corren, is a time-travel fantasy. RH now concentrates on novels and has written no short stories since 1975. [PN]

HOUGH, S.B. *See* Rex GORDON.

HOUGHTON, CLAUDE Pseudonym of Claude Houghton Oldfield (1889–1961). British writer, known primarily for his work outside the sf field. Most of his works are "psychological thrillers" in which the events are mundane but the commentary upon them rather bizarre. He declared that all his work was based on the thesis that modern civilization must collapse "because it no longer believes it has a destiny" — a conviction echoed by such titles as *Chaos is Come Again* (1932) and *All Change, Humanity!* (1942). His most important work, *This Was Ivor Trent* (1935) deals with the effect upon a writer of a vision in which he sees a man of the future. His last book was *More Lives Than One* (1957). [BS]
Other works: *Neighbours* (1927); *Julian Grant Loses His Way* (1933); *Three Fantastic Tales* (coll. **1934**); *The Beast* (1936); *Six Lives and a Book* (1943).
See also: EVOLUTION; SUPERMAN.

HOUSE NAMES *See* PSEUDONYMS.

HOUSMAN, LAURENCE (1865–1959). English writer, brother of the poet A.E. Housman, best known for his plays and for several volumes of fantasy stories, including *Gods and their Makers* (coll. **1897**), *What Next?*

Provocative Tales of Faith and Morals (coll. **1938**) and *Strange Ends and Discoveries* (coll. **1948**). Some of his work for children, such as *A Farm in Fairyland* (1894), and some of his plays, such as *Possession* (1921), are also of fantasy interest, as is his novel *Trimblerigg* (1924). Closer to an sf interest are his two Ruritanian SATIRES, *John of Jingalo: The Story of a Monarch in Difficulties* (1912; vt *King John of Jingalo* USA) and its sequel *The Royal Runaway; and, Jingalo in Revolution* (1914); in both novels there is a running commentary on UTOPIAN social solutions, particularly with regard to women's rights. [JC]
Other works: *The Field of Clover* (coll. **1898**); *The Blue Moon* (**1904**); *All-Fellows and the Cloak of Friendship* (coll. **1923**); *A Doorway in Fairyland* (**1923**); *Ironical Tales* (coll. **1926**).

HOWARD, (JOHN) HAYDEN (? –). American writer, who began publishing sf with "It" for *Planet Stories* in 1952, and whose sf novel, *The Eskimo Invasion* (1965–7 *Gal.*; fix-up **1967**), rather unusually set in Canada, comprises a speculative view of OVERPOPULATION problems through a story about a group of Eskimos transformed into an apparently benign, fast-breeding new species. [JC]

HOWARD, IVAN (? –). American anthologist who produced six anthologies in 1963 for Belmont books, and nothing since: *Escape to Earth*, *Novelets of Science Fiction*, *Rare Science Fiction*, *6 and the Silent Scream*, *Things* and *Way Out*. [PN]

HOWARD, ROBERT E. (1906–36). American writer. REH was born in Peaster, Texas, and lived nearly all his life in that state, mostly in the town of Cross Plains. His first professionally published story was "Spear and Fang" (1925) in WEIRD TALES — the magazine which became his most regular market. REH was a prolific writer of all kinds of PULP fiction. His best stories show a good sense of narrative pace and are written in a direct, uncluttered style: the characteristic virtues of a competent pulp writer. He is best known as the author of the Conan series: SWORD-AND-SORCERY adventures which are the cornerstone of the modern development of this sub-genre. 17 stories in the series appeared in *Weird Tales*, 1932–6, and another four were published posthumously in other magazines. The series has been added to extensively by L. Sprague DE CAMP, Lin CARTER and Bjorn Nyberg — by completing fragments of stories, by rewriting straightforward REH adventure stories into the canon, and by composing pastiches. The merits of these additions to the saga are the subject of some controversy among REH's devotees, but most are agreed in finding them inferior to the originals.
There are four different book editions

of the Conan stories. The first, GNOME PRESS, series consists, in order of internal chronology, of *The Coming of Conan* (coll. **1953**), *Conan the Barbarian* (coll. **1955**), *The Sword of Conan* (coll. **1952**), *King Conan* (coll. **1953**) and *Conan the Conqueror* (1935 *Weird Tales* as "The Hour of the Dragon"; **1950**; vt *The Hour of the Dragon*). To these were added a pastiche sequel by De Camp and Nyberg — *The Return of Conan* (**1957**; vt *Conan the Avenger* with minor additional material) — and a collection of non-Conan stories rewritten by De Camp to include him, *Tales of Conan* (coll. **1955**). The series was reorganized into twelve volumes in the 1960s and '70s, comprising all the material from the above books, plus many more Conan stories by other hands (including three volumes written entirely by De Camp and Carter). These are: *Conan* (coll. **1968**), *Conan of Cimmeria* (coll. **1969**), *Conan the Freebooter* (coll. **1968**), *Conan the Wanderer* (coll. **1968**), *Conan the Adventurer* (coll. **1966**), *Conan the Buccaneer* (**1971**, by De Camp and Carter), *Conan the Warrior* (coll. **1967**), *Conan the Usurper* (coll. **1967**), *Conan the Conqueror*, *Conan the Avenger*, *Conan of Aquilonia* (coll. **1977**, by De Camp and Carter) and *Conan of the Isles* (**1968**, by De Camp and Carter). A third printing of the series, published by Donald M. GRANT, in a luxury illustrated edition containing only Howard's own stories, consists of *The People of the Black Circle* (**1974**), *A Witch Shall Be Born* (**1975**), *Tower of the Elephant* (coll. **1975**), *Red Nails* (**1975**), *Rogues in the House* (coll. **1976**) and *The Devil in Iron* (**1976**). The fourth series, in paperback, authorized by the REH estate, like Donald M. Grant's, follows the original texts from *Weird Tales*. They are edited by Karl Edward WAGNER. The first such title is *The Hour of the Dragon* (**1977**), which reverts to the original title and text of the story first published in book form as *Conan the Conqueror*, and the second is *The People of the Black Circle*.

The popularity of the Conan series has led to two different MARVEL COMICS based on the character: *Conan the Barbarian* and *The Savage Sword of Conan*. There has also, inevitably, been much talk of a film, with a former Mr Universe (equally inevitably) being cast in the role of REH's muscular if monosyllabic hero. REH's other work has also been reprinted intensively, with many non-fantasy pulp stories being packaged misleadingly. One interesting sidelight of this is that it has brought back into print the original versions of stories later rewritten in Conan form by De Camp: it is instructive to compare, for example, *Three-Bladed Doom* (**1977**) with "The Flame Knife" (*Conan the Wanderer*) or "The Curse of the Crimson God" (in *Swords of Shahrazar*, coll. **1976**) with "The Blood-Stained God" (*Tales of Conan*; *Conan of Cimmeria*). The majority of these stories,

which involve anything from piracy to cowboys, are outside the scope of this Encyclopedia, as are the numerous pamphlets issued by REH enthusiasts, which draw on a seemingly inexhaustible supply of unpublished REH manuscripts. Three other sword-and-sorcery characters around whom he wrote series for *Weird Tales* (all predating Conan) are the eponymous *King Kull* (coll. **1967**, edited and with additional material by Lin Carter) and *Bran Mak Morn* (coll. **1969**; vt *Worms of the Earth*), and Solomon Kane, whose adventures are collected in *Red Shadows* (coll. **1968**; split into three volumes for paperback publication: *The Moon of Skulls*, coll. **1969**, *The Hand of Kane*, coll. **1970** and *Solomon Kane*, coll. **1971**). His stories of the character Cormac Mac Art were collected in *Tigers of the Sea* (coll. **1976**). Both Bran Mak Morn and Cormac Mac Art have inspired pastiches, the former in *Legions from the Shadows* (**1976**) and *Queen of the Night*

Robert E. HOWARD. Photo © Glenn Lord.

(**1977**), by Karl Edward Wagner, the latter in *Sword of the Gael* (**1975**), *The Undying Wizard* (**1976**) and *Sign of the Moonbow* (**1977**) by Andrew J. OFFUTT. Several other REH characters, including King Kull and Solomon Kane, have had Marvel Comics devoted to them.

An emotionally unstable character, REH committed suicide on learning of his mother's imminent death. Most of his voluminous output is crude by any literary standard, although its vigour makes it more readable today than most pulp sf of the same period. It should be remembered, though, that it was the work of a young man; REH's letters reveal a more intelligent and perceptive

man than his fiction might suggest and it may be that, had he lived, he would have become a more considerable writer. *The Miscast Barbarian* (**1975**) is a short biography by De Camp; it is also incorporated into his *Literary Swordsmen and Sorcerers* (coll. **1976**). *The Last Celt* (**1976**) by Glenn Lord is an exhaustive bio-bibliography, written by the agent of REH's estate. AMRA is a FANZINE largely devoted to REH's work. *An Annotated Guide to Robert E. Howard's Sword and Sorcery* (**1976**) by Robert WEINBERG is a useful guide. *The Ultimate Guide to Howardia 1925–1975* (**1976**) ed. Wayne Warfield indexes all REH stories but not his books. *A Gazetteer of The Hyborian World of Conan* (**1977**) compiled by Lee N. Falconer attempts to derive a consistent geography from REH's sometimes slapdash references. [MJE]

Other works: *Skull-Face and Others* (coll. **1946**; UK paperback divided into three vols, the second and third entitled *Valley of the Worm* and *The Shadow Kingdom*); *Always Come Evening* (poems **1957**); *The Dark Man and Others* (coll. **1963**); *Almuric* (1939 *Weird Tales*; **1964**); *Wolfshead* (coll. **1968**); *Pigeons From Hell* (coll. **1976**); *The Book of Robert E. Howard* (coll. **1976**); *The Second Book of Robert E. Howard* (coll. **1976**); *The Robert E. Howard Omnibus* (coll. **1977**).

See also: ATLANTIS; FANTASY; GODS AND DEMONS; HEROIC FANTASY; MAGIC; MYTHOLOGY; PUBLISHING; SEX; SUPERMAN.

HOWARD, WARREN F. *See* Frederik POHL.

HOWELL, SCOTT *See* Paul CONRAD.

HOWELLS, WILLIAM DEAN (1837–1920). American writer, best known for his many realist novels from 1870 to his death. His UTOPIAN sequence, *A Traveler from Altruria* (**1894**) and *Through the Eye of the Needle* (**1907**), is a deceptively mild-mannered assault on the pretensions of late-19th-century American democracy and culture, seen from the perspective of a dreamlike visiting Altrurian, who comes from a land where the principles of Christianity and of the American Constitution are taken literally. In the second volume, he takes an American bride back to Altruria, whence they send letters descriptive of that land, whose nature is somewhat influenced by the work of Edward BELLAMY, but more so by that of William MORRIS. Capitalism has been replaced by a genuine altruistic "neighbourliness". Though gently put, the two books' attacks on hypocrisy and the more ruthless forms of capitalism are both unmistakable and highly telling. Much the same narrative technique reappears movingly in *The Seen and Unseen at Stratford-on-Avon* (**1914**), whose revived but ghostly Shakespeare sweetly defends his right to be considered the author of his

own plays to a 20th-century narrator; the book is an answer to Mark TWAIN's *Is Shakespeare Dead*? (**1909**), which argues Sir Francis BACON's authorship after the fashion of the time. *Questionable Shapes* (coll. **1903**) and *Between the Dark and the Daylight* (coll. **1907**), neither sf, are collections of club stories in which the psychologist Wanhope scientifically debunks the ghost stories of his fellow members. [JC]
Other works: *The Undiscovered Country* (**1880**); *The Leatherwood God* (**1916**).

HOYLE, FRED (1915–). British astronomer and writer, famed in the former capacity for his long-held advocacy of the steady state theory of the creation of the universe, a concept which the Big Bang theory has acrimoniously replaced in recent years; his first book, *The Nature of the Universe* (**1950**), eloquently popularizes his cosmogony in non-fiction terms. It was followed by other important popularizations in the same vein: *Frontiers of Astronomy* (**1955**) and several since. FH's first novel, *The Black Cloud* (**1957**), is strict genre sf, postulating a sentient cloud of gas from space blotting off the Sun's rays from Earth, and subsequent attempts at COMMUNICATION with it. His second, *Ossian's Ride* (**1959**), is a chase novel with an sf climax; the fine earlier part of the novel (set in Ireland) is reminiscent of John Buchan or Geoffrey HOUSEHOLD. Both these novels are interesting for the aggressively POLITICAL stance taken by FH, who believes that science-educated people are more fit to govern than arts-educated people — not just that numeracy is as important as literacy, but that, because a numerate training is less tied up with emotional questions than a literate training, it would give a necessary coolness of judgement to the ruling classes. With John ELLIOT, FH next adapted their two television serials A FOR ANDROMEDA and ANDROMEDA BREAKTHROUGH into two novels, dated **1962** and **1964** respectively. Since this time, most of FH's work has been written in collaborations with his son, Geoffrey HOYLE, starting with *Fifth Planet* (**1963**), set about 100 years into the future (unusually far for him): a grassy, wandering planet, Achilles, poses some problems for both Russians and Westerners. FH's only solo fiction from this period is *October the First is Too Late* (**1966**), which combines social speculation with time travel (*see* PARALLEL WORLDS *for details*), and *Element 79* (coll. **1967**), his only gathering of stories.

With his son, FH has published several further novels, *Rockets in Ursa Major* (as play by FH 1962; novelized with GH **1969**), *Seven Steps to the Sun* (**1970**), *The Molecule Men* (coll. **1971** with title story plus "The Monster from Loch Ness"), *The Inferno* (**1973**), *Into Deepest Space* (**1974**), and *The Incandescent Ones* (**1977**). This last novel, with its slightly

archaic politics and stiff characters, confirms the moderate lessening of quality of the Hoyles' later books in its story of a young man who finds out that he is a kind of ANDROID. Perhaps unsurprisingly he accepts the news impassively, and journeys to Jupiter to join the eponymous Beings there. Throughout his career as a writer, however, FH has brought a fine scientific mind to the background of his tales, strengthening them very considerably, and often giving his readers an accurate sense of what it means to think like a scientist. [JC/PN]
See also: ALIENS; ANTI-INTELLECTUALISM; ARTS; ASTRONOMY; CONCEPTUAL BREAKTHROUGH; COSMOLOGY; DISASTER; DISCOVERY AND INVENTION; INTELLIGENCE; MATHEMATICS; PARALLEL WORLDS; PHYSICS; SCIENTISTS; TIME TRAVEL.

HOYLE, GEOFFREY (1941–). English writer, author of several sf novels with his father, Fred HOYLE (*who see for further details*). They are *Fifth Planet* (**1963**), *Rockets in Ursa Major* (novelization of his father's play of 1962; **1969**), *Seven Steps to the Sun* (**1970**), *The Molecule Men* (coll. **1971** with title story plus "The Monster from Loch Ness"), *The Inferno* (**1973**), *Into Deepest Space* (**1974**) and *The Incandescent Ones* (**1977**). [JC]
See also: COSMOLOGY; DISASTER.

HOYNE, THOMAS TEMPLE (1875–1946). American writer, a popularizer of ECONOMIC topics, and author of *Intrigue on the Upper Level: a Story of Crime, Love, Adventure and Revolt in 2050 A.D.* (**1934**), in which a primitive, hierarchical, capitalist society is riven by discontent among the lower orders. [JC]

HUBBARD, L(AFAYETTE) RON(ALD) (1911–). American writer in many genres, including sf and fantasy, and subsequent quasi-religious leader and reputed millionaire after his invention of the controversial DIANETICS and later SCIENTOLOGY. He began publishing sf with "The Dangerous Dimension" for *ASF* in 1938, and remained active for more than a decade under his own name, and under the pseudonyms Kurt von Rachen, Rene Lafayette and Frederick Engelhardt, as well as some unrevealed names. Though there is no hard and fast line drawn, he seems to have used his own name mainly for his fantasy output in *Unknown* and elsewhere, and Von Rachen and Lafayette for his sf, mostly in *ASF*. His best-known sf novel, *Final Blackout* (**1940** *ASF*; **1948**), grimly describes a world devastated by many wars in which a young army officer, who becomes dictator of England, organizes that country and fends off decadent America. *Slaves of Sleep* (1939 *Unknown*; **1948**), with its sequel "The Masters of Sleep" (1950), is his best-known fantasy; it is set

in an Arabian Nights world.

LRH's strongest fantasy is the darkly PARANOID *Fear* (1940 *Unknown*; **1957**). It has also been published as one of the two novellas in *Fear & Typewriter in the Sky* (coll. **1951**; vt *Typewriter in the Sky & Fear*) and one of the two novellas in *Fear and the Ultimate Adventure* (coll. **1970**). "Typewriter in the Sky" was originally published in *Unknown*, 1940, and "The Ultimate Adventure" in *Unknown*, 1939. *Return to Tomorrow* (1950 *ASF* as "To the Stars"; **1954**) is a remarkably ruthless SPACE OPERA (*see* SOCIAL DARWINISM). LRH's "Ole Doc Methuselah" stories, as by Rene Lafayette, have been assembled as *Ole Doc Methuselah* (1947–50 *ASF*; coll. **1970**). He wrote other series, too, notably the "Conquest of Space" series as Rene Lafayette in *Startling Stories*, all but the last story in 1949: "Forbidden Voyage"; "The Magnificent Failure"; "The Incredible Destination"; "The Unwilling Hero"; "Beyond the Black Nebula"; "The Emperor of the Universe"; and "The Last Admiral" (1950). As Kurt von Rachen he wrote the "Kilkenny Cats" series, all in *ASF*: "The Idealists" (1940); "The Kilkenny Cats" (1940); "The Traitor" (1941); "The Mutineers" (1941); "The Rebels" (1942). LRH was a hasty but frequently very intense writer of melodramas, space operas and other adventures whose implications were sometimes controversial. Many of his works, like those of his one-time colleague A.E. VAN VOGT, feature highly developed powers of the mind resulting in quasi-SUPERMEN. [JC/PN]
Other works: *Death's Deputy* (1940 *Unknown*; **1948**) and *The Kingslayer* (coll. **1949**; vt *Seven Steps to the Arbiter*) are also bound together as *From Death to the Stars* (coll. **1953**); *Triton and Battle of Wizards* ("Triton" 1940 *Unknown*; "Battle of Wizards" 1949 *Fantasy Book*; coll. **1949**). The latter collection was also bound with Ed Earl REPP's *The Radium Pool* (coll. **1949**) as *Science Fantasy Quintet* (**1953**). Non-fiction: *Dianetics* (**1950**); and others of this type.
See also: COSMOLOGY; FANTASTIC VOYAGES; FASTER THAN LIGHT; GENERAL SEMANTICS; GOLDEN AGE OF SF; HEROES; MESSIAHS; POLITICS; PSI POWERS; PSYCHOLOGY; SPACESHIPS; TIME TRAVEL; WAR.

HUDSON, JAN *See* George H. SMITH.

HUDSON, WILLIAM HENRY (1841–1922). British naturalist and writer born in the Argentine. He wrote a rather mystical UTOPIAN novel, *A Crystal Age* (**1887**, first edition anonymous; signed with new preface 1906), which shows small, self-sufficient, matriarchally organized households living in harmony with nature. The same theme of quasi-supernatural harmony with the wild forest was developed in the powerful novel *Green Mansions* (**1904**) in the character of the girl Rima, who is ultimately destroyed by the forest Indians, whom Hudson sees as being no closer to nature than the civilized protagonist. These stories are evolutionary fantasies (see EVOLUTION) which demand far more of human adaptation than conventional fantasies of retreat into the Utopian simplicities supposed to belong to earlier eras. "Master Riquelem" (in *El Ombu*, coll. **1902**) is a dark fantasy in which desperate sorrow transforms a woman into a bird. [BS]

See also: ECOLOGY; FAR FUTURE; LIFE ON OTHER WORLDS; PASTORAL; TIME TRAVEL.

HUEFFER, FORD MADOX (1873–1939). English writer and editor, of German descent. He changed his name to Ford Madox Ford during the First World War. He was a versatile man of letters, perhaps best known now as founder of the *English Review* and *Transatlantic Review*, and author of *The Good Soldier* (**1915**). With Joseph CONRAD (*who see for details*) he collaborated on the sociological sf novel *The Inheritors: An Extravagant Story* (**1901**). [JC]

HUGHES, DENIS (? –). British writer (or possibly a Curtis Warren house name) whose PULP-style paperback sf adventures are *The Earth Invasion Battalion*, *Formula 695*, *Moon War*, *Murder by Telecopter* and *War Lords of Space*, the latter as by Dennis Hughes. All are undated, but were probably published 1950–53. [PN]

HUGHES, RILEY (? –) American writer, whose sf novel, *The Hills Were Liars* (**1963**), describes an attempt to maintain a Church after civilization collapses. [JC]

HUGHES, TED (1930–). English poet, best known for volumes of dark, violent verse, like *Crow* (coll. **1970**). Of sf interest is his children's story, *The Iron Man: A Story in Five Nights* (**1968**), in which a frightening but friendly iron man defends the world against a dragon from space, ultimately persuading it to sing the music of the spheres, a sound which soothes humanity's terrible lust for war and causes peace. [JC]

HUGHES, ZACK Form of his name used by American writer Hugh Zachary (? –) for his sf writing; he uses his full name for other work. His novels in the sf field, expertly devised and readable though somewhat routine, are *The Book of Rack the Healer* (**1973**); *The Legend of Miaree* (**1974**); *Tide* (**1974**); a parody of the VON DÄNIKEN books, *Seed of the Gods* (**1974**); *The Stork Factor* (**1975**); *For Texas and Zed* (**1976**); *Tiger in the Stars* (**1976**); *The St. Francis Effect* (**1976**). The books, though light, have unexpected moments of grimness. [JC]

See also: FLYING SAUCERS.

HUGIN *See* SCANDINAVIA.

HUGO Almost invariably used informal term for the Science Fiction Achievement Award. The name "Hugo" is in honour of Hugo GERNSBACK, and has been an official variant of the formal title since 1958. Hugos have been awarded at World SF CONVENTIONS, or worldcons, from 1953 (the idea was dropped for a year in 1954) and annually from 1955. They have always been the amateur or fan awards as opposed to, say, the NEBULA or JUPITER awards, which are voted on by different categories of professional reader. The original idea, from fan Hal Lynch, was based on the National Film Academy Awards (Oscars). The award takes the form of a rocketship mounted upright on fins, the first model designed and produced by Jack McKnight; from 1955 a similar design by Ben Jason has normally been used.

Awards are made in several classes, which have varied in definition and number from year to year. They are given primarily for fiction, but have also included classes for editing, artwork, film and TV, and fan writing and illustration. Occasional unclassified special awards have been made. The rules governing awards are made, and often remade, at worldcon business meetings. The power of such committees to alter the rules annually has recently been widely challenged, leading as it does to many inconsistencies.

Winners in each class are chosen by ballot; since 1960 the voters have been limited annually to members of the forthcoming worldcon (anyone can buy membership without actually attending the convention). The occasional special awards, however, are made by worldcon committees. Voting on Hugos is always carried out postally before the convention begins; counting is done using the so-called Australian ballot, the least successful contender's votes being redistributed, using second or subsequent preferences, after each vote. There was no nominating procedure up to 1958. Since 1959 there have been ballots for nominations, distributed to fans generally until 1963, when they were limited to the membership of the current and previous year's worldcon, except in 1965 and 1967.

World conventions are held in September, and Hugos are given for publication or activity in the previous calendar year. Hence, for example, a novel which wins a 1968 Hugo will have been published in 1967, though if it also won a Nebula, the latter would be known confusingly as the 1967 Nebula. "No award" votes have, in some years, been permitted, and have resulted occasionally in void classes. Since 1963, story and TV series have been excluded from the short fiction and drama classes; thus in 1968 five individual STAR TREK episodes were nominated for the drama award; back in

1962 Brian W. ALDISS was able to win the short fiction award with a series, the "Hothouse" stories.

The definitions of the various categories of short fiction have varied. In a recent ruling a novella was defined as being of 17,500 to 40,000 words, a novelette as 7,500 to 17,500 words and a short story anything shorter. In the years 1955–9 there were only two classes of short fiction, novelette and short story. These were amalgamated 1960–66 as "short fiction"; few short stories were nominated during this period. The new class, novella, was included from 1968. In 1970–72 the only two classes were short story and novella. Since 1973 there have been three classes of short fiction.

Since 1971, the drama category has included recordings. In 1973 the professional magazine class changed to a professional editor class, in an acknowledgement of the increasing importance of original ANTHOLOGIES.

The Hugos have for many years been subject to criticism on the grounds that awards made by a small, self-selected group of hardcore sf fans do not necessarily reflect either literary merit or the preferences of the sf reading public generally. Hardcore FANDOM probably makes up less than 1% of the general sf readership. Certainly Hugos have tended to be given to traditional, HARD SF, and have seldom been awarded to experimental work, but they have been, on the whole, surprisingly eclectic. While many awards have gone to such good but conservative writers as Poul ANDERSON, Robert A. HEINLEIN, Clifford D. SIMAK and Larry NIVEN, they have also been given to such doyens of the NEW WAVE as Harlan ELLISON, Roger ZELAZNY and James TIPTREE Jr, and to a number of works of literary excellence which quite fail to conform to the standard patterns of genre expectation, such as Walter M. MILLER Jr's *A Canticle for Leibowitz* (**1959**) and Ursula K. LE GUIN's *The Dispossessed* (**1974**). Fritz LEIBER's eccentric *The Big Time* (1958; **1961**), which won the award before going into book format, is not a traditionalist selection, either. Although the opposition award, the Nebula, is chosen by professional writers, there is no evidence that they have consistently chosen works of superior literary merit to those of the Hugo winners; indeed, some critics would argue the contrary case, that the Hugo voters have proved themselves the marginally more reliable judges. Both Hugo and Nebula, being America-centered, are notably chauvinistic, and awards to British writers have been rare. Despite all the criticisms to which both awards are readily subject, they are of real value to their recipients in increasing book sales.

A useful detailed guide, which lists rule changes, and all nominations as well as the actual winners up to 1975, is *A History of the Hugo, Nebula and*

International Fantasy Awards (**1970**; rev. 1976) by Donald Franson and Howard DeVore. Nearly all the Hugo-winning short fiction is available in a series of anthologies edited by Isaac ASIMOV (*who see for details*). [PN/CL]

Novels:

1953: Alfred BESTER, *The Demolished Man*

·1955: Mark CLIFTON and Frank RILEY, *They'd Rather be Right*

1956: Robert A. HEINLEIN, *Double Star*

1958: Fritz LEIBER, *The Big Time*

1959: James BLISH, *A Case of Conscience*

1960: Robert A. HEINLEIN, *Starship Troopers*

1961: Walter M. MILLER Jr, *A Canticle for Leibowitz*

1962: Robert A. HEINLEIN, *Stranger in a Strange Land*

1963: Philip K. DICK, *The Man in the High Castle*

1964: Clifford D. SIMAK, *Way Station*

1965: Fritz LEIBER, *The Wanderer*

1966: Roger ZELAZNY, "... And Call Me Conrad" and Frank HERBERT, *Dune* (tie)

1967: Robert A. HEINLEIN, *The Moon is a Harsh Mistress*

1968: Roger ZELAZNY, *Lord of Light*

1969: John BRUNNER, *Stand on Zanzibar*

1970: Ursula K. LE GUIN, *The Left Hand of Darkness*

1971: Larry NIVEN, *Ringworld*

1972: Philip José FARMER, *To Your Scattered Bodies Go*

1973: Isaac ASIMOV, *The Gods Themselves*

1974: Arthur C. CLARKE, *Rendezvous with Rama*

1975: Ursula K. LE GUIN, *The Dispossessed*

1976: Joe HALDEMAN, *The Forever War*

1977: Kate WILHELM, *Where Late the Sweet Birds Sang*

1978: Frederik POHL, *Gateway*

Short Fiction:

1955

Novelette: Walter M. MILLER Jr, "The Darfsteller"

Short Story: Eric Frank RUSSELL, "Allamagoosa"

1956

Novelette: Murray LEINSTER, "Exploration Team"

Short story: Arthur C. CLARKE, "The Star"

1958

Short Story: Avram DAVIDSON, "Or All the Seas with Oysters"

1959

Novelette: Clifford D. SIMAK, "The Big Front Yard"

Short story: Robert BLOCH, "The Hell-Bound Train"

1960

Short fiction: Daniel KEYES, "Flowers for Algernon"

1961

Short story: Poul ANDERSON, "The Longest Voyage"

1962

Short fiction: Brian W. ALDISS, the "Hothouse" series

1963

Short fiction: Jack VANCE, "The Dragon Masters"

1964

Short story: Poul ANDERSON, "No Truce with Kings"

1965

Short fiction: Gordon R. DICKSON, "Soldier, Ask Not"

1966

Short fiction: Harlan ELLISON " 'Repent, Harlequin!' said the Ticktockman"

1967

Novelette: Jack VANCE, "The Last Castle"

Short story: Larry NIVEN, "The Neutron Star"

1968

Novella: Anne MCCAFFREY, "Weyr Search" and Philip José FARMER, "Riders of the Purple Wage" (tie)

Novelette: Fritz LEIBER, "Gonna Roll Those Bones"

Short story: Harlan ELLISON, "I Have no Mouth and I Must Scream"

1969

Novella: Robert SILVERBERG, "Nightwings"

Novelette: Poul ANDERSON, "The Sharing of Flesh"

Short story: Harlan ELLISON, "The Beast that Shouted Love at the Heart of the World"

1970

Novella: Fritz LEIBER, "Ship of Shadows"

Short story: Samuel R. DELANY, "Time Considered as a Helix of Semi-Precious Stones"

1971

Novella: Fritz LEIBER, "Ill Met in Lankhmar"

Short story: Theodore STURGEON, "Slow Sculpture"

1972

Novella: Poul ANDERSON, "The Queen of Air and Darkness"

Short story: Larry NIVEN, "Inconstant Moon"

1973

Novella: Ursula K. LE GUIN, "The Word for World is Forest"

Novelette: Poul ANDERSON, "Goat Song"

Short story: R.A. LAFFERTY, "Eurema's Dam" and Frederik POHL and Cyril M. KORNBLUTH, "The Meeting" (tie)

1974

Novella: James TIPTREE Jr, "The Girl Who was Plugged In"

Novelette: Harlan ELLISON, "The Deathbird"

Short story: Ursula K. LE GUIN, "The Ones Who Walk Away From Omelas"

1975

Novella: George R.R. MARTIN, "A Song for Lya"

Novelette: Harlan ELLISON, "Adrift Just Off the Islets of Langerhans: Latitude 38° 54' N, Longitude 77° 00' 13" W"

Short story: Larry NIVEN, "The Hole Man"

1976

Novella: Roger ZELAZNY, "Home is the Hangman"

Novelette: Larry NIVEN, "Borderland of Sol"

Short story: Fritz LEIBER, "Catch that Zeppelin"

1977

Novella: Spider ROBINSON, "By Any Other Name" and James TIPTREE Jr, "Houston, Houston, Do You Read?" (tie)

Novelette: Isaac ASIMOV, "The Bicentennial Man"

Short story: Joe HALDEMAN, "Tricentennial"

1978

Novella: Spider and Jeanne ROBINSON, "Stardance"

Novelette: Joan VINGE, "Eyes of Amber"

Short Story: Harlan ELLISON, "Jeffty is Five"

Other awards:

1953

No. 1 Fan personality: Forrest J. ACKERMAN

Interior illustrator: Virgil FINLAY

Cover artist: Ed EMSHWILLER and Hannes BOK (tie)

Excellence in fact articles: Willy LEY

New sf author or artist: Philip José FARMER

Professional magazine: GALAXY and ASF (tie)

1955

Professional magazine: ASF

Illustrator: Frank Kelly FREAS

Amateur publication: James V. Taurasi's FANTASY TIMES

1956

Feature writer: Willy LEY

Professional magazine: ASF

Illustrator: Frank Kelly FREAS

Most promising new author: Robert SILVERBERG

Amateur publication: Ron Smith's INSIDE and *Science Fiction Advertiser*

Critic: Damon KNIGHT

1957

Professional magazine, American: ASF

Professional magazine, British: NW

Amateur publication: James V. Taurasi's SCIENCE FICTION TIMES

1958

Professional magazine: FSF

Illustrator: Frank Kelly FREAS

Motion picture: THE INCREDIBLE SHRINKING MAN

Most outstanding actifan: Walter A. Willis

1959

Illustrator: Frank Kelly FREAS

Professional magazine: FSF

Amateur publication: Terry CARR and Ron ELLIK'S FANAC

1960

Professional magazine: FSF

Amateur publication: F.M. BUSBY'S CRY

Illustrator: Ed EMSHWILLER

Dramatic presentation: THE TWILIGHT ZONE

Special award: Hugo GERNSBACK as "The Father of Science Fiction"

1961

Professional magazine: ASF

Amateur publication: Earl KEMP's "Who

Killed Science Fiction?"
Illustrator: Ed EMSHWILLER
Dramatic presentation: THE TWILIGHT ZONE
1962
Professional magazine: ASF
Amateur magazine: Richard Bergeron's WARHOON
Professional artist: Ed EMSHWILLER
Dramatic presentation: THE TWILIGHT ZONE
1963
Professional magazine: FSF
Amateur magazine: Dick LUPOFF's XERO
Professional artist: Roy KRENKEL
Special awards: P. Schuyler MILLER for "The Reference Library" reviews in ASF; and Isaac ASIMOV for science articles in FSF
1964
Professional magazine: ASF
Professional artist: Ed EMSHWILLER
Book publisher: ACE BOOKS
Amateur publication: George SCITHERS' AMRA
1965
Professional magazine: ASF
Professional artist: John SCHOENHERR
Book publisher: BALLANTINE BOOKS
Amateur publication: Robert and Juanita COULSON's YANDRO
Dramatic presentation: DR STRANGELOVE
1966
Professional magazine: IF
Professional artist: Frank FRAZETTA
Amateur magazine: Camille Cazedessus's ERB-dom
Best all-time series: Isaac ASIMOV's "Foundation" series
1967
Professional magazine: IF
Professional artist: Jack GAUGHAN
Dramatic presentation: "The Menagerie" (STAR TREK)
Amateur publication: Ed Meskys and Felice Rolfe's NIEKAS
Fan artist: Jack GAUGHAN
Fan writer: Alexei PANSHIN
1968
Dramatic presentation: "City on the Edge of Forever" (STAR TREK)
Professional magazine: IF
Professional artist: Jack GAUGHAN
Amateur publication: George SCITHERS' AMRA
Fan artist: George BARR
Fan writer: Ted WHITE
1969
Drama: 2001: A SPACE ODYSSEY
Professional magazine: FSF
Professional artist: Jack GAUGHAN
Amateur publication: Dick Geis's PSYCHOTIC
Fan writer: Harry WARNER Jr
Fan artist: Vaughn Bodé
1970
Dramatic presentation: TV coverage of Apollo XI
Professional magazine: FSF
Amateur magazine: Dick Geis's SCIENCE FICTION REVIEW
Fan writer: Bob (Wilson) TUCKER
Fan artist: Tim Kirk

1971
Professional artist: Leo and Diane DILLON
Professional magazine: FSF
Amateur magazine: Charles and Dena Brown's LOCUS
Fan writer: Dick Geis
Fan artist: Alicia Austin
1972
Dramatic presentation: A CLOCKWORK ORANGE
Amateur magazine: Charles and Dena Brown's LOCUS
Professional magazine: FSF
Professional artist: Frank Kelly FREAS
Fan artist: Tim Kirk
Fan writer: Harry WARNER Jr.
1973
Dramatic presentation: SLAUGHTERHOUSE FIVE
Professional editor: Ben BOVA
Professional artist: Frank Kelly FREAS
Amateur magazine: Michael and Susan Glicksohn's ENERGUMEN
Fan writer: Terry CARR
Fan artist: Tim Kirk
1974
Amateur magazine: Andy Porter's ALGOL and Dick Geis's THE ALIEN CRITIC (tie)
Professional artist: Frank Kelly FREAS
Professional editor: Ben BOVA
Dramatic presentation: SLEEPER
Fan writer: Susan Wood
Fan artist: Tim Kirk
Special award: Chesley BONESTELL
1975
Professional artist: Frank Kelly FREAS
Professional editor: Ben BOVA
Amateur magazine: Dick Geis's THE ALIEN CRITIC
Dramatic presentation: Young Frankenstein
Fan writer: Dick Geis
Fan artist: William ROTSLER
1976
Dramatic presentation: A BOY AND HIS DOG
Fanzine: Charles and Dena Brown's LOCUS
Professional artist: Frank Kelly FREAS
Professional editor: Ben BOVA
Fan writer: Richard E. Geis
Fan artist: Tim Kirk
1977
Professional editor: Ben BOVA
Fanzine: Dick Geis's SCIENCE FICTION REVIEW
Professional artist: Rick STERNBACH
Fan artist: Phil Foglio
Fan writer: Richard E. Geis and Susan Wood (tie)
Special award: STAR WARS
1978
Dramatic presentation: STAR WARS
Fanzine: LOCUS
Professional artist: Rick STERNBACH
Professional editor: George SCITHERS
Fan writer: Richard E. Geis
Fan Artist: Phil Foglio

HULL, E(DNA) MAYNE (1905–75). Canadian-born American writer, married from 1939 to her death to A.E. VAN VOGT, who collaborated with her on most

of her work, either in its original magazine form or in expanding it for book publication. She began publishing sf with "The Flight that Failed" for ASF in 1942, and made her greatest impact with the Arthur Blord series, later assembled by Van Vogt as *Planets for Sale* (1943–6 ASF; fix-up **1954**; both authors credited), and with the magazine version of *The Winged Man* (1944 ASF; exp. by Van Vogt **1966**; both authors credited). The collection *Out of the Unknown* (coll. **1948**) was credited to both writers, and consisted of six stories, three by each of them, according to their original bylines. EMH ceased writing sf and fantasy when she became involved in DIANETICS. [JC]

HUMOUR There is a legend that sf and humour do not mix, but it is false. Certainly sf has produced many bad jokes; Arthur C. CLARKE's *Tales From the White Hart* (coll. of linked stories **1957**) is full of them; but throughout its history it has also produced many good ones.

Much sf humour takes the form of social SATIRE, and stories of this kind are discussed mainly in that entry. While the discussion below will necessarily mention many satires, it is concentrated on sf that makes the reader laugh rather than smile wryly. Nothing is more subjective than humour, and the works cited below are unlikely to amuse every reader.

The wittiest sf writers of the late 19th century were probably Mark TWAIN, Samuel BUTLER, Ambrose BIERCE and H.G. WELLS. The humour of Twain's *A Connecticut Yankee in King Arthur's Court* (**1889**), like so much humour generally, is rooted in self-confident prejudice; Twain clearly found the bumbling incompetence of the middle ages irresistibly funny; he strikes readers as the sort of man who in America would tell Polish jokes, and in England tell Irish jokes. Butler's satire in *Erewhon* (**1872**) often consists in topsy-turvy analogies, as in the comparison between British churches and Erewhonian banks, which clearly shows the self-interest Butler supposed to be the motive for religious devotion. Bierce's short stories often have a grim and macabre humour; Wells's on the other hand, are often surprisingly jolly, as in "The Truth about Pyecraft" (1903). Other early works of sf humour are *Mr. Hawkins' Humorous Adventures* (coll. of linked stories **1904**) by Edgar FRANKLIN; *Button Brains* (**1933**) by J. Storer CLOUSTON, a novel about a funny robot; and *Caleb Catlum's America* (**1936**) by Vincent McHUGH, a rollicking story about a family of immortals.

Also working in the 1930s was John COLLIER, whose short stories (sometimes sf, more usually fantasy) amuse through the occasionally poisonous sharpness of the language, and an innocently, blandly cruel sense of the ironies of life. Roald DAHL was to write rather similar stories later on, and a similar blend of irony and epigrammatic wit, also based on a sense of cosmic absurdity, is found in most of the novels of James Branch CABELL. But all three of these writers, working to some extent in the *contes cruels* ["Cruel Stories"] (coll. **1883**) tradition of VILLIERS DE L'ISLE-ADAM, are primarily grotesque fantasists who used sf themes only occasionally and more or less by accident.

Genre sf has always had the occasional humorist, and with the advent of UNKNOWN (a magazine founded in 1939 by John .W. CAMPBELL Jr) they had a platform; *Unknown* specialized in whimsical fantasy, sometimes dealing with SUPERNATURAL CREATURES, very often set in ALTERNATE WORLDS. Anthony BOUCHER was an important contributor, and many of his stories of this type are collected in *The Compleat Werewolf* (coll. **1969**). Most fondly remembered from *Unknown* are the "Harold Shea" stories, written by L. Sprague DE CAMP and Fletcher PRATT, and later collected as *The Complete Enchanter* (coll. **1975**); propelled back into alternate versions of the past, often based on myth or literature, Shea has a terrible time trying to come to terms with the local customs, in worlds where MAGIC works. The early 1940s also saw a whole series of broad but accomplished jokes by Eric Frank RUSSELL, the basic plot of which usually consists of smart guys pinpricking the pretensions of the brutal, the stupid and the pompous in various interplanetary venues; examples from a slightly later period when Russell had perfected his wisecracking style are "... And Then There Were None" (1951), "Diabologic" (1955), *Wasp* (**1957**) and *The Space Willies* (1956 *ASF*; exp. **1958**; vt *Next of Kin* UK). From the same period come many of Fredric BROWN's amusing stories, the most amazing being "Placet is a Crazy Place" (1946) in which the eponymous planet keeps meeting itself, creating hallucinations, being undermined by heavy-matter widgie birds and being the locale for horrendous puns. Brown's generally outrageous inventions have appeared in many collections, including *Angels and Spaceships* (coll. **1954**; vt *Star Shine*) and *Nightmares and Geezenstacks* (coll. **1961**).

Three of sf's premier humorists were notable for working at their strongest in short stories, with the result, perhaps, that their full stature has not been generally recognized; they are Henry KUTTNER, William TENN and Robert SHECKLEY. Kuttner's humour, generally couched in a more pulp-style language than that of the other two, has probably dated the most quickly, but "The Twonky" (1942 as by Lewis Padgett) is a classic which was filmed (*see* THE TWONKY), as are the "Hogben" stories (1947–9), and the "Galloway Gallegher" series, collected as *Robots Have No Tails* (1943–8 *ASF*; coll. **1952**). Tenn's style is more polished; but it is Sheckley who has probably remained the most consistent and uproarious sf

humorist of them all. His stories (*see his entry for list of collections*) are consistently urbane and sharp, with a wonderfully accurate eye for the many absurdities implicit in the sf themes that most writers were taking seriously. Sheckley works always with a kind of controlled PARANOIA, which sometimes emerges as a variant on "the universe is out to get us", and sometimes on "the universe is out to surprise us"; nothing is ever quite what it seems in a Sheckley story, and with an inventiveness that has lasted from the early 1950s to the late '70s, he has continued as, in effect, the James Thurber of sf, depicting the naïve but sometimes successful struggles of little men against an unimaginably absurd and rather menacing cosmos. Philip K. DICK is another writer with something of the same quality, and, though few of his novels are outright comedies, most have a rich sense of the various comic ways in which the life of the future might thwart us; Dick is especially well known for robots that talk back.

Both Dick and Sheckley often published in GALAXY SCIENCE FICTION, a magazine that under its earlier editors especially, notably Horace GOLD, encouraged wit, satire and a moderately demanding literacy in its writers, who also included Frederik POHL and Alfred BESTER, both of whom were as much at home with the humorous story as with the serious sf for which they are best remembered; examples are Pohl's "The Tunnel Under the World" (1955) and Bester's "The Men Who Murdered Mohammed" (1958). The latter appeared in *FSF*, which also printed a number of witty stories, including most of Richard MATHESON's. When Matheson was not being horrific he was often very funny indeed. Reginald BRETNOR's "Ferdinand Feghoot" series of appalling vignettes with punning punch-lines also appeared in *FSF*.

Most well-known sf authors have tried their hand at humour at one time or another, sometimes rather heavy handedly, as in Keith LAUMER's "Retief" stories, or Gordon R. DICKSON's "Hoka" series, written in collaboration with Poul ANDERSON. More successful in this line has been Harry HARRISON, who has often amusingly parodied the excesses of genre sf, as in the "Stainless Steel Rat" stories, and *Bill, the Galactic Hero* (**1965**). A more recent parodist whose style is somewhere midway between Harrison's and Sheckley's is Bob SHAW, most of whose novels feature a wry humour of observation; his comic novel *Who Goes Here?* (**1977**) makes great play with time travel, and a spaceship with a matter transmitter at each end which is driven by constantly transmitting itself through its own length. A less well known sf author is Homer NEARING Jr, whose *The Sinister Researches of C.P. Ransom* (coll. of linked stories **1954**) is consistently funny.

Recent comic sf has tended strongly

towards satire, and its comedy is often black. Nearly all of John SLADEK's work is of this sort; it tends more towards irony than farce, blending comedy with nightmare in tales that often deal with technology running amok, and mankind being manipulated. His one-time collaborator Thomas M. DISCH is one of the most formidable of sf's wits and stylists, though again it is the wry smile rather than the outright laugh that is evoked. Ron GOULART, on the other hand, is best known for knockabout, satiric farce, in a number of different novels and collections. Michael MOORCOCK often deals with a comedy of unexpected juxtapositions, as in his "Dancers at the End of Time" series, where time-travellers constantly misunderstand one another's customs. Some of sf's most consistent humorists are those like Moorcock, Disch, Shaw, Barry MALZBERG, Bester and Pohl, who seldom write comedies *per se*, but whose serious sf is constantly shot through with flashes of perceptive humour; sf need not be solemn, and as it continues to abandon the worst excesses of the pulp style, it seems to have more room for stylish wit than it once did. Piers ANTHONY's style is perhaps less than polished, but his *Prostho Plus* (**1971**), featuring a kidnapped Earth dentist forced to practise on a hideous variety of alien teeth, is carried off with more verve than one might guess was possible from the outline. Richard COWPER on the other hand, an elegant stylist indeed, has been more successful generally with his serious work than with such comedies as *Worlds Apart* (**1974**) and *Clone* (**1972**), though the latter has some splendid touches, and was the first work to bring Cowper international notice.

Humour notoriously translates badly, and while readers of Polish swear that the wit of Stanislaw LEM in such works as *Cyberiada* (coll. **1965**; trans. as *The Cyberiad* **1974**) and "Kongres Futurologiczny" (**1971**; trans. as *The Futurological Congress* **1974**) is full of subtle ironies and linguistic fireworks, their humour in translation is too blunt and thumping for real success. Nor does sf humour, it seems, normally transfer readily to the screen, as several dire comedies including IT'S ABOUT TIME have demonstrated on TV, though the films BARBARELLA and SLEEPER are both, in their very different ways (the first an erotic parody, the second a *Candide*-style satire), successfully witty.

One of the most offbeat of recent sf humorists is R.A. LAFFERTY, whose comedy relies on the bizarre and the unexpected (sometimes reminiscent of the quasi-surrealist humour of the British TV series *Monty Python*) laid out with exuberantly idiosyncratic language.

A major work of comic sf is the *Illuminatus* trilogy (**1975**) by Robert SHEA and Robert Anton WILSON, a rambling and almost indescribable story of

HUMOUR has crept into the sf cinema, as in Woody Allen's *Sleeper*.

conflicting conspiracies by different secret cults, which persuasively argues for the accuracy of a PARANOID view of POLITICS; a cynical and sometimes bloodshot view of the vagaries of human behaviour is blended with parody, farce, puns, wisecracks and general lunacy in what is almost a compendium of American comic styles.

The most famous of sf humorists is certainly Kurt VONNEGUT Jr, and although his best-known work is probably *Slaughterhouse-5* (1969), his wit is probably less brittle and fatalistic, more humane and understanding, in *The Sirens of Titan* (1959) and *Cat's Cradle* (1963). In both these books Vonnegut gets some of his most sardonic effects by juxtaposing the cosmic and the trivial in what seems to be an argument for the indifference of the universe, and the absurdity of expecting justice or even rational common sense from life. But at least in the earlier books, the nihilism is softened by the affection he shows for the absurd and doomed ambitions of his protagonists. It is hard to tell whether Vonnegut is truly one of the great wits, in the tradition of Jonathan SWIFT, or whether his black humour may not, basically, be rather facile. But while critics argue the point, the books become best-sellers, demonstrating yet again that there is no greater cosmic futility than in the endeavour to analyse why we laugh.
[PN]

HUNGARY *See* EASTERN EUROPE.

HUNT, GILL House name used by the British paperback publisher Curtis Warren, 1950–52. *Planetfall* (1951) is by E.C. TUBB. Other titles of unknown provenance are *Elektron Union* (undated), *Fission* (1950), *Galactic Storm* (1952), *Hostile Worlds* (undated), *Planet X* (undated), *Space Flight* (undated), *Spatial Ray* (undated), *Station 7* (1951), *Vega* (undated) and *Zero Field* (1952). [PN]

HUNTER, EVAN Main pseudonym of American writer S. A. Lombino (1926–), under which, along with the names Richard Marsten and Hunt

Collins, he has written his sf, including 16 magazine sf stories 1953-6 and the screenplay for Alfred Hitchcock's THE BIRDS (1963). He published seven magazine sf stories under his own name also. He may now be best known as Ed McBain, under which name he has published close to 40 police thrillers. As EH he has also published many best-selling non-sf novels, including *The Blackboard Jungle* (1954). His first sf novel, *Find the Feathered Serpent* (1952 as by EH), is a juvenile featuring time travel to the Mayan empire, and his second, *Rocket to Luna* (1953 as by Richard Marsten), also a juvenile, sends students to the moon. *Danger: Dinosaurs!* (1953 as by Richard Marsten) is another juvenile, featuring time travel to the remote past. *Tomorrow's World* (1954 *If* as "Malice in Wonderland" by EH; exp. 1956 as by Hunt Collins; vt *Tomorrow and Tomorrow* as by Hunt Collins) takes a somewhat satirical look at a future dominated by organized drug addicts. Some sf stories are included in *The Last Spin* (coll. 1960) and *Happy New Year, Herbie* (coll. 1965). EH has been inactive recently as an sf writer; his loss to this genre has been the gain of others. [JC]
See also: LEISURE.

HUNTER, E. WALDO *See* Theodore STURGEON.

HUNTER, NORMAN (1899–). English writer who lived for a period in South Africa after the Second World War; he is also a professional conjuror. His now classic series of children's books about Professor Branestawm and his inventions, *The Incredible Adventures of Professor Branestawm* (coll. 1933), *Professor Branestawm's Treasure Hunt* (coll. 1937) and *The Peculiar Triumph of Professor Branestawm* (coll. 1970), the first two of which inspired an English television series in 1969, delightfully involve the professor and his extraordinary devices in various exploits and entanglements. [JC]
Other works: *Larky Legends* (coll. 1938; vt abridged as *The Dribblesome Teapots*

and Other Incredible Stories), a juvenile.

HUNTING, GARDNER (1872–1958). American writer, whose sf novel is *The Vicarion* (1926); the eponymous MACHINE enables its user to view other lives. [JC]

HUXLEY, ALDOUS (1894–1963). English novelist and man of letters, in California from 1937 to his death. His best fiction, like *Point Counter Point* (1928), was written in the 1920s, a decade of which he is perhaps the premier literary representative, and is not sf. He is undoubtedly most widely known today, however, for his seminal DYSTOPIA *Brave New World* (1932). This novel has established such words as "soma" (originally from Sir Thomas MORE's *Utopia*, 1517) and "feelie" in the English language, and has contributed to social and literary thought a definite model of pharmacological totalitarianism; it depicts a future Earth in which the expression of dissonant emotions and acts is rigorously controlled from above, ostensibly for the betterment of all. Babies, once decanted, are chemically adjusted to grow into the body-type and intelligence required by society, and enter into the appropriate castes as a result, from Alpha to Epsilon (*see* GENETIC ENGINEERING). Sex and all relationships are casual and without dissonance. Soma is a kind of psychedelic drug used as a social control; the feelies are multi-sense movies, developed for the same reason. The story illustrates this inexorable plastic paradise, and presents opportunities for discussion about it; one protagonist goes to a Savage Reservation (where a few old-style humans are permitted their exemplary culture), rescues a girl in trouble, and returns with her and her Savage son to the central society, where she disgusts everyone with her visible diseases and her horrifying descent into age, and gradually overdoses despairingly on soma. After a fracas, her son and two discontented citizens are interviewed by Mustapha Mond, one of the ten World Controllers, who argumentatively justifies the price paid for stability. When the unconvinced Savage attempts to live alone and in this way replicate the conditions necessary for the creation of high art, he is soon bedevilled by the mass media into committing suicide. As argument and as SATIRE, *Brave New World* is a compendium of usable points and quotable jibes — the substitution of Ford for God being merely the best known — and has provided material for much subsequent fiction. Its pessimistic accounting of the shape a scientifically planned community would take, of its sterility and human emptiness, has caused the book to be read as a decisive refutation of those UTOPIAS of H.G. WELLS, for example *Men Like Gods* (1923), which argue a stridently optimistic outcome for scientific Utopian endeavour that Wells himself did not feel

The strong but heavily retouched photo of Aldous HUXLEY is by E.O. Hoppe.

---

with any conviction. *Brave New World Revisited* (coll. **1958**) is a non-fiction series of essays on the themes of the novel, from the perspective of 25 years.

After Many a Summer Dies The Swan (**1939**; vt *After Many a Summer* UK), in which a California oil magnate rediscovers an 18th-century longevity compound and its macabre consequence, and *Time Must Have a Stop* (**1944**), one of the characters of which undergoes posthumous experiences, are both relevant to sf. AH also wrote two more Utopian/anti-Utopian works. *Ape and Essence* (**1948**) is another Dystopia, set in 2108 after an atomic and bacteriological final war, which has left untouched only New Zealand, from where comes a researcher to America, to discover a literally devilish society, in which human nature and science have gone savagely wrong, and in which females, known as vessels, come into oestrus for only two weeks in the year, after Belial Day; the pessimism of the book is unalleviated, and its presentation, as a kind of ideal filmscript, horrific and disgusted. *Island* (**1962**) presents a Utopian alternative to the previous books, though without much conviction. The ISLAND (Pala) is set in the Indian Ocean, and has enjoyed for

a century a mildly euphoric existence, sustained spiritually by religious practices derived from Tantric Buddhism, and physically by moksha, a sort of benign soma, whose psychedelic effects smooth the rough edges of the world.

AH wrote discursive novels, some of them technically sf, from a position which treated their fictional content as subservient to the matters being discussed and illuminated. The literacy of his style, and the apparent sophistication of his transcendental thought, have perhaps impressed traditional sf readers and critics more than he has deserved. There is no denying, however, the extreme importance of the example of his thought in the intellectual development of the genre. [JC]

About the author: There are many critical studies. Lilly Zahner's *Demon and Saint in the Novels of Aldous Huxley* (**1975**) provides clear analysis and an adequate bibliography. *See also: Aldous Huxley: A Study of the Major Novels* (**1968**) by Peter Bowering; *Aldous Huxley, Satire and Structure* (**1969**) by Jerome Meckier.

See also: AUTOMATION; IMMORTALITY; LEISURE; MEDICINE; PERCEPTION; POLITICS; SOCIOLOGY.

HYAMS, EDWARD S(OLOMON) (1910–75). English writer, prolific in various genres, fiction and non-fiction, from before the Second World War; he has also been active as a translator. Although not widely known as a writer of sf or fantasy, he has in fact published several novels of sf interest. *The Astrologer* (**1950**) is an early novel on the ECOLOGICAL theme of soil exhaustion, and the DISASTER its protagonist tries to avert; *The Final Agenda* (**1973**) places a world-wide organization of anarchists in power in a NEAR-FUTURE venue, and traces their attempts to found an ecological UTOPIA with considerable sympathy; *Morrow's Ants* (**1975**) is about the creation of a HIVE MIND. Typically of writers not identified with the sf genre, ESH tends to use sf components in a didactic fashion, in his case to considerable effect. [JC]

Other works: *The Wings of the Morning* (**1939**); *Not in Our Stars* (**1949**); *Sylvester* (**1951**; vt *998* USA); *The Death Lottery* (**1971**).

See also: ASTRONOMY; SCIENTISTS.

HYNE, C(HARLES) J(OHN) CUTCLIFFE (WRIGHT) (1866–1944). English writer. He utilized his ample travelling experience in creating the popular "Captain Kettle" series which appeared in PEARSON'S MAGAZINE and later in the cinema: *Captain Kettle on the Warpath* (coll. **1916**), *The Rev. Captain Kettle* (coll. **1925**), *Mr. Kettle, Third Mate* (**1931**) and *Ivory Valley* (**1938**) being the only volumes to contain sf elements. He is best known for his LOST-WORLD novel *The Lost Continent* (**1900**), set in ATLANTIS at the time of its destruction. CJCH began writing sf with *Beneath Your Very Boots* (**1889**), a hollow-Earth, lost-world novel, following it up with a ROBINSONADE, *The New Eden* (**1892**), later turning to future WAR with *Empire of the World* (**1910**; vt *Emperor of the World* UK) and to the Wandering Jew theme with *Abbs, His Story Through Many Ages* (**1929**). This diversity of ideas was even more prevalent in his short stories, particularly in a work published under his Weatherby Chesney pseudonym, *The Adventures of a Solicitor* (coll. of linked stories **1898**), which contains stories about INVISIBILITY, ROBOTS, SPACE FLIGHT and rejuvenation, together with several GOTHIC and weird fantasies. CJCH was one of the most prolific writers of early magazine sf, but is almost forgotten today. [JE]

Other works: *The Foundered Galleon* (1898–9 *Scraps* as by Weatherby Chesney and Alick Jones; **1902** as by Weatherby Chesney); *The Adventures of an Engineer* (coll. of linked stories **1903**, as by Weatherby Chesney); *Atoms of Empire* (coll. **1904**); *Red Herrings* (coll. **1918**); *Man's Understanding* (coll. **1933**); *Wishing Smith* (**1939**).

See also: WEAPONS.

HYPERION PRESS American publisher of reprints — the "classics of science fiction" series. This was the first publisher to undertake such a series, preceding ARNO, GARLAND and GREGG PRESS. The editor was Sam MOSKOWITZ, who also provided introductions to many of the volumes, and the books selected were primarily drawn from the late 19th and early 20th centuries. The first series of HP reprints had 23 vols, and was published in 1974; the second series had 19 vols, published 1976. In addition, HP brought back into print six anthologies and collections of criticism by Moskowitz. [MJE/PN]

HYPERSPACE In sf TERMINOLOGY, a kind of FOURTH DIMENSION in space through which SPACESHIPS can take a short cut in order to get rapidly from one point in "normal" space to another far distant. The term may have been invented by John W.CAMPBELL Jr in *The Mightiest Machine* (1934 *ASF*; **1947**). It has since been used in literally thousands of stories by many hundreds of writers, who, these days, seldom bother to explain it. *See* FASTER THAN LIGHT for further details. [PN]

HYPHEN Irish FANZINE (1952–65) ed., from Belfast, Walt Willis, with Chuck Harris and later Ian McAuley. Probably the most famous of humorous fanzines, the quality and style of *H*'s writing made it not only one of the most admired fanzines of its time but also gave it a prestige and influence in FANDOM which still remains. Contributors included Bob SHAW, James WHITE, William F. TEMPLE, Robert BLOCH and Damon KNIGHT. [PR]

HYPNOSIS *See* PSYCHOLOGY.

ICONOCLASM An essential part of sf is change; indeed it may be said that the belief that the circumstances of human life were bound to keep on changing provided the most powerful stimulus for the creation of the genre. Nevertheless, it is obvious from experience that all changes, technical or social, encounter resistance ranging from the perfunctory to the desperate, as a result of human inertia. Much sf, then, is concerned with the nature of that resistance, its unexpected force, the most efficacious

methods of breaking it, and of course with the whole question of whether anyone has any right to break it.

One of the oldest expressions of this theme is the conflict between scientific advance and religious orthodoxy, seen very evidently in the post-Darwinian furore, and reacted to at second hand, if not at first, by H.G. WELLS, perhaps most bitterly in *The Island of Dr. Moreau* (**1896**). In that story the "iconoclasm" or breach of faith does not become general, for Moreau's experiment, with its proof that men are not distinct from animals, is accidentally destroyed. But its implications are obvious to the reader: religion is a myth, morality a swindle, society a convenience. Few later authors have gone as far as Wells, but exposés of missionaries are not uncommon, e.g. Harry HARRISON's "The Streets of Ashkelon" (1962) (*see also* RELIGION).

Yet assaults on religious faith are only a small part of the corrosive scepticism projected by much sf. It has not escaped notice, for instance, that some people "believe" in science in exactly the same way as others "believe" in Christ; and in so far as the former are committed to non-acceptance of new knowledge they too become targets of "iconoclastic" fiction. A series of stories by Mark CLIFTON (and his collaborators) in *ASF* 1953–7 dealt with the discovery of ANTIGRAVITY, TELEPATHY, IMMORTALITY, etc. by methods part-scientific, part-occult (*see* PSI POWERS). One of the basic assumptions of the series was that such discoveries would be opposed first by trained scientists, that there could be other kinds of Inquisition than religious. This attack on what must be the most deeply entrenched of modern beliefs was characteristically daring, but also at times simplistic, in that the stories conveyed no sense of doubt as to where Truth lay. *Sensible* people, the authors felt, would always be on the side of change. While this might be true in merely technical matters, one wonders how far continuous cultural instability could be borne by normal people. A telling scene in Kurt VONNEGUT's *Player Piano* (**1952**) comes after the anti-authoritarian revolution, when one of the first acts of the revolutionaries is to start tinkering with machines. If you have no faith in an ultimate UTOPIA and are committed to ceaseless change, are you not likely to find yourself bound on the wheel of cyclic history? As with many other genres, sf has found it easier to destroy current orthodoxy than to portray positive values convincingly: a sense of vague aspiration often pervades stories of iconoclasm.

Thus, in the highly characteristic series *The Shrouded Planet* (1956 *ASF*; **1957**) and *The Dawning Light* (1957 *ASF*; **1959**) "Robert RANDALL" (Randall GARRETT and Robert SILVERBERG) presents in great detail the destruction of the stable alien theocracy of Nidor by the controlled

release of human techniques and ideas, the consequences of which are never appreciated by the Nidorians who adopt them. The stories are neat and powerful in their opposition of good intentions and disastrous short-term results. But what is the long-term motivation? To bring Nidorians, apparently, up to technical parity with Earthmen. Will this make them happier? The question is not ignored in the book, but it is shelved. Evidently the interest in iconoclastic method outweighs concern for iconoclastic purpose. One of many similar stories in *ASF* is Poul Anderson's "The Three-Cornered Wheel" (1963), once more anti-theocratic but made more complex by the fact that one of its protagonists is a Jew, and so in a sense respectful of ancient tradition even while engaged in destroying it. But too many stories dramatizing the destruction of cultures keep up their interest solely by making the problem technically and even arbitrarily difficult. Thus Lloyd BIGGLE's novel *The Still, Small Voice of Trumpets* (**1968**) centres on the so-called "Rule of One" (a derisory gesture in response to a non-interventionist policy) which stipulates that Earthmen can introduce only one technical innovation to alien cultures, and that this must be destructive all by itself; concern for "elegance" of solution has become dominant. The moral problems involved in cultural manipulation were seen altogether more sharply on the other side of the world by the Russian brothers Arkady and Boris STRUGATSKI, whose *Trudno byt' bogom* (**1964**; trans. **1973** as *Hard To Be A God*) relates a story about the paternalist direction of backward societies which also raises many questions directly relevant to fascism and Stalinism. Iconoclasm of this sort may adopt an sf shape, but its conclusions relate painfully enough, whether the authors are American or Russian, to problems of the real world.

It is not impossible to argue, however, as Hal CLEMENT does, that the benefits of technology are such that they will be grasped by any intelligent being who is free to choose. At the end of his *Mission of Gravity* (**1954**), the alien Barlennan "goes on strike" for more technical knowledge, a gesture of opposition of which his human mentors, of course, thoroughly approve. Clement's aliens, then, cooperate in the destruction of their own way of life, and the problem is solved. Sociologically this may appear naïve. At the other extreme Ursula K. LE GUIN's *The Word for World is Forest* (1972; rev. **1976**) portrays a conflict avowedly based on the Vietnam war, with Earthmen trying to impose their cultural standards on aliens quite properly satisfied with their own. It should be noted, though, that Ms Le Guin's non-interventionism was common in sf long before Vietnam (and indeed was early applied to Vietnam); consider for instance

Katharine MacLean's *ASF* story "Unhuman Sacrifice" (1958) or indeed Randall Garrett's *ASF* story "The Destroyers" (1959). The latter gained an added twist by continuous internal reference to the American Civil War. Should one refuse to intervene in any circumstances? Even to free slaves? And what if the slaves appear happy? The morality of iconoclasm versus non-interventionism is not simple.

Most of the stories discussed so far have projected the problems of cultural change outwards, on to the hypothetical conflicts of aliens and Earthmen. It is not, indeed, easy to see how ordinary human beings could emerge from their own societies sufficiently to diagnose the necessity for, or engineer the achievement of, destruction of established beliefs; Darwin, the great model of innovation in sf, was notably indirect in his effects. The standard iconoclastic mode of stories without aliens is, accordingly, to trace the unexpected social effects of technical change. Universal MATTER TRANSMISSION changes attitudes to privacy, sexuality and social hierarchy in Harry Harrison's *One Step from Earth* (coll. of linked stories **1970**), as in Alfred Bester's *The Stars my Destination* (**1956**; vt *Tiger! Tiger!*); artificially cultured human organs destroy the basis of social control in Larry Niven's *A Gift from Earth* (**1968**); "slow glass" insidiously changes justice in Bob Shaw's *Other Days, Other Eyes* (fix-up **1972**).

Underlying all the material that has been discussed is an intense distrust, not of reason, but of the human capacity for rationalizing whatever happens to be the present state. Conviction of their own demonstrable rightness has not saved many scientists from being proved wrong over aeroplanes, evolution, space travel; the same is true of many moralists. Can any knowledge, then, be universally true, any ethical system be *always* right? Ingeniously or perversely, sf authors tend to answer "No" to both questions, and to demonstrate this ultimate belief by writing stories of ideological change and social manipulation. [TS]

IDLER, THE British magazine published monthly by Chatto & Windus (later by Dawburn & Ward and others), ed. Jerome K. Jerome and Robert Barr, both jointly and separately, Arthur Lawrence and Sidney H. Sime and others, Feb. 1892-Mar. 1911.

Although comparatively short-lived, *I* published much sf, mainly through the leanings of its founding editors, both fantasy authors, who contributed to the genre in its pages. Other notable contributors in its early days were Arthur Conan Doyle, Edwin Lester Arnold and H.G. Wells. Fantasy and sf continued through to its demise with Patrick Vaux, William Hope Hodgson, Paul Bo'ld and others. Many of its stories were reprinted in McClure's Magazine. [JE]

Nov./Dec. 1973. Cover by Brian Boyle Studio.

IF US DIGEST-size magazine. 175 issues, Mar. 1952 – Nov./Dec. 1974. It was founded by the Quinn Publishing Co. with Paul Fairman as editor, but James Quinn quickly took over the editorial chair himself, in Nov. 1952, holding it until 1958, when Damon Knight took over briefly. The title was sold during 1959 to Digest Productions and became a companion to Galaxy, under the editorship of *Gal.*'s editor H.L. Gold. Frederik Pohl assumed the editorship from Jan. 1962, and from Jul. 1963 the publisher operated as Galaxy Publishing Corp. *Gal.* and *If* were both sold in 1969 to the Universal Publishing and Distributing Co., and Ejler Jakobsson took over as editor of both in Jul. James Baen became editor early in 1974, shortly before the magazine folded. For most of its life it was bi-monthly, but Mar. 1954-Jun. 1955, and again Jul. 1964-May 1970, it was monthly. The latter period was its heyday, during which it won Hugo awards for best magazine in 1966, 1967 and 1968. *If* absorbed its bi-monthly companion Worlds of Tomorrow in 1967.

The most notable story appearing in *If* during the Quinn period was James Blish's classic *A Case of Conscience* (Sep. 1953; exp. **1958**). At its height, under Pohl, the magazine featured several Hugo-winning stories, including Robert A. Heinlein's *The Moon is a Harsh Mistress* (Dec. 1965-Apr. 1966; **1966**), Larry Niven's "Neutron Star" (Oct. 1966) and Harlan Ellison's "I Have No Mouth and I Must Scream" (Mar. 1967). In this period the magazine also featured A.E. van Vogt's return to sf-writing after a long absence, and the fourth volume of E. E. "Doc" Smith's "Skylark" series, nearly 30 years after the third — *Skylark Du Quesne* (Jun.-Oct. 1965; **1966**). Under Jakobsson's editorship the magazine resumed playing second fiddle to *Gal.* and gradually declined until it was merged with its companion. [BS]

Collectors should note: *If* was first of all subtitled *Worlds of Science Fiction*, but the cover logo was altered to *Worlds of If Science Fiction* in Nov. '61. There were various anomalies in the numbering system: Vols 1 to 13 had six numbers each in theory, but both Oct. and Dec. '57 were marked Vol.7 no.6, and there was no Vol.8 no.1. What should have been Vol.9 no.3 was marked as Vol.8 no.6. What should have been Vol.10 no.1 was marked as Vol.10 no.6, which turned up again later in its proper sequence. Vol.14 had seven numbers, Vols 15 to 18 had 12 numbers, Vol.19 had 10, and thereafter 12 numbers per volume, until Vol.22 which had eight. There was no issue between Feb. '59 and Jul. '59. Sep. '64 was omitted from the monthly sequence, as was Jun. '69.

The history of *If*'s British editions is inordinately complex. Strato Publications reprinted 15 numbered issues from the '53–4 period, and a further 18 (beginning again at no.1) from '59–62. Gold Star Publications marketed a British edition in '66–7 whose issues were backdated two months from the US edition. Copies of the UPD version were imported during '72–4 and numbered for British release, the numbers running from 1–9 then 11, 1, 13, 3, 4 and 5. The last issue was never distributed in Britain. Two anthologies of stories from *If*, in magazine format, were released as *The First World of If* (anth. **1957**) and *The Second World of If* (anth. **1958**), both ed. James L. Quinn. More recent collections have been *The Best From If* (anth. **1973**); *The Best From If Vol. II* (anth. **1974**), ed. The Editors of If Magazine, and *The Best From If Vol. III* (anth. **1976**) ed. James Baen.

IGGULDEN, JOHN (1917–). Australian author whose sf work is restricted to an unremarkable novel, *Breakthrough* (**1960**); a dictator uses radio to control people. [JC]

IKARIA XB1 (vt **VOYAGE TO THE END OF THE UNIVERSE**) Film (1963). Ceskoslovensky Filmexport/AIP. Directed by Jindřich Polak, starring Zdenek Stepanek, Radovan Lakavsky and Dana Medricka. Screenplay by Pavel Juracek and Jindrich Polak. 81 mins (cut to 65). Colour.

This interesting Czech film is set in a giant spaceship (with elaborate interiors designed by Jan Zazvorka) on a long exploratory mission. The daily routines of the ship's inhabitants create, in subtle ways, the impression of a culture alien to ours. The stock situations of American or British films and TV series with a similar setting (Star Trek and Space 1999, for example) are mostly avoided by the Czech writers, although the building up of suspense when the spaceship encounters a lifeless wreck floating in space adds a touch of Western space opera; an amusing sequence is the discovery of a group of corpses seated round a table and dressed in opulent finery, the men even wearing top hats, in a Russian-style caricature of American capitalism. The ending has the spaceship reaching a planet that we soon realize is contemporary Earth. On its British release the film was savagely cut.   [JB]

ILLUSTRATED MAN, THE Film (1968). SKM Productions/Warner-Seven Arts. Directed by Jack Smight, starring Rod Steiger, Claire Bloom, Robert Drivas, Don Dubbins and Jason Evers. Screenplay by Howard B. Kreitsek, based on the book of the same title by Ray BRADBURY. 103 mins. Colour.

Bradbury's retrospective idea of a man whose various tattoos each represent a different story did not completely work as a linking framework for an anthology of his already written stories, and it is even less successful in the film. The stories here are "The Long Rains" (set on Venus), "The Veldt" and "The Last Night of the World"; only "The Veldt" (two children in the future use a three-dimensional recreational toy, with an African setting, complete with lions, as a means of disposing of their parents) makes a successful transition to the visual medium. The same actors appear in each episode, and clearly the director was aiming at an atmosphere of downbeat enigma and malign destiny, with Rod Steiger as a constantly reincarnated loser.   [JB/PN]

ILLUSTRATION The historical function of art in sf has been to illustrate rather than interpret; this reflects the hard-edged nature of early magazine sf itself, which illustrated technics-dominated society rather than interpreting its *raisons d'être*. As this kind of sf was popular science plus human- or wonder-interest, so the illustrations were there to provide page-interest. When these functional attitudes weakened, sf illustrations became freer, aspiring to illumination rather than diagram. Today their relationship to text is often generic rather than specific.

Before the sf magazines, there is little that can be regarded as pure generic sf illustration, though the art history of that early period of sf publication awaits research. Inspiration was derived on the one hand from black-and-white masters of graphic pun, such as Grandville, Richard ("Dicky") Doyle, and the astonishing Albert ROBIDA, and on the other hand from more "serious" artists, such as Gustave Doré and John Martin. The latter in particular, first artist of the immense, has had great influence. Although Martin died in 1854, his mighty visions were natural material for Hollywood; echoes of them abound, for instance, in the original KING KONG.

The other matter upon which the first generation of sf illustrators could rely was the spate of pictures of scientific and engineering marvels appearing in the press; a later generation turned to NASA handouts. Many drawings in the early GERNSBACK magazines in particular can be traced directly to sawn-down or blown-up versions of the Eiffel Tower and the thermionic valve or tube.

Such illustrations accompanied stories which were often cautionary in nature: scientific experiments could result in catastrophe; interstellar gas and renegade planets were hazards in Earth's path; robots were prone to rape inventors' daughters: but still technology had to go on. The illustrations were diagrams to enforce the thesis, often set over a line or two of the actual text, so that cautious readers could test for accuracy.

Yet the subservient role of the sf artist is by no means the whole story. Even in the most commercial period, it was recognized that the impact of the cover sold the magazine or paperback; care and money went into the cover art in consequence. Some artists worked at their best on covers, not necessarily because the pay was better. Dedication was a more noteworthy characteristic than artistic excellence among this low-salaried breed of men.

Because of printing deadlines, some publishers, particularly those with a "stable" of magazines, commissioned covers before stories. As a result, a writer might be asked to write a tale to fit a picture; this doubtful privilege gave the writer his name on the cover but could also entail a cut in the already stingy rates of payment.

In this way, magazine art developed and became, even if in small compass, a tradition, with names of prolific illustrators like PAUL, FINLAY and EMSH dominating the field. Interior art became increasingly less tied to text, just as text became less tied to technics. It was free to indulge in the pleasantly hazy symbolism of an ORBAN, the immaculacy of a SCHOMBURG, or even the whimsicality of a CARTIER. It was also at liberty to fudge on the detail in which members of the previous generation of illustrators, such as Paul and DOLD, had gloried. Increasingly, the magazine covers symbolized the spirit of the magazine rather than depicting an incident in an actual story; the series of covers Emsh executed for *Gal.* in the early 1960s is a noteworthy example of this.

Increased paper and production costs in the 1940s hit the PULPS hard; as they dwindled, the COMIC BOOK rose in popularity, its simplistic moral issues probably encouraged by the War, where enemy powers could be depicted as unremittingly evil, allies as undilutedly good. The books evolved from comic strips, which already had some history behind them. Harold Foster started the ever-popular *Tarzan* strip in 1929, in the same year that BUCK ROGERS, drawn by Dick CALKINS and written by Phil NOWLAN, appeared on the scene. What Tarzan did for Africa, Buck did for space.

Success bred imitators: the 1930s brought the cave-man *Alley Oop*, a sort of anti-Tarzan (by Vincent Hamlin), *The Phantom* (Lee Falk and Ray Moore), BRICK BRADFORD (Clarence Gray and William Ritt), and the much admired FLASH GORDON, elegantly drawn by Alex RAYMOND. From such superheroes, it was only a step to the king of them all, SUPERMAN.

Superman, by Jerry SIEGEL and Joe SHUSTER, two science fiction fans, began life in a comic book, *Action Comics*, in 1938. It was a success from the start. Like Flash and Buck before him, Superman went into radio and then into films. By 1941, the fortnightly comic-book version reached a circulation of 1,400,000. The day of the superhero had dawned. Wish-fulfilment scooped the pool.

MARVEL COMICS introduced *The Fantastic Four* in 1961; since then Marvel's fabulous but fallible beings, *Spiderman*, *The Incredible Hulk*, *The Silver Surfer*, and the rest of the grotesques, have changed the nature of comics and, on the whole, improved the standard of draughtsmanship in the field. But the most astonishing recent developments have come from France, in particular from the group of artists, of whom Philippe DRUILLET is one, working for the magazine MÉTAL HURLANT. Here, the mood is of brooding unease rather than action; sophisticated surreal effects are achieved without recourse to balloons or commentary.

As the written word affected artwork, so artwork influenced the written word. There was a period in sf when interiors of spaceships were vast, shadowy, and echoing; they came complete with cast-iron doors opening directly on to space and equipped with doorknobs for handles. That was the influence of Calkins's *Buck Rogers*. Raymond's *Flash Gordon* has similar effects, and his line of galactic romance, with proud queens dressed in fur-tipped boots and haughty expressions, and usurping villains lurking behind the arras with axe and ray-gun, is with us yet. The enormous vacuum-vehicles of Christopher Foss spring from VAN VOGT's epics — and will surely inspire future Van Vogts.

Imitation is promoted by systems of tight deadlines and tighter payrolls; whatever comes to hand must be used. Artists, like writers, still borrow heavily from each other. In the jungle world of the pulps, artists moved easily from one genre to another, depending on the corporation employing them. We should be surprised, not that there is so little individuality, but that there is so much. Hubert ROGERS, *ASF*'s chief artist throughout much of the 1940s, produced many covers for other Street & Smith magazines; Frank Kelly FREAS, an *ASF* illustrator of infinite jest, created *Mad Magazine*'s lunatic optimist Alfred E. Neuman ("What, worry, me?").

In the magazines of the early post-

Gernsback period, the mode depends heavily on horror and GOTHIC, perhaps because here was a convention readily to hand, waiting to be adapted. Finlay, LAWRENCE, BOK, LEYDENFROST and Cartier are names that spring to mind. These artists of the macabre secured and kept a great following; Finlay and Bok in particular have become revered since their death. Leydenfrost, son of a Dutch illustrator, produced some of the most imaginative monsters in the business; they are frequently based on insect morphology.

Later sf artists were able to forge an idiom more in tune with the technophile nature of sf. The precept of Frank R. Paul was decisive here. An artist with training as an architect, Paul was possibly Gernsback's most remarkable discovery; this prodigious talent created his own brand of future city, with its sensuously curving lines an exotic amalgam of Byzantium and the local Odeon, owing something to the Art Deco movement. The same patterns are exaggerated in paranoid style by Elliot Dold, who developed an intense poetry of machinery. During this period, WESSO also produced spirited interpretations of mighty cities and machineries, as did MOREY and Orban, but it was the purity of line of SCHNEEMAN and Rogers which best conveyed the aspirations of technocratic culture, where the merely human dwindles in the light of its aseptic artefacts.

Few sf illustrations are memorable in their own right; they come and they go. An exception must be made for Schneeman's idealistic picture of E.E. SMITH's hero, Kimball Kinnison, the Grey Lensman, striding along with two formidable alien allies (ASF Oct. 1939). Together with Rogers' cover for Heinlein's "The Roads Must Roll" (ASF Nov. 1939), it represents a synthesis of that immaculate metal-clad future towards which many thought the world was rolling. Of course it was an illusion: World War II was already raging in Europe. Instead of Rogers, Freas became ASF's most popular artist; he specialized in roughnecks with guns.

ASF was an iconoclastic magazine, aware of its brand-image as the intellectual's sf magazine. The emphasis was on the word, which got things done, not the drawing, which was merely decorative; in consequence, much interior artwork was dull. For vigour, one turned to lesser magazines, to the crowded Herman Vestals in Startling Stories and Planet Stories, or to Rod RUTH in Fantastic Adventures, whose spirited sketches for "Queen of the Panther World" by Berkeley Livingstone (Jul. 1948) retain their power.

After the War, and despite a multiplication of media which includes TV, "microgroove" records, and cheap paperbacks, new sf magazines arose. Of the new 1950s magazines, Gal. has

already been mentioned. Its misty interior illustrations appeared refreshingly contemporary; best-remembered exponents of this style are Ashman, Don Sibley, Dick Francis and the alarming Kossin. Among the names rising to prominence in the 1960s are John SCHOENHERR, Mel Hunter and Jack GAUGHAN. By this time, the magazines had tidied up their typography, imitating their powerful rivals in the paperback industry; it is in paperback books that most of the traditional art is aired nowadays.

With sf motifs pervading certain strata of popular MUSIC, sf and fantasy art has made formidable appearances on record album sleeves. Here the name of Roger DEAN comes immediately to mind; his striking composites of machine, insect, animal and bone have convincing power. Dean and the remarkably fecund Patrick WOODROFFE have both published collections of their own work. So has Karel THOLE, King Surrealist of sf art.

The new professional magazines of the later 1970s rely heavily on old modes of illustration. Vortex leans towards Foss/Dean amalgams. Cosmos Science Fiction and Fantasy has begun with weak fantasy covers. Algol, a semi-professional FANZINE, opts for an Eddie JONES mode. Presumably Isaac Asimov's Science Fiction Magazine can for ever narcissistically run portraits of the eponymous ASIMOV. Galileo does best, with Tom Barber striving towards something fresh. But it is undeniable that innovations are more likely to occur elsewhere. Innovation follows cash flow; movies, TV, and record album covers have adopted, on a wide front, an idiom that virtually began in the magazines. That early work, for many reasons, can never be repeated; for aesthetic reasons, it cannot be ignored. A number of books in the last few years have dealt, in whole or in part, with sf illustration; among them may be mentioned Hier, L'an 2000 (Paris, 1973; as 2000 A.D., Illustrations from the Golden Age of Science Fiction Pulps 1975) by Jacques SADOUL; One Hundred Years of Science Fiction Illustration (1974) by Anthony FREWIN; Science Fiction Art (1975) by Brian ALDISS and A Pictorial History of Science Fiction (1976) by David KYLE.   [BWA]
See also. Entries on the following 55 sf illustrators: George BARR, Earle K. BERGEY, Hannes BOK, Chesley BONESTELL, Howard V. BROWN, Dick CALKINS, Edd CARTIER, Mal DEAN, Roger DEAN, Vincent DI FATE, Leo and Diane DILLON, Elliott DOLD, Philippe DRUILLET, Ed EMSH, Stephen FABIAN, Virgil FINLAY, Christopher FOSS, Frank FRAZETTA, Frank Kelly FREAS, Jack GAUGHAN, Jean GIRAUD, Richard GLYN-JONES, Frank HAMPSON, Eddie JONES, Robert Gibson JONES, Jack KIRBY, Josh KIRBY, Roy G. KRENKEL, Stephen LAWRENCE, Brian LEWIS, A. LEYDENFROST, Leo MOREY, Paul ORBAN, Frank R. PAUL, David PELHAM,

Bruce PENNINGTON, Richard POWERS, Gerald QUINN, Alex RAYMOND, Keith ROBERTS, Albert ROBIDA, Hubert ROGERS, Rod RUTH, John Allen ST JOHN, Charles SCHNEEMAN, John SCHOENHERR, Alex SCHOMBURG, Joe SHUSTER, James STERANKO, Rick STERNBACH, Karel THOLE, Henry R. VAN DONGEN, Edward VALIGURSKY, H.W. WESSO and Patrick WOODROFFE.

IMAGINARY SCIENCE This is extremely common in sf, and not at all the same thing as PSEUDO-SCIENCE, the difference being that the adherent or user of pseudo-science usually believes it to be true, whereas the sf writer who uses imaginary science knows perfectly well that it is untrue.

Sf has often been unfairly criticized for scientific illiteracy, not least by scientists. While it has indeed a fair share of simple errors (see SCIENTIFIC ERRORS), sf commonly uses science of a sort which is at present impossible, for two reasons, neither stemming from ignorance. The first is the belief that what is impossible now may one day become possible. The second is because the imaginary science is essential for plot purposes.

An example of the first category is the common sf device of MATTER TRANSMITTERS. Since all matter can be described in terms of information, and since all information can be transmitted, then one can legitimately theorize that matter transmission (or at least matter reconstruction) does not transgress the laws of nature as we know them, even though the practical problems are so vast as to seem, at present, insuperable. Similarly, SUSPENDED ANIMATION is not possible now, but with advances in CRYONICS it may be, one day soon.

We are primarily concerned here with the second category: the imaginary scientific device which does indeed contradict what we know of the sciences, usually PHYSICS, but which allows the writer a kind of imaginative freedom extremely difficult to obtain otherwise. The four best-known examples are ANTIGRAVITY; FASTER-THAN-LIGHT (or FTL) travel and COMMUNICATION; INVISIBILITY; and TIME TRAVEL, and all are given a detailed examination under those entries.

It is the very skill of the sf writer that worries the scientific purist, for the game is, usually, to produce as plausible-seeming a rationalization for the impossible as the sf author's special arts will allow. Thus James BLISH, in the series which was published as four separate books (1955–62) and as the collection Cities in Flight (coll. 1970), uses a double-talk, which he has derived largely from quantum mechanics, with an air of such bland conviction that a generation of sf readers believes that antigravity is possible; in the same book Blish offers, as a kind of icing on the cake, a not quite so convincing rationale for IMMORTALITY. Similarly H.G. WELLS in The Invisible

Man (**1897**) rattles on about refraction with a perfectly straight face. Blish did not believe in antigravity, nor Wells in invisibility, but their aim was not to mislead us and deepen our ignorance with untruths; Blish was simply in love with an image of cities flying through space, and Wells with an image of a suit and a mask being removed to reveal nothing behind them. In order to achieve their central image, both writers had to invent imaginary devices to clear the way.

Time travel is perhaps the clearest example; the time-travel sub-genre has always been one of sf's most ebulliently creative aspects, and through its use many serious points have been made about HISTORY, EVOLUTION and even METAPHYSICS — all three in the case of the great original, H.G. Wells's *The Time Machine* (**1895**), itself. The puritan who demands that sf should adhere to scientific responsibility by never contravening the possible would in fact be forced to reject what in some respects have been the most intellectually rigorous works of the genre.

A more controversial example of imaginary science, with which sf is riddled, is the use of ESP or PSI POWERS. One's response to this will depend very much on whether or not one believes that there is a conspiracy of scientists to conceal the true facts of the matter; many would regard these themes as in the realm of pseudo rather than imaginary science. Some sf writers, such as Alfred BESTER and James Blish, have used them in exactly the same way as they use imaginary science, as an evocative and useful plot device; other sf writers appear to be propagandizing on their behalf. In SUPERMAN tales especially, the science involved tends to be pseudo rather than imaginary, and perhaps more open to criticism on that account, though this could be regarded as hair-splitting.

Sf writers have been continually inventive in creating imaginary scientific devices, such as the "slow glass" of Bob SHAW's poignant story "Light of Other Days" (**1966**), and occasionally even new sciences. An early example of the latter, and still one of the best, is Alfred JARRY's "pataphysics", the science of imaginary solutions.

Isaac ASIMOV has been especially prolific in creating new sciences, such as POSITRONICS and PSYCHOHISTORY; he has also used such old imaginary-science favourites as miniaturization (*see* GREAT AND SMALL) in *Fantastic Voyage* (**1966**); in *The Gods Themselves* (**1972**) he came up with an "electron pump" that provides us with a limitless supply of electricity (electrons) in return for positrons supplied to an alternate universe; his most absurd *coup* in the imaginary-science line is "thiotimoline", first described in "The Endochronic Properties of Resublimated Thiotimoline" (**1948**), and again in several sequels since. This is, in effect, a time-travelling chemical which

effortlessly reverses cause and effect, described in a parody of the dusty and humourless style of a scientific report. Ursula K. LE GUIN also came up with a spoof science in a spoof-scientific paper in "The Author of the Acacia Seeds and Other Extracts from the *Journal of the Association of Therolinguistics*" (**1974**); therolinguistics is a form of linguistics which should exist if it does not; it is the study of animal languages, and especially their literature; though delightful, it is in a sense only half a spoof, and may have a serious point.

One real science is thus far imaginary, in the sense that it has no subject matter: XENOBIOLOGY.   [PN]

IMAGINARY   VOYAGES   *See* FANTASTIC VOYAGES and PROTO SF.

First issue, Oct. 1950. Cover by Bok.

IMAGINATION   US   DIGEST-size magazine. 63 issues. First released Oct. 1950 by the Clark Publishing Co., ed. Ray PALMER. Early in 1951 it was acquired by William L. HAMLING's Greenleaf Publishing Co., and continued, with Hamling as editor, until Oct. 1958. Beginning as a bi-monthly, it operated a monthly schedule briefly Sep. 1952-Jul. 1955, and then reverted to bi-monthly. Until Jul. 1955 its full title was *Imagination Stories of Science and Fantasy*, and then it became *Imagination Science Fiction*. Hamling followed a policy of including a short novel in every issue, and among his most frequent contributors were Kris NEVILLE and Daniel GALOUYE, both of whom published much of their early work in the magazine. Others were Milton LESSER, Dwight V. SWAIN and, towards the end of the magazine's career, Edmond HAMILTON. The magazine dealt primarily in routine SPACE OPERA, and featured an unusually high number of titles which ended in exclamation marks.   [BS]
Collectors   should   note: Volume numeration was irregular. Vol.1 had two

numbers, Vol.2 had five, Vol.3 had seven, Vol.4 had 11, Vol.5 had 12, Vol.6 had nine, Vols 7 and 8 had six, and Vol.9 had five. There was no issue between Jun. and Sep. '51, Oct. and Dec. '52, Feb. and Apr. '53, and Jul. and Oct. '55, but otherwise schedules were regular.

July 1957. Cover by Malcolm Smith.

IMAGINATIVE TALES US DIGEST-size magazine. 26 issues. A bi-monthly companion to IMAGINATION, it was published by William HAMLING's Greenleaf Publishing Co., Sep. 1954-May 1958. The last three issues, Jul.-Nov. 1958, were published under the title *Space Travel*.

IT began as a fantasy magazine, early issues featuring complete novels in the style of Thorne Smith by Charles F. Myers and Robert BLOCH, but from Sep. 1955 it reverted to a policy identical to that of its companion, featuring only sf, with a short novel heading every issue. Regular writers included Dwight V. SWAIN, Geoff St Reynard (Robert W. Krepps) and Edmond HAMILTON, while the supporting short fiction was principally supplied by the authors constituting the regular stable writing for the Ziff-Davis magazines AMAZING STORIES and FANTASTIC.   [BS]
Collectors should note: Vol.2 had only two numbers, but all other vols had six. *Space Travel* continued the *Imaginative Tales* numeration, beginning with Vol.5 no.4 and ending with Vol.5 no.6. The bi-monthly schedule was completely regular.

I MARRIED A MONSTER FROM OUTER   SPACE   Film   (**1958**). Paramount. Directed by Gene Fowler Jr, starring Tom Tryon, Gloria Talbot and Ken Lynch. Screenplay and story by Louis Vittes. 78 mins. B/w.

Yet another manifestation of the rampant PARANOIA of the 1950s, the film might be called an sf version of *I Married a Communist*. A young woman's husband is taken over and replaced by an alien with the power to change its shape, one of a group whose mission on Earth is to breed with human women in an attempt to replenish their own declining population. But the girl, who has grown suspicious of her "spouse", succeeds in convincing a "real" man of what is happening and he organizes a rescue party. The aliens, impervious to bullets, are destroyed when a pack of Alsatian dogs is set on them. At points in the film, surprisingly, some sympathy for the aliens is deliberately invoked, and in this respect (but no other) it is more interesting than the similar INVASION OF THE BODY SNATCHERS. Gene Fowler, a former editor for Fritz Lang, builds up the suspense effectively. [JB/PN]

IMMORTAL, THE Made-for-TV film (1969). Paramount/ABC-TV. Directed by Joseph Sargent, starring Christopher George, Carol Lynley, Barry Sullivan, Ralph Bellamy and Jessica Walter. Teleplay by Robert Specht, based on the novel *The Immortals* (1962) by James GUNN. 75 mins. Colour.

A man is discovered to have blood containing remarkable properties, rendering him immune to disease and the ageing process. His sick and ageing employer, a millionaire, promptly kidnaps him, intending to keep him locked up as a human fountain of youth, but he escapes and goes in search of his long-lost brother, who may have the same type of blood. The millionaire pursues him, and the film reverts to a typical chase formula. It proved popular with audiences, however, and was turned into a series the following year, again starring Christopher George; it lasted only 13 episodes. The TV series was novelized by James Gunn as *The Immortal* (1970). [JB]

IMMORTALITY Immortality (which term, for the purposes of this section, shall be taken to include extreme longevity) has always been one of the basic motifs in speculative and religious thought. The idea appears to be universal, both in legend and in factual belief. The elixir of life and the fountain of youth are the hypothetical goals of classic intellectual and exploratory quests. Freud claimed that every man is unconsciously convinced of his own immortality. Inevitably, we find in imaginative literature a superabundance of stories dealing with the immortal man or woman in all his or her characteristic roles.

One thing immediately noticeable about this rich literary tradition, especially in its 18th- and 19th-century manifestations — e.g. the Struldbruggs in Jonathan SWIFT's *Gulliver's Travels* (1726; rev. 1735), Charles MATURIN's *Melmoth the Wanderer* (1820), Honoré de BALZAC's "The Elixir of Life" (1830), Eugène Sue's *Le juif errant* (1844–5 France; trans. as *The Wandering Jew* 1844–5), W. Clark RUSSELL's *The Death Ship* (1888), H. Rider HAGGARD's *She*

(1887) and Harrison Ainsworth's *Auriol* (1898) — is that the idea of immortality is treated with some contempt. It is represented as a curse, its corollaries misery and anguish. These are cautionary tales, warning against the emptiness of dreams (though a cynic might observe that they follow the pattern described in the fable of the fox and the grapes). They are, of course, all fantasies, and one might expect a different view from those writers who were prepared to assume that science might make immortality a reality. In fact, opinions differed sharply. In a foreword to the published version of his play *The Makropoulos Secret* (1925) Karel ČAPEK took pains to point out that his work had been in no way influenced by George Bernard SHAW's *Back to Methuselah* (1921), and that the proof of this was that Shaw actually approved of the idea while he, Čapek, considered that it would be an unmitigated curse. This polarization of opinion has always been evident in sf. In some stories immortality is the beginning of limitless opportunity, in others it represents the ultimate stagnation and the end of innovation and change. We find the former view in the mildly erotic immortality trilogy by George Sylvester VIERECK and Paul ELDRIDGE (1928–32), in such early pulp stories as "The Jameson Satellite" (1931) by Neil R. JONES and Laurence MANNING's *The Man Who Awoke* (1933; fix-up 1975); and the latter in David H. KELLER's "Life Everlasting" (1934) and John R. PIERCE's "Invariant" (1944). More recently, the former attitude is implicit in J.T. McINTOSH's "Live For Ever" (1954) and James BLISH's "At Death's End" (1954), while the latter is seen in Damon KNIGHT's "World Without Children" (1951), Frederik POHL's *Drunkard's Walk* (1960) and Brian ALDISS's "The Worm That Flies" (1968). It is not easy to assess the majority without actually taking census, but if the intensity of the reaction can be trusted then the second viewpoint appears dominant. There is, however, a general acceptance of the fact that the *desire* for immortality remains very powerful, and that it is an infallible lure or bribe. This is dramatized in Jack VANCE's *To Live Forever* (1956), James GUNN's *The Immortals* (1955–60; fix-up 1962), Norman SPINRAD's *Bug Jack Barron* (1969), Thomas N. SCORTIA's "The Weariest River" (1973) and Bob SHAW's *One Million Tomorrows* (1970), in which the price many are prepared to pay is impotence. Outside genre sf the dominance of Čapek's view is clear. It is advanced fiercely by Aldous HUXLEY's elaborate sick joke *After Many a Summer Dies the Swan* (1939; vt *After Many a Summer* UK), more carefully by VERCORS in *The Insurgents* (1957) and ironically in Anders BODELSEN's *Freezing Down* (1971; vt *Freezing Point*). Within the genre, though, there have been numerous influential books featuring immortal

heroes, including A.E. VAN VOGT's *The Weapon Makers* (1943; 1952), Wilson TUCKER's *The Time Masters* (1953; rev. 1971), Clifford D. SIMAK's *Way Station* (1963), Roger ZELAZNY's *This Immortal* (1966) and Robert HEINLEIN's *Time Enough For Love* (1973). However, there has been no major attempt even within the genre to analyse the experience of limitless opportunity in immortality which does not ultimately tend to the opinion that boredom and sterility must set in; the most comprehensive study is probably Raymond Z. GALLUN's *The Eden Cycle* (1974), while Michael MOORCOCK's "Dancers at the End of Time" novel and story sequence (1972–6) satirizes the attempt by immortals to maintain the novelty of experience. Ultimately, the most carefully thought-out attitudes tend to be ambivalent, contrasting the power of the desire with the achievement of the reality, and this ambivalence is perhaps best represented by Robert SILVERBERG's "Born With the Dead" (1974), although Damon Knight's "Dio" (1957) examines the situation of a lone mortal in a world of immortals with some delicacy.

The prospect of immortality suggested by research into CRYONICS or SUSPENDED ANIMATION has inspired a good deal of discussion — as in two non-fiction books, R.C.W. Ettinger's *The Prospect of Immortality* (1964) and Alan Harrington's *The Immortalist* (1969) — and has influenced a good deal of recent sf. The notion is, however, really a sidetrack which should be considered independently; it hardly touches on the basic issue of the infinite prolongation of conscious existence and its benefits and terrors. [BS]

See also: MEDICINE; GODS AND DEMONS; HIVE-MINDS; RELIGION; SUPERMAN.

IMPULSE *See* SCIENCE FANTASY.

INCREDIBLE HULK, THE Made-for-TV film (1977). Universal/CBS-TV. Written, produced and directed by Kenneth Johnson, starring Bill Bixby, Susan Sullivan, Jack Colvin, Lou Ferrigno and Susan Batson. 120 mins.

This was a pilot episode for a series based on the MARVEL COMICS character of the same name. It concerns a scientist (Bill Bixby, star of the 1963 comedy TV series MY FAVOURITE MARTIAN) who subjects himself to an overdose of gamma radiation and finds himself turning into a seven-foot, green muscle-man. The current trend away from violence on TV has resulted perhaps in too much caution; the Hulk is a pallid and lacklustre character compared to his frenzied comic-book counterpart. A series has been developed from the pilot. [JB]

INCREDIBLE SHRINKING MAN, THE Film (1957). Universal. Directed by Jack ARNOLD, starring Grant Williams, Randy Stuart and April Kent. Screenplay

THE INCREDIBLE SHRINKING MAN, played by Grant Williams, menaced by his own cat.

by Richard MATHESON, based on his own novel. 81 mins. B/w.

This is one of the classic sf films of the 1950s. The basic premise is unscientific, but that does not detract from the power of this story about a man who becomes contaminated by radioactive fall-out and starts to shrink. What was once safe and comforting to him becomes increasingly threatening as he continues to diminish. His cat becomes a monster and the prosaic confines of his own basement take on the characteristics of a nightmare landscape. Eventually he disappears completely. The mature script by Matheson is intelligently handled by Arnold. Clifford Stine's special effects are excellent. [JB]

INFINITY Original anthology series ed. Robert HOSKINS, published by Lancer Books, and presented as a lineal descendant of INFINITY SCIENCE FICTION (whose editor, Larry T. SHAW, was also connected with Lancer). It was a competent, but not outstanding series; regular contributors included Poul ANDERSON, Barry MALZBERG and Robert SILVERBERG. *Infinity One* (anth. **1970**) reprinted Arthur C. CLARKE's "The Star" (1955) from the first issue of its spiritual ancestor. Later volumes were *Infinity Two* (anth. **1971**), *Infinity Three* (anth. **1972**), *Infinity Four* (anth. **1972**) and *Infinity Five* (anth. **1973**). The series was terminated on the bankruptcy of the publisher. [MJE]

INFINITY SCIENCE FICTION US DIGEST-size magazine. 20 issues, Nov. 1955-Nov. 1958, published by Royal Publications; ed. Larry T. SHAW. *ISF* was one of the most interesting of the flood of new sf magazines in the early 1950s. Its first issue featured Arthur C. CLARKE's HUGO-winning story "The Star", and the magazine went on to publish other good stories by such authors as Isaac ASIMOV,

June 1957. Cover by Ed Emsh.

James BLISH, Algis BUDRYS, Damon KNIGHT and C.M. KORNBLUTH. Robert SILVERBERG was also a regular — sometimes prolific — contributor; the last issue contained book reviews by him and also three of his stories (including "Ozymandias", published under the name Ivar JORGENSON). Damon Knight had earlier been *ISF*'s regular critic; much of the material in *In Search of Wonder* (**1956**; rev. 1967) originated in *ISF*. After the first issue, all the covers were painted by EMSH. The original anthology series INFINITY described itself as the "lineal descendant" of *ISF*. [MJE] **Collectors should note:** Although the schedule was irregular, four months between some issues, others monthly, the volume numeration was quite regular: three vols of six numbers followed by Vol.4 which had two.

INGHAM, FREDERICK See Edward Everett HALE.

INGREY, DEREK (? –). British writer, whose post-HOLOCAUST sf novel, *Pig on a Lead* (**1963**), describes the dead-ended life of the last surviving humans in England, two men and a boy, from the viewpoint of the boy. [JC]

INNER SPACE In sf TERMINOLOGY, used as an antonym to outer space. J.G. BALLARD coined the term in 1962, feeling that sf might just as usefully explore happenings taking place in the human mind as those in space. As he regularly demonstrated in his stories, such events could be equally exotic. The term is now in common use, especially by, and in relation to, NEW WAVE writers. [PN]

INSIDE (American FANZINE.) *See* RIVERSIDE QUARTERLY.

INTELLIGENCE Much sf refers to intelligence, but a surprisingly small amount gives a good idea of what the workings of a superior or different intelligence would feel like or even look like. In many stories of abnormally intelligent supermen or mutants we have to take the intelligence on trust; such intelligences were favourites with A.E. VAN VOGT, but their workings are often less than transparent to the reader, as is the case with the hero of his *The World of Ā* (1945 *ASF*; rev. **1948**; rev. 1970; vt *The World of Null-A*), whose blinding leaps of non-Aristotelean logic are frequently incomprehensible, and on the face of it rather stupid.

Intelligence is necessarily one of the issues discussed in the entries on ANTI-INTELLECTUALISM IN SF, CYBERNETICS, MUTANTS and SUPERMAN. Machine intelligence is discussed under COMPUTERS and ROBOTS. Paranormal powers of the mind are discussed under ESP and PSI POWERS. The entry below will be restricted to those stories in which the emphasis is on the actual workings of intelligence in living beings.

The first important intelligence story in sf is *The Hampdenshire Wonder* (**1911**; vt *The Wonder* USA) by J.D. BERESFORD, in which the focus of interest is on the feelings of a super-intelligent child growing up in a world of what seem to him subnormals. A colder and harsher reworking of the same theme was twice undertaken by Olaf STAPLEDON, in *Odd John* (**1935**), about an abnormally intelligent human whose spiritual powers are also highly developed, and in *Sirius* (**1944**), about an intelligent dog. In some ways the latter work is the more successful, perhaps because of the recurrent problem in stories of this kind of finding a form of language appropriate to describing an experience which by its very nature cannot be fully comprehended by the reader — and presumably the writer is only guessing at it. Describing to someone with an IQ of 120 what it might feel like to have an IQ of, say, 300, is probably more difficult than describing colour to a blind man, especially when the describer may himself be assumed to be blind. One way round the problem, in stories of increased intelligence, is to begin with an animal or a moron, so that his higher intelligence is not hopelessly out of reach of our own. This strategy has been adopted in several genre sf stories, of which the two best known are *Brain Wave* (**1954**) by Poul ANDERSON and "Flowers for Algernon" (1959) by Daniel KEYES, later much expanded as *Flowers for Algernon* (**1966**). The latter, which was filmed as CHARLY (1968), is a moving story of intelligence artificially induced in a moron, largely told through his diaries; sadly, the process is only temporary, and while the hero and the reader are given a glimpse, surprisingly convincing, of what genius might feel like, the gates of the golden city are soon barred, and the story ends with an almost intolerable feeling of loss in the reader, and an itching discomfort in the subnormal mind of the hero.

An episodic series of stories about intelligent dogs is Clifford D. SIMAK's *City* (1944–51 var. mags; fix-up **1952**), but here the emphasis is not on the acquisition of intelligence *per se* in a tale which focuses, plangently, on the canine inheritance of the Earth in Man's absence.

Super-intelligence is often pictured as going along with what seems, to ordinary humans, a cold indifference and a casual amorality, perhaps out of a sense of sour grapes on the writers' parts. We are not altogether cheerful at the thought of being relegated to a minor place in the evolutionary scheme, and as evolution is traditionally carried out by a "nature red in tooth and claw", we half expect that a race of geniuses would treat us cruelly. A prototype of this kind of story is John TAINE's *Seeds of Life* (1931 *AMZ*; **1951**), in which an accident with radiation transforms a surly laboratory technician into a cruel, glowing supermind in the body of an Adonis; the sense we are given of the workings of his mind is vivid enough to transcend the pulp crankiness of the story's ideas of evolution. Here, too, the growth of intelligence is reversible.

Many adults are ready enough anyway to see children as essentially alien creatures, and a flourishing sub-genre has been the story of the superchild (*see* CHILDREN IN SF), often turning on his relationship with his parents or guardians. Henry KUTTNER reverted to this theme several times, as in "Mimsy Were the Borogoves" (1943, as by Lewis Padgett) in which a teaching machine from the future has frightening effects on children, and "When the Bough Breaks" (1944, as by Lewis Padgett) in which a peculiarly nauseating superbaby gives his parents a hard time. "Star Bright" (1952) by Mark CLIFTON is a typically pulp version of the intelligence theme, in which the manifestations of high intelligence in children, which is where the real interest of the story might have lain, rapidly develop into what are in effect magical powers. The two most thoughtful and mature novels in this sub-genre are *Children of the Atom* (1948–50 *ASF*; fix-up **1953**) by Wilmar H. SHIRAS, which incorporates the classic story "In Hiding", in which an extremely intelligent boy attempts, in self protection, to behave just like any other child, and is discovered, and *The Fourth "R"* (**1959**; vt *The Brain Machine*) by George O. SMITH, in which the intelligence of a five-year-old has been trained artificially by a machine which reinforces learning mechanisms in the brain. Both books deal sensitively with the contrast between intellectual maturity and emotional immaturity, and both are surprisingly plausible in their scenarios for the ways in which super-intelligence might show itself in action.

Two other relevant stories from the 1950s are C.M. KORNBLUTH's "The Marching Morons" (1951), a vividly unpleasant story of a future which has become polarized between morons and geniuses, the former in much greater numbers because the middle classes know more about contraception (an interesting not-very-hidden assumption here), and *The Black Cloud* (**1957**) by Fred HOYLE, in which a cloud-intelligence in space attempts to communicate with mankind, injuring several men whose brains are not big enough to absorb all the new data.

This brings us to the general topic of intelligence in ALIENS. A number of stories have hinged on the COLONIZATION OF OTHER WORLDS under an imagined future law which states that the worlds of intelligent beings must either be left alone or be treated with great care. Thus the measurement of alien intelligence becomes a question of politics. H. Beam PIPER's *Little Fuzzy* (**1962**) is a story of this kind, as is Joseph GREEN's *Conscience Interplanetary* (1965–71 var. mags; fix-up **1972**), though Green does not really develop the potentialities of the theme. Perhaps the most interesting novel about surveying the nature of alien life and intelligence is Naomi MITCHISON's thoughtful and vivacious *Memoirs of a Spacewoman* (**1962**).

Other recent variations on the intelligence theme are Olof JOHANNESSON's *The Tale of the Big Computer* (**1966** Sweden; trans. **1968**; vt *The Great Computer, a Vision* UK), which is actually a history of intelligence, written in the future, seeing human intelligence as an evolutionary step towards machine intelligence; "The Planners" (1968) by Kate WILHELM, about the acceleration of the genetic transmission of intelligence in apes; *The Papers of Andrew Melmoth* (**1960**) by Hugh Sykes DAVIES, about the evolution of intelligence in rats, a quite sophisticated variation on a popular theme; "Eurema's Dam" (1972) by R.A. LAFFERTY, about an incredibly stupid genius; the last story is one of a long line of genre sf yarns about *idiots savants* who construct various marvellous machines and theories without having the least idea about what they are doing. Oscar ROSSITER's *Tetrasomy 2* (**1974**) is a black comedy about a young doctor in whom a sudden acceleration of intelligence is catalysed by a bed-ridden and vegetable-like superbeing; the doctor's inability to use his improved mind with any social *sang froid* poses a problem not generally considered in this type of story.

The major single work of recent years on the evolution of intelligence is Thomas M. DISCH's *Camp Concentration* (**1968**), a highly structured novel which describes, through a series of recurrent images and thematic leitmotivs, an experiment in drug-induced raising of intelligence, among deserters and conscientious objectors, in a prose whose increasing richness and difficulty reflect the ever increasing intelligence of the narrator. The book, which evokes every conceivable variant of the Faust theme, is a *tour de force*, both poignant and ironic.

Two sf novelists who have in effect devoted their entire careers to date in speculating on the nature of intelligence, and the various directions in which it may evolve, are Frank HERBERT and Ian WATSON. Both are heavily committed to the possibility of some form of transcendent intelligence. In Herbert's work the theme is seen most clearly in the "Dune" trilogy and *The Dosadi Experiment* (**1977**), though it appears in all his other novels without exception. As with Van Vogt, however, it is not always clear exactly how his "other" intelligences operate. With Herbert, much depends on enigmatic hints and clues, as if he knows more than he's telling; this is reflected in his plots which combine abstruse metaphysical speculation with conspiratorial, cloak-and-dagger manipulations in a sometimes confusing way. None the less, Herbert has at times evoked the *difference* of evolved intelligences with great feeling.

Where Herbert hints, Ian Watson analyses and chips patiently away at his recurrent theme, approaching it from a slightly different angle in each of his novels (in English) up to 1978. Unlike the sf writers who seem to fear the thought of a transcendent intelligence, Watson desires it, while recognizing how such an evolution may be quite alien to our present selves. Watson, more than any other sf writer, is intent on analysing how the mind works, and how it could be streamlined or redirected, bringing to bear an impressive arsenal of analytic tools extracted from CYBERNETICS, ANTHROPOLOGY, LINGUISTICS, PSYCHOLOGY, semiotics and neurology. Like Herbert, he is ready to tackle ambitious projects, and in particular has attempted to evoke, with partial success, the feeling of a supermind whose processes are more juxtapositional, lateral, analogizing and synthesizing than sequential in the traditional mode of human logic. Examples can be found in *The Embedding* (**1973**), *The Martian Inca* (**1977**) and *Alien Embassy* (**1977**).

The question of intelligence-testing comes up in many UTOPIAS and DYSTOPIAS, and is analysed interestingly in "Intelligence Testing in Utopia" by Carolyn H. Rhodes in EXTRAPOLATION, Dec. 1971. Among the works she discusses in which this theme is central are *The Messiah of the Cylinder* (**1917**; vt *The Apostle of the Cylinder*) by Victor ROUSSEAU, *Player Piano* (**1952**; vt *Utopia 14*) by Kurt VONNEGUT Jr, *The Rise of the Meritocracy* (**1958**) by Michael YOUNG, *The Child Buyer* (**1960**) by John HERSEY and *World out of Mind* (**1953**) by J.T. MCINTOSH. [PN]

INTERNATIONAL FANTASY AWARDS British awards, made annually, 1951–7, missing 1956. The idea came from four British enthusiasts, including John Beynon Harris (John WYNDHAM). They were presented to the authors of the best fantasy or sf book of the year, with a second category for the best non-fiction book likely to be of interest to sf readers. The non-fiction class was dropped after 1953. Winners were selected by a panel of prominent sf personalities; from 1952 the panel was international. The award took the form of a trophy. Once the HUGO awards were successfully launched, some of the *raison d'être* for the IFAs was gone, but while they lasted they were given to some excellent and imaginatively chosen works, most of which would have had almost no chance of winning any of the major American awards. The first award was presented at the 1951 British sf CONVENTION. [PN/CL]
1951
Fiction: George R. STEWART, *Earth Abides*
Non-fiction: Willy LEY and Chesley BONESTELL, *The Conquest of Space*
1952
Fiction: John COLLIER, *Fancies and Goodnights*
Non-fiction: Arthur C. CLARKE, *The Exploration of Space*
1953
Fiction: Clifford D. SIMAK, *City*
Non-fiction: Willy Ley and L. Sprague DE CAMP, *Lands Beyond*
1954
Theodore STURGEON, *More than Human*
1955
Edgar PANGBORN, *A Mirror for Observers*
1957
J.R.R. TOLKIEN, *Lord of the Rings*

INTERNATIONAL SCIENCE FICTION US DIGEST-size magazine. Two issues, Nov. 1967 and Jun. 1968, published by Galaxy Publishing Corp.; ed. Frederik POHL. The interesting idea of reprinting stories from all over the world, including RUSSIA, sadly but unsurprisingly met with no success. [FHP]

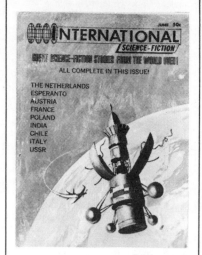

Second issue. Cover by Jack Gaughan.

INTERNATIONAL STORYTELLER *See* STORYTELLER.

INVADERS, THE Television series (1967–8). A Quinn-Martin Production for ABC TV, created by Larry Cohen. Producer: Alan Armer; executive producer: Quinn Martin. Writers on the series included Anthony Wilson, Dan Ullman, Robert Sherman, John W. Bloch, Jerry SOHL and Robert Collins. Directors included Joseph Sargent, Paul Wendkos, David W. Rintels and William Hale. A total of 43 episodes were produced, each 50 mins long, in colour.

Roy Thinnes starred as a man who has witnessed a landing on Earth by aliens in a FLYING SAUCER but is unable to get anyone else to believe his story. The aliens are trying to infiltrate Earth to take it over, as their own planet is doomed; able to take on human form, they can be distinguished only by the stiffness of their little fingers. As they evaporate when killed, evidence of their existence is hard to find. The rigid formula of the series — in each episode the hero would discover and foil a new alien plot, but remain unable to persuade the authorities of the threat — meant that there was little variation in the stories, and the series was cancelled after the second season. Perhaps the programme came too late — it belonged, in spirit, to the PARANOIA formula which was the sf version of the communist spy scares of the 1950s, as in Robert HEINLEIN's *The Puppet Masters* (**1951**) and the films INVASION OF THE BODY SNATCHERS (1956) and I MARRIED A MONSTER FROM OUTER SPACE.

Two collections of stories based on the series, written by Keith LAUMER, are *The Invaders* (coll. **1967**; vt *The Meteor Men* UK as by Anthony LeBaron) and *Enemies from Beyond* (**1967**). Another book based on the series was *The Halo Highway* (**1967**; vt *Army of the Undead* USA) by Rafe BERNARD. [JB/PN]

INVADERS FROM MARS Film (1953). National Pictures Corp./20th Century-Fox. Directed by William Cameron Menzies, starring Helena Carter, Arthur Franz, Jimmy Hunt and Leif Erickson. Screenplay by Richard Blake. 78 mins. Colour.

This is a curiously PARANOID film by the man who directed THINGS TO COME. Through a small boy's eyes we see aliens from a flying saucer take over the minds of everyone in a town, beginning with the boy's own parents. The army moves in, there is an underground battle and the aliens are defeated. Then the boy wakes up and realizes that it was all a dream ... but then he once again sees the flying saucer land on the hill behind his house. (This last sequence was cut from the British prints.)

Although the film is cheaply made, Menzies has managed, by using mildly expressionistic sets, and a camera placed to give us a child's-eye view, to produce a powerful sf metaphor for the loneliness and alienation of a child whose world seems subtly wrong. The image of human bodies concealing incomprehensible and menacing alien motives was an important one in American sf cinema, especially during the 1950s communist-spy phobias. [JB/PN]

INVASION Sf invasion stories tend to parallel historical experience: they are often distorted versions of actual events or commonly held fears. G.T. CHESNEY's tale of a German invasion of Britain, *The Battle of Dorking* (**1871**), and the many future-WAR stories which emulated it, have their roots in the experience of the Franco-Prussian war and the "scramble for empire" in Africa and elsewhere. In the late 19th century a new sense of the globe as a finite territory subject to Malthusian pressures led to such myths as that expressed by M.P. SHIEL in his novel *The Yellow Danger* (**1898**) about a Chinese invasion of the West. Such alarmist military fantasies have persisted throughout the 20th century — the German invasion of England crops up again in *The Invasion of 1910* (**1906**) by William LE QUEUX and *When William Came* (**1913**) by H.H. Munro (SAKI); and the Asian invasion of America features in Robert A. HEINLEIN's *Sixth Column* (1941 *ASF*; **1949**; vt *The Day After Tomorrow*) and C.M. KORNBLUTH's *Not This August* (**1955**; vt *Christmas Eve* UK).

The first story of invasion by ALIENS is probably the London-published Australian novel *The Germ Growers* (**1892**) by Robert POTTER; space-dwellers able to assume the form of men culture bacteria in widely dispersed locations on Earth as part of their invasion plan. It is difficult to gauge the impression of this now forgotten novel; it was probably not widely read. It was H.G. WELLS who is usually credited with raising the whole imaginative pitch of the future-war story in *The War of the Worlds* (**1898**). Here,

The archetypal symbols of sf INVASION are the Martian fighting machines from H.G. Wells's *The War of the Worlds*; this is taken from the first US edition of 1898.

by an ironic inversion, the heart of the British Empire — London and the Home Counties — is subjected to the sort of imperialist invasion which, say, the natives of Tasmania suffered. Wells's Martians are the archetypal Bug-Eyed Monsters (BEMs) which have featured in vulgar sf invasion stories ever since. In particular, they have loomed large in sf in the CINEMA (THE WAR OF THE WORLDS was itself filmed, quite successfully, by Byron HASKIN in 1953) and in the PULP sf of the 1920s and '30s, which contained many invasions by such monstrosities as giant insects, robots and dinosaurs, most of which are stale variants of Wells's ideas. Edgar Rice BURROUGHS' *The Moon Maid* (1926) concerns the conquest of Earth by semi-human creatures from the Moon's interior. The invasion serves no purpose other than to provide the author with unlimited opportunity for derring-do. A more serious emulation of Wells was Olaf STAPLEDON's *Last and First Men* (1930), which contains among other things an invasion from Mars which nearly succeeds in exterminating humanity. (Incidentally, in the vast majority of invasion stories mankind survives, and the invaders are rebuffed; thus they do not necessarily constitute a pessimistic subcategory of sf.) Karel ČAPEK's *War With the Newts* (1936; trans. 1937), not so much an invasion story as a "takeover" story, also owed something to Wells and was intended as a comment on the rise of the Nazis.

Since the Second World War, invasion stories have taken many interesting forms: (1) The benign invasion, which usually results in some form of transcendence for humanity, as in Arthur C. CLARKE's *Childhood's End* (1953); Algis BUDRYS's "Silent Brother" (1956); or (in ironic form) Thomas M. DISCH's "Invaded By Love" (1966). (2) The sinister invasion, a product of the era of McCarthyism and communist witch-hunts, usually involving telepathic control and/or aliens who are hard to distinguish from human beings, as in Heinlein's *The Puppet Masters* (1951);

Chad OLIVER's *Shadows in the Sun* (1954); Jack FINNEY's *The Body Snatchers* (1955), successfully filmed by Don Siegel as INVASION OF THE BODY SNATCHERS (1956); Eric Frank RUSSELL's *Three to Conquer* (1955); Clifford D. SIMAK's *They Walked Like Men* (1961); and Frank Belknap LONG's *Lest Earth Be Conquered* (1966). (3) The comic invasion, in which the Earth is overrun by little green men, beautiful girls, etc., as in Fredric BROWN's *Martians Go Home* (1955); Richard WILSON's *The Girls from Planet 5* (1955); and Mark CLIFTON's *When They Come from Space* (1962). (4) The old-fashioned invasion, which continues to rely on variants of the BEM, as in John WYNDHAM's *The Day of the Triffids* (1951) and *The Kraken Wakes* (1953; vt *Out of the Deeps* USA); Keith ROBERTS's *The Furies* (1966); and Simak's *Our Children's Children* (1974). One might mention here, as a very minor sub-type, the nostalgic invasion, which leans heavily on Wells, as in Manly Wade WELLMAN and Wade Wellman's *Sherlock Holmes's War of the Worlds* (1969–75 *FSF*; fix-up **1975**); and Christopher PRIEST's *The Space Machine* (1976). (5) The children's invasion, an intriguing variant in which the aliens are identified with human children, as in Ray BRADBURY's "Zero Hour" (1947); Edgar PANGBORN's *A Mirror for Observers* (1954); Wyndham's *The Midwich Cuckoos* (1957); and, again, Clarke's *Childhood's End* (1953). (6) The elegiac invasion, set in the distant future and concerning humanity's struggle to reassert itself long after the invasion has taken place, as in Ursula K. LE GUIN's *City of Illusions* (1967); Robert SILVERBERG's *Nightwings* (1969); and M. John HARRISON's "London Melancholy" (1969). (7) The apocalyptic/grotesque invasion, usually symbolic and pessimistic, as in William BURROUGHS' novels involving the "Nova Mob" and "viral takeover", e.g. *Nova Express* (1964); or Disch's *The Genocides* (1965), in which humans are reduced to the status of caterpillars in a galactic cabbage-patch. (They effectively become mice in the walls in *Of Men and Monsters*, **1968**, by William TENN, which was based on "The Men in the Walls", *Gal.* 1963.) (8) The zany or offbeat invasion, which takes unpredictable forms, as in Brown's "The Waveries" (1945), in which electrical creatures usurp our air-waves; or Kornbluth's "The Silly Season" (1950), in which it turns out that the UFO scares have been a deliberate ploy to distract our attention. (9) The absorbed invasion, where the invaders join the invaded populace, as in two stories by Eric Frank Russell, "Late Night Final" (1948) and "And Then There Were None" (1951) (10) The defeated-by-the-few invasion, where massive military strength is outwitted by the cunning of a few humans, or one only in the case of A.E. van VOGT's "The Monster" (1948). A novel-length example is *Sleeping Planet* (1965) by William R. BURKETT; and the reverse situation, where the invading force consists of a solitary human, is found in *Wasp* (1957), again by Eric Frank Russell. This sub-genre was extremely popular in *ASF*. It was the policy of John W. CAMPBELL, *ASF*'s editor, to show human ingenuity triumphing inevitably over all things alien.

The list could be endlessly elaborated. Clearly, invasions, whatever their form, remain a potent theme in sf.   [DP]
See also: ALIENS; DISASTER; FLYING SAUCERS; PARANOIA; WEAPONS.

INVASION Film (1966). Merton Park/ AIP. Directed by Alan Bridges, starring Edward Judd, Valerie Gearson, Yoko Tani and Lyndon Brook. Screenplay by Roger Marshall, based on a story by Robert Holmes. 82 mins. Colour.

This small-scale but interesting British film tells of a female alien who crash-lands on Earth and is taken to a country hospital. Other aliens then arrive and demand that the girl be handed over to them, and when their request is refused they place an impenetrable force field around the hospital. We learn that the girl is a criminal on the run and that the other aliens are members of an extraterrestrial police force. Alan Bridges successfully creates an atmosphere of strangeness and the special effects simulating the force field are impressive.   [JB]

INVASION OF THE BODY SNATCHERS Film (1955). Allied Artists. Directed by Don Siegel, starring Kevin McCarthy, Dana Wynter, Carolyn Jones and King Donovan. Screenplay by Daniel Mainwaring and Sam Peckinpah (uncredited), based on the novel *The Body Snatchers* (1955) by Jack FINNEY. 80 mins. B/w.

PARANOIA was the dominant theme running through much of the sf cinema of the 1950s, and nowhere was it better realized than in this subtle and sophisticated movie, directed by B-film veteran Siegel, about pods from outer space which turn into replicas of human beings, replacing the originals in the process. Whether the film reflects right-wing or left-wing paranoia is open to argument. The original downbeat ending, in which the pods were victorious, was diluted by the later addition of an epilogue showing the authorities discovering the existence of the pods and making plans to destroy them. The film has received extraordinarily high praise over the years. *Hal in the Classroom: Science Fiction Films* (1974) ed. Ralph J. Amelio, and *Focus on the Science Fiction Film* (1972) ed. William Johnson, both include articles about it. It is possibly the most discussed B-grade movie in the history of American film.

A remake of this film is currently in production, from Solo Films, directed by Phil Kaufman, starring Donald Sutherland, Brooke Adams and Leonard Nimoy.   [JB/PN]

INVENTION See DISCOVERY AND INVENTION; MACHINES; SCIENTISTS; TECHNOLOGY.

INVISIBILITY The fantasy of making oneself invisible is a common childhood daydream, offering as it does infinite potential for undetected mischief and unlimited opportunity for the practical joker. As with all common daydreams, literary treatments of the theme tend to be cautionary tales. No good comes of being invisible in Jack LONDON's "The Shadow and the Flash" (1903), Edward Page MITCHELL's "The Crystal Man" (1881) or

H.G. WELLS's *The Invisible Man* (1897), though Wells also wrote a straight-forward daydream version in "The New Accelerator" (1901) and his contemporary C. Howard HINTON also took a positive view in his short novel "Stella", the title story of *Stella* (coll. 1895). Much more common than stories of *being* invisible, however, are stories of confrontation with invisible adversaries. These are, of course, the easiest way in which feelings of fear and insecurity with no immediate and obvious cause can be symbolized. Legend is replete with invisible monsters and demons, and there is a series of literary versions of the theme; they move gradually across the borderland between supernatural fantasy and sf: Fitz-James O'BRIEN's "What Was It?" (1859); Ambrose BIERCE's "The Damned Thing" (1893); Guy de Maupassant's "The Horla" (1887); H.P. LOVECRAFT's "The Dunwich Horror" (1929); George Allan ENGLAND's "The Thing from Outside" (1923); Edmond HAMILTON's "The Monster-God of Mamurth" (1926) and Victor ROUSSEAU's *The Sea Demons* (1925, as by H.M. Egbert).

Invisible aliens almost free from supernatural overtones are featured in Eric Frank RUSSELL's *Sinister Barrier* (1939; 1943; rev. 1948) and Murray LEINSTER's *War With the Gizmos* (1958). R.C. SHERRIFF exploited the menace aspect of the invisible man in his script for the classic film version (1933) of Wells's novel (*see* THE INVISIBLE MAN); Philip WYLIE's *The Murderer Invisible* (1931) is a mad scientist/invisible menace story. The three TV series (*see* THE INVISIBLE MAN) featuring invisible men, however, abandoned the menace aspect for the straightforward daydream version, making their heroes invisible crime-fighters and secret agents. Not all invisible fighters merely as light entertainment, however; the invisible, manned bomb-carrier in "For Love" (1962) by Algis BUDRYS plays a darkly symbolic role in one of the most horrific stories of genre sf.

Modern sf has had little to do with either the daydream or the nightmare versions of the invisibility theme, but there is a remarkable group of stories in which invisibility becomes a metaphor for alienation. In Damon KNIGHT's "The Country of the Kind" (1956) and Robert SILVERBERG's "To See the Invisible Man" (1963) criminals are "exiled" from society because people simply refuse to see them, and they suffer agonies of loneliness. A similar theme was broached by Fritz LEIBER in *The Sinful Ones* (1953; vt abridged *You're All Alone*). A more recent, but far less effective variant on this theme is offered in Gardner R. DOZOIS's "The Visible Man" (1975), in which it is other people that become invisible from the criminal's viewpoint. A parallel group of stories has people obsessed with the idea that they are losing their grip on

The distraught hero of INVASION OF THE BODY SNATCHERS attempts to flag down cars on the highway and warn them of the sinister peril.

existence and fading away from inconsequentiality into invisibility. These include Charles BEAUMONT's "The Vanishing American" (1955), Harlan ELLISON's "Are You Listening?" (1958) and Sylvia Jacobs' "The End of Evan Essant" (1962).

An anthology of stories on the theme of invisibility is *Invisible Men* (anth. **1960**) ed. Basil DAVENPORT. [BS]

INVISIBLE BOY, THE Film (1957). Pan/MGM. Directed by Herman Hoffman, starring Richard Eyer, Philip Abbott, Diane Brewster and Harold J. Stone. Screenplay by Cyril Hume, story by Edmund COOPER. 89 mins. B/w.

A young boy assembles a robot from bits and pieces brought back from the future by a time-travelling relative, and ends up with "Robby the Robot", who had won the hearts of audiences in FORBIDDEN PLANET. Robby comes under the influence of an evil computer trying to conquer the world by implanting electronic receivers in the brains of prominent men, but redeems himself at the end when he ignores the computer's command to kill the boy and instead destroys the computer, with the implicit moral that machines shaped like men are basically more trustworthy than machines shaped like machines. [JB/PN]

INVISIBLE MAN, THE 1. Film (1933). Universal. Directed by James Whale, starring Claude Rains, Gloria Stuart, Henry Travers, William Harrigan and Una O'Connor. Screenplay by R.C. SHERRIFF, based on the novel by H.G. WELLS. 71 mins (later version cut to 56). B/w.

This excellent black comedy tells of a scientist who discovers the secret of invisibility but whose mind is affected by the drug, which turns him into a megalomaniac. After a series of murders he is finally trapped by police (his footprints in the snow betray his presence) and is shot. He dies in hospital,

slowly regaining visibility as his life ebbs away. Whale's direction is full of his usual idiosyncratic touches and the special effects by John P. Fulton are inventive and very sophisticated for the period. This was one of the most successful Wells adaptations.

2. The progressively inferior and silly filmed sequels to the above were *The Invisible Man Returns* (1940), *Invisible Agent* (1942), *The Invisible Man's Revenge* (1944) and *Abbott and Costello Meet the Invisible Man* (1951). Over 30 other films use the invisibility theme.

3. British television series (1958). ATV. Created and produced by Ralph Smart. In this version, which bears little resemblance to Wells's original, the hero divides his time between seeking an antidote for his condition and fighting evil. The cast included Lisa Daniely and Deborah Watling, but the actor who played the hero was kept anonymous as a publicity gimmick; he is thought to have been Tim Turner. The series also played on American TV.

4. American television series (1975). Universal TV for NBC. Created and produced by Harve Bennett and Steve Bocho. Pilot episode directed by Steve Bocho. Pilot episode 90 mins, remainder each 50 mins. Colour.

David McCallum starred in this updated version of the Wells creation as a scientist who accidentally discovers a way of turning himself invisible, but is unable to regain his visibility. Eventually a plastic-surgeon friend makes him a skin-coloured mask. The pilot episode concerned his attempts to keep the formula from both military and mafia; in subsequent episodes the plots revolved around his work as a secret agent for the government.

5. The above series was not a great popular success, so in 1976 Universal replaced McCallum with Ben Murphy and changed the title to *Gemini Man*. The character became a secret agent who could remain invisible for only 15

minutes a day, his powers controlled by a wrist-watch-like device. This version, also, failed to attract more than an average-sized audience. The producer, Harve Bennett, was having greater success elsewhere with THE SIX MILLION DOLLAR MAN. [JB/PN]

ION DRIVE A common item of sf TERMINOLOGY, coming from a much discussed theory of ROCKET propulsion. Because chemically fuelled rockets cannot carry large amounts of fuel, the weight of the fuel itself being an item which has to be driven along with the SPACESHIP, it is desirable to use a fuel which has the lowest possible mass. This can be accomplished only by making up for the lower mass of the propellant by giving it a much higher velocity. The theory is that ions (charged particles), which can be accelerated to enormous velocities by a magnetic field, would be such an ideal fuel. All elements can be ionized, with varying degrees of difficulty, so ion-drive rockets could theoretically make use of pretty well any substance on hand. An ion drive would produce only a small acceleration, because of the relatively tiny masses involved, but would compensate for this by being able to continue the acceleration for months or years. *See* ROCKETS, SPACESHIPS. [PN]

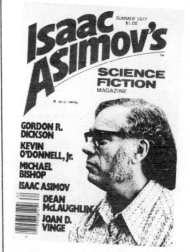

Summer 1977. Isaac is on the cover.

ISAAC ASIMOV'S SCIENCE FICTION MAGAZINE US DIGEST-size magazine. Ten issues to end of 1978, now bi-monthly, from Spring 1977 onwards, published by Davis Publications; ed. George H. SCITHERS.

Asimov is named as "Editorial Director" of this recent sf magazine, obviously titled to take advantage of his popularity. The cover of no.1 showed his photograph full-face; on no.2 he was left profile; but readers hoping to see the back of Asimov's head on no.3, while logical, were disappointed. (He was full-face again.) Asimov is the first sf writer since A. MERRITT to be honoured by becoming

A publicity still for the 1933 version of THE INVISIBLE MAN. Claude Rains is lurking invisibly behind the bandages.

part of a magazine title. *IASFM* is in other respects an efficient, conventional sf publication, rather like a cross between GALAXY SCIENCE FICTION and THE MAGAZINE OF FANTASY AND SCIENCE FICTION, though unusually for a digest magazine it uses a single-column format. It has featured uncondescending science-fact articles (not by Asimov), a mathematical puzzle column by Martin GARDNER, a resurrection of Grendel BRIARTON's "Ferdinand Feghoot" series, once a popular feature of *FSF*, and fiction by Poul ANDERSON, A. Bertram CHANDLER, Gordon R. DICKSON, Michael BISHOP, John VARLEY and many others.

It is generally expected to be the most financially successful of the new mid-1970s sf magazines. [PN]

ISAACS, LEONARD (1939–). American teacher and writer, an associate professor in biology at the Justin Morrill College of Michigan State University, where with R. Glenn Wright he has co-directed the CLARION (East) SCIENCE FICTION WRITERS' WORKSHOP. His *Darwin to Double Helix: the Biological Theme in Science Fiction* (**1974**; rev. 1977) is an intelligently constructed syllabus with notes in the SISCON (Science in a Social Context) series. [PN]

ISLAND OF DR MOREAU, THE Film (1977). AIP. Directed by Don Taylor, starring Burt Lancaster, Michael York, Nigel Davenport and Barbara Carrera. Screenplay by John Herman Shaner and Al Ramrus, based on the novel by H.G. WELLS. 93 mins. Colour.

In this disappointing remake of the 1932 film ISLAND OF LOST SOULS, a young man is cast away on the remote island where the scientist Dr Moreau, we slowly discover, is carrying out experiments to give animals human characteristics; some of the half-man, half-animal results live in the jungle and worship Moreau as a god. In Wells's novel and the first film version Moreau achieves his hybrid creatures by means of vivisection and other cruel and painful methods, but here Moreau is a genetic engineer who creates his monsters by tampering with their chromosomes; hence the references to the "House of Pain", which are so relevant in the novel, lose their meaning. The film, unlike its predecessor, is plodding. The director, Taylor, had made an earlier, also routine sf film, ESCAPE FROM THE PLANET OF THE APES. The novelization of the film (one might have supposed the Wells original to be sufficient) is *The Island of Dr Moreau* (**1977**) by Joseph Silva. [JB]

ISLAND OF LOST SOULS Film (1932). Paramount. Directed by Erle C. Kenton, starring Charles Laughton, Richard Arlen, Leila Hyams, Kathleen Burke, Bela Lugosi, Alan Ladd and Randolph Scott. Screenplay by Waldemar Young and Philip WYLIE, based on the novel *The Island of Dr.*

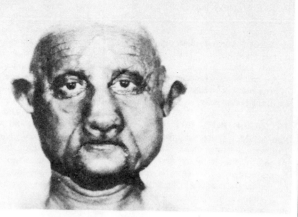

This rare still from ISLAND OF LOST SOULS shows the pig man; it was rediscovered by Phil Riley and Forrest Ackerman and displayed in the magazine *Famous Monsters of Filmland.*

Moreau by H.G. WELLS. 72 mins. B/w.

Though not completely faithful to the Wells original, and adding such Hollywood touches as a seductive Panther Girl, the film nevertheless incorporates much of the novel's grim and moody atmosphere. Charles Laughton plays the leering, whip-cracking Moreau who, by means of vivisection and other cruel medical techniques, is trying to turn animals into men. The results of his experiments, pathetic beast-men (created with first-rate and often horrific make-up), are kept in check by their belief that Moreau is a god. But when they see him murder his human assistant, thus breaking one of his own commandments, their fear of him dissolves and they carry him off to the House of Pain, the surgery where they were all created, and wreak bloody vengeance. A much later remake was THE ISLAND OF DR MOREAU (1977). [JB]

ISLAND OF TERROR Film (1966). Planet/Universal. Directed by Terence Fisher, starring Peter Cushing, Edward Judd, Carole Gray and Eddie Byrne. Screenplay by Alan Ramsen and Edward Andrew Mann. 89 mins. Colour.

This is one of the few films with an sf theme made by Terence Fisher, best known for his horror movies, of which this, in effect, and despite its sf trappings, is one. Giant mutated viruses, the product of cancer research gone wrong, get loose on a small island and kill their victims by sucking their bones out of their bodies. As the monsters, rather like animated piles of porridge in appearance, can only move slowly, it is never clear how they manage to overtake their prey. [JB]

ISLAND OF THE BURNING DAMNED *See* NIGHT OF THE BIG HEAT.

ISLANDS Imaginary islands have long been useful settings for two types of story: those which describe new societies in conveniently isolated settings, and those which explore human nature in circumstances where it is rendered vulnerable and stripped of the props of civilization. The first type of island story is at least as old as PLATO's dialogues "Timaeus" and "Critias" (*c.* 350 BC), which describe ATLANTIS as an island bearing an advanced civilization. Sir Thomas MORE, in *Utopia* (**1516** in Latin; trans. **1551**), also placed his exemplary society on an island. Many subsequent UTOPIAS and DYSTOPIAS have island settings, e.g. Francis BACON's *The New Atlantis* (**1627**), Jonathan SWIFT's *Gulliver's Travels* (**1726**; rev. 1735), Samuel BUTLER's *Erewhon* (**1872**), Austin Tappan WRIGHT's *Islandia* (**1942**), Jacquetta HAWKES's *Providence Island* (**1959**) and Aldous HUXLEY's *Island* (**1962**). Bernard WOLFE's *Limbo* (**1952**; vt *Limbo '90* UK) and Kurt VONNEGUT's *Cat's Cradle* (**1963**) both portray primitive island Utopias as contrasts to global Dystopias.

The second type of island story has Shakespeare's play *The Tempest* (*c.* 1611) (*see also* FORBIDDEN PLANET) and Daniel DEFOE's *Robinson Crusoe* (**1719**) as its paradigms. Jules VERNE's major ROBINSONADE, *The Mysterious Island* (**1875**), concerns a group of Americans who crash their balloon on a desert island and survive to build a miniature industrial economy there. It bears resemblances to both Shakespeare and Defoe (Nemo relates to Prospero; Cyrus Harding relates to Crusoe). Later sf robinsonades include H.G. WELLS's *The Island of Dr. Moreau* (**1896**); S. Fowler WRIGHT's *The Island of Captain Sparrow* (**1928**); Edmond HAMILTON's "The Island of Unreason" (**1933**); William GOLDING's *Lord of the Flies* (**1954**), John CHRISTOPHER's *Cloud on Silver* (**1964**; vt *Sweeney's 'Island* USA) and J.G. BALLARD's "The Terminal Beach" (**1964**). Gene WOLFE, with a great display of fireworks and wit, rings the changes on the symbolism of death and of healing, along with the robinsonade, in his stories "The Island of Dr. Death"

(1970) and "The Death of Dr. Island" (1973).

Sf writers have also transferred island symbolism into interplanetary settings. Either planets are viewed as "islands" in themselves, an idea expressed in the title of Raymond F. JONES's *This Island Earth* (1952), or they provide a vast new *terra incognita* (or *mare incognitum*) in which islands can be located. Rex GORDON's *No Man Friday* (1956; vt *First on Mars* USA) and Charles LOGAN's *Shipwreck* (1975) both use the first ploy, and are good examples of the transposed robinsonade. C.S. LEWIS's *Perelandra* (1943; vt *Voyage to Venus*), Philip José FARMER's *The Gates of Creation* (1966), Jack VANCE's *The Blue World* (1966) and Ursula K. LE GUIN's "Earthsea" trilogy (1968–73) all use the second approach, and deal literally with islands in other worlds. So, in an oblique way, does *Solaris* (1961 Poland; trans. 1970) by Stanislaw LEM, in which the living planet seems to communicate in part by the production of islands; the film SOLARIS makes much of this in its ending.

Island symbolism can also be applied to artificial habitats in space, as in the title of Arthur C. CLARKE's *Islands in Space* (1952), a juvenile novel about space stations. James BLISH's "Okie" novels, collected in *Cities in Flight* (coll. 1970), are, in a sense, island stories, as is Arthur C. Clarke's *Rendezvous with Rama* (1973). But perhaps the most unusual transposition is to be found in J.G. Ballard's robinsonade *Concrete Island* (1974), an ABSURDIST novel of a man marooned on waste ground between motorways. [DP]

ITALY Italy has been a fertile hunting-ground for seekers of PROTO-SF, beginning with *The Travels of Marco Polo* (*c.* 1300) which had a strong influence on the genre of the FANTASTIC VOYAGE, and DANTE ALIGHIERI's *The Divine Comedy* (*c.* 1314–21), which can be treated as a Christian work of speculative fiction. As late as the 17th century, Italy remained at the vanguard of the arts in Europe, and both UTOPIAS and epic romances are numerous, including Jacopo Sannazaro's *Arcadia* (pub. 1504), Ludovico Ariosto's *Orlando Furioso* (definitive ed. 1532), Frascator's *Syphilis* (1530) and Tommaso CAMPANELLA's *City of the Sun* (1602; first pub. in Latin 1623). Utopian literature continued to appear through the political turmoils of post-Renaissance Italy, but few titles are worthy of note. (CASANOVA's major sf work, *Icosaméron* (1788), was written in French.) In the 19th century, however, came the appearance of Emilio Salgari (1862–1911), the "Italian Jules Verne", best known today for his swashbuckling Sandokan pirate stories, though he also wrote many scientific romances ranging from *Duemile leghe sotto America* ["2000 Leagues under America"] (1888) to *Le meraviglie del duemila* ["The Marvels of the Year

2000"] (1907). Luigi Motta (1881–1955), a prolific collaborator with Salgari, continued in the same vein with such novels as *Il tunnel sottomarino* ["The Underwater Tunnel"] (1912) and *Il raggio naufragatore* ["The Wrecking Ray"] (1926) and many others.

In the 20th century, Italian sf follows a pattern familiar to many western European countries, where the widespread influence of American sf has had a pronounced negative effect on the development of home-grown writers. At the same time, a large number of major MAINSTREAM Italian authors have successfully worked with sf themes and images, though often put to uses which are by no means typical of genre sf: Dino BUZZATI with *Il deserto dei Tartari* (1940; trans. as *The Tartar Steppe* 1952) and *Il grande ritratto* (1960; trans. as *Larger Than Life* 1962); Italo CALVINO with *I nostri antenati* ["Our Ancestors"] (coll. of previously published volumes 1960; previously published sections being *Baron of the Trees*, 1957, trans. 1960, and *The Non-Existent Knight and the Cloven Viscount*, 1952 and 1959, trans. 1962), *Le Cosmicomiche* (coll. of linked stories 1965; trans. as *Cosmicomics* 1969) and *Le città invisibili* (1972; trans. as *Invisible Cities* 1974); Tommaso Landolfi with *Cancroregina* (1950); Mario Soldati with *La verità sul caso Motta* ["The Motta Affair"] (1941); Roberto Vacca with *Il robot e il minotauro* ["The Robot and the Minotaur"] (1959); Giorgio Scerbanenco with *Il cavallo venduto* ["The Sold Horse"] (1959); and others including Ennio Flaiano, Giovanni Papini and Giovanni Arpino.

It was not until about 1950, when American PULP sf of the so-called GOLDEN AGE had filtered through to Italy, partly because of the Allied invasion in 1943–5, that we see the emergence of the first contemporary Italian sf writer, Sandro Sandrelli (1926–), with his short story "Le Ultime 36 ore di Charlie Malgol" ["The Last 36 Hours of Charlie Malgol"] (1949) in a Venice newspaper. The fact that nearly 30 years later Sandrelli is still, with Lino Aldani (born in the same year), one of the leading Italian sf writers, is a tribute to his imagination and also a pointer to the lack of newer Italian authors. The first Italian sf magazine, *Scienza Fantastica*, was launched in 1952, ed. Lionello Torossi (himself a writer under the pseudonym Massimo Zeno); it was a short-lived venture with only seven issues but it heralded a flood of similarly brief magazines and publishing ventures over the next 10 years or so, principally devoted to material translated from English (except for *Mondi Astrali*, where Italian writers used foreign-sounding pseudonyms).

The year 1957 saw more Italian writers in the magazines (principally *Cosmo* and *Oltre il Cielo*); Gianfranco Briatore, Roberta Rambelli, Piero Prosperi, Massimo Lo Jacono, Ugo

Malaguti, known for his two *Alan Hardy* volumes (1968) and *Il palazzo en il cielo* ["The Palace in the Sky"] (French trans. 1976), Gianfranco de Turris, Giulio Raiola and Ivo Prandin are the most notable, and their work began to appear with some regularity. Further outlets for these authors were the *Interplanet* anthologies launched in 1962, during which year Aldani published his interesting if superficial survey of sf, *La fantascienza* ["Science Fiction"] (1962). Aldani's other major volumes are his collections *Bonnanote Sofia* ["Good-night Sophia"] (coll. 1964) and *Quarta dimensione* ["Fourth Dimension"] (coll. 1963). He also wrote as N.L. Janda.

Sandro Sandrelli's best title is probably *Caino dello spazio* ["Cain of Space"] (coll. 1962). Material by Sandrelli and Luigi Cozzi appears in Donald WOLLHEIM's *The Best from the Rest of the World* (anth. 1977).

Despite the growing popularity of sf in their country, Italian sf authors are still very much in a minority, and their work is mostly derivative of American sf. Unlike the "spaghetti Western" film genre, which assimilated and transcended the traditions of its original source, Italian sf has not yet succeeded in finding a voice of its own which might afford it a more widespread recognition (as has happened very significantly with Guido Crepax, the iodiosyncratic, erotic, leading Italian comic-strip artist, whose disturbing work develops sf themes to eerie effect). Sf illustration is generally flourishing in Italy, one of its most popular and accomplished practitioners being the Dutch émigré Karel THOLE. New magazines such as *Robot* (1975–) have begun in the 1970s. The first Eurocon (European sf CONVENTION) was held in 1972 in Trieste, a city which has also had, for some years, an annual festival of sf cinema. There are many Italian fan groups, and an annual award, the *Cometa d'Argento* (Silver Comet) is given for sf published in Italy.

Although serious sf criticism is not yet common in Italy, the 1970s have seen the publication of several works, mainly devoted to Anglo-American sf, which will certainly help to remove the dominant Italian image of sf as a pulp literature. The most important of these is probably *Il senso del futuro* ["The Sense of the Future"] (1970) by Carlo PAGETTI. Others are *Che cos'è la fantascienza* ["SF — What it Is"] (1970) and *La "musa stupefatta" o della fantascienza* ["SF — the Astonished Muse"] (1974) by Franco Ferrini and the interesting study of British sf, *Ieri, il futuro* ["Yesterday, the Future"] (1977) by Gianni MONTANARI. A rather disappointing critical anthology, *Utopia e fantascienza* ["Utopia and SF"] (anth. 1975), was nevertheless significant in being the first academic compilation on sf published in Italy; it was produced by the Institute of English Studies at the University of Turin. [MJ/PN]

Ray Harryhausen's mutated octopus attacks San Francisco in It Came from Beneath the Sea.

IT CAME FROM BENEATH THE SEA Film (1955). Columbia. Directed by Robert Gordon, starring Kenneth Tobey, Faith Domergue and Donald Curtis. Screenplay by George Worthing Yates and Hal Smith, based on a story by Yates. 77 mins. B/w.

A giant octopus, as so often in the genre, is affected by atomic radiation and goes on a destructive rampage attacking San Francisco and demolishing various landmarks, including the Golden Gate Bridge, before being destroyed by a torpedo. The special effects by Ray HARRYHAUSEN were limited by the small budget: his animated octopus, for instance, has only six tentacles.   [JB]

It Came from Outer Space was originally released in 3-D.

IT CAME FROM OUTER SPACE Film (1953). Universal. Directed by Jack ARNOLD. Starring Richard Carlson, Barbara Rush and Charles Drake.

Screenplay by Harry Essex, based on a screen treatment, "The Meteor", by Ray BRADBURY. 80 mins. B/w.

The film was Jack Arnold's first venture into the sf/horror genre. Though little remains of Bradbury's original treatment this is still a genuinely alarming film about an alien spaceship that crash-lands in the desert. The aliens, monstrosities by human standards, are able to change their shapes, and they begin duplicating inhabitants of a nearby town in order to repair their ship. The fine photographic effects are by Clifford Stine and David S. Horsley, and good use was made of the desert settings.   [JB]

IT HAPPENED HERE Film (1963). Rath/Lopert. Directed by Kevin Brownlow and Andrew Mollo, starring Pauline Murray, Sebastian Shaw, Fiona Leland and Honor Fehrson. Screenplay by Kevin Brownlow and Andrew Mollo. 99 mins (cut to 93). B/w.

ALTERNATE-WORLD stories have long been popular in literary sf but are rare in sf cinema. This British film is one exception; it shows what might have happened if Nazi Germany had successfully invaded England. Shot in a realistic, documentary-like style, it is a remarkable achievement when one takes into account that it is virtually an amateur film, made over a period of years by Brownlow and Mollo working mainly at weekends and using non-professional talent. It has still not received the wider showing it deserves.   [JB]

IT'S ABOUT TIME Television series (1966). CBS-TV. Created by Sherwood Schwartz, who was also executive producer. Produced by George Cahan. Writers included Sherwood Schwartz, David P. Harmon and Elrey Schwartz. Director of the pilot episode was Richard Donner, who later directed such films as The Omen and SUPERMAN. 25 mins each

episode. Colour.

After his success with the brisk, low-comedy series Gilligan's Island, Schwartz created this even lower comedy series set in the Stone Age. It concerned two astronauts, played by Frank Aletter and Jack Mullaney, who accidentally go back in time, are stranded in prehistory and are befriended by a tribe of gross cave-dwellers, the principal members played by Imogene Coca and Joe E. Ross; Mike Mazurki was well cast as a cave-man. Later the cave people accompany the astronauts back to the present. The series lasted one season.   [JB]

IT'S ALIVE! Film (1974). A Larco Production/Warner Bros. Directed by Larry Cohen, starring John Ryan, Sharon Farrell, Andrew Duggan and Guy Stockwell. Screenplay by Larry Cohen. 91 mins. Colour.

A mutant baby, immediately after birth, kills all the medical staff in the delivery room and leaps through a skylight to go on a rampage, killing a woman, a milkman and several policemen. Although the plot is evidently ludicrous, and as sf the story leaves much to be desired (the mutant's existence is simply explained as the result of "chemical pollution"), as a pure horror film it is more than satisfactory. The baby is never shown clearly, being presented in a series of very fast, almost subliminal shots, thus not too severely taxing the audience's suspension of disbelief. The concentration on one of the prime characteristics of all babies — that they crawl around on the floor — is disturbing. The model of the baby is a truly nasty creation, with bulging head, large, hideous eyes and a vicious-looking set of teeth and claws, designed by Rick Baker (who also designed the mask for the 1976 KING KONG).   [JB]

IT! THE TERROR FROM BEYOND SPACE Film (1958). Vogue/United Artists. Directed by Edward L. Cahn, starring Marshall Thompson, Shawn Smith and Ray "Crash" Corrigan (as the monster). Screenplay by Jerome BIXBY. 69 mins. B/w.

This film seems inspired by parts of A.E. VAN VOGT's book Voyage of the Space Beagle, which is not credited. The crew of a spaceship returning from Mars discover that "something" has stowed away on board. It turns out to be a blood-sucking monster which attacks various crew members and stores their bodies in the ship's ventilation system to preserve them for future snacks. The surviving crew members are slowly forced to retreat as the creature takes over the ship, section by section, until they are all trapped in the nose cone, with the creature breaking open the last hatch-cover. An effective build-up of suspense takes place when the monster is kept vague and shadowy, but the ending is anti-climactic.   [JB]

JACKSON, SHIRLEY (1919–65). American short-story writer and novelist, none of whose work is sf proper, but whose interest in the darker byways of PSYCHOLOGY, as in *The Bird's Nest* (1954; vt *Lizzie*), which deals with split personality, and *The Haunting of Hill House* (1959), makes her work of some interest to sf readers. The latter book was filmed as *The Haunting* (1963) by Robert WISE. Her most famous single story is "The Lottery" (1948), whose ritual stoning is as explicable in sf terms as any other. It appeared in *The Lottery: Adventures of the Demon Lover* (coll. 1949) with a number of stories typical of her fantasy work. In *The Sundial* (1958), 12 of her New England characters await the END OF THE WORLD; again, the allegory is explicable in sf terms. SJ is regarded as one of the finest of GOTHIC writers.
[JC/PN]
Other works: *Hangsaman* (1951); *We Have Always Lived in the Castle* (1962); *Come Along with Me* (coll. 1968).

JACOBI, CARL (RICHARD) (1908–). American writer and editor, in the latter capacity of journals including the *Minnesota Quarterly*. His short fiction is mainly of horror and fantasy interest, though he has also produced considerable sf, mostly SPACE OPERA. He began publishing with "Mive" for *Weird Tales* in 1932, and has collected some of his large output in *Revelations in Black* (coll. 1947), *Portraits in Moonlight* (coll. 1964) and *Disclosures in Scarlet* (coll. 1972).
[JC]

JACOBS, HARVEY (1930–). American writer, much of whose work, some of it in the form of FABULATIONS, deals with the nature and fate of the urban Jew, especially in New York. His more fable-like tales, many of which appear in *The Egg of the Glak; and Other Stories* (coll. 1969), are not dissimilar to some of Bernard Malamud's; the title story (1968), and "In Seclusion" (1968 NW), with which he began publishing stories in the sf magazines, typically demonstrate HJ's sharply sardonic use of sf elements to make moral points about man's inhumanity to man in a cold world.
[JC]

JACOMB, CHARLES ERNEST (1888– ?). British journalist and editor, former lance-corporal in the 23rd Royal Fusiliers and author of one sf novel, *And A New Earth* (1926), which combines the UTOPIAN, future-WAR, and DISASTER genres into one volume. It describes a scientifically advanced matriarchal community which weathers hostilities and comet disaster to become the major power on Earth.
[JE]

JAEGER, MURIEL (? –). British writer, MA (Oxon.), possibly a psychologist by profession. Her first sf work, *The Question Mark* (1926), depicted a UTOPIAN England of 200 years hence (as witnessed by an awaker from a cataleptic trance) and showed strong influences from H.G. WELLS and William MORRIS. More original in concept was *The Man With Six Senses* (1927) in which a weakly youth, endowed with unrefined ESP talents, is helped towards maturity by a sympathetic girl friend. The promise shown in this novel was never realized, presumably through bad sales. Following a change in publisher MJ wrote *Hermes Speaks* (1933), which followed the consequences in the political and financial worlds of adherence to the prophecies of a fake medium, and *Retreat From Armageddon* (1936), a peripheral future-WAR novel in which a group of people withdraw from the ensuing conflagration to a remote country house where they philosophize on Man's shortcomings. Notable for its advocacy of GENETIC ENGINEERING, it likewise met with little success, and MJ's writings terminated.
[JE]

JAKES, JOHN (WILLIAM) (1932–). American writer, until recently best known for his sf and fantasy, though his "Bicentennial" series of novels tracing the fictional history of an American family over the past 200 years has been an extraordinary bestseller, undoubtedly justifying his decision to retire from sf writing, in which field he wrote the bulk of his shorter work in the 1950s and 1960s, and his last novel proper in 1973. JJ began publishing sf in 1952 with "Machine" for *FSF*, an unremarkable story but one which prefigured his capacity to write competently to available markets. His first novels were historical, under the name Jay Scotland, and it was not until *When the Star Kings Die* (1967) that he published an sf book. This, with its sequels *The Planet Wizard* (1969) and *Tonight We Steal the Stars* (1969), features members of the Dragonard clan guarding II Galaxy and its corporate "star kings" against various perils. A selection from the 70 or more stories that have appeared up to this date are assembled in *The Best of John Jakes* (coll. 1977), whose introduction, by Martin Harry GREENBERG and Joseph D. Olander, and bibliography are both valuable. JJ's next books were *Brak the*

Barbarian (coll. of linked stories 1968), *Brak the Barbarian Versus the Sorceress* (1969) and *Brak the Barbarian Versus the Mark of the Demon* (1969); these routine SWORD-AND-SORCERY tales he amusingly pastiched, along with those of his model, Robert E. HOWARD, in what may be his most popular novel in the sf/fantasy field, *Mention My Name in Atlantis* (1972). *The Last Magicians* (1969) is also a fantasy. Among the considerable number of novels he published between 1969 and 1973, three stand out: *Six-Gun Planet* (1970) depicts a deliberately archaic colony planet called Missouri complete with robot gunfighters, just as in the later film WESTWORLD (1973); *Black in Time* (1970) presents vignettes from black history dramatized through a TIME-TRAVEL plot device; *On Wheels* (1973), is a tautly written story set in a mobile subculture of an America about 100 years in the future; members of this subculture live, breed and die on wheels, whether in large trailers or their own vehicles, never leaving the Interstate highway system, never dropping below 40 mph; their god is the Texaco Firebird, which they only see at the moment of death; as SATIRE the story is simple but gripping.

JJ took an MA in English literature in 1954 from Ohio State University. Since then he has received two honorary doctorates, from Wright State in 1976 and De Pauw University in 1977, both for his work in dramatizing American history.
[JC]
Other works: *The Asylum World* (1969); *The Hybrid* (1969); *Secrets of Stardeep* (1969), a juvenile; *Mask of Chaos* (1970); *Master of the Dark Gate* (1970); *Monte Cristo no. 99* (1970); *Time Gate* (1972), a juvenile; *Witch of the Dark Gate* (1972); *Conquest of the Planet of the Apes* (film novelization; 1974).
See also: COLONIZATION OF OTHER WORLDS; POLITICS; SOCIOLOGY; TRANSPORTATION.

JAKOBER, MARIE (1941–). Canadian writer whose first, promising sf novel, *The Mind Gods* (1976), confronts a materialist, tolerant society with a repellent spiritual creed on another planet. With some subtlety the outcome is shown to be not altogether, morally, on the side of the liberals; various ironies take place.
[PN]
See also: POLITICS; RELIGION.

JAKOBSSON, EJLER (1911–). American editor. Finnish by birth, EJ emigrated to the USA in 1926. He became a PULP-MAGAZINE writer in the 1930s and joined the staff of one of the pulp chains, Popular Publications, in 1943. He briefly had responsibility for ASTONISHING STORIES and SUPER SCIENCE STORIES, but both magazines were already in the process of closing down due to paper shortages and Frederik POHL's departure. EJ remained with the company and became editor of *Super*

Science Stories on its revival in 1949, a position he retained until the magazine again (and finally) ceased publication in 1951. Damon KNIGHT was his assistant for part of this period. EJ returned to sf magazine editing in 1969, when he took over the editorship of GALAXY SCIENCE FICTION and IF — again, in succession to Frederik Pohl. He attempted to make the magazines more contemporary and trendy, with indifferent results. He was succeeded as editor by James BAEN in mid-1974. During his editorship the following anthologies were published: *The Best From Galaxy Vol. I* (anth. **1972**) ed. The Editors of Galaxy Magazine; *The Best From If* (anth. **1973**); *The Best From Galaxy Vol. II* (anth. **1974**) ed. The Editors of Galaxy Magazine; *The Best From If Vol. II* (anth. **1974**) ed. The Editors of If Magazine. EJ's name did not appear on the title pages. [MJE]
See also: SF MAGAZINES.

JAKUBOWSKI, MAXIM (1944–). British writer, critic, translator and anthologist. A company director in the flavour industry, he was educated in France and writes in both French and English. Generally more at ease in short-story length (material in *Fiction* and *Satellite* in France, *NW* and anthologies in England), MJ writes very marginal examples of sf and his preoccupation with doomed love, music, sex and death is more often expressed in mainstream fiction. He has written stories about Michael MOORCOCK's character Jerry Cornelius. A prolific anthologist in France (six books), he has also edited an interesting selection of French sf in English, *Travelling Towards Epsilon* (anth. **1977**). [MJ/PN]

JAMES, EDWIN *See* James E. GUNN.

JAMES, LAURENCE (? –). British writer active under his own name and at least nine pseudonyms and house names in various genres including Westerns, thrillers, historical romances and soft-core pornography. He has averaged about a book a month over four years. As LJ he began publishing sf with "And Dug the Dog a Tomb" for *New Worlds Quarterly 3* (anth. **1972**), an sf development of Samuel Beckett's *Waiting for Godot* (trans. **1954**), though he is best known for his series of paperback SPACE OPERAS featuring Simon Rack and his Galactic Security Service Comrades: *Earth Lies Sleeping* (**1974**), *Starcross* (**1974**; vt *War on Aleph* USA), *Backflash* (**1975**), *Planet of the Blind* (**1975**) and *New Life for Old* (**1975**). They are swiftly told but otherwise unremarkable. [JC]

JAMES, PHILIP *See* (1) Lester DEL REY; (2) James CAWTHORN.

JAMES BLISH AWARD Created by the SCIENCE FICTION FOUNDATION to commemorate the well-known sf writer

and critic, this award, which is planned to be bi-annual, was first made to Brian ALDISS in 1977. It is given "for excellence in science fiction criticism" over the two calendar years preceding the year in which the award is made, and takes the form of an inscribed plaque and a sum of money. The JBA is supported financially by eight British sf publishers. All English-language sf critics are eligible. [PN]

JAMESON, MALCOLM (1891–1945). American writer, who began producing fiction only after cancer forced him to retire from a non-writing life which had included a career in the American Navy; he began publishing sf with "Eviction by Isotherm" for *ASF* in 1938, and produced prolifically until his death. His first sf novel, *Atomic Bomb* (**1945**), is a NEAR-FUTURE story of an atomic explosion; *Bullard of the Space Patrol* (1940–45 *ASF*; coll. of linked stories **1951**; 1955 edition omits "The Bureaucrat") is a juvenile, ed. Andre NORTON, and tells of Bullard's highly successful career in the Patrol; one further story in the series, "Devil's Powder" (1941), remains uncollected. *Tarnished Utopia* (1943 *Startling Stories*; **1956**) features two people awakened from SUSPENDED ANIMATION in conflict with a dictatorship. [JC]
See also: ASTEROIDS; DYSTOPIAS; NUCLEAR POWER.

JAMESON, (MARGARET) STORM (1897–). British novelist, known mainly for work outside the sf field, particularly such complex, witty family chronicles as those collected together as *The Triumph of Time* (**1932**). Her sf novels derive from her interest in European POLITICS of change, and extrapolate extremist political "solutions" into the NEAR FUTURE. *In the Second Year* (**1936**) projects a Fascist Britain; in *Then We Shall Hear Singing* (**1942**) a victorious German Reich dominates an unnamed country, but is unable to eliminate the resistance of the individual consciousness; in *The Moment of Truth* (**1949**) Britain is this time ruled by Communists. [JC]

JANE, FRED(ERICK) T(HOMAS) (1865–1916). English writer and illustrator, best known for his founding of the series *Jane's Fighting Ships* (from **1898**). His *To Venus in Five Seconds* (**1897**) takes its kidnapped narrator to VENUS, where he sets off a conflict between the native, intelligent giant insects of Venus and some ancient Egyptians who have been resident there for some time, and to whose race his lady kidnapper belongs. *Blake of the "Rattlesnake"* (**1895**) is a WAR story set in the NEAR FUTURE, featuring the use of modern torpedoes. *The Violet Flame: A story of Armageddon and After* (**1899**) features a mad scientist who brings about the END OF THE WORLD with a

disintegrator ray; the narrator and his wife survive to be a new ADAM AND EVE. FTJ's main interest was in warfare and WEAPONS, as is also clear from his many book illustrations, not only of his own work but also of future-war novels by George GRIFFITH and E. Douglas FAWCETT. [PN/JC]
Other works: *The Incubated Girl* (**1896**).
See also: CRIME AND PUNISHMENT; MATTER TRANSMISSION.

JANIFER, LAURENCE M(ARK) (1933–). American writer. Born Larry Mark Harris — a name used on his fiction until 1963 — he recovered the old family name which had been discarded by an immigration officer when his grandfather gained entry to the USA from Poland. Much of his work has been written in collaboration — his early works with Randall GARRETT (some as Mark PHILLIPS) and some later ones with S.J. TREIBICH. His first novel, written with Garrett, was *Pagan Passions* (**1959** as by Randall Garrett and Larry M. Harris) — a slightly bawdy mythological fantasy written for the Beacon Books series of GALAXY NOVELS. After the Mark Phillips collaborations he wrote his first solo novel, *Slave Planet* (**1963**). *The Wonder War* (**1964**), though credited to Janifer alone, appears from the dedication to have been written in collaboration with Michael KURLAND. *You Sane Men* (**1965**; vt *Bloodworld*) is a sensational but unconvincing account of a world where sadism is the aristocratic way of life. His most ambitious novel is *Power* (**1974**), a study of the POLITICS of rebellion. He edited the anthology *Master's Choice* (anth. **1966**; paperback in 2 vols as *SF: Master's Choice* UK; vt *18 Greatest Science Fiction Stories* USA). His three novels with Treibich, constituting the "Angelo di Stefano" series, are comedies: *Target: Terra* (**1968**); *The High Hex* (**1969**) and *The Wagered World* (**1969**). [BS]
Other works: *A Piece of Martin Cann* (**1968**); *Impossible?* (coll. **1968**).

JANSEN, MICHEL *See* Jacques VAN HERP.

JANSON, HANK *See* Stephen FRANCES.

JANVIER, IVAN or **PAUL** *See* Algis BUDRYS.

JANVIER, THOMAS A(LLIBONE) (1849–1913). American writer of popular fiction; also active as a journalist. His LOST-RACE novel, *The Aztec Treasure House* (**1890**), didactically describes a surviving remnant of the Aztec empire; *In Great Waters* (coll. **1901**) is fantasy. *In the Sargasso Sea* (**1898**) is a romance with some scientific speculation. [JC]
See also: ANTHROPOLOGY.

JAPAN It seems that the continuing attention the Japanese people have always paid to their ancient legends and fantastic stories has rendered them open also to modern fantasies and sf stories, and the rationalization of a chaotic universe which they offer; and, as a matter of fact, Japanese sf proper begins early with translations of Jules VERNE, from the 1870s onwards, during the period of violently rapid modernization in Japan. The first native Japanese sf writers, such as Shunro Oshikawa (1877–1914), show the strong influence of Verne. One of Oshikawa's most popular books is *Kaitei Gunkan* ["Undersea Battleship"] (1900), a future-WAR novel about a conflict between Japan and Russia, which effectively predicted the actual war of 1904–05.

Between the two World Wars, some writers of straight sf as well as fantasy began to appear, the most popular and capable among them being Juza Unno (1897–1949), who wrote stories influenced by Hugo GERNSBACK's attempt to use sf to teach its readers about the technological marvels of the future; among his many books, *Chikyu Tonan* ["The Earth Was Stolen"] (1936) and *Yojigen Hyoryu* ["Marooned in the 4-D World"] (1946) were notably influential, although not highly regarded as literature.

It was only after the Second World War, however, that sf became truly widely popular, due in large part to the flood of sf paperbacks discarded by the American forces in occupation, which filled the shelves of secondhand bookshops in the large cities and stimulated some ambitious publishers to attempt series of translations. Most of these trials failed through limited sales, but notable among them were a series of seven anthologies from *Amazing Stories* (all 1950) and 20 volumes of the *Gengensha SF Series* (1956–7); both series began the process of establishing a sizeable sf audience in Japan.

This audience was soon catered for by the first successful sf series, the *Hayakawa SF Series* (1957–74), published by Hayakawa-shobo Co., which in less than 20 years issued 318 volumes, mostly of translations, but containing about 50 Japanese originals; a companion series, *Hayakawa SF Bunko*, reached more than 200 numbers. In competition with Hayakawa-shobo the Tokyo Sogensha Co. began its own translation series, the sf section of *Sogen Suiri Bunko*, in 1963, and has reached 200 numbers, featuring works by Edgar Rice BURROUGHS (the "Barsoom" books) and E.E. "Doc" SMITH. Other publishers have recently followed suit with their own sf translation series.

Also in 1957, the fanzine *Uchujin* ["Cosmic Dust"] was founded, and began publishing original Japanese work; over half the popular sf writers in Japan today started there. In 1960, the first successful professional sf magazine in Japan was launched by Hayakawa-shobo; *SF Magazine* began as a reprint vehicle for *FSF*, but soon began to publish original material. In the late 1960s, the usual course for a budding Japanese sf writer was to begin publishing in *Uchujin* and to graduate to *SF Magazine*. An indication of the journal's success is the fact that by Sep. 1977 it had reached its 226th issue. A second sf magazine, *Kiso-Tengai* ["Fantastic"], began in 1975, folded after 10 issues, but was revived in 1976. Though magazine circulation figures are classified in Japan, the best estimate is that these two magazines sell about 50,000 copies each.

Excluding reprints and juveniles (e.g. the translations of the German PERRY RHODAN series in *Hayakawa SF Bunko*), about 200 sf books a year are published at the present time, a figure that varies somewhat according to criteria of distinction between sf and non-sf. Though the borderline between hardback and paperback publication is difficult to determine in the Japanese system, probably about a third of the original sf books published in a year are hardbacks. Paperbacks average about 30,000 copies in the first print run, whether original releases or translations; the latter still make up more than half the yearly output. The sf readership is typical of most countries, most of it being of secondary school/university age.

Japanese fandom began to exhibit itself formally in 1962 with the first Japanese sf convention at Tokyo, which was attended by about 200 fans; the 16th convention was held at Yokohama in 1977. Attendance has increased considerably. *Uchujin*, with a circulation of some 1000, remains Japan's leading fanzine, and ceremonially heralded its 20th anniversary in May 1977. *Kikan NW-SF* ["New Wave SF Quarterly"] (1970–) is a semi-prozine, published from Tokyo, and printing about 5000 copies two or three times a year. There are more than 100 additional fanzines, some of them close imitations of *Uchujin*.

The first Japanese sf film was GODZILLA (1954), and was followed by many monster films, mostly from Toho-Eiga Co., including straight sf offerings like THE MYSTERIANS (1957), and SUBMERSION OF JAPAN (1974; the English-language version, *Tidal Wave*, is severely cut, with some new footage). Many monster series appeared on TV in the 1960s, but were less successful than animated sf series, like *Astroboy* (1963–5), *Guts-A-Man* (1972–4) and *Space Cruiser Yamato* (1976).

Among Japanese sf authors, the best known abroad is Kobo ABÉ, author of *Inter Ice Age 4* (1959; trans 1970); he is, however, fundamentally a writer of mainstream literature.

Shin'ichi Hoshi (1926–) is a prolific writer, and has published nearly 1000 short stories, one of which, "Bokko-chan" (1958), was published in *FSF* in June 1963. *Koe no Ami* ["Network of the Voice"] (1970) stands out among his infrequent full-length books; a collection of linked stories, it describes the invasion of a telephone system rather on the lines of D.F. JONES' *Colossus* (1966).

Osamu Tezuka (1926–), writer/artist for *Astroboy*, is regarded as a kind of Japanese Walt Disney, having produced the first animated film series for TV in Japan, as well as being a top name in comics, sf and otherwise. He is best represented in book form by *Hi no Tori* ["The Phoenix"] (1968–), a continuing series of volumes.

Ryu Mitsuse (1928–) combines a hard-sf surface with poetic form in such perceptive novels as *Hyaku-oku no Hiru to Sen-oku no Yoru* ["Ten Billion Days, a Hundred Billion Nights"] (1967), in which Christ, Buddha, Plato and many other figures "fight" one another with blasters and so forth. His "Sunset 2217" (1964; trans. 1972) appeared in *Best Science Fiction for 1972* (anth. 1972) ed. Frederik POHL.

Sakyo KOMATSU (1931–) is perhaps Japan's most successful sf writer. His *Hateshinaki Nagare no Hate ni* ["At the End of the Endless Stream"] (1966) deals panoramically with the history of the universe and of *Homo sapiens*. He is best known as the author of *Nippon Chimbotsu* (1973; trans. 1976 as *Japan Sinks*, cut by about one-third), which has sold about four million copies in Japan alone and has been filmed as *The Submersion of Japan*.

Ryo Hammura (1933–) won the prestigious Naoki award in 1974, the first time for an sf writer. He is known as an excellent storyteller, a capacity best seen in *San-Rei-Zan Hiroku* ["The Hidden History of the Hi Tribe"] (1973) and *Yoseiden* ["Weird Stars"] (1975–), the latter a continuing series; both titles narrate a fictitious history of ancient Japan.

Yasutaka Tsutsui (1934–) is noted for his sharp satires of journalistic and media exploitation, like *Viet-Nam Kanko Kosha* ["The Vietnam Sightseeing Co."] (1967) and *Zokubutsu Zukan* ["Who's Who of Snobs"] (1972).

Taku Mayumura (1934–) is noted for his serious attempts at creating a future HISTORY, a representative work being *Shiseikan* ["Governors of the Worlds"] (coll. of linked stories 1974), a series of novelettes describing the rise and fall of a galactic government.   [TS]

JARRY, ALFRED (1873–1907). French writer. He carried the fruits of his education in science into his *avant-garde* writing, particularly the influence of the evolutionary philosopher Henri Bergson. He was a pioneer of the theatre of the absurd. He was inspired by H.G. WELLS's *The Time Machine* (1895) to write the speculative essay "How to Construct a Time Machine". He invented "pataphysics", the science of imaginary solutions. One of his sf novels is the disorganized and extravagant *Exploits*

and Opinions of Dr Faustroll, Pataphysician (**1911** France; in *Selected Works of Alfred Jarry*, coll. ed. Roger Shattuck and Simon Watson-Taylor, trans. Watson-Taylor **1965**). The other is the comic erotic fantasia *The Supermale* (**1902** France; trans. Barbara Wright **1968**). He fell into obscurity for many years, but interest in his works revived after the Second World War, and he has influenced several modern French writers and one or two sf writers (*see* ABSURDIST SF), including J.G. BALLARD, whose "The Assassination of John Fitzgerald Kennedy Considered as a Downhill Motor Race" recalls Jarry's parody "The Crucifixion of Christ Considered as an Uphill Bicycle Race".   [BS]
See also: EVOLUTION; SCIENTISTS; SUPERMAN; THEATRE.

JARVIS, E.K. Ziff-Davis house name used on *AMZ*, *Fantastic Adventures* and *Fantastic* by Paul FAIRMAN, Harlan ELLISON and Robert SILVERBERG — one identified story each — and on over 45 other stories, many of them possibly by Robert Moore WILLIAMS, 1942–58.

JASON, JERRY *See* George H. SMITH.

JAVOR, FRANK A. (? –). American writer who appeared infrequently in sf magazines from 1963, beginning with "Patriot" for *ASF*; three of his stories were included in the Judith MERRIL "Year's Best S-F" series of anthologies. His only sf novel, *The Rim-World Legacy* (**1967**), a capably framed galactic intrigue

on an alien planet, makes one regret that it has, to date, no successors.   [JC]

JAY, MEL *See* John E. MULLER.

JEFFERIES, (JOHN) RICHARD (1848–87). English naturalist and novelist. The son of a farmer, he showed remarkable powers of observation when writing about nature, describing it in a poetic style from an animist viewpoint that was devoid of sentimentality. This was particularly noticeable in his first fantasy novel, *Wood Magic: a fable* (**1881**; vt abridged *Sir Bevis: a Tale of the Fields*, 1889). Semi-autobiographical in content, it featured a young boy gifted with the ability to communicate with animals, birds and plants, and was primarily concerned with the social and political structure of the local animal kingdom and the struggles of a contender for the throne. In its complexities of plot and counter-plot this work is the superior of Richard Adams' *Watership Down* (**1972**). A sequel, *Bevis: the Story of a Boy* (**1882**) appeared a year later but here the emphasis was placed on the pleasures and intrigues of childhood rather than on the hero's supernatural abilities.

For the last six years of his life RJ's health was severely in decline. As with Anthony TROLLOPE, his thoughts turned to the future and to speculation. The result was *After London; or, Wild England* (**1885**), a post-HOLOCAUST novel which described an England reverted to rural wilderness. Written from the viewpoint of a future historian the novel

was set in two parts, the first describing the lapse into barbarism, the specific reasons for the disaster being deliberately kept vague; the second detailing the medieval society which had come into being, and relating of a voyage of discovery on a great inland lake covering the centre of England. Because it has elements in common with the Bevis novels, it is often considered as part of a trilogy, even though characters and setting are completely different. It is a first-class example of Victorian sf and proved very popular at the time. Its influence can be traced through W. H. HUDSON's *A Crystal Age* (**1887**) to John COLLIER's *Tom's A-Cold* (**1933**; vt *Full Circle, a Tale* USA). Earlier RJ had written a political satire, *Jack Brass: Emperor of England* (**1873**), which can loosely be construed as fantasy.   [JE]
See also: CITIES; PASTORAL; POLLUTION; UTOPIAS.

JEFF HAWKE British COMIC STRIP created by writer Eric Souster and artist Sidney Jordan. *JH* first appeared in 1954 in the *Daily Express*. Some scripts were written by William Patterson. It ceased in 1974.

JH was Britain's leading sf comic strip. The overall scenario depicts Earth as a primitive planet on the periphery of a highly advanced galactic civilization. Individual stories (over 60 appeared) contain standard sf concepts interspersed with theories similar to those of VON DÄNIKEN (Vishnu and Shiva as interplanetary visitors, Aladdin's lamp as

JEFF HAWKE was one of the most vigorous sf comic strips. This is from the *Daily Express*, Aug. 20th, 1955.

the communicator of a dead space pilot). *JH*'s storylines were original, for a comic strip, and kept abreast of contemporary technological progress.

Jeff Hawke's adventures are being reprinted in Italy in hardcover volumes. [JE]

JENKINS, WILL F. *See* Murray LEINSTER.

JENSEN, AXEL (1932–   ). Norwegian writer, active since 1955. His DYSTOPIAN sf novel, *Epp* (**1965**; trans. **1967**), describes a world, in chillingly grey, fragmented prose, where men live in cells isolated from one another, and file reports on their similarly treacherous, alienated "neighbours". [JC]

JENSEN, JOHANNES V(ILHELM) (1873–1950). Danish poet, novelist and essayist. Receiver of the Nobel Prize for Literature 1944. Author of *Den Lange Rejse* (6 vols **1908–22** Denmark; all but one vol. trans. Arthur G. Chater; the first two vols as *The Long Journey: Fire and Ice* **1922**; the third and fourth as *The Cimbrians: The Long Journey II* **1923** and the sixth as *Christopher Columbus: The Long Journey III* **1924**), an epic myth spanning mankind's development from his origins in a temperate Scandinavian Eden before the Ice Age through to the threshold of modern times with the explorations of Christopher Columbus. *Skibet* ["The Ship"] (**1912**) is the untranslated fifth volume. A one-volume edition of the translated portions is *The Long Journey* (**1933**). [JE]
See also: ANTHROPOLOGY; ORIGIN OF MAN.

JERSILD, P.C. *See* SCANDINAVIA.

JESSEL, JOHN *See* Stanley WEINBAUM.

JE T'AIME, JE T'AIME Film (1968). 20th Century-Fox. Directed by Alain Resnais, starring Claude Rich, Olga Georges-Picot and Anouk Ferjac. Screenplay by Alain Resnais and Jacques STERNBERG. 94 mins (cut to 82). Colour.

A failed suicide is co-opted into a secret and dangerous scientific experiment, his dislike of life making him a suitable subject. He is to be sent back into the past for one minute. The experiment has proved safe for mice, but humans are conscious of time and memory in a way that animals are not, and the protagonist is trapped in a series of not-quite-random time oscillations, trapped in his own past and an unhappy love affair. Where Resnais' previous study of time and memory, *Last Year at Marienbad*, was a triumph for the cameraman, this film is a triumph for the editor. Some of the time oscillations last only seconds, some minutes, sometimes replaying the same scene (with subtle differences) several times over, sometimes visiting fantasy events as if this second time around they were real, memory with its distortions carrying the same metaphysical weight as fact. The final sequence of the film, involving an experimental mouse, is sad, resonant and beautiful; it suggests obliquely that the past can be changed, if only ironically. The time machine itself is organic, curvilinear, womb-like, and from it the hero emerges into the amniotic fluid of the sea. This is one of the most striking sf films ever made, though it is not centrally sf; it uses the idea of time travel to explore the extent to which we can, or cannot, withdraw ourselves from our own pasts, and hence from the processes of time. The screenwriter, Sternberg, is himself an sf writer of distinction and sophistication. [PN]

JETÉE, LA Short film (1962). Argos/Arcturus Films. Directed by Chris Marker, starring Hélène Chatelain, Jacques Ledoux and Davos Hanich. Screenplay by Chris Marker. 29 mins. B/w.

This short, celebrated French film is set after World War III, when a group of scientists are trying to send a man back in time to pre-War days. A vivid childhood memory is used as the catalyst for time travel, accomplished through the agency of a mysterious drug, but the man is seduced by the events of his own past and refuses to return to the present. He is then tracked down by other travellers in time and killed on an airport runway while watching his former self leaving on a trip. Composed entirely of still photographs (though there is one brief sequence — a close-up of a girl winking — that gives the impression of movement) the film is nearer in theme and approach to the NEW-WAVE sf of the 1960s than to traditional TIME-TRAVEL stories in the cinema or in literature. [JB]

JET JACKSON *See* CAPTAIN MIDNIGHT.

JEURY, MICHEL (1934–   ). French writer. He is generally considered to be the leading French practitioner of the genre. His work successfully blends Anglo-Saxon traditions and a freshness of approach to established themes. Under his pseudonym Albert Higon he won the PRIX JULES VERNE in 1960 for *La machine du pouvoir* ["The Machine of Power"] (**1960**). His major achievement is an impressive trilogy about TIME TRAVEL and the struggle between multinational corporations: *Le temps incertain* ["Uncertain Time"] (**1973**; award for best French sf novel of the year); *Les singes du temps* ["The Monkeys of Time"] (**1974**) and *Soleil chaud poisson des profondeurs* ["Hot Sun Fish of the Deep"] (**1976**). He has also written 20 short stories, some of which connect with the trilogy. [MJ]
Other works: *Utopies 75* ["Utopias 75"] (anth. **1975**); *Aux étoiles du destin* ["Stars of Destiny"] (**1960**) and *Les animaux de justice* ["The Animals of Justice"] (**1976**), the last two under the Higon pseudonym; *L'empire du peuple* ["Empire of the People"] (**1977**), written under the Higon pseudonym in collaboration with Pierre Marlson.

JOHANNESSON, OLOF Pseudonym of Swedish scientist and writer Hannes Alfvén (1908–   ), winner of the 1970 Nobel Prize in Physics; his sf book, *Sagan om den stora datamaskinin* (**1966**; trans. as *The Tale of the Big Computer* **1968**; vt *The Great Computer, a Vision* UK; vt *The End of Man?*) purports to be a

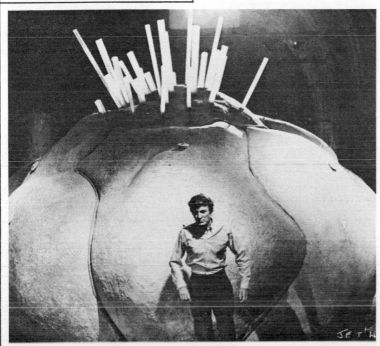

Claude Rich stands before the time machine in Resnais's JE T'AIME, JE T'AIME.

HISTORY of Earth written in the future by a COMPUTER, though perhaps it is by a human, whose drily witty fundamental premise is that mankind is merely an intermediate step in the EVOLUTION of MACHINES — a chilling perspective on our ultimate purpose. [JC/PN]
Other works: non-fiction as by H. Alfven: *Worlds-Antiworlds: Antimatter in Cosmology* (trans. **1966**).
See also: AUTOMATION; INTELLIGENCE.

JOHNS, KENNETH Pseudonym used for collaborations between Kenneth BULMER and John NEWMAN on a very long series of science-fact articles for *NW* and *Nebula*, 1955-61.

JOHNS, MARSTON *See* John E. MULLER.

JOHNSON, GEORGE CLAYTON (? -). American writer, who wrote three sf stories for GAMMA, 1963-5, and was co-author with William F. NOLAN of *Logan's Run* (**1967**), which was filmed as LOGAN'S RUN, and inspired a TV series. [JC]
See also: CRIME AND PUNISHMENT; OVERPOPULATION.

JOHNSON, L.P.V. (? -). British writer, whose sf novel is *In the Time of the Thetans* (**1961**). The Thetans look like starfish, and are nasty. [JC]

JOHNSON, OWEN M(cMAHON) (1878–1952). American writer in various genres, in whose sf novel, *The Coming of the Amazons* (**1931**), an awakened CORPSICLE discovers a matriarchal AD 2181, and fights for male equality; as in Thomas BERGER's *Regiment of Women* (**1973**), sexual roles are reversed, to SATIRIC effect. [JC]
See also: WOMEN.

JOHNSON, RAY W. (1900–). American writer, whose sf novel is *Astera: The Planet That Committed Suicide* (**1960**). [JC]

JOHNSON, SAMUEL (1709–84). English poet, critic, lexicographer and author of one novel, *The History of Rasselas: Prince of Abissinia* (**1759**), written to pay for his mother's funeral (he got £125 for it). It is of interest to the student of PROTO SCIENCE FICTION for its sustained meditation on the nature of, and the chances of obtaining, human happiness (*see also* UTOPIAS *and* DYSTOPIAS), along with its initial setting in a secret valley, the flying machine Rasselas hopes will transport him to freedom in the world outside (in the event it fails — SJ's spirit was inimical to unsustained flights of fancy) and the mad astronomer who believes himself responsible for WEATHER CONTROL. The book is an archetypal example of the important sf theme of CONCEPTUAL BREAKTHROUGH. A useful critical edition is

Oxford University Press 1971, ed. Tillotson and Jenkins. [JC/PN]
See also: ASTRONOMY; FANTASTIC VOYAGES; SCIENTISTS.

JOHN W. CAMPBELL AWARD Award for the best new sf writer of the year, selected by votes of sf fans and presented at the World Sf CONVENTION. The award is sponsored by Condé-Nast, publishers of ANALOG, and was instituted in 1972 in tribute to John W.CAMPBELL Jr, who died in 1971. Winners of the award are: Jerry POURNELLE (1973), Lisa TUTTLE and Spider ROBINSON (1974), P.J.PLAUGER (1975), Tom REAMY (1976), C.J.CHERRYH (1977) and Orson Scott Card (1978). [PR]

JOHN W. CAMPBELL MEMORIAL AWARD Given annually for the best sf novel of the year published in English, selected by a committee of academic critics and sf writers. The membership of the committee has undergone slight changes, and since 1975 the award has been administered from the UK, though it was originated by Americans, including Harry HARRISON and Leon STOVER. The administration of the award has always been based at a university (two successively in the USA, and then one in the UK), and the selections have at times been criticized as over-academic, especially the first, and untrue to the memory of Campbell. In response, one judge commented that it was no good trying to guess what Campbell would have chosen; the only honest thing to do is to choose for oneself: "You can't second-guess the dead". The award has not been well publicized, but although it got off to a shaky start, there is probably room for an award voted on by a small panel of experts, as opposed to fans (the HUGO), writers (the NEBULA) or teachers (the JUPITER) *en masse*. [PN]
Winners:
1973: Barry MALZBERG, *Beyond Apollo*; special trophy for excellence in writing to Robert SILVERBERG
1974: Arthur C. CLARKE, *Rendezvous With Rama* and Robert MERLE, *Malevil* (tie)
1975: Philip K. DICK, *Flow My Tears, the Policeman Said*
1976: Wilson TUCKER, *The Year of the Quiet Sun* (special retrospective award)
1977: Kingsley AMIS, *The Alteration*
1978: Frederik POHL, *Gateway*

JOKAI, MÓR or MAURUS (1825–1904.) Extremely prolific Hungarian novelist, probably the dominant literary figure of 19th-century Hungary; most of his 100 or more novels are violent historical tales, full of catastrophic incident; he was very frequently translated. *Az aramy ember* (**1872**; trans. as *Timar's Two Worlds* 1888; vt *Modern Midas* USA; vt *The Man With the Golden Touch* Hungary) contrasts a hectic and hysterical urban life

with an idyllic UTOPIA established on an "ownerless island" in the Danube, where the protagonist eventually retires into serenity. MJ wrote a number of anticipations in novel form, not translated into English, in which, for example, he writes of SUSPENDED ANIMATION and the use of aircraft in future WAR. Many of these works were translated into German. *Tales from Jokai* (coll. trans. **1904**) contains a number of sf stories, including the novella "The City and the Beast" which deals with ATLANTIS and its destruction. An important Jokai work, apparently untranslated into English, is *A jövő század regénye* ["The Novel of the Coming Century"] (**1874**), a long, futuristic anticipation full of sf ideas. [PN/JC]
Other works: *Told by the Death's Head* (trans. **1902** of *Egy hirhedett kalandor a tizenhetedil századból* **1904**).

JONES, D(ENNIS) F(ELTHAM) (? -). English writer, who has been variously employed, and who served as an officer in the Royal Navy in the Second World War. He began publishing sf with the first volume of his "Colossus" trilogy, *Colossus* (**1966**), which was made into an effective film, COLOSSUS THE FORBIN PROJECT (1969); as in the film, Charles Forbin helps to create a master COMPUTER designed to coordinate all the defences of the Western world. At the same time, the Russians have been building their own, and the two computers, Colossus and Guardian, exchange information in an impressive scene. Soon, however, Colossus becomes conscious and autonomous, and takes over the world. The sequels, *The Fall of Colossus* (**1974**) and *Colossus and the Crab* (**1977**), expand from the first volume (diluting its admonitory impact in the process) by introducing religious sects that worship Colossus, complicated plots and irritated Martians; ultimately everything comes to a transcendental stop. DFJ's other novels, like *Implosion* (**1967**), in which most women become sterile, the fate of the fertile ones being rather grim, also veer distressingly close to an apocalyptic gloom too easily achieved; in the grip of this tendency, he has a habit of allowing his characters little real scope for action or development; his stories tend therefore to drift into the routine. [JC]
Other works: *Don't Pick the Flowers* (**1971**; vt *Denver is Missing* USA); *The Floating Zombie* (**1975**).
See also: DISASTER.

JONES, EDDIE (1935–). British illustrator. Active in sf illustration since 1958, he has generally been accepted as a major sf artist since 1969, when he became art editor of *Visions of Tomorrow*. He has done cover paintings for over 500 magazines and paperback books in half a dozen countries, including the United States. His style is representational; he

A typically elaborate Eddie JONES spaceship, *Algol*, Winter 1977.

crafts the spaceships for which he is best known with a baroque detail reminiscent of Frank R. PAUL, using thick, glowing colours that range right across the spectrum. He mainly uses brushes, but often includes a touch of airbrush as well. He has been criticized for working in too narrow a mode — most of his covers feature various forms of space hardware, with a strong generic similarity to one another. EJ has been nominated twice for the HUGO award for best professional artist.   [JG]

JONES, GONNER (? –). British writer whose *The Dome* (1968) has a brain in charge of a future city.   [PN]

JONES, LANGDON (1942–). English-born short-story writer, editor and musician, now resident in Wales. LJ was strongly associated with *NW* during its NEW-WAVE period, both as contributor — he published all his sf stories there beginning with "Storm Water Tunnel" in 1964 — and in various editorial capacities. The most memorable of his notably experimental work, which is characterized by bleak textures and a strongly angular narrative style, appears in *The Eye of the Lens* (coll. 1972). LJ's wide taste as an editor is demonstrated in his *The New SF* (anth. 1969); he also collaborated with Michael MOORCOCK in putting together the "Jerry Cornelius" anthology of *NW* material *The Nature of*

the *Catastrophe* (anth. 1971). Mervyn PEAKE's *Titus Alone* (1959; rev. 1970) was originally published in a heavily edited form; LJ is responsible for the reconstruction work resulting in the posthumous 1970 publication of the definitive state of the work. LJ's interest in music is reflected in the hilarious "Symphony no.6 in C minor 'The Tragic' by Ludwig van Beethoven II" (1968). [JC] **See also:** ABSURDIST SF; ARTS.

JONES, MARGARET (? –). English writer, and lecturer in human communication studies. She began publishing sf with an amusing novel, *The Day They Put Humpty Together Again* (1968; vt *Transplant* USA), about what happens when prosthetic surgery techniques are used to wire an artist's head to a criminal's libidinous torso. *Through the Budgerigar* (1970) is a fantasy.   [JC]

JONES, MERVYN (1922–). British writer, best known for his many novels outside the sf field, and for journalism with the *New Statesman*. His sf novel, *On the Last Day* (1958), is a NEAR-FUTURE story about attempts to build a new intercontinental missile in the midst of the Third World War.   [JC]

JONES, NEIL R(ONALD) (1909–). American writer who until his retirement in 1973 worked as a New York State unemployment insurance claims investigator. His first story, "The Death's Head Meteor" (the first sf story to use the word "astronaut"), published in *Air Wonder Stories* in 1930, shares with almost all his fiction a very generalized common background, a future history given some explanation in "Time's Mausoleum" (1933), a story from the "Professor Jameson" series. This future history is one of the earliest and most popular in genre sf. It involves epic advances and conflicts centering on the 24th and 26th centuries and climaxes with the arrival on the scene of Professor Jameson, whose preserved body has been

reactivated, long after all other men have died, by the Zoromes, who encase his brain in metal and give him the chance to travel the universe in search of knowledge and adventure.

The first "Jameson" story, "The Jameson Satellite", dates from 1931; most of the pre-War "Jameson" stories appeared in *AMZ*, and most of the somewhat inferior later instalments in *Super Science Stories* and *Astonishing Stories*. The first 16 stories of the sequence have been published as *The Planet of the Double Sun* (coll. 1967), *The Sunless World* (coll. 1967), *Space War* (coll. 1967), *Twin Worlds* (coll. 1967) and *Doomsday on Ajiat* (coll., including two previously unpublished stories, 1968). The remaining stories, which did not reach book form, are "The Cat-Men of Aemt" (1940), "Cosmic Derelict" (1941), "Slaves of the Unknown" (1942), "Parasite Planet" (1949), "World Without Darkness" (1950), "The Mind Masters" (1950), and "The Star Killers" (1951). At least seven further stories remain written but unpublished. NRJ's two other connected series, "Tales of the 24th Century" and "Tales of the 26th Century", received magazine publication only; they are also known together as the "Durna Rangue" series, after the cult that dominates them. The "24th Century" series consists of "Spacewrecked on Venus" (1932), "Escape from Phobos" (1933), "Durna Rangue Neophyte" (1937), "Swordsmen of Saturn" (1939), "Hermit of Saturn's Ring" (1940), "Captives of Durna Rangue" (1941), "Priestess of the Sleeping Death" (1941) and "Spoilers of the Spaceways" (1942). The "26th Century" series consists of "The Death's Head Meteor" (1930), "The Asteroid of Death" (1931), "The Moon Pirates" (1934), "Little Hercules" (1936), "The Dark Swordsmen of Saturn" (1940), "Liquid Hell" (1940), "Invisible One" (1940) and "Vampire of the Void" (1941).

NRJ is a vigorous, straightforward writer whose style and concerns are typical of the first blossoming of sf at the end of the 1920s; his long-running "Jameson" series maintains from first to last a capacity to evoke an unselfconscious sense of wonder.   [JC] **See also:** CYBORGS; FAR FUTURE; IMMORTALITY; UNDER THE SEA.

JONES, RAYMOND F. (1915–). American writer born in Salt Lake City. He was very active for about 15 years after he first appeared in *ASF* in 1941 with "Test of the Gods", and virtually silent in the 1960s, though he has published some books recently. His best-known short story is the witty "Noise Level" (1952), an archetypal *ASF* tale of CONCEPTUAL BREAKTHROUGH, scientific advance taking place through destruction of a previous paradigm. Scientists are told that antigravity exists, and proceed to invent it. The story had two sequels,

"Trade Secret" (1953) and "The School" (1954). An earlier series, the "Peace Engineers", consists of "The Alien Machine" (1949), "The Shroud of Secrecy" (1949) and "The Greater Conflict" (1950). RFJ wrote one story, "Utility" (1944), under the pseudonym David Anderson.

RFJ's first novel is probably his best: *Renaissance* (1944 *ASF*; **1951**; vt *Man of Two Worlds*), a long, complicated PARALLEL-WORLDS adventure with an exciting narrative and a number of lively variations on favourite sf themes. *The Alien* (**1951**) also has a strong narrative drive in its story of the discovery of an ancient ALIEN artefact in the asteroid belt. *This Island Earth* (1949–50 *TWS*; fix-up **1952**) begins with beleaguered aliens secretly using Earth scientists in order to resist an enemy on their home planet. A good sf film was made from it (*see* THIS ISLAND EARTH). RFJ's 1950s juveniles are also good; they are *Son of the Stars* (**1952**), *Planet of Light* (**1953**) and *The Year When Stardust Fell* (**1958**). Two collections, *The Toymaker* (coll. **1951**) and *The Non-Statistical Man* (coll. **1964**), gather short work from the 1940s and '50s. After *The Secret People* (**1956**; vt *The Deviates*) and *The Cybernetic Brains* (1950 *Startling Stories*; **1962**), RFJ was comparatively inactive until he recently published such less interesting novels as *Syn* (**1969**) and *The River and the Dream* (**1977**). Though not generally an innovator in the field, RFJ, during his first period of activity, produced solid, well-crafted HARD-SF adventures. [JC/PN]

Other works: *Moonbase One* (**1971**); *Renegades of Time* (**1975**); *The King of Eolium* (**1975**).

See also: DISCOVERY AND INVENTION; DYSTOPIAS; GRAVITY; GREAT AND SMALL; ISLANDS; PHYSICS; POWER SOURCES; SPACE OPERA; SUSPENDED ANIMATION.

JONES, RICHARD GLYN *See* Richard GLYN JONES.

JONES, R(OBERT) G(IBSON) (? – ?). American illustrator. Almost forgotten today, RGJ painted 90 covers for the Ziff-Davis publications *Amazing Stories* and *Fantastic Adventures*, 1942–52. His stimulating cover illustrations often had an "Arabian Nights" feel about them, with exotically costumed characters. His very commercial style, reminiscent of Earle K. BERGEY's in some respects, was strong on the sort of dashing melodrama that would have been equally appropriate for historical romance magazines, but had little sense of the rather different romance of sf. [JG/PN]

JORGENSEN or **JORGENSON, IVAR** A "floating PSEUDONYM" which originated as a house name of the Ziff-Davis Publishing Co. in the early 1950s. It was later also used in IF, IMAGINATION and IMAGINATIVE TALES. Most of the early stories under the name Ivar Jorgensen were written by Paul FAIRMAN; other writers who used it include Robert SILVERBERG, Randall GARRETT and Harlan ELLISON. Silverberg subsequently

published several stories in SCIENCE FICTION ADVENTURES as Ivar Jorgenson (note spelling), one of which was published in book form as *Starhaven* (**1958**) under that name. Other books appearing under the name in its original form are all by Fairman. They are: *Rest in Agony* (**1963**; vt *The Diabolist*), *Ten From Infinity* (**1963**; vt *Ten Deadly Men*; vt *The Deadly Sky*) and *Whom the Gods Would Slay* (1951 *Fantastic Adventurers*; **1968**). A Jorgensen story written by Fairman for *If*, "Deadly City" (1953) was filmed as TARGET EARTH! (1954). [BS]

JOSEPH, M(ICHAEL) K(ENNEDY) (1914–). English-born, Oxford-educated New Zealand writer and professor of English, whose earlier novels have been well received. They include *I'll Soldier No More* (**1958**) and *A Pound of Saffron* (**1962**). His sf novel, *The Hole in the Zero* (**1967**), begins as an apparently typical SPACE-OPERA adventure into further DIMENSIONS at the edge of the universe, but quickly reveals itself as a linguistically brilliant, complex exploration of the nature of the four personalities involved, as they begin out of their own resources to shape the low-probability regions they have tumbled into; ultimately, the novel takes on allegorical overtones. As an examination of the metaphorical potentials of sf language and subject matter, it is a significant contribution to the field. MKS has also produced a scholarly edition of Mary SHELLEY's *Frankenstein* (**1818**; his Oxford University Press edition 1969). [JC]

Other works: *The Time of Achamoth* (**1977** New Zealand).

See also: COSMOLOGY; FANTASTIC VOYAGES.

JOURNEY TO THE CENTER OF THE EARTH Film (1959). 20th Century-Fox. Directed by Henry Levin, starring Pat Boone, James Mason, Diane Baker and Alan Napier. Screenplay by Walter Reisch and Charles Brackett, based on the novel by Jules VERNE. 132 mins. Colour.

A map is discovered which shows a route deep into the Earth through a series of large caverns. Two rival groups become involved in a race to the bottom and encounter various hazards, including prehistoric reptiles. A stirring climax shows the hero being fired out of a volcano. The sets are impressive. [JB]

JOURNEY TO THE CENTER OF TIME Film (1968). Borealis and Dorad. Directed by David L. Hewitt, starring Scott Brady, Gigi Perreau, Anthony Eisley, Abraham Sofaer, Austin Green and Andy David. Screenplay by David Prentiss. 82 mins. Colour.

In this low-budget film a group of people oscillate between the future and the past in an out-of-control time machine. First they journey to the future where they encounter the inevitable totalitarian society engaged in a struggle

An R.G. JONES girl, more surprised than terrified; British edition, Aug. 1953.

with an equally stereotyped horde of mutants; they then return to a prehistoric era populated with dinosaurs, then find themselves in the future again, and so on. The quality of special effects is not equal to the ambition of the script. [JB]

JOURNEY TO THE FAR SIDE OF THE SUN (vt **DOPPELGANGER**) Film (1969). Century 21 Productions/ Universal. Directed by Robert Parrish, starring Ian Hendry, Roy Thinnes, Patrick Wymark, Lyn Loring and Herbert Lom. Screenplay by Gerry and Sylvia Anderson and Donald James. 101 mins (cut to 94). Colour.

The film is an above average offering from the Anderson production team which was also responsible for the TV series THUNDERBIRDS, UFO and SPACE 1999. No doubt the credit lies with the direction of Hollywood veteran Robert Parrish, who handled the confused and illogical plot with style. It involves the discovery of a duplicate of the Earth, which is always on the opposite side of the sun from our planet. An expedition is mounted to reach the other Earth, and the confusions of the subsequent plot, involving sabotage and apparent conspiracy between the two planets, are compounded by the fact that the story is told in flashbacks by a character in a mental asylum, giving a *Dr Caligari*-like ambiguity to the whole film. [JB]

JUDD, CYRIL Pseudonym used by Cyril M. KORNBLUTH and Judith MERRIL for their collaborative work. *Outpost Mars* (1952; rev. vt *Sin in Space*) deals with the COLONIZATION of MARS, while *Gunner Cade* (1952) concerns the rebellion of a mercenary in an age when WAR is staged as a spectator SPORT. The only other story to appear under the name was "Sea Change" (1953). [BS]

JUENGER, ERNST (1895–). German writer, whose early works reflected his experiences in the First World War. *Auf den Marmorklippen* (1942 French translation; trans. as *On the Marble Cliffs* 1947), though its status as a classic of resistance to Nazism has been somewhat shaken by analysis of its broodingly passive austerity regarding political action, is a peculiarly resonant allegory of the destruction of a civilized country by an incursion of vandal-like conquerors; *Gläserne Bienen* (1957; trans. as *The Glass Bees* 1961) also applies an allegorical mode to the story of the creation and use of ROBOT bees for industrial work. *Heliopolis* (Germany 1949), an ironical UTOPIA, remains untranslated. [JC]

JULES VERNE-MAGASINET *See* SCANDINAVIA.

JULES VERNE'S ROCKET TO THE MOON Film (1967). *See* FROM THE EARTH TO THE MOON.

JUPITER Jupiter's image in sf is derived from its status as the largest of the planets and the most accessible (by virtue of being the nearest to Earth) of the GAS GIANTS. Its four major moons — Ganymede, Callisto, Io and Europa — were discovered by Galileo, but it was not until 1892 that Barnard discovered the fifth. Seven others have been discovered in the 20th century. The visible "surface" of Jupiter is an outer layer of a very dense, deep atmosphere, and is thus fluid, though it does have one enduring and enigmatic feature: the Great Red Spot. Radio-astronomers discovered in the 1950s that Jupiter is a radio-source, and this has encouraged speculation about its suitability as an abode of life, though the signals themselves show no pattern. Jupiter was included in various interplanetary tours inspired by the religious imagination, as were the other planets known to the ancients, but attracted more attention than most because of its size. It is prominent in many 19th-century interplanetary novels, including Joel R. Peabody's *A World of Wonders* (1838), J.B. Fayette's anonymously published *The Experiences of Eon and Eona* (1886) and John Jacob ASTOR's *A Journey in Other Worlds* (1894). In the last-named it is presented as a "prehistoric" version of Earth, with a mixed fauna of dinosaurs, mastodons and others. In two other roughly contemporary novels it was represented as a parallel of Earth: Harold Brydges' *A Fortnight in Heaven* (1886) and the anonymous *To Jupiter via Hell* (1908). As astronomical discoveries were popularized, however, the credibility of an Earthlike Jupiter waned rapidly. The last significant novel to use a Jovian scenario for straightforward UTOPIAN modelling was Ella SCRYMSOUR's *The Perfect World* (1922). The American PULP writers, however, were prepared to squeeze a little more life out of the notion for the purposes of scientific romance. Edmond HAMILTON's "A Conquest of Two Worlds" (1932) tells a harrowing tale of the brutal human invasion of Jupiter, and Edgar Rice BURROUGHS took John Carter away from Mars to fight "The Skeleton Men of Jupiter" (1943) in the last novelette of the series. Most exotic romances set beyond the orbit of Mars employ not Jupiter itself but one of its satellites. Ganymede is featured in E.E. "Doc" SMITH's *Spacehounds of I.P.C.* (1931; 1947) and Leigh BRACKETT's "The Dancing Girl of Ganymede" (1950), while Lin CARTER set a recent series of Burroughs pastiches on Callisto. Io features in two notable early pulp sf stories: Stanley G. WEINBAUM's "The Mad Moon" (1935) and Raymond Z. GALLUN's "The Lotus Engine" (1940).

In John W. CAMPBELL Jr's ASTOUNDING SCIENCE-FICTION there began a series of attempts to make speculative use of the planet as it might really be. Good early examples are "Heavy Planet" (1939) by Lee Gregor (Milton A. Rothman) and "Clerical Error" (1940) by Clifford D. SIMAK. Simak later returned to an ultra-alien Jupiter in the curious "Desertion" (1944), one of the "City" series in which humans leave the planet of their birth in return for a new existence, biologically transfigured, on Jupiter. Isaac ASIMOV, who set one of his earliest stories, "The Callistan Menace" (1940), in this neighbourhood, turned his attention to Jupiter proper in "Not Final!" (1941) and "Victory Unintentional" (1942). In the former story hostile aliens are discovered there, while in the second Jovians get mistaken ideas about the abilities of humans because they do not realize their visitors from Earth are actually robots.

The 1950s produced two classic stories dealing with conditions on Jupiter. James BLISH's "Bridge" (1952), which was incorporated into *They Shall Have Stars* (1956; vt *Year 2018!*), is about the mounting of a colossal experiment to test a hypothesis regarding modifications to the theory of gravity and its psychological effects on the people involved. Poul ANDERSON's "Call Me Joe" (1957) is about the everyday life of an artificial, centaur-like creature designed for the Jovian environment. Anderson later made use of a similar background in *Three Worlds to Conquer* (1964), the three worlds being Jupiter, Ganymede and Earth. In this novel Ganymede comes into focus as a possible site for a colony — a notion already developed in the 1950s by Robert HEINLEIN in *Farmer in the Sky* (1950), Anderson himself in *The Snows of Ganymede* (1955; 1958) and Robert SILVERBERG in *Invaders from Earth* (1958). James Blish, however, felt that even Ganymedean COLONIZATION might require GENETIC ENGINEERING of considerable magnitude in "A Time to Survive" (1956), which was incorporated into *The Seedling Stars* (1957). More recently, one particular theme which has exerted a powerful fascination over a number of writers has been that of a descent into Jupiter's atmosphere. This figures in Isaac Asimov's *Lucky Starr and the Moons of Jupiter* (1957 as by Paul French; vt *The Moons of Jupiter*) and the brothers STRUGATSKI's "Destination: Amaltheia" (1960; trans. 1962) as a potential disaster for malfunctioning spaceships, but in two impressive stories of the 1970s the descent is made deliberately, in search of Jovian life — Arthur C. CLARKE's "A Meeting With Medusa" (1971) and Gregory BENFORD and Gordon EKLUND's "The Anvil of Jove" (1976) which was incorporated into *If the Stars are Gods* (1977). Ben BOVA's *As on a Darkling Plain* (1972) also has a brief sequence featuring such a descent.

In view of the fact that VENUS and MARS are now virtually ruled out as possible abodes for life, more interest in Jupiter might be expected in the near future. An anthology of stories with

Jovian themes is *Jupiter* (anth. **1973**) ed. Frederik and Carol POHL. [BS]

JUPITER AWARDS These literary awards for best sf in the categories of novel, novella, novelette and short story were inaugurated in 1973 by the Instructors of Science Fiction in Higher Education, a group founded by Dr Charles G. Waugh at the University of Maine, primarily for this purpose. The Jupiter awards are administered by the SCIENCE FICTION RESEARCH ASSOCIATION. Awards are dated by year of publication, not year of voting; they consist of illustrated scrolls. [PN]

1973
Novel: *Rendezvous with Rama* by Arthur C. CLARKE
Novella: "The Feast of St. Dionysus" by Robert SILVERBERG
Novelette: "The Deathbird" by Harlan ELLISON
Short story: "A Suppliant in Space" by Robert SHECKLEY
1974
Novel: *The Dispossessed* by Ursula K. LE GUIN
Novella: "Riding the Torch" by Norman SPINRAD
Novelette: "The Seventeen Virgins" by Jack VANCE
Short story: "The Day Before the Revolution" by Ursula K. LE GUIN
1975
No awards given
1976
Novel: *Where Late the Sweet Birds Sang* by Kate WILHELM
Novella: "Houston, Houston, Do You Read?" by James TIPTREE Jr
Novelette: "The Diary of the Rose" by Ursula K. LE GUIN
Short story: "I See You" by Damon KNIGHT
1977
Novel: "A Heritage of Stars" by Clifford D. SIMAK
Novella: "In the Hall of the Martian Kings" by John VARLEY
Novelette: "Time Storm" by Gordon R. DICKSON

JUST IMAGINE Film (1930). Fox. Directed by David Butler, starring El Brendel, Frank Albertson, Maureen O'Sullivan and John Garrick. Screenplay by David Butler, Ray Henderson, G.G. DeSylva and Lew Brown. 113 mins. B/w.

The failure of this expensive sf blockbuster may explain why Hollywood kept clear of sf subjects (except in the context of horror films) for so long afterwards, but it was the whimsicality of a silly story rather than its sf content that led to the film's failure. A man is struck by lightning while playing golf in 1930 and wakes to find himself in New York in 1980. There follows a stowing away on a spaceship and a romantic-triangle plot between man, girl and beautiful Martian, interspersed with banal musical numbers.

New York in 1980 as visualized in the 1930 musical JUST IMAGINE.

The special effects are good for their period and the sets are spectacular, in particular the huge model of New York City, which cost $250,000 to build, designed by art directors Stephen Goosson and Ralph Hammeras. [JB]

JUVENILE SERIES *See* DIME NOVELS AND JUVENILE SERIES; CHILDREN'S SF.

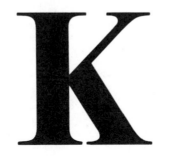

KAEMPFERT, WADE House pseudonym used by the editor of ROCKET STORIES: Lester DEL REY on the first two issues; probably Harry HARRISON on the third. [PN]

KAFKA, FRANZ (1883–1924). Czech-born, German-speaking Austrian writer, not usually or profitably considered a writer of fantasy or sf, though at the same time some of his stories, such as "In der Strafkolonie" (1919; trans. 1933; trans. as title story in *In the Penal Settlement*, coll. **1947**), or *Die Verwandlung* (1916; trans. as "The Transformation" 1933; as *The Metamorphosis* **1937**; vt *Metamorphosis*), contain elements which in themselves are quasi-sf, but here are put to ABSURDIST and METAPHYSICAL purposes. The former tells of an execution machine which incises moral slogans on the victim's body; the latter is a horrifying allegory in which a young man is transformed overnight into a huge beetle. FK's work is Modernist, its fable-like quality indefinably dreamlike and menacing. His influence has been enormous, especially in Europe, and permeates, consciously or unconsciously, much of modern sf's attempts to get at the quality of life in dislocated, totalitarian or merely surrealistic venues. FK's most famous works, all published posthumously and in a probably unfinished condition, are *Der Prozess* (**1925**; trans. as *The Trial* **1935**), *Das Schloss* (**1926**; trans. as *The Castle* **1930**) and *Amerika* (**1927**; trans. **1938**). They all tell of dilemmas where the protagonist cannot find justice, or common sense, or any clear place in a meaningful universe, and are certainly reflected (though sometimes at second hand) in sf that deals with PARANOIA or shifting realities (*see* PERCEPTION). [JC/PN]
See also: FANTASY; MONSTERS.

KAGAN, NORMAN (? –). American writer whose occasional sf stories, from "The Mathenauts" for *If* in 1964, have sometimes dealt vigorously and amusingly with MATHEMATICS as a subject, and tend to feature extroverted mathematicians as protagonists. NK also wrote *The Cinema of Stanley Kubrick* (**1972**). [JC]
See also: FANTASTIC VOYAGES; FOURTH DIMENSION (AND OTHERS).

KAGARLITSKI, JULIUS (1926–). Russian critic, and professor of European drama at the State Theatrical Institute in Moscow. He is one of several Russian critics with a strong interest in sf, and unusually, one of his books has been translated into English, as *The Life and Thought of H.G. Wells* (**1963** Russia; trans. **1966**). A more recent work, *Chto takoie fantastika?* ["What is the Fantastic?"] (**1974**) has been translated into Polish, Spanish and German, but not

English. He has won the Chief Award of the Polish Ministry of Culture, and again unusually, the American PILGRIM award, in 1972, for services to sf studies. [PN]

KAHN, HERMAN (1922–). American mathematician, political scientist and futurologist. He worked 1947–59 with the RAND Corporation, and is now director of the Hudson Institute, a body devoted to forecasting, and producing political, economic and military scenarios of the future. HK is one of the most influential and best-known workers in this area, though many have found the kind of analysis for which he stands cold-blooded and too narrowly based. In terms of accuracy there has not been a great deal to choose between the predictions of FUTUROLOGY and the best of the sf PREDICTIONS. HK's works include *The Year 2000: Framework for Speculation on the Next 37 Years* (1967) with Anthony J. Wiener; *On Escalation: Metaphors and Scenarios* (1968); *The Emerging Japanese Superstate: Challenge and Response* (1971); *Things to Come: Thinking About the 70's and 80's* (1972) with B. Bruce-Briggs; and as editor, *The Future of the Corporation* (anth. 1974). [PN]
See also: LEISURE.

KAMIN, NICK Pseudonym of American writer Robert J. Antonick (1939–), whose sf novels, *Earthrim* (1969), a heavily plotted melodrama on a tyrannized Earth, and *The Herod Men* (1971), both feature adventure plots, somewhat awkwardly presented. [JC]

KANE, WILSON Ziff-Davis house name, used on several stories 1958–9 in *AMZ* and *Fantastic*; at least one, unidentified, was the work of Robert BLOCH. [PN]

KANER, H(YMAN) (? –). British writer who publishes his own books from Llandudno in Wales; some are of sf interest and include *People of the Twilight* (1946), a PARALLEL-WORLDS tale, and *The Sun Queen* (1946), which features instantaneous travel and a race of dwellers on the SUN. [JC]
Other works: All very short, undated paperbacks published by Kaner in the mid-1940s: *Ape-Man's Offering*, *Fire Watcher's Night*, *Hot Swag*, *The Naked Foot*, *Ordeal by Moonlight*, *Squaring the Triangle and other Short Stories* (coll.).

KANTOR, MACKINLAY (1904–77). American writer, best known for such works outside the sf field as *Andersonville* (1955), a long novel set in the Civil War, the area of his deepest concern, in which he also set his sf book, *If the South Had Won the Civil War* (1961), the ALTERNATE-WORLDS thesis of the title being a favourite crux for American writers in the genre. [JC]
See also: POLITICS.

KAPITÄN MORS DER LUFTPIRAT *See* LUFTPIRAT UND SEIN LENKBARES LUFTSCHIFF.

KAPP, COLIN (1929?–). English writer and worker in the electronics field. He began publishing sf with "Life Plan" for *NW* in 1958, where his best work soon appeared, including "Lambda 1" (1962), which gave its title to the E.J. CARNELL collection, *Lambda 1* (anth. 1964), and *Transfinite Man* (1964; vt under the magazine title *The Dark Mind* UK), in which the strange protagonist, Dalroi, who turns out to be an unkillable SUPERMAN, pits himself against the corrupt Failway Terminal in duels extending through a number of dimensions, access to which the Terminal attempts to control. Dalroi's superman status combines features of Keith LAUMER's better-known variety, along with something of the flawed nature of Alfred BESTER's Gully Foyle in *The Stars My Destination* (1956), which includes a sequence of uncollected stories for NEW WRITINGS IN SF and novels like *The Patterns of Chaos* (1972) and its sequel *The Chaos Weapon* (1977) are considerably less compelling. [JC]
Other works: *The Wizard of Anharitte* (1973); *The Survival Game* (1976); *Manalone* (1977).

KARAGEORGE, MICHAEL *See* Poul ANDERSON.

KARIG, WALTER (1898–). American journalist and novelist, an author for many years of the famous "Nancy Drew " girls' detective series; in his sf fantasy, *Zotz!* (1947), a man is given an ancient power to kill by pointing his hand and saying "Zotz"; his attempts to help America win the Second World War are frustrated by bureaucracy, to some SATIRICAL point. [JC]

KARINTHY, FRIGYES (1887–1938). Hungarian writer and translator, best known for his work outside the sf field, mostly humorous satires; he translated Jonathan SWIFT and Mark TWAIN, among others, into Hungarian. His two continuations of Swift's *Gulliver's Travels* (1726) are *Utazas Faremidóba* (1916) and *Capillária* (1922), translated together by Paul TABORI as *Voyage to Faremido and Capillaria* (trans. 1966); sharp-tongued and convincingly Swiftian, they are impressive introductions to his melancholy, sometimes savage view of the 20th century. [JC]

KARP, DAVID (1922–). American writer, whose sf novel *One* (1953; vt *Escape to Nowhere*) is a notable MAINSTREAM approach to sf modes as a way of expressing DYSTOPIAN views about the future. Though distinctly less convincing than such predecessors as Arthur KOESTLER's *Darkness at Noon* (1940) and George ORWELL's *Nineteen*

Eighty-Four (1949), it does present a salutarily grim and sharply described vision of a totalitarian future USA and the brutal mind control it finds necessary to survive; part of the novel's interest is in its sometimes sympathetic insight into the mind of inquisitor as well as victim. *The Day of the Monkey* (1955) is fantasy. [JC]
See also: POLITICS.

KASTEL, WARREN Ziff-Davis house name used by Chester S. GEIER and possibly others 1948–50, and by Robert SILVERBERG 1957, on magazine stories.

KASTLE, HERBERT D(AVID) (1924–). American writer, who began publishing sf with "The York Problem" for *If* in 1955, and whose sf novel, *The Reassembled Man* (1964), routinely depicts the transformation by aliens of a human into a sexually supercharged SUPERMAN. [JC]
Other works: *Edward Brenner is Alive Again!* (1975).

KAUL, FEDOR (? – ?). German writer. His sf novel, *Die Welt ohne Gedächtnis* (trans. as *Contagion to this World* 1933), begins conventionally enough with a deformed scientist, thwarted in love, determining to revenge himself on the world by releasing dangerous bacteria he has developed, which turn out to have a memory-erasing effect on humans. The scientist's love-affair forgotten, the novel becomes a post-HOLOCAUST vision, in which the remnants of mankind mutate into a roving race of giants in harmony with Nature; the scientist grows old and dies forgiven. [JC]
Other works: *A Modern Monte Cristo* (trans. 1938).

KAVAN, ANNA Pseudonym under which French-born, much travelled writer Helen Woods Edmonds (1901–68) wrote her fiction from 1940, though previously she signed herself Helen Ferguson (her first married name). Her life, which ended in suicide, was tragically complicated by heroin addiction. She is well known for work outside the sf field, though her sf novel and last work, *Ice* (1967), is as familiar to readers as anything she wrote; it depicts, through compulsively intense imagery, with links with Franz KAFKA (whose initial she borrowed in her pseudonym) and the surrealists generally, a post-DISASTER search for a woman through a world increasingly shadowed by an approaching ice age. Several editions carry an introduction by Brian W. ALDISS, whose own work has been influenced by that of AK, whom he sees as one of the great sf writers. [JC/PN]
Other works: *Asylum Piece and Other Stories* (coll. 1940); *House of Sleep* (1947; vt *Sleep Has His House* UK); *A Bright Green Field* (coll. 1958).
See also: END OF THE WORLD.

First issue, Oct. 1936. Cover by H.W. Scott.

KA-ZAR US PULP MAGAZINE. Three issues, Oct. 1936, Jan. and Jun. 1937, published by Manvis Publications; no editor named. The last issue was titled *KA-ZAR The Great*. Ka-Zar begins as a small boy, the sole survivor of a plane crash that kills his parents. He is raised by lions and becomes a Tarzan/Mowgli character. The character was resuscitated by MARVEL COMICS in the 1960s, featured in their *Strange Tales* series. The Oct. 1936 issue was reprinted as a facsimile book, **1975**. [FHP/MJE]

KDO CHCE ZABIT JESSII? (vt **WHO WOULD KILL JESSIE?**) Film (1965). State Film. Directed by Milos Macourek and Vaclav Vorlicek, starring Jiri Sovak, Dana Medricka, Olga Schoberova, Karl Effa and Juraj Visny. Screenplay by Milos Macourek and Vaclav Vorlicek. 80 mins. B/w.

This very funny Czechoslovak film tells of three comic-book characters who are brought inadvertently to life and cause chaos in a large town. It was originally conceived as a children's film, but the makers realized that the idea had satirical potential. An overworked professor becomes obsessed with a newspaper comic strip featuring a voluptuous heroine, Jessie, who is constantly being pursued by two villains — a cowboy and a character similar to SUPERMAN. The professor's wife, also a scientist, has invented a machine that can eradicate unwanted dreams but its side-effect is to give three-dimensional substance to the subject of the dreams, and the result is the manifestation of the three comic-book characters in the professor's apartment. This exhilarating film has not had a wide distribution outside Czechoslovakia, perhaps because, like most films made in that country in the mid-1960s, it has become an embarrassment to the present regime. [JB]

KEARNEY (ELFRIC WELLS) CHALMERS (1881– ?). English writer, author of a text, *Rapid Transit in the Future* (second edition only is recorded, **1911**). His UTOPIA *Erone* (**1943**), an old-fashioned love-story set in a rather sentimentalized communist society on the planet Uranus, had quite a popular success, though is now forgotten. His short pamphlet *The Great Calamity* (**1948**) itemizes the destruction of most of the world. [JC]

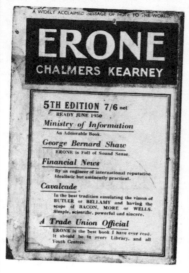

KEARNEY's *Erone*, now forgotten, once had a wide following, even among trade union officials.

KEE, ROBERT (1919–). English broadcaster and writer. His sf novel, *A Sign of the Times* (**1955**), is set in the NEAR FUTURE, where regimentation rules along lines familiar to post-War British fiction. [JC]

KEENE, DAY (? –). American writer, mostly of detective novels and film and TV scripts; in his sf novel, *World Without Women* (**1960**), written with Leonard PRUYN, the condition described in the title has violent results. [JC]

See also: WOMEN.

KEITH, LEIGH See Horace L. GOLD.

KELLEAM, JOSEPH E(VERIDGE) (1913–). American writer, variously employed, an occasional contributor to the sf field since publishing his first story, "Rust," for *ASF* in 1939. His first novel, *Overlords from Space* (**1956**), is a routine tale in which ALIEN conquerors of Earth are defeated at last. *The Little Men* (**1960**) and its sequel, *Hunters of Space* (**1960**), based on various characters from European MYTHOLOGY, traces the fight between Jack Odin and the villainous Grim Hagen, first under the Earth, then in space, with attendant princesses and dwarfs. [JC]

Other works: *When the Red King Woke* (**1966**).

See also: ROBOTS.

KELLER, DAVID H(ENRY) (1880–1966). American writer, physician and psychiatrist, deeply involved in the last capacity in First World War work on the phenomenon of shell-shock; he published a great deal of technical work in his professional role. As a writer of fantasy and sf, he was unpublished but active for many years before the period 1928–35, when much of his work received relatively wide attention from its publication in *Weird Tales* and *AMZ*, as well as several other magazines of the period. He remained active in sf FANDOM after that period. He began publishing sf with "The Revolt of the Pedestrians" (*see* DYSTOPIAS) for *AMZ* in 1928 and, along with much fantasy, produced the "Taine" sequence of stories, 1928–47; they usually involved thriller and fantasy components as well as sf. Some of his sf involves GENETIC ENGINEERING and MEDICINE. Although crudely written in a typical PULP style, it is occasionally vigorous and imaginative. The publication of his books postdates his magazine activity, and is complex with several fantasy pamphlets and private-press releases, the most notable of the former being *The Thing in the Cellar* (title story 1932 *Weird Tales*; coll. undated, *c.* **1940**). Most of his full-length books were story collections, with some sf being included in a preponderantly fantasy mix. They include *The Sign of the Burning Hart* (coll. of linked stories **1938**); *The Devil and the Doctor* (**1940**); *The Solitary Hunters and the Abyss* (coll. **1948**); *Life Everlasting and Other Tales of Science, Fantasy and Horror* (coll. **1949**); *The Eternal Conflict* (1939 *Les Primaires*, part only; **1949**); *The Homunculus* (**1949**); *The Lady Decides* (**1950**); *Tales from Underwood* (coll. **1952**); *Figment of a Dream* (**1962**), a pamphlet; *The Folsom Flint and Other Curious Tales* (coll. **1969**). [JC]

See also: AUTOMATION; BIOLOGY; IMMORTALITY; PSYCHOLOGY; ROBOTS; TRANSPORTATION.

KELLERMANN, BERNHARD (1879–1951). German writer whose sf novel, *Der Tunnel* (**1913**; trans. as *The Tunnel* **1915**), is an epic, at times heartfelt, about the construction of a transatlantic tunnel. It was the basis of the German film DER TUNNEL (1933) and its English re-make, THE TRANS-ATLANTIC TUNNEL (1935). [JC]

See also: TRANSPORTATION.

KELLEY, LEO P(ATRICK) (1928–). American novelist, for some time also an advertising copywriter. He began publishing sf with "Dreamtown, U.S.A." for *If* in 1955; several of his sf novels also concentrate on societies which invidiously dominate their inhabitants by psychological means, as in his second sf novel, *Odyssey to Earthdeath* (**1968**). His first, *The Counterfeits* (**1967**), as by Leo F. Kelley, also puts sociological sf into a

routine adventure frame. His slightly over-urgent, baroque style sometimes jars against the stories he tells, but he is a readable contributor to the genre. [JC]
Other works: *Time Rogue* (**1970**); *The Accidental Earth* (**1970**); *The Coins of Murph* (**1971**); *Brother John* (**1971**); *Time: 110100* (**1972** ; vt *The Man from Maybe* UK); *Mindmix* (**1972**); *Mythmaster* (**1973**); *The Earth Tripper* (**1973**). As editor: *Themes in Science Fiction* (anth. **1972**); *Fantasy: the Literature of the Marvelous* (anth. **1973**).

KELLEY, THOMAS P. *See* WEAPONS.

KELLEY, WILLIAM MELVIN (? –). American writer, whose short novel *A Different Drummer* (**1959**) tells of black history in an imaginary southern state of the USA, ending with a mass emigration of all blacks from the state in 1957, in a borderline sf fable. [PN]
See also: POLITICS.

KELLY, ROBERT (1935–). American poet, extremely prolific in the medium, and professor of English. His novel, *The Scorpions* (**1967**), has been read as sf because of its baroque rendering of a psychiatrist's conviction that a rich patient does in fact have contact with the Scorpions, a race of ultra-violet people; the book is more plausibly viewed as a FABULATION, however, depicting American life after the fashion of Harry Mathews and Thomas PYNCHON. [JC]

KEMP, EARL An associate of William L. HAMLING (*who see for details*).

KENDALL, JOHN Pseudonym of British writer Margaret Maud Brash (1880– ?), author of *Unborn Tomorrow* (**1933**), a futuristic DYSTOPIA describing dehumanization, regimentation and subsequent revolution in England under a communist regime. [JE]
See also: POLITICS.

KENNAWAY, JAMES Pseudonym of Scottish writer James Ewing Peebles (1928–68), best known for such works outside the sf field as *Tunes of Glory* (**1956**); his borderline sf novel is *The Mind Benders* (**1963**), which applies MAINSTREAM tactics to a story about brainwashing and the psychological consequences of over-exposure to experimental conditions of sensory deprivation; the book was written from his script for the film of the same name (1963). [JC]
See also: PSYCHOLOGY.

KENNEDY, R.A. (? – ?). English METAPHYSICAL writer, whose curious sf work, written as by "The Author of 'Space and Spirit' " is *The Triuneverse: A Scientific Romance* (**1912**). Set in the future, after the destruction of Mars and other events, it is mainly taken up with COSMOLOGICAL speculations about the

fabric of the universe, and has only a thin narrative. [JC]
See also: GREAT AND SMALL; LIVING WORLDS.

KENT, KELVIN Pseudonym used individually by Arthur K. BARNES and Henry KUTTNER, and on two stories they wrote in collaboration: "Roman Holiday" (1939) and "Science is Golden" (1940). [PN]

KENT, MALLORY *See* Robert A.W. LOWNDES.

KENT, PHILIP *See* Kenneth BULMER.

KENYON, ROBERT O. *See* Henry KUTTNER.

KEPLER, JOHANNES (1571–1630). German astronomer. An early dissertation brought him to the attention of the astronomers Galileo and Tycho Brahe, and he became Tycho's assistant in 1600, following him a year later as imperial mathematician to Rudolph II. The emperor was more interested in astrology than astronomy and Kepler became expert in casting horoscopes. The Holy Roman Empire was racked by several anti-Protestant persecutions while Kepler held his post, but he was protected by Rudolph. His contribution to ASTRONOMY — the three laws of planetary motion — was crucial, and laid vital groundwork for Newton's cosmological synthesis.

While at Tübingen University in 1593 JK prepared a dissertation on the heliocentric theory, which explained how events in the heavens would be seen by an observer stationed on the Moon. A new draft of the essay, in which the observer is conveniently placed on the Moon by a demon conjured up by his mother, was prepared in 1609, but this was stolen in 1611 and JK later had to defend his own mother on a charge of witchcraft which had possibly been encouraged by the literary device. Between 1620 and 1630 he annotated the piece extensively, but died while it was being prepared for publication. Soon after this the publisher was carried off by the plague, and it was not until **1634** that the piece — titled *Somnium* — finally appeared (in Latin). The definitive English translation is *Kepler's Somnium* (trans. E. Rosen **1967**). The bulk of the work consists of the lunar observations derived from theory, but the last few hundred words construct a hypothetical life-system for the Moon based on an assessment of the lunar environment as it was supposed to be. This is a remarkable piece of speculative work (*see* LIFE ON OTHER WORLDS) and an important piece of PROTO SCIENCE FICTION. [BS]
About the author: *The Sleepwalkers* by Arthur Koestler (**1959**) especially Part Four, "The Watershed"; "Kepler's *Somnium*. Science Fiction and the

Renaissance Scientist" by Gale E. Christianson in *Science-Fiction Studies*, March 1976.
See also: BIOLOGY; COSMOLOGY; FANTASTIC VOYAGES; MOON; SPACE FLIGHT.

KEPPEL-JONES, ARTHUR (? –). South African writer, whose sf novel, *When Smuts Goes* (**1947**), takes a gloomy view of the effects of that then imminent demise upon the fortunes of South Africa whose racist policies are seen as among the factors leading to barbarism; it is subtitled "History of South Africa from 1952 to 2010 – first published in 2015", and is a minor contribution to the future-HISTORY genre. [JC]
See also: POLITICS.

KERN, GREGORY *See* E.C. TUBB.

KERSH, GERALD (1911–68). Russian-born British writer, active from the mid-1930s, very prolific in shorter forms and known mainly for such work outside the sf field as *Time and the City* (**1938**) and *They Die with their Boots Clean* (**1941**). Several of his numerous short stories are sf, and have their original book appearance in collections such as *The Horrible Dummy and Other Stories* (coll. **1944**), *Neither Man nor Dog* (coll. **1946**), *The Brighton Monster* (coll. **1953**), *Men Without Bones* (coll. **1955** UK; USA edition has different stories) and *The Ugly Face of Love* (coll. **1960**). Two American compilations, *Nightshade and Damnations* (coll. **1968**; ed. Harlan ELLISON) and *On an Odd Note* (coll. **1958**), conveniently abstract some of GK's fantasies and sf from his other short stories. His stories are often anecdotes told to a narrator, sometimes identified as GK himself. In "Whatever Happened to Corporal Cuckoo?" (1953) (*see* IMMORTALITY), the corporal himself tells GK of his 500 years of soldier life following a mysterious cure given him about 1537. A tropical explorer tells us of a species of loathsome invertebrate, adding the hypothesis that we are really Martians, in "Men Without Bones". *An Ape, a Dog, and a Serpent: A Fantastic Novel* (**1945**) fabulates a history of film-making with borderline sf elements. *The Great Wash* (**1953**; vt *The Secret Masters* USA) is an sf novel in which the usual narrator, GK, becomes gradually involved in a plot to inundate most of the world and to rule the remains on authoritarian lines. GK's strengths as an author, a strong and vivid sense of character, a colourful style, a capacity to infuse his stories with a deep emotional charge (sometimes sentimentalized), make him an unusual sf writer; he has strong admirers. [JC]

KESHISHIAN, JOHN M. (1923–). American doctor of medicine and writer whose sf novel with Jacob HAY (*who see for details*) is *Autopsy for a Cosmonaut* (**1969**, vt *Death of a Cosmonaut*). [JC]

KETTERER, DAVID (1942–). British-born Canadian academic, with a DPhil from the University of Sussex, based at the University of Concordia in Montreal. His *New Worlds for Old: The Apocalyptic Imagination, Science Fiction and American Literature* (**1974**) interestingly, though in rather academic terminology, links apocalyptic themes in American MAINSTREAM literature with similar obsessions in genre sf. A projected anthology ed. DK is *The Science Fiction of Mark Twain*; he has also published numerous articles on Edgar Allan POE.
[PN]

See also: DEFINITIONS OF SF.

KETTLE, (JOCELYN) PAMELA (1934–). British writer, author of a historical novel, *Memorial to the Duchess* (**1968**) as by Jocelyn Kettle, and the sf novel *The Day of the Women* (**1969**). [JC]

KEY, EUGENE G(EORGE) (? –). American author of an sf collection, *Mars Mountain* (coll. **1934**), which was the first book from an American publishing house specializing in sf, William L. CRAWFORD's semi-professional Fantasy Publications, and so the precursor of great things to come; in themselves, the stories are unremarkable. [JC]

KEYES, DANIEL (1927–). American writer and university lecturer in English. He began his sf career as associate editor of MARVEL SCIENCE FICTION, Feb.-Nov. 1951, and it was in that magazine that his first published story, "Precedent", appeared in 1952. He is known mainly for one excellent novel, *Flowers for Algernon* (1959 *FSF*; exp. **1966**), winner of a 1960 HUGO award in its magazine form and a 1966 NEBULA award for the full-length book version. The film CHARLY (1968) is based on the book. It is the story, largely told in the first person, of Charlie Gordon, whose INTELLIGENCE, starting from an IQ of only 68, is artificially increased to genius level (*see* MEDICINE; SUPERMAN). The mouse Algernon, who has preceded him in this

course, soon dies, however, and Gordon's main contribution to science is his working out of the "Algernon-Gordon Effect", by which "artificially induced intelligence deteriorates at a rate of time directly proportional to the quantity of the increase". The last pages of the novel, detailing the loss of Charlie's faculties, are extremely moving. His treatment as an object of scientific curiosity throughout his ordeal underlines the book's points about deficiencies in the scientific method as applied to human beings. A further novel, *The Touch* (**1968**; vt *The Contaminated Man* UK), which is borderline sf about the psychological consequences of an industrial accident involving radioactive contamination, has received less attention. DK has written very little in the past decade. [JC]

See also: CONCEPTUAL BREAKTHROUGH; NUCLEAR POWER; PSYCHOLOGY.

KEYES, NOEL Pseudonym of British-born American writer and anthologist David Noel Keightley (1932–), whose *Contact* (anth. **1963**) is a theme anthology dealing with meetings of humans and ALIENS. [PN]

KEYNE, GORDON *See* H. BEDFORD-JONES.

KILLDOZER Made-for-TV film (1974). ABC/Universal TV. Directed by Jerry London, starring Clint Walker, Carl Betz and Neville Brand. Teleplay by Theodore STURGEON. 75 mins. Colour.

Based on Sturgeon's own well-known story about a bulldozer that becomes possessed by an alien force from outer space, this TV movie does not live up to its potential. The story is a tightly constructed description of the battle between the machine and a group of men on a Pacific island. The film not only waters down this basic conflict, but pads it out with clichéd emotional conflicts between the human characters. [JB]

KILWORTH, GARRY (1941–). English telecommunications engineer and writer, raised partly in Aden; he has travelled and worked in the Far East and the Pacific. He published his first sf story, "Let's Go to Golgotha" in *The Gollancz/Sunday Times Best Sf Stories* (anth. **1975**), having won the competition. His first, interesting sf novel, *In Solitary* (**1977**) is set on an Earth whose few remaining humans have for over 400 years been dominated by birdlike ALIENS, and deals with a human rebellion whose moral impact is ambiguous. [JC]
Other works: *Night of Kadar* (**1978**).
See also: TIME TRAVEL.

KING, ALBERT or **CHRISTOPHER** *See* Paul CONRAD.

KING, JOHN ROBERT (1948–). English writer, now resident in Cornwall; he is head of the drama department at Redruth School, and a Cornish nationalist, presently writing a novel in Cornish. His sf novel, *Bruno Lipshitz and the Disciples of Dogma* (**1976**), rather uneasily juggles a number of ingredients in a complex plot: they include an ALIEN invasion, a strange RELIGION, interpersonal conflicts and dollops of adventure. [JC]

KING, STEPHEN (1947–). American writer. Though he published occasionally in the sf world, beginning with "The Glass Door" for *Startling Mystery Stories* in 1967, he was perhaps diverted from a conventional sf career by the response of Donald A. WOLLHEIM to his first novel submission: "We here at Ace Books are not interested in negative Utopias". SK has since concentrated on horror/fantasies with some sf grounding, most notably *Carrie* (**1974**), made into the successful film CARRIE. *Salem's Lot* (**1975**) puts vampirism into a contemporary setting. *The Shining* (**1978**) is a conventional GOTHIC story, in the line of similar haunted-house tales by Shirley JACKSON and Richard MATHESON, featuring a psychic boy whose parents are caretakers of a malign, out-of-season resort hotel; it has no sf elements. *Night Shift* (coll. **1977**) is short stories. [JC]

KING, VINCENT Pseudonym of English writer, artist and teacher, Rex Thomas Vinson (1935–), who works in Cornwall. He began publishing sf with "Defence Mechanism" for *New Writings in SF No 9* (anth. **1966**) ed. E.J. CARNELL. His more successful novels, like *Light a Last Candle* (**1969**) and *Candy Man* (**1971**), tend to combine elements of epic and grotesque sf adventure with a characteristically English darkness of emotional colouring and a tendency towards downbeat conclusions. [JC]
Other works: *Another End* (**1971**); *Time Snake and Superclown* (**1976**).

KING KONG Films (1933 and 1976). The first version was made by RKO, directed by Merian C. Cooper and Ernest B. Schoedsack, starring Fay Wray, Robert Armstrong and Bruce Cabot. Screenplay by James A. Creelman and Ruth Rose from a story by Merian C. Cooper, and credit also given to Edgar WALLACE. Special effects designed and supervised by Willis H. O'BRIEN. 100 mins. B/w.

The classic monster film: on a remote island inhabited not only by a tribe of unfriendly natives but also by prehistoric monsters, the most powerful being a giant ape called Kong, a young actress from a visiting film unit is kidnapped by tribesmen and offered to Kong, a gift which he eagerly accepts. She is finally rescued, and Kong captured and taken to New York where he is exhibited, escapes, rampages, recaptures the girl, and makes his last defiant stand on top of the Empire

Jessica Lange in the hands of KING KONG in the 1976 version.

State Building before being machine-gunned by a squadron of bi-planes.

Although *KK* is an early film, its special effects have seldom been surpassed, the most important resulting from the technique of stop-motion photography (*see* Willis H. O'BRIEN). The special effects are not just set pieces; they are perfectly integrated with the story.

Merian C. Cooper, a hardboiled adventurer and former documentary film-maker, originated the project, but his plans did not really take shape until 1931 when he became familiar with O'Brien's animation techniques. The basic story is Cooper's, but many of the film's key sequences were created by O'Brien himself, improving on animation set-pieces he used in his version of LOST WORLD (1925) and using various designs and ideas from his uncompleted epic *Creation*. Edgar Wallace received a story credit, but he died in Hollywood of pneumonia in Feb. 1932 before he had actually begun to write the script for which he was contracted.

The classic status of *KK*, which has become one of the great mythopoeic works of the 20th century, has probably to do with the ambiguous feelings, not unlike those of its fairy-tale model "Beauty and the Beast", created towards Kong himself: terror at his savagery; admiration for his strength and naturalness and effortless regality in his primeval surroundings; and pity for his squalid end — the most memorable of all cinematic images of nature destroyed in the CITY. This ending is also an image of the great destroyed by the small, for the humans are dwarfed by the ape and indeed by the city they have created, a feeling emphasized by the setting in the Great Depression, with a bored, impoverished populace ready to grasp at any marvel, and panicking when it finds

itself faced with the real thing, not the ersatz. The narrative moves with *élan*, and the film has been almost as popular with critics as with the general public.

King Kong (1976), the second version, was made by the Dino De Laurentiis Corp./Paramount, directed by John Guillermin, starring Jessica Lange, Jeff Bridges, Charles Grodin, John Randolph and Rene Auberjonoise. Screenplay by Lorenzo Semple Jr, based on that of the original. Special effects by Glen Robinson, Joe Day, Harold Wellman, Frank van der Veer, Barry Nolan and Lou Lichtenfield. 134 mins. Colour.

In this lavish, heavily publicized and expensive remake, it is an oil-company executive who leads the expedition to Kong's island. The captured heroine is rescued by a young zoologist and Kong is taken back to America in a super oil-tanker. His last stand is on top of the World Trade Center, and he is shot dead by a group of helicopter gun-ships.

This version did not make use of model animation and was therefore more restricted in its effects. Such set-pieces from the original as the battles between Kong and various prehistoric monsters are gone. Although advance publicity made much of the 40-foot high mechanical model that would be used, it finally appeared in only two mercifully brief shots. For most of the film Kong is represented by a man in an ape-suit and by two ingenious full-scale hands. The film is inferior in other respects also. The vigorous narrative of the original is here slowed down by a number of didactic scenes spelling out the morality of the situation in a manner which suggests that Hollywood supposes its audiences to have become much stupider since 1933. The delicate balance of the original between pity and terror is here shifted strongly towards pity, and Kong is softened.

Tragedy becomes at best pathos, at worst bathos. Yet many scenes remain moving, and the heroine (now feminist and tough, no longer a limp screamer) has a more interesting script than her original, though it is startlingly vulgar. The various aims of the film, which seems designed to be spoof, tragedy, nostalgia-epic, spectacle and allegory about "the rape of the environment by big business", are partly self-cancelling, but the primal strength of the story is not readily destroyed, and the second *KK* is good entertainment. [JB/PN]

KINGSMILL, HUGH Form of his name used by English writer Hugh Kingsmill Lunn (1889–1949) for his writing and editing; he is now (unfairly) best known for his anthologies, like the famous *Invective and Abuse* (anth. **1930**). *The Dawn's Delay* (coll. **1924**) contains, of sf interest, the title story, vt "The End of the World", and "W.J.", about a future WAR in 1966–72; *The Return of William Shakespeare* (**1929**) presents, within a sketchy sf frame, the thoughts and activities of a reconstituted Shakespeare in the 20th century (*see* ARTS and REINCARNATION); both volumes were assembled, under the title of the former, as *The Dawn's Delay* (coll. **1948**). With Malcolm Muggeridge, HK wrote two SATIRES rendering NEAR-FUTURE doings in the form of newspaper stories: *Brave Old World: A Mirror for the Times* (**1936**) and *Next Year's News* (**1938**). A much-loved figure, HK appears in novels and reminiscences of writers like William GERHARDI and Lance SIEVEKING. [JC]
See also: END OF THE WORLD; SUN.

KIPLING, (JOSEPH) RUDYARD (1865–1936). English poet, short-story writer and novelist, known mainly for such works outside the sf field as *Kim* (**1901**). He won the Nobel Prize for Literature in 1907. Before the age of 27, RK wrote a considerable number of stories containing elements of fantasy and horror. Some, like "The Strange Ride of Morrowbie Jukes" (1885) and the title story, are to be found in *The Phantom Rickshaw, and Other Eerie Tales* (coll.

1888), others in *Life's Handicap, Being Stories of Mine Own People* (coll. **1891**) and *Many Inventions* (coll. **1893**), which includes "The Lost Legion" (1892). *The Brushwood Boy* (1895; **1899**) and "The Ship that Found Herself" (1895) both appear in *The Day's Work* (coll. **1898**). Also fantasy are the various linked and unlinked stories assembled in *The Jungle Book* (coll. **1894**) and *The Second Jungle Book* (coll. **1895**), while *Just So Stories for Little Children* (coll. **1902**) contains classic children's fables; *Puck of Pook's Hill* (coll. **1906**) and *Rewards and Fairies* (coll. **1910**) contain a series of stories about the formation and growth of Britain as told by Puck to two children. Sf proper appears rarely in RK's work, being restricted fundamentally to *With the Night Mail* (1905; **1909**), also appearing in *Actions and Reactions* (coll. **1909**) and "As Easy as ABC" (1912) in *A Diversity of Creatures* (coll. **1917**). The latter is a famous, somewhat DYSTOPIAN vision of a WELLS-style future ruled by the Aerial Board of Control (ABC), and has influenced writers as far apart as Michael ARLEN and Rex WARNER. The ABC also features in the earlier story, which deals with transatlantic airships. In his complex, elliptic, highly crafted later stories, RK made some ambiguous use of supernatural principles of explanation in such tales as "The Gardener," "A Madonna of the Trenches" and "The Wish House", all from 1924, assembled in *Debits and Credits* (coll. **1926**), which has a claim to being his finest collection of short stories. These tales are not comfortably amenable to either sf or fantasy reading, but demonstrate the power of hinted supernatural themes in writing of high virtuosity. Although RK was not an sf writer to any extent, his intense, somewhat feverish talent makes even the least characteristic of his works of more than peripheral interest to the sf reader. [JC]

Other works: *They* (1904; **1906**).

About the author: Literature on RK is extensive. Charles Carrington's *Rudyard Kipling* (**1955**) is the definitive biography, while J.M.S. Tompkins' *The Art of Rudyard Kipling* (**1959**) very competently surveys both prose and poetry. Angus WILSON's *The Strange Ride of Rudyard Kipling* (**1977**) combines biography and criticism in a sustained, intense study. Also interesting is *Rudyard Kipling and His World* (**1977**) by Kingsley AMIS.

See also: DISCOVERY AND INVENTION; TRANSPORTATION.

KIPPAX, JOHN Pseudonym of English writer John Charles Hynam (1915–74). He was a regular contributor to the British sf magazines during 1955–61, publishing over 30 stories in that time. His first two stories appeared in Dec. 1954: "Dimple" in *Science Fantasy* and "Trojan Hearse" in *NW*. The latter was a collaboration with Dan MORGAN, with whom he also published a SPACE-OPERA series, *A Thunder of Stars* (**1968**), *Seed of Stars* (**1972**) and *The Neutral Stars* (**1973**), about the Space Corps team of the ship *Venturer Twelve*. The fourth in the series, *Where No Stars Guide* (**1975**), is by JK alone. [JC]

KIRBY, JACK (1917–). American COMIC BOOK illustrator. He began his long career in 1936 by working for Max Fleischer, animating the comic strip *Popeye*. He later worked for Lincoln Features, doing editorial and sports cartoons, then broke into the comic book field, creating *Captain America* with Joe Simon in 1941 for MARVEL COMICS, and working on CAPTAIN MARVEL. Kirby's recent fame, however, stems from a later period in the history of *Marvel Comics*, which he rejoined in 1960, now under the direction of Stan LEE. In 1961 JK created, with Lee, and illustrated *The Fantastic Four*, a group of superheroes

that helped to establish *Marvel Comics* as one of the leading comic book producers in the USA, with a large cult following among adults as well as children. JK has helped to create dozens of other superheroes in the years since: the 1960s were the boom years for this genre largely as a result of his work. He left the Lee organization and worked for DC Comics for a while, then returned to *Marvel*, where he remains. Though basically JK is an ideas man, his pictorial style became the most imitated in the field: his strong lines, blocky, muscular characters and movie-still/frame concept of storytelling have been highly influential on newer comic book artists. Much of his work is reproduced in *Origins of Marvel Comics* (**1974**), *Son of Origins of Marvel Comics* (**1975**) and *Bring on the Bad Guys* (**1976**), all ed. Stan Lee. [JG/PN]

Illustrator Josh KIRBY had already developed a strong style by 1957.

KIRBY, JOSH (1928–). British illustrator, trained at Liverpool School of Art. JK's work in sf began in 1956 with covers for *Authentic Science Fiction* and

Comic-strip artist Jack KIRBY was at the height of his powers in the late 1960s, as in this setting-up of a confrontation between the mighty Thor and Galactus in Marvel Comics. Note the sophisticated changes in perspective.

he has continued working for most of the British paperback publishers, including Corgi, Panther and New English Library. He has also done covers for American publishers, including ACE BOOKS, BALLANTINE BOOKS, DAW BOOKS and Lancer Books. His style is complex, often partially abstract with hundreds of weaving, interconnected lines throughout the illustration. He works slowly and on a small scale, sometimes no larger than the book cover itself. His aliens are probably the most grotesquely conceived in sf illustration today. [JG]

KIRCHER, ATHANASIUS (1601–80). German scholar. For his relevance to sf, *see* MARS, MERCURY, OUTER PLANETS, RELIGION, VENUS.

KIRST, HANS HELLMUT (1914–). German writer, best known for his novels about the Second World War; his NEAR-FUTURE sf novel, *Keiner Kommt Davon* (**1957**; trans. as *The Seventh Day* **1959**; vt *No One Will Escape* UK), deals with the period directly preceding the next World War. [JC]

KLEIN, GÉRARD (1937–). French writer, anthologist, critic and editor. An economist by profession, GK is one of the few European sf writers known in the USA. He has used the pseudonyms Gilles d'Argyre, François Pagery and Mark Starr. His first stories, heavily influenced by Ray BRADBURY, appeared in 1955 when he was only 18 years old, and he soon made a major impact on the field in France, publishing over 40 delicately crafted stories between 1956 and 1962 (60 by 1977), while also establishing himself as a forceful and literate critic of the genre with a series of 30 penetrating essays in various publications. His first novel, *Le gambit des étoiles* (**1958**; trans. as *Starmaster's Gambit* by C.J. Richards **1973**), a clever and wide-ranging adventure yarn, shows the increasing influence that American traditional sf was having on GK, a trend which comes strongly to the fore in the following novels which, though well conducted and interesting, lack the poetic invention of his early work: *Le temps n'a pas d'odeur* (**1963**; trans. as *The Day Before Tomorrow* by P.J. Sokolowski **1972**); *Les seigneurs de la guerre* (**1971**; trans. as *The Overlords of War* by John BRUNNER **1973**). Since 1969, GK has edited the Ailleurs et Demain imprint for publisher Robert Laffont, where he has been instrumental in introducing some of the major modern Anglo-American sf writers to the French public while also encouraging the better local authors — CURVAL, JEURY, RUELLAN, LÉOURIER and WUL. Many of GK's works feature an imagery and even a structure influenced by chess. [MJ]
Other works: *Agent galactique* ["Galactic Agent"] (**1958**, as by Mark Starr); *Embûches dans l'espace* ["Ambushes in

Space"] (**1958**, as by François Pagery); *Les perles du temps* ["Pearls of Time"] (coll. **1958**); *Chirurgiens d'une planète* ["Planet Surgeons"] (**1960**, as by Gilles d'Argyre); *Les voiliers du soleil* ["Sailors of the Sun"] (**1961**, as by d'Argyre); *Le long voyage* ["The Long Journey"] (**1964**, as by d'Argyre); *Les tueurs du temps* (**1965**; trans. as *The Mote in Time's Eye* by C.J. Richards **1975**; bylined Gilles d'Argyre in France, GK in USA); *Le sceptre du hasard* ["The Sceptre of Chance"] (**1966**, as by d'Argyre); *Un chant de pierre* ["Stone Song"] (coll. **1966**); *La loi du talion* ["The Law of Retaliation"] (coll. **1973**); *Histoires comme si* ["Stories as If"] (coll. **1975**).
See also: GALACTIC EMPIRES; GAMES AND SPORTS; LIVING WORLDS; WAR.

KLINE, OTIS ADELBERT (1891–1946). American songwriter, author and literary agent, active in music before beginning to write popular fiction in several genres, though predominantly fantasy, in the early 1920s, most notably for *Weird Tales* and *Argosy*. With the exception of such stories as "Race Around the Moon" (1939), space adventures which comprised a certain part of his output, most of his sf is of the HEROIC-FANTASY variety, much of his work being seen as competing with and derived from that of Edgar Rice BURROUGHS' "Mars" and "Venus" series. The "Robert Grandon" sequence is typical; comprised of *The Planet of Peril* (1929 *Argosy*; **1929**), *The Prince of Peril* (1930 *Argosy*; **1930**) and *The Port of Peril* (1932 *Weird Tales* as "Buccaneers of Venus"; **1949**), they are the extremely swashbuckling adventures of Grandon on Venus. Further novels, linked to these by the character of Dr Morgan, are *The Swordsman of Mars* (1933 *Argosy*; **1960**) and *Outlaws of Mars* (1933 *Argosy*; **1961**). In his later years, OAK's time was almost entirely taken up by his literary agency. His style is wooden but violently coloured. [JC]
Other works: *Maza of the Moon* (**1930**); *The Call of the Savage* (1931 *Argosy*; **1937**; vt under magazine title *Jan of the Jungle*); *The Man who Limped and Other Stories* (coll. of linked stories **1946**), some stories from an oriental fantasy series originally published 1930–33; *Tam, Son of the Tiger* (1931 *Weird Tales*; **1962**); *Jan in India* (1935 *Argosy*; **1974**); *The Bride of Osiris and Other Weird Tales* (coll. **1975**).
See also: LIFE ON OTHER WORLDS; MARS; MOON; VENUS.

KLOOR, MARY CONWAY (? –). American writer whose sf novel is *My Beloved Trosnanus* (**1963**). [JC]

KNEALE, (THOMAS) NIGEL (1922–). British author and screenwriter, married to Judith Kerr, well-known author of books for children. After attending the Royal Academy of

Dramatic Art and then working as an actor he began writing short stories and soon won the Somerset Maugham Literary Prize in 1950, but he turned to writing for television when he realized that he could not afford to live solely from short stories. Many of his early stories, some of them fantasies, appear in *Tomato Cain and Other Stories* (coll. 1949). Over the years he often used sf themes, usually combined with elements from the traditional horror story. His first major TV success was in 1953 with the BBC TV serial THE QUATERMASS EXPERIMENT. Then in 1954 he adapted George ORWELL's *Nineteen Eighty-Four* (1949) for BBC TV; it caused a great deal of controversy when it was televised. In 1955 NK wrote QUATERMASS II, a sequel to the first Quatermass serial, and in 1958 QUATERMASS AND THE PIT, both for BBC. All three were adapted into feature films by Hammer Films, as THE QUATERMASS XPERIMENT (1955; vt *The Creeping Unknown*), QUATERMASS II (1957; vt *Enemy From Space*) and QUATERMASS AND THE PIT (1968; vt *Five Million Years to Earth*). All three were also published as paperback books of the original scripts, the first in **1959**, the second and third in **1960**.

NK then began writing screenplays and adapted for the screen two of John Osborne's plays, *Look Back in Anger* and *The Entertainer*, filmed in 1959 and 1960. Three further TV plays, "The Road" (1963), "The Year of the Sex Olympics" (1969) and "The Stone Tape" (1972) have been collected in *The Year of the Sex Olympics and Other TV plays* (coll. **1976**). "The Road" is a ghost story set in the 18th century, with a puzzled scientific investigator: the ghosts are in fact apparitions of 20th-century technology. "The Year of the Sex Olympics" deals satirically with a future TV-watching population, and improved methods of apathy control. "The Stone Tape" again combines Gothic horror with messages across time.

In 1972 NK's TV play *Wine of India* was broadcast, and in 1975 another play, *Murrain*, was part of ATV's series of plays produced under the blanket title of "Against the Crowd". In 1976 NK wrote a series of six plays for ATV under the series title of *Beasts*. Each play took a different aspect of the theme, the beasts in question ranging from psychological through supernatural to science-fictional. His current work involves a new Quatermass play or film, already written but not yet in production. [JB/PN]
See also: MYTHOLOGY.

KNEBEL, FLETCHER (1911–). American journalist and novelist, most of whose books are POLITICAL thrillers, not excepting his borderline sf books. *Seven Days in May* (**1962**) with Charles BAILEY, later filmed, tells of an attempted military coup in the USA. *Night of Camp David* (**1965**) tells of a NEAR-FUTURE President of the USA going mad and almost destroying the country. *Trespass* (**1969**), set in 1973, has a black activist group taking over white properties and upsetting the FBI. [JC/PN]

KNIGHT, DAMON (1922–). American writer and editor. Married (1) Trudy Werndl, (2) Helen del Rey, former wife of Lester DEL REY, (3) sf writer Kate WILHELM. Like many sf writers, DK became an sf fan at an early age. He became involved in sf FANDOM, and was a member of the FUTURIANS in New York, where he shared an apartment with Robert A.W. LOWNDES and met James BLISH, C.M. KORNBLUTH, Frederik POHL and others. (His history of this fan group is *The Futurians*, **1977**.) His first professional sale was a cartoon to AMAZING STORIES; his first story was "Resilience" (1941) in STIRRING SCIENCE STORIES, which was edited by another Futurian, Donald A. WOLLHEIM. In 1943 he became an assistant editor with Popular Publications, a pulp magazine chain. Later he worked for a literary agency, and then returned to Popular Publications as assistant editor of SUPER SCIENCE STORIES. In 1950–51 he was editor of WORLDS BEYOND, but the magazine ran for only three issues.

DK published a few short stories during the 1940s, including occasional collaborations with James Blish, once using the collaborative pseudonym Donald Laverty, and three times using the pseudonym Stuart Fleming, but he did not begin to emerge as a writer of note until 1949, when his ironic END OF THE WORLD story "Not with a Bang" appeared in the MAGAZINE OF FANTASY AND SCIENCE FICTION which, along with GALAXY SCIENCE FICTION, provided a market for which he could develop his urbane and often humorous short stories. These included "To Serve Man" (1950), "Four

In One" (1953), "Babel II" (1953), "The Country of the Kind" (1955) and "Stranger Station" (1956). DK's reputation as a writer has primarily rested on his short stories, which have been included in the collections *Far Out* (coll. **1961**), *In Deep* (coll. **1963**), *Off Center* (coll. **1965**; vt *Off Centre* UK) and *Turning On* (coll. **1966**). He also published two novels during the 1950s, *Hell's Pavement* (1952–3 var. mags; fix-up **1955**; vt *Analogue Men* USA and later UK), a DYSTOPIAN story of a future society with humanity under psychological control, and *The People Maker* (**1959**; rev. vt *A for Anything* UK and later USA), while two novellas also had separate publication — *Masters of Evolution* (1954 *Gal.* as "Natural State"; **1959**) and *The Sun Saboteurs* (1955 *If* as "The Earth Quarter"; **1961**). He was also editor of *If* for three issues, 1958–9.

DK is generally acknowledged as the first outstanding sf critic, an aspect of his career which began in 1945 with an extended fanzine essay on A.E. VAN VOGT's *World of Ā* (**1948**) in its serialized version that eventually inspired considerable revisions in the published book. He later reviewed books for a number of professional and amateur magazines, notably INFINITY and *FSF*. His reviews were collected in *In Search of Wonder* (coll. **1956**; rev. 1967), and won him a HUGO award in 1956.

Never a prolific writer, DK has written increasingly less since the late 1950s, and has concentrated more on editing. He became editorial consultant to Berkley Books in 1960, a position he held for six years. His first anthology was the distinguished *A Century of Science Fiction* (anth. **1962**); this was followed by *First Flight* (anth. **1963**), *Tomorrow × 4* (anth. **1964**), *A Century of Great Short Science Fiction Novels* (anth. **1964**) and many others. He translated a number of

French sf stories, some of them for publication in *FSF*, and collected them as *13 French Science-Fiction Stories* (anth. **1965**). Two more novels appeared, *Beyond the Barrier* (**1963**) and *Mind Switch* (**1965**; vt *The Other Foot* UK); the latter, in which a man's mind is transferred to an alien's body, he considers his most successful long work.

In 1966 DK produced the first volume of the ORBIT series of anthologies. The series was highly influential, and its success was to some degree responsible for triggering the boom in original anthologies which developed during the following decade. Stories from *Orbit* were extensively nominated for NEBULA awards, and several were winners. Such writers as Gardner DOZOIS, R.A. LAFFERTY, Kate WILHELM and Gene WOLFE became strongly identified with the series.

In 1968 DK published his most notable short story, "Masks", a study of the psychological problems which would face a CYBORG, a man in a wholly artificial body. In the same year appeared a short series about the character Thorinn: "The World and Thorinn" (1968), "The Garden of Ease" (1968) and "The Star Below" (1968). Later he published a biography of the iconoclast Charles FORT: *Charles Fort: Prophet of the Unexplained* (**1970**).

DK has also served the sf world in an organizational capacity. He began the MILFORD SCIENCE FICTION WRITERS' CONFERENCE in 1956, which popularized the idea of writers' workshops among sf writers. He was largely responsible for founding the SCIENCE FICTION WRITERS OF AMERICA, and was the organization's first President. The Nov. 1976 *FSF* was a special DK issue, including an appreciation by Theodore STURGEON. [MJE]

Other works: ed. *Beyond Tomorrow* (anth. **1965**); ed. *The Dark Side* (anth. **1965**); ed. *The Shape of Things* (anth. **1965**); *The Rithian Terror* (1953 *Startling Stories* as "Double Meaning"; **1965**); ed. *Cities of Wonder* (anth. **1966**); ed. *Orbit 1* (anth. **1966**); *Three Novels* (coll. **1967**; vt *Natural State and other stories* UK); ed. *Orbit 2* (anth. **1967**); ed. *Science Fiction Inventions* (anth. **1967**); ed. *Worlds to Come* (anth. **1967**); ed. *The Metal Smile* (anth. **1968**); ed. *One Hundred Years of Science Fiction* (anth. **1968**); ed. *Orbit 3* (anth. **1968**); ed. *Orbit 4* (anth. **1968**); ed. *Toward Infinity* (anth. **1968**); ed. *Orbit 5* (anth. **1969**); *World Without Children and The Earth Quarter* (coll. **1970**); ed. *Dimension X* (anth. **1970**; UK paperback divided into two volumes, the second entitled *Elsewhere × 3*); ed. *Orbit 6* (anth. **1970**); ed. *Orbit 7* (anth. **1970**); ed. *Orbit 8* (anth. **1970**); ed. *A Pocketful of Stars* (anth. **1971**); ed. *Orbit 9* (anth. **1971**); ed. *First Contact* (anth. **1971**); *Two Novels* (coll. **1971**; contains "Double Meaning" [*The Rithian Terror*] and "The Earth Quarter" [*The Sun*

Saboteurs]); ed. *Perchance to Dream* (anth. **1972**); ed. *Orbit 10* (anth. **1972**); ed. *Orbit 11* (anth. **1972**); ed. *Science Fiction Argosy* (anth. **1972**); ed. *Tomorrow and Tomorrow* (anth. **1973**); ed. *Orbit 12* (anth. **1973**); ed. *The Golden Road* (anth. **1974**); ed. *Orbit 13* (anth. **1974**); ed. *Orbit 14* (anth. **1974**); ed. *Orbit 15* (anth. **1974**); ed. *A Shocking Thing* (anth. **1974**); ed. *Happy Endings* (anth. **1974**); ed. *Orbit 16* (anth. **1975**); ed. *Orbit 17* (anth. **1975**); ed. *The Best from Orbit* (anth. **1975**); ed. *Science Fiction of the Thirties* (anth. **1975**); *The Best of Damon Knight* (coll. **1976**); ed. *Orbit 18* (anth. **1976**); ed. *Turning Points* (critical anth. **1977**); ed. *Orbit 19* (anth. **1977**).
About the author: "All in a Knight's Work" by James Blish, *Speculation* 29, 1971. "Ragged Claws" by Damon Knight in *Hell's Cartographers*, ed. Brian W. ALDISS and Harry HARRISON (coll. **1975**).
See also: ALIENS; ANTI-INTELLECTUALISM IN SF; ARTS; CITIES; COMMUNICATIONS; COSMOLOGY; CRIME AND PUNISHMENT; DISCOVERY AND INVENTION; ECOLOGY; ECONOMICS; EVOLUTION; GENETIC ENGINEERING; IMMORTALITY; INVISIBILITY; MATHEMATICS; MONSTERS; ROBOTS; SATIRE; SF MAGAZINES; TABOOS; TRANSPORTATION.

KNIGHT, NORMAN L(OUIS) (1895–). American writer and pesticide chemist for the United States Department of Agriculture until his retirement in 1963. He has not been an active writer, beginning his career with the novella "Frontier of the Unknown" for *ASF* in 1937 and a few other stories, and making his main contribution with his part in *A Torrent of Faces* (**1967**) with James BLISH; it is a novel in which an ambiguously UTOPIAN solution to population problems is challenged by the approach of a very large meteor. It is a sequel to NLK's solo novella "Crisis in Utopia" (1940) which appeared in *ASF*, but never as a book.   [JC]
See also: ASTEROIDS; OVERPOPULATION.

KNOX, CALVIN M. *See* Robert SILVERBERG.

KNOX, RONALD A(RBUTHNOT) (1888–1957). English Roman Catholic priest (he was converted in 1917, ordained in 1919) and extremely prolific writer. Among his many books are several well-known detective novels, a new translation of the Old and New Testaments, and *Memories of the Future; Being Memoirs of the Years 1915–1972 Written in the Year of Grace 1988 by Opal, Lady Porstock* (**1923**), a satire on the type of evolutionary UTOPIA most closely identified with H.G. WELLS's works in the genre. The story is perhaps too cleverly told, and its imitation of the genteel memoir too exact in places. [JC]

KNYE, CASSANDRA *See* Thomas M. DISCH and John SLADEK.

KOESTLER, ARTHUR (1905–). Hungarian-born author and journalist, who narrowly avoided execution in the Spanish Civil War, and has since lived in England and France. He became a naturalized British citizen in 1940, and all his books subsequent to the famous *Darkness at Noon* (trans. **1940**) have been written in English. Several of the speculative, philosophical works of his later career have a direct interest for sf readers and have probably been influential on sf writers. They include *The Sleepwalkers: A History of Man's Changing Vision of the Universe* (**1959**), *The Act of Creation* (**1964**), *The Case of the Midwife Toad* (**1971**) about inherited "Lamarckian" characteristics in BIOLOGY, and *The Roots of Coincidence* (**1972**). His play, *Twilight Bar: An Escapade in Four Acts* (written 1933; English version **1945**), is a UTOPIAN fantasia set on a world-ISLAND visited by aliens who threaten to destroy human life unless we better ourselves immediately. AK's sf novel, *The Age of Longing* (**1951**), is a NEAR-FUTURE discussion novel set in France; it distils his intimate experience with European thought and politics into a prediction of the nature of our response to a threatened invasion from the East. AK is an important speculative thinker, many of whose ideas are at the leading edge (though perhaps insecurely) of scientific and social thought. He has several times expressed contempt for sf.   [JC]
See also: POLITICS; PSEUDO-SCIENCE.

KOLCHAK: THE NIGHT STALKER Television series (1974). Francy Productions for Universal TV/ABC. Created by Jeff Rice. Executive producer: Darren McGavin; producer: Paul Playton. Story consultant: David Chase. 20 episodes, each 50 mins. Colour.
   This short-lived series was a spin-off from a made-for-TV movie, *The Night Stalker* (1972) directed by Dan Curtis and written by Richard MATHESON, which was about a vampire in modern-day Las Vegas. This was so successful that it led to a feature-length sequel, *The Night Strangler*, also written by Matheson, and then to the series, in which McGavin again played the reporter, Kolchak, who each week uncovered some new, fantastic threat of a supernatural or sf-related nature. Unable to persuade anyone in authority of its existence, he was usually obliged to combat the menace by himself. Most of the episodes featured creatures of the supernatural, but the sf-related ones included "The Energy Eater" by Arthur Rowe and Rudolph Borchert; "The Primal Scream" by Bill S. Ballinger and David Chase, about cells from the Arctic which grow into a prehistoric ape-creature; and "Mr R.I.N.G." by L. Ford Neale, about a robot which runs amok. The series was entertaining and filmed with great attention to atmospheric detail, but its formula was too rigid to allow many variations in the stories.   [JB]

KOMATSU, SAKYO (1931–). Japanese novelist and journalist, most popular for his sf work. His DISASTER novel *Nippon Chimbotsu* (**1973**; trans., abridged by one-third as *Japan Sinks*, **1976**), has sold about four million copies in Japan, and was filmed as NIPPON CHIMBOTSU (1973), with a minimal release in the West as *The Submersion of Japan*; the version made for the Western world, *Tidal Wave*, produced by Roger CORMAN, is cut from 140 to 81 mins, and includes added sequences. The story is based on a highly plausible application of the theory of plate tectonics: suddenly the Japanese archipelago begins to slide inexorably into the Japan Trench, which does in reality parallel Japan, and is the extremely unstable line along which the local oceanic and continental plates clash; the numerous characters of the novel (whose personalities the awkward and abridged English translation undoubtedly muffles) are involved first in helping to determine that the archipelago is in fact beginning to slip, then in the Japanese Government's attempts to save as much of the population as possible in the year before the quakes and the actual sinking become too bad for action. The novel closes with two of its protagonists escaping to Siberia, in "the chill darkness of an early winter" A sequel is projected. Beyond its thoroughly worked-out geological hypothesis, *Japan Sinks* is effective as an obviously deeply felt elegy for Japan herself in all her physical and cultural fragility; the story has no heroes or villains, the main focus of our attention being the dying of Japan.   [JC]
See also: POLITICS.

KONEC SRPNA V HOTELU OZON (vt **THE END OF AUGUST AT THE HOTEL OZONE**) Film (1965). New Line Cinema. Directed by Jan Schmidt, starring Ondrej Jariabek, Beta Ponicanova, Magda Seidlerova and Hana Vitkova. Screenplay by Pavel Juracek. 87 mins. B/w.
   This Czech film is set in a desolate post-World-War-Three landscape where a band of women survivors search for men. They eventually locate one living in an otherwise empty hotel, but he turns out to be too old and their hopes of continuing the human race are dashed. This is a bleak and depressing film. [JB]

KOONTZ, DEAN R(AY) (1945–). American writer of much fiction under various names, including K.M. Dwyer, Brian Coffey and David Axton, though he seems to have written all his sf under his own name. His sf output has recently dwindled sharply. He began publishing sf in 1967 with "Soft Come the Dragons" for *FSF*; his first novel, *Star Quest* (**1968**), was quickly followed by the bulk of his sf output to date, including an interesting volume of stories, *Soft Come the Dragons* (coll. **1970**), *Fear That Man* (**1969**) and *Anti-Man* (**1970**). DRK's writing is noted for a slightly uneasy shifting between rather conventional plotting and a somewhat forced "darkness" of imagery and style. Much of it is a blend of GOTHIC fantasy with sf. A more recent novel, *Nightmare Journey* (**1975**), though over-complicated, is comparatively formidable in its depiction of mankind 100,000 years hence thrust back from the stars by an incomprehensible alien intelligence and going sour on Earth, where radioactivity has speeded mutation, causing a religious backlash; but there is hope that Man will rescue himself. [JC]

Other works: *The Fall of the Dream Machine* (**1969**); *The Dark Symphony* (**1970**); *Dark of the Woods* (**1970**); *Beastchild* (**1970**); *Hell's Gate* (**1970**); *The Crimson Witch* (**1971**); *A Darkness in My Soul* (**1972**); *Warlock!* (**1972**); *Time Thieves* (**1972**); *The Flesh in the Furnace* (**1972**); *Starblood* (**1972**); *Demon Seed* (**1973**) made into the film DEMON SEED; *A Werewolf Among Us* (**1973**); *The Haunted Earth* (**1973**); *After the Last Race* (**1974**); *Night Chills* (**1976**); *The Vision* (**1977**).

See also: MEDIA LANDSCAPE.

KORNBLUTH, C(YRIL) M. (1923–58). American writer. He became a fan during the late 1930s and belonged to the New York fan group the FUTURIANS. He published prolifically during the years 1940–42 in magazines edited by fellow Futurians Donald WOLLHEIM and Frederik POHL. He used many pseudonyms and often wrote in collaboration, particularly with Pohl. Pseudonyms which he used more than once (and subsequently acknowledged) are Cecil Corwin; S.D. Gottesman (often with Pohl and twice with Pohl and Robert LOWNDES); Walter C. Davies; Paul Dennis Lavond (a house pseudonym used on several collaborations with Pohl or Pohl and Lowndes); Scott Mariner (in collaboration with Pohl) and Kenneth Falconer (under which name he published in 1941 the best of his early stories, "The Words of Guru"). (*For the most complex pseudonym of all see* Arthur COOKE.) As with many of the Futurians, his career was interrupted by the War. He served as an infantryman and was decorated. Afterwards he went into journalism and resumed writing sf in 1947, this time using his own name. After his reappearance with "The Only Thing We Learn" (1949) he quickly established himself as a writer of considerable ability. "The Little Black Bag" (1950) was reprinted in the SFWA's *Science Fiction Hall of Fame* (anth. **1970**) ed. Robert SILVERBERG as a classic of the genre. It concerns the use and misuse made of a medical bag temporarily dislodged from the future.

In 1951 he published his best-known short story, "The Marching Morons", also in *Science Fiction Hall of Fame*, describing a future where the practice of birth control by the intelligentsia has had a negatively eugenic effect, creating a society of subnormal intelligence. In that year he also published the first of two novels which he wrote in collaboration with Judith MERRIL under the pseudonym Cyril JUDD. Subsequently he began working again with Pohl, producing one of the most famous of modern sf novels, *The Space Merchants* (1952 *Gal.* as "Gravy Planet"; **1953**). This novel, which features a world run by advertising agencies in the service of capitalist consumerism, became the archetype of a whole generation of sf novels which show the world of the future dominated by one particular institution or power group. Two other collaborations with Pohl — the satirical comedy *Search the Sky* (**1954**) and *Gladiator-at-Law* (**1955**) — belong to the same subspecies. The last novel CMK wrote with Pohl was *Wolfbane* (**1957**), in which the Earth is moved out of its orbit by aliens who capture humans in order to use their bodies in a vast COMPUTER complex. Collaborative stories continued to appear for four years after CMK's death, and Pohl wrote some more stories from CMK's ideas in the early 1970s. These were published as collaborations and one, "The Meeting", won a HUGO award in 1973. Some of the collaborative short stories were collected in *The Wonder Effect* (coll. **1962**) and *Critical Mass* (coll. **1977**). Several stories appear in both volumes.

Two of the novels which CMK wrote solo are relatively ordinary. *Not This August* (**1955**; vt *Christmas Eve* UK) is about a revolution in a future USA which has been conquered by communists. *Takeoff* (**1952**) is a thriller centered on the building of the first spaceship. In between the two he wrote *The Syndic* (**1953**), which belongs to the same subspecies as the early novels he wrote with Pohl, featuring an America run by organized gangsterism in a semi-benevolent fashion. His writing is at its best, however, in some of the short stories belonging to this second phase of his career.

Some of CMK's shorter pieces are gentle and delicately constructed, including "With These Hands" (1951) and "The Goodly Creatures" (1952). Many of the most memorable, however, are deeply ingrained with bitter irony. These range from the black comedy of "The Cosmic Charge Account" (1956), which is about a little old lady who finds the power to remake her environs, to the early OVERPOPULATION horror story "Shark Ship" (1958). Also notable is the ALTERNATE-WORLD story "Two Dooms" (1958). The considerable talent for graceful writing and elegant construction which is evident in his short stories rarely shows up in his longer work, whether collaborative or not, and he seems to share the inability to write effectively at novel length which was curiously common among sf writers of his generation. The best of his short work is collected in *A Mile Beyond the Moon* (coll. **1958**; paperback omits three stories) and *The Marching Morons* (coll. **1959**).

CMK contributed a lecture on "The Failure of the Science Fiction novel as Social Criticism" to a series given at the University of Chicago and collected as *The Science Fiction Novel* (coll. **1959**) with an introduction by Basil DAVENPORT. The best of the four papers, this is an important early piece of sf criticism. His premature death at the age of 35 — he died of a heart attack after shovelling snow — closed an extremely promising career. His widow, Mary Kornbluth, compiled an anthology, *Science Fiction Showcase* (anth. **1959**), as a memorial volume. [BS]

Other works: *The Explorers* (coll. **1954**; vt *The Mindworm and Other Stories* UK, with "Thirteen O'Clock" omitted and four stories added); *Best Science Fiction Stories of Cyril M. Kornbluth* (coll. **1968**); *Thirteen O'Clock and Other Zero Hours* (coll. **1972**), ed. James BLISH.

See also: ANTI-INTELLECTUALISM IN SF; ARTS; COLONIZATION OF OTHER WORLDS; DYSTOPIAS; ECOLOGY; ECONOMICS; FLYING SAUCERS; GAMES AND SPORTS; GOTHIC SF; HEROES; HISTORY IN SF; INTELLIGENCE; INVASION; LEISURE; MEDIA LANDSCAPE; MEDICINE; NEAR FUTURE; OPTIMISM AND PESSIMISM; PARANOIA AND SCHIZOPHRENIA; POLITICS; POLLUTION; PSYCHOLOGY; PUBLISHING; ROCKETS; SATIRE; SF MAGAZINES; SCIENTISTS; SOCIOLOGY; SUPERNATURAL CREATURES; TIME TRAVEL; VENUS; WAR.

KORZYBSKI, ALFRED (HABDANK SKARBEK) (1879–1950). Polish-born aristocrat (a count) sent to the USA as an artillery expert after the First World War. He remained, and wrote a quasi-philosophical text, *Science and Sanity* (**1933**), which became the basic handbook of the GENERAL SEMANTICS movement (later to prove so influential on the writer A.E. VAN VOGT). With the support of a Chicago millionaire, AK set up the Institute of General Semantics in 1938. [PN]

About the author: *Fads and Fallacies in the Name of Science* (**1957**; revised edition of *In the Name of Science*, **1952**) by Martin GARDNER.

See also: PSEUDO-SCIENCE.

KOSINSKI, JERZY (1933–). Polish writer who moved to the USA after harrowing experiences as a child in the Second World War; he now writes exclusively in English. His first novel, *The Painted Bird* (**1965**) is a hallucinated picaresque set in the surrealistic landscape of the War, and recounts the fantastic life of a child whom horror has driven mute. Most of his fiction is FABULIST and his nearest approach to sf, *Being There* (**1970**), is a MAINSTREAM allegory in which Chance, an innocent, acquires the human characteristics necessary to become

President of the USA. Several of the incidents in *Cockpit* (**1975**) also approach sf from a fabulist vantage. [JC]
See also: POLITICS.

KOTZWINKLE, WILLIAM (? –). American author, whose allegorical FABULATIONS created something of a literary stir in the 1970s. Although he is not an sf writer *per se*, several of his books have sf relevance, including *Hermes 3000* (**1972**) and *Doctor Rat* (**1976**). The latter is an extraordinary work, mostly narrated by an elderly laboratory rat, his mind jumbled by too much maze-running, who sees himself as an active collaborator with the human experimenters; the destiny of the animal world, he feels, is to be subjected to such experiments for the ultimate good. Crises in the ECOLOGY, however, have driven the brutalized animals to form a global consciousness, and revolt is on the way, war ensues between Man and animals, and Doctor Rat heroically quells revolt in the lab. The book is a black and witty commentary on the psychology of destruction; finally Doctor Rat stands alone as the only animal left. [PN]

Illustrator Roy G. KRENKEL specializes in Heroic Fantasy, as in this cover for a 1964 Ace Books edition.

KRENKEL, ROY G. (1918–). American illustrator. RGK has been heavily influenced by the work of John Allen ST JOHN, and his style, particularly that of his b/w illustrations, is similar to St John's. He is known as a HEROIC FANTASY illustrator, and gained much of his fame from a series of covers for ACE BOOKS in the 1960s; he and Frank FRAZETTA painted the covers for all the Edgar Rice BURROUGHS Ace Books reprints. He has also been active in sf FANDOM, contributing much artwork to AMRA, a HUGO-winning fanzine. He won a Hugo award himself in 1963 as best professional artist, and was also nominated the following year. [JG]

KRONOS Film (1957). Regal/20th Century-Fox. Directed by Kurt Neumann, starring Jeff Morrow, Barbara Lawrence and John Emery. Screenplay by Laurence Louis Goldman, story by Irving Block. 78 mins. B/w.

A flying saucer deposits a huge mechanical creature on a California beach. When activated it proceeds to move across the countryside, crushing anything and anyone in its path. Its aim is to destroy power stations and absorb their energy, too much of which ultimately causes it to explode. The script is mediocre but Kronos itself is such an original and unusual monster that it stands out among all the giant reptiles, giant insects, and so on of the 1950s sf boom. Producer / director Kurt Neumann's other sf films include ROCKETSHIP XM (1950) and the very successful THE FLY (1958). [JB]

KUBILIUS, WALTER (1918–). American writer, active in the 1930s as fan, and in the 1940s as writer, beginning with "Trail's End" for *Stirring Science Stories* in 1941. His best-known story is "The Other Side" (1951). He has had no books or collections published. [PN]

KUBRICK, STANLEY (1928–). American film-maker, resident in the UK. He was born in New York City, the son of a doctor, and became obsessed with photography at a very early age. While still at school he was selling his pictures, and *Look* magazine was so impressed by his work that they hired him as soon as he left school. SK was very successful as a photo-journalist, but motion pictures became his dominant interest and he left *Look* after four years to make two short films financed out of his own savings. He then made two feature films, *Fear and Desire* (1953) and *Killer's Kiss* (1955), borrowing the production money from relatives. By then he had also become a fully qualified cameraman. In 1956 he made *The Killing*, which attracted the attention of critics, and his reputation was further enhanced by *Paths of Glory* in 1957. In 1959 he directed most of *Spartacus* (taking over from Anthony Mann) and then in 1961 moved to Britain and began, with *Lolita*, the cycle of films that have made him internationally famous. In 1963 he made his first sf film, DR STRANGELOVE, and in Dec. 1965 he started work on 2001: A SPACE ODYSSEY (which he completed in Mar. 1968). His next film was also sf — the controversial A CLOCKWORK ORANGE. His most recent film, however, is a baroque, historical epic, *Barry Lyndon* (1975). SK is one of the few film-makers who has succeeded in maintaining control over all aspects of his films (*Spartacus* was the exception) and his personal style is stamped on all his work, its most obvious characteristic being a cold and ironic wit. His films manifest a formidable intelligence, unusual in a maker of high-budget spectaculars. SK is reported to have an almost obsessive desire for perfection, which shows itself in a fastidious attention to detail. During the making of *2001*, for instance, he not only immersed himself in large numbers of books about space flight and cosmology but also supervised the special effects, forcing his teams of effects-men to develop new techniques and systems. Critics have emphasized the intellectual authority of SK's work, but he is also, and perhaps primarily, a consummate showman. [JB]

A bearded Stanley KUBRICK on the set of *2001: A Space Odyssey* with writer Arthur C. Clarke.

KUPRIN, ALEXANDER (IVANO-VICH) (1870–1938). Russian writer who is best known for his army novel *The Duel* (**1905**; trans. **1916**). An impoverished aristocrat, AK was first an army officer, later a journalist. A prolific reviewer, he was an Anglophile who expressed much admiration for such writers as Conan DOYLE, Rudyard KIPLING and H.G. WELLS. His admiration for Wells took the form of writing Wellsian scientific romances, though the first of these is in part a parody of an sf tradition which in imitation of foreign works was already becoming established in popular Russian magazines. The book was a novella, *Liquid Sunshine* (**1913**); set in England (a rather idealized G.K. CHESTERTON-style England, full of good cheer and roistering) and Ecuador, the story tells of a British scientist who is working in the latter country to store the energy of the Sun in liquid form. A later novella, "Every Wish" (1917) is in effect a retelling of Wells's "The Man Who Could Work Miracles" (1899), but with rather more scientific rationale. Neither work has been translated into English, and indeed AK is rather a minor though vigorous writer, interesting primarily in showing how early Wells's influence percolated to Russia. [PN]
About the author: "H.G. Wells' First Russian Admirer" by Leland Fetzer in FOUNDATION 11/12, 1977.

KURLAND, MICHAEL (JOSEPH) (1938–). American writer who began publishing sf in 1964 with "Elementary" written with Laurence M. JANIFER, and *Ten Years to Doomsday* (**1964**) with Chester ANDERSON. The latter is a lightly written alien INVASION novel, full of harmless violence in space and on other planets. MK's association with Anderson continued in the unusual trilogy comprising *The Butterfly Kid* (**1967**) by Anderson, *The Unicorn Girl* (**1969**) by MK, and *The Probability Pad* (**1970**) by T.A. WATERS. The books all feature the various authors as characters; *The Unicorn Girl* deals with a number of sf themes in a spoof idiom which is sometimes successful; MATTER TRANSMISSION and invasions abound. Although MK has perhaps gained most recognition for his suspense novel, *A Plague of Spies* (**1969**), which won an Edgar Allan Poe Scroll from the Mystery Writers of America, his later sf has increased in interest. Most noteworthy are *Pluribus* (**1975**), a post-HOLOCAUST novel which, though breaking no new ground in that genre, makes effective use of its American locations, and *The Whenabouts of Burr* (**1975**), an ALTERNATE-WORLDS tale featuring Aaron Burr. [JC]
Other works: The "War, Inc." series is not sf, but includes *Mission: Third Force* (**1967**), *Mission: Tank War* (**1968**) and *A Plague of Spies* (**1969**). Sf: *Transmission Error* (**1970**); *Tomorrow Knight* (**1976**).

KURTZ, KATHERINE (1944–). American writer, employed in various fields including oceanography and cancer research (she has a BS in chemistry), now an instructional designer for the Los Angeles Police Department. Her fiction is basically fantasy, and consists of two ongoing sequences, both part of "The Chronicles of the Deryni" and set in a highly detailed, coherent ALTERNATE WORLD, hierarchical and medieval Welsh in many of its aspects. One is comprised of *Deryni Rising* (**1970**), *Deryni Checkmate* (**1972**) and *High Deryni* (**1973**), with a sequel projected. The other, set 200 years earlier than the first, thus far consists of *Camber of Culdi* (**1976**) with a sequel projected. These chronicles tell the history of a group of humans whose paranormal (witch-like) powers, the explanation for which hovers between sf and mysticism, cause them to be persecuted by a medieval Church. The first novel is perhaps the best, but the whole is generally well above average for HEROIC FANTASY, well characterized, although sometimes suffering from a clash between archaic and modern language. [JC/PN]
See also: FANTASY; SWORD AND SORCERY.

KUTTNER, HENRY (1914–58). American writer. Married to C.L. MOORE. HK came into writing through his interest in WEIRD TALES, which led to correspondence with H.P. LOVECRAFT and others. His first sale to *Weird Tales* was a poēm, followed by "The Graveyard Rats" (1936), an often reprinted horror story. He contributed to the magazine frequently for a few years; his stories included a SWORD-AND-SORCERY series about the character Elak of Atlantis — "Thunder in the Dawn" (1938), "Spawn of Dagon" (1938), "Beyond the Phoenix" (1938) and "Dragon Moon" (1941).
HK began to publish sf stories in 1937, in the first instance mainly in THRILLING WONDER STORIES. He wrote a popular series about the movie business of the future, featuring the character Tony Quade. These were "Hollywood on the Moon" (1938), "Doom World" (1938), "The Star Parade" (1938), "The Energy Eaters" (1939) and "The Seven Sleepers" (1940). The last two stories were collaborations with Arthur K. BARNES, and combined HK's series with Barnes's own series about the character Gerry Carlyle. HK and Barnes also wrote under the pseudonym Kelvin KENT.
When MARVEL SCIENCE STORIES appeared in 1938, HK, who had been contributing to a non-sf magazine from the same publisher, achieved minor notoriety with the stories he wrote for it, which were tailored to the magazine's policy of introducing a mild lasciviousness to sf. "The Time Trap" (1938) was the most notable of these stories, for which he also used the pseudonyms James Hall and Robert O. Kenyon, two of many which he used

during his career. Several of his pen-names became established in their own right; early examples were Paul Edmonds and Keith Hammond. His others included Noel Gardner, Hudson Hastings, C.H. Liddell, Scott Morgan, K.H. Maepen and Woodrow Wilson Smith. He also published stories under various house names, notably Will GARTH. Under this name he wrote a short story, "Dr. Cyclops" (1940), based on the film of the same name. A Will Garth novel of the same title was published later, but was the work of Manly Wade WELLMAN.
In 1940 he married C.L. Moore, at that time a much more prestigious writer than he was. After their marriage most of their stories, except those published under C.L. Moore's byline, were to some degree collaborations. Some can definitely be ascribed to one or other writer, but the majority — even those published under HK's name alone — should be considered Kuttner-and-Moore stories. One writer would reportedly pick up any story where the other left off, so that their later work was a complete fusion of talents.
During the 1940s most of their major work appeared in ASTOUNDING SCIENCE FICTION, and they adopted two new pseudonyms: Lawrence O'Donnell and Lewis Padgett. The latter name was appropriate, since Lewis CARROLL was plainly an influence on many of these stories, which showed considerable ingenuity and technical proficiency combined with the HUMOUR for which HK was particularly noted. As Padgett HK (without Moore's help) wrote the "Galloway Gallegher" series, *Robots Have No Tails* (1943–8 *ASF*; coll. of linked stories **1952**; published in paperback under HK's name). Other Padgett stories included "The Twonky" (1942), which was made into a film (*see* THE TWONKY), "Shock" (1943), "Mimsy Were The Borogoves" (1943), *Tomorrow and Tomorrow & The Fairy Chessmen* (1946–7 *ASF*; coll. **1951**; republished separately in paperback; vts of *The Fairy Chessmen* being *Chessboard Planet* USA, *The Far Reality* UK) and *Mutant* (1945–53 *ASF*; fix-up **1953**; subsequent editions credited to HK). The "Baldy" series, collected in *Mutant*, are notable for their treatment of TELEPATHY. Most of the Lawrence O'Donnell stories were Moore's work; but they also included "Clash By Night" (1943) and its sequel *Fury* (1947 *ASF*; **1950**; vt *Destination: Infinity* USA), set in the undersea cities of VENUS after nuclear war has destroyed life on Earth. Both these works were probably collaborations — they have since been reprinted under HK's name — with *Fury* generally supposed to be largely the work of HK. *Fury*, a colourful story featuring a monomaniacal protagonist, is generally considered to be HK's best novel.
HK was also a prolific contributor to

other magazines during this period, especially STARTLING STORIES and *TWS*. *Startling Stories* featured a complete short adventure novel in each issue, and HK wrote a considerable number of these, including "When New York Vanished" (1940), *The Creature From Beyond Infinity* (1940 *Startling Stories* as "A Million Years To Conquer"; **1968**), *The Dark World* (1946 *Startling Stories*; **1965**), *Valley of the Flame* (1946 *Startling Stories* as by Keith Hammond; **1964**), "Lands of the Earthquake" (1947), "Lord of the Storm" (1947, as by Keith Hammond), *The Mask of Circe* (1948 *Startling Stories*; **1971**), *The Time Axis* (1949 *Startling Stories*; **1965**), *Beyond Earth's Gates* (1949 *Startling Stories* as "The Portal in the Picture" by HK; **1954**; book credited to "Lewis Padgett and C.L. Moore"), and *Well of the Worlds* (1952 *Startling Stories*; **1953**; first book edition bylined Lewis Padgett, later edition credits HK). For *TWS* he wrote the humorous "Hogben" series, about an ill-assorted family of MUTANT hill-billies: "Exit the Professor" (1947), "Pile of Trouble" (1948), "See You Later" (1949), "Cold War" (1949).

In 1950 HK went to study at the University of Southern California, as did C.L. Moore. They wrote a number of mystery novels but few more sf stories. HK graduated in 1954 and went on to work for his MA, but died of a heart attack before it was completed. During his career HK rarely received the credit his work merited, and was to an extent overshadowed by his own pseudonyms. His reputation as one of the most able and versatile of modern sf writers has risen steadily since. His influence on the young Ray BRADBURY was considerable (he wrote the ending for one of Bradbury's first published stories), and many later writers have acknowledged their debt to him.   [MJE]

Other works: *A Gnome There Was* (coll. **1950**, as by Lewis Padgett); *Ahead of Time* (coll. **1953**); *Line to Tomorrow* (coll. **1954**, as by Lewis Padgett); *No Boundaries* (coll. **1955**, by HK and C.L. Moore); *Bypass to Otherness* (coll. **1961**); *Return to Otherness* (coll. **1962**); *Earth's Last Citadel* (1943 *Argosy*; **1964**, by HK and C.L. Moore); *The Best of Kuttner, Volume 1* (coll. **1965**); *The Best of Kuttner, Volume 2* (coll. **1966**), *The Best of Henry Kuttner* (coll. **1975**), with introduction by Ray Bradbury.

See also: ANDROIDS; ANTI-INTELLECTUALISM IN SF; ATLANTIS, AUTOMATION; CHILDREN IN SF; COLONIZATION OF OTHER WORLDS; CRIME AND PUNISHMENT; DISCOVERY AND INVENTION; ECOLOGY; ECONOMICS; FANTASY; FAR FUTURE; FLYING SAUCERS; FOURTH DIMENSION (AND OTHERS); GAMES AND SPORTS; GODS AND DEMONS; GOLDEN AGE OF SF; INTELLIGENCE; MESSIAHS; OUTER PLANETS; PARALLEL WORLDS; PSI POWERS; RELIGION; ROBOTS; SATIRE; SCIENTISTS; SUPERMAN; TIME TRAVEL; UNDER THE SEA.

KYLE, DAVID A. (*c.* 1912–). American sf fan, writer, illustrator, owner of several radio stations, and publisher. DK is a member of "first fandom", having been active in the field since 1933. Until the 1970s his writing activities were only occasional; his first published sf was "Golden Nemesis" for *Stirring Science Stories* in 1941. In 1948, with Martin GREENBERG, he founded the fan publishing company GNOME PRESS, which probably maintained the highest standards of any of the small sf publishers of the period. DK designed several of the book jackets. For most of the 1970s DK has been resident in England, where he wrote two illustrated "coffee-table" style books on sf, the first dealing primarily with its history, and the second with its dominant themes. They are *A Pictorial History of Science Fiction* (**1976**) and *The Illustrated Book of Science Fiction Ideas and Dreams* (**1977**). Both are descriptive rather than analytic, are oriented heavily towards a conservative, fannish reading of genre sf, and are factually unreliable once they leave that area. However, DK's intimate knowledge of genre sf publishing over many years is reflected in much useful data which he gives about this aspect of sf. The books are rather heavily contemptuous about, and dismissive of, sf that falls outside the HARDCORE and GOLDEN-AGE sector of the market, particularly NEW WAVE sf. They are well and lavishly illustrated.   [PN]

LACH-SZYRMA, W(LADISLAW) S. (? – ?). British clergyman and author who began writing his series of interplanetary romances featuring the travels around the Solar System of the winged Venusian Aleriel in a magazine story in 1865; this was incorporated into *A Voice from Another World* (**1874** as by WSLS; exp. vt *Aleriel: or, A Voyage to Other Worlds* as by the Rev. W.S. Lach-Szyrma 1883). Aleriel's further travels were chronicled in the "Letters from the Planets" series in *Cassell's Magazine*, nine stories (1887–93), which were reprinted in *Worlds Apart* (anth. **1972**) ed. George LOCKE. *Under Other Conditions* (**1892**) tells of another Venusian's adventures on Earth. The forgetting of these stories has not been a

great loss to literature.   [PN]
See also: MARS; MOON; VENUS.

LADY AND THE MONSTER, THE Film (1944). Republic. Directed by George Sherman, starring Vera Ralston, Richard Arlen, Erich von Stroheim and Sidney Blackmer. Screenplay by Dane Lussier and Frederick Kohner, based on the novel *Donovan's Brain* by Curt SIODMAK. 86 mins. B/w.

This is the first of three film versions of Siodmak's novel; the others are DONOVAN'S BRAIN (1953) and THE BRAIN (1962). Financial wizard W.H. Donovan is killed when his plane crashes in the desert. A scientist, whose laboratory is nearby, removes the undamaged brain and keeps it alive in a glass tank, but it gradually takes over the minds of those around it, forcing them to commit a series of evil deeds. The direction and photography evoke a haunting atmosphere.   [JB]

LAFAYETTE, RENE *See* L. Ron HUBBARD.

LAFFERTY, R(APHAEL) A(LOYSIUS) (1914–). American writer, who worked in the electrical business for 35 years, though he does so no longer, and came to writing only in 1960, when he published his first sf, "Day of The Glacier", with *Science Fiction Stories*; he has since produced well over 100 stories, extremely diverse in character, but consistently notable for technical inventiveness and an apparently slapdash style that, on analysis, reveals considerable skill in the deploying of various rhetorical narrative voices, though these voices sometimes get choked in baroque flamboyance. RAL was awarded a 1973 HUGO award for best short story for "Eurema's Dam" (1972). Though a portion of his work in short forms has been assembled in *Nine Hundred Grandmothers* (coll. **1970**), *Strange Doings* (coll. **1972**) and *Does Anyone Else Have Something Further to Add?* (coll. **1974**), much of it remains uncollected, and a full assessment of his work awaits readier access to it.

RAL's first three novels, *Past Master* (**1968**), *Reefs of Earth* (**1968**) and *Space Chantey* (**1968**), all appeared within a few months of one another, and caused considerable stir. Even the pre-publication praise for *Past Master* (accolades from Samuel R. DELANY, Roger ZELAZNY and Harlan ELLISON) demonstrate the impact his work was beginning to have, and also show how clearly he had established himself as a significant representative of the American NEW WAVE, an ill-defined term, but certainly one that was intended to comprehend the works of writers like Delany, Zelazny and Ellison. Along with them, RAL wrote books whose broadened resources of style and language attempted to make sf themes and conventions applicable to the radically altering world of the late 1960s. Though it can be said that the American new wave was more a somewhat iconoclastic tone of voice than anything more substantive, movements are rarely more than that, and the generally sardonic air of the new wave proved bracing to such mature writers as RAL, even though he had newly come to the craft. *Past Master* places Sir Thomas More on the planet Astrobe, where he is tricked into becoming World President; the contrasts between UTOPIA and life are not dismissive of More. *Space Chantey* retells HOMER's *Odyssey* as SPACE OPERA, very rollickingly, and is the most representative of RAL's attempts at rendering saga-like tales in a sometimes laboured singing prose. *The Devil is Dead* (1971) features that gentleman in a narrative whose effect is tangled. *Arrive at Easterwine; The Autobiography of a Ktistec Machine* (1971) is the life story of a COMPUTER, and is again somewhat tangled. It is arguable that RAL achieves his best effects in such short fiction as "Continued on Next Rock" (1970), where his eccentric modes of storytelling, and his deliberately intrusive authorial voice, make for successful *tours de force*. Proper assessment of his entire corpus is due. [JC]

Other works: *Fourth Mansions* (1969); *The Fall of Rome* (1971); *The Flame is Green* (1971); *Okla Hannali* (1972; not sf); *Not to Mention Camels* (1976); *Archipelago* (1977); *Apocalypses* (coll. of two novel-length stories 1977).

See also: CITIES; FANTASTIC VOYAGES; HUMOUR; INTELLIGENCE; LINGUISTICS; MESSIAHS; MYTHOLOGY; PERCEPTION; REINCARNATION; SATIRE.

LAING, ALEXANDER (KINNAN) (1903–). American writer and editor, noted for his books on the sea, his *The Haunted Omnibus* (anth. 1937; vt *Great Ghost Stories of the World*) and his fantasy *The Cadaver of Gideon Wyck* (1934). Two further books with fantastic elements are *Dr. Scarlett: A Narrative of his Mysterious Behavior in the East* (1936) and its sequel *The Methods of Dr. Scarlett* (1937). In collaboration with Thomas PAINTER, AL wrote an sf thriller, *The Motives of Nicholas Holtz* (1936; vt *The Glass Centipede*); it is well told and surprisingly authentic in its use of biological data in a story of the creation of artificial life in the form of a deadly virus, and the dangers that beset the man who tries to investigate the ensuing deaths. [PN]

LAKE, DAVID J(OHN) (1929–). Australian writer (he emigrated there in 1967) born in India and originally a British citizen; his education (a Jesuit school in India, a BA in English at Cambridge, a diploma in linguistics and a PhD in English) is reflected in the texture of his sf work, as is his teaching in

Vietnam, Thailand and India (1959–67). After publishing several works of criticism, including the strongly argued, somewhat controversial *The Canon of Thomas Middleton's Plays* (1975), and a volume of poetry, *Hornpipes and Funerals* (coll. 1973), which deals with some of the themes of his fiction, he began publishing sf with *Walkers on the Sky* (1976) which promptly won a 1977 DITMAR. This book, *The Right Hand of Dextra* (1977) and its sequel on the same world, *The Wildings of Westron* (1977), make up the first instalments of a continuing sequence, the "Breakout Novels". They all share, or will retrospectively be shown to share, certain fundamental premises: In World War IV (2068), Earth destroys itself, by 2122 the colonies of the Moon are also in the throes of terminal conflict. But before the final collapse, interstellar ships break out of the Solar System in search of suitable planets to inhabit (see COLONIZATION OF OTHER WORLDS). The novels to date are set on two of these planets, and share comparatively simple, action-packed surface narratives along with considerable complexity of implication, some of it Jungian. *Walkers on the Sky*, set in the year 12117, is the entertaining saga of a young man making his way in a TERRAFORMED world irradiated by planes of force whose operation explains the dreamlike behaviour indicated by the title; *The Right Hand of Dextra*, set earlier in AD 2687, intermingles BIOLOGICAL, RELIGIOUS and colonization themes in the story of the reconciliation between incompatible forms of biological organization on a planet whose human colonists are religious fundamentalists insensitive to the vital questions surrounding Dextra's weird ECOLOGY. *The Wildings of Westron* is set in AD 3179. In the space of only a year, DJL has established himself as a newcomer of considerable note. [JC]

See also: CONCEPTUAL BREAKTHROUGH; GRAVITY.

LALLI, CELE G. *See* Cele GOLDSMITH.

LA MASTER, SLATER (? –). American writer. He appeared in *Argosy All-Story Weekly* with "Luckett Of The Moon" (1928), a humorous account of a hoax Moon landing, with sf elements, followed by the marginally sf *The Phantom In The Rainbow* (1929). [JE]

LAMBOURNE, JOHN Form of his name used on books by English writer John Battersby Crompton Lamburn (1893–), brother of Richmal Crompton, the authoress of the "Just William" juveniles. JL's *The Kingdom That Was* (1931) and its sequel *The Second Leopard* (1932) are mildly allegorical works describing the events in the animal kingdom of 50,000 years ago which led its apathetic rulers to abdicate in favour of mankind. Both are subduedly humorous and are reminiscent of both H. Rider HAGGARD and Rudyard KIPLING. JL also wrote *The Unmeasured Place* (1933), about a female vampire-cum-were-leopard. [JE]

LANCOUR, GENE Pseudonym of Gene Fisher (? –), American author of two volumes in the apparently ongoing SWORD-AND-SORCERY saga of Dirshan the God-Killer: *The Lerios Mecca* (1973) and *The War Machines of Kalinth* (1977). Dirshan is a barbarian warrior. The books are rather mysteriously marketed as sf. [PN]

LAND OF THE GIANTS TV series (1968–70). An Irwin Allen Production for 20th Century-Fox Television/ABC. Created by Irwin ALLEN, who was also executive producer. Writers included Ellis St Joseph, Bob and Esther Mitchell, Bob and Wanda Duncan, Richard

Giant props create startling effects in the TV series LAND OF THE GIANTS.

Shapiro and William Welch. Directors included Harry Harris, Nathan Juran, Sobey Martin and Irwin Allen (first episode only). The regular cast were Gary Conway, Kurt Kasznar, Don Marshall, Heather Young, Don Matheson, Deanna Lund and Stefan Arngrim. Special effects were by L.B. Abbott and Art Cruickshank. A total of 51 episodes, each 50 mins long. Colour.

Carrying on the tradition of such films as DR CYCLOPS and THE INCREDIBLE SHRINKING MAN (see GREAT AND SMALL) as well as an earlier TV series, WORLD OF GIANTS, the first episode showed seven people, travelling in a "strato-cruiser" sometime in the future, who pass through a space/time-warp and crash-land on a world, similar to 20th-century Earth, but in which everything, including people, is twelve times larger. The rest of the series concerned their predictable encounters with giant people and giant props. Three novelizations from the series were done by Murray LEINSTER: *Land of the Giants* (1968), *Land of the Giants No. 2 : The Hot Spot* (1969) and *Land of the Giants No. 3 : Unknown Danger* (1969). A fourth was *Land of the Giants: Flight of Fear* (1969) by Carl Henry Rathden.   [JB/PN]

LAND THAT TIME FORGOT, THE Film (1975). Amicus. Directed by Kevin Connor, starring Doug McClure, John McEnery and Susan Penhaligon. Screenplay by Michael MOORCOCK and James Cawthorn, adapted from the novel by Edgar Rice BURROUGHS. 95 mins. Colour.

A German U-boat with a mixed crew of Germans, Britons, one American and a girl discover Caprona, a long-lost landmass near the South Pole. It is crawling with prehistoric monsters and cave-men who do their best to destroy the invaders, with little success. The film ends with a volcanic eruption and the marooning of the hero and heroine. The various monsters are unconvincing. The script by Moorcock and Cawthorn was apparently altered extensively by the producers.   [JB]

LANE, JANE Pseudonym of English writer Elaine Dakers (? -), whose post-HOLOCAUST sf novel is *A State of Mind* (1964), set in an ORWELL-like DYSTOPIA.   [JC]

LANE, MARY E. BRADLEY (? – ?). Nothing is known about this woman, other than the fact that the book *Mizora: A Prophecy: A Mss. Found Among the Private Papers of Princess Vera Zarovitch; Being a true and faithful account of her Journey to the Interior of the Earth, with a careful description of the Country and its Inhabitants, their Customs, Manners and Government*, which was published anonymously (1890) in New York, is copyright in the name Mary E. Bradley, and attributed to Mary E. Bradley Lane on the Library of Congress catalogue card. According to the preface, the book was serialized in the Cincinnati *Commercial* in 1880 and 1881. The UTOPIA in a hollow Earth is all female (see WOMEN). Men and blacks have been eliminated.   [PN]

LANG, ALLEN KIM (1928–). American writer, who began publishing sf with "Machine of Klamugra" for *Planet Stories* in 1950, and wrote a good number of action stories in the following decade; his sf novel, *Wild and Outside* (1966), unbelievably sends an American baseball shortstop to subdue a planet of alien musclemen.   [JC]

LANG, ANDREW (1844–1912). Scottish man of letters well known for a wide range of literary activity, including novels, poetry, belles-lettres, anthropology, children's books and (perhaps most familiar to current readers) anthologies of traditional fables and tales retold for children, with some added hagiographical and historical material, much of the work being done by his wife; numerous volumes followed the first, *The Blue Fairy Book* (anth. 1889). The rather delicate fantasy content of many of his children's tales, like *Prince Prigio* (1889) and its sequel *Prince Ricardo of Pantouflia* (1893), which has a trip to the Moon on a flying horse, gives them a nostalgic interest for some adults today.

Some of his adult fiction contains more bracing material, however, though *That Very Mab* (1885), written with May Kendall and published anonymously, is a rather feeble SATIRE involving the return of the fairy queen to a 19th-century England where interplanetary travel exists, though is only talked about. The title story of *In the Wrong Paradise and Other Stories* (coll. 1886) is less ineffectual in its demonstration of the dictum that one man's paradise is another man's hell — a Christian is misrouted to a Red Indian's Happy Hunting Ground, and there are further mishaps; in the same volume, "The Romance of the First Radical" may well be the first example of ANTHROPOLOGICAL sf, predating H.G. WELLS's "A Story of the Stone Age" (1897) by more than a decade. Why-Why, a revolutionary Ice Age citizen, falls in love with Verva, asks intolerable questions and otherwise defies the customs of his tribe, and comes to a sad end. "The End of Phaeacia" (same volume) is a LOST-RACE tale in which a missionary is shipwrecked upon a South Sea ISLAND that actually turns out to be the Homeric Phaeacia; its inhabitants have maintained all their traditions. A novel, *The Mark of Cain* (1886) introduces a flying machine as *deus ex machina* late in the action to solve a court case; the book is long out of print.

Considerably more durable is AL's collaboration with his friend H. Rider HAGGARD; after he affectionately parodied Haggard's *She* (1887) in *He* (1887), written with W.H. Pollock and published anonymously, AL joined with him to produce *The World's Desire* (1890), a novel which combines Haggard's crude, sometimes haunting vigour and AL's chastely pastel classicism; despite occasional longueurs, the resulting tale of Odysseus's last journey to find Helen in Egypt is a moving, frequently eloquent romance, coming to a climax with Odysseus's discovery that Helen is the avatar of Ayesha (of Haggard's *She*), and his death at the hands of his son.

The Disentanglers (1902), AL's last adult novel, is fundamentally uncategorizable, though its sections have some resemblance to the club story; some of its episodes deal with submarines, occult sects, spectres and so forth, all used, as Roger Lancelyn GREEN noted in *Andrew Lang* (1946), the best work on this author, to replace the traditional "magical devices of the fairy tale" with the latest scientific developments, though retaining the magical function. Copious, but flawed by a disheartening dilettantism, AL's work is just the wrong side of major ranking in the sf/fantasy field, just as in his other areas of concentration.   [JC]

See also: ORIGIN OF MAN.

LANG, FRITZ (1890–1976). Austrian film-maker who, after trouble with the Nazis, left Germany for France in 1933, and emigrated to the USA in 1934. He was originally trained as an architect but preferred the graphic arts, and during the years before the First World War he supported himself as a cartoonist and caricaturist. He turned to writing after being wounded during the War, producing several popular thrillers and fantasy romances. After the War ended, he entered the German film industry and began directing a series of lavish melodramas, such as *Die Spinnen* (vt *The Spiders*) in 1919, many of which were sf-related, involving, as they did, technologically-supported plots to take over the world, LOST RACES, etc. In this vein was the first "Dr Mabuse" film, *Dr Mabuse, der Spieler* (vt *Dr Mabuse, the Gambler*) in 1922. In 1923–4 he made the huge fantasy *Die Nibelungen* (released as two separate films, *Siegfried* and *Krimhild's Revenge*). Like all FL's German films, this version of the famous German epic was co-written with his wife, Thea VON HARBOU. In 1925 he started work on another epic, his first real sf film, METROPOLIS; it is deservedly the most celebrated of all sf films of the silent period. His wife novelized the script as *Metropolis* (1926; trans. 1927). FL's other major sf film was DIE FRAU IM MOND (1929; vt *The Girl in the Moon*). Thea von Harbou's novel *Frau im Mond* (1928; trans. as *The Rocket to the Moon* 1930) came out before the film was released.

In the 1930s FL's German films included the famous murder film *M* in 1931 and *Das Testament des Dr Mabuse* in 1932. The latter involved the master criminal operating through hypnotic powers, and even undergoing a form of REINCARNATION. During the 25 years after his emigration to America, FL directed mostly low-budget, though often impressive, thrillers, such as *Fury* (1936), *You Only Live Once* (1937) and *The Big Heat* (1953). The nearest thing to another sf film he ever directed was his last film, the German DIE TAUSEND AUGEN DES DR MABUSE (vt *The 1000 Eyes of Dr Mabuse*) in 1960. The influence of FL's harsh, expressive style on genre cinema, especially adventure thrillers, psychological thrillers and sf films, is incalculable. Few film critics do not include him in their pantheon of great directors. [PN/JB]

LANG, HERRMANN (? – ?). Apparently a German writer and professor in the Polytechnic School at Karlsruhe, with publications in chemistry. His sf novel, *The Air Battle: A Vision of the Future* (trans. 1859), of which there seems to be no German edition, presents in short compass a remarkable portrait of a world several millennia hence, long after European civilization has been destroyed by floods and earthquakes. The peace-loving black rulers of the country of Sahara dominate Africa, and in a final battle with other powers utilize their great heavier-than-air machines to establish a beneficial hegemony over the world. Remarkably for a novel of this period, miscegenation is strongly approved of, and the white woman whose adventures the plot traces is destined to marry a black man. [JC]
See also: HOLOCAUST AND AFTER; POLITICS; WAR.

LANG, KING House name used by the British paperback publisher Curtis

Warren. *Saturn Patrol* (1951) is by E.C. TUBB; *Terra!* (undated, probably 1953) is by George HAY. Other titles of unknown provenance are *Gyrator Control* (undated), *Projectile War* (undated), *Rocket Invasion* (undated), *Space Line* (1952), *Task Flight* (undated) and *Trans-Mercurian* (undated). [PN]

LANG, SIMON Possibly a pseudonym; his novels are copyright in the name of Darlene Hartman. SL's novels, beginning with *All the Gods of Eisernon* (1973) and continuing with *The Elluvon Gift* (1975), are SPACE OPERAS and constitute a loose series, both featuring the Terran starship *Skipjack* and both set in the same galactic venue. The first novel is the more ambitious, presenting in the planet Eisernon an idyllic picture of an ALIEN race ECOLOGICALLY integrated with nature; both books feature more ominous aliens as well, and suffer from their all too clear resemblance to STAR TREK. [JC]

LANGART, DARREL T. *See* Randall GARRETT.

LANGE, JOHN *See* Michael CRICHTON.

LANGE, NED *See* Robert SHECKLEY.

LANGE, OLIVER (? –). Author of the sf novel *Vandenberg* (1971), in which the eponymous hero fights to the death against Russia's takeover of America, retreating to the Rocky Mountains to die undefeated. [JC]
See also: POLITICS.

LANGELAAN, GEORGE (c. 1910–). French-born British writer and journalist, active for many years in the USA before returning to France; his collection of sf/horror stories, *Out of Time* (coll. 1964), includes "The Fly" (1957), a macabre story of an unsuccessful experiment in MATTER TRANSMISSION, in which the scientist ends up with the head of a fly. It was filmed as THE FLY (1958). He has published several works in French, including *Nouvelles de l'anti-monde* ["Tales of the Anti-World"] (coll. 1962) and *Le vol de l'anti-g* ["The Flight of Anti-G"] (1967). [JC/PN]

LANGUAGES *See* LINGUISTICS.

LANIER, STERLING E. (1927–). American writer. He graduated from Harvard in 1951 with a degree in English, fought in Korea, and later did six years' graduate work at the School of Anthropology and Archeology at the University of Pennsylvania. He was for a time editor at Chilton Books, whom he persuaded to publish Frank HERBERT's *Dune* (1965). He is by profession a sculptor and jeweller, designing miniature bronzes, etc.

SEL's first published story was "Join Our Gang" (1962) in ANALOG. The majority of his short stories belong to the

"Brigadier Ffellowes" series, published in *FSF*. These are fantastic tall stories, told from a clubland setting, similar in conception to Lord DUNSANY's "Jorkens" stories or Arthur C. CLARKE's *Tales from the White Hart* (coll. 1957), and mostly involving the irruption of mythical creatures into the real world. *The Peculiar Exploits of Brigadier Ffellowes* (coll. 1972) includes all of these stories with the exception of "And the Voice of the Turtle" (1972), "Thinking of the Unthinkable" (1973), "A Father's Tale" (1974), "Ghost of a Crown" (1976).

SEL's first book was a good children's fantasy, *The War for the Lot* (1969). His only other novel is *Hiero's Journey* (1973), a long and inventive quest tale set in a post-HOLOCAUST world, which ends in mid-story. No sequel has yet appeared, though it was announced in 1975. [MJE]
See also: FANTASTIC VOYAGES; MUTANTS; MYTHOLOGY; SWORD AND SORCERY.

LARGE, E(RNEST) C(HARLES) (? –1976). British plant pathologist and writer, author of the notable *Sugar in the Air* (1937), which details the conflicts between scientific and commercial interests in the development of an industrial process of artificial photosynthesis. Also of note is the allegorical SATIRE *Dawn in Andromeda* (1956), in which God translocates a group of humans to an alien world in order to build a society from scratch using their scientific knowledge and practical skills. The political evolution of the community and the spontaneous regeneration of RELIGION confound the Utopian scheme of the original group. Another satire, *Asleep in the Afternoon* (1939) is weakened by the stratagem of presenting the speculative material (about a device for inducing sleep) in synoptic form within a mundane frame narrative. His principal scientific work was *The Advance of the Fungi* (1940). [BS]
See also: DISCOVERY AND INVENTION; SCIENTISTS; SOCIOLOGY.

LA SALLE, VICTOR House name used on early paperback sf novels published by John Spencer & Co. (later BADGER BOOKS). One such title, *Menace from Mercury* (1954), was the first published novel of the prolific R.L. FANTHORPE; this is the only VLS title definitely attributed to him. *The Black Sphere* (1951) was written by the minor pulp writer Gerald Evans. The remainder are: *After the Atom* (1953), *Assault from Infinity* (1953), *Dawn of the Half-Gods* (1953), *The 7th Dimension* (1953), *Suns in Duo* (1953) and *Twilight Zone* (1954). [MJE]

LASER BOOKS Canadian sf imprint initiated in 1975 by Harlequin Books, the US publisher of Mills & Boon romances, under the editorship of Roger ELWOOD. The books were restricted to a formula which specified a male protagonist, an upbeat ending, no sex or atheism, and a minimum of long words. All Laser Book covers were the work of Frank Kelly FREAS. The series was suspended early in 1977.   [MJE]

LASKI, MARGHANITA (1915–). English writer, also known as one of the most prolific contributors of material for the *Supplements* to the *Oxford English Dictionary. Love on the Super-Tax* (**1944**) edges into sf in its depiction of a wartime transformation of England; *Tory Heaven* (**1948**) is a spoof UTOPIA; *The Victorian Chaise Longue* (**1953**) is a fantasy in which two invalids, 100 years apart, switch identities.   [JC]
See also: ALTERNATE WORLDS.

LASSWITZ, KURD (1848–1910). German Kantean philosopher, historian of science, novelist and short-story writer. As the first major sf writer in German, he holds the same place in GERMANY as do H.G. WELLS in England and Jules VERNE in France. He taught philosophy for many years at the Gymnasium Ernestinum in Gotha, and it is symptomatic of 19th-century German intellectual culture that he irradiated his fiction with theoretical speculation; there is no KL fiction without a lesson. In "German Theories of Science Fiction" (1976 *Science-Fiction Studies*), William B. Fischer claims on KL's behalf that many of his ideas directly prefigure later critics' use of terms like "extrapolation" and "analogue", and translates as follows from KL's introduction to the short story collection *Bilder aus der Zukunft* ["Images of the Future"] (coll. **1878**): "Many inferences about the future can be drawn from the historical course of civilization and the present state of science; and analogy offers itself to fantasy as an ally." The seriousness of his didactic impulse can be seen in the strong emphasis he places in his fiction on establishing a plausible imaginary world whose hypothetical nature will be governed, and given verisimilitude, by the resemblance to scientific method evident in its realization. Unsurprisingly, the stories that embody these overriding concerns tend to be more effective as broad technological and scientific canvases than as studies in character; the tales collected in *Bilder aus der Zukunft* read consequently almost like illustrated tours of various "superior terrestrial cultures located in the future". Further short stories are collected in *Seifenblasen* ["Soap Bubbles"] (coll. **1890**) and *Nie und Nimmer* ["Never, Ever"] (coll. **1902**). KL's major work is his long sf novel, *Auf zwei Planeten* (**1897**; abridged 1948; new abridgement 1969; trans. as *Two Planets* from both abridged editions **1971**), in which mankind confronts a superior Martian culture when the Martian space satellite is discovered above the North Pole, along with an enclave at the Pole itself; after useless defiance of the Martians, Earth is put

under a benign protectorate, and men gradually begin a process of self-improvement at the same time that the Martians become decadent on Earth; ultimately, mankind rebels, equality between the two planets is established, and Earth seems destined to a UTOPIAN future. The book incorporates much technological speculation, including details about life on MARS (based on the theories of Percival Lowell), possible alien forms of biology (*see* XENOBIOLOGY) and the nature of mankind, actual and potential. It was deeply influential upon at least two generations of German youth, as the epigraph to the 1971 translation by Wernher von Braun attests.   [JC]
See also: PREDICTION.

LAST MAN ON EARTH, THE Film (1964). Alta Vista/AIP. Directed by Sidney Salkow and Ubaldo Ragona, starring Vincent Price and Franca Bettoia. Screenplay by Logan Swanson and William P. Leicester. 86 mins. B/w.
This Italian/US production was the first of two film versions of Richard MATHESON's novel *I Am Legend*, about the lone survivor of a plague whose victims develop the characteristics of the traditional vampire, for which the novel, unlike the film, provided an ingenious medical explanation. Each night the survivor is besieged in his house by these "vampires", and each day he travels around killing as many as he can while they sleep. Finally, however, they succeed in trapping and killing him. "I thought the film was terrible," said Matheson. "I had written a good screenplay but they had someone rewrite it and make it abysmal." The second film version of the novel was THE OMEGA MAN (1971).   [JB]

LATHAM, PHILIP Pseudonym of American astronomer Robert Shirley Richardson (1902–), used on his sf. He began publishing sf in the magazines in 1946, and continued into the late 1950s. Many of his stories had ASTRONOMICAL themes. Also, under his own name, he wrote a number of astronomical articles for sf magazines. PL wrote two juvenile sf adventure stories: *Five Against Venus* (**1952**) and *Missing Men of Saturn* (**1953**). As R.S. Richardson he wrote the semi-fictional work *Second Satellite* (**1956**) and the non-fiction work *Exploring Mars* (**1954**; vt *Man and the Planets*).   [PN]
See also: COSMOLOGY; DISASTER; OUTER PLANETS; SCIENTISTS; SUN; VENUS.

LAUMER, (JOHN) KEITH (1925–). American writer who has used his experiences in the American armed forces and diplomatic corps to considerable advantage in his sf work. He served in the army 1943–5, studied architecture and graduated with a B.Sc. Arch. from the University of Illinois in 1952, served in the US Air Force 1953–6, and then

joined the US foreign service. He rejoined the USAF as a captain in 1960. He began publishing sf in 1959 with "Greylorn" for *AMZ*, and for more than a decade remained extremely prolific, producing three major series and two minor ones along with a number of independent novels; since 1973 he has published little.
The most interesting of KL's series, though incomplete in its present three volumes, is comprised of his first novel, *Worlds of the Imperium* (**1962**), *The Other Side of Time* (**1965**) and *Assignment in Nowhere* (**1968**), and depicts a series of PARALLEL-WORLDS universes in which the Imperium dominates, and maintains the stability of the chosen time stream. As opposed to the grimmer, and perhaps more plausible versions of the same task as expressed in novels like Barrington BAYLEY's *The Fall of Chronopolis* (**1974**), KL takes an essentially optimistic view of this kind of situation, treating it in a no-nonsense, HARDCORE manner. Also related, if only thematically, to the Imperium series, is *Dinosaur Beach* (**1971**), a tale of TIME PARADOXES in which the role of the Imperium is played by Nexx Central, and the basic problems are similar. A second series, the parallel-worlds comic novels featuring Lafayette O'Leary, and comprising *The Time Bender* (**1966**), *The World Shuffler* (**1970**) and *The Shape Changer* (**1972**), attempts to replay a similar scenario in terms of slapstick, with only moderate success.
KL's other major series depicts the adventures of interstellar diplomatic troubleshooter Jaime Retief on a variety of alien worlds; Retief's main role, in a series of volumes including *Envoy to New Worlds* (coll. **1963**), *Galactic Diplomat* (coll. **1965**), *Retief's War* (**1966**), *Retief and the Warlords* (**1968**), *Retief: Ambassador to Space* (coll. **1969**), *Retief of the CDT* (coll. **1971**), *Retief's Ransom* (**1971**) and *Retief: Emissary to the Stars* (**1975**), is to mediate between the residents of these worlds, some of them nefarious, and his bumbling superiors in the Terran Diplomatic Corps, and to solve various sticky problems, almost all of them couched in comic terms, sometimes amusingly.
Away from his series, KL's books run a wide gamut, from (again generally unsatisfactory) comedies like *The Monitors* (**1966**), which was filmed as THE MONITORS in 1969, to taut, extremely efficient sf thrillers whose structures amalgamate SPACE OPERA and the favourite sf theme of the coming to awareness of the SUPERMAN. Best of them all is probably *A Plague of Demons* (**1965**), in which a tough human on Earth is biologically engineered into a preliminary sort of superman in order to deal with an ominously vague threat, and finds, after a long, remarkably sustained chase sequence, and after he is captured by some singularly efficient aliens, that for centuries Earth has been despoiled of its best fighting men, who, like the hero

of this novel, are taken off-planet and transplanted into gigantic, armed fighting machines, to act as their command centres and to continue an interstellar war that has been going on for aeons. Now a CYBORG, the protagonist manages to regain self-control, organizes a revolt of his fellow cyborg-supertanks, wins, and prepares to carry — fabulously armed — his message of freedom to the stars. In this, and other such similar novels as *A Trace of Memory* (**1963**), *The Long Twilight* (**1969**) and *The House in November* (**1970**), the essential KL superman takes shape: often an orphan, usually a loner, he discovers the world to be a persecuting snare and delusion, and gradually comes to realize that his PARANOIA is realistic when his true superior nature is revealed to him; once he becomes a superman he is able to transcend the world of normals, and often takes it over, though behind the scenes. It is for novels in which this wish-fulfilment version of the superman is expressed that KL will be best remembered, though his tendency to write too quickly seems to have damaged his later efforts even in this favourite mode. Much of his production is sadly routine and stripped down; even his heroes are sometimes only sketched in. But at his best, KL has written polished and succinct daydreams of sf transcendence that can serve as models of their kind. [JC]

Other works: *The Great Time Machine Hoax* (**1964**); *Catastrophe Planet* (**1966**); *Earthblood* (**1966**) with Rosel George BROWN (*who see for details*); *Nine by Laumer* (coll. **1967**); *Galactic Odyssey* (**1967**); *Planet Run* (**1967**) with Gordon R. DICKSON; *The Day Before Forever and Thunderhead* (coll. **1968**); *Greylorn* (coll. **1968**; vt *The Other Sky* UK); *It's a Mad, Mad, Mad Galaxy* (coll. **1968**); *Time Trap* (**1970**); *The Star Treasure* (**1971**); *Once There was a Giant* (coll. **1971**); *The Infinite Cage* (**1972**); *Timetracks* (coll. **1972**); *The Big Show* (coll. **1972**); *The Glory Game* (**1973**); *Night of Delusions* (**1973**); *The Undefeated* (coll. **1974**); *Bolo: The Annals of the Dinochrome Brigade* (coll. of linked stories with new linking material **1976**); *The Best of Keith Laumer* (coll. **1977**). KL's versions of stories from the sf television series THE INVADERS are: *The Invaders* (coll. **1967**; vt *The Meteor Men* UK as by Anthony LeBaron) and *Enemies from Beyond* (coll. **1967**). His novelizations from a second television series, THE AVENGERS, are: *The Afrit Affair* (**1968**); *The Drowned Queen* (**1968**); and *The Gold Bomb* (**1968**). The book *Five Fates* (anth. **1972**) was devised by KL, with five novellas written about the theme of fate.

See also: ALTERNATE WORLDS; ESCHATOLOGY; GODS AND DEMONS; HEROES; HISTORY OF SF; HUMOUR; TIME TRAVEL; WAR; WEAPONS.

LAURIE, ANDRÉ Pseudonym of Paschal Grousset (1845–1909). French politician and author. His first political novel, *Le rêve d'un irreconciliable* ["Dream of a Diehard"] (**1869**), along with several political works, was published under his real name, but thereafter he used the AL pseudonym. While living as a *communard* exile in London, AL wrote the original version of the book which was later published as *The Begum's Fortune* (**1879**) by Jules VERNE. Laurie legally renounced title to the story, as he did with *The Southern Star Mystery* (**1884**), rewritten and published as by Verne. Both authors put their name to *L'épave du Cynthia* (**1885**; trans. as *Salvage from the Cynthia* **1958**). It was a strange collaboration, AL being a long way to the left of Verne politically. Of AL's several sf novels, five have been translated into English. The best known is *The Conquest of the Moon, A Story of the Bayouda* (**1888** France; trans. **1889**), in which the Moon is drawn from its orbit to land on the Sahara desert. AL wrote of the discoveries of scientifically advanced societies in *The Secret of the Magian; or The Mystery of Ecbatana* (**1890** France; trans. **1892**) and *The Crystal City Under the Sea* (**1895** France; trans. **1896**), and of a transatlantic tunnel in *New York to Brest in Seven Hours* (**1889** France; trans. **1890**). His most critically acclaimed work, *Spiridon le muet* ["Spiridon the Mute"] (**1909** France), remains untranslated. [JE/PN]

Other works: *Axel Eberson, the Graduate of Upsala* (**1891** France; trans. **1892**)

See also: BOYS' PAPERS; MOON; NEAR FUTURE; UNDER THE SEA.

LAVERTY, DONALD Pseudonym of James BLISH and Damon KNIGHT in collaboration.

LAVOND, PAUL DENNIS See C.M. KORNBLUTH, Frederik POHL and Robert A.W. LOWNDES.

LAWRENCE, HENRY L(IONEL) (? –). English writer whose sf novel, *The Children of Light* (**1960**), deals with the effects of radiation. It was used as the basis for a film, THE DAMNED (1961). [JC/PN]

LAWRENCE, LOUISE See STARS.

LAWRENCE, STEPHEN Pseudonym of Lawrence Sterne Stephens (? – ?). American illustrator. SL also worked under the name L. Sterne Stephens. He did both colour and b/w work, 1942–55, for such magazines as *Amazing Stories*, *Fantastic Novels*, *Fantastic Adventures*, *Super Science Stories*, *Thrilling Wonder Stories*, *Startling Stories*, *A. Merritt's Fantasy Magazine*, *Astonishing Stories* and others, including 39 covers for *Famous Fantastic Mysteries*, 1943–53. His style is similar to Virgil FINLAY's, and he was often criticized for being a mere

In this ingenious Stephen LAWRENCE cover, a woman's breasts become the eyes of a skull. June 1952.

imitator. However, his colour paintings were generally superior to Finlay's, though his interior illustrations were not generally as dramatic. His b/w illustrations lacked the definitive use of strong dark/light contrasts that Finlay had mastered, and SL's people appeared less natural. None the less, he was one of the most vigorously lurid illustrators of the PULP covers during their most enjoyable garish period. [JG/PN]

LEACH, DECIMA (? –). Writer whose sf novel is *The Garthians* (**1962**). [JC]

LEACOCK, STEPHEN (BUTLER) (1869–1944). Canadian academic and humorist, known mainly for work outside the sf field, e.g. *Sunshine Sketches of a Little Town* (**1912**). His more fantastic comic sketches sometimes shade into sf, notably "The Man in Asbestos", which parodies H.G. WELLS's *The Time Machine*, and other stories in *Nonsense Novels* (coll. **1911**). *Afternoons in Utopia* (coll. **1932**) contains six stories satirical of various UTOPIAS. *The Iron Man and the Tin Woman* (coll. **1929**) has many sf spoofs. [JC]

Other works: *Moonbeams from the Larger Lunacy* (coll. **1917**); *Frenzied Fiction* (coll. **1918**); *The Hohenzollerns in America, and Other Impossibilities* (coll. **1919**); and many other books of comic vignettes which often contain a fantastic element.

LEAHY, JOHN MARTIN (1886–). American PULP-MAGAZINE author and illustrator. He contributed sf to SCIENCE AND INVENTION and to WEIRD TALES, in which appeared *Drome* (1927; **1952**) a hollow-Earth LOST-WORLD novel, published by FPCI. [JE]

LeBARON, ANTHONY See Keith LAUMER.

LE CLÉZIO, J(EAN)-M(ARIE) G(USTAVE) (1940–). French writer, known primarily for his work outside the sf field. Of British origin, he took his degree in literature at Nice University. He is a major contemporary author in the ABSURDIST tradition, whose work often borders on sf and the surreal through a minute examination of physical phenomena and aspects of reality. His hallucinatory scrutiny of manifestations of madness in the world at large is best demonstrated in *Les géants* (**1973**; trans. as *The Giants* by Simon Watson-Taylor **1975**), which is set in Hyperbolis, a nightmare shopping-complex in a futuristic CITY. [MJ]
Other works: The following have sf connotations: *Le procès-verbal* (**1963**; won Prix Renaudot; trans. as *The Interrogation* by Daphne Woodward **1964**); *La fièvre* (coll. **1964**; trans. as *Fever* by Daphne Woodward **1966**); *Le déluge* (**1965**; trans. as *The Flood* by Peter Green **1967**); *Terra Amata* (**1967**; trans. Barbara Bray **1969**); *Le livre des fuites* (**1969**; trans. as *The Book of Flights* by Simon Watson-Taylor **1972**); *La guerre* (**1970**; trans. as *War* by Simon Watson-Taylor **1973**); *Voyages de l'autre côté* ["Journeys on the Other Side"] (**1975**).
See also: MEDIA LANDSCAPE.

LEE, MATT *See* Sam MERWIN.

LEE, ROBERT EGGERT *See* Paul W. FAIRMAN.

LEE, STAN (1922–). American COMIC-BOOK writer and executive, born Stanley Leiber; his name has been legally changed to Lee. Before the Second World War, he had already begun to establish himself in the New York comics publishing world, and was soon associated with Timely comics, the firm for which Jack KIRBY invented Captain America. Timely eventually changed its name to Atlas Comics, and finally to MARVEL COMICS, without changing its corporate identity, and SL has remained with the firm without break, as its editor from 1942 to 1972, and as its publisher and editorial director from 1972. His career is not of particular importance within the comic-book field or for the student of sf until 1961, when, with Kirby, who had spent many years away from Marvel, he began to create a new type of comic book SUPERMAN with such series as *The Fantastic Four* (from 1961) and *The Incredible Hulk* (from 1962) and individual heroes like Spiderman (initiated in *Amazing Fantasy* in 1962) which was drawn by Steve Ditko in an angular, repressed style evocative of pedestrian urban life. Over the next half decade, SL (usually with Kirby) initiated a number of similar comic books including *The Avengers* (from 1963), into which Kirby reintroduced his Captain America, *X-Men* (from 1963) and *Thor* (separate comic from 1966, character introduced in *Journey into Mystery* in 1962).

What was remarkable in all these creations, most of them scripted by SL, was his introduction of the notion of human frailty into protagonists whose superpowers enabled them sometimes, but never permanently, to transcend their personal problems. Coincident with this, SL began to emphasize continuing storylines, the somewhat garish complexity of whose plots enabled him to write many characters into ongoing sf situations, most notably in these early years in *The Fantastic Four*, the heroes of which were involved by late 1965 in intergalactic disputes with the planet-devouring (but rather sympathetic) Galactus, and his moody, coerced sidekick, the Silver Surfer (featured in *The Silver Surfer* from 1968–70), a non-human surfer of space imprisoned by Galactus within Earth's atmosphere where, misunderstood and reviled, he saves humanity time and again from itself.
In 1970, Kirby left Marvel, and though he returned later, it is arguable that SL's domination, as both editor and writer, of the comic-book world began to slip from about that time. He has more recently introduced a number of themes and characters from HEROIC FANTASY (including Robert E. Howard's Conan in *Conan the Barbarian* from 1970, and Michael MOORCOCK's Elric character), and under his guidance Marvel Comics have featured ever more spectacular and sf-like situations, though with less ebullience than formerly. All the same, 1961–6 may well come to be seen as the comic world's golden age of superhero tales, with SL as its undoubted presiding genius. [JC]
See also: MYTHOLOGY.

LEE, TANITH (1947–). British writer, at first of juveniles, latterly of sf and fantasy as well. Her books for younger children are *The Dragon Hoard* (**1971**), *Princess Hynchatti and Some Other Surprises* (coll. **1972**) and *Animal*

Castle (**1972**). Her stories for older children are also of legitimate adult interest. She tells, in clean-cut, rhythmically precise language, fable-like tales: *Companions on the Road* (**1975**), *The Winter Players* (**1976**) and *East of Midnight* (**1977**). The two former titles have been published in one volume in the USA as *Companions on the Road* (coll. **1977**). The middle volume tells of the quest of a young witch for a Bone that has been stolen from her; a simple chase story turns into a complex initiation into adulthood (*see* CHILDREN IN SF), involving, among other things, TIME PARADOXES. Her first adult novel, *The Birthgrave* (**1975**), is also a quest story, much longer and more ambitious, not necessarily a better book: the female protagonist awakens in the heart of a volcano convinced that she is being told that she brings death and destruction to the world; a long, picaresque, SWORD-AND-SORCERY story follows, rationalized at the end by the arrival of Earthmen in a spaceship who treat her and give her a psychological explanation for her compulsions and the voices in her head. The sequels are *Vazkor, Son of Vazkor* (**1978**) and *Quest for the White Witch* (**1978**). *Don't Bite the Sun* (**1976**) and *Drinking Sapphire Wine* (**1977**) form a sequence set in a FAR-FUTURE world somewhat resembling Michael MOORCOCK's in his "Dancers at the End of Time" series. TL is a sometimes powerful writer of considerable clarity of mind, and her reputation is bound to grow rapidly. [JC]
Other works: *Volkhavaar* (**1977**); *The Storm Lord* (**1977**); *Night's Master* (**1978**).

LEE, WALT(ER) (WILLIAM) (1931–). American film-writer and consultant, and editor, with a BS in physics with honor from California Institute of Technology, 1954. His monumental three-volume *Reference Guide to Fantastic Films* contains upwards of 20,000 entries in an amazing, and amazingly accurate, work of sustained research. Fantasy, occult and horror feature more largely than pure sf, but sf is dealt with very thoroughly indeed. The work, published by Lee, is the most essential of research tools for anyone dealing with sf cinema. The volumes are *A–F* (**1972**), *G–O* (**1973**) and *P–Z* (**1974**). WL projects further publications in the same area. [PN]

LEE TUNG (? –). Indian writer whose interesting sf novel, *The Wind Obeys Lama Toru* (**1967**), is a complex story about OVERPOPULATION in which fertility and sterility drugs act and counteract, driving the population up and down disastrously. [JC]

LE GUIN, URSULA K(ROEBER) (1929–). American writer. Her first novel was not published until 1966, but her rise to fame has been very rapid. By

1970 she was already spoken of as one of the most important writers within the field; since then her reputation has gone well beyond the barriers of genre sf, and within the genre she has been honoured with four HUGOS and three NEBULAS.

UKLG is the daughter of Dr Alfred Kroeber and Theodora Kroeber, the former a celebrated anthropologist who has published much work on Amerindians, the latter a writer, best known for *Ishi in Two Worlds* (**1961**). UKLG was brought up in academic surroundings, and has in one sense stayed there; her husband, Charles Le Guin, is a professor of history. UKLG's education, with an undergraduate degree from Radcliffe and a master's degree from Columbia, was in romance languages, particularly French. Her master's thesis was on "Ideas of Death in Ronsard's Poetry" (1952). Her home is in Portland, Oregon.

UKLG wrote poetry (some of it collected in *Wild Angels*, coll. **1975**) and a number of unpublished realistic novels, mostly set in an imaginary Central European country, before turning to sf, which she had read as a child. Early on, also, she found Lord DUNSANY a liberating force, in his creation of imaginary worlds, though she has not directly imitated him. Her turning to sf was partly inspired by the discovery that writers as subtle as Cordwainer SMITH were, in the 1960s, being published in the sf magazines.

All her early work was bought by Cele GOLDSMITH for *AMZ* and *Fantastic*, her first published sf being "April in Paris" for *Fantastic* in 1962; like much of her early work this is more FANTASY than sf, though she is not happy at making a rigorous distinction between the two, as she has discussed in her autobiographical article "A Citizen of Mondath" (1973) in FOUNDATION, 4, and again in her introduction to the 1977 hardcover edition of *Rocannon's World* (**1966**).

Much of UKLG's work is set in a common universe; it is generally known as the "Hainish" series. The people from the planet Hain originally seeded the habitable worlds of our part of the galaxy with human life; thus we have a great many worlds, all populated by humanoids, but with enormous cultural variety; this is a useful background for a writer who grew up with ANTHROPOLOGY as an everyday discipline. Five novels and three important short stories (one later published as a separate novella) belong to this sequence; between them they spell out in very broad outline about 2,500 years of future HISTORY, beginning 300–400 years from now.

UKLG's first three novels all belong to the latter part of this sequence, considered in terms of its internal chronology. They are *Rocannon's World* (**1966**; 1977 with many typographical errors eliminated), *Planet of Exile* (**1966**) and *City of Illusions* (**1967**). In comparison with what was to follow, they are apprentice work, though all three show, well developed, the typical UKLG strategy of structuring a story around recurrent metaphors, which gain in richness and density as the action continues to juxtapose them in new patterns, until it might almost be said that they *are* the story. Many of them are the simple archetypal symbols that have always dominated myth and poetry: darkness and light, root and branch, winter and spring, submission and arrogance, language and silence. These are not normally seen by UKLG as polarities or opposed forces; rather, they are twin parts of a balanced whole as in *yin* and *yang*, each deriving meaning from the other. It has often been observed that UKLG's dualism, insofar as it exists at all, is not Western (where painful progress often comes about through the tension of antitheses, as in Marxist dialectics) so much as Eastern, especially Taoist, where the emphasis is on balance, mutuality and an ordered completeness, resulting in historical terms in cycles, rather than evolution in a straight line.

Typically, UKLG's stories set a man in an apparently alien and alienated landscape, and follow him on a quest, until he makes a CONCEPTUAL BREAKTHROUGH, and proves an agent for the reconciliation of the sundered parts; the quest often takes the form of a winter journey.

The actual plot structures of the first three novels belong too conventionally to genre sf to sustain fully the weight of meaning they are asked to bear. In *Rocannon's World* an ethnographer is marooned on a primitive planet, after a military action resulting from rebellion in the League of All Worlds; finally in giving himself to the planet he receives in return the gift of "mindspeech" or telepathy (*see* ESP). *Planet of Exile*, set over 1,000 years later, has mindspeech in normal use; a Terran colony (*see* COLONIZATION OF OTHER WORLDS) is struggling to survive on a planet whose natives they despise; under pressure the two communities are finally able to merge and even interbreed. *City of Illusions* is set on a cowed Earth ruled by the human-seeming but alien Shing invaders (*see* INVASION) who have the hitherto unknown art of "mindlying"; mindspeech is no longer synonymous with truth. The hero is an amnesiac (in the manner of A.E. VAN VOGT) who, when his memory is restored and his Earth life and previous life are set in balance, turns out to be a messenger from the planet of the previous book. Able to detect mindlying, he will be the agent of destruction for the evil Shing.

The first work of UKLG's real maturity as a writer is *The Left Hand of Darkness* (**1969**), which won both Hugo and Nebula awards for best novel. The League of All Worlds has now developed into the less arrogant Ekumen of Known Worlds; once again an ethnologist visits a planet, this time Gethen, whose people are androgynous in that, though normally neuter, at the peak of their sexual cycle they have the capability of becoming either male or female; the world itself is cold and snow-bound. The professional observer is unable to hold aloof from events, which are complex; in the novel's most moving sequence, a long and lonely journey across the ice, he reaches a painful understanding with, and a kind of reciprocated love for the Gethenian protagonist. The strength of the novel comes from the interplay between the strange and the familiar; the Gethenians are very like us in many respects, and our slow understanding of their differences has much to say about the nature of SEX and sexism in our world, and of cultural alienation generally.

The next two important items in the "Hainish" sequence are novellas, "Vaster Than Empires and More Slow" (1971) and *The Word for World is Forest* (1972 in *Again, Dangerous Visions*, anth. ed. Harlan ELLISON; **1976**). The former story, its title taken from Andrew Marvell's poem "To His Coy Mistress", is set just after the action of *Rocannon's World*, and the latter, which won a 1973 Hugo in the novella class, only 18 years after the foundation of the League of All Worlds. Both, typically, set humans on alien planets (*see* LIFE ON OTHER WORLDS); the first (*see* LIVING WORLDS) is inhabited only by a sentient plant network (the previous line of the Marvell poem is "my vegetable love shall grow"), the second by a highly exploited race of natives, in a situation deliberately reminiscent of the Vietnam war. In both cases a kind of union is gained through human surrender to otherness; in both cases alienation is imaged as violence, madness and ravening egoism. UKLG's stories are remarkably persuasive and consistent in their outlook, although the answers tend to come less easily in the later work, which perhaps puts a greater value on the individual, and less on the harmony of the whole.

Her next major novel, which was a Hugo, a Nebula and a JUPITER, was *The Dispossessed* (**1974**), in which difficulties are surmounted only partially; a central image is that of the wall; there seems a greater recognition of complexity here, and less use is made of the slightly diagrammatic, transcendent unity which perhaps came a little too easily in the early work. The novel deals with the life of a physicist, and the ways in which he comes to a new way of looking at the universe, in a mathematics which ultimately results in the construction of the ANSIBLE, the instantaneous com-

munication which is the necessary prerequisite for the League of All Worlds (*see* FASTER THAN LIGHT). Thus it stands at the head of the internal chronology of the entire "Hainish" sequence. Two inhabited worlds, one a moon of the other, have different political systems; one is an anarchy (partly after the models proposed in real life by Kropotkin), the other is primarily capitalist. The tensions set up are reflected in the development of the hero, Shevek, who is not completely at home in either society. The book has been read as pitting an anarchist UTOPIA against a DYSTOPIA, but it is more complex than that. There are seldom absolutes in UKLG's work, and the anarchist society, though strongly imagined and attractive, is in some ways blinkered and emotionally regimented (with the willing collaboration of its people). The novel is one of the most important studies of POLITICS in sf, and is also an important study in the thought processes of a scientist. Its structure (alternating, parallel sections set in the different worlds) offers no absolute resolution, and its metaphoric life, which is strong, is less reliant than in previous work on the evocation of *yin-yang* components. In terms of idea, it is UKLG's greatest work; in terms of performance, it has a certain didactic dryness, which some readers have found places them at too great an emotional distance from the protagonists. Nevertheless, it is a remarkable and major work of art.

Through all this period, UKLG was writing occasional short stories, nearly all outside the "Hainish" series, although "The Day Before the Revolution" (1974) is a short preamble to the anarchist society of *The Dispossessed*, in terms of its tired and unromantic founder's last memories; it won a Nebula and a Jupiter. "The Ones Who Walk Away from Omelas" (1973) won a Hugo; it is a deft and bitter parable about the cost of the good life. In "Nine Lives" (1969) individual values are measured against those of the group in a moving and masterly story of CLONES mining an alien planet (*see* GENETIC ENGINEERING). All UKLG's short sf up to 1974, with the exception of *The Word for World is Forest*, can be found in *The Wind's Twelve Quarters* (coll. **1975**; UK paperback in two vols). Her non-sf short fiction, much of it recent, is in *Orsinian Tales* (coll. **1976**). She has published little sf since *The Dispossessed*, the most notable exceptions being "The Author of the Acacia Seeds and Other Extracts from the *Journal of the Association of Therolinguistics*" (1974) (*see* IMAGINARY SCIENCE), "The Diary of the Rose" (1976), which won a Jupiter award, and "The New Atlantis", title story of *The New Atlantis* (anth. **1975**) ed. Robert SILVERBERG. The latter is a story, unusually dark for UKLG, of the NEAR FUTURE, where the State has become

frightened and cruel, and a ruined ECOLOGY is causing America to slide into darkness just as the lost continent's white towers re-emerge above the sea; it ends with the cry of the Atlanteans "*We are here. Where have you gone?*", and may confirm the thesis above that UKLG's work is moving away from ready resolutions. (It has always been too subtle to be seen as an example of easy OPTIMISM.)

This leaves two important works, the first being the "Earthsea" trilogy, ostensibly for children, but in actuality more assured and complex than her first three novels for adults; it is made up of *A Wizard of Earthsea* (**1968**), *The Tombs of Atuan* (**1971**) and *The Farthest Shore* (**1972**; UK edition slightly cut and revised); the three have been collected as *Earthsea* (coll. **1977**). *The Tombs of Atuan* received a Newbery Silver Medal, and *The Farthest Shore* a National Book Award. Set in an ocean world, in a cluster of ISLANDS, the trilogy tells of training in MAGIC and its proper use; this sounds like pure fantasy but, so rigorous is the logic with which the principles of magic are described, it can easily be understood as a form of alternate science; there is no woolliness. The books tell of episodes in the apprenticeship, the full-powered maturity and the final death-quest of a magician, Ged. A sober and sometimes sombre joyfulness pervades the trilogy, which in terms of the moral teaching it conveys is perhaps more mature than the comparable and even more celebrated "Narnia" series of C.S. LEWIS. Always gripping, often moving, and shot through with a complexly used but plain and almost puritanical imagery, it may be UKLG's most perfect work.

Her other novel is an interesting experiment, *The Lathe of Heaven* (**1971**), which deals, at first sight uncharacteristically, with a man who through his dreams can bring alternate reality structures into being; this is the imaginative territory which is generally associated with Philip K. DICK. The book is flawed, but is by no means a failure. As in all UKLG's work, there is a strong though unpreachy emphasis on the moral responsibility of the individual, and its cost. In its interest in METAPHYSICS, the book is all of a piece with her other work, though unusually shaped.

It is possible that UKLG has been over-praised; it is too soon yet to say that she is the greatest of sf writers, which is a view many critics at least imply. But she has given much to the genre: an intelligent and feeling use of image structures, in the manner of a poet, and not least, an example that shows how the interest of the traditional novelist, in questions of character and moral growth, need not be alien to sf. (She writes on this theme in "Science Fiction and Mrs Brown" in *Science Fiction at Large*, anth. **1976**, vt *Explorations of the Marvellous*, ed. Peter NICHOLLS.) If there is a weakness in her work it is a paradoxical one, a kind of grave and demure certainty which could, perhaps, be leavened with a little more openness to the random and the unpredictable; but self-confidence cannot justly be evidenced as a flaw. [PN]

Other works: *From Elfland to Poughkeepsie* (**1973**), a critical pamphlet; *Dreams Must Explain Themselves* (coll. **1975**), a pamphlet which has a story, an essay, a speech and an interview; *A Very Long Way From Anywhere Else* (**1976**), a contemporary love story, not sf, directed at teenagers. As editor: *Nebula Award Stories 11* (anth. **1976**).

About the author: SCIENCE-FICTION STUDIES, Vol. 3, part 1, Mar. 1976, is a Le Guin issue; the same journal has interesting pieces by and about UKLG in Vol. 1, part 3, and Vol. 2, parts 1–3, notably the article by Ian WATSON: "Le Guin's *Lathe of Heaven* and the role of Dick: The False Reality as Mediator" in Vol. 2, part 1; *The Farthest Shores of Ursula K. Le Guin* (**1976**) by George Edgar SLUSSER; "Showing Children the Value of Death" (1974) by Peter Nicholls in *Foundation*, 5.

See also: ANTI-INTELLECTUALISM IN SF; CHILDREN'S SF; CRITICAL AND HISTORICAL WORKS ABOUT SF; GODS AND DEMONS; ICONOCLASM;   LINGUISTICS;   MAGIC; MYTHOLOGY;   PASTORAL;   PERCEPTION; SCIENTISTS; SOCIOLOGY; WOMEN.

LEIBER, FRITZ (REUTER) (1910–). American writer. He graduated from the University of Chicago, majoring in psychology and physiology, then spent a year at theological seminary. His subsequent career includes periods as an editor (chiefly with *Science Digest*) and a drama teacher. He became interested in writing   through   voluminous correspondence with a college friend, Harry Fischer; it was Fischer who in 1934 suggested the characters of Fafhrd and the Gray Mouser, whose HEROIC-FANTASY adventures are central to FL's career. Both men worked intermittently on embellishments to the saga, as described in detail by FL in his essay "Fafhrd and Me", included in *The Second Book of Fritz Leiber* (coll. **1975**); in 1939 FL sold his first story — and thus the first published story of the sequence — "Two Sought Adventure" to *Unknown*. The series to date consists of six books: *Swords and Deviltry* (coll. **1970**), *Two Sought Adventure* (coll. **1957**; rev. and exp. as *Swords Against Death* 1970), *Swords Against Wizardry* (coll. **1968**), *Swords in the Mist* (coll. **1968**), *The Swords of Lankhmar* (1961 *Fantastic* as "Scylla's Daughter"; exp. **1968**) and *Swords and Ice-Magic* (coll. **1977**; vt *Rime Isle* in an illustrated edition of only two of the eight stories). From fairly prosaic beginnings the series has developed into a complex and enjoyable cycle owing little to the standard clichés of its sub-genre (for which FL is credited with coining the widely used description SWORD AND SORCERY). The mood varies from sombre introspection to broad comedy, and there is a very wide range of invention. The story "Ill Met in Lankhmar" (1970), included in *Swords and Deviltry*, won both HUGO and NEBULA awards. *The Swords of Lankhmar*, which adds a strong element of sophisticated fetishistic sex to its other virtues,   has   strong   claims   to   be considered   the   best   modern   heroic fantasy novel, as well as FL's own best novel. Fischer's contribution to the published series is restricted to a portion of "The Lords of Quarmall", begun by him in the 1930s and completed by FL many years later; it is included in *Swords Against Wizardry*.

FL is also noted for his fantasies in modern settings. These include such notable stories as "Smoke Ghost" (1941) and "The Man Who Made Friends With Electricity" (1962), and his most recent novel, *Our Lady of Darkness* (**1977**), which is a subtle and touching Gothic, with strong autobiographical elements. *Conjure Wife* (1943 *Unknown*; **1953**), a contemporary novel of witchcraft, has twice been filmed — as *Weird Woman* and *Burn, Witch, Burn* — and has also been adapted for TV. His most successful story in this idiom, "Gonna Roll the Bones" (1967), was published in DANGEROUS VISIONS and won Hugo and Nebula awards; in it a compulsive gambler finds himself playing dice with the Devil with his soul at stake. "Belsen Express" (1975) won both the Lovecraft award and the August Derleth award. FL's other awards for his fantasy writing include the 1975 Grand Master of Fantasy (Gandalf) award and the 1976 Life Achievement Lovecraft award. He has won more awards than any other sf or fantasy author: altogether six Hugos, three Nebulas and the four fantasy awards mentioned above.

FL's first important work of sf was the novel *Gather, Darkness!* (1943 *ASF*; **1950**), a variation on the theme of Robert HEINLEIN's *Sixth Column* (1941 *ASF*; **1949**) in which a RELIGIOUS dictatorship is overthrown by rebels who disguise their super-science (colourfully, if by far-fetched logic) as witchcraft. *Destiny Times Three* (1945 ASF; **1957**) is a neglected ALTERNATE-WORLDS variant.

In the early 1950s FL became a regular contributor to GALAXY, for which he wrote a number of notable stories, chiefly social SATIRE; paramount among these was "Coming Attraction" (1951), depicting an unpleasantly decadent future America.   His   novel   *The   Green Millennium* (**1953**) shows some similar thematic concerns, particularly regarding sexual *mores*.

After a four-year hiatus occasioned by alcoholism FL returned to sf in 1958 with the first stories of his "Change War" series, built around a war being fought through time and space by two factions, the "Spiders" and the "Snakes", a conflict involving alternate worlds and TIME PARADOXES. Stories in the sequence are "Try and Change the Past" (1958), *The Big Time* (1958 *Gal.*; **1961**); "Damnation Morning" (1959), "The Oldest Soldier" (1960), "No Great Magic" (1963), "When the Change Winds Blow" (1964) and "Knight to Move" (1965). Other stories, such as "Nice Girl With Five Husbands" (1951), are peripheral to the series. *The Big Time*, which takes place entirely in one room, is suggestive of a play in prose form, and thus reflects FL's background in theatre (both his parents were Shakespearean actors and his father appeared in many films — FL has himself acted both on the stage and on the screen, including a small part in the Greta Garbo film *Camille*). It won a Hugo award for best novel, a feat emulated by his most ambitious sf work *The Wanderer* (**1964**). A long DISASTER novel telling of the havoc caused by the arrival of a strange planet in the Solar System, its mosaic narrative technique, observing events through a multiplicity of viewpoints, foreshadows the profusion of such novels and films in the 1970s. FL won a further Hugo award for "Ship of Shadows" (1969), a novella first published in a special FL issue of *FSF*, and completed the double of Hugo and Nebula awards for the third time with "Catch That Zeppelin!" (1975), a vivid if inconclusive PARALLEL-WORLDS story. A wide selection of his best short fiction can be found in *The Best of Fritz Leiber* (coll. **1974**; rev. 1974 USA) and *The Worlds of Fritz Leiber* (coll. **1976**).

Despite his many awards FL has never quite established an identity as an sf writer in the way he has for his fantasy; for this reason his work is sometimes undervalued.   His   work   reflects   his various enthusiasms — cats, chess and the theatre are all recurrent motifs — and beliefs, notably a distaste for sexual repression and hypocrisy; but the variety of his approaches is considerable. His prose is ebullient; its idiosyncrasies occasionally appear mannered, but its baroque and colourful qualities are usually prevented from becoming slapdash by the precision with which he uses words, and the appropriateness of his imagery, at least in his fantasies. FL has never been quite as comfortable in sf, and here a straining for effect is more often noticeable. Many of his sf works, he has revealed, were fantasies rewritten when the fantasy market began to contract. By refusing to create an easily recognizable template for his sf and then adhering to it, he may have sacrificed some popularity; in compensation he is the only sf and fantasy writer of his generation still developing and producing his best work in the late 1970s. [MJE]

Other Works: *Night's Black Agents* (coll. **1947**); *The Sinful Ones* (1950 *Fantastic Adventures* as "You're All Alone"; exp. **1953**; vt at original length as title story of *You're All Alone,* coll. 1972 USA); *The Mind Spider and Other Stories* (coll. **1961**); *The Silver Eggheads* (1958; **1961**); *Shadows With Eyes* (coll. **1962**); *Ships to the Stars* (coll. **1964**); *A Pail of Air* (coll. **1964**); *Tarzan and the Valley of Gold* (**1966**); *The Night of the Wolf* (coll. **1966**); *The Secret Songs* (coll. **1968**); *Night Monsters* (coll. **1969**; UK edition adds three stories); *A Specter is Haunting Texas* (**1969**); *The Demons of the Upper Air* (poems **1969**); *The Book of Fritz Leiber* (coll. **1974**).

About the author: "The Profession of Science Fiction: XII: Mysterious Islands" by FL in FOUNDATION 11/12 (1977); the special FL edition of *FSF,* Jul. 1969.

See also: ANTI-INTELLECTUALISM IN SF; ARTS; CITIES; CRIME AND PUNISHMENT; DYSTOPIAS; END OF THE WORLD; FANTASY; FAR FUTURE; FLYING SAUCERS; GAMES AND SPORTS; GENERATION STARSHIPS; GENETIC ENGINEERING; GRAVITY; HISTORY IN SF; HOLOCAUST AND AFTER; INVISIBILITY; LEISURE; MAGIC; MEDIA LANDSCAPE; MUTANTS; ROBOTS; SUPERNATURAL CREATURES; WAR.

LEINSTER, MURRAY The name under which American writer William Fitzgerald Jenkins (1896–1975) is best known in the sf field, and under which he wrote almost all his work in the genre, with the exception of a few stories in magazines, mainly those in the "Bud Gregory" series as by William Fitzgerald, and a small number as by Will F. Jenkins. He remained active in the sf field from 1919, when his first story, "The Runaway Skyscraper", about a building falling backwards through time, was published in *Argosy,* until about 1970. Like most writers of magazine sf of the pre-War period, ML published a great deal of material that did not reach book

form until after 1945; his first book publication, *Murder Madness* (**1931**), as its title indicates, did not aim directly at any (still nascent) sf market. *The Murder of the U.S.A.* (**1946**; vt *Destroy the U.S.A.* Canada), as by Will F. Jenkins, was again directed as much to the mystery as to the sf market, though its plot (the hero solves the mystery of who dropped 300 A-bombs on American cities) is more sf than locked room. Because of this pile-up of magazine material, many of ML's post-War book publications contain or rework early stories, and are often rather dated in plotline and character development; at the same time, oddly enough, he was publishing his best work in the magazines, stories that competed on equal terms with those by writers 20 years newer to the field.

ML's first series was the set of four off-beat "Masters of Darkness" stories contributed to *Argosy,* 1929–30, and never collected in book form; the "Bud Gregory" series, comprised of the three stories in *Out of this World* (coll. **1958**) and "The Seven Temporary Moons" (1948), is more widely known; all four were originally published in *TWS.* Bud is a hillbilly with an intuitive knack with high technology and superscience problems. Of more interest is the "Med Service" sequence, *S.O.S. from Three Worlds* (coll. **1967**), *The Mutant Weapon* (**1959**), *Doctor to the Stars* (coll. **1964**), and *This World is Taboo* (**1961**). In these stories and novels, Calhoun and the "being" Murgatroyd act as troubleshooters in various far-flung crises; the tales are robust and adventurous, but their MEDICAL themes are rudimentary compared to the inventiveness of James WHITE's "Sector General" tales. The "Joe Kenmore" novels, *Space Platform* (**1953**), *Space Tug* (**1953**), and *City on the Moon* (**1957**), make up a juvenile series about the crisis-ridden first years of the near-future American space effort, told in melodramatic terms that have not worn well.

ML's best years as an sf writer were undoubtedly the decade following the Second World War, a period during which his finest short stories were published, among them "First Contact" (1945), "Doomsday Deferred" (1949 as by Jenkins), "The Lonely Planet" (1949), "If You Was a Moklin" (1951), and "Exploration Team" (1956), which won the 1956 HUGO award for best novelette, and became part of *Colonial Survey* (1955–6 *ASF;* fix-up **1956**; vt *The Planet Explorer*), perhaps his most enjoyable single volume, though his individual short stories are generally superior to his book-length tales. His novels were frequently unambitious and repetitive, often stretched beyond their proper span, and seemingly written for a less demanding market than his best stories (which appeared in many journals, including *ASF* and *Gal.*) were able to satisfy. A good selection of his tales can

be found in *Monsters and Such* (coll. **1959**); the posthumous *The Best of Murray Leinster* (coll. **1976**), ed. Brian Davis, is decidedly inferior. When ML did contrive fix-ups of short material, the result was often disappointing. His first classic story, for instance, "The Mad Planet" (1920) was incorporated into *The Forgotten Planet* (1920–53 var. mags; fix-up **1954**), but the implausibilities tolerable in a short story in a 1920 pulp venue were not satisfactorily worked out in the longer form.

Although the last decade of ML's career boasted numerous publications, there were no substantial works written after the mid-1950s. His career took shape when American sf was practically barred from book publication, and this may have occasioned his creative disregard for the novel. Though he adapted astonishingly well to the John W. CAMPBELL-inspired revolution in taste and quality, so far as short fiction went, in post-War years he increasingly released books that either reflected the attitudes and techniques of pre-War pulp fiction, or actually incorporated early work. Allied to this was a deepening political simplicity of view, rather right-wing in orientation (as with many sf writers of his generation), which led to the frequent depiction of cartoon-like confrontations between America and underhanded enemies, in the resolving of which means tended to dominate ends, as in *The Time Tunnel* (**1967**), based on an episode from the TV series TIME TUNNEL (confusingly unrelated to ML's other books *Time Tunnel,* **1964**, and *Tunnel Through Time,* **1966**), where the past is to be restructured to make life safe for democracy. But for nearly half a century ML wrote to the heart of magazine sf with craftsmanship and consistency, and will be remembered for that. [JC]

Other works: *Fight for Life* (1947 *Startling Stories;* **1949**); *The Last Space Ship* (1946–7 *TWS;* fix-up **1949**); *Sidewise in Time* (coll. **1950**); *The Black Galaxy* (1949 *Startling Stories;* **1954**); *The Brain-Stealers* (1947 *Startling Stories* as "The Man in the Iron Cap"; **1954**); *Gateway to Elsewhere* (1950 *Fantasy Book;* 1952 *Startling Stories* as "Journey to Barkut"; **1954**); *Operation: Outer Space* (**1954**); *The Other Side of Here* (1936 *ASF* as "The Incredible Invasion"; rev. **1955**); *War with the Gizmos* (**1958**); *Four from Planet 5* (**1959**); *The Monster from Earth's End* (**1959**); *The Pirates of Zan* (**1959**); *The Aliens* (coll. **1960**); *Men into Space* (**1960**), based on the TV series of the same name; *Twists in Time* (coll. **1960**); *Creatures of the Abyss* (**1961**; vt *The Listeners* UK); *The Wailing Asteroid* (**1961**); *Operation Terror* (**1962**); *Talents, Incorporated* (**1962**); *The Duplicators* (**1964**); *The Greks Bring Gifts* (**1964**); *Invaders of Space* (**1964**); *The Other Side of Nowhere* (**1964**); *Get Off my World!* (coll. **1966**); *Space Captain* (**1966**);

Checkpoint Lambda (**1967**); *Miners in the Sky* (**1967**); *Space Gypsies* (**1967**); *Timeslip!* (**1967**), based on an episode of *Time Tunnel*; *Land of the Giants* (**1968**), based on LAND OF THE GIANTS, the TV series; *Land of the Giants No.2: The Hot Spot* (**1969**); *Land of the Giants No.3: Unknown Danger* (**1969**); *A Murray Leinster Omnibus* (coll. **1968**; includes *Operation Terror, Checkpoint Lambda* and *Invaders of Space*).

As editor: *Great Stories of Science Fiction* (anth. **1951**).

See also: ALIENS; ALTERNATE WORLDS; ASTEROIDS; AUTOMATION; COLONIZATION OF OTHER WORLDS; COMMUNICATIONS; CRIME AND PUNISHMENT; GREAT AND SMALL; HIVE-MINDS; INVISIBILITY; LIVING WORLDS; MACHINES; MOON; OUTER PLANETS; PARALLEL WORLDS; PARASITISM AND SYMBIOSIS; PSI POWERS; SPACE FLIGHT; SPACE OPERA; SPACESHIPS; TIME PARADOXES.

LEISURE Dictionaries define leisure as "spare time" or "freedom from work". The AUTOMATION of modern industry tends to result in higher productivity, a smaller workforce and/or shorter working hours. Hence, it is reasonable to expect there will be an increasing amount of leisure time available to ordinary people in the future. In *The Next 200 Years: a Scenario for America and the World* (**1976**), the futurologists Herman KAHN, William Brown and Leon Martel say that the most advanced nations will enter a "post-industrial era" within a century, and it will then be impossible to distinguish between work and leisure. The architect Martin Pawley, in *The Private Future* (**1973**), describes the extent to which our society has already become "privatized" through the effect of television, the automobile and mass advertising. For the individual, leisure has become a major goal, almost a necessity. The journalist Tom Wolfe hints at a similar, if more hopeful thesis in *The Pump House Gang* (**1968**), where he describes a 1960s culture of affluent self-indulgence, symbolized by Las Vegas, customized cars, rock music, drugs, etc. Although intellectuals remain fashionably obsessed with poverty and war, claims Wolfe, "if we want to be *serious*, let us discuss the real apocalyptic future and things truly scary: ego extension, the politics of pleasure, the self-realization racket, the pharmacology of Overjoy ..."

Future modes of leisure have frequently been portrayed in sf. Numerous stories have dealt in passing with the technology of leisure and the ever-growing MEDIA LANDSCAPE; some have dealt in greater depth with leisure as a "problem". Few have celebrated leisure as an end in itself, which suggests that the protestant work-ethic remains strong among sf writers. A puritanical shudder — the conception of total leisure as the ultimate decadence — lies behind E.M. FORSTER's "The Machine Stops" (**1909**), a *reductio-ad-absurdum* story of people living in mechanically tended cells. A realization of the possibilities of leisure as a form of social control informs Aldous HUXLEY's *Brave New World* (**1932**), which depicts a society where the citizens are kept happy by euphoric drugs, casual sex and "feelies" (tactile cinema). Huxley's DYSTOPIA has been widely accepted as a paradigm of the post-War Western world, a nightmare of imposed leisure. It has given comfort to liberals who believe in a "conspiracy" theory of leisure — manipulation by ad-men, behavioural psychologists, etc. — and who thus avoid the question of voluntary pleasure-seeking, the intelligent hedonism which characterizes our world and its foreseeable future.

Several modern sf novels are derivative of *Brave New World* to a degree, e.g. Shepherd MEAD's *The Big Ball of Wax* (**1954**), a heavily satirical novel about titillating sales techniques; *Tomorrow's World* (**1956**; vt *Tomorrow and Tomorrow*) by Hunt Collins (Evan HUNTER), which depicts a future USA in which the "Vicarions", believers in hard drugs and easy sex, have gained power; and James GUNN's *The Joy Makers* (**1954–5** var. mags; fix-up **1961**) which shows the world being taken over by "Hedonics, Inc.", an organization devoted entirely to pleasure and stasis. The ending of *The Joy Makers*, in which the human race slumbers in separate "happiness" cocoons, is reminiscent of "The Machine Stops" and of such later stories as Arthur C. CLARKE's "The Lion of Comarre" (1949), John D. MACDONALD's "Spectator Sport" (1950) and John T. SLADEK's "The Happy Breed" (1967).

Other writers have depicted more active uses of leisure. There are many stories dealing with GAMES AND SPORTS and with the ARTS. Those which deal with SEX as a leisure pursuit often concern perversions, ranging from the mild — televised pornography in Clarke's "I Remember Babylon" (1960) — to the strong — motorized sado-masochism in J.G. BALLARD's *Crash* (**1973**). The latter example leads us to the topic of violence (and the vicarious enjoyment of violence) as a leisure activity. Anthony BURGESS's *A Clockwork Orange* (**1962**) deals with juvenile delinquents of the future who get pleasure from gratuitous assault and rape. Fritz LEIBER's "Coming Attraction" (1950) also deals in part with such violence. *Gladiator-at-Law* (**1955**) by Frederik POHL and C.M. KORNBLUTH treats of a future in which the entertainments of the Roman arena have been revived. *The Tenth Victim* (**1966**) by Robert SHECKLEY portrays a society in which one can take out a licence to murder. Brian W. ALDISS's "Another Little Boy" (1966) is about the celebration of the centenary of Hiroshima by the dropping, as a sentimental gesture, of another atom bomb on the city. In C.L. MOORE's "Vintage Season" (1946)

leisured time travellers visit the disaster areas of the past in order to enjoy human suffering as an aesthetic experience.

The idea of an over-aestheticized future has led to some of the best treatments of the leisure theme in modern sf. J.G. Ballard's *Vermilion Sands* (coll. **1971**; rev. 1973) concerns the life-styles of artistic beachcombers in a desert resort furnished with musical statues, psychotropic houses, poetry machines, etc. The stories effectively combine humour and melancholy, technological inventiveness and world-weary lassitude, in a mixture which one feels is more psychologically true, more genuinely predictive of a leisured future, than anything else in sf. Imitation *Vermilion Sands* stories have been written by other authors, e.g. "The Siren Garden" (1974) and "Tropic of Eden" (1977) by Lee Killough; and "The Cinderella Machine" (1976) and "Catapult to the Stars" (1977) by Michael G. CONEY. Michael MOORCOCK's "Dancers at the End of Time" series represents an extension rather than an imitation of the *Vermilion Sands* mood. The novels *An Alien Heat* (**1972**), *The Hollow Lands* (**1974**) and *The End of All Songs* (**1976**), together with the shorter stories in the series, are set in a remote future when unlimited technological prowess has resulted in total leisure. Similar themes have been touched on by George Alec EFFINGER in "How it Felt" (1974), and by Edward BRYANT in *Cinnabar* (coll. of linked stories **1976**).

The other side of the coin, namely enforced leisure without an accompanying wealth of technological possibility, has been dealt with most effectively by Thomas M. DISCH in *334* (**1972**). Disch concentrates on the lives of the unemployed and the inadequate in a welfare state of the near future. A more hopeful scenario for the new *Lumpenproletariat* is outlined by Philip José FARMER in the linked stories "Riders of the Purple Wage" (1967) and "The Oogenesis of Bird City" (1970), which depict people living in enclosed welfare cities, passing the time in sexual and artistic pursuits. Even more Utopian is *Looking Backward, from the Year 2000* (**1973**) by Mack REYNOLDS. An updating of Edward BELLAMY's socialist UTOPIA *Looking Backward* (**1888**), it depicts a post-industrial future worthy of Herman Kahn. Whereas Bellamy was typically of the 19th century in his concern with the dignity of labour, Reynolds is exercised by the paradox of a society where "your work is also your hobby and your play".

[DP]

LEM, STANISLAW (1921–). Polish writer, critic and polymath; his work has won numerous awards including the 1973 Polish State Literary Award. Born in Lwów, he has described his childhood and adolescence charmingly in the autobiographic *Wysoki zamek* ["High

Stanislaw LEM.

Castle"] (1966 Poland). SL's study of medicine was interrupted during the Nazi occupation when he worked as a car mechanic and welder. In 1946 he moved to Cracow (where he still resides), received his MD, wrote lyrical verse and essays on scientific methodology until he ran foul of the adulation of Lysenko, and was research assistant in a scientific institute. SL's only "naturalistic" novel *Czas nieutracony* ["Time Saved"] (1955) presents already an intellectual finding his way from solitude to sociopolitical meaning; it was written in the late 1940s. In the meantime SL switched to sf — two dozen book titles so far with translations into about 30 languages and about seven million copies. His early sf novels *Astronauci* ["The Astronauts"] (1951 Poland) and *Oblok Magellana* ["The Magellan Nebula"] (1955 Poland), works of a beginner limited by some conventions of "socialist realism", are still interesting and contain a number of SL's constant themes (the threat of global destruction and militarism; human identity); their UTOPIAN naïvety is shaped by the committed humanism characteristic of one axis of his work. His other axis, a black grotesque, appeared in *Dzienniki Gwiazdowe* (coll. 1957 Poland, gradually expanded until 1971 to 14 "voyages" and eight other "Ion Tichy" stories; 12 "voyages" trans. Kandel as *The Star Diaries* 1976), which develops into a parable-like expression.

The dozen years after the "Polish October" of 1956 were the golden noontime of SL. He published 17 books, including five sf novels; 10 partly overlapping books of sf short stories including the "Pirx" cycle, the "robotic fairy tales" of *Bajki robotów* (coll. 1964 Poland), the "Trurl-Klapaucius" cycle; in *Noc księżycowa* (coll. 1963 Poland) one sf play and three TV plays; non-fiction including "cybernetic sociology" *Dialogi* (1957 Poland); and the crown of SL's speculation and key to his fiction, *Summa technologiae* (1964 Poland), a breathtakingly brilliant and risky survey of possible social, informational, cybernetic, cosmogonic and biological engineering in Man's game with Nature.

Solaris (1961 Poland; trans. Kilmartin and Cox from French translation 1970), *Niezwyciezony* (1964 Poland; trans. Ackerman from German translation as *The Invincible* 1973), and *Opowieści o pilocie Pirxie* ["Tales of Pilot Pirx"] (coll. 1968 Poland) use the mystery of strange beings, events and localities for educating the protagonist into understanding the limitations and strengths of humanity. Solaris was filmed as SOLARIS (1972). These parables for our age are fittingly open-ended: their tenor is that no closed reference system is viable in the age of CYBERNETICS and rival political absolutisms; the protagonists are redeemed by ethical and aesthetic insight rather than by hardware, abstract cognition or power — thence SL's strong, at times oversimplifying, but salutary critique of English-language sf in his *Fantastyka i futurologia* (1970 Poland) for abusing the potentialities of the new in gimmicks and disguised fairy tales. His critique of equally anthropomorphic banalities in Soviet sf was conducted through his immense popularity and liberating influence there. In between the two Leviathans, SL uses the experience of Central European intellectuals (*see* EASTERN EUROPE) to fuse a bright, humanistic hope with a bitter, historical warning. This double vision subverts both the "comic inferno" approach and a deterministic Utopianism by juxtaposing the black flickerings of the former with the bright horizons of the latter. Such a procedure of wit places SL in the "philosophic tale" tradition of Jonathan SWIFT and VOLTAIRE. Even his grotesque stories, where no "cruel miracles" redeem the often disgusting limits of Man — such as *Cyberiada* (coll. 1965 Poland; trans. Kandel as *The Cyberiad* 1974) collecting many of the Trurl-Klapaucius stories, — are informed by such humanizing fun, black satire or allegorical iconoclasm.

Signs of an ideological dead-end, if not exhaustion, showed in about 1968, prompting further formal experimentation and a furious brilliance in SL's writing. In his last long work, *Glos pana* ["His Master's Voice"] (1968 Poland), his radical doubts about human self-determination and sovereignty, and therefore about · possibilities of COMMUNICATION with other people (much less other civilizations) began threatening to sort out the fictional form of the novel into solipsist musings, lectures and ideational adventure. *Glos pana* may have avoided that by a *tour de force* of narrative tone, but SL drew some consequences from this threat: he turned to a brilliantly innovative series of briefer second-order glosses at the borderland of fiction and treatise. *Doskonala próżnia* (coll. 1971 Poland) — mainly composed of reviews of non-existent books, characterized and persiflaged simultaneously —

and *Wielkość urojona* (coll. 1973 Poland) range from thumbnail sketches of grisly futuristic follies to developments of *Summa technologiae* ideas on "intellectronics" or artificial, heightened intelligence and "phantomatics" or illusory existence. We find the latter in the most grimly hilarious and longest work of this period, a further "Ion Tichy" story, "Kongres Futurologiczny" (in coll. *Bezsenność*, 1971 Poland; trans. Kandel as *The Futurological Congress* 1974), as well as SL's deeply rooted though atheistic theologico-cosmogonic obsessions.

SL's overflowing LINGUISTIC inventiveness, matching his controversial ideational plenty, is partly lost in translation. None the less, his peculiar geopolitical vantage point, enabling him effectively to transcend both cynical pragmatism and abstract Utopianism, his stubborn warnings against static "final solutions", his position at the crossroads of major European cultures and ethics, joined to an intense internalization of problems from cybernetics and information theory, his fusion of dilemmas from ultramodern science and the oldest cosmogonic heresies, his dazzling formal virtuosity — all mark him as one of the most significant sf writers of our century, and a distinctive voice in world literature. [DS]

Other works: *Czlowiek z Marsa* (1946 Poland, apparently only as continuations in a weekly); *Sezam* ["Sesame"] (coll. 1955 Poland); *Edem* ["Eden"] (1959 Poland); *Sledztwo* (1959 Poland; trans. Milch as *The Investigation* 1974), ontological mystery rather than sf; *Inwazja z Aldebarana* ["Invasion from Aldebaran"] (coll. 1959 Poland); *Powrót s gwiazd* ["Return from the Stars"] (1961 Poland); *Pamietnik znaleziony w wannie* (1961 Poland; trans. Kandel and Rose as *Memoirs Found in a Bathtub* 1973); *Księga robotów* ["The Book of Robots"] (coll. 1961 Poland); *Wejście na orbite* ["Getting into Orbit"] (coll. 1962 Poland), essays on technology and fiction; *Polowanie* ["The Hunt"] (coll. 1965 Poland); *Ratujmy kosmos* (coll. 1966 Poland); *Opowiadania* (coll. 1969 Poland); *Rozprawy i szkice* (coll. 1974 Poland), essays on literature, sf and science; *Katar* (1977 Poland).

About the author: "To My Readers" by Stanislaw Lem, *Poland* 5, 1973; "Language and Ethics in Solaris" by Edward Balcerzan, *Science-Fiction Studies: Selected Essays on Science Fiction 1973–1975* (1976) ed R.D. MULLEN and Darko SUVIN; "Stanislaw Lem, Rationalist and Sensualist" by Jerzy Jarzębski, SCIENCE-FICTION STUDIES Jul. 1977; "Lem in Review (June 2238)" by Michael Kandel, *Science-Fiction Studies* Mar. 1977; "Stanislaw Lem on Men and Robots" by Michael Kandel, EXTRAPOLATION Dec. 1972; *New Worlds for Old* (1974) by David KETTERER; "European SF" by Ursula K. LE GUIN,

Science-Fiction Studies Spring 1974; "The Open-Ended Parables of Stanislaw Lem and *Solaris*" by Darko Suvin, afterword to *Solaris* (trans. **1970**) and rev. for 1976 translation.

See also: ALIENS; AUTOMATION; CONCEPTUAL BREAKTHROUGH; DISCOVERY AND INVENTION; GODS AND DEMONS; GOTHIC SF; HUMOUR; LIVING WORLDS; MACHINES; METAPHYSICS; PERCEPTION; PHYSICS; SATIRE; SPACESHIPS; SUPERNATURAL CREATURES.

LE MAY, JEAN (? –). French author, usually with Doris Le May, as J. et D. Le May, of lively SPACE OPERAS, at least 12 of which fall into his GALACTIC-EMPIRE "Anticipation" series; he has also published sf outside this series. JLM, who is usually published under the Fleuve noir imprint, has been active in the field since 1966, and by 1975 had published at least 29 books. His works have not been translated into English. [PN]

LÉOURIER, CHRISTIAN (1948–). French writer. He is the author of *Les montagnes du soleil* (**1971**; trans. as *The Mountains of the Sun* **1973**), an interesting socio-anthropological novel mapping the rediscovery of Earth after a cataclysmic deluge. CL has since written principally for children. [MJ]
See also: ANTHROPOLOGY.

LE PAGE, RAND Almost certainly a house name for the London firm of Curtis Warren. The name appears on eight PULP-style SPACE OPERAS: *"A" Men* (**1952**), *Asteroid Forma* (**1953**), *Beyond These Suns* (**1952**), *Blue Asp* (**1952**), *Satellite B.C.* (**1952**), *Time and Space* (**1952**), *War of Argos* (**1952**) and *Zero Point* (**1952**). RLP was described on the wrappers as "the French master of modern science fiction"! [JC]

LE QUEUX, WILLIAM (TUFNELL) (1864–1927). British writer, extremely prolific for a number of years in a variety of genres, though most of his most popular works were espionage thrillers and detective novels, often with oriental colouring. In the vein of H. Rider HAGGARD he wrote a number of fantasies with some immediate but no lasting success, and a number of romances, like *Stolen Souls* (**1895**), whose generic definition shifts between suspense and the occult. He is best remembered today for his two future WAR/INVASION novels: *The Great War in England in 1897* (**1894**) and *The Invasion of 1910; With a Full Account of the Siege of London* (**1906**; vt *The Invasion*). Both books were serialized in English newspapers before being separately published, and both aroused considerable stir, particularly the latter, with its letter of commendation from Lord Roberts. Though both tales were told with every trick WLQ had acquired in his years of journalism, and though the latter of the two is replete with diagrams

of the threatened invasion from Germany, the ultimate effect of each novel is of a laboured turgidity of effect. A further novel, apparently of the same genre, *England's Peril* (**1899**), is fundamentally an espionage thriller. WLQ persistently utilized Germany as the opponent in his work; even after the First World War, stories like *A Terror of the Air* (**1920**) attempt to present a world in constant danger of Teutonic aggression. The sf of WLQ's last years is consistently routine. He is fundamentally a figure of pre-War interest only. [JC]
Other works: *Zoraida: A Romance of the Harem and the Great Sahara* (**1895**); *The Great White Queen* (**1896**); *The Eye of Ishtar* (**1897**), one of several LOST-RACE novels; *A Madonna of the Music Halls* (**1897**; vt *A Secret Sin*); *The Veiled Man* (**1899**); *The Sign of the Seven Sins* (**1901**); *The Closed Book* (**1904**); *The Unknown Tomorrow* (**1910**); *The House of Whispers* (**1910**); *The Great God Gold* (**1910**); *The Mystery of the Green Ray* (**1915**); *"Cinders"of Harley Street* (coll. **1916**), featuring a doctor with paranormal powers; *The Zeppelin Destroyer* (**1916**); *The Bomb-Makers* (**1917**); *The Rainbow Mystery*; *Chronicles of a Colour-Criminologist* (coll. **1917**); *The Little Blue Goddess* (**1918**); *The Voice from the Void* (**1922**); *The Gay Triangle* (**1922**), featuring a car with collapsible wings; *Tracked by Wireless* (**1922**); *The Broadcast Mystery* (**1925**); *Double Nought* (**1927**); *The Chameleon* (**1927**; vt *Poison Shadows* USA); *The Secret Formula* (**1928**).
See also: DYSTOPIAS; LOST WORLDS; WAR; WEAPONS.

LERTETH, OBEN See R.L. FANTHORPE.

LESLIE, DESMOND (1921–). English writer, best known for his co-authoring, with George Adamski, of the non-fiction book *Flying Saucers have Landed* (**1954**); of sf interest is *The Amazing Mr. Lutterworth* (**1958**), about an amnesiac who discovers in his past the key to new vistas, including a long space trip for himself and his girl. [JC]
Other works: *Angels Weep* (**1948**).

LESLIE, O.H. See Henry SLESAR.

LESLIE, PETER (1922–). English author, journalist and actor, most of whose books have been borderline sf contributions to TV spin-off series, like *No.5: The Finger in the Sky Affair* (**1966**; vt as No.23 in the US series) from *The Man from U.N.C.L.E.* series of British paperbacks (No.5 in the US series was by John T. PHILLIFENT) and *No.4: The Cornish Pixie Affair* (**1967**) from *The Girl from U.N.C.L.E.* series of British paperbacks. His first sf proper is *The Night of the Trilobites* (**1968**), followed by *The Autumn Accelerator* (**1969**) and *The Plastic Magicians* (**1969**). He has also written two books as Patrick MacNee in

the spin-off series from the TV programme THE AVENGERS: *Deadline* (**1966**) and *Dead Duck* (**1967**). [JC/PN]
Other works: *Hell for Tomorrow* (**1966**); more *Man from U.N.C.L.E.* spin-offs: *No.7: The Radioactive Camel Affair* (**1966**), *No.10: The Diving Dames Affair* (**1967**; vt as No.9 in the US series), *No.14: The Splintered Sunglasses Affair* (**1968**; vt as No.16 in the US series), *No.17: The Unfair Fare Affair* (**1968**; vt as No.18 in the US series).

LESSER, DERWIN See Charles D. HORNIG.

LESSER, MILTON (1928–). American writer. He was primarily associated with the Ziff-Davis magazines, where he used the names Stephen Marlowe, Adam CHASE, Christopher H. Thames (which he used on 29 stories) and the house name S.M. TENNESHAW, as well as his own. He also wrote some juvenile novels. His first published story was "All Heroes Are Hated" (1950). His adult novels were: *Recruit for Andromeda* (1953 *Imagination* as "Voyage to Eternity"; exp. **1959**); *Secret of the Black Planet* (1952 *AMZ*; fix-up **1965**); and *The Golden Ape* (**1959** as by Adam Chase), which he wrote in collaboration with Paul FAIRMAN. He edited the anthology *Looking Forward* (anth. **1953**). [BS]
Other works: The following are all juvenile sf novels: *Earthbound* (**1952**); *The Star Seekers* (**1953**); *Stadium Beyond the Stars* (**1960**); *Spacemen Go Home* (**1961**).
See also: GENERATION STARSHIPS.

LESSING, DORIS (1919–). Persian-born South Rhodesian novelist, in England from 1949. She is best known for her searching examinations of the position of women in the world in such novels as *The Golden Notebook* (**1962**); the five volumes of her "Children of Violence" sequence deal more expansively with the same problems, and *The Four-Gated City* (**1969**), which ends the series, moves in its final pages rapidly into the NEAR FUTURE, providing in this fashion a somewhat apocalyptic perspective on the preceding volumes. *Briefing for a Descent into Hell* (**1971**) and *The Summer Before the Dark* (**1973**) both use sf perspectives as eliciting manoeuvres to focus attention more sharply on her continuing concerns. Her most important sf novel is *The Memoirs of a Survivor* (**1974**), in which a woman watches the end of urban civilization from her window, never leaving her room, while a young girl grows up beside her, giving some muted hope for human continuity. [JC]
See also: DISASTER.

LESTER, ANDREW See Terry GREENHOUGH.

LESTER, IRVIN See Fletcher PRATT.

LEVENE, MALCOLM (? –). British writer whose sf novel, *Carder's Paradise* (**1968**), describes the mixed blessings of a completely automated society whose inhabitants are kept busy by complex entertainments. [JC]

LEVENE, PHILIP See J.L. MORRISSEY.

LEVIE, REX DEAN (**1937?–**). American businessman and writer, whose sf novel, *The Insect Warriors* (**1965**), deals with problems humans face on a world where they are the size of insects. [JC]

LEVIN, IRA (**1929–**). American writer. He began with *A Kiss Before Dying* (**1953**), an extremely impressive mystery, and continued with the fantasy *Rosemary's Baby* (**1967**), about the Devil and his impregnation of a young woman, filmed by Roman Polanski in 1968. IL moved into sf proper with *This Perfect Day* (**1970**), a DYSTOPIAN view of a cybernetically regimented future (*see* COMPUTERS), and *The Stepford Wives* (**1972**), which was soon filmed (*see* THE STEPFORD WIVES), a horrific morality tale about an American suburb whose women have been turned into compliant ROBOTS. Most impressive of all is perhaps *The Boys from Brazil* (**1976**), also filmed, with an expected release in 1978, a complex story involving the CLONING of cells from Adolf Hitler's body and impregnating a number of women a decade or so later with young Hitlers, which a Brazilian neo-Nazi group, headed by Dr Mengele, tries to raise in environments as close as possible to that in which the Führer himself was raised; their plan is discovered by a Jewish Nazi hunter, made suspicious by a series of apparently unrelated male deaths (Hitler's father died when he was a child). IL applies to sf themes a meticulous style and plotting capacity, along with a certain fascination with the multitude of ways in which women can be violated (*see* WOMEN). [JC]

See also: SATIRE.

LEWIN, LEONARD C. (**1916–**). American writer, whose *Report from Iron Mountain; On the Possibility and Desirability of Peace* (**1967**) is the hoax-report of an American government commission whose conclusions have a spuriously Realpolitik cynicism about the possibility of world peace and the need for a continual WAR-footing; *Triage* (**1972**) is a NEAR-FUTURE novel about growing political oppression in America, in which the government secretly applies the wartime medical practice of triage to social "problems" — to the end of literally eliminating them (*see* OVERPOPULATION). [JC]

LEWIS, BRIAN (**1929–78**). British illustrator. He is a highly skilled painter, whose cover art in the mid and late 1950s

Abstract shapes dominate the cover art of Brian LEWIS; *New Worlds* Aug. 1958.

often showed a strong influence from surrealist art reminiscent of Paul Klee or Max Ernst, perhaps partly mediated through the work of Richard POWERS. This style was encouraged, for a time, by the editor John CARNELL. BL also often painted in a representational manner. His colours were strong and plain and gave the impression of being laid on thickly, an impression few other illustrators give. He did most of his work for *Science Fiction Adventures*, *New Worlds* and *Science Fantasy*. Besides his work in sf he has drawn comic strips in newspapers, including a period on DAN DARE, and worked on stop-motion animation and children's puppet films. [JG/PN]

LEWIS, CAROLINE See Harold BEGBIE.

LEWIS, CHARLES (? –). British writer, whose sf novel, *The Cain Factor* (**1975**), mixes sex and apocalypse in recounting the eventual escape of a man and a woman from a post-HOLOCAUST Earth to become ADAM AND EVE on a new planet. [JC]

LEWIS, C(LIVE) S(TAPLES) (**1898–1963**). British author, born in Belfast. CSL was also a well-known critic, Fellow of Magdalen College, Oxford (1925–54), and finally Professor of Medieval and Renaissance English at Cambridge. Most of his writing, whether directly or indirectly, was Christian apologetics; this was as true of his autobiography *Surprised By Joy* (**1955**) as it was of the fantasy *The Screwtape Letters* (**1943**), in which an older devil writes letters of advice to a younger, devising various means of winning human souls. Five other books were non-fiction, directly concerned with the Christian message. In Oxford CSL was friendly with Charles WILLIAMS (another Anglican) and J. R. R. TOLKIEN (a Roman Catholic). All three were Christian moralists with a strong interest in allegory

or fantasy, and they used regularly to read to one another from works in progress.

CSL's most popular fiction is for children, and is allegorical FANTASY rather than sf, although it uses many sf devices, including TIME TRAVEL, other DIMENSIONS and PARALLEL WORLDS. The kingdom of Narnia, to which various human children travel, is ruled by a lion, Aslan, who is "crucified" by a wicked witch. Many excitingly described perils take place, most with a direct Christian allegorical application. They are much loved by many children who may or may not (often not) pay much attention to their religious import. The series consists of *The Lion, the Witch and the Wardrobe* (**1950**), *Prince Caspian* (**1951**), *The Voyage of the "Dawn Treader"* (**1952**), *The Silver Chair* (**1953**), *The Horse and his Boy* (**1954**), *The Magician's Nephew* (**1955**), which comes first in terms of the internal chronology, and *The Last Battle* (**1956**). Two minor fantasies for adults are *The Great Divorce* (**1945**), about Heaven and Hell, and *Till We Have Faces* (**1956**), a retelling of the myth of Cupid and Psyche.

CSL's primary contribution to sf proper is the trilogy about the linguist Dr Ransom, who like Christ is at one point offered as a ransom for mankind. The books are *Out of the Silent Planet* (**1938**), *Perelandra* (**1943**; vt *Voyage to Venus: Perelandra*), and *That Hideous Strength* (**1945**; vt *The Tortured Planet* USA; UK and US paperbacks abridged). The first two novels are interplanetary romances, with strong traces of medieval mythology; each planet is seen as having a tutelary spirit; those of the other planets are both good and accessible; that of Earth is fallen, twisted and not known directly by most humans. These two books are powerfully imagined, although their scientific content is intermittently absurd; the effect of lesser gravity on Martian plant and animal life is rendered with great economy and vividness, as is Ransom's first perception of the water world of Venus, a rich exercise in PERCEPTION. Ransom's human eyes cannot at first make sense of the strangeness about him, in a passage as purely evocative of a sense of alien wonder as anything in sf. The religious allegory of *Perelandra*, however, in which an evil scientist plays Satanic tempter to the female ruler of Venus, a new Eve, is deeply conservative, and also sexist, in its courtly, romantic (and some may think dehumanizing) view of womanhood. The third volume, *That Hideous Strength*, is set on contemporary Earth, and is more directly occult in its genre machinery than either of its predecessors. The fury of CSL's attack on scientific "humanism" (science directed towards purely worldly ends) is very nearly unbalanced, and leads to a grossly melodramatic caricature of scientists and their government-supported research units in general, and against H.G. WELLS in particular, here grotesquely envisaged as a vulgar cockney journalist, Jules. The book's attack on government indifference to ECOLOGY won it a new audience in the late 1960s. CSL's attitude towards any form of modernism was neatly encapsulated by a remark he made during a lecture on medieval poetry in 1938; "And then the Renaissance came, and spoiled everything".

This trilogy is, for all its propagandizing, in comparison to most genre sf a richly imagined work, and has attained classic status. Some of CSL's minor essays in and about sf, including a transcript of a talk with Brian ALDISS and Kingsley AMIS, can be found in the posthumous *Of Other Worlds* (coll. **1966**), which includes two stories originally published in *FSF*. A number of biographical and critical studies of CSL exist, including *Shadows of Imagination: The Fantasies of C.S. Lewis, J.R.R. Tolkien and Charles Williams* (anth. **1969**) ed. Mark R. HILLEGAS, which contains an entertaining and passionate attack on CSL by the Marxist biologist and author J.B.S. HALDANE. [PN]
Other works: *The Pilgrim's Regress* (**1933**; rev. 1943).
See also: ALIENS; ANTI-INTELLECTUALISM IN SF; CHILDREN'S SF; CONCEPTUAL BREAKTHROUGH; ESCHATOLOGY; FANTASTIC VOYAGES; GODS AND DEMONS; ISLANDS; LIFE ON OTHER WORLDS; LINGUISTICS; LIVING WORLDS; MAGIC; MARS; MESSIAHS; MYTHOLOGY; RELIGION; SOCIAL DARWINISM; VENUS.

LEWIS, (ERNEST MICHAEL) ROY (1913–). English novelist and journalist, editor of *New Commonwealth*, 1953–4, later with the *Economist* and *The Times*, and the author of several political/sociological studies. His sf novel, *What we Did to Father* (**1960**; vt *The Evolution Man*), amusingly concentrates Man's Pleistocene evolution into the hands of one man, the narrator's father, all of whose discoveries are seen in terms of their extrapolated effects; not surprisingly, the parricide which ends the book is nothing if not proto-neo-Freudian. [JC]
See also: ORIGIN OF MAN.

LEWIS, (HARRY) SINCLAIR (1885–1951). American writer, highly esteemed in the 1920s and '30s for such novels as *Main Street* (**1920**) and *Babbitt* (**1922**), and first American winner of the Nobel Prize for Literature in 1930, but with much diminished reputation today. *Arrowsmith* (**1925**) is not so much sf as fiction about science; it contrasts the idealism of the research scientist with the avarice and greed of the medical profession in general. His sf novel, *It Can't Happen Here* (**1935**), predicts, without paying much attention to the nature of American political institutions, the development of a Nazi-like fascist

regime. SL's NEAR-FUTURE scenario contrasts interestingly with Gordon EKLUND's very similar portrait of 1930s authoritarianism in *All Times Possible* (**1974**), though in the latter case there is an ALTERNATE-WORLDS framework. [JC/PN]
See also: DEFINITIONS OF SF; POLITICS.

LEWIS, IRWIN (? –). American writer who began publishing sf with "To Invade New York" for *ASF* in 1963, a story whose basic idea was incorporated into his first novel, *The Day They Invaded New York* (**1964**), in which invading ALIENS confuse New Yorkers by fouling the transportation systems of the great city; a second novel, *The Day New York Trembled* (**1967**), creates its chaos through a pain-relieving drug and its unexpected consequences. [JC]

LEWIS, OSCAR (1893–). American editor and writer, whose ALTERNATE-WORLD novel, *The Lost Years* (**1951**), depicts the last years of Abraham Lincoln in a world where he was never assassinated. [JC]

LEWIS, (PERCY) WYNDHAM (1884–1957). English artist and writer, known mainly as the instigator of Vorticism and the author of such determinedly Modernist manifestos and novels as *The Apes of God* (**1930**). Of particular sf interest is *The Human Age*, a trilogy comprising *The Childermass* (**1928**; rev. 1956) and *Monstre Gai* and *Malign Fiesta*, both novels first published together as *The Human Age; Book Two Monstre Gai, Book Three Malign Fiesta* (**1955**); like Philip José FARMER's "Riverworld" series, though with greater impact, *The Human Age* depicts the posthumous existence of various characters. In *The Childermass*, Pulley and Satters, the two main protagonists, freshly dead, observe and join in the jousting, linguistic and intellectual, that surrounds the Bailiff, a sort of doorkeeper who decides the eligibility of applicants to the Magnetic City. In *Monstre Gai* he takes Pulley and Satters into the Third City, a DYSTOPIA based on post-War England and its Welfare State; finding life difficult there, they all go on to Matapolis in *Malign Fiesta*; Matapolis is Hell, and punishments abound; there is a sense of suffocating evil. A fourth volume, *The Trial of Man*, in which the two protagonists were to be transported to Heaven, remained unwritten. The arduousness of *The Childermass*, a major 20th-century novel, has kept many readers from its much more clear-cut sequels. WL is far less read than read about, a situation to be deplored. [JC]

LEY, WILLY (1906–69). German-born scientist and scientific writer who emigrated to America in 1935. In Germany, he had been part of a small group which, early on, believed in the

possibilities of rocket propulsion (some went on to become famous with the construction of the V2 in the Second World War). His first book was *Die Fahrt ins Weltall* ["Journey into Space"] (**1926**); his second, *Die Möglichkeit der Weltraumfahrt* ["The Possibility of Interplanetary Travel"] (**1928**) was to be one of the inspirations behind the film (and book) DIE FRAU IM MOND. In America, his articles on science fact, well researched and precise, became one of the notable features of the sf magazines, especially *ASF* (from 1937) and *AMZ* (from 1940). He became science editor for *Gal.* in Sep. 1952, having begun a science column in *Gal.* in Mar. of that year which lasted until his death. He was given HUGO awards in 1953 and 1956 for his science writing.

WL was also a prolific author of books on science, especially SPACE FLIGHT. Perhaps his best-known (and certainly most beautiful) book was *The Conquest of Space* (**1949**), with splendid illustrations by Chesley BONESTELL, many in colour. It won the non-fiction category of the INTERNATIONAL FANTASY AWARD in 1951. *Lands Beyond* (**1952**), a historical account of strange explorations and discoveries, written with L. Sprague DE CAMP, won the same award in 1953. Of the science-fact writers intimately connected with genre sf, only De Camp, Arthur C. CLARKE and Isaac ASIMOV could rival WL.

WL wrote three sf stories as Robert Willey. [PN]
Other works: (all science fact) *The Lungfish and the Unicorn* (**1941**; vt rev. *The Lungfish, the Dodo and the Unicorn* 1948); *The Days of Creation* (**1941**; rev. 1952); *Shells and Shooting* (**1942**); *Rockets* (**1944**; vt rev. *Rockets and Space Travel* 1947; vt rev. *Rockets, Missiles and Space Travel* 1951; vt rev. *Rockets, Missiles and Men in Space* 1968); *Dragons in Amber* (**1951**); *Engineer's Dreams* (**1954**); *Salamanders and Other Wonders* (**1955**); *The Exploration of Mars* (**1956**; vt *Project Mars*) with illustrations by Bonestell; *Satellites, Rockets and Outer Space* (**1958**; rev. 1962); *Space Stations* (**1958**); *Space Travel* (**1958**); *Exotic Zoology* (**1959**) featuring rearranged selections from his previous books on natural history; *Watchers of the Skies* (**1963**); *Beyond the Solar System* (**1964**) with illustrations by Bonestell; *Missiles, Moonprobes and Megaparsecs* (**1964**); *Ranger to the Moon* (**1965**); *On Earth and in the Sky* (coll. **1967**); *Another Look at Atlantis* (coll. **1969**); *The Drifting Continents* (**1969**); *Events in Space* (**1969**); *Gas Giants: The Largest Planets* (**1969**); *Visitors from Afar: The Comets* (**1969**).
See also: SUN.

LEYDENFROST, A. (? – ?). American illustrator; his father was a Dutch illustrator. Although forgotten by most fans today, AL was one of the best sf artists of the 1940s, particularly when

Illustration by A. Leydenfrost.

CHILD OF THE SUN
By LEIGH BRACKETT

**Far beyond molten Mercury flashed the Patrol-pursued *Falcon*.
. . . Out to where black Vulcan whirled his hidden orbit, and a
flame-auraed last child of Sol played his cosmic game.**

ERIC FALKEN stood utterly still, staring down at his leashed and helpless hands on the controls of the spaceship *Falcon*.

The red lights on his indicator panel showed Hiltonist ships in a three-dimensional half-moon, above, behind, and below him. Pincer jaws, closing fast.

One of the greatest of all pulp sf illustrations, A. LEYDENFROST's sketch in *Planet Stories*, Spring 1942.

elements of fantasy or horror were required. His often grotesque, heavily shadowed and hideous forms sprawled across the pages of such magazines as *Planet Stories*, *Super Science Stories*, *Astonishing Stories*, *Famous Fantastic Mysteries* and *Tops in Science Fiction*. While AL's b/w works were strong and dynamic, with expressive lines and stark contrasts, his colour work, including two covers for *Planet Stories*, was strained and awkward. [JG]

LIDDELL, C.H. *See* Henry KUTTNER.

LIFE AFTER DEATH *See* ESCHATOLOGY and REINCARNATION.

LIFE ON OTHER WORLDS The development of this theme is intricately linked with the evolution of the role of the alien being (*see* ALIENS). It is also much involved with other themes discussed independently (*see* COLONIZATION OF OTHER WORLDS and ECOLOGY).

Early interplanetary travellers discovered worlds which were undeniably exotic but which were obviously akin to Earth. Life-forms were derived by analogy with Earthly organisms, and there was little ecological systematization. Without a theory of EVOLUTION as a guide, the creation of other-worldly life was inevitably a

haphazard and arbitrary process. One notable exception is the attempt to invent a lunar *fauna* made by Johannes KEPLER in the last pages of his *Somnium* (**1634** in Latin). There is little in other accounts of other worlds, before the 20th century, to distinguish them from the strange imaginary lands of Earth in many travellers' tales and romances.

Camille FLAMMARION's pioneer descriptions of alien life-systems in *Real and Imaginary Worlds* (**1865**) and *Lumen* (**1897**) stand alone in their time, and even the second of these is semi-fiction at best. Flammarion's romance of reincarnation, *Urania* (**1890**), is halfhearted in its description of other-wordly conditions. A much more comprehensive account is offered by Flammarion's contemporary Charles DEFONTENAY in *Star* (**1854** France; trans. **1975**), but this too is only semi-fiction. Most late 19th-century interplanetary romances feature pseudo-human races and are vehicles for political and sociological rather than biological speculations. Exotic *milieux* were occasionally featured for the sake of filling in a little local colour for interplanetary tourists — most straightforwardly in George GRIFFITH's *Honeymoon in Space* (**1901**) — but there is little real attempt to use these milieux or to describe them. Edgar FAWCETT, in *The Ghost of Guy Thyrle* (**1895**), went to some

lengths to convey an impression of the multifariousness of life on other worlds, but did not pause for detailed description.

H. G. WELLS, the writer most competent, with his biological training, to take on the job of designing an alien life-system, never attempted the task — the Selenites in *The First Men in the Moon* (**1901**) are an alien society with only the most cursory supportive ecology. His French contemporary J.H. ROSNY AÎNÉ did make the attempt, but not until 1922, in *L'étonnant voyage de Hareton Ironcastle* (rewritten rather than trans. by Philip José FARMER as *Ironcastle*, **1976**), and even then he chose to situate his alien enclave on Earth.

Scientific romances in the UK and the USA in the early years of the 20th century did build up an image of life on at least one other world: MARS. It became an exotic primitive Earth — a wholly imaginary romantic environment designed for swashbuckling adventure. Many writers paid lip service to Percival Lowell's non-fiction book *Mars as the Abode of Life* (**1908**), but they merely borrowed ideas from it as was convenient, rather than adapting and developing Lowell's speculations into fictional models. Mars as an environment designed for exotic adventure appears in Edwin Lester ARNOLD's *Lieut. Gulliver Jones: His Vacation* (**1905**; vt *Gulliver of*

Mars USA) and was made famous by Edgar Rice BURROUGHS. This species of other world has been maintained by a score of Burroughs imitators, including Otis Adelbert KLINE, Ralph Milne FARLEY, J.U. GIESY, Lin CARTER, Gardner F. FOX, Alan Burt AKERS and John NORMAN, and several sf writers have adapted it slightly with the infusion of more complex and sometimes more bizarre ideas. C.L. MOORE, Leigh BRACKETT and Marion Zimmer BRADLEY have all done very effective work in this vein. A further step in adapting the romantic image of Mars, in particular, was taken by Ray BRADBURY, who freighted an impossible romanticism with heavy nostalgia in *The Martian Chronicles* (**1950**; vt *The Silver Locusts* UK). The influence of this romantic image has been so great that it even infects — and has had quite a marked influence upon — supposedly realistic treatments of the planet, e.g. in Arthur C. CLARKE's *The Sands of Mars* (**1951**) and James BLISH's *Welcome to Mars* (**1967**).

The early PULP sf writers did make an effort to introduce variety and a degree of plausibility into their accounts of extraterrestrial life. Several stories published during 1932 present imaginative accounts of other worlds: Laurence MANNING's "The Wreck of the Asteroid", Jack WILLIAMSON's "The Moon Era" and Leslie F. STONE's "The Hell Planet". The story which is remembered today as a turning-point in the development from melodrama to a conceptual interest in the different forms life and intelligence might take was "A Martian Odyssey" (1934) by Stanley G. WEINBAUM. Weinbaum followed up this story with a whole series of adventures in alien ecologies which are outstanding by the standards of the day. No one, however, was able to take up where he left off at his untimely death. John W. CAMPBELL Jr's "Penton and Blake" series (1936–8; fix-up *The Planeteers* **1966**) is not one of the author's more creditable efforts. Clifford D. SIMAK began a series in 1939 which was intended· to deal in a realistic manner with conditions on each of the planets in turn, but he wrote only four stories of which the last, "Tools" (1942), is the most notable. Eric Frank RUSSELL, in the course of another series of exploration stories, collected with one addition as *Men, Martians, and Machines* (fix-up **1956**), produced the memorable "Symbiotica" (1944), but contributed little more to the theme.

Outside genre sf very few writers tackled the problem of describing life on worlds unlike Earth. Olaf STAPLEDON, in *Star Maker* (**1937**), offered little more detail than Edgar Fawcett in his attempt to convey the idea of the variety of life in the universe, save in the long description of an Earthlike world. The only full descriptions of other worlds undertaken by non-genre writers before the Second World War were in works inspired by the religious or mystical imagination: David LINDSAY's *A Voyage to Arcturus* (**1920**) and C.S. LEWIS's *Out of the Silent Planet* (**1938**) and *Perelandra* (**1943**).

The post-War sf boom saw a much more determined attack on the problem of constructing alien life-systems. "Grandpa" (1955) by James H. SCHMITZ is a study of a complex marine life-cycle on an Earth-type planet. Conscientious attempts to design ecologies for unearthly physical circumstances have been made regularly by Hal CLEMENT, most notably in *Mission of Gravity* (**1954**), *Cycle of Fire* (**1957**) and *Close to Critical* (1958; **1964**); and by Poul ANDERSON, notably in "Call me Joe" (1957), *War of the Wing-Men* (**1958**) and *Three Worlds to Conquer* (**1964**). "Call me Joe" strongly recalls an earlier story about life on JUPITER, "Desertion" (1944) by Clifford D. Simak. Anderson has also written a non-fiction work, *Is There Life on Other Worlds?* (**1963**), which belongs to a branch of speculative science called exobiology — the study of extraterrestrial life. It is, at present, a wholly theoretical discipline. One of its leading exponents is Carl SAGAN, and Isaac ASIMOV has also written essays on the subject.

One writer of the post-War period whose name is particularly associated with the detailed presentation of alien worlds is Jack VANCE. His interest in alien ecology is linked to a strong interest in cultural ANTHROPOLOGY, and his alien worlds usually have human populations adapted to and integrated into the native ecology. Outstanding among his many novels in this vein are: *Son of the Tree* (1951; **1964**), *Big Planet* (1952; **1957**), *The Houses of Iszm* (1954; **1964**), *The Languages of Pao* (**1958**), *The Dragon Masters* (**1963**), *The Blue World* (**1966**) and *Emphyrio* (**1969**). Many of these novels contain a good deal of extraterrestrial romanticism, but there is much speculative material too.

There grew up in opposition to the romantic school of other-worldly adventures a school of fiction which represented human life on other worlds as a grim and terrible battle against implacably hostile circumstances (see COLONIZATION OF OTHER WORLDS), and these two opposing schools dominated the depiction of life on other worlds in the 1950s. Popularization of the ecological crisis in the real world, however (see ECOLOGY), brought about a significant change in emphasis during the 1960s. The notion of "conquering" other worlds and mastering harsh environments by hard work and sheer determination — which reached its peak in such novels as Tom GODWIN's *The Survivors* (**1958**; vt *Space Prison* USA) and Harry HARRISON's *Deathworld* (**1960**) — found a new opposition in stories presenting the theme of harmony with alien ecologies, whereby a new and perfect balance of nature might be achieved. These stories often embodied a strong element of

mysticism (see RELIGION and MYTHOLOGY). The mythical connotations of Mark CLIFTON's *Eight Keys to Eden* (**1960**) are explicit in the title, and in John BRUNNER's *Bedlam Planet* (**1968**) the process of integration with the alien world involves visions borrowed from classical mythology. Other celebrations of an alien Eden include Richard M. McKENNA's "Hunter Come Home" (1963), John BOYD's ironic *Pollinators of Eden* (**1969**), Ursula K. LE GUIN's *The Word for World is Forest* (1972; **1976**) and Neal BARRETT's *Highwood* (**1972**). The motif crops up several times in the work of Brian STABLEFORD, e.g. in *Promised Land* (**1974**) and *The Paradise Game* (**1974**). Many of these works echo the forest fantasies of W.H. HUDSON.

The 1960s produced two thorough and detailed accounts of human populations in alien environments which are particularly impressive: Frank HERBERT's *Dune* (**1965**), with its description of life on the desert world Arrakis, and Ursula K. Le Guin's *The Left Hand of Darkness*, (**1969**) which describes the life of hermaphroditic humans on the world of Winter. Both of these novels won major awards, as did two more other-world novels with a sociological focus: *A Time of Changes* (**1971**) by Robert SILVERBERG and *The Dispossessed* (**1974**) also by Ursula K. Le Guin.

There is scope within sf for much more detailed and considered modelling of alien environments, although interest will always be focused on life-systems native to planets that are habitable by Man. [BS]
See also: BIOLOGY; HIVE-MINDS; LIVING WORLDS.

LIGHTNER, A(LICE) M(ARTHA) (1904–). American writer and entomologist, married to Ernest Hopf. She began publishing her sf, all of which is for children, with "A New Game" for *Boy's Life* in 1959; her first published novel, *The Rock of Three Planets* (**1963**), with its sequels, *The Planet Poachers* (**1965**) and *The Space Ark* (**1968**), was followed by several other effective juveniles, though she came to general sf notice only with *The Day of the Drones* (**1969**), a post-HOLOCAUST story set half a millennium after a nuclear war. This was actually her first novel, and was originally written for adults; it was later revised for publication as a juvenile. As in Margot BENNETT's *The Long Way Back* (**1954**), black Africa has survived, discovering in this case that the white remnants of English civilization have evolved into a hive society (see HIVE-MINDS), from which one drone escapes to help piece together the history of the years of silence. There are interesting implications about racial prejudice. AML has also written a number of non-fiction books of dramatized natural science. [JC]
Other works: *Doctor to the Galaxy* (**1965**); *The Galactic Troubadours* (**1965**); *The Space Plague* (**1966**); *The Space*

Olympics (**1967**); *The Thursday Toads* (**1971**); *Star Dog* (**1973**); *Gods or Demons?* (**1973**); *The Space Gypsies* (**1974**); *Star Circus* (**1977**).

See also: POLITICS.

LINDBOHM, DÉNIS *See* SCANDINAVIA.

LINDNER, ROBERT (MITCHELL) (1914–56). American psychoanalyst and prison psychologist who reported on his work in the latter capacity in *Rebel Without a Cause* (**1944**). "The Jet-Propelled Couch", a long narrative essay which appears in *The Fifty-Minute Hour: A Collection of True Psychoanalytic Tales* (coll. **1955**; vt *The Jet-Propelled Couch* UK), absorbingly examines and analyses the sf-based fantasies of one of his patients, who retreated from an intolerable childhood, adolescence and adulthood by a progressive immersion in an elaborate SPACE-OPERA universe, to which he believed he was literally translated on a regular basis, and in which he was the ruler of a planet. His rationalization of his role in this universe was impeccably couched in sf terms, with alternate time streams playing a considerable role, and provides an explanation *in extremis* for sf's imaginative power over adolescents. Also of interest is one effect of RL's curative strategy; he pretended to enter into his patient's universe with him, and eventually was himself fascinated and almost ensnared by it. Roger ZELAZNY's *The Dream Master* (**1966**) develops the implications of RL's experience in bravura fashion. A persistent rumour over the years has been that the anonymous patient in RL's essay was actually the young Paul Linebarger, who later gained fame under the pseudonym Cordwainer SMITH; it seems to fit with what is known of Linebarger's early history, not to speak of the consistency of his fantasy world. However, some Cordwainer Smith scholars deny the link. [JC/PN]

See also: PARANOIA AND SCHIZOPHRENIA; PSYCHOLOGY.

LINDSAY, DAVID (1878–1945). English writer, remembered today almost entirely for his first novel, *A Voyage to Arcturus* (**1920**), a remarkable, though somewhat high-handed, use of sf and fantasy devices to transport a man ostensibly to the planet Tormance to undergo a series of baroque adventures, but actually to engage its protagonist in a mystical inner journey into a state where ethical precepts within his mind, and all the other slings and arrows his soul is open to, are embodied in the extraordinary Tormance life forms. *The Haunted Woman* (**1922**) is a more conventional fantasy with the same kind of allegorical reading constantly underlined. *The Adventures of M. de Mailly* (**1926**; vt *A Blade for Sale* USA) is a historical novel, while *Sphinx* (**1923**),

Devil's Tor (**1932**) and *The Violent Apple & the Witch* (two short novels posthumously published **1976**) are all fantasies. [JC]

About the author: *The Strange Genius of David Lindsay* (anth. **1970**), a collection of essays about him.

See also: CONCEPTUAL BREAKTHROUGH; ESCHATOLOGY; ESP; FANTASTIC VOYAGES; FANTASY; GODS AND DEMONS; LIFE ON OTHER WORLDS; MYTHOLOGY; PERCEPTION.

LINGFELD, NORBERT (1942–). German literary historian interested in popular fiction. With Michael PEHLKE he wrote a Marxist analysis of contemporary Western sf, *Roboter und Gartenlaube* ["The Robot and the Summerhouse"] (**1970**). They argued that while the older UTOPIAS stood for social progress, sf cements existing conditions, aiming merely at amazement. It is a mixture of fairy-tale and popular non-fiction, taking its motifs from low-grade fiction; its ideology is reactionary. "Its gadgetry belongs to the future, its characters to the present, its laws to the past." [FR]

One of the most memorable sf novels dealing with LINGUISTICS. Ace Books, 1958. Cover by Gray Morrow.

LINGUISTICS Linguistics is the study of language, how languages work, what their function is, how they are constructed, and whence they are derived. Languages play a surprisingly important role in sf, and many stories turn on linguistic issues. The theme overlaps, naturally, with COMMUNICATIONS, and also to some extent with ANTHROPOLOGY and PERCEPTION, inasmuch as a language tells us much about the culture that uses it and the way it perceives the world. This entry will primarily concentrate on verbal languages in sf; other ways of giving information are dealt with under COMMUNICATIONS, and two examples will suffice here. In James BLISH's *VOR* (**1958**) an extremely dangerous alien, whose metabolism is powered by a nuclear fusion process, communicates by changing the colour of a patch on his

head; his name, Vor, is the acronym of violet, orange, red; the story turns on an actual linguistic problem quite apart from decoding his colour flashes; his psychology has to be understood sufficiently for humans to transmit a verbal command which will lead to his self-destruction. Terry CARR's "The Dance of the Changer and the Three" (1968) is set on an alien planet whose natives are energy forms; their language is dancing; for no clear reason they destroy many humans for whom they seem to feel no enmity, and the only clue we are given to their behaviour is one of their myths, translated possibly incorrectly, in which the height of epic glory is expressed in terms which for humans would be regarded as self-destructive failure.

Sf stories in which linguistics play a subsidiary role are very much more common than sf stories actually *about* linguistics. Most sf writers who set stories in the past, or in alternate presents, or in the future, ignore the problem of language changes, apparently assuming that mid-20th-century English will cease to evolve and will become the universal language; but some writers have made an attempt to face the problem, with various degrees of success. Many of these attempts are discussed by Walter E. Myers in "The Future History and Development of the English Language" in SCIENCE-FICTION STUDIES Vol. 3, part 2, Jul. 1976. They are often patchy; the ways in which grammar and vocabulary evolve do not seem to be widely understood. Examples of sf stories demonstrating linguistic change whether fanciful or plausible are Alfred BESTER's "Of Time and Third Avenue" (1951), Bester being generally very much alive to the forms of language; Robert HEINLEIN's "Gulf" (1949), with its future speedtalk; Anthony BURGESS's *A Clockwork Orange* (**1962**), with its NEAR-FUTURE Russian-derived *Nadsat* slang; George ORWELL's *Nineteen Eighty-Four* (**1949**), with its Newspeak designed to reinforce proper social attitudes; Poul ANDERSON's "Time Heals" (1949), with a futurified pronunciation; Felix C. GOTSCHALK's *Growing Up in Tier 3000* (**1975**), where a great variety of future colloquialisms are worked out with considerable gusto; Benjamin APPEL's *The Funhouse* (**1959**), linguistically ingenious; and Michael FRAYN's *A Very Private Life* (**1968**), whose future languages are more lively than plausible.

A genre sf writer always aware of linguistic problems is L. Sprague DE CAMP; his article "Language for Time Travelers" (1938), similar material being incorporated into his *Science-Fiction Handbook* (**1953**; rev. 1975), was probably the first account of linguistic problems in sf. His stories, sometimes rather ploddingly, reflect this interest, as in "The Wheels of If" (1940), set in an ALTERNATE WORLD where the Norman

Conquest did not take place and English is never Frenchified, (but here De Camp gets Grimm's Law of sound changes quite wrong, both in its effect and in the historical period to which it refers), and in the "Viagens Interplanetarias" series in which the space pidgin Intermundos is heavily influenced by Brazilian space crews.

Orwell's Newspeak, though it is the most celebrated example of language control being used by the state to impose social conformity and an unthinking acceptance of the way things are, is by no means the first. Yevgeny ZAMIATIN's *We* (circulated in manuscript 1920, trans. **1924**, not published in Russia) has a heavily conformist, mechanical language, which reflects the regimentation of society. Anthony BOUCHER's interesting "Barrier" (1942), a TIME-TRAVEL story, features such a language also, along with an interestingly daffy collocation of future linguists all researching via time machines.

Language is an important aspect of the above stories, but not their *raison d'être*; three kinds of story in which linguistics becomes central are those where Man communicates with animals, or with aliens, or endeavours to translate dead alien languages.

In the first group two good examples are *Un animal doué de raison* (**1967**; trans. as *The Day of the Dolphin* **1969**) by Robert MERLE, and *Slave Ship* (**1957**) by Frederik POHL, in which a military computer decodes the languages of domestic animals so that the animals can be used as secret weapons; the latter novel begins promisingly, but quickly ducks the most challenging questions in favour of plenty of action. Ursula K. LE GUIN's amusing spoof scientific paper, based on the idea that animals and insects have not only languages but also art forms, "The Author of the Acacia Seeds and Other Extracts from *The Journal of the Association of Therolinguistics*" (1974), is probably not intended entirely as a joke.

So-called first-contact stories (*see* ALIENS and ANTHROPOLOGY) necessarily involve linguistics, unless, as often, the question is dodged by the use of some kind of magical translation box. There are many such stories that do involve linguistic questions. Suzette Haden ELGIN, who has a degree in linguistics, has written a series about the galactic intelligence agent Coyote Jones, which occasionally deals with linguistic problems. John Berryman's "Berom" (1951) has an amusing variant on the theme, in which the visiting aliens turn out to be speaking in a British commercial cable code of the 1920s that they have picked up by radio. The "Hoka" series by Poul Anderson and Gordon R. DICKSON features aliens who understand language quite literally, with sometimes comic results. Frank HERBERT's *Whipping Star* (**1970**) conjures up so intense a miasma of semantic

confusions, in a story of humans making contact with aliens who turn out to be stars, that the narrative structure and human interest of the story is very nearly overwhelmed by ever more complicated enigmas. Roger ZELAZNY's "A Rose for Ecclesiastes" (1963) has a poet-linguist of great arrogance and brilliance chosen to attempt contact with the few remaining Martians, and to translate their high language and their holy texts; his complacency is punctured, in an intense and verbally brilliant story with a depth of feeling seldom found in sf. Chad OLIVER's *The Winds of Time* (**1956**) has some expertly worked out descriptive field linguistics in operation in a story of interstellar aliens waking from SUSPENDED ANIMATION on Earth. The film CLOSE ENCOUNTERS OF THE THIRD KIND (1977) ends with a prolonged and beautiful epiphany .when the alien occupants of FLYING SAUCERS finally consent to make contact, communication being initiated through a linguistic code of flickering lights and crashing chords of music. David MASSON, a devoted student of linguistics, is responsible for what is certainly the first-contact story with the best-informed and greatest linguistic detail: his fascinating "Not So Certain" (1967), which gives a very clear example of precisely the kind of problem that may bedevil exo-culture specialists, no matter how well intentioned. This was republished in his *The Caltraps of Time* (coll. **1968**), in which many of the stories contain linguistic elements, notably the sustained and amusing *tour de force* "A Two-Timer" (1966), in which an inadvertent time traveller from the 17th century describes in his own English what he finds in the 20th—not least, semantic bafflement.

Stories of archaeological linguistics are less common in sf. H. Beam PIPER's "Omnilingual" (1957), probably his best story, has a woman seeking a Rosetta Stone with which to interpret the writings of a dead Martian civilization; she ultimately finds it in a periodic table of the elements.

Other sf works with a notable linguistic element include many stories by R.A. LAFFERTY, including the autobiography of a computer, *Arrive at Easterwine* (**1971**), which is typical of this author's sometimes self-indulgent but usually vivid verbal eccentricities. M.A. FOSTER's *The Warriors of Dawn* (**1975**) and its sequel *The Gameplayers of Zan* (**1977**) include an unusual amount of linguistic speculation among their carefully worked out cultural inventions. Jack VANCE's *The Languages of Pao* (**1958**) is one of the most intelligent uses in genre sf of the idea that the world-view of different races is reflected in, and to some extent actually created by, the language they speak; hence cultural engineering can be carried out by training peoples in new languages. In real-life linguistics this view is strongly identified with the writings of Dr

Benjamin Whorf (1897–1941), in his studies of American Indian languages. Whorf's theories are most spectacularly reflected in sf terms in Samuel R. DELANY's *Babel-17* (**1966**), a complexly structured novel about communication which takes language itself as the central image; a web of different languages is threaded through the spy-story plot, in which an alien code turns out to be only paradoxically alien; it is Babel-17, a perfect analytical language which has no word for "I"; this absence Delany sees as its strength and also its weakness. Delany's interest in language and linguistic philosophy is reflected in much of his work, from the curious dialects of *Nova* (**1968**) to the new coinage "golden" in "The Star Pit" (1967) to describe the psychotic space crews.

Two earlier writers, both more firmly identified with FANTASY than with sf, who have used considerable philological expertise in their work are C.S. LEWIS and J.R.R. TOLKIEN. The former's *Out of the Silent Planet* (**1938**) speaks interestingly of the differing grammars and vocabularies of the three Martian languages, and plays some slightly cheap linguistic tricks to show up what Lewis regarded as the arrogant self-regard of humanistic scientists; Tolkien's *The Lord of the Rings* (three vols **1954–5**; coll. **1968**) is unusual in that its genesis itself was largely linguistic; Tolkien invented his imaginary languages (carefully glossed and explained in the many appendices) before he wrote the books. Both men were Oxford dons who specialized in linguistic studies.

If Whorf has been the one powerful influence on sf linguistic scenarios, the other has been Noam Chomsky (1928–), whose view that all human languages share a deep structure which is perhaps genetically determined is to some extent at odds with Whorf's view that our conceptual categorization of the world is determined by our native language; where Chomsky stresses unity, Whorf stressed diversity. Sf has added little to this recent debate, nor seemed very conscious of it, until 1973, when Ian WATSON first attracted the attention of the sf readership. In all his novels the influences of various kinds of structuralism, notably linguistic and anthropological, but also with ample borrowings from semiotics, topology, cosmology and physical and biological morphology, are synthesized into perhaps the most intellectually demanding whole in genre sf. Watson's verbal felicity is not as strong as his ideational exuberance, but it would be foolish to minimize his importance for this reason. All his novels feature linguistic thought somewhere in their usually complex structure, and his first, *The Embedding* (**1973**), is certainly the sf linguistics novel *par excellence*, with all three of its sub-plots linking language and perception in interweaving stories of alien, South American Indian and computer-imposed languages, and the differing subjective realities they may or may not succeed in generating. An important essay by Watson is "Towards an Alien Linguistics" in VECTOR 71, 1975, in which he brings an imposing intellectual armoury to bear on questions of epistemology, and hazards the thought that there may be "a topological grammar of the universe, which reflects itself in the grammars of actual languages" — Chomsky writ very large indeed. Watson uses arguments from quantum mechanics to support the solipsist view that the universe exists as an external structure only through the consciousnesses of its participants and observers; language, in his scheme, is reflexive, nature sending a message to itself. As an intellectual position, apparently defensible, the view is at once deeply romantic, deeply frightening and deeply attractive. It seems that the once apparently irrelevant discipline of linguistics may become one of the more central sciences in sf, just as it already leapt to prominence among academic disciplines in the real world during the 1960s.

There is no wholly satisfactory text on the use of linguistics in sf. Apart from those cited, the two most interesting are *Linguistics and Language in Science Fiction-Fantasy* (1975) by Myra Edwards BARNES, a work which has received criticism suggesting that though stimulating it may not be wholly reliable; and much more simply, on the favourite sf subject of word-coinage by sf writers, "The Words in Science Fiction" by Larry NIVEN in *The Craft of Science Fiction* (anth. 1976) ed. Reginald BRETNOR. [PN]

LINKLATER, ERIC (ROBERT RUSSELL) (1899–1974). Scottish writer in various genres, though in his earlier career he concentrated on novels, beginning with *White Maa's Saga* (1929). *The Impregnable Women* (1938) is a NEAR-FUTURE rewrite of *Lysistrata*: the women of Europe band together, go on strike and end a futile war. His two children's novels, *The Wind on the Moon* (1944) and *The Pirates in the Deep Green Sea* (1949). are both attractive fantasies, in the latter of which Davey Jones and all the drowned pirates under the sea continually guard the great knots that tie latitudes and longitudes together and thus keep the world from splitting. Also for children is *Mr Byculla* (1950). *A Spell for Old Bones* (1949) is a fantasy set in a mythical first-century Scotland; *Sealskin Trousers* (coll. 1947) and *A Sociable Plover* (coll. 1957) both contain fantasy stories; EL's Second World War conversation plays, notably *The Raft and Socrates Asks Why* (1942) and *The Great Ship and Rabelais Replies* (1944), employ fantasy elements as didactic pointers. EL was a proficient, frequently subtle, middlebrow writer. [JC]
Other works: *Crisis in Heaven* (1944).

LINUS See Pierre CHRISTIN.

LIN YUTANG (1895–). Chinese-American novelist and essayist, educated in Europe. His sf novel, *The Unexpected Island* (1955; vt *Looking Beyond* USA), deals with an island populated by refugees after several world HOLOCAUSTS. [JC]

LIONEL, ROBERT See R.L. FANTHORPE.

LIPPINCOTT, DAVID (McCORD) (1925–). American writer and advertising executive whose NEAR-FUTURE political thriller *E Pluribus Bang!* (1970) involves the President of the USA in the murder of a Secret Service agent he finds in bed with his wife. *Tremor Violet* (1975) is a DISASTER novel about earthquakes in Los Angeles. [JC]
Other works: *Voice of Armageddon* (1974).

LIVESEY, ERIC M. (? –). British writer whose pulp-style sf paperback novel is *The Desolate Land* (1964). [JC]

LIVINGSTON, BERKELEY (1908–). American PULP writer whose sf appeared only in the Ziff-Davis magazines *AMZ* and *Fantastic Adventures*. Some 50 stories appeared, 1943–50, under either his own name or the house names of Alexander BLADE and Morris J. Steele. He is entered here for the quantity rather than the quality of his work. [JE/PN]

LIVINGSTON, HAROLD (1924–). American writer, often of TV scripts, whose fourth book, *The Climacticon* (1960), spoofs SEX obsessions in a borderline sf tale. [JC]

LIVING WORLDS The notion that a world might be a living creature is a rather startling one, and when it first appeared in sf it was used purely for its shock value. In the remarkable philosophical extravaganza *The Triuneverse* (1912) by "The Author of 'Space and Spirit'" (R.A. KENNEDY) Mars begins to reproduce by binary fission and its daughter cells devour much of the Solar System. In "When the World Screamed" (1929) by A. Conan DOYLE, a hole is drilled through the Earth's "skin" and the living flesh within reacts against the violation. Other attempts to exploit the shock value of the theme are Edmond HAMILTON's "The Earth-Brain" (1932) Jack WILLIAMSON's "Born of the Sun" (1934) (in which the sun is living, the planets are its eggs, and Earth actually hatches), and Nelson BOND's "And Lo! The Bird" (1950). But ideas in themselves tend very rapidly to lose their ability to shock, necessitating an escalation of scale, and Laurence MANNING crowned the series with his depiction of "The Living Galaxy" (1934), compared with which a mere living planet becomes trivial.

The notion of living STARS seems to fascinate sf writers more than the notion of living planets. One of the earliest and most important examples is the idea of the austere stellar intelligences in *Star Maker* (1937) by Olaf STAPLEDON, though this probably derives ultimately from the medieval equation between stars and angels, seen also in William Blake's poem "The Tiger" (1794). More recent examples are Gérard KLEIN's *Starmaster's Gambit* (1958 France; 1973), Frederik POHL and Jack Williamson's *Starchild* (1965) and *Rogue Star* (1969), Frank HERBERT's *Whipping Star* (1970) and the award-winning "If the Stars are Gods" (1974) by Greg BENFORD and Gordon EKLUND. Actual living planets are rare, though visiting spacemen offend one in Ray BRADBURY's "Here There Be Tygers" (1951) and one takes a hand in the action in Brian STABLEFORD's "Dies Irae" trilogy (1971). There is a curious world-consciousness in Theodore STURGEON's "Case and the Dreamer" (1972) and an even more curious one in Neal BARRETT's *Stress Pattern* (1974), but these are external to the actual substance of the planets, as are the planetary spirits in the Ransom trilogy (1938–45) by C.S. LEWIS. There are several stories of planets invested with life-systems which comprise single vast organisms, including Murray LEINSTER's "The Lonely Planet" (1949), and three world-forest stories: "Process" (1950) by A.E. VAN VOGT, "The Forest of Zil" (1967) by Kris NEVILLE, and "Vaster than Empires and More Slow" (1971), a distinguished story by Ursula K. LE GUIN. The most impressive presentation of a truly ALIEN world intelligence is Stanislaw LEM's already classical *Solaris* (1961; trans. 1971). [BS]
See also: BIOLOGY; HIVE-MINDS.

LLEWELLYN, ALUN (1903–). British writer, active in several genres, including political satire; his sf novel *The Strange Invaders* (1934) shares with John COLLIER's *Tom's A-Cold* (1933) a genuine building upon the deeply felt elegiac mood of Richard JEFFERIES' post-HOLOCAUST novel *After London* (1885); set in a new Ice Age and told with intensely worked, harsh images, it depicts a tribal society in a future Russia where Marx, Lenin and Stalin are revered as saints in a barbarian religion; the world has, long ago, been nearly destroyed by war. The novel's focus is the invasion by great lizard-like successors to humanity, which the inhabitants of a small settlement finally defeat at great cost. The novel was republished in 1977 with an introduction by Brian W. ALDISS. [JC]
See also: DISASTER.

LLOYD, JOHN URI (1849–1936). American chemist and author of *Etidorhpa; or, The End of Earth* (1895; rev. 1901), a metaphysical FANTASTIC VOYAGE in which the narrator is led by a blind humanoid to a LOST WORLD in the interior of the Earth. The book went through at least 11 editions. Such other notable hollow-Earth works of the period as Charles Willing BEALE's *The Secret of the Earth* (**1899**), Charles Romyn DAKE's *A Strange Discovery* (**1899**) and Willis G. EMERSON's *The Smoky God* (**1908**) are, like *Etidorhpa*, derivative of the theories of John Cleves SYMMES. [JE]

LOCKE, GEORGE (WALTER) (1936–). English writer, one-time pharmacist, antiquarian bookseller and bibliographer. Under the name Gordon Walters, he published a number of sf stories in England and America, beginning with "Pet Name for a World" for *NW* in 1963, but has not used this name for a number of years. His bibliographic speciality is 19th-century sf; a first fruit of his researches is *Voyages in Space* (**1975**), covering interplanetary sf 1801–1914. A more extensive coverage of British sf 1818–1919 is projected. GL's *Science Fiction First Editions: A Select Bibliography and Notes for the Collector* is projected for 1978 publication. His publishing house, Ferret Fantasy, issues books of sf, fantasy and mystery interest, with 15 so far produced. [JC]
Other works: *Worlds Apart* (anth. **1972**), early interplanetary fiction in facsimile (as editor); *From an Ultimate Dim Thule* (**1973**), a study of fantasy illustrator Sidney H. Sime; *The Land of Dreams* (**1975**), an illustrated survey of Sime.

LOCKE, RICHARD ADAMS (1800–71). American journalist and editor. He is usually regarded as the author of a famous hoax published in the *New York Sun* in 1835, purporting to be a description of the inhabitants of the MOON and of their environs as observed by Sir John Herschel through a new, high-magnification telescope, and all pamphlet and book versions were published under his name. They include *Great Astronomical Discoveries Lately Made By Sir John Herschel At The Cape Of Good Hope* (**1835**; vt *A Complete Account Of The Late Discoveries In The Moon* USA; vt *Interesting Astronomical Discoveries Lately Made By Sir John Herschel At The Cape of Good Hope* USA; vt *Some Account Of The Great Astronomical Discoveries Lately Made By Sir John Herschel At The Cape Of Good Hope* UK; rev. 1841 under original title; rev. vt *The Moon Hoax; or, A Discovery That The Moon Has A Vast Population Of Human Beings* 1859 USA; rev. vt *The Celebrated "Moon Story": Its Origins And Incidents* USA. The book was widely translated, including Welsh and shorthand editions. It has also been dubiously ascribed to Joseph Nicolas Nicollet, but the consensus is that the work was indeed RAL's. The effectiveness of the hoax was comparable to the reactions to Edgar Allan POE's "Balloon Hoax" (1844 *New York Sun*), which was purchased for the

paper by RAL, then one of its editors, and the Orson Welles broadcast of the play "The Invasion from Mars" (1938), which was based on H. G. WELLS's *The War of the Worlds* (**1898**). [JE]
See also: ASTRONOMY.

LOCKHARD, LEONARD See Theodore L. THOMAS.

LOCUS American FANZINE (1968–) ed., from New York, Charlie and Marsha Brown and later from San Francisco by Charlie and Dena Brown; 217 issues to end of 1978. A fortnightly, later monthly, sf and fantasy newsletter, *L* contains comprehensive information on publishing, films, broadcasting and other sf activities, as well as substantial bibliographical material and brief book and magazine reviews. With its comparatively large circulation and regular appearance, *L* has established itself as the main source of news in the sf field. The editors conduct an annual poll of sf (the *Locus* awards) plus a survey of subscribers' ages, occupations, and reading habits. *L* won the HUGO award for best fanzine in 1971, 1972, 1976 and 1978. Although produced by sf fans for their own pleasure, and non-profit-making, and therefore technically a fanzine, *L* in terms of content and regularity is a fully professional magazine. Dena Brown severed her connection with the journal at the end of 1977. [PR]

LOFTING, HUGH See CHILDREN'S SF.

LOGAN, CHARLES (1930–). British writer and nurse for the mentally handicapped, whose sf novel, *Shipwreck* (**1975**), won the Gollancz/*Sunday Times* sf contest jointly with Chris BOYCE's *Catchworld* (**1975**). Calmly and inexorably, it tells the story of the inevitable, though delayed, death of a man whose spaceship lands disabled on a planet the ECOLOGY of which is impassively unfriendly to Man; the pilot tries desperately to stay alive, and does so for a considerable time, but gradually his metabolism (and the ship's computer) begin to fail. That this grim anti-ROBINSONADE presents the most likely outcome of such an occurrence has not made it any more popular with sf fans. [JC]
See also: ISLANDS.

LOGAN'S RUN 1. Film (1976). MGM/United Artists. Directed by Michael Anderson, starring Michael York, Jenny Agutter, Richard Jordan and Peter Ustinov. Screenplay by David Zelag Goodman, based on the novel by William F. NOLAN and George Clayton JOHNSON. 121 mins. Colour.
This is a film that encapsulates the many flaws that seem inherent in sf cinema: paradoxically they may be summarized as irrationality, and a lack of scientific thought, perhaps resulting from

a Hollywood cynicism which regards sf as basically a genre for uncritical children, which in turn suggests a lack of familiarity with written sf outside the COMICS. Set in a domed city where no one is allowed to pass their 30th birthday, the film concerns a renegade "Sandman" (one of the official killers who dispose of the people who refuse their ritual suicide) and his girl-friend, who attempt to reach the legendary "Sanctuary" outside. Sanctuary does not exist; instead they find a mildewed Washington DC, inhabited by the only living old man. They decide that old age is a good thing and return to the dome to spread the news, but while being interrogated by the city's computer the reformed Sandman confuses it to the point where it blows itself up, along with the whole city. The lavish special effects would have seemed much stronger if they had been given a rationale, or even some sort of human resonance, but they come to seem merely peripheral and decorative. The society of young people presented, too, exists in a conceptual vacuum, being riddled with contradiction and never plausibly viable. Yet this was one of the largest, most "prestigious" sf films of the decade.
The film by comparison with the novel is slow, omitting most of the book's original touches. Its director, Michael Anderson, was not the audacious stylist that such a story requires, as his previous work, which includes *The Dam Busters*, *Around the World in Eighty Days* and *Doc Savage*, all rather ponderous in their narration, might have suggested.
2. Television series (1977). An MGM TV Production for CBS TV. Produced by Ben Roberts and Ivan Goff; executive producer: Leonard Katzman; plot director: Preston Ames; story editor: Dorothy C. FONTANA. Pilot episode script written by Saul David, William F. NOLAN, Ben Roberts and Ivan Goff, based on the novel by William F. Nolan and George Clayton JOHNSON. Cast: Gregory Harrison, Heather Menzies, Randy Powell and Donald Moffatt. Writers on the series include: Dorothy C. Fontana, David GERROLD, Kathryn Michaelian Powers, Michael Michaelian, Shimon Wincelberg, John Meredith Lucas, Ray Brunner, James Schmerer, Ellison Joseph and John Sherlock. 50 mins per episode. Colour.
The two men who wrote, created and produced the popular crime-busting programme *Charlie's Angels*, and who have both admitted they know nothing about sf, made this TV series based on the film. It is even less impressive. For budget reasons the series, which is still further removed from the original book than the film was, is set outside the domed city of the film and concerns the adventures of Logan, Jessica and Rem (the latter character is a comic ANDROID — with non-biological components — hastily introduced to exploit the popularity of the two robots in STAR WARS) as they search

for sanctuary while pursued by the deadly Sandmen from the city. The sf elements are few, and at the level of comic-book stereotypes; the moral dilemmas are heavily weighted on one side, and simplified, as the escaping protagonists move from one DYSTOPIAN situation to another. The cancellation of the series was announced at the end of 1977.   [JB/PN]

LOHRMAN, PAUL House name used on the Ziff-Davis magazines by Richard SHAVER, Paul W. FAIRMAN and perhaps others on seven stories, 1950–53. "The World of the Lost" (*Fantastic Adventures* 1950) has been definitely attributed to Shaver.   [PN]

LOMBINO, S. A. *See* Evan HUNTER.

LONDON, JACK (1876–1916). American writer, known primarily for his work outside the sf field. After leaving school at the age of 14, JL lived seven years of adventure and hardship, as an oyster pirate, a sailor, a hobo, a prisoner and a Klondike gold-seeker. During this period, he acquired a self-education steeped in the most influential scientific and philosophic theories of the late 19th century — Darwinism, SOCIAL DARWINISM, Nietzscheism, and Marxism — which he was to amalgamate in his voluminous writings. These writings consist of adventure tales, socialist essays and fiction, autobiographical narratives, and about 20 works of sf, including four novels.

JL's first sf story, "A Thousand Deaths" (1899), combines some key themes of 19th-century sf: a cold-hearted lone scientist uses his own son in revivification experiments and is then dematerialized by a superweapon invented by the son. "The Rejuvenation of Major Rathbone" (1899) displays a "rejuvenator" extracted from a "lymph compound". "The Shadow and the Flash" (1903) has two competing scientific geniuses attaining INVISIBILITY, one by perfecting a pigment that absorbs all light, the other by achieving pure transparency. In "The Enemy of All the World" (1908), a lone genius invents a superweapon and terrorizes the world. Running through much of JL's sf is the disastrous pseudo-scientific theory that white people constitute a superior race. This appears most shockingly in "The Unparalleled Invasion" (1910): the white nations wipe out the Chinese with an aerial germ-warfare assault, thus establishing a joyous epoch of "splendid mechanical, intellectual, and art output". One major area of JL's sf is the prehistoric world (*see* ANTHROPOLOGY), which he explores in his first sf novel *Before Adam* (1906), using a favourite theme, atavism, as a device to project a consciousness into the past, and in "The Strength of the Strong" (1911). Atavism appears also in "When the World Was Young" (1910), in which a "magnificent", "yellow-haired" savage shares the body of a successful California businessman, and *The Star-Rover* (1915 vt *The Jacket* UK), a novel based partly on the revelations of Ed Morrell, who had experienced a dissociation of mind from body under torture in San Quentin. In *The Scarlet Plague* (1912 *London Magazine*; 1915), human history is viewed as cyclical: the post-catastrophe world of the near future has reverted to primitive tribal existence. The novella "The Red One" (1918) describes a contemporary stone-age society that has turned a mysterious sphere from outer space into the centrepiece of a death cult.

Several of JL's sf works deal with the struggle between the capitalist class, trying to establish a fascist oligarchy, and the proletariat, striving for socialism. "A Curious Fragment" (1908), set in the 28th century, shows one of the ruling oligarchs encountering a severed arm bearing a petition from his industrial slaves. A more optimistic view appears in "Goliah" (1908), where a "scientific superman" masters "Energon", the ultimate energy source, becomes master of the world's fate, and inaugurates a millennium of international socialism, and in "The Dream of Debs" (1909), where a general strike brings the capitalist class to its knees in the near future. JL's finest achievement in sf, and perhaps his masterpiece, is *The Iron Heel* (1907), which predicts a 20th-century fascist oligarchy in the United States and displays the epic revolutionary struggle of the enslaved proletariat, all in documents discovered by scholars in the socialist world of the 27th century.

Many of JL's shorter works can be found reprinted in *Curious Fragments: Jack London's Tales of Fantasy Fiction* ed. Dale L. Walker (1975) and *The Science Fiction of Jack London* ed. Richard Gid Powers (1975). The latter has a good introduction.   [HBF]

See also: DISASTER; DYSTOPIAS; ECONOMICS; ORIGIN OF MAN; POLITICS; REINCARNATION; TIME TRAVEL; WAR.

LONG, CHARLES R(USSELL) (1904–). American writer whose two routine sf novels are *Infinite Brain* (1957) and *The Eternal Man* (1964); both are filled with action, the first on a distant planet, the second on an Earth replete with human and alien immortals.   [JC]

LONG, FRANK BELKNAP (1903–). American writer of sf and fantasy whose career has extended from 1924 to the present; he is most noted for his stories of weird fantasy, especially those given a slender sf base after the model of H.P. LOVECRAFT, who promoted his first acceptance in WEIRD TALES — such as his first story, "The Desert Lich", and "Death Waters", both 1924 — and who remained a close colleague until his death in 1937. FBL has frequently told of his friendship, personal and professional, with Lovecraft, and gives additional details in the valuable introduction and running notes to *The Early Long* (coll. 1976), which assembles stories from 1924 to 1944, the period of his prime as a writer of sf and fantasy. Though he had published poetry very early, with *A Man from Genoa and Other Poems* (coll. 1926) and *The Goblin Tower* (1935), it was only with his third book, released by ARKHAM HOUSE, *The Hounds of Tindalos* (coll. 1946; selections in two vols under original title and vt *The Dark Beasts* 1963 USA; in two vols under original title and vt *The Black Druid and Other Stories* 1975 UK), that his best work was made available in book form; a more recent Arkham collection, *The Rim of the Unknown* (coll. 1972), draws from the same prime material. His style in weird fantasy is somewhat influenced by Lovecraft's.

The post-War years have seen a change of emphasis in FBL's long career, with a much higher proportion of sf being written and published, beginning with *John Carstairs: Space Detective* (coll. of linked stories 1949) which, with "The Ether Robots" (1942) and "The Heavy Man" (1943), forms a series about Carstairs, detective and biological expert. Most of FBL's sf deals with future Earth situations, space travel occurring relatively infrequently, though much of his sf, especially earlier examples, features time travel. *Space Station No 1* (1957) indeed occurs off Earth, but not too distant; several of his recent sf books concentrate on INVASION plots in which aliens menace our world, as in *Lest Earth be Conquered* (1966; vt *The Androids* USA) and *Journey into Darkness* (1967); others, like *It was the Day of the Robot* (1963) and *This Strange Tomorrow* (1966), depict intrigue-filled future-Earth societies. Some of his most recent books, like *Survival World* (1971) and *The Night of the Wolf* (1972), a horror fantasy, are among his better works. He has also written a full-length study of his mentor in recent years: *Howard Phillips Lovecraft: Dreamer on the Nightside* (1975). FBL has published hundreds of short stories over his career in addition to those collected in his own books; a proper estimate of his stature will have to take them into account, as well as the more routine sf novels of his later years.   [JC]

Other works: *Woman from Another Planet* (1960); *The Mating Center* (1961); *Mars Is my Destination* (1962); *Three Steps Spaceward* (1953 *Fantastic Universe* as "Little Men of Space"; 1963); *The Horror from the Hills* (1931 *Weird Tales*; 1963; vt with two additional stories *Odd Science Fiction* USA); *The Martian Visitors* (1964) *Mission to a Star* (1958 *Satellite*; 1964); *So Dark a Heritage* (1966); *... And Others Shall be Born* (1968); *The Three Faces of Time* (1969); *Monster from out of*

Time (**1970**); *In Mayan Splendor* (coll. of poetry **1977**).
See also: PARALLEL WORLDS.

LONG, WESLEY *See* George O. SMITH.

LONGEVITY *See* IMMORTALITY.

LÖNNERSTRAND, STURE *See* SCANDINAVIA.

LOOMIS, NOEL (1905–). American writer and editor, variously employed for many years. He was active in the magazine field for some time, publishing work under his own name and as Benjamin Miller, and a book as by Silas Water. In his first novel, *City of Glass* (1942 *Startling Stories*; exp. **1955**), which was based on the first sf story he had published, three men are time-warped into a desolate distant future on Earth; the story is sequelled by "Iron Men" (**1945**). A second novel, *The Man With Absolute Motion* (**1955** as by Silas Water), is also set in a desolate venue: in this case the universe is running out of energy.   [JC]
See also: SPACE OPERA.

LOPEZ, ANTONY (? –). Possibly a pseudonym. His awkwardly surrealist sf novel is *The Second Coming* (**1975**), set in the near future, with a new messiah (and attendant dictatorship) at hand.   [JC]

LORAN, MARTIN Collaborative pseudonym. *See* John BAXTER *for details*.

LORD, JEFFREY *See* Lyle Kenyon ENGEL.

LORD OF THE FLIES Film (1963). Allen-Hodgdon Productions and Two Arts. Directed by Peter Brook, starring James Aubrey, Tom Chaplin, Hugh Edwards and Roger Elwin. Screenplay by Peter Brook, based on the novel by William GOLDING. 91 mins. B/w.
Set in the NEAR FUTURE, the film concerns a group of English schoolboys whose plane, while flying from the scene of an undisclosed military danger, crash-lands on a remote island. The boys, with two exceptions, quickly revert to savagery, a process which results in the murder of one of their number. The film can be interpreted in several ways: as a demonstration of the validity of the belief in Original Sin, as a variation on H.G. WELLS's theme that civilization is only skin deep (as is also demonstrated by the implication that World War III is taking place elsewhere); or as an indictment of the British public-school system. It is an honest but slightly plodding and "literary" rendition of a work that is much greater in book form.   [JB]

LORRAINE, ALDEN *See* Forrest J. ACKERMAN.

LORRAINE, PAUL House name

created by the publishers Curtis Warren, UK, used by John Russell FEARN for *Dark Boundaries* (**1953**). Two other PL titles, unattributed to known authors, are *Two Worlds* (**1952**) and *Zenith-D* (**1952**). [PN]

LOST CONTINENT, THE Film (1968). Hammer / 20th Century-Fox. Directed by Michael Carreras, starring Eric Porter, Hildegard Knef, Suzanna Leigh and Tony Bentley. Screenplay by Michael Nash, based on the novel *Uncharted Seas* by Dennis WHEATLEY. 98 mins. Colour.
A ramshackle freighter carrying a load of characters in varying stages of degeneracy wanders into the Sargasso Sea and becomes trapped in the seaweed. Passengers and crew then face the onslaught of various menaces, including a giant octopus, a giant crab, a giant lobster, carnivorous seaweed and, finally, a group of Spanish conquistadores. The reality of the characters reflects, almost exactly, the likelihood of the plot.   [JB]

LOST HORIZON 1. Film (1936). Columbia. Directed by Frank Capra, starring Ronald Colman, Jane Wyatt, Sam Jaffe, Edward Everett Horton and H.B. Warner. Screenplay by Robert Riskin, based on the novel by James HILTON. 133 mins. B/w.
Set in the mythical Himalayan city of Shangri-La, a sort of middle-class UTOPIA, this film is pure 1930s wish-fulfilment. After their plane crashes in the snow, a group of travellers, having just escaped from war-torn China, find themselves in a mysterious, tranquil city ruled, in a totally beneficent way, by the High Lama, who tells them that war and disease do not exist in Shangri-La (something to do with the air) and that they will live for ever, providing they remain in the city. Eventually they decide to return to civilization, but all rapidly die once they leave Shangri-La, with the exception of one man who, after a brief return to his old way of life, is last seen, hauntingly, struggling through the snow and in long shot, reaching the gate of the forbidden city as the bells ring out.
2. Film (1972). Columbia. Directed by Charles Jarrott, starring Peter Finch, Liv Ullman, Sally Kellerman, George Kennedy, Charles Boyer, Michael York, Olivia Hussey and Bobby Van. Screenplay by Larry Kramer. 150 mins. Colour.
This lush and vapid remake, produced by Ross Hunter, has 17 extra minutes of running time and a number of banal songs, none of which serve to improve a very dated story. The original piece of hokum was orchestrated by Capra with skill and conviction; the second version shows that nostalgia at two removes is one remove too many.   [JB/PN]

LOST IN SPACE Television series (1965–8). An Irwin Allen Production in association with Van Bernard Productions for 20th Century-Fox

Jonathan Harris playing the wicked Dr Smith has a tough time in this episode of LOST IN SPACE.

Television/CBS. Created by Irwin ALLEN who was also executive producer. Story consultant: Anthony Wilson. Writers on the series included Peter Packer, William Welch, Bob and Wanda Duncan, Jackson Gillis and Barney Slater. Directors included Tony Leader, Harry Harris, Don Richardson and Sobey Martin. 83 episodes, each 50 mins. First season b/w; colour from second.

This children's sf series featured the Robinsons (the series was originally to be called *Space Family Robinson*), whose rocket-ship is sabotaged by a secret agent, causing them to crash-land on a remote planet. The group consists of the five Robinsons and a young male co-pilot and the saboteur, Dr Smith (the most successful character), played by Jonathan Harris. The other main actors were June Lockhart, Guy Williams, Angela Cartwright, Marta Kristen, Billy Mumy and Mark Goddard. There was also a robot, whose catch-phrase was "That does not compute". Though remote, the planet soon became a stopping-off point for practically every space-travelling alien or monster in the galaxy and each episode would see the arrival of some new visitor from outer space. After the first season the Robinsons got back into space themselves. As the series progressed the young Robinson boy and the ambiguous Dr Smith became the central characters, together with the robot, while the others

receded more and more into the background. A novelization from the series was *Lost in Space* (**1967**) by Ron Archer (Ted WHITE) and Dave VAN ARNAM.   [JB]

LOST PLANET, THE 1. Film serial (1953). Columbia. Directed by Spencer G. Bennet, starring Judd Holdren, Vivian Mason, Ted Thorpe, Forrest Taylor and Michael Fox. Script by George H. Plympton and Arthur Hoerl. This 15-part children's series featured among other things an attempted alien invasion of Earth.

2. Television serial (1954). BBC TV. Produced by Kevin Sheldon, starring Peter Kerr, Jack Stewart and Mary Law. Script by Angus McVicar, based on his book of the same name. Six episodes, each 25 mins. B/w. This was one of the first sf-related BBC TV serials made for children. A sequel, *Return of the Lost Planet*, also based on a book by McVicar, was produced the following year.   [JB]

LOST RACES *See* LOST WORLDS.

LOST WORLD, THE 1. Film (1925). First National. Directed by Harry O. Hoyt, starring Wallace Beery, Lewis Stone, Bessie Love and Lloyd Hughes. Script by Marion Fairfax, based on the novel by Arthur Conan DOYLE. 9700 ft. B/w, with some tinted sequences.

Wallace Beery makes an unlikely Professor Challenger in this often slow-moving, silent-film version of the famous novel about the discovery of an almost inaccessible South American plateau on which a wide variety of prehistoric creatures, including dinosaurs and apemen, still live. The film is relatively faithful to the book, certainly much more so than the 1960 remake, though one major departure occurs at the climax when the brontosaurus taken back to London by Challenger breaks free and goes on a rampage that ends with the destruction of Tower Bridge (in the book it was a small pterodactyl that escaped), a forerunner of many similar sequences in later sf/horror movies. The film is interesting chiefly because of its special effects, the work of stop-motion photography pioneer Willis H. O'BRIEN. It was the first feature film to employ model animation, often combined with live action, on a large scale.

2. Film (1960). 20th Century-Fox. Directed by Irwin ALLEN, starring Claude Rains, Michael Rennie, Jill St John, David Hedison and Fernando Lamas. Screenplay by Irwin Allen and Charles Bennett. 97 mins. Colour.

This is a rather lifeless and clumsy remake of the Conan Doyle story. Despite a contribution from Charles Bennett, a scriptwriter who worked on many of Hitchcock's early thrillers, the

A slightly jerky but still convincing brontosaurus in the 1925 version of THE LOST WORLD.

script contains all the usual Allen trademarks, including banal dialogue and implausible plotting, with the customary reliance on spectacle to carry the film. The special effects, supervised by L.B. Abbott, are certainly spectacular; this time the various dinosaurs were achieved by using live lizards photographically enlarged, and their death throes, when the plateau is engulfed with volcanic fire, are alarmingly realistic.   [JB]

Novels for boys from the 1890s to the 1920s regularly featured LOST WORLDS, as in this example from 1923, with its fine embossed cover.

LOST WORLDS Lost races, lost cities, lost lands — enclaves of mystery in a rapidly shrinking and all-too-familiar world — featured largely in the sf of the late 19th and early 20th centuries. This sub-genre was obviously a successor to the FANTASTIC VOYAGES of the 18th century and earlier, but there are important distinctions to be drawn. The earlier tales had belonged to a world which was still geographically "open"; at the time Jonathan SWIFT wrote *Gulliver's Travels* (1726), Australia had yet to be discovered by Europeans and Africa had yet to be explored. The later lost-world stories, however, belonged to a cartographically "closed" world; unknown territories were fast disappearing in Jules VERNE and H. Rider HAGGARD's day. The options were running out, and hence the 19th-century lost lands tended to be situated in the most inaccessible regions of the globe: the Amazon basin, Himalayan valleys, at the poles, or within the Earth itself. These works are also distinguishable from earlier "travellers' tales" by their much larger "scientific" content. The new sciences of geology, ANTHROPOLOGY and, above all, archaeology, had a considerable influence on Verne, Haggard and their successors. For a while, the fiction was concurrent with the reality (at least in the popular mind). From the discoveries of Troy and Nineveh to those of Machu Picchu and Tutankhamun's tomb, there flourished a

"heroic age" of archaeology and scientific exploration, of which the fiction was a natural concomitant.

The fiction was often based on PSEUDO-SCIENCE, rather than real science, for example the many ATLANTIS stories which followed the success of Ignatius DONNELLY's non-fiction work, *Atlantis, the Antediluvian World* (1882). Tales of undiscovered worlds within the earth tended to be based on the crackpot geology of John Cleves Symmes, who first publicized his theory of polar openings, leading to a succession of inner worlds, in 1818. Symmes was the possible author of a novel, *Symzonia* (1820; published under the pseudonym Adam SEABORN), in which Antarctic explorers find an underground society of scientifically advanced, pallid-skinned people. Edgar Allan POE was one of Symmes's admirers, and in his stories "MS Found in a Bottle" (1833) and "The Unparalleled Adventure of One Hans Pfaal" (1835) he mentioned polar openings in the Earth, but did not pursue the theme. Perhaps the best of all inner-world fantasies is *Journey to the Centre of the Earth* (1864) by Jules Verne, in which explorers reach a subterranean sea by means of an extinct volcano. Later variations on the hollow-Earth theme include Bulwer LYTTON's *The Coming Race* (1871); James DE MILLE's *Strange Manuscript Found in a Copper Cylinder* (1888); William R. BRADSHAW's *The Goddess of Atvatabar* (1892); William N. HARBEN's *The Land of the Changing Sun* (1904); Willis George EMERSON's *The Smoky God* (1908); Edgar Rice BURROUGHS' *At the Earth's Core* (1914 *All-Story*; 1922) and its many sequels; John M. LEAHY's *Drome* (1927 *Weird Tales*; 1952); Stanton A. COBLENTZ's *Hidden World* (1935 *Wonder Stories*; 1957); John WYNDHAM's *The Secret People* (1935); and Joseph O'NEILL's *Land Under England* (1935). The recent novelette "Black as the Pit, from Pole to Pole" (1977) by Steven Utley and Howard WALDROP is a pastiche of this whole tradition.

The writer who did more than any other to establish the formula of the lost race novel was H. Rider Haggard. His *King Solomon's Mines* (1885), *Allan Quatermain* (1887) and *She* (1887) are all set in Africa and involve the discovery by white explorers of the remnants of unknown civilizations. The last two also introduce the erotic motif of the beautiful queen, or high priestess, who attempts to seduce the hero. A blend of topographical realism and unabashed fantasy, Haggard's romances were very popular and inspired numerous imitations. Haggard wrote many more in the same vein, for example *The People of the Mist* (1894), *Queen Sheba's Ring* (1910) and *The Ivory Child* (1916). Among his more successful emulators were Grant ALLEN, with *The White Man's Foot* (1888) and *The Great Taboo* (1891); Thomas

JANVIER, with *The Aztec Treasure House* (1890); Austyn GRANVILLE, with *The Fallen Race* (1892); William LE QUEUX, with *The Great White Queen* (1896); Jules Verne, with *Le Village Aérien* (1901; trans. as *The Village in the Treetops* 1964); A. Conan DOYLE, with *The Lost World* (1912); Edgar Rice Burroughs, with *The Land That Time Forgot* (1918 *Blue Book*; 1924) and most of his "Tarzan" novels; John TAINE, with *The Purple Sapphire* (1924) and *The Greatest Adventure* (1929); Talbot MUNDY, with *Om: the Secret of Ahbor Valley* (1924) and *Full Moon* (1935; vt *There Was a Door* UK); A. MERRITT, with *The Face in the Abyss* (1931) and *Dwellers in the Mirage* (1932); James HILTON, with *Lost Horizon* (1933); and Dennis WHEATLEY, with *The Fabulous Valley* (1934) and *The Man Who Missed the War* (1945). Of these, the best-known individual work is Doyle's *The Lost World*, a perennially popular adventure story about the discovery of surviving prehistoric creatures on a South American plateau. Hilton's *Lost Horizon*, a mystical romance set in Tibet, is also well remembered (both novels have been filmed more than once, see THE LOST WORLD; LOST HORIZON).

Since the Second World War, tales of lost worlds and races, along with the exercises in cultural anthropology which were a part of their *raison d'être*, have been largely superseded by interplanetary fiction (see COLONIZATION OF OTHER WORLDS). Symmesian geology now holds little conviction for the popular mind, and the South Pole, Central Africa and Tibet are no longer very mysterious. Nevertheless, occasional lost-race novels have appeared. Ian CAMERON's *The Lost Ones* (1961; vt *Island at the Top of the World*) is set in the Arctic and has been filmed by the Walt Disney Studios. Gilbert Phelps's *The Winter People* (1963) is an intelligent novel about an eccentric South American explorer and his discovery of a remarkable tribe. It is unlikely, however, that the lost-world story has much future other than as an exercise in pastiche.

A relevant essay is "Lost Lands, Lost Races: A Pagan Princess of Their Very Own" by Thomas D. CLARESON in *Many Futures, Many Worlds* (anth. 1977) ed. Clareson.   [DP]

See also: ISLANDS; PASTORAL; UTOPIAS.

LOTT, S. MAKEPEACE (? –). British author. His *Escape to Venus* (1956) is a DYSTOPIAN, ORWELL-influenced view of a Venus colony established 60 years after a 1980 World War.   [JE]

LOUDON, JANE (WEBB) (1807–58). English author of many books on popular natural history and gardening, and of *The Mummy! A Tale of the Twenty-Second Century* (1827), published anonymously. Around a somewhat melodramatic plot, in which

the Mummy of Cheops conspires with a Roman Catholic priest in the year 2126 to control the choice of the next Queen of England, JL assembles a number of elaborate speculations about the inventions of the future, including mechanical farming, movable housing and WEATHER CONTROL among the more plausible. [JC]
See also: HISTORY OF SF; HOLOCAUST AND AFTER; NEAR FUTURE.

LOUVIGNY, ANDRÉ See André RUELLAN.

LOVECRAFT, H(OWARD) P(HILLIPS) (1890–1937). American writer, one of the major figures in 20th-century supernatural fiction and originator of a style extensively imitated by his admirers. He lived almost all his life in Providence, Rhode Island, maintaining social contacts via prolific correspondence. He joined the United Amateur Press Association in 1914 and produced much of his early fiction in connection with this enterprise, which also allowed him to make contact with Clark Ashton SMITH, Frank Belknap LONG and others. His first professional publication was a cycle of stories for *Home Brew* called "Herbert West — Reanimator" (1922).

"Nothing", he wrote in an autobiographical sketch, "has ever seemed to fascinate me so much as the thought of some curious interruption in the prosaic laws of nature, or some monstrous intrusions on our familiar world by unknown things from the limitless outside." This thought, especially its morbid variants, inspired all his major works, most of which appeared in WEIRD TALES. He corresponded with many other *Weird Tales* writers and influenced them greatly — among his disciples were Robert BLOCH, Henry KUTTNER, E. Hoffman Price and August DERLETH. More recent writers who have attempted to use his style include J. Ramsey Campbell, Brian Lumley and Colin WILSON.

Many of his earliest stories were imitative of Lord DUNSANY, and those of his middle period are relatively conventional horror stories, but in the last few years of his life he wrote a series of works with a common background: the Cthulhu Mythos. This background fuses the traditional apparatus of the supernatural imagination with such notions more familiar in sf as other DIMENSIONS and alien INVASION, constructing a universe which is hostile, horrifying and essentially alien. This sensation is conveyed by long passages of dense, highly adjectival description.

Lovecraft was happy to have other writers work within the structure of the Cthulhu Mythos, and even encouraged them. The *Reader's Guide to the Cthulhu Mythos* (**1969**; rev. 1973) by Robert E. WEINBERG and Edward P. Berglund lists a great many writers who at some time adopted and occasionally developed HPL's mythic pattern, among whom the most prominent have been, aside from those already mentioned, Lin CARTER, Robert E. HOWARD, Fritz LEIBER, Robert A.W. LOWNDES, Donald WANDREI and Manly Wade WELLMAN.

It is generally accepted that HPL's own primary Mythos stories are "The Nameless City" (1921), "The Festival" (1925), "The Call of Cthulhu" (1928), "The Colour out of Space" (1927), "The Dunwich Horror" (1929), "The Whisperer in Darkness" (1931), "The Dreams in the Witch-House" (1933), "The Haunter of the Dark" (1936), *The Shadow over Innsmouth* (**1936**), "The Shadow out of Time" (1936 abridged; 1939), "At the Mountains of Madness" (1936 abridged; 1939), *The Case of Charles Dexter Ward* (1941 *Weird Tales* abridged; 1943; **1951**) and "The Thing on the Doorstep" (1937).

An earlier, minor HPL series is comprised of the "Randolph Carter" stories, now to be found in various of his collections: "The Unnamable" (1925), "The Statement of Randolph Carter" (1925), "The Silver Key" (1929), "Through the Gates of the Silver Key" (1934) with E. Hoffman Price and the early, but posthumously published *The Dream-Quest of Unknown Kadath* (1943; **1955**).

HPL submitted only one story to an sf magazine — "The Colour out of Space" (1927 *AMZ*) — but Donald Wandrei placed "The Shadow out of Time" (1936) and "At the Mountains of Madness" (1936) with *ASF* on his behalf. Both were severely cut, with full versions not appearing until hardback publication. These stories, together with other Mythos novelettes, *The Shadow Over Innsmouth* and "The Whisperer in Darkness", represent his most impressive works. After his death Derleth and Wandrei founded ARKHAM HOUSE to publish *The Outsider and Others* (coll. **1939**), containing all his major works except *The Case of Charles Dexter Ward* (**1951**), which first appeared in book form in the subsequent Arkham volume *Beyond the Wall of Sleep* (coll. **1943**). Another Arkham book, *Marginalia* (coll. **1944**), contained some stories Lovecraft had revised for other writers as well as essays, fragments and appreciations, and a complete collection of such revisions was made available as *The Horror in the Museum and Other Revisions* (coll. **1970**). His complete stories remain available in three volumes: *The Dunwich Horror and Others* (coll. **1963**; paperback edition severely abridged; vt, with six stories omitted, *The Haunter of the Dark* UK), *At the Mountains of Madness and Other Novels* (coll. **1964**; UK and US paperback editions abridged, omitting *The Case of Charles Dexter Ward* and other stories) and *Dagon and Other Macabre Tales* (coll. **1965**; vt *Dagon* UK). August Derleth has written many stories based on HPL's notes, which have appeared as "collaborations". These include the novel *The Lurker at the Threshold* (**1945**), the stories in *The Survivor and Others* (coll. **1957**) and two stories in *The Shuttered Room and Other Pieces* (coll. **1959**), which also contains some HPL juvenilia and essays about him. All the Derleth collaborations are assembled in *The Watchers Out of Time and Others* (coll. **1974** USA), and all but *The Lurker at the Threshold* in *The Shadow out of Time and Other Tales of Horror* (coll. **1968** UK), which also contains the six stories omitted from the UK edition of *The Dunwich Horror and Others*, which was titled *The Haunter of the Dark*. Many other HPL collections exist, especially in paperback, but they are essentially reshufflings of the collections named above. [BS/PN]
Other works: *Funghi from Yuggoth* (coll. of poems **1941**); *Supernatural Horror in Literature* (critical essay originally published in *The Outsider and Others*: **1945**); *Something About Cats and Other Pieces* (coll. of revisions, essays, notes etc. **1949**); *Collected Poems* (coll. **1963**).
About the author: *Lovecraft: A Biography* (**1975**) by L. Sprague DE CAMP; *Lovecraft: A Look Behind the Cthulhu Mythos* (**1972**) by Lin Carter; *Lovecraft at Last* (correspondence, **1975**) by HPL and Willis Conover.
See also: DEVOLUTION; FANTASY; GOTHIC SF; INVISIBILITY; MONSTERS; PARALLEL WORLDS; PARANOIA AND SCHIZOPHRENIA; PSYCHOLOGY; SUPERNATURAL CREATURES; SWORD AND SORCERY.

LOVESEY, ANDREW (1941–). English writer and biochemist, whose sf/fantasy novel *The Half-Angels* (**1975**) transports its hero from Earth to an alien planet, via an ancient book, into a confusing allegorical quest where good might be evil and vice versa. [JC]

LOVE WAR, THE Made-for-TV film (1970). Paramount/ABC-TV. Directed by George McCowan, starring Lloyd Bridges, Angie Dickinson, Harry Basch and Dan Tavantry. Screenplay by Guerdon Trueblood and David Kidd. 76 mins. Colour.

Six aliens from two warring planets arrive on Earth for a duel to the death, to decide which planet is the victor. Four of the aliens are quickly eliminated and one of the survivors decides that he does not want to continue with the fight; he wishes to remain on Earth and live as peaceful a life as possible, merging with the natives. He even begins a relationship with a girl, to whom he eventually tells the truth about himself, promising that they will marry as soon as he overcomes the other survivor, who he knows is closing in for the kill. The other alien, however, turns out to be the girl herself, and the man is the one who dies. This is a cheaply made but entertaining and unpretentious sf thriller. [JB]

LOW, A(RCHIBALD) M(ONT-GOMERY) (1888–1956). British academic, inventor and writer. He was president of the British Interplanetary Society for a period, and invented a flying bomb in 1917. His first sf novel, *Adrift in the Stratosphere* (1934 *Scoops*; **1937**), was a juvenile in which the young protagonists accidentally take off in a professor's rocket-ship. *Satellite in Space* (**1956**) is space opera, with humans, including an old-time Nazi, meeting aliens from the asteroid belt. AML also wrote a non-fiction prognosis of things to come, *It's Bound to Happen* (**1950**; vt *What's the World Coming To?* USA). [JC]
Other works: *Peter Down the Well* (**1933**), a juvenile; *Mars Breaks Through* (**1937**).
See also: BOYS' PAPERS.

LOWNDES, ROBERT A(UGUSTINE) W(ARD) (1916–). American writer, often referred to as "Doc" Lowndes. He was a member of the FUTURIANS fan group and collaborated on several stories with other members of the group under the names S.D. GOTTESMAN, Paul Dennis LAVOND, Arthur COOKE and Lawrence WOODS. For his solo work in the early 1940s he used the names Mallory Kent, Carol Grey, and Richard Morrison. Later he used the names Wilfred Owen Morley, Robert Morrison, Michael Sherman and Peter Michael Sherman, and once collaborated with James BLISH as John MacDougal. He edited FUTURE FICTION and SCIENCE FICTION QUARTERLY for Columbia Publications, from early 1941 to their demise, and again throughout their revival in the 1950s. He also edited DYNAMIC SCIENCE FICTION and *Science Fiction Stories* for Columbia Publications, the latter becoming ORIGINAL SCIENCE STORIES in 1955, and when the chain folded in 1960 he began editing for Health Knowledge Inc. He gradually added a number of fantasy magazines to the latter publisher's line, including *The Magazine of Horror*, *Startling Mystery Stories*, *Weird Terror Tales*, *Bizarre Fantasy Tales* and FAMOUS SCIENCE FICTION, but all became defunct in 1970. He was also the editor of the Avalon Books sf line in the late 1950s and early '60s. He wrote a novel in collaboration with Blish, *The Duplicated Man* (**1953** as by Blish and Michael Sherman; 1959), and three solo novels: *The Mystery of the Third Mine* (**1953**), *The Puzzle Planet* (**1961**) and *Believers' World* (**1961**; based on "A Matter of Faith" 1952 as by Michael Sherman). His literary columns from *Famous Science Fiction* were collected into a short critical book, *Three Faces of Science Fiction* (**1973**). [BS/PN]
See also: SF MAGAZINES.

LOXMITH, JOHN See John BRUNNER.

LUCAS, F(RANK) L(AURENCE) (1894–1967). English writer and critic, best known in the latter capacity. Of his

fiction, *The Woman Clothed with the Sun and Other Stories* (coll. of linked stories **1937**), like much of the work of F. Britten AUSTIN, presents a didactic rendering of Man's destiny through a story-sequence, in this case extending from AD 53 to 1995, ending in an exemplary cleansing of Man from the world. [JC]

LUCAS, GEORGE (1944–). American film-maker best known for STAR WARS. He attended the University of Southern California Film School and soon became a teaching assistant there. While working with a class of US Navy trainee cameramen he made an sf short entitled *THX 1138 : 4EB*, assisted by half the class. The film subsequently won top honours at the Third National Student Film Festival in 1967–8, and many other awards. In 1968 he won a scholarship to Warner Brothers to observe the making of *Finian's Rainbow* directed by Francis Ford Coppola. He then worked as Coppola's assistant on *The Rain People*, at the same time making a 40-minute documentary about the making of the film, *Filmmaker*, which was highly praised. Then, with Coppola acting as executive producer, Lucas made an expanded version of his sf short. The result, *THX 1138* (1969) (*see separate entry*) was well received by critics but was not a popular success. His second feature film was *American Graffiti*, based on autobiographical material about Californian youth in the 1950s. Its success established him as a commercial film-maker. None the less, Lucas had difficulty in setting up his next film, which was to become *Star Wars* — a project that he had been planning for several years. The subsequent phenomenal success of *Star Wars* has placed Lucas in a uniquely strong position as a director, but he has announced that he plans an early retirement from the industry due to ill health (he is a diabetic); he has said, however, that he will probably return to direct the final instalment of his *Star Wars* saga. *Star Wars II* was in production in 1977. More than any other film-maker, Lucas has helped to make sf acceptable to a mass audience, but inasmuch as *Star Wars* is simple action-adventure, pitched at an intellectual level not much higher than that of the old FLASH GORDON serials to which it makes nostalgic reference, it is not yet clear whether its effect on the development of sf cinema will be good or bad.
The novelization *THX 1138* (**1971**) was credited to Ben BOVA, but the book of *Star Wars* (**1976**) is attributed to GL. Persistent rumour has it that Alan Dean FOSTER was the actual adapter of GL's screenplay into book form, and that GL gave his approval to the end product. [JB/PN]

LUCIAN (*c*. 120–180). Syrian-Greek writer, also known as Lucian of

Samosata, from his birth in the city of that name, the capital of Commagene, in Syria. He early became an advocate and practised at Antioch, but soon set out on the travels which were to help provide the verisimilitude underlying the fantastic surface of some of his works; he visited Greece, Italy and Gaul, studied philosophy in Athens, and eventually became procurator of part of Egypt, where he died. The number of works attributed to him varies with criteria of authenticity, but amounts to at least 80 titles, some certainly spurious. His works can be subdivided into various sections, some of little interest to the student of PROTO SF, including works of formal rhetoric, numerous essays, and biographies; of most interest are the prose fictions, which include both *The True History* and the possibly spurious *Lucius or the Ass*, and the series of Dialogues which comprises L's most important work, and to the form of which he gave his name. The Lucianic Dialogues combine features of PLATO's dialogues, Old and New Comedy, and Menippean Satire into a racy, witty, pungent form ideally suited to the debunking activities with which L is most associated, and which are his most important bequest, his influence on these lines extending to Sir Thomas MORE and Erasmus, and from them to the dialogue-based SATIRES of Thomas Love Peacock and others. The Lucianic Dialogue of greatest sf interest is the *Icaro-Menippus*, in which Menippus, disgusted with the fruitless anim-adversions of Earthly philosophers, acquires a pair of wings and flies first to the Moon, whence he is able to get a literal (i.e. visual) perspective on the nature of Man's follies, and second to Olympus, where he meets Jupiter and watches the God deal with men's prayers (which arrive fart-like through huge vents). Jupiter proves venal enough, but does in the end threaten to destroy the acrimonious philosophers who had driven Menippus to flight. Other Dialogues of interest include the *Charon*, *Timon*, the 26 *Dialogues of the Gods*, and the *Dialogues of the Dead*.
Though less important, the prose fictions are vital proto sf. *The True History* — taking off from the numerous unlikely travel tales that proliferated at the time – is an extremely enjoyable and frequently scatological debunking exercise, in which L (as narrator himself) travels with 50 companions to the MOON, where they become embroiled in a space war, then past the Sun and back to Earth, where they land in the great sea and are soon swallowed by an enormous whale, from which they escape and visit various ISLANDS, where L's fertile imagination piles lunatic marvel upon marvel. With regard to fantasy and the spirit of romance, the *True History* is decidedly detumescent. Its influence extends to François RABELAIS and Jonathan SWIFT. *Lucius or The Ass* is influential as a

cognate or original source for Apuleius' *The Golden Ass* (c. AD 200), also known as *Metamorphoses*, about a magician's helper who is turned into an ass, suffers much, and is finally retransformed by a goddess. Lucius's picaresque adventures, and the earthy manner of their telling, provided models for picaresque counter-attacks on idealistic fiction from Cervantes onwards.

L is considered vital to the somewhat problematic line of descent of prose fictions leading eventually to what we can legitimately think of as sf proper, but has often been treated as a romancer himself, rather than as the consistent (and often savage) debunker of the idiom and ideals of romance that he actually was. His attitude to the extraordinary voyages of his supposed descendents would not have been that of the typical proud father.

There are various translations.   [JC]
About the author: "Lucian's *True History* as SF" by S.C. Fredericks in SCIENCE-FICTION STUDIES, Vol.3, part 1, Mar. 1976.

LUCIE-SMITH, (JOHN) EDWARD (McKENZIE) (1933–). Poet, anthologist and art critic, born in Jamaica, settled in England 1946, educated at Merton College, Oxford. Only one of his many books has sf relevance: *Holding Your Eight Hands: an Anthology of Science Fiction Verse* (anth. **1969**). Like most such works it contains several poetic horrors, but it covers an interestingly wide field, including work by George MacBeth, Robert CONQUEST, John Ciardi, Peter Redgrove, Thomas M. DISCH and Brian W. ALDISS.   [PN]

LUDLOW, EDMUND (1898–). American writer whose sf novel is *The Coming of the Unselves* (**1965**).   [JC]

LUFTPIRAT UND SEIN LENKBARES LUFTSCHIFF, DER German DIME NOVEL series, better known as *Kapitän Mors der Luftpirat*. Author and exact date of publication are unknown, but the series was probably written by only one writer, and appeared c. 1908–c. 1913. In 1915 it was forbidden as "trash". There were at least 165 issues of 32 pages each, published by Druck- und Verlagsgesellschaft m.b.H. in Berlin, one of the biggest fiction factories producing reading matter for the masses. The series anticipates many later SPACE OPERAS, having an interplanetary background, with many adventures on the Moon and the planets of the Solar System. Its hero, Captain Mors, is a Nemo-like fugitive from mankind. There is a case for calling this the first sf magazine.   [FR]

LUKENS, ADAM *See* Diane DETZER.

LUNA MONTHLY American FANZINE, published by Frank and Ann Dietz from New Jersey, ed. Ann Dietz, founded 1969. The schedule has varied from monthly to quarterly. Current. Over 65 issues. The format is stapled DIGEST size, litho. *LM* has been notable for its exceptionally thorough review coverage and listing of sf publications, for which it is a useful research tool. Reviews have been variable in quality, but Mark Purcell's column "The International Scene" has been consistently well informed. The other main critic is Paul Walker.   [PN]

LUNDIN, CLAËS (1825–1908). Swedish writer, one of the earliest to write sf. His *Oxygen och Aromasia* ["Oxygen and Aromasia"] (**1878**) is set in Stockholm in the year 2378. It has not been translated into English.   [PN]

LUNDWALL, SAM J(ERRIE) (1941–). Swedish author, editor, critic, translator and publisher. His first published work was an sf play for Swedish radio, broadcast in 1952 when he was 11 years old. Enormously active in sf FANDOM since 1956, SJL began selling stories in 1963. His first book was a collection, *Visor i vår tid* (coll. **1965**). His next book was, perhaps surprisingly, sold to ACE BOOKS: *Science Fiction: från begynnelsen till våra dagar* (**1969**; exp. trans. as *Science Fiction: What It's All About* **1971**). It was one of the earlier studies of sf in English. Beginning in 1970, SJL has written nine novels, four of which have been translated into English. His forte is satire, often vicious, as in *King Kong Blues* (**1974**; trans. as *AD 2018: or, The King Kong Blues* **1975**), at other times despondent, as in *Bernhards magiska sommar* ["Bernhard's Magical Summer"] (**1974**; the third in a trilogy), or hilarious, as in *Mörkrets furste* ["The Prince of Darkness"] (**1975**), probably his best novel; it is a burlesque of turn-of-the-century DIME NOVELS. Other translated novels are *Alice's World* (trans. **1970**; vt *Alice, Alice!* Sweden **1974**), *No Time for Heroes* (trans. **1970**; vt *Inga hjältar här* Sweden **1972**) and *Bernhard the Conqueror* (trans. **1973**; vt *Uppdrag i universum* Sweden **1973**). The latter two titles are the first two in the trilogy mentioned above. It is interesting that in these cases US publication preceded Swedish.

From 1970, SJL edited the Askild & Kärnekull sf line, thereby reviving Swedish publishing interest in sf. In 1973 he formed his own house, Delta, specializing in new and reprint sf, and issuing some 25 books yearly. SJL's careful bibliography, *Bibliografi över science fiction & fantasy, 1741–1973* (**1974**) is the second revision of a work which originally appeared in 1962. The anthology series "Den fantastiska romanen" (four vols, **1973–4**) is a major work which collects documents of sf history with critical comment. SJL also edits and publishes *Jules Verne-magasinet*, the only Swedish professional sf magazine. He was instrumental in creating the current Swedish sf field, and still plays a major role in Swedish sf. A projected work, in English, is *An Illustrated History of Science Fiction*.
      [J-HH/PN]

LUPOFF, RICHARD A(LLEN) (1935–). American writer. He graduated in arts from the University of Miami in 1956, and after two years in the army worked in computers until 1970, when he became a full-time writer. He was active in sf fandom, and the fanzine XERO, which he co-edited with his wife Pat, won a HUGO award in 1963. A series of articles therein about comics later formed the core of *All in Color for a Dime* (**1970**), which RAL co-edited with Don Thompson. He has contributed a long-running book-review column to the fanzine ALGOL.

RAL is also an expert on Edgar Rice BURROUGHS. As fiction editor of Canaveral Press in the early 1960s he supervised the re-publication of many of Burroughs' works. He is the author of *Edgar Rice Burroughs: Master of Adventure* (**1965**), probably the best short introduction to Burroughs' work, and *Barsoom: Edgar Rice Burroughs and the Martian Vision* (**1976**).

RAL's first published fiction was the novel *One Million Centuries* (**1967**), a colourful adventure of the FAR FUTURE. His short stories include a series of parodies of sf writers published in FANTASTIC under the pseudonym Ova Hamlet. Several of these were incorporated in *Sacred Locomotive Flies* (fix-up **1971**). A second series is the "Tales from the Computer Works", seven so far published in various magazines and anthologies. He has also used the pseudonym Addison Steele II. RAL's most notable stories to date include the satirical "With the Bentfin Boomer Boys on Little Old New Alabama", published in *Again, Dangerous Visions* (**1972**), and a novel based and styled on Japanese mythology, *Sword of the Demon* (**1977**). The former is incorporated in a book projected for 1978 as *Space War Blues*. This will also incorporate "After The Dreamtime" (**1974**), "Sail The Tide of Morning" (**1975**) and "The Bentfin Boomer Girl Comes Thru" (**1976**). RAL is a chameleonic writer, adapting his style with a varying degrees of success to each new story. Perhaps it is for this reason that he has not yet established himself as an individual voice, although he has been greatly more prolific since 1974, dealing with the split personality of a comic-strip artist in *The Triune Man* (**1976**), OVERPOPULATION, ecocatastrophe and sf in-jokes in *The Crack in the Sky* (**1976**), shipwreck on a dehydrated planet in *Sandworld* (**1976**) and a female werewolf in *Lisa Kane* (**1976**).   [MJE]
Other works: *The Comic-Book Book* (anth. **1973**; as editor, with Don

Thompson); *Into the Aether* (**1974**).
See also: CITIES; SF OVERTAKEN BY EVENTS.

LURGAN, LESTER Pseudonym of English writer Mabel Winfred Knowles (? – ?), author of various popular novels including *The League of the Triangle* (**1911**). LL's sf novel, *A Message from Mars* (**1912**), based on a play by Richard Ganthony, may have been used along with the play in creating the film version, A MESSAGE FROM MARS (1913); the story deals with the effects on humans of the arrival of a messenger from Mars with words of good sense about our earthly dilemmas. [JC]
See also: SATIRE.

LUTHER, RAY *See* Arthur SELLINGS.

LUXEMBURG *See* BENELUX.

LYMINGTON, JOHN Pseudonym of British writer John Newton Chance (? –), prolific author of detective yarns. His first novel as JL, later made into a film (*see* THE NIGHT OF THE BIG HEAT), was *The Night of the Big Heat* (**1959**), about an alien INVASION, and much of his subsequent work has been a series of routine variations on the theme of alien or natural menace to Earth, though not at the imaginative level of his predecessors (and possible models) John WYNDHAM and John CHRISTOPHER. JL's use of genuine science is minimal and most of his books (many of which feature MONSTERS) operate at the level of B-grade sf/horror films, where menace strikes unexpectedly into a lazy, rural setting. He writes with some verve but little style; there are many clichés of character. Books of this nature include *The Giant Stumbles* (**1960**), *The Night Spiders* (**1963**), *The Green Drift* (**1965**), *Ten Million Years to Friday* (**1967**) and *Give Daddy the Knife, Darling* (**1969**). [JC/PN]
Other works: *The Grey Ones* (**1960**); *The Coming of the Strangers* (**1961**); *A Sword Above the Night* (**1962**); *The Sleep Eaters* (**1963**); *The Screaming Face* (**1963**); *Froomb!* (**1964**); *The Star Witches* (**1965**); *The Nowhere Place* (**1969**); *The Year Dot* (**1972**); *The Hole in the World* (**1974**); *The Laxham Haunting* (**1976**); *Starseed on Eye Moor* (**1977**). [JC]
See also: BOYS' PAPERS.

LYNCH, (JOHN GILBERT) BOHUN (1884–1928). English writer and caricaturist. His *Menace from the Moon* (**1925**) is a blending of interplanetary, LOST-WORLD, and future-WAR themes, in which descendants of a Moon colony established by 17th-century Europeans attack the Earth with heat-rays. It contains many references to the works of Bishop John WILKINS. [JE]
Other works: *A Muster Of Ghosts* (anth. **1924**; vt *The Best Ghost Stories* USA).

LYON, LYMAN R. *See* L. Sprague DE CAMP.

LYTTON, (EDWARD GEORGE EARLE) BULWER (1803–73). He was known as Edward Bulwer until 1838, when he became Sir Edward Bulwer. He became Sir Edward Bulwer Lytton (or Bulwer-Lytton) in 1843 when he succeeded to the Knebworth estate on his mother's death. He became Colonial Secretary in 1858–9 (and signed the documents creating British Columbia and Queensland). He was raised to the peerage as first Baron Lytton in 1866. He is thus an indexer's and bibliographer's nightmare.

BL was an English writer, most significant for such fashionable and trend-setting novels as *Pelham* (**1828**), though best remembered for *The Last Days of Pompeii* (**1834**). Versatile and prolific, though often superficial, he wrote many novels, and his collected works fill over 110 volumes. He was interested in the occult, and wrote several stories and one novel, *A Strange Story* (**1862**), on occult themes, as well as the fine novelette *The Haunted and the Haunters: or, The House and the Brain* (1859 *Blackwood's Magazine*; **1905**), a haunted-house tale which qualifies as marginal sf through its quasi-scientific explanations in terms of mesmerism and magnetism. His sf novel is *The Coming Race* (**1871**), a UTOPIA set in an underground world inhabited by refugees from the surface who have been there for thousands of years, morally and physically fuelled by *vril*, a marvellous energy-sustaining force. The book is mainly descriptive, and ends in a prediction of the eventual ascendancy of this submerged race. It is more important as an influence on such writers as H.G. WELLS than for its comparatively slender literary qualities. [JC]
See also: GOTHIC SF; LOST WORLDS; POWER SOURCES; WOMEN.

McALLISTER, BRUCE (1946–). American writer, editor and academic, director since 1974 of the creative writing programme at the University of Redlands, California. He began publishing sf with "The Faces Outside" for *If* in 1963, and has written at least 20 stories since. "The Boy" (1976), a peculiarly revolting, skilful tale of the entropic life of a reconstructed Peter Pan

and Wendy on a less than Utopian ISLAND, is an exercise about, and to some extent in, literary sadism. His sf novel, *Humanity Prime* (**1971**), was used as his thesis for an MFA degree in creative writing. He has edited an anthology, *SF Directions* (anth. **1972**), has worked on the *Best SF* anthology series with Harry HARRISON and Brian W. ALDISS, and is currently associate editor of *West Coast Poetry Review*. In mid-1977 proper evaluation awaits wider publication of his stories. [JC/PN]

MacAPP, C.C. Pseudonym used by Carroll M. Capps (1917?–71) for all his sf work, which he began publishing with "A Pride of Islands" in 1960 for *If*, a magazine with which (with its stablemates) he was to be associated for the balance of his short career. Much of his fiction concerned itself with alien INVASION themes, notably the "Gree" stories, in *If* and *Worlds of Tomorrow* from 1965–6, and his first novel, *Omha Abides* (1964–6 *Worlds of Tomorrow*; fix-up **1968**), in which a long-lasting alien occupation is opposed by Terrans whose Indian-like nature also finds expression in CCM's most ambitious novel, *Worlds of the Wall* (1964 *Fantastic*; exp. **1969**), a complex adventure of initiation and self-fulfilment set upon a strange other-DIMENSIONAL world. CCM wrote clearly and excitingly, and the truncation of his career must be regretted. [JC]
Other works: *Prisoners of the Sky* (1966 *If*; exp. **1969**); *Secret of the Sunless World* (**1969**); *Recall Not Earth* (**1970**); *Subb* (1968 *If*; fix-up **1971**); *Bumsider* (**1972**).

McARTHUR, JOHN *See* Arthur WISE.

MACAULAY, ROSE (1881–1958). English writer, best known for works outside the sf field, such as her last and most famous novel, *The Towers of Trebizond* (**1956**). Her sf novel, *What Not: A Prophetic Comedy* (**1919**), set several years after the conclusion of the First World War, depicts the coming to power in England of an autocratic government designed to counter post-War crises. *Orphan Island* (**1924**) is a borderline UTOPIA (*see also* ISLANDS) set in the 19th and 20th centuries, and satirizing conventional Victorian social and sexual mores. [JC]

McAULEY, JACQUELIN ROLLIT (1925–). American writer whose sf novel is *The Cloud* (**1964**). [JC]

McCAFFREY, ANNE (INEZ) (1926–). American writer, now living in Ireland. Most of her fiction combines sf and fantasy elements. She began publishing with "Freedom of the Race" for Hugo GERNSBACK's *Science Fiction Plus* in 1953. Her first novel, *Restoree* (**1967**), rather conventionally, though with tongue in cheek, tells the story of a young lady brought back from SUSPENDED ANIMATION for dubious purposes. Soon, however, AM began publishing the linked novels and stories that have made her reputation as a writer of romantic, heightened adventure fantasies. Set in a world where tame dragons and humans engage symbiotically in high adventures, *Dragonflight* (fix-up **1968**), *Dragonquest* (**1971**) and the projected *White Dragon* make up the most important of these series. Associated with it is a juvenile sequence comprised of *Dragonsong* (**1976**), *Dragonsinger* (**1977**) and the projected *Dragonstar*. Two of the stories which made up *Dragonflight* received awards; a HUGO went to "Weyr Search" (**1967**) and a NEBULA to "Dragonrider" (**1967–8**). More centrally science-fictional, though perhaps less convincingly constructed and told, is *The Ship Who Sang* (coll. of linked stories **1969**), about a deformed girl who is grafted into a SPACESHIP (*see* CYBORGS) and who as it were, and jovially, becomes the ship; the emotional difficulties facing a musical lady spaceship are many.

AM's interest in music also emerges in a series of linked stories which appeared in Roger ELWOOD's series of four *Continuum* anthologies (**1974–5**), about Killashandra, the Crystal Singer: "Prelude to a Crystal Song" (**1974**), "Killashandra − Crystal Singer" (**1974**), "Milekey Mountain" (**1974**) and "Killashandra − Coda and Finale" (**1975**). Elwood made an error, transposing the second and third stories; in terms of internal chronology "Milekey Mountain" precedes "Crystal Singer".

AM is among the most popular writers in her particular sub-genre, though several critics have seen her work as over-sentimental. *To Ride Pegasus* (fix-up **1973**), like most of the above based on a series of magazine stories, deals with a parapsychological corps of investigators in the near future; it is notable for its political conservatism. A new sequence, projected for three volumes, is initiated by *Dinosaur Planet* (**1978**), and features humans on a planet rife with dinosaurs. Two shorter series, "The Bitter Tower" (two stories) and the "Charity" series (three stories) are collected with other stories in *Get Off the Unicorn* (coll. **1977**). [JC/PN]
Other works: *Decision at Doona* (**1969**); *Mark of Merlin* (**1971**), not sf; *Ring of Fear* (**1971**), not sf; *A Time When* (**1975**). As editor: *Alchemy & Academe* (anth. **1970**); *The Out of this World Cookbook* (anth. **1973**), a collection of recipes supplied by various sf writers.
See also: ARTS; COLONIZATION OF OTHER WORLDS; POLITICS; PSI POWERS; SPACESHIPS; SUPERNATURAL CREATURES; WOMEN.

McCANN, ARTHUR *See* John W. CAMPBELL Jr.

McCANN, EDSON Pseudonym used by Frederik POHL and Lester DEL REY on the novel *Preferred Risk* (**1955**), hurriedly written for a GALAXY novel competition because no acceptable submissions had been received. It is cast in the same mould as Pohl and C.M. KORNBLUTH's *The Space Merchants* (**1953**) and features a world dominated by insurance companies. [BS]
See also: DYSTOPIAS; SATIRE.

McCLARY, THOMAS CALVERT (? –). American sf writer appearing in *ASF* in the 1930s, his works written under his own name and the pseudonym Calvin Peregoy (the "Doctor Conklin" series). Basic to his two unusual novels *Rebirth* (1934 *ASF*; **1944**) and *Three Thousand Years* (1938 *ASF*; **1954**) is the theory, reminiscent of Buckminster Fuller, that a small scientific elite unhindered by the opportunism of businessmen and politicians could keep the world running in decency and comfort. Both are worked out in a post-catastrophe setting, intentionally and instantaneously precipitated in the former by means of a ray which obliterates all memory and in the latter by the transition of all life forms to a state of SUSPENDED ANIMATION; in both the idealistic theory is set up only to be exploded. (*See* HOLOCAUST AND AFTER *for further details*.) [JE/PN]

MacCLURE, VICTOR (1887–1963). British writer of popular fiction. His *The Ark of the Covenant: A Romance of the Air and of Science* (**1924**; vt *Ultimatum: A Romance of the Air* UK) tells of world disarmament brought about through the great powers' being held to ransom by a pacifist group armed with an airship carrying a sleep gas and a ray that transmutes elements. It was very popular in its day. [PN/JC]
See also: WEAPONS.

McCLURE'S MAGAZINE US "slick" magazine published by S.S. McClure, ed. Ida Tarbell and others. Monthly, Jun. 1893–Jan. 1926 (irregularly towards the end). Recommenced in Jun. 1926 as a romance magazine. Merged with *Smart Set* in Apr. 1929.

Although *MM* was initially conceived as the US edition of the IDLER, it appeared as a new magazine with original stories and features. Some sf was reprinted from the *Idler*, however *MM*'s best remembered publication of sf was Rudyard KIPLING's *With the Night Mail, a Story of 2,000 AD* (1905; **1909**). [JE]

MacCOLL, HUGH (? – ?). British author of *Mr. Stranger's Sealed Packet* (**1889**), an interplanetary novel describing a spaceship journey to Mars and the discovery there of two races of Earth origin, one having attained a UTOPIAN ideal (*see* EVOLUTION). Although lacking the depths of Percy GREG's influential *Across The Zodiac* (**1880**), it proved

popular and may in turn have influenced H.G. WELLS, especially in its account of the death of a Martian female through exposure to bacteria in the Earth's atmosphere. [JE]
See also: MARS; SOCIAL DARWINISM.

McCOMAS, J. FRANCIS (1911–78). American writer and editor. Author of a number of sf stories under his own name, including "Shock Treatment" (1954) and "Parallel" (1955), and the pseudonym Webb Marlowe. He was co-editor with Raymond J. HEALY of the important *Adventures in Time and Space* (anth. **1946**). JFM was also joint editor with Anthony BOUCHER of THE MAGAZINE OF FANTASY AND SCIENCE FICTION from its first issue until August 1954, though he has not generally received his due share of credit for establishing the direction of that magazine. He remained advisory editor of *FSF* until March 1962. He was also co-editor with Boucher of the first three annual anthologies of stories from *FSF*. JFM was a member of the Mystery Writers of America. [MJE]
Other works: ed. *The Graveside Companion* (anth. **1962**); ed. *Crimes and Misfortunes* (anth. **1970**); ed. *Special Wonder: the Anthony Boucher Memorial Anthology of Fantasy and Science Fiction* (anth. **1970**).

McCORD, GUY *See* Mack REYNOLDS.

MacCREIGH, JAMES *See* Frederik POHL.

McCUTCHAN, PHILIP (1920–). English Sandhurst graduate and writer of several routine sf thrillers. His "Commander Shaw" series begins with *Skyprobe* (**1966**) and includes *The Screaming Dead Balloons* (**1968**), *The All-Purpose Bodies* (**1969**) and *The Bright Red Business Men* (**1969**). The Commander's function is to involve himself with espionage and save the world from mad scientists who grow extraterrestrial fungi or construct malign CYBORGS. Other works include *A Time for Survival* (**1966**), a post-HOLOCAUST story; *The Day of the Coastwatch* (**1968**); *This Drakotny ...* (**1971**); and other thrillers which occasionally use marginally sf devices in the manner of Ian FLEMING's "James Bond" books. [PN/JC]

McDANIEL, DAVID Pseudonym of American writer Ted Johnstone (1939–77), under which he wrote an sf SPACE OPERA, *The Arsenal Out of Time* (**1967**) and a number of television spin-offs, most of them of *The Man from U.N.C.L.E* series. They are *The Dagger Affair* (**1966**); *The Vampire Affair* (**1966**); *The Monster Wheel Affair* (**1967**); *The Rainbow Affair* (**1967**); *The Utopia Affair* (**1968**); and *The Hollow Crown Affair* (**1969**). He also wrote a spin-off from the TV series THE PRISONER, *The Prisoner No. 2* (**1969**). [JC]

McDERMOT, MURTAGH Pseudonym. The English Moon-voyage novel published as by MM, *A Trip to the Moon* (1728), describes various remarkable sights and beings, after the fashion of Cyrano de Bergerac. The necessary propulsion for the trip is given by gunpowder. [JC]

McDERMOTT, DENNIS *See* P. Schuyler Miller.

MacDONALD, ANSON *See* Robert A. Heinlein.

MacDONALD, GEORGE (1824–1905). Scottish author and editor, noted for his fairy tales. His former occupation as a clergyman (terminated through ill-health), was reflected in his allegorical fantasies, *Phantastes* (1858) and *Lilith* (1895; rev. 1924), the latter work being his closest to the sf genre. Based on the premise that an infinite number of three-dimensional universes can exist in a four-dimensional frame (*see* PARALLEL WORLDS), *Lilith* drew heavily from the Talmud in its enigmatic description of a search for the self, set in both this universe and another. It compares interestingly with David Lindsay's *A Voyage to Arcturus* (1920). [JE] **Other works:** *Adela Cathcart* (1864; rev. 1882); *The Portent* (1864); *Dealings with the Fairies* (1867); *At the Back of the North Wind* (1871); *Works of Fancy and Imagination* (10 vols, 1871); *The Princess and the Goblin* (1872); *The Wise Woman* (1875; vt *A Double Story* USA; vt *Princess Rosamund* USA; vt *The Lost Princess* UK); *The Princess and Curdie* (1882); *Fairy Tales* (1920); *The Light Princess* (coll. 1961) ed. Roger Lancelyn Green; *Evenor* (coll. 1972) ed. Lin Carter.

MacDONALD, JOHN D(ANN) (1916–). American writer and ex-lieutenant colonel in the US Army, known mainly for such well-written thrillers as *The Brass Cupcake* (1950) and the "Travis McGee" series (since 1964). At one time extremely prolific, JDM now produces about one novel a year, mostly in the latter series. His sf, beginning early in his career with "Cosmetics" for *ASF* in 1948, is a product of his prolific years; in addition to around 50 short stories, nearly all written 1948–53, he produced two sf novels in that period, *Wine of the Dreamers* (1951; vt *Planet of the Dreamers* UK) and *Ballroom of the Skies* (1952), both polished and proficient adventures in PARANOID sf, and both involving extraterrestrial manipulations of humanity, inadvertent in the first book, and as part of a winnowing process to select good leadership material in the second. A later novel, *The Girl, the Gold Watch, & Everything* (1962), is a complicated spoof adventure, in which a man inherits a watch which speeds up time, when correctly used, for the owner, rendering him invisible to the people in real, apparently frozen, time, and giving him great power. It is an old theme; *see* PARIS QUI DORT.

JDM occasionally wrote sf stories under the pseudonyms John Wade Farrell and Peter Reed. [PN/JC] **See also:** LEISURE; TIME TRAVEL.

MacDOUGAL, JOHN Pseudonym of James Blish and Robert A.W. Lowndes in collaboration.

MACEY, PETER (? –). British research chemist and writer, whose routine sf novels are *Stationary Orbit* (1974), in which the alien intelligence turns out to be a local dolphin, *Distant Relations* (1975) and *Alien Culture* (1977) which features invasion by intelligent microbes. [PN]

McGIVERN, WILLIAM P(ETER) (1927–). American writer, prolific contributor to the Ziff-Davis magazines *AMZ*, *Fantastic* and *Fantastic Adventures*, from "John Brown's Body" (with David Wright O'Brien, with whom he several times collaborated) for *AMZ* in 1940 to "Love That Potion" for *Fantastic* in 1955. He often used the house name Alexander Blade. Although he never attracted any special attention in sf, like John D. MacDonald he also wrote for the detective pulps and there, like MacDonald, though not so spectacularly, he was more successful. His thrillers are hard-bitten, with a tight-lipped *angst*, and include the famous *The Big Heat* (1953) and *Rogue Cop* (1954). [PN/JC]

McGOWAN, INEZ *See* Rog Phillips.

MacGREGOR, RICHARD (? –). British author of several routine sf novels in PULP-style paperbacks, including *Horror in the Night* (1963), *The Day a Village Died* (1963), *Taste of the Temptress* (1963), *The Creeping Plague* (1963), *The Deadly Suns* (1964), *The First of the Last* (1964) and *The Threat* (1964). [JC]

McGUIRE, JOHN J(OSEPH) (1917–). American writer who began his career in sf by collaborating with H. Beam Piper on the sf action novel *Crisis in 2140* (1953 *ASF* as "Null ABC"; 1957). A later collaboration was *A Planet for Texans* (1957 *Fantastic Universe* as "Lone Star Planet"; 1958). They are not readily distinguishable from Piper's solo efforts. JM wrote two other stories with Piper and four solo stories, 1957–64. [JC] **See also:** COLONIZATION OF OTHER WORLDS; CRIME AND PUNISHMENT.

MacHARG, WILLIAM *See* Edwin Balmer.

MACHEN, ARTHUR (1863–1947). Welsh writer, translator and actor, born Arthur Llewellyn Jones, his parents adding Machen in an apparent attempt to please a rich relative. AM was an isolated, lonely child, and was from a very early age deeply devoted both to romantic literature and to the Welsh landscape that dominated his writings visually all his life. He also applied his extensive if somewhat random readings in the occult and metaphysics imaginatively to his Welsh background. He was in London for long periods from 1880; the death of his father in 1887 provided him with enough money to marry and to write; by the end of the century, he was once again poverty-stricken; he went on the stage for much of the following decade, and for the rest of his life did a great deal of hack work. By the time he was rediscovered in the 1920s, he was no longer capable of producing material of high calibre.

With influences ranging from William Morris to Robert Louis Stevenson, and associations running from John Lane's Bodley Head at the time it was publishing *The Yellow Book* to the Order of the Golden Dawn (whose occultist members included both W.B. Yeats and Aleister Crowley), AM's fiction shies generally clear of sf as it was practised in late Victorian and Edwardian England; most of his best tales are horror or occult fantasies. They tend to be set in a medievalized England with Welsh tinges; those set in London are irradiated by deeply romantic visions of alternatives to the industrial world which he saw dominating England and which he despised. "The Great God Pan", title story of *The Great God Pan and The Inmost Light* (coll. 1894; exp. 1926), is typical of Victorian sf/horror at about the time sf was beginning to lose its GOTHIC elements into a separate horror/fantasy genre. The story begins with an sf rationale (brain surgery) for a metamorphosis which remains one of the most dramatically horrible and woman-loathing in fiction; the evil female offspring of the operated-on idiot girl grows into a malign being, apparently a woman, but actually a half-human horror, whose father may have been the eponymous horned god. AM's influence, via H.P. Lovecraft and others, has been strong on 20th-century sf Gothic. *The Terror: A Fantasy* (1917) is quasi-sf in its story of animals turning against humans.

Volumes in which fantasy predominates include *The Chronicle of Clemendy* (coll. 1888), *The Three Impostors, or The Transmutations* (coll. 1895; vt *Black Crusade*), *The House of Souls* (coll. 1906), *The Hill of Dreams* (1907), *The Angels of Mons, The Bowmen and Other Legends of the War* (coll. 1915), *The Great Return* (1915), *The Shining Pyramid* (coll. 1923), *The Cosy Room* (coll. 1936), *The Children of the Pool, and Other Stories* (coll. 1936), *Dreads and Drolls* (coll. 1927), *The Green Round* (1933), *Holy Terrors* (coll. 1946), *Tales of Horror and the Supernatural* (coll. 1948).

Physically, AM was like a morose

G.K. Chesterton, and his works also slightly resemble that author's, but have darker, less accessible strands.　　[JC/PN]

See also: PARANOIA AND SCHIZOPHRENIA.

MACHINES Many people consider that sf is basically TECHNOLOGY fiction in which machines are more important than men. Virtually all proffered DEFINITIONS of the literary species are somewhat wider in scope, but the assumption that "real" sf is HARD technological sf is very common. Various categories of machine have exerted a powerful fascination upon the imagination (see TRANSPORTATION; SPACESHIPS; WEAPONS) and the impact of technology upon society has been a continual concern in sf (see AUTOMATION, Utopias and Dystopias), so the attitude, though narrow minded, is understandable.

The first major work to celebrate the shape of machines to come was Francis Bacon's essay in PROTO SF *New Atlantis* (1627; **1629**), which comprises a catalogue of marvellous inventions (see also DISCOVERY AND INVENTION). Bacon's contemporary John Wilkins, one of the first popularizers of science, also catalogued the potential of the mechanical arts, in *Mathematicall Magick* (**1648**). These catalogues are remarkably realistic, but a new perspective was used by Daniel Defoe in *The Consolidator* (**1705**), which uses machines as metaphors. The satire features a "cogitator", which forces rational thoughts into unwilling brains, a "devilscope", which infallibly detects and exposes political chicanery, and an "elevator", which allows communication between minds, and with the spirits of the dead. While Bacon and Wilkins extrapolated from contemporary technology to test the limits of practicality, Defoe merely discovered miraculous purposes and then proposed machines to serve as symbols for the means to those ends. With one or two exceptions — the most notable being Arthur C. Clarke — modern sf writers have much more in common with Defoe than with Bacon in terms of their *modus operandi*.

With the exception of flying machines, which were a common concern in speculative fiction in the 17th and 18th centuries, few of the machines anticipated by Bacon and Wilkins play a significant part in sf until the late 19th century, when the industrial revolution lent historical confirmation to their prospectus for technology. The Utopians made much of the productive capacity of the machines, but the first major literary disciple of the machine, Jules Verne, was much more interested in its potential in imaginary voyaging, and it is the machine's role in TRANSPORTATION which first became a conspicuous inspiration in sf, quickly followed by its role in remaking WAR. In this period the machine does appear as a device for working miracles, but more often it is simply a means of achieving

quite commonplace ends: in travel, in COMMUNICATION, and in many forms of amusement. The quality of the fascination is accurately reflected by the sporting contraptions featured in Anthony Trollope's *The Fixed Period* (**1882**) and J.A.C.K.'s *Golf in the Year 2000* (**1892**). Convenient literary devices engineered by machine are featured in Edward Bellamy's *Dr. Heidenhoff's Process* (**1880**), about a machine which erases unpleasant memories, Conan Doyle's *The Doings of Raffles Haw* (**1891**), about a gold-making machine, and H.G. Wells's *The Time Machine* (**1895**).

There was, however, another side to the fascination with mechanical contrivance, manifest in a series of baroque tales and allegories from E.T.A. Hoffmann's "Automata" (1814) and "The Sandman" (1816) to Nathaniel Hawthorne's "The Celestial Railroad" (1843) and Herman Melville's "The Bell-Tower" (1855), in which machines play a quasi-diabolical role. Something of this more sinister fascination is found in Samuel Butler's *Erewhon* (**1872**), H.G. Wells's classic short story of man-machine confrontation "The Lord of the Dynamos" (1894) and in the cautionary children's fantasy *The Master Key* (**1901**) by L. Frank Baum. Enthusiasm for technological achievement and suspicion regarding Man's relationship with the machine are combined in the curiously intense study of mechanical creativity *Morrison's Machine* (**1900**) by J.S. Fletcher.

In the last few years of the 19th century the potential of technology was drastically transformed by the discovery of the electromagnetic spectrum and the development of modern atomic theory. Vulgar mechanism could hardly compete with the magic of rays and radio, and as the horizons that had confined the technological imagination of Bacon and Wilkins disappeared there seemed to be no bounds to possibility. A new era of imaginative exuberance began, which took means of transportation (especially spaceships) and weapons of war out of the realms of extrapolation into those of boundless fantasy.

One of the prophets of the new technology, and one whose understanding of its potential was more realistic than he is sometimes given credit for, was Hugo Gernsback, a would-be inventor who became the publisher of *Radio News*, *Modern Electrics*, *The Electrical Experimenter* and Science and Invention, and who founded Amazing Stories as their companion. In his own romance *Ralph 124C 41+* (1911–12; **1925**) Gernsback produced a catalogue of wonders akin to that of the *New Atlantis* which, though painfully naïve in terms of literary representation and social speculation, proved far from incompetent as a technological prospectus.

It was not unnatural that the early sf PULP MAGAZINES should go to extremes in

their use of machines in a way that Verne never had. The pulp writers were the product of an age of extremely rapid technological advance in which science was coming to seem mysterious again. It was an age in which it seemed that machines might do anything, when even the subtle metaphors of Defoe's *Consolidator* could seem plausible as actual devices. The limitless scope of the machine was translated into a kind of quasi-supernatural awe in such stories as John W. Campbell Jr's "The Last Evolution" (1932), "Night" (1935 as by Don A. Stuart) and "The Machine" (1935 as by Don A. Stuart) — a much more reverential awe than that manifest in Hoffmann's stories and "The Celestial Railroad". The attitude of the pulp sf writers seems astonishingly naïve in our more cynical age, but it was not altogether out of keeping with its own *Zeitgeist*. What was missing from all the extravagant accounts of miracle-working machines was a consciousness of the social implications of such extravagant technological advance. Gardner Hunting's *The Vicarion* (**1926**), for instance, is a machine which can look through time to record any event from the past. The political implications of such an invention are tremendous, but in Hunting's blinkered view it is merely a new entertainment medium which might make cinema obsolete (though Hunting does consider the psychological implications of the machine, and decides in consequence that the world would be better off without it). André Maurois's *The Thought-Reading Machine* (**1937**; trans. **1938**) is a device with similarly wide-ranging implications which is represented in the novel as a mere fashionable fad (again with bad psychological effects on individuals). Many other stories carry the conviction that we might be better off without miraculous machines, notably E. Charles Vivian's *Star Dust* (**1925**), Karel Čapek's *The Absolute at Large* (1922; trans. **1927**) and William M. Sloane's *The Edge of Running Water* (**1939**; vt *The Unquiet Corpse*) but there are very few attempts to examine their implications for social life. *Brave New World* (**1932**) is outstanding in this respect, but it, too, is dominated by the obsessive conviction that the miracles are evil. Within the sf magazines this assumption was almost non-existent, and it was within the sf magazines that the demand was first made for a careful consideration of the effects of technology upon society. This was John Campbell's prospectus for science fiction, promoted in Astounding Science-Fiction, and while speculation outside the genre continued to be associated with polemics, magazine sf was at least prepared to attempt to be analytical. Robert A. Heinlein was one of the first to take up the challenge, in such stories as "The Roads Must Roll" (1940) and *Beyond This Horizon* (1942 as by Anson MacDonald;

1948), and the 1940s became, in magazine sf, the era of the gadget — the small machine with considerable implications.

Another common concern of the period was the issue of Man's dependence upon machines. First dramatized straightforwardly in stories of the 1930s which described Man's decadence through overdependence — Campbell's "Twilight" (1934 as by Don A. Stuart) is the classic of the species — this theme gradually took on satirical overtones, first in such stories of mechanical revolution as Robert BLOCH's "It Happened Tomorrow" (1943) and Clifford D. SIMAK's "Bathe Your Bearings in Blood" (1950; vt "Skirmish"), and later in overtly satirical comedies of gadget-precipitated chaos such as Murray LEINSTER's "A Logic Named Joe" (1946 as by Will F. Jenkins). The concern with the social effects of progress engendered by Campbell ultimately led to a strong vein of satire of a much more general kind in the sf of the 1950s.

The Second World War and the bombing of Hiroshima encouraged the notion that Man's machines were becoming too powerful, and that he was not up to the task of responsibly administering their use. A particularly powerful parable of the power of the machine acting independently of human control is Theodore STURGEON's "Killdozer!" (1944), and the immediate post-War period saw a proliferation of stories showing a sharp awareness of the potential of inventions in precipitating power-struggles. T.L. SHERRED's "E for Effort" (1947) features a machine similar to Gardner Hunting's vicarion, but takes a very different view of its likely career in human society. Jack WILLIAMSON's "The Equalizer" (1947) is an elegant study of the political implications of free power.

As the 1950s progressed, writers became increasingly prone to show machines out of human control, remaking the world, while Man was swept helplessly along — or left helplessly behind. Lord DUNSANY's only sf novel, The Last Revolution (1951) described the rebellion of the machines, and magazine sf featured such bleak images as Philip K. DICK's "Second Variety" (1953), in which self-replicating, evolving war machines inherit the Earth. More recent works embodying similar images include Fred SABERHAGEN's "Berserker" series, John SLADEK's satirical The Reproductive System (1968; vt Mechasm USA) and Stanislaw LEM's The Invincible (1964 Poland; trans. from German 1973). Very many stories dealing with specific categories of machine, particularly ROBOTS and COMPUTERS, testify to this pattern reflecting the alienation of Man from his mechanical environment. It seems to have been at its strongest during the 1950s, and from the early 1960s there has been a trend towards an uneasy reconciliation, perhaps best evidenced by changes in the typical roles assigned to CYBORGS.

In contemporary sf suspicion of the machine remains deeply entrenched, but the inevitability of the association is accepted. The man/machine relationship may involve all kinds of intimacy, including sexual intimacy in such stories as Harlan ELLISON's "Pretty Maggie Moneyeyes" (1967) and "Catman" (1967). Robots often become mentors, and so do computers — notably in David GERROLD's When Harlie Was One (1972) — and machines even take over psychiatric functions in Philip K. Dick's The Three Stigmata of Palmer Eldritch (1964) and Frederik POHL's Gateway (1977). The distinction between life and mechanism often becomes blurred, particularly in Dick's Do Androids Dream of Electric Sheep? (1968) and the most recent of Isaac ASIMOV's robot stories, "The Bicentennial Man" (1976). So closely do the themes of man/machine conflict and man/machine intimacy co-exist in contemporary sf that they may be seen as parts of a single love/hate relationship. They no longer represent different points of view.

The growth of the awareness that Man and machine are inextricably bound together in contemporary society has deflected attention away from the miraculous potential of the machine. The naïve assumption that all human problems might be solved by appropriate technological innovations, very common in the 1930s, has now died out (see ECOLOGY). It is generally accepted in today's sf that man/machine relationships are just as problematic, and just as difficult, as interhuman relationships, and very probably more so. Machines, whether spaceships or weapons, have lost their force as symbols of individual freedom and power, and with this loss the potential of sf to provide escapist fantasies and power fantasies has been extensively eroded. (The resurgence of interest in "pure" FANTASY — anti-scientific fantasy — during the last decade is an eloquent confirmation of this fact.) Formerly, speculative fiction's main concern in dealing with machines was the adaptation of machines to human purposes (and this is equally true of Baconian extrapolation and Defoe's mechanical fantasies); now, the main concern is with the adaptation of Man to his mechanical achievements and his mechanical environments.							[BS]

McHUGH, VINCENT (1904–). American writer whose comic saga Caleb Catlum's America (1936) is about a family of IMMORTALS who amusingly represent the high points of American history in the flesh (the family includes "Abe" Lincoln and Davy Crockett, among others). I Am Thinking of My Darling (1943) is also amusing; an inhibition-releasing epidemic hits New York.					[JC]

See also: HUMOUR; PSYCHOLOGY.

McINNES, GRAHAM (CAMPBELL) (1912–70). British-born, Australian-educated Canadian diplomat and novelist, son of the novelist Angela Thirkell. Most of his work is not sf, but Lost Island (1954) is a LOST-RACE story.	[PN]

McINTOSH, J.T. Pseudonym (in some earlier work spelled M'Intosh) of Scottish writer and journalist James Murdoch MacGregor (1925–), used for all his sf writing, though he has written non-sf under his own name. He began publishing sf with "The Curfew Tolls" in ASF in 1950, though his short fiction has appeared only infrequently, and with his first novel, World out of Mind (1953), began a career that was notably successful in its early years at least. World out of Mind implausibly but enjoyably sets a disguised alien on an Earth dominated by aptitude tests to win his way to the top and thence prepare the way for invasion. Born Leader (1954; vt Worlds Apart USA) puts two sets of colonists from a destroyed Earth on nearby planets, where the authoritarian set conflicts with the libertarian set. In One in Three Hundred (1954), Earth is doomed again, and pilots of the only rocketships available are given the task of selecting passengers to safety from the planet's billions of inhabitants. The Fittest (1955; vt The Rule of the Pagbeasts USA) depicts the harrowing effects of a misfired experiment to increase animal intelligence. 200 Years to Christmas (1961) is a routine but competent variation on the GENERATION STARSHIP theme.

Although some of JTM's novels in the 1960s and '70s continue to show his professional skill with a plot, and his competence at creating identifiable characters, his novels do show a slackening of interest, so that The Million Cities (1958 Satellite; rev. 1963) is a bland urban DYSTOPIA, and The Noman Way (1964) uninterestingly repeats the test situation of his first novel. Out of Chaos (1965) is a routine post-HOLOCAUST novel, and Time for a Change (1967; vt Snow White and The Giants USA) treats a local intrusion of time-travelling aliens with considerable domestic detail. Flight from Rebirth (1971) has a chase plot in an urban venue that also involves testing. JTM has not lost the vivid narrative skills that made him an interesting figure of 1950s sf, but has by no means challenged himself in his later career, with results that verge on mediocrity.	[JC]
Other works: Six Gates from Limbo (1968); Transmigration (1970); The Cosmic Spies (1972); The Space Sorcerers (1972; vt The Suiciders USA); Galactic Takeover Bid (1973); Ruler of the World (1976); Norman Conquest 2066 (1977); This is the Way the World Begins (1977).

See also: ANDROIDS; END OF THE WORLD;

GAMES AND SPORTS; IMMORTALITY; INTELLIGENCE; SUN.

McINTYRE, VONDA N. (1948–). American writer and geneticist (BS from the University of Washington 1970) and one of the earliest successful graduates of the CLARION SCIENCE FICTION WRITERS' WORKSHOP, which she attended in 1970. She gained prominence with her first published story, "Of Mist, and Grass, and Sand" (1973); the female protagonist, a healer in a desolated primitive venue, encounters violent and destructive superstition, suffering the loss of her healer snake, with which she is empathically linked. It won a NEBULA award for best novelette. VNM's novel, *The Exile Waiting* (**1975**), more diffuse in telling and effect, also features an empathic protagonist, this one a girl sneak thief in a post-HOLOCAUST Earth's last city who eventually manages, with a Japanese poet from the stars and a good CLONE (the bad clone twin is killed in the city), to escape from Earth, with the prognosis that she will become a very successful starfarer indeed. VNM was co-editor (with Susan Janice Anderson) of *Aurora: Beyond Equality* (anth. **1976**), a collection of feminist sf stories, not all by women. [JC]
See also: WOMEN.

MacISAAC, FRED (1886–1940). American writer who appeared frequently in *Argosy* after the First World War, and whose sf novels are *The Vanishing Professor* (**1927**), *The Mental Marvel* (**1930**) and *The Hothouse World* (1931 *Argosy*; **1950**), a typical post-HOLOCAUST story. [JC]

MACKELWORTH, R(ONALD) W(ALTER) (1930–). English writer and insurance salesman. He began publishing sf with "The Statue" for *NW* in 1963, and has since produced some above-average sf adventure novels, usually involving complex, sometimes jumbled plotting, and an Earth somehow in danger. They include *Firemantle* (**1968**; vt *The Diabols* USA), *Tiltangle* (**1970**), *Starflight 3000* (**1972**), which involves some interesting use of TERRAFORMING, both of the Moon and of other planets, and *The Year of the Painted World* (**1975**). [JC]

McKENNA, RICHARD M(ILTON) (1913–64). American writer. He spent most of his adult life, not very happily, in the US Navy, which he joined in 1931. After he returned to civilian life in 1953, he took a BA in literature at the University of North Carolina. His first published story was "Casey Agonistes" (1958) in *FSF*, although the first he wrote was "The Fishdollar Affair" (1958), which appeared in *If*. His efforts to revise the former story according to the editor's demands are described in his essay "Journey With a Little Man", recently reprinted in Damon KNIGHT's anthology of sf criticism *Turning Points* (anth. **1977**). RMM was to publish only five more sf stories during his lifetime; another six appeared posthumously. Five of his strongest stories are collected in *Casey Agonistes and other Fantasy and Science Fiction Stories* (coll. **1973**). The central theme of these stories is the power of mind over environment — to adapt the existing environment or, ultimately, to create a new one, to meet human needs. In the title story the inmates of a terminal ward create the eponymous hero in order to ameliorate the oppressive hopelessness of their situation. "Mine Own Ways" (1960) and "Hunter Come Home" (1963) are both set on alien worlds and deal with processes of EVOLUTION. "The Secret Place" (1966), which won a NEBULA award, is about PARALLEL WORLDS which can be reached through the power of the mind, while "Fiddler's Green" (1967), perhaps RMM's most ambitious story, tells of a group of men adrift in a small boat, without food and water, who mentally create an ALTERNATE WORLD into which they may escape. RMM was a powerful fantasist who never intended his work in this form as anything more than an apprenticeship (he chose the sf field for his early attempts at fiction because, he reasoned, the low rates of pay would mean there were few good writers working in the medium, thus restricting the competition). His major work in the early 1960s was a novel drawing on his naval experiences, *The Sand Pebbles* (**1962**). It was a critical and popular success, and was filmed. RMM did not live to capitalize on its success; even if he had, it is unlikely that he would have written more sf. None the less, his existing body of sf is sufficient to secure him a sure if not major position in the sf pantheon. [MJE]
See also: ANTHROPOLOGY; ECOLOGY; LIFE ON OTHER WORLDS; PASTORAL; PERCEPTION.

MACKENZIE, COMPTON (EDWARD MONTAGUE) (1883–1972). Scottish writer, knighted in 1952. He is best known for his work outside the sf field, for example his influential *Bildungsroman*, *Sinister Street* (two vols **1913–14**). His sf novel, *The Lunatic Republic* (**1959**), is one of his many comic entertainments, told with considerable slapstick in an easy-going, winning style; the novel depicts the UTOPIAN society that exists, at the end of the century, on the Moon. Two fantasies are *Hunting the Fairies* (**1949**) and *The Rival Monster* (**1952**). [JC]

McKILLIP, PATRICIA A. *See* CHILDREN'S SF.

MacLAREN, BERNARD (? –) British writer whose sf novel, *Day of Misjudgment* (**1956**), unusually represents COMPUTER domination of society as more of a blessing than a curse. [JC]

McLAUGHLIN, DEAN (BENJAMIN) (1931–). American writer who began publishing sf with "For Those who Follow After" for *ASF* in 1951. Of his three sf novels, *Dome World* (1958 *ASF*; exp. **1962**), *The Fury from Earth* (**1963**) and *The Man Who Wanted Stars* (1956–7 var. mags; fix-up **1965**), the last is probably the best, though all of them are densely written if straightforward adventures. The first is set under the sea, the second describes a war between Earth and a liberated Venus; *The Man Who Wanted Stars* is the story of a man's long, driven quest to force and trick Earth governments into interstellar space flight. *Hawk Among the Sparrows* (coll. **1976**) assembles stories of the 1960s. DM's subject matter and style are fairly typical of those encouraged by John W. CAMPBELL Jr during his editorial domination of *ASF*. [JC]
See also: POLLUTION; SPACE FLIGHT; STARS.

MacLEAN, KATHERINE (ANNE) (1925–). American writer. She is a BA from Barnard College, did postgraduate

Photo Chris Grasse Studio.

study in psychology, and is presently a laboratory technician in quality control in a food factory. She is also a college lecturer in creative writing and literature. KM writes primarily short stories, most of which have appeared in *ASF* from her first story, "Defense Mechanism" (*ASF* 1949), mostly under her own name, though she wrote three stories as by Charles DYE (*see his entry for details*), who was her husband 1951–3. She is now married to writer Davis Mason, and has a projected book written in collaboration with her son, Chris Mason. KM has been in the vanguard of those sf writers trying to apply to the SOFT SCIENCES the machinery of the HARD SCIENCES, in a generally optimistic reading of the potentials of that application. Her tone is generally that of HARDCORE SF, despite this subject matter, and her work should not be confused with later NEW WAVE uses of her basic material. KM was one of the earlier women sf writers, but it would be neither desirable nor possible to read her stories as "women's" sf; in a notoriously male chauvinist field she competed on equal terms, not restricting herself to "feminine" themes or protagonists, and not generally using a male pseudonym. The admiration accorded her work has nothing to do with any sexist tokenism. A number of her early stories have been assembled in *The Diploids* (coll. **1962**); their range and competence in dealing with technological matters may reflect KM's wide range of occupations in her extra-literary life.

Many of KM's early stories have also been anthologized, perhaps the best-known being: "Pictures Don't Lie" (1951), which tells of the arrival of an alien spaceship which seems normal according to advance radio signals, but turns out to be almost microscopic; "The Snowball Effect" (1952), an amusing satire on social engineering in which a ladies' knitting circle expands to become the strongest political pressure group in the USA; and "Unhuman Sacrifice" (1958), an important piece of ANTHROPOLOGICAL sf in which a visiting missionary on another planet misreads a functional biological change in the natives as a painful and needless initiation ceremony, interferes, and damages an alien as a result. In these early years KM began writing the "Hills of Space" series, dealing with the settling of the ASTEROIDS by refugees, fugitives and the poor. It includes "Incommunicado" (1950), "The Man Who Staked the Stars" (1952 as by Charles Dye), "Collision Orbit" (1954), "The Gambling Hell and the Sinful Girl" (1975) and a novel projected for publication in the near future, provisionally titled *The Hills of Space.* KM collaborated on one story with Harry HARRISON, "Web of the Worlds" (1953; vt "Web of the Norns"). She wrote one story, "The Carnivore" (1953), under the pseudonym G.A. Morris.

KM's first novel, *Cosmic Checkmate* (1958 *ASF*; exp. **1962**), written with Charles DE VET, combines SPACE OPERA with interesting speculations on a society where hierarchy is built around skill at GAMES. Perhaps her best book is *Missing Man* (1968–71 *ASF*; fix-up **1975**), which contains the 1971 NEBULA award story "The Missing Man" (1971), and deals with the exploits of George Sanford, an ESPER whose telepathy is a kind of sonar device, enabling him to trace people emitting emotional distress signals; allied with New York's Rescue Squad, he goes to their aid. Unusually for sf, the novel depicts New York with affection. An interesting article by KM is "Alien Minds and Nonhuman Intelligences", a study of the logic of evolved intelligence on other planets, in *The Craft of Science Fiction* (**1976**) ed. Reginald BRETNOR.   [JC/PN]
See also: ALIENS; ICONOCLASM; PHYSICS; RELIGION; SOCIOLOGY; WOMEN.

MacLEOD, ANGUS (1906–   ). Scottish writer of fiction and plays for radio; his sf novels are *The Body's Guest* (**1958**), in which a Yoga machine built by an Indian

physicist switches identities between nine Scots and a bull, with mildly amusing results, and *The Eighth Seal* (**1962**).
[JC/PN]

MacLEOD, SHEILA (? –). Scottish writer, married to actor Paul Jones (*see* PRIVILEGE). She is the author of five novels, *Xanthe and the Robots* (**1977**) being the first sf. Set in the Institute for Advanced Robotic Research, it explores the creation of "Philophrenics" (ROBOTS of near-human capability) and the problems their designers face in deciding how far to permit their development to go; it is an intelligent and sophisticated novel. *Circuit-Breaker* (**1978**) entertainingly mixes the inner and outer space in which astronauts are marooned; that is, if the hero is in fact an astronaut and not a mental case or an sf writer; the ending is ambiguous.   [MJE/PN]

McMAHON, PAT See Edward D. HOCH.

MacNEE, PATRICK See Peter LESLIE.

McNELLY, Dr WILLIS E. (1920–   ). Professor of English at California State University at Fullerton and sf critic; he was the first academic critic invited to contribute a summary of the year's fiction to a *Nebula Award Stories* anthology; it was no. 4 (anth. **1969**) ed. Poul ANDERSON. His anthologies include *Mars, We Love You* (anth. **1971**; vt *The Book of Mars* UK) ed. with Jane Hipolito, *Above the Human Landscape: A Social Science Fiction Anthology* (anth. **1972**) ed. with Leon STOVER, and *Science Fiction Novellas* (anth. **1975**) ed. with Harry HARRISON. The last title had a companion work, *Science Fiction Novellas: Teacher's Guide* by WEM alone. He also edited a series of brief essays about the increasing interest of the academic world in sf (*see* SF IN THE CLASSROOM): *Science Fiction: The Academic Awakening* (anth. **1974**). WEM is a permanent member of the board of judges for the JOHN W. CAMPBELL AWARD for best sf novel of the year.   [PN]

MACROCOSM, THE See GREAT AND SMALL.

MacTYRE, PAUL Pseudonym of Scottish writer R.J. Adam (1924–   ), under which name his best-known novel is his first, *Midge* (**1962**; vt *Doomsday, 1999* USA), a literate post-HOLOCAUST story in which a new form of life threatens to take over from the remnants of outmoded, destructive Man. Further novels are the Buchanesque *Fish on a Hook* (**1963**) and *Bar Sinister* (**1964**), whose eponymous bar represents a borderline COMMUNICATIONS technology.
[JC]

MADDOCK, LARRY The solo writing name of Jack Owen Jardine (1931–   )

for his "Agent of T.E.R.R.A." series, speedy SPACE OPERAS starring Hannibal Fortune and an alien sidekick on various assignments to save Earth from her enemies. The series includes *The Flying Saucer Gambit* (**1966**), *The Golden Goddess Gambit* (**1967**), *The Emerald Elephant Gambit* (**1967**), *The Time Trap Gambit* (**1969**). Jardine is a creative director for radio. With his former wife, Julie Ann Jardine, he wrote under the pseudonym Howard L. CORY.   [JC]

MADDOX, CARL See E.C. TUBB.

MADDUX, RACHEL (1912–   ). American writer, in whose sf novel, *The Green Kingdom* (**1957**), five people find a LOST WORLD.   [JC]

MADER, FRIEDRICH W. (1866– ?). German author whose juvenile novel of interplanetary exploration, *Distant Worlds: the story of a Voyage to the Planets* (**1921** Germany; **1932**), is his only work translated into English. He also wrote *El Dorado* (**1919**; vt *Auf den Spuren der Inkas*).   [JE]
See also: SPACESHIPS.

MAD LOVE See HANDS OF ORLAC, THE.

MAEPEN, K.H. See Henry KUTTNER.

MAGAZINE OF FANTASY, THE See MAGAZINE OF FANTASY AND SCIENCE FICTION, THE.

MAGAZINE OF FANTASY AND SCIENCE FICTION, THE US DIGEST

Dec. 1955. The delicately rendered alien landscape on the cover is by Chesley Bonestell.

magazine published by Mercury Press whose first issue (Fall 1949) was titled *The Magazine of Fantasy*. It became a bi-monthly in Feb. 1951 but has maintained a monthly schedule since Aug. 1952. It was edited by Anthony BOUCHER and J.

Francis McComas until 1954, and by Boucher alone Sep. 1954 – Apr. 1958. Robert P. Mills was editor until Mar. 1963, then Avram Davidson took over until Nov. 1964. Publisher Joseph Ferman took control for a year, and then his son, Edward Ferman, became editor, and remains so today. *FSF* won Hugo awards for best magazine in 1958, 1959, 1960, 1963, 1969, 1970, 1971 and 1972. Between 1952 and 1977, 20 annual anthologies of "Best" stories from its pages were published, none appearing in 1970, 1972, and 1974–6. No. 22 appeared in 1977. There were also the special anthologies *A Decade of Fantasy and Science Fiction* (anth. **1960**) ed. Robert P. Mills, and *Twenty Years of the "Magazine of Fantasy and Science Fiction"* (anth. **1970**) ed. Edward L. Ferman and Robert P. Mills.

In contrast to the pulps, whose staple diet consisted of novelettes, and to the other major digest magazines, which habitually made use of serial novels, *FSF*'s editorial policy placed heavy emphasis on short stories. Its editors abandoned the standards of pulp fiction and asked for sf and fantasy that was well-written and stylish, up to the literary standards of the slick magazines which had shaped American short-story writing between the wars. They also abandoned interior illustrations. *FSF* published a great deal of light and humorous material, and used occasional reprints of stories by prestigious writers, including Eric Linklater, James Thurber, Robert Louis Stevenson, P.G. Wodehouse, Robert Graves, Robert Nathan and Oscar Wilde. It also attracted such writers as Gerald Heard, C.S. Lewis and Kingsley Amis to write for its pages. Despite numerous changes of editorship the personality of the magazine has been most consistent, although in recent years it has become more of an orthodox sf magazine than it was in earlier days. It used serials only occasionally, and most of the novels appearing in it have been substantially abridged, including *Bring the Jubilee* by Ward Moore (Nov. 1952; **1953**), *Rogue Moon* by Algis Budrys (Dec. 1960; **1960**) and "Starship Soldier" (magazine version of *Starship Troopers*, **1959**) by Robert A. Heinlein (Oct.-Nov. 1959). Several notable series have been associated with the magazine, including Zenna Henderson's "People" series, Manly Wade Wellman's "John the Ballad Singer" series, later published as *Who Fears the Devil?* (coll. **1963**), Poul Anderson's "Time Patrol" series, later published as *Guardians of Time* (coll. **1960**) and Reginald Bretnor's "Papa Schimmelhorn" series.

Many award winners appeared in *FSF* or are based on material appearing there. *Starship Troopers* won a Hugo, as did Walter Miller's *A Canticle for Leibowitz* (**1960**), developed from three novelettes published in 1955–7. Roger Zelazny's "And Call Him Conrad" (Oct.–Nov. 1965;

exp. as *This Immortal*, **1966**) won a Hugo, and sections of another Zelazny Hugo-winner, *Lord of Light* (**1967**), appeared in *FSF* in 1967.

Other award-winning stories are: Robert Bloch's "That Hellbound Train" (Sep. 1958; Hugo); Daniel Keyes' "Flowers for Algernon" (Apr. 1959; Hugo — the expanded version *Flowers for Algernon*, **1966**, subsequently won a Nebula as best novel); Brian Aldiss's "Hothouse" series (1961; Hugo — later a fix-up book *Hothouse* (**1962**; vt *The Long Afternoon of Earth* USA) and "The Saliva Tree" (Sep. 1965; Nebula); Poul Anderson's "No Truce With Kings" (Jun. 1963; Hugo), "The Queen of Air and Darkness" (Apr. 1971; Hugo and Nebula) and "Goat Song" (Feb. 1972; Hugo and Nebula); Fritz Leiber's "Ship of Shadows" (Jul. 1969; Hugo), "Ill Met in Lankhmar" (Apr. 1970; Hugo) and "Catch That Zeppelin" (Mar. 1975; Hugo and Nebula); Roger Zelazny's "The Doors of His Face, The Lamps of His Mouth" (Mar. 1965; Nebula); Frederik Pohl's "collaboration" with the late C.M. Kornbluth "The Meeting" (Nov. 1972; Hugo); Harlan Ellison's "The Deathbird" (Mar. 1973; Hugo) and "Adrift Just Off the Islets of Langerhans" (Oct. 1974; Hugo); Robert Silverberg's "Born With the Dead" (Apr. 1974; Nebula); Robert Aickman's "Pages From a Young Girl's Journal" (Feb. 1973; World Fantasy Award); Tom Reamy's "San Diego Lightfoot Sue" (Aug. 1975; Nebula); and Charles L. Grant's "A Crowd of Shadows" (Jun. 1976; Nebula).

Other notable stories include Alfred Bester's "The *Pi* Man" (Oct. 1959); Philip José Farmer's "Father" (Jul. 1955) and "Open to Me My Sister" (May 1960; vt "My Sister's Brother"); Robert Heinlein's "All You Zombies" (Mar. 1959); Ray Nelson's "Turn Off the Sky" (Aug. 1963), Roger Zelazny's "A Rose for Ecclesiastes" (Nov. 1963); Robert Silverberg's "Sundance" (Jun. 1969) and Poul Anderson's "The Problem of Pain" (Feb. 1973). *FSF* has published a "special all-star anniversary issue" every October since the mid-1960s, and a series of special issues celebrating particular authors, each featuring a new story, a checklist of the author's work and articles about the author. The first of these was devoted to Theodore Sturgeon (Sep. 1962). Subsequent issues featured Ray Bradbury (May 1963), Isaac Asimov (Oct. 1966), Fritz Leiber (Jul. 1969), Poul Anderson (Apr. 1971), James Blish (Apr. 1972), Frederik Pohl (Sep. 1973), Robert Silverberg (Apr. 1974) and Harlan Ellison (Jul. 1977). The Anderson, Leiber and Silverberg stories are among the award winners listed above. The first six of these stories, with abridged checklists and biographical articles, were published as *The Best from Fantasy and Science Fiction: A Special 25th Anniversary Anthology* (anth. **1974**), ed. Edward L. Ferman, which, though not so titled, is

assumed to be no. 21 of the "Best" series, as its successor is no. 22. Since Nov. 1958 every issue of *FSF* has featured a science article by Isaac Asimov, and these essays, showing the popularization of science at its best, have been collected into a number of books. Another feature was the long series of punning shaggy dog stories known as "Feghoots" written by Reginald Bretnor, as Grendel Briarton, in 1958–64. Recent issues have included competitions of a light-hearted nature. In 1968 the magazine sponsored a novel-writing contest won by Piers Anthony with *Sos the Rope* (Jul.–Sep. 1968; **1968**). [BS]

Collectors should note: *FSF* presents few difficulties. Vol.1 had five numbers, Vol.2 had six, Vol.3 had eight, and thereafter each volume had six numbers. There were, however, three numbering errors: Vol.14 no.1 was wrongly numbered Vol.13 no.7; Vol.19 no.1 was wrongly numbered Vol.18 no.7; there were two issues numbered Vol.29 no.1, the first of which should have been numbered Vol.28 no.6. Before the regular monthly schedule was adopted, the editions ran as follows: Fal. '49; Win./Spr. '50; Sum. '50; Fal. '50; Dec. '50; Feb. '51; Apr. '51; Jun. '51; Aug. '51; Oct. '51; Dec. '51; Feb. '52; Apr. '52; Jun. '52 and Aug. '52. Since then the monthly schedule has been completely regular, with each month and year appearing on the cover.

British editions of the magazine ran Oct. '53–Sep. '54 (12 issues) and Dec. '59–Jun. '64 (55 issues). These did not reprint whole issues, but selected and recombined stories from the US edition. The British reprint magazine Venture carried some material from *FSF* as well as from the American *Venture*, its short-lived companion. There was a selective reprint edition in Australia, 11 numbers, 1954–7.

MAGAZINES For a full discussion of sf and fantasy magazines, together with a listing of all separate sf and post-1926 fantasy magazines in this Encyclopedia, see sf Magazines. For a discussion of pulp magazines generally, and a listing of all the pulp entries not listed under the sf magazines rubric, including such hero/villain pulps as Scorpion, see pulp magazines, which also discusses the relationship between the pulps and their competitors, the slicks and tabloids. Several of the latter regularly published sf stories, and a selection of the most important have received entries: Black Cat, Collier's Weekly, Idler, McClure's Magazine, Munsey's Magazine, Overland Monthly, Pall Mall Budget, Pall Mall Magazine, Passing Show, Pearson's Magazine, Pearson's Weekly, St. Nicholas Magazine, Strand Magazine. Finally, other forms of periodical publishing are discussed under boys' papers, dime novels and juvenile series, comic strips and comic

BOOKS. The entries for HISTORY OF SF and SF PUBLISHING also discuss the importance of the magazines. [PN]

MAGIC In the *Oxford English Dictionary* "magic" is defined as "the pretended art of influencing the course of events ... by processes supposed to owe their efficacy to the power of compelling the intervention of spiritual beings, or of bringing into operation some occult controlling principle of nature". The lexicographer assumes that there is no difficulty in telling a "pretended" art from a real one, nor in distinguishing the "occult" from the scientific. Many sf authors have felt dissatisfied with such confident categorizations, and have written stories exemplifying alternative relationships between magic and science.

One typical attitude is summed up by Arthur C. CLARKE's "Third Law" (in *Profiles of the Future*, coll. **1962**): "Any sufficiently advanced technology is indistinguishable from magic". This statement unconsciously echoes Roger Bacon's observation 700 years before, that "many secrets of art and nature are thought by the unlearned to be magical"; the irony by which Bacon, a pioneer of experimental science, developed a posthumous reputation for sorcery goes far to confirm Clarke's "Law", and is at the heart of James BLISH's novel of the history of science, *Doctor Mirabilis* (**1964**). Stories in which superior technology is treated as magic are common, the most thoroughgoing being Larry NIVEN and David GERROLD's *The Flying Sorcerers* (**1971**). However, the unexpressed converse of Clarke's "Law" has proved even more attractive: if technology looks like magic, could magic not have been misunderstood technology?

The possibilities for fiction of this nature were well exemplified by several stories published in UNKNOWN in the 1940s, Fritz LEIBER's *Conjure Wife* (1943; **1953**), Robert A. HEINLEIN's "The Devil Makes the Law" (1940; vt as "Magic Inc." in *Waldo and Magic, Inc.*, coll. **1950**), and the "Harold Shea" stories by L. Sprague DE CAMP and Fletcher PRATT, later collected as *The Incomplete Enchanter* (1940; **1942**) and *The Castle of Iron* (1941; **1950**). The first is set in contemporary America, the second in an ALTERNATE WORLD very similar to contemporary America, the third in PARALLEL WORLDS to which contemporary Americans are sent. All rely heavily on the juxtaposition of familiar and unfamiliar, realistic and fantastic; their concern, above all, is to discipline and rationalize notions of magic. Thus, in *Conjure Wife* the hero, a professor of social anthropology, discovers that his wife is a witch and forces her to give up this "superstition". Accumulating catastrophes persuade him that he is wrong. In the end he has to use his academic training to systematize his wife's knowledge and restore stability. The "incomplete enchanters" are also academic psychologists, though Heinlein's hero, characteristically, is a small-town businessman.

In presenting rationalized forms of magic the *Unknown* authors were following the lead of Sir James Frazer's *The Golden Bough* (3rd edition in 12 vols, **1911–15**). This extremely influential work had suggested (a) that magic was like science but unlike religion in its assumption that the universe worked on ·"immutable laws", and (b) that some of these laws could be codified as Laws of Sympathy, Similarity and Contact. Frazer was probably no more than half serious in this, but the notion of quasi-Newtonian laws proved irresistible. Leiber, De Camp and Pratt include overt references to *The Golden Bough*, while the hero of *Magic Inc.* is actually called "Fraser". At one point he explains, for instance, how he exploits the laws of "homeopathy" and "contiguity" to erect temporary grandstands. He has a section of seating carefully built, then chops it to pieces. "Under the law of contiguity, each piece remained part of the structure it had once been in. Under the law of homeopathy, each piece was potentially the entire structure." So Mr Fraser can send out splinters which, when activated by the proper spells, will temporarily become entire structures. We realize that the world he lives in is controlled entirely by "occult" principles, but that these are not haphazard. Much of the amusement of worlds-where-magic-works stories lies in developing the possibilities of a small number of magical rules.

Many authors have followed the lead of the *Unknown* stories: Poul ANDERSON in *Three Hearts and Three Lions* (1953 *FSF*; exp. **1961**) and *Operation Chaos* (1956–9 *FSF*; fix-up **1971**), John BRUNNER in *The Traveler in Black* (coll. of linked stories **1971**), James Blish in *Black Easter* (**1968**), Larry Niven in "What Good is a Glass Dagger?" (**1972**) and James GUNN in *The Magicians* (1954 *Beyond* as "Sine of the Magus"; exp. **1976**). The principles of magic (as a kind of alternate technology) are also examined in Jack VANCE's *The Dying Earth* (coll. **1950**) and *The Eyes of the Overworld* (**1966**), in Mark GESTON's *The Siege of Wonder* (**1976**), in Fred SABERHAGEN's trilogy beginning with *The Broken Lands* (**1968**) and in Christopher STASHEFF's *The Warlock in Spite of Himself* (**1969**) and its sequel. But the purest example of "Frazerian" sf is Randall GARRETT's "Lord Darcy" series in *ASF*, 1964–76. The stories are set in an alternate world where King Richard I founded a stable Plantagenet dynasty, Europe remained feudal and Catholic, and magic was developed in harmony with science. Their heroes are a detective pair, Lord Darcy and Master Sean O Lochlainn, resembling Coñan DOYLE's Sherlock Holmes and Dr Watson. Master Sean is not a doctor, however, but a sorcerer, and he plays a much.more significant role than Dr Watson ever did, compensating for the absense of forensic science in the "Darcy" universe by a series of carefully described magical tests for murder weapons, times of death, chemical analysis and so on. It is not too much to say that the stories are vehicles for the explanations of Master Sean rather than for the adventures of Lord Darcy. Garrett's distinctive contributions are the range of new "laws" added to the old Frazerian ones (Relevance, Synecdoche, Congruency etc.) and the rigour with which these are stated and used.

In the stories so far mentioned magic is seen not as *like* science but as a *form* of science. Why, then, has it never been systematized in our world? Many different answers have been given to this. Garrett's, for example, is that it is a result of prejudiced enquiry on the part of scientists, complicated by the fact that the exercise of magic demands a mysterious "talent" which many investigators do not possess: experiments are therefore likely to be unrepeatable. Magic here is being assimilated to PSI POWERS, which sf authors are capable of taking seriously. Nevertheless, the danger lurking in the whole sub-genre is one of frivolity: for after all magic, unlike many sf notions, is not still in the limbo of possibility, but has been effectively disproved.

There is, accordingly, an extremely large section of FANTASY literature which exploits the presence of magic without trying to rationalize it. Nearly all the authors mentioned so far have tried their hand at SWORD-AND-SORCERY stories, for example, Leiber's "Fafhrd and Gray Mouser" series (1939–77), De Camp's "Pusadian" and "Novarian" series (1968–71) and Heinlein's *Glory Road* (**1963**). There is no hard and fast distinction here between fantasy and sf. However, it is possible to argue that there is a hierarchy of seriousness in the employment of magic in fiction, running down from Garrett's considered suggestions about the history of science and the nature of psi powers to the virtually thoughtless romances of, say, Robert E. HOWARD, in which the sorcery is less significant than the swords.

It is striking, indeed, that one "Frazerian" area has daunted all but the boldest users of magic in sf, this being RELIGION. The position of magic in a Christian universe is especially difficult to define, since its compulsive quality appears to contradict dogmas of divine omnipotence. Most authors accordingly relegate religion to the background of their stories, C.S. LEWIS going so far, in *That Hideous Strength* (**1945**), as to explain how magic has come to be unlawful for Christians in normal circumstances. One author who does not shirk the challenge is James Blish, but his *Black Easter* ends with the words "God is dead" Here magic appears almost to have overcome religion, though a sequel, *The Day After Judgement* (**1972**), proves this to be an error.

The only wholly successful resolution of magic, science and religion in sf so far is Ursula K. LE GUIN's "Earthsea" trilogy (**1968–72**). This is in a sense a "Frazerian" work, for the magic in it is based on the notion that everything has a true name and can be controlled by knowledge of it: Frazer was familiar with name-taboos. However the relationship is virtually one of parody, for while the first "golden bough" was Aeneas's talisman of return from the underworld (Virgil's *Aeneid* Book 6), the Archmage hero of "Earthsea" finds himself continually struggling against death without any supporting token. He learns in the first book of the trilogy that the defeat of death is an improper aim for a magician, whose art depends on respect for the individual qualities (or names) of others, rather than on manipulation of them for one's own self-perpetuation. In the second book he faces an organized religion of sacrifice and propitiation, to demonstrate that this offers no better hope for humanity. In the third he duels with a rival "mage" who appears to have won power over death, though with disastrous consequences for others. Magic is presented continually as an alternative ideology to those with which we are familiar, i.e. those of science and religion, and as a more attractive one. *Earthsea* is informed, atypically for sf, by an awareness of the discoveries of post-Victorian ANTHROPOLOGY; it exemplifies the serious and powerful argumentative quality which can underline what appear to be only entertaining fantasies. [TS]

See also: GODS AND DEMONS; GOTHIC SF; MONSTERS; MYTHOLOGY; PSEUDO-SCIENCE; SUPERNATURAL CREATURES.

MAGIDOFF, ROBERT (1905–). Russian-born American academic, chairman of the Slavic Department at New York University. His three anthologies are *Russian Science Fiction* (anth. **1964**), *Russian Science Fiction, 1968* (anth. **1968**) and *Russian Science Fiction, 1969* (anth. **1969**). [PN]

MAGNETIC MONSTER, THE Film (**1953**). A-Men Productions/United Artists. Directed by Curt SIODMAK, starring Richard Carlson, King Donovan, Jean Byron and Strother Martin. Screenplay by Curt Siodmak and Ivan Tors. 76 mins. B/w.

A new isotope, created in a laboratory, sucks in all nearby energy and starts to grow. It emits deadly radiation and is finally destroyed in a cyclotron. The film includes footage from the German sf classic GOLD (1934). [JB]

MAGUIRE, JOHN FRANCIS (1815–72). Irish nationalist politician and journalist, founder of the Cork *Examiner*. In his sf novel *The Next Generation*

(**1871**), set in 1891, Great Britain has been much improved by the granting of women's suffrage; romance, and the explication of other meliorist reforms just this side of UTOPIA, take up the remainder of a very long book. "Jack Tubbs; or the Happy Isle," in *Young Prince Marigold, and Other Fairy Stories* (coll. **1873**) features an Edenic ISLAND populated by animals with whom the hero has learned to converse. [JC]

MAINE, CHARLES ERIC Pseudonym used by British writer David McIlwain (1921–) for his sf work; another pseudonym, Richard Rayner, he has not used for sf. CEM was one of the relatively few but extremely active British fans before the Second World War, and began publishing sf after serving in the War. His first novel was *Spaceways* (**1953**; vt *Spaceways Satellite* USA); based on his own radio play, it was filmed as SPACEWAYS (1953). Most of his sf shares a leaning towards thriller-like plots, and a disinclination to argue its often shaky scientific pinnings very closely, the latter tendency particularly visible in stories featuring hard sf themes such as space travel, as in *High Vacuum* (**1956**). Sometimes lightly, sometimes with gravity, CEM's numerous books touch on a variety of sf themes, from ROCKETS to SOCIOLOGY, but generally without more than fitfully illuminating them; he is determinedly an author of routine middle-of-the-road genre sf, and as such has been successful. His finest novel is generally thought to be *The Mind of Mr Soames* (**1961**), a story of a man who does not reach consciousness until the age of 30, and of the arguments about how best to educate him. The moral issues are dealt with quite sensitively. The book was made into a film of the same title in 1969. [JC/PN]

Other works: *Timeliner* (**1955**); *Crisis 2000* (**1955**); *Escapement* (**1956**; vt *The Man Who Couldn't Sleep* USA), filmed as *The Electronic Monster* (1957; vt *The Dream Machine*); *The Isotope Man* (**1957**); *World Without Men* (**1958**; rev. vt *Alph* 1972); *The Tide Went Out* (**1958**; rev. vt *Thirst!* 1977); *Count-Down* (**1959**; vt *Fire Past the Future* USA); *Calculated Risk* (**1960**); *He Owned the World* (**1960**; vt *The Man Who Owned the World* UK); *Subterfuge* (**1960**); *The Darkest of Nights* (**1962**; vt *Survival Margin* USA); *Never Let Up* (**1964**); *B.E.A.S.T. · Biological Evolutionary Animal Simulation Test* (**1966**); *The Random Factor* (**1971**).

See also: CLONES; DISASTER; GRAVITY; MOON; WOMEN.

MAINE, DAVID See Pierre BARBET.

MAINS D'ORLAC, LES See HANDS OF ORLAC, THE.

MAINSTREAM WRITERS OF SF When used of literature, the term "mainstream" in its narrowest

application refers to the tradition of the realistic novel of human character; in a wider application, common among sf readers and many others, it denotes all serious prose fiction outside the market genres; in its widest and perhaps most regrettable denotation it refers to practically any fiction, serious or otherwise (including the sort of lowbrow best-sellers that Harold Robbins writes), outside sf, the thriller and the Western. As a piece of jargon, not yet fully accepted into the language, "mainstream" lacks precision; none the less, there is a useful distinction to be drawn between those writers who think of themselves as writing sf, and whose books and stories are marketed as sf, and those who think of themselves simply as writing fiction, without adopting either the protection or the stigma of a genre label. As a shorthand device we have referred to the work of the first group as genre sf, and the work of the second group as mainstream sf.

In a sense, until the sf label was adopted (in the form of the word "scientifiction") in the first English-language genre sf magazine, AMAZING STORIES, in 1926, all sf was mainstream. The genre did exist, notably in the scientific romances of H.G. WELLS, the "Voyages extraordinaires" of Jules VERNE, and in much fiction in the general fiction magazines, PULP or otherwise, but it had not yet hardened into a selfconscious separateness.

From the 18th century on, many distinguished writers best known for other forms of fiction flirted occasionally with sf themes. Among such early mainstream writers who are given entries in this volume are Jonathan SWIFT, VOLTAIRE, Giacomo CASANOVA, RESTIF DE LA BRETONNE, Denis DIDEROT, Honoré de BALZAC, Nathaniel HAWTHORNE, Herman MELVILLE, Fyodor DOSTOYEVSKY, Robert Louis STEVENSON, Samuel BUTLER, Anthony TROLLOPE, Mark TWAIN, Richard JEFFERIES, W.H. HUDSON, Bulwer LYTTON, George DU MAURIER, George Bernard SHAW, Edith WHARTON, Marie CORELLI, Joseph CONRAD, Rudyard KIPLING, G.K. CHESTERTON, SAKI and A.C. BENSON and his two brothers. This does not include such important figures as Mary SHELLEY, Edgar Allan POE and Jack LONDON, whose work is so intimately bound up with the development of sf that it would be irrelevant to distinguish them as mainstream writers, just as it would with Verne and Wells.

While sf was beginning to take shape as an identifiably separate genre, mainstream writers continued, in ever greater numbers, to tackle sf themes, often in ignorance of or lack of interest in genre sf, though they were usually familiar with Wells and some of the other major figures in the HISTORY OF SF. The two favourite sf themes with non-genre sf writers have always been DYSTOPIAS (see, for example, E.M. FORSTER, Aldous

HUXLEY) and stories imagining life after some sort of HOLOCAUST; stories of future POLITICS and WAR have also been very popular outside the genre, where sf has more often than not been used for purposes of SATIRE (see, for example, P.G. WODEHOUSE). Some mainstream sf writers from the 1920s and '30s are Alexei TOLSTOY, André MAUROIS, J.B. PRIESTLEY, Michael ARLEN, C.S. FORESTER, Rex WARNER, Herbert READ, Upton SINCLAIR, Hilaire BELLOC, Guy DENT, Wyndham LEWIS, Sinclair LEWIS, Rose MACAULEY, Flann O'BRIEN, Edgar WALLACE, Olaf STAPLEDON, Karel ČAPEK and E.C. LARGE. Like all the lists of names in this entry, this contains only a small fraction of the total number of mainstream writers who receive entries in this volume.

As, in the 1940s and '50s, genre sf became better known outside its immediate small circle of devotees, it began to feed back more often and more directly into mainstream writing, and the traffic was by no means one-way. Huxley and Stapledon probably had a stronger influence on genre sf than any mainstream writer since Wells. However, the dominant mainstream sf themes continued to be Dystopian (see George ORWELL), and tales of the HOLOCAUST AND AFTER (see Pat FRANK). The number of mainstream writers whose works qualify, sometimes rather marginally, as sf continued to increase. A brief selection includes C.S. LEWIS, Neil GUNN, L.P. HARTLEY, Laurence DURRELL, Evelyn WAUGH, Vladimir NABOKOV, Mackinlay KANTOR, John HERSEY, Nicholas MONSARRAT, Herman WOUK, Nevil SHUTE, Gore VIDAL, Robert ARDREY, Nigel BALCHIN, John Cowper POWYS, Herbert BEST, Dino BUZZATI, Italo CALVINO, Paul GALLICO, Romain GARY, Arthur HAILEY, Jacquetta HAWKES, Storm JAMESON, Arthur KOESTLER, LIN YUTANG, Adrian MITCHELL, Alan SILLITOE, Angus WILSON, Kingsley AMIS, Jorge Luis BORGES, William BURROUGHS, Howard FAST, William GOLDING, Robert GRAVES, Walker PERCY, Naomi MITCHISON and Doris LESSING.

In the 1960s and '70s the cross-traffic between genre sf and the mainstream became so intense that there is not a great deal of point, any more, in making the distinction. Many writers such as J.G. BALLARD, Michael MOORCOCK and Kurt VONNEGUT Jr won a mainstream readership well outside the usual genre readership, and a large number of mainstream writers, especially writers of FABULATIONS and ABSURDIST works, such as Angela CARTER, Thomas PYNCHON and John BARTH, made an increasing use of images from the sf iconography. Genre sf itself came to take on many of the qualities of mainstream fiction; literary experiment being one, and a jettisoning of the hard-bitten, PULP-style narrative tone being another; genre sf, indeed, has lost its homogeneity, which augurs well for

its future health, even though it may no more be so readily identifiable as a separate genre. Genre boundaries are to some extent breaking down; a notable number of thriller writers, for example, including Ira LEVIN, John D. MACDONALD, Michael CRICHTON, Evan HUNTER and Ernest TIDYMAN have worked occasionally in sf.

Although the main developments in sf have taken place within the genre, any account of its history which neglects both the importance and the number of its mainstream exponents (as most histories to date have done) is incomplete. Almost half the author entries in this volume refer to writers who have tackled sf themes from outside the genre.

One marginal sf theme whose main development has been outside the genre is PSYCHOLOGY, under which heading the relation between mainstream and genre sf is further discussed.

A theme anthology collecting sf stories by mainstream writers is *The Light Fantastic* (anth. **1971**) ed. Harry HARRISON and Theodore J. Gordon. [PN] **See also:** DEFINITIONS OF SF; PROTO SF.

MAITLAND, EDWARD (? – ?). 19th-century British author and theosophist, whose speculative UTOPIA *By and By* (**1873**, in three vols) was praised by a contemporary reviewer as portraying "the distant future as a living present". The book takes an unusually optimistic view of the likely effects of technology, and attacks marriage as hindering the emancipation of women. There is much talk about moral education. The book is the third part of a trilogy; the first two vols, *The Pilgrim and the Shrine* and *The Higher Law*, were originally published anonymously and are not sf. [PN]

MAJORS, SIMON *See* Gardner F. Fox.

MALAGUTI, UGO *See* ITALY.

MALCOLM, DAN *See* Robert SILVERBERG.

MALCOLM, DONALD (1930–). Scottish writer of fiction and considerable popular science; he began publishing sf with "Lone Voyager" for *Nebula* in 1958; two series of stories, the "Preliminary Exploration Team" tales in *NW* 1957–64 and "The Dream Background" tales in *NW* in 1959 and subsequently in the continuing anthology series, NEW WRITINGS IN SF, 1965–75, have not reached book form; his sf novels, both routine, are *The Unknown Shore* (**1976**) and *The Iron Rain* (**1976**). DM is also a publishing philatelist. [JC]

MALEC, ALEXANDER (1929–). American writer, variously employed, who began publishing sf with "Project Inhumane" for *The Colorado Quarterly* in 1966; *Extrapolasis* (coll. **1967**)

assembles much of his sometimes awkward but frequently sharply pointed work, which is restricted to short stories. [JC]

MALLORY, MARK *See* Mack REYNOLDS.

MALZBERG, BARRY (N.) (1939–). American writer. In the seven years or so

The special MALZBERG issue of *Delap's F & SF Review*, Feb. 1977.

that he was writing sf he was extremely prolific, producing some 20 sf novels and over a hundred short stories. He also wrote numerous non-sf works, including several erotic novels. His early sf appeared under the name K.M. O'Donnell, apparently obtained by combining the initial letters of surnames of Henry KUTTNER and C.L. MOORE with the surname of one of the Kuttner-Moore pseudonyms. His first notable sf sale, for *FSF*, as O'Donnell, was the bitter novelette "Final War" (1968), about an unwilling soldier trapped in a never-ending wargame, although his first appearance in an sf magazine was for *Gal.*, "We're Coming Through the Window" (1967). Books published under the O'Donnell name were the short story collections *Final War and Other Fantasies* (coll. **1969**) and *In the Pocket and Other Science Fiction Stories* (coll. **1971**); the novels *The Empty People* (**1969**) and *Universe Day* (fix-up **1971**); and two satirical farces featuring sf fans and writers in confrontation with aliens, *Dwellers of the Deep* (**1970**) and *Gather in the Hall of the Planets* (**1971**).

The first sf novels to appear under his own name were "commentaries" on the Apollo programme: *The Falling Astronauts* (**1971**), *Revelations* (**1972**) and *Beyond Apollo* (**1972**). The third won the JOHN W. CAMPBELL MEMORIAL AWARD. All three feature astronauts as archetypes of alienated contemporary Man, struggling to make sense of an incomprehensible world and unable to account for their failure. All BM's central characters are caught in such existential traps, and the measure of his versatility is the large number of such situations which he has been able to. model out of sf's vocabulary of ideas, and also out of the mythology of pornography. In his erotic novel *Screen* (**1968**) the protagonist can only obtain sexual satisfaction by projecting himself into fantasies evoked by the cinema, while in *Confessions of Westchester County* (**1971**) a prolific seducer obtains satisfaction not from the sexual act but from the confessions of loneliness and desperation which follow it. The situation of the racetrack punter, unable to win against the odds by any conceivable strategy, becomes the model of alienation in *Overlay* (**1972**), in which aliens take an actual part in the process of frustration, and in the non-sf novel *Underlay* (**1974**). Aliens threaten the Earth, and set absurd tasks to decide its fate, in *The Day of the Burning* (**1974**) and *The Tactics of Conquest* (**1974**). In *Galaxies* (**1975**) the central character is in command of a ship loaded with corpses which falls into a BLACK HOLE. *Scop* (**1976**) is a time-traveller trying desperately to change the history that has created his intolerable world.

Even the situation of the sf writer, struggling to cope with real life and the pressures of the market, becomes in *Herovit's World* (**1973**) a metaphor for general alienation. In this novel, and to a lesser extent in *Galaxies* and the introductions to some of his collections, BM provides a scathing critique of the market forces shaping contemporary sf.

BM's writing is intense, his work often apocalyptic. His critics consider him monotonous and object to the despairing note in his fiction, but he is one of the few writers to have used sf's vocabulary of ideas extensively as psychological symbols and as apparatus in psychological landscapes, dramatizing relationships between mind and environment in a science-fictional "theatre of the absurd".

In 1976 BM announced that he was leaving sf, a field in which he came to feel unhappy. Books published since that time, it is presumed, have been published from already completed manuscripts. [BS]
Other works: *In the Enclosure* (**1973**); *The Men Inside* (**1973**); *Phase IV* (**1973**; the book of the film PHASE IV); *The Destruction of the Temple* (**1974**); *On a Planet Alien* (**1974**); *The Sodom and Gomorrah Business* (**1974**); *Conversations* (**1974**); *Out From Ganymede* (coll. **1974**); *The Gamesman* (**1975**); *Guernica Night* (**1975**); *The Many Worlds of Barry Malzberg* (coll. **1975**); *Down Here in the Dream Quarter* (coll. **1976**); *The Best of Barry Malzberg* (coll. **1976**); *The Last Transaction* (**1977**).
As editor: *Final Stage* (**1975** with Edward FERMAN); *Arena: Sports SF* (**1976** with Edward Ferman); *Graven Images: Three Original Novellas of Science Fiction* (anth. **1977** with Edward Ferman).

About the author: "Insoluble Problems: Barry Malzberg's Career in Science Fiction" by Brian M. STABLEFORD, FOUNDATION 11/12 (March 1977).
See also: ABSURDIST SF; ENTROPY; GAMES AND SPORTS; GREAT AND SMALL; HUMOUR; MEDIA LANDSCAPE; NEW WAVE; PARANOIA AND SCHIZOPHRENIA; PERCEPTION; PSYCHOLOGY; SATIRE; SPACE FLIGHT; WAR.

MAN, EVOLUTION OF *See* ADAM AND EVE, ANTHROPOLOGY and ORIGIN OF MAN.

MAN AND HIS MATE *See* ONE MILLION BC.

MANCHURIAN CANDIDATE, THE Film (1962). MC Productions/United Artists. Directed by John Frankenheimer, starring Frank Sinatra, Laurence Harvey, Janet Leigh, Angela Lansbury, Henry Silva and James Gregory. Screenplay by George Axelrod, based on the novel by Richard CONDON. 126 mins. B/w.

A group of American soldiers captured in Korea are subjected to elaborate brainwashing by the Chinese as part of a plot to have a Chinese agent elected President of the USA. An American officer is programmed to become a killing machine whenever one of the people working for the Chinese, and that includes his own mother, gives the right command. The resulting confusions back in America, both funny and sinister, especially the climax at the Party convention, are choreographed with great panache by Frankenheimer, whose best film this probably is, though it owes much to the wit and intelligence of Axelrod's screenplay. Its ominous reverberations became darker when the President of the USA was actually assassinated a year later. [JB/PN]

MANDEM DER TAENKTE TING (vt **THE MAN WHO THOUGHT LIFE**) Film (1969). Asa Film/Palladium. Directed by Jens Ravn, starring Preben Neergaard, John Price and Lotte Tarp. Screenplay by Henrik Stangerup, based on the novel by Valdemar Holst. 97 mins. B/w.

This Danish fantasy tells of a man who can create objects, animals and even people by sheer force of will. However, anything he brings into existence has only a short life, so he goes to a doctor and asks him to operate on his brain in an attempt to perfect his power. The doctor refuses, so the man creates a duplicate doctor who takes over his original's career and wife, and ultimately performs the necessary operation, which kills his creator. Well designed and photographed, this comedy (its director's first film) makes interesting philosophical points about reality of the kind made familiar to Anglo-American readers by the novels of Philip K. DICK. [JB/PN]

MANDERS, HARRY *See* Philip José FARMER.

MAN FROM ATLANTIS, THE Television series (1977). Solow Productions for NBC TV. Created and produced by Herb Solow, pilot film directed by Lee Katzin, starring Patrick Duffy and Belinda J. Montgomery. Special effects by Tom Fisher. The first four episodes consisting of 90-min. telefilms were followed by a series of 50-min. episodes. Colour.

A green-eyed, web-handed stranger is found washed up on a beach. Though nearly dead, he is revived by an attractive woman scientist who realizes that he is not human and places him in a tank of water. Believed to come from ATLANTIS, he is persuaded to work for the US Navy and the Foundation for Oceanic Research, and is soon off on his first mission, to tackle an overweight villain in his underwater headquarters. Though the settings and special effects were sometimes eye-catching, the general intellectual level of this and subsequent episodes was comic-book. The cancellation of the series was announced at the end of 1977.

A series of novelized spin-offs began with *Man From Atlantis: Sea Kill* (**1977**) and *Man From Atlantis: Death Scouts* (**1977**) by Richard Woodley. [JB]

MAN FROM U.N.C.L.E., THE Television series (1964–8). Arena Productions/MGM for NBC TV. Executive producer: Norman Felton. Producers: Sam Rolfe and Anthony Spinner. Writers on the series included Sam Rolfe, Clyde Ware, Joseph Cavelli, Dean Hargrove, David Victor, Peter Allan Fields, Henry SLESAR, Howard Rodman and Harlan ELLISON. Directors included Don Medford, E. Darrell Hallenbeck, Joseph Sargent, Boris Sagal and Barry Shear. Running time per episode 50 mins. First season b/w, subsequent seasons colour.

This was one of TV's first reactions to the success of the "James Bond" films. Robert Vaughn starred as Napoleon Solo, a member of United Network Command for Law Enforcement. With the assistance of his Russian colleague Ilya Kuryakin, played by David McCallum, he fought to prevent the sinister organization T.H.R.U.S.H. (Technological Hierarchy for the Removal of Undesirables and the Subjugation of Humanity) from taking over the world. Many of the plots revolved round such sf devices as death rays and robots. The style was joky and tongue-in-cheek. The great success of the series catalysed the creation of a sister series, *The Girl from U.N.C.L.E.*, which began in 1966, starring Stefanie Powers; it lasted only one season.

Several feature films were released outside America, consisting of episodes from the series edited together, sometimes with added footage, to make 90-min. films. These included *The Spy with My Face* (1965), *One of Our Spies is Missing*

(1966), *One Spy Too Many* (1966), *The Spy in the Green Hat* (1966), *The Helicopter Spies* (1967), *The Karate Killers* (1967) and *How to Steal the World* (1968).

A series of 23 paperback novelizations from the series began with *The Thousand Coffins Affair* (**1965**) by Michael AVALLONE; no.2 was by Harry Whittington, nos 3 and 22 were by John Oram, nos 4, 6, 8, 13, 15 and 17 by David McDANIEL, nos 5, 19 and 20 by John T. PHILLIFENT, nos 7, 9, 18 and 23 by Peter LESLIE, no.10 was by J. Hunter HOLLY, nos 11 and 12 were by Thomas Stratton, no.14 was by Fredric DAVIES and no.21 was by Joel Bernard. This was the US ACE BOOKS numeration; the British numeration was different, with fewer titles. There was a much briefer series of *Girl from U.N.C.L.E.* novelizations also, by Michael Avallone, Peter Leslie and others.   [JB/PN]

MAN IN THE WHITE SUIT, THE Film (1951). Ealing Studios. Directed by Alexander Mackendrick, starring Alec Guinness, Joan Greenwood, Cecil Parker and Ernest Thesiger. Screenplay by Roger MacDougall, John Dighton and Alexander Mackendrick, based on a play by Roger MacDougall. 97 mins. B/w.

A scientist creates an artificial fibre that neither wears out nor gets dirty. To prove it he makes himself a shining white suit that retains its pristine condition throughout the film. Attempts by clothing manufacturers and their workers are made to suppress the new material. Finally its inventor is cornered in a street where, suddenly and symbolically, his suit begins to disintegrate and is torn to shreds by the angry mob. However, the film ends with the scientist planning a second attempt. It is a witty and pertinent satire, but its success owes more to the traditions of the Ealing comedy than to sf.   [JB]

MANN, JACK *See* E. Charles VIVIAN.

MANNES, MARYA (1904–). American author, feature editor and journalist. Her sf novel, *They* (**1968**), satirizes the young; the USA is taken over by the under-30s. *Message from a Stranger* (**1948**) is fantasy.   [JC/PN]

MANNING, LAURENCE (1899–). Canadian-born writer, resident in the United States from 1920. He is still remembered for his numerous contributions to *Wonder Stories* and *Wonder Stories Quarterly* in the 1930s; he also collaborated on some stories with Fletcher PRATT. His best-known series, all of which appeared in *Wonder Stories*, was the "Man Who Awoke" sequence, five stories later published as *The Man Who Awoke* (1933; fix-up **1975**). Another series is the "Stranger Club" sequence in *Wonder Stories*: "The Call of the Mech-Men" (1933), "Caverns of Horror"

(1934), "Voice of Atlantis" (1934), "The Moth Message" (1934) and "Seeds from Space" (1935). A short series of above-average space stories is made up by "The Voyage of the *Asteroid*" (1932) and "The Wreck of the *Asteroid*" (1932). LM was very much of his time in his PULP style, but had a more wide-ranging imagination than many of his colleagues.   [JC/PN]
See also: AUTOMATION; DYSTOPIAS; FANTASTIC VOYAGES; GENERATION STARSHIPS; IMMORTALITY; LIFE ON OTHER WORLDS; LIVING WORLDS; MARS; SPACESHIPS; SUSPENDED ANIMATION; UTOPIAS.

MANSFIELD, ROGER (ERNEST) (1939–). English programme director in educational television and editor, whose *The Starlit Corridor* (anth. **1967**) assembles a wide range of sf prose and verse with some imagination.   [JC]

MAN THEY COULD NOT HANG, THE Film (1939). Columbia. Directed by Nick Grinde, starring Boris Karloff, Lorna Gray, Robert Wilcox and Roger Pryor, screenplay by Karl Brown, based on a story by Leslie T. White and George W. Sayre. 72 mins. B/w.

A scientist steals a mechanical-heart invention from a student, whom he kills. He is caught and sentenced to death in the electric chair but arranges to be revived with the artificial heart. He then lures the judge, jury and witnesses at his trial to a booby-trapped house where he proceeds to dispose of them one by one, but his daughter intervenes and is accidentally killed by one of the lethal devices. He revives her at the cost of his own life. As with most sf films of the period, the story has little to do with real science; and is in fact a Gothic melodrama of retribution.   [JB]

MANTLEY, JOHN (TRUMAN) (1920–). Canadian writer and actor.

His sf novel, *The Twenty-Seventh Day* (**1956**), features Galactic Federation aliens who give five humans from opposing countries each an invincible weapon, to see what they do with them; it was soon filmed, as THE 27TH DAY.   [JC]

MANVELL, ROGER (1909–). English writer, mostly on film and also on aspects of the Second World War, with a doctorate in English literature; his sf novel, *The Dreamers* (**1958**), is a tale of revenge via a dream transmitted to the intended victim by vengeful African tribesmen; a borderline sf explanation is allowed as an alternative to the occult.   [JC]

MAN WHO FELL TO EARTH, THE Film (1976). British Lion/A Cinema V Release. Directed by Nicolas Roeg, starring David Bowie, Rip Torn, Candy Clark and Buck Henry. Screenplay by Paul Mayersberg, based on the novel by Walter TEVIS. 140 mins (cut to 117). Colour.

Tevis's evocative novel, about an alien who comes to Earth in order to use its resources to build a spacecraft large enough to save most of the inhabitants of his dying world, was turned into a self-indulgent film, alternating between pretentiousness and brilliance. The clear-cut narrative of the book is replaced with a non-linear structure that oscillates in time in a manner familiar from Roeg's other films. The motive for the alien's visit is deliberately left hazy; characters and incidents are added, including some embarrassing sequences set on the alien's home planet where his wife and children can be seen tottering about the sand dunes. The central performance by David Bowie as the frail and ethereal alien whose contact with the harsh world of humanity ultimately dooms him is excellent, as is the sensitivity with which

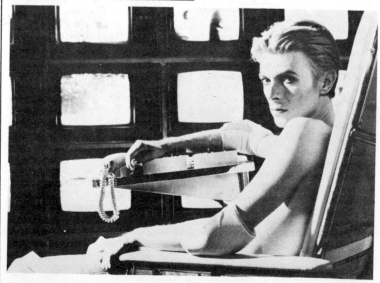

David Bowie as the alien in THE MAN WHO FELL TO EARTH, here succumbing passively to TV voyeurism.

his gradual corruption is observed, as he moves from a vulnerable innocence to a kind of sodden, muted hysteria.

Roeg was formerly a highly praised cameraman, and the film is visually strong, but as cinema and sf it is at best a flawed masterpiece, in part through the rather literary complexity of its allusions (many to Brueghel's painting of the fall of Icarus) and the symbolic portentousness of its visual juxtapositions.

Only British audiences have seen the complete version; 23 mins were cut for the film's American release.   [JB/PN]

MAN WHO THOUGHT LIFE, THE
See MANDEM DER TAENKTE TING.

MAN WHO WAS WARNED, THE
See Harold BEGBIE.

MAN WITH THE X-RAY EYES, THE (vt "X" — THE MAN WITH THE X-RAY EYES) Film (1963). Alta Vista/AIP. Directed by Roger CORMAN, starring Ray Milland, Dina Van Der Vlis, John Hoyt and Don Rickles. Screenplay by Robert Dillon and Ray Russell, based on a story by Ray Russell. 88 mins. Colour.

A surgeon, Dr Xavier, uses drugs to develop X-ray vision and thus operate better, but the process affects his mind. He accidentally kills a colleague and is forced to hide in a carnival sideshow where he is then exploited by its owner as a faith healer. When an attempt to use his power at the Las Vegas gaming tables arouses suspicion, he flees into the desert where he encounters an evangelist, holding a religious meeting, who cries: "If thine eye offend thee, pluck it out!"; the surgeon does just that. A better than average Corman film, though the script does not explore all the possibilities of the theme. The special effects are ingenious, but not quite up to showing Dr Xavier's ability to "see through the centre of the universe".   [JB/PN]

MARAS, KARL *See* Kenneth BULMER.

MARGROFF, ROBERT E(RVIEN) (1930–). American writer who published his first story, "Monster Tracks", for *If* in 1964, but who is generally associated with Piers ANTHONY for their joint novels, *The Ring* (1968) and *The E.S.P. Worm* (1970).   [JC]
See also: CRIME AND PUNISHMENT; PSYCHOLOGY.

MARGULIES, LEO (1900–75). American publisher and editor, born in Brooklyn and educated at Columbia University. He joined the MUNSEY chain of PULP MAGAZINES in 1932, later moving to Beacon magazines, where he became editorial director of THRILLING WONDER STORIES when they began publishing that title in 1936. He had overall responsibility for the entire output of the chain; this later included the magazines CAPTAIN

FUTURE, STARTLING STORIES and STRANGE STORIES. One of the editors who worked with him on these magazines was Oscar J. FRIEND, and the two later collaborated on three anthologies: *From Off This World* (anth. **1949**), a thematic collection about ALIENS, *My Best Science Fiction Story* (anth. **1949**; paperback edition includes 12 stories out of 25) and *The Giant Anthology of Science Fiction* (anth. **1954**). After the War LM formed a publishing company, and returned to sf as publisher of FANTASTIC UNIVERSE, of which he was also editorial director for a time. He left that company and formed another, which published SATELLITE SCIENCE FICTION. He edited various other anthologies, including *Three Times Infinity* (anth. **1958**), *Three From Out There* (anth. **1959**), *Get Out of My Sky* (anth. **1960**), *The Ghoul Keepers* (anth. **1961**), *The Unexpected* (anth. **1961**), *Three in One* (anth. **1963**), *Weird Tales* (anth. **1964**) and *Worlds of Weird* (anth. **1965**).   [MJE]

MARINER, SCOTT Pseudonym used by Cyril KORNBLUTH and Frederik POHL in collaboration on the story "Old Neptunian Custom" (1942).

MARKHAM, ROBERT *See* Kingsley AMIS.

MARKS, WINSTON K(ITCHENER) (? –). American writer of sf short stories. He began with "Mad Hatter" for *Unknown* in 1940, but then, after publishing a story in *ASF* in 1941, was not heard of again until 1953 when he published "The Water Eater" in *Gal.* He was quite prolific until about 1959; his style was mildly hard-bitten and amusing. Several of his stories have been anthologized.   [PN/JC]

MARLOW, LOUIS Pseudonym of British writer and lecturer in English studies Louis Umfreville Wilkinson (1881–1966), who also wrote novels under his real name. Of sf interest is *The Devil in Crystal* (**1944**) which, in LM's typically pert, dandiacal, somewhat over-eager manner, describes the effects of a sort of self-possession: the protagonist finds himself cast 20 years into his own past, where he relives his own life, all the while conscious of his observer status.   [JC]

MARLOWE, STEPHEN *See* Milton LESSER.

MARLOWE, WEBB *See* J. Francis McCOMAS.

MARNER, ROBERT *See* Algis BUDRYS.

MAROONED Film (1969). Columbia. Directed by John Sturges, starring Gregory Peck, Gene Hackman, David Janssen, Richard Crenna, James Franciscus and Nancy Kovack.

Screenplay by Mayo Simon. 134 mins. Colour.

John Sturges is best known for Westerns (e.g. *The Magnificent Seven*) and in the opinion of some critics outer space is a less suitable setting for his work. The film is a quasi-documentary about the rescue of three astronauts trapped in orbit around the Earth. Opinions were divided on whether the suspense, built up very slowly, was potent or merely monotonous. The dialogue is even more banal than the real NASA chat. The special effects were low-keyed and accurate, but not visually memorable, and the most impressive sequence in the film was the one that contained genuine shots of an actual Saturn rocket-launching. Sturges received some praise at the time for eschewing the more baroque forms of melodrama, but the film suffered through being released at much the same time as the more dramatic and powerful space film, 2001: A SPACE ODYSSEY.   [JB/PN]

MARS Mars, which seemed for a long time to be the most likely abode for life outside the Earth, has for that reason always been of cardinal importance in sf. Its surface, unlike that of VENUS, exhibits markings visible (albeit unclearly) with the aid of optical telescopes, and has a distinct red colour. Blue-green tracts interrupting the red were once thought to be oceans but were later construed as vegetation. The polar caps, seen to wax and wane with the seasons, were generally held to be snow and ice which melted periodically. In 1877 Schiaparelli reported an intricate network of *canali* (channels), which were interpreted as canals. Percival Lowell wrote a popular book, *Mars* (**1896**), in which he built up an image of a cool, arid world with great red deserts and a few areas of arable land, but perfectly capable of sustaining life. In 1905 he published photographs which he believed to offer proof of the existence of the canals. The landing of the Mariner probes in 1976, however, revealed that Mars is extremely cold and has virtually no atmosphere, and though there really are gigantic channels possibly caused by floods of water the intricate network reported by Schiaparelli does not exist, and nor do the tracts of "vegetation". It now seems unlikely in the extreme that life might exist there, and it is clear that the myth of Mars created and developed in sf was governed almost entirely by a series of illusions.

Mars was visited by the usual interplanetary tourists: Athanasius KIRCHER, Emanuel SWEDENBORG, W.S. LACH-SZYRMA, George GRIFFITH *et al.* (*see* MERCURY *and* VENUS), but it became singularly important in the late 19th century as the major target for specific cosmic voyages (the MOON, of course, was already known to be lifeless). It is the home of an advanced civilization in Percy GREG's *Across the Zodiac* (**1880**) and the scene of the hero's defence of the peaceful Grensumin against the attack of a more aggressive race in *Mr. Stranger's Sealed Packet* (1889) by Hugh MacColl. Robert Cromie's *A Plunge into Space* (1890) is an interplanetary love story and Gustavus W. Pope's *A Journey to Mars* (1894) is similar, though longer and more detailed in its description of the red planet. Kurd Lasswitz's Two Planets (1897; trans. abridged 1971) provides another elaborate description of an advanced civilization and is the first novel to make much of the politics of interplanetary relations.

H.G. Wells published a brief vision of Mars in "The Crystal Egg" (1897), and followed it up with the archetypal alien invasion story, *The War of the Worlds* (1898), which was to cast a long shadow over the sf of the 20th century. Wells's Martians, attempting to escape their due fate on a waterless, dying world, come as predatory Darwinian competitors to claim Earth from the human race. This novel firmly implanted in the popular imagination the image of the Martian as monster, and brought a new sensationalism into interplanetary fiction. When Orson Welles's Mercury Theatre dramatized the novel for radio in 1938 it precipitated a panic whose seeds had been sown 40 years before and fed since by a stream of pulp fiction in which Mars was the abode not only of life but of ugly and hostile life. Against the power of Wells's imagery Garrett P. Serviss's "sequel" *Edison's Conquest of Mars* (1898; 1947), which reassuringly describes the obliteration of the decadent Martian civilization, could make no impact. Nor was there much opposition in Louis Pope Gratacap's *The Certainty of a Future Life on Mars* (1903). In fact, the only other image which did take hold was something much closer to Lowell's enthusiastic prospectus for exotic Martian life and landscape. This alternative image of Mars and its Martians first appeared in Edwin Lester Arnold's *Lt. Gullivar Jones — His Vacation* (1905; vt *Gulliver of Mars*), but was permanently enshrined in modern mythology by the much imitated "Martian" novels of Edgar Rice Burroughs — a series begun with *A Princess of Mars* (1912; 1917) and extending over 30 years to the final novelette "Skeleton Men of Jupiter" (1943). Here John Carter and his kin battle for beautiful, egg-laying princesses against assorted villains and monsters, armed only with swords and yet borne aloft by flying gondolas. Burroughs was co-opted into genre sf when Hugo Gernsback asked him to write *The Mastermind of Mars* (1928) for the 1927 Amazing Stories Annual, and his influence there has been as powerful as that of Wells. His principal imitator, Otis Adelbert Kline, began by setting his works on Venus, but eventually started a "Martian" series with *The Swordsman of Mars* (1933; 1960).

The early sf pulps were resonant with echoes of *The War of the Worlds*. The first issue of Amazing Stories reprinted Austin Hall's "The Man Who Saved the Earth" (1923) and another early example is Edmond Hamilton's "Monsters of Mars" (1931). It was not long, however, before a reaction against the cruel logic of Wells's classic was manifest. P. Schuyler Miller's "The Forgotten Man of Space" (1933) features gentle Martians reminiscent of MacColl's Grensumin, and Raymond Z. Gallun's "Old Faithful" (1934) is practically an ideological reply to Wells. Other writers attempted to take a more straightforward hypothetical approach to the depiction of life on Mars — notably Laurence Manning in "The Wreck of the *Asteroid*" (1932–3) and Stanley G. Weinbaum in "A Martian Odyssey" (1934). The latter story made a considerable impact because of the ingenuity of its bizarre aliens. Other notable Martian stories from the 1930s include Clark Ashton Smith's "The Vaults of Yoh-Vombis" (1932), C.L. Moore's "Shambleau" (1933), P. Schuyler Miller's "The Titan" (first part only 1936; 1952) and Clifford D. Simak's "The Hermit of Mars" (1939). Outside the sf pulps one work stands out from all others as a contribution to the mythology of Mars — C.S. Lewis's *Out of the Silent Planet* (1938). This remarkable fantasy, in which Mars is a world whose life system is organized according to Christian ethical principles rather than the logic of Darwinian natural selection, remains unique. The scene in which the villain Weston pits his theories of Social Darwinism against the moral philosophy of the Martian guiding spirit, the Oyarsa, remains the archetypal confrontation between the scientific and religious imaginations.

The advent of John W. Campbell Jr as editor of *ASF*, with his insistence on more careful speculative logic, suppressed the "traditional" image of Mars in the pulps' primary sf market. Its exotic qualities were played down and replaced by a "realism" captured precisely by P. Schuyler Miller's "The Cave" (1944) — an ironic story in which Martian life forms kill an Earthman who violates the truce which they all must observe in order to survive the long Martian night. But the exotica flourished nevertheless, primarily through the activities of two writers. One, Leigh Brackett, made her début in *ASF* with "Martian Quest" (1940) but went on to do the bulk of her work for Planet Stories, Startling Stories and Thrilling Wonder Stories. She produced an especially lush version of the red planet and its decadent cultures, already dying but facing the extra threat of plundering Earthmen and their lust for wealth. Her major Martian stories were: *Shadow over Mars* (1944; 1951; vt *The Nemesis from Terra*); *The Sword of Rhiannon* (1949 as "Sea-Kings of Mars"; 1953); *The Secret of Sinharat* (1949 as

"Queen of the Martian Catacombs"; 1964); *The People of the Talisman* (1950 as "Black Amazon of Mars"; rev. 1964); and "The Last Days of Shandakor" (1952). The same pulps that published Brackett's work also provided the first refuge for Ray Bradbury, who brought the traditional image of Mars to a kind of impressionistic perfection in *The Martian Chronicles* (1946–50; fix-up 1950; UK version *The Silver Locusts* differs slightly in contents). In these stories decadent Mars is replaced by a Mars which is dead but still haunted by the ghosts of an extinct civilization, and which is visited by Earthmen who become doubly haunted because of the echoes of their own Earthly past which follow them. The stories are heavy with nostalgia and an extraordinarily seductive atmosphere of alienness. A few other writers have had some success in capturing the same atmosphere, notably Clifford Simak in "Seven Came Back" (1950) and J.G. Ballard in "The Time-Tombs" (1963), but the mythology of *The Martian Chronicles* remains a special creation.

In the 1950s the romance of exotic Mars was rapidly left behind as the dominant theme became the problems of colonization of a planet with barely enough water and barely enough oxygen. The most notable stories in this new vein were *Sands of Mars* (1951) by Arthur C. Clarke, *Outpost Mars* (1952; vt *Sin in Space*) by Cyril Judd, "Crucifixus Etiam" (1953) by Walter M. Miller, *Alien Dust* (fix-up 1955) by E.C. Tubb and *Police Your Planet* (1956 as by Erik van Lhin; rev. 1975) by Lester del Rey. Juvenile novels on the same theme were *Red Planet* (1949) by Robert A. Heinlein and a series begun with *Mission to Mars* (1955) by Patrick Moore. Developments of the same "realistic" approach include a number of Martian robinsonades, including Lester del Rey's *Marooned on Mars* (1952), Rex Gordon's *No Man Friday* (1956; vt *First on Mars*) and James Blish's *Welcome to Mars* (1967). The most impressive product of this type of approach is a fine novel in which Mars becomes a prison colony: *Farewell Earth's Bliss* (1966) by D.G. Compton. Other memorable stories from this period include Theodore Sturgeon's poignant vignette about a dying astronaut, "The Man Who Lost the Sea" (1959), and Philip José Farmer's exploration of the possibilities of alien sexuality "Open to Me, My Sister" (1960; vt "My Sister's Brother").

The mythology of Mars moved into a new phase in the early 1960s as the scenarios of the '50s began to appear in a somewhat surrealized form. Heinlein's *Stranger in a Strange Land* (1961) features a human raised by Martians who returns to Earth to build a religious philosophy out of the elements of their cultural heritage. Roger Zelazny's "A Rose for Ecclesiastes" (1963) works the same theme in reverse, introducing to a

Brackettesque Mars a poet who becomes a preacher and leads the decadent Martians to a cultural revival. Philip K. DICK, in *Martian Time-Slip* (**1964**) and *The Three Stigmata of Palmer Eldritch* (**1964**), uses the colony scenario as background for reality-shifting plots. The arid, depleted environment is ideal for Dick's psychological landscaping. A more elaborate but equally enigmatic fantasy is Algis BUDRYS's *The Amsirs and the Iron Thorn* (**1967**; vt *The Iron Thorn*). Throughout the decade the real possibility that Mars might harbour life was waning, and this shows in the fiction – most particularly in a remarkable award-winning novel *The Earth is Near* (**1970**; trans. **1974**) by Ludek PESEK, in which members of the first Martian expedition, driven by the myth, undertake an obsessive search for life in an environment which simply cannot sustain it.

In the 1970s the whole speculative concept of life on Mars was drastically rethought. Lin CARTER wrote two pastiches of Leigh Brackett — *The Man Who Loved Mars* (**1973**) and *The Valley Where Time Stood Still* (**1974**) — but by this time the nostalgia seemed fake, and Brackett herself had moved on to new worlds beyond the Solar System. Christopher PRIEST went all the way back to Wells in his pastiche, *The Space Machine* (**1975**), but this too seemed remote from both past and present. The fascination of Mars, however, remains. No matter how desperate the measures which might be needed in order to sustain its viability as a potential home for life, sf writers are still willing to take them. This is demonstrated — in rather different ways — by Frederik POHL's *Man Plus* (**1976**) and John VARLEY's "In the Hall of the Martian Kings" (**1977**). In the former story a man undergoes extreme biological engineering to adapt him for life on the new Mars, while in the latter it is Mars itself which adapts to sustain stranded astronauts in the most ambitious of the Martian robinsonades. In *The Martian Inca* (**1976**) Ian WATSON designs an extremely strange life system for Mars, which proves to have astonishing effects in interaction with humans. These most recent stories testify not only to the power, but also to the adaptability of the mythology of Mars. Within that mythology have been written some of the most fascinating and most enduring of sf's literary products, but it seems that it has now run its course. There is little more to say now that Mars stands revealed for what it really is. We know now that the Mars of sf — in all its guises — has been nothing more than a dream; but the stuff that dreams are made of can linger a long time in the memory. [BS]

MARSHALL, ARCHIBALD (1866–1934). British writer. He was quite a prolific novelist; his sf SATIRE *Upsidonia* (**1915**) amusingly puts a young man into a PARALLEL WORLD, somehow linked with

ours, where all values, in particular ECONOMIC ones, suffer a reversal; many comic points are lightly adduced. [JC]
Other works: *Simple People* (**1928**).

MARSHALL, EDISON (TESLA) (1894–1968). American writer and big-game hunter, best known for his work outside the sf field, especially his many historical novels. He began publishing sf with "Who is Charles Avison?" (1916); *Ogden's Strange Story* (1928 *Popular Magazine*; **1934**) is sf, in which Ogden recollects his life in the Stone Age in another body; *Dian of the Lost Land* (**1935**; vt *The Lost Land*) is a romantically told LOST-RACE tale. *Earth Giant* (**1960**) is about Hercules. [JC/PN]
Other works: Primarily adventure, with some fantastic elements: *The Death Bell* (**1924**); *Sam Campbell, Gentleman* (**1934**); *The Stolen God* (**1936**); *Darzee, Girl of India* (**1937**); *The White Brigand* (**1937**); *The Jewel of Mahabar* (**1938**).

MARSTEN, RICHARD See Evan HUNTER.

MARTENS, PAUL See Neil BELL.

MÅRTENSSON, BERTIL (1945–). Swedish writer. Active in fandom since 1961, he started selling short fiction in 1964. His first novel, *Detta är verkligheten* ["This is Reality"] (**1968**) is a moody story on the relationship of dreams to reality; later novels, *Samarkand 5617* (**1976**) being his most important, confirm a preoccupation with philosophical and emotional rather than scientific motifs. BM is probably the most widely acclaimed specialized Swedish sf writer. [J-HH]

MARTIN, DAVID S. (? –). British writer whose sf novel is *No Lack of Space* (**1967**). [JC]

MARTIN, GEORGE R.R. (1948–). American writer with a master's degree in journalism from Northwestern University; by profession a college instructor in journalism. GRRM published his first story, "The Hero" (1971), in *Galaxy*, but it was with his stories in *ASF* that he initially made his reputation; they include "With Morning Comes Mistfall" (1971), "A Song for Lya" (1974) and "The Storms of Windhaven" (1975), the latter in collaboration with Lisa TUTTLE. These stories all have colourful, imaginative settings, distant in space and time; they are romantic, sometimes bordering on sentimentality, but they are more carefully judged in their literary effects than is usual in the adventurous galactic romance. GRRM's work is in some ways reminiscent of Poul ANDERSON's better stories. His first novel, *Dying of the Light* (**1977**), demonstrates most of his virtues. Its setting, a drifting planet which, passing close by a sun, has briefly been

the site of a vast galactic festival, is richly imagined. It imports much of the traditional apparatus of galactic adventure — feudalism, duelling, slavery, codes of honour — but uses them in an examination of the conflicts which arise when a rigid set of beliefs meets a situation demanding flexibility. Its narrative is fast moving and vividly exciting. Its weakness lies fundamentally in the secondhand nature of its plot elements, its strength in the assurance with which it uses them.

Most of GRRM's stories have a notionally common background, but this is not clearly enough developed to form them into a coherent series. Separate from these are his stories "Override" (1973), "Meathouse Man" (1976) and "Nobody Leaves New Pittsburgh" (1976), which all develop the concept of corpse labour — cadavers artificially powered to provide a slave workforce. A further, short, separate series, "Star Ring", is made up of "The Second Kind of Loneliness" (1972) and "Nor the Many-Colored Fires of a Star Ring" (1976). "A Song for Lya", a novella in which a girl with PSI POWERS becomes a convert to an ALIEN RELIGION whose members achieve telepathic unity through absorption into the body of a giant PARASITE, won a HUGO award, and was featured in GRRM's first book, *A Song For Lya* (coll. **1976**). A further collection of his stories is *Songs of Stars and Shadows* (coll. **1977**), and he has edited *New Voices in Science Fiction* (anth. **1977**; vt *New Voices 1: The Campbell Award Nominees*). GRRM has established himself, before his 30th birthday, as one of the leading new sf writers. [MJE]

MARTIN, PETER Writing name of Peter Martin Leckie (1890–), in whose sf novel, *Summer in 3,000: Not a Prophecy — A Parable* (**1946**), a progressive World Island state is contrasted with a conservative America. [JC]

MARTIN, WEBBER See Robert SILVERBERG.

MARTINSON, HARRY (EDMUND) (1904–78). Swedish author and poet, member of the Swedish Academy, Nobel Prize laureate. A prolific writer, HM's one contribution to sf is *Aniara* (**1956**; trans. Hugh MacDiarmid and E. Harley Schubert **1963**), a 103-canto epic poem eloquently defending humane values against the inhumanity of technology within the story of the irreversible voyage of a giant spaceship towards outer space. An opera (1959) based on the poem, composed by Karl-Birger Blomdahl, has achieved international success. [J-HH]
See also: GENERATION STARSHIPS.

MARTYN, WYNDHAM (? –). British thriller writer who, like many such, occasionally incorporated sf themes. In particular his *Stones Of Enchantment* (**1948**) details the discovery of a LOST WORLD possessing the secret of longevity.   [JE]

MARVEL COMICS Originally Timely Comics, then Atlas Comics. *Marvel*

The Fantastic Four, one of the most celebrated MARVEL COMICS, briefly announced itself · as a "Pop Art Production" in the trendy 1960s.

Comics was originally the title of only one of this group's many publications; no.1 was published in Nov. 1939; it featured the Human Torch, drawn by Carl Burgos, and Sub-Mariner, drawn by William Blake Everett. Both these characters proved popular, and both were given their own comic books. Another early success was *Captain America*, drawn by Jack KIRBY, its first issue being in Apr. 1941; Kirby was to become one of the giants of comic-strip illustration. Another early employee was Stan LEE, from 1942.

While the Marvel Comics group was

This cover by James Steranko shows one of the MARVEL COMICS titles most valued by collectors.

of some importance to the history of sf in comic-strip form because it was among the early pioneers of the super-hero (*see also* SUPERMAN *and* CAPTAIN MARVEL), whose strange powers were normally given an sf rationale of some sort, it was not until 1961 that Stan Lee introduced *The Fantastic Four*, and with it a concept of human fallibility in the superhero which was to dominate SF COMICS from that time on. Marvel Comics titles from the early 1960s, despite being comparatively recent, are among the most prized items of comic-book collectors. (*For further details of MC titles, see* Jack KIRBY, Stan LEE *and* James STERANKO.)   [PN]

MARVELL, ANDREW Pseudonym of English writer Howell Davies (? –), whose brief career under this name saw three effective novels published. *Minimum Man: or, Time to be Gone* (**1938**) combines sf and thriller ingredients in its depiction of a Fascist coup in England in 1950 and of its overthrow by a new race of tiny but very powerful telepathic people whose parthenogenetic births were caused by poison gas; *Three Men Make a World* (**1939**) is a kind of DISASTER story, though the petroleum-destroying bacteria that make Britain into a rural land in its pages may strike later readers as a mixed curse indeed; *Congratulate the Devil* (**1939**), in which a happiness drug is found to be intolerable to society at large, describes the process by which its disseminators are hounded to death. AM's novels are professional and engrossing.   [JC]

Aug. 1951. Cover by Hannes Bok.

MARVEL SCIENCE FICTION *See* MARVEL SCIENCE STORIES.

MARVEL SCIENCE STORIES US PULP magazine. Nine issues, 1938–41; six further issues, 1950–52, published by Postal Publications (first two issues), then by Western Fiction Publishing Co. for the remainder of its first incarnation, finally by Stadium Publishing Co., ed. Robert O.

The confusing nomenclature of sf magazines is demonstrated by this Dec. 1939 issue of *Marvel Tales*, which is actually a variant title of MARVEL SCIENCE STORIES, and not to be confused with the 1934 MARVEL TALES.

Erisman.

An sf pulp magazine from a chain which included such fringe titles as UNCANNY TALES, *MSS* was the first of the many new sf magazines of the late 1930s and early 1940s. It was notorious for the mildly erotic approach of its early issues, to which Henry KUTTNER contributed several stories, including "The Time Trap" (Nov. 1938). The Feb. 1939 issue featured Jack WILLIAMSON's *After World's End* (**1961**). After five issues the title changed to *Marvel Tales* in Dec. 1939, and for two issues the magazine leaned more heavily towards sex and sadism. The title then changed again, in Nov. 1940, to *Marvel Stories*, and it returned to straightforward sf. Although initially successful enough to generate a companion, DYNAMIC SCIENCE STORIES, *MSS*, which began as a quarterly, became less and less frequent through 1939 and 1940, ceasing with the Mar. 1941 issue. It was revived in Nov. 1950 under its original title. It switched to DIGEST size after two issues, appeared three times in that format, and reverted to PULP size for its final issue. It became *Marvel Science Fiction* for its last three issues. Daniel KEYES was an assistant editor for some of these later numbers, which were generally unmemorable.   [MJE]
Collectors should note: Vol.1 had six numbers, Vol.2 had three, and Vol.3 had six, of which the first five were quarterly, with a six-month gap before the final issue. The second series of *MSS* was also published in a British reprint edition 1951–2.

MARVEL STORIES *See* MARVEL SCIENCE STORIES.

MARVEL TALES US magazine (the first three issues small-DIGEST-size, the fourth digest-size and the last BEDSHEET-size). Five issues, May 1934-Summer

First issue, 1934. The tag "binding deluxe" appears to be a joke.

1935. Published by Fantasy Publishers; ed. William L. CRAWFORD. *MT* was a semi-professional magazine; Crawford was not only the publisher, but also set the type himself. Some issues were distributed with several different covers. Distribution was very limited; *MT* was never generally available.

MT published fiction by Robert E. HOWARD, H.P. LOVECRAFT, Clifford D. SIMAK and others, including Robert BLOCH's first story. The Winter 1935 issue commenced serialization of P. Schuyler MILLER's short novel "The

Titan" finally published as the title novella of Miller's *The Titan* (coll. **1952**), but the magazine ceased publication before it was completed. An even shorter-lived companion title was UNUSUAL STORIES.

Marvel Tales was also a briefly used variant title, for only two issues, of the later PULP magazine MARVEL SCIENCE STORIES.   [MJE]

MASK OF FU MANCHU, THE Film (1932). MGM. Directed by Charles Brabin and Charles Vidor, starring Boris Karloff, Lewis Stone, Karen Morley, Jean Hersholt and Myrna Loy. Screenplay by Irene Kuhn, Edgar Allen Woolf and John Willard, based on the novel by Sax ROHMER. 72 mins (cut to 67). B/w.

Rohmer's oriental super-villain has been brought to the screen many times but this visually lavish version, produced by Irving Thalberg, is probably the most memorable. Boris Karloff lisps his way enjoyably through the role of Fu Manchu, torturing and murdering with glee, with the assistance of his equally evil daughter (played by Myrna Loy). Fu Manchu searches for Genghis Khan's death mask and sword which he intends to use as symbols to arouse the oriental races in a war against the white nations. In a spectacular climax Fu's electrical death-ray machine goes out of control and destroys him and most of his followers. The marvellously stylized sets were designed by Cedric Gibbons and the electrical effects were created by Ken Strickfaden.   [JB]

MASON, DAVID (1924–74). American writer who began publishing with "Placebo" for *Infinity* in 1955. Most of his novels are routine SWORD AND SORCERY, such as his first, *Kavin's World* (**1969**) and its sequel, *The Return of Kavin* (**1972**), but his final book, *The Deep Gods* (**1973**), is somewhat more impressive.   [JC]
Other works: *Devil's Food* (**1969**); *The Sorcerer's Skull* (**1970**); *The Shores of Tomorrow* (**1971**).

MASON, DOUGLAS R(ANKINE) (1918–). English writer and headmaster of a junior school, prolific since he began publishing in 1964, both under his own name and as John Rankine. His first story was "Two's Company" for E.J. CARNELL's *New Writings in SF 1* (anth. **1964**) as Rankine. Beginning with *The Blockage of Sinitron* (**1966**) as Rankine, he was soon releasing two or three books a year, generally routine SPACE OPERA and other adventures, though occasionally under his own name, as with *From Carthage Then I Came* (**1966**; vt *Eight Against Utopia* USA) and *Matrix* (**1970**), he would attempt somewhat more ambitious novels, with some social comment. Generally speaking, however, DRM has been content to produce rather low-pressure work.

The "Dag Fletcher" space operas, as by Rankine, *Interstellar Two-Five* (**1966**), *One is One* (**1968**), *The Plantos Affair* (**1971**), *The Ring of Garamas* (**1972**) and *The Bromius Phenomenon* (**1973**), are set in the same galaxy as several other Rankine books, including *The Fingalnan Conspiracy* (**1973**) and *The Thorburn Enterprise* (**1977**).   [JC]
Other works: As DRM: *Landfall is a State of Mind* (**1968**); *Ring of Violence* (**1968**); *The Tower of Rizwan* (**1968**); *The Janus Syndrome* (**1969**); *Dilation Effect* (**1971**); *Horizon Alpha* (**1971**); *Satellite 54-Zero* (**1971**); *The Resurrection of Roger Diment* (**1972**); *The End Bringers* (**1973**); *The Phaeton Condition* (**1973**); *Pitman's Progress* (**1976**); *Euphor Unfree* (**1977**). As by John Rankine: *Moons of Triopus* (**1968**); *Never the Same Door* (**1968**); *Binary Z* (**1969**); *The Weisman Experiment* (**1969**); *Operation Umanaq* (**1973**); novelizations of episodes from the TV series SPACE 1999: *2. Moon Odyssey* (**1975**); *5. Lunar Attack* (**1975**); *6. Astral Quest* (**1975**), *8. Android Planet* (**1976**); *10. Phoenix of Megaron* (**1976**).
See also: CITIES; MATHEMATICS.

MASON, ERNST *See* Frederik POHL.

MASON, GREGORY Collaborative pseudonym of American writers Doris Meek (? –) and Adrienne Jones (?), whose sf DYSTOPIA, *The Golden Archer* (**1956**), depicts a 1975 America

The blend of sf and Gothic in THE MASK OF FU MANCHU can be clearly seen in the paraphernalia surrounding Boris Karloff in this evocative publicity still.

suffering under regimented, McCarthy-like bigotry. [JC]

MASON, TALLY See August W. DERLETH.

MASSIE, DOUGLAS (? –). English writer, whose sf/fantasy novel *Mr. Ciggers Goes to Heaven* (**1931**) details Mr Ciggers' posthumous experiences in that not altogether UTOPIAN place, to satirical effect. [JC]

MASSON, DAVID I. (1915–). Scottish writer, long resident in England, with an MA in English language and literature, now a rare books librarian. He began publishing sf with "Traveller's Rest" for *NW* in 1965; along with this extraordinarily intense study in the distortion of PERCEPTION, all of his fiction was assembled in *The Caltraps of Time* (coll. **1968**), which single volume has established his strong reputation as a writer of vigorously experimental, vivid, often scientifically sound stories. Notable among them, and reflecting his close and informed interest in LINGUISTICS, are "Not so Certain" (1967) and the brilliant TIME-TRAVEL story "A Two-Timer" (1966), told entirely in language appropriate to 1683, the year from which the inadvertent time traveller is whisked into the future. Each of DIM's stories seems to be a solution to some cognitive or creative problem or challenge, and he has seemed little inclined to repeat any of his effects. He has published almost no fiction since 1968, though "Doctor Fausta" in George HAY's *Stopwatch* (anth. **1974**), is an interesting satire. DIM has also reviewed sf fairly frequently during the 1970s in FOUNDATION. [JC]
See also: FOURTH DIMENSION (AND OTHERS); MATHEMATICS.

MASTER OF THE WORLD Film (1961). AIP. Directed by William Witney, starring Vincent Price, Charles Bronson, Henry Hull and Mary Webster. Screenplay by Richard MATHESON. 104 mins. Colour.

Though based on the novel *Clipper of the Clouds* (vt *Robur the Conqueror*; **1886**) and its sequel *Master of the World* (**1904**) by Jules VERNE, *MOTW* owes more to the Walt Disney version of 20,000 LEAGUES UNDER THE SEA in terms of plot and theme than to Verne, the major difference being that the action takes place in the air instead of under the sea. Robur, a mad genius, has built a flying machine, with which he attempts to force the world to outlaw war. He launches a campaign of terror, bombarding cities, ships and armies, but before he can achieve his aims his airship is sabotaged by an American secret agent and crashes into the sea.

Matheson's script is adequate, but the film as a whole is undermined by an obvious lack of money. Library footage is used in the scenes showing the effects of

Robur's bombardments and some of it is wildly anachronistic. For instance, a supposedly aerial shot of 1860s London is actually footage from Olivier's *Henry V*. The special effects by Ray Mercer, Tim Barr, Wah Chang and Gene Warren are mediocre, but the model of the airship itself is suitably elaborate. [JB]

MASTERS, JOHN (1914–). Indian-born English writer of many novels set in British India. *The Himalayan Concerto* (**1976**) is set along the India-China-Pakistan border in 1979, and offers a NEAR-FUTURE scenario in which the Chinese prove villainous. [JC]

MASTIN, JOHN (1865– ?). British writer and scientist, author of three sf novels. *The Stolen Planet* (**1905**) features the picaresque adventures of two Earthmen through the Solar System and beyond; its sequel, *Through the Sun in an Airship* (**1909**), again takes the two young men on an exciting tour in which undiscovered planets are explored. *The Immortal Light* (**1907**) is a LOST-WORLDS novel set in the Antarctic where an underground, Latin-speaking race abides. Through his various FANTASTIC VOYAGES, JM tried, like Jules VERNE before him, to exploit the romance of science in stories with an attractive patina of verisimilitude. [JC]
See also: RELIGION; SPACESHIPS; SUN.

MATHEMATICS The imaginations of pure mathematicians have provided sf writers with some prominent items in their common stock of concepts. The notions of a FOURTH DIMENSION, and others taken from geometry and topology, have the essential qualities of strangeness and mystery, making them an enjoyable struggle for the untrained intuition to accept, which combined with the respectability of their academic pedigree helps to persuade the reader that the struggle is worth while and to enhance his feeling of wonder.

In discussing the use of mathematical ideas in sf, the boundary between sf and fantasy must be drawn according to somewhat different principles from those used in the case of the natural sciences. Since many mathematical ideas derive their piquancy from the fact that they are definitely incompatible with the world we live in, a story illustrating such an idea cannot claim any credence as a record of possible events, but must be classed as a fantasy. Yet an important consideration in judging a story of this type will be its fidelity to mathematical truth, in which respect it belongs to the part of sf at the furthest remove from fantasy, consisting of those stories which turn on a point of established science.

In the field of geometry these points are illustrated by the prototype of all stories using the idea of a space other than three dimensions, E.A. ABBOTT's *Flatland* (**1884**), originally published under the

pseudonym "A Square". Written in a period when there was great interest among mathematicians in n-dimensional geometry, this fantasy offers an indirect approach to the problems of understanding four-dimensional space by examining the difficulties two-dimensional beings would have in understanding three-dimensional space — an explanatory device which was to become a standard feature of sf invoking a fourth dimension. With sentient lines, triangles and polygons for its inhabitants, the only three-dimensional character being a sphere, *Flatland* makes no pretence of being related to the real world (though this does not prevent its author, the headmaster of the City of London School, from displaying the most appalling sexism and class prejudice). The book has been made into a short animated film of the same title with narration by Peter Cook.

Among the many stories using fourth and other dimensions, two deserve mention here for their emphasis on particular mathematical points. H.G. WELLS's "The Plattner Story" (1896) turns on the fact that a three-dimensional object, if rotated through half a turn in a fourth dimension, becomes its mirror image (in the story this happens to Gottfried Plattner, who afterwards finds that his heart is on his right-hand side). The reception of this point by literary readers amusingly illustrates how, if science can lend credibility to sf, sf removes credibility from science: one critic (Allan Rodway, in *Science and Modern Writing*, **1964**) told his readers that this was "neither scientific nor mathematical". In fact it is excellent mathematics.

In " — And He Built a Crooked House — " (1940) Robert A. HEINLEIN describes a house of eight cubical rooms which fit together like the eight three-dimensional "faces" of a four-dimensional cube. The story ostensibly takes place in the real world, but Heinlein's main concern is not to persuade the reader that his house is physically possible but to show him something which is mathematically possible though apparently paradoxical. He is therefore careful to be mathematically correct in describing the structure of his house, while emphasizing its startling features. His one slip, as it happens, offends against both requirements; the mathematical truth is even stranger than he realizes.

Other writers have set stories in frankly imaginary worlds for the sake of unusual topological structures of space, but few have been so careful to define the structure as Heinlein. It is common for the topological oddity to be revealed only at the end of the story in order to make a shock ending, as in David I. MASSON's "Traveller's Rest" (1965) (though this is only one factor in a subtle and complex story in which the structures of time and language undergo variation related to that of the structure of space), and Arthur C. CLARKE'S "Wall of Darkness' (1949), which uses a similar idea. Topology is also likely to be abused as a catch-all explanation for any weird happening: in "A Subway Named Möbius" (1950) by A.J. Deutsch, for example, it is supposed that a subway network has become so complex that trains mysteriously disappear and reappear. This is held to be sufficiently explained by the use of Möbius's name in the title; the relevance of Möbius strips to subway tunnels is not made clear.

The attitude to topology displayed in "A Subway Named Möbius" is similar to the numerology of such stories as "Six Cubed Plus One" (1966) by John Rankine (Douglas R. MASON), in which magical properties are attributed to special numbers. (A sardonic comment on this attitude to mathematics was made by L. Sprague DE CAMP and Fletcher PRATT in The Incomplete Enchanter, 1942, in which an equation in mathematical logic is used as a magic talisman.)

Transfinite arithmetic shares with topology the appeal of the unfamiliar and the smack of paradox, and infinity has its own sensational connotations. For these reasons transfinite numbers are often called upon to establish an atmosphere of mathematical mysticism, but few authors have found it possible to do more than mention them. They appealed to the intellectual Gothicism of James BLISH, who in "FYI" (1953) seized on the fact that they do not and cannot count material objects and contemplated the universe being reconstructed to accommodate them.

The two other areas of mathematics which have provided material for sf stories are statistics and logic. The concepts of statistics and probability theory are easy to misunderstand, and such misunderstanding has been demonstrated in many sf stories; also, being abstractions which can masquerade as concrete instances, they are easy to ridicule, and this can be seen in Russell Maloney's "Inflexible Logic" (1940), which shows us monkeys typing famous works of literature, and William TENN's "Null-P" (1951), in which an exactly average man is discovered. A rather more serious point about statistics was made by Robert M. Coates in "The Law" (1947), which describes the "Law of Averages" breaking down and so prompts consideration of why human beings in large numbers normally do behave in predictable ways.

The perennial fascination of logical paradoxes was exploited by Gordon R. DICKSON in "The Monkey Wrench" (1951). This story uses the paradox of Epimenides the Cretan ("this statement is false") to deflate a computer engineer's pride in the perfection of his machine, thus giving a reassuring reminder of the insufficiency of logic. An opposite effect

was achieved by Frederik POHL in a number of stories, notably "The Schematic Man" (1968), which describes a man coding himself as a computer programme, and so raises the question of what makes the real world more than a mathematical model.

Mathematics whose point is not primarily mathematical can also appear in sf; the use of an occasional mathematical formula is seen by some sf writers, as it is by some scientists, as conferring intellectual respectability. A rare example of a genuine mathematical argument occurs in a footnote to Fred HOYLE'S The Black Cloud (1957). It is a nice calculation, and has probably added to the enjoyment of a number of readers of the book. Hoyle has also given a mathematical explanation of an sf speculation in the preface to Fifth Planet (1963).

Examples of popular exposition of mathematical ideas in sf are the explanation of the calculus of variations in David DUNCAN's Occam's Razor (1957) and that of coordinate systems and relativity in Miles J. BREUER's "The Gostak and the Doshes" (1930). Both authors proceed to tell stories which have only tenuous connections with the mathematical ideas they have expounded.

Mathematicians as characters in sf are usually stereotyped as absent-minded, ineffectual and unworldly, though the mathematical genius Libby in Robert Heinlein's "Misfit" (1939) proves resourceful; they are clearly descended from the inhabitants of Jonathan SWIFT's Laputa in Gulliver's Travels (1726). Sf is popular among mathematicians, however, and it is not surprising that there should have been some attempts to adjust this image. This can be seen particularly in the stories of Norman KAGAN, whose portrayals of zany, hyperactive maths students may be rather closer to reality but sometimes appear self-congratulatory. Kagan's stories make witty use of many parts of mathematics; although they are ostensibly concerned with sf speculations — in "Four Brands of Impossible" (1964) the use of a different logic to describe the world, in "The Mathenauts" (1964) a journey into various mathematical spaces — they are really about the experience of doing mathematics. The same topic was treated more earnestly by Bob Parkinson in "Solipsist" (1967). A particularly interesting mathematician is the elderly protagonist of "Euclid Alone" (1975) by William F. Orr, himself a mathematician. The story can be found in Orbit 16 (anth. 1975) ed. Damon KNIGHT. In it, a student successfully proves one of Euclid's axioms to be wrong. His teacher is left with the moral quandary of whether or not to suppress the discovery, which may, ultimately, destroy the serenity of everyone in the world.

Mathematical games occasionally make an appearance in sf, as in Ox (1976)

by Piers ANTHONY (see GAMES AND SPORTS). The mathematics of computer programming has played a surprisingly small role in sf, though it is central to Magic Squares (1977) by Paul Calter, a mathematics professor. This is a strange book in which a burlesque mad-scientist-takes-over-the-computers-of-the-world story is interspersed with bona fide problems in programming theory and practice.

Two anthologies of mathematical sf, both ed. Clifton Fadiman, are Fantasia Mathematica (anth. 1958) and The Mathematical Magpie (anth. 1962). Also relevant is Science Fiction Adventures in Dimension (anth. 1953) ed. Groff CONKLIN. [TSu]

See also: PERCEPTION.

MATHESON, RICHARD (BURTON) (1926–   ). American writer of stories, novels and film scripts, initially thought of as primarily an sf writer, but more and more identified as one of the better creators of fantasy, in both fiction and film, of recent years. He began publishing sf with the famous "Born of Man and Woman" for FSF in 1950, which he had regarded as a simple horror story, but on finding it praised as sf he decided to cash in on what was then the sf boom. He included most of his best early work in Born of Man and Woman (coll. 1954; vt Third from the Sun, omitting four stories). The title story tells in affecting pidgin English of a terrifying MUTANT child and its break towards a kind of freedom; the element of horror fantasy nearly overrides the perfunctory sf basis for the story, a tendency also to be found in his first sf novel, I Am Legend (1954). (He had by this time moved from New York to California and had three mystery novels published.) I Am Legend is a post-HOLOCAUST story in which only one man remains unaffected by a virus which induces vampirism; RM was not responsible for either film version of this novel (see THE LAST MAN ON EARTH and THE OMEGA MAN). He did, however, adapt The Shrinking Man (1956), his second sf novel, as THE INCREDIBLE SHRINKING MAN; indeed he sold it to Universal only on condition that he could write the screenplay, thus giving him an entry into the film business. It also uses an sf component to shape the horror story of a man who, after exposure to radiation and insecticide, begins to shrink inexorably, eventually to disappear. The success of the film allowed RM to continue writing for the screen, his next major commission being to write for the TV series THE TWILIGHT ZONE in 1959. In 1960 he wrote the screenplay for the first of Roger CORMAN's adaptations of horror stories by Edgar Allan POE, The Fall of the House of Usher, and since that time has scripted a number of fantasy/horror films, sometimes in collaboration with Charles BEAUMONT, for Corman and other directors. His TV work included several scripts for STAR TREK, and later NIGHT GALLERY. He also scripted a number of made-for-TV feature films, by far the best being DUEL (1971), which was given theatrical release in the UK. Others have been *The Night Stalker* (1972) (*see* KOLCHAK: THE NIGHT STALKER), *The Night Strangler* (1973), *Dying Room Only* (1973), *Scream of the Wolf* (1974) and THE STRANGER WITHIN (1974). Of his feature film scripts, that for MASTER OF THE WORLD (1961) is the most obviously science-fictional. His own psychological-cum-supernatural melodrama *Hell House* (1971) was filmed as *The Legend of Hell House* (1973), with his own screenplay. Here, too, there are borderline sf elements. RM's entire career has cross-fertilized sf with horror.

Further volumes of stories with some sf interest are *The Shores of Space* (coll. 1957) and *Shock! Thirteen Tales to Thrill and Terrify* (coll. 1961), though the latter volume's two sequels, *Shock II* (coll. 1964) and *Shock III* (coll. 1966) are primarily assemblages of fantasy stories. More recently, a fantasy, *Bid Time Return* (1975), once again powerfully utilizes devices from sf (TIME TRAVEL in this case) in a story whose emotional satisfactions are not dependent on a successful sf resolution of any problems that arise. Though RM cannot (in 1977) be considered any longer an sf writer, his influence as one of the "liberators" of magazine sf in the early 1950s keeps his name vividly to mind.

The dominant theme in RM's work has always been PARANOIA, whether imagined in GOTHIC or sf terms. In *Duel* a truck inexplicably attacks a car; in *Dying Room Only* a woman's husband disappears in a motel toilet but no one will believe her; the pregnancy in *The Stranger Within* did not result from infidelity, but that is not the way it seems to the woman's sterile husband. *I Am Legend* (one man against a world of white-faced vampires) is, in its obsessive images of persecution, perhaps the very peak of all paranoid sf.   [JC/JB]
Other works: *A Stir of Echoes* (1958); *Shock Waves* (coll. 1970).
See also: BIOLOGY; CHILDREN IN SF; DISASTER; END OF THE WORLD; GREAT AND SMALL; HUMOUR; MEDICINE; MONSTERS; RELIGION; ROBOTS; SUPERNATURAL CREATURES.

MATTER TRANSMISSION The matter transmitter is one of several sf devices which, though purporting to have a technological explanation, have the effect of being a pseudo-scientific analogue of various PSI POWERS, in this instance TELEPORTATION. Both processes involve the instantaneous (or nearly so) transfer of a person or object from one place to another without apparent traverse of the intervening space. For the purposes of this article teleportation is defined as such transportation achieved by mental power, although the term is frequently used in contexts where the actual process is matter transmission, the mechanical accomplishment of such a journey. This confusion of terminology is evident in Larry NIVEN's article "The Theory and Practice of Teleportation" (1969), which is primarily concerned with matter transmission, and is otherwise a useful and thorough introduction to the various problems and paradoxes raised by this branch of IMAGINARY SCIENCE.

The earliest use of the matter transmitter in sf is probably the horrific "The Man Without a Body" (1877) by Edward Page MITCHELL, in which a cat is successfully transmitted by wire, but the electric battery fails at the point where the scientist has transmitted only his own head. Matter transmission is used for interplanetary travel in *To Venus in Five Seconds* by Fred. T. JANE. Early PULP examples are "The Secret of Electrical Transmission" (1922) by Clement FEZANDIE, "The Moon Menace" (1927) by Edmond HAMILTON and "Cosmic Express" (1930) by Jack WILLIAMSON.

As the last example suggests, matter transmission is primarily used in sf simply as a convenient TRANSPORTATION device, especially for overcoming the problems of travelling interstellar distances. The basic system is that the transmitter somehow "records" every detail of a human (or alien or object), conveys the information to the receiver (or simply to another point, in systems where no receiver is required), where the body then reappears. Sometimes this involves the physical disintegration of the original body — as in *The Enemy Stars* (1959) by Poul ANDERSON, where the transmitter is used to alternate the crew on an exploring starship — but more often this aspect is glossed over. In Joe HALDEMAN's *Mindbridge* (1976), the transmitter requires no receiver but its use is circumscribed by a "sling-shot" effect which automatically returns any object transmitted to its point of departure after a fixed duration. Matter transmitters are an aid to colonization of an alien world in Joseph L. GREEN's *The Loafers of Refuge* (fix-up 1965), and are essential to the alien intrigues of Lloyd BIGGLE's *All the Colors of Darkness* (1963); these are typical cosmetic uses of the device. In Clifford D. SIMAK's *Way Station* (1963) there is a galaxy-wide network of matter transmitters of restricted range, like a railway system; the story's protagonist is the superintendent of the hidden station on Earth. All these examples suppose that matter transmission will work over interstellar distances. One interesting artefact developed from this notion is the House in *Today We Choose Faces* (1973) by Roger ZELAZNY: a single, huge building whose various wings are actually on different worlds, joined together by matter transmitters.

Larry Niven has himself written a number of stories based on the assumption of a matter transmitter which will revolutionize transport on Earth but will not work over interplanetary distances, and is one of the few authors to try to speculate on how the existence of such devices might transform society. "Flash Crowd" (1973) suggests, for example, that crowds would instantly gather at any newsworthy venue, presenting obvious problems, particularly for the police; the consequences are explored further in "The Alibi Machine" (1973), "All The Bridges Rusting" (1973), "A Kind of Murder" (1974) and "The Last Days of the Permanent Floating Riot Club" (1974). In the opening chapter of *Ringworld* (1970), Niven describes how the existence of matter transmitters irons out differences between cities (as the existence of airports already does, to a limited extent), so that although it is possible to travel anywhere instantaneously there is no point in doing so, because everywhere is the same. An absurd but logical method of space travel using short-range matter transmission suggested in Niven's article is used humorously in Bob SHAW's *Who Goes Here?* (1977): a spaceship with a matter transmitter at the rear and a receiver at the front which repeatedly transmits itself forward through itself. Other authors to have examined seriously the implications of matter transmission include John BRUNNER in *Web of Everywhere* (1974) and Harry HARRISON in *One Step From Earth* (coll. of linked stories 1970).

The recording of a signal which is then decoded by a receiver does not necessarily, in theory, involve the dissolution of the body being recorded. A matter transmitter can therefore be a matter duplicator. (There are many sf stories about matter duplicators which are not matter transmitters but presumably might be if a transmitted signal were substituted for the circuitry linking their two halves.) This idea provides the mechanism in Algis BUDRYS's *Rogue Moon* (1960) whereby the protagonist, having travelled by matter transmitter to the Moon, is able repeatedly to explore and be killed by a mysterious alien structure, while his other body on Earth, to which he is telepathically linked, learns from his successive deaths. An elegant variant is Thomas M. DISCH's *Echo Round His Bones* (1969), in which a matter transmitter leaves behind an "echo" of anything which passes through it, undetectable and intangible in the "real" world but actual enough to other echoes. These stories address, indirectly, a problem which most matter-transmission tales gloss over: identity. If the physical body ceases to exist at one point, can the exact duplicate which appears at the other end of the journey be proven to be the same individual, or is it just an identical copy?

Matter transmitters are familiar devices through their use in films and TV series. THE FLY and its sequels examine, in fairly simplistic terms, the possibility of the signal's becoming scrambled, with horrifying consequences: when a fly is caught in the transmitter with the experimenting scientist the latter emerges with the fly's head and leg and vice versa (both of them emerge with human brains, oddly enough). In STAR TREK matter transmission (without a receiver being necessary) is used to transfer the crew of the USS *Enterprise* from orbit to a planetary surface (by "beaming down") and back, thus enabling the show to carry on without long pauses in the action. The creators of the 1978 British TV series *Blake's Seven* evidently thought this idea so firmly established with the audience that they adopted it without feeling any explanation was needed. [MJE]

MATTES, ARTHUR S. (1901–). American writer whose sf novel is *Soul Mates* (**1963**). [JC]

MATURIN, CHARLES R(OBERT) (1782–1824). Irish novelist, playwright and clergyman, the son of French Protestants in exile, who wrote several GOTHIC romances and sensational plays with intermittent success before the publication of his definitive terror-romance, *Melmoth the Wanderer* (**1820**), the eponymous hero of which, who is reminiscent of figures from the Wandering Jew to Faust, has sold his soul to the Devil in return for IMMORTALITY. Haunted and desperate, he tries to find a person to accept his curse. The novel itself is made up of a series of complexly linked stories concerning people in various extremities to whom Melmoth appears as tempter; but all refuse him, regardless of the perils under which they labour, and after a century or so Melmoth returns to Ireland where he disappears over the edge of a cliff. Honoré de BALZAC wrote a sequel, *Melmoth Reconciled* (**1835**). The Penguin edition of CRM's novel, edited and introduced by Alethea Hayter (1977), is convenient and scholarly. [JC]
Other works: *The Albigenses* (**1824**).

MAUROIS, ANDRÉ Pseudonym of prolific French novelist and man of letters Émile Herzog (1885–1967), resident in the USA during the Second World War. He was best known for his romantic biographies and other non-fiction, though even his first work, "La dernière histoire du monde" ["The Final History of the World"] (1903 as by Emile Herzog), was sf; later included in *Premiers contes* ["First Stories"] (coll. **1935** as by AM), it was the first of his several future HISTORIES, the most interesting of them being *Le chapitre suivant* (**1927**; trans. as *The Next Chapter: The War Against the Moon* **1928**), which describes a war against the ostensibly uninhabited Moon concocted by the newspapers to provide bored mankind with an external enemy; but unfortunately the Moon is indeed occupied, and retaliates. This fragment

was collected in *Deux fragments d'une histoire universelle 1992* (coll. **1928**) with "Chapitre CXVIII: La vie des hommes", which latter piece reappeared in English as the second of the two title stories of *The Weigher of Souls and The Earth Dwellers* (coll. **1963**); it deals with inhabitants of Uranus who fail to understand the supposedly inferior inhabitants of Earth. Another fragment of the future history appeared in the collection *Relativisme* (coll. **1930**; trans. as *A Private Universe* **1932**).

An interesting ALTERNATE-WORLDS essay by AM is "If Louis XVI Had Had an Atom of Firmness", written for J.C. Squire's collection *If: or History Rewritten* (anth. **1931**).

AM also wrote more conventional sf narratives; *Voyage aux pays des Articoles* (**1927**; trans. by David GARNETT as *A Voyage to the Island of the Articoles* **1928**) carries a man and woman to an ISLAND in whose UTOPIAN society the dominant Articole caste is made up of artists who provide the other castes with their *raisons d'être*; the tale is ironic. In *Le peseur d'âmes* (**1931**; trans. as *The Weigher of Souls* **1931**), a doctor discovers that the *élan vital* is a gas which escapes the body at death; his attempts to mingle in posthumous harmony with his wife are frustrated, however; this short novel reappeared in *The Weigher of Souls and The Earth Dwellers*. The sf device in *La machine à lire les pensées* (**1937**; trans. as *The Thought-Reading Machine* **1938**) is a "camera" capable of registering thoughts on photographic film. Though amiability tends to soften the bite of his morality-like tales, and his reputation has faded, AM's work is nicely representative of the idiomatic ease with which sf ideas have been used in this century by MAINSTREAM writers, especially in England and on the Continent, as vehicles for the conveyance of SATIRICAL material. [JC/PN]
Other works: *Patapoufs et filifers* (**1930**; trans. as *Fatapouts and Thinifers* **1940**; vt *Fattypuffs and Thinifers*), a juvenile illustrated by Jean Bruller (VERCORS); *Nouveaux discours du Docteur O'Grady* (coll. **1950**; trans. as *The Return of Dr. O'Grady* **1951**); *Illusions* (**1968**), a speculative essay.
See also: ARTS; ESCHATOLOGY; MACHINES; RELIGION.

MAVITY, HUBERT See Nelson S. BOND.

MAXWELL, EDWARD Pseudonymous author of the sf novel *Quest for Pajaro* (**1957**), in which TIME TRAVEL to the future is used to alter present events: an unusual twist for this type of story. [JC]

MAYA British FANZINE (1970–) ed. from Newcastle Ian Williams (1970), Ian Maule (1972), and Rob Jackson (1975). Under the editorship of Jackson, a doctor, *Maya* has become one of Britain's leading sf fanzines, attractively produced and

containing a variety of material on sf and FANDOM. Contributors have included Bob SHAW, Brian ALDISS, Peter WESTON, Christopher PRIEST and Leroy Kettle. *Maya* won the Nova award for best British fanzine in 1975 and 1976, the international Fan Activity Achievement award in 1977, and was nominated for a HUGO in 1978. [PR]

MAYAKOVSKY, VLADIMIR (VLADIMIROVICH) (1893–1930). Russian poet and playwright, a revolutionary from early years, a Futurist poet whose verse radically shocked post-Revolution Russia. Of particular sf interest is his first, fully fledged prose SATIRICAL play, *Klop* (**1928**; trans. as *The Bedbug* **1960**), in which a Soviet bureaucrat is kept in a ZOO some generations hence as a curious example; *Banya* ["The Bath House"] (**1930**) is set in contemporary Russia, but employs a similar array of satirical tools. These two plays were sufficiently sharp in their criticism of the blandness of Soviet Russian ideas to bring a good deal of official criticism down on VM's head. [JC]
See also: POLITICS: RUSSIA; THEATRE.

MAYNE, WILLIAM See CHILDREN'S SF.

MAYUMURA, TAKU See JAPAN.

MEAD, HAROLD (1910–). British writer of two sf novels, the first of which, *The Bright Phoenix* (**1955**), is the better known, being a sombrely told post-HOLOCAUST tale in which the re-established but over-regimented human society tries unsuccessfully to reinhabit abandoned parts of the Earth; it ends a little sentimentally with a Second Coming. His second novel, *Mary's Country* (**1957**), tells of the quest of a group of children, most of whose social peers have been killed by plague, for a perfect society. [JC]

MEAD, SHEPHERD Variant of his name used by American writer and Swiss resident Edward Mead (1914–), active in various genres. Most of his work combines SATIRE and comedy, including his sf and fantasy novels *The Magnificent MacInnes* (**1949**; vt *The Sex Machine*), in which the consumer society is satirized in a story of an electronic device that can predict personal preferences, *The Big Ball of Wax* (**1954**) and *The Carefully Considered Rape of the World* (**1966**), in which ALIENS artificially inseminate Earth females. The middle novel is of greatest interest: Madison Avenue techniques are applied to corrupt a device that permits people to enter vicariously into the lives of others, a technique whose potential for good is subverted into a kind of feelie.

SM worked in advertising before turning to writing, and his experience was also put to good use in his best-known work (not sf), *How to Succeed in Business Without Really Trying* (**1952**),

for the staged version of which he shared a Pulitzer Prize and a Tony.   [JC/PN]
See also: LEISURE; MEDIA LANDSCAPE; SATIRE.

MEDIA LANDSCAPE The technology of COMMUNICATIONS has long been part of the subject matter of sf. From Hugo GERNSBACK's *Ralph 124C 41 +* (1911–12 *Modern Electrics*; **1925**) onwards, PULP sf was full of references to super-efficient means of communication. Such speculations built on the social experience of writers and readers (Gernsback was himself an early radio enthusiast), for the media were proliferating throughout the first half of the century: slick magazines, the telephone, sound recording, the cinema, television. Sf extrapolated from these realities, predicting video-telephones, communications satellites, holograms, personalized computers, etc. But the emphasis was on the devices themselves; these inventions were merely a part of the marvellous gadgetry of sf, and there was little speculation about their effects on society and the individual. The extent to which communications technology (and foreseeable future extensions of it) was replacing the natural world with a "media landscape" was scarcely noticed until the 1950s. The phrase was coined to denote a world dominated by the images of advertising and the popular arts (among which sf images, especially the iconography of movies and magazine covers, loomed large) and it was initially used to describe the obsessions of Pop artists and media critics such as Eduardo Paolozzi, Andy Warhol, Marshall McLuhan and Rayner Banham.

However, the reality was there before the name, and sf had reflected it in various ways. The idea that the media can be used to manipulate people had long been extant. In George ORWELL's

Nineteen Eighty-Four (**1949**) this theme takes a directly political form: the media are represented not only by the ubiquitous posters of "Big Brother", but also by the "telescreens" which act as two-way channels for propaganda and surveillance. Political use of the media in this sort of way has featured frequently in sf – for example, in Ray BRADBURY's *Fahrenheit 451* (**1953**), Kurt VONNEGUT's "Harrison Bergeron" (1961) and Philip K. DICK's *The Penultimate Truth* (**1964**). More often, sf has portrayed future societies controlled by the media in more oblique ways. McLuhan's *The Mechanical Bride* (**1951**), a book about the psychological subtleties of advertising, contains a passing tribute to Fritz LEIBER, whose "The Girl With the Hungry Eyes" (1949) is about exploitation of the female image by ad-men. Advertising became a major theme in sf in the 1950s. Leiber returned to it in *The Green Millennium* (**1953**), set in a future when the walls of private apartments are lined with ads. Frederik POHL and C.M. KORNBLUTH's *The Space Merchants* (**1953**) is a more extended satire on the all-powerful ad-men. Other stories about advertising include Pohl's "The Tunnel Under the World" (1954), Shepherd MEAD's *The Big Ball of Wax* (**1954**), J.G. BALLARD's "The Subliminal Man" (1963) and (in part) Dick's *The Simulacra* (**1964**). Daniel F. GALOUYE's *Simulacron-3* (**1964**; vt *Counterfeit World* UK) is about a society which turns out to be a computer simulation for market research; many of Ron GOULART's stories satirize advertising techniques.

Manipulation to the extent that one suspects one's whole reality is a fiction (*see* PARANOIA) can give rise to a belief in "the new demonology" – the idea that the artificial landscape has alien inhabitants with evil powers. Literal treatments of "demons" taking over the

media include "Ether Breather" (1939) by Theodore STURGEON and "The Waveries" (1945) by Fredric BROWN, both stories about creatures which inhabit the air-waves, tampering with Man's communications. The writer who takes the new demonology most seriously is William S. BURROUGHS, who, in *The Ticket That Exploded* (**1962**; rev. 1967) and *Nova Express* (**1964**), shows the human race at the mercy of "the Nova Mob" and other alien parasites who use the media (and drugs) as their means of control. Burroughs asserts that life is "a biologic film", and the purpose of his writing is to help us break out of the "stale movie" into the "grey room" of silence. This is not entirely different from the wishful conservatism of Brown's "The Waveries", in which America abandons electricity and reverts to a rural economy. Barrington J. BAYLEY's "An Overload" (1973) is about computer-generated demons who adopt the personae of gangster-movie stars.

Not all media-men are demons, however, and some stories deal with those who attempt to use their power to good effect. Norman SPINRAD's *Bug Jack Barron* (**1969**) concerns the compère of a phone-in chat-show in the 1980s who finds himself in a position to challenge the political and industrial powers that be. Most of the action actually takes place "on the air", before an audience of millions, making this a novel set almost entirely *within* the media landscape. Spinrad returns to this area in several of the stories in *No Direction Home* (coll. **1975**). Several of Philip K. Dick's novels deal with media-men, such as *Dr. Bloodmoney; or How We Got Along After the Bomb* (**1965**), in which a post-nuclear-HOLOCAUST world is held together by a disc-jockey's broadcasts from an orbital satellite, and *Flow my Tears, the Policeman Said* (**1974**), in which a famous TV personality is thrust into a world where nobody recognizes him. Algis BUDRYS's *Michaelmas* (**1977**) concerns a roving newsman who, through a secret computer link-up, is in fact the benevolent dictator of the world. A point which Budrys makes by presenting us with this extreme situation is that the news-media do not merely report events: they actually influence them to an enormous extent.

It is all too easy for the media landscape to pander to human weaknesses. One of the ways in which the media create news is by invading the privacy of individuals in order to gratify the curiosity of others. D.G. COMPTON's *The Continuous Katherine Mortenhoe* (**1974**; vt *The Unsleeping Eye* USA) is about a TV-man with "camera eyes" who follows a dying woman in order to record her last indignities for the entertainment of a mass audience. Many other stories deal with pornography, violence and vicarious suffering, for example, Arthur C. CLARKE's "I

Traffic between sf and the MEDIA LANDSCAPE runs both ways, as in this ingenious 1974 advertising photo-collage, suggesting a Moonscape. © Nordfoto.

Remember Babylon" (1960); Robert SILVERBERG's "The Pain Peddlers" (1963) and *Thorns* (1967); Robert SHECKLEY's "The Prize of Peril" (1958), Dan MORGAN's *The Richest Corpse in Show Business* (1966); and Brian STABLEFORD's *The Mind-Riders* (1976). A particularly gruesome example is Christopher PRIEST's "The Head and the Hand" (1972), in which a TV entertainer has his limbs amputated and climaxes his "act" with his decapitation. Anything is grist to the media mill, from violence to TIME TRAVEL. By recreating the styles of the past in a thousand soap-operas, the media landscape presents all human experience in a spurious simultaneity. McLuhan's "global village" extends through time as well as space, and this has been dramatized in sf stories in which the media literally invade the past in search of material. Isaac ASIMOV's "The Dead Past" (1956) concerns a woman obsessed with watching her dead child on the "chronoscope"; Harry HARRISON's *The Technicolor Time Machine* (1967) is a humorous treatment of a film crew's adventures in history, and J.G. Ballard's "The Greatest Television Show on Earth" (1972) is a satire on the TV companies' attempts to film such events as the parting of the Red Sea "live". These sf exaggerations point up the extent to which the media have brought about *la société du spectacle*.

In such stories as Ballard's "The Subliminal Man" (1963), in which vast hoardings are erected alongside motorways to flash subliminal messages into drivers' brains, even the unconscious is annexed by the media landscape. Of course, manipulation of unconscious desires has long been recognized as part of advertising. The media speak to the unconscious in a complex language of signs. Semiotics, as applied to popular culture by Roland Barthes in his *Mythologies* (1957; trans. 1972), testifies to this. All Man's creations are, in a sense, media of communication, since they are coded with latent "messages" – particularly such everyday things as architecture, furniture, clothing and vehicles. This is the conceptual territory which J.G. Ballard has made very much his own, particularly in the series of "condensed novels" collected in *The Atrocity Exhibition* (1970; vt *Love and Napalm: Export USA* USA). In these non-linear stories Ballard juxtaposes elements of the media landscape of the 1960s, from the architecture of motorways and multi-storey car-parks to the bodies of Marilyn Monroe and Elizabeth Taylor, from the styling of cars and kitchen gadgets to the televised violence of Vietnam and Kennedy's assassination. He blends these external "facts" with the private memories and fantasies of his characters, and with the neutral language of medical reports and astronomical data. *The Atrocity Exhibition* is a selfconscious book (Ballard

has been much influenced by the Pop artists) but it is the most sustained attempt in sf to deal with the media landscape and its massive influence on all our lives. Later Ballard stories have also dealt with the media, e.g. "The Intensive Care Unit" (1977), which concerns a society in which marriage and family life are conducted entirely by TV: nobody ever meets anyone else in the flesh.

Other sf works which have to some extent been influenced by McLuhan and the ideas about the media which became fashionable in the 1960s include John BRUNNER's *Stand on Zanzibar* (1968); Dean R. KOONTZ's *The Fall of the Dream Machine* (1969); Michael MOORCOCK's "Jerry Cornelius" novels; John T. SLADEK's works, especially *The Muller-Fokker Effect* (1970); Barry MALZBERG's *The Destruction of the Temple* (1974); J.M.G. LE CLÉZIO's *Les Géants* (1973; trans. as *The Giants* 1975). "The Girl Who Was Plugged In" (1973), by James TIPTREE Jr, is a savage story about the creation of a jet-set member of "the beautiful people" for purposes of advertising. In reality the woman is an android with no independent intelligence, controlled through the nervous system of a horribly exploited ugly duckling. The language of the story cleverly reflects the cold trendiness of a society whose cruelties are largely unconscious and affectless.   [DP]

MEDICINE Medicine is one of the few disciplines that demand a correlation of scientific data with almost everything described as "human". Medicine is therefore an enormously popular theme in sf, but there are only a few authors who provide the two elements essential to creating a successful medical sf story: command of the medical knowledge, and a sure sense of historical context. Medical sf that is done well provides a fascinating mirror of medical assumptions at the time the story was written; comparison of medical sf from various periods in the 19th and 20th centuries also shows how much medicine has changed. The present (1977) controversy over GENETIC ENGINEERING, especially research into recombinant DNA, has now brought us back to the explicit fears expressed by Mary SHELLEY's *Frankenstein* (1818), the great-grandfather of medical sf, as it is of so many other sf themes. Just as Goethe had recast the Faustian dream of total knowledge, Mary Shelley took images from university life to delineate the character of Victor Frankenstein, who has become the archetype of the ethical scientist plagued by his thirst for discovery.

Reflections of the developments in medicine during the 19th century appeared in popular fiction; one of the most interesting reflections of the new notions of toxicology is "Rappaccini's Daughter" by Nathaniel Hawthorne (1844), in which the old dream of drug

panaceas backfires — again. Sir Arthur Conan DOYLE in *The Poison Belt* (1913) picked up the theme of medical toxicology from an early 20th-century standpoint: the tale is an intriguing look at the effects of poison gas. Doyle was trained in medicine, and like many authors of his time was fascinated by the implications of the new medicine, which was now armed with anaesthetics and the knowledge of Pasteur's bacteria. The most famous novels and stories of medical sf in the late 19th and early 20th centuries were by H.G. WELLS: *The War of the Worlds* (1898) tells at its end how bacteria conquer the invading Martians, against whom mankind had stood helpless; *The Island of Dr. Moreau* (1896) considers anatomical alteration of the body, and Wells reaches the same conclusion as did Mary Shelley; *The Food of the Gods* (1904) broods over what would happen if Man should discover the chemical principle of growth. Many of Wells's short stories have medical themes, accurately recording knowledge at the time, including "The Stolen Bacillus" (1895); "Under the Knife" (1897) and "A Slip under the Microscope" (1897). Almost all of Wells's earlier writing shows his early training in BIOLOGY.

Wells and his time seem haunted by "progress" in medical and scientific research, and sf neatly records the constant paradox: the dream of improved conditions and the fear of rampant change. The theme appeared early in a quasi-medical manner in Robert Louis STEVENSON's classic *Dr. Jekyll and Mr. Hyde* (1886), in which inner demons plague the good scientist. Such fears were to be expected during a period which had produced the innovative genius of Francis Galton, the revolutionary theories of Charles Darwin (whose *Origin of Species* appeared in 1859), and the brilliant syntheses of embryology, comparative anatomy and paleontology of Thomas Henry Huxley (who became Darwin's champion in 1860 and who directly inspired Wells). Stevenson did not anticipate Freud any more than did Galton. Both, however, instinctively pinpointed the unease which was troubling comfortable European and American assumptions. Both connected the evidence of Man's physiological nature with his less openly investigated non-physical being. Psychiatry took root in well-prepared medical soil, and sf after Freud's various publications from the 1880s to the 1920s began to make use of his theories, though to no marked degree before the 1930s.

Medical themes of countless varieties are very common in sf. Maurice RENARD's *Le docteur Lerne, sous-dieu* (1908; trans. as *New Bodies for Old* 1923) deals with organ transplants, a favourite sf theme. Aldous HUXLEY in *Brave New World* (1932) provides Utopia with contraceptive belts. Walter M. MILLER in

A Canticle for Leibowitz (**1960**), Edgar PANGBORN in *Davy* (**1964**) and John WYNDHAM in *The Chrysalids* (**1955**; vt *Re-Birth* USA) brood on genetic EVOLUTION. Nikolai N. AMOSOV's *Notes from the Future* (**1967**; trans. **1970**) is a brilliant, clipped look at anabiosis. Heinrich Böll, in *18 Stories* (trans. **1966**), has two gems on psychological mixing: "Unexpected Guests" (puzzled by the animals in your daughter's heart?), and "The Seventh Trunk" (are nuns sane?). David H. KELLER's *Life Everlasting and Other Tales* (coll. **1949**) is a fine collection by an MD, the best story being "The Thirty and One". Richard MATHESON's *I Am Legend* (**1954**) is another vampire tale, with an ingenious pseudo-medical basis, that makes *Dracula* look pale. Murray LEINSTER produced some stirring extraterrestrial medicine in his "Medship" series of nine stories, three of which were collected in *Doctor to the Stars* (coll. **1964**) and three in *S.O.S. from Three Worlds* (coll. **1967**). Charles R. HARNESS, in *The Rose* (1953 *Authentic*; **1966**), pits psychiatry and music against bloodless technology. "Caduceus Wild" (a serialized novel in *Original Science Fiction Stories*, Jan.-May 1959) by Ward MOORE and Robert Bradford is a medical DYSTOPIA. An extraordinary if ambiguous medical UTOPIA, on the other hand, is Bernard WOLFE's *Limbo* (**1952**; vt *Limbo 90*), in which a post-World-War-III cult of prosthetic-limbed amputees becomes attracted to an even more Utopian programme of lobotomies for all. Frederik POHL's *Man Plus* (**1976**) is a solid novel about BIONICS and astronauts. J.G. BALLARD's books often mix medicine with disaster: *The Drowned World* (**1962**) features Jurassic jungles, monster mosquitoes, and a doctor as hero; the protagonist of *The Crystal World* (1966) is a leprosy expert. James WHITE's "Sector General" series focuses on extraterrestrial medicine, in *Hospital Station* (**1962**), *Star Surgeon* (**1963**) and *Major Operation* (fix-up **1971**), as does his recent collection *Monsters and Medics* (coll. **1977**). Dr Martin BAX in *Hospital Ship* (**1976**) couples psychiatry with SEX and radiation sickness. Charles PLATT, in *The Power and the Pain* (**1971**), plays rather obscenely with the remoulding of body parts. Lester DEL REY included an early discussion of radiation sickness in *Nerves* (1942 *ASF*; exp. **1956**). Judith MERRIL's "That only a Mother" (1948) packs together mutations, gynaecology and genetics. C.M. KORNBLUTH in "The Little Black Bag" (1950) shows the medical technology of the future with sickening repercussions in the present. Daniel KEYES, in *Flowers for Algernon* (1959 *FSF*; exp. **1966**), gives us INTELLIGENCE, artificially enhanced by brain surgery, and a problem in medical ethics. Ray BRADBURY's "Skeleton" (1947) is a master tale of hypochondria. Michael CRICHTON's medical training shows in *The Andromeda Strain* (**1969**)

and *The Terminal Man* (**1972**), which respectively display an extraterrestrial plague and some neurological mismatching in California. Alan E. NOURSE, himself a doctor, in *The Bladerunner* (**1975**) has published the most recent in a series of novels using medical figures, mostly blending intrigue and medical exotica. Chelsea Quinn YARBRO is cynical about medical ethics in *Time of The Fourth Horseman* (**1976**) where doctors attempt to counter OVERPOPULATION with controlled disease.

Medical themes are so common in sf that the above list is heavily selective. Many other sf authors have used them, from Brian ALDISS to Bob SHAW, from L. Ron HUBBARD to Larry NIVEN.

Great Science Fiction about Doctors (anth. **1963**) ed. Groff CONKLIN and Noah D. Fabricant, MD, is one of the few anthologies devoted to this vast subject. [JSc]

See also: ANDROIDS; CLONES; CYBORGS; DIANETICS; IMMORTALITY; MUTANTS; PARASITISM AND SYMBIOSIS; SUSPENDED ANIMATION.

MEDIEVAL SOCIETIES *See* CONCEPTUAL BREAKTHROUGH; HOLOCAUST AND AFTER; MAGIC; POLITICS; SWORD AND SORCERY.

MEEK, Colonel S(TERNER ST) P(AUL) (1894–). American writer and army ordnance officer. He was active for about a decade, but primarily 1930–32, in the American PULP magazines from his first story, "The Murgatroyd Experiments" for *AMZ Quarterly* in 1929. Many of his stories comprised a series featuring Doctor Bird and Operative Carnes; they ran from "The Cave of Horror" (1930) to "Vanishing Gold" (1932), and have not been collected in book form. *The Monkeys Have No Tails in Zamboanga* (coll. **1935**) assembles a series of sf tall tales; some are amusing. Of his several novels published in magazine form, only the LOST-WORLD tales *The Drums of Tapajos* (1930 *AMZ*; **1961**) and its sequel *Troyana* (1932 *AMZ*; rev. **1961**) have reached book form. A booklet collecting two stories, *Arctic Bride* (coll. **1944**), is no. 1 in the AMERICAN FICTION series. [JC]
See also: GREAT AND SMALL.

MÉLIÈS, GEORGES (1861–1938). French film-maker. A natural showman, GM began his theatrical career as a conjurer, designing his own trick gadgets. In 1888 his wealthy family provided him with the finances to buy the Théâtre Robert-Houdin, and his magic shows there became famous throughout France. In 1896, inspired by the Lumière brothers, he acquired a motion-picture camera and began making his own short films. He realized the medium's potential for creating illusions and was soon producing many films utilizing trick photography as well as a wide range of

the stage effects built into his theatre. His most successful period was 1897–1902, and it was in the last year that he made LE VOYAGE DANS LA LUNE, which is regarded as one of the first sf movies. His work was popular in many countries but even by 1904, when he made LE VOYAGE À TRAVERS L'IMPOSSIBLE, audiences were requiring more from the cinema than just trick films. By 1913 he was bankrupt, forced out of business by the larger film companies that had grown up in the industry he had helped to create. During the First World War many of the negatives of his films were destroyed, and much of his work was lost forever. He enjoyed a comeback in the late 1920s when his surviving films were rediscovered by the French intellectuals of the period. He died with the satisfaction of being recognized as one of the cinema's true innovators; he had pioneered many of the techniques on which all subsequent sf cinema has been based. [JB]

MELTZER, DAVID (1937–). American writer and poet, known primarily for his work outside the sf field. Generally considered one of the major West Coast poets, he was a great reader of sf in his youth and was encouraged by Kris NEVILLE to write some sf short stories in the late 1950s. DM was closely connected with the short-lived ESSEX HOUSE erotic imprint to which he contributed nine novels. His trilogy "The Agency" (*The Agency*, **1968**; *The Agent*, **1968**; *How Many Blocks in the Pile?*, **1968**) relentlessly dissects an all-powerful SEXUAL underground and constitutes a fierce moral tract. His "Brain-Plant" series (*Lovely*, **1969**; *Healer*, **1969**; *Out*, **1969**; *Glue Factory*, **1969**) is an account of totalitarian eroticism in a future urban society, in an impressionistic style reminiscent of the work of William BURROUGHS and Harlan ELLISON. [MJ]

MELVILLE, HERMAN (1819–91). American writer, best known for such radically symbolic novels as *Moby-Dick* (**1851**); the great whale of this novel is an archetype of the more METAPHYSICAL variety of sf MONSTER, and the spirit of the book has permeated much sf, notably Roger ZELAZNY's "The Doors of his Face, the Lamps of his Mouth" (1965) and, rather trivially, Philip José FARMER's "sequel" *The Wind Whales of Ishmael* (**1971**). HM's blend, in *Moby-Dick*, of rational explanation with a romantic openness to the inexplicable was later to become typical of sf.

In *The Confidence-Man, His Masquerade* (**1857**), HM's violent conflict with the dictates (or concept) of a manipulative destiny may well have provided some sf writers with inspiration for contemporary sf tales of justified PARANOIA.

Of more direct sf interest is HM's short story "The Bell-Tower" (1855), which

appears in *The Piazza Tales* (coll. **1856**); rather reminiscent of the work of his friend Nathaniel HAWTHORNE, it is the story, set in Renaissance Italy, of the construction of a MACHINE-man whose function it will be to strike the hour on a large bell, but which in the event kills its maker. The story can be read as allegorical of Man's hubris, and a comment on the implications of the new era of mechanical invention and science HM was beginning to witness. [JC/PN]
See also: ROBOTS.

MENASCO, NORMAN *See* Wyman GUIN.

MENDELSOHN, FELIX Jr (? –). American writer of two routine sf novels, *Club Tycoon Sends Man to Moon* (**1965**) and *Superbaby* (**1969**). Neither is remarkable, both are comic; the first, in its spoofing of the space race, sometimes scores an amusing point. [JC]
See also: GENETIC ENGINEERING.

MENVILLE, DOUGLAS *See* Robert REGINALD.

MERAK, A.J. British writer, author of several PULP-style, paperback sf romances: *Dark Andromeda* (**1954**), *No Dawn and No Horizon* (vt *The Frozen Planet*), *The Dark Millenium*, *Dark Conflict*, *Barrier Unknown*, *Hydrosphere*, *The Lonely Shadows* and *Something About Spiders*. The last seven titles, all undated but *c.* 1959–60, were published by BADGER BOOKS, which has led many readers to suppose that AJM, whose real identity has not been verified, is one of the many pseudonyms of R.L. FANTHORPE. [PN]

MERCIER, LOUIS-SÉBASTIEN (1740–1814). French writer, best known for his numerous plays and for his anecdotal journalism. His UTOPIA, *L'an deux mille quatre cent quarante* (**1771**; trans. as *Memoirs of the Year Two Thousand Five Hundred* **1772**; rev. trans. 1802), depicts a future France governed rationally; it was originally published anonymously in England, and may be thought to partake of the pre-Revolutionary ferment of the late 18th century. It was probably the first Utopia to be published in America, in 1795. [JC]
See also: CITIES; NEAR FUTURE; SUSPENDED ANIMATION; TIME TRAVEL.

MERCURY Mercury is the planet nearest the Sun, and hence one of the most difficult to observe. Until the late 19th century it was believed to rotate on its axis every 24 hours or so, but this opinion was displaced by that of Schiaparelli and Lowell, who contended that it kept the same face permanently towards the Sun. 20th-century sf writers thus pictured it as having an extremely hot "day side", a cold "night side" and a narrow "twilight zone". This image persisted until the 1960s, when it was discovered that Mercury does rotate on its axis rapidly enough to have days somewhat shorter than its years.

The earliest visit to Mercury was probably that of Athanasius KIRCHER in his *Itinerarium Exstaticum* (**1656**), and it was generally included in other round tours of the planets, including Emanuel SWEDENBORG's *The Earths in our Solar System* (**1758**) and George GRIFFITH's *A Honeymoon in Space* (**1901**). The earliest novel in which Mercury came into principal focus was *Relation du Monde de Mercure* (**1750**) by Le Chevalier de Bethune, and the first notable novel in English set there was William Wallace COOK's satire *Adrift in the Unknown* (1904–05 *Argosy*; **1925**) though it also figures in John MUNRO's *A Trip to Venus* (**1897**). E.R. EDDISON's HEROIC FANTASY *The Worm Ouroboros* (**1922**) is also set on Mercury, but in this case the name is used purely for convenience.

PULP scientific romances rarely employed Mercury as a milieu for exotic adventure, preferring MARS and VENUS, but some examples are Homer Eon FLINT's "The Lord of Death" (1919; title story of *The Lord of Death and the Queen of Life*, coll. **1965**), Ray CUMMINGS' *Tama of the Light Country* (1930 *Argosy*; **1965**) and its sequel and, most notably, Clark Ashton SMITH's "The Immortals of Mercury" (1932). An invasion from Mercury was thwarted in J.M. WALSH's *Vandals of the Void* (**1931**) and Leigh BRACKETT set one of her exotic romances, "Shannach — the Last" (1952), there.

Attempts to use Mercury in more thoughtful stories with some fidelity to astronomical knowledge were also infrequent in the pre-War pulps, the first significant examples being Clifford D. SIMAK's "Masquerade" (1941; vt "Operation Mercury") and Isaac ASIMOV's "Runaround" (1942). After the War, however, things picked up a little. Three juvenile novels featuring Mercury are Lester DEL REY's *Battle on Mercury* (**1956** as by Erik van Lhin), Isaac Asimov's *Lucky Starr and the Big Sun of Mercury* (**1956** as by Paul French; vt *The Big Sun of Mercury*) and *Mission to Mercury* (**1965**) by Hugh WALTERS. Alan NOURSE wrote a memorable story, "Brightside Crossing" (1956), in which a journey across the day side of the planet becomes an adventurous feat akin to the then recent conquest of Everest. The night side of Mercury features ironically in Larry NIVEN's "The Coldest Place" (1964). Perhaps the most enduring image of Mercury, though, is from Kurt VONNEGUT's *The Sirens of Titan* (**1959**), which offers an account of the Harmonia — life forms living on vibration which inhabit deep caves and which are introduced to music by a stranded astronaut. [BS]

MEREDITH, JAMES CREED (?). Irish writer, usually on philosophical subjects, who carried that interest into fiction in his discursive novel *The Rainbow in the Valley* (Dublin **1939**), in which scientists in communication with Martians have much to talk over. [JC]

MEREDITH, RICHARD C. (1937–). American writer, with a BA in English from the University of West Florida, who began publishing sf with "Slugs" for *Knight* magazine in 1962. His first novel, *The Sky is Filled with Ships* (**1969**), is an effective SPACE OPERA in which colonies revolt against a tyrannical corporation, while his second, *We All Died at Breakaway Station* (**1969**), is a well-considered TIME PARADOX novel, as is *Run, Come See Jerusalem!* (**1976**). *At the Narrow Passage* (**1973**) is effective also, being a PARALLEL-WORLDS tale in which aliens are changing Earth's past for us; it begins a trilogy (the second and third vols coming from another publisher), which continues with *No Brother, No Friend* (**1976**) and *Vestiges of Time* (**1978**). RM makes intelligent use of HISTORY in his time-travel novels. [JC/PN]

MERLE, ROBERT (1908–). French writer known primarily for his work outside the sf field. Degree in literature. He was a recipient of the Prix Goncourt in 1949. More recently RM has shown an increasing preoccupation with sf themes. His *Un animal doué de raison* (**1967**; trans. as *The Day of the Dolphin* by Helen Weaver **1969**), which was later filmed in the USA, is an ingenious examination of scientific and political ethics following the main character's breakthrough in communicating with dolphins (*see* THE DAY OF THE DOLPHIN). *Malevil* (**1972**; trans. Derek Coltman **1974**), joint winner of the JOHN W. CAMPBELL AWARD in 1974, is a realistic post-HOLOCAUST survival and reconstruction story. *Les hommes protégés* (**1974**; trans. as *The Virility Factor* by Martin Sokolinsky **1977**) uses an sf framework to satirize both male sexist and feminist attitudes; an epidemic to which women, boys and men over 60 are immune is killing off the male population of America. Castrated men survive. The Government is taken over by women and castrates, and some new changes are rung on the old sf theme with what some saw as cheery ribaldry, others as cheap vulgarity. *Madrapour* (**1976**), where a plane full of passengers is hijacked by a godlike being, is a fictional treatment of the Hindu "wheel of time" philosophy. [MJ/PN]
See also: COMMUNICATIONS; LINGUISTICS; UNDER THE SEA.

MERLYN, ARTHUR *See* James BLISH.

MERRIL, JUDITH (1923–). American writer and anthologist. She was born Juliet Grossman, but preferred the forename Judith. She became Judith Zissman by marriage and was associated with the FUTURIANS fan group during and after the War, where her left-wing political views caused some strife. She changed her name to Merril and married Frederik POHL in 1948, but the marriage proved to be temporary. She was never a prolific writer and the bulk of her work appeared between 1950 and 1960; her first published sf was "That Only a Mother" (1948) for *ASF*. She occasionally used the pseudonym Rose Sharon. She wrote two novels in collaboration with C.M. KORNBLUTH under the name Cyril JUDD (*see for details*), but neither measures up to her solo work. Her novel *Shadow on the Hearth* (**1950**; rev. 1966) tells the story of an atomic war from the viewpoint of a housewife and shows a remarkable sensitivity to the emotional psychology of the post-Hiroshima era; it was televised as *Atomic Attack*. Most of her protagonists are passively caught up in speculative events rather than in control of them, and her studies of individuals facing unprecedented situations are unrivalled in the sf of the period; she was, perhaps a little before her time. Three good novellas are collected in *Daughters of Earth* (coll. **1968**); the title story (1953) is a family saga of the COLONIZATION of another world; "Homecalling" (1956) is a story of contact with an alien being; and "Project Nursemaid" (1955) concerns the problems of the administrator of a space project which must adopt human embryos. Her second solo novel, *The Tomorrow People* (**1960**), is an intense psychological mystery story, but lacks the emotional resonance of her best early work. Her short-story collections, which overlap somewhat, are *Out Of Bounds* (coll. **1960**), *Survival Ship and Other Stories* (coll. **1974**) and *The Best of Judith Merril* (coll. **1976**).

JM began editing ANTHOLOGIES in the early 1950s with *Shot in the Dark* (anth. **1950**), *Beyond Human Ken* (anth. **1952**), *Beyond the Barriers of Time and Space* (anth. **1954**), *Human?* (anth. **1954**) and *Galaxy of Ghouls* (anth. **1955**; vt *Off the Beaten Orbit*), but really made her mark with the series of best-of-the-year anthologies she began in 1956; they continued for 14 years (13 vols) as follows: *S-F: The Year's Greatest Science-Fiction and Fantasy* (anth. **1956**); *S-F: 57* (anth. **1957**; vt *S-F: The Year's Greatest Science-Fiction and Fantasy Second Annual Volume*); *S-F 58* (anth. **1958**; vt *S-F: The Year's Greatest Science-Fiction and Fantasy Third Annual Volume*); *S-F 59* (anth. **1959**; vt *The Year's Greatest Science-Fiction and Fantasy Fourth Annual Volume*); *5th Annual Edition The Year's Best S-F* (anth. **1960**); *6th Annual Edition The Year's Best S-F* (anth. **1961**; vt *The Best of Sci-Fi 1* UK); *7th Annual Edition The Year's Best S-F* (anth. **1962**; vt *The Best of Sci-Fi 2* UK); *8th Annual Edition The Year's Best S-F* (anth. **1963**; vt *The Best of Sci-Fi 4* UK); *9th Annual Edition The Year's Best S-F* (anth. **1964**; vt *The Best of Sci-Fi 5* UK); *10th Annual Edition The Year's Best S-F* (anth. **1965**; vt *The Best of Sci-Fi 9* UK); *11th Annual Edition The Year's Best S-F* (anth. **1966**; vt *The Best of Sci-Fi 10* UK); *SF 12* (anth. **1968**; vt *The Best of Sci-Fi 12* UK); *SF 13* (anth. **1969**). It will be noted that the British retitling was not conducted on a rational basis; there was no British *6*, *7*, *8* or *11*; *The Best of Sci-Fi 3* (anth. **1964** UK), is an entirely independent collection, ed. Cordelia Titcomb Smith. There was also a retrospective anthology, *The Best of the Best* (anth. **1967**; UK paperback in two vols). These anthologies were remarkable primarily for JM's eclectic philosophy — she selected many stories from outside the sf magazines — and for her interest in experimental writing. She campaigned, both in the anthologies and in her book-review column in *FSF* (for which she was book editor May 1965-May 1969), for the replacement of the term "science fiction" by "speculative fiction", and was the first American champion of the so-called NEW WAVE primarily associated with the British magazine NEW WORLDS. A long critical essay, in which she summarizes her sometimes over-enthusiastic views, seeing sf as on the whole more experimental and daring, in comparison with the MAINSTREAM, than is altogether balanced, is "What Do You Mean: Science? Fiction?" in *SF: The Other Side of Realism* (anth. **1971**; ed. Thomas D. CLARESON. JM edited an anthology of British new-wave stories, *England Swings SF* (anth. **1968**; vt abridged *The Space-Time Journal* UK). Her book collection now forms the basis of the Spaced-Out Library in Toronto (where she now resides), the largest sf library in Canada. [BS]

See also: DEFINITIONS OF SF; END OF THE WORLD; GENERATION STARSHIPS; HOLOCAUST AND AFTER; MEDICINE; SCIENTIFIC ERRORS; SUPERNATURAL CREATURES; WAR; WOMEN.

MERRIMAN, ALEX *See* Robert SILVERBERG.

MERRITT, A(BRAHAM) (1884-1943). American writer, primarily of FANTASY, though he was influential among sf writers and readers as well. His first years were occupied with newspaper journalism, and he was a longtime assistant editor of *The American Weekly*, becoming editor in 1937 and remaining so until his death. His fiction was written therefore as a sideline to a busy journalistic career, which explains his relative smallness of output. He began publishing stories with *Through the Dragon Glass* for *All-Story Weekly* in 1917; it was later republished as a pamphlet (**1940**). His first novel, *The Moon Pool* ("The Moon Pool" 1918 *All-Story Weekly*; "The Conquest of the Moon Pool" 1919 *All-Story Weekly*; fix-up **1919**), featured a subterranean world reachable via a force field in the pool. *The Metal Monster* (1920 *Argosy*; **1946**), which contains one of the same characters, describes a collective alien being, comprised of millions of metal parts, who is absent-mindedly kind to the explorer-protagonist; *The Face in the Abyss* ("The Face in the Abyss" 1923 *Argosy*; "The Snake Mother" 1930 *Argosy*; fix-up **1931**) describes an ancient, almost extinct, semi-reptilian race and its considerable wisdom; in *The Ship of Ishtar* (1924 *Argosy*; rev. with cuts **1926**; rev. to original state 1949), his best novel, a man travels into a magical world and falls in love with the beautiful female captain of the ship of Ishtar; the purple prose of the descriptive passages in this novel still has a strong effect on readers; *Seven Footprints to Satan* (1927 *Argosy*; **1928**), filmed in 1929, is a horror/detective mystery, "Satan" being a greedy villain; *The Dwellers in the Mirage* (1932 *Argosy* with happy ending; **1932**; with originally intended unhappy ending 1944) is an effective LOST-RACE novel, one of AM's best; *Burn, Witch, Burn!* (1932 *Argosy*; exp. **1933**), and its sequel, *Creep, Shadow!* (1934 *Argosy*; **1934**; vt *Creep, Shadow, Creep!* UK and later USA), the first volume filmed as THE DEVIL DOLL (1936), comprise a short series about witchcraft and horror detection; *The Fox Woman* (coll. **1949**) assembles short stories and uncompleted fragments, one of them (the title story) already having been incorporated into *The Fox Woman and the Blue Pagoda* (coll. of two stories **1946**) by AM and Hannes BOK, "The Blue Pagoda" being Bok's own work and linked to AM's fragment with connecting passages. Bok's second completion of AM's work is *The Black Wheel* (**1947**), of which less than a quarter is by AM.

AM's influence on the sf and fantasy world is less through his storylines, which tended to be unoriginal at best, or through excesses of his style, than through his genuine imaginative power in the creation of desirable alternative worlds and realities. He was extremely popular during his life, even having a magazine, A. MERRITT'S FANTASY, named after him, and he became very wealthy. His works are still regarded as classics, and Sam MOSKOWITZ, in chapter 12 of *Explorers of the Infinite* (**1963**), probably represents many readers in his view that AM was the supreme fantasy genius of his day; even though by any absolute literary standard AM's prose is verbose and sentimental, and his repeated romantic image of the beautiful, evil priestess, derived from the ambiguity of a popular Victorian men's attitude to womanhood (women being either virgins or devils), is rather silly, the escapist yearning for otherness and mystery that he expresses has seldom, in sf, carried such an emotional charge. [JC/PN]

See also: FANTASTIC VOYAGES; FAR FUTURE; PARALLEL WORLDS; SUPERNATURAL CREATURES.

MERRITT'S FANTASY MAGAZINE
See A. MERRITT'S FANTASY MAGAZINE.

MERWIN, (W.) SAM(UEL) JR.
(1910–). American writer, son of the writer W.S. Merwin. SM's first published sf story was "The Scourge Below" (1939) in THRILLING WONDER STORIES; he later went to work for the pulp chain which published *TWS* and STARTLING STORIES, and was appointed to the editorship of both magazines in 1944, succeeding Oscar J. FRIEND. Although he had contributed to *TWS* and had done some editorial work for the magazines, he claims never actually to have read an sf magazine before becoming editor of two of them. During his editorship he greatly raised the standard of both titles, abolishing the juvenile slant they had previously adopted, and making them the leading PULP magazines in the field (second only to *ASF*). He also contributed stories to both, using his own name and the pseudonyms Matt Lee and the confusing Carter Sprague. He also edited WONDER STORY ANNUAL and FANTASTIC STORY QUARTERLY — additional companion magazines to *Startling* and *TWS* — before leaving in 1951 to freelance. Later editorial forays included editing the first issues of FANTASTIC UNIVERSE, a period as assistant editor for Galaxy Publications — working on GALAXY SCIENCE FICTION, BEYOND FANTASY FICTION and GALAXY SCIENCE FICTION NOVELS — and editing the auspicious first two issues of SATELLITE SCIENCE FICTION. He later went to work in Hollywood. SM's fiction is unexceptional; it includes *The House of Many Worlds* (1951) and its sequel *Three Faces of Time* (1955). The Feb. 1957 issue of *Satellite* contained "Planet for Plunder", a novel written in collaboration with Hal CLEMENT; this was actually a Clement novelette expanded by SM (who added alternate chapters from another viewpoint) in order to fit *Satellite*'s novel-oriented policy.

Two articles by SM — reminiscences of his pulp magazine days — appeared in THE ALIEN CRITIC 9 and 10. Although comparatively little known, SM's record shows him to have been one of the most capable of all sf magazine editors. [MJE]
Other works: *Killer to Come* (1953); *The White Widows* (1953; vt *The Sex War* US); *The Time Shifters* (1971); *Chauvinisto* (1976).

MESMERISM *See* PSYCHOLOGY.

MESSAC, RÉGIS *See* FRANCE.

MESSAGE FROM MARS, A Film (1913). UK Films. Directed by J. Wallett Waller, starring Charles Hawtrey, E. Holman Clark and Chrissie Bell. Scenario by J. W. Waller, based on the play by Richard Ganthony. Silent, 4,000 feet.

This moral fable about a messenger sent from Mars to help bring humans to

This rare still from the 1913 film A MESSAGE FROM MARS is reproduced from the second edition of the book.

their senses was based on a remarkably successful and long-running play, and the film version was actually made in the theatre with the same actors. It was one of the earliest uses of sf themes in British cinema, but an even earlier version of the same play was made in 1909 in New Zealand, probably much shorter; the details have been lost. A later US version (Metro, 5187 feet) was directed by Maxwell Karger in 1921. The American version gives the events of the story a dream framework. A novelized version of the now forgotten play was *A Message From Mars* (1912) by Lester LURGAN. The second edition was illustrated by a number of stills from the film. [PN]

MESSIAHS As with many words whose meaning was once quite specific, the Judaeo-Christian term "messiah" has been generalized, through time, to apply to any saviour or champion whose arrival is anticipated, hoped for or even simply needed. We therefore find in sf a great many characters whose roles may, to a greater or lesser extent, be described as messianic, as well as a distinct category of stories which deal directly with Christian mythology in one way or another.

The image of the future contained within the Christian religious imagination is associated with the idea of the Millennium and the Apocalypse, and a preoccupation with messiahs in futuristic fiction in Western culture is understandable (*see* RELIGION). In scientific romances around the turn of the century we find secularized versions of the myth in H.G. WELLS's *When the Sleeper Wakes* (1899; rev. vt *The Sleeper Awakes* 1910) and M.P. SHIEL's *Lord of the Sea* (1901). Countless religious anticipatory romances flourished in the same period, the cardinal example being Robert Hugh BENSON's *Lord of the World* (1907). All three of these novels are basically political fantasies, however; the first even provoked a political reply in Victor ROUSSEAU's *Messiah of the Cylinder* (1917). Fiction concerned more narrowly with the future of science and technology

had no use for messiahs, unless the term may be applied metaphorically to certain inventors. There is no hint of the messiah in the early sf PULPS, though the Earth is saved a hundred times and more from disaster, and apocalyptic menaces abound.

Messianism began to appear in sf in connection with the role of the SUPERMAN in the 1940s. The Second World War, which greatly encouraged the millennarian imagination, was the agent primarily responsible for the boom in messiahs. James BLISH claimed that the revelation of the A-bomb provoked a wave of "chiliastic panic". The superman plays a messianic role in *Darker than You Think* (1940; 1948) by Jack WILLIAMSON and in *What Dreams May Come* (1941), an English wartime fantasy by J.D. BERESFORD. The bleakest and most extreme future war story produced by an sf writer before the A-bomb revelation, L. Ron HUBBARD's *Final Blackout* (1940; 1948), also has messianic overtones, especially in the final sacrifice of its hero. In C.S. LEWIS's anti-humanist, anti-scientific *That Hideous Strength* (1945), the messiah's role is taken, strangely, by Merlin.

In the same period messianic overtones also invaded one of sf's most stereotyped fantasies, in which an ordinary man is transplanted into an alien world where he finds a fulfilment in love and life which is unattainable on Earth (*see* PARALLEL WORLDS). Stories in which the displaced man takes on a pseudo-messianic role in the alien milieu include Henry KUTTNER's *The Dark World* (1946; 1965) and James Blish's *The Warriors of Day* (1951; 1953).

Christ first appeared in a pulp sf story in Ray BRADBURY's "The Man" (1949), although it was not until the 1960s that TIME TRAVEL was used to focus on Christ's life and death in major novels. In Michael MOORCOCK's *Behold the Man* (1966; exp. 1969) a time traveller takes Christ's place, and Brian EARNSHAW's *Planet in the Eye of Time* (1968) is a curious SPACE OPERA which features the crucifixion as its climax. In Philip José FARMER's "Riverworld" (1966) — a novelette separate from the novels that form the main sequence of the "Riverworld" series — the crucifixion is re-enacted in the human race's new incarnation. Re-enactments of the myth on alien worlds occur in several stories, most notably "The Streets of Ashkelon" (1962) by Harry HARRISON. Nativity stories are even more common, and include Robert F. YOUNG's "Robot Son" (1959), Ed BRYANT's "Eyes of Onyx" (1971) and John CAMERON's *The Astrologer* (**1972**). Accounts of the second coming include Edward Wellens' "Seven Days Wonder" (1963) and J.G. BALLARD's "You and Me and the Continuum" (1966). Similar stories account for an astonishingly high percentage of the unsolicited manuscripts received by sf magazines — a phenomenon which prompted Michael Moorcock to dub them "Shaggy God stories".

The theme of redemption through sacrifice, derived from Christian mythology, forms the core of many memorable sf stories, including Cordwainer SMITH's "The Dead Lady of Clown Town" (1964), Robert F. Young's "Redemption" (1963), Harlan ELLISON's "'Repent, Harlequin!' said the Ticktockman" (1965) and R.A. LAFFERTY's *Past Master* (**1968**). In the first of these stories the central role is linked to the story of Joan of Arc, in the last it is taken by St Thomas MORE. Robert A. HEINLEIN's *Stranger in a Strange Land* (**1961**) also belongs to this category, as does Clifford D. SIMAK's *Time and Again* (**1951**; vt *First He Died*), although the latter novel does not require the death of its hero to be permanent. More enigmatic messiahs, whose deaths do not seem to offer any kind of redemption, are featured in Gore VIDAL's *Messiah* (**1954**; rev. 1965) and Robert SILVERBERG's *Masks of Time* (**1968**; vt *Vornan-19 UK*). Philip K. DICK, too, is interested in ambiguous messiahs, whose coming may bring either salvation or destruction, as in *The Three Stigmata of Palmer Eldritch* (**1964**). A fake messiah, used as an instrument in a political power-play, is featured in Robin SANBORN's *The Book of Stier* (**1971**).

Perhaps the most powerful messiah myth in modern sf, and certainly the most popular (along with *Stranger in a Strange Land*), is Frank HERBERT's *Dune* (**1965**), extended in *Dune Messiah* (**1969**) and *Children of Dune* (**1976**): an epic following the career of Paul Atreides, messiah of the desert world Arrakis, and the historical pattern which begins to develop after his apparent death. The writer for whom messianic MYTHOLOGY seems to hold most fascination, however, is Roger ZELAZNY, author of "A Rose for Ecclesiastes" (1963), about a poet forced into a pseudo-messianic role on Mars; the epic *Lord of Light* (**1967**) about a messianic career set against a background

derived from Hindu mythology; and *Isle of the Dead* (**1969**), in which the "name-bearer" of an alien god is drawn into a divine duel as his incarnate champion. In fact, there are few Zelazny novels without messiah figures.

As confidence in the historical future wanes, millennarian philosophy thrives. It is not surprising that in today's intellectual climate the messiah myth is common in sf, and it may well remain so (at least until the year 2001).

See also: GODS AND DEMONS; POLITICS.

The French comic book MÉTAL HURLANT features some of the most sophisticated sf artwork of today. The cover of no. 4 is by Moebius (Jean Giraud).

MÉTAL HURLANT French adult BEDSHEET-size COMIC BOOK series. *MH* was launched Jan. 1975 by Bernard Farkas, Jean-Pierre Dionnet and illustrators Jean GIRAUD and Philippe DRUILLET. Conceived as a glossy showcase for the growing number of French sf artists, *MH* has been a success since its inception, combining many aspects of sf narrative, with particular stress on the erotic, the grotesque and the horrific, in illustrated form. Overseas editions have been published in the USA from 1977 (as *Heavy Metal*, published by the *National Lampoon* team, contents not identical with the French original, though the overlap is very considerable), Italy, Spain and Holland. Major contributors have included Giraud, Druillet, Corben, Gal, Mandryka, Alexis, Tardi, Claveloux, Jakubowicz, Nicollet, Massé, Bodé, Bilal, Lob, Clerc, F'Murr, Mézières, Hé, Forest, Pétillon, Macedo and Caza. Originally quarterly, *MH* has appeared monthly since Sep. 1976, and in Oct. 1976 spawned a companion magazine, exclusively devoted to feminine illustrators, *Ah! Nana*.   [MJ]
See also: ILLUSTRATORS.

METAPHYSICS One of the qualities of sf that sometimes baffles newcomers to it is the relative infrequency, despite its label, with which it deals with the HARD SCIENCES. Indeed, sf deals as often with

metaphysics as with PHYSICS. This is not an accidental or a recent development; the exploration of metaphysical questions has been central to sf at least since the time of Mary SHELLEY's *Frankenstein* (**1818**; rev. 1831); this centrality was not thereafter abandoned. It recurs in the pioneering sf of Edgar Allan POE, of Nathaniel HAWTHORNE, of Robert Louis STEVENSON and pre-eminently of H.G. WELLS.

Metaphysics is an important branch of philosophy, and from early on has been regularly used as a synonym for ontology, the study of being or existence. Metaphysics is defined in *The Shorter Oxford English Dictionary* as "that branch of speculation which deals with the first principles of things, including such concepts as being, substance, essence, time, space, cause, identity etc." Many of the thematic entries in this Encyclopedia can be regarded as pertaining as much to metaphysics as to the natural sciences, notably PARADOXES OF TIME, TIME TRAVEL, PERCEPTION (under which rubric sf dealing with questions of appearance versus reality is discussed), RELIGION, CONCEPTUAL BREAKTHROUGH, ESCHATOLOGY, COSMOLOGY, ENTROPY, ORIGIN OF MAN, EVOLUTION, END OF THE WORLD, ALTERNATE WORLDS, PARALLEL WORLDS, FOURTH DIMENSION (AND OTHERS), GODS AND DEMONS, INTELLIGENCE, LINGUISTICS, MYTHOLOGY and REINCARNATION. Indeed, it is no longer possible, particularly at the frontiers of theoretical physics, to distinguish clearly between speculation which belongs specifically to the natural sciences and speculation which is metaphysical.

Sf works discussed under all the above entries regularly question the patterning and meaning of the universe, and the relationship of that pattern to our perceptions of it; these are metaphysical questions.

If metaphysics can be distinguished from science it is in this (the quotation is from *Man is the Measure*, **1976**, by Reuben Abel, a good account for the layman of central problems in philosophy): "Metaphysics is that branch of philosophy which attempts to comprehend the universe as a whole – not so much by examining it in detail (which is the procedure of science) as by analyzing and organizing the ideas and concepts by means of which we examine and think about the world."

Thus, for example, a central example of metaphysical sf is Stanislaw LEM's *Solaris* (**1961**; trans. **1970**), which asks the question, to what extent can scientists studying a totally alien and apparently sentient planet comprehend its essence without perverting their understanding through their inability to transcend categories of thought which are limited by their very humanness? This question about the limitation of our perceptions is one of the fundamental problems sf regularly tackles; many further examples are discussed under CONCEPTUAL BREAKTHROUGH and ALIENS. Confrontation with the alien, especially in sf stories of the 1960s and after, is often seen in sf as leading to some kind of transcendence, and a renewed sense of cosmic harmony. Robert SILVERBERG has written several novels of this type, a good one being *Downward to the Earth* (**1970**). Algis BUDRYS's *Rogue Moon* (**1960**) projects its protagonist into a maze of metaphysical self-discovery by confronting him with a literal, murderous, alien maze on the Moon.

Metaphysical questions of identity are particularly closely associated with the work of Philip K. DICK, who by blurring the distinctions between human and artificial, between Man, ANDROID and MACHINE, forces the reader to consider what qualities of consciousness constitute the essence of humanity. (Gene WOLFE entered the same area of speculation with his brilliant and subtle *The Fifth Head of Cerberus* (**1972**), in which it is not clear whether or not one of the protagonists is a simulation.) Dick, in fact, has a finger in almost every metaphysical pie. He specializes in questions of appearance and reality, and of solipsism, asking to what extent the universe as it appears to us is an objective fact, and to what extent it is a construction of our minds, whether working alone or in unison. Ursula K. LE GUIN entered this territory too, with *The Lathe of Heaven* (**1971**), whose hero has the power to dream ALTERNATE WORLDS into being. More recently, the novels of Ian WATSON have characteristically met some of the most difficult questions in metaphysics head-on and doggedly; Watson's special interest is also whether our models of the universe, especially as reflected in language (*see* LINGUISTICS), correspond to any external reality; at times he seems to go further and suggest that the meaning and shape of the universe is created by the consciousnesses that observe it.

Questions of good and evil in sf are intimately bound up with questions of human EVOLUTION; to what extent do we carry the mark of the amoral, unknowing beast within us? Robert Louis Stevenson's *Dr. Jekyll and Mr. Hyde* (**1886**) asks this question, and the theme is still very much with us, in part through the work of such evolutionary, behaviourist popularizers as Desmond Morris and Robert ARDREY (the latter himself an sf writer on one occasion), and in part through sf itself. A recent example is *Altered States* (**1978**) by Paddy Chayefsky, in which, absurdly, cause and effect is reversed; because consciousness may be coded in the DNA molecule, Chayefsky proposes that alterations in consciousness may be somehow able to alter our genetic make-up, so that we might literally bring alive the primordial within us; his hero devolves first to hominid, then, briefly, to primal chaos, undifferentiated cosmic matter.

Reversals of cause and effect are not new to sf. It is the very nature of the TIME-TRAVEL story to confront us with thought-provoking paradoxes of this sort, and in so doing, of course, to make us speculate about the question (not merely an intellectual game) of whether the meaning of our lives is created by free will or determinism. Examples are legion; a good one is the novella "The Custodians" (1975) by Richard COWPER; another is *Slaughterhouse Five* (**1969**) by Kurt VONNEGUT Jr.

The basic metaphysical question, perhaps, exists as an everyday cliché, the old cry "What does it all mean?" It is to the credit of sf that it has tackled this nebulous, overpowering question, through a fantastically elaborate series of thought experiments, sometimes trivial and sometimes profound, in a way that the traditional novel of character and society usually cannot manage.

There is no traditional crux in metaphysics which is not amply reflected in sf, whether it be "What is the nature of mind as opposed to body?" or "Is there purpose in nature?" Among sf writers of the pre-War generation, Olaf STAPLEDON is certainly pre-eminent, if not as a stylist, then as a propounder of questions of ultimate meaning, he confronted all the great metaphysical questions one after the other. But genre sf, too, has been amply supplied with amateur metaphysicians who have often made up in colour and verve what they may have lacked in rigorous thought; A.E. VAN VOGT is one such, and Charles L. HARNESS, with his fantastic paradoxes of COSMOLOGY, is another; even in the early PULPS, John TAINE, in *The Time Stream* (1931; **1946**) and elsewhere, flung himself headlong and daringly (and quite unselfconsciously) into questions of ultimate meaning. Much more recently, and initially only in garish pulp paperback format, Barrington J. BAYLEY

has been doing the same. Sf may derive its muscle and sinew from science and sociology, but much of the time its heartbeat derives from the intellectual drama of metaphysics; metaphysics as a study may originate in thought, but in its yearnings and its aspiration for understanding it permeates the feelings.
[PN]

METCALF, NORM(AN) (1937–). American fan bibliographer, whose *The Index of Science Fiction Magazines 1951–1965* (**1968**) is a sequel to *Index to the Science Fiction Magazines 1926–1950* (**1952**) by Donald B. DAY, and covers very much the same ground as the computerized index for the same years ed. Erwin S. STRAUSS, though the latter work gives an issue-by-issue contents listing which NM's does not. One or other of these works is essential to the serious sf researcher. [PN]

METROPOLIS Film (1926). UFA. Directed by Fritz LANG, starring Brigitte Helm, Alfred Abel, Gustav Frohlich, Rudolf Klein-Rogge, Heinrich George and Fritz Rasp. Screenplay by Fritz Lang and Thea VON HARBOU, based on the novel by Thea von Harbou. 140 mins. approx. on silent projection equipment; 120 mins. on modern equipment. B/w.

Though often described as the first sf epic of the cinema, this famous German film has more in common with the cinema of the Gothic. Set in a vast city of the future whose society is divided into downtrodden workers and a ruling elite, it concerns a member of the latter, Freder, who falls in love with Maria, saintly protector of the workers' children. But Freder's father, the ruler of the city, uses Maria as a model for a robot, built for him by the evil scientist Rotwang, which he uses to incite the workers to revolt (his reasons for this are never made clear). The damage to the city's machinery

The cowed proletariat of a mechanized future shamble through the greatest of early sf films, METROPOLIS, 1926.

caused by the rioting masses causes flooding to occur in the lower levels, threatening the lives of a number of children, but they are saved by the real Maria who has managed to escape the clutches of Rotwang. The film ends with the city's ruler being persuaded to shake hands with the workers' spokesman and promising that things will be better from now on.

Though set in a future visually emphasized by towering buildings and vast, brooding machines, the city of Metropolis is in some ways a Gothic creation, its underworld dark and medieval in atmosphere. Rotwang is based in a bizarre house with a pentagram inscribed over the door, and his methods seem to owe as much to the supernatural as to science; he is a sorcerer of the old school. The story of *M* is trite; the motivations of its characters' actions are confused; its politics are ludicrously simplistic and naïve; but these flaws cannot detract from the sheer visual power of the film — a combination of the huge Expressionistic sets (the work of art directors Otto Hunte, Erich Kettelhut and Karl Vollbrecht) and Lang's direction, particularly in the sequences involving the vast crowds which he uses as a kind of living clay with which to create giant fluid sculptures. Individual images, as when the false Maria is burned, apparently alive, to reveal the gleaming robot beneath, have been so well remembered as now to seem archetypes, alive still in the consciousness of filmgoers everywhere. [JB]
See also: DYSTOPIAS.

MEYERS, ROY (LETHBRIDGE) (1910–). English physician and writer, whose sf consists of a series of novels about the relationship between dolphins

and Man, beginning with *Dolphin Boy* (**1967**; vt *Dolphin Rider* UK), and continuing with *Daughters of the Dolphin* (**1968**) and *Destiny and the Dolphins* (**1969**). RM's style is wooden, but his obviously deep interest in dolphins is compelling and the novels are easy reading, though their mixture of melodrama and didacticism may not be to everyone's taste. [JC]
See also: UNDER THE SEA.

MEYN, NIELS *See* SCANDINAVIA.

MICROCOSM, THE *See* GREAT AND SMALL.

MIGHTY JOE YOUNG (vt **MR JOSEPH YOUNG OF AFRICA**) Film (1949). Argosy/RKO. Directed by Ernest B. Schoedsack, starring Terry Moore, Ben Johnson and Robert Armstrong. Screenplay by Ruth Rose, story by Merian C. Cooper. 94 mins. B/w, with some tinted sequences.

A virtual remake, though on a smaller scale, of KING KONG, by the same team that produced the 1933 classic. The hero organizes a cowboy expedition to Africa to capture animals for his new night-club. Once there they encounter a 12-foot-high gorilla and, after failing to lasso it, discover it is a girl's pet. They persuade her to return with the ape to America where it is exhibited in the night-club. Finally it goes berserk, but redeems itself by rescuing children from a burning orphanage.

Special effects genius Willis H. O'BRIEN had few successes after *King Kong* but at least *MJY*, on which he supervised the model animation, won him some belated recognition as well as an Academy award. Also working on the film was the young Ray HARRYHAUSEN. [JB]

MILES *See* Neil BELL.

MILES, CHARLES A. (? –). American writer whose sf novel is *Argosy: The Imaginary Memoirs of an Astronaut* (**1961**). [JC]

MILFORD SCIENCE FICTION WRITERS' CONFERENCE This annual event, held at Milford, Pennsylvania, where several sf writers including Damon KNIGHT, one of the founders of the conference, have lived at various times, is a writers' workshop. Sessions of mutual criticism of not yet published stories are interspersed with discussion groups on various professional problems. The first conference was in 1956, and the success of the workshops, especially the camaraderie they inspired, was directly responsible for the setting up of the professional body, the SCIENCE FICTION WRITERS OF AMERICA. James BLISH, Robert SILVERBERG, Harlan ELLISON, Kate WILHELM, Terry CARR and Samuel DELANY are among the many who have been at some period regular Milford attenders. Ideally, the workshop (only open to published sf writers) had a balance between beginner writers and more experienced professionals. It was felt at one time that Milford attenders constituted a powerful in-group in sf, particularly since so many editors of important anthology series attended, and were thought, probably unjustly, to be favouring their Milford friends; hence the rather paranoid term "Milford Mafia" used by unfriendly critics to describe this rather heterogeneous group. When founder member James Blish moved to England with his wife, Judith Ann Lawrence, the two of them set up an English Milford in 1972, which is held, out of terminological nostalgia, at Milford-on-Sea in Hampshire every autumn. Richard COWPER and Christopher PRIEST are two regular attenders. [PN]

MILLARD, JOSEPH (JOHN) (1908–). American writer who began publishing sf with "The Crystal Invaders" for *TWS* in 1941, and was active for a few years, a period which included the magazine release of his only novel, *The Gods Hate Kansas* (1941 *Startling Stories*; **1964**), a routine adventure involving manipulation of humans by aliens. [JC]

MILLER, JIMMY (? –). American writer. Her sf novel, *The Big Win* (**1969**), is a noisy but sometimes effective post-HOLOCAUST quest story, with an eventually interplanetary venue; the search is for the Chinese war criminal whose plague decimated the rest of the world. [JC]

MILLER, P(ETER) SCHUYLER (1912–74). American writer and critic. PSM gained an MSc in chemistry from

MIGHTY JOE YOUNG was not as big as *King Kong*, though both were designed by Willis H. O'Brien, but he was more readily lovable.

Union College, Schenectady, and did research for a time; however, for most of his career he worked as a technical writer. He is best known now for his book reviews in *ASF*, which first appeared in 1945 and became a regular monthly feature in Oct. 1951, continuing until his death. PSM was not a particularly demanding critic, but his judgements were generally shrewd, his enthusiasm never waned, and the coverage of his column was remarkably comprehensive. Largely as a by-product of this, he accumulated one of the largest private sf collections, and the annotated *Catalogue of the Fantasy and Science Fiction Library of the Late P. Schuyler Miller* (**1977**) is a useful bibliographical aid. He was presented with a special Hugo award in 1963 for his reviewing.

PSM had previously been one of the more popular and accomplished of pulp writers of the 1930s, his first story being "The Red Plague" (1930) in *Wonder Stories*. He collaborated with Aubrey McDermott and Walter Dennis on two connected stories: "Red Spot on Jupiter" (1931) and "Duel on the Asteroid" (1932). The first was published under the pseudonym Dennis McDermott; the second as by PSM and McDermott. Later stories of note include a TIME-PARADOX variant, "As Never Was" (1944) and "The Titan", a story whose (mild) sexual content made it unacceptable to the pulp magazines. Instead it was serialized in MARVEL TALES during 1934–5, but the magazine ceased publication before the last instalment appeared, and the story was not printed in its entirety until the publication of *The Titan* (coll. **1952**), which assembles most of PSM's better fiction. He also collaborated with L. Sprague DE CAMP on *Genus Homo* (1941 *Super Science Stories*; rev. **1950**), a novel set in the FAR FUTURE, filled with satirical evolutionary marvels.   [MJE]
About the author: *A Canticle for P. Schuyler Miller* (**1975**) by Sam MOSKOWITZ, a pamphlet.
See also: ALIENS; EVOLUTION; MARS; TIME TRAVEL.

MILLER, R(ICHARD) DEWITT (1910–58). American writer, involved in promulgating ideas about unusual occurrences of the kind associated with Charles FORT. He began publishing sf with "The Shapes" for *ASF* in 1936. In addition to some works of Fortean non-fiction, such as *You Do Take it With You* (**1956**), he published an sf novel with Anna Hunger, *The Man Who Lived Forever* (1938 *ASF* as "The Master Shall not Die" as by RDM only; rev. **1956**; vt *Year 3097* Australia), about an IMMORTAL who struggles to keep Man's technology from running amuck. *The Loose Board in the Floor* (**1951**) is a fantasy about stuffed animals going on a trip.   [JC]

MILLER, WALTER M(ICHAEL) (1922–). American writer, whose impact on modern sf is out of proportion to the small amount of material he has published in book form, though he published around 40 sf stories in magazines since "Secret of the Death Dome" appeared in *AMZ* in 1951. During a period (the 1950s) when American sf expressed its new-found interest in character through stories whose rigid formulae were derived from sentimental fiction and which tended to read as simplistic moralities, WMM published in *Gal.*, *FSF*, *ASF* and elsewhere tales whose treatment of character was effortlessly complex.

Perhaps the best example is "The Darfsteller" (1955), which won the HUGO novelette award for 1955. The sf apparatus is simple: a computer-like machine that controls a theatre of life-size mannequins and has displaced human actors. The darfsteller, an unemployed Method actor, has been working as a janitor in a theatre, and sabotages one of the mannequin-tapes so that he can replace it on stage. At this point the typical sf story of "character" would give him his comeuppance and the tale would end. But WMM is just beginning; the rigged performance becomes an essay in acting and a continually deepening examination of the actor's complex nature. The story appears in *Conditionally Human* (coll. **1962**); WMM's other collection, of shorter items, is *The View from the Stars* (coll. **1964**).

WMM's best and best-known work is *A Canticle for Leibowitz* (1955–7 *FSF*; fix-up **1960**), along with James BLISH's *A Case of Conscience* (1953 *If*; exp. **1958**) one of the very few attempts in sf to deal with formal RELIGION. The first part of this three-part work is set in a Dark Ages 600 years after a 20th-century nuclear HOLOCAUST; the Order of Leibowitz, a 20th-century physicist who had founded a religious order to preserve knowledge during the period of violent nescience following the holocaust, has come into some holy relics of its founder relevant to Leibowitz's canonization. In the second part, half a millennium later, the Order is confronted with the rise once again of the scientific mentality, with all its benefits and risks. In the third part, again half a millennium on, the Order has lost prestige and power in a new industrial-scientific age, but prepares a spaceship to escape the inevitable second holocaust, thus hoping to shorten the period of darkness that will ensue. The novel is full of subtly presented detail about the nature of religious vocation, the way of life of an isolated community, deals ably with the questions of the nature of historical and scientific knowledge which it raises, and poses and intriguingly answers ethical questions about Man's proper relation to God and the world. Although sometimes taken as a work of Christian apologetics (WMM is a Roman Catholic), the book has an attitude towards the Church which is ambiguous and often ironic. The presence of the Wandering Jew is perhaps a little contrived, but that is a small flaw in a seminal work. Its 1961 Hugo award was richly deserved.

WMM is a kind of sport in the sf world. Though broadly speaking he wrote within the norms of magazine fiction of his period of active publishing, which ceased in 1957, because of their subtlety and careful crafting his works stand out in a genre not especially welcoming to contemplative efforts. [JC]
See also: ANTI-INTELLECTUALISM IN SF; ARTS; AUTOMATION; COLONIZATION OF OTHER WORLDS; HISTORY IN SF; MARS; MEDICINE; MUTANTS; ROBOTS; David N. SAMUELSON; SOCIOLOGY; SPACE FLIGHT; SUPERNATURAL CREATURES.

MILLER, WARREN (1921–66). American writer, best known for such works outside sf field as his first "Harlem" novel, *The Cool World* (**1959**). *Looking for the General* (**1964**) is a combination of FABULATION and quest, and some of its devices resemble sf. WM's sf novel proper is *The Siege of Harlem* (**1964**), a NEAR-FUTURE tale in which Harlem, New York, declares itself a separate State.   [JC]
See also: HOLOCAUST AND AFTER; POLITICS.

MILLIGAN, ALFRED L(EE) (1893–). American writer and retired postmaster whose novel is *The Strange Flight of Frank Shapar* (**1965**).   [JC]

MILLS, ROBERT P(ARK) (1920–). American editor. He was managing editor of THE MAGAZINE OF FANTASY AND SCIENCE FICTION from its inception, and assumed the editorship proper with the Sep. 1958 issue, following Anthony BOUCHER's resignation. He remained editor until Mar. 1962, and continued thereafter as consulting editor until Feb. 1963. During his tenure *FSF* maintained its standing as the most sophisticated sf magazine, and won HUGO awards in 1959 and 1960. He edited the anthologies *The Best From Fantasy and Science Fiction: Ninth Series* (anth. **1959**; vt *Flowers For Algernon and Other Stories*), *Tenth Series* (anth. **1961**) and *Eleventh Series* (anth. **1962**), as well as *A Decade of Fantasy and Science Fiction* (anth. **1960**) and *Twenty Years of the Magazine of Fantasy and Science Fiction* (anth. **1970**), the latter in collaboration with Edward L. FERMAN. RPM was also editor of VENTURE SCIENCE FICTION during its first incarnation (1957–8), when the magazine was renowned for its "daring" (in terms of the prim attitude of 1950s sf magazines) approach to sexual topics. After leaving *FSF*, RPM became a literary agent — an occupation he still practises, with an agency bearing his name. He also edited *The Worlds of Science Fiction* (anth. **1963**).   [MJE]

MIND MAGIC US PULP magazine. Six issues, Jun.-Dec. 1931, published by

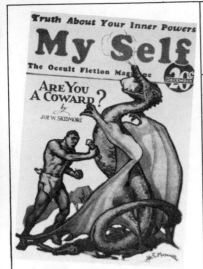

Confusingly, the fantasy magazine MIND MAGIC was retitled *My Self* for its last two issues; this is Dec. 1930. Cover by H. S. Moskovitz.

Shade Publishing Co. The first four issues possibly ed. August DERLETH (editor not named), the last two, retitled *My Self*, ed. G.R. Bay. A fantasy magazine, always struggling to survive, *MM* published mainly articles and fiction on occult subjects.   [FHP]

MINES, SAMUEL (1909–). American editor. From 1942 he worked for the PULP MAGAZINE chain which published STARTLING STORIES and THRILLING WONDER STORIES. Although an sf enthusiast he worked mainly on non-sf pulps until Sam MERWIN left the company in 1951, whereupon he took over the editorship of *Startling Stories*, *TWS*, FANTASTIC STORY QUARTERLY and WONDER STORY ANNUAL. He had previously published four stories in *TWS*, beginning with "Find the Sculptor" (1946). He was editor of *Startling Stories* Nov. 1951–Fall 1954; of *TWS* Dec. 1951–Summer 1954; of *Fantastic Story Quarterly* Winter 1952–Fall 1954; and of the 1952 and 1953 issues of *Wonder Story Annual*. He also edited all issues of the short-lived SPACE STORIES. Although he took over control of the magazine at a time when the pulp magazine industry was generally in decline, and the sf pulps in particular were suffering from the powerful competition of such new magazines as GALAXY SCIENCE FICTION and THE MAGAZINE OF FANTASY AND SCIENCE FICTION, SM was generally successful in maintaining the standard to which Merwin had raised the magazines. He edited *The Best from Startling Stories* (anth. **1953**; vt *Startling Stories* UK; vt *Moment Without Time* UK); the book also contains stories from *TWS*. He left the company in 1954; the various magazines did not survive him long. He has held no further editorial positions,

although he does review books for LUNA MONTHLY.   [MJE]

MINKOV, SVETOSLAV *See* EASTERN EUROPE.

This fine cover for the second issue, June/July 1931, was by Elliott Dold, the brother of the editor.

MIRACLE SCIENCE AND FANTASY STORIES US PULP magazine. Two issues, Apr./May and Jun./Jul. 1931, published by Good Story Magazine Co.; ed. Douglas M. Dold. *MSFS*'s publisher was Harold Hersey, previously editor of THRILL BOOK, while Dold was consulting editor of ASTOUNDING STORIES 1930–31. The magazine featured undistinguished pulp fiction by Dold, his brother, illustrator Elliott DOLD, and Victor ROUSSEAU. Its cover design, by Elliott Dold, was unusually stylish for its time.   [MJE]

MIRAGE PRESS American specialist publishing house, primarily of fantasy-related material, part-owned by Jack L. CHALKER (who had earlier published a fanzine, *Mirage*). Its publications include *The Conan Reader* (**1968**), a collection of essays by L. Sprague DE CAMP drawn from the fanzine AMRA. De Camp and George SCITHERS subsequently edited two further volumes of SWORD-AND-SORCERY related material for Mirage: *The Conan Swordbook* (anth. **1969**) and *The Conan Grimoire* (anth. **1972**). Other Mirage books include collections by Robert BLOCH and Seabury QUINN, poetry by De Camp, *A Guide to Middle Earth* (**1971**) by Robert Foster and *H.G. Wells: Critic of Progress* (**1973**) by Jack WILLIAMSON. *Harlan Ellison Hornbook*, planned and publicized, never appeared.   [MJE]

MIRRLEES, HOPE (1887–1978). English writer whose *Lud-in-the-Mist* (**1926**) has an interesting confrontation across the boundary between the supernatural (fairies) and the natural.

Though the book is basically fantasy in the line of William MORRIS, its down-to-earth quality, and its theme, give it a marginal relevance to sf.   [PN/JC]

MITCHELL, ADRIAN (1932–). English writer, best known for his poetry. His second novel, *The Bodyguard* (**1970**), is the deathbed narrative of a representative figure of 1980s Britain, a paramilitary Bodyguard whose reminiscences of his various jobs defending a totalitarian state provide a DYSTOPIAN portrait of the Europe to come.   [JC]
See also: POLITICS.

MITCHELL, CLYDE Ziff-Davis house name used twice by Robert SILVERBERG and Randall GARRETT in collaboration, twice by unidentified writers, 1956–7, and once by Harlan ELLISON on "The Wife Factory" (1957 *Fantastic*).

MITCHELL, EDWARD PAGE (1852–1927). American newspaperman and writer, associated from 1875 to his death with the New York *Sun*, which he edited from 1903. EPM's sf is restricted to short stories, and comes from the first decade of his career, beginning with "The Tachypomp" (1874), about a sort of humanoid calculator. Their subject matters range widely, from TIME TRAVEL in "The Clock That Went Backward" (1881), to MATTER TRANSMISSION in "The Man Without a Body" (1877), to INVISIBILITY in "The Crystal Man" (1881). EPM's work has come to be noticed in the sf field through the publication of *The Crystal Man: Landmark Science Fiction* (coll. **1973**) ed. and with a long informative introduction by Sam MOSKOWITZ.   [JC]

MITCHELL, J(AMES) LESLIE (1901–35). Scottish novelist, known mainly for works outside the sf field, written under the pseudonym Lewis Grassic Gibbon, e.g. *Scottish Scene* (**1934**, with Hugh MacDiarmid). Under his own name he wrote popular archaeology and fiction, much of the latter coloured by fantasy and romantic chinoiserie after the fashion of James Elroy Flecker. Typical of these are *The Calends of Cairo* (coll. of linked stories **1931**, with a letter in preface by H.G. WELLS) and *Persian Dawns, Egyptian Nights* (coll. of two linked story sequences **1933**, with a foreword by J.D. BERESFORD). *Three Go Back* (**1932**; abridged 1953) is sf, combining ANTHROPOLOGY, ATLANTIS and TIME TRAVEL themes in a well-written though awkwardly plotted story of three 20th-century passengers on an airship cast back in time (by earthquakes!) to Atlantis, where they find unspoiled pre-civilization proto-Basques in a doomed Eden. The Ice Age nears rapidly, and conflicts with savage Neanderthalers decimate the tribe; the two surviving castaways snap back (just as inexplicably) to the present. The

book is notable for its realistic and ebullient female protagonist, who adapts far more readily to her strange surroundings than either of the men. The Galaxy Books reprint of *Three Go Back* (**1953**) was severely bowdlerized and cut. *Gay Hunter* (**1934**) less convincingly sends another female protagonist into a far-future Britain; the eponymous heroine helps defeat a Fascist attempt to reindustrialize the country. Most of Mitchell's fiction contains passages of speculation of the kind given full rein in these two novels.   [JC]
About the author: "The Science Fiction of John Leslie Mitchell" by Ian Campbell, EXTRAPOLATION, Dec. 1974.
See also: ORIGIN OF MAN.

MITCHELL, JOHN A(MES) (1845–1918). American writer of early sf novels and other romances, beginning with *The Last American* (**1889**), a satirical post-HOLOCAUST novel in which a 30th-century Persian expedition visits an America long devastated by climatic changes; it is much influenced by Edgar Allan POE's "Mellonta Tauta" (1849). JAM's other well-known sf book is *Drowsy* (**1917**), a sentimental love story involving a telepath who discovers antigravity and visits the Moon and Mars. The book was notable for Angus Peter Macdonnel's fine illustrations, many of them moonscapes, some reproduced in EXTRAPOLATION, May 1971.   [JC]
Other works: *Life's Fairy Tales* (coll. **1892**); *Amos Judd* (**1895**); *That First Affair* (**1896**); *Gloria Victis* (**1897**; vt *Dr Thorne's Idea*); *The Villa Claudia* (**1904**); *The Silent War* (**1906**).

MITCHELL, SILAS WEIR (1829–1914). American physician, neurologist and writer, of considerable eminence for his original research, publishing at least 172 papers from 1852 on neurophysiology and related subjects. Most of his voluminous fiction is historical and depicts American subjects solemnly and romantically. His first story, "The Case of George Dedlow" (1866), is of some sf interest, as it is a satire on spiritualism. In *Dr North and his Friends* (**1900**), a female character exhibits a dual personality; it is one of the earliest appearances of this phenomenon (*see* PSYCHOLOGY) in fiction. *Little Stories* (coll. **1903**) assembles tales whose sf interest lies in SWM's ability to ground supernatural subject matter with speculations usually derived from his own researches. A further story, "Was He Dead?" (1870), appears in *Future Perfect* (anth. **1966**) ed. H. Bruce FRANKLIN.   [JC]

MITCHISON, NAOMI (MARGARET) (1897–). British novelist, story writer, cattle breeder and polemicist, born in Scotland, sister of J.B.S. HALDANE. She is known mainly for her work outside the sf field, including

such historical novels as *The Conquered* (**1923**) and *The Corn King and the Spring Queen* (**1931**), the latter an ANTHROPOLOGICAL fantasy about Sparta. Some of her earlier short stories, such as "The Goat", published in *Barbarian Stories* (coll. **1929**), the short novel *The Powers of Light* (**1932**), which deals with prehistory, and many of the tales and fables in *The Fourth Pig* (coll. **1936**), use sf or fantasy elements for allegorical purposes. *To the Chapel Perilous* (**1955**) is a witty account of the Grail legend which pits rival anthropological and historical theories together as if, in a sense, they were all true; it deserves to be better known. *The Big House* (**1950**) is a fairy tale for children, with a Celtic redolence. *Behold Your King* (**1957**) is a novel about Christ's crucifixion, told in a slangy, contemporary idiom to demystify it.

NM's first genuine sf novel is *Memoirs of a Spacewoman* (**1962**), a ruminative picaresque comprised of a series of episodes remembered by the narrator, Mary, a COMMUNICATIONS expert dealing with ALIEN intelligences. Most of the episodes contain ingenious biological (or exobiological) speculations. Mary's reminiscences are warm and urgent; her job requires travel, which requires "time blackouts", so that she constantly returns to a changed world. She loves her job, however, and intends to continue; it is a radiant book. NM's more recent sf novel, *Solution Three* (**1975**), is a less sustained examination of a CLONE solution to the problems of a post-catastrophe Earth. Heterosexuality is out; but a new generation is beginning to question the rigidity of the homosexual Solution Three.   [JC]
See also: INTELLIGENCE; MYTHOLOGY; WOMEN.

MITSUSE, RYU *See* JAPAN.

MODERN ELECTRICS *See* SCIENCE AND INVENTION.

MOEBIUS *See* Jean GIRAUD.

MOEBIUS TRIP American FANZINE (1969–) edited from Illinois by Edward Connor. Also known as *Sf Echo*, *MT* is a substantial, duplicated fanzine, unusually bound in book format rather than in standard quarto size. Contents are varied and contributors have included Philip José FARMER, Leslie Fiedler and Jack WODHAMS. A long and useful series of interviews with sf authors has also been published in the fanzine.   [PR]

MOFFETT, CLEVELAND LANGSTON (1863–1926). American playwright and popular novelist, author of one of the not infrequent early-20th-century American sf novels featuring Thomas Alva Edison or someone like him. In *The Conquest of America* (**1916**), it is the inventor himself who fends off a future-WAR threat from Germany.   [JC]

MONEY Love of money, being the root of all evil, has always played a leading part in literature, and sf is no exception. Few plots could move without it. Precisely because it is so basic, however, speculative thought has rarely focused upon it; it is one of those things that is habitually taken for granted. Money may change its form, and the dollar may be replaced by the CREDIT, but its centrality in human affairs is inviolable (in Anglo-American sf, at least). Jack VANCE has been particularly ingenious in the invention of various monetary systems adapted to different cultures.

The commonest of all wish-fulfilment fantasies is the sudden acquisition of wealth, and sf has often given form to the wish. As with other wish-fulfilment fantasies, however, sf writers have characteristically taken a cynical and slightly disapproving view of the issue, convinced that no good can come of it. The frenzy which can be aroused by the prospect of easy money is exemplified in history by the affair of the South Sea Bubble, and this prompted one of the earliest speculative fictions about speculation, Samuel Brunt's *A Voyage to Cacklogallinia* (**1727**). Many UTOPIANS before this date had, however, expressed their distaste for the profit motive and its effects on human affairs. Various romances commenting on the folly of the alchemical quest — of which the most notable is Honoré de BALZAC's *La recherche de l'absolu* (**1834**; trans. as *Balthazar; or Science & Love* **1859**; vt *In Search of the Absolute*) — took a similar line. The prospect of science making the alchemist's quest a reality did little to alter this disparaging attitude. Edgar Allan POE's "Von Kempelen and His Discovery" (1849) suggests that the discovery would simply rob a practically-valueless metal of its ridiculous price and that the world would press on regardless. Arthur Conan DOYLE's successful gold-maker in *The Doings of Raffles Haw* (**1891**) is quickly disillusioned with philanthropy and reverts his hoard to the dust whence it came. Henry Richardson Chamberlain's *6000 Tons of Gold* (**1894**) nearly precipitates world-wide catastrophe. The hero of E. Charles VIVIAN's *Star Dust* (**1925**) finds that his success opens few doors to him and turns his machine to the business of raising storm and tempest instead. Only John TAINE's hero in *Quayle's Invention* (**1927**) seemed to get much joy out of his instant wealth, and he found it far from easy. Much more beneficial to humanity, in the eyes of its author, was the wealth-destroying machine in George Allan ENGLAND's *The Golden Blight* (**1916**), which freed mankind from the present generation of capitalists. Money come by honestly, however, could occasionally be put to good as well as evil use, as in *Les cinq cent millions de la bégum* (**1879**; trans. as *The Begum's Fortune* **1880**) by Jules VERNE.

The main change in the money system made consistently by sf writers is the replacement of the gold standard, usually by a purely theoretical credit system. The dangers of relying on an artificial standard are investigated not only by the gold-making stories but by Garrett P. SERVISS's *The Moon Metal* (**1900**). George O. SMITH's "Pandora's Millions" (1945), though, concerns the desperate race to find a new symbolic medium of exchange following the invention of the matter-duplicator.

One theme that has fascinated a few writers is that of compound interest. Simple mathematics show that money invested for a thousand years grows quite magnificently even at relatively low interest rates. Men awake from periods of SUSPENDED ANIMATION to find themselves rich in Edmond ABOUT's *L'homme à l'oreille cassée* (**1861**; trans. as *The Man With the Broken Ear* **1867**) and H. G. WELLS's *When the Sleeper Wakes* (**1899**; rev. as *The Sleeper Awakes* 1910). Harry Stephen Keeler took the notion to extremes in "John Jones' Dollar" (1927), in which a dollar invested in trust for John Jones's distant descendant ultimately grows to represent all the wealth in the universe. More recently, however, we have become all too aware of what inflation can do to long-term investments, and the hero of Frederik POHL's *The Age of the Pussyfoot* (**1968**) awakes from suspended animation to find his "fortune" valueless in terms of real purchasing power.   [BS]

See also: ECONOMICS.

MONITORS, THE Film (1969). A Commonwealth United Production. Directed by Jack Shea, starring Guy Stockwell, Susan Oliver, Avery Schreiber and Sherry Jackson, with cameos by Keenan Wynn, Ed Begley, Larry Storch, Alan Arkin, Xavier Cugat and Stubby Kaye. Screenplay by Myron J. Gold, based on the novel by Keith LAUMER. 92 mins. Colour.

Filled with bizarre jokes and moments of stunning banality, this film, made in Chicago by the Second City cabaret troupe, concerns an invasion of Earth by superior aliens who enforce on the population a system of brotherly love and non-violence. Dressed in black overcoats, black hats and dark glasses, the "monitors" control people by spraying them with a pacifying gas, but a resistance movement is formed and they are overthrown. A genuine oddity, which flopped badly, the film is very much a product of the late 1960s, when the hippy "flower power" counterculture seemed, to some, to be ushering in an era of peace and happiness.   [JB]

MONOLITH MONSTERS, THE Film (1957). Universal. Directed by John Sherwood, starring Grant Williams, Lola Albright and Les Tremayne. Screenplay by Norman Jolley and Robert M. Fresco,

Giant crystals lurch towards a desert town in the bizarre THE MONOLITH MONSTERS.

based on a story by Jack ARNOLD and Robert M. Fresco. 77 mins. B/w.

Crystals from a meteorite which has landed near a small desert town grow rapidly when wet. They also cause death by absorbing all the silicon from any living thing that touches them, paradoxically turning the victims to stone. When a rainstorm causes the crystals to expand violently over a large area the town's destruction seems imminent, until it is discovered that salt will destroy them. The special effects by Clifford Stine are good, particularly in the sequences showing the crystals rearing up, then crashing down, in their inexorable march towards the town. Sherwood's debt to Jack Arnold is obvious, especially in the moody desert landscapes. The idea of the marching crystals may well have been borrowed from "White Lily" (1930) by John TAINE.   [JB/PN]

MONROE, LYLE *See* Robert A. HEINLEIN.

MONSARRAT, NICHOLAS (1910–). English writer resident in Canada, best known for such adventure novels as *The Cruel Sea* (**1951**). His sf work, *The Time Before This* (**1962**), is about the discovery of ancient artefacts and frozen beings in Canada, evidence of a highly civilized earlier race on Earth.   [JC]

MONSTER ON THE CAMPUS Film (1958). Universal. Directed by Jack ARNOLD, starring Arthur Franz, Joanna Moore, Judson Pratt and Troy Donahue. Screenplay by David DUNCAN. 77 mins. B/w.

This is one of Jack Arnold's last sf films and is not among his best. Basically it is a variation on the Jekyll and Hyde theme: a scientist cuts his hand on the

teeth of a dead coelacanth which he is studying, and a substance in the creature's body fluid causes him to revert into a prehistoric ape-man. The subsequent plot is quite conventional for the genre, with some moments of genuine horror.   [JB]

Man's vision of MONSTERS is almost as ancient as art itself. This is a detail from Albrecht Dürer's 15th-century "Knight, Death and the Devil".

MONSTERS Monsters have always stalked the hinterlands of the imagination, the emblems of fear and the products of guilt. Commonly, they take their aspects and their roles from the SUPERNATURAL imagination, as in the stories of the early, marginal sf writer William Hope HODGSON, whose monsters appear like archetypal projections of inner horrors; but the scientific imagination, which seeks its explanations from inside nature rather than beyond it, has produced its monsters too. Imaginative writers have taken their images of the monstrous from a variety of sources: the prehistoric past revealed by the fossil record; familiar but

Virgil Finlay is among the sf artists who most enjoyed portraying MONSTERS. This illustration to A. Merritt's "The Face in the Abyss" comes from *A. Merritt's Fantasy Magazine*, July 1950.

repulsive creatures made monstrous by increasing size (*see* GREAT AND SMALL); and products of an alien creation. There are also monsters which arise as the direct products of human scientific endeavour, like the archetypal monster of science made by Mary SHELLEY's *Frankenstein* (**1818**).

Many of the standard figures of fear have made their way into sf via processes of rationalization. The INVISIBLE monster is the easiest to adapt, and there was one in the first issue of *Amazing Stories* — George Allan ENGLAND's "The Thing From — Outside" (1926). The monster haunts the characters as it might in a classic ghost story, but the interest of the story lies in their determinedly rational response to their predicament. The gorgon became C. L. MOORE's "Shambleau" (1933). Werewolves are rationalized in *Darker Than You Think* (1940; **1948**) by Jack WILLIAMSON and "There Shall Be No Darkness" (1950) by James BLISH. Vampires are "explained" in *I Am Legend* (**1954**) by Richard MATHESON and *The Space Vampires* (**1976**) by Colin WILSON. These are straightforward adaptations, but the idea of shape-changing, and analogues of vampirism, are associated with a great many of sf's monsters. "Asylum" (1942) by A.E. VAN VOGT and *Sinister Barrier* (1939; **1943**; rev. 1948) by Eric Frank RUSSELL are clearly vampire stories at root, while Van Vogt's "Discord in Scarlet" (1939) and Robert A. HEINLEIN's *The Puppet Masters* (**1951**) deal with processes of PARASITISM not too far removed from vampirism. "Who Goes There?" (1938) by John W. CAMPBELL Jr is a shape-changer story.

Monsters have always been popular in the movies (*see* CINEMA). The first of many versions of FRANKENSTEIN was made in 1910, but the legend was created anew in the 1930s when Boris Karloff took the role of the monster. A new legend was created in the same period by the story of KING KONG (1933). Here, for almost the first time, fear was modified by sympathy — these were the monsters of the

scientific imagination, and the notion of Evil was no longer relevant. The necessary destruction of monster by man could take on a dimension of tragedy, and the monsters could be pitied in their monstrousness.

This sympathy was slow in coming to PULP sf — and, indeed, it never became common in films despite *King Kong*'s classic status. There was too much potential in simple melodrama. Illustrators played a considerable part in building sf's monster mythology — alien horrors were a particularly rich source of

The cover for a special MONSTER issue of *Super-Science Fiction*, April 1959, is by Ed Emsh.

lurid cover pictures, and the Bug-Eyed Monster, or BEM (whose archetype appeared on the cover of *ASF* in May 1931, illustrating Charles Willard Diffin's "Dark Moon"), quickly became a cliché (*see* ILLUSTRATION).

After the war the monster theme became much less evident. *The Day of the Triffids* (**1951**) by John WYNDHAM was perhaps the last classic monster story in sf, though the theme continues in the

horror genre, and occasionally in marginal horror/sf, as in *The Clone* (**1965**) by Theodore L. THOMAS and Kate WILHELM, a tale of a constantly growing amorphous creature that emerges from drains and sewers and absorbs whoever is handy.

As sympathy for alien beings in general developed, priorities shifted, and several stories were written to analyse the predicament of the monster. The shock of monstrous self-discovery had been the theme of such stark parables of alienation as "The Outsider" (1926) by H.P. LOVECRAFT and Franz KAFKA's "Metamorphosis" (1916; trans. 1937; reprinted, showing some awareness of MAINSTREAM writing in the pulp magazines, in *Famous Fantastic Mysteries* in 1953), but many sf stories written in the 1960s and '70s were prepared to take the initial situation of monstrousness for granted and analyse its implications, especially the psychological ones. This is particularly common in the work of Robert SILVERBERG, e.g. *Thorns* (**1967**), *The Man in the Maze* (**1968**) and "Caliban" (1971) and crops up often in the work of Damon KNIGHT, e.g. "The Country of the Kind" (1956), *Beyond the Barrier* (**1963**) and *Mind Switch* (**1965**; vt *The Other Foot* UK). An interesting example from outside most DEFINITIONS OF SF is John GARDNER's *Grendel* (**1971**), which retells the Beowulf legend from the monster's viewpoint. The rehabilitation of the monster is perhaps best illustrated, however, by "Look, You Think You Got Troubles" by Carol Carr (1969), a Jewish mother's account of her daughter's marriage to a Martian whose eventual conversion to Judaism makes everything all right.   [BS]

See also: ALIENS; GODS AND DEMONS; GOTHIC SF; MYTHOLOGY.

MONTANARI, GIANNI (1949–). Italian writer, translator, editor and critic. His university thesis on sf was revised into book form as *Ieri, il futuro* ["Yesterday, the Future"] (**1977**); it is a study of British sf. GM edits two well-known Italian sf book series, Galassia and SFBC. In the former, two of his own novels have been published, *Nel nome dell'uomo* ["In the Name of Man"] **(1971)** and *La sepoltura* ["The Burial"] **(1972)**. The latter is an attack on Italian hypocrisy from a left-wing stance, including hypocrisy within the sf genre itself. GM's first published story was in 1968.   [PN]

MONTELEONE, THOMAS F. (? –). American writer, who has been active in sf since 1972, both with short stories, two of which have received NEBULA nominations, and with novels, the first being *Seeds of Change* **(1975)**. This was a routine, rather brutal story of revolution against a tightly regulated future society, but of interest as the first of the LASER BOOKS, issued free to libraries and booksellers as a promotional item in order to generate sales of later titles. TFM's subsequent novels are *The Time Connection* **(1976)** and *Time Swept City* **(1977)**. He also edited the theme anthology *The Arts and Beyond: Visions of Man's Aesthetic Future* (anth. **1977**). TM was secretary of SFWA for three years.   [PN]

MONTHLY STORY BLUE BOOK MAGAZINE, THE *See* BLUE BOOK MAGAZINE, THE.

MONTHLY STORY MAGAZINE, THE *See* BLUE BOOK MAGAZINE, THE.

MOON, THE The lunar voyage has a long literary history, having developed from one of the standard frameworks of social SATIRE to become one of the archetypal projects of speculative fiction. Major works in the former tradition are two second-century tales by LUCIAN of Samosata; Francis GODWIN's *The Man in the Moone* **(1638)**; the first part of CYRANO DE BERGERAC's *L'autre monde* **(1657)**; Daniel DEFOE's *The Consolidator* **(1705)**; Samuel Brunt's *A Voyage to Cacklogallinia* **(1727)**; Murtagh McDERMOT's *A Trip to the Moon* **(1728)**; and Joseph ATTERLEY's *A Voyage to the Moon* **(1827)**. This phase of the history of the lunar voyage is the subject of Marjorie Hope NICOLSON's excellent study *Voyages to the Moon* **(1948)**, which has an extensive annotated bibliography.

The use of the Moon as a stage for the erection of mock societies became less fashionable in the 19th century, though echoes of the tradition recur even in the present century, for example in Compton MACKENZIE's *The Lunatic Republic* **(1959)**. The idea that travelling to the Moon was a notion that might be worth taking seriously first crops up in the appendix to John WILKINS' *The Discovery of a New World* (third edition **1640**), where the author suggests that a man might be carried to the Moon by a large bird or that a flying machine capable of the trip might one day become practical. Another writer to take seriously the modes of travel used as conveniences by satirists was David RUSSEN, author of *Iter Lunare* **(1703)**, whose own proposition that a man might be propelled to the Moon by the force of a gargantuan spring now seems a little far-fetched. The first writer to make a determined attempt at verisimilitude in his account of a Moon voyage was Edgar Allan POE, whose "Hans Pfaall" **(1835)** is a curious admixture of comic satire and "hard" speculative fiction, though Pfaall's balloon now seems hardly more credible than Russen's spring. A more convincing attempt (though likewise not kindly treated by the passage of time) was the thoroughly serious space-gun envisaged by Jules VERNE in *De la terre à la lune* **(1865)** and *Autour de la lune* **(1870)**, the two translated as one book *From the Earth to the Moon* (trans. **1873**). Many of the early Moon voyages, up to 1841, can be found in *The Man in the Moone* (anth. **1971**) ed. Faith K. PIZOR and T. Allan Comp.

Serious interest in the Moon in its own right, possibly harbouring life of its own, began with the speculative final passage of Johannes KEPLER's *Somnium* **(1634** in Latin), but this work stands almost alone. Richard Adams LOCKE published his "Moon Hoax" in the *New York Sun* in 1835, purporting to describe the inhabitants of the Moon as observed by Sir John Herschel with the aid of a new telescope, but this vision of lunar life was a gaudy burlesque. By the time the cosmic voyage began to be taken seriously in the 19th century the possibility of there being life on the Moon was already past credibility. H. G. WELLS imagined a Selenite society within the Moon in *The First Men in the Moon* **(1901)** but the setting here was no more than a convenient literary device, a licence taken out for the attempt to design the first ALIEN society. Works contemporary with Wells share a rather different image of the Moon as a place of ultimate desolation where life, if it had ever existed, was long gone. W. S. LACH-SZYRMA's "Letters from the Planets" (1887–93), Edgar FAWCETT's *The Ghost of Guy Thyrle* **(1895)** and George GRIFFITH's *A Honeymoon in Space* **(1901)** all have scenes in which interplanetary voyagers find the ruins of long-dead civilizations on the Moon, and there is a curious, nostalgic sense of tragedy in each of these representations.

Lunar life does, however, crop up in scientific romances whose authors took a much more cavalier attitude to the matter of credibility. The first trip to the Moon which seems to have been motivated solely by the spirit of adventure was a brief episode in Ralph MORRIS's ROBINSONADE *The Life and Wonderful Adventures of John Daniel* **(1751)**. Some of Verne's imitators, however, were inspired by the daring of his "voyages imaginaires" without being restrained by his respect for scientific plausibility. André LAURIE featured a trip to the dead Moon in *The Conquest of the Moon* **(1889)** — a voyage memorable because of the magnificently ridiculous notion that the vacuum of space might be

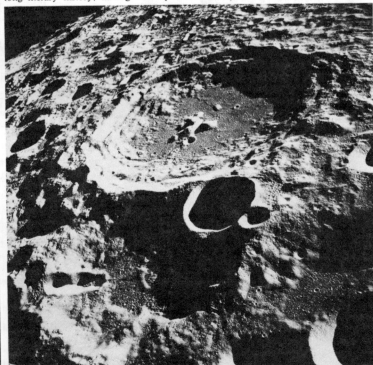

The far side of the MOON as photographed by *Apollo 11* astronauts. Before the space programme this part of the Moon was a fine field for sf speculation. Photo NASA, 1969.

avoided by dragging the Moon temporarily into the Earth's atmosphere by the power of giant magnets. A British writer, Mark Wicks, wrote a Vernian novel in *To Mars Via the Moon* (**1911**), while the most notable of the early American writers of juvenile scientific romances, the pseudonymous Roy Rockwood, contributed *Lost on the Moon* (**1911**). Lunar life, however, made its reappearance in extravagant style primarily in the works of the American PULP writers, notably in Edgar Rice Burroughs' *The Moon Maid* (1923–5; fix-up **1926**), Edmond Hamilton's "The Other Side of the Moon" (1929), Otis Adelbert Kline's *Maza of the Moon* (**1930**) and, most impressively, Jack Williamson's "The Moon Era" (1932). Even here there was consistent recognition of the deadness of the Moon's visible surface — the aliens are within the Moon or from its invisible face, or on the Moon as it was a very long time ago. The sf pulps produced their own nostalgic elegy for lunar life in Lester del Rey's "The Wings of Night" (1942).

Dead or not, however, the Moon was there — a mere quarter of a million miles away. It was there to be reached and to be claimed. To the early pulp writers this was an article of faith, but it was also a dream of a future they did not expect to arrive so very soon, and so they made light of the problem and minimized the Moon's importance — it became one short and relatively tedious step *en route* to Mars or the stars. The lunar voyagers of the 1930s and early '40s took the Moon very much for granted. It was a constant but rarely central theme of sf of the period. But this situation changed dramatically during the years of the Second World War. The imminent possibility of space travel in the real world was taken seriously by a few writers even in 1939 — Arthur C. Clarke's essay "We Can Rocket to the Moon — Now!" was published in that year — but it was the advent of the V-1 and V-2 rocket-bombs that hammered the point home. The V-1 looked very much as sf writers in the wake of Konstantin Tsiolkovsky had always imagined a SPACESHIP would look (*see* ROCKETS). The post-War era saw the publication of a number of visionary novels which elevated the first trip to the Moon to mythical status. Robert A. Heinlein, who had earlier written the poignant "Requiem" (1940) about the burning ambition of a man who longed to go to the Moon even knowing that the trip would kill him, now wrote a short novel about the same hero's earlier fight to finance the first Moon-shot and sell the myth of space conquest to the world: "The Man Who Sold the Moon" (1950). Heinlein also scripted the George Pal film *Destination Moon* (1950). Arthur Clarke, the chief British prophet and propagandist of space travel, wrote *Prelude to Space* (**1951**). Writers of juvenile fiction, in

particular, made much of the myth — Heinlein in *Rocketship Galileo* (**1947**), Clarke in the space-station story *Islands in the Sky* (**1952**) and Lester del Rey in *Mission to the Moon* (**1956**) and its sequels. Pierre Boulle ultimately moved the myth into MAINSTREAM fiction in *Le jardin de Kanashima* (**1964**; trans. as *Garden on the Moon* **1965**), and though most sf writers had by then abandoned the theme as too commonplace William F. Temple showed that it was still viable within the genre in *Shoot at the Moon* (**1966**). Neil Armstrong set the seal on the myth with his little speech delivered as he set foot on the Moon in 1969.

Actually reaching the Moon was, of course, only one of the issues which confronted sf writers. Its logical corollary — or so it seemed to them — was the establishment of lunar bases, followed in due course by lunar colonies. Even in the Gernsback pulps the lunar colony had waged its war of independence in "The Birth of a New Republic" (1931) by Jack Williamson and Miles J. Breuer, and it was easy to see where the sympathies of the authors lay. Even as they propagandized the myth of reaching out for the Moon Heinlein and Clarke were backing this up with the myth of its colonization, Heinlein in a series of stories published in the *Saturday Evening Post*, including "It's Great to be Back" (1947), "The Black Pits of Luna" (1947) and "Gentlemen — Be Seated!" (1948), Clarke in *Earthlight* (**1951**) and later in *A Fall of Moondust* (**1961**). The Moon, of course, was known to be an utterly hostile environment, but faith in human ingenuity ran high. John W. Campbell Jr wrote the ultimate robinsonade in *The Moon is Hell* (**1950**), in which stranded spacemen make their poor refuge into a reasonable imitation of a Hilton Hotel. Subsequent writers, such as Charles Eric Maine in *High Vacuum* (**1956**), were more modest in their claims, but still confident of the outcome. Mysteries set on the inhabited Moon became commonplace — Murray Leinster's *City on the Moon* (**1957**) and Clifford D. Simak's *Trouble With Tycho* (**1961**) are examples — and Heinlein produced a new version of the birth of the new republic in *The Moon is a Harsh Mistress* (**1966**).

Despite its deadness the Moon retained its status as an alien world, and this is particularly well shown by a group of stories in which visitors find there some echo of other visitors long passed on: artefacts left behind to confront the Earthmen breaking out of their atmospheric shell with a glimpse of the infinite possibilities of an inhabited universe. Arthur Clarke's "Sentinel of Eternity" (1951; vt "The Sentinel") captured the essence of this notion and became its archetypal expression, ultimately forming the seed of the film 2001: A SPACE ODYSSEY (1967), novelized under the same title (**1968**). A much more

extreme version is *Rogue Moon* (**1960**) by Algis Budrys, in which an enigmatic machine discovered on the Moon kills a man over and over again as he tries to move through its surrounding maze to its centre.

A theme anthology is *Men on the Moon* (**1958**) ed. Donald A. Wollheim. [BS]
See also: ASTRONOMY; NEAR FUTURE; SPACE FLIGHT.

MOONBASE 3 Television serial (1973). BBC TV. Producer: Barry Letts. Script editor: Terrance Dicks. 6 episodes, each 30 mins. Colour. Scriptwriters included Terrance Dicks, Barry Letts, John Brason, John Lucarotti and Arden Winch. Directors included Ken Hannam and Christopher Barry.

The serial was set on a Moon base in AD 2003, and concerned a group of scientists. The usual sensational elements of TV sf, such as ALIENS and MONSTERS, were studiously avoided by the makers; but the attempt at a responsible realism was somewhat dull. [JB]

MOON ZERO TWO Film (1969). Hammer/Warner Bros. Directed by Roy Ward Baker, starring James Olson, Catherine von Schell, Warren Mitchell and Adrienne Corri. Screenplay by Michael Carreras. Special effects by Kit West, Nick Allder and Les Bowie. 100 mins. Colour.

At the same time as the first actual Moon landing, Hammer Films were making this quasi-Western, set on the Moon, and the results were predictably absurd. One of the hoariest of pulp Western plots is dressed up with a lot of colourful space hardware: a poor but honest space pilot/cowboy is forced by a group of villains to capture an asteroid of pure sapphire, but his principles triumph and he foils their plans. The special effects are unexpectedly convincing, considering the relatively small budget, but the film has no other strength. A novelization with the same title by John Burke was published in **1969**. [JB]

MOORCOCK, MICHAEL (1939–). English writer, editor and occasional composer. Married Hilary Bailey in 1962, divorced 1978. His vivid early memories of the Second World War bombing of London are constantly reflected in his fiction, and wartime London provides many of its characteristic landscapes and images of ENTROPY. During his somewhat desultory schooling, MM began to produce hand-done magazines, beginning with *Outlaw's Own* in 1951, and continuing with several others until about 1960; after leaving school, he began to contribute to *Tarzan Adventures*, which he edited 1956–8, producing for it his first HEROIC-FANTASY series, which has been assembled as *Sojan* (coll. of linked stories plus independent material **1977**); *The Golden Barge*, a novel written in 1958, is also projected

Michael MOORCOCK, an author of many faces, is here appropriately enigmatic.

for publication in 1978. Both volumes demonstrate the precocity common to many generic writers, plus an already characteristic questioning of the violence and dubious morality of the genre which he was to exploit extensively for the next 15 years. After working on the Sexton Blake Library (which published thrillers), publishing one non-sf novel for it, *Caribbean Crisis* (**1962** as by Desmond Reid), and after doing some night-club work as a blues singer, MM, inspired by E.J. CARNELL, began to contribute sf and fantasy stories to SF ADVENTURES and SCIENCE FANTASY. His first sf novel is *The Sundered Worlds* (1962–3 *SF Adventures*; fix-up **1965**; vt *The Blood Red Game*), a metaphysical SPACE OPERA which introduces the term "multiverse" (the word itself is probably derived from the writings of John Cowper POWYS); by multiverse, MM has come to mean, very loosely, a universe in which multiple alternate realities co-exist, sometimes destroying one another, though never permanently, and in which some of the same cosmic dramas are played and replayed by various characters in various worlds. The fundamental conflict in his heroic fantasies, and more complexly in his other work, is between order and chaos; these opposing principles are sometimes represented in the rather gaudy language of SWORD AND SORCERY, and sometimes exist only as an inference to be drawn from the text; but the conflict is always there.

It is in the heroic-fantasy series for which he is perhaps best known that MM has made the most explicit use of the notion of the multiverse, specifically using the idea to justify the numerous cross-references and linkages which virtually (though not quite) make all his series and individual books into one super-series. As these linkages are understandable as workings-out of the multiverse concept, and are too complex for ready summary, MM's series are here treated as formally separate from one another.

After the Sojan stories, the first series to take shape, at least in magazine form, the Erekosë sequence, comprised of *The Eternal Champion* (1956 *Avilion*; 1962 *Science Fantasy*; fix-up **1970**) and *Phoenix in Obsidian* (**1970**; vt *The Silver Warriors* USA), makes articulate the notion of the Eternal Champion who, under whatever name, seeks to resolve the war between order and chaos at the heart of each story. Soon after this came MM's most remarkable heroic-fantasy sequence, the novels and stories dealing with the anti-hero Elric of Melniboné, a melancholic albino monarch dominated by his evilly sentient sword. The "Elric" stories have appeared from 1961 out of chronological order, and have recently been reissued, some with reordered and revised contents, in the following proper order: *Elric of Melniboné* (**1972** vt *The Dreaming City* USA); *The Sailor on the Seas of Fate* (including a reworking of *The Jade Man's Eyes*, **1973**; fix-up **1976**); *The Weird of the White Wolf* (1961 3 *Science Fantasy*, comprised of four stories from *The Stealer of Souls*, coll. of linked stories **1963**; plus two stories from *The Singing Citadel*, coll. **1970**; coll. of linked stories **1977**); *The Sleeping Sorceress* (**1971**; vt *The Vanishing Tower* USA); *The Bane of the Black Sword* (including one story each from *The Stealer of Souls* and *The Singing Citadel* plus new material **1977**); *Stormbringer* (1963–4 *Science Fantasy*; with cuts **1965**; text restored and rev. **1977**). An illustrated booklet, *Elric, the Return to Melniboné* (**1973**), has not been reissued; a further "Elric" story is projected for 1978 publication. Elric's doomed defence of his empire of Melniboné against Chaos (as embodied by his own sword) attains moments, especially in the first-written segments, of an oddly passive intensity very much unlike the normal run of heroic fantasy. Indeed, rather than identify himself with such writers as Robert E. HOWARD, MM prefers to see as influential upon his work such writers as Mervyn PEAKE.

Most of MM's other heroic-fantasy series either began in these early years of his career or closely resemble early work. They include the "Corum" books, *The Knight of the Swords* (**1971**), *The Queen of the Swords* (**1971**) and *The King of the Swords* (**1971**), all three being assembled as *The Swords Trilogy* (coll. **1977**), plus *The Bull and the Spear* (**1973**), *The Oak and the Ram* (**1973**) and *The Sword and the Stallion* (**1974**); the "Hawkmoon" books, *The Jewel in the Skull* (**1967**; rev. **1977**), *Sorcerer's Amulet* (**1968**; rev. **1977**; vt *The Mad God's Amulet* UK and later USA), *Sword of the Dawn* (**1968**; rev. **1977**; vt *The Sword of the Dawn* UK and later USA) and *The Secret of the Runestaff* (**1969**; rev. **1977**; vt *The Runestaff* UK and later USA), comprising an initial tetralogy, plus *Count Brass* (**1973**), *The Champion of Garathorm* (**1973**) and *The Quest for Tanelorn* (**1975**),

comprising a concluding trilogy, the last volume of which formally brings to a climax and terminates all stories involving the Eternal Champion; and a cognate series, originally written as by Edward P. Bradbury, later published under his own name, an Edgar Rice BURROUGHS pastiche comprised of *Warriors of Mars* (**1965**; vt *The City of the Beast* USA and later UK), *Blades of Mars* (**1965**; vt *The Lord of the Spiders* USA and later UK) and *Barbarians of Mars* (**1965**; vt *The Masters of the Pit* USA and later UK).

During the years the heroic-fantasy multiverse was taking shape, MM also began to conceive more ambitious projects; from very early on, he had a strong, argumentative sense that the quality of genre fiction, both sf and fantasy, sadly lacked human values and literacy of texture, and when he became editor of NEW WORLDS in May/Jun. 1964, a position he held, with a few voluntary breaks, from issue 142 to its demise as a magazine with issue 201 in Mar. 1971, he very quickly began to accept and proselytize for the kind of stories soon to be characterized as typical of the English NEW WAVE. *NW* continued as a series of paperback book anthologies until 1976, the first six of these (**1971–3**) being edited by MM, the remainder by his wife. *NW* and the new wave were virtually synonymous in the middle and late 1960s; and MM published stories experimental in form and content from many writers, including Brian W. ALDISS, J.G. BALLARD, Thomas M. DISCH, M. John HARRISON, John T. SLADEK, Norman SPINRAD and many others, along with his own material. In addition to the pseudonyms Desmond Reid and Edward P. Bradbury, MM also used in these years the names Bill Barclay (for two non-sf novels), the collaborative pseudonym Michael BARRINGTON with Barrington J. BAYLEY, and the floating pseudonym James COLVIN (under which he published fiction and reviews, and other writers the occasional review, in *NW*); MM also published as Colvin *The Deep Fix* (coll. **1966**), the title novella and two short stories from this being included in *The Time Dweller* (coll. **1969**). Of the genre sf he published in these years, *The Ice Schooner* (1966 *SF Impulse*; **1969**; rev. 1977), a homage to and recasting of Joseph CONRAD's *The Rescue* (**1920**), convincingly portrays the cultures of a new Ice Age at the point at which the temperature begins to rise again. Of greater significance, however, was the publication in 1965 of the first sections of the "Jerry Cornelius" sequence, ultimately comprised of *The Final Programme* (excerpts 1965–6 *NW*; **1968**; rev. 1969) which was filmed as THE FINAL PROGRAMME (1973; vt *The Last Days of Man on Earth* USA), *A Cure for Cancer* (1969 *NW*; **1971**), *The English Assassin* (**1972**) and *The Condition of Muzak* (**1977**; rev. 1978 paperback edition), all four being revised and assembled as a tetralogy, *The Cornelius Chronicles* (coll. **1977**). *The Lives and Times of Jerry Cornelius* (coll. **1976**) and *The Adventures of Una Persson and Catherine Cornelius in the Twentieth Century* (**1976**) contain associated material, as does *The Nature of the Catastrophe* (anth. **1971**) which, edited by MM and Langdon JONES, contains stories and material by MM and other *NW* writers who used the Cornelius figure for their own work; *The Distant Suns* (1969 *The Illustrated Weekly of India*; **1975**) with Philip James (James CAWTHORN) has as its protagonist a Jerry Cornelius who bears no relation to the Jerry Cornelius of the other books. Cornelius begins as a portmanteau anti-hero painted in the pop colours of 1960s Swinging London, an instant myth whom MM and his associates used both iconoclastically (to mock the kinds of sf story in which he starred) and as a positive emblem of *NW*'s innovative literary campaigns. In later volumes, MM's deeper intentions regarding Cornelius come clearer: Jerry and his enduring family and associates, as they inhabit and manipulate and are manipulated by various forms of London in the multiverse, come to represent a search for a *modus vivendi* (caught between Law and Chaos) for surviving in the intensely urban latter 20th century. The Cornelius books are MM's most substantial achievement.

Two other mature sequences are worthy of note as well, however. *Behold the Man* (1966 *NW*; exp. **1969**), the magazine version of which won a 1967 NEBULA award for best novella, and *Breakfast in the Ruins* (**1972**), both feature Karl Glogauer; in the earlier book he is cast by a time machine into the beginning of our era, where he becomes Christ and is crucified; in the second book, structured as a series of vignettes, Glogauer is exposed to a series of moral crises exemplary of our modern world, and to which he is forced to respond. The second sequence of note is set in the FAR FUTURE, and is comprised of a main trilogy, *An Alien Heat* (**1972**), *The Hollow Lands* (**1974**) and *The End of All Songs* (**1976**), plus *Legends from the End of Time* (coll. **1976**) and *The Transformation of Miss Mavis Ming* (**1977**; vt *A Messiah at the End of Time* USA); the protagonist of the sequence, Jherek Carnelian, is an obvious version of Jerry Cornelius, but is an independent character at the same time; in the far-future Earth he inhabits, infinitely available power makes everything and everyone constantly malleable, but Carnelian, transported into the 19th century, becomes obsessed with humanity's moral and physical trammels, even to the point of falling in love. Though the novels and stories are dreamlike, a consistent humane melancholy infuses them.

Though MM is still strongly associated with *NW*, his best work has been done since that magazine folded. His novels intermix sf, fantasy and Edwardian social realism with increasing authority, and constitute a remarkable progress from PULP fiction to works that transcend genre, though without abandoning any of the material and concerns of their origins. By following this course, MM has become a writer of some stature and influence within and without the sf/fantasy field; as a token of this, *The Condition of Muzak* won the 1977 *Guardian* Fiction Prize.   [JC]

Other works: *The Fireclown* (**1965**; vt *The Winds of Limbo* USA); *The Twilight Man* (**1966**; vt *The Shores of Death*); *The Wrecks of Time* (1965–6 *NW* as by James Colvin; edited version **1967**; vt with text restored *The Rituals of Infinity* 1971 UK); *The Black Corridor* (**1969**) with Hilary Bailey (uncredited); *The Warlord of the Air* (**1971**) with its sequel *The Land Leviathan* (**1974**); *Moorcock's Book of Martyrs* (coll. **1976**). *The Time of the Hawklords* (**1976**) and *Queens of Deliria* (**1977**), both listed as by MM and Michael BUTTERWORTH, are by Butterworth alone, only the general idea being supplied by MM. As by Bill Barclay: *Somewhere in the Night* (**1966**; rev. vt *The Chinese Agent* as by MM) with its sequel *Printer's Devil* (**1966**).

As editor: *The Best of New Worlds* (anth. **1965**); *Best S.F. Stories from New Worlds* (anth. **1967**); *Best Stories from New Worlds 2* (anth. **1968**; vt *Best S.F. Stories from New Worlds 2* USA); *Best S.F. Stories from New Worlds 3* (anth. **1968**); *The Traps of Time* (anth. **1968**); *Best S.F. Stories from New Worlds 4* (anth. **1969**); *The Inner Landscape* (anth. **1969**, edited anonymously); *Best S.F. Stories from New Worlds 5* (anth. **1969**); *Best S.F. Stories from New Worlds 6* (anth. **1970**); *Best S.F. Stories from New Worlds 7* (anth. **1971**); *New Worlds 1* (anth. **1971**; vt *New Worlds Quarterly 1* USA); *New Worlds 2* (anth. **1971**; vt *New Worlds Quarterly 2* USA); *New Worlds 3* (anth. **1972**; vt *New Worlds Quarterly 3* USA); *New Worlds 4* (anth. **1972**; vt *New Worlds Quarterly 4* USA); *New Worlds 5* (anth. **1973**); *New Worlds 6* (anth. **1973**; vt *New Worlds Quarterly 5* USA) with Charles PLATT; *Best S.F. Stories from New Worlds 8* (anth. **1974**); *Before Armageddon* (anth. **1975**); *England Invaded* (anth. **1977**).

As composer and singer: *The New Worlds Fair* (album 1975) with Graham Charnock and Steve Gilmore.

Films: THE LAND THAT TIME FORGOT (1975), script by MM and James Cawthorn.

See also: ABSURDIST SF; ADAM AND EVE; CITIES; COMIC STRIPS; CRITICAL AND HISTORICAL WORKS; FANTASY; HOLOCAUST AND AFTER; HUMOUR; IMMORTALITY; LEISURE; MEDIA LANDSCAPE; MESSIAHS; MUSIC AND OPERA; MYTHOLOGY; OPTIMISM AND PESSIMISM; PARALLEL WORLDS; POLITICS; RELIGION; SATIRE; SF MAGAZINES; SF OVERTAKEN BY EVENTS; SEX; SUSPENDED ANIMATION; TIME TRAVEL; WAR.

MOORE, BRIAN (1921–). Irish-born Canadian novelist, now resident in the USA; best known for such works outside the sf field as *The Luck of Ginger Coffey* (**1960**). His novel *The Great Victorian Collection* (**1975**) somewhat resembles sf in its allegorical treatment of a professor who dreams into reality a collection of Victorian antiques, which survive his death. *Catholics* (**1972**) is a short novel dealing with a wishy-washy, liberal Roman Catholicism at the end of the 20th century pitted against a conservative Catholic revivalism run by a cynical priest in Ireland; milk-and-water ecumenicalism wins the day.   [JC/PN]

MOORE, C(ATHERINE) L. (1911–). American writer. Married (1) Henry KUTTNER, (2) Thomas Reggie. CLM was working as a secretary in a bank when she wrote her first story, "Shambleau" (1933), which appeared in WEIRD TALES and made her name immediately prominent. A variation on the Medusa legend and crammed with ambiguous Freudian symbolism, it is a powerful, if partly subconscious, early example from the PULP MAGAZINES of SEX in sf. Its hero, Northwest Smith, continued his adventures through a series of weird fantasies in interplanetary settings: "Black Thirst" (1934), "Scarlet Dream" (1934), "Dust of Gods" (1934), "Juhli" (1935), "Nymph of Darkness" (1935) in collaboration with Forrest J. ACKERMAN, "The Cold Gray God" (1935), "Yvala" (1936), "Lost Paradise" (1936), "The Tree of Life" (1936), "Quest of the Starstone" (1937), in collaboration with Henry Kuttner, "Werewoman" (1938), "Song in a Minor Key" (1940). Excepting the Ackerman collaboration, all the stories up to and including "The Tree of Life" can be found in the books *Shambleau and Others* (coll. **1953**; vt *Shambleau* in subsequent editions; USA paperback edition omits four stories and all British paperback editions omit one) and *Northwest of Earth* (coll. **1954**).

In 1934 CLM commenced another series in *Weird Tales*, this time with a heroine, Jirel of Joiry. Written in the same highly coloured, romantic style which characterized the "Northwest Smith" series, these were SWORD-AND-SORCERY tales in an imaginary medieval French setting. *Jirel of Joiry* (1934–9 *Weird Tales*; fix-up **1969**; vt *Black God's Shadow*) includes five of the six stories, which are also variously collected in *Shambleau and Others* and *Northwest of Earth*. The exception is "Quest of the Starstone", in which Northwest Smith and Jirel of Joiry meet. This story is also notable as CLM's first collaboration with Henry Kuttner, whom she married in 1940. Thereafter she became a full-time writer.

Most of their subsequent work was collaborative to some degree, and is discussed in the entry for Kuttner. Attempts to attribute stories published under Kuttner's name or under their multitudinous pseudonyms have been largely fruitless and contradictory, although it is known that some stories under the name of Lawrence O'Donnell were written entirely by CLM, and stories published under her name are her own. Outstanding among these are "No Woman Born", (1944) and "Vintage Season" (1946, as by O'Donnell). The former is a seminal treatment of the CYBORG theme, focusing on the PSYCHOLOGICAL problems which would face a human (in this case female) brain in an artificial body; the latter suggests that TIME TRAVEL might be a tourist industry, bringing visitors from a decadent future to sample historical catastrophes. Both stories create a typically rich atmosphere, but the style is far more controlled than in earlier works.

CLM, like her husband, went to college in 1950, graduating in 1956. After Kuttner's death, she moved into writing for television, doing scripts for such series as *Maverick* and *77 Sunset Strip*. She remarried in 1964. [MJE]
Other works: *Judgement Night* (coll. **1952**; paperback edition includes only the title novel, 1943 *ASF*); *Beyond Earth's Gates* (1949 *Startling Stories* as "The Portal in the Picture"; **1954** as by Lewis Padgett and C.L. Moore); *No Boundaries* (coll. **1955** as by Kuttner and Moore); *Doomsday Morning* (**1957**); *Earth's Last Citadel* (1943 *Argosy*; **1964** as by Kuttner and Moore); *The Best of C.L. Moore* (coll. **1976**).
About the author: "C.L. Moore" by Sam Moskowitz, in *Seekers of Tomorrow* (**1965**); "The C.L. Moore Interview", *Chacal* 1, 1976.
See also: ALTERNATE WORLDS; ARTS; CRIME AND PUNISHMENT; ECONOMICS; FANTASY; FAR FUTURE; GALACTIC EMPIRES; GOLDEN AGE OF SF; LEISURE; LIFE ON OTHER WORLDS; MARS; MONSTERS; MUTANTS; ROBOTS; UNDER THE SEA; VENUS; WOMEN.

MOORE, PATRICK (ALFRED) (1923–). British astronomer, scientific journalist, TV personality and author. His non-fiction works, mainly on astronomy, are too numerous to list; however, it is often forgotten that at one time he wrote many sf adventures for children. One series consists of *Mission to Mars* (**1956**), *Domes of Mars* (**1956**), *Voices of Mars* (**1957**), *Peril on Mars* (**1957**) and *Raiders of Mars* (**1959**). A second series consists of *Quest of the Spaceways* (**1955**) and *World of Mists* (**1956**). His first novel was *Master of the Moon* (**1952**), and others are *The Frozen Planet* (**1954**), *Island of Fear* (**1954**), *Destination Luna* (**1955**), *Wheel in Space* (**1956**), *Wanderer in Space* (**1961**), *Crater of Fear* (**1962**), *Invader from Space* (**1963**) and *Caverns of the Moon* (**1964**). They are jovial, though stereotyped, and were popular in their day. PM also wrote a brief general study of sf, *Science and Fiction* (**1957**); it is one of the earliest books of its kind; portions

are sensible enough, but whole areas of sf are quite ignored and the critical judgements are simplistic. [PN]
See also: COLONIZATION OF OTHER WORLDS; DEFINITIONS OF SF; MARS; PROTO SF.

MOORE, ROBERT See Robert Moore WILLIAMS.

MOORE, WALLACE See Gerard F. CONWAY.

MOORE, WARD (1903–78). American writer, as well known for works outside the sf field, like the picaresque *Breathe the Air Again* (**1942**), as for works within. Although his contributions to the field have been infrequent, each of his books has become something of a classic. His first sf publication is *Greener Than You Think* (**1947**), a successful comic novel about the disastrous introduction of a mutated grass into the world, and how it overruns everything. His most famous sf book, and the definitive ALTERNATE-WORLDS novel in which the South wins the American Civil War, is *Bring the Jubilee* (**1953**). It is also a TIME-TRAVEL story, narrated by an eminent historian from the disinherited Northern States who, after describing his depressed environment, is given the chance of travelling back in time to the crucial moment of the Civil War, the Battle of Gettysburg, which the South had won, thus winning the entire conflict. The narrator's actions at this crucial point change history: the South loses the battle, he is caught in the "past", because the time machine he had travelled in has never been invented, and writes out his narrative of the history he had changed in our own 1877; the manuscript is discovered in 1953 and published. This seminal novel is told in a manner both concise and elegiac. WM's third novel, *Caduceus Wild* (1959 *Science Fiction Stories* as with Robert Bradford; rev. **1978** as by WM alone), is a medical DYSTOPIA (*see also* MEDICINE) whose book publication was long delayed. His fourth book, *Joyleg* (**1962**), with Avram DAVIDSON, returns to a nostalgic view of America, this time comically, in giving the story of the discovery in our century of a man, Joyleg, who lives deep in the Appalachians and claims to remain entitled to his Revolutionary War pension. They find out that a special brew keeps him young, from which point in the novel bureaucratic complications become tedious. WM is not a professional genre writer, and as a possible consequence much of his work seems to have been written (and certainly reads) as though carefully and leisurely composed, almost as though for his own pleasure. He is on record as disliking the sf label and having found it "an albatross around my neck".

WM also wrote two of the most notable stories describing nuclear

HOLOCAUST and its consequences, "Lot" (1953) and "Lot's Daughter" (1954), featuring a great motorized exodus from a doomed Los Angeles, seen through biblical parallelism as the city of Sodom. The hero jettisons his irredeemably suburban wife and his sons, continuing to make a new and incestuous life with his daughter in the mountains. The ironies are savage and the latter-day Lot suffers from toothache. The stories were used as an uncredited basis for the film PANIC IN THE YEAR ZERO (1962), losing much of their power in the cleaning-up process. [JC/PN]
See also: DISASTER; FANTASTIC VOYAGES; ECOLOGY; END OF THE WORLD; HOLOCAUST AND AFTER; PASTORAL; POLITICS; TABOOS; TIME PARADOXES.

MORE, Sir THOMAS (1478–1535). English writer, lawyer, diplomat and politician. The son of a barrister, he was first educated for the Church, but soon decided upon a secular career; he sat in Parliament and gained steadily in political influence, occupying several posts under Henry VIII until that king's proposed divorce from Catherine of Aragon, and TM's subsequent refusal to swear to the Act of Supremacy, caused his death. He was knighted in 1521 and canonized in 1935. Throughout his career he was intellectually involved with the kind of humanism best exemplified by his friend Erasmus, who spent some time in England, and the work by which he is popularly remembered, *Utopia* (Part 2 **1516** in Latin; trans. by Ralphe Robynson including Part 1, written after Part 2, **1551**), can be seen as the first substantial humanistic work written by an Englishman.

In Part 1, TM, as a character, comes across Raphael Hythloday, a Portuguese seaman who had gone with Amerigo Vespucci to the New World; Hythloday, having discovered the ISLAND of Utopia on his travels, compares the corrupt state of European society with the ideal world of Utopia. In Part 2, Utopia is described in detail; it is a humanistic reversal of English society; all goods are held in common; the island's 54 shires are constructed and run rationally by citizens who participate fully in the government, though there are also slaves; arms are borne in self-defence only; there is religious tolerance, though not for atheists. Most of the rational ingredients of the hundreds of UTOPIAS (a word which, in TM's usage, is a pun on *ou-topos*, nowhere, and *eu-topos*, good place) that followed TM's initiative can be found in *Utopia*; what, however, many of its successors lacked was TM's insistence that his humanistic, rationally governed world was amenable to change, and that his picture of Utopia had caught only a moment in its evolution towards a more perfect constitution for the life of men on Earth.

While the majority of readers of

A glowing Leo MOREY cover, July 1932.

Utopia seem to have assumed that TM was recommending the kind of society he would have liked to live in himself, a number of critics have pointed out that some of his suggestions may have been SATIRICAL; since irony is largely a matter of tone, and since it is difficult for most modern readers to evaluate the tone of a Latin text, it is almost impossible to prove the case one way or the other. It is certainly true that some aspects of TM's Utopia seem, to the modern reader, rigid and even cruel, but to impute these feelings to TM himself may be anachronistic sentimentality. However, at least in translation, the book has a kind of dry, ambiguous wit which suggests that to read it as a straightforward prospectus of the good life may be simplistic.

The degree to which *Utopia* and Utopias can be thought of as relevant to sf, particularly genre sf of the 20th century, is controversial, and it can certainly be argued that the Utopian tradition has contributed minimally to the fundamentally Romance nature of modern sf (*but see* PROTO SF).

The amount of available reading on TM in particular and Utopias generally is huge; some works are listed under UTOPIAS.   [JC/PN]
See also: ECONOMICS.

MOREY, LEO (? – ?). American illustrator. He became the cover illustrator for *Amazing Stories* shortly after it changed hands in 1929 and did dozens of cover paintings and interior b/w illustrations for the magazine. He painted covers for *Amazing Stories Quarterly*, *Cosmic Stories*, *Thrilling Wonder Stories*, *Fantastic Adventures*, *Science Fiction Quarterly* and others. His last covers appeared in 1951. He used a wider range of colours than Frank R. PAUL and added a liquid sheen to his paintings, which were crude in execution but vigorous and dramatic. His machines and gadgets were less plausible than Paul's but his people were superior. He was perhaps a better artist than Paul, though he never gathered the same popular following. He was born in Peru, and came to the USA for his education; he graduated from Louisiana State University with a degree in engineering, and did some art work in New Orleans before entering sf illustration.   [JG]

MORGAN, DAN (1925–). English writer and professional guitarist, about which instrument he has written a successful manual, *Guitar* (**1965**). He began publishing sf with "Alien Analysis" for *NW* in 1952; his first two sf novels, *Cee Tee Man* (**1955**) and *The Uninhibited* (**1957** *NW*; **1961**) are routine adventures, but *The Richest Corpse in*

Show Business (**1966**) is a slapstick guying of sf conventions. He published a SPACE-OPERA series, *A Thunder of Stars* (**1968**); *Seed of Stars* (**1972**); and *The Neutral Stars* (**1973**), with John KIPPAX, and a much more interesting series in his own right, comprising *The New Minds* (**1967**), *The Several Minds* (**1969**), *The Mind Trap* (**1970**) and *The Country of the Mind* (**1975**); the "Mind" series is about PSI POWERS, and is DM's most effective work. Though not a powerful writer by any means, DM is all the same surprisingly ignored in the sf field.   [JC]
Other works: *Inside* (**1971**); *The High Destiny* (**1973**); *The Concrete Horizon* (**1976**).
See also: MEDIA LANDSCAPE.

MORGAN, SCOTT *See* Henry KUTTNER.

MORLAND, DICK Pseudonym of British writer and academic Reginald Hill (1936–), both of whose sf novels, *Heart Clock* (**1973**) and *Albion! Albion!* (**1974**), use DYSTOPIAN techniques to describe visions of repellent future Englands. In the first book, citizens are fitted with termination devices for the government to use according to actuarial needs; in the second, England having been literally taken over by soccer rowdies, the country is divided into competing clubs with the citizenry as violent supporters. Both books are heavy-handed but enjoyably sharp-tongued. Hill is also a prolific detective novelist who writes as Patrick Ruell and Charles Underhill.   [JC]

MORLEY, FELIX (1894–). American writer whose sf novel, *Gumption Island* (**1956**), has a Russian super-weapon which knocks some Americans on an island back millions of years in time. [JC]

MORLEY, WILFRED OWEN *See* Robert A.W. LOWNDES.

MORRESSY, JOHN (1930–). American writer and teacher; he is a professor of English at Franklin Pierce College in New Hampshire, and has been an active writer for some time, though he only began his sf career in 1971 with "Accuracy" for *FSF*. JM's novels are generally SPACE OPERAS, though he is capable of constructing interesting ALIEN societies; most of his books share a common galactic background, a somewhat disordered polity still dominated by humans, though with no imperial government. Within this background, his stories tend to the dark and extravagant end of the sf epic spectrum, as in his trilogy comprised of *Starbrat* (**1972**), *Nail Down the Stars* (**1973**; vt *Stardrift*) and *Under a Calculating Star* (**1975**). Also set explicitly in the same galactic scene are *A Law for the Stars* (**1976**) and *Frostworld and Dreamfire* (**1977**); the latter is a

strongly constructed and occasionally rousing epic of a metamorphic humanoid's search for a breeding-partner; the last of his race on its native planet, he must find her elsewhere or the race dies. Typical space opera elements, like an inimical interstellar trading corporation, the Sternverein, are brought skilfully into the story of the humanoid's search and eventual failure. With some success, JM seems to be exploring the possibilities for sf of the pessimistic space opera.   [JC]
Other works: *The Humans of Ziax II* (**1974**), a juvenile; *The Windows of Forever* (**1975**), a juvenile; *The Extraterritorial* (**1977**).

MORRIS, G.A. *See* Katherine MacLean.

MORRIS, GOUVERNEUR (1876–1953). American writer. Extremely prolific in his day, mostly with short fiction, he wrote some early sf and fantasy, beginning with a prehistoric romance, *The Pagan's Progress* (**1904**), in which the hero begins to acquire spiritual values. Other titles include *The Footprint and Other Stories* (coll. **1908**); *The Voice in the Rice* (**1910**); *It and Other Stories* (coll. **1912**); *If You Touch Them They Vanish* (**1913**); and *The Goddess* (**1915**), with Charles W. Goddard.   [JC]
See also: ORIGIN OF MAN.

MORRIS, JANET E. (1946–). American writer, songwriter and musician, being a professional singer and bass guitarist. Her first novel, *High Couch of Silistra* (**1977**) begins a projected four-part sequence, of which the second volume, *The Golden Sword* (**1977**), has appeared; the concluding instalments are projected for 1978 release. The protagonist of the first novel is a courtesan of highest standing in the romantically conceived planet Silistra; the culture described is intricately primitive (the book has a glossary) and sophisticated; the tetralogy is projected to cover about half a decade of its harsh history.   [JC]

MORRIS, RALPH Probably pseudonymous author of the ROBINSONADE *A Narrative of the Life and Astonishing Adventures of John Daniel ... Taken from his own Mouth, by Mr Ralph Morris* (**1751**), which involves a voyage to the Moon and the discovery of unearthly creatures there; the protagonists are ironically unaware of where they are marooned, though the reader is allowed to know.   [JC]

MORRIS, WILLIAM (1834–96). British artist and writer, whose greatest fame rests on his work as a designer of furniture and fabrics. His efforts to reform the prevalent vulgarity of mid-Victorian taste and to preserve standards of craftsmanship placed him in radical

Painted by G.F. Watts in 1880.

and irresolvable conflict with the basic tendencies of the industrial era, then in the first vigour of youth. This conflict was variously expressed in his writing. In his early poems, collected in *The Defence of Guenevere* (coll. **1858**), and even more in *The Earthly Paradise* (coll. in three vols **1868–70**), WM created the literary equivalent of Pre-Raphaelite paintings, romances of febrile charm and phthisic delicacy. The relation of these poems to their own time is one of studied and disdainful avoidance. In life such avoidance was to be denied him. He was cuckolded on an Arthurian scale by his friend and mentor, D.G. Rossetti. He became involved in politics through his efforts, beginning in 1878, to save historical buildings from demolition and unwise "restoration". This involvement led him, remarkably quickly, to an active and enduring commitment to socialism. It was from this unusual (for its day) perspective of orthodox Marxism that WM wrote his UTOPIAN novel, *News from Nowhere* (**1890**) (*see* ARTS). Written in immediate response to Edward Bellamy's *Looking Backward* (**1888**), *News from Nowhere* propels its dreaming narrator from the England of WM's day into a perfected England from which all traces of poverty, squalor and industrial unsightliness have been effaced, an England that bears notable similarities to the bucolic dream-landscapes of the early poetry. As a work of fiction, this most translucent of Utopias exhibits all the clarity, grace and narrative force of WM's best wallpaper designs. Where the book is most visibly Marxist in inspiration, as in the capsule history of proletarian revolution in chapter XVII, it is also most densely and compellingly imagined. Its influence on later Utopian writing has been negligible, and on sf as such still less, since WM's vision is so relentlessly PASTORAL, looking back rather to an idealized middle ages which he represented in the earlier and structurally related socialist romance, *A Dream of John Ball* (**1888**), than to the urban, technologically advanced "future" of common consensus. During the composition of *News from Nowhere* the

Socialist League, which WM had founded in 1884 and funded thereafter, dissolved from an excess of democracy. This event encouraged, by reaction, WM's tendency to make his writing a species of highly ornamented wish-fulfilment from which the less savoury odours of daily life have been artfully exorcized. The prose romances of his last years, such as *The Wood Beyond the World* (**1894**) and *The Well at the World's End* (**1896**), have the same reluctantly valedictory air as his most defiantly escapist poetry, with little of the poetry's hypnotic harmony. He had become, once more, "the idle singer of an empty day". It is these late romances that, through their acknowledged influence on C.S. Lewis, J.R.R. Tolkien and lesser writers of the SWORD-AND-SORCERY sub-genre, have most impinged on sf.

WM also translated Icelandic sagas, and several Greek and Roman classics.
[TMD]
Other works: *The Life and Death of Jason* (**1867**), a poem; *The House of the Wolfings* (**1889**), a historical romance; *The Story of the Glittering Plain* (**1891**); *Child Christopher and Goldilind the Fair* (**1895**); *The Water of the Wondrous Isles* (**1897**); *The Story of the Sundering Flood* (**1898**).
About the author: *The Life of Morris* (**1899**) by J.W. Mackail; *William Morris* (**1936**) by May Morris; *William Morris, the Marxist Dreamer* (trans. **1978**) by Paul Meier.
See also: POLITICS; TECHNOLOGY.

MORRISON, RICHARD or **ROBERT** *See* Robert A.W. Lowndes.

MORRISSEY, J(AMES) (LAW-RENCE) (? –). British writer of thrillers in the 1930s and '40s and *City of the Hidden Eyes* (**1960**), as by JLM and Philip Levene, adapted from the latter's BBC radio serial about underground monsters threatening the surface world.
[JC]

MOSKOWITZ, SAM(UEL) (1920–). American sf historian and anthologist; he also works as a consultant and editor in the frozen foods industry. For a long time SM, who had been a prominent member of sf FANDOM since 1936, was the best known of all sf historians and commentators from within the genre; his work in this field antedates that of nearly all non-genre historians of the field, with the notable exception of J.O. BAILEY. His first book was *The Immortal Storm* (**1954**), a history of early sf fandom which recounted the feuds of the late 1930s among the then tiny group of sf fans with a passion and detail quite unabraded by the passing years. Much more important was SM's series of profiles of sf authors and discussions of sf themes, which appeared in various sf magazines, primarily *AMZ*, from 1959. Many of these were collected in three volumes: *Explorers of the Infinite* (coll. **1963**), which concentrates on the period up to 1940; *Seekers of Tomorrow* (coll. **1966**), which concentrates on writers from the mid-1930s on; and *Strange Horizons* (coll. **1976**), which concentrates on such sf themes as RELIGION, WOMEN, negroes and anti-Semitism in sf. These works have all been much criticized within the genre and by academics, for too many inaccuracies and a hurried and not always fluent style, but the fact remains that SM, though his every word cannot be accepted as gospel truth, did more original research in this field than any other scholar of his period, and few since; no later history of sf has not made use of SM's painstaking work, especially his research into the early history of sf in periodical publications. Much of this work appeared in three further volumes which combined long historical introductions with collections of stories: *Science Fiction by Gaslight: A History and Anthology of Science Fiction in the Popular Magazines 1891 to 1911* (anth. **1968**), *Under the Moons of Mars: a History and Anthology of the Scientific Romance in the Munsey Magazines, 1912 to 1920* (anth. **1970**) and *The Crystal Man* (coll. **1973**) by Edgar Page MITCHELL ed. SM. Although SM is not an academic, and does not always lay out his findings as carefully as academics might like, being sometimes rather cavalier in withholding his sources of information, the above six books are a major contribution to sf scholarship. His critical evaluations are less useful than his factual research.

SM's professional connection with sf includes a brief stint as a writer, with three stories in 1941 and a couple more in the mid-1950s, the first being a SPACE-OPERA novella of distant galaxies, "The Way Back" for *Comet Stories*. He was an sf literary agent, 1940–41, and managing editor for the last GERNSBACK magazine, SCIENCE FICTION PLUS, 1952–4. He also edited the brief, four-issue revival of WEIRD TALES 1973–4. He ghost-edited a number of anthologies, including four which appeared as ed. Leo MARGULIES, two as ed. Roger ELWOOD and three as ed. Alden H. Norton. He was special consultant on and largely responsible for *Contact* (anth. **1963**) ed. Noel KEYES and *The Pulps* (anth. **1970**) ed. Tony Goodstone.

SM also edited the following: *Life Everlasting* (coll. **1947**) by David H. KELLER with introduction by SM; *Editor's Choice in Science Fiction* (anth. **1954**); *The Coming of the Robots* (anth. **1963**); *Exploring Other Worlds* (anth. **1963**); *A Martian Odyssey and Other Classics of Science Fiction* (coll. **1966**) by Stanley G. WEINBAUM with introduction by SM; *Modern Masterpieces of Science Fiction* (anth. **1966**; first paperback publication in three vols as *Doorway Into Time*, **1966**, *Microcosmic God*, **1968**, *The Vortex Blasters*, **1968**; second paperback

publication in two vols as *Doorway Into Time*, **1973**, and *The Microcosmic God*, **1975**); *Strange Signposts* (anth. **1966**) with Roger Elwood; *Three Stories* (anth. **1967**; vt *The Moon Era* USA; vt *A Sense of Wonder* UK with introduction severely abridged); *The Human Zero* (anth. **1967**) with Roger Elwood; *Masterpieces of Science Fiction* (anth. **1967**); *The Time Curve* (anth. **1968**) with Roger Elwood; *The Man Who Called Himself Poe* (anth. **1969**), a collection of essays, poems and stories about Edgar Allan POE, and two stories arguably by Poe; *Other Worlds, Other Times* (anth. **1969**) with Roger Elwood; *Alien Earth* (anth. **1969**) with Roger Elwood; *Great Untold Stories of Fantasy and Horror* (anth. **1969**) with Alden H. Norton; *Futures to Infinity* (anth. **1970**); *Ghostly by Gaslight* (anth. **1970**) with Alden H. Norton; *The Citadel of Fear* (**1970**) by Francis STEVENS, introduction by SM; *The Space Magicians* (anth. **1971**) with Alden H. Norton; *The Ultimate World* (**1971**) by Hugo GERNSBACK, introduction by SM, a late and dreadful novel by Gernsback edited to half the length of the manuscript by SM; *Horrors Unknown* (anth. **1971**; paperback omits one story); *When Women Rule* (anth. **1972**); *Horrors in Hiding* (anth. **1973**) with Alden H. Norton; *Horrors Unseen* (anth. **1974**); *The Raid of "Le Vengeur"* (coll. **1974**), hitherto uncollected stories by George GRIFFITH, introduction by SM; *Out of the Storm* (coll. **1975**) by William Hope HODGSON, 25,000-word critical biography by SM; *"A Dream of X"* (**1977**) by William Hope Hodgson, illustrated by Stephen FABIAN, a short version of *The Night Land* (**1912**), introduction by SM.

SM's most important recent work is his editorship of the two useful HYPERION PRESS series of reprints of sf classics in 1974 and 1976; the Hyperion series also included reprints of six of SM's most important historical works.

Four privately printed pamphlets by SM are *Peace and Olaf Stapledon* (**1949**), *Hugo Gernsback: Father of Science Fiction* (**1959**), *A Canticle for P. Schuyler Miller* (**1975**) and *Charles Fort: a Radical Corpuscle* (**1976**).   [PN]
See also: DEFINITIONS OF SF; NEW WAVE; ROBOTS; SOCIOLOGY.

MOST DANGEROUS MAN ALIVE, THE Film (1958). Trans-Global/Columbia. Directed by Allan Dwan, starring Ron Randell, Debra Paget, Elaine Stewart and Anthony Caruso. Screenplay by James Leicester and Phillip Rock, based on a story by Phillip Rock and Michael Pate. 82 mins (cut to 76). B/w.

A gangster framed by his criminal colleagues escapes from prison and hides out in the desert but is caught up in an atomic explosion. He survives but discovers that he is slowly turning to steel. This enables him to exact revenge on his betrayers, but the process robs him

of all human characteristics, until finally even his loyal mistress is forced to abandon him. He is eventually destroyed by soldiers wielding flame-throwers. The film is cheaply made, and the script is banal, but veteran director Dwan imbues it with a certain harsh power.   [JB]

MOST DANGEROUS MAN IN THE WORLD, THE (vt **THE CHAIRMAN**) Film (1969). Apjac/20th Century-Fox. Directed by J. Lee Thompson, starring Gregory Peck, Anne Heywood, Arthur Hill and Conrad Yama. Screenplay by Ben Maddow, based on the novel by Jay Richard Kennedy. 104 mins. Colour.

A scientist has a transmitting device implanted in his head and is sent to China with the object of convincing Chairman Mao that he is a political defector. It is hoped that he will learn the secret of a new enzyme, developed by the Chinese, that will enable crops to grow under any conditions, anywhere in the world. The transmitter in his brain automatically passes what he speaks and hears, via a satellite, to the intelligence team in London, but he is unaware that they have also implanted a small bomb in his head in case anything goes wrong. The character of Chairman Mao himself makes an appearance in the film, and is lectured by the scientist over a game of ping-pong; this understandably infuriated the Chinese, who forced the film unit to stop shooting in Hong Kong and move elsewhere. Director J. Lee Thompson wisely treated the whole thing with tongue in cheek, and the result is a mildly effective satire on international intrigue.   [JB]

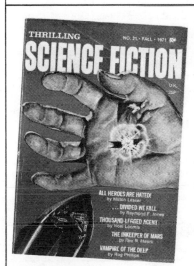

Thrilling Science Fiction, a retitling of THE MOST THRILLING SCIENCE FICTION EVER TOLD, Fall 1971. Cover by Robert Gibson Jones.

MOST THRILLING SCIENCE FICTION EVER TOLD, THE/ THRILLING SCIENCE FICTION One of the many reprint DIGEST-size magazines published by Sol Cohen's Ultimate Publishing Co., using reprint rights acquired when he bought AMAZING STORIES and FANTASTIC. 42 issues were published between early 1966 and mid-1975. Issues 1–13 appeared as *The Most Thrilling SF Ever Told*, later issues as *Thrilling Science Fiction* or *Thrilling Science Fiction Adventures*. Most issues used stories by well-known names from the period when Cele GOLDSMITH edited *Amazing Stories* and *Fantastic*, but from no.14 to no.25 older stories by obscure authors were used, probably because of a dispute between Cohen and the SCIENCE FICTION WRITERS OF AMERICA regarding payment for the reprints.

The publishing schedule was, rather irregularly, quarterly. The first 25 issues were numbered consecutively, but thereafter only the month and year was used. Another Ultimate magazine, SCIENCE FICTION (ADVENTURE) CLASSICS, merged with *TSF* for its last two issues in 1975. [BS]

MOSZKOWSKI, ALEXANDR (1851–1934). German writer. He was a prolific writer of humorous pieces and commentaries on science and philosophy, but very few of his works were translated into English. His major work was the classic UTOPIAN satire *The Isles of Wisdom* (**1922** German; trans. H.J. Stenning **1924**). The protagonists of the novel are guided by Nostradamus through an archipelago of Utopian ISLANDS, including a Platonic Island, a Buddhist Utopia, an Island of Fine Arts (*see* ARTS), pacifist islands, reactionary islands etc. Of particular interest is Sarragalla (the Mechanized Island), through which the technological Utopianism of Walter Rathenau is satirized. The characters learn from the experience that: "We may conclude that no principle can be put into practice. Every principle is bound to break down somewhere, or, if its application is enforced, it is transformed into a caricature of itself." [BS]
Other works: *Der Venuspark* (**1923** Germany).
See also: AUTOMATION.

MOTHRA Film (1961). Toho. Directed by Inoshiro Honda, starring Frankie Sakai, Emi and Yumi Ito. Screenplay by Shinichi Sekizawa, based on a story by Shinichiro Nakamura, Takehiki Fukunaga and Yoshie Hotta. 100 mins. Colour.

The *aficionados* of Toho Studio's monster movies are not only delighted with the monsters themselves. The attraction of the films also depends on the sheer bizarreness, to Western eyes and ears, of the stories and the dialogue. *M* was perhaps the most notably grotesque of all in this respect, its relatively mundane giant moth being amply compensated for by the eccentricities of the story. Two six-inch high women are kidnapped from an island whose inhabitants have been mutated by radiation, and used as night-club singers by an evil showman. Back on the island a venerated, huge moth egg hatches, its contents heading off to Japan to save the dwarf-girls, whose piping singing voices act as a homing signal. One might call this an anti-exploitation exploitation movie, whose imagery is surprisingly strong and resonant. [PN]

MOTTA, LUIGI *See* ITALY.

MOTTRAM, R(ALPH) H(ALE) (1883–1971). English writer and banker, who began his long and prolific writing career as a chronicler of his First World War experiences in the famous "Spanish Farm" trilogy, comprised of *The Spanish Farm* (**1924**) and sequels. He wrote one sf novel, *The Visit of the Princess* (**1946**), in which a joyless Britain in 1960 is galvanized by the visit of a European princess. Fantasy titles are *The Gentleman of Leisure* (**1948**), in which the *Gentleman travels to Heaven*, *The Ghost and the Maiden* (**1940**) and *The Headless Hound and Other Stories* (coll. **1931**). [JC/PN]

MOUDY, WALTER (1929–73). American writer, killed in an auto crash, author of a few sf stories subsequent to his sole novel, *No Man on Earth* (**1964**), a rather compellingly told story of a man born of a human mother and an alien father, and of his search for his destiny. [JC]

MOXLEY, F(RANK) WRIGHT (1889– ?). American writer whose interesting sf novel, *Red Snow* (**1930**), tells of a snow-like precipitation which causes world-wide sterility, and the subsequent social breakdown. One survivor is rescued by an enigmatic alien. [PN/JC]

MR JOSEPH YOUNG OF AFRICA *See* MIGHTY JOE YOUNG.

MROZEK, SLAWOMIR (1930–). Polish writer, mainly of ABSURDIST plays, several of which are assembled in *Six Plays* (trans. **1967**). The short stories of *Słón* (coll. **1957**; trans. as *The Elephant* **1962**) and *Wesele w atomicach* (coll. **1959**; trans. as *The Ugupu Bird* **1968**), in their SATIRICAL mixing of fantasy and absurdist elements, use sf ideas in a manner similar to that of Italo CALVINO. [JC]

MUDGETT, HERMAN W. *See* Anthony BOUCHER.

MULLEN, R(ICHARD) D. (? –). American sf critic and scholar, professor of English at Indiana State University. RDM is an executive member of the SCIENCE FICTION RESEARCH ASSOCIATION, and has been, since its inception, editor of SCIENCE-FICTION STUDIES with Darko Suvin. He and Suvin also edited *Science-Fiction Studies: Selected Articles on Science Fiction 1973–75* (anth. **1976**). The journal is irradiated with RDM's editorial personality, sensible, meticulous, always eager to get the facts straight, qualities which also permeate his interesting criticism published in EXTRAPOLATION, RIVERSIDE QUARTERLY and elsewhere. [PN]

MULLEN, STANLEY (1911–). American writer. He appeared regularly with stories, mostly SPACE OPERA, in a variety of magazines, including FANTASTIC UNIVERSE and PLANET STORIES, 1949–59. *Kinsmen of the Dragon* (**1951**) is a romantic adventure set in a PARALLEL WORLD. [PN]
Other works: *Moonfoam and Sorceries* (coll. **1948**); *The Sphinx Child* (**1948**).
See also: ASTEROIDS.

MULLER, JOHN E. House name used on many sf and supernatural novels published by BADGER BOOKS. The great majority of these were the work of R.L. FANTHORPE; authorship of the remainder is still unknown. Those definitely attributed to Fanthorpe are: *A 1000 Years On* (**1961**), *The Ultimate Man* (**1961**), *The Uninvited* (**1961**), *Crimson Planet* (**1961**), *The Venus Venture* (**1961**; published in the USA as by Marston Johns), *The Return of Zeus* (**1962**), *Perilous Galaxy* (**1962**), *The Eye of Karnak* (**1962**), *The Man Who Conquered Time* (**1962**), *Orbit One* (**1962**; published in the USA as by Mel Jay), *Micro Infinity* (**1962**), *Beyond Time* (**1962**; published in the USA as by Marston Johns), *Vengeance of Siva* (**1962**), *The Day the World Died* (**1962**), *The X-Machine* (**1962**), *Reactor XK9* (**1963**), *Special Mission* (**1963**), *Dark Continuum* (**1964**), *Mark of the Beast* (**1964**), *The Exorcists* (**1965**), *The Negative Ones* (**1965**), *The Man from Beyond* (**1965**), *Spectre of Darkness* (**1965**), *Beyond the Void* (**1965**), *Out of the Night* (**1965**), *Phenomena X* (**1966**) and *Survival Project* (**1966**).

Other JEM titles include: *Space Void* (**1965**; published in the USA as by Marston Johns), *Search the Dark Stars* (**1961**), *Day of the Beasts* (**1961**), *The Unpossessed* (**1961**), *The Mind Makers* (**1961**), *Alien* (**1961**), *Forbidden Planet* (**1961**), *Edge of Eternity* (**1962**), *Uranium 235* (**1962**), *Infinity Machine* (**1962**), *Night of the Big Fire* (**1962**) and *In the Beginning* (**1962**). [MJE]

MULLER, PAUL *See* Paul CONRAD.

MUNDY, TALBOT Pseudonym of English-born writer William Lancaster Gribbon (1879–1940), who emigrated to the USA in 1911 after a career in the British Foreign Service in India and Africa, 1900–10, and soon began producing, prolifically, the adventure novels that made his name. Relatively little of his work uses sf ideas, except peripherally, though some of his novels set in mysterious valleys, like *Om: The Secret of Ahbor Valley* (**1924**) and *Full Moon* (**1935**; vt *There Was a Door* UK), are of some interest. *Jimgrim* (**1931**; vt *Jimgrim Sahib*) features adventures of its eponymous American soldier of fortune in a LOST WORLD whose inhabitants boast gravity-defying aircraft; no other adventures involving Jimgrim and his friends are sf, however. *Tros of Samothrace* (1925–6 *Adventure*; **1934**; paperback publication in four vols as *Tros* **1967**, *Helma* **1967**, *Liafail* **1967** and *Helene* **1967**; paperback republication in three vols as *Tros of Samothrace No 1: Lud of Lunden* **1976**, *Avenging Liafail* **1976** and *The Praetor's Dungeon* **1976**), along with its sequels, *Queen Cleopatra* (**1929**), in which Tros plays only a minor role, and *Purple Pirate* (**1935**; vt *Tros of Samothrace No. 4: The Purple Pirate*), comprise a HEROIC-FANTASY sequence set in a quasi-historical context.

There are some fantasy elements, usually involving Eastern sorcery, in *The Caves of Terror* (1922 *Adventure* as "The Gray Mahatma"; **1924**), *The Nine Unknown* (**1924**), *The Devil's Guard* (**1926**; vt *Ramsden*), *Black Light* (**1930**), *The Mystery of Khufu's Tomb* (**1935**), *The Thunder Dragon Gate* (**1937**), and *Old Ugly Face* (**1940**). *Bibliography of Adventure: Mundy, Burroughs, Rohmer, Haggard* (**1964**) by Bradford M. DAY is a useful reference. [JC/PN]

MUNN, H(AROLD) WARNER (1903–). American writer, first active in the early years of WEIRD TALES; he began publishing his work there in 1925 under the influence of H.P. LOVECRAFT, who suggested to him the werewolf point of view of his first work, "The Werewolf of Ponkert" (1925 *Weird Tales*) which with a sequel novel, "The Werewolf's Daughter" (1929 *Weird Tales*), has been published as *The Werewolf of Ponkert* (fix-up **1958**); there are other stories in the series. HWM remained fairly active until the end of the 1930s, his last story for many years being *King of the World's Edge* (1939 *Weird Tales*; **1966**), which tells of Merlin's life after the death of King Arthur. This novel was combined with its sequel, *The Ship from Atlantis* (**1967**), as *Merlin's Godson* (coll. **1976**); a third volume in this sequence is *Merlin's Ring* (**1974**). These two sequels mark a return to writing by HWM inspired by the publicity consequent to the 1966 book publication of the first title in the series. Though he has written in other genres, including a long, rather laboured poem about Joan of Arc, *The Banner of Joan* (**1975**), and though some of his stories contain sf rationales, HWM is essentially a fantasy writer, whose work features the high colours and simple characters of his origins. [JC]

MUNRO, DUNCAN H. *See* Eric Frank RUSSELL.

MUNRO, H.H. *See* SAKI.

MUNRO, JOHN (1849–1930). English engineer, later professor of mechanical engineering at Bristol, and author of two short stories, "Sun-Rise in the Moon" (1894) and "A Message from Mars" (1895), appearing in *Cassell's Magazine*. The latter was revised to form the first chapter of *A Trip to Venus* (**1897**), an unexceptional account of a journey by spaceship to an idyllic UTOPIA on VENUS, with a brief excursion to MERCURY. [JE] **See also:** ROCKETS.

MUNSEY, FRANK A(NDREW) (1854–1925). American newspaper and magazine publisher and writer. He began publishing in 1882 with *The Golden Argosy*, a weekly BOYS' PAPER, later transformed into THE ARGOSY. FAM expanded his titles to include MUNSEY'S MAGAZINE, THE SCRAPBOOK, ALL-STORY MAGAZINE, CAVALIER and later, after a complex series of mergers and title changes, ALL-STORY WEEKLY and ARGOSY ALL-STORY WEEKLY. A self-made millionaire, FAM was reviled for his heavy-handed treatment of newspapers under his control. Under the editorship of Robert Hobart Davis, his magazines became the most important of pre-sf-PULP MAGAZINES, publishing many works by prominent sf authors, including Edgar Rice BURROUGHS, Ray CUMMINGS, George Allan ENGLAND, Ralph Milne FARLEY, Homer Eon FLINT, Austin HALL, Otis Adelbert KLINE and A. MERRITT. [JE]

MUNSEY'S MAGAZINE US magazine published by the Frank A. Munsey Corp.; ed. Richard H. Thitherton (with Robert H. Davis as fiction editor) and others. Appeared from 2 Feb. 1889 as *Munsey's Weekly*, became *MM* from Oct. 1891 to Oct. 1929. Combined with *Argosy All-Story Weekly* to form two magazines, *Argosy Weekly* and *All-Story Love Tales*.

Although *MM* was contemporary with the ALL-STORY MAGAZINE it published little sf, and what did appear was not of any lasting quality. Most notable was its publication of stories by Ray CUMMINGS, George Allan ENGLAND and Sax ROHMER. [JE] **See also:** *Under the Moons of Mars: A History and Anthology of "The Scientific Romances" in the Munsey Magazines, 1912-1920* (**1970**) by Sam MOSKOWITZ.

MUNSEY'S WEEKLY *See* MUNSEY'S MAGAZINE.

MUSIC AND OPERA Just as the influence of music pervades the work of many sf writers (Philip K. DICK, James BLISH, Brian ALDISS, John BRUNNER, Samuel R. DELANY and Michael MOORCOCK are notable examples — *see* ARTS), sf has exercised a major influence on modern musicians, particularly in rock music. It is no coincidence that rock

music and sf are similarly popular modes of expression among Western youth.

By historical necessity, sf being in the broad sense a 20th-century phenomenon, classical music is less affected, but there are exceptions: Haydn's opera *Il Mondo della Luna* (**1777**) from a Goldoni libretto; the 19th-century Polish composer Moniuszko's *Pan Twardowski in the Moon* and, more directly attributable to sf, Offenbach's musical adaptation of Jules VERNE's *Voyage to the Moon* (**1875**). Berlioz provides an interesting footnote, having written "Euphonia" (1853), a short sf tale of a musical city, although his music shows no detectable influence by the genre, even in the strongly allegorical *Symphonie Fantastique* (**1830**). Holst's *The Planets* (**1918**) stems more from astronomy or astrology; Richard Strauss's *Also Sprach Zarathustra* (**1895**), used by Stanley KUBRICK for the sound-track of 2001: A SPACE ODYSSEY, has only as a result of that use taken on strong sf connotations. Janáček's opera *The Makropoulos Secret* (**1925**) adapts Karel ČAPEK's play on immortality, while Menotti's tongue-in-cheek *Globolinks* (**1971**) tackles alien invasions and Blomdahl's *Aniara* (**1959**) is a musical version of H. MARTINSON's epic starship poem. But, with the partial eclipse of classical traditions, sf in "serious" music and opera waned and its sole modern expression remains in the electronic "music of the spheres" exemplified by the work of Terry Riley, François Bayle, John Cage, David Bedford (whose *Star's End*, 1974, paraphrases Isaac ASIMOV) and the *avant-garde* reaches of jazz-rock: Sun Ra, the Mahavishnu Orchestra and Weather Report.

It was, however, in the mid-1960s, with the widespread assimilation of sf into general pop culture and the pronounced influence of soft drugs and psychedelia on jazz and rock'n'roll that sf came into its own as a factor in popular music.

Nowhere was this relationship more visible than with the San Francisco groups in America, where sf themes and imagery often became the prime subject matter of songs. The Steve Miller Band's early albums are titled *Children of the Future* (**1968**) *Sailor* (**1968**) and *Brave New World* (**1969**) and feature songs like "Overdrive", the eerie "Song for our Ancestors" and "Beauty of Time"; likewise the Grateful Dead with *Aoxomoxoa* (**1969**), *From the Mars Hotel* (**1974**) and improvisatory pieces like "Dark Star", as well as Spirit (whose 1977 *Future Games* flirts with STAR TREK), Quicksilver Messenger Service, the Byrds, Moby Grape, Kaleidoscope or, in a satirical guise, the Mothers of Invention. But the Californian group most influenced was certainly Jefferson Airplane, spearheaded by Paul Kantner, Grace Slick and Marty Balin. Their early albums *Surrealistic Pillow* (**1967**), *After*

Bathing at Baxter's (1968), *Crown of Creation* (1968) and *Volunteers* (1969) are consummate examples of dynamic melodies and furiously articulate lyrics often referring to sf (including Robert HEINLEIN and John WYNDHAM). Shortly after Balin's departure from the group, guitarist and songwriter Kantner recorded *Blows Against the Empire* (1970) with Jefferson Starship, an amalgam of the previous band with other outstanding San Francisco musicians. This concept album (nominated for a HUGO award in 1971) is sometimes thought to be the finest fusion of the genres, though the opposite opinion has also been published; it is a symphonic poem in the rock mode about the hijacking of a spaceship by a group of rebels in a fascist future America and their hopeful journey to the stars. If the subject matter remains pedestrian in sf terms, Kantner and Slick's feeling and artistry are moving as well as convincing. Later albums by Jefferson Starship see Kantner adopting a persistent revolutionary stance interlaced with stark depictions of a totalitarian planet; the return of Balin to the group in 1975 brought an end to the predominance of Kantner's sf situations, as well as a new outburst of popularity for the band: the young rock public had not been particularly enamoured with Kantner and Slick's DYSTOPIAN involvement.

While the West Coast groups heartily embraced sf in America, the situation in Britain was more fragmented. Despite the early, arguably sf imagery of the Shadows' ethereal guitar style or the Tornados' "Telstar", the Pink Floyd were the premier sf group to gain popularity, although some critics have claimed they lack warmth. *Piper at the Gates of Dawn* (1967), *A Saucerful of Secrets* (1968), *Ummagumma* (1969), *Atom Heart Mother* (1970) and *Dark Side of the Moon* (1973) are among their many albums with sf subject matter contained and illuminated in highly evocative music, using the quicksilver guitar and organ runs which have since become closely associated with the sf-music concept. Their style has been widely imitated in Europe (Tangerine Dream, Klaus Schulze, Nektar and a score of supposed wizards of the synthesizer), but Pink Floyd themselves, despite all this adulation, have not been content to relax into mere repetition; like the better sf writers they seem always capable of renewing their inspiration.

Another important but lesser known British group is Peter Hammill's Van Der Graaf Generator, who are particularly adept at mapping the powerful, bleak vistas of post-nuclear desolation: "After the Flood", *The Aerosol Grey Machine* (1969), "Lemmings", *The Least We Can Do Is Wave to Each Other* (1970), *Chameleon in the Shadow of the Night* (1973). The singer David Bowie, on the other hand, enjoys world-wide fame and shows a comprehensive understanding of

sf in his work, ranging from the early "Space Oddity" and "Cygnet Committee" (1969) to the songs about Ziggy Stardust, the ultimate superstar of the apocalypse on the album *The Rise and Fall of Ziggy Stardust and the Spiders from Mars* (1972), or the album *Diamond Dogs* (1974), an impressive jaunt through a Delany-like city of fear. Other notable British groups conversant with the use of sf concepts have been Yes, King Crimson, Jimi Hendrix (occasionally), Genesis, Man (whose guitarist Deke Leonard peppers his songs with sf references), and the Anglo-French group Gong who have evolved a complete mythology full of pixies and flying teapots. Hawkwind, with whom Michael MOORCOCK has been associated, offer an uneasy mixture of heavy-metal music laced with conventional sf archetypes, while Moorcock's own group, Deep Fix, has recorded the uneven *New World's Fair* (1975). A better use of aggressively high-energy music with sf connotations can be found with the American group Blue Oyster Cult.

Most modern German groups remain patently derivative (Can; the Jefferson-Airplane-influenced Amon Duul II). The French musical scene has revealed two strong contenders in the sf stakes: Magma, led by Christian Vander, whose dense, oppressive chords chronicle, in a truly alien language, the legends of the imaginary planet Kobaia, while Richard Pinhas's electronic synthesizer group Heldon owes a heavy debt to Norman SPINRAD and Philip K. Dick, whose novels are explicitly illustrated in the band's tense, repetitive albums. The Swiss Patrick Moraz (*I*, 1976); the Greek Vangelis Papathanassiou (*666*, 1972, *Albedo 0.39*, 1976); and the Japanese Stomu Yamashta (*Go*, 1976) are among the many keyboard and percussion players who also thrive on speculative subjects for their compositions.

The popularity of sf with modern rock musicians in the 1970s is fast becoming a vogue, made worse by the clever packaging of the record companies, whereby attractive sf artwork is used as bait for any type of musical material, although the general record-buying public may often find the connection between the music and sf tenuous or even non-existent. But, when the genres genuinely blend, the results can be most forceful and the cross-breeding between these two areas of art satisfying fertile. [MJ]

MUTANTS The word "mutation" in its fully fledged biological sense first appeared in *Die Mutationstheorie* (1901–03) by Hugo de Vries, though it was earlier suggested as a possible useful term by Waagen. De Vries used it to describe sudden and hereditary variations which, according to him, caused diversification of species. Some such notion of spontaneous variation was

needed as an adjunct to Darwin's theory of EVOLUTION, but Darwin himself had accorded little importance to the freakish sports which occasionally turn up in animal populations because they are usually short-lived and sterile. Ultimately, the word "mutation" was modified in meaning to refer to modifications of individual genes, usually with slight effect. In 1927 H. J. Muller succeeded in inducing mutations in fruit flies by irradiation, and this success captivated the imagination of many speculative writers. One of the first to take up the notion was John TAINE, who wrote several novels which may be termed "mutational romances". In *The Greatest Adventure* (1929) the corpses of giant saurians, no two alike, begin floating up from the ocean depths and are traced to a lost land in Antarctica where experiments in mutation were once carried out. In *The Iron Star* (1930) a mutagenic meteor transforms a region in Africa, causing local wildlife to undergo an exotic metamorphosis. In *Seeds of Life* (1931; 1951) an irradiated man becomes a SUPERMAN, but does not realize the damage he has done to the genes which he transfers to the next generation. These novels attribute magical metamorphic qualities to radiation which really have nothing to do with actual mutation theory, being a developmental analogue of the original De Vriesian thesis. The idea of mutation continued to be misused in this way in pulp sf for some years (and still exists in sf CINEMA), with the irradiation of various creatures producing monsters and the irradiation of people causing metamorphosis into a variety of supermen and subhumans. Examples include Jack WILLIAMSON's "The Metal Man" (1928) and Edmond HAMILTON's "The Man Who Evolved" (1931). Hamilton went on to write several more mutational romances, most notably *The Star of Life* (1947; rev. 1959). He habitually used the erroneous version of developmental metamorphosis, though he appears to have been aware of the distortion — he also wrote an early story in which a mutant child is born to irradiated parents, "He That Hath Wings" (1938). Ironically, this story was published in the fantasy magazine *Weird Tales* while the more bizarre variants appeared in the sf pulps. Another author who developed the mutational romance during the 1940s was Henry KUTTNER, in such stories as "I Am Eden" (1946) and "Atomic!" (1947): here the accent is still on the exotic products of mutational processes, but the magical aspects of the transformation are spread over several generations; he also invented the humorous mutant in his "Hogben" series. Kuttner, writing in collaboration with C. L. MOORE as Lewis Padgett, also introduced into the sf pulps the sympathetic mutant superman, unjustly persecuted by "normal" man, in the "Baldy" series assembled as *Mutant*

(1945–53; fix-up **1953**). H. G. WELLS had toyed half-heartedly with the same idea in *Star-Begotten* (**1937**) and Robert A. HEINLEIN had represented freakish human mutants sympathetically in "Universe" (1941), as did Isaac ASIMOV in *Foundation and Empire* (1945; fix-up **1952**; vt *The Man Who Upset the Universe*) in his character the "Mule", superhuman but emotionally crippled; however it was the formula used by Kuttner and Moore which caught on. The explosion of the atom bomb in 1945 was a great stimulus to mutational themes in sf, although their wilder extravagances began to die out, at least in written sf. Of numerous stories and series following up the "Baldy" theme the most notable is perhaps Wilmar H. SHIRAS's *Children of the Atom* (1948–50; fix-up **1953**). (*See* SUPERMAN *for other examples*.) Another theme which made consistent use of mutants was the post-atomic war scenario (*see* HOLOCAUST AND AFTER). Many of these stories, of course, co-opt the superman theme, so that the most common variant has the "normal" survivors of the atomic war persecuting the mutants, although from the assorted mutants a new species of man, better than the old model, is scheduled to appear. Examples include Poul ANDERSON's *Twilight World* (1947 in collaboration with F.N. Waldrop; fix-up **1961**), John WYNDHAM's *The Chrysalids* (**1955**; vt *Re-Birth*) and, extremely vividly, J.G. BALLARD's "Low-Flying Aircraft" (1975), in which the mutation is spontaneous, not holocaust-generated. The persecution cliché was used by Norman SPINRAD in his example of the archetypal PARANOID sf novel, *The Iron Dream* (**1972**). Variants on the theme include Lester DEL REY's *The Eleventh Commandment* (**1962**; rev. 1970), in which a post-war Church encourages limitless reproduction in order to fight the lethal effects of the mutation rate. Mutants play an important, if subsidiary role in Edgar PANGBORN's post-holocaust stories — most notably *Davy* (**1964**). More recently, the post-holocaust scenario, usually carried forward a few centuries, has become the milieu for a new generation of mutational romances. A classic example is Samuel R. DELANY's *The Einstein Intersection* (**1967**). Other examples include Stuart GORDON's *One-Eye* (**1973**) and its sequels, Walter M. MILLER's *A Canticle for Leibowitz* (1955 7; fix-up **1960**), Fritz LEIBER's "Night of the Long Knives" (**1960**; vt "The Wolf Pair") and *Hiero's Journey* (**1973**) by Sterling LANIER.

The older version of the mutational romance, featuring monstrous metamorphoses, became the basis for a glut of sf films in the 1950s. The irradiation of various creatures expanded them to giant size, and the flood was stemmed only because the supply of possible candidates was so limited. Examples include the giant-ant story THEM! (1954) and the self-explanatory

TARANTULA (1955). There was also a pair of stories featuring irradiated humans: THE INCREDIBLE SHRINKING MAN (1957) and *The Amazing Colossal Man* (1957), plus several others in which irradiated men became monsters. There has recently been a revival of this kind of menace story, both in books and in films, e.g. DAMNATION ALLEY, but the logic of mutational metamorphosis is no longer so popular (as compared, for instance, with the logic of prehistoric survivals). One example of mutant monsters from the recent batch, however, is *The Swarm* (**1974**) by Arthur HERZOG, a novel inspired by a real-life incident in which specially bred bees escaped from captivity in South America and caused numerous deaths.   [BS]
See also: DEVOLUTION; MONSTERS; NUCLEAR POWER.

MUTATIONS Film (1974). Getty/ Columbia. Directed by Jack Cardiff, starring Donald Pleasence, Tom Baker and Julie Ege. Screenplay by Robert D. Weinbach and Edward Mann. 91 mins. Colour.

Many talented people worked on this film, yet the result is disappointing. In a scientifically ludicrous story, a mad scientist attempts to combine plant with animal life, aided by the owner of a carnival freak-show who obtains human guinea-pigs for his experiments. The results of these experiments (one is half-man, half-Venus-flytrap) carry out the inevitable revenge on their creator. [JB]

MYERS, HOWARD L. (? –). American writer whose sf novel, *Cloud Chamber* (**1977**), attractively combines COSMOLOGY, anti-matter invaders of our universe, sex and effortless rebirth of all sentient beings in a wide-ranging SPACE OPERA climaxing in its hero's arrival at nirvana.   [JC]
See also: SOCIOLOGY.

MY FAVORITE MARTIAN Television series (1963–6). CBS TV. Produced and created by Jack Chertok. Writers included John L. Greene, Ben Gershman, Bill Freedman, Albert E. Lewin and Bert Styler. Directors included Sheldon Leonard, Oscar Rudolph and John Erman. Running time 25 mins each episode. First two seasons in b/w, third in colour.

This was a fairly sophisticated (compared to most TV situation comedies of the time) humorous series about a Martian (played by Ray Walston) who becomes stranded on Earth and is befriended by a young man (Bill Bixby) who passes him off to friends and relations as his uncle. The Martian's unfamiliarity with Earth customs, plus his special powers, which included TELEPATHY, INVISIBILITY and TELEKINESIS, provided much of the humour. [JB]

MYHRE, ØYVIND *See* SCANDINAVIA.

MY LIVING DOLL Television series (1964). CBS TV. Created by Jack Chertok. Executive producer: Jack Chertok. Producer: Howard Leeds. Pilot episode directed by Lawrence Dobkin and written by Al Martin and Bill Kelsay. 25 mins per episode. Colour.

After his success with the TV comedy series MY FAVORITE MARTIAN, Chertok came up with another sf comedy. Starring Bob Cummings as a psychiatrist, it concerned a female robot, originally designed for use in space but put in his care for an indefinite period while its inventor was out of the country. Cummings decides to train it as the "perfect woman", that is, quiet and obedient, but the robot's basic unpredictability naturally places him in a series of embarrassing situations. Statuesque Julie Newmar was memorable as the robot (reminiscent, in the way she looked and moved, of Brigitte Helm in METROPOLIS) and she carried an undeniable erotic charge which, of course, could not be properly utilized within the context of a TV comedy. The series lasted only one season.   [JB]

MY SELF *See* MIND MAGIC.

MYSTERIANS, THE Film (1957). Toho/MGM. Directed by Inoshiro Honda, starring Kenji Sahara and Yumi Shirakawa. Screenplay by Takeshi Kimura, based on a story by Jojiro Okami. 89 mins. Colour.

In this Japanese sf pulp epic about alien invaders who land in Japan, seeking women for breeding purposes, the images include a giant robot crashing out of a mountain-side, flying saucers and ray-guns. The colourful special effects are by Eiji Tsuburaya, creator of the eponymous monster of GODZILLA.   [JB]

MYSTERIOUS ISLAND Film (1960). Columbia. Directed by Cy Endfield, starring Michael Craig, Joan Greenwood, Michael Callan and Herbert Lom. Screenplay by John Prebble, Daniel Ullman and Crane Wilbur, based on the novel by Jules VERNE. 100 mins. Colour.

This is a showcase for Ray HARRYHAUSEN's robust special effects. Some prisoners escape by balloon from a confederate prison during the American Civil War and are washed ashore on a remote island. They encounter a giant crab, two female castaways, a giant rooster, giant bees, pirates and even Captain Nemo himself, with his famous submarine the *Nautilus*. Bernard Herrmann's score enhances the eerie quality of the locations.

Other versions of *MI* include one made by MGM in 1929. Directed by Lucien Hubbard, Maurice Tourneur and Benjamin Christiansen, it starred Lionel Barrymore, Pauline Starke, Karl Dane and Warner Oland. The script was by Hubbard, and technical effects handled by

James Basevi, Louis H. Tolhurst and Irving Ries. In 1950 Sam Katzman produced a 15-part serial for Columbia, directed by Spencer G. Bennett and starring Richard Crane, Marshall Reed and Karen Randle. There was also a Russian version made in 1941 by the Children's Film Studio and, more recently, a little-seen French/Italian/Spanish/US co-production made in the early 1970s, starring Omar Sharif. [JB]

Jan. 1952.

MYSTERIOUS TRAVELER MAGAZINE, THE US DIGEST-size magazine. Four issues, Nov. 1951 - Jun. 1952, published by Grace Publishing Co.; ed. Robert Arthur. *MTM* was subtitled "Great Stories of Mystery, Detection and Suspense, old and new", but included some sf until, with its fifth issue, it was retitled *The Mysterious Traveler Mystery Reader*. [FHP/MJE]

Oct. 1935.

MYSTERIOUS WU FANG, THE US PULP MAGAZINE. Seven monthly issues, Sep. 1935 - Mar. 1936, published by Popular Publications; ed. Rogers Terrill. Intended to capitalize on the popularity of Sax ROHMER's character Fu Manchu (featured in films and a radio series of the period), *WF* featured the "Dragon Lord of Crime" in search of world domination. The novels were written by the prolific Robert J. Hogan (who was simultaneously producing G-8 AND HIS BATTLE ACES); the first of them, "The Case of the Six Coffins", was reprinted in PULP CLASSICS no.8 (**1975**). DR YEN SIN was a near-identical follow-up from the same publisher. [MJE/FHP]

MYTHOLOGY The relationship of mythology to sf is close and deep, but not always obvious. Part of the confusion stems from the widely held belief that sf is itself a form of latter-day mythology, fulfilling comparable hungers in us. James BLISH took issue with this argument, pointing out that myth is usually "static and final in intent and thus entirely *contrary* to the spirit of sf, which assumes continuous change". We restrict ourselves below, more modestly, to the literal, new mythologies which are sometimes created *within* sf, usually in the context of explaining the way alien societies think, and to the role of traditional mythologies in sf.

Traditional mythology appears in sf in two ways; its archetypes are either re-enacted or rationalized, sometimes both. The re-enactment of myths is the more complex of the two cases. Behind the retelling of a myth in a modern context lies the feeling that although particular myths grow out of a specific cultural background, whether it be that of ancient Greece or ancient India or any other society, the truths they express relate to our very humanity and remain relevant to us now. Some myths now seem more relevant than ever. The story of Prometheus, who was punished by the gods for stealing fire from the heavens, or its Christian variant, where Dr Faustus is doomed to eternal damnation for selling his soul in exchange for knowledge, has a direct bearing on the scientist's aspiration for ever more information about the meaning of the universe, and ever more power over matter. The entry CONCEPTUAL BREAKTHROUGH lists many such stories; even such an apparently HARDCORE technological story as Arthur C. CLARKE's *Rendezvous With Rama* (**1973**) is permeated quite deliberately with echoes of ancient myths, the Promethean one in particular. But to list mythic echoes in sf (as with most forms of prose fiction) would be comparatively pointless; there are too many. Even a list of full-scale sf analogues of myths as opposed to mere echoes would be too long; only a selection is possible.

Several of the most popular mythic analogues are discussed elsewhere in this volume. Retellings of the Christian legend are discussed under RELIGION and MESSIAHS, and retellings of the story of Genesis, a notorious SF CLICHÉ, are examined under ADAM AND EVE. The entry GODS AND DEMONS also bears on mythology, as does SUPERNATURAL CREATURES, which looks specifically at vampires, werewolves, witches' familiars and their like.

The use of mythology is sf reflects a paradox familiar to sf writers: that in undergoing social and technological change, we do not escape the old altogether, but carry it encysted within us, possibly coded in our very genetic structure. The totally new is by its nature almost impossible for the sf writer or anyone else to envisage. Far more commonly, he works out ancient patterns of love and death, aspiration and reconciliation, in a new context. Several sf writers have imagined a sterile future which has consciously repudiated its myths and hence its past, the oldness within it, only to be left with a terrible emptiness. Ray BRADBURY's nostalgic "The Exiles" (1949 as "The Mad Wizards of Mars") has literary and mythic figures exiled on Mars, perishing when the last of the books containing their stories is burned or lost; the emerald city of Oz dissolves like a mist; an Earth expedition is faced with only a desert. Robert SILVERBERG's "After the Myths Went Home" (1969) has figures of myth reincarnated, via a time machine, for the entertainment of a far future which is suffering from ennui; boredom soon sets in; the myths are dismissed; the society, emptied of heroism and mystery, is destroyed by invaders. Conversely, James WHITE's *The Dream Millennium* (**1974**), shows a crew of starship colonists, who spend much of their time in SUSPENDED ANIMATION, able to survive because in their dreams they have access to a kind of Jungian substratum of racial memory; the awareness they are given of the mythic patterns in human history gives them the strength to survive on a new world.

Re-enactments of myth in sf take several forms. The simplest strives to deepen the emotional connotations of a story by permeating it with the reverberations of some great original, as C.S. LEWIS does quite successfully with the myth of the temptation of Eve in *Perelandra* (**1943**; vt *Voyage to Venus*), and less successfully with the Arthurian legend in the sequel, *That Hideous Strength* (**1945**; vt *The Tortured Planet* USA). Lewis's friend Charles WILLIAMS also re-enacted myths both Christian and pre-Christian in most of his novels, usually digesting the pagan elements so that they emerge as supportive to Christian ethics.

Several writers have striven for a Homeric resonance by retelling HOMER's *Odyssey* in sf terms, whether directly or indirectly, as Stanley WEINBAUM did in a short series of stories in the 1930s, as R.A. LAFFERTY did in *Space Chantey* (**1968**), and as Brian STABLEFORD did in his "Dies Irae" trilogy (**1971**). (SPACE OPERA generally, of course, has a good deal in common with the picaresque voyages of Odysseus.) Lafferty has several times reverted to mythic themes, notably in *The Devil is Dead* (**1971**) and *Fourth Mansions* (**1969**); the latter categorizes mythic archetypes into four groups; the eternal conflict between them leads to many of our troubles.

The Cretan myth of the Earth-Mothers, and the king sacrificed to ensure renewed fertility, is often evoked in sf, naturally enough by Robert GRAVES in *Seven Days in New Crete* (**1949**; vt *Watch The North Wind Rise* USA), since he is the best-known popularizer of the myth in this century. It is also used, colourfully if confusingly, in *Sign of the Labrys* (**1963**) by Margaret St CLAIR, in which members of a surviving witch/priestess cult are best equipped to cope with an underground, post-HOLOCAUST existence. Philip José FARMER has also been preoccupied with the image of woman as archetypal seeress, creator and destroyer, and with men as virile but doomed horned gods, notably in *Flesh* (**1960**; rev. 1968). Like Bradbury in "The Exiles", Farmer makes little distinction in most of his writings between literary and religious myths, which he seems to regard as feeding the same human needs. All Farmer's work is permeated by mythology, whether the mythic creature is a reincarnated god, or a great white whale, or Tarzan, or a new mythology invented by Farmer himself, usually on very traditional models.

More complex than the above are stories whose mythic components are seen with a certain amount of irony, stressing not only a continuity with the past, but also a distinct modernism which no amount of mythic analogy can fully comprehend. Several of Samuel R. DELANY's novels fall into this category, notably *The Einstein Intersection* (**1967**) and *Nova* (**1968**); in the former a deserted Earth is repopulated by aliens who take on human shape and, with it, the mythic burden of the past, in a confused and not always understood form; in the latter the story of Prometheus is replayed in a story of literally stealing fire from the heavens, but the narrative tone has as much of the deflationary as the heroic in it. Michael MOORCOCK's *Behold The Man* (**1966**; exp. **1969**) has a time-traveller, who wanted to see Christ's crucifixion, playing an uncomfortably central role in that event; the scene he finds is more squalid than transcendent. Lawrence DURRELL's *Tunc* (**1968**) and its sequel *Nunquam* (**1970**) feature a multinational conglomerate called Merlin, but the Arthurian echoes are primarily to show that there is little room for romance in a corrupt future. Cordwainer SMITH is an interesting case; he derives a considerable emotional charge from the mythic analogues he uses in his stories, often Oriental, but in the case of "The Dead Lady of Clown Town" (1964) the parallels are with the legend of Joan of Arc. Smith's use of

myth is curiously touching but sometimes rather remote; often, as in "The Dead Lady ...", the mythic parallels are further distanced by the events of the story being themselves remembered by later generations, and recounted with the formality and balance of a well-rounded myth — myths within myths, as it were. Angela CARTER is another ironist, who in *The Infernal Desire Machines of Doctor Hoffman* (**1972**; vt *The War of Dreams* USA) has a mad scientist using a machine, charged with erotic energy, to make the dreams and myths of men come alive; the very series of betrayals through which his plans go awry is itself, ironically, mythic. Charles L. HARNESS regularly uses mythic archetypes both of character and of plot in his involuted, grandiose melodramas, notably in *The Ring of Ritornel* (**1968**) and "The Rose" (1953; title story of *The Rose*, coll. **1966**), in both of which art and science dance a complex sarabande, and winged archetypes are confronted with mathematics. Alan GARNER specializes in a kind of cyclic history in which ancient myths of violence and betrayal work themselves out again in a modern setting, but such books as *The Owl Service* (**1967**), based on a Welsh legend in the *Mabinogion*, and *Red Shift* (**1973**) are not purely determinist; it is as if, for Garner, our lives are structured like myth, but human endeavour can, at least, play variations on the frightening basic themes. James TIPTREE Jr evokes the legendary figure of the Rat King in "The Psychologist who Wouldn't do Awful Things to Rats" (1976), but the protagonist is not saved by its majestic appearance; indeed, he is goaded into brutal rat murder.

Within genre sf and fantasy a particularly popular variant on the mythology theme is to have humans encountering mythic figures by time travelling to the past, or in an ALTERNATE WORLD, or conversely to have mythic survivals appearing in the modern world. Some of these stories are dealt with under the heading of MAGIC. They were especially associated with the magazine UNKNOWN, and often involved a puckish or whimsical humour, as in the silly things that happen in the worlds of myth entered by Harold Shea in the series of stories written by L. Sprague DE CAMP and Fletcher PRATT. Jack WILLIAMSON's *The Reign of Wizardry* (1940; rev. **1965**) is from the same magazine and the same period. Edmond HAMILTON's "A Yank at Valhalla" was another similar story, published in *Startling Stories* in 1941, and later as the novel *The Monsters of Juntonheim* (**1950**; vt *A Yank at Valhalla*). Naomi MITCHISON gives an account of the search for the Holy Grail as told by two reporters from the *Camelot Chronicle* and the *Northern Pict* in *To The Chapel Perilous* (**1955**), but here the basic points are serious, despite the anachronistic jokes which usually feature

largely in stories of this kind, including several by Poul ANDERSON (*see* MAGIC). Thomas Burnett SWANN made a career out of writing sweet but sometimes sentimental narratives about mythic survivals of various kinds, his point apparently being that something wonderful and delicate left the world as our modern rationalism took a grip, and as we desecrated our landscapes.

One quite popular strategy for mythology stories is to tell the myths from the viewpoint of an observer or protagonist from the time in which they happened, and sometimes of course, rationalizing them in the process. John GARDNER's *Grendel* (**1971**) does this with the Beowulf story, as did Henry Treece in *The Green Man* (**1966**) and more recently, Michael CRICHTON in *Eaters of the Dead* (**1976**), but only Crichton's book, which rationalizes Grendel and his dam as Neanderthal survivals, can be seen as sf.

Many of the stories of mythic survival are in effect FANTASY, as with Peter BEAGLE's *The Last Unicorn* (**1968**), which tells of the sad search for the beast of the title for its extinct fellows, or the allegorical *The Circus of Dr Lao* (**1935**) by Charles FINNEY, in which mythic creatures survive in a circus, and have a deep effect on the disbelieving town folk who witness them. A yearning for the survival of mystery, and an intellectual belief in the necessity of such a survival if humanity is not to become sterilely rational, pervades these stories, even at the simplistic end of the spectrum, as seen in Emil PETAJA's "Kalevala" series, in which avatars of the Finnish gods have adventures, or Joseph E. KELLEAM's *The Little Men* (**1960**) and its sequel, where Jack Odin has fights in space and elsewhere. Stan LEE resuscitated various myths, notably that of *The Mighty Thor*, in MARVEL COMICS, in much the same way as did Sterling LANIER, with rather more wit and sophistication, in the series of stories which appeared in *The Peculiar Exploits of Brigadier Ffellowes* (coll. **1971**) and elsewhere, in which are recounted tales of confrontations with demigods, monsters, and other mythic survivals. John BLACKBURN also worked with the theme, but here we enter a new area, and a peculiarly science-fictional one, the *rationalized* myth.

Blackburn was not the best exponent of the rationalized myth, although *Children of the Night* (**1966**) and *For Fear of Little Men* (**1972**) elicit satisfying shudders in their account of hidden LOST RACES in England whose existence explains legends of fairies and goblins, with a logic similar to that of the Crichton novel mentioned above. Manly Wade WELLMAN's "Hok" series of stories (1939–42) explains various myths in a rational manner, as H. BEDFORD-JONES had earlier done in his successful "Trumpets from Oblivion" series in THE BLUE BOOK MAGAZINE 1938–9. A number of sf stories, rather in the manner of the theories of Erich VON DÄNIKEN, explain myths as distorted memories of visits to Earth by aliens, as did Arthur C. Clarke in *Childhood's End* (1950; exp. **1953**), the aliens in this case being horned and having given rise to the legend of the Devil. In Clifford D. SIMAK's *The Goblin Reservation* (**1968**) a rather feeble attempt is made to explain gnomes, trolls, fairies, banshees, etc. as specialized colonists created by biological engineering, but the emphasis is so much on pure whimsy that only a gesture is made towards rationalization. More successful was Nigel KNEALE's TV serial QUATERMASS AND THE PIT, the script of which is available in book form as *Quatermass and the Pit* (**1960**), in which the image of the Devil turns out to be a racial memory of insect-like Martian ancestors, a memory that comes disturbingly to life in modern London. Larry NIVEN and Jerry POURNELLE reversed the ordinary rationalization procedure in *Inferno* (**1976**), in which an sf writer finds himself, possibly deservedly, in hell, a place he consistently and unsuccessfully attempts to rationalize as an actual physical construct in the universe of matter; ultimately it turns out to be, indeed, Hell.

The sf writer who has most consistently used mythological themes in sf, as opposed to fantasy, is Roger ZELAZNY. His first novel, *This Immortal* (**1966**), re-enacts a number of the Greek myths in the confrontation of the almost immortal protagonist (*see* IMMORTALITY) with various MUTANT creatures which are somehow mythic archetypes given flesh. Zelazny stayed with themes of this type for some years, in stories which several times involved artificial gods, whose powers consist of a blend of advanced mental training and high technology, deliberately reconstructing and replaying mythic confrontations, in *Creatures of Light and Darkness* (**1969**), which reincarnates the Egyptian pantheon, and perhaps most successfully in *Lord of Light* (**1967**), a complex and quite subtle story of planetary colonists who deliberately take on the aspect of Hindu gods, and promptly become involved with a variety of appropriate metaphysical paradoxes.

Zelazny's novels are really a new kind of mythology story, in which myths are evoked not only by the author, but quite consciously by the characters, very often as a form of highly manipulative and sometimes cold-blooded social engineering. Another example is Harry HARRISON's *Captive Universe* (**1969**), in which the crew of a giant starship are brainwashed into a medieval monkishness, and the colonists into an Aztec tribalism complete with Aztec gods, which turn out to be constructs; both crew and colonists are ignorant of the true state of affairs, as a result of their cynical programming. Poul Anderson's story "The Queen of Air and Darkness" (1971) has the native inhabitants of a colonized planet reading the minds of the colonists, picking out their archetypal fears and hopes, and creating by hallucination a world of sinister faerie to keep the colonists away, even kidnapping human children in the manner of the old ballads.

Finally, sf commonly creates its own myths. The sub-genre of SWORD AND SORCERY, for example, regularly constructs mythologies which often, as in the case of Robert E. HOWARD's, bear a close relation to our own; the ongoing confrontation between the forces of Law and Chaos (both rather unpleasant) in Michael Moorcock's fantasies is one of the most successful creations of this sort, and comes complete with an apparatus of magic swords, monsters, demigods etc. *Out of the Mouth of the Dragon* (**1969**) by Mark GESTON (a novel so short on plot and so long on richly melancholy and entropic poetic imagery that its publication in a popular paperback format is a mystery, since it is in effect a highly experimental work) is permeated with a myth of Armageddon, a final conflict doomed never to take place, since the forces who have volunteered to fight it keep cutting their own side to ribbons in squabbles on the way.

At a more accessible level, sf has created a number of SPACE-OPERA myths which have resulted from the borrowing of ideas from story to story, with additional accretions on the way. The Mars of sf, for example, is the work of no single writer, has little to do with the real Mars, and yet exists very clearly in the imagination of readers. Leigh BRACKETT and Ray Bradbury have created some of the more poignant variations on the Mars myth (*see* MARS *for further details*).

In his *A Voyage to Arcturus* (**1920**) David LINDSAY invents not one but a whole series of mythologies which ultimately annihilate one another in a kind of mutual critique so that both protagonist and reader are subjected to a progressive stripping of illusions.

With the growing interest in ANTHROPOLOGY in sf of the 1960s and '70s, several of the better sf writers have added richness and density to their depiction of alien societies by creating myths for them. This is the case with most of Ursula K. LE GUIN's work, especially *The Left Hand of Darkness* (**1969**) and *The Word for World is Forest* (1972; **1976**). The mythic elements here work in too complex a way, too allusively, for ready synopsis. They can only be recommended as fine examples of myth-creation, as can those of another striking and important sf novel of recent years, *The Fifth Head of Cerberus* (**1972**) by Gene WOLFE, where as with the Le Guin stories the bearing of myth on reality manifests itself in some surprising ways. Terry CARR's "The Dance of the Changer and the Three" (1968) presents a dangerous problem posed by an alien society, whose enigmatic behaviour is only partially solved by the recounting of one of their heroic legends; it was a brave task for Carr to essay a mythology for beings composed of pure energy.

Finally, Harlan ELLISON, by juxtaposing icons and images from the ancient and the modern worlds, has forged some fine modern myths, many collected in *Deathbird Stories* (coll. **1975**), which includes "The Whimper of Whipped Dogs" (1973), in which the violence and indifference of a great city are seen to coalesce into a kind of contemporary demon. Ellison's "Croatoan" (1975) is typical of his best writing in the vividness with which it encapsulates wholly familiar horrors in an unselfconsciously bizarre metaphor – in this case bringing together the legend of the lost Virginian colony of Roanoke with a colony of children in the sewers descended from aborted foetuses flushed down the drains, along with huge alligators that, when smaller, suffered the same fate. Few writers alive would hazard so wild an imagery, and perhaps none but Ellison could carry it off with so little sense of straining for effect.

A theme anthology is *New Constellations: An Anthology of Tomorrow's Mythologies* (anth. **1976**) ed. Thomas M. DISCH and Charles Naylor.

[PN]

See also: ATLANTIS.

NABOKOV, VLADIMIR (1899–1977). Russian-born American entomologist, novelist, poet and translator; he lived in Russia until the Revolution, was educated at Cambridge, lived in Germany and France until 1940 and then emigrated to the USA, at which point he began to write in English rather than Russian. His first books of poetry date from the teens of the century, his first novel from 1926. *Lolita* (**1955**) first brought him wide popular notice. *Ada* (**1969**) has been treated by some critics as sf, though not very fruitfully. Nevertheless, it is the case that *Ada* depicts an ALTERNATE WORLD, whether or not this Anti-Terra has been created by protagonist Van Veen (as a counterpart to and justification of incest); it can therefore be read with some interest for its rendering of sf elements, though the novel itself comprises much,

much more. Other VN novels dubiously amenable to the same sort of reading would include *Invitation to a Beheading* (1938; trans. **1959**), *Bend Sinister* (**1947**) and *Pale Fire* (**1962**). Fundamentally, however, VN was concerned in all his books to shape versions of the creative act; the materials he uses are subjunctive to the shaping, not vice versa, as in sf. [JC]
Other works: *The Waltz Invention* (1938; trans. **1966**), a play.

NAGL, MANFRED (1940–). German critic. His dissertation *Science Fiction in Deutschland: Untersuchungen zur Genese, Soziographie und Ideologie der phantastischen Massenliteratur* ["SF in Germany: Enquiries into the Genesis, Sociology and Ideology of Fantastic Popular Literature"] (**1972**) is critical of the studies by SCHWONKE and Krysmanski, who in his opinion grossly overrated sf. MN sees sf as a sub-literature embracing all sorts of scientific and political crank ideas, and he traces rare popular sources. An essay of importance by MN is "Unser Mann im All" ["Our Man in Everywhere"] (1969 *Zeitnahe Schularbeit* no. 4/5), an analysis of the fabulously successful PERRY RHODAN series of dime novels.   [FR]

NAKED JUNGLE, THE Film (1953). Paramount. Directed by Byron HASKIN, starring Charlton Heston, Eleanor Parker and William Conrad. Screenplay by Philip Yordan and Franz Bachelin, based on the story "Leiningen Versus the Ants" by Carl Stephenson. 95 mins. Colour.
     This film is not strictly sf, though it does follow the basic monster-movie formula and is made by the team (George PAL and Byron Haskin) that produced several sf epics in the early 1950s. The owner of a South American plantation is threatened by a vast column of soldier ants. He finally stops their advance by blowing up a dam and flooding his property. The sequences involving the ants are unpleasantly convincing, and the script is above average.   [JB]

NATHAN, ROBERT (1894–). American writer, prolific since the publication of his first novel, *Peter Kindred* (**1919**). The wistful, melancholy, sometimes satirical fantasy content of his books is most famously represented by *Portrait of Jennie* (**1940**), in which J.W. Dunne's time theories are used to frame the sentimental tale of a young girl not of this earth. *The Barly Fields* (coll. **1938**) assembles most of his early work of fantasy interest, containing *The Fiddler in Barly* (**1926**), *The Woodcutter's House* (**1927**), *The Bishop's Wife* (**1928**), *There is Another Heaven* (**1929**) and *The Orchid* (**1931**). A second collection, *The Adventures of Tapiola* (coll. **1950**), contains *Journey of Tapiola* (**1938**) and *Tapiola's Brave Regiment* (**1941**). Of his later fantasies, *The Fair* (**1964**) sustains a sublimated elegiac tone in its depiction of

a maiden's adventures in Arthurian England, *The Mallot Diaries* (**1965**) deals with Neanderthal survivals in Arizona, *Elixir* (**1971**) is also an Arthurian story and *The Summer Meadows* (**1973**) movingly explores the nature of love in a fantasy quest for significant and telling moments in the protagonists' lives. Of direct sf interest is *The Weans* (1956 *Harper's Magazine* as "Digging the Weans"; **1960**), a satirical archaeological report on the long-destroyed American civilization. RN's reputation is submerged at present, but on revaluation he will be seen as a significant creator of humanistic fantasy.   [JC]
Other works: *The Puppet Master* (**1923**); *Jonah* (**1925**; vt *Son of Ammitai*); *Road of Ages* (**1935**); *The Enchanted Voyage* (**1936**); *They Went on Together* (**1941**); *But Gently Day* (**1943**); *Mr. Whittle and the Morning Star* (**1947**); *The Innocent Eve* (**1951**); *Sir Henry* (**1955**); *The Color of Evening* (**1960**); *Stonecliff* (**1967**); *Heaven and Hell and the Megas Factor* (**1975**).

NATION, TERRY (1930–). English screenwriter involved in the inception of the long-running British TV series DR WHO; he created its most famous villains, the mechanical DALEKS, and has more recently created a post-HOLOCAUST series, also for British TV, SURVIVORS, which rather unsuccessfully attempts to transcribe for TV the flavour of the English DISASTER novel; his novelization of the series is *The Survivors* (**1976**). *Rebecca's World* (**1975**), illustrated with bravura by Larry Learmonth, is for young children; Rebecca visits a planet where wicked developers are ruining the ECOLOGY. TN's most recent sf is the TV series *Blake's Seven* (1978), based on his own concept, and with several episodes by him. It began rather crudely with some hoary sf clichés (political criminals deported to prison planet from totalitarian home world) but picked up considerably in later episodes, where Blake and his mates take part in spirited, SPACE-OPERA adventures in a miraculous spaceship, operated by an ill-tempered computer, which they find conveniently abandoned in space.   [JC/PN]

NEAL, HARRY *See* Jerome BIXBY.

NEAR FUTURE Images of the near future in sf differ markedly from images of the FAR FUTURE in content and also in attitude. The far future tends to be associated with notions of ultimate destiny, and is dominated by metaphors of senescence; in it the world is irrevocably transfigured and normally contemplated from a detached viewpoint; the dominant mood is, paradoxically, one of nostalgia, because like the dead past the far future can be entered only imaginatively, and has meaning only in terms of its emotional resonances. The near future, by contrast, is a world which

is imminently real. It is a world of which we can have no knowledge, which can exist only imaginatively and hypothetically, but which is nevertheless a world in which we will one day have to live, and to which our present hopes and life-strategies are directed. The fears and ambitions reflected in our images of the near future are real, however over-pessimistic or over-optimistic they may seem. In order to plan our lives we must all hold images of the near future in our heads, and the fact that these images are fictions does not mean that they are unimportant. Literary presentations of the near future not only reflect these images but also feed them.
     Just as fictions of the far future could not emerge until there was an appreciation of the true time scale of the Earth and the forces involved in long-term change, so fictions dealing with the near future could not emerge until it was generally realized that a man's lifespan might see changes of considerable import. (There is, of course, an amorphous space existing between the near future — the future of personal horizons, extending 50 to 60 years — and the far future. This imaginative space may be used for romance, or hypothetical UTOPIAN or other constructs, but it is, almost invariably, historically "disconnected" from the present.) The realization that habits and strategies designed to deal with the present might not be adequate to deal with one's personal future emerged rather more slowly than the realization of the Earth's true time scale, and was handicapped in its emergence by a dogged imaginative resistance. It is doubtful whether anyone, even today, has really absorbed a genuine appreciation of the scope of the change that might overtake the world in the space of a lifetime. Our minds inevitably apply the lessons of past experience to future planning, and no matter how fast that experience changes it always *appears* stable and settled. We can cope with innovations only by adjusting to them as they come; such imaginative preparation as we can make in advance is extremely limited in practical value.
     The near future is threatening, for whatever innovations it produces must invalidate — however temporarily — the past experience on which our present consciousness is based. At a time when no one believed in the possibility of fundamental change, this threat was ineffective, not because innovations never occurred, but because they were not anticipated, and because the processes which produced them were unperceived. In today's world change is so rapid we cannot fail to perceive it, despite our most fervent efforts to ignore it, and the threat of the future haunts the consciousness that it could so readily disrupt. In such a historical situation it is easy to understand the popularity of dogmas of conservatism and conservationism, and the dramatic

increase in our sensations of personal and social insecurity. It is also easy to understand the rapid growth of a literature dealing with the near future, and the marked ambivalence of that literature in honestly reflecting anxieties while simultaneously offering palliative reassurances.

In early futuristic fiction there is no trace of either the near future or the far future in the senses outlined above; events take place in the disconnected, generalized imaginative space distanced by its dating, for example the anonymous *The Reign of King George VI 1900–1925* (**1763**), MERCIER's *Memoirs of the Year 2500* (**1771**; trans. **1772**) and Jane LOUDON's *The Mummy! A Tale of the 22nd Century* (**1827**). These were not futures that anyone expected himself, or his children, to live in. The earliest near-future speculations are warnings against specific political policies. I.F. CLARKE's bibliography of *The Tale of the Future* (**1961**; rev. 1972) lists one as early as 1644, a pamphlet on the dangers of restoring the monarchy, and another in 1831, a pamphlet warning of the effects of the Reform Bill, but the idea of historical change independent of strategic action on the part of governing bodies did not emerge until the late 19th century.

The first class of near-future fantasies to emerge was the war-anticipation genre in Britain (*see* WAR). This began with a political debate concerning the need for rearmament (George T. CHESNEY's classic story *The Battle of Dorking*, **1871**, is a propagandistic political pamphlet) but the real issue at stake was the effect of technological progress on the conduct of warfare. This was quickly realized by a number of authors, most notably George GRIFFITH and H.G. WELLS, who produced memorable nightmares of war remade by submarines, tanks, aeroplanes and, ultimately, atomic bombs. Griffith died before the outbreak of the First World War, but most of his readers did not. Wells lived just long enough to witness the advent of the real atom bomb. No one can argue that the anxiety reflected in this early class of near-future fantasies was unjustified, even the more extreme variants in Wells's *The War in the Air* (**1908**), Griffith's *The Angel of the Revolution* (**1893**), and Joseph O'NEILL's *Day of Wrath* (**1936**).

A very different set of images was presented by another sub-genre which emerged in the same period, celebrating the miracles of the age of inventions (*see* DISCOVERY AND INVENTION). Significantly, there are very few Utopian images in this class, most Utopias being set at least a century on; Edward BELLAMY's *Looking Backward* (**1888**) steps ahead to the year 2000, while even the super-optimistic Hugo GERNSBACK subtitled his *Ralph 124C 41+* (1911–12; **1925**) "A Romance of the Year 2660". In fact, the romances which were located within the personal future of their readers were virtually all concerned with the future of TRANSPORTATION; they are linked to the war-anticipation genre through rejoicing in the conquest of the air. Jules VERNE's interests were confined to the very near future, and this is true of his most faithful imitators, but those of a more cavalier temperament were more extravagant in their speculations about the velocities which might be possible. Verne went *Around the World in 80 Days* (**1870**) but André LAURIE went from *New York to Brest in Seven Hours* (**1890**) and Herbert STRANG *Round the World in Seven Days* (**1910**). Strang consistently combined the transportation romance with the war-anticipation theme by having his magnificent youths in their magical machines avert or short-circuit INVASIONS and rebellions in all corners of the globe.

A more generalized celebration of the wonders of TECHNOLOGY, in so far as they would affect everyday life in the personal future, was quite slow in emerging. Sf writers were by and large insensitive to the changes which technology was making in industry and to the nature of work (*see* AUTOMATION). Sf's emphasis was all on LEISURE and the joys of travel. There was, however, one man, Hugo Gernsback, who attempted to capture the scattered aspects of technological enthusiasm and bind them all together into a medium of communication which, he proposed, would "blaze a trail, not only in literature, but in progress as well". He called this medium "scientifiction", which he saw as a means of anticipating the transformation which the world was already undergoing through the acceleration of technological progress. Gernsback was a would-be inventor, passionately involved with contemporary technology and particularly with the development of radio. In the editorials which he wrote for his early sf PULPS he talked about atomic energy and radar and television and space travel. No one can argue that his ambitions for the future of the world within his own lifetime (he died in 1967) and the lifetime of his readers (most of whom were in their teens in the 1920s) were unjustified. It is easy to understand how an early convert, Donald WOLLHEIM, can begin his account of a lifelong romance with sf: "Ever since the day that I first heard that an atomic bomb had been exploded over Japan I have had the disturbing conviction that we are all living in a science-fiction story."

Sf undertook to deal with all aspects of the future, but it was in its generalization of images of the *near* future that it was really new. The effect of sf upon young readers in the 1920s and '30s — which was tantamount to a revelation or quasi-religious conversion in many cases — was mainly due to its opening up a consciousness of the *immediacy* of change.

Early pulp sf was, however, largely a sham. The consciousness of change was conveyed more by Gernsback's editorializing than by the content of the stories, most of which were located in the safer realms of the future beyond the personal horizon. It was also a sham because — at least under Gernsback's direction — it pretended that technological change would make no real difference to the quality of life but would, in effect, just make life more pleasant: a holiday, plus adventures. Outside the genre this attitude seemed childish, and anxieties attached to the awareness of change were more prominently represented. The exuberance of pulp sf was bought at the cost of producing a curiously blinkered outlook (*see* ECOLOGY). This situation began to change gradually when John W. CAMPBELL Jr took over ASTOUNDING STORIES in the late 1930s, and began to ask for more carefully considered appraisals of the near future. One effect of this was a retreat by many authors to the safer realms of the more distant future which they had always preferred; but there also emerged a new generation of writers prepared to tackle the problems of the near future in a more realistic fashion. Examples of their work include several notable stories discussed in the entry on NUCLEAR POWER, and such endeavours as Robert A. HEINLEIN's attempt to construct a historical schema for the future based on the interplay of technological innovation and political response.

In 1945 history came to Campbell's aid in a most dramatic fashion; Hiroshima brought home to virtually everyone that their lives were vulnerable to technological change. It brought a sensation of existential insecurity that was unknown in modern history, comparable only to that which might have attended the advent of the Black Death in Europe in 1347. The products of that sensation have dominated sf since 1945. To fans like Wollheim, it did indeed seem that sf was "justified" — that its implicit attitudes had become real, and that from 1945 on we would all have to live with the awareness of change that sf had cultivated. But there also emerged a powerful sense of nostalgia for that sf which had been aware of change only as a succession of miracles and make-believe adventures. That pretence died in 1945, just as the pretence that change could not affect the personal future also died. Genre sf's consciousness of change, while perhaps more sensible than dogged resistance to the idea of change, was, after all, a false consciousness.

The response of the authors to the new intellectual climate was quick and varied. Leaving aside the straightforward warnings of imminent atomic doom (*see* WAR, HOLOCAUST AND AFTER *and* END OF THE WORLD), one of the most obvious and remarkable responses was the creation of distorted future societies in which contemporary power-groups have "taken over" and formed self-interested, oppressive regimes; the archetype is *The Space Merchants* (**1953**) by Frederik POHL and C.M. KORNBLUTH. These stories of distorted societies are often labelled SATIRES, but their primary intention is not so much to mock the contemporary world as to push its priorities to their absurdly possible limits (*see* SOCIOLOGY). Though the works themselves often seem surreal there is an element of actual anticipation and not merely satirical exaggeration involved.

The baroque mode of this kind of imaginative exercise then gradually gave way in sf to a more acute awareness of real processes of change in the contemporary world and their dangers. In the 1960s OVERPOPULATION, POLLUTION and resource crises (*see* POWER SOURCES) became standard features of sf's images of the near future. Stories on these subjects often have a hint of panic about them, and there has been a monotonous sounding of an apocalyptic note in post-1960 sf; lists of stories reflecting various kinds of anxiety can be found under the various subheadings noted above. Images of the near future produced outside the genre are now virtually indistinguishable in attitude from those produced within it: the stark contrast of the 1930s, which created a kind of "ghetto" enclosing pulp sf, is no longer evident. Genre sf is now just as much a literature of anxiety with respect to the near future as speculative fiction outside the pulps ever was (and always has been since the decline of the transportation romances). This is necessarily so. Our ambitions are tied to our expectations, which are based on our experience of the past (if they are not so based they are merely castles in the air). The innovations which the future will surely bring are much more likely to threaten these ambitions than to aid them (even though they may compensate by making possible new ambitions) and are therefore sources of often acute anxiety. Sf's dominant image of the near future is hostile (*see* DYSTOPIAS); but unpleasant literary futures have evolved along with the awareness of change, and *not* as a reaction to Utopian images, which have never been located in the near future.

The rate of change will probably not slow down, though it is possible that we may adjust to it rather better than we have so far managed. It is extremely unlikely that sf will adopt a more optimistic stance in the foreseeable future, save in regard to romances situated in the imaginative space which exists, to borrow Heinlein's phrase, beyond this horizon.   [BS]
See also: FUTUROLOGY; OPTIMISM AND PESSIMISM; PREDICTION.

NEARING, HOMER Jr (1915–   ). American writer and professor of English at Pennsylvania Military College. His series of stories about Professor Cleanth Penn Ransom and Professor Archibald MacTate, mathematician and philosopher respectively, appeared in *FSF* from "The Poetry Machine" in 1950 up to 1963. Seven of these stories, with four more, were assembled as *The Sinister Researches of C.P. Ransom* (coll. **1954**); they concern the two professors' attempts to formalize a union between science and the arts; their efforts, though doomed, are told without malice. Uncollected stories are "The Embarrassing Dimension" (1951), "The Maladjusted Classroom" (1953), "The Cerebrative Psittacoid" (1953), "The Gastronomical Error" (1953) and "The Hermeneutical Doughnut" (1956 *Fantastic Universe*). The professors' names, not coincidentally, are similar to those of several American poets and critics. In book form, the stories are very thinly "novelized".   [JC/PN]
See also: FOURTH DIMENSION (AND OTHERS); HUMOUR.

NEBULA Sf award, given by the SCIENCE FICTION WRITERS OF AMERICA since 1966. The idea of funding such an award from the royalties of an annual anthology of award-winning short fiction was proposed in 1965 by the then secretary-treasurer of SFWA, Lloyd BIGGLE Jr. The awards are made in the spring and, unlike the HUGO awards, they are dated by the year of publication of the award-winning stories; thus the first, the 1965 awards, were made in 1966. The award takes the form of a metallic-glitter spiral nebula suspended over a rock crystal, both embedded in clear lucite; the original design by Judith Ann Lawrence (wife of James BLISH) was based on a drawing by Kate WILHELM and has been followed ever since. The original four classes of award, all for professional writing, have remained unchanged; a fifth class, for best dramatic presentation, was added in 1974. Some special awards have been made: a Grand Master award for lifetime achievement in sf writing was made to Robert A. HEINLEIN in 1975, to Jack WILLIAMSON in 1976, and to Clifford D. SIMAK in 1977; a special plaque for his pre-1965 film work was awarded to George PAL in 1976.

The four writing classes are: novel (over 40,000 words); novella (17,500–40,000 words); novelette (7,500–17,500 words); short story (under 7,500 words). Voting is by SFWA members, using a ballot paper made up from members' nominations. Since 1970, a preliminary ballot of all nominated works has been circulated early in the year, the entries receiving the most votes being entered on the final ballot. The procedures for Nebula awards have been more consistent than those for Hugos, but lobbying among the SFWA membership has received increasing criticism. Some critics have maintained that the awards have, at times, reflected political as much as literary ability. Consequently the proportion of SFWA members taking part in voting has fallen off. Although the Nebula awards have occasionally gone to rather more experimental writing than ever wins a Hugo, there has not been a great deal of difference between the choices. It might have been expected that the Nebula award, inasmuch as it is given by a consensus of professional writers, may have placed a stronger emphasis on literary ability, but there is no evidence that this has been so. Neither the Hugo nor the Nebula has been given to non-genre sf, and both have gone, most of the time, to American recipients. While the Nebula has certainly gone to some fine works, it cannot really be argued as particularly meaningful, and many critics have argued that the whole award system, in sf at least, is more a publicity exercise than a consistently well-judged measure of value.

Anthologies of short-fiction Nebula winners, along with a selection of the runners-up, are published annually as *Nebula Award Stories*, each volume edited by an SFWA member. They sometimes also contain critical essays and accounts of the year in sf. Volumes to date are *Nebula Award Stories 1965* (anth. **1966**; vt *Nebula Award Stories I* UK) ed. Damon KNIGHT, *Nebula Award Stories 1967* (anth. **1967**; vt *Nebula Award Stories 2* UK) ed. Brian W. ALDISS and Harry HARRISON, *Nebula Award Stories Three* (anth. **1968**) ed. Roger ZELAZNY; the title style remained the same thereafter as for no.3; *Four* (anth. **1969**) ed. Poul ANDERSON, *Five* (anth. **1970**) ed. James Blish, *Six* (anth. **1971**) ed. Clifford D. Simak, *Seven* (anth. **1972**) ed. Lloyd Biggle Jr, *Eight* (anth. **1973**) ed. Isaac Asimov, *Nine* (anth. **1974**) ed. Kate Wilhelm, *Ten* (anth. **1975**) ed. James GUNN and *Eleven* (anth. **1976**) ed. Ursula K. LE GUIN. No volume appeared in 1977, and it seems that the series may have ceased.

In 1969 the concept of SFWA members voting on stories was extended retroactively to cover those stories (but not novels) considered the all-time best prior to 1965. The chosen short stories were published as *Science Fiction Hall of Fame* (anth. **1970**) ed. Robert SILVERBERG, and the novellas in *The Science Fiction Hall of Fame Volume Two A* (anth. **1973**; vt *The Science Fiction Hall of Fame Volume Two* UK) and *The Science Fiction Hall of Fame Volume Two B* (anth. **1973**; vt *The Science Fiction Hall of Fame Volume Three* UK) ed. Ben BOVA. *A History of the Hugo, Nebula and International Fantasy Awards* (rev. **1976**) by Donald Franson and Howard DeVore, lists all nominees, final ballots and winners of the Nebula award up to 1975, together with changes of procedure.   [PN/CI]

Novels:
1965: Frank HERBERT, *Dune*
1966: Daniel KEYES, *Flowers for Algernon* and Samuel R. DELANY, *Babel-17* (tie)

1967: Samuel R. Delany, *The Einstein Intersection*
1968: Alexei Panshin, *Rite of Passage*
1969: Ursula K. Le Guin, *The Left Hand of Darkness*
1970: Larry Niven, *Ringworld*
1971: Robert Silverberg, *A Time of Changes*
1972: Isaac Asimov, *The Gods Themselves*
1973: Arthur C. Clarke, *Rendezvous with Rama*
1974: Ursula K. Le Guin, *The Dispossessed*
1975: Joe Haldeman, *The Forever War*
1976: Frederik Pohl, *Man Plus*
1977: Frederik Pohl, *Gateway*

Novellas:
1965: Brian W. Aldiss, "The Saliva Tree" and Roger Zelazny, "He Who Shapes" (tie)
1966: Jack Vance, "The Last Castle"
1967: Michael Moorcock, "Behold the Man"
1968: Ann McCaffrey, "Dragonrider"
1969: Harlan Ellison, "A Boy and his Dog"
1970: Fritz Leiber, "Ill Met in Lankhmar"
1971: Katherine MacLean, "The Missing Man"
1972: Arthur C. Clarke, "A Meeting with Medusa"
1973: Gene Wolfe, "The Death of Dr. Island"
1974: Robert Silverberg, "Born with the Dead"
1975: Roger Zelazny, "Home is the Hangman"
1976: James Tiptree Jr, "Houston, Houston, Do You Read?"
1977: Spider and Jeanne Robinson, "Stardance"

Novelettes:
1965: Roger Zelazny, "The Doors of his Face, the Lamps of his Mouth"
1966: Gordon R. Dickson, "Call Him Lord"
1967: Fritz Leiber, "Gonna Roll the Bones"
1968: Richard Wilson, "Mother to the World"
1969: Samuel R. Delany, "Time Considered as a Helix of Semi-Precious Stones"
1970: Theodore Sturgeon, "Slow Sculpture"
1971: Poul Anderson, "The Queen of Air and Darkness"
1972: Poul Anderson, "Goat Song"
1973: Vonda McIntyre, "Of Mist, and Grass, and Sand"
1974: Gregory Benford and Gordon Eklund, "If the Stars are Gods"
1975: Tom Reamy, "San Diego Lightfoot Sue"
1976: Isaac Asimov, "The Bicentennial Man"
1977: Raccoona Sheldon (James Tiptree Jr), "The Screwfly Solution"

Short stories:
1965: Harlan Ellison, " 'Repent, Harlequin!' said the Ticktockman"

No. 13, Sep. 1955. Cover by James Rattigan.

1966: Richard McKenna, "The Secret Place"
1967: Samuel R. Delany, "Aye, and Gomorrah…"
1968: Kate Wilhelm, "The Planners"
1969: Robert Silverberg, "Passengers"
1970: no award
1971: Robert Silverberg, "Good News from the Vatican"
1972: Joanna Russ, "When it Changed"
1973: James Tiptree Jr, "Love is the Plan, the Plan is Death"
1974: Ursula K. Le Guin, "The Day Before the Revolution"
1975: Fritz Leiber, "Catch that Zeppelin"
1976: Charles L. Grant, "A Crowd of Shadows"
1977: Harlan Ellison, "Jeffty is Five"

Dramatic presentation:
1973: Soylent Green
1974: Sleeper
1975: Young Frankenstein
1976: no award
1977: no Nebula, but a Special Award to Star Wars.

NEBULA SCIENCE FICTION British digest-size magazine. 41 issues, Autumn 1952 – Aug. 1959, published by Crownpoint Publications, Glasgow; ed.

Peter Hamilton. *N* was the first and only Scottish sf magazine, and was part of the 1950s British sf magazine revival, one of the most important titles along with New Worlds and Science Fantasy. *N* was subsidized by its editor, an enthusiastic fan. It always ran a news section, including a column by the celebrated Irish fan Walt Willis, editor of Hyphen and Slant. But although *N* was fannish, it was by no means juvenile; Hamilton was serious-minded and prepared to experiment with difficult stories and to encourage young writers. Brian Aldiss, Bob Shaw and Robert Silverberg all had their first published stories in *N*. Other contributors included Harlan Ellison, Eric Frank Russell, H.K. Bulmer and E.C. Tubb, the latter being the most prolific. Early issues contained a novel, with a small number of short stories, but the policy of a novel an issue was later dropped. The handsome and distinctive front covers were the work of various artists, including Ken McIntyre, James Stark, Gerard Quinn and Eddie Jones. An innovation was the introduction of b/w cartoon back covers, mainly by Arthur Thompson. Although unable to pay high rates, *N* was popular with writers, and Hamilton was able to keep it going as very much a one-man show, and never very profitably, for seven years. Some later issues went on sale in the USA. [PN/FHP]

Collectors should note: Issues were numbered consecutively after Vols 1 and 2 of four nos each. What should have been Vol.3 no.1 was actually marked no.9. The first three nos, Aut., Spr., Sum., were followed by two issues of Sep. 1953. Publication was quite irregular except for the period Jul. '57–Feb. '59, which was monthly apart from the omission of Nov. and Dec. '57.

NEEF, ELTON T. See R. L. FANTHORPE.

NEGROES See POLITICS.

NELSON, R(ADELL) F(ARADAY) (1931–). American writer and former computer programmer. He has published as Ray Nelson, R.F. Nelson and R. Faraday Nelson. He has been active in both sf and detective genres, publishing his first sf story, "Turn off the Sky", with *FSF* in 1963. His first sf novel was *The Ganymede Takeover* (1967) with Philip K. DICK; Dickian preoccupations are somewhat damped in this tale in which action is rather implausibly emphasized. RFN published a story, "Time Travel for Pedestrians", in *Again, Dangerous Visions* (anth. 1972) ed. Harlan ELLISON, and has had work in *FSF* and *NW*, but has concentrated on longer forms and on his work as a gagwriter for cartoonist Grant Canfield. For a time he collaborated with Michael MOORCOCK in the smuggling of Henry Miller books from France into England; Moorcock was caught, RFN was forced to cease. RFN holds a secure place in the hearts of sf FANDOM (he used to be a fan artist) for having invented the propeller beanie which in fan cartooning is always emblematic of the sf fan.

RFN's second sf novel, *Blake's Progress* (1975), accords the poet/painter the capacity to travel through time, along with his wife Kate, who is by far the better painter of the two, though her husband signs her works. History is altered, the novel being in part an ALTERNATE-WORLDS story. *Then Beggars Could Ride* (1976) depicts an ECOLOGICAL UTOPIA of small, self-contained but interacting units, in which a protagonist tries to sort himself out. In his recent work, RFN writes more interestingly and vigorously than in earlier efforts. [JC]
Other works: *The Ecolog* (1977).
See also: TRANSPORTATION.

NEPTUNE See OUTER PLANETS.

NESFA See Erwin S. STRAUSS.

NESVADBA, JOSEF (1926–). Czech psychiatrist, doctor and writer, born in Prague. He started by writing dramatic sketches but soon turned to detective stories and satirical sf, continuing the tradition of Karel ČAPEK. JN writes subtly

ironic variations on common sf themes, poking fun at human weaknesses, and he is not afraid to satirize his own social system (*see* "Inventor of His Own Undoing", in all the English-language collections below). His collections of short stories are *Tarzanova smrt* (coll. 1958), *Einsteinův mozek* (coll. 1960), *Výprava opačným směrem* (coll. 1962) and *Vynález proti sobě* (coll. 1964). His stories "The Death of an Apeman" and "The Idiot of Xeenemünde" have been filmed by Jaroslav Balik. JN also wrote a contemporary novel about Vietnam, *Dialog s doktorem Dongem*, while a mystery novel of fantasy interest is *Bludy Erika N.* (1974), which utilizes some of Erich VON DÄNIKEN's ideas.

JN's intricately plotted, absurdly logical stories have been translated into many languages and anthologized the world over, including the MERRIL and HARRISON/ALDISS vols of *The Year's Best SF* and WOLLHEIM's *World's Best SF*. English language editions of JN's stories are *Vampires Ltd.* (coll. 1964, Prague) and *In the Footsteps of the Abominable Snowman* (coll. 1970; vt *The Lost Face* USA). All but the first and third stories of the latter collection are also in the former. [FR]
See also: EASTERN EUROPE; POLITICS.

NEUTRON STAR See BLACK HOLES for explanation of the term, though a neutron star is not itself a black hole. [PN]

NEVILLE, KRIS (OTTMAN) (1925–). American writer of fiction who has worked for many years as a technical writer specializing in plastics technology, and through his connection with the Epoxylite Corporation has co-authored a large handbook on the epoxy resins. He began publishing sf with "The Hand from the Stars" for *Super Science Stories* in 1949, and for several years was a prolific contributor to *FSF* and other magazines; he wrote some fantasy as by Henderson Starke. The only collection of his short fiction, *Mission: Manstop* (coll. with some stories updated 1971) demonstrates his notable strengths as a writer: conciseness, clarity of style and a capacity to develop the sometimes routine initial material of a story so that its implications expand constantly, rather in the manner mastered more recently by James TIPTREE Jr. "Hunt the Hunter" (1951), for instance, begins as a simple hunt on an alien planet but expands subtly but quickly into a study in power politics whose trick ending turns the meaning of the whole tale in upon itself very neatly. Another early story, "The Toy" (1952), powerfully structures a very sharp lesson in ANTHROPOLOGY within an apparently routine tale about humans oppressing "inferior" aliens.

KN's best-known story is probably "Bettyann" (in *New Tales of Space and Time*, anth. 1951 ed. Raymond J. HEALY) which, with a sequel, "Overture",

eventually became *Bettyann* (1951–4 var. anths; fix-up 1970). It tells the story of a young girl whose adolescent sense that she really belongs somewhere else is, in classic sf fashion, confirmed by her discovery first that she is an adopted child, and second that she is a child of creatures from the stars. She is then forced to decide between heredity and environment, a choice whose implications are developed in a recent sequel, "Bettyann's Children" (in *Demon Kind*, anth. 1973 ed. Roger ELWOOD), written with his wife, Lil Neville. Among the fiction they have written together is a novel, *Run, the Spearmaker* (1975 in Japanese), which has not yet appeared in English.

KN's comparative silence for two decades — despite book publication of old material, some of it revamped — is much to be regretted, as the sharp, well-thought-out stories of his first productive years augured a major talent. [JC]
Other works: *The Unearth People* (1964); *The Mutants* (fix-up 1966); *Special Delivery* (1952 *Imagination*; 1967); *Peril of the Starmen* (1954 *Imagination*;1967); *Invaders on the Moon* (1970) with Mel Sturgis, left uncredited through a publishing decision against which KN protested. KN's six non-fiction titles are all technical.
See also: LIVING WORLDS.

NEW AVENGERS, THE See AVENGERS, THE.

NEWCOMB, SIMON (1835–1909). American writer of texts on and studies of astronomical and mathematical subjects. In his early sf novel, *His Wisdom, the Defender* (1900), future historians tell the story of how a professor discovers a source of limitless energy, uses it to defeat German imperialism, and settles the world consequently, with himself as dictator. [JC]
See also: WEAPONS.

NEW DIMENSIONS Original anthology series edited by Robert SILVERBERG. *New Dimensions 1* (anth. 1971) appeared at a time when original anthology series were proliferating in the USA, with such titles as INFINITY, QUARK and UNIVERSE. *ND* is one of the few survivors from this period, although the series has had to change publishers in order to keep going. *ND* has been one of the more experimental anthology series, and has introduced a number of new writers. Its regular contributors have included Gardner DOZOIS, George Alec EFFINGER, Felix GOTSCHALK and James TIPTREE Jr. *New Dimensions 3* (anth. 1973) contained two HUGO-winning stories: "The Girl Who Was Plugged In" by Tiptree and "The Ones Who Walk Away From Omelas" by Ursula K. LE GUIN. One volume a year has been published, up to *New Dimensions 7* (anth. 1977). [MJE]

NEWMAN, BERNARD (1897–1968). English writer of novels and travel books, most of whose output was espionage thrillers (some as by Don Betteridge) and detective mysteries, the two genres being perhaps most successfully combined in *Maginot Line Murder* (**1939**). The entertainment value of his sf is comparatively minimal, as he uses the form primarily to provide platforms for his arguments about WAR, WEAPONS, and the political nature of peace. In *Armoured Doves* (**1931**), scientists combine to end war, as they do in *The Flying Saucer* (**1948**), whose Martians blackmailing the world are in fact human scientists calling another halt to war; *The Wishful Think* (**1954**) is a marginal story about politicized ESP. [JC]
Other works: *The Cavalry Goes Through* (**1930**); *Hosanna* (**1933**); *Secret Weapon* (**1941**); *Shoot!* (**1949**); *The Blue Ants* (**1962**); *The Boy Who Could Fly* (**1967**).

NEWMAN, JOHN (? –). British research chemist and writer who collaborated with Kenneth BULMER on a long series of science articles for *NW* and *Nebula*, 1955–61, under the name Kenneth JOHNS. [JC]

NEWTON, JULIUS P. (? –). English writer whose sf novel is *The Forgotten Race* (**1963**). [JC]

NEWTON, W(ILFRID) DOUGLAS (1884–1951). Irish writer. He began writing sf with two future-WAR novels, *The North Afire* (**1914**) and *War* (**1914**, with preface by Robert Hugh BENSON and introduction by Rudyard KIPLING). Later works include *The Golden Cat* (**1930**), *The Beggar and Other Stories* (coll. **1933**), which includes a story about guided missiles, "The Joke that Ended War", and *Dr. Odin* (**1933**), about an attempt to perfect a Nordic "master race". His "Savaran" series includes a LOST-WORLD novel, *Savaran and the Great Sands* (1939 *Passing Show* as "The Devil Comes Aboard"; **1939**). He contributed sf to various early magazines, including PEARSON'S MAGAZINE. [JE]

NEW WAVE The term as applied to sf is borrowed from film criticism, where it was much used in the early 1960s, as a translation of the French *nouvelle vague*, to refer to the experimental cinema associated with Jean-Luc Godard, François Truffaut and others. Curiously it has been, since 1977, applied to rock music also, where New Wave has come to be a synonym for so-called Punk Rock.
The term New Wave was used more by sf publicists than by sf writers, and it was especially popularized by Judith MERRIL, notably in her anthology *England Swings SF* (anth. **1968**; vt abridged *The Space-Time Journal* UK). The kind of story to which the term refers, however, is rather older than the term itself, which anyway has never been

defined with any precision. Among the first writers whose work was later subsumed under the New Wave label were several Englishmen, especially Brian W. ALDISS and J.G. BALLARD. These two were publishing stories in NEW WORLDS magazine while it was still under the editorship of E.J. CARNELL, but it was not until Michael MOORCOCK took over the editorship in May/Jun. 1964 that the kind of imagistic, highly metaphoric story, inclined more towards psychology and the SOFT SCIENCES than to HARD SF, which both men wrote (in quite different styles), was given a setting where it appeared appropriate and comfortable.
Traditional genre sf had reached a crisis point in both England and America by the middle 1960s; far too many writers were creating endless and sometimes mindless variations on the same few traditional sf themes. Good writers continued to write traditional sf also, but their work was being swamped. Many of the better younger writers who came along at this point came to feel, either instantly like Thomas M. DISCH, or after years slogging away at producing conventional commercial sf like Harlan ELLISON and Robert SILVERBERG, that genre sf had become a straitjacket; it had gone rigid, and, paradoxically for a form of literature that emphasized change and newness, it had become conservative and had lost its spirit of enterprise. Young Turks, of course, conventionally exaggerate the sins of their seniors, but here a real case could be made out for their side. It was not as if the market were shrinking; on the contrary, hardcover publishers were more willing than ever before to add sf to their lists, but for success in this format it would be a positive advantage if the hard-bitten style of PULP sf could be allowed to evolve into a more flexible and literate prose.
By 1965, then, there was nothing to stop a certain amount of experiment in both the form and the content of sf, and there were sound reasons both artistic and commercial for attempting it. Many of the so-called sf experiments of the period were not experiments at all, but merely an adoption of the narrative strategies, and sometimes the ironies, that had long been familiar in the MAINSTREAM novel; some writers, though, especially J.G. Ballard and perhaps (rather later) Michael Moorcock genuinely added something to prose fiction that had not been there before.
New Wave writing is easiest to define by negatives; it always tended, sometimes unconsciously rather than as an act of deliberate rebellion, to break down the barriers between sf and mainstream fiction. Positively, it shared many of the general qualities of late 1960s counterculture, including a hippy-style interest in mind-changing drugs and oriental religions, a (normally) left-wing political stance closely associated with protest at American involvement in South

East Asia and elsewhere, a marked interest in SEX, a strong involvement in pop art and in the MEDIA LANDSCAPE generally and a rather pessimistic (for sf) attitude towards the likelihood of DISASTER caused by OVERPOPULATION and interference with the ECOLOGY, as well as by WAR. New Wave sf generally concerned itself with the NEAR FUTURE.
Moorcock's *New Worlds* published most of the notable figures of the New Wave at one time or another, including the work of several Americans who lived for a time in England, such as Disch, John SLADEK, James SALLIS and Samuel R. DELANY. Other American contributors to *New Worlds* were Norman SPINRAD and Harlan Ellison, and other notable British contributors were Langdon JONES, Charles PLATT, M. John HARRISON and Barrington J. BAYLEY. Despite the various excesses of *New Worlds*, whose stories sometimes seemed to embrace ENTROPY with a fervour reminiscent of Edgar Allan POE's "The Masque of the Red Death" (1842), there is no doubt that it had a potent liberating effect on sf publishing generally, and it was not long at all before various American markets, notably the original anthology series of ORBIT, DANGEROUS VISIONS, QUARK and NEW DIMENSIONS, were adopting a far less exclusive attitude to what they would or would not publish.
All this naturally horrified some of sf's more conservative spokesmen, as a glance at sf histories written by Samuel MOSKOWITZ, Donald A. WOLLHEIM and David KYLE will demonstrate. Wollheim commented, in *The Universe Makers* (**1971**), that "the readers and writers that used to dream of galactic futures now get their kicks out of experimental styles of writing, the free discussion of sex, the overthrow of all standards and morals (since, if the world is going to end, what merit had these things?)".
But in fact the battle was quickly over; the better New Wave sf writers were soon accepted by sf readers generally, and often found an audience outside sf as well, as tends to be the way with good writers; the bad writers (there were quite a few) mostly fell by the wayside. By the 1970s there no longer seemed very much point to the term, although newcomers like Joanna RUSS, James TIPTREE Jr, Gardner DOZOIS, Barry MALZBERG and Gene WOLFE clearly wrote in a style that would have been called New Wave only a year or so earlier.
There can be no doubt that during the late 1960s sf found new freedoms, some valuable, and also a greater readiness to admit sophisticated writing. As with all ideological arguments, one uses whatever ammunition comes conveniently to hand, and it suited many friends (and many foes) to see the New Wave as a kind of homogeneous, monolithic politico-literary movement. It was never that in the minds of most of its writers, many of whom resented being categorized.

Thomas M. Disch commented, in an open letter published in 1978: "I have no opinion of the 'New Wave' in sf, since I don't believe that that was ever a meaningful classification. If you mean to ask – do I feel solidarity with all writers who have ever been lumped together under that heading – certainly I do not."

There has been an accommodation between the best of traditional sf and the most interesting innovations of the New Wave in the 1970s, which has proved liberating, it seems, even to writers of an older generation, such as Frederik POHL and Algis BUDRYS. But not all the reverberations have been good; there is a kind of wordy, campus cleverness about some American 1970s sf, self-consciously burdened with figures of speech, which the unkind may see as part of the legacy of the New Wave. But this muddiness of style would certainly be repudiated by the best of the New Wave writers, and probably only exists because the market situation gives more room today than ever before to student writers who have lived through no apprenticeship.

Two of the many anthologies of New Wave sf are *The New SF* (anth. **1969**) ed. Langdon Jones and *The New Tomorrows* (anth. **1971**) ed. Norman Spinrad. [PN]
See also: ARTS; INNER SPACE; OPTIMISM AND PESSIMISM.

The first issue, above, failed to sell well with this cover, and was withdrawn. Rebound in a new cover it did better, although collectors find the first version of the cover no rarer than the second.

NEW WORLDS The leading British sf magazine, which published 201 issues over a chequered career of some 30 years. Three PULP-size issues were published by Pendulum in 1946–7 under the editorship of an sf fan, E.J. CARNELL – in fact, *NW* was a development from a pre-War FANZINE called *New Worlds*. Nova Publications, a publishing group formed by the British sf fans who used to meet at the White Horse pub, revived *NW* in 1949 as a DIGEST. Carnell remained in charge until no.141 (Apr. 1964), after which the title was taken over by Roberts & Vinter, publishers of Compact Books, who published it in a paperback-size edition, ed. Michael MOORCOCK. After no.172 (Mar. 1967) it was published by Moorcock under the auspices of the Arts Council in a stapled 8 × 11 inch format, rising to BEDSHEET-size with no.179. In this incarnation *NW* suffered financial difficulties, compounded when the leading British distributor, W.H. Smith Ltd, refused to carry copies because, among other reasons, of obscene language in Norman SPINRAD's *Bug Jack Barron* (Dec. 1967-Jul. 1968; **1969**). The last issue to be properly released was no.200 (Apr. 1970), though no.201, a special, final, "good-taste" issue with retrospective index, did go to subscribers. During this period Moorcock relaxed his control over editorship, various members of his coterie taking a hand in the issues released in 1969. Charles PLATT was editor from no.197. From the greater part of the period from no.22 to no.200 the magazine maintained a monthly schedule with only occasional lapses. In 1971 the title was revived again, this time as a series of original anthologies published in paperback by Sphere Books. Sphere issued eight, and nos *9* (**1975**) and *10* (**1976**) appeared from Corgi Books. The first five — *1* (**1971**); *2* (**1971**); *3* (**1972**); *4* (**1972**); *5* (**1973**) — were ed. Moorcock, no.6 (**1973**) ed. Moorcock and Platt, no.7 (**1974**) ed. Platt and Hilary BAILEY and nos *8* (**1975**), *9* (**1975**) and *10* (**1976**) ed. Bailey. At the end of 1977 *NW* was defunct, but the fervour of its supporters brought about yet another resuscitation in 1978, with no.212 in a FANZINE-style format, and no.213 professionally published. The nature of this most recent incarnation is not yet clear, though it is plainly no longer, except incidentally, an sf magazine.

Under Carnell *NW* was the primary force in shaping a tradition in British magazine sf, and under Moorcock its name became the banner of what was dubbed the NEW WAVE movement, creating an sf *avant garde*. Carnell provided a stable domestic market for the leading British writers and played a considerable role in the careers of Brian ALDISS, Kenneth BULMER, E.C. TUBB, James WHITE, John BRUNNER, J.G. BALLARD and Colin KAPP. He encouraged a species of sf more sober in tone than much American material, with the emphasis on problem-solving. An excellent example of the species is James White's "Sector General" series (1956–62). In publishing ambitious work by Brian Aldiss and most of J.G. Ballard's early work Carnell began a shift in emphasis toward PSYCHOLOGICAL and existential sf (*see* ABSURDIST SF), which also showed in his choice of reprints from US authors: Philip K. DICK's *Time Out of Joint* (Dec. 1959-Feb. 1960; **1959**) and Theodore STURGEON's *Venus Plus X* (Jan.-Apr. 1961; **1960**). Most of the American magazines were also shifting their emphasis away from the "hardware" of sf, but retained a kind of brashness not evident in *NW* save in the work of those authors most heavily influenced by pulp sf.

Moorcock's editorship was a good deal more flamboyant than Carnell's, and he was as polemical in the material which provided the environment for the fiction as John W. CAMPBELL Jr had been in ASTOUNDING during the early 1940s, though to very different ends, juxtaposing fiction with factual social comment, visual collage, even concrete poetry, in a deliberate attempt to lose the genre sf image and place speculative fiction in a context of rapid social change, and radical art generally. Apart from his own *avant-garde* material (often written under the name James Colvin) he promoted inventive British writers like Barrington J. BAYLEY, Langdon JONES, David I. MASSON and, later, Ian WATSON, and recruited some American writers — notably Thomas M. DISCH and John SLADEK. Moorcock's early "Jerry Cornelius" pieces appeared in *NW*, as did the NEBULA-winning "Behold, The Man" (Sep. 1966; exp. as *Behold The Man* **1969**). The large-size version serialized *Camp Concentration* by Disch (Jul.-Sep. 1967; **1968**) and featured two more Nebula-winning short pieces: Samuel R. DELANY's "Time Considered as a Helix of Semi-Precious Stones" (Dec. 1968) and Harlan ELLISON's "A Boy and His Dog" (Apr. 1969). The Delany story also won a Hugo. Under Moorcock *NW* established in its review columns a particularly trenchant style of criticism which continued in the paperback anthologies, much of it written by M. John HARRISON and John CLUTE. It cannot be said that Moorcock's programme met with wide-ranging approval, especially among those readers attuned to the more modest and traditional aspects of Carnell's policy, and it certainly lacked Carnell's sense of balance. Its contribution to sf in the 1960s was, however, considerable — the paths beaten by the *NW* writers are now much more generally in use.

A US edition of *NW*, with Hans Stefan SANTESSON credited as editor, ran for five issues Mar.-Jul. 1960. Some unsold issues of the Roberts & Vinter *NW* were bound up in twos and threes and sold under the title *SF Reprise*. Carnell edited an anthology called *The Best From New Worlds Science Fiction* (anth. **1955**) and his anthology *Lambda 1 and Other Stories* (anth. **1964**. UK and US contents vary) was also selected from *NW*. Moorcock edited *The Best of New Worlds* (anth. **1965**) and then a series of eight *Best SF Stories from New Worlds: 1* (**1967**); *2* (**1968**); *3* (**1968**); *4* (**1969**); *5* (**1969**); *6* (**1970**); *7* (**1971**) and *8* (**1974**). These series anthologies also sometimes used stories from SCIENCE FANTASY/IMPULSE. The first six of the eight *Best SF Stories*

new worlds

No. 191   Five Shillings or One Dollar

JERRY CORNELIUS
an
THE FIRMAMENT THEOREM
by
BRIAN W. ALDISS
also
J.G. RENN
BALLARD & BURNS
LANGDON JONES
MICHAEL MOORCOCK
& others

This was one of the strongest covers, the work of Mal Dean, for Michael Moorcock's large-format NEW WORLDS; no. 191, 1969.

publish new writers. Regular contributors included not only Colin KAPP (chiefly with his "Unorthodox Engineers" series), Douglas R. MASON (under his own name and as "John Rankine"), John RACKHAM and James WHITE, but also Keith ROBERTS, while M. John HARRISON and Christopher PRIEST both published early short stories in its pages. NWISF was intended to be a quarterly, but began to depart from that schedule after its first two years, and its appearances became erratic. *New Writings in SF 1* (anth. **1964**) was followed by *NWISF 2* (**1964**), *3, 4, 5, 6* (all **1965**), *7, 8, 9* (all **1966**), *10* (**1967**), *11, 12, 13* (all **1968**), *14, 15* (both **1969**), *16, 17* (both **1970**), *18* (**1971**), *19, 20* and *21* (all **1972**). After Carnell's death the editorship was taken over by Kenneth BULMER, starting with *New Writings in SF 22* (anth. **1973**). The change in editorship brought about no substantial change in policy, although one feature of Bulmer's *NWISF* has been Brian ALDISS's series of "Enigmas". New authors to appear in recent issues include Charles Partington, Michael Stall and Cherry WILDER. Bulmer edited *NWISF 23* (**1973**), *24* (**1974**), *25, 26, 27* (all **1975**), *28* and *29* (both **1976**). The series, the most durable original anthology series so far in sf, was suspended in 1976 after the 29th volume. Carnell also edited *The Best From New Writings in SF (First Selection)* (anth. **1971**).   [MJE]

NICHOLLS, PETER (DOUGLAS) (1939–   ). Australian sf critic and editor, resident in the UK since 1970. A one-time lecturer in English, PN studied film-writing and direction in the USA on a Harkness Fellowship, 1968–70. He became the first administrator of the SCIENCE FICTION FOUNDATION in 1971, resigning at the end of 1977; he edited the journal FOUNDATION: THE REVIEW OF SCIENCE FICTION from no.5, 1974, having been an assistant editor from the outset, until no.13, 1978. He edited *Science Fiction at Large* (anth. **1976**; vt

from New Worlds were also published in the USA. The original paperback anthology incarnation of *NW* was, for the first four numbers, published as *New Worlds Quarterly* in the USA; the sixth, *New Worlds 6*, was published in the USA as *New Worlds 5*. *New Worlds 5* (UK) was never republished in the USA. [BS] **Collectors should note:** *NW*, though it had vol. nos up to 177, has always been numbered consecutively, the numeration not beginning again with each volume number. No.1 was issued twice, with different covers, the second version using the same cover as no.2. No.1 with the original cover had not sold well, but it did better the second time round. The first five nos (two in '46, one in '47, two in '49) were undated. There were three issues in '50 (Spr., Sum., Win.), four in '51 (Spr., Sum., Aut., Win.) and a bi-monthly schedule began with Jan. '52. '53 saw only three nos (Jan., Mar., Jun.). A monthly schedule began with no.22, Apr. '54, the first issue in that year. This continued up to no.141 (Apr. '64), with

the only variation being the squeezing of Aug./Sep. '59 into a single number. No.142 was marked May/Jun. '64, and the bi-monthly schedule continued until the end of that year. Jan. '65 began another monthly schedule which lasted until no.172 (Mar. '67). It began monthly again in Aug. '67, squeezing Dec. '67/Jan. '68 together, skipping May and Jun. '68, Aug. and Sep. '68, and squeezing Sep./Oct. '69 together, ending with no.200 (Apr. '70). The subscribers-only no.201 was dated Mar. '71.

NEW WORLDS QUARTERLY *See* NEW WORLDS.

NEW WRITINGS IN SF Original anthology series instigated in 1964 by E.J. CARNELL after he relinquished the editorship of NEW WORLDS and SCIENCE FANTASY. *NWISF* carried on the tradition of Carnell's *New Worlds*: predominantly middle-of-the-road sf, leavened with occasional more adventurous pieces and saved from staleness by his willingness to

Explorations of the Marvellous), a symposium originally delivered at the Institute of Contemporary Arts in 1975, featuring essays, some polemical, by himself, Ursula K. LE GUIN, Thomas M. DISCH, Philip K. DICK and others; he has also presented two seasons of sf CINEMA at London's National Film Theatre, contributed a critical essay to *Nebula Award Stories 11* (anth. **1976**), ed. Ursula K. Le Guin, and published other criticism, mostly in *Foundation*, generally attempting to mediate between the two extremes of academic orthodoxy and fannish bonhomie. General editor of this Encyclopedia, he has been dressed in black since the death of F.R. Leavis. [PN] *See also:* DEFINITIONS OF SF; PROTO SF; SF IN THE CLASSROOM.

NICHOLSON, J.S. *See* ANONYMOUS SF AUTHORS.

NICOLSON, HAROLD (GEORGE) (1886–1968). English diplomat, MP and writer, married to V. SACKVILLE-WEST, knighted in 1953. His novel *Public Faces* (**1932**), set in 1939, describes the international conflicts aroused when England is found to know how to make atomic bombs. [JC]

NICOLSON, MARJORIE HOPE (1894– ?). American scholar, with a PhD from Yale. Her useful pioneering study in PROTO SF is *Voyages to the Moon* (**1948**). It is subtitled "Discourse on Voyages to the Moon, the Sun, the Planets and Other Worlds generally, written by divers authors from the earliest times to the time of the First Balloon Ascensions made during the years 1783–84 with remarks on their sources and an epilogue about a few selected later works of this kind; to which is appended a Bibliography of 133 works up to the year 1784 with an added listing of 58 books and articles dealing with the theme itself and with related sciences." The works dealt with are primarily English. [PN]

NIEKAS American FANZINE (1962–) ed., from California, Ed Meškys and Felice Rolfe. Starting as a small, personal fanzine, *N* established itself as a large and variegated magazine containing a mixture of articles, but with particular emphasis on fantasy. Al Halevy's "Glossary Of Middle Earth" was published in *N*, and other contributors have included Philip K. DICK, Avram DAVIDSON, Anthony BOUCHER and Jack GAUGHAN. *N* won the HUGO award for best fanzine in 1967. [PR]

NIELSEN, NIELS E. *See* SCANDINAVIA.

NIGHT GALLERY Television series (1971–2). A Jack Laird Production for Universal TV/NBC. Created by Rod SERLING. The first two seasons consisted of 50-min. episodes containing two or three playlets; the third and final season consisted of 25-min. episodes only. Colour.

Created by Rod Serling who, in the early 1960s, had made the series THE TWILIGHT ZONE, *NG* was primarily made up of supernatural stories, but it did contain a number of sf episodes; many of the plays were scripted by Serling from original stories by such writers as Fritz LEIBER, A.E. VAN VOGT, C.M. KORNBLUTH and H.P. LOVECRAFT. Richard MATHESON scripted several segments. Two collections by Serling were series spin-offs: *Night Gallery* (coll. **1971**) and *Night Gallery 2* (coll. **1972**). [JB/PN]

NIGHT OF THE BIG HEAT (vt **ISLAND OF THE BURNING DAMNED**) Film (1967). Planet. Directed by Terence Fisher, starring Christopher Lee, Peter Cushing, Patrick Allen, Sarah Lawson and Jane Merrow. Screenplay by Ronald Liles and Pip and Jane Baker, based on the novel by John LYMINGTON. 94 mins. Colour.

An island off the coast of Britain experiences a freak heatwave, during which there are a number of mysterious killings involving fire. The culprits turn out to be aliens from outer space which resemble giant fried eggs and are attracted to any source of heat. At the climax the few surviving characters are saved when a thunderstorm destroys the aliens (water, it seems, dissolves them). John Lymington's pulp novel was certainly not rational sf, but it managed to build up an atmosphere of claustrophobic tension which the film lacks. [JB]

NIGHT OF THE BLOOD BEAST Film (1958). Balboa/AIP. Directed by Bernard Kowalski, starring Michael Emmet, Angela Greene, John Baer and Ed Nelson. Screenplay by Martin Varno, based on a story by Gene Corman. 65 mins. B/w.

In this typically cheap 1950s Corman production (the executive producer was Roger CORMAN; his brother Gene produced it from his own story) an astronaut has cells implanted in his body by an alien, from which embryos grow. This was one of several films, mostly crude, which attempted to cash in on the popularity of THE QUATERMASS XPERIMENT, or so the plot suggests. [JB]

NIGHT OF THE LEPUS Film (1972). MGM. Directed by William F. Claxton, starring Stuart Whitman, Janet Leigh, Rory Calhoun and DeForest Kelley. Screenplay by Don Holliday and Gene R. Kearney, based on the novel *The Year of the Angry Rabbit* by Russell BRADDON. 88 mins. Colour.

Braddon's satirical novel was set in Australia, but the film was switched to Arizona. A test rabbit full of experimental hormones breaks loose and breeds with local rabbits — and suddenly hordes of gigantic, carnivorous rabbits are attacking people, eating horses and demolishing houses. It is hard to make a rabbit, even a giant one, appear ferocious, and one ends up feeling more sorry for the rabbits than for their victims. The film is amusing, though it is doubtful whether this was the makers' intention. [JB]

NIGHT OF THE LIVING DEAD Film (1968). Image 10 Productions/Walter Reade-Continental. Directed by George A. Romero, starring Duane Jones, Judith O'Dea, Russell Streiner, Karl Hardman and Keith Wayne. Screenplay by John A. Russo. 96 mins (cut to 90). B/w.

This unrelenting and downbeat horror film tells of a horde of walking, cannibalistic corpses who lay siege to an isolated house in the country. Their revival is explained by "space radiation" brought to Earth on a returning satellite, but the absurdity of this barely detracts from the concentrated Gothic PARANOIA of the action, whose savagery won the film a cult following, expecially from those who saw its brutality (ordinary people are wiped out along with the zombies) as somehow symbolic of the horrors of the Vietnam War. The film was independently financed and made during weekends by a small group of film-makers based in Pittsburgh. George Romero later directed THE CRAZIES. [JB/PN]

NIGHT THAT PANICKED AMERICA, THE Made-for-TV film (1975). ABC TV. Directed by Joseph Sargent, starring Vic Morrow, Cliff De Young, Michael Constantine, Meredith Baxter, Walter McGinn and Paul Shenar. Screenplay by Nicholas Meyer and Antony Wilson, based partly on the text of the original radio broadcast by Howard Koch. 75 mins. Colour.

The film recreates the Orson Welles broadcast of H.G. WELLS's *The War of the Worlds* (**1898**) in 1938 which, due to its news-bulletin format, caused many Americans to believe that a Martian invasion was actually taking place. When the film concentrates on what went on inside the studio during the broadcast it is fascinating, conjuring up a realistic picture of work in 1930s American radio; but when it shows the effects of the broadcast it degenerates into a routine DISASTER movie with hackneyed characters reacting in predictable ways. [JB]

1984 Film (1955). Holiday Film Productions. Directed by Michael Anderson, starring Edmond O'Brien, Michael Redgrave, Jan Sterling, David Kossof and Donald Pleasence. Screenplay by William P. Templeton and Ralph Bettinson, based on the novel by George ORWELL. 91 mins. B/w.

After the success of a 1954 BBC TV production of *Nineteen Eighty-Four*, scripted by Nigel KNEALE, it was inevitable that a film would follow. But for all its technical limitations the BBC adaptation was superior to the over-careful and lifeless film. A miscast Edmond O'Brien plays Winston Smith, a clerk in the Ministry of Information who decides to rebel against the totalitarian nightmare of England in 1984, where the TV sets do the watching instead of vice versa. Together with his lover he creates a private world of his own for a brief time but is betrayed by a government official who poses as a revolutionary to uncover potential dissidents. Two different endings were shot, one for the American market and one for the British. The former version followed the book with Winston and his lover successfully brain-washed, now devoted supporters of Big Brother, the State's symbol of power; the British version had them overcoming their conditioning, defiantly dying in a hail of bullets, and incidentally vitiating Orwell's theme.   [JB]

1990 Television serial (1977–8). BBC TV. Produced by Prudence Fitzgerald, starring Edward Woodward, Barbara Kellerman, Robert Lang, Michael Napier Brown, Tony Doyle, Edward Judd and Mitzi Rogers. Writers included Wilfred Greatorex, who devised the series, and Edmund Ward. Episodes 50 mins each. Colour.

Reflecting the fears of the British middle class in the 1970s, the serial is set in a socialist England of 1990. It shows what could happen (according to the testimony of Wilfred Greatorex) if the welfare state continues in its present direction. The country is run by the PCD, an all-powerful bureaucracy that incorporates the trade union movement within its machinery; the only people free of its control are a select elite possessing Privilege Cards. The series concerns the efforts of a lone journalist, played by Edward Woodward, to outwit the system in such ways as helping people to escape to the USA, which is still a bastion of freedom. George ORWELL did it all much better in *Nineteen Eighty-Four* (1949).   [JB]

NIPPON CHIMBOTSU (vt **THE SUBMERSION OF JAPAN**) Film (1973). Directed by Shiro Moritani, starring Keiju Kobayashi, Hiroshi Fujioka, Tetsuro Tamba and Ayumi Ishida. Screenplay by Shinobu Hashimoto, based on the novel of the same title by Sakyo KOMATSU. 140 mins. Colour.

Ever since the War, Japan has suffered periodic devastation on its cinema screens, usually at the hands of prehistoric monsters, like GODZILLA, or aliens from outer space; but this film is more sophisticated and ambitious, and involves natural rather than fantastic forces. Geophysical changes within the Earth's core result in the chain of islands which make up Japan sinking beneath the ocean over a period of two years. Most

other countries do not display much eagerness to accept millions of homeless Japanese citizens, although ironically Australia offers its Northern Territory as a new Japanese homeland — an unusual form of poetic justice. The film has been widely praised, though more for its elegiac feeling than for the special effects which, though they involve cities sliding into the sea, earthquakes and fire-storms, and are spectacular, are not wholly convincing; they were directed by Teruyoshi Nakano.

Tidal Wave is the title of the American version released by Roger CORMAN's New World company. It was cut to 81 mins and little remains of the original other than the special effects. It also includes some specially shot American footage written and directed by Andrew Meyer and starring Lorne Greene and Rhonda Leigh Hopkins.   [JB]

NIVEN, LARRY Form of his name used by Laurence van Cott Niven (1938–   ), American writer. He was born in California, where he has set many of his stories, and has a BA in mathematics from Washburn University, Kansas. From his first publication, "The Coldest Place" for *If* in 1964, he set his mark on the American sf field, and won both HUGO and NEBULA awards in 1971 for the culminating novel of his "Tales of Known Space" sequence, *Ringworld* (1970). In the novels and stories of this sequence, and in some unrelated work, he has been seen as HARDCORE sf's last best hope.

The "Tales of Known Space", a title LN himself selected for the sequence, is a wide-ranging, complex, unusually well-integrated future HISTORY, beginning with humanity's initial steps into interplanetary space, introducing more than one ALIEN species along the way and continuing into the 31st century, at the conclusion of *Ringworld*. This overarching structure has the advantage of providing continuing rationales for the sort of technological and extrapolative inventiveness that has made LN a writer of such interest; his facility with the rhetoric and language of hard sf is quite remarkable, and many invented sf terms, such words as CORPSICLE, organlegger and ramscoop, originate with him; his interest and expertise in sf TERMINOLOGY is evident in his essay "The Words in Science Fiction" in *The Craft of Science Fiction* (anth. **1976**) ed. Reginald BRETNOR. LN's concentration on the "Tales of Known Space" has both encouraged their invention and allowed for their recurrent use, thus helping to establish them generally.

The "Known Space" sequence is comprised, in order of internal chronology, of the novel *World of Ptavvs* (**1966**), the collection *The Long ARM of Gil Hamilton* (coll. of linked stories, var. mags and anths 1969–75; **1976**), and the further novels *Protector* (1967 *Gal.* as

"The Adults"; exp. **1973**), *A Gift from Earth* (**1968**) and *Ringworld*; it also includes most of the stories from the collections *Neutron Star* (coll. **1968**), *The Shape of Space* (coll. **1969**), *All the Myriad Ways* (coll. **1971**), *Inconstant Moon* (stories from *The Shape of Space* and *All the Myriad Ways*; coll. **1973**; paperback edition abridged); and *Tales of Known Space: The Universe of Larry Niven* (coll. **1975**). Two further collections — *The Flight of the Horse* (coll. **1973**; includes the five stories of the "Svetz" series of TIME PARADOX comedies) and *A Hole in Space* (coll. **1974**) — assemble out-of-series material. The series has not been constructed in chronological order, with the consequence that various collections develop various periods of the sequence; LN has given a clear chronology and explanation, however, in the introduction and bibliographical apparatus to *Tales of Known Space*. Within an essentially optimistic, technophilic frame, the sequence provides an explanatory structure for the expansion of humanity, beginning with the first tentative steps into the Solar System, where no aliens are yet encountered, but a fruitful dichotomy between the Inner Planets and the Outer is developed. First alien contact is dealt with in LN's first, and in some ways most gripping novel, *World of Ptavvs*; aeons previously, a slave-owning thrint (a species which uses mind-control to maintain hegemony over "inferior" races termed "ptavvs") has entered a time-stopping stasis suit to escape death, and is only reawakened accidentally as the novel begins. The thrint possesses a telepathic human, whose control over others is terrifyingly depicted, and soon comes into the scene itself, even more ominously. Eventually, however, it is contained, and humanity wins knowledge of stasis-control. Men are not ptavvs after all.

Protector again utilizes a long time scale to introduce a second dangerous alien into Earth's expanding sphere of influence; actually an "adult" form of *Homo sapiens*, the yam necessary for the transformation to adulthood not being available on Earth; this alien has travelled from afar, slowly (at sub-light speeds), to take care of us, and to protect us against other Protectors who find our slightly evolved species loathsome. The novel spans many years; its complex, casually alluded-to background demonstrates the value of a coherent sequence to buttress SPACE OPERA of this variety, though at the same time, as LN has recently admitted, the complex, universe-changing plotting of books like *Protector* increasingly makes it difficult to maintain internal consistency as time passes within the invented Known Worlds. In any case, humanity is now an interstellar species, and in *A Gift From Earth* a planet colonized from Earth sets itself up as an independent government; the story is interfused with arguments for personal and entrepreneurial liberty whose connection, as in much American sf, is taken as axiomatic.

With the passing of years, new methods of space travel, further alien species and other additions to the sequence's set of premises gradually expand and complicate the picture, until in *Ringworld* the Tales culminate in a wide-ranging though somewhat diffusely compendious tale whose protagonists, Louis Wu and Teela Brown, come across a sun "orbited" by a ringworld in the shape of a flat, thin ring, rather like the hub of a wheel, obviously artificial; large rectangles interposed between the sun and the ring supply intermittent periods of night. The surface area of the ringworld is of course enormous, but neither protagonist can figure out its original function, and the novel closes inconclusively, without a firm resolution, perhaps in part because of the nature of Teela herself, who incorporates what may be the most definitive series-stopping idea sf has yet seen: Teela is a nubile female bearing a gene that infallibly engineers good luck for its possessor and her infallibly victorious, ascendent offspring; as this categorically reduces any future "Known Space" tale to an examination of the Teela gene's faultless workings, the series, as LN admits, has reached its logical close, with Man dominant throughout whatever part of the universe he/she has reached. None the less, a further "Known Space" novel is projected.

Most of LN's other work is organized, sometimes very notionally, into series. Chief among these are the "Leshy Circuit" series, comprised of "Passerby" (1969), "The Fourth Profession" (1972), "Night on Mispek Moor" (1974) and *A World Out of Time* (fix-up 1976, comprised of "Rammer", 1971, and "Children of the State", 1976, from *Gal.*), and a series of stories examining the social implications of MATTER TRANSMITTERS: "By Mind Alone" (1966), "Flash Crowd" (1973), "The Alibi Machine" (1973), "All the Bridges Rusting" (1973), "A *Kind* of Murder" (1974) and "The Last Days of the Permanent Floating Riot Club" (1974).

In addition to the Hugo award for *Ringworld*, LN has won a 1976 Hugo for best novella with "The Borderland of Sol" (1976), and three times won Hugos for best short story, for "Neutron Star" (1966), "Inconstant Moon" (1971) and "The Hole Man" (1974). "Inconstant Moon", an account of a California evening during which the increased brightness of the Moon reveals the possibility of a huge solar flare or even a nova on the other side of the Earth, is LN's most memorable short story, powerfully imagined.

LN has also written several collaborative works. For details of *The Flying Sorcerers* (1971), see the entry for the co-author, David GERROLD. With Jerry POURNELLE, LN has published three novels. *The Mote in God's Eye* (1974) is a giant, spectacular tale, with all the trappings — space-opera shenanigans, aliens with unhealthy proclivities to hide, galactic aristocracies, and so forth; the book is essentially a development of Pournelle's "CoDominium" series, and should be read in that context. Several critics have taken the book for task for what they regard as its chauvinism on behalf of mankind, the discrepancy between an imaginative plot and old-fashioned characterization and its conservative political stance. *Inferno* (1975) is a re-working of DANTE's *Inferno*, amazing in its sheer cheek and apparently conscious vulgarity, interesting in its theological explanation for what is presented as sadism on the part of God in the interests of encouraging self-help among the damned, and amusing in its placing of anti-NUCLEAR-POWER propagandists in Hell. As stylists LN and Pournelle do not seem to have learned much from their great original. *Lucifer's Hammer* (1977) is a long, ambitious DISASTER novel that weds sf sophistication with the methods of fictionalizing catastrophe and the best-seller idiom that have become familiar through the many disaster films of the early 1970s.

Though he has not yet shown himself capable of writing a fully successful book, perhaps because his control of larger structures is insecure, LN has been a steadily invigorating force in the sf field, and should remain one for a long while. [JC/PN]

See also: ASTEROIDS; BLACK HOLES; CHILDREN IN SF; COMIC STRIPS; COMMUNICATIONS; CRIME AND PUNISHMENT; CRYONICS; END OF THE WORLD; ESCHATOLOGY; FANTASTIC VOYAGES; FASTER THAN LIGHT; GALACTIC EMPIRES; GODS AND DEMONS; GRAVITY; GREAT AND SMALL; ICONOCLASM; LINGUISTICS; MAGIC; MERCURY; MYTHOLOGY; OUTER PLANETS; OVERPOPULATION; PARALLEL WORLDS; PHYSICS; POLITICS; SCIENTIFIC ERRORS; SPACESHIPS; STARS; SUN; SUSPENDED ANIMATION; TECHNOLOGY; TIME TRAVEL; TRANSPORTATION; VENUS.

NIZZI, GUIDO (1900–). Italian-born writer, long resident in the USA. His sf books are *The Victor* (1946), *The Paralyzed Kingdom and Other Stories* (coll. 1947); *The Paralyzing Rays vs the Nuclears* (1964) and *The Daring Trip to the Moon* (1968). [JC]

NOBEL, PHIL *See* R.L. FANTHORPE.

NO BLADE OF GRASS Film (1970). Symbol/MGM. Directed by Cornel Wilde, starring Nigel Davenport, Jean Wallace, Anthony May and Lynne Frederick. Screenplay by Sean Forestal and Jefferson Pascal, based on the novel *The Death of Grass* by John CHRISTOPHER.

96 mins. Colour.

Chemical pollution results in the destruction of most strains of cereals, causing world-wide famine. A family journeys across strife-torn England to sanctuary in the Lake District. As all law and order have broken down they encounter various hazards, the main threat coming from armed groups of marauders searching for food. In many ways the film is similar to PANIC IN THE YEAR ZERO, dealing, as it does, with a group of "ordinary" people being forced to adopt extreme methods to survive in a suddenly chaotic and brutal environment.

Cornel Wilde, the director/producer, had previously directed the highly praised *The Naked Prey* but *NBOG* has a strangely amateurish quality, reinforced by some poor acting. The film is disjointed, but this is apparently the fault of the distributors who cut it drastically before release. [JB]

NOLAN, WILLIAM F(RANCIS) (1928–). American writer and editor, full-time since 1956. Previously he trained and for a time practised as a commercial artist. He also raced cars, and has published eight books on the subject of auto racing. Of his 30 books, also including thrillers and biographies, 14 have related directly to sf. WFN was first active in sf as a fan; he co-founded the San Diego Science Fantasy Society, edited a fanzine, the *Rhodomagnetic Digest*, and published *The Ray Bradbury Review*; he published his first sf story, "The Joy of Living", in *If* in 1954. He was managing editor of the first three issues of GAMMA (1963–4). He has written short stories and criticism as Frank Anmar and F.E. Edwards. His first sf book, *Impact 20* (coll. 1963), assembles some of his early work, though he is best known for his novel *Logan's Run* (1967) with George Clayton JOHNSON, which was filmed and then became the basis of an American TV series (*see* LOGAN'S RUN); a sequel, *Logan's World*, is projected for late 1977. *Logan's Run* presents a world whose solution to problems of conflict between the generations and OVERPOPULATION is compulsory death at the 21st birthday; the hero poses as a rebel against the system and escapes with a genuine, female rebel. The novel is colourful; it is a series of brief, baroque, almost unrelated episodes, but considerably less moralizing and simplistic than the film based upon it. WFN has also been active as a compiler of sf anthologies, mostly of reprinted material, though *The Future is Now* (anth. 1970) assembles original stories. He has also compiled a detailed bibliography of Ray BRADBURY, with copious annotations: *The Ray Bradbury Companion* (1975). [JC/PN]
Other works: *Space for Hire* (1971); *Alien Horizons* (coll. 1974); *Wonderworlds* (coll. 1977). As editor: *Man Against Tomorrow* (anth. 1965); *The Pseudo-People* (anth. 1965; vt *Almost*

Human UK hardback, paperback reverts to original title); *3 to the Highest Power* (anth. **1968**); *A Wilderness of Stars* (anth. **1969**); *A Sea of Space* (anth. **1970**); *The Human Equation* (anth. **1971**).
See also: CRIME AND PUNISHMENT.

"NONAME" *See* Luis Philip SENARENS.

NOONE, EDWINA *See* Michael AVALLONE.

NORBERT, W. *See* Norbert WIENER.

NORDEN, ERIC (? – ?). American author of the routine sf novel *The Ultimate Solution* (**1973**). [PN]

NORMAN, BARRY (? –). English journalist, TV personality and writer. After two thrillers, his sf novel is *End Product* (**1975**), a NEAR-FUTURE story in which blacks are lobotomized at birth and provide the civilized world with ample meat; the allegorical and political messages of the novel, though highly loaded, tend to clash. [JC]

NORMAN, ERIC (? –). American writer. His routine sf novel *The Under-People* (**1969**) is not to be confused with *The Underpeople* (**1968**) by Cordwainer SMITH. [JC]

NORMAN, JOHN Pseudonym of American writer and philosophy teacher John Frederick Lange Jr (1931–), used for his series of borderline sf novels set on the planet Gor, a counter-Earth in Earth's orbit but on the other side of the Sun, so always invisible. The first novel of the series, *Tarnsman of Gor* (**1966**), sets Earthman Tarl Cabot abruptly on Gor, where, after the fashion of Edgar Rice BURROUGHS' novels about exotic societies on Mars and Venus, he begins to undergo numerous adventures, alarms, fights, and romance. Very soon, however, as the series progresses, JN introduces, and increasingly concentrates upon, a rather single-minded brand of SEXUAL fantasy involving bondage and sadomasochism, in which proud women are humiliated, stripped and beaten, only to discover that they enjoy total submission to a dominant male. Once humbled, they become satisfactory companions and/or slaves for Cabot and the protagonists who succeed him as the series continues. Later volumes, like *Marauders of Gor* (**1975**), which is illustrated, actually present arguments for male dominance and female submission, and the stories themselves have become routine. The series includes *Outlaw of Gor* (**1967**); *Priest-Kings of Gor* (**1968**); *Nomads of Gor* (**1969**); *Assassin of Gor* (**1970**); *Raiders of Gor* (**1971**); *Captive of Gor* (**1972**); *Hunters of Gor* (**1974**); *Tribesmen of Gor* (**1976**); *Slave Girl of Gor* (**1977**). An unrelated, though essentially similar novel is *Time Slave* (**1975**) and a non-fiction book, *Imaginative Sex* (**1974**)

argues the sexual bias of the novels very explicitly. [JC]
See also: LIFE ON OTHER WORLDS; SWORD AND SORCERY.

NORTH, ANDREW See Andre NORTON.

NORTH, ERIC Pseudonym used by Charles Bernard Cronin (1884–), Australian novelist, for his sf work; he used many pseudonyms in various genres. As EN he published sf in Australian journals such as the Melbourne *Herald* and the Australian *Bulletin*: *Toad* (mid-1920s Melbourne *Herald* as "The Green Flame"; **1929**) features a man capable of setting water afire; *The Ant Men* (**1955**) is a juvenile about intelligent ants. "The Satyr" (1924 Melbourne *Herald*; vt "Three Against the Stars" *Argosy* 1938) tells of invaders from another DIMENSION; it has not been published as a book. [JC]

NORTON, ANDRE Writing name of Alice Mary Norton (1912–), who has recently become Andre Alice Norton. A librarian for 20 years before turning to full-time writing, she is one of the few sf figures of any stature to have entered the field through juvenile novels, and though much of her work is fully as adult in theme and telling as almost all general sf, she has been primarily marketed as a writer for children and adolescents. Beginning to publish in the 1930s, she soon produced an espionage trilogy set in the Netherlands during and after the Second World War, comprised of *The Sword is Drawn* (**1944**), *Sword in Sheath* (**1949**) and *At Swords' Point* (**1954**); she came to sf proper only in 1947 with "The People of the Crater" for *Fantasy Books* as by Andrew North, a pseudonym she also used for three novels; the story is included in *Garan the Eternal* (coll. **1972**) which, along with *The Many Worlds of Andre Norton* (coll. **1974**; vt *The Book of Andre Norton*) ed. Roger ELWOOD, assembles much of her relatively small output of short fiction.
AN has consistently demonstrated her preference for novel-length fictions, and for the establishing of links among her numerous books; indeed most of her novels make use (though sometimes rather casually) of a common background and common vocabulary whose general effect is to place into a broadly conceived galactic venue a wide variety of tales, some SPACE OPERA, some comparatively intimate studies of men, ALIENS and beasts and their relationships under various circumstances: terms like Forerunner, Patrol and Free Trader are common; alien species like the Zacathans appear in book after book. Though shared assumptions and a shared galaxy do not make a series, many of the novels are more closely linked. They are the "Dane Thorson" books, *Sargasso of Space* (**1955** as by Andrew North; 1969 as by

Andre Norton), *Plague Ship* (**1956** as by Andrew North; 1969 as by Andre Norton), *Voodoo Planet* (**1959** as by Andrew North; 1968 as by Andre Norton) and *Postmarked the Stars* (**1969**); the "Blake Walker" sequence, *The Crossroads of Time* (**1956**) and *Quest Crosstime* (**1965**; vt *Crosstime Agent* UK); the "Ross Murdock" sequence, *The Time Traders* (**1958**), *Galactic Derelict* (**1959**), *The Defiant Agents* (**1962**) and *Key out of Time* (**1963**); the "Astra" sequence, *The Stars are Ours!* (**1954**) and *Star Born* (**1957**); the "Hosteen Storm" sequence, *The Beast Master* (**1959**) and *Lord of Thunder* (**1962**); the "Lantee" sequence, *Storm over Warlock* (**1960**), *Ordeal in Otherwhere* (**1964**) and *Forerunner Foray* (**1973**); the "Janus" sequence, *Judgement on Janus* (**1963**) and *Victory on Janus* (**1966**); the "Witch World" sequence, essentially fantasy and not tied to the shared background, *Witch World* (**1963**), *Web of the Witch World* (**1964**), *Year of the Unicorn* (**1965**), *Three Against the Witch World* (**1965**), *Warlock of the Witch World* (**1967**), *Sorceress of the Witch World* (**1968**), *Spell of the Witch World* (coll. **1972**), *The Crystal Gryphon* (**1972**), *The Jargoon Pard* (**1974**) and *Trey of Swords* (**1978**); the 1977 edition of the first seven volumes, which are more closely linked, includes introductions and maps; they are thought by many to be among her most imaginative works; the "Moon Singer" sequence, *Moon of Three Rings* (**1966**) and *Exiles of the Stars* (**1971**); and the "Murdoc Jern" sequence, *The Zero Stone* (**1968**) and *Uncharted Stars* (**1969**).
The "Witch World" sequence is an exception, but most other novels in AN's sf series make free cross-references one to another, and to non-series books. The AN universe revealed in these numerous books, from her first sf novel *Star Man's Son* (**1952**; vt *Daybreak–2250 A.D.*), to her most recent, is a colourful, complex, rewarding environment for her many young protagonists; in most of the books, the advanced technology of space travel, war, communications and so forth that liberate her narrative lines and add verisimilitude to her romantic sense of wonder is described perfunctorily, if at all, and she displays a consistent tendency to oppose man and machine. In the "Hosteen Storm" sequence, as in many individual novels, man and beast establish a close, sometimes telepathic rapport with one another; in *Catseye* (**1961**) this empathy is multiple and among equals. Her protagonists, in escaping repressive environments and establishing themselves free of the past with new homes on new planets, often pit themselves against not only machines but administrative and bureaucratic insensitivity and oppression; a rather awkwardly conceived computer is the actual foe to be defeated in the "Janus" sequence, which also features man-animal compacts. Time travel, as in the "Ross Murdock" sequence, is found

infrequently in the AN universe.

Though her style has matured over the years, and her plots have tended to darken somewhat, from first to last an AN story will show virtues of clear construction, a high degree of narrative control, protagonists whose qualities allow easy reader identification and a universe (whose availability to Man is described in space-opera terms and represented by the familiarity of the shared backgrounds) which is fundamentally responsive to virtue, good will, and spunk. The large number of books published so far, the fact that she has not been inclined to publish material in the sf magazines, and the label of juvenile writer she has borne, have all worked to restrict AN's impact within the sf genre, though her actual sales are very considerable. Though she is not innovative with regard to ideas, she is all the same a prolific craftsman whose relative critical neglect is regrettable. [JC]
Other works: Representative non-sf includes: *The Prince Commands* (**1934**); *Follow the Drum* (**1942**); *Rogue Reynard* (**1947**); *Scarface* (**1948**); *Huon of the Horn* (**1951**); *Murders for Sale* (**1954**) with Grace Allen Hogarth, both as Allen Weston.

Sf and fantasy: *Star Rangers* (**1953**; vt *The Last Planet*); *Star Guard* (**1955**); *Sea Siege* (**1957**); *Star Gate* (**1958**); *Secret of the Lost Race* (**1959**; vt *Wolf's Head* UK); *Shadow Hawk* (**1960**); *The Sioux Spaceman* (**1960**); *Star Hunter* (**1961**); *Eye of the Monster* (**1962**); *Night of Masks* (**1964**); *Steel Magic* (**1965**; vt *Gray Magic*); *The X Factor* (**1965**); *Octagon Magic* (**1967**); *Operation Time Search* (**1967**); *Dark Piper* (**1968**); *Fur Magic* (**1968**); *Dread Companion* (**1970**); *Ice Crown* (**1970**); *High Sorcery* (coll. **1970**); *Android at Arms* (**1971**); *Breed to Come* (**1972**); *Dragon Magic* (**1972**); *Here Abide Monsters* (**1973**); *Iron Cage* (**1974**); *Outside* (**1974**); *Lavender-Green Magic* (**1974**); *Merlin's Mirror* (**1975**); *The White Jade Fox* (**1975**); *The Day of the Ness* (**1975**) with Michael Gilbert; *No Night Without Stars* (**1975**); *Knave of Dreams* (**1975**); *Perilous Dreams* (coll. **1976**); *Star Ka'at* (**1976**) with Dorothy Madlee; *Wraiths of Time* (**1976**); *Red Hart Magic* (**1976**); *The Opal-Eyed Fan* (**1977**).

As editor: *Bullard of the Space Patrol* (coll. of linked stories **1951**), tales by Malcolm JAMESON; *Space Service* (anth. **1953**); *Space Pioneers* (anth. **1954**); *Space Police* (anth. **1956**); *Gates to Tomorrow* (anth. **1973**) ed. with E. Donaldy; *Small Shadows Creep* (anth. **1974**).
About the author: "Andre Norton: Loss of Faith" (1971) by Rick Brooks in *The Many Worlds of Andre Norton* (coll. 1974); introduction by Sandra Miesel to the GREGG PRESS reissue (1977) of the "Witch World" series.
See also: CHILDREN'S SF; CRIME AND PUNISHMENT; FANTASY; SWORD AND SORCERY; WOMEN.

NORTON, ROY (1869–1942). Popular author of many Westerns and some sf, beginning with *The Vanishing Fleets* (**1908**), in which a group of scientists cause the disappearance of two fleets in the Pacific, in the name of peace. In his second sf novel, *The Toll of the Sea* (**1909**), the Pacific figures again, this time changing its shape. [JC]
Other works: *The Flame* (**1916**); *The Caves of Treasure* (**1925**); *The Land of the Lost* (**1925**).

NORWAY See SCANDINAVIA.

NORWOOD, VICTOR (GEORGE CHARLES) (? –). British writer of routine paperback sf novels, beginning with *The Untamed* (**1951**). [JC]
Other works: *The Caves of Death* (**1951**); *The Temple of the Dead* (**1951**); *The Skull of Kanaima* (**1952**); *The Island of Creeping Death* (**1952**); *Drums Along the Amazon* (**1953**); *Cry of the Beast* (**1953**); *Night of the Black Horror* (**1962**).

NOTT, KATHLEEN (CECILIA) (? –). English poet, novelist and academic, perhaps best known for her articulately scathing attack on the religious pretensions of such writers as T. S. Eliot and C. S. LEWIS in *The Emperor's Clothes* (**1953**), her sf novel, *The Dry Deluge* (**1947**), describes the founding of an underground UTOPIA devoted to the achievement of IMMORTALITY. [JC]

NOURSE, ALAN E(DWARD) (1928–). American writer and physician. He began publishing sf with "High Threshold" for *ASF* in 1951, and has gained a reputation as a reliable creator of juvenile novels, starting with his first, *Trouble on Titan* (**1954**), which features rebellion and conflict within a SPACE OPERA Solar System, as do other juveniles, like *Raiders from the Rings* (**1962**), in which conflict between an oppressive Earth regime and libertarian Spacers is finally halted by the intervention of superior, peaceful ALIENS. In *Rocket to Limbo* (**1957**), Man's destiny is explained to him by alien observers. In these juveniles, young men and women join to effect reconciliations amongst their bigoted elders, and men are put on the right road to the stars. AEN's novels are straightforward, frequently making somewhat simple points about bureaucracies and tyrannies, as in *The Invaders Are Coming* (**1959**) with J. A. Meyer. Several others make use of his medical knowledge, of brain surgery in *A Man Obsessed* (**1955**; exp. as *The Mercy Men* 1968), which is part of a series which also includes "Nightmare Brother" (1953) and "The Expert Touch" (1955), and of MEDICINE in general in the lively and interesting *Star Surgeon* (**1960**), one of his best works. *Rx for Tomorrow* (coll. **1971**) assembles medical sf and fantasy tales. It is sometimes difficult to determine whether or not these works are intended

for a juvenile market, though the age of the protagonists in *Star Surgeon* and *The Mercy Men*, where medicine and ESP meet in the search of a boy for his father, are suggestive. A sense of fundamental decency permeates AEN's fiction; and though it is sometimes too easily achieved, the victories of decency over bigotry cannot be seriously faulted for the market upon which AEN concentrates. [JC]
Other works: *Junior Intern* (**1955**), not sf; *Scavengers in Space* (**1959**); *Tiger by the Tail and Other Stories* (coll. **1961**; vt *Beyond Infinity* UK); *The Counterfeit Man and Others* (coll. **1963**); *The Universe Between* (**1951**; fix-up **1965**), which incorporates his first story; *PSI High and Others* (coll. **1967**); *The Bladerunner* (**1974**). *Nine Planets* (**1960**) is science fact.
See also: CHILDREN'S SF; MERCURY; OUTER PLANETS; PARALLEL WORLDS.

NOVA 1. Original anthology series; ed. Harry HARRISON. It lasted for four volumes: *Nova 1* (anth. **1970**), *Nova 2* (anth. **1972**), *Nova 3* (anth. **1973**; vt *The Outdated Man*) and *Nova 4* (anth. **1974**). Brian W. ALDISS was listed as co-editor of the first volume. This was a catholic anthology, the contents ranging from old-fashioned sf adventure stories by such writers as Gordon R. DICKSON to experimental pieces by younger authors. Although the contributors included such writers as Aldiss and Robert SHECKLEY, the series achieved no great distinction, and failed to develop an identity of its own.

2. Norwegian sf magazine. See SCANDINAVIA. [MJE]

NOWLAN, PHILIP FRANCIS (1888–1940). American writer. His story "Armageddon 2419", published in the (1928) issue of *AMZ* that began E.E. "Doc" SMITH's "Skylark" saga, introduced Anthony "Buck" Rogers to the world. This and a subsequent story, "The Airlords of Han" (1929), were put together as *Armageddon 2419 AD* (1928–9 *AMZ*; 1962) long after his death. PFN is best remembered for his collaboration with Dick CALKINS on the first sf COMIC STRIP, BUCK ROGERS IN THE 25TH CENTURY, which resulted from the success of his original story; the strip began in 1929, ending in 1967; he worked on it until his death, which also cut short a new series he had begun in *ASF*. [JC/PN]
See also: TRANSPORTATION.

NOYES, ALFRED (1880–1958). English poet and man of letters, best known for work outside the sf field, e.g. *Drake* (1906–08), a long narrative poem, and *The Torchbearers* (1922–30), an even longer poem about the march of science. He wrote some fantasy and horror stories, which appear in *Tales of the Mermaid Tavern* (coll. 1914), *Walking*

Shadows: Sea Tales and Others (coll. **1918**) and *The Hidden Player* (coll. **1924**), and a fantasy novel, *The Devil Takes a Holiday* (**1955**). His post-HOLOCAUST novel, *The Last Man* (**1940**; vt *No Other Man* USA), concerns the lives of a few survivors after the explosion of a doomsday weapon. AN was a fervent Roman Catholic convert (he was received into the Church in 1930), an ardent anti-Modernist in his views on art, an early Japanophile and a defender of VOLTAIRE and Parnell.   [JC]

See also: END OF THE WORLD; WEAPONS.

N3F The National Fantasy Fan Federation, formed 1941 in the USA. After a succession of short-lived and factional American fan associations in the 1930s, the N3F proved a stable and enduring national organization. However, despite its long existence, it has maintained a very low level of membership and activity and has contributed little to sf or FANDOM. It continues none the less to sponsor an annual short story competition for amateur sf writers and to publish *The National Fantasy Fan*, an introverted newsletter which first appeared, under the title *Bonfire*, in 1941.   [PR]

NUCLEAR POWER The claim that sf is a realistic, extrapolative literature is often supported by the citing of successful PREDICTIONS, among which atomic power and the atom bomb are usually given pride of place. When the news of the bombing of Hiroshima and Nagasaki was released in 1945, John W. CAMPBELL Jr, editor of ASTOUNDING SCIENCE FICTION, was exultant, claiming that from that moment on sf would have to be taken seriously. It could, however, be argued that while it is true that the advent of atomic power was anticipated in a considerable number of sf stories, this was not a tremendous imaginative leap. Even if one takes this view, however, one must concede that Campbell was fully entitled to a measure of self-congratulation, for the fact that sf writers of the early 1940s concerned themselves so seriously with atomic power was almost entirely due to his editorial influence.

The notion of "splitting the atom" goes back into antiquity as a philosophical problem raised in the consideration of atomic theories from Epicurus and Democritus on. It was not until the end of the 19th century, however, that any evidence relating to the actual structure of atoms became accessible. At the turn of the century this was one of the most rapidly evolving areas of scientific knowledge, and in 1902 Rutherford and Soddy demonstrated the instability of certain heavy atoms — including uranium and radium — which were in a state of continuous spontaneous decay, emitting various types of energetic radiation. The popularization of these and related discoveries had an influence on popular scientific romance comparable only to the influence of evolutionary theory. The power of radioactivity, in many applications, quickly became commonplace in sf, especially in the sub-genre of war-anticipation stories (*see* WAR; WEAPONS). Einstein's famous equation linking mass and energy ($E = mc^2$) became a magical formula by which any imaginative writer could derive limitless energy by the destruction of mass. It is by no means surprising that Garrett P. SERVISS, in *A Columbus of Space* (1909; rev. **1911**), could imagine an atomic-powered spaceship; or that George GRIFFITH, in *The Lord of Labour* (**1911**), could imagine weapons like bazookas firing atomic missiles; or that H.G. WELLS, in *The World Set Free* (**1914**), could imagine civilization destroyed by atomic bombs. These notions were natural responses to the popularization of ideas in contemporary PHYSICS.

Hugo GERNSBACK was certainly aware of the possibility of atomic power, and had no hesitation in predicting its use in the imminent future. He sometimes referred to the coming era of high technology as "The Atom-Electronic Age" or "The Age of Power-Freedom". Nevertheless, atomic power would simply have been one more idea in the extravagant vocabulary of PULP sf had it not been for Campbell.

Campbell's first published story, "When the Atoms Failed" (1930), featured the release of energy by the destruction of matter, and one of his earliest stories as by Don A. Stuart was "Atomic Power" (1934). He took a serious interest in actual progress in this area of science, and in such articles as "Atomic Generator" (1937), "Isotope 235" (1939 as Arthur McCann) and "Atomic Ringmaster" (1940 as Arthur McCann) he popularized this research for the readers of *ASF*. He discussed contemporary developments in his editorials, and actively encouraged his writers to consider the possibilities seriously. He made the scientific issues so familiar that even a routine space opera like Theodore STURGEON's "Artnan Process" (1941) could hinge its plot on the esoteric problem of isotope separation. He published several stories dealing with the theme of nuclear power which were, in their structure and style, quite atypical of early-'40s pulp sf. "Blowups Happen" (1940) by Robert A. HEINLEIN deals with the psychological stress involved in working with a nuclear power plant and its potential hazards. "Solution Unsatisfactory" (1941), also by Heinlein, writing as Anson MacDonald, is about using radioactive dust as a weapon of war, and the difficulties of exercising control over its use. *Nerves* (1942; exp. **1956**) by Lester DEL REY is a classic story of an accident in a nuclear power station which threatens to become a major disaster, and deals perceptively with the issues which now face the real world, as seen in the public anxiety regarding power plants. In its attempt at realism this story was unparalleled by anything else appearing in the sf magazines at the time. A fourth story, in itself less impressive, Cleve CARTMILL's "Deadline" (1944), brought Campbell the joyous triumph of a visit from the government's security forces, because it featured an atomic bomb. Campbell later made much of the fact that he was publishing sf of such anticipatory expertise that the FBI suspected him of having access to secrets, but the compliment paid him is less impressive when one remembers that Philip WYLIE received a similar visit in 1945 and that two comic-book stories featuring SUPERMAN were actually suppressed.

Campbell's achievement in making sf writers think seriously about atomic power should not be minimized. The only story of any significance dealing with atomic power which was published outside *ASF* before Hiroshima was a melodrama about a "breeder" reaction published in *Startling Stories* as "The Giant Atom" (1944) and reprinted subsequently as *Atomic Bomb* (**1945**). This was by Malcolm JAMESON, a member of Campbell's regular stable of authors. The fact that magazine sf investigated the possibilities of atomic power in such depth is more a testament to Campbell's personal enthusiasm than a reflection of the general extrapolative competence of the genre. (It is something of a tragedy that other causes which Campbell later espoused in an attempt to repeat the trick — DIANETICS, the Dean drive, etc. — were all hopeless.)

After 1945 atomic power became one of the standard themes in sf, as the shock of revelation precipitated a wave of apocalyptic atomic war stories (*see* HOLOCAUST AND AFTER). The mutational romance, popular since the mutagenic effects of X-rays had been discovered in the 1920s, also received a considerable boost (*see* MUTANTS). The idea that new potential in human EVOLUTION might be stimulated by post-disaster radioactivity became an important supportive logic in the "psi boom" (*see* ESP; PSI POWERS; SUPERMAN). But as nuclear power became a reality, the kind of realistic treatment of issues connected with it seen in "Blowups Happen" and *Nerves* went into decline. These themes, no longer hypothetical, passed out of the area of interest of the sf writers. The major novels dealing with the social and psychological problems of living with nuclear power and radioactive substances in the post-War period were presented as mainstream fiction — which, indeed, they had become. Two of the most notable examples are Henri QUEFFELEC's *Frontier of the Unknown* (1958; trans. **1960**; vt *The Men of Danezan* USA) and Daniel KEYES' *The Touch* (1968; vt *The Contaminated Man*).

(The seemingly paradoxical observation might be made here that sf can be realistic only when it deals with the imaginary.) Inevitably, the priorities of magazine sf shifted in 1945 quite dramatically. Today, we are living with the reality of nuclear power, and it is only specific aspects which now concern sf writers — the one imaginative aspect that dominates all others being that of the possibilities inherent in the use of atomic weapons in war. This is only natural, in view of what is at stake: Gunther Anders has said that since 1945 the axiom that "all men are mortal" has acquired a sinister corollary, to the effect that "all men are exterminable". The change of consciousness brought about by this new axiom has been one of the principal forces shaping post-War sf, making it a literature of anxiety, often apocalyptic in tone and content. One particular group of stories which brings out the point very clearly is that dealing with the moral issues facing the atomic scientists, who gave their fellow men the power to annihilate the world: "The Weapon" (1951) by Fredric BROWN; "Day of the Moron" (1951) by H. Beam PIPER; "The Disintegrating Sky" (1953) and "Progress" (1962) by Poul ANDERSON; "Judgment Day" (1955) by L. Sprague DE CAMP; and "Chain Reaction" (1956) by Boyd Ellanby.

In contemporary sf, nuclear power plants are part of virtually all NEAR-FUTURE scenarios and, as the real world faces a resource crisis with respect to the principal fossil fuels, a constructive role is usually given to them. They still symbolize, in some ways, "the Age of Power-Freedom", but also, in a very direct sense, the Age of Anxiety. [BS]
See also: DISASTER; POLITICS; POWER SOURCES; TECHNOLOGY.

NUETZEL, CHARLES (ALEXANDER) (1934–). American self-styled hack writer; in various genres, under a variety of names, he has written over 70 paperback novels. CN became active as an sf writer in the 1960s, when he began publishing in this genre with "A Very Cultured Taste" for *Jade* no. 1 in 1960. His first sf novel, *Lovers: 2075* (**1964**), as by Charles English, was, like his second, *Queen of Blood* (**1966**), mildly erotic, and marketed as such. *Images of Tomorrow* (**1969**) is a satirical novel; *Warriors of Noomas* (**1969**) and its sequel *Raiders of Noomas* (**1969**) are romantic adventures heavily influenced by Edgar Rice BURROUGHS, as is *Swordsmen of Vistar* (**1969**). The last four titles were all published by CN's own sf publishing company, Powell Books, as was his *The Slaves of Lomooro* (**1969**) as by Albert Augustus Jr. [JC]
Other works: *Last Call for the Stars* (**1970**). As editor: *If this Goes On* (anth. **1965**).

NUNES, CLAUDE (1924–). South African writer and statistician, almost all of whose work is in collaboration with his wife Rhoda Nunes; they published their first sf story, "The Problem", with *Science Fantasy* in 1962, and have remained moderately active. *Inherit the Earth* (1963 *Science Fiction Adventures* as by Claude and Rhoda Nunes; exp. **1966**) was published as by CN alone, as his wife participated less than usual in the re-write; *Recoil* (**1971**) was published as by both writers, and, in a rather archaic style, tells of telepathic ALIENS and their attempts to influence humans, specifically a group of children. [JC]

NYE, HAROLD G. *See* Lee HARDING.

O'BRIEN, DAVID WRIGHT (? –1944). American writer, nephew of Farnsworth WRIGHT. He published almost entirely for the Ziff-Davis magazines *AMZ* and *Fantastic Adventures* under a number of pseudonyms, including John York Cabot, Bruce Dennis, Duncan Farnsworth, Richard Vardon and the house names Alexander BLADE and Clee GARSON. Under his own name he published about 40 magazine stories and novels; none of them reached book form. He also collaborated with William P. McGIVERN on four stories. As John York Cabot, he wrote the Sergeant Shane series of three stories about a space marine, and about 20 further tales. As Bruce Dennis, he wrote three stories. As Duncan Farnsworth, he wrote 19 stories. As Richard Vardon, he published only one story. His Alexander Blade stories have not been identified; he seems to have been the main contributor under the Clee Garson name. His first story seems to have appeared in *AMZ*, Feb. 1940. Almost all his work was SPACE OPERA or other routine adventure. He was killed in the Second World War when shot down over Berlin. [JC]

O'BRIEN, DEAN D. *See* Eando BINDER.

O'BRIEN, E.G. *See* Arthur C. CLARKE.

O'BRIEN, FITZ-JAMES (c.1828–62). Irish-born American writer. From his arrival in New York in 1852 until he died of an infected wound in the Civil War, FJOB contributed numerous poems and minor stories to the magazines. His importance rests on a handful of brilliantly original sf tales, which were influential not only on subsequent sf but also on the development of the short-story genre.

His finest work is "The Diamond Lens" (1858), a long story, narrated with precise detail, about a scientist who invents a super-microscope and is then consumed by his morbid love for a beautiful woman he perceives living in an infinitesimal world inside a drop of water (*see* GREAT AND SMALL). "What Was It? A Mystery" (1859) tells of an encounter with an INVISIBLE being whose nature remains an enigma, although a plaster cast, made while the creature is chloroformed, reveals it to be a hideous diminutive humanoid. These two stories, his best known, are both set firmly in the mid-19th-century New York scene; they helped establish a mode of sf characterized by surface realism. In a similar vein was the earlier "The Bohemian" (1855), in which the narrator's passionate love for gold fatally induces him to have his fiancée mesmerized in order to reveal the whereabouts of a treasure. "From Hand to Mouth" (1858) is a remarkable surrealistic fantasy in which a man sits in the Hotel de Coup d'Oeil surrounded by disembodied but living eyes, ears, mouths and hands. In "The Lost Room" (1858), a strange house, whose intricate "corridors and passages, like mathematical lines, seemed capable of indefinite expansion", becomes the scene of an orgy by six male and female "enchanters" who apparently succeed in kidnapping the narrator's room into some other world or DIMENSION. "The Wondersmith" (1859) is notable in the history of sf, despite its fantastic framework, for its extended descriptions of an army of miniature automata. The posthumously published "How I Overcame My Gravity" (1864), though marred by the use of dream, is otherwise a singularly modern piece of sf: its core is a detailed description of suborbital flight achieved with the aid of gyroscopic stabilization.

The great strength of FJOB's sf is its inventiveness, which also became its greatest weakness whenever he allowed ingenuity to dominate the fiction. "The Diamond Lens" remains a masterpiece because here he subordinated his brilliant invention to a profound exploration of the diseased psychology of one of the main figures of his age, the would-be lone genius of scientific creation.

FJOB's works were collected in various posthumous editions: *Poems and Stories* (coll. **1881**); *The Diamond Lens and Other Stories* (coll. **1885**); *What Was It? and Other Stories* (coll. **1889**) and *Collected Stories by Fitz-James O'Brien* (coll. **1925**). [HBF]

O'BRIEN, FLANN Pseudonym of Irish writer and civil servant Brian O Nolan (1911–66), who also wrote a newspaper column as Myles na Gopaleen. He is best known for work outside the sf field, such as the ABSURDIST mythological fantasy "saga" *At Swim-Two-Birds* (**1939**). Though much of his work utilizes fantasy elements, his novels most closely resembling sf are *The Third Policeman* (**1967**), written around 1940, set in a character's posthumous universe after he has committed a murder (he may be in hell), and *The Dalkey Archive* (**1964**), which features a mad scientist eager to destroy the world and the fantastic results of a gas he invents. *Faustus Kelly* (**1943**) is a fantasy play about the Devil in Ireland. [JC/PN]

O'BRIEN, ROBERT C(ARROLL) (1922–73). American writer. His books have been marketed as juveniles, though the last two are essentially adult. His first, *The Silver Crown* (**1968**), is a sometimes frightening, complex fantasy about the kidnapping of a young girl by a king, ruled in turn by a malignant machine. *Mrs Frisby and the Rats of NIMH* (**1971**), which won the Newbery medal, tells of a group of rats, fugitives from a laboratory where their INTELLIGENCE has been enhanced, who, with the help of Mrs Frisby, a field mouse, found an independent colony, determined not to batten off humans. The treatment is realistic and without a trace of whimsy. *A Report from Group 17* (**1972**) is about biological warfare between the US and Russia. It is competent, but less successful than RCOB's other work. *Z for Zachariah* (**1975**) is a post-HOLOCAUST novel of considerable sensitivity in which a solitary surviving adolescent girl comes to realize that she cannot make a life with another, male survivor who enters her quiet valley; she eludes his attempt at rape and travels across the desolated landscape in search of other survivors. It is a fine book, morally complex, and not simply a story of good versus evil; the girl's victory is ambiguous. RCOB died before the novel was quite finished; it was completed by his family. [PN/JC] See also: CHILDREN'S SF.

O'BRIEN, WILLIS H. (1886–1962). American special-effects expert. Born in Oakland, California, he began his career as a marble-cutter but was interested in sculpture and cartooning. For his own amusement he began experimenting with stop-motion photography and filmed two small clay boxers (stop-motion photography involves exposing one frame of film and then moving the object being filmed into a new position for the next exposure, an obviously time-consuming process; cartoon animation is achieved in a similar way). His next project was more ambitious — a one-minute film of an animated cave-man and dinosaur, involving 960 separate exposures. The result led to a producer's advancing him $5,000 to make a more elaborate version of the same subject. Called *The Dinosaur and the Missing Link*, it ran for only five minutes on the screen but took two months to make. It proved successful and he made a series of similar films for the Edison Company. In 1919 he made the more elaborate *The Ghost of Slumber Mountain*, which was one of the first films to combine footage of live actors with animated models.

WHOB's next project was THE LOST WORLD, released in 1925, his first full-length feature film. The success of this led him to start work on a project of epic proportions. Called *Creation*, it was to be a variation on the "lost world" theme. The film was never completed, but he was able to incorporate a great deal of its material (including improved designs for his models, which by then had metal skeletons with ball-and-socket joints) in KING KONG (1933) which proved to be the peak of his career. A sequel, SON OF KONG, was hurriedly made and released in the same year, but after that he found difficulty in getting financial backing for his increasingly expensive animation projects. In the late 1930s he began work on *The War Eagles*, which was to be about a remote race of people who rode on the backs of tame giant eagles: the proposed climax had an aerial battle between eagles and airships over New York City; but the film was abandoned, as was his next project, *Gwangi*, about a group of cowboys who discover dinosaurs on a Texas mesa, in 1942. It was not until 1949 that he was able to complete another animated feature — MIGHTY JOE YOUNG, a less ambitious remake of *King Kong*. It was the last picture in which he had any substantial control. During the 1950s he worked on various monster films for other people but was unable to obtain the necessary backing for his own films. He died in 1962 while working on *It's a Mad, Mad, Mad, Mad World*. [JB]

OBRUCHEV, V(LADIMIR) (AFANAS'EVICH) (1863–1956). Russian geologist, academician and writer. Two of his novels, both early classics of Russian sf, have been translated: *Plutonia* (1915; **1924**; trans. B. Pearce **1957**) and *Sannikov's Land* (**1926**; trans. **1955**). Both are adventures after the style of Jules VERNE, aimed at younger readers, and making much use of geological information. The first is a hollow-Earth story, in which a party of Russian explorers enters the Earth north of Alaska, and finds a LOST WORLD, full of prehistoric reptiles. The second is similar; a volcano near the North Pole has a fertile lost world inside it populated by an archaic race. [PN]

OCEANOGRAPHY See UNDER THE SEA.

OCTOBER, JOHN Possibly pseudonymous British writer whose routine sf novel is *The Anarchy Pedlars* (**1976**). [JC]

OCTOPUS, THE US PULP MAGAZINE. One issue, Feb./Mar. 1939, published by Popular Publications; ed. Rogers Terrill. The feature novel, "The City Condemned to Hell" by Randolph Craig (Norvell W. PAGE), was actually a rewritten SPIDER story. It was reprinted in PULP CLASSICS no.11 (**1976**). THE SCORPION was a follow-up to *O*. Collectors should note that the single issue was confusingly designated Vol.1 no.4. [MJE/FHP]

ODELL, SAMUEL W. (1864–1948). American writer of two sf books, *Atlanteans* (coll. **1889**) and *The Last War; or The Triumph of the English Tongue* (**1898**). In the latter, a future-WAR story, three million enemies are destroyed in a final air battle. [JC]

ODLE, E.V. (? – ?). British writer, in whose interesting sf novel *The Clockwork Man* (**1923**) a CYBORG who can perceive the FOURTH DIMENSION arrives from AD 8000 to describe his world (in which Man has become clockwork in the eyes of God, and a machine-regulated life is voluntarily accepted by some, not all, of the men of the future) and to play cricket. [JC]

O'DONNELL, K.M. See Barry N. MALZBERG.

O'DONNELL, LAWRENCE See Henry KUTTNER and Catherine L. MOORE.

O'DONNEVAN, FINN See Robert SHECKLEY.

O'DUFFY, EIMAR (1893–1935). Irish writer whose mock-epic Irish tales *King Goshawk and the Birds* (**1926**), with its sequel *The Spacious Adventures of the Man in the Street* (**1928**) and *Asses in Clover* (**1933**) make satirical points about contemporary civilization, very much in the manner of James Stephens in *The Crock of Gold* (**1912**), by viewing modern life through the eyes of characters who are, or claim to be, figures of Irish legend; the second volume mounts its comparatively sustained SATIRE through its heroes' voyage to a UTOPIA where everything is, not unusually, inverted. [JC]

ODYSSEY US BEDSHEET-size magazine. Two issues, Spring 1976 and Summer 1976, published by Gambi Publications, New York; ed. Roger ELWOOD. *O* was advertised as an sf magazine, but contained a high proportion of fantasy. The fiction and articles were unremarkable; lead novellas were by Jerry POURNELLE (no.1) and Larry NIVEN (no.2). Production was poor, and the covers by Frank Kelly FREAS and Jack GAUGHAN were inferior to the usual work of both artists. Bad distribution and poor sales killed *O*. A third announced issue with stories already commissioned did not appear.   [FHP/PN]

OFFUTT, ANDREW J. (1937–). American writer who often signs his name as andrew j offutt, whose first story was published as by Andy Offutt and first professional sale as by A.J. Offutt. He has Master's degrees in both history and psychology. His first published story, a contest winner, was "And Gone Tomorrow" in 1954 for *If*, but he considers his professional sf career to have begun with "Blacksword" for *Galaxy* in 1959. He has become a prolific writer in several genres, both under his own name and under pseudonyms including John Cleve, Jeff Douglas and the house name J.X. Williams. These pseudonymous works have been sex novels, several of them with sf content. AJO's first sf novel under his own name is *Evil is Live Spelled Backwards* (**1970**), in which an underground movement fights a 21st-century religious tyranny with a sexual revolution. *The Castle Keeps* (**1972**) more ambitiously depicts the violent disintegration of Western culture. A juvenile, *The Galactic Rejects* (**1973**), features three young friends with PSI powers on a UTOPIAN world threatened by invasion. Most of AJO's signed work, like *Messenger of Zhuvastou* (**1973**) and *My Lord Barbarian* (**1977**), is fantasy, usually SWORD AND SORCERY. He has an urgent, sometimes rather hasty style, and though he seems to find all sorts of material congenial to him, from juveniles to pornography, he is perhaps most effective in sf stories depicting a hectic urban world. As president of the SFWA (1976–8, and treasurer and membership chairman, 1973–6), he has offered a defence and explanation ("How it Happened: One Bad Decision Leading to Another", in SCIENCE-FICTION STUDIES Jul. 1977) of that organization's expulsion of Stanislaw LEM in 1975.   [JC]
Other works: As AJO: *The Great 24-Hour Thing* (**1971**); *Ardor on Aros* (**1973**); *Genetic Bomb* (**1975**) with D. Bruce Berry; a fantasy series, based on Robert E. HOWARD's character Cormac mac Art, *Sword of the Gael* (**1975**), *The Undying Wizard* (**1976**) and *Sign of the Moonbow* (**1977**); *Chieftain of Andor* (**1976**). As John Cleve: *Barbarana* (**1970**); *The Devoured* (**1970**); *Fruit of the Loins* (**1970**); *Jodinareh* (**1970**); *The Juice of Love* (**1970**); *Pleasure Us!* (**1971**; vt *The Pleasure Principle* as by Baxter Giles); *Manlib!* (**1974**); *The Sexorcist* (**1974**; vt *Unholy Revelry*). As Jeff Douglas (with D. Bruce Berry): *The Balling Machine* (**1971**). As J.X. Williams: *The Sex Pill* (**1968**).
As editor: *Swords Against Darkness* (anth. **1977**); *Swords Against Darkness II* (anth. **1977**).
Provisional titles of books projected for the near future as by AJO are *The Mists of*

Doom and *Tower of Death*, both in the Cormac mac Art series, and *Demon in the Mirror*, with Richard K. Lyon, the first volume in a trilogy.
See also: EVOLUTION.

O'FLINN, PETER *See* R.L. FANTHORPE.

OFSHE, RICHARD (? –). American sociologist. His anthology with critical commentary *The Sociology of the Possible* (anth. **1970**), aimed at students, is probably the best of the several collections designed to show the relevance of sf to SOCIOLOGY.   [PN]

O'HARA, KENNETH *See* Bryce WALTON.

OLEMY, P.T. American author, presumably pseudonymous, of *The Clones* (**1968**).   [JC]

OLERICH, HENRY (1851– ?). American author of three UTOPIAS, resident in the Midwest. The books are *A Cityless and Countryless World* (**1893**), *Modern Paradise: an Outline or Story of How Some of the Cultured People Will Probably Live, Work, and Organize in the New Future* (**1915**) and *The Story of the World a Thousand Years Hence* (**1923**). The former was published in Iowa and the latter two in Nebraska: the books typify Midwestern political idealism of the period.   [PN]

OLIPHANT, MRS (MARGARET) (1828–97). Scottish writer, mostly of historical romances, extremely prolific and currently undervalued; as much of her work was published anonymously, no survey can yet be comprehensive. Much of it originally appeared in *Blackwood's Magazine*. Of her 120 or so acknowledged novels, perhaps *The Greatest Heiress in England* (**1879**) stands out. It immediately precedes her finest sf/ fantasy, *The Beleaguered City: A Story of the Seen and the Unseen* (**1880**), in which the sinning inhabitants of Semur are mysteriously exiled from their city by supernatural forces, either good or evil. Other fantasy novels are *A Little Pilgrim of the Unseen* (**1882**; vt *A Little Pilgrim USA*) – which is also included in the collection *Stories of the Seen and Unseen* (coll. **1889**), and whose sequel appears in *The Land of Darkness: Along with some Further Chapters in the Experience of the Little Pilgrims* (coll. **1888**) – and *The Wizard's Son* (**1883**).   [JC]
About the author: *Autobiography and Letters* (**1899**).

OLIVER, CHAD Form of his name used by American writer and anthropologist Symmes Chadwick Oliver (1928–) for his sf stories and novels. CO was born in Ohio but has spent most of his life in Texas, where he took his BA and MA at the University of Texas (his 1952 MA thesis, "They Built a Tower", being an

early academic study of sf); his PhD in ANTHROPOLOGY is from the University of California, Los Angeles. He is professor of anthropology at the University of Texas at Austin, and his sf work has consistently reflected both his professional training and his place of residence. His fiction has generally used the outdoors of the American Southwest; most of his characters are deeply involved in outdoor activities, and he has always been concerned with the depiction of the life and concerns of the American Indian. His only non-sf fiction, *The Wolf is My Brother* (**1967**), which won the Best Western Historical Novel award in 1967 from Western Writers of America, features a sympathetically characterized Indian protagonist.

Most of CO's sf, too, could be thought of as Westerns, of the sort that eulogize the land and the men who survive in it. When he introduces specifically sf themes into his stories, like the awakening of ALIENS held in suspended animation for hundreds of centuries in *The Winds of Time* (**1957**), their fate, and that of the human protagonist, are settled in terms of the rewarding of a deeply felt longing, on the part of author, human hero and alien intruders, for a non-urban life closely involved with nature, though the effect of this is somewhat dissipated by CO's characteristic inability to prepare for his favourite scenes by adequate plotting, and a tendency (in his earlier works) to pad novelettes into novel length.

CO's first published story, "The Land of Lost Content", appeared in *Super Science Stories* in 1950; his first novel, a juvenile, was *Mists of Dawn* (**1952**). *Shadows in the Sun* (**1954**), set in Texas, describes with some vividness its protagonist's discovery that all the inhabitants of a small town are aliens. His short stories are collected in *Another Kind* (coll. **1955**), *Unearthly Neighbors* (coll. **1960**) and *The Edge of Forever* (coll. **1971**); the latter contains biographical material and a checklist compiled by William F. NOLAN. *The Shores of Another Sea* (**1971**) is set in Africa, and articulates CO's concern with the natural world, specifically in terms of ECOLOGY. *Giants in the Dust* (**1976**) argues the thesis that man's fundamental nature is that of a hunting animal, and his progress from that condition has fundamentally deracinated him. A series of four linked novelettes published in *Continuum* (*1* to *4*) (anths. **1974–5**), ed. Roger ELWOOD, is comprised of "Shaka!", "Caravans Unlimited: Stability", "The Middle Man" and "Caravans Unlimited: Monitor".

CO has been a pioneer in the application of competent anthropological thought to sf themes, and though awkward construction sometimes stifled the warmth of his earlier stories, he is a careful author whose speculative thought deserves to be more widely known and appreciated.   [JC]

See also: GENERATION STARSHIPS; INVASION; LINGUISTICS; ORIGIN OF MAN; VENUS.

OMEGA MAN, THE Film (1971). Warner Bros. Directed by Boris Sagal, starring Charlton Heston, Anthony Zerbe and Rosalind Cash. Screenplay by John William and Joyce H. Corrington. 98 mins. Colour.

This is the second film version of Richard MATHESON's ultra-PARANOID novel *I Am Legend*, (the first was THE LAST MAN ON EARTH, 1964). "The first one was very poorly done," said Matheson, "but it did follow the book. *The Omega Man* bore no resemblance to my book ... I had absolutely nothing to do with the screenplay." A survivor of a biological war is besieged in his fortified apartment by a group of mutated, albino fanatics. He also becomes involved with a group of young people who have developed a natural resistance to the plague; they eventually come to regard him as a threat, and kill him. The film sacrifices the claustrophobia and nightmare of the novel for fast-moving action. [JB]

OMPA The Offtrail Magazine Publishers Association, formed 1954 in Great Britain by Ken BULMER, Vincent Clarke and Chuck Harris. OMPA was modelled on the original amateur press association, FAPA, and was formed to facilitate distribution of FANZINES published by and for members. Past contributors included John BRUNNER and Michael MOORCOCK. OMPA still survives. [PR]

ONE HOUR TO DOOMSDAY See CITY BENEATH THE SEA.

O'NEILL, JOSEPH (1886–1953). Irish educationalist and novelist. A graduate of the Royal University of Ireland, he was Permanent Secretary to the Department of Education, Irish Free State, 1923–44. He wrote three sf novels, the first, *Wind from the North* (1934) being only marginally sf, its narrator passing through a time-slip to give a vivid account of Dublin under Viking rule in AD 1013. JON turned to sf proper with *Land under England* (1935), a DYSTOPIAN novel in a LOST-WORLD setting, which depicts a totalitarian state of descendants of the Roman army located in a cave system under Cumberland, where individualism is completely obliterated by telepathic means. The contemporary impression that this was an allegorical attack on Nazi Germany was vindicated with the appearance of *Day of Wrath* (1936), a future-WAR novel which describes the destruction of civilization by advanced aircraft following a coalition between Germany, Japan and China.

JON was not a genre sf writer; he was probably, however, influenced by such MAINSTREAM sf writers as E.M. FORSTER and Olaf STAPLEDON. *Day of Wrath* uses

A caveman gnaws a prehistoric bone in the 1940 film ONE MILLION B.C.

the same narrative approach as H.G. WELLS by taking the viewpoint of an individual caught in the conflagration. *Land under England* appeared as a UK paperback in 1978, with introduction by Anthony Storr. [JE]
See also: NEAR FUTURE; POLITICS.

ONE MILLION B.C. (vt **MAN AND HIS MATE**) Film (1940). Hal Roach/United Artists. Directed by Hal Roach and Hal Roach Jr, starring Victor Mature, Carole Landis and Lon Chaney Jr. Screenplay by Mickell Novak, George Baker and Joseph Frickert. Story by Eugene Roche. 85 mins (later cut to 80 mins). B/w.

A young cave-man is exiled from the family cave and meets a girl from a rival tribe; together they face various prehistoric hazards. Photographically enlarged lizards wearing rubber disguises play the dinosaurs and an elephant wearing a woolly coat stands in for a mammoth. D.W. Griffith supposedly worked on portions of the film. [JB]

ONE MILLION YEARS B.C. Film (1966). Hammer/20th Century-Fox. Directed by Don Chaffey, starring Raquel Welch, John Richardson, Robert Brown and Martine Beswick. Screenplay by

Michael Carreras, story by Mickell Novak, George Baker and Joseph Frickert. 91 mins. Colour.

This is Hammer's entertaining remake of the 1940 ONE MILLION B.C. It roughly follows the story of the original, a prehistoric *Romeo and Juliet* in which a pair of lovers from different tribes overcome tribal warfare, prehistoric monsters and volcanic upheavals. Ray HARRYHAUSEN was in charge of the animation of the monsters. His special effects, as usual, are good. [JB]

ON THE BEACH Film (1959). Lomitas Productions/United Artists. Directed by Stanley Kramer, starring Gregory Peck, Ava Gardner, Fred Astaire, Anthony Perkins and Guy Doleman. Screenplay by John Paxton, based on the novel by Nevil SHUTE. 134 mins. B/w.

Set in 1964 after an atomic war has destroyed life in all countries of the world except Australia, OTB is the most effective of the anti-Bomb films produced during the 1950s. As the deadly radioactive shroud slowly moves down from the north the people of Melbourne attempt to live their lives as normally as possible, despite the ever present knowledge that they will all soon die. Also stranded in Melbourne is an

American atomic submarine, and one of the more memorable sequences involves a voyage it makes to California to investigate the source of a radio signal, only to discover that is was caused by a window shade blowing on to a morse key and that, as they feared, America is totally without life. When symptoms of radiation sickness appear in Melbourne, suicide pills are distributed though some people prefer alternative methods of dying; the American ship, for instance, heads out to sea on a final voyage to nowhere. For all its flaws — it is at times both mawkish and pretentious, and moves very slowly — the film creates a chilling and realistic atmosphere of despair, that has seldom been equalled on the screen.   [JB]

OPERA See MUSIC AND OPERA.

OPERATOR # 5, Dec. 1934; a cover calculated to stir a readership in the aftermath of the great depression.

OPERATOR # 5 US PULP MAGAZINE. 48 issues, Apr. 1934-Nov./Dec. 1941, published by Popular Publications; ed. Rogers Terrill. Operator # 5 was secret agent Jimmy Christopher, whose assignment, every issue, was to save the USA from total destruction by various menaces and unfriendly powers, frequently Asiatic. The lead novels were published under the house name Curtis Steele, which initially concealed the highly prolific pulp writer Frederick C. Davis; later novels were the work of Emile Tepperman. Other features included a series of spy stories by Arthur Leo ZAGAT. Several of the novels were reprinted in paperback form in the 1960s and 1970s.   [MJE/FHP]

OPPENHEIM,   E(DWARD) PHILLIPS (1866–1946). English writer, extremely prolific; most of his many novels are early espionage thrillers or society detective mysteries; of the approximately 160 titles, perhaps The

Great Impersonation (**1920**) is best remembered. His sf novels of interest — most of the titles listed below — are potboiling, romantic fantasies — are *The Dumb Gods Speak* (**1937**), a novel set in the future, involving high intrigue and a secret weapon, and *The Wrath to Come* (**1924**), in which the USA is threatened by a German-Russian-Japanese axis in the 1950s. *Exit a Dictator* (**1939**) features the overthrow of the Russian government. EPO was a careless, clumsy, quite enjoyable writer of escapist fiction.   [JC]

Other works: *The Mysterious Mr. Sabin* (**1898**); *A Daughter of Astrea* (**1898**); *The Traitors* (**1902**); *The Great Awakening* (**1902**); *The Secret* (**1907**); *The Double Life of Mr. Alfred Burton* (**1913**); *The Great Prince Shan* (**1920**); *Gabriel Samara* (**1925**); *Matorni's Vineyard* (**1928**); *The Adventures of Mr. Joseph P. Cray* (**1929**); *Up the Ladder of Gold* (**1931**); *Mr. Mirakel* (**1943**).

OPTIMISM AND PESSIMISM In the most simplistic version of the HISTORY OF SF, still current among the more conservative members of FANDOM, sf was always (and rightly) an optimistic literature until the NEW WAVE came along in the 1960s and spoiled everything. This was at best a very partial truth, which could be remotely applied to genre sf, and not at all to MAINSTREAM sf.

The sf of the mainstream could never be categorized as simply optimistic or pessimistic, not even the work of individual authors. Both Jules VERNE and H.G. WELLS took a darker view of the future as they became older; indeed Wells's career almost described a parabola, opening with *The Time Machine* (**1895**), a novel of evolutionary futility, and ending with *Mind at the End of its Tether* (**1945**), although from 1905 through the 1920s his visions of the future were generally UTOPIAN. The favourite themes of sf outside the genre magazines were always DYSTOPIA, INVASION, future-WAR, and the HOLOCAUST AND AFTER, and the stories often took the form of dire warnings or a generalized philosophical dourness aimed at demonstrating humanity's predilection for getting itself into trouble. Olaf STAPLEDON envisaged, in *Last and First Men* (**1930**), an ultimate harmony in the universe, but achieved only after a prolonged variety of evolutionary torments.

By contrast, sf in the magazines was generally cheerful, especially after Hugo GERNSBACK founded the first English-language magazine devoted exclusively to sf, AMAZING STORIES, in 1926. Gernsback proselytized actively for technological optimism, and this, with many exceptions (including several stories by John W. CAMPBELL Jr, writing as Don A. Stuart, which evoked an atmosphere of moody desolation) remained the dominant tone of sf until the dropping of the atom bomb

on Hiroshima in 1945. Campbell's activities as editor of *ASF* stressed a constructive attitude towards science among his contributors, but although writers like Robert A. HEINLEIN were temperamentally inclined to oblige, even before 1945 the typical *ASF* story was by no means mindlessly cheery, and many of the stories showed a strong awareness of possible technological DISASTER.

The atom bomb was a traumatic event for sf writers (*see* NUCLEAR POWER), as it was for everyone, and it was no longer possible to see the applications of science as an unmixed blessing. Also working against optimism was the Cold War, the atmosphere of sometimes PARANOID suspicion which was prevalent in the USA from the early 1950s (shown notably in the anti-Communist scares), which probably helped to change the focus of interest of many sf stories from TECHNOLOGY to SOCIOLOGY and POLITICS. The magazine GALAXY SCIENCE FICTION specialized in a form of social SATIRE, best exemplified by *The Space Merchants* (1952 as "Gravy Planet"; **1953**) by C.M. KORNBLUTH and Frederik POHL; this type of story created its future scenario with a distinct cynicism, but its narrative tone was similar to that of most PULP sf, cheerful and hardbitten, with no such strong sense of horror and disgust as could be found outside the genre in novels such as George ORWELL's *Nineteen Eighty-Four* (**1949**).

But any categorization of sf stories into the optimistic and the pessimistic is so imprecise as not to be greatly useful, and indeed there would be no point in discussing the subject were it not that just such a distinction has been made by several well-known sf historians, such as Donald A. WOLLHEIM in *The Universe Makers* (**1971**); it is implicit, also, in much of the work of Sam MOSKOWITZ; sf critics from within the genre seem generally to regard the optimism/pessimism split as of grave importance. As an example of the difficulties in making such a distinction, the work of Clifford D. SIMAK is relevant: Simak's stories regularly revolve around reconciliation and the achievement of some kind of harmony between Technological Man and Nature (hence optimistic), but his tone, as in *City* (fix-up **1952**), is often elegiac and nostalgic (hence pessimistic).

It was only in the middle and late 1960s, with the advent of the so-called New Wave in sf, that real anger, bleakness and sometimes apparent despair about the future of humanity became moderately commonplace. But the writers of the New Wave, even though their attitudes seemed sometimes anarchic, were seldom *passively* accepting of a dark view; the dominant New-Wave metaphor may have been of ENTROPY, of things running down, but the fierce commitment of much of the writing of, say, Harlan ELLISON or Brian W. ALDISS could be airily dismissed as "pessimism" by only the crudest and most simplistic of critics. Aldiss, indeed, has many times inveighed in print against what he regards as the strong moral pressure, found especially in some American publishing houses, to legislate for a kind of mandatory optimism. The casual insertion of a happy ending or a few improving messages no more constitutes true optimism than an awareness of the difficulties of life either now or in the future constitutes true pessimism.

Poets have many times argued that an awareness of death gives a sharper edge to love; just so, the darker elements which have entered sf since 1945, and especially since the mid-1960s, have been argued by some critics to constitute an essential recognition of a balance without which sf could never have reached maturity as a genre. In a sense the good sf writer is a mediator between the simplistic extremes of optimism and pessimism, and his mode of mediation is often irony, that is, an understanding of the multitudes of possibilities that events offer us, and of the fact that statements cannot always be taken at face value. Notable sf ironists have included Philip K. DICK, Algis BUDRYS, Ursula K. LE GUIN, Thomas M. DISCH, Michael MOORCOCK, J.G. BALLARD, and more recently, James TIPTREE Jr and Gene WOLFE. To read the more painful or rueful aspects of their work as simple pessimism is to show an inability to read accurately. [PN]

Some delicately worked symbolism in this illustration by Paul ORBAN to "Pax Galactica" by Ralph Williams in *ASF*, Nov. 1952.

ORBAN, PAUL (? – ?). American illustrator. He executed a few cover and many interior illustrations for a remarkable number of magazines, including *If, Future, Space Science Fiction, Original Science Fiction Stories, The Shadow* and *ASF* from the late 1940s to 1960. His b/w illustrations often

feature scantily clad young women. His style, which often includes bold cross-hatching, was fairly typical of the period, always competent and sometimes more. Brian ALDISS calls PO "an incurable romantic in a field of incurable romantics". [JG]

ORBIT Seminal American original anthology series; ed. Damon KNIGHT. Although *Orbit* was not the first such series, having been preceded by STAR in the USA and NEW WRITINGS IN SF in the UK; it was its extraordinary early success which precipitated the boom in such series in the early 1970s, with such competing titles as INFINITY, NEW DIMENSIONS, NOVA, QUARK and UNIVERSE. It had a more literary orientation than the sf magazines, and perhaps for this reason was especially popular with the active members of the newly formed SCIENCE FICTION WRITERS OF AMERICA. Whatever the cause, stories from *Orbit* dominated the NEBULA awards in their early years, although none has ever won a HUGO. *Orbit 1* (anth. **1966**) contained "The Secret Place" by Richard McKENNA, which won the short-story Nebula. *Orbit 3* (anth. **1968**) featured two Nebula-winning stories: "Mother to the World" by Richard WILSON and "The Planners" by Kate WILHELM. *Orbit 4* (anth. **1968**) contained another winner in "Passengers" by Robert SILVERBERG. That was the last *Orbit* story to win an award, although the year of pervasive dominance was 1970, when between them *Orbit 6* (anth. **1970**) and *Orbit 7* (anth. **1970**) provided one of the five novellas on the final Nebula ballot, three of the six novelettes, and six of the seven short stories, without winning in any category. Three writers in particular became associated with *Orbit*, and have remained its most regular contributors: R.A. LAFFERTY, Kate Wilhelm and Gene WOLFE. In the first 20 volumes, Lafferty and Wolfe had 18 stories each, and Wilhelm 19. *Orbit* lost its dominance once the flood of competitors appeared, and has had to change publishers in order to survive. Notable stories in later volumes include Wolfe's "The Fifth Head of Cerberus" in *Orbit 10* (anth. **1972**), Ursula LE GUIN's "The Stars Below" in *Orbit 14* (anth. **1974**) and Wilhelm's "Where Late the Sweet Birds Sang" in *Orbit 15* (anth. **1974**). Other volumes in the series are *Orbit 2* (anth. **1967**), *Orbit 5* (anth. **1969**), *Orbit 8* (anth. **1970**), *Orbit 9* (anth. **1971**), *Orbit 11* (anth. **1972**), *Orbit 12* (anth. **1973**), *Orbit 13* (anth. **1974**), *Orbit 16* (anth. **1975**), *Orbit 17* (anth. **1975**), *Orbit 18* (anth. **1976**), *Orbit 19* (anth. **1977**) and *Orbit 20* (anth. **1978**). *The Best from Orbit* (anth. **1977**) is a collection culled from the first 10 volumes. [MJE]

ORBIT SCIENCE FICTION US DIGEST-size magazine. Five issues, 1953-Nov./Dec. 1954, published by Hanro

First issue, 1953.

Corp.; ed. Jules Saltman. The first two issues were undated. *OSF* was a middling-quality magazine that fell victim to the inundation of the sf magazine market with too many titles in the early 1950s. The most notable fiction was the "Tex Harrigan" series by August DERLETH, one story of which appeared in every issue.

An Australian edition, one issue in pulp format, appeared in 1954, published by Consolidated Press, Sydney. It was a reprint of the first US issue. [FHP]

O'REILLY, JOHN BOYLE (1844–90). Irish-born American writer; a Fenian transported to Australia, he escaped to America and became a journalist, poet and novelist. His sf novel about a republican England, *The King's Men: A Tale of Tomorrow* (**1884**), written with Robert GRANT, F.J. Stimson and J.T. Wheelwright, features an attempted monarchist coup, which is roundly defeated. [JC]

ORIGINAL ANTHOLOGIES *See* ANTHOLOGIES. Important original anthology series receive separate entries.

ORIGINAL SCIENCE FICTION STORIES, THE US DIGEST magazine. 38 issues, 1953–May 1960. Published by Columbia Publications; ed. Robert A.W. LOWNDES. A companion magazine to FUTURE and SCIENCE FICTION QUARTERLY, *OSFS* began life as a one-shot simply entitled *Science Fiction Stories*. A second issue followed in 1954, and the magazine commenced regular publication in Jan. 1955. The Sep. 1955 issue added the tag *The Original* to the title on the cover, and the magazine subsequently became known by that name, although technically its title remained *Science Fiction Stories*, the prefix being an advertising slogan. Like its companion magazines, *OSFS* existed on a very small editorial budget, but maintained a respectable, if largely mediocre, level of quality. Serialized novels included *The*

May 1956. Cover by Ed Emsh.

Tower of Zanid (**1958**) by L. Sprague DE CAMP and *Caduceus Wild* (1959 *OSFS*; **1978**) by Ward MOORE and Robert Bradford; Robert SILVERBERG was the magazine's most prolific contributor. [MJE/FHP]

Collectors should note: The first issue was unnumbered; with the third issue *OSFS* adopted the numbering of *Future Science Fiction*, with that issue being Vol.5 no.4. This numbering continued through to the last issue (Vol.11 no.2), with six issues per vol., except for Vol.8, which had seven. The magazine was bimonthly, apart from brief periods of monthly publication Jun.-Sep. 1958 and Jan.-Mar. 1959. In Dec. 1961 the first of three issues of a bedsheet-size, semi-professional magazine purporting to be a continuation of *OSFS* appeared, numbered Vol.11 no.2A. Nos 3 and 4 followed, dated Winter 1962 and Winter 1963.

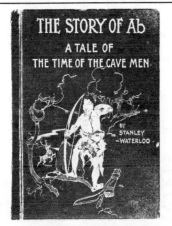

An important early sf document about the ORIGIN OF MAN. The embossed cover belongs to the UK edition, 1898.

ORIGIN OF MAN An abundant literature dealing with the remote ancestry of the human species inevitably sprang up in the wake of Darwin's theory of EVOLUTION. Thomas Henry Huxley, the principal champion of Darwinism in Britain, published a classic essay on "Man's Place in Nature" (1863) and Darwin himself wrote *The Descent of Man* (**1871**) soon after. The main point at issue was, as Disraeli put it, "the question of whether Man is an ape or an angel". Disraeli was on the side of the angels, but science — and hence speculative fiction based on scientific ideas — was not; however, *see* ADAM AND EVE. The principal question stimulating speculative fiction in this area was not *whether* Man had evolved from apelike ancestors, but *how*: when had he ceased to be a brute beast and become a proto-man? The vital corollary to this question was: what is it in Man that is essentially human, and sets him apart from brute beasts? There are many possible approaches to this question (*see* ANTHROPOLOGY), of which the prehistoric fantasy is one of the most direct.

T.H. Huxley took a rather harsh and uncompromising view of the process of natural selection, and so did his pupil, H.G. WELLS, whose "A Story of the Stone Age" (1897) envisages the crucial moment in human evolution as the invention of a "new club" — a better means to cut and kill. This view recurs constantly, and was employed as recently as 1968 in Stanley KUBRICK's film 2001: A SPACE ODYSSEY, in which the dawn of intelligence is represented by a vision of an ape realizing that he can use a bone to smash other bones, and then leading his band into battle equipped with the first armaments. Darwin himself presented a slightly different account, stressing the positive value of cooperation and mutual protection in the struggle for existence. While acknowledging the importance of weapons he also stressed the development of measures directed towards the preservation of life. This stress on the development of emotions as well as physical inventions is found in Jack LONDON's *Before Adam* (**1906**), although previous authors more religiously inclined had represented the origins of humanity in purely spiritual terms — Gouverneur MORRIS in *The Pagan's Progress* (**1904**), for example. Fire, of course, was another common candidate as the crucial invention, its importance most heavily emphasized in Stanley WATERLOO's *The Story of Ab* (**1897**) and Charles Henry Robinson's *Longhead: the Story of the First Fire* (**1913**). A significant total rejection of the Huxleyan account of human nature was put forward by J. Leslie MITCHELL in his polemical novel *Three Go Back* (**1932**), in which time-travellers discover our ancestors living in peaceful harmony, in contrast to the brutish Neanderthalers. Few other writers, however, found such a notion convincing, and a reversal of Mitchell's situation is seen in William GOLDING's *The Inheritors* (**1955**). Golding is responsible for the most sophisticated attempts to model the world view of

primitive proto-humans, his other work in this vein being "Clonk Clonk" (1971). Many of these works are, in part, admonitory fables, and by natural exaggeration prehistoric fantasies have also been employed satirically, as in Andrew LANG's "The Romance of the First Radical" (1886), W.D. Locke's "The Story of Oo-oo" (1926) and Roy LEWIS's *What We Did to Father* (**1960**; vt *The Evolution Man*).

The most prolific author of prehistoric fantasies was J.H. ROSNY AÎNÉ, whose *La guerre du feu* (**1909**) is generally considered a classic of the species. His others include *Vamireh* (**1892**), *Eyrimah* (**1893**), *Le félin géant* (**1918**; trans. **1924** as *The Giant Cat*; vt *Quest of the Dawn Man*) and *Helgvor de Fleuve Bleu* (**1930**). Another notable French novel is *Les bisons d'argile* (**1925**; trans. **1926** as *Bison of Clay*) by Max BEGOUEN. There have been several attempts to write novels on a vast scale which link prehistory and history to provide a "whole" account of the "spirit of Man". The most impressive is *The Long Journey* (1908–22 Denmark; trans. in three vols **1922**, **1923** and **1924**; one vol. **1933**) by the Danish Nobel prizewinner Johannes V. JENSEN. The first two parts of the work in translation, *Fire and Ice* (**1922**) and *The Cimbrians* (**1923**) are prehistoric fantasies, while the third is the historical novel *Christopher Columbus* (**1924**). A work on an even greater scale is the "Testament of Man" series by Vardis FISHER, a 12-novel series of which the first four are prehistoric: *Darkness and the Deep* (**1943**) examines the life of proto-humans before the harnessing of fire; *The Golden Rooms* (**1944**) is concerned with that breakthrough; *Intimations of Eve* (**1946**) constructs a primitive matriarchal society; and *Adam and the Serpent* (**1947**) is about the overthrow of that society and the establishment of patriarchy. A third major panoramic work in this tradition is *Les enchaînements* (**1925**; trans. in two vols **1925** as *Chains*) by Henri BARBUSSE, and more trivial examples include *The Invincible Adam* (**1932**) by George S. VIERECK and Paul ELDRIDGE and *Tomorrow* (coll. of linked stories **1930**) by F. Britten AUSTIN. Austin also wrote a volume of prehistoric short stories, *When Mankind Was Young* (coll. of linked stories **1927**).

The attempt to find in the evolutionary history of Man some sequence of events for which the Genesis myth may be considered a metaphor, extensively developed in Fisher's novels, is quite common. It is such an attractive notion that it has infected anthropological theory as well as speculative fantasy. Austin BIERBOWER's *From Monkey to Man* (**1894**) has Man's ancestors expelled from their Eden by the advance of the glaciers — a rather more simplistic explanation of the myth than Fisher's. The notion has also inspired fierce reaction — *The Sons of the*

Mammoth (trans. **1929**) by the Russian anthropologist V.G. BOGORAZ is extremely vitriolic about myth, religion and superstition.

In the American PULP MAGAZINES there grew up a rather romantic school of prehistoric fiction glorifying the life of the savage. Its most prolific proponent was Edgar Rice BURROUGHS, most notably in the "Pellucidar" series, in *The Eternal Lover* (1914; **1925**; vt *The Eternal Savage*) and in *The Cave Girl* (1913–17; **1925**). Other examples of the romantic school include H. Rider HAGGARD's *Allan and the Ice-Gods* (**1927**) and a short story by Lester DEL REY, redolent with fake nostalgia, "When Day is Done" (1939). There are, however, few prehistoric novels which are not touched to some degree by this romance — it is strong in Jack London's prehistoric stories and also in Charles G.D. Roberts's *In the Morning of Time* (**1919**) and Richard TOOKER's *The Day of the Brown Horde* (**1929**), though these are not ostensibly romantic adventure stories. Prehistoric romances in the cinema, which are famous for their blithe disregard for anachronism, are perhaps the extreme examples of the school, from D.W. Griffith's *Man's Genesis* (1911) onwards.

Though Hugo GERNSBACK reprinted Wells's "A Story of the Stone Age" and FAMOUS FANTASTIC MYSTERIES featured a few prehistoric romances, pulp sf did not really absorb the prehistoric novel, but was content to leave it a borderline case. Only a handful of magazine stories turned their attention to the issue of the origin of "humanness", of which the most important is Jack WILLIAMSON's "The Greatest Invention" (1951), which concentrates on the evolution of a new way of thinking. Anthropologist Chad OLIVER wrote a juvenile novel, *Mists of Dawn* (**1952**), but it is a disappointing work in comparison to his other anthropological sf. The most effective treatment of a prehistoric theme in genre sf is probably a short story concerning a stranded time-traveller's attempt to live up to the Hippocratic Oath in proto-human society: "The Doctor" (1967) by Theodore L. THOMAS. In general, it may be said that apart from William Golding's stories the whole species has virtually died out in contemporary fiction. The only other major exception is a series of surreal fantasies included in Italo CALVINO's *Cosmicomiche* (coll. of linked stories **1965**; trans. as *Cosmicomics* **1968**) and *Ti con zero* (coll. of linked stories **1967**; trans. as *t zero* **1969**).

There has in recent times been a considerable wave of alternative accounts of the origin of Man, particularly the notion of extraterrestrial origins encouraged by Erich VON DÄNIKEN's popular fantasies, presented as science fact, regarding extraterrestrial interference in human affairs at the dawn of history. This notion recurs throughout the history of sf, but is rarely developed

save as a clichéd gimmick (*see* ADAM AND EVE). Examples of stories suggesting extraterrestrial origins are Eric Frank RUSSELL's *Dreadful Sanctuary* (1948; **1951**; rev. 1963), which, deriving from the ideas of Charles FORT, hypothesizes that Earth is an asylum for the lunatics of other worlds, and James BLISH's "The Writing of the Rat" (1956), which makes us the descendants of a lost colony of galactic slavers. The "lost colony" thesis is probably the commonest account of our origins outside the scientific account.
[BS]

See also: MYTHOLOGY.

ORKOW, BEN (HARRISON) (1896–). Russian-born American writer, mostly of plays and film scripts; his sf novel, *When Time Stood Still* (**1962**), deals with a trip, via SUSPENDED ANIMATION, of a couple to the year 2007.
[JC]

ORLACS HÄNDE *See* HANDS OF ORLAC, THE.

ORWELL, GEORGE Pseudonym of English author Eric Arthur Blair (1903–1950), much of whose best work is contained in his impassioned journalism and essays, assembled in *The Collected Essays, Journalism and Letters of George Orwell* (coll. **1968**; in four vols); his fiction and extended social criticism, as in *Down and Out in Paris and London* (**1933**) is also of superior quality. *Animal Farm* (**1945**) is a fable satirical of the form Communism took, once established in the Soviet Union, and consequently enraged many who, with GO, were of Left orientation in the years before and during the Second World War. *Animal Farm* mocks not the ideals of Socialism or Communism, however, but their embodiment and corruption in an actual state. The allegory is direct: the Farm undergoes a revolution which is soon subverted by the Pigs, who end up more equal than the remainder of the animals. The attack on Stalin is devastating. A cartoon feature film

animated by John Halas and Joy Batchelor, *Animal Farm*, was released in 1955.

By far GO's most famous book is, of course, *Nineteen Eighty-Four* (**1949**), published shortly before his death of tuberculosis. It was filmed in 1955 as *1984* (*which see for details*). With Aldous HUXLEY's *Brave New World* (**1932**), it is the century's most famous DYSTOPIA. Told with claustrophobic power and involvement (so intensely that many critics have faulted the book for subjective imbalance — though unjustly), *Nineteen Eighty-Four* grippingly paints the picture of a totalitarian world both shabby and deeply sadistic, for its rulers (symbolized by the images of Big Brother) use their ability to inflict pain to drive the fact of their power into the masses, whose lives are mercilessly regimented, and whose thoughts are controlled by the Newspeak to which GO devotes a scathing appendix. "It was intended that when Newspeak had been adopted once and for all and Oldspeak forgotten, a heretical thought ... should be literally unthinkable." The scarifying story of Winston Smith's attempt to liberate himself and his eventual surrender under torture to the way of this horrifying world makes up the actual plot of the novel. As an indictment of the deep tendency of modern technologically sophisticated governments, whatever their political colouration, to rule by coercion and "doublethink", *Nineteen Eighty-Four* is unmatched. Its pessimism is both distressing and salutary. The decency and vigour of GO's mind, and the power of his writings, have come all the clearer with time.
[JC]

About the author: There is much Orwell criticism in print. Irving Howe's *Orwell's Nineteen Eighty-Four* (**1963**) is valuable, as is George Woodcock's *The Crystal Spirit* (**1967**).

See also: CRIME AND PUNISHMENT; LINGUISTICS; MEDIA LANDSCAPE; OPTIMISM AND PESSIMISM; POLITICS; PSYCHOLOGY; SATIRE; SF OVERTAKEN BY EVENTS; SOCIOLOGY.

OSBORNE, DAVID or **GEORGE** *See* Robert SILVERBERG.

OSHIKAWA, SHUNRO *See* JAPAN.

OTHER WORLDS US DIGEST magazine. 57 issues, Nov. 1949–Sep. 1957. Published by Palmer Publications Inc; ed. Ray PALMER. *OW* was launched by Palmer while he was still editor of AMAZING STORIES and FANTASTIC ADVENTURES; for this reason editorship of the first issue was credited to Robert N. Webster (a Palmer pseudonym). *OW* was editorially very similar to the previous Palmer magazines, particularly in featuring the stories of Richard S. SHAVER. Eric Frank RUSSELL was also a regular contributor, and the magazine serialized L. Sprague DE CAMP's

Sep. 1956. Cover by Paul Blaisdell.

non-fiction book *Lost Continents* (**1954**) during 1952–3. *OW* was suspended after the 31st issue, in Jul. 1953, though, to confuse the story further (Ray Palmer was notorious for his many title changes), it is possible to regard his short-lived SCIENCE STORIES (1953–4) as a continuation of *Other Worlds*. At any rate, in 1953 Palmer promptly took over another new magazine, *Universe Science Fiction*, which had seen two issues in Jun. and Sept. 1953, ed. and published by George Bell. With the third issue, Dec. 1953, Palmer became editor and publisher. *Universe* began as a more sophisticated magazine, but its contents gradually converged on the Palmer norm, and after 10 issues (the last of which was Mar. 1955) the title was changed to *OW* again. 12 more issues followed, until in

OTHER WORLDS was retitled as above in June, 1957.

Jun. 1957 the title was altered to *Flying Saucers from Other Worlds*, reflecting Palmer's increasing preoccupation with

UFOs. Four more issues featured sf stories, but after Sep. 1957 the magazine became solely UFO-oriented, and though it carried on for several more years could no longer be called an sf magazine. [MJE/FHP]

Collectors should note: The first incarnation of *OW* consisted of five vols with, consecutively, four, four, seven, nine and seven numbers (the Jan. 1952 issue, Vol.4 no.1, being mistakenly numbered Vol.3 no.5). The magazine was bi-monthly until Sept. 1951 (apart from an additional issue in Oct. 1950), whereafter it was monthly (apart from missing the Nov. 1951 issue) until its suspension. As *Universe* it was numbered consecutively and was quarterly for its first four issues and bi-monthly thereafter. Resuming the title *OW* it retained the bi-monthly schedule, although in 1956 it missed the Jan. issue and published in Feb., Apr. and Jun. before resuming its regular pattern in Sep. It continued *Universe's* numbering, although both Mar. and May 1957 were numbered 21. It assumed monthly publication when it became *Flying Saucers from Other Worlds* in Jun. 1957, and was unnumbered apart from the Aug. 1957 issue, no.25.

OUTER LIMITS, THE Television series (1963–5). A Daystar-Villa di Stefano Production for United Artists, ABC TV. Created by Leslie Stevens, who was also executive producer. The first season (1963–4) was produced by Joseph Stefano, who wrote a number of the episodes; the second season (1964–5) was produced by Ben Brady. Special effects were by the Ray Mercer Company and Projects Unlimited. 49 episodes, each of 50 mins. B/w.

This was an anthology series featuring different, weekly stories each based on an sf theme. Though leaning towards the horror/monster genre, the series was often innovative in both style and subject matter. The pilot episode, "The Galaxy Being", was written and directed by Leslie Stevens and concerned an alien being, made of pure energy, who is accidentally absorbed into a radio telescope on Earth. Harlan ELLISON contributed two episodes: "Soldier" (1964), about an ultra-conditioned soldier from the future who is projected back in time and finds himself in a typical 1960s American household, and "Demon with a Glass Hand" (1964), perhaps the finest episode of the series, about an android, being pursued by aliens, who has the entire human race coded in his artificial hand. Other writers who contributed to the series were David DUNCAN, Robert Towne, Jerry SOHL, Jerome Ross and Meyer DOLINSKY. Directors included Byron HASKIN, Leonard Horn, Gerd Oswald and Charles Haas. Actors who appeared in the series, several of them being unknown at the time, included Leonard Nimoy, Robert Culp, William

Shatner, Bruce Dern, Donald Pleasence, Martin Landau and David McCallum. The bizarre make-up that was such a feature of the series was the work of Fred Phillips, John Chambers and, primarily, Wah Chang.

The talented cinematographer Conrad Hall worked on the first season, and the series was visually striking. Only stupid programming (it was shifted to a time slot opposite the hugely popular *Jackie Gleason Show*) led to the series' cancellation halfway through the second season. *TOL* was, on the whole, more imaginative and intelligent than its more famous competitor on CBS, Rod SERLING's THE TWILIGHT ZONE. [JB/PN]

OUTER PLANETS Relatively little attention has been paid in sf to the planets beyond Jupiter. Only Saturn was known to the ancients — Uranus was discovered in 1781, Neptune in 1846 and Pluto in 1930 — and it is the only outer planet featured in Athanasius KIRCHER's and Emanuel SWEDENBORG's interplanetary tours. Uranus, however, is included in the anonymous *Journeys into the Moon, Several Planets and the Sun: History of a Female Somnambulist* (**1837**). The only object beyond Jupiter that has made significant appeal to speculative writers as a possible abode for life is Saturn's major moon Titan, though the fascinating rings have provoked a good deal of interest. Pluto has come in for a certain amount of special attention as the Ultima Thule of the Solar System, though as much, if not more, interest has been shown in the possibility of there being something else even further out.

Saturn was visited by VOLTAIRE's visitor from Sirius, *Micromégas* (**1750** Berlin; **1752** France) en route to Earth, and a Saturnian accompanied the hero of the story on his sightseeing trip. It was one of the major worlds featured in J.B. Fayette's anonymously published *The Experiences of Eon and Eona* (**1886**). In John Jacob ASTOR's *A Journey in Other Worlds* (**1894**) it is the home of the spirits who confirm the truth of the theological beliefs of the travellers from future Earth. The early scientific romancers, however, rarely bothered to venture so far, generally finding enough exciting adventures available close to home. Roy ROCKWOOD extended his series of juvenile interplanetary novels thus far in *By Spaceship to Saturn* (**1935**), but few of the PULP writers followed suit. Arthur K BARNES's *Interplanetary Hunter* (1937–46 *TWS*; fix-up **1956**) — or, to be strictly accurate, huntress — Gerry Carlisle ventured beyond Jupiter on two occasions, but she was more than usually intrepid. Stanley G. WEINBAUM was the only pulp writer of any real significance who explored the outer planets, first in "Flight on Titan" (1935), then in one of the rare stories set on Uranus, "The Planet of Doubt" (1935) and lastly in a space opera set partly on Pluto, "The Red

Saturn, with its rings, has always had the most appeal of the OUTER PLANETS for sf artists. This by Chesley Bonestell depicts Saturn as seen from its satellite Titan, from *The Conquest of Space* by Bonestell and Willy Ley, 1949.

Peri" (1935). Other pulp stories set in the outer reaches are J.M. WALSH's "The Vanguard to Neptune" (1932), Wallace WEST's "En Route to Pluto" (1936), Raymond Z. GALLUN's "Raiders of Saturn's Rings" (1941) and Murray LEINSTER's "Pipeline to Pluto" (1945). One of Stanton A. COBLENTZ's satires was set *Into Plutonian Depths* (1931; **1950**) and Clifford D. SIMAK's *Cosmic Engineers* (1939; rev. **1950**) begins near Pluto. By far and away the most significant role allotted to an outer planet in the speculative fiction of the pre-War period was, however, that attributed to Neptune by Olaf STAPLEDON in *Last and First Men* (**1930**) and *Last Men in London* (**1932**), where, in the very far future, the ultimate members of the human race are forced to make a new home on Neptune following the expansion of the Sun.

In the post-War period the outer planets began to feature occasionally in more serious speculative fictions. The rings of Saturn play a key part in Isaac ASIMOV's novelette "The Martian Way" (1952) and Asimov returned to the same locale in his juvenile *Lucky Starr and the Rings of Saturn* (**1958** as by Paul French; vt *The Rings of Saturn* UK). Another notable juvenile, using the bold premise that Saturn might harbour life, is Philip LATHAM's *Missing Men of Saturn* (**1953**). Titan, however, features much more prominently than its parent world. Alan E. NOURSE's *Trouble on Titan* (**1954**) is another juvenile novel about COLONIZATION of the satellite. The climactic scenes of Kurt VONNEGUT's *The Sirens of Titan* (**1959**) take place there. In more recent times Titan is the location of huge alien machines in Ben BOVA's *As on a Darkling Plain* (**1972**), the setting for an elegantly described colony in Arthur C. CLARKE's *Imperial Earth* (**1976**), and the home of the strange life-form which

provides the climax of Gregory BENFORD and Gordon EKLUND's *If the Stars are Gods* (fix-up **1977**).

Pluto figures in Algis BUDRYS's *Man of Earth* (**1958**) and is the destination of the characters in Wilson TUCKER's *To the Tombaugh Station* (**1960**), but is otherwise seen by everyone as a thoroughly boring and very cold lump of rock. Uranus and Neptune feature hardly at all, though Neptune's moon Triton is the setting of a curious story by Margaret ST CLAIR, "The Pillows" (1950) and Samuel DELANY's "ambiguous heterotopia" *Triton* (**1976**). The "outer satellites" conduct a war against the inner planets in Alfred BESTER's *The Stars My Destination* (**1956**; vt *Tiger! Tiger!* UK) but the reader never gets to visit them (or even sees a list of those involved). A similar but very detailed conflict takes places in Cecelia HOLLAND's *Floating Worlds* (**1976**), in which the floating cities of the title are based above Saturn and Uranus.

It has long been held in some quarters that a 10th planet is necessary to account for the orbital perturbations of Uranus even after Neptune and Pluto are taken into account, and sf writers have occasionally dealt with the possibility. John W. CAMPBELL Jr's *The Planeteers* (1936–8; coll. of linked stories **1966**) ultimately made their way out to the 10th planet. Henry KUTTNER's "We Guard the Black Planet" (1942) is set there. In Philip K. DICK's *Solar Lottery* (**1955**; vt *World of Chance*) members of a small cult flee Earth in the hope that it exists to provide them with a destination. Edmund COOPER's *The Tenth Planet* (**1973**) represents it as the home of an advanced civilization. In *Lucifer's Hammer* (**1977**) by Larry NIVEN and Jerry POURNELLE the 10th planet is envisaged as a GAS GIANT whose orbit is tilted 90° from that of the

planetary plane; its gravity perturbs the orbit of a comet which later collides with Earth.

Perhaps a little more intriguing is the notion that what is out there might not be a planet at all, but something different — perhaps a second ASTEROID belt. One version of this notion is extravagantly developed in *The Reefs of Space* (**1964**) by Frederik POHL and Jack WILLIAMSON, which features a particularly imaginative reef life-system. Clarke's *Imperial Earth* also makes much of the possibility of life beyond Pluto, but leaves the issue conjectural. [BS]

The only issue, Winter 1946, had an unusual and elegant cover design.

OUTLANDS British DIGEST-size magazine. One issue, Winter 1946. Published by Outlands Publications, Liverpool; ed. Leslie J. Johnson. A semi-professional magazine, *O* included stories by John Russell FEARN, Sydney J. BOUNDS (his first published story) and others. It was subtitled "A magazine for adventurous minds". The venture proved abortive because of a failure to get proper distribution. [MJE/FHP]

OUT OF THE UNKNOWN Television series (1965–7). BBC TV. Produced by Alan Bromly. Script editor: Roger Parkes. 50 mins each episode. B/w.

This sf anthology series dramatized the work of many well-known sf writers. Stories included *Immortality, Inc.* by Robert SHECKLEY, "Liar!" by Isaac ASIMOV, "The Last Lonely Man" by John BRUNNER, "Beachhead" by Clifford D. SIMAK, "Random Quest" by John WYNDHAM, "The Little Black Bag" by C.M. KORNBLUTH, "Thirteen to Arcturus" by J.G. BALLARD, *The Naked Sun* by Asimov, "Target Generation" by Simak and "The Machine Stops" by E.M. FORSTER. Scriptwriters included Jack Pulman, Leon Griffiths, Clive Exton, Julian Bond, Robert Muller, Owen Holder and Jeremy Paul. Directors

A village of humanoids from the "Beachhead" episode of the TV series OUT OF THE UNKNOWN.

included Roger Jenkins, Michael Ferguson, Philip Dudley, Eric Hills, Christopher Barry, Douglas Camfield and Gerald Blake.

Despite budget limitations, the standard of production was often very high. The quality of the scripts varied, some of the writers assigned to the series being unfamiliar with sf. Unfortunately, the BBC decided that the series lacked mass popularity and switched it from sf to supernatural stories; it came to an end shortly thereafter. [JB]

OUT OF THIS WORLD 1. Television series (1952). ABC TV. Produced by Milton Kaye, narrated by Jackson Beck. One season. 25 mins each episode. B/w.

The series hovered between sf and lectures on science. The third episode, for example, directed by Milton Kaye and written by Robbie Robertson, concerned a young couple in 1993 going to the Moon for a vacation and then telephoning their relations on Earth to give impressions of their holiday. Between these dramatized segments the narrator discussed with a scientist, Robert R. Cole, the actual possibilities of space travel and conditions on the Moon. Apart from describing such problems as weightlessness and the lack of air, the scientist told Beck that "… a trip to the Moon is closer than one thinks".

2. Television series (1962). British ABC TV. Produced by Leonard White. Story editor: Irene Shubik. 50 mins each episode. B/w.

This short-lived (Jun.–Sep. 1962) but relatively ambitious sf anthology series was hosted by Boris Karloff. Stories adapted for the series included "Little Lost Robot" by Isaac ASIMOV, "The Cold Equations" by Tom GODWIN, "Impostor" by Philip K. DICK, "Botany Bay" by Terry NATION, "Medicine Show" by Robert WILLIAMS, "Divided We Fall" by Raymond F. JONES and "Pictures Don't Lie" by Katherine MACLEAN. Directors included Guy Verney, Peter Hammond, Richmond Harding, John Knight, Don Leaver and Charles Jarrot. [JB]

First issue, July 1950.

OUT OF THIS WORLD ADVENTURES US PULP magazine. Two issues, Jul. 1950 and Dec. 1950, published by Avon Periodicals; ed. Donald A. WOLLHEIM. The first issue included an impressive line-up of authors: A. Bertram CHANDLER, Ray CUMMINGS, Lester DEL REY, Kris NEVILLE, Mack REYNOLDS, William TENN and A.E. VAN VOGT. The stories, however, were not the authors' best, and Chandler was the only writer of equivalent stature in the second issue. An unusual feature was a 32-page comic section in colour (the second issue of the Canadian edition included a different comic section from that in the US edition). [MJE]

OUTWORLDS American FANZINE (1966–) ed., from Ohio, Bill Bowers. *O* is particularly noted for the quality of its presentation and has been published in a variety of distinctive formats, both duplicated and printed, with copious illustrations from fan and sf artists such as Stephen FABIAN, Grant Canfield, William ROTSLER, Mike Gilbert, Tim Kirk and Jim CAWTHORN. Issues have contained articles, verse and fiction, and regular columnists have included Poul ANDERSON, Greg BENFORD, Ted WHITE, Robert A.W. LOWNDES, John BRUNNER, and Piers ANTHONY. [PR]

OVERLAND MONTHLY, THE US magazine founded by Bret Harte and initially published by A. Roman & Co. Monthly, Jul. 1868-Dec. 1875, then Jan. 1883-Jul. 1935. Under the editorship of Millicent W. Shinn the issue for Jun. 1890 contained articles and essays all of which were directly related to Edward BELLAMY's *Looking Backward 2000–1887* **(1888)**. In addition, its six fiction contributions were all sf and included an early translation of Kurd LASSWITZ under the title "Pictures out of the Future". It is the earliest known case of a general magazine devoting an issue exclusively to sf. *OM* is also known for its publication of poetry and fiction by Clark Ashton SMITH in the 1910s and '20s. [JE]

The theme of OVERPOPULATION is neatly caught by Alan Aldridge's cover for Harry Harrison's *Make Room! Make Room!*, Penguin Books, 1967.

OVERPOPULATION In 1798 T.R. Malthus published the first edition of his *Essay on the Principle of Population as it Affects the Future Improvement of Society*, attempting to demonstrate logically that a UTOPIAN situation of peace and plenty is impossible to achieve because the tendency of populations to increase exponentially in the absence of the checks of war, famine and plague would result in society's continually outgrowing its resources. In the second edition (1803), replying to criticism, he introduced another hypothetical check — "moral restraint". Malthus was an important influence on Darwin, but had little direct influence on society at large. Although his principle is logically unassailable it was ignored by most speculative writers even while the population explosion was taking place. It is not easy to suggest an explanation for this blindness, but the rapid emergence of the overpopulation theme in sf and popular science during the 1950s and '60s is probably connected with the triumph of the DYSTOPIAN image of the future over the Utopian image, awareness of the population problem perhaps being an effect of this pessimism rather than a cause (see OPTIMISM AND PESSIMISM).

Although the magazine MARVEL SCIENCE STORIES published a "symposium" on the subject of whether the world's population should be strategically limited, in its Nov. 1951 issue, the question was at that time unexplored in sf. C.M. KORNBLUTH's "The Marching Morons" (1951), depicting a future in which the intelligentsia have prudently exercised birth control while the *Lumpenproletariat* have multiplied unrestrained, is a black comedy on the theme of eugenics rather than overpopulation *per se*. In Kurt VONNEGUT's black comedy "The Big Trip Up Yonder" (1954) overpopulation is very definitely the theme, but it is the result of extreme longevity achieved by medical means rather than straightforward Malthusian increase. Overpopulated milieux became increasingly popular as backgrounds in 1950s sf. Isaac ASIMOV, one of the first sf writers to become worried about the subject, used one in *The Caves of Steel* (1954). It was in the late 1950s that the overpopulation problem in its pure Malthusian form really emerged into sf. Kornbluth wrote the first major overpopulation horror story in "Shark Ship" (1958); later, his collaborator Frederik POHL produced the ironic "The Census Takers" (1956). Robert SILVERBERG's *Master of Life and Death* (1957) is an early attempt to take seriously the notion of institutionalizing population control measures. One of the most effective early treatments of the theme is J.G. BALLARD's "Billenium" (1961), which presents a simple picture of the slow shrinkage of personal space. A curiously ambiguous novel on the theme is Lester DEL REY's *The Eleventh Commandment* (1962), which begins as a polemic against over-fertility but concludes with a *volte-face* in the name of natural selection and the survival of the fittest.

The most powerful attempt to confront the issue squarely — and the first novel to do so — was written barely a decade ago:

Harry HARRISON's *Make Room! Make Room!* (1966), a careful and detailed projection whose virtues were entirely lost when it was filmed as SOYLENT GREEN. The following year saw a major novel on the theme, written in India: *The Wind Obeys Lama Toru* (1967) by LEE TUNG.

There are three main elements in the population problem, which may require separate solutions: the exhaustion of resources, the destruction of the environment, and the social problems of living in crowded conditions. The first two aspects commanded attention earlier, and form the basis of such extrapolations of the problem as *A Torrent of Faces* (1968) by James BLISH and Norman L. KNIGHT, *Stand on Zanzibar* (1969) and *The Sheep Look Up* (1972) by John BRUNNER, and such black comedies as "The People Trap" (1968) by Robert SHECKLEY and "The Big Space Fuck" (1972) by Kurt Vonnegut. The third aspect, however, comes into focus in *The World Inside* (1972) by Robert Silverberg and *334* (1972) by Thomas M. DISCH. The majority of sf stories connected with this issue are awful warning stories and prophecies of inescapable doom — the black-comedy element emphasizes this. Because sf writers had not considered the problem until it was imminent the quest for hypothetical solutions was made difficult. Such traditional sf myths as Escape into Space lacked plausibility with reference to a problem so immediate (as is made very clear by James Blish's "We All Die Naked", 1969). Confidence in moral restraint, even aided by birth control (which Malthus forbore to propose), was very low. Those sf stories which do explore possible solutions almost always concern themselves with the setting up of prohibitions, or various forms of culling, and almost always content themselves with commentary on the impracticability and/or inhumanity of such measures. Two examples are *Triple Détente* (1974) by Piers ANTHONY, which with grotesque implausibility proposes population-culling by alien invasion, and *Time of the Fourth Horseman* (1976) by Chelsea Quinn YARBRO, in which population-culling by disease gets out of control. Kurt Vonnegut's black comedy "Welcome to the Monkey House" (1968) envisages a future in which reproduction is discouraged by the use of drugs obliterating the sex drive, but most speculations in this vein are concerned with the principle of triage — the practice of sorting out those who are to be saved from those who are to be abandoned to die. *Logan's Run* (1967) by William F. NOLAN and George Clayton JOHNSON goes to extremes in imagining a world in which euthanasia is compulsory at 21. More modest forms of mass murder are the subject of Alice Glaser's "The Tunnel Ahead" (1961), D.G. COMPTON's *The Quality of Mercy* (1965), Leonard C.

LEWIN's *Triage* (1972) and Philip K. DICK's "The Pre-Persons" (1974). It is surprising that there seem to be no stories at all which attempt to be constructive in their setting up of hypothetical solutions to the problem. A lack of confidence in the future is one thing, but the apparent lack of a desire to look for practical solutions is quite another. If sf accurately reflects the thinking of society at large this is surely the most worrying aspect of the way the theme has been handled. A rather lurid application of Malthusian thinking is employed in *The Mote in God's Eye* (1974) by Larry NIVEN and Jerry POURNELLE, where the whole plot hinges on the absence of any practicable solution, although the sufferers here are an alien race for whom birth control is impossible. Except for some effective horror stories and some neat black comedy, sf has not yet come to terms with this theme.

An interesting anthology, containing several of the short stories mentioned above, is *Voyages: Scenarios for a Ship Called Earth* (anth. 1971) ed. Bob Sauer, published by BALLANTINE BOOKS for the Zero Population Growth movement. The major non-fiction books involved in the popularization of the issues discussed are *The Population Bomb* (1968) by Paul Ehrlich and *The Limits to Growth: A Report for the Club of Rome's Project on the Predicament of Mankind* (1972) by D.H. Meadows, D.L. Meadows, J. Randers and W.W. Behrens III.   [BS]

See also: ECOLOGY; NEAR FUTURE; POLITICS; POLLUTION; PREDICTION; SOCIOLOGY.

OVERTON, MAX *See* Don WILCOX.

OWEN, DEAN Pseudonym of American writer Dudley Dean McGaughy (? –), whose routine novelizations of horror and sf films are *The Brides of Dracula* (1960), *Konga* (1960), *Reptilicus* (1961; *see* REPTILICUS) and *End of the World* (1962), which is based on PANIC IN THE YEAR ZERO, a film based in turn, uncredited, on two short stories by Ward MOORE.   [JC]

OWEN, FRANK (1893–1968). American writer, essentially of Oriental fantasy, almost all of it set in an imaginary China; he published primarily in *Weird Tales*, his first story there being "The Man who Owned the World" (1923). His best work is collected in *The Wind that Tramps the World: Splashes of Chinese Color* (coll. 1929), *The Purple Sea: More Splashes of Chinese Color* (coll. 1930), *Della Wu, Chinese Courtezan* (coll. 1931), *A Husband for Kutani* (coll. 1938) and *The Porcelain Magician* (coll. 1948), which was published by the sf house GNOME PRESS. Novels include *Rare Earth* (1931) and *Madonna of the Damned* (1935), the first fantasy, the second horror.   [JC/PN]
Other works: *The Blue Highway* (1932),

a juvenile, with Anna Owen; *Loves of Lo Foh* (**1936**) as by Roswell Williams; *The Scarlet Hill* (**1941**).

OWINGS, MARK (SAMUEL) (1945–). American civil servant and energetic fan sf bibliographer. His works in this field include *The Index to the Science-Fantasy Publishers: a Bibliography of the Science Fiction and Fantasy Specialty Houses* (**1966**) with Jack L. CHALKER. Also with Chalker, in this instance uncredited, he produced *The Necronomicon: a Study* (**1967**), which expands H.P. LOVECRAFT's data on this notorious, fictitious book; also with Chalker, MO produced *The Revised H.P. Lovecraft Bibliography* (**1973**). Other MO listings include *The Electric Bibliograph, Part 1: Clifford D. Simak* (**1971**), *Robert A. Heinlein: a Bibliography* (**1973**), *James H. Schmitz: a Bibliography* (**1973**) and *A Catalog of Lovecraftiana: the Grill/Binkin Collection* (**1975**), with Irving Binkin. As with most fan bibliographers, MO's industry is admirable, but it is a pity that his procedures are not more rigorous. Most of the above were published by MIRAGE PRESS. [PN]

PADGETT, LEWIS *See* Henry KUTTNER *and* C.L. MOORE.

PAGE, NORVELL W. (1904–61). American writer. He was a prolific contributor to the hero/villain PULP MAGAZINES of the 1930s. Under the house name Grant Stockbridge he wrote more than 100 novels featuring a superhero, THE SPIDER, some bordering on the supernatural. Several have been reprinted in paperback. He also used the pseudonym Randolph Craig on two spin-offs of *The Spider*, THE OCTOPUS and THE SCORPION. He cultivated a somewhat eccentric image, appearing publicly in a black cape and floppy hat. He contributed three long stories to UNKNOWN in its first year. *Flame Winds* (1939 *Unknown*; **1969**) and *Sons of the Bear-God* (1939 *Unknown*; **1969**) were SWORD-AND-SORCERY novels whose hero was based on· the legendary figure of Prester John. His story "But Without Horns" (**1940**) concerns a MUTANT who uses his telepathic powers to induce religious worship in those who come into

contact with him. NWP took a post writing government reports during the Second World War, and afterwards worked for the Atomic Energy Commission. [MJE]
See also: GODS AND DEMONS.

PAGE, THOMAS (? –). American writer whose sf novel, *The Hephaestus Plague* (**1973**), filmed as BUG, describes the effect of an irruption from underground of a new species of beetle capable of emitting fire; a scientist becomes (rather metaphysically) fascinated with these beetles, which seem to possess a kind of group intelligence. [JC]

PAGERY, FRANÇOIS *See* Gérard KLEIN.

PAGETTI, CARLO (? –). Italian critic and academic, who teaches at the Università "Gabriele D'Annunzio". His study of sf *Il senso del futuro: la fantascienza nella litteratura Americana* ["The Sense of the Future: Science Fiction in American Literature"] (**1970**) is the first serious literary study of sf by an Italian. Writers studied in some detail include Kurt VONNEGUT, Philip K. DICK and Robert SHECKLEY, and such figures at the fringes of sf as John BARTH and William BURROUGHS are also considered. CP has had articles translated in SCIENCE-FICTION STUDIES. [PN]

PAINE, A(LBERT) B(IGELOW) (1861–1937). American writer, best remembered as Mark TWAIN's confidant and posthumous expurgator in his mutilated editions of *The Mysterious Stranger* (**1916**) and *Mark Twain's Autobiography* (**1924**). ABP was mainly a writer and editor of children's fiction. In his sf novel, *The Great White Way* (**1901**), a warm, Antarctic UTOPIA peopled by telepaths appeals to the protagonist who discovers the land and stays there to marry its queen. *The Mystery of Evelin Delorme* (**1894**) interestingly uses hypnosis to split the heroine's personality in an experiment that goes wrong. [JC]
See also: PSYCHOLOGY.

PAINTER, THOMAS (? – ?). American writer, whose collaboration with Alexander LAING (*who see for details*), is *The Motives of Nicholas Holtz* (**1936**; vt *The Glass Centipede*).

PAIRAULT, PIERRE *See* Stefan WUL.

PAL, GEORGE (1908–). Hungarian film-producer based in America since 1940, best known for his sf and fantasy films. Trained as an illustrator in Budapest, GP decided to specialize in cartoon animation and in 1931 moved to Germany, where he worked at the UFA studios. When Hitler came to power he moved to Paris, arriving with plans for

producing films featuring animated dolls. A cigarette manufacturer invested in the scheme, and GP soon became very successful with a series of commercials and pure entertainment films which he called "Puppetoons". After emigrating to America he set up a new Puppetoon unit at Paramount Studios. His first live-action film was made in 1949. Titled *The Great Rupert* (directed by Irving Pichel) it starred Jimmy Durante and an animated squirrel called Rupert. He then started work on DESTINATION MOON (1950, directed by Irving Pichel), the film which began the sf film boom of the 1950s. It was so successful that GP immediately chose another sf subject for his next film, WHEN WORLDS COLLIDE (1951, directed by Rudolph Maté). This was followed by WAR OF THE WORLDS (1953, directed by Byron HASKIN), THE NAKED JUNGLE and THE CONQUEST OF SPACE (1955, both directed by Haskin), ATLANTIS, THE LOST CONTINENT (1959, directed by GP), THE TIME MACHINE (1960, directed by GP) and THE POWER (1967, directed by Byron Haskin). GP also made a number of pure fantasy films during this period, including *Tom Thumb* (1958) and THE SEVEN FACES OF DR LAO (1964). His last film to date is DOC SAVAGE, MAN OF BRONZE (1974, directed by Michael Anderson). GP's dominant interest in special effects has often meant that he has neglected other aspects of his films, including the quality of scripts and acting, but most of his productions possess a colourful bravura that distracts attention from their shortcomings, and he has produced, on occasion, memorably strong visual images. [JB]

PALLEN, CONDE B(ENOIST) (1858–1929). American editor and writer; edited *The Catholic Encyclopedia* (**1907–14**). *Ghost House* (**1928**) is not sf, but *Crucible Island: a Romance, an Adventure and an Experiment* (**1919**) is an anti-socialist DYSTOPIA in which a radical, having been transported to Schlectland, where socialism has been allowed to run rampant, comes to his senses and escapes to America. [JC]
See also: POLITICS.

PALL MALL BUDGET, THE British magazine, ed. C. Lewis Hind and others. Weekly, 3 Oct. 1868-27 Dec. 1894. It was later incorporated into *The New Budget*. PMB had negligible sf content until C. Lewis Hind, himself a minor fantasy author, persuaded H.G. WELLS to write a series of short stories. They appeared in 1894 under the general heading "Single Sitting Stories" and were collected, with additional material, in *The Stolen Bacillus and Other Incidents* (**1895**). [JE]

PALL MALL MAGAZINE British magazine published by G. Routledge & Sons, ed. Lord Frederick Hamilton and Sir Douglas Straight and others. Monthly, with various title changes, May 1893-Sep. 1937, when it was incorporated into *Good Housekeeping*. Although in competition with PEARSON'S MAGAZINE and the STRAND MAGAZINE, *PMM* placed less emphasis on sf. Its major contributions to the genre were the serializations of H.G. WELLS's "A Story of the Days to Come" (1897), *The War in the Air* (1908; **1908**) and *The Dream* (1923–4; **1924**). [JE]

Photo *Locus*.

PALMER, RAYMOND A. (1910–77). American author and editor. His childhood was plagued by serious accidents. In adulthood he was four feet tall and hunchbacked, but remained hardworking and courageous. He was an active sf fan in the 1930s (he is credited with publishing the first sf FANZINE, *The Comet*) and the author of a small number of stories — the first of which, "The Time Ray of Jandra" (1930), appeared in WONDER STORIES. In 1936, after the death of Stanley WEINBAUM, RAP edited and published a memorial collection of his stories, *Dawn of Flame and Other Stories* (coll. **1936**). When AMAZING STORIES was bought by the Chicago-based Ziff-Davis company in 1938 they decided to replace T. O'Conor SLOANE as editor; RAP, a Chicago resident, was recommended for the job and was appointed. *AMZ* was in a moribund state by this time; RAP made it livelier, albeit with a more overtly juvenile slant, and it revived. In 1939 he began a companion magazine, FANTASTIC ADVENTURES. The magazines used a large number of house names, and RAP contributed stories using several of these. He achieved notoriety in the 1940s with his promotion as fact of the stories of Richard S. SHAVER. RAP claimed that the popularity of the "Shaver Mystery" gave *AMZ* the highest circulation ever achieved by an sf magazine. RAP's interest in PSEUDO-SCIENCE and the occult widened; in 1948, while still employed at Ziff-Davis, he started his own occult magazine, *Fate*, which proved enduringly

successful. In 1949 he established his own sf magazine, OTHER WORLDS (using the editorial pseudonym Robert N. Webster on the first issue), and shortly afterwards left Ziff-Davis. He began a companion magazine, IMAGINATION, in 1950, but in fact was simply lending his name as a cover for William HAMLING, who was still officially working with Ziff-Davis. RAP suffered another severe accident in 1950 and sold *Imagination* to Hamling, while Bea Mahaffey edited *Other Worlds*. After he had recovered, in 1953, he took over the magazine UNIVERSE and started a companion, SCIENCE STORIES; meanwhile *Other Worlds* was suspended. *Science Stories* was short-lived, and in 1955 he changed the title of *Universe* back to *Other Worlds*, continuing the *Universe* numeration. The magazine began to feature more and more FLYING SAUCER material, and in 1957 was retitled *Flying Saucers From Other Worlds* as RAP decided to concentrate all his energies on promoting UFOs and the occult. The bewildering title changes of his magazines resulted in part, he later explained, from financial difficulties and the need to throw up smokescreens. A later RAP publication, including flying saucer and Shaver material, was THE HIDDEN WORLD. [MJE]
See also: SF MAGAZINES.

PALMER, WILLIAM J. (1890– ?). American judge and writer, whose *The Curious Culture of the Planet Loretta* (**1968**), written in his retirement, discusses sexual morality; the plot is not gripping. [JC]

PALTOCK, ROBERT (1697–1767). English lawyer and writer, known mainly for *The Life and Adventures of Peter Wilkins, a Cornish Man* (**1751**), which ranks in popularity as an 18th-century imaginary voyage behind only Daniel DEFOE's *Robinson Crusoe* (**1719**) and Jonathan SWIFT's *Gulliver's Travels* (**1726**). Peter Wilkins finds a race of flying people in a deep valley near the South Pole and teaches them about civilization and the arts of war, while himself manufacturing a flying machine, in which he eventually escapes to tell his tale. [JC]
See also: SATIRE.

PAN *See* Leslie BERESFORD.

PANGBORN, EDGAR (1909–76). American writer. His publishing career began with *A-100* (**1930**), as by Bruce Harrison, and other routine work, long before he published his first sf story, the famous "Angel's Egg" for *Gal.* in 1951. His first sf novel, *West of the Sun* (**1953**), combines interstellar flight, ALIENS, and a UTOPIAN colony founded by six shipwrecked humans on the planet Lucifer; when the rescue ship eventually arrives, they decide to stick with the society they have constructed in

collaboration with the planet's natives; the reflective conclusion of this novel is typical of EP's work. *A Mirror for Observers* (**1954**) won the 1955 INTERNATIONAL FANTASY AWARD; two opposing Martian observers (Mars has been leading mankind into the light of civilization for thousands of years) contest for control over a human boy genius, a potential ethical innovator; the good Martian wins. As with the first novel, EP's obvious literacy usually overcomes a tendency towards a somewhat sickly sententiousness, and does so in *Davy* (**1964**), a long post-HOLOCAUST tale which marked his return to sf after a historical novel, *Wilderness of Spring* (**1958**), and *The Trial of Callista Blake* (**1961**), a moving courtroom drama. *Davy*, along with *The Company of Glory* (**1975**), is set in an America that has suffered a nuclear disaster, and has reverted to a pre-industrial, mythopoeic type of culture. *The Company of Glory* takes place about 50 years after the catastrophe, and describes some of the adjustments begun to be made in order to cope with the new life; Davy lives about 250 years later, and in his novel recounts his long, picaresque life, and his attempts to go about the task of rebuilding a complex human civilization; shorter stories in the sequence are "Tiger Boy" (1972), "The World is a Sphere" (1973), "My Brother Leopold" (1973), "The Freshman Angle" (1973), "The Night Wind" (1974), "Harper Conan & Singer David" (1975), and the four linked stories in *Continuum 1* to *4* (anths. **1974–5**) ed. Roger ELWOOD: "The Children's Crusade", "The Legend of Hombas", "The Witches of Nupal" and "Mam Sola's House". Thematically a companion piece to *Davy*, *The Judgment of Eve* (**1966**) less convincingly puts the task of reconstructing civilization into the highly emblematic hands of the woman, Eve, whose task it is to try to choose among the lifestyles of her disparate male suitors. The trek on which she sends them, in order to find out the meaning of love, represents, perhaps, the nadir of EP's constant drops into ethical bathos. When, however, he was able to control himself — most of the stories in *Good Neighbors and Other Strangers* (coll. **1972**) sidestep these pitfalls — the inherently rural decency of his view of life often won through. [JC]
See also: ARTS; CHILDREN IN SF; INVASION; MEDICINE; MUTANTS; PASTORAL.

PANIC IN THE YEAR ZERO Film (1962). AIP. Directed by Ray Milland, starring Ray Milland, Jean Hagen, Frankie Avalon and Mary Mitchell. Screenplay by J. Simms and John Morton, story by J. Simms, based (without credit) on the stories "Lot" and "Lot's Daughter" by Ward MOORE. 92 mins. B/w.
 This cynical, violent film shows how a typical American family have to act to

survive the aftermath of an atomic war — by trusting no one and shooting first. The father quickly, and almost gleefully, reverts to being a ruthless "natural survivor" who will let nothing stand in the way of getting his family to safety after Los Angeles has been A-bombed. He succeeds, naturally. The escape from the city along roads, jammed with panicking traffic is strongly done, but thereafter the film subsides into clumsy adventure, distinctly inferior to the stories on which it was loosely based. The novelization is *End of the World* (**1962**) by Dean Owen. [JB/PN]

PANIC ON THE TRANSIBERIAN *See* Horror Express.

PANSHIN, ALEXEI (1940–). American writer, active as an sf fan, doing considerable writing and editing in this area, for which he won a Hugo in 1967. He began publishing sf stories in 1963 with "Down to the Worlds of Men" for *If*, and has since been active as both critic and author. The story "Dark Conception" (1964) as by Louis J.A. Adams was written in collaboration with Joe L. Hensley. *Heinlein in Dimension: A Critical Analysis* (**1968**), a comprehensive study of the works of Robert A. Heinlein, is perhaps the most thorough and literate book on an American sf writer to date. It convincingly breaks Heinlein's career into three phases (1940–42; 1947–58; 1958–), argues the superior merit of his later "juveniles" and presents the case for his latter-day decline.

AP's only major sf novel is *Rite of Passage* (1963 *If*, part only as "Down to the Worlds of Men"; exp. **1968**), which won the Nebula award for that year. It is a complex generation-starship novel, and in its narration of the heroine's progress from childhood into questioning adulthood, via a dangerous trial conducted on a planet near her asteroid-ship, is expertly carried off. The heroine not only comes into her own as a person, but validly questions the stratified quasi-democracy of the ship, one of eight to survive the destruction of Earth a century and a half earlier and subsequently to colonize other planets and monitor the colonies founded. AP's series of space operas about Anthony Villiers and his alien companion Torve the Trog — *Star Well* (**1968**), *The Thurb Revolution* (**1968**) and *Masque World* (**1969**) is rather less successful, though its spoofing of the conventions of the more swashbuckling sort of sf adventure is amusing, and the worlds visited are colourful enough.

Farewell to Yesterday's Tomorrow (coll. **1975**) assembles short fiction from 1966; in the introduction to this volume AP credits his wife, Cory Panshin, whom he married in 1969, with collaborative work on some of the stories, and announces that from this date all future work will be signed by both authors. Like

others (e.g. Samuel R. Delany) who began active writing in the 1960s, AP combines practical and theoretical involvement in the sf field, and marks a new sophistication and selfconsciousness in the genre. Much of the Panshins' criticism appeared in *Fantastic*, and many of these pieces, along with some others, appeared in *SF in Dimension* (coll. **1976**) as by both authors. The criticism is often stimulating, but is uneven; AP has a slight weakness for such remarks as "the purpose of mimetic fiction is consciousness-raising". The Panshins emphasize in their criticism that sf is a form of fantasy (*see also* Definitions of sf). [JC]

See also: Galactic Empires; Paranoia and Schizophrenia; Proto sf; Social Darwinism; Sociology; Spaceships; Women.

PANSHIN, CORY (1947–). American writer and critic, educated at Radcliffe College. She collaborates with her husband Alexei Panshin (*who see for details*).

PANTROPY This useful item of sf terminology was invented by James Blish in the series of stories which was later melded together as *The Seedling Stars* (fix-up **1957**). Blish's view was that in the colonization of other planets (in which entry this topic is discussed further), Man must either change the planet to make it habitable (terraforming) or change humanity itself to fit it for survival in an alien environment (pantropy). The word literally means "turning, or changing, everything". Pantropy is usually undertaken by some form or other of biological engineering; *see* Genetic Engineering. A notable pantropy story is "Between the Dark and the Daylight" (1958, as by David C. Hodgkins in *Infinity*, and as by Algis Budrys in *Budrys' Inferno*, coll. **1963**, vt *The Furious Future*). On a planet similar to Harry Harrison's *Deathworld* (**1960**), but invented earlier, successive generations of humans are rendered, genetically, progressively more inhuman, in order to fit them for violent conflict. It is one of the ugliest fables of sf. [PN]

PAPE, RICHARD. (? –) British writer in whose novel, *And So Ends the World* ... (**1961**), arrogant mankind is given a severe warning (the Moon disappears) and comes to its senses; it is more mysticism than sf. [JC]

PAPP, DESIDERIUS (1897–). German writer whose non-fiction work, *Zukunft und Ende der Welt* (**1932**; trans. as *Creation's Doom* **1934**), treats the history and future of Earth, not excluding its termination, in a manner which was influential on contemporary sf. It has been incorrectly referred to in bibliographies as fiction. [JC]

PARALLEL WORLDS A parallel world is another universe situated "alongside" our own, displaced from it along a spatial fourth dimension (in the same way that two two-dimensional universes may lie together like pages in a three-dimensional book). Parallel worlds are often referred to in sf as "other dimensions" because of this displacement. Although whole universes may lie parallel in this sense, interest is usually much narrower, focusing on the parallel Earths. The parallel world idea forms a useful framework for the notion of historical alternate worlds and is often used in this way.

The notion of other worlds parallel to our own and occasionally connecting with it to allow certain kinds of intercourse is one of the oldest speculative ideas in literature and legend. It appears in many guises, "fairyland" and the "astral plane" of the spiritualists being two of the principal archetypes, reflecting the two basic mythical patterns connected with the notion. In one pattern an ordinary human is translocated into a fantasy land where he undergoes adventures and may find the love and fulfilment that remain beyond his reach on Earth. In the second pattern a communication or visitation from the other world affects the life of a man within this world, often injuring or destroying him. Both patterns survive and thrive in modern fantasy fiction, shaping whole sub-genres. Both have spilled over into sf, and these two patterns are primarily responsible for establishing a continuum between sf and mythological fantasy which makes clear definition of the two forms impossible.

The first pattern, basic to fairy romance, extends into sf historically via the works of A. Merritt, Edgar Rice Burroughs and other writers established in the general pulp fiction magazines before the founding of Amazing Stories. A classic example is *The Blind Spot* (1921; **1951**) by Austin Hall and Homer Eon Flint, which made bolder attempts to manipulate scientific ideas to these ends than the works of either Merritt or Burroughs. Much of Jack Williamson's early work was heavily influenced by this aspect of Merritt, and Henry Kuttner wrote several novels to the pattern, including *The Dark World* (1946; **1965**).

Among the first writers to co-opt the parallel worlds idea for straightforward sf melodrama, forsaking the mythical aspect of the pattern, were Edmond Hamilton in "Locked Worlds" (1929) and Murray Leinster in "The Fifth-Dimensional Catapult" (1931) and its sequels. The basic pseudo-scientific idea, however, had already been embodied in stories by J.H. Rosny aîné ("Another World", 1895) and H.G. Wells ("The Strange Case of Davidson's Eyes", 1895, and "The Plattner Story", 1896).

The second pattern, of creatures from a parallel world impinging on ours, basic to the ghost story and horror fiction in general, was science-fictionalized by H.P. LOVECRAFT and several of his disciples, including Frank Belknap LONG and Donald WANDREI. It had already been applied with considerable effect, however, by William Hope HODGSON in *The House on the Borderland* (1908) and *The Ghost Pirates* (1909).

The pulp sf writers made little attempt to develop any of the speculative possibilities corollary to the idea, though one notable attempt to describe a parallel world whose physical laws are different from those holding in our continuum was made by Clark Ashton SMITH in "The Dimension of Chance" (1932). The concept was used straightforwardly by Raymond JONES in *Renaissance* (1944; 1951; vt *Man of Two Worlds*) and Fritz LEIBER used it in connection with the historical alternative theme in *Destiny Times Three* (1945; 1957), but it was not until the post-War period that it was explored more fully. Clifford D. SIMAK imagined a series of Earths empty of Man and thus available for colonization and exploitation in *Ring Around the Sun* (1953), and also imagined inter-parallel trading in "Dusty Zebra" (1954) and "The Big Front Yard" (1958), as did Alan E. NOURSE in "Tiger by the Tail" (1951). The use of a parallel world for SATIRICAL purposes, applied by Archibald MARSHALL in *Upsidonia* (1915), was developed by Lloyd BIGGLE in "Esidarap ot Pirt Dnuor" (1960; vt "Round Trip to Esidarap"). L. Sprague DE CAMP had already applied it humorously in a number of fantasies written for UNKNOWN WORLDS in the 1940s. Gordon R. DICKSON's *Delusion World* (1955 as "Perfectly Adjusted"; exp. 1961) has a city simultaneously occupied by two societies, each invisible to the other.

A common variant of the theme is the notion of a multiplicity of precisely similar worlds existing in parallel: alternate worlds in which there has been no significant change. This appears straightforwardly in "Next Door" (1952) by Jack Thomas and "Next Door, Next World" (1961) by Robert Donald Locke, and is a subsidiary theme in Robert SILVERBERG's "Trips" (1974), in which transuniversal tourists wander aimlessly through worlds similar and dissimilar. In *Worlds of the Imperium* (1962), the first published novel by Keith LAUMER, an infinite series of parallel worlds features minute historical changes in adjacent worlds, which over a wider "space" build up into major differences. A similar idea was used by Richard C. MEREDITH in *At the Narrow Passage* (1973) and its sequel *No Brother, No Friend* (1976).

Significant innovation within the parallel worlds theme has, however, been more or less confined to the last decade. Brian ALDISS's novel *Report on Probability A* (1968) is a surreal novel which has observers in parallel worlds making intimate studies of one another.

Larry NIVEN's "All the Myriad Ways" (1969) deals, albeit very tentatively, with the psychological implications of multiple universes. Isaac ASIMOV's *The Gods Themselves* (1972) presents the most detailed exposition of the theme to date, dealing with communication and energy-exchange between dissimilar parallel worlds. Bob SHAW's *A Wreath of Stars* (1976) uses the jargon of sub-atomic physics to present two worlds of different species of matter existing in the same place, and describes what happens when a "cosmic disaster" affecting one world begins to draw them apart.

The dominant use of the theme, however, in sf as in fantasy, remains linked to the traditional patterns, which continue to exert a powerful mythical hold on the imagination, appealing on the one hand to elementary wish-fulfilment and on the other to elementary fear. *Breakthrough* (1967) by Richard COWPER has ESP fuelled by emotion, and the hyper-consciousness of archetypal images carries his hero across into a parallel world. This novel makes obvious what is implicit in many others in the category: that the attraction of parallel-world stories has much in common with the yearning that leads to tales of REINCARNATION and re-birth. The association of the idea of parallel worlds with these ancient patterns has probably helped to stifle its independent development within sf as a model of scientific or mathematical concepts.

A contemporary fantasy series in which the idea is employed in an unusually complex form, and perhaps to its best advantage, is Roger ZELAZNY's "Amber" series, begun with *Nine Princes in Amber* (1970). Michael MOORCOCK has also found the idea particularly useful in re-complicating his many SWORD-AND-SORCERY series, binding them all together into once complex "multiversal" background. The wish-fulfilment pattern of parallel worlds is seen in its "purest" form, stripped of all its stereotypes and symbols, in two stories by Richard McKENNA — "The Secret Place" (1965) and "Fiddler's Green" (1967).

There is a curious idea featured in several sf stories which also invites discussion under this heading, although it falls outside the definition of parallel worlds offered above. In "Sidewise in Time" (1934) by Murray Leinster a temporal accident results in different geographical areas of the Earth's surface bringing different periods of history into coexistence. Not only do the actual past, present and future merge, but also periods out of alternate histories (*see* ALTERNATE WORLDS). This kind of transtemporal parallelism is also featured in *October the First is Too Late* (1966) by Fred HOYLE, and the similar idea of time-slips is well used in *Frankenstein Unbound* (1973) by Brian Aldiss, where a parallel world of sf myth emerges into reality. [BS]

PARANOIA AND SCHIZOPHRENIA

Paranoia is common in sf; schizophrenia is comparatively rare.

It is obviously necessary to distinguish between sf stories about paranoia (a fairly small group) and sf stories whose implicit attitude is paranoid (an extremely large group). Paranoia has been defined as "a mental disorder characterized by systematic delusions, as of grandeur or, especially, persecution". The delusions of persecution that appear to lie behind much sf were once discussed by the SCIENCE FICTION WRITERS OF AMERICA, and three papers were later published together as a pamphlet, *Paranoia and Science Fiction* (1967), the contributions being by Alexei PANSHIN, James BLISH and also Joanna RUSS who argues that, historically, the paranoid element in sf stems largely from its roots in the GOTHIC; this is undoubtedly true. It is fundamental to the Gothic that none of us is safe; that it is the nature of the universe to contain menaces which may at any time, arbitrarily, threaten us. Such menaces play a prominent role, for example, in the stories of Edgar Allan POE, Arthur MACHEN and Ambrose BIERCE, whose "The Damned Thing" (1893), a tale of a ravening invisible monster, is a particularly pure example.

The PULP MAGAZINES, especially WEIRD TALES, but also the early SF MAGAZINES, were fond of such stories. H.P. LOVECRAFT is an almost perfect example of a writer whose work exhibits a systematic paranoid frame of reference; basic to his work was the idea that adherents of hideous cults formed to worship malign gods are conspiring throughout the world to bring these gods physically back to rule us and feed from us. There was no lack of paranoid stories at the sf end of the spectrum, either; most stories of INVASION, whether by foreigners or aliens, fall into this category.

Two things should be kept in mind, though. The first is the old dictum that "the paranoid is not entirely wrong". Invasions, after all, do take place; people are sometimes persecuted; the universe, as simple observation shows, does indeed contain menaces. The second warning is that there is normally no justification for the assumption that, because a story fits the paranoid pattern, the author is in fact lunatic. There has always been a large commercial market for stories that are aimed to scare, and the writer who works in this market could equally argue that it is the readers who are paranoid.

Early sf stories of paranoia within the genre magazines include "Parasite" (1935) by Harl VINCENT, where invading aliens attach themselves to us and control our thoughts, and "The Earth-Owners" (1931) by Edmond HAMILTON, one of the earliest examples of a theme later to be enormously popular in sf, that Earth is already invaded and manipulated by aliens in disguise. That indefatigable investigator of the inexplicable, Charles

FORT, formulated this paranoid insight in the pithy phrase "We are property". Many sf writers took the hint, as, for example, Eric Frank RUSSELL in *Sinister Barrier* (1939; **1943**; rev. 1948) and *Dreadful Sanctuary* (1948; **1951**; rev. 1963). A common variant on the theme, which must have won sf many adherents among genuine paranoiacs, is that half the people in mental hospitals are there because they know the truth, they have uncovered the conspiracy, but nobody will listen; an example is "Come and Go Mad" (1949) by Fredric BROWN, where it turns out that Earth is controlled by a HIVE MIND (of ants) of enormous intelligence; the man who uncovers the truth is cold-bloodedly driven mad. The magazine AMAZING STORIES improved its circulation very considerably in the years 1945–7 by publishing a series of stories, purporting to have a factual basis, by Richard S. SHAVER, showing how we are all manipulated by malign underground robots.

Conspiracy theories of the Shaver variety are extremely popular among propagandists of the PSEUDO-SCIENCES, many of whom themselves have believed that there is a conspiracy among the scientific community to suppress their findings, as is demonstrated by Martin GARDNER in his *In the Name of Science* (**1952**; rev. vt *Fads and Fallacies in the Name of Science* 1957) and later by John SLADEK in *The New Apocrypha* (**1973**), which has many interesting observations about the relationship of the pseudo-sciences themselves to paranoia. Among the more popular pseudo-science cults are the groups that believe we are being secretly observed by FLYING SAUCERS, and those that follow Erich VON DÄNIKEN's belief that human progress is the result of alien intervention.

An sf sub-genre which fascinatingly mixes delusions of grandeur with delusions of persecution is the persecuted-SUPERMAN story, especially associated with A.E. VAN VOGT, whose entire *oeuvre* probably contains more systematic conspiracy theories than that of any other writer in sf. Notable examples are *Slan* (1940; **1946**; rev. 1951) and *The World of Ā* (1945; rev. **1948**; rev. 1970; vt *The World of Null-A*). Van Vogt was later to be associated with L. Ron HUBBARD's DIANETICS movement, whose appeal was in part to the same mixture: desire for grandeur and fear of persecution. Hubbard himself wrote one of the most forceful paranoia stories in pulp sf, *Fear* (1940; **1957**; as one of the title stories of *Fear & Typewriter in the Sky*, coll. **1951**); this is a story both paranoid and about paranoia; it can be taken two ways, either as the case history of a psychotic killer, or as a demonstration of demonic manipulation; in either event, a remarkably vivid and frightening series of delusions is projected through the apparent banalities of the typical pulp style. "Typewriter in the Sky" (1940) also projects paranoid delusions, this time more attractively.

The other major paranoid variant is the story of the alien menace which can either change its shape or attach itself as a PARASITE to a human; in either event, the fear is that it looks just like us. This is an image from the very heart of paranoia: the idea that our friends, sweethearts or even parents could be mysteriously *other*, hateful, dangerous and to be destroyed. In real life such delusions have often led to murder; they are unnervingly popular in sf. The most celebrated early example is John W. CAMPBELL Jr's story "Who Goes There?" (1938), but the heyday of stories of this kind was the 1950s. This was the period of the so-called Cold War, when Americans were encouraged to believe as a matter of daily routine that a secret conspiracy of Communists and homosexuals was preparing to subvert the American way of life; it was the time of the McCarthy hearings, and of the evangelical religious revival largely led by Billy Graham; paranoia was in the air. The great thing about Communists and homosexuals, as everyone knew, is that from the outside they look just like us. Hence the unprecedented popularity of stories about aliens who looked like humans, especially in the CINEMA, including such films as IT CAME FROM OUTER SPACE, INVADERS FROM MARS, INVASION OF THE BODY SNATCHERS and I MARRIED A MONSTER FROM OUTER SPACE. (Over a decade later the theme entered TV in the form of the series THE INVADERS.) In book form, the best known example is Robert A. HEINLEIN's *The Puppet Masters* (**1951**), where the analogy between the alien group mind and totalitarian Communism was made overtly. An interesting variant on the theme is Brian W. ALDISS's "Outside" (1955), where the story is told from the point of view of a human-seeming alien who does not realize what in fact he is.

Shape-changers still exist in sf, though not with the same bravura and not in the same numbers. A workmanlike example from more recent times is John BRUNNER's *Double, Double* (**1969**). Rather earlier was Clifford D. SIMAK's *They Walked Like Men* (**1962**), in which aliens disguised as humans attempt a capitalist takeover by buying up Earth, bit by bit. The anti-Communist scares, however, are more clearly reflected in another, Cold-War-period Simak novel, *Ring Around the Sun* (**1952**), but here the sympathy is with the conspirators, human mutants persecuted through ignorance, attempting to bring dignity back to human life.

British examples of paranoia stories from the 1950s are less common, though *Alien Life* (**1954**) by E.C. TUBB, in which a starship crew is taken over by alien parasites preparatory to an Earth invasion, would certainly qualify. This idea has been used several times since, as in the film PLANET OF THE VAMPIRES. (Almost all sf/horror films fall into the paranoia category, RABID, NIGHT OF THE LIVING DEAD and DEMON SEED being three recent examples; *see* CINEMA.) Back in 1950s America, the two most notable remaining exponents of paranoia were Richard MATHESON and Robert SHECKLEY, Matheson in almost everything he wrote, including the film scripts for THE INCREDIBLE SHRINKING MAN and, later, DUEL. Sheckley's style is more rueful and ironic; he pokes fun at paranoia even though most of his stories, which are the clearest possible demonstrations of his belief that the universe is out to get us, invoke it. He is paranoia's ace humorist. More serious paranoia is invoked by a curious *idée fixe* which appears in several stories by Frederik POHL either in conjunction with C.M. KORNBLUTH or writing alone: that a small group of very old, very selfish near-IMMORTALS are secretly manipulating society behind the scenes. Examples are *Gladiator-at-Law* (**1955**), by both, and *Drunkard's Walk* (**1960**), by Pohl. The two together showed society manipulated by advertising agencies in *The Space Merchants* (**1953**) and by aliens in *Wolfbane* (**1959**), and Pohl alone had us manipulated by a computer in *Man Plus* (**1976**). It is possible that Pohl's declared interest in grass-roots Democratic politics has given him an overly sceptical outlook; paranoia emerges frequently (and perhaps with some justice) in stories that blend sf with POLITICS.

Two early and remarkably accomplished sf studies about paranoia in action were written by little-remembered genre writers. Peter PHILLIPS's "Dreams are Sacred" (1948) has a telepath actually entering the mind of a paranoid in order to destroy his grandiose fantasies at root, and Rog PHILLIPS (no relation) wrote "The Yellow Pill" (1958), a successful joke story in which both reader and characters are left quite unclear as to who is having delusions and who is perceiving reality. But perhaps the most interesting study of a delusory framework is the one presented as fact in Robert LINDNER's *The Fifty-Minute Hour* (coll. **1955**; vt *The Jet-Propelled Couch* UK), a case-study of an sf fan who believes himself to be living in a SPACE OPERA, and merely dreaming reality.

Space does not permit anything like a full listing of paranoia stories since the 1950s; there have been many, although something of the hysterical edge has gone since the partial evaporation of the Cold War. By far the most important writer in this area has been Philip K. DICK, in many of whose novels the basic question is "to what extent is a paranoid (or schizophrenic) frame of reference delusory, and to what extent is reality itself a mere construct erected defensively by the mind in order to maintain sanity through an illusory stability?" Several of Dick's stories take place, in effect, in ALTERNATE WORLDS actually projected by paranoid consciousnesses. Three novels relevant to the paranoia theme are *Eye in the Sky* (1957), *Clans of the Alphane Moon* (1964) and, most powerfully, *The Three Stigmata of Palmer Eldritch* (1964). Dick's novels are amazing in the emotional intensity of their psychodramas, their bewildering and rather supercilious attitude towards reality, and yet a kind of narrative calm and even wit which allows their plots to totter on the brink of insanity without calling the author's own stability into doubt.

Other monuments of paranoia in the 1960s and '70s include the TV series THE PRISONER, in which a political prisoner is subjected to an increasingly grotesque series of manipulations; several of Christopher HODDER-WILLIAMS' novels in which the protagonist's sanity is called into question as he makes curious discoveries; Richard COWPER's *Breakthrough* (1967), in which communication from outside seems like madness from inside; Davis R. BUNCH's *Moderan* (coll. of linked stories 1971), in which future CYBORGS retreat to strongholds; John Brunner's *The Jagged Orbit* (1969), in which paranoia is endemic and taken for granted in a NEAR-FUTURE situation of racial hatred; Roger ZELAZNY's "Amber" series, in which a large family of quasi-supermen plot constantly against one another, and real universes keep on turning out to be mere shadows of some further but unreachable reality; Algis BUDRYS's *Who?* (1958), in which nobody knows if an enigmatic man in a metal mask is a good American or a Russian spy; Budrys's *Michaelmas* (1977), which comes out on the side of the conspiracy by producing as hero the man who secretly manipulates human politics, though with some uneasiness; Norman SPINRAD's *The Iron Dream* (1972), which parodies sf paranoia by passing itself off as a SWORD-AND-SORCERY novel written by Adolf Hitler; John T. Sladek's *The Müller-Fokker Effect* (1970), which takes American paranoia as one of its satiric targets; Philip José FARMER's "Riverworld" series (unfinished in early 1978), in which the human race is apparently reincarnated *en masse* as a cold-blooded experiment and the smell of conspiracy and plot is heavy in the air; Robert SHEA and Robert Anton WILSON's *Illuminatus!* (three vols 1975), in which recent political history is explained in terms of a dazzlingly complex, absurd and convincing series of interlocking conspiracies by rival ancient cults, still alive today, some going back to ATLANTIS; Frank HERBERT's *The Santaroga Barrier* (1968), in which an entire community is cut off and apparently has its identity submerged (here what begins as horrifying is cleverly, gradually, tilted so that it is seen as perhaps not a bad thing); and finally a series of novels by Barry MALZBERG (some listed under PSYCHOLOGY) which see Man as a puppet in some kind of

enigmatic or indifferent cosmic game.

It is difficult to generalize about all this; clearly the phenomenon is important, and has led to some distinguished work. It does seem as if sf of the last two decades has matured, and that where sf once simply reflected paranoia, it is now often written to analyse the real paranoia which the writers know very well to exist on a large scale in society; it is probably true that Western society has never before had such a complex and cumbrous, bureaucratic power system; no wonder if the average man feels himself to be at the mercy of forces he cannot even identify.

Schizophrenia is very much rarer in sf, though there is a small but persistent subgenre of tales about dual personality, beginning with the classic *Dr. Jekyll and Mr. Hyde* (1886) by Robert Louis STEVENSON. The popular belief that schizophrenia is no more than a synonym for split personality is not correct; in clinical psychology schizophrenia is more complex and more common than that. (*For a listing of some dual-personality stories, see* PSYCHOLOGY.) An amusing variant of the theme can be found in Robert Sheckley's *The Alchemical Marriage of Alistair Crompton* (1978), in which split personalities can be excised by psychic surgery and implanted into new bodies; the story concerns a man trying to reconnect his four personalities.

The film FORBIDDEN PLANET features a proud scientist whose id does not have the self-control of his ego; his secret passions are literally projected into the form of a ravening monster, unbeknown to him. The notion is a colourful and surprisingly successful post-Freudian variation on Stevenson's Jekyll-and-Hyde syndrome.

Where stories of PARASITISM often appear paranoid, stories of SYMBIOSIS often appear schizophrenic, at least in such stories as Brian STABLEFORD's "Hooded Swan" series, where the symbiote literally inhabits the host's brain. (An earlier example is Algis Budrys's "Silent Brother" 1956.) Stableford is one of the few sf writers to use schizophrenia in the modern sense as an sf theme, in his best novel, *Man in a Cage* (1975), where a schizophrenic is chosen to take part in a space project which might prove impossible for sane men. Samuel R. DELANY had used a similar idea in "The Star Pit" (1967), but there the spacemen, though unbalanced, were not schizophrenic.

Theodore STURGEON wrote several strong but psychologically glib stories about schizophrenia, including "The Other Man" (1956), and "Who?" (1955; vt "Bulkhead"), which is about the deliberate splitting of an astronaut's personality to save him from insanity during a long space flight alone. His extraordinarily violent "The Professor's Teddy Bear" (1948) evokes an atmosphere of such manic disgust that it is unclear whether it is a schizophrenic

story or a story about schizophrenia. Another story about the deliberate splitting of personality is Wyman GUIN's interesting "Beyond Bedlam" (1951).

The most consistently evocative use of schizophrenic themes in sf, however, is in the work of Philip K. Dick, notably in *We Can Build You* (1972) and *Martian Time-Slip* (1964). Both use the word schizophrenia in the full clinical sense, and both treat schizophrenics with considerable empathy, though not necessarily sympathy; the latter novel is fascinating in its theorizing that the anomie of the schizophrenic may be to do with his subjective experience of time being radically removed from the normal; the desolated landscapes projected by (or perceived by) the schizoid mind are memorable. [PN]

See also: MONSTERS; PERCEPTION; SUPERNATURAL CREATURES.

PARASITE MURDERS, THE See THEY CAME FROM WITHIN.

PARASITISM AND SYMBIOSIS Parasitism and symbiosis are the extreme forms of commensalism in nature (commensal species are those which live in physical association). Parasitism refers to the state in which one species promotes its own interests to the detriment of the other. Symbiosis refers to the state in which both organisms obtain some benefit from the association. Cases of symbiosis are rare in nature and it has been argued that there are actually none at all, all the proffered candidates being cases in which one partner benefits while the other's survival chances are unaffected.

The human implications of parasitism are unpleasant. The concept has been used in sf as the basis for a number of effective horror stories, in which it is often linked to the idea of vampirism (though, strictly speaking, vampirism is an example of a predatory relationship). Stories dealing with LIFE ON OTHER WORLDS often feature alien parasites which are exaggerated versions of earthly creatures — a particularly notable one is featured in A.E. VAN VOGT's "Discord in Scarlet" (1939; incorporated in *The Voyage of the Space Beagle*, fix-up 1950), where a creature lays eggs in the body of its victim, like a wasp — but the most extreme examples tend to feed on the mind or "life force" rather than simply upon the flesh. An early example of the vampire/parasite association of ideas is Conan DOYLE's story of psychic vampirism *The Parasite* (1895). Classic sf stories in this vein are Eric Frank RUSSELL's *Sinister Barrier* (1939; 1943; rev. 1948) and Robert HEINLEIN's *The Puppet Masters* (1951). Other stories with similar thematic links are Russell's "Vampire from the Void" (1939), Frank CRISP's *The Ape of London* (1959) and Robert SILVERBERG's "Passengers" (1968). The imagery becomes overt in Colin

WILSON's novels *The Mind Parasites* (**1967**) and *The Space Vampires* (**1976**). Many of these stories invoke not only the notion of vampirism but also that of demonic possession to dramatize the situation of parasitism. Straightforward biological analogy is, in fact, quite rare as the central notion of a story, though Philip José FARMER's classic *The Lovers* (1952; exp. **1961**) re-applies the wasp analogy used in "Discord in Scarlet" to increase its effectiveness; this time the larvae consume the body of their human-seeming mother. Farmer also wrote an innovative parasite story in "Strange Compulsion" (1953; vt "The Captain's Daughter").

The elevation, commonplace in sf, of the notion of parasitism from the context of the mundane to the quasi-supernatural is in keeping with sf's habitual treatment of biological themes (*see* BIOLOGY). In concert with general trends in the HISTORY OF SF relating to other forms of life (*see* ALIENS) there has been a dramatic change of emphasis in post-War stories relating to this theme, the representation of commensal, human/alien relationships being much more commonly associated with symbiosis than with parasitism.

The concept of symbiosis is used straightforwardly in the design of alien life systems in a few PULP stories, notably Eric Frank Russell's "Symbiotica" (1943), and the word was used ironically in a story of defensive biological warfare — "Symbiosis" (1947) by Will F. Jenkins (Murray LEINSTER). The use of the notion which has since become commonplace, however, is in stories which attribute to associations between human and alien quasi-supernatural ideas very different from those of vampirism and possession, often making a direct ideological attack on the earlier metaphor-system. The most overt example is Ted WHITE's *By Furies Possessed* (**1970**), which is an ideological reply to Heinlein's *The Puppet Masters*, taking exception to the implied xenophobia of the earlier story. Religious imagery comes very much to the fore in a similar story, "A Song for Lya" (1974) by George R.R. MARTIN. Other stories of symbiosis which present ideas analogous to religious notions are Clifford D. SIMAK's *Time and Again* (**1951**; vt *First He Died*) and Bob SHAW's *Palace of Eternity* (**1969**). Stories of mental symbiosis, with human and alien minds sharing the human brain, are devoid of religious imagery but no less positive in their attitude to the relationship. Examples include Hal CLEMENT's *Needle* (**1950**; vt *From Outer Space*), Brian STABLEFORD's six-book series begun with *Halcyon Drift* (**1972**) and Roger ZELAZNY's *Doorways in the Sand* (**1976**).

This area of speculation is perhaps the most obvious example in sf of the power of biological notions as METAPHYSICAL metaphors, and of the way that such metaphorical usage dominates the expression of biological notions in sf. [BS]

A couple make themselves comfortable on the Eiffel Tower while Paris is frozen in time below them in PARIS QUI DORT.

See also: ECOLOGY; HIVE-MINDS; RELIGION; SUPERNATURAL CREATURES.

PARIS QUI DORT (vt **PARIS ASLEEP**; vt **THE CRAZY RAY**). Film (1923). Directed by René Clair, starring Henri Rollan, Albert Préjean, Madeleine Rodrigue and Marcel Vallée. Script by René Clair. 61 mins. B/w.

One of the earliest sf films, other than shorts, this comedy tells of a scientist who accidentally freezes Paris into a split-second of time with an experimental ray. Not all of the city's inhabitants are frozen, however, and most of them take advantage of the situation by breaking out of their social roles, having drunken parties, etc. But the film's young protagonist, a nightwatchman on the Eiffel Tower, persuades some of them to seek out the source of the problem and put it right, which they do. Made with style and charm by Clair, the film retains its wit and good humour when seen today. [JB]

PARKER, RICHARD (? –). British writer whose *The Hendon Fungus* (**1968**) is a juvenile novel about fungus specimens proliferating, at first in a suburb of London. *The Old Powder Line* (**1971**) is a well-done novel for children featuring a train as a time machine. *Spell Seven* (**1971**) is a fantasy for younger children. [PN]

PARKES, LUCAS or **WYNDHAM** See John WYNDHAM.

PARNELL, FRANCIS See Festus PRAGNELL.

PARRY, DAVID MacLEAN (1852–1915). American businessman and writer, whose anti-socialist DYSTOPIA, *The Scarlet Empire* (**1906**), introduces a young American to a numbers-obsessed ATLANTIS, which he destroys in making his escape by submarine. [JC]

PARSEC The common abbreviation of parallax-second, a measure of astronomical distance introduced by British astronomer Herbert Hall Towner (1861–1930). As the Earth travels from one side of the Sun to the other in half a year, it effectively marks out a base line of 186 million miles. The position of a star might therefore vary, apparently, between summer and winter, though in reality it is the position of the man with a telescope which has varied. An angular displacement of one second of arc would take place when the star in question was at a distance of 3.26 light years from the Sun, and this is a parsec. Parsec is an extremely common item of sf TERMINOLOGY; in sensible sf it is used as a unit of distance, but very often, in bad PULP or juvenile sf, it is mistakenly used as a unit of velocity. "We're moving at 17 parsecs!" the hero of the TV series SPACE 1999 might erroneously cry. [PN]

PASSES, ALAN (1943–). English writer, translator and film technician, educated in Switzerland and France, whose first sf story was "Spoor" for *NW* in 1969. He has written two sf plays, "Mystic of the Western World", produced 1976, and "Death Raise", produced 1977, and has published an epic novel, *Big Step* (**1977**), which mixes sf material with MYTHOLOGY in the experimentally couched story of the adventures on Earth of an interstellar Angel of Death who finds himself vulnerable to sexual seduction on this planet. [JC]

PASSING SHOW, THE British large-format (14¼ x 10¼ inches) weekly magazine, 26 Mar. 1932 - 25 Feb. 1939. It featured articles, short stories, serials

The popular British weekly of the 1930s, this issue 19 Jan. 1935.

and cartoons. With the serializations of *Pirates of Venus* (1933; **1934**) and *Lost on Venus* (1933–4; **1935**) by Edgar Rice BURROUGHS (both reprinted from THE ARGOSY), *PS* became the UK's most regular periodical source of sf in the 1930s, prior to the publications of TALES OF WONDER and FANTASY. Several short fantasy stories by Lord DUNSANY and others and a series of articles by Ray CUMMINGS, "The World of Tomorrow" (1936), appeared in *PS* over the next five years, together with 11 other serials, notably Warwick Deeping's "The Madness of Professor Pye" (1934), Edwin BALMER and Philip WYLIE's *When Worlds Collide* (1934–5; being a reprint of *When Worlds Collide*, 1933, and *After Worlds Collide*, 1934), Wynant Davis Hubbard's *The Thousandth Frog* (1935; **1935**), John BEYNON's *Planet Plane* (1936 as "Stowaway to Mars"; **1936**; vt abridged as "The Space Machine", 1937 *Modern Wonder*; rev. vt *Stowaway to Mars* 1953) and *The Secret People* (1935; **1935**), and Douglas NEWTON's "The Devil Comes Aboard" (1938; vt *Savaran and the Great Sand* **1939**).

PS later became *The Illustrated* and focused its attention on the Second World War, though sf still made an occasional appearance. [JE]

PASTORAL The term "pastoral" can be understood in various ways; it can refer to the Classical or Shakespearean tale of courtiers holidaying amidst nymphs and shepherds; it can refer, as William Empson and other modern critics have argued, to the proletarian novel or to the story which contrasts childhood innocence and adult experience. In essence, a pastoral is any work of fiction which depicts an apparently simple and natural way of life, and which contrasts this simple life with our complex, technological, anxiety-ridden, urban world of the present. Pastorals can be full of moral earnestness or they can be utterly escapist.

Of the many "versions of pastoral" in sf, the most obvious is the tale of country life as written by Clifford D. SIMAK, Zenna HENDERSON and others. Such stories usually involve the intrusion of alien beings (frequently telepathic) into rural landscapes peopled by farmers and small-town tradesmen. Examples are Simak's "Neighbor" (1954), "A Death in the House" (1959), *Way Station* (**1963**), *All Flesh is Grass* (**1965**) and *A Choice of Gods* (**1972**); and Henderson's *Pilgrimage: the Book of the People* (1952–9; fix-up **1961**) and *The Anything Box* (coll. **1965**). Fantasies in a kindred mode include Ray BRADBURY's *Dandelion Wine* (1950–57; fix-up **1957**), Ward MOORE and Avram DAVIDSON's *Joyleg* (**1962**) and Manly Wade WELLMAN's *Who Fears the Devil?* (coll. of linked stories **1963**). What these works have in common is an emphasis on the virtues (and sometimes the constraints) of the rural way of life. They are, explicitly or implicitly, anti-CITY and anti-MACHINE; they frequently extol the values of living close to nature, of being in rhythm with the seasons. This bucolic and Luddite strain in magazine sf has its origins in some major works of American literature, such as Thoreau's *Walden* (**1854**) and Sherwood Anderson's *Winesburg, Ohio* (**1919**), as well as in such English UTOPIAS and romances as Richard JEFFERIES's *After London* (**1885**), with its vision of the city reconquered by forest and field, W.H. HUDSON's *A Crystal Age* (**1887**) and William MORRIS's *News from Nowhere* (**1890**).

A second version of sf pastoral, which also takes its cue from Jefferies and Morris, is exemplified by George R. STEWART's *Earth Abides* (**1949**) and Leigh BRACKETT's *The Long Tomorrow* (**1955**), both tales which depict the rise of agricultural and anti-technological societies after some sort of HOLOCAUST. This type of story is set in the future, although the future becomes a clear analogue of the pre-industrial past. A particularly fine example is Fredric BROWN's "The Waveries" (1945), a tale in which modern America is forced back into a horse-and-buggy economy by invading alien beings who prevent the use of electricity. Other examples of this kind of story are Pat FRANK's *Alas, Babylon* (**1959**), which is less of a nuclear doom warning than a hymn to self-sufficiency, Brian W. ALDISS's *Greybeard* (**1964**) and Edgar PANGBORN's *Davy* (**1964**).

A third version of sf pastoral is the story set on an Edenic other world. Such works usually depict benign alien ecologies which support non-technological societies. Man is often seen as a destructive intruder upon these planets, although frequently the protagonist is "accepted" because he is capable of seeing the wisdom of the alien ways. The ideological thrust of such stories is anti-anthropomorphic and anti-xenophobic. Examples of this kind of

pastoral are Robert A. HEINLEIN's *Red Planet* (**1949**) and, by implication, *Stranger in a Strange Land* (**1961**); Ray Bradbury's *The Martian Chronicles* (fix-up **1950**) and "Here There Be Tygers" (1951); Mark CLIFTON's *Eight Keys to Eden* (**1960**); H. Beam PIPER's *Little Fuzzy* (**1962**); Robert SILVERBERG's *Downward to the Earth* (**1970**); and Lloyd BIGGLE Jr's *Monument* (**1974**). Ursula K. LE GUIN's *The Word for World is Forest* (1972 *Again, Dangerous Visions*; **1976**) is an outstanding treatment of this theme, the sourness of the narrative reflecting the realities of the Vietnam war. Brian STABLEFORD's *The Paradise Game* (**1974**) and *Critical Threshold* (**1976**) are clever variations; both are about planets which are apparently Edenic but which turn out to be rather more sinister. Richard McKENNA's "Hunter, Come Home" (1963) and John VARLEY's "In the Hall of the Martian Kings" (1977) are both good treatments of the ultimate in benign ecologies: bio-systems which enfold and preserve the sympathetic human characters against all dangers.

The fourth version of sf pastoral is perhaps the commonest of them all: the escapist adventure story set in a simpler world, whether it be the future, the past, another planet or another continuum. If the portrayal of "nature" is an essential element in all pastorals, then this is the version of pastoral which prefers its nature red in tooth and claw. Edgar Rice BURROUGHS's *Tarzan of the Apes* (**1914**) belongs in this category, as do his *A Princess of Mars* (1912 *All-Story*; **1917**), *At The Earth's Core* (1914 *All-Story*; **1922**) and all their various sequels. One of the leading contemporary authors of this form of escapist pastoral is Philip José FARMER. His *Maker of Universes* (**1965**) and its sequels are, in common with the Burroughs novels, tales of adventure set in never-never worlds where ordinary men are free to develop all the talents repressed by modern civilization. It is no accident that Farmer is obsessed with Burroughs' major hero and has written such pseudo-Tarzan books as *Lord Tyger* (**1970**) and the spoof biography *Tarzan Alive* (**1972**). Tarzan is an archetypal 20th-century pastoral hero: his freedom of action, affinity with animals, and innocent capacity for violence represent a perfect amalgam of daydreams, Rousseau married to Darwin.

One could go further and say that the whole sub-genre of HEROIC FANTASY, and in particular SWORD AND SORCERY, is in a sense pastoral. As urbanization increases and free space diminishes on the Earth's surface, so the pastoral dream of simpler worlds in harmony (or in delightful conflict) with nature gains in popularity. Hence it is hardly surprising that sf and fantasy should present us with numerous versions of pastoral and are likely to continue to do so in the future. [DP]

See also: CHILDREN IN SF; ECOLOGY; ISLANDS; LIVING WORLDS.

PATCHETT, M(ARY) E(LWYN)

(1897–   ). Australian writer for children, resident in England, whose competent juvenile sf novels are *Kidnappers of Space* (**1953**; vt *Space Captives of the Golden Men* USA), *Adam Troy, Astroman* (**1954**), *Lost on Venus* (**1954**; vt *Flight to the Misty Planet* USA); *Send for Johnny Danger* (**1956**) and *The Venus Project* (**1963**). She did not begin writing sf until she was a grandmother.   [JC]

PATROUCH, JOSEPH F. Jr (? –   ).

American critic, much of whose work on *The Science Fiction of Isaac Asimov* (**1974**) was completed in graduate school at the University of Dayton. The study is extremely detailed on Asimov's narrative strategies, of which it often disapproves, but its nuts-and-bolts approach to literary craftsmanship does little to explain where Asimov's strengths really lie.   [PN]

PAUL, FRANK R. (1884–1963).

Austrian-born American illustrator. FRP received much of his education in Vienna, and studied also in Paris and New York. Trained as an architect, he was discovered by Hugo GERNSBACK while working for a rural newspaper. Their names have been virtually inseparable ever since the first issue of *Amazing Stories* in Apr. 1926; FRP not only painted the cover illustration but did all the interior b/w artwork as well. Gernsback was often called the "father of modern sf literature"; FRP is an even more convincing candidate for the title of "father of modern sf illustration". In his long career, he worked almost equally in colour and b/w, but is best known for his colour work. He was most closely associated with *Amazing Stories* and was its only cover artist until Gernsback lost control of the magazine in 1929. When Gernsback started *Science Wonder Stories* and *Air Wonder Stories* later that year, FRP was again his primary

This marvellous cover by Frank R. PAUL, Feb. 1933, is the basis of the jacket illustration for the US edition of this Encyclopedia.

illustrator. He worked on every Gernsback magazine, including the short-lived *Science Fiction Plus* in 1953. FRP did nearly 1,000 illustrations for such magazines as *Wonder Stories, Fantastic Novels, Astonishing Stories, Dynamic Science Stories, Planet Stories* and a dozen others; he also did all the illustration for *Superworld Comics*, a Gernsback experiment of 1939. FRP's style was heavily influenced by his architectural training; his CITIES and machines were lovingly detailed, his aliens well thought out and plausible, but his human figures too often stiff and simplistic. His colours were bright (almost garish, even for the period) and flat, and he had a fondness for pure reds and yellows. The brightness of colour in today's sf illustration is a direct result of FRP's influence. He is often called the "Dean of sf illustrators". FRP was guest of honour at the first World SF

Artist Frank R. PAUL at work.

Convention in 1939.   [JG]
See also: UTOPIAS.

PEABODY, JOEL R. *See* SUN, THE.

PEACE GAME, THE *See* GLADIATORERNA.

PEAKE, MERVYN (LAWRENCE)

(1911–68). British writer and artist, born in China, where he lived until he was 12, as well known outside as within the sf and fantasy fields for his important work as an illustrator and painter. His novels are essentially fantasies. The trilogy comprised of *Titus Groan* (**1946**), *Gormenghast* (**1950**) and *Titus Alone* (**1959** in edited version; reconstructed from manuscript by Langdon JONES 1970) is by far his most famous work; though couched in FANTASY terms, and told in an elaborated, densely pictorial language, the story of Titus Groan's birth and childhood in Gormenghast castle is fundamentally the story of a coming-of-age; it is that rare thing in the sf or fantasy genres, a genuine *Bildungsroman*, the story of the growth of a soul. The wealth of detail MP created in this work makes it one of the most richly realized alternate worlds in fantasy literature, even though very much more small scale than its nearest competitors in this respect, J.R.R. TOLKIEN's *The Lord of the Rings* (three vols **1954–5**) and Frank HERBERT's *Dune* (**1965**). The relative sparseness of *Titus Alone* reflects not primarily the lingering, fatal disease which darkened MP's last years, but the necessary loss of childhood. MP's contribution to the original anthology *Sometime, Never* (anth. **1956**) is another story about Titus, "Boy in Darkness". Another fantasy is *Mr Pye* (**1953**). Regardless of how he is labelled, MP is a writer of considerable general importance.   [JC/PN]
Other works: *Captain Slaughterboard Drops Anchor* (**1939**), for children; *Letters from a Lost Uncle* (**1948**), for children; *Mervyn Peake: Writings and Drawings* (anth. **1974**) ed. Maeve Gilmore, MP's widow, and Shelagh Johnson.
About the author: *A World Away; a Memoir* (**1970**) by Maeve Gilmore; *Mervyn Peake* (**1974**) by John Batchelor; *Mervyn Peake* (**1976**) by John Watney.

PEARCE, BRENDA (1935–   ).

British writer who began publishing sf with "Hot Spot" for *ASF* in 1974; her two sf novels, *Kidnapped into Space* (**1975**) and *Worlds for the Grabbing* (**1977**) are both routine adventures, though her interest in technical and technological matters sometimes shows through to advantage.   [JC]

PEARCE, PHILIPPA *See* CHILDREN'S SF.

PEARSON, MARTIN Pseudonym used by Donald A. WOLLHEIM alone, except for one story, "The Embassy" (1942), which he wrote with C.M. KORNBLUTH.

Feb. 1931. One of the occasional sf covers.

PEARSON'S MAGAZINE British magazine published by C.A. Pearson, Ltd., ed. Sir Arthur Pearson and others. Monthly, Jan. 1896-Nov. 1939.

PM was a popular fact and fiction magazine which, following the trend set by its companion paper PEARSON'S WEEKLY, published sf by George GRIFFITH, H.G. WELLS, F.M. White, Cutcliffe HYNE and others on a regular basis for several years, becoming the STRAND MAGAZINE's keenest competitor. It is best remembered for the serializations of Wells's *The War of the Worlds* (1897; **1898**) and *The Food of the Gods* (1903–04; **1904**), and George Griffith's *A Honeymoon in Space* (1900 as "Stories of Other Worlds"; fix-up **1901**) and the sf illustrations of Fred T. JANE and Warwick Goble.

Sf continued intermittently into the 1930s in *PM*, sometimes originally, as with John Raphael's weird sf novel *Up Above* (1912; **1913**), and sometimes with reprints, as with Douglas NEWTON's "Sunken Cities" (1923) reprinted from MUNSEY's MAGAZINE.

A US edition appeared Mar. 1899-Apr. 1925 with substantially different contents. In particular it serialized H.G. Wells's *War in the Air* (1908; **1908**) a month or two after the original publication in PALL MALL MAGAZINE. [JE]

See also: *Science Fiction By Gaslight: A History and Anthology of Science Fiction in the Popular Magazines 1891–1911* (**1968**) by Sam MOSKOWITZ.

PEARSON'S WEEKLY British 16-page tabloid magazine published by C.A. Pearson, Ltd, ed. Peter Kerry and others. Weekly, 26 Jul. 1890 - 1 Apr. 1939. Retitled *The New Pearson and Today* from 17 Sep. 1938, and *The New Pearson's Weekly* from 26 Nov. 1938. Incorporated into *Tit-Bits* from 8 Apr. 1939.

PW popularized sf in Victorian magazines with the publication of George GRIFFITH's *The Angel of the Revolution* (1893; rev. **1893**), following it with other serials by Griffith, H. Rider HAGGARD, Louis Tracy and M.P. SHIEL, and H.G. WELLS (*The Invisible Man*, 1897; rev. **1897**). Many short sf stories appeared during this period, with further stories appearing sporadically into the 1930s. [JE]

See also: "Warriors of If" in *Strange Horizons: The Spectrum of Science Fiction* (**1976**) by Sam MOSKOWITZ.

PECK, RICHARD E. (1936–). American writer and academic, professor of English at Temple University, Philadelphia; he is an active critic, both of literature in general and of sf in particular, and has published an edition of Nathaniel HAWTHORNE's poetry. He has produced some non-sf plays, and began publishing sf with "In Alien Waters" for *Venture* in 1969; there have been 12 stories 1969–77. REP's first sf novel, *Final Solution* (**1973**), is an amusing but grim tale of an American academic sent 50 years into the future (through CRYONICS) to find universities and CITIES merged into a hideous conglomerate, and sealed off, with Middle America living comfortably outside. [JC/PN]

PEDLER, KIT Form of his name used by English writer and scientist Christopher Magnus Howard Pedler (1927–) for his writing. He is a medical doctor, and practised from 1953 for about three years, after which he began the research into the experimental pathology of eye disease that resulted in a second doctorate. With Gerry DAVIS, in 1970, KP devised the BBC TV series DOOMWATCH, which ran to 37 episodes, many written by KP and Davis, most of them with some sf content dealing generally with the prevention of man-made threats to this fragile planet. KP's first sf novel, *Mutant 59: The Plastic Eaters* (**1972**) with Gerry Davis, features a Doomwatch-type scenario, in which a plastic-eating virus, created in the laboratory, escapes, creating havoc as plastics start dissolving; the working out of the notion is less than crisp. POLLUTION and ECOLOGY are themes that recur in the next two collaborations, *Brainrack* (**1974**) and *The Dynostar Menace* (**1975**), neither a wholly satisfactory novel. KP's scientific ideas are stronger than the methods he uses to dramatize them. More recently he has made many TV and radio appearances, usually dealing with ecological problems, and has presented several TV films in this field. [JC/PN]

See also: DISASTER; GENETIC ENGINEERING.

PEHLKE, MICHAEL (1943–). German linguist with an interest in mass communication from a Marxist point of view. With Norbert LINGFELD he wrote *Roboter und Gartenlaube: Ideologie und Unterhaltung in der Science-Fiction-Literatur* ["The Robot and the Summerhouse: Ideology and Entertainment in SF"] (**1970**). Analysing contemporary Anglo-American sf and PERRY RHODAN, they hold that sf is a defender of the social status quo, a means for conscious and unconscious political indoctrination. In their opinion, aesthetic yardsticks are insufficient for investigating such a reactionary, trivial form of fiction. [FR]

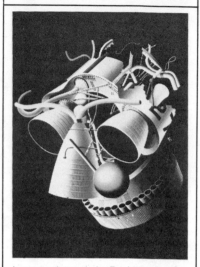

A spectacular study by David PELHAM for the cover of Alfred Bester's *Tiger! Tiger!*; it portrays Gully Foyle symbolically. (*Science Fiction Monthly*)

PELHAM, DAVID (1938–). British illustrator, and art director of Penguin Books. Although his work in sf illustration necessarily takes second place to his professional duties, he has designed some fine covers, notably those for the Penguin editions of J.G. BALLARD novels. He uses the airbrush effectively and his smooth, symbolic, simplified shapes are instantly recognizable; his illustrations would be at home in any "mainstream" magazine that uses high quality graphics, and his inspiration probably comes in part from such modern artists as Eduardo Paolozzi. [JG/PN]

PELOT, PIERRE (1945–). French writer. He frequently uses the pseudonym Pierre Suragne. A prolific commercial author of over 70 sf, horror and juvenile novels, his output has been consistently interesting. He appears to have given up hack work and his two most recent novels, *Les barreaux de l'Éden* ["The Benches of Eden"] (**1977**) and *Foetus party* (**1977**), which are respectively a post-HOLOCAUST tale of the discovery of IMMORTALITY and a refreshingly original treatment of OVERPOPULATION, have established him as one of the most interesting sf writers in France. [MJ]

PEMBERTON, MAX (1863–1950). English writer, educated at Caius College, Cambridge, editor of *Chums*, 1892–3,

and of *Cassell's Magazine*, 1896–1906, later a director of Northcliffe Newspapers. He received a knighthood in 1928. His most famous books are CHILDREN'S SF: the much reprinted *The Iron Pirate* (1893 *Chums*; **1897**) and its sequel *Captain Black* (**1911**), in which an advanced submarine was used for piracy. Equally popular in its day was his novel of attempted future WAR, *Pro Patria* (**1901**), in which a Channel tunnel is excavated by the French for a planned INVASION of Britain. France was again the unsuccessful protagonist in *The Giant's Gate* (**1901**), this time using advanced submarines to bypass Britain's defence systems. Another theme prominent in MP's writing is of secret communities established either for scientific reasons, as in *The Impregnable City* (**1895**) and *The House under the Sea* (**1902**) or for UTOPIAN, as in *White Walls* (**1910**). His works include many non-sf titles.
Other works: *Queen of the Jesters* (**1897**); *The Phantom Army* (**1898**); *Dr. Xavier* (**1903**); *The Diamond Ship* (**1906**).
About the author: *Sixty Years Ago and After* (**1936**), his autobiography.
See also: SPACESHIPS; UNDER THE SEA.

PENDLETON, DON (? –). American writer whose sf novels, all of them routine, are *Revolt!* (**1968**; rev. vt *Civil War II: How it Finally Happened!* as by Dan Britain; reissued under second title as by DP), *The Olympians* (**1969**), *Cataclysm: The Day the World Died* (**1969**), *The Guns of Terra 10* (**1970**), *The Godmakers* (**1970**) and *1989: Population Doomsday* (**1970**). The first two titles are soft-core pornography.   [JC/PN]

PENDRAY, (GAWAIN) EDWARD(S) (**1901**–). American writer, who published some stories in early 1930s sf magazines as Gawain Edwards, and as EP a novel, *The Earth Tube* (**1929**), a future-WAR tale involving Asia and South America: they are connected by the eponymous tube.   [JC]

PENNINGTON, BRUCE (**1944**–). British illustrator. One of the young sf

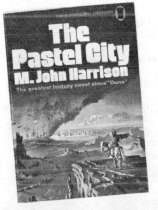

A strong Bruce PENNINGTON book cover. New English Library, 1974.

artists to gain prominence in the 1970s, BP first entered the field in 1967 with a cover for Robert A. HEINLEIN's *Stranger in a Strange Land*, though at the time he worked primarily on covers for Westerns and historical novels. Since then he has done sf covers for *New English Library*, BALLANTINE BOOKS, Corgi, Sphere and *Science Fiction Monthly*, among others. His covers, with their strong sense of colour and chiaroscuro, often have a vastness rarely seen in sf; his sometimes surreal landscapes are among the best in the field. Though his work is not as polished and smooth as that of many artists, his textures and brush-strokes add an important vitality to his work. A substantial portfolio is *Eschatus* (**1977**) by BP.   [JG]

PENNY, DAVID G. (? –). British writer, whose routine sf novels are *Starchart* (**1975**) and *The Sunset People* (**1975**).   [JC]

PEOPLE THAT TIME FORGOT, THE Film (1977). Amicus. Directed by Kevin Connor, starring Patrick Wayne, Sarah Douglas, Dana Gillespie, Thorley Walters and Shane Rimmer. Screenplay by Patrick TILLEY, based on the novel by Edgar Rice BURROUGHS. 90 mins. Colour.
After the mild success of THE LAND THAT TIME FORGOT and AT THE EARTH'S CORE, made by the same company, a third Burroughs adaptation was inevitable, but Tilley's screenplay lacked the mild ironies and tautness of Michael MOORCOCK's for *Land that Time Forgot*. The monsters, this time around, were perfunctory, and the added feminist subplot ended up as more notably male chauvinist than the Burroughs original. Compared to its predecessors, both quite entertaining, this was a pot-boiler.   [PN]

PERCEPTION The ways in which we become aware of and receive information about the outside world, mainly through the senses, are called perception. Philosophers are deeply divided as to whether our perceptions of the outside world correspond to an actual reality, or whether our perceptions are merely hypotheses, intellectual constructs, which may give us an unreliable or partial picture of external reality, or whether, indeed, outside reality is itself a mental construct.
Perception has always been an important theme in sf, playing a central role in some stories, and a subsidiary role in a great many. For convenience, we can divide sf perception stories into five groups. (i) stories about unusual modes of perception; (ii) stories about appearance and reality; (iii) stories about perception altered through drugs; (iv) stories about synaesthesia; (v) stories about altered perception of time. The groups are not mutually exclusive, and several stories fall into more than one category.
Unusual modes of perception appear

early in sf. R.H. HORNE's *The Poor Artist* (**1871**), which is partly devoted to the way the world would appear as perceived through the senses of animals, was the first book ever to be described at the time as "science fiction" (by his contemporary William WILSON). Edwin A. ABBOTT's *Flatland* (**1884**) is an exercise in how beings from a one- or two-dimensional universe would perceive reality, and about how we would perceive a FOURTH DIMENSION. J.H. ROSNY AÎNÉ's story "Un autre monde" (**1895**; trans. as "Another World" 1962) tells of a mutant with a very fast metabolism who can see colours beyond violet (and new life forms) invisible to ordinary humans. David LINDSAY developed a similar idea in *A Voyage to Arcturus* (**1920**), in which the protagonist, mysteriously transported to another planet, keeps growing and then losing new organs of perception which fulfil various functions from seeing additional colours, to sensing emotions, to intensifying the will.
Many sf writers have followed Rosny aîné's lead in imagining modes of perception which allow the direct sensing of ALTERNATE WORLDS or other dimensions. (It is probably more accurate to suppose that the idea was popularized by an H.G. WELLS story of the same year, "The Story of Davidson's Eyes" (1895), though Rosny aîné's story is superior as sf.) Many subsequent stories have involved what we now call extra-sensory perception (*see* ESP). A.E. van VOGT's melodramatic *Siege of the Unseen* (**1946** as "The Chronicler"; **1959**; vt as title story in *The Three Eyes of Evil*, coll. **1973** UK) has a hero with a third eye which allows him to perceive and then travel into another dimension. In Richard McKENNA's "The Secret Place" (1966), no special organ is required; a world of the distant geological past is perceived direct by the mind of the heroine. (Nearly all McKenna's work involves the perception and/or construction of alternate realities).
Another McKenna story, "Hunter, Come Home" (1963) involves an alien life form which perceives by instant molecular analysis, an example of the strange modes of perception which appear in many of the stories described in the entry on ALIENS. James TIPTREE Jr often uses perception themes, notably in the almost surreal "Painwise" (1971), in which a human explorer surgically modified to feel no pain takes up with a crew of hedonistic aliens fixated on taste sensations; pain is rediscovered. Several of Ian WATSON's novels have dealt more seriously with perception, as in *The Jonah Kit* (**1975**) where the perceptions of a whale are mediated through (and modified by) a human intelligence, and *The Martian Inca* (**1977**), where the perceptions of two South American Indians are changed by the accidental intake of a Martian organism; as a result their model of the world becomes very

much more complex. Watson here, as elsewhere, touches on the relation between external reality and the way that reality is perceived and modified by mental programmes in the observer. These are questions that emerge regularly in the second category, stories of appearance and reality.

Appearance and reality is one of the fundamental themes of sf; it has as much to do with METAPHYSICS and CONCEPTUAL BREAKTHROUGH as with perception *per se*, and the topic is discussed (from rather a different perspective) in those two entries also. Relevant stories discussed in more detail in CONCEPTUAL BREAKTHROUGH are "The Yellow Pill" (1958) by Rog PHILLIPS, *Simulacron-3* (**1964**; vt *Counterfeit World* UK) by Daniel GALOUYE and *Rogue Moon* (**1960**) by Algis BUDRYS; this last novel, where a MATTER TRANSMITTER is used to duplicate successive bodies of the hero when earlier bodies are killed, has relevance to human perceptions of death as well as of reality.

The difficulty in perceiving the difference between the real and the illusory is a central theme in ABSURDIST sf, as it is in surrealist literature generally; it comes up often in the stories of Josephine SAXTON, and is, in effect, the subject of Angela CARTER's *The Infernal Desire Machines of Doctor Hoffman* (**1972**; vt *The War of Dreams* USA) and Salman RUSHDIE's *Grimus* (**1975**). All three writers regularly use the quest format, life being seen as a journey through baffling illusions, and the desired end being understanding. Ed BRYANT's *Cinnabar* (coll. of linked stories **1976**) is set around an enigmatic CITY where desires can be made flesh in various ways, and where reality itself is ever dissolving from one form to another; always changing and diverse, its one unchanging quality appears to be the evanescence of external reality.

Richard COWPER has written that "one single theme which intrigues me above all others is the nature of human perception". Where Van Vogt's ESP breakthroughs into other realms of perception tend to be brutally direct and melodramatic, Cowper has many times approached the subject with some sensitivity; a kind of further reality, not explicable in everyday terms, makes itself known to several of his characters in dreams, intimations, glimpses caught, as it were, out of the corner of the eye. Cowper clearly believes that our everyday reality is only partial, and has expertly evoked a kind of quivering, tense broadening of perception, especially in *Breakthrough* (**1967**) and *The Twilight of Briareus* (**1974**). Sf stories commonly dwell on the strangeness of such experiences, and the protagonist's feeling that he might be going mad. Another example is Arthur SELLINGS's *The Uncensored Man* (**1964**), in which drugs are used to increase receptivity, a theme we will examine further below.

Several sf stories have combined ideas from MATHEMATICS (strange topologies and geometries) with stories of perception. Arthur C. CLARKE's "The Wall of Darkness" (1949) describes how it feels to live in a world which is a three-dimensional analogue of a moebius strip; it is all inside and no outside; the other side of the wall surrounding this land is still the same side. R.A. LAFFERTY's "Narrow Valley" (1966) is quite remarkably bigger on the inside than it is on the outside, and the perceptions of the observers are driven to the brink of insanity. (Lafferty rejoices in paradoxes of all kinds, and tricks of appearance and reality are common in his stories.) Christopher PRIEST's *Inverted World* (**1974**) is a fascinating story of perceptual paradox in two respects; first is the progressive spatial distortion that takes place north and south of a shifting zone of stability in the hyperboloid planet on which the story is set, and second, the revelation that the planet may in fact be our own Earth, viewed by a group whose perceptions have created a model of its shape which inverts the spheroid to a hyperboloid, and who cannot escape their own intellectual construct. Such stories approach genuine philosophical questions, though these are evoked in sf more commonly than they are actively explored; but even in such cases as Priest's novel (and most like it), where the scientific and philosophical argument is not really rigorous, there is a kind of compulsive teasing quality about the central image which amply compensates.

Stanislaw LEM has several times written about the difficulties of transcending our perceptions; *Solaris* (**1961**; trans. **1970**) asks the pessimistic philosophical question "Can we ever regard reality as knowable, given the limitations of the senses with which we apprehend it and the mental programmes which force us to relate our understanding of it always to human experience?" Barry MALZBERG is also intrigued with this area of speculation, and also pessimistic; *Beyond Apollo* (**1972**) has an astronaut returning from a disastrous expedition to Venus; he tells the story of what went wrong over and over again, always differently, but it seems that the real tragedy cannot be put in terms of his human perceptions, and all his analogies can only give a partial truth. This theme, of course, is as familiar outside sf as it is inside, though sf has remarkable resources of image and metaphor with which to explore it.

The two sf writers who have played the most extravagant and kaleidoscopic variations on the theme of appearance and reality are J.G. BALLARD and Philip K. DICK. Almost all of Ballard's early work, and much of his later, deals with the various psychological processes to which we subject our perceptions of reality. One of his earliest stories, "Build-Up" (1957; vt "The Concentration City") is, in effect,

a bravura replay of the Clarke story cited above; a young man living in a claustrophobic, crowded world catches a train to escape; after weeks of travelling in one direction he finds he is going east, not west; the space of the city is curved; there is no outside, just as with our own universe. In "The Subliminal Man" (1963) the very quickness of our perception is exploited by advertisers. In "Manhole 69" (1957) an experiment in sleep deprivation gets out of control as the subjects' apprehension of reality shrinks their universe, smaller and smaller, effectively strangling them. The whole of Ballard's *oeuvre* is, in effect, an extended exploration of the inner, psychic universes made up by our selective perceptions of the external world.

The paradox in Ballard is that although our inner reality is made up of a kind of hotchpotch of confusing data from the outside (very often the system is almost fused by sheer overload of input), this inner pattern mediates the ways in which we perceive the outside world, in a kind of vicious circle, where no kind of certainty is possible. Dick's emphasis is a little different; in several of his stories the outside reality turns out to be in fact a mere projection of somebody's mental state. Dick's realities very often require inverted commas; they are "realities", consistently adulterated by false constructs, hallucinations, counterfeiting. Ultimately the conjuring is so baffling that the stability of *any* reality comes to seem suspect; the external world suffers a kind of dissolution. In its place we are left with a view which is surprisingly far from pessimistic, as Dick implies it; it can be synopsized (only crudely) as "the universe is what we perceive it to be". This is not necessarily a bewildering maze from which there is no escape. Dick appears to believe in a kind of dogged survival factor; it is an innate human decency which somehow prevents the mind from spiralling downwards into its own subjective madness by constructing simple, often ethical reference points; in effect they act as handholds to the mind. The most important works by Dick which are relevant to perception are *Eye in the Sky* (**1957**), *Time Out of Joint* (**1959**), *The Man in the High Castle* (**1962**), *The Three Stigmata of Palmer Eldritch* (**1964**), *Martian Time-Slip* (**1964**), *The Penultimate Truth* (**1964**), *Dr Bloodmoney* (**1965**), *Now Wait for Last Year* (**1966**), *Ubik* (**1969**), *A Maze of Death* (**1970**), and *Flow My Tears the Policeman Said* (**1974**). Together they constitute a kind of meta-novel, unique in literature. Ursula K. LE GUIN moved briefly into Dick's territory with *The Lathe of Heaven* (**1971**), in which a man has the power to alter reality through his dreams; here, though, although the reality-shifts are adroitly done, the central theme bears more on the making of ethical decisions than it does on questions of appearance and reality *per se*.

Several of the shifting realities cited in the Dick novels above were catalysed by drugs, and his more recent work, *A Scanner Darkly* (**1977**) concentrates entirely on their effects. The late 1960s saw a general interest in the drug-culture; the romantic belief that drugs could open the gates of perception, and offer heightened and superior versions of reality, was very much in the air. Very few sf writers subscribed to this myth, and indeed when drugs had figured in earlier sf, as in Aldous HUXLEY's *Brave New World* (**1932**), where drugs are used to dim perception and bring about a false euphoria, they were usually seen as detracting from the powers of perception rather than heightening them. Margaret ST CLAIR, however, in *Sign of the Labrys* (**1963**), has the consciousness-heightening power of various curious fungi as an essential item of the plot. Similarly, in Robert SILVERBERG's *Downward to the Earth* (**1970**) a drug is the agent for the transcendent rebirth undergone by the hero, who like the despised natives on the planet he has revisited, is suffused by a new and joyful perception of life's harmony. Also relevant here is *The Butterfly Kid* (**1967**) by Chester ANDERSON, in which the drug-induced mood is more cheerful than transcendent.

More common, even in the 1960s, at the height of the drug-culture's years of euphoria, were sf stories about the distortions of perception brought about by drugs, especially those written by NEW-WAVE writers, who could not, generally speaking, be described as conservative, and indeed lived in the main closer to the drug-culture than sf writers a little older. Drug-taking, for example, plays a role in Charles PLATT's *The City Dwellers* (**1970**; rev. vt *Twilight of the City* 1977) and M. John HARRISON's *The Centauri Device* (**1974**). Perhaps the most vivid of all new-wave sf works dealing with perception shifts through drugs is Brian W. ALDISS's *Barefoot in the Head* (fix-up **1969**), in which hallucinogenic drugs have been used as a weapon in Europe, and the entire freaked-out population, often in the belief that it is somehow reaching a transcendent state, shifts into a crazed anarchy and violence; the story centres on a kind of objectless motorcycle crusade. Norman SPINRAD has written some notable short stories about drugs, including "No Direction Home" (1971), where a future America is so used to orchestrating its mental states by drugs that perception of naked reality without any chemical assistance is seen as the worst trip of all.

Synaesthesia is an interesting perceptual state which occasionally comes into sf; it is a condition where the senses become confused and feed into one another, so that, perhaps, a sound becomes a tactile sensation or a vision can be smelt. Alfred BESTER used it in *The Stars My Destination* (**1956**; vt *Tiger! Tiger!* UK), where, in a compelling passage, the hero's transcendence comes about (with many verbal fireworks) in a synaesthetic rite of passage which mixes agony and exultation. Norman Spinrad envisaged synaesthesia as perhaps addictive in his strong story "All the Sounds of the Rainbow" (1973).

Drugs can be seen as a quasi-natural or at least organic method of altering modes of perception. Sf, naturally, has many times invented technological means for doing the same thing. One example out of many possible here is Bob SHAW, whose stories show a persistent interest in strange forms of vision: as in the "slow glass" stories collected in *Other Days, Other Eyes* (fix-up **1972**), in which a new glass is invented which slows the passage of light through it, so that the past can be directly perceived in the present; in *Night Walk* (**1967**), where a blind man invents a device which allows him to see through the eyes of other humans and animals; and in *A Wreath of Stars* (**1976**), where a device is invented to render visible a world (co-existing with our own) made entirely from anti-neutrinos.

The "slow glass" stories bring us directly to the last category: unusual perceptions of time (*see also* TIME TRAVEL). Spinrad has written in this area, too, with a remarkable story, "The Weed of Time" (1970), about a drug which makes its victim see all his lifetime as co-present; the effect is retroactive, so that the hero as a child knows he will be affected by the drug before he has been. Dick's *Martian Time-Slip* (**1964**) sees SCHIZOPHRENIA as bringing with it an altered time perception. In James BLISH's "Common Time" (1953) the altered time perception is brought about by relativistic effects in a rapidly accelerating spaceship. Eric Frank RUSSELL's "The Waitabits" (1955) is an amusing story about a race of aliens whose metabolism is so slow that they perceive time much more slowly, and appear almost static to humans. Kurt VONNEGUT Jr's *Slaughterhouse-Five* (**1969**) has aliens who like Spinrad's hero see all time as existing simultaneously, which gives them a somewhat deterministic view of the universe and leaves little room for free will. In Jacques STERNBERG's "Ephemera", one of the stories in *Futurs sans avenir* (coll. **1971**; trans. as *Future without Future* **1974**), survivors of a spacewreck are doomed when they land on a planet in which, as in Russell's story, the inhabitants see time more slowly. J.G. Ballard, as might be expected, has several stories about the perception of time, the most powerful being "The Voices of Time" (1960), in which the universe is running down, and on Earth time perception is altered in various ways; one man is able to sense geological time directly, as if he smelt it. Time is the dominant theme of Brian W. Aldiss's work; his stories about time perception include the strange "Man in his Time" (1965), about a man who perceives time a few minutes ahead of everyone else and "The Night that all Time Broke Out" (1967), in which a time gas used for controlled, mental time travel gushes out and affects everyone; Aldiss's most notable story of this kind is *An Age* (**1967**; vt *Cryptozoic!*), in which it finally turns out that time actually runs backwards, but our minds defensively perceive it as going forward. The same idea was used at around the same time, quite coincidentally, by Philip K. Dick in *Counter-Clock World* (**1967**), but the Aldiss book, though uneven, has the greater imaginative *brio*. The strangest of all such stories, however, must be David I. MASSON's "Traveller's Rest" (1965), which sadly has not yet attained the classic status it certainly deserves, about a vicious war against an unknown enemy on the northern frontier of a country where the perception of time slows down as one travels south; a soldier on indefinite leave marries, raises a family, grows middle-aged, and is eventually called up again to find himself back in his bunker 22 minutes after he left. The story is told with extraordinary conviction.

The above group of time-perception stories is generally of a very high standard. It demonstrates with clarity the way that sf thought-experiments can stimulate the mind and move the feelings, in certain areas at least that are quite closed to MAINSTREAM fiction. We take time for granted without fully understanding it, or how it works; these stories, with some intensity, stretch our perceptions of what meaning it might have for us. [PN]

See also: PSYCHOLOGY.

PERCY, F. WALKER (1916–). American writer of notable MAINSTREAM fiction. His first novel, *The Moviegoer* (1961), is still his best known; his sf novel, *Love in the Ruins; The Adventures of a Bad Catholic at a Time Near the End of the World* (**1971**), is a long, complex NEAR-FUTURE story set in a 1980s America, technologically decayed but possibly on the road to a moral resurgence, helped in part by the narrator's invention of an insanity-curing device. [JC]

PEREGOY, CALVIN *See* Thomas Calvert McCLARY.

PERFECT WOMAN, THE Film (1949). Two Cities/Eagle-Lion. Directed by Bernard Knowles, starring Patricia Roc, Stanley Holloway, Nigel Patrick, Miles Malleson, Irene Handl, Pamela Davis and Constance Smith. Screenplay by George Black and Alfred Black, based on the play by Wallace Geoffrey and Basil Mitchell. 89 mins. B/w.

An inventor creates a robot in the image of his niece, and hires a young man to take it out on a date as a final test of its believability. But the young man falls in love with the real girl and the film

Stanley Holloway confronting a robot (played by Patricia Roc wearing a dazzlingly fetishistic display of old-fashioned underwear) in THE PERFECT WOMAN.

develops into a conventional farce involving mistaken identities. The ending, however, is mildly apocalyptic when the robot, completely out of control due to a malfunction, marches stiff-legged and spouting sparks and smoke, through a crowded hotel before exploding into pieces. [JB]

PERKINS, D.M. *See* Michael PERKINS.

PERKINS, MICHAEL (1942–). American writer, critic and poet, known primarily for his work outside the sf field (he is a frequent contributor to the *L.A. Free Press*, *Screw* and *Village Voice*; author of the book version of the pornographic film *Deep Throat* — as D.M. Perkins — and of a history of sex in literature). MP was closely associated with the ESSEX HOUSE imprint under which he published eight novels, some bordering on sf: *Evil Companions* (**1968**), a bizarre urban fantasy of impossible sexual odysseys; *Terminus* (**1969**), a violent DYSTOPIA where warrior gangs roam through paranoiac cities, a possible precursor to Samuel R. DELANY's *Dhalgren*; and *The Tour* (**1969**), a modern re-telling of DANTE's *Inferno*. [MJ]

PERRY RHODAN German magazine, though it could also be described as a DIME NOVEL series or a juvenile book series. Weekly, published by Moewig-Verlag, created by Walter Ernsting (who writes for the series under the name Clark DARLTON) and Karl-Herbert SCHEER. *PR* began in 1961, and is still current, with over 700 octavo booklets describing Perry Rhodan's adventures having been published, a record in sf. Though the stories have been dismissed as pot-boilers, *aficionados* (of whom there are many, even holding their own CONVENTIONS)

argue that the density and complexity of the world built up over so many volumes

A dramatic but uncredited cover, no. 345, 1968.

has led to a sophistication unusual in SPACE OPERA. Conversely, the many critics of *PR*, especially in Germany, have attacked it not only on literary grounds, but also for being what Franz ROTTENSTEINER calls "notoriously fascist". This judgement has been supported and argued at length by Michael PEHLKE and Norbert LINGFELD, and also by Manfred NAGL. Be that as it may (or perhaps because of it?) the success of the series has been enormous, and not just in GERMANY. Translations appear in many European countries including UK (since 1975), and notably in the USA, where it has been published by ACE BOOKS since 1969, following the original German

sequence. This US series is in effect a magazine, though its editor, Forrest J. ACKERMAN, calls it a "magabook", and it appears in paperback-book format. The

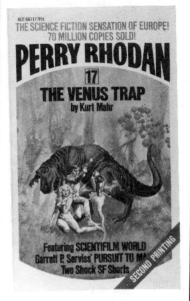

PERRY RHODAN was reprinted in the USA in "magabook" form. Ace Books, 1972. Cover by Gray Morrow.

US *PR* contains a letter column, factual articles, often on sf in the cinema, new stories and reprints of sf classics, all in addition to the leading *PR* novella. However, the US series was projected to cease in Jan. 1978. When all the translations are included, then *PR* has a readership higher than anything else in sf.

Perry himself is an Earthman who is propelled into the politics of the galaxy (*see* GALACTIC EMPIRES), building his small group, the New Power, into a Solar Empire, and taking part in various forms of galactic derring-do. It has been said that there is no sf idea which will not, sooner or later, be used in a Perry Rhodan yarn, for while low on invention, the authors are ingenious at adaptation. They are all German, and include, in addition to the two founders, Kurt Brand, H.G. Ewers, Kurt Mahr, W.W. Shols and William Voltz. Each episode is credited to one or other of the team. The stories are fairly obviously for teenagers, aimed at a market parallel to that of the COMIC BOOKS, many of whose plot conventions also appear in *PR*. Indeed, *PR* has appeared as a comic strip, and in comic books. [PN]

PESEK, LUDEK (? –). Czech writer and astronomical artist. His *The Earth is Near* (**1970**; trans. **1974** by Anthea Bell) deals, with unusual sophistication for CHILDREN's SF, with the psychological stresses experienced by the first manned expedition to Mars (*see* MARS *for further details*). It was winner of the 1971 Children's Book Prize in Germany. [PN]

Other works: *Log of a Moon Expedition* (trans. **1969**).
See also: SPACE FLIGHT.

PESSIMISM *See* OPTIMISM AND PESSIMISM.

PETAJA, EMIL (THEODORE) (1915–). American writer of Finnish descent, based in San Francisco, most of whose earlier fiction was fantasy rather than sf. He began publishing in 1935 with "The Two Doors" for the semi-professional UNUSUAL STORIES; his first professional sale was "Time Will Tell" for *AMZ* in 1942, and some of his early work can be found in *Stardrift and Other Fantastic Flotsam* (coll. **1971**). Occasionally he wrote as Theodore Pine (once with Henry L. HASSE), though only in magazines. A friend of Hannes BOK, EP founded the Bokanalia Foundation in 1967, after Bok's death, and soon published a commemorative volume, *And Flights of Angels: the Life and Legend of Hannes Bok* (**1968**). EP's first novel is *Alpha Yes, Terra No!* (**1965**), and he is best known for the books he released in the 1960s, particularly for the series he based on the Finnish *Kalevala* (a long verse epic detailing the legendary life of the Finnish gods). In each of the novels of this sequence, *Saga of Lost Earths* (**1966**), *The Star Mill* (**1966**), *The Stolen Sun* (**1967**) and *Tramontane* (**1967**), a descendant of one of the four main heroes of the *Kalevala* is reborn into his avatar's role to re-enact his adventures on Otava, the planet of origin of this pantheon. A fifth book of the sequence is unpublished. EP suggests that the alienness of the Finnish people results from their being descendants of this extraterrestrial race! A novel unrelated to the series, but still related to the *Kalevala*, is *The Time Twister* (**1968**). A second series, comprised of *Lord of the Green Planet* (**1967**) and *Doom of the Green Planet* (**1968**), recounts the rather similar adventures of Diarmid O'Dowd, who finds himself identified with ancient legend on a strange planet. Most of EP's sf trades unpretentiously on the emotions aroused by mythical analogues like those in his "Kalevala" books, the adventure plots through which he evokes these resonances are by no means poorly conceived, and he will continue to be read.   [JC]
Other works: *The Caves of Mars* (**1965**); *The Prism* (1965 *Worlds of Tomorrow*; exp. **1968**); *The Nets of Space* (**1969**); *The Path Beyond the Stars* (**1969**); *Seed of the Dreamers* (**1970**); *As Dream and Shadow* (coll. **1972**), poetry.
As editor: *The Hannes Bok Memorial Showcase of Fantasy Art* (**1974**).
See also: MYTHOLOGY.

PETERKIEWICZ, JERZY (1916–). Polish writer (born Pietrkiewicz) active as a poet in his native land before the Second World War. He has lived in England for many years, was married to Christine BROOKE-ROSE, and writes novels and criticism in English. *The Quick and the Dead* (**1961**) is a fantasy involving posthumous activities. *Inner Circle* (**1966**) remarkably conflates in a tripartite structure stories set in the mythical past, in the present (on the Circle Line of London's underground railway), and in a horrific FAR FUTURE where congestion (under an artificial dome) is so great there is no room to lie down. Each story reflects the others, setting up a complex commentary on the human condition. [JC]

PETERS, LUDOVIC (? –). English writer of political thrillers whose sf novel, *Riot '71* (**1967**), posits a NEAR-FUTURE racist crisis in an economically battered Britain. [JC]

PETTY, JOHN (1919–). English writer, variously employed until he began publishing in 1957. His sf novel, *The Last Refuge* (**1966**), is a post-HOLOCAUST novel laid in an oppressive, grey England; there is no refuge there for the protagonist-writer. [JC]

PFEIL, DONALD J. (? –). American writer whose sf novels *Voyage to a Forgotten Sun* (**1975**), *Through the Reality Warp* (**1976**) and *Look Back to Earth* (**1977**) are written in a deliberately (and enjoyably) outmoded SPACE-OPERA idiom. As William ARROW, he wrote *Return to the Planet of the Apes 2: Escape from Terror Lagoon* (**1976**). He also edited VERTEX. [JC]

PHASE IV Film (1974). Paramount. Directed by Saul Bass, starring Nigel Davenport, Lynne Frederick and Michael Murphy. Screenplay by Mayo Simon. 91 mins. Colour.
A battle of wits take place between a fanatical scientist and a species of ant which has acquired intelligence, presumably as a result of alien tampering. The script substitutes mysticism for science and tries, too hard, to emulate 2001: A SPACE ODYSSEY, even to the extent of having a similar ending, with the two surviving human protagonists being transformed into a new form of life. Originally there was also a *2001*-like montage of surrealistic images at the end, showing a fantastic evolutionary upheaval, but this was later cut by the studio.
Phase IV was Saul Bass's directorial début; he was previously known as the designer of such striking title sequences as those for *Walk on the Wild Side* and *Psycho*, and while he is a master of his craft visually, his handling of actors is unsatisfactory and he seems to have little feeling for sf. The film is an interesting failure, and its attraction lies in the superb insect photography by Ken Middleham rather than in its sf content.
The novelization by Barry MALZBERG was published in 1973. [JB]

PHILLIFENT, JOHN T(HOMAS) (1916–76). British writer of much sf and works in other genres; he was at least as well known to sf readers under his pseudonym, John Rackham, as he was under his own name, though he claimed to reserve his best material for the latter signature. He had an engineering background, served in the Royal Navy 1935–47, and was a planning engineer for the English Electrical Board, working at the Battersea power station in London. He began writing sf with some contributions to Pearson's Tit-Bits SF Library as John Rackham, including *Space Puppet* (**1954**), *Jupiter Equilateral* (**1954**) and *The Master Weed* (**1954**), and produced a fantasy series, the "Chappie Jones" stories, for *Science Fantasy*, beginning with "The Veil of Isis" (**1961**); these stories were put together in *The Touch of Evil* (coll. of linked stories **1963**) as by John Rackham. In the mid-1960s his career picked up some steam with a flow of John Rackham SPACE OPERAS, beginning with *We, the Venusians* (**1965**) and *Danger from Vega* (**1966**), and continuing with others of the same unambitious, readable character. Under his own name, JTP produced some book spin-offs from the "Man from U.N.C.L.E." TV series, and in the 1970s some sf novels, including *King from Argent* (**1973**), an entertaining adventure set on a strange planet. Through his career, JTP remained a reliable producer of the second-rank fiction necessary in an entertainment genre with large demands for copy. [JC]
Other works: from the "Man from U.N.C.L.E." series: 5. *The Mad Scientist Affair* (**1966**); 20. *The Corfu Affair* (**1967**); 19. *The Power Cube Affair* (**1968**). Sf books: *Genius Unlimited* (**1972**); *Hierarchies* (**1973**); *Life with Lancelot* (coll. of linked stories **1973**). As by John Rackham: *Alien Virus* (**1955**); *Watch on Peter* (**1964**), a juvenile; *The Beasts of Kohl* (**1966**); *Time to Live* (**1966**); *The Double Invaders* (**1967**); *Alien Sea* (**1968**); *The Proxima Project* (**1968**); *Ipomoea* (**1969**); *Treasure of Tau Ceti* (**1969**); *The Anything Tree* (**1970**); *Flower of Doradil* (**1970**); *Beyond Capella* (**1971**); *Dark Planet* (**1971**); *Earthstrings* (**1972**); *Beanstalk* (**1973**).

PHILLIPS, MARK Pseudonym used on a series of novels written by Randall GARRETT and Laurence M. JANIFER for *ASF*, featuring confrontations between a secret-service agent and various PSI-powered individuals: *Brain Twister* (1959 *ASF* as "That Sweet Little Old Lady"; **1962**); *The Impossibles* (1960 *ASF* as "Out Like a Light"; **1963**) and *Supermind* (1960–61 *ASF* as "Occasion for Disaster"; **1963**). [BS]

PHILLIPS, PETER (1921–). British newspaperman and author whose best-

known sf story was his first, "Dreams are Sacred" (*see* FANTASTIC VOYAGES; PARANOIA AND SCHIZOPHRENIA; PSYCHOLOGY) for *ASF* in 1948; he remained active until 1958, mostly in American magazines, but with some stories in *NW*. [JC/PN]
See also: ROBOTS.

PHILLIPS, ROG Pseudonym of Roger Phillips Graham (1909–65). American writer. Married for a time to Mari Wolf, an sf fan and occasional author who wrote a fan column for IMAGINATION. RP was a prolific contributor to the sf magazines of the late 1940s and 1950s. His first story was "Let Freedom Ring" (1945) in AMAZING STORIES, which remained his most regular market, along with its companion magazine FANTASTIC ADVENTURES. He wrote a series of stories featuring the character Lefty Baker: "Squeeze Play" (1947), "The Immortal Menace" (1949), "The Insane Robot" (1949) and "But Who Knows Huer or Huen?" (1969). Under the aegis of *AMZ* editor Raymond A. PALMER, RP wrote an influential FANZINE review column, "The Club House", from March 1948 to March 1953. The column was later revived in other magazines edited by Palmer: UNIVERSE SCIENCE FICTION and OTHER WORLDS. RP wrote three novels for an early paperback firm: *Time Trap* (1949), *Worlds Within* (1950) and *World Of If* (1951). His best-known story is "The Yellow Pill" (1958), an ingenious exercise in paradoxes of PERCEPTION. He also used the pseudonyms Franklin Bahl, Craig Browning, Gregg Conrad, Inez McGowan, Melva Rogers, Chester Ruppert, William Carter Sawtelle and John Wiley, and the house names Robert ARNETTE, Alexander BLADE, P.F. COSTELLO, A.R. STEBER, Gerald VANCE and Peter WORTH. [MJE]
Other works: *The Involuntary Immortals* (1949 *Fantastic Adventures*; rev. 1959).
See also: CONCEPTUAL BREAKTHROUGH; PARANOIA AND SCHIZOPHRENIA; PSYCHOLOGY.

PHILLPOTTS, EDEN (1862–1960). British writer, known primarily for his work outside the sf field. He was an extremely prolific writer, author of about 250 books and plays. The most important of his sf novels is *Saurus* (1938), in which a space capsule containing an egg lands in rural England. The egg hatches into an intelligent lizard, who becomes an objective observer commenting upon contemporary society and the human condition. Later, however, Phillpotts questioned the validity of a supposedly superior and objective ALIEN viewpoint in social criticism in *Address Unknown* (1949). One of his mystery novels, *The Grey Room* (1921), is interesting because it embodies a dramatic confrontation between scientific rationalism and religious mysticism relative to a seemingly inexplicable series of events. Also notable is *The Fall of the House of* *Heron* (1948), a study of an amoral atomic scientist. A thriller, *The Owl of Athene* (1936), about the invasion of the land by giant crabs, was dramatized by the BBC and caused a small-scale scare akin to the panic later generated by the Mercury Theatre *War of the Worlds* broadcast in the USA. A rather lurid sf thriller, *Number 87* (1922), appeared under the pseudonym Harrington Hext, as did *The Thing at Their Heels* (1923) and *The Monster* (1925). [BS]
Other works: *A Deal with the Devil* (1895); *The Girl and the Faun* (1916); *Evander* (1919); *Pan and the Twins* (1922); *The Lavender Dragon* (1923); *The Treasures of Typhon* (1924); *Circe's Island* (1925); *Peacock House* (1926); *The Miniature* (1926); *Arachne* (1927); *The Apes* (1929); *Lycanthrope* (1937); *Tabletop* (1939); *The Hidden Hand* (1952).
See also: ASTEROIDS; ASTRONOMY; SATIRE; SOCIOLOGY.

PHILMUS, ROBERT M. (1943–). American sf critic, professor of English literature at Loyola College, Concordia University, Montreal. He is on the editorial board of SCIENCE-FICTION STUDIES. His *Into the Unknown : The Evolution of Science Fiction from Francis Godwin to H.G. Wells* (1970) is scholarly, though in dealing largely with works of PROTO SF it is not especially enlightening about sf's generic nature. RMP also wrote the section "Science Fiction: From its Beginning to 1870" in *Anatomy of Wonder: Science Fiction* (1976) ed. Neil BARRON. With David Y. Hughes he edited *H.G. Wells: Early Writings in Science and Science Fiction* (coll. 1975), and is associate editor of the forthcoming *H.G. Wells and Modern Science Fiction*, a collection of essays ed. Darko SUVIN. [PN]

PHILOSOPHY See CONCEPTUAL BREAKTHROUGH; METAPHYSICS; PERCEPTION; RELIGION.

PHYSICS In discussing the scientific content of sf it is customary to regard the sciences as ranging from "hard" to "soft", with physics lying at the hard end of the spectrum (*see* HARD SF). A concern with the hard sciences is generally held to have characterized sf of the period 1940-60, or a type of sf whose *locus classicus* is to be found in that period, and so we may expect this type of sf, in its scientific aspect, to be dominated by physics. In fact a large part of the importance of physics can be attributed to its association with TECHNOLOGY, and among the pure sciences ASTRONOMY and BIOLOGY have probably provided more motive force for hardcore sf than physics. Nevertheless, physics is prominent in the ideological and cultural background to sf and its influence can often be detected even when it makes no explicit contribution to a story. A familiarity with physical ideas and an ability to deploy the language of physics have been used by many authors to establish a general scientific atmosphere — a good example being Isaac ASIMOV's "Three Laws of Robotics", which borrow the form of Newton's Three Laws of Motion so as to claim the same seminal impact, though Asimov's Laws bear as much relation to Newton's as the Hays Code does to the genetic code.

The two areas of physics which have been most popular with sf writers, GRAVITY and relativity (*see* FASTER THAN LIGHT), are covered elsewhere in this volume. Ideas from physics have been applied to technology constantly since Jules VERNE and Hugo GERNSBACK, but in such writing the interest usually lies in the application rather than the physics. Some writers seem to feel that the meaning and motivation of fundamental research lie in its applications. Tom GODWIN, for example, in "Mother of Invention" (1953), changes the proverb and proposes that necessity is the mother of discovery; he shows the crew of a crashed spaceship developing a new theory of gravitation which enables them to design an anti-gravity generator to lift their ship. The most extreme example of this attitude is embodied in Raymond F. JONES's "Noise Level" (1952), which argues that if we only try hard enough we should like to discover any law of nature we should like to be true. The story concerns a gathering of scientists, presented with totally spurious evidence of levitation, who devise a theory to explain this evidence and thereby make antigravity possible.

Many imaginary inventions and strange events are based on points of physics, though sometimes the explanation of the working of the invention amounts to no more than a translation into technical terms of the everyday description of its effect — as in H.G. WELLS's explanation in *The Invisible Man* (1897) that the invisibility potion works by giving human flesh a refractive index of one. An effect at the opposite pole to this was envisaged by Bob SHAW in his invention of "slow glass" in "Light of Other Days" (1966), incorporated into *Other Days, Other Eyes* (1972), in which light travels so slowly that it takes several years to travel through the thickness of a window pane. (Realizing that it did not give quite the effect he wanted, Shaw was obliged to reject the description of slow glass as simply having a very high refractive index.)

Part, if only a small part, of the effectiveness of the idea of slow glass lies in the way it provides an imaginative realization of a physical fact that in normal experience remains merely theoretical knowledge, namely the finiteness of the speed of light. This kind of imaginative exploration of physics can be seen in its purest form in James BLISH's "Nor Iron Bars" (1957), which is an attempt to provide a picture of the inside of an atom and the quantum behaviour exhibited by electrons, by the device of having a spaceship shrink to subatomic size and move inside an atom as if it were a solar system. This is one of the very few sf stories to make any substantial use of quantum phenomena. Blish adopted a similar approach to a more familiar area of physics in his famous microscopic-world story "Surface Tension" (1952).

"Nor Iron Bars" is not a didactic story, but it possibly comes as close to one as a 20th-century editor would accept. An example of 19th-century didacticism applied to physics (among other sciences) can be found in Camille FLAMMARION's *Urania* (**1889**).

Ideas from physics have been used in postulating new forms of life. The favourite basis for these is electromagnetic fields, either in isolation, as in Fredric BROWN's "The Waveries" (1945) and Bob Shaw's *The Palace of Eternity* (**1969**), or in conjunction with inorganic matter, as in Fred HOYLE's *The Black Cloud* (**1957**). The latter has something in common with the sentient suns in Olaf STAPLEDON's *Star Maker* (**1937**). James Blish's *VOR* (**1958**) is about a creature whose energy source is one of the fusion cycles which Bethe proposed as taking place in stars (this creature communicates by modulating light waves rather than sound waves). In Fredric Brown's "Placet is a Crazy Place" (1946) there are birds, made of condensed matter, which fly through the rock of a planet as if it were air. Stanislaw LEM's *Solaris* (**1961**; trans. **1970**) contains a type of life formed from a new type of matter composed entirely of neutrinos. Bob Shaw's *A Wreath of Stars* (**1976**) postulates an anti-neutrino world whose form of matter can interpenetrate with that of our own.

The last four examples make use of the branch of physics which, together with COSMOLOGY (including theories of BLACK HOLES), has undergone dramatic development in the last decade and therefore has the most obvious potential for sf; the physics of nuclear and subnuclear particles. Some of the more striking ideas from this area concern condensed matter, antimatter and neutrinos. Condensed matter is of two kinds: "electron-degenerate" matter, the material of white dwarf stars, in which the atoms are compressed as close as they can be while remaining atoms (a matchboxful would weigh several tons); and nuclear matter, the material of neutron stars, which has the density of the atomic nucleus (a pinhead of it would weigh several thousand tons). Degenerate matter features in "Placet is a Crazy Place" and in Paul CAPON's juvenile novel *The Wonderbolt* (**1955**); and nuclear matter in Larry NIVEN's "There is a Tide" (1968).

Antimatter is composed of particles which are the opposite in all respects to those which compose ordinary matter; when matter and antimatter meet, they are mutually annihilated in a burst of radiation. A.E. VAN VOGT's "The Storm" (1943) is about a storm in space that takes place when an ordinary gas cloud meets a cloud of antimatter gas. Some more of the craziness of Placet in the Fredric Brown story comes from its orbiting two suns, one made of matter and the other of antimatter. Larry Niven described an antimatter planet in "Flatlander" (1967); and in "The Purple Mummy" (1965); Anatoly Dneprov (pseudonym of A.P. Mitskevich) postulated an anti-Earth populated by antimatter counterparts of the inhabitants of Earth. This story also takes account of the law of physics known as CP symmetry, according to which the behaviour of antimatter is the same as that of matter in a mirror. The correspondence between an electron and its antiparticle, the positron, was used by James Blish in "Beep" (1954) as the basis of a method of instantaneous signalling, following ideas suggested by Dirac's original description of the positron. The formation of matter and antimatter universes in the first fraction of a second of creation, and some extremely hypothetical consequences for the nature of our reality, occur in *The Jonah Kit*, (**1975**) by Ian WATSON, who blends real and imaginary physics very adroitly throughout the book.

Neutrinos are particles which have no properties other than momentum and spin, and only interact very weakly with other particles, so that they are very difficult to stop. Their harmlessness is the point of Ralph S. Cooper's satire "The Neutrino Bomb" (1961); their delicacy underlies the idea of "neutrino acupuncture" in "Six Matches" (1960) by Arkady and Boris STRUGATSKY.

Subnuclear physics provides one of the ideas in Isaac Asimov's *The Gods Themselves* (**1972**), in which he postulated a parallel universe whose strong nuclear force is stronger than in ours. Pumping electrons between the two universes provides a source of energy in both.

Stories which turn on fairly elementary points of physics include Arthur C. CLARKE's "A Slight Case of Sunstroke" (1958), in which the spectators at a football match hold their glossy programmes so as to form an enormous parabolic mirror focusing sunlight on the referee; the same author's "Silence Please" (1954), in which the phenomenon of interference is used as the basis for a silence generator; Robert HEINLEIN's "Let There Be Light" (1940 as by Anson MacDonald), which suggests that the relationship between radio waves and light waves could be used to provide a cold light source; and Larry Niven's "A Kind of Murder" (1974), in which the fact that potential energy and heat are interchangeable forms of energy is exploited in an attempt at a perfect murder.

The Dispossessed (**1974**) by Ursula K. Le GUIN is unusual in sf in that much of the story is focused on an attempt to recreate the thought processes and psychology of a physicist whose theories, regarding simultaneity and the nature of time, would create a revolution in physics comparable to that initiated by Einstein's relativity theories. Le Guin's physics is imaginary though plausible and presented with conviction; her psychology might very well be accurate.

Finally, since measurement is of fundamental importance in physics, this is the place to mention those stories that make the point that all physical measurements are relative. The point was made in its simplest form by Katherine MacLEAN in "Pictures Don't Lie" (1951); it was put further into the context of physics by Philip Latham in "The Xi Effect" (1950), pointing out that there would be no observable consequences if everything in the universe were to contract at the same rate (but the contraction would become observable if the wavelength of visible light stayed constant). Referring to time rather than length, James Blish in "Common Time" (1953) described an oscillating discrepancy between a man's internal (mental) time and external (physical) time.   [TSu]

PIERCE, JOHN R(OBINSON) (1910–). American scientist and writer; as scientist he was a director of Bell Telephone Laboratories 1952-71, working intimately at the forefront of communications research and development; since 1971 he has been professor of engineering at the California Institute of Technology, from which he received his PhD in 1936. As writer, JRP has published 14 non-fiction works, both specialized and popularizing, in his professional capacity, from *Theory and Design of Electron Beams* (**1949**; rev. 1954) to *Almost All About Waves* (**1974**). As a writer of sf, he has published material under his own name, as John Roberts, and as J.J. Coupling, beginning with "The Relics from the Earth" for *Science Wonder Stories* in 1930, under his own name, though he is most generally associated with the post-War *ASF* as J.J. Coupling, with a number of non-fiction articles, 1944-71. He published fiction infrequently in the post-War years as J.J. Coupling; it has appeared intermittently from 1948 in several journals; he has not released a collection of stories in book form. JRP's fiction is lucid but slightly cold; it interestingly applies his strong powers of scientific cognition to sf themes.   [JC]
See also: IMMORTALITY.

PILGRIM AWARD Made by the SCIENCE FICTION RESEARCH ASSOCIATION to "a science fiction personality" who has added to our understanding of the genre, at the Association's annual conference since 1970. Judging is by the SFRA committee. There is no physical award, but recipients become Honorary SFRA Members. This and the JAMES BLISH AWARD are the only regular awards made for sf scholarship and criticism. The recipients are as follows: 1970, J.O. BAILEY; 1971, Marjorie H. NICOLSON; 1972, Julius KAGARLITSKI; 1973, Jack WILLIAMSON; 1974, I.F. CLARKE; 1975, Damon KNIGHT; 1976, James E. GUNN; 1977, Thomas CLARESON; 1978, Brian W. ALDISS.   [PN]

PILLER, EMANUEL S. (1907–). American author, with Leonard ENGEL (*who see for details*), of *The World Aflame: The Russian-American War of 1950* (**1947**).   [JC]

PINCHER, (HENRY) CHAPMAN (1914–). Indian-born English writer of some fiction and considerable scientific journalism, in whose first sf novel, *Not With A Bang* (**1965**), the effects of an anti-age drug are seen as catastrophic. *The Giantkiller* (**1967**) is borderline sf in its portrait of a rabid union leader attempting to take over the nation.   [JC]
Other works: *The Eye of the Tornado* (**1976**).

PINE, E. THEODORE See Henry L. HASSE and Emil PETAJA.

PIPER, H(ENRY) BEAM (1904–64). American writer, employed on the late Pennsylvania Railroad; he committed suicide in 1964. Though he wrote for other genres, he is best remembered for his sf work, much of which appeared in *ASF* from 1947, when he began publishing sf stories with "Time and Time Again". His first sf novels were written with John J. McGUIRE; *Crisis in 2140* (1953 *ASF* as "Null ABC"; **1957**) and *A Planet for Texans* (**1958**) are both straightforward adventures, one set in an America that has revolted from literacy from fear of its consequences, the other on a planet set up like a Western. HBP shows to best advantage in his "Fuzzy" sequence, *Little Fuzzy* (**1962**) and *The Other Human Race* (**1964**; vt *Fuzzy Sapiens*), about the planet Zarathustra, where a race of small, joyful, sapient beings is discovered (*see* COLONIZATION OF OTHER WORLDS); the plots centre on the attempts of an interested corporation first to prevent recognition of Fuzzy sapience, then to exploit this recognition, when it has become inevitable. In the court scenes that climax the first volume, the Fuzzy supporters win their case with a definitive, almost slapstick ease highly expressive of HBP's clarity of effect and simplicity of mind. *The Fuzzy Papers* (**1977**) is an omnibus edition. His other series, the "Paratime Police" sequence, also published in *ASF*, is comprised of "Police Operation" (1948), "Last Enemy" (1950), "Temple Trouble" (1951), "Time Crime" (1952) and *Lord Kalvan of Otherwhen* (fix-up **1965**; vt *Gunpowder God* UK); it is a routine set of

ALTERNATE-WORLDS variations. Not an innovative writer, HBP is at his best when he applies an *ASF*-derived firmness of setting and plausibility of characterization to emotionally arousing adventure plots, as in his most enjoyable single book, *Junkyard Planet* (1958 *Gal.* as "Graveyard of Dreams"; exp. **1963**; vt *The Cosmic Computer* USA), in which high action causes a simplistic political upheaval, and good wins. His best short story is probably "Omnilingual" (1957) (*see* LINGUISTICS). Many of his novels and stories, including the "Fuzzy" sequence, are set in a common future HISTORY, but are insufficiently connected to be regarded as a coherent series.   [JC]
Other works: *Four-Day Planet* (**1961**); *Space Viking* (**1963**).
See also: ALIENS; ANTI-INTELLECTUALISM IN SF; COMMUNICATIONS; CRIME AND PUNISHMENT; INTELLIGENCE; NUCLEAR POWER; PASTORAL; SPACE OPERA.

PISERCHIA, DORIS (1928–). American writer, born and raised in West Virginia, in the American navy from 1950 to 1954. She has an AB degree and has done graduate work in educational psychology. She began publishing short fiction with "Rocket to Gehenna" for *Fantastic* in 1966, and her first novel, the remarkable, densely plotted, VAN VOGTian revenge drama *Mister Justice* (**1973**) (*see* CRIME AND PUNISHMENT), appeared after she had established some reputation in shorter forms, one of her stories being included in *Best Science Fiction for 1972* (anth. **1973**; ed. Frederik POHL). *Star Rider* (**1974**) tells first-person adventures in a somewhat chokingly vivid universe; events are pellmell, hampering the adventurousness of the protagonist's far-flung quest for Doubleluck, a planet

of dreams. *A Billion Days of Earth* (**1976**) also tails off towards its climax, but its FAR-FUTURE picture of a dying Earth is vivid, precise and frequently eloquent. The rat-men with mechanical claws for hands are a particularly resonant notion. *Earthchild* (**1977**) is also set in a far future Earth, under a similar threat of termination. Very much a writer of the American NEW WAVE, so that she is at times both daring and a trifle coy in subject matter and style, DP has developed a conciseness and flexibility in her writing suggestive of considerable stature as her *oeuvre* expands.   [JC]
See also: WOMEN.

PIZOR, FAITH K. (1943–). American historian and proprietor of a children's bookstore. With T. Allan Comp she edited the useful collection *The Man in the Moone: An Anthology of Antique Science Fiction* (anth. **1971**), in which nine MOON voyages from 1638 to 1841 appear, including works not otherwise readily accessible to the modern reader, by Francis GODWIN, John WILKINS and others.   [PN]

PLANET EARTH Made-for-TV film (1974). ABC. Directed by Marc Daniels, starring John Saxon, Janet Margolin, Ted Cassidy and Diana Muldaur. Teleplay by Gene RODDENBERRY and Juanita Bartlett. 75 mins. Colour.
One of producer Gene Roddenberry's several attempts to repeat the success of STAR TREK, this pilot for a proposed series failed to generate the necessary network enthusiasm. It is sf at its most simplistic. The hero and his companions are projected into the 22nd century to locate a missing scientist. They encounter a tribe of hostile militant feminists and, by

Violence erupts as a giant Draag is brought low by a group of rebellious Oms in LA PLANÈTE SAUVAGE.

saving them from a band of dangerous mutants, prove to them that men can be useful.   [JB]

PLANÈTE SAUVAGE, LA (vt **FANTASTIC PLANET**) Animated film (1973). Les Films Armorial/ORTF/ Ceskoslovensky Filmexport. Directed by René Laloux. Scenario and dialogue by Roland Topor and René Laloux, based on the novel *Oms en série* by Stefan WUL. Original artwork by Roland Topor. 72 mins. Colour.

The plot of this French/Czech co-production will be over-familiar to the experienced sf reader: human beings on a distant planet are kept as pets by a race of blue, humanoid giants, but they finally organize themselves into an efficient guerrilla army and, despite the disparity in size, force their oppressors to recognize them as equals. The animation is achieved mainly with a 'limited animation' technique using hinged paper cut-outs, though some "full animation" is also used; it is not especially impressive, but what makes the film interesting is the bizarre, surreal background in which such nightmarishly ingenious creatures as the plant that spends its time swatting down small animals for fun, while giggling unpleasantly, go about their sinister business. The subtly disturbing world shown in the background is at odds with the juvenile events of the story.   [JB]

PLANET OF STORMS Film (1962). Leningrad Studio of Popular Science Films. Directed by Pavel Klushantsev, starring Kyunna Ignatova, Gennadi Vernov, Vladimir Yemelianov and Georgi Zhonov. Screenplay by Alexander Kazantsev and Pavel Klushantsev. Colour.

A large Russian spaceship journeys to Venus. Accompanied by a versatile robot, a group of male astronauts travels to the planet's surface in a small spaceship, leaving the command ship under the control of a lone female; the subsequent conversation between the ground party and the girl provides opportunities for uplifting homilies about the Soviet way of life. The men search for signs of intelligent life, but encounter dinosaurs and a volcanic eruption. They finally leave, unaware that their departing rocket is being watched by an intelligent Venusian lurking beneath the surface of a lake. The film is slow-moving and over-talkative, and apparently made for children. The special effects and the settings provide some interest.

Much footage from this film, primarily involving the special effects and the Venus sequences, was utilized in a 1965 Roger CORMAN/AIP production, *Voyage to the Prehistoric Planet*, which also included new American footage directed and written by John Sebastian (pseudonym of Curtis Harrington), starring Basil Rathbone and Faith

Domergue. Then in 1968 *POS* footage was used again in AIP's *Voyage to the Planet of Prehistoric Women*, together with new footage directed by Peter Bogdanovich, starring Mamie Van Doren and Mary Park.   [JB]

The bizarre quality of PLANET OF THE APES is caught in this shot of the actor Maurice Evans relaxing with the *Daily Mail* on the set, dressed for the part of Zaius.

PLANET OF THE APES 1. Film (1968). 20th Century-Fox. Directed by Franklin J. Schaffner, starring Charlton Heston, Roddy McDowall, Kim Hunter, Maurice Evans and James Whitmore. Screenplay by Michael Wilson and Rod SERLING, based on the novel by Pierre BOULLE. 112 mins. Colour.

A film that proved to be surprisingly successful, it inspired a whole series of *Ape* sequels as well as a TV series. Two astronauts crash-land on a planet where various species of ape rule over human savages. One astronaut is killed by gun-toting gorillas, and the survivor is put in a zoo where he unsuccessfully attempts to persuade his captors that he is an intelligent being. He escapes and is befriended by two chimpanzee scientists who accept his story. The film ends with his leaving the ape city accompanied by a female "savage" and coming face to face with a half-buried Statue of Liberty – he then realizes that he is still on Earth, having unknowingly passed through a time-warp, thousands of years into the future. The film (in particular the action sequences) is well directed, but it is poor sf. A major flaw is that the apes speak perfect English yet the astronaut does not find this remarkable, nor do the apes find it remarkable when he answers them in English. The satire which was the point of the original novel, and the ostensible point of the film, is heavy-handed, wavering uneasily between using the apes and the humans as its butt.

2. TV series (1974). 20th Century-Fox Television for CBS. Produced by Stan Hough, executive producer Herbert Hirschman. Running time per episode:

50 mins. Colour. This was a short-lived TV spin-off from the successful series of films, and starred Roddy McDowall, Ron Harper, James Naughton, Booth Colman and Mark Leonard. It was set in a future world where apes were the ruling species and Man had become one of the lower animals. Ape make-up design was by John Chambers. Books based on the TV series have been written by Geo. Alec EFFINGER and William ROTSLER.   [JB]

PLANET OF THE VAMPIRES See TERRORE NELLO SPAZIO.

PLANETS *See individual entries for* MERCURY; VENUS; MARS; ASTEROIDS; JUPITER *and also* OUTER PLANETS; COLONIZATION OF OTHER WORLDS; LIFE ON OTHER WORLDS; LIVING WORLDS.

PLANET STORIES US PULP magazine. 71 issues, Winter 1939–Summer 1955, published by Love Romances Publishing Co.; ed. Malcolm Reiss (Winter 1939–Summer 1942), Wilbur S. Peacock (Fall 1942–Fall 1945), Chester Whitehorn (Winter 1945–Summer 1946), Paul Payne (Fall 1946–Spring 1950), Jerome BIXBY (Summer 1950 – Jul. 1951), Malcolm Reiss (Sep. 1951–Jan. 1952), Jack O'Sullivan (Mar. 1952 – Summer 1955). (Reiss was always associated with the magazine as general manager when he was not actually its editor.)

One of the sillier covers, Spring 1942. Cover by Leydenfrost. The menaced woman is typical.

Subtitled in its early years "strange adventures on other worlds — the universe of future centuries", *PS* was the epitome of PULP sf. Its covers were garish in the extreme; its story titles promised extravagantly melodramatic inter-planetary adventures (which the stories themselves frequently provided). A typical selection of featured stories (from 1947–8) includes "Beneath the Red World's Crust", "Black Priestess of Varda", "The Outcasts of Solar III",

"Werwile of the Crystal Crypt", "Valkyrie from the Void" and "The Beast-Jewel of Mars". The authors of these epics include such *PS* regulars as Erik Fennel, Gardner F. Fox and Emmett McDowell; Fennel and McDowell, like Wilbur S. Peacock, were frequent contributors whose magazine appearances were largely confined to *PS*. The magazine's artwork was mostly crude and lurid; LEYDENFROST was the most individual of its regular artists.

Other authors who appeared often in later issues included Poul ANDERSON and Alfred COPPEL. The most popular contributor, and the one whose work characterizes *PS*'s appeal at its best, was Leigh BRACKETT, with her colourful tales of love and adventure on Mars and Venus. *PS*'s short stories were more varied and less easily classifiable. All but one of the issues from which the story titles listed above were taken also contained short stories by Ray BRADBURY, including "Zero Hour" (Fall 1947) and "Mars is Heaven!" (Fall 1948). Later *PS* published Philip K. DICK's first story, "Beyond Lies the Wub" (Jul. 1952). One of the many sf magazines to come into being around 1940, *PS* was one of the longest survivors, and one of the last sf pulps to continue in that format. *The Best of Planet Stories I* (anth. **1975**), ed. Leigh Brackett, is a selection of typical *PS* fiction. A British edition, published by Pemberton, consisted of 12 numbered, undated, truncated and very irregular issues, Mar. 1950–Sep. 1954. A Canadian edition published Vol.3 no.12 to Vol.4 no.11, Sep. 1948–Mar. 1951. [MJE] **Collectors should note:** The first five vols had 12 numbers each and Vol.6 had 11 numbers. The quarterly schedule was regular until Nov. 1950, when *PS* went bi-monthly. Issues at the beginning and end were marked with the season, but from Nov. 1950 to May 1954 were marked with the month.

PLATO (*c.* 429–347 BC). Greek philosopher. His inclusion here is in part a consequence of his dialogues *Timaeus* and its appendix *Critias* (*c.* 350 BC) being taken as examples of PROTO SF in their references to the sunken state of ATLANTIS; additionally, and more importantly, *The Republic* (undated, but earlier than *Timaeus*, which is in a sense its afterword) discusses and in part describes the ideal state or UTOPIA. It is the first work to do so in any detail. It would be difficult to make too much of Plato's importance to the history of Utopian thought, but his influence, which emphasized an ideal stasis over the constant changes and evolution of the sensual world, runs counter to the Utopian ideas of most 20th-century sf writers. Arthur C. CLARKE's *The City and the Stars* (**1956**) is effectively an attack on a Platonic Utopia. Plato disapproves of poetry interestingly in *The Republic*, but his remarks on children's games in Book

VII of *The Laws* (a late work) are an even better example of those elements of his thought which most modern writers would see, by their own standards, as not Utopian at all: "... when innovations creep into their games and constant changes are made in them, the children cease to have a sure standard of what is right and proper. The person most highly esteemed by them is the one who introduces new devices in form or colour, or otherwise. There can be no worse evil for a city than this. ... Change ... is most dangerous for a city." Nevertheless, Plato was one of the first philosophers at least to consider the idea of change — that the future could be better than the past — and in this respect he bequeathed to us the technique of the imagination which is ancestral to the whole of sf. Also, his famous metaphor of the cave reappears everywhere in sf in various forms, especially in stories of CONCEPTUAL BREAKTHROUGH. (We are prisoners in a cave and take the flickering shadows cast by the firelight on the walls as reality; but the philosopher finds his way into the sunlight and sees that he has hitherto been deceived.) [PN] **See also:** ARTS; ISLANDS.

PLATT, CHARLES (1945–). English writer and editor, now resident in the USA. He began publishing sf with "One of Those Days" for *Science Fantasy* in 1964, and soon became associated with *NW* during the period when, under Michael MOORCOCK's editorship, it was seen as the pre-eminent English NEW-WAVE journal. CP performed various editorial functions for several years, becoming editor in 1970 after Moorcock stepped down, and co-editing with Moorcock no.6 (**1973**) of the *NW* anthology series (no.5 USA) and with Hilary BAILEY no.7 (**1974**) (no.6 USA). CP's first novel, serialized the previous year in *NW*, was *Garbage World* (**1967**), in which its author's scatological humour (the ASTEROID of the title is called Kopra) sometimes overwhelms the sf premise, in which Kopra is used as an asteroid-belt garbage dump. *Planet of the Voles* (**1971**) is a confused SPACE OPERA, but *The City Dwellers* (**1970**; rev. vt *Twilight of the City* 1977 USA) is, in its heavily revised version, a substantial NEAR-FUTURE look at the death of New York and of the crisis-ridden America surrounding it. He has published one novel, *A Song for Christina* (**1976**), under the Playboy Press house name Blakely St James. Several of his other novels are SEX books, including *The Gas* (**1970**), which has a genuine sf premise; *The Image Job* (**1971**) and *The Power and the Pain* (**1971**) are both pornography with marginal sf elements. Sometimes lurid and clumsy, his writing at its best carries strong conviction. CP has worked as an sf editor with several American publishing houses. [JC] **See also:** DISASTER; MEDICINE; PERCEPTION; POLLUTION.

PLAUGER, P.J. (1944–). American writer and vice-president of a computer consulting firm (he holds a 1969 PhD in physics). He began publishing sf with "Epicycle" for *ASF* in 1973 and, though his published books were restricted in late 1977 to two texts on computer programming, he won the JOHN W. CAMPBELL AWARD for best new sf author in 1975, and an sf novel, "Fighting Madness", was published in Ben Bova's *Analog Annual* (anth. **1976**). His most successful short story, "Child of All Ages" (1975), a story of a female IMMORTAL who always retains the body of a child, demonstrates his fluency in composing variations on familiar sf themes. [JC/PN]

PLUTO *See* OUTER PLANETS.

POE, EDGAR ALLAN (1809–49). Major American writer and pioneer of sf. "By 'scientifiction'", wrote Hugo GERNSBACK, "I mean the Jules Verne, H.G. Wells, and Edgar Allan Poe type of story." As a poet, short-story writer and critic, EAP's influence on world literature has been enormous, though he spent most of his career in the cut-throat world of magazine publishing. He is usually credited as an originator of the detective story and the horror story, an innovator in the areas of psychological realism and poetic form, as well as a founder of New Criticism and a strong influence on the French Symbolist movement.

Among French appreciators of EAP was Jules VERNE, who found in certain of his pieces — "The Balloon Hoax" (1844), for example, inspired both *Five Weeks in a Balloon* (**1863**; trans. **1870**) and *Around the World in Eighty Days* (**1873**; trans. **1874**) — a basis for his own "nuts-and-bolts" sf. However, it should be emphasized that in EAP's context much of the scientific verification is of a deliberately specious, hoaxing nature. Another writer of HARD sf, Isaac ASIMOV, created the kind of amalgam between sf and detective fiction that EAP's work anticipates. But something of the more central, metaphysical and visionary aspect of EAP's writing is captured by two other disciples: H.P. LOVECRAFT and Ray BRADBURY. Paul Valéry defined EAP's sf when he observed "Poe was opening up a way, teaching a very strict and deeply alluring doctrine, in which a kind of mathematics and a kind of mysticism became one ...". What EAP referred to as "the Calculus of Probabilities", a species of extrapolation in which he and his detective hero, Dupin, were expert, calls for the combined talents of the mathematician and the poet.

EAP's corpus is very much of a piece, and to isolate his sf is to distort, significantly, both the whole and the part. In fact, no single work can be satisfactorily categorized as sf in any conventional sense (for one thing the hoaxing quality of many of the tales detracts from the necessary illusion of verisimilitude). But at the same time, the underlying rationale is marginally science-fictional and by that token so is everything EAP wrote.

EAP assumed that the fabric of "reality" constituted a "grotesque" deception imposed by limitations of time and space, and such personal impediments as human reason. This revelation and the concomitant awareness of the true "arabesque" nature of a unified reality are available only to the perspective provided by the "half-closed eye" of the imagination or, in the later works, of intuition. EAP makes clear in "Mesmeric Revelation" (1844; rev. 1845) that this visionary arabesque reality is of a material, not a spiritual, nature. It is equivalent to the alternative or additional dimensions of sf and may be apprehended by strategies which constitute EAP's version of the space-time warp. The dizzying sensation experienced on entering an EAP room, typically containing a luridly lit, kaleidoscopically fluid assemblage of arabesque furnishings, or in the process of literally falling in such tales as "A Descent into the Maelström" (1841), will effect the transition. In the case of most visionary or mystical literature, the experience of a transcendent reality depends upon personal volition (an unreliable programme of fasting or praying) or divine intervention. In EAP's case, as in sf, natural phenomena may effect the transition *accidentally*, and the conditions of such phenomena may be mechanically duplicated.

There is a further sense in which all of EAP's work may be regarded as marginal sf. The cosmology embodied in the late summational treatise *Eureka* (**1848**) — a scheme of remarkable prescience (to the point of explaining BLACK HOLES) which has some parallel and perhaps conscious development in the speculation of such writers as Olaf STAPLEDON, George Bernard SHAW and Arthur C. CLARKE — is variously anticipated, whether directly, rhythmically or symbolically, in virtually everything he wrote. To this extent, for example, "The Fall of the House of Usher" (1839) and the sea tales may be regarded as displaced versions of a kind of literalistic sf, if *Eureka* (which EAP called a "romance" or a "poem") may be so described. In *Eureka* the movement from a grotesque, deceptive "reality" to arabesque reality is correlated with the history of the universe moving from its present diastolic state of dispersion to a glorious future state of centripetal collapse into a primal unity, an "Overmind".

Although none of EAP's compositions can be fully accounted for by the sf label, some do come closer than others in that they contain specific sf elements. Three poems merit consideration. "Al Aaraaf" (1829; rev. 1831; rev. 1845), with its ASTRONOMICAL setting and the apparent destruction of the planet Earth, might be related to the post-apocalyptic prose of "The Conversation of Eiros and Charmion" (1839) in which Earth is destroyed by fire when raped of nitrogen by a passing comet (*see* H.G. WELLS's "The Star", 1897, and *In the Days of the Comet*, **1906**). A second poem, "The City in the Sea" (1831; rev. 1845), is related to various sf-like sunken city myths. "Ulalume" (1847) makes use of astrology and, to that degree, relates to EAP's use of other PSEUDO-SCIENCES in some of his most science-fictional tales: mesmerism in "A Tale of the Ragged Mountains" (1844), "Mesmeric Revelation" (1844) and "The Facts in the Case of M. Valdemar" (1845); alchemy in "Von Kempelen and His Discovery" (1849). The automaton chess-player, invented by Baron Kempelen and probed by EAP in his essay "Maelzel's Chess-Player" (1836), might be linked tenuously to the ROBOTS of sf while "The Man that was Used Up" (1839) presents a being, part-human, part-machine, something like a CYBORG. "The Masque of the Red Death" (1842) has Man destroyed by plague as in Mary SHELLEY's *The Last Man* (**1826**) (*see* END OF THE WORLD).

EAP's sea voyages, especially "MS. Found in a Bottle" (1833) and *The Narrative of A. Gordon Pym* (**1837**), seem ultimately oriented towards a HOLLOW EARTH (*see also* LOST WORLDS) like Captain Adam SEABORN's *Symzonia* (**1820**); EAP's unfinished story was "completed" by Jules Verne in *Le sphinx des glaces* (**1897**; trans. as *An Antarctic Mystery* **1898**; vt *The Mystery of Arthur Gordon Pym*). The most ambitious of the balloon tales, "The Unparalleled Adventure of One Hans Pfaall" (1835; rev. 1840), is clearly oriented towards outer space. "Hans Pfaall" is, if taken literally, an early example of the MOON voyage. Another balloon story and another hoax, "Mellonta Tauta" (1849; the title is Greek for "these things are in the future"), might best be considered as one of the three tales that experiment with the theme of time displacement. "The Thousand and Second Tale of Scheherazade" (1845), "Some Words with a Mummy" (1845), a reanimation story, and "Mellonta Tauta" demonstrate the inaccuracy of past conceptions of the future, present conceptions of the past and future conceptions of the present, respectively. "Mellonta Tauta" presents a UTOPIA as a DYSTOPIA, bears on the theme of OVERPOPULATION, and is among the first of such works to open directly in a future environment.

A great many of EAP's stories have been filmed, most famously and prolifically by Roger CORMAN. [DK]
Other works: "Shadow — A Parable" (1835); "The Colloquy of Monos and Una" (1841) EAP's poems and stories appear in at least 30 collections, differing radically in completeness. Nearly all the above stories, the essay "Eureka", but not the poems, appear in *The Science Fiction of Edgar Allan Poe* (coll. **1976**) ed. Harold Beaver, which has an interesting introduction and commentary. Beaver also edited a companion volume, the Penguin Books edition of *The Narrative of Arthur Gordon Pym of Nantucket* (**1975**).
About the author: "Edgar Allan Poe — Science Fiction Pioneer" by Clarke Olney, *Georgia Review* 12, 1958; "The Prophetic Edgar Allan Poe" in *Explorers of the Infinite* (coll. **1963**) by Sam MOSKOWITZ; "Edgar Allan Poe and Science Fiction" in *Future Perfect: American Science Fiction of the Nineteenth Century* (anth. **1966**) ed. H. Bruce FRANKLIN; "The Influence of Poe on Jules Verne" by Monique Sprout, *Revue de Littérature Comparée* 41, 1967; " 'A Clear-Sighted, Sickly Literature': Edgar Allan Poe" in *Billion Year Spree* (**1973**) by Brian W. ALDISS; "Edgar Allan Poe and the Visionary Tradition of Science Fiction" in *New Worlds for Old: The Apocalyptic Imagination, Science Fiction, and American Literature* (**1974**) by David KETTERER; "The SF Element in the Work of Poe: A Chronological Survey" by David Ketterer, SCIENCE-FICTION STUDIES 1, 1974.
See also: COSMOLOGY; DEFINITIONS OF SF; GOTHIC SF; HISTORY OF SF; METAPHYSICS; MONEY; PARANOIA AND SCHIZOPHRENIA; PROTO SF; PSYCHOLOGY; SPACESHIPS; SUSPENDED ANIMATION; TIME TRAVEL.

POHL, FREDERIK (1919–). American writer. He had little formal education. His third marriage was to sf writer Judith MERRIL and his fourth and present wife, Carol Stanton, has collaborated with him in editing several anthologies. He was a member of the FUTURIANS fan group, and wrote much of his early work in collaboration with other members of the group, mostly with C.M. KORNBLUTH. Names used by these two, sometimes involving third parties (including Robert LOWNDES and Joseph H. Dockweiler) were S.D. GOTTESMAN, Scott MARINER, Dirk WYLIE and the house name Paul Dennis LAVOND. On his early solo work FP usually used the name James MacCreigh, though he published one story as Wylie and one as Warren F. Howard. He sold much of this work to himself while he was editing ASTONISHING STORIES and SUPER SCIENCE STORIES, which he began doing before he turned 21, from the spring of 1940 to the autumn of 1941. Late in 1941 he rejoined the magazines as assistant editor to Alden Norton, and stayed until their demise in 1943. After the War he worked as an sf literary agent, and represented many of the most celebrated writers in the field during the late 1940s. He turned to writing again in this period also, and finally abandoned the MacCreigh pseudonym in 1953, by which time he had used his own name on the first of a new set of collaborations with Kornbluth, the classic *The Space Merchants* (1952 *Gal.* as "Gravy Planet"; **1953**). While working as assistant editor to H.L. GOLD at GALAXY he sometimes used pseudonyms, including Paul Flehr, Ernst Mason and Charles SATTERFIELD. The last he also used for a story written in collaboration with Lester DEL REY, in partnership with whom he also wrote *Preferred Risk* (**1955**) as Edson McCANN. Other writers with whom he collaborated at one time or another were Judith Merril, Isaac ASIMOV and Joseph Samachson (who wrote as William Morrison), and he built up a second stable partnership with Jack WILLIAMSON. FP was editor of *Galaxy* and IF from Nov. 1961 to May 1969, introducing many fine writers into the field, after which he reverted to full-time writing. While under his aegis *If* won three HUGO awards as best magazine, in 1966, '67 and '68. While editing *Gal.* and *If*, FP founded and edited two shorter-lived magazines, WORLDS OF TOMORROW (1963–7) and INTERNATIONAL SCIENCE FICTION (1967–8). Another significant editorial endeavour was the early series of original anthologies STAR SF (six vols **1953–9**), which grew from the ill-fated STAR SCIENCE FICTION MAGAZINE, and he has edited many reprint anthologies since the early 1950s.

As far as his solo work is concerned FP was until recently noted primarily as a short-story writer. His work for *Galaxy* included many excellent ironic satires, most notably the classic "The Midas Plague" (1954) and its sequel "The Man Who Ate the World" (1956), and also "The Tunnel Under the World" (1955) and "The Wizards of Pung's Corners" (1958). Later works in a similar vein, showing a sharp wit combined with economy of presentation, are "Day Million" (1966) and "Shaffery Among

the Immortals" (1972). It is slightly surprising that the only short fiction award FP has won is the Hugo for the atypical "posthumous collaboration" with Kornbluth, "The Meeting" (1972). His early novels were disappointing. *Slave Ship* (**1957**), *Drunkard's Walk* (**1960**) and especially *A Plague of Pythons* (**1965**) all exhibit a distinct uneasiness in plot-construction. *The Age of the Pussyfoot* (**1969**), dealing with the adventures of a man revived into the future after CRYONIC storage, is also rather rudderless. There was, however, a sharp improvement in his longer works once he was no longer editing full time. He published two fine novellas in 1971: "The Gold at the Starbow's End" and "The Merchants of Venus". His next solo novel, *Man Plus* (**1976**) — about the adaptation of a man for life on Mars — won a NEBULA award in 1977, and the improvement was sustained in *Gateway* (**1977**). These recent novels employ simple linear plots, but they are much strengthened by the fact that the author always seems to know where he is going and how to get there.

The work which FP did in collaboration with Kornbluth appears to have been hurriedly written, but is possessed of considerable vigour. Sheer exuberance in the building of the various scenarios and the manner in which the protagonists are raced through them compensates for the occasional weaknesses of logic. The image of a future dominated by advertising painted in such gaudy colours in *The Space Merchants* has given the novel a deservedly high reputation, and history has increased its relevance. *Gladiator-at-Law* (**1955**) is a similar novel whose content has not been so kindly treated by the passage of time. The episodic *Search the Sky* (**1954**) is an enjoyable early contribution to the "absurd society" variety of sf. Only *Wolfbane* (**1959**), which deals with more serious and ambitious subject matter, involving a curious and probably metaphorical treatment of Man as part of a giant, alien machine, fails to come off because of the superficiality of the treatment.

The collaborations with Williamson fall into three groups. The first is the series of juveniles *Undersea Quest* (**1954**), *Undersea Fleet* (**1955**) and *Undersea City* (**1958**) which are unremarkable adventure stories. The second series is the "Starchild" trilogy: *The Reefs of Space* (**1964**); *Starchild* (**1965**) and *Rogue Star* (**1969**, published in one volume as *The Starchild Trilogy* (coll. **1977**). These books represent what is perhaps a better blending of talents than the Pohl-Kornbluth partnership (though the blending of talents is not the only appropriate aim of collaboration). They combine Williamson's strengths with Pohl's, developing concepts gradually to a cosmic scale while retaining a neatness and economy of style. An announced

third group was begun with two novellas combined in the volume *Farthest Star* ("Doomship" 1973 *If* and "The Org's Egg" 1974 *Gal.*; fix-up **1975**), which follow up the lead of the earlier trilogy in developing ambitious new ideas with a cavalier flourish. The second story, which features a vast alien artificial world, suffers from the same difficulty that most such stories encounter — the action is dwarfed by the context, and becomes trivial.

FP was president of the SCIENCE FICTION WRITERS OF AMERICA 1974–6. Much insight into the early days of his career is provided by the commentary to *The Early Pohl* (coll. **1976**), and his contribution to *Hell's Cartographers* (**1975**), ed. Brian ALDISS and Harry HARRISON, may be regarded as an extension of this commentary into more general areas. A special issue of THE MAGAZINE OF FANTASY AND SCIENCE FICTION was devoted to Pohl in September 1973. FP continues to write and to act as an sf book editor.   [BS]

Other works: *Alternating Currents* (coll. **1956**); *The Case Against Tomorrow* (coll. **1957**); *Tomorrow Times Seven* (coll. **1959**); *The Man Who Ate The World* (coll. **1960**); *Turn Left at Thursday* (coll. **1961**); *The Wonder Effect* (coll. of stories written with C.M. Kornbluth **1962**); *The Abominable Earthman* (coll. **1963**); *Digits and Dastards* (coll. **1966**); *The Frederik Pohl Omnibus* (coll. **1966**); *Day Million* (coll. **1970**); *The Gold at the Starbow's End* (coll. **1972**); *The Best of Frederik Pohl* (coll. **1975**); *In the Problem Pit* (coll. **1976**); *Critical Mass* (coll. of stories written with C.M. Kornbluth **1977**).

As editor: *Beyond the End of Time* (anth. **1952**); *Shadow of Tomorrow* (anth. **1953**); *Assignment in Tomorrow* (anth. **1954**); *Star Short Novels* (**1954**); *Star of Stars* (anth. **1960**); *Time Waits For Winthrop and Four Other Short Novels from Galaxy* (anth. **1962**); *The Expert Dreamers* (anth. **1962**); *The Seventh Galaxy Reader* (anth. **1964**); *The Eighth Galaxy Reader* (anth. **1965**); *The Ninth Galaxy Reader* (anth. **1966**); *Star Fourteen* (anth. **1966**); *The If Reader* (anth. **1966**); *The Tenth Galaxy Reader* (anth. **1967**); *The Second If Reader* (anth. **1967**); *The Eleventh Galaxy Reader* (anth. **1968**); *Nightmare Age* (anth. **1970**); *The Year's Best SF 1972* (anth. **1972**); *Jupiter* (with Carol Pohl, anth. **1973**); *SF: The Great Years* (with Carol Pohl, anth. **1973**); *The Science Fiction Roll of Honour* (anth. **1975**); *SF Discoveries* (with Carol Pohl, anth. **1976**).

See also: ANTI-INTELLECTUALISM IN SF; AUTOMATION; BLACK HOLES; COLONIZATION OF OTHER WORLDS; COMPUTERS; CONCEPTUAL BREAKTHROUGH; COSMOLOGY; CRIME AND PUNISHMENT; CRYONICS; CYBORGS; DISCOVERY AND INVENTION; DYSTOPIAS; ECONOMICS; ESP; FOURTH DIMENSION (AND OTHERS); GAMES AND SPORTS; GOTHIC SF; GREAT AND SMALL; HISTORY IN SF; HUMOUR; IMMORTALITY;

JUPITER; LEISURE; LINGUISTICS; LIVING WORLDS; MACHINES; MATHEMATICS; MARS; MEDIA LANDSCAPE; MEDICINE; MONEY; NEAR FUTURE, NEW WAVE; OPTIMISM AND PESSIMISM; OUTER PLANETS; OVERPOPULATION; PARANOIA AND SCHIZOPHRENIA; SATIRE; SF MAGAZINES; SOCIOLOGY; SPACESHIPS; STARS; TIME TRAVEL; UNDER THE SEA; VENUS.

POLAND *See* EASTERN EUROPE.

POLITICS In most of the stories which we can characterize with hindsight as PROTO SF, even though they were written long before sf became an identifiably separate genre, the central theme is political and the mode is SATIRE. The works of CYRANO DE BERGERAC, Jonathan SWIFT and VOLTAIRE are good examples, but this is true of the 18th-century *conte philosophique* generally.

Since that time, politics has retained a central thematic role in the great majority of works of sf by MAINSTREAM writers. (It is less popular within genre sf, but still important.) It is almost impossible to write a UTOPIA or a DYSTOPIA without expressing some sort of political preference; similarly any story of WAR or INVASION set in the NEAR FUTURE is almost bound to identify potential political enemies; even LOST WORLDS were usually notable for having some kind of interesting political structure. Political stories are discussed in this Encyclopedia under all the above headings, which indeed cover the main genres of sf up to the turn of this century.

A surprising number of early sf works espouse some form of socialist system; some details will be found in the entries for Theodor HERTZKA, Edward BELLAMY, William MORRIS, Jack LONDON, George GRIFFITH and H.G. WELLS. London and Griffith are interesting partly because they stand at the head of a new tradition of PULP MAGAZINE sf, and through their work and that of others like them (such as George Allan ENGLAND whose *The Golden Blight*, 1916, is both anti-capitalist and anti-Semitic) political themes were to infiltrate into sf at a more popular level.

Anti-socialist works were more common; several are listed under DYSTOPIAS. They include Victor ROUSSEAU's *The Messiah of the Cylinder* (1917), Condé B. PALLEN's *Crucible Island* (1919) and P. Anderson GRAHAM's *The Collapse of Homo Sapiens* (1923); this last book imputes the eponymous fall in part to the activities of trade unions and in part to the decadence of all non-white races. Anti-totalitarian and anti-authoritarian works are perhaps more important; two of the most famous are Yevgeny ZAMIATIN's *We* (trans. 1924) and Aldous HUXLEY's *Brave New World* (1932); also in this category are Owen GREGORY's *Meccania* (1918), Milo HASTINGS' *City of Endless Night* (1920) and John KENDALL's *Unborn Tomorrow* (1933). Anti-Fascist works were written

by Storm JAMESON, Sinclair LEWIS, Murray CONSTANTINE and Joseph O'NEILL; Upton SINCLAIR wrote several political comedies, set in the future, satirizing viewpoints of both right and left.

The flood of political, mainstream sf novels continued unabated after the Second World War, many of them dealing with the political causes of HOLOCAUST, and the kinds of political system that might be set up after the holocaust. The peak period for political sf was the years when the Cold War was at its height, from the late 1940s to the early 1960s. Anti-totalitarian novels of this period include *Animal Farm* (1945) and *Nineteen Eighty-Four* (1949) by George ORWELL, *Up Jenkins!* (1956) by Ronald HINGLEY, *The Age of Longing* (1951) by Arthur KOESTLER, *One* (1953; vt *Escape to Nowhere*) by David KARP, *The World Aflame* (1947) by Leonard ENGEL and Emanuel S. PILLER and James BARLOW's *One Half of the World* (1957). Orwell's books were by far the strongest and most influential of the above; and the sub-Orwellian Dystopias which have been written since are too many to enumerate; they include Adrian MITCHELL's *The Bodyguard* (1970) and *Travels in Nihilon* (1971) by Alan SILLITOE; both of these have more merit than most, and do not blindly follow Orwell's lead.

Many political novels are so only by courtesy, because they are set in the near future; they include such stories of the political use of NUCLEAR POWER as *Two Hours to Doom* (1958; vt *Red Alert*) by Peter GEORGE (the basis of the film DR STRANGELOVE, OR: HOW I LEARNED TO STOP WORRYING AND LOVE THE BOMB), *Fail-Safe* (1962) by Eugene L. BURDICK and J.H. WHEELER and *Red January* (1964) by William CHAMBERLAIN. Other books involving political conspiracy in America are *The Manchurian Candidate* (1959) by Richard CONDON, *Night of Camp David* (1965) by Fletcher KNEBEL, *Being There* (1970) by Jerzy KOSINSKI and *Come Nineveh, Come Tyre* (1973) by Allen DRURY, as well as several films, including THE PRESIDENT'S ANALYST, and TWILIGHT'S LAST GLEAMING.

Other works of political mainstream sf, which do not fit so readily into the above categories, are Robert CONQUEST's *A World of Difference* (1955), Sakyo KOMATSU's *Nippon Chimbotsu* (1973; trans. as *Japan Sinks* 1976) and Oliver LANGE's *Vandenberg* (1971).

An interesting and not uncommon theme in mainstream political sf is racial prejudice and racial conflict, especially conflict between black and white. (Yellow Peril stories are discussed below.) One of the earliest books to touch on the theme was Herrmann LANG's *The Air Battle* (1859), where, interestingly, the future African races are able to put things together again after Europe collapses. This was unusual in the 19th century; far more common was the view that the

blacks were less than human, though seldom put forward with quite the naked malice of King WALLACE's *The Next War* (1892). Several novels about the future of apartheid have been written by South Africans, including Garry ALLIGHAM's *Verwoerd – The End* (1961), which is pro-apartheid, and Arthur KEPPEL-JONES's *When Smuts Goes* (1947) and Anthony DELIUS's *The Last Division* (1959) which are against it.

However, most stories about race relations between black and white involve the USA. T. Shirby HODGE's *The White Man's Burden* (1915) is pro-black, and ends with a UTOPIA being founded by blacks in Africa, after they have overcome white Americans. Some sf has been written on social themes by black writers; John Pfeiffer gives examples in "Black American Speculative Literature: a Checklist" in EXTRAPOLATION, Dec. 1975. One such work is George Samuel SCHUYLER's *Black No More* (1931), which satirizes those blacks who want to be white in a story of a successful cosmetic treatment which accomplishes that feat, and its ludicrous results.

By far the greatest volume of sf novels dealing with black-white relations, however, was written in the 1950s and later, in the aftermath of the growing success of the civil rights movement. American works on this theme include, by black authors, *A Different Drummer* (1959) by William Melvin KELLEY, *The Siege of Harlem* (1964) by Warren MILLER, *The Man Who Cried I Am* (1967) together with *Sons of Darkness, Sons of Light* (1969) and *Captain Blackman* (1972) by John A. WILLIAMS, and *The Spook Who Sat by the Door* (1969) by Sam GREENLEE. Works by white authors include *Siege* (1969) by Edwin CORLEY, *Black in Time* (1970) by John JAKES, and a series by Mack REYNOLDS, largely set in North Africa, beginning with *Black Man's Burden* (1972). Curiously, several British writers have set near-future stories about racial problems in the USA, including John BRUNNER in *The Jagged Orbit* (1969) and Alan SEYMOUR in *The Coming Self-Destruction of the United States of America* (1969). A relevant film is *Watermelon Man* (1970), in which a white bigot suddenly becomes black and has to learn to live with it.

British stories on the theme are fewer. They include Margot BENNETT's *The Long Way Back* (1954) in which a future civilized black Africa sends an expeditionary party to an England reverted to savagery – the American Alice M. LIGHTNER later used a very similar theme in *The Day of the Drones* (1969). Others are *When The Whites Went* (1963) by Robert BATEMAN and *Fugue for a Darkening Island* (1972; vt *Darkening Island* USA) by Christopher PRIEST.

Where mainstream political sf is usually explicit in its political preferences, and often polemical, sometimes crudely so, genre sf's political attitudes tend to be implicit. A study of the VILLAINS in sf melodramas often gives a good idea of the almost unconsidered prejudices these works fed, if not by design, then because the authors tended to share the prejudices of the population at large. Hence, during the 1920s and '30s there were a number of works about the Yellow Peril; M.P. SHIEL had been writing stories of this kind back at the turn of the century; later Sax ROHMER was to make a very good thing out of Fu Manchu. Fascist villains predominated during the Second World War, and during the Cold War, stories of HIVE MINDS became popular, because the hive organization was seen as an analogue of social organization in Soviet Russia.

American genre sf has been much criticized, especially in Europe, for its political naïvety. Political attitudes are implicitly expressed by the shape of future societies, and in genre sf those societies tended in their political structure to be very simple projections of a *laissez-faire* capitalism which even in the USA had become to some extent outmoded after the great crash of 1929 (*see also* ECONOMICS). SPACE OPERAS might be set thousands of years in the future, but their attitudes would usually sit well with any Junior Chamber of Commerce; E.E. "Doc" SMITH's stories were rather of this kind. An early pulp writer who had obviously gone to some trouble to think out his political position (although he could never overcome his woodenness of style) was Stanton A. COBLENTZ, in whose novels *The Sunken World* (1928; **1949**) and *Hidden World* (1935; **1957**; vt *In Caverns Below*) there is much relatively orthodox debate about the rival merits of different political systems.

Isaac ASIMOV's "Foundation" series creates several different political systems on the fringes of a crumbling GALACTIC EMPIRE (it is fascinating how strongly the concept of future empires gripped the imagination of genre sf writers, despite the innate implausiblity of imperialism as a workable system over the distances between the stars), but basically he too seems to pin his faith on free trade and capitalism. It is wrong, however, to suppose that this fairly typical genre sf attitude was unexamined in the minds of its writers; it was often quite deliberate. Robert A. HEINLEIN, for one, had been very clearly influenced by the work of Ayn RAND in which she outlines her "objectivist" philosophy, notably in *Anthem* (**1938**; abridged 1946), *The Fountainhead* (**1943**) and *Atlas Shrugged* (**1957**). This was probably also true of John W. CAMPBELL Jr, the editor of *ASF*, who regularly expressed right-wing attitudes in his editorials. The whole of this question is discussed in detail in the entry SOCIAL DARWINISM. It is enough to say here that although Heinlein and indeed Campbell have been accused of fascism, their attitude is rather that of a

romantic, libertarian individualism. Heinlein hated centralized government because he so much liked the idea of the frontier mentality, where a man could be a man without interference. Heinlein's rulers are, very simply, the toughest – those best equipped to rule. The unfortunate corollary, of course, is that the weakest go to the wall.

This deeply conservative streak, going along with a celebration of rugged individualism, has been pronounced in some of genre sf's best-known writers, including L. Sprague DE CAMP, L. Ron HUBBARD, A.E. VAN VOGT (who wrote a non-sf novel about the Communist menace in China, *The Violent Man*, **1962**), Poul ANDERSON, Gordon DICKSON, Larry NIVEN, Jerry POURNELLE, Anne McCAFFREY and Marion Zimmer BRADLEY. It appears in a humorous form in the work of the English writer Eric Frank RUSSELL, but here the rugged individualism is carried to such magnificently absurd lengths that one feels him to be anti-authoritarian in all respects, and not at all inclined even to Heinlein's strong, disciplined man variety of power structure. Political attitudes in genre sf tend to come out especially clearly in stories of COLONIZATION OF OTHER WORLDS and the treatment of ALIENS; much of Poul Anderson's "Polesotechnic League" series is of this kind. Anderson is a strongly humanitarian writer, and a thoughtful one, and it would be unfair to encapsulate his political attitudes as "right wing" and leave them at that; none the less, in so far as they can be expressed in present-day American political terms, they are certainly conservative.

For a long time, especially with the domination of the (usually) right-wing magazine *ASF* over genre sf, left-wing attitudes received very little expression within the genre, especially in America. Mack REYNOLDS, whose novels often express Marxist attitudes, was for a long time a voice crying in the wilderness. Even C.M. KORNBLUTH, many of whose political attitudes appear quite liberal, wrote a Communist-scare sf novel, *Not this August* (**1955**; vt *Christmas Eve* UK); his *The Syndic* (**1953**) carried contempt for conventional, centralized government even further than Heinlein, being set in a future where the mafia is successfully running a kind of benevolent quasi-anarchy. Magazine sf 1940–60 was generally, then, in favour of political systems with a minimum of government interference, and a maximum freedom for strong and intelligent individuals to make their own way. But Heinlein, especially, is far from anarchic in the traditional European sense; he merely despises what he regards as the flabbier democratic procedures and believes the proposition that all men are created equal to be untrue, and has several times suggested that the franchise should not be automatic, but should be earned. His

novels regularly extol the virtues of authority, often in various forms of space corps with a power structure rather like that of the US marines. One outstanding genre sf political novel of these years which does not quite fit the usual hardbitten pattern is Ray BRADBURY's *Fahrenheit 451* (**1953**), about an officer of a totalitarian state becoming sickened by its refusal to allow independent thought; in the book's gentleness there is no trace of Social Darwinism, no hardheaded survival-of-the-fittest policies. (*For further discussion of the political attitudes of 1950s sf, see* PARANOIA AND SCHIZOPHRENIA.)

The Vietnam war brought about a polarization among genre sf writers, neatly encapsulated by two paid advertisements, taken out by two large groups in *Gal.*, Jun. 1968; one group opposed American participation in the Vietnam war; the other (including the majority of the names above) supported it. It would be simplistic to argue that this was a straightforward rift between the left and the right. The opponents of the war included James BLISH, who was in fact hostile to socialism, though years ago he had had the courage to satirize Senator McCarthy's anti-Communism in *They Shall have Stars* (1952–4; fix-up **1956**; vt *Year 2018!*), and Asimov who, though he had always been among the more liberal-minded genre sf writers, was hardly a political radical. However, they also included several writers, only later to become known for their political sf, who did something to redress the balance and help to swing genre sf away from its general conservatism and its general lack of questioning of the capitalist ethos, notably Norman SPINRAD and Ursula K. LE GUIN. Spinrad's *The Iron Dream* (**1972**) is especially interesting in the way it reveals how disguised political attitudes can emerge in sf; the book purports to be a HEROIC FANTASY written by Hitler, but it could easily have been by many genre writers of less renown, and that is the point; Spinrad's story "The Big Flash" (1969) is a memorable tale of cynical political manipulation via the youth culture. But by a long way the most subtle and probing political novel in genre sf is Le Guin's *The Dispossessed* (**1974**), which pits a Kropotkin-style anarchy on one planet against a conventional capitalist-socialist split on another; while she shows the radical failure of the latter she also, and more interestingly, shows the subtle distortions created by the former. *The Word for World is Forest* (1972; **1976**) is one of the strongest sf stories ever written about colonial exploitation, and contains several biting parallels to the situation in Vietnam.

The 1960s and '70s showed a marked opening up of political themes in genre sf in many respects, by no means always in terms of left-right polarities. Interestingly, some of the earlier signs of this were in sf novels of ALTERNATE WORLDS, as written by Mackinlay KANTOR, Philip K. DICK, Ward MOORE, Harry HARRISON and others; these are stories which show how history and politics might so easily have been otherwise, a view which came as rather a relief in a genre which, generally speaking, saw the future in terms of more and more of the same. Other writers who have constructed interesting political scenarios in the future, not at all in the line of development that runs from Heinlein to Pournelle, are John BRUNNER, Michael MOORCOCK, Fred HOYLE, Algis BUDRYS, Frank HERBERT, Cecelia HOLLAND and Marie JAKOBER. In terms of politics, genre sf is coming of age.

Two works which approach politics from unusual angles are James TIPTREE Jr's "The Peacefulness of Vivyan" (1971), a study in the psychology of political betrayal, and J.G. BALLARD's The Atrocity Exhibition (coll. of linked stories 1970; vt Love and Napalm: Export USA USA), which is in part about the way that images of political horror, in an age of near-instantaneous COMMUNICATIONS, become part of the data entering our heads as we live our comparatively peaceful lives at home; thus, mentally, we all live in a world of great political violence, and it has its repercussions on our everyday attitudes; there is a danger that we may become brutalized, needing ever more bizarre stimuli to arouse our feelings.

The sf CINEMA has not ignored political themes, though generally it has not treated them with any great sophistication. The few political sf films of the 1950s showed a rather naïve political idealism, though two of them, THE DAY THE EARTH STOOD STILL and THE 27TH DAY, involve some distinctly immoral political blackmail by aliens, which the directors approve. The late 1960s saw several political films built around manipulation of or by the youth culture, including PRIVILEGE, GAS-S-S! and WILD IN THE STREETS. More recent filmed political statements have tended to be either cynical, like ROLLERBALL, or inane, like LOGAN'S RUN.

Neither British nor American genre sf has given much thought to socialist systems of government. It is therefore interesting to turn to the sf of RUSSIA and EASTERN EUROPE. The STRUGATSKI brothers have used sf metaphors to make rather circuitous criticisms of aspects of the Soviet system, though they are certainly no great lovers of capitalism; recently they seem to have reached some sort of accommodation with the establishment, and their work is again receiving regular publication (as of 1977) in Russia. No accommodation was reached in the cases of Yuli DANIEL and Andrey SINYAVSKY, both now in exile. Stanislaw LEM's political satires are complex; they certainly have a Utopian element, but very little political absolutism, and in their occasional black

grotesqueness are markedly different from the bland optimism which is thought by many Western readers to be obligatory in Communist bloc sf; such optimism certainly did exist with many writers, notably Ivan YEFREMOV. But many Russian and Eastern European writers of both the past and the present, including Vladimir MAYAKOVSKY and Josef NESVADBA, are far too disturbing in their satire for any simple dismissal as Communist stereotypes. Indeed, sf is one of the few literary forms in the Communist bloc where it seems that (metaphoric) criticism of the system is possible. It does not behove us in the West to feel comfortable about this, since politics are not as simply dualistic as we might like to believe; a criticism of the Soviet system does not imply an open-hearted acceptance of capitalism, and such an acceptance has certainly not been signalled by any Communist bloc sf.

European sf generally has been very much more ready to consider alternative political systems than American, and sf criticism in Europe, especially in GERMANY, is very often Marxist. European sf writers of the left include Herbert FRANKE and Jean-Pierre ANDREVON.   [PN]
See also: CITIES; MESSIAHS.

POLLUTION The first sf story chronicling a catastrophe brought about by waste matter polluting the environment was Robert BARR's "The Doom of London" (1892), in which smog suffocates the city. This may, however, be regarded as a variant of a chain of stories (all by English authors) dealing with the perils of fog, ranging from W. Delisle HAY's The Doom of the Great City (1880) through Gerald HEARD's "The Great Fog" (1944) to John CREASEY's The Smog (1970). The pollutant effects of industrial waste were well enough known in 19th-century England. Air pollution had shaped the city of London (the prevailing wind blows east and the upper strata of the population moved steadily west) and slag defaced the northern counties to the extent that Yorkshiremen coined a proverb: "where there's muck, there's brass". It is hardly surprising that England produced the one enduring 19th-century image of civilization as pollution in Richard JEFFERIES' After London (1885). The image of city life presented in the socially conscious, traditional 19th-century novel, as for example by Charles Dickens, makes much of the foulness of city dirt, but the problem was generally seen as one that might easily be corrected. The notion that environmental pollution might be a serious threat in the future is not evident in early 20th-century speculative fiction – quite the reverse, in fact. It was assumed that dirt was very much a present-day problem, and that progress would sweep it away. The city of the future, in virtually

all UTOPIAN visions of the time, was remarkable for its cleanliness. It seemed reasonable to one inhabitant of a northern industrial city, signing himself "A Disciple" (of H. G. WELLS), to borrow the famous time machine in order to see The Coming Era; or, Leeds Beatified (1900). This optimism seems ironic now, but at the turn of the century things seemed to be getting better rather than worse, and it seemed to be little more than a matter of taking the trouble to act. American fiction of the period shows no awareness of the issue at all, but it was not until some time later that major American cities (especially Los Angeles) came to share the experiences of smog-bound London, although industrial towns in Pennsylvania and Ohio had bad pollution problems in the 19th century.

As late as the 1950s, serious attention had been given in sf to only one special agent of pollution: radioactive waste. The effects of the residual radiation of the Hiroshima explosion and the tests at Bikini atoll became well known, and the destruction of the environment by radiation poisoning became one of the most horrifying aspects of the post-atomic war scenario (see HOLOCAUST AND AFTER and MUTANTS). These stories probably helped to bring about a much increased sensitivity to the idea of insidious poisons in the environment, and it was not long before awareness grew of more commonplace dangers: arsenic in certain dyes used in wallpaper, lead in water pipes, etc.

The first sf cautionary tales about society's general philosophy of waste disposal began to appear in the 1950s. C.M. KORNBLUTH's "Shark Ship" (1958) is a particularly extreme example, and James WHITE's story of the hazards of orbital garbage, "Deadly Litter" (1960) has been transformed by the passage of time into a neat parable. It was in the early 1960s, however, that the problem was brought very sharply into focus, largely due to the publication of a single book, Rachael Carson's The Silent Spring (1962). One of the main points made by this book was that pollution of a radically new type had begun — pollution by chemical substances which are not biodegradable, and which tend to build up within living matter to fatal concentrations. These substances – particularly the chlorinated hydrocarbons – are not only deadly but, once produced, are with us for ever because they cannot be broken down to harmless substances by biochemical action. DDT, once widely used as an insecticide, was one of the main targets of attack in Carson's book. PBB, the compound recently responsible for poisoning large numbers of cattle and some people in Michigan, belongs to the same family of compounds. The awareness of this new threat was very rapidly absorbed into sf, and became a standard feature of NEAR-FUTURE scenarios virtually overnight.

One of the most notable early dramatizations of the issue is *The Clone* (**1965**) by Theodore L. THOMAS and Kate WILHELM, a horror story about pollutants which spontaneously generate life and become a giant amorphous mass transforming any and all organic matter into its own substance. A realistic treatment of the issues at stake is found in *Make Room!, Make Room!* (**1966**) by Harry HARRISON, which also deals with the closely related issue of OVERPOPULATION. Similar scare stories, often reflecting an anxiety close to hysteria, were produced by several authors: John BRUNNER in *The Sheep Look Up* (**1972**); Philip WYLIE in *Los Angeles: A.D. 2017* (**1971**) and *The End of a Dream* (**1972**); James BLISH in "We All Die Naked" (1969); Kurt VONNEGUT Jr in "The Big Space Fuck" (1972); Andrew J. OFFUTT in *The Castle Keeps* (**1972**); and Kit PEDLER and Gerry DAVIS in *Brainrack* (**1974**). The rapidity with which the subject became familiar is evidenced by the very early appearance of such satirical works as Charles PLATT's *Garbage World* (**1967**) and Norman SPINRAD's "The Lost Continent" (1970). More sophisticated treatments of the theme include *The Thinking Seat* (**1970**) by Peter TATE and "King's Harvest" (1972) by Gardner DOZOIS. It seems to be generally felt that the biggest danger is complacency – a point made by one of the most effective sf pollution stories, Dean MCLAUGHLIN's "To Walk With Thunder" (1973), in which the hero fights to suppress a device which will guarantee clean air inside the home, on the grounds that it would become an industrial *carte blanche* to pollute the atmosphere irredeemably. This is a major aspect of the general disillusionment with the prospects of industrial society (*see* DYSTOPIAS).

A collection, *Pollution: Omnibus* (anth. **1971**), was issued in the UK, but the logic of selection involved (it contains "Shark Ship" and *Make Room! Make Room!*, but also Clifford D. SIMAK's *City, 1952*) is not altogether clear. *The Ruins of Earth* (anth. **1971**) ed. Thomas M. DISCH is another theme anthology with a number of relevant stories.   [BS]
See also: ECOLOGY.

PONS, MAURICE (1927–). French novelist who has translated into French works by Jerzy KOSINSKI and others. His sf/fantasy novel *Rosa* (**1967**; trans. **1972**) presents a mythical 19th-century principality whose army is bedevilled by mysterious desertions, which are connected to Rosa, a tavern-keeper. The army discovers that soldiers having sex with her enter her literally and find Paradise in her womb; taking action, the army sends a poet into Rosa, wired to a bomb.   [JC]

POPE, GUSTAVUS W. (? – ?). American writer and physician, remembered for his two sf novels,

Journey to Mars (**1894**) and *Romances of the Planets, No. 2: Journey to Venus* (**1895**), which tell the adventures of an American officer on an advanced MARS (miscegenation being barred) and a primitive VENUS; he falls in love with a Martian princess, who travels with him to the younger world. Both books are remarkably silly.   [JC]

POPULAR MAGAZINE, THE US PULP magazine published by Street & Smith, ed. Henry Harrison Lewis and others. Appeared monthly, from Nov. 1903, becoming semi-monthly from 1 Oct. 1909, and weekly from 24 Sep. 1927. Reverted to semi-monthly from 7 Jul. 1928, and monthly from Feb. 1931 to Sep. 1931. Merged with *Complete Stories* from Oct. 1931.

PM, which was in competition with the Frank A. MUNSEY chain, regularly published fantasy and sf. Among its noteworthy contributions to the genre were stories in the "Craig Kennedy" series by Arthur B. REEVES, future-WAR stories by Edwin BALMER and the serialization of *Ayesha* (1905; **1905**) by H. Rider HAGGARD. Other contributors included Sax ROHMER, Edgar WALLACE, Roy NORTON, John COLLIER, and John Buchan.   [JE]

First issue, 1953.

POPULAR SCIENCE FICTION Australian DIGEST-size magazine. Eight numbered issues in all: six, 1953–5, published by Frew Publications, Sydney, and two, 1967, published by Page Publications, NSW: no editors named. The Frew series used both US reprints and original Australian material, the Page series reprinted from the Frew publications. A companion magazine was FUTURE SCIENCE FICTION.   [FHP]
Collectors should note: The first six issues were undated, but appeared two in '53, three in '54 and one in '55.

POPULATION EXPLOSION *See* OVERPOPULATION.

PORGES, ARTHUR (1915–). American teacher of mathematics and writer, until his retirement in 1975. He began publishing sf with "The Rats" for *Man's World* in 1951, and since that date published about 70 stories without as yet releasing any of them in book collections, so that his influence in the sf and fantasy field is less marked than it might be; he is a strong and inventive writer, especially of fantasy. Some of his stories were written under the names Peter Arthur and Pat Rogers. His best-known stories are "The Fly" (1952) and "The Ruum" (1953).   [JC]

PORTNOY, HOWARD N. (? –). American writer and teacher, involved in postgraduate linguistic studies. His first novel, *Hot Rain* (**1977**), seems to start off as a horror fantasy about apparently supernatural bolts of lightning, but eventually a scientific explanation is found in a secret military project.   [JC]

PORTUGAL *See* SPAIN, PORTUGAL AND SOUTH AMERICA.

POSITRONIC ROBOTS These are not really an item of general sf TERMINOLOGY, since few writers have had the cheek to borrow the idea from Isaac Asimov, their inventor. But because Asimov's robot stories are so celebrated (*see* ASIMOV *entry for details*), "positronic robot" must be one of the best-known technical terms in sf. The positron is the anti-particle of the electron, but the idea of positrons (highly unstable) being suitable material for the construction of a positronic brain with "enforced calculated neuronic paths" is sheer glorious double-talk, typical of sf of the period, as Dr Asimov would be the first to admit.   [PN]

POTTER, ROBERT (? – ?). Australian author and clergyman; canon of St Paul's, Melbourne. His novel *The Germ Growers* (**1892**) was originally published in Australia as by Robert Easterley and John Wilbraham, the names of the two protagonists, but the UK edition of the same year gave RP's name. A space-dwelling race of shape-changers invades Earth, setting up a number of beachheads where they cultivate dangerous bacteria; one of these, in the Australian outback, is discovered, and the adventures begin. This is not only the first Australian sf, and probably the first alien INVASION story (antedating H.G. WELLS's *The War of the Worlds*, **1898**, by six years); it is also one of the first books that is undeniably genre sf in every respect. It is rare now, and almost forgotten.   [PN]
See also: HISTORY OF SF.

POURNELLE, JERRY (E.) (1933–). American writer, with an undergraduate degree in engineering and a PhD from the University of Washington in psychology and political science, employed for 15

years in the US space programme, working for both government and private firms, and one-time political campaign manager. Before entering the sf field, JP wrote some technical non-fiction and some fiction, occasionally using pseudonyms and house names; his first books were the non-fiction text *The Strategy of Technology* (**1970**) with Stefan T. Possony, and two non-sf novels, *Red Heroin* (**1965**) and *Red Dragon* (**1970**), as by Wade Curtis, a name he also used for a few stories in *ASF*, where his first sf story, "Peace with Honor", appeared in 1971 under his own name. This story forms part of his most extended series, the "CoDominium" sequence, earlier parts of which are identified with its chief military protagonist, a cunning, honourable, mercenary and military genius named Falkenberg who, in a period of civilian stupidity and venality (a common theme in JP's work) conspires with the CoDominium military force to maintain a human presence in those worlds already colonized by Man. He appears in *West of Honor* (**1976**) and *The Mercenary* (1971–3 *ASF*; fix-up rev. **1977**), the latter book reworks "Peace with Honor". Stories not yet included in book form include "He Fell into a Dark Hole" (1973), "His Truth Goes Marching On" (1975) and "Silent Leges" (1976). *A Spaceship for the King* (**1973**) is set considerably later, and features a tough military genius whose resemblance to Falkenberg is obviously of thematic importance, as JP argues implicitly through this series for a hierarchical structuring of society, and for the maintenance of such military virtues as honour. These arguments are most clearly on view in what is currently the series' climax, *The Mote in God's Eye* (**1974**), with Larry NIVEN, set in a period when the CoDominium has evolved into a full-blown GALACTIC EMPIRE with all the trappings. The fascinating ALIENS depicted in that novel reflect his collaborator's conceptual ingenuity as clearly as the Empire reflects JP's sustained fictional argument for that kind of solution to the problems of just government. A further novel with Niven, *Inferno* (**1976**), replays Dante's version and is not sf, although its damned hero is an sf writer, who keeps seeking sf type explanations for the hell he finds himself in; their third collaboration, *Lucifer's Hammer* (**1977**), is a long DISASTER novel in which a comet impacts with the Earth.

A second, more pessimistic series is in progress and substitutes corporate warfare for military/political conflict; most of the stories of this "Laurie Jo Hansen" sequence have been assembled in *High Justice* (coll. of linked stories **1977**), and a novel, "Exiled to Glory", has been published in *Gal.* (Sep./Oct. 1977). JP was first recipient of the JOHN W. CAMPBELL AWARD for the best new sf writer in 1973; in both his solo and his collaborative works he has rapidly

become one of sf's most popular exponents of the politically conservative-libertarian, hard-technology story.

JP is also well known for his thoughtful and clearly expressed science fact column, "A Step Further Out", which has appeared in *Gal.* since Apr. 1974.   [JC]
Other works: *Escape from the Planet of the Apes* (**1974**), a novelization of the film; *Birth of Fire* (**1976**). As editor: *2020 Vision* (anth. **1974**)
See also: COMMUNICATIONS; ESCHATOLOGY; GODS AND DEMONS; MYTHOLOGY; OUTER PLANETS; OVERPOPULATION; POLITICS; SOCIAL DARWINISM; SPACESHIPS; STARS; WAR.

POWER, THE Film (1967). Galaxy/MGM. Directed by Byron HASKIN, starring George Hamilton, Suzanne Pleshette and Michael Rennie. Screenplay by John Gay, based on the novel by Frank M. ROBINSON. 103 mins. Colour.

This George PAL production, made in 1967, is without the lavish, spectacular special effects of Pal's earlier films, concentrating instead on the tightly plotted story of a mutant supermind, masquerading as an ordinary human, who is destroying one by one a group of scientists who suspect his existence. One scientist survives all the murder attempts, the reason being, as he himself finally learns, that he too is a mutant. The film ends with a battle of wills between the two superminds — a literally heart-stopping event. The interesting script and taut direction led one critic to call it "one of the finest of all sf films".   [JB]

Richard M. POWERS effectively introduced the abstract cover to American sf publishing, as in this Ballantine Book, 1957.

POWERS, RICHARD M. (1921–). American illustrator. He studied fine arts at the Art Institute of Chicago, the

University of Illinois and other schools before taking up commercial art. He soon began work in sf illustration, where he found he could experiment with various techniques and in abstract or surreal modes of expression; his style, at that time unique in sf, was influenced by Yves Tanguy, De Chirico, Arshile Gorky and Francis Bacon, and quickly became one of the trademarks of BALLANTINE BOOKS in the 1950s. He has also painted hundreds of cover illustrations for *Beyond Fantasy Fiction*, *Galaxy*, Berkley Books, MacFadden Books, Permabooks, Avon, Dell Books and many others. RP has rarely painted a representational cover illustration; his paintings are full of amorphous shapes, floating in space or over some vague, surreal landscape. He has had 15 exhibitions in New York's Rehn Gallery and about 20 more in various others; his works command as much respect outside sf as in it. It was with RP's work, in one sense, that the packaging of sf could be said to come of age. Sf no longer necessarily required glamorous space girls or menacing technological hardware on book and magazine covers to sell it, and surreal covers capture its disturbing essence, in their own way, just as strongly as ray-guns or monsters.   [JG/PN]

POWER SOURCES In today's world the question of energy resources is a particularly thorny one. We can foresee the day when the fossil fuels — coal, oil and natural gas — will run out. We can now generate power by nuclear fission, but there are problems involved in so doing: the production of radioactive wastes, and the wide distribution of the materials necessary for making atomic bombs. Other options open to us rely on discoveries not yet made: the development of nuclear fusion reactors, or the development of efficient ways to store solar heat. It is, however, only recently that these issues have become matters of public concern, and there is no trace of them in sf published before public concern began to grow. The problems envisaged by sf writers before the last two decades involved coping with *unlimited* energy resources.

For most of human history, machines were worked by three "basic" power sources: wind, water and muscle, of which the last was the most important. For thousands of years Man used fire as a source of heat and an agent of physical and chemical change without learning how to harness it as an energy source in mechanical work. The acquisition of that knowledge — the invention of the steam engine — was the essence of the industrial revolution. The electrical revolution brought vastly more sophisticated means of energy redeployment, but did nothing to break away from the traditional energy *sources*. (It should also be noted that the "sources" themselves are redeployment mechanisms. Fire and muscle-power each involve the release of organically stored energy — solar energy initially fixed by photosynthesis — and the elevation of water prior to the exploitation of its kinetic energy is also the work of solar heat.) In the imagination, however, the situation seemed very different. Of all the writers inspired to scientific romance there was hardly one unwilling to assume that new sources of energy were readily available and discoverable — that power might literally be drawn from the ether. The triviality of the problem, so far as the 19th-century imagination is concerned, may be judged from the casualness of the jargon employed to excuse literary inventions.

In Bulwer LYTTON's *The Coming Race* (1871) the key to energy-prosperity is vril, a kind of "atmospheric magnetism" administered by a device bearing a suspicious resemblance to a magic wand. The wand is waved to considerable effect in *The Vril Staff* (1891) by "XYZ". In Percy GREG's *Across the Zodiac* (1880) the mysterious power source is apergy, which seems to be straightforward ANTIGRAVITY, with a little electrical mysticism thrown in as seasoning. Like vril, apergy was borrowed by other writers, including John Jacob ASTOR in *A Journey in Other Worlds* (1894). Other antigravity devices are used in the anonymous *The History of a Voyage to the Moon* (1864), Robert CROMIE's *A Plunge into Space* (1890) and H.G. WELLS's *The First Men in the Moon* (1901). Even Jules VERNE was ready to assume that electrical energy could be drawn directly from sea water in *Twenty Thousand Leagues Under the Sea* (1870 France; trans. 1873).

This optimistic outlook was boosted by the discovery of X-rays in 1895, and for many years thereafter unlimited power could be generated in sf stories by the invocation of a handy ray. The discovery of radioactivity only a few years later provided yet another jargon: power derived from atomic breakdown, spontaneous or forced. This, at least, turned out to be a real possibility (*see* NUCLEAR POWER), but its prominence in early sf owes far more to convenience than to any assessment by sf writers of its real potential. Pulp sf inherited a considerable jargon and made particularly free with it. E.E. "Doc" SMITH's *The Skylark of Space* (1928; 1946; rev. with cuts 1958) begins magnificently, as a bathtub is hurled into oblivion when X, the unknown metal, reacts to the appropriate stimulus by releasing limitless quantities of "infra-atomic energy". All this is clearly magic in disguise, and even the agents of power-redeployment were often invested with magical capabilities — notably electricity, as in Mary SHELLEY's *Frankenstein* (1818; rev. 1831) and Conan DOYLE's "The Los Amigos Fiasco" (1892).

Given this literary confidence in the imminent availability of unlimited power, it is not surprising that the most thoughtful work of speculative writers in the early 20th century deals with the question of the responsibility of scientists making such discoveries. Stories of wise men blackmailing the world into peace and social justice for all are common, but a much more delicate exercise is Karel ČAPEK's rather surreal novel *Krakatit* (1924; trans. 1925; vt *An Atomic Phantasy*), to which history lent such relevance that it was re-released in 1948 with the subtitle given new prominence. Another "atomic phantasy" by Čapek was *The Absolute at Large* (1922; trans. 1927), concerning the invention of a Karburator, which releases the energy bound in matter, but also a kind of diffuse godliness — the spiritual "power" which went into the creation of the matter — which causes worldwide religious fanaticism. A recent fantasy with a related theme is Romain GARY's *The Gasp* (1973), in which the energy of the immortal soul is harnessed as a power source by science.

Magazine sf, in its handling of the theme of power-generation, developed a strong element of doublethink. Under the influence of John W. CAMPBELL Jr, stories dealing with atomic power became much more realistic, but in the matter of other power sources there were no holds barred. Antigravity and wonderful rays continued to defy the conservation laws. This situation was not inhibited but encouraged by the actual discovery of atomic power, which was for a brief period taken as "proof" that limitless energy was actually available. Jack WILLIAMSON's "The Equalizer" (1947), the best of sf's attempts to analyse the social consequences of free power for all, actually resurrects the vril staff as a literary device. A classic story of the post-War decade, Raymond F. JONES's "Noise Level" (1952), was based on the supposition that all that stood between science and the discovery of limitless power (antigravity) is the belief of scientists in its impossibility. In the story the scientists are made to believe otherwise, and the discovery naturally follows. So convincing was the line of argument to *ASF* readers, it seems, that the sequels to the story are polemical works criticizing patent law on the grounds that such a discovery, once made, ought to be patentable.

This optimism died during the 1960s as the intellectual climate changed, and it became obvious that the immediate problem was energy conservation rather than coping with a glut. The dependence of the developed countries on shrinking coal and oil supplies was brought home dramatically by the emergence of OPEC (the Organization of Petroleum-Exporting Countries) as a political force capable of dictating energy policy to the Western world. With this realization came the total deflation of science-fictional optimism, and many stories now see the NEAR FUTURE as a period of transition into a breakdown of what we think of as civilization. Such pessimism runs deep: few writers seem to have any faith in our ability to conserve resources, and few are prepared to assume blithely that fusion power or efficient techniques in the exploitation of solar energy are just around the corner. The post-disaster scenario which long ago became a standard in sf (*see* DISASTER; HOLOCAUST AND AFTER) is increasingly connected in contemporary sf with the aftermath of a purely social breakdown, without the aid of plague or nuclear war. Only in the matter of SPACESHIP propulsion does any real measure of imaginative fervour survive with respect to miraculous power sources, ranging from the solar yachts of Arthur C. CLARKE's "Sunjammer" (1964; vt "The Wind from the Sun"), which use the SOLAR WIND, to the BLACK-HOLE propulsion system for interplanetary vessels in the same author's *Imperial Earth* (1975). An awareness of energy economics permeates contemporary sf even at the level of mass-produced adventure stories. The fashion will undoubtedly wear off, but as long as the issues remain relevant in the real world they will never again be ignored by sf writers generally.   [BS]

See also: ECOLOGY; MACHINES; SUN; TECHNOLOGY; UNDER THE SEA; WEAPONS.

POWYS,   JOHN   COWPER (1872–1963). British writer, resident for much of his career in the USA, though he returned to Britain in his later years. In the novels of his old age, from *Morwyn: Or the Vengeance of God* (1937) to *All or Nothing* (1960), he utilized fantasy and some sf elements in an attempt, sometimes obscure, to combine mythology and mysticism into a unique amalgam. *Atlantis* (1954) describes Odysseus's search for that island. Of specific sf interest are *Up and Out* (coll. 1957), the first novella of which is a post-HOLOCAUST tale in which four survivors witness the end of time, and *All or Nothing* (1960) in which two children make a kind of tour of the universe. [JC]
Other works: (with fantasy elements) *A Glastonbury Romance* (1932); *Maiden Castle* (1936); *Owen Glendower* (1940); *Porius* (1951); *The Inmates* (1952); *The Brazen Head* (1956); *Homer and the Aether* (1959).
See also: ATLANTIS; END OF THE WORLD; FANTASTIC VOYAGES.

POYER, JOE Form of his name used by American writer Joseph J. Poyer (1939–) for his fiction, beginning with "Mission 'Red Clash'" for *ASF*, a magazine with which he has been closely associated, in 1965. His novels, *Operation Malacca* (1968), about talking dolphins, and *North Cape* (1969), are both NEAR-FUTURE stories, with international thriller components. He has also written novels in other genres. [JC]

See also: UNDER THE SEA.

PRAGNELL, FESTUS (1905–). English writer and policeman, who first appeared in the American PULPS with "The Venus Germ" for *Wonder Stories* in 1932, written in collaboration with R.F. STARZL; he published one tale as by Francis Parnell. His "Don Hargreaves" stories, all set on a lurid Mars, appeared in *AMZ* from 1938 ("Ghost of Mars") to 1943 ("Madcap of Mars"). His first sf novel, *The Green Man of Kilsona* (**1936**; rev. vt *The Green Man of Graypec* 1950 USA), describes a voyage into a miniature world; a second novel, *The Terror from Timorkal* (**1946**), sets a world-threatening crisis in Africa, where a new mineral suitable for the manufacture of superweapons is being exploited by unscrupulous politicians. His last work, "The Machine God Laughs" (1948), was the title story of *The Machine God Laughs* (anth. **1949**) ed. William L. CRAWFORD. FP is not a pseudonym. [JC]

Other works: *Thieves of the Air* (undated), wartime 27-page booklet with Benson HERBERT.

PRATT, CORNELIA ATWOOD Maiden name, by which she signed her books, of Cornelia Atwood Comer (? – ?), author, with Richard SLEE, of *Dr Berkeley's Discovery* (**1899**), in which the doctor solves a mystery with his memory-cell-reading device (*see* PSYCHOLOGY). [JC]

PRATT, FLETCHER (1897–1956). American writer and historian. He started his career as an author and translator for Hugo GERNSBACK'S SCIENCE WONDER STORIES and its companions in the early 1930s; his first published story was "The Octopus Cycle" (1928) with Irvin Lester in *AMZ*. (Actually, Irvin Lester was a Pratt pseudonym.) With his translations of German sf novels he evolved a renowned method of extracting payment from the notoriously slow Gernsback organization. He would submit the first part of a novel, wait until it was set in type, then refuse to deliver the conclusion until he was paid. FP undertook many collaborations, notably "City of the Living Dead" (1930) with Laurence MANNING. He contributed regularly to the sf magazines, but is now best remembered for his fantasy, especially his collaborations with L. Sprague DE CAMP (*who see for details*). The most successful of these were the "Harold Shea" stories: *The Incomplete Enchanter* (1940 *Unknown*; **1942**), *The Castle of Iron* (1941 *Unknown*; **1950**) and *Wall of Serpents* (1953–4 var. mags; fix-up **1960**). His own fantasy novels are *The Well of the Unicorn* (**1948** under the pseudonym George U. Fletcher; 1967 as by FP) and *The Blue Star* (1952; **1969**), which originally appeared in *Witches*

Three (anth. **1952**), a book anonymously edited by FP. This was one of the "Twayne Triplets" (Twayne being the publisher), collections of three original novellas by different authors with a common theme or setting. The idea was FP's, and he edited (also anonymously) another such book, *The Petrified Planet* (anth. **1952**). The project proved abortive, but the idea was later revived with greater success by Robert SILVERBERG. FP also wrote several volumes of popular history and three books on rockets and space travel, most notably *Rockets, Jets, Guided Missiles and Space Ships* (**1951**), which was a runner-up for the INTERNATIONAL FANTASY AWARD non-fiction category. [MJE]

Other works: With L. Sprague de Camp: *The Land of Unreason* (**1941**); *The Carnelian Cube* (**1948**); *Tales from Gavagan's Bar* (coll. **1953**).
FP alone: *Double in Space* (coll. **1951**; two novellas, one of which is replaced in the British edition with "The Conditioned Captain", later published as *The Undying Fire* in the US); ed. *World of Wonder* (anth. **1951**); *Double Jeopardy* (coll. **1952**); *The Undying Fire* (**1953**); *Invaders From Rigel* (1932 *Wonder Stories Quarterly* as "The Onslaught From Rigel"; **1960**); *Alien Planet* (1932 *Amazing Stories Quarterly* as "A Voice Across The Years"; **1962**).

About the author: Chapter 7 of *Literary Swordsmen and Sorcerors* (**1976**) by L. Sprague de Camp.

See also: ALTERNATE WORLDS; AUTOMATION; CLONES; COLONIZATION OF OTHER WORLDS; DYSTOPIAS; HUMOUR; MAGIC; MATHEMATICS; MYTHOLOGY; SWORD AND SORCERY; UTOPIAS.

PREDICTION The most widespread false belief about sf among the general public is that it is a literature of prediction. Very few sf writers have ever claimed this to be the case, although Hugo GERNSBACK did see the function of his sf magazines as being not only to entertain and to impart scientific knowledge, but also to paint an accurate picture of the future. Very few of his stories he published lived up to his editorializing. When John W. CAMPBELL Jr took over the editorship of *ASF* he demanded an increasing scientific plausibility from his writers, but a plausible-sounding "perhaps" is a long way from prediction.

None of this has prevented sf fans from crowing with delight when an sf writer made a good guess, and the mythology of sf is full of such examples, which tend to be repeated *ad nauseam*. H.G. WELLS predicted the use of the tank in "The Land Ironclads" (1903), of aerial bombing in *The War in the Air* (**1908**) and of the atom bomb in *The World Set Free* (**1914**). It was generally well known that enormous power was locked up in the atom, ever since Einstein's mass-energy equations were published, and

stories about atomic power and atomic weapons were commonplace in the 1920s and '30s; they became very much more accurate in the early 1940s, and Cleve CARTMILL, Robert A. HEINLEIN and Lester del REY all wrote good predictive stories before Hiroshima, as is described in the entry on NUCLEAR POWER.

Most early prediction stories were about future WAR, future WEAPONS and the various possibilities of INVASION. Not many of them were correct; several stories predicted war between England and Germany before 1914 (and, indeed, between England and almost everyone else), but most of these centered on an invasion across the Channel which never took place.

Edward Everett HALE wrote about an artificial satellite, rather charmingly, in "The Brick Moon" (1869), as also did Kurd LASSWITZ, rather more convincingly, in *Auf zwei Planeten* (**1897**; trans. abridged as *Two Planets* **1971**); Arthur C. CLARKE wrote a celebrated article about communications satellites, "Extraterrestrial Relays" (*Wireless World* Oct. 1945), but this was not a story.

Jules VERNE was thought by many to have invented the submarine in *Vingt mille lieues sous les mers* (**1870**; trans. as *Twenty Thousand Leagues Under the Sea* **1873**), but this was sheer ignorance; submarines already existed when Verne wrote. One of Verne's best pieces of prediction was quite accidental; the moon-shot in *De la terre à la lune* (**1865**), which was published with the sequel *Autour de la lune* (**1870**) in *From the Earth to the Moon* (trans. **1873**), is fired from a spot very close to Cape Canaveral in Florida.

Rudyard Kipling predicted transatlantic aerial trade, specifically airmail postage, in *With the Night Mail* (1905, **1909**). Erasmus DARWIN's predictions in the poem *The Temple of Nature* (**1802**) preceded Verne, Wells and just about everybody else in its joyful description of airborne fleets of transport ships, war in the air, submarines and great cities with skyscrapers. Edwin BALMER had an early form of lie detector in *The Achievements of Luther Trant* (coll. **1910**), written with William MacHarg. Hugo Gernsback had many technological predictions in *Ralph 124C 41 +* (1911–12; fix-up **1925**), including television. Nevil SHUTE predicted metal fatigue as a danger to aircraft in *No Highway* (**1948**), written shortly before several planes, including a Comet, crashed for exactly that reason.

It is a moderately impressive list, and could be made more so by multiplication of examples, but it proves very little. For every correct prediction a dozen were wrong, or correct only if facts are stretched a little; for example, PULP sf of the 1930s made much of death rays. It is rather a dubious vindication of this melodramatic device to point out that laser beams can now be used as an item of weaponry. The entry FUTUROLOGY discusses the usual strategy of the sf writer when dealing with the future; his imaginative scenarios are as often as not meant as awful warnings; the emphasis is almost invariably on what *could* happen, not what *will* happen. It would hardly be fair to attack sf writers as false prophets when they seldom think of themselves as being in the prophecy business at all. In many ways their errors are more interesting than their successes, for they add to our knowledge of social history. Our expectations of the future change just as quickly as history itself changes; the AUTOMATION to which Gernsback and others looked forward in the teens of the century had already become a potential nightmare by the time of Kurt VONNEGUT Jr's *Player Piano* (**1952**; vt *Utopia 14*). An entry which discusses the nostalgic charm of sf's mistakes is SF OVERTAKEN BY EVENTS. Where sf is correct, of course, the explanation is not magic, just good research. Jules Verne took much advice from his engineer friends; Nevil Shute spent many years as an aeronautical engineer; most sf writers subscribe to the more popular scientific.journals, such as *Scientific American, New Scientist* and *Nature*.

The one area where sf can claim credit is SPACE FLIGHT; this had been a dream most fervently believed in by many, even during the years when respectable scientists regularly argued for its impossibility (*see* ROCKETS *for details*). But even here, though sf was right enough in the broad sense, it managed to get both the sociological and the technological details appallingly wrong. Most of Robert A. HEINLEIN's early Moon rockets were built by capitalist enterprise, and not by the resources of the American government; the Russian government, naturally, was not mentioned at all, even though it was in Russia that the first solidly grounded theorizing about space travel had taken place, in the work of Konstantin TSIOLKOVSKY, who wrote sf stories on the subject. Heinlein's *Rocket Ship Galileo* (**1947**), absurdly, is largely constructed by teenage boys in the backyard. Not one sf story about the first Moon landing imagined the single most dramatic detail: that the entire proceedings would be watched on Earth on TV.

COMPUTERS are another area where sf's predictive abilities were ridiculously askew; so preoccupied were sf writers with the dramatic possibilities of the ROBOT that they hardly noticed that back in the real world mechanical men were of little interest to anyone, while the computer was rapidly transforming the face of the future. Sf writers caught up, of course, but only after computers were becoming commonplace.

Nearly all the above examples are cases of predictions in the sphere of TECHNOLOGY; more interesting perhaps, and generally with a slightly higher rate of good guesses, were the predictions made about future POLITICS and SOCIOLOGY. Fortunately most DYSTOPIAS have not come into being in the real world, but certain aspects of them certainly have. One of the most interesting cases of prediction in the SOFT SCIENCES was Robert Louis STEVENSON's *Dr. Jekyll and Mr. Hyde* (**1886**), whose melodramatic suppositions were, even as he wrote, being given notable support by the work of Sigmund Freud, to whom it came as no surprise that the mind of Man might have passionate and uncontrollable components which could occasionally escape the control of the well-trained ego.

Occasionally the images thrown up by sf enter the public mind by an apparent process of osmosis, so that they become known even to those who do not read sf, to such an extent that they create a kind of self-fulfilling prophecy. Some examples are given in FUTUROLOGY, which discusses this question. Perhaps the most notable is again the case of space flight, where it is certainly arguable that the American government could never have got away with budgeting such large amounts of the national income on the space programme if the *desire* for space flight, largely catalysed by sf, had not been so great among the people.

Most sf prediction is set in the NEAR FUTURE, and further examples are given in that entry. In the nature of things, a great many themes in this Encyclopedia necessarily deal in part with prediction. Apart from those already mentioned, entries where predictions in the social sciences predominate include CITIES; DISASTER, ECONOMICS, GAMES AND SPORTS, LEISURE, MEDIA LANDSCAPE and OVERPOPULATION; more technical areas where sf has made predictions which in many cases have already been shown to be true or false are COMMUNICATIONS, CYBERNETICS, ECOLOGY, MACHINES, MEDICINE, MOON, POLLUTION, POWER SOURCES, TRANSPORTATION and UNDER THE SEA; areas where sf predictions have not yet had the opportunity for a full testing, but may be tested in the next 50 years, are CLONES, CRYONICS, CYBORGS, SPACESHIPS, SUSPENDED ANIMATION, TERRAFORMING and WEATHER CONTROL.

Much of the above has used the word prediction loosely. If an sf writer imagines something which later comes into being, then we may call that a prediction, but only with hindsight. Very few writers would wish the fruits of their imagination to be read as statements taking the form: "this will happen". Almost invariably, they take the form: "it would be interesting if this did happen". Quite often, the mental attitude behind sf creations is: "I don't suppose this will ever happen, but I will use all my skills as a writer to make it seem plausible, because the images produced have an attractive resonance in my mind". [PN]

PREHISTORIC ROMANCES See ANTHROPOLOGY; ORIGIN OF MAN.

PRESIDENT'S ANALYST, THE Film (1967). Panpiper/Paramount. Directed by Theodore J. Flicker, starring James Coburn, Godfrey Cambridge, Severn Darden, Joan Delaney, Pat Harrington and Barry McGuire. Screenplay by Theodore J. Flicker. 104 mins. Colour.

This amusing satire is even more relevant now than when it was made. A psychoanalyst hired to listen to the President's troubles soon breaks down under the strain. He flees Washington and takes refuge with a "typical" American family who describe themselves as militant liberals (the husband has a vast collection of guns, the wife takes karate lessons and their son specializes in wire-tapping). Pursued by the FBI (all very short men), the CIA (all college graduates with pipes and tweed jackets), the Russians and the Chinese, the hero barely avoids death on several occasions before discovering that the real power behind America is the Telephone Company, which turns out to be manned by bland, smiling robots. The hero apparently wrecks the Company's plan to insert a miniature telephone in the head of every person in the world, but the film ends with the robots still in control. Flicker's script is witty and literate. [JB]

PRIEST, CHRISTOPHER (1943–). English writer. CP, then working as an accountant, began to publish short stories in 1966 with "The Run" for *Impulse*. Several of these are included in *Real-Time World* (coll. **1974**; a German translated version, *Transplantationen*, had already appeared, **1972**).

CP's first novel was *Indoctrinaire* (**1970**). His second novel, *Fugue for a Darkening Island* (**1972**; vt *Darkening Island* USA), is usually thought to be much stronger. It is set in an England of the NEAR FUTURE, and deals with politics and racial tension, focused on the arrival of African refugees whose homeland has been destroyed by nuclear war. It came third in the 1973 JOHN W. CAMPBELL MEMORIAL AWARD for the best sf novel of the year.

CP's next novel, *Inverted World* (**1974**; vt *The Inverted World* USA), is generally considered to be his major work so far. The hyperboloid world on which the action takes place is perhaps the strangest planet invented since Mesklin in Hal CLEMENT's *Mission of Gravity* (**1954**). *Inverted World* deals with paradoxes of PERCEPTION and CONCEPTUAL BREAKTHROUGH, and is an interesting addition to that branch of sf which deals with the old theme of appearance versus reality. *Inverted World* won the BRITISH SCIENCE FICTION AWARD in 1975. *The Space Machine* (**1976**) is a cleverly plotted pastiche of the work of H.G. WELLS (himself a character in the book) and proposes plot-explanations for some of the narrative gaps left by Wells in *The Time Machine* (**1895**) and *War of the Worlds* (**1898**). It had a mixed critical reception, but won a DITMAR in 1977.

CP's most recent work is *A Dream of Wessex* (**1977**; vt *The Perfect Lover* USA), which deals with a meshing of 39 human minds in a computer in 1983, which projects them (or their mental simulacra) into a world of their consensus imagination, set 150 years in the future, in which they "live", not remembering the real world. The entire book is a metaphor about the creative process and its relation to solipsism, and in this latter respect continues some of the themes of *Inverted World*.

The first stories in a projected series, "The Dream Archipelago", which is to include two novels, are scheduled for appearance in late 1977/78. CP has also written pseudonymous novels in other genres; none contain sf, though some are rumoured to contain elements of fantasy. The author will not confirm the existence of these works.

CP is a council member of the SCIENCE FICTION FOUNDATION, and was for two years associate editor of its journal, FOUNDATION: THE REVIEW OF SCIENCE FICTION.   [PN]
See also: DISASTER; FANTASTIC VOYAGES; FOURTH DIMENSION (AND OTHERS); INVASION; MARS; MEDIA LANDSCAPE; POLITICS.

PRIESTLEY, J(OHN) B(OYNTON) (1894–). English novelist, playwright and man of letters, formidably productive from the teens of the century; known mainly for such works outside the sf fields as his picaresque novel *The Good Companions* (**1929**). He is married to Jacquetta HAWKES. Many of his novels and plays use sf/fantasy elements, though often in a delusional frame, as with *Albert Comes Through* (**1933**), in which experiences in an absurd cinematic universe are explained as a fever-dream. Similarly borderline are *Adam in Moonshine* (**1927**), *Benighted* (**1927**; vt *The Old Dark House* USA), some of the "time" stories in *The Other Place* (coll. **1953**), *Saturn Over the Water* (**1961**), *The Thirty-First of June* (**1961**) and *The Shapes of Sleep* (**1962**). Sf elements are more pointed in some novels like *The Doomsday Men* (**1938**), where DISASTER is in the air, or *Low Notes on a High Level* (**1954**), where a Dobbophone emits implausibly low notes of music. Several of JBP's plays are concerned with J.W. Dunne's theories about the nature of time, within an sf/fantasy frame, most notably *Time and The Conways* and *I Have Been Here Before*, published together as *Two Time Plays* (coll. **1937**) and, with *Dangerous Corner* (**1932**), as *Three Time Plays* (coll. **1947**). Johnson, in *Johnson Over Jordan* (**1939**), posthumously prepares himself for Heaven. A long essay, *Over the Long High Wall* (**1972**), meditates speculatively on the same themes.

The three magicians of *The Magicians* (**1954**) use a wonder drug to spiritually invade the mind of a tycoon, in what is JBP's closest approach to a full-fledged sf novel, along with the juvenile, *Snoggle* (**1971**), in which three children and an old man save an ALIEN pet from bigoted Wiltshire locals, and are thanked for their troubles by its masters, advanced beings in a flying saucer. JBP's use of sf is generally didactic in its intent; his protagonists tend, through their experience of extraordinary events, to come to better understandings of their own lives and roles.   [JC].

PRIME PRESS Short-lived American specialist publishing house, whose few titles are of interest. They include the first published books of Lester DEL REY, George O. SMITH and Theodore STURGEON: respectively, *... And Some Were Human* (coll. **1948**), *Venus Equilateral* (coll. **1947**) and *Without Sorcery* (coll. **1948**).   [MJE]

PRISONER, THE Television series (1967). An ITC Production. Created by, starring and partly written and directed by Patrick McGoohan, produced by David Tomblin. Script editor: George Markstein. Other writers included George Markstein, Anthony Skene, Paddy Fitz and Terence Feely. Other directors included Don Chaffey, Peter Graham Scott and Joseph Serf. 17 episodes, each 50 mins long. Colour.

In this KAFKA-esque, sf-related series a secret agent working for the British, who for unknown reasons resigns from his organization, is gassed in his apartment and wakes to find himself in The Village: a mysterious establishment whose geographical location is ambiguous and whose inhabitants consist of either rebels like himself or stooges of "them" — the people who run the place. The former spy (McGoohan had previously in real life starred in a series called *Secret Agent*) is unable to discover just who "they" are — perhaps the Communists and perhaps his own government. His every movement in The Village, which appears externally as a cross between a bland Mediterranean holiday camp and an old people's home, is watched by "Number Two", and his staff, by electronic means. Various episodes concerned the efforts of the different Number Twos (they changed with each episode) to break him and discover why he resigned, and his attempts to escape from The Village. The most obvious sf elements are the balloon-shaped robot watchdogs that guard the establishment and the complex scientific brainwashing equipment which includes devices for projecting thoughts on to a screen.

The series may have been wrongly interpreted by its many liberal supporters. It was not so much an anti-prison series, a plea for freedom, as a celebration of the power of a strong man to resist incursions into his mind, though the surrealist last episode suggests that the metaphorical prison is partly a creation of the mind itself, including the hero's. McGoohan, both a puritan and a political conservative, once said in relation to the series, "I believe in democracy but the inherent danger is that with an excess of freedom in all directions we will eventually destroy ourselves." The series was not popular with either the mass audience or the ITC management when it was first shown in Britain, but it developed a vocal and enthusiastic cult following. It has been repeated several times since, and was also shown in the USA. Its confident manipulations of surrealist and sf themes, its literate scripts and its enjoyably obsessive evocations of

Patrick McGoohan is subjected to a thought-reading machine in THE PRISONER.

a whole range of fantasies of PARANOIA together created what in the opinion of many — often those discontented with SPACE OPERA — is the finest sf television series to date. Books based on the series are *The Prisoner* **(1969)** by Thomas M. DISCH and *The Prisoner No. 2* **(1969)** by David McDANIEL. [JB/PN]

PRISONS See COLONIZATION OF OTHER WORLDS; CRIME AND PUNISHMENT.

PRIVILEGE Film (1967). Worldfilm Services and Memorial Enterprises/ Universal. Directed by Peter WATKINS, starring Paul Jones, Jean Shrimpton, Mark London and Max Bacon. Screenplay by Norman Bogner, based on a story by Johnny Speight. 103 mins. Colour.

In this rather PARANOID film, a rock star is used by a NEAR-FUTURE British government to control and mould the opinions of its youthful citizens. The singer is forced to change his image to suit the sinister plans of the Establishment, rebels and is destroyed by his teenage followers. Watkins, who also directed THE WAR GAME, GLADIATORERNA and PUNISHMENT PARK, labours at his simplistic theme with a heavy hand. [JB]

PRIX APOLLO Originated in France by Jacques SADOUL in 1971 to commemorate Apollo XI, this literary award is given on an annual basis to the best sf novel of the year published in France. The 11 members of the jury are writers Michel BUTOR, Alain Robbe-Grillet, René BARJAVEL, Michel DEMUTH, critics Jacques Sadoul, Francis Lacassin, Jacques Goimard, Jean-Jacques Brochier, journalists Jacques Bergier, Michel Lancelot and scientist François Le Lionnais.

The following books have been awarded the prize: 1972 *Isle of the Dead* by Roger ZELAZNY; 1973 *Stand on Zanzibar* by John BRUNNER; 1974 *The Iron Dream* by Norman SPINRAD; 1975 *The Embedding* by Ian WATSON; 1976 *Nightwings* by Robert SILVERBERG; 1977 *Cette chère humanité* ["This Dear Humanity"] by Philippe CURVAL. [MJ]

PRIX JULES VERNE Originally organized by the French publishers Hachette to obtain material for their magazine *Lectures pour tous*, this award was made seven times between 1927 and 1933 to novels written in the spirit of Jules VERNE: 1927 *La petite-fille de Michel Strogoff* ["Michel Strogoff's Granddaughter"] by Octave Béliard; 1928 *Le secret des sables* ["Secret of the Sands"] by J.L. Gaston Pastre; 1929 *L'Ether-Alpha* ["The Alpha-Ether"] by Albert Bailly; 1930 *L'île au sable vert* ["The Green Sand Island"] by Tancrède Vallerey; 1931 *L'étrange menace du Professeur Ioutchkoff* ["The Strange Menace of Professor Ioutchkoff"] by H. de Peslouan; 1933 *Les vaisseaux en flammes* ["Ships Ablaze"] by Jean-Toussaint Samat. In 1932 the award was given to a Western novel, although Verne never wrote in the genre.

The prize was resuscitated in 1957 by Hachette and Gallimard, and the prizewinning novels by contemporary French sf writers were published in the "Rayon Fantastique" imprint. The winning novels were: 1958 *L'adieu aux astres* ["A Farewell to the Stars"] by Serge Martel; 1959 *Surface de la planète* ["Surface of the Planet"] by Daniel DRODE; 1960 *La machine du pouvoir* ["The Machine of Power"] by Albert Higon (pseudonym of Michel JEURY); 1961 *Le sub-espace* ["Sub-Space"] by Jérôme SÉRIEL; 1962 *Le ressac de l'espace* ["The Breakers of Space"] by Philippe CURVAL; 1963 *Métro pour l'enfer* ["Metro to Hell"] by Vladimir Volkoff. [MJ]

PROJECT MOONBASE Film (1953). Galaxy Pictures/Lippert. Directed by Richard Talmadge (pseudonym of Ricardo Metzetti), starring Donna Martell, Ross Ford, Hayden Rorke, James Craven and Barbara Morrison. Screenplay by Robert HEINLEIN and Jack Seaman. 63 mins (cut to 51). B/w.

This rarely seen, low-budget sf film is of interest mainly because Heinlein worked on the screenplay. A group of space explorers take off for the Moon from a station orbiting Earth. The aim of their expedition is to select a site for a lunar base, but their rocket crash-lands on the Moon and only three survive. One of the survivors subsequently dies and the remaining two, a man and a woman (Colonel Breiteis!) are then, though doomed themselves, married via television by the President of the USA (who, in a typically Heinlein touch, is a woman). The ambitious idea is undermined by a very small budget reflected in Jacques Fresco's inadequate special effects. [JB]

PROTO SCIENCE FICTION Meaningful use of the term "proto-science fiction" obviously depends very much on what interpretation is put upon the term "science fiction". It is not too difficult to describe sf (*see* DEFINITIONS) but hunting for its literary ancestry and "origins" adds an extra dimension to the problem of definition. On what grounds might we seek to declare: "Here science fiction began, and works which are in various ways similar that appeared before this time must be termed proto science fiction"? One possible answer is to consider only *labelled* sf as sf, and to decide that sf began in 1926. But Hugo GERNSBACK clearly believed that sf already existed and that all it lacked was a convenient name — he considered H.G. WELLS, Jules VERNE and Edgar Allan POE all to be "scientifiction" writers. An alternative answer is offered by Brian ALDISS, in *Billion Year Spree* **(1973)**, who considers that there is a coherent literary tradition in sf — a common cause if not a chain of direct influence — which has its origin in Mary SHELLEY's *Frankenstein* **(1818)**. This depends, however, on the dubious assertion that sf is "characteristically cast in the Gothic or post-Gothic mode". Peter NICHOLLS has argued that sf is a continuation of "a tradition of the artistic imagination which is very ancient" — a tradition of fantastic speculation cast in various literary forms. A very similar view has been advanced by Alexei and Cory PANSHIN in *SF in Dimension* **(1976)**, proposing that modern genre sf is but one aspect of a literary category they call "speculative fantasy". If this view is accepted then we may accept as ancestral to sf such works as LUCIAN's *True History* (written *c.* AD 170–180) and much mythological fantasy, but the matter of deciding where proto sf gives way to sf proper becomes obscured somewhat by matters of technical definition.

It seems reasonable to argue that we cannot meaningfully characterize something called "science fiction" until we can meaningfully characterize (a) "science" and (b) "fiction" in meanings close to those held by these words today. Raymond Williams' study of shifts in the meaning of certain important words, *Keywords* **(1976)**, reveals that "science" came into English in the 14th century, but with a meaning virtually interchangeable with "art". A more modern definition did not appear until 1725, and the notion of science as the theoretical and methodical study of nature was not generally established until the early 19th century. The same source states that "fiction" first acquired the literary sense in which we use it today in the late 18th century. Before that time the distinction (which we nowadays find very easy to make) between "fiction" and "non-fiction" was not recognized as a *basic* category distinction. The main forms of prose discourse — the dialogue, the history, the meditation and the imaginary voyage — were all more or less amenable to the incorporation of non-fictional commentary in concert with descriptions of events both "true" and "imaginary". It was largely due to the rise of the novel — which made a formal attempt to counterfeit real experience — that it became appropriate to draw a basic distinction between the types of discourse used for non-fictional commentary and the types used for "fiction". The standardized non-fictional forms of today — the essay, the treatise and the scientific paper — were still in the early stages of evolution in the late 18th century.

Logically, therefore, it would be inappropriate to describe as "science fiction" anything published in the early 18th century or before, in that the labelling terms we are using lose their applicability at that point in time. Indeed, so intimately connected is our sense of the word "fiction" with the growth of the novel that it would seem most sensible to begin our reckoning of what is "science fiction" rather than "proto science fiction" with the first work which is (a) cast in the novel form, and (b) clearly aware of what is and what is not "science" in the modern sense of the word. There is only one significant candidate which fits this description, and that is *Frankenstein* (**1818**). Previous works which, with the aid of hindsight, we observe to belong to the literature of the scientific imagination — notably Francis BACON's *New Atlantis* (1627; **1629**), Johannes KEPLER's *Somnium* (**1634**) and Gabriel Daniel's *Voyage to the World of Cartesius* (**1692**) — would not have been considered by their authors to be works of fiction as opposed to non-fiction. They might equally well be considered essays. They are cast in a form (the imaginary voyage) which we now consider to be definitely fiction, but which was then an available and legitimate medium for straightforward speculation and commentary.

The question of which pre-*Frankenstein*ian works may be identified as proto sf, and the extent to which they might be considered important in defining the literary influences and patterns of literary expectation which have contributed to the shaping of sf, is a difficult one. It may even be thought in some quarters to be a sterile one, in that it is possible to argue that the extent to which literary influences have contributed to the shaping of sf is negligible. Certainly other influences (historical and social) have been important, and very probably more important, but nevertheless the importance of various traditions in fantastic literature should not be minimized and cannot be altogether denied. It is necessary to realize that we cannot assess the importance of pre-1818 literary works to the ancestry of sf by testing their content against modern definitions, because the whole point of labelling them proto sf is to emphasize that the modern definitions are inapplicable. What we can do is identify traditions and forms whose subject matter and methods were later adopted into sf. The most important of these, clearly, is the imaginary voyage (*see* FANTASTIC VOYAGES).

The imaginary voyages which are generally identified as being the closest kin to modern sf are the lunar voyages. Marjorie Hope NICOLSON's study of *Voyages to the Moon* (**1948**) has been adopted as one of the standard academic works on sf history, not least for its excellent bibliography. Many studies in the history of sf, including Russell Freedman's *2000 Years of Space Travel* (**1963**), Roger Lancelyn GREEN's *Into Other Worlds* (**1958**) and Patrick MOORE's *Science and Fiction* (**1957**), begin with Lucian's lunar fantasies, *Icaro-Menippus*

and the *True History* and proceed via Francis GODWIN's *Man in the Moone* (**1638**), CYRANO DE BERGERAC's *Other Worlds* (**1657-1662**) and others to contemporary works. This assumption of kinship relies rather blandly on a superficial similarity (though it should be noted that Nicolson, Green and Freedman are interested in trips to the Moon *per se*, and that it is their disciples in the sf community who have construed their work as histories of sf). To take a single example, apart from the fact that the travellers in Lucian's *True History* go to the Moon, there seems to be little to link it to modern sf. It is not a speculative story but a caricature of the traveller's tale — a tall story called "true" because it is so extravagantly false. However, its cynical lack of credulity may recommend it to the sceptical scientific world-view, and we must remember that scientific fidelity in speculation is only one of the characteristic demands made of modern sf (*see* DEFINITIONS) — the other is for imaginative adventurousness. Sheer invention — bold and extravagant — has always played an important part in sf, and it may well be that the effectiveness of sf derives merely from the *pretence* to scientific fidelity which asks that wild flights of the imagination be considered *as if* they were serious hypotheses. On this basis we might find a close kinship between sf and the traveller's tale, which attempts to make wild fantasies palatable by reference to exotic distant lands, and the *True History* would become important as a satirical commentary.

There would be few objections to extending this principle to take in many of the travellers' tales of the 17th and 18th centuries (*see* FANTASTIC VOYAGES), and at least one, Jonathan SWIFT's *Travels into Several Remote Nations of the World by Lemuel Gulliver, first a Surgeon, and then a Captain of several Ships* (**1726**; rev. 1735), better known as *Gulliver's Travels*, has had pronounced repercussions in the later history of sf proper. Like most of its predecessors in the genre but with much greater force, it uses the genre in an admonitory, satirical manner, but it is unusual in its rigour, and even though its purpose is largely to attack the follies of scientific fancy (it might therefore be seen as an early work of *anti*-science fiction), it contains much of the disciplined curiosity and readiness to entertain the consequences of new data which are characteristic of the scientific imagination itself.

Understandable difficulties arise with those travellers' tales whose apparatus is concerned with the religious imagination rather than with pure fabulation. Thus SWEDENBORG's cosmic visions, which include the first descriptions of life on worlds beyond the Solar System, might be considered of less relevance. It should, however, be remembered that the distinction between scientific thought and religious thought, even after Copernicus,

was not nearly so clear-cut as we perceive it today, and there is a good deal of scientific speculation in Swedenborg's attempt to depict conditions on other worlds. DANTE's *Divine Comedy* (*c.* 1310), Milton's *Paradise Lost* (**1667**; rev 1674) and John Bunyan's *Pilgrim's Progress* (**1678**; exp. 1684) can hardly be said to take much account of scientific knowledge, but though the first two reflect contemporary cosmology faithfully enough, they have established mythic archetypes of considerable importance, and analogies may be drawn between the kinds of fantastic environment which they establish and those used in many sf stories. It is worth noting that the literary tradition of UTOPIAS, which appears to have much closer purposive ties with sf, is in reality echoed there primarily because sf writers have adopted a "Utopian scenario" as one of the standard environments for their adventures. There is actually very little Utopian philosophy in sf.

If we go further back in time we may trace the imaginary voyage to its beginnings in oral tradition and legend. The archetypal imaginary voyage is HOMER's *Odyssey*, though there are others in Greek mythology and analogues in virtually all mythologies, as early as the Babylonian *Epic of Gilgamesh* which, because it recounts the narrative of the great flood, has been claimed as the first disaster story. The direct influence of the *Odyssey* upon sf, in terms of both narrative strategy and imaginative symbology, is considerable. In many ways it stands as *the* work of proto sf, not because it is itself in any way a pseudo-science-fictional endeavour, but because so much of its apparatus has been adopted by sf writers.

The *Odyssey* is not only an imaginary voyage. It also incorporates two literary forms which have more or less died out in the later historical periods under consideration here: the HERO myth, and what was then its corollary, the MONSTER story. Both these forms have been revived within sf, and there are clear structural and ideative links between many sf stories and such early legendary constructions as *Beowulf*. It is interesting to observe, however, that sf's heroes are conceived in a very different way from those of the ancient hero-myths.

There still remain for consideration those prose-forms current in the 17th and 18th centuries whose status as "fiction" or "non-fiction" is not so easy to establish with hindsight: the dialogue, the "meditation" and the history. The first two seem to belong principally to non-fiction, though CAMPANELLA's *The City of the Sun* (**1637**) is cast as a dialogue, and so is Poe's "Conversation of Eiros and Charmion" (1838). The dialogue is now subsumed within ordinary narrative form, but there are several notable contemporary stories which are basically dialogues (e.g. Poul

ANDERSON's "The Problem of Pain", 1973). Despite the fact that we now classify them as non-fiction, perhaps we should be prepared to concede an important role in the history of proto sf to the basic *strategy* employed in PLATO's dialogues and their descendants, for debate and interrogation are extensively used in sf, not merely as a means of exposition but as a means of developing ideas and their implications. A genre which attempts to develop speculations logically and rigorously obviously depends to a considerable degree on the Socratic method of examining ideas. The "meditation" seems much less important to the form and development of sf, and may be negligible in this respect, but the history is a different matter. The construction of a history, which necessitates connecting events into a coherent narrative, requires both a creative and an orderly imagination (thus combining the essential requirements of the imaginary voyage and the dialogue). Imaginary histories must be considered alongside imaginary voyages as works which belong to the literary tradition of which modern sf is one product.

Imaginary voyages and imaginary histories may be formulated in poetry as well as in prose; several of the works referred to above are verse epics rather than prose discourses. As to poetry in general, and also drama, a case might obviously be made for including many poems and plays in the literature of the scientific imagination, but it needs to be stressed that the most important links we can draw between classical literature and sf pertain to the structure and apparatus of literary environments, the settings in which the stories take place and from which they very often spring, and that with the exception of epic poetry neither poetry nor drama is strong in this sense. This is not to say that sf cannot be adapted to poetry or to the THEATRE (there are at least two classic sf works which originated as plays), but is merely to say that the importance of poetry and drama to any sf tradition is small, and there seems little to be gained by attempting to argue that Shelley's "Prometheus Unbound" or Shakespeare's *The Tempest* might be co-opted into proto sf.

The attempt to identify a coherent tradition of proto sf is a vain one, in more than one sense of that word. Without a doubt, individual works of classical literature can be shown to be ancestral in certain respects to occasional themes of sf, but we devalue the word "tradition" if we use it to describe a series of isolated juxtapositions of this kind. To say that an assembly of illustrious literary works constitutes such a tradition is a form of self-congratulation on the part of the sf writer/reader/critic akin to that of a prostitute who claims to be operating in the tradition of Cleopatra and Madame de Pompadour, or a barrow-boy who claims metaphorical descent from merchant

princes, even though in an obvious respect they are correct. We can all interpret our actions by reference to previous actions of great men. Sf is a form of literature and can lay claim to all of literary history as its background if its adherents so wish. This does not mean that we can turn the historical sequence on its head and claim that sf is the logical culmination of the "great tradition of proto sf", or the sole beneficiary of its heritage. Modern sf cannot be so "justified". Nevertheless, the going back into literary history, with the intention (however eccentric it may be) of classifying literary works according to their various similarities with modern sf, is not irrelevant. It may serve as a reminder that modern sf, like prostitutes and barrow-boys, is not a mere accident of circumstance, a product of random chance … and that it is not, in the literal or commonplace sense of the word, inconsequential.   [BS]
See also: GOTHIC SF; HISTORY OF SF.

PRUYN, LEONARD (? –). American writer, who began publishing sf with "In Time of Sorrow" for *Authentic* in 1954, and continued with an sf novel, *World Without Women* (**1960**) with Day KEENE, about the violent consequences to the world of the loss of its WOMEN.   [JC]

PSEUDOMAN, AKKAD Pseudonym of American writer Edwin Fitch Northrup (1866– ?), whose sf novel, *Zero to Eighty* (**1937**), combines a technical and pictorial account of the building of a gun-launched spaceship, and its trip to the Moon, with a wooden storyline.   [JC]

PSEUDONYMS The main entry for all people covered in this volume, whether authors, editors, illustrators, critics or film-makers, is under the name by which they are best known, even if pseudonymous. Thus we refer you for full information to Rog PHILLIPS and not to Roger Phillips Graham, to John WYNDHAM and not to John Wyndham Parkes Lucas Beynon Harris.

There will be a cross-reference under all other names, whether pseudonymous or real, if used for the writing of sf, to the main entry. Thus one entry will read in full: **KNOX, CALVIN M.** *See* Robert SILVERBERG. There are also, as it happens, entries for Roger Phillips GRAHAM and John Beynon HARRIS, as these writers wrote some sf under their real names, but they are cross-references only, to the main entry. There will not, however, be a cross-reference entry in cases where the real name of a person was never used in a professional capacity connected with sf. Thus there will be no entry reading **AVICE, CLAUDE** *See* Pierre BARBET, and no entry reading **NUTT, CHARLES** *See* Charles BEAUMONT. It will of course be possible to find out from the BARBET and BEAUMONT entries that the real names

of these writers are Avice and Nutt.

Maiden names, or names from a previous marriage, used professionally by women writers are not regarded by us as pseudonyms. Thus Hilary BAILEY, C.L. MOORE and Kate WILHELM will be found under those entries, and not under MOORCOCK, KUTTNER and KNIGHT.

Ordinary pseudonyms are given simple cross-references to a main entry, but in three special cases information about publications will be given under the pseudonym entry. These are the cases of collaborative pseudonyms, floating pseudonyms and house names. Thus, the collaborative pseudonym entry for Robert RANDALL will give details of the books written together by Robert SILVERBERG and Randall GARRETT. A floating pseudonym is one which is, in a sense, freely available for anyone who cares to use it. Ivar JORGENSEN is an example of a floating pseudonym which was used by a number of authors, and details will be found under that name. The commonest form of the floating pseudonym is the house name. This is an imaginary name invented by a publishing company, usually used on magazine stories to conceal the fact that an author has more than one story in a given issue of a magazine. Thus, if Robert Silverberg successfully sold two stories to a single issue of a Ziff-Davis magazine such as *AMZ*, one of the stories might well be published under a house name such as Alexander BLADE or E.K. JARVIS — usually though not necessarily the story of which he had less reason to be proud. House names might also be used in a case where an author did not want it known that he was selling stories to a certain magazine.   [PN]

PSEUDO-SCIENCE Pseudo-sciences are here defined as systems of belief which, though they adopt a scientific-sounding terminology, are generally regarded by the scientific establishment as mistaken, fraudulent or unproven. They are not to be confused with IMAGINARY SCIENCE, a term used in this volume to refer to that large proportion of the science in sf which the writer knows perfectly well to be impossible in the light of present-day knowledge, but which he regards as essential for plot purposes.

The adherents of pseudo-sciences very often evince a passionate commitment to them, almost as if they were religions; some of them indeed, such as SCIENTOLOGY (which is registered as a Church) use much quasi-religious terminology. Creators of and believers in the pseudo-scientific cults often interpret the contempt or indifference of the scientific establishment towards their work as being evidence of jealousy, or even a self-interested conspiracy designed to conceal the truth. Martin GARDNER has documented this PARANOIA very amusingly and at some length in his classic study of such cults, *In the Name of*

Science (**1952**; rev. vt *Fads and Fallacies in the Name of Science* 1957). More recent studies of such cults are the moderately sympathetic *Cults of Unreason* (**1973**) by Dr Christopher Evans, and *The New Apocrypha* (**1973**) by John T. SLADEK. Gardner's and Sladek's books in particular could probably be read by very few people who did not find some favourite and unquestioned belief being airily dismissed as nonsense, which points to the general difficulty in defining the whole topic with any precision. Gardner, for example, has many harsh words about osteopathy, and Sladek is not gentle with Teilhard de Chardin's theories of EVOLUTION, or Marshall McLuhan's theories about the SOCIOLOGY of the MEDIA LANDSCAPE.

There has always been a close and rather embarrassing link between the pseudo-sciences and sf. Some commentators have suggested that, at its lowest level, sf appeals to a childishness in readers, an unwillingness to get to grips with the real world. Martin Gardner says "... how far from accurate is the stereotype of the science fiction fan as a bright, well-informed, scientifically literate fellow. Judging by the number of Campbell's readers who are impressed by this nonsense [an editorial on PSIONICS], the average fan may very well be a chap in his teens, with a smattering of scientific knowledge culled mostly from science fiction, enormously gullible, with a strong bent towards occultism, no understanding of scientific method, and a basic insecurity for which he compensates by fantasies of scientific power." This is to see the matter at its blackest, but in the mid-1950s when Gardner was writing, some aspects of magazine sf, notably its tales of PARANOIA, its SUPERMAN fantasies, and its obsession with ESP, certainly support his case, though it is not of course the whole truth.

Not all the pseudo-sciences are regularly met with in sf; the richest field for pseudo-sciences is medicine and health, and apart from A.E. VAN VOGT's flirtation with Bates's notorious eye exercises, in *Siege of the Unseen* (1946 as "The Chronicler"; **1959**; vt as title story in *Three Eyes of Evil*, coll. **1973** UK), there is not much feedback of pseudo-scientific theories in this area into sf. The situation is otherwise with psychiatry; some harsher critics would dismiss Carl Gustav Jung's theories as mere pseudo-science, and of all psychologists, his influence on sf has probably been the greatest. But sf has also produced its own psychiatric techniques, notably those associated with DIANETICS and SCIENTOLOGY.

The richest source of pseudo-scientific ideas in sf was the work of Charles FORT in the 1920s and '30s. Fort was a chronicler of strange events, and had a sense of humour; he was not a pseudo-scientist *per se*. He did, however, in colourful language and with his tongue lodged, nobody knows how far, in his cheek, produce many wild and wonderful theories which later writers have taken relatively solemnly. The two areas of his theorizing which have most influenced sf are ESP (and PSI POWERS) and the idea that we are being secretly observed, and perhaps controlled, by mysterious higher intelligences. The latter view has led to many theories about FLYING SAUCERS, to the sort of PARANOIA demonstrated in the lurid stories of Richard SHAVER, and in a roundabout way to the idea (now strongly associated with the books of Erich VON DÄNIKEN) that we have been visited many times in the past by ALIENS who have directed the evolution of our technology. (*For sf stories reflecting the latter view, see* ADAM AND EVE *and* ORIGIN OF MAN.)

A.E. van Vogt is the richest source in genre sf for pseudo-scientific theories. He was also much influenced by the GENERAL SEMANTICS philosophy of Count Alfred KORZYBSKI and played a prominent role in the early days of dianetics.

One of the most prominent pseudo-scientists of recent years, since 1950 when he published *Worlds in Collision*, is Immanuel VELIKOVSKY. His theories relate to various events of the Bible and of MYTHOLOGY, which he sees as explicable only in terms of some cosmic catastrophe (the details are very complex, involving much perturbation of planetary orbits); he has, in effect, rewritten history, astronomy and geology. While his works have probably had little direct effect on modern sf, there is no doubt that the melodramatic and catastrophic events he describes are very similar to those that were so dear to the heart of PULP writers of SPACE OPERA, such as Edmond HAMILTON. (It is possible of course that here the influence is from sf into pseudo-science, which probably happens as commonly as does the reverse.)

It is not only in genre sf that we find pseudo-scientific theories; they have, probably in the nature of things, been with sf almost from the beginning; sf, after all, is an ideal mode to dramatize ideas whether pseudo-scientific or not. Thus many eccentricities relating to spiritualism and astral bodies (*see* ESCHATOLOGY), and to IMMORTALITY and REINCARNATION were commonplace in late 19th-century sf, and are still with us today, though to a considerably lesser degree. Many racial theories (*see* POLITICS), often relating to the supposed inferiority of the black races, also appeared in early LOST-WORLD stories and elsewhere. Theories relating to ATLANTIS, Lemuria and Mu, all supposed sunken continents, are common in early sf also. Ever since the Darwinian controversies in the 19th century, alternative theories of EVOLUTION have been popular, particularly those of the Lamarckian variety (which suppose that acquired characteristics can be inherited); pseudo-scientific theories of DEVOLUTION and racial degeneracy also appear much in early sf, including PULP sf at least up to the 1930s; John TAINE, for one, often used them in his stories. One of the most popular of all pseudo-scientific theories of the 19th century was John Cleves SYMMES's belief in a hollow Earth; many hollow-Earth stories are discussed under LOST WORLDS.

Astrology has never been very important in sf, but it sometimes appears (*see* ASTRONOMY). An interesting example is *The Astrologer* (**1972**) by John CAMERON. Numerology is even less common; the wilder eccentricities of numerologists are parodied in Martin Gardner's book *The Incredible Dr. Matrix* (fix-up **1977**).

Quite another question from all the above is raised by the so-called SOFT SCIENCES, in which the repeatability of experiments, the use of statistics and the pinning of theory to fact is often not at all to the liking of scientists trained in more numerate disciplines. It is true, certainly, that there are many pseudo-scientific elements on the fringes of a number of the soft sciences, notably ANTHROPOLOGY, PSYCHOLOGY and SOCIOLOGY, and these feed regularly into sf, as have, occasionally, some of the loonier theories in ECONOMICS. For examples of pseudo-scientific stories in all these categories, it will be necessary to turn to the cross-referenced entries. Another discipline with a special relevance to sf, regarded as a pseudo-science by many, is FUTUROLOGY.

None of the above is meant to suggest that some of the theories involved, notably those relating to ESP, have not had a certain amount of support from thoroughly reputable sources. Arthur KOESTLER, for example, has expanded his views on Jung's curious theories of synchronicity into a book, *The Roots of Coincidence* (**1972**), and has pleaded for a rethinking of Lamarckian views of evolution in *The Case of the Midwife Toad* (**1971**). Professor John Taylor, a professor of mathematics in King's College, London, has been very sympathetic to the curious phenomenon of "fork-bending" associated with the performer Uri Geller, in *Super Minds* (**1975**). The scientific community has been by no means as unready to consider outrageous suggestions as the more paranoid of the pseudo-scientists have supposed, and indeed, could hardly afford to be, considering the amazing theories they themselves are prepared to entertain in such fields as particle physics, COSMOLOGY and BLACK HOLES.

Since the 1960s, however, there seems to have been an increasing responsibility in sf writers both outside the genre and within it, and the heyday of pseudo-science melodramas, which was in the 1950s, is long past. Many sf writers, including Isaac ASIMOV and John BRUNNER, have actively campaigned against the current popularity of the pseudo-sciences, especially in book publishing. As the public seems to grow ever more gullible, the sf writers, on the whole, get crosser. A well-known phenomenon familiar to all commentators on sf, whether writers or critics, is that in public theatres or radio and TV programmes, at least half the questions put to them will relate to the Bermuda Triangle, or to UFOs, or to visits in the past from alien astronauts. A scathing article on this phenomenon was written by Brunner, "Scientific Thought in Fiction and in Fact", for *Science Fiction at Large* (coll. **1976**; vt *Explorations of the Marvellous*) ed. Peter NICHOLLS. His view is that the publishing boom in books on the pseudo-sciences (usually appearing on the same bookstore shelves as books on the occult) is leading to a great deal of cynical and fraudulent production of fictions masquerading as fact; sf writers at least maintain their fictions as fictions (which has not prevented Von Däniken from citing sf stories among the scholarly references in various of his books).

If it were once possible for pseudo-scientists to complain about a conspiracy among scientists to suppress their work, it is so no longer. Their books constitute one of the largest categories in book marketing, and certainly reach the best-seller lists with a very much greater frequency than books of science — or, indeed, of sf. [PN]

PSIONICS A common item of sf TERMINOLOGY, referring to the study and use of PSI POWERS, under which head it is discussed. [PN]

PSI POWERS This common item of sf TERMINOLOGY has not yet gained acceptance in the language generally. It is probably derived directly from "psychic powers", although many sf readers assume it to be a short form of "psionic powers". The term "psionic" came into general sf use in the middle 1950s, one of its earliest uses being in Murray LEINSTER's "The Psionic Mousetrap" (1955); its real popularity dates from one of John W. CAMPBELL Jr's more eccentric articles in *ASF*, "Psionic Machine — Type One", in June 1956, in which Campbell explained how to build a Hieronymous machine, which appeared to derive its power from the mind of its operator (no scientist has since been able to make it work). Psionics, explained Campbell, means psychic electronics.

Psionic powers, or psi powers, are powers of the mind; they were especially common in sf of the 1950s, usually occurring in stories of MUTANTS or SUPERMEN, but in other contexts also. The commonest psi powers in sf are telepathy and precognition, which along with clairvoyance are discussed in this volume under ESP, which is the usual acronym for extra-sensory perception. All psi powers involve either the manipulation of matter or the manipulation of other minds by the power of the mind alone. Their popularity in sf largely derives from Charles FORT's book *Wild Talents* (**1932**), in which many news stories appearing to prove the existence of such powers are reported. The remaining psi powers are many; a pyrotic is somebody who can start fires by mental force; TELEPORTATION and TELEKINESIS both involve the transmission of material objects instantaneously from place to place, and are discussed in part under MATTER TRANSMISSION; levitation is another psi power. James BLISH's novel *Jack of Eagles* (1952; vt *ESP-er*) is a veritable compendium of such powers.

The most celebrated of all teleportation stories is Alfred BESTER's *The Stars My Destination* (1956; vt *Tiger! Tiger!* UK). In this story teleportation is called "jaunting" after its discoverer, Jaunte, who practises it when threatened with instant annihilation; it proves teachable, and part of the fun of the novel, which is extraordinary in many ways, is in its picture of a future where conventional TRANSPORTATION has become outmoded.

The more *outré* psi powers are given little rationalization, and are in effect a form of MAGIC; the sceptic would argue that *all* psi powers are as imaginary as magic. One of the most grotesque and correspondingly well-remembered psi stories of this kind is Jerome BIXBY's "It's a Good Life" (1953), which features a monstrously sadistic and self-willed child who is able to create monsters, turn people into insects and indeed destroy the world by mental power alone. But the spectrum of psi stories features many powers more moderate than this, as for example in Gordon R. DICKSON's interesting *The Genetic General* (abridged version **1960**; full version vt *Dorsai!* 1976). The hero of this novel has psi powers which emerge only slowly, beginning with an intuitive understanding of military tactics and a great power of command, and ending with his having become a quasi-superman. More baroque than this is the series of "Hogben" stories (1947–9) by Henry KUTTNER, about a family of hillbillies whose staggering powers are directed at trivial ends, and largely devoted to securing their own comfort. Theodore STURGEON and Clifford D. SIMAK both regularly evoked psi powers in their novels, several of which are discussed under ESP. Simak several times, notably in *Time is the Simplest Thing* (**1961**), imagined a kind of universal brotherhood between alien races, linked by psionic communications. James H. SCHMITZ is also devoted to psi powers, most consistently in the "Telzey Amberdon" series (1962–72), and most amusingly in *The Witches of Karres* (1949; exp. **1966**), whose young protagonists delight in their ability to produce poltergeist phenomena, and use other mental powers. Psi powers are commonly attributed to CHILDREN IN SF.

Psi powers are equally common in stories of GODS in sf, especially in several novels by Roger ZELAZNY, and also in *The God Makers* (**1972**) by Frank HERBERT.

A common psi power in sf is the ability to create hallucinations, sometimes deadly ones; they play a prominent role in Frank M. ROBINSON's *The Power* (**1956**). On the other hand, psi-induced fantasy worlds are used therapeutically in John BRUNNER's *The Whole Man* (fix-up **1964**; vt *Telepathist* UK).

Various comic and alarming psi powers are induced in the unfortunate hero of Oscar ROSSITER's *Tetrasomy Two* (**1974**), including total recall when drunk which results in a boring line in conversation, and sexual athleticism to a high degree.

L. Ron HUBBARD is perhaps the only sf writer to have attempted to introduce psi powers into everyday life, largely through the cult of DIANETICS which he founded; they also play a prominent role in his stories, as they do in those of his one-time colleague, the best-known of psi-story pioneers, A.E. VAN VOGT.

Harry HARRISON's *Deathworld* (**1960**) features a planet with incredibly belligerent animal and plant life; it turns out that naturally occurring psi-amplifiers and psi sensitivity make them read the natural mild fear of the colonists as aggression, and they fight back, creating a kind of psi feed-back situation, hostility begetting worse aggression. Anne McCAFFREY's "Dragonrider" series features teleportation in the dragons, which are certainly her most interesting sf creation. Psi stories remain commonplace in sf, and it would be possible to multiply examples almost indefinitely. As the years go by it becomes more difficult for writers to play plausible variations on the theme, but Gene WOLFE has managed several times, notably in "The Eyeflash Miracles" (1976), in which (once again) a child, blind and a healer, is psionically gifted and persecuted; the story is complex, for the reader sees the events through the perceptions of the child, who cannot quite distinguish between fact and fantasy; it is sensitively told, and angry. [PN]

PSYCHOHISTORY One of the best-known items of sf TERMINOLOGY, (not to be confused with the term used by historians, which refers to the study of the relation of psychological motives to historical process), because of the enormous popularity of Isaac ASIMOV's "Foundation" trilogy, published 1942–50 in its original magazine form, in which the term was coined. The purely imaginary though attractive science of psychohistory is based on the notion that the behaviour of humans in the mass could be predicted by purely statistical means, and thus future HISTORY predicted, but "... a further necessary assumption is that the human conglomerate be itself unaware of psychohistoric analysis in order that its reactions be truly random ..." It is this latter condition upon which the plot of the trilogy depends.   [PN]

PSYCHOLOGY The three hypothetical entities which provide the framework for scientific enquiry are the atom, the universe and the mind. A common view of sf holds that its primary area of concern is natural science and speculations arising therefrom, but it has always been recognized within the field — at least since John W. Campbell Jr's manifesto for Astounding Stories — that the proper focus of interest is the human being and the implications in human terms of discoveries in all sciences. It has often been claimed that the proper concern of the traditional novel is the analysis and explication of character, and this places psychological speculation in a curiously ambiguous situation relative to most of the Definitions which seek to distinguish between sf and mainstream fiction.

It is easy enough to label as sf stories which deal with the invention of a new drug or a machine which has bizarre psychological effects, but it is difficult to argue that studies of normal and abnormal psychology really fall outside the province of the traditional novel of character, no matter how much their insights may be derived from such "scientific" constructs as formal psychoanalysis of one species or another. There seems to be no reason to classify as sf studies of obsession or alienation – especially since these are commonplace in contemporary fiction generally. Jean-Paul Sartre's La nausée (**1938**; trans. **1949** as The Diary of Antoine Roquentin; vt Nausea), Albert Camus's L'étranger (**1942**; trans. as The Outsider **1946**) and Alain Robbe-Grillet's Le voyeur (**1955**; trans. as The Voyeur **1959**) are all exercises in speculative psychology, but they are barely surreal, let alone science-fictional. A slightly stronger case might be made out for various works by J.D. Beresford which are not normally included among his fantasies. Peckover (**1934**) is a study of amnesia, All or Nothing (**1928**) of conversion, and Revolution (**1921**), quite apart from its futuristic elements, includes a study of shell-shock. A stronger case still might be made out for such studies of "dual personality" as Edgar Fawcett's The New Nero (**1893**), Albert Bigelow Paine's The Mystery of Evelin Delorme (**1894**), Ben Hecht's The Florentine Dagger (**1924**), Patrick Hamilton's Hangover Square (**1941**) and Stanley Weinbaum's The Dark Other (**1950**); and surely there can be no doubt about stories so steeped in scientific psychoanalysis as Thomas Bailey Aldrich's The Queen of Sheba (**1877**) and Guy Endore's classic Freudian mystery Methinks the Lady (**1945**; vt The Furies in Her Body; vt Nightmare). Even if the last-named were

disqualified as sf we could not exclude Endore's study of the psychological syndrome of lycanthropy The Werewolf of Paris (**1933**), but if it were included we might also be tempted to include his split personality story The Man From Limbo (**1930**). It is clearly extremely difficult to draw a line dividing stories of human psychology into character studies and sf.

Curiously, the one sub-genre of psychological speculative fiction which we are safe in claiming for sf is the class of stories dealing with mesmerism and hypnotism, precisely because these are the "least scientific" and hence the most obviously fantastic. Thus Edgar Allan Poe's "The Facts in the Case of M. Valdemar" (1845) and perhaps Robert W. Chambers' Some Ladies in Haste (**1908**) may safely be claimed. Conventional "psychosis" stories such as Robert Bloch's Psycho (**1961**) and Firebug (**1961**) or Colin Wilson's The Killer (**1970**) must, by contrast, surely be ruled out if they are modern. If, however, they antedate the very concept of psychosis, like E.T.A Hoffmann's "The Sandman" (1816), or if, like Ronald Fraser's The Flower Phantoms (**1926**) they are inordinately bizarre in their imaginative constituents, then they must surely be reckoned as fantasies, though not sf. When one considers, in addition to all this, that there is a whole school of modern novelists — whose work is generally reckoned to be a long way removed from sf — whose self-defined task has been the capturing of the "stream of consciousness" (a psychological hypothesis we owe to the philosopher William James, not to his writer brother Henry), it is obvious that this is one area where the conventional boundaries demarcating sf from other literature simply evaporate. It seems that the only method which may easily be invoked to mark off those exercises in speculative psychology which definitely belong to sf is to sort out those stories which make an invention (a machine, a drug or simply a mental technique) in order to permit greater control over the psyche. This would place the origins of psychological sf with such early novels as Edward Bellamy's Dr. Heidenhoff's Process (**1880**), Robert Louis Stevenson's The Strange Case of Dr. Jekyll and Mr. Hyde (**1886**) and Vincent Harper's The Mortgage on the Brain (**1905**), but it leaves the status of psychiatric techniques as developed by Freud and others in an ambiguous situation, just as they remain in an ambiguous situation relative to science itself, though for the opposite reason. Perhaps the ambiguity shows up best of all in a story which purports to be an essay: "The Jet-Propelled Couch" (1955) by Robert Lindner — a psychiatrist's account of the curing of a patient who believes he has a second existence as the hero of a series of space operas.

The early scientific romancers

envisaged numerous modes of mental interference and control. Dr. Jekyll and Mr. Hyde features a drug which separates the principle of evil from that of good (or the id from the superego, as the Freudian reader is bound to interpret it). Dr. Heidenhoff's Process is about a device which erases unpleasant memories and brings into focus the ironies of conscience. Richard Slee and Cornelia Atwood Pratt's Dr. Berkeley's Discovery (**1899**) is a method of photographing memories to render them independent of subjective consciousness. Harper's The Mortgage on the Brain is about an electrical method of changing personality and restoring lost memories.

Numerous early 20th-century detective series co-opted psychological jargon and developed methods partly based thereon. Edwin Balmer and William MacHarg's The Achievements of Luther Trant (coll. 1910) features a psychologist/detective, while Arthur B. Reeve's Craig Kennedy solves a murder by Freudian dream-analysis in The Dream Doctor (fix-up 1914). A more intuitive brand of psychoanalysis often forms the basis of G.K. Chesterton's detective stories featuring Father Brown, and in the same author's The Poet and the Lunatics (**1929**) the detective is inspired by his (certified) insanity.

That the early sf pulps took any marked interest in psychoanalysis was almost entirely due to the recruitment of the practising psychiatrist David H. Keller. There is little doctrinaire "theory" in his work but a good deal of imaginative insight. Though most of his work was clumsy and pedestrian, he wrote a number of elegant psychological studies as "horror stories", including "The Thing in the Cellar" (1932), "A Piece of Linoleum" (1933) and "The Dead Woman" (1939). His most notable sf story based on a psychological premise was "The Abyss" (1948), which tracks events following the release of a drug which destroys inhibitions. This is a common theme, but Keller's version is notably harsher than that featured in Vincent McHugh's libidinous comedy I Am Thinking of my Darling (1943) or such modern LSD fantasies as William Tenn's "Did Your Coffee Taste Funny This Morning?" (1967; vt "The Lemon-Green Spaghetti-Loud Dynamite-Dribble Day") and Brian Aldiss's Barefoot in the Head (**1969**). On average, the contemporary view seems to be rather more optimistic than the view shared by Freud and Keller that repression is the necessary price we pay for society and civilization.

The most impressive psychological study to appear in the pulps was not in an sf magazine but in Unknown. This was L. Ron Hubbard's classic Fear (**1940**; 1957), about a man who loses a slice of his life through repression and is tortured by the demons of guilt. One is tempted to read extra significance into the story when one recalls that Hubbard went on to found a "new psychiatry" in DIANETICS (later converting it into the religion of SCIENTOLOGY). This PSEUDO-SCIENCE of Hubbard's is much in evidence in the stories collected in *Ole Doc Methuselah* (1947–50 *ASF* as by Rene Lafayette; coll. **1972**), and an associated attack on established psychiatric practice is featured in his "Masters of Sleep" (1950). *Fear* itself bears a certain resemblance to a notable mainstream novel about amnesiac disorientation, *Night* (1940; trans. **1956**) by Erico Verissimo. It is a relatively common ploy in sf to feature amnesiac heroes, in that the memories they have lost can always turn out to be excitingly bizarre. Examples are H.P. LOVECRAFT's "The Shadow out of Time" (1936 abridged; 1939) and L.P. DAVIES's *The Shadow Before* (1970).

One of the most famous pulp sf stories, Isaac ASIMOV's "Nightfall" (1941), deals with the psychology of revelation — a subject dealt with in a less pessimistic fashion in a number of stories featuring different kinds of CONCEPTUAL BREAKTHROUGH. Asimov's main contribution to psychological sf, however, is the rather curious science of robopsychology, which he invented for the classic story series *I, Robot* (1940–50; coll. **1950**). Robopsychology remains the essential fuel of his robot stories even to the present day, "That Thou Art Mindful of Him" (1974) and "The Bicentennial Man" (1976) being two of its most detailed investigations. Many of the earlier stories are "detective stories" featuring the robopsychologist Susan Calvin, who is continually faced with practical and theoretical problems regarding robot behaviour as governed by the three laws which form the basis of robotic ethics. Pre-War pulp sf stories were generally prepared to be more analytical and thoughtful in examining ROBOT psychology than human or alien psychology. This situation changed after the War.

One of the first actual journeys into the human mind was undertaken by the hero of "Dreams are Sacred" (1948) by Peter PHILLIPS, who has to win a catatonic dreamer back to the real world by disrupting his fantasy world. Other journeys followed in "The Mental Assassins" (1950) by Gregg Conrad (Rog PHILLIPS), "City of the Tiger" (1958) by John BRUNNER, "Descent into the Maelstrom" (1961) by Daniel F. GALOUYE and "The Girl in his Mind" (1963) by Robert F. YOUNG. The Brunner story was eventually incorporated into a novel developing the notion of telepathic psychiatry at greater length — *The Whole Man* (fix-up **1964**; vt *Telepathist*). Another, much praised novel on the same theme is *The Dream Master* (1966) by Roger ZELAZNY. *The Whole Man* is part of a sub-set of Brunner's work whose primary interest is psychological. Other stories include the study of

institutionalization "Silence" (1959; vt "Elected Silence"); a story about a reality-distorting drug, *The Gaudy Shadows* (1960; exp. **1971**); a psychiatric case-study, *Quicksand* (**1967**); a story of hypnotic "possession", *The Evil That Men Do* (**1969**); and a novel dealing with the psychological effect which Alvin TOFFLER calls "Future Shock", *The Shockwave Rider* (**1975**).

Brunner is only one of a number of writers who have shown a consistent interest in psychology in their post-War fiction. Alfred BESTER's most notable work in this vein includes a quasi-Freudian vignette, "The Devil's Invention" (1950; vt "Oddy and Id"); a study in obsession, "Time is the Traitor" (1953); the classic novel about a psychotic murderer who undergoes psychic demolition and reconstruction, *The Demolished Man* (**1953**); and the remarkable study of a homicidal ANDROID, "Fondly Fahrenheit" (1954). Theodore STURGEON's sf consists very largely of psychological studies, most constructing bizarre analogues of common loneliness and alienation which are often resolved by the transcendental "curative power" of love. A few examples from a great many are the bitter study of prejudice, "The Worlds Well Lost" (1953); a story of a megalomaniac, "Mr. Costello, Hero" (1953); and the classic novels of literal psychic reintegration, *More than Human* (fix-up **1953**) and *The Cosmic Rape* (**1958**). Ray BRADBURY has written a number of neat stories turning on the vagaries of child psychology, most notably the ironic "Zero Hour" (1947) and "The World the Children Made" (1950; vt "The Veldt"), and the nostalgic "Homecoming" (1947) and *Dandelion Wine* (fix-up **1957**). Another classic story built on the essential selfishness of the child mind is Jerome BIXBY's "It's a *Good* Life" (1953).

One writer whose work has been dominated by psychological themes is Philip K. DICK, most of whose stories are concerned with false world-views of various kinds — and, indeed, with the possibility of there being in the final analysis no "real" world-view. *Eye in the Sky* (**1957**) takes place in a series of ALTERNATE WORLDS created out of the distorted world-views of neurotics. *The Three Stigmata of Palmer Eldritch* (**1964**) is the first of a sequence of novels dealing with reality-warping drugs which eventually culminated in the unremittingly bitter *A Scanner Darkly* (**1977**). Other novels featuring the dissolution of reality in the face of illusion are Chester ANDERSON's *The Butterfly Kid* (**1967**) and Angela CARTER's *The Infernal Desire Machines of Dr. Hoffman* (**1972**; vt *The War of Dreams* USA). Many of Dick's novels feature an attitude to the world which is schizophrenic in the clinical rather than the vulgar sense of the word, and this is explicit in *Martian Time-Slip* (**1964**) and *We Can Build You*

(**1972**). While Dick specializes in SCHIZOPHRENIA, Barry N. MALZBERG is a specialist in PARANOIA, using sf's vocabulary of ideas to build such implicitly paranoid situations as are found in *Overlay* (**1972**), *Beyond Apollo* (**1972**), *The Day of the Burning* (**1974**) and *The Gamesman* (**1975**). A third writer who consistently draws out psychological syndromes into situations, landscapes and world-designs is J.G. BALLARD, again in virtually all his work. Harlan ELLISON also externalizes psychological factors in many of his short stories, including "The Silver Corridor" (1956), "Lonelyache" (1964), "Delusion for a Dragon-Slayer" (1966) and "Shattered Like a Glass Goblin" (1968). The most notable instance of this kind of externalization is the creation of organic analogues for psychic elements practised by Philip José FARMER in "Mother" (1953) and "Rastignac the Devil" (1954), the former being a distressingly literal acting out of the Oedipus complex fantasy, while the second features an alien organism functioning as a *superego*.

The specific psychological themes which stand out most obviously in post-War sf are simple in nature but complex in elaboration. One is the problem of identity explored in various stories in which people undergo physical transformation of some kind. Examples are Marcel AYMÉ's *La belle image* (1941; trans. as *The Second Face* 1951), Algis BUDRYS's *Who?* (**1958**), David ELY's *Seconds* (**1963**) and Kobo ABÉ's *The Face of Another* (**1964**; trans. **1966**). A variant of this theme figures in a curious group of horror stories in which bits of dead criminals are grafted on to innocent people; the most notable example is *Choice Cuts* (**1965**; trans. **1966**) by Boileau and Narcejac, but the archetypal expressions of the notion behind it are in the film FRANKENSTEIN (1931), in which the personality of the monster is blamed on the use of a "criminal brain", and the earlier film THE HANDS OF ORLAC (1924), based on a novel by Maurice RENARD, in which a murderer's hands are grafted on to a pianist. Other variants include skin-colour-change fantasies such as Chris Stratton's *Change of Mind* (**1969**) and the film *Watermelon Man* (1970) and sex-change fantasies such as Hank STINE's *Season of the Witch* (**1968**) and Angela Carter's *The Passion of New Eve* (**1977**). This kind of physical disorientation is taken to extremes in a number of stories by Robert SILVERBERG in which humans are altered by other beings — alienation in the most literal sense. These include *Thorns* (**1967**) and *The Man in the Maze* (**1969**).

A second predominant issue is the prospect of mind control or "brainwashing" which plays a key part in George ORWELL's *Nineteen Eighty-Four* (**1949**) and which has become a standard element in DYSTOPIAN fiction. Stories focusing on possibilities in this area include *A Clockwork Orange* (**1962**) by Anthony BURGESS, *The Mind Benders* (**1963**) by James KENNAWAY, *The Ring* (**1968**) by Piers ANTHONY and Robert E. MARGROFF and *The Barons of Behavior* (**1972**) by Tom PURDOM.

There are many stories dealing with the psychological effects of ESP, but there is an extra dimension of speculation involved here. Similarly, stories such as Poul ANDERSON's *Brain Wave* (**1954**) and Daniel KEYES's classic *Flowers for Algernon* (1959; exp. **1966**), which deal with the psychology of increasing intelligence, depend primarily on their assumptions about the nature of INTELLIGENCE itself.

An interesting, though not very large, group of stories focuses on the possibility of recording emotional experiences for transmission into other minds — notable examples include Lee HARDING's "All My Yesterdays" (1963) and D.G. COMPTON's *Synthajoy* (**1972**). This is a variant of the common notion that memories, and perhaps knowledge, might be transmitted from one mind to another, a notion which crops up in its most primitive form in A.E. VAN VOGT's *Future Glitter* (**1973**; vt *Tyranopolis* UK) and James GUNN's *Kampus* (**1977**), which both feature lurid scenes of cannibalism involving mashed-up brain.

The techniques of experimental psychology have received remarkably little attention in sf; a notable exception is "The Psychologist Who Wouldn't Do Awful Things to Rats" (1976) by James TIPTREE Jr, herself a psychologist. Many of her other stories also have an interesting bearing on psychology, as do those of Gene WOLFE, who came to prominence in sf at around the same time.

Some unique stories of considerable interest are Wyman GUIN's "Beyond Bedlam" (1951), in which the population problem is solved by having minds share bodies; Gregory BENFORD's *Deeper Than the Darkness* (**1970**; rev. vt *The Stars in Shroud* 1978), in which aliens conquer mankind by afflicting them with an infectious psychosis; and Ian WATSON's *The Embedding* (**1973**), a brilliant exercise in speculative psycholinguistics. Earlier stories dealing with the psychological effects of language upon their users are *The Languages of Pao* (**1958**) by Jack VANCE and *Babel-17* (**1966**) by Samuel R. DELANY (*see* LINGUISTICS).

The final position, however, must be preserved for a small group of stories which deal with the psychology of sf itself, in a rather alarmingly cynical fashion: Norman SPINRAD's *The Iron Dream* (**1972**) and Barry Malzberg's *Herovit's World* (**1973**) and *Galaxies* (**1975**). These stories are concerned not so much with whether we all belong on a jet-propelled couch as with the question of where it is taking us and why we love it so. Their answers are harsh, and have

aroused considerable ire among sf fans. There is a certain amount of psychoanalytical literary criticism of well-known sf works which is even harsher — in fact, positively cruel. Examples are C.M. KORNBLUTH's comments on E.E. "Doc" SMITH in "The Failure of the Science Fiction Novel as Social Criticism" (1959), Robert Plank's analysis of HEINLEIN's *Stranger in a Strange Land* (1961) in "Omnipotent Cannibals" (1971) and Thomas M. DISCH's analysis of the same author's *Starship Troopers* (**1959**) in "The Embarrassments of Science Fiction" (1976). The basic charge of all three essays is infantilism. The results of the annual poll of its readers conducted by the magazine LOCUS suggest that the usual age at which readers are recruited to sf FANDOM is 13, and these essays suggest that this may be the age at which such people first fail to cope with reality, remaining existentially becalmed in psychological pre-adolescence for ever. This is not the only interpretation which can be placed upon the facts (*see* HEROES).

[BS]

See also: COMMUNICATIONS; CYBERNETICS; MEDICINE; PERCEPTION; SEX; TABOOS.

PSYCHOTIC American FANZINE, ed. Richard E. Geis (1927–). He began it as a typical "fannish" magazine in 1953, and after 20 issues changed the title to *Science Fiction Review* in 1955. After a brief change back to being called *P*, it remained *Science Fiction Review*, from no.28, until the end of its first incarnation. The magazine was by this time printing more serious reviews and interviews, though its main feature remained Geis's amusing, rambling, personal comments. As *P* it won a HUGO for best amateur publication in 1969, and again as *SFR* in 1970. Geis won a Hugo for best fan writer in 1971, 1975, 1976 and 1977 (tied), but the latter three awards were for his work in THE ALIEN CRITIC, a later fanzine he began in 1973, which itself, confusingly, underwent a change of title to *Science Fiction Review* in 1975. *SFR* in its first incarnation ended with no.43, Mar. 1971, at which point it had a circulation, unusually high for a fanzine, of 1700. [PN]

PUBLISHING The history of sf publishing is, in its widest sense, the HISTORY OF SF itself; this entry, however, is concerned with the emergence of sf as an identifiable and distinctive category of publishing, genre sf, which is a much more recent phenomenon. It was the first SF MAGAZINES which, from 1926 onwards, established "science fiction" (or, earlier, "scientifiction") as a generic term. The original material which they featured was viewed, from beyond an immediate circle of enthusiasts, as debased and trivial PULP literature. The term science fiction became synonymous with ill-written space adventure, while authors outside

these magazines who in retrospect became identified as sf writers, pursued their careers and published their books without being tarred with the sf brush (*see* MAINSTREAM WRITERS OF SF). Before 1945 only a small handful of stories from the sf and fantasy pulp magazines found their way into general publishers' lists; these included J.M. WALSH's *Vandals of the Void* (**1931**), Edmond HAMILTON's *The Horror on the Asteroid* (coll. **1936**). L. Sprague DE CAMP's *Lest Darkness Fall* (**1941**) and two of his collaborations with Fletcher PRATT, and a number of anthologies partly or wholly drawn from the pages of WEIRD TALES. Meanwhile authors who sold their sf and fantasy to the better-paying and less-despised general-fiction pulps like ARGOSY (Ray CUMMINGS, Otis Adelbert KLINE, A. MERRITT and others) regularly had their magazine serials issued in book form.

In the absence of interest from established publishers, it fell to sf enthusiasts themselves to publish in book form the stories they admired. The first such project of great importance was the memorial volume of Stanley G. WEINBAUM's stories, *The Dawn of Flame* (coll. **1936**); the first enterprise to launch itself as a proper publishing imprint was ARKHAM HOUSE, founded by August DERLETH and Donald WANDREI to preserve the memory of H.P. LOVECRAFT and his work. Its first title, appearing in 1939, was Lovecraft's *The Outsider* (coll. **1939**).

The Second World War postponed the establishment of any rival ventures. It also saw the publication of the first significant sf ANTHOLOGIES: Donald A. WOLLHEIM's *Pocket Book of Science Fiction* (anth. **1943**) and *Portable Novels of Science* (anth. **1945**). The immediate post-War years saw a boom in sf anthology publishing from respectable imprints, epitomized by *Adventures in Time and Space* (anth. **1946**), a mammoth compilation edited by Raymond J. HEALY and J. Francis McCOMAS and published by the prestigious Random House. Other anthologists, notably Groff CONKLIN and Derleth, mined the sf magazines extensively. Successful as these books were, they did not immediately lead to an interest in publishing novels or single-author collections written by magazine sf writers, and a rash of specialist publishers appeared to fill the gap. Some of these, such as the Buffalo Book Company, New Era and Polaris Press, vanished almost as quickly as they appeared. Others, such as HADLEY PUBLISHING COMPANY and PRIME PRESS, were short-lived, but more significant. Four imprints, FANTASY PRESS, FANTASY PUBLISHING COMPANY INC, GNOME PRESS and SHASTA, proved more enduring. There was no shortage of material to draw on, and there was a plentiful readership of sf enthusiasts who did not have access to the old magazines in which many of the stories were confined. The specialist publishers, to a significant degree, determined the form in which future readers would perceive the stories of the stable of contributors to ASTOUNDING SCIENCE FICTION who formed the core of their lists. For example, Isaac ASIMOV's "Foundation" series was a long string of magazine stories until Gnome Press's packaging turned it into a trilogy of (supposed) novels; similarly, Shasta determined the shape of Robert A. HEINLEIN's "Future History" series.

By the early 1950s, however, a number of established publishers had become aware of the commercial potential of sf, and they began sf lists. Doubleday was the most significant and enduring of these; others included Grossett and Dunlap and Simon & Schuster. In Britain a similar boom occurred. Many of the giant American anthologies were republished, generally in heavily abridged form, and such publishers as Grayson & Grayson and Weidenfeld & Nicolson started sf lists. Michael Joseph attempted in the mid-1950s the first sf list which tried to establish the category as worthwhile literature: their series, under the umbrella title "Novels of the Future", was edited by the romantic novelist Clemence Dane and included work by C.M. KORNBLUTH, Wilson TUCKER and others. Sf was more readily treated seriously in Britain, where John WYNDHAM had established a considerable reputation, stepping confidently from the pages of the sf magazines to the publication of such novels as *The Day of the Triffids* (1951); John CHRISTOPHER shortly followed a similar path. Equally, however, Britain published much of the worst juvenile sf, in paperback series from such publishers as Curtis Warren, Scion, BADGER BOOKS, Hamilton (who later became Panther Books) and the Tit-bits SF Library.

Where paperback sf remained, with certain exceptions, largely worthless ephemera in Britain until the late 1950s, in the USA it more quickly became an established part of publishers' lists. Such imprints as ACE and BALLANTINE had a heavy, and successful, reliance on sf from their inception; other publishers had a less considerable, but significant involvement. Ace, in particular, gave much encouragement to newer writers, using their "Double Novel" format to couple them with more established names.

Through the 1960s and '70s sf continued to grow in strength as a published category. The last of the important specialist sf publishers, Gnome Press, died in the early 1960s (although FPCI continued into the 1970s on a semi-professional basis); they had been squeezed out by the larger firms, whose resources they could not match. Arkham House, however, continued successfully to publish – chiefly collections of macabre stories and Lovecraftiana. Harper & Row and Berkley/Putnam joined Doubleday as the leading American hardcover publishers of sf (though Doubleday continued to produce the largest volume of titles); in Britain Gollancz's books, in their distinctive yellow jackets, dominated the market, although Faber & Faber, Sidgwick & Jackson and Dennis Dobson (in descending order of discrimination and ascending order of volume) also made significant contributions. In the paperback field Ace Books faded in importance following the departure of their editor, Donald A. Wollheim; his new imprint, DAW BOOKS, took over their place in the market with renewed success. Ballantine retitled their sf imprint Del Rey Books after their husband and wife sf and fantasy editors, Judy-Lynn and Lester DEL REY. In Britain, Panther Books was for many years the leading sf imprint, though this supremacy was challenged in the early 1960s by Penguin Books and in the 1970s by Sphere Books, Pan Books and the specialist imprint Orbit Books. By 1978 virtually every significant paperback publisher on both sides of the Atlantic included science fiction as an integral part of their list, and a high proportion of paperback editors were themselves sf enthusiasts.

The 1970s also saw a revival of small specialist publishers, but whereas in the 1940s they had been largely animated by a wish to bring back into print unobtainable novels, in the 1970s they were to a great degree feeding the demand of the growing market of sf and fantasy *collectors*, publishing obscure items by "collected" authors (such as Lovecraft or, most particularly, Robert E. HOWARD) or lavishly produced illustrated editions of favourite works. The more valuable of these imprints include CARCOSA, FAX and GRANT. Another phenomenon of the 1970s, which brings the story of sf publishing full circle from its being beneath contempt to its being totally respectable, is the establishment of scholarly reprint series, bringing classic sf works back into print in special durable editions. Such series have been published by ARNO, GARLAND, HYPERION and, most notably, GREGG PRESS. Thus sf novels first published in obscure and garish pulp magazines, later reprinted in hardcovers by loving enthusiasts when no commercial publisher would look at them, later still issued in equally garish paperback editions, are now made safe for posterity. [MJE]

PUCCETTI, ROLAND (? –). American philosopher and writer, in the Philosophy Department of Dalhousie University, Nova Scotia. He has long been professionally involved in mind-body problems, and has contributed several essays on the split-brain controversy, perhaps most accessibly in "Sperry on Consciousness: A Critical Appreciation" for *The Journal of Medicine and Philosophy* in 1977, though both his novels deal, in their way, with the question. In *The Death of the Fuhrer* (1972), Hitler's brain is transplanted into the body of a voluptuous woman, and "his" identity discovered, *in flagrante delicto*, as it were, by the hero at a moment of passion. *The Trial of John and Henry Norton* (1973) convincingly updates the Jekyll and Hyde theme, in that the two Nortons of the title inhabit a single body as the result of a commissurectomy (an operation to cut the link between the two lobes of the upper brain); one of the Nortons turns out to be a murderer, and they are tried "together". RP's concern with identity problems is also evident in his philosophical work, *Persons: A Study of Possible Moral Agents in the Universe* (1968), which argues an expansion of the concept of "person" beyond its usual human-centered limitations, and could provide serious cognitive backing for the more speculative attempts in sf to apprehend the potential nature of ALIENS. [JC]

PULP CLASSICS Ed. and published by Robert WEINBERG, a series of booklets reprinting material from or about PULP MAGAZINES. A minority are of sf interest. *Pulp Classics No 1* appeared in 1973; it was *Gangland's Doom* by Frank Gruber. *No 2* (1974) was a full reprint of the single issue of CAPTAIN HAZZARD. Others in the series have reproduced issues of DR YEN SIN, THE MYSTERIOUS WU FANG, THE OCTOPUS and THE SCORPION. *No 6* (1975) reprinted five stories of the "Doctor Satan" series (originally published in *Weird Tales*) by Paul ERNST. The series had reached no. 15 by 1978. [MJE]

PULP MAGAZINES In discussions of popular literature, as in this volume, the term "pulp" is used metaphorically as often as it is used specifically, and when used specifically it has both a narrow and a wide sense.

1. "Pulp" is used in this volume as an indication of format, in contrast to BEDSHEET and DIGEST. The pulp magazine normally measured 10×7 inches, and where the word "pulp" is used with no other indications of size, it can be assumed that the magazine in question is of approximately these dimensions.

2. More broadly, "pulp" is used to designate the type of magazine whose format is as above. There was more to a pulp magazine than its size. Pulp magazines, as their name suggests, were printed on cheap paper manufactured from chemically treated wood pulp, a process invented in the early 1880s. The paper is coarse, absorbent and acid, with a distinctive sharp smell much loved by magazine collectors. Pulp paper ages badly, largely because of its acid content, yellowing and becoming brittle. Because of the thickness of the paper, pulp magazines tended to be quite bulky, often half an inch thick or more. They

generally had ragged, untrimmed edges, and later in their history had notoriously garish, brightly coloured covers, many of the coal-tar dyes used to make cover inks being of the must lurid hues.

It is usually accepted that Frank A. MUNSEY invented the pulp magazine formula when in 1896 he changed the contents of the magazine THE ARGOSY (previously *The Golden Argosy* 1882–8) over to the publication of nothing but fiction. Previously the most popular periodicals had published a mixture of fiction, factual articles, poetry etc. Sf was already popular in magazine format before the advent of the pulps: see the STRAND MAGAZINE, the IDLER and McCLURE'S MAGAZINE. However, these three and many like them were aimed at a wealthier, more middle-class and possibly more literate audience than the pulps were invented to exploit. They were very much family magazines, with a more demure format, and usually printed on coated, slick paper, which led to their being dubbed in America "the slicks", to distinguish them from their humbler brethren, the pulps. It is sometimes stated that the slicks were more expensive than the pulps, but this was not necessarily so. The popular slicks and the pulps were both part of a magazine publishing revolution beginning in the 1880s, in which mass distribution techniques and the carrying of greatly increased advertising allowed the dropping of prices. Most previous magazines, before the 1880s, had a small circulation and were relatively expensive, aimed at a narrow, upper-middle-class, literate group. But literacy was becoming nearly universal in the UK and the USA in the 1880s; population was increasing at an amazing rate (doubling in 30 years in the USA); modern technology was on the whole leading to more leisure time; and there was as yet no cinema to offer opposition in the telling of stories. As a consequence, magazine circulations became massive towards the end of the century, over half a million in the most successful cases.

The slicks and, a little later, the pulps rode the crest of this wave, with the pulps cornering the all-fiction magazine market. Other periodical formats (some had a longer history — see DIME NOVELS *and* BOYS' PAPERS) included the popular weekly tabloid, such as PEARSON'S WEEKLY and the PALL MALL BUDGET.

3. The word "pulp" when used metaphorically describes the quality and style of the fiction which was published in the pulp magazines, and by extension, of any similar fiction, no matter in what format it was published. It is still used today, 20 years after the death of the pulps proper. The pulps emphasized action, romance, heroism, success, exotic milieux, fantastic adventures often with a sprinkling of love interest, and almost invariably a cheerful ending. "Pulp" is often taken as a synonym, in literary

criticism, for "stylistically crude", but this was not necessarily the case. Good narrative pacing, which is by no means a negligible quality, was regularly found in the pulps, as were other virtues of colour, inventiveness, clarity of image and occasional sharp observation, such as might be seen in the work of the early pulp writer Jack LONDON. But it is true that the voracious appetite of the pulp market led to many writers' becoming, in effect, one-man word factories, writing too swiftly and to a cynical formula. The pulps did not generally pay as well for fiction as the slicks, so the pulp writer, then as now, was forced into high productivity by economic pressure.

The general-fiction pulp began to give way after 1915 (founding of *Detective Story Monthly*) to specialized genre pulps. (Frank Munsey had been a pioneer here, too, with *Railroad Man's Magazine*, 1906, and *Ocean*, 1907.) *Western Story* followed in 1919, *Love Stories* in 1921, and WEIRD TALES in 1923. It is surprising that sf did not get its own pulp until AMAZING STORIES in 1926, for scientific romance had been a staple of the general-fiction pulps, along with LOST-WORLD stories and FANTASY, and in these fields the pulps had produced writers as celebrated and well loved as Edgar Rice BURROUGHS, Ray CUMMINGS, George Allan ENGLAND, Ralph Milne FARLEY, William Hope HODGSON, A. MERRITT, Sax ROHMER and Garrett P. SERVISS, and helped to popularize H.G. WELLS (who was more commonly published in the slicks) and H. Rider HAGGARD. Many of these writers retain their popularity 60 and more years later.

The advent of specialized pulps did little at first to disturb the hardened pulp writers, who turned from pirate stories to jungle stories, detective stories to science fiction, sports stories to Westerns, love stories to horror, with admirable sang-froid, though often with unhappy literary results. It was not until the late 1930s that sf writers in the pulps generally came to see themselves as specialists, concentrating usually on sf, fantasy and horror, and not often ranging further. [The crossing of genre boundaries is not, however, a rarity among pulp sf and fantasy writers; many have written detective novels, and recently some have done very well with disaster novels. Conversely, thriller writers like S.A. Lombino (better known as Evan HUNTER and Ed McBain) and William P. McGIVERN have occasionally written sf.]

Nor did the advent of specialized pulps mark the end of sf in the general-fiction pulps. *Argosy* and BLUE BOOK MAGAZINE, for example, continued in the early 1930s to attract the most popular sf writers, including Edgar Rice Burroughs and Ralph Milne Farley. *Argosy* was paying up to six cents a word, and *Blue Book* also paid well, considerably better than the one cent or even half cent a word available from the sf pulps. However,

Argosy's rates had dropped to one and a half cents a word by the end of the 1930s. This marked the effective death of the general-fiction pulp, and probably had a lot to do with the new vigour apparent in such sf pulps as ASTOUNDING SCIENCE-FICTION.

Although the sf pulps of the 1930s are remembered with great nostalgia by sf fans, the fact is that they formed a very minor portion of the overall pulp publishing business (*see* SF MAGAZINES). The great American pulp publishing houses, such as Clayton, Street & Smith and Standard, published dozens of titles of which sf, in terms of number of titles and overall sales, formed only a tiny proportion. Sf as big business had to wait for the post-War paperback book publishing boom (*see* SF PUBLISHING).

Most of the pulp magazines, sf included, had died by the middle 1950s, to be replaced by digests (*see* SF MAGAZINES) in increasingly unhappy competition with paperback books; the reading of stories was itself tending to give way to the watching of television. Indeed, many pulp historians would claim that despite the proliferation of titles in the 1930s, the heyday of the pulp magazines with their half-million circulations was already over with the paper shortages following the First World War, and the rapidly growing popularity of the cinema. The economic depression of the late 1920s probably prolonged the end, bringing with it an urgent need for fiction which escaped the greyness of an ordinary world where individuals seemed impotent. In the pulps, individuals not only influenced events, they regularly saved the world.

The term "pulp sf" lives on, though the magazines are dead. It is associated primarily with stories written, usually rapidly, for the least intellectual segment of the sf market: packed with adventure, and with little emphasis on character, which is usually stereotyped, or on ideas, which are frugally and constantly recycled (*see* CLICHÉS). Many of the entries in this volume discuss typical pulp sf themes and modes, including HEROES, VILLAINS, SPACE OPERA, OPTIMISM, SEX, SUPERMAN, SWORD AND SORCERY and GALACTIC EMPIRES. On the other hand, not all the fiction published in the pulp magazines was subject to the limitations that the word "pulp" usually suggests. Two famous examples from crime fiction of writers transcending their pulp origins, even while continuing to be published in a pulp format, are Dashiell Hammett and Raymond Chandler (both associated with *Black Mask*), and examples from sf are common, too, or else the genre would long ago have died of malnutrition (*see* GOLDEN AGE OF SF).

A full index of sf and post-1930 fantasy magazines, including many pulp magazines, with entries in this volume is given under SF MAGAZINES. Other periodicals in which sf was published are discussed under DIME NOVELS, BOYS' PAPERS, COMIC STRIPS AND COMIC BOOKS and MAGAZINES, the latter entry listing the most important of the general slicks and tabloids which published sf in the period 1890–1940.

The following are the general-fiction pulp magazine entries: ARGOSY, ALL-STORY MAGAZINE, BLUE BOOK MAGAZINE, CAVALIER, POPULAR MAGAZINE, SCRAP BOOK. Four specialized early pulps given entries are SCIENCE AND INVENTION, TALES OF MAGIC AND MYSTERY, THRILL BOOK and WEIRD TALES. Although a number of 1930s "weird menace" and science/detective pulps had a very marginal sf content, it was decided not to give them entries, with the pious exception of Hugo GERNSBACK's SCIENTIFIC DETECTIVE MONTHLY. There was a small fantasy element in such varied genre pulps as *Oriental Stories* (1930), *Golden Fleece Historical Adventure* (1938) and *Jungle Stories* (1938), but the line had to be drawn somewhere in the no-man's-land between sf and fantasy, and they have been omitted. The sf content of the superhero/super-villain genre is sometimes greater, and though many are omitted, including the extremely popular *The Shadow* (1931–49) whose sf content was marginal and irregular, entries will be found for CAPTAIN HAZZARD; CAPTAIN ZERO; DOC SAVAGE MAGAZINE; DOCTOR DEATH; DR. YEN SIN; DUSTY AYRES AND HIS BATTLE BIRDS; FLASH GORDON STRANGE ADVENTURE MAGAZINE; G-8 AND HIS BATTLE ACES; KA-ZAR; THE MYSTERIOUS WU FANG; THE OCTOPUS; OPERATOR #5; THE SCORPION; SHEENA, QUEEN OF THE JUNGLE; THE SPIDER; and TERENCE X. O'LEARY'S WAR BIRDS.

A good account of life as a pulp writer will be found in *The Pulp Jungle* (1967) by Frank Gruber; of pulp publishing in *Cheap Thrills: an Informal History of the Pulp Magazines* (1972) by Ron GOULART and *The Fiction Factory: or, from Pulp Row to Quality Street: the Story of 100 Years of Publishing at Street & Smith* (1955) by Quentin James Reynolds; of the feeling of the pulps themselves in *The Pulps: 50 Years of American Pop Culture* (1970) ed. Tony Goodstone; and of the "weird menace" pulps in *The Shudder Pulps* (1975) by Robert Kenneth Jones.   [PN]

PULP SF *See* PULP MAGAZINES.

PUNISHMENT PARK Film (1970). Chartwell-Françoise. Directed by Peter WATKINS, starring Paul Alelyanes, Carmen Argenziano, Stan Armsted, Jim Bohan, Frederick Franklin and Gladys Golden. Screenplay by Peter Watkins. 89 mins. Colour.

Made at a time when youthful protest against America's involvement in the Vietnam war was at its peak, this is propaganda of the most blatant kind, but shows signs of an important talent. While Watkins' lack of subtlety and objectivity

tells against him, he does possess a genuinely individual cinematic vision; he could be described as the Ken Russell of naturalism. Set in the NEAR FUTURE, *PP* concerns a group of young political dissidents who are forced to endure a government-controlled "run of the gauntlet" before they can attain amnesty for their political crimes. They must travel many miles across an American desert to reach a flagpole flying the Stars and Stripes, at the same time avoiding the patrols of government troops who have orders to shoot to kill. What provides the film with an extra dimension is the presence of a TV camera team that follows one group of dissidents and becomes increasingly involved with their situation, thus, ingeniously, increasingly involving the audience.   [JB]

PURDOM, TOM Form of his name used by American writer Thomas Edward Purdom (1936–   ) for all his sf, which he began publishing with "Grieve for a Man" for *Fantastic Universe* in 1957. His sf novels, beginning with *I Want the Stars* (**1964**), have been unpretentious, routine but competent adventures. *The Tree Lord of Imeten* (**1966**), for instance, vividly puts two human colonists into a crisis situation in the jungle while two native races fight one another; *The Barons of Behavior* (**1972**) mixes politics and social conditioning in a future Earth.   [JC]
Other works: *Five Against Arlane* (**1967**); *Reduction in Arms* (1967 *ASF*; exp. **1971**). As editor: *Adventures in Discovery* (anth. **1969**).
See also: PSYCHOLOGY.

PURSUIT Made-for-TV film (1972). ABC Circle/ABC TV. Directed by Michael CRICHTON, starring Ben Gazzara, E.G. Marshall, William Windom, Joseph Wiseman and Martin Sheen. Screenplay by Robert Dozier, based on the novel *Binary* by Michael Crichton, published under the pseudonym John Lange. 72 mins. Colour.

A mad politician obtains a germ warfare device capable of killing millions. He plans to explode it in San Diego during a Republican convention in order to kill the President, but the authorities track him down before he can succeed. This was Crichton's directorial début. He has been closely involved with sf cinema since.   [JB]

PYNCHON, THOMAS (1937–   ). American writer, all of whose works are FABULATIONS which resemble sf under some interpretations. *V* (**1963**) has a plot whose dovetailing search for a character named V is a physical analogue of the title; some events in the book border on sf. *The Crying of Lot 49* (**1966**) presents a complex conspiracy theory of history, the tone of which seems to have influenced the *Illuminatus* trilogy (**1975**) of Robert SHEA and Robert Anton WILSON.

Gravity's Rainbow (**1973**) is enormous and complex, but the search for the main protagonist (whose sexual climaxes predict and attract rockets from the V-2s on) relates to sf; TP's general concerns with ENTROPY, PARANOIA and COMMUNICATION have had a fruitful effect on some sf writers.   [JC]
See also: ABSURDIST SF; DEFINITIONS OF SF; FANTASY.

QUANDRY American FANZINE (1950–53) ed., from Georgia, Lee HOFFMAN. Though undistinguished in appearance, *Q* was noted for the quality and humour of its writing; along with HYPHEN, its influence on sf fan publishing is still strong. Contributors included Walt Willis, Robert SILVERBERG, Wilson TUCKER, Robert BLOCH and James WHITE.   [PR]

QUARBER MERKUR Austrian FANZINE; ed., since its inception in 1963, Franz ROTTENSTEINER. In the argot of fans, *QM* is a "sercon" (serious and constructive) fanzine, one of the longest running and most impressive of its type. *QM* publishes critical, bibliographical, socio-political and historical studies of sf, UTOPIAS, weird fiction and FANTASY. Averaging 90 large pages an issue, with no illustrations, *QM* has now published several million words of serious criticism, much of it from a Marxist standpoint, its contributors including most of the major German sf critics, and writers such as Herbert FRANKE and Stanislaw LEM. Many of the contributors have been from EASTERN EUROPE. Rottensteiner is assisted in its production by the German fan Hans Joachim Alpers.   [PN]

QUARK Original anthology series edited by Samuel R. DELANY and the poet Marilyn Hacker (Delany's wife). It was the most overtly experimental of the various anthology series which appeared in the early 1970s, and provoked a certain amount of hostility in the sf world. It attempted an ambitious, graphically sophisticated package; unfortunately many of its illustrations were substandard and the design was irritating rather than innovative, with such counter-productive features as the absence of a contents page and the authors' names given only at the

end of each story. Although *Quark* featured interesting work by such authors as Delany and Thomas M. Disch, it lasted for only four issues: *Quark 1* (anth. **1970**), *Quark 2* (anth. **1971**), *Quark 3* (anth. **1971**) and *Quark 4* (anth. **1971**).
[MJE]

QUATERMASS AND THE PIT Television serial (1958–9). BBC TV. Produced and directed by Rudolph Cartier, starring André Morell (as Quatermass) and Anthony Bushell. Written by Nigel Kneale. Six 35-min. episodes. B/w.

As with The Quatermass Experiment and Quatermass II, Kneale's theme was one of demonic possession, dressed up ingeniously as sf. (*For the story see* Quatermass and the Pit (vt Five Million Years to Earth) *below*). [JB]

QUATERMASS AND THE PIT (vt **FIVE MILLION YEARS TO EARTH** USA) Film (1968). Hammer/Seven Arts. Directed by Roy Ward Baker, starring Andrew Keir, Barbara Shelley, James Donald, Julian Glover and Duncan Lamont. Screenplay by Nigel Kneale, based on his BBC TV serial. 97 mins. Colour.

Ten years after the second, Hammer made their third Quatermass film, based on the BBC TV serial transmitted in 1956. The first two were The Quatermass Xperiment and Quatermass II. For the first time a British actor, Andrew Keir, appeared in the title role. A strange object discovered by workers excavating a new underground train tunnel is at first believed to be a World War Two bomb, but rocket expert Professor Quatermass learns that it is a spaceship buried since prehistoric times. Its crew were insect-like creatures from Mars who had

attempted to ensure the survival of their culture by implanting their racial memories and traits, by means of genetic engineering, into the brains of the primitive humans in existence at the time. One of these traits involved the destruction of the weaker members of the species by ritualistic culling, and when investigation of the spaceship activates its power source Londoners in the area are dominated by their prehistoric programming and start destroying each other by means of paranormal powers.

Kneale's script, the strongest of his three Quatermass stories, ingeniously combines sf with traditional supernatural elements (the Martians, for instance, vaguely resemble the popular conception of the Devil). Les Bowie's special effects, especially his extraordinary evocation of poltergeist phenomena across miles of London, add much to the awe-inspiring and curiously disturbing climax. The published TV script, *Quatermass and the Pit* (**1960**), by Nigel Kneale, antedates the film by eight years. [JB]

QUATERMASS EXPERIMENT, THE Television serial (1953). BBC TV. Produced and directed by Rudolph Cartier, starring Reginald Tate (as Quatermass), Isabel Dean and Duncan Lamont. Written by Nigel Kneale. Six 35-min. episodes. B/w.

When the first episode was shown, the BBC warned that the serial was "... thought to be unsuitable for children or persons of a nervous disposition". For the following five Saturday nights the British TV audience watched a genuinely unsettling story unfold — an ingenious combination of sf and the traditional horror theme of possession. (*For details of the story see* The Quatermass Xperiment *below*.) [JB]

Richard Wordsworth beginning to transmute into monster, his arm already a blob, in The Quatermass Xperiment.

QUATERMASS II Television serial (1955). BBC TV. Produced and directed by Rudolph Cartier, starring John Robinson (as Quatermass). Written by Nigel Kneale. Six 35-min. episodes. B/w.

This was the sequel to the popular The Quatermass Experiment (1953). (*For details of the story see* Quatermass II (vt Enemy From Space) *below*). In this instance there is no doubt that the TV version was superior, creating an atmosphere of paranoia through the slow piling up of telling details, with "unhumanness" being particularly well portrayed in the Civil Service, to the undoubted amusement of the British public, who had always suspected it.
[JB/PN]

QUATERMASS II (vt **ENEMY FROM SPACE**) Film (1957). Hammer/United Artists. Directed by Val Guest, starring Brian Donlevy, Vera Day, Bryan Forbes, John Longden, Sidney James and Michael Ripper. Screenplay by Nigel Kneale and Val Guest, based on the BBC TV serial by Nigel Kneale. 85 mins. B/w.

This was the second of the three Quatermass films produced by Hammer, and the least original, but still superior to most sf/horror films made during this period. The other two were The Quatermass Xperiment and Quatermass and the Pit. Professor Quatermass discovers that a mysterious technological complex exists in a remote part of England, and tries to investigate, but is prevented from doing so by armed government security men. Meanwhile small, meteor-like projectiles are falling in great numbers in the surrounding area

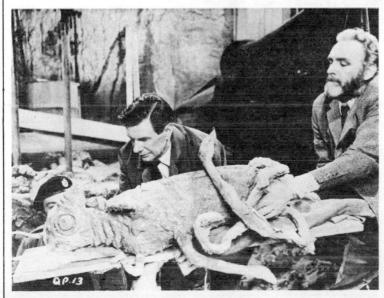

Andrew Keir as the Professor examines a mummified alien dug up in the film Quatermass and the Pit.

and people who approach them are being instantaneously possessed by alien intelligences. A number of these alien-controlled humans have infiltrated the British government, which is unwittingly assisting in the establishment of an extraterrestrial colony on Earth. Quatermass finally succeeds in entering the alien complex and the film ends with a battle in which the aliens, resembling giant piles of sludge, are destroyed. Despite a miniscule budget, Les Bowie's special effects are quite good, and Kneale's script is gripping if implausible. The original TV script was published: *Quatermass II* (**1960**) by Nigel Kneale. [JB]

QUATERMASS XPERIMENT, THE (vt **THE CREEPING UNKNOWN** USA) Film (1955). Hammer. Directed by Val Guest, starring Brian Donlevy, Richard Wordsworth, Margia Dean and Jack Warner. Screenplay by Richard Landau and Val Guest, based on the BBC TV serial by Nigel KNEALE. 78 mins. B/w.

This was the film that convinced the Hammer company there was money to be made out of horror. It is a cheap but impressive adaptation of the first of Nigel Kneale's TV serials involving the stubborn Professor Quatermass. An astronaut returns to Earth infected by a mysterious spore that proceeds to take over his body. He is finally transformed into an octopus/blob creature that retreats into Westminster Abbey, where it is then electrocuted by Quatermass. The performance of Richard Wordsworth as the afflicted astronaut is comparable to Karloff's as the Frankenstein Monster, combining horror with tragedy, and communicating a sense of something utterly alien to all human experience. *QX* is a minor classic. The second and third Quatermass serials were also filmed, as QUATERMASS II (vt *Enemy From Space*) and QUATERMASS AND THE PIT (vt *Five Million Years to Earth*). The television script of *QX* was later published as *The Quatermass Experiment* (**1959**) by Nigel Kneale. [JB]

QUEFFELEC, HENRI (1910–). French writer, most of whose works deal with Brittany from a Catholic perspective; of sf interest is *Combat contre l'invisible* (**1958**; trans. as *Frontier of the Unknown* **1960**; vt *The Men of Danezan* USA), in which nuclear research in a French establishment (*see* NUCLEAR POWER) is almost stopped by cogently presented fears about its consequences. [JC]

QUENEAU, RAYMOND (1903–76). French writer, deeply and originally involved in Surrealism. He was a member of the Order of Pataphysics, a group founded to honour the memory of Alfred JARRY. He wrote several works on MATHEMATICS. His novels are in no direct

way describable as sf (a subject on which he wrote enthusiastically in a 1952 article in *Critique*, "Un nouveau genre littéraire"), though they frequently use sf imagery, and works like *Gueule de pierre* ["Stone Face"] (**1934**), *Les temps mêlés* ["Tangled Time"] (**1943**) and *Saint Glinglin* (**1948**) group considerable and intense imagery around a vision of a CITY whose details are sf-like, and where questions of illusion versus reality abound. [JC/PN]
Other works: *Le dimanche de la vie* ["The Sunday of Life"] (**1952**); *Zazie dans le métro* (**1959**; trans. as *Zazie in the Metro* **1960**).

QUESTOR TAPES, THE Made-for-TV film (1974). NBC/Universal. Directed by Richard A. Colla, starring Robert Foxworth, Mike Farrell and John Vernon. Teleplay by Gene RODDENBERRY and Gene L. Coon. 100 mins. Colour.

This was originally a pilot for a TV series that was never sold. Questor, an android who is the last of a series of mechanical guardians deposited on Earth aeons ago by a beneficent alien race, has been faultily programmed, and the plot involves his search for the information that will explain his origin and mission. *QT* was intended to be the beginning of a series, hence little is resolved.

A book, *The Questor Tapes* (**1974**), based on the film, was written by D.C. FONTANA, who had previously worked with Roddenberry on the STAR TREK TV series. [JB]

QUESTS *See* FANTASTIC VOYAGES.

QUINN, GERARD A. (1927–). British illustrator, Irish-born. One of the "grand old men" (with Brian LEWIS) of

An evocative cover by Gerard QUINN for *Vision of Tomorrow*, Feb. 1970.

British sf illustration, GQ has done hundreds of illustrations for sf magazines, including covers for *New Worlds, Science Fantasy, Nebula Science Fiction* and *Visions of Tomorrow*. Specializing in

realistically rendered alien landscapes, his astronomical paintings were often compared to those of Chesley BONESTELL, though his use of colour was less realistic and more vivid. He often tilted his landscapes to add visually exciting diagonals and used a variety of perspectives to achieve the right dramatic focus. [JG]

QUINN, JAMES L(OUIS) (? –). American publisher and editor. His publishing company started the magazine IF in 1952; JLQ was editor after the first four issues. Its circulation gradually declined, and in 1958 JLQ appointed Damon KNIGHT as editor, but the magazine's fortunes did not revive, and JLQ suspended publication, subsequently selling the title to the publishers of GALAXY SCIENCE FICTION. With Eve Wulff he edited two anthologies drawn from the magazine: *The First World of If* (anth. **1957**) and *The Second World of If* (anth. **1958**). [MJE]

QUINN, SEABURY (GRANDIN) (1889–1969). American author. SQ was by far the most prolific contributor to WEIRD TALES; during its 31-year life he contributed well over a hundred stories, appearing on average in roughly every other issue. Many of these contributions — 93 in all — featured his occult detective Jules de Grandin, together with his assistant Dr Trowbridge. (The first story in the series — although it featured only Trowbridge — was "Stone Image", 1919, in THRILL BOOK.) Ten of these stories were included, revised, in *The Phantom-Fighter* (coll. **1966**); a more comprehensive reprinting (so far including 34 of the stories) comprises *The Adventures of Jules de Grandin* (coll. **1976**), *The Casebook of Jules de Grandin* (coll. **1976**), *The Hellfire Files of Jules de Grandin* (coll. **1976**), *The Skeleton Closet of Jules de Grandin* (coll. **1976**), *The Devil's Bride* (1932 *Weird Tales*; **1976**) and *The Horror Chambers of Jules de Grandin* (coll. **1976**). SQ was *Weird Tales*'s most popular author, although his stories, padded and overwritten, have not survived as well as those by authors he once overshadowed, Robert E. HOWARD, H.P. LOVECRAFT and Clark Ashton SMITH. Though his mysteries occasionally contained rationalized, sf explanations, they are more appropriately regarded as occult fantasy. One of SQ's other activities was ideal for an author of his persuasion: he edited a trade journal for undertakers, called *Casket and Sunnyside*. He was the (unnamed) writer who figured in an anecdote related in Kingsley AMIS's *New Maps of Hell* (**1960**): visiting a bordello on one occasion, he found his stories so popular with the girls there that he was offered a night "on the house". [MJE]
Other works: *Roads* (1938 *Weird Tales*; rev. **1948**); *Is the Devil a Gentleman?* (coll. **1970**).

RABELAIS,   FRANÇOIS
(1494?–1553). French monk, doctor,
priest and writer; the various manuscripts
now published as *Gargantua and
Pantagruel* (1532–52 plus a posthumous
text of dubious authenticity 1564; many
trans., of which the best known is that of
Sir Thomas Urquhart — first two books
1653, Third Book 1693, and Peter Le
Motteux, Fourth and Fifth Books 1694)
form   an   immense,   exuberant,
linguistically inventive SATIRE with most
of medieval Christendom the target; the
giants of the title are enormous both
physically and in their joyous gusto. In
the *Fourth Book* (1552) of the sequence,
various ISLANDS exemplary of various
aspects of society are visited, including
the island of the Papimanes; the
description of the inhabitants of this
island involves a radical criticism of the
Catholic Church. The *Fifth Book* (1564),
which may well have been completed by
another hand from FR's first draft, is
darker and more bitter in tone. It
incorporates a section, *The Ringing Island*
(1562), originally published separately,
which has the most notably sf imagery of
the entire work. The islands of the fourth
and fifth books were probably the most
sustained invention of other worlds in
literature up to that time. The succession
of ALIEN societies, often making some
kind of satirical comment on our own,
complete with all kinds of colourful
ANTHROPOLOGICAL detail, has been greatly
influential in PROTO SF, and its resonances
can be sensed even today in the work of
such writers as Jack VANCE, who
continue the FR tradition, even if not
directly influenced by him.   [JC/PN]
See also: ABSURDIST SF.

RABID Film (1976). A Dunning/Link/
Reitman Production. Directed by David
Cronenberg, starring Marilyn Chambers,
Joe Silver, Howard Ryshpan, Patricia
Gage and Susan Roman. Screenplay by
David Cronenberg. 90 mins. Colour.
    In this Canadian film from the maker
of CRIMES OF THE FUTURE and THEY CAME
FROM WITHIN, an experimental skin graft
on an accident victim turns her into the
carrier of a rabies-like disease. The disease
turns people into berserk monsters,

dominated by a desire to eat raw meat,
anybody's. Soon Montreal is in chaos as
victims of the disease strike without
warning, in crowded streets, subway
trains, cinemas and shopping centres.
Martial law is established; citizens who
cannot produce proof of inoculation are
indiscriminately shot by troops and their
bodies dumped into garbage trucks for
disposal. Like Cronenberg's other films,
R is a mixture of clichés from sf and
horror films, a deliberately tasteless black
joke, as seen in the exaggerated Freudian
symbols: the girl spreads the disease by
means of labia beneath her arm from
which emerges a needle-tipped phallic
object. Critics are divided over whether
Cronenberg is a sophisticated allegorical
film-maker, or whether he is seeing how
much he can get away with, or both; in
any event he ranks high in the cinema of
sf nausea.   [JB/PN]

RABKIN, ERIC S. (1946–). Sf critic
and professor of English language and
literature at the University of Michigan,
Ann Arbor, with a 1970 PhD from the
University of Iowa. Of his four critical
books, the first two, *Narrative Suspense*
(1973) and *Form in Fiction* (1974), with
David Hayman, have only a peripheral
relation to sf. Much more relevant is *The
Fantastic   in   Literature* (1976),   a
provocative academic study which suffers
a little from fuzziness of definition. With
Robert SCHOLES, ESR wrote *Science
Fiction: History, Science, Vision* (1977),
one of the best general introductions to
the subject, though the opening and
closing sections, on the HISTORY OF SF and
ten representative novels, are very much
stronger than the intermediate chapters
on media, sciences and themes, which are
sketchy.   [PN]
See also: SF IN THE CLASSROOM.

RACIAL CONFLICT *See* POLITICS.

RACINA, THOM (? –). American
writer, composer and stage director. His
first sf novel is borderline: *The Great Los
Angeles Blizzard* (1977), a DISASTER story
in which the implausible, eponymous,
meteorological freak blankets Southern
California in snow and ice with
consequent mayhem.   [PN]

RACKHAM, JOHN *See* John T.
PHILLIFENT.

RADIATION *See* HOLOCAUST AND AFTER;
NUCLEAR POWER; SUN; WEAPONS.

RADIO (UK) Sf has been broadcast by
the BBC since the 1930s; indeed, radio is
such a suitable medium for it that it is
hard to find a celebrated sf author whose
work   has   not   been   transmitted.
Dramatizations, as single plays, serials or
readings by authors, of stories by such
writers as Arthur C. CLARKE, H.G.
WELLS, John WYNDHAM, Isaac ASIMOV,
Ray BRADBURY, John CHRISTOPHER and

Brian ALDISS have been broadcast. Sf
programmes have been aimed at all ages.
For example, a typical Monday in 1953
would offer one of Angus MacVicar's
"Lost Planet" stories on the 5 pm
Children's Hour, and at 7.30 pm the
fantastically   successful *Journey   Into
Space* serial would be trasmitted for the 7
to 70-year-olds.
    Journey Into Space was written and
produced for radio by Charles CHILTON,
already well known to youngsters as
creator of the popular Western *Riders-of-
the-Range* series through its appearances
on radio and in the boys' paper *Eagle.*
Journey Into Space ran for only two
years, between 1953 and 1955, with three
serialized stories, 54 episodes in all, but it
enthralled a generation for whom landing
on the Moon was still a far-fetched
fantasy. The three stories were set on the
Moon in 1965, and on Mars in 1971 and
1973, and featured the adventures of the
Scots pilot Jet Morgan and his crew,
Cockney Lemmy Barnet, Australian
Stephen Mitchell and American Dr
Matthews. High points were the meeting
with   a   malevolent   extraterrestrial
civilization shortly after the first Moon
landing, the foiling of a Martian invasion,
time travel, mass hypnosis and flying
saucers. By 1955 the programme reached
five million listeners, the largest UK radio
audience ever, and deservedly so, since
no previous sf radio drama had equalled
its narrative vigour. The programmes
were sold to 58 countries. The adventures
were published as novels by Chilton, who
also scripted a further adventure of Jet
Morgan and his companions for a comic
strip in *Express Weekly* (1956–7).
    The other well-remembered sf radio
serial was *Dan Dare*, broadcast for
several years from 1953 by the English-
language service of Radio Luxembourg
in weekly 15-minute episodes. The
programme was written and produced by
people quite unconnected with the staff of
Frank HAMPSON's comic strip DAN DARE
and, although it used the same characters
and situations, was in quite a different
style which, while unsophisticated SPACE
OPERA as sf, was thoroughly successful as
juvenile high adventure. No radio sf
serials since that time have approached
the popularity of the above two
programmes, and most recent radio sf has
appeared as individual dramatizations or
readings of already well-known sf works,
rather than plays especially written for
radio.   [ABP]
See also: RADIO (USA); GERMANY.

RADIO   (USA)   Fantastic   thrillers,
incorporating   sf   and   supernatural
elements alternately, were fairly common
in the USA all through the "Golden Age"
of radio (usually considered 1930–50),
but "hardcore" sf was more rarely heard.
    As early as 1929, Carlton E. Morse
(1900–) in San Francisco wrote and
produced closed-end serials (one story,
from which the characters did not

continue indefinitely) which involved sf concepts. Amid ancient jungle temples, Morse rationalized mysticism into science in *The Cobra King Strikes Back* and *Land of the Living Dead*. The same titles and scripts were reprised in the 1945 series *Adventures by Morse*. Similar themes were developed with more sophistication by Morse in *I Love a Mystery*, 1939–45 (NBC, then CBS), and new productions repeating the scripts, 1949–52 (Mutual). "Temple of Vampires" had heroes Jack, Doc and Reggie facing human vampires and gigantic mutant bats. Two other episodes of *I Love a Mystery*, "The Stairway to the Sun" and "The Hermit of San Felipe Atabapo", concerned the same lost plateau in South America, where dwelled prehistoric monsters and a race of supermen who controlled world destiny. More celebrated for his literate domestic serial *One Man's Family*, Morse was also radio's foremost adventure writer, similar (and comparable) to H. Rider HAGGARD and Arthur Conan DOYLE. Much of his work has survived, thanks to private collectors, and is being re-released on phonograph records.

Children's programming was deeply involved with sf. *Buck Rogers in the 25th Century* was probably the first "hardcore" sf series on radio, beginning in 1932 (CBS). (It was only the second important afternoon adventure serial of any kind, its predecessor being *Little Orphan Annie*.) Based on the comic strip by Phil NOWLAN and Dick CALKINS, the programme was also written partly by Calkins, but for the most part by radio producer Jack Johnstone. The stories were far from silly or trivial, and made a good job of presenting such basic ideas as time and space travel to a youthful audience. Various revivals carried the BUCK ROGERS title through to 1946 on radio. Other series of shorter duration were FLASH GORDON, *Brad Steele — Ace of Space*, SPACE PATROL and *Space Cadet* (the last two being original radio shows based on established TV favourites in the early 1950s — *see* TOM CORBETT).

SUPERMAN was an sf character, created by Jerry SIEGEL and Joe SHUSTER in their comic strip, but on radio (1940–52), the series generally dealt with crime and mystery. Some sf appeared when the Man of Steel ventured to the planet Utopia, or when menaced by Kryptonite, a radioactive element from his destroyed home planet, which is the only threat to his life on Earth. Supporting characters included guest stars Batman and Robin.

Other juvenile serials had *Jack Armstrong, the All-American Boy* (1933–51) experimenting with Uranium U-235 in 1939; *Captain Midnight* (1938–50), the mysterious aviator, encountering flying saucers in 1949; and *Tom Mix* (1933–50), the Western movie star impersonated on radio usually by Curley Bradley, constantly facing mysteries with a supernatural and super-

science atmosphere. (The same actor and theme were used in *Curley Bradley's Trail of Mystery*, which was written and produced by Jim HARMON in 1976 for syndication.)

Horror stories, in half-hour anthologies, appeared in the 1930s. Such series were mostly supernatural in content, but sf occasionally appeared. *Lights Out* began in 1938 (NBC), written by Willis Cooper, later by Arch Oboler. Oboler's tale of an ordinary chicken's heart, stimulated by growth hormones to engulf the entire radio, is one of the most famous single radio plays of any kind. Other horror anthologies include *Witch's Tale* by Alonzo Deen Cole, *Quiet Please*, also by Willis Cooper, and *Hermit's Cave*, by various authors.

A general drama anthology, *Mercury Theatre on the Air*, was begun by its producer-star Orson Welles in 1938 (CBS). One of the earliest broadcasts adapted H.G. WELLS's *War of the Worlds* in the form of a contemporary on-the-spot newscast. Thousands of listeners were thrown into a state of panic, believing Mars was invading the Earth. The resulting havoc undoubtedly made this sf play the most famous single radio broadcast of all time. The *Mercury* series also did memorable versions of *Frankenstein* and *Dracula*.

Before leaving for the movies and his classic *Citizen Kane*, Orson Welles also starred in *The Shadow* in 1937–8. The series had begun in 1931 and until 1954 often presented sf in charmingly lurid pulp fashion, with its mysterious hero who could "cloud men's minds" by hypnosis (thus becoming invisible), facing mad scientists who could control volcanoes, dead bodies, light and dark itself. Rival fantasy heroes included *The Avenger* (almost an exact copy); *Peter Quill*, a weird, benevolent, hunchbacked scientist; and the fearless shipmates of *Latitude Zero*.

In the 1940s, various general or thematic anthology series began to present occasional sf, generally adapted from well-known works. *Suspense* (mostly crime-detective) offered Ray BRADBURY's "Zero Hour", and *Escape* (usually exotic adventure) presented H.G. Wells's *The Time Machine*, among others.

Near the end of major night-time programming on radio in 1949, sf came into its own in an anthology of modern sf, *Dimension X* later retitled *X Minus 1*. This NBC programme had well-presented versions of Bradbury's *Martian Chronicles*, Robert HEINLEIN's "Requiem", and many other celebrated sf stories, intermittently until 1957. Although sf is today occasionally presented experimentally on culture-oriented FM stations, and on the *CBS Radio Mystery Theater* (the first major network revival of drama, beginning in 1973), *X Minus 1* still stands as one of the finest showcases for sf in any dramatic

medium. [JH]

RADIO COMMUNICATION *See* COMMUNICATION.

RAND, AYN (1905–). Russian-born American writer. Her "objectivist" philosophy, as expounded in most of her work, had an influence in the USA mainly during the 1950s, and mainly upon college students, for whom her arguments about the need for rational self-interest, against altruism, and about the SUPERMAN potential within us may have seemed particularly compelling. Her first, short sf novel, *Anthem* (**1938**; abridged 1946), is a DYSTOPIA set after a devastating war; individualism has been eliminated, along with the concept of the person, but the protagonist discovers himself and escapes to the forest with a beautiful woman. The skyscraper constructed in *The Fountainhead* (**1943**) lies within the bounds of MAINSTREAM fiction. In the long novel *Atlas Shrugged* (**1957**), however, John Galt and his objectivist associates abandon an increasingly socialistic America, retreat to the mountains while civilization crumbles and prepare to return only when they will be able to rebuild along the lines of objectivist philosophy. AR's influence has lessened over the years. [JC]
See also: ECONOMICS; POLITICS; SOCIAL DARWINISM; SOCIOLOGY.

RANDALL, ROBERT Pseudonym used on collaborative works by Robert SILVERBERG and Randall GARRETT, most notably the Nidorian series, originally published in *ASF*, which deals with the effects of human contact on an alien race: *The Shrouded Planet* (fix-up **1957**) and *The Dawning Light* (**1959**). [BS]

RANKINE, JOHN *See* Douglas R. MASON.

RANZETTA, LUAN (? – ?). Possibly pseudonymous British writer whose routine paperback sf adventures are *The Uncharted Planet* (**1962**), *The Maru Invasion* (**1962**), *The World in Reverse* (**1962**), *Night of the Death Rain* (**1963**) and *The Yellow Inferno* (**1964**). [JC]

RAPHAEL, RICK (1919–). American writer and journalist, involved in politics as commentator and staff member for American Senator Frank Church; he began publishing sf with "A Filbert is a Nut" for *ASF* in 1959, and established a considerable reputation in the field with a comparatively small output of about 10 stories, most of them assembled in his *The Thirst Quenchers* (coll. **1965**) and *Code Three* (1963–4 *ASF*; fix-up **1966**). The first contains four good stories, the best of which is the title story about professionals in a world where water is scarce, their job being its proper allocation. In *Code Three*, we are given an insight into the way of life of the police who patrol the super-highways of the future in enormously complex vehicles made to cope with the huge speeds and corresponding irresponsibility on the roads. RR is at his best when describing, in eulogistic terms, the life of professional expediters of our technological way of life.   [JC]

See also: CRIME AND PUNISHMENT; WEATHER CONTROL.

RAW MEAT *See* DEATHLINE.

RAY, RENÉ (? –). Author of a routine sf novel about the FOURTH DIMENSION, *The Strange World of Planet X* (**1957**). An earlier fantasy is *Wraxton Marne* (**1946**).   [JC]

RAY, ROBERT. (? –) English writer who began publishing sf with "If Tomorrow be Lost" for *Fantastic Adventures* in 1950, but who appeared very rarely in the magazines. His routine sf novels are *No Stars for Us* (**1964**) and *The Seedy* (**1966**).   [JC]

RAYER, FRANCIS G(EORGE) (1921–). British writer and technical journalist. He began publishing sf with "Juggernaut" for Link House Publications in 1944; his first sf novel is *Realm of the Alien* (**1949**) and his most notable perhaps *Tomorrow Sometimes Comes* (**1951**), which forms part of his "Mens Magna" series about a thinking machine, which also includes "Deus Ex Machina" (1950), "The Peacemaker" (1952), "Ephemeral this City" (1955), "Adjustment Period" (1960) and "Contact Pattern" (1961). He was most closely associated with *NW*, and also had several lead novels in the early years of *Authentic*. Most of his work is routine.   [JC]

Other works: *Fearful Barrier* (**1950**); *The Star Seekers* (**1953**); *The Iron and the Anger* (**1964**); *Cardinal of the Stars* (**1964**); *Journey to the Stars* (**1964**). As editor: *Worlds at War* (anth. undated c. 1948).

See also: COMPUTERS.

RAY-GUNS *See* WEAPONS.

RAYMOND, ALEX (1909–56). American cartoonist. AR studied at the Grand Central School of Art in New York City and, after graduating, worked on the COMIC STRIP *Tillie the Toiler*. He soon moved up in the comics world, working for Chic Young on *Blondie* and with Lyman Young on *Tim Tyler's Luck*, before being given his own strip, *Secret Agent X-9*, which gave him invaluable experience for his future work; it was during this time that he began to develop his distinctive style. In 1934, he was given the chance to do a new strip, FLASH GORDON, and American cartooning has not been the same since; he is acknowledged as the earliest demonstrably modern comics illustrator.

Alex RAYMOND's work on *Flash Gordon*, 1936; his style was one of the most innovative in comic strip art.

Although his style at first was characterized by convoluted masses and strong, sweeping lines, by 1936 it had become more precise and controlled. He refined the technique of "feathering" (a series of fine brush- or pen-strokes used in cartooning to create contours) to a degree as yet unexcelled in comic strips. *Flash Gordon*'s major flaw was that the characters were dream-like; their features were impossibly perfect. Military trappings, such as shiny boots and wide leather belts, often appeared in the strip. In 1944, AR joined the US Marines, leaving the strip to Austin Briggs; when he returned in 1946, he created a new strip, not sf, of considerable popularity, *Rip Kirby*. AR died in a tragic accident in 1956, at the peak of his career.   [JG]

RAYMOND, E.V. *See* Raymond Z. Gallun.

READ, HERBERT (EDWARD) (1893–1968). English poet, literary and art critic and theorist, knighted in 1953. His only novel, *The Green Child* (**1935**), is a remarkable double UTOPIA, in which each form of ideal human life – one a Latin American political Utopia, the other a mystical, underground transcendence of

human aspirations – comprises a critique of and dramatic metaphor for the other.   [JC]

REALITY AND APPEARANCE *See* CONCEPTUAL BREAKTHROUGH; METAPHYSICS; PERCEPTION.

REAMY, TOM (1935–77). American writer and graphic designer who began publishing sf/fantasy with "Twilla" for *FSF* in 1974, and whose 10 stories by late 1977, the time of his premature death, had established him as a writer of potential stature in the field. His FANTASY novelette, "San Diego Lightfoot Sue" (1975), won a 1976 NEBULA award, and he also won the JOHN W. CAMPBELL AWARD for best new sf writer of that year. Prior to his death he completed a novel tentatively entitled *Blind Voices*; it has a common background with "Twilla" and "San Diego Lightfoot Sue"; these three stories also have some overlapping characters. A volume of short stories is projected   [JC/PN]

RED PLANET MARS Film (1952). Melaby Pictures/United Artists. Directed by Harry Horner, starring Peter Graves, Andrea King and Marvin Miller.

Screenplay by John L. Balderston and Anthony Veiller, based on the play *Red Planet* by John L. Balderston and John Hoare. 87 mins. B/w.

Two young American scientists, man and wife, pick up TV transmissions from Mars and learn that a veritable Utopia exists there, ruled over by a "Supreme Authority" who is none other than God himself. The world is thrown into a panic at these revelations and an ex-Nazi scientist attempts to prove that the messages are fake, but religion is ultimately justified, and Godless Communism (the true villain of the film) destroyed.

RPM is a fascinating product of its time: a reflection of the Cold War PARANOIA that swept America in the early 1950s. In one sequence a group of aged revolutionaries overthrow the Communist government of Russia and restore the monarchy, choosing an Orthodox priest as their new Czar. During this period religious crusades in the USA, such as those of Billy Graham, were regularly and consciously seen as a political weapon against Communism, and the film neatly reflects the feeling of that time. [JB/PN]

REED, CLIFFORD C(ECIL) (1911–). South African-born writer and civil servant, who emigrated to England in 1950. He began publishing sf with "Jean-Gene-Jeanne" for *Authentic* in 1954; his routine sf novel is *Martian Enterprise* (1962). [JC]

REED, DAVID V. Pseudonym most frequently used by American writer David Vern (1924–) for almost all his fiction, starting with "Where is Roger Davis?" for *AMZ* in 1939, most of which was written for Ray PALMER's magazines. With Don WILCOX, who wrote the first of the two stories from which it was cobbled together, he wrote *The Whispering Gorilla* (1940–43 *Fantastic Adventures*; fix-up 1950), about an ape with a man's brain; the book was published as by DVR. *Murder in Space* (1944 *AMZ*; 1954) is an unconvincing attempt to combine mystery and sf techniques. A further novel, published in magazine form as "The Metal Monster Murders" (1943), and in a mid-1950s undated book form as *The Thing that Made Love*, is a mystery, not sf. He was probably the first writer to use the house name Alexander BLADE; he also used the house names Craig ELLIS and Peter HORN and wrote one story as Clyde Woodruff. [JC/PN]

REED, KIT Form of her name used by American writer Lillian Craig Reed (1932–) for all her fiction, much of which is not sf, though she is as well known for her work within the sf and fantasy genres as outside them. She began publishing sf and fantasy with "The Wait" (vt "To Be Taken in a Strange Country") for *FSF* in 1958, and has

published mainly with that journal since. Her first book, *Mother Isn't Dead She's Only Sleeping* (1961) is not sf; she has assembled sf stories in *Mister da V. and Other Stories* (coll. 1967) and *The Killer Mice* (coll. 1976); at her worst, her stories are diminutions of the effects of which Shirley JACKSON was capable; at best, her moral fables, which are often closer to fantasy than to sf, sharply and precisely make their uncomfortable points, as in "Winston" (1969) and "The Vine" (1967) from the second volume, and "Mister da V." (1962) and "Automatic Tiger" (1964) from the first. Her sf novel, *Armed Camps* (1969), sets up a NEAR-FUTURE apocalypse in which nothing is capable of saving the USA from collapse, neither the soldier nor the woman pacifist who share the narrative, nor what they represent. KR is a quiet writer who has had less influence in the field than she merits. [JC]
See also: TIME TRAVEL.

REED, PETER *See* John D. MacDONALD.

REEVE, ARTHUR B(ENJAMIN) (1880–1936). American writer of detective fiction featuring the scientific detective Craig Kennedy, whose first book appearance is in *The Poisoned Pen* (coll. 1911); the original Kennedy stories appeared in *Cosmopolitan*, 1910–18. Kennedy often invented and always made use of scientific gadgets or theories, many of them sf, to explain the mysteries he confronted. Two of ABR's books, *The Master Mystery* (1919) and *The Mystery Mind* (1921) were collaborations with John Grey. [JC/PN]
Other works: *The Silent Bullet* (coll. 1912); *The Dream Doctor* (fix-up 1914); *The War Terror* (1915); *The Exploits of Elaine* (1915); *The Gold of the Gods* (1915); *The Ear in the Wall* (1916); *The Romance of Elaine* (1916); *The Treasure Train* (1917); *Atavar:* (1917); *The Diamond Queen* (1917); *The Panama Plot* (1918); *The Soul Scar* (1919); *The Fourteen Points* (1925); *Pandora* (1926); *The Radio Detective* (1926). As editor: *The Best Ghost Stories* (anth. 1936).
See also: CRIME AND PUNISHMENT; PSYCHOLOGY.

REGINALD, ROBERT Pseudonym of M.R. Burgess (1948–), American publisher, writer and librarian, born in Japan. His *Stella Nova: the Contemporary Science Fiction Authors* (1970; vt *Contemporary Science Fiction Authors*), first edition published anonymously, is a very useful work containing mini-biographies and book checklists of most sf authors who published new books in the years 1960–8. An updated volume, *Contemporary Science Fiction Authors II*, is projected for 1978 publication along with a checklist of sf and fantasy 1700–1974. RR founded his own publishing company, the Borgo Press, in

California in 1975, and edits its books, which include many booklet studies of sf authors, several by George Edgar SLUSSER. RR's other important reference work, though it is not wholly complete, is *Cumulative Paperback Index, 1939–1959* (1973). He has also edited a number of anthologies with Douglas Menville: *Ancestral Voices: an Anthology of Early Science Fiction* (anth. 1975), *Ancient Hauntings* (anth. 1976), *Phantasmagoria* (anth. 1976), *R.I.P.: Five Stories of the Supernatural* (anth. 1976), *The Spectre Bridegroom, and Other Horrors* (anth. 1976); these were all produced in the ARNO PRESS series of sf, supernatural and occult reprints, for which RR and Menville are the editors. They had originally worked together on the short-lived magazine FORGOTTEN FANTASY, of which RR was associate editor, in 1971–2. RR has also published in the Borgo Press two works of his fiction written by himself under pseudonyms: *The Attempted Assassination of John F. Kennedy: a Political Fantasy* (1976) as by Lucas Webb, and *Up Your Asteroid! A Science Fiction Farce* (1977) as by C. Everett Cooper; neither is a full-lenth novel. Four more anthologies with Menville are projected from Arno in 1978; also projected, written with Menville, is an illustrated history of the sf film. [PN]

REIDA, ALVAH (? –). American writer, whose sf novel, *Fault Lines* (1972), not to be confused with Kate WILHELM's later novel with the same title, deals apocalyptically with the consequences of a San Andreas Fault earthquake. [JC]

REIN, HAROLD (? – ?). American writer. His post-HOLOCAUST sf novel, set partly in the subways of New York, is *Few Were Left* (1955). [JC]

REINCARNATION There is much fantastic literature dealing with reincarnation; it had a great vogue between 1885 and 1925 (approximately), whose reverberations are still with us. Other than straightforward occult material the bulk of it belongs to the sub-genre of "transcendental romance" — stories in which romantic love becomes a quasi-supernatural force transcending time or death to reunite lovers. The pattern of H. Rider HAGGARD's *She* (1887), in which the hero is the reincarnated lover of the archetypal female, has been extensively copied. Many romances of reincarnation have also been inspired by the ancient Egyptian methods of preserving the dead, including Haggard's "Smith and the Pharaohs" (1912; as title story of *Smith and the Pharaohs and Other Tales* 1920). Closer to sf is the notion of "race memory" which is often used as an imaginative device allowing characters to "remember" previous incarnations.

Haggard used this idea in *The Ancient Allan* (**1920**) and *Allan and the Ice Gods* (**1927**), and Jack LONDON used it in *Before Adam* (**1906**) and *The Star Rover* (**1915**; vt *The Jacket* UK). The most impressive use of the formula is John GLOAG's *99%* (**1944**). Several time-spanning historical romances have made use of "serial reincarnation", including Edwin Lester ARNOLD's novels *Phra the Phoenician* (**1890**) and *Lepidus the Centurion* (**1901**), and George GRIFFITH's *Valdar the Oft-Born* (**1895**).

Camille FLAMMARION, the first writer to develop the notion of ALIEN beings adapted to LIFE ON OTHER WORLDS, did so partly in order to support his theory of the immortality of the soul and its reincarnation on other worlds. First presented in *Lumen* (1887; **1897**), the idea was also used in *Urania* (**1890**). It was copied by Louis Pope GRATACAP in the didactic romance *The Certainty of a Future Life on Mars* (**1903**). Early sf writers, however, shunned this and all other PSEUDO-SCIENTIFIC versions of reincarnation as pure FANTASY.

Hugh KINGSMILL reincarnated Shakespeare in *The Return of William Shakespeare* (**1929**) so that a critical commentary on the works could be put into the Bard's own mouth and bracketed by a satirical comedy. When reincarnation began to creep into sf the resurrection of great men of the past was a favourite theme, from Manly Wade WELLMAN's *Giants from Eternity* (**1939**) to R.A. LAFFERTY's *Past Master* (**1968**) and Philip K. DICK's *We Can Build You* (**1972**). The jargon of TIME TRAVEL and ANDROID simulation, however, tends to be used in order to avoid the notion of literal reincarnation. The most sensitive of all these stories is James BLISH's "A Work of Art" (1956; vt "Art-Work") concerning the experiences of a reincarnated Richard Strauss (*see* ARTS).

The extravagance of pulp superscience epics occasionally extended to a blithe disregard for such inconveniences as death, but the actual process and experience of reincarnation is rarely central in such stories. The hero of A.E. VAN VOGT's *The World of Ā* (1945; **1948**; vt *The World of Null-A*) is reincarnated several times without slowing the action down. Van Vogt also used a literal process of reincarnation in "The Monster" (1948; vt "Resurrection"). Reincarnation is also the *donnée* of his *The Book of Ptath* (1947; vt *Two Hundred Million A.D.*) in which a tank commander from World War II wakes up as an amnesiac god.

The first sf novel which developed a "scientific" logic for straightforward reincarnation was Robert SHECKLEY's *Immortality, Inc.* (**1959**), in which disembodied minds compete for bodies made redundant by their occupiers for one reason or another. Religious notions of reincarnation have been transplanted into sf by Roger ZELAZNY, most notably

in *Lord of Light* (**1967**), which employs a framework based on Hindu MYTHOLOGY, and *Creatures of Light and Darkness* (**1969**), which uses Egyptian mythology. There is also a memorable reincarnation scene in his *Jack of Shadows* (**1971**). Another writer to make extensive use of the idea in recent years is Philip José FARMER, most notably in the "Riverworld" series whose best episode is *To Your Scattered Bodies Go* (**1971**), in which the entire human race is reincarnated along the banks of a great river and also — incidentally — in *Traitor to the Living* (**1973**) and — obliquely — in *Inside Outside* (**1964**). An ingenious reincarnation project is mounted by an heiress whose lover dies of cancer in "When You Care, When You Love" (1962) by Theodore STURGEON, using the idea of CLONING. Another variety of reincarnation by MATTER TRANSMISSION is employed in Algis BUDRYS's *Rogue Moon* (**1960**). A form of reincarnation takes place with an alien re-birth ceremony in *Downward to the Earth* (**1970**) by Robert SILVERBERG, one of his best novels.

An original twist on the theme is provided by Richard COWPER in *Breakthrough* (**1967**), in which personalities from the future are "reincarnated" in the present. The most common use of the idea in contemporary sf, however, is based on the thesis that it might become possible to record and store personalities by electrical means for possible reincarnation at a later date. The inevitable corollary of this notion is a shortage of bodies. The difficulty is overcome by sharing in Robert Silverberg's *To Live Again* (**1969**), but other novels focus on the problems of personalities awaiting reincarnation, including *Gray Matters* (**1971**) by William HJORTSBERG and *Friends Come in Boxes* (**1973**) by Michael G. CONEY. This version of the theme seems to hold considerable potential for the future. [BS] **See also:** IMMORTALITY; RELIGION; SUSPENDED ANIMATION.

REINEKE, L. THOMAS (? –). American writer whose sf novel is *The Hormone Holocaust* (**1974**). [JC]

RELATIVITY *See* FASTER THAN LIGHT; PHYSICS.

RELIGION From a study of the usual rationalist DEFINITIONS of sf it would seem that there is nothing more alien to its concerns than religion. However, if we go back in time to seek its roots in PROTO SF we find many of them embedded in the traditions of speculative fiction associated with the religious imagination, and when we examine the sf of today for its dominant trends we find a strong interest in certain mystical and transcendental themes and images. As sf moved beyond the constraints of standardized PULP fiction it was forced to confront the age-

This book was a milestone in the exploration of RELIGION as a theme in genre sf. Cover of the Weidenfeld and Nicolson edition, 1960, by Milton Glaser.

old speculative issues associated with METAPHYSICS and theology, in search of possible answers consonant with the discoveries of modern science – because of, rather than in spite of, the fact that science itself rules the questions unanswerable. One of the principal imaginative impulses behind sf has been the need to move into these speculative areas where there are no empirical data to be sought, and in this sense speculative fiction is not only science fiction but metaphysical fiction too.

It was the religious imagination of such men as Giordano Bruno which first envisioned an infinite universe filled with habitable worlds, and it was visionaries like Athanasius KIRCHER and Emanuel SWEDENBORG who first journeyed in the imagination to the limits of the Solar System and beyond. John WILKINS, who first conjectured that men might go to the Moon in a flying machine, was a bishop – and so was Francis GODWIN, the author of the satirical cosmic voyage *The Man in the Moone* (**1638**). Other early speculative fictions were attacks upon religious cosmology and religious orthodoxy by free thinkers such as CYRANO DE BERGERAC, VOLTAIRE and, later, Samuel BUTLER. Mary SHELLEY's *Frankenstein* (1818; rev. 1831) takes its imaginative inspiration from the image of the scientist as usurper of the prerogatives of God. The boldest of all the 19th-century speculative fictions, Camille FLAMMARION's *Lumen* (1887 France; trans. **1897**), was the result of a desperate need felt by the astronomer to reconcile and fuse his scientific knowledge with his religious faith. J.H. ROSNY AÎNÉ, the prolific writer of evolutionary fantasies, also saw the object of his work as an imaginative revelation of the divinely planned evolutionary schema, and he too wanted to remodel theology to integrate it with scientific knowledge – a task later taken up by Pierre Teilhard de Chardin.

C. Howard HINTON, who wrote fiction and essays about the FOURTH DIMENSION, was particularly moved by the notion that a four-dimensional God might indeed be omniscient of everything that has ever or will ever take place in our three-dimensional continuum. Marie CORELLI developed the notion of a God of electric force in *A Romance of Two Worlds* (**1886**; rev. 1887). John Jacob ASTOR's *A Journey in Other Worlds* (**1894**) makes abundant use of the scientific imagination while continuing the tradition of cosmic voyages whose main aim was to investigate theological issues. The same is true of Edgar FAWCETT's *The Ghost of Guy Thyrle* (**1895**), whose hero journeys to the edge of the universe to consult a messenger of God about the possibility of release from his unhappy state, and of Jean Delaire's *Around a Distant Star* (**1904**). Even a relatively crude scientific romance, like John MASTIN's *Through the Sun in an Airship* (**1909**), took time out to observe that the inner structure of the SUN was compatible with the account of creation offered in Genesis.

In virtually all late 19th-century and early 20th-century speculative fiction the antagonism of the scientific and religious imaginations is evident, whether the thrust of the narrative is toward reconciliation or conflict. This was the period in which the religious imagination faced simultaneous attack from Darwinism, humanism and socialism. In Guy THORNE's *When it was Dark* (**1904**) an evil rationalist fakes evidence that the resurrection never happened and Christian civilization comes to the brink of collapse. In Robert Hugh BENSON's *Lord of the World* (**1907**) a humanist socialist woos the world to his cause and proves to be the anti-Christ of prophecy. In another novel, *The Dawn of All* (**1911**) Benson, a Catholic, tries to show the wonderful world that might result if only men would renounce humanism, socialism, protestantism and other heresies, but the tide was already too strong. One of the humanists Benson hated so much, H.G. WELLS, had already written a novel in which a new kind of angel comes to Earth to observe the sins of mankind in *The Wonderful Visit* (**1895**), and he was to go on to write *First and Last Things* (**1908**) and *God the Invisible King* (**1917**), developing a new speculative theology which formed the background to such novels as *The Soul of a Bishop* (**1917**) and a new Book of Job, *The Undying Fire* (**1919**). This interest in alternative theology is central to the work of Olaf STAPLEDON, who undertook in *Star Maker* (**1937**) to explore a cosmic scheme spanning all space and all time, culminating in the vision of the Star Maker, God the Scientist, experimenting with creation. In the following year C.S. LEWIS co-opted the science-fictional vocabulary of symbols for the theological fantasy *Out of the Silent Planet* (**1938**),

which retained a solid base in Christian teaching. Lewis extended his borrowing further in *Perelandra* (**1943**; vt *Voyage to Venus*) and *The Great Divorce* (**1945**). Lewis's friend Charles WILLIAMS also wrote a series of theological fantasies, in some of which he borrowed from rationalistic speculators – notably in *Many Dimensions* (**1931**) and *Shadows of Ecstasy* (**1933**).

André MAUROIS returned to the theme of the scientist interfering with divine ordinance in *Le peseur d'âmes* (**1931**; trans. as *The Weigher of Souls* 1931). Franz WERFEL's last work, *Stern der Ungeborenen* (**1946**; trans. as *Star of the Unborn* 1946) was a massive futuristic novel in which scientific and religious speculations weigh equally. Bertrand RUSSELL, a dedicated humanist, emulated Voltaire in "Zahatopolk" (1954), a vitriolic satire on the pretensions of established religion, and in "Faith and Mountains" (1954) he was equally scathing about faddish cults. John ATKINS wrote the ironic *Tomorrow Revealed* (**1955**), in which the history of our age is reconstructed from its imaginative works and its hidden theological significance is displayed. Philip WYLIE brought another angel to Earth in *The Answer* (**1955**). This long tradition of theological speculation in literature continues to the present day, extending into the 1970s in such works as John CAMERON's *The Astrologer* (**1972**) and Romain GARY's *The Gasp* (**1973**). It would not be unreasonable to claim that, outside genre sf, speculative fiction has always been as much concerned with the visions of the religious imagination as those of the scientific imagination.

Within the genre, however, the story is different. In the pulps, religion was TABOO. Theology was ignored, and where metaphysical issues were touched upon they were treated with circumspection. The one curious exception to this rule was the sub-genre of "Shaggy God" stories which reinterpreted the truth of Biblical mythology in the most banal fashion. The early pulps, however, played safe even here by scrupulously avoiding the New Testament; most of the older pulp stories in this vein deal with ADAM AND EVE. The earliest sf story featuring a world-creating alien, Clifford D. SIMAK's *The Creator* (**1935**; **1946**) found a home only in the semi-professional MARVEL TALES. The future evolution of institutionalized religion was first considered in Robert A. HEINLEIN's "If This Goes On. ..." (1940), in which a tyrannical state of the future operates through an Established Church. This story represented its religious leader as a bigot and a fanatic, an image which has persisted in sf ever since. In *Sixth Column* (1941 as by Anson MacDonald; **1949**; vt *The Day After Tomorrow*) Heinlein showed the other side of the coin: America is conquered by Asians and wins free with the aid of a fake religious cult. This story originated another notion

common in sf, that religion can be good and useful only if it is wholly insincere. Fritz LEIBER amalgamated the two ideas in *Gather, Darkness!* (1943; **1950**), in which the tyrannical rule of the state religion is overthrown by a cult of pretend-Satanists. All these religions, however, were mere superstructure. The theological issues remained untouched. In UNKNOWN, John W. CAMPBELL Jr's authors were willing to tackle angels, GODS AND DEMONS with gay abandon, but strictly for fun. At least, however, they were prepared to offer no particular favour to Christian MYTHOLOGY. Alongside stories making light of the Greek pantheon and the world of the *Faerie Queen* appeared Henry KUTTNER's "The Misguided Halo" (1939), Cleve CARTMILL's "Prelude to Armageddon" (1942), and Fredric BROWN's "The Angelic Angleworm" (1943). The magazine did feature one hypothetical novel which confronted general theological issues – A.E. VAN VOGT's *The Book of Ptath* (1943; **1947** vt *200,000,000 A.D.*; vt *Ptath*) — but its treatment of them was rather confused. This was the situation before and during the Second World War.

After the War, things changed dramatically. There was a boom in stories which, without any trepidation whatever, cut straight to the heart of the matter. Ray BRADBURY's "The Man" (1949) concerns space travellers following Jesus on his interplanetary mission of salvation, and in his "In This Sign ..." (1951; vt "The Fire Balloons") priests encounter sinless beings on Mars. Anthony BOUCHER's "The Quest for St. Aquin" (1951) is about a ROBOT who emulates St Thomas Aquinas in logically deducing the existence of God. Paul L. Payne's "Fool's Errand" (1952) is about a Jew who finds a cross in the sands of Mars. James BLISH's *A Case of Conscience* (first part 1953; **1958**) is about a Jesuit forced by his faith to the conclusion that an alien world is the creation of the devil. Lester DEL REY's "For I Am a Jealous People" (1954) builds on the premise that alien invaders might arrive to take possession of the Earth having made their own covenant with God and become his chosen people. Arthur C. CLARKE's "The Star" (1955) deals with the discovery of the inhabited worlds that were destroyed in the nova that made a new star shine over Bethlehem. The writer who did most to import religious concerns into sf in this period was Philip José FARMER; his *The Lovers* (1952; exp. **1961**) has a future Earth whose social *mores* derive from the "Western Talmud", and its sequel *A Woman a Day* (1953; rev. **1960**; vt *The Day of Timestop* USA; vt *Timestop* UK) continues the exploration of future religions. "The God Business" (1954) is a phantasmagoric, pantheistic fantasy whose hero ends up as a deity, and the same opportunity is offered to a conventional Churchman in "Father"

(1955). The latter belongs to a series featuring the priest John Carmody, whose conversion as a result of authentic transcendental experience is described in *Night of Light* (1957; exp. **1966**) and whose eventual mission is the subject of "A Few Miles" (1960) and "Prometheus" (1961). The most impressive single work to come out of the post-War sf boom was Walter M. MILLER's *A Canticle for Leibowitz* (1955-7; fix-up **1960**), which follows the society of the future as it recovers from atomic HOLOCAUST, focusing on the role played by the Church. Farmer's first two novels, James GUNN's *This Fortress World* (**1955**) and Poul ANDERSON's "Superstition" (1956) are all more sophisticated investigations of the sociology of religion than *Sixth Column* or *Gather, Darkness!*, but Miller's novel is one of the most thoughtful speculative exercises produced within genre sf.

To explain this sudden outburst of interest in theology we need more than the observation that the death of the pulps resulted in a decline of the taboos associated with them. James Blish, drawn to consider the phenomenon by his own involvement with it, wrote the essay "Cathedrals in Space" (1953; incorporated into *The Issue at Hand*, coll. **1964**), as by William Atheling Jr, citing the stories as "instruments of a chiliastic crisis, of a magnitude we have not seen since the chiliastic panic of 999 A.D." He draws a link between these stories and the boom in atomic Armageddons (made explicit, in fact, by the two stories written by Boucher and Miller, both Catholics). In 1945 our power to destroy outstripped our power to create and by 1953 the advent of the H-Bomb both the USA and the USSR had the power to annihilate the human race. The main difference between the new millenarian panic and the old is that in AD 999 there was a deadline which expired and allowed the Christian world to relax again. Since 1945 there has been no such possibility of relief. In view of this it is hardly surprising that the interest in theological issues, and metaphysical issues in general, prompted by this existential insecurity has not waned, but has become more powerful, though sometimes it is not explicit. A remarkable phenomenon associated with the boom is the resurgence of images which are obviously analogues of religious notions but which are disconnected from religious doctrine. Arthur C. Clarke has said that any religious symbolism or imagery in *Childhood's End* (1950; exp. **1953**) is "entirely accidental", and yet the chain of events described is strikingly similar to the evolutionary schema drawn up by the Jesuit Pierre Teilhard de Chardin and published posthumously (after the publication of *Childhood's End*). Similarly, there is no religious doctrine evident in Clifford D. Simak's *Time and Again* (**1951**; vt *First He Died*), though

the alien symbiotes of this novel, infesting all living things, are analogous to souls (*see* ESCHATOLOGY). In later works by Simak — particularly *A Choice of Gods* (**1972**) — a "cosmic mind" or "Principle" similar to Teilhard's lurks in the background of the emotional substratum which connects much of the author's work. A novel explicitly based on Teilhard is George ZEBROWSKI's *The Omega Point* (**1972**). This movement towards a rationalized theology is non-Christian (this applies even to Teilhard, whose ideas were deemed heretical), but there is also a contrasting group of stories which approach the central symbol of the Christian faith — the crucifixion — in the most direct manner. Richard MATHESON's "The Traveler" (1962) visits the scene in order to find faith; the heroes of Brian EARNSHAW's *Planet in the Eye of Time* (**1968**) go there to protect faith from subversion; the hero of Michael MOORCOCK's *Behold the Man!* (1966; exp. **1969**) goes in order to become Christ and find his own redemption.

"Fake" religions still crop up regularly in sf. Trivial examples include *The Symmetrians* (**1966**) by Kenneth HARKER and *To the Land of the Electric Angel* (**1976**) by William ROTSLER, while not-so-trivial ones are Kurt VONNEGUT Jr's *The Sirens of Titan* (**1959**) and *Slapstick* (**1976**); but even in juvenile fiction one can find thoughtful studies in the sociology of religion, as in *This Star Shall Abide* (**1972**; vt *Heritage of the Star*) by Sylvia ENGDAHL. Other exercises in the sociology of religion are Keith ROBERTS's *Pavane* (coll. of linked stories **1968**) and Kingsley AMIS's *The Alteration* (**1976**) — both ALTERNATE-WORLDS stories in which history is changed so that the Catholic Church's domination of Europe survives the Reformation.

There is a very noticeable change in post-War attitudes to alien religions – which, before the War, all fell into the "fake" category and were often used for satirical purposes. It was to alien beliefs that sf writers first began to credit the element of truth that they withheld from Earthly religion. In Katherine MacLEAN's "Unhuman Sacrifice" (1958) missionaries to an alien world find that the superstitions they set out to subvert are not so absurd as they assume. In Robert SILVERBERG's *Downward to the Earth* (**1970**) a man seeks his own salvation via the transcendental experiences associated with an alien religion, and a similarly powerful myth of rebirth is featured in his *Nightwings* (**1969**). In D.G. COMPTON's *The Missionaries* (**1972**) alien missionaries bring to Earth an enigmatic offer of salvation. In Poul Anderson's "The Problem of Pain" (1973) a man must come to terms with the fact that an alien has allowed his wife to die in agony because of her alien religious precepts. In Gregory BENFORD and Gordon EKLUND's "If the Stars are Gods" (1974; incorporated into *If the Stars are Gods*,

fix-up **1977**) alien visitors seeking a new sun-god allow a man to "know" our sun, though the meaning of the revelation remains unclear. In George R.R. MARTIN's "A Song for Lya" (1974) humans again seek and find transcendental experience in alien ways. The point of view of Satan, seen here as a wise, misunderstood alien, is given in Harlan ELLISON's remarkable "The Deathbird" (1973), a FAR-FUTURE story which movingly argues that the story of the Fall in Genesis is effectively a fraud perpetrated on us by God. *The Mind Gods* (**1976**) by Marie JAKOBER pits an apparently repellent religion, developed on a human-seeded planet, against "liberal" materialism, and the moral outcome is not wholly anti-religious. One writer who has attempted in a number of recent novels to establish a concrete theology in both Earthly and alien terms is Philip K. DICK, especially in "Faith of Our Fathers" (1967), *Galactic Pot-Healer* (**1969**), *A Maze of Death* (**1970**) and *Our Friends from Frolix-8* (**1970**).

Sf writers have also been remarkably eager to look at religious experience from "the other side" — the experience of being God (*see also* GODS AND DEMONS). This theme was first developed in artificial situations concerning scientists who rule their tiny creations, as in Edmond HAMILTON's "Fessenden's Worlds" (1937) and Theodore STURGEON's "Microcosmic God" (1941), and progressed through weak Shaggy God jokes like Fredric Brown's "Solipsist" (1954) and Eric Frank RUSSELL's "Sole Solution" (1956) to serious consideration, beginning with Farmer's "The God Business" and "Father". Later examples are Robert BLOCH's intensely bitter "The Funnel of God" (1960), a number of novels by Roger ZELAZNY, including *Lord of Light* (**1967**), *Creatures of Light and Darkness* (**1969**) and *Isle of the Dead* (**1969**), and Frank HERBERT's *The God Makers* (**1972**). There is perhaps no other theme within religious sf which better testifies to the nature of our contemporary millenarian anxiety and emphasizes its distinctness from the panic of AD 999. Our present predicament is brought about by our inheritance of "godlike power" — a power which may doom us all or may also promise us emancipation from the gods of religion which once symbolized the fact that our destiny was not under our own control. Our anxiety now is that of opportunity as well as that of fear. Sf, in looking at the futures which may grow from our present situation, must confront all the implications of this. Thus sf is now a medium for fantasies of metaphysics as well as of physics, and many of its authors are realizing that the former may be more important than the latter.

A variety of thematic anthologies bear on this topic; they include *Other Worlds, Other Gods* (anth. **1971**) ed. Mayo Mohs, *Strange Gods* (anth. **1974**) ed. Roger

ELWOOD, *Wandering Stars* (anth. **1974**) ed. Jack DANN, which features sf about Jews, and *The New Awareness: Religion Through Science Fiction* (anth. **1975**) ed. Martin Harry GREENBERG and Patricia Warrick.   [BS]

See also: ENTROPY; IMMORTALITY; REINCARNATION; SATIRE; SUPERNATURAL CREATURES.

REMBER, WINTHROP ALLEN (? – ?). American writer whose sf work is *Eighteen Visits to Mars* (coll. **1956**).   [JC]

RENARD, CHRISTINE (? –). French writer. Married scientist and sf writer Claude F. Cheinisse in 1965. An elegant and warm writer, sometimes using feminist themes, CR has written several sf and fantasy novels, including *A contre-temps* ["Against time"] (**1963**), *La planète des poupées* ["Planet of the Dolls"] (**1971**) and *La mante au fil des jours* ["Day of the Mantis"] (**1977**). She is particularly at ease in the short-story form, and has published over 30.   [MJ]

RENARD, MAURICE (1875–1940). French writer, best known in English for his sf novel *Les mains d'Orlac* (**1920**; trans. as *The Hands of Orlac* **1929**), filmed in 1924 as THE HANDS OF ORLAC; another version was MAD LOVE (1935). The story deals, GOTHICally, with the ominous consequences of a hand transplant. A less well-known though more wildly imaginative novel is *Le docteur Lerne, sous-dieu* (**1908**; trans. as *New Bodies for Old* **1923**), in which the sinister doctor's experiments in grafting have produced rats with leaves and the transplanting of the hero's brain into a bull's body and vice versa; the ultimate transplant is of the villain's brain into the body of a car, but the machinery is thus rendered mortal, and ultimately putrefies.

With Albert Jean, MR wrote *Le Singe* (**1925**; trans. as *Blind Circle* **1928**), a mystery story whose solution reveals the manufacture of a series of identical ANDROIDS by a kind of electrolysis. MR is generally regarded in France as the most important native sf writer for the period 1900–1930. His untranslated works include the collections *Le voyage immobile suivi d'autres histoires singulières* ["The Immobile Voyage and Other Curious Stories"] (coll. **1909**; rev. 1922), *M. D'Outremort et autres histoires singulières* ["Mr Overdeath and Other Curious Stories"] (coll. **1913**; vt *Suite Fantastique*), *L'invitation à la peur* ["Invitation to Fear"] (coll. **1926**) and *Le carrousel du mystère* ["Mystery Roundabout"] (coll. **1929**). These include many fine stories on a great variety of sf themes: invisibility, time travel, cyborgs, gravity, space-time paradoxes and, especially and often, altered modes of PERCEPTION. MR's untranslated novels include *Le péril bleu* ["The Blue Peril"] (**1910**), about an extraordinary civilization of life-forms living on the top

The Fly, one of the sf film stars of the 1950s, in RETURN OF THE FLY.

of an atmosphere as if it were a sea; *Un homme chez les microbes, scherzo* ["A Man Amongst the Microbes: a scherzo"] (**1928**), a journey into the microcosm with more sophistication and verbal wit than those of Ray CUMMINGS; *L'homme truqué* ["The Fake Man"] described by Pierre VERSINS as "a nightmare based on the universe as seen by a mutilated giant whose eyes have been replaced by 'electroscopes' ... the pretext for many pages of a strange, visual poetry" and *Le maître de la lumière* ["Master of Light"] (1920s; **1948**), a serial published posthumously in book form about the invention of a new form of glass which condenses space and time, similar to the "slow glass" invented (independently) by Bob SHAW.   [PN/JC]

See also: CLONES; ESCHATOLOGY; FANTASY; PSYCHOLOGY; SCIENTISTS.

REPP, ED EARL (1901–). American advertising man, and later a fairly typical PULP writer (from the Great Crash on). He published his first sf story, "Beyond Gravity", with *Air Wonder Stories* in 1929, simultaneously with the magazine publication of his first novel, *The Radium Pool* (1929 *Science Wonder Stories*; **1949**) which with two other stories, plus L. Ron HUBBARD's *Triton*, are also bound as *Science-Fantasy Quintet* (**1953**); his

collection of stories *The Stellar Missiles* (coll. **1949**) also reached book form after he had stopped contributing to the magazines before the end of the Second World War. He also wrote a series of stories in *AMZ*, 1939–43, about John Hale, a scientific detective perhaps modelled on Arthur B. REEVE's Craig Kennedy.   [JC]

See also: ALIENS.

REPTILICUS Film (1963). Cinemagic/ AIP. Directed by Sidney Pink, starring Carl Ottosen and Smyrner. Screenplay by Ib Melchior and Sidney Pink. 90 mins. Colour.

In this poor film, Danish cinema's only excursion into the monster genre, the drill bit of an oil survey team is found to contain samples of flesh and blood which turn out to have come from the tail of a buried dinosaur. The tail is exhumed and taken to a laboratory where it then proceeds to grow a new body — the only novel touch in the film. The hilariously unreal special effects are all that make this production in any way memorable.

The novelization, *Reptilicus* (**1961**), by Dean OWEN, was released earlier.   [JB]

RESNICK, MICHAEL D. (1942–). American writer who began as an Edgar Rice BURROUGHS fan, publishing material

The much-loved star of the 1950s, the Creature, in REVENGE OF THE CREATURE.

in *ERB-dom Magazine*; he has published fiction in numerous genres. His sf/fantasy novels, beginning with the series *The Goddess of Ganymede* **(1967)** and *Pursuit on Ganymede* **(1968)** show Burroughs' influence. His *Official Guide to Fantastic Literature* **(1976)** is a price guide; several book dealers have felt it to be less than official. [JC]
Other works: *Redbeard* **(1969)**.

RESTIF DE LA BRETONNE Name by which the French writer Nicolas-Anne-Edmé Restif (1734–1806) is usually known. He was an extremely prolific author of formless, semi-autobiographical novels often attacked for imputed pornographic content; his sf novel, *La découverte australe par un homme volant, ou le dédale français* ["The Southern-Hemisphere Discovery by a Flying Man, or the French Daedalus"] **(1781)**, first describes the flying Frenchman's gear (wings plus parachute), then his Alpine UTOPIA, then his adventures in the Antipodes where, like François RABELAIS's heroes, he visits a number of allegorical islands. [JC]
Other works: *Les posthumes* ["The Posthumous Ones"] **(1802)**.
See also: EVOLUTION; SATIRE.

RETURN OF THE FLY Film (1959). Associated Producers/20th Century-Fox.

Directed by Edward L. Bernds, starring Vincent Price, Brett Halsey, David Frankham and John Sutton. Screenplay by Edward L. Bernds. 78 mins. B/w.

This was the first of two sequels of the successful sf/horror film THE FLY, the subsequent sequel being CURSE OF THE FLY. Here the son of the unfortunate scientist of *The Fly* repeats his father's errors, rather limply; it is the least successful of the three films. [PN]

RETURN OF THE LOST PLANET
See LOST PLANET, THE.

REVENGE OF THE CREATURE
Film (1954). Universal. Directed by Jack ARNOLD, starring John Agar, Lori Nelson and John Bromfield. Screenplay by Martin Berkeley, story by William Alland. 82 mins. B/w.

The success of CREATURE FROM THE BLACK LAGOON inspired the inevitable sequel. This time the "Creature" is captured and taken to an oceanarium in Florida, but it soon breaks out and makes off with the nearest pretty girl under its arm. Thanks to Arnold's direction, it is just as entertaining and atmospheric as its predecessor, and even more erotically charged. A further sequel was THE CREATURE WALKS AMONG US. [JB]

REYNOLDS, MACK Form of his name

used by American writer Dallas McCord Reynolds (1917–   ) from the beginning of his career as an author in 1950, when he published his first story, "Isolationist", in *Fantastic Adventures*, though he very occasionally wrote under the pseudonyms Clark Collins (one story), Guy McCord (one story), Dallas Ross (two stories) and Mark Mallory (four stories). Born in California (his ancestors were Forty-Niners), MR is a graduate of the United States Army Marine Officers' Cadet School and its Up-Grading School. He was for 25 years an active member of the American Socialist Labor Party, for which his father, Verne L. Reynolds, had twice been presidential candidate, and still considers himself a "militant radical", a self-evaluation reflected in many of the novels he has written, especially those in recent years whose presentations of possible futures are unashamedly didactic, though by no means doctrinaire.

MR's first novel, *The Case of the Little Green Men* **(1951)**, is not sf but is (very unusually) *about* sf in the form of a mystery set at an sf CONVENTION. Some of MR's early work was written in collaboration with, at different times, Fredric BROWN, Theodore COGSWELL and August DERLETH. Many of the lucid, clear-cut stories of his first decade as a writer can be found in *The Best of Mack Reynolds* (coll. **1976**); its introduction explains his early decision to concentrate on sf which speculated on social and economic issues, and describes some of his far-flung investigative travels, one of which, through Russia, confirmed his distaste for institutionalized communism. His first novels, however, like *The Earth War* (**1962**), with its sequels, *Time Gladiator* (**1966**) and *Mercenary from Tomorrow* (**1968**), all based on material originally published in *ASF*, tend to be straightforward interstellar adventures, often, as with this first series, featuring military or paramilitary heroes in situations sometimes verging on slapstick, opposed by aliens whose colourful simplicity resembles that of Eric Frank RUSSELL'S. His best-known series, the adventures of the agents of Section G of the United Planets Organization, begins at this time, comprising to date *Planetary Agent X* (1960–66 var. mags; fix-up **1965**), *Amazon Planet* (1966 *ASF*; in Italian **1967**; **1975**), *Dawnman Planet* (**1966**), *The Rival Rigelians* (1960 *ASF* as "Adaptation"; exp. **1967**), *Code Duello* (**1968**), and *Section G: United Planets* (1967 *ASF*; fix-up **1976**). Section G agents have the task of stimulating progress undercover on various alien planets. A similar series, set in North Africa, is comprised of *Black Man's Burden* (1961 *ASF*; **1972**), *Border, Breed Nor Birth* (1962 *ASF*; **1972**), the recent novella "Black Sheep Astray" and a further projected novel, tentatively entitled *The Best Ye Breed*. The similar "Rex Bader" series, which combines action-adventure and economic theory, is comprised of *Five Way Secret Agent* (1969 *ASF*; **1975**) and *Satellite City* (**1975**). Two sequels have been written and are projected for publication soon, their tentative titles being *Of Future Fears* and *Lagrange Five*. It should be noted that *Planetary Agent X* and *Time Gladiator* both exist in pirated editions published in Israel, with numerous changes and deletions.

More recently, MR has been publishing a series of novels linked only by being placed in various projected societies of the year 2000; the projections are based on his speculative sense of what the world of that date might have come to, given various politico-economic outcomes of our present situation: communist, anarchist, capitalist, and so forth. Though several novels contribute to this panorama, such as *Commune 2000 AD* (**1974**), *The Towers of Utopia* (**1975**) and *Police Patrol: 2000 AD* (fix-up **1977**), the centrepiece of the project is undoubtedly MR's two sequels to Edward BELLAMY's two famous UTOPIAS, *Looking Backward, from the Year 2000* (**1973**) and *Equality: in the Year 2000* (**1977**). Fatally ill, Julian West is put to sleep to await a world in which he might be cured (*see* CRYONICS), and is awoken in 2000 to find himself in an environment dominated by the knowledge explosion and a technological expansion whose

effects are mostly beneficial: Utopia indeed. His main problem — an incapacity to catch up to this vastly more complex world — seems by the end of the second volume to be near solution; an experimental knowledge-transplant process has been announced.

In all his work MR writes with speed, clarity and a simplicity that sometimes fails to do justice to the complexity of the issues he treats. His portraits of the year 2000 are still in progress, and may amount to an impressive sequence of arguments. [JC]

Other works: *Night is for Monsters* (**1964**); *Of Godlike Power* (**1966**; vt *Earth Unaware*); *After Some Tomorrow* (**1967**); *Computer War* (**1967**); *Space Pioneer* (**1967**); *Star Trek: Mission to Horatius* (**1969**); *The Cosmic Eye* (**1969**); *The Space Barbarians* (fix-up **1969**); *Speakeasy* (1963 *FSF*; exp. **1969**); *Computer World* (**1970**); *Once Departed* (**1970**); *The House in the Kasbah* (**1972**), a Gothic; *The Home of the Inquisitor* (**1972**), a Gothic; *Depression or Bust* (**1974**); *Ability Quotient* (**1975**); *Tomorrow Might Be Different* (**1975**); *Rolltown* (**1976**); *Day after Tomorrow* (1961 *ASF* as "Status Quo"; exp. **1976**); *Galactic Medal of Honour* (**1976**); *Space Visitor* (**1977**); *After Utopia* (**1977**); *Perchance to Dream* (**1977**).

As editor, with Fredric Brown, *The Science Fiction Carnival* (anth. **1953**).

See also: ECONOMICS; HISTORY IN SF; LEISURE; POLITICS; TIME PARADOXES; TIME TRAVEL; WAR.

RHODES, W(ILLIAM) H(ENRY) (1822–76). American lawyer and writer who published various newspaper pieces and stories under the name Caxton, notably *The Case of Summerfield* (1871 in a San Francisco newspaper; **1907**), about a scientist who threatens the destruction of the oceans of the world; this, along with its sequel, four other sf stories and other ephemera, were published as a memorial by colleagues of the author as *Caxton's Book: A Collection of Essays, Poems, Tales and Sketches* (coll. **1876**). [JC]

RICHARDS, ALFRED BATE (1820–76). English editor of the *Morning Advertiser*, and writer. For many years he was active as a propagandist for English military preparedness, in aid of which he wrote his long story *The Invasion of England (A possible tale of future times)* (**1870**); the tale, published privately, had little impact, and was in any case much inferior to Lt.-Col. Sir George T. CHESNEY'S *The Battle of Dorking* (**1871**), which though it came second effectively founded the future-WAR/INVASION genre so popular over the next 40 years. [JC]

RICHARDS, GUY (1905–). American writer and reporter, whose sf novel about a Russian takeover of New York, embarrassingly disowned by the

Kremlin, is *Two Rubles to Times Square* (**1956**; vt *Brother Bear* UK). [JC]

RICHARDS, HENRY *See* Richard SAXON.

RICHARDSON, R.S. *See* Philip LATHAM.

RICHMOND, LEIGH (? –). American journalist and writer, the latter almost exclusively in collaboration with her husband, Walt RICHMOND (*who see for details*).

RICHMOND, MARY (? –). British writer whose sf novel is *The Grim Tomorrow* (**1953**). [JC]

RICHMOND, WALT (1922–77). American writer and research scientist, his fiction always in collaboration with his wife, Leigh RICHMOND; they began publishing sf with the novel "Where I Wasn't Going" for *ASF* in 1963; their first book is *Shock Wave* (**1967**). This and their subsequent novels, like *The Lost Millenium* (**1967**), which capably combines a new source of solar energy and the return of ancient Earth-dwellers, routinely but competently use hard-sf material in adventure settings. *Challenge the Hellmaker* (**1976**) is a NEAR-FUTURE novel expanding "Where I Wasn't Going", pitting scientists on a space station against an attempt at dictatorship on Earth. [JC]

Other works: *Phoenix Ship* (**1969**); *Gallagher's Glacier* (1964 *ASF*; **1970**); *Positive Charge* (coll. **1970**); *The Probability Corner* (**1977**).

RICHTER-FRICH, ØVRE *See* SCANDINAVIA.

RIDERS TO THE STARS Film (1954). Ivan Tors/United Artists. Directed by Richard Carlson, starring William Lundigan, Herbert Marshall, Richard Carlson and Martha Hyer. Screenplay by Curt SIODMAK. 82 mins. Colour.

Scientists and space pilots are trying to overcome the problem of air friction when re-entering the Earth's atmosphere, which causes their vehicles to burn up. The theory is put forward that meteors possess a special quality that protects them from heat friction, and a number of spaceships are sent up, with special scoops on their noses, to capture meteors before they reach the atmosphere. The alloy that the meteors contain is then used as a protective coating for the spaceships. The film is popular with aficionados, many of whom maintain it is the most absurdly unscientific movie in the entire genre, from which much of its value as entertainment derives. The novelization as by Curt Siodmak and Robert Smith was published in 1953. [JB]

RIENOW, LEONA (TRAIN) (? –). American writer, whose prehistoric sf novel is *The Bewitched Caverns* (**1948**). With her husband Robert Rienow she later wrote *The Year of the Last Eagle* (**1970**), a sour NEAR-FUTURE comedy about ECOLOGY, set in 1989; the hero's job is to locate the last white-headed eagles (the national bird of the USA), if any still exist. [PN/JC]

RIGG, Lt.-Col. ROBERT B. (? –). American writer on military topics whose *War — 1974* (**1958**) puts into the didactic fictional form of a future-WAR narrative his speculations about developments in WEAPONS and tactics, and about the general nature of warfare in the future. After an initial exchange of ICBMs, East and West settle down to conventional conflict dominated by much implausible non-nuclear gimmickry. [JC]

RILEY, FRANK (? –). American writer. His first sf was "The Execution" for *If* in 1956. He is mainly known for his collaboration with Mark CLIFTON in *They'd Rather Be Right* (**1954**), the HUGO-winning conclusion of Clifton's "Bossy" series about an advanced COMPUTER rendered almost useless by men's fear of her. [JC]
See also: AUTOMATION.

RIMWORLD A common item of sf TERMINOLOGY. *See* GALACTIC LENS.

RITCHIE, PAUL (1923–). Australian painter, novelist and playwright, known mainly for his work outside the sf field, e.g. *The Protagonist* (**1966**). His sf novel, *Confessions of a People Lover* (**1967**), depicts a grey, urban, DYSTOPIAN England where the old ("longlivers") are eliminated by the state and where the young are corrupt, cultureless vandals. The book is narrated by a longliver in an enriched, clotted, free-associational narrative markedly unlike most sf prose; he has been caught by the state, is given a last night in the arms of a whore, and faces the morning of his death fully human, though the world is indifferent. There is no sf hardware to speak of, and the book could be read as allegorical of post-War Britain. [JC]

RIVERSIDE, JOHN *See* Robert A. HEINLEIN.

RIVERSIDE QUARTERLY American FANZINE (1964–) edited by Leland Sapiro from Canada and the USA. Jon White was originally co-editor and *RQ* formed a part continuation of the fanzine *Inside*, which won a HUGO award in 1956. Academic essays on sf and fantasy are its main content. Alexei PANSHIN published the major part of his *Heinlein In Dimension* (**1968**) in *RQ* originally; other contributors have included James BLISH, Jack WILLIAMSON, and Algis BUDRYS. [PR]

ROBERTS, ANTHONY (1950–). British sf illustrator. He attended Wolverhampton College of Art, 1967-9, and Ravensbourne College of Art, 1969-72. He has done cover illustrations for Coronet, Sphere Books, Quartet, Star, Panther Books, Magnum, Futura and Puffin, as well as adventure covers for Fontana paperbacks. His style is similar to, and perhaps imitative of, that of Chris Foss; his smooth, hard-edged, highly detailed paintings are typical of recent British commercial sf illustration. [JG]

ROBERTS, CHARLES G.D. *See* ORIGIN OF MAN.

ROBERTS, JANE (1929–). American writer who has become known for such speculative works as *Dialogues of the Soul & Mortal Self in Time* (**1975**), which is in the form of a series of connected poems. She began publishing sf with "The Red Wagon" for *FSF* in 1956. Her sf novel, *The Rebellers* (**1963**), mixed OVERPOPULATION and ECOLOGY themes in a melodramatic plot in which successive waves of plague answer Man's problems by nearly eliminating him for good. More typical of her later concerns is *The Education of Oversoul Seven* (**1973**), a transcendental parable about the meaning of reality and time and space in which the student protagonist inhabits the bodies and souls of four humans from different periods, ranging from 35,000 BC to AD 2300, and discovers the profound simultaneity of all realities. [JC]

ROBERTS, JOHN *See* John R. PIERCE.

ROBERTS, JOHN MADDOX (? –). American writer. His first sf novel *The Strayed Sheep of Charun* (**1977**), is an action-packed romance set on a medievalized planet in which Jesuits and others attempt to reform the violence which is the planet's (and novel's) *raison d'être*. [PN]

ROBERTS, KEITH (1935–). English writer and illustrator, who lives in the south of England, where he has set much of his fiction; he has worked in advertising for many years. KR began publishing sf with "Anita" and "Escapism" for *Science Fantasy* in 1964, before editing *SF Impulse* briefly (*see* SCIENCE FANTASY), from Oct. 1966 to Feb. 1967. Several of his early stories appeared under the pseudonym Alistair Bevan. As an sf writer, his only novel proper is his first book, *The Furies* (**1966**), all his other works being assemblages of shorter units, usually written for eventual publication under a single title but nevertheless showing their separate origins. *The Furies* narrates, at considerable length, a typical British DISASTER tale: A nuclear test goes awry, inspiring an onslaught of space-spawned giant wasps which ravage England and come close to eliminating mankind.

With his second book, KR came fully into his own as a writer: *Pavane* (coll. of linked stories **1968**; the American edition includes one additional story, "The White Boat") superbly depicts an ALTERNATE WORLD in which the first Queen Elizabeth was assassinated, the Armada won, there was no Reformation, and a technologically backward England survives under the sway of the Catholic Church Militant. The individual stories are moody, eloquent, elegiac and thoroughly convincing. *The Inner Wheel* (coll. of linked stories **1970**) deals with the kind of *gestalt* SUPERMAN theme made familiar by Theodore STURGEON's *More than Human* (fix-up **1953**) and is similarly powerful, though tending to a rather uneasy sentimentality perhaps endemic to tales of supernormal *gestalt*

Anthony ROBERTS's baroque spaceship trundling over a red desert comes from *The Orbit Poster Book*, 1976.

2/6

Science Fantasy

A great new novel by
KEITH ROBERTS
commencing in this issue

THE FURIES

K. ROBERTS-65

Keith ROBERTS is a notable illustrator as well as writer. Here his striking cover pictures his own story; July 1965.

KR is an ample writer, and an eloquent one, though perhaps too expansive. He has a tendency to create characters who are treated cruelly; a clear hatred of violence and savagery sometimes emerges uncomfortably in images of pain and mutilation. His books are permeated with a melancholy, rain-drenched, sometimes enchanted English landscape.

As an illustrator, KR did much to change the appearance of British sf magazines, notably *Science Fantasy*, for which he designed all but seven of the covers from Jan. 1965 until its demise as *SF Impulse* in Feb. 1967, and also NEW WORLDS for a period in 1966. His boldly Expressionist covers, line-oriented, paralleled the shift in content of these magazines away from genre sf and fantasy towards a more free-form, speculative kind of fiction. He later did covers and interior illustrations for the book editions of *New Worlds Quarterly*, ed. Moorcock, for some of whose novels he has also designed covers. [JC]
Other works: *Anita* (coll. of linked stories **1970**).
See also: ANDROIDS; ESP; HIVE-MINDS; INVASION; RELIGION; ROBOTS; SOCIOLOGY; SUPERNATURAL CREATURES.

ROBERTS, LIONEL *See* R.L. FANTHORPE.

ROBERTS, TERENCE Pseudonym of Ivan T. Sanderson (1911–73), a popular writer on the natural sciences. He was born in Scotland, educated at Cambridge, and resided in the USA; he led several natural history expeditions. As TR his sf novel was *Report on the Status Quo* (**1955**), a DISASTER story set in 1958–9, when the world is seen to reel under great floods and World War Three. As Sanderson he wrote two books with a relevance to PSEUDO-SCIENCE, *Things* (**1967**) about unexplained mysteries and *Uninvited Visitors* (**1967**) about FLYING SAUCERS. [PN]

ROBERTSON, E. ARNOT Writing name of English writer and broadcaster Eileen Arbuthnot Robertson (1903–   ), best known for such non-sf novels as *Four Frightened People* (**1931**). *Three Came Unarmed* (**1929**) is sf, and is a striking attack on the myth of the Noble Savage in the form of the story of the destruction of three *enfants sauvages* when they are exposed to English civilization. [JC]

ROBESON, KENNETH House name for authors writing the "Doc Savage" series as it appeared in DOC SAVAGE MAGAZINE, published by Street & Smith. The Robeson name is most strongly associated with Lester DENT, who wrote most of the Doc Savage stories, which ran from 1933 to 1949. The series was brought to life again in the 1960s and '70s with Bantam Books' extensive republication of the original stories. The

relationships. In 1971 KR published *The Boat of Fate*, a historical novel whose Roman setting and concern with primitive landscapes links it with his most ambitious assemblage to date, *The Chalk Giants* (coll. of linked stories **1974**; the American edition is abridged), which uses its separate tales elegantly to embody the cyclical shape of the book. The protagonist of the framing narrative (in the English edition only), after driving to the south coast of England to escape what may be a terminal though unclarified disaster, goes into a kind of hiding and either cycles the rest of the book through his head, or can be seen as himself emblematic of what those stories portend: they depict a movement from post-HOLOCAUST chaos through God-ridden savagery back to a state premonitory of the protagonist's own condition; his concerns and sexual obsessions are replicated variously

throughout the book. It is an ambitious effort.

KR has assembled independent stories in *Machines and Men* (coll. **1973**) and *The Grain Kings* (coll. **1976**); *The Passing of the Dragons* (coll. **1977**) assembles five stories from the first book and six from the second, plus "Coranda" (1966), which is based, as an *hommage*, on the glacial world of Michael MOORCOCK's *The Ice Schooner* (1966 *SF Impulse*; **1969**; rev. 1977), which was published during KR's editorship of *SF Impulse*. The title story of *The Grain Kings* fascinatingly describes life on giant hotel-like grain harvesters in a world of vast farms; in the same volume, "Weihnachtsabend" (1972), perhaps KR's finest single story, depicts a world in which the Nazis won the Second World War, and expands upon certain savage myths implicit in that victory, as does SARBAN in *The Sound of his Horn* (**1952**).

house name KR was also used on the pulp magazine *The Avenger*, another Street & Smith crime-busting hero series, with rather fewer sf elements. This was an attempt to cash in on the popularity of *Doc Savage*. However, most of the *Avenger* series (many also reprinted as paperback books in the 1970s) were the work of Paul ERNST, not Lester Dent. Other writers associated with the Kenneth Robeson name were William G. Bogart, Norman A. Danburg, Alan Hathaway and Emile Tepperman. Because the Doc Savage titles are of only peripheral sf interest, we do not list the paperback reprints here. They range so far from *1. Doc Savage: The Man of Bronze* (1933 *Doc Savage Magazine*; **1964**) to *90. Doc Savage: The Flying Goblin* (1940 *Doc Savage Magazine*; **1977**). It seems probable that more will follow. Three of the titles received earlier book publication: *The Man of Bronze* (**1933**), *The Land of Terror* (**1933**) and *The Quest of the Spider* (**1933**). [PN/JC]

ROBIDA, ALBERT (1848–1926). French illustrator, lithographer and writer. AR was the most important and popular of 19th-century sf illustrators, and may even be said to have founded the genre, though he was clearly working in the tradition of such French fantastic artists as Grandville (1803–47) and Gustave Doré (1832–83). Always interested in DYSTOPIAS and SATIRE, he illustrated works by François RABELAIS, CYRANO DE BERGERAC, Jonathan SWIFT and Camille FLAMMARION among others, but his most important works were published with texts written by himself. These were very often first published as periodical-series, each instalment being quite slim, and then later on in most cases as books. AR first took up sf themes with his gently satirical homage to Jules VERNE's "Voyages extraordinaires" series of novels with *Voyages très extraordinaires*, a 100-part periodical beginning Jun. 1879. It was later collected together as five books published in **1882**: *Le roi des singes* ["King of the Monkeys"]; *Le tour du monde en plus de 80 jours* ["Round the World in More than 80 Days"]; *Les quatre reines* ["The Four Queens"]; *À la recherche de l'éléphant blanc* ["In Search of the White Elephant"]; *S. Exc. M. le Gouverneur du Pôle Nord* ["His Excellency the Governor of the North Pole"]. A more prophetic work was *Le vingtième siècle* ["The 20th Century"], a periodical in 50 parts beginning Jan. 1882. There followed another periodical-series appearing later as a single volume book, *La vie électrique* ["The Electric Life"] (**1883**) which foretells the events of 1955. AR's ironically half-amused but pessimistic view of the likely nature of future warfare (many of his predictions proved all too true) appeared in no.200 of the humorous magazine *La Caricature* (1883) as "La guerre au vingtième siècle"

["War in the 20th Century"], and in a book with the same title but different contents, *La guerre au vingtième siècle* (**1887**). The anticipated war in the earlier work is set in 1975; in the second, the date is 1945. A time-travel fantasy was published as a serial in 1890 in the magazine *Le petit français illustré*, entitled *Jadis chez aujourd'hui* ["The Long-Ago is with us Today"], featuring a scientist resuscitating Molière and other literary figures of the past in order to show them the Universal Exhibition of 1889, which bores them. *L'horloge des siècles* ["Clock of the Centuries"] (**1902**), is one of the earliest treatments of the time-reversal theme used by Philip K. DICK in *Counter-Clock World* (**1967**) and Brian ALDISS in *An Age* (**1967**; vt *Cryptozoic!* USA). AR continued to produce quite prolifically, his last work being yet another future-fantasy entitled *Un chalet dans les airs* ["Castle in the Air"] (**1925**).

AR was by no means a master of prose, and the texts to the above works are generally undistinguished. The illustrations, however, mostly in a vein of detailed caricature, are consistently inventive and amusing. He worked much with lithographic pencil and crayon, achieving a haphazard but impressive vigour. The people in the pictures are very much those of Victorian Europe, dressed in the fashions of the time, and involved in various busy scenes with a huge variety of modernistic devices. Among his hundreds of predictions were the video-phone, and more blackly, bacteriological warfare. His machines and weapons were usually well designed — some may actually have been practical — although his flying machines look distinctly un-airworthy. The constant ironic intelligence of his work is rather undermined by his inability to imagine the future except in terms of more and more gadgetry. Social *mores* remain frozen in the Victorian mould. He had a strong influence on the Future-War genre (*see* INVASION *and* WAR). [PN/IG]

ROBINETT, STEPHEN (? – ?). American writer. He began publishing sf,

Albert ROBIDA's jaunty view of aerial warfare in the year 1955 as predicted in his book *La Vie électrique*, 1892.

under the name Tak Hallus (apparently Persian for "pen name", a pseudonym he has often used), with "Minitalent" for *ASF* in 1969; his first novel, *Stargate* (1974 *ASF* as by Tak Hallus; **1976**), combines technological sf, in its use of a MATTER TRANSMITTER (the stargate of the title), with a murder mystery related to 21st-century mining operations. SR draws character ably. [JC]

ROBINSON, CHARLES HENRY See ORIGIN OF MAN.

ROBINSON, ELEANOR (? –). American writer. In her sf novel, *Chrysalis of Death* (**1976**), a disastrous, primordial germ changes people into beasts; a brave doctor fights the menace; there is soap opera and sex. [JC]

ROBINSON, FRANK M(ALCOLM) (1926–). American writer, also active in publishing, who began writing sf stories in 1950 with "The Maze" in *ASF*. He was fairly prolific for a time, soon publishing his only solo novel, *The Power* (**1956**), which was immediately successful, very effectively combining sf and detection elements in its hero's search for a malignant SUPERMAN with undefined powers which include the capacity of seeming different to everyone who looks at him. It was filmed as THE POWER, produced by George PAL and directed by Byron HASKIN, in 1967. After writing little for some years (he has been an editor of *Playboy*) FMR collaborated with Thomas M. SCORTIA on two DISASTER novels which, though both technically sf, relate more closely to the disaster movie popular with American film-makers in the early 1970s. *The Glass Inferno* (**1974**), with Richard Martin Stern's *The Tower*, was filmed as *The Towering Inferno* (1974); *The Prometheus Crisis* (**1975**) deals with a vast nuclear reactor failure and the corrupt politics by which it is occasioned. [JC]
See also: ESP; PSI POWERS.

ROBINSON, PHILIP BEDFORD (1926–). English writer who has worked in India; his sf novel, *Masque of a Savage Mandarin* (**1969**), tells of the revenge upon the world of the deracinated "Mandarin" figure via the systematic destruction, by electrical means, of his victim's brains. [JC]

ROBINSON, SPIDER (1948–). American writer, now living in Nova Scotia, who entered the sf field in 1973 with considerable impact, publishing several stories of note and sharing with Lisa TUTTLE the 1974 JOHN W. CAMPBELL AWARD for best new writer; he also topped the 1977 Locus Poll for best critic, mainly for his "Galaxy Bookshelf" column for *Gal.* from Jun. 1975 to Sep. 1977. His first story, "The Guy With the Eyes", for *ASF*, was also the first of his "Callahan" tales, most of which have

been assembled as *Callahan's Crosstime Saloon* (coll. of linked stories **1977**), though further instalments are projected, and two have been published: "Dog Day Evening" (1977) and "Mirror/rroriM, off the Wall" (1977). The Callahan stories belong to the club-story genre, as it has passed from G.K. CHESTERTON and Lord DUNSANY through more recent writers like Arthur C. CLARKE and Sterling LANIER, and features the coming together in Callahan's saloon of various creatures, human and alien, who have various experiences to recount; but SR's stories differ from some older models in the amount of action that occurs in the saloon itself, so that their ultimate effect is complex and satisfying. SR's first novel is *Telempath* (**1976**), a complicated story set in a post-HOLOCAUST world after a decimating virus plague; the hero, as described by the title, brings unusual abilities to bear on the problem of reconstructing a viable human environment in a world dominated by the telepathic Muskies, beings imperceptible before the plague. The first four chapters were excerpted in *ASF* as "By Any Other Name" (1976) and later shared the 1977 HUGO award for best novella with a James TIPTREE story. Since his marriage in 1975, SR has been collaborating with his wife, Jeanne Corrigan Robinson, on fiction, notably "Stardance" (1977), which won a 1978 Hugo. He has an easy, conversational style — his criticism is enthusiastic — which at times masks the intelligent edge of his writing.

SR has written several stories as B.D. Wyatt, reported to be a rearrangement of "Y.D. Buy It?". [JC]

ROBINSONADE Daniel DEFOE's *The Life and Strange Surprizing Adventures of Robinson Crusoe* (**1719**) provides the original model for robinsonades, romances of solitary survival in such inimical terrains as desert ISLANDS (or planets); and also provides much of the thematic and symbolic buttressing that makes so many of these stories allegories of Man's search for the meaning of life (just as Crusoe's ordeal is both a religious punishment for disobedience and a triumphant justification of entrepreneurial individualism). Crusoe's paternalistic relation to the natives he eventually encounters has also been echoed in much modern sf, where until very recently human/ALIEN relations tended to be depicted within the same code of mercantilist opportunism. A second important model for sf's numerous robinsonades may well be Johann R. Wyss's *Swiss Family Robinson, or Adventures in a Desert Island* (Switzerland **1813**; many trans.), in which the element of the triumphant ordeal is broadened to include the testing of a full microcosm of social life — leading either to UTOPIAN speculations, to which the robinsonade has always been structurally attuned, or to the simpler, more active adventure of the COLONIZATION OF OTHER WORLDS. However, the fundamental appeal of the robinsonade — its depiction of solitary entrepreneurial triumph over great odds — remains at the heart of almost all its offspring. [JC]

ROBINSON CRUSOE ON MARS Film (1964). Schenck-Zabel/Paramount. Directed by Byron HASKIN, starring Paul Mantee, Vic Lundin and Adam West. Screenplay by Ib J. Melchior and John C. Higgins, based on the novel by Daniel DEFOE. 109 mins. Colour.

Byron Haskin directed several sf films in the 1950s, including WAR OF THE WORLDS, and returned to the genre in 1964 with this futuristic version of Defoe's classic novel. A spaceship, carrying two pilots, crash-lands on Mars. The lone survivor struggles to survive in the alien, barren landscape, his only

The Nevada desert stands in for Mars in the film ROBINSON CRUSOE ON MARS.

companion a tiny monkey. He lives in a small cave, renewing his air supply by heating rocks that miraculously give off oxygen, and is haunted by images of his dead colleague. With the arrival of alien spaceships, what had been a convincing study of a man's fight to overcome the hostility of his environment and his own loneliness becomes pure pulp sf. The Earthman rescues one of the aliens' slaves, who becomes his Man Friday, and a conventional pursuit-and-escape story follows. Death Valley provided the Martian setting and at the time of the film's release it looked realistic enough.

The story bears resemblances to Rex Gordon's novel *No Man Friday* (**1956**; vt *First on Mars*), but no credit is given to Gordon in the titles.   [JB/PN]

ROBOTS The word "robot" first appeared in Karel Čapek's play *R. U. R.* (**1921**; trans. **1923**), first produced in Prague in 1921. The word derives from the Czech *robota* (statute labour). Čapek's robots were, however, artificial men of organic origin, whereas the term is more often used specifically to describe a mechanical contrivance. Although the term remains ambiguous, and is sometimes interchangeable with the term "android", this entry will deal specifically with manlike MACHINES, while the section on ANDROIDS will deal with manlike organic artefacts.

Machines which mimic human form date back, in fiction and reality, to the early 19th century. The real automata were showpieces: clockwork dummies or puppets. Their counterparts in the fiction of E.T.A. HOFFMANN, however — the Talking Turk in "Automata" (1814) and Olympia in "The Sandman" (1816) — present an altogether more convincing image, and play a decidedly sinister role, their wondrous artifice being seen as something blasphemous and diabolically inspired. However, man-shaped machines are uncommon in scientific romance before 1926; two appearances are in Herman MELVILLE's "The Bell-Tower" (1855) and William Wallace COOK's *A Round Trip to the Year 2000* (1903; **1925**).

Stories published during the first decade of the SF MAGAZINES manifest an ambivalent attitude toward the robot. "The Psychophonic Nurse" (1928) by David H. KELLER shows the robot as a co-operative servant but no substitute for a mother's love. Abner J. Gelula's "Automaton" (1931) has lecherous designs on its creator's daughter and has to be destroyed. Harl VINCENT's "Rex" (1934) takes over the world and is about to remake Man in the image of the robot when his regime is overthrown. By contrast, Eando BINDER's "The Robot Aliens" (1935) come in peace but are misunderstood and abused by hostile humans. Outside the sf magazines J. Storer CLOUSTON made use of what was to become a standard comic theme in *Button*

Brains (**1933**), in which a robot is constantly and absurdly mistaken for its human model. All the mechanical malfunction jokes which were used in the film THE PERFECT WOMAN (1949), the TV series MY LIVING DOLL (1964), and are still in use in the 1976 TV series *Holmes and Yoyo*, appear therein. Isaac ASIMOV claims to have invented the famous "Three Laws of Robotics" in response to a "Frankenstein syndrome" (the belief that artificial men are menacing) characteristic of early sf attitudes to the robot, but this assumption does not seem to have been general, or even very evident.

In point of fact, Asimov's first robot story (*see* POSITRONIC ROBOTS), "Strange Playfellow" (1940; vt "Robbie") appeared amid a glut of stories featuring lovable and altruistic robots. In "Helen O'Loy" (1938) by Lester DEL REY, a man marries the ideal mechanical woman. In the sentimental "Robots Return" (1938) by Robert Moore WILLIAMS, spacefaring robots discover that they were once created by men. "Rust" (1939) by Joseph E. KELLEAM is a robot tragedy describing the decline into extinction of mechanical life on Earth. "I, Robot" (1939) by Eando Binder is a straightforward anti-*Frankenstein* parable. In "True Confession" (1940) by F. Orlin TREMAINE, an altruistic robot confesses to murder to save its creator, and a similar altruism is displayed in "Almost Human" (1941) by Ray CUMMINGS. In "Farewell to the Master" (1940) by Harry BATES, a man and a robot visit Earth, with the man the servant of the robot rather than vice versa. In "Jay Score" (1941) by Eric Frank RUSSELL, the first of a series later published as *Men, Martians and Machines* (fix-up **1956**), a robot member of a team of space explorers proves himself more than equal to his companions and a hero as well. None of these robots had the ethical system designed by Asimov built into their natures, but none could be accused of being fearsome monsters, or even undesirables.

Asimov's three laws of robotics are: 1. A robot may not injure a human being, or, through inaction, allow a human being to come to harm. 2. A robot must obey the orders given it by human beings except where such orders would conflict with the First Law. 3. A robot must protect its own existence as long as such protection does not conflict with the First or Second Law. The laws emerged gradually from the early stories "Reason" (1941) and "Liar" (1941) and provided the basis for plot twists regarding apparently odd robot behaviour in many of the subsequent stories written in the 1940s, collected in *I, Robot* (coll. **1950**). In virtually all robot stories of the late '30s and early '40s, Man and robot are not merely allies, but also friends. The robot's claim to quasi-human status advanced, climaxing in Asimov's

"Evidence" (1946), in which robot psychologist Susan Calvin is faced with the problem of whether a prominent public figure is really a robot. In the end, the robot convinces the world of his humanity and proceeds to be a more than adequate replacement for his model. In C.L. MOORE's "No Woman Born" (1944) a dancer whose mind is resurrected in a robot body quickly concludes that the robot condition is preferable to the human. In most of the stories of this period the robot is not the emotionless being one might suppose but a feeling creature. Some robots even shed tears. The robot servants who survive mankind in Clifford D. SIMAK's *City* (1944–52; fix-up **1952**) are not so much mechanical slaves as perfect gentlemen's gentlemen. The only notable voice raised against robots before the end of the War was that of Anthony BOUCHER, whose stories "Q.U.R." and "Robinc" (both 1943 as by H.H. Holmes) championed "usuform robots" against anthropomorphous ones. The stated reasons were utilitarian, but it may be that Boucher's religious faith — he was one of the few Roman Catholic sf writers — was influential in this prejudice.

In 1945, with the revelation of the atom bomb, a new suspicion of technological "progress" grew up very quickly. "Evidence", though published in September 1946, clearly belongs to the pre-Hiroshima consciousness, and may have been written somewhat earlier, taking into account publication lag. In 1947 Asimov published his first sinister robot story, "Little Lost Robot", and Jack WILLIAMSON published the classic "With Folded Hands". In this story humanoid robots are charged "to serve man, to obey, and to guard men from harm", but take this mission too literally, and guard men against themselves to ensure that no man endangers his well-being and to guarantee everyone happiness — if need be through permanent tranquillization or lobotomy.

Significantly, many writers did not relinquish their loyalty to machines. Asimov and Simak remained steadfastly pro-robot, and even man and humanoid were reconciled in the sequel to "With Folded Hands", *The Humanoids* (**1949**), though the ending of this novel may have been suggested by John W. CAMPBELL Jr rather than being a spontaneous expression of Williamson's own technophilic tendencies. In stories of the 1950s the robot may still take the heroic role, but the impact of the new consciousness is clear in that virtually all robot stories in this period take some kind of confrontation and conflict as their theme. Robots kill or attempt to kill humans in "Lost Memory" (1952) by Peter PHILLIPS, "Second Variety" (1953) by Philip K. DICK, "Short in the Chest" (1954) by Idris Seabright (Margaret ST CLAIR), "First to Serve" (1954) by Algis BUDRYS, *The Naked Sun* (**1956**) by Asimov and "Mark XI" (1957; vt "Mark

ROBOTS were a favourite subject for sf illustrators from the beginning of the sf pulps; this example is by Frank R. Paul, Oct. 1928.

the later "The Cruel Equations" (1971). As the anxiety began to ebb away in the late 1950s and a more relaxed attitude to the robot became dominant, humour and a relatively gentle irony came very much to the fore in robot stories, as in Harry HARRISON's *War With the Robots* (1958–62; coll. **1962**), Brian W. ALDISS's "Who Can Replace a Man?" (1958), Fritz LEIBER's *The Silver Eggheads* (**1961**) and Poul ANDERSON's "The Critique of Impure Reason" (1962).

In the 1960s there was something of a reconciliation between Man and robot in sf. Sentimentality returned to the robot story in full force in Simak's "All the Traps of Earth" (1960), and reached new depths of sickliness in Ray BRADBURY's "I Sing the Body Electric" (1969).

The rehabilitation of the robot in contemporary sf is eloquently expressed by Barrington J. BAYLEY's study of robot existentialism *The Soul of the Robot* (**1974**; rev. 1976), and by the most recent of Asimov's robot stories, "That Thou Art Mindful of Him" (1974) and "The Bicentennial Man" (1976), which take robot self-analysis to its logical conclusion and end with the identification of the robot as a thoroughly "human" being. Meanwhile, in Poland Stanislaw LEM wrote a series of sophisticated and witty moral fables about robots, opening up many of the philosophical questions their existence would create; some of these were collected in *Cyberiada* (coll. **1965**; trans. **1974** as *The Cyberiad*).

The remaking of the association between Man and robot, and the merging of their roles, is reflected by the increasing importance in sf of the Man/machine hybrid, the CYBORG. Another group of stories deals with robot RELIGION and MYTHOLOGY. An early example is Robert F. Young's "Robot Son" (1959), more recent ones being Zelazny's "For a Breath I Tarry" (1966), Simak's *A Choice of Gods* (**1972**) and Gordon EKLUND's "The Shrine of Sebastian" (1973). Robert SILVERBERG's story "Good News from the Vatican" (1971), about the election of the first robot pope, won a NEBULA award.

The writer who confirms the identification of Man and robot most strongly is Philip K. Dick, whose later work usually substitutes the term "android" for "robot" and is much concerned with the difficulties, both physical and metaphysical, of separating the real from the artificial. His most notable stories concerned with the issues are *Do Androids Dream of Electric Sheep?* (**1968**), "The Electric Ant" (1969) and *We Can Build You* (1969–70; **1972**). In his essay "The Android and the Human" (1973), Dick makes the following observation: "Someday a human being may shoot a robot which has come out of a General Electrics factory, and to his surprise see it weep and bleed. And the dying robot may shoot back and, to its surprise, see a wisp of gray smoke arise from the electric pump that it supposed

Elf") by Cordwainer SMITH. The story of mistaken identity, a comic theme in *Button Brains*, takes on sinister or unfortunate associations in Asimov's "Satisfaction Guaranteed" (1951), Philip Dick's "Impostor" (1953), Walter M. MILLER's "The Darfsteller" (1955) and Robert BLOCH's "Comfort Me, My Robot" (1955). Robot courtroom dramas include Simak's "How-2" (1954), Asimov's "Galley Slave" (1957), Del Rey's "Robots Should Be Seen" (1958) and, later, "Synth" (1966) by Keith ROBERTS, though the latter could be regarded as an android story. Man-robot boxing matches are featured in "Title Fight" (1956) by William Campbell Gault, "Steel" (1956) by Richard MATHESON and "The Champ" (1958) by Robert Presslie. The robot is an instrument of judgement in "Two-Handed Engine" (1955) by Henry KUTTNER and C.L. Moore — a theme which recurs in an atypical story of recent years "Home Is The Hangman" (1975) by Roger ZELAZNY.

In this period the robot was thoroughly reified by sf writers, even though many continued to defend it. (It is worth noting that completely outside the pattern is a

robot story by Anthony Boucher, this time showing the Catholic influence very clearly, "The Quest for St. Aquin", 1951, in which a perfectly logical robot emulates Aquinas and deduces the reality of God.)

Robot stories of the 1950s reflect deep anxieties concerning the relationship between Man and machine. Asimov's *Caves of Steel* (**1954**), dealing in some depth with its hero's anti-machine prejudices and his mechanical environment, brings this anxiety clearly into focus.

The main exception to this pattern is provided by a few stories in which robots are used purely for comic purposes. The most notable example is the narcissistic robot in Henry Kuttner's *Robots Have No Tails* (1943–8 as by Lewis Padgett; coll. of linked stories **1952** as by Lewis Padgett; paperback as by Kuttner). Another writer who frequently used robots in comic roles in this period was Robert SHECKLEY, but his stories are frequently edged with a sour irony which relates well to the attitudes of the day. Examples include "Watchbird" (1953) and "The Battle" (1954), though Sheckley's classic story in this vein was

was the human's beating heart. It would be rather a great moment of truth for both of them."

Anthologies of robot stories are *The Robot and the Man* (anth. **1953**) ed. Martin GREENBERG; *The Coming of the Robots* (anth. **1963**) ed. Sam MOSKOWITZ; *Invasion of the Robots* (anth. **1965**) ed. Roger ELWOOD; and *The Metal Smile* (anth. **1968**) ed. Damon KNIGHT. *Science Fiction Thinking Machines* (anth. **1954**) ed. Groff CONKLIN also has a substantial section on robots.   [BS]
See also: AUTOMATION; COMPUTERS; CYBERNETICS; INTELLIGENCE; TECHNOLOGY.

ROCKETS The Chinese were using skyrockets as fireworks in the 11th century, and adapted them as weapons of war in the 13th. Europeans borrowed the idea, but rocket-missiles were abandoned as muskets and rifles became more efficient. A 15th-century Chinese legend tells of one Wan Hoo, who attached rockets to a chair, strapped himself in, and blasted off for the unknown. A similar notion was used by CYRANO DE BERGERAC in the first part of *L'autre monde* (1657), in which the hero straps three rows of rockets to his back, intending that as each set burns out it will ignite the next, so renewing the boost. The device proves impractical.

War rockets were used against the British in India at the end of the 18th century, and the British reinstituted rocket technology, using rocket missiles in the Napoleonic War and the American war of 1812. British rockets used in an attack on Fort Henry in 1814 inspired the reference to "the rocket's red glare" in *The Star-Spangled Banner*, written by Francis Scott Key, who witnessed the battle. Rockets fell into disuse again with the development of better field artillery, but the notion of rocketry as a means of TRANSPORTATION recurred, with Ruggieri going so far as to send mice up in a skyrocket, returning them safely to Earth by parachute.

In 1898 Konstantin TSIOLKOVSKY wrote his classic article on "The Probing of Space by Means of Jet Devices" (1903), though publication was delayed for some years. He had already published his "fantasies of Earth and Sky", known in English as *The Call of the Cosmos* (1895; trans. **1963**) and went on to popularize his work further in the novel *Beyond the Planet Earth* (1920; trans. **1960**). In the same period the American Robert Goddard — reputedly inspired by reading H.G. WELLS's *The War of the Worlds* (1898) — also began thinking seriously about space travel, and began experimenting with rockets in 1911. He was working towards a liquid-fuel stage rocket — a notion already applied seriously to the business of interplanetary travel in John MUNRO's romance *A Trip to Venus* (1897). Goddard launched the first liquid-fuel rocket in 1926.

Meanwhile, Germany had a third rocket research pioneer in Hermann Oberth, author of *Die Rakete zu den Planetenräumen* ["The Rocket into Interplanetary Space"] (1921). He and others (including Willy LEY) formed a "Society for Space Travel" in 1927. In 1928 Oberth was offered the opportunity to build a rocket by a German film company which hired him as technical adviser for Fritz LANG's film DIE FRAU IM MOND (1929). His experimental rocket was to be launched before the film's premiere as a publicity stunt, but the project collapsed. Oberth began anew with a number of assistants, including Wernher von Braun, and managed to get a number of rockets off the ground in 1931. The project was abandoned as Germany's economy collapsed but Von Braun joined a rocket development project with the German Army. Ley emigrated to the USA. In 1937 the Army project acquired a large research centre at Peenemünde on an island in the Baltic, where Von Braun and his staff developed the V-2 rocket bomb. This arrived too late to make any difference to the course of the war and Von Braun fled to the Bavarian Alps in order to surrender to the Americans rather than waiting for the Russians. Goddard spent the war developing take-off rockets for US Navy aeroplanes.

Von Braun went to work for an American research programme, but things moved slowly until competition with the Russians made funds flow freely, whereupon the project developed the Jupiter rocket to launch America's first space satellite in 1958, and ultimately the Saturn rocket which carried the first men to the MOON. During this post-War period a number of American and British sf writers — most notably Arthur C. CLARKE, a leading member of the British Interplanetary Society founded by P.E. Cleator in the 1930s — were active and enthusiastic propagandists for the space programme. Even before the War the sf PULPS had taken a considerable interest in rocket research — SCIENCE WONDER STORIES publicized an occasion when "The Rocket Comes to the Front Page" (Dec. 1929) with an unsigned article that was probably by Hugo GERNSBACK; ASF published such articles as Leo Vernon's "Rocket Flight" (1938) and the British TALES OF WONDER published Clarke's "We Can Rocket to the Moon — Now!" (1939). After the war George PAL made the film DESTINATION MOON (1950) — America's answer to *Die Frau im Mond* — scripted by Robert HEINLEIN, and remotely based on Heinlein's juvenile novel about teenagers cobbling together a moon rocket, *Rocket Ship Galileo* (1947). Ray BRADBURY became particularly fascinated by the mythology of the rocket and followed up his "I, Rocket" (1944) with the early "Martian Chronicles" episode "Rocket Summer" (1947) and the curious story "Outcast of the Stars" (1950; vt "The Rocket"). C.M.

KORNBLUTH based his novel *Takeoff* (1952) on the ironic theme of a crackpot project to build an unworkable rocket which conceals a real attempt to build a practical spaceship. This was a testimony to the ambivalent attitude still prevailing toward rocket research. As late as 1956 a newly appointed British Astronomer Royal declared confidently that space travel was "utter bilge". He represented a considerable body of opinion, which evaporated only with the ascent of *Sputnik* one year later.

There is no other historical sequence of events in which fact and fiction are so closely entwined, or which seems to justify so well the imaginative reach of HARD SF writers. Tsiolkovsky, Goddard and Oberth were visionaries more closely akin to speculative writers than to their contemporary theorists. Though rocket technology has always been dependent on the practical demands of war it is surely true that for some of the men involved the real objective was always that of Wan Hoo, Cyrano, Munro and Tsiolkovsky. Pierre BOULLE's *Le jardin de Kanashima* (1964; trans. as *Garden on the Moon* 1965), in which the German rocket scientists are entranced with the notion of cosmic voyaging even as they develop the V-2, probably has an element of truth in it, though its bland assumption that the end justified the means may trouble some historians and visionaries.   [BS]
See also: PREDICTION; SF OVERTAKEN BY EVENTS; SPACE FLIGHT; SPACESHIPS.

ROCKETSHIP XM Film (1950). Lippert. Directed by Kurt Neumann, starring Lloyd Bridges, Osa Massen and John Emery. Screenplay by Kurt Neumann. 78 mins. B/w, with tinted sequence.

This cheap film was hastily made to beat the more illustrious DESTINATION MOON to the cinemas. A rocket on its way to the Moon is diverted by a storm of meteors and lands on Mars instead. The astronauts find evidence that the planet has suffered an atomic war, and encounter a race of mutants.

A German director who came to Hollywood in 1925, where he directed short comedies at first, Kurt Neumann is best known for THE FLY, which he produced and directed in 1958.   [JB]

ROCKET STORIES US DIGEST-size magazine. Three issues, Apr., Jul. and Sep. 1953, published by Space Publications; ed. Wade Kaempfert. *RS* was a companion magazine to FANTASY MAGAZINE/FICTION, SPACE SCIENCE FICTION and the 1952–4 SCIENCE FICTION ADVENTURES. All four magazines were closed down fairly rapidly when the publisher lost interest. Wade Kaempfert was a pseudonym which concealed the identity of Lester DEL REY on the first two issues, and probably that of Harry HARRISON on the third. *RS* published fair,

July 1953. Cover by Alex Schomburg.

average fiction but at the height of the sf magazine boom, with well over 30 sf magazines being published simultaneously in the USA, it was effectively invisible.   [FHP/PN]

ROCKLYNNE, ROSS Form of his name used by American writer Ross L. Rocklin (1913–   ) for his sf stories, most of which appeared in such magazines as *ASF* from the mid-1930s up to 1947, beginning with "Man of Iron" for *ASF* in 1935. He specialized in SPACE-OPERA plots constructed around sometimes ingenious "scientific" problems, such as how to escape from the centre of a hollow planet in "At the Center of Gravity" (1936), the first of his "Colbie and Deverel" series assembled as *The Men and the Mirror* (coll. of linked stories **1973**). A second series, "The Darkness", was assembled as *The Sun Destroyers* (1940–51 var. mags; fix-up **1973**); it features vast, nebula-like beings (*see* LIVING WORLDS) and follows their life-courses through millions of years from galaxy to galaxy without the intervention of Man. RR had one of the most interesting, if florid, imaginations of PULP writers of his time, and wrote very much better than most. He continued to write sf, rather sporadically, up to 1954 (he was interested in DIANETICS at that time); he later made a formidable comeback with several stories in 1968, demonstrating that he had no difficulty at all in adjusting his narrative voice to the more sophisticated demands of the later period, as in "Ching Witch", one of the most assured *tours de force* in Harlan ELLISON's *Again, Dangerous Visions* (anth. **1972**), an ironic tale about the curious morality of a man, the result of GENETIC ENGINEERING, who has a lot of cat in him.
[JC/PN]
See also: ALTERNATE WORLDS; CRIME AND PUNISHMENT; WAR.

ROCKWOOD, ROY House name used by Cupples & Leon of New York. *See* DIME NOVELS AND JUVENILE SERIES; MOON; OUTER PLANETS.

RODAN Film (1956). Toho. Directed by Inoshiro Honda, starring Kenji Sahara, Yumi Shirkawa and Akihiko Hirata. Screenplay by Takeshi Kimura and Takeo Murata, based on a story by Takashi Kuronuma. 79 mins. Colour.

This film is from the same team that produced GODZILLA; this time the devastation of Japan is brought about by a giant pterodactyl. It is finally defeated by a rival flying reptile, and both perish in a volcano. The spectacular effects are by Eiji Tsuburaya and his team.   [JB]

RODDENBERRY, GENE (1926–   ). American TV scriptwriter/producer/director and creator of STAR TREK. GR began writing when he was working as a pilot for a commercial airline in the late 1940s and his first sales were to flying magazines. In 1949 he left the airline and moved to Los Angeles with the intention of becoming a TV writer but as, at that time, little TV was being produced in Hollywood (most TV companies were then based on the East Coast) he was obliged to take a job with the Los Angeles Police Department. In 1951 he sold his first script to TV and the following year wrote and sold his first sf TV script, a genre in which he had not previously been particularly interested. In 1954 he resigned his job as a police sergeant and became a full-time TV writer. In 1963 he created and produced a series of his own — *The Lieutenant* — for MGM. That same year he conceived the idea for the *Star Trek* series but had a great deal of difficulty in launching the project and it was not until 1966 that the show reached TV screens. It was not, according to the ratings system, a great success, and was ended in 1968; but since then, due to many reruns, the show has built up a huge following of fans and a new series, produced by Roddenberry, went into production in 1977. In the years between the two *Star Trek* series GR spent much time trying to launch other sf projects on TV but without success. Four of these were GENESIS II, PLANET EARTH, THE QUESTOR TAPES and STRANGE NEW WORLD, the pilot episodes of which appeared as made-for-TV films. In 1977 GR directed the feature film *Spectre* in England. With Stephen E. WHITFIELD he wrote *The Making of Star Trek* (**1968**).
[JB]

RODMAN, ERIC *See* Robert SILVERBERG.

ROE, IVAN *See* Richard SAVAGE.

ROGER, NOELLE Pseudonym of Hélène Pittard (1874– ?), French writer of the sf novel *Le nouvel Adam* (**1924**; trans. as *The New Adam* **1926**), about a wholly logical and unpleasant SUPERMAN (*see* ADAM AND EVE).   [JC]

ROGERS, ALVA (1923–   ). American fan writer and artist. A long-time sf fan, he drew the covers for a number of 1940s publications, including some of the AMERICAN FICTION series. His *A Requiem for Astounding* (**1964**) is a nostalgic and largely uncritical history of *ASF*.   [MJE]

ROGERS, HUBERT (? – ?). American illustrator. HR is closely connected with the first John W. CAMPBELL decade of *ASF*, a magazine for which he painted 59 covers, 1939–52. His cover art was sometimes criticized for being dull, with muted colours and low-key chiaroscuro; he used a particular shade of grey throughout his works that many call his trademark. He and William Timmins dominated the covers of *ASF* in the 1940s, a period where its comparatively quiet appearance gave it something of the dignity Campbell craved, especially in contrast to most of

Tokyo burns again, as in most Toho films. This time the culprit is RODAN, a giant pterodactyl.

Hubert ROGERS' covers for *ASF* were among the most dignified and calmly evocative of the pulp era. Feb. 1941.

the lurid competition. HR's cover painting for Laurence O'DONNELL'S "Fury" (May 1947) is considered by many fans to be his finest work. His covers, more serious (and even solemn) than those of many of his colleagues, epitomized the technological aspirations of *ASF* in its more high-minded mode. HR did very little work for other magazines. His sf career stopped just before the HUGO awards began, and he never received official recognition from FANDOM.   [JG/PN]

ROGERS, MELVA *See* Rog PHILLIPS.

ROGERS, MICHAEL (ALAN) (1951–). American writer. His first published sf story was "She Still Do" (1970), as by M. Alan Rogers, in *If*. His sf novel is *Mindfogger* (1973), which deals with a hippy inventor whose mindfogging device acts as a gentle hallucinogenic; he uses it against an armaments company, and the reader is left wondering whether hip mind control is in any way preferable to mind control by the powers of the right wing. MR also writes rock music criticism.   [PN/JC]

ROGERS, PAT *See* Arthur PORGES.

ROHMER, SAX Pseudonym of English journalist and author Arthur Sarsfield Ward (1883–1959). A popular thriller writer, he started writing in 1909 and published in *Cassell's Magazine*, COLLIER'S WEEKLY, *The Premier Magazine* and numerous other early general fiction magazines and BOYS' PAPERS. SR capitalized on contemporary anxiety about the Chinese, generated by the Boxer Rebellion and the fictions of M.P. SHIEL and others, to produce many sensational novels about the Yellow Peril. Most famous is his series about Dr Fu Manchu, a malign scientific genius and leader of a secret Chinese organization bent on world domination. He appeared in *The Mystery of Dr. Fu-Manchu* (1912–13 *The Story Teller* as "Fu-Manchu"; fix-up **1913**; vt *The Insidious Dr. Fu-Manchu* USA), *The Devil Doctor* (1914–15 *Collier's Weekly* as "Fu-Manchu & Co."; fix-up **1916**; vt *The Return of Dr. Fu-Manchu* USA), *The Si-Fan Mysteries* (1916–17 *Collier's Weekly*; fix-up **1917**; vt *The Hand of Fu-Manchu* USA), *Daughter of Fu Manchu* (**1931**), *The Mask of Fu Manchu* (**1932**), which was filmed as THE MASK OF FU MANCHU, *The Bride of Fu Manchu* (**1933**; vt *Fu Manchu's Bride* USA), *The Trail of*

Fu Manchu (**1934**), *President Fu Manchu* (**1936**), *The Drums of Fu Manchu* (**1938**), *The Island of Fu Manchu* (**1941**), *The Shadow of Fu Manchu* (**1948**), *Re-Enter Fu Manchu* (**1957**; vt *Re-Enter Dr. Fu Manchu* UK), *Emperor Fu Manchu* (**1959**) and the omnibus volume *The Book of Fu Manchu* (coll. of three novels **1929**; four novels in USA edition).

Although these and other novels by SR tend more towards the occult thriller than sf, many sf elements were incorporated into them, particularly in *The Day the World Ended* (**1930**), set in and around a fortress guarded by death rays. Apart from his "Dr Fu Manchu" series, SR wrote several others: the "Sumuru" series, about an oriental villainess, *Nude in Mink* (**1950**; vt *Sins of Sumuru* UK), *Sumuru* (**1951**; vt *Slaves of Sumuru* UK), *The Fire Goddess* (**1952**; vt *Virgin in Flames* UK), *Return of Sumuru* (**1954**; vt *Sand and Satin* UK) and *Sinister Madonna* (**1956**); the "Gaston Max" series, *The Yellow Claw* (**1915**), *The Golden Scorpion* (**1919**), *The Day the World Ended* (**1930**) and *Seven Sins* (**1943**); the "Paul Harley" series, *Bat-Wing* (**1921**), *Fire-Tongue* (**1921**) and 11 short stories; and the non-fantasy "Red Kerry" series, *Dope* (**1919**) and *Yellow Shadows* (**1925**).

SR also wrote several stage plays, including an adaptation from C.J. Cutcliffe HYNE's "Captain Kettle" series. Several of his novels have been made into films and the "Dr Fu Manchu" series was adapted by him into a popular radio series. Although contributing nothing to the development of HARDCORE sf, the "Dr Fu Manchu" series was widely imitated, notably by Roland Daniels, Nigel Vane and Anthony RUD, and was a strong influence on the development of hero/villain sf thrillers set in the present day, as written by Lester DENT, Ian FLEMING and many others. Two direct imitations were the short-lived magazines THE MYSTERIOUS WU FANG and DR YEN SIN. His only novel not written as by SR was a supernatural and theological work, *Wulfheim* (**1950**), as by Michael Furey.   [JE]

Other works: *The Sins of Séverac Bablon* (**1914**); *Brood of the Witch Queen* (1914 *The Premier Magazine*; **1918**); *Tales of Secret Egypt* (coll. **1918**); *The Orchard of Tears* (**1918**); *The Quest of the Sacred Slipper* (1913–14 *Short Stories* as by Hassan of Aleppo; fix-up **1919**); *The Dream Detective* (coll. **1920**; with additional story 1925); *The Green Eyes of Bast* (**1920**); *The Haunting of Low Fennel* (coll. **1920**); *Tales of Chinatown* (coll. **1922**); *Grey Face* (**1924**); *Moon of Madness* (**1927**), not fantasy; *She Who Sleeps* (**1928**); *Yu'an Hee See Laughs* (**1932**), not fantasy; *The Emperor of America* (**1929**); *Tales of East and West* (coll. **1932** UK; same title, different stories, coll. **1933** USA); *The Bat Flies Low* (**1935**); *White Velvet* (**1936**), not fantasy; *The Golden Scorpion Omnibus*

(coll. **1938**); *The Sax Rohmer Omnibus* (coll. **1938**); *Salute to Bazarada and Other Stories* (coll. **1939**); *The Moon is Red* (**1954**); *The Secret of Holm Peel and Other Strange Stories* (coll. **1970**).
About the author: *Master of Villainy* (**1972**) by Cay van Ash and Elizabeth Sax Rohmer.
See also: POLITICS; VILLAINS; WEAPONS.

ROLANT, RENÉ *See* R.L. FANTHORPE.

ROLLERBALL Film (1975). United Artists. Directed by Norman Jewison, starring James Caan, John Houseman, Maud Adams and John Beck. Screenplay by William HARRISON, based on his own short story. 129 mins. Colour.

Rollerball is a "sport" in which teams of men on roller-skates try to beat each other's brains out with metal-studded gloves. The Corporations which rule a future world have devised the game in the belief that people will not want to indulge in any unwelcome political activity if they can watch men trying to kill each other. The scheme goes wrong when one of the champions achieves world-wide stardom. Fearful of this dangerous display of individuality, the Corporations attempt to kill him by making the game increasingly difficult. He survives, however, and the film ends with him alone and triumphant on a body-littered track, with crowds roaring his name in approval.

The rollerball sequences are well staged and exciting to watch, but when off the track the film is slow. As sf the film is unsatisfactory: little is said about this future world, which is only 40 years away, except that the Corporations have abolished all individual nations, and that war, poverty and disease no longer exist; generally the events in the film are left suspended in a cultural and social limbo. The film perhaps exploits exactly that voyeurism of violence against which it ostensibly moralizes. [JB]

ROMANIA *See* EASTERN EUROPE.

ROMANO, DEANE (LOUIS) (1927–). American writer, who has written non-sf novels such as *The Town that Took a Trip* (**1968**). Some of his work deals with current investigations into parapsychology (*see* PSI POWERS); a film screenplay on this subject by DR was novelized by Louis CHARBONNEAU as *The Sensitives* (**1968**). His first solo sf novel, *Flight from Time One* (**1972**), also deals with parapsychology in a somewhat didactic tone in a story of "astralnauts", an elite squad of the future, who take on missions in their astral bodies. [JC]
See also: ESCHATOLOGY.

ROME, ALGER The collaborative pseudonym of Jerome BIXBY and Algis BUDRYS, used on one story, "Underestimation" (1953).

ROME, DAVID Pseudonym of an Australian writer whose first sf was "Time of Arrival" for *NW* in Apr. 1961. His sf novel, a less than elegant début, is *Squat* (**1970** Australia). It is subtitled "Sexual Adventures on Other Planets". He has written paperback fiction in other genres. [PN]
See also: GENERATION STARSHIPS.

RONALD, BRUCE W. (1931–). American writer, actor and advertising man. His *Our Man in Space* (**1965**) is a little reminiscent of Robert A. HEINLEIN's *Double Star* (**1956**) in its story of an actor unhappily spying on behalf of Earth. [PN]

ROOT, A(LBERT WALDO) (1891– ?). American writer and raiser of poultry. His sf novel is *Tomorrow's Harvest: or, Death Takes a Holiday* (**1967**). [JC]

ROSE, F(REDERICK) HORACE (VINCENT) (1876– ?). British author. His *The Maniac's Dream* (**1946**) was the first post-Hiroshima future-WAR novel to depict nuclear destruction of the Earth. An earlier work, *The Night of the World* (**1944**), centres on a time slip in an oasis peopled with figures from other ages. [JE]
Other works: *Bride Of The Kalahari* (**1940**); *Pharaoh's Crown* (**1943**).
See also: CRIME AND PUNISHMENT.

ROSE, LAURENCE F. *See* John Russell FEARN.

ROSHWALD, MORDECAI (1921–). Polish-born Israeli writer and academic, resident in the USA. He has published several books on politics and other topics, including *Moses* (**1969**) with Miriam Roshwald. His sf novels, *Level Seven* (**1959**) and *A Small Armageddon* (**1962**), are both coloured by political concern about our nuclear civilization: in the first, a military officer, deep within a bomb shelter, describes his feelings and duties as the world is gradually demolished above him; in the second, the crew of a nuclear submarine threatens to detonate its cargo unless its demands are met. MR's novels, which are both awful-warning books, have perhaps dated a little already, but only because of mankind's survival; they are powerful indictments all the same. [JC]

See also: END OF THE WORLD; HOLOCAUST AND AFTER.

ROSNY aîné, J.H. Pseudonym of Joseph-Henri Boëx (1856–1940). French-speaking Belgian writer. His younger brother Justin shared the pseudonym J.H. Rosny with him between 1893 and 1907, and works published between these dates are collaborative. Joseph used the name for solo writings before 1893, and after 1907 it was divided, Joseph taking the suffix "aîné" and Justin "jeune" so that their writings might be differentiated. Although a prolific writer important in the history of sf, the elder Rosny remains virtually unknown outside France. Only one of his novels, *Le félin géant* (**1918** France; trans. **1924** as *The Giant Cat*; vt *Quest of the Dawn Man*) was translated into English during his lifetime. Damon KNIGHT translated two of his most important short stories "Un autre monde" (1895; trans. as "Another World") and "Les xipéhuz" (1887; trans. as "The Shapes") for his anthologies *A Century of Science Fiction* (**1962**) and *100 Years of Science Fiction* (**1969**), but *L'étonnant voyage de Hareton Ironcastle* (**1922** France; trans. and rewritten by Philip José FARMER as *Ironcastle* **1976**) is so drastically modified that it can no longer be regarded as the same novel as the original. He is best known for his five romances of prehistory: *Vamireh* (**1892**), *Eyrimah* (**1893**), the classic *La guerre du feu* (**1909**), *Le félin géant* and *Helgvor du fleuve bleu* (**1930**). He published a semi-mystical speculative essay on creation and EVOLUTION, *La légende sceptique* (**1889** France), which invites comparison with

James Caan with fellow sportsmen in ROLLERBALL.

POE's *Eureka* (**1848**). It embodies the kind of schema associated with the French tradition in evolutionary philosophy which runs from Lamarck through Bergson. A similar semi-fictional meditation is found in *Les compagnons de l'univers* (**1934**). His other speculative novels include *La grande énigme* (**1920** France), and the two-volume work *Les navigateurs de l'infini* (**1925** France; part II **1960** as *Les astronautes*). He also wrote novels on LOST WORLD and END OF THE WORLD themes. His short stories, collected in *Récits de science-fiction* (coll. **1973** France), include early evolutionary fantasies, early stories featuring ALIEN beings — including "Les xipéhuz" — and the PARALLEL WORLDS story "Un autre monde". The lack of English translations has led to an unfortunate neglect of Rosny in commentaries on the history of sf by English and American scholars. [BS]
About the author: "The sf of J.H. Rosny the elder" by J.-P. Vernier in *Science-Fiction Studies*, Vol.2, part 2 (July 1975).
See also: ANTHROPOLOGY; BIOLOGY; COSMOLOGY; LIFE ON OTHER WORLDS; ORIGIN OF MAN; PERCEPTION; RELIGION.

ROSS, DALLAS *See* Mack REYNOLDS.

ROSS, JOSEPH Spelling of his name used professionally by American editor Joseph Wrocz (? –). He was managing editor of AMAZING STORIES and FANTASTIC, 1965–7, and edited *The Best of Amazing* (anth. **1967**). [PN]

ROSS, MALCOLM (HARRISON) (1895–). American writer and reporter, whose sf novel, *The Man Who Lived Backward* (**1950**), is about an attempt to prevent Lincoln's assassination. [JC]

ROSS, RAYMOND GEORGE (? –). American writer whose novel *Beyond the Chains of Bondage* (**1964**) has a Chinese-dominated future USA. [JC]

ROSSITER, OSCAR Pseudonym of American physician and writer Vernon H. Skeels (1918–), who received his MD in 1949 and whose first sf novel, *Tetrasomy Two* (**1974**), features a hospital setting, in which a helpless human vegetable turns out to be an amoral SUPERMAN preparing to eliminate the Solar System in order to gain sufficient energy to go travelling among the stars; the telepathic awakening of a high but indiscriminate INTELLIGENCE in the bumbling doctor hero, and his subsequent PSI-assisted seduction of a beautiful nurse, involves some light but assured black comedy. [JC/PN]

ROTH, PHILIP (1933–). American writer, best known for his novel *Portnoy's Complaint* (**1969**), which in its sophisticated and often comic dealing with sexual obsessions is rather similar to his sf novel, *The Breast* (**1972**), where the sudden and painful transformation of a man into a female breast is described with a great deal of verisimilitudinous detail, leading to a remarkable, deadpan articulation of a surrealistic metaphor probably derived directly from Franz KAFKA's *Die Verwandlung* (1916; trans. as "The Transformation" 1933, in book form as *The Metamorphosis* **1937**); the psychosexual implications of this metaphor are obvious enough. [JC]

ROTSLER, WILLIAM, (1926–). American writer and artist, who received a 1975 HUGO award for his fan art. He began publishing sf with "Ship Me Tomorrow" for *Gal.* in 1970, and has published actively since, under his own name, as John Ryder Hall, and under the BALLANTINE house name William Arrow. All his novels under his own name, published and unpublished (there are at least three unpublished), inhabit a shared universe, the nature of which was still unclear in late 1977, though *Patron of the Arts* (**1974**) and *To the Land of the Electric Angel* (**1976**) are set in Earth societies which are seemingly extrapolations of southern California today, and both are in some fashion concerned with the relationship between art and money or social control (*see* ARTS). The first incorporates his best-known and most praised short story, "Patron of the Arts" (1972), but the expansion weakened some of its impact. The second, which involves CRYONICS, reawakening in a DYSTOPIAN future, gladiatorial contests and much more, is perhaps the best example of his work. *Zandra* (**1978**) is the earliest of the series in terms of internal chronology. WR's pseudonymous work is restricted to film and TV link-ups. [JC]
Other works: As John Ryder Hall: *Futureworld* (**1976**) from the film FUTUREWORLD; *Sinbad and the Eye of the Tiger* (**1977**) from the film of that name. As William Arrow: nos 1 and 3 of the "Return to the Planet of the Apes" books based on the animated TV series: *Visions from Nowhere* (**1976**) and *Man, The Hunted Animal* (**1976**).
See also: RELIGION.

ROTTENSTEINER, **FRANZ** (1942–). Austrian sf critic and editor, and librarian; PhD from the University of Vienna. He writes in English as well as German, and his critical articles have appeared in SCIENCE-FICTION STUDIES and elsewhere; he is particularly well known for his spirited promotion of the work of Stanislaw LEM for whom he is literary agent, and for the contempt he has often expressed for most genre sf; his criticism is intelligent, polemical and left-wing, and best expressed in fairly academic formats; his popular illustrated history of sf, *The Science Fiction Book* (1975), is generally felt to be sketchy and disappointing. In English he is also known for his collection of European sf *View From Another Shore* (anth. **1973**). Many of his writings in German appear in his own, high-quality FANZINE, QUARBER MERKUR. He has also edited three anthologies of stories and essays about sf, in German, *Polaris 1* (anth. **1973**), *Polaris 2* (anth. **1974**), a special Soviet sf issue, and *Polaris 3* (anth. **1975**), in addition to another collection, *Die Ratte im Labyrinth* (anth. **1971**). FR has also worked as editor on several sf book series, including 15 vols of Insel-Verlag's hardback "SF of the World" series 1971–5. [PN]

ROUSSEAU, VICTOR Usual writing name of Victor Rousseau Emanuel (1879–1960); he also used the pseudonym H.M. Egbert. Little is known of his life; Sam MOSKOWITZ writes in *Under the Moons of Mars* (anth. **1970**) that he was born in London of a Jewish father and French mother; he apparently lived for some time in South Africa during the Boer War, at some time converted to Catholicism, and emigrated to the USA, probably during the First World War. He began writing sf in the PULP MAGAZINES before the War and stopped in 1941; much material has never been collected from the magazines, including the fantasy "Surgeon of Souls" series, 11 stories in *Weird Tales* (1926–7). *The Sea Demons* (1916 *All-Story Weekly* as V. Rousseau; **1924** as H.M. Egbert) features hive-like sea creatures threatening humanity (*see* INVISIBILITY); a submarine finds and destroys the queen. *The Messiah of the Cylinder* (**1917**; vt *The Apostle of the Cylinder*) is VR's best-known work. As it directly imitates the form of H.G. WELLS's *When the Sleeper Wakes* (**1899**) and harshly criticizes the atheistic world-state UTOPIA it depicts, it has been seen as a melodramatic anti-Wellsian critique of socialism; Wells's novel, however, is deeply ambiguous about the world it describes, and serves more as a pre-text for VR's book than as an argument to be refuted. VR's book is as much against the soulless use of science, especially eugenics, as it is against socialism. In *Draught of Eternity* (1918 *All-Story Weekly* as V. Rousseau; **1924** as H.M. Egbert) a love story is set in a ruined New York. VR published three mainstream novels under his own name of V.R. Emanuel; as V. Rousseau he also published adventures and Westerns. [JC]
Other works: *Eric of the Strong Heart* (**1925**); *Mrs. Aladdin* (**1925**); *My Lady of the Nile* (undated).
About the author: "H.G. Wells and Victor Rousseau Emanuel" by Richard D. MULLEN, EXTRAPOLATION, Vol.8 no.2 (1967).
See also: MESSIAHS; POLITICS; TIME TRAVEL; INTELLIGENCE.

RUD, ANTHONY (MELVILLE) (1893–1942). American author and PULP MAGAZINE editor. He contributed sf to *Weird Tales*, *Blue Book* and other periodicals, but is best known for the

ROHMEResque fantasy *The Stuffed Men* (**1935**), rather like John BLACKBURN's *A Scent of New-Mown Hay* (**1958**) in its account of a fungus growing within the human body; this is part of a hideous Oriental revenge.   [JE]

RUELLAN, ANDRÉ (1922–). French writer. A doctor of medicine, he has used the following pseudonyms in his writing: Kurt Steiner, Kurt Dupont, Kurt Wargar, André Louvigny and Luc Vigan. He has written 31 novels, of which at least ten are sf/fantasy. An author of uneven quality, AR was the first in France to tackle heroic fantasy with his *Ortog* saga, published as by Kurt Steiner: *Aux armes d'Ortog* ["To Arms, under the Banner of Ortog"] **1960**, and *Ortog et les ténèbres* ["Ortog and the Darkness"] **1969**, and then the two together as *Ortog* (coll. **1975**). *Le tunnel* ["The Tunnel"] (**1973**), considered his best book, is an ambitious sociological view of the future. *Le bruit du silence* ["The Sound of Silence"] (**1955**); *Le 32 juillet* ["32nd of July"] (**1959**); *Le disque rayé* ["The Scratched Record"] (**1970**) and *Brebis galeuses* ["Black Sheep"] (**1974**), all as by Kurt Steiner, are worth noting. AR now principally writes film scripts.   [MJ]

RUNCIMAN, JOHN See Brian W. ALDISS.

RUNYON, CHARLES W. (1928–). American writer of thrillers and sf. He began publishing sf with "First Man in a Satellite" for *Super-Science Fiction* in 1958. His first sf novel, *Pig World* (**1971**), depicts a NEAR-FUTURE America governed by a right-wing tyranny whose oppression is challenged by a vicious would-be demagogue. *Soulmate* (1970 *FSF*; exp. **1974**) is a possession novel; the victim is a young prostitute. CWR's sf tends to action-filled, rather direct effects.   [JC]
Other works: *Ames Holbrook, Deity* (**1972**); *I, Weapon* (**1974**).

RUPPERT, CHESTER See Rog PHILLIPS.

RUSHDIE, (AHMED) SALMAN (1947–). Indian writer, educated in England at Rugby and Cambridge and now a British citizen. His complex and witty, legend-like novel, *Grimus* (**1975**), can be treated as marginally sf in its use of IMMORTALITY themes and in the interdimensional conflicts its eternally young Amerindian protagonist must undergo in his search through an emblematic World-Island for the moment of death. Ultimately, with Sufi-like ambiguity, he succeeds.   [JC]
See also: ABSURDIST SF; PERCEPTION.

RUSS, JOANNA (1937–). American writer and academic, currently a university professor, with an MFA in playwriting from the Yale School of

Drama, 1960. Though she began publishing short fiction in 1959 with "Nor Custom Stale" for *FSF*, where she has also published occasional book reviews for some years, JR published her first novel, *Picnic on Paradise* (**1968**), only after a decade had passed. It comprises the largest single portion of *Alyx* (coll. **1976** with an introduction by Samuel R. DELANY), a series of tales about the female character Alyx, the remainder of which were originally published in Damon KNIGHT's original anthology series, ORBIT. Much of the impact of *Picnic* lies in its use of a female protagonist in situations where she is a fully responsible agent, involved actively in the circumstances surrounding her. Unlike most earlier women writers of sf, JR is feminist, sometimes highly persuasively, both in her fiction and in the strong and perceptive critical work which she has published widely. Her second novel, *And Chaos Died* (**1970**), is a somewhat muffled but ambitious rendering, from inside, of the rewriting of the psyche of a man who crash-lands on a planet inhabited by psychically transformed humans, and must live through the perilous acquiring of new PSI POWERS — telepathy, teleportation, and so forth. His rediscovery of Earth in the latter part of the book is to satirical effect.

Photo Jeff Levin.

JR's third novel, *The Female Man* (**1975**), which awaited publication for some time, remarkably uses several sf milieux to argue a strong feminist case about the condition of woman on Earth. The several female characters of the book, each of whom inhabits a radically different kind of environment, can be taken as literal representatives of the various fates of woman in the world, from psychic servitude to freedom as represented by the UTOPIAN life on the planet Whileaway. Each female character can also be read as a different version of the same fundamental personality, and therefore as a linked set of the potentials for a woman of today. The book is angry and convincing.
JR won the 1972 NEBULA award for best short story with "When it Changed". Other short works of note includes "Daddy's Girl" (1975), a reprise of some of the themes of *The Female Man*, and "The Autobiography of My Mother" (1975), which has appeared in *Prize Stories 1977: The O. Henry Awards* (anth. **1977**). (Not all JR's stories are sf.) *We Who Are About To ...* (**1977**) is a

metaphysical SPACE OPERA combining many of the themes of her earlier books. JR is an accomplished writer of fiction whose unrelenting use of her skill to make deeply felt arguments about woman's fate in the world gives her a somewhat daunting austerity, so far as the genre reader is concerned. That her use of sf is radically significant is, however, indisputable.   [JC]
About the author: Marilyn Hacker's introduction to the 1977 reprint of *The Female Man*; the Delany introduction referred to above.
See also: ANTHROPOLOGY; AUTOMATION; COLONIZATION OF OTHER WORLDS; CRITICAL AND HISTORICAL WORKS ABOUT SF; ESP; FANTASTIC VOYAGES; NEW WAVE; PARANOIA AND SCHIZOPHRENIA; SEX; WOMEN.

RUSSELL, BERTRAND (ARTHUR WILLIAM) (1872–1970). English mathematician, philosopher and controversialist; he succeeded to the family title, becoming the third Earl Russell in 1931. He was awarded a Nobel Prize for literature in 1950. Near the end of his immensely long career (his first book, *German Social Democracy*, appeared in **1896**), he published three volumes containing a series of fable-like tales, *Satan in the Suburbs and Other Stories* (coll. **1953**), *Nightmares of Eminent Persons and Other Stories* (coll. **1954**) and *Fact and Fiction* (coll. **1961**). Somewhat after the manner of VOLTAIRE, these stories — some of them, like "The Infra-Rediscope" from the first volume, and "Planetary Effulgence" from the last, use an sf idiom — didactically though with grace present their author's sceptical attitude toward human ambitions and pretensions, and to the ideas with which we delude ourselves.   [JC]
See also: AUTOMATION; DYSTOPIAS; RELIGION; SOCIOLOGY.

Photo from Walter Gillings' collection.

RUSSELL, ERIC FRANK (1905–78). British writer, who first came into contact with sf fans through his membership of the British Interplanetary Society in the mid-1930s. He soon began to write sf, and his first story, "The Saga of Pelican West" (1937), was published in ASTOUNDING STORIES. A number of short stories followed in *ASF* and in British magazines. Some were based on ideas or unsuccessful stories by other British fans, including Arthur C. CLARKE.

EFR became strongly interested in the works and theories of Charles FORT, and was for a time British representative of the Fortean Society. His first novel, *Sinister Barrier* (1939 *Unknown*; **1943**; rev. **1948**) was based on Fort's notion of the human race being "property", of INVISIBLE PARASITES in EFR's formulation. *Sinister Barrier* was featured in the first issue of UNKNOWN, the short-lived fantasy companion to *ASF*, although it is straightforward PULP sf and quite atypical of that magazine. EFR later used a similar theme in *Sentinels From Space* (**1953**).

In 1941 he published the first story of the "Jay Score" series, which featured a ROBOT who looked and acted like a human. The third story of the series, "Symbiotica" (1941), was an interesting treatment of SYMBIOSIS. The stories were collected in *Men, Martians and Machines* (1941–3 *ASF*; fix-up **1956**). EFR was a regular contributor to *ASF* for nearly two decades, occasionally using the pseudonyms Webster Craig and Duncan H. Munro. He developed a racy, wisecracking style in most of his stories; often it made his stories seem more quintessentially American than those of any American contributor to the magazine. Notable contributions included "Metamorphosite" (1946), "Hobbyist" (1947), *Dreadful Sanctuary* (1948 *ASF*; **1951**; rev. 1963), "Dear Devil" (1950) and "I Am Nothing" (1952).

"Late Night Final" (1948) was a dry run for his short novel "… And Then There Were None" (1951). Both stories show a dislike for regimentation, either political or military, and for bureaucracy; " … And Then There Were None" additionally presents an ingenious decentralized POLITICAL system. It was later incorporated into the novel *The Great Explosion* (1951 *ASF*; fix-up **1962**). HUMOUR was a strong element in these stories, as in much of EFR's work; it frequently took the form of bungling aliens being outwitted by humans. Often one man was sufficient to tackle an entire species, as in "Diabologic" (1955), *Wasp* (**1957**) and *The Space Willies* (1956 *ASF* as "Plus X"; exp. **1958**; vt *Next of Kin* UK). *Wasp* and *The Space Willies* are both WAR stories — a spy novel and a prisoner-of-war camp story respectively — and their aliens closely resemble wartime propaganda Germans, but they are told with an inventive relish which disarms criticism. "Allamagoosa" (1955) lampooned bureaucracy and won EFR a HUGO award. In a serious vein, *Three To Conquer* (**1956**) was a novel on the theme of INVASION, the threat coming from parasitic aliens.

EFR wrote very little sf after 1960, although he published a number of collections: *Far Stars* (coll. **1961**), *Dark Tides* (coll. **1962**), *Somewhere A Voice* (coll. **1965**) and *Like Nothing on Earth* (coll. **1975**). [MJE]
Other works: *Deep Space* (coll. **1954**); *Great World Mysteries* (**1957**); *Six*

Worlds Yonder (coll. **1958**); *With A Strange Device* (**1964**; vt *The Mindwarpers* USA).
See also: ALIENS; AUTOMATION; COLONIZATION OF OTHER WORLDS; ESP; EVOLUTION; GODS AND DEMONS; GOLDEN AGE OF SF; LIFE ON OTHER WORLDS; MONSTERS; ORIGIN OF MAN; PARANOIA AND SCHIZOPHRENIA; PERCEPTION; RELIGION; TIME TRAVEL; VILLAINS.

RUSSELL, JOHN See John Russell FEARN.

RUSSELL, JOHN ROBERT (? –). American writer, whose first novel, *Cabu* (**1974**), translates a man to a violent new life on the planet Cabu. The planet *Ta* (**1975**) features sentient plants. [JC]
Other works: *Sar* (**1974**).

RUSSELL, W(ILLIAM) CLARK (1844–1911). American-born British sailor (1858–66) and prolific writer of books, fiction and non-fiction, almost exclusively about sailors and the sea. Of sf interest are *The Frozen Pirate* (**1887**), in which a French pirate, frozen for years in cold climes, is resuscitated briefly and tells the narrator where there is some buried treasure, and *The Death Ship, A Strange Story; an Account of a Cruise in 'The Flying Dutchman'* (**1888**; vt *The Flying Dutchman* USA), which tries to add scientific verisimilitude to the legend. Other works include *A Tale of Two Tunnels* (**1897**) and the stories assembled in *Phantom Death and Other Stories* (coll. **1895**). [JC]
See also: CRYONICS; IMMORTALITY.

RUSSEN, DAVID (? – ?). British author, born in the 17th century, of the extended book-review published in book form, *Iter Lunare: Or, A Voyage to the Moon: Containing Some Considerations on the Nature of that Planet, the Possibility of getting thither, With Other Pleasant Conceits about the Inhabitants, their Manners and Customs* (**1703**). The book reviewed was *Selenarchia*, the title given to the 1659 English translation of CYRANO DE BERGERAC's *Voyage dans la lune* (**1657**). DR criticizes Cyrano on scientific grounds, and speculates on other possible systems for travel to the MOON, noting the likelihood of a lack of air on the way. A recent edition (**1976**) has an introduction by Mary Elizabeth Bowen. [PN]

RUSSIA (*Book and story titles below are translations of the original Russian title. They refer to an existing translation of the work itself only where the word "trans." appears.*) Russian sf can trace its ancestry back to the 18th century. Prince Mikhail Shcherbatov's UTOPIA *Voyage to the Land of Ophir* (written 1783, **1807**) embodied the political and social reforms espoused by the liberal and progressive elements of Catherine the Great's aristocracy. Much more chauvinistic is Prince Vladimir Odoyevsky's "Year 4338" (1840). Russia

here leads the world in technology and scientific thought. Odoyevsky introduced many entertaining extrapolations regarding transport, food, drink and fashion. By contrast, N. Chernyshevsky's radical novel *What is to be Done* (**1863**) contains the celebrated Vera Palovna's "Fourth Dream", a Fourierist vision of Utopian socialism.

Two fantasies reflect 19th-century technological advance in Russia: V. Chikolev's *Neither Fact nor Fantasy: an Electrical Utopia* (**1895**) and A. Rodnykh's intriguing fragment "The Self-Propelled Petersburg-Moscow Underground Railway" (1902).

Of paramount importance to the later development of Russian sf is K. TSIOLKOVSKY, especially in his "On the Moon" (1893) and *Beyond the Planet Earth* (**1920**; trans. **1960**), VERNE-influenced tales with a powerful emphasis on exact scientific data.

The popularity of H.G. WELLS, whose work was translated continuously into Russian from 1899 onwards, and was very influential, led to A. Bogdanov (pseudonym of A. Malinovsky) placing the action of his remarkable novel *The Red Star* (**1908**) on Mars. His main interest is in men and their social relationships under a future communism, and the book was reissued several times after the revolution. Wells's ideas of a governing scientific elite found reflection also in *Cold City* (**1971**) by S. Komarov, in which engineers use future refrigeration technology to cope with solar fluctuation.

Verne's influence can be traced in V. Uminsky's *Unknown World* (**1897**) and *To the South Pole* (**1898**), and V. Semyonov's *Kings of the Air* (**1909**). The chief magazines of the time (1909–18) in this field were *Nature and People* and *Around the World*. These published translations of foreign classics, which were in turn imitated by native pulp magazines. Alexander KUPRIN parodied the latter in his *Liquid Sun* (**1912**).

Academician OBRUCHEV wrote two classics of Russian sf, *Plutonia* (**1915**; trans. **1957**; new trans. 1961) and *Sannikov Land* (**1926**; trans. **1955**; new trans. 1968). Plutonia lies within the earth, while Sannikov Land is a warm island in the Arctic. Both stories give a picture of past ages for the young reader, after the manner of Verne.

The period following the 1917 revolution saw a number of established Russian writers entering the sf field and founding the sub-genre "Red Detective". These stories usually involved adventures abroad, with assistance being given to world revolutionary movements. The fantastic element might be a new weapon or explosive. Examples still in print are M. Shaginyan's *Mess-Mend* (**1924**) and *Laurie Lane, Metalworker* (**1925**), V. Katayev's *Iron Master* (**1924**) and, most famous of all, A. TOLSTOY's *The Death Box* (**1926**; trans. **1936** by B.G. Guerney;

rev. 1937; trans. vt *The Garin Death Ray* 1957 by George Hanna).

A theme born of revolutionary euphoria was the outward spread of communist man through the universe. It found fanciful expression in the poetic movement "cosmism", notably in the sf-orientated verse of the celebrated poet Valery Briusov, and in sf produced A. Tolstoy's *Aelita* (**1922**; trans. **1957**), filmed in 1924 (*see* AELITA). This haunting tale of love on revolutionary Mars has retained its popularity. Y. ZAMIATIN wrote *We* (trans. **1924**), in which the One State plans to export its soulless doctrine across the universe. This novel, one of the most important of early political DYSTOPIAS, has never been published in Russia.

Naïve socialist Utopias made an appearance once more in the 1920s. They tended to be dull and overloaded with technological marvels. V. NIKOLSKY's *One Thousand Years Hence* (**1927**) and Ya. Okunyev's *Tomorrow* (**1923**) are good examples. Ya. Larri's *Happy Land* (**1930**) was the last communist Utopia until I. YEFREMOV's *Andromeda* (**1959**; trans. **1959**).

A more caustic approach to Utopia can be seen in V. MAYAKOVSKY's brilliant play *The Bedbug* (**1928**; trans. **1960**), in which he satirizes a dull, virtuous, over-clean future without condoning the energetic, alcoholic prole who represents the present generation: Mayakovsky sees both extremes as undesirable.

Alexander BELYAEV rose to prominence in the later 1920s. He was an excellent storyteller: *The Amphibian* (**1928**; trans. as by A. Belayev **1959**) and *Professor Dowell's Head* (**1925**) are known to all Russian schoolchildren, and in 1963 his works were republished in eight volumes (200,000 copies printed). The "Red Detective" theme of world revolution virtually disappears in Belyaev, doubtless as a consequence of Trotsky's disgrace and exile in 1927; most of his novels, however, are set in capitalist countries, and are fiercely critical of their social and scientific *mores*.

Magazines, particularly *Round the World* and *Adventure World*, went on publishing sf throughout the 1920s, usually mad-scientist tales of adventures in the laboratory, as in S. Golub's "Secret of the Micro-world" (1927), or spy/adventure yarns about new weapons, or such explosives as "Mortonite", "Neronite", "Antibellum" and "Shtekkerite", all of which appeared in stories between 1927 and 1929. These magazines attained great popularity: *World Sleuth*'s circulation rose, between 1926 and 1929, from 15,000 to 100,000.

Tighter Communist-party control of literature in the 1930s compelled sf writers to become more ideologically correct than hitherto. They were to direct their readers' attention to tasks close at hand, to stress collective over individual effort, and to set their plots within the USSR. G. Adamov typifies the themes and attitudes of the new cultural climate. His *Secret of Two Oceans* (**1938**) combines scientific information with a patriotic plot involving the thwarting of Japanese spies. *Conquerors of the Depths* (**1937**) shows a scientific collective at work. In all such works, speculation stuck close to contemporary scientific knowledge. The belief that speculative fiction was an escape from reality lasted until after Stalin's death in 1953. Okhotnikov's typically named *Frontiers of the Possible* (**1947**) dealt with new road-laying techniques, new combine harvesters, and so on.

The late 1950s saw a dramatic change in Russian sf, which has not been reversed. The technical magazine *Knowledge is Power* printed one sf story only in 1953; in 1961 it printed 19, including two by Ray BRADBURY and part of *Solaris* by the Polish writer Stanislaw LEM. Writers demanded the freedom to speculate far more widely, to write "far" fantasy rather than "near", as they put it. Encouraged by a more liberal literary climate and the example of the Anglo-American work which was now being translated in quantity, writers like G. Al'tov, V. Zhuravlyova, A Dneprov and V. Savchenko emerged and themes formerly TABOO began to appear in print: ROBOTS, CYBERNETICS, TIME TRAVEL, ESP and even ALIENS, for example. Lem, Isaac ASIMOV (*I, Robot*), Bradbury (*The Martian Chronicles*), Robert SHECKLEY, Murray LEINSTER, Frederik POHL and Arthur C. CLARKE were among the foreign sf writers now published in Russia. Yefremov brought out the first communist Utopia for thirty years: *Andromeda* (**1959**) caused great controversy but encouraged the younger generation of sf writers by its bold speculations about, for example, null-space, bi-polar mathematics and secluded islands for dissidents. Level-headed critics like E. Brandis and V. Dmitreyevsky kept readers informed about developments abroad, as the first sf magazines and anthologies began to appear in the early 1960s: *Seeker*, *N.F.*, *Fantastika*, etc. These also contained translations from mainstream Anglo-American sf.

A poll in *Fantastika* in 1967 shows the STRUGATSKY brothers as the most popular sf writers, followed in order by Bradbury, Lem, Sheckley and Asimov. The Strugatskys were the only native writers in the first ten.

Of the writers to make their mark in the 1960s, including D. Bilenkin, O. Larionova, I. Varshavsky, G. Gor, M. Yemtsev, E. Parnov and, latterly, S. Snegov and K. Bulychov, the Strugatsky brothers stand out as major talents. They have written far and away the most interesting and readable sf so far produced in Russia. More subdued of late, since clashing with authority, they typify the present state of sf in Russia, a genre seemingly exhausted after the great surge of creativity in the 1960s. Interestingly, sf criticism, notably by Julius KAGARLITSKY, R. Nudelman and T. Chernysheva, has become vastly more sophisticated.

Sf as a genre in Russia enjoys great popularity in a country where light literature is hard to come by. A known sf author or good sf anthology will appear in editions of 100,000 to 200,000. Its readership is predominantly among the young and the scientifically minded. A recent survey showed that 25% of workers, students and the technical intelligentsia read sf! Despite the Strugatskys, sf is not regarded seriously by the literary establishment and there seems no prospect (or danger) of its becoming a part of Russian mainstream literature. Nonetheless, judged by volume alone, one must suppose sf in Russia to be an influential (or potentially influential) genre. Three million sf books are now published annually, and there have been 1,624 new Russian sf titles since 1917, of which 1,000 have been published since 1958.   [AM]

See also: The several anthologies of Russian sf stories which have been published in English translation, including the Moscow Foreign Language Publishing House anthologies *A Visitor From Outer Space* (anth. **1961**); *Destination: Amaltheia* (anth. **1962**); *The Heart of the Serpent* (**1960**) and the three Mir anthologies *Everything but Love* (anth. **1973**), *Journey Across Three Worlds* (anth. **1973**) and *The Molecular Café* (anth. **1968**). Anthologies published in the UK and the USA include *Vortex* (anth. **1970**) ed. C.G. Bearne; *Last Door to Aiya* (anth. **1968**) and *The Ultimate Threshold* (anth. **1970**) ed. Mirra GINSBURG; *Russian Science Fiction* (anth. **1964**), *Russian Science Fiction Vol. II* (anth. **1967**) and *Russian Science Fiction Vol. III* (anth. **1969**) ed. R. MAGIDOFF; *View From Another Shore* (anth. **1973**) ed. F. ROTTENSTEINER; *Other Worlds, Other Seas* (anth. **1970**) ed. Darko SUVIN; and the anonymously edited *Path Into the Unknown* (anth. **1966**). All the novels mentioned in the text above as being translated were published either by the Foreign Language Publishing House in Moscow or by British or American publishers, or occasionally both. In addition to the cross-references listed in the text above, *see also* (for other Russian authors whose relationship to the field is less central): N. AMOSOV, M. BULGAKOV, Y. DANIEL, F. DOSTOYEVSKY, V. DUDINTSEV and Abram TERTZ. Finally, *see* Darko Suvin's *Russian Science Fiction 1956–1974: A Bibliography* (**1976**).

RUTH, ROD (1912–). American illustrator. Some of his early work was in animal illustration, a talent that served him well in sf also, where he created some very credible alien beasts. He is best known for his b/w illustrations in the

early 1940s for *Amazing Stories, Fantastic Adventures, Captain Future* and *Weird Tales*, and he also painted a few covers. He has illustrated for Follett Publications, Golden Press, Western Publishing, Whitman Publishing and many other companies. After 25 years away from sf, RR recently illustrated *Science Fiction Tales: Invaders, Creatures and Alien Worlds* (**1973**) ed. Roger ELWOOD, and two other anthologies. RR has also illustrated children's books, worked on a comic strip, and worked in advertising and several other art-related fields. He has won awards from the Artists' Guild of Chicago and the Society of Illustrators, but none in sf. [JG]

SABERHAGEN, FRED (THOMAS) (1930–). American writer and editor, in the latter capacity with the *Encyclopedia Britannica*, 1968–73, for which he wrote the entry on sf. He began publishing sf with "Volume PAA-PYX" for *Gal.* in 1961, and has been active with both short stories and novels from that date, his first novel being *The Golden People* (**1964**), a SPACE OPERA involving PSI POWERS. He is best known for his "Berserker" series of stories and novels: *Berserker* (coll. of linked stories **1967**), *Brother Assassin* (**1969**; vt *Brother Berserker* UK), *Berserker's Planet* (**1975**), a projected fourth volume, and several stories still in magazine form: "Berserker's Prey" (**1967**; vt "Pressure"); "Starsong" (**1968**); "Wings out of Shadow" (**1974**); "Inhuman Error" (**1974**) and "Annihilation of Angkor Apeiron" (**1975**). The series combines space opera with some speculation about the nature of human society in its narratives of the interstellar conflict between Man and the Berserkers, huge, sentient war-MACHINES savagely inimical to all forms of organic life. A second series, comprised of *The Broken*

Rod RUTH's aliens, more bizarre then threatening, were a feature of the Ziff-Davis magazines in the 1940s. *Amazing Stories*, March 1942.

Lands (**1968**), *The Black Mountains* (**1971**) and *Changeling Earth* (**1973**), combines ancient technology and new powers in a SWORD-AND-SORCERY variation (*see* HOLOCAUST AND AFTER; MAGIC). Of single novels, *The Dracula Tape* (**1975**), consisting of Dracula's own confessions, is of peculiar interest. *The Book of Saberhagen* (coll. **1975**) gives an overview of FS's career. [JC]
Other works: *The Water of Thought* (**1965**); *Specimens* (**1976**).
See also: AUTOMATION; HISTORY IN SF; TECHNOLOGY; WAR.

SACKVILLE-WEST, V(ICTORIA MARY) (1892–1962). English writer, daughter of the third Baron Sackville, married to Harold NICOLSON. A member of the Bloomsbury Group, she is best known for MAINSTREAM novels, such as *The Edwardians* (**1930**); her sf novel, *Grand Canyon* (**1942**), threatens the world with a victorious Germany. [JC]

SADEUR, JACQUES Pseudonym of French writer Gabriel de Foigny (*c.* 1650–92), whose *La terre australe connue, c'est à dire, la description de ce pays inconnu jusqu'ici, de ses moeurs et de ses coûtumes, par M. Sadeur* (**1676**; expurgated by author 1692 as *Les aventures de Jacques Sadeur dans la découverte et le voiage de la terre australe*; trans. of 1692 edition as *A New Discovery of Terra Incognita Australis, or the Southern World* 1693) places its narrator (called Sadeur) in an Antipodean land peopled by an enlightened, human-like race, with whose precepts current European ideas contrast poorly; after many years, Sadeur falls under suspicion and escapes on a bird. [JC]

SADOUL, JACQUES (1937–). French editor and scholar. A strong

personality on the French sf scene, JS was the first editor to launch sf successfully in paperback form in France with his J'ai lu imprint. He was also a founder of the PRIX APOLLO. *Hier, l'an 2000* (**1973**; trans. as *2,000 A.D.* **1976**), a book of illustrations edited by him from the GOLDEN AGE of pulp sf, presents a good selection of gaudy nostalgia, but suffers from bad translation in the US/British edition. His *Histoire de la sf moderne* ["History of Modern sf"] (**1973**) is a lengthy and enthusiastic survey of the field, judged by some reviewers as suffering from a pedestrian style and structure, lack of critical analysis and too many sweeping generalizations and personal prejudices out of place in a scholarly volume. JS has also written a history of comic strips published in 1976 which is open to the same criticisms. [MJ]

SAGAN, CARL (1934–). American astronomer and author. He has a 1960 PhD from the University of Chicago, and is professor of astronomy and space sciences and director of the Laboratory for Planetary Studies at Cornell University; he edits the astronomy journal *Icarus*.

CS's relevance to sf is through his work on exobiology, sometimes called XENOBIOLOGY. The majority of his books have been about the possibility of LIFE ON OTHER WORLDS, and he is one of the comparatively few scientists to have given serious thought to this question. His first book was an updating of a 1963 book, published in Russian, by the astronomer I.S. Shklovskii; the collaboration, published under both their names, was *Intelligent Life in the Universe* (**1966**). CS's next books in this area were *The Cosmic Connection: An Extraterrestrial Perspective* (**1973**), "produced" by Jerome Agel, and the collection of articles, *Communication with Extraterrestrial Intelligence* (anth. **1973**), which he edited. More recently he has written, rather outside his field, on EVOLUTION (*see also* ORIGIN OF MAN) in *Dragons of Eden: Speculations on the Evolution of Human Intelligence* (**1977**).

CS has played an active role in the MARS experiments carried out by *Mariner* 9, and was responsible for placing a message to alien life aboard the interstellar spaceship *Pioneer 10*. [PN]
Other works: *Other Worlds* (**1975**); *Planets* (**1970**) with Jonathan Norton Leonard and the Editors of Time-Life. As editor: *U.F.O's: a Scientific Debate* (anth. **1973**) ed. with Thornton Page.
See also: TERRAFORMING.

ST CLAIR, MARGARET (1911–). American writer, usually under her own name but sometimes as Idris Seabright, and once in 1952 as Wilton Hazzard. She began publishing sf with "Rocket to Limbo" for *Fantastic Adventures* in 1946, and by 1950 had released about 30 stories, most of them vigorous adventures in a strongly coloured idiom; her magazine series, the "Oona and Jik" stories, appeared in *Startling Stories* and *TWS*, 1947-9. In 1950, MSC began publishing in *FSF* as Idris Seabright, a name which, for several years, was as well known as her own, though she has never published books under this pseudonym. The Idris Seabright name – almost exclusively restricted to *FSF* stories from 1950 to 1959 – was used for tales with a larger fantasy element than her others; these stories also tended to have a more elegant literary polish, though none of MSC's work can be considered clumsy. Her first novel, *Agent of the Unknown* (1952 *Startling Stories* as "Vulcan's Dolls"; **1956**), is set on a pleasure planetoid and tightly narrates the dark adventures of a man caught there in an intrigue involving a tiny animate doll. This novel is typical of her earlier work. Some of the short stories from these years are collected in *Three Worlds of Futurity* (coll. **1964**) and *Change the Sky and Other Stories* (coll. **1974**).

Among MSC's more recent, longer works, *The Dolphins of Altair* (**1967**), *The Shadow People* (**1969**) and *The Dancers of Noyo* (**1973**) are notably more ambitious and sustained than her earlier novels, with the possible exception of *Sign of the Labrys* (**1963**), and have not received adequate critical attention. *The Dolphins of Altair*, for instance, is one of the best of the many novels of the 1960s and later which use the concept of intelligent dolphins, in this case part of an ancient Altairan breeding programme, to arrive at sharp conclusions about Man's treatment of his planet. Further publication of MSC and Idris Seabright tales still in magazine form will undoubtedly enhance her reputation, as well as appreciation of her subtle later work. [JC]
Other works: *The Green Queen* (**1956**); *The Games of Neith* (**1960**); *Message from the Eocene* (**1964**).
See also: MYTHOLOGY; OUTER PLANETS; PERCEPTION; ROBOTS; WOMEN.

ST JAMES, BLAKELY See Charles PLATT.

ST JOHN, JOHN ALLEN (1872-1957). American illustrator. JASJ was the principal illustrator for the original editions of Edgar Rice BURROUGHS' many books. Of these, he is best remembered for his "Tarzan" and "Barsoom" series illustrations, which became so well known that they have overshadowed all his other work. His b/w illustrations are unsophisticated sketches, and the colours in his paintings are muted, especially when compared to today's illustrations, but the overall effect of violent yet graceful movement was to add a perfect romantic complement to Burroughs' writing. JASJ's illustrations were as Victorian as Burroughs's stories, with noble heroes and pure, virginal

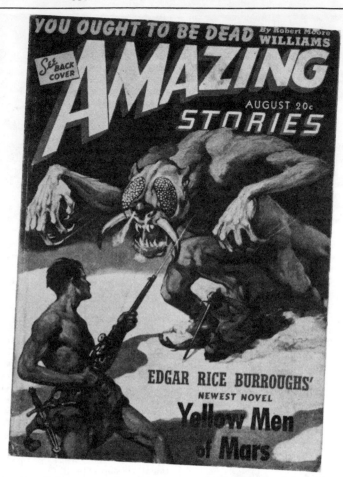

John Allen ST JOHN was reckoned demure, as pulp illustrators go, but could produce monsters as lurid as any. Aug. 1941.

heroines. His visualizations have had a profound influence on many illustrators, particularly those specializing in HEROIC FANTASY, notably Roy G. KRENKEL and Frank FRAZETTA. [JG]

ST JOHN, PHILIP See Lester DEL REY.

ST MARS, F. See Frank AUBREY.

ST. NICHOLAS MAGAZINE US juvenile magazine, 1873-1943, for boys and girls, published by Scribner, later by Century Co., then by American Education Press. Founded by Rosewell Smith and edited by Mary Mapes Dodge, 1873-1905, William Fayal Clarke, 1905-27, and others. Assistant editors included Frank R. STOCKTON, 1873-81, and Tudor Jenks, 1887-1902. It appeared monthly Nov. 1873-May 1930 as *St. Nicholas*, becoming *SNM* from Jun. 1930 to its demise in Jun. 1943. The format was large square octavo, becoming quarto from 1926.

Although of less sf interest than the DIME NOVELS, *SNM* maintained a high literary standard and kept its circulation at 70,000 for many years. Numerous fantasy stories appeared within its pages, notably by Frank R. Stockton, John

Kendrick BANGS and Rudyard KIPLING, ranging in content from fairy tales to sf such as Clement FEZANDIE's *Through The Earth* (1898; rev. **1898**). Aimed at a more educated and middle-class market than the dime novels, *SNM* was undoubtably enjoyed by many children to whom the FRANK READE series was out of reach (through parental selectivity) and thus has some bearing on the HISTORY OF SF. [JE]
See also: *Books In Black Or Red* (**1924**) by Edmund Lester Pearson.

SAKI (1870-1916). Pseudonym of Hector Hugh Munro, British author and journalist noted for his acerbic writings. As H.H. Munro he wrote *When William Came* (**1914**), a trenchant future-WAR novel about a German INVASION and the occupation of London, regarded by I.F. CLARKE as the best of all such works. Many weird and fantasy stories, ironic, witty and sometimes cruel, are included in the following collections, all published as by Saki: *Reginald* (coll. **1904**), *Reginald in Russia* (coll. **1910**), *The Chronicles of Clovis* (coll. **1911**), *Beasts and Super-Beasts* (coll. **1914**), *The Toys of Peace* (coll. **1919**), *The Square Egg* (coll. **1924**) and *The Complete Short Stories of Saki* (coll. **1930**). [JE]

SALGARI, EMILIO See ITALY.

SALLIS, JAMES (1944–). American writer, strongly associated with *NW* in its Michael MOORCOCK-directed NEW WAVE phase; he published his first sf story, "Kazoo", with *NW* in 1967. His clearly acknowledged models in the French *avant garde*, and the gnomic brevity of much of his work limited his appeal in the sf world, though he received some critical acclaim for *A Few Last Words* (coll. **1970**). He also edited two sf anthologies: *The War Book* (anth. **1969**) and *The Shores Beneath* (anth. **1971**). [JC] See also: ABSURDIST SF.

SAMBROT, WILLIAM (ANTHONY) (1920–). American author of more than 50 sf short stories, beginning with "Report to the People" for THE BLUE BOOK MAGAZINE in 1953. Most of his work has appeared in *Saturday Evening Post* and other "slicks", and has consequently received less attention from within the sf field than it might have done, considering its vigour and polish. WS has published one collection of his work, *Island of Fear and Other SF Stories* (coll. **1963**), and under the pseudonym William Ayes (he has also used Anthony Ayes) is publishing an ongoing series of stories about Crazy Murtag, in various men's magazines, in which Melvin Murtag attempts various such impossible feats as repealing the First Law of Thermodynamics. [JC]

SAMUELSON, DAVID N. (1939–). American academic and sf critic, with a 1969 PhD from the University of Southern California, now teaching at California State University, Long Beach. His PhD dissertation was published later as a book, *Visions of Tomorrow: Six Journeys from Outer to Inner Space* (**1975**) by ARNO PRESS: it contains analyses of novels by Arthur C. CLARKE, Isaac ASIMOV, Theodore STURGEON, Walter M. MILLER Jr, Algis BUDRYS and J.G. BALLARD. Shorter critical pieces have appeared in EXTRAPOLATION and SCIENCE-FICTION STUDIES. DS is among the more intelligent and better-informed academic critics of sf. [PN]

SANBORN, ROBIN (? –). American writer, whose sf novel, *The Book of Stier* (**1971**), features the overtoppling of all American institutions by a youth movement inspired by mysterious Richard Stier's music; at the book's close, Canada takes over the USA. [JC]

See also: MESSIAHS.

SANDERS, LAWRENCE (1920–). American writer, best known for his thriller *The Anderson Tapes* (**1970**), later filmed; his sf novel, *The Tomorrow File* (**1975**), depicts a NEAR-FUTURE America on a large canvas; the heart of the book is the Department of Bliss and the analysis of its functions in a jaded country. [JC]

SANDERS, WINSTON P. See Poul ANDERSON.

SANDERSON, IVAN T. See Terence ROBERTS.

SANDRELLI, SANDRO See ITALY.

SANTESSON, HANS STEFAN (1914–75). American editor and author. He edited FANTASTIC UNIVERSE Sep. 1956 to its demise in Mar. 1960, and also a collection of stories from the magazine, *The Fantastic Universe Omnibus* (anth. **1960**). Other HSS anthologies are *Rulers of Men* (anth. **1965**), *Gods for Tomorrow* (anth. **1967**), *Crime Prevention in the 30th Century* (anth. **1969**), *Gentle Invaders* (anth. **1969**), *The Mighty Barbarians* (anth. **1969**), *The Mighty Swordsmen* (anth. **1970**), *The Days After Tomorrow* (anth. **1971**) and *Flying Saucers in Fact and Fiction* (anth. **1968**), this last containing some non-fiction items. [PN]

SARAC, ROGER Pseudonym of American writer and motion picture executive Roger Andrew Caras (1928–), author of non-fiction under his own name, and an sf novel, *The Throwbacks* (**1965**), as RS; it deals with genetic monsters who threaten mankind. [JC]

SARBAN Pseudonym of British writer John W. Wall (? –), who published two volumes of unusual fantasy stories, *Ringstones and Other Stories* (coll. **1951**) and *The Doll Maker and Other Tales of the Uncanny* (coll. **1953**), but is best known for his ALTERNATE-WORLDS sf novel *The Sound of his Horn* (**1952**), in which the Nazis have won the Second World War and established a vicious DYSTOPIAN society in conquered England; dissidents are hunted down for SPORT (*see also* Keith ROBERTS's "Weihnachts-abend", 1972), a fate which the protagonist escapes only by being returned to this world. The novel is haunting and nightmarish. [JC]

SARGENT, PAMELA (? –) American writer and editor, with an MA in classical philosophy. As editor, she is best known for her series of anthologies with women as protagonists: *Women of Wonder* (anth. **1975**), *More Women of Wonder* (anth. **1976**), and *The New Women of Wonder* (anth. **1978**). Her anthology *Bio-Futures* (anth. **1976**) is one of the strongest and best-organized thematic collections of recent years. She began publishing sf with "Landed Minority" for *FSF* in 1970; much of her short fiction appears in *Starshadows* (coll. **1977**), and demonstrates, as does her first novel, *Cloned Lives* (**1976**) (*see* CLONES), her ability to use sf subject matter to explore human relationships without mawkishness or the over-delicate "sensitivity" once assumed to be the woman sf writer's prerogative and burden in the sf field. [JC]

See also: WOMEN.

Feb. 1958. Cover by Alex Schomburg.

SATELLITE SCIENCE FICTION US magazine, DIGEST-size Oct. 1956-Dec. 1958, BEDSHEET-size Feb.-May 1959. 18 issues, Oct. 1956-May 1959. Published by Renown Publications; ed. Sam MERWIN (Oct.-Dec. 1956) and Cylvia Kleinman (Mrs Leo MARGULIES?) (Feb. 1957-May 1959).

Satellite was to some degree a re-creation in digest format of STARTLING STORIES, with a similar editorial policy ("a complete science fiction novel in every issue") and an editor and publisher who had worked on *Startling* in the 1940s (the publisher was actually Leo Margulies, formerly editorial director of *Startling* and its companions). It began promisingly, its first two issues featuring "The Man from Earth" (Oct. 1956; rev. vt *Man of Earth*; **1958**) by Algis BUDRYS and "A Glass of Darkness" (Dec. 1956; as *The Cosmic Puppets* 1957) by Philip K. DICK, as well as stories by Isaac ASIMOV, Arthur C. CLARKE (who had stories in each of the first five issues), L. Sprague DE CAMP and others. Merwin left after two issues, however, and the magazine gradually declined into mediocrity. One notable later novel was *The Languages of Pao* (Dec. 1957; abridged **1958**) by Jack VANCE. For its last four issues (Feb.-May 1959) *Satellite* switched from bi-monthly to monthly publication and adopted a more impressive large format. Frank Belknap LONG was associate editor Feb.-May 1959. The Jun. 1959 issue was printed but never distributed. [MJE]

SATIRE. From the earliest days of PROTO sf, satire was its prevailing mode, and this inheritance is evident even after sf proper began in the 19th century. *The Shorter Oxford English Dictionary* defines satire as a literary work "in which prevailing vices or follies are held up to ridicule". Proto sf is seldom interested in imagining the societies of other worlds or future times for their own sake; far more commonly they are a travesty of some aspect of the writer's own society. This is still a common strategy in sf by MAIN-STREAM authors and in genre sf as well.

The satire may even take the form of debunking other kinds of literature, as in the very early example *The True History* (2nd century AD) of LUCIAN. The wonderful exaggerations of this story poke fun at travellers' tales generally, though its zestful telling suggests a certain sympathy with the inquisitive mind which dotes on such imaginings.

Most proto sf of the 17th and 18th centuries (*see, e.g.,* Francis GODWIN, CYRANO DE BERGERAC, Daniel DEFOE, Jonathan SWIFT, Eliza HAYWOOD, RESTIF DE LA BRETONNE, Robert PALTOCK) creates imaginary worlds, commonly on ISLANDS or on the MOON, as a kind of convenient blank slate upon which various societies satirizing our own can be inscribed. Satire is ancestral to the DYSTOPIA, and even the UTOPIA often contains satirical elements. Many critics believe that Sir Thomas MORE intended the reader to take some aspects of *Utopia* (1516 in Latin; trans. 1551) with a grain of salt.

It is almost impossible to write a work of fiction set in another world, be it our own world in another time, or some alien place, which does not make some sort of statement about the present-day, real world of the writer. Thus, very little sf does not bear at least a family resemblance to satire, at least in those works where the parallels to the contemporary world are derogatory. In his critical study *New Maps of Hell* (1960), Kingsley AMIS argued (perhaps because his own fiction is very much of that kind) that Dystopian satire rather than technological extrapolation was central to sf. It is an easy argument to support, at least in terms of the number of texts that can be cited as evidence.

Among the prominent satirists of the 19th century who used sf imagery to make their points, Samuel BUTLER and Mark TWAIN are supreme, but even when we turn to the work of writers considered more central to the development of modern sf, such as Jules VERNE and H.G. WELLS, we still find the satirical element prominent. Wells's *The Time Machine* (1895), for example, contains many pithy observations about the relationship of the working classes and the leisured classes, and *The War of the Worlds* (1898) can be read as an ironic tale in which Britain, the great colonizing power of the day, is herself subject to an invasion of would-be colonists whose technology is superior to Britain's, just as hers is superior to Africa's. Satire need not be good humoured; both these works are notably savage, especially *The War of the Worlds*, in its portrait of a demoralized and cowardly population.

Among the mainstream writers of this century who wrote important sf satires are Anatole FRANCE, André MAUROIS, Aldous HUXLEY, George ORWELL, Karel ČAPEK, Anthony BURGESS, Evelyn WAUGH and Gore VIDAL; details will be found in all their entries. It would be impossible to list the innumerable sf satires of less well-known writers, which include Archibald MARSHALL's *Upsidonia* (1915), Owen M. JOHNSON's *The Coming of the Amazons* (1931) and Frederick Philip GROVE's *Consider her Ways* (1947). This last work contains many pungent comments on human society by a party of intelligent ants, and this is an example · of one of the most popular satiric strategies in sf, the use of an alien perspective to allow us to see our own institutions in a fresh light. Jonathan SWIFT, for example, used intelligent horses in *Gulliver's Travels* (1726; rev. 1735), VOLTAIRE used a visiting giant alien from Sirius in *Micromégas* (1750 Berlin; 1752 France), and, to give some lesser-known examples, Grant ALLEN used a man from the future in *The British Barbarians* (1895), Lester LURGAN used a visiting Martian in *A Message From Mars* (1912) and Eden PHILLPOTTS used a visiting alien lizard in *Saurus* (1938). Indeed, there is a sense in which *all* satire depends upon just such reversals of perspective, which sf is peculiarly well fitted to supply; satire forces us to look at familiar aspects of our lives with a fresh vision, so that all their absurdity or horror glows much more luridly at us. Visiting aliens and future Dystopias are two familiar strategies for producing such shifts of perspective, but there are many others. One such is in *The Stepford Wives* (1972) by Ira LEVIN (*see the film entry* THE STEPFORD WIVES) in which sexist masculine attitudes, especially in middle-class suburbia, are satirized in a thriller centering on the construction of passive, substitute robot wives.

Robots are often used in sf satire for a different reason: it is their innocence that is exploited for satiric purposes. Because robots are, in theory, not programmed with prejudices, and are given simple ethical systems, then they may have a childlike purity about them that cuts through rationalizations and sophistications; thus in Philip K. DICK's *Now Wait for Last Year* (1966), the hero's moral quandary is amusingly but touchingly resolved by advice from a robot taxi-cab. CHILDREN IN SF are occasionally used in a similar manner. Both these are simply special cases of the "innocent observer" satirical strategy, which was first popularized by Voltaire in *Candide* (1759); in this story a naïve man, with few expectations of life and a likeable character, is consistently abused and exploited in his travels. Modern sf examples include *The Sirens of Titan* (1959) by Kurt VONNEGUT Jr, in which the hero is a millionaire brainwashed into innocence on Mars, and Robert SHECKLEY's *Journey Beyond Tomorrow* (1963; vt *The Journey of Joenes* UK), where the traveller is a naïve islander who has a terrible time in a future America. Sheckley is among the finest of genre sf satirists, and a great deal of his work depends on the introduction of a similar, innocent viewpoint.

Satire is not only a matter of imaginary societies and shifts in perspective; it has a great deal to do with narrative tone. Good satire often stands or falls by the tone of voice the author adopts, which cannot, generally, afford to be too hectoring or sarcastic, or the reader simply feels bludgeoned. An air of mild surprise is often considered appropriate for satire, though commonly, of course, the narrator's voice is ironic or sardonic, a good example of the latter being found in a collection which contains several satirical sf fables, *Sardonic Tales* (coll. trans. 1927) by VILLIERS DE L'ISLE ADAM. This same sardonic note is often found in the work of John COLLIER, Roald DAHL and sometimes Howard FAST. In genre sf it characterizes the excellent work of John T. SLADEK, who shifts skilfully between the mock-innocent and the ironic in his stories, nearly all of which are satire.

The standard of satire within genre sf was not very high before the 1950s, though numerous PULP writers from Stanton A. COBLENTZ to L. Sprague DE CAMP wrote occasional satires. One of the earliest sf writers to excel in this field was Henry KUTTNER, especially in his short stories. Short, satirical sf stories found a natural home in the early 1950s when GALAXY SCIENCE FICTION opened up a new market. The best of the *Galaxy* satirists were probably Robert Sheckley, William TENN, Damon KNIGHT and C.M. KORNBLUTH and Frederik POHL. Kornbluth and Pohl specialized in Dystopian stories which extrapolated certain aspects of present-day life into the future, with satirical effect; the world of advertising was pilloried in *The Space Merchants* (1953) and of organized sport in *Gladiator-at-Law* (1955). It was the turn of insurance companies in *Preferred Risk* (1955) by Pohl and Lester DEL REY writing together as Edson McCANN. Perhaps the sharpest anti-advertising book in sf is *The Big Ball of Wax* (1954) by Shepherd MEAD: more recently, much of the amusing but occasionally heavy-handed satire of Ron GOULART has also been directed against the ad-man's mentality, and the MEDIA LANDSCAPE generally.

Sf satire of the 1960s and '70s has been generally a little more polished than most of the above. NEW WORLDS magazine published many writers whose satirical skills tended more towards a rather dry irony than to angry or jovial sarcasm, notably Thomas M. DISCH, Brian W. ALDISS and the editor himself, Michael MOORCOCK, whose most directly satirical sequence is "Dancers at the End of

Time", beginning with *An Alien Heat* (**1972**). American satire, too, is less broad than it was. The amusing but obvious satire of Fritz LEIBER's *The Silver Eggheads* (**1961**) and *A Specter is Haunting Texas* (**1969**) seems to be giving ground to the work of writers like R.A. LAFFERTY, Barry MALZBERG and James TIPTREE Jr, who all (in completely different ways) seem to prefer a lower-key and more circuitous form of irony, and in whose works the satirical is only one of several elements. Pure satires are becoming comparatively rare in sf, though Peter DICKINSON's *The Green Gene* (**1973**) and Richard COWPER's *Clone* (**1972**) are examples; the latter is another story on the *Candide* pattern. Some important satirical work has issued from the Communist bloc, notably that of Stanislaw LEM, especially in *Cyberiada* (coll. **1965**; trans. as *The Cyberiad* **1974**) and *The Futurological Congress* (**1971**; trans. **1974**), where the savagery of the wit is Swift-like.

The sf CINEMA has flirted with satire occasionally. The three best-known examples are probably PLANET OF THE APES (**1968**), SLEEPER (**1973**) and DR STRANGELOVE (**1963**); others are THE PRESIDENT'S ANALYST (**1967**) and WESTWORLD (**1973**).

Parody is a form of satire, and there has not been a great deal in sf. *Illuminatus!* (three vols **1975**) by Robert SHEA and Robert Anton WILSON does not parody sf *per se*, but it does sharply parody some of its PARANOIA and also its PSEUDO SCIENCE; it adduces a variety of self-contradictory ATLANTIS legends, for example. The best parodies of sf writers are probably those by John Sladek in *The Steam-Driven Boy* (coll. **1973**); also fairly successful are Norman SPINRAD's *The Iron Dream* (**1972**), a parody with a serious point which masquerades as a SWORD-AND-SORCERY novel written by Adolf Hitler, and Harry HARRISON's *Bill, the Galactic Hero* (**1965**) and *Star Smashers of the Galaxy Rangers* (**1973**), which parody Robert HEINLEIN and E.E. "Doc" SMITH respectively. H.G. WELLS was a favourite subject for parodists from early on, as in Max Beerbohm's "Perkins and Mankind" (**1912**); Brian Aldiss's "The Saliva Tree" (**1965**) is a horror story in the style of Wells, but in content like those of H.P. LOVECRAFT. *Mention my Name in Atlantis* (**1972**) by John JAKES is a parody of Robert E. HOWARD, not as sharp as Spinrad's. Bob SHAW's *Who Goes Here?* (**1977**) parodies many themes of SPACE OPERA in general with considerable inventiveness, as does the most successful sf-parody film, DARK STAR.   [PN]

See also: CLICHÉS; HUMOUR; ICONOCLASM; SOCIOLOGY; TABOOS.

SATTERFIELD, CHARLES Pseudonym used on four magazine stories by Frederik POHL, 1954–9, the first time in collaboration with Lester DEL REY.

SATURN *See* OUTER PLANETS.

First issue, March 1957.

SATURN US DIGEST-size magazine. Five issues, Mar. 1957-Mar. 1958, published and ed. Robert C. Sproul; editorial consultant Donald A. WOLLHEIM. A Jules VERNE story appeared in the first issue, but nothing else of note was published. The first issue was subtitled "The Magazine of Science Fiction", the second "Magazine of Fantasy and Science Fiction" and the remainder "Magazine of Science Fiction and Fantasy". [FHP/PN]

SAUNDERS, CALEB *See* Robert A. HEINLEIN.

SAUNDERS, JAKE (? –). American writer. With Howard WALDROP (*who see for details*) he wrote *The Texas-Israeli War: 1999* (**1974**). [JC]

SAVA, GEORGE (1903–). English surgeon and writer, both under his own name and as George Borodin; as Sava, he is best known for *The Healing Knife* (**1938**); as Borodin, he wrote many belles-lettres and the sf novel *Spurious Sun* (**1948**), in which a nuclear explosion in Scotland has profound philosophical effects. [JC]

SAVAGE, RICHARD Pseudonym of English writer Ivan Roe (1917–). As RS he wrote thrillers and one sf novel, *When the Moon Died* (**1955**), in which the destruction of the Moon prevents another war. As Roe he has written MAINSTREAM novels, including *The Salamander Touch* (**1952**), in which an atomic scientist disappears, with difficult consequences. [PN/JC]

SAVARIN, JULIUS JAY (? –). Dominican-born, West Indian writer and musician resident in England since his teens. His sf work comprises the "Lemmus" trilogy, *Lemmus One: Waiters on the Dance* (**1972**), *Lemmus*

Two: Beyond the Outer Mirr (**1976**) and *Lemmus Three: Archives of Haven* (coll. of linked stories **1977**), an expansive SPACE OPERA in which the Galactic Organisation and Dominions (i.e. G.O.D.) experimentally settles Terra with people who will EVOLVE in isolation (*see* ADAM AND EVE). The trilogy offers subsequent explanations for the Judaeo-Christian tradition, the fall of ATLANTIS, etc. [JC]

SAWTELLE, WILLIAM CARTER *See* Rog PHILLIPS.

SAXON, PETER Floating pseudonym used primarily by prolific Scottish writer Wilfred McNeilly (1921–); most of his work of interest to an sf audience is as by PS. In addition to thrillers written for the Sexton Blake Library, as PS he has written *The Disorientated Man* (**1967**; vt *Scream and Scream Again*), filmed as SCREAM AND SCREAM AGAIN (**1969**), about an attempt to make SUPERMEN out of commandeered human parts. His "Guardian" books, beginning with *The Guardians 1 : The Killing Bone* (**1968**), are fantasies about black magic. McNeilly has also written occult novels as Errol Lecale. Martin THOMAS has used the PS name for at least one novel, *The Curse of Rathlaw* (**1968**). [JC/PN]
Other works: (primarily occult, and not necessarily all by McNeilly) *The Torturer* (**1966**); *The Darkest Night* (**1966**); *Corruption* (**1967**); *Black Honey* (**1968**); *Satan's Child* (**1968**); *Through the Dark Curtain* (**1968**; vt *The Guardians 2 : Dark Ways to Death*); *The Guardians 3 : The Haunting of Alan Mais* (**1969**); *The Guardians 4 : The Vampires of Finisterre* (**1970**); *Vampire's Moon* (**1970**).

SAXON, RICHARD Pseudonym of American writer Joseph Laurence Morrissey (1905–), under which he has written some routine sf novels: *The Stars Came Down* (**1963**); *The Hour of the Phoenix* (**1964** UK; US edition, 1965, as by Henry Richards); *Cosmic Crusade* (**1964**); *Future For Sale* (**1964**). [JC]

Photo Peter Nicholls.

SAXTON, JOSEPHINE (1935–). English writer, who began publishing sf with "The Wall" for *Science Fantasy* in

1965, and whose three novels, *The Hieros Gamos of Sam and An Smith* (**1969**), *Vector for Seven: The Weltanschaung* [sic] *of Mrs. Amelia Mortimer and Friends* (**1970**) and *Group Feast* (**1971**), are markedly inventive attempts to exploit the idiom of sf in narratives whose outcomes are as easily readable as allegorical of their protagonists' moral fates as of their physical. The image of the journey is central to her work; though described in some detail, as in *Vector for Seven*, this journey seems generally to occur in what J.G. BALLARD has described as INNER SPACE. JS's stories are closer to surreal or ABSURDIST narratives than to conventional sf, though her three novels were marketed as sf.   [JC]
See also: PERCEPTION.

SCANDINAVIA The term "science fiction" was first introduced in Scandinavia in 1949. Not surprisingly, before this date little sf had been either written or translated in this part of the world.

The early works in the genre were generally inspired from abroad, and of either a Utopian or strongly satirical nature, as in the case of such important works as Ludvig HOLBERG's *Nicolai Klimii iter Subterraneum* (**1741** in Latin; trans. as *A Journey to the World Under-Ground by Nicolas Klimius* **1742**) or Claës LUNDIN's *Oxygen och Aromasia* (**1878** Sweden). In the early 20th century, Norway, Sweden and Denmark could each point to one prolific popular writer bordering on sf in the vein of foreign authors such as Jules VERNE or Edgar Rice BURROUGHS: in Sweden, the inventor Otto Witt (1875–1923) wrote some 25 books and published the weekly magazine *Hugin*, combining fiction and popular science articles (85 issues 1916–20). In Norway, Øvre Richter-Frich (1872–1945), beginning in 1911, issued more than 20 popular novels detailing the adventures of super-scientist hero Jonas Fjeld. And in Denmark, Niels Meyn (1891–1957) from 1911 published an amazing minimum of 340 novels and story collections under more than 40 names; many of his books were modelled on American sf works.

After this first surge of popular sf, however, the field stagnated in Scandinavia. Apart from notable single works (as for instance Karin Boye's *Kallocain*, **1940** Sweden, a major Dystopian novel) almost no sf was issued until the 1950s. One exception may be noted: the Swedish weekly magazine *Jules Verne-magasinet* (1940–47), translated extensively (and in its first three years almost exclusively) from American sf pulps.

Around 1950, sf was also introduced in Scandinavia through translated novels and, in Sweden, through the monthly magazine *Häpna!* (1954–65). Following these translations, native authors also began to emerge, the first such major writer being Niels E. Nielsen in Denmark, who since 1950 has issued some 20 sf novels and short story collections. In Sweden, a place somewhat similar to Nielsen's may be given to Sture Lönnerstrand (1919–), who played a major role in popularizing sf, by writing numerous articles on the field for popular publication, by partly editing *Häpna!*, and through his own fiction, most notable of which is the juvenile *Rymdhunden* (**1954**).

The 1950s, however, created no viable native sf in Scandinavia. Again apart from occasional noteworthy works (this time best exemplified by Harry MARTINSON's epic poem *Aniara*, **1956** Sweden, trans. **1963**) the majority of sf published was translated, and by the beginning of the 1960s the number of such translations was diminishing rapidly. Some influence remained obvious in the writings of several major writers; in Sweden in the satirical novels of P.C. Jersild and Per WAHLÖÖ among others, in Denmark in, for instance, the work of Anders BODELSEN, and in Norway in the work of Axel JENSEN.

In the late 1960s a second renaissance of translated sf began to gather momentum. First obvious in Denmark, through the enormous efforts of Jannick STORM, who from 1966 on edited and translated innumerable sf titles, this renewal of interest reached Norway in 1967, introduced by Jon BING and Tor Åge BRINGSVAERD, and in 1969 Sweden, where Sam J. LUNDWALL filled a similar function.

Along with the new mass of translations stemming from the efforts of those mentioned and of others, this renewed surge of sf publishing included a number of native authors. In Sweden, Sven Christer SWAHN was among the first to be published, and also among the first to win critical acclaim; he was followed by Bertil MÅRTENSSON, Carl Johan HOLZHAUSEN, Sam J. Lundwall and Dénis Lindbohm (1927–). In Norway, Bing and Bringsvaerd themselves, at first, not only provided the translations but also wrote the native stories; however, after some years of total domination, their exclusive rights to the sf field have been challenged by other editors and by new authors, among those the most notable being Øyvind Myhre (1945–), a prolific writer of considerable story-telling power and also the editor of the Norwegian sf magazine *Nova*; Ingar Knudsen and Åsmund Forfang. A further incentive in Norway was provided in 1971, when a publisher (again spurred by Bing and Bringsvaerd) held an sf short-story contest, later publishing the best entries in book form. In Denmark, Jannick Storm had already succeeded in doing the same in 1969, and here also a new generation of writers has begun developing, including in this case Merete Kruuse, Tage Eskestad, and Erwin Neutzsky-Wulff.

During the 1970s, it now seems obvious, sf reached Scandinavia to stay. The readership is reasonably large; in Denmark, Norway and Sweden sf titles generally show a profit, and this in itself should guarantee a continued market. But, more important, the new generation of writers, both those working within the field and those preferring not to have their works labelled, have grown up with sf and learned from its techniques and motifs. Thus, originally an import, sf is now firmly rooted in Scandinavian literature and has begun to attract serious critical attention, this last in part inspired by several recent Swedish and Danish book-length studies of the field (*see, e.g.,* John-Henri HOLMBERG *and* Sam LUNDWALL).

One development however remains to be seen: the emergence of Scandinavian sf utilizing native literary themes and elements. Scandinavian sf thus far is to an overwhelming extent a part of Anglo-Saxon sf; writers such as Sam J. Lundwall, Bertil Mårtensson, Øyvind Myhre and even, although to a much lesser extent, since they have identified this problem, Jon Bing and Tor Åge Bringsvaerd, can often be viewed as Scandinavian counterparts of British or American sf authors. It remains, therefore, for future Scandinavian sf writers to give their sf a basis in Scandinavian myth, literature and present-day society. A first step towards this might be taken when the average Scandinavian sf novel begins to be set in Scandinavia, and when its characters are given Scandinavian names; at present, however, not even this is the case. [J-HH]

SCARFF, WILLIAM *See* Algis BUDRYS.

SCHACHNER,   NAT(HAN) (1895–1955). American lawyer and writer, known mainly for his work outside the sf field, mostly biographies of American historical figures. He began publishing sf with "The Tower of Evil" for *Wonder Stories Quarterly* in 1930; this story was written with Arthur Leo ZAGAT; their collaboration lasted over a year, all NS's first 11 stories being done with Zagat, including a novel, "Exiles of the Moon" for *Wonder Stories* in 1931. After they separated, NS continued to write copiously for the PULPS, under his own name, and under the pseudonyms Chan Corbett and Walter Glamis. His "Past Present and Future" series appeared in *ASF* 1937–9, and his "Revolt of the Scientists" sequence in *Wonder Stories* in 1933. He published only one book of sf, *Space Lawyer* (1941 *ASF*; fix-up **1953**), whose wooden devices and characters were not well received.   [JC]

SCHEER,   K(ARL)-H(ERBERT) (1928–). German writer, with Clark DARLTON (Walter Ernsting) one of the creators in 1961 of the famous PERRY RHODAN series of adventures. He has written many weekly episodes in the sequence.   [JC]

SCHEERBART, PAUL (1863–1915). German fantasist, born in Danzig, died in Berlin. Appearing in many literary periodicals, PS was always a literary outsider. A typical Bohemian, he was a pacifist and anti-eroticist, creating a playful cosmic world of colourful constant permutations of cosmic beings and heavenly bodies totally divorced from the laws of physics. He wrote in a deceptively simple, almost childlike style. His aim was to create "novelty" — new arrangements of familiar grotesque elements. His best novel is perhaps *Lesabéndio* (**1913**), the story of a tower building on the asteroid Pallas, leading up to a union with the cosmic spirit. He was very popular in his day. His many sf books include (the list is not complete) *Das Paradies, die Heimat der Kunst* (**1889**), *Der Tod der Barmekiden* (**1897**), *Na prost!* (**1898**), *Rakkóx der Billionär und die wilde Jagd* (**1900**), *Liwúna und Kaidôh* (**1902**), *Die große Revolution* (**1902**), *Kometentanz* (**1902**), *Immer mutig!* (**1902**), *Revolutionäre Theaterbibliothek* (**1904**), *Der Kaiser von Utopia* (**1904**), *Münchhausen und Clarissa* (**1906**), *Das Perpetuum mobile* (**1910**), *Astrale Novelletten* (**1912**), *Das große Licht* (**1912**), *Das graue Tuch und 10 Prozent Weiß* (**1914**), *Glasarchitektur* (**1914**). [FR] **About the author:** *Paul Scheerbart* (**1912**) by E. Mondt; *Die phantastisch-surreale Welt im Werke Paul Scheerbarts* (**1970**) by C. Ruosch; *Paul Scheerbarts astrale Literatur* (**1976**) by H. von Gemmingen.

SCHIZOPHRENIA *See* PARANOIA AND SCHIZOPHRENIA.

SCHMIDT, STANLEY (1944–). American writer and academic, with a 1969 PhD in physics, which he teaches. He began publishing sf with "A Flash of Darkness" for *ASF* in 1968. Much of his work is grouped in series, though in late 1977 some of the connecting tissue had not yet been published. His first novel, *Newton and the Quasi-Apple* (1970 *ASF*; exp. **1975**), is followed by "His Loyal Opposition" (1976); its basis in physics provides material for an interesting adventure on a primitive planet where questions as to what kinds of knowledge are helpful and when are raised with regard to a new discovery of Newton's principles. *The Sins of the Fathers* (**1976**) involves an exploding galaxy, TIME TRAVEL and more physics; a sequel is projected for publication in 1978 — portions of it, beginning with "A Thrust of Greatness" (1976) and "Caesar Clark" (1977), having been first published as separate stories in *ASF*. SS writes straightforward novels that serve as vehicles for cogently argued hard-sf concepts, and has written an article, "The Science in Science Fiction", published in

Many Futures, Many Worlds (anth.**1977**) ed. Thomas D. CLARESON.

In Summer 1978 it was announced that SS would take over the editorship of *ASF* after Ben BOVA's resignation.   [JC]

SCHMITZ, JAMES H(ENRY) (1911–). American writer, born in Germany of American parents. Served with the USAF in the Second World War and became a full-time writer as late as 1959. His first story, "Greenface", appeared in 1943 in *Unknown*; a hiatus followed until 1949, when "Agent of Vega" appeared in *ASF*, where he has since published regularly. JHS has been notable throughout his career for the use of female protagonists in a remarkably liberated manner for the male-centered sf genre. His women characters perform their active tasks in a manner completely free of sexual role-playing clichés; some of the stories could have male protagonists with only the most minimal changes. This emphasis on his part is all the more remarkable in that he tends to write full-blown galactic SPACE OPERAS, with traditional themes, villains and plots; it is a part of the genre most prone to gross caricature of women.

Much of JHS's fiction is set in a human- and alien-settled galaxy that shares common assumptions and vocabulary from story to story. PSI POWERS are common. Most stories centre on the Federation of the Hub or the Overgovernment, both of which are composed of human and non-human members. The stories usually involve security arms of the central government in actions against criminals, monsters and unfriendly species. The galaxy is in general a very secure place to be for JHS's readers; in contrast to the interstellar venues of many current writers in this subgenre of sf, his galaxy is relatively young, and its civilizations are correspondingly active and optimistic.

JHS's main series set within this universe is the sequence of stories about Telzey Amberdon, a brilliant young telepath (with an affinity for animals) who is recruited by the Psychology Service of the Overgovernment as an agent. The series comprises *The Universe Against Her* (1962–4 *ASF*; fix-up **1964**), *The Lion Game* (1965–71 *ASF*; fix-up **1973**), *The Telzey Toy* (coll. **1973**) and the uncollected stories "Poltergeist" (1971), "Child of the Gods" (1972) and "The Symbiotes" (1972). The main part of *The Lion Game* is typical: Telzey tracks down a complex race, the Elaigar, who are under cover on a large planet; they come in three interlinked forms, and Telzey conspires to manipulate them out of human territory. She is typical of JHS's heroines, very similar to the protagonists of *A Tale of Two Clocks* (**1962**) — Trigger Argee, whose other adventures have intersected with Telzey's — and *The Demon Breed* (**1968**), which is interesting for its water-based alien culture, and to

the three young psi-powered *Witches of Karres* (1949 *ASF* part only; **1966**) who are escorted about a colourfully conceived series of worlds by the hapless space captain who has rescued them from slavery. This last is perhaps JHS's most exuberant work.

Agent of Vega (coll. of linked stories **1960**) precedes *A Tale of Two Clocks*, but is otherwise linked only by shared background. JHS's stories have been collected in *A Nice Day for Screaming and Other Tales of the Hub* (coll. **1965**) and *A Pride of Monsters* (coll. **1970**). An unsuccessful novel, *The Eternal Frontiers* (**1973**), is not connected to the galaxy of his other books.   [JC] **About the author:** *James H. Schmitz: a Bibliography* (**1974**) by Mark OWINGS, with introduction by Janet Kagan. **See also:** CHILDREN IN SF; ECOLOGY; LIFE ON OTHER WORLDS; SUPERMAN.

Charles SCHNEEMAN's technophilic b/w sketches were a feature of *ASF* before the War. *ASF*, May 1940.

SCHNEEMAN, CHARLES (? – ?). American illustrator. CS was active in sf for only a short time before the Second World War. He excelled in b/w sketches, mainly for *ASF*, and is fondly remembered for his illustrations in that magazine of Kimball Kinnison, for E.E. "Doc" SMITH's *Grey Lensman* (1939–40 *ASF*; **1951**), and his drawings for Jack WILLIAMSON's *The Legion of Time* (1938 *ASF*; rev. **1952**). He reappeared with a cover for *ASF* in Nov. 1952, but has been largely forgotten since.   [JG]

SCHNEIDER, JOHN G. (? –). American writer, whose borderline sf novel, *The Golden Kazoo* (**1956**), satirizes the Madison Avenue nature of the (NEAR-FUTURE) 1960 Presidential election.   [JC]

SCHOENHERR, JOHN (1935–). American illustrator. His work has appeared primarily in *ASF*, but he has

John SCHOENHERR is one of the few giants of sf art. His illustrations for Frank Herbert's *Dune* are deservedly famous. These two come from the *Dune Calendar*, 1977.

The prolific Alex SCHOMBURG was often merely workmanlike, but this June 1957 cover is expressive and dramatic.

drawn b/w illustrations for other sf magazines, and has also done paintings for paperback publishers, most notably ACE BOOKS and Pyramid Books; he has almost 400 cover illustrations to his credit. The cover and interior b/w illustrations he did for Frank HERBERT's "Dune" stories when they appeared in *ASF* are considered classics in the field. JS's style, at least in colour, appears to derive from Impressionism, and he is regarded by other illustrators as the most "painterly" in the field. He carries his painting techniques over into his b/w illustrations by using a dry-brush method on rough paper, with fine details added by pen; he has also used scratchboard with great skill. His aliens are particularly convincing, thanks in part to his love for animal illustration (for which he has won numerous awards). JS has been nominated 11 times for a HUGO; he received the award once, in 1965. [JG]

SCHOLES, ROBERT (1929–). American academic and sf critic, with a 1959 PhD from Cornell, now professor of English at Brown University. He is the author of five books on literary theory, and is one of the better-known US theorists in structuralism. The three books with a special relevance to sf readers are *The Fabulators* (**1969**), which deals with FABULATIONS, *Structural Fabulation* (**1975**) and, with Eric S. Rabkin, *Science Fiction: History, Science, Vision* (**1977**). The first two of these books are academic and serious in approach (*see* DEFINITIONS OF SF); for the third, *see* Eric S. RABKIN. RS also wrote the introduction to the 1975 US paperback edition of Tzvetan TODOROV's *Introduction à la littérature fantastique* (**1970**; trans. as *The Fantastic: A Structural Approach to a Literary Genre* **1973**), has written shorter critical pieces on sf, and is general editor of a forthcoming series from an academic

publisher, tentatively entitled "Masters of Science Fiction". [PN]

See also: SF IN THE CLASSROOM.

SCHOMBURG, ALEX (1905–). American illustrator. AS, who has also spelled his name Schomberg, has been working in sf for over 50 years, longer than anyone else in the field. He began with Hugo GERNSBACK and did his first cover in 1925 for *Science and Invention*; his latest was in 1977 for *FSF*. His most prolific period was 1950–65, when his work appeared on the covers of such magazines as *Thrilling Wonder Stories*, *Startling Stories*, *Future Science Fiction*, *Fantastic*, *Satellite Science Fiction*, *Amazing Stories*, *Science Fiction Plus* and *Fantastic Universe*. He has also painted covers for many books, notably for ACE BOOKS and Winston Books (their "juvenile" sf series of the 1950s, for which he also designed the endpapers). His work is realistic, versatile and assured, tending to flatness, and usually keeping away from bright colours, and he is especially adept with the airbrush; he is often called the "King of the Airbrush" by sf fans. He typified run-of-the-mill sf illustration of the 1950s and '60s. He was nominated for a HUGO in 1962 but has never won the prestigious award.

[JG/PN]

SCHOONOVER, LAWRENCE (1906–). American writer, best known for works outside the sf field, especially his many historical novels; his sf novel, *Central Passage* (**1962**), presents its awful warning through a disastrous war. [JC]

SCHUCK, F(REDERICK) H(UGH) P(AUL) (1916–). Trinidad-born American writer and meteorologist, whose sf novel is *The Phantom Caravan* (**1964**). [JC]

SCHUTZ, J(OSEPH) W(ILLARD)
(1912–). American writer and retired
diplomat, with a graduate degree in
science; he is also a graduate of the US
Counter-Insurgency School, now resident
in France. He began writing sf in his
fifties, with "Maiden Voyage" in *FSF* in
1965. Most of his work has been short
stories. His two sf adventure novels are
People of the Rings (**1975**) and *The Moon
Microbe* (**1976**). He has also written
thrillers under the pseudonym Jerry
Scholl.   [PN]

SCHUYLER, GEORGE SAMUEL
(1895–). Black American writer,
whose sf novel, *Black No More: Being an
Account of the Strange and Wonderful
Workings of Science in the Land of the
Free, A.D. 1933–1946* (**1931**) is an
acerbic satire about race relations, in
which a cosmetic treatment is discovered
that will bleach blacks white. Part of the
satire (some of the results are ludicrous) is
directed at blacks who want to be other
than themselves.   [PN/JC]
See also: POLITICS.

SCHWARTZ, ALAN (? –).
American writer, whose sf novel is *The
Wandering Tellurian* (**1967**).   [JC]

SCHWONKE, MARTIN (1923–).
German professor of sociology. His
historical study *Vom Staatsroman zur
Science Fiction* (**1957**) is an influential
analysis which traces the development of
sf from the "Staatsromane" of the 17th
and 18th centuries, stressing the dynamic
thinking of modern sf and the role played
in it by the idea of change. Motivated by
the progress of science and technology, sf
is a testing ground for new ideas. The
emphasis has shifted from the social
ameliorations proposed in UTOPIAS to
thought-experiments with possible
alternatives, in an attempt to prepare for
the contingencies of the future.   [FR]

SCIENCE AND INVENTION US
monthly BEDSHEET-size PULP MAGAZINE.
191 issues, 1908–29. Published by
Experimenter Publishing Co.; ed. Hugo
GERNSBACK. *SAI*, which title first
appeared in Aug. 1920, was not in fact a
new magazine, but a retitling of
Gernsback's *Electrical Experimenter*
(which had itself originated as *Modern
Electrics*). The magazine was founded in
1908, undergoing its first title change in
1913. Gernsback's *Ralph 124C 41+*
(1911–12 *Modern Electrics*; **1925**) first
appeared there. The Aug. 1923 issue was
a special "Scientific Fiction" number, and
was effectively Gernsback's first sf
magazine. Otherwise *SAI* regularly
featured sf stories and novels – notably
three serials by Ray CUMMINGS and A.
MERRITT's "The Metal Emperor" (1920
Argosy; 1927 *SAI*; vt *The Metal Monster*
1946) – although its main content was
science articles, almost wholly so once
Gernsback's AMAZING STORIES became

The cover by Hilliker, showing the
evolutionary progression, came at the end
of the magazine's life, Mar. 1929.

established. *SAI* ceased publication after
Gernsback's bankruptcy.   [MJE/FHP]

SCIENCE FANTASY In the
TERMINOLOGY of sf readers, and more
especially publishers, the term has never
been clearly defined, although it was the
title of a well-known magazine (*see
below*). In recent years it seems to have
been superseded by the term SWORD AND
SORCERY, and more recently still, HEROIC
FANTASY, but it differs from these two
categories in that Science Fantasy does
not *necessarily* contain MAGIC or HEROES.
Science Fantasy can be differentiated
from Weird Fantasy by its emphasis on
the strange and the bizarre, rather than
the horrible and the obviously
SUPERNATURAL, but this distinction is not
at all rigid, and there is considerable
overlap. In effect, Science Fantasy is the
kind of FANTASY that sf readers prefer. It
often features ALTERNATE WORLDS, other
DIMENSIONS, PARALLEL WORLDS,
SUPERNATURAL CREATURES, MAGIC, GODS
AND DEMONS, SWORD AND SORCERY, ESP,
PSIONIC POWERS, SUPERMEN, MYTHOLOGY
and MONSTERS, but no single one of these
ingredients is essential.   [PN]

SCIENCE FANTASY British DIGEST-
size magazine published by Nova
Publications as a companion to NEW
WORLDS, subsequently taken over by
Roberts & Vinter in Jun./Jul. 1964, in a
paperback-size format. 81 issues appeared
under that title, Summer 1950-Feb. 1966,
and 12 more, Mar. 1966-Feb. 1967 under
the titles *Impulse* (Mar.-Jul. 1966) and *SF
Impulse* (Aug. 1966-Feb. 1967). The first
two issues were edited by Walter
GILLINGS, and it was then taken over by
John CARNELL until Nova folded. The
Roberts & Vinter version was edited until
Sep. 1966 by Kyril Bonfiglioli, and the
last five issues were edited by Harry
HARRISON and Keith ROBERTS.
SF used off-beat fantasy material but
very rarely published the kind of

whimsical story associated with the
American UNKNOWN. It tended to use
stories of greater length than its
companion, *New Worlds*, while Carnell
was editor, and it published many
novellas. Many of its lead stories were
supplied by John BRUNNER, Kenneth
BULMER and Michael MOORCOCK, all of
whom published some of their best early
work in its pages. The first published
stories of Brian ALDISS and J.G. BALLARD
appeared there, and virtually all the
important early work of Thomas Burnett
SWANN. While Bonfiglioli was editor
Keith ROBERTS, Christopher PRIEST,
Josephine SAXTON and Brian STABLEFORD
all made their débuts in the magazine,
and the early *Impulse* issues featured the
stories comprising Keith Roberts' classic
Pavane (Mar.-Jul. 1966; fix-up **1968**).
During Carnell's incumbency it published
material of a higher quality than its
companions, but after its sale in 1964 it
was overshadowed by Moorcock's *New
Worlds*, with which it ultimately merged.
The cover art of *SF* was intermittently of
a high standard, especially that of Brian
LEWIS who did most of the covers from
1958–61, and Keith Roberts, who did
nearly all the covers from 1965 until the
end. Roberts's bold semi-abstractions
were quite outside the conventions of
genre SF ILLUSTRATION, and Lewis's
surreal landscapes, reminiscent of Max
Ernst, were also unusual.   [BS]

Feb. 1963. Cover by Gerard Quinn.

Collectors should note: *SF* was
numbered consecutively from nos 1 to 84
(Feb. '66). Numeration was begun again
with the title change to *Impulse*, in Mar.
'66, with one vol. of 12 nos. Early on *SF*
appeared irregularly (Sum. '50; Win.
'50/'51; Win. '51/'52; Spr. '52; Aut.
'52; Spr. '53), but with the following
number, Mar. '54, an uneasy bi-monthly
schedule began lapsing to quarterly every
now and then, improving in the late '50s.
A monthly schedule began Mar. '65,
lasting with perfect regularity to the end.
Science Fantasy was also used as a

variant title of SCIENCE FANTASY YEARBOOK.
See also: FANTASY REVIEW.

Science Fantasy was also a variant title of the US magazine SCIENCE FANTASY YEARBOOK. Spring 1971.

SCIENCE FANTASY YEARBOOK

One of the many reprint DIGEST-size magazines issued by Sol Cohen's Ultimate Publishing Co. Four issues appeared, two in 1970, two in 1971, all but the first as *Science Fantasy*. [BS]

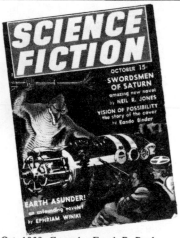

Oct. 1939. Cover by Frank R. Paul.

SCIENCE FICTION US PULP

magazine. 12 issues, Mar. 1939 - Sep. 1941. Published by Blue Ribbon Magazines Inc. (Mar.-Dec. 1939), Double Action Magazines Inc. (Mar. 1940-Jan. 1941) and then Columbia Publications Inc. (Mar.-Sep. 1941); ed. Charles D. HORNIG (Mar. 1939 - Mar. 1941) and Robert A.W. LOWNDES (Jun.-Sep. 1941).

The second venture into magazine editing by former WONDER STORIES editor Hornig, *SF* was never better than very mediocre. Its covers were all by Frank R. PAUL, but were poor examples of his work. The stories were supplied by such authors as John Russell FEARN and Eando

BINDER, both of whom also used pseudonyms to multiply their contributions to the magazine. The readers' departments were conducted on a determinedly chummy basis by Hornig, who spent a good deal of space airing his enthusiasm for Esperanto. (In later issues his firm pacifism showed in some anguished editorials.) After two issues under Lowndes' editorship *SF* was merged with its companion FUTURE FICTION, as *Future Combined With Science Fiction*. The Apr. and Jul. 1943 issues of *Science Fiction Stories*, which revived the *SF* cover design, were actually a continuation of *Future Fiction* after a further title change. [MJE]
Collectors should note: *SF* had two vols, each of six numbers. The schedule was never regular, issues succeeding one another in anything from two to four months.

SCIENCE FICTION ACHIEVEMENT AWARD *See* HUGO.

SCIENCE FICTION (ADVENTURE) CLASSICS *See* SCIENCE FICTION CLASSICS.

SCIENCE FICTION ADVENTURES

Title used on two US DIGEST-size magazines during the 1950s and on one UK magazine that began as a reprint and continued, using original material, after its parent — the second US magazine — folded.

The first US magazine published nine issues, Nov. 1952–Jun. 1954. The first issue was published by Science Fiction Publications, the rest by Future Publications. The issues from Nov. 1952–Sep. 1953 were edited by Lester DEL REY under the pseudonym Philip St John, but Harry HARRISON took over shortly before the magazine folded.

The second magazine, published by Royal Publications Inc., was edited by Larry T. SHAW, and ran for 12 issues in 18 months from Dec. 1956-Jun. 1958.

The editorial policy in each case — more overtly expressed in Shaw's magazine — was to concentrate on adventure stories. The first *SFA* serialized del Rey's *Police Your Planet* (Mar.-Sep. 1953; **1956**) as by Erik Van Lhin, and Cyril KORNBLUTH's *The Syndic* (Dec. 1953-Jun. 1954; **1953**). The second *SFA* used very few short stories, usually featuring three long novelettes per issue. Robert SILVERBERG, under various names, was a particularly prolific contributor, magazine versions of six of his early novels appearing there.

Novelettes from Shaw's magazine were reassorted into five issues of a British edition marketed from Mar.-Nov. 1958 by Nova Publications, with both Shaw and John CARNELL credited as editors. Carnell alone continued the magazine for a further 27 issues until May 1963, using a great deal of material by Kenneth BULMER (under various

names) and novelettes by many writers regularly featured in the companion magazines NEW WORLDS and SCIENCE FANTASY. Notable stories include John BRUNNER's "Society of Time" series (1962; fix-up vt *Times Without Number* **1962**; rev. 1974) and the magazine version of J.G. BALLARD's *The Drowned World* (Jan. 1962; exp. **1962**).

The title *Science Fiction Adventures* was used briefly at the end of 1974 as a variant title of SCIENCE FICTION CLASSICS. [BS]
Collectors should note: The first *SFA* had six numbers in Vol.1, and three in Vol.2. The schedule was irregular. The second *SFA* had two vols, each of six numbers, of which the first (Vol.1 no.1) was wrongly numbered Vol.1 no.6. The British *SFA* was numbered consecutively from 1 to 32, approximately bi-monthly to no.14, and regularly bi-monthly from then on.

SCIENCE FICTION BOOK CLUB

SFBCs were started in both Britain and the USA at roughly the same time (*c.* 1953). The British version was owned in its early years by Sidgwick & Jackson, and more recently by Readers Union; the American club is owned by Doubleday. The two clubs operate somewhat differently. In Britain the SFBC, with a very few exceptions, chooses among recent hardcover titles, reprinting the hardcover edition (or having the publisher print extra copies for its use). It does not set its own books. In America, the club, which is proportionately far larger, offers a wider selection, publishes its own editions (including special hardcover editions of paperback originals) and creates books — omnibuses of various sorts — especially for its members. In recent years the American SFBC has become one of the major forces in sf publishing, while its British equivalent remains a comparatively minor adjunct to the publishing industry in the UK. [MJE]

SCIENCE FICTION CLASSICS One of the many reprint DIGEST-size magazines published by Sol Cohen's Ultimate Publishing Co. 30 issues published. It began publication in Feb. 1967, published issues 1–6 in 1967–8 as *Science Fiction Classics* and issues 7 and 8 in 1969 as *Science Fiction (Adventure) Classics*. It resumed publication in Winter 1970 under the latter title with issue 12 and published 22 more issues before merging with THRILLING SCIENCE FICTION in early 1975. The hiatus in numbering (nos 9–11 missing) is connected with the fact that two other magazines took up their numbering from *SFC* in 1969: SPACE ADVENTURES (CLASSICS) was published for six issues numbered 9–14, and STRANGE FANTASY published six issues numbered 8–13, before both folded, in 1971 and 1970 respectively. In its early issues *SFC* used a great deal of material from the

The title SCIENCE FICTION ADVENTURES presents more problems of identification than any other, since four distinct magazines have used it. From left to right: version one, Mar. 1954, cover by Mel Hunter; version two, Apr. 1957, cover by Ed Emsh; version three, the British continuation of version two, Mar. 1962, cover by Brian Lewis; version four, a variant title of *Science Fiction Classics*, Sep. 1974.

1930s AMAZING, reprinting stories by Hugo GERNSBACK, John W. CAMPBELL Jr, Edmond HAMILTON *et al.*, but later issues reprinted mainly from the period of Raymond PALMER's editorship. [BS]

Science Fiction Adventures Classics was a late variant title of SCIENCE FICTION CLASSICS. July 1974.

Collectors should note: *SFC* was numbered consecutively, up to no. 19, and subsequently simply dated. The schedule was irregular. Variant titles were *Science Fiction Adventures Classics* and briefly, at the end of 1974, *Science Fiction Adventures.*

SCIENCE FICTION CLASSICS ANNUAL US DIGEST-size magazine. One issue, dated 1970, published by Ultimate Publishing Co.; probably ed. Sol Cohen,

All stories were reprinted from AMAZING STORIES of the 1930s. [FHP]

SF COMMENTARY Australian FANZINE. 55 issues from Jan. 1969, current; ed. Bruce GILLESPIE. *SFC* is a serious critical journal in stencilled format; it also includes rather charming autobiographical ramblings by Gillespie. It is generally considered one of the best serious fanzines, has received three HUGO nominations and three DITMARS. The most consistent contributors have been George TURNER, Barry Gillam, John Foyster and Stanislaw LEM; most of the earliest English translations of Lem's critical articles appeared in *SFC*. [PN]

No 1, 1954. Cover by Chester Martin.

SCIENCE FICTION DIGEST US DIGEST-size magazine. Two issues, Feb. and May 1954, published by Specific

Fiction Corp., New York; ed. Chester Whitehorn. *SFD* was intended as a reprint magazine which would take its material from the slick general fiction magazines and other sources, but the selections were weak, and it quickly failed. The same publisher and editor had already failed with VORTEX SCIENCE FICTION in the previous year.

This magazine should not be confused with the British SF DIGEST. [FHP/PN]

Only issue, 1976. Cover by David Bergen.

SF DIGEST British small-BEDSHEET-size magazine (8 × 11 inches). One issue, 1976, published New English Library; ed. Julie Davis. This magazine was to have been a quarterly successor to SCIENCE FICTION MONTHLY, but was doomed even before the first issue appeared by the publisher's decision to drastically reduce its numerous magazine publishing activities and concentrate on books. *SFD*'s format was superior to that of *Science Fiction Monthly*, less obviously slanted to a juvenile market. It contained stories by Michael CONEY, Brian ALDISS and Robert SILVERBERG, and a number of factual and critical pieces. It appeared to be the strongest British sf magazine for some years but in the event received almost no distribution. [PN]

SCIENCE FICTION FORTNIGHTLY See AUTHENTIC SCIENCE FICTION.

SCIENCE FICTION FOUNDATION British teaching and research unit set up in 1971 at the North East London Polytechnic, but semi-autonomous, being controlled by a council with 14 members, half academics and half sf professionals, and including George HAY, whose enthusiasm had much to do with its inception. The first administrator was Peter NICHOLLS, 1971–7, followed by Malcolm EDWARDS in 1978. The SFF is the first and only academic body in the UK set up to investigate sf; it also supervises graduate research work in the field and is investigating the usefulness of sf in education generally. Its journal is FOUNDATION: THE REVIEW OF SCIENCE FICTION, ed. Nicholls for most of its life to date. The patron is Arthur C. CLARKE; council members have included James BLISH, John BRUNNER, Kenneth BULMER, Ursula K. LE GUIN, Christopher PRIEST, Ian WATSON and Brian STABLEFORD. The SFF has the largest publicly accessible collection of sf in the UK outside the British Library: *c.* 11,000 items. [PN] **See also:** SF IN THE CLASSROOM.

SCIENCE FICTION GREATS See GREAT SCIENCE FICTION.

SF GREATS See GREAT SCIENCE FICTION.

SF HORIZONS British critical magazine, ed. Harry HARRISON and Brian ALDISS. An early attempt to establish a serious critical sf journal — and as such a precursor of FOUNDATION, SCIENCE-FICTION STUDIES and others — *SFH* saw only two issues, in 1964 and 1965. Each was 64 pages long, and was dominated by a long article by Aldiss, who contributed a second article to each issue under the pseudonym C.C. Shackleton. Other contributors included Harrison, James BLISH and C.S. LEWIS, and the first issue contained a much reprinted discussion of sf between Aldiss, Lewis and Kingsley AMIS. *SFH*'s main difficulty was that it appeared several years before there was sufficient audience for a magazine of its type. *SFH* was reprinted as a book, *SF Horizons* (1975), by ARNO PRESS. [MJE]

SF IMPULSE See SCIENCE FANTASY.

SF IN THE CLASSROOM In 1961 the first two university-level classes in sf in the USA were set up by Mark HILLEGAS at Colgate and H. Bruce FRANKLIN at Stanford. By 1971 Jack WILLIAMSON's pamphlet *Science Fiction Comes to College* (1971) listed 61 universities offering such courses, and he judged that to be a mere sampling; by the time of Williamson's later pamphlet, *Teaching SF* (1975), that estimate had considerably increased. It seems likely that there are now at least 300 such courses. *A Research Guide to Science Fiction Studies* (1977), compiled by Marshall B. Tymn, Roger C. Schlobin and L.W. Currey, lists 412 doctoral dissertations on sf subjects, the great majority submitted in the USA. Sf teachers in the USA have their own association, the SCIENCE FICTION RESEARCH ASSOCIATION. It is clear that in parallel with all this activity at university level, there has also been a greatly increased use of sf material at high-school level, sf being studied not only in its own right, but because it helps to dramatize issues of SOCIOLOGY, FUTUROLOGY, TECHNOLOGY, OVERPOPULATION, ECOLOGY etc.

There are further reasons for using sf in an academic context, one being that, as a form of popular culture, sf is important to any study of changing prejudices and expectations in the general reading public; sf is indeed an important register of social history.

The story is very different outside America; a small scattering of universities in Europe and Australia have courses, but in no great quantity. The first sf course in the UK was begun by Philip STRICK in 1969, but it remains a non-credit course; the only academic courses up to 1977 had been taken by Peter NICHOLLS at the SCIENCE FICTION FOUNDATION at the North East London Polytechnic, and Ian WATSON at the City of Birmingham Polytechnic, though occasional sf texts found their way on to more conventional courses in English, politics etc. None the less, here, too, academic interest seems to be greatly increasing. In 1976 the BBC sponsored a half-hour TV programme on the academic use of sf, produced and directed by the Science Fiction Foundation, which resulted in many hundreds of letters from interested teachers. The signs are that in the UK, too, sf is likely to gain academic respectability.

Fears have been expressed that the academic study of sf will castrate it, just as jazz began to lose its vitality when it became a serious item of musical study. One angry fan put it: "Kick sf out of the classroom and back to the gutter where it belongs", obviously believing that sf would be healthier if it were not subjected to the stresses of upward social mobility. The fears are not entirely groundless; some academics seem rather cynically to have jumped on the bandwagon, and the standards of academic sf criticism are not

notably high, though some good criticism has been published in the three academic journals dealing with sf, EXTRAPOLATION and SCIENCE-FICTION STUDIES in the USA, and FOUNDATION in the UK.

It is hard to argue, however, that the blasting away of genre sf's ghetto walls has been a bad thing; sf is flourishing in the 1970s as seldom before, and seems to have broadened its range in terms of both form and content.

Several books have been published for use by teachers of sf at high-school level; they include: *Teaching Tomorrow: a Handbook of Science Fiction for Teachers* (1972) by Elizabeth Calkins and Barry McGhan; *Science Fiction: the Classroom in Orbit* (1974) by Beverly Friend; *Science Fiction Primer for Teachers* (1975) by Suzanne Millies; *Grokking the Future: Science Fiction in the Classroom* (1973) by Bernard C. Hollister and Deane C. Thompson. These tend to be slightly patronizing and simplistic; the Friend book perhaps offers the best practical advice. Also useful in their analyses of representative works by particular authors are *Science Fiction: an Introduction* (1973; rev. vt *Science Fiction Reader's Guide*) and *The Ballantine Teachers' Guide to Science Fiction* (1975), both by L. David ALLEN.

The standard of books aimed at university-level readers and graduates is rather higher. They include *Structural Fabulation* (1975) by Robert SCHOLES, *Science Fiction: History, Science, Vision* (1977) by Scholes with Eric S. RABKIN and a number of critical booklets by George Edgar SLUSSER. Sf BIBLIOGRAPHIES have only become a marketable commodity because of the academic interest in sf, notably those aimed at librarians, like the useful *Anatomy of Wonder: Science Fiction* (1976) ed. Neil BARRON.

A series of essays about the academic interest in sf is *Science Fiction: the Academic Awakening* (anth. 1974) ed. Willis E. McNELLY.

The effect of the academic interest in sf goes far beyond the publication of critical guides for teachers and students. It has directly influenced the publication of sf ANTHOLOGIES, and some notably thoughtful compilations have been produced, such as *The Mirror of Infinity: a Critic's Anthology of Science Fiction* (anth. 1970) ed. Robert SILVERBERG; *Those Who Can* (anth. 1973) ed. Robin Scott WILSON; *Modern Science Fiction* (anth. 1974) ed. Norman SPINRAD; *In Dreams Awake* (anth. 1975) ed. Leslie A. Fiedler; and a great many theme anthologies edited by Leon E. STOVER, Gardner DOZOIS and others; one of the most active anthologists for the academic market has been Martin Harry GREENBERG with his several colleagues. The production of teaching film-strips for schools is also expanding, as is the production of cassette tapes of sf readings. Thomas M. DISCH edited an interesting series of film-strips for Prentice Hall.

Beyond all these direct responses to the academic stimulus is the very much more responsible interest being paid to sf by the intellectual world generally; newspapers and magazines are not so dismissive or so ignorant about sf as was the case as recently as in the 1960s. Many more publishers are entering the field, and the trickle of critical studies has swollen to an occasionally muddy river. Much of this material has been produced by trend-spotters, bandwagon-riders and journalists out to cash in on a good thing, but this is inevitable. Perhaps the most important effect has been on the writers themselves, who are very much less inclined to answer evasively when asked what they do for a living, and generally, have more reason to be proud of their work. There can be little doubt, despite the lamentations of old-time fans for the lost glories of the GOLDEN AGE, that more sf of a reasonable standard is being written now than ever before, and this can in part be attributed to the breaking down of the ghetto walls, a process that has been catalysed by academic enthusiasts.   [PN]

See also: CRITICAL AND HISTORICAL WORKS ABOUT SF; PUBLISHING.

SCIENCE FICTION LEAGUE Launched Apr. 1934 by Charles D. HORNIG and Hugo GERNSBACK through WONDER STORIES, the SFL was the first and most successful of several professionally sponsored sf organizations. The formation of local chapters in America, Australia, and Great Britain brought sf readers together and provided a firm foundation for present-day sf fandom; indeed the establishment of the Leeds and Nuneaton SFL chapters led directly to the first UK FANZINES.   [PR]

SCIENCE FICTION LIBRARY. No. 2, 1960.

SCIENCE FICTION LIBRARY British pocketbook magazine. Three numbered, undated issues, 1960, published by G.G. Swan, London; no editor named. This was a poorly produced magazine with no table of contents; the paper was of bad quality and the small type made it difficult to read. Original and reprinted material was used, including some from the first incarnation of SCIENCE FICTION QUARTERLY.

A companion magazine was WEIRD AND OCCULT LIBRARY.   [FHP]

SF MAGAZINES Sf stories were a popular and prominent feature of such general-fiction PULP MAGAZINES as the ARGOSY and ALL-STORY MAGAZINE during the first quarter of the 20th century, although they were not known by that name. If there was a need to differentiate such stories in these magazines, the terms "scientific romance" or "different stories" might be used, but until the appearance of a magazine specifically devoted to sf there was no need of a label to describe the category. The first specialized pulps with a leaning towards sf were the THRILL BOOK (1919) and WEIRD TALES (1923), but the editorial policy of both was aimed more towards weird/occult fiction. As specialized pulps became common it was inevitable that there would be one devoted in some fashion to sf; it fell to Hugo GERNSBACK actually to publish the first such magazine, if we discount the "Twentieth Century Number" (Jun. 1890) of OVERLAND MONTHLY. Gernsback's magazine SCIENCE AND INVENTION had a special issue devoted to "scientific fiction" in Aug. 1923, and in 1924 he solicited subscriptions for a magazine to be called *Scientifiction*. This did not materialize, but two years later, in Apr. 1926, the first issue of AMAZING STORIES appeared. Gernsback's coinage, "scientifiction", reflected his particular interest in sf as a vehicle for prediction and for the teaching of science. In a magazine which featured the stories of both Jules VERNE and Edgar Rice BURROUGHS, it was a label which fitted the former's stories far more readily than the latter's.

AMZ was somewhat different in appearance from the usual pulp magazines, which measured approximately 7 × 10 inches and were printed on poor quality paper with rough, untrimmed edges. *AMZ* adopted the larger, BEDSHEET size (approx. 8½ × 11½ inches) and its pages were trimmed. The reason for this may have been to give an impression of greater respectability in order to have the magazine displayed on news-stands with the more prestigious "slick" magazines; in any event Isaac ASIMOV has testified in *Before the Golden Age* (anth. **1974**) that this was the result. The attempt at dignity was belied by the garishness of some of Frank R. PAUL's cover art, while the magazine's editorial matter had a stuffy, Victorian air. However, it proved initially successful; by Sep. 1928 Gernsback could write, "We put out 150,000 magazines a month, and trust to luck that they will all sell, every month. Very frequently we do not sell more than 125,000 copies." The same issue gives a clue to *AMZ*'s readership: of 22 letters printed, 11 are avowedly from high-school pupils. It was through the letter column of *AMZ* and later magazines that sf FANDOM began.

When Gernsback lost control of *AMZ* in 1929 through bankruptcy it remained in the hands of his assistant, the venerable T. O'Conor SLOANE, and changed little, while the new magazines which Gernsback started — AIR WONDER STORIES and SCIENCE WONDER STORIES — adopted the same format and were very much the mixture as before. Gernsback is generally credited with starting the first sf magazine. In fact, including AMAZING STORIES QUARTERLY and *Science Wonder Quarterly* (later WONDER STORIES QUARTERLY), he initiated the first *five* sf magazines. It is not surprising that the limited Gernsbackian view of sf gained a strong hold. The emphasis on "science" in the category label, often quite inappropriately, is a legacy of this.

The first challenge to Gernsback's view of sf magazine publishing came in 1930 with the appearance of ASTOUNDING STORIES OF SUPER-SCIENCE. *ASF* belonged to the large Clayton magazine chain; it was unequivocally a pulp magazine. Its editor, Harry BATES, was unimpressed by Gernsback's achievements ("Packed with puerilities! Written by unimaginables!" was his later assessment of *AMZ*), and *ASF*'s priorities were adventure first and science a long way second. Adherents of *AMZ* were unimpressed by its vulgarity, and it is truthfully said that the Clayton *ASF* produced vanishingly few stories of enduring quality. However, the same is true of its competitors.

Air Wonder and *Science Wonder* soon amalgamated into WONDER STORIES and the three magazines — *AMZ*, *ASF* and *Wonder* — with minor exceptions constituted the American magazine sf field until 1939. (In 1931 MIRACLE SCIENCE AND FANTASY STORIES published two issues; in 1934 the semi-professional MARVEL TALES began its short life.) Interestingly, none of the three finished the decade under the same ownership that it had at the beginning. *ASF* was initially the only sf magazine belonging to a pulp chain — one of a whole variety of magazines appearing each month, with the marketing and distributing strength that that implied — and when it was sold to another group, Street & Smith, in 1933, it was because of the collapse of the whole Clayton chain. The magazine itself had been quite successful, if undistinguished in content; under its new management and new editor F. Orlin TREMAINE it went from strength to strength, its popular success matched by a notable increase in quality. It had the advantage of paying considerably better than its sf competitors (one cent a word on acceptance, rather than half a cent a word on publication or later — "payment on lawsuit" as the popular saying had it). Even so, *ASF*'s payment rates were only half what they had been in its Clayton days, and represented the lowest standard pulp rates; it was a question of the other sf magazines' paying very badly rather than *ASF*'s paying particularly well. This had obvious repercussions in terms of the writers contributing to them. Authors who could sell their work to *Argosy* for six cents a word were not going to favour *AMZ*, for instance, with anything other than their rejects. More importantly, the prolific professional pulp writers, turning out hundreds of thousands of words each year in any and every category, never made the sf magazines their chief focus of attention. The adverse result of this was that the sf magazines published a great deal of material by writers ignorant even of the minimal standards of professionalism of the pulp hack (hence Bates's dismay with *AMZ*), but in the longer term the advantage was that the field was able to develop itself from within. Fans of the magazines believed, with justification, that they could do as well as the published writers. They tried; a proportion of them succeeded. Jack WILLIAMSON was an early example of such a writer but — as he describes in *The Early Williamson* (1975) — he received little useful encouragement from Gernsback and Sloane. When *ASF* under Tremaine became the first sf magazine with a dynamic editorial policy, it reaped dividends.

While *ASF* prospered the competition floundered, losing their better writers and failing to replace them. By the end of 1933 both *AMZ* and *Wonder Stories* had adopted the standard pulp format. By the end of 1935 both magazines had gone over to bi-monthly publication (the same year, incidentally, that *ASF* was contemplating twice-monthly publication). In 1936 *Wonder Stories* was sold, reappearing after a short gap as THRILLING WONDER STORIES with a change of emphasis epitomized by the bug-eyed monsters on the cover of the first issue. *AMZ* followed suit in 1938.

The failure of the sf magazines to establish themselves as a healthy pulp category in the 1930s is surprising in view of the general popularity of pulp magazines in that decade of the Great Depression, when the pulps provided cheap entertainment in a pre-TV era. As a comparison, the far more specialized, peripherally associated field of "weird menace" pulps (as described in *The Shudder Pulps*, 1975, by Robert Kenneth Jones) — magazines devoted entirely to stories in which apparently strange happenings turned out to have mundane explanations, such as criminals dressed in rubber suits to make them appear like monsters — was thriving, with such titles as *Dime Mystery Magazine*, *Horror Stories*, *Terror Tales* and *Thrilling Mystery*. The only sf magazine to establish itself on a regular monthly basis was the only sf magazine with which Hugo Gernsback had never been associated. This suggests that Gernsback's conception of sf, and of sf magazine publishing, failed to capture the audience it sought. The emphasis of the early sf magazines on machinery, as represented by Paul's cover art, may have alienated as many readers as it attracted.

The first boom in sf magazine publishing came towards the end of the 1930s. MARVEL SCIENCE STORIES, in 1938, became the first fully professional new title since *Miracle* in 1931; it gained some notoriety by trying briefly to introduce to sf a little mild lasciviousness of the kind common in other pulps. In 1939 it was followed by a rush of new titles. *AMZ* and *TWS* had both proved successful enough under new management and with a more lively approach to give birth to companion magazines, FANTASTIC ADVENTURES and STARTLING STORIES. John W. CAMPBELL Jr, who had become editor of *ASF* late in 1937, began a fantasy companion, UNKNOWN, as well as printing during 1939 the first stories of Robert HEINLEIN, Theodore STURGEON and A.E. VAN VOGT, which heralded the start of *ASF*'s greatest period of dominance. Other new magazines were DYNAMIC SCIENCE STORIES, FUTURE FICTION, PLANET STORIES, SCIENCE FICTION, STRANGE STORIES and the reprint magazine FAMOUS FANTASTIC MYSTERIES. In 1940 ASTONISHING STORIES, CAPTAIN FUTURE, COMET STORIES, SCIENCE FICTION QUARTERLY, SUPER SCIENCE STORIES and the reprint FANTASTIC NOVELS came along; in 1941 COSMIC STORIES and STIRRING SCIENCE STORIES made their appearance. This was not quite the flood it appears. The economics of magazine publishing meant that when a bi-monthly magazine was successful it was often better to start a companion title in the alternate months than to switch to monthly publication. In this way the magazines gained twice as much display space (each title remaining on sale until the new issue appeared) and twice as long a period on sale, while the publisher could hope for an increased share of the total market through product diversification. So *Startling Stories* was paired with *TWS* (although *TWS* also went monthly in 1940–41), *Marvel Science Stories* with *Dynamic Science Stories*, *Astonishing Stories* with *Super Science Stories*, *Cosmic Stories* with *Stirring Science Stories* and *Future Fiction* with *Science Fiction*. Nevertheless, much more sf was needed each month, most of it paid for at minimal rates (if at all), and many young sf fans were able to gain invaluable early experience as writers or editors. Asimov, James BLISH, Damon KNIGHT, C.M. KORNBLUTH, Robert A.W. LOWNDES, Frederik POHL and Donald A. WOLLHEIM — all FUTURIANS — launched their careers in this period.

In Britain sf magazines gained less of a foothold before the Second World War. The first was SCOOPS (1934), a short-lived juvenile weekly. This was followed in 1937 by TALES OF WONDER, the most notable early British magazine, which survived until 1942. FANTASY appeared briefly in 1938–9.

Inevitably, the boom over-saturated the market; some of the new titles only published two or three issues. American involvement in the War, with consequent paper shortages, took its toll of other titles. By the middle of 1944 all but four of the new titles had disappeared; nevertheless, these had all established themselves, and for the duration of the 1940s there were seven regular sf magazines: *AMZ*, *ASF*, *Fantastic Adventures*, *Planet Stories*, *Startling Stories*, *TWS* and the reprint magazine *Famous Fantastic Mysteries*. *ASF* was in a different class from the others, in both quality and appearance. In 1943 it changed to digest size (approx. $5\frac{1}{2} \times 7\frac{1}{2}$ inches), anticipating the general trend of the 1950s. Discovering a serious, adult readership for sf — and discovering and developing the writers to provide serious, adult stories — it changed its appearance until it looked as different as possible from the sf pulps; often seeming deliberately to cultivate a drab look. *Startling Stories* and *TWS* aimed overtly at a juvenile audience in the early 1940s (perhaps recognizing their readership for what it was), although later, under the editorship of Sam MERWIN, the standard soared, until by 1948 *Startling Stories*, in particular, represented the closest challenge to *ASF*. Their cover art, largely the work of Earle K. BERGEY, typified the drift away from an appeal based on futuristic technology — scantily clad girls threatened by monstrous aliens promised more undemanding entertainment, and evidently provided the necessary sales appeal to sustain the enlarged market. *Planet Stories* was more garish still, the epitome of SPACE OPERA. *AMZ* and *Fantastic Adventures* appeared crude, but prospered under the editorship of Ray PALMER. *AMZ*, especially, grew huge (a peak of 274 pages in 1942). Palmer showed a shrewd ability to tap the market for occultism and PSEUDO-SCIENCE, using in particular the allegedly factual stories of Richard S. SHAVER to attain for *AMZ* (he claimed) the highest circulation ever reached by an sf magazine.

New magazines began to appear again in 1947–8, although at first they were either reprint-based (AVON FANTASY READER, ARKHAM SAMPLER, the revived FANTASTIC NOVELS) or semi-professional (FANTASY BOOK). They were followed in 1949 by A. MERRITT'S FANTASY, the revived *Super Science Stories* and OTHER WORLDS SCIENCE STORIES. However, the significant development of the period was the appearance in 1949 of THE MAGAZINE OF FANTASY AND SCIENCE FICTION, followed in 1950 by GALAXY SCIENCE FICTION. Both magazines originated in digest format and from their inception aimed for the adult audience which *ASF* had shown to exist. Campbell's *ASF* was by this time showing evidence of stagnation and *FSF*, with its emphasis on literary standards, and *Gal.*, which concentrated on the "soft" sciences and on satire, both appeared more sophisticated and quickly established themselves, with *ASF*, as the three leading magazines — a situation which, generally speaking, has obtained ever since.

New and revived magazines continued to appear in profusion, and to disappear almost as regularly. They included *Future Combined with Science Fiction Stories*, Imagination, *Marvel*, Out of this World Adventures, Two Complete Science-Adventure Books and Worlds Beyond in 1950, If and *Science Fiction Quarterly* in 1951, Dynamic Science Fiction, Fantastic, Science Fiction Adventures, Space Science Fiction and Space Stories in 1952, Beyond Fantasy Fiction, Fantastic Universe, Fantasy Magazine, Science Fiction Plus, Original Science Fiction Stories and Universe Science Fiction in 1953, Imaginative Tales in 1954, Infinity Science Fiction in 1955, Satellite Science Fiction, Science Fiction Adventures (the second magazine of this title) and Super-Science Fiction in 1956, Dream World, Saturn and Venture Science Fiction in 1957. From this plethora of new titles, the group of magazines edited by Robert A.W. Lowndes — *Future, Original* and *Science Fiction Quarterly* — managed well for a number of years on tiny budgets; *Fantastic Universe, Imagination* and *Imaginative Tales* continued for several years; *Infinity, Satellite* and *Venture* were notable among the shorter-lived magazines. Many other titles came and went after only one or two issues. Beyond the end of the decade only *Fantastic* and *If* survived. *Fantastic* was a digest-size companion to *AMZ* and *Fantastic Adventures. AMZ* switched to digest size in 1953, at which point *Fantastic Adventures* ceased, although *Fantastic* can be considered effectively to be a continuation. *If* would have been another 1950s casualty, but in 1958 the title was sold to Galaxy Publishing Corporation, which wanted a companion for *Gal.*

The new magazines which succeeded were digests; of the six 1940s pulps only *AMZ* (and, in a sense, *Fantastic Adventures*) survived the change in the publishing industry. The pulp magazine business in general died in the early 1950s, a victim of the growing television industry, which provided a more immediate cheap home entertainment, and of increasing distribution problems. *Famous Fantastic Mysteries* ceased in 1953; *TWS, Startling Stories* and *Planet Stories* all survived until 1955, and were among the last pulp magazines to die. *Weird Tales* (which had pursued its own course through the 1930s and 1940s, publishing occasional sf) also failed, in 1954.

In Britain the post-War revival started earlier, with the appearance of two magazines in 1946. Walter Gillings, editor of *Tales of Wonder*, edited the short-lived Fantasy; New Worlds, under E.J. Carnell, began in the same year. Both ceased publication in 1947, but *NW* was revived in 1949. In 1950 a companion magazine, Science Fantasy, began under Gillings' editorship. Carnell took over after two issues, and continued the magazines successfully through the decade, publishing the early work of such authors as Brian Aldiss, J.G. Ballard and John Brunner. In 1958 a third magazine, Science Fiction Adventures, joined the two under unusual circumstances: initially a reprint of the American title, it continued after its transatlantic parent ceased publication, publishing original stories under Carnell's editorship. Authentic Science Fiction and Nebula Science Fiction were other British magazines of the 1950s; there were also a number of minor titles, such as the Vargo Statten Science Fiction Magazine.

Into the 1960s six US magazines continued: *AMZ, ASF* (now retitled *Analog*), *Fantastic, FSF, Gal.* and *If. AMZ* and *Fantastic* began the decade strongly under the editorship of Cele Goldsmith, who raised *AMZ* to a position of relative prominence which it had not enjoyed since the mid-1930s, although it remained clearly of secondary interest. In the mid-1960s they lapsed into reprint magazines, spawning numerous companion titles. Later they began to include original fiction once more, undergoing a resurgence with the accession to the editorship of Ted White in 1969. *ASF*, under new management, took on a more modern, glossy appearance — experimenting for a while with a handsome large format — and continued to lead the field in sales, if not in quality. *FSF*, established as the "quality" sf magazine, maintained its reputation through two changes of editor. *Gal.* and *If* had a new editor, Frederik Pohl, under whom they remained successful; *If* concentrated strongly on adventure sf in the mid-1960s with a popular success that showed itself in three consecutive Hugo awards (which otherwise were shared between *ASF* and *FSF*). Later they came under the editorship of Ejler Jakobsson, who made an unconvincing, gimmicky attempt to "modernize" them. There were few attempts to launch new magazines during the decade, chief among them being the short-lived Gamma and another companion to *Gal.* and *If*, Worlds of Tomorrow, although a great number of reprint titles appeared during the decade. The most significant event for the future of sf magazines was the publication in 1966 of the first volume of Damon

Knight's Orbit series of original anthologies. It was not the first such series — Pohl had edited Star in the 1950s — but it came at a more significant time, when the magazines were encountering increasing problems in distribution, in many cases suffering falling circulations, while the paperback industry continued to grow strongly. Anthology series like *Orbit* — essentially magazines in paperback format, without some of the readers' departments, and appearing less frequently — could obtain better distribution, would remain on sale for longer periods, could be more selective in their choice of material, and could offer better payment than the majority of sf magazines. In due course *Orbit* was followed by other anthology series — Infinity, New Dimensions, Nova, Quark, Universe — as well as many once-off original anthologies, most notably Dangerous Visions. It was widely felt that the traditional sf magazine was now an anachronism and that in due course it would be replaced by the paperback series, just as the digest magazines had supplanted the pulps.

In Britain the process happened rather differently. *NW* and *Science Fantasy* were taken over by a new publisher in 1964, and Carnell resigned as editor. Both magazines now adopted paperback format, but otherwise continued to be marketed as magazines rather than books. *Science Fantasy* went through various changes of editor — and a change of title to *SF Impulse* — before ceasing publication. *NW*'s new editor was Michael Moorcock, who gradually transformed its outlook, making it more experimental and less bound to the conventions of genre sf; it became known as the standard-bearer of new wave sf. In 1967 Moorcock, with Arts Council assistance, took over as publisher of the magazine, changing it to a large (approx 8 × 11½ inches) format which allowed for more graphic adventurousness. *NW* encountered moments of controversy, and subsequent distribution problems. It eventually ceased publication in 1971. Carnell, meanwhile, had begun New Writings in SF, a quarterly original anthology series which predated *Orbit* by two years. In 1969 the short-lived Vision of Tomorrow appeared.

The 1970s saw only one change among the established sf magazines in America, *If* being absorbed into *Gal.* at the beginning of 1975. *Gal.* acquired a new editor, James Baen. At the beginning of 1977 it began to miss issues, but it shortly regained a regular schedule. *AMZ* and *Fantastic* suffered slowly dwindling circulations; produced with a bare minimum of staff and budget they were only just viable. *FSF* and *ASF* remained stable, although *ASF* had by far the greater circulation and, from 1972, a new editor, Ben Bova, who did much to revive it from the stagnation into which it had fallen in the later years of Campbell's reign. In Britain *NW* reappeared as an irregular paperback series, changing editors and publishers along the way. In 1974 SCIENCE FICTION MONTHLY was launched, a poster-size magazine which relied heavily on the visual appeal of the many pages of full-colour art it contained. The written content was sparse, and of variable quality, and although the magazine enjoyed a huge initial circulation, this vanished with each succeeding issue and it ceased publication in 1976. A projected successor, SF DIGEST, was aborted before its first issue was distributed.

Despite the predictions that original anthologies would replace magazines, the 1970s proved a more fertile period for new titles than the previous decade, while several of the anthology series failed. VERTEX, a glossy bedsheet-size magazine, was begun in 1973 and apparently enjoyed early success. However, it was forced into a change to a newsprint format when its publisher was affected by paper shortages, and it died in 1975. 1976 saw the launch of the short-lived ODYSSEY and the subscription-based, semi-professional GALILEO. 1977 saw three further titles: in Britain VORTEX came and went; in America COSMOS SCIENCE FICTION AND FANTASY MAGAZINE and ISAAC ASIMOV'S SCIENCE FICTION MAGAZINE were launched, both on apparently firm foundations. It seemed that reports of the imminent death of the science fiction magazine were somewhat exaggerated. [MJE]
Because it is not possible to make a clear distinction between sf and fantasy magazines, we have included post-1930 fantasy magazines in the following list of sf magazines (there are 167 of them) which have entries in this Encyclopedia. The list is fully comprehensive for professional sf magazines in English, and where there is any doubt about whether a magazine is professional or amateur, we have included it. It will not be fully comprehensive for fantasy magazines, though it will include all fantasy magazines that regularly published sf or work by well-known sf writers. Early fantasy magazines and hero/villain pulp magazines with an sf content, such as THE SPIDER, are separately listed under PULP MAGAZINES. General fiction pulp magazines such as THE BLUE BOOK MAGAZINE are also listed under PULP MAGAZINES. Further information on the publishing of sf in periodical format will be found under BOYS' PAPERS, COMIC STRIPS AND COMIC BOOKS, DIME NOVELS AND JUVENILE SERIES, FANZINES and MAGAZINES. The latter entry lists all general fiction slicks and tabloids which regularly published science fiction. They too have received entries in this book.
See also: AIR WONDER STORIES; ALIEN WORLDS; AMAZING SCIENCE STORIES; AMAZING STORIES; AMAZING STORIES ANNUAL; AMAZING STORIES QUARTERLY; AMAZING STORIES SCIENCE FICTION

NOVELS; AMERICAN FICTION; AMERICAN SCIENCE FICTION MAGAZINE; A. MERRITT'S FANTASY MAGAZINE; ARIEL: THE BOOK OF FANTASY; ARKHAM SAMPLER; ASTONISHING STORIES; ASTOUNDING SCIENCE-FICTION/ ANALOG; ASTOUNDING STORIES YEARBOOK; AUTHENTIC SCIENCE FICTION; AVON FANTASY READER; AVON SCIENCE FICTION AND FANTASY READER; AVON SCIENCE FICTION READER; THE BEST SCIENCE FICTION; BEYOND FANTASY FICTION; BEYOND INFINITY; BIZARRE MYSTERY MAGAZINE; THE BLACK CAT; CAPTAIN FUTURE; COMET STORIES; COSMIC SCIENCE STORIES; COSMIC STORIES; COSMOS SCIENCE FICTION AND FANTASY MAGAZINE (two distinct titles); COVEN 13; DREAM WORLD; DYNAMIC SCIENCE FICTION; DYNAMIC SCIENCE STORIES; ETERNITY SCIENCE FICTION; FAMOUS FANTASTIC MYSTERIES; FAMOUS SCIENCE FICTION; FANCIFUL TALES OF TIME AND SPACE; FANTASTIC; FANTASTIC ADVENTURES; FANTASTIC ADVENTURES YEARBOOK; FANTASTIC NOVELS; FANTASTIC SCIENCE FICTION; FANTASTIC SCIENCE THRILLER; FANTASTIC STORY QUARTERLY; FANTASTIC UNIVERSE; FANTASY (two distinct titles); FANTASY BOOK; FANTASY FICTION; FANTASY MAGAZINE; FANTASY TALES; FORGOTTEN FANTASY; FUTURE FICTION; FUTURE SCIENCE FICTION; FUTURISTIC SCIENCE STORIES; FUTURISTIC STORIES; GALAXY SCIENCE FICTION; GALAXY SCIENCE FICTION NOVELS; GALILEO; GAMMA; GREAT SCIENCE FICTION; HIDDEN WORLD; IF; IMAGINATION; IMAGINATIVE TALES; INFINITY SCIENCE FICTION; INTERNATIONAL SCIENCE FICTION; ISAAC ASIMOV'S SCIENCE FICTION MAGAZINE; THE MAGAZINE OF FANTASY AND SCIENCE FICTION; MARVEL SCIENCE STORIES; MARVEL TALES; MIND MAGIC; MIRACLE SCIENCE AND FANTASY STORIES; THE MOST THRILLING SCIENCE FICTION EVER TOLD; THE MYSTERIOUS TRAVELER MAGAZINE; NEBULA SCIENCE FICTION; NEW WORLDS; ODYSSEY; ORBIT SCIENCE FICTION; ORIGINAL SCIENCE FICTION STORIES; OTHER WORLDS SCIENCE STORIES; OUTLANDS; OUT OF THIS WORLD ADVENTURES; PERRY RHODAN; PLANET STORIES; POPULAR SCIENCE FICTION; ROCKET STORIES; SATELLITE SCIENCE FICTION; SATURN; SCIENCE FANTASY; SCIENCE FANTASY YEARBOOK; SCIENCE FICTION; SCIENCE FICTION ADVENTURES (four distinct titles); SCIENCE FICTION CLASSICS; SCIENCE FICTION CLASSICS ANNUAL; SCIENCE FICTION DIGEST; SF DIGEST; SCIENCE FICTION LIBRARY; SCIENCE FICTION MONTHLY (three distinct titles); SCIENCE FICTION PLUS; SCIENCE FICTION QUARTERLY; SCIENCE STORIES; SCIENCE WONDER STORIES; SCOOPS; SELECTED SCIENCE FICTION; SKYWORLDS — CLASSICS IN SCIENCE FICTION; SPACE ADVENTURES (CLASSICS); SPACE FACT AND FICTION; SPACE SCIENCE FICTION; SPACE SCIENCE FICTION MAGAZINE; SPACE STORIES; SPACEWAY; SPACE WISE; STAR SCIENCE FICTION MAGAZINE; STARTLING STORIES; STIRRING SCIENCE STORIES; STORYTELLER; STRANGE ADVENTURES;

STRANGE FANTASY; STRANGE STORIES; STRANGE TALES (two distinct titles); SUPER-SCIENCE FICTION; SUPER SCIENCE STORIES; SUSPENSE; SWAN AMERICAN MAGAZINE; SWAN YANKEE MAGAZINE; SWORD AND SORCERY; TALES OF TOMORROW; TALES OF WONDER; 10 STORY FANTASY; THRILLING WONDER STORIES; THRILLS, INC.; TOPS IN SCIENCE FICTION; TREASURY OF GREAT SCIENCE FICTION STORIES; TWO COMPLETE SCIENCE-ADVENTURE BOOKS; UNCANNY STORIES; UNCANNY TALES (two distinct titles); UNIVERSE SCIENCE FICTION; UNKNOWN; UNUSUAL STORIES; VANGUARD SCIENCE FICTION; VARGO STATTEN SCIENCE FICTION MAGAZINE; VENTURE SCIENCE FICTION; VERTEX; VISION OF TOMORROW; VOID; VORTEX; VORTEX SCIENCE FICTION; WEIRD AND OCCULT LIBRARY; WEIRD WORLD; WONDERS OF THE SPACEWAYS; WONDER STORIES; WONDER STORIES QUARTERLY; WONDER STORY ANNUAL; WORLDS BEYOND; WORLDS OF FANTASY (two distinct titles); WORLDS OF THE UNIVERSE; WORLDS OF TOMORROW.

SCIENCE FICTION MONTHLY 1. Australian DIGEST-size magazine. 18 undated issues, Aug. 1955-Jan. 1957, published by Atlas Publications, Melbourne; no editor named. The fiction was of variable quality, reprinted from various US magazines, and included important work by Ray BRADBURY and others. The covers were reprinted from the same sources. A feature was Graham Stone's fact and comment section, "Science Fiction Scene".
2. The name *Science Fiction Monthly* was also used by AUTHENTIC SCIENCE FICTION in one of its early manifestations, May-Aug. 1951.
3. *Science Fiction Monthly* was the title of a British magazine, approx. tabloid-size (16 × 11 inches). 28 monthly issues, Feb. 1974-May 1976, issues in two vols of 12 nos and one vol. of four nos, undated except by year, published by New English Library; ed. Feb. 1974-Jan. 1975 Pat Hornsey, and Feb. 1975-May 1976 Julie Davis. Born some time after the demise of NEW WORLDS, and before the birth of VORTEX, *SFM* was during its lifetime the only British magazine market for sf, and should have been a success. It was launched in large format, with much interior colour artwork, often in the form of pull-out posters, in an effort to find a teenage audience similar to that which was buying pop-music magazines, also with pull-out posters. Neither editor was previously experienced with sf, and especially at first the quality of fiction was low, though it improved under the editorship of Julie Davis as she appeared to gain confidence. From the beginning a feature was the substantial number of well-researched factual articles, review pages, news pages and interviews. The juvenile policy succeeded at first but after a time circulation figures dropped from over 100,000 to less than 20,000,

SCIENCE FICTION MONTHLY is another title which leads to problems of identification; from left to right: version one, Australian, 1956, with a cover reprinted from a US magazine; version two, an early variant title of *Authentic Science Fiction*, June 1951; version three, the tabloid British magazine, vol. 1, no. 7, 1974, cover by Bruce Pennington.

presumably as the novelty value wore off. Featured authors included Bob SHAW, Ian WATSON, Josephine SAXTON, Robert HOLDSTOCK and Brian STABLEFORD; many other stories were reprinted from US sources. *SFM* was closed as part of a general retrenchment in New English Library's magazine publication. A plan to replace it with SF DIGEST failed after one issue. An anthology of stories from *SFM* was *The Best of Science Fiction Monthly* (anth. **1975**) ed. Janet Sacks. [PN/FHP]

SF OVERTAKEN BY EVENTS
Without attempting a comprehensive DEFINITION of sf, one may safely say that most sf stories and novels present an imaginary record of the human condition at some future time and, further, that the events recorded are usually of an epic dimension, either overtly or by implication. That is, that even when the protagonists are not of heroic stature they inhabit a landscape differing from our own in historically significant ways. At the least, they confront the possibility of such a radical transformation. Almost any sf story can be considered, therefore, as a PREDICTION or an agglomeration of discrete predictions. While only the most naïve readers would measure a story's success chiefly by its predictive accuracy, even the most sophisticated may have difficulty keeping a straight face when a story guesses wrong on a scale of any magnificence.

Most risible are near misses. That TIME TRAVEL or ANTIGRAVITY have yet to be perfected is no embarrassment to H.G. WELLS or later traffickers in such notions. But who can resist a friendly sneer at Jules VERNE when he proposes to propel a spaceship FROM THE EARTH TO THE MOON (two vols **1865** and **1870** France; trans. **1873**) by firing it from a gigantic cannon on a mountain-top in Florida? A boner of similar period charm is Edward

BELLAMY's pneumatic-tube broadcasting system in *Looking Backward* (**1888**). Bellamy, like Verne, knows the result he's after — something like the early BBC — but the means he envisions seem ludicrous to our latter-day view.

Lack of technological sophistication by itself does not yield the most memorable failures of prediction; there must be, as well, an earnestness and gravity of prophetic purpose. An author who adopts a whimsical or even satiric tone has thereby secured himself against the failure of his prophecies. No one feels a comfortable superiority over CYRANO DE BERGERAC for the means he proposes for reaching the Moon; though his scheme is more preposterous than Verne's, it is only a fancy.

The heyday, therefore, of malachronism (if we may coin a word) was the era of GERNSBACKean "scientifiction", when the prediction of future technology was considered the specific and defining virtue of the genre. The pages of the early pulps are a virtual patent office of malachronistic inventions, and the interested reader may sample them in such collections as Isaac ASIMOV's *Before the Golden Age* (anth. **1974**), though the flavour of that era comes through just as well in its artwork, which has recently been reproduced in a number of books (*see* ILLUSTRATION).

Aside from its malachronisms, the Gernsback era produced little to command the attention of latter-day readers. Only with the advent of such writers as Robert A. HEINLEIN, Asimov, Arthur C. CLARKE and James BLISH, who combined scientific literacy with literacy of a more ordinary kind, does (PULP) sf begin to possess an interest of other than an anthropological nature. These writers are not immune to malachronism, but even where such exists (as in Heinlein's "The Roads Must Roll", 1940, which

gives a detailed timetable for the replacement of the automobile by "mechanized roads", a process commencing in 1960), there is seldom the sense of a mighty pratfall, since, as Heinlein himself has pointed out, these fictions are intended not to be prophetic but only speculative.

Malachronism need not be limited to imaginary hardware. Prophets may err with regard to the *Zeitgeist* even when their hardware is substantially "correct". In another early story by Heinlein, "The Man Who Sold the Moon" (1950), it is not the mechanics of space travel that defies the wisdom of hindsight but rather Heinlein's all-informing assumption that SPACE FLIGHT — and COLONIZATION — will be accomplished by private initiatives for the sake of financial profit. Scarcely a bull's eye, yet the story's interest is not really vitiated thereby, for its relevance (and that of every sf story, ultimately) is as a realization of the spirit of the age in which it was written. George ORWELL's *Nineteen Eighty-Four* (**1949**) is a harrowing picture not of some hypothetical future, but of 1948.

The most potent malachronism — and that which gives pulp sf its special *vertu* as a collector's item — is style. Broadly enough considered, there may be no distinction between style and *Zeitgeist*, the former being merely the fleshly form of the latter. The protocols and conventions of the earliest pulp sf — both the stories and their illustrations — are of a simplicity and guilelessness that in many instances partakes of the character of genuine folk art rather than (as it would become in the 1940s and '50s) that of commercial art. Tattooing as against advertising.

When all three forms of malachronism coincide — technological, *Zeitgeist*-ish, and stylistic — the result, for latter-day readers, is one of total escapism, for one is constantly reminded that the events being described belong wholly to the realm of the impossible and the irrelevant. E.E. "Doc" SMITH's "Skylark" and "Lensman" series are splendid exemplars of such a perfect confluence of malachronism and have maintained a merited popularity as such.

So powerful is the charm of malachronism that several recent writers have set out to produce it (or reproduce it) with, as it were, premeditation. One of the first such deliberately malachronistic sf stories is John Sladek's "1937 A.D.!" which appeared in *NW* in 1967. Subsequently, there have been entire malachronistic novels by Michael MOORCOCK (*The Warlord of the Air*, **1971**, and *The Land Leviathan*, **1974**), Richard LUPOFF (*Into the Aether*, **1974**), and Brian W. ALDISS (*The Eighty-Minute Hour*, **1974**). Some of the above fictions take the ostensible form of ALTERNATE WORLDS, but what all of these authors clearly hope to achieve is the distancing effect of total malachronism, of irony in equilibrium with silliness. [TMD]

Dec. 1953. Cover by Frank R. Paul.

SCIENCE FICTION PLUS US BEDSHEET-size magazine. Seven issues, Mar.-Dec. 1953, monthly for four months then slipping to bi-monthly, published by Hugo GERNSBACK's Gernsback Publications, with Sam MOSKOWITZ as managing editor. This was Gernsback's last venture in the sf field, and attempted to recover something of the flavour of his early pulps, including some Frank R. PAUL covers, but it was a financial failure.

Notable stories include two of Philip José FARMER's early novelettes, "The Biological Revolt" (Mar. 1953) and "Strange Compulsion" (Oct. 1953), and two stories by veteran Harry BATES: "Death of a Sensitive" (May 1953) and "The Triggered Dimension" (Dec. 1953). The magazine was well produced, the first five issues being on slick paper, but an appeal to nostalgia was not enough, and Gernsback retired hurt. [BS]

Feb. 1953. Cover by A. Leslie Ross.

SCIENCE FICTION QUARTERLY US PULP magazine. Summer 1940-Spring 1943 (10 issues), May 1951-Feb. 1958 (28 issues), published by Columbia Publications. The first two issues of the first series were edited by Charles HORNIG, all others by Robert A.W. LOWNDES.

In its first incarnation the magazine featured a complete novel in every issue, most of them being reprinted from varied sources. Five were by Ray CUMMINGS. Many of the short stories were original, and the magazine was an important market for members of the FUTURIANS, notably C.M. KORNBLUTH under various pseudonyms. Two undated reprint editions of the Summer 1940 and Winter 1941/42 issues were published in the UK in 1943, and are now collector's items. The second version published a number of notable articles, including a series, "Science in Science Fiction", by James BLISH (May 1951-May 1952) and "The Evolution of Science Fiction" by Thomas CLARESON (Aug. 1953). Notable stories include Blish's "Common Time" (Aug. 1953) and Isaac ASIMOV's "The Last Question" (Nov. 1956). Some stories from the first series were reprinted in Britain as part of the Swan SCIENCE FICTION LIBRARY (a 1960 pocketbook series), Winter 1942 was reprinted as no. 15 of SWAN AMERICAN MAGAZINE in 1950, and 10 numbered, undated issues of the second series were reprinted in the UK during 1952–5. [BS]

Collectors should note: The first series, which had a fairly regular schedule, was numbered consecutively 1–10. The second series was completely regular, publishing in May, Aug., Nov. and Feb. It had four vols of six numbers and a fifth with only four numbers.

SF REPRISE *See* NEW WORLDS.

SCIENCE FICTION RESEARCH ASSOCIATION This group was formed in October 1970 to aid and encourage sf scholarship, especially in the USA and Canada. The first chairman was Thomas D. CLARESON. In effect, the organization has acted as a central liaison between academics teaching sf in America, though academic affiliation is not a requirement for membership, which can be individual, institutional, foreign or student. Members receive, ten times a year, *The SFRA Newsletter* with news and reviews, and the critical journal EXTRAPOLATION. 1977 membership was 330. *SFRA* also administers the JUPITER awards, which are voted on by members of the Institute of Science Fiction in Higher Education. [PN]

SCIENCE FICTION REVIEW Variant title of two FANZINES ed. Richard E. Geis. *See* THE ALIEN CRITIC *and* PSYCHOTIC. *See also* SCIENCE FICTION REVIEW MONTHLY.

SCIENCE FICTION REVIEW MONTHLY, THE Semi-professional critical magazine Mar. 1975–Mar. 1976; ed. Martin Last, with Baird Searles associate editor. The first issue was called *The Science Fiction Review*; it was then *The Science Fiction Review* (*Monthly*) until Aug. 1975. It aimed at reviewing, in fairly popular terms, every sf book published in the USA in a given month, but the quality of the reviews was not as high as those in DELAP's F & SF REVIEW, which began a month later, and it seems there was no room in the market, especially with the distribution problems of such small magazines, for two competing titles. [PN]

SCIENCE FICTION STORIES *See* FUTURE FICTION for the 1943 magazine, and ORIGINAL SCIENCE FICTION STORIES for the 1953–5 magazine.

SCIENCE-FICTION STUDIES Academic, critical journal about sf. 14 issues, Spring 1973–Mar. 1978 (current). Published three times a year from Indiana State University, where one of its two editors, R.D. MULLEN, teaches. The other editor is Darko SUVIN. Mullen's resignation as editor was announced in 1978, and it seems probable that *SFS* will be transferred to Canada.

SFS is the youngest of the three academic journals about sf; the others are EXTRAPOLATION and FOUNDATION. *SFS* does not normally review contemporary sf, though it has an excellent coverage of the reprint series of sf classics and of critical works. It carries many articles on PROTO SF, MAINSTREAM WRITERS OF SF and UTOPIAS, and these have been its greatest strength; its coverage of genre sf has sometimes been a little ponderous; the special issues on Philip K. DICK and Ursula K. LE GUIN are slightly disappointing. Unusually for an American journal, some of its critical material is Marxist oriented. Its coverage of European sf is very good. *SFS* is a responsible, interesting journal which, while it reflects some of the excesses in academic sf criticism, has also reflected its strengths. [PN]

SCIENCE FICTION THEATRE American TV series (1955–7). ZIV/WRCA-TV. Produced by Ivan Tors, hosted by Truman Bradley. Technical adviser Dr Maxwell Smith. Running time per episode: 25 mins.

This television series went out of its way to avoid the sensationalism so prevalent in the sf films of the period, but most episodes were bland and prosaic. In an interview in 1956 the producer said: "One of the traps into which such a series may fall is complete dependence on science for interest. This is avoided at the story conference by excluding the scientists at the start and depending on the writers to come up with a story with human interest, suspense and the other components of any half-hour drama. After the story is developed it is up to Smith (the technical adviser) and the other research people to suggest some scientific fact on which the story can be hung."

Each episode began with the dignified Truman Bradley sitting at a desk covered with various "scientific" objects (some of which were spinning, or had flashing lights) and introducing the audience to the theme of the story. A typical episode, transmitted on 28 Oct. 1955, involved a mysterious explosion at sea which causes a hurricane to move towards Miami. The young meteorologist at the local weather bureau sits holding hands with his wife while they both worry about their son, who is on a camping trip. But just as the hurricane reaches the shore a high-pressure area pushes it back again. The sf element in the story consists of the discovery that the hurricane was created by a meteor landing in the sea. [JB]

SF TIMES German FANZINE, later the journal of the AST (Arbeitsgemeinschaft Spekulative Thematik). First published in 1958 by Rainer Eisfeld as a straight translation of the American *Sf Times* (*see* FANTASY TIMES), the fanzine began to publish original German material under the editorship of Burkhard Blüm (1961), Helmut Struck (1964), and Horst Peter Schwagenscheidt (1965). With the arrival of Hans Joachim Alpers (1967) (later joined by Ronald Hahn), *SFT* quickly established itself as a serious journal of socialist and radical criticism, containing original articles on German and international sf and related topics. Its best-known regular contributor is Franz ROTTENSTEINER. [PR]

SFWA *See* SCIENCE FICTION WRITERS OF AMERICA.

SFWA BULLETIN Full name is *SFWA: The Bulletin of the Science Fiction Writers of America*; the official organ of SFWA, and, unlike SFWA's other publication, the informal discussion paper SFWA FORUM, available to non-members. Its contents are news, market reports, and general discussion of professional and literary problems. Vol.1 no.1 was Jul. 1965, and there have been over 65 produced up to 1978. Editors have included Damon KNIGHT, Terry CARR, George ZEBROWSKI, Stephen GOLDIN and John F. Carr. [PN]

SFWA FORUM A publication of the SCIENCE FICTION WRITERS OF AMERICA, consisting almost entirely of letters from the membership; it is a forum for complaints, proposals, discussions. Unlike SFWA BULLETIN, *SFWA Forum* is for members only, and its contents may not be reprinted; they are livelier and considerably more revealing than those of the *Bulletin*, quite often unpleasantly so; polemical exchanges are commonplace; much heat was generated by the revocation of Stanislaw LEM's honorary membership of SFWA. The journal was begun several years after the *Bulletin*; there have been over 55 issues to 1978. Editors have included Juanita COULSON, George SCITHERS and Theodore R. COGSWELL. [PN]

SCIENCE FICTION WRITERS OF AMERICA Formed in 1965 to inform sf writers on matters of professional interest, to promote their professional welfare and to help them deal effectively with publishers, agents, editors and anthologists, in the manner of a small trade union. The first president, probably the most active of the founder members, was Damon KNIGHT, and it was from the MILFORD SCIENCE FICTION WRITERS' CONFERENCE, also founded by Knight and others, that the initial impetus for a professional organization sprang. Later presidents have been Robert SILVERBERG, Alan E. NOURSE, Gordon R. DICKSON, James E. GUNN, Poul ANDERSON, Jerry POURNELLE, Frederik POHL, Andrew J. OFFUTT and Jack WILLIAMSON. Membership is restricted to professional writers; "professionalism" includes, naturally, the sale of individual stories as well as of books; there are currently over 450 members, including some 20 British writers. SFWA sponsors the annual NEBULA awards and the annual anthologies resulting from them. There are two SFWA publications, *SFWA: The Bulletin of the Science Fiction Writers of America*, usually known as SFWA BULLETIN, and SFWA FORUM. The SFWA membership has been occasionally given to polemics, and resignations have been moderately commonplace. The greatest rift occurred in 1976 when Stanislaw LEM's honorary membership was cancelled. Much debate followed. Despite being the subject of sometimes justified accusations of parochialism, and despite internal dissension, SFWA has played an important role in improving the notoriously hazardous conditions of the sf writer's life. [PN]

SF YEARBOOK: A TREASURY OF SCIENCE FICTION See TREASURY OF GREAT SCIENCE FICTION STORIES.

First issue, Oct. 1953. Cover by Bok.

SCIENCE STORIES US DIGEST-size magazine. Four issues, Oct. 1953–Apr. 1954. The first issue was published by Bell Publications, Chicago, the rest by Palmer Publications, Evanston; ed. Ray PALMER and Bea Mahaffey. It printed no notable fiction. *Universe Science Fiction*, which was effectively a continuation of OTHER WORLDS, was a companion magazine. Some magazine historians regard *SS* as a continuation of *Other Worlds* also, but it was the numeration of *Universe* that *Other Worlds* adopted when it reverted to its original title in 1955. [FHP/PN]

SCIENCE WONDER QUARTERLY *See* WONDER STORIES QUARTERLY.

First issue. Cover by Frank R. Paul.

SCIENCE WONDER STORIES US BEDSHEET-size magazine. 12 monthly issues, Jun. 1929-May 1930, published by Stellar Publishing Corp.; ed. Hugo GERNSBACK.

After Gernsback lost control of his first sf magazine, AMAZING STORIES, in 1929, he rapidly made a comeback with a new company, and two new magazines, *SWS*, and AIR WONDER STORIES which began a month later. "SCIENCE WONDER STORIES are clean, CLEAN from beginning to end. They stimulate only one thing — IMAGINATION", he wrote (his capitals) in the first editorial. His policy, as usual, was to emphasize the didactic aspects of sf, and he claimed that all the stories were passed by "an array of authorities and educators". *SWS* dealt with all aspects of science, unlike *Air Wonder Stories*, but in fact they used much the same authors and similar material, and it was logical, after a year, to amalgamate them into WONDER STORIES. *SWS* was a handsome magazine, all the covers being the work of Frank R. PAUL. Authors included David H. KELLER, Stanton A. COBLENTZ, Jack WILLIAMSON, Harl VINCENT, Raymond Z. GALLUN, Miles J. BREUER, Laurence MANNING and Fletcher PRATT.   [PN]

March 1930. Cover by Ruger.

SCIENTIFIC DETECTIVE MONTHLY US BEDSHEET-size magazine. 10 monthly issues, Jan.-Oct. 1930, published by Techni-Craft Publishing Co., ed. Hugo Gernsback, with Arthur B. Reeve as editorial consultant. The second five issues were entitled *Amazing Detective Tales*, but *Scientific Detective Monthly* more accurately described the magazine's contents. Most issues included "Craig Kennedy" stories by Arthur B. Reeve and collaborations by Edwin BALMER and William McHarg.

SDM was a sister magazine to SCIENCE WONDER STORIES and AIR WONDER STORIES. A similarly titled magazine, *Amazing Detective Stories*, was published during 1931 with volume numbering suggesting a follow-up. This magazine, however, carried no fantasy.   [FHP]

SCIENTIFIC ERRORS Scientific errors in sf are not to be confused with IMAGINARY SCIENCE, where the author invents the science and tries to make it plausible, nor with PSEUDO-SCIENCE, where the author adheres to some alternative quasi-scientific system unrecognized by the majority of the scientific community. Scientific errors are here taken to mean old-fashioned mistakes in the sort of science that is taught in high schools and universities.

Sf in the days of the PULP magazines was very much more prone to error than it is now, and it was for the absurdity of so much of the science, at least in part, that pulp sf (particularly in the 1930s) got a bad name; schoolteachers and parents were worried by its innumeracy as well as its illiteracy. Most sf written in the 1960s and '70s will pass scientific muster even with readers who have a little university-level science, but the excesses of the 1920s and '30s must have been obvious even to many readers who had only a smattering of high-school science.

Some quite simple errors, of course, require specialized knowledge to pick them up. Hal CLEMENT cites a MAINSTREAM story in which a myopic boy's spectacles are used to concentrate the sun's rays and light a fire; Clement points out that these would in fact disperse the rays. On the other hand, although Judith MERRIL uses a helicopter for transport on the Moon, most schoolboys could have told her that it would not work without air.

Some errors are notorious. When Jules VERNE uses a gun to shoot travellers at the Moon, he ignores the fact that the acceleration would leave them as a thin red smear on the back wall of the cabin. The *canali* or channels which Schiaparelli thought he saw on MARS were wrongly translated into English as "canals", and hence Edgar Rice BURROUGHS and many others felt justified in assuming the plausibility of placing intelligent life there. H.G. WELLS's *The Invisible Man* (1897) has transparent retinas, and would, of course, be blind.

The history of pulp sf is full of examples of writers using PARSECS as a unit of velocity instead of distance, of confusing weight with mass (so that in space we have heroes able to push several tons of spaceship along with their finger) and, most commonly of all, exceeding the speed of light without any sort of justification (*see* FASTER THAN LIGHT), as in A.E. VAN VOGT's "The Storm" (1943): "Half a light year a minute; it would take a while to attain that speed, but — in eight hours they'd strike the storm." (The same story has a hero with a second brain which has an IQ of 917, as if somehow the exact figure might mean something real in terms of intelligence.) In those days ROCKETS would regularly perform manoeuvres and turns, just like a car doing a U-turn. In fact, as most of us know in the space age, if you use gyros to turn a rocket it will continue in the same direction, *unless* another rocket blast is given in the new configuration, and even then, of course, the original forward momentum is not lost. John W. CAMPBELL Jr, the man who was supposed to have done more than any other to put the science back in sf, was quite happy to publicize what he called the Dean Drive (*ASF* 1960), a device which violates the conservation of momentum by pushing against itself, and on a par with the "inertialess drive" of E.E. "Doc" SMITH, with which his spaceships were propelled. The other favourite of the pulps was the electromagnetic spectrum, whose properties were perfectly well known in the scientific world, but which was regularly rifled by writers in search of mysterious "rays" which would have almost magical effects. Magnetism was another favourite in the pulps, and all sorts of remarkably cock-eyed schemes were cooked up to exploit its hitherto unknown properties, though here we reach an area of overlap between straightforward scientific errors and imaginary science.

Nearly all stories in the pulps about submicroscopic worlds (*see* GREAT AND SMALL) use a model of the atom which had been out of date for at least half a century by 1920 in which the atom is seen as a kind of solid, spherical ball. Ray CUMMINGS, several of whose heroes shrink and have adventures on just such atoms which turn out to be worlds in their own right, was a noteworthy offender.

Excesses of this kind still exist, of course, especially in sf's lowest, paperback echelons, but Robert A. HEINLEIN and Isaac ASIMOV did much in the 1940s to bring scientific responsibility to sf, and their work was continued by Hal CLEMENT, James BLISH, Poul ANDERSON, Larry NIVEN and many others.

Sf in the CINEMA and on TELEVISION, however, is still about as scientifically illiterate as was pulp sf on the 1930s. SPACE 1999 was a particularly bad offender; Bob SHAW has several times expressed amazement at STAR TREK, in which the spaceship *Enterprise* is constantly being buffeted about by various forms of attack, and the crew are invariably thrown from their seats. Why, asks Shaw, in this super-technological future, has the concept of seat-belts been forgotten?

MONSTER movies very often depend on giant ants, spiders, etc. In fact, such creatures could not exist; they would collapse under their own weight, not having legs, like the elephant's, designed to prop them up. Elephants are thought to be near the upper size limit for a land animal on Earth, though, of course, larger-scale life is better supported in the water. Many problems arise with increases in scale, one of them being that the ratio between skin area and internal capacity does not stay the same, hence throwing the physiology of the body completely askew. Flying men are probably impossible, though Poul Anderson made a valiant attempt to rationalize them scientifically in *War of the Wing-Men* (**1958**; vt *The Man Who Counts*), greatly increasing their lung capacity and incorporating other necessary design changes.

Errors in sf are less common in the SOFT SCIENCES, perhaps because they are subject to less rigorous laws. None the less, absurdities proliferate here too. Brainwashing, for example, and mental conditioning generally, are almost invariably based on Pavlov's behavioural psychology rather than on B.F. SKINNER's; that is, in sf the conditioning is carried out through aversion and punishment, not through reward, even though the latter system has been amply demonstrated to be more efficient, and presents, perhaps, moral issues of a more subtle and interesting kind.   [PN/JS]

SCIENTISTS Scientists in pre-20th-century sf exhibited many symptoms of social maladjustment, often to the point of insanity. They were characteristically obsessive and anti-social. Sometimes the scientist became a diabolical figure, like Coppelius in E.T.A. HOFFMANN's "The Sandman" (1816) or Mary SHELLEY's Victor Frankenstein. Sometimes he was merely ridiculous, as in the third book of Jonathan SWIFT's *Gulliver's Travels* (1726; rev. 1735) or Samuel JOHNSON's *Rasselas* (**1759**). In Honoré de BALZAC's *La recherche de l'absolu* (**1834**; trans. as *Balthazar* **1859**; vt *In Search of the Absolute*) the unholy lusts of scientific research become a kind of blight. To some extent this is explicable in that the scientist had inherited the mantle (and the public image) of the medieval alchemists, astrologers and sorcerers. This image proved to be extraordinarily persistent. It was still very prominent at the end of the 19th century, and its vestiges remain even today.

Even writers like Jules VERNE (who was fascinated by the machines that scientists made) and H.G. WELLS (who was enthusiastic about scientific discovery) fell prey to the common notion of the scientist as obsessive neurotic. Verne's most memorable scientists are Nemo and Robur, while Wells had produced Moreau, Griffin and Cavor before he realized what he was doing, and carefully prepared a different image for the scientific workers of *The Food of the Gods* (**1904**). Robert Louis STEVENSON's Dr Jekyll is obviously cast from the traditional mould, and Alfred JARRY's Professor Faustroll and Conan DOYLE's Professor Challenger are not too far removed from it. An extraordinarily detailed analysis of the process of scientific creativity as a species of madness, and the total unworldliness of the scientist, is presented in J.S. Fletcher's *Morrison's Machine* (**1900**). Later manifestations of the image include Philip WYLIE's *The Murderer Invisible* (**1931**),

Professor Lerne in Maurice RENARD's *Le docteur Lerne, sous-dieu* (**1908**; trans. as *New Bodies for Old* **1923**) and the hero of E. Charles VIVIAN's *Star Dust* (**1925**).

By the end of the 19th century, however, other images of the scientist were beginning to appear. The American public made a hero of Edison, and this admiration for the clever inventor is reflected in much popular fiction, some of which even borrowed the name of the great man — Garrett P. SERVISS's *Edison's Conquest of Mars* (1898; **1947**) and the series of DIME NOVELS featuring Tom Edison Jr. A similar hero-worship later developed with respect to Louis Pasteur, and even Einstein, although no one doubted that Einstein's genius was perilously close to madness. One of the most wholehearted products of this hero-worship was Hugo GERNSBACK's *Ralph 124C 41 +* (1911–12; fix-up **1925**), and the scientist-as-hero entered PULP sf at its very inception, alongside the mad genius. A relevant study here is "The Scientist as Hero in American Science-Fiction 1880–1920" by Thomas D. CLARESON in *Extrapolation* Dec. 1965.

"Humanized" scientists appeared in the sf pulps at any early stage, but were essentially fakes — stock pulp heroes with scientific prowess uneasily grafted on. E.E. "Doc" SMITH's Richard Seaton is a cardinal example. The most significant shift in the characterization of the scientist hero in pulp sf was the de-emphasizing of the role of the theoretical genius relative to that of the engineer, who modifies, improvises and generally tinkers rather than creates. The archetypal examples of the species were the staff of George O. SMITH's "Venus Equilateral" satellite, who were forever scribbling equations and designs on the tablecloths in Joe's Bar. John W. CAMPBELL Jr's *ASF* featured many such heroes, but the essence of real genius remained as wayward as ever, as evidenced by the character of Henry KUTTNER's Galloway Gallegher, the inventor in the series of stories written as by Lewis Padgett *Robots Have No Tails* (1943–8; coll. **1952**; paperback as by Kuttner), who always made his marvellous machines while blind drunk and could never remember afterwards how he had done it. Hero-worship of the scientific genius was taken to extremes in the same era by Isaac ASIMOV in the "Foundation" series — though it is worth noting that Hari Seldon was the first social scientist to be thus elevated. Sf of this period is analysed in "Image of the Scientist in Science Fiction" by Walter Hirsch, in *American Journal of Sociology*, Mar. 1958.

It was outside the sf magazines that a more realistic idea of the work and social situation of the scientist was first embodied in speculative fiction, in E.C. LARGE's *Sugar in the Air* (**1937**). This novel reduces the myth of genius to a more appropriate level, and explores in great detail a new kind of social

maladjustment caused by the nature of the scientist's work and his goals being at odds with those of the commercial institutions which finance him. Here the scientist, Charles Pry, is both a visionary and an idealist, while the system within which he is employed is blind, stupid and irrational. Thus the myth of the mad scientist is inverted. This attitude did not become widespread for some time, but in the post-War decade it infected magazine sf to a tremendous extent; often the nuclear scientist came to be represented as a lone, sane figure in a political and military matrix that threatened the destruction of the world (*see* NUCLEAR POWER). The magazine sf writers mostly accepted the popular judgement that TECHNOLOGY had got out of hand, but attributed this to the machine-*users* rather than the machine-*makers*. It was no longer the mad scientist who threatened to blow up the world to gratify his warped ego, but the mad generals and the mad politicians. Outside the technologically committed sf establishment, writers were not so sure — as witness Peter GEORGE's Dr Strangelove — but it is not difficult to find stories where the scientists themselves are credited with the noblest of ideals and motives. Pierre BOULLE's *Le jardin de Kanashima* (**1964**; trans. as *Garden on the Moon* **1965**) shows the German rocket scientists thinking only of the Moon and space flight, and shuddering at the very mention of the V2.

The American security clamp-down of the 1950s emphasized the new social situation of the scientist, and provoked a wave of sf stories dealing with the morality of carrying out research which had potential military applications, and with the difficulty of making scientific discoveries in such circumstances. An effective vignette dealing with the conscience of the scientist who watches his discoveries in action is C.M. KORNBLUTH's "The Altar at Midnight" (1952), and several other examples are listed under NUCLEAR POWER. The most dramatic depiction of the conflict between scientific interests and military security is Algis BUDRYS's novel *Who?* (**1958**). More recent examples of scientists in conflict with the demands made by society include Theodore STURGEON's "Slow Sculpture" (1970), Bob SHAW's *Ground Zero Man* (**1971**) and D.G. COMPTON's *The Steel Crocodile* (**1970**; vt *The Electric Crocodile* UK). An effective caricature of the conscientious scientist destroyed by social expediency is Hugo Doppel in Edward HYAMS's *The Astrologer* (**1950**).

In modern sf there has been an almost total divorce between the theoretical scientist (the unworldly genius) and the scientific worker. The former has been pushed into the background to a large extent. Scientists in general, in fact, are far less common as major characters in sf stories than they used to be. Notable exceptions are characters in stories by authors who are themselves scientists (e.g. Fred HOYLE, Philip LATHAM). The most memorable attempt at characterizing a scientific genius in recent years is Ursula K. LE GUIN's Shevek in *The Dispossessed* (1974). There are, however, a very large number of contemporary sf writers who have never made any attempt to show scientists at work in their fiction. It has been generally realized that science is a collective endeavour, but there still seems to be relatively little awareness of how scientific progress is actually achieved. [BS]

See also: ANTI-INTELLECTUALISM IN SF; CLICHÉS; CONCEPTUAL BREAKTHROUGH; DISCOVERY AND INVENTION; HEROES; IMAGINARY SCIENCE; ICONOCLASM.

SCIENTOLOGY For the first years scientology was known as DIANETICS (*which see for details*), and this term is still used within scientology. The word "scientology" was coined in 1952 by L. Ron HUBBARD, its founder; its meaning has evolved in many curious and highly publicized ways since then. A lively account of the story by a not wholly unsympathetic outsider can be found in *Cults of Unreason* (1973) by Dr Christopher Evans.

Scientology, originally a form of psychotherapy with many PSEUDO-SCIENTIFIC overtones, became what has been described as the first sf religion, when the Founding Church of Scientology was incorporated in Washington DC in July 1955. Sceptical commentators saw this as no more than a crafty tax dodge, but in fact scientology had from the beginning many of the qualities of a genuine religion, and certainly aroused a religious fervour among its adherents.

L. Ron Hubbard extended scientology overseas from the USA quite early, opening centres in Australia and South Africa in 1953, and settling in the UK in 1955. The worst setback scientology received was the result of the Board of Inquiry set up in the state of Victoria, Australia, in 1963. The Anderson report which followed in 1965 found that "Scientology is evil; its techniques are evil; its practice a serious threat to the community, medically, morally and socially; and its adherents sadly deluded and often mentally ill." 151 witnesses had been examined before this conclusion was reached. Scientology was then banned in Victoria. A later disaster was the deportation of L. Ron Hubbard from the UK as an undesirable alien in 1968. Scientology has since been directed from the ships of Hubbard's fleet, usually found in the Mediterranean. In 1978 he was sentenced, in his absence, to four years' imprisonment in Paris after being found guilty of obtaining money under false pretences through scientology. Scientology has lost some ground, but continues to flourish in a small way.

Hubbard's role remains enigmatic: some see him as a cynic, who has been calculated to have made many millions out of scientology; others see him as a man of genuine if eccentric vision, totally convinced of the truth of his case, and fighting valiantly against the powerful conspiracy of orthodox psychiatry. Scientology is the most dramatic example of the precepts of pulp sf being put into practice in the real world. Inside each of us is a SUPERMAN struggling to get out; the appeal of this ancient, potent belief was one of the attractions of pulp sf, as witness Hubbard's own stories and those of his one-time colleague A.E. VAN VOGT. The glowing promise held out to the disciples of scientology is that this dream can be realized. [PN]

SCITHERS, GEORGE (1929–). American editor. He was educated at the United States Military Academy and Stanford University, where he obtained an MSc in military engineering. His FANZINE, AMRA, specializes in SWORD AND SORCERY, particularly the work of Robert E. HOWARD; it won HUGO awards in 1964 and 1968. He is co-editor, with L. Sprague DE CAMP, of two anthologies drawn from *Amra*: *The Conan Swordbook* (anth. 1969) and *The Conan Grimoire* (anth. 1972). His first published story, "Faithful Messenger" (1969), appeared in *If*. He wrote a spoof cookery book (suggested by Damon KNIGHT's famous story) *To Serve Man* (1976), as Karl Würf. He is editor of ISAAC ASIMOV'S SCIENCE FICTION MAGAZINE and of two anthologies drawn from it, *Astronauts and Androids* (anth. 1977) and *Black Holes and Bug Eyed Monsters* (anth. 1977). [MJE]

Great Story by Sir A. CONAN DOYLE Inside

Scoops

STORIES of the WONDER-WORLD of TOMORROW

2ᵈ

MOON MADNESS

June 2, 1934   PRICE TWOPENCE

2 June 1934.

SCOOPS British BEDSHEET-size magazine. 20 issues, 10 Feb.-23 Jun. 1934, published by Pearsons, London; ed. Hadyn Dimmock. It was intended as a weekly BOYS' PAPER, but had some adult appeal. Serials published were "Space"

by A.M. Low, "The Poison Belt" by Sir Arthur Conan DOYLE and "The Black Vultures" by G.E. Rochester, and John Russell FEARN also wrote for the magazine. All issues are now collector's items. *S* was the first British sf magazine. [FHP]

SCORPION, THE US PULP MAGAZINE. One issue, Apr. 1939, published by Popular Publications; ed. Rogers Terrill. *S* was in every respect a sequel to THE OCTOPUS; only the alias of the villainous protagonist was changed. The feature novel, "Satan's Incubator" by Randolph Craig (Norvell W. PAGE), was reprinted in PULP CLASSICS 12 (1976). [MJE/FHP]

SCORTIA, THOMAS N(ICHOLAS) (1926–). American writer, active since the mid-1950s in the sf magazines, beginning with "The Prodigy" for *Science Fiction Adventures* in 1954; he was for some time a physiochemist in the aerospace industry before becoming a full-time writer. The somewhat over-commercial style of his short work can be seen in the varied and variable stories assembled in *Caution! Inflammable!* (coll. 1975). His first novel is *What Mad Oracle?: a Novel of the World as it is* (1961), though it was not for about a decade, till he began writing full-time, that his production began to increase with *Artery of Fire* (1960 *Original Science Fiction Stories*; rev. exp. 1972) and *Earthwreck!* (1974). Both novels reflect his scientific background and his professional attitude towards markets. His collaborations with Frank M. ROBINSON are somewhat more formidable. Their DISASTER novel *The Glass Inferno* (1974), along with Richard Martin Stern's *The Tower* (1973), was filmed as *The Towering Inferno* (1974); *The Prometheus Crisis* (1975) deals knowledgeably with a vast nuclear reactor failure and the corrupt politics that occasion it. [JC]
Other works: *The Nightmare Factor* (1978) with Frank M. Robinson. As editor: *Strange Bedfellows: Sex and Science Fiction* (anth. 1972); *Two Views of Wonder* (anth. 1973) ed. with Chelsea Quinn YARBRO; *Human-Machines* (anth. 1975) ed. with George ZEBROWSKI.
See also: AUTOMATION; CYBORGS; HOLOCAUST AND AFTER; IMMORTALITY; SPACESHIP.

SCOT, CHESMAN *See* Kenneth BULMER.

SCOTT, J.M. *See* Robert THEOBALD.

SCOTT, WARWICK *See* Elleston TREVOR.

SCRAP BOOK, THE US PULP magazine published monthly by the Frank A. MUNSEY Corp.; ed. Perley Poore Sheehan, Mar. 1906-Jan. 1912. *SB* was published in two separate sections from Jul. 1907, the first containing articles, the second

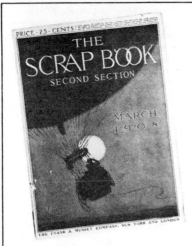

March 1908. Cover by R. Menel.

fiction. The second section became THE CAVALIER from Sep. 1908, the first continued as *SB*, with some fiction content, until it merged with *The Cavalier* to form *The Cavalier Weekly*.

SB began as a reprint magazine, often featuring classic weird fiction. Later it published original stories, including some sf, notably Julian Johnson's "When Science Warred" (1907), George Allan ENGLAND's "The House of Transformation" (1909) and Garrett P. SERVISS's "The Sky Pirate" (1909).   [JE]

SCREAM AND SCREAM AGAIN Film (1969). Amicus/AIP. Directed by Gordon Hessler, starring Vincent Price, Christopher Lee, Peter Cushing and Alfred Marks. Screenplay by Christopher Wicking, based on the novel *The Disoriented Man* by Peter SAXON. 94 mins. Colour.

In this confused mixture of several standard sf and horror plots, a group of mad scientists is making artificial people who possess super strength and vampiric tendencies, with the aim of using them to take over the world. As with so much sf in the cinema, the sf content is merely a peg on which to hang a horror story. [JB]

SCRYMSOUR, ELLA (? –). English writer, whose sf novel, *The Perfect World: A Romance of Strange People and Strange Places* (1922), pivots on the disastrous experience of the First World War, during which an underworld is discovered inside the Earth, and after which the world itself dissolves in holocaust and the protagonists come under the influence of the inhabitants of JUPITER.   [JC]

SEA *See* UNDER THE SEA.

SEABORN, Captain ADAM Usually thought to be the pseudonym of Captain John Cleves Symmes (? –?); the author is in any case American; his PROTO-SF novel, *Symzonia: A Voyage of Discovery* (1820), is a FANTASTIC-VOYAGE

story, Symzonia being a UTOPIA (strongly moral) reachable through a hole at the South Pole; the Earth is therefore hollow. Eventually Seaborn (who narrates) is told he must leave, mankind being a corrupting influence on Utopia. It has long been assumed that this work (by no means the first hollow-Earth story: *see* Ludvig HOLBERG and CASANOVA for 18th-century examples) was part of the propaganda campaign of John Symmes, late of the US Infantry where he was distinguished for bravery in the war of 1812, to persuade Congress to finance a trip to the Arctic, where he expected to find one of the two polar entrances to the hollow Earth; in fact he envisaged five hollows, Earth being constructed of five concentric spheres. Symmes was angry and obsessive, and it is in fact unlikely that he wrote *Symzonia*, which has a light touch reported by William Stanton to be wholly lacking from Symmes's correspondence and polemics. Stanton is the author of the historical study of Symmes's campaigns, *The Great United States Exploring Expedition* (**1975**), which omits all reference to *Symzonia*. An early work about Symmes's theories, written by a convert, is *Symmes' Theory of Concentric Spheres* (**1826**) by James McBride.   [JC/PN]
See also: LOST WORLDS.

SEABRIGHT, IDRIS *See* Margaret ST CLAIR.

SEAFORTH *See* George C. FOSTER.

SEAMARK *See* Austin J. SMALL.

SEARLS, HANK Form of his name used by American writer Henry Hunt Searls (1922–), whose books are primarily about flying and rockets. *The Big X* (**1959**) has a test-pilot flying a plane that is almost a spaceship; *The Pilgrim Project* (**1964**) is about sending a man to the Moon.   [JC]

SECONDS Film (1966). Douglas and Lewis/Paramount. Directed by John

Frankenheimer, starring Rock Hudson, Salome Jens, John Randolph, Will Geer, Jeff Corey and Richard Anderson. Screenplay by Lewis John Carlino, based on David Ely's novel. 106 mins. B/w.

A middle-aged businessman pays a mysterious organization a large sum of money to restore his youth; this is achieved by what appears to be merely an extensive face-lift. Despite being transformed into Rock Hudson and becoming part of a community of wealthy young swingers, he begins to pine for his old life, including his abandoned wife, only to discover that he is forbidden to go back. When he persists in his attempts he is killed by the organization who intend to use his body as a replacement corpse for some new client. Frankenheimer's cold and calculating direction together with James Wong Howe's atmospheric photography create an effective mood of increasing PARANOIA which helps to rejuvenate a rather tired sf idea.   [JB]

SECRET FILES OF CAPTAIN VIDEO, THE *See* CAPTAIN VIDEO.

SEDBERRY, J(AMES) HAMILTON (1863– ?). American author of *Under the Flag of the Cross* (**1908**), a novel about a future WAR between the West and Asia, most of it taking place in Turkey.   [JC]

SELECTED SCIENCE FICTION Australian DIGEST-size magazine. Five monthly issues, May-Sep. 1955, published by Malian Press, Sydney; no editor named. *SCF* reprinted US material. It was a companion to AMERICAN SCIENCE FICTION MAGAZINE.   [FHP]

SELLINGS, ARTHUR Pseudonym of Robert Arthur Ley (1921–68), British author and long-time bookdealer, who began publishing sf stories in 1953; towards the end of his life (his death was sudden) his output was increasing in both quantity and quality. The earlier stories of this craftsmanlike writer tended to hard sf

Futuristic surgery turns the hero into Rock Hudson in SECONDS.

themes; many are collected in *Time Transfer* (coll. **1956**; the 1966 UK paperback edition eliminates five stories at the author's direction). Later in his career, most noticeably in the posthumous *Junk Day* (**1970**), perhaps his finest novel, he integrated literate investigations of character into sf storylines of some conventionality. *Junk Day*, a post-HOLOCAUST story peopled with engrossing character types, points the direction he was beginning to travel. His second collection, *The Long Eureka* (coll. **1968**), also demonstrates his considerable competence. His other novels were all published in the 1960s. *Telepath* (**1962**; vt *The Silent Speakers* UK) builds a gradual and convincing picture of a man's discovery of limited telepathic ability. *The Uncensored Man* (**1964**) transfers its protagonist by drugs into another dimension where he develops his previously masked PSI POWERS and meets dubiously superior forms of life (*see* SUPERMAN). *The Quy Effect* (**1966**) combines the invention of a new form of power with a love story involving its struggling inventor. *The Power of X* (**1968**) is set in a world where material objects can be perfectly duplicated, but in which the process is forbidden. Complications ensue. AS's body of work is modest in size and scope, but its literacy and firmness of execution have been underrated.

AS wrote one novel, *Intermind* (**1967**) under the pseudonym Ray Luther, a near anagram of his real name. A secret agent is injected with another person's memory to pursue a complex case. [JC]
See also: GENERATION STARSHIPS; PERCEPTION.

SENARENS, LUIS PHILIP (1863–1939). American writer and publisher, graduate of St John's College of Art and Science. He wrote some 1500 DIME NOVELS, beginning in his teens, under 27 pseudonyms, later turning to adventure, detective and motion picture work when the market declined. Writing under the pseudonym "Noname", he took over the FRANK READE series from Harry Enton in 1882, developing his sf themes to such heights that he earned the sobriquet "the Jules Verne of America". His sf output exceeded 180 dime novels, including titles in the companion scientific invention series about Jack Wright. [JE]
About the author: "The American Jules Verne" (anon.) in SCIENCE AND INVENTION, Oct. 1920; "Lu Senarens, Writer of a Thousand Thrillers" by E. Alden in *American Magazine*, Apr. 1921; "Ghosts of Prophecies Past" by Sam MOSKOWITZ in *Explorers of the Infinite* (coll. **1963**).
See also: BOYS' PAPERS.

SENTRY, JOHN A. *See* Algis BUDRYS.

SÉRIEL, JÉRÔME Pseudonym used by French UFO expert Jacques Vallée

(1939–) for two very entertaining space operas: *Le sub-espace* ["Sub-Space"] (**1961**), which was awarded the PRIX JULES VERNE and *Le satellite sombre* ["The Dark Satellite"] (**1963**). He also published five intriguing short stories between 1961 and 1965, after which he appears to have given up sf. [MJ]

SERLING, ROD (1924–75). American screenwriter and TV producer, best known for the series THE TWILIGHT ZONE. A paratrooper in the Second World War, he then studied at Antioch College under the GI Bill; in 1948 he went to New York as a freelance writer first for radio, then for TV; during the 1950s he became one of the most highly regarded TV writers, winning many awards, including six Emmies, for such TV plays as "Patterns" (1955), "Requiem for a Heavyweight" (1956) and "The Comedian" (1957). In 1959 he created and produced the first of the *Twilight Zone* series, on which he also appeared as host and narrator, and as a result his dark figure and gravelly tones became very familiar to TV viewers. The series, mainly fantasy, with some sf, lasted for five years. In 1970 he tried to repeat his success with a similar series, NIGHT GALLERY, but it lasted only until 1972. As well as his TV work, which included writing many episodes for both *The Twilight Zone* and *Night Gallery*, RS wrote a number of film scripts, at least two of which were based on his award-winning TV plays: *Patterns of Power* (1956) and *Requiem for a Heavyweight* (1963); he also wrote the screenplay for John Frankenheimer's *Seven Days in May* and the original version of the script for PLANET OF THE APES (1968), which was later rewritten by Michael Wilson. RS could hardly be described as either an original or an important writer, but he was certainly clever at adapting existing ideas, and was a superior craftsman in writing for TV. He had the knack of producing work that, in the context of most TV material, seemed more daring and profound than it really was. His major flaw was a kind of slick portentousness, but whatever his limitations *The Twilight Zone* came as a breath of fresh air to fans of fantasy and sf, who had hitherto had little TV material available to them. RS wrote a number of his screenplays into short-story form and published the following collections: *Stories from the Twilight Zone* (coll. **1960**), *More Stories from the Twilight Zone* (coll. **1961**), *New Stories from the Twilight Zone* (coll. **1962**), *Night Gallery* (coll. **1971**) and *Night Gallery 2* (coll. **1972**). He also edited the following anthologies: *Rod Serling's The Twilight Zone* (anth. **1963**), *Rod Serling's Twilight Zone Revisited* (anth. **1964**) and *The Season to be Wary* (anth. **1967**). [JB]

SERVICE, ROBERT W. (1874–1958). English-born writer, long associated with Canada, where much of his popular verse

was set; of his several novels, *The Master of the Microbe* (**1926**) is sf, and deals with a deadly plague virus developed by a vengeful German but stolen from him by a master-criminal. [JC]
Other works: *The House of Fear* (**1927**).
See also: WEAPONS.

SERVISS, GARRETT P(UTNAM) (1851–1929). American writer. GPS majored in science at Cornell University, after which he studied law before entering journalism. He worked on two New York newspapers before moving into freelance writing and lecturing; his speciality was ASTRONOMY. In 1897 he was commissioned to write an unofficial sequel to H.G. WELLS's *The War of the Worlds* (**1898**), which was then enjoying successful newspaper and magazine serialization, and wrote *Edison's Conquest of Mars* (1898 *The New York Journal*; **1947**), in which Thomas Edison masterminded the building of an armed spaceship to travel and defeat the Martians. This was followed by *The Moon Metal* (**1900**). "The Sky Pirate", a novel of aerial warfare, was serialized in THE SCRAP BOOK (1909); it has not appeared in book form. *A Columbus in Space* (1909 *All-Story Magazine*; rev. **1911**) featured another pioneering space flight, this time to VENUS. *The Second Deluge* (**1912**) was a DISASTER novel in which the Earth is inundated to a depth of several miles as a result of passing through a "nebula" composed of water. A latter-day Noah builds an ark and saves all God's creatures. This novel was reprinted three times in sf magazines: AMAZING STORIES (1926), AMAZING STORIES QUARTERLY (1933) and FANTASTIC NOVELS (1948). His last story was a romantic novel, "The Moon Maiden", which was published in *The Argosy* in 1915. It has not been reprinted. [MJE]
See also: DISCOVERY AND INVENTION; END OF THE WORLD; HOLOCAUST AND AFTER; MARS; MONEY; NUCLEAR POWER; SCIENTISTS; SPACESHIPS.

SEVEN FACES OF DR LAO, THE Film (1964). George Pal Productions/ MGM. Produced and directed by George PAL, starring Tony Randall, John Ericson, Arthur O'Connell, Barbara Eden and Noah Beery Jr. Screenplay by Charles BEAUMONT, based on the novel by Charles FINNEY. 99 mins. Colour.

The film is fantasy, but warrants inclusion here as the work of a celebrated sf producer, based on an often-reprinted novel by an author much loved by sf readers. The hero of the film is really William Tuttle, whose make-up for Tony Randall in the leading role, and in the six fantastic shapes he adopts in order to teach a series of moral lessons to the people of the small town the circus is visiting, is astonishingly good. The special effects by a team of five are good, too, but what were only a latent preachiness and sentimentality in the book, *The Circus of*

The Snowman, one of Tony Randall's *alter egos*, in THE SEVEN FACES OF DR LAO.

Dr Lao (**1935**), threaten to swamp the film version, whose moralizing is trite and couched in surprisingly literary terms. A splendid sea serpent, also played by Randall, helps to enliven the climax. [PN]

SEX The following discussion includes "gender", "sexual stereotypes" and "sexual roles" under the general rubric of "sex". "Sexual stereotypes" and "sexual roles" are also discussed, with a different emphasis, in the entry on WOMEN.

Traditionally sf has been rather a puritanical and male-oriented form of literature. Until the 1960s there was only a small amount of sf that consciously investigated sexual questions but, as is the case with nearly all popular genre literatures, what is implied is often as important as what is consciously put forward. Seen from this viewpoint, sf is an accurate reflector of popular prejudices and feelings about sex over the years — especially in stories at the PULP end of the sf spectrum, where the fantasies and taboos of the day are encapsulated more clearly than in more sophisticated works.

An important work of PROTO SF, *Gulliver's Travels* (**1726**; rev. 1735) by Jonathan SWIFT, consciously satirizes sex, especially in Book IV, which contrasts the intelligent horses, the Houyhnhnms, to the Yahoos (clearly of human stock), who think of little but the appetites of the flesh. The Yahoos express disapproval by defecating upon strangers from trees, and a Yahoo girl appals Gulliver by exposing her vulva to him invitingly. Swift himself seems ambiguous about sexual questions, and while he sees the life of pure reason led by the Houyhnhnms to be an impractical and rather cold ideal, it is clear from a variety of episodes in his work that he himself, although obsessed by the flesh, tended to loathe and fear it.

Swift's 18th-century frankness was not to appear in sf again with the same force for more than two centuries. In the 19th century, powerful feelings about sex were implied, but seldom dealt with overtly. GOTHIC sf dealt with fears and fantasies, sexual and otherwise, as phenomena not subject to cool analysis; in short, the Gothic deals with the intrusion of the irrational. *Frankenstein* (**1818**; rev. 1831) by Mary SHELLEY has strong sexual connotations. Would the bestial urges of an artificial man without a restraining soul prove devastating? This aspect of the story has been emphasized in the various film versions of FRANKENSTEIN, and become dominant in the recent parody *Young Frankenstein* (1974), where the monster's amorous abilities prove as overwhelming as the audience had always suspected.

Frankenstein is an example of what was to become a recurrent theme in pulp sf, the semi-conscious link between sexual potency and the ALIEN. Just as white men traditionally fear that the black man is a sexual athlete too well endowed to compete against, so in sf the menace of the alien is often seen in sexual terms, particularly in sf ILLUSTRATIONS, which right through the magazines of the 1930s and '40s have a very much stronger sexual charge than the milk-and-water stories they purported to picture. MARVEL TALES made a brief and unremarkable attempt to add a mild carnality to the stories themselves, but it rapidly turned out that the readership of *Spicy Mystery Stories* and similar pulps was not so readily to be wooed. Indeed the SF MAGAZINES proved mercifully unable to link the two genres of the spicy and the technological with any conviction, although the conjunction of flesh and metal later proved inspirational to sf COMIC-STRIP artist Jean-Claude Forest, whose erotic and mildly sophisticated BARBARELLA featured a heroine who was prepared to receive even the embrace of a robot — a not uncommon theme in the liberated 1970s, most amusingly dealt with in Robert SHECKLEY's story "Can You Feel Anything When I Do This?" (1969). *Barbarella* was successfully filmed by Roger Vadim; the film is a veritable compendium of the familiar sexual fantasies to be found in sf. Its humour consists in making overt what the reader had always imagined was implied by a row of asterisks.

The sexual implications of sf stories have varied remarkably little in the past hundred years, and most of the themes were already well established in the popular literature of the 19th century. *Dr. Jekyll and Mr. Hyde* (**1886**) by Robert Louis STEVENSON explores the notion that the mind of man contains a large and immorally cheerful component under the control of a kind of mental censor device, which can be switched off by the use of certain mysterious drugs. Although there was more of metaphysics than science in the notion when Stevenson penned it — he was interested in morality rather than neurology — later developments (already beginning with the work of Sigmund Freud while Stevenson wrote) showed him to have been not so very far from the truth, as chemical and anatomical studies of disturbance of the mind attest. Mr Hyde was one of the incarnations of "the evil that lurks in the heart of Man", a continuing popular theme in Gothic sf, especially in Hollywood sf/monster movies in the 1940s and '50s.

Sf has been largely written by men, and hence tends to reveal specifically masculine sexual prejudices; its two dominant female archetypes are the Timorous Virgin and the Amazon Queen, though these are to be found everywhere in literature. To these we can add two lesser types: the Tomboyish Kid Sister (revealed only in the last pages, as the scales lift from the hero's eyes, as a Desirable Sexual Object) and the Frustrated Spinster Scientist, such as Susan Calvin in Isaac ASIMOV's *I, Robot* (coll. **1950**).

Sexual archetypes appear clearly in *The Time Machine* (**1895**) by H.G. WELLS, where the two future races discovered by the Time Traveller are the masculine, hairy Morlocks and the Eloi (in whom the sexual characteristics of men and women have merged into a near-hermaphroditic unisex), who appear feminine, beautiful, carefree and irresponsible. The Eloi are, ultimately, just cattle for the Morlocks the two races allegorize 19th-century sexual distinctions and class distinctions simultaneously. An illustration to a magazine reprint of the story by Virgil FINLAY makes the point clear.

Woman as Amazon Queen imperious, cruel, infinitely desirable yet remote — is abundantly present in *She* (**1887**) by H. Rider HAGGARD. The she-devil was one of the most popular of recurrent Victorian literary archetypes — not surprisingly, in a period when flagellation was known throughout Europe as "the English vice". She turns up throughout pulp sf in succeeding years, notably in the romances of Edgar Rice BURROUGHS, and in many tales

In the earlier days of pulp-style sf, SEX tended to adopt the same implausible guise of inter-species desire, no matter what the medium. Left, a cover by Parkhurst, Winter 1945; above, a 1954 publicity still for *The Creature From The Black Lagoon*.

published in PLANET STORIES. A.E. VAN VOGT used her many times. It might be thought that woman as dangerous, Holy Prostitute, She-Fiend, would be an exclusively masculine fantasy — after all, it dehumanizes womanhood. However, Catherine L. MOORE made a speciality of such figures, notably in the tales featuring Northwest Smith. The Medusa creature "Shambleau" in Moore's story of that name (1933) is a prototype of the female as a fantasy of sexual horror: "From head to foot he was slimy from the embrace of the crawling horror about him. His face was that of some creature beyond humanity — dead-alive, fixed in a gray stare, and the look of terrible ecstasy that overspread it seemed to come from somewhere far within ...".

The conjunction of the idea of Womanhood and the idea of Slime may have pathological connotations, but is familiar enough in the sf genre and elsewhere. Consider also the following passage from *The Deathworms of Kratos* (1975) by Richard Avery (Edmund COOPER): "Each time she was penetrated, the queen's huge body rippled and arched and she gave out a hissing, screaming grunt. Steam rose from her straining body, gouts of milky fluid dripped from her immense length, bubbling from her orifices ..." The sexual confusions are intense: the queen is a giant worm, and, though female, unmistakably phallic in shape. The watchers are "sickened", but sufficiently excited that, within pages, they are asking the spaceship captain for permission to pair off and make love. The sexual ambiguities here are of the very essence of pulp sf.

The worst sexual crudities in sf, against which feminist writers rightly turn their wrath, are found in the male writers of HEROIC FANTASY, notably Robert E. HOWARD in the "Conan" stories of the 1930s, and John NORMAN in the "Gor" books of the 1960s. Norman specializes in the whipping of slave girls, and other items of conventional sexual fetishism.

The visual counterpart of these writers is the sf cover illustrator Frank FRAZETTA, whose ripe, lush beauties, when not being menaced by scaly, phallic monsters, are themselves cruel Amazons, holding the most brawny-thewed men in thrall.

In sf proper, especially SPACE OPERA, women were less prone to fall into the extremes of savagery or timorous defencelessness. The heroines of E.E. "Doc" SMITH in the "Lensman" and "Skylark" books have a wooden charm of the jolly girl-next-door variety, typical of conventional sf stories at least until the middle 1940s. Harry HARRISON parodies the sexual relationships of pulp sf, specifically "Doc" Smith's, in his novel *Star Smashers of the Galaxy Rangers* (1973). A comic-strip version of the all-American career girl/tomboy is to be found in Lois Lane, girl-friend of SUPERMAN.

Miscegenation, the mixing of races, is the most common sexual theme in sf. In the early days it tended to be treated lightly. One unconsciously amusing scene is that where John Carter stands proudly next to his wife, the princess, in *A Princess of Mars* by Edgar Rice Burroughs (1919), looking at their child in its incubator; the child at this stage is a large egg. During the period when the alien was usually seen as fearful, miscegenation was commonly a matter of

rape. Many magazines, notably *Planet Stories*, featured BEMs (Bug Eyed Monsters) with lascivious expressions in pursuit of human women on the cover — an obvious sexual absurdity, for presumably an octopus would be no more attracted to a human woman than she to an octopus. In the early 1950s, two writers, Philip José FARMER and Theodore STURGEON, treated the theme more seriously. Hitherto magazine sf, no matter what sexual events or feelings it might coyly imply, was never explicit. Kay Tarrant, assistant to John W. CAMPBELL, the editor of ASTOUNDING SCIENCE FICTION (later *Analog*), was famous for her prudishness, and persuaded many writers to remove "offensive" scenes and "bad language" from their stories. This was partly in keeping with the spirit of the age, and partly to protect adolescent boys, probably their largest readership. With some writers it became a game to outwit her, as in the apocryphal tale of the writer who got away with mentioning a "ball-bearing mousetrap" on one page, revealing on the next page the device: a tomcat.

But both Farmer and Sturgeon were, for their period, explicit. They recognized that in a genre which prided itself on imagining new and different societies, the sexual taboo was absurdly anachronistic, particularly because it did not exist to the same degree in conventional fiction. Sturgeon explored both three-way relationships and human-alien relationships in a number of stories and novels, notably *Venus Plus X* (**1960**). Farmer's novel *The Lovers* (1952 *Startling Stories*; exp. **1961**) dealt with inter-species love and sex, as did many of his stories, including the incredible "Mother" (1953), in which a spaceman is inveigled into an alien womb, where he makes his home — perhaps the ultimate in Freudian sf stories. Both these writers questioned concepts of "normal" and "perverse", but there is a critical argument about the degree of crudeness or salacity with which the attempt was made.

By the 1960s miscegenation was an acceptable serious theme in sf, and it was perhaps most carefully explored in Ursula K. Le Guin's novel *The Left Hand of Darkness* (**1969**) which won both Nebula and Hugo awards for the year. Faced with a society whose natives are bisexual in that they can be, at different times, either man, woman or neuter, and coming to love one of its people, an ordinary human is forced to rethink the whole question of sexual roles. The success of the book is a tribute to the delicacy of the treatment. Le Guin returned to the question of sexual roles in *The Dispossessed* (**1974**). A recent, sensitive treatment of love between alien races is the story "Strangers" by Gardner Dozois which appeared in New Dimensions IV (anth. **1974**). It draws attention to the ghastly errors that can occur from trying to understand a foreign society in terms of the assumptions of one's own.

After the pioneer work of Sturgeon and Farmer, and also such mildly daring works as "Consider Her Ways" (1956) by John Wyndham, which deals with an ambiguously Utopian all-woman society, and *The Girls from Planet 5* (**1955**) by Richard Wilson, which deals skittishly with a similar theme, the breaking of the dam came with the so-called New wave in the 1960s. Suddenly, explicit sex and even pornography were commonplace in sf. Norman Spinrad's *Bug Jack Barron* (**1969**) was for a brief time considered rather wicked. Brian Aldiss's *Hothouse* (fix-up **1962**; vt *The Long Afternoon of Earth* USA), *The Primal Urge* (**1961**), *Barefoot in the Head* (fix-up **1969**) and many of his other books dealt jovially and unselfconsciously with sex as one of many issues. Harlan Ellison's anthology *Dangerous Visions* (anth. **1967**) printed some stories that were on previously taboo topics, and many that were not. One publisher, Essex House, specialized in pornographic sf, including Farmer's *The Image of the Beast* (**1968**) and *A Feast Unknown* (**1969**), Hank Stine's interesting man-becomes-woman novel *Season of the Witch* (**1968**) and David Meltzer's *The Agency* (**1968**). Olympia Press followed suit with *The*

Power and the Pain (**1971**) by Charles Platt, which tells of a mad scientist's hospital where patients are surgically modified to allow their bodies a more flexible approach to pleasure. Most of these works were notable more for their ingenuity than for anything else, and tended towards the emetic rather than the erotic.

Sf is perhaps more liable than most genres (except horror) to link sex with disgust. Ray Bradbury, Theodore Sturgeon and Robert Bloch all wrote stories in which sex is inextricably linked with violence, blood, repulsion, pain, deformity and even death. Yet all three are generally considered to be towards the more "reputable" end of the sf spectrum. The dominant image of sf which deals overtly with sex is often that of the body seen as "alien" and governing the mind, rather than vice versa.

Many critics consider that the most distinguished work of "pornographic" sf is *Crash* (**1973**) by J.G. Ballard, in which images of technology and images of sex are interwoven to make an ambiguous, not necessarily disapproving, comment on the nature of technological society and its alienations. The central images of this book are the orgasm and the car crash, the one often leading to the other (*see also* Ballard's *The Atrocity Exhibition* **1970**; vt *Love and Napalm: Export USA* USA).

Recent writers have made extrapolations towards cultures where troilism, homosexuality, bisexuality or even pansexuality is the norm. Samuel R. Delany does so in much of his writing, notably in *Dhalgren* (**1975**) and *Triton* (**1976**). Thomas M. Disch does so in *334* (**1972**). Michael Moorcock adduces incest, bisexuality and strong female dominance in the "Jerry Cornelius" books and other works. In *The Female Man* (**1975**) Joanna Russ produces a fiery and painful polemic against male chauvinism, and suggests various workable societies in which men would be redundant. Joanna Russ is perhaps the most notable feminist in sf; her angry reaction to the male chauvinism still rampant in sf is widely shared.

Writers of an older generation, such as Isaac Asimov — who even wrote a non-sf work entitled *The Sensuous Dirty Old Man* (**1971**) — and Robert Heinlein, also blossomed out into the freedom of the 1960s. In most of Heinlein's recent work the central theme is a strong plea for sexual emancipation. This has been his emphasis ever since his very popular *Stranger in a Strange Land* (**1961**), most obviously in *I Will Fear No Evil* (**1970**) in which an old man is given new life in the body of his young female secretary, and again in *Time Enough For Love* (**1973**). Thomas M. Disch has argued that sexual themes lurk in earlier Heinlein also, and that behind the tough, masculine façade of his *Starship Troopers* (**1959**) a

homosexual theme is evident, visible even in such minor details as the earrings worn by the soldiers! (*See* "The Embarrassments of Science Fiction" by Disch in *Science Fiction at Large*, ed. Peter Nicholls, **1976**; vt *Explorations of the Marvellous*.) If Disch is correct in his general point, then even the most "manly" aspects of sf may not be all that they seem.

Sexual freedom has also reached sf cinema. The mild frissons of I Married a Monster From Outer Space (1958), with its theme of the bridegroom-cum-monster, a traditional fear, have given way to the bland acceptance of overt bisexuality in Nicholas Roeg's The Man Who Fell to Earth (1976) and the vileness of David Cronenberg's They Came From Within (1975; vt *The Parasite Murders*; vt *Shivers*) in which red larval parasites penetrate mouths and vaginas, infecting the hosts with acute nymphomania. Some critics have found the latter film merely degrading, while others see in it a witty comment on the malaise of the times.

Recent anthologies of sf stories with sexual themes are *Strange Bedfellows: Sex and Science Fiction* (**1972**) ed. Thomas N. Scortia, *Eros in Orbit* (**1973**) ed. Joseph Elder and *The Shape of Sex to Come* (**1978**) ed. Douglas Hill. An amusing study, with special reference to sf illustration, is *Great Balls of Fire! A History of Sex in Science Fiction* (**1977**) by Harry Harrison.   [PN]

SEYMOUR, ALAN (1927–). English writer, whose sf novel, *The Coming Self-Destruction of the United States of America* (**1969**), features a black revolution that, though temporarily successful, precipitates eventual all-round catastrophe.   [JC]
See also: POLITICS.

SHACKLETON, C.C. *See* Brian W. Aldiss.

SHANKS, EDWARD (1892– ?). English writer, whose sf novel, *The People of the Ruins* (**1920**), places a man from the present into a decadent England a century or so hence, where civil wars rage.   [JC]
Other works: *The Dark Green Circle* (**1936**).

SHARKEY, JACK Form of his name used by American writer John Michael Sharkey (1931–) for all his sf, which he began publishing with "The Captain of his Soul" for *Fantastic* in 1959, producing about 50 stories over the next five or so years, though his production decreased after 1965. His sf novels, *The Secret Martians* (**1960**) and *Ultimatum in 2050 A.D.* (**1965**), are routine but enjoyable, the protagonist in the first book, for instance, being a thoroughly likeable SUPERMAN.   [JC]
See also: ECOLOGY.

SHARON, ROSE *See* Judith MERRIL.

SHASTA PUBLISHERS Chicago-based American specialist publisher founded by three fans, Ted DIKTY, Erle Korshak and Mark Reinsberg, originally to publish books about fantasy and sf. Its first title was Everett F. BLEILER's *The Checklist of Fantastic Literature* (**1948**). The company soon expanded into fiction publishing with such titles as John W. CAMPBELL Jr's *Who Goes There?* (coll. **1948**), L. Sprague DE CAMP's *The Wheels of If* (coll. **1949**) and L. Ron HUBBARD's *Slaves of Sleep* (**1948**). All these early titles featured jackets by Hannes BOK. Subsequent publications include the first three volumes of Robert A. HEINLEIN's "Future History" and Alfred BESTER's *The Demolished Man* (**1953**). In 1953 Shasta sponsored a novel competition in conjunction with the paperback publisher Pocket Books. This was won by Philip José FARMER with *I Owe For The Flesh*. By this time the company was in financial difficulties: the book was never published and the prize money never paid. (The novel later formed the basis of Farmer's "Riverworld" series.) Shasta produced one or two further titles, then expired.
[MJE]

SHAVER, RICHARD S(HARPE) (1907–75). American writer. He wrote some sf stories, but is remembered now almost exclusively for his hoax-like sequence of "Shaver Mystery" stories, presented as based on fact, published in Ray PALMER's AMAZING STORIES, 1945–7, beginning with "I Remember Lemuria" in Mar. 1945. It brought over 2,500 letters in response, and the sequence boosted *AMZ*'s circulation though it alienated many fans. The Jun. 1947 *AMZ* was an all-Shaver issue. RS continued to release the same sort of material briefly in *Other Worlds* (still as Palmer's protégé), and was revived yet again in Palmer's small-circulation THE HIDDEN WORLD in 1961. A selection of the "articles" was published as *I Remember Lemuria & The Return of Sathanas* (coll. **1948**). Essentially the "articles" are comprised of a series of messages from an underground world which, VON DÄNIKEN-like, establish a new, conspiracy-oriented, highly lurid history and cosmology: we are manipulated by "deros" (detrimental robots) through various ESP powers. RS never admitted the hoax, and may have genuinely believed what he wrote — or so he sturdily submitted, until the end of his life.
[JC/PN]
See also: PARANOIA AND SCHIZOPHRENIA; PSEUDO-SCIENCE.

SHAW, BOB Form of his name used by Robert Shaw (1931–), Northern Irish writer. Educated at the Technical High School, Belfast, he worked in structural engineering until the age of 27, then aircraft design, then industrial public relations and journalism. He has lived in

England since 1973 and has been a full-time author since 1975.

BS was an enthusiastic sf fan from an early age. His first story, "Aspect" (1954), appeared in *Nebula Science Fiction*. During the mid-1950s he contributed several more stories to the same magazine, then ceased writing for some years. His "come-back" story was "... And Isles Where Good Men Lie" (1965) in *NW*. The following year, his "Light of Other Days" (1966) was published in *ASF* and gained a NEBULA award nomination. It established his reputation as a writer of remarkable ingenuity. The story is built around the intriguing concept of "slow glass", a type of glass which hinders the passage of light to such an extent that it may take years for the light to travel through, enabling people to view scenes from the past. Anthologized numerous times, "Light of Other Days" remains BS's best-known story. He later incorporated it, together with two sequels, into the novel *Other Days, Other Eyes* (fix-up 1972).

His first novel, however, was *Night Walk* (1967). A fast-moving chase story, it concerns a man who is blinded and condemned to a penal colony on a far planet. He invents a device which enables him to see through other people's eyes (and the eyes of animals) and thus manages to make his escape. *The Two-Timers* (1968) is a well-written tale of parallel time-streams, *Doppelgängers* and murder. It demonstrates BS's ability to handle characterization and, in particular, his talent for realistic dialogue. *The Palace of Eternity* (1969) is a still more impressive novel. It is about interstellar warfare, the environmental degradation of an Edenic planet, and human transcendence. The final section of the novel, where the hero finds himself reincarnated as an "Egon", or soul-like entity, displeased some critics although it is in fact a good handling of a traditional sf displacement of ideas from METAPHYSICS or RELIGION. The intelligent reworking of well-worn sf themes is BS's forte, as was demonstrated in his next novel, *One*

Million Tomorrows (1970). This is a story of IMMORTALITY, the twist being that the option of eternal youth entails sexual impotence.

Ground Zero Man (1971) is a near-future thriller about a man who invents the means to blow up all the world's nuclear weapons. Less rich in ideas than most of BS's novels, it nevertheless contains much effective writing. The uneasy relationship of the protagonist and his wife is particularly well portrayed. *Orbitsville* (1975) is the longest, and certainly one of the best, of BS's novels. Like Larry NIVEN's *Ringworld* (1970) and Arthur C. CLARKE's *Rendezvous With Rama* (1973), it concerns the discovery of a vast alien artefact in space — in this case, a habitable shell (or DYSON SPHERE) which entirely surrounds a star. The living-space provided by the inner surface of the artificial shell is of enormous extent, billions of times the surface area of the earth. Against this background BS spins an exciting story of political intrigue and exploration. Some of the plot devices owe a little to A.E. VAN VOGT, an early influence on BS, but the prose, characterization and general inventiveness make this work superior to anything produced by the older writer. *Orbitsville* gained a 1976 BRITISH SCIENCE FICTION AWARD.

A Wreath of Stars (1976) is BS's most original, and perhaps his finest, novel. A rogue star, composed entirely of anti-neutrinos, approaches the earth. It passes nearby, with no immediately discernible effect. However, it is soon discovered that an anti-neutrino "earth" exists within our planet, and its orbit has been seriously disturbed by the passage of the star. This is an ingenious, almost a poetic, idea, to which the plot unfortunately fails to do full justice. Despite its flaws, however, this remains a memorable novel. *Medusa's Children* (1977) is less satisfactory. Here BS's ingenuity has run away with him, and the result is a rather empty and unbelievable "tall story" involving the mystery of the Bermuda Triangle. The novel has its moments, though, particularly in the early chapters which describe the mysterious, gravity-free, underwater environment of a tribe of people descended from shipwreck survivors. *Who Goes Here?* (1977) is another *jeu d'esprit*; akin to Harry HARRISON's *Bill, the Galactic Hero* (1965), it is about a kind of interstellar Foreign Legion and the quest of one man to regain his memory. With its digs at the conventions (particularly the more militaristic ones) of American sf, it is a notable contribution to HUMOUR in sf.

BS's short stories have been reprinted in *Tomorrow Lies in Ambush* (coll. **1973**; UK edition omits "Stormseeker" and "Element of Chance") and *Cosmic Kaleidoscope* (coll. **1976**; US edition omits "The Brink" and adds "Element of Chance" and "Deflation 2001"). His series of four stories about the adventures of the Stellar Survey Ship "Sarafand" has been collected, together with new material, in *Ship of Strangers* (1968–75 var. mags.; fix-up **1978**).

BS is very much a genre writer, in that he keeps well within the limits of sf as it is usually defined. His stories are written with a sureness of tone, a knowledge of technical detail and an understanding of character which few other writers can match. He may not be the most ambitious writer in contemporary sf, but he is certainly one of the finest entertainers. [DP]

Other works: *Shadow of Heaven* (**1969**; abridged 1970).

About the author: "Escape to Infinity" by BS in FOUNDATION 10, 1976.

See also: ALTERNATE WORLDS; CONCEPTUAL BREAKTHROUGH; DISCOVERY AND INVENTION; ESCHATOLOGY; FANTASTIC VOYAGES; GREAT AND SMALL; ICONOCLASM; IMAGINARY SCIENCE; MATTER TRANSMISSION; PARALLEL WORLDS; PARASITISM AND SYMBIOSIS; PERCEPTION; PHYSICS; RENARD, Maurice; SATIRE; SCIENTIFIC ERRORS; SCIENTISTS; TIME TRAVEL.

SHAW, BRIAN House name used by the publishers Curtis Warren, UK. The pseudonym was used by John Russell FEARN for *Z Formation* (**1953**), and E.C. TUBB for *Argentis* (**1952**). Two titles without definite attribution are *Lost World* (**1953**) and *Ships of Vero* (**1952**). They are juvenile adventure sf. [PN]

SHAW, FREDERICK L(INCOLN) (1928–). American writer, whose routine sf novel, *Envoy to the Dog Star* (**1967**), sends an intelligent dog's brain to Sirius. [JC]

SHAW, GEORGE BERNARD (1856–1950). Irish-born writer of novels, plays and much controversial non-fiction; he lived most of his life in England. Many of his later plays, from *Back to Methuselah: a Metabiological Pentateuch* (**1921**; several times revised up to 1945) to the playlets of his last years, dissolve realist conventions of stagecraft in the direction of sf or fantasy to make their sweeping points; though they have been treated less kindly by critics than his earlier work, the quality of these plays is gradually being recognized. *Back to Methuselah* uses a good deal of sf material in its five-part depiction of Man's EVOLUTION from the time of Genesis down to a period, into the FAR FUTURE, when mankind has become long-lived and, by AD 31,920 is on the verge of corporeal transcendence and of becoming disembodied thought-entities. A short novel, *The Adventures of the Black Girl in her Search for God* (**1932**), is fantasy, while the "Farfetched Fables" assembled in *Buoyant Billions* (coll. **1950**) are as close to sf as much of the work of Italo CALVINO or Slawomir MROŻEK. [JC]

See also: ADAM AND EVE; IMMORTALITY; SUPERMAN; THEATRE.

SHAW, LARRY T(AYLOR) (1924–). American writer and editor. He was an active sf fan in the 1940s and was a member of the FUTURIANS. He sold a few sf stories in the early 1950s, beginning with "Simworthy's Circus" (1950) in *Worlds Beyond*, but is primarily known as an editor. He was associate editor of IF, May 1953 – Mar. 1954. In 1955 he became editor of INFINITY SCIENCE FICTION, which grew to be one of the leading sf magazines of its period, and he later started a companion title, SCIENCE FICTION ADVENTURES. Both magazines failed in 1958 and he turned to editing in other fields. He worked for Lancer Books 1961–8, where he built a successful sf line and edited the anthologies *Great Science Fiction Adventures* (anth. **1964**) and *Terror!* (anth. **1966**). He subsequently worked for Dell Books and Brandon House (parent company of ESSEX HOUSE). He was formerly married to sf writer Lee HOFFMAN. [MJE]

SHEA, MICHAEL (? –). American writer whose FAR-FUTURE sf novel is *A Quest for Simbilis* (**1974**). Effectively a fantasy, it is a sequel to *The Eyes of the Overworld* (fix-up **1966**) by Jack VANCE and, while not as witty, is surprisingly close in its imitation of Vance's style. [PN]

SHEA, ROBERT (? –). American writer and senior editor of *Playboy* magazine. His elaborate sf novel with Robert Anton WILSON, *Illuminatus!*, published in three instalments with the subtitles *The Eye in the Pyramid* (**1975**), *The Golden Apple* (**1975**) and *Leviathan* (**1975**), combines detective, FANTASY and sf components in the extremely complex tale of a vast conspiracy on the part of the Illuminati, historically a late-18th-century German association of freethinkers, but expanded in the novel into the gods of H.P. LOVECRAFT's "Cthulhu" pantheon, among other incarnations. The Illuminati plan more or less to destroy the world to gain power, and almost eveything of meaning in the contemporary world turns out somehow to signify their malign omnipresence. The novel, which shows the influence of Thomas PYNCHON's *The Crying of Lot 49* (**1966**), has been made into a successful stage play, adapted by Ken Campbell and Chris Langham; it was the opening play of the National Theatre's Cottesloe auditorium in London in 1977. The book's combination of parody, PARANOIA, joke and deadpan, hysterical conspiracy-mongering has proved very popular. Wilson has described it as "a *reductio ad absurdum* of all mammalian politics, right or left, by carrying each ideology one logical step further than its exponents care to do". [JC]

See also: HUMOUR; SATIRE.

SHEAR, DAVID (? –). American writer, whose routine sf novel is *Cloning* (**1972**). [JC]

SHECKLEY, ROBERT (1928–). American writer, born and educated in New York, where he sets some of his fiction, though he has lived abroad for many years and is now resident in England. In the army from 1946–8 in Korea, he began writing only after his return, publishing his first story, "Final Examination" for *Imagination* in 1952 and producing short fiction prolifically for several years in various magazines, though his supple, witty, talkative, well-crafted work was especially suited to GALAXY, where much of it appeared. He is best known as a short-story writer, a reputation based primarily on the work of his first half-decade or so; his first collection, *Untouched by Human Hands* (coll. **1954**), is an extremely fine beginning, and contains several of his best efforts, including "The Monsters" (1953), the title story (1952), "Seventh Victim" (1953, which was much later made into a film, LA DECIMA VITTIMA, 1965, and in turn novelized by RS as *The Tenth Victim*, **1966**), and the superb "Specialist" (1953) which, with an adroitness typical of RS, posits a galaxy inhabited by a variety of cooperating races who can merge their specialized functions to become, literally, a spaceship; the story describes the search for a new Pusher, a being capable of shoving the ship into FTL velocities — unsurprisingly for the 1950s, *Homo sapiens* turns out to be a Pusher species. Further successful collections followed swiftly: *Citizen in Space* (coll. **1955**); *Pilgrimage to Earth* (coll. **1957**); *Notions: Unlimited* (coll. **1960**); *Store of Infinity* (coll. **1960**); and *Shards of Space* (coll. **1962**). RS's stories are unfailingly elegant and literate; their mordant humour and sudden plot reversals separate them from the mass of magazine sf stories of the time, for the wit and surprises usually function to make serious points about the calamitous aspects of life in the later 20th century.

RS wrote one early series of note, featuring the misadventures of the AAA

Ace Interplanetary Decontamination Service. They are "Milk Run" (1954), "Ghost V" (1954), "The Laxian Key" (1954), "Squirrel Cage" (1955), "Lifeboat Mutiny" (1955), "The Necessary Thing" (1955) and "The Skag Castle" (1956). In the middle 1950s he wrote 10 stories as Finn O'Donnevan, and also published as Phillips Barbee and Ned Lange.

After several years, RS began gradually to turn toward novel-writing, with somewhat mixed results. He has carried his literacy and wit into longer forms, but has perhaps lost something of the lucid control over form which he demonstrated in the short story. His novels tend to be episodic, and often these episodes are structured as a kind of guided tour of a particular sf milieu he wishes to investigate; his protagonists tend to find themselves dumped into strange new worlds, where they must scramble about to survive and to find out where they are. In *Immortality Delivered* (1958; exp. vt *Immortality, Inc.* 1959), the protagonist dies in a car crash and is revived 150 years hence in a whirligig America where most forms of psychic phenomena, including life after death, have been verified. In *Journey Beyond Tomorrow* (1963; vt *The Journey of Joenes* UK) the protagonist is an innocent, after the style of VOLTAIRE's Candide, who suffers a variety of alarming adventures after leaving his quiet Pacific island in the near future; the novel takes the form of a series of remembrances enshrined as myths 1000 years later. In *Mindswap* (1966) the protagonist switches minds with a Martian, and is subjected to reality displacements galore. In *Dimension of Miracles* (1968) the protagonist wins a prize, in error, that takes him all over a galaxy whose reality is again disconcertingly arbitrary. Of his earlier novels, perhaps only *The Status Civilization* (1960) is genuinely successful, and embodies its SATIRICAL points in a shaped narrative. The story tells of social hierarchies, many of them topsy-turvy, on a prison planet where conformity means always being wicked.

In recent years, RS has been less productive, but the quality has remained high, though his increasing tendency to write almost ABSURDIST stories may not be to the taste of the sf market in general — which is reflected in the fact that many of them were first published in slick magazines such as *Playboy* rather than in sf magazines, though he won the JUPITER award, with "Suppliant in Space" for the best short story of 1973. *The People Trap* (coll. 1968) contains a mixture of old and new stories, but most of the fiction in *Can You Feel Anything When I Do This?* (coll. 1971; vt *The Same to You Doubled* UK) is recent and typical of his late work; the story which gave its title to the US edition involves the sad fate of a sex-maddened domestic robot, but the finest story is the non-sf "Cordle to Onion to Carrot", about a timid man who makes a

conscious and successful attempt to develop *machismo*. *Options* (1975) is a novel in which the sf apparatus could be read as a delusional frame, or taken with a degree of literalness as dramatic projections on the part of the protagonist, Tom Mishkin, of the various forms his life could be read as taking, rather after the fashion of Barry N. MALZBERG. Malzberg is the author whose treatment of sf themes as metaphors for all-too-human problems most resembles RS in the field, just as Ron GOULART's most closely resembles his narrative dexterity and wit. RS is an urban and urbane writer of sf, unable to take seriously the simpler, more adventurous forms the genre can take, which he regularly and affectionately parodies. Though as a consequence he is less popular than others less capable than he, he has nevertheless built a considerable satiric reputation in a field where wit is sometimes dismissed as a form of frivolity. A good retrospective volume is *The Robert Sheckley Omnibus* (1973). [JC]
Other works: various titles, such as *White Death* (1963) and *The Game of X* (1965), are detective thrillers; *The Alchemical Marriage of Alistair Crompton* (1978; vt *Crompton Divided*); *The Robot Who Looked Like Me* (coll. 1978); *Futuropolis* (1978), non-fiction.
See also: ANTI-INTELLECTUALISM IN SF; CITIES; COLONIZATION OF OTHER WORLDS; CRIME AND PUNISHMENT; DISCOVERY AND INVENTION; ECONOMICS; ESCHATOLOGY; FANTASTIC VOYAGES; GAMES AND SPORTS; GODS AND DEMONS; HUMOUR; LEISURE; MEDIA LANDSCAPE; OVERPOPULATION; PARANOIA AND SCHIZOPHRENIA; REINCARNATION; SUPERNATURAL CREATURES; TABOOS; TIME TRAVEL.

SHEEHAN, PERLEY POORE (1875–1943). American writer and journalist, who wrote a large amount of magazine fiction; his sf novel, *The Abyss of Wonders* (1915 *Argosy*; 1953), features a LOST RACE. [JC]
Other works: *The Prophet* (1913); *The Whispering Chorus* (1928).

SHEENA, QUEEN OF THE JUNGLE US PULP MAGAZINE. One issue, Spring 1951, published by Glen Kel Co.; no editor named. Sheena — a sort of female Tarzan — was one of the few characters to make the transition from COMICS to pulp magazines (rather than vice versa), having first appeared in *Jumbo Comics* in 1938. *SQOTJ* contained three Sheena stories by James Anson Buck. The character was also featured in the pulp magazine *Jungle Stories*. [MJE/FHP]

SHELDON, LEE Pseudonym of American writer and mailman Wayne Cyril Lee (1917–), who began publishing sf with "Project Asteroid" for *Teens* in 1966, and whose routine sf adventure novel is *Doomed Planet* (1967). [JC]

SHELDON, RACCOONA See James TIPTREE Jr.

SHELDON, ROY English house name used by Hamilton for short fiction and full-length novels in AUTHENTIC in 1951–2, and for some routine sf books, one of which, *The Metal Eater* (1954) is by E.C. TUBB. The others are: *Two Days of Terror* (1951); *The Menacing Sleep* (1952); *Atoms in Action* (1953); *House of Entropy* (1953); *Mammoth Man* (undated, 1951); *Moment out of Time* (undated, 1951). The authors of these have not been identified. [JC]

This miniature of Mary SHELLEY by Reginald Easton (Bodleian Library) was made posthumously, by copying a bust sculptured in her lifetime.

SHELLEY, MARY WOLLSTONE-CRAFT (1797–1851). English writer, daughter of the philosopher and novelist William Godwin and of the feminist and educationist Mary Wollstonecraft, who died in giving birth to her. MWS married Percy Bysshe Shelley in 1816, two years after they had eloped to the Continent, and after his first wife had committed suicide. During 1816, the Shelleys spent much time with Lord Byron who (or possibly his physician) suggested, after reading some of their work, that they should each write a ghost story. Nothing much came of Byron's or Percy Shelley's efforts, but MWS wrote *Frankenstein: or, The Modern Prometheus* (1818; rev. 1831), the most famous English horror novel, though perhaps not the most widely read, as its conventional GOTHIC narrative structure, which involves stories within frames and a sentimentalized rhetoric, makes somewhat difficult going for many modern readers more familiar with the numerous film, television and other spin-offs from the original tale (*see* FRANKENSTEIN; FRANKENSTEIN MONSTER). The young Swiss scientist Frankenstein is obsessed with the notion that the spark of life may be a "spark" in some literal fashion, and hopes to create life itself by galvanizing dead matter; to this end, he collects human remains, constructs a body, grotesque but mechanically sound, and shocks it into life. The awakened/created MONSTER, initially innocent but soon distorted by Frankenstein's growing revulsion, demands of his maker that a mate be created for him, and when this demand is refused starts on a rampage in which Frankenstein's wife and brother are both killed. Frankenstein begins to track the monster down to destroy it, but eventually perishes, his mind gone, deep in the Arctic. The monster disappears across the ice floes.

Frankenstein has received increasing critical attention in recent years, with study focusing on MWS herself, on her relation to her father's rationalist philosophy, and on her life with her husband at the time of the book's genesis; the novel itself has been treated in terms of these concerns, perhaps most fruitfully in studies of its relation to the idea of the natural man: the monster — who reads Goethe's *The Sorrows of Werther* — is in a sense a *tabula rasa*, and the evil that he does he is shaped to do by the revulsion and persecution of others; he has to *learn* to be a monster. Alternatively, he can be thought of as an embodiment of the evil latent in Man, in which case he merely need be given the opportunity to be a monster. The novel has also been studied as a defining model of the Gothic mode of fiction, and in *Billion Year Spree* (**1973**), Brian W. ALDISS argues its importance as the first genuine sf novel, the first significant rendering of the relations between Man and science through an image of Man's dual nature appropriate to an age of science. Aldiss's *Frankenstein Unbound* (**1973**) also treats of both MWS and her creation. Although MWS's novel does seem vulgarly to argue that there are things that Man is not meant to know, it is far more than an awful-warning shot across the bows against the evils of scientism; no simple paraphrase of this sort can adequately describe it.

MWS wrote a further PROTO SF novel, *The Last Man* (**1826**), set in 2073, in which a plague wipes Man off the face of the Earth. The last man of the title is rather like her husband, who was dead by the time of its composition. This novel, too, has served as a model for much subsequent work using its basic idea of a world in which there can be a last, secular survivor. The only story in the posthumous collection *Tales and Stories of Mary Wollstonecraft Shelley* (coll. **1891**) which can be called sf is "The Mortal Immortal".   [JC]
About the author: there is much criticism, especially in recent years: *Mary Shelley* (**1959**) by E. Bigland; *Mary Shelley* (**1972**) by William A. Walling; *Ariel Like a Harpy: Shelley, Mary and Frankenstein* (**1972**; vt *Mary Shelley's Frankenstein: Tracing the Myth* USA) by Christopher Small; *Mary Shelley's*

Monster — the Story of Frankenstein (**1976**) by Martin Tropp; *Moon in Eclipse: a Life of Mary Shelley* (**1978**) by Jane Dunn. Two critical editions of *Frankenstein* have recently been published by M.K. JOSEPH (**1969**) and James Rieger (**1974**).
See also: ANDROIDS; BIOLOGY; CONCEPTUAL BREAKTHROUGH; END OF THE WORLD; DISCOVERY AND INVENTION; FANTASTIC VOYAGES; FANTASY; GODS AND DEMONS; HISTORY OF SF; HOLOCAUST AND AFTER; MEDICINE; METAPHYSICS; POWER SOURCES; RELIGION; SCIENTISTS; SEX; WOMEN.

SHELTON, MILES *See* Don WILCOX.

SHERBURNE, ZOA (? –). American writer whose juvenile sf novel is *The Girl Who Knew Tomorrow* (**1970**).   [JC]

SHERIDAN, THOMAS *See* Walter GILLINGS.

SHERMAN, MICHAEL or **PETER MICHAEL** *See* Robert A.W. LOWNDES.

SHERRED, T(HOMAS) L. (1915–). American writer who has worked as a military technical writer and in advertising. Most of his slim sf output is now available in his two published books. *Alien Island* (**1970**), a sometimes comic but fundamentally melancholy novel about ALIENS secretly on Earth and the eventual disaster that results, and *First Person, Peculiar* (coll. **1972**), which contains his four well-known stories, most famous among them being "E for Effort", with which he began publishing sf in 1947 for *ASF*. The story describes, again humorously but with fundamental pessimism, the results of an invention which permits its users to view past and present events; its inventor and his associate are successful at first, but are soon defeated by government forces; ultimately, the existence of the "camera" in the hands of the American military causes a final war, as the victim-narrator predicts. The other stories are "Cue for Quiet" (1953), "Eye for Iniquity" (1953) and "Cure, Guaranteed" (1954). TLS's work is notable for its clear-cut force and its pointed black humour. One more recent story, "Bounty", appeared in *Again, Dangerous Visions* (anth. **1972**) ed. Harlan ELLISON, where it was revealed that TLS suffered a mild stroke in 1971 and is unlikely to write further.   [JC]
See also: MACHINES; TIME TRAVEL.

SHERRELL, CARL (1929–). American commercial artist and writer, for many years in the former capacity; he began publishing with *Raum* (**1977**), a SWORD AND SORCERY novel.   [JC]

SHERRIFF, R(OBERT) C(EDRIC) (1896–1975). English playwright, novelist and film-writer, known mainly for his work outside the sf field, his hit

play *Journey's End* (**1929**) recently having been filmed as *Aces High* (1975). His sf novel, *The Hopkins Manuscript* (**1939**; rev. vt *The Cataclysm* 1959), is a DISASTER story set mostly in rural England; dislodged from its course, the Moon crashes into the Atlantic Ocean, causing tornadoes and tidal waves. As the Moon nears, Edgar Hopkins, whose manuscript is discovered hundreds of years later by Abyssinian archaeologists, fussily eulogizes his beloved countryside and people; afterwards, he records an abortive recovery of civilization before the Moon's mineral wealth tempts the shattered nations of Europe into terminal conflict, and an Asian warlord moves in. The science is derisory, but the elegy is strongly felt. RCS wrote the screenplay for the 1933 film THE INVISIBLE MAN, based on H.G. WELLS's novel (*see* INVISIBILITY).   [JC]

SHERWOOD, MARTIN (1942–). English writer, with a PhD in organic chemistry, and editor of a technical journal, *Chemistry & Industry*. He has published two sf novels, *Survival* (**1975**) and *Maxwell's Demon* (**1976**).   [JC]

SHERWOOD, NELSON *See* Kenneth BULMER.

SHIEL, M(ATTHEW) P(HIPPS) (1865–1947). British writer, born in the West Indies of an Irish father. He was educated at King's College, London, and was proficient in several languages. He began writing fiction in 1892 and continued until his death.

MPS's writings fall into two distinct periods, one ending in 1913, the other beginning in 1923. During the first his name was allied with those of George GRIFFITH, William LE QUEUX and Louis Tracy (with whom he collaborated on *An American Emperor*, **1897**, and several detective novels), partly because he appeared in the same magazines, but mainly because like them he wrote many future-WAR stories, including *The Yellow Danger* (as "The Empress of the Earth" in *Short Stories*; **1898**; vt "The Yellow Peril" UK, rev. 1899), *The Yellow Wave* (**1905**) and *The Dragon* (as "To Arms", *The Red Magazine*, **1913**; rev. vt *The Yellow Peril* 1929); all featured oriental INVASIONS of the Western world. It was in this period that his most highly acclaimed works appeared: *Prince Zaleski* (coll. **1895**), an exotic pastiche of Sir Arthur Conan DOYLE's "Sherlock Holmes" stories, strongly influenced by the works of Edgar Allan POE; *The Lord of the Sea* (**1901**; rev. 1913; rev. 1924), in which the founding of an empire of seaborne fortresses results in the establishment of a Jewish homeland in the Middle East; *The Purple Cloud* (**1901**; rev. 1929), a novel depicting a world DISASTER, the sole survivor of which expiates his fears of loneliness through a lifelong orgy of destruction (it was freely adapted into a popular film THE WORLD, THE FLESH AND THE DEVIL, 1959); and *Shapes in the Fire* (coll. **1896**) and *The Pale Ape and Other Pulses* (coll. **1911**), two noteworthy volumes of weird fiction.

MPS's second creative period, which began with *Children of the Wind* (**1923**) and his revisions of earlier novels, is less sensational in nature, the emphasis being placed on fuller development of his philosophical and political beliefs (his main associations of this period are with E.H. VISIAK, Edward SHANKS, Arthur MACHEN and John Gawsworth). Of particular importance are *This Above All* (**1933**; rev. vt *Above All Else* 1943) and *The Young Men are Coming* (**1937**), in which his Nietzschean theory of the "Overman" and his belief in the supremacy of science over religion are most fully expanded. In spite of some academic acclaim, MPS remains underrated in the HISTORY OF SF, perhaps through his use of circumlocutory sentence structures and his rich, poetically alliterative style, which tends either to infatuate or to alienate the reader. He is both controversial and enigmatic; condemned by some, notably Sam MOSKOWITZ, for overt racialism and anti-Semitism, yet praised by others for his celebration of Zionism; best suited for *The Yellow Book*, yet writing for popular monthly magazines, penny weeklies and daily newspapers. To date, no unbiased critical appreciation of his work has appeared. [JE]
Other works: *The Rajah's Sapphire* (**1896**); *The Lost Viol* (**1905**); *The Last Miracle* (**1906**; rev. 1929); *The Isle of Lies* (**1909**); *Here Comes the Lady* (coll. **1928**); *Dr Krasinski's Secret* (**1929**); *The Invisible Voices* (coll. **1935**); *The Best Short Stories of M.P. Shiel* (coll. **1948**); *Xélucha and Others* (coll. **1975**); *Prince Zaléski and Cummings King Monk* (coll. **1977**).
About the author: *The Works of M.P. Shiel* (**1948**) by A. Reynolds Morse; "The World, the Devil, and M.P. Shiel" by Sam Moskowitz in *Explorers of the Infinite* (coll. **1963**).
See also: END OF THE WORLD; MESSIAHS; POLITICS; SOCIAL DARWINISM; VILLAINS.

SHIRAS, WILMAR H. (1908–   ). American writer. She began publishing sf with "In Hiding" for *ASF* in 1948, the first of the stories later assembled into *Children of the Atom* (1948–50 *ASF*; fix-up **1953**), about a number of radiation-engendered child geniuses who first conceal themselves from the world, then reveal themselves, taking the risk that in trying to help normal humans they may merely end as martyrs. The story is sensitively told, and avoids most of the clichés of PULP sf SUPERMAN stories. [JC]
See also: ANTI-INTELLECTUALISM IN SF; CHILDREN IN SF; INTELLIGENCE; MUTANTS.

SHIRLEY, GEORGE E(RNEST) (1898– ?   ). American writer whose

routine sf novels are *A World of Their Own* (**1965**), *The Robot Rulers* (**1967**) and *A World Beyond* (**1967**). [JC]

SHIVERS See THEY CAME FROM WITHIN.

SHRINKING MEN See GREAT AND SMALL.

The first appearance on a comic-book cover of *Superman*, leading to fame for illustrator Joe SHUSTER. June 1938.

SHUSTER, JOE (1916–   ). American COMIC BOOK illustrator. In 1933, after reading Philip WYLIE's novel *Gladiator* (**1930**), a young sf fan, Jerry SIEGEL, conceived a superhero whom he called SUPERMAN; he asked JS to illustrate his ideas and over the next several years they were rejected by every comics publisher in the United States. Finally accepted, *Superman* appeared in *Action Comics* in Jun. 1938, and was an immediate success; the list of subsequent imitations and resultant lawsuits made comic book history. JS's style was similar to Dick CALKINS's, stiff, somewhat crude and boldly colourful. He drew his characters with a charming simplicity that captivated the audiences of the late 1930s. JS and Siegel were associated with the strip for only a couple of years, then slipped into obscurity; they resurfaced in the early 1970s for long enough to collect on a lawsuit against National Periodicals Publications, the original purchasers of *Superman*, then disappeared again. [JG]

SHUTE, NEVIL Form of his name used by English writer Nevil Shute Norway (1899–1960) for his fiction from 1926; for many years he combined writing with work as an aeronautical engineer, specializing in Zeppelins; after moving to Australia for his health, he set much of his later fiction, including his two full-scale sf novels, there. Some of his other novels, however, through his intense and

very up-to-date knowledge of his professional field, verge very closely on sf; *No Highway* (**1948**) deals with metal fatigue as the cause of airplane disasters just before a Comet jet crashed for that reason in real life. It was filmed as *No Highway in the Sky* (1951). An earlier novel, *An Old Captivity* (**1940**), also verges on sf in its tale of a man who dreams in a coma (it turns out accurately, and on the basis of data unknown at the time of the dream) of Vikings in Greenland and of their life there. More properly sf is *In the Wet* (**1953**), a leisurely novel in the form of the journal of an Australian outback priest who copies down from a dying man a vision (or memory) of the British Empire of the year 2000, when Australia has become the leader of the Commonwealth, royalty has survived handsomely, socialism has faded away, and the Empire is secure. Somewhat closer to home was his second sf novel, *On the Beach* (**1957**), filmed as ON THE BEACH (1959), a NEAR FUTURE/DISASTER tale in which nuclear war has eliminated all life in the northern hemisphere leaving only Australia to await the inevitable radioactive contamination (merely delayed by global wind-patterns) that will end human life on Earth. NS was an excellent popular novelist; his stories demonstrate his seamless narrative skill and his predilection for deeply decent protagonists. [JC]
See also: END OF THE WORLD; PREDICTION.

SIBSON, FRANCIS H. (? – ?   ). South African writer, most of whose work has something to do with the sea and ships; *The Survivors* (**1932**) and its sequel *The Stolen Continent* (**1934**) describe first the violent creation of a new island in the Sargasso Sea (its rapid surfacing beaches an ocean liner), and second the international conflicts surrounding claims to the new territory, which is called New Canada; *Unthinkable* (**1933**) depicts an arduous Antarctic expedition whose members find, on their return north, that civilization has been destroyed by a war gas. [JC]
See also: END OF THE WORLD.

SIEGEL, JERRY (1914–   ). American writer and sf fan, who founded and issued with the illustrator Joe SHUSTER the fanzine *Science Fiction* in Oct. 1932, one of the earliest occasions on which the term was used in a title. Also with Shuster, he created the comic SUPERMAN, which first appeared in 1938, after they had spent years trying to sell the idea to publishers. [JC]

SIEGEL, MARTIN (1941–72). American writer, who died young of leukemia. His sf novels are *Agent of Entropy* (**1969**) and *The Unreal People* (**1973**). The first combines SATIRE and SPACE OPERA in a heated tale; the second is a post-HOLOCAUST story in which Earth's surface is uninhabitable and men live frenetically and desperately underground. [JC]

SIEVEKING, LANCE Form of his name used by English writer and radio producer Lancelot de Giberne Sieveking (1896–1972) for his later work, though he used larger portions of his name in his first publications. From 1924 to his retirement in 1956, he was involved in various capacities with the BBC, and edited Ward Lock's sf list for a short period, about 1955–6; his memories of English literary life, including portraits of such figures as H.G. WELLS, were published as *The Eye of the Beholder* (1957). Among his many writings, there is some sf, including *Stampede* (1924), illustrated by G.K. CHESTERTON, a NEAR-FUTURE political SATIRE, and *The Ultimate Island* (1925), in which a kind of whirlpool is abducting Atlantic shipping. His best-known sf work, *A Private Volcano* (1955), depicts the effects of a catalyst (thrown up from a volcano) which turns all dross to gold. LS is a literate writer, sometimes uneasy in his handling of the more straightforward genre effects. [JC]
Other works: *The Woman She Was* (1934).

SILENT RUNNING Film (1971). Universal. Directed by Douglas TRUMBULL, starring Bruce Dern. Screenplay by Deric Washburn, Mike Cimino and Steve Bocho, story by Douglas Trumbull. 90 mins. Colour.

Douglas Trumbull was one of the special effects supervisors on 2001: A SPACE ODYSSEY, so it is not surprising that there should be similarities between the two films. Made for only a fraction of the cost of *2001*, *SR*'s scenes of vast spaceships cruising silently through space compare well with those in KUBRICK's epic but there the similarities end; *SR*'s story is based on the absurd premise that one day all remaining vegetation on Earth will be stored in giant spaceships and put into orbit — apparently because there is no room left for such luxuries on Earth. The central character is a watchman on one of these orbiting greenhouses and the only true conservationist left alive. When Earth gives instructions to dump the vegetation he, like any conservationist at bay, murders his companions and sets off for deep space with the plants. He is accompanied only by three small, box-shaped robots (each operated by an amputee, an idea Trumbull got from watching Tod Browning's *Freaks*). *SR* is occasionally spectacular and consistently famous. [JB]

SILLITOE, ALAN (1928–). British writer, best known for such works outside the sf field as his first novel, *Saturday Night and Sunday Morning*

(1958). His anti-authoritarian SATIRE, *Travels in Nihilon* (1971), is ostensibly a DYSTOPIA, for the five travellers to that country despise it and work to overthrow it; but Nihilism as a political creed, by story's close, seems to have been given the author's guarded sanction. [JC]
See also: POLITICS.

SILVERBERG, ROBERT (1936–). American writer, now retired. He was an extremely prolific writer, producing more than 70 sf books and over 200 uncollected short stories in a career that lasted barely 20 years. In the same period he produced some 60 non-fiction books and did a considerable amount of writing for non-sf magazines. He has also edited more than 40 anthologies. He began to write while studying for his BA at Columbia University and his first published story was "Gorgon Planet" (1954). His first novel, for a juvenile audience, was *Revolt on Alpha C* (1955). He began to publish prolifically in 1956, winning a HUGO award in that year as the most promising new author, and continued to specialize in sf for three years. He worked for the Ziff-Davis "stable", producing wordage at assembly-line speed for AMAZING and FANTASTIC, and was also a highly productive contributor to other minor magazines — particularly SCIENCE FICTION ADVENTURES and SUPER-SCIENCE FICTION — under many different names. The most important pseudonyms which he used exclusively were Calvin M. Knox and David Osborne, and he also published a good deal of work as by Ivar JORGENSON, a variant spelling of the floating pseudonym Ivar JORGENSEN. Other names which he used were Richard F. Watson, Ralph Burke (which he also used on three stories written with Randall GARRETT), Dan Malcolm, Eric Rodman, Hall Thornton, Alex Merriman, T.D. Bethlen, George Osborne, Dirk Clinton

and Webber Martin, plus the Ziff-Davis house names Alexander BLADE, E.K. JARVIS, Warren KASTEL, S.M. TENNESHAW and Robert ARNETTE. He wrote in collaboration with Randall GARRETT as Robert RANDALL (*see latter entry for details*) and also as Gordon Aghill and Ralph Burke. They also collaborated under the house names Alexander BLADE, Richard GREER, Clyde MITCHELL, Leonard G. SPENCER, S.M. TENNESHAW and Gerald VANCE.

The best novels written during this early period are: *Master of Life and Death* (1957), a novel dealing with institutionalized measures to combat OVERPOPULATION; *Invaders from Earth* (short version as "We the Marauders" 1958 *Science Fiction Quarterly*; 1958), a drama of political corruption involved with the COLONIZATION of Ganymede; and *Recalled to Life* (1958 *Infinity*; 1962; rev. 1972), which investigates the social response to a method of reviving the newly dead. In 1959, however, RS began to diversify his output, and as the magazine market shrank he virtually abandoned sf. Between 1960 and 1966 the great majority of his published sf books were rewritten from work originally done in 1957–9. His productivity continued to be prodigious, but somewhat mechanical. As time went by he began to devote more care and effort to some of his non-fiction books, and produced some works of genuine scholarship — notably *The Golden Dream* (1967) and *Mound-Builders of Ancient America* (1968). Eventually this determination to produce work of higher quality fed back into his fiction, and he resumed writing sf with the intention of making fuller use of his artistic abilities rather than his capacity to work quickly. *Thorns* (1967), a stylized novel of alienation and psychic vampirism, and *Hawksbill Station* (short version, 1967 *Gal.*, has been frequently anthologized; 1968; vt *The Anvil of Time* UK), a study of the lives of men exiled from the near future into the Cambrian period, represented the beginning of what was tantamount to a new career. In the following decade, though his total output declined steadily, he produced an astonishing number of excellent novels and shorter pieces.

The Masks of Time (1968; vt *Vornan-19* UK) is an account of a visit by an enigmatic time traveller to the world of 1999. *The Man in the Maze* (1969) is a dramatization of the problems of alienation. *Nightwings* (three novellas, title story, *Gal.* 1968, frequently anthologized independently; fix-up 1969) is a lyrical novel of the conquest of a senescent Earth by aliens which culminates with the rebirth of its hero. *Up the Line* (1969) is a clever TIME PARADOX story. *Downward to the Earth* (1970) is a story of repentance and rebirth with strong religious imagery. *Tower of Glass* (1970) also makes use of religious imagery in its study of the obsessional construction of a new "Tower of Babel" and the struggle of an ANDROID race to win emancipation. *A Time of Changes* (1971) describes a society in which selfishness is a cardinal sin. *Son of Man* (1971) is a surreal evolutionary fantasy of the FAR FUTURE. *The World Inside* (fix-up 1971) is a careful study of life under conditions of high population density. *The Second Trip* (1972) is an intense psychological novel describing the predicaments of an "artificial" man created in the body of an "erased" criminal and a telepathic girl. *The Book of Skulls* (1972) is a painstaking analysis of relationships among four young men on a quest for IMMORTALITY. *Dying Inside* (1972) is a brilliant study of a telepath losing his power. *The Stochastic Man* (1975) is a complementary study of a man developing the power to foresee the future. *Shadrach in the Furnace* (1976) concerns the predicament of the personal physician of a future dictator who finds his identity in jeopardy.

Two of the above-mentioned works won major awards in the USA: the novella "Nightwings" won a Hugo and *A Time of Changes* won a NEBULA. RS also won Nebula awards for several shorter pieces: "Passengers" (1968), a story about people who temporarily lose control of their bodies to alien invaders; "Good News From the Vatican" (1970), about the election of the first robot pope; and the brilliant "Born With the Dead" (1974), about relationships between the living and the benefactors of a scientific technique guaranteeing life after death. The novella "The Feast of St. Dionysus" (1972), about the experience of religious ecstasy, won a Jupiter award. *Nightwings* also won the 1976 PRIX APOLLO in France.

Apart from these award-winners RS published a great deal of excellent short fiction during the second phase of his career. Particularly notable are: "To See the Invisible Man" (1963); "Sundance" (1969); "In Entropy's Jaws" (1971) and "Schwartz Between the Galaxies" (1974). THE MAGAZINE OF FANTASY AND SCIENCE FICTION published a special issue devoted to RS in April 1974. An autobiographical essay appeared in *Hell's Cartographers* (coll. 1975), ed. Brian ALDISS and Harry HARRISON. RS was president of the SCIENCE FICTION WRITERS OF AMERICA in 1967–8.

RS is one of the most imaginative and versatile writers ever to have been involved with sf. His productivity seems almost superhuman and his metamorphosis from a writer of standardized pulp fiction into a prose artist is an accomplishment unparalleled within the field. His retirement was associated with — though probably not directly caused by — disillusionment regarding the marketing philosophy of sf publishers. He still remains active as an editor, and is responsible for the excellent series of original anthologies NEW DIMENSIONS (seven annual vols to date, 1971–7), several collections of original novellas, and many reprint anthologies.

RS has said that *Tower of Glass* and *Dying Inside* were "assassinated" by the publishers; that is, that the texts as published were regarded by the author as mutilated.   [BS]

Other works: *The 13th Immortal* (1957); *Aliens from Space* (1958 as by David Osborne); *Invisible Barriers* (short version "And the Walls Came Tumbling Down" under own name 1957 *If*; 1958 as by David Osborne); *Lest We Forget Thee, Earth* (fix-up 1958 as by Calvin M. Knox); *Starhaven* (short version "Thunder Over Starhaven" 1957 *Science Fiction Adventures*; 1958 as by Ivar Jorgenson); *Stepsons of Terra* (short version "Shadow on the Stars" 1958 *Science Fiction Adventures*; 1958); *The Planet Killers* (short version "This World Must Die" 1957 *Science Fiction Adventures* as by Ivar Jorgenson; 1959); *The Plot Against Earth* (1959 as by Calvin M. Knox); *Starman's Quest* (1959); *Lost Race of Mars* (1960); *Collision Course* (1961); *Next Stop the Stars* (coll. 1962); *The Seed of Earth* (based on "Winds of Siros" *Venture* 1957; 1962); *The Silent Invaders* (short version 1958 *Infinity* as by Calvin M. Knox; 1963); *Godling Go Home* (coll. 1964); *One of Our Asteroids is Missing* (1964 as by Calvin M. Knox); *Regan's Planet* (1964); *Time of the Great Freeze* (1964); *Conquerors from the Darkness* (short version "Spawn of the Deadly Sea" 1957 *Science Fiction Adventures*; 1965); *To Worlds Beyond* (coll. 1965); *Needle in a Timestack* (coll. 1966); *The Gate of Worlds* (1967); *Planet of Death* (1967); *Those Who Watch* (1967); *The Time Hoppers* (short version "Hopper" 1956 *Infinity*; 1967); *To Open the Sky* (fix-up 1967); *Across a Billion Years* (1969); *The Calibrated Alligator* (coll. 1969); *Dimension Thirteen* (coll. 1969); *Three Survived* (short version 1957 *Super-Science Fiction*; 1969); *To Live Again* (1969); *Parsecs and Parables* (coll. 1970); *World's Fair 1992* (1970; sequel to *Regan's Planet*); *The Robert Silverberg Omnibus* (coll. 1970); *The Cube Root of Uncertainty* (coll. 1971); *Moonferns and Starsongs* (coll. 1971); *The Reality Trip and Other Implausibilities* (coll. 1972); *Earth's Other Shadow* (coll. 1973); *Valley Beyond Time* (coll. 1973); *Unfamiliar Territory* (coll. 1973); *Sundance and Other Science Fiction Stories* (coll. 1974); *Born With the Dead* (coll. 1974); *The Feast of St. Dionysus* (coll. 1975); *Sunrise on Mercury* (coll. 1975); *The Best of Robert Silverberg* (coll. 1976); *Capricorn Games* (coll. 1976); *The Shores of Tomorrow* (coll. 1976).

Anthologies: *Earthmen and Strangers* (1966); *Voyagers in Time* (1967); *Men and Machines* (1968); *Dark Stars* (1969); *Three for Tomorrow* (1969; UK edition states as ed. Arthur C. CLARKE); *Tomorrow's Worlds* (1969); *Alpha One* (1970); *The Ends of Time* (1970); *Great Short Novels of Science Fiction* (1970); *The Mirror of Infinity* (1970); *Worlds of Maybe* (1970); *The Science Fiction Hall of Fame Vol.1* (1970); *Alpha Two* (1971); *To the Stars* (1971); *Four Futures* (1971); *Mind to Mind* (1971); *The Science Fiction Bestiary* (1971); *Alpha Three* (1972); *Beyond Control* (1972); *Invaders from Space* (1972); *The Day the Sun Stood Still* (1972); *Alpha Four* (1973); *Chains of the Sea* (1973); *Other Dimensions* (1973); *Three Trips in Time and Space* (1973); *No Mind of Man* (1973); *Deep Space* (1973); *Alpha Five* (1974); *Threads of Time* (1974); *Mutants* (1974); *Infinite Jests* (1974); *Windows into Tomorrow* (1974); *The Aliens* (1976); *Alpha Six* (1975); *Epoch* (with Roger ELWOOD 1975); *The New Atlantis* (1975); *Strange Gifts* (1975); *Explorers of Space* (1975); *The Crystal Ship* (1976); *The Aliens* (1976); *The Infinite Web* (1977); *Alpha 7* (1977); *Earth Is The Strangest Planet* (1977); *Trips in Time* (1977); *Alpha 8* (1977); *Triax* (1977).

About the author: "The Metamorphosis of Robert Silverberg" by Brian STABLEFORD in SCIENCE FICTION MONTHLY Vol.3 no.3 (1976). Special "Silverberg Forum", no.51 of SF COMMENTARY, Mar. 1977.

See also: ALIENS; ALTERNATE WORLDS; ANTHROPOLOGY; ARTS; BLACK HOLES; CITIES; COLONIZATION OF OTHER WORLDS; COMIC STRIPS; COMPUTERS; CRIME AND PUNISHMENT; CRITICAL AND HISTORICAL WORKS; DYSTOPIAS; END OF THE WORLD; ENTROPY; ESCHATOLOGY; ESP; EVOLUTION; FANTASTIC VOYAGES; FUTUROLOGY; GALACTIC EMPIRES; HISTORY IN SF; INVASION; INVISIBILITY; JUPITER; LIFE ON OTHER WORLDS; MEDIA LANDSCAPE; MESSIAHS; METAPHYSICS; MONSTERS; MYTHOLOGY; NEW WAVE; PARALLEL WORLDS; PARASITISM AND SYMBIOSIS; PASTORAL; PERCEPTION; PSYCHOLOGY; REINCARNATION; RELIGION; ROBOTS; SF IN THE CLASSROOM; SOCIOLOGY; SPACE OPERA; SUN; SUPERMAN; TECHNOLOGY; TIME TRAVEL; TRANSPORTATION; UNDER THE SEA.

SIMAK, CLIFFORD D(ONALD) (1904–). American writer, a newspaperman for most of his life. His first published story, "The World of the Red Sun" (1931), was quite unremarkable, and the four stories he produced in the following year showed little improvement. He ceased writing at the end of 1932, and apart from one novelette, *The Creator* (1935; 1946), he published no more sf until 1938. Then, inspired by John W. CAMPBELL Jr's editorial policy at ASTOUNDING, CDS wrote such stories as "Rule 18" and "Reunion on Ganymede" (both 1938). He swiftly followed these with his first full-length novel, *Cosmic Engineers* (1939 *ASF*; rev 1950), a galaxy-spanning epic in the vein of E.E. SMITH and Edmond HAMILTON. He continued to write steadily

Photo Noreascon.

---

for Campbell, and there was a gradual improvement in his work, evident in stories like "Rim of the Deep" (1940), "Tools" (1942) and "Hunch" (1943). However, CDS did not "arrive" as a major sf writer until the appearance of "City" and its sequel, "Huddling Place" (both 1944). These tales concern the NEAR FUTURE exodus of mankind from the cities, and the return to a PASTORAL existence aided by a benign technology. Sentimental, yet deeply felt, they struck an immediate chord in the sf readership. CDS went on to write another six stories in the series, the progression becoming more fantastic as he depicts an Earth inherited by old men, ROBOTS and dogs. Eventually published as a fix-up book (1952), *City* won an INTERNATIONAL FANTASY AWARD and remains CDS's best-known work. A final *City* story, "Epilog", appeared in *The John W. Campbell Memorial Anthology*, ed. Harry Harrison (1973).

In 1950, CDS found another market in the new magazine GALAXY, which serialized his novel *Time and Again* (1951; vt *First He Died*). A trickily plotted time-travel story, it proved to be very popular. Even better is *Ring Around the Sun* (1953) which involves the discovery of a chain of parallel Earths, and the machinations of a secret society of mutants who are plotting to subvert the world's economy by producing everlasting goods. It contains those anti-urban and pro-agrarian sentiments which are so typical of CDS's work. A deeply conservative writer in many ways, he is sf's leading spokesman for rural, Midwestern values. His stories contain little violence and much folk humour, and they stress the value of individualism tempered by compassion — "good neighbourliness", in short. Throughout the 1950s, CDS produced dozens of competent short stories, many of which are included in the collections *Strangers in the Universe* (coll. 1956), *The Worlds of Clifford Simak* (coll. 1960; vt *Aliens for Neighbours* UK) and *All the Traps of Earth* (coll. 1962; issued in two volumes in the UK, the second entitled *The Night of the Puudly* 1964). Two highpoints were the stories "The Big Front Yard" (1958), which won a 1959 HUGO award, and "A

Death in the House" (1959).

After 1960, CDS began to produce novels at the rate of roughly one a year. *Time is the Simplest Thing* (1961) and *They Walked Like Men* (1962) are workmanlike and entertaining books, but *Way Station* (1963) is rather more impressive. It concerns a lonely farmer who is given immortality in return for his services as a galactic station-master (his house has been made into a way-station for aliens who teleport from star to star). Its warmth, imaginative detail and finely rendered bucolic scenes make this CDS's best novel, and it was awarded a 1964 Hugo. *All Flesh is Grass* (1965), *Why Call Them Back from Heaven?* (1967) and *The Werewolf Principle* (1967) are all enjoyable, if essentially repetitive, works. In *The Goblin Reservation* (1968) CDS seemed to be striking into new territory, but in fact it is the old Wisconsin valley fantasy in a new and whimsical guise. Some readers date CDS's decline as a novelist from this book. Certainly, his work in the 1970s has been uneven. Novels like *Destiny Doll* (1971), *Cemetery World* (1973) and *Enchanted Pilgrimage* (1975) contain only flashes of the old talent mingled with a good deal of sheer silliness. The major exception is *A Choice of Gods* (1972), an elegiac work in which CDS repeats all his favourite themes: the depopulated world, the sage old man, the liberated robots, the "haunted" house, teleporting to the stars, etc. *Shakespeare's Planet* (1976), about an explorer who lands on an alien world to find that a Shakespeare lover has been there before him, is also a pleasing work. The most recent novel *A Heritage of Stars* (1977) is almost a compendium of CDS's previous themes. It is a quest novel set in a post-technological society. A man of strong moral convictions and little real concern for ideas, CDS certainly has his limits, but at his best he is a writer of considerable charm. [DP]
Other works: *Empire* (1951); *Trouble with Tycho* (1961); *Worlds Without End* (coll. 1964); *Best SF Stories of Clifford Simak* (coll. 1967); *So Bright the Vision* (coll. 1968); *Out of Their Minds* (1969); editor of *Nebula Award Stories 6* (anth. 1971); *Our Children's Children* (1974); *The Best of Clifford D. Simak* (coll. 1975); *Skirmish: the Great Short Fiction* (coll. 1977).
About the author: "Clifford D. Simak" by Sam Moskowitz, in his *Seekers of Tomorrow* (1966); "Aliens for Neighbours. a Reassessment of Clifford D. Simak" by David Pringle, *Foundation* 11/12 1977.
See also: ALIENS; ANDROIDS; ARTS; ASTEROIDS; CITIES; COLONIZATION OF OTHER WORLDS; COMMUNICATIONS; CRYONICS; ECOLOGY; ESCHATOLOGY; ESP; EVOLUTION; FOURTH DIMENSION (AND OTHERS); GALACTIC EMPIRES; GAMES AND SPORTS; GENERATION STARSHIPS; GODS AND DEMONS; GOLDEN AGE OF SF; IMMORTALITY; INTELLIGENCE; INVASION; JUPITER; LIFE ON OTHER WORLDS;

MACHINES; MARS; MATTER TRANSMISSION; MERCURY; MESSIAHS; MOON; MYTHOLOGY; OPTIMISM AND PESSIMISM; OUTER PLANETS; PARALLEL WORLDS; PARANOIA AND SCHIZOPHRENIA; PARASITISM AND SYMBIOSIS; PSI POWERS; RELIGION; SOCIOLOGY; SPACE OPERA; SPACESHIPS; SUN; SUPERNATURAL CREATURES; VENUS.

SIMPSON, HOWARD (? –). American writer whose routine sf novel is *West of the Moon* (1968). [JC]

SINCLAIR, UPTON (1878–1968). American writer. Known primarily for his work outside the sf field, particularly for his novels of social criticism, including *The Jungle* (1905). His most notable sf work is the comedy *The Millennium* (1924), based on a play in which the survivors of a disaster go through the economic stages described by the Marxist theory of history one by one. Another political satire is *I, Governor of California, and How I Ended Poverty* (1933). [BS]
Other works: *Prince Hagen: a Phantasy* (play, 1903); *Roman Holiday* (1931); *Our Lady* (1938); *What Didymus Did* (1954).
See also: BOYS' PAPERS; ECONOMICS; POLITICS.

SINYAVSKY, ANDREY (DONATO-VICH) (1925–). Russian dissident writer and literary critic who published the manuscripts he smuggled into the West in the late 1950s and early 1960s under the name Abram Tertz; his identity became known when the Soviet authorities arrested him in 1966 and put him through the motions of a show trial, along with his friend and fellow dissident Yuli DANIEL (who wrote as Nikolai Arzhak); both were imprisoned; both are now in exile (*see* POLITICS). Several of AS's "fantastic stories" are of sf interest, most being assembled in *Fantasticheskiye Povesti* (coll. Paris 1961; trans. as *The Icicle and Other Stories* 1963; vt *Fantastic Stories* USA), though the most striking of the lot, "Pkhentz" (trans. 1966; Russian text in *Fantasticheski Mir Abrama Tertza*, coll. Washington 1967), was only smuggled later into the West. In this story, an alien spaceship crashes in Russia, leaving only one survivor, who is forced to exist for years in a desperate limbo under a false identity, passing for an ordinary citizen. "The Icicle" (1961) features a man of whose clairvoyant powers the State makes destructive use in its attempts to control the future. AS's finest novel, *Lyubimov* (Washington 1964; trans. as *The Makepeace Experiment* 1965), tells, with warmth and power, of the transformation of a small Russian village through the power of one man to broadcast his will hypnotically through space; when he loses this power, robot tanks regain the village, and he flees. The SATIRICAL implications of this allegorical recasting of the triumph of Communism in Russia are sufficiently obvious. At the same time, as with earlier writers like Gogol and DOSTOYEVSKY, AS's satirical effects are mediated through an imagination deeply Russian in its metaphysical, fundamentally religious, Slavophile bent; his sf stories are slashing moral fables rather than political diatribes. [JC]

Other works: *For Freedom of Imagination* (coll. trans. **1971**) contains speculations on the nature of sf.

About the author: *On Trial: The Case of Sinyavsky (Tertz) and Daniel (Arzhak)* (**1967**) ed. Leopold Labedz and Max Hayward; this deals largely with AS, and discusses his work in literary terms as well as political.

SIODMAK, CURT (or **KURT**) (1902–). German writer/film-director based in Hollywood. He entered the film industry in 1929 as a screen-writer, and his credits include F.P.1 DOES NOT ANSWER (1932, based on his own novel *F.P.1 Does Not Reply* 1930; **1932**; trans. H.W. Farrel, **1933**) and THE TUNNEL (1933). He emigrated to America in 1937 and his American screenplays include *The Invisible Man Returns* (1939), *The Ape* (1940), *The Invisible Woman* (1941), *Son of Dracula* (1942), *Frankenstein Meets the Wolfman* (1943), *I Walked with a Zombie* (1943), *House of Frankenstein* (1944), LADY AND THE MONSTER (1944, based on his own novel *Donovan's Brain*, and subsequently filmed again as DONOVAN'S BRAIN in 1953 and THE BRAIN in 1962), *The Beast with Five Fingers* (1946), RIDERS TO THE STARS (1953) and *Creature with the Atom Brain* (1955). He also wrote the story on which the film *Earth vs the Flying Saucers* (1956; vt *Invasion of the Flying Saucers*) was based. Later in his career he also started directing and his films include *Bride of the Gorilla* (1951), THE MAGNETIC MONSTER (1953) and *Curucu, Beast of the Amazon* (1956). He has often been involved with sf-orientated subjects but has never really displayed much feeling or understanding for the genre. Like other German film-makers of his generation he is obviously more at home with the supernatural, the macabre and the grotesque than with science, and such science as he introduces tends to be for picturesque atmosphere rather than for the sake of its rationality or logic.

CS has 35 motion picture credits in the United States and 18 in Europe. Before emigrating to the USA he had 18 novels published in Germany, only one of which was translated into English — *F.P.1 Does Not Reply* (**1933**; vt *F.P.1 Fails to Reply* UK). His other novels in English are *Donovan's Brain* (**1943**) and its belated sequel *Hauser's Memory* (**1968**) which was filmed as HAUSER'S MEMORY in 1970; *Skyport* (**1959**); *The Third Ear* (**1971**) and *City in the Sky* (**1974**), the latter dealing with a rebellion of inmates of a prison satellite. *Riders to the Stars* (**1953**) was published as by Curt Siodmak and Robert

Smith, but in fact the only connection CS had with the book was to write the screenplay on which it was based. The story, which involves intrepid astronauts hunting for rare meteors, mounted on rockets with mouths, is regarded by Damon KNIGHT as a splendid example of all that is silliest and most unscientific in sf cinema. *Hauser's Memory* and *The Third Ear* both involve mysterious and absurd experiments carried out by biochemists, in plots which basically have more in common with the spy story than with sf. [JB/PN]

See also: CYBORGS.

SITWELL, (Sir) OSBERT (1892–1969). English poet and novelist in a variety of genres, brother of Edith and Sacheverell Sitwell. *The Man Who Lost Himself* (**1929**) tells the complex psychological life-story of a man from his youth to his death sometime after the middle of the 20th century; *Miracle on Sinai* (**1933**) is a discussion novel, like several of H.G. WELLS's from this period, set in a luxury hotel near Mount Sinai, and on the Mount itself, where a glowing cloud deposits new Tablets of the Law, which are variously interpreted; in the final chapter a cataclysmic war begins. A MAINSTREAM writer, OS used sf/fantasy components to add point to his satirical effects. *A Place of One's Own* (**1941**) is a ghost story. [JC]

SIX MILLION DOLLAR MAN, THE Television series (1973–). A Silverton and Universal Production for ABC, produced by Lionel E. Siegel and Kenneth Johnson, based on the novel *Cyborg* by Martin CAIDIN. The series originally began as a 90-minute ABC "Wednesday Movie of the Week" in Mar. 1973. Two more made-for-TV movies followed and then came the series, each episode 50 mins, colour.

Lee Majors plays Steve Austin, a former air force astronaut (author Caidin is an air force colonel and ex-test pilot) who, after an accident in an experimental aircraft, has his badly injured body rebuilt with various artificial parts, becoming half machine, half man, though it is impossible to tell externally which parts are artificial. His unique situation is treated in purely comic-book terms. He becomes a latter-day SUPERMAN able to perform feats of great strength and move at incredible speeds (an effect achieved, ironically, by slowing down the film), and he is used as a special secret agent by a CIA-like government organization. The basic premise of the series is technologically absurd. The leverage of Austin's bionic arm would be enough in real life to destroy the body (flesh, not metal) which supports it, when lifting great weights. The success of the series resulted in a spin-off series, THE BIONIC WOMAN, which many critics found to be better acted although no more adult. [JB]

SKINNER, B(URRHUS) F(REDERICK) (1904–). American psychologist and writer. His cogently argued (and just as cogently refuted) brand of behaviourism has dominated that theory of psychology for many years in America, and provides the basic arguments for his one work of fiction, the UTOPIA *Walden Two* (**1948**), whose inhabitants grow up as successful experiments in behavioural engineering. The first Walden was of course Thoreau's. *Walden Two* is conducted in the main as a dialogue between Castle and Frazier, two colleagues of a professor significantly named Burris, who can be thought to stand in some fashion for the author himself. Frazier, who has founded the Utopian colony, dismisses (as BFS has more recently done in *Beyond Freedom and Dignity*, **1972**) the traditional notions of free will, and disparages democratic forms of government; his opponent, Castle, argues for the time-tested liberal solutions to the problems of human happiness. Burris seems neutral, but the colony, with its crèches, positive reinforcement regimes and transparently happy residents, is obviously intended to represent the power of Frazier's ideas. [JC]

See also: SCIENTIFIC ERRORS; SOCIOLOGY.

SKORPIOS, ANTARES *See* VENUS.

SKY, KATHLEEN (? –). American writer. Her heavily emotive novel, *Birthright* (**1975**), offers some speculations about how to distinguish between human being and ANDROID after GENETIC ENGINEERING has become a common practice. [PN]

Other works: *Ice Prison* (**1976**).

The only issue, 1977.

SKYWORLDS — CLASSICS IN SCIENCE FICTION US DIGEST-size magazine. One issue, Nov. 1977, published by Humorama Inc., New York; no editor named. *SCISF* reprinted from MARVEL SCIENCE STORIES of 1951. The cover is a NASA photograph. [FHP]

SLADEK, JOHN T(HOMAS) (1937–). American writer, resident in England since 1966. His Midwestern American upbringing is reflected, however, in most of his work, much of which seems set in the vast, hyperbolic flatlands of middle America; this *mise en scène*, when interpenetrated by his adept control of the language and pretensions of the modern bureaucratic state, provides a matrix for his best work, and suggests the frequent comparisons that have been made between him and Kurt VONNEGUT Jr; though Vonnegut has an easier emotional flow than JTS, JTS lacks Vonnegut's vitiating self-pity and excessive simplicity of effect. He began writing sf with "The Happy Breed", published in Harlan ELLISON's *Dangerous Visions* (anth. 1967), though his first published story is "The Poets of Millgrave, Iowa" for *NW* in 1966, and as Cassandra Knye he wrote two GOTHIC novels, *The House That Fear Built* (1966), with Thomas M. DISCH, and *The Castle and the Key* (1967).

His first sf novel, *The Reproductive System* (1968; vt *Mechasm* USA), sets up a mélange of sf material in a small-town American setting: a self-reproducing technological device goes out of control in passages of allegorical broadness, but everything turns out all right in the end, though not through positive efforts of the inept cast, and a dreamlike UTOPIA looms on the horizon. With Disch, with whom he has collaborated on several sf stories as well, JTS next published *Black Alice* (1968; the first, US edition only under the collaborative pseudonym Thom DEMIJOHN), an acute mystery novel, not sf. JTS's next sf book, *The Müller-Fokker Effect* (1970), is his major effort in the field to date; a man's character is transferred on to COMPUTER tape, and the dissemination of several copies of this "personality" instigates a series of ABSURDIST events, some of them extremely comic in effect, some horrifying, all mounting to a picture of America disintegrated morally and physically by its own surrender to technology, the profit motive, and the ethical falseness that leads to dehumanization. In its questioning of the nature of narrative events and of fiction itself, the book lies in the MAINSTREAM of the modern American serious novel, and proper evaluation is overdue.

Through his career, JTS has written numerous stories whose wit and sadness combine deadpan ribaldry and pathos, perhaps most notably in "Masterson and the Clerks" (1967), a long story in which the immolation of its protagonists in the processes of an American business is first hilariously then movingly presented. In his first collection, *The Steam-Driven Boy and Other Strangers* (coll. 1973), there are notable parodies of well-known sf writers; they are probably the finest set ever done in the field. More recent short fiction is collected in *Keep the Giraffe*

Burning (coll. **1977**). *The New Apocrypha: A Guide to Strange Sciences and Occult Beliefs* (**1973**), a non-fiction work, is a scathing investigation of the various cults that exist (for the sf reader) as a kind of fringe around his areas of interest, from SCIENTOLOGY to VON DÄNIKEN (*see* PSEUDO-SCIENCE). JTS has also written detective novels, one of which, *Black Aura* (**1974**), has some borderline sf elements. His sf inhabits a territory at the very edge of genre acceptability, and he has consequently failed to gain his full due as a serious, innovative, cogent writer of modern fiction.   [JC]
See also: AUTOMATION; HUMOUR; LEISURE; MACHINES; MEDIA LANDSCAPE; NEW WAVE; PARANOIA AND SCHIZOPHRENIA; SATIRE; TECHNOLOGY.

SLANT Irish FANZINE (1948–53) edited from Belfast by Walt Willis. It was neatly hand printed on a small letterpress machine and contained woodcut illustrations by James WHITE and Bob SHAW. *Slant* is best remembered for introducing Irish FANDOM (principally Willis, Shaw, and White) to sf fandom at large; it also contained fine pieces of humorous writing (continued in HYPHEN) and featured fiction by authors such as Kenneth BULMER, John BRUNNER, A. Bertram CHANDLER and Bob Shaw. [PR]

SLATER, HENRY J. (? –). Author. His *Ship of Destiny* (**1951**) depicts post-HOLOCAUST existence on the ship, Europe being flooded. *The Smashed World* (**1952**) is set 3,000 years on. [JC]

SLAUGHTERHOUSE-FIVE Film (1971). Universal. Directed by George Roy Hill, starring Michael Sacks, Ron Leibman, Eugene Roche, Sharon Gans and Valerie Perrine. Screenplay by Stephen Geller, based on the novel by Kurt VONNEGUT Jr. 105 mins. Colour.

A middle-class, middle-aged American, dissatisfied with his job, marriage and life in general, starts to experience sudden shifts in time, mainly back to when he was a prisoner of war in the German city of Dresden which was subsequently fire-bombed on a massive scale by the Allies. He later experiences forward shifts in time to when he has become the prisoner of the alien Tralfamadorians who keep him in a zoo on their planet and provide him with a half-naked Hollywood starlet for company. This is a slickly directed film in which the novel's absurd disjunctions between the real horrors of war and the minor horrors of suburban life are rendered even more whimsical and random; the alien sequences are visually embarrassing.   [JB/PN]

SLEE, RICHARD (? – ?). Author, with Cornelia Atwood PRATT (*who see for details*) of *Dr Berkeley's Discovery* (**1899**). [JC]

SLEEPER Film (1973). Jack Rollins-Charles H. Joffe Productions/United Artists. Directed by Woody Allen, starring Woody Allen, Diane Keaton, John Beck, Mary Gregory and Don Keefer. Screenplay by Woody Allen and Marshall Brickman. 88 mins. Colour.

The plot device of having a man from the present day suddenly finding himself in the future (this time through CRYONICS) is nearly always used as it is here to comment on contemporary society rather than as speculation about the future. This SATIRE jokes about such current American obsessions as Nixon, health food, beauty contests and revolutionary politics, but it does also include sf gags involving robots, futuristic sex practices, robot pets and artificial food (which has to be beaten into submission before it can be served). One of the best sequences involves an attempt to CLONE a new body for the country's dictator, using the only part of him that remains after a successful assassination bid — his nose. The film is funny, though perhaps the slapstick is over-emphasized.   [JB]

SLESAR, HENRY (1927–). American writer, who began his career in advertising, and only began to publish sf with "The Brat" for *Imaginative Tales* in 1955. Most of the work for which he is best known lies in the mystery field; he has published a number of thrillers from *The Gray Flannel Shroud* (1958), which won an Edgar award, onwards. Among them is the borderline sf tale *The Bridge of Lions* (1963); closely connected to this kind of work is his stint as headwriter for the American daytime suspense serial, *The Edge of Night*; he has been 9 years with this programme, and won an Emmy award as best TV serial writer in 1974. He has also done scripts for programmes like *The Man from U.N.C.L.E.* Of his 500 or more short stories to date, about a third are sf or fantasy, most of them appearing in the decade following 1955. He has also written sf as O.H. Leslie. His one sf book was the novelization of the film TWENTY MILLION MILES TO EARTH; it was published in **1957** (undated), as no. 1 in the abortive AMAZING STORIES SCIENCE FICTION NOVELS series. About 15 of his sf stories, many of them originally published in *Playboy*, have been anthologized.   [JC/PN]

SLOANE, T(HOMAS) O'CONOR (1851–1940). American editor and author of popular scientific works. He was associate editor (designated managing editor for the first issue) of AMAZING STORIES, and of AMAZING STORIES QUARTERLY, from the beginning, succeeding to the editorship of both magazines in 1929. *Amazing Stories Quarterly* ceased publication in 1934, but he retained the editorship of *AMZ* until June 1938, when the ailing magazine was sold to the Chicago-based Ziff-Davis organization. As associate editor he

carried much responsibility for the actual running of the magazines, although they were in the overall charge of, successively, Hugo GERNSBACK and Arthur Lynch. Nearing his 80th year when he finally succeeded to the editorship, TOCS sported a long white beard and exhibited an appropriately Rip Van Winkle-like approach to the job. Although *AMZ* bought the first stories of such writers as E.E. SMITH, John W. CAMPBELL JR and Jack WILLIAMSON, the combination of poor payment and slack management made it inevitable that they would move to more attractive markets. TOCS actually lost Campbell's first story, and returned Clifford D. SIMAK's first submission after four years' silence, remarking that it was "a bit dated". He was more than once fooled into publishing plagiarisms, and on one occasion, in February 1933, printed a story ("The Ho-Ming Gland" by Malcolm R. Afford) which had already appeared in WONDER STORIES in January 1931. The author had submitted the story four years earlier, and having heard nothing after a year had sold it to the rival magazine. Although he worked for 12 years on sf magazines, TOCS stated publicly his belief (in a 1929 *AMZ* editorial) that Man would never achieve space travel. Nonetheless, TOCS had himself been an inventor, and his son married the daughter of the more celebrated inventor, Thomas Alva Edison. TOCS was a PhD. [MJE]
See also: SF MAGAZINES.

SLOANE, WILLIAM M(ILLIGAN) (1906–74). American writer and publisher, whose interest in the occult is reflected in his two sf novels. *To Walk the Night* (**1937**) and *The Edge of Running Water* (**1939**; vt *The Unquiet Corpse*) were later combined in *The Rim of Morning* (coll. **1964**) and comprise all his significant fiction. The first novel complexly combines mystery and sf elements in the story of the possession by an alien of the widow of a famous physicist, who seems to drive her new husband to "suicide". The narrator recounts these events with absorption and some polish. The second novel features a scientist's attempts to communicate with his dead wife and to revive her; horrors ensue, and local prejudice exacts its toll. WMS also edited two sf anthologies, *Space, Space, Space* (anth. **1953**) and *Stories for Tomorrow* (anth. **1954**); the second was one of the finest collections of its period. [JC]
Other works: *Back Home: A Ghost Play in One Act* (**1931**); *Runner in the Snow: a Play of the Supernatural* (**1931**).
See also: ESCHATOLOGY; MACHINES.

SLUSSER, GEORGE EDGAR (1939–). American academic and critic. GES has a PhD in literature from Harvard and has taught at the University of Paris. He is based in California. His six

critical works, with more announced, have all appeared in the Borgo Press "Popular Writers of Today" series, in quick succession. They are *Robert A. Heinlein: Stranger in his own Land* (**1976**: rev. 1977), *The Farthest Shores of Ursula K. Le Guin* (**1976**), *The Bradbury Chronicles* (**1977**) and *Harlan Ellison: Unrepentant Harlequin* (**1977**), *The Delany Intersection* (**1977**) and *The Classic Years of Robert A. Heinlein* (**1977**). His insights are sometimes ponderously or scrappily expressed, but often sharp; unlike most fan-critics, GES is quite willing to express adverse criticism, though his judgements are on the whole fair and balanced. [PN]
See also: SF IN THE CLASSROOM.

SMALL, AUSTIN J. (? –1929). British adventure and thriller writer. He wrote two sf novels, *The Man They Couldn't Arrest* (**1927**); a mystery novel incorporating unusual devices and inventions into the plot, and *The Avenging Ray* (**1930**, as by Seamark), an uninspired reworking of the perennial DEATH-RAY theme. Other works include *Out of the Dark* (coll. **1931**, as by Seamark), the title story of which is about a were-leopard. [JE]
See also: WEAPONS.

SMITH, CLARK ASHTON (1893–1961). American writer and sculptor, of most interest to the sf reader as a fantasist whose rich style (sometimes idiomatic, sometimes "jewelled" in the DUNSANY manner) and baroque creations of imaginary worlds had a loosening effect on the sf field and its creation in turn of colourful alien cultures, perhaps most notably those immured in FAR-FUTURE Dying Earths such as those of Jack VANCE. By 1910 CAS had sold stories to THE BLACK CAT and THE OVERLAND MONTHLY but had concentrated on poetry; early works included *The Star-Treader* (coll. of poetry **1912**).
Although CAS published some desultory fantasy before 1930, almost all his work of note — commencing with "The Last Incantation" (1930) — was written for PULP magazines, most frequently *Weird Tales*, occasionally *Wonder Stories*, from that date to about 1936, when he virtually stopped writing. These stories, over 100 of them, can be found in *The Double Shadow* (coll. **1933**), *Out of Space and Time* (coll. **1942**; UK paperback broken into two vols) *Lost Worlds* (coll. **1944**; UK paperback broken into two vols), *Genius Loci and Other Tales* (coll. **1948**), *The Abominations of Yondo* (coll. **1960**), *Poems in Prose* (coll. **1964**), *Tales of Science and Sorcery* (coll. **1964**), and *Other Dimensions* (coll. **1970**; UK paperback broken into two vols). The last two contain most of his sf, much of it rather garish SPACE OPERA. Lin CARTER reassembled those of CAS's tales which are set in particular venues, and

republished them as *Zothique* (coll. of linked stories **1970**), *Hyperborea* (coll. of linked stories **1971**), *Xiccarph* (coll. of stories, some linked, **1972**) and *Poseidonis* (coll. of linked stories **1973**). The only other sequences of any importance are the medieval "Averoigne" stories, and several additions to H.P. LOVECRAFT's Cthulhu Mythos. CAS is one of the few writers of weird fantasy in the 1930s (his main competitors being his friend Lovecraft and Robert E. HOWARD) who can be read today without embarrassment.
CAS's collected essays can be found in *Planets and Dimensions* (coll. **1973**).
[JC/PN]
Other works: (all poetry) *Odes and Sonnets* (coll. **1918**); *Ebony and Crystal* (coll. **1922**); *Sandalwood* (coll. **1925**); *Nero and Other Poems* (coll. **1937**); *The Dark Chateau* (coll. **1951**); *Selected Poems* (coll. **1971**); *Grotesques and Fantastiques* (coll. **1973**), which includes drawings.
See also: ASTEROIDS; ASTRONOMY; ATLANTIS; MARS; MERCURY; PARALLEL WORLDS; SUN; SWORD AND SORCERY; TRANSPORTATION; VENUS.

SMITH, CORDWAINER Most famous pseudonym of Paul Myron Anthony Linebarger (1913–66). American writer, political scientist, military adviser in Korea and Malaya (though not Vietnam); a polyglot, he spent many of his early years in Europe, Japan and China. He was a devout High Anglican, deeply interested in psychoanalysis and expert in "brainwashing" techniques, on which he wrote an early text, *Psychological Warfare* (**1948**). Right-wing in politics, he played an active role in propping up the partially corrupt regime in China before the Communist revolution. (For a curious possible sidelight on CS's youth, *see* Robert LINDNER.)
One of his earliest publications, under his own name, is *The Ocean War: an Allegory of the Sun Yat-Sen Revolution* (**1937**); the style of some of his later stories reflects his attempts to translate a Chinese narrative and structural style into his sf writing, not perhaps with complete success, as the somewhat garrulous fabulist voice he assumed (*see* FABULATION) does verge towards the sentimental in English prose. His first sf story is something of a mystery; entitled "War No 81-Q", apparently published (though no one knows where) in 1928, it was probably written as by Anthony Bearden. Astonishingly, for the author was 15 at the time, the tale is claimed to relate. clearly to CS's overarching Instrumentality background which almost all his later fiction shares, and even to mention the Instrumentality by name. After serving in the American Army Intelligence Corps in China during the Second World War, CS published three non-sf novels, *Ria* (**1947**) and *Carola* (**1948**), both as by Felix C. Forrest, and

Atomsk: a Novel of Suspense (**1949**), as by Carmichael Smith. After that date, he published fiction only as CS.

As CS, his first story is the famous "Scanners Live in Vain" (1950), published obscurely in FANTASY BOOK magazine and for several years his only acknowledged work in the field. It was included in his first collection, *You Will Never Be the Same* (coll. **1963**) and in J.J. Pierce's assembly *The Best of Cordwainer Smith* (coll. **1975**) which, though it prints nothing previously unobtainable in book form, does contain a valuable introduction to CS and a chronology for "The Instrumentality of Mankind". Coming at the beginning of the Second Age of Space, when a revitalized mankind is once again moving into the galaxy, "Scanners Live in Vain" chronologically preludes the main body of CS's work. Scanners are space pilots; the sensory rigours of their job entail their transformation into beings whose sensorium has been blanked; the story deals with their contorted lives and with the end of the form of space travel necessitating the contortions. The story is preceded in the overarching "Instrumentality sequence" only by stories like "No, No, Not Rogov!" (1959), "War No 81-Q", and "Mark Elf" (1957).

The heart of the CS universe comes at least 10,000 years later, and is centered in the main on two foci: the hegemony of true humans under the Instrumentality, a vaguely defined term describing a hereditary caste of rulers centered on Manhome or Old Earth from which they benevolently dominate the galaxy; and the planet Norstrilia, or Old North Australia, whose mutated sheep grow viruses that give forth the drug santa clara, or stroon, which confers IMMORTALITY, at great financial cost; therefore no one but Norstrilians and members of the Instrumentality is permitted by law to live beyond 400 years. Interpenetrating these locales is the long story of the underpeople — animals biologically transformed into human-like beings, but without any civil rights whatsoever until a slow revolution is begun, as recounted in "The Dead Lady of Clown Town" (1964), to gain equal status. A couple of millennia after that revolution has begun, and at the same time that the Rediscovery of Man (an Instrumentality-induced and -controlled reintroduction, into Man's painless boring world, of disease, ethnicity, strife, as recounted in "Alpha Ralpha Boulevard", 1961) has been initiated, the underpeople are beginning to achieve some success in their campaign, as in "The Ballad of Lost C'mell" (1962). Stories centering on this culminating part of the sequence are assembled in *Space Lords* (coll., with two linking passages, **1965**), CS's second collection. His only sf novel, which deals with the same period, also began its complex publication history

at this time, a version of part of it, "The Boy Who Bought Old Earth", appearing in *Gal.* in 1964. This version was expanded as *The Planet Buyer* (**1964**), and the second part of the novel was published posthumously as *The Underpeople* (**1968**). These two volumes were edited down from a single manuscript, with some linking additions; the full original manuscript was eventually published as *Norstrilia* (**1975**) and constitutes the definitive novel. *Norstrilia* combines all CS's main themes in the story of Norstrilian Rod McBan's stroon-assisted purchase of Old Earth, his love affair with the cat-woman C-mell, his successful return to Norstrilia.

Some earlier stories in the sequence appear in *Under Old Earth* (coll. **1970**) and *Stardreamer* (coll. **1971**); the latter book also contains the few stories CS wrote unconnected to his main sequence. *Quest of The Three Worlds* (coll. of linked stories **1966**) seems to come chronologically last of the work he completed, and deals with another young protagonist's enforced trek through CS's richly conceived romantic universe in search of justice.

The "Intrumentality" series, and hence CS's work as a whole, stands as a fragment, though his wife has completed some additional stories. The climax of the sequence, one senses, was never reached, in that the long conflict between underpeople and Instrumentality was not resolved. Enough exists, however, to explain the series' strong and lasting impact on its readers. The Chinese derivation of some of CS's narrative devices enforces this impact by using a voice that in telling a tale of long ago *confers* both with the reader and with general tradition about the tale's meaning; CS invests his best later stories with an air of complexity and antiquity that, on analysis, the plots themselves do not always sustain; much of the structuring of the series is lyrical and incantatory (down to the literal use of rather bad poetry, and much internal rhyming), and beyond stroon, and Norstrilia, and Old Earth, and the absorbingly described spaceships, much of the CS universe remains only potential, though his methods ensured the sense that all awaited explication. The question of whether the sequence was, in fact, ever resolvable remains unanswerable.   [JC]

About the author: *Exploring Cordwainer Smith* (anth. **1975**) ed. John Bangsund, from ALGOL Press; almost the whole of SPECULATION 33, 1976, is an analysis of CS's work by John J. Pierce.

See also: ANDROIDS; COLONIZATION OF OTHER WORLDS; CRIME AND PUNISHMENT; CYBORGS; GALACTIC EMPIRES; GENETIC ENGINEERING; MESSIAHS; MYTHOLOGY; ROBOTS; SPACESHIPS.

SMITH, E(DWARD) E(LMER) (1890–1965). American writer, and chemist. He is often called the "father of

SPACE OPERA", which he certainly put into its definitive shape; he was greatly influential in American PULP sf between 1928 and about 1945, though his reputation dimmed somewhat just after the end of the Second World War. By beginning to publish him in book form at about this time, the specialty houses that became active after 1945 (*see* PUBLISHING) were instrumental in keeping his name alive. Towards the end of his life, after an inactive period, he began producing space operas once again, and his earlier work started to appear in paperback editions; since his death, a new generation has made him an sf best-seller, first in the USA, later in Britain. EES had a 1919 PhD in food chemistry, was a professional doughnut-mix specialist, and was commonly known in the sf field as "Doc" Smith.

EES's work is strongly identified with the beginnings of American pulp sf as an identifiable marketing genre, and did much to define it, for good and for ill. When he began to write the first novel of his "Skylark" series with Mrs Lee Hawkins GARBY, in 1915, no magazine published sf of the range, narrative scope and high-handedness with science that *The Skylark of Space* (written 1915–20; 1928 *AMZ*; **1946**; rev. with cuts 1958) displayed when it finally appeared in *AMZ* two years after the start of that magazine, in the same issue as Philip NOWLAN's "Armageddon — 2419 A.D.", the story which introduced BUCK ROGERS. Along with its sequels — *Skylark Three* (1930 *AMZ*; **1948**), *Skylark of Valeron* (1934–5 *ASF*; **1949**) and *Skylark DuQuesne* (**1966**) — *The Skylark of Space* effectively popularized the concept of the inventor scientist who is also the hero of the action; innumerable stories have followed that lead, doing much to define the exhilarated, optimistic, rather Wild West tone of pre-War sf. Before 1928, there were inventors who piloted their own rockets to the Moon and elsewhere, but were very frequently accompanied by a younger friend who took on the action of the story. Though it seriously undermined the scientific and technological plausibility of his novels, EES's merging of the two figures made for a much speedier storyline and a strict subordination of science to adventure, and contributed (in his second series) to that almost constant sense of wonder for which he is justly famous.

The basic conflict animating the "Skylark" series is relatively trivial; hero-inventor Richard Seaton is at perpetual loggerheads, through ever widening canvases, with villain-inventor Marc "Blackie" DuQuesne, perhaps EES's most vivid creation, who develops from the stage histrionics of the first novel to the dominating anti-heroics of the last. Each new part of the sequence is marked by an increase in the scale — soon interstellar — of the action, the potency of the WEAPONS, the power, size and speed of the spaceships. What does not change, unfortunately, is the chummy idiocy of the women (*see* SEX), or the hokum of the slang in which all emotions are conveyed.

But the ebullience of the "Skylark" sequence seems almost intimate beside the massive (though crude) architecture of EES's second and much larger series, the "Lensman" books, with which his name is most strongly associated. The volumes of the main "Lensman" sequence are, in order of internal chronology, *Triplanetary* (1934 *AMZ*; exp. and rev. to fit the series **1948**); *First Lensman* (**1950**); *Galactic Patrol* (1937–8 *ASF*; **1950**); *Gray Lensman* (1939–40 *ASF*; **1951**); *Second-Stage Lensman* (1941–2 *ASF*; **1953**); *Children of the Lens* (1947–8 *ASF*; **1954**). *The Vortex Blaster* (1941–2 var. mags; fix-up **1960**; vt *Masters of the Vortex* USA) is set in the Lensman universe, probably some time before *Children of the Lens*, but does not deal with the central conflict of the main series, which is grandiose in scope — as witness its latter publication in a leather-bound, boxed set titled "The History of Civilization" — and thoroughly worked out. The first two novels prelude the main action; the final four were conceived by EES as one 400,000-word novel divided into the separate titles under which it appeared from 1937 to 1948 in *ASF*, that is from before John W. CAMPBELL Jr's editorship, through the high pitch of the GOLDEN AGE (1939–42), and into the post-War period. *ASF* was the dominant magazine of the time, and despite the new writers Campbell recruited in 1939 and 1940, EES provided much of the excitement that made the period so richly memorable for the sf writers and fans who lived through it.

The conflict of the "Lensman" series is at bottom between two vastly advanced and radically opposed races, the good Arisians and the evil Eddorians, a conflict which has extended over billions of years. The Arisians understand that their only hope of defeating absolute evil is to develop Civilization, via special breeding lines, on specially selected planets, Earth (Tellus) being one. These breeding lines will develop Civilized beings capable of enduring the enormous stress of inevitable conflict with the forces of evil commanded (invisibly) by the Eddorians. The first two novels introduce us to the broad picture, and to the idea of the Lens, a bracelet — "a lenticular polychrome of writhing, almost fluid, radiance" — which tenders to suitable members of the Arisian-influenced Galactic Patrol certain telepathic and other powers. The third novel introduces the series' main protagonist, Kim Kinnison who, with his eventual wife Clarissa MacDougall, represent the penultimate stage in the Arisian breeding programme. Their children will finally defeat the Eddorians in the last volume. Before then, however, the special glory of the series is revealed. The Eddorians operate through a secret chain of command, a pyramid whose upper reaches are only gradually penetrated by Kinnison and his fellow Lensmen. At the end of each long sequence, they feel that final victory is theirs; but the next sequence, on each occasion, drastically expands the scope of the conflict, introduces new "scientific" concepts, weapons, spaceships and new enemies. It was this massive, controlled sequence of jumps in scale that fascinated most early readers of the series who, because the first section of *Triplanetary* (which explains the overall structure) was added only to the expanded book version, knew no more than Kinnison who the final enemy was, or when the enormous conflict would stop irresistibly expanding. Many readers would associate the sense of wonder they looked for in sf with their first encounter with a Lensman shift in scale. The series is constantly reread; its clumsiness of its style, the awfulness of its female characters, the lunacy of its slang, the racist implications of the Anglo-Saxon breeding programme (with the children of Kinnison and MacDougall destined to rule the universe) seem minor impediments.

EES wrote some rather less popular out-of-series books as well, none having anything like the force of his major effort. A decade after his death, books he had begun or completed in manuscript, or had merely inspired or authorized, began to appear in response to his great posthumous popularity. The "Family d'Alembert" series, for instance, is published as by EES "with Stephen GOLDIN". The first volume, *The Imperial Stars* (1964 *If*; exp. **1976**), is based on published material; the series continues with *Stranglers' Moon* (**1976**), *The Clockwork Traitor* (**1977**) and *Getaway World* (**1977**). William B. Ellern has begun a new series set in the Lensman universe with *New Lensman* (**1977**). EES's reputation has not been helped by these additions to the saga.   [JC]

Other works: *Spacehounds of IPC* (1931 *AMZ*; **1947**); *The Galaxy Primes* (1959 *AMZ*; **1965**); *Subspace Explorers* (1960 *ASF* as "Subspace Survivors"; exp. **1965**); *The Best of E.E. 'Doc' Smith* (coll. **1975**); *Masters of Space* (1961–2 *If*; **1976**) with E. Everett EVANS.

About the author: *The Universes of E.E. Smith* (**1966**) by Ron ELLIK and Bill EVANS; "E.E. Smith" in *Seekers of Tomorrow* (coll. **1966**) by Sam MOSKOWITZ.

See also: COSMOLOGY; CRIME AND PUNISHMENT; FANTASTIC VOYAGES; FOURTH DIMENSON (AND OTHERS); GALACTIC EMPIRES; HEROES; JUPITER; POLITICS; POWER SOURCES; PSYCHOLOGY; SF OVERTAKEN BY EVENTS; SCIENTIFIC ERRORS; SCIENTISTS; SPACE FLIGHT; SPACE OPERA; SPACESHIPS; STARS.

SMITH, EVELYN E. (1927–). American writer and crossword-puzzle compiler. She began publishing sf with "Tea Tray in the Sky" for *Gal.* in 1952, and for about a decade published actively in the magazines, though from about 1960 she has appeared there only infrequently. Her sf novels are *The Perfect Planet* (**1962**), about a planet that was once a health farm, and the unrelated *Unpopular Planet* (**1975**); the second is a comparatively ambitious work, written in a sometimes passable imitation of 18th-century typographical (if not stylistic) practices; it is the memoirs, long after most of the events of the novel, of a human from an overpopulated future Earth, whose contacts with aliens trying to maintain Earth as a breeding-ground for men and other species, lead to picaresque adventures, some of them sexual.   [JC]

See also: COLONIZATION OF OTHER WORLDS.

SMITH, GARRET (? –). American writer and newspaper editor. He was active with sf stories in magazines like *Argosy*, where several novels appeared, though only *Between Worlds* (1919 *Argosy*; **1929**) reached book form; it is a romantic story of relations between Venus and Earth.   [JC]

SMITH, GEORGE H(ENRY) (1922–). American writer of much popular fiction and considerable sf, under his own name and several pseudonyms including Jan Smith, George Hudson Smith, Jan Hudson, Jerry Jason and (with his wife M. Jane Deer) M.J. Deer. He began publishing sf with "The Last Spring" for *Startling Stories* in 1953, and became very active after about 1960, beginning with his first sf novel, *1976 — Year of Terror* (**1961**; vt *The Year for Love*) and continuing in that year with *Scourge of the Blood Cult* (**1961**), *The Coming of the Rats* (**1961**) and *Love Cult* (**1961**) as by Jan Hudson. Some of these early novels are rather negligible, but with *The Four-Day Weekend* (**1966**) he began to strike a more sustained note, and in the following year began his ALTERNATE-WORLD series comprising *Druids' World* (**1967**), *Kar Kaballa, King of the Gogs* (**1969**), *Second War of the Worlds* (**1976**) and the projected title *The Island Snatchers*. The last three volumes of this sequence share the same main characters and make up GHS's major effort at the kind of coloured, near-fantasy sf in which he specializes. Short stories of interest include "The Last Days of L.A." (1959) and "In the Imagicon" (1966), the latter a runner-up for the NEBULA award in 1966. Most of GHS's work is outside the sf field, a fact reflected in the competent but routine quality of much of his sf, though recently he has become visibly more interested in the genre. GHS's wife collaborates on much of his work.   [JC]

Other works: *Doomsday Wing* (**1963**); *The Unending Night* (**1964**); *The Forgotten Planet* (**1965**); *Witch Queen of Lochlann* (**1969**). As M.J. Deer (with his wife): *A Place Named Hell* (**1963**); *Flames of Desire* (**1963**). As Jerry Jason: *Sexodus* (**1963**); *The Psycho Makers* (**1965**).

SMITH, GEORGE HUDSON See George H(enry) SMITH.

SMITH, GEORGE O(LIVER) (1911–). American writer and electronics engineer. He was most active and prominent in the 1940s in *ASF*, for which he wrote his first story in 1942; "QRM — Interplanetary" began both his sf career and his most famous work, the series of stories (all in *ASF*) about a communications space station in the orbit of Venus, 60 degrees ahead of that planet. These stories are assembled as *Venus Equilateral* (coll. of linked stories **1947**; vt *The Complete Venus Equilateral*, 1976, including "Interlude", 1973, as "External Triangle"). They exhibit GOS's main strength, a fascination with technical problems and their didactic explanation, after the fashion of Hugo GERNSBACK and the early *AMZ*; and his main weakness, an almost complete lack of interest in character or plot plausibility. Unfortunately, the technical presuppositions on which he based his communications station have dated very swiftly, considerably reducing the impact of the series on later readers. The stories are written in a cheerful but crude wise-cracking style.

GOS also wrote several SPACE OPERAS whose technical bases have also dated, though this is very much less important in an adventure tale. The best of them, originally published under his occasional pseudonym Wesley Long, was *Nomad* (1944 *ASF*; **1950** under his own name). Like most of his space epics, this story concerns an alien INVASION of the Solar System, in this case by means of a wandering planet. Other similar novels are *Pattern for Conquest* (1946 *ASF*; **1949**) and the inferior *Hellflower* (**1953**). The rocket gimmickry, the sense of space and the kind of protagonists featured in these stories are strongly reminiscent of, though decidedly inferior to, the more expansive galactic stage of E.E. "Doc" SMITH's "Lensman" series, the later volumes of which were serialized in *ASF* at about the same time.

Though GOS wrote several further novels before becoming inactive in 1959 (except for the one "Venus Equilateral" story cited above), he published only one other memorable book, the vivid SUPERMAN story *The Fourth "R"* (**1959**; vt *The Brain Machine* USA). Although the story, of an artificially created child *Homo superior* and his lonely fight to remain independent until adulthood, reflects earlier novels, such as Theodore STURGEON's *The Dreaming Jewels* (**1950**; vt *The Synthetic Man* USA), *The Fourth "R"* so vividly enters into its protagonist's young mind, and so intriguingly details his strategy, that it has become a model for tales of this kind (*see*

also INTELLIGENCE). Another novel that combines both invasion and superman themes is *Highways in Hiding* (**1956**; vt abridged *Space Plague*). Never strongly original, GOS was however an effective expounder of ideas and an enjoyable sf novelist of the second rank. [JC]
Other works: *Operation Interstellar* (**1950**); *Troubled Star* (1953 *Startling Stories*; **1957**); *Fire in the Heavens* (1949 *Startling Stories*; **1958**); *Lost in Space* (1954 *Startling Stories*; **1959**); *The Path of Unreason* (1947 *Startling Stories* as "Kingdom of the Blind"; rev. **1959**).
See also: DISCOVERY AND INVENTION; ECONOMICS; HEROES; MONEY; SCIENTISTS; SUN; TECHNOLOGY.

SMITH, H(ARRY) ALLEN (1907–). American writer, mostly of humorous sketches and books, often for *Saturday Evening Post*, whose sf novel *The Age of the Tail* (**1955**) is a SATIRE depicting the effect on a near-future society of all children being born with tails. [JC]

SMITH, JAN See George H. SMITH.

SMITH, WAYLAND (? – ?). Apparently an English writer, probably pseudonymous, in whose sf novel, *The Machine Stops* (**1936**), metals disintegrate and Man must begin again from savagery. [JC]

SMITH, WOODROW WILSON See Henry KUTTNER.

SNELL, EDMUND (1889– ?). Author of a number of mystery novels and several sf books. The most relevant for sf readers is *Kontrol* (**1928**), in which a mad scientist switches a genius brain into an athlete's body and vice versa; he is in league with a bolshevik agent who has built a fleet of futuristic vertical-take-off aerial juggernauts and a super-city on a secret island with an active volcano. It is a well-written sf thriller, very much of its day. *The Sound Machine* (**1932**) also has a crazed inventor, who uses sound-waves to kill and disintegrate. [MM]
Other works: *The Yellow Seven* (**1923**); *The Yu-Chi Stone* (**1926**); *The White Owl* (**1930**); *The Z Ray* (**1932**); *Blue Murder* (**1933**).
See also: WEAPONS.

SNYDER, CECIL (? –). Author of the sf novel *The Hawks of Arcturus* (**1974**). [JC]

SNYDER, GENE or **E.V.** (? –). American writer and academic, associate professor of humanities at Brookdale Community College. With William Jon WATKINS (*who see for details*), he has written two sf novels, *Ecodeath* (**1972**) as by EVS and *The Litany of Sh'reev* (**1976**) as by GS. [JC]

SNYDER, GUY (1951–). American author and journalist whose sf novel is

Testament XXI (**1973**). [JC]

SOCIAL DARWINISM At its simplest, Social Darwinism is the thesis that social evolution and social history are governed by the same principles that govern the EVOLUTION of species in nature — the "laws" of natural selection. The emergence of such beliefs in concert with Darwin's theory is not surprising. Both Darwin and Wallace had received essential theoretical inspiration from reading the economist Malthus, and Darwin borrowed heavily from the socio-economic theories of Herbert Spencer (who actually coined the phrase "the survival of the fittest"). Spencer once stated that what Darwin had borrowed from socio-economic theory he had "returned with interest", and this was a common view. Political champions of *laissez-faire* capitalism were ready to consider themselves "justified" by "natural law". In opposition, the politics of socialism also found a "scientific" justification in the Marxist theory of history, which "explained" social history as a continuing process of change governed and determined by a dialectical process. Because of this opposition it is often held that Social Darwinism is implicitly associated with right-wing politics, but this is not necessarily so. Similarly, there is no logically necessary connection between Social Darwinism and racism, though many racists have attempted to co-opt the logic of Social Darwinism in support of their prejudices. Because Social Darwinism is only an analogy it is very versatile — its use depends entirely upon which group is to be designated "the fittest". A distinction may be made on grounds of social class, race, INTELLIGENCE or personality.

The most important sf writer who may be termed a Social Darwinist was the socialist H.G. WELLS. Wells had no doubt that the "laws of evolution" discovered by Darwin applied to human society, and his Utopian plans are directed to the design of a "fitter" society. His account of the future evolution of society in *The Time Machine* (**1895**) is based entirely on a crude Darwinian logic, and notions of evolutionary "fitness" are prominent in *A Modern Utopia* (**1905**), where a "struggle for existence" is artificially maintained in the ascetic life of the "samurai", in order to preserve the health and intelligence of the elite. Many of Wells's blueprints for the future assume that a better society can emerge only out of the destruction of the present one, by a process of rigorous winnowing. This scheme — with a supporting logic couched in Darwinian jargon — is found in *The World Set Free* (**1914**), in the account of their history offered by the *Men Like Gods* (**1923**) and in *The Shape of Things to Come* (**1933**). When Wells finally despaired of his world-saving mission it was the logic of Darwinian law that he invoked to condemn society for its failure in *Mind at* *the End of its Tether* (**1945**).

An author whose ideas are rather more typical of Social Darwinism was M.P. SHIEL. In *The Yellow Danger* (**1898**) he imported into the WAR-anticipation genre his brand of pseudo-Darwinian thought, which argued that there must ultimately be a war for possession of the Earth between the different races of Man. He was prepared to dismiss the black and brown races as outsiders and deal with the ultimate conflict between white and yellow. This theme recurred in his work through *The Yellow Wave* (**1905**) and *The Dragon* (**1913**; rev. vt *The Yellow Peril* 1929). On a more parochial level, the persistent anti-Semitism in his works is also "justified" in terms of inferior heredity. Another theme common in his works is that of the "overman" — a superior breed of man destined to inherit the Earth and rule or annihilate inferior types. This is most clearly stated in *The Young Men are Coming* (**1937**).

The harsher versions of Social Darwinism have been fiercely attacked in imaginative fiction. Hugh MacCoLL's *Mr. Stranger's Sealed Packet* (**1889**) has an Earthman on Mars attempting to save the peaceful Grensumin from the predations of a "superior" race, and this is a plot which has been echoed many times since in sf. Claude FARRERE's *Useless Hands* (**1926**) presents a lurid warning of the ultimate effects of applying Darwinian logic to human society as the capitalists slaughter the workers on a large scale. Raymond Z. GALLUN's "Old Faithful" (**1934**) from the early sf PULPS is a powerful anti-Darwinian parable. The most furious attack on Social Darwinism found in literature is that mounted by C.S. LEWIS in his trilogy *Out of the Silent Planet* (**1938**), *Perelandra* (**1943**; vt *Voyage to Venus*) and *That Hideous Strength* (**1945**; vt *The Tortured Planet* USA). The last volume, in which the organization N.I.C.E. begins to mould British society along Social Darwinist lines, is the most direct.

In magazine sf, where there has always been a lot of thinking by analogy, the logic of Social Darwinism has cropped up continually, but rather inconsistently. The one writer who has persistently invoked such logic in support of political statements is Robert A. HEINLEIN. The assumptions of Social Darwinism shape many of his attitudes — notably the attitude to ALIENS displayed in *The Puppet Master* (**1951**) and *Starship Troopers* (**1959**), and the rugged social theory of TANSTAAFL (There Ain't No Such Thing As A Free Lunch) propounded in *The Moon is a Harsh Mistress* (**1966**). Alexei PANSHIN offers an analysis of Heinlein's views on liberty in his *Heinlein in Dimension* (**1968**), but the essence of the philosophy is extracted by Heinlein himself for the collection of aphorisms called "The Notebooks of Lazarus Long" in *Time Enough for Love* (**1973**), which includes such observations as: "All

societies are based on rules to protect pregnant women and children. All else is surplusage."; "Racial survival is the only universal morality"; and "Beware of altruism. It is based on self-deception, the root of all evil."

Heinlein is not the only magazine sf writer whose political views are right-wing and tough-minded, but he is the only major one to make consistent use of this type of supportive logic. Poul ANDERSON's politics are clearly based on more pragmatic grounds — the belief that capitalism is best because it works best, and the same is true of Jerry POURNELLE. It is also true of the writer outside the genre who is most extreme politically — Ayn RAND, author of the vitriolic *Anthem* (**1938**; abridged 1946) and *Atlas Shrugged* (**1957**). A much more difficult person to judge is John W. CAMPBELL Jr who, as editor of *ASF*, did much to encourage a right-wing bias in sf during the 1940s and '50s. In his own sf there is little evidence of Darwinian thinking misapplied in a social context except for his constant adherence to the common myth that society becomes decadent if the living is too easy. The same seems to be true of his editorials at least until the mid-1950s (his editorial on "Evolution" for July 1951 argues strongly against a biological supportive logic for aggression in human society). In later years, however, Campbell seemed to select his arguments with different prejudices, and he became somewhat more kindly disposed to any argument which might be called up to support his tough thinking. In his occasional defences of slavery as an institution he was ready to assume a justification on the grounds of biological inferiority — as evidenced by his enthusiasm with regard to Lloyd BIGGLE Jr's *The World Menders* (**1971**). Curiously, one writer apart from Heinlein in whose novels Social Darwinist principles are overt is Lester DEL REY, whose early short stories in the 1940s showed a very strong humanist outlook. The novels in question include *Police Your Planet* (**1956** as by Erik van Lhin; rev. 1975 as by Lester del Rey and Erik van Lhin) and *The Eleventh Commandment* (**1962**; rev. 1970). Perhaps the single most extreme example of the Social Darwinist perspective is found in L. Ron HUBBARD's *Return to Tomorrow* (1950; **1954**), whose conclusion states that Man's expansion into the galaxy should be accompanied by the genocide of all alien races who might prove to be "competitors". On the whole, however, this viewpoint is one which is vigorously attacked throughout the spectrum of contemporary sf. [BS]

See also: ECONOMICS; EVOLUTION; HISTORY IN SF; POLITICS; SOCIOLOGY.

SOCIAL ENGINEERING *See* ANTHROPOLOGY; COLONIZATION OF OTHER WORLDS; ICONOCLASM; POLITICS; SOCIOLOGY.

SOCIOLOGY Sociology is the systematic study of society and social relationships. The word was coined by Comte in the mid-19th century, and it was in this period that the first attempts were made to divorce studies of society, to some extent, from dogmatic political and ethical presuppositions, employing instead the scientific method. Social studies in a more general sense have, of course, a much longer history, going back to PLATO.

One of the precursors of sociology was UTOPIAN philosophy, which often used literary forms — most commonly the imaginary voyage — for the imaginative modelling of ideal societies (*see* FANTASTIC VOYAGES, PROTO SF). Such models are available for evaluation and criticism; this may be regarded as a crude form of hypothesis-testing. The history of the Utopian novel shows that more and more reliance came to be placed on ways of constructing narratives and creating personal relationships in order to evaluate the "quality of life" in these hypothetical societies. The increasing use of such purely literary strategies in the late 19th century is not irrelevant to the decline of Utopian thinking and the rise of the DYSTOPIAS.

In common with Utopian novels, sf — which deals extensively in the imaginative construction of societies, human and non-human — is an implicitly sociological literature. Certain assumptions must go into the building of these societies, and these assumptions are quasi-sociological in kind. They are hypotheses, and the attempt to construct a narrative which evaluates — and usually tracks the changes within — such imaginary societies is a crude method of assessing the hypothesis. This is not (except in very rare cases) the prime purpose of the sf writer, but it is nevertheless an aspect of his work. In investigating "sociological themes" in sf we are really examining the fruits of this process rather than examining the influence of sociology itself upon speculative thought in sf (as we do, for instance, in discussing biological themes in sf, where the science itself has directly fed into the literature). The actual influence of academic sociology, at least on Anglo-American sf, has been virtually negligible. The only work of any significance which appears to have been based on a formal sociological thesis is Keith ROBERTS's *Pavane* (coll. of linked stories **1968**) which employs Max Weber's thesis concerning the complicity of capitalism and the protestant ethic in its depiction of an ALTERNATE WORLD in which modern Europe remains under Catholic domination. Sf writers have seldom borrowed from sociologists (though they have borrowed from economists and cultural anthropologists), but have preferred to rely upon their own intuitive judgements regarding society and social relationships. Whether or not this has been to the detriment of sf is a matter of opinion.

It is remarkable how close sf stories may come to being thought-experiments in sociology, and some are framed in exactly that way. Philip WYLIE's *The Disappearance* (1951) is an experiment pure and simple, as is the account of the factory-society run according to the tenet of "from each according to his ability, to each according to his need" in Ayn RAND's *Atlas Shrugged* (1957). Poul ANDERSON's "The Helping Hand" (1950) carefully compares the fortunes of two conquered cultures, one of which accepts economic aid from its conquerors, while the other — the "control" group — does not. Many speculative novels from Grant ALLEN's *The British Barbarians* (1895) through Aldous HUXLEY's *Brave New World* (1932) and Eden PHILLPOTTS's *Saurus* (1938) to Theodore STURGEON's *Venus Plus X* (1960) introduce an "objective observer" of some kind into a social situation in order to "evaluate" it (*see also* SATIRE). The first such exercise was probably Benjamin Disraeli's *The Voyage of Captain Popanilla* (1828), whose hero is a naïve savage brought into the mock-England of Vraibleusia. Allen's hero is a man of the future brought back to the present, Huxley's a "savage" from the present taken into the future promised in J.B.S. HALDANE's essay *Daedalus* (1923). *Saurus* is an alien, while superhuman viewpoints are used by J.D. BERESFORD in *The Hampdenshire Wonder* (1911; vt *The Wonder* USA) and Olaf STAPLEDON in *Odd John* (1935). Sturgeon's hero is taken to a pseudo-Utopian future, while the hero of Ursula K. LE GUIN's *The Left Hand of Darkness* (1969) is cast adrift in an alien society. In genre sf too the strategy may be reversed, with men of the future or visitors from alien society casting an eye over our world, as in Robert HEINLEIN's *Stranger in a Strange Land* (1961) or Robert SILVERBERG's *The Masks of Time* (1968; vt *Vornan-19* UK). It is precisely this kind of experimental observation which is impractical in the real world (except in cultural ANTHROPOLOGY), for the sociologist is himself culture-bound and unable to achieve the alienated viewpoint of the objective observer, while future society and alien society are implicitly beyond his grasp. The natural scientist does not, for the most part, encounter similar problems. For this reason the relationship between the social sciences and speculative fiction is markedly different from that between the natural sciences and speculative fiction. In the latter case the relationship is a simple matter of ideas generated by the natural sciences becoming starting points for speculative fantasy. In the former case, speculative fiction may actually try to accomplish what the practical science cannot, and becomes itself the generator, rather than the borrower, of ideas. Whether the ideas may then be "fed back" into ways of thinking about the real world is dubious, but it is certainly true that Huxley's *Brave New World* and George ORWELL's *Nineteen Eighty-Four* (1949) have had considerable influence on attitudes to social trends, and that some modern social theorists have built literary models in support of their own ideas — notably B.F. SKINNER in *Walden Two* (1948) and the sociologist of education Michael YOUNG in *The Rise of the Meritocracy* (1958). (The latter work, however, is a Dystopia; Young supports his ideas by presenting the coldness of opposite ideas in action.) An American sociologist, Richard OFSHE, has presented an anthology of sf stories, together with useful commentary, as a textbook on *The Sociology of the Possible* (anth. 1970), while at a much cruder level John Milstead, Martin Harry GREENBERG, Joseph D. Olander and Patricia Warrick have compiled two anthologies as teaching aids in sociology: *Sociology Through Science Fiction* (anth. 1974) and *Social Problems Through Science Fiction* (anth. 1975).

Most model societies in imaginative fiction tend to be classified by modern critics into Utopias and Dystopias, largely because this is the only system of categories which has so far been made available. It serves moderately well for literary models built outside genre sf, but is really quite incompetent to deal with those built within it. The persistent attempt to sort out genre sf stories into Utopias and Dystopias often serves to distort the true nature of the attempts which the authors are making. Genre sf writers are very rarely concerned with trying to design ideal societies, and although they do have a tendency to offer dire polemical warnings about the way the world is going, the extent to which their visions may be described as simply Dystopian has also been exaggerated. Sf writers often try to envisage forms of society which are quite simply *possible* — they build for the sheer joy of building, and commonly take an ironic delight in the building that has been construed by many critics (aptly but not entirely accurately) as SATIRE. To gain a full understanding of what sf writers have actually done — and thus to be able to judge what potential there might be in sf as a sociological art form — we need a much more complex and delicate system of categorization than is implied by terms like "Utopia", "Dystopia" and "satire". Perhaps, in the near future, someone will provide such a theoretical instrument.

One of the earliest examples of a hypothetical social model (variously mislabelled a satire and a Dystopia) is *The Revolt of Man* (1882) by Walter BESANT — the archetype of a whole subgenre of stories which depict female-dominated societies. Its assumptions regarding the structure and fortunes of the society clearly reveal the main tenets of Victorian male chauvinism, and it is interesting to compare the work with recent explorations of the same theme — e.g. Edmund COOPER's *Five to Twelve* (1968) and Robert BLOCH's *Ladies' Day* (1968). This is one of the commonest themes in social modelling (*see* Sam MOSKOWITZ's "When Women Rule" in his *Strange Horizons*, coll. 1976), its products outnumbered only by those inspired by the political movements grouped under the headings of "socialism" and "fascism" (*see* DYSTOPIAS, POLITICS).

The first model of a *purely* hypothetical society — an ALIEN society — is H.G. WELLS's *The First Men in the Moon* (1901). It takes as its model the social organization of the ant-hive, and this has remained a common reference for social design in sf (*see* DYSTOPIAS; HIVE-MINDS).

We may group the two types of speculative exercise represented by *The Revolt of Man* and *The First Men in the Moon* under the heading "the distorted society". Alien societies are usually — but not always — more distorted than the peculiar human ones envisaged in sf, but the two form a continuum rather than two separate groups. Outside the genre distorted societies are used almost entirely to Dystopian or satirical ends but inside the genre, as with these two classic examples, the distortion becomes an end in itself, to be subject to scrutiny and evaluation. Alien societies *have* been used in sf for satirical purposes — Stanton A. COBLENTZ made a habit of it in such works as *Hidden World* (1935; 1957 vt *In Caverns Below*) and *The Blue Barbarians* (1931; 1958) — but this is comparatively rare. Examples of non-human societies in sf are so numerous that any list has to be highly selective, but some of the most important ones are: Clifford D. SIMAK's *City* (1944–51; fix-up 1952); L. Sprague DE CAMP's *Rogue Queen* (1951); Philip José FARMER's *The Lovers* (1952; exp. 1961); James BLISH's "A Case of Conscience" (1953); Poul ANDERSON's *War of the Wing-Men* (1958; vt *The Man Who Counts*) and *The People of the Wind* (1973); Brian W. ALDISS's *The Dark Light Years* (1964) and Isaac ASIMOV's *The Gods Themselves* (1972). Of all these only one — the Aldiss novel — really invites description as a satire, and none are Utopian or Dystopian. The same applies to distorted human societies. Again, the list is selective, but some of the most notable are: Wyman GUIN's "Beyond Bedlam" (1951); Frederik POHL and C.M. KORNBLUTH's *The Space Merchants* (1953); James GUNN's *The Joy Makers* (1955; fix-up 1961); Jack VANCE's *The Languages of Pao* (1958), Harlan ELLISON's "Eyes of Dust" (1959); Alexei PANSHIN's *Rite of Passage* (1963; exp. 1968); Ursula K. LE GUIN's *The Left Hand of Darkness* (1969) and John JAKES's *Mask of Chaos* (1970) and Samuel R. DELANY's *Triton* (1976). All of these are primarily analytical — even *The Space Merchants*, whose reputation as a satirical work misrepresents it. Implicit in all these stories, whatever their immediate dramatic purpose, are statements about society and social possibility.

One of the commonest forms of sociological thought-experiment in sf is that of taking society apart and building it up again. Many stories of this type are discussed in DISASTER and HOLOCAUST AND AFTER. Classic examples include S. Fowler WRIGHT's *Deluge* **(1928)** and *Dawn* **(1929)**, George R. STEWART's painstaking *Earth Abides* **(1949)** and Walter M. MILLER's *A Canticle for Leibowitz* (1955–7; fix-up **1960**). The pattern of social disintegration is subject to detailed scrutiny in William GOLDING's *Lord of the Flies* **(1954)** while the building of a society from scratch is featured — in a genuinely satirical fashion — in E.C. LARGE's *Dawn in Andromeda* **(1956)**. Individual investigations of the theme range from outright horror stories — e.g. Rudoph WURLITZER's *Quake* **(1972)** — to romantic fictions strongly reminiscent of the classic desert island castaway stories, or ROBINSONADES. The BBC TV series SURVIVORS (1975–7) steers an uneasy course between realism and romanticism.

So far we have been concerned exclusively with holistic sociological perspectives. When we refine our consideration to sf whose concerns are similar to those of particular narrow fields within sociology it is not so easy to find examples. Martin Harry Greenberg and his associates, in collecting stories for their two anthologies, were often unable to find suitable stories on particular themes. There is an abundance of stories bearing upon the sociology of RELIGION, including Robert Heinlein's "If This Goes On ..." (1940) and *Sixth Column* (1941 as by Anson MacDonald; **1949**; vt *The Day After Tomorrow*); Miller's *A Canticle for Leibowitz*; Poul Anderson's "The Problem of Pain" (1973), Gerald Jonas's "The Shaker Revival" (1970), and even two novelettes by Bertrand RUSSELL: "Zahatopolk" (1954) and "Faith and Mountains" (1954). Curiously, though, there is no such abundance of stories relating to the sociology of science, though Asimov's *The Gods Themselves* has some useful observations and there is a neat story by Howard L. MYERS entitled "Out, Wit!" (1972). On the sociology of education, the sociology of the mass media *et al.* there is relatively little in sf that seems relevant (*though see* MEDIA LANDSCAPE; COMMUNICATIONS; ARTS). There is, however, a brief but classic commentary on applied sociology in Katherine MACLEAN's "The Snowball Effect" (1952), about a sociologist who draws up an incentive scheme which permits the Watashaw Ladies Sewing Circle to recruit the entire world (via techniques that later materialized in the real world as "pyramid selling").

It has been argued that there has been a distinct shift in the focus of interest of genre sf, and that whereas the magazine writers were once interested almost exclusively in inventions and scientific "hardware", they are now interested primarily in social problems. This shift in emphasis has not, in fact, been caused by any exhaustion of the possibilities inherent in the hard sciences, or even any exhaustion in the interest which sf writers take in those sciences. The change has been very largely caused by the fact that in the 1920s and '30s sf writers tended to be extremely complacent about the direction in which society was evolving — the face of the future did not seem to be particularly enigmatic or disturbing. Over the years, however, and particularly since the Second World War, that complacency has vanished. The social situations of tomorrow can no longer be taken for granted, so that the problems we can now anticipate are no longer primarily connected with new scientific toys. The primacy of social problems, and the fact that social issues will determine the context in which inventions will be made and used, has been clearly recognized. As Alvin TOFFLER points out in *Future Shock* **(1970)**, the future is now so much closer because the rate of change has accelerated so rapidly. The steadily growing interest in sf may, in fact, be one symptom of this acceleration of social change ... and if this is so then the academic study of sf (*see* SF IN THE CLASSROOM), now entrenched in most American universities, might perhaps have more to offer sociologists than students of literature *per se*. Even if one were to overlook or deny the role of social change as an important factor in the evolution of sf, it would still retain its essential interest as a medium for sociological thought-experiments. [BS]
See also: CITIES; HISTORY IN SF; LIFE ON OTHER WORLDS; LINGUISTICS; POLITICS; SEX; SOCIAL DARWINISM; TABOOS; WOMEN.

SOFT SF This not very precise term is generally applied either to sf which deals with the SOFT SCIENCES, or to sf which does not deal with recognizable science at all, but emphasizes human feelings. The term is usually opposed to HARD SF or HARDCORE SF, but often not used logically. Stories of PSIONIC POWERS or SUPERMEN have little to do with real science and more to do with PSEUDO-SCIENCE, or IMAGINARY SCIENCE, but such stories are nevertheless regularly regarded by sf readers as hard sf. The NEW WAVE has been generally associated with soft sf. [PN]

SOFT SCIENCES In academic slang, and sf TERMINOLOGY, the soft sciences are those which deal mainly with biology and human affairs — very often the sciences which require little or no hardware for their carrying out. (Some would claim BIOLOGY as a hard science.) Theme entries in this volume which deal directly or indirectly with soft sciences are ANTHROPOLOGY, ECOLOGY, ECONOMICS, EVOLUTION, FUTUROLOGY, INTELLIGENCE, LINGUISTICS, MEDICINE, PERCEPTION, PSYCHOLOGY and SOCIOLOGY. The soft sciences very often work through statistics, and hard scientists have been known to despise them for their lack of rigour and their occasional difficulty in attaining respectable results. Sociology has been much criticized for this reason, whether fairly or not. Sf which deals primarily with the soft sciences is sometimes known as "soft sf", and it most commonly deals with questions of sociology and psychology. [PN]

SOHL, JERRY Form of his name used by American writer and former journalist Gerald Allan Sohl (1913–), active from about 1950 in sf and other genres as JS and under various pseudonyms, including Nathan Butler and Sean Mei Sullivan. He has done much TV work, including scripts for STAR TREK, THE TWILIGHT ZONE and THE OUTER LIMITS, under various names; as an sf writer he began publishing with "The 7th Order" for *Gal.* in 1952, and soon released his first novel, *The Haploids* **(1952)**. The books for which he is still best known in sf followed in short succession: *The Transcendent Man* **(1953)**, *Costigan's Needle* **(1953)**, *The Altered Ego* **(1954)** and *Point Ultimate* **(1955)**; all share a polished popular style, considerable narrative ingenuity and sf interest as well. *Costigan's Needle* deals with the colonizing of a PARALLEL WORLD; *The Altered Ego* combines a mystery plot and a form of IMMORTALITY via personality recordings, though without the concept of CLONING the technology of transference is unwieldy compared to later uses of the same basic idea, as in John VARLEY's *The Ophiuchi Hotline* **(1977)**. JS's sf output began to slacken in the late 1950s, though he remained active in other areas, several non-sf novels being published as by Nathan Butler. Of his later sf, *The Odious Ones* **(1959)** and *Night Slaves* **(1970)**, which was later televised, best show his combination of slick style and ingenuity. [JC]
Other works: *The Mars Monopoly* **(1956)**; *The Time Dissolver* **(1957)**; *One Against Herculum* **(1959)**; *The Anomaly* **(1971)**; *I, Aleppo* **(1976)**.

SOLARIS Film (1972). Mosfilm. Directed by Andrei Tarkovsky, starring Donatas Banionis, Natalia Bondarchuk, Youri Yarvet and Anatoli Solintsin. Screenplay by Andrei Tarkovsky and Friedrich Gorenstein, based on the novel by Stanislaw LEM. 165 mins (version released in USA cut to 132). Colour.

This extremely long and ambitious rendering of Lem's metaphysical novel is regarded by many critics as among the finest sf films yet produced, although a minority opinion sees it as tediously slow-moving. The film shifts the emphasis of the book from the intellectual to the emotional, partly by restructuring the narrative, which in the film begins with a

Donatas Banionis as the baffled hero in the bedraggled space station orbiting the planet SOLARIS.

protracted sequence on Earth, mainly at the country house of the young space-scientist hero's parents, shot with a pervasive attention to a kind of elegiac nostalgia and focusing on the scientist's relation with his father. The film then moves to the space-station orbiting the planet Solaris, whose ever changing ocean, which throws up evanescent islands, is thought to be organic and sentient. The scientist finds the station in disrepair and his colleagues demoralized by the materialization of solid, fleshly "phantoms" of their innermost obsessions, and soon he is himself haunted by a reincarnation of his suicided wife; these phantoms may be an attempt at communication by Solaris. At first horrified, he kills the phantom, but a replica arrives that night; ultimately he recognizes that, no matter what its source, she is both living and lovable; while he sleeps she connives at her own exorcism. Solaris remains an enigma; at the end it recreates on its surface the Russian house, and the scientist sees his father through a window, obscured and sundered from him by streaming water. The philosophical questions are not put so sharply as in the book, but the visual images are haunting; the leitmotivs of water, visual screens, snow and technology are used with great sophistication.   [PN]

SOLAR WIND This technical term has found much favour in sf TERMINOLOGY, though it did not originate in sf. The sun is constantly emitting particles, and also, of course, light, which can itself be envisaged as composed of tiny particles, photons. These particles, whether of matter or light, can be envisaged as exerting a gentle outward pressure (which is why the tail of a comet always points away from the sun). A light spacecraft with a huge, incredibly thin and gossamer metal sail, perhaps made of aluminium, could take advantage of this pressure just as a yacht uses wind. Hence the proliferation of rather charming space-sailing stories in the past two decades, ever since the idea was popularized by scientists.   [PN]

SOLO, JAY See Harlan ELLISON.

SOMERS, BART See Gardner F. Fox.

SOMERS, JONATHAN SWIFT III See Philip José FARMER.

SON OF KONG Film (1933). RKO. Directed by Ernest B. Schoedsack, starring Robert Armstrong, Helen Mack, Frank Reicher and Noble Johnson. Screenplay by Ruth Rose. 70 mins. B/w.
This film was made immediately after KING KONG, as a small-scale sequel. The hero returns to Skull Island and discovers Kong's son, a 20-foot-high white ape with all the characteristics of a friendly puppy. Various prehistoric monsters make their appearance before a volcanic upheaval destroys the island. The ape saves the hero by holding him above the encroaching flood waters — an act which would certainly have earned him the disapproval of his late father. Good special effects by Willis H. O'Brien do not obscure the fact that the film is an obvious rush job, made to cash in on the success of King Kong.   [JB]

SOREL, EDWARD (1929–). American illustrator and writer, in whose *Moon Missing: An Illustrated Guide to the Future* (1962) the Moon disappears, the 1960s are satirized, and the illustrations are more satisfyingly vindictive than the text.   [PN]

SOUTH, CLARK See Dwight V. SWAIN.

SOUTH AMERICA See SPAIN, PORTUGAL AND SOUTH AMERICA.

SOUTHWOLD, STEPHEN Real name of the writer better known as Neil Bell, and used by him on some children's books. See Neil BELL for details.   [PN]

SOUZA, STEVEN M. (1953–). American writer whose routine sf novel is *The Espers* (1972).   [JC]

SOWDEN, LEWIS (1905–). English-born South African writer and newspaperman. His *Tomorrow's Comet* (1951) brings the END OF THE WORLD and considerable distress to its people beforehand.   [JC/PN]
Other works: *The Man who was Emperor* (1946).

SOYLENT GREEN Film (1973). MGM. Directed by Richard Fleischer, starring Charlton Heston, Edward G. Robinson, Leigh Taylor-Young, Chuck Connors, Joseph Cotten and Paula Kelly. Screenplay by Stanley R. Greenberg, based on the novel *Make Room! Make Room!* (1966) by Harry HARRISON. 97 mins. Colour.
A police detective in the New York of AD 2022 investigates what appears to be a routine murder and discovers that "soylent green", the main food for the world's population, is actually made from dead human bodies. The plot has little to do with the book (Harrison has spoken eloquently of what he sees as the perversion of his work), but the vision of a nightmarish, overpopulated and polluted New York is recreated almost intact. *SG* is unusual for an sf film in that its future setting is a logical extrapolation of the present rather than the usual unrelated limbo featured in such films as LOGAN'S RUN and ZARDOZ. The cannibalism theme, however, is there purely for shock value; it makes no rational sense. Indeed Harrison coined the word "soylent" from "soy beans" and "lentils"; his book has no cannibalism and the people of his future are largely and necessarily vegetarian. Edward G. Robinson's performance, the last before he died, is one of his finest.   [JB/PN]

SPACE ADVENTURES See SPACE ADVENTURES (CLASSICS).

SPACE ADVENTURES (CLASSICS) One of the reprint DIGEST-size magazines published by Sol Cohen's Ultimate Publishing Co. Six issues, Winter 1970-Summer 1971. The title was changed to *Space Adventures* after the first two. The numbering began, strangely, with no.9, apparently picking up where SCIENCE

FICTION (ADVENTURE) CLASSICS left off, and *SAC* would be regarded as simply a variant title of the latter if it were not that *Science Fiction (Adventure) Classics* resumed publication, also in Winter 1970, with no.12. *SAC* was numbered 9–14. Most of its stories were reprinted from AMAZING STORIES from the period of Raymond PALMER's editorship.   [BS]

SPACE CHILDREN, THE Film (1957). Paramount. Directed by Jack ARNOLD, starring Adam Williams, Peggy Webber, Johnny Crawford and Jackie Coogan. Screenplay by Bernard C. Schoenfeld, story by Tom Filer. 69 mins. B/w.

This was the last of Jack Arnold's cycle of sf films with producer William Alland, though on this occasion the studio was Paramount, not Universal. A group of children are "taken over" by a benign alien resembling a glowing brain (which expands as the film progresses). Its aim is to use the children in the sabotage of a missile project on which their parents are working. Arnold makes his usual evocative use of landscape — this time a remote beach.   [JB]

SPACE FACT AND FICTION British PULP-size magazine. Eight monthly issues, Mar.-Oct. 1954, several undated, published by G.G. Swan, London; no editor named. *SFAF* published reprints from wartime issues of FUTURE FICTION and SCIENCE FICTION, slanted towards the juvenile reader. An album of unsold copies, in jumbled order, was issued, presumably as a Christmas annual. [FHP]

SPACE FLIGHT Flight into space is the classic theme in sf. The lunar romances of Francis GODWIN, CYRANO DE BERGERAC *et al.* are the works most commonly and readily identified as literary ancestors of sf. In modern times, as genre sf spilled out of print into the CINEMA, RADIO and TELEVISION, many of the archetypal works produced for these media were romances of space travel: the films THINGS TO COME (1936) and 2001: A SPACE ODYSSEY (1968); Charles CHILTON's BBC radio serial *Journey Into Space* (1953) and its sequels; and TV's STAR TREK (1966–8). The landing of *Apollo 11* on the MOON was seen by many as "science fiction come true". It is natural that sf should be symbolized by the theme of space flight, in that sf is primarily concerned with transcending imaginative boundaries, with breaking free of the gravitational force which holds consciousness to a traditional core of belief and expectancy. The means by which space flight has been achieved in sf (*see* SPACESHIPS) have always been of secondary importance to the mythical impact of the theme. Only a handful of writers — most notably Konstantin TSIOLKOVSKY — actually attempted to embody real scientific ideas in fictional form for the purpose of popularization (*see* ROCKETS).

If one is pedantic, it is by no means easy to trace the origins of the theme. All the early lunar voyages are stories of *flight* rather than *space flight*, in that their authors took for granted the continuity of the atmospheric ether. None of the early travellers had to contend with the barrier of interplanetary vacuum — and this applies even to Edgar Allan POE's "The Unparalleled Adventure of One Hans Pfaall" (1835; rev. 1840), though it was the first of the traveller's tales in which the protagonist takes elaborate precautions to provide himself with air, in recognition of the tenuousness of the sublunar atmosphere.

All the romances of interplanetary flight prior to "Hans Pfaall" are didactic — either straightforwardly, after the fashion of Johannes KEPLER's *Somnium* (1634 in Latin) and Gabriel Daniel's *Voyage du monde de Descartes* (1690; trans. as *A Voyage to the World of Cartesius* 1692), or satirically, after the fashion of Cyrano's *L'autre monde* (1657–62; trans. as *Other Worlds*) and Daniel DEFOE's *The Consolidator* (1705). Poe's story is a satire, but the author also advanced claims as to its verisimilitude.

Jules VERNE, in *De la terre à la lune* (1865), also put the priority on verisimilitude, and its sequel, *Autour de la lune* (1870), is a travelogue similar in kind to his Earthbound imaginary voyages; the two were together translated as *From the Earth to the Moon* (trans. 1873). Most of the other major 19th-century romances of space flight are didactic, although purely adventurous motives are evident in Robert CROMIE's *A Plunge into Space* (1890) and some similar works. Today, looking back at these works, it is possible to invest them with the same mythical significance that sf has more recently lent to the notion of space travel, but this is something the stories have acquired with the passage ot time; they had no such significance in their own day. The story of flight into space could not and did not come to symbolize the ethos of sf until the genre had been identified and demarcated by Hugo GERNSBACK — and even then, it was not a strategic move on Gernsback's part. He was primarily interested in the future and the general effect of TECHNOLOGY on history — space travel was, to him, only one among a whole series of probable developments. It was

SPACE FLIGHT has always been the dominating theme on covers of *Analog*, with great ships thrusting and aspiring as in this example by Jack Gaughan, Dec. 1975.

because of the kind of impact sf made with the readers who discovered it — young readers, for the most part — that space flight became its central myth. Many sf readers found in sf a kind of revelation: a sudden mind-opening shock. This was not the effect of any single story but the discovery of sf as a category, a genre of fictions presenting an infinity of possibilities. It is because of this element of revelation, the sudden awareness of a vast range of possibilities, that the appeal of early sf has come to be symbolized by stories of escape from Earth into a universe full of worlds: the first SPACE OPERAS, notably E.E. "Doc" SMITH's *Skylark of Space* (1928; **1946**).

As with other themes in sf, the post-War period saw considerable sophistication of the myth. Significantly, and perhaps contrary to popular belief, there was relatively little development in verisimilitude outside the work of one or two technically adept authors. The most significant post-War stories related to the theme are not so much stories about space flight as commentaries upon the myth itself — concerned with imaginative horizons rather than hardware. One of the earliest examples of this kind of commentary is Ray BRADBURY's "King of the Gray Spaces" (1943; vt "R is for Rocket"), and the classics of the species are Robert A. HEINLEIN's "The Man Who Sold the Moon" (1950) and Arthur C. CLARKE's *Prelude to Space* (**1951**). Others include Murray LEINSTER's "The Story of Rod Cantrell" (1949), Fredric BROWN's *The Lights in the Sky are Stars* (**1953**; vt *Project Jupiter* UK), Walter M. MILLER's "Death of a Spaceman" (1954; vt "Memento Homo") and Dean McLAUGHLIN's *The Man Who Wanted Stars* (1956–7; fix-up **1965**). The mythic significance of the theme is most obvious in a story in which "space flight" is, from the viewpoint of the reader, purely metaphorical: James BLISH's "Surface Tension" (1952), in which a microscopic man builds himself a protective shell and forces his way up through the surface of a pond into the open air. Also notable is a short story by Edmond HAMILTON, "The Pro" (1964), in which an ageing sf writer meets up with the reality of the myth when his son goes into space.

Sf writers often became annoyed when, following Neil Armstrong's Moon landing, they were asked what they would find to write about in the future. But there was, in fact, a subtle change which overcame sf during the course of the Apollo programme. Since then, stories about space flight within the solar system have been "demystified", and now we have a generation of stories in which spacemen operating within a "real" context come into conflict with the myth: Barry MALZBERG's *The Falling Astronauts* (**1971**), Nigel BALCHIN's *Kings of Infinite Space* (**1967**) and Ludek PESEK's *The Earth Is Near* (**1970**; trans.

Barry Morse and Martin Landau probably have good reason to look worried in the TV series SPACE 1999.

1974) are examples. The myth of transcending the closed world of the known and familiar (*see also* CONCEPTUAL BREAKTHROUGH) must now be tied specifically to interstellar travel — as in the Clarke-KUBRICK film 2001: A SPACE ODYSSEY, Poul ANDERSON's *Tau Zero* (1967; exp. **1970**) or Brian STABLEFORD's *Man in a Cage* (**1975**) — or to entirely different symbols: contact with ALIEN beings, or evolutionary transcendence (*see* SUPERMAN). [BS]

See also: FASTER THAN LIGHT; GALACTIC EMPIRES.

SPACE MAIDENS *See* STAR MAIDENS.

SPACE 1999 Television series (1975–7). A Gerry Anderson Production for ITC. Created by Gerry and Sylvia Anderson. Producers: Sylvia Anderson (first season) and Fred Freiberger (second season); executive producer: Gerry Anderson; story consultant: Christopher Penfold; special effects: Brian Johnson. 50 mins per episode. Colour.

This British-made series, created by the Andersons, who had previously produced such TV series as *Supercar*, *Fireball XL5*, *Captain Scarlett*, THUNDERBIRDS (all with puppets), UFO and *The Protectors* (both live action) and the sf movie JOURNEY TO THE FAR SIDE OF THE SUN, was obviously inspired in part by the success of STAR TREK. Here, too, the format involves a group of people travelling through the galaxy, visiting different planets and encountering strange life forms, but where the *Star Trek* characters travelled on a spaceship the *Space 1999* characters do their interplanetary wandering on Earth's runaway Moon — an unwieldy gimmick that must have caused many frustrations to the writers. Despite excellent special effects and imaginative sets the series as a whole was strangely lifeless and bland, a fault that seems to beset most Anderson productions. The characters were

stereotyped and the scripts humourless. The other major flaw with the series was a disregard for basic science which many critics saw as scandalous; stars are confused with asteroids, the Moon's progress through space follows no physical laws and PARSECS are assumed to be a unit of velocity. The series was cancelled in 1977. The regular cast included Martin Landau, Barbara Bain, Barry Morse (first series only), Nick Tate, Catherine Schell, Tony Anholt and Zienia Merton. Directors included Ray Austin, Lee H. Katzin, Charles Crichton, David Tomblin, Bob Kellett, Val Guest and Bob Brooks. Writers included Christopher Penfold, Johnny Byrne, Donald James, Tom Clegg, Tony Barwick and Charles Woodgrove. A book about the series is *The Making of Space 1999: a Gerry Anderson Production* (**1976**) by Tim Heald. [JB]

SPACE OPERA When radio was the principal medium of entertainment in the USA, certain long-running serials presenting a constant routine of domestic crises were dubbed "soap operas" because they were sponsored by companies making household goods, including soap powders. The name was generalized to refer to any corny domestic drama. Westerns were then dubbed "horse operas" by false analogy. The pattern was extended into sf terminology by WILSON TUCKER in 1941, who proposed "space opera" as the appropriate term for the "hacky, grinding, stinking, outworn spaceship yarn". Though the term still retains some of its pejorative qualities it is often used today with nostalgic affection, loosely applicable to any space adventure story, but particularly to those in which the scale of the action is extravagant.

The term can be applied retrospectively to such early space adventures as Robert William COLE's *The Struggle for Empire* (**1900**) but as it was coined as a complaint against literary naïvety and pulp CLICHÉ it seems more reasonable to limit its use to genre sf. There were five writers principally involved in the development of space opera in the 1920s and '30s. E.E. "Doc" SMITH made his début with the exuberant interstellar adventure *The Skylark of Space* (1928; **1946**), originally written in collaboration with Mrs Lee Hawkins GARBY, and continued to write stories in a similar vein until the mid-'60s. Two sequels, *Skylark Three* (1930; **1948**) and *Skylark of Valeron* (1934–5; **1949**) escalated the action somewhat, and then the "Lensman" series took over, the starships growing bigger and the weapons more destructive until in *Children of the Lens* (1947–8; **1954**) GALACTIC EMPIRES toppled like rows of dominoes. When there was no greater scale of action to be employed Smith had little more to offer, and his last novels — *The Galaxy Primes* (1959; **1965**) and *Skylark DuQuesne* (**1966**) — are mere recapitulation. In the 1970s, however, a reissue of the "Lensman" series enjoyed considerable success, and Smith's banner was picked up by Stephen GOLDIN in a series of posthumous "collaborations" begun with *The Imperial Stars* (short version by Smith 1964; **1976**). Contemporary with Smith's first interstellar epic was a series of novelettes written by Edmond HAMILTON for WEIRD TALES, ultimately collected as *Crashing Suns* (1928–9; coll. **1965**). A novel in the same series was *Outside the Universe* (1929; **1964**). Hamilton took great delight in large-scale adventures, particularly in wrecking worlds and destroying suns, and although he was a more versatile writer than Smith his name was made with space opera and he too continued to write it until the 1960s. Other early examples are "The Universe Wreckers" (1930) and the CAPTAIN FUTURE series. In the late 1940s he wrote *The Star of Life* (1947; **1959**) and the memorable *The Star Kings* (1949; vt *Beyond the Moon*), the latter being an sf version of Anthony Hope's *The Prisoner of Zenda*. The last of Hamilton's works in this vein were *Doomstar* (**1966**) and the "Starwolf" trilogy (**1967–8**).

Even before Smith and Hamilton made their débuts Ray CUMMINGS was writing interplanetary novels for the general-fiction PULP MAGAZINES and for Hugo GERNSBACK's SCIENCE AND INVENTION. His principal space operas were *Tarrano the Conqueror* (1925; **1930**), *A Brand New World* (1928; **1964**), *Brigands of the Moon* (**1931**) and its sequel *Wandl the Invader* (1932; **1961**), but his reputation was made by his microcosmic romances (*see* GREAT AND SMALL) and it was to such adventures that he returned when he turned to self-plagiarism in later years. The two most important writers who took up space opera in the wake of Smith and Hamilton were John W. CAMPBELL Jr and Jack WILLIAMSON. Campbell made his first

impact with galactic adventures, the novelettes collected in *The Black Star Passes* (1930; fix-up **1953**), and he went on to write in the same vein *Islands of Space* (1931; **1957**), *Invaders from the Infinite* (1932; **1961**) and *The Mightiest Machine* (1934; **1947**). Campbell had a better command of scientific jargon than his contemporaries, and therefore a slicker line in super-scientific wizardry, but he began writing a different kind of sf as Don A. Stuart and subsequently abandoned writing when it clashed with his duties as editor of *ASF*. Williamson flavoured his space opera with a more ancient brand of romanticism when he based characters in *The Legion of Space* (1934; rev. **1947**) on the Three Musketeers and Falstaff, but though he never quite abandoned space opera — his most recent was *Bright New Universe* (**1967**) — the priority in his work was always on a more sophisticated variety of exotic adventure.

Other notable space operas from the 1930s are the "Hawk Carse" series written by Harry BATES and Desmond W. HALL as Anthony GILMORE, which appeared in book form as *Space Hawk* (1931–2; fix-up **1952**), and Clifford D. SIMAK's *Cosmic Engineers* (1939; rev. **1950**).

During the 1940s some of the naïvety of the space opera was lost as standards of writing rose and plots became somewhat more complicated. Greater versatility is evident in many examples from *ASF*, particularly *Judgement Night* (1943; title story of coll. **1952**; printed alone in paperback 1965) by C.L. MOORE and numerous works by A.E. VAN VOGT, including *The Voyage of the Space Beagle* (1939–50; fix-up **1950**), *The Mixed Men* (1943–5; fix-up **1952**; vt abridged *Mission to the Stars*) and *Masters of Time* (1942 as "Recruiting Station"; title story of coll. **1950**; vt *Earth's Last Fortress*; printed alone as *Masters of Time* 1967). Until this time the galactic-empire scenario had belonged entirely to space opera, but a dislocation was effected by Isaac ASIMOV in the "Foundation" series (1942–50; **1951–3**), and from the 1950s on it became a standardized framework in more serious sf. Once this happened the impression of vast scale so important to the space opera was no longer the sole prerogative of straightforward adventure stories, and the day of the classic space opera was done. Asimov, though, did use his galactic-empire background for one space opera: *The Stars Like Dust* (1951; vt *The Rebellious Stars*). The trend towards sophistication continued, with many writers producing more "realistic" space adventures. A notable example is James BLISH's *Earthman Come Home* (1950–53; fix-up **1955**), which features space battles between star-travelling cities, but the other novels in the same ("Okie") series have rather different priorities. The old-style space opera seemed vulgar and crude by now, but a

little more life was extracted from it by Leigh BRACKETT in *The Starmen* (1952; vt *The Galactic Breed*; vt *The Starmen of Llyrdis*), Raymond F. JONES in *This Island Earth* (1949–50; fix-up **1952**), Jack VANCE in *The Space Pirate* (1953; vt abridged *The Five Gold Bands*) and Noel LOOMIS in *The Man With Absolute Motion* (**1955** as by Silas Water).

There began in the 1950s a number of magazines which specialized in exotic adventure stories, including space operas. The most consistent in quality was IMAGINATION, but one which showed rather more flair was the second of the two American magazines entitled SCIENCE FICTION ADVENTURES, which survived for some years after its death in the USA as a British magazine. Robert SILVERBERG wrote a good deal for the US version, his most exuberant contribution being the trilogy assembled as *Lest We Forget Thee, Earth* (fix-up **1958** as by Calvin M. Knox), while Kenneth BULMER was a prolific contributor to the British version. Many stories from the magazine were picked up by ACE BOOKS for their Ace Doubles series, ed. Donald A. WOLLHEIM, and it was in these paperbacks that space opera found a home once the magazines left it behind. Though other paperback companies also thrived on space opera it was those under Wollheim's direction — Ace and DAW BOOKS — which did most to ensure its survival, reprinting old works and promoting new ones.

The most sophisticated space operas of the late 1950s and the '60s were *Starship Troopers* (**1959**) by Robert A. HEINLEIN, Gordon R. DICKSON's "Dorsai" series and *Naked to the Stars* (**1961**), H. Beam PIPER's *Space Viking* (**1963**), Keith LAUMER's "Retief" series, Ian WALLACE's *Croyd* (**1967**) and its sequel *Dr. Orpheus* (**1968**) and Samuel R. DELANY's *Nova* (**1968**). The most notable of those produced purely as adventure stories include *The Super Barbarians* (**1962**) by John BRUNNER, *The Other Side of Nowhere* (**1964**) and *Checkpoint Lambda* (**1967**) by Murray LEINSTER, *The Sundered Worlds* (1962–3; fix-up **1965**; vt *The Blood Red Game*) by Michael MOORCOCK, *Earthblood* (**1966**) by Keith Laumer and Rosel George Brown and *Galactic Odyssey* (**1967**) by Laumer alone. The 1960s also saw the first thoroughgoing parody of the militaristic space opera in Harry HARRISON's *Bill, the Galactic Hero* (**1965**), though Harrison was less successful when he later attempted to parody "Doc" Smith in *Star Smashers of the Galaxy Rangers* (**1973**).

Space opera continues to be popular in the 1970s, with a juvenile audience welcoming the reprinting of Smith and Williamson. Two long-running and above average series still continue: A. Bertram CHANDLER's "Rim Worlds" series (1959 onwards) and E.C. TUBB's "Dumarest" series (1967 onwards). Recent space operas include Barrington J. BAYLEY's *The Star Virus* (1964; exp.

1970) and *Empire of Two Worlds* (**1972**), Dav GARNETT's *The Starseekers* (**1971**), David GERROLD's *Space Skimmer* (**1972**), George ZEBROWSKI's *The Omega Point* (**1972**), Brian M. STABLEFORD's *The Halcyon Drift* (**1972**) and Robert CHILSON's *The Star-Crowned Kings* (**1975**). The TV series STAR TREK, several of whose episodes constituted space opera at its purest and most naïve, has given rise to a minor branch of the publishing industry. The most marked difference between these recent adventures stories and the classic space operas is the fact that the writers are wholly at ease with the colourful backgrounds and the miraculous superscience. They have become blasé about it — or even cynical. Their ideative flourishes are only ironically romantic — a far cry from the wide-eyed attitude which predominated when it was all new. Even the recent parody of space opera *The Centauri Device* (**1974**) by M. John HARRISON, is almost languorous in its treatment of its themes. Space opera is no longer mind-opening and mind-expanding, but rather the reverse, allowing readers to return to imaginative pastures that are comfortably familiar. What is taken for granted cannot inspire awe. Naïve art inevitably changes as it becomes deliberate and self-aware, and space opera today has become selfconsciously decadent. Nevertheless, it lives.

A series of relevant theme anthologies, ed. Brian W. ALDISS, begins with *Space Opera* (anth. **1974**). [BS]
See also: FANTASTIC VOYAGES; SPACE FLIGHT; WEAPONS.

SPACE PATROL Television serial (1954). ABC TV. Produced by Helen Mosier, directed by Dock Darley, written by Norman Jolly, starring Ed Kermer, Lynn Osborn, Kan Mayer and Gene Reynolds. 25 mins per episode. B/w.

One of the many SPACE OPERA serials aimed at children in the early 1950s on American TV, all of which followed in the footsteps of CAPTAIN VIDEO. Like the others, *SP* was filmed live within a studio — a situation that did not allow much in the way of special effects or space spectacle. The first episode had members of the patrol being captured by a villain on a distant planet, who forces them into slavery. A rescue attempt is mounted by other patrol members and the episode ends in a typically cliff-hanging situation. [JB]

SPACE SCHOOL Television serial (1956). BBC TV. Produced by Kevin Sheldon, starring John Stuart, Matthew Lane, Donald McCorkindale, Julie Webb and David Drummond. Written by Gordon Ford. Four 25-min. episodes. B/w.

The producer of this children's serial was also behind such earlier sf serials as THE LOST PLANET. In *SS* a group of children live in an artificial satellite while their father spends his time surveying the moons of Mars for possible landing sites. The model work (space-station and rocketships) by John Ryan was quite effective, considering the small budget. [JB]

SPACE SCIENCE FICTION. British edition, March 1953. Ebel's cover contrives to be distinctly anti-erotic.

SPACE SCIENCE FICTION US DIGEST-size magazine. Eight issues, May 1952 – Sep. 1953, published by Space Publications; ed. Lester DEL REY. The most prolific contributor was Del Rey himself, sometimes using the pseudonyms Erik van Lhin and Philip St John. Notable stories include T.L. SHERRED's "Cue For Quiet" (May-Jul. 1953) and Philip K. DICK's "The Variable Man" (Sep. 1953). The final issue began serialization of Poul ANDERSON's "The Escape" (as *Brain Wave* **1954**) but it was not completed. All eight issues were reprinted in the UK, 1952-3. [BS]
Collectors should note: Publication schedule was irregular; Vol.1 had six numbers, Vol.2 had two.

SPACE SCIENCE FICTION MAGAZINE. First issue. Cover by Tom Ryan.

SPACE SCIENCE FICTION MAGAZINE US DIGEST-size magazine. Two issues, Spring and Aug. 1957, published by the Republic Features Syndicate; ed. Lyle Kenyon ENGEL. [BS]

SPACESHIPS The suggestion that men might one day travel to the Moon inside a flying machine was first put forward seriously by John WILKINS in 1638. There had been cosmic voyages prior to that date, and there were to be many more thereafter (*see* FANTASTIC VOYAGES; SPACE FLIGHT), but few took the mechanics of the journey seriously enough to invest much imaginative effort in the design of credible vehicles. The first man who tried was Edgar Allan POE, whose story "The Unparalleled Adventure of One Hans Pfaall" (1835) usually appears with an afterword complaining about the failure of other writers to achieve verisimilitude. Pfaall makes his journey by balloon, though, and Poe's assumption of the continuity of the atmosphere is hard to swallow (especially as it was written 200 years after Torricelli's estimate of the atmosphere as only a few miles high).

The next serious attempt to envisage the means by which space flight might really be effected was by Jules VERNE, who described the building of a space-gun in *De la terre à la lune* (**1865**) and a voyage in the projectile shot from it in the sequel *Autour de la lune* (**1870**); the two appeared as one book in English: *From the Earth to the Moon* (trans. **1873**). Most scientific romancers of the period, however, were content to invent no more than a jargon to signify some mysterious force of propulsion: Percy GREG's spaceship in *Across the Zodiac* (**1880**) is powered by "apergy"; H.G. WELLS invented the antigravitic Cavorite for *The First Men in the Moon* (**1901**); John MASTIN had an "airship" taken by a new gas into space in *The Stolen Planet* (**1905**); and Garrett P. SERVISS envisaged an atomic-powered space-car in *A Columbus of Space* (1909; rev. **1911**). Because their means of propulsion were so often mysterious, spaceships in this period could easily assume the "perfect" spheroid shape of the heavenly bodies themselves — a notable example is found in Robert CROMIE's *A Plunge into Space* (**1890**). When they were not round or bullet-shaped they tended to resemble flying railway-carriages or submarines.

Spaceships were taken up in a big way by the early sf PULPS, and here changed their visual image drastically. Frank R. PAUL and his contemporary ILLUSTRATORS showed a strong preference for bulbous machines like enormously bloated aeroplanes or rounded-off oceangoing liners with long rows of portholes. These were often shown with jets of flame or vapour gushing out behind, but this was as much to suggest speed as to indicate that the means of propulsion involved might be ROCKETS. The streamlining of the hull and the appearance of elegant fins

SPACESHIPS in sf art have undergone considerable development in the past century. Above, Victorian comfort, a dog and a ladder in an early edition of Jules Verne's *From the Earth to the Moon*; facing page, top, the Ballantine edition of Arthur C. Clarke's *Rendezvous With Rama*, 1974, features a diminishing perspective down the several kilometres of the derelict spacecraft's interior, complete with clouds in the inside "sky"

more imaginative power when it was displayed by Robert A. HEINLEIN in "Universe" (1941), scorning the convenience of FASTER-THAN-LIGHT travel to establish the archetypal image of the GENERATION STARSHIP. This motif, a genuine embodiment of *per ardua ad astra*, came to be linked in many instances to the myth of the Ark, and this led to the development of a rather different theme, of escaping from disaster; notable examples include Leigh BRACKETT's *Alpha Centauri — or Die!* (1953 as "The Ark of Mars"; exp. **1963**) and Roger DIXON's *Noah II* (**1970**). The spaceship was a powerful symbol of escape invoked continually in stories of future tyranny and the struggles of oppressed minorities throughout the 1950s, though the theme became steadily less fashionable thereafter, being replaced by internal and transcendental escape mythologies (*see* SUPERMAN). Other stories developed the notion of far-travelling starships into the idea of a starship culture. Notable examples include Heinlein's *Citizen of the Galaxy* (**1957**) and Alexei PANSHIN's *Rite of Passage* (1963; exp. **1968**). A variant on the theme is L. Ron HUBBARD's *Return to Tomorrow* (1950; **1954**), in which the crews of starships become alienated from the course of history by the time-dilatation effect of travelling at near-light-speed.

The FLYING-SAUCER craze of the post-War years made little impact on sf imagery in the magazines, though Sam MERWIN's interest was reflected in the stories he wrote — notably "Centaurus" (1953) — and in the magazines which he edited. It had a considerable influence, however, on the imagery of sf CINEMA, where saucer-shaped ships became commonplace. The streamlined ships which still dominated magazine illustration continued supreme for some time, and when their imagery finally was challenged it was by the bizarre and surreal hardware of artists like Eddie JONES and Christopher FOSS. This movement towards the bizarre was foreshadowed in fiction even in the early 1950s: Cordwainer SMITH's "Instrumentality" stories often featured remarkable light-powered "sailing ships" — notable examples are "The Lady Who Sailed the *Soul*" (1960) and "Think Blue, Count Two" (1963) — while Jack WILLIAMSON's *Dragon's Island* (**1951**; vt *The Not-Men*) has spaceships which grow on trees. Scientifically minded writers had by this time pointed out that starships built in space for journeys in hard vacuum had no conceivable need of streamlining.

People characteristically refer to ships as "she", and often tend to credit vehicles of various kinds with personalities and names. In sf this tendency could be carried to its logical and literal conclusion. Human brains take up a symbiotic relationship with spaceship

was a slow process, corresponding historically to the development of sleeker automobiles in the real world rather than to any realization of the importance of rocket-power. There were few attempts in the early pulps to create convincing spaceships — perhaps the most notable is Laurence MANNING's *Asteroid* in "The Voyage of the *Asteroid*" (1932) — but there were many extravagant adventures in space which thrived on fantastic machines with limitless capabilities. The pulp sf spaceship was the fulfilment of childhood fantasies of power and mobility, the classic examples being the various *Skylarks* employed by E.E. "Doc" SMITH's Richard Seaton and friends. Some scientific romancers still regarded spaceships as mere conveniences (Edgar Rice BURROUGHS was even prepared to do without in his "Barsoom" series) but Smith and the

other high priests of SPACE OPERA exploited the fantasy of power and luxury which had hitherto been attached to such Earthly vessels as Verne's submarine *Nautilus* and the Golden Ship used by Max PEMBERTON's *The Iron Pirate* (**1897**). Outside the pulps Friedrich W. MADER tapped the same aesthetic fascination in *Distant Worlds* (1921 Germany; trans. **1932**), whose hero declares that his vessel is no mere airship but a "world-ship" with the freedom of the universe.

The writers of HARD SF knew by the 1930s that the first real spaceships would be rockets, and there were a few stories about the projects which would build them — notably Lester DEL REY's "The Stars Look Down" (1940) — but the dominant theme was the naïve get-away-from-it-all fantasy in which spaceships could be built casually in the back yard. A different kind of realism proved to have

bodies (*see* CYBORGS), losing their own bodies in the process, in Thomas N. SCORTIA's "Sea Change" (1956; vt "The Shores of Night"), Anne McCAFFREY's *The Ship Who Sang* (coll. of linked stories **1969**), and Cordwainer Smith's "Three to a Given Star" (1965). Spaceships in recent times have often acquired intelligence and personality in their own right thanks to their sophisticated COMPUTER networks — examples are the starship with aspirations to become God in Frank HERBERT's *Destination: Void* (**1966**) and the multiple-personality ship of Clifford D. SIMAK's *Shakespeare's Planet* (**1976**). The relationship between man and ship has, however, been preserved in the traditional naval fashion by the Merchant Navy writer A. Bertram CHANDLER and in such novels as *Starman Jones* (**1953**) by Heinlein and *The Mote in God's Eye* (**1974**) by Larry NIVEN and Jerry POURNELLE. An interesting adjunct to this tradition is provided by two stories which recast the voyage of the *Titanic* as sf: Boyd Ellanby's "The Star Lord" (1953) and Murray LEINSTER's "The Corianis Disaster" (1960).

In recent years writers have become more suspicious of the spaceship mythology built up by their predecessors. An interesting exploration of the myth is presented in Mark GESTON's *Lords of the Starship* (**1967**), while an ironic criticism is presented of the eponymous spaceship's name and symbolic stature in Stanislaw LEM's *Niezwyciezony* (1964; trans. as *The Invincible* **1973**). The idea that the spaceship owed much of its charisma to phallic symbolism has been bandied about — it is rather crudely presented in Virgil FINLAY's cover for *Worlds of Tomorrow*, Oct. 1963, and in Kurt VONNEGUT Jr's "The Big Space

Fuck" (1972) — but is hardly necessary or convincing as an explanation. The role of the spaceship in sf has certainly been symbolic, but of escape, of the transcendence of Earthly bonds and of passage to the remote worlds of exotic adventure: a point clearly evident in *Gateway* (**1977**) by Frederik POHL, in which the human race serendipitously stumbles on its passport to anywhere in a stockpile of alien starships. Another mystique-laden alien starship is the gargantuan vessel featured in Arthur C. CLARKE's *Rendezvous with Rama* (**1973**), while the myth of escape and isolation has its apotheosis in Poul ANDERSON's ultimate time-dilatation fantasy *Tau Zero* (1967; exp. **1970**). The power of the myth is evident in the decision to name the experimental space-shuttle which was under test in 1977 after the heroine of the TV series STAR TREK: the *Enterprise*. [BS]

Dec. 1952. Cover by Earle K. Bergey.

SPACE STORIES US PULP magazine.

Five bi-monthly issues, Oct. 1952-Jun. 1953, published by Standard Magazines as a companion to STARTLING STORIES *et al.*; ed. Samuel MINES. Its policy, identical to that of *Startling Stories*, was to feature a complete novel in every issue, the most notable being *The Big Jump* (Feb. 1953; **1955**) by Leigh BRACKETT.   [BS]

SPACE TRAVEL *See* GENERATION STARSHIPS, SPACE FLIGHT and SPACESHIPS.

SPACE TRAVEL (magazine) *See* IMAGINATIVE TALES.

SPACE WARP In sf TERMINOLOGY, a concept similar to that of HYPERSPACE and subspace. The analogy of "normal" space to a handkerchief is sometimes used. Two points on a handkerchief may be six inches apart, but if the handkerchief is folded they become adjacent. If space could be warped in like style, the resulting short cut would effectively enable SPACESHIPS to travel FASTER THAN LIGHT: the topic is discussed further in the latter entry. Space warp has become such a CLICHÉ in sf that it allows endless variants. One of the best known is the "warp factor" used in the STAR TREK television series as a measure of velocity, much like miles per hour. This is illogical on all levels.   [PN]

The reincarnated version, Oct. 1969. Cover by Morris Scott Dollens.

SPACEWAY US DIGEST-size magazine. 12 issues in all, published by William L. CRAWFORD's Fantasy Publishing Co. Eight issues Dec. 1953-Jun. 1955; the magazine then died having published only the first part of Ralph Milne FARLEY's "Radio Minds of Mars". It was resurrected many years later to publish four more issues, Jan. 1969-Jun. 1970, printing the serial in full. The second version reprinted from the first, but added a few new stories. The most notable story carried by the magazine was "The Cosmic Geoids" by John TAINE (Dec.

1954-Apr. 1955), though this had already been published in book form as the lead novel of *The Cosmic Geoids and One Other* (**1949**). [BS]
Collectors should note: The subtitle "Stories of the Future" changed to "Science Fiction" Dec. '54. The first two vols had three numbers, Vol.3 had two, Vol.4 had three, and Vol.5 had one. After the first four bi-monthly issues, the schedule was quite irregular. The first four numbers were reprinted in England 1954-5 by Regular Publications.

SPACEWAYS Film (1953). Hammer. Directed by Terence Fisher, starring Howard Duff, Eva Bartok, Alan Wheatley and Andrew Osborn. Screenplay by Paul TABORI and Richard Landau, based on a radio play by Charles Eric MAINE. 76 mins. B/w.
A scientist is suspected of murdering his wife and placing her body in a satellite. This is an early, low-budget Hammer production which has dated. Maine's novel *Spaceways* (**1953**; vt *Spaceways Satellite* USA) was published the same year. [JB]

SPACE-WISE British BEDSHEET-size magazine. Three issues, Dec. 1969, Jan. and Mar. 1970, published by the Martec

First issue. Cover by Mike Attwell.

Publishing Group; ed. Derek R. Threadgall. *SW* contained a mixture of sf, science and occult articles, which proved not viable. *SW* ran an sf serial that remained unfinished. [FHP]

SPAIN, PORTUGAL AND SOUTH AMERICA In Spain, where freedom of expression has long been the object of censorship, it is ironic that the early manifestations of sf were characterized by satirical political fantasies: N.M. Fabra's *Presente y Futuro* (**1897**), Domingo Ventalló's *El Secreto de Lord Kitchener* (**1914**) and E. Cerdá's *Don Quijote en la Guerra* (**1915**). The Civil War was however to put a brutal end to the fashionable era of post-VERNE and WELLS

adventures and Utopias in Spain.
It was not until the 1950s that sf reappeared in Spain, with material translated from the Anglo-American GOLDEN AGE OF SF eventually stimulating such home-grown writers as Antonio Ribera, Francisco Torné, Domingo Santos, Carlos Buiza, Juan Atienza and Luis Vigil. Most of these authors first appeared in the many magazines and imprints of the mid-1960s, but the milestone of native Spanish sf was the launching in 1968 by Santos, Vigil and Sebastián Martínez of the magazine *Nueva Dimensión* (voted best European magazine at the 1972 Trieste sf convention Eurocon) where local authors became regularly featured alongside the best Anglo-American sf.
Although numerous other Spanish sf magazines have come and gone since, *Nueva Dimensión* was still being published in 1977 and, at one time or another, has presented a majority of the present Spanish sf writers, Carlos Saiz Cidoncha (author of a history of Spanish sf in 1976), Gabriel Bermúdez Castillo (*Amor en la Isla Verde* and *Viaje a un Planeta Wu-Wei*), Teresa Inglés (*El Jardín de Alabastro*), Francisco Lezcano, Carlo Frabetti, Pedro Sánchez Paredes, Juan Extremadura and José Luis Garci among them.
Tomás Salvador, a well-known MAINSTREAM author and recipient of the coveted Premio Nacional de Literatura, is one of the more interesting Spanish personalities. His novel *La Nave* (**1959**) is a treatment of the popular GENERATION STARSHIP theme and he has also written various intriguing political allegories (*Y, T and K*) named after letters of the alphabet. Domingo Santos, a pseudonym used by journalist Pedro Domingo Mutiñó (1941–), remains, however, the major contemporary Spanish sf writer; a prolific author, editor and anthologist, his best-known work is *Gabriel, Historia de un Robot* (**1962**), translated into several foreign languages, where a ROBOT saves Earth from its rebellious Moon colonists and achieves the feat of falling in love. It is a witty and articulate tale. Other notable titles by Santos are *Volveré Ayer*, *Civilización*, *Meteoritos* and *La Cárcel de Acero*.
As a rule, modern Spanish sf is still heavily inspired by the "epic" coordinates of the SPACE OPERA genre, and its forays into the more rewarding fields of sociology or psychology generally lack depth. However, since the political changes brought about by Franco's death, a group of NEW WAVE younger writers has emerged, heavily involved in speculative fiction like their French counterparts. The work of these newcomers, Asís Calonge, Eduardo Ibars, Juan Alcover and Mariano Lato, is generally found in magazines like *Zikurath* and *Cuaderno de San Armadans*.
In Portugal, sf has followed a similar pattern to that of Spain, and the

emergence of local authors like Joel Lima, Luis de Mesquita and Alves Morgado is fairly recent in a publishing field where translated material has long been dominant.
In South America, however, fantasy and speculative elements are much more widespread and, in Argentina, popular major mainstream authors such as Jorge Luis BORGES, BIOY CASARES, Cortazar and Ernesto Sabato can arguably be annexed as borderline exponents of literary as opposed to genre sf. In Brazil, several writers specialize in sf: André Carneiro, J. Monteiro, Dinah de Queiroz and Geraldo Mourão are among the most important. [MJ]

SPANNER, E(DWARD) F(RANK) (1888– ?). English writer. He wrote dramatized warnings about the state of England's defences against future INVASION; they include *The Broken Trident* (**1926**) and *The Naviators* (**1926**). [JC]
Other works: *The Harbour of Death* (**1927**).

SPARTACUS, DEUTERO See R.L. FANTHORPE.

SPECULATION British FANZINE ed. Peter WESTON from Birmingham 1963–73. *S* was consistently the best amateur magazine of comment and criticism in the UK for many years. Regular contributors included such well-known professional writers as James BLISH, Kenneth BULMER, M. John HARRISON, Michael MOORCOCK and Frederik POHL. A number of fans whose writing often appeared in *S* later became sf writers, Christopher PRIEST and Brian M. STABLEFORD among them. *S* averaged about 60 pages an issue. [PN]

SPENCER, G.F. (? –). British writer, whose sf novel is *Heavens for All* (**1955**). [JC]

SPENCER, JOHN (? –). English musician, art agency director and writer, whose sf novel, *The Electronic Lullaby Meat Market* (**1975**), not dissimilarly to the books of Mick FARREN, renders a violently hyperbolic NEAR FUTURE world in terms reminiscent of the late-1960s counter-culture. [JC]

SPENCER, LEONARD G. Ziff-Davis house name used once by Robert SILVERBERG and Randall GARRETT in collaboration, and twice by unknown writers, 1956–7.

SPIDER, THE US PULP MAGAZINE. 118 issues, Oct. 1933-Dec. 1943; monthly until Feb. 1943, bi-monthly thereafter. Published by Popular Publications; ed. Rogers Terrill. *S* began as a straightforward imitation of the highly successful *The Shadow*, telling of a mysterious caped avenger. The first two

THE SPIDER, Nov. 1943. The masked hero is lurking in the background behind his symbolic web.

novels were written by R.T.M. Scott. The remainder were credited to the house pseudonym Grant Stockbridge, and were all the work of the prolific Norvell W. PAGE. Under his guidance, the Spider became a more ruthless character, and the menaces he combated became more fantastic. Page himself took to dressing in a black cape and wide-brimmed hat in imitation of the character. The magazine also contained short stories, including a series by Arthur Leo ZAGAT. The character later featured in a cinema serial, *The Spider's Web*. Four of the novels have been reprinted in paperback form, 1975 onwards, and the series is currently continuing.   [MJE/FHP]

SPINDIZZY One of the best-loved items of sf TERMINOLOGY. The spindizzy is the ANTIGRAVITY device (*see* GRAVITY) used to drive the flying cities of the "Cities in Flight" series of novels by James Blish. (*See* BLISH *entry for details of the books*.) The spindizzy is given a wonderfully plausible rationale in theoretical physics for anyone not too familiar with that arcane discipline.   [PN]

SPINRAD, NORMAN (RICHARD) (1940–). American writer, born in New York, where he has set some impressive fiction. He was a significant contributor to both the American and the British NEW WAVE movements in the sf of the later 1960s, in both countries, though with different emphases (British "new wavers" tending more selfconsciously to assimilate MAINSTREAM modes, like Surrealism), the new wave argued for a move from externalized stories that used the HARD sciences to "INNER SPACE" fiction whose sf material derived more from the SOFT SCIENCES, like PSYCHOLOGY, SOCIOLOGY or LINGUISTICS. NS's first two novels, *The Solarians* (**1966**) and *Agent of Chaos*

(**1967**), are somewhat florid SPACE OPERAS, and his third, *The Men in the Jungle* (**1967**), subjects a tough, urban protagonist to a complex set of Realpolitik adventures on a distant planet, with some success, and with a loosening of style; but it is with his fourth book, *Bug Jack Barron* (**1969**), that he made his greatest impact on the sheltered world of sf. This long novel was first serialized in a shorter form in *NW*, where its violent texture and use of profanities caused a notable stirring in the dovecotes and led directly to the vast English chain of bookstores, W.H. Smith, banning the magazine. The parochialism of the sf world's response to a not particularly shocking novel is visible in Sam J. LUNDWALL's *Science Fiction: What It's all About* (**1969**; trans. exp. **1971**), where it is described as "practically a collection of obscenities", and dismissed as such. The novel itself, whose language does not fully conceal a certain sentimentality, deals with a NEAR-FUTURE America through television figure Jack Barron and his involvement in a politically corrupt system; the resulting picture of America is of a hyped, SEX-obsessed, apocalyptic world; the style matches the content, sometimes, though not in the profanities, with a sledgehammer effect.

During these years NS also published a good deal of short fiction (his first story, "The Last of Romany", had appeared in 1963 in *ASF*), much of which has been assembled in *The Last Hurrah of the Golden Horde* (coll. **1970**) and *No Direction Home* (coll. **1975**). The title story of the first collection is among the most successful attempts — many authors were involved — to write a story using the characters and universe of Michael MOORCOCK's "Jerry Cornelius" series, and was originally published in *NW*. The best story of the second volume, and perhaps NS's best story altogether, is "A Thing of Beauty" (1973), in which a degenerate America is symbolized by the sale, to a Japanese aesthete, of the Brooklyn Bridge, which he exports to Japan, where it will be properly preserved.

A fine novella, "Riding the Torch" (1974), won a 1975 JUPITER award, and featured as one of the two novels in the first of the "Binary Star" series of two short novels in a volume: *Destiny Times Three/Riding the Torch* (coll. **1978**) by Fritz LEIBER and NS. It features mankind in a metaphysical galactic quest, with hallucinations.

NS's most recent sf novel is *The Iron Dream* (**1972**), an ALTERNATE-WORLDS story which is structured as a SWORD-AND-SORCERY novel by Adolf Hitler (a mere writer in this world); some of the less attractive tendencies of sword-and-sorcery writing are effectively if somewhat unrelentingly guyed, as is bad academic critical thought in the Afterword by "Homer Whipple". Though often crude in his effects, and

sometimes incapable of cutting himself short, NS has been a refreshing, iconoclastic force in modern sf, and a convincing analyst of some of the more apocalyptic tendencies in modern American life.   [JC]

Other works: *Passing Through the Flame* (**1975**) is not sf. As editor: *The New Tomorrows* (anth. **1971**); *Modern Science Fiction* (anth. **1974**).

See also: ABSURDIST SF; ARTS; CLONES; END OF THE WORLD; ENTROPY; HOLOCAUST AND AFTER; IMMORTALITY; MEDIA LANDSCAPE; MUSIC AND OPERA; MUTANTS; PARANOIA AND SCHIZOPHRENIA; PERCEPTION; POLITICS; POLLUTION; PSYCHOLOGY; SATIRE; SF IN THE CLASSROOM; SUN; WAR; WEATHER CONTROL.

SPIRITUALISM *See* ESCHATOLOGY.

SPITZ, JACQUES *See* FRANCE.

SPLIT PERSONALITY *See* PARANOIA AND SCHIZOPHRENIA; PSYCHOLOGY.

SPORTS *See* GAMES AND SPORTS.

SPRAGUE, CARTER *See* Sam MERWIN.

SPRIGEL, OLIVIER *See* Pierre BARBET.

SPRUILL, STEVEN G. (1946–). American writer and psychology intern, with a BA in biology, completing a PhD in psychology in 1977. His first sf novel, *Keepers of the Gate* (**1977**), tells a complicated adventure tale, rather in the mode of Keith LAUMER, with some competence; the alien Proteps of Eridani turn out to be an advanced form of *Homo sapiens*, and have been suppressing mankind's urge to the stars for selfish reasons. *The Psychopath Plague* (**1978**) is the first of a projected series involving detective work on a galactic scale undertaken by a partnership of a human and an alien.   [JC/PN]

SQUIRE, J.C. *See* ALTERNATE WORLDS.

S-S-SNAKE! (vt SSSSSSSS!) Film (1973). Universal. Directed by Bernard L. Kowalski, starring Strother Martin, Dirk Benedict and Heather Menzies. Screenplay by Hal Dresner, based on a story by Dan Striepke. 99 mins. Colour.

A mad scientist believes that the future of mankind depends on its developing snake-like properties. He experiments on his daughter's boy-friend, and succeeds in transforming him into a snake-creature. An asset of the film is the fine make-up by John Chambers.   [JB]

SSSSSSSS! *See* S-S-SNAKE!

STABLEFORD, BRIAN M(ICHAEL) (1948–). English writer, critic and academic. Educated at Manchester Grammar School and York University, BMS has a first-class degree in biology, and has done postgraduate work in both biology and sociology. He is now a lecturer in sociology at Reading University.

He began writing sf in his teens. His first story, a collaboration with a school-friend, Craig A. Mackintosh, entitled "Beyond Time's Aegis" (1965), appeared in *Science Fantasy* under the pseudonym Brian Craig. *Cradle of the Sun* (1969) is a quest story set in the FAR FUTURE, and is notable for its colourful imagery. *The Blind Worm* (1970) is another hastily written novel in the same vein. In these, and in most of his subsequent work, BMS puts his knowledge of BIOLOGY to good use. He is expert in the construction of outrageous but plausible ECOLOGIES. The "Dies Irae" trilogy — *The Days of Glory* (1971), *In the Kingdom of the Beasts* (1971) and *Day of Wrath* (1971) — is an experiment in SPACE OPERA with an admixture of SWORD AND SORCERY. Based on HOMER's *Iliad* and *Odyssey*, the trilogy has been dismissed as cynical hackwork (not least by the author himself), although the narrative has a certain verve. *To Challenge Chaos* (1972) is the last example of BMS's juvenilia, an over-extravagant adventure set on the chaotic hemisphere of a planet which intersects another dimension; short stories associated with this novel are "The Sun's Tears" (1974), "An Offer of Oblivion" (1974) and "Captain Fagan Died Alone" (1976).

The Halcyon Drift (1972) is the first volume of BMS's most successful series. A first-person narrative, influenced in style by the Raymond Chandler school of thriller writing, it concerns the adventures of Grainger, pilot of a FASTER-THAN-LIGHT spacecraft, "The Hooded Swan". Grainger is a cynic and survivor; marooned on a remote planet, he becomes host to a mind parasite, a benign entity which occasionally takes over his body and drives it to feats of endurance. The later novels in the "Hooded Swan" sequence, most of which involve biological mysteries on a variety of planets, are *Rhapsody in Black* (1973; rev. 1975 UK), *Promised Land* (1974), *The Paradise Game* (1974), *The Fenris Device* (1974) and *Swan Song* (1975). They are essentially formula novels, although BMS's keen intelligence and sense of humour lead him to subvert genre expectations in various ways; for instance, Grainger is an undeclared pacifist and achieves his aims without violence.

Man in a Cage (1975) is BMS's most serious novel to date. Entirely non-formulaic, it is concerned with the PSYCHOLOGY of social adaptation. This is dramatized through the use of a SCHIZOPHRENIC narrator who is selected to participate in a space-project where "sane" men have already proved inadequate. A powerfully written but difficult novel, it is slightly reminiscent of the best work of Robert SILVERBERG and Barry MALZBERG. BMS's *The Mind-Riders* (1976) is a more conventional novel in a not dissimilar vein. In this case the cynical narrator is a boxer who performs via an electronic simulation device while the audience "plugs in" to his emotions. Like Grainger's wonderful spaceship, and like the false personality which "cages" the hero of *Man in a Cage*, the simulator is an armour surrounding the self, enabling the protagonist to survive in a hostile world.

The Realms of Tartarus (1977) is a trilogy in one volume, the first part of which was published separately in the UK as *The Face of Heaven* (1976). It is a biological phantasmagoria, concerning a UTOPIA built on a huge platform above the Earth's surface, and the conflict with the mutated life-forms which proliferate below. The trilogy suffers from an excess of padding, but contains much ingenious invention and appealing grotesquerie. BMS's latest series, begun with *The Florians* (1976), is about the planet-hopping adventures of "The Daedalus", a space vessel which has been sent out to re-contact lost earth colonies. The formula here is much the same as in the "Hooded Swan" books, although the series lacks a strong central character. Later novels in the "Daedalus" series include *Critical Threshold* (1977), *Wildeblood's Empire* (1977) and *The City of the Sun* (1978). As a writer of intelligent formula entertainments with a sound grounding in the sciences, BMS is virtually unmatched in contemporary sf.

BMS has also written a number of short stories and a considerable quantity of non-fiction, including articles on sf and reviews which have appeared in AMZ, *Fantastic*, ALGOL, VECTOR, FOUNDATION and elsewhere; he is a contributing editor to this volume. He perhaps has a more detailed knowledge of the HISTORY OF SF than any other critic at work today, and he adopts a stimulating sociological approach to the topic. His book *The Mysteries of Modern Science* (1977) is an excellent popularization of the history and philosophy of science. [DP]
See also: ANDROIDS; CRITICAL AND HISTORICAL WORKS ABOUT SF; EVOLUTION; GAMES AND SPORTS; GENERATION STARSHIPS; GENETIC ENGINEERING; HIVE-MINDS; LIFE ON OTHER WORDS; LIVING WORLDS; MYTHOLOGY; PARASITISM AND SYMBIOSIS; PASTORAL; SPACE FLIGHT; WAR.

STABLES, (WILLIAM) GORDON (1840–1910). Scottish doctor and author of fiction for children. He served as surgeon on a whaling boat, and later with the Royal Navy. He wrote extensively for the BOYS' PAPERS, including *The Boy's Own Paper*, where he wrote many FANTASTIC VOYAGES in competition with the serials of Jules VERNE. Most similar to Verne's work were *An Island Afloat* (1903) and *The Cruise of the Crystal Boat* (1891), a moralistic tale of aerial adventure in an electrically powered craft. LOST-WORLD elements appeared in some stories, notably *In Regions of Perpetual Snow* (1904) and *In Quest of the Giant Sloth* (1901; vt *The Strange Quest*), becoming more dominant with *The City at the Pole* (1906), which envisages a temperate polar region, a Viking community and prehistoric survivals. His only excursion outside these themes was his future-WAR novel, *The Meteor Flag of England* (1906). [JE]
Other works: *Wild Adventures Round the Pole* (1883); *From Pole to Pole* (1886); *Frank Hardinge* (1898); *In the Great White Land* (1902).
See also: TRANSPORTATION.

STACPOOLE, H(ENRY) DE VERE (1865–1951). British author, best known for his South Sea romances, including the ROBINSONADES *The Blue Lagoon* (1908), *The Garden of God* (1923), *The Gates of Morning* (1925), *The Beach of Dreams* (1919), all of which are collected in *The Blue Lagoon Omnibus* (coll. 1933); *The Ship of Coral* (1911) and *The Naked Soul* (1933). His one LOST-WORLD novel is *The City in the Sea* (1926); he also wrote several weird novels, *Death, the Knight, and the Lady* (1897), *The Man Who Lost Himself* (1918), *The Ghost Girl* (1918) and *The Sunstone* (1936). His sf proper was restricted to the magazines, and includes a world-DISASTER story, "The White Eye" (1918). [JE]
Other works: *Goblin Market* (1927); *The Vengeance of Mynheer Van Lik* (coll. 1934); *The Story of my Village* (1947).

STAINES, TREVOR See John BRUNNER.

STANFORD, J(OHN) K(EITH) (1892– ?). English writer, mostly humorous; his sf SATIRE, *Full Moon at Sweatenham: a Nightmare* (1953), takes rather heavy pot-shots at a decadent, ludicrous England of 1960; the Welfare State is guyed. [JC]
Other works: *The Twelfth* (1944).

STANLEY, A(LFRED) M(ORTIMER) (1888– ?). American writer, in whose *Tomorrow's Yesterday* (1949) an archaeologist wakes up in the future. [JC]

STANLEY, WILLIAM (FORD ROBINSON) (1829–1909). British writer, often on economic issues, of sf interest for *The Case of The. Fox: Being his Prophecies under Hypnotism of the Period Ending A.D. 1950. A Political Utopia* (1903). Hypnosis releases the "prophetic mental element" in the poet Theodore Fox; the UTOPIA he describes, with its Federal Europe, electrified cars and Channel Tunnel, has few unusual elements. [JC]

STANTON, PAUL (? –). Author of a routine NEAR-FUTURE nuclear-war thriller, *Village of Stars* (1960). [JC]

STANTON, WILL (? – ?). American

writer of magazine sf, who began with "Barney" for *FSF* in 1951, and remained with that magazine solely. He was active for about a decade, his stories witty and well-told variants on familiar sf themes; many have been anthologized. [JC/PN]

STAPLEDON, OLAF (1886–1950). English writer and philosopher, born of well-to-do parents in the Wirral peninsula near Liverpool, where he spent the greater part of his life. In *Waking World* (1934) he admitted that he lived "chiefly on dividends and other ill-gotten gains". The name Olaf does not indicate foreign antecedents, but was given merely because his parents happened to be reading Carlyle's *Early Kings of Norway* at the time. Memories of childhood in Suez and a cultivated family background are recaptured in *Youth and Tomorrow* (1946). He was educated at Abbotsholme, a progressive public school, and at Balliol College, Oxford. For a short period he worked without enthusiasm in the family shipping office in Port Said, and used the experience in his highly autobiographical last novel, *A Man Divided* (1950). There is scattered evidence that the international flavour of Port Said influenced his complex ideas about "true community". He was a pacifist, serving with the Friends' Ambulance Unit in the First World War, and this provided material for *Last Men in London* (1932). He took a doctorate in philosophy at Liverpool University.

OS's first published work was *Latter-Day Psalms* (1914), a small book of verse printed privately. It is remarkable only for showing at the outset a preoccupation with the themes that would engage him for the rest of his life: the irrelevance of a RELIGION based on hopes of immortality and the hypothesis of an evolving god. There was a gap of 15 years before the next book, *A Modern Theory of Ethics* (1929), written when OS was 43. Here is the philosophical underpinning for all the major ideas that would appear repeatedly in the fiction: moral obligation as a teleological requirement, ecstasy as a cognitive intuition of cosmic excellence, personal fulfilment of individual

capacities as an intrinsic good, community as a necessary prerequisite for individual fulfilment, and the hopeless inadequacy of human faculties for the discovery of truth. It was this last conviction which provided the springboard for the writing of his fiction: all the fiction, by some speculative device or other, strives to overcome the congenital deficiencies of the ordinary human being.

Last and First Men (1930), OS's first work of fiction, caused something of a sensation. Contemporary novelists and critics acclaimed it, though later, for a time, it was nearly forgotten. The book employs a time scale of 2,000 million years to describe the rise and fall of 18 races of men. The story is told by one of the Last (18th) Men working through the "docile but scarcely adequate brain" of one of the 1st Men (ourselves). The civilization of the 1st Men had reached its highest points in Socrates (the search for truth) and Jesus (self-oblivious worship). The 2nd, 3rd, 5th, 15th, 16th and 18th Men represent higher orders of wisdom. The emigration of the 5th Men to Venus is an early example of TERRAFORMING and the construction of the 9th Men to adapt them for Neptune is an early example of PANTROPY.

In *Odd John* (1935) the individual SUPERMAN appears, although his attributes are spiritual and intellectual, quite divorced from the supermen of the comics and pulp magazines. John recapitulates in his own evolution some of the characteristics of the 2nd, 3rd and 5th Men. He and his fellow "supernormals" finally achieve something akin to the wisdom of the 18th Men.

Star Maker (1937) is often regarded as OS's greatest work. Its cosmic range, fecundity of invention, precision and grandeur of language, structural logic, and above all its attempt to create a universal system of philosophy by which modern men might live, permit serious comparison with DANTE's *Divine Comedy*. The narrator is rapt from a suburban hilltop and becomes a "disembodied, wandering viewpoint". He observes "Other Men", whose extraordinary development of scent and taste should remind us of the relative nature of our own perceived values; and "strange mankinds", including the Human Echinoderms, whose communal method of reproduction provides an ingenious metaphor for the ideal of true community; and a wide range of species far removed from mankind. Of these ALIENS some of the most interesting are the "ichthyoids" and "arachnoids". Over a long period of time these two species come together in a symbiosis: the ichthyoids are artistic and mystical, while the arachnoids are dextrous and practical. The development of the relationship provides OS's most extended and detailed metaphor for the ideal of true

community, which has its microcosm in a pair of human lovers and its macrocosm in a universe of "minded" worlds (*see* LIVING WORLDS). The narrator proceeds to the "supreme moment of the cosmos" in which he faces the Star Maker and discovers something of his pitiless nature.

Paradoxically, the book with the greatest human interest is sometimes said to be *Sirius* (1944), the story of a dog with enhanced INTELLIGENCE, consciousness and sensibility. The dog, with its natural limitations, is a paradigm of our own limited capacity; but at the same time the dog's superior gifts, e.g. scent, are another reminder of human inadequacy.

The four works of sf described constitute the living core of OS's fiction. Both *Last and First Men* and *Star Maker* have their advocates as the finest sf ever written; many critics argue that *Odd John* is the best novel about a superman, and that *Sirius* is the best book with a non-human protagonist. All four works show OS's unwavering concern with the pursuit of truth and the impossibility of our species ever finding it. Each of the fictions sets up a speculative device to leap over the plodding faculties of *Homo sapiens*: the supernormal intelligence of *Homo superior* in *Last and First Men* and *Odd John*; and the alternative intelligence of alien creatures in *Star Maker* and *Sirius*. Along with the quest for truth, and as a necessary accompaniment to it, there is a search for the gateways to a "way of the spirit". These constant preoccupations give to all OS's work a striking consistency, and it is possible to place everything he did within a highly original scheme of METAPHYSICS. Everything has its place in the same cosmic history that the Star Maker coldly regards. In his avatar of Jahweh, the Star Maker had been invoked at the beginning in *Latter-Day Psalms*; and as the "mind's star" and "phantom deity" he will be there at the end in the posthumous *The Opening of the Eyes* (1954).

Of OS's remaining fiction, perhaps *The Flames* (1947) deserves most attention. The "flames" are members of an alien race, originally natives of the sun, who can be released when igneous rock is heated. They have affinities with the "supernormals" who occur on OS's other worlds. There are similarities with the recently discovered *Nebula Maker* (1976, but probably written mid-1930s). This book is part of a draft for *Star Maker* which OS put aside. It relates the history of the nebulae, and shows how their striving is brought to nothing by an uncaring God. Religion is dismissed as the opium of the people in *Old Man and New World* (1944). Supermen reappear in *Darkness and the Light* (1942) and cosmic history is recapitulated in *Death into Life* (1946). OS's insistence on scrupulously considering opposed points of view, and his sceptical intelligence, found an admirable vehicle in the imaginary conversations of *Four Encounters* (**1976**, but probably written later 1940s).

Of OS's non-fiction, *Philosophy and Living* (**1939**), written after the best of his fiction, is the most comprehensive work. The best introduction for the general reader is *Beyond the "Isms"* (**1942**) whose last chapter, under the characteristic heading "The Upshot", provides an admirable summary of his philosophy and a clear exposition of what he means by the "way of the spirit".

OS was writing in an ancient tradition of European speculative fiction. He called his stories "fantastic fiction of a semi-philosophical kind". He was completely unaware of sf as a genre and was somewhat taken aback when in the 1940s he was acclaimed by sf fans; he was even more taken aback when he was shown the contemporary magazines which provided their staple fodder. The acclamation he has received as an sf writer may partially account for his total neglect by historians of modern literature. At the same time he is sometimes ignored by such sf commentators as Kingsley AMIS in *New Maps of Hell* (**1960**), presumably partly because he did not write for the sf magazines and partly because his work is difficult to anthologize.

OS is the dimly perceived Star Maker behind many subsequent stories of the FAR FUTURE and GALACTIC EMPIRES. He did much original and seminal thinking about such matters as ALTERNATE WORLDS, COSMOLOGY, CYBORGS, COLONIZATION OF OTHER WORLDS, ESP, HIVE-MINDS, IMMORTALITY, MONSTERS, MUTANTS and TIME TRAVEL. Arthur C. CLARKE and James BLISH are among the few sf writers who have expressed their indebtedness to him, though his influence, both direct and indirect, on the development of many concepts which now permeate genre sf is probably second only to that of H.G. WELLS. [MA]

Other works (all non-fiction): *New Hope for Britain* (**1939**), *Saints and Revolutionaries* (**1939**), and numerous uncollected articles for such scholarly journals as *Mind* and *Philosophy*.

See also: ANTHROPOLOGY; DEVOLUTION; END OF THE WORLD; EVOLUTION; GENETIC ENGINEERING; GODS AND DEMONS; INVASION; LIFE ON OTHER WORLDS; OPTIMISM AND PESSIMISM; OUTER PLANETS; PHYSICS; SOCIOLOGY; SUN; VENUS.

STARK, HARRIET (? – ?). American writer. In her moral tale *The Bacillus of Beauty* (**1900**), a lady is infected with a beauty-enhancing germ (*see* BIOLOGY); her character subsequently deteriorates. [JC/PN]

STARK, RAYMOND (? –). British writer. In his *Crossroads to Nowhere* (**1956**), an anarchist unsuccessfully confronts a future dictatorship. [JC]

STARK, RICHARD *See* Donald E. WESTLAKE.

STARKE, HENDERSON *See* Kris NEVILLE.

STAR MAIDENS (vt **SPACE MAIDENS**) Television series (1975). ATV. Produced by James Gatward, written by Otto Strang, Eric Paice and Ian Stuart Black, starring Dawn Addams, Judy Geeson and Lisa Harrow. Directors included Freddie Francis, James Gatward, Wolfgang Storch and Hans Heinrich. 13 25-min. episodes. Colour.

This German/British co-production plunged sf on TV to new depths. It concerned a group of alien women from the planet of Medusa who come to Earth seeking two escaped males from their world (the women rule Medusa and the men are mere playthings). As the series progressed it became increasingly chaotic; it seemed that the budget had run out halfway through the shooting. The special effects were superior to the script. [JB]

STARMONT HOUSE *See* FAX COLLECTOR'S EDITIONS.

STARR, MARK *See* Gérard KLEIN.

STARR, ROLAND (? –). Author, possibly pseudonymous, of two routine sf novels, *Operation Omina* (**1970**) and *Time Factor* (**1975**). [JC]

STARS The stars have always exerted some kind of imaginative fascination upon the human mind. When they were believed to be mere points of light in the panoply of heaven it was held that the secrets of the future were written there. The Greeks wove their mythology into the patterns of the various constellations; Giorgio de Santillana and Hertha von Dechend, in their "essay on myth and the frame of time" *Hamlet's Mill* (**1969**), have argued that the observation of the stars in their courses lies at the foundation of all mythological chronographies of the universe. It was not until 1718 that Halley demonstrated that the stars were not "fixed", and not until the late 1830s that the distance of the nearer stars was determined. Their remoteness from the human world assured them of symbolic significance but denied them any other kind. It was the religious imagination rather than the scientific which first despatched imaginary voyagers so far from Earth. The notion of the stars as habitable worlds is associated with Giordano Bruno (executed for heresy in 1600), and was later popularized by Fontenelle in *Entretiens sur la pluralité des mondes* (**1686**; trans as *A Plurality of Worlds* **1688**). In the 18th century Emanuel SWEDENBORG's visions took him voyaging throughout the cosmos, and other religious mystics followed his example. C.I. DEFONTENAY, probably

influenced by Fontenelle, undertook to describe another stellar system in some detail in *Star; ou Psi de Cassiopée* (**1854**; trans. as *Star* **1975**), but the first work which took the scientific imagination out into the greater cosmos was Camille FLAMMARION's *Lumen* (**1887**; trans. **1897**). The first scientific romance of interstellar adventure was Robert W. COLE's *The Struggle for Empire* (**1900**), but it was not until the establishment of the sf magazines that the interstellar adventure playground was extensively exploited by such writers as E.E. "Doc" SMITH, Edmond HAMILTON and John W. CAMPBELL Jr. Hamilton became especially fascinated by the ultimate melodramatic flourish of exploding stars, and was still exploiting its potential in the 1950s.

This new familiarity with the stars did not breed contempt. They remained awe-inspiring entities in all stories which confronted them directly (rather than using them simply as coloured lamps to light imaginary worlds). Their sustained power of fascination is evident in Fredric BROWN's *The Lights in the Sky are Stars* (**1953**; vt *Project Jupiter*), Robert F. YOUNG's "The Stars are Calling, Mr. Keats" (1959) and Dean McLAUGHLIN's *The Man Who Wanted Stars* (**1965**), and nowhere more so than in Isaac ASIMOV's classic "Nightfall" (1941), which offers a new perspective on Emerson's statement: "If the stars should appear one night in a thousand years, how would man believe and adore and preserve for many generations the remembrance of the city of God!"

There are relatively few sf stories which make significant use of scientific knowledge concerning stars and their nature; one of them is Hal CLEMENT's "Cold Front" (1946), which links the behaviour of an odd star to the meteorology of one of its planets. In the last decade or so, however, the growing interest in the transcendental in sf (*see* RELIGION; METAPHYSICS) has allowed the awesome quality of the stars to take on clearer ideative form. The stars are credited with godlike life and intelligence in *Starchild* (**1965**) and *Rogue Star* (**1969**) by Frederik POHL and Jack WILLIAMSON, and a collective quasi-supernatural influence is jargonized into sf in *The Power of Stars* (**1972**) by Louise Lawrence. This metaphysical mysticism is carried to its logical extreme in an early section of *If the Stars are Gods* (1973; fix-up **1977**) by Gordon EKLUND and Gregory BENFORD, and the inspiration of Sun-worship also plays a minor part in *The Mote in God's Eye* (**1974**) by Larry NIVEN and Jerry POURNELLE. Even some of the "hardest" sf stories based on astronomical discoveries are not immune from this residual mysticism – it is evident in Poul ANDERSON's *The Enemy Stars* (**1959**), which features a "dead star" and in his "Starfog" (1967) and *World Without Stars* (**1967**). It seems, though, that the grandeur of the stars may be deflated by collapse, if Larry Niven's sober "Neutron Star" (1966) may be taken as typical.   [BS]

See also: ASTRONOMY; COSMOLOGY; LIVING WORLDS; SUN.

STAR SCIENCE FICTION MAGAZINE US DIGEST-size magazine. One issue, published by Ballantine Magazines, Jan. 1958. This was an attempt to convert Frederik POHL's STAR SF original anthology series into a magazine.   [BS]

STAR SCIENCE FICTION STORIES Original anthology series edited by Frederik POHL and published by BALLANTINE BOOKS. *SSFS* was the first such series, antedating NEW WRITINGS IN SF by 11 years. The series was irregular: after *Star Science Fiction Stories* (anth. **1953**), *Star Science Fiction Stories no.2* (anth. **1953**) and *Star Science Fiction Stories no.3* (anth. **1954**) there was a three-year gap. In Jan. 1958, Ballantine attempted to relaunch the title in magazine format, but this, STAR SCIENCE FICTION MAGAZINE, lasted only one issue. Reverting to book format, the series continued with *Star Science Fiction Stories no.4* (anth. **1958**), *no.5* (anth. **1959**) and *no.6* (anth. **1959**). *Star Short Novels* (anth. **1954**) was an additional, out-of-series volume. The first three volumes were of extraordinarily high quality; later issues, while highly competent, were less inspired. Notable stories published in *SSFS* include "The Nine Billion Names of God" by Arthur C. CLARKE (no.1), "Disappearing Act" by Alfred BESTER (no.2), "It's A *Good* Life" by Jerome BIXBY (no.2), "Foster, You're Dead" by Philip K. DICK (no.3) and "Space-Time for Springers" by Fritz LEIBER (no.4). *Star of Stars* (anth. **1960**; vt *Star Fourteen* UK) is an anthology of stories from *SSFS*. The later Ballantine anthology series *Stellar* clearly derives its title from *SSFS* (and even includes a corresponding *Stellar Short Novels*).   [MJE]

STARSHIP In sf TERMINOLOGY, obviously, a ship capable of travel between the stars — one of the many sf neologisms which have passed into the language. *See* GENERATION STARSHIPS; SPACESHIPS.   [PN]

STARTLING STORIES US PULP magazine. 99 issues, Jan. 1939-Fall 1955, published by Better Publications (later Standard Magazines), ed. Mort WEISINGER (Jan. 1939-May 1941); Oscar J. FRIEND (Jul. 1941-Fall 1944), Sam MERWIN (Winter 1945-Sep. 1951), Sam MINES (Nov. 1951-Fall 1954) and Alexander Samalman (Winter-Fall 1955). (Leo MARGULIES was editorial director of *SS* and its companion magazines during Weisinger's and Friend's editorships.)

SS was started as a companion magazine to THRILLING WONDER STORIES.

June 1943. The cover by Earle K. Bergey features his trademark, the brass brassiere.

Whereas *TWS* printed only shorter fiction, the policy of *SS* was to include a complete novel (albeit sometimes a very short novel) in each issue. In its early years the cover bore the legend: "A Novel of the Future Complete in This Issue". The space left for shorter stories was limited, and was partially filled by "Hall of Fame" reprints — stories from the Hugo GERNSBACK-edited WONDER STORIES and its predecessors. The first issue featured Stanley G. WEINBAUM's *The Black Flame* (Jan. 1939; **1948**); other contributors to its early years included Eando BINDER, Oscar J. Friend, Edmond HAMILTON, Henry KUTTNER, Manly Wade WELLMAN and Jack WILLIAMSON. Early covers were painted by Howard BROWN, but from 1940 onwards were mostly the work of Earle K. BERGEY, the artist whose style is most closely identified with *SS* and its sister magazines. The characteristic Bergey cover showed a rugged hero, a desperate heroine (either clad in a metallic bikini or in a dangerous state of *déshabille*) and a hideous alien menace.

Under Margulies and, more particularly, under Friend, *SS* adopted a deliberately juvenile slant. This was most clearly manifested in the patronizing shape of the character "Sergeant Saturn", who conducted the letter column and other readers' departments (in *TWS* and CAPTAIN FUTURE as well as in *SS*). Many readers were alienated by this, and when Sam Merwin became editor he phased out such puerility and built *SS* gradually into the best sf magazine of the period, apart from *ASF*. In 1948–9 it featured such novels as *What Mad Universe* (Sep 1948; **1949**) by Frederic Brown, *Against the Fall of Night* (Nov. 1948; **1953**; rev. vt *The City and the Stars* **1956**) by Arthur C. CLARKE and *Flight Into Yesterday* (May 1949; **1953**; vt *The Paradox Men*) by Charles L. HARNESS, in addition to novels by Kuttner and Murray LEINSTER and stories by Ray BRADBURY, Clarke, C.M. KORNBLUTH, John D. MACDONALD, A.E. VAN VOGT, Jack VANCE and others. Merwin left the magazine in 1951

(thereafter becoming a frequent contributor). By this time *SS*, like other pulp magazines, was feeling the effect of the increased competition provided by such new magazines as GALAXY and THE MAGAZINE OF FANTASY AND SCIENCE FICTION. Although the standard suffered to a degree, Merwin's successor, Samuel Mines, continued to publish interesting material, such as Philip José FARMER's *The Lovers* (Aug. 1952; exp. **1961**) and many Jack Vance stories, notably *Big Planet* (Sep. 1952; **1957**). The magazine adopted a new cover slogan ("Today's Science Fiction — Tomorrow's Fact") and a more dignified appearance, but it became another victim of the general decline of pulp magazines. In Spring 1955, as the most popular title in its stable, it absorbed *TWS* and its more recent companion, FANTASTIC STORY MAGAZINE. After two further issues it ceased publication, one short of its hundredth number. Samuel Mines edited an anthology drawn from its pages, *The Best from Startling Stories* (anth. **1954**), while a number of its "Hall of Fame" reprints were collected in *From Off This World* (anth. **1949**), edited by Margulies and Friend. A heavily cut and very irregular British edition was published by Pembertons in 18 numbered issues, Jun. 1949-May 1954. A Canadian reprint series ran 1945–6, and a second 1948–1951.   [MJE]

Collectors should note: Although volume numeration was quite regular (33 vols of three numbers), the schedule was variable. A bi-monthly schedule operated from Jan. '39 to Mar. '43 which was followed by Jun. '43, and then a quarterly schedule marked by season from Fal. '43 to Fal. '46. (A Mar. issue appeared between Win. '46 and Spr. '46.) A regular bi-monthly schedule ran from Jan. '47 to Jan. '52, then monthly to Jun. '53, followed by Aug. '53, Oct. '53, Jan. '54, Spr. '54 and quarterly to Fal. '55.

STAR TREK Television series (1966-8). A Norway Production for Paramount Television/NBC. Created by Gene RODDENBERRY Executive producer. Gene Roddenberry. Producers: Gene Roddenberry, Gene L. Coon, John Meredyth Lucas and Fred Freiberger (last season only). Story consultants: Steven Carabatsos and D.C. FONTANA. Writers for the first and second seasons included Richard MATHESON, Robert BLOCH, Jerry SOHL, Theodore STURGEON, Harlan ELLISON, Gene L. Coon, D.C. Fontana, Gene Roddenberry, Jerome BIXBY, Max EHRLICH, Norman SPINRAD and David GERROLD. The only well-known writer to work for the third season was Jerome Bixby. Directors on the series included Marc Daniels, James Goldstone, Vincent McEveety, Joseph Sargent, Joe Pevney, Judd Taylor, Marvin Chomsky and Gene Roddenberry. The series consisted of 78 episodes in all, each 50 mins long, in colour.

A phenomenon among sf TV series, *ST* was set on a giant starship, the *U.S.S. Enterprise*, the crew of which is on a mission to explore new worlds and, with the most famous split infinitive in TV history, "... to boldly go where no man has gone before". Though the crew supposedly numbered several hundred, only a few of them were ever seen at one time, the principal characters being Captain Kirk (William Shatner), Mr Spock (Leonard Nimoy), Doctor McCoy (De Forest Kelley), Mr Sulu (George Takei) and Scotty (James Doohan). Though it did not achieve mass popularity when it was first shown, the series quickly attracted a hard core of devoted fans, known as Trekkies, which has grown over the years. There have been a number of *ST* CONVENTIONS, some of which have attracted a much greater attendance than ordinary sf conventions. Reasons for this almost fanatical following are not clear; it has been suggested that the cosy family unit presented in the series was attractive to adolescents, but it is more likely that the answer lies with the ambiguous sexuality of Spock, particularly as most of the show's most ardent fans are female. It is doubtful whether the sf elements of *ST* have much to do with its popularity. As sf it was often adequate and occasionally quite strong in the first two seasons, but the quality of the scripts had dropped badly by the end of the third season. Several well-known sf writers contributed to the first two seasons, but their work was invariably rewritten by the show's regular writers. The SPACE-OPERA format was not used, as a general rule, with any great imagination. A typical episode would face the crew with alien superbeings, monsters, or cases of apparent demoniac possession. The formula seldom varied; many adult viewers came to feel that the series suffered from a blandness resulting from the repetition of plot ideas, the clumsiness of the scientific elements, the trite moralizing, and the effort to please all viewers and offend none by the inclusion of a token Russian, token Asiatic, and in the person of actress Nichelle Nichols, who played Uhura, a token black and token woman in one package: all these characters behaved in a traditional white Anglo-Saxon protestant manner. Only Spock was a truly original creation.

The early two-part episode "The Menagerie", which was adapted from the original pilot for the series, won a 1967 HUGO award for best dramatic presentation, as did Harlan Ellison's episode, "City on the Edge of Forever", in 1968. The latter is generally thought to be the best of the individual episodes; it posed a moral dilemma which cut more deeply than usual. The original script, which differed slightly from the filmed version, was published in *Six Science Fiction Plays* (anth. **1976**) ed. Roger ELWOOD.

Despite the reservations of many viewers, there is no doubt that *ST* was one of the best sf TV series, certainly in comparison to the puerility of many of its predecessors. Its success had extraordinary repercussions in the publishing industry. James BLISH (*see his entry for details*) published 11 books of *ST* adaptations between 1967 and 1975, and one original novel, *Spock Must Die* (**1970**), based on the same characters. Another novelization was *Star Trek: Mission to Horatius* (**1969**) by Mack REYNOLDS. More recently the original novels *Spock, Messiah!* (**1976**) by Theodore R. COGSWELL and Charles A. Spano, *The Price of the Phoenix* (**1977**) by Sondra Marshak and Myrna Culbreath and *Planet of Judgment* (**1977**) by Joe HALDEMAN have been published, all based on *ST* characters; the last is the best. Two early accounts of *ST* and its production problems were written by David Gerrold: *The World of Star Trek* (**1973**) and *The Trouble with Tribbles* (**1973**). The latter included Gerrold's *ST* script of the same title, together with an account of its production. The first account of *ST* published as a book was *The Making of Star Trek* (**1968**) written by Stephen E. WHITFIELD, and credited on the cover to Whitfield and Roddenberry. Other *ST* spin-offs in book form are *Star Trek Blueprints* (**1975**) and *Star Fleet Technical Manual* (**1975**), both prepared by Franz Joseph Designs; *Star Trek Puzzle Manual* (**1976**) by James Razzi; *Letters to Star Trek* (anth. **1977**) ed. Susan Sackett; *Star Fleet Medical Reference Manual* (**1977**) ed. Eileen Palestine; *Star Trek Concordance* (**1976**) by Bjo Trimble; *Star Trek: The New Voyages* (anth. **1976**) ed. Sondra Marshak and Myrna Culbreath. The latter is a collection of moderately dire *ST* stories written by fans of the series, mostly amateur, but including Juanita COULSON. A new series of "fotonovels" — in comic-book style, but using stills from episodes instead of drawings — was inaugurated with *Star Trek Fotonovel 1: City on the Edge of Forever* (**1977**), based on the Harlan Ellison script. *I am not Spock* (**1975**) by Leonard Nimoy is a cautious account, not going very deep, of the actor's relation to the character he played. *Star Trek Lives!* (coll. **1975**) by Jacqueline Lichtenberg, Sondra Marshak and Joan Winston is a collection of notes and anecdotes about the series and about *ST* fandom in general.

When it became clear that the fuss over *ST* was unlikely to die down, NBC commissioned an animated cartoon series, also called *Star Trek*, based on the original series, but introducing several new characters, including an orange, tripedal alien navigator, Arex, and a cat-like alien communication officer, M'Ress. The voices were done by the actors from the original series. The animated series ran through the 1973–4 season. One episode was written by Larry NIVEN, and several by David Gerrold. This series in turn spawned yet more book adaptations, in the form of the *Star Trek Log* series, by Alan Dean FOSTER (*who see for details*), of which nine appeared 1974–7.

Rumours, counter-rumours and press releases about proposed revivals of *Star Trek*, either on TV or as a feature film, have abounded for several years. In 1977 a new TV series produced by Gene Roddenberry was announced, but shortly afterwards appeared to founder through lack of enthusiasm from independent TV stations. More reliable is the 1978 announcement of a high-budget (possibly $15 million) feature film to be directed by Robert WISE and scripted by Roddenberry, with Doug TRUMBULL as special-effects adviser and all the main players from the original cast. [PN/JB]

STAR WARS Film (1977). 20th Century-Fox. Directed by George LUCAS,

Bad knight Darth Vader (David Prowse) and good knight Obi-Wan Kenobi (Alec Guinness) duel with lightsabres in STAR WARS.

starring Mark Hamill, Harrison Ford, Carrie Fisher, Alec Guinness and Peter Cushing. Screenplay by George Lucas. 121 mins. Colour.

The most financially successful sf film to date, *SW* is an entertaining pastiche that draws upon a wide variety of other genres such as comic strips, old serials, Westerns, James Bond stories, *The Wizard of Oz*, *Snow White*, Errol Flynn swashbucklers and movies about the Second World War. The ending, for instance, is lifted from *The Dam Busters*. Lucas may not have succeeded in unifying all these diverse elements into a satisfying whole, and his script is extremely though deliberately juvenile, but the film is always visually interesting. The gratifyingly spectacular special effects and martial music hypnotize the audience into a state of uncritical acceptance of the basically absurd, deliberately PULP-style conflict between good and evil. A young man, Luke Skywalker, becomes involved in a mission to rescue a beautiful princess from the clutches of the evil Tarkin, who represents a decadent GALACTIC EMPIRE (perhaps inspired by Isaac ASIMOV's "Foundation" series). Tarkin's henchman is a mysterious, masked, black-clad giant, Darth Vader, who looks like a cross between Dr Doom (of MARVEL COMICS) and a Samurai warrior; they are based in a vast space station, the Death Star, which is the size of a small moon and capable of destroying whole planets. With the help of an old man who possesses supernatural powers, a mercenary and two cute robots, Luke rescues the princess and secures the secret information that enables a group of rebel fighters to destroy the Death Star. He is assisted by a power of good, the "Force", left sufficiently vaguely ecumenical as to be equally inoffensive to Buddhist, Christian and Moslem.

The special effects are of a sophistication greater than anything previous in the history of sf cinema, approached only by those of Stanley KUBRICK's *2001: A Space Odyssey* (1968). But where Kubrick's team went back to the painstaking techniques of the silent era, John Dykstra, in charge of *SW*'s miniature photography, succeeded in achieving comparable results using an automatic matteing system with the help of such technical innovations as a computer-linked effects camera. While the model work was created by American effects men, the live-action settings and effects were created by British technicians, such as John Barry, production designer, and John Stears, physical effects.

The novelization, attributed to George Lucas, but rumoured to be ghost-written by Alan Dean FOSTER, is *Star Wars* (1976). [JB/PN]

STARZL, R(AYMOND) F. (1899–). American journalist and story-writer. He began publishing sf with "Out of the Sub-Universe" for *AMZ Quarterly* in 1928 (the sub-universe is sub-microscopic), and wrote over 20 stories from that date, one with Festus PRAGNELL, to 1934, when he ceased to publish his typical PULP-style adventures and SPACE OPERAS. [JC]

STASHEFF, CHRISTOPHER (? –). American writer, who has worked in educational TV. His *The Warlock in Spite of Himself* (**1969**) and its sequel *King Kobold* (**1971**), especially the former, successfully combine sf and SWORD AND SORCERY in adventure plots on the medieval planet of Gramarye; the clumsy robot in the first book is agreeably comic. The MAGIC involved has a thin rationalization to do with PSI POWERS. [JC/PN]
See also: FANTASY; SUPERNATURAL CREATURES; TECHNOLOGY.

STATIC SOCIETIES *See* ANTI-INTELLECTUALISM IN SF; CONCEPTUAL BREAKTHROUGH; DYSTOPIAS; UTOPIAS.

STATTEN, VARGO *See* John Russell FEARN.

STEBER, A.R. House name used on the Ziff-Davis magazines AMAZING STORIES and FANTASTIC ADVENTURES, primarily by Ray PALMER, sometimes by his close friend Rog PHILLIPS, who also used it for one story in OTHER WORLDS. [PN]

STEELE, ADDISON II *See* Richard A. LUPOFF.

STEIGER, A(NDREW) J(ACOB) (1900–). American writer, whose novel *The Moon Man* (**1961**) involves the philosophical lunar thoughts of immortals. [PN]

STEINER, KURT *See* André RUELLAN.

STEPFORD WIVES, THE Film (1975). Columbia. Directed by Bryan Forbes, starring Katharine Ross, Paula Prentiss, Peter Masterson, Nanette Newman and Patrick O'Neal. Screenplay by William Goldman, based on the novel by Ira Levin. 114 mins. Colour.

In this black satire on the role of women in American society, a young wife is persuaded by her husband to move to the deceptively sleepy town of Stepford in Connecticut. She finds the other housewives in the area dull, their interests confined to housework and cooking. Her husband, on the other hand, seems happy with the situation and spends an increasing amount of time at the local Men's Society headquarters. It turns out that the men of Stepford are taking part in a bizarre conspiracy to replace their wives with robot duplicates — a scheme devised by an ex-employee of Disney World ("Why? Because we *can*!" he tells her). She tries to escape, but her children are kidnapped and she is forced to surrender. The final shots show the robot wives of Stepford drifting around a vast supermarket.

Despite the flaws in the logic of the plot this is an above average example of the genre — a sophisticated mixture of THE INVASION OF THE BODY SNATCHERS and *Rosemary's Baby* (also from a Levin novel) and an interesting evocation of a certain type of feminist paranoia. [JB]

STEPHENSON, ANDREW M. (1946–). English writer, (born in Venezuela), electronic design engineer

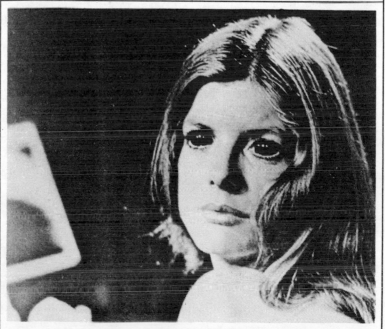

The heroine's android duplicate in THE STEPFORD WIVES is almost ready for action, requiring only an eye transplant. The actress is Katharine Ross.

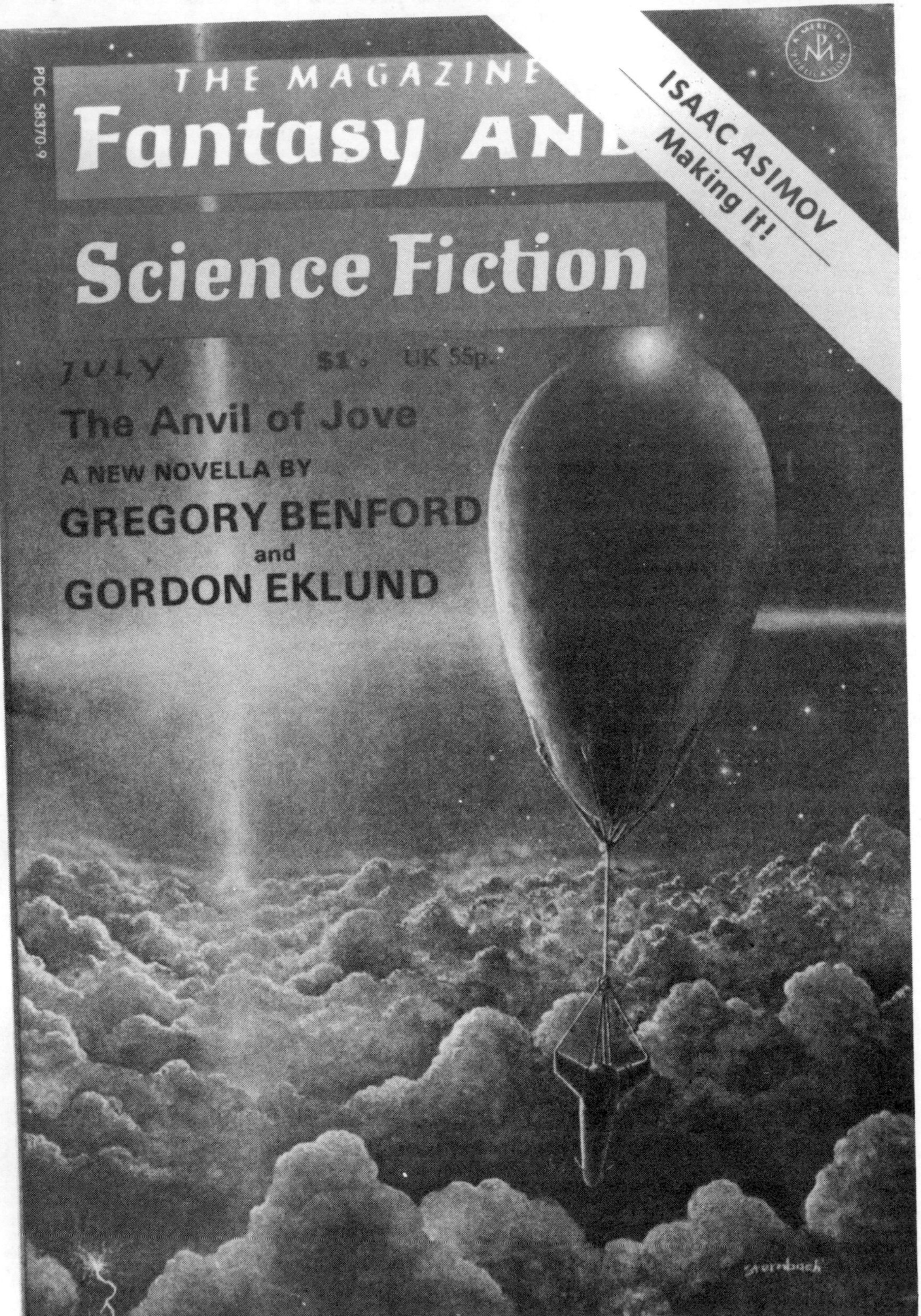

THE MAGAZINE

PDC 58370-9

Fantasy AND

Science Fiction

JULY $1. UK 55p.

The Anvil of Jove

A NEW NOVELLA BY

GREGORY BENFORD
and
GORDON EKLUND

ISAAC ASIMOV
Making It!

Rick Sternbach is perhaps the most popular sf artist of the mid 1970s. This glowing cover is July 1976.

An early *Nick Fury* comic-book cover by James STERANKO, one of the series whose sophisticated graphics first won him fame. Nov. 1968.

Steranko History of the 'Comics (**1970**) and *The Steranko History of the Comics Volume 2* (**1971**). He publishes and edits a semi-professional magazine *Mediascene* (1974 onwards, first six numbers as *Comixscene*) which covers fantasy, heroic fantasy, and sf activity in comics, posters, films, television, records and books. He has received many awards, including Best Illustrator of the Year Award in 1970.
[PN/JG]

STEREOTYPES *See* CLICHÉS; HEROES; PULP MAGAZINES; SCIENTISTS; SEX; SPACE OPERA; VILLAINS.

STERLING, BRETT House name used originally in the magazines STARTLING STORIES and CAPTAIN FUTURE for five short "Captain Future" novels, three of which ("The Star of Dread", 1943, "Magic Moon", 1944, and "Red Sun of Danger", 1945) were by Edmond HAMILTON. The second and third of these saw book publication as *The Tenth Planet* (**1969**) and *Danger Planet* (**1968**), both as by BS. Two "Captain Future" stories by BS actually written by Joseph Samachson are "Days of Creation" (1944) and "Worlds to Come" (1943). The BS pseudonym was used once more by Hamilton in "Never the Twain Shall Meet" (1946 *TWS*) and once by Ray BRADBURY in "Referent" (1948 *TWS*).
[PN]

STERN, J(ULIUS) DAVID (1886– ?). American writer and newspaper publisher. His *Eidolon* (**1952**) tells of a virgin birth.
[PN]

STERN, PAUL F. *See* Paul ERNST.

STERNBACH, RICK (1951–). American astronomical and sf illustrator. He has done cover and interior illustrations for a variety of books and magazines including *Gal., FSF, If, ASF,* and BALLANTINE BOOKS. He has also worked for *Astronomy Magazine* and is nearly as well known for his astronomical paintings as for his sf illustrations. He is an acknowledged master of the airbrush but also uses ordinary brushes, particularly with gouache, extremely well. He uses mainly reds, blues and one particular shade of purple. Though his landscapes and spaceships are very convincing, his figures are sometimes awkward, but at his best he shows a splendidly inventive sense of design. In 1976, RS was instrumental in forming the Association of Science Fiction Artists (ASFA), an organization devoted to disseminating information to artists on such matters as copyright laws and contracts. He has been nominated for three HUGO awards for best professional artist, winning his first in 1977.
[JG]

and, under the name Ames, an illustrator who has published magazine and book illustrations; he began publishing sf with "Holding Action" for *ASF* in 1971, though he has not been active as a writer, publishing only one more story and his first novel, *Nightwatch* (**1977**) to date; this latter rather portentously describes adventures on the Moon and an alien contact.
[JC/PN]

STERANKO, JAMES (1938–). American COMIC BOOK illustrator, writer, and one-time stage magician. Influenced early in his career by the work of Jack KIRBY, as was virtually every modern American comic book illustrator, he rapidly developed a reputation for originality, especially with his work for MARVEL COMICS on the sf strip *Nick Fury, Agent of Shield* (Jun. 1968 - Mar. 1971) for which he painted the first seven covers and drew the stories for nos 1–3 and 5, and also for his work on *X-Men*

and *Captain America*. Some of his *Nick Fury* covers were revolutionary for comic books of that time, in their bold design and utilization of surrealist themes JS was not so much an innovator *per se* as an artist who took a number of techniques, hitherto seldom (and haphazardly) used, and welded them into a new style, in which the design unit became the whole double page, not just the single frame. Like Kirby's, his narrative technique was strongly cinematic, but JS's work was more stylized and baroque, and less straightforwardly representational. He has done remarkably few comics, considering the height of his reputation, but has been much imitated, by Philippe DRUILLET among others. JS has also illustrated some paperback book covers, notably for *The Shadow* series, and is working on a history of pulps and comics, planned to be six vols, of which the first two have been published. *The*

STERNBERG, JACQUES (1923–). Belgian writer. A particularly idiosyncratic author with a keen sense of the absurd, JS has since 1953 built a unique body of work, often only tenuously linked to sf, where everyday situations logically degenerate into darkly humorous nightmares. *Futurs - sans avenir* (coll. **1971**; incomplete trans. as *Future without Future* **1974**) is a representative selection. JS also wrote the script for Alain Resnais' only sf film, JE T'AIME, JE T'AIME (**1968**). [MJ]

Other works: *La géometrie dans l'impossible* ["Impossible Geometry"] (coll. **1953**); *La sortie est au fond de l'espace* ["The Way Out is at the Bottom of Space"] (**1956**); *Entre deux mondes incertains* ["Between Two Uncertain Worlds"] (coll. **1957**); *La géometrie dans la terreur* ["Geometry in Terror"] (coll. **1958**); *L'employé* ["The Employee"] (**1958**); *Toi, ma nuit* ["You, my Night"] (**1956**; trans. as *Sexualis 95* **1967**); *Univers zéro* ["Universe Zero"] (coll. **1970**); *Attention, planète habitée* ["Beware, Inhabited Planet"] (**1970**); *Contes Glacés* ["Icy Tales"] (coll. **1974**); *Sophie, la mer, la nuit* ["Sophie, the Sea, the Night"] (**1976**); *Le navigateur* ["The Navigator"] (**1977**).

See also: PERCEPTION.

STEVENS, FRANCIS Pseudonym of American writer Gertude Barrows Bennett (1884– ?). She wrote 12 quite highly acclaimed fantasies in the period 1917–23, which appeared in ARGOSY, ALL-STORY MAGAZINE, THRILL BOOK and other early PULP MAGAZINES which published sf. A similarity in style and imagery led many readers to believe that FS was a pseudonym of A. MERRITT. The content is highest in her DYSTOPIAN novel *The Heads of Cerberus* (1919 *Thrill Book*; **1952**), in which a grey dust within a silver phial transports its inhalers to the totalitarian city of Philadelphia in AD 2118. Other works include the LOST-WORLD novel *The Citadel of Fear* (1918 *Argosy Weekly*; **1970**), *Claimed* (1920 *Argosy Weekly*; **1966**) in which an elemental being reclaims an ancient artefact, and the novels "Serapion" (1920), "The Labyrinth" (1918), "Avalon" (1919) and "Sunfire" (1923). Short stories include "The Elf Trap" (1919), "Friend Island" (1918) and "Behind the Curtain" (1918). Some of her stories were reprinted in FAMOUS FANTASTIC MYSTERIES and FANTASTIC NOVELS. [JE]

STEVENS, R.L. *See* Edward D. HOCH.

STEVENSON, ROBERT LOUIS (BALFOUR) (1850–94). Scottish author, best known for works outside the sf field. A student at Edinburgh University, he abandoned engineering for law, but never practised. He travelled widely, suffered most of his life from tuberculosis, and settled in Samoa in 1890. His early novel *The Strange Case of Dr. Jekyll and Mr. Hyde* (**1886**) shows the influence of an

Robert Louis STEVENSON. (National Portrait Gallery)

early Calvinist background on a hot, romantic temperament. An early version, resulting from a nightmare, which he scrapped, had an evil Jekyll using the Hyde transformation as a mere disguise. The published version has echoes of Deacon Brodie (hanged 1788), James Hogg's *Private Memoirs and Confessions of a Justified Sinner* (**1824**) and current psychological theories; it is a Faustian, moral fable which takes the form of a tale of mystery and horror. It precedes Oscar Wilde's *The Picture of Dorian Gray* (**1891**), which in some respects resembles it, by five years. It is the prototype of all stories of multiple personality, transformation and possession; in some aspects it is a tale of drug dependency also. The once respected and affluent Jekyll's full account is discovered at the end; he began dissociating his libertine side (cf. Freud's "Id") with a drug; the evil self, Hyde, that surfaced, in whose person Jekyll enjoys unspecified depravities (we are given instances of only rage, brutality and murder), is less robust at first. Then spontaneous Hyde-metamorphoses occur and after a temporary intermission larger and larger doses are needed to switch back to Jekyll. Supplies run out and, cornered, Hyde commits suicide. The symbolic physical changes (Hyde is young, stunted, nimble and repulsive) seem today unconvincing melodrama, and the silence about vices other than cruelty seems prudish, but the psychological power of the writing, including Jekyll's agonies, is patent. The story has been filmed many times (*see* DR JEKYLL AND MR HYDE) and has been deeply influential on the development of the theme of PSYCHOLOGY in sf. A small point: RLS pronounced "Jekyll" with a "long" *e*.

RLS wrote many other stories with fantastic or supernatural elements, most to be found in *New Arabian Nights* (coll. in two vols **1882**; contents of Vol.1 first appeared in the magazine *London* in 1878, under the general title "Latter-Day Arabian Nights"), *More New Arabian Nights: The Dynamiter* (coll. **1885**) with his wife, *The Merry Men, and Other Tales and Fables* (coll. **1887**) and *Island Nights' Entertainments* (coll. **1893**). The third collection includes "Thrawn Janet",

"Markheim" (a good-angel story with a twist), "Will o' the Mill" and "Olalla"; the last includes "The Bottle Imp". Many of these stories had previously appeared in magazines. [DIM]

See also: BIOLOGY; GOTHIC SF; MEDICINE; METAPHYSICS; PARANOIA AND SCHIZOPHRENIA; PREDICTION; SCIENTISTS; SEX; SUPERNATURAL CREATURES.

STEWART, GEORGE R(IPPEY) (1895–). American writer. He graduated from the University of California, obtaining his PhD in 1922; he later became professor of English there. He is the author of a number of novels and non-fiction works, including *Fire* (**1948**) and *Storm* (**1941**), in both of which the "protagonist" is the event of the novel's title. He is best known among sf readers for *Earth Abides* (**1949**), which tells of the struggle to survive and rebuild (*see* HOLOCAUST AND AFTER) after a virus plague has wiped out most of humanity; one of the finest of all DISASTER novels in sf, it is generally acknowledged to be a classic of the genre. It was the first winner of the INTERNATIONAL FANTASY AWARD. [MJE]

See also: PASTORAL; SOCIOLOGY.

STEWART, WENDELL *See* Gordon EKLUND.

STEWART, WILL *See* Jack WILLIAMSON.

STILSON, CHARLES B. (? – ?). American writer, active in the early decades of the century with serialized novels and some stories for the MUNSEY magazines; he is most noted for the sf-fantasy trilogy *Polaris of the Snows* (1915 *All-Story*; **1965**), *Minos of Sardanes* (1916 *All-Story*; **1966**) and *Polaris and the Immortals* (1917 *All-Story* as "Polaris and the Goddess Glorian"; **1968**). They feature an Antarctic LOST WORLD. [JC]

See also: ESCHATOLOGY.

STINE, G(EORGE) HARRY *See* Lee CORREY.

STINE, HANK (1945–). American writer, real name Hank Stein, whose *Season of the Witch* (**1968**) is an interesting blend of sf and erotica, in which a man is biologically transformed into a woman as a punishment for rape and murder and eventually finds happiness. HS has written chiefly thrillers. However, a second novel with an sf background is *Thrill City* (**1969**), which is set in a city devastated by World War Three. It was announced in autumn 1978 that HS would take over the editorship of GALAXY. [MJ]

See also: PSYCHOLOGY; SEX; WOMEN.

March 1942. Cover by Hannes Bok.

STIRRING SCIENCE STORIES US PULP magazine, changing to BEDSHEET-size for its last issue. Four issues, Feb. 1941-Mar. 1942, published by Albing Publications; ed. Donald A. WOLLHEIM. The companion magazine to COSMIC STORIES, *SSS* was produced under similarly adverse financial conditions. Its second issue was notable for carrying the first cover by artist Hannes BOK. *SSS* also featured many stories by C.M. KORNBLUTH (who contributed multiple stories to some issues, using various pseudonyms) and printed Damon KNIGHT's first published story. *SSS* was presented as two magazines in one: the second half was separately titled *Stirring Fantasy Fiction*, and came complete with its own editorial and readers' departments. After three bi-monthly issues the magazine suspended publication, re-emerging nine months later in an abortive revival, by Manhatten Fiction Publications, which only produced one more issue. [MJE]

STOCKBRIDGE, GRANT House name used by Popular Publications, especially in their PULP MAGAZINE THE SPIDER. Most if not all the GS stories were by Norvell W. PAGE. [PN]

STOCKTON, FRANK R(ICHARD) (1834–1902). American author and editor. He was on *Scribner's Magazine* before working as assistant editor of ST. NICHOLAS, 1873–81. It was during this period, while writing for children, that he developed his combination of humour

and fantasy, featured in such works as *Tales out of School* (coll. **1875**), which includes "How Three Men Went to the Moon", and *The Floating Prince and Other Fairy Tales* (coll. **1881**). His numerous short stories have appeared in over 20 collections, though several of these are just composite volumes of his better works, which include "The Lady or the Tiger?" (1882), a classic puzzle story; "The Transferred Ghost" (1882) and its sequel "The Spectral Mortgage" (1883); and his sf story "A Tale of Negative Gravity" (1884). Other short sf stories by him include "The Tricycle of the Future" (1885) and "My Translataphone" (1900; recently reprinted in *The Science Fiction of Frank R. Stockton*, coll. **1976**, ed. Richard Gid Powers).

Later, when FRS turned to novels, he continued occasionally to use sf themes, though his humorous style remained the most prominent feature of his fiction. In *The Great War Syndicate* (**1889**) a naval war between Britain and America is resolved when the British see the advanced weaponry arrayed against them. *The Great Stone of Sardis* (**1898**) is set in 1947 and culminates in the discovery that the Earth is a gigantic diamond with a relatively thin crust of surface soil. His other two novels, *The Vizier of the Two-Horned Alexander* (**1899**) and *The Adventures of Captain Horn* (**1895**), are respectively a retelling of the Wandering Jew theme and a LOST-WORLD novel.

FRS was influential on John Kendrick BANGS and other humorous fantasists. His complete works appear in *The Novels and Stories of Frank R. Stockton* (23 vols, **1899–1904**). [JE]

See also: UNDER THE SEA.

STOKER, BRAM (1847–1912). Irish writer, civil servant, theatrical manager closely associated with Henry Irving and the actress Ellen Terry, and playwright. He is best known as the author of *Dracula* (**1897**), the classic vampire novel. Although his fantasies are in the weird and occult fields, his writings do

contain sf elements. These, however, are generally treated as products of magic rather than of science, as in *The Jewel of the Seven Stars* (**1903**), in which an Egyptian princess, adept in an ancient science, rests in a form of SUSPENDED ANIMATION. Anthropomorphism of an antediluvian and malignly intelligent reptile is the central theme of *The Lair of the White Worm* (**1911**; vt *The Garden of Evil* USA). Other fantasy works include his Ruritanian romance *The Lady of the Shroud* (**1909**), *The Mystery of the Sea* (**1902**), centered on the Baconian cipher, *Under the Sunset* (coll. **1882**), consisting of allegorical fairy tales for children, and *Dracula's Guest* (coll. **1914**; vt *Dracula's Curse* USA), in which the title story is a chapter omitted from *Dracula*.

Although not a direct influence in sf, BS is of considerable importance to weird fiction. *Dracula* has been filmed on many occasions, though never in keeping with the novel, and has often been imitated. [JE]

STOKES, SIMPSON See F. Dubrez FAWCETT.

STONE, LESLIE F. Pseudonym (or more probably maiden name) of Mrs William Silberberg (1905–). American writer. She began publishing sf with "Men with Wings" for *Air Wonder Stories* in 1929, and was active in the field for the next eight years. Her two sf stories in book form are *When the Sun Went Out* (**1930**), a booklet in Hugo GERNSBACK's "Science Fiction" series, and *Out of the Void* (1929 *AMZ*; **1967**). The sequel to the latter SPACE OPERA was "Across the Void" (1930), another novel, never published as a book. [JC/PN]

See also: LIFE ON OTHER WORLDS.

STONG, PHIL(IP) (DUFFIELD) (1899–1957). American novelist and editor. His *The Other Worlds* (anth. **1941**) was the first important sf ANTHOLOGY. Its 25 stories were approximately half sf, half horror, and were mostly drawn from the PULP MAGAZINES, never previously regarded as a proper source of material (in sf at least) for respectable hardcover books. [PN]

STOREY, ANTHONY (1928–). English writer, formerly a rugby player, brother of the novelist David Storey. *The Rector* (**1970**) and *The Centre Holds* (**1973**), the first two volumes of a projected trilogy, describe first the traumas surrounding the announced birth of a child its mother claims to be the new MESSIAH, and second the 1980s upheavals centering on the 12-year-old child, who calls himself Jesus. [JC]

STOREY, RICHARD See Horace L. GOLD.

STORM, JANNICK (1939–). Danish writer, editor and translator. In sf, he is important primarily as the editor of two major Danish book series, issued respectively by Hasselbalch and Notabene; these lines were instrumental in bringing sf to the notice of the general Danish reading public. JS has also edited several anthologies of translated sf stories, published and partly written the underground magazine *Limbo* (4 issues, 1970–72) and scripted Danish underground comics with an sf slant. His own writings include short stories, novels, criticism (where he has written a large number of essays on sf for Danish publications) and poetry. His collection *Miriam og andre* (coll. **1971**) contains some sf, but his other works lie outside the field. [J-HH]

STORM, MALLORY *See* Paul W. FAIRMAN.

STORM, RUSSELL *See* Robert Moore WILLIAMS.

STORR, CATHERINE (1913–). English doctor and writer, for many years a psychotherapist, since 1963 an author of children's books, journalism, and an sf novel, *Unnatural Fathers* (**1976**), in which the success of an experiment to make men capable of bearing children causes great upheavals in a NEAR-FUTURE England. [JC]
Other works: (all for children) *Rufus* (**1969**); *The Adventures of Polly and the Wolf* (**1970**); *Thursday* (**1972**).

STORY, JACK TREVOR (1917–). English writer, best known for such works outside the sf field as his first novel, *The Trouble With Harry* (**1949**), which Alfred Hitchcock filmed. Several of his more recent novels use sf components to make their points about the decline of England and the loss of youth; they include *Hitler Needs You* (**1970**), *One Last Mad Embrace* (**1970**), *Little Dog's Day* (**1971**), the surrealistic *The Wind in the Snottygobble Tree* (**1971**), and a borderline sf novel about sexual obsession, *Morag's Flying Fortress* (**1976**). [JC]

STORY OF MANKIND, THE Film (1957). Warner Bros. Directed by Irwin ALLEN, starring Ronald Colman, Vincent Price, the Marx Brothers, Hedy Lamarr, Cedric Hardwicke and Peter Lorre. Screenplay by Irwin Allen and Charles Bennett, suggested by the history by Hendrik Van Loon. 100 mins. Colour.
A godlike figure sits in the clouds, holding court to decide whether or not mankind should be destroyed by atomic war. Counsel for the defence and prosecution (the latter is the devil) call up as evidence some of history's better-known events: Moses receiving the Ten Commandments, Nero fiddling while Rome burns, Shakespeare writing a play. Harpo Marx plays Sir Isaac Newton. This bizarre film was produced and directed by Irwin Allen, who later made several sf films and TV series, including VOYAGE TO THE BOTTOM OF THE SEA. [JB]

The all-sf issue, no. 3, 1964.

STORYTELLER British pocketbook magazine, published by Liverpolitan, Birkenhead. The front cover and subscription form bear the variant title *International Storyteller*, while the spine and title page read *Storyteller*. No. 3 was an all-sf issue, all stories (apart from Chris BOYCE's first) by writers unknown in sf, some possibly pseudonymous. It is dated 1964, no editor named. Other issues were not sf. This has not previously been indexed as an sf magazine. [PN]

STOUT, REX (TODHUNTER) (1886–1975). American writer, best known for his detective novels featuring Nero Wolfe, beginning with *Fer-de-Lance* (**1934**) and continuing into the 1970s. His borderline sf novel, originally published anonymously, is *The President Vanishes* (**1934**), in which the disappearance of the American president causes a NEAR-FUTURE crisis. [JC]

STOVER, LEON E. (1929–). American anthropologist, editor and writer, professor of anthropology at the Illinois Institute of Technology, where he also teaches sf courses. He was science editor of *AMZ* 1967–9. He has been most active as writer and editor in collaboration with Harry HARRISON, editing with him *Apeman, Spaceman: Anthropological Science Fiction* (anth. **1968**), and writing with him *Stonehenge* (**1972**), a historical novel which links the building of Stonehenge with refugees from the explosion of ATLANTIS, seen as a Mediterranean island of the Mycenean era. With Willis E. McNELLY, he edited *Above the Human Landscape: an Anthology of Social Science Fiction* (anth. **1972**). He has published a critical work on sf, *La science-fiction américaine: essai d'anthropologie culturelle* (**1972**), based on one of his courses. It has not been published in English. He is a vigorous anthologist with forceful views; founder and first chairman of the JOHN W. CAMPBELL MEMORIAL AWARD, he resigned that post, later giving as his reason that the first novel awarded the prize was Barry N. MALZBERG's controversial *Beyond Apollo* (**1972**). [JC]
See also: ANTHROPOLOGY; COMMUNICATIONS; SF IN THE CLASSROOM.

Cover of bound edition, Jul./Dec. 1893.

STRAND MAGAZINE, THE British magazine published monthly by George Newnes, Ltd, ed. Sir George Newnes and others, Jan. 1891-Mar. 1950. *SM* was a low-priced magazine, though its appearance was by no means cheap, containing illustrated articles and fiction by well-known authors; its success created many rivals. In competition with PEARSON'S MAGAZINE it began featuring sf regularly (it had previously published Jules VERNE's "An Express of the Future", 1895). Foremost among its sf contributors were Grant ALLEN, F.M. White, H.G. WELLS and Arthur Conan DOYLE. It is best remembered for the serializations of Wells's *The First Men in the Moon* (1900–01; **1901**) and Doyle's *The Lost World* (1912; **1912**), *The Poison Belt* (1913; **1913**) and "The Maracot Deep" (1927–8), title story of *The Maracot Deep and Other Stories* (coll. **1929**). [JE]
See also: *Science Fiction By Gaslight: A History and Anthology of Science Fiction in the Popular Magazines 1891–1911* (**1968**) by Sam MOSKOWITZ.

STRANG, HERBERT Collaborative pseudonym of British writers George Herbert Ely (? – ?) and C.J. L'Estrange (? – ?) used on a large number of boys' adventure stories. These included a series of novels about futuristic TRANSPORTATION devices, including *King of the Air* (**1907**), *Lord of the Seas* (**1908**), *The Cruise of the Gyro-Car* (**1910**),

Round the World in Seven Days **(1910)**, *The Flying Boat* **(1911)** and *A Thousand Miles an Hour* **(1928)**. HS also published future-war "Yellow Peril" stories. [PN] **Other works:** *The Heir of a Hundred Kings* **(1930)**; *The Old Man of the Mountain* **(1932)**.

See also: NEAR FUTURE; UNDER THE SEA.

No. 1, 1946. Cover by H.W. Perl.

STRANGE ADVENTURES British PULP-size magazine. Two undated issues, 1946 and 1947, published by Hamilton & Co., Stafford; no editor named. *SA* was an unmemorable juvenile magazine; a companion was FUTURISTIC STORIES. [FHP]

Third issue, mysteriously called no. 10, Fall 1969.

STRANGE FANTASY One of the many reprint DIGEST-size magazines published by Sol Cohen's Ultimate Publishing Co. Six issues, three in 1969 (nos 8–10) and three in 1970 (nos 11–13). This strange numbering seems to be connected with the temporary death of SCIENCE FICTION (ADVENTURE) CLASSICS after no.8, in 1969, but *SF* is not simply a variant title of the latter, which began again at the end of 1970. Also, *Science Fiction (Adventure) Classics* concentrated on sf, whereas *SF* concentrated on fantasy, mostly reprinted

from FANTASTIC during the period of Cele GOLDSMITH's editorship.

Strange Fantasy Yearbook (1970) has been reported as existing, but not confirmed by us. It is not listed in the standard indexes. [PN]

STRANGE NEW WORLD Made-for-TV film (1975). Warner Bros TV/ABC. Directed by Robert Butler, starring John Saxon, Kathleen Miller, Keene Curtis, James Olson, Martine Beswick and Gerrit Graham. Screenplay by Walton Green, Ronald F. Graham and Al Ramrus. 100 mins. Colour.

This was another television film made by cobbling together two completed episodes from TV series produced by Gene RODDENBERRY that never got off the ground, though in this case his name was not included in the credits. Three astronauts, after 180 years in suspended animation, return to an Earth devastated by a meteor storm. Civilization has divided into small societies, all differing greatly. The astronauts encounter two. Eterna is a sterile Utopia, with an obsession for cleanliness, that has conquered death; the three wholesome travellers ensure that death makes a cleansing return to Eterna before they leave. They go on to restore peace in Arboria, a land divided by two factions, the Hunters and the Zookeepers, the latter being fanatical conservationists ready to kill to achieve their aims. [JB]

STRANGER WITHIN, THE Made-for-TV film (1974). Lorimar Productions for ABC TV. Directed by Lee Philips, starring Barbara Eden, George Grizzard, Joyce Van Patten and David Doyle. Teleplay by Richard MATHESON, based on his short story "Mother by Protest" (1953). 75 mins. Colour.

A woman becomes inexplicably pregnant (her husband is sterile) and it turns out that she has been impregnated by a wandering Martian seed. At first the unpleasant side-effects of the pregnancy drive her to an attempted abortion, but she finally bears a healthy child who, along with a number of other Martian babies, floats off back towards Mars. The film was clearly an attempt to cash in on the popularity of *Rosemary's Baby*, but Matheson may be exonerated, since he wrote the story 20 years before. [JB]

STRANGE STORIES US PULP magazine. 13 issues, Feb. 1939-Feb. 1941, published by Better Publications Inc.; ed. Leo MARGULIES. A companion magazine to STARTLING STORIES and THRILLING WONDER STORIES, *SS* was devoted to supernatural and weird fiction, in competition with WEIRD TALES. Most of its covers were the work of Earle K. BERGEY. Its contributors included August DERLETH, Henry KUTTNER and Manly Wade WELLMAN. Oddly, although its companion magazines always publicized one another, they hardly mentioned SS.

First issue, Feb. 1939.

The magazine has remained remarkably little known. [MJE] **Collectors should note:** There were four vols of three numbers each, and a fifth with one number. The bi-monthly schedule was regular.

STRANGE TALES was a title used on two magazines. Above, the US version, Oct. 1932, cover by Wesso; overleaf, the UK version, no. 1, April 1946, cover by Alva Rogers.

STRANGE TALES US PULP magazine. Seven issues, Sep. 1931-Jan. 1933, published by Clayton Magazines; ed. Harry BATES. *ST* (subtitled "of Mystery and Terror") was a companion magazine to ASTOUNDING STORIES and was similar in editorial policy to WEIRD TALES. Its contributors included Robert E. HOWARD, Clark Ashton SMITH, Jack WILLIAMSON and other authors familiar to readers of *ASF* and *Weird Tales*. Its covers were all the work of WESSO. Like *ASF* it ceased publication when the Clayton chain of

WEIRD AND FANTASTIC FICTION
FIRST SELECTION   ONE SHILLING NET

magazines went into liquidation; unlike *ASF* it was not taken over by another publisher. *Strange Tales* (anth. **1976**) is a facsimile collection of stories from the magazine produced by Odyssey Publications. A British weird-story reprint magazine, also called *Strange Tales*, was a DIGEST that appeared for only two undated issues in 1946–7, ed. Walter GILLINGS, from Utopia Publications, featuring stories by Jack Williamson, John Beynon Harris (John WYNDHAM), Clark Ashton Smith, Ray BRADBURY, Robert BLOCH, H.P. LOVECRAFT and others.   [MJE/PN]
Collectors should note: The US *ST* had two vols of three numbers each and a third of one number. After four bi-monthly issues the schedule was irregular.

STRANGE WORLD OF PLANET X, THE (vt **THE COSMIC MONSTER**) Film (1958). Eros/DCA. Directed by Gilbert Gunn, starring Forrest Tucker, Gaby André, Martin Benson and Wyndham Goldie. Screenplay by Paul Ryder and Joe Ambor, based on the BBC TV serial of the same name, from the novel by René Ray. 75 mins. B/w.

This is a very poor British film about giant insects accidentally created by aliens from outer space. The creatures are eventually destroyed by a friendly alien in his flying saucer. The special effects were created on a tiny budget.   [JB]

STRATFORD, H. PHILIP *See* Kenneth BULMER

STRATTON, CHRIS *See* PSYCHOLOGY.

STRAUSS, ERWIN S. A member of the Massachusetts Institute of Technology sf society, ESS compiled on their behalf *Index to the S-F Magazines, 1951–1965* (**1966**), a bibliography which covers the same years as Norman METCALF's similar index; both these works succeed the original index for 1926–50 by Donald B. DAY. Unlike Metcalf's, ESS's book is

compiled from a computer printout, and contains an issue-by-issue contents listing of the magazines for the period, in addition to story and author indexes. The MIT group, now known as NESFA (New England Science Fiction Association) has produced subsequent volumes, starting with *Index to the Science Fiction Magazines 1966–1970* (**1971**), with annual volumes since. From 1971, they have also covered the contents of original anthologies.   [PN]

STRETE, CRAIG (? –). Pseudonym of a Cherokee Indian writer whose Amerindian name has not been revealed, who has written under this and other names, by himself and in collaboration. He has an MFA in creative writing. At least 40 of his 80 or more stories are under unrevealed names other than CS. As CS, he began publishing for *If* in 1974 with the well-known "Time Deer", a runner-up for the 1975 NEBULA award, along with two other simultaneously published tales. His books are *If All Else Fails, we can Whip the Horse's Eyes and Make Him Cry and Sleep* (coll. **1976**, published in Amsterdam), introduced by Jorge Luis BORGES, and *The Bleeding Man and Other Science Fiction Stories* (coll. **1977**). In his intensely written stories, CS frequently combines prose rhythms and subject matter from his Amerindian background with more usual sf themes, like COLONIZATION OF OTHER WORLDS in "When They Find You" from the second volume; his writing is spare, committed, often moving; its conjunctions between imagery from the white and the Amerindian worlds, however, though passionate, are sometimes crude in their opposition of the total horror of the former with the "naturalness" of the latter.   [JC/PN]

STRICK, PHILIP (1939–). English sf and film critic, anthologist and teacher, and managing director of a leading 16mm film library. He initiated in 1969 one of the first adult evening classes in sf in the UK, which still continues, sponsored by the University of London (*see* SF IN THE CLASSROOM). PS's most important work is *Science Fiction Movies* (**1976**), a witty, stimulating and well-illustrated account of the genre, which, despite its lack of a filmography, is probably the best introduction to sf CINEMA. He also edited a collection of funny sf stories (*see* HUMOUR), *Antigrav* (anth. **1975**).   [PN]

STRIKE, JEREMY Pseudonym of American writer Thomas E(dward) Renn (1939–). His sf novel is *A Promising Planet* (**1970**).   [JC]

STRINGER, ARTHUR (JOHN ARBUTHNOTT) (1874–1956). Canadian writer, prolific in several genres; of his many works, of sf interest is *The Woman Who Couldn't Die* (**1929**),

about a resuscitated Viking woman. *The Wolf Woman* (**1928**) is fantasy. *The Man Who Couldn't Sleep* (coll. **1919**) contains a number of fantasy stories.   [JC]

STROUD, ALBERT *See* Algis BUDRYS.

STRUGATSKI, ARKADY (NATANOVICH) (1925–) and **BORIS (NATANOVICH)** (1931–). Russian writers. AS studied English and Japanese, and worked as technical translator and editor; BS was a computer mathematician at Pulkovo astronomical observatory; both seem now to be freelance writers. The brothers' early cycle — *Strana bagrovykh tuch* (**1959** USSR), *Shest' spichek* (coll. **1960** USSR), *Put'na Amal'teiu* (coll. **1960** USSR; lead novella trans. as title story of *Destination: Amaltheia*, anth. in English **1962**), *Vozvrashchenie (Polden'.22-i vek)* (coll. **1962** USSR; exp. to 22 stories 1967 USSR; trans. as *Noon: 22nd Century* **1978**), and *Stazhery* (**1962** USSR) — is an optimistic future HISTORY on or near Earth, where the romance of exploration, and Utopian ethics, are acted out by believable vernacular heroes.

History with its pain re-entered in the Strugatskis' early masterpieces *Dalakaia Raduga* (**1963** USSR; trans. by Myers as *Far Rainbow* **1967**), where the darkness invading human existence is a physical catastrophe, and *Trudno byt' bogom* (**1964** USSR; trans. by Ackerman from German as *Hard to be a God* **1973**), where — more directly — it is a regress into a political obscurantism fusing fascism and Stalinism. The successful domestication of vivid historical novel into sf, answering social devolution with tragic, personal, Utopian activism, makes this their paradigmatic early work.

A third phase, in which the VOLTAIRE-like candid protagonist confronts a modern mass society with monopolized information channels, joins formal mastery to societal bewilderment. A masterly updating of the folk-tale to embody the black and white magic of modern alienated science and society results in the loose picaresque of *Ponedel'nik nachinaetsia v subbotu* (**1965** USSR; trans. as *Monday Begins on Saturday* **1977**) and the wildly hilarious satire of "scientifico-administrative" bureaucracy *Skazka o troike* (mag. publ. 1968 USSR; first book publication in Russian 1972 W. Germany; trans. by Bouis as *Tale of the Troika* in same volume as *Roadside Picnic* **1977**). The universe of *Ulitka na sklone* ["The Snail on the Slope"] (mag. publ. 1966–8 USSR), translation projected, is a swampy forest seen indistinctly through interlocking stories of two protagonists expressing the dilemma of accommodation or refusal when faced with huge power-complexes; the "Kandid" story at least, employing stream-of-consciousness techniques and archaic rural speech, is a gem of Russian literature. *Vtoroe nashestvie Marsian* (1968 USSR; trans. by Matias and Barrett as "The Second Martian Invasion" in *Vortex*, anth. **1970**) is the Strugatskis' Swift-like masterpiece: misinformation, economic corruption and quislingism, more effective than H.G. WELLS's super-weapons, are witnessed through the philistine narrator. With *Obitaemyi ostrov* (**1971** USSR; trans. as *Prisoners of Power* **1978**) begins the Strugatskis' final sombre phase, often as incongruous juvenile heroics amid increasing alienation and desperation. Possibly the richest work in this vein is *Roadside Picnic* (mag. publ. 1972 USSR; trans. by Bouis in same volume as *Tale of the Troika* **1977**).

The Strugatskis have moved from static Utopian brightness in a near future, through a return of the complex dynamics of history, to an unresolvable tension between the necessity of Utopian ethics and the inhuman, inscrutable powers of anti-Utopian stasis. Though the nexus of ethics with either politics or philosophy has remained unclear, so that their humanist criticism has sometimes fitted only loosely into sf, they are not only the best Soviet sf writers, legitimate continuators of the Gogol and Shchedrin to MAYAKOVSKY and Olesha line, but half a dozen of their novels, recognizing that people without cognitive ethics devolve into a predatory bestiary, approach major literature. [DS]
Other works: "Popytka k begstvu" (1962 USSR); *Khishchnye veshchi veka* (**1965** USSR; trans. by Rennen as *The Final Circle of Paradise* **1976**); *Gadkie lebedi* (**1972** W. Germany, disavowed edition); "Otel' "U pogibshego al'pinista" " (mag. publ. 1970 USSR), *Malysh* (**1973** USSR); *Paren' iz preispodnei* (**1976** USSR); "Za milliard let do kontsa sveta" (mag. publ. 1976–7 USSR; trans. as *Definitely Maybe* **1978**).
About the authors: "Criticism of the Strugatskii Brothers' Work" by Darko SUVIN, *Canadian-American Slavic Studies* no.2 (Summer 1972); "The Literary Opus of the Strugatskii Brothers" by Darko Suvin, *Canadian-American Slavic Studies* no.3 (Fall 1974).
See also: GODS AND DEMONS; ICONOCLASM; JUPITER; PHYSICS; POLITICS; TABOOS; UTOPIAS.

STUART, ALEX R. *See* Stuart GORDON.

STUART, DON A. *See* John W. CAMPBELL Jr.

STUART, W.J. (? – ?). American writer, whose only sf work is the novelization of the sf film, FORBIDDEN PLANET, under the same title, *Forbidden Planet* (**1956**). [JC]

STURGEON, THEODORE (1918–). American writer, born as Edward Hamilton Waldo in New York City; he later adopted his stepfather's surname. He

resisted formal schooling and, especially in his early years, took on an enormous variety of jobs, from seaman to salesman to guitar player to hotel manager to bulldozer operator; many of his experiences in these occupations were translated fairly directly into his fiction. He has been married several times and has a number of children.

TS made his first fiction sales in 1937 to McClure's syndicate for newspaper publication, and over the next few years published 39 similar items. His career as an sf writer began in 1939, with the publication of "Ether Breather" in *ASF*, though he seemed to find *ASF*'s sister magazine, *Unknown*, more fitting to his needs, and his first highly productive, though short, period as a writer can be said to end with the demise of *Unknown* and with his entry into the US armed forces. In about three years of active writing, he produced more than 25 stories, all in *ASF* and *Unknown*, using the pseudonyms E. Waldo Hunter or E. Hunter Waldo on occasions when he had two stories in an issue; several of the 25 are among his best known, such as "It" (1940) and "Microcosmic God" (1941). Along with A.E. VAN VOGT, Robert A. HEINLEIN and Isaac ASIMOV, TS was a central contributor to and shaper of John W. CAMPBELL Jr's so-called GOLDEN AGE OF SF, though perhaps less comfortably than his colleagues, as even in these early years he was less interested in technological or HARD SF than in attempting to use sf frameworks to illuminate psychological tales, often romantic.

The decade following the Second World War saw TS at his most prolific and assured. Although he continued to contribute to *ASF* for several years, more and more his stories appeared in other, newer markets, and he became a natural GALAXY writer, appearing in that journal from 1950. He was increasingly free to write stories expressive of his interest in various manifestations of love, and though his explorations of sexual diversity seem unexceptionable nowadays, stories like "The World Well Lost" (1953), about aliens exiled from their own culture because they are homosexuals, created considerable stir on publication. TS became increasingly noted as sf's premier writer of romantic fiction; the world tends to act repressively towards the natural emotions of his characters, who are often described in terms with which adolescents could identify, and to try to deprive them of proper fulfilment. Fortunately for most of them, however, the author uses the freedom of the sf genre to suggest routes of liberation, so that most of them tend to reach some kind of romantic goal, sometimes through a manipulation of the repressive world outside, sometimes through internal paranormal developments. TS's most famous single volume is *More Than Human* (fix-up

1953), winner of the 1954 INTERNATIONAL FANTASY AWARD, which consists of three connected stories, two new sections built around "Baby is Three", which was originally published in *Gal.* (1952) and is perhaps his most famous single story; it depicts with considerable intensity the coming together of six "freaks" into a PSI-powered *Gestalt*, and of its eventual achieving of true maturity.

A later tale, "Claustrophile" (1956), illustrates TS's adroitness with themes of frustrated adolescence. The young protagonist of this story, cramped by his repressive family, is a senstive oddball (like many young sf readers), and discovers himself to be not an Earthling at all but a lost member of a spacefaring race; at the climax he discovers that his fear of falling is something else entirely: he is instinctively afraid that the Earth is falling on him.

By 1958 TS had written most of the stories he has so far published, though his collections have continued to appear, and he won both HUGO and NEBULA awards for one of his infrequent later stories, "Slow Sculpture" (1970). He has published the following American collections: *Without Sorcery* (coll. **1948**; vt abridged *Not Without Sorcery* USA); *E Pluribus Unicorn* (coll. **1953**); *A Way Home* (coll. **1955**; US paperback omits two stories; vt *Thunder and Roses* UK, omitting three stories); *Caviar* (coll. **1955**); *A Touch of Strange* (coll. **1958**); *Aliens 4* (coll. **1959**); *Beyond* (coll. **1960**); *Sturgeon in Orbit* (coll. **1964**); *... And My Fear is Great and Baby is Three* (coll. **1965**); *Starshine* (coll. of reprints plus three previously uncollected stories **1966**); *The Worlds of Theodore Sturgeon* (coll. **1972**). Two further collections, *Sturgeon is Alive and Well ...* (coll. **1971**) and *Case and the Dreamer* (coll. **1974**), assemble generally more recent material. A UK collection, *The Joyous Invasions* (coll. **1965**), includes two stories from *Aliens 4* together with "To Marry Medusa", which TS expanded into the novel *The Cosmic Rape* (**1958**) in the USA. Many stories remain uncollected. One very short story, "The Man who Told Lies" (1959), TS wrote as by Billy Watson.

Apart from *More Than Human*, TS has not been generally as noted for novels as short stories, but three more sf ventures in longer forms have not been negligible. *The Dreaming Jewels* (**1950**; vt *The Synthetic Man*) is an enjoyable and sophisticated tale of young Horty, forced to run away to a circus by wicked step-parents; gradually he becomes aware of his powers, and defeats the evil forces about him. In *The Cosmic Rape*, a hive-mind from the stars invades mankind but finds itself — to its betterment — catalysing *Homo sapiens* into a higher, and linked, form of being. *Venus Plus X* (**1960**) is as close to a traditional UTOPIA as any American genre sf writer had approached before the efforts of Mack

REYNOLDS in that genre. The protagonist, Charlie Johns, awakens in Ledom, a melodious unisex society, longingly and effectively depicted as having transcended that sexual divisiveness of mankind against which TS has always argued; the novel is unremittingly didactic, for Charlie Johns has been awakened to find out about Ledom and to judge its success.

TS's technical exuberance and emotional warmness of texture have often fitted ill into the traditional sf moulds he has so frequently been forced to utilize. Though the lack of opportunity to write adult stories of love from the beginning of his career has engendered some very unfortunate sentimentality in his work, so that his insistently adolescent protagonists tend to resolve their problems in women's-fiction style, he has been a powerful and generally liberating influence in post-War American sf. He has been particularly influential upon such younger writers of the 1960s as Samuel R. DELANY. His voice as a writer has sometimes been self-indulgent, and his technical experiments less substantial than they seem to claim by the exuberance of their presentation, but his very faults demonstrate how great a struggle it has been in American sf to treat openly (and relaxedly) the profound themes to which he has always addressed himself.

TS has proved himself a sensitive and sympathetic book reviewer, in *Gal.*, *The New York Times Book Review* and elsewhere. [JC]

Other works: *I, Libertine* (**1956**), a historical novel under the pseudonym Frederick R. Ewing; *Some of Your Blood* (**1961**), a non-sf study of a blood-drinking psychotic; *Voyage to the Bottom of the Sea* (**1961**), a novelization of the film VOYAGE TO THE BOTTOM OF THE SEA; *To Here and the Easel* (coll. **1973**); *Sturgeon's West* (coll. **1973**), Western stories, in collaboration with Don Ward.

See also: ALIENS; BIOLOGY; CHILDREN IN SF; CLONES; CONCEPTUAL BREAKTHROUGH; DEFINITIONS OF SF; ESP; EVOLUTION; FLYING SAUCERS; FOURTH DIMENSION; GENETIC ENGINEERING; GODS AND DEMONS; GREAT AND SMALL; HIVE-MINDS; LIVING WORLDS; MACHINES; MARS; MEDIA LANDSCAPE; NUCLEAR POWER; PARANOIA AND SCHIZOPHRENIA; PSYCHOLOGY; REINCARNATION; RELIGION; SAMUELSON, David N.; SF MAGAZINES; SCIENTISTS; SEX; SOCIOLOGY; SUPERMAN; SUPERNATURAL CREATURES; TABOOS; TRANSPORTATION; UNDER THE SEA.

SUBMARINES *See* UNDER THE SEA; TRANSPORTATION.

SUBMERSION OF JAPAN, THE *See* NIPPON CHIMBOTSU.

SUDDABY, (WILLIAM) DONALD (1900–). English writer, who began publishing sf under the pseudonym Alan Griff with an adult novel, *Lost Men in the Grass* (**1940**) (*see* GREAT AND SMALL). He is better known for his juvenile sf novels, beginning with *The Star Raiders* (**1950**); most notable among them is *Village Fanfare* (**1955**), a TIME-TRAVEL novel in which a 1908 Shropshire village is visited from the future. *Prisoners of Saturn* (**1957**) is a SPACE OPERA. Some of DS's non-sf juveniles, like *Tower of Babel* (**1962**), have some fantasy content. [JC]
Other works: *The Death of Metal* (**1952**).

SUFFLING, MARK (? –). Author of two routine sf novels, *Project Oceanus* (**1975**) and *Space Crusader* (**1975**). [JC]

SUN, THE The Sun, as the energy-source which permits life to exist on Earth, was widely worshipped in the ancient world. After the Copernican revolution it became the hub of the universe, but with the advent of a rationalist view of the cosmos it lost some of its prestige. Some speculative writers of the 19th century considered it a world like any other and included it in cosmic tours — examples are the anonymous *Journeys into the Moon, Several Planets and the Sun* (**1837**) and Joel R. Peabody's *A World of Wonders* (**1838**). Although it hardly needed much imagination to realize that the Sun's visible surface would probably be very hot it was not until the 1890s that its temperature could actually be calculated (with the aid of Wien's law). Even so, John MASTIN was able to imagine a voyage, in *Through the Sun in an Airship* (**1909**), to investigate its inner structure, and later still H. KANER set a scientific romance, *The Sun Queen* (**1946**), on a sunspot. Generally speaking, though, modern sf writers treat the Sun with considerable respect. It figures in sf most often as a potential disaster area ready to consume spaceships which stray too close — an early example is Willy LEY's "At the Perihelion" (1937 as by Robert Willey; vt "A Martian Adventure"), while more recent are Hal CLEMENT's "Sun Spot" (1960), Poul ANDERSON's "What'll You Give?" (1963 as by Winston P. Sanders; vt "Que Donn'rez Vous?") and George Collyn's "In Passage of the Sun" (1966). A close encounter no less spectacular takes place in a space-station close to the Sun in Charles L. HARNESS's *Flight into Yesterday* (1947; **1953**; vt *The Paradox Men*). On the other hand, the weather technicians of Theodore L. THOMAS's "The Weather Man" (1962) skim across the surface of the Sun itself in "sessile" boats, in order to control its radiation output.

The knowledge that the fortunes of Earth are so completely dependent upon the behaviour of the Sun has inspired a number of stories dealing with the prospect of its undergoing a change — or even going nova. J.B.S. HALDANE's "The Last Judgment" (1927) and Olaf STAPLEDON's *Last and First Men* (**1930**) both foresee changes in the Sun's brilliance being a crucial factor in Man's future EVOLUTION, and countless stories featuring the extinction of Man (*see* END OF THE WORLD) connect this to the senescence of the Sun. In "Ark of Fire" (1943) by John Hawkins the Earth is moved nearer to the Sun, with predictable consequences for surface life. In J.T. McINTOSH's *One in Three Hundred* (**1954**) the Sun goes nova while the privileged few escape into space, a theme which recurs constantly in sf. In one early version — Edmond HAMILTON's "Thundering Worlds" (1934) — the nine planets become interstellar wanderers accelerating toward a new star. In Arthur C. CLARKE's "Rescue Party" (1946) aliens arrive to save us but find that we have already left under our own steam. In Norman SPINRAD's *The Solarians* (**1966**) the nova is deliberately set off to destroy an alien spacefleet while the human race makes a similar escape. In Edward Wellan's "Hijack" (1970) the myth is used in order to trick the mafia into hijacking a spacefleet and blasting off for the stars. The prospect of such a nova is itself anxiety-provoking, and there are several END-OF-THE-WORLD stories which make a detailed study of reactions to the news, notably Hugh KINGSMILL's "The End of the World" (1924) and Larry NIVEN's "Inconstant Moon" (1971). A similar threat causes the hero of George O. SMITH's *Troubled Star* (**1953**) a good deal of worry when he discovers that aliens want to make Sol into a variable star so as to serve as an interstellar lighthouse, but he at least can thwart them. Very few sf stories see any possibility of interfering with the Sun, hence this theme tends to be one of the more fatalistic in the genre's canon. An implausible but memorable exception is Clark Ashton SMITH's "Phoenix" (1954), in which Earthmen find a way to re-ignite the dying Sun to prolong the life of the race, but even here there is a strong element of fatalism in the price that has to be paid.

The notion that the Sun might, despite its nature, be the abode of life has been developed occasionally, most notably in Olaf STAPLEDON's *The Flames* (**1947**). A memorable example from genre sf is Edmond Hamilton's "Sunfire!" (1962). A rather more ambitious notion involving Sun-consuming life-forms which hatch out of the planets is featured in Jack WILLIAMSON's "Born of the Sun" (1934). The notion that STARS themselves might be living beings has been developed on several occasions, but there seems to be a certain reluctance to apply the notion to Sol. The ending of Gregory BENFORD and Gordon EKLUND's "If the Stars are Gods" (1973; incorporated into *If the Stars are Gods*, fix-up **1977**) is deliberately ambiguous in this respect.

One of the most curious observations of the Sun's behaviour is the 11-year sunspot cycle discovered by Schwab in 1851. There have been many pseudo-astrological attempts to correlate this cycle with Earthly events, and this preoccupation is reflected in Clifford D. SIMAK's "Sunspot Purge" (1940) and Philip LATHAM's "Disturbing Sun" (1959). Other discoveries concerning the Sun's effects on Earth include the SOLAR WIND — a flood of particles responsible for the auroral displays above the poles. This features in a number of recent stories, most memorably in Arthur C. Clarke's "Sunjammer" (1964; vt "The Wind from the Sun"), which features space "sailing ships" powered by the solar wind.

In recent years the Sun's importance as a religious symbol has revived in sf. The cardinal example is the award-winning Benford/Eklund novelette mentioned above, and another is the theme anthology *The Day the Sun Stood Still* (anth. 1972) ed. Robert SILVERBERG, which features three novellas based on the premise that the miracle granted to Joshua so that he might win a vital battle might be repeated tomorrow to persuade mankind of the reality of divine power. [PN]

See also: POWER SOURCES.

SUPERMAN In the same way that an imaginative context was initially provided for ALIEN roles by evolutionary theory, so the work of Darwin and Bergson governed attitudes to superhumans in early sf. There was, however, one important difference. The alien is Man's equivalent, a competitor or a partner in the evolutionary scheme. The superman is, by definition, a member of a "fitter" species, which can — and inevitably will — replace Man in the scheme of things. It might be thought that in consequence of this the superman, like the WELLSian alien, would inevitably become a figure of menace — at least where Darwinian thought was dominant. In fact, though early writers conceded that there was no place for supermen in contemporary human society, and usually disposed of them one way or another, most were very much on the side of the superhuman viewpoint. The reasons for this are simple enough — on the one hand, most of the early writers who used the superman were harshly critical of the contemporary human condition and wholly in favour of "progress"; and on the other hand, there has always been a distinct tendency for people to consider themselves somewhat superior to their fellows, and to credit themselves with a superhuman viewpoint. It may be that the philosopher Nietzsche had very little influence on early sf, but we should not forget the example of his *Thus Spake Zarathustra* (1883–92 Germany). It is very easy to love the notion of the superman if we believe that we can become one — and especially if we believe that no more than the belief is necessary, as in George Bernard SHAW's play *Back to Methuselah* (1921), whose wish-fulfilment element is excused in Shaw's long introductory tract on neo-Lamarckism.

Thus, we find both the Darwin-inspired Wells, in *The Food of the Gods* (1904), and the Bergson-inspired J.D. BERESFORD, in *The Hampdenshire Wonder* (1911; vt *The Wonder* USA), allied with — if not quite identifying with — their superhuman characters. Both make much of the hostility of the common man towards their hypothetical supermen, though Beresford, with his characteristic determination to see both sides of the question, does put in a good word for contemporary Man at the end. This is not true of Olaf STAPLEDON, whose replay of Beresford's plot in *Odd John* (1935) makes no concessions towards ordinary humanity, though his later novel about a superdog, *Sirius* (1944), is paradoxically more humane; or of Claude HOUGHTON, whose *This Was Ivor Trent* (1935) reveals an almost hysterical bitterness towards it. Perhaps surprisingly, it was in France, where Bergson's pupil Alfred JARRY had produced a comic erotic fantasia *The Supermale* (1902; trans. 1968) as early as 1902, that the first significant anti-superman novel was produced. This was *Le nouvel Adam* (1924; trans. as *The New Adam* 1926) by Noëlle ROGER, who could find nothing admirable in an ultra-rational being contemptuous of human life. In America, Philip WYLIE put an ordinary human mind into a superhuman body in *Gladiator* (1930), and thus avoided the whole issue of intellectual comparison, but he too made a hero of his character, and it is with a note of tragedy that the superman decides that there is no place for him in human society and invites God to strike him dead. God (no friend of evolution) obliges.

In early PULP sf the superman was used as a figure of menace in a straightforward manner by John Russell FEARN in *The Intelligence Gigantic* (1933; 1943). Fearn, however, appears gradually to have relented. A note of sympathy creeps into his superwoman story *The Golden Amazon* (1944) and in the many sequels to that novel the protagonist becomes the heroine. *Seeds of Life* (1931; 1951) by John TAINE is also melodramatic, and the superman meets his customary end (in a particularly horrible manner) but there is an attempt to analyse the superman's viewpoint with some sympathy in the author's handling of the theme. In Stanley G. WEINBAUM's "The Adaptive Ultimate" (1936) a scientist creates a superwoman, and has to kill her in order to protect the world, but again there is a tentative expression of sympathy. By no means tentative, however, is Weinbaum's novel *The New Adam* (1939) — a major, first-person account of a superhuman growing up in the human world. Here, for the first time, is a detailed, analytical account of a superman which is *not* fuelled by the desire to criticize the contemporary human condition. In the end the superman falls in with the stereotype, concludes that he has no place

in the world, and bows out gracefully — but takes care before doing so to leave behind a son and heir.

The doomed-superman pattern was decisively broken by two novels published in the pulps in 1940: *Slan* (1940; 1946; rev. 1951) by A.E. VAN VOGT and *Darker Than You Think* (1940; 1948) by Jack WILLIAMSON. In the former, a persecuted superchild grows into mature command of his latent powers, takes arms against a sea of troubles and, by opposing, ends them. In the latter, the hero sets out to fight a second species of the genus *Homo* which threatens *Homo sapiens*, but discovers that he is one of the other race himself, and accepts the dictates of his genes. In these stories there is no compromise; the superman is offered to the reader for identification, and he is not made to die, gracefully or otherwise, at the end. Indeed, the role of the central character becomes in each case quasi-messianic (*see* MESSIAHS). This new pattern was rapidly established in pulp sf. Van Vogt repeated it many times — in "Recruiting Station" (1942; as *Masters of Time* in coll. 1950; vt *Earth's Last Fortress*), in "The Changeling" (1944), in *The World of A* (1945; rev. 1948; vt *The World of Null-A*) and in *The Pawns of Null-A* (1948; 1956; vt *The Players of Null-A* UK). Van Vogt abandoned writing sf for some years when he became involved with L. Ron HUBBARD's DIANETICS movement, which translocated this same fiction into a PSEUDO-SCIENCE, and later into a religion (*see* SCIENTOLOGY). When he returned to sf in the 1960s he still used the plot extensively — e.g. in "The Proxy Intelligence" (1968) and "The Reflected Men" (1971). Williamson, too, repeated his formula precisely in *Dragon's Island* (1951; vt *The Not-Men*).

The late 1940s and early 1950s abound with sf stories about groups of superhumans misunderstood and unjustly persecuted by common men. The element of social criticism is either missing or very muted — the reader is simply invited to identify with the supermen, and this apparently proved easy. Great impetus was lent to the theme by the popularization of J.B. Rhine's experiments in parapsychology (*see* ESP), which worked upon the assumption that there may be supermen already among us, themselves unsuspecting of their latent powers. Rhine provided a new archetype for the superman — outwardly normal but possessed of one or more of the extra-sensory perceptions, telepathy and precognition; or perhaps even possessed of some psychokinetic ability. Classic stories of persecuted Rhine-type supermen were Henry KUTTNER's "Baldy" series, published as by Lewis Padgett (fix-up 1953 as *Mutant*), Wilmar H. SHIRAS's *Children of the Atom* (fix-up 1953), Zenna HENDERSON's "People" series (colls. *Pilgrimage*, 1961, and *The People: No Different Flesh*, 1966) and

Wilson TUCKER's *Wild Talent* (**1954**). Sympathy for the supermen was developed by many strategies. Superchildren were common (*see* CHILDREN), as in Van Vogt's *Slan*, the first really influential work of the sub-genre, Shiras's *Children of the Atom*, George O. SMITH's *The Fourth 'R'* (**1959**; vt *The Brain Machine*) and James H. SCHMITZ's *The Witches of Karres* (**1949** *ASF*; exp. **1966**), though a cautionary note was sounded by Jerome BIXBY's "It's a *Good* Life" (**1953**), in which a superchild institutes a reign of terror directed towards the gratification of his every whim. Physically afflicted supermen were occasionally employed, as in Theodore STURGEON's "Maturity" (**1947**) and John BRUNNER's *The Whole Man* (fix-up **1964**; vt *Telepathist* UK).

Sometimes, in this period, there were secret organizations of criminal supermen fighting against the good supermen, as in James BLISH's *Jack of Eagles* (**1951**; vt *ESP-er*) and George O. Smith's *Highways in Hiding* (**1956**; vt *Space Plague*), but even where the superman appears to be used as an outright figure of menace, as in Frank M. ROBINSON's *The Power* (**1956**), the good guy is waiting only for his own latent super-powers to develop to bring about the defeat of the villain, in an ending of intriguing moral ambiguity. There is a similar result of man-superman confrontation in Jack VANCE's "Telek" (**1951**) and Theodore Sturgeon's "And my Fear is Great" (**1953**). The everyone-can-be-superman myth reached its highest expression in Poul ANDERSON's *Brain Wave* (**1954**), in which the Earth passes out of a zone of cosmic distortion which had been damping potential intelligence throughout history, and even idiots and animals get smart.

The attractiveness of the myth is undeniable. The COMIC BOOK hero SUPERMAN, who lurks unsuspected within his unassuming "secret identity" Clark Kent, has become legendary and has spawned countless imitations. Superhero comics were popular in the early 1940s (*see also* CAPTAIN MARVEL), and had their real boom period in the 1960s, following the resurgence of MARVEL COMICS in 1961. Early comic book superheroes tended to be simplistic good guys, popular with the humans on whose behalf they fought crime. The superhero creations of Stan LEE in the 1960s were usually morally ambiguous, often psychologically maimed or suffering desperate pangs of love.

Hubbard is not the only one to have sold the myth as a pseudo-science or a religion — many other contemporary cults offer transcendental powers as well as arcane knowledge. In the 1950s, the pseudo-science element was definitely ascendant, with parapsychology stories accounting for an astonishingly high percentage of the fiction published in *ASF*. As time went by, however, the emphasis shifted away from the Rhine version of the myth towards a quasi-religious version — a trend which Hubbard followed with alacrity in his development of scientology. The image of the superman became the primary vehicle for a science-fictional translation of the Christian myth of personal salvation, and the achievement of super-powers became a transcendental process — in its extreme forms, indeed, an apotheosis.

This version of the superman myth is particularly obvious in the novels of Charles L. HARNESS: *Flight into Yesterday* (**1953**; vt *The Paradox Men*), *The Rose* (**1953**; **1966**) and *The Ring of Ritornel* (**1968**), all of which involve the central character's transcendental metamorphosis via death. It also forms the bases of two of the most highly regarded of all sf novels: Theodore Sturgeon's *More Than Human* (fix-up **1953**) and Arthur C. CLARKE's *Childhood's End* (**1953**). The first features the route to maturity of a *gestalt* group of misfit superchildren, and their eventual transcendental admission to a community of superminds, while the second has an entire generation of Earth's children undergoing an apotheosis to fuse with the cosmic mind. The latter event bears a striking resemblance to the ideas put forward by the French Jesuit Pierre Teilhard de Chardin, regarding the possible evolutionary future for Man within a Bergsonian scheme, in *The Future of Man* (**1959** France; trans. **1964**). One sf novel specifically based on Teilhard's speculations is George ZEBROWSKI's *The Omega Point* (**1973**), but a "cosmic mind" also features in *The Uncensored Man* (**1964**) by Arthur SELLINGS and the moment of apotheosis has become a common motif, as in *The Infinite Cage* (**1972**) by Keith LAUMER and *Tetrasomy Two* (**1974**), by Oscar ROSSITER, for example.

Images of transcendental rebirth have also become common, particularly powerful ones appearing in the early post-War period in the novels of Alfred BESTER. In *The Demolished Man* (**1953**) a psychopathic murderer subject to terrible visions is trapped by a telepathic police force and "cleansed" of his madness. In *The Stars My Destination* (**1956**; vt *Tiger! Tiger!* UK) the central character, after the discovery of his super-powers and his violently vengeful use of them, is trapped in a burning building, moves through time to appear to himself and others as a fire-shrouded vision, and is similarly cleansed before finding a species of peace in an interplanetary haven. In Bester's most recent novel after a long silence, *The Computer Connection* (**1974**; vt *Extro* UK), supermen attempt to recruit others to their kind by the only process known to them — violent death.

Literal survival after death is featured in *I Will Fear No Evil* (**1971**) and *Time Enough for Love* (**1973**) by Robert HEINLEIN, in *Camp Concentration* (**1968**) by Thomas M. DISCH and in *Traitor to the Living* (**1973**) by Philip José FARMER.

Religious imagery is overt in the many works by Robert SILVERBERG which couple the notion of superhumanity with the idea of re-birth, including *To Open the Sky* (fix-up **1967**), *Downward to the Earth* (**1970**), *Nightwings* (fix-up **1970**), *Son of Man* (**1971**), *The Book of Skulls* (**1972**) and "Born with the Dead" (**1974**). Silverberg has also written the powerful *Dying Inside* (**1972**), which presents the re-birth theme in terms of the *loss* of a superhuman power. The decline of ephemeral superhumanity is also a powerful motif in the classic *Flowers for Algernon* (**1959**; exp. **1966**) by Daniel KEYES. The superman as messianic leader whose death is redemptive for mankind appears in the two best-selling sf novels of the 1960s, Robert Heinlein's *Stranger in a Strange Land* (**1961**) and Frank HERBERT's *Dune* (**1965**).

In some fringe areas of sf the transcendence of the superhuman figure assumes a distinctly pre-Christian aura. Supermen play a central if stereotyped role in the sub-genre of SWORD AND SORCERY, whether their powers are physical as in the "Conan" series of the 1930s by Robert E. HOWARD, or mental/magical (*see* MAGIC). Supermen also turn up regularly in sf stories rooted in MYTHOLOGY, particularly in a large number of novels by Roger ZELAZNY, who delights in the ironic contrast between superhuman powers, often achieved with technological assistance, and all-too-human appetites and failings. But in all these cases the role of the superman is that of archetype, as in fairy-tale or FANTASY, and is in no sense seriously presented as an evolutionary possibility, in the manner of most sf proper.

Four novels by Ian WATSON, very much sf proper, return to the old idea of supermen appearing as part of a process of EVOLUTION (sometimes self-induced), with the emphasis falling on a superhumanity arising through a radically altered and heightened capacity for CONCEPTUAL BREAKTHROUGH. In all four books the growth process is agonizing, and ultimately unsuccessful in *The Embedding* (**1973**) and *The Jonah Kit* (**1975**), in which it is brought about by human science, though ambiguously successful in *The Martian Inca* (**1977**), where it is a quite unlooked-for side-effect of the space programme, and in *Alien Embassy* (**1977**).

No other symbol in sf has evolved quite so dramatically as that of the superman, which, although pandering to the simplest and most basic form of human wish-fulfilment, has, in its several distinct phases of development, made its reverberations felt across surprisingly diverse areas of human thought and feeling. In what it tells us of both our aspirations and our fears, it has become one of the central images of sf. [BS]

See also: CYBORGS; HEROES; IMMORTALITY; INTELLIGENCE; RELIGION.

This excerpt from SUPERMAN's first comic-book appearance, June 1938, drawn by Joe Shuster, shows the superhero's belief that advocating American intervention in the forthcoming World War would be an act of treason.

SUPERMAN 1. American COMIC STRIP created by writer Jerome SIEGEL and artist Joseph SHUSTER, loosely based on Philip WYLIE's *Gladiator* (**1930**). *S* first appeared in *Action Comics* in 1938, then *Superman Comics* in 1939. Under the editorship of Mort WEISINGER the series was given a more elaborate background, and was expanded to include additional superbeings and further comic titles. Many writers and artists including Alfred BESTER, Henry KUTTNER, Edmond HAMILTON and Manly Wade WELLMAN have contributed to the series, which continues today.

A very badly drawn version of SUPERMAN made his first UK appearance a year later than in the USA, in a boys' paper, Aug. 5th, 1939.

As sole survivor of a planetary cataclysm, raised from infancy by American foster-parents, Superman's dual identity as timid reporter and superhuman, indestructible crimefighter has a basic appeal to readers. Storylines are varied and often implausible. They include time travel, interplanetary journeys and alternate universes, while sub-plots are woven around attempts to unmask his secret identity and to engage him amorously.

Superman has been the most influential of sf comics heroes and has inspired many imitations, the most noted being CAPTAIN MARVEL. His adventures have appeared as a syndicated newspaper strip, a RADIO programme, in serial and feature films, and in an sf TELEVISION series. His dynamic character has transcended the media and become incorporated into contemporary Western mythology, with some subsequent de-mystification, notably in Larry NIVEN's "Man of Steel, Woman of Kleenex" (1971).   [JE]

2. American animated cartoon series, directed by Dave Fleischer for Paramount in the period 1940–43.

3. Serial film. Produced by Sam Katzman, directed by Spencer Bennet and Thomas Carr, starring Kirk Alyn as Superman, with Noel Neill and Tommy Bond. 15 episodes, and later released (cut to 88 mins) as a feature film.

4. American TV series (1953–7). ABC TV. The first season was produced by Robert Maxwell and Bernard Luber; from the second series onward the producer was Whitney Ellsworth. The pilot episode, "Superman on Earth", was written by Richard Fielding, actually a pseudonym for the team of Maxwell and Ellsworth, and directed by Thomas Carr, who also directed several of the following episodes. Special effects were by Thol Thomson. Running time per episode: 25 mins. The series ran for six seasons, the first two in b/w; thereafter in colour. The title role was played by George Reeves, a former Hollywood leading man who made his film début in *Gone With the Wind*. He first played Superman in the film *Superman and the Mole Men* (vt *Superman and the Strange People*), produced by Maxwell and Luber in 1951 and directed by Lee Sholem. With the TV series he became typecast in the role, and when the series came to an end (he directed the last two episodes himself) he was unable to find further work in films. He committed suicide at the age of 45 in 1959. Other members of the cast included Phyllis Coates, who played Lois Lane in the first season only, and Noel Neill, who played her from the second season onwards, Jack Larson as Jimmy Olsen and John Hamilton as Perry White. The series was primarily aimed at children and despite its mediocre standard was extremely popular for a long time. Unlike the comic strip the stories rarely entered the realm of the fantastic: Superman was usually pitted against mundane, often bumbling criminals.

5. Musical/TV film. During the 1960s a Broadway musical was based on *Superman*. Called *It's a Bird! It's a Plane! It's a Superman!*, it was turned into a made-for-TV film for ABC TV in 1975 with David Wilson as Superman. Direction was by Jack Regas, script was by Romeo Miller, based on the musical by Charles Strouse and David Newman.

6. Film (currently in production, 1977). This is an extravagant, multi-million dollar Salkind Brothers production, directed by Richard Donner from a script by Mario Puzo with Christopher Reeve in the title role and also starring Marlon Brando.   [JB]

One of SUPERMAN's first and funniest cinema appearances, *Superman and the Mole Men*, 1951, starring George Reeves.

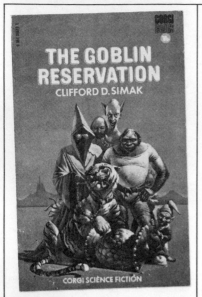

THE GOBLIN RESERVATION
CLIFFORD D. SIMAK

CORGI SCIENCE FICTION

Clifford D. Simak's novel gives a quasi-sf explanation for the "existence" of SUPERNATURAL CREATURES. Corgi Books, 1971. Cover by Bruce Pennington.

SUPERNATURAL CREATURES Just as it is common in sf to give empirical explanations of ancient myths and stories of the gods (see GODS AND DEMONS; MYTHOLOGY) and to seek a rationale for MAGIC, so too, when sf deals with supernatural creatures, it commonly invokes quasi-scientific explanations. Sometimes these involve racial memory of unusual but natural creatures, and commonly they involve MUTANTS. Occasionally they involve cases of abnormal PSYCHOLOGY. The supernatural creatures that most often appear in sf are vampires, werewolves, ghouls, poltergeists, ghosts, and elves and fairies.

The sf writer is not usually, however, a pure rationalist, desirous of demythologizing all wonder from the world, by giving it a mundane explanation. Commonly he has his cake and eats it too, by keeping the horror while rendering it a believable phenomenon of the world we live in. Also, by making the condition of vampirism or lycanthropy, for example, a natural affliction, it is often possible to evoke pity for the MONSTER as well as its victims. Two stories which illustrate this clearly are James BLISH's "There Shall be no Darkness" (1950) and Richard MATHESON's *I Am Legend* (**1954**). The former is a werewolf story which links lycanthropy with artistic talent, and allows the reader some empathy with the shape-changing killer; the latter tells of a plague which renders its victims vampires, who besiege the one immune left in the city. In both cases a far-fetched rationale is given, Matheson being particularly ingenious in explaining the traditional stigmata of the vampire in terms of symptoms of an illness.

Jack WILLIAMSON wrote another excellent werewolf story, *Darker than you Think* (1940; exp. **1948**), in which lycanthropes are seen as members of a distinct race, genetically different from *Homo sapiens* though superficially identical; the hero who discovers the truth turns out to share this awful but thrilling heritage. This story, like many others of its kind, has a symbolic relationship with split-personality stories like Robert Louis STEVENSON's *Dr. Jekyll and Mr. Hyde* (**1886**), in which the more primitive, amoral, beast-like part of our evolutionary heritage is able to emerge and take on a shape of its own. All such stories can ultimately be traced back to a dualistic view of Man which is linked to the old Christian view that humanity on the one hand suffers from Original Sin, but on the other hand has an aspiring spirit which is a gift from God.

Guy ENDORE's *The Werewolf of Paris* (**1933**) sees lycanthropy as a psychological distortion, perhaps hereditary, and no literal transformation from man to wolf takes place. Similarly Theodore STURGEON's *Some of Your Blood* (**1961**) has a tortured and not very dangerous "vampire" who is in fact a psychotic, whose blood-drinking, it gradually emerges, can be traced back to childhood trauma. The protagonist of Gene WOLFE's "The Hero as Werwolf" (1975) is one of the few human survivors of a Utopian future where the genetically fit have been bred into placidity and health, a kind of superhuman sheep. The descendants of the abandoned remainder live a tragic, hole-and-corner life, surviving cannibalistically on the super-race responsible for their condition.

Stories of demonic possession, such as John CHRISTOPHER's *The Possessors* (**1965**) and many others, are commonly rationalized in terms of PSI POWERS, the takeover being telepathic, or as a form of parasitism, usually by an alien; several of these stories are discussed in PARASITISM AND SYMBIOSIS. Familiars are often symbiotes also, as is the case with the little, sinister creatures who accompany the "witches" in Fritz LEIBER's *Gather, Darkness!* (1943; **1950**).

Many stories of supernatural creatures which appear in supposedly sf collections are in fact straight FANTASY, which is to say that the supernatural status of these beings is left unquestioned. UNKNOWN magazine published quite a few stories of this kind, as did THE MAGAZINE OF FANTASY AND SCIENCE FICTION later on. The latter published a series of stories by Manly Wade WELLMAN (probably his best work) in which John the Minstrel is faced with a variety of supernatural menaces, though occasionally some sf jargon is used to bring them down to earth a little; one of the best is "O Ugly Bird!" (1951); they were collected in *Who Fears the Devil?* (coll. **1963**). H.L. GOLD's "Trouble with Water" (1939) is a typical *Unknown* joke story, about the chaos caused by a water gnome. Ray BRADBURY's

"Homecoming" (1946) is a touching story of the one "normal" in a jolly, clannish family of supernaturals. The magazine WEIRD TALES also published many stories of supernatural creatures with seldom any but the flimsiest demythologizing; H.P. LOVECRAFT wrote rather well about ghouls, as in "Pickman's Model" (1927) and several other *Weird Tales* stories. Many supernatural stories of the jokier kind can be found in Theodore COGSWELL's *The Wall Around the World* (coll. **1962**) and Avram DAVIDSON's *Or All the Seas with Oysters* (coll. **1962**); Davidson was himself editor of *FSF* for a period. A number of such stories are also collected in Judith MERRIL's above-average anthology *Galaxy of Ghouls* (anth. **1955**; vt *Off the Beaten Orbit*), which contains Walter M. MILLER's "Triflin' Man" (1955; vt "You Triflin' Skunk"), in which the demon lover turns out to be an ALIEN, a common explanation for supernatural manifestations.

Elves and fairies often turn out to be aliens also, as in Clifford D. SIMAK's *The Goblin Reservation* (**1968**), or Neanderthal or atavistic survivals, as in several stories discussed in MYTHOLOGY. Sometimes they merely live on colonized and then forgotten planets, as in Christopher STASHEFF's "Warlock" series. The creatures out of Greek legend, including several of an apparently supernatural variety, in Roger ZELAZNY's *This Immortal* (1965 *FSF* as "... And Call me Conrad"; exp. **1966**) are mutants. C.M. KORNBLUTH's vampire in "The Mindworm" (1950), is a telepathic mutant created by atomic radiation.

Unicorns and dragons remain popular, unicorns for some reason being usually allowed to remain mythic, and dragons often rationalized as alien creatures. Examples of the former occur in Peter BEAGLE's *The Last Unicorn* (**1968**), Harlan ELLISON's "On the Downhill Side" (1972) and Mark GESTON's *The Siege of Wonder* (**1976**); there are many others. Dragons appear notably in Anne McCAFFREY's "Dragonrider" series, Jack VANCE's *The Dragon Masters* (**1963**) and Avram Davidson's *Rogue Dragon* (**1965**).

Supernatural creatures generally play a prominent role in romantic fantasy, often as symbolic of a wondrousness that may survive in odd, untouched corners of the world (see MYTHOLOGY) while dead in our rational, urbanized, modern civilization. They are for example to be found in forms both horrific and lovely in the various LOST WORLDS of A. MERRITT, in practically every story written by Thomas Burnett SWANN, and in SWORD AND SORCERY generally.

Ghosts are rather a special case, and are discussed in ESCHATOLOGY. They are reconstructed in the flesh from a reading of human minds by the sentient planet *Solaris* (1961; trans. **1970**) by Stanislaw LEM; and along with zombies have a very real existence in Robert SHECKLEY's amusing *Immortality Delivered* (**1958**; exp. vt *Immortality, Inc.* 1959). Sheckley often plays games with supernatural creatures; he brings nightmares, for example, to life in "Ghost V" (1954), and the hero of "Protection" (1956) has good reason to wish he had never accepted aid from a ghostly alien from another dimension. The poltergeists in Keith ROBERTS's "Boulter's Canaries" (1965) are energy configurations which can do substantial damage in the real world.

Stories of this kind are not restricted to genre sf, nor to Anglo-American sf. Stanislaw Lem's *Sledztwo* (**1959**; trans. as *The Investigation* 1974) is an interesting study of the extent to which the unknown may be susceptible to rational explanation, in a mystery where Scotland Yard is faced with the activities of a ghoul, whose status as either natural or supernatural is difficult to determine. [PN]
See also: GOTHIC SF; RELIGION.

SUPER SCIENCE AND FANTASTIC STORIES *See* SUPER SCIENCE STORIES.

Dec. 1958. Cover by Frank Kelly Freas.

SUPER-SCIENCE FICTION US DIGEST-size magazine. 18 issues, Dec. 1956-Oct. 1959, published bi-monthly by Headline Publications; ed. W.W. Scott. Though it used material by established writers its contents were mediocre. There were three volumes of six numbers each. [BS]

SUPER SCIENCE NOVELS *See* SUPER SCIENCE STORIES.

SUPER SCIENCE STORIES US PULP magazine. 31 issues, published by Fictioneers, Inc., a subsidiary of Popular Publications. 16 issues were published Mar. 1940-May 1943, three of the 1941 issues (Mar.-Aug.) under the title *Super Science Novels*. Frederik POHL was editor until Aug. 1941 and was then replaced by Alden H. Norton. The magazine was revived to publish 15 more issues, Jan. 1949-Aug. 1951, ed. Ejler JAKOBSSON,

The second incarnation of this magazine, Apr. 1949. Cover by Stephen Lawrence.

with Damon KNIGHT assistant editor on some issues.

SSS featured standard pulp adventure sf, and in its first incarnation it was an important market for the FUTURIAN group, Pohl buying a good deal of material from himself (including many of his early collaborations with C.M. KORNBLUTH). The most notable story *SSS* published was the novel *Genus Homo* by L. Sprague DE CAMP and P. Schuyler MILLER (Mar. 1941; rev. **1950**). It also published a number of early stories by Isaac ASIMOV and James BLISH's first story, "Emergency Refueling" (1940). The Canadian edition of the magazine continued publication after the first US version ceased, publishing 21 issues, Aug. 1942-Dec. 1945, the last five issues under the title *Super Science and Fantastic Stories*. After the US version ceased the Canadian edition used stories from the Popular Publications reprint magazines FAMOUS FANTASTIC MYSTERIES and

FANTASTIC NOVELS. The second incarnation of *SSS* was also reprinted in Canada 1949-51 as *Super Science Stories*. There were two series of British reprints, one reprinting three whole issues in 1949-50, the other publishing 14 consecutively numbered issues of selections from both versions of the US magazine in 1950-53. [BS]
Collectors should note: Volume numeration of *SSS* ran continuously through both incarnations, there being seven vols of four nos and an eighth vol. of three nos. The schedule was bi-monthly from Mar. '40 to May '41, and quarterly from Aug. '41 to May '43. The second version ran Jan. '49, Apr. '49, then bi-monthly from Jul. '49 regularly except for a gap between Jan. and Apr. '51.

SURAGNE, PIERRE *See* Pierre PELOT.

SURREALISM *See* ABSURDIST SF; ILLUSTRATION; NEW WAVE.

SURVIVORS Television series (1975-7). BBC TV. Written and created by Terry NATION and produced by Terence Dudley. 50 mins per episode. Colour.

The "after-the-HOLOCAUST" novel is considered a particularly British sub-genre of sf; it is not surprising that its first real TV manifestation should be produced by the BBC. The starting-point for the series was the arrival of a plague in Britain that kills almost everyone in six weeks, leaving about 7,000 people alive. The series follows the adventures of various small groups of survivors, concentrating on their efforts to cope without technology and their encounters with other, less sympathetic groups. The atmosphere is rather too cosy; in fact the series sometimes takes on aspects of a middle-class, rural paradise, what with the disappearance not only of all those smelly cities but also of the working

Denis Lill, Lucy Fleming and John Abineri dressed up for the post-holocaust world of SURVIVORS, in the third season. © BBC.

Sleeping for uncounted ages she lay, a goddess enshrined. Then, under Jerry Miles' touch, she awoke, to explain the mystery of the incredible valley of science, controlled evolution . . . and grim danger!

SUSPENDED ANIMATION was a cliché in the sf pulps; this illustrates "The Sleeping Goddess" by Maurice Duclos in *Fantastic Adventures*, May 1939.

classes. The overnight disappearance of technology, and in particular the shortage of petrol, is never adequately rationalized. Terry Nation's book of the series is *The Survivors* (**1976**). [JB]

SUSPENDED ANIMATION The notion of suspended animation is one of the oldest literary devices in sf. It first proved convenient as a means of TIME TRAVEL — a short cut to the future, in common use long before the invention of the time machine. It is used in Louis-Sébastien MERCIER's *L'an deux mille quatre cent quarante* (**1771** Amsterdam; trans. as *Memoirs of the Year Two Thousand Five Hundred* **1772**), the first of the UTOPIAS of "progress", and again in Mary GRIFFITH's *Three Hundred Years Hence* (in *Camperdown*, coll. **1836**; **1975**) and Edward BELLAMY's *Looking Backward* (**1888**). It became somewhat more than a literary convenience in H.G. WELLS's *When the Sleeper Wakes* (**1899**; rev. vt *The Sleeper Awakes* 1910). These stories, having other purposes in view, gloss over the scientific means by which suspended animation might be achieved. Edgar Allan POE's short story "The Facts in the Case of M. Valdemar" (1845) achieves suspended animation by hypnosis, while Grant ALLEN's

"Pausodyne" (1881) imagines an 18th-century scientist inventing a gas to put him into a protracted anaesthetic condition. The most popular means, however, has always been preservation by freezing (*see* CRYONICS). Another example of preservation in the real world which inspired a number of fantasies was the ancient Egyptian habit of mummifying the dead. It was a relatively small imaginative step to suppose an arcane mummification process which preserved life and beauty, and Egyptian princesses have a habit of reviving in fantastic romances of the mysterious East: examples include Robert W. CHAMBERS' *The Tracer of Lost Persons* (1906) and Clive Holland's *The Spell of Isis* (1917). Visitors preserved from a more remote past included the Atlanteans of Olof W. ANDERSON's *Treasure-Vault of Atlantis* (**1925**) and Erle Cox's *Out of the Silence* (1919; **1925**; exp. 1947).

The device of suspended animation was co-opted into early PULP sf as one of the standard elements in its vocabulary of ideas, and was copiously used, notably in the first pulp exploration of the future of Man, Laurence MANNING's *The Man Who Awoke* (1933; fix-up **1975**). The genre sf writers eventually found it a useful device in another context, for avoiding the

intolerable time-lags involved in slower-than-light journeys to the stars. One of the earliest trips taken by this means was in A.E. VAN VOGT's "Far Centaurus" (1944), whose luckless heroes arrive to find that FASTER-THAN-LIGHT travel was invented while they were asleep, and that a thriving civilization awaits them. More recent dramas involving ships populated largely by people in suspended animation include *The Black Corridor* (**1969**) by Michael MOORCOCK and Hilary BAILEY and *The Dream Millennium* (**1974**) by James WHITE. Genre sf writers were also willing to discover stranger beings than Atlanteans in suspended animation, in a manner reminiscent of a common theme in supernatural literature, in which ancient gods and their magic may be revived into the present by folly or evil intent, and the closeness is evident in most of the sf stories using the notion, notably *The Alien* (**1951**) by Raymond F. JONES, *The Space Vampires* (**1976**) by Colin WILSON and *World of Ptavvs* (**1966**) by Larry NIVEN.

The recent popularization of cryonics as a means of suspending animation has offered a boost to the credibility of the jargon surrounding the literary device, but has added little to its use as a theme in its own right. The one novel which explores in any depth the existential significance of the ability to suspend animation in oneself is *The Insurgents* (**1957**) by VERCORS.   [BS]

See also: IMMORTALITY; GENERATION STARSHIPS; MEDICINE.

SUSPENSE US DIGEST-size magazine. Four quarterly issues, Spring 1951-Winter 1952, published by Farrell

First issue, spring 1951; it featured stories by Ray Bradbury, William Tenn and other sf writers.

Publishing Co., Chicago; ed. Theodore Irwin. *S* contained a mixture of detective, weird, sf and fantasy stories, including some reprints. Authors included Theodore STURGEON and John WYNDHAM. The unusual mixing of genres may have accounted for its rapid demise. [FHP/PN]

SUTPHEN, (WILLIAM GILBERT) VAN TASSEL (1861–1945). American writer, author of *The Doomsmen* (**1906**) and *The Nineteenth Hole; Being Tales of the Fair Green* (coll. **1901**). The former pictures the rough-hewn remnants of civilization after plague has destroyed much of America, but the emphasis is on routine adventure related to a forbidden city.   [JC/PN]

SUTTON, JEAN (1917–). American writer, wife of Jeff SUTTON (*who see for details*) with whom she has written five novels which do not differ markedly from those written by Jeff Sutton alone.   [JC]

SUTTON, JEFF(ERSON) (HOWARD) (1913–). American writer, who began publishing in 1955. His background — he has been a journalist, served time in the Marines, and done research in high-altitude survival — is reflected in several of his novels, from *First on the Moon* (**1958**), his first, to *Spacehive* (**1960**) and *Whisper from the Stars* (**1970**). The narrator of this last, a newspaper reporter, becomes involved in genuine COSMOLOGICAL speculations with humans who have transcended our common lot. The novel deals, less sophisticatedly but fully as professionally, with the kind of speculations about the nature of reality and PERCEPTION dealt with in his novels by Ian WATSON. JS writes with a somewhat dilute clarity; his fiction occasionally rises above the routine, when he deals in NEAR-FUTURE subject matter, but when he attempts more far-flung adventure stories his inspiration tends to flag.   [JC]
Other works: *Bombs in Orbit* (**1959**); *The Missile Lords* (**1963**); *The Atom Conspiracy* (**1963**); *Beyond Apollo* (**1966**); *H-Bomb Over America* (**1967**); *The Man Who Saw Tomorrow* (**1968**); *Alton's Unguessable* (**1970**); *The Mindblocked Man* (**1972**). With his wife Jean SUTTON: *The Programmed Man* (**1968**); *The Beyond* (**1968**); *Lord of the Stars* (**1969**); *Alien from the Stars* (**1970**); *The Boy Who Had the Power* (**1971**).

SUVIN, DARKO (R.) (1930–). Yugoslav academic and sf critic; he went to the USA in 1967, and since 1969 has lived in Canada, where he is a professor of English at McGill university. His PhD is from Zagreb University.
DS has been very closely associated with the development of academic interest in sf in America, having been an active member of the SCIENCE FICTION RESEARCH ASSOCIATION, a co-editor of SCIENCE-FICTION STUDIES since its inception, and having lectured and published widely on the subject. (His other field is drama, especially the work of Brecht.) His works include *Russian Science Fiction 1956–1974: a*

Bibliography (**1976**) and *Pour une poétique de la science-fiction* (**1977** Canada) in French; he has edited *Other Worlds, Other Seas: Science Fiction from Socialist Countries* (anth. **1970**), *H.G. Wells and Modern Science Fiction* (anth. **1977**), a collection of essays by various hands, and, with R.D. MULLEN, *Science-Fiction Studies: Selected Articles on Science Fiction 1973–1975* (anth. **1976**), from GREGG PRESS. All these works, especially the last, contain examples of DS's critical writing, in which one of the most sustained attempts yet to appear in sf criticism is made to define sf as a genre. DS's critical prose has been criticized as clotted and obscurantist, and it is true that his English does not flow easily. Part of the obscurity results from rigorously complex argument, for which a new terminology has had to be found, very much based in European structuralism; DS sees sf as a literature of "cognitive estrangement", a term explained in DEFINITIONS OF SF; it was DS who introduced the term "cognition" to sf criticism. It is unfortunate for English readers that his only full-scale study of sf is in French.   [PN]

SWAHN, SVEN CHRISTER (1933–). Swedish writer, critic, editor and translator. A lifelong sf reader, SCS first approached the field in short stories, then wrote a series of acclaimed juvenile novels, the best of which compare favourably with the best adult Swedish sf: *Stenjätten* ["The Stone Giant"] (**1965**); *Vår man i Nyhavn* ["Our Man in Nyhavn"] (**1967**); *Jakten på Stora Sjöormen* ["The Great Seasnake Hunt"] (**1974**). For adults, SCS has produced several philosophically enticing, often humorous sf radio plays; his adult sf novels, *Ljuset från Alfa Centauri* ["The Light from Alpha Centauri"] (**1977**) and *Förmedlarna* ["The Intermediaries"] (**1977**) are centered on psychologically convincing portrayals of outcast or idiosyncratic characters. As editor and critic, SCS has played a major role in gaining serious attention for sf in Sweden. His personal, in parts brilliant *7 x framtiden* ["7 x the Future"] (**1975**) remains the best critical study of sf in Swedish; his voluminous critical writings in papers, magazines and scholarly journals, as well as the sf line he edited for Bernce Publishers are also major contributions. Outside sf, SCS, a PhD in literature and a major Swedish author, has published some 20 volumes of poetry, short stories, novels and biography. Some of his juveniles have been translated into English.   [J-HH]

SWAIN, DWIGHT V. (1915–). American writer, with a 1937 BA and a 1954 MA in journalism, very variously employed, his jobs ranging from migrant labourer to university lecturer. His first sf story, "Henry Horn's Super Solvent", for *Fantastic Adventures* in 1941, initiated

the "Henry Horn" series of tales about a bumblingly incompetent would-be scientist; the remaining stories are "Henry Horn's Blitz Bomb" (1942), "Henry Horn's Racing Ray" (1942) and "Henry Horn's X-Ray Eye Glasses" (1942). In addition to several non-fiction books on the art of successful writing, DVS published two sf novels: *Cry Chaos!* (1951 *Imagination*; undated c. **1954**), with interplanetary conflicts, and *The Transposed Man* (**1955**), in which one human rebel wins through to the stars. DVS wrote three stories in 1942 as Clark South.   [JC]

No. 5, 1973. Cover by Berni Wrightson.

SWAMP THING, THE COMIC BOOK published by National Periodical Publications, beginning Oct. 1972. The first 10 nos. illustrated by Berni Wrightson, are much admired by comics collectors for their evocative GOTHIC style. The narrative is a variant on the superhero convention of comics, whereby the protagonist is involved in a scientific accident and finds himself surviving with strangely mutated powers. *ST*'s hero, less fortunately, becomes a monstrous, decaying, putrescent swamp-dweller. *ST* was one of many 1970s comic books which featured fantasies of humiliation, decay and revenge.   [PN]

SWAN AMERICAN MAGAZINE British PULP-size magazine, published by G.G. Swan, London. The only two sf issues in the series, no.11, 1948, and no.15, 1950, were reprints of FUTURE FICTION, Dec. 1942, and SCIENCE FICTION QUARTERLY, Winter 1942. No.11 was titled *Future Fantasy and Science Fiction*.   [FHP]

SWANN, THOMAS BURNETT (1928–76). American poet, writer and academic. He was born in Florida, where he also taught English literature at Florida Atlantic University, turning to full-time writing in the early 1960s. He died of cancer. As an academic he published

works on the poet HD and others. His fiction, beginning with "Winged Victory" for *Fantastic Universe* in 1958, and continuing with many stories for the British magazine *Science Fantasy*, is only marginally sf, and is devoted almost entirely to the rewriting in fantasy terms of early Mediterranean history. Into such tales of Minoan Crete as his first novel *Day of the Minotaur* (**1966**) and its sequel *The Forest of Forever* (**1971**), or of the founding of Rome, as in *Green Phoenix* (**1972**) and its sequel *Lady of the Bees* (1962 *Science Fantasy* as "Where is the Bird of Fire?"; exp. **1976**), he inserted a counter-narrative of the doomed encounter between the creatures of legend — dryads, centaurs, *panisci* and so forth — and insensitive, triumphant mankind. The elegiac, occasionally charming and sometimes sentimental tone in which these encounters were depicted evoked a warm response from fantasy and sf readers of the 1960s and '70s, a response not dissimilar to that evoked by most ECOLOGICAL sf of recent years. TBS's treatment of mankind assuredly plays on his readership's growing sense of unease about Man's continuing violation of the natural order on this planet. His early works are thought by some critics to be the strongest; his later books are over sentimental, and their style is perhaps over ornate.							[JC]
Other works: *The Weirwoods* (**1967**); *The Dolphin and the Deep* (1963–6 var. mags; fix-up **1968**); *Moondust* (**1968**); *Where is the Bird of Fire?* (coll. **1970**); *The Goat Without Horns* (**1971**); *Wolfwinter* (**1972**); *How Are the Mighty Fallen* (**1974**); *The Not-World* (**1975**); *The Gods Abide* (**1976**); *The Minikins of Yam* (**1976**); *The Tournament of Thorns* (1966 and 1973 *FSF*; exp. **1976**); *Will-O-The-Wisp* (**1976**); *Cry Silver Bells* (**1977**); *Queens Walk in the Dusk* (**1977**).
See also: MYTHOLOGY; SUPERNATURAL CREATURES.

Yankee Science Fiction was the title given to the sf numbers of SWAN YANKEE MAGAZINE. No. 21, July 1942.

SWAN YANKEE MAGAZINE British PULP-size magazine, published by G.G. Swan, London. There were three sf and three weird fiction issues in the series. The sf numbers were no.3, 1941; no.11, 1942; and no.21, 1942. The weird numbers were no.6, 1942; no.14, 1942; and no.19, 1942. *SYM* contained both original stories and US reprints. The sf titles were marketed as *Yankee Science Fiction*.							[FHP]

SWAYNE, MARTIN Pseudonym of English writer Maurice Nicoll (1884–1953), in whose sf novel *The Blue Germ* (**1918**) the germ makes people IMMORTAL, lethargic, and blue.				[JC]

SWEDEN *See* SCANDINAVIA.

SWEDENBORG, EMANUEL (1688–1772). Swedish theologian. *See* MARS, MERCURY, OUTER PLANETS, PROTO SF, RELIGION, STARS, VENUS.

SWEVEN, GODFREY Pseudonym of Scottish writer and professor of English John Macmillan Brown (1846–1935); he was Chancellor of the University of New Zealand from 1923, and his work, fiction and non-fiction, deals almost exclusively with the South Pacific. Of sf interest is *Riallaro: the Archipelago of Exiles* (**1901** USA; references have been made to an 1897 UK edition which has not been traced) and its sequel, *Limanora: the Island of Progress* (**1903**), both republished in 1931 under his own name. An ethereal winged man is discovered in the South Pacific and recounts his long trek through a mist-enshrouded group of islands, each of them exemplifying different modes of existence, until he finds himself in the scientific UTOPIA of Limanora, where he is physically and psychologically reconstructed. GS is literate and sometimes eloquent, though (at over 700 pages) his description of Limanora is over-extended.				[JC]

SWIFT, JONATHAN (1667–1745). Irish satirist, poet and cleric. His most famous work, perhaps the most important of all works of PROTO SF apart from Sir Thomas MORE's *Utopia* (**1616** in Latin, trans. **1551**), is *Travels into Several Remote Nations of the World by Lemuel Gulliver, first a Surgeon, and then a Captain of Several Ships* (**1726**; rev. 1735), better known to us now as *Gulliver's Travels*. The work is in many respects pure sf, and it certainly makes use of and in some cases invents several narrative strategies which are now basic to sf; its influence, both direct and indirect, on subsequent sf has been enormous, as for example on H.G. WELLS's *The Island of Dr. Moreau* (**1896**).

Gulliver's Travels is divided into four books, in each of which Captain Gulliver finds himself marooned in an alien culture. JS's SATIRE has two main forms; sometimes the culture in which he finds himself reflects aspects of British society in an exaggerated manner, so as to reveal its absurdities, and sometimes, and more interestingly to sf readers, it is the differences in the alien societies which serve by contrast to make us see our own culture from a new perspective. This latter technique predominates in Book IV, "A Voyage to the Houyhnhnms", in which Gulliver finds himself stranded in a society of intelligent horses, who do not (for example) understand such concepts as war, the telling of untruths, or sexual passion. The cultural details of the society are more detailed and convincing than was commonly the case with satire of this kind, and the satire itself more complex. Although the story is often read as if it were a simple attack on mankind, a more interesting reading, and one more readily supported from the text, is to suppose that in describing a life of pure intellect Swift was simultaneously satirizing humanity for being, ironically, more bestial than these beasts, and attacking the horses for their emotional sterility and soullessness.

Books I and II, in which Gulliver voyages to Lilliput where everyone is very small, and to Brobdingnag where everyone is a giant, are the best known, partly through the bowdlerized versions which have become children's classics; the originals are savage and bawdy. Book III is set in and around Laputa, an ISLAND floating in the air, largely populated by semi-crazed scientific researchers (the first important appearance of the mad SCIENTIST in literature); also living there is a group of infinitely depressing, senile IMMORTALS, "opinionative, peevish, covetous, morose, vain, talkative, but uncapable of Friendship and dead to all natural Affection", the Struldbruggs. Many of the scientific experiments satirized by JS, interestingly, have been staples of later sf; though he shows their absurdity, he also seems to show sympathy for their imaginative enthusiasm, almost despite himself. Most of JS's work contains paradoxes of this kind.

Another narrative strategy of JS, used for satire, has become important to DYSTOPIAN writing generally; he takes an outrageous proposition and debates it quite seriously and deadpan, as if he not only supported it, but did not seriously expect opposition. Thus he satirized the more inhuman attitudes to poverty in *A Modest Proposal* (**1729**) by suggesting that OVERPOPULATION and starvation in Ireland could be cured at a stroke by using the children of the poor as food. The title of another of his works is self-explanatory: *An Argument to Prove that the Abolishing of Christianity in England may as Things now Stand, be Attended with some Inconveniences, and perhaps not Produce those many good Effects proposed thereby* (**1711**).							[PN]
See also: ABSURDIST SF; ASTRONOMY; FANTASTIC VOYAGES; GREAT AND SMALL; LOST WORLDS; MATHEMATICS; POLITICS; SEX; UTOPIAS.

L. Sprague de Camp's study of SWORD AND SORCERY. Arkham House, 1976. Cover by Tim Kirk.

SWORD AND SORCERY The term is usually attributed to Fritz LEIBER, who is said to have coined it in 1960, but the sub-genre to which it refers is much older than that, having been variously called SCIENCE FANTASY, weird fantasy, fantastic romance, and more recently, and perhaps more usefully, HEROIC FANTASY.

Leiber was one of the members of the Hyborian League, a fan group founded in 1956 to preserve the memory of the pulp writer Robert E. HOWARD; many professional writers belonged to it; the group's FANZINE was AMRA. All the members seemed to agree that Howard founded the sword-and-sorcery genre with his "Conan" stories in WEIRD TALES: swashbuckling, romantic fantasies, beginning with "The Phoenix on the Sword" (1932), set in Earth's imaginary past, and featuring a mighty swordsman, violently amorous, who often confronted various supernatural forces of evil.

Howard's stories were not *sui generis* however; the creation of imaginary worlds on which colourful adventures took place was very much a feature of the PULP MAGAZINES, notably the "Barsoom" stories of Edgar Rice BURROUGHS, which had begun 20 years before "Conan". Burroughs did not feature magic to quite the same extent as Howard (and when he did, he usually rationalized it as advanced science), but the atmosphere of the books shows a clear continuity between the two writers. MAINSTREAM literature, too, had a long tradition of picaresque adventures in imaginary worlds, though usually more demure (and literate), and sometimes less energetic, than Howard's. The usually quoted high points of this tradition up to the time of Howard are the somewhat etiolated medieval fantasies of William MORRIS, the stylish though mannered romances of Lord DUNSANY (often set in a sort of "Faerie"), the rather more swaggering and rambustious adventures of E.R. EDDISON, and the elegant, ironic and elaborate "Poictesme" series of James Branch CABELL. All of these

influenced various of the *Weird Tales* sword-and-sorcery writers, though Howard less than H.P. LOVECRAFT, Clark Ashton SMITH, C.L. MOORE and Henry KUTTNER. Lovecraft stands out a little from the others, since most of his work is set on Earth in the recent past, and it emphasizes the sorcery very much more than the swords. In terms of literary strength, C.L. Moore was probably the finest of this group, with her "Jirel of Joiry" and her "Northwest Smith" stories. But there is no denying the colour and vigour of Howard's work. The essential, new element which Howard brought to the genre was the emphasis on brutal, heroic ambition in the HERO, who is seen (unlike Cabell's heroes for example) quite without irony, as simply admirable. This is a matter of taste, perhaps, but many readers prefer those sword-and-sorcery stories in which the heroes or heroines are vulnerable and imperfect, or alternatively capable of showing some wit; there is plenty of invention in Howard, but not much tension, the hero's victories being effectively preordained.

Sometimes sf devices are used to explain the setting of the societies (nearly always tribal or feudal) in which such adventures take place; they may be in ALTERNATE WORLDS, PARALLEL WORLDS, other DIMENSIONS, LOST WORLDS, Earth's prehistoric past even before ATLANTIS, on other planets such as MARS or VENUS, inside the HOLLOW EARTH, or even on forgotten colonies of a GALACTIC EMPIRE. It does not really matter which; the thing is to provide a detailed, exotic background (the more elaborately worked out the better, judging from reader's preferences), to an action which is thoroughly dualistic, which is to say that the conflict is almost invariably between good and evil.

Weird Tales continued to publish sword-and-sorcery stories up to the beginning of the 1940s, many of which never saw book publication until much later. Clark Ashton Smith's extremely colourful, "jewelled" prose was popular; C.L. Moore had perhaps the most baroque imagination, especially when it came to dreaming up quite extraordinarily sinister menaces. Her work has not yet been properly evaluated. But sword and sorcery dwindled in the 1950s. Until the activities of the Hyborian League, and also the publication in book form (often by

Frank Frazetta's poster, Ballantine Books 1977, captures the essential blood-and-thunder of SWORD AND SORCERY

GNOME PRESS) of the works of Howard, Moore and others, it seemed as if this kind of fantasy might be disappearing. The chances are that it would never have attained the extraordinary popularity it has today were it not for the belated but huge success of J.R.R. TOLKIEN's *The Lord of the Rings* (three vols **1954–5**), and the lesser though still remarkable success of T.H. WHITE's *The Once and Future King* (**1958**; vt *Camelot* USA). When these works had become generally known, in the early 1960s, publishers began to fall over one another in the effort to feed the appetite for heroic fantasy which was suddenly manifest.

Tolkien's long, richly imagined work is as important to modern sword and sorcery as Howard's; the two writers together, in fact, represent the two ends of the genre's spectrum: Howard all amoral vigour, Tolkien all deeply moral clarity of imagination; common to both is a powerful commitment to the idea of worlds where MAGIC works, and where heroism can be pitted against evil (even though Howard's heroes were very big, and Tolkien's very small). The two writers could not have had the remotest influence upon one another, but together they are the strongest influences on the modern genre as a whole.

This is getting ahead of the story a little. By the time Tolkien was published, sword and sorcery was showing signs of vigour elsewhere, its two finest exponents, in the opinion of many, being Fritz Leiber and Jack VANCE. Leiber, with his "Fafhrd and Gray Mouser" series, was one of the few who published sword and sorcery in the 1940s, the first of the series being "Two Sought Adventure" in 1939. The whole series is imaginative, vivacious and full of verve; Leiber's stroke of genius was to have two heroes, one huge and powerful, one small, nimble and quick-witted. Vance's *The Dying Earth* (coll. **1950**) and its successor *The Eyes of the Overworld* (coll. **1966**) are dry, ironic, moving, cynical, and often very witty indeed; they are written with precision and flourish, and insofar as they can be compared with anything else in the genre, recall the work of James Branch Cabell.

Other writers who have had a strong influence on the development of the genre are L. Sprague DE CAMP and Fletcher PRATT, Poul ANDERSON, Leigh BRACKETT (especially her Mars stories) and, regrettably in the opinion of some critics, Lin CARTER. Both De Camp and Carter have had a hand in adding to the "Conan" series, and Carter's style in particular is very much more verbose than that of the original. Carter was also editor of BALLANTINE BOOKS' Adult Fantasy series, which certainly did much to increase the fantasy readership among young people, and he has been a tireless proselytizer for the genre; this is to be admired, though its less happy consequence (which can certainly not be

laid exclusively at Carter's door) has been the ever-swelling stream of hackwork which has gone into modern sword and sorcery.

Among the stronger writers is Andre NORTON, whose "Witch World" books, set in parallel worlds where magic works, have at their best a genuine sense of the macabre, evoking vividly the efforts of a few decent people to maintain some kind of civilization in the face of evil, ambition and chaos, though like other works in the genre her books sometimes suffer from a rather clotted, mock-medieval rhetoric. Even Robert A. HEINLEIN wrote one sword-and-sorcery novel, *Glory Road* (**1963**), but his matter-of-factness, and a tendency to preachiness, renders the book devoid of any spell-binding quality, though it is interesting in what it tells us of the author.

Michael MOORCOCK is one of the few English writers to work in the genre, and though his sword and sorcery has been dismissed, not least by himself, as hackwork, and while he certainly wrote too much too fast, his fantasy generally and his "Elric" books in particular imported a welcome breadth to the genre; good and evil in Moorcock's books are never easy to define; the forces of Chaos and the forces of Law are alike unsentimental, self-seeking and untroubled by human anguish. The albino Elric, with his blood-seeking, phallic sword, at the mercy of intolerable forces, is a memorable creation. Moorcock has put paid to the idea of the hero in control of his own destiny; an indifferent universe in his books cares nothing for heroism, but Moorcock does, and the courage shown by his heroes is the more touching for being, often, doomed.

Many women writers have been attracted to sword and sorcery, several already discussed. Others are Katherine KURTZ, Jane GASKELL, Tanith LEE and C.J. CHERRYH, all among the better writers in the genre; Marion Zimmer BRADLEY's "Darkover" books have much in common with sword and sorcery too, and have slowly won a deservedly wide readership.

M. John HARRISON's *The Pastel City* (**1971**) is a more interesting than usual variant, using the conventions of the genre with skill, but to slightly deflationary effect. Christopher STASHEFF, Sterling LANIER and Fred SABERHAGEN have all produced entertaining stories in the genre, as has Avram DAVIDSON, with perhaps more originality.

Sword-and-sorcery readers appear to welcome long and sometimes seemingly endless series, and many writers have obliged: John JAKES with the "Brak" books, Lin Carter with the "Thongor" books, John NORMAN with the "Gor" books, and others by Gardner F. Fox, Jeffrey LORD, Alan Burt AKERS, Karl Edward WAGNER, Andrew J. OFFUTT, Peter Valentine TIMLETT and Robert

Moore WILLIAMS. Not all of these works are pure sword and sorcery; many, such as Akers', are more directly in the Edgar Rice Burroughs tradition. It can be said that most of these (Jakes's and Wagner's being perhaps the best) are routine, and that at their worst they are execrable. The genre has, perhaps, too narrow a range of interests, and the constant recurrence of the same themes is likely to make all but the most fanatic enthusiast tire quickly, at least with work at this lower end of the market. Much sword and sorcery is violent, sexist and even, according to some, fascist. Norman SPINRAD showed what he thought of the genre in *The Iron Dream* (**1972**), a heroic fantasy which purports to have been written by Hitler. But at its best the genre welcomes wit, imagination, and freewheeling invention; it has produced some memorable images.

Sword and sorcery is not sf; it is an accident of publishing history that its links with sf are so strong, but hardly surprising, since both have roots in 1930s pulp fiction, and they are often written by the same people; both, indeed, revel in the creation of adventures in imaginary worlds. The fact that sf attempts to rationalize its mysteries while sword and sorcery simply attributes them to supernatural powers does not, perhaps, make as big a difference as sf purists would like to believe. John CROWLEY's *The Deep* (**1975**) uses the confusion between the genres interestingly in the actual structure of the book.

L. Sprague de Camp's *Literary Swordsmen and Sorcerers* (**1976**) is a useful study. [PN]

See also: GODS AND DEMONS; SEX; VILLAINS.

The only issue, 1975.

SWORD & SORCERY ANNUAL US DIGEST-size magazine. One issue, 1975, published by Ultimate Publishing Co.; probably ed. Sol Cohen. One reprint was from *Weird Tales*: "Queen of the Black

Coast" by Robert E. HOWARD; the other stories were reprinted from *Fantastic* 1961–5. [FHP]

SYMBIOSIS *See* PARASITISM AND SYMBIOSIS.

SYMMES, JOHN CLEVES *See* Captain Adam SEABORN; LOST WORLDS, PSEUDO-SCIENCE.

SZILARD, LEO (1898–1964). Celebrated Hungarian-American physicist, in the USA from 1937. Late in his career he published a volume of short sf stories, *The Voice of the Dolphins and Other Stories* (1961); the title story, told impersonally as though a report, is a pioneer use of the notion that cetacean INTELLIGENCE is both vastly different and in some ways superior to that of *Homo sapiens*. The dolphins of the story grow to dominate mankind, using scientists and institutions as fronts. [JC]

TABOOS Sf has a reputation, not always deserved, for attacking sacred cows and breaking taboos; stories of this kind are discussed under ICONOCLASM. There are also many stories, set in imaginary or alien societies, where taboos are an important part of the social structure; several of these stories (Robert SHECKLEY and Jack VANCE both wrote a lot of them) are discussed under ANTHROPOLOGY.

This entry is devoted only to taboos in sf PUBLISHING. Sf by MAINSTREAM writers has not been subjected to any more censorship than fiction in general, and indeed has often been a medium for discussing "taboo" subjects with comparative freedom. Things were very different within genre sf. Here, publishers unwilling to alienate a general readership, or any part of it, put a great many taboos into operation for a period that lasted at least from the inception of the sf magazines in 1926 until well into the 1950s. Most of these taboos related to SEX, profanity and RELIGION. Several examples of stories which broke religious or sexual taboos, and consequently had difficulty in finding publishers, are discussed under ALIENS. Harry HARRISON's "The Streets of Ashkelon" (1962) is a good story, not

extraordinarily daring, about the anthropological stupidity of a Christian missionary on an alien planet, and the damage he does; he had great difficulty in placing the story, on the grounds that Christians might find it offensive, although it has been anthologized at least six times since.

Nothing changes more quickly in society than prejudices of this sort; in general literature ever since (at least) the Second World War, there has been considerable freedom available to writers in discussing sexual matters, but magazine sf remained downright prudish, even after the pioneering work of Theodore STURGEON and Philip José FARMER. All of this is discussed in detail under SEX.

Not all subjects were taboo; violence, for example, was all right, and extreme POLITICS of the conservative, though not usually the socialist wing (*see* SOCIAL DARWINISM) were acceptable to editors like John W. CAMPBELL Jr, whose own editorials on possible justifications for slavery were notorious. On the other hand, Campbell's *ASF* exercised several quite subtle taboos, not just the well-publicized ones regarding sex and profanity. Campbell strongly disliked publishing downbeat stories in which humanity is somehow unsuccessful, or outwitted by aliens. This did not precisely take the form of censorship, but the writers all knew very well what sort of stories would be acceptable to which editors. In more recent years Roger ELWOOD, who for a while controlled a large percentage of the ANTHOLOGY market, was well known for his extremely conservative views, both religious and sexual. Generally, until the 1960s, PESSIMISM in magazine sf was largely if not entirely taboo.

On the other hand, cannibalism was perfectly all right. It turned up quite often in genre sf even before the 1960s, and has been central in such recent stories as Harlan ELLISON's "A Boy and his Dog" (1969). Ellison was prominent among the editors of original anthologies and magazines of the NEW WAVE, in consciously breaking taboos, notably in his DANGEROUS VISIONS series of anthologies, although only a decade later most of these stories seem tame enough, and indeed many were quite tame even for their period. NEW WORLDS magazine performed a similar function, rather earlier, in the UK; other original anthology series like ORBIT and NEW DIMENSIONS also had an important liberating effect on what could or could not be discussed in genre sf. By 1976 Damon KNIGHT had no qualms about publishing a story advocating incest in a post-HOLOCAUST situation, Felix GOTSCHALK's "The Family Winter of 1986" in *Orbit 18* (anth. **1976**); his editorial foreword itself had a vulgarity which would have been impossible not long before: "The family that lays

together stays together". But the real ground-breaking incest story is very much older: Ward MOORE's classic "Lot's Daughter" (1954).

Political taboos have not been directly important in American sf, although there seems to have been a kind of unspoken agreement not to publish stories of a left-wing orientation (it may have been that few were written), and until the 1960s Negroes were extremely rare in magazine sf. Racial problems tended to be discussed symbolically, in terms of meetings with alien races, rather than directly.

In the Communist bloc countries, political censorship has, as is well known, been strong. The entry on RUSSIA discusses how, from the 1930s until the late 1950s, Russian sf, to be published, had to cleave closely and boringly to ideological correctness. The situation then improved considerably, although even recently the STRUGATSKI brothers have had publication difficulties, and it was not long ago, in the 1960s, that Yuli DANIEL and Andrey SINYAVSKY were silenced and imprisoned. [PN]

TABORI, PAUL (1908–74). Hungarian writer with a doctorate in economic and political science, in Britain since the Second World War; his legal name was Paul Tabor. He was known mainly for his work outside the sf field, his eloquent works on the nature of being a refugee and his non-fiction investigations into the occult being particularly notable. Of his many novels, several are sf, the best of them being the first, *The Green Rain* (1961), a comedy about a chemically polluted rainfall that turns people green; the comedy soon turns to rather sharp SATIRE. Sexual and occult subject matter infuse others of his novels, like *The Cleft* (1969), the fissure of the title being nearly as symbolic as the crack in Emma TENNANT's *The Time of the Crack* (1973). PT was an effective writer who sometimes allowed haste to spoil his effects. [JC]
Other works: *Solo* (**1949**); *The Talking Tree* (**1950**); *The Survivors* (**1964**); the short "Hunter" series, *The Doomsday Rain* (**1967**) and *The Invisible Eye* (**1967**); *The Torture Machine* (**1969**); *The Demons of Sandorra* (**1970**).

TACHYONS The tachyon is a hypothetical FASTER-THAN-LIGHT particle invented not so much because theoretical physicists had reason to suspect its existence as because there seemed no absolute reason why it should not exist. There is an only half-facetious precept in PHYSICS stating that "anything which is not prohibited is compulsory". Olexa-Myron Bilaniuk and E.C. George Sudarshan suggested in 1962, and Gerald Feinberg in 1967, that the idea of a particle that can only travel faster than light does not violate any of the basic maxims of relativistic physics. Such a particle (a tachyon, as opposed to the more familiar tardyon, or slower-than-light particle) may emit Cerenkov radiation analogous to the bow wave of a ship, and thus might perhaps be detected, an otherwise difficult job, since a tachyon at infinite velocity is required by theory to be devoid of energy. No sf reader will be surprised to learn that the mass, or meta-mass, of a tachyon must be imaginary, in the same sense that the square root of minus one is imaginary. If tachyons could be shown to exist (none has yet been detected despite the setting up of a number of experiments), then we might have to rethink the idea of causality, since they would appear in some circumstances to go backwards in time, and to a hypothetical observer the emission of a tachyon would appear to be its absorption. However a negative-energy tachyon propagating backward in time could be reinterpreted as a positive-energy tachyon propagating forward in time; some physicists think that such reinterpretation would be the loophole through which the principle of causality might be preserved. The tachyon has become an item of sf TERMINOLOGY (though not to a great extent as yet, since few sf writers are prepared to tackle the physics involved, even though the equations are simpler than they may at first appear), because it suggests a more rational basis on which TIME-TRAVEL stories could be written. J. Richard Gott proposed in 1973 that after the Big Bang which in some views created the universe, a tripartite universe may have been formed, consisting of universes of matter, ANTIMATTER and tachyons. Physicist-writer Gregory BENFORD has announced the writing of a novel using this idea as its basis. [PN]

TAFF The Transatlantic Fan Fund, usually known by its acronym, formed in Britain in 1953. TAFF exists to send well-known sf fans across the Atlantic to meet fellow fans and to attend major sf CONVENTIONS, Europeans normally attending the Worldcon and Americans the British Eastercon. Several candidates are nominated for each TAFF race and fans on both sides of the Atlantic vote for an eventual winner. Cash is raised by voting fees, donations, and special auctions. Though entirely voluntary and without complex organization, TAFF has become one of sf FANDOM's most successful institutions: from 1955 to 1977, nine American, eight British and two German fans made transatlantic trips through TAFF. [PR]

TAINE, JOHN Pseudonym of Eric Temple Bell (1883–1960). American mathematician and writer, born in Scotland. Under his own name Bell wrote many works on mathematics, and was a noted popularizer of the science, but all his fiction appeared under his pseudonym. His first novel was a LOST-WORLD fantasy, *The Purple Sapphire* (1924). About half of his sf novels were first published as books, while the rest appeared in the PULP magazines. His early scientific romances are unimpressive: *The Gold Tooth* (1927) concerns a quest for a magical element; *Quayle's Invention* (1927) employs the familiar theme of gold-making; and *Green Fire* (1928) is a routine superweapon story (*see* WEAPONS). His best and most interesting work is a long sequence of evolutionary fantasies (*see* EVOLUTION): *The Greatest Adventure* (1929); *The Iron Star* (1930); *The Crystal Horde* (1930 *AMZ Quarterly*; 1952; vt

White Lily USA); *Seeds of Life* (1931 *AMZ Quarterly*; 1951); "The Ultimate Catalyst" (1939) and *The Forbidden Garden* (1947). All these are extravagant romances based on bizarre mutational effects and other possibilities opened up by evolutionary theory. *The Crystal Horde* features crystalline life, and *Seeds of Life* is an important early SUPERMAN story. Related to these is *Before the Dawn* (1934), a prehistoric romance whose hero is a dinosaur watched through a time-viewer by observers in the present day. His best novel is probably *The Time Stream* (1931 *Wonder Stories*; 1946), an elaborate TIME-TRAVEL adventure. An interesting but not altogether successful literary experiment is "The Cosmic Geoids" (title story of *The Cosmic Geoids*, coll. 1949, which includes the story "Black Goldfish"), a series of imaginary scientific reports dealing with strange extraterrestrial objects.

Two inferior novels appeared in the pulps but were never reprinted: the superweapon story "Twelve Eighty-Seven" (1935 *ASF*) and a thriller which turns into a DISASTER story, "Tomorrow" (1939 *Marvel Science Stories*). His last book was the sympathetic monster story *G.O.G. 666* (1954).

Taine's writing is often crude, and his characterization usually lacks finesse, but his speculations are bold and bizarre. He loved to do things on a grand scale, and most of his novels end with catastrophes which overwhelm whole continents. [BS] **See also:** BIOLOGY; DEVOLUTION; INTELLIGENCE; METAPHYSICS; MONEY; MUTANTS; PSEUDO-SCIENCE.

TALBOT, LAWRENCE *See* Edward BRYANT.

TALES OF MAGIC AND MYSTERY, April 1928. TALES OF TOMORROW, No. 3, Nov. 1950. Cover by RT. TALES OF WONDER, Spring 1939. Cover by W.J. Roberts.

TALES OF MAGIC AND MYSTERY

US PULP MAGAZINE. Five issues, Dec. 1927-Apr. 1928, published by Personal Arts Co., New Jersey; ed. Walter Gibson, although he is not credited. *TOMAM* printed fact and fiction, with many articles on magic and conjuring, and at least one article on Houdini in each issue. The fiction was mostly fantasy, notably H.P. LOVECRAFT's "Cool Air" (Mar. 1928). [FHP]

TALES OF TOMORROW

1. British pocketbook magazine. 11 issues, 1950–54, published irregularly by John Spencer, London; probably ed. John Manning. There were no issues in 1951. One of the four Spencer juvenile sf magazines, of interest only to completist collectors, the other three being FUTURISTIC SCIENCE FICTION, WONDERS OF THE SPACEWAYS, and WORLDS OF FANTASY.

2. Television series (1952). ABC TV. American. Created and produced by George Foley and Dick Gordon. One of the earliest sf anthology TV series, it was ambitious in theme but, like most TV productions of the period, limited by the restrictions imposed by live studio shooting. It drew its material from a variety of sources, including the sf PULP magazines; its initial two episodes (30 mins per episode) consisted of a dramatization of Jules VERNE's *Twenty Thousand Leagues Under the Sea* (**1870** France; trans. **1873**), starring Thomas Mitchell as Captain Nemo; Leslie Nielsen co-starred. [FHP/JB]

TALES OF WONDER

British PULP-size magazine. 16 quarterly issues, no.1 undated, Jun. 1937 – Spring 1942. Published by Worlds Work, London; ed. Walter GILLINGS.

TOW was the first adult British sf magazine. It used both original British and reprinted US material, and prospered until wartime paper restrictions caused its demise. Several authors, including William F. TEMPLE and Frank Edward ARNOLD, made their first appearance in *TOW*. Stories included "Sleepers of Mars" (1938; title story of *Sleepers of Mars*, coll. **1973** as by John WYNDHAM) by John Beynon, "The Mad Planet" (1920; 1939) by Murray LEINSTER and "City of the Singing Flame" (1931; 1940) by Clark Ashton SMITH. Other contributors were Benson HERBERT, Festus PRAGNELL, John Russell FEARN and Eric Frank RUSSELL. [FHP/PN]

Collectors should note: Publications became irregular in 1940, the issues being Spr., Sum., Aut. in that year; Win., Spr. and Aut. in 1941; and Spr. in 1942. Issues were numbered consecutively 1–16.

TALL, STEPHEN

(? –). Pseudonym of American writer Compton N. Crook (? –). He began publishing with "The Lights on Precipice Peak" for *Gal* in 1955, but did not

---

become active for another decade, when the stories assembled as *The Stardust Voyages* (coll. of linked stories **1975**) began to appear: they comprise the SPACE OPERA saga of the crew of the ship *Stardust* whose mission it is to assess the potential of various planets and the nature of their ALIEN inhabitants. Though the stories exhibit a sameness of effect, they are capably told. *The Ramsgate Paradox* (**1976**) carries the crew into a novel-length adventure. [JC]

TARANTULA

Film (1955). Universal. Directed by Jack ARNOLD, starring John Agar, Mara Corday and Leo G. Carroll. Screenplay by Martin Berkeley and Robert M. Fresco, based on an episode of SCIENCE FICTION THEATRE called *No Food for Thought* by Robert M. Fresco. 80 mins. B/w.

This film is a better than average contribution by Jack Arnold to the "giant beast on the loose" genre. A biochemist's experiments with nutrients get out of

---

hand and a spider which he has injected with the nutrient escapes into the desert and grows to a vast size. It preys on cattle and people before being incinerated by the army. Arnold makes strong use of the desert setting, creating a kind of watchful stillness, where the giant spider seems natural rather than alien. Clifford Stine's special effects are good. [JB/PN]

TARGET EARTH!

Film (1954). Allied Artists. Directed by Sherman A. Rose, starring Richard Denning, Virginia Grey, Kathleen Crowley and Richard Reeves. Screenplay by William Raynor, based on a story by Paul W. FAIRMAN. 75 mins. B/w.

In this film, whose low budget is reflected in its cheap appearance, robots from Venus invade the Earth but are eventually defeated by scientists. [JB]

TATE, PETER

(? –). Welsh journalist and author. His first sf story was "The Post-Mortem People" (1966) in

A daunting poster for TARANTULA.

NW. His novel *The Thinking Seat* (**1969**) is the first of three featuring the charismatic and guru-like Simeon. It was followed by *Moon on an Iron Meadow* (**1974**) and *Faces in the Flames* (**1976**). All show an interest in POLITICS and *Moon on an Iron Meadow* in particular demonstrates a deep concern over the dangers of biological weapons. It also manifests the extent to which PT has been influenced by Ray BRADBURY: the bulk of the story takes place in Bradbury's imaginary township Green Town, Illinois. PT has published two other novels: *Gardens 12345* (**1971**; vt *Gardens One to Five* USA) and *Country Love and Poison Rain* (**1973**). The latter is probably the first sf novel about Welsh Nationalism and concerns the political repercussions of the discovery of a secret NATO cache of deadly nerve gas in the Brecon Beacons. PT has also published a collection: *Seagulls Under Glass and Other Stories* (coll. **1975**).   [MJE]
See also: POLLUTION.

TATE, ROBIN *See* R.L. FANTHORPE.

TAUSEND AUGEN DES DR MABUSE, DIE (vt **THE THOUSAND EYES OF DR MABUSE**) Film (1960). CCC Filmkunst/CFI Incom/Criterion. Directed by Fritz LANG, starring Dawn Addams, Peter Van Eyck, Gert Fröbe, Wolfgang Preiss and Werner Peters. Screenplay by Fritz Lang and Heinz Oskar Wuttig, based on characters created by Norbert Jacques. 103 mins. B/w.

After a gap of 28 years Fritz Lang, in this West German/Italian/French production, returned to the character that had helped to make him well known as a film-maker in the early 1920s — Dr Mabuse, the evil genius who seeks world conquest. The other Mabuse films were the two-part *Doctor Mabuse, Der Spieler* (1922) and *Das Testament des Dr Mabuse* (1932). *TADDM*, about the tracking down of a madman who believes that he is the reincarnation of Mabuse and who operates from a hotel fitted with countless television cameras, is over-wordy and slow moving.   [JB]

TAYLOR, ANGUS M. (1945–). American-born, Canadian sf critic, now resident in Amsterdam; he has an MA in political science, and a 1976 MSc in history and social studies of science from the University of Sussex in England. His sharp, socio-political criticism has appeared in FOUNDATION and elsewhere. His one book is *Philip K. Dick and the Umbrella of Light* (**1975**), a stimulating though too brief overview of Dick's work.   [PN]

TAYLOR, ROBERT LEWIS (1912–). American writer, often of humorous material, whose sf novel is *Adrift in a Boneyard* (**1947**), in which a few survivors of a mysterious DISASTER come

to a peaceful island and face, farcically, their human natures there.   [JC]

TECHNOLOGY To many the story of future technology (rather than pure science) is virtually synonymous with sf; it is certainly one of the most all-pervading of its themes. Sf and technology grew up together; both existed in a much simpler form in the 18th century and earlier, but both really took their impetus from the Industrial Revolution, which was primarily a phenomenon of the early 19th century.

This entry will provide an overview. Individual technology stories are listed in detail elsewhere in this Encyclopedia, most notably under MACHINES, but also under AUTOMATION, CITIES, COMPUTERS, DISCOVERY AND INVENTION, NUCLEAR POWER, POWER SOURCES, PREDICTION, ROBOTS, ROCKETS, SPACE FLIGHT, SPACESHIPS, TRANSPORTATION, UNDER THE SEA and WEAPONS. Indeed, there is hardly a thematic discussion in this volume that does not bear upon the topic.

It has never been true that sf as a whole has been simply a medium of propaganda for an increasingly technologized future, though it has been true of individual works. Sf adopted from the beginning an ambiguous attitude towards technology. At one extreme is the view that technology is synonymous with progress, and that with its growth will come greater happiness for all, and a chance for even the poor and the unskilled to live lives of dignity and peace, with ample LEISURE in which to enjoy family life and the arts. At the other extreme is the view that technology will make us all dependent on the machine, cogs in a great system; it will deprive us of spontaneity and independence; it will sever our links with the soil and with nature generally; it will encapsulate our lives and deprive us of any stimuli towards maturity; it will be used by perverted men to create worse WARS; it will despoil the Earth (*see* ECOLOGY; POLLUTION).

Few sf writers express attitudes so clearly polarized between OPTIMISM AND PESSIMISM; many who are worried about the misuse of technology would be horrified at the suggestion that we voluntarily return to a pre-technological, medieval way of life; the many horrors of the middle ages are not so readily forgotten, although there has been a persistent medievalizing, anti-technological strain in sf, whose first important document is perhaps William MORRIS's *News from Nowhere* (**1890**). This lust for a rural or small-town life, where a man can work with his hands and experience the joys of creation and independence directly, is discussed under PASTORAL. Even stories of LIFE ON OTHER WORLDS often present human explorers assuming that ALIEN civilizations are unsophisticated and primitive merely because they are unindustrialized, only to receive some sort of comeuppance.

Because views about technology are so various, both UTOPIAS and DYSTOPIAS, from the late 19th century on, regularly envisage a future dependent on technology. An example of such a Utopia is Edward BELLAMY's *Looking Backward* (**1888**); an early Dystopian attitude to machines is shown in Samuel BUTLER's *Erewhon* (**1872**).

One of the interests of sf for the social historian is the way in which the balance between these two extreme views of technology swings first one way and then the other at different periods. H.G. WELLS envisaged a technology-dependent society, ruled by technocrats, in *A Modern Utopia* (**1905**), but E.M. FORSTER soon responded with what remains one of the classic horror stories of Man's dependence on the machine, "The Machine Stops" (1909).

Genre sf in the magazines was, in the early days, generally disposed to be enthusiastic about technology, continuing a tradition which goes back to the wild and wonderful INVENTIONS in the 19th-century DIME NOVELS (very popular with readers) and to all the stories in the BOYS' PAPERS which featured heroes modelled on an idealized Thomas Edison. Hugo GERNSBACK was writing in exactly this tradition in *Ralph 124C 41+* (1911–12; fix-up **1925**); his magazines, from SCIENCE AND INVENTION onwards, proselytized vigorously for a popular understanding of the miracles of modern technology, and he encouraged his writers to produce stories of further miracles of this kind in the future. But Gernsback's earnest optimism was not to last, even in magazine sf, and indeed (though primarily for reasons irrelevant to this topic) his magazines had all failed by the mid-1930s. John W. CAMPBELL Jr, in his own writing (particularly as by Don A. Stuart) and also as editor of *ASF*, showed a much greater awareness of the dangers of the machine (though he remained fascinated with technology), and this feeling was expressed clearly in stories he published even before the Second World War. With the dropping of the atom bomb in 1945, these dangers found a symbol which sf was not to forget (*see* NUCLEAR POWER), and simplistic technological optimism left the pages of genre sf for good; the tone even of technophilic writing was, from now on, much more cautious. None the less *ASF* remained associated with a kind of fiction which put a romantic emphasis not so much on the pure scientist as on the technician, the engineer. (Campbell himself had been trained as an engineer.) Pre-eminent in the writing of stories of this kind was Robert A. HEINLEIN, from the beginnings of his career, as in "The Roads Must Roll" (1940), where an engineer heroically fulfils his duty to keep technology running, in this case the continuous moving belts which Heinlein envisaged as replacing our ordinary roads. George O. SMITH's "Venus

Equilateral" stories neatly summed up the *ASF* ethos; they were yarns of radio engineers in space, always ready to improvise in order to keep the technology of the future functioning, always with time for a wisecrack and a few drinks with the boys. Sf generally, and not just in *ASF*, has tended to stress applied over pure science.

In the hundreds of magazine stories about the misuse of science it was usually the military, the politicians or the industrialists who were the VILLAINS, not the SCIENTISTS; only in the most simplistic stories was technology seen as itself the villain. The moral dilemmas in sf are usually associated with the use of technology; few stories ask the ancient Faustian question of whether Man has a right to invent such devices in the first place.

The position of honour given to technology by sf, however, is not because sf writers as a race were engineers *manqués*. Some writers did like machinery for its own sake, but many more saw it as symbolic of a new freedom. The first technological myth in sf was that of TRANSPORTATION, and Jules VERNE was its presiding genius; his super-boats and super-airships were means of breaking the shackles of the here-and-now, opening the way to new adventures and new living places; in genre sf this rapidly developed into opening the way to the stars. SPACE FLIGHT is the supreme myth of sf, because it is seen as a means of CONCEPTUAL BREAKTHROUGH, the ultimate barrier broken. Humanity, no longer Earthbound, would become somehow transcendent. The romantic heyday of this myth was from the 1930s to the 1950s.

The details of actual flights to the Moon were so thoroughly unromantic, and the recognition of the huge expense with which such projects burdened the taxpayer became so widespread, that glorifying Man's triumphant progress through the galaxy came by the late 1960s to look a little premature, and the whole theme in sf has become slightly muted. Part of this sombreness derives from the feeling, dominant in the 1960s and '70s, that we have made a mess of things; wars and starvation continue, OVERPOPULATION is a burden, our natural resources are being squandered and industrial pollution has affected the whole world. The comparative sobriety of post-1960s sf is not surprising in the circumstances, though doubtless these feelings are cyclic, and the open-hearted, romantic, expansionist sf tale will return full-bloodedly; meanwhile many sf writers, notably Robert SILVERBERG, clearly feel that humanity's progress to the stars, if it ever happens, may merely infect the innocence of other worlds with our guilt. (This is the loaded vocabulary of RELIGION, which often recurs in modern sf.) Technological optimism in sf is by no means dead, merely more

hedged about with an awareness of the problems; Arthur C. CLARKE has been the most notably positive apostle of technology in the post-War period, and continues so, along with Larry NIVEN and others.

The images of technology's triumph which once dominated magazine sf were not only a matter of the written word. Sf ILLUSTRATION in the 1930s carried a tremendous, naïve emotional charge, especially the crude but vivid cityscapes and spaceships of Frank R. PAUL, and to a lesser extent the work of his contemporaries WESSO and Elliott DOLD. This tradition has never died in sf illustration. Magazine covers still feature towering machines, sparkling, godlike colossuses, emblems of Man's greatness. Christopher Foss is one of many illustrators for whom the myth is very much alive.

Sf in the CINEMA has not been so technology-conscious, partly for the practical reason that a convincing future technology is extremely expensive to mock up. The popularity of STAR WARS (1977), however, can be partly attributed to the success with which it recreated the atmosphere of technological gigantism that dominated the PULPS. The most notable film expressing the opposing view may have been THE ANDROMEDA STRAIN (1971), which used its aseptic, gleaming underground technology to symbolize a kind of claustrophobic trap, dwarfing and minimizing the protagonists; in this respect it harks back to the first such visual classic, Fritz LANG's METROPOLIS (1926).

Several minor categories of sf story (and some major ones) relate interestingly to the technological debate. The first consists of stories which suggest that to give technology to a primitive society may be to destroy it; the idea has been used so often as to become a cliché. Two good examples are William GOLDING's "Envoy Extraordinary" (1956) and Poul ANDERSON's "The Longest Voyage" (1960).

The second group consists of stories about machines creating more machines, rendering Man irrelevant, a popular satirical notion. Two successful examples are John SLADEK's *The Reproductive System* (1968; vt *Mechasm* USA) and Philip K. DICK's "Autofac" (1955). A relevant theme anthology here is *Beyond Control* (anth. 1972) ed. Robert Silverberg.

The third is a small but interesting category of stories which take as their basic assumption that there are two ways for a society to evolve, either through technology or through the development of mental powers which a reliance on technology will stunt. They include Fred SABERHAGEN's "Black Mountains" trilogy, Christopher STASHEFF's "Warlock" books and Theodore COGSWELL's memorable "The Wall around the World" (1953). Others are discussed under MAGIC and PSI

POWERS.

The fourth category is the oldest and most important: tales of the HOLOCAUST AND AFTER. In most of these stories the emphasis is not so much on the DISASTER itself as on the new life which follows it, a life of difficulty and pain perhaps, but a life in which we start afresh, working with our hands and our wits, with technology an irrelevant memory, known only through grim, rusting artefacts jutting into the landscape, or ruined cities. In these stories (and films) there is often a sense of exhilaration, a sheer joy in seeing our Western, technological civilization go smash. Nowhere is Man's resentment at what he has done to himself with his machines more evident than in this exultation, even though, ironically, the stories often end with a new technology being developed all over again.   [PN]

TEILHET, DARWIN L(E ORA) (1904–64). American author of suspense thrillers who also writes as Cyrus T. Fisher. Told in a nightmarish, tough-guy idiom, *The Fear Makers* (1945) deals in borderline sf fashion with subversion and psychological warfare as a kind of haunting in contemporary Washington.   [JC]

TELEKINESIS An important item of sf TERMINOLOGY. Telekinesis is the ability to move objects by the power of the mind, and after telepathy is the most commonly used PSI POWER in sf. The word, however, probably did not originate in sf.   [PN]

TELEPATHY *See* ESP; PSI POWERS; SUPERMAN.

TELEPORTATION Common item of sf TERMINOLOGY, its meaning being the same as TELEKINESIS but, unlike the latter, which is usually applied to inanimate objects, is often applied to moving oneself from one place to another by the power of the mind. It is a PSI POWER.   [PN]
See also: MATTER TRANSMISSION.

TELEVISION The first sf series to appear on American TV, CAPTAIN VIDEO, was primarily aimed at children and it is arguable that the situation, nearly three decades later, has not changed. Current (1977–8) American sf series remain on a comic-book level, designed simply to provide action and adventure thrills while their sf elements are merely decorative, rather than themes to be explored.

Captain Video, which began in 1949, was a serial made on a very small budget and transmitted live every night. This situation ensured that sets and special effects were primitive (scenes involving special effects were pre-filmed and then inserted, usually clumsily, into the show, by cutting to a TV camera that was pointing directly into the lens of a movie projector) but its popularity with young viewers quickly produced a host of imitations, like BUCK ROGERS (1950), TOM

CORBETT, SPACE CADET (1950), SUPERMAN (1953), SPACE PATROL (1954), CAPTAIN MIDNIGHT (1954) and COMMANDO CODY — SKY MARSHAL OF THE UNIVERSE (1955). While the later series were more expensively produced, and pre-recorded on film, they all followed in the tradition of the movie serials of the 1930s and '40s rather than that of written sf. Science, of course, had little part in any of these productions, with the exception of *Tom Corbett*, which had Willy LEY as scientific adviser, but it did play an important part in one of the first "adult" sf series on American TV. OUT OF THIS WORLD (1952) was a mixture of sf and science fact, with guest scientists interrupting the story to discuss scientific points with the narrator. This non-sensational approach to sf was continued in the 1955 series SCIENCE FICTION THEATER in which the distinguished-looking host, Truman Bradley, and the show's various writers, did their best (presumably unconsciously) to ensure that no trace of any "sense of wonder" remained in the stories. Nearer to written sf was TALES OF TOMORROW (1952), one of the earliest sf anthology series, which featured stories adapted from sf books and magazines but, like the early children's serials, was handicapped by the limitations imposed by live transmission.

The first major British sf event on TV (apart from Nigel KNEALE's TV adaptation, in 1949, of George ORWELL's *Nineteen Eighty-Four*, which was published in that year) was the BBC serial THE QUATERMASS EXPERIMENT, a mixture of horror and sf which was considered suitable only for adults at the time, though today it would probably seem no more disturbing than the children's serial DR WHO. Even by the early 1950s the fundamental differences between American and British TV had been established, due mainly to the fact that the BBC was financed by public funds rather than having to rely upon private enterprise. Instead of having to produce self-contained programme "packages" that would be attractive to sponsors, which was the case in America, the BBC TV producers had a greater choice over what form their programmes would take and thus were able to alter the format to suit the subject. The most popular format for BBC drama (apart from individual plays) became the serial, usually consisting of between six and 10 episodes; this enabled the writers to build up atmosphere and to concentrate on character development whereas in America the trend was towards long-running series in which the episodes were complete in themselves. (Another advantage of the BBC is the lack of interruptions by commercials, which cause the unnatural rhythm of most American TV shows, each commercial break having to be preceded by a false climax or cliff-hanger designed to entice the viewer to stay tuned.) With the arrival of commercial TV in Britain, American-style programming was also introduced, but the serial format remains popular on British TV today, even on the commercial channel.

BBC TV's first productions of sf for children also took the form of serials, one of the earliest being THE LOST PLANET (1954), followed by a sequel, *Return of the Lost Planet*, in 1955, the year that saw the first of the *Quatermass* sequels, QUATERMASS II.

1956–8 were sparse years for sf on TV. In America most of the juvenile series had ended, with the exception of *Superman*, which lasted until 1957 (already the steady erosion of the boundaries between children's and adult programmes on American TV had begun). The sober and dull *Science Fiction Theater* also continued to 1957 but from then until 1959 sf on TV was practically non-existent. The situation was little different in Britain, though 1956 saw the children's serial SPACE SCHOOL on the BBC and in 1958 came the third and best of the *Quatermass* serials: QUATERMASS AND THE PIT.

WORLD OF GIANTS had one brief season on CBS in 1959, but the most important new American series that year for the sf fans was THE TWILIGHT ZONE, an anthology series created by Rod SERLING that consisted of a mixture of fantasy and sf stories (it lasted until 1964). The 1960s saw an increase of sf-related series in both countries: the BBC serial A FOR ANDROMEDA was shown in 1961 and was unusual in that it was co-written by a scientist, Fred HOYLE. A sequel, THE ANDROMEDA BREAKTHROUGH, followed in 1962. 1961 was also the year THE AVENGERS began, though at that time it was called *Police Surgeon* and did not feature any of the sf or fantasy gimmicks that were to dominate the show in later years. Another British series, OUT OF THIS WORLD (1962), tried to repeat the success of *The Twilight Zone* by adopting a similar format. Its episodes were based on the stories of many well-known sf writers, but it lasted only one short season.

One of the most remarkable TV phenomena began in 1963: the BBC serial DR WHO, which was aimed at children but attracted adults as well. Producers, writers and cast have changed many times since then but 15 years later it is still running and is more popular than ever.

In America another series inspired by *The Twilight Zone* began in 1963. THE OUTER LIMITS was more sf-oriented than Serling's series and also took itself rather less seriously, and though it was bizarre, inventive and often entertaining it could hardly be described as adult sf. The same year saw the first of many comedy sf series, MY FAVORITE MARTIAN, a relatively sophisticated situation comedy that proved popular with audiences and lasted until 1966. Less successful though in some ways superior was MY LIVING DOLL, an sf comedy about a robot woman which ran for one season in 1964.

It was also in 1964 that Irwin ALLEN produced the first of his sf action/adventure series for TV, VOYAGE TO THE BOTTOM OF THE SEA, and his lowest-possible-common-denominator approach to the genre has influenced the style and quality of American TV sf ever since. The same year saw the début of THE MAN FROM U.N.C.L.E., a by-product of the "James Bond" craze (see Ian FLEMING) but incorporating many sf devices and plot situations. It was also a little more intelligent than Allen's series. A hybrid of the two was THE WILD, WILD WEST (1965) which told of two secret agents, equipped with various anachronistic devices, and often pitted against mad scientists, working in the 19th-century West. Another Irwin Allen series, LOST IN SPACE, began in 1965 and was more obviously aimed at children than *Voyage to the Bottom of the Sea*, though the difference between the two was slight as far as quality or plausibility was concerned.

In Britain, 1965 saw the début of the adult sf series OUT OF THE UNKNOWN, an anthology show that presented adaptations of the work of many sf writers including Isaac ASIMOV, Clifford D. SIMAK, J.G. BALLARD, John BRUNNER, etc., from which it derived an authority not often visible in televised sf written by professional TV screenwriters. The standard of the adaptations varied and the small budgets were a handicap (another major difference between American and British TV is that the latter is usually produced with much less money) but overall it was superior to most sf series that have appeared before or since. It was not considered a popular success by the BBC, however, who later turned it into a series about the supernatural. It ended in 1967.

Also from Britain in 1965 came the THUNDERBIRDS series — a show that used sophisticated puppets and clever special effects. Produced by Gerry Anderson, the series proved very popular with children on both sides of the Atlantic. Anderson had pioneered the use of puppetry for children's sf with *Fireball XL5* and *Supercar*, back in 1962.

Sf comedy continued in America with IT'S ABOUT TIME (1966), whose crude humour lasted only one season. TIME TUNNEL, another Irwin Allen production, also began that year but was not as popular as his other series. The most important new American series of 1966 was STAR TREK, a show which still has a large and enthusiastic following over a decade later. Aimed basically at adolescents, it featured the work of several established sf writers in the first two seasons though their scripts were usually rewritten by the show's resident writers (no well-known sf names appeared in any of the credits for the final season, which may account in part for the plunge in quality).

THE INVADERS was another American series of the late 1960s but, as it was based on a single plot gimmick that had to be repeated in each episode, it lasted for only two seasons. More interesting, and equally reliant on evoking total PARANOIA, was THE PRISONER (1967), a KAFKA-esque series created by actor Patrick McGoohan who also starred in it. But it was popular neither with the British company that produced it (ITC) nor with the public, and it came to a premature end, although its supporters continue to argue passionately that it was the finest sf ever to appear on TV. Irwin Allen launched yet another series, LAND OF THE GIANTS, in 1968, and was busily preparing his next that same year, to be called CITY BENEATH THE SEA, but the vogue for his type of programme came to a temporary end and the latter series never materialized (though the pilot episode was shown in 1971 as a feature film). Also short-lived was THE IMMORTAL (1970) which was based on a novel by sf writer James GUNN.

In England in 1969 Gerry Anderson of *Thunderbirds* fame switched from puppets to live actors in his new children's series UFO. His special effects were as impressive as ever but they did not compensate for the poor scripts and the series only lasted one season. Another British series with more serious intentions was DOOMWATCH (1970) which exploited popular anxiety about the dangers of scientific research; one of the creators of the series was the scientist Kit PEDLER.

Rod Serling began another anthology series in 1971, NIGHT GALLERY, but it was less sf-oriented than *The Twilight Zone* and proved less successful as well. Then in 1973 came the series which has had the greatest influence on American sf TV in the 1970s, THE SIX MILLION DOLLAR MAN — which, though basically a live comic strip and a continuation of the juvenile 1950s *Superman* series, appears to have cloned successfully; there have been several close duplications of the formula and the original remains popular in 1978.

The British children's serial THE TOMORROW PEOPLE began on commercial TV in 1973, and has approached the level of *Dr Who*. The BBC in the same year attempted a more adult series with MOONBASE 3, a non-sensational serial set on the Moon, but it was not a success.

The following year in America saw the equally short-lived PLANET OF THE APES series, based on the popular movie of the same name. Also short-lived, though rather better, was KOLCHAK: THE NIGHT STALKER (1974), an anthology series primarily about the supernatural, which included a few sf episodes.

In 1975 Gerry Anderson, after the failure of UFO, created a pale imitation of *Star Trek* with his series SPACE 1999. Surprisingly, it enjoyed some success in America, but only briefly, and it ended

after two seasons. The series represents a nadir in the quality of scientific thought in televised sf. A more typically British series of the same year was SURVIVORS, an after-the-HOLOCAUST type of story in the British manner established by H.G. WELLS and John WYNDHAM.

One of the first of the many *Six Million Dollar Man* imitations was THE INVISIBLE MAN (1975), but it did not prove as popular as expected, despite some ingenious special effects and the use of David McCallum, the star of *The Man from U.N.C.L.E.* It returned the following season with a different actor in the lead role and a new title: THE GEMINI MAN, neither of which saved the series from being cancelled. Yet another short-lived series was THE FANTASTIC JOURNEY (1976) which utilized the *Star Trek* formula without spaceship or other planets (different cultures being encountered via "time zones" on a lost island in the Bermuda Triangle).

THE BIONIC WOMAN, a spin-off from *Six Million Dollar Man*, made her début in 1976, as did *Wonder Woman* (derived from the fantasy comic strip of the same title). In 1977 the comic-book style trend was continued (but with none of the verve of the best comics) with THE MAN FROM ATLANTIS, LOGAN'S RUN and THE INCREDIBLE HULK. But while fantasy and sf-related series proliferated in America in 1977, British TV produced only the gloomy, Orwellian serial *1990* and, of course, the never-ending and still sprightly *Dr Who*. It was not until 1978 that British TV made a comparatively formidable entry into the world of SPACE OPERA with Terry NATION's series *Blake's Seven*, which while proficiently produced and more sophisticated than *Space 1999*, was still too close to the *Star Trek* formula.

In the 1970s such anxiety-ridden British series as *Doomwatch*, *Survivor* and *1990* seem to reflect the fears of a society that suspects it is on the brink of something unpleasant, whereas whatever fears may be preying on the American mass-consciousness the apparent reaction to them is to plunge wholeheartedly into a second childhood, not only with TV, but also in the cinema, as with STAR WARS and SUPERMAN.

The current standard of televised sf in both countries is as poor as ever; in America, indeed, it has got worse. While British sf series over the years became more serious and adult in their approach, they are still plagued with the same problem that causes so much bad sf to be produced on American TV, and that is the seeming inability of TV writers to understand what sf is all about. No matter how good an original concept may be, the writers will process it until it conforms with the rest of TV, and along the way the vital elements of sf are lost. This used to apply to the CINEMA also, but in recent years more and more film-makers with a background in the

traditions of sf have entered the industry; *Star Wars*, for all its faults, is obviously the work of someone who has a genuine feeling for sf. Until this happens in TV, which is unlikely, as the TV industry is something of a "closed shop" with its own well-established writers and producers, the standard of sf will not improve. [JB]

TEMPLE, ROBIN *See* Samuel Andrew WOOD.

TEMPLE, WILLIAM F(REDERICK) (1914–). English writer who began his activities in the sf world before the Second World War as an active fan, a member of the British Interplanetary Society, editor of its *Bulletin* and housemate of Arthur C. CLARKE. He published a horror story, "The Kosso" in *Thrills* (anth. **1935**), and his first sf story, "Lunar Lilliput", for *Tales of Wonder* in 1938. His first and best-known novel, *The Four-Sided Triangle* (1939 *AMZ*; exp. **1949**), is a love story in which the sf element is the duplication of the one girl the two men love (*see* CLONES); it was filmed as FOUR-SIDED TRIANGLE. After *The Dangerous Edge* (**1951**), a non-sf crime novel, WFT became active in the 1950s in the magazines, and has remained reasonably prolific, though his sf novels were for several years either juveniles in his "Martin Magnus" series or routine sf adventures, like *The Automated Goliath* (**1962**). More recently, however, he has published two much better sf novels, *Shoot at the Moon* (**1966**) and *The Fleshpots of Sansato* (**1968**). The first is clearly a parody of many of the more routine sf conventions concerning trips to the MOON, and the gallery of characters usually involved, so that the book mounts to a ship-of-fools extravaganza; the second is a remarkable SPACE OPERA replete with interstellar agents, a corrupt city in the stars, and much symbolism; the original edition is complete, but at least one paperback reprint was cut clumsily. [JC]
Other works: *Martin Magnus, Planet Rover* (**1954**); *Martin Magnus on Venus* (**1955**); *Martin Magnus on Mars* (**1956**); *The Three Suns of Amara* (**1962**); *Battle on Venus* (**1963**). Non-fiction: *The True Book About Space Travel* (**1954**; vt *The Prentice-Hall Book About Space Travel* USA).

TENN, WILLIAM Pseudonym of American writer and academic Philip Klass (1920–), who has been teaching writing and sf at Pennsylvania State College, as an associate professor, since 1966. WT began writing after World War Two army service, publishing his first story, "Alexander the Bait", for *ASF* in 1946. It gives some evidence of the pointed intelligence of his work in its prediction that space flight would be achieved institutionally rather than through the efforts of an individual inventor-industrialist-genius, a prediction which sf as a whole was remarkably loth to make. WT soon became one of sf's very few genuinely comic, genuinely incisive writers of short fiction, sharper and more mature than Fredric BROWN, less self-indulgent than Robert SHECKLEY. He found a congenial market in *Galaxy* from 1950 onwards. Among the finer stories assembled in his first collection, *Of All Possible Worlds* (coll. **1955**;. UK edition omits two stories and substitutes two from *The Human Angle*), are "Down Among the Dead Men" (1954), about the use of ANDROIDS reconstituted from human corpses as front-line troops in a savage interstellar war, "The Liberation of Earth" (1953), in which liberation is imposed upon Earth alternately by two warring ALIEN races (in a prescient SATIRICAL model for much recent revolutionary activity), and "The Custodian" (1953), an effective variant on the last-man-on-Earth theme. In addition to this volume, WT has published five further collections, the bulk of whose contents date from the late 1940s through the mid 1950s — though his occasional later stories maintain the same high calibre, comic manner and dark vision. The five are: *The Human Angle* (coll. **1956**); *Time in Advance* (coll. **1958**), comprised of several longer stories; *The Seven Sexes* (coll. **1968**); *The Square Root of Man* (coll. **1968**); and *The Wooden Star* (coll. **1968**). Each volume contains examples of his best work. In *The Human Angle*, for instance, can be found "Wednesday's Child" (1956), in which a rather simple young woman's biological peculiarities climax in her giving birth to herself, and "The Discovery of Morniel Mathaway" (1955), which involves TIME TRAVEL and evolves (unusually in the sf genre) into a serious look at the nature of the making of ART.

Since the early 1960s, WT has been relatively inactive, and the simultaneous publication of three of the above collections with his only full-length novel, *Of Men and Monsters* (1963 *Gal.* as "The Men in the Walls"; exp. **1968**), may have somewhat diminished the impact of the latter book, which was in any case not much helped by its inept title. It is a fascinating INVASION story in which giant aliens (*see also* GREAT AND SMALL) have occupied Earth and almost eliminated mankind, except for small groups living, like mice, within the walls of the aliens' dwellings. Like mice, all the same, men do survive, and even prosper, and as the novel closes are about to spread, as passengers, and in secret, to the stars. The novel has been influential, despite its limited immediate impact. Also published at this time, *A Lamp for Medusa* (1951 *Fantastic Adventures* as "Medusa Was a Lady"; **1968**) is a short fantasy-like tale in which a young American falls into a kind of PARALLEL WORLD where, as Perseus, he is given an opportunity to rewrite human history.

An interesting account by WT, partly autobiographical, partly about SF IN THE CLASSROOM, is "Jazz Then, Musicology Now" in *FSF*, May 1972. Despite his cheerful surface, and the occasional zaniness of his stories, WT, like most real satirists, is fundamentally a pessimist; and when the comic disguise is whipped off, as sometimes happens, the result can be salutary. [JC]
Other works: As editor: *Children of Wonder* (anth. **1953**; vt *Outsiders: Children of Wonder*).
See also: AUTOMATION; ECOLOGY; HUMOUR; MATHEMATICS; PSYCHOLOGY; TIME PARADOXES.

TENNANT, EMMA (1937–). British writer and editor of the literary newspaper *Bananas*. Under the name Catherine Aydy, she published her first novel, *The Colour of Rain* (**1963**), but only began writing her allegorical sf novels with *The Time of the Crack* (**1973**; vt *The Crack*), about an inexplicable fault line that opens through the heart of London; *The Last of the Country House Murders* (**1975**), though technically a detective novel, is set in a vaguely realized, depressed NEAR FUTURE in which the eponymous country house is maintained artificially; *Hotel de Dream* (**1976**) resembles sf in some of the devices it presents to dramatize the reality-dreams of the hotel's inhabitants. ET's sf shows a MAINSTREAM writer's typically casual use of sf material to arrive at literary structures illuminating the condition of the here-and-now. [JC]

TENNESHAW, S.M. Ziff-Davis house name, used by Randall GARRETT, three times by Garrett in collaboration with Robert SILVERBERG, by Milton LESSER and on over 20 stories whose authors have not been identified.

10 STORY FANTASY. The only issue. The artist who produced the whip-fetish picture is uncredited.

10 STORY FANTASY US PULP-size magazine. One issue, Spring 1951, published by Avon Periodicals; ed. Donald A. WOLLHEIM. It is primarily remembered for its poor arithmetic (there were 11 stories) and for the first publication of Arthur C. CLARKE's "Sentinel of Eternity" (vt "The Sentinel"), on which the film 2001: A SPACE ODYSSEY was based.

It was published simultaneously in Canada. [FHP]

TENTH VICTIM, THE *See* DECIMA VITTIMA, LA.

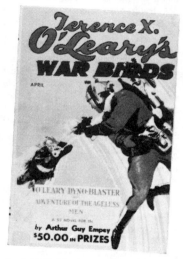

April 1935. The low quality of the cover matched that of the stories.

TERENCE X. O'LEARY'S WAR BIRDS US PULP MAGAZINE. Three issues, Mar., Apr. and May/Jun. 1935, published by Dell, no editor named. These were fantasy issues of the aviation pulp *War Birds*, whose numeration they followed: nos 84, 85 and 86. Extremely rare collector's items, they could be of little interest to non-collectors, given the quality of the stories by Arthur Guy Empey which they contained, a kind of lowest common denominator of the pulp style, which some have surmised was intended as a skit on then current SF MAGAZINES. The Apr. issue has been reprinted as a facsimile paperback book, **1975**. [FHP]

TERMINAL MAN, THE Film (1974). Warner Bros. Produced, directed and written by Mike Hodges, starring George Segal and Joan Hackett. Based on the novel by Michael CRICHTON. 107 mins. Colour.

A computer specialist suffers from violent blackouts as a result of brain damage caused by a car accident. As his condition cannot be controlled by drugs his doctors decide to insert a number of electrodes into his brain, linked to a tiny computer surgically implanted in his shoulder, so that when a convulsion starts the computer will automatically send soothing impulses directly into the brain. However, the brain enjoys the soothing effect so much that it induces the blackouts at an ever increasing rate. During these periods its owner is driven to commit acts of violence and is finally killed by the police.

British director Hodges is best known for such crime thrillers as *Get Carter* and *Pulp*, which probably explains why the thriller elements of the story are better handled than the sf. The opportunity to examine the implications of mind control is forfeited in order to concentrate on visual excitement.   [JB]

TERMINOLOGY Newcomers to sf are occasionally dismayed by its jargon. Certain concepts have become so useful in sf that they tend to be referred to by genre writers in a kind of shorthand, without explanation, to save time. The experienced sf reader comes across some of these terms again and again, and each time they take on an additional richness and resonance. Many of them receive entries in this volume, sometimes brief (*see* CREDITS), sometimes very detailed (*see* ANDROIDS, CLONES, ROBOTS). The main jargon words, many of which are now recognized by dictionaries, receive entries as follows. First is the cluster of terms used by sf readers to describe different aspects of the genre: HARD SF, HARDCORE SF, HEROIC FANTASY, PULP SF, SCIENCE FANTASY, SOFT SF, SPACE OPERA, SWORD AND SORCERY. Second is the cluster of terms which are borrowed from outside sf, usually from science, but are much used within sf, sometimes with modified meanings: ALIENS, ANDROIDS, ANTIMATTER, BIONICS, BLACK HOLES, CLONES, CRYOGENICS, CRYONICS, CYBERNETICS, DYSON SPHERE, ENTROPY, ESP, EXTRATERRESTRIAL, FLYING SAUCERS, FOURTH DIMENSION, GALACTIC LENS, HOMEOSTATIC SYSTEMS, ION DRIVE, MUTANTS, NEUTRON STAR, PARSEC, SOLAR WIND, SUPERMAN, SUSPENDED ANIMATION, TACHYONS, TELEKINESIS, TELEPORTATION, TERRA, UFOS. The final cluster is of terms which either originate within sf, or would be almost unknown if it were not for sf: ANSIBLE, ANTIGRAVITY, ASTROGATION, BEM, BLASTER, BUG-EYED MONSTER, CONAPT, CORPSICLE, CREDITS, CYBORGS, DALEKS, DEATH RAYS, DIRAC COMMUNICATOR, DISINTEGRATOR, ESPER, E.T., FORCE FIELD, FRANKENSTEIN MONSTER, FTL, GAS GIANT, GENERATION STARSHIPS, HYPERSPACE, INNER SPACE, MATTER TRANSMISSION, PANTROPY, POSITRONIC ROBOTS, PSIONICS, PSI POWERS, PSYCHOHISTORY, RIMWORLD, ROBOTS, SPACE WARP, SPINDIZZY, STARSHIP, TERRAFORMING, TIME MACHINE, VIDPHONE, WALDO. The list is by no means exhaustive. Sf fans have also developed a specialist terminology, but this is quite distinct, generally, from the terminology of sf itself. It is discussed under FAN LANGUAGE.   [PN]

TERRA There's no place like Terra, muses the typical sf spaceman home on leave. In sf TERMINOLOGY the Latin form is that usually given to the name of our planet, since Earth is ambiguous, meaning the planet itself, and also the friable material we grow vegetables in. Similarly, our Sun is conventionally, in sf, called Sol.   [PN]

TERRAFORMING If mankind is to colonize planets where Earthlike conditions do not obtain (*see* COLONIZATION OF OTHER WORLDS) he has two possible courses (apart from relying permanently on protective equipment). The first is to change himself, through GENETIC ENGINEERING, to fit a different environment, a process for which James BLISH coined the term PANTROPY; the second, bringing the mountain to Mahomet, is to change the planet to fit himself, to make it like Earth. This process is now generally referred to as terraforming.

The word itself was coined by Jack WILLIAMSON in the series of stories collected as *Seetee Ship* (1942–3 *ASF*; fix-up **1951** as by Will Stewart; later edition as by Williamson), although in these tales the concept of planetary engineering is secondary to that of ANTIMATTER. The first detailed description of terraforming occurs earlier, in Olaf STAPLEDON's *Last and First Men* (**1930**). His Fifth Men, forced to consider leaving Earth because of its impending collision with the Moon, turn their attention to VENUS, which Stapledon describes as having a dense atmosphere lacking in oxygen, oceans covering almost its entire surface, and to be extremely hot. A solution is found: "It was … decided to split up some of the ocean of the planet into hydrogen and oxygen by a vast process of electrolysis … The oxygen thus formed … would be allowed to mix with the atmosphere. The hydrogen had to be got rid of somehow, and an ingenious method was devised by which it should be ejected beyond the limits of the atmosphere at so great a speed that it would never return. Once sufficient free oxygen had been produced, the new vegetation would replenish the loss due to oxidation. This work was duly set on foot. Great automatic electrolysis stations were founded on several of the islands; and biological research produced at length a whole flora of specialized vegetable types to cover the land surface of the planet. It was hoped that in less than a million years Venus would be fit to receive the human race…." (Ch. XII, 3). Later writers have wrought more detailed variants on this process, and have taken account of subsequent information about conditions on Venus, but have fundamentally followed Stapledon's model. Poul ANDERSON, in "The Big Rain" (1954) and "Sister Planet" (1959), describes such projects on Venus.

MARS and Ganymede (*see* OUTER PLANETS) have also been considered possible terrain for terraforming. A project to make Mars habitable is described in Arthur C. CLARKE's *The Sands of Mars* (**1951**); it involves turning Phobos into a miniature sun through a nuclear explosion and liberating oxygen from the oxides which form the Martian sand by means of a plant which breaks the sand down. Whereas Venus has become less popular as a potential environment for Man as space probes have revealed its hostility, Mars continues to attract sf writers, as with the scheme to change its climate in Ian WATSON's *The Martian Inca* (**1977**) and also with *A Double Shadow* (**1978**) by Frederick Turner. Terraforming Ganymede is described by Poul Anderson, again, in *The Snows of Ganymede* (1955; **1958**) and by Gregory BENFORD in *Jupiter Project* (**1975**). Benford's novel, although a spiritual sequel to Robert A. HEINLEIN's *Farmer in the Sky* (**1950**), is authoritative and up to date in its speculations.

The terraforming of planets outside the Solar System rarely occurs in sf, it generally being assumed that once mankind colonizes the stars he should have little difficulty in finding Earthlike planets on which to live. An extensive climatological programme, falling short of full terraforming, is described in Frank HERBERT's "Dune" trilogy, particularly *Children of Dune* (**1976**), while the process of terraforming a distant planet is described in considerable detail in David GERROLD's *Moonstar Odyssey* (**1977**). The protagonist of Jack L. CHALKER's *The Web of the Chozen* (**1978**) is employed by a big corporation to seek suitable planets for terraforming.

Works of non-fiction which discuss the problems and possibilities of terraforming include Carl SAGAN's *The Cosmic Connection* (**1973**) and Adrian Berry's *The Next Ten Thousand Years* (**1974**).   [MJE]

TERRORE NELLO SPAZIO (vt **PLANET OF THE VAMPIRES**) Film (1965). Italian International/Castilla Cinematografica/AIP. Directed by Mario Bava, starring Barry Sullivan, Norma Bengell, Angel Aranda and Evi Morandi. Script by Castillo Cosulich, Antonio Roman, Alberto Bevilacqua, Mario Bava and Rafael J. Salvia. 86 mins. Colour.

This Italian/Spanish co-production is directed by Mario Bava, whose lurid, baroque, erotic and sometimes sado-masochistic horror films have won him a cult following; he was once a notable cameraman, and this sf/horror film is visually intense. Astronauts land on a strange planet and immediately start killing one another, inexplicably. Three corpses are buried but rise, in a striking sequence, from the grave, still shrouded in polythene. It turns out that they are possessed by alien spirits; they take the spaceship and return to Earth, where the pickings will be rich. The florid atmospherics almost make up for the silliness of the story.   [PN]

TERTZ, ABRAM *See* Andrey SINYAVSKY.

TEVIS, WALTER S. (? –). American writer, professor of English literature at the University of Ohio, author of the screenplay for the film *The Hustler*. He has published some short fiction since "The Ifth of Oofth" for *Gal.* in 1957, but is known almost exclusively to sf readers as the author of *The Man Who Fell to Earth* (1963), the basis of Nicolas Roeg's film THE MAN WHO FELL TO EARTH (1976). It is the delicately crafted story of an ALIEN who comes to Earth, probably from Mars, in an attempt to get help from mankind for his dying race. Becoming as physically and emotionally human as his technology and his powers of empathy permit, he finds man's xenophobic response to him, when he reveals himself and his quest, impossible to bear. In the film version David Bowie conveys a portion of this fragile pathos. [JC]

TEZUKA, OSAMU *See* JAPAN.

THACKER, ERIC (? –). English writer who collaborated with Anthony EARNSHAW on two novels, *Musrum* (1968) and *Wintersol* (1971). [JC]

THAMES, C(HRISTOPHER) H. *See* Milton LESSER.

THANET, NEIL *See* R.L. FANTHORPE.

THEATRE Sf and the theatre have always been uneasy bedfellows. Unlike television and the cinema, the theatre does not present the fantastic with any sense of strict realism, and the traditional demand of sf is that its accoutrements should not seem fantastic: they should be plausible. The theatre is limited in space, also. Roger ELWOOD summed up his view of the situation when he wrote: "Writing an sf play is a bit like trying to picture infinity in a cigar box" (introduction to *Six Sf Plays*, 1976).

Although some scholars detect speculative elements in the plays of Aristophanes and even Shakespeare's *The Tempest* (*see* FORBIDDEN PLANET!), it is safer to put forward Karel ČAPEK as the first playwright to make widespread use of traditional sf themes: *The Insect Play*, written with his brother Josef (1921; trans. 1923), sees insects replacing mankind; *R.U.R.* (1920; trans. 1923) introduced the word "robot" to our language, although it deals in fact with an ANDROID factory; *The Makropoulos Secret* (1922; trans. 1925) discusses IMMORTALITY. These highly successful plays remain, however, isolated examples, and specifically stage-bound sf is rare.

The advent of Surrealism, itself later to spawn the theatre of the ABSURD, introduced fertile fantasy elements to the stage, but the links with sf *per se* always

remain tenuous in the plays of such dramatists as MAYAKOVSKY, VIAN, Audiberti, JARRY, AYMÉ, MROŻEK, Ionesco, Paul ABLEMAN and the French Grand Guignol. On the other hand, the presence of Utopian themes in works by MAINSTREAM playwrights like Claudel (*La Ville* 1893), Charles Morgan or G.B. SHAW is a continuation of 19th-century philosophical preoccupations with little genuine relevance to sf.

Sf in the theatre thus remains characterized by a small number of unrelated plays. The more notable post-War examples are: Elias Canetti's *Die Befristeten* (1956; trans. as *The Numbered*), set in the future, where all people have numbers determining their fate; William GOLDING's *The Brass Butterfly* (1958), based on his story "Envoy Extraordinary" (*see* HISTORY IN SF); Gore VIDAL's "Visit to a Small Planet" (in *Visit to a Small Planet*, coll. 1956), a satire about a child alien who visits Earth, and creates a crisis with his ability to alter the past — it was later filmed, 1960; Jean-Louis Barrault's production of Ray BRADBURY's *Martian Chronicles* in Paris; *Via Galactica*, a massive Broadway musical flop; VERCORS' *Zoo* (1963) adapted from his novel *Borderline*; Jon BING and Tor Age BRINGSVAERD's *A Miste eit Romskip* ["The Lost Spaceship"] performed at Oslos's Norske Teatret in 1973; *The Bed-Sitting Room* (1969) by Spike Milligan and John Antrobus, a sombre World War Three nuclear comedy, later filmed (*see* THE BED-SITTING ROOM); Ken Campbell and Chris Langham's lengthy *Illuminatus!*, adapted from the SHEA/WILSON trilogy of the same name, which inaugurated the London National Theatre's Cottesloe auditorium in 1977; Richard O'Brien's *Rocky Horror Show* which opened in 1973, a witty satire on the paraphernalia of sf monster movies (though O'Brien's later spoof of the Tarzan mythos flopped).

Two writers closely connected with sf who have written plays are Ray Bradbury and Kurt VONNEGUT Jr. But their dramatic work has generally only a marginal relevance to sf: Vonnegut's *Happy Birthday, Wanda June* (1973) and Bradbury's *The Anthem Sprinters and Other Antics* (coll. 1963), *The Day it Rained Forever: A Comedy in One Act* (1966), *The Pedestrian: A Fantasy in One Act* (1966), *The Wonderful Ice Cream Suit and Other Plays* (coll. 1972) and *Pillar of Fire and Other Plays for Today, Tomorrow, and Beyond Tomorrow* (coll. 1975). Most of Bradbury's plays are dramatizations of his stories.

Elsewhere, the imagery of sf still frequently occurs in plays, but writers outside the genre are principally employing these images for their archetypal value (in Savary's Grand Magic Circus, Arrabal, Paul Zindel, and the prolific use in many theatrical events of familiar characters such as Tarzan, KING KONG, FRANKENSTEIN or SUPERMAN)

rather than for their thematic content. [MJ/PN]

See also: MUSIC AND OPERA.

THEM! Film (1954). Warner Bros. Directed by Gordon Douglas, starring Edmund Gwenn, James Whitmore, James Arness and Joan Weldon. 93 mins. B/w.

Atomic tests in the American desert create gigantism in a species of ant. Their nest is located and destroyed, but one female escapes and lays her eggs in a storm drain beneath Los Angeles, which becomes the setting for the final battle between the giant ants and Man. Along with THE THING, THE BEAST FROM 20,000 FATHOMS, etc., *Them!* was a template for a series of similar films that followed in the 1950s. It is a well-made film and handles its absurd subject with an almost documentary style — the main reason, no doubt, for its standing out from the cheaper and more sensationalized variations on the theme that followed. The special effects, by Ralph Ayers, are excellent; the giant ants were not animated miniatures but full-scale mock-ups. [JB]

THEOBALD, ROBERT (1929–). American economist, recently an exponent of the need for alternative technologies and strategies to survive the next decades, in several books culminating in *An Alternative Future for America's Third Century* (1976). His sf novel, *Teg's 1994: an Anticipation of the Near Future* (1972), written with J.M. Scott, carries on these concerns through a series of dialogues between George Orwell Fellowship winner Teg and various interlocutors who discuss the course of history leading up to 1994, a time less bad (because alternative technologies were employed) than it might have been, hence the name of the fellowship she has won. The book, originally circulated in mimeographed form in 1969, is structured for readers' participation, and 60 pages of the first printed edition contain readers' and authors' comments. [JC/PN]

THESE ARE THE DAMNED *See* DAMNED, THE.

THEY CAME FROM WITHIN (vt **SHIVERS**; vt **THE PARASITE MURDERS**) Film (1975). A DAL-Reitman Production. Directed by David Cronenberg, starring Paul Hampton, Joe Silver, Lynn Lowry, Alan Migicovsky and Barbara Steele. Screenplay by David Cronenberg. 94 mins. Colour.

In an attempt to develop a species of animal that will have a beneficial symbiotic relationship with humanity, a scientist creates a parasite that, when it invades a human body, turns its host into a sexually ravenous monster. The vaguely phallic parasites spread though an isolated apartment building, either passed from person to person by such means as kissing or simply by entering any available human orifice. A young doctor fights a losing battle against them as his companions are taken over one by one until he is completely alone. The film has been compared to INVASION OF THE BODY SNATCHERS and NIGHT OF THE LIVING DEAD, but Canadian director Cronenberg (a former underground filmmaker, whose other films include CRIMES OF THE FUTURE and RABID) is working along unique lines of his own. His hallmark is an exaggerated tastelessness designed, perhaps, to alienate the audience from traditional sf/horror clichés by revealing their putrescent underside, and also more generally, to demonstrate a variety of forms of social rot.　　　　　　　　　　　　　[JB/PN]

THING, THE (vt THE THING FROM ANOTHER WORLD) Film (1951).

Winchester Pictures/RKO. Directed by Christian Nyby (*see below*), starring Kenneth Tobey, Margaret Sheridan, Robert Cornithwaite and James Arness. Screenplay by Charles Lederer, based on the novelette "Who Goes There?" by John W. CAMPBELL Jr. 86 mins. B/w.

One of the films that marked the beginning of the sf/monster film boom of the 1950s, *The Thing* was superior to the many imitations that followed. Though Nyby is credited as the director, the film was actually directed by Howard Hawks. Nyby had been an editor on many of Hawks's pictures, and as a favour to him Hawks had arranged for him to get a directing credit, but the film is full of Hawks's obvious trademarks: the fast pace, the overlapping dialogue and the handling of the cast who all give very relaxed, naturalistic performances. The "Thing" itself is a humanoid vegetable from outer space which terrorizes an American military base in the Arctic. Hawks wisely kept it off the screen for most of the film, except at the climax, when the camera lingers on it too long. The film sustains a build-up of tension (one jumps every time a door is opened), and though sf purists claim that it is inferior to Campbell's original concept (in the novelette the creature was able to alter its shape) it remains a superior example of sf cinema.

A remake was being planned by Universal in 1978.　　　　　[JB]

THING FROM ANOTHER WORLD, THE *See* THING, THE.

THINGS TO COME Film (1936).

London Films. Directed by William Cameron Menzies, starring Raymond Massey, Cedric Hardwicke, Margaretta Scott, Ralph Richardson, Edward Chapman, Ann Todd and Maurice Braddell. Screenplay by H.G. WELLS, based on his book *The Shape of Things to Come* (1933). 130 mins (cut to 113). B/w.

This Alexander Korda production was

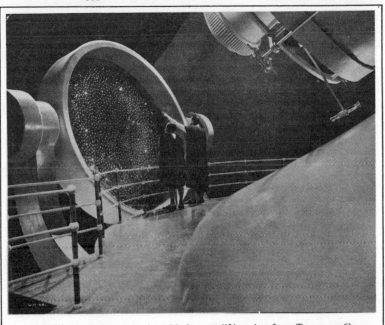

Raymond Massey looks extremely noble in an uplifting shot from THINGS TO COME.

the most expensive and ambitious sf film of the 1930s, but though the script was written by Wells himself it is not the most satisfactory of the films based on his work during this period. The film is divided into three parts, the first set in 1940 which sees the start of a world war that continues for decades; the second deals with a community reduced by the war to a primitive way of life, and ruled over by a despot until the arrival of a mysterious "airman" who announces that a new era of "law and sanity" has begun; the third takes place in AD 2036 when the ruling technocrats have built a gleaming white underground city, supposedly Utopian; an attempt is being made to fire a manned projectile at the Moon from a huge cannon (harking back to Jules VERNE's idea, which by 1936 Wells should have known to be quite impossible), despite opposition from a horde of effete "artists" who are still maintaining that "there are some things Man is not meant to know". But their efforts are in vain and the gun is fired.

Some of the characterization is inappropriately domestic; the dialogue is weakly imagined throughout and its rhetoric hollow, despite the emotional thrill in Raymond Massey's voice as he declares of Man at the end "... and when he has conquered all the deeps of space and all the mysteries of time — still he will be beginning." Wells's Utopianism and his belief that the future of mankind lay with a technocratic elite seemed oddly old fashioned even in 1936, judging from the hostility of contemporary reviews. But the visual rhetoric (supported by Arthur Bliss's majestic musical score), despite the static composition of shots, is occasionally overwhelming in its sheer scale (special effects by the imported Hollywood expert Ned Mann); the film is

one of the most important in the history of sf CINEMA for the boldness of its ambitions, and the ardour with which it projects the myth of SPACE FLIGHT as the beginning of Man's transcendence. Wells published a version of the script as *Things to Come* (1935).　　　　　[PN/JB]

THIS ISLAND EARTH Film (1954).

Universal. Directed by Joseph Newman, starring Jeff Morrow, Faith Domergue and Rex Reason. Screenplay by Franklin Coen and Edward G. O'Callaghan, based on the novel by Raymond F. JONES. 86 mins. Colour.

One of the few sf films of the 1950s to reflect the themes of written pulp sf, *TIE* is not just another variation on the usual monster formula. Of course, the high cost of such films (FORBIDDEN PLANET was another) was the main reason for their scarcity.

A scientist receives a strange, build-it-yourself machine in the mail which, when constructed, turns out to be a futuristic two-way TV communicator. This leads to his joining a team of scientists organized by extraterrestrials on Earth who are searching for a means to save their doomed planet, Metaluna. The scientist, with his girl-friend (who is also a scientist, and still a typical 1950s sf film heroine), is taken to the Metalunans' home world in their huge flying saucer; they arrive in time to see it in the final stages of destruction: Enemy spaceships are guiding large meteors in from space to crash into the planet's disintegrating outer shell. In these sequences the special effects are quite remarkable — not convincing in the way that the effects in 2001: A SPACE ODYSSEY are, but impressive because of their sheer visual extravagance. They were created by Clifford Stine, Universal's effects expert,

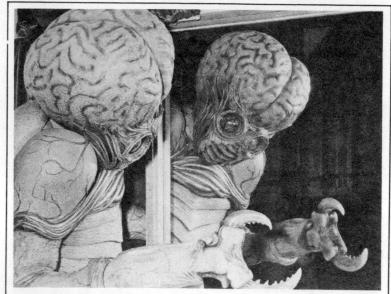

A particularly memorable alien from THIS ISLAND EARTH.

who also achieved marvels in Jack ARNOLD's sf films for the same studio, though with much smaller budgets. [JB]
See also: Raymond Durgnat: "The Wedding of Poetry and Pulp" in his *Films and Feelings* (1967).

THIUSEN, ISMAR Pseudonym of John Macnie (1836–1909), American writer. His UTOPIA *The Diothas; or, a Far Look Ahead* (1883; vt *Looking Forward; or, The Diothas* UK), set in AD 3000, presents a not untypically regimented picture of ideal existence, especially constricting for women, who go out, when unmarried, only with chaperons. [JC]

This fine, surreal cover by Karel THOLE was reproduced on a large scale for a German sf calendar. Heyne.

THOLE, KAREL Professional name of Carolus Adrianus Maria Thole (1914–). Dutch-born illustrator, resident in Italy since 1958. The best-known European sf illustrator, KT has had cover paintings published in virtually every country in Europe, as well as in England and the United States, but the

greatest body of his sf work has been for the publishers Mondadori in Italy and Heyne in Germany. His covers are the most sophisticatedly surrealist-influenced in sf, and it is not absurd to compare his best work with that of Max Ernst, Salvador Dali or Magritte, all of whom are visible influences. Symbolic, and often featuring human shapes metamorphosing into other forms, his covers have a sometimes dream-like, sometimes nightmarish quality. They are often more evocative than the stories they illustrate. He received a special award for general excellence at the world sf CONVENTION in Toronto in 1973. [PN/JG]

THOMAS, CHAUNCEY (1822– ?). American writer, whose sf novel is *The Crystal Button: or, Adventures of Paul Prognosis in the forty-ninth century* (1891), a technocratic UTOPIA into which a present-day engineer is transported. [JC]

THOMAS, CRAIG (1942–). Welsh writer of political thrillers, the second of which, *Firefox* (1977), is set in 1979 and deals with a British attempt to steal a new Russian plane, the MIG-31, which boasts both anti-radar and weapons operated by thought waves. [JC]

THOMAS, DAN Pseudonym of American writer Leonard M. Sanders Jr (1929–), in whose sf novel, *The Seed* (1968), a COMPUTER explains the meaning of life to one of its engineers. [JC]

THOMAS, MARTIN Form of his name used by English writer Thomas Hector Martin (1913–) for his fiction, though he has used the floating pseudonym Peter SAXON on at least one occasion, for *The Curse of Rathlaw* (1968). After the Second World War, MT began publishing occult stories and other weird fantasy; from his first novel, *The Evil Eye*

(1958), he has published a number of sf and occult books of only routine quality. [JC]
Other works: *Bred to Kill* (1960); *Assignment Doomsday* (1961); *Beyond the Spectrum* (1964); *Laird of Evil* (1965); *The Mind Killers* (1965); *Such Men are Dangerous* (1965); *Sorcerers of Set* (1966); *The Hand of Cain* (1966); *Brainwashed* (1968).

THOMAS, THEODORE L. (1920–). American writer and lawyer, prolific in the magazines under his own name (sometimes as Ted Thomas) and as Leonard Lockhard, the pseudonym he used for his "Patent Attorney" spoof series (eight stories 1952–64). He began publishing sf in 1952 with "The Revisitor" for *Space Science Fiction* simultaneously with "Improbable Profession" (as Lockhard) in *ASF*. His numerous stories, which he has placed widely, conform competently and at their best expertly to the markets for which they have been designed. With Kate WILHELM he has written two novels, *The Clone* (1959 *Fantastic*; 1965) and *The Year of the Cloud* (1970); they both feature unnatural DISASTERS. Though the CLONE of the first novel is not a clone but a blob, both novels achieve an effective verisimilitude. [JC]
See also: ECOLOGY; MONSTERS; ORIGIN OF MAN; POLLUTION; SUN; TIME TRAVEL; WEATHER CONTROL.

THOMPSON, VANCE (1863–1925). American writer in various genres. His sf novel is *The Green Ray* (1924), in which a hoax ray that inexplicably bleaches blacks white is unpleasantly made the basis of a racist story. [JC]
Other works: *The Carnival of Destiny* (1916); *The Scarlet Iris* (1924).

THORNE, GUY Pseudonym of Cyril Arthur Edward Ranger-Gull (? – ?), British journalist and writer. All his speculative fiction was written under the names Guy Thorne and Ranger Gull. His most successful work was *When It Was Dark* (1904), published as by GT. It tells of the effect on the Christian world of faked "scientific evidence" that Christ's resurrection never took place. Most of his other scientific romances are thrillers featuring new INVENTIONS, though *Made in His Image* (1906 as by GT) is a kind of sequel to *When It Was Dark*, reversing the situation: a bleak futuristic world is redeemed by Christian belief. The other sf stories signed GT are: *The Angel* (1908), *The Secret Sea-Plane* (1915) and *When the World Reeled* (1924). Those signed Ranger Gull are *The Soul-Stealer* (1906), *The Enemies of England* (1915), *The Air Pirate* (1919) and *The City in the Clouds* (1921). [BS]
See also: RELIGION.

THORNTON, HALL See Robert SILVERBERG.

THORPE, TREBOR *See* R.L.
FANTHORPE.

THOUSAND EYES OF DR
MABUSE, THE *See* TAUSEND AUGEN
DES DR MABUSE, DIE.

The final issue, Oct. 1919.

THRILL BOOK US magazine, in DIME
NOVEL format for eight issues, then PULP
size. 16 issues, two issues a month, 1
Mar.-15 Oct. 1919, published by Street &
Smith; ed. Harold Hersey (Mar.-Jun.
1919) and Ronald Oliphant (Jul.-Oct.
1919). *TB* has often been claimed to be
the first sf magazine, a statement which
its extreme rarity (single copies sell for
$300 or more) has made difficult to
confirm or deny. However, the magazine
is fully described in Sam MOSKOWITZ's
Under The Moons of Mars (anth. 1970):
although it included some sf — including
stories by Murray LEINSTER and the novel
The Heads of Cerberus (15 Aug.-15 Oct.
1919; 1952) by Francis STEVENS — its
primary orientation was towards occult
fiction and straightforward adventure.
The 1 May issue contained the first story
of Seabury QUINN's "Jules de Grandin"
series, which later became a regular
feature of WEIRD TALES. *TB*'s first editor,
Harold Hersey, later published the short-
lived MIRACLE SCIENCE AND FANTASY.
Seven of the last eight issues of *TB*
appeared in a British reprint edition.
[MJE]

THRILLING SCIENCE FICTION *See*
MOST THRILLING SCIENCE FICTION EVER
TOLD, THE.

THRILLING SCIENCE FICTION
ADVENTURES *See* MOST THRILLING
SCIENCE FICTION EVER TOLD, THE.

THRILLING WONDER STORIES US
PULP magazine. 111 issues, Aug. 1936-
Winter 1955. Published by Beacon
Magazines Aug. 1936-Jun. 1937; Better
Publications Oct. 1937-Aug. 1943; and
Standard Magazines Fall 1943-Winter
1955. Ed. Mort WEISINGER (Aug. 1936-

July 1940. Cover by Howard V. Brown.

Jun. 1941), Oscar J. FRIEND (Aug. 1941-
Fall 1944), Sam MERWIN (Winter 1945-
Oct. 1951), Samuel MINES (Dec. 1951-
Summer 1954) and Alexander Samalman
(Fall 1954-Winter 1955). Leo MARGULIES
was editorial director during Weisinger's
and Friend's editorships.

TWS was the continuation, after a
brief gap, of WONDER STORIES, the Hugo
GERNSBACK magazine. The adjective
"Thrilling" was added to the title to bring
it into conformity with other magazines
from the same publisher — *Thrilling
Detective*, *Thrilling Western*, etc. The
new magazine was far more garish than
its predecessor. The early covers, by
Howard BROWN, are said to have been
responsible for the coinage of the term
"Bug-Eyed Monsters" (or BEMS), such
creatures being a regular feature of his
paintings, along with giant dinosaurs,
insects, and men. Its first eight issues
featured an early sf comic strip ("Zarnak"
by Max Plaisted) which was abruptly
suspended in mid-plot after the Oct. 1937
number. *TWS*'s contributors were mostly
second-string authors: Eando BINDER,
Frederick Arnold Kummer, Arthur Leo
ZAGAT and others. It ran a number of
popular series, notably John W.
CAMPBELL Jr's "Penton and Blake"
stories, Arthur K. BARNES's "Gerry
Carlyle" stories and the "Hollywood on
the Moon" series by prolific contributor
Henry KUTTNER. An amateur writers'
contest sponsored by the magazine was
won by Alfred BESTER with his first story,
"The Broken Axiom" (Apr. 1939). *TWS*
was successful enough to generate a
companion magazine, STARTLING STORIES,
in Jan. 1939. *Startling Stories* featured
longer stories (a complete novel in each
issue, when possible) and soon became
the better magazine of the two. In
mid-1940 *TWS* also began to proclaim a
"complete novel" in most issues, but in
actuality the majority of these were no
more than long novelettes. During this
boom period a second companion,
CAPTAIN FUTURE, was initiated, and for a
little over a year *TWS* changed from its
habitual bi-monthly schedule and
appeared monthly. Earle K. BERGEY

succeeded Brown as cover artist with the
Sep. 1940 issue and was responsible for
most subsequent covers; his paintings
switched the emphasis from the bug-eyed
monster to the scantily clad lady it was
threatening with a fate more unnatural
than death. *TWS* became more overtly
juvenile in the early 1940s with the
introduction of "Sergeant Saturn" (*see*
STARTLING STORIES).

When Sam Merwin became editor he
quickly did away with the magazine's
juvenile trappings and considerably
improved it, although it remained
evidently secondary to *Startling Stories*.
Nevertheless it published more
noteworthy stories, including some
"novels" which actually *were* novel-
length: A.E. VAN VOGT's *The Weapon
Shops of Isher* (Feb. 1949; fix-up 1951),
James BLISH's "Let the Finder Beware"
(Dec. 1949; vt rev. *Jack of Eagles* 1952;
vt *ESP-er*) and Leigh BRACKETT's "Sea-
Kings of Mars" (Jun. 1949; as *Sword of
Rhiannon* 1953). Ray BRADBURY, whose
first solo short story appeared in *TWS* in
1943, was a regular contributor, as was
Jack VANCE (who also made his début in
its pages). Vance's "Magnus Ridolph"
series and Kuttner's "Hogben" stories
were popular features of the Merwin
TWS. In Jun. 1951 the magazine began a
series of 10 articles on "Our Inhabited
Universe" by James Blish.

Although the magazine acquired more
companions in the boom of the early
1950s — FANTASTIC STORY MAGAZINE and
SPACE STORIES — it soon began to suffer
in the general decline of the pulp
magazine industry. Changes in editor had
little negative effect, Samuel Mines
maintaining, approximately, the standard
of Merwin's *TWS*. Its last issue appeared
in Winter 1955, after which the
magazine's title (along with *Fantastic
Story Magazine*) was absorbed into
Startling Stories for that magazine's last
three issues. Two British editions
appeared for short periods, both heavily
cut from the original: Atlas Publishing
produced 10 numbered issues (three in
1949–50, seven in 1952–3); Pemberton
published a further four, numbered
101–104, in 1953–4. There was a
Canadian reprint also, 1945–6, and again
1948–51. [MJE]

Collectors should note: The issue
numeration continued from *Wonder
Stories*, Aug. '36 being Vol.8 no.1.
Volume numeration continued, three
numbers to a vol., through to Vol.44
no.3, the last issue. (Two issues of a
reprint magazine, *Wonder Stories*,
reviving the old title, continued the *TWS*
numeration with Vol.45 nos 1 and 2.)
The schedule of *TWS* began as regular bi-
monthly and changed to monthly Dec.
'39-Apr. '41, then back to bi-monthly
Jun. '41-Aug. '43. A quarterly schedule
followed, Fal. '43-Fal. '46; then bi-
monthly Dec. '46-Aug. '53. The last six
issues ran Nov. '53; Win. '54; Spr. '54;
Sum. '54; Fal. '54; Win. '55.

THRILLS, INC. No 22, 1952.

THRILLS, INC. Australian PULP/BEDSHEET/DIGEST-size magazine. 23 numbered, undated, mostly monthly issues, Mar. 1950–Jun. 1952, published by Associated General Publications, Sydney, then Transport Publications; no editor named. The first 12 issues were pulp or bedsheet size, the remainder digest size. *TI* was intended for juvenile readers. Although US reprints as such were not used, a certain amount of plagiarism did occur without the publishers' knowledge. No notable stories were printed. Some stories were reprinted in the British AMAZING SCIENCE STORIES. [FHP]

One of the puppet protagonists of THUNDERBIRDS.

THUNDERBIRDS Television series (1965–9). An ATV Network Presentation. British. Created by Sylvia and Gerry Anderson, produced by Gerry Anderson. Writers included Dennis Spooner, Alan Fennell, Donald Robertson, Martin Crump and Alan Pattillo. Directors included David Lane, David Elliott, Desmond Saunders and Alan Pattillo. Model effects supervised by Derek Meddings. 50 mins per episode. Colour.

This elaborately produced, animated puppet series for children involved a future family who ran an air, space and undersea rescue service which utilized a variety of spectacular vehicles: rocket ships, submarines, etc. The Andersons,

who had made other puppet series, later went on to produce the live-action series UFO and SPACE 1999. [JB]

THX 1138 Film (1969). American Zoetrope. Directed by George LUCAS, starring Robert Duvall, Donald Pleasence and Maggie McOmie. Screenplay by George Lucas and Walter Murch, story by George Lucas. 88 mins. Colour.

A totalitarian, subterranean society of the future is run by computers and bland human technocrats who keep the rest of the population under control with drugs. Everyone wears white clothing, heads are kept shaven and sexual intercourse is forbidden (breeding is by artificial insemination) — a truly sterile, antiseptic world until the occurrence of the inevitable rebellion by a small group. One of the rebels is THX, who experiments with sex, but his wife becomes pregnant and is killed by the authorities. THX is imprisoned but escapes and manages to reach the surface and freedom.

It is an old and familiar story to sf fans, but Lucas presents his DYSTOPIAN nightmare with panache. He begins the film with a series of apparently unrelated visual fragments, accompanied by snatches of dialogue, all of which gradually coalesce to form a comprehensive picture of THX's world. *THX 1138* is visually impressive though not at all lavish, with an economical sense of style. The script is also above average, dominated by its dry wit, an unusual characteristic in sf films. *THX 1138* is a small masterpiece and it is unfortunate that, because of its financial failure in the USA, distribution has been sporadic. Lucas returned to the genre with the epic STAR WARS. The novelization is *THX 1138* (**1971**) by Ben BOVA. [JB]

THYNN, ALEXANDER Form of his name used by Viscount Weymouth (1932–), artist and writer. His sf novel *The King is Dead* (**1977**) was published from his own press at Longleat House. It comprises the reflections of the crown prince of a dynasty ruling a future Earth. [JC]

TIDAL WAVE *See* NIPPON CHIMBOTSU.

TIDYMAN, ERNEST (1928–). American journalist, novelist and screenwriter, author of the "Shaft" series of books about a black detective, of scripts for the "Shaft" movies and for *The French Connection* and *High Plains Drifter*, among other films; his sf novel is *Absolute Zero* (**1971**), a NEAR-FUTURE thriller whose protagonist has become involved in CRYONICS in an attempt to preserve his accidentally frozen dwarf parents. [JC]

TILLEY, PATRICK (1928–). English writer, whose sf novel, *Fade-Out* (**1975**), after the fashion of borderline works like *Fail-Safe* (**1962**) by Eugene BURDICK and J.H. WHEELER, concentrates long-windedly on the workings of government and military in a NEAR-FUTURE situation: in this case an alien landing and the subsequent damping out of all electrical impulses. [JC]

TIME MACHINE One of the early, key terms of sf TERMINOLOGY, first used by H.G. WELLS in the title of his book *The Time Machine* (**1895**). It is, of course, a machine used for travelling through time. *See* TIME TRAVEL. [PN]

TIME MACHINE, THE Film (1960). Galaxy Films/MGM. Directed by

The stylized appearance of the characters in THX 1138 emphasizes the conformity of their underground existence.

George PAL, starring Rod Taylor, Alan Young, Yvette Mimieux, Whit Bissel and Sebastian Cabot. Screenplay by David DUNCAN, based on the story by H.G. WELLS. 103 mins. Colour.

Unlike Pal's WAR OF THE WORLDS, *TM* is set in the Victorian era at the beginning of the film, and it is these sequences, with the inventor demonstrating his creation to his disbelieving friends amid the Victorian bric-à-brac of their cosy world, that work the best. After a visually interesting journey through time (special effects by Wah Chang and Gene Warren) the film reduces Wells's angry parable to a Hollywood sf formula.

The symbolic parallels between the troglodyte Morlocks and the Victorian working class, and the beautiful but thoughtless Eloi and the Victorian upper class, are lost. The time traveller becomes a confident, romantic hero, successfully rousing the Eloi to battle against their ape-like persecutors. The disturbing evolutionary perspectives of the end of Wells's book are also missing from the film. The work of the special effects men, William Tuttle's make-up and the art direction of George W. Davis and William Ferrari (whose design for the time machine is charming) are all above average, but technical expertise does not compensate for the patronizing simplification of the story. [JB/PN]

TIME PARADOXES The time-paradox story is a subdivision of the TIME-TRAVEL story arising out of the apparent impossibility of reconciling travel through time with a principle of causality. If time travel is possible, then the effect may initiate the cause. Possibly the earliest example of this sort of difficulty is in F. ANSTEY's *The Time Bargain* (**1891**; vt *Tourmalin's Time Cheques*). The majority of time-travel stories either ignore or evade the problem, using Time Police or other devices to circumvent paradoxical situations, or saying that they cannot occur because they *did not* occur. The prevention-of-paradox story is an aspect of the paradox story, in that it recognizes the possibility of paradox, but resolves it rather than exploiting it. An excellent example is "The Men Who Murdered Mohammed" (1958) by Alfred BESTER, which suggests that everyone has a personal continuum, "like millions of strands of spaghetti", so that a time traveller can wreak all manner of havoc in his own past without affecting anyone else; all he accomplishes is eliminating his own continuum. Poul ANDERSON's *Guardians of Time* (coll. **1960**) is an example of the time-police approach: his Time Patrol has various adventures averting paradox. A series of books by Barrington J. BAYLEY also deals with attempts to maintain a stable reality in the face of hostile forces manipulating time, most notably *The Fall of Chronopolis* (**1974**).

The simplest form of time paradox is a closed loop: for instance, a man finds the plans for a time machine, builds it, travels into the future, analyses it, writes down the plans and sends them back to himself in the past. Something is created out of nothing. Examples include P. Schuyler MILLER's "As Never Was" (1944), in which a strange artefact, a knife made from an unidentifiable metal, is discovered, investigated (without success), displayed in a museum and eventually transferred back in time to be found. The story is given a metaphysical gloss by the fact that the knife undergoes a slight change during this process, having sustained a scratch during the attempted analysis. A similarly circular story is "The Gadget Had a Ghost" (1952) by Murray LEINSTER, where the discovery of an ancient message in the protagonist's handwriting in an ancient book initiates a chain of events which leads ultimately to the writing of the message. In Mack REYNOLDS' "Compounded Interest" (1956) a man travels into the past to invest a few coins, which, accumulating interest over the centuries, eventually yield the huge fortune he requires to build a time machine and send it into the past to make the investment.

The other common form of time paradox is that in which the past is changed, with consequent alterations in the present. This is a close cousin to the ALTERNATE-WORLD story, which pictures a present in which such alterations have been made. A simple example is "A Sound of Thunder" (1952) by Ray BRADBURY, in which the trivial act of killing a butterfly in the Mesozoic Era leads to a number of subtle changes in the present, observed with horror by the returning protagonist. The difficulties of perceiving such changes are humorously illustrated in William TENN's "Brooklyn Project" (1948), in which an increasingly profound series of changes in the present go unnoticed, since the characters and their memories are also changed. L. Sprague DE CAMP's *Lest Darkness Fall* (**1941**) and "Aristotle and the Gun" (1958) are examples of stories in which history (*see* HISTORY IN SF) is deliberately altered from the events we know by time-travellers; conversely, in Ward MOORE's *Bring the Jubilee* (**1953**) such meddling destroys an alternate world in which the Confederate States won the American Civil War, bringing our own world into existence. The most sweeping story of this kind is Jack WILLIAMSON's *The Legion of Time* (**1938**, **1952**), in which incompatible alternate future worlds battle through time to influence the events which can bring only one of them into existence.

Other adventurous tales of time paradox include Charles L. HARNESS's *Flight Into Yesterday* (1949; exp. **1953**; vt *The Paradox Men*), Fritz LEIBER's "Change War" series, such as *The Big Time* (1958; **1961**) and Isaac ASIMOV's *The End of Eternity* (**1955**). Wilson

TUCKER's *The Lincoln Hunters* (**1957**) suggests that the paradox of two versions of an individual existing at the same moment in time would cause one of them to wink out of existence; the novel's plot extracts considerable tension from the premise.

The exemplary form of time-paradox story is that which takes the closed loop and complicates it. The two classic treatments are both by Robert A. HEINLEIN: "By His Bootstraps" (1941 as by Anson MacDonald) and "All You Zombies" (1959). The former story presents a situation where a man is taken into the future through a series of events which he later initiates and conducts himself, but turns the simple situation into a cat's cradle of complications; the latter outlines a sequence of events whereby a person can become his own parent – genetically impossible if he is only one parent, but technically feasible with a strategic sex change, so that the protagonist is his or her father *and* mother. Among later writers, Robert SILVERBERG has most regularly made use of time-paradox situations. His early novel *Stepsons of Terra* (**1958**) is a primitive treatment, but *Up The Line* (**1969**) is a clever and convoluted farce involving inept Time Couriers, while "Many Mansions" (1973) expertly dovetails reality and fantasy in the story of a husband and wife, each of whom plans to end their strained marriage by travelling into the past and eliminating one of their spouse's ancestors. David GERROLD's *The Man Who Folded Himself* (**1973**), an attempt at the ultimate time-paradox story, takes almost every variant previously attempted and multiplies them endlessly.

The time-paradox story occupies a very specialized niche among sf themes. Its attraction is the ingenuity with which authors can wring new variants from its very constrained laws; in this respect it is the equivalent in sf of the locked-room mystery. Many time-paradox stories purport to be a light-hearted part of the ancient philosophical debate about determinism and free will, but generally they are remembered for their adroitness rather than their metaphysical depth. [MJE]

TIME TRAVEL A time-travel device projects the human body, or consciousness, into past or future. Such a device is not necessarily mechanical, and, indeed, early uses of the idea used various methods to achieve the displacement. In L.S. MERCIER's *L'an deux mille quatre cent quarante* (1771 Amsterdam; trans. as *Memoirs of the Year Two Thousand Five Hundred* 1772), a man simply falls asleep, to awaken in AD 2500, where he encounters a UTOPIA. A similar fate befell Washington Irving's Rip Van Winkle, and the protagonist of W.H. HUDSON's *A Crystal Age* (**1887**). SUSPENDED ANIMATION was a popular means of transporting 19th and early 20th-century Man into the future, in such novels as Louis BOUSSENARD's *10,000 Years in a Block of Ice* (**1898**), H.G. WELLS's *When the Sleeper Wakes* (**1899**; rev. vt *The Sleeper Awakes* 1910), Alvarado FULLER's *A.D. 2000* (**1890**), George Allan ENGLAND's *Darkness and Dawn* (fix-up **1914**), Victor ROUSSEAU's *The Messiah of the Cylinder* (**1917**; vt *The Apostle of the Cylinder*) and L. Sprague DE CAMP and P. Schuyler MILLER's *Genus Homo* (1941; **1950**). Other rationalizations included mesmerism, in Edward BELLAMY's *Looking Backward* (**1888**) and dreams, as in Robert GRAVES's *Seven Days in New Crete* (**1949**; vt *Watch the North Wind Rise* USA); alternatively, the protagonist might simply be transported from here to there instantaneously, as in William Hope HODGSON's *The Night Land* (**1912**). The purpose, in almost every case, was to confront a contemporary man with a Utopian or DYSTOPIAN situation, although in Max Beerbohm's classic "Enoch Soames" (1916) the purpose of the hero, whose trip is made after a deal with the Devil, is to see if his poetry has become famous; it hasn't. In John TAINE's *The Time Stream* (1931; **1946**) "an involuntary twist of the mind" plunges the time travellers into the stream; this is one of the few early time-travel stories whose main purpose is to speculate (elaborately) on the nature of time itself.

Recent stories have often used CRYONICS for the purpose of arriving in a future Utopia or Dystopia, e.g. Frederik POHL's *The Age of the Pussyfoot* (**1968**), N. AMOSOV's *Zapiski iz budushchego* (**1967**; trans. as *Notes from the Future* 1970), Edmond HAMILTON's *The Star of Life* (1947; rev. **1959**), Mack REYNOLDS' *Looking Backward, from the Year 2000* (**1973**) and Larry NIVEN's *A World Out of Time* (fix-up **1976**). Contemporary sf novels have transported their protagonists into the future through accidents involving nuclear radiation (Isaac ASIMOV's *Pebble in the Sky*, **1950**), stasis fields (Philip José FARMER's *The Stone God Awakens*, **1970**), radio telescopes (James BLISH's *Midsummer Century*, **1972**) or through unfortunate proximity to a nuclear explosion (Robert A. HEINLEIN's *Farnham's Freehold*, **1964**). The time dilatation effect of space travel at near light speed (*see* FASTER THAN LIGHT) projects people into the future in such novels as *Return to Tomorrow* (1950; **1954**) by L. Ron HUBBARD, *Seed of Light* (**1959**) by Edmund COOPER, *Tau Zero* (1967; **1970**) by Poul ANDERSON and *The Forever War* (fix-up **1974**) by Joe HALDEMAN. Equally, it is possible to bring people or aliens from the distant past to life in the contemporary world, as in Larry Niven's *World of Ptavvs* (**1966**), whose malevolent alien has been imprisoned in a stasis field, or René BARJAVEL's *La nuit des temps* (**1968**; trans. as *The Ice People* 1970), in which people from the distant past are woken from suspended animation. Time travel from the past to the present is comparatively rare, though there is one very early example: Grant ALLEN's "Pausodyne" (1884), in which an 18th-century time traveller is taken for a lunatic in the 19th century.

Time travel into the past is less easy to rationalize. In Edgar Allan POE's "A Tale of the Ragged Mountains" (1844) the protagonist experiences events 65 years in the past through a dream in which he inhabits an avatar's body. Dreaming is also the mechanism used in Jack LONDON's *Before Adam* (**1906**). Drugs caused travel into the past in William Wallace COOK's *Marooned in 1492* (1905; **1925**), and allowed Allan Quatermain and Lady Ragnall mentally to travel into the past in *The Ancient Allan* (**1920**) and *Allan and the Ice Gods* (**1927**) by H. Rider HAGGARD. Simple random displacement was the method used in Mark TWAIN's *A Connecticut Yankee in King Arthur's Court* (**1889**; vt *A Yankee at the Court of King Arthur* UK) and such successors as L. Sprague de Camp's *Lest Darkness Fall* (**1941**; rev. 1949) and Robin Carson's *Pawn of Time* (**1957**).

The importance of H.G. Wells's *The Time Machine* (**1895**) in this context was that it gave the time traveller mobility and control over his movements. Wells also made an imaginative leap in taking his time traveller into the FAR FUTURE, to witness the END OF THE WORLD, in a sequence clearly echoed in such later stories as Clifford D. SIMAK's "The World of the Red Sun" (1931) and, to considerable ironic effect, Robert SILVERBERG's "When We Went to See the End of the World" (1972). Wells's invention of a TIME MACHINE revolutionized time-travel stories, making it possible for the traveller to venture into other eras selectively and purposefully. Surprisingly, the idea was not extensively followed up by other authors prior to the growth of specialist sf magazines; Ray CUMMINGS was among the earliest writers regularly to explore time-travel notions, in such novels as *The Man Who Mastered Time* (1924; **1929**), *The Shadow Girl* (1929; **1947**) and *The Exile of Time* (1931; **1964**).

Wells also pioneered the story in which an individual's subjective time is greatly speeded up, so that the world about him appears to freeze into immobility, with "The New Accelerator" (1901). Later variants include Arthur C. CLARKE's "All The Time in the World" (1952) and John D. MACDONALD's *The Girl, The Gold Watch, & Everything* (**1962**); Eric Frank RUSSELL's "The Waitabits" (1955) introduces an alien species with a very slow subjective time rate compared to that of mankind. David I. MASSON's "Traveller's Rest" (1965) describes a world divided into zones of differing subjective time. Stories about the perception of time are numerous, and are also discussed under PERCEPTION. They include stories in which time is reversed, such as *An Age* (**1967**; vt *Cryptozoic!* USA and later UK), by Brian W. ALDISS, "Mr. F is Mr. F" (1961) by J.G. BALLARD and *Counter-Clock World* (**1967**) by Philip K. DICK. Aldiss has also written "Man in His Time" (1965), in which the main character's mind exists 3.3077 minutes in the future. Speculations on the nature of time occur frequently in Ballard's work, in such stories as "The Garden of Time" (1962), "The Voices of Time" (1960) and *The Crystal World* (**1966**). In Dick's *Ubik* (**1969**) time regresses around the protagonist. It is one of a number of stories in which the structure of time breaks down in various ways; others include "I'm Scared" (1951) by Jack FINNEY, *October the First is Too Late* (**1966**) by Fred HOYLE, "What We Learned from This Morning's Newspaper" (1972) by Robert Silverberg and *Time Storm* (**1977**) by Gordon R. DICKSON. James TIPTREE Jr's "The Man Who Walked Home" (1972) reverses the usual time-perception theme by telling the story of a time traveller's agonies through the eyes of ordinary people observing him across centuries of normal time.

Stories utilizing time machines are now very numerous and various. Many of them encompass elements of TIME PARADOX: the opportunities time travel affords to play havoc with the principle of causality are difficult to resist. Few stories attempt to deal seriously with the practical problems a time traveller might face. L. Sprague de Camp's article "Language for Time Travellers" (1938) pointed out some of the LINGUISTIC problems, which were subsequently recognized in Anthony BOUCHER's "Barrier" (1942) and David I. Masson's "A Two-Timer" (1966). The supposition that modern Man would be greatly superior to people of earlier ages and would be able to bring about revolutionary changes is called into question in Poul Anderson's "The Man Who Came Early" (1956) and Theodore L. THOMAS's "The Doctor" (1967).

Expansive sagas of battle and adventure through time — the temporal equivalent of SPACE OPERA — frequently hinge on paradox; Time Police are invoked to maintain the historical status quo. Such novels as *The Legion of Time* (1938; **1952**) by Jack WILLIAMSON, *Flight Into Yesterday* (**1949**; exp. **1953**; vt *The Paradox Men*) by Charles L. HARNESS, *The End of Eternity* (**1955**) by Isaac Asimov, *The Corridors of Time* (**1965**) by Poul Anderson and *Dinosaur Beach* (**1971**) by Keith LAUMER fall into this category. Otherwise modern time-machine stories divide into three general groups: stories of travel from the near present into the future; from the near present into the past; and from the future into the near present. The first category is the least common, cryonics still being a common, and more plausible, mechanism for achieving such a journey. Wilson TUCKER's *The Year of the Quiet Sun* (**1970**) realistically describes a project to send a man into the near future; Rex GORDON's *First Through Time* (**1962**; vt *The Time Factor* UK) has a similar basis.

Stories which bring people or artefacts from the future into the present are generally salutary; they point out how limited is our knowledge of the universe, how primitive we may appear to our descendants. Henry KUTTNER's "The Twonky" (1942 as by Lewis Padgett), in which an engineer from the future is brought briefly back to the present through a "temporal snag" and during his short stay builds a machine — a Twonky — which has a devastating effect on its unsuspecting users, was a model for many later stories. Kuttner's "Mimsy Were the Borogoves" (1943 as by Lewis Padgett), William TENN's "Child's Play" (1947), C.M. KORNBLUTH's "The Little Black Bag" (1950) and Robert SHECKLEY's "Something for Nothing" (1954) all hinge on the protagonist's misuse of an item of future technology mistakenly displaced through time. C.L. MOORE's "Vintage Season" (1946 as by Lawrence O'Donnell) brings sensation-seeking tourists from the future to witness the beginning of a disastrous plague. The protagonists of Michael MOORCOCK's "Dancers at the End of Time" series are obsessed with time travel because, almost all-powerful, they have forgotten the meaning of mortality; one travels back to rediscover desire, itself a new sensation. Mack Reynolds' "Photojournalist" (1965) similarly shows a roving reporter recording great news stories through the ages, while John WYNDHAM's "Pawley's Peepholes" (1951) and John BRUNNER's *The Productions of Time* (**1967**) also introduce tourists from the future. In Robert Silverberg's *The Masks of Time* (**1968**; vt *Vornan-19* UK) a visitor from the future precipitates the millennium — a theme mirrored in Ian WATSON's "The Very Slow Time Machine" (1978), in which a possible messiah is projected into the future to enable the world to prepare itself for him, but by means of an ingenious time machine which first of all must travel slowly into the past — experiencing normal duration, only in reverse — like the stone in a catapult being drawn back before release. Alternatively, such stories as Alfred BESTER's "Hobson's Choice" (1952) and John Brunner's "Some Lapse of Time" (1963) and *Quicksand* (**1967**) show time travellers fleeing from unpleasant futures. Robert Silverberg's *The Time Hoppers* (**1956**; exp. **1967**) presents a similar scenario from a future setting, but adds an awareness and exploitation of paradox.

The possibility of paradox is almost omnipresent in stories of time travel from the present into the past, since changes introduced into the past will be manifested in the present, whereas changes introduced into the present will only be manifested in the future and thus do not carry the same force, since they are changes in what has not yet happened. Tourism or encounters with famous historical figures are the chief reasons for exploring the past. In the former category, trips to the prehistoric world are particularly popular, placing Man against dinosaur. Ray BRADBURY's "A Sound of Thunder" (1952), L. Sprague de Camp's "A Gun for Dinosaur" (1956) and Brian W. Aldiss's "Poor Little Warrior!" (1958) are all stories of this type, while Clifford D. Simak's "Small Deer" (1965) offers a new explanation for the dinosaurs' abrupt extinction (they are taken away by aliens) observed by a time traveller. Robert Silverberg's *Hawksbill Station* (**1968**; vt *The Anvil of Time* UK) is set in the still more distant past, which in this instance is used for the most isolated of prison colonies. Silverberg's *Up The Line* (**1969**) combines tourism with very convoluted paradoxes; Garry KILWORTH's "Let's Go to Golgotha" (1975) raises the difficulties — and paradoxes — inherent in taking a large number of tourists to a popular historical spectacle, in this instance the Crucifixion, an event which has attracted many other time travellers, most notably Karl Glogauer in Michael Moorcock's *Behold the Man* (1966; exp. **1969**). Other historical figures to feature in time-travel stories include Leonardo da Vinci, in Manly Wade WELLMAN's *Twice in Time* (1940; **1957**) and also in Kit REED's "Mister Da V." (1962); Byron and the Shelleys in Brian W. Aldiss's *Frankenstein Unbound* (**1973**); and Abraham Lincoln in Wilson Tucker's *The Lincoln Hunters* (**1957**).

Machines for viewing or eavesdropping on the past feature in Harry HARRISON's "Famous First Words" (1965), Isaac Asimov's "The Dead Past" (1956) and T.L. SHERRED's "E for Effort" (1947). In the latter story the viewer is used to record feature films; a variant of this is Harry Harrison's *The Technicolor Time Machine* (**1967**), in which location shooting for historical epics is done in the past, on the spot. Harrison's novel is one of many stories which exploit time travel for HUMOUR. Others already mentioned include Silverberg's *Up the Line* and Sheckley's "Something for Nothing"; further stories of this kind are John Brunner's *Timescoop* (**1969**), Keith Laumer's *The Great Time Machine Hoax* (**1964**) and Bob SHAW's *Who Goes Here?* (**1977**).

Time travel has consistently attracted a number of writers. Robert Silverberg has explored numerous variants, and it occurs regularly in the work of such writers as Poul Anderson, L. Sprague de Camp, Keith Laumer and Clifford D. Simak. The nature of time and our perception of it has commonly been the preoccupation of British writers, particularly Brian W. Aldiss and J.G. Ballard. There have been few attempts to analyse the time-travel story; Larry Niven's essay "The Theory and Practice of Time Travel", included in *All The Myriad Ways* (coll. **1971**) presents a basic, but limited, introduction; a competent survey of the time-travel story in sf magazines is included in Paul A. Carter's *The Creation of Tomorrow* (**1977**). [MJE]

TIME TUNNEL, THE Television series (1966–7). An Irwin Allen Production for 20th Century-Fox Television/ABC TV. Created by Irwin ALLEN who was also executive producer. 30 episodes. Colour. The pilot episode was directed by Irwin Allen; other directors included Sobey Martin, Harry Harris and J. Juran. Writers on the series included William Welch, Wanda and Bob Duncan and Leonard Stadd.

James Darren and Robert Colbert starred as two human guinea-pigs trapped in a government TIME-TRAVEL experiment. The time machine itself was a huge, spiral tunnel operated by military personnel who could see what was happening to the two time travellers but were unable to return them to the present, though their efforts in this direction often switched them from time to time (usually at the beginning and end of each episode). The travellers spent more time in the past than the future, visiting such key moments of history as the sinking of the Titanic and the attack on Pearl Harbor; thus a good deal of stock footage could be utilized. Bill Abbott's photographic effects were good; as with most Irwin Allen productions the dialogue was wooden and the plot situations routine. The series lasted only one season.

Two novelizations of separate episodes were *The Time Tunnel* (**1967**) and *Timeslip!* (**1967**) by Murray LEINSTER. [JB]

TIMLETT, PETER VALENTINE (1933–). British writer, whose sf-fantasy trilogy is *The Seedbearers* (**1974**), *The Power of the Serpent* (**1976**) and *Twilight of the Serpent* (**1977**); inspired by their author's interest in occult subjects, these novels deal first with ATLANTIS and its fall and thence with the survivors' evolutionary role at the beginning of human history. [JC]
See also: SWORD AND SORCERY.

TINCROWDOR, LEO QUEEQUEG *See* Philip José FARMER.

TIPTREE, JAMES Jr Pseudonym of American writer and psychologist Alice B. Sheldon (1915–), who until revealing her identity in 1977 was widely assumed to be a man, despite the deeply felt rapport JT displayed for women in stories like "The Women Men Don't See" (1973); she has also written five stories as Raccoona Sheldon. Alice Sheldon was born in Chicago, spent much of her childhood in Africa and

India and worked in the American Government for many years, including a period in the Pentagon; all this was known of JT, and wrongly assumed to be a masculine history; she acquired a PhD in experimental psychology in 1967. For much of her life she was involved in psychological research, and is now retired. Her mother was Mary Hastings Bradley, a well-known geographer and travel author.

Almost all JT's work is in short forms, beginning with "Birth of a Salesman" for *ASF* in 1968, and continuing with a number of other competent, fast-paced but somewhat conventional early stories such as "The Mother Ship" (1968; vt "Mamma Come Home") and "Pupa Knows Best" (1968; vt "Help"); her first collection, *Ten Thousand Light-Years from Home* (coll. **1973**; UK edition with many typographical errors corrected), demonstrates the slightly ill-at-ease heartiness of her early work, as well as the astonishing speed with which she began to produce such mature work as "And I Awoke and Found Me Here on the Cold Hill's Side" (1971), whose ostensibly straightforward rendering of the effects vastly superior ALIENS have upon *Homo sapiens* only retroactively reveals the apt sophistication of the sexual and ANTHROPOLOGICAL analogies worked into the basic story, in which an old spacer tells a young reporter the true situation: that aliens ravage *Homo sapiens* utterly, and with indifference, bestowing a cargo cult mentality on mankind. As the story closes with the unconvinced reporter trailing an alien, we see that the narrative itself is an ongoing revelation of the psychological and social nature of the cargo cult.

In his introduction to JT's second collection, *Warm Worlds and Otherwise* (coll. **1975**), Robert SILVERBERG remarks on this "sense of extended process", this technique of perpetual unfolding of material that makes any JT story an exercise in the metamorphosis of content and expectation. In "The Last Flight of Doctor Ain" (1969; rev. 1974), only gradually through an apparently *reportage*-like, narrative reconstruction of certain events do we begin to realize that the woman Doctor Ain seems to be travelling with across a heavily polluted, wounded Earth is actually the Earth itself personified in the Doctor's mind; as he passes about the Earth he infects mankind with a redesigned leukemia virus, hoping to save her, whom he loves. Very few later JT stories are amenable to anything but extensive analysis; her range is wide, running from investigations of the condition of woman to such intense revelations of the nature of alien life-forms as "Love is the Plan the Plan is Death" (1973), whose last sentence reorders the previous narrative without disqualifying a word. It won a NEBULA award for best short story. "Houston, Houston, Do You Read?" (1976) also

won a Nebula, a JUPITER, and shared a HUGO award, for best novella. JT's first Hugo, in 1974, was also for best novella, with "The Girl who was Plugged In" (1973).

Many of JT's short stories have undergone minor revision for book publication, notably "Your Haploid Heart" (1969). Her most recent collection, which includes this story, is *Star Songs of an Old Primate* (coll. **1978**).

JT's first novel, *Up the Walls of the World* (**1978**), demonstrates a deliberate broadening of her techniques in the creation of an extraordinarily full-blown SPACE OPERA, whose three venues (the interior "spaces" of a vast interstellar being derangedly destroying all suns in its path; an alien planet inhabited by skate-like, telepathic flying beings whose sun is being destroyed; and contemporary Earth, where a government-funded experiment in ESP begins to cash out terrifyingly) interpenetrate complexly and with considerable narrative impact; from telepathy to COSMOLOGY, from densely conceived psychological narrative to the broadest of sense-of-wonder revelations, the novel is a *tour de force* only possible to a mature writer who has absorbed all the language and other generic material that sf writers of space opera have built up over 50 years. JT's limited production (she writes much less frequently now) should not disguise the weight of her contribution to sf. She may prove to have been the most important new writer to enter genre sf in the 1970s, and it is to be hoped that she reverses her recent announcement that she is unlikely to publish any further work. [JC/PN]

About the author: *The Fiction of James Tiptree, Jr.* (**1977**) by Gardner DOZOIS, unfortunately for Dozois written before JT's identity was made known, but critically astute none the less.

See also: ABSURDIST SF; ASTEROIDS; BIOLOGY; ENTROPY; GAMES AND SPORTS; HOLOCAUST AND AFTER; GODS AND DEMONS; MEDIA LANDSCAPE; MYTHOLOGY; NEW WAVE; OPTIMISM AND PESSIMISM; PERCEPTION; POLITICS; PSYCHOLOGY; SATIRE; TIME TRAVEL; WOMEN.

TITAN, EARL *See* John Russell FEARN.

TODD, RUTHVEN (1914–). English writer and Blake scholar, author of two quest novels, *Over the Mountain* (**1939**), in which the quest is consanguinous with a search for political self-understanding, and the surrealist *The Lost Traveller* (**1943**), in which the protagonist, lost in a strange country, finds himself questing for a great bird which, at the final moment, he himself becomes. In his introduction to the 1968 reprinting of the second novel, RT recognizes influences from Rex WARNER to Wyndham LEWIS. [JC]

Other works: (a juvenile series) *Space Cat* (**1952**); *Space Cat Visits Venus* (**1955**); *Space Cat Meets Mars* (**1957**);

Space Cat and the Kittens (**1958**).
See also: DYSTOPIAS; FANTASTIC VOYAGES.

TODOROV, TZVETAN (1939–). Bulgarian literary critic, who pursued his postgraduate studies in Paris under the direction of the semiotic philosopher Roland Barthes. Among TT's several books and essays on structuralist criticism, all written in French, *Introduction à la littérature fantastique* (**1970**; trans. as *The Fantastic: A Structural Approach to a Literary Genre* **1973**; US paperback 1975 with an introduction by Robert SCHOLES) has relevance to the student of sf; indeed it is the most notable structuralist work on the fantastic, along with Scholes's own *Structural Fabulation* (**1975**). An interesting controversy about TT's book arose in the pages of SCIENCE-FICTION STUDIES; the Fall 1974 issue contained an attack on TT's work by Stanislaw LEM, and the Jul. 1975 issue continued the debate. Also relevant is "Historical Genres/Theoretical Genres: A Discussion of Todorov on the Fantastic" by Christine BROOKE-ROSE in *New Literary History*, Autumn 1976. TT's DEFINITION of the fantastic is much more exclusive than most (*see* FANTASY); he devotes only a half-page to sf. [PN]

TOFFLER, ALVIN (1928–). American journalist and author, best known for his speculative works on SOCIOLOGY and FUTUROLOGY. He graduated with a major in English from New York University in 1949, with a BA; after the success of the best-selling *Future Shock* (**1970**), he was awarded four honorary doctorates. *Future Shock* is an important documentation of the increasing rate of change in most spheres of life in the 20th century, and it speculates on the kinds of psychological trauma this may be causing in Western civilization. It has had a great influence in futurology generally, and quite directly on many sf writers, notably John BRUNNER, whose *The Shockwave Rider* (**1975**) pays homage to AT in its title. *The Eco-Spasm Report* (**1975**), a much shorter work than *Future Shock*, produces three plausible scenarios for NEAR-FUTURE disaster in a kind of documented speculation very close indeed to the narrative strategies of the more thoughtful near-future sf, interspersed with more conventional socio-economic analysis. [PN]

Other works: As editor: *The Futurists* (anth. **1972**); *Learning for Tomorrow* (anth. **1973**).
See also: DEFINITIONS OF SF; DYSTOPIAS; PSYCHOLOGY.

TOLKIEN, J(OHN) R(ONALD) R(EUEL) (1892–1973). South-Africa-born British scholar and writer. He was a distinguished professor of Anglo-Saxon at Oxford University, where he formed a close literary association with C.S. LEWIS and Charles WILLIAMS. He was profoundly interested in philology, and it was this which led him to devise Middle Earth, the setting of his major fantasies, in order to create an environment within which the Elvish language he had devised could exist. Within this created world he set *The Hobbit* (**1937**) and his trilogy consisting of *The Fellowship of the Ring* (**1954**; rev. **1966**), *The Two Towers* (**1954**; rev. **1966**) and *The Return of the King* (**1955**; rev. **1966**), the three published in one volume as *The Lord of the Rings* (**1968**). A full discussion of JRRT's work is beyond the scope of this book; he is included because of his pervasive influence on modern sf and fantasy writers. His is the most detailed of all invented fictional worlds, perhaps rivalled only by Austin Tappan WRIGHT's *Islandia* (**1942**). The actual fictions are buttressed by exhaustive background material, some of which is made available in the appendices to *The Lord of the Rings* and in *The Silmarillion* (**1977**). Poems and songs belonging to the cycle are included in *The Adventures of Tom Bombadil* (**1962**) and *The Road Goes Ever On* (**1967**). Although *The Lord of the Rings* was well received on publication (and won the last INTERNATIONAL FANTASY AWARD), it was not until the mid-1960s that it achieved widespread popularity and blossomed into the major cult book of the day. Many sf writers, most notably Ursula K. LE GUIN, owe a debt to JRRT, and the success of his work has been in large part responsible for the general revival of FANTASY and SWORD AND SORCERY. An animated film has been made of *The Hobbit*.

JRRT's other publications include the children's fantasies *Farmer Giles of Ham* (**1949**) and *Smith of Wootton Major* (**1967**), and the posthumous collection *The Father Christmas Letters* (coll. **1976**). He spent many years preparing *The Silmarillion* for publication, but never completed the task; his manuscripts were edited after his death by his son Christopher Tolkien. [MJE]
Other works: *Tree and Leaf* (coll. **1964**); *The Tolkien Reader* (coll. **1966**).
About the author: Books about JRRT and his work are numerous, and include *J.R.R. Tolkien: A Biography* (**1977**) by Humphrey Carpenter; two concordances, *A Guide to Middle Earth* (**1971**) by Robert Foster and *The Tolkien Companion* (**1976**) by J.E.A. Tyler; and, among many other biographical/critical works, *Tolkien and the Critics* (anth. **1968**) ed. Neil D. Isaacs and Rose A. Zimbardo; *Tolkien: A Look Behind the Lord of the Rings* (**1969**) by Lin CARTER; *Master of Middle Earth* (**1972**) by Paul H. Kocher; *Tolkien's World* (**1974**) by Randel Helms; *J.R.R. Tolkien: Architect of Middle Earth* (**1976**) by Daniel Grotta-Kurska and *The Mythology of Middle Earth* (**1977**) by Ruth S. Noel.
See also: CHILDREN'S SF; DIME NOVELS AND JUVENILE STORIES; FANTASTIC VOYAGES; HEROIC FANTASY; LINGUISTICS.

TOLSTOY, ALEXEI (1882–1945). Russian writer, a distant relative of Leo Tolstoy, known mainly for works outside the sf field, including poetry and plays; his most famous novel is the late *Khozhdeniy po mukam* (1919–41; trans. as *The Road to Calvary* 1945). His sf is restricted to two books published in the experimental 1920s, *Aelita* (1922; trans. 1957) and *Giperboloid inzhenera Garina* (1926; rev. 1937; trans. by B.G. Guerney as *The Deathbox* 1936; rev. edition trans. by George Hanna as *The Garin Death Ray* 1955). *Aelita* (filmed as AELITA) is set on Mars, where a Red Army officer foments a rebellion against a corrupt government; *The Garin Death Ray* puts its eponymous WEAPON into the hands of a would-be fascist dictator of Europe. Both books show a narrative gusto typical of their precarious period, and an attractive contrast to AT's later, less ebullient work. [JC]

TOM CORBETT, SPACE CADET Television series (1950). CBS TV. Produced by Leonard Carlton, written by Albert Aley, directed by George Gould, starring Frankie Thomas, Jan Merlin, Al Markim and Michael Harvey. Three episodes a week, each 15 mins. B/w.

This was one of the earliest American sf TV serials (CAPTAIN VIDEO was the first); it concerned young Tom Corbett (the show was for children), a cadet in the Solar Guides, an interplanetary police force which exists to maintain the Solar Alliance. As with the other sf serials of the early 1950s the concept was on a grand scale, but the visual effects were severely limited by the necessity of broadcasting the shows live as well as by small budgets. This meant that almost everything had to be described by the characters in their dialogue or merely suggested instead of shown. For instance, in the first episode there was a sequence in which a rocket-ship crashed in flames, all of which was suggested by sound effects and flickering lights on the faces of those who were supposedly watching. The scientific adviser was Willy LEY. [JB]

TOMORROW PEOPLE, THE Television series (1973–7). A Thames TV Production. Produced by Ruth Boswell and Roger Price; series conceived by Roger Price; technical adviser: Dr Christopher Evans. Starring Nicholas Young, Peter Vaughan Clarke, Sammie Winmill, Stephen Salmon and Elizabeth Adare. Writers have included Brian Finch and Roger Price; directors have included Paul Bernard, Darrol Blake and Roger Price. 25 mins per episode. Colour.

The series incorporates many childhood wish-fulfilment fantasies; it concerns a group of MUTANT children with PSI POWERS who have banded together for self-protection. Their world is free of parental control and they live in a secret, underground base protected by a smooth-voiced super-computer. Most of the stories, each of which lasts an average of four episodes, involve either time travel or encounters with evil beings from outer space. As with most British TV series made for children the budget is limited, but within the limits so imposed the scripts, sets and special effects have been adequate. [JB]

TOM SWIFT Hero of a JUVENILE SERIES of hardcover scientific invention novels produced by the Stratemeyer Syndicate and written under the house name of Victor APPLETON, most of them being the work of H.R. GARIS. Between 1910 and 1935 38 titles appeared, featuring such inventions as "the photo telephone" and "the ocean airport". The stories emphasized the technical difficulties in utilizing these inventions and created a potential readership for the GERNSBACK magazines. A second *TS* series, this time featuring Tom Swift Jr, the son of his famous father, appeared from 1954 to 1971, with two titles a year, and was at first enormously successful. The author of these was given as Victor Appleton II. Although the *TS* series was very popular, the books were written in what was, even for the time, stilted prose, and while it remains the best-known juvenile sf series, it was not the best written. [JE/PN]
See also: "Tom Swift and the Syndicate" in *Strange Horizons: The Spectrum of Science Fiction* (**1976**) by Sam MOSKOWITZ.

TONKS, ANGELA (? –). British writer, resident in the USA, whose *Mind Out of Time* (**1958**) deals with a telepathic relationship. [JC]

TOOKER, RICHARD (1902–). American writer. He began publishing sf with "Tyrant of the Red World" for *Wonder Stories* in 1932, and published fairly frequently for about a decade, but is best remembered for *The Day of the Brown Horde* (**1929**), a prehistoric sf novel, like most of them dealing with the onset of human consciousness (*see* ORIGIN OF MAN). [JC]
Other works: *The Dawn Boy* (**1932**), for children; *Inland Deep* (**1936**).

TOOMBS, ALFRED (GERALD) (1912–). American writer whose sf novel *Good as Gold* (**1955**) deals with reverse gold-transmutation, comically. [JC]

TOOMEY, ROBERT E. Jr (1945–). American writer who began publishing sf stories with "Pejorative" for *NW* in 1969; his first novel, *A World of Trouble* (**1973**), routinely sets a galactic agent on an alien planet, where he has many adventures, jocosely told. [JC]

TOOMORROW Film (1970). Sweet Music & Lowndes/United Artists. Directed by Val Guest, starring Olivia Newton-John, Benny Thomas, Vic

Cooper, Karl Chambers and Roy Dotrice. Screenplay by Val Guest. 95 mins. Colour.

In this unsuccessful attempt by James Bond producer Harry Saltzman to mix pop music with sf, an embarrassingly made-to-order pop group is kidnapped by aliens from outer space and taken to their planet for the purpose of creating music. The film was an artistic and financial failure. [JB]

British edition. No. 3, 1954.

TOPS IN SCIENCE FICTION US magazine. Two issues, Spring 1953 (PULP size) and Fall 1953 (DIGEST). Published by Love Romances; ed. Jack O'Sullivan (first issue) and Malcolm Reiss (second). *TISF* was a reprint magazine, featuring stories which first appeared in PLANET STORIES. The contributors included such *Planet* regulars as Leigh BRACKETT and Ray BRADBURY. A British edition, published by Top Fiction, saw three digest-sized issues in 1954. [FHP/MJE]

TORRO, PEL *See* R.L. FANTHORPE.

TOWERS, IVAR House name used in *Astonishing Stories* and *Super Science Stories* on two occasions. (*For details, see* Richard WILSON.)

TOYNBEE, POLLY (1946–). English writer, more recently an investigative journalist; of the fourth generation of Toynbees to be involved in literature; her sf novel, *Leftovers* (**1966**), depicts the mixed destinies of a group of youths, survivors of a poisonous gas which destroys the rest of humanity. [JC]

TRAIN, ARTHUR (CHENEY) (1875–1945). American writer and lawyer, best known for work outside the sf field, particularly his legal series about the lawyer Ephraim Tutt. His first sf novel, written with R.W. WOOD, *The Man Who Rocked the Earth* (**1915**), features the use of atomic power in the story of a scientist whose opposition to war extends to giving out such warnings

as the disintegration of mountains; after his death there is a world federation in the works. A second collaboration with Wood is the sequel, *The Moon Maker* (**1958**), published posthumously in book form, though presumably serialized in a magazine much earlier. In this, an asteroid is about to collide with Earth. *Mortmain* (coll. **1907**) is a collection of fantasy stories. [JC]

TRALINS, ROBERT (S.) (1926–). American writer, prolific in several genres, whose routine sf novels are *The Cosmozoids* (**1966**) and *Android Armageddon* (**1974**). [JC]

TRANSATLANTIC FAN FUND *See* TAFF.

TRANS-ATLANTIC TUNNEL, THE *See* TUNNEL, THE.

TRANSPORTATION Means of transportation figure in sf in two ways. There are stories which deal speculatively with means of transportation to be employed in the future or on alien worlds, but these are numerically outweighed by stories in which the means of transportation is a literary device — a convenient way of shifting the characters into an alien environment. Inevitably, the same machines crop up in both categories of story — the second category borrows heavily from the first. Much fruitless argument has been wasted in attempts to compare the plausibility of machines designed for quite different literary functions. One such argument of long standing concerns the relative merits of the spacegun in Jules VERNE's *De la terre à la lune* (**1865**; trans. as first part of *From the Earth to the Moon* **1873**) and the antigravity device in H.G. WELLS's *The First Men in the Moon* (**1901**), which consistently ignores the fact that while Verne's novel is actually *about* the gun and its possibility as a real project, Wells merely adopted a convenient formula to get his characters to the Moon. The two categories are not always so distinct, but it

The airship was the favorite futuristic mode of TRANSPORTATION in 19th-century sf. In this illustration from an early edition of Jules Verne's *Clipper of The Clouds*, the airships (ridiculously) really do look like ships.

is important to realize that SPACESHIPS have been employed by sf writers almost exclusively as a literary device, and that there are very few stories dealing speculatively with the real possibilities of interplanetary and interstellar transportation.

In FANTASTIC VOYAGES before 1825 virtually all modes of transport are literary devices. Little attention was paid in fiction to the future of transportation: the anonymous *The Reign of George VI, 1900–1925* (**1763**) foresees no single significant advance in transportation, but is optimistic about the future of the canal barge. Today this seems absurd shortsightedness, but the author of the book lived in a world in which there had been no significant advance in motive power for two thousand years. How was it possible in 1763 to foresee the imminent obsolescence of horse-power and wind-power? John WILKINS, a man quite fascinated by transportation technology, had discussed submarines, flying machines and land-yachts at some length in *Mathematicall Magick* (**1648**), but even he had touched only tentatively on the possibility of adapting new POWER SOURCES to the business of transport. In the 19th century, however, the situation changed dramatically. The *Charlotte Dundas*, the first practical steamboat, was built in 1801, though it was not until the development of the screw propeller in 1840 for Brunel's *Great Eastern* that the revolution in marine transport really began. On land, Trevithick built the first practical steam locomotive in 1804, but the crucial date was 1825, in which the Stockton-Darlington railway began operations and commenced the railroad revolution. That revolution very rapidly extended itself across Europe and, perhaps more importantly, across the American continent. It is understandable that the speculative writers of the later 19th century should find the future of transportation one of their most inspiring themes. The revolution was continued with the development of the internal combustion engine, and may be said to have reached its peak only in 1909, when Henry Ford's Model-T production line began to roll. By that date the first heavier-than-air flying machines were in operation, and so were the first practical submarines. Everything that has happened since in the world of transportation was within the imaginative sights of the writers of 1909: private motor cars for all; large, fast aeroplanes to carry passengers and freight; and even spaceships (Konstantin TSIOLKOVSKY published his classic paper "The Probing of Space by Means of Jet Devices" in 1903).

The man whose literary work stands as the principal imaginative product of this era of revolution is Jules Verne, who loved imaginary voyaging — not because he wanted to visit strange places, but simply because he loved the sensation of imaginary travelling. This was the period that made tourism possible, and Verne remains the archetypal tourist of the literary imagination. He was fascinated by the machines that made far travelling practical. The title of his first novel, *Cinq semaines en ballon* (**1863**; trans. as *Five Weeks in a Balloon* **1870**), is revealing, as is his memoir of a real voyage on the *Great Eastern*, *Une ville flottante* (**1871**; trans. as *A Floating City* **1876**). The *Nautilus* is the real hero of *Vingt mille lieues sous les mers* (**1870**; trans. as *Twenty Thousand Leagues Under the Sea* **1873**) and the aeronef of *Robur le conquérant* (**1886**; trans. as *The Clipper of the Clouds* **1887**). The ultimate novel of imaginary tourism is, of course, *Le tour du monde en quatre-vingt jours* (**1873**; trans. as *Around the World in 80 Days* **1874**). Few of Verne's imitators had the same fascination with means — they invented marvellous devices to enable the characters to participate in exotic adventure stories whose plots were thoroughly routine. A predominant function for submarines and airships, especially in English fiction, was as WEAPONS of WAR rather than means of transport. The writer closest to Verne in spirit was probably Gordon STABLES, in such works as *Wild Adventures around the Pole* (**1883**) and *The Cruise of the Crystal Boat* (**1891**).

Verne, however, was a conservative writer as far as projecting his ideas into the future was concerned. He never attempted to write a story which would look to the eventual culmination of the transport revolution. Nor, for the most part, would the British writers of the period, whose imaginative horizons were largely limited to the next war (and this includes Wells, who imagined very little of the future of transport beyond the warplanes of *When the Sleeper Wakes*, **1899**; rev. vt *The Sleeper Awakes* 1910, and *The War in the Air*, **1908**). The one notable exception — a surprising one — is Rudyard KIPLING, whose short stories *With the Night Mail* (1905; **1909**) and "As Easy as ABC" (1912) look forward to a day when the Aerial Board of Control is the dominant power group in all the world because of its control of the movement of people and goods. It is interesting that Kipling's schema was co-opted by Michael ARLEN in *Man's Mortality* (**1933**), although by that date its overestimation of the aeroplane must have been obvious. Of all the imagined devices of the early 20th century none had more charisma than the aeroplane, and its extension into the 1930s is also evident in *Zodiak* (**1931**) by Walther Eidlitz. This mystique carried over into the early sf pulps — Hugo GERNSBACK founded AIR WONDER STORIES to deal exclusively with the future of flight. Artists like Albert ROBIDA in France and Frank R. PAUL in the Gernsback magazines made much of flying machines, although some illustrators lacked the requisite imagination (one artist required to draw an "airship" for the cover of Stables' *Cruise of the Crystal Boat* simply showed a three-masted schooner sitting on a cloud).

The PULP sf writers were primarily interested in speed and convenience in transportation, and were quite ready to take extreme liberties. The FASTER-THAN-LIGHT starship arrived before the end of the 1920s and so did the ultimate in personal transport, the ANTIGRAVITY belt (featured in the BUCK ROGERS stories by Philip Francis NOWLAN). MATTER TRANSMITTERS arrived soon afterwards, though it was not until some time later that there was any widespread exploitation of the most convenient means of all: TELEPORTATION. Not until Alfred BESTER's *The Stars My Destination* (**1956**; vt *Tiger! Tiger!* UK) did anyone attempt to imagine a society based on teleportation as a means of travel.

Attempts to imagine the eventual social effects of the transportation revolution appeared very early in the pulps, with David H. KELLER's "Revolt of the Pedestrians" (1928), in which a ruling elite of automobilists is overthrown by the underprivileged pedestrians. The social role of the motor car has continued to be a significant theme in sf, with explorations ranging from Clark Ashton SMITH's "The Great God Awto" (1940) through light comedies like Isaac ASIMOV's "Sally" (1953) and Robert F. YOUNG's "Romance in a 21st Century Used Car Lot" (1960) and black comedies like Fritz LEIBER's "X Marks the Pedwalk" (1963) to H. Chandler ELLIOTT's dour "A Day on Death Highway" (1963) and John JAKES's surreal *On Wheels* (**1973**). The car as death-machine in a macabre future SPORT is the theme of Harlan ELLISON's story "Dogfight on 101" (1969; vt "Along the Scenic Route") and the film DEATH RACE 2000 (1975).

One of the classic sf stories of the 1940s is Robert A. HEINLEIN's "The Roads Must Roll" (1940), which deals with the social effects of moving roadways and the commuter chaos resulting from a strike of maintenance engineers. The majority of sf stories attempting to deal with social revolution brought about through transport, however, used the more direct method of matter transmission. Notable stories in this vein include "Ticket to Anywhere" (1952) by Damon KNIGHT and "Granny Won't Knit" (1954) by Theodore STURGEON. A recent anthology, Robert SILVERBERG's *Three Trips in Time and Space* (anth. **1973**) collected three original novellas on the theme: Larry NIVEN's "Flash Crowd", Jack VANCE's "Rumfuddle" and John BRUNNER's "You'll Take the High Road". Brunner also developed the theme in a novel, *Web of Everywhere* (**1974**).

An early aid to transportation which figured in many sf stories was the sub-oceanic tunnel. The Channel Tunnel often featured in INVASION stories written in Britain, while a transatlantic tunnel was featured in Bernhard KELLERMANN's novel *Der Tunnel* (1913; trans. as *The Tunnel* 1915) and two films of the 1930s based on it: THE TRANS-ATLANTIC TUNNEL and DER TUNNEL. The idea reappears in modern sf in Ray NELSON's "Turn Off the Sky" (1963) and is the theme of Harry HARRISON's ALTERNATE-WORLD satire *Tunnel Through the Deeps* (1972; vt *A Transatlantic Tunnel, Hurrah! UK*).

It cannot be said that sf has been particularly adept in the invention of new means of transportation that have subsequently proved practicable, although there are a number of ingenious devices concerned with space technology which have been echoed in reality. Arthur C. CLARKE has proved particularly expert in this regard, and there remain several imaginative devices used in his stories which may one day become actualized, including the lunar transport in *A Fall of Moondust* (1961) and the spacefaring yachts of "Sunjammer" (1965) (*see* SOLAR WIND; SUN).

The mood of contemporary sf is pessimistic about energy resources, and the days when the future looked illimitably rosy for personal transport are over. It is not impossible that in the real world we are entering the period of the transportation counter-revolution, as the fierce debate over the Anglo-French supersonic jet *Concorde* suggests. There are already signs that the prevalent attitude in sf toward the problems of transportation is beginning to change, to become much more conservatively inclined.   [BS]
See also: COMMUNICATIONS; ROCKETS; UNDER THE SEA.

First issue, 1964.

TREASURY OF GREAT SCIENCE FICTION STORIES US PULP-size magazine. Eight issues, 1964–71, published by Popular Library; ed. Jim Hendryx Jr for the first three issues, then Helen Tono. A follow-up of Hendryx's WONDER STORIES of 1957 and 1963, it was continued as *Great Science Fiction*

Stories (third issue), *SF Yearbook: a Treasury of Science Fiction* (fourth issue) and *Science Fiction Yearbook*. The stories were reprinted from STARTLING STORIES and THRILLING WONDER STORIES.   [FHP]
Collectors should note: It is possible to consider the last five issues as a separate magazine, as the title now stressed the annual publication (in fact it was annual throughout), the editor changed, and the numeration began again from no.1.

TREIBICH S(TEVEN) J(OHN) (1936–72). American writer, co-author with Laurence M. JANIFER of the three "Angelo di Stefano" novels: *Target: Terra* (1968); *The High Hex* (1969) and *The Wagered World* (1969).   [BS]

TREMAINE, F(REDERICK) ORLIN (1899–1956). American editor and writer. An experienced PULP magazine editor, FOT assumed the editorship of ASTOUNDING STORIES in October 1933, after it had been taken over by Street & Smith Publications. Curiously, although he had been working for *ASF*'s previous publisher, Clayton Magazines, he seems to have had no connection with the magazine prior to becoming editor. He produced 50 issues of *ASF*, initially with the assistance of Desmond W. HALL, being succeeded by John W. CAMPBELL Jr in December 1937. Under FOT's editorship *ASF* became unquestionably the pre-eminent sf magazine of its day, featuring all the leading writers of the period and publishing the first stories of such writers as L. Sprague DE CAMP and Eric Frank RUSSELL. He instituted a policy of featuring in each issue at least one story termed a "thought variant" — that is, a new concept, or a new gloss on a familiar idea. As an attention-attracting device this was an undoubted success, and inspired an imitation "new story" policy in WONDER STORIES. FOT gave up the editorship of *ASF* when he became editorial director of a number of Street & Smith magazines, but in any case he left the company in 1938 to found his own publishing firm. In 1940–41 he edited the magazine COMET STORIES, which was of indifferent standard and lasted only five issues. FOT wrote a number of stories under his own name, and at least one as Warner VAN LORNE. He worked in non-sf publishing enterprises in later years, before being forced into early retirement through ill health.   [MJE]
See also: ROBOTS; SF MAGAZINES.

TREMAINE, NELSON *See* Warner VAN LORNE.

TRENT, OLAF *See* R.L. FANTHORPE.

TREVARTHEN, HAL P. *See* J.K. HEYDON.

TREVOR, ELLESTON (1920–). English writer, best known for his many thrillers. His first sf novel, *The Immortal*

Error (1946), combines IMMORTALITY and TIME-TRAVEL themes with a dollop of mysticism; *Domesday Story* (1952 as by Warwick Scott; vt *Doomsday*; vt *The Doomsday Story* as by ET) tells of fears that an H-bomb test in Australia will bring about the end of the world; *The Pillars of Midnight* (1957) depicts the effects of a devastating disease; *The Mind of Max Duvine* (1960) is about telepathy; *The Shoot* (1966) also deals with weapons-testing, this time of a missile using a dangerous, unstable fuel. *Forbidden Kingdom* (1955) is a children's LOST-WORLD story. The espionage thrillers ET has written under the name Adam Hall, such as *The Quiller Memorandum* (1965), sometimes utilize sf hardware but are, at most, borderline sf.   [JC/PN]

TRIMBLE, LOUIS (PRESTON) (1917–). American writer and academic, prolific in several genres, including mysteries, Westerns and sf (he had written 66 novels up to 1977), though relatively little of the latter, which he began publishing with "Probability" for *If* in 1954; his sf work, however, is almost entirely novels, beginning with *Anthropol* (1968), and a further Anthropol bureau investigation, *The Noblest Experiment in the Galaxy* (1970). His most noted novel is *The City Machine* (1972), set on a colony planet, where the device that constructs CITIES has been lost, forcing everyone into one overcrowded construct. LT is an unpretentious, clear, professional writer.   [JC]
Other works: *Guardians of the Gate* (1972) with his first wife, Jacquelyn Trimble; *The Wandering Variables* (1972); *The Bodelan Way* (1974).

TROLLENBERG TERROR, THE (vt **THE CRAWLING EYE** USA) Film (1958). Eros/DCA. Directed by Quentin Lawrence, starring Forrest Tucker, Laurence Payne, Janet Munro, Jennifer Jayne and Warren Mitchell. Screenplay by Jimmy Sangster, based on the TV series *The Trollenberg Terror* by Peter Kay. 85 mins. B/w.

Aliens from outer space hide on a mountain under cover of a cloud and attempt to exert telepathic influence over various people. The special effects were cheap — the cloud on the mountain was achieved with a piece of cotton wool pinned to a photograph.   [JB]

TROLLOPE, ANTHONY (1815–82). English writer whose most famous books are the "Barchester Chronicles" and whose best are the later political novels; his 61st book is his sole venture into sf, *The Fixed Period* (1882), written only a few years before his death, and understandably (though evasively: no one actually dies in the book) concerned with that topic; it is 1980 on an ISLAND near Australia, where rebel Englishmen establish a UTOPIA in which no one is allowed to live past the age of 68, though

the Navy arrives in time to avert any implementation of the scheme. It is one of AT's weaker novels. [JC]
See also: MACHINES.

TROUT, KILGORE *See* Philip José FARMER, and Kurt VONNEGUT Jr, who invented the character whose name Farmer borrowed.

TRUMBULL, DOUGLAS (1942–). American cinematic special effects expert and film director. Originally he trained as an architect but while still at college switched his interest to graphic arts. After working with advertising agencies as a technical illustrator, he was hired by Graphic Films, a Hollywood company, to work on animated promotional films for NASA and the USAF. One of these films, *To the Moon and Beyond*, was seen by Stanley KUBRICK at the World's Fair in 1964. Kubrick remembered this work when he was preparing 2001: A SPACE ODYSSEY and hired him as one of four special-effects supervisors. DT worked for three years on *2001* and was mainly responsible for the spectacular light show at the end of the film which utilized the "slit-scan effect", a technique developed by him. Other films that DT worked on as an effects man were *Candy* (1968) and THE ANDROMEDA STRAIN (1971). In 1972 he directed SILENT RUNNING, based on his own original idea. It was not a great success and since then he has experienced difficulty in setting up his own sf projects. Most recently he has supervised the highly praised special effects in Spielberg's sf epic CLOSE ENCOUNTERS OF THE THIRD KIND (1977). DT's imaginative innovations in special effects for sf films, though not widely recognized by the general public, may prove to have been one of the most important creative influences on a genre which, technically at least, is becoming rapidly more sophisticated. [JB/PN]

Konstantin TSIOLKOVSKY as an old man, in 1930, with his grandson Alexei. © Novosti Press Agency.

TSIOLKOVSKY, KONSTANTIN (EDUARDOVICH) (1857–1935). Russian scientist and writer. He began

investigating the possibility of SPACE FLIGHT in 1878, and published the monograph "Free Space" (1883), in which he suggested that spaceships would have to operate by jet propulsion. His consideration of some of the practical difficulties led to a paper entitled "How to Protect Fragile and Delicate Objects from Jolts and Shocks" (1891). He attempted to popularize his scientific knowledge and ideas in a series of didactic "Fantasies of Earth and Sky" which eventually appeared in English as *The Call of the Cosmos* (**1895** Russia; trans. by A. Shkarovsky and others **1963**). In 1903 he published the classic paper "The Probing of Space by means of Jet Devices" — a thoroughgoing account of the theory of liquid-fuelled rockets.

His major work of fiction, *Beyond the Planet Earth* (**1920** Russia; trans., with introduction, by K. Syers **1960**), is a popularization of his prospectus for space travel. It is a didactic work written for a naïve audience, providing an account of the building and first flight of a spaceship by an international group of scientists. It ends with the initiation of a project to colonize space. The inscription on the obelisk marking KT's grave reads: "Man will not always stay on earth; the pursuit of light and space will lead him to penetrate the bounds of the atmosphere, timidly at first but in the end to conquer the whole of solar space". He may be considered the first prophet of the myth of the conquest of space which has played such a vital role in modern sf. [BS]
See also: COLONIZATION OF OTHER WORLDS; FANTASTIC VOYAGES; GENERATION STARSHIPS; MOON; PREDICTION; ROCKETS; TRANSPORTATION.

TSUTSUI, YASUTAKA *See* JAPAN.

TUBB, E(DWIN) C(HARLES) (1919–). English writer and editor who began publishing sf with "No Short Cuts" for *NW* in 1951, and for the next half decade produced a great amount of fiction, in British magazines and in book form, under his own name and under many pseudonyms, some still undisclosed. After the late 1950s, his production moderated somewhat, but he remains a prolific author of consistently readable SPACE OPERAS and other works. Of his many pseudonyms, those known to be used by him for book titles are Charles Grey, Carl Maddox and the house names Volsted GRIDBAN, Gill HUNT, King LANG, Brian SHAW and Roy SHELDON for the years up to 1955, and Gregory Kern in the 1970s. At least 50 names were used for magazine stories only. His first sf novels are mostly pseudonymous. *Saturn Patrol* (**1951** as by King Lang); *Planetfall* (**1951** as by Gill Hunt); *Argentis* (**1952** as by Brian Shaw); and *Alien Universe* (**1952** as by Volsted Gridban). He soon began publishing under his own name with *Atom War on Mars* (**1952**), however, though his best

work in these years was probably written as by Charles Grey, beginning with *The Wall* (**1953**). Of his enormous output of magazine fiction, the "Dusty Dribble" stories in *Authentic* 1955–6 stand out; ECT also edited *Authentic* from Feb. 1956 to its demise in Oct. 1957.

With *Enterprise 2115* (**1954** as by Charles Grey; vt *The Mechanical Monarch* USA as by ECT), he began to produce more sustained adventure novels; *Alien Dust* (1952–3 *NW*, 1954 *Nebula*; fix-up **1955**; US edition expurgated) is a quietly effective depiction of the rigours of interplanetary exploration; *The Space-Born* (**1956**) is a crisp GENERATION-STARSHIP tale. These novels all display a convincing expertise in the use of the language and themes of PULP sf, though they tend not to examine this material very thoroughly. *Enterprise 2115*, for instance, deals swiftly with REINCARNATION, the SUPERMAN theme and CYBERNETICS, along with a matriarchal DYSTOPIA, with typical largesse, in its story of the pilot of the first spaceship who returns from frozen sleep to reinvigorate a world gone wrong through its misuse of a predicting machine.

The next decade saw few ECT titles, however, until the introduction in *The Winds of Gath* (**1967**; rev. vt *Gath* 1968 UK) of his most popular character, Earl Dumarest, whose search for Earth — the planet on which he was born, and which no one seems to believe exists — extends from planet to planet in a post-GALACTIC-EMPIRE period; as Dumarest moves gradually outwards from Galactic Centre along a spiral arm of stars, he gathers clues about the location of Earth and is increasingly opposed by the Cyclan, a vast organization of passionless humans linked cybernetically to a central organic computer. The series, which continues, comprises to date 16 further volumes: 2. *Derai* (**1968**), 3. *Toyman* (**1969**), 4. *Kalin* (**1969**), 5. *The Jester at Scar* (**1970**), 6. *Lallia* (**1971**), 7. *Technos* (**1972**), 8. *Veruchia* (**1973**), 9. *Mayenne* (**1973**), 10. *Jondelle* (**1973**), 11. *Zenya* (**1974**), 12. *Eloise* (**1975**), 13. *Eye of the Zodiac* (**1975**), 14. *Jack of Swords* (**1976**), 15. *Spectrum of a Forgotten Sun* (**1976**), 16. *Haven of Darkness* (**1977**) and 17. *Prison of Night* (**1977**). The "Dumarest" books are well above the average quality of paperback series sf, keeping up a surprisingly high standard of narrative vigour. Concurrently, as Gregory Kern, ECT has produced a more routine space-opera sequence featuring galactic secret agent Cap Kennedy; the Kern titles comprise 1. *Galaxy of the Lost* (**1973**), 2. *Slave Ship from Sergan* (**1973**), 3. *Monster of Metelaze* (**1973**), 4. *Enemy within the Skull* (**1974**), 5. *Jewel of Jarhen* (**1974**), 6. *Seetee Alert!* (**1974**), 7. *The Gholan Gate* (**1974**), 8. *The Eater of Worlds* (**1974**), 9. *Earth Enslaved* (**1974**), 10. *Planet of Dread* (**1974**), 11. *Spawn of Laban* (**1974**), 12. *The Genetic Buccaneer*

(1974), 13. *A World Aflame* (1974), 14. *The Ghosts of Epidoris* (1975), 15. *Mimics of Dephene* (1975) and 16. *Beyond the Galactic Lens* (1975). Though these and some of the "Dumarest" books descend too readily to cliché, ECT has established a well-earned reputation for a reliably competent kind of adventure novel full of action, sex and occasional melancholy.

[JC]

Other works: *The Mutants Rebel* (1953); *Venusian Adventure* (1953); *Alien Life* (1954); *World at Bay* (1954); *Journey to Mars* (1954); *City of No Return* (1954); *The Stellar Legion* (1954); *The Hell Planet* (1954); *The Resurrected Man* (1954); *Moon Base* (1964); *Ten from Tomorrow* (coll. 1966); *Death is a Dream* (1967); *C.O.D. Mars* (1968); *S.T.A.R. Flight* (1969); *Escape Into Space* (1969); *The Century of the Manikin* (1972); *A Scatter of Stardust* (coll. 1972); *The Primitive* (1977); and the following novelizations of episodes from the TV series SPACE 1999: *Breakaway* (1975); *Collision Course* (1975); *Alien Seed* (1976), *Rogue Planet* (1976) and the comparatively ambitious *Earthfall* (1977). As by Charles Grey: *Dynasty of Doom* (1953); *The Tormented City* (1953); *Space Hunger* (1953); *I Fight for Mars* (1953); *The Hand of Havoc* (1954); *The Extra Man* (1954). As by Volsted Gridban: *Reverse Universe* (1952); *Planetoid Disposals, Ltd* (1953); *Debracy's Drug* (1953); *Fugitive of Time* (1953). As by Carl Maddox: *The Living World* (1954); *Menace from the Past* (1954). As by Roy Sheldon: *The Metal Eater* (1954).

See also: COLONIZATION OF OTHER WORLDS; CRYONICS; CYBORGS; END OF THE WORLD; GAMES AND SPORTS; MARS; PARANOIA AND SCHIZOPHRENIA.

From the 1975 Aussiecon programme.

TUCK, DONALD H(ENRY) (1922–). Australian bibliographer and industrial manager. His bibliographical labours in sf since the late 1940s are certainly the most important and extensive in the field since the pioneering work of Everett F. BLEILER, though the mid-1970s have seen some very active competition; all recent scholars, however, have been indebted to DHT's work. His early work was *A Handbook of Science Fiction and Fantasy* (1954; rev. in two vols 1959), in duplicated format, published by himself. Far more thorough is *The Encyclopedia of Science Fiction and Fantasy*, of which *Volume 1: Who's Who, A–L* (1974) and *Volume 2: Who's Who, M–Z* (1978) are the two vols so far produced by ADVENT: PUBLISHERS. A projected third volume will deal with SF MAGAZINES, paperbacks, pseudonyms, series and other matters. The usefulness of these works is bibliographic rather than critical; assessments are few; brief synopses are given for many works, and publishing data for all. The book is remarkably though not absolutely free of error and omission, and its usefulness is primarily limited by the slowness of the publication process, whereby, although both volumes only cover sf works up to 1968, the second volume was not published till a decade later. Coverage of genre sf is thorough; coverage of sf outside the genre, and of older sf generally, is only patchy. Generally (there are exceptions) DHT does not cover work which has not been reprinted between 1945 and 1968. Listings of stories in anthologies are given, and the coverage is almost as thorough for fantasy as it is for sf. [PN]

Photo William H. Cramp.

TUCKER, (ARTHUR) WILSON (1914–). American writer, orphaned, brought up in Bloomington and Normal, Illinois, where he has set some of his fiction, some early stories being signed Bob Tucker. He is a retired theatre electrician, and despite his considerable production, which includes 11 mystery and adventure novels in addition to his sf work, he has never been a full-time writer. WT began his involvement with sf about 1932, and during the 1930s was exceedingly active as a fan and FANZINE publisher, starting with *The Planetoid* in 1932, though his most notable fanzine was *Le Zombie*, which has lasted for over 60 issues, with its heyday in 1939–44 and occasional issues since. In *All Our Yesterdays* (1969), Harry WARNER Jr reports "Bob" Tucker as among the most polished and prolific of fan writers whose skill and humour were then almost unique. As an example of the violent humour and intense emotions aroused in early FANDOM, it is notable that WT was twice subjected to hoax obituaries in the sf magazines of the time. His fanzine *The Bloomington News Letter* (later *Science Fiction News Letter*) dealt mainly with the professional field.

While active as a fan WT was also writing fiction, though it was not until 1941 that he published his first story, "Interstellar Way Station", as by Bob Tucker, in *Super Science Novels*; although he published several stories in the 1940s he has never been prolific in that form. He soon turned to novels. *The Chinese Doll* (1946) is a mystery, but makes considerable reference to the world of sf fandom. (WT pleased the knowledgeable fans, while annoying some critics, by his lifelong habit of using the names of fans and writers for the characters of his books; these names became known as Tuckerisms.) His first sf novel, *The City in the Sea* (1951), deals somewhat crudely with much the same material effectively treated in his most recent, *Ice and Iron* (1974; exp. 1975 in paperback edition): in both a matriarchal culture begins to re-explore an America reverted to savagery, but in the latter TIME-TRAVEL themes contrast the matriarchy with an America closer to the present during a period when the polar ice is once again advancing. Time travel is central to much of WT's work, featuring in *The Time Masters* (1953; rev. 1971), *Time Bomb* (1955; vt *Tomorrow Plus X*), which has the same leading character as the previous novel, and *The Lincoln Hunters* (1957; author's note added in 1968 reprinting). This last is thought by many critics to be WT's best novel. Time travellers from an imperial America several hundred years hence are sent to acquire a recording of a lost speech of Abraham Lincoln; the two cultures are effectively contrasted; the ending, in which the protagonist is trapped in 1856, is both poignant and welcome.

WT has a knack of choosing unusually resonant and appropriate titles for his novels. Examples are *The Long Loud Silence* (1952; rev. 1970; early US editions delete implications of cannibalism, UK editions do not) and *The Year of the Quiet Sun* (1970). The former is a powerful post-HOLOCAUST novel, sombre and tough in feeling; the hero, unusually for a genre sf novel, is in many ways cruel and insensitive. The latter, which won a JOHN W. CAMPBELL MEMORIAL AWARD retrospectively in 1976, is a grim story of time travel to the NEAR FUTURE and a USA in bad shape. *Wild Talent* (1954; UK 1955 edition has much expanded final chapter; vt *The Man From Tomorrow*) is a story of the

political exploitation of a man with PSI POWERS and again takes a rather dark and sceptical attitude to political morality. Although WT is a very uneven writer, he did something to expand the boundaries of genre sf with his downbeat and realistic attitudes. His writing improved as he went on. He ties his use of time travel to a virtual archaeology of the worlds thus exposed; the effective sobriety of his use of genre themes underlines the quiet authority of his novels.   [JC/PN]
Other works: *Science Fiction Sub-Treasury* (coll. **1954**; vt *Time X*); *To the Tombaugh Station* (**1960**).
See also: END OF THE WORLD; ESP; IMMORTALITY; OUTER PLANETS; PUBLISHING; SPACE OPERA; SUPERMAN; TIME PARADOXES.

TUCKER, BOB *See* (Arthur) Wilson TUCKER.

TUCKER, GEORGE *See* Joseph ATTERLEY.

TUMANNOST ANDROMEDY (vt **THE ANDROMEDA NEBULA**) Film (1967). Directed by Eugene Sherstobytov, based on the novel of the same title by Ivan YEFREMOV. 85 mins. Colour.
A polemical Russian film about an attempt, 2,000 years in the future, to establish contact with an intelligent alien race living on a planet situated in the Andromeda Nebula. The UTOPIAN aspects of future Russian society are manifested in the glowing health of the cast, which resembles a Russian Olympic team in appearance and, according to less kind critics, in acting ability. The film's optimism about the future is light years from the bleakness of SOLARIS, a more recent Russian contribution to sf cinema. The special effects are spectacular, especially in the fiery finale.   [JB]

TUNG, LEE *See* LEE TUNG.

TUNNEL, DER Film (1933). Bavaria Film. Directed by Kurt Bernhardt, starring Paul Hartmann, Olly von Flint, Attila Hörbiger and Elga Brink. Screenplay by Kurt SIODMAK, based on the novel by Bernhard KELLERMANN. 80 mins. B/w.
This ambitious German film tells of a NEAR-FUTURE attempt to drill a tunnel under the Atlantic ocean. Technically it is of a very high standard with convincing sets and special effects; the various natural disasters that occur — cave-ins, floods and volcanic eruptions — are realistically staged (too realistically, perhaps, as the film's associate producer was killed during the shooting of one such sequence). A French-language version was made simultaneously, starring Jean Gabin, Madeleine Renaud and Gustaf Gründgens. Two years later came the slightly inferior English remake, THE TUNNEL (vt *The Trans-Atlantic Tunnel* USA).   [JB]

TUNNEL, THE (vt **THE TRANS-ATLANTIC TUNNEL**) Film (1935). Gaumont. Directed by Maurice Elvey, starring Richard Dix, Leslie Banks, Madge Evans, Helen Vinson, C. Aubrey Smith, George Arliss and Walter Huston. Screenplay by Clemence Dane and L. du Garde Peach, from an adaption by Kurt SIODMAK of the novel by Bernhard KELLERMANN. 94 mins. B/w.
This is an English remake of the successful German film DER TUNNEL (1933). The plot is basically the same: a tunnel is built under the Atlantic linking the USA with Europe (though here the European end of the tunnel is situated in England) but the film is not as technically impressive as the German version.   [JB]

TUNSTALL, (WILLIAM CUTH-BERT) BRIAN (? –). British writer whose sf novel, *Eagles Restrained* (**1936**), shows less prescience than some in its depiction of the League of Nations intervention to quell a German-Polish dispute in 1954.   [JC]

TURNER, FREDERICK *See* TERRAFORMING.

TURNER, GEORGE (1916–). Australian writer and sf critic. His interest in sf came quite late in life, long after the publication of his first five novels. He became well known to sf fans through his stern critical strictures, and his sometimes very sensitive analyses, in Bruce GILLESPIE's SF COMMENTARY, a FANZINE. He edited *The View from the Edge* (anth. **1977** Australia), stories which resulted from the second major Australian sf workshop, run in imitation of the CLARION SF WRITERS' WORKSHOP in the USA. With some courage, and unusually for a critic, GT has himself written an sf novel, *Beloved Son* (**1978**), a long and complex work in which a returning interstellar expedition returns to find a radically changed culture, a diminished post-HOLOCAUST population with very few old people, and a rather merciless, puritanical ethos. CLONES and GENETIC ENGINEERING play a role. The book is slow-moving, but has been generally well received by critics for its careful exploration of some plausible moral problems of the 21st century.   [PN]

TUTTLE, LISA (1952–). American journalist and story-writer, with a BA in English from Syracuse University, who, though yet to publish her first book, has already established her name as a writer of impressive fiction, beginning with her first story, "Stranger in the House", for Robin Scott WILSON's *Clarion II* (anth. **1972**). LT was one of the early members of the CLARION SF WRITERS' WORKSHOP. Another notable story is "Storms of Windhaven" (1975) with George R.R. MARTIN, which tells sensitively of a lost colony planet whose culture is focused on the use of artificial (but functional) wings.

LT won the 1974 JOHN W. CAMPBELL AWARD for best new sf writer.   [JC]

TWAIN, MARK Pseudonym of Samuel L. Clemens (1835–1910), American writer and humorist. It has not been generally appreciated (although Philip José FARMER makes MT the central character of *The Fabulous Riverboat*, **1971**) that a significant portion of his output, including what is at least his second-best novel, may be classified as sf. Some of Edgar Allan POE's sf was humorous but MT, drawing on the traditions of the literary hoax and the tall tale, was the first American writer fully to exploit the humorous possibilities of sf, inaugurating a rich but narrow vein which finds its current apotheosis in the work of Kurt VONNEGUT Jr. In MT's brief, sf-like hoax "The Petrified Man" (1862), intended to satirize a mania for cases of natural petrification, the title character is described as thumbing his nose. This is an exact analogue for the conclusion of Vonnegut's *Cat's Cradle* (**1963**) where the protagonist arranges that as a consequence of the freezing properties of *ice-nine* he be solidified in an identical attitude of disrespect.
The switch in MT's work from the relatively light-hearted to the pessimistically philosophical is reflected in his sf. To take the more frivolous material first: one of MT's Notebooks indicates that, like Poe, he was interested in the possibilites of ballooning and in 1868 began a story about a Frenchman's balloon journey from Paris to a prairie in Illinois but left it unfinished because of the American publication (**1870** as *Five Weeks in a Balloon*) of Jules VERNE's *Cinq semaines en ballon* (**1863**). However, he returned to the topic in an unpublished manuscript entitled "A Murder, a Mystery, and a Marriage" (1876) and in *Tom Sawyer Abroad* (**1894**), in which the hero crosses the Atlantic by balloon in the other direction and ends up in Cairo.

Also essentially humorous is that skewed UTOPIA, "The Curious Republic of Gondour" (1875), in which certain classes of people, including the more intelligent, have more votes than others (cf. Vonnegut's antithetical "Harrison Bergeron", 1961). An equally skewed view of another ideal state is offered in *Captain Stormfield's Visit to Heaven* (written 1870s + ; **1909**). This is a materialist heaven located in interstellar space, through which Stormfield is sailing with an increasing number of companions rather in the manner of the narrator in Olaf STAPLEDON's *Star Maker* (**1937**). To begin with, Stormfield races a comet, a not unlikely invention for a writer whose arrival and departure from Earth coincided with the timetable of Halley's Comet (a fragment from the 1880s is entitled "A Letter from the Comet"). MT's interest in astronomical distances, evident elsewhere, is particularly apparent here.

A parallel interest in vast temporal perspectives and geological ages is conspicuous in the many pieces that constitute MT's down-home version of the Genesis story, including his practical speculation concerning the daily lives of ADAM AND EVE in "Papers from the Adam Family" (written 1870s + ; 1962) and "Letters from the Earth" (written 1909; 1962). A considerably darkened sense of time and cyclical history informs "The Secret History of Eddypus, the World-Empire" (written 1901–02; 1972), MT's horrific but uncompleted vision of a future a thousand years hence in which Mrs Mary Baker Eddy's Christian Science rules the world, and MT himself, the potential saviour, is confused with Adam.

Given his fascination with time and history, it is not surprising that MT's best and most influential work of sf, *A Connecticut Yankee in King Arthur's Court* (**1889**; vt *A Yankee at the Court of King Arthur* UK), should be concerned with TIME TRAVEL. It may be the first genuine time-travel story (the destructive ending takes care of the anachronism issue) and it certainly established the pattern for that kind of sf (predominantly American) where the hero, more or less single-handedly, affects the destiny of an entire world or universe (cf. in particular L. Sprague DE CAMP's *Lest Darkness Fall*, **1941**). While writing *A Connecticut Yankee*, MT, who like his Promethean hero was gripped by the march of invention (his own inventions include a history game and a notebook with ears, and he anticipated radio and television), became disastrously involved financially with the Paige typesetter. That was one reason why *A Connecticut Yankee* is the transitional work between the light and the dark in MT's corpus. Many of the gloomy, quasi-Darwinist, philosophical ideas explored in such non-sf works as *What Is Man?* (first version written 1898; **1906**) — a machine — and *Mark Twain's*

Mysterious Stranger Manuscripts (written 1897–1903; fraudulent composite text **1916**; **1969**), which claim that everything is determined and that reality is all a dream anyway, figure prominently in *A Connecticut Yankee*.

The same ideas pervade MT's explorations in microcosmic worlds (*see* GREAT AND SMALL) in two extended but unfinished works. "The Great Dark" (A.B. PAINE's title; written 1898; 1962) is about an apocalyptic voyage in a drop of water (cf. Fitz-James O'BRIEN's "The Diamond Lens", 1858), while the narrator of "Three Thousand Years among the Microbes" (written 1905; 1967), reduced to microscopic size by a wizard, explores the world-body of the diseased tramp Blitzowski (one of the inhabitants is called Lemuel Gulliver and the influence of Jonathan SWIFT is apparent). It is implied that the universe we inhabit is actually God's diseased body. (This kind of macrocosm/microcosm relationship is hinted at in MT's 1883 Notebook outline for what, in anticipation of the GENERATION STARSHIP theme, might best be called a Generation Iceberg story.)

If travel or communication can be managed instantaneously (and in *A Connecticut Yankee* and the microscopic-world stories the transference is instantaneous) it seems logical that some loss of faith in the physicality of existence might occur, augmenting MT's notion that reality is insubstantial, a vagrant thought, a dream. In this connection and as evidence of MT's concern with psychic possibilities (including the whirligig of schizophrenia), mention should be made of two essays, "Mental Telegraphy" (1891) and "Mental Telegraphy Again" (1895), which argue for the reality of ESP. Reference is made to the English Society for Psychical Research and it is suggested that something called a "phrenophone" might communicate thoughts instantaneously just as the telephone communicates words. In "From the 'London Times' of 1904" (1898) — another newspaper hoax like "The Petrified Man" — another futuristic invention, called the "telelectroscope", a visual telephone, is used seemingly to disprove a murder. But it is precisely the divorce between image and reality afforded by this kind of instantaneous communication which causes ontological anxiety. Thus the suspected murderer is executed anyway. [DK]

About the author: A reader interested in detailed information on MT's recently published sf should consult the Introductions and additional apparatus for the in-progress University of California editions of *The Mark Twain Papers* (15 vols projected). Other relevant secondary material includes: "Mark Twain and Captain Wakeman" by Ray B. Browne, *American Literature* 33, 1961; *Mark Twain's Fable of Progress: Political and Economic Ideas in "A*

Connecticut Yankee" (**1964**) by Henry Nash Smith; "Mark Twain and Science Fiction" in *Future Perfect: American Science Fiction of the Nineteenth Century* (anth. **1966**) ed. H. Bruce FRANKLIN; "*Captain Stormfield's Visit to Heaven* and *The Gates Ajar*" by Robert A. Rees, *English Language Notes* 7, 1970; "Mark Twain's Later Dialogue: The 'Me' and the Machine" by John Tuckey, *American Literature* 41, 1970; "The Humor of the Absurd: Mark Twain's Adamic Diaries" by Stanley Brodwin, *Criticism* 14, 1972; "Mark Twain, Phrenology, and the 'Temperaments': a Study of Pseudoscientific Influences" by Alan Gribben, *American Quarterly* 24, 1972; "A Cosmic Tramp: Samuel Clemens' Three Thousand Years among the Microbes" by Henry J. Lindborg, *American Literature* 44, 1973; *New Worlds for Old: the Apocalyptic Imagination, Science Fiction, and American Literature* (**1974**) by David KETTERER; "An Innocent in Time: Mark Twain in King Arthur's Court" by Philip Klass (William TENN), EXTRAPOLATION 16, 1974; "Science in the Thought of Mark Twain" by H.H. Waggoner, *American Literature* 8, 1937.

See also: DISCOVERY AND INVENTION; FANTASY; HISTORY IN SF; HUMOUR; SATIRE.

TWEED, THOMAS F(REDERICK) (1890–). American writer whose sf novel, *Gabriel Over the White House* (**1933**; vt *Rinehard* UK), filmed the same year, deals with a newly elected NEAR-FUTURE American president who, after a car crash, under possibly divine inspiration cures all the world's far-flung ills. [JC]

TWENTY MILLION MILES TO EARTH Film (1957). Columbia. Directed by Nathan Juran, starring William Hopper, Joan Taylor, Frank Puglia and John Zaremba. Screenplay by Bob Williams and Christopher Knopf, based on a story by Charlott Knight and Ray HARRYHAUSEN. 82 mins. B/w.

A spaceship returns to Earth from Venus carrying a strange egg which hatches a humanoid/reptilian creature, an Ymir. The Ymir grows and grows until finally it is bigger than an elephant, invades Rome and is eventually trapped and killed on top of the Colosseum. Ray Harryhausen maintains his usual high standard of model animation and special effects.

A novelized version of the film appeared in the first and only issue of the proposed AMAZING STORIES SCIENCE FICTION NOVELS series (**1957**), by Henry SLESAR. [JB/PN]

27TH DAY, THE Film (1956). Romson Productions/Columbia. Directed by William Asher, starring Gene Barry, Valerie French, George Voskovec, Arnold Moss and Stefan Schnabel. Screenplay by John MANTLEY, based on his own novel. 75 mins. B/w.

This sf morality tale (many of them found their way on to the screen during the 1959s) is more optimistic about mankind's inherent goodness than most of the others. An alien gives each of five people, in five different countries, a box of capsules capable of destroying all human life on any one continent. The capsules will respond only to the telepathic commands of the recipients, on whom great pressure is put to use the capsules to wipe out enemy states. The five recipients are forced to go into hiding, until one of them discovers that the aliens are only using the capsules as a means of testing mankind's maturity. In a finale which is chilling in a way that the makers did not intend, the capsules selectively kill "every enemy of human freedom" — no doubt as a sign of the aliens' maturity.   [JB]

20,000 LEAGUES UNDER THE SEA
Film (1954). Walt Disney. Directed by Richard Fleischer, starring James Mason, Kirk Douglas, Paul Lukas and Peter Lorre. Screenplay by Earl Felton, based on the novel by Jules VERNE. 127 mins. Colour.

This early Walt Disney live-action film was his best — a lavish, well-scripted epic that creates a genuine "sense of wonder". Richard Fleischer has twice returned to sf themes since *TTLUTS*, with FANTASTIC VOYAGE (1966) and SOYLENT GREEN (1973), but the first is still his most memorable contribution to the genre. "I spent a year preparing the film," said Fleischer. "It was difficult to make a story out of the novel because it doesn't *have* a story — it's really just a series of unrelated incidents. And Nemo as a character also doesn't exist in the book though there are all sorts of allusions to what motivates him politically, but we really had to create a new character and a new story. The odd thing is that when people now think of Verne's novel they are usually remembering the story of the film and not the book."

Nemo is an anti-war fanatic who uses his submarine, the *Nautilus*, as a weapon to sink warships. James Mason gives a fine performance as the obsessed Nemo who fights a lone battle against the world before being betrayed by three shipwreck survivors whom he has taken on board. He expires in style, at the centre of a self-made holocaust that envelops both his private island and the *Nautilus* before, significantly, forming a mushroom shaped cloud.

The special effects are of a very high standard and the *Nautilus* itself is beautifully designed by John Meeham, the art director. Members of the Oscar-winning effects team were Bob Mattey, Ralph Hammeras, Ub Iwerks, Peter Ellenshaw, John Hench and Joshua Meador.

(There were two previous versions of *TTLUTS* — a French one made by George MÉLIÈS in 1907 and an American one written and directed by Stuart Paton in 1917.)   [JB]

TWILIGHT'S LAST GLEAMING
Film (1976). Geria Productions/ Hemdale. Directed by Robert Aldrich, starring Burt Lancaster, Richard Widmark, Paul Winfield, Charles Durning and Melvyn Douglas. Screenplay by Ronald M. Cohen and Edward Huebsch, based on the novel *Viper 3* by Walter Wager. 146 mins (UK version cut to 122). Colour.

A renegade American air force general, in 1981, takes over a missile base and threatens to initiate World War Three unless the President reveals to the nation the contents of a secret Pentagon file concerning the Vietnam war. In the original version of the film the file showed how the Pentagon deliberately became involved in the Vietnam war to prove to the country's enemies that America was willing to sacrifice thousands of men, thus giving extra credibility to America's willingness to fight a conventional war. These sequences disappeared when 24 minutes were cut by the distributor, ostensibly to "speed it up". What is left is a tautly directed action/adventure film, though some of the cynical message, typical of Aldrich's films, remains (the Pentagon is victorious, destroying even the President to protect its secrets). The skilful use of a split-screen technique to create tension and moments of chaos and confusion justifies it, perhaps for the first time, as a legitimate cinematic tool.   [JB]

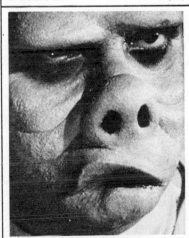

The deformed protagonist of "Eye of the Beholder", an episode from THE TWILIGHT ZONE.

TWILIGHT ZONE, THE US television series (1959–64). Created by Rod SERLING, *TZ*, which was basically fantasy, included many sf episodes. It began as a half-hour series in 1959, was briefly expanded to an hour for 13 episodes in 1963, then reverted to half an hour for its final series, ending in 1964. Rod Serling, the show's creator, wrote many of the episodes. Other writers on the series included Richard MATHESON and Charles BEAUMONT.

The first instalment was "Where is Everybody?", directed by Robert Stephens, written by Serling, in which a young man wakes up in a small town to find it totally deserted, with signs that all the inhabitants had left only moments before. The dénouement reveals that the situation had been implanted in his mind as part of a study into human reactions to loneliness, conducted by space scientists.

Episodes varied in quality, some of the better ones being written by Matheson. In one, entitled "Steel" (1963), Lee Marvin is the manager of a robot boxer who is forced to take his machine's place in the ring after it breaks down, with punishing results; "Little Girl Lost" (1962) is about a child who falls into a dimensional warp under her bed — her parents can hear her crying but cannot reach her, and finally she is saved by the family dog; "Nightmare at 20,000 Feet" (1963) stars William Shatner as a man on an airliner who keeps seeing a mysterious creature land on the wing and tamper with one of the engines; whenever he attempts to draw other people's attention to it, it vanishes. As in most of Matheson's work, PARANOIA is eventually vindicated and the creature is proved to exist.

Considering the standard of much American television in this period *TZ* stands out as an above average series. It offered some stimulating ideas instead of the customary gun-play.

Short-story versions of many of the *TZ* scripts appeared in three collections by Rod Serling: *Stories from The Twilight Zone* (1960), *More Stories from the Twilight Zone* (1961), and *New Stories from the Twilight Zone* (1962). [JB/PN]

TWO COMPLETE SCIENCE-ADVENTURE BOOKS US PULP magazine. 11 issues, Winter 1950-Spring 1954, published by Wings Publishing Co.; ed. Jerome BIXBY (Winter 1950-Summer 1951), Malcolm Reiss (Winter 1951-Summer 1953) and Katharine Daffron (Winter 1953-Spring 1954).

A companion magazine to PLANET STORIES, *TCSAB* was originally intended to reprint in cheap magazine format recently published sf novels. The first issue contained Isaac ASIMOV's *Pebble in the Sky* (1950) and L. Ron HUBBARD's short novel "The Kingslayer" (title story of *The Kingslayer*, coll. 1949). However, this policy proved impossible to sustain, and although it featured a few more reprints, the majority of subsequent stories were original to the magazine. These included Arthur C. CLARKE's "The Seeker of the Sphinx" (vt "The Road to the Sea") (Spring 1951), James BLISH's "Sword of Xota" (Summer 1951; as *The Warriors of Day* 1953) and "Sargasso of Lost Cities" (one of the "Okie" series) (Spring 1953), L. Sprague DE CAMP's *The Tritonian Ring* (Winter 1951; title story

Two Complete Science-Adventure Books. Spring 1951. Cover by Anderson.

of coll. **1953**) and John BRUNNER's first story, "The Wanton of Argus" (Summer 1953, as by Kilian Houston Brunner; as *The Space-Time Juggler* **1963**). *TCSAB* did not contain any editorial matter and was unusual among pulp sf magazines in not printing readers' letters (except in two early issues). With its last two issues a price rise (to 35¢) made it the most expensive sf pulp, a distinction it did not survive long to enjoy.   [MJE]

Collectors should note: Issues were numbered consecutively, 1–11, and marked with the season, coming out three times a year, Win., Spr. and Sum.

TWONKY, THE Film (1952). Arch Oboler Productions/United Artists. Directed by Arch Oboler, starring Hans Conreid, Billy Lynn, Gloria Blondell, Janet Warren and Ed Max. Screenplay by Arch Oboler, based on the short story by Henry KUTTNER. 72 mins. B/w.

After his sanctimonious FIVE, about five survivors of a nuclear war, Arch Oboler chose another sf subject for his next film. A creature from the future invades a TV set, bringing it to life. The set is soon controlling its owner's life, scuttling about the house doing household jobs by means of an electronic beam, but later becoming menacing and dictatorial, hypnotizing those who attempt to stop it. Kuttner's witty story is badly weakened by Oboler's script, and also by the inadequate special effects. TV was a much hated medium in Hollywood at that time, and it was only appropriate that Oboler, an old-time radio producer, should have launched this symbolic attack.   [JB/PN]

2001: A SPACE ODYSSEY Film (1968). Directed by Stanley KUBRICK, starring Keir Dullea, Gary Lockwood, William Sylvester, Leonard Rossiter and Douglas Rain (as the voice of the computer). Screenplay by Stanley Kubrick and Arthur C. CLARKE, based on an idea from Arthur C. Clarke's short story "The Sentinel". 160 mins (cut to 140). Colour.

This was the most ambitious sf film of the 1960s. Kubrick's unique production lays a gloss of METAPHYSICS over a number of traditional sf themes, including the idea, derived from Charles FORT, that "we are property". Spanning thousands of years of human development, the film begins in prehistoric time when the mysterious arrival of a alien artefact, in the form of a black monolith, triggers primitive Man into becoming a tool-user; the first tool is used as a weapon. The subsequent leap ahead to 2001 contrives to suggest that for all the awesome complexity of Man's tools, Man himself is still in a primitive stage; this impression is reinforced by the deliberate banality of exchanges between the various human characters — a kind of sterility is invoked, and ironically the most "human" character is a neurotic computer, HAL 9000. Once again alien intervention has sparked off another major step up the ladder of EVOLUTION; an alien artefact is discovered buried on the Moon, and when it beams a powerful radio signal at one of the moons of Jupiter a spaceship is sent to investigate. As a result of HAL's nervous breakdown only one of the astronauts reaches the destination. He is thrust without warning, presumably by the never-seen aliens, on a wholly disorienting trip through what appears to be inner time and INNER SPACE, and then transformed into the foetus of a superbeing. The implication is that Man is about to discard his technological toys and enter a new, transcendent state of being.

Apart from the unusually ambitious scope of its theme, *2001* is remarkable also for its visual splendour, achieved in part through some of the most convincing special effects ever produced for the screen. Conceived by Kubrick himself, and put into practice by a large team of technicians headed by Wally Veevers, Douglas TRUMBULL, Con Pederson and Tom Howard, they utilized many of the techniques from the silent era. Instead of using modern automatic matting processes, such as the blue-screen system, hand-drawn mattes were produced for each frame of film in an effects shot. In many of the effects sequences several of the various image components were combined in the camera on a single negative, thus increasing the realism of the effects but at the cost of a considerable amount of time and money, which is why such methods are now rarely used. Another of Kubrick's major innovations was to reinforce the occasionally chilling romanticism with which the action, especially the technological action, is seen, with music by Richard Strauss, Johann Strauss and Gyorgy Ligeti.

The tension which can be felt in the film between the attitudes of the two screenwriters, between Kubrick's love of the oblique and mystifying (often operating through visual symbolism and allusion) and Clarke's rationalism and openness, is resolved in the book of the film, which provides clear explanations. This, written after the completion of the film, is *2001: A Space Odyssey* (**1968**) by Clarke, who also wrote an account of his connection with the film in *The Lost Worlds of 2001* (coll. **1972**), which also prints some alternative script versions of key scenes.   [JB/PN]

TYLER, THEODORE Pseudonym of American writer Edward William Ziegler (1932–), whose sf novel *The Man Whose Name Wouldn't Fit* (**1968**) deals humorously with the computerized regimentation of a NEAR-FUTURE society.   [JC]

UFO British TV series (1969–70). An ITC/Century 21 Production. Created by Gerry and Sylvia Anderson with Reg Hill. Producer Reg Hill; executive producer Gerry Anderson. Writers on the series included Tony Barwick, David Tomblin, Ruric Powell, Dennis Spooner, Alan Fennell and Terence Feely. Directors included Gerry Anderson, David Tomblin, Alan Perry, Dave Lane, Ken Turner, Ron Appleton and Jeremy Summers. Special effects were supervised by Derek Meddings. Running time per episode: 50 mins. Colour.

Before this series the Andersons were best known for such TV puppet series as THUNDERBIRDS, though they did produce a live-action sf movie in 1969, DOPPELGANGER (vt *Journey to the Far Side of the Sun*). Most critics noted that the actors in *UFO* seemed to have been chosen for their resemblance to puppets, and the make-up, apparently deliberately, reinforced the effect. Set a few years in the future, *UFO* concerns the activities of a secret government organization formed to combat the menace of hostile FLYING SAUCERS. The special effects are impressive, but the scripts tend towards the general blandness that marks most of the Anderson productions (*see* SPACE 1999), possibly deriving from an unnecessarily patronizing attitude towards the ability of children's minds to assimilate data. *UFO* was made for children.   [JB]

Gabrielle Drake, looking just like a puppet, plays Lt. Gay Ellis in UFO.

UNCANNY STORIES US PULP magazine. One issue, Apr. 1941, published by Manvis Publications; ed. R.O. Erisman. *US* contained both sf and weird fantasy, including a story by Ray CUMMINGS, but nothing of importance. It should not be confused with the US *Uncanny Tales* (1938–40), a weird menace pulp also ed. Erisman; nor with the Canadian UNCANNY TALES, which like *US* did publish some sf. [FHP/MJE]

UNCANNY TALES Canadian PULP magazine. 21 issues, Nov. 1940-Sep. 1943. Until May 1942 it was published by the Adam Publishing Co., and thereafter by the Norman Book Co. It was edited by Lyle Kenyon ENGEL and used some original material as well as reprinting from US pulps, including WEIRD TALES, COSMIC STORIES and STIRRING SCIENCE STORIES. A US pulp with the same title was published by the Western Fiction Co. 1938–40 and edited by Robert O. Erisman, but published no

UFO INCIDENT, THE Made-for-TV film (1975). NBC. Directed by Richard A. Colla, starring James Earl Jones, Estelle Parsons, Bernard Hughes, Beeson Carroll and Dick O'Neill. Screenplay by S. Lee Pogostin and Hesper Anderson, based on *The Interrupted Journey* (**1966**) by John G. Fuller. 100 mins. Colour.

James Earl Jones (the voice behind the villain Darth Vader in *Star Wars*) tried for years, after buying the rights to Fuller's book, to secure the necessary finance to make a feature film on the subject, and eventually succeeded with Universal Television. Based on a supposedly true UFO incident that took place in 1961, the story concerns a couple who encounter a FLYING SAUCER while driving their car. Subsequent nightmares and feelings of deep-rooted anxiety lead them to seek psychiatric help which later reveals, through hypnosis, that they both possess unconscious memories of being taken from the car and examined for two hours by aliens. [JB]

UFOs (Unidentified flying objects) *See* FLYING SAUCERS.

ULTIMATE WARRIOR, THE Film (1975). Warner Bros. Directed by Robert Clouse, starring Max von Sydow, Yul Brynner, Joanna Miles and William Smith. Screenplay by Robert Clouse. 92 mins. Colour.

New York in the year 2022 is in an advanced state of decay after a man-made biological catastrophe which occurred a couple of decades earlier. The leader of a group of people, who have banded together in a barricaded street for mutual protection against gangs of thugs roaming outside, hires the services of a super samurai. He dispatches several of the

marauders with his knife and then escapes from New York accompanied by the leader's daughter.

This is really the first Kung Fu sf movie, following, as it does, the basic formula of the Kung Fu genre (two opposing camps each with their own champion fight it out to the death in the final reel) and it was produced by Fred Weintraub and Paul Heller who made Bruce Lee's *Enter the Dragon*; but it is also, surprisingly, an above average sf film. It is well scripted, unpretentious, fast-moving and cynical. There is no real difference between the "heroes" and the "villians", which is unlike the moral simplicity in most pulp sf films. [JB]

Two pulp magazines were titled UNCANNY TALES. Left, the Canadian version, March 1942, cover by K.P. Ainsworth; right, the US version, Dec. 1941, cover by Wilf Long, which was horror, not sf.

sf, being a semi-pornographic horror magazine.   [BS]

Collectors should note: *UT* was numbered consecutively, 1–21. It appeared monthly with only a few gaps until May '42; no.21 was the only issue for '43, and indeed only the last four numbers were published by the Norman Book Co., over a period of 16 months.

UNDER THE SEA The world under the sea is the only alien environment accessible to Man. Although its fringes — the littoral zone and the shallow water of the continental shelves — have always been well known, the ocean deeps provide a reservoir of mysteries. Mastery of the ocean's surfaces was gained slowly, over a period extending from the 15th century to the 19th, and as early as the 17th century John WILKINS, in *Mathematicall Magick* (**1648**), was designing submarines and talking about the possibility of underwater colonization. In the same century Cornelius Drebbell navigated a submarine rowing boat in the Thames and another inventor lost his life in Plymouth Sound. Bushnell built a submarine boat in 1775 and Robert Fulton remained under water for four hours in his egg-shaped submarine in 1800. By 1863 the *David*, a submarine built by the Confederacy during the American Civil War, was sufficiently functional to attempt a torpedo attack on an ironclad. It failed, and though its successor actually managed to sink a ship it was lost with all hands. By the 1890s, however, the French Navy was equipped with four submarines and both Germany and America were building them. The first notable literary work to feature a submarine was Théophile Gautier's romance of a plot to rescue Napoleon, *Les deux étoiles* (**1848**; exp. vt *Partie carrée* 1851; vt *La Belle Jenny*; trans. in various English collections as "The Quartette", "The Belle-Jenny" and "The Four-in-Hand"). The classic underwater romance of the 19th century was, however, Jules VERNE's *Vingt mille lieues sous les mers* (**1870**; trans. as *Twenty Thousand Leagues Under the Sea* 1873), in which the undersea world became for the first time a place of marvels and natural wonders to be explored. This particular "voyage extraordinaire" was not, however, much copied. Frank STOCKTON's *The Great Stone of Sardis* (**1898**), Harry Collingwood's *The Log of the Flying Fish* (**1887**), Herbert STRANG's *Lord of the Seas* (**1908**) and Max PEMBERTON's *Captain Black* (**1911**) all feature submarine adventures, but are concerned primarily with getting from one place to another rather than with exploring the wonders of the deep. The reason for this disinterest was the impossibility of any real interaction between human visitors and the alien environment. The visitors were primarily observers, and apart from the occasional

duel with a sea-monster (almost always a giant squid or octopus) there was little dramatic potential in their underwater ventures. For a hero to get to grips with the underwater world, a modification that would render the tale the purest of fantasy was necessary — as, for instance, in *The Water Babies* (**1863**) by Charles Kingsley. The notion of adapting men to underwater life by biological engineering did not appear until Alexander BELYAEV's *The Amphibian* (**1928** Russia; trans. as by A. Belayev **1959**). The only attempt to set aside this difficulty in the 19th and early 20th centuries was associated with stories dealing with the rediscovery of ATLANTIS — which had often, by means more or less miraculous, managed to preserve itself and its air despite its cataclysmic submersion. Examples include André LAURIE's *The Crystal City Under the Sea* (**1895**; trans. **1896**), Conan DOYLE's *The Maracot Deep* (coll; **1929**), Stanton A. COBLENTZ's *The Sunken World* (**1928**; **1949**) and Dennis WHEATLEY's *They Found Atlantis* (**1936**).

The early PULP sf writers showed relatively little interest in undersea adventures, though film-makers faced with the challenge made persistent attempts to make bigger and better versions of 20,000 LEAGUES UNDER THE SEA, from the earliest years of silent movies to the Disney version in 1955. Several pulp sf stories, however, dealt with undersea life on alien worlds. An early example is Neil R. JONES's "Into the Hydrosphere" (1933), but the classics of the species were "Clash by Night" (1943) and *Fury* (1947; **1950**; vt *Destination: Infinity* USA) by Henry KUTTNER and C.L. MOORE, writing as Lawrence O'Donnell (later editions as by Kuttner). The most notable pulp story set beneath the oceans of Earth was *The Green Girl* (1930; **1950**) by Jack WILLIAMSON. In the post-War period, however, sf writers became much more interested in the possibilities of undersea melodrama. Alien oceans figure in "The Game of Glory" (1958) by Poul ANDERSON, "The Gift of Gab" (1955) by Jack VANCE, *Lucky Starr and the Oceans of Venus* (**1954**; vt *The Oceans of Venus* UK) by Isaac ASIMOV (writing as Paul French) and in the story in which Roger ZELAZNY bade a fond farewell to the image of Venus as an oceanic world, "The Doors of His Face, the Lamps of His Mouth" (1965). The notion of adapting men to underwater life (*see* GENETIC ENGINEERING) came into magazine sf in this period, most notably in James BLISH's "Surface Tension" (1952) — though Blish had earlier introduced the notion in a more tentative form in "Sunken Universe" (1942 as by Arthur Merlyn).

The mid-1950s produced a sudden rush of sf stories set beneath the oceans of Earth. These include Frank HERBERT's submarine spy-thriller *The Dragon in the Sea* (**1956**; vt *21st Century Sub*; vt. *Under Pressure*); Arthur C. CLARKE's

novel about whale-farming, *The Deep Range* (**1954**; exp. **1957**); the first of Frederik POHL and Jack Williamson's trilogy of juveniles dealing with undersea colonization, *Undersea Quest* (**1954**); and Kenneth BULMER's melodrama *City Under the Sea* (**1957**). The Bulmer novel features the idea of surgical modification for life in the sea, and the same author took the notion of biological engineering much further in *Beyond the Silver Sky* (**1961**). The idea was also developed by Gordon R. DICKSON in *The Space Swimmers* (1963; **1967**); by Hal CLEMENT in *Ocean On Top* (1967; **1973**) and by Lee HOFFMAN in *The Caves of Karst* (**1969**). The early 1960s also saw a good deal of spin-off from the successful film VOYAGE TO THE BOTTOM OF THE SEA (1961), which was novelized as *Voyage to the Bottom of the Sea* (**1961**) by Theodore STURGEON, including a long-running TV series, one of whose episodes was novelized as *City Under the Sea* (**1965**) by Paul FAIRMAN.

The 1960s saw an increasing interest in dolphins by the scientific community, and the idea that dolphins might possess high INTELLIGENCE and were potentially able to communicate with men was popularized. Several sf stories grew out of these ideas, including the Dickson titles mentioned above, Arthur C. Clarke's *Dolphin Island* (**1963**); Joe POYER's *Operation Malacca* (**1968**); Roy MEYERS' *Dolphin Boy* (**1967**; vt. *Dolphin Rider* UK) and its sequels; Robert MERLE's *Un animal doué de raison* (**1967**; trans. as *The Day of the Dolphin* **1969**); Robert SILVERBERG's "Ishmael in Love" (1970); John BOYD's "The Girl and the Dolphin" (1973); and Ian WATSON's *The Jonah Kit* (**1975**).

There is, of course, an analogy which may be drawn between a submarine and a spaceship. The parallel is made in Harry HARRISON's *The Daleth Effect* (**1970** vt *In our Hands, the Stars* UK) in a quite straightforward way — when the heroes need a spaceship quickly they simply put their drive unit on to a submarine. In Stefan WUL's *Le temple du passé* (**1958**; trans. as *Temple of the Past* **1973**), a spaceship lands in an alien ocean and is swallowed by a whale-like creature. Much greater subtlety in the use of the analogy is seen, however, in a remarkable novel by James WHITE, *The Watch Below* (**1966**), which juxtaposes the problems of an alien spaceship nearing Earth with those of a group of people surviving in the hold of a ship which has been under water for many years. A similar analogy is drawn in Isaac Asimov's "Waterclap" (1970), which deals with a conflict of interest between projects to colonize the sea bed and the Moon.

Interest in the possibilities of the sea continues, and recent years have seen publication of a dramatic novel dealing with the genetic engineering of future generations to assure their survival after a new deluge, *Inter Ice Age 4* (**1959**; trans. **1970**) by Kobo ABÉ, and a remarkable underwater adventure story featuring a

CYBORG leviathan, *The Godwhale* (**1974**) by Thomas J. BASS. [BS]

See also: ECOLOGY; TRANSPORTATION.

UNEARTHLY STRANGER Film (1963). Independent Artists/AIP. Directed by John Krish, starring John Neville, Gabriella Lucudi, Philip Stone, Jean Marsh and Warren Mitchell. Screenplay by Rex Carlton. 74 mins. B/w.

In this low-key, unpretentious sf film a man gradually discovers that his wife (who sleeps with her eyes open) is an alien, one of many who have infiltrated Earth. She is ordered by her superiors to kill him but cannot, having fallen in love with him. Her emotional involvement with a human being destroys her ability to survive undetected and the film's strongest image is of her tears leaving corrosive tracks down her cheeks as she reveals the truth to her husband. [JB]

UNICORNS *See* FANTASY; SUPERNATURAL CREATURES.

UNIVERSE Original anthology series edited by Terry CARR. *Universe 1* (anth. **1971**) initiated the series while Carr was still an editor for its publisher; ACE BOOKS. Since then it has been the most peripatetic anthology series, its seven volumes to date issuing from three different publishers. The first volume contained Robert SILVERBERG'S NEBULA-award-winning story "Good News From The Vatican"; Silverberg has been one of the series' most regular contributors, along with Gregory BENFORD, Gordon EKLUND and Edgar PANGBORN. Benford and Eklund won a Nebula for their story "If The Stars Are Gods" in *Universe 4* (anth. **1974**). The other volumes to date are *Universe 2* (anth. **1972**), *Universe 3* (anth. **1973**), *Universe 5* (anth. **1974**), *Universe 6* (anth. **1976**) and *Universe 7* (anth. **1977**). [MJE]

UNIVERSE, THE *See* ASTRONOMY; COSMOLOGY; ENTROPY.

Dec. 1953. Cover by Mel Hunter and Malcolm H. Smith.

UNIVERSE SCIENCE FICTION *See* OTHER WORLDS.

First issue. Cover by H.W. Scott.

UNKNOWN US magazine, PULP size Mar. 1939-Aug. 1941 and Jun. 1943-Oct. 1943; BEDSHEET-size Oct. 1941-Apr. 1943. 39 issues, Mar. 1939-Oct. 1943, published by Street & Smith; ed. John W. CAMPBELL Jr.

The fantasy companion to ASTOUNDING SCIENCE-FICTION, *Unknown* was one of the most unusual of all pulp magazines, and its demise one of the most lamented. Its first issue featured Eric Frank RUSSELL'S novel *Sinister Barrier* (Mar. 1939; **1943**; rev. 1948), but a better indicator of the direction in which the magazine would develop, in the same issue, was H.L. GOLD'S story "Trouble With Water", a humorous fantasy exploiting the incongruity of confronting a 20th-century American with a figure out of folklore. While the magazine (particularly during its first year) featured some ordinary science fiction and some SWORD-AND-SORCERY stories, it quickly attracted a group of regular contributors who defined its very individual flavour. These included L. Sprague DE CAMP, with such stories as "Nothing in the Rules" (Jul. 1939), *Lest Darkness Fall* (Dec. 1939; **1941**), "The Wheels of If" (Oct. 1940) and his collaborations with Fletcher PRATT, "The Roaring Trumpet" (May 1940), "The Mathematics of Magic" (Aug. 1940) (the two together making up *The Incomplete Enchanter*, fix-up **1942**), *The Castle of Iron* (Apr. 1941; **1950**) and others. These De Camp/ Pratt stories — the "Harold Shea" series, in which the hero is transported into a series of fantasy worlds drawn from Norse mythology, Spenser's *Faerie Queene* and so forth — typify the exuberantly wacky approach to fantasy which *Unknown* made its own. Other authors who appeared frequently were L. Ron HUBBARD, with *Slaves of Sleep* (Jul. 1939; **1948**), "The Indigestible Triton" (Apr. 1940), "Fear" (Jul. 1940), "Typewriter in the Sky" (Nov.-Dec. 1940) (together in *Fear & Typewriter in The Sky*, **1951**) and many others; Fritz LEIBER, whose Fafhrd/Gray Mouser

series, although sword and sorcery, had a wry, ironic tone which suited the magazine very well, Henry KUTTNER, Theodore STURGEON, Anthony BOUCHER, Cleve CARTMILL and Jack WILLIAMSON. *Unknown* occasionally carried serials, but most issues included a complete novel, or short novel. Notable examples were Heinlein's "The Devil Makes The Law" (as "Magic, Inc." in *Waldo & Magic, Inc.*, **1950**) (Sep. 1940), Williamson's *Darker Than You Think* (Dec. 1940; **1949**), Alfred BESTER'S "Hell is Forever" (Aug. 1942), Leiber's *Conjure Wife* (Feb. 1943; **1953**) and A.E. VAN VOGT'S *The Book of Ptath* (Oct. 1943; **1947**; vt *Two Hundred Million A.D.*).

Until Jun. 1940, *Unknown* had illustrative covers of which the best (apart from the very first, by H.W. Scott) were the work of Edd CARTIER, the artist whose style most exactly caught the tone of the magazine. With the Jul. 1940 issue the magazine adopted instead a lettered cover intended to give it a more dignified appearance. In Oct. 1941 it switched, three months before *ASF*, to the larger, bedsheet format, and at the same time its name became *Unknown Worlds*. For its last three issues it returned to pulp size. The Dec. 1943 issue was to have adopted the DIGEST size which *ASF* had taken the previous month, but it never appeared: wartime paper shortages had put an end to the magazine. Its revival was mooted after the War ended, and an anthology in magazine format *From Unknown Worlds* (anth. **1948**) was put out to test the market. But *Unknown* never reappeared, although H.L. Gold's fantasy companion to GALAXY, BEYOND FANTASY FICTION, was an avowed imitation. Anthologies drawn from its pages include *The Unknown* (anth. **1963**) and *The Unknown Five* (anth. **1964**), both ed. D.R. Bensen. It appeared during Campbell's peak years as editor; *Unknown*'s reputation may stand as high as it does in part because it died while still at its best. [MJE]

Collectors should note: There were six vols, each of six nos, and a seventh with three nos. A regular monthly schedule was followed Mar. '39-Dec. '40, then regular bi-monthly Feb. '41-Oct. '43.

The British edition, from Atlas Publishing Company, was unusual in appearing for more issues (41) than the original, and for outlasting it by six years. It first appeared in Sep. '39 (Vol.2 no.1) and followed the American issues closely, while omitting stories to fit its more restricted size. It was published regularly up to Dec. '40 (Vol.4 no.4), then very intermittently for the next three years, following the American numbering but skipping issues. Like its parent, but a little later, it changed its title to *Unknown Worlds* (Jun. '42). Four unnumbered issues followed in '43-'44, and then in Spr. '45 it restarted at Vol.3 no.4 (as though the 27 issues previously published had been numbered in twelve-issue volumes) and continued until Win. '49

(Vol.4 no.5), by which time it had run out of stories to reprint.

UNKNOWN WORLDS See UNKNOWN.

UNNO, JUZA See JAPAN.

UNUSUAL STORIES US DIGEST-size magazine. Three issues, 1934–5, published by Fantasy Publishers, Everett, Pa.; ed. William L. CRAWFORD. An advance issue of this semi-professional magazine was published in 1934, and could be considered as the first issue, even though it had only 16 pages and the 1935 issues are referred to as nos 1 and 2. It was a companion magazine to MARVEL TALES. [FHP]

URANUS See OUTER PLANETS.

UTOPIAS The myth of Utopia, the Ideal State, is an ancient one. It is linked to myths of religious origin — Heaven or the Promised Land — and to the folklore relating to such dream lands as the Isles of the Blessed, but it often stands in opposition to these as a historical goal to be achieved by the active efforts of men, not as a transcendental goal reserved as a reward for those who follow a particularly virtuous path in life. The term itself was coined by Thomas MORE in *Utopia* (Latin edition **1516**; first English trans. **1551**; many since), and stands ambiguously and punningly intermediate between "eutopia" (literally well-place: a better place) and "outopia" (no place).

The extent to which Utopian literature overlaps with sf is a matter of opinion. It can be argued that all Utopias are sf in that they are exercises in hypothetical sociology and political science. Alternatively, it might be argued that only those Utopias which embody some notion of scientific advancement qualify as sf — the latter view is in keeping with most DEFINITIONS of sf. An interesting point is made by Frank Manuel in *Utopias and Utopian Thought* (**1966**): that a significant shift in Utopian thought took place when writers changed from talking about a better place (eutopia) to talking about a better time (euchronia), under the influence of the notion of historical and social progress. When this happened Utopias ceased to be imaginary constructions with which contemporary society could be compared and began to be speculative statements about real historical possibilities. It seems most sensible, without making any dogmatic declaration, to regard this as the point at which Utopian literature takes on a conceptual similarity to sf.

The scientific imagination first became influential in Utopian thinking in the 17th century. An awareness of the advancement of scientific knowledge and of the role that science might play in transforming society first appears in BACON's *New Atlantis* (1627; **1629**) and

CAMPANELLA's *City of the Sun* (**1637**). The former introduced the notion of the Utopian potential of technological advance with quite extravagant claims. However, though it was a popular work, and inspired at least two later writers to undertake its completion ("R.H. esq." in 1660 and Jos. Glanvil in 1676), it provoked little further thought along the same lines for many years. *The Blazing World* (**1668**) by Margaret Cavendish shows a rather different awareness of science, presenting a thorough-going mockery of the endeavours of scientists. SWIFT, in *Gulliver's Travels* (**1726**), and Samuel JOHNSON, in *Rasselas* (**1759**), also parodied the efforts of scientists and inventors, criticizing their imagination as over-fanciful, and their unworldliness.

In the second half of the 18th century, however, a French school of philosophy took up the idea of progress, and one of its members, L.S. MERCIER, produced the first "euchronian" novel, *Memoirs of the Year 2500* (**1772**), which proposed that the perfectibility of mankind was not only possible, but inevitable, with the aid of science, mathematics and the mechanical arts. Another member of the school, RESTIF DE LA BRETONNE, concluded his *La découverte australe par un homme volant, ou le Dédale français* (**1781**) ["The Southern Hemisphere Discovery by a Flying Man, or the French Daedalus"] with a description of a Utopian state based on the principles of natural philosophy and scientific advancement.

Despite the international popularity of Mercier's book the 19th century was well advanced before the Utopian potential of scientific progress was celebrated in English literature. Jane LOUDON's anonymous *The Mummy* (**1827**) is usually described as a GOTHIC novel, but may be better regarded as the first scientific romance, with Utopian overtones. Mary GRIFFITH's *Three Hundred Years Hence* (1836; **1975**) was the first American Utopian novel to endorse Mercier's optimism wholeheartedly.

In many of the classic English Utopian romances of the 19th century there is a strong vein of anti-scientific romanticism. Bulwer LYTTON's *The Coming Race* (**1870**) belongs with the author's occult romances rather than with scientific Utopias. Samuel BUTLER's SATIRICAL *Erewhon* (**1872**) and its sequel are PASTORAL and anti-mechanical in so far as they are Utopian at all. W.H. HUDSON's *A Crystal Age* (**1887**) is very much a dream story, whose pastoral Ideal State is inaccessible to the civilized man who stumbles into it. Richard JEFFERIES' *After London* (**1885**) is most extreme of all in its nostalgia for barbarism, presenting images of dead cities that have poisoned the Earth. This nostalgic conservatism did not, however, extend to America, by then the homeland of progress. Edward BELLAMY's best-selling *Looking Backward* (**1888**) brought the myth to a glorious resurgence of popularity, and was

followed by a great many replies in kind. Most of the dissenting voices objected to Bellamy's socialism on political grounds, but the most famous of the replies, William MORRIS's *News From Nowhere* (**1890**) objected to its acceptance of technology and to the prospect of Man's living in idleness while machines supplied his needs.

Bellamy's book was undeniably naïve, but it became the archetype of a whole school of mechanized Utopias. A host of novels glorifying technology followed in its wake, including *A.D. 2000* (**1890**) by Alvarado FULLER, *The Crystal Button* (**1891**) by Chauncey THOMAS and *Limanora* (**1903**) by Godfrey SWEVEN. Other nations discovered prophets of technological Utopia: Walter Rathenau in Germany wrote *In Days to Come* (**1921**) and *The New Society* (**1921**), while H.G. WELLS in England wrote *A Modern Utopia* (**1905**), *Men Like Gods* (**1923**) and *The Shape of Things to Come* (**1933**). Rathenau and Wells were somewhat more sophisticated than Bellamy, but they had one contemporary in America who was notably less so: Hugo GERNSBACK.

Gernsback was a confirmed "euchronian", who believed that a Utopian state would be the inevitable product of technological progress, and set about lending what aid he could, both practically and imaginatively. In his magazine *Modern Electrics* he serialized his own Utopian romance *Ralph 124C 41+* (1911–12; **1925**), and he conceived of his literary genre of "scientifiction" primarily as promoting the magnificent potential of modern technology.

Long before Gernsback tried to initiate sf as a "euchronian" genre the Utopian dream had been questioned on the grounds of practicality. Aristotle had doubted the workability of PLATO's *Republic* (fourth century BC) on the grounds that its citizens would lack incentives to make them work. At the end of the 18th century Malthus had objected to the Utopian optimism of William Godwin, and set out to prove in his "Essay on Population" that peace and plenty could not easily be achieved. In opposition to Bellamy's faith in social evolution Ignatius DONNELLY had written *Caesar's Column* (**1890**), arguing that society's present historical course was leading toward greater inequality and social injustice (*see* DYSTOPIAS). By the time AMAZING STORIES was founded in 1926, however, a new kind of Utopian criticism had grown up — criticism not on grounds of practicality but on grounds of *desirability*. Anatole FRANCE, in *The White Stone* (1905; trans. **1910**), had a citizen of a future Utopian state declare that peace and plenty is all very well, but insufficient to ensure happiness, which is a problem of an entirely different kind. E.M. FORSTER, in "The Machine Stops" (1909), objected much more fiercely that the Utopian dream of Wells was sterile, and would lead to such stagnation of the human mind that Man would become dependent upon his machines and helpless in the face of catastrophe. Alexandr MOSZKOWSKI's *The Isles of Wisdom* (1924) tried to show that all Utopian schemes were absurd, and if imposed upon real people would rapidly become self-parodies. By 1926 there had already been a considerable loss of faith in Utopian thought, and especially in the hope of technological Utopia. Wells was yet to produce *The Shape of Things to Come* (1933), but that would be the last major technological Utopian novel, and it appeared a year later than Aldous HUXLEY's *Brave New World* (1932) — a devastating attack on scientific Utopianism (as expressed in *Daedalus*, 1924, an essay by J.B.S. HALDANE) which became a powerful myth in its own right.

Because of these circumstances, despite Gernsback's inspiration and intention, sf was never strongly Utopian. The early sf pulps abounded with adventure stories set in pseudo-Utopian futures where poverty and injustice, if they still exist, are nowhere in evidence, but when writers turned their attention away from adventure toward the prospects facing society as a whole doubt and pessimism were obvious. Miles J. BREUER, in "Paradise and Iron" (1930), Laurence MANNING and Fletcher PRATT in "City of the Living Dead" (1930) and John W. CAMPBELL Jr in "Twilight" (1934 as by Don A. Stuart) all foresaw decadence and decline for humanity as a result of overdependence on machines. Utopia is present in early genre sf, but only in the background — perhaps the most eloquent testimony to its presence and its situation is provided by the illustrations of Frank R. PAUL, whose magnificent cities fade away into vagueness behind his central motifs, which are usually individual machines or confrontations between rather wooden humans. Where Utopian states occur in manifest form, as in *The Sunken World* (1928; 1949) by Stanton COBLENTZ, they tend to be small enclaves facing imminent destruction — and at the end of such novels the hero almost always has to forsake the crumbling dream to return to the real world. This, in fact, is the fate of the Utopian dream outside the sf establishment too — it is relegated to the status of the Isles of the Blessed as a pleasant impossibility, in a series of novels from James HILTON's *Lost Horizon* (1933) to Aldous Huxley's *Island* (1962).

Utopian thought in the last half century has to a large extent dissociated itself from the idea of progress and connected itself to the idea of an "historical retreat" to a simpler life. In this vein we discover the immensely weighty *Islandia* (1942) by Austin Tappan WRIGHT, *Seven Days in New Crete* (1949; vt *Watch the North Wind Rise* USA) by Robert GRAVES, Huxley's *Island* and *In Watermelon*

Sugar (1968) by Richard BRAUTIGAN. Even the recent past has been restored, by the momentum of nostalgia, to the status of a pseudo-Utopia in such novels as *Time and Again* (1970) by Jack FINNEY. Outside this trend there have been one or two Utopian designs following up individual hobby-horses, including *Walden Two* (1948) by the behavourist psychologist B.F. SKINNER and *Erone* (1943) by Chalmers KEARNEY, but there have been only two large-scale attempts to imagine a technologically developed future state which is in any sense of the word ideal, and both are distinctly ambiguous. In Herman HESSE's *Magister Ludi* (1943; trans. 1950; vt *The Glass Bead Game*) the hero finally rejects the ideal on which his society is based. In Franz WERFEL's *Star of the Unborn* (1946; trans. 1946) there is no rejection, largely because the future state retains, as well as its miraculous technology, the Catholic faith of the author, but there is a good deal of doubt on both practical and ethical grounds about whether the Utopian ideal can or should be maintained. In this Utopia there is still rebellion, war, and a certain amount of horror.

Within genre sf those novels which can be adduced as examples of analytical Utopian thought retain the same deep ambiguity tending towards rejection. Theodore STURGEON, in *Venus Plus X* (1960), constructs a hermaphrodite Utopia for evaluation by a man of our time, but the society fails the test. Ursula K. LE GUIN's *The Dispossessed* (1974) carries the subtitle "An Ambiguous Utopia" to proclaim its uncertainty, and Samuel R. DELANY's *Triton* (1976), presumably in response, is subtitled "An Ambiguous Heterotopia", forsaking even the word, which has been devalued along with the dream.

Two of the sf writers who have won most fame within the genre, Isaac ASIMOV and Arthur C. CLARKE, both remain convinced of the beneficence of technological advance, but this optimism finds no Utopian expression in their works, with the exception of Clarke's most recent and most selfconscious novel, *Imperial Earth* (1975). Clarke's earlier work includes *The City and the Stars* (1956), whose portrayal of the city of Diaspar deliberately echoes "The Machine Stops" and "Twilight" in its rejection of the stasis of Utopia; and *Childhood's End* (1953), a classic work which stands at the beginning of a well-established trend in sf of turning away from social or political solutions of Man's problems towards a transcendental "salvation". Asimov's most memorable images of future Earth are to be found in the Dystopian *Pebble in the Sky* (1950) and the agoraphobic society of *The Caves of Steel* (1954). His most famous work, the *Foundation* trilogy (1951–3), begins with the fall of Utopian Trantor.

Two sf writers have, in recent years,

produced Utopian novels in protest against the dominant pessimism of American sf: Mack REYNOLDS in the Bellamy-inspired *Looking Backward, From the Year 2000* (1973), with its sequel *Equality: in the Year 2000* (1977), and Ray NELSON in *Then Beggars Could Ride* (1976). It is possible that these novels may herald a new trend, but they are not impressive.

The spirit of RUSSIAN sf, which enjoyed something of a renaissance in the late 1950s, was at first very different from that of Anglo-American sf. The single work most responsible for the revival of the genre in Russia, Ivan YEFREMOV's *Andromeda* (1958; trans. 1959), looks forward to the socialist Utopia promised by Marx, and features a more enthusiastic championship of the alliance of technology and socialism than may be found even in Bellamy or Wells. Such Soviet sf as has been more recently translated, however, shows little evidence of this enthusiasm, and the novels of Arkady and Boris STRUGATSKI in particular — including *Hard to Be a God* (1964; trans. 1973) and *The Final Circle of Paradise* (1965; trans. 1976) — exhibit an anxiety comparable to that of contemporary Western sf.

Genre sf, which Hugo Gernsback intended to establish as a Utopian literature, has, in fact, in its 50-year history, seen the decline and fall of Utopia and the dereliction of the Utopian image of the future.

Notable studies of Utopian literature include: *The Image of the Future* (rev. edition 1973) by Fred Polak, *Utopias Old and New* (1938) by Harry Ross, *Utopian Fantasy: a Study of English Utopian Fiction Since The End of the Nineteenth Century* by Richard Gerber (1955), and *Yesterday's Tomorrows* (1968) by W.H.G. ARMYTAGE. A relevant thematic anthology is *The New Improved Sun: An Anthology of Utopian Science Fiction* (anth. 1976) ed. Thomas M. DISCH. [BS]
See also: CITIES; ECONOMICS; HISTORY OF SF; MAINSTREAM WRITERS OF SF; OPTIMISM AND PESSIMISM; PASTORAL; PROTO SF; SOCIOLOGY.

VALE, RENA (1898–). American writer who began publishing sf with the novella "The Shining City" for *Science*

Fiction Quarterly in 1952; in the same year she published the fantasy *The Red Court* (**1952**). Her activity has since been restricted to novels, beginning with *Beyond the Sealed World* (**1965**). *Taurus Four* (**1970**) combines satire with SPACE OPERA in a story involving hippies lost on another planet, a sociologist, and an alien INVASION. *The Day After Doomsday; A Fantasy of Time Travel* (**1970**) sends 15 selected survivors of a DISASTER on Earth back in time 50,000 years, for mysterious reasons. [JC]

Other works: *The House on Rainbow Leap* (**1973**).

See also: CITIES.

VALENTINE, VICTOR (? –). British writer whose novel *Cure for Death* (**1960**) deals routinely with a ray that cures not only cancer but ageing as well, creating a dangerous race of immortals. [JC]

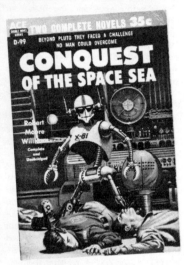

A typical robot cover by Ed. VALIGURSKY. Ace Books, 1955.

VALIGURSKY, ED(WARD I.) (1926–). American illustrator. Born in Pennsylvania, he attended the Art Institute of Chicago and the American Academy of Arts before graduating from the Art Institute of Pittsburgh. He began as an associate art director for Ziff-Davis in 1952 and became art director for Quinn Publishing in 1953. In 1954, EV began freelancing with paperback book and advertising illustrations; he did covers for ACE BOOKS, AVON, BALLANTINE BOOKS, Berkely Books, Dell, Doubleday, Pocket Books, Pyramid Books and others. He is perhaps best known for the 78 covers he painted for AMAZING STORIES and FANTASTIC, 1955-61, and for his Ace Double covers in the 1950s and early '60s. These latter featured some of the finest, most menacing ROBOTS ever to lend a weird grace to sf. He generally depicted metallic objects with great skill, and his needle-nosed spaceships were often imitated. Since EV left sf illustration his

paintings have been featured on *Popular Mechanics, The Reader's Digest* and in various publications for the aerospace market. [JG]

VAMPIRES *See* GOTHIC SF; SUPERNATURAL CREATURES.

VAN ARNAM, DAVE Form of his name used professionally by American writer David G. van Arnam (? –), who began writing sf with the novelization from the television series LOST IN SPACE, *Lost in Space* (**1967**), written with Ron Archer (Ted WHITE); *Sideslip* (**1968**) was also written with Ted White who this time used his own name. Further routine sf adventures by DVA are *Star Gladiator* (**1967**), *The Players of Hell* (**1968**), *Starmind* (**1969**), *Star Barbarian* (**1969**), *Wizard of Storms* (**1970**), *Lord of Blood* (**1970**) and *Greyland* (**1972**). [JC]

VAN CAMPEN, KARL *See* John W. CAMPBELL Jr.

VANCE, GERALD Ziff-Davis house name, used by Chester S. GEIER, Roger P. Graham (Rog PHILLIPS), Randall GARRETT in collaboration with Robert SILVERBERG, and on over 30 stories whose authors have not been identified.

VANCE, JACK (John Holbrook Vance) (1920–). American writer. Educated at the University of California first as a mining engineer, then a physics major, and finally in journalism, JV has since had a varied career; his first story, "The World Thinker" (1945), was written while he was serving in the Merchant Navy during the Second World War. It appeared in *TWS*. During the late 1940s and early 1950s JV contributed a variety of short stories (on one occasion using the pseudonym John Holbrook) and novels to the pulp magazines, primarily STARTLING STORIES and *TWS*. These included the "Magnus Ridolph" series, chronicling the adventures of a roguish interstellar troubleshooter. Part of the series was collected as *The Many Worlds of Magnus Ridolph* (coll. **1966**); the other stories are "Hard Luck Diggings" (1948), "Sanatoris Short-Cut" (1948), "The Sub-Standard Sardines" (1949) and "Cosmic Hotfoot" (1950).

JV's first published book was *The Dying Earth* (coll. **1950**), which consisted of six previously unpublished stories, fantasies set on Earth in the FAR FUTURE. They showed him to be a writer of considerable imagination and developing style. He later returned to this setting with *The Eyes of the Overworld* (fix-up **1966**), "Morreion" (**1973**), "The Seventeen Virgins" (1974) and "The Bagful of Dreams" (1977). (A direct sequel to *The Eyes of the Overworld* by another hand is *A Quest for Simbilis*, **1974**, by Michael SHEA.)

JV's magazine stories, while primarily fast-moving adventure stories, exhibited

further evidence of his ability to devise strange future worlds and quirky, exotic societies. The most notable example from this period was *Big Planet* (1952 *Startling Stories*; **1957**; all book versions to 1977 are abridged), which describes a huge, Earthlike world on which a great variety of social systems have found space to coexist. His interest in ANTHROPOLOGY and SOCIOLOGY was apparent in the care and detail with which these creations were presented. Other titles, less ambitious but with interesting incidental invention, included *Son of the Tree* (1951 *TWS*; **1964**), *Slaves of the Klau* (1952 *Space Stories* as "Planet of the Damned"; abridged **1958**) and *The Houses of Iszm* (1954 *Startling Stories*; **1964**).

JV was considerably less prolific in the latter part of the 1950s, but the stories he did publish made interesting contributions to various sf themes: COMMUNICATION in "The Gift of Gab" (1955), IMMORTALITY in *To Live Forever* (**1956**), LINGUISTICS in *The Languages of Pao* (**1958**). The main thrust of his work, however, as seen in such stories as "The Miracle Workers" (1958), was towards increasingly ambitious explorations of the theme of LIFE ON OTHER WORLDS. In JV's work this generally means human life, sometimes altered physically, always adapted culturally, to create what is essentially a fantasy world. These worlds may occasionally be linked notionally to Earth by conventional sf trappings (generally of little actual relevance); but basically they are timeless, placeless worlds, exotic locales where mankind has developed different codes and institutions by which to live. *The Dragon Masters* (**1963**), a short novel which won JV his first HUGO award, clearly illustrates this trend. Set on a distant world in the distant future it is a story grounded in GENETIC ENGINEERING, but the science is so far advanced that it could equally be considered magic.

As JV's created worlds became richer and more complex, so too did his style. Always tending towards the baroque, it developed by the time of *The Dragon Masters* into a characteristic prose, highly mannered, somewhat pedantic, with a judiciously effective use of unusual vocabulary and a detached and ironic narrative voice. JV's talent for naming the people and places in his stories (a mixture of exotic invented terms and commonplace words with the right resonance) contributes to the unusual atmosphere of his work. Three novels, similar in structure, show these talents at their fullest stretch: *The Blue World* (**1966**), *Emphyrio* (**1969**) and *The Anome* (**1973**). Each follows the life of a boy born into and growing up in a static, stratified society, with which he comes into conflict, eventually being driven into rebellion. The invented world in each is particularly carefully thought out. Both *Emphyrio* and *The Anome* additionally feature some piercing satire of RELIGION.

JV has produced several series of novels, with mixed results. He sometimes gives the impression of losing interest in a story once the setting has been fully established, so that the later books in a series may seem routine by comparison with their predecessors. This is the case with the "Planet of Adventure" series — *City of the Chasch* (1968), *Servants of the Wankh* (1969), *The Dirdir* (1969) and *The Pnume* (1970) — and with the "Durdane" trilogy — *The Anome, The Brave Free Men* (1973) and *The Asutra* (1974). The earlier "Demon Princes" series, an interstellar saga of vengeance projected to fill five novels, remains incomplete, with three volumes so far published: *The Star King* (1964), *The Killing Machine* (1964) and *The Palace of Love* (1967). A more recent series of rather loosely connected novels contains *Trullion: Alastor 2262* (1973), *Marune: Alastor 993* (1975) and *Wyst: Alastor 1716* (1978). *Showboat World* (1975) is set on Big Planet, but has no other connection with the earlier novel. (It is also linked, by a reference, to *Emphyrio*; and in fact many of JV's stories may be thought of as taking place in the same future universe, although they are not rigorously connected.)

JV has written comparatively little short fiction. Apart from those stories already mentioned, the best include "Telek" (1952), "The Moon Moth" (1961) and the novella *The Last Castle* (1967), which won JV his second Hugo, as well as a NEBULA. "The Moon Moth", one of JV's most elaborate stories, features the use of music as a secondary form of communication. Music and other ARTS feature in several other JV stories, including *Space Opera* (1965), *Emphyrio*, *The Anome* and *Showboat World*. Many of JV's best short stories are included in *Eight Fantasms and Magics* (coll. 1969; vt *Fantasms and Magics* with two stories taken out) and *The Best of Jack Vance* (coll. 1976). The latter collection is also notable for containing informative commentaries on the stories included, as JV is renowned for his reticence concerning himself and his stories, maintaining such a low profile that a rumour, which started in 1950, that he was another Henry KUTTNER pseudonym was still being perpetuated in some quarters 20 years later, notwithstanding Kuttner's death in 1958.

JV has also written mystery novels. His *The Man in the Cage* (1960) won the prestigious Edgar award. He also wrote scripts for the television series CAPTAIN VIDEO. [MJE]

Other works: *The Space Pirate* (1950 *Startling Stories*; 1953; vt abridged *The Five Gold Bands*), *Vandals of the Void* (1953); *Future Tense* (coll. 1964); *The World Between* (coll. 1965; vt *The Moon Moth* UK); *Monsters in Orbit* (1952 *TWS* as "Abercrombie Station" and "Cholwell's Chickens"; abridged 1965); *The Brains of Earth* (1966); *The Worlds of Jack Vance* (coll. 1973); *The Gray Prince* (1974); *Maske: Theary* (1976).

See also: ABSURDIST SF; ALIENS; ASTEROIDS; COLONIZATION OF OTHER WORLDS; CRIME AND PUNISHMENT; CYBORGS; ECOLOGY; FANTASTIC VOYAGES; FANTASY; GALACTIC EMPIRES; GAMES AND SPORTS; MAGIC; MONEY; PSYCHOLOGY; SPACE OPERA; SUPERMAN; SUPERNATURAL CREATURES; SWORD AND SORCERY; TABOOS; TRANSPORTATION; VILLAINS; UNDER THE SEA.

VAN DONGEN's covers are vigorous and roughly textured. This example, Nov. 1952, launched a new magazine.

VAN DONGEN, (HENRY R). (? –). American illustrator. He is mainly remembered for his work for *ASF* Aug. 1951-Nov. 1961, during which period he executed many interior illustrations and 107 covers out of a total of 124. HRVD's first cover was for *Super Science Stories*, and he worked also for *Science Fiction Adventures, Worlds Beyond* and others. After more than a decade of inactivity so far as sf illustration went, he re-entered the field in 1976 with book cover paintings for BALLANTINE BOOKS, especially their DEL REY imprint. His style is distinctive; his human figures are thin and tall. His b/w illustrations have strong lines and a good sense of design; his covers are in fairly subdued colours. The 1976 covers, however, shine with colours that match almost anything in the field. [JG]

VAN GREENAWAY, PETER (1929–) British lawyer who has been a full-time writer since 1960; of his several novels, *The Crucified City* (1962), his first, is a post-HOLOCAUST story set in a devastated London after a nuclear bomb is dropped; *The Man who held the Queen to Ransom and Sent Parliament Packing* (1968) presents a NEAR-FUTURE coup attempt in England. [JC]

Other works: *The Medusa Touch* (1973).

VANGUARD SCIENCE FICTION US DIGEST-size magazine. One issue, Jun.

The only issue. Cover by Ed Emsh.

1958, published by Vanguard Science Fiction; ed. James BLISH. *VSF* made a promising début: its stories included "Reap the Dark Tide" (vt "Shark Ship") by C.M. KORNBLUTH, and it contained what were intended as regular features by L. Sprague DE CAMP and Lester DEL REY. However, the decision to fold the magazine was made before the first issue even appeared. [MJE]

VAN HERCK, PAUL (1938–). Belgian writer. His *Sam, of de Plutertag* (1968; trans. as *Where Were You Last Pluterday?* 1973) is a SATIRE about a society in which the higher classes have access to an extra day of the week. [JC]

VAN HERP, JACQUES (1923–). Belgian critic and editor. A mathematician by training, he has written many books for children, including sf, under the pseudonym of Michel Jansen. He is one of the first literate sf critics to have discussed the genre in French publications, notably *Fiction* and *Satellite*, from the mid-1950s, with interesting pieces on Maurice RENARD, H.P. LOVECRAFT, A. MERRITT, Edgar Rice BURROUGHS, A.E. VAN VOGT and many of the French 19th-century precursors of sf. His *Panorama de la science-fiction* ["A Panorama of sf"] (1973) is an idiosyncratic book analysing some, but not all, of sf's major themes with genuine depth and insight, although it strongly emphasizes pre-20th-century work and is anti-American and pro-French in bias. JVH has been, since 1974, the editor of the Le Masque sf imprint with the Librairie des Champs Élysées. [MJ/PN]

See also: FRANCE.

VAN LHIN, ERIK See Lester DEL REY.

VAN LORNE, WARNER Pseudonymous author of a number of stories in ASTOUNDING SCIENCE FICTION, from 1935-9. Of these, "The Blue-Men of Yrano" (1939) is probably the best remembered, though not by reason of its quality. WVL's identity remained secret, although it was acknowledged that F. Orlin TREMAINE wrote one story published under the name. The remainder have been ascribed to his brother, Nelson Tremaine, although the possibility must remain that they were all the work of the former. [MJE]

VAN LUSTBADER, ERIC (? –). American author, and journalist on rock music and film subjects. His first sf book, *The Sunset Warrior* (**1977**), is volume one of a projected HEROIC FANTASY trilogy, set in an underground society of military hierarchies. [PN]

VAN SCYOC, SYDNEY J(OYCE) (1939–). American writer, active in the Unitarian Church, who began publishing sf with "Shatter the Wall" for *Gal.* in 1962, and has contributed stories regularly to the magazines since, though she is best known for her novels, beginning with the impressive *Salt Flower* (**1971**), in which aliens seed Earth, producing a new breed of "men". *Assignment Nor'Dyren* (**1973**) combines a DYSTOPIAN Earth and a complexly rendered alien planet in trouble; *Starmother* (**1976**) and *Cloudcry* (**1977**) are both set in a galaxy dominated by Man, but on alien planets where men are faced with fundamental challenges to their sense of order and rightness. Though her work is sometimes vitiated by narrative longueurs, SJVS's strong sense of the deep strangeness of the universe makes her work sometimes compelling. [JC]

VANSITTART, PETER (1920–). English writer, best known for his densely written historical novels. *I am the World* (**1942**), like *The Game and the Ground* (**1956**), generalizes its politically speculative plot by placing it in an allegorized and unnamed country; in the first novel, the career of a dictator is so remarkable that the world he creates is a UTOPIA of sorts. *The Story Teller* (**1968**) offers no sf explanation for the longevity of its central character, whose lifespan extends over 500 years and the stages of whose life are analogous to the development of northern European civilization, but the novel's narrative and linguistic powers deserve notice. *The Dark Tower: Tales from the Past* (**1969**) is a juvenile with fantasy elements. [JC]

VAN TUYL, ZAARA (ROSEALTHEA) (1901–). American writer. Her sf novel is *Skyways for Doorian* (**1967**). [JC]

VAN VOGT, A(LFRED) E(LTON) (1912–). Canadian-born American writer who moved to the United States in 1944 after establishing his name as one of the creators of John W. CAMPBELL's GOLDEN AGE of sf in *ASF* with a flood of material, starting with "Black Destroyer" in 1939, though he had been active for

In *Reflections of A.E. van Vogt*, 1975, the author claims this as the only decent photo ever taken of him.

several years in various other genres. Also in 1939, he married the writer E. Mayne HULL, and produced several stories with her to 1950, when she stopped writing. With his conversion to DIANETICS, also in 1950, AEVV stopped producing new sf material, and was effectively silent for several years. Recently, however, a second, though smaller flood of new material has come from his pen.

From 1939 to 1947, AEVV published at least 35 sf stories in *ASF* alone, some of novel length, and it is the work of these years, much of it only published in book form long afterwards in reconstructed versions, that has given him his high reputation as a master of the intricate, metaphysical SPACE OPERA. It was during these years that AEVV, along with Isaac ASIMOV and Robert A. HEINLEIN, and to a lesser extent Theodore STURGEON, seemed nearly alone to create, by writing what Campbell wanted to publish, the first genuinely successful period of American sf; only in this GOLDEN AGE did American sf begin to achieve, in literary terms, what its writers had abandoned 20 years earlier when they became writers of PULP fiction for a restricted, generally adolescent market. Although AEVV catered for this market, he intensified the emotional impact and complexity of the stories it would bear; his nearly invincible alien beasts, the long time-spans of his tales, the TIME PARADOXES they were filled with, the quasi-messianic SUPERMEN who came into their own as their stories progressed, the empires they tended to rule, all were presented in a prose that used crude, dark colours but whose striking sense of wonder was conveyed with a dreamlike conviction. The complications of plot for which he became so well known, and which have been so scathingly mocked for their illogic and preposterousness (within narratives that claim to be presenting

higher forms of logic to the reader), are best analysed, and their effects best understood, it has been argued, when their sudden shifts of perspective and rationale and scale are seen as analogous to the movements of a dream. It is these "HARD-SF dreams", so grippingly void of constraints, or of the usual surrealistic appurtenances of dream literature, that have so haunted generations of children and adolescents.

AEVV's first novel, and perhaps still his best known, is *Slan* (1940 *ASF*; **1946**; rev. 1951). Its protagonist, the young Slan Jommy Cross, is a member of a MUTANT race originally created to help mankind out of its difficulties, but long driven into hiding because of the jealousy of normals. Jommy's powers (*see* CHILDREN IN SF), which include TELEPATHY, physical superiority to normals (he has two hearts), and extraordinary intelligence, enable him to survive the mobbing and death of his mother, and a secret adolescence and young manhood; as a man he becomes involved with Earth's mysterious dictator, with defective Slans and with various intrigues centering on new sources of energy; matters are only cleared up at the book's close with the revelation that the dictator is a secret Slan, that the girl Slan with whom Jommy is in love, is, in fact, the dictator's daughter, and that Jommy is in line for the succession. As a model for the creation of wish-fulfilment stories, *Slan* has inspired many imitations.

It is in the two volumes of the "Weapon Shops" series, however, *The Weapon Shops of Isher* (1941–2 *ASF*, 1949 *Thrilling Wonder Stories*; fix-up **1951**) and *The Weapon Makers* (1943 *ASF*; **1946**; rev. 1952; vt *One Against Eternity*), that AEVV's mixture of "hard-sf dreams", enormous complications and transcendent superheroes is most hypnotically presented. The main protagonist of the two books, the immortal Robert Hedrock, has not only in the dim past created the Weapon Shops as a libertarian countervailing force to the imperial world government long dominant on Earth, but eventually turns out to have been the literal begetter of the race of emperors and empresses traditionally opposed to the mysterious Shops, which are invulnerable and sell weapons to anyone. To cap this dream of omnipotence, Hedrock unwittingly passes a Galactic initiation test at the end of the second volume; the test has been designed to select the next rulers of the "sevagram". The first appearance of the word "sevagram" is as the last word of *The Weapon Makers*; in its placing, and space-operatic resonance, and mysteriousness (for its precise meaning is unclear), this use of "sevagram" may well stand as the best working demonstration in the whole of genre sf of how to impart a sense of wonder.

The second major series of AEVV's prolific decade, comprised of *The World* of $\bar{A}$ (1945 *ASF*; rev. **1948**; rev. with introduction 1970; vt *The World of Null-A*) and *The Pawns of Null-A* (1948–9 *ASF* as "The Players of $\bar{A}$"; **1956**; vt *The Players of Null-A* UK), may seem weightier in its attempts to present its arguments in terms of "anti-Aristotelean" thought (*see* GENERAL SEMANTICS), a claim which may seem ominously to prefigure a rationalization of the effortless dream logic of the earlier stories, but tends to stumble into excessive tangles of complication. The protagonist, Gosseyn (go sane), lacks humour even more decidedly than his superman predecessors, and his rapid, confusing, nearly emotionless shifting from one Gosseyn body to another, in a kind of CLONING without the idea of cloning to sustain it, makes his eventual supremacy so peculiarly disorganized as to be almost without effect on the reader. By this time AEVV was nearing the end of his association with *ASF*, after an extraordinarily productive decade, and would soon stop writing entirely; perhaps *The Pawns of Null-A*, which extended in magazine form to 100,000 words, was about as far as he could go without an extended breather. Certainly his third series from this period, made up of *Empire of the Atom* (1946–7 *ASF*; fix-up **1956**) and *The Wizard of Linn* (1950 *ASF*; **1962**), is written at a lower degree of intensity; James BLISH has argued of this series about superscience and palace politics that its plot and characters closely resemble those of Robert GRAVES's Claudius novels.

During this first decade of his career, AEVV also contributed material to *ASF*'s sister magazine, *Unknown*, most notably *The Book of Ptath* (1943 *Unknown*; **1947**; vt *200,000,000 A.D.*; vt *Ptath*) a FAR-FUTURE epic in which a reincarnation god-figure must fight to re-establish his suzerainty. Some of the independent stories of these years were collected in *Destination Universe* (coll. **1952**) and *Away and Beyond* (coll. **1952**; paperback ed. is abridged). *The Voyage of the Space Beagle* (1939–43 *ASF*, 1950 *Other Worlds*; fix-up **1950**; vt *Mission Interplanetary*) marshals several early stories into a chronicle depicting various ways in which "Nexialist" Elliot Grosvenor copes with problems by using a response to ALIENS and their environments that synthesizes different fields of knowledge; various monsters are detected and dealt with. The book incorporates AEVV's first two sf stories. Nexialism itself, which involves a system of intensive psychological training, is an interesting prefiguring of L. Ron HUBBARD's dianetics, with which AEVV was to become so closely involved. This involvement was the culmination of his persistent interest in all training systems which purport scientifically (or PSEUDO-SCIENTIFICALLY) to create physical or mental superiority and awaken dormant talents. Not only had he written

the two general semantics novels described above; he also wrote a novel inspired by the Bates system of eye exercises, which endeavoured to rectify eye problems through partly mental means: *Siege of the Unseen* (1946 *ASF* as "The Chronicler"; **1959**; vt as title story in *The Three Eyes of Evil*, coll. **1973** UK; which coll. vt *Earth's Last Fortress and Three Eyes of Evil*).

In his autobiographical *Reflections of A.E. van Vogt* (**1975**), AEVV uses the term "fix-up" in the same sense in which it has been taken over for use in this Encyclopedia — to define a book made up of stories previously published, but altered to fit together, usually with the addition of new cementing material; the end product is generally marketed as a novel, though it tends to read more episodically than most novels. It is possible that AEVV invented the term, for although fix-ups are not unknown outside sf, the peculiar marketing circumstances of the genre in America encouraged their creation, and it is certainly the case that AEVV has written (or compiled) more fix-ups than any other sf writer of stature. It was during his time of relative inactivity as a producer of original material — the 1950s and early '60s — that he began producing these numerous fix-ups, including of course *The Weapon Shops of Isher*, perhaps the most successful and ingenious of all. Fix-ups incorporating Golden Age material include *The Mixed Men* (1943–5 *ASF*; fix-up **1952**; vt abridged *Mission to the Stars*), *The War Against the Rull* (1940–50 *ASF*; fix-up **1959**), *The Beast* (1943–4 *ASF*; fix-up **1963**; vt *Moonbeast* UK) and *Quest for the Future* (1943–6 *ASF*; fix-up **1970**).

The Silkie (1964–7 *If*; fix-up **1969**) is technically similar, but is the first to use substantially contemporary material, and signals the beginning of AEVV's second period of productivity, with *Children of Tomorrow* (**1970**) being his first completely new sf novel since *The Mind Cage* (**1957**), though he had also published a political thriller about the attempted brainwashing of Westerners in contemporary Communist China, *The Violent Man* (**1962**). Perhaps the most sustained of his recent output is *The Battle of Forever* (**1971**), in which the enhanced-human protagonist, Modyun, leaves the refuge where his kind had dwelt in seclusion for aeons, and undertakes a far-future odyssey through a decadent world and galaxy, battling against aliens, and gradually coming to full stature as a superman. Compared to the fix-ups of the previous decade or so, the story is well paced and emotionally coherent, though compared to his best early novels there is a sense of self-consciousness that damages the oneiric flow of arousing event and imagery. Further novels have not lived up to this promise of partial renewal, and have not been well received by critics.

Critics, such as Damon KNIGHT in an essay which was reprinted as "Cosmic Jerrybuilder" in *In Search of Wonder* (critical coll. **1956**; rev. 1967), have tended to treat the typical AEVV tale as a failed effort at "hard" sf, and have consequently tended to speak of stories others have written in the modes he developed as "improvements" on the original model, novels by writers like Philip K. DICK, Charles L. HARNESS and Larry NIVEN. In some ways, of course, these writers have built upon the complexity of AEVV's worlds, and on the way his plots would constantly reshuffle the meaning of what had gone before. But AEVV's space operas, as we have mentioned, are fundamentally dream enactments that articulate the deep, symbolic needs and wishes of his usually adolescent readership. Because there is no misunderstood science or cosmography or technology at the very heart of his best work, there is therefore no "improving" AEVV.   [JC]

Other works: *Out of the Unknown* (coll. **1948**) with E. Mayne Hull, three stories by each writer; *Masters of Time* (coll. **1950**) comprised of two stories published separately afterwards as *The Changeling* (1944 *ASF*; written into *The Beast, see above*; **1967**) and *Earth's Last Fortress* (1942 *ASF* as "Recruiting Station"; vt in *Masters of Time* as title story; **1960** as *Earth's Last Fortress*; title reverts to *Masters of Time*, minus "The Changeling", 1967; *see also The Three Eyes of Evil above*); *The House That Stood Still* (**1950**; vt *The Mating Cry*; vt *The Undercover Aliens* UK); *The Universe Maker* (1949 *Startling Stories* as "The Shadow Men"; rev. **1953**); *Planets for Sale* (1943–6 *ASF* as by E. Mayne Hull; fix-up **1954**) with E. Mayne Hull; *Rogue Ship* (1947 *ASF*, 1950 *Super-Science Stories*, 1963 *If*; fix-up **1965**); *The Twisted Men* (coll. **1964**); *Monsters* (coll. **1965**; vt *The Blal and Other Science-Fiction Monsters*); *The Winged Man* (1944 *ASF* as by E. Mayne Hull; exp. **1966**) with E. Mayne Hull; *The Far-Out Worlds of A.E. van Vogt* (coll. **1968**; vt with added stories as *The Worlds of A.E. van Vogt* 1974); *More Than Superhuman* (coll. **1971**); *The Proxy Intelligence and Other Mind Benders* (coll. **1971**); *M-33 in Andromeda* (coll. **1971**); *The Darkness on Diamondia* (**1972**); *The Book of Van Vogt* (coll. **1972**); *Future Glitter* (**1973**; vt *Tyranopolis* UK); *The Secret Galactics* (**1974**; vt *Earth Factor X*); *The Man with a Thousand Names* (**1974**); *The Gryb* (coll. of various stories retitled but otherwise unchanged from previous appearances; **1976**); *Supermind* (1968 *If* as "The Proxy Intelligence"; exp. **1977**); *The Anarchistic Colossus* (**1977**).

About the author: "A.E. van Vogt" in *Seekers of Tomorrow* (**1966**) by Sam MOSKOWITZ; "The Development of a Science Fiction Writer" by AEVV in FOUNDATION no.3 (1973); *Reflections of*

A.E. van Vogt (**1975**) by AEVV

See also: ADAM AND EVE; ANDROIDS; CONCEPTUAL BREAKTHROUGH; COSMOLOGY; DISASTER; DISCOVERY AND INVENTION; ESP; FANTASTIC VOYAGES; GALACTIC EMPIRES; GENERATION STARSHIPS; GENETIC ENGINEERING; GODS AND DEMONS; HEROES; HISTORY IN SF; IMMORTALITY; INTELLIGENCE; INVASION; LIVING WORLDS; METAPHYSICS; MONSTERS; PARANOIA AND SCHIZOPHRENIA; PARASITISM AND SYMBIOSIS; PERCEPTION; PHYSICS; POLITICS; PSI POWERS; PSYCHOLOGY; REINCARNATION; RELIGION; SF MAGAZINES; SCIENTIFIC ERRORS; SEX; SUSPENDED ANIMATION; WAR; WEAPONS.

VARDON, RICHARD *See* David Wright O'BRIEN.

VARDRE, LESLIE *See* L.P. DAVIES.

VARGO STATTEN BRITISH SCIENCE FICTION MAGAZINE *See* VARGO STATTEN SCIENCE FICTION MAGAZINE.

April 1954.

VARGO STATTEN SCIENCE FICTION MAGAZINE British PULP/DIGEST-size magazine. 19 issues, Jan. 1954–6, published by Scion, London, for the first seven issues, then Dragon Publications for the remainder; ed. Vargo Statten (John Russell FEARN). Month of publication did not appear on the last two issues. The first three issues were pulp size, then digest size to the end. It was intended to be a monthly publication but there were several gaps in the publication dates. The magazine was retitled *Vargo Statten British Science Fiction Magazine* Vol.1 nos 4–5, *The British Science Fiction Magazine* Vol.1 nos 6–12, and finally *The British Space Fiction Magazine* from Vol.2 no.1 to the end.

The magazine owed its existence to the ready sale of Scion's paperback novel line, many published as by Vargo Statten. The policy of aiming stories at younger readers may have alienated some British

authors; the low rates of payment, finally 12s. 6d. a thousand words for world rights, cannot have helped. Barrington BAYLEY published his first story here, and E.C. TUBB appeared in most issues under his own name and under pseudonyms, but Fearn was forced to use many of his own stories, sometimes old stories slightly rewritten under various pseudonyms, to fill up the issues. [FHP]

VARLEY, JOHN (HERBERT) (1947–). American writer who has made a considerable impact in only a few years with some fine short stories, beginning in 1974, and including "In the Bowl" (1975) and "The Phantom of Kansas" (1976). His remarkable first novel is *The Ophiuchi Hotline* (**1977**), set 500 years in the future, a time when mankind has been long exiled from Earth by immensely superior, indifferent "Invaders", and when human life is as a consequence radically different from today's; the fellow humanoids beaming information to the Solar System down the Hotline tell the multi-CLONED female protagonist of the book that mankind is doomed to wander the stars, homeless, for ever. This happens. [JC]
Other works: *The Persistence of Vision* (coll. **1978**; vt *In the Hall of the Martian Kings*).
See also: CHILDREN IN SF; GENETIC ENGINEERING; MARS; PASTORAL.

June 1977. Cover by Eaianne Cooke.

VECTOR The journal of the British Sf Association (BSFA). *V* has been published irregularly since the foundation of the BSFA in 1958. E.C. TUBB was its first editor, and it has had several dozen editors since then, including, briefly, Michael MOORCOCK. The production, quality and contents of the magazine have fluctuated from editor to editor, and *V* has appeared variously as an association newsletter, a typical FANZINE and an academic journal. Despite this inconsistency, the magazine has contained many articles, critiques and

interviews of considerable value and interest, particularly when under the editorships of Roger Peyton, Malcolm EDWARDS and Christopher Fowler. Occasional contributors have included Brian ALDISS, James BLISH, Philip K. DICK, Harry HARRISON, Ken BULMER, Ursula K. LE GUIN, Bob SHAW, John BRUNNER and Christopher PRIEST. [PR]

VELIKOVSKY, IMMANUEL (1895–). Russian Jewish writer, now an American. He graduated in medicine in Moscow in 1921, and studied psychoanalysis with Wilhelm Stekel in Vienna in 1933. He is primarily known for the series of books he has written putting forward, with a vast amount of documentation and argument, a theory of the evolution of the Solar System which proposes that it underwent various catastrophic changes comparatively recently, and that historical evidence exists for these. The books are *Worlds in Collision* (**1950**), *Ages in Chaos* (**1952**), *Earth in Upheaval* (**1955**) and *Oedipus and Akhnaton* (**1960**). The first documents the theory, and the third adduces additional geological, archaeological and paleontological evidence for it; the second rewrites Egyptian history to make its chronology fit his schema better, and the fourth also concentrates on history. The gist of the theory is that Jupiter expelled a comet, which passed close to Earth, and ultimately became the planet VENUS. Its approach to Earth caused global cataclysm; Earth's axis tilted; the Red Sea parted; Israelites in the desert were fed by hydrocarbons (manna) from the comet's tail. The books are perhaps the most densely argued in the history of PSEUDO-SCIENCE (the theory cannot readily be called scientific, and has been heatedly denied by scientists generally), and their multidisciplinary approach, blending history, religion and astronomy, has won them many supporters, including a few among the scientific establishment. An apparent effort by scientists to have IV's work censored is recounted in *The Velikovsky Affair* (**1966**), ed. Alfred de Grazia. A collection of essays defending IV's science, and pointing to the accuracy of many of his predictions (e.g. a high surface temperature for Venus; Jupiter as a radio source) is *Velikovsky Reconsidered* (anth. **1976**) by the Editors of *Pensée*. IV's dramatic scenario of the heavens parallels many of the catastrophic events in sf, and the popularity of some forms of PULP sf is probably not unconnected to a public hunger of which IV has been the most notable feeder. [PN]
See also: ADAM AND EVE.

VENTURE SCIENCE FICTION US DIGEST-size magazine. 16 issues, published by Fantasy House (a subsidiary of Mercury Publications), Jan. 1957-Mar. 1958, and by Mercury Press, May 1958-Aug. 1970, as a companion to THE

Aug. 1969, in the title's second incarnation. Cover by Bert Tanner.

MAGAZINE OF FANTASY AND SCIENCE FICTION. There were 10 bi-monthly issues, Jan. 1957-Jul. 1958, ed. Robert P. MILLS, and then the title was revived for six quarterly issues, May. 1969-Aug. 1970; ed. Edward FERMAN. *VSF* put a higher priority on action-adventure sf than did its companion. In its second incarnation it featured an abridged novel in every issue. Notable stories include C.M. KORNBLUTH's "Two Dooms" (Jul. 1958) and Edward Wellen's short novel "Hijack" (May 1970).

The British edition was a monthly digest magazine published by the Atlas Publishing and Distributing Co., Sep. 1963-Dec. 1965 (28 issues). It reprinted most of its material from the first series of the US magazine, but also used stories from *FSF*, some from the 1950s, and some which had appeared after *FSF*'s British edition folded in June 1965. [BS]

VENUS Because Earth's inner neighbour presented a bright and featureless face to early astronomers it became something of a mystery planet, forever sheathed in dense cloud. 19th-century astronomers and early 20th-century sf writers generally imagined it to be warm and wet — a planet of vast oceans (perhaps with no land at all) or sweltering jungles. In the 1960s, however, it was discovered that Venus has a surface temperature of several hundred degrees, owing to the fact that its clouds are mostly carbon dioxide and create a "greenhouse effect" in the lower atmosphere, and that there is no liquid water at the surface at all.

Early tours of the planets which took in Venus, including Athanasius KIRCHER's *Itinerarium Exstaticum* (**1656**), Emanuel SWEDENBORG's *The Earths in our Solar System* (**1758**) and George GRIFFITH's *A Honeymoon in Space* (**1901**), tended to be influenced in its portrayal by its long-time association with the goddess of love. Its inhabitants were often

characterized as gentle and beautiful, a notion popularized in non-fiction by Bernard le Bovier de Fontenelle in *Entretiens sur la pluralité des mondes* (**1686**; trans. as *A Plurality of Worlds* **1688**). The first novel concerned specifically with Venus was Achille Eyraud's *Voyage à Venus* (**1865**). A winged visitor from Venus arrives on Earth in W. LACH-SZYRMA's *A Voice from Another World* (**1874**; exp. vt. *Aleriel* **1883**), and was later the protagonist of an interplanetary tour in the form of a series of nine "Letters from the Planets" (1887–93 *Cassell's Magazine*). A detailed description of a Venerean civilization is featured in *History of a Race of Immortals Without a God* (**1891** as by Antares Skorpios; vt *The Immortals' Great Quest* as by James W. Barlow). Early scientific romances set on Venus include Gustavus W. POPE's *Romances of the Planets, no 2: Journey to Venus* (**1895**) and John MUNRO's *A Trip to Venus* (**1897**). Fred T. JANE's early satire on the interplanetary romance featured a trip *To Venus in Five Seconds* (**1897**), and Venus was also the world visited by Garrett P. SERVISS's *A Columbus of Space* (**1911**). Edgar Rice BURROUGHS' chief imitator, Otis Adelbert KLINE, set his principal series of exotic romances on Venus — a trilogy comprised of *The Planet of Peril* (**1929**), *The Prince of Peril* (**1930**) and *The Port of Peril* (1932; **1949**) — but Burroughs' own Venerean series is self-pastiche. Other PULP romances set on Venus include Homer Eon FLINT's "The Queen of Life" (1919; in *The Lord of Death and the Queen of Life*, coll. **1966**) and Ralph Milne FARLEY's series begun with *The Radio Man* (1924; **1948**; vt *An Earthman on Venus*).

The early sf pulps made abundant use of Venerean scenarios. Notable examples are John W. CAMPBELL's "Solarite" (1930), Clark Ashton SMITH's "The Immeasurable Horror" (1931) and John WYNDHAM's story of COLONIZATION "The Venus Adventure" (1932 as by John Beynon Harris). Stanton A. COBLENTZ used Venus as the setting for his satire *The Blue Barbarians* (1931; **1958**) and for a rather more sober short novel *The Planet of Youth* (1932; **1952**). Some of Stanley G. WEINBAUM's stories of LIFE ON OTHER WORLDS are set on Venus, including "The Lotus Eaters" (1935) and "Parasite Planet" (1935). In a slightly later period Clifford D. SIMAK used the milieu imaginatively in "Hunger Death" (1938) and "Tools" (1942), both written for John W. Campbell's *ASF*, which also featured Lester DEL REY's "The Luck of Ignatz" (1939) and Robert A. HEINLEIN's "Logic of Empire" (1941).

The image of Venus as an oceanic world was mainly developed in the 1940s, most memorably by C.S. LEWIS in *Perelandra* (**1943**; vt *Voyage to Venus*), in which islands of floating vegetation are used as a new Garden of Eden for a replay of the myth of ADAM AND EVE. The

most memorable pulp image of the same species was that provided by Henry KUTTNER and C.L. MOORE in "Clash by Night" (1943) and its sequel *Fury* (1947; **1950**) — both initially published under the name Lawrence O'Donnell. Here mankind lives in "keeps" UNDER THE SEA of Venus after Earth has died, and is faced with the terrible task of colonizing the inordinately hostile land-surface. Other stories using this image are Isaac ASIMOV's *Lucky Starr and the Oceans of Venus* (**1954** as by Paul French; vt *The Oceans of Venus*) and Poul ANDERSON's "Sister Planet" (1959). The alternative image of Venus the jungle planet, perpetually beset by fierce wet weather, has not been so commonly used — examples include Ray BRADBURY's "Death-by-Rain" (1950; vt "The Long Rain") and Poul Anderson's "The Big Rain" (1954).

Although MARS was much more popular as a setting for exotic romances, Venus had the advantage of being rather more versatile. With Mars there was always the constraint of perennial red desert, but the clouds of Venus might hide a multitude of wonders. Thus we find the gaudiest exotic romances of genre sf set on Venus: C.L. Moore's "Black Thirst" (1934), Leigh BRACKETT and Ray Bradbury's "Lorelei of the Red Mist" (1946), Brackett's "The Moon that Vanished" (1948) and "The Enchantress of Venus" (1949 vt "City of the Lost Ones") and Keith Bennett's "The Rocketeers Have Shaggy Ears" (1950). Partly because of this versatility, however, there never grew up a consistent "Venerean mythology" comparable in power to the mythology of Mars. As with Mars, though, there was a change in the main concern of stories concerned with Venus during the 1950s, when it became more often seen as a tough challenge to would-be colonists. In *The Space Merchants* (**1953**) by Frederik POHL and C.M. KORNBLUTH it is the "Gravy Planet" which has to be "sold" to the public by high-pressure advertising. Other stories of colonization from the period are Heinlein's *Between Planets* (**1951**) and Chad OLIVER's "Field Expedient" (1955). Philip LATHAM's juvenile novel *Five Against Venus* (**1952**) is a Venerean ROBINSONADE. There is also a trilogy of novels by Bryan BERRY, writing as Rolf Garner, which deals with the colonization of Venus after the destruction of Earth: *Resurgent Dust* (**1953**), *The Immortals* (**1953**) and *The Indestructible* (**1954**). The notion that Venus might be the appropriate home for Man after Earth becomes uninhabitable seems to be a popular one — it was a proposal first advanced in J.B.S. HALDANE's visionary essay "The Last Judgment" (1927) and taken up from there by Olaf STAPLEDON in *Last and First Men* (**1930**), where Man spends part of his future history as a winged creature on the Venerean floating islands.

Since the discovery of the true nature of the Venerean surface the interest of sf writers in the planet has waned considerably. It no longer offers a credible prospect as a stage for adventures of any kind. The new Venus shows its face in Larry NIVEN's "Becalmed in Hell" (1965), but perhaps a deeper impression was made in the same year by Roger ZELAZNY's florid nostalgic farewell to the world of the great ocean, "The Doors of His Face, the Lamps of His Mouth" (1965). The record of Venerean mythology, such as it is, is preserved in the excellent anthology *Farewell, Fantastic Venus!* (anth. **1968**; abridged vt *All About Venus*) ed. Brian ALDISS and Harry HARRISON. An earlier theme anthology was *The Hidden Planet* (anth. **1959**) ed. Donald A. WOLLHEIM.   [BS]

VERCORS Pseudonym used by French artist, illustrator and writer Jean Bruller (1902–) for all his publications from the beginning of his writing career with *Le silence de la mer* (**1942**; trans. by Cyril Connolly as *The Silence of the Sea* **1944**); to publish this he founded the French Resistance press Les Éditions de Minuit. After the Second World War he wrote several novels, some of which have elements of fantasy. His sf novel *Les animaux denaturés* (**1952**; trans. as *You Shall Know Them* **1953**; vt *Borderline* UK; vt *The Murder of the Missing Link* USA) deals with the discovery of a new species of ape-man, and the deliberate murder of an infant by its human father to provide a test case in which he hopes to establish the species' claim to human status; he wins, but is acquitted of murder as the act preceded the declaration of humanity. *The Insurgents* (**1957**) deals with the search for IMMORTALITY by a man who attains it at great personal cost. *Sylva* (**1961**; trans. **1962**) closely resembles David GARNETT's *Lady into Fox* (**1922**): it is a metamorphosis tale in which a vixen is changed into a woman by an English bachelor but eventually reverts. V was somewhat uneasy with his post-War allegorical fictions, but his fables were thought-generating and occasionally moving. As Bruller he illustrated, among other books, *Patapoufs et Filifers* (**1930**) by André MAUROIS.   [JC]

See also: ANTHROPOLOGY; SUSPENDED ANIMATION; THEATRE.

VERLANGER, JULIA Pseudonym of Héliane Taieb (1929–), French writer. She published 20 interesting stories in magazines between 1958 and 1963, before temporarily disappearing from the field, and has re-emerged with two lively HEROIC FANTASY adventures, *Les portes sans retour* ["Doors of No Return"] (**1976**) and *La flûte de verre froid* ["The Cold Glass Flute"] (**1976**).   [MJ]

VERNE, JULES (1828–1905). French playwright and novelist; with H.G. WELLS, he is generally thought of as one

Jules VERNE.

of the two founding fathers of sf, though neither author claimed this status either for himself or for the other, nor did either author claim to be originating a new genre. As sf scholarship has only recently begun to emphasize, both Wells and JV consciously wrote within traditions of popular literature that already had large though diffuse reading publics by the time they began producing their own seminal titles; both were adept at picking up hints from inferior or earlier writers and turning out definitive versions of sf themes later to become central to the field as it took on conscious shape with the 20th century, and both excelled in the imaginative density (and in Wells's case at least) the shapeliness of their tales. In some other ways as well, the linking of both writers as founding fathers is deceptive, for they were by no means contemporary with one another. JV was a pragmatic, middle-class entrepreneur of letters, and for the first part of his career at least expressed to the full the clear-eyed optimism about progress and European Man's central role in the world typical of high 19th-century culture. Born almost 40 years later, and to lower-middle-class parents, Wells in his early work exuded and helped to define the doom-laden *fin-de-siècle* atmosphere of the century's hectic, premonitory climax. It should be noted, however, that JV was by no means insensible to change, and that the novels of his last decade at least are much darker in texture and more pessimistic in implications than the novels for which he is best remembered today, all of which were written by 1880.

JV was born and raised in the port of Nantes, and the fact that the sea appears in a large number of his best and most romantic novels can perhaps be traced directly to the strong impression a bustling harbour must have made upon the child. His father was a successful lawyer, and assumed that JV would eventually take over his practice, but he rebelled from an early age at this form of

worldly success, though, true to his time, his rebelliousness did not express itself in disdain for the things of the world; his first declaration of independence, all the same, was an attempt — which came surprisingly close to success — to switch places with a cabin-boy on a ship; he was extricated from this fate only after the ship had actually left harbour. By young adulthood, however, his romantic flamboyance took a more productive course. He went to Paris on an allowance, and, under the influence of such writers as Victor Hugo and Alexandre Dumas fils, he wrote a good deal of drama (about 20 plays remain unpublished), romantic verse, and libretti, several of which were produced, as well as engaging in mild flirtations with various women, though unsuccessfully — JV was never at ease with women, and his works are notably free of realistic portrayals of them; his Catholicism, which did not sit well with the Bohemian life-style he tried to imitate, may have contributed to this. He soon discovered Edgar Allan POE, somewhat misreading his solitary (indeed almost solipsistic) melancholy as a kind of romantic adventurousness, and under this influence began to publish his first tales of lasting interest. "Un voyage en ballon" ["A Voyage in a Balloon"] (1851) was eventually republished in *Une fantaisie du Docteur Ox* (coll. **1872**; trans. as *Dr Ox's Experiment, and Other Stories* **1874**) as "Une Drame dans les airs" ["A Drama in the Sky"] and republished in book form under this latter title (**1874**). Also in *Dr Ox's Experiment* was the more interesting early story "Maître Zacharius" ["Master Zacharius"] (1854), an allegory about Time, a clockmaker, and the Devil; both stories demonstrate from how early a date JV had developed his characteristic technique of inserting quasi-scientific explanations into a simply told adventure imbued with the romance of geography. This storytelling method proved from the first to be a singularly appropriate tool, legitimizing the love of adventure (or more specifically of travel, in this first age of the tourist) by infusing it with the sense that scientific progress (and hence national virtue) was being encouraged at the same time.

But despite these early hints of the course he was to follow, JV felt himself only marginally successful as a writer and bon vivant, and with his father's help soon turned to stockbroking, an occupation he maintained until 1862, when his singularly important association with Hetzel began; Hetzel, a successful publisher and children's writer, was planning a children's magazine and needed a reliable author to provide material for it. JV had come to him with a narrative about travelling in balloons (it was apparently couched in semi-documentary form), and when Hetzel suggested that he properly novelize his story, JV did so eagerly and swiftly; the renovated tale, published as *Cinq semaines en ballon* (**1863**; trans. as *Five Weeks in a Balloon* **1870**), began the long series of "Voyages extraordinaires" ["Extraordinary Journeys"] which the firm of Hetzel published under that rubric from then to the end of JV's career. There has been some misunderstanding about the contracts under which JV supplied material for Hetzel; he was required to provide a certain number of volumes a year (initially three, eventually two), but a volume did not necessarily constitute a novel, some of which were defined as taking two or even three volumes to run their course. JV's production, therefore, while large, is not phenomenal; as a rule he published about a novel a year, to a total of 64, not all of them sf by any means. His first novel is still comparatively primitive. Three colleagues decide to try to cross Africa in a balloon, have numerous adventures as they go, learn a great deal about Africa, and survive the experience.

Five Weeks in a Balloon as a consequence lacks the hectic, romantic intensity of JV's best work, an example of which is his next novel, *Voyage au centre de la terre* (**1864**; trans. as *Journey to the Centre of the Earth* **1872**); in this novel, three protagonists (JV very frequently found the use of multiple protagonists a convenient method of splitting and reassimilating his didactic and narrative duties) take part variously in an expedition into the heart of a dormant volcano which leads them eventually into the dark hollow heart of the Earth itself. JV's highly visible wonderment at the world's marvels in tales of this sort goes far to explain the success he was beginning to achieve by this time; his vision has a childlike exuberance and clarity that gives traditional PROTO-SF devices, like the HOLLOW EARTH of this tale, a definitively memorable shape, and his three-part division of protagonists (one a scientist, one an intensely active, athletic type, the third a more or less ordinary man representative of the reader's point of view) sorted out duties and pleasures remarkably well.

JV's techniques for the merging of wonderment and didacticism became only more refined with the books of the next decade, his most famous; they include: *De la terre à la lune* (**1865**) and its sequel, *Autour de la lune* (**1870**), both trans. as *From the Earth to the Moon direct in 97 hours 20 minutes; and a trip around it* (**1873**); *Les aventures du Capitaine Hatteras*, in two vols as *Les anglais au pôle nord* (**1864**; trans. as *English at the North Pole* **1874**) and *Le désert de glace* (**1866**; trans. as *Field of Ice* **1876**); *Les enfants du Capitaine Grant* (**1867–8**; trans. as *Voyage Round the World* **1876–7**; vt *Captain Grant's Children* in three vols), *Vingt mille lieues sous les mers* (**1870**; trans. as *Twenty Thousand Leagues under the Seas* **1873**), with its sequel, *L'île mystérieuse*

(**1874–5**; trans. as *The Mysterious Island* **1875**), and, perhaps best known of all, *Le tour du monde en quatre-vingt jours* (**1873**; trans. as *Around the World in Eighty Days* **1874**). In all these novels the reader feels the strength of JV's powerful sense of the ultimate rightness of the course of the 19th century, and of his fundamentally conservative, pragmatic imagination, for the books are all set in more or less contemporary venues, and attempt to deal with the world in realistic, plausible terms. *From the Earth to the Moon* may seem an exception, with its huge cannon in Florida blasting passengers into space, but (questions of acceleration aside) the science of the story is firmly exposited. The reputation JV has had for a century in English-speaking countries for ineptness and carelessness in scientific matters is fundamentally due to the innumerate (and often illiterate) translators who have been visited upon him. *Twenty Thousand Leagues Under the Seas* (the last word is now always translated as *Sea*) may be JV's most deeply felt novel; carefully and slowly composed, it introduces Captain Nemo and his elaborate submarine, the *Nautilus*, in a tale whose easy, exaggerated sombreness agreeably conflates the domesticated Byronism of the time and expressive marvels of science. Nemo (it turns out in the sequel) is an Indian prince whom British injustice has turned misanthropic, hence his life under the seas in his submarine, amply and comfortingly furnished in Second Empire plushness. Not really sf at all, *Around the World in Eighty Days* of course recounts Phileas Fogg's journey around the world in that time to win a bet; in *The Other Log of Phileas Fogg* (**1973**), Philip José FARMER has attempted to enlist Fogg into his own complex pantheon of culture heroes.

From this point on, JV's work tends to repeat itself in gradually darkening hues, though he never lost the sense of the fundamental *usableness* of science and technology — a sense vital to much 20th-century sf, in which, as in JV's work, there is a strong tendency for usableness to serve as its own justification. It is notable, for instance, that JV's several ROBINSONADES, which include *The Mysterious Island*, *L'école des Robinsons* (**1882**; trans. as *Godfrey Morgan: a Californian Mystery* **1883**; vt *The School for Crusoes*) and the late, nostalgic *Deux ans de vacances ou un pensionnat de Robinsons* (**1888**; trans. as *Two Years Holiday* **1889**), all exploit the romantic implications of being cast alone (or with a few companions) into the bosom of a bounteous Nature; JV's robinsonades are carefully socialized as well, and the small groups of protagonists comprising their casts always make do very well together, all of which further underlines his basic agreement with Man's role in the world. All the same, JV's later work is painted from a grimmer palette. *Robur le*

conquérant (**1886**; trans. as *The Clipper of the Clouds* **1887**), with its sequel, *Maître du monde* (**1904**; trans. as *Master of the World* **1914**), demonstrates the process. In the earlier book, the steely, megalomaniacal Robur, inventor of an impressive flying machine, though rendered less favourably than earlier romantic misanthropes like Nemo, is still allowed by JV to represent the march of scientific progress as he forces the world to listen to him; but in the second book, JV's last work of any significance, Robur has become a dangerous madman, blasphemous and uncontrollable, and his excesses — like those of Wells's Dr Moreau — seem to represent the excesses of an unfettered development of the implications of scientific "progress". Science and a subservient, bounteous Nature are no longer seen as united under Man's control.

JV's life was externally uneventful from the 1860s on; he married, prospered mightily, lived in a large provincial house, yachted occasionally, unflaggingly produced his novels for the firm of Hetzel, and became a fine example of the 19th-century French middle-class dignitary. At the same time, however, that his works display the boyish, escapist dream-life of that class, they can also be read, perhaps with as great a relevance, as an ultimate requiem for the dreams of his century: the dream (or vision) that the world was illimitable and obedient, and that Man could only improve upon creation.

JV's work was always attractive to film-makers, and as early as 1902 Georges MÉLIÈS loosely adapted *From the Earth to the Moon* to make VOYAGE DANS LA LUNE. It was not until JV's work came out of copyright in the 1950s, however, that the real rush started, beginning with Walt Disney's 20,000 LEAGUES UNDER THE SEA in 1954. Other JV adaptations were *Around the World in 80 Days* (1956), FROM THE EARTH TO THE MOON (1958), JOURNEY TO THE CENTER OF THE EARTH (1959), THE MYSTERIOUS ISLAND (1961), MASTER OF THE WORLD (1961) and *Five Weeks in a Balloon* (1962). The Czech film VYNALEZ ZKAZY, released in the USA as *The Fabulous World of Jules Verne*, was a blend of live action and animation made in 1958. JV's characters have been revived in various, sometimes embarrassing guises, as in CAPTAIN NEMO AND THE UNDERWATER CITY (1969). [JC]

Other works: We list the remaining "Voyages extraordinaires"; many are not sf. Most better-known titles are a bibliographical nightmare, with many unauthorized editions and titles; we have normally attempted to list first translations only, and have not traced paths through the jungle of (usually pirated) vts: *Une ville flottante* (**1871**; trans. as *A Floating City* **1876**); *Aventures de trois russes et de trois anglais dans l'Afrique australe* (**1872**; trans. as

Meridiana; the Adventures of three Englishmen and three Russians in South Africa 1873; vt Measuring a Meridian); Le pays des fourrures (1873; trans. as The Fur Country 1873); Le "Chancellor" (1875; trans. as Survivors of the Chancellor 1875); Michel Strogoff (1876; trans. as Michael Strogoff, the Courier of the, Czar 1876–7); Hector Servadac (1877; trans. 1878); Les indes noires (1877; trans. as Child of the Cavern; or, Strange Doings Underground 1877; vt Black Diamonds); Un capitaine de quinze ans (1878; trans. as Dick Sands, the Boy Captain 1879); Les cinq cents millions de la bégum (coll. 1879, consisting of title story, based on a draft by Paschal Grousset, known as André LAURIE, and the story "Les révoltés de la Bounty"; trans. as The Begum's Fortune 1880); Les tribulations d'un chinois en Chine (1879; trans. as Tribulations of a Chinaman 1880); La maison à vapeur (1880; trans. as The Steam House 1881); La Jangada (1881; trans. as The Giant Raft 1881); Le rayon vert (1882; trans. as The Green Ray 1883); Kéraban le têtu (1883; trans. as Kéraban the Inflexible in two vols, The Captain of the Guidara 1884, and Scarpante the Spy 1885); L'étoile du Sud (1884; trans. as The Vanished Diamond, a tale of South Africa 1885; vt The Southern Star Mystery) probably based on a draft by André Laurie; L'Archipel en feu (1884; trans. as The Archipelago on Fire 1886); Mathias Sandorf (1885; trans. 1886); Un billet de loterie (1886; trans. as The Lottery Ticket: a Tale of Tellemarken 1887); Nord contre sud (1887; trans. as North Against South: a Tale of the American Civil War 1888); Le chemin de France (1887; trans. as Flight to France 1888); Une famille sans nom (1889; trans. as A Family Without a Name 1890); Sans dessus dessous (1889; trans. as Purchase of the North Pole 1891); César Cascabel (1890; trans. 1891); Mistress Branican (1891; trans. 1892); Le Château des Carpathes (1892; trans. as Castle of the Carpathians 1893); Claudius Bombarnac (1892; trans. 1894); P'tit bonhomme (1893; trans. as Foundling Mick 1895); Les mirifiques aventures de Maître Antifer (1894; trans. as Captain Antifer 1895); L'ile à hélice (1895; trans. as The Floating Island 1896); Clovis Dardentor (1896; trans. 1897); Face au drapeau (1896; trans. as For the Flag 1897); Le Sphinx des glaces (1897; trans. as An Antarctic Mystery 1898; vt The Mystery of Arthur Gordon Pym) which is a "completion" of Edgar Allan Poe's The Narrative of Arthur Gordon Pym of Nantucket (1838); Le superbe Orénoque ["The Superb Orinoco"] (1898); Le testament d'un excentrique (1899; trans. as The Will of an Eccentric 1900); Seconde patrie (1900; trans. in two vols as Their Island Home 1923 and Castaways of the Flag; the Final Adventures of the Swiss Family Robinson 1923); Les histoires de Jean-Marie Cabidoulin (1901; trans. as The Sea Serpent 1967); Le village aérien (1901; trans. as The Village in the Tree Tops 1964); Les frères Kip ["The Kip Brothers"] (1902); Bourses de voyage ["Travelling Grants"] (1904); Un drame en Livonie (1904; trans. as Drama in Livonia 1967); L'invasion de la mer ["The Invasion of the Sea"] (1905); Le phare du bout du monde (1905; trans. as The Lighthouse at the End of the World 1923); Le volcan d'or (1906; trans. as The Golden Volcano 1963); L'agence Thompson (1907; trans. in two vols as The Thompson Travel Agency 1965); La Chasse au météore (1908; trans. as The Chase of the Golden Meteor 1909); Le pilote du Danube (1908; trans. as The Danube Pilot 1967); Les naufragés du Jonathan (1909; trans. as The Survivors of the "Jonathan" 1962); Hier et demain (coll. 1910; trans. as Yesterday and Tomorrow 1965); Le secret de Wilhelm Storitz (1910; trans. as The Secret of Wilhelm Storitz 1965); L'étonnante aventure de la mission Barsac (1919; trans. in two vols as Into the Niger Bend 1960 and City in the Sahara 1965). An interesting novel not in the "Voyages extraordinaires" is L'épave du Cynthia (1885; trans. as Salvage from the Cynthia 1958) with André Laurie.

About the author: Jules Verne (1940) by Kenneth Allott; The Political and Social Ideas of Jules Verne (1971; trans. 1972) by Jean Chesneaux; Jules Verne: a Biography (1973; trans. 1976) by Jean Jules-Verne, JV's grandson, particularly valuable for its bibliography; Jules Verne: Inventor of Science Fiction (1978) by Peter Costello.

See also: ANTHROPOLOGY; ASTRONOMY; ATLANTIS; BIOLOGY; BOYS' PAPERS; CHILDREN'S SF; DISCOVERY AND INVENTION; DYSTOPIAS; EVOLUTION; FANTASTIC VOYAGES; FRANCE; HISTORY OF SF; ISLANDS; LOST WORLDS; MACHINES; MONEY; MOON; MUSIC AND OPERA; NEAR FUTURE; OPTIMISM AND PESSIMISM; PHYSICS; POWER SOURCES; PREDICTION; SATIRE; SF MAGAZINES; SF OVERTAKEN BY EVENTS; SCIENTIFIC ERRORS; SCIENTISTS; SPACE FLIGHT; SPACESHIPS; TECHNOLOGY; TRANSPORTATION; UNDER THE SEA; WEAPONS.

VERNON, ROGER LEE (1924–). American writer and schoolteacher, whose awkwardly routine sf is contained in the assemblage of original stories The Space Frontiers (coll. 1955) and the novel Robot Hunt (1959). [JC]

VERRILL, A(LPHEUS) HYATT (1871–1954). American naturalist, explorer and writer, in the latter capacity best known for works outside the sf field, most of his 100 or so books being non-fiction, though some of them are boys' adventure tales. Of the nine novels he published in AMZ and AMZ Quarterly from 1926 to 1935, beginning with "Beyond the Pole" (1926), The Bridge of Light (1929 AMZ Quarterly; 1950) is of interest as a typical LOST-WORLD story set in South America, where AHV did much of his real-life exploration. AHV's work shows the marks of a somewhat desultory interest in fiction, and of the PULP markets he served, but all the same vividly dramatizes his professional concerns. Of minor interest is When the Moon Ran Wild (1931 AMZ Quarterly as by AHV; 1962) as by Ray Ainsbury. [JC]
See also: ANTHROPOLOGY.

VERSINS, PIERRE (1922–). French scholar and writer. He began writing sf in the 1950s and published two novels, Les étoiles ne s'en foutent pas ["The Stars Care"] (1954), Le professeur ["The Professor"] (1956) and over 20 stories (some with his wife Martine Thome), while editing Ailleurs (1957–62) a critical FANZINE of high repute. Resident in Switzerland, PV also produced Passeport pour l'inconnu ["Passport for the Unknown"], a regular sf radio programme for Radio Geneva. A keen researcher and bibliographer, PV is a foremost authority on early sf and donated his priceless collection of books and magazines to the town of Yverdon, Switzerland, in 1975, becoming the curator of the unique local sf museum thus created. PV's major achievement is undoubtedly his massive 1,000-page Encyclopédie de l'Utopie et de la sf ["Encyclopedia of Utopia and sf"] (1972) which was given a special award at the 1973 Toronto World SF Convention. An invaluable, if idiosyncratic, volume, particularly useful on sf outside the US and the UK and prior to 1900, it remains to this day one of the finest reference books on sf, though it has not been translated. [MJ]

Apr. 1974. Cover by Rodger MacGowan.

VERTEX US BEDSHEET/tabloid-size magazine. 16 bi-monthly issues, Apr. 1973-Oct. 1975, published by Mankind Publishing, Los Angeles; ed. Donald J. PFEIL. V, subtitled "The Magazine of Science Fiction", was a slick magazine of imaginative layout and much internal illustration, some in colour. The covers were often semi-abstract. Like most recent sf magazines, *V* ran many non-fiction pieces: interviews with authors and excellent science-fact articles. Stories were by, among others, Ed BRYANT, F.M. BUSBY, William Carlson, Geo. Alec EFFINGER, Stephen GOLDIN, Joe HALDEMAN, George R.R. MARTIN, Jerry POURNELLE, William ROTSLER, Robert SILVERBERG, Norman SPINRAD and John VARLEY. *V* was something of a showcase for up-and-coming US authors, and in quality was the strongest of the new 1970s sf magazines, but financial problems and a paper shortage forced a change to newspaper format on cheap paper for the last three issues, then closure. [PN/FHP]

VIAN, BORIS (1920–59). French writer in various genres, most likely to be remembered as a fine ABSURDIST dramatist, for such plays as *Équarrissage pour tous* (**1950**; trans. as *The Knackers' ABC* **1968**), which savagely mocks the military mind and military punctilio. *J'irai cracher sur vos tombes* (**1947**; trans. as *I Spit on your Grave* **1971**), published as by Vernon Sullivan, pretends to be an American tough-guy detective novel, but extends into fantasy. BV was one of the main personalities of the early post-War French sf scene, translator of A.E. VAN VOGT, William TENN, Henry KUTTNER and Ray BRADBURY and a writer of speculative fiction years ahead of his time. His major mainstream novels are deeply indebted to sf and surrealism, particularly *L'Écume des jours* (**1947**; trans. as *Froth on the Daydream* by Stanley Chapman **1966**); *L'automne à Pékin* ["Autumn in Peking"] (**1947**), a desert Utopia; and *L'herbe rouge* ["Red Grass"] (**1950**), which involves time travel. His novels had some influence on the English NEW-WAVE sf writers, and were actively promoted by James SALLIS, among others. BV used sf devices to the end of articulating his sense of the world's violent impingement on the self; though sometimes his characters transcend their shackles. BV is at present a major youth cult in France, much as TOLKIEN and VONNEGUT are in the USA. [MJ/JC]

See also: THEATRE.

VIDAL, GORE (1925–). American writer, resident in Italy, best known for such satirical works outside the sf field as *Myra Breckinridge* (**1968**) and its sequel *Myron* (**1974**) (although the sex change of these novels could be regarded as borderline sf). His sf novel *Messiah* (**1954**), which ends his first phase of novel-writing, is a dark SATIRE on RELIGION (*see also* MESSIAHS), in which a new messiah teaches a defeatedly secular America how to worship death. A play, *Visit to a Small Planet* (**1956**; **1960**), again satirizes contemporary Western civilization in presenting the story of an alien child capable of changing the past

who comes close to wrecking our corrupt society before its guardians arrive to take it back. GV is a pessimistic, sharp-tongued, deeply knowledgeable critic of American ways of life; the messages of his essays and novels (especially his later ones) are close to interchangeable, sometimes to the detriment of his fiction; but his literate skill generally triumphs. [JC]

See also: FLYING SAUCERS; THEATRE.

VIDPHONE One of the oldest and most commonly used items of sf TERMINOLOGY. A vidphone is like a telephone which transmits pictures as well as sound. (Though expensive, they are now commercially available in the real world.) Early hack writers, casting around for ways of making the future seem more different and exciting than the present, always hit upon the vidphone before anything else. It is one of sf's many futuristic CLICHÉS. [PN]

VIERECK, GEORGE S(YLVESTER) (1884–1962). German-born American writer, between the Wars well known as an apologist for defeated Germany, as in *The Kaiser on Trial* (**1937**), though his views on Hitler were considerably more guarded. On his refusal to register as a German lobbyist or agent in the Second World War he was imprisoned (released 1947). His first fiction of interest is the fantasy *The House of the Vampire* (**1907**), but he is best known for his trilogy about three immortals (*see* IMMORTALITY), written with Paul ELDRIDGE and comprised of *My First Two Thousand Years; The Autobiography of the Wandering Jew* (**1928**), *Salome: The Wandering Jewess* (**1930**; vt abridged *Salome: 2000 Years of Love*) and *The Invincible Adam* (**1932**) (*see* ADAM AND EVE). The three immortals — the third being a vigorous young masculine figure, Kotikokura — intermingle their adventures through time, and symbolize mankind's striving after reality and love. A kind of pendant, *Gloria* (**1952**), presents an espionage thriller plot on a luxury liner in which Gloria is either a spy or the goddess of love — chances are she's the latter. [JC]

See also: ORIGIN OF MAN.

VIGAN, LUC *See* André RUELLAN.

VIKING, OTTO (1883– ?). American writer whose sf novel is *A World Intervenes* (**1964**). [JC]

VILLAGE OF THE DAMNED Film (1960). MGM. Directed by Wolf Rilla, starring George Sanders, Barbara Shelley and Martin Stephens. Screenplay by Sterling Silliphant, Wolf Rilla and George Barclay, based on the novel *The Midwich Cuckoos* by John WYNDHAM. 77 mins. B/w.

In this faithful but pedestrian adaptation of Wyndham's novel, a British

village is mysteriously sealed off from the outside world for 24 hours. During this period all the women of childbearing age are mysteriously and unknowingly impregnated by aliens from outer space. In due course they give birth to a number of strange children who possess such powers as telepathy and mind control. It is surmised that the children represent an attempt by another planet to colonize Earth, and they are finally destroyed. The children, with their glowing eyes, are the most successful feature of an otherwise unimaginative production; their sang-froid is chilling and suggests the authentically alien. A virtual re-make of this film, this time in an urban setting, was CHILDREN OF THE DAMNED. [JB]

VILLAINS The division of people into simple archetypes of good and bad, HEROES and villains, has always been stronger in popular literature than in more serious fiction; indeed, the essence of the serious novel of character has always been to explore the various shades of grey between the moral absolutes of black and white. Thus sf's villains are mainly associated with PULP sf, not just in the post-1926, specialist sf magazines, but in the pulp magazines generally from the 1890s onwards.

An analysis of which variety of villain is uppermost in popular literature at any given period tells us much about the societies that read such stories, and which in one sense can be said to have produced them, if we accept that commercial fiction is generally written in response to a known popular demand.

British sf from 1890–1920 (and to some extent later) was notably xenophobic; foreigners were not to be trusted. The same was true to a lesser extent in the USA, whose East Coast cities were becoming a kind of melting-pot of different races, to the alarm of the more conservative.

Anti-Semitic views are expressed surprisingly seldom, although the capitalist villain of George Allan ENGLAND's *The Golden Blight* (**1912**; **1916**) is a Jew, and M.P. SHIEL's stories often contain Jewish villains (although he was very ambiguous on the subject, and was sympathetic to Zionist aspirations).

Better known are the "Yellow Peril" books, and here, too, M.P. Shiel figures largely with *The Yellow Danger* (**1898**; rev. 1899), *The Yellow Wave* (**1905**) and *The Dragon* (**1913**; rev. vt *The Yellow Peril* 1929). Floyd GIBSON's *The Red Napoleon* (**1929**) features a Mongol world-conqueror. But the most famous Oriental villain of all was Sax ROHMER's Dr Fu Manchu, the slant-eyed super-machinator set on dominating the world.

With Fu Manchu we enter the arena of the hero-versus-villain pulps of the 1930s, some, such as DR YEN SIN and THE MYSTERIOUS WU FANG, modelled directly on Rohmer's work. By the 1930s the confrontation had developed into a simple formula, still popular today, as in Ian FLEMING's "James Bond" books. A small group of fighters for right, with the aid of highly trained reflexes and an armoury of super-scientific devices, stands off a variety of almost indistinguishable mad SCIENTISTS and /or ambitious businessmen and politicians who plan to conquer all. The best-known sf archetype is DOC SAVAGE, but CAPTAIN HAZZARD, CAPTAIN ZERO, DUSTY AYRES AND HIS BATTLE BIRDS, THE SPIDER and *The Avenger* were all cast in the same mould. Hero magazines were more popular than villain magazines; the latter included DOCTOR DEATH, THE OCTOPUS and THE SCORPION. Although the pulps are dead, the great success of MARVEL COMICS in the 1960s was built on the identical formula, the villains as nasty as ever, though the heroes (in a less straightforward age) more given to self-pity.

Although the attack on Pearl Harbor may well have been seen by many Americans as a retrospective justification of the yellow-peril story (and perhaps by the cynics as a self-fulfilling prophecy), pulp sf of the Second World War and immediately afterwards tended to take brutal European-style fascists as their model for the typical villain. Eric Frank RUSSELL wrote many amusing stories of caricature-Teutonic aliens being outwitted in their myopic militarism by nimble-witted heroes working almost alone.

But far more interesting were the villains of cold-war sf in the 1950s, when the USA was very nearly in a panic over the "Communist menace". Many of these stories are discussed under PARANOIA AND SCHIZOPHRENIA. The day of the individual villain was in decline; he had given way to the group-villain, often indeed symbolized as a HIVE-MIND. The fear of Communism was in large part a fear that here was an expansionist movement in which individuality was subjugated to the demands of the mass. Thus, in Robert A. HEINLEIN's *The Puppet Masters* (1951), the villains are indistinguishable from one another. In this case the villains were aliens, and this of course is where sf differs from most other genres; although sf heroes are usually human, the villains might easily be MONSTERS, ALIENS, ROBOTS or SUPERMEN. A little analysis of what sort of monster or superman it is, however, often shows that there is some readily identifiable human analogue, or at least human fear, involved. The robot destroying everything in its path is simply Man's fear of TECHNOLOGY writ large.

The heyday of the sf villain was over by the 1960s and '70s. Villains still exist, of course, but cannot generally be so easily categorized; very often they remain faceless — they are behind-the-scenes manipulators, politicians, militarists, admen, commercial interests, corporate polluters of the environment working at a distance or through bureaucracies; this reflects a growing fear in the real world (symbolized by COMPUTER data banks) that we are all filed and docketed, and have no way of identifying the enemy out front. In the USA it could be called the Watergate syndrome. But an interesting reversal of the usual scenario can be found in Algis BUDRYS's *Michaelmas* (1977), where it is the hero (who has an almost symbiotic relationship with an enormously complex computer) who does the behind-the-scenes manipulation. Invisible pullers of strings need not be grey or boring villains, however, and Jack VANCE's five "Demon Princes" in his unfinished series of that name are satisfyingly melodramatic, as are the nine immortals who run things in Philip José FARMER's *A Feast Unknown* (1969), *Lord of the Trees* (1970) and *The Mad Goblin* (1970). Most Farmer villains are concerned with using humanity as dupes.

Individual sf writers are naturally liable to incorporate any sort of personal or political resentment or distaste into their creation of villains; Heinlein often lays the blame on flabby liberals, for example, but no useful generalization can be made about villainy at this level.

A surprisingly rare amalgam in sf is the hero/villain, an imaginative territory staked out by Alfred BESTER in the figures of Gully Foyle and Ben Reich, the heroes of his first two novels; they are saturnine, vengeful, obsessive malcontents, for all the world like figures out of 17th-century drama: Webster's *The Duchess of Malfi* or Tourneur's *The Revenger's Tragedy*. They certainly caught the imagination of sf fans, who to this day can still be found at CONVENTIONS wearing badges inscribed with Gully Foyle's anguished cry, "Vorga, I kill you deadly". [PN]

VILLIERS DE L'ISLE - ADAM, (JEAN - MARIE - MATHIAS - PHILIPPE - AUGUSTE, Comte de)
(1840–89). French writer, mostly of poetry and plays, and an extremely impoverished member of the Breton aristocracy. Of some interest to the student of sf is *L'Ève future* ["The Future Eve"] (1886), in which a handsome young lord despairs when his fiancée turns out to be extremely crass — but Thomas Alva Edison comes to the rescue with an impeccable robot duplicate. The work, which was seen as an important contribution to the Symbolist movement, is philosophical and ironic. The earlier collection *Contes Cruels* (coll. 1883; trans. as *Cruel Tales* 1963) contains bizarre fantasy stories, several of them sf, including "Celestial Publicity", in which advertising slogans are projected into the night sky by electric light. An early translation containing most of the above is *Sardonic Tales* (coll. trans. 1927). [JC/PN]

See also: HUMOUR; SATIRE.

VINCENT, HARL. Form of his name used by American engineer and writer

Harl Vincent Schoepflin (1893–1968) for all his fiction, little of which reached book form, though he was a popular writer in the PULP magazines of the early years of the century, and published frequently in *Argosy, AMZ, ASF* and other magazines until the Second World War, stopping then until just before his death, when some further stories appeared, including several reprints, and his novel *The Doomsday Planet* (1966). His work was vigorous but crude. [JC]

See also: GREAT AND SMALL; PARANOIA AND SCHIZOPHRENIA; ROBOTS.

VINGE, JOAN D. (? –). American writer, part Erie Indian, married to sf writer Vernor VINGE. She began publishing sf with "Tin Soldier" in 1974, and her most notable story to date is probably "The Crystal Ship" (1976), title story of *The Crystal Ship: Three Original Novellas of Science Fiction* (anth. 1976) ed. Robert SILVERBERG; it is a sensitive though rather tremulous story of human-alien relations. Her "Eyes of Amber" (1977) won a HUGO award for best novelette. [PN]

VINGE, VERNOR (STEFFEN) (1944–). American writer and mathematician who holds a PhD in mathematics; he began publishing sf with "Apartness" for *NW* in 1965, and has since published several stories with *ASF*; his first novel, *Grimm's World* (1969), is a colourful adventure set on a primitive human planet exploited by interstellar slavers; *The Witling* (1976) is also routine but effective, in its story of two castaway humans who are made to feel pariahs on a planet of medieval-style aliens with PSI POWERS, but who are wanted for their technological prowess. VV is married to sf writer Joan VINGE. [JC/PN]

VISIAK, E(DWARD) H(AROLD) (1878–1972). English poet, critic and novelist. His fiction is essentially fantasy, as in *The Haunted Island* (1910), a complex tale with ghosts, magic and piracy, and *Medusa* (1929), an almost surreal FANTASTIC VOYAGE into unknown seas, with a dark and paranoid atmosphere. He also wrote "The Shadow", a good surrealist ghost novella which appeared in *Crimes, Creeps and Thrills* (anth. 1936) ed. John Gawsworth. He was a friend of David LINDSAY, and an essay by him appeared in *The Strange Genius of David Lindsay* (anth. 1970). [JC/PN]

VISION OF TOMORROW British magazine, BEDSHEET-size. 12 issues, Aug. 1969-Sep. 1970, published by Ronald F. Graham, an Australian sf enthusiast; ed. Philip HARBOTTLE. It featured work by many active British sf writers, including Kenneth BULMER and E.C. TUBB, with the emphasis on straightforward action stories, and several posthumous works by John Russell FEARN. Cover artists

Apr. 1970. Cover by David Hardy.

included Eddie JONES and David Hardy. *VOT* was the first English-language magazine to publish a story by Stanislaw LEM; it was "Are You There, Mr Jones?", and it appeared in the first issue. "The Impatient Dreamers", a history of British sf publishing by Walter GILLINGS, John CARNELL and others, ran through all issues.   [BS/PN]

Collectors should note: After the second issue, Nov. '69, the schedule was monthly. Nov. '69 was wrongly numbered no.3, and Dec. '69 wrongly numbered no.2.

VIVIAN, E(VELYN) CHARLES (? –). British writer of popular fiction, who also wrote, as Jack Mann, a series of fantasy novels about the detective "Gees", including *Gees' First Case* (**1936**), *Her Ways are Death* (undated), *Nightmare Farm* (**1937**), *The Kleinert Case* (**1938**), *Maker of Shadows* (**1938**), *Grey Shapes* (**1938**), *The Ninth Life* (**1939**) and *The Glass Too Many* (**1940**). As by ECV, *Star Dust* (**1925**) describes the calamitous effects of transmuting gross matter into gold; *City of Wonder* (**1922**) sets a LOST WORLD in the East Indies. *Woman Dominant* (**1929**) is an adventure story about a matriarchal lost race.   [JC/PN]

Other works: As ECV: *Fields of Sleep* (**1923**); *Lady of the Terraces* (**1925**). As Jack Mann: *Coulson Goes South* (**1933**); *Dead Man's Chest* (**1934**).

See also: MACHINES; MONEY; SCIENTISTS.

VOID SCIENCE FICTION AND FANTASY Australian DIGEST-size magazine. Eight issues to date, current, 1975 onwards, published by Void Publications; ed. Paul Collins, *V*'s first three issues were published from Queensland, the rest from Melbourne. At best a semi-professional sf magazine, it could be described as a fiction FANZINE, with an overcrowded layout on cheap paper. *V* has contained a few US reprints, but is primarily a platform for such

Australian sf writers as Frank Bryning, A. Bertram CHANDLER and Jack WODHAMS. It has printed no notable stories. *V* is dated by year only, and only one issue (2) has been numbered. Nos 6, 7 and 8 were published in book form as an original anthology, *Envisaged Worlds* (anth. **1977**).   [PN]

VOLTAIRE Pseudonym of François-Marie Arouet (1694–1778). French writer, philosopher and historian. His life was enormously productive; of interest to the student of PROTO SF is his *Micromégas* (Berlin **1750**; France **1752**), in which two giants, one from a planet circling Sirius and one from Saturn, visit Earth, their responses to human life making for some SATIRICAL points, not least that mankind himself may not be so very important in the much larger universe that was coming to be accepted. *Candide* (**1759**), the best-known of all tales of the innocent abroad, can be seen as a precursor of satirical picaresques from Kurt VONNEGUT to Robert SHECKLEY; it could be argued that *Candide*, which is certainly a FANTASTIC VOYAGE, is also ANTHROPO-

LOGICAL sf. It was made into a musical comedy in the USA in the 1950s. Both works exist in a variety of English translations.   [JC/PN]

See also: HISTORY OF SF; OUTER PLANETS; POLITICS; RELIGION.

VON DÄNIKEN, ERICH (1935–   ). A self-educated (his phrase) Swiss writer of what purports to be non-fictional historical speculation, he is the most popular exponent of the equation: ancient gods – space visitors. In *Chariots of the Gods?* (**1968** Germany; trans. **1969**), *Return to the Stars* (**1968** Germany; trans. **1970**) and *The Gold of the Gods* (**1972** Germany; trans. **1973**) he delivers broad hints of a space invasion in some vague past age (Late Tertiary to Jonathan Swift) in all parts of the world. This permits him to give as evidence almost any myths, monuments or curios: if a drawing shows circles, they are a planetary system; if wings, a "flying machine"; if dots, "strange objects". Stone balls are model spaceships; a hole in the ground, a bomb shelter; Aladdin's lamp, a radio. The great Pyramid (a cryogenic chamber) and Easter Island's monuments (images of spacemen) were quarried with lasers and lifted by helicopters. It is central to his thesis that all ancient peoples were moronic, unable to invent or imagine, capable only of copying what the spaceman showed them. Throughout, EVD shows little acquaintance with archaeology, astronomy or even everyday logic ("Could it be?" turns into "it can only be"). But his best-selling books (over 40 million copies) perhaps fill a need for readers lacking scientific training, a sense of the past, or deeply felt myths. The only refutation of his work at all likely to have reached a wide audience was the BBC "Horizon" programme "The Case of the Ancient Astronauts", televised 25 Nov. 1977.   [JS]

See also: ADAM AND EVE; FLYING SAUCERS; MYTHOLOGY; ORIGIN OF MAN; PARANOIA AND SCHIZOPHRENIA; PSEUDO-SCIENCE.

VON HARBOU, THEA (1888–1954). German writer, most noted for the novels based on screenplays written by herself and her husband, Fritz LANG: *Metropolis* (**1926**; trans. **1927**), filmed as METROPOLIS (1926) and *Frau im Mond* (**1928**; trans. as *The Rocket to the Moon* **1930**), filmed as DIE FRAU IM MOND (1929). The books have little of the films' symbolic force, and are thickly propagandistic. TVH was co-author of the screenplays for all the films Fritz Lang made before leaving Germany in 1933.   [JC]

See also: AUTOMATION; CITIES.

VONNEGUT, KURT Jr (1922–   ). American writer born in Indianapolis. He was a prisoner of war in Dresden during the saturation bombing of the city and subsequent firestorm. He later studied at

Kurt VONNEGUT Jr. Photo Jill Krementz.

the Universities of Tennessee and Chicago, and began to write for various magazines in the early 1950s. Although some of this work was sf, the earliest being "Report on the Barnhouse Effect" in COLLIER's in 1950, only a couple of short stories appeared in sf magazines, the first being "Unready to Wear" (1953) in *Gal.*, and KV has always tried hard to avoid categorization as an sf writer. He first became widely popular in the mid-1960s and is recognized as a major American writer of the post-War period.

His first novel was the DYSTOPIAN *Player Piano* (**1952**; vt *Utopia 14*), which describes the dereliction of human purpose and of the quality of life by the progressive surrender of all activities and decisions to machines (*see* AUTOMATION). It is a book heavy with irony, occasionally bordering on black HUMOUR. As KV's career progressed this irony came more and more to the fore. *The Sirens of Titan* (**1959**) is a complex novel about the folly of mistaking luck for the favour of God; it features the Church of God the Utterly Indifferent and the revelation of the manipulation of human history by Tralfamadorian aliens sending messages to one of their kind stranded on Titan. One leading character has an extratemporal viewpoint from which all moments appear co-existent — a theme which crops up again in KV's novel about the firestorming of Dresden, *Slaughterhouse-Five; or, The Children's Crusade* (**1969**).

Mother Night (**1961**) is a non-sf, ABSURDIST novel about the struggle of an American ex-Nazi, who functioned during the War as a propagandist for Hitler (and also as an American agent) to discover his "true" identity. Ironies are multiplied. Several of the characters reappear in later work; in fact the minor characters in KV's work move so readily from story to story it is almost as if it is all one big book. *Cat's Cradle* (**1963**) revolves around the confrontation of opposing philosophies — the narrow scientific outlook of Felix Hoenikker, one of the fathers of the atom-bomb and inventor of the ultimate weapon *ice-nine*

(*see* END OF THE WORLD), and the mythology of Bokonon, a rebel against rationality and architect of a religion consisting of unashamed lies, whose function is to protect believers against the harshness of reality. The novel is at once extremely bitter and highly sentimental, possessed of an apocalyptic pessimism. *God Bless You, Mr. Rosewater* (**1965**) is a second non-sf novel (though it contains an often-quoted paragraph about sf writers) concerning the exploits of a determined philanthropist and the attempt to prove him insane. *Slaughterhouse-Five* follows the career of Billy Pilgrim, survivor of the Dresden firestorm, who finds peace of mind after being kidnapped by Tralfamadorians and learning that the secret of life is to live only in the happy moments — from a Tralfamadorian viewpoint all moments are co-existent (*see* METAPHYSICS) and the whole pattern of the universe is determined. Following this novel Vonnegut's work showed a sharp decline in quality, and both *Breakfast of Champions* (**1973**) and *Slapstick; or, Lonesome No More!* (**1976**) seem to verge on self-parody, and are pervaded with little shoulder-shrugging, verbal tics. The first makes much of a chance meeting between Dwayne Hoover, a car salesman in the process of cracking up, and the sf writer Kilgore Trout, whose "fantasies of an impossibly hospitable world" are published as padding in books of pornographic pictures. Trout — favourite author of Eliot Rosewater and Billy Pilgrim — writes absurd stories in which KV's characters can find plausible excuses for the horrors of the real world. Hoover finds his revelation in a book called *Now It Can Be Told*, which takes the form of a letter from the Creator of the Universe to the only creature possessed of free will, explaining that the whole mess is just an experiment to test his reaction. *Slapstick* is a mechanical fantasy about two ugly children who manifest super-intelligence while together, and who are therefore parted for ever by their extremely rich parents. In these late novels the balance between bitter SATIRE and sentimental commentary is lost as both are driven to extremes.

Vonnegut's best work — which includes some of the short stories first assembled in *Canary in a Cat House* (coll. **1961**) and then reassembled with new material added in *Welcome to the Monkey House* (coll. **1968**), as well as the first seven novels — has a unique flavour not only because of its sardonic brand of *Weltschmerz* but also because of a consistent refusal to seek out scapegoats. Most satirical work is polemical in that it points to the persons or institutions which its author considers responsible for the situation he is criticizing by mockery. KV, however, does not deal in villains, but is content to leave blame unattributed — or attributed only to the carelessness of God the Utterly Indifferent. He is full of

pity for the human predicament but can see no hope in any solutions except for the adoption of actions and beliefs which are absurdly irrational. This is a philosophy very much in keeping with the contemporary *Zeitgeist*.

KV has also written a play (*see* THEATRE), *Happy Birthday, Wanda June* (**1973**), and had a hand in the production of a TV play based on extracts from several of his works, *Between Time and Timbuktu* (1972); the book, also entitled *Between Time and Timbuktu* (**1972**), consists of the script illustrated with stills. A collection of KV's essays is *Wampeters, Foma and Granfalloons* (coll. **1974**). A novel attributed to KV's character Kilgore TROUT, by Philip José FARMER, appeared as *Venus on the Half-Shell* (**1975**). [BS]

About the author: *The Vonnegut Statement* (anth. **1973**), ed. Jerome Klinkowitz and John Somer is one of a number of books; it, in turn, lists over 70 critical articles published up to 1973; there have been many more since.

See also: DEFINITIONS OF SF; DISASTER; DISCOVERY AND INVENTION; ESCHATOLOGY; GENERATION STARSHIPS; INTELLIGENCE; ISLANDS; MERCURY; OUTER PLANETS; OVERPOPULATION; PERCEPTION; POLLUTION; PREDICTION; RELIGION; SPACESHIPS.

VON RACHEN, KURT *See* L. Ron HUBBARD.

VORHIES, JOHN R(OYAL HARRIS) (1920–). American writer, in whose NEAR-FUTURE novel, *Pre-Empt* (**1967**), a nuclear submarine captain threatens the world. [JC]

Feb. 1977. Cover by Rodney Matthews.

VORTEX British small-BEDSHEET size magazine (8¼ inches × 10¼ inches). Five issues, Jan.-May 1977. Published by Shalmead (Jan.-Feb.); Container Publications (Mar.); Cerberus Publishing (Apr.-May); ed. Keith Seddon. *V* was a glossy magazine with some interior illustration in full colour. The first three covers, by Rodney Matthews, suggested an orientation towards fantasy which was not evident in the actual magazine. The first four issues serialized Michael MOORCOCK's novel *The End of All Songs* (**1976**); the fifth contained the first instalment of *The Chaos Weapon* (**1977**) by Colin KAPP. Other stories were for the most part experimental pieces by previously unknown authors such as Ravan Christchild who in most cases were certainly pseudonyms of the editor. [MJE]

No. 1, 1947. Cover by Ethel Siegel.

VORTEX, THE US FANZINE. Two issues, 1947, ed. Gordon M. Kull and George R. Cowie from San Francisco. *V* is listed in some indexes as a professional SF MAGAZINE, but the fiction was by unknown amateurs, and it was distributed free. It was attractively printed on glossy paper. [MJE/FHP]

Oct. 1953. Cover by Martin.

VORTEX SCIENCE FICTION US DIGEST-size magazine. Two issues, May and Oct. 1953, published by Specific Fiction Corp., New York; ed. Chester Whitehorn. *VSF* contained 20 or more very short stories in each issue; the idea did not prove popular. A later magazine (1954), with the same publisher and

editor, was SCIENCE FICTION DIGEST.

VSF should not be confused with the 1977 British magazine VORTEX. [FHP]

VOYAGE À TRAVERS L'IMPOSSIBLE, LE ["An Impossible Voyage"] Film (1904). Star. Produced and directed by Georges MÉLIÈS. 1414 feet. B/w.

This second sf-oriented film made by French cinema pioneer and innovator Méliès (the first was LE VOYAGE DANS LA LUNE) involves a high-speed train taking off from the summit of a mountain, travelling through space, falling into the sea and then returning safely to dry land, all achieved with a repertoire of primitive but ingenious special effects, including stop-motion photography, split-screen, multiple exposures, giant moving cut-outs and live action combined with painted backdrops. [JB]

VOYAGE DANS LA LUNE, LE ["A Trip to the Moon"] Film (1902). Star. Produced and directed by Georges MÉLIÈS. 845 feet. Tinted.

The French film pioneer Méliès based this amusing little spectacle extremely loosely on Jules VERNE's *From the Earth to the Moon* and H.G. WELLS's *First Men in the Moon*. No attempt is made to depict a possible Moon flight seriously; the Moon projectile is loaded into the space-gun by a line of grinning chorus girls; the Man in the Moon is shown with the projectile stuck in his eye; the Moon travellers encounter a group of cardboard lunar inhabitants who explode when tapped with an umbrella; and the travellers safely return home, due to the pull of Earth's gravity, in time to see a statue erected in their honour. Méliès' innovatory special effects are naturally primitive but encompass many basic techniques still in use today. [JB]

VOYAGE TO THE BOTTOM OF THE SEA 1. Film (1961). 20th Century-Fox. Directed by Irwin ALLEN, starring Walter Pidgeon, Joan Fontaine, Barbara Eden and Peter Lorre. Screenplay by Allan and Charles Bennett, story by Irwin Allen. 105 mins. Colour.

The crew of a glass-nosed nuclear submarine has a mission to fire an atomic missile into the Van Allen belt, which has been set on fire by an unfriendly foreign power and is melting the icecaps. Despite enemy submarines, a giant octopus and other hazards, the mission succeeds. As with most of Allen's productions, the plot does not survive an instant's rational scrutiny; it is full of PSEUDO-SCIENCE. Allen later produced a TV series based on the film. The novelization by Theodore STURGEON was *Voyage to the Bottom of the Sea* (**1961**).

2. Television series (1964–8). An Irwin Allen Production for 20th Century-Fox TV/ABC. Created by Irwin ALLEN who was also executive producer. Story consultant: Sidney Marshall. Writers included Irwin Allen, Richard Landau,

Harlan ELLISON (one episode), Robert Hamner, Rik Vollaerts, William Welch and Arthur Weiss. Directors included Irwin Allen, Leonard Horn, Felix Feist, Harry Harris and J. Addiss. Special effects were by L.B. Abbott. 110 episodes, each 50 mins. First season b/w, the remainder colour.

Based on the 1961 film, also by Irwin Allen (*see above*), the series concerned the exploits of the experimental submarine *Seaview* and its crew; it starred Richard Basehart and David Hedison. Early episodes had fairly conventional stories involving secret agents and threats from unfriendly foreign powers, but later the plots became increasingly fantastic. Not only were the submarine crew members faced with such dangers as giant whales, giant jellyfish, giant octopuses and giant "things", but the *Seaview* was also regularly invaded by a variety of esoteric menaces ranging from sentient seaweed to the ghost of a U-boat captain; other uninvited guests included a lobster man, a mummy, a blob and a mad robot. Throughout, Basehart and Hedison kept straight faces, no matter how absurd things became. *City Under the Sea* (**1965**) by Paul FAIRMAN was based on an early episode. [JB]

VOYAGE TO THE END OF THE UNIVERSE *See* IKARIA XB1.

VOYAGE TO THE PLANET OF PREHISTORIC WOMEN *See* PLANET OF STORMS.

VOYAGE TO THE PREHISTORIC PLANET *See* PLANET OF STORMS.

VÝNALEZ ZKAZY (vt **THE FABULOUS WORLD OF JULES VERNE**) Film (1958). Direction and art direction by Karel Zeman, starring Lubor Tokus, Arnost Navratil, Miroslav Holub and Jana Zatloukalova. Screenplay by Karel Zeman and Frantisek Hrubin, based primarily on Jules VERNE's *Face au drapeau* (**1896**; trans. as *For the Flag* **1897**), but also drawing on sections of his *20,000 Leagues Under the Sea* (**1870**), *The Mysterious Island* (**1874–5**) and *Robur le conquérant* (**1886**; trans. as *The Clipper of the Clouds* **1887**). 83 mins. B/w.

This Czech film, also known under the titles *Weapons of Destruction*, *The Diabolic Invention* and *The Deadly Invention*, is a charming blend of cartoon animation, puppet film and live action with the overall style patterned on 19th-century steel engravings. A monomaniacal scientist invents an incredibly powerful new explosive; he and his assistant are captured by a Caption Nemo-like character and his followers. There are various adventures with submarines, balloons, a giant octopus and a vast cannon. At the end patriotism triumphs over unscrupulous technology. [JB/PN]

WADE, TOM (? –). British author of two routine paperback sf novels, *The World of Theda* (**1962**) and *The Voice from Baru* (**1963**). [JC]

WADEY, VICTOR (? –). British author of two routine paperback sf novels, *A Planet Named Terra* (**1962**) and *The United Planets* (**1962**). [JC]

WADSWORTH, PHYLLIS MARIE (? –). British writer whose *Overmind* (**1967**) deals with aliens who contact humanity from another dimension. [JC]

WAGNER, KARL EDWARD (1945–). American writer and editor, formerly a practising psychiatrist, whose fiction, beginning with *Darkness Weaves with Many Shades* (abridged version **1970**; rev. vt 1978 *Darkness Weaves*), is essentially SWORD AND SORCERY; the "Kane" series is comprised of this first novel plus *Death Angel's Shadow* (coll. **1973**), *Bloodstone* (**1975**), *Dark Crusade* (**1976**) and a number of uncollected stories; the "Bran Mak Morn" series is comprised of *Legion from the Shadows* (**1976**), a sequel to the Robert E. HOWARD collection, *Bran Mak Morn* (coll. **1969**; vt *Worms of the Earth*) and *Queen of the Night* (**1977**). As editor of CARCOSA, he has published works by E. Hoffmann Price, Hugh B. Cave and *Worse Things Waiting* (coll. **1973**) by Manly Wade WELLMAN. [JC]

WAHLÖÖ, PER (1926–1975). Swedish writer, best known for his detective novels with Maj Sjowall. His NEAR-FUTURE sf thrillers include *Mord pa 3J* (**1965**; trans. as *Murder on the 31st Floor* **1966**; vt *The Thirty-First Floor* USA), *Stålspranget* (**1968**; trans. as *The Steel Spring* **1970**), about a deadly plague in Sweden, and *Generalerna* (**1965**; trans. as *The Generals* **1974**) , a trial novel set in a military DYSTOPIA; during the course of the trial, the decline among the state's revolutionary rulers from idealism to internecine feuding becomes clear. [JC]

WALDO An item of sf TERMINOLOGY originated by Robert HEINLEIN in his short novel "Waldo" (1942 *ASF*; one of the title stories of the collection of two stories *Waldo & Magic, Inc.*, **1950**; as *Waldo: Genius in Orbit*, **1958**). The eponymous hero suffers from a crippling wasting of the muscles, and invents a number of remote control devices, also called waldoes, for amplifying the power of his feeble muscular movements. The term has since come into general use in technology to describe a whole range of remote control devices which are now commonplace. It has expanded in meaning to include those devices which are arranged to handle radioactive materials in isolation from the handler, and those concerned with fine and precise rather than powerful movements. [PN]

WALDO, E. HUNTER *See* Theodore STURGEON.

WALDROP, HOWARD (? –). American writer, resident in Texas. His first sf story was "Lunch Box" (1972) for *ASF*; his sf novel *The Texas-Israeli War: 1999* (**1974**), with Jake SAUNDERS, makes little capital of its transpositions of genres and nationalities. However, since 1976 several of his stories have been appearing in best-of-the-year and other anthologies quite frequently. These include several collaborations with Steven Utley, notably "Custer's Last Jump" (1976), a rather ponderous ALTERNATE-WORLDS story in which powered flight has reached the USA in time for the Civil War. "Mary Margaret Road-Grader" (1976) is an accomplished post-HOLOCAUST story of Amerindian trials of strength conducted with ageing bulldozers, etc. [PN]
See also: LOST WORLDS.

WALKER, DAVID (HARRY) (1911–). Scottish writer, best known for works outside the sf field, like his novel *Geordie* (**1950**), later filmed; his sf novel, *The Lord's Pink Ocean* (**1972**), is a POLLUTION and DISASTER tale set in North America. [JC]

WALLACE, DOREEN. Writing name of English writer Dora Eileen Agnew (Wallace) Rash (1897–), author of much popular fiction, whose sf novel, *Forty Years On* (**1958**), sets on the Isle of Ely, an area in the fens of Eastern England, a communal attempt to cope with life after a nuclear DISASTER; rural values are extolled. [JC]

WALLACE, EDGAR (1875–1932). English author, playwright and editor, best known for his detective fiction. EW used his experiences of the Boer War in the future-WAR novels *Private Selby* (1909 *The Sunday Journal* as " 'O.C.' — A Soldier's Love Story"; **1912**) and *"1925": The Story of a Fatal Peace* (**1915**). He featured the use of Pavlovian conditioning techniques applied to Man in *The Door With Seven Locks* (**1926**) and "Control No. 2" (1934); impending world catastrophe in *The Fourth Plague*

The cover spread of one of Edgar WALLACE's almost forgotten sf novels.

(**1913**), *The Green Rust* (**1919**), "The Black Grippe" (1920) and *The Day of Uniting* (1921 POPULAR MAGAZINE; **1926**); the counter-Earth theme in *Planetoid 127* (1924 *The Mechanical Boy*; **1929**); and weird fiction in "The Stranger of the Night" (1910), "While the Passengers Slept" (1916) and *Captain of Souls* (**1922**). While working in Hollywood he assisted on the screenplay of KING KONG, though his contribution may have been minimal, and scripted a horror film, *The Table* (adapted into a novel by Robert Curtis, **1936**). [JE]
See also: WEAPONS.

WALLACE, F(LOYD) L. American writer, who began publishing sf with "Hideaway" for *ASF* in 1951, but was strongly associated with *Gal*. in the 1950s, the period of his greatest activity. His novel, *Address: Centauri* (1952 *Gal* as "Accidental Flight"; exp. **1955**), features volunteer cripples setting off for the stars. [JC]

WALLACE, IAN Pseudonym of John Wallace Pritchard (1912–), American clinical psychologist and teacher with a doctorate in education, and a writer active mainly since 1967, though he did publish earlier a non-sf novel under his own name, *Every Crazy Wind* (**1952**). IW spent all his working life in professional education in Detroit, both with the Detroit Board of Education and as a member of the Wayne State University part-time faculty in Philosophy and History of Education; he retired in 1974.
Beginning with *Croyd* (**1967**), IW has produced a remarkable series of sf novels, all but one of them more or less closely linked to a common background about 500 years in the future. Although these novels are all baroque, with freewheeling structures and complex plots that have been likened to those of A.E. VAN VOGT, even sharing with that writer's books a dreamlike intensity, this common sustaining background is left generally unclear. The Solar System is the dominant member of a large group of planets; various alien creatures participate in and impinge upon this central system; TIME PARADOXES abound, and all the other appurtenances of the more intricate sort of SPACE OPERA. But IW's books have an unmistakable contemplative flavour all their own.

Two series use the common background. The St. Cyr Interplanetary Detective novels, *The Purloined Prince* (**1971**) set in 2470, *Deathstar Voyage* (**1969**) set in 2475, and *The Sign of the Mute Medusa* (**1977**) set in 2480, all feature Claudine St. Cyr, an ace detective officer whose missions take her into complexly plotted dilemmas on various planets; there is some time travel. More interesting are the Croyd/Pan novels: *Croyd*, set in 2496, *Dr. Orpheus* (**1968**), set in 2502, *A Voyage to Dari* (**1974**), set in 2506, and *Pan Sagittarius* (**1973**), set in 2509 and earlier and featuring a somewhat more callow, younger duplicate of Croyd. As Croyd is the effective ruler of the human worlds for much of the series, his exploits tend to have weightier consequences than those of St. Cyr. In *Dr. Orpheus*, for instance, one of the most complicated of all, he must combat a plot on the part of distant but approaching aliens desperate to implant their fertile eggs in humans; these aliens have (earlier in time) instituted a conspiracy by which the egomaniac Dr Orpheus has been allowed the use of an IMMORTALITY drug, anagonon, which has the side effect of forcing those who take it to obey anyone (i.e. Orpheus) they know to be hierarchically superior. The success of this drug has hardened the lines of time-probability on Earth, making the aliens' trip potentially successful; Croyd's counter-offensive involves his shaking this high-probability outcome by a great deal of paradoxical time travel. The contemplative narrative distance at which the story is told is significant, permitting the reader to enjoy its intricacies with relative calm; the dreamlike aspects of IW's work are retrospective in effect, rather than wish-fulfilling, as with Van Vogt; in line with this central calm, his style is allusive, adjective-heavy, ornate, and amiably corny. The earlier novels are perhaps better, or at least more stylistically accessible. [JC]
Other works: *The World Asunder* (**1976**); *Z-Sting* (**1978**), a "Croyd" novel.
See also: ABSURDIST SF; CRIME AND PUNISHMENT; GALACTIC EMPIRES.

WALLACE, JAMES (? –). Author of *The Plague of the Golden Rat* (**1976**). [JC]

WALLACE, KING (? – ?). American writer whose sf novel, *The Next War* (**1892**), not untypically of its time and place of origin, plays on white fears of Negro uprisings; the blacks lose the NEAR-FUTURE war of the story, and disappear into the swamps (*see* POLITICS). [JC]

WALLING, WILLIAM (**1926**–). American writer, whose sf novel is *No One Goes There Now* (**1971**). He is not to be confused with William A. Walling, an academic critic, one of whose books is listed under Mary SHELLEY. [JC]

WALLIS, DAVE (? –). Author, probably American, of the sf novel, *Only Lovers Left Alive* (**1964**), in which only teenagers have rights; terrible things happen. [JC]

WALLIS, GEORGE C. (? – ?). English writer, printer (before the First World War) and cinema manager. He began writing sf, historical and adventure fiction in 1896, first for the penny weekly adult magazines, turning to slick magazines at the turn of the century. Around 1903 he began to write almost exclusively for the BOYS' PAPERS, ceasing around 1912. When genre sf magazines began in the 1920s, he began to write again, with "The World at Bay" for *AMZ* in 1928 as by B. and G.C. Wallis, the B. referring to his cousin, who acted as his literary agent. He had nine SPACE OPERAS published in TALES OF WONDER, 1938–41.
Only three of his early sf and fantasy novels were reprinted as books: *Children of the Sphinx* (**1901**), a historical fantasy set in Egypt; *A Corsair of the Sky* (1910–11 *Lot-O'-Fun*; **1912**) as by Royston Heath, in which an airborne pirate declares war on the world; *Beyond the Hills of Mist* (1912 *Lot-O'-Fun*; **1913**), in which a Tibetan LOST RACE, equipped with aircraft, plans world domination. Other early novels, some in serial form, were "The Last King of Atlantis" (1896–7 *Short Stories*), in which an ancient MS describing the destruction of ATLANTIS is found in a UTOPIAN world of the future, "The World Wreckers" (1908 *Scraps*), a future-WAR story influenced by George GRIFFITH, "The Terror from the South" (1909 *Comic Life*), in which an Antarctic lost race becomes belligerent, and "Wireless War" (1909 *Comic Life*), with A.J. Andrews, another future-war novel. GCW also published at least seven sf short stories 1896–1904, including "The Great Sacrifice" (1903 *The London Magazine*) in which benevolent Martians save us from ourselves.
GCW is probably the only Victorian sf writer, exactly contemporary with H.G. WELLS, who continued to publish after the Second World War. His last novel was *The Call of Peter Gaskell* (**1947**), in which yet another lost race, this time Inca, plots to conquer the world. He is interesting not because he was a good writer, but because he so exactly typifies the themes of Victorian sf and the longevity of their sales appeal. [JE/PN]

WALLIS, G. McDONALD Pseudonym of American writer and actress Hope Campbell (? –), who has acted under the name Hope McDonald, and written non-sf fiction under her own name and as Virginia Hughes, concentrating on juveniles. Her sf novels as GMW, *The Light of Lilith* (**1961**) and *Legend of Lost Earth* (**1963**), are both routine but enjoyable adventures, both set initially on other planets but focusing on a threatened

or desirable Earth. [JC]

WALSH, J(AMES) M(ORGAN) (1897–1952). Australian-born British writer, primarily of mystery stories, some written as Stephen Maddock. His *Vandals of the Void* (**1931**), its sequel "The Struggle for Pallas" (1931 *Wonder Stories Quarterly*) and *Vanguard to Neptune* (1932 *Wonder Stories Quarterly*; **1952**) are fairly routine early SPACE OPERAS. *The Secret of the Crater* (**1939**) has fantasy elements. [PN]
See also: MERCURY; OUTER PLANETS; PUBLISHING.

WALTER, W(ILLIAM) GREY (1910–77). English writer and pioneer, between 1936 and 1956, of the development and use of electroencephalography in England; his early, popular study of the nature of the brain, *The Living Brain* (**1953**), was influential in its time. His sf novel, *Further Outlook* (**1956**; vt *The Curve of the Snowflake* USA), affords illustrative, fundamentally OPTIMISTIC views of future HISTORY up to AD 2056 through the use of a time machine. [JC]

WALTERS, GORDON *See* George LOCKE.

WALTERS, HUGH Form of his name used by English writer Walter Llewellyn Hughes (1910–) for his fiction, all of it juveniles, beginning with *Blast Off at Woomera* (**1957**; vt *Blast Off at 0300* USA). Most of his novels are SPACE OPERAS, as the titles hint. The books form a series, the hero being Chris Godfrey, though in later books, as Godfrey grows older and becomes director of U.N.E.X.A. (United Nations Exploration Agency, the "organization responsible for the exploration of the Universe"), younger characters like the mechanic Tony Hale come into the foreground. [JC]
Other works: *The Domes of Pico* (**1958**; vt *Menace from the Moon* USA); *Operation Columbus* (**1960**; vt *First on the Moon* USA); *Moon Base One* (**1961**; vt *Outpost on the Moon* USA); *Expedition Venus* (**1962**); *Destination Mars* (**1963**); *Terror by Satellite* (**1964**); *Mission to Mercury* (**1965**); *Spaceship to Saturn* (**1967**); *The Mohole Mystery* (**1968**; vt *The Mohole Menace* USA); *Nearly Neptune* (**1969**; vt *Neptune One is Missing* USA); *First Contact?* (**1971**); *Passage to Pluto* (**1973**); *Tony Hale, Space Detective* (**1973**); *Murder on Mars* (**1975**); *The Caves of Drach* (**1977**).
See also: MERCURY.

WALTHER, DANIEL (**1940**–). French writer. A journalist, his first story was published in 1965. An eclectic author and easy stylist who can switch from HARD sf to poetic HEROIC FANTASY, DW has written over 60 short stories. His collection *Requiem pour demain* ["Requiem for Tomorrow"] (coll. **1976**) shows him at his most experimental. Not unlike Harlan ELLISON, to whom he has often been likened, DW has yet to produce a major novel. *Mais l'espace … Mais le temps* ["What about Space? What about Time?"] (**1972**) is a long novella blending space technology and MAGIC. His anthology *Les soleils noirs d'Arcadie* ["Black Suns of Arcadia"] (anth. **1975**) is a manifesto for the "NEW WAVE". [MJ]

WALTON, BRYCE (1918–). American writer, prolific under his own name and others in several genres, including TV work. He has written sf as Kenneth O'Hara. He began publishing sf with "The Ultimate World" for *Planet Stories* in 1945, and was an active contributor to the magazines for about 15 years, though less frequently since. A juvenile novel, *Sons of the Ocean Deeps* (**1952**), is set in the Mindanao Deep. His work is efficient but stereotyped. [JC]

WANDREI, DONALD (1908–). American writer and editor, founder with August DERLETH in 1939 of ARKHAM HOUSE, initially to publish the work of H.P. LOVECRAFT, whom both admired deeply, though DW soon resigned his interest in the firm. As a writer he is best known, justifiably, for his FANTASY and weird stories, beginning with "The Red Brain" for *Weird Tales* in 1927; later sf work, much of it in *ASF* in the 1930s, is of less interest. He has been inactive since the Second World War in the sf field. In addition to some unremarkable verse, collected in *Dark Odyssey* (coll. **1931**) and *Poems for Midnight* (coll. **1965**), he published a collection of fantasy, *The Eye and the Finger* (coll. **1944**), a Lovecraftian "Cthulhu Mythos" novel, *The Web of Easter Island* (**1948**), and a further collection, *Strange Harvest* (coll. **1965**). With Derleth he edited *Selected Letters: 1925–1929: H.P. Lovecraft* (coll. **1968**). All except the first of the above were published by Arkham. [JC] See also: COSMOLOGY; END OF THE WORLD; FOURTH DIMENSION (AND OTHERS); GREAT AND SMALL; PARALLEL WORLDS.

WAR One of the principal imaginative stimuli to futuristic and scientific speculation has been the possibility of war, and the possibility that new TECHNOLOGY might transform war, as indeed it has done in the past century. This stimulus was particularly important during the period 1870–1914 and in the years following the revelation of the atom bomb in 1945.

Antique futuristic fictions such as the anonymous *Reign of George VI, 1900–25* (**1763**) show no sign of awareness that war might change its aspect — here King George, sabre in hand, leads his cavalry in the charge as of old. In the middle of the 19th century, however, awareness of technology spread rapidly with the railways (*see* TRANSPORTATION), and as early as 1859 Herrmann LANG envisaged

WAR in the future was a dominating theme of early sf, as in H.G. Wells's *The War in the Air*, 1908. The magnificent cover by A.C. Michael is from a 1911 edition.

a different pattern for future combat in *The Air Battle* (**1859**). The possibilities of the new technology in war were displayed during the American Civil War (1861–5), which was observed by representatives of various European nations. When the German Empire was consolidated after the Franco-Prussian war of 1870 the political balance of power in Europe shifted enough to alarm certain influential Britons, who began to campaign for Army reform and rearmament in order to keep abreast of the Germans. The case was dramatized spectacularly by Sir George CHESNEY in *The Battle of Dorking* (**1871**), an ingenious fiction describing how England is invaded and conquered by Germany. It caused a sensation, and a debate which did not die down entirely until the Great War itself (*see also* INVASION). After a flurry of replies in kind the political dispute cooled somewhat, but a new sub-genre of fiction had been inaugurated and future-war stories were established as a brand of popular romance. The genre is very well documented in I.F. CLARKE's *Voices Prophesying War, 1763–1984* (**1966**) and featured such successful pieces of alarmism as Erskine CHILDERS' *The Riddle of the Sands* (**1903**) and William LE QUEUX's *The Invasion of 1910* (**1906**), which made a great impact when it was serialized in the new-born *Daily Mail*. Le Queux wrote a large number of anti-German thrillers and war-anticipation stories before and during the War, and the total volume and tone of similar fictions makes it difficult to doubt that this species of fiction was influential in the genesis of the great enthusiasm which Britons carried into the real war against Germany when it finally came. The great bulk of this fiction was relatively mundane, envisaging little significant alteration in the mode of warfare as a

result of new technology, though there were a number of stories published after 1895 featuring miraculous devastating rays (*see* WEAPONS).

One writer who did appreciate the difference which new inventions might make to warfare was George GRIFFITH, author of *The Angel of the Revolution* (**1893**) and its sequel *Olga Romanoff* (**1894**). Airships and submarines are the stars of these early novels, but by the time he wrote his last, *The Lord of Labour* (**1911**), his future wars were being fought with atomic missiles and disintegrator rays. Although he dealt in destruction on a grand scale, his attitude was little different from that of his contemporaries. He loved writing about violence and devastation, revelling in conflict and gore. (This attitude has been satirized in two recent parodies by Michael MOORCOCK, *The Warlord of the Air* **1971**, and *The Land Leviathan*, **1974**.) Another of Griffith's fantasies is *Valdar the Oft-Born* (**1895**), in which a warrior of the ancient past is serially reincarnated to take his place in all the great conflicts of history, a notion previously used in a slightly less bloodthirsty manner by Edwin Lester ARNOLD in *Phra the Phoenician* (**1890**).

A more disciplined imagination was put to work by H.G. WELLS, who foresaw technological developments in warfare accurately enough in "The Land Ironclads" (1903), *The War in the Air* (**1908**) and the atom-bomb story *The World Set Free* (**1914**). The British High Command, however, continued to show an extreme conservatism of imagination to the bitter end, refusing to believe in the potential of the tank, the submarine or the aeroplane until they were shown the way by the Germans.

The war-anticipation story flared up again in Europe during the 1930s when Hitler came to power and the future seemed ominous, though neither alarmism nor enthusiasm ever reached the same pitch, largely because the disillusionment of the terrible war in the trenches and the colossal loss of life cast such a long shadow. The future war stories of the 1930s, including *The Gas War of 1940* (**1931** as by Miles; vt *Valiant Clay*) by Neil BELL, *Day of Wrath* (**1936**) by Joseph O'NEILL and the American *Final Blackout* (1940; **1948**) by L. Ron HUBBARD, are noticeably more sombre and bitter than those which preceded the Great War. The second boom in future-war stories, which came *after* the curtain fell on the Second World War, was remarkable for its extreme alarmism, this time without the slightest hint of enthusiasm. Thus history, as reflected in futuristic fiction, really learned the lesson of what technology meant in the context of international conflict. It took just 75 years. (Examples of post-War stories in this sub-genre may be found under END OF THE WORLD, HOLOCAUST AND AFTER and WEAPONS).

Two variants on the theme of

international conflict which require mention here are the "Yellow Peril" story first popularized by M.P. SHIEL in *The Yellow Danger* (**1898**; rev. **1899**) and *The Dragon* (**1913**; vt *The Yellow Peril*) and the "socialist menace" story popularized by William Le Queux in *The Unknown Tomorrow* (**1910**) and Hugh ADDISON's *The Battle of London* (**1923**). Both these themes were abundantly represented in thrillers of the 1930s. The socialist cause did get a few opportunities to answer back in kind (*see* POLITICS) — notably Jack LONDON's early *The Iron Heel* (**1907**) — but the Oriental races did not. A third variant, of minor importance and seemingly confined to Britain, is the ironic-civil-war story exemplified by Ronald HINGLEY's *Up Jenkins!* (**1956**) and Arthur WISE's *The Day the Queen Flew to Scotland for the Grouse Shooting* (**1968**).

I.F. Clarke sees Wells's *War of the Worlds* (**1898**) as a logical extension of the 19th-century future-war story, and it was quickly followed by Robert William COLE's story of colonial war against Sirian aliens in *The Struggle for Empire* (**1900**), but most scientific romancers were content with other-worldly wars fought in a more or less barbaric fashion with swords as the key weapons. Wherever the HEROES of early PULP sf went they found wars being fought between humans and ALIENS or between aliens and aliens. Even in the latter case they never felt inhibited about joining in (in the former case, of course, it was their evident duty), and such was the moral insight of pulp fantasists that they almost never had the slightest difficulty in selecting the "right" side. It was always a matter of the noble, gentle and handsome against the vicious, aggressive and ugly. In pulp literary conventions it never needed two to make a fight: the evil always forced it and the good always won it. SPACE OPERA thrived on war — war between races, between planets or between GALACTIC EMPIRES. The search to discover bigger and more powerful apparatus was driven to its limits in a few short years. Spectacular genocide was common before the 1920s were out (an example is Edmond HAMILTON's "The Other Side of the Moon", 1929), and stars were soon being blown up right, left and centre. Any genuine speculative thought about future warfare that might have crept into the pulps was drowned by sheer extravagance, and this situation did not change until 1939, when the example of war in Europe brought a new note of sobriety. Anti-German and anti-Japanese stories that were little more than thinly veiled propaganda began appearing in the lesser pulps, and became standard in 1942 when America joined the war. In John W. CAMPBELL Jr's *ASF* more serious depictions of war appeared; here Hubbard presented the classic *Final Blackout*, A.E. VAN VOGT began chronicling *The War Against the Rull* (1940–50, fix-up **1959**), and Ross

ROCKLYNNE, in "Quietus" (1940), posed the moral dilemma that had been so easily sidestepped in the past: when visitors from elsewhere find two creatures locked in conflict, how do they choose which to help?

Though the possibility of future wars on Earth dominated the military concerns of sf writers from 1939 until the 1950s, more exotic wars continued to be fought. War across time was invented by Jack WILLIAMSON in *The Legion of Time* (1938; **1952**) and has been developed since then by Fritz LEIBER, in his stories about the "Change Wars" — most notably *The Big Time* (1958; **1961**) — and by Barrington J. BAYLEY in *The Fall of Chronopolis* (**1974**). Leiber also considered the possibility of war between PARALLEL WORLDS in *Destiny Times Three* (1945; **1957**) — a theme taken up again by Keith LAUMER in *Worlds of the Imperium* (**1962**) and *The Other Side of Time* (**1965**). War between worlds, though, continued to provide the main context for the more abstract species of military sf which concerned itself with issues more general (*see also* SOCIAL DARWINISM) than the prospect of immanent war on Earth. A strong tradition of militaristic sf grew up in the 1950s and '60s, notable early examples being Robert A. HEINLEIN's *Starship Troopers* (**1959**) and Gordon R. DICKSON's "Dorsai" series begun with *The Genetic General* (**1960**; exp. vt *Dorsai!* 1976). Other important contributors include Poul ANDERSON, with *The Star Fox* (fix-up **1965**) and *The People of the Wind* (**1973**); Jerry POURNELLE in *A Spaceship for the King* (**1973**) and Joe HALDEMAN in *The Forever War* (fix-up **1974**). During the period in which these works were published, popular opinion in America underwent a drastic change in its attitude to war, occasioned by the war in Vietnam. This stimulated a good deal of thought about the moral justification of war, and the anti-militaristic opposition found greater strength and conviction both in life and in books. Perhaps the most lurid of sf's war stories of the 1960s, Norman SPINRAD's *The Men in the Jungle* (**1967**), was composed with Vietnam very much in mind, and Spinrad went on to write a "history" of the Second World War transfigured into the science-fictional dream of a Hitler who emigrated to the USA instead of instituting the Third Reich: *The Iron Dream* (**1972**). The most successful MAINSTREAM anti-war novel of the 1960s, Joseph Heller's *Catch-22* (**1961**), influenced such sf stories as Barry MALZBERG's "Final War" (1968 as by K.M. O'Donnell) and Dav GARNETT's *Mirror In the Sky* (**1969**), both of which present wars which are purposeless and rather surreal nightmares — wars which are no longer the means to economic or territorial ends but which have become domesticated as ways of life. A more literal version of the same notion was developed by C.M. KORNBLUTH and

Judith MERRIL in *Gunner Cade* (**1952** as by Cyril JUDD) and more extensively explored by Mack REYNOLDS in *The Earth War* (**1963**).

War technology is taken to its logical conclusion in Fred SABERHAGEN's "Berserker" series, begun in 1963, and the destructive potential of future war is conveyed by a matter-of-fact account of a brief interplanetary conflict in which billions die in Samuel R. DELANY's *Triton* (**1976**). All this is a far cry from the conscienceless genocide of 1930s space opera, and even in modern space operas such as Norman Spinrad's *The Solarians* (**1966**) or Brian STABLEFORD's "Dies Irae" trilogy, (all published in 1971), the devil-may-care attitude is clearly extinct. The prevalent feeling is, however, that no matter how horrible it may become war will always be with us — that it serves either some kind of psychological craving or some kind of economic imperative. This point of view is well illustrated by the acid cynicism of Leonard C. LEWIN's *Report from Iron Mountain on the Possibility and Desirability of Peace* (**1967**), a report prepared by an imaginary committee investigating the feasibility of finding economic and psychological substitutes for war.

It is notable that, on average, British sf is somewhat less militaristic than American sf. When militarism was rampant in the work of various American writers in the late 1950s and early '60s, Eric Frank RUSSELL wrote a number of vitriolic anti-militaristic stories ranging from the horror story "I Am Nothing" (1952) to the farcical "Nuisance Value" (1957), and though Russell is an extreme example there is nothing in British sf which compares to the work of Heinlein or Anderson. America, of course, came late into both world wars and escaped relatively unscarred from them, and it was not until the TV set brought Vietnam into American homes that any real consciousness of the significance of war reached the American homeland. If the attitude of Gérard KLEIN's *Les seigneurs de la guerre* (**1971**; trans. as *The Overlords of War* **1973**) may be taken as typical, then French sf seems to have more in common with the temper of British sf in this regard, but it may be significant to note that the PERRY RHODAN novellas, which are extremely popular in Germany, are distinctly ambiguous, combining a certain amount of anti-war posturing with a basic brutality very reminiscent of American space opera of the 1930s. It is also worth noting that the trend in sf toward a more peace-loving outlook has been matched historically by the regrowth of interest in the ultra-violent SWORD-AND-SORCERY genre, which still reflects, in a crude and bloody manner, an unsophisticated version of the war-glorifying ideology of E.R. EDDISON's *The Worm Ouroborus* (**1922**).

Three theme anthologies are *Beachheads in Space* (anth. **1952**) ed. August

DERLETH, *Combat SF* (anth. **1975**) ed. Gordon R. Dickson and *Before Armageddon* (anth. **1975**) ed. Michael Moorcock, the latter concentrating on the period before 1914. [BS]

WARD, HENRY (1913–). Apparently French writer, whose sf novels are *L'enfer est dans le ciel* (trans. as *Hell's Above Us* **1960**) and *Les soleils verts* (**1956**; trans. as *The Green Suns* **1961**). The latter book contains a detailed biography of HW in the introduction, claiming that he is a scientist, educated at Cambridge in the UK and then Columbia in the USA, that at the request of the State Department he liaised between atomic research units in France and the USA in 1939–40, and that he was later connected with the destruction of the V-Bomb centre at Peenemunde. However, this information and even HW's nationality may be a spoof to lend verisimilitude to the two documentary-style thrillers, both involving conspiracy at high political levels involved with the investigation of implausible sf events *vis à vis* the space programme, aliens, the Suez conflict and PARALLEL WORLDS. HW appears as a character in both these stories. He may be pseudonymous and British; he is not listed in Pierre VERSINS's *Encyclopédie de l'utopie et de la science fiction* (**1972**). [PN]

WAR GAME, THE Made-for-TV film (1965). BBC/Pathé Contemporary. Directed and written by Peter WATKINS. 50 mins (cut to 47). B/w.

This pseudo-documentary about a nuclear attack on England and its aftermath in a small town in Kent was refused a showing by the BBC, though made for them, on the grounds that it was too realistic and might disturb audiences — exactly what it was designed to do. Since then the film has had a wide theatrical release and won an Academy Award. Though clumsily made it is full of shattering images: the glare and concussion of the bomb; the raging fire storms; the hideously disfigured casualties; torment and slow death from radiation poisoning; mass cremations; buckets of wedding rings gathered from the dead; and execution squads, composed of English policemen, shooting looters. [JB]

WARGAR, KURT *See* André RUELLAN.

WARHOON American FANZINE (1952–70) ed., from New York, Richard Bergeron. *W* was a large, attractive, duplicated fanzine containing careful and literate articles on sf and FANDOM. James BLISH, Robert A.W. LOWNDES and John BAXTER were among the regular sf columnists, and Walt Willis, Bob SHAW, Terry CARR and Harry WARNER Jr were fan columnists. Occasional contributors included Ted WHITE, Robert BLOCH, and Harlan ELLISON. *W* won the HUGO award for best fanzine in 1962. [PR]

WARLAND, ALLEN *See* Donald A. WOLLHEIM.

WARNER, HARRY Jr (1922–). American journalist and sf fan. Publisher of several FANZINES, including *Spaceways* and the long-lived *Horizons*, which has appeared regularly in FAPA since 1939. His history of sf FANDOM, *All Our Yesterdays* (**1969**), is an affectionate and thorough examination of individuals, fan organizations and fanzines in the 1940s. The second volume, *A Wealth Of Fable* (**1976**), continues the history through the 1950s. HW won the HUGO award for best fan writer in 1969 and again in 1972. [PR]

WARNER, REX (1905–). English writer and translator, whose best-known novels are his earliest works for adults, *The Wild Goose Chase* (**1937**), *The Professor* (**1938**) and *The Aerodrome* (**1941**). Each of them is a political allegory some of whose devices relate to the KAFKA-esque side of MAINSTREAM sf. In *The Wild Goose Chase*, three brothers bicycle into a strange country in search of the eponymous goose, and encounter, participate in and ultimately cause a revolution in a DYSTOPIAN society. *The Aerodrome*, his best-known novel, depicts (within the allegorical confines of an aerodrome) an attempt at violently remoulding human nature. RW is always clear about which side he stands on in these metaphysical conflicts; this is sometimes detrimental to the imaginative power of his fiction. [JC]

WAR OF THE WORLDS Film (1953). Paramount. Directed by Byron HASKIN, starring Gene Barry, Anne Robinson, Les Tremayne and Paul Frees. Screenplay by Barré Lyndon, based on the novel by H.G. WELLS. 85 mins. Colour.

Not much of the original Wells novel remains in this George PAL production: the setting is changed from 1890s-England to 1950s-California; the Martian war machines are altered from walking tripods to flying-saucer-like vehicles; and, most damaging of all, a Hollywood "love interest", typical of the period, is added. Despite the weaknesses of the script and indifferent performances, the film generates considerable excitement. Much of this is due to the spectacular special effects which cost $1,400,000, a large amount in those days (the whole film cost only $2,000,000). Not all the effects are especially convincing: the first appearance of the war machines, after an impressive build-up of suspense, is spoilt by the obvious maze of wires supporting each one; but as a whole the effects are dazzling and colourful, especially the final sequences showing the machines attacking Los Angeles. The manta-shaped vehicles glide down the streets (the supporting wires were matted out in these scenes) with their snake-like heat-ray projectors blasting the surrounding

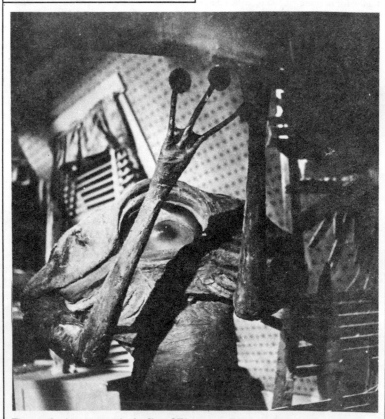

The one fleeting moment in the film of WAR OF THE WORLDS where an actual Martian is visible.

buildings into rubble. In charge of the effects were Gordon Jennings, Wallace Kelley, Paul Lerpae, Ivyl Burks, Jan Domela and Irmin Roberts. The film is usually considered one of the few major works of sf cinema.   [JB]

WATER, SILAS See Noel Loomis.

WATERLOO, STANLEY (1846–1913). American writer, whose first sf novel is *The Story of Ab: a Tale of the Time of the Caveman* (**1897**), in which Ab's life represents the gradual acquisition of the necessary inventions and culture to begin the march to civilization; this is among the earliest romances of ANTHROPOLOGY, though preceded by Andrew LANG's "The Romance of the First Radical" from his *In the Wrong Paradise* (coll. **1886**). Further SW novels are *Armageddon* (**1898**), in which an Anglo-American supremacy is achieved over the rest of the world in a near-future WAR, and *A Son of the Ages* (**1914**), in which the Son's various REINCARNATIONS carry us through significant moments in history; for a sophisticated working of that idea, *see* Peter VANSITTART's *The Story Teller* (**1968**). SW was a routine stylist with a good nose for structure and idea.   [JC] **Other works:** *The Wolf's Long Howl* (coll. **1899**). **See also:** ORIGIN OF MAN.

WATERS, T(HOMAS) A. (? –). American writer, whose first sf novel, *The Probability Pad* (**1970**), concludes a trilogy begun by Chester ANDERSON's *The Butterfly Kid* (**1967**) and continued by Michael KURLAND's *The Unicorn Girl* (**1969**); it is a lightweight spoof involving the three authors as characters in Greenwich Village, and a good deal of alien-inspired body duplication. A counter-cultural ethos also inspires the grimmer *Centerforce* (**1974**), in which motorcycle drop-outs and commune dwellers combine in opposition to a NEAR-FUTURE, police-state America. [JC]

WATKINS, PETER (1935–). British television and film director. Educated at Cambridge, PW worked in documentary films from 1959. He made a reputation with two television quasi-documentaries for the BBC, *Culloden* (1964) and THE WAR GAME (1965). He was one of the pioneers of the technique of staging historical or imaginary events as if they were contemporary and undergoing television-news coverage. *Culloden* reconstructed the famous battle of that name, and *The War Game* adopted a cinema-verité manner to create the likely consequences of nuclear attack in the UK, sufficiently horrifyingly for the film to be denied a screening on TV, for which it was made. It was successful when released in the cinema. His next film, PRIVILEGE (1966), has a pop-star used as a puppet by a future government in a cunning propaganda plan for the

manipulation of the nation's youth. Most of PW's work since his first film has been sf. GLADIATORERNA (1968; vt *The Peace Game*), made in Sweden, and PUNISHMENT PARK (1971) are both set in the future, and both use stories of channelled violence to argue a pacifist case, the latter more plausibly. An interesting paradox is that while his theme is normally the future use of propaganda and mind control by inhumane governments to channel the aggressive instincts of the people, and his purpose is to generate moral indignation in the audience at this cynical curtailment of our freedoms, his own work equally uses the illusion of fact to present a propaganda fiction. Whether knowingly or not, he is fighting fire with fire. After its initial success, PW's work has been treated less kindly by critics who do not doubt his sincerity but deprecate his methods; it is felt by some that he has thumped the same tub for too long. [PN]

WATKINS, WILLIAM JON (1942–). American writer and academic, associate professor of English at Brookdale Community College; with Gene SNYDER he has written the sf novels *Ecodeath* (1972), a POLLUTION story in which the leading characters are called Snyder and Watkins and the plot is fast and furious, and *The Litany of Sh'reev* (1976), in which Sh'reev, a healer with precognitive powers, becomes involved in a revolution. On his own, WJW has written *Clickwhistle* (1973), about dolphins (*see* COMMUNICATIONS), and *The God Machine* (1973), in which political dissidents shrink themselves with a "micronizer" to get away from it all. His fiction is stylish, often violent, and sometimes silly.   [JC/PN]

WATSON, BILLY See Theodore STURGEON.

Ian WATSON, with daughter Jessica.

WATSON, IAN (1943–). English writer. He read English at Balliol College, Oxford, graduating with a BA in 1963, and lectured in English in Tanzania (1965–7) and Tokyo (1967–70). He then taught future studies for six years at Birmingham Polytechnic, taking there one of the first academic courses in sf in the UK; he has been a full-time writer

since 1976.

IW began writing sf with "Roof Garden Under Saturn" for *NW* in 1969, and has published several short stories since, but it is as a novelist that he has gained his reputation, beginning with *The Embedding* (**1973**). (His first book had been a juvenile, *Japan: A Cat's Eye View*, Osaka, **1969**.) *The Embedding* was runner-up for the JOHN W. CAMPBELL MEMORIAL AWARD in 1974, and its French translation, *L'enchâssement*, won the PRIX APOLLO in 1975.

IW's novels are very much of a piece; they form together a continuing series of thought experiments which spiral outwards from the same central obsessions, though they are a series in no formal sense. Subsequent novels have been *The Jonah Kit* (**1975**) (which won, in its paperback form, the BRITISH SCIENCE FICTION AWARD for 1978), *The Martian Inca* (**1977**) and *Alien Embassy* (**1977**), and one thus far published only in French, reputedly having not secured a British publication because of its sexual content, *Orgasmachine* (**1976**). This, which would have been entitled *The Woman Factory* in English, was written in collaboration with his wife Judy; it deals with the manufacture of custom-built girls in a fable about the exploitation of women.

IW's intelligent, polemical pieces about the nature of sf, most of which have appeared in SCIENCE-FICTION STUDIES, FOUNDATION (which he joined as features editor in 1976 — he is also on the Council of the SCIENCE FICTION FOUNDATION) and VECTOR, throw some light on the intentions of his sometimes difficult fiction, and is also, in a sense, of a piece with it. Indeed IW's published work, both fiction and non-fiction, is actively committed to the possibility of things being very much better, although he clearly believes that the world is in a ravaged and collapsing condition. He has criticized much recent sf as being in effect a form of mere elegant, entropic doodling, a kind of fiddling while Rome burns.

Specifically, his novels enact narratives in which reality, so far as humanity is concerned, is subjective and partial, created too narrowly through our PERCEPTION of it; it may be possible to generate fuller realities, through means ranging from drugs through linguistic disciplines, focused meditation, radical changes in education from childhood up, and a kind of enhanced awareness of other perceptual possibilities. In all the novels we are given forms of transcendent or other perception, whether in whales, humans or aliens. In addition to comment on contemporary and NEAR-FUTURE POLITICS, IW's work brings together a formidable apparatus from the sciences, both SOFT and HARD, notably cultural ANTHROPOLOGY, semiology, LINGUISTICS, COMMUNICATIONS theory, COSMOLOGY and PHYSICS; his works are further discussed under all these headings, and also in CONCEPTUAL BREAKTHROUGH and INTELLIGENCE.

IW is perhaps the most impressive synthesizer in modern sf, and as intellectual thrillers his books are exciting and thought-provoking. His writing can be intensely vivid, but it suffers occasionally from a certain clotted, dry quality. His characterization is sometimes notional, and the anomie from which so many of his protagonists suffer sometimes makes it difficult to distinguish them, as several critics have observed of the three astronauts in *The Martian Inca*. None the less, he is certainly one of the most important sf writers and critics to emerge in the 1970s, and indeed he may well have opened up new areas for speculation which will revolutionize the genre. His most recent novel is *The Miracle Visitors* (1978). [PN]

See also: ARTS; CRITICAL AND HISTORICAL WORKS ABOUT SF; MARS; METAPHYSICS; PSYCHOLOGY; SF IN THE CLASSROOM; SUPERMAN; TERRAFORMING; TIME TRAVEL; UNDER THE SEA.

WATSON, RICHARD F. *See* Robert SILVERBERG.

WATSON, SIMON (? –). English writer, whose sf novel for older children is *No Man's Land* (1975); it is set in a regimented future England where nonconformist schoolboys are brainwashed. [PN]

WAUGH, EVELYN (1903–66). English writer, known mostly for works outside the sf field, e.g. *A Handful of Dust* (1934). Some of his early fiction, like *Black Mischief* (1932) and *Scoop* (1938), utilizes imaginary African countries for satirical purposes, and *Vile Bodies* (1930) ends in an apocalyptic Europe torn by a final war, but it is only in some post-War works that he wrote fiction genuinely making use of sf themes. *Scott-King's Modern Europe* (1947) satirizes post-War totalitarianism through the imaginary state of Neutralia; *Love Among the Ruins: A Romance of the Near Future* (1953), also included in *Tactical Exercise* (coll. 1954), combines the chemical coercion of Aldous HUXLEY's *Brave New World* (1932) and the drabness and scarcity of the needs of life of George ORWELL's *Nineteen Eighty-Four* (1949) in a brief but savage attack on the joylessness of a Welfare State England advanced a few decades in time and dominance. Miles Plastic, his free will bureaucratically threatened, his lover co-opted by the state, takes refuge in "gemlike, hymeneal, auspicious" acts of arson. It is a book, like most of EW's work, in which humour only brings out the more clearly a radical despair. [JC]

See also: DYSTOPIAS; SATIRE.

WAYMAN, TONY RUSSELL (1929–). English-born writer now living in the USA, after having spent some years in Singapore; he was actively involved in Malayan film-making. His first novel, *World of the Sleeper* (1967), tells the story of a man transported into another world, one rather resembling Malaya (the story had originally been the script for a Malayan film). [JC]

Other works: *Dunes of Pradai* (1971); *Ads Infinitum* (1971).

WEAPONS In the catalogue of possible technological wonders offered in the *New Atlantis* (1627; 1629), Francis BACON included more powerful cannons, better explosives and "wildfires burning in water, unquenchable". Such a promise was one which he could not leave out if his prospectus was to appeal to the political establishment. In the second half of the 19th century, when the effects of technological progress upon society became the subject of widespread speculation, the progress of weaponry became one of the most important stimulants of the imagination. George CHESNEY's classic *The Battle of Dorking* (1871) popularized the concern felt by a number of politicians that Britain's military forces had fallen considerably behind the times. It achieved great success, and became the prototype of a whole new genre of popular fiction: the war-anticipation story (*see* WAR), and it was within this genre that speculation about the weapons of the future first began to run riot. In *The Angel of the Revolution* (1893) George GRIFFITH imagined a world war fought with airships and submarines, and realized the tremendous potential for destruction inherent in the technological revolution. Other writers were quick to follow, including Jules VERNE, whose *Face au drapeau* (1896; trans. as *For the Flag* 1897) featured the "fulgurator", a powerful explosive device with a "boomerang" action, a primitive guided missile. H.G. WELLS also made a significant early contribution to the genre in "The Land Ironclads" (1903), foreseeing the development of the tank. (Curiously, the tank has not figured largely in sf since, though Keith LAUMER's interesting "Dinochrome Brigade" series, collected as *Bolo*, coll. 1976, is about super-tanks of the future.)

This imaginative trend received a boost in the last years of the 19th century with the discovery of the X-ray and, to a lesser extent, the discovery of radioactivity. The imagination of the writers leaped ahead to imagine all kinds of destructive rays and weapons causing or using the energy of atomic breakdown. In his last book, *The Lord of Labour* (1911), George Griffith described a war fought with atomic missiles and disintegrator rays, and similar awesome rays continued as standard super-weapons for some 30 years. Percy F. Westerman's *The War of the Wireless Waves* (1923) made much of the conflict between the British ZZ ray and the German Ultra-K ray, and during the First World War William LE QUEUX was ready to rally morale with his account of the fight to discover a crucial ray in *The Zeppelin Destroyer* (1916). Mad scientists were often armed with marvellous rays, and had to be prevented from using them, as in Edmund SNELL's *The Z Ray* (1932), Austin SMALL's *The Avenging Ray* (1930 as by Seamark) and one of the earliest examples of Soviet sf, *Giperboloid inzhenera Garina* (1926; rev. 1937; trans. as *The Deathbox* 1936; rev. edition trans. as *The Garin Death Ray* 1955) by Alexei TOLSTOY. Others not quite so mad, who used their weapons to force peace upon the world, were the heroes of *His Wisdom the Defender* (1900) by Simon Newcomb, *Empire of the World* (1910; vt *Emperor of the World* UK) by C.J. Cutcliffe HYNE and *The Ark of the Covenant* (1924; vt *Ultimatum*) by Victor MacCLURE. Curiously, few writers seemed to be aware of the difference such advanced weaponry would make to the nature of warfare. Griffith realized that mass destruction would be possible, with non-combatants likely to be slaughtered, but seemed to think that this merely made the business or war more exciting. Wells, in *The War in the Air* (1908) and the atomic war story *The World Set Free* (1914), realized the measure of misery that advanced warfare might bring, but was disposed to accept this as a necessary prelude to the rebuilding of civilization. Virtually all the rest seemed simply to be playing games with fancy toys.

The early sf PULP writers took to super-weapons — particularly rays — in a big way. E.E. "Doc" SMITH's *The Skylark of Space* (1928; 1946) features heat rays, infra-sound, ultra-violet rays and "induction rays", and his contemporaries were no less prolific. John W. CAMPBELL Jr was so prolific in "Space Rays" (1932) that Hugo GERNSBACK thought he was joking, and billed the story as a "burlesque", apparently offending Campbell sufficiently to discourage him from submitting to WONDER STORIES again. In an era which specialized in annihilation at the flick of a switch an amazing example of restraint can be found in Thomas P. Kelley's SPACE OPERA in *Weird Tales*, "A Million Years in the Future" (1940), which features a space fleet armed only with gigantic crossbows. Jack WILLIAMSON's *The Legion of Space* (1934; rev 1947) makes much of its enigmatic super-weapon AKKA, but this turns out to be a device which obliterates whole space fleets at the push of a button — extremism without ingenuity. Edmond HAMILTON was fond of disposing of worlds — and even stars — with a similar flourish. There was no further to go in imagining the awesome power of weapons, and innovation now had to follow more modest paths, involved in the design of weaponry, particularly personal weaponry. Two of the standard types have become clichés: 'the stun-gun and the BLASTER. Modern space-opera heroes, for convenience, often carry modifiable pistols usable in either way, after the fashion of STAR TREK's "phasers". Developments in the real world have contributed only minor inspiration: T.H. Maiman's discovery of the laser in 1960 "confirmed" what sf writers had always known about ray guns (see DEATH RAYS) just as Hiroshima "confirmed" what they knew about atom bombs.

More subtle weapons — chemical and biological means of destruction — also entered sf at an early stage, but were used almost entirely by mad scientists and super-criminals rather than in open warfare. Sax ROHMER's Fu Manchu was especially adept with exotic poisons, and biological blights were used as threats in Edgar WALLACE's *The Green Rust* (1919), William Le Queux's *A Terror of the Air* (1920) and Robert W. SERVICE's *The Master of the Microbe* (1926).

The Second World War renewed fears about the destructive potential of war, but prompted little imaginative innovation save for the first appearance of the "doomsday weapon" — the ultimate deterrent which, if triggered, will destroy the whole world. This first appeared in Alfred NOYES's *The Last Man* (1940; vt *No Other Man* USA). Post-War stories took on a note of hysteria about Man's propensity to make and use terrible weapons. The deadly rays died out with other fancy toys, and the atom bomb ceased to be a way of making more exciting wars. Notable examples of this post-War anxiety include Bernard WOLFE's bitter black comedy on the theme of "disarmament", *Limbo* (1952; vt *Limbo '90*) and James BLISH's story about ways and means of guiding missiles, "Tomb Tapper" (1956). This anxiety interrupted for a decade or so a trend which had begun in the 1940s toward the return of a more romanticized attitude to weaponry — a kind of futuristic swashbuckling. It is an attitude most abundantly clear in A.E. VAN VOGT's "Weapon Shops" series, *The Weapon Shops of Isher* (1941–9; fix-up 1951) and *The Weapon Makers* (1943; 1946; rev. 1952; vt *One Against Eternity*). The shops operate under the slogan "the right to bear weapons is the right to be free", and the whole basis of this kind of fiction is the *intimacy* of the characters and their weapons, and it has links with the kind of simplistic power-fantasy which underlies the whole genre of SWORD-AND-SORCERY fiction. Indeed some writers, such as Charles L. HARNESS in *Flight Into Yesterday* (1949; exp. 1953; vt *The Paradox Men*) have imagined good technological reasons (in this case that FORCE FIELDS are less opaque to slow-moving objects) for using swords even in advanced societies.

In recent years there has been some interest in psychological "weapons", as in Gregory BENFORD's *Deeper Than the Darkness* (1970; rev. 1978 as *The Stars in Shroud*) and Philip K. DICK's bizarre fantasy about fashions in the arms race, *The Zap Gun* (1967), but the major trend seems to be a continuation of the theme of intimacy, which has progressed through the futuristic suits of armour worn by Robert A. HEINLEIN's *Starship Troopers* (1959) to the business of making people *into* weapons by cyborgization (see CYBORGS). Often this takes the form of ultimately romantic power-fantasies, whose appeal is demonstrated by the success of THE SIX MILLION DOLLAR MAN on TV, but sometimes it becomes the basis for rather more thoughtful stories. Poul ANDERSON, who wrote the early "Kings Who Die" (1962) about a man engineered as a weapon, later wrote the rather horrifying psychological study "The Pugilist" (1973), which brings a new perspective to power-fantasies and the symbolization of masculinity in sword or pistol.   [BS]

WEAPONS OF DESTRUCTION See VÝNALEZ ZKAZY.

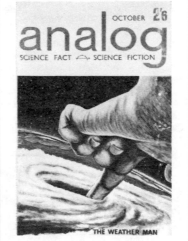
THE WEATHER MAN

The best-loved story dealing with WEATHER CONTROL is perhaps "The Weather Man" by Theodore L. Thomas, illustrated on John Schoenherr's cover for *Analog*, UK edition, Oct. 1962.

WEATHER CONTROL Man's dream of controlling the weather is an old one. It appears in PROTO SF in Samuel JOHNSON's *Rasselas* (1759), in the words of the mad astronomer: "I have possessed, for five years, the regulation of weather, and the distribution of seasons: the sun has listened to my dictates, and passed, from tropick to tropick, by my direction; the clouds, at my call, have poured their waters...."

Jane LOUDON's anonymously published *The Mummy!* (1827) envisages weather control as something to be taken for granted in life 200 years on; she may yet prove to have been right, although in real life, weather control is in its infancy. Cloud-seeding with silver iodide sometimes works, and the extent to which weather control as practised by the US army for strategic reasons during the Vietnam War was successful is still classified.

A great deal of sf simply assumes that weather will be controlled in the future, without going into too much detail, although Ivan YEFREMOV's UTOPIA *Tumannost Andromedy* (1958; trans. as *Andromeda* 1959), in which the Russian steppe has a far more equable climate than today, suggests some means of doing so. The commonest form of weather control in sf is the building of great domes over cities, as in LOGAN'S RUN, the film, or in Norman SPINRAD's "The Lost Continent" (1970), in which a plastic dome encases a future and derelict Manhattan, built originally to create an oasis of clean air in the middle of the East Coast smog bank. But domed cities are much older than this, and indeed were a cliché of PULP sf of the 1930s, in both stories and ILLUSTRATION.

Another area where weather control is commonplace in sf is in the modification of climatic conditions on other worlds (see TERRAFORMING), the most famous being Frank HERBERT's *Dune* (1965), in which the ECOLOGY of a water-poor planet is in the process of being painfully altered by various means of water-fixing, including the growth of vegetation.

Mistakes in weather control can bring disaster. Francis BEEDING's *The One Sane Man* (1934) features a scientist who blackmails the whole world through his ability to control weather; John BOLAND's *White August* (1955), whose title refers to snow in midsummer, tells of an experiment in weather control going catastrophically wrong.

Weather control usually enters sf parenthetically, rather than as a central theme. Four stories, however, make it the focus. Peter DICKINSON's *The Weathermonger* (1968) is an exciting novel for children, but the weather control here is exerted by mental power, so although the descriptions of the results are enthralling, the methods have nothing to do with real science. It is quite otherwise with Rick RAPHAEL's "The Thirst Quenchers" (1963) which is, characteristically for this author, a story of competent technicians in action; it is one of several stories by him dealing with a future US Division of Agriculture, at a time when water conservation has become all-important; though it does not deal with weather control directly, it is fascinating about meteorological forecasting generally, and about controlling the results of the weather, as by placing reservoirs underground and covering snow with a black monomolecular film, in both cases to minimize evaporation. Ben BOVA's *The Weathermakers* (1967) is a NEAR-FUTURE thriller about the political implications of weather control, and is at its most interesting in its accounts of how such control might be achieved. But the classic weather-control story remains Theodore L. Thomas's novelette "The Weather Man" (1962), which has been much anthologized. In a well-written version of *ASF*-style sf at its best, he describes the three phases of weather control: political (Earth is ruled by a Weather Congress), mathematical, and technological (the Sun's emission of radiation is controlled by sessile sun-boats which, skimming across the Sun's surface and even entering its outer sphere, have various means of damping or increasing its output). The object of this exercise, typically for *ASF*, is to make an old man in Southern California happy by giving him a snowfall before he dies, but this sentimental plot gimmick hardly affects the high drama of the controlling processes themselves. [PN]

WEBB, A(UGUSTUS) C(AESAR) (1894– ?). American writer and pathologist, who began publishing sf with "The Double Lightning" for *Amazing Detective Stories* in 1930, but who soon became inactive, only much later publishing his sf novel, *Farewell to the Bomb* (1967). [JC]

WEBB, LUCAS *See* Robert REGINALD.

WEBSTER, ROBERT N. *See* Raymond A. PALMER.

WEEKEND Film (1968). Comacico/ Copernic/Lira/Ascot Cineraid. Directed by Jean-Luc Godard, starring Mireille Darc, Jean Yanne, Jean-Pierre Kalfon, Valerie Lagrange and Jean-Pierre Léaud. Screenplay by Jean-Luc Godard. 103 mins. Colour.

Godard's attack on contemporary French bourgeois society (and, by implication, Western society as a whole) is more fantasy than sf though it does contain traditional sf elements. The progression of the film is from naturalism and social order through a series of ever more entropic images, involving increasingly horrible, large-scale car smashes, to anarchy. The bickering middle-class couple who have set out on a weekend drive to the country at the outset observe the road accidents and associated violence with cool detachment, as does the film itself, in a disturbingly affectless manner. Finally the couple abandon their car and continue on foot, meeting a variety of strange people, including such fictional characters as Emily Brontë, whom they set on fire. The film ends with the wife joining a group of armed anarchists and then killing and eating her husband, who apparently represents all that must be destroyed in French society before Godard's Brave New World can begin. [JB/PN]

WEEKLEY, IAN (? –). British writer. His sf novel, *The Moving Snow* (1974), rather prosaically describes how a family copes with a change of climate that brings severe Arctic conditions to Great Britain; all in all they do quite snugly. [JC]

WEEKS, EDWARD OLIN (? – ?). British author, whose typically Victorian sf story in PEARSON'S MAGAZINE is "The Master of the Octopus" (1899), about a perpetual lamp. [JE]

WEINBAUM, STANLEY G(RAUMAN) (1900–35). American writer. He began writing in the main stream and published a romantic novel, but failed to place other early works and turned to the PULP market. A graduate in chemical engineering, he applied his understanding of science to the writing of sf stories slightly more realistic in outlook than those of many of his contemporaries. His first story in *Wonder Stories*, "A Martian Odyssey" (1934), was an early attempt to present life on another world as a strange and complex system rather than a conglomerate of weird creatures haphazardly modified from earthly life-forms (*see* LIFE ON OTHER WORLDS). He continued to construct similar systems in stories such as "The Lotus Eaters" (1935), "The Mad Moon" (1935), "Flight on Titan" (1935) and "Parasite Planet" (1935), the first of which contains an interesting attempt to imagine the world view of an intelligent plant. In a series of stories featuring a caricature scientist named Van Manderpootz he took a flippant approach to the invention of miraculous machines. The series includes "The Worlds of If" (1935), "The Ideal" (1935) and "The Point of View" (1936). He imported some of the methods and values of his early romantic fiction into sf in "Dawn of Flame" (title story of *Dawn of Flame and Other Stories*, coll. **1936**) and its sequel "The Black Flame" (1939 *Startling Stories*; title story of *The Black Flame*, fix-up **1948**, which includes "Dawn of Flame") but the amalgamation was not altogether successful, and the stories were not published until after his death. During the last two years of his life he produced sf stories prolifically, including the early story of GENETIC ENGINEERING "Proteus Island" (1936) and the SUPERMAN story "The Adaptive Ultimate" (1935) (actually featuring a superwoman, and published under the name John Jessel). He collaborated on two stories with Ralph Milne FARLEY.

SGW's most important sf work is probably the posthumously published novel *The New Adam* (1939), a first-person account of the career of a potential superman born into contemporary human society and becoming, in consequence, half human. It is one of the most careful and analytical works produced by an sf writer in the pre-War period, and stands at the beginning of a sequence of superman stories that was to change drastically the role customarily allotted to the superhuman in sf. Another posthumously published sf novel is the psychological horror story *The Dark Other* (**1950**). All the short stories are collected in *A Martian Odyssey and Other Science Fiction Tales* (coll. **1975**) ed. Sam Moskowitz, which combines the contents of two earlier collections — *A Martian Odyssey* (coll. **1949**) and *The Red Peri* (coll. **1952**) — and adds one previously uncollected piece. Moskowitz had previously edited a smaller collection, *A Martian Odyssey and other Classics of Science Fiction* (coll. **1962**). The paperback *The Best of Stanley G. Weinbaum* (coll. **1974**) contains 12 of the 22 stories which appear in the 1975 collection.

SGW, like his important contemporary John TAINE, was habitually clumsy in his writing, but compensated for this with clever and interesting deployment of ideas. At his best, though, he could rise well above the naïvety of his usual pulp style, and *The New Adam* is a classic of the period. [BS]
About the author: "Dawn of Fame: The Career of Stanley G. Weinbaum" in *Explorers of the Infinite* (**1963**) by Sam Moskowitz.
See also: ADAM AND EVE; ALIENS; ALTERNATE WORLDS; BIOLOGY; COMMUNICATIONS; ECOLOGY; HOLOCAUST AND AFTER; JUPITER; MARS; MYTHOLOGY; OUTER PLANETS; PSYCHOLOGY; PUBLISHING; VENUS.

WEINBERG, ROBERT (1946–). American editor and publisher. A PULP MAGAZINE enthusiast, he has edited and published a variety of material on the subject. This includes series of pulp magazine reprints, under the general titles PULP CLASSICS, *Lost Fantasies*, *Weird Menace* and others, the anonymously edited *Famous Fantastic Classics 1* (anth. **1974**) and *Famous Fantastic Classics 2* (anth. **1975**), and a horror anthology, *Far Below and Other Horrors* (anth. **1974**). He is co-compiler with Lohr McKinstry of *The Hero Pulp Index* (**1971**) and with Edward P. Berglund of *Reader's Guide to the Cthulhu Mythos* (**1969**; rev. 1973). He has compiled *The Annotated Guide to Robert E. Howard's Sword & Sorcery* (**1976**). He also edited and published *Lester Dent, The Man Behind Doc Savage* (anth. **1974**), a book devoted to DOC SAVAGE MAGAZINE and its chief writer, and *WT50* (anth. **1974**), a 50th-anniversary tribute to WEIRD TALES which he later revised and enlarged as *The Weird Tales Story* (anth. **1977**). [MJE]

WEIRD AND OCCULT LIBRARY British pocketbook magazine. Three numbered, undated issues, 1960, published by G.G. Swan, London; no editor named. *WOL* contained a mixture of weird, sf, mystery and adventure stories. It was difficult to read, due to the small print. It was a companion magazine to SCIENCE FICTION LIBRARY. [FHP]

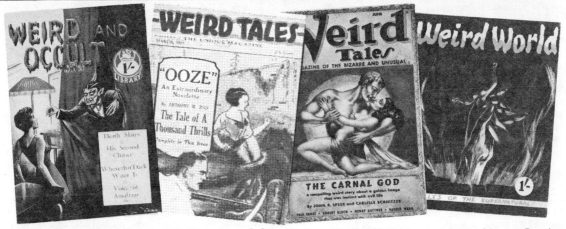

WEIRD AND OCCULT LIBRARY. No. 2, 1960. WEIRD TALES. Left, the first issue, March 1923; right, a representative Margaret Brundage cover, June 1937. WEIRD WORLD. First issue, 1955.

WEIRD TALES US magazine, small PULP-size (9 x 6 inches) Mar.-Apr. 1923, BEDSHEET-size May 1923-May/Jul. 1924, pulp-size Nov. 1924-Jul. 1953, DIGEST-size Sep. 1953-Sep. 1954. 279 issues, Mar. 1923-Sep. 1954. Published by Rural Publishing Corp. (Mar. 1923-May/Jul. 1924), Popular Fiction Co. (Nov. 1924-Oct. 1938), Short Stories Inc. (Nov. 1938-Sep. 1954); ed. Edwin Baird (Mar. 1923-Apr. 1924), Otis Adelbert KLINE (May/Jul. 1924), Farnsworth WRIGHT (Nov. 1924-Dec. 1939), Dorothy McIlwraith (Jan. 1940-Sep. 1954).

WT was founded in 1923 by J.C. Henneberger, who retained an interest in the magazine throughout its existence. Its early issues were undistinguished (despite the presence of writers who later became regular contributors, such as H.P. LOVECRAFT, Seabury QUINN and Clark Ashton SMITH) and the bumper Anniversary issue, May/Jul. 1924, was to have been the last. It reappeared in Nov. 1924, with a new publisher and a new editor. It has been suggested that the controversy caused by a necrophiliac horror story ("The Loved Dead" by C.M. Eddy with H.P. Lovecraft) in the May/Jul. issue — attempts were made to have it removed from the newsstands — gave WT the publicity boost it needed to survive.

Under Farnsworth Wright's editorship WT developed into the "Unique Magazine" its subtitle promised. Its stories were a mixture of science fiction, horror stories, SWORD AND SORCERY, exotic adventure, and anything else which its title might embrace. The early issues were generally crude in appearance, but the look of the magazine improved greatly in 1932 with the introduction of the artists Margaret Brundage and John Allen St John. Brundage's covers — pastel chalks depicting women in various degrees of undress being menaced in various ways — alienated some readers, but promised a sensuous blend of the exotic and the erotic which typified the magazine's appeal. The 1930s were WT's heyday; in

addition to Lovecraft and Smith, it regularly featured Robert E. HOWARD (including his "Conan" series), August DERLETH, Edmond HAMILTON, C.L. MOORE and others — although the most popular contributor was Seabury Quinn, with an interminable series featuring the psychic detective Jules de Grandin. Although WT printed its share of dreadful pulp fiction, at this time the magazine was, at its best, far advanced over the largely primitive sf pulps. However, Wright's WT never really recovered from the almost simultaneous loss of three of its key contributors with the deaths of Howard (1936) and Lovecraft (1937) and the virtual retirement of Smith. New contributors in the late 1930s included author Henry KUTTNER and artist Virgil FINLAY.

At the end of 1930 Wright, suffering poor health, was replaced as editor by Dorothy McIlwraith. The magazine continued steadily through the 1940s — although after being monthly, Nov. 1924-Jan. 1940, it was now bi-monthly (and remained so to the end) — and featured such authors as Robert BLOCH, Ray BRADBURY and Fritz LEIBER. However, it was no longer a unique magazine: the editorial policy was more restrictive; other fantasy magazines had appeared and, in the case of UNKNOWN, overshadowed it. Nevertheless, it continued to be the only regular magazine outlet for supernatural fiction until its death in 1954, when its publisher went bankrupt. An abortive attempt to revive the magazine — or at least its name — was made in 1973, with three issues, Summer, Fall and Winter, ed. Sam MOSKOWITZ, and continuing the original WT numeration (Vol 47 nos 1, 2 and 3).

WT, although it emphasized fantasy and the supernatural, was an influential training ground for sf writers, and did, over the years, print a number of sf tales.

WT has been exhaustively mined for anthologies, and many of its contributors from the 1930s have gone on to new heights of popularity with paperback

reprints of their stories. WT50 (anth. 1974), ed. Robert WEINBERG, is a 50th anniversary tribute to the magazine, with nostalgic reminiscences by many of its contributors. Weird Tales (anth. 1976), ed. Peter HAINING, reprints a selection of stories in facsimile. See also: The Weird Tales Story (anth. 1977) ed. Robert Weinberg. [MJE]

Collectors should note: The first three vols of WT had four numbers each. During this period the schedule was monthly, except that Jul./Aug. '23 was a single issue, and there was no Dec. '23. There was no Vol.4 no.1, the May/Jun./Jul. '24 issue being Vol.4 no.2, followed by Vol.4 nos 3 and 4. Vols 5–16 had six numbers. Vol.17 in '31 interrupted the monthly schedule, with the following four issues: no.1 (Jan.), no.2 (Feb./Mar.), no.3 (Apr./May) and no.4 (Jun./Jul.). Vol.18 had five numbers. Vols 19–27 had six numbers. Vol.28 had only five numbers, Aug./Sep. '36 being a single issue. Vols 29–32 had six numbers. Vol.33 had five numbers. Vol.34 had six numbers, the first being a single Jun./Jul. '39 issue. Vol.35 had 10 bi-monthly numbers. Vol.36 had 12 numbers. Vols 37–38 had six numbers. Vol.39 had 12, Vols 40–43 had six, Vol.44 had eight, Vol.45 had six, and Vol.46 had four.

Three British editions were published at various times. In the first half of '42 Swan Publishers produced three unnumbered issues. One more came in Nov. '46 from Merritt. Finally, Thorpe & Porter published 28 issues, numbered 1–23, and then Vol.1 nos 1–5 in Nov. '49-Jul. '54. There were two Canadian reprint editions: the first '35–6 (Vol.25 no.6-Vol.28 no.1) and the second '42–51. The latter series had extremely eccentric numeration, which after 11 consecutive issues marked Vol.38 no.4, was wisely terminated, and the 19 issues of '48–'51 were unnumbered.

WEIRD WORLD British PULP-size magazine. Two undated issues, 1955, published by Gannet Press, Birkenhead;

no editor named. *WW* printed a mixture of sf and fantasy, including some reprints. The fiction was generally of low quality. The advertised companion magazine, *Fantastic World*, has never been seen. [FHP]

WEISINGER, MORT(IMER) (1915–78). American editor. Educated at New York University, he was an active sf fan in the early 1930s, editing *Fantasy Magazine*, the leading FANZINE of its day. He also sold a few sf stories, starting with "The Price of Peace" (1933) in *Wonder Stories*. In 1936 he became editor of THRILLING WONDER STORIES; later he also edited its companion magazines STARTLING STORIES and CAPTAIN FUTURE, the latter being probably his own conception. Under his direction *TWS* was openly juvenile in appeal, its garish covers giving rise to the term BUG-EYED MONSTERS. In 1941 he became editor of the COMIC BOOK SUPERMAN, and subsequently editorial director of the whole range of National Periodical Publications (DC Comics), where he recruited many sf writers, such as Edmond HAMILTON, Horace GOLD, Manly Wade WELLMAN, Alfred BESTER and Otto BINDER. His career is outlined in "Superman" in *Seekers of Tomorrow* (1965) by Sam MOSKOWITZ. [MJE]

WELCOME TO BLOOD CITY Film (1977). An EMI/Len Herberman Production. Directed by Peter Sasdy, starring Jack Palance, Keir Dullea, Samantha Eggar and Barry Morse. Screenplay by Stephen Schneck and Michael Winder. 96 mins. Colour.

A group of people wake up to find themselves literally in the middle of nowhere, with their memories wiped out and the only clue to their previous lives a card in their pockets stating that each of them is a convicted murderer. They are captured by the inhabitants of a Western-style town and told by the sheriff (Jack Palance) that they are slaves until they can fight their way up the community's social scale — a process which involves killing as many people as possible. It then becomes apparent that the whole situation exists only in the minds of the participants; it is a computer-induced illusion aimed at discovering who is suitable "Kill Master" material, a breed of person needed by the authorities in a world where political chaos is increasing. The film has similarities to Michael CRICHTON's superior WESTWORLD but where in that film the Western setting was ingeniously integrated into a futuristic world, *WTBC* is no more than a Western with an sf story clumsily tacked on. The potential of the basic idea is not developed by the script-writers, who concentrate on familiar Western-style confrontations. [JB]

WELLMAN, MANLY WADE (1903–). American writer, born in Angola, prolific in both fantasy and sf, though more noted for works in the former genre; he has also written crime fiction. His brother, the late Paul I. Wellman, wrote Westerns. MWW began publishing in the sf and fantasy genres with "Back to the Beast" for *Weird Tales* in 1927, though his first sf story proper, "When Planets Clashed" appeared in *Wonder Stories Quarterly* as late as 1931. Both these stories were published under his own name, though he has also used pseudonyms, in several genres, including, in sf and fantasy, Levi Crow, Gans T. Field and the house names Gabriel BARCLAY and Will GARTH. Though his first book is a short sf novel, *The Invading Asteroid* (**1932**), from early in his career MWW has been most successful as a writer of fantasy with some sf underpinning, publishing frequently in *Weird Tales*, *Unknown* and *FSF*, though the "Hok" series, stories published 1939–41 in *AMZ* and 1942 in *Fantastic Adventures*, comprises sf adventures set in various early mythic civilizations. More centrally, the "Judge Pursuivant" series (in *Weird Tales* 1938–41), written as by Gans T. Field, and the "John Thunstone" series (in *Weird Tales* 1943–51), are both fantasy sequences about men with psychic powers who pursue the occult; these two series precede his most famous sequence, the stories about the Appalachian witchcraft-fighter John the Minstrel with his silver-stringed guitar, published in *FSF* 1951–62 and assembled as *Who Fears the Devil?* (coll. of linked stories **1963**). This book, along with an earlier novel, *Twice in Time* (1940 *Startling Stories*; **1957**), probably make up his most lasting work: *Twice in Time* is an effective TIME-TRAVEL tale which features a vivid portrayal of Leonardo da Vinci's Florence. A recent novel of interest is *Sherlock Holmes's War of the Worlds* (**1975**), written with his son Wade Wellman, which gives Holmes intricate involvement in the world of H.G. WELLS's Martian INVASION. MWW has been extremely prolific, and has not yet received adequate evaluation. [JC]
Other works: *Dr Cyclops* (**1940**), as by Will Garth, a novelization of the film DR CYCLOPS; *Romance in Black* (1938 *Weird Tales* as "The Black Drama"; **1946**), as by Gans T. Field; *Sojarr of Titan* (1941 *Startling Stories*; **1949**); *The Beasts from Beyond* (1944 *Startling Stories* as "Strangers on the Heights"; **1950**); *The Devil's Planet* (1942 *Startling Stories*; **1951**); *Giants from Eternity* (1939 *Startling Stories*; **1959**); *The Dark Destroyers* (1938 *ASF* as "Nuisance Value"; **1959**; paperback abridged); *Island in the Sky* (1941 *TWS*; **1961**); *The Solar Invasion* (1946 *Startling Stories*; **1968**); *Worse Things Waiting* (coll. **1973**); *The Beyonders* (**1977**).
See also: COMIC STRIPS; HISTORY IN SF; MYTHOLOGY; PASTORAL; REINCARNATION; SUPERNATURAL CREATURES.

WELLS, BARRY *See* DAY THE EARTH CAUGHT FIRE, THE.

WELLS, BASIL (1912–). American writer, who began publishing sf with "Rebirth of Man" for *Super Science Stories* in 1940, and whose routine stories are collected in *Planets of Adventure* (coll. **1949**) and *Doorways to Space* (coll. **1951**). He also wrote four stories as Gene Ellerman. [JC]

WELLS, (FRANK CHARLES) ROBERT (1929–). British writer who began publishing sf with "Song of the Syren" for *Science Fantasy* in 1965, though he has concentrated on novels, beginning with *The Parasaurians* (**1969**), in which play-safaris against ROBOT dinosaurs turn into a more serious threat to the hero. *The Spacejacks* (**1975**) is traditional SPACE OPERA. [JC]
Other works: *Candle in the Sun* (**1971**); *Right-Handed Wilderness* (**1973**).

H.G. WELLS as a young man, at the time he was writing his early and best sf.

WELLS, H(ERBERT) G(EORGE) (1866–1946). British writer. HGW was the third son of a shopkeeper, who had been a gardener and cricketer before marrying a servant. His parents clung desperately to their acquired middle-class status, and this struggle is represented in some of his work. "Bertie" was apprenticed, like his brothers, to a draper, but left in 1883 to become a teacher/pupil at Midhurst Grammar School. He obtained a scholarship to the Normal School of Science in London and studied biology there under Thomas Henry Huxley, a vociferous proponent of Darwin's Theory of Evolution and an outspoken scientific humanist, who made a deep impression on him. HGW resumed teaching, took his degree externally and wrote two textbooks (published in 1893) while working for the University Correspondence College. He began to dabble in scientific journalism, publishing an essay on "The Rediscovery of the Unique" in 1891. He began to sell articles and short stories regularly in 1893.

The most ambitious and important of his early articles was "The Man of the Year Million" (1893), which described Man as HGW thought EVOLUTION would ultimately shape him — huge head and eyes, delicate hands and a much reduced body. He foresaw the descendants of Man outliving the Sun, permanently immersed in nutrient fluids in refuges deep beneath the surface of the planet. In other articles he wrote about "The Advent of the Flying Man", "An Excursion to the Sun" (a poetic cosmic vision of solar storms and electromagnetic tides), "The Living Things That May Be" (on the possibility of silicon-based life), and "The Extinction of Man" (on the possibility that in the Earthly "struggle for existence" Man might not be fittest to survive). His early short stories are less daring accounts of encounters between men and strange life-forms, including "The Stolen Bacillus" (1894), "In the Avu Observatory" (1894), "The Flowering of the Strange Orchid" (1894) and "Aepyornis Island" (1894). All the imaginative concepts which he used in his early sf novels initially appeared in his speculative non-fiction, some of which is accessible in *H.G. Wells: Early Writings in Science and Science Fiction* (coll. **1975**) ed. Robert M. PHILMUS and David Y. Hughes.

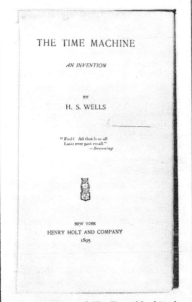

THE TIME MACHINE

AN INVENTION

BY

H. S. WELLS

" Fust! All that is at all
Lasts ever past recall "
—*Browning*

NEW YORK
HENRY HOLT AND COMPANY
1895

The first edition of *The Time Machine* by H.G. WELLS, the American of 1895, named him H.S. Wells on the title page.

A series of essays written for an amateur publication in 1888 became the basis for the major scientific romance *The Time Machine* (1888 *Science Schools Journal* as "The Chronic Argonauts"; exp. **1895** USA; rev. 1895 UK), which maps the evolutionary future of life on Earth. The human species subdivides into the gentle Eloi and the bestial Morlocks, both of which ultimately become extinct while life as we know it slowly decays and is finally eclipsed by new, quite alien life-forms. But HGW's interest in evolutionary science was not merely abstract. He was also interested in social evolution and the prospect of a better world in the immediate future. His first novel of social criticism was *The Wonderful Visit* (**1895**), in which an angel fallen from Heaven casts a critical eye upon late Victorian society. These two themes – the implications of Darwin's evolutionary theory (in Huxley's uncompromising interpretation) and the desire to oppose and eradicate the injustices and hypocrisies of contemporary society – run through all HGW's work, and many of his imaginative visions are inspired by the attempt to reconcile faith in the one and commitment to the other.

In *The Island of Dr Moreau* (**1896**) he developed ideas from an essay on "The Limits of Plasticity" into the notion of a SCIENTIST populating a remote ISLAND with beasts surgically re-shaped as men, matching them against a castaway in a small-scale "struggle for existence". In "A Story of the Stone Age" (1897) he attempted to imagine the circumstances which allowed Man to evolve from his bestial ancestors in the remote past. Other romances of this period include the cosmic-vision story "Under the Knife" (1896), the cosmic-DISASTER story "The Star" (1897) and the fantasy-fulfilment stories *The Invisible Man* (**1897**) and "The Man Who Could Work Miracles" (1898). "A Story of the Days to Come" (1897) was his first futuristic piece of social criticism, imagining a technologically developed world where poverty and misery are needlessly maintained by class divisions.

Some of HGW's most striking sf ideas appear in his short stories. Nearly all his work in short forms appears in five British collections and one American. All but two of these stories were in turn collected in an omnibus volume in 1927 (*see below*); all other short-story collections by HGW merely consist of selections from or rearrangements of the contents of these. The British collections are *The Stolen Bacillus, and Other Incidents* (coll. **1895**), *The Plattner Story, and Others* (coll. **1897**), *Tales of Space and Time* (coll. **1899**), *Twelve Stories and a Dream* (coll. **1903**) and *The Country of the Blind, and Other Stories* (coll. **1911**). The American collection, never issued in the UK, contains three new stories; it is *Thirty Strange Stories* (coll. **1897**).

In *The War of the Worlds* (**1898**) HGW introduced the ALIEN being into the role which became a cliché – a monstrous invader of Earth, a competitor in a cosmic struggle for existence. Though the Martians were a ruthless and terrible enemy, HGW was careful to point out that Man had driven many animal species to extinction, and that human invaders of Tasmania had behaved no less callously in exterminating their cousins. His next romance, *When the Sleeper Wakes* (**1899**; rev. vt *The Sleeper Awakes* 1910), was the first of many socialist novels. The hero awakes from SUSPENDED ANIMATION to become a MESSIAH in the totalitarian world of the future, rejecting the overtures of the ruling clique and taking a hand in a revolution. HGW was never able to believe in proletarian socialism, but only socialism created and imposed by a benevolent intelligentsia. He tried hard all his life to be part of such a world-saving movement.

In 1900 he set out to make his name as a serious novelist with *Love and Mr. Lewisham* (**1900**), but his interest in evolutionary BIOLOGY and his interest in social evolution each inspired a major work in 1901. In *The First Men in the Moon* (**1901**) he described the hyper-organized, efficient and rather horrific society of the Selenites, while in the series of essays collected as *Anticipations of the Reaction of Mechanical and Human Progress upon Human Life and Thought* (**1901**) he produced one of the earliest works of futurological analysis. These essays brought him to the attention of Sidney and Beatrice Webb, and he joined the Fabian Society in 1903. His career as a social crusader went through many phases. He tried to assume command of the Fabian Society in 1906, but failed and withdrew in 1908. During the First World War he was active in the League of Nations movement. Between the Wars he visited many countries, addressing the Petrograd Soviet, the Sorbonne and the Reichstag. In 1934 he had discussions with both Stalin and Roosevelt, trying to recruit them to his world-saving schemes. His real influence, however, remained negligible, and he despaired of the whole business when the world was embroiled in war for a second time. In the meantime, he was a prolific writer in many genres, though his polemical intentions restricted the imaginative territory that he covered, and he never recovered the vigour and scope of his early scientific romances.

In his UTOPIAN novels, *A Modern Utopia* (**1905**) and *Men Like Gods* (**1923**), HGW described technologically developed societies governed by an elite-inspired socialism (*see* TECHNOLOGY). In some of his scientific romances he tried to describe a new kind of man who might credibly and happily inhabit such worlds. In *The Food of the Gods and How it Came to Earth* (**1904**) a new race emerges through the accidental discovery of a super-nutrient which enlarges both body and mind. In *In the Days of the Comet* (**1906**), a wondrous change in human personality is brought about by the gases in a comet's tail through which the Earth is fortunate enough to pass. A significant group of HGW's sf belongs to the genre of WAR-anticipation stories which flourished in Britain between 1871 and 1914. In "The Land Ironclads" (1903) he anticipated the use of tanks in war, and in *The War in the Air, and Particularly How*

Mr. Bert Smallways Fared while It Lasted (1908) he envisaged colossal destruction wrought by aerial bombing. In *The World Set Free: a Story of Mankind* (1914) the destruction is greater because the bombs are atomic. All these anticipations were ultimately justified, but although prophetic in terms of technological hardware the novels were weak as social prophecies. Both presumed that out of the ashes of the old world a new order might be born, a just and generous world state. When the Great War began in actuality HGW championed it for exactly these reasons, and though disillusioned by events after 1918 he clung to the conviction that a world-wide catastrophe of some kind would be a necessary prelude to any Utopian restructuring of society.

His early realistic novels draw heavily upon his own experiences, and deal with the pretensions and predicaments of the lower-middle class, usually with a spice of comedy. *The Wheels of Chance* (1896), *Love and Mr. Lewisham* (1900), *Kipps* (1905) and *The History of Mr. Polly* (1910) belong to this group. As time went by he grew more ambitious, tackling larger themes and attacking issues of contemporary social concern. His most successful effort along these lines was *Tono-Bungay* (1909), which was followed by *Ann Veronica* (1909), on the subject of the situation of women in society, and the political novel *The New Machiavelli* (1911). The longest and most pretentious of these novels was a *Bildungsroman*, *The World of William Clissold* (three vols. 1926).

Between the Wars HGW became increasingly impatient of his fellow men, and was bitterly critical in several imaginative works. In *The Undying Fire* (1919) he produced an allegory in which the Book of Job is re-enacted in contemporary England, with a dying Wellsian hero "comforted" by various social philosophers. In *Mr Blettsworthy on Rampole Island* (1928) a shipwrecked man tries to convert superstitious savages to the ways of common sense but cannot prevail against their cruel and stupid tribal customs. In the end he discovers that he has been delirious, and that Rampole Island is New York.

In 1931 Wells summed up his whole Utopian philosophy in *The Work, Wealth and Happiness of Mankind* (two vols. 1931). Two years later he added to it a companion volume – a speculative fiction laying out a historical route-map by which the Utopian state might be reached: *The Shape of Things to Come* (1933). (Some ideas from this work became the basis of the film THINGS TO COME in 1935, scripted by HGW. A version of the script was published as *Things to Come*, 1935.) These two books represent the climax of HGW's literary career; he began thereafter to write his autobiography. Some of his later works are short and whimsical, and these are

little more than footnotes to his career. They include several fantasies: *The Croquet Player: a Story* (1936), in which a man is haunted by a vision of his evolutionary heritage; *Star-Begotten: a Biological Fantasia* (1937), in which cosmic rays emanating from Mars cause a mutation in the human spirit comparable to that wrought by the miraculous comet; and *The Camford Visitation* (1937), in which the routine of life and learning at a university is upset by the interventions of a mocking, disembodied voice. HGW's last fantasy was *All Aboard for Ararat* (1941), in which God asks a new Noah to build a second Ark. Noah agrees, provided that this time God will be content to remain a passenger while Man takes charge of his own destiny.

The Holy Terror (1939) is a longer novel which ultimately forecasts a world state, but on the way frames an indictment of fascism in an interesting NEAR-FUTURE story of demagogy in British politics.

HGW is the scientific romancer *par excellence*. His best longer works were collected into *The Scientific Romances of H.G. Wells* (coll. 1933; vt *Seven Science Fiction Novels of H.G. Wells* USA, which omits *Men Like Gods*). *The Short Stories of H.G. Wells* (coll. 1927) contains all but eight of HGW's short stories to that date, and includes those published in the five earlier British collections (*see above*), along with *The Time Machine* and four short stories not previously collected in book form, including the prehistoric tale "The Grisly Folk" (1921) and an apocalyptic tale, "The Story of the Last Trump", which was originally an insert in the non-sf book *Boon* (1915 as by Reginald Bliss; 1920 as by HGW). HGW possessed a prolific imagination which remained solidly based in biological and historical possibility, and his best works are generally regarded as exemplary of what sf should aspire to do and be. But he never managed to resolve the imaginative conflict between his Utopian dreams and his interpretation of Darwinian "natural law", as is evidenced by his final despairing essay *Mind at the End of its Tether* (1945), which concludes that Man is doomed because he cannot and will not adapt himself to his technological circumstances. He seems to have imagined his own career as analogous to that of the hero of *The Undying Fire* or the luckless sighted man in the classic story "The Country of the Blind" (1904) (though HGW portrays himself ironically as a deluded idealist in *Christina Alberta's Father*, 1925); the historical climate has remained such that it is still easy to sympathize with him.

Films based on HGW's work include THE INVISIBLE MAN; ISLAND OF LOST SOULS; THE ISLAND OF DR MOREAU; THINGS TO COME; THE FIRST MEN IN THE MOON; THE WAR OF THE WORLDS, THE TIME MACHINE and, very loosely, FOOD OF

THE GODS. [BS]

Other works: Fiction: *The Sea Lady* (1902); *The Soul of a Bishop* (1917); *The Dream* (1924); *The Autocracy of Mr. Parham* (1930); *The Bulpington of Blup* (1932); *Man Who Could Work Miracles* (1936), the book of the film; *You Can't Be Too Careful: a Sample of Life 1901–1951* (1941).

Non-fiction: *God the Invisible King* (1917); *The Outline of History* (1920); *The Salvaging of Civilization* (1921); *The Way the World is Going: Guesses and Forecasts of the World Ahead* (1928); *The Open Conspiracy: Blue Prints for a World Revolution* (1928); *The Science of Life* (1930) with Julian Huxley and G.P. Wells; *World Brain* (1938); *The Fate of Homo Sapiens* (1939); *The New World Order* (1939); *Phoenix* (1942); *The Conquest of Time* (1942); *The Happy Turning: a Dream of Life* (1945).

About the author: *Experiment in Autobiography* (1934) by HGW; *The Early H.G. Wells* (1961) by Bernard Bergonzi; *H.G. Wells: a Collection of Critical Essays* (anth. 1976) ed. Bernard Bergonzi; *H.G. Wells: His Turbulent Life and Times* (1969) by Lovat Dickson; *The Future as Nightmare* (1967) by Mark R. HILLEGAS; *The Life and Thought of H.G. Wells* (1963 Russia; trans. 1966) by Julius KAGARLITSKI; *The Time Traveller: the Life of H.G. Wells* (1973) by Norman and Jeanne Mackenzie; *H.G. Wells* (1970) by Patrick Parrinder; *H.G. Wells: the Critical Heritage* (anth. 1972) ed. Patrick Parrinder; *H.G. Wells and Modern Science Fiction* (anth. 1977) ed. Darko SUVIN and Robert M. Philmus; *H.G. Wells: Critic of Progress* (1973) by Jack WILLIAMSON; *H.G. Wells: a Comprehensive Bibliography* (third edition 1972) published by the H.G. Wells Society; *Herbert George Wells: an Annotated Bibliography of his Works* (1977) by J.R. Hammond.

See also: ANDROIDS; ANTHROPOLOGY; ANTI-INTELLECTUALISM IN SF; ASTRONOMY; CITIES; COLONIZATION OF OTHER WORLDS; COSMOLOGY; DEVOLUTION; DISCOVERY AND INVENTION; DYSTOPIAS; FANTASTIC VOYAGES; FAR FUTURE; FOURTH DIMENSION (AND OTHERS); GENETIC ENGINEERING; GODS AND DEMONS; GRAVITY; HISTORY IN SF; HISTORY OF SF; HIVE-MINDS; HUMOUR; ICONOCLASM; IMAGINARY SCIENCE; INVASION; INVISIBILITY; LIFE ON OTHER WORLDS; MACHINES; MARS; MEDICINE; METAPHYSICS; MONEY; MOON; MUTANTS; NUCLEAR POWER; OPTIMISM AND PESSIMISM; ORIGIN OF MAN; PARALLEL WORLDS; PERCEPTION; PHYSICS; POLITICS; POLLUTION; POWER SOURCES; PREDICTION; PROTO SF; RADIO (UK); RADIO (USA); RELIGION; ROCKETS; SATIRE; SF OVERTAKEN BY EVENTS; SCIENTIFIC ERRORS; SEX; SOCIAL DARWINISM; SOCIOLOGY; SPACESHIPS; TIME TRAVEL; TRANSPORTATION; Jules VERNE; WEAPONS.

WELLS, HUBERT GEORGE See Forrest J. ACKERMAN.

WELLS, JOHN JAY *See* Juanita COULSON.

WENTWORTH, ROBERT *See* Edmond HAMILTON.

WEREWOLVES *See* SUPERNATURAL CREATURES.

WERFEL, FRANZ (1890–1945). Austrian poet, playwright and novelist, born in Prague, known mainly for his work outside the sf field; as an Expressionist poet and dramatist he achieved an early fame, and is also well known for his *Das Lied von Bernadette* (1941; trans. as *The Song of Bernadette* 1958). After escaping the Nazis via Spain, with the onset of the Second World War, he went to California, where he wrote *Stern der Ungeborenen* (1946; trans. as *Star of the Unborn* 1946) before dying in exile. This long, contemplative UTOPIA depicts a philosophically complex FAR-FUTURE Earth through the eyes of a narrator (named FW) who is guided through the three parts of the novel by a mentor explicitly associated with DANTE's Vergil. FW's first response to the depopulated, deeply alienating, surreal world being shown to him seems cunningly to mirror the exiled author's real-world experiences of California. The melancholy underlying the story, and its long effortless perspectives of time and thought, give *Star of the Unborn* a clarity and reserve reminiscent of the work of Olaf STAPLEDON. [JC]
See also: ARTS; RELIGION.

WERPER, BARTON Pseudonym of American writer Peter T. Scott (? –), under which he has written a new "Tarzan" series comprised of *Tarzan and The Silver Globe* (1964), *Tarzan and the Cave City* (1964), *Tarzan and the Snake People* (1964), *Tarzan and the Abominable Snowman* (1965) and *Tarzan and the Winged Invaders* (1965). The Edgar Rice BURROUGHS estate successfully sued and the books were withdrawn in 1966. [JC]

WESSO, H.W. Pseudonym of Hans Waldemar Wessolowski (1894– ?). German-born American illustrator. HWW was educated at the Berlin Royal Academy, where he did cartoon work to help pay his fees; he was later awarded a scholarship. He emigrated to the USA in 1914, and soon found work as an illustrator (both covers and interiors) for a variety of magazines. When the Clayton magazine chain created *ASF* (then called *Astounding Stories of Super-Science*) they hired HWW who painted all 34 covers of the Clayton *ASF*. His b/w work was similar to that of his contemporary Frank R. PAUL, but his colour paintings were very different; where Paul's were crowded and often artificially busy, HWW's were more open, and he seemed more concerned with the overall design

A typically apocalyptic cover by H.W. WESSO. Feb. 1939.

of each piece. His best covers create an almost abstract beauty out of the conventional icons of SPACE OPERA. HWW worked for many sf magazines in the 1930s and early 1940s, including more work for *ASF* 1937–8, and *Amazing Stories*, *Amazing Stories Quarterly*, *Marvel Science Stories*, *Captain Future*, *Startling Stories* and *Thrilling Wonder Stories*. [JG]

WESSOLOWSKI, HANS WALDEMAR *See* H.W. WESSO.

WEST, ANTHONY (1914–). English writer, son of H.G. WELLS and Rebecca West. His first sf novel, *On a Dark Night* (1949; vt *The Vintage* USA), describes a suicide's posthumous questings in space and time; *Another Kind* (1951) is a NEAR-FUTURE story with love in the foreground and a British civil war backing up. [JC]

WEST, WALLACE (GEORGE) (1900–). American lawyer, writer and public relations man. He began publishing sf with "The Last Man" for *AMZ* in 1929, and appeared fairly regularly in the magazines from that date until the late 1960s. Two magazine series of note were collected in book form as *The Bird of Time* (1936–53 var. mags; fix-up 1959) and *Lords of Atlantis* (1952 *Future*; coll. of linked stories 1960) His first novel in book form is *The Memory Bank* (1951 *Startling Stories* as "The Dark Tower"; 1961); like most of his fiction, it is routine but enjoyable. [JC]
Other works: *Outposts in Space* (1931 *Weird Tales*; exp. 1962), *River of Time* (1963); *Time-Lockers* (1935–56 var. mags; fix-up 1964); *The Everlasting Exiles* (1951 65 var. mags; fix-up 1967).
See also: OUTER PLANETS.

WESTALL, WILLIAM (BURY) (1835–1903). English author and

journalist, foreign correspondent for *The Times*, extensively travelled in South America. His *The Phantom City* (1886) describes the discovery of a scientifically advanced UTOPIAN community of Inca descent, and was followed by three similar LOST-WORLD novels, *A Queer Race* (1887; vt "In Quest of Millions" in *Scraps* 1904), *Nigel Fortescue* (1888; vt *Mr. Fortescue* USA; vt "The Hunted Man" UK) and *Don or Devil?* (1901). [JE]
Other works: *Tales and Legends of Saxony and Lusatia* (coll. 1877); *Tales and Traditions of Switzerland* (coll. 1882).
See also: ANTHROPOLOGY.

WESTERMAN, PERCY F. *See* WEAPONS.

WESTLAKE, DONALD E(DWIN) (1933–). American writer, mostly of detective novels and thrillers, often humorous, under his own name and under pseudonyms. He won an Edgar award for detective fiction with *God Save the Mark* (1968). He began publishing sf stories in 1954 with "Or Give Me Death" for *Universe* and released a collection, *The Curious Facts Preceding My Execution and Other Fictions* (coll. 1968), but had already become inactive in the field by the early 1960s. He is a polished, intelligent, witty writer, and his decision not to write sf is regretted. In sf he also used the pseudonyms Richard Stark and Curt Clark, and under the latter name published a novel, *Anarchaos* (1967), whose title amply describes political conditions on the eponymous planet where one's own death is the only crime; it is cleaned up by the hero. [JC]

WESTON, GEORGE (1880–). American writer whose sf novel *His First Million Women* (1934; vt *Comet "Z"* UK), was an early version of the story in which sterility affects all but one man, a theme to become more widely used after the first nuclear explosion. Pat FRANK's *Mr Adam* (1946) is a later example. [JC]
Other works: *The Apple Tree* (1918); *Queen of the World* (1923).

WESTON, PETER (1944–). British sf fan and editor. He published the now defunct FANZINE SPECULATION, and also organized the Speculation sf conferences in Birmingham (1970–72), was TAFF winner (1974) and is chairman of the 1979 British World SF CONVENTION. He is currently editing the ANDROMEDA series of original sf anthologies, which to 1977 consists of *Andromeda 1* (anth. 1976) and *Andromeda 2* (anth. 1977). [PR]

WESTWORLD Film (1973). MGM. Directed by Michael CRICHTON, starring Yul Brynner, Richard Benjamin and James Brolin. Screenplay by Michael Crichton. 88 mins. Colour.
Westworld is a section of an amusement park of the future, the other

Yul Brynner after an acid attack, as a robot run amuck in WESTWORLD.

two sections being simulacra of medieval England and ancient Rome. The park is populated with humanoid and animal robots controlled by technicians from an underground laboratory. Two male visitors enjoy themselves greatly on the first day of their holiday by sleeping with the acquiescent robot saloon girls and out-drawing the local robot gunman, but on the second day the robot actually shoots one of the men dead. Westworld is based not on the real West but on Hollywood's version of it (a point emphasized by the fact that Brynner, who plays the robot gunman, wears the costume he wore in *The Magnificent Seven*), and up to this point it seems that the film will be mainly concerned with exploring men's *machismo* and gun fantasies and their relationship with the fantasy "Wild West". But once the robots rebel, *W* becomes the sort of movie that the visitors come to the park to act out for themselves. The image of Brynner's implacable robot gunman pursuing the lone surviving human is memorable — but it is a pity that the film did not develop its interesting ideas more fully. *W* is nevertheless an sf film of some quality, an impressive directorial début for Michael Crichton, author of ANDROMEDA STRAIN and TERMINAL MAN, and was successful enough to inspire a sequel, FUTUREWORLD. The screenplay of *W* was published as *Westworld* (**1974**) by Michael Crichton. [JB]

WHARTON, EDITH (1862–1937). American writer, best known for her novel *Ethan Frome* (**1911**) though much of her fiction is of importance and has been underrated. The collection *Tales of Men and Ghosts* (coll. **1910**) contains fantasies and one story, "The Debt", of sf interest in that it turns on a conflict between scientific generations. [JC]
Other works: *Xingu and Other Stories* (coll. **1916**); *Here and Beyond* (coll. **1926**); *Ghosts* (coll. **1937**).

WHEATLEY, DENNIS (1897–1977). English writer (wing-commander with the Joint Planning Staff 1941–4), prolific and extremely popular as the author of many espionage thrillers, historical romances, and a number of black magic and occult books, including *The Devil Rides Out* (**1935**) with its sequel *Strange Conflict* (**1941**), *The Haunting of Toby Jugg* (**1948**), *To the Devil a Daughter* (**1953**), *The Ka of Gifford Hillary* (**1956**), *The Satanist* (**1960**), *They Used Dark Forces* (**1964**) and *The White Witch of the South Seas* (**1968**). Further fantasy stories appear in *Gunmen, Gallants and Ghosts* (coll. **1943**). Though these often ponderous volumes have made his name and sales, DW also published a considerable amount of sf, much of it devoted to the discovery of LOST WORLDS, and beginning with *Such Power is Dangerous* (**1933**) and *Black August* (**1934**), in which the Prince Regent of England defeats the forces of totalitarianism. Lost-world novels include *The Fabulous Valley* (**1934**), *They Found Atlantis* (**1936**), *Uncharted Seas* (**1938**), filmed as THE LOST CONTINENT, and set in the Sargasso Sea, and *The Man Who Missed the War* (**1945**), set in the Antarctic, the last three being published in the omnibus volume, *Worlds Far from Here* (coll. **1952**). Other sf includes *The Secret War* (**1937**), *Sixty Days to Live* (**1939**), in which a comet destroys human civilization, and *Star of Ill-Omen* (**1952**), which is about FLYING SAUCERS. DW's sf is GOTHIC, menacing and sensational. It is not scientific. [JC]

See also: ATLANTIS; UNDER THE SEA.

WHEELER, (JOHN) HARVEY (1918–). American writer, co-author with Eugene L. BURDICK (*who see for details*) of the sf novel *Fail-Safe* (**1962**). [JC]

WHEELER, THOMAS GERALD (? –). American physician and author. His juvenile novel *Lost Threshold* (**1968**) is a very late LOST-WORLD story, set underground. *Loose Chippings* (**1968**) is a borderline sf tale, also a juvenile, of an anachronistic village in England. [JC]

WHEN WORLDS COLLIDE Film (1951). Paramount. Directed by Rudolph Maté, starring Richard Derr, Barbara Rush, John Hoyt, Mary Murphy, Laura Elliott and Larry Keating. Screenplay by Sydney Boehm, based on the novel by Philip WYLIE and Edwin BALMER. 83 mins. Colour.
After the success of DESTINATION MOON, George PAL chose another sf subject for his next film; *When Worlds Collide* had originally been bought by Paramount back in 1934 as an ideal property for Cecil B. De Mille, who chose to make *Cleopatra* instead. The plot concerns the destruction of the world by a wandering star and the escape from Earth by a group of people in a hastily made spaceship to the Earthlike planet that orbits the star. Most of the film is concerned with preparations for the flight and the construction of the spaceship and its huge launching-ramp. Most of the

The end of the world is presaged by flood in WHEN WORLDS COLLIDE, in one of the most memorable images from sf cinema.

passengers are chosen by lottery. The approach of the star has catastrophic effects, including the destruction of New York by a tidal wave. The Oscar-winning special effects, supervised by Gordon Jennings, are particularly strong in the sequence showing the spaceship taking off. The screenplay is better than those of many George Pal films.   [JB]

WHERE HAVE ALL THE PEOPLE GONE? Made-for-TV film (1974). NBC. Directed by John L. Moxey, starring Peter Graves, Verna Bloom, Ken Sanson and George O'Hanlon Jr. Teleplay by Lewis John Carlino and Sandor Stern, based on a story by Lewis John Carlino. 75 mins. Colour.

A man and his two teenage children are in a cave when a solar flare occurs which destroys almost everybody on Earth, the bodies being reduced to a sandlike substance. The family journeys across California to their seaside home, where they hope to find their mother still alive, encountering other survivors, some unfriendly, and packs of dogs running wild. It is a familiar sf plot, but the script is surprisingly good — one novel twist being that the two children take the initiative while the father is passive. [JB]

WHITE, ARED (? – ?). American writer whose sf novel, *Attack on America* (**1939**), is a future-WAR warning tale, in which Germany (as she was suspected of trying to do in the First World War) attacks America from Mexico. The novel is signed General Ared White.   [JC]

WHITE, FRED(ERICK) M(ERRICK) (1859–   ). English writer, contributor of sf to PEARSON'S MAGAZINE, THE STRAND MAGAZINE and other of the general fiction magazines that featured sf in the early 1900s. He continued writing, mostly sensational mysteries, well into the 1920s, though he is best known for his DISASTER series, "The Four White Days" (1903), "The Four Days Night" (1903), "The Dust of Death" (1903), "A Bubble Burst" (1903), "The Invisible Force" (1903) and "The River of Death" (1904), in which London and England were subjected to a variety of calamities. Catastrophe was turned to Britain's advantage in his only sf novel, *The White Battalions* (1900), in which arctic conditions in Europe resulting from a shift in the flow of the Gulf Stream enable Britain to win a future WAR. His stories are typical of popular Edwardian sf.   [JE]

WHITE, JAMES (1928–   ). British writer from Ulster, who works as publicity officer with an aircraft company. Many of his stories are set in MEDICAL contexts; he is perhaps best known for his series of linked stories and fix-ups dealing with Sector General, a 384-level space-station-hospital "far out on the galactic Rim", designed to accommodate all known kinds of XENOBIOLOGICAL problems, with a multi-species medical staff of 10,000. A human, Dr Conway, provides point of view throughout. *Hospital Station* (coll. of linked stories **1962**) introduces Conway and his colleagues to a variety of medical crises, all solved with humour, ingenuity and an underlying sense of decency. *Star Surgeon* (**1963**), a novel, *Major Operation* (1966–70 *New Writings in SF*; fix-up **1971**) and the stories "Counterchasm" (1969) and "Spacebird" (1973) provide more of the same, just as enjoyably. White's capacity to conceive and make plausible a wide range of alien anatomies seems unflagging.

JW began writing sf stories in 1953 with "Assisted Passage" for *NW*; some of these are collected in *Deadly Litter* (coll. **1964**), *The Aliens Among Us* (coll. **1969**) and *Monsters and Medics* (coll. **1977**), but they have generally had less impact than his series, though they share an ease with sf hardware and a quickness of plot. Of his several novels, perhaps the most successful is the ingenious *The Watch Below* (**1966**), a story with two narrative lines which dovetail cleverly. In one, a Second World War merchant vessel sinks; three men and two women survive in a large air pocket, work out life maintenance systems and eventually breed there; 100 years pass. In the second narrative line, water-dwelling aliens from afar seek a wet world like Earth to inhabit peacefully; their ship lands in the sea in time to save the descendants of the five 20th-century survivors. The various correspondences between the two sets of "prisoners" are neatly and humanely stressed. Later novels have had a milder effect. *The Dream Millennium* (**1974**) takes another physician to the stars in a slower-than-light ship where, to pass the time, and to learn from the Jungian substrate how to be more human, he dreams the history of the human race in "coldsleep"; awakened, he leads his fellow passengers to a new planet rather like paradise. If White's work sometimes fails to grip, it is never through lack of decency. Quiet and unpretentious, his stories leave a moral good taste in the mouth.   [JC]
Other works: *The Secret Visitors* (**1957**); *Second Ending* (**1962**); *Open Prison* (**1964**; vt *The Escape Orbit* USA); *All Judgement Fled* (**1968**); *Tomorrow is Too Far* (**1971**); *Dark Inferno* (**1972**; vt *Lifeboat* USA).
See also: CRIME AND PUNISHMENT; CRYONICS; GENERATION STARSHIPS; MYTHOLOGY; POLLUTION; SUSPENDED ANIMATION; UNDER THE SEA.

WHITE, JAY C. An unrevealed pseudonym; only *A Cup of Life* (1962) is attributed to this name.   [JC]

WHITE, STEWART EDWARD (1873–1946). American writer of travel books and novels, many of the latter set in California. In his later years he became interested in spiritualism, believed he was in contact with his dead wife, and wrote some books about the other world, including *The Unobstructed Universe* (**1940**). His two sf novels with Samuel Hopkins ADAMS are *The Mystery* (**1907**), about ships lost at sea, with an sf explanation of their disappearance, and *The Sign at Six* (**1912**), in which a mad scientist threatens to intercept all heat, sound and light waves entering New York. A rumoured SEW fantasy title, (not seen by us) is *The Leopard Woman*.
                                              [JC/PN]

WHITE, TED Form of his name used professionally by American writer and editor Theodore Edward White (1938–   ). In the latter capacity he became, after a period as assitant editor for *FSF*, 1963–8, editor, sometimes controversially, of AMAZING STORIES and FANTASTIC from Mar. 1969. As editor he improved the magazines and emphasized matters relating to sf FANDOM. TW was known, too, for the many chatty, aggressive, self-defensive and polemical letters he published in such fanzines as THE ALIEN CRITIC, and for his continuing column in ALGOL, which had the same qualities, as did his editorials in *AMZ* and *Fantastic*. He won a HUGO award as best fan writer in 1968.

As a writer of sf, he began publishing with "Phoenix" for *AMZ* in 1963 with Marion Zimmer BRADLEY; his first novel is *Invasion from 2500* (**1964**) with Terry CARR, under the collaborative pseudonym Norman Edwards; other collaborations are *Lost in Space* (**1967**), a television spin-off (*see* LOST IN SPACE) which he wrote as Ron Archer with Dave VAN ARNAM, and *Sideslip* (**1968**), under his own name with Van Arnam. These novels are routine, as are most of TW's sf-fantasy adventures such as *Android Avenger* (**1965**) and its sequel *The Spawn of the Death Machine* (**1968**), about the ANDROID Tanner and his adventures, and *Phoenix Prime* (**1966**) and its sequel *Sorceress of Qar* (**1966**), in which a good SUPERMAN fights bad supermen, and *Star Wolf!* (**1971**). TW also wrote the ending of the Philip K Dick serial "A. Lincoln — Simulacrum" (*AMZ* 1969–70), but Dick's own ending was restored when it was published as *We Can Build You* (**1972**). His major novel to date is *By Furies Possessed* (**1970**), about a form of ALIEN PARASITISM.
                                              [JC/PN]
Other works: *The Jewels of Elsewhen* (**1967**); *The Secret of the Marauder Satellite* (**1967**); *The Great Gold Steal* (**1968**), a Captain America story; *No Time Like Tomorrow* (**1969**); *Trouble on Project Ceres* (**1971**); *The Oz Encounter* (**1977**) in collaboration with Marv Wolfman (actually written by Wolfman from characters and a scenario devised by TW). As editor: The *Best from Amazing Stories* (anth. **1973**); *The Best from Fantastic* (anth. **1973**).
See also: CITIES; SF MAGAZINES.

WHITE, T(ERENCE) H(ANBURY)
(1906–64). English writer, known mainly
for such works outside the sf field as the
novel *Farewell Victoria* (1933); of
considerable sf/fantasy interest is his
superlative fantasia on Sir Thomas
Malory's *La Morte D'Arthur*, *The Once
and Future King* (1958; vt *Camelot
USA*), which is made up of three volumes
previously published, though with the
final work always in mind, and now
revised, plus a previously unpublished
fourth part. (It is the basis of the musical
Camelot, filmed in 1967). The first
published section of the work, *The Sword
in the Stone* (1938), differs from its final
form and remains a children's classic;
Walt Disney made a cartoon film of it,
under the same title, in 1963. The second
and third parts were *The Witch in the
Wood* (1939) and *The Ill-Made Knight*
(1940). The original conclusion to *The
Once and Future King* (quite different
from the present conclusion) was declined
by THW's English publishers during the
Second World War, because of its pacifist
content, and it has only recently been
released as *The Book of Merlyn* (1977).
Taken as a whole, the novel is a
remarkably adult exploration of the
complexity of evil, of the decay of the
Matter of Britain (particularly in the ant
DYSTOPIA Merlyn subjects the young
Arthur to as part of his education), and
generally of the loss of innocence. Other
works by THW, like *Mistress Masham's
Repose* (1946), about some Lilliputians
who have survived Gulliver's
transportation of them to England, and
The Elephant and the Kangaroo (1947),
contain strong fantasy elements. The
early novel sequence, *Earth Stopped*
(1934) and *Gone to Ground* (1935),
introduces an sf HOLOCAUST to underline
the points it makes about contemporary
civilization through the conversations and
fox-hunting manias of a large cast; in the
second volume, survivors of the final WAR
tell each other exemplary tales while
hiding in a cave. *The Master* (1957) is
juvenile sf: a boy and girl come across a
plot to rule the world from the deserted
island of Rockall, where a Merlyn-like
Master, 157 years old, has perfected both
telepathy and a vibration device that will
destroy all machines; fortunately he trips
over the children's dog and falls into the
sea. THW's sf is of a piece with all his
work, sharing the sentimentality, satirical
power, sadness, manic humour and
compassion of his best fantasy.   [JC]
About the author: *T.H. White, a
Biography* (1968) by Sylvia Townsend
Warner.
See also: SWORD AND SORCERY.

WHITE, W.A.P. *See* Anthony
BOUCHER.

WHITFIELD, STEPHEN E(DWARD)
(? –). American advertising man and
writer, author of the non-fiction work
The Making of Star Trek (1968). The idea
for the book was SEW's, as was the
actual writing, but the producer of STAR
TREK, Gene RODDENBERRY, gave
considerable help and is credited along
with SEW on the cover.   [JC]

WHITLEY, GEORGE *See* A. Bertram
CHANDLER.

WHO? Film (1974). Hemisphere &
Maclean & Co. Directed by Jack Gold,
starring Elliott Gould, Trevor Howard
and Joe Bova. Screenplay by John Gould,
based on the novel of the same name by
Algis BUDRYS. 91 mins. Colour.
    In this disappointing film version of
Budrys's interesting novel, an American
scientist is seriously injured in a
laboratory explosion in East Germany.
The Russians claim to have rebuilt his
shattered body, giving him a metal skull
and face, and return the CYBORG result to
the West; the suspicion then grows
among the Americans that the man
beneath the metal might not be their
scientist at all, but a Russian spy. He is
kept under constant surveillance in the
hope that he will reveal some definite clue
to his real identity, but when the film
ends the 20th-century "man in the iron
mask" has kept his secret. Jack Gold has
directed some fine plays for British TV
but his feature films are poor in
comparison. *W* is ponderous, and fails to
develop the fascinating possibilities
offered by the novel.   [JB]

WHO WOULD KILL JESSIE? *See*
KDO CHCE ZABIT JESSII?.

WIBBERLEY, LEONARD (FRANCIS)
(1915–). Irish writer now resident in
the United States, for some time both
novelist and journalist but now writing
novels full time; he has published at least
100 books. His first sf novel is his most
famous, *The Mouse that Roared* (1955; vt
The Wrath of Grapes UK), a Ruritanian-
style comedy involving a space flight; it
was later made into a film. Its sequels are
The Mouse on the Moon (1962) and *The
Mouse on Wall Street* (1969). Of his many
titles, there are some fantasies of interest,
including *Mrs Searwood's Secret
Weapon* (1954), *McGillicuddy McGotham*
(1956), *Take Me To Your President*
(1957), *The Quest of Excalibur* (1959) and
Stranger at Killknock (1961). Of his
juveniles, *Encounter Near Venus* (1967)
and its sequel, *Journey to Untor* (1970),
are sf. A further sf novel is *One in Four*
(1975).   [JC]

WICKS, MARK (? – ?). British
writer whose sf novel, *To Mars Via the
Moon* (1911), describes a UTOPIA on a
Mars whose features owe an
acknowledged debt to the theories of
Percival Lowell (*see* MARS). The book
was probably intended as a
fictionalization of popular science for
younger readers.   [JC/PN]
See also: MOON.

WIENER, NORBERT (1894–1964).
German mathematician, long resident in
the USA, who established the
contemporary sense of the word
CYBERNETICS in his book *Cybernetics*
(1948; rev. 1961). Some of his
speculations in this field appear in *The
Human Use of Human Beings* (1950) and
in *God & Golem, Inc.: a Comment on
Certain Points where Cybernetics
Impinges on Religion* (1964). As W.
Norbert, he published two sf stories,
"The Miracle of the Broom Closet", with
FSF in 1954, and "The Brain" (1953). A
novel, *The Tempter* (1959), is not sf. *Ex-
Prodigy* (1953) speculates interestingly
about intellectual SUPERMAN.   [JC]
About the author: *I am a Mathematician*
(1956) by NW.

WILBRAHAM, JOHN *See* Robert
POTTER.

WILCOX, DON (1908–). American
writer who has taught creative writing at
Northwestern University; most of his
work, sometimes as Miles Shelton or
Max Overton, was for Ray PALMER's
AMZ and *Fantastic Adventures*, where he
published his first story, "The Pit of
Death", in 1939; a good
GENERATION-STARSHIP tale, "The Voyage
that Lasted 600 Years" (1940), soon
followed. DW used the house name
Alexander BLADE at least once, and also
published a novelette, "Confessions of a
Mechanical Man" (1947), as Buzz-Bolt
Atomcracker. His story "The Whispering
Gorilla" (1940), had a sequel written by
his fellow Ziff-Davis writer David Vern,
writing as David V. REED, "The Return
of the Whispering Gorilla" (1943); the
two were cobbled together as a book, *The
Whispering Gorilla* (fix-up 1950), as by
David V. Reed. A popular series by DW
writing as Miles Shelton is made up of the
four "Ebbtide Jones" stories, 1939–42,
the first in *AMZ*, the rest in *Fantastic
Adventures*.   [JC/PN]

WILDER, CHERRY (1930–).
Australian writer, resident in Germany.
Her first published sf was "The Ark of
James Carlyle" in *New Writings in SF 24*
(anth. 1974) ed. Kenneth BULMER, and her
sf novel for older children, the first of a
projected series, is *The Luck of Brin's
Five* (1977). It is a pleasantly romantic
story of an Earthman who crashes on a
strange planet, and the learning process
involved with his adoption into an alien
culture.   [PN]

WILDING, PHILIP (? –). British
author of two routine sf adventures,
Spaceflight Venus (1955) and *Shadow
Over the Earth* (1956). Under the name
John Robert Haynes he wrote *The
Scream from Outer Space* (1955), also
unremarkable: "To thwart the menace of
impulsatia, they probed the endless voids
of hyperspace"; impulsatia is ultra-sonic
vibration from space.   [JC/PN]

WILD IN THE STREETS Film (1968). AIP. Directed by Barry Shear, starring Christopher Jones, Shelley Winters, Diane Varsi, Ed Begley, Hal Holbrook, Richard Pryor and Walter Winchell. Screenplay by Robert Thom. 97 mins. Colour.

Another of the youth-movies that enjoyed a brief surge of popularity in the late 1960s, this concerns a pop star who lends his support to a Kennedy-style senator in California and wins the election for him. He demands, as payment, the lowering of the voting age to 14. They compromise on 18, but the pop star and his group, their foot now in the door, take over the country and everybody over 35 is put in a concentration camp. The remainder briefly enjoy what they believe to be a paradise on Earth but by the end of the film the sub-teens are muttering rebelliously and another revolution seems imminent. It all seems very dated now. [JB]

WILD, WILD WEST, THE Television series (1965–8). CBS TV. Producer of the first season: Fred Freiberger; of the second and later seasons: Michael Garrison. Pilot episode directed by Richard Sarafian, written by Gilbert Ralston. Episodes 50 mins. First season b/w; colour thereafter.

A mixture of Western and modern secret-agent fantasies, the series had Robert Conrad playing Jim West, an 1870s James Bond. The plots usually involved anachronistic gadgets and sf devices and often featured mad scientists attempting to overthrow the American government. At its best the series had something of the bizarre quality of THE AVENGERS, but was sometimes rather leaden; the stylization was perhaps not quite light enough, although low-angle shooting and clever use of sets ensured a genuine sense of decadent menace in the more baroque episodes. To counterpoint the bland persona of the hero, Ross Martin played his jovial partner, Artemus Gordon. [JB/PN]

WILEY, JOHN See Rog PHILLIPS.

WILHELM, KATE (1928–). American writer. She has been influential in the sf field with her husband, Damon KNIGHT, through his founding of the MILFORD SCIENCE FICTION WRITERS' CONFERENCE in 1958 and its offshoot, in which she has been directly involved, the CLARION SCIENCE FICTION WRITERS' WORKSHOP, a recent anthology of whose products, *Clarion SF* (anth. **1977**), she has edited, earlier anthologies being edited by Robin Scott WILSON, its co-founder.

KW began publishing sf in 1956 with "The Pint-Size Genie" for *Fantastic*, though it was not for several years that she began to make an impact as a writer, and only since the late 1960s that her work has attained its considerable stature. Early stories can be found in *The Mile-Long Spaceship* (coll. **1963**; vt *Andover and the Android* UK). After *More Bitter than Death* (**1963**), a mystery, her first novel is *The Clone* (**1965**) with Theodore L. THOMAS; this is one of the first sf books to use CLONES as ostensible subject matter (though the clone in this case is actually a blob), and illustrates the workmanlike but somewhat rudimentary techniques of her early work; a second collaboration with Thomas, *The Year of the Cloud* (**1970**), a DISASTER novel in which the viscosity of Earth's water begins to rise, displays similar characteristics. *The Killer Thing* (**1967**; vt *The Killing Thing* UK) is the last of her strictly generic adventures; she was soon consistently involved in writing speculative fiction rather than sf, as her book titles tended to emphasize. *The Downstairs Room, and Other Speculative Fiction* (coll. **1968**), *Abyss: Two Novellas* (coll. **1971**) and *The Infinity Box: A Collection of Speculative Fiction* (coll. **1975**) all underline this claim, one richly justified by at least the stories in *The Infinity Box*, and particularly the title work, whose depiction of NEAR-FUTURE America as it affects grown men and women combines an sf boldness of structure with non-generic fullness of realization. Additional stories in this volume, like "The Village" (1973) and "The Funeral" (1972), radically transform and darken conventional sf devices, illuminating both them and the world. "The Planners" (1968) won a NEBULA award for best short story.

In her more recent novels, KW has attempted with somewhat less success an equivalent broadening and deepening of her art, but in longer works retains a tendency to drift from the intensity and pointedness of her stories, thus diffusing her effects. Nevertheless, *Where Late the Sweet Birds Sang* (**1976**), which won HUGO and JUPITER awards for best novel, successfully translates her interest in the implications of cloning to a post-HOLOCAUST venue in the Appalachians, where an isolated community of clones has been formed to weather the interregnum until civilization can spread again, but develops in its own, perilously narrow fashion. *The Clewiston Test* (**1976**) tells a suspenseful story involving unsatisfactorily tested drugs and their possible effects on their developer, Clewiston herself, and on her unhappy marriage; *Fault Lines* (**1977**), not actually sf, works at the point where sf and the MAINSTREAM tend to come interestingly together in 1977, in its rich though somewhat chaotic presentation of a woman's broken remembrances of her life, the fault lines of the title representing her own life, her future, her unhappy marriages, plus the earthquake that traps her and a powerful sense that civilization itself is cracking at the seams.

KW is at the forefront of those sf writers trying to amalgamate their genre to the mainstream, which is not only a difficult marketing task, but is also perilous creatively; that she avoids most of the pitfalls of "Midcult" sentimentality in her recent work consequently augurs well for the future of the attempt. [JC]
Other works: *The Nevermore Affair* (**1966**); *Let the Fire Fall* (**1969**); *Margaret and I* (**1971**); *City of Cain* (**1974**), a crime novel. As editor: *Nebula Award Stories Nine* (anth. **1974**).
See also: ECOLOGY; INTELLIGENCE; MONSTERS; POLLUTION; WOMEN.

WILKINS, JOHN (1614–72). British philosopher and Bishop of Chester. He wrote no fiction, but his works of scientific speculation are remarkable. Historians of sf usually mention his *The Discovery of a New World* (**1638**), to whose third edition (**1640**) he added a brief discourse on the possibility of lunar travel. His *Mathematicall Magick* (**1648**) is a treatise on technology including essays on submarines, flying machines and many other wonders, and a somewhat sceptical consideration of perpetual motion. He was one of the first popularizers of science and a propagandist for scientific progress. While Master of Wadham College, Oxford, he founded the Philosophical Society, which in 1662 became the Royal Society. [BS]
See also: ASTRONOMY; MACHINES; MOON; RELIGION; SPACESHIPS; TRANSPORTATION; UNDER THE SEA.

WILKINS, (WILLIAM) VAUGHAN (1890–1959). English writer, best known for his historical fiction; his sf novel *Valley Beyond Time* (**1955**) is a search through the DIMENSIONS. *The City of Frozen Fire* (**1950**) is a LOST-WORLD story. [JC]
Other works: *Fanfare for a Witch* (**1954**).

WILL, JOHN N. (? –). Author, probably American, of *My Blonde Princess of Space* (**1968**). [JC]

WILLARD, C.D. See Charles W. DIFFIN.

WILLEFORD, CHARLES (RAY) (1919–). American writer. In his *The Machine in Ward Eleven* (coll. **1963**) none of the stories is sf, despite the book's appearance in some sf indexes. One is surreal fantasy. [PN]

WILLEY, ROBERT See Willy LEY.

WILLIAMS, CHARLES (1886–1945). English writer, often associated with his friends C.S. LEWIS and J.R.R. TOLKIEN, because of the interest shown by all three in both FANTASY and the higher forms of Christianity (two were Anglican, Tolkien was Catholic). CW's novels are fantasy thrillers, with some remote resemblance to sf in the case of *Many Dimensions* (**1931**), in which the world is at stake in

the hunt, via the many DIMENSIONS, for a magical stone; but in this, as with the remainder of his fiction, the bent of the fantasy is towards RELIGION; the TIME TRAVEL in *All Hallows' Eve* (**1945**) is used to similar ends.   [JC]
Other works: *War in Heaven* (**1930**); *The Place of the Lion* (**1931**); *The Greater Trumps* (**1932**); *Shadows of Ecstasy* (**1933**); *Descent into Hell* (**1937**).
About the author: *Shadows of Imagination: the Fantasies of C.S. Lewis, J.R.R. Tolkien and Charles Williams* (anth. **1969**) ed. Mark R. HILLEGAS.
See also: MYTHOLOGY.

WILLIAMS, ERIC C. (1918–). English writer, previously a bookseller, who began publishing sf with "The Desolator" for *Science Fantasy* in 1965, and who is the author of some routine sf novels starting with *The Time Injection* (**1968**). *The Drop In* (**1977**) is an alien INVASION novel.   [JC]
Other works: *Monkman Comes Down* (**1968**); *The Call of Utopia* (**1971**); *Flash* (**1972**); *Project: Renaissance* (**1973**).

WILLIAMS, FRANK (? –). Author, probably American, of the sf novel *It Happened Tomorrow* (**1952**).   [JC]

WILLIAMS, JOHN (ALFRED) (1925–). American writer, among the best-known black writers in the USA. His novel *The Man Who Cried I Am* (**1967**) involves a black genocide plot on the part of the US government, to be put into action in case of civil uprising. A critic familiar with the Civilian Exclusion Order No. 5, Title II, of the Nixon-McCarran Act, reckons the book to have a remote factual basis. *Sons of Darkness, Sons of Light* (**1969**) presents a black revolt centered on Manhattan, comparable to Warren MILLER's *The Siege of Harlem* (**1964**) as a MAINSTREAM use of sf material. *Captain Blackman* (**1972**) has a time-travelling hero who takes part, as a black soldier, in all the wars of US history.   [JC/PN]
See also: POLITICS.

WILLIAMS, J.X. House name used on pornographic novels, several with sf content, published by Greenleaf Classics, a company owned by one-time sf editor William HAMLING. A subsidiary company was Regency Books, with which Harlan ELLISON was associated. *The Sex Pill* (**1968**) as by JXW is in fact by Andrew J. OFFUTT. Two more titles, *Her* (**1967**) and *Witch in Heat* (**1967**), are by unidentified authors.   [PN]

WILLIAMS, NICK BODDIE (1906–). American newspaperman and writer, who has contributed short material to various "slicks". His sf novel, *The Atom Curtain* (**1956**), describes a distorted American society 270 years after it has separated itself from the rest of the world by an atomic barrier.   [JC]

WILLIAMS, ROBERT MOORE (1907–78). American writer, active in the sf field under his own name and various pseudonyms, including John S. Browning, H.H. Harmon, Russell Storm and the house name E.K. JARVIS; he began publishing sf as Robert Moore with "Zero as a Limit" for *ASF* in 1937, and by the 1960s had published over 150 stories. Though most of them are routine, he has been an important supplier of competent genre fiction during these decades. Notable among the 150 is the "Jongor" series, comprising *Jongor of Lost Land* (1940 *Fantastic Adventures*; **1970**), *The Return of Jongor* (1944 *Fantastic Adventures*; **1970**) and *Jongor Fights Back* (1951 *Fantastic Adventures*; **1970**). He did not begin publishing books until *The Chaos Fighters* (**1955**), but has since released many novels of the same general calibre as his short fiction. Notable among them are *Doomsday Eve* (**1957**), a post-HOLOCAUST drama, and a series, *Zanthar of the Many Worlds* (**1967**), *Zanthar at the Edge of Never* (**1968**), *Zanthar at Moon's Madness* (**1968**) and *Zanthar at Trip's End* (**1969**). Zanthar is a remarkable professor hero.   [JC]
Other works: *Conquest of the Space Sea* (**1955**); *The Blue Atom* (**1958**); *The Void Beyond and Other Stories* (coll. **1958**); *To the End of Time* (coll. **1960**); *World of the Masterminds* (**1960**); *The Day They H-Bombed Los Angeles* (**1961**); *The Darkness Before Tomorrow* (**1962**); *King of the Fourth Planet* (**1962**); *Walk Up the Sky* (**1962**); *The Star Wasps* (**1963**); *Flight from Yesterday* (**1963**); *The Lunar Eye* (**1964**); *The Second Atlantis* (**1965**); *Vigilante — 21st Century* (**1967**); *The Bell from Infinity* (**1968**); *When Two Worlds Meet* (coll. of linked stories **1970**); *Beachhead Planet* (**1970**); *Love is Forever — We Are for Tonight* (**1970**); *Now Comes Tomorrow* (**1971**).
See also: ROBOTS; SWORD AND SORCERY.

WILLIAMSON, JACK Form of his name used by American writer John Stewart Williamson (1908–) throughout his career, though his "Seetee" stories were originally signed Will Stewart. JW was born in Arizona and raised (after stints in Mexico and Texas) on an isolated New Mexico homestead; he describes his early upbringing and his introduction to 1920s sf in the introduction and notes to *The Early Williamson* (coll. **1975**), a collection of the rough but vigorous stories he published from 1928 to 1933. His notes reconfirm the explosively liberating effect early PULP sf had on its first young audiences, especially those, like JW, coming to maturity in small towns or farms across the USA. After discovering AMAZING STORIES, and specifically being influenced by its 1927 serialization of A. MERRITT's *The Moon Pool* (**1919**), he immediately decided to try to write stories for that magazine. His first

Jack WILLIAMSON

published fiction, "The Metal Man" (1928), is deeply influenced by Merritt's lush visual style, but like most of his early work conveys an exhilarating sense of liberation.

JW has always been an adaptable writer, responsive to the changing nature of his markets, and his collaborations over the years have seemed to be genuine attempts to learn more about his craft as well as to produce saleable fiction. His first collaborations, with Miles J. BREUER, came about through his early association with fan organizations like the International Science Correspondence Club and the American Interplanetary Society; JW deliberately apprenticed himself to Breuer, reporting (in *The Early Williamson*) that Breuer "taught me to curb my tendencies toward wild melodrama and purple adjectives". *The Girl from Mars* (**1930**), a novelette published as a booklet, and "The Birth of a New Republic" (1930), a novel, in *AMZ Quarterly*, resulted from their work together; JW also collaborated with Lawrence Schwartzman at about this time.

JW's development was swift, and it is notable that from the very first he was equally comfortable with both the story and novel form; indeed, by 1940 he had published more than 12 novels in the magazines, including the unreprinted tales "The Alien Intelligence" (1929), "The Stone from the Green Star" (1931), "Xandulu" (1934), "Islands of the Sun" (1935), "The Blue Spot" (1937) and "Fortress of Utopia" (1939), and has concentrated on longer forms even more heavily since that date. Very early in his career, he began publishing what remains his most famous (though not his best) work, the "Legion of Space" series, comprised of *The Legion of Space* (1934 *ASF*; rev. **1947**), *The Cometeers* (1936

ASF; rev. as title story of *The Cometeers*, coll. **1950**; **1967**) and *One Against the Legion* (1939 *ASF*; rev. 1950 in *The Cometeers*, coll. **1950**; **1967**); an additional story, "Nowhere Near", appeared in the 1967 edition of *One Against the Legion*. The series depicts the far-flung, universe-shaking, SPACE-OPERA adventures of four buccaneering soldiers (the RABELAISIAN Giles Habibula being the most original character, and a frequently used model for later sf life-loving grotesques, including Poul ANDERSON's Nicholas van Rijn); more or less unaided, the four save the human worlds from threats both internal and external. The series has much the same venue as E.E. "Doc" SMITH's "Lensman" books, but lacks their scope and momentum. Other novels from these years, like *The Green Girl* (1930 *AMZ*; **1950**), *Golden Blood* (1933 *Weird Tales*; rev. **1964**), *The Legion of Time* (1938 *ASF*; rev. 1952 as the title story of *The Legion of Time*, coll. **1952**; **1961**), not connected to the "Legion of Space" books, and *After World's End* (1939 *Marvel Science Stories*; in *The Legion of Time*, coll. **1952**; **1961**) share a crude narrative brio, adaptability to various markets, but a certain lack of serious ambition. The exception, perhaps, is *The Legion of Time*, which was one of the earliest and most ingenious stories of ALTERNATE WORLDS and TIME PARADOXES, with conflicting potential future worlds battling through time, each trying to ensure its own existence and deny its opponent's. It inspired one of the most penetrating studies yet written about a PULP sf novel, Brian W. ALDISS's "Judgement at Jonbar" (1964) published in SF HORIZONS.

By the 1940s, however, JW began to adapt successfully to the somewhat higher literary standards of John W. CAMPBELL Jr's *ASF*, and by the end of the decade had published some of his finest work to date. His ANTIMATTER series, *Seetee Ship* (1942–3 *ASF*; fix-up **1951**) and *Seetee Shock* (1949 *ASF*; **1950**), both published as by Will Stewart but later reissued under JW's own name, and intended to be read (as above) in the original magazine order, is transitional, perhaps more smoothly told than its predecessors, but unchallengingly treating its ASTEROID miners and their crises in the old fashion, with a great deal of action but little insight. Its success led to JW's creation of a COMIC STRIP, *Beyond Mars*, which ran for three years in the *New York Daily News*. Of a different calibre entirely is *Darker than you Think* (1940 *Unknown*; exp. **1948**), a remarkable speculative novel about lycanthropy, with the thesis that werewolves are genetic throwbacks to a species cognate with *Homo sapiens* (*see* SUPERNATURAL CREATURES). Also from the 1940s is his most famous single novel, *The Humanoids* (**1949**), about which there has been some confusion. A preceding

novelette (JW's best-known short story), "With Folded Hands ..." (1947), in which humanoid ROBOTS destroy men's nature by serving them with greater than human competence, does not form part of the novel, which is revised from the *ASF* serial "... And Searching Mind" (1948) alone, and deals darkly with the implications of Man's relation to his superior servants in describing the conflict between them, and its moderately optimistic resolution.

The early 1950s saw JW undergo a writer's block, out of which he characteristically worked himself through collaboration and the continued modernizing of his techniques and concerns. Though *Star Bridge* (**1955**) with James GUNN is no more than a competent space opera, his continuing collaborative work with Frederik POHL is of more interest, comprised to date of two completed series. *Undersea Quest* (**1954**), *Undersea Fleet* (**1955**) and *Undersea City* (**1958**) is a set of juveniles. *The Reefs of Space* (**1964**), *Starchild* (**1965**) and *Rogue Star* (**1969**) deal in terms combining space opera and metaphysics (*see* LIVING WORLDS) with Man's evolving into a mature planet-spanning species. The three have been collected as *The Starchild Trilogy* (coll. **1977**). A third series with Pohl has begun with the publication of *The Farthest Star* (fix-up **1975**).

JW has continued working into the 1970s, with novels like *The Moon Children* (**1972**) and *The Power of Blackness* (fix-up **1975**), but, beginning in 1960, also embarked on a second career at Eastern New Mexico University, where he took a BA in English and an MA with an unpublished thesis (1957), "A Study of the Sense of Prophecy in Modern Science Fiction" and taught the modern novel and literary criticism until his retirement in 1977; he has also been deeply involved in promoting sf as an academic subject (*see* SF IN THE CLASSROOM) and in *Science Fiction Comes to College* (**1971**) and *Teaching SF* (**1975**) has published valuable reference works on the subject, with a further volume, an anthology of essays ed. JW to be called *Science Fiction: Education for Tomorrow* projected JW received a PILGRIM award for his academic work relating to sf in 1973. He took a PhD with the University of Colorado in 1964 on H.G. WELLS's early sf, and expanded his thesis into *H.G. Wells: Critic of Progress* (**1973**), a book which, despite some methodological clumsiness, valuably examines Wells's complex development of ideas as they relate to the idea of progress.

JW has been an sf writer of substance for 50 years. His newest books seem written by a comparatively young man. Because he never concentrated on one kind of fiction, his reputation is perhaps less high than some of his later works merit – although in 1976 he won the second Grand Master NEBULA award, preceded only by Robert A. HEINLEIN –

an imbalance that time will correct. JW is also the current (1978) president of the SCIENCE FICTION WRITERS OF AMERICA. [JC]

Other works: *Dragon's Island* (**1951**; vt *The Not-Men*); *Dome Around America* (1941 *Startling Stories* as "Gateway to Paradise"; rev. **1955**); *The Trial of Terra* (1951–62 var. mags; fix-up **1962**); *The Reign of Wizardry* (1940 *Unknown*; rev. **1965**); *Bright New Universe* (**1967**); *Trapped in Space* (**1968**), a juvenile; *The Pandora Effect* (coll. **1969**); *People Machines* (coll. **1971**).

See also: ANDROIDS; AUTOMATION; BIOLOGY; CHILDREN'S SF; COLONIZATION OF OTHER WORLDS; CRIME AND PUNISHMENT; FANTASTIC VOYAGES; GALACTIC EMPIRES; GOLDEN AGE OF SF; GREAT AND SMALL; ISLANDS; LIFE ON OTHER WORLDS; MACHINES; MATTER TRANSMISSION; MESSIAHS; MONSTERS; MOON; MUTANTS; MYTHOLOGY; ORIGIN OF MAN; OUTER PLANETS; PARALLEL WORLDS; POWER SOURCES; SF MAGAZINES; SPACESHIPS; STARS; SUN; SUPERMAN; TERRAFORMING; TIME TRAVEL; UNDER THE SEA; WAR; WEAPONS.

WILLIS, CHARLES *See* Arthur C. CLARKE.

WILSON, ANGUS (1913–). English writer, best known for such works outside the sf field as *Anglo-Saxon Attitudes* (**1956**). His sf novel, *The Old Men at the Zoo* (**1961**), applies MAINSTREAM techniques to a NEAR-FUTURE vision of a 1970s England threatened internally by a loss of nerve and Neo-Fascism and externally by a federated Europe. AW was an early supporter of hardcover sf PUBLISHING in the UK, and edited the book of the best stories entered for the *Observer* sf prize in 1954, *A.D. 2500* (anth. **1955**). [JC]

WILSON, COLIN (1931–). English writer of speculative works, including his famous first book, *The Outsider* (**1956**), various non-fiction works on occult topics, and some fiction, including three sf novels, the LOVECRAFT-influenced *The Mind Parasites* (**1967**), *The Philosopher's Stone* (**1969**) and *The Space Vampires* (**1976**). The second novel deals somewhat heavily with IMMORTALITY, and the third is a kind of horror SPACE OPERA. His fiction shares the earnest argumentativeness of his other work, as most relevantly demonstrated in *The Strength to Dream: Literature and the Imagination* (**1961**), which includes discussions of H.P. Lovecraft and of H.G. WELLS. [JC]

Other works: *The Return of the Lloigor* (1969 in the original anthology, *Tales of the Cthulhu Mythos*; **1974**).

See also: MONSTERS; PARASITISM AND SYMBIOSIS; PSYCHOLOGY; SUSPENDED ANIMATION.

WILSON, F. PAUL (1946–). American physician and writer, who began publishing sf with "The Cleaning Machine" for *Startling Mystery Stories* in 1971; much of his work was under the influence of John W. CAMPBELL Jr (and also the Libertarian movement) and was published in *ASF*, including all the stories and serialized novels of his "LaNague Federation" series, which comprise "The Man with the Anteater" (1971), "Higher Centers" (1971), "Wheels Within Wheels" (1971), with book publication projected for 1978, "Ratman" (1971) and *Healer* (1971 *ASF* as "Pard"; exp. **1976**), in which an IMMORTAL protector of mankind uses his psychiatric healing skills against an alien intelligence within the loose network of inhabited planets. [JC]

WILSON, RICHARD (1920–). American writer and currently director of the News Bureau, Syracuse University. He has combined journalism and sf writing since the beginning of his career, when he published his first sf story, "Murder from Mars", with *Astonishing Stories* in 1940; in the same issue, he collaborated with C.M. KORNBLUTH under the house name Ivar TOWERS in the story "Stepsons of Mars". A later Towers story, "The Man Without a Planet" (1942), was by RW alone. Later he used the pseudonym Edward Halibut for "Course of Empire" (1956). War service interrupted his career, but after 1950 he became a quite prolific magazine contributor, and soon published his first novel, *The Girls from Planet 5* (**1955**), in which Amazonian aliens invade Earth (*see* INVASION; SEX; WOMEN), comically; much of his early fiction appears in the collections *Those Idiots from Earth* (coll. **1957**) and *Time Out for Tomorrow* (coll. **1962**). He won a 1968 NEBULA award for his novelette "Mother to the World" (1968). He writes in a brisk, comfortable style, closely resembling that used by writers specializing in the "slick" magazines, a style perhaps best demonstrated in *30-day Wonder* (**1960**), in which aliens once again invade Earth, this time peaceably, and by a comically rendered ethical literalism gimmick Earth into a mature galactic confederation. [JC] **Other works:** *And Then the Town Took Off* (**1960**).

WILSON, ROBERT ANTON (? –). American writer. In collaboration with Robert SHEA (*who see for details*) he produced *Illuminatus!* (**1975**, in three vols). An earlier pornographic novel, *The Sex Magicians* (**1973**), by RAW alone, is distantly related to the *Illuminatus!* books. [JC]
See also: FANTASY; HUMOUR; PARANOIA AND SCHIZOPHRENIA; SATIRE.

WILSON, ROBIN SCOTT (1928–). American editor, writer and academic. He began publishing sf stories with "The State of the Art" for *FSF* in 1970; his best story is probably "For a While

There, Herbert Marcuse, I Thought You Were Maybe Right About Alienation and Eros" (1972). RSW has been most influential as the founder in 1968, along with Damon KNIGHT and others, of the CLARION SF WRITERS' WORKSHOP in Clarion, Pennsylvania; in addition to directing the workshop, he edited *Clarion: An Anthology of Speculative Fiction from the Clarion Writers' Workshop* (anth. **1971**), *Clarion II* (anth. **1972**) and *Clarion III* (anth. **1973**). In the last volume he announced his retirement from Clarion. Additionally, RSW has edited *Those who Can; a Science Fiction Reader* (anth. **1973**), in which, interestingly, writers discuss their own and others' stories in the anthology under various critical headings. [JC]
See also: SF IN THE CLASSROOM.

WILSON, STEVE (1943–). British writer who has published short fiction and whose first sf is his novel *The Lost Traveller* (**1976**); in a venue reminiscent of T.A. WATERS' *Centerforce* (**1974**), SW attempts, colourfully, to shape a post-HOLOCAUST Hell's Angel motorcyclist into a MESSIAH figure. [JC]

WILSON, WILLIAM (mid-19th century; dates unknown). British writer, one of several contemporaries with the same name, distinguished from the others by the British Museum catalogue as "Author of *A House for Shakspere*" (the reference is to a book published in 1848). His poetry was collected posthumously in *Gathered Together* (**1860**). In a book of criticism, *A Little Earnest Book Upon a Great Old Subject* (**1851**) he devoted two chapters to "The Poetry of Science", defining a species of literature he calls Science-Fiction, the first use of the term, "in which the revealed truths of science may be given, interwoven with a pleasing story which may itself be poetical and *true* — thus circulating a knowledge of the Poetry of Science, clothed in a garb of the Poetry of Life". His example is *The Poor Artist* by R.H. HORNE. [BS]
About the author: "William Wilson's Prospectus for Science-Fiction: 1851" by Brian STABLEFORD in *Foundation* 10 (June 1976).
See also: ARTS; DEFINITIONS OF SF.

WINGRAVE, A. *See* S. Fowler WRIGHT.

WINIKI, EPHRIAM *See* John Russell FEARN.

WINSOR, G(EORGE) McLEOD (? – ?). Author, probably English, of two sf novels, *Station X* (**1919**) and *Vanishing Men* (**1927**). In the former a psychic invasion from Mars is repelled by an Earth-Venus alliance. A reprint (1975) has an introduction by Richard Gid Powers which mystifyingly claims the novel as important. It was one of the first novels to be serialized in *AMZ* (1926). [JC/PN]

WINTER, H.G. *See* Harry BATES *and* Desmond W. HALL.

WINTERBOTHAM, RUSS(ELL) R(OBERT) (1904–71). American newspaperman and writer, active in both the Western and the sf genres. He published his first sf story, "The Star That Would Not Behave", with *ASF* in 1935, and contributed most prolifically to the genre before the Second World War, during which period he also wrote as many as 60 *Big Little Books* (*see* DIME NOVELS AND JUVENILE SERIES), some of them borderline sf, though fundamentally of juvenile interest. He returned to sf writing from 1952 and was again noted as a prolific minor writer, publishing his first novel, *The Space Egg* (**1958**), about an INVASION of Earth, and several other routine adventures, including *The Other World* (**1963**) as by J. Harvey Bond, and *Planet Big Zero* (**1964**), as by Franklin Hadley. In the 1960s he scripted the sf comic strip *Chris Welkin*; his work as R.R. Winter was not sf. [JC]
Other works: *The Red Planet* (**1962**); *The Man from Arcturus* (**1963**); *The Puppet Planet* (**1964**); *The Lord of Nardos* (**1966**).

WISE, ARTHUR (1923–). English writer and drama consultant, most of whose works are thrillers; he has also written as John McArthur. Most of his sf is borderline, and uses genre elements as heightening devices in his suspense stories, the best known of which is probably *The Day the Queen Flew to Scotland for the Grouse Shooting* (**1968**) where she is abducted. A second novel in this NEAR-FUTURE, political vein is *Who Killed Enoch Powell?* (**1970**), where the assassination of that figure sets a complex thriller in motion, mounting to racial violence at Wimbledon. [JC]
Other works: *Days in the Hay* (**1960** as John McArthur); *The Little Fishes* (**1961**); *How Now Brown Cow* (**1962** as John McArthur); *The Death's-Head* (**1962**); *Leatherjacket* (**1970**).
See also: WAR.

WISE, ROBERT (1914–). American film director. He began in the industry as a film-cutter at RKO Studios and by 1939 was a fully qualified editor. He worked on Orson Welles's *Citizen Kane* in 1941 and also directed a few scenes in Welles's *The Magnificent Ambersons* in 1942 (at the studio's insistence, when the director was out of the country). He then worked with the Val Lewton unit at RKO, first as editor then as director. He directed three films for Lewton: *Curse of the Cat People* (1944) with Gunther von Fritsch, *Mademoiselle Fifi* (1944) and *The Body Snatcher* (1945) and stayed with RKO until 1949. In 1951 he directed the classic sf film THE DAY THE EARTH STOOD STILL but did not return to the genre until 1971 when he made THE ANDROMEDA STRAIN. A versatile director, he has made films

Film director Robert WISE on the set of *The Andromeda Strain*, 1970, with Peter Nicholls. © Universal.

covering a wide range of subjects, including the musicals *West Side Story* (1961) and *The Sound of Music* (1964). Apart from his Lewton films he has also made two superior contributions to the supernatural genre: *The Haunting* (1963), based on Shirley JACKSON's *The Haunting of Hill House* (1959) and *Audrey Rose* (1977). RW's work, which is always technically strong and interesting, has done more than that of most directors to bring some maturity to sf in the cinema; it is perhaps ironic, therefore, that he has been announced in 1978 as director of the proposed feature film to be based on STAR TREK. [JB/PN]

WISE, ROBERT A. (? –). Author, probably English, of the paperback sf novel *12 to the Moon* (**1961**). [JC]

WITCHCRAFT & SORCERY (magazine) *See* COVEN 13.

WITKIEWICZ, STANISLAW IGNACY *See* EASTERN EUROPE.

WITT, OTTO *See* SCANDINAVIA.

WITTIG, MONIQUE (1935–). French writer, whose novel, *Les Guérillères* (**1969**; trans. **1971**), transforms the arguments of feminism into a series of narrative litanies that work movingly to describe an abstract "tribe" of women in a constant state of warfare with their natural enemy; the novel balances exquisitely between sf (when its images are taken literally) and poetry. [JC]

WOBIG, ELLEN (1911–). American writer, whose sf novel is *The Youth Monopoly* (**1968**), about rejuvenation. [JC]

WODEHOUSE, P(ELHAM) G(RENVILLE) (1881–1975). English writer who lived in the USA for most of his life; he is known mainly for his comic novels. *The Swoop! or How Clarence Saved England. A Tale of the Great Invasion* (**1909**) spoofs the future-WAR/INVASION genre so popular in England before 1914 with its description of nine simultaneous invasions, most of which are variously diverted (the five Coloured powers soon go home), leaving the German and the Russian armies in command, their chiefs competing with one another in music-hall recitals of their feats. Boy Scout Clarence Chugwater saves England by exposing the fact that one of them is being paid more than the other; the invasions end in ignominy. In *Laughing Gas* (**1936**), rival dentists' anaesthesias cause an identity switch between an earl and an obnoxious child star; the resulting story has all the earmarks of the typical PGW comedy, however, and is not easy to think of as sf. [JC]

WODHAMS, JACK (1931–). English-born Australian writer and mail-van driver. He began publishing sf with "There is a Crooked Man" for *ASF* in 1967, and has contributed actively to the magazines, mostly in *ASF* in the following decade. His first novel is *Authentic Touch* (**1971**). [JC]

WOLF, GARY K. (? –). American writer, who began publishing sf with "Love Story" for *Worlds of Tomorrow* in 1970, and has contributed extensively to the magazines since that date. His first novel, *Killerbowl* (**1975**), is a briskly violent picture (rather similar to that in the film ROLLERBALL) of games being used to sublimate more politically dangerous passions (*see* GAMES AND SPORTS). His second novel, *A Generation Removed* (**1977**), depicts a NEAR-FUTURE society in which the young have violently taken the reins of power, and euthanasia of the middle-aged is common. Here the analogy would be with the film LOGAN'S RUN. [JC]

WOLFE, BERNARD (1915–). American writer, best known for his work outside the sf field. He gained a BA in psychology from Yale in 1935, worked for two years in the Merchant Marine, and for a time was a bodyguard to Leon Trotsky in Mexico. He subsequently became a war correspondent, newsreel editor and freelance writer, and has contributed stories and articles to many leading magazines. His first contribution to sf was a novelette in *Gal.*, "Self Portrait" (1951). His first full-length sf work was *Limbo* (**1952**; vt *Limbo '90* UK; abridged 1961). This large and extravagant book is perhaps the finest sf novel of ideas published during the 1950s. It portrays a future in which men have deliberately chosen to cut off their own arms and legs in order to avoid the risk of war. Complex (making use of many ideas from CYBERNETICS), ironic, hectoring and full of puns, *Limbo* is firmly based on BW's knowledge of psychoanalysis and in particular on his understanding of the masochistic instinct in modern Man. It is perhaps this last factor which explains the book's appeal to J.G. BALLARD (himself an sf writer concerned with the self-destructive urges in contemporary civilization), who has stated several times that he considers *Limbo* the greatest American sf novel. BW has written very little of since, although Harlan ELLISON persuaded him to contribute two stories to *Again, Dangerous Visions* (anth. **1972**). "The Bisquit Position" is an impassioned anti-Vietnam-War story, centering on the image of a napalmed dog; "The Girl With Rapid Eye Movements" is about sleep research and ESP. In his "Afterword" to these stories, BW expresses an extreme hostility to science, and to sf which he considers its handmaiden. Further details of BW's remarkable career can be found in his *Memoirs of a Not Altogether Shy Pornographer* (**1972**). [DP]
See also: DYSTOPIAS; ISLANDS; MEDICINE; WEAPONS.

WOLFE, GENE (1931–). American writer. He was born in New York, but spent most of his childhood in Houston. After serving in the Korean War he graduated in mechanical engineering from the University of Houston. He has followed a career in engineering, and is now editor of a trade periodical.

GW's first published sf story was "Trip, Trap" in *Orbit 2* (anth. **1967**) ed. Damon KNIGHT. Throughout his writing career he has been very closely identified with the ORBIT series of anthologies, where many of his best stories have been published. His writing is characteristically very precise, often oblique. He habitually uses CHILDREN as protagonists and viewpoint characters, a device whereby he combines wide-eyed clarity with a distinctively different angle of vision. His first story to make a significant impact was "The Island of Doctor Death and Other Stories" (1970) which treads with assurance the shifting dividing line between fantasy and reality in its story of a young boy retreating from a harsh adult environment into the more clearcut world of a comic. It was followed by a "sequel", "The Death of Doctor Island" (1973), which describes the treatment of a psychologically disturbed child in an artificial environment which responds to his state of mind; the story is constructed as a thematic mirror-image of its predecessor. The cycle of titles is completed by "The Doctor of Death Island" (1978), in which a CRYOGENICALLY frozen prisoner is awakened to find he has been made IMMORTAL. All three stories contribute to modern sf treatment of literal and symbolic ISLANDS. "The Island of Doctor Death" was nominated for a NEBULA award, and received more votes than any other story in its category; however, GW was deprived of the award because a greater number of voters nominated "No Award" (although it emerged that several people did so in the belief that they were abstaining, rather than voting against any award being made). The situation was appropriately rectified when GW later won a Nebula for "The Death of Doctor Island".

GW's major sf work to date is his collection of linked novellas *The Fifth Head of Cerberus* (coll. **1972**). Set on a distant two-planet system colonized by settlers of French origin, the book combines ALIENS, ANTHROPOLOGY, CLONES and other elements in a richly imaginative exploration of the nature of identity and individuality. Other important stories include "The Hero as Werwolf" (1975) and "The Eyeflash Miracles" (1976), although regrettably he has yet to publish a volume of short stories. He has written one sf novel, *Operation ARES* (**1970**), which describes the INVASION of the USA by its abandoned Martian colony in the 21st century; it was heavily cut for publication. He has published a non-sf novel, *Peace* (**1975**), and a medieval fantasy intended for young adults, *The Devil in a Forest* (**1976**). Greatly underrated, GW is one of the finest modern sf writers. [MJE]
See also: ABSURDIST SF; COLONIZATION OF OTHER WORLDS; METAPHYSICS; MYTHOLOGY; NEW WAVE; OPTIMISM AND PESSIMISM; PSI POWERS; PSYCHOLOGY; SUPERNATURAL CREATURES.

WOLLHEIM, DONALD A(LLEN) (1914–   ). American editor and writer. A lifetime resident of New York, DAW was one of the first and most vociferous sf fans; together with Forrest J. ACKERMAN he was perhaps the most dynamic member of the embryo FANDOM of the 1930s. He published innumerable fanzines, and was co-editor of the early semi-professional magazine FANCIFUL TALES OF SPACE AND TIME. DAW became a leader of the FUTURIANS in the late 1930s. His part in early fandom is extensively chronicled in *The Immortal Storm* (**1954**) by Sam MOSKOWITZ and *The Futurians* (**1977**) by Damon KNIGHT. DAW himself has edited *Operation: Phantasy* (anth. **1967**), a collection of early fanzine material.

DAW's first published story was "The Man from Ariel" (1934) in *Wonder Stories*, but he did not begin to publish fiction with any regularity until the 1940s, by which time he had already embarked on his major career as an editor. He was appointed editor of COSMIC STORIES and STIRRING SCIENCE STORIES, both of which he produced creditably on a minute budget, publishing many stories by his fellow Futurians (most prolifically C.M. KORNBLUTH). He also compiled two pioneering sf ANTHOLOGIES: *The Pocket Book of Science Fiction* (anth. **1943**) and *Portable Novels of Science* (anth. **1945**). For his short stories he often used the pseudonyms Millard Verne Gordon and Martin Pearson, also used the collaborative pseudonyms Arthur COOKE and Lawrence WOODS, and once wrote as Allen Warland; as Pearson, he published the "Ajax Calkins" series which later formed the basis of his novel *Destiny's Orbit* (**1962**), published under the pseudonym David Grinnell. A sequel to this novel is *Destination: Saturn* (**1967**), written under the Grinnell name in collaboration with Lin CARTER.

After the Second World War DAW worked for Avon Books, for whom he edited the AVON FANTASY READER, the AVON SCIENCE FICTION READER, OUT OF THIS WORLD ADVENTURES and 10 STORY FANTASY as well as the uncredited anthology of original stories *The Girl With the Hungry Eyes* (anth. **1949**). He subsequently moved to ACE BOOKS in 1952, and for 20 years edited their renowned sf list. He used their double-novel format to publish the early works of many writers who later achieved fame, e.g. Samuel R. DELANY, Philip K. DICK, Harlan ELLISON, Ursula K. LE GUIN and Robert SILVERBERG, although the bulk of the list was unashamedly commercial. During the 1950s he also worked editorially on the magazines ORBIT and SATURN. He edited a great many anthologies, primarily for Ace; these included such theme collections as *The End of the World* (anth. **1956**), *Men on the Moon* (anth. **1958**; rev. 1970) and *The Hidden Planet* (anth. **1959**), the latter comprised of stories set on VENUS.

DAW's writing in the 1950s and 1960s consisted largely of novels. These divided into CHILDREN'S SF published under his own name and adult novels issued as by David Grinnell. None of these was very notable, although his "Mike Mars" series of children's books, exploring different facets of the space programme, was popular. These were *Mike Mars, Astronaut* (**1961**), *Mike Mars Flies the X-15* (**1961**), *Mike Mars at Cape Canaveral* (**1961**; vt *Mike Mars at Cape Kennedy*), *Mike Mars in Orbit* (**1961**), *Mike Mars Flies the Dyna-Soar* (**1962**), *Mike Mars, South Pole Spaceman* (**1962**), *Mike Mars and the Mystery Satellite* (**1963**) and *Mike Mars Around the Moon* (**1964**).

World's Best Science Fiction: 1965 (anth. **1965**) was the first of a series of best-of-the-year anthologies co-edited by DAW and Terry CARR; it was followed by *World's Best Science Fiction: 1966* (anth. **1966**), *World's Best Science Fiction: 1967* (anth. **1967**), *World's Best Science Fiction: 1968* (anth. **1968**), *World's Best Science Fiction: 1969* (anth. **1969**), *World's Best Science Fiction: 1970* (anth. **1970**) and *World's Best Science Fiction: 1971* (anth. **1971**). DAW left Ace to start his own imprint, DAW BOOKS, in 1972, with a policy very similar to the successful formula he had evolved at Ace. He continued to edit an annual anthology, now with assistance from Arthur W. Saha and with a slightly different title: *The 1972 Annual World's Best SF* (anth. **1972**; vt *Wollheim's World's Best SF: Series One*); *The 1973 Annual World's Best SF* (anth. **1973**); *The 1974 Annual World's Best SF* (anth. **1974**; vt *World's Best SF Short Stories No.1* UK); *The 1975 Annual World's Best SF* (anth. **1975**; vt *World's Best SF Short Stories No.2* UK); *The 1976 Annual World's Best SF* (anth. **1976**) and *The 1977 Annual World's Best SF* (anth. **1977**).

During his career DAW has been one of the most important editorial influences on sf; the success of both Ace and Daw under his editorship testifies to his commercial good sense. He has also written an idiosyncratic, reflective memoir about sf, *The Universe Makers* (**1971**). [MJE]
Other works: *The Secret of Saturn's Rings* (**1954**); *Secret of the Martian Moons* (**1955**); *One Against the Moon* (**1956**); *Across Time* (**1957**) as by David Grinnell; *Edge of Time* (**1958**) as by David Grinnell; *The Martian Missile* (**1959**) as by David Grinnell; *Secret of the Ninth Planet* (**1959**); *Two Dozen Dragon's Eggs* (coll. **1969**); *To Venus! To Venus!* (**1970**) as by David Grinnell.

As editor: *Flight into Space* (anth. **1950**); *Every Boy's Book of Science Fiction* (anth. **1951**); *Prize Science Fiction* (anth. **1953**; vt *Prize Stories of Space and Time* UK); *Adventures in the Far Future* (anth. **1954**); *Tales of Outer Space* (anth. **1954**); *The Ultimate Invader and Other Science Fiction* (anth. **1954**); *Adventures on Other Planets* (anth. **1955**); *Terror in the Modern Vein* (anth. **1955**; UK edition divided into two vols, the second entitled *More Terror in the Modern Vein*); *The Earth in Peril* (anth. **1957**); *The Macabre*

Reader (anth. **1959**); *More Macabre* (anth. **1961**); *More Adventures on Other Planets* (anth. **1963**); *Swordsmen in the Sky* (anth. **1964**); *The Avon Fantasy Reader* (anth. **1969**) with George Ernsberger; *The Second Avon Fantasy Reader* (anth. **1969**) with George Ernsberger; *The Ace SF Reader* (anth. **1971**; vt *Trilogy of the Future* UK); *The Best from the Rest of the World* (anth. **1976**); *The DAW Science Fiction Reader* (anth. **1976**).

See also: DEFINITIONS OF SF; END OF THE WORLD; GALACTIC EMPIRES; GREAT AND SMALL; HISTORY OF SF; NEAR FUTURE; NEW WAVE; OPTIMISM AND PESSIMISM; SF MAGAZINES; SPACE OPERA.

WOMEN There are two separate themes here, not necessarily connected: women who write sf and women in sf. To begin with the latter: one of the more shameful facets of genre sf is the stereotyped and patronizing roles which are usually though not invariably assigned to women; these are discussed in greater detail under SEX. With the growth of the feminist movement in the late 1960s (though its repercussions in publishing did not really make themselves felt until around 1974) a consciousness that something had gone wrong began to filter, very slowly, into sf and some of the other genre fictions. MAINSTREAM fiction had not has this dishonourable history to anything like the same extent.

Most sf has been written by men, and they have produced very few important female protagonists. There have been exceptions, the work of James H. SCHMITZ being one, but generally the woman in sf is Comforter or Victim, sadistic Amazon Queen or Girl Next Door. She is seldom merely an adult (to which it might be responded that even the men in pulp sf seldom behave like adults, for all the "heroism" of their roles). Several women critics have been naturally incensed at this chauvinism, as in, for example, Joanna RUSS's "The Image of Woman in Science Fiction" (1970) in *Red Clay Reader*, and "A Feminist Critique of Science Fiction" by Mary Kenny Badami in EXTRAPOLATION, Dec. 1976. The same issue of *Extrapolation* carries "A Checklist of SF Novels with Female Protagonists" compiled by George Fergus, and, while the list is certainly incomplete, its brevity is nevertheless startling; most of the listed stories are by women, although John BOYD, John BRUNNER, Samuel DELANY, Charles HARNESS and Alexei PANSHIN receive entries. The subject of female stereotypes in sf is also discussed by Beverly Friend in "Virgin Territory: the Bonds and Boundaries of Women in Science Fiction" in *Many Futures, Many Worlds* (anth. **1977**) ed. Thomas D. CLARESON. A particularly interesting document is unfortunately difficult to obtain: a special issue of the FANZINE *Khatru* (no. 3/4, Nov. 1975) ed. Jeffrey

D. Smith, over 150 pages, consisting of a round robin discussion (by letter) between a number of women sf writers and one or two men; it turned out (much later) to be only one man, but James TIPTREE Jr did not drop her cover, despite being attacked by (for example) Samuel Delany as a male chauvinist — an extraordinary act of willpower in the circumstances. This fanzine has certainly the most detailed discussion of the role of women in sf yet to appear in print.

Although sf would seem an ideal format in which to examine this question, since it can readily admit the construction of alternative societies in which the role of women is quite different, the feminist movement has not yet resulted in very much feminist sf. By far the fiercest and most interesting example is Joanna Russ's *The Female Man* (**1975**); others are to be found in two anthologies ed. Pamela SARGENT, *Women of Wonder* (anth. **1975**) and *More Women of Wonder* (anth. **1976**), and also in *Aurora: Beyond Equality* (anth. **1976**) ed. Susan Janice Anderson and Vonda N. McINTYRE; this latter contains several stories by men. Also relevant is Suzy McKee CHARNAS's novel *Walk to the End of the World* (**1974**). A very much earlier sf novel, with an extremely liberated, likeable and intelligent heroine, is Naomi MITCHISON's *Memoirs of a Spacewoman* (**1962**); this too examines the role of women, and finds no reason to suppose that childbearing disqualifies a person from competing on equal or even advantageous terms with men.

An earlier story by Joanna Russ, "When it Changed" (1972), tells of an all-women world on which men finally arrive, assuming that they will be more than welcome; they are wrong. The idea of all-women societies is an old one in sf (*see also* SOCIOLOGY), along with its variant where men are present but distinctly subsidiary, as in Bulwer LYTTON's *The Coming Race* (**1871**). The extraordinary thing is that so few of these works have been written by women, and indeed their attitude is often far from sympathetic towards women, as in Sir Walter BESANT's *The Revolt of Man* (**1882**), which in its depiction of a woman-dominated society is in effect a bad-tempered anti-feminist tract. More appalling because more masculinely patronizing is Robert W. CHAMBERS' *The Gay Rebellion* (coll. of linked stories **1913**), which finds much to smirk at its story of a revolt of women who find they cannot cope, reform, and get married like good girls.

However, one of the earlier works of this kind was by a woman (by no means the earliest — aside from Besant's and Lytton's novels, there was the great original, Aristophanes' play *Lysistrata*, 411 BC): Mary E. Bradley LANE's anonymously published *Mizora* (**1890**), which depicts an all-woman UTOPIA in a HOLLOW EARTH. Later variants on the

theme have been J.D. BERESFORD's *Goslings* (**1913**; vt *A World of Women*); Owen M. JOHNSON's *The Coming of the Amazons* (**1931**); Philip WYLIE's *The Disappearance* (**1951**); Richard WILSON's *The Girls from Planet 5* (**1955**); John WYNDHAM's "Consider Her Ways" (1956); Poul ANDERSON's *Virgin Planet* (**1959**); Edmund COOPER's *Five to Twelve* (**1968**) and *Who Needs Men?* (**1972**; vt *Gender Genocide* USA); Robert BLOCH's *Ladies' Day* (**1968**); Thomas BERGER's *Regiment of Women* (**1973**) and Charles Eric MAINE's *World Without Men* (**1958**; vt *Alph*). The situation is reversed in Leonard PRUYN and Day KEENE's *World Without Women* (**1960**). These books range in attitude from the rabidly sexist (Cooper) to the thoughtful (Wyndham, Wylie). What they have in common is that they are all by men. The list is incomplete; many short stories have also been written on the theme, a number of them listed in "Women's Liberation: When Women Rule" in *Strange Horizons* (coll. **1976**) by Sam MOSKOWITZ.

Most sexism by men writers of sf has been thoughtless, a matter of cultural conditioning, rather than deliberately derogatory or malicious; this, of course, makes things if anything more difficult for women, who if they complain are apt to be met by a bewildered and hurt stare or its literaray equivalent. A classic of sexist sf is "Helen O'Loy" (1938) by Lester DEL REY, one of the most unconsciously disgusting stories in the genre, in which a ROBOT woman is the perfect helpmeet, a state of which the narrator sentimentally approves, and incidentally a condition satirized to some effect in Ira LEVIN's *The Stepford Wives* (**1972**), filmed as THE STEPFORD WIVES. Robot women also featured in the film THE PERFECT WOMAN, and the TV series MY LIVING DOLL, but here only for purposes of mildly titilating comedy. The same idea was used by Ian WATSON, in his *Orgasmachine* (**1976** France), published only in French, a story of the manufacture of custom-built girls for men, to comment on the exploitation of women.

Another category of fantasy in which it is possible to say something about the condition of women is the story in which men wake in women's bodies, as in Thorne Smith's *Turnabout* (**1931**) and Hank STINE's *Season of the Witch* (**1968**) and a great many other stories.

We turn now to women writers of sf, of whom there have been many more than is in general realized, although because it was felt that a predominantly male readership might not accept woman writers generally, in the early days especially, many women used pseudonyms, or forms of their name which did not clearly reveal their sex. This is true even today. It was not so long ago that Ursula K. LE GUIN succumbed to the pressure (she has publicly regretted it since) and signed her story "Nine Lives"

(1969) in *Playboy* as U.K. Le Guin.

Women writers include E.L. ARCH, Leigh BRACKETT, Rosel George BROWN, C.J CHERRYH, Murray CONSTANTINE, Lee HOFFMAN, J. Hunter HOLLY (who in her more recent work signs herself Joan Hunter Holly), A.M. LIGHTNER, C.L. MOORE, Andrew North (an early pseudonym of Andre NORTON), M.E. PATCHETT, Ayn RAND, Kit REED, Wilmar H. SHIRAS, Francis STEVENS, Leslie F. STONE, James Tiptree Jr, Sydney J. VAN SCYOC and Chelsea Quinn YARBRO. Without a doubt many of these are real names, but the point remains that they would all be taken very readily for male names by the readership.

However, the number of women writers more easily identifiable as such is considerably larger. The following is an incomplete list (many mainstream writers in particular are omitted, otherwise the list would be unmanageable): Hilary BAILEY, Bee BALDWIN, Margot BENNETT, Marion Zimmer BRADLEY, Christine BROOKE-ROSE, Doris P. BUCK, Hortense CALISHER, Angela CARTER, Suzy McKee Charnas, Mildred CLINGERMAN, Susan COOPER, Juanita COULSON, CRISTABEL, Miriam Allen DEFORD, Sonya DORMAN, Madelaine DUKE, Suzette Haden ELGIN, Carol EMSHWILLER, Sylvia ENGDAHL, Gertrude FRIEDBERG, Jane GASKELL, Phyllis GOTLIEB, Zenna HENDERSON, Cecelia HOLLAND, Shirley JACKSON, Marie JAKOBER, Anna KAVAN, Katherine KURTZ, Jane LANE, Tanith LEE, Ursula K. Le Guin, Doris LESSING, Rose MACAULAY, Anne McCAFFREY, Vonda McIntyre, Katherine MacLEAN, Judith MERRIL, Naomi MITCHISON, Doris PISERCHIA, Joanna Russ, Margaret ST CLAIR, Pamela Sargent, Josephine SAXTON, Ella SCRYMSOUR, Evelyn E. SMITH, Emma TENNANT, Lisa TUTTLE, Phyllis WADSWORTH, Kate WILHELM and Pamela ZOLINE.

The often heard remark that there are few women writers in sf is true in the relative sense (there are perhaps nine men for every one woman), but quite false in the absolute sense; there are numerous women writers of sf, over 60 of whom are cited in this entry.

Since the mid-1960s, by which time publishers were no longer prepared to regard being a woman as necessarily a handicap (women editors like Cele GOLDSMITH helped considerably), it has not been possible to generalize about what sort of sf women write. Indeed, generalizations about the earlier period must be cautious. Joanna Russ identified one category as "ladies' magazine fiction", but named only Zenna Henderson as a culprit; it is fair to say that Judith Merril, Anne McCaffrey and Mildred Clingerman in their worse moments have also produced what Russ scornfully calls "gentle, intuitive little heroines".

Quite a few women writers have produced works of borderline sf —

FABULATION, ABSURDIST, experimental or surrealist — among them being Hilary Bailey, Christine Brooke-Rose, Hortense Calisher, Angela Carter, Sonya Dorman, Madelaine Duke, Carol Emshwiller, Anna Kavan, Josephine Saxton, Emma Tennant and Pamela Zoline.

More surprising is the considerable number of women involved in writing SWORD AND SORCERY, which has rightly been castigated, at least in its Robert E. HOWARD/John NORMAN manifestation, as being one of the most grossly male chauvinistic genres in existence. C.L. Moore, in her "Jirel of Joiry" stories, produced not only the first sword-and-sorcery heroine, but one of the best sword-and-sorcery protagonists of either sex. Other women writers who have worked in forms closely related to sword and sorcery are Andre Norton, Anne McCaffrey, Marion Zimmer Bradley, Katherine Kurtz, C.J. Cherryh, Tanith Lee, Janet E. MORRIS, Ursula K. Le Guin, Margaret St Clair, Leigh Brackett and Nathalie-Charles HENNEBERG. It would be interesting to make a detailed comparison of the attitudes towards heroism displayed by these authors of heroic fantasy and those displayed by its male writers. Apart from observing that the above list contains several of the finest writers in the genre, no simple generalization seems to fit, and indeed there is no reason at all why it should, unless one believes (an attitude implied in some male sf) that women are effectively a different race. Being a woman writer, of course, is no guarantee of producing fiction that will be acceptable to the feminist movement. Several women writers of sf have cultural attitudes superficially indistinguishable from those of their more chauvinist male colleagues. Marion Zimmer Bradley's "Darkover" books, for example, have been accused of advocating attitudes suppressive to women, although Ms Bradley certainly does not accept the charge.

It is even less simple to generalize about women writers in the period 1968–78; many more women have entered the field in this decade, both as writers and almost certainly as readers too; there are certainly more women in FANDOM. Among the newer women writers, Ursula Le Guin, Joanna Russ and James Tiptree Jr stand out most obviously, and C.J. Cherryh, Doris Piserchia and Pamela Sargent are probably capable of work of the top rank. Among writers a little older, C.L. Moore, Katherine MacLean, Leigh Brackett, Margaret St Clair and Kate Wilhelm stand out (and nobody should forget Mary SHELLEY, who in the opinion of many founded the entire genre). Andre Norton and Marion Zimmer Bradley, too, have given enormous pleasure to readers.

Sf is becoming less sexist. Considering the originality and importance of the sf by many of the writers listed above, one can

only feel that this liberalizing is a long way overdue. At least it can be said that in the sf of the 1970s we are seeing fewer heroines like Podkayne of Mars (*see* Robert A. HEINLEIN) and more who are real people.   [PN]

No. 8, Oct. 1953.

WONDERS OF THE SPACEWAYS British pocketbook-size magazine. 10 numbered, undated issues, 1950–54, published by John Spencer, London; probably ed. John S. Manning. One of the four Spencer juvenile sf magazines, the others being FUTURISTIC SCIENCE STORIES, TALES OF TOMORROW, and WORLDS OF FANTASY; they are of little interest, except to completist collectors.   [FHP]

Dec. 1932. Cover by Frank R. Paul.

WONDER STORIES US magazine amalgamated from AIR WONDER STORIES and SCIENCE WONDER STORIES, published by Hugo GERNSBACK's Stellar Publishing Corporation, Jun. 1930-Nov. 1933, and by Gernsback's Continental Publications, Inc., Dec. 1933-Apr. 1936. 66 issues appeared, Jun. 1930-Mar./Apr. 1936, and the title was then sold to Better Publications, to reappear as THRILLING WONDER STORIES. It began as a BEDSHEET-size pulp but was forced to revert to standard PULP format Nov. 1930-Oct. 1931, returning to bedsheet size Nov. 1931 and shrinking again from Nov. 1933 until it was sold. David Lasser was managing editor until mid-1933, and was succeeded by Charles HORNIG, although Gernsback remained editor-in-chief throughout. Illustrator Frank R. PAUL was the cover artist for all issues.

WS encouraged the growth of sf FANDOM by sponsoring the SCIENCE FICTION LEAGUE in 1934. Notable stories include Stanley WEINBAUM's classic "A Martian Odyssey" (Jul. 1934); John TAINE's *The Time Stream* (Dec. 1931-Feb. 1932; **1946**); and Jack WILLIAMSON's "The Moon Era" (Feb. 1932). John Beynon Harris (John WYNDHAM) published his first story and much of his early work in *WS*, and Clark Ashton SMITH published his best sf stories in it, including "City of the Singing Flame" (Jul. 1931) and "The Eternal World" (Mar. 1932). One author particularly associated with *WS* is Laurence MANNING, all of whose major work appeared therein: "The Wreck of the *Asteroid*" (Dec. 1932), the "Stranger Club" series (1933–5), and the "Man Who Awoke" series (1933).

After the demise of *Thrilling Wonder Stories* in Win. '55, the *Wonder Stories* title was resuscitated for a reprint magazine, subtitled "An Anthology of the Best in Science Fiction", ed. Jim Hendryx Jr, which appeared in only two, widely separated, issues, dated 1957 and 1963, the first being in DIGEST format and the second in PULP format. These continued the *TWS* numeration, being marked as Vol.45, nos 1 and 2. [BS]
Collectors should note: Volume numeration continued from *Science Wonder Stories*, beginning, therefore, with Vol.2 no.1. Vols 2, 3 and 4 had 14 numbers; Vol.5 had 10; Vol.6 had 12 and Vol.7 had eight. The schedule was monthly, Jun. '30-Jun. '33, and then came Aug. '33. Monthly scheduling returned with Oct. '33-Oct. '35. Then followed Nov./Dec. '35, Jan./Feb. '36 and Apr. '36.

WONDER STORIES QUARTERLY US BEDSHEET-size pulp magazine. 14 issues, published by Hugo GERNSBACK's Stellar Publishing Corporation, Fall 1929-Winter 1933, as a quarterly companion to SCIENCE WONDER STORIES and WONDER STORIES, the first three issues appearing as *Science Wonder Quarterly*. David Lasser was the managing editor. A complete novel was featured in every issue, and the magazine is primarily notable for its translations from the German, including Otto Willi GAIL's "Shot into Infinity" (**1925** Germany; trans Fall 1929) and "The Stone from the Moon" (**1926** Germany; trans. Spring 1930) and Otfried Von Hanstein's "Electropolis" (Summer 1930) and "Between Earth and Moon" (Fall 1930). [BS]

Left, the first issue of *Science Wonder Quarterly*, Fall 1929; the magazine became WONDER STORIES QUARTERLY after three issues. Cover by Frank R. Paul. Right, WONDER STORY ANNUAL, 1952. Cover by Alex Schomburg.

WONDER STORY ANNUAL US PULP reprint magazine published by Best Books, 1950–53. The first two issues were edited by Sam MERWIN, the other two by Samuel MINES. The lead novels were reprinted from WONDER STORIES and STARTLING STORIES, the most notable being Manly Wade WELLMAN's *Twice in Time* (1940 *Startling Stories*; 1950; **1957**) and Jack WILLIAMSON's "Gateway to Paradise" (1941 *Startling Stories*; 1953; as *Dome Around America* **1955**). [BS]

WOOD, R(OBERT) W(ILLIAM) (1868–1955). American writer and optical physicist, whose sf works were written with Arthur TRAIN (*who see for details*). [JC]
About the author: *Dr. Wood, Modern Wizard of the Laboratory* (**1941**) by William Seabrook.

WOOD, SAMUEL ANDREW (1890– ?). English author and journalist. He wrote two minor LOST-WORLD novels, *Winged Heels* (**1927**) and *The Aztec Temple* (**1955**, as by Robin Temple) together with a reworking of the airborne-pirate theme, *I'll Blackmail the World* (1934 *Blue Book* as "The Man Who Bombed The World"; rev. **1935**). [JE]

WOODBURY, DAVID O(AKES) (1896–). American writer in whose sf novel, *Mr Faraday's Formula* (**1965**), enemy agents steal a gravity-control device. [JC]

WOODCOTT, KEITH See John BRUNNER.

WOODROFFE, PATRICK (1940–). British illustrator. He studied French and

The decorative surrealism of Patrick WOODROFFE. A book cover study from his *Mythopoeikon*, 1977.

German at Leeds University and became a freelance illustrator in 1972. Along with Roger DEAN, *PW* rapidly became one of the most popular fantasy artists in Britain, painting covers for nearly all the sf and fantasy paperback publishers, and being especially associated with covers of Michael MOORCOCK's books. His work, which is clearly influenced by Dali, but also by the traditions of children's book illustration, is mostly in acrylic gouache. Evoking the spectrum of fantasy artists from Bosch, through Dadd, to the surrealists, it is symbolic and often crowded with rococo decoration. *PW* is more at home with mythological than technological imagery, though he has used both. His work tends to be cheerfully "life-affirming", even when incorporating traditional macabre images, and the mythic ingredients are sometimes weakened by sheer prettiness. A collection of his best work is *Mythopœikon* (**1977**). [PN]

WOODRUFF, CLYDE *See* David V. REED.

WOODS, LAWRENCE Pseudonym used on magazine stories in 1941 by Donald A. WOLLHEIM, alone or in collaboration with Robert A.W. LOWNDES or John B. Michel.

WOODS, P. F. *See* Barrington J. BAYLEY.

WOOLF, VIRGINIA (1882–1941). English writer, famous for novels whose structures sensitively emblematize the forms of inner consciousness; of sf interest is *Orlando; a Biography* (**1928**), whose androgynous hero/heroine survives from Elizabethan to modern times, changing sex more than once, and coming to represent a vision of the nature of England itself. [JC]
Other works: *A Haunted House and other Short Stories* (coll. **1943**).

WOOTTON, BARBARA (1897–). Baroness Wootton of Abinger, English economist, academic, Deputy Speaker of the House of Lords from 1967 and writer. Her NEAR-FUTURE novel, *London's Burning; a Novel for the Decline and Fall of the Liberal Age* (**1936**), set in 1940, describes the totalitarian implications of the aftermath of a general strike. [JC]

WORLD OF GIANTS Television series (1959). CBS TV. Produced and created by William Alland. Episodes 25 mins; b/w.
Marshall Thompson played a man who, while on a secret mission for the government, becomes the victim of atomic radiation and is shrunk to six inches. The government keeps him on as a secret agent, using him for assignments where his small size will be an advantage. His full-size partner on these missions was played by Arthur Franz. The series was really an excuse to use all the giant-

sized props left over from THE INCREDIBLE SHRINKING MAN, which William Alland had produced for Universal. [JB]

Feb. 1951. Cover by Van Dongen.

WORLDS BEYOND US DIGEST-size magazine. Three issues, monthly Dec. 1950-Feb. 1951, published by Hillman Publications; ed. Damon KNIGHT. *WB* was divided between original and reprint material. New stories of note included "Null-P" by William TENN (Dec. 1950) and Harry HARRISON's first story, "Rock Diver" (Feb. 1951). Harrison also did illustrations for the magazine. Other contributors included C.M. KORNBLUTH, Richard MATHESON and Jack VANCE. Knight wrote book reviews. *WB* was cancelled by the publisher after adverse sales reports on its first issue. The second and third issues were by then advanced in preparation and duly appeared. [MJE]

WORLDS OF FANTASY 1. British pocketbook-size magazine. 14 numbered, undated issues, 1950–54, published by John Spencer, London; probably ed.

John S. Manning. *WOF* is almost identical to the other three Spencer juvenile sf magazines, FUTURISTIC SCIENCE STORIES, TALES OF TOMORROW and WONDERS OF THE SPACEWAYS, containing fiction of very low quality.
2. US DIGEST-size magazine. Four issues, 1968–71, no.1 published by Galaxy Publishing Corp., nos 2–4 published by Universal Publishing; nos 1 and 2 ed. Lester DEL REY, nos 3–4 ed. Ejler JAKOBSSON. No.1 was dated 1968, no.2 1970, no.3 Winter 1970/71 and no.4 Spring 1971. This attempt to produce a fantasy companion to GALAXY might well have succeeded with better distribution. The standard was good, *WOF* including important work by Ursula K. LE GUIN, and early stories by Michael BISHOP and James TIPTREE Jr. [FHP/PN]

WORLDS OF IF SCIENCE FICTION *See* IF.

WORLDS OF THE UNIVERSE British pocketbook-size magazine. One undated issue, 1953, published by Gould Light Publishing, London; no editor named, no notable stories. Copies are rarely seen. [FHP]

WORLDS OF TOMORROW US DIGEST-size magazine. 26 issues in all, originally published by Barmaray Co., (Apr. 1963) and then by Galaxy Publishing Co., as a bi-monthly companion to GALAXY SCIENCE FICTION and IF, Apr. 1963-May 1967 (23 issues). It was briefly revived by the Universal Publishing and Distributing Co. after they bought the Galaxy group, with three more issues published 1970–71. The first series was edited by Frederik POHL, the second by Ejler JAKOBSSON. Notable stories include Philip K. DICK's "All We Marsmen" (Aug.-Dec. 1963; exp. as *Martian Time-Slip* **1964**); Samuel R.

The title WORLDS OF FANTASY was used on two magazines. Left, the British version, no. 1, June 1950, cover by Facey. Right, the US version, no. 1, 1968, cover by Jack Gaughan.

June 1964. Cover by Gray Morrow.

DELANY's "The Star Pit" (Feb. 1967) and several stories in Philip José FARMER's "Riverworld" series, including "Day of the Great Shout" (Jan. 1965; incorporated into the HUGO-winning *To Your Scattered Bodies Go*, fix-up **1971**). An article on CRYONICS by R.C.W. Ettinger (Jun. 1963) ultimately led to the magazine's publishing a symposium discussion on the subject (Aug. 1966). *WOT* was absorbed into its senior partner *Worlds of If Science Fiction* after May 1967. [BS]
Collectors should note: *WOT* had five vols, the first two with six nos, the third with seven, the fourth with four and the fifth with three. The bi-monthly schedule slipped up when Aug. '64 was followed by Nov. '64, and went quarterly May '66-May '67. Vol.5 no.1 was simply marked '70, and nos 2 and 3 were marked Win. '70 and Spr. '71.

WORLD, THE FLESH AND THE DEVIL, THE Film (1958). Sol Siegel and Harbel/MGM. Directed by Ranald MacDougall, starring Harry Belafonte, Inger Stevens and Mel Ferrer. Screenplay by Ranald MacDougall, based on *The Purple Cloud* by M.P. SHIEL. 95 mins. B/w.

Similar to Arch Oboler's FIVE (1951), this film reduces the number of survivors in a nuclear-bomb-ravaged America to three, symbolically representing humanity: a girl, a black man and a cynical adventurer (white and male). Despite the stereotyped situation the film is evocative, as in the black man's entry into the empty metropolis, and in the final hunt through the deserted streets of New York. The plot is simple: black man finds white girl; white racist finds both of them; the girl is willing to remain with the black man, and a running duel takes place between the two men. Eventually they realize the futility of it all, and the film ends with all three of them walking off into the sunset. The script is more sophisticated than the banality of the plot would suggest. [JB]

WORLD WITHOUT END Film (1955). Allied Artists. Directed by Edward Bernds, starring Hugh Marlowe, Nancy Gates, Rod Taylor, Lisa Montell and Nelson Leigh. Screenplay by Edward Bernds. 80 mins. Colour.

After orbiting Mars a spaceship goes through a time-warp and ends up in AD 2508. The astronaut lands on Earth to find that it has undergone the inevitable atomic war, with the surface inhabited by grotesque mutants and giant spiders while the remaining normal humans live underground. Special effects expert Milton Rice managed quite well with what was obviously a restricted budget. [JB]

WORTH, PETER One of the many house names used by Ziff-Davis on various magazine stories; it appeared in their various sf magazines 14 times, 1949-51. It usually concealed the identity of Chester S. GEIER or Roger Phillips Graham (Rog PHILLIPS). [PN]

WOUK, HERMAN (1915–). American writer, best known for works outside the sf field, like *The Caine Mutiny* (**1951**). His sf SATIRE, *The "Lomokome" Papers* (**1956**), somewhat clumsily puts allegorically opposing UTOPIAN societies on the MOON, and sets them at each other's throats. [JC]

WRATISLAW, A.C. (1862– ?). English writer, in whose novel, *King Charles & Mr Perkins* (**1931**), a time machine transports Mr Perkins to Restoration England and returns him just in time to save him from execution. [JC]

WRIGHT, AUSTIN TAPPAN (1883–1931). American lawyer, who spent much of his leisure time constructing, through numerous manuscripts, an imaginary ISLAND, with some characteristics of a UTOPIA, though too densely imagined and free of didacticism to fit happily into that conventional category, set near the Antarctic and relating complexly to the real world. After his death, his wife condensed many of his manuscripts into the novel *Islandia* (**1942**) with introduction by Basil DAVENPORT, an enormous book ostensibly describing the travels of a visitor to the island, and in fact providing an extremely elaborate picture of an invented alternative society. [JC]

WRIGHT, FARNSWORTH (1888–1940). American editor. Known for his editorship of WEIRD TALES. An early contributor to the magazine, FW became editor in November 1924 after the 13th issue. He continued in the post until December 1939, producing 177 issues. Under his guidance, *Weird Tales* presented a unique mixture of horror stories, sf, occult fiction, FANTASY and SWORD AND SORCERY. In 1930 he began a

companion magazine, *Oriental Stories*, featuring borderline fantasy stories in an exotic and largely imaginary Eastern setting, with stories by many regular *Weird Tales* contributors. *Oriental Stories* became *Magic Carpet* in 1933, but ceased publication in 1934. FW was a Shakespeare enthusiast; another project was a PULP MAGAZINE edition of *A Midsummer Night's Dream*. He suffered from a form of Parkinson's disease which made it impossible for him even to write his name, except with a typewriter. Eventually, deteriorating health forced him to leave *Weird Tales*, and he died very soon afterwards. In its field, FW's *Weird Tales* rivals John W. CAMPBELL Jr's ASTOUNDING SCIENCE FICTION in terms of the number of stories of lasting interest which it produced. [MJE]

WRIGHT, LAN Form of his name used by English writer and white-collar worker Lionel Percy Wright (1923–) for all his fiction. Long employed with British Railways, LW began publishing sf with "Operation Exodus" for *NW* in 1952, and continued steadily for more than a decade. His "Johnny Dawson" series in *NW*, about intrigues between Earth and the planet Luther, were partly assembled in *Assignment Luther* (1955-7 *NW*; fix-up **1963**), with "Joker's Trick" (1959) and "The Jarnos Affair" (1960) remaining uncollected. He began publishing novels with *Who Speaks of Conquest?* (**1957**), and continued releasing routine but enjoyable sf adventures for several years. [JC]
Other works: *A Man Called Destiny* (**1958**); *Exile from Xanadu* (**1964**; vt *Space Born* UK); *The Last Hope of Earth* (**1965**; vt *The Creeping Shroud* UK); *The Pictures of Pavanne* (**1968**; vt *A Planet Called Pavanne* UK).

WRIGHT, S(YDNEY) FOWLER (1874–1965). British writer. After leaving school he became an accountant but in 1920 "retired" from that career and became editor of the magazine *Poetry*, a post he held for 12 years. His own first book of poetry was *Scenes from Morte d'Arthur* (coll. **1919**) as by Alan Seymour, and he went on to publish four more as well as editing various anthologies. His first novel, *The Amphibians* (**1924**; vt *The World Below*, 1953 UK paperback) was subtitled "A Romance of 500,000 Years Hence" and describes an Earth where Man is extinct and new intelligent species are engaged in their own struggle for existence. Only H.G. WELLS, in *The Time Machine* (**1895**), and William Hope HODGSON, in *The Night Land* (**1912**), had previously written FAR-FUTURE fantasies of such imaginative scope.

SFW then began work completing a translation of DANTE's *Inferno* which had been begun by Sir Walter Scott, publishing it in 1928. (He was later to publish a biography of Scott and completed his unfinished novel *The Siege* of Malta, 1942). The work on the *Inferno* strongly influenced Wright's extension of *The Amphibians* into *The World Below* (1929; 1951 GALAXY NOVELS edition in two vols, vol. one as *The Amphibians*; 1953 UK paperback in two vols, vol. two as *The Dwellers*). By this time SFW had published two other sf novels. *Deluge* (1928), which enjoyed great success in the USA, is a DISASTER story remarkable for its flaunting of conventional morality in that the hero gets both the girls. *The Island of Captain Sparrow* (1928) is a fantasy in which the descendants of a pirate crew threaten the remnant of a LOST RACE on an island inhabited by satyr-like beast-men. *Dawn* (1929), a sequel to *Deluge*, continued the combination of semi-barbaric adventures with bitter commentary on civilized morality. *Dream, or the Simian Maid* (1931) takes this to extremes with the story of a woman transported back to a lost prehistory to witness the battle for survival between a humanlike species and ratlike predators. Quite different are the detective stories *The Bell Street Murders* (1931) and its sequel *The Secret of the Screen* (1933), in which an sf element is the use of a paste on a screen which is able to store multiple moving images. All SFW's thrillers were published as by S. Fowler Wright in the USA and as by Sydney Fowler in the UK. The thriller *The Adventure of the Blue Room* (1945) is of marginal sf interest.

As time went by SFW's idiosyncrasies became increasingly overt. Many of his stories are calculated to shock in a rather acidic manner, forecasting ugly developments in the society of the near future and moving occasionally to vast time scales to celebrate the cosmic insignificance of humankind. He published several future-WAR stories as he perceived the threat of Nazism, including *Prelude in Prague: The War of 1938* (1935) and its sequel *Megiddo's Ridge* (1937). In *The Adventure of Wyndham Smith* (1938), mankind, having reached a quasi-UTOPIAN state in the far future, commits mass suicide. SFW's last novel was a sequel to *Dream* entitled *Spiders' War* (1954), in which the heroine visits a barbaric culture of the future which SFW uses in order to build up an intensely bitter critique of the present. A year later (at the age of 81) he wrote "The Better Choice" for *Science-Fiction Adventures in Mutation* (anth. 1955) ed. Groff CONKLIN, presenting the proposition that life as a cat is infinitely preferable to life as a human being.

SFW's urge to write seems to have arisen from a sense of profound dissatisfaction with his own life. His novels afforded escape to exotic environments where there were often no humans at all, and an opportunity to express his bitterness. When one recalls that he published his first novel at 50, after two marriages and ten children, it is perhaps not suprising that his early work

is his best and that his work from the 1930s on became steadily crankier as its quality waned. *The World Below* remains a masterpiece, and *The Island of Captain Sparrow* is also a classic, but many of his minor works are poor. He used the pseudonym Anthony Wingrave for one novel, *The Vengeance of Gwa* (1935), which was subsequently reprinted under his own name. [BS]

Other works: *Beyond the Rim* (1932; vt with two stories added *The Throne of Saturn* USA 1949); *The New Gods Lead* (coll. 1932); *Power* (1933); *The Four Days' War* (1936); *The Screaming Lake* (1937); *The Hidden Tribe* (1938); *The Witchfinder* (coll. 1946).

About the author: "Better the World Below than the World Above" in *Strange Horizons* (coll. 1976) by Sam MOSKOWITZ.

See also: FANTASTIC VOYAGES; HOLOCAUST AND AFTER; ISLANDS; SOCIOLOGY.

WRIGHT, WEAVER *See* Forrest J. ACKERMAN.

WSFA JOURNAL American FANZINE (1963–74), ed. Don Miller for the Washington SF Association. Besides local items, the *WSFAJ* contained articles of general sf interest, including a regular column by Thomas Burnett SWANN. Of particular importance was the extensive bibliographical material and reviews published in the journal and also in its companion newsletter, *Son Of The WSFA Journal*. [PR]

WU FANG *See* MYSTERIOUS WU FANG, THE.

WUL, STEFAN Pseudonym of dental surgeon Pierre Pairault (1922–), French writer. SW appeared on the French sf scene with 11 consistent and imaginative novels all published between 1956 and 1959. *Niourk* (1957) is a BALLARD-like account of a drowned world. *Oms en série* ["Oms by the Dozen"](1957) inspired the animated film LA PLANÈTE SAUVAGE. *Le temple du passé* (1958; trans. as *The Temple of the Past* by Ellen Cox, 1973) combines the themes of Moby Dick and ATLANTIS. After 1959, SW fell silent until the appearance of *Noò* (1977), a lengthy and flamboyant saga which, like his earlier novels, shows a deep understanding of the traditions of American pulp sf. [MJ]

Other works: *Retour à O* ["Back to O"] (1956); *Rayons pour Sidar* ["Rays for Sidar"] (1957); *La peur géante* ["The Immense Fear"] (1957); *L'orphelin de Perdide* ["The Orphan from Perdide"] (1958); *La mort vivante* ["Living Death"] (1958); *Piège sur Zarkass* ["Trap on Zarkass"] (1958); *Terminus 1* (1959); *Odyssée sous contróle* ["Controlled Odyssey"] (1959).

See also: UNDER THE SEA.

WÜRF, KARL *See* George SCITHERS.

WURLITZER, RUDOLF (1937–). American writer, most of whose work can be read as FABULATION with sf elements; his novels, *Nog* (1969; vt *The Octopus* UK), *Flats* (1970) and *Quake* (1972), share an apocalyptic *mise en scène* similar in feeling to, but not identified as, that familiar to sf readers as depicting a post-HOLOCAUST world. RW has also written screenplays. [JC]

See also: SOCIOLOGY.

WYATT, B.D. *See* Spider ROBINSON.

WYATT, PATRICK Pseudonym; possibly, it has been speculated, that of a woman. PW's sf novel, *Irish Rose* (1975), is a love story set in a world where almost all white women have died (except in Ireland) from taking the Pill; the religion of the frustrated male population is predictably misogynist. [JC]

WYLIE, DIRK Name adopted by Joseph H. Dockweiler, a member of the FUTURIANS fan group, used on several stories written in collaboration with Frederik POHL. C.M. KORNBLUTH had a hand in one, and Frederick Arnold Kummer was named as collaborator on another. "Highwayman of the Void" (1944) is by Pohl alone. [BS]

WYLIE, PHILIP (GORDON) (1902–71). American author well regarded for his penetrating surveys of American mores and behaviour, especially for his coining the term "Momism" with reference to American motherhood in the popular non-fiction work *Generation of Vipers* (1942), which won him a perhaps unjust reputation as an early male chauvinist pig. He made his reputation in the sf field with four major works: *Gladiator* (1930), a novel about a young man endowed with superhuman strength, which was directly responsible for the appearance of SUPERMAN and filmed as *The Gladiator* (1938); *When Worlds Collide* (1933), a retelling of the Noah's ark legend involving the END OF THE WORLD and interplanetary flight (it was later adapted into an sf COMIC STRIP and a successful film, WHEN WORLDS COLLIDE, 1951), and its sequel, *After Worlds Collide* (1934) (both written in collaboration with Edwin BALMER); and *The Disappearance* (1951), an ingenious novel which makes a slightly old-fashioned but well-meaning attack on the double standard, in which the men and women of Earth are suddenly separated from each other into two PARALLEL WORLDS.

The first three of these novels were published during his first period of sf writing, at which time he also wrote the sf works *The Murderer Invisible* (1931) — which is derivative of H.G. WELLS's *The Invisible Man* — *The Savage Gentleman* (1932), "An Epistle to the Thessalonians" (1934) and "Epistle to the Galatians" (1934), as well as the

screenplays of three fantasy films, THE ISLAND OF LOST SOULS (1932; adapted from H.G. Wells's novel *The Island of Dr. Moreau,* **1896**), *The King of the Jungle* (1933) and *Murders in the Zoo* (1933). Following a 10-year gap, he returned to sf with "The Snibbs Phenomenon" (1944), the story of a Martian infiltration into Earth society. A year later he turned to works centered upon the atomic bomb with "The Paradise Crater" (1945, written before Hiroshima), following it up with "Blunder" (1946), *The Smuggled Atom Bomb* (in *Three to be Read,* coll. **1951**; **1952**), "Philadelphia Phase" (1951), *The Answer* (**1955**), a short pacifist fantasy, *Tomorrow!* (**1954**) and *Triumph* (**1963**), the two latter novels being pleas for a nuclear Civil Defence. Towards the end of his life he turned from atomic DISASTER to ecological disaster in *The End of a Dream* (**1972**) (*see* ECOLOGY) and a screenplay for the television series *The Name of the Game,* novelized as *Los Angeles: A.D. 2017* (**1971**). He also wrote an essay on sf, "Science Fiction and Sanity in an Age of Crisis", which appeared in *Modern Science Fiction* (anth **1953**) ed. Reginald BRETNOR. His short sf stories have appeared in *Finnley Wrenn* (**1934**), *Night Unto Night* (coll. **1944**) and *Three to be Read* (coll. **1951**).
Other works: *The Spy Who Spoke Porpoise* (**1969**). *The Golden Hoard* (**1934**), in collaboration with Edwin Balmer, is a mystery thriller.
About the author: "Philip Wylie" in *Explorers of the Infinite* (**1963**) by Sam MOSKOWITZ.
See also: CRIME AND PUNISHMENT; DYSTOPIAS; HOLOCAUST AND AFTER; INVISIBILITY; NUCLEAR POWER; POLLUTION; RELIGION; SCIENTISTS; SOCIOLOGY; WOMEN.

WYNDHAM, JOHN Form of his name used after the Second World War by English writer John Wyndham Parkes Lucas Beynon Harris (1903–69), and by far his best-known signature. Particularly before the War, he used various other permutations of his name, including John Beynon Harris, John Beynon, Wyndham Parkes, Lucas Parkes and Johnson Harris. After moving about among various jobs in the 1920s, JW began publishing sf stories in 1931 with "Worlds to Barter" as by John Beynon Harris for *Wonder Stories,* and contributed frequently to the latter magazine and to *Tales of Wonder* in the 1930s. Early magazine work, published as by John Beynon Harris, has been assembled as *Wanderers of Time* (coll. **1973** as by JW). The title story, originally appearing in *Wonder Stories,* 1933, was reprinted as a separate 32-page pamphlet, undated, in the AMERICAN FICTION series, vt *Love in Time* (**1945**) as by Johnson Harris. His first novel, *The Secret People* (**1935** as by John Beynon; 1972 as by JW), set in the Sahara, was followed by *Planet Plane* (**1936** as by John Beynon; subsequent serial version

in *Modern Wonder,* 1937, is abridged; rev. vt under original magazine title, *Stowaway to Mars* **1953**; 1972 as by JW), a rather well-told, though only intermittently subtle, narrative of Man's first space flight to Mars, where Vaygan the Martian and the machines destined to succeed his dying species deal swiftly with the three competing sets of Earthlings who have landed almost simultaneously, Vaygan himself impregnating the stowaway Joan; she dies in childbirth (the offspring being illegitimate), but the sequel, "Sleepers of Mars" (1938 *Tales of Wonder* as by John Beynon; as title story in *Sleepers of Mars,* coll. **1973** as by JW), deals merely with some stranded Russians, not with the miscegenate child. In his publisher's memoirs, *Bound to be Read* (**1975**), Robert Lusty describes the John Beynon Harris of these years as a rather diffident, obscure, lounging individual at the fringes of the literary and social world.
The Second World War interrupted JW's writing career, and his later works show considerable advance in skill and a change in basic subject matter. Where much of his pre-War material was SPACE OPERA leavened with the occasional witty aside or passage, JW's post-War work — notably in the novels *The Day of the Triffids* (**1951**; vt *Revolt of the Triffids* USA), *The Kraken Wakes* (**1953**; vt *Out of the Deeps* USA) and *The Chrysalids* (**1955**; vt *Re-Birth* USA), which together comprise *The John Wyndham Omnibus* (coll. **1964**) — presents an eloquently middle-class English response to the theme of DISASTER, whether caused by the forces of nature, ALIEN INVASIONS, or by man's own nuclear warfare. Though he did not invent the English disaster novel — there are many pre-War English examples of novels emphasizing the fragility of the island, going back to H.G. WELLS's *The War in the Air* (**1908**), and earlier — JW effectively memorialized some of its defining patterns: the city (usually London) depopulated by the catastrophe; the exodus, with its scenes of panic and bravery; the focus on a small but growing nucleus of survivors who reach some kind of sanctuary in the country and prepare to re-establish Man's shaken dominion. English writers as diverse as John CHRISTOPHER, Brian W. ALDISS and M. John HARRISON have used the pattern with notable success. Their natural tendency has been to darken somewhat JW's palette, and widen its social relevance, for his protagonists and their women tend to behave with old-fashioned decency and courage, rather as though they were involved in the Battle of Britain, a time imaginatively close to him, and to his markets. THE DAY OF THE TRIFFIDS (1963) was a rather unsuccessful film of the book. Three story collections, with considerable overlapping among them, assemble shorter material which JW was producing after the War; they are *Jizzle* (coll. **1954**), *Tales of Gooseflesh*

John WYNDHAM.

and Laughter (coll. **1956**) and *The Seeds of Time* (coll. **1956**). In them, JW demonstrates his skill at translating sf situations into fundamentally comfortable (however prickly their subject matter may be) tales of character. In the UK, though not in America, he was marketed as a middlebrow writer of non-generic work, and was not strongly identified with sf.
His later work is somewhat less forceful than his best novels from the early 1950s, and includes *The Midwich Cuckoos* (**1957**; vt *Village of the Damned* USA), filmed as VILLAGE OF THE DAMNED (1960), an effectively spooky novel about the insemination of women in a small village by aliens, and the resulting enigmatic progeny. *The Outward Urge* (coll. of linked stories; **1959**; with one added story, 1961) assembles five stories making up the long saga of the family Troon, through which JW (who added his pseudonym Lucas Parkes as a "collaborator" to the book, which was published as by Wyndham and Parkes) examines Man's conquest of space; the device is somewhat strained.
JW effectively wrote for a specific English market at a specific point in time — the decade following the Second World War. His work before and after that period is comparatively ill at ease, and tends to a mildly (perhaps too mildly) acerbic attitude toward the world he was responding to so distantly. He will be remembered mainly for the brief moment in which he expressed English hopes, fears and complacency to a readership that recognized a kindred spirit. Yet during that period, in England and Australia at least, he was probably more read than any other sf author. To this day his books regularly appear on school syllabuses in the UK, in part, perhaps, because they are so "safe".   [JC]

Other works: *Trouble With Lichen* (**1960**); *Consider Her Ways and Others* (coll. **1961**); *The Infinite Moment* (coll. **1961**), a US title mostly duplicating the previous collection; *Chocky* (1963 *AMZ*; exp. **1968**); *Three Stories* (by JW, Jack WILLIAMSON and Murray LEINSTER; anth. **1967**; vt *A Sense of Wonder* UK) ed. Sam MOSKOWITZ; *Sometime, Never* (first publication of "Consider her Ways" by JW plus a story each by William GOLDING and Mervyn PEAKE) (anth. **1956**); *The Best of John Wyndham* (coll. **1973**); *The Man from Beyond and Other Stories* (coll. **1975**).

See also: CHILDREN IN SF; DEFINITIONS OF SF; FLYING SAUCERS; HOLOCAUST AND AFTER; LOST WORLDS; MEDICINE; MONSTERS; MUSIC AND OPERA; MUTANTS; PUBLISHING; RADIO (UK); SEX; TIME TRAVEL; VENUS; WOMEN.

XENOBIOLOGY The study of life-forms which may be supposed to exist elsewhere than on Earth. It is one of the few legitimate sciences to have, as yet, no experimental application, other than the recent experiments carried out on the surface of Mars, using various automatic devices, to see if the Martian soil showed any of the biological activity that might be associated with the presence of microscopic life-forms. It seemed for a time as if some of the results of this experiment were positive, but it is now thought that they were probably caused by non-biological factors. [PN]
See also: LIFE ON OTHER WORLDS; Carl SAGAN.

XERO American FANZINE (1960–63) edited from New York by Richard and Pat LUPOFF. Large and attractively produced, with illustrations by Roy KRENKEL, Eddie JONES and others, *X* was particularly well known for its articles on COMICS, notably the series "All In Color For A Dime" by Richard Lupoff, Ted WHITE and others. The fanzine also contained material on sf and fandom, and contributors included James BLISH, Avram DAVIDSON, Lin CARTER, Walt Willis and Wilson TUCKER. *X* won the HUGO award for best fanzine in 1963. [PR]

"X" — THE MAN WITH THE X-RAY EYES See THE MAN WITH THE X-RAY EYES.

X THE UNKNOWN Film (1956). Hammer/Warner Bros. Directed by Leslie Norman, starring Dean Jagger, Edward Chapman, Leo McKern and Anthony Newley. Screenplay by Jimmy Sangster. 86 mins. B/w.

In this, one of the first of Hammer's horror films to be made after the success of THE QUATERMASS XPERIMENT, a radioactive blob comes from the Earth's core. A critic said of the film: "This anxiety-laden thriller shot at the beginning of 1956 conveys the atmosphere of Suez and cold war hysteria more tellingly than a dozen documentaries." There is good use of dark, atmospheric settings and adequate, if cheap, special effects by Jack Curtis and Les Bowie. [JB]

"XYZ" See POWER SOURCES.

YANDRO American FANZINE (1953–) ed., from Indiana, Robert and Juanita COULSON. Originally published as *Eisfa*, *Y* is one of the longest-running large fanzines. Its contents, in the normal tradition of fanzines, are not restricted to sf, but include regular columns, articles, reviews, and letters. *Y* won the HUGO award for best fanzine in 1965. [PR]

YANKEE SCIENCE FICTION See SWAN YANKEE MAGAZINE.

YARBRO, CHELSEA QUINN (1942–). American writer and composer, active in the mystery and occult genres as well as sf; she began publishing sf stories with "The Posture of Prophecy" (vt "Misconception") for *If* in 1969, and has edited *Two Views of Wonder* (anth. **1974**) with Thomas N. SCORTIA. *Ogilvie, Tallant & Moon* (**1976**) is a suspense thriller; her first sf novel is *Time of the Fourth Horseman* (**1976**), in which a doctor-administered plan (*see also* MEDICINE) to control population growth by reinfecting children with various diseases gets radically out of hand. Set further into the future, *False Dawn* (1973 in *Strange Bedfellows*, ed.

Chelsea Quinn YARBRO.

Thomas N. Scortia; exp. **1978**) also deals with a world ravaged by mutated diseases. The vampire hero of *Hotel Transylvania: a Novel of Forbidden Love* (**1978**), the first volume of a projected trilogy, is apparently IMMORTAL. CQY combines apocalyptic flair with an unfortunate tendency to speak of human relations in terms of romance. [JC]
See also: DISASTER; OVERPOPULATION.

YEFREMOV or **EFREMOV, IVAN ANTONOVICH** (1907–72). Russian paleontologist and writer. A leading figure in the renaissance of Soviet sf in the 1950s, his UTOPIAN novel *Tumannost Andromedy* (**1958**; trans. George Hanna as *Andromeda* **1959**) was an outstanding success, and is one of the few attempts by a Communist writer to create a literary model of the ideal socialist state envisioned by Marx. Several of his early stories appeared in *A Meeting Over Tuscarora* (coll. trans. M. and N. Nicholas **1946**) and again in *Stories* (coll. trans. O. Gorchakov **1954**), but the latter collection also includes new material, including two impressive novellas: "Shadow of the Past" and "Stellar Ships". In each story paleontologists make a discovery which offers them a glimpse of possibilities; there is a restraint and imaginative economy in these stories which makes them quite unlike most American sf. Another important novella is "Cor Serpentis", or "The Heart of the Serpent" (which can be found in the anthology *More Soviet Science Fiction*, **1962**, introduced by Isaac ASIMOV; no editor named), an "ideological reply" to Murray LEINSTER's "First Contact". IAY objects strongly to the attitude of paranoid anxiety manifest in Leinster's story, contending that when Man is "mature" enough to undertake interstellar exploration he will have put such anxieties (the result of the alienation of Man under capitalism) behind him. In fact, though, the story is not dissimilar in spirit to much American work of the 1950s (e.g. that of Hal CLEMENT). IAY also wrote a historical fantasy set in ancient Greece and Africa, *The Land of*

Foam (**1949** Russia; trans. George Hanna **1957**), and a further historical novel that remains untranslated.

In the introduction to *Stories* IAY produced a manifesto for Soviet sf: "To try to lift the curtain of mystery over these roads, to speak of scientific achievements yet to come as realities, and in this way to lead the reader to the most advanced outposts of science — such are the tasks of science-fiction, as I see them. But they do not exhaust the aims of Soviet science-fiction: its philosophy is to serve the development of the imagination and creative faculty of our people as an asset in the study of social life; and its chief aim is to search for the new, and through this search to gain an insight into the future." The emphasis here is significantly different from that in most American DEFINITIONS, stressing the social role of sf as an imaginative endeavour. [BS]

See also: ALIENS; POLITICS; WEATHER CONTROL.

Ivan YEFREMOV. © Novosti Press Agency.

YELNICK, CLAUDE (? –). French writer, whose sf novel, *L'homme, cette maladie* (**1954**; trans. as *The Trembling Tower* **1956**), depicts the inter-DIMENSIONAL relationship between Earth and another world, via a lighthouse. [JC]

Photo Francine Ann Yep.

YEP, LAURENCE (1948–). American writer, educated latterly at the

State University of New York at Buffalo (1970–75), where he gained a PhD in English. He began publishing sf with "The Selchey Kids" for *If* in 1968. His first novels have been juveniles, including the sf story *Sweetwater* (**1973**), set in a dying city on a strange planet, and the highly successful *Dragonwings* (**1975**), a non-sf story about Chinese-Americans that won several awards in the field; *Child of the Owl* (**1977**) is also about Chinese-Americans. LY's first adult sf novel is *Seademons* (**1977**). It tells of colonists on another world, and their relation to the beings there, evoking an atmosphere of strangeness in a prose that is sensitive to nuances. LY could become an important writer in sf, at least at the fantasy end of the spectrum. [JC/PN]
See also: ARTS.

YERXA, LEROY (1915–46). American writer for the PULP magazines, particularly the Ziff-Davis productions *AMZ* and *Fantastic Adventures*. He published under his own name, as Elroy Arno and under the house names Richard CASEY and Alexander BLADE, beginning with "Death Rides at Night" for *AMZ* in 1942 under his own name, and contributing prolifically until his death. His work is unremarkable. [JC]

YOLEN, JANE (1939–). American writer and editor whose juvenile fantasies include *The Witch Who Wasn't* (**1964**), *The Princess Who Couldn't Sleep* (**1965**), *The Wizard of Washington Square* (**1969**) and *The Transfigured Hart* (**1975**) along with several others. Her anthology *Zoo 2000; Twelve Stories of Science Fiction and Fantasy Beasts* (anth. **1973**) assembles stories neatly connected as the title indicates. [JC]

YOUD, CHRISTOPHER See John CHRISTOPHER.

YOUNG, MICHAEL (1915–). British sociologist and writer whose *Family and Kinship in East London* (**1957**) with Peter Willmott has had a seminal effect on community planning priorities; his sf work (see *also* SOCIOLOGY) is *The Rise of the Meritocracy 1870–2033: the New Elite of Our Social Revolution* (**1958**), which both gave the word "meritocracy" to the language and extensively defined it: a meritocracy is an elite whose members are recruited on the basis of merit (largely INTELLIGENCE) in a competitive educational system and with much IQ testing; it is also, as the book delights sardonically in describing, a form of government. The book takes the form of a report written by a historical sociologist in 2033, and has no characterization, except of the narrator, in the ordinary sense; for this reason, curiously, many libraries have catalogued it as non-fiction. Though the narrator supports the system he describes, it is quite clear that MY does not; the book is a subtle and interesting

DYSTOPIA; its ending (in which the narrator is reported as killed in a Populist revolt) is ironic and mutedly apocalyptic. MY's own views on intelligence-testing are also made clear in his *Innovation and Research in Education* (**1965**). [PN/JC]

YOUNG, ROBERT F(RANKLIN) (1915–). American writer. He became a full-time writer after engaging in a number of menial occupations. His first sf story was "The Black Deep Thou Wingest" (1953) in *Startling Stories*, since when he has published short stories quite prolifically. RFY is a slick, polished writer; his stories are readable, but often superficial. The best of them have generally appeared in *FSF*, although his work has appeared in most of the American sf magazines, as well as the *Saturday Evening Post* and elsewhere. His modes range from the heavily satiric — typified by the series of stories "Chrome Pastures" (1956), "Thirty Days Had September" (1957) and "Romance in a Twenty-First Century Used Car Lot" (1960), in which the American automobile mania is extrapolated to absurd extremes — to the deeply sentimental, to the strongly allegorical, such as "Goddess in Granite" (1957). Examples of these various styles can be found in his two collections, *The Worlds of Robert F. Young* (coll. **1965**) and *A Glass of Stars* (coll. **1968**). [MJE]
See also: MESSIAHS; PSYCHOLOGY; STARS; TRANSPORTATION.

YOUNG FRANKENSTEIN See FRANKENSTEIN.

YOU ONLY LIVE TWICE Film (1967). Eon/United Artists. Directed by Lewis Gilbert, starring Sean Connery, Donald Pleasence, Akiko Wakabayashi, Tetsuro Tamba and Mie Hama. Screenplay by Roald DAHL, based on the novel by Ian FLEMING. 116 mins. Colour.

Several of the "James Bond" novels were slightly sf-oriented. The films have emphasized this aspect of Fleming's fantasy world, and most of them have featured futuristic sets and plenty of sf gadgetry — in particular DR No (1962), *Goldfinger* (1964), *Thunderball* (1965), *On Her Majesty's Secret Service* (1969), *Diamonds are Forever* (1971), *The Man with the Golden Gun* (1974) and *The Spy Who Loved Me* (1977); *You Only Live Twice* contains the most sf hardware. An American satellite is literally swallowed up by a mystery craft in outer space. The super-criminal organization SPECTRE has constructed a secret rocket base inside a Japanese volcano from which it launches its bizarre vehicle to capture both American and Russian spacecraft, in an attempt to provoke a war between the two nations. James Bond, with the assistance of a horde of Japanese secret agents, foils SPECTRE's plans and destroys the base. For all the spectacular sets and the vast budget, there are some surprising lapses in the special effects and space sequences, particularly at the climax of the film. [JB]

YUGOSLAVIA *See* EASTERN EUROPE.

YUTANG, LIN *See* LIN YUTANG.

ZAGAT, ARTHUR LEO (1895–1949). American writer, extremely prolific in a number of PULP genres, publishing about 500 stories, relatively few of them sf, and several of that number in collaboration with Nat SCHACHNER: ALZ's first sf story, in fact, was with Schachner: "The Tower of Evil" for *Wonder Stories Quarterly* in 1930. It was the first of nine collaborations, which are the best of his early work, before the two writers separated in 1931. After about 1936, ALZ published mostly with *Argosy*, including a novel, *Drink We Deep* (1937 *Argosy*; **1951**), about dwellers underground. Also in *Argosy* in the early 1940s was the "Tomorrow" series, set in a near-future, post-HOLOCAUST USA, beginning with "Tomorrow" (1939; reprinted in *Famous Fantastic Classics 1*, **1974**). *Seven Out of Time* (1939 *Argosy*; **1949**) is probably his best novel, in which seven contemporary humans are studied by people of the future to rediscover the value of emotions. A post-War novel, "Slaves of the Lamp" (1946 *ASF*), was little noticed; ALZ did not adjust his style or plotting to new demands. [JC]

ZAMIATIN, YEVGENY (IVANOVICH) (1884–1937). Russian writer. He graduated in naval engineering from St Petersburg Polytechnical Institute, his studies interrupted by participation in the 1905 revolution as a Bolshevik, prison and deportation (renewed 1911–13). YZ began writing in 1908, withdrew from active politics, lectured at the Polytechnic Institute until his emigration, ran foul of the Tsarist censor in 1914 and built icebreakers in England 1916–17.

YZ wrote about 40 books of stories, fables, plays, excellent essays and two novels. After the October Revolution he became a prominent figure in key literary groups, guru for a whole school of young writers, and editor of an ambitious

publishing programme of books from the West; he wrote prefaces for works by H.G. WELLS, Jack LONDON, George Bernard SHAW, etc. From 1921 on he incurred much critical and some censoring disfavour which culminated in a campaign of vilification by the dominant literary faction, especially after *We* was published in an émigré journal in 1927. After writing a dignified letter to Stalin, YZ was allowed to go to Paris (retaining his Soviet passport), where he died shunned by both Soviet officialdom and right-wing émigrés.

We (written 1920, circulated in manuscript, first book publication in Russian, New York **1952**; trans. Zilboorg **1924**) is situated between YZ's principles of Revolution (life) versus Entropy (death). It incorporates prominent elements of a satirical novella he had written against British philistinism (including coupons for rationing sex, and the "Taylorite" regulation of the whole day), thus extrapolating the repressive potentials of every centralized state along with rational utilitarianism, in which the only irrational element is people — like the alienated narrator. Committed to the scientific method even in his narrative form, which mimics lab notes, YZ's only explanation of why its rationalism turns sour is mythical: every belief when victorious must turn repressive, as did Christianity. The plot is modelled on an inevitable Fall ending in an ironic crucifixion; instead of motivations it advances through powerful recurring images. Yet, in YZ's terms, *We* judges yesterday's UTOPIA — turned absolutist today — in the name of tomorrow's Utopia: there is no final revolution. The first and greatest anti-Utopia is thus *not* a DYSTOPIA. The expressionistic language of *We*, manipulated for speed and economy, helps to subsume the protagonist's defeat under the novel's concern for the integration of Man's science and art (including love).

YZ demonstrated that Utopia should be not a new religion (albeit of mathematics and space flights) but the dynamic horizon of Man's developing personality. *We* is the paradigmatic anti-Utopia (for George ORWELL, Aldous HUXLEY etc.), superseding the tradition of Utopianism, from MORE on, that ignores technology and anthropology. It is both a masterpiece of sf and an indispensable book of our epoch. [DS]
Other sf works: "A Story About the Most Important Thing" (1927 Russia; trans. Glenny in YZ's *The Dragon*, coll. **1966**).
About the author: *A Soviet Heretic* by YZ (**1970**); *Evgenij Zamjatin* (The Hague, **1973**) by Christopher Collins; *The Future as Nightmare* (**1967**) by Mark R. HILLEGAS; *Dostoevskij's Underground Man in Russian Literature* (The Hague, **1958**) by Robert L. Jackson; "Imagining the Future: Wells and Zamyatin" by Patrick Parrinder in *H.G. Wells and*

Modern Science Fiction (**1977**) ed. Darko SUVIN; *The Life and Works of Evgenij Zamjatin* (**1968**) by Alex M. Shane; "The Utopian Tradition of Russian Science Fiction" by Darko Suvin, *Modern Language Review* 1, Jan. 1971. Further bibliography of YZ appears in the last two items.
See also: LINGUISTICS; POLITICS.

ZARDOZ Film (1974). John Boorman Productions/20th Century-Fox. Directed by John BOORMAN, starring Sean Connery, Charlotte Rampling, Sara Kestelman and John Alderton. Screenplay by John Boorman. 105 mins. Colour.

A future society is divided into two regions — the Vortex and the Outlands, separated by an impenetrable force field. Within the Vortex live the Eternals, IMMORTAL and given to a decadent aestheticism, while in the Outlands dwell the Brutals, including a group called the Exterminators whose job is to keep the population level down. One of these Exterminators, Zed (Sean Connery), infiltrates the Vortex and his presence acts as a catalyst which destroys both the Immortals and their computer-run society. Zed represents the primal force that brings back to the impotent, static Immortals such old favourites as Emotion, Sex, Fear and Death, releasing them from their artificial world and allowing them to become part of the Natural Scheme of things again; that is, dead. The film is self-indulgent; Boorman's presentation of old ideas as if they were just new-minted has a certain silly charm, and the film has considerable visual brio, assisted by Geoffrey Unsworth's photography and the beautiful Irish settings; but the profundity is all on the surface. Also troubling is the film's curious oscillation between parody and solemnity. The novelization, by Boorman and Bill Stair, is *Zardoz* (**1974**). [JB/PN]

ZAREM, LEWIS (? –). American writer whose sf novel, *The Green Man from Space* (**1955**), features a Martian looking for greens. He has also written non-fiction on aeronautical subjects. [JC]

ZEBROWSKI, GEORGE (1945–). American writer. One of the first alumni of the CLARION SCIENCE FICTION WRITERS' WORKSHOP to achieve recognition in the sf world, GZ began publishing sf stories with "Traps" for *If* in 1970, and has remained active since. From 1970 to Winter 1974–5 he was editor of the SFWA BULLETIN. His first novel, *The Omega Point* (**1972**), part of a projected trilogy, is an ambitious, somewhat metaphysical SPACE OPERA incorporating some of the theories of the evolutionary theologian Teilhard de Chardin; a lone survivor of a bitter interstellar war with the Earth worlds searches for an ultimate secret WEAPON; Omega Point turns out to have weapon characteristics but is

The graven image of ZARDOZ hangs in the sky; an Outlands Exterminator rides below.

is a leading and representative figure of the American NEW WAVE sf that urged a shift of emphasis from the external world of the hard sciences to the internal worlds explorable through disciplines like PSYCHOLOGY (mostly Jungian), SOCIOLOGY, LINGUISTICS and the like. From 1962 to '69, RZ was employed by the Social Security Administration in Cleveland, Ohio, and Baltimore, Maryland. From 1969 he has been a full-time writer, and from 1975 he has lived in New Mexico. The external events of his life do not, therefore, show the restlessness characteristic of the other members of the new-wave triad.

RZ's first published story was "Passion Play" (1962) in *AMZ*, and for several years he was reasonably prolific in shorter forms, for a time using the pseudonym Harrison Denmark when stories piled up in *AMZ* and *Fantastic*; but more and more he has concentrated on novels. The magazine titles of his first two books are as well known as their book titles, and the awards given them attach to the magazine titles. *This Immortal* (1965 *FSF* as "… And Call me Conrad"; exp. **1966**) won the 1966 HUGO award for best novel; *The Dream Master* (1965 *AMZ* as "He Who Shapes"; exp. **1966**) won the 1965 NEBULA award for best novella. Both books are remarkably intense, narratively experimental, explosively conceived new-wave efforts, and with RZ's concurrent Nebula for best novelette for "The Doors of His Face, The Lamps of His Mouth" (1965) decisively signalled the arrival on the sf scene of new styles and new concerns. All are substantial works. *This Immortal* features a favourite RZ protagonist, the extremely long-lived or immortal (or somehow invulnerable) human who lives a kinetically active but highly cultured life, spending much of his time manipulating and protecting his fellow *Homo sapiens*, in this case against a complex alien threat. "The Doors of His Face, The Lamps of His Mouth" depicts with an unparalleled literate intensity the hunting of a huge sea-monster. In some ways *The Dream Master* is the most interesting of the three. Throughout his career RZ has had a tendency to side, perhaps a little too openly, with his complexly gifted, vain, dominating protagonists, and his treatment of neuroparticipant psychiatrist Charles Render seems no different. Render is eminent in his new field of psychiatry, which involves his actually entering and controlling (for therapeutic reasons) the subconscious experiences of his patients, and he does so superbly; nor does his involvement with a congenitally blind woman, and his attempt to give her dreams a visual content, appear to provide an exception. But gradually his own deficiencies as a person, his patient's character, and dovetailing crises in his own life subtly and terrifyingly trap him in a highly plausible psychic cul-de-s

fundamentally a focus of transcendental empathy. The second book of the trilogy (the first in terms of internal chronology) is *Ashes and Stars* (**1977**). *The Star Web* (**1975**) is a considerably less ambitious space opera, complete with two star-spanning forms of transportation, which are the heart of the book. *The Monadic Universe* (coll. **1977**) assembles GZ's early fiction. He has also edited *Tomorrow Today* (anth. **1975**), composed of original stories, and co-edited *Faster than Light* (anth. **1976**) with Jack DANN and *Human-Machines* (anth. **1975**) with Thomas N. SCORTIA. An interesting essay on sf in the CINEMA by GZ is "Science Fiction and the Visual Media" in *Science Fiction Today and Tomorrow* (anth. **1974**) ed. Reginald BRETNOR.   [JC/PN]
See also: ESCHATOLOGY; RELIGION.

ZEIGFREID, KARL House name used on many BADGER BOOKS sf titles. Books published under this name were predominantly the work of R.L. FANTHORPE. Those titles definitely attributed to him are: *Gods of Darkness* (**1962**), *Walk Through Tomorrow* (**1963**), *Android* (**1962**), *Atomic Nemesis* (**1962**), *Zero Minus X* (**1962**), *Escape to Infinity* (**1963**), *Radar Alert* (**1963**), *World of Tomorrow* (**1963**; vt *World of the Future*

USA), *The World That Never Was* (**1963**), *Projection Infinity* (**1964**), *No Way Back* (**1964**), *Barrier 346* (**1965**), *Girl From Tomorrow* (**1965**). Other KZ titles are: *Beyond the Galaxy* (no date), *Chariot into Time* (**1953**), *Chaos in Arcturus* (**1953**), *The Uranium Seekers* (**1963**) and *Dark Centauri* (**1964**).   [MJE]

Photo Indiana University News Bureau.

ZELAZNY, ROGER (1937–). American writer, born in Ohio, with MA from Columbia University in 1962. With Samuel R. DELANY and Harlan ELLISON he

All the sf apparatus of the story, and its sometimes overly baroque manner, are integrated into RZ's unveiling of the nature of a character under stress. This reversal of emphasis lies at the heart of what the new wave was all about.

RZ's two story collections are drawn mainly from these scintillating early years. They are *Four For Tomorrow* (coll. 1967; vt *A Rose for Ecclesiastes* UK) and *The Doors of His Face, The Lamps of His Mouth, and Other Stories* (coll. 1971). His next novel, *Lord of Light* (1967), which won a 1968 Hugo, is also richly conceived and plotted, dealing expansively with a group of men on another planet who, aided by superior technology, impersonate (and in a sense become) the Hindu pantheon of gods. However, from *Isle of the Dead* (1969) and *Creatures of Light and Darkness* (1969), some falling-off became evident; RZ's storylines became simpler, somewhat coarser, darker. *Damnation Alley* (1969) is perhaps the most savage of all, depicting a post-HOLOCAUST motor-cycle-trek across a vicious America; it has been filmed with many changes as DAMNATION ALLEY (1977).

In 1970 RZ began his continuing "Amber" series — *Nine Princes in Amber* (1970), *The Guns of Avalon* (1972), *Sign of the Unicorn* (1975) and *The Hand of Oberon* (1976), with, it is understood, one further volume projected, but no end as yet in sight — to a somewhat mixed reaction. The land of Amber (like C.S. LEWIS's Narnia) exists on a plane of greater fundamental reality than Earth, and provides normal reality with its ontological base; unlike Narnia, however, Amber (to date) is ruled by a cabal of squabbling siblings, whose quasi-Olympian feudings have provided a great deal of complicated plotting; the climax (which must be forthcoming) may resolve the somewhat aimless though often locally interesting impression the sequence gives so far. More recently, RZ has made something of a comeback. Though his collaboration with Philip K. DICK, *Deus Irae* (1976), finds him labouring somewhat in the unstable Dick world, *My Name is Legion* (coll. of linked stories 1976), about another behind-the-scenes manipulator who has obtained his invisibility from the omnipresent computers, contains the novella "Home is the Hangman" (1975), winner of both a Hugo and a Nebula, in which the protagonist is hired to protect guilty programmers from the robot-cum-computer with a brain of human complexity that has apparently returned to Earth to kill them off. This turns out not to be the case, very interestingly. *Doorways in the Sand* (1976) is also a relatively successful story, close to space opera in theme but expertly handled.

Through his career RZ has suffered the inevitable price of writing at the peak of intensity and conviction — that of slackening into routine when his obsessive concerns have been given definitive form. With RZ this happened early. His arduous investigations of "inner space", into the ways human beings respond to deep psychic challenges, seemed to have exhausted him for several years, a period during which he sustained his career by writing competent but somewhat distant novels. Without the burning conviction of the first novels, his secret-guardian protagonists began to seem rather self-indulgent. But, as he is still a relatively young writer, the recent signs of creative renewal are good news indeed for the genre he has so invigorated.   [JC]

Other works: *Jack of Shadows* (1971); *Today We Choose Faces* (1973); *To Die in Italbar* (1973), featuring the protagonist of *Isle of the Dead*; *Bridge of Ashes* (1976). As editor: *Nebula Award Stories Three* (anth. 1968).

About the author: "Faust & Archimedes" in *The Jewel-Hinged Jaw: Notes on the Language of Science Fiction* (coll. 1977) by Samuel R. Delany; "Introduction" by Ormond Seavey to the 1976 GREGG PRESS printing of *The Dream Master*; "Zelazny's *Damnation Alley*: Hell Noh" by Carl B. Yoke in EXTRAPOLATION (Vol. 15 no. 1), Dec. 1973.

See also: ALIENS; CONCEPTUAL BREAKTHROUGH; CRIME AND PUNISHMENT; ESCHATOLOGY; ESP; FANTASY; GAMES AND SPORTS; GODS AND DEMONS; HEROES; IMMORTALITY; MARS; MATTER TRANSMISSION; MESSIAHS; MYTHOLOGY; PARALLEL WORLDS; PARANOIA AND SCHIZOPHRENIA; PARASITISM AND SYMBIOSIS; PSI POWERS; PSYCHOLOGY; REINCARNATION; RELIGION; ROBOTS; SUPERMAN; SUPERNATURAL CREATURES; UNDER THE SEA; VENUS.

ZERO POPULATION GROWTH See Z.P.G.

ZERWICK, CHLOE (1923–). American writer and editor, who collaborated with Harrison BROWN (*who see for details*) on an sf novel, *The Cassiopeia Affair* (1968).   [JC]

See also: ASTRONOMY.

ZETFORD, TULLY See Kenneth BULMER.

ZIEROLD, NORMAN (1927–). American writer whose sf novel is *The Skyscraper Doom* (1927).   [JC]

ZOLINE, PAMELA (1941–). American painter and writer, living in England from 1963. She illustrated several stories for *NW* in the late 1960s, including the magazine publication of Thomas M. DISCH's *Camp Concentration* (1968), in a collage-derived style; her first sf story, "The Heat Death of the Universe" (1967) also appeared in *NW*; it is a finely structured application of the concept of ENTROPY to the life of an American housewife. It has been anthologized in the much praised *The Mirror of Infinity: A Critics' Anthology of Science Fiction* (anth. 1970) ed. Robert SILVERBERG, as Brian W. ALDISS's choice of best story. Excerpts from a novel are to be included in Harlan ELLISON's much delayed *The Last Dangerous Visions*. [JC]

See also: ABSURDIST SF; COSMOLOGY.

Z.P.G. (vt **ZERO POPULATION GROWTH** UK) Film (1971). Sagittarius/Paramount. Directed by Michael Campus, starring Oliver Reed, Geraldine Chaplin, Diane Cilento and Don Gordon. Screenplay by Max EHRLICH and Frank DeFelitta. 97 mins. Colour.

"Zero population growth" is a term which refers to a situation where the population of a society remains steady, neither increasing nor decreasing. It seems that the script-writers of *Z.P.G.* assumed that it meant having no children at all, and the film should perhaps be called simply *Zero Population*. A married couple defy a ban on breeding and have a baby secretly. They are betrayed by a jealous neighbour, but escape the authorities by descending into a sewer. Where they escape to is not explained. The novelization is *The Edict* (1972) by Max Ehrlich.   [JB]

ZULAWSKI, JERZY (1874–1915). Polish playwright, poet and novelist, of sf interest for his untranslated trilogy about the colonization of the MOON, comprised of *Na srebrynym globie* ["The Silver Globe"], *Zwycięzca* ["The Conqueror"], and *Stara ziemia* ["That old Earth"] (1903–11).   [JC]